Webster's

Icelandic
–
English

Thesaurus Dictionary

PROCEEDS BENEFIT

Webster's Online Dictionary
(www.websters-online-dictionary.org)

EDITED BY

Philip M. Parker, Ph.D.
INSEAD (Fontainebleau & Singapore)

Published by ICON Group International, Inc.
7404 Trade St
San Diego, CA 92122 USA
Phone: (858) 635-9410
Fax: (858) 635-9414
iconsubs@san.rr.com

www.icongrouponline.com

This edition published by ICON Classics in 2008
Printed in the United States of America.

Webster's Icelandic – English Thesaurus Dictionary

ISBN 0-497-83518-5

PREFACE

This is an English thesaurus designed for Icelandic speakers who wish to better understand the ambiguities and richness of the English language. The first chapter is a full English thesaurus organized by 10565 Icelandic subject words. For each Icelandic subject word, one or more corresponding English subject words (translations) are provided. Synonyms are then given for the English translations for all relevant parts of speech (even in cases where the Icelandic subject word has a unique part of speech). This process results in over 23799 English synonyms.

The second chapter gives an index of these English synonyms back to the Icelandic subject words (a potentially useful chapter to English speakers interested in basic Icelandic vocabulary). The third chapter has short vocabulary lists organized by parts-of-speech. English teachers or students can use these bilingual lists to create flash cards, basic lesson plans, and English as a Second Language (ESL) study lists.

While creating an English thesaurus for Icelandic speakers seems simple enough, it can be tricky. What's the problem? Translations do not always follow strict transitivity. Normally, if *a=b* and *b=c*, then *c=a*. This is not necessarily true in linguistics when *b* is an English word that has more than one part of speech. For example, "test" is a verb, noun and adjective. What is the correct English synonym for "a" (in Icelandic) when "b" (in English) has synonyms ("c") having many parts of speech? Furthermore, what if "a" (in Icelandic) is ambiguous and has several translations into English ("b")? This thesaurus embraces this ambiguity by giving as much information to the reader as possible. This was accomplished in two phases. In the first phase, maximum-likelihood English translations of the Icelandic subject words are given. For all the languages covered in Webster's Online Dictionary translations are determined using rather massive content analyses of translations from various sources including translations of United Nations documents, translations of the Holy Bible (and similar sources), training manuals, popular works, and academic sources. An English translation having the highest probability of being used is reported first, then the second most probable is reported second, and so on.

Reference: Webster's Online Dictionary (www.websters-online-dictionary.org)

In the second phase, English synonyms for all parts of speech, including those not related to the original Icelandic subject, are given for each English translation generated by the first phase. If an English entry is most used as a certain part of speech (estimated based on an English language corpus), then English synonyms for that part of speech are listed first. This indicates to the speaker of Icelandic how the English subject word is most used. Other parts of speech are listed based on their frequency of usage in English. Within each part of speech, synonyms most likely to be used in English are listed first. Readers who seek further information on any of the words in this book, including translations to other world languages, can freely refer to Webster's Online Dictionary (www.websters-online-dictionary.org).

The goal of Webster's Online Dictionary is to give all people of the world free access to a complete mapping of all known words to and from all written languages. In fulfillment of this goal, Webster's Online Dictionary (www.websters-online-dictionary.org) also offers as much information as possible for each word, including definitions, translations, images, trade name usage, quotations, and encyclopedic knowledge. The proceeds generated by the sale of this Icelandic–English thesaurus dictionary as well as other books extracted from the project will be used to augment the contents of the Webster's Online Dictionary.

This book may be the first Icelandic-English thesaurus ever published. All the errors and omissions are mine. I will certainly revise and improve this book at some later date, so if you wish to see better editions published in the future, please send any suggestions, corrections, or translations to webstersedits2@hotmail.com. Thank you for purchasing this book and supporting Webster's Online Dictionary.

Philip M. Parker, Ph.D., editor
Chair Professor of Management Science
INSEAD (Singapore & Fontainebleau, France)

CONTENTS

ICELANDIC TO ENGLISH THESAURUS 1

A 1
Á 20
Æ 26
B 28
C 51
D 51
Ð 59
E 59
É 74
F 74
G 104
Ĝ 124
H 125
I 161
Í 166
J 168
Ĵ 172
K 172
L 193
M 216
N 238
O 247
Ó 250
Ö 258
P 261
R 266
S 283
Ŝ 364
T 364
Þ 382
U 394
Ú 403
V 409

Reference: Webster's Online Dictionary (www.websters-online-dictionary.org)

W..435
X..435
Y..435
Ý..438
Z..438

INDEX OF ENGLISH SUBJECTS TO ICELANDIC SUBJECTS.........................439

A..439
B..450
C..457
D..470
E..477
F..483
G..488
H..491
I...496
J...501
K..502
L...503
M...507
N..513
O..515
P...518
Q..528
R..529
S...536
T...549
U..557
V..558
W...560
X..563
Y..563
Z..563

VOCABULARY STUDY LISTS...565

Verbs (Icelandic - English)...565
Verbs (English - Icelandic)...570
Nouns (Icelandic - English)..573
Nouns (English - Icelandic)..665
Adverbs (Icelandic - English)..707
Adverbs (English - Icelandic)..707
Adjectives (Icelandic - English)...707
Adjectives (English - Icelandic)...719

Icelandic to English Thesaurus

A

aangström angstrom; *synonyms* (*n*) a, amp, ampere, axerophthol.

abakus abacus; *synonyms* (*n*) aback, (*v*) logometer, slipstick, tallies.

aborri perch; *synonyms* (*v*) roost, light, abide, lodge, (*adj*) dwell.

að 1. a; *synonyms* (*n*) amp, ampere, angstrom, axerophthol, (*adj*) cream, 2. at; *synonyms* (*prep*) in, a, (*adv*) on, along, (*prf*) all, 3. on; *synonyms* (*prep*) at, about, concerning, (*adj*) forward, aboard; *antonym* (*adv*) off, 4. in; *synonyms* (*prep*) during, between, by, through, (*adj*) stylish; *antonyms* (*prep*) out, outside, 5. inside; *synonyms* (*n*) interior, middle, (*adj*) inner, internal, indoor; *antonyms* (*n*) exterior, (*adj*) free.

aðal primary; *synonyms* (*adj*) chief, basic, elementary, essential, (*n*) paramount; *antonym* (*adj*) secondary.

aðalbláber bilberry; *synonyms* (*n*) blaeberry, whortleberry, whinberry.

aðalbláberjalyng bilberry; *synonyms* (*n*) blaeberry, whortleberry, whinberry.

aðalbraut highway; *synonyms* (*n*) road, highroad, way, course, path.

aðaleinkunn aggregate; *synonyms* (*n*) total, agglomerate, whole, (*v*) accumulate, cluster; *antonyms* (*n*) individual, part.

aðalframleiðsluvara staple; *synonyms* (*n*) pin, material, (*v*) nail, (*adj*) basic, fundamental.

aðalhnöttur primary; *synonyms* (*adj*) chief, basic, elementary, essential, (*n*) paramount; *antonym* (*adj*) secondary.

aðalhringur deferent; *synonyms* (*adj*) deferential, regardful, submissive, bearing, slavish.

aðalhvatamaður protagonist; *synonyms* (*n*) hero, booster, champion, exponent, supporter.

aðallögn main; *synonyms* (*adj*) chief, grand, great, head, leading; *antonyms* (*adj*) minor, auxiliary, secondary, supplementary.

aðalmerking denotation; *synonyms* (*n*) sense, indication, character, meaning, reference.

aðalskip nave; *synonyms* (*n*) chancel, choir, hub, omphalos, transept.

aðalskuldabréf indenture; *synonyms* (*n*) bond, indent, agreement, contract, covenant.

aðalstjarna primary; *synonyms* (*adj*) chief, basic, elementary, essential, (*n*) paramount; *antonym* (*adj*) secondary.

adamsepli larynx; *synonyms* (*n*) spiracle, tonsils, windpipe.

aðbúð nurture; *synonyms* (*v*) foster, cherish, grow, (*n*) education, breeding; *antonym* (*v*) neglect.

aðburður presentation; *synonyms* (*n*) donation, exhibition, demonstration, display, introduction.

aðdrættir supplies; *synonyms* (*n*) food, provisions, stores, (*v*) equipment, outfit.

aðdragandi preamble; *synonyms* (*n*) introduction, prelude, foreword, preface, overture.

aðdráttarafl 1. attraction; *synonyms* (*n*) allure, enticement, invitation, affinity, allurement; *antonyms* (*n*) repulsion, disgust, revulsion, 2. gravitation; *synonyms* (*n*) attraction, gravity, graveness, habit, soberness.

aðdráttarkraftur 1. pull; *synonyms* (*v*) drag, draw, draught, pluck, attract; *antonyms* (*v*) push, repel, 2. attraction; *synonyms* (*n*) allure, enticement, invitation, affinity, allurement; *antonyms* (*n*) repulsion, disgust, revulsion.

aðdráttur attraction; *synonyms* (*n*) allure, enticement, invitation, affinity, allurement; *antonyms* (*n*) repulsion, disgust, revulsion.

adenín adenine; *synonym* (*n*) aminopurine.

adenósíneinfosfat amp; *synonyms* (*n*) ampere, a, amplifier, loudspeaker, speaker.

aðfærandi afferent; *synonym* (*adj*) sensory.

aðfærsla 1. supply; *synonyms* (*n*) provision, (*v*) furnish, stock, afford, fill, 2. adduction, 3. input; *synonyms* (*n*) contribution, incoming, data, advice, feed.

aðfall 1. tide; *synonyms* (*n*) current, flow, stream, course, (*v*) wave, 2. flow; *synonyms* (*n*) flood, discharge, (*v*) flux, jet, run.

aðfallandi incident; *synonyms* (*n*) event, fact, adventure, case, circumstance.

aðfallsfasi diastole; *synonyms* (*n*) distension, dropsy, intumescence, swelling, tumefaction.

aðfari preparation; *synonyms* (*n*) arrangement, concoction, provision, readiness, training.

aðfella 1. regression; *synonyms* (*n*) regress, lapse, setback, degeneration, deterioration, 2. asymptote.

aðfelldur asymptotic; *synonym* (*v*) asymptotical.

aðfenginn 1. passive; *synonyms* (*adj*) inactive, apathetic, inert, submissive, indifferent; *antonyms* (*adj*) active, assertive, spirited, working, 2. heterogenous; *synonyms* (*adj*) heterogeneous, heterogene, heterogenetic.

aðferð 1. strategy; *synonyms* (*n*) dodge, plan, scheme, strategics, (*v*) tactics, 2. procedure;

synonyms (*n*) process, formula, practice, routine, fashion, **3**. process; *synonyms* (*n*) operation, proceeding, method, procedure, (*v*) action, **4**. methodology; *synonyms* (*n*) attitude, line, organization, slant, style, **5**. mode; *synonyms* (*n*) means, manner, form, way, condition.

aðferðafræði methodology; *synonyms* (*n*) method, attitude, line, organization, slant.

aðferðarlýsing protocol; *synonyms* (*n*) etiquette, manners, ceremony, bill, formality.

aðfinnslur protest; *synonyms* (*n*) demonstration, objection, (*v*) dissent, assert, complain; *antonym* (*v*) support.

aðflug approach; *synonyms* (*n*) access, entry, (*v*) advance, accost, address; *antonym* (*v*) leave.

aðflugsgreining briefing; *synonyms* (*n*) instruction, announcement, communication, direction, instructions.

aðflugshringviti locator; *synonym* (*n*) locater.

aðföng 1. stores; *synonyms* (*n*) supplies, provisions, commissariat, equipment, food, **2**. supply; *synonyms* (*n*) provision, (*v*) furnish, stock, afford, fill, **3**. input; *synonyms* (*n*) contribution, incoming, data, advice, feed.

aðgæta check; *synonyms* (*v*) bridle, stop, (*n*) control, arrest, curb.

aðgætinn vigilant; *synonyms* (*adj*) alert, attentive, observant, watchful, cautious; *antonym* (*adj*) inattentive.

aðgangsorð password; *synonyms* (*n*) countersign, catchword, parole, watchword, (*v*) key.

aðgangur 1. admission; *synonyms* (*n*) acceptance, access, acknowledgment, confession, admittance; *antonym* (*n*) denial, **2**. access; *synonyms* (*n*) admission, approach, entrance, entry, entree; *antonym* (*n*) exit, **3**. entrance; *synonyms* (*v*) enchant, captivate, charm, bewitch, enrapture; *antonyms* (*n*) departure, (*v*) bore.

aðgát precaution; *synonyms* (*n*) forethought, foresight, care, discretion, prevention.

aðgengi accessibility; *synonyms* (*n*) friendliness, approachability, availability, access, approachableness.

aðgengilegur 1. available; *synonyms* (*adj*) accessible, free, possible, attainable, (*adv*) present; *antonyms* (*adj*) unavailable, occupied, suppressed, concealed, engaged, **2**. accessible; *synonyms* (*adj*) approachable, available, open, convenient, amenable; *antonyms* (*adj*) inaccessible, out-of-the-way.

aðgengileiki 1. accessibility; *synonyms* (*n*) friendliness, approachability, availability, access, approachableness, **2**. availability; *synonyms* (*n*) accessibility, handiness, availableness, opening, supply.

aðgerð 1. dressing; *synonyms* (*n*) bandage, bandaging, binding, fertilization, stuffing, **2**. operation; *synonyms* (*n*) execution, movement, act, agency, effect, **3**. measure; *synonyms* (*n*) amount, criterion, extent, beat, benchmark.

aðgerðaleysi inertia; *synonyms* (*n*) inactivity, idleness, lethargy, inaction, apathy; *antonym* (*n*) momentum.

aðgerðarmaður operator; *synonyms* (*n*) driver, hustler, manipulator, agent, doer.

aðgerðir measure; *synonyms* (*n*) amount, criterion, extent, beat, benchmark.

aðgöngumerki ticket; *synonyms* (*n*) pass, card, label, certificate, ballot.

aðgöngumiði ticket; *synonyms* (*n*) pass, card, label, certificate, ballot.

aðgönguspjald ticket; *synonyms* (*n*) pass, card, label, certificate, ballot.

aðgreina 1. resolve; *synonyms* (*v*) determine, decide, (*n*) purpose, determination, decision; *antonyms* (*n*) indecision, weakness, **2**. segregate; *synonyms* (*v*) isolate, detach, discriminate, divide, (*adj*) detached, **3**. distinguish; *synonyms* (*v*) discern, describe, know, perceive, discover; *antonym* (*v*) confuse.

aðgreinandi diagnostic; *synonyms* (*adj*) characteristic, individual, (*n*) criterion, (*v*) demonstrative, diacritical.

aðgreining 1. resolution; *synonyms* (*n*) decision, determination, answer, conclusion, firmness; *antonym* (*n*) indecisiveness, **2**. separation; *synonyms* (*n*) detachment, disjunction, disunion, division, partition; *antonyms* (*n*) amalgamation, closeness, connection, marriage, unification, **3**. segregation; *synonyms* (*n*) dissociation, separation, elimination, discrimination, sequestration; *antonyms* (*n*) integration, inclusion, **4**. disaggregation, **5**. division; *synonyms* (*n*) department, disagreement, allotment, branch, break; *antonyms* (*n*) convergence, estimation.

aðgreiningargeta discrimination; *synonyms* (*n*) discernment, difference, differentiation, distinction, (*v*) judgment; *antonym* (*n*) tolerance.

aðhæfing 1. accommodation; *synonyms* (*n*) adjustment, compromise, loan, lodging, (*v*) advance, **2**. adjustment; *synonyms* (*n*) adaptation, accommodation, alteration, control, fit, **3**. adaptation; *synonyms* (*n*) version, reworking, adaption, conversion, fitness.

aðhaldssamur restrictive; *synonyms* (*adj*) prohibitive, restraining, exclusive, restricted, (*v*) limitary; *antonym* (*adj*) encouraging.

aðhneiging convergence; *synonyms* (n) confluence, meeting, concentration, concourse, convergency; *antonyms* (n) divergence, division.

aðhvarf regression; *synonyms* (n) regress, lapse, setback, degeneration, deterioration.

aðhverfa convergence; *synonyms* (n) confluence, meeting, concentration, concourse, convergency; *antonyms* (n) divergence, division.

aðhverfing convergence; *synonyms* (n) confluence, meeting, concentration, concourse, convergency; *antonyms* (n) divergence, division.

aðhverfur 1. ventral; *synonyms* (adj) abdominal, adaxial, front, forward, intestinal, **2.** convergent; *synonyms* (adj) concurrent, converging, (v) confluent.

aðhyllast endorse; *synonyms* (v) defend, approve, back, certify, confirm; *antonyms* (v) disapprove, oppose.

aðild involvement; *synonyms* (n) entanglement, concern, interest, implication, inclusion; *antonym* (n) disconnection.

aðili 1. party; *synonyms* (n) gang, band, company, assembly, association, **2.** entity; *synonyms* (n) being, existence, object, thing, whole, **3.** member; *synonyms* (n) limb, part, supporter, extremity, phallus.

aðkomandi extrinsic; *synonyms* (adj) exterior, external, extraneous, exotic, alien; *antonym* (adj) intrinsic.

aðkominn adventitious; *synonyms* (adj) accidental, casual, random, additional, adventive.

aðkomuleið access; *synonyms* (n) admission, approach, entrance, entry, admittance; *antonym* (n) exit.

aðkomumaður alien; *synonyms* (adj) foreign, strange, unknown, (n) foreigner, (v) alienate; *antonyms* (adj) familiar, (n) native, citizen.

aðkomusteinn erratic; *synonyms* (adj) capricious, changeable, eccentric, irregular, freakish; *antonyms* (adj) consistent, constant, certain, dependable, predictable.

aðkvæni exogamy; *synonyms* (n) intermarriage, endogamy, inmarriage.

aðlægur 1. adjacent; *synonyms* (adj) abutting, adjoining, close, contiguous, (adv) near; *antonym* (adj) distant, **2.** afferent; *synonym* (adj) sensory, **3.** contiguous; *synonyms* (adj) adjacent, conterminous, nearby, bordering, immediate.

aðlaga 1. adjust; *synonyms* (v) temper, accommodate, adapt, align, acclimatize, **2.** adapt; *synonyms* (v) adjust, acclimate, fashion, alter, arrange.

aðlagast 1. tune; *synonyms* (n) melody, song, strain, air, (v) adjust, **2.** place; *synonyms* (n) position, (v) post, arrange, fix, lay; *antonym* (v) remove, **3.**

adapt; *synonyms* (v) accommodate, acclimate, fashion, alter, assimilate, **4.** accommodate; *synonyms* (v) adapt, fit, oblige, contain, (adj) suit; *antonym* (v) evict, **5.** attune; *synonyms* (v) tune, modulate, reconcile, coordinate, harmonize.

aðleiðir feeder; *synonyms* (n) eater, affluent, feed, filler, tributary.

aðleiðsla induction; *synonyms* (n) inauguration, deduction, initiation, beginning, elicitation.

aðleiðsluaðferð induction; *synonyms* (n) inauguration, deduction, initiation, beginning, elicitation.

aðleitni convergence; *synonyms* (n) confluence, meeting, concentration, concourse, convergency; *antonyms* (n) divergence, division.

aðlifun 1. acculturation; *synonyms* (n) assimilation, civilization, culture, absorption, socialisation, **2.** assimilation; *synonyms* (n) acculturation, incorporation, integration, addition, amalgamation.

aðlífun anabolism; *synonyms* (n) catabolism, metabolism.

aðliggjandi 1. afferent; *synonym* (adj) sensory, **2.** contiguous; *synonyms* (adj) adjacent, adjoining, close, abutting, conterminous; *antonym* (adj) distant, **3.** adjacent; *synonyms* (adj) contiguous, nearby, neighboring, next, (adv) near.

aðlögun 1. adaptation; *synonyms* (n) accommodation, adjustment, alteration, version, reworking, **2.** adjustment; *synonyms* (n) adaptation, control, fit, settlement, (adj) adaption, **3.** accommodation; *synonyms* (n) compromise, loan, lodging, agreement, (v) advance, **4.** assimilation; *synonyms* (n) absorption, acculturation, incorporation, integration, addition, **5.** agreement; *synonyms* (n) accord, acquiescence, concord, accordance, coincidence; *antonyms* (n) disagreement, argument, conflict, discord, rejection.

aðlögunarhæfileiki adaptability; *synonyms* (n) flexibility, efficiency, adaptableness, adaptivity, usefulness.

aðlögunarhæfni adaptability; *synonyms* (n) flexibility, efficiency, adaptableness, adaptivity, usefulness.

aðlögunarörðugleikar maladjustment; *synonym* (n) neurosis.

aðmíráll admiral; *synonyms* (n) admiralty, administration.

adrenalín 1. adrenaline; *synonyms* (n) epinephrin, epinephrine, **2.** epinephrine; *synonym* (n) adrenaline.

adrenergur adrenergic; *synonym* (adj) sympathomimetic.

aðrennslisrör penstock; *synonyms* (*n*) floodgate, sluice, penchute, pentrough, sluicegate.

adrenvirkur adrenergic; *synonym* (*adj*) sympathomimetic.

aðrenvirkur adrenergic; *synonym* (*adj*) sympathomimetic.

aðsetur residence; *synonyms* (*n*) abode, dwelling, home, house, accommodation.

aðseygur adsorbent; *synonym* (*adj*) adsorptive.

aðskilið split; *synonyms* (*v*) crack, cut, fracture, (*n*) break, rip; *antonyms* (*v*) join, unite, merge.

aðskilinn 1. separate; *synonyms* (*v*) detach, divorce, part, insulate, scatter; *antonyms* (*adj*) connected, (*v*) unite, merge, mix, combine, **2.** discrete; *synonyms* (*adj*) separate, distinct, different, detached, diverse, **3.** disjoint; *synonyms* (*v*) dislocate, disarticulate, disjoin, dismember, dissociate.

aðskilja 1. separate; *synonyms* (*v*) detach, divorce, part, insulate, scatter; *antonyms* (*adj*) connected, (*v*) unite, merge, mix, combine, **2.** segregate; *synonyms* (*v*) isolate, discriminate, divide, separate, (*adj*) detached.

aðskilnaðarkennd alienation; *synonyms* (*n*) estrangement, abalienation, disaffection, dislike, separation.

aðskilnaðarstefna 1. separatism; *synonyms* (*n*) segregation, autonomy, independence, **2.** segregation; *synonyms* (*n*) dissociation, separation, elimination, discrimination, (*v*) detachment; *antonyms* (*n*) integration, inclusion.

aðskilnaður 1. segregation; *synonyms* (*n*) dissociation, separation, elimination, discrimination, (*v*) detachment; *antonyms* (*n*) integration, inclusion, **2.** separation; *synonyms* (*n*) disjunction, disunion, division, partition, disconnection; *antonyms* (*n*) amalgamation, closeness, connection, marriage, unification, **3.** disjunction; *synonyms* (*n*) disjuncture, break, disconnectedness, discontinuance, **4.** exclusion; *synonyms* (*n*) exception, banishment, debarment, expulsion, ejection; *antonyms* (*n*) addition, entitlement.

aðskotaefni 1. dope; *synonyms* (*n*) dolt, boob, booby, ass, (*v*) drug, **2.** contaminant; *synonyms* (*n*) pollutant, contamination, poison, pollution, taint.

aðsóp accretion; *synonyms* (*n*) increment, accumulation, increase, augmentation, accession.

aðstaða 1. facility; *synonyms* (*n*) ability, dexterity, adroitness, ease, readiness, **2.** facilities; *synonym* (*n*) equipment.

aðstæður 1. situation; *synonyms* (*n*) place, employment, position, post, job, **2.** context; *synonyms* (*n*) circumstance, environment, setting, surroundings, background.

aðstandendur relative; *synonyms* (*adj*) related, comparative, proportionate, (*n*) relation, (*v*) kinsman; *antonym* (*adj*) absolute.

aðstoð assistance; *synonyms* (*n*) aid, assist, support, boost, encouragement; *antonym* (*n*) hindrance.

aðstoða assist; *synonyms* (*v*) aid, support, abet, serve, (*n*) help; *antonym* (*v*) hinder.

aðsveigður inclining; *synonyms* (*n*) inclination, disposition, leaning, tendency, (*adj*) oblique.

aðsvif syncope; *synonyms* (*n*) swoon, faint, syncopation, fainting, deliquium.

aðverminn endothermic; *synonym* (*adj*) endothermal.

aðvífandi exogenous; *synonyms* (*adj*) endogenous, exogenetic, extogenous, secondary.

aðvörunarhljóð buzz; *synonyms* (*n*) hum, rumor, hearsay, (*v*) call, drone.

AEF amp; *synonyms* (*n*) ampere, a, amplifier, loudspeaker, speaker.

afæta predator; *synonyms* (*n*) marauder, vulture, piranha, destroyer, scavenger.

afbaka distort; *synonyms* (*v*) contort, deform, falsify, bend, buckle; *antonym* (*v*) untwist.

afbjögun rectification; *synonyms* (*n*) correction, amendment, improvement, redress, revision.

afborgun 1. amortization; *synonyms* (*n*) amortisation, payment, **2.** instalment; *synonyms* (*n*) episode, installment, installation, installing, facility, **3.** installment; *synonyms* (*n*) deposit, instalment, part, section, earnest.

afbrigði 1. version; *synonyms* (*n*) reading, translation, construction, interpretation, rendering, **2.** variation; *synonyms* (*n*) alteration, change, difference, divergence, mutation; *antonym* (*n*) similarity, **3.** variant; *synonyms* (*n*) variation, version, (*adj*) different, divergent, changeable, **4.** variety; *synonyms* (*n*) kind, sort, species, form, (*adj*) class; *antonym* (*n*) uniformity, **5.** anomaly; *synonyms* (*n*) abnormality, aberration, anomalousness, deviation, abnormity.

afbrigðilegur 1. anomalous; *synonyms* (*adj*) abnormal, irregular, aberrant, atypical, deviant; *antonym* (*adj*) normal, **2.** abnormal; *synonyms* (*adj*) anomalous, monstrous, odd, perverted, strange; *antonyms* (*adj*) typical, usual, **3.** heterologous; *synonyms* (*adj*) heterologic, heterological, different.

afbrigðileiki 1. abnormality; *synonyms* (*n*) aberration, anomaly, abnormalcy, deviation, eccentricity; *antonym* (*n*) normality, **2.** anomaly; *synonyms* (*n*) abnormality, anomalousness, abnormity, peculiarity, exception.

afbrot crime; *synonyms* (*n*) offense, blame, guilt, injustice, transgression.

afbrotaiðni crime; *synonyms* (*n*) offense, blame, guilt, injustice, transgression.

afdragi 1. puller; *synonyms* (*n*) dragger, anchor, tugger, trawler, **2**. extractor; *synonyms* (*n*) centrifuge, exhauster, separator, plunger, (*v*) pliers.

afdráttarþvinga puller; *synonyms* (*n*) dragger, anchor, tugger, trawler.

afdráttur annealing; *synonym* (*n*) tempering.

afefni derivative; *synonyms* (*adj*) derived, (*n*) derivate, derivation, differential, offshoot; *antonym* (*n*) original.

afeinangrunartæki stripper; *synonyms* (*n*) ecdysiast, peeler, stripteaser, extractor, remover.

afeitra detoxify; *synonym* (*v*) detoxicate.

afeitrun detoxification; *synonym* (*n*) detoxication.

afeitur 1. toxoid; *synonyms* (*n*) anatoxin, poison, **2**. anatoxin; *synonym* (*n*) toxoid.

afero things; *synonyms* (*n*) gear, stuff, belongings, equipment, garb.

affall 1. shunt; *synonyms* (*n*) bypass, (*v*) shift, avert, move, remove, **2**. abscission; *synonyms* (*n*) abscision, apocope, (*v*) rescission, recision.

affallssegulmagnaður shunt; *synonyms* (*n*) bypass, (*v*) shift, avert, move, remove.

afferma unload; *synonyms* (*v*) discharge, drop, empty, unlade, clear; *antonyms* (*v*) load, fill.

afferming unloading; *synonyms* (*v*) discharge, unload, absolve, acquit, acquittal; *antonym* (*n*) loading.

afflæði regression; *synonyms* (*n*) regress, lapse, setback, degeneration, deterioration.

afföll 1. discount; *synonyms* (*n*) deduction, rebate, (*v*) reduce, disregard, ignore; *antonym* (*v*) increase, **2**. mortality; *synonyms* (*n*) fatality, death, flesh, humanity, mankind; *antonym* (*n*) immortality.

affræflun emasculation; *synonyms* (*n*) castration, (*adj*) orchotomy, orchiotomy.

affrysta defrost; *synonyms* (*v*) melt, thaw, soften.

afgangur 1. residual; *synonyms* (*adj*) remaining, leftover, (*v*) remnant, residue, balance, **2**. residue; *synonyms* (*n*) remainder, rest, end, (*adj*) remains, residual, **3**. reserve; *synonyms* (*n*) backup, (*v*) keep, save, book, maintain; *antonyms* (*n*) openness, friendliness, informality, warmth, **4**. surplus; *synonyms* (*adj*) extra, (*n*) excess, overabundance, surfeit, glut; *antonyms* (*n*) necessary, lack, shortage, scarcity, **5**. balance; *synonyms* (*n*) poise, symmetry, (*v*) counterbalance, adjust, offset; *antonyms* (*n*) imbalance, (*v*) unbalance.

afgerandi determinant; *synonyms* (*n*) clincher, determiner, (*adj*) crucial, determinative, conclusive.

afgjald rent; *synonyms* (*n*) breach, cleft, fissure, lease, (*v*) hire.

afglóðun tempering; *synonyms* (*n*) annealing, hardening, toughening, change, drawing.

afgreiðsla discharging; *synonyms* (*n*) unloading, discharge, acquittal, fulfillment.

afhelgun secularization; *synonyms* (*n*) secularisation, temporality.

afhending delivery; *synonyms* (*n*) childbirth, birth, consignment, discharge, rescue; *antonyms* (*n*) death, dispatch.

afhjúpun exposure; *synonyms* (*n*) display, exposition, detection, peril, (*v*) disclosure.

afhlaða discharge; *synonyms* (*n*) release, dismissal, (*v*) acquit, clear, absolve; *antonyms* (*v*) capture, hire.

afhleðsla discharge; *synonyms* (*n*) release, dismissal, (*v*) acquit, clear, absolve; *antonyms* (*v*) capture, hire.

afhleyping releasing; *synonyms* (*adj*) cathartic, evacuant, psychotherapeutic, purgative, (*n*) acquittal.

afhleypir trigger; *synonyms* (*v*) activate, initiate, spark, start, incite.

afhol pocket; *synonyms* (*n*) cavity, pouch, (*v*) bag, take, appropriate.

afhröðun deceleration; *synonyms* (*n*) retardation, slowdown, backwardness, slowing, lag.

afhvarf abstract; *synonyms* (*adj*) theoretical, (*v*) abridge, (*n*) synopsis, abridgement, digest; *antonym* (*adj*) concrete.

afhverfa abstract; *synonyms* (*adj*) theoretical, (*v*) abridge, (*n*) synopsis, abridgement, digest; *antonym* (*adj*) concrete.

afhverfing abstraction; *synonyms* (*n*) abstract, abstractedness, reverie, engrossment, extraction; *antonyms* (*n*) addition, attentiveness.

afhverfur 1. divergent; *synonyms* (*adj*) different, differing, dissimilar, distinct, conflicting; *antonyms* (*adj*) similar, convergent, **2**. abstract; *synonyms* (*adj*) theoretical, (*v*) abridge, (*n*) synopsis, abridgement, digest; *antonym* (*adj*) concrete.

afi grandfather; *synonyms* (*n*) gramps, grandad, granddad, grandpa, grandpapa.

afisingarbúnaður defroster; *synonym* (*n*) deicer.

afkastageta 1. capacity; *synonyms* (*n*) capability, aptitude, capacitance, function, (*adj*) ability; *antonyms* (*n*) inability, incapability, **2**. performance; *synonyms* (*n*) act, discharge, achievement, execution, (*v*) action; *antonyms* (*n*) omission, practice.

afkastamælir dynamometer; *synonyms* (*n*) dynameter, (*v*) bathometer, galvanometer, heliometer, interferometer.

afkastamikill 1. efficient; *synonyms* (*adj*) effectual, competent, effective, able, capable; *antonyms* (*adj*) incompetent, inefficient, **2**. effective; *synonyms* (*adj*) beneficial, practical, efficacious, operative, strong; *antonyms* (*adj*) ineffective, useless, weak, inoperative.

afkóðun decoding; *synonyms* (*n*) decipherment, decryption, translation.

afkoma 1. survival; *synonyms* (*n*) existence, relic, life, endurance, selection; *antonym* (*n*) extinction, **2**. subsistence; *synonyms* (*n*) being, entity, maintenance, food, livelihood, **3**. performance; *synonyms* (*n*) act, discharge, achievement, execution, (*v*) action; *antonyms* (*n*) omission, practice.

afkomandi progeny; *synonyms* (*n*) issue, posterity, breed, child, (*v*) offspring.

afkomendur progeny; *synonyms* (*n*) issue, posterity, breed, child, (*v*) offspring.

afköst 1. throughput; *synonyms* (*n*) bandwidth, offtakes, **2**. power; *synonyms* (*n*) force, ability, potency, (*v*) influence, might; *antonyms* (*n*) powerlessness, helplessness, weakness, **3**. capability; *synonyms* (*n*) capacity, aptitude, capableness, competence, faculty; *antonyms* (*n*) inability, failure, incapability, **4**. capacity; *synonyms* (*n*) capability, capacitance, function, intelligence, talent, **5**. output; *synonyms* (*n*) crop, harvest, turnout, yield, (*v*) outcome.

afkóta decode; *synonyms* (*v*) decipher, crack, interpret, translate, decrypt.

afkótari decoder; *synonym* (*n*) decipherer.

afkrækja unhook; *synonyms* (*v*) liberate, loosen, undo, disengage, unbolt; *antonym* (*v*) hook.

afkúpling decoupling; *synonym* (*n*) uncoupling.

afkvæmi progeny; *synonyms* (*n*) issue, posterity, breed, child, (*v*) offspring.

afkynjun castration; *synonyms* (*n*) emasculation, eviration, bowdlerisation, bowdlerization, expurgation.

afl 1. power; *synonyms* (*n*) force, ability, potency, (*v*) influence, might; *antonyms* (*n*) powerlessness, helplessness, weakness, **2**. watt; *synonyms* (*n*) tungsten, w, west, wolfram, **3**. demand; *synonyms* (*n*) claim, request, (*v*) ask, command, need; *antonym* (*v*) supply, **4**. effect; *synonyms* (*n*) consequence, (*v*) accomplish, achieve, create, cause; *antonym* (*n*) reason, **5**. output; *synonyms* (*n*) crop, harvest, turnout, yield, (*v*) outcome.

afla 1. provide; *synonyms* (*v*) give, contribute, furnish, offer, accommodate, **2**. catch; *synonyms* (*v*) arrest, capture, hook, apprehend, get; *antonym* (*v*) release.

aflaga deform; *synonyms* (*v*) distort, deface, bend, contort, disfigure; *antonym* (*v*) straighten.

aflagaður deformed; *synonyms* (*adj*) crooked, bent, distorted, malformed, misshapen.

aflauki booster; *synonyms* (*n*) admirer, friend, patron, promoter, protagonist.

aflausn 1. acquittal; *synonyms* (*n*) absolution, discharge, acquittment, acquittance, justification; *antonym* (*n*) conviction, **2**. absolution; *synonyms* (*n*) pardon, remission, exemption, exoneration, (*v*) excuse; *antonym* (*n*) blame.

afleggjari cutting; *synonyms* (*adj*) sharp, biting, keen, acute, bitter; *antonyms* (*adj*) blunt, mild, (*n*) extension, freedom.

afleiða derivative; *synonyms* (*adj*) derived, (*n*) derivate, derivation, differential, offshoot; *antonym* (*n*) original.

afleiðandi derivative; *synonyms* (*adj*) derived, (*n*) derivate, derivation, differential, offshoot; *antonym* (*n*) original.

afleiddur derivative; *synonyms* (*adj*) derived, (*n*) derivate, derivation, differential, offshoot; *antonym* (*n*) original.

afleiðing 1. result; *synonyms* (*n*) consequence, fruit, issue, outcome, (*v*) ensue; *antonym* (*v*) cause, **2**. effect; *synonyms* (*v*) accomplish, achieve, create, complete, do; *antonym* (*n*) reason.

afleiðsla 1. deduction; *synonyms* (*n*) allowance, conclusion, discount, abatement, decrease; *antonym* (*n*) addition, **2**. derivation; *synonyms* (*n*) ancestry, origin, birth, cause, derivative.

Afleikur blunder; *synonyms* (*n*) fault, mistake, error, (*v*) stumble, fail.

aflestur 1. playback, **2**. reading; *synonyms* (*n*) recital, learning, construction, interpretation, (*v*) read.

aflétta relieve; *synonyms* (*v*) assuage, comfort, ease, allay, (*n*) alleviate; *antonyms* (*v*) worsen, burden.

aflétting rebound; *synonyms* (*n*) bound, kick, (*v*) bounce, recoil, glance.

afleysingamaður 1. replacement; *synonyms* (*n*) exchange, substitute, alternate, deputy, renewal, **2**. relief; *synonyms* (*n*) comfort, aid, consolation, ease, (*v*) assistance.

aflfræði mechanics; *synonyms* (*n*) mechanism, workings, procedure.

aflfræðilegur 1. dynamic; *synonyms* (*adj*) active, aggressive, dynamical, energetic, forceful; *antonyms* (*adj*) dull, static, **2**. mechanical; *synonyms* (*adj*) automatic, instinctive, unthinking, automated, (*v*) involuntary; *antonym* (*adj*) manual.

aflgeta performance; *synonyms* (*n*) act, discharge, achievement, execution, (*v*) action; *antonyms* (*n*) omission, practice.

aflgjafi propellant; *synonyms* (*n*) propellent, fuel, explosive, (*adj*) propelling, propulsive.

aflhjól pinion; *synonyms* (*n*) feather, pennon, (*v*) fetter, bind, (*adj*) tie.

afli catch; *synonyms* (*v*) arrest, capture, hook, apprehend, get; *antonym* (*v*) release.

aflimun amputation; *synonyms* (*n*) deletion, elimination, exclusion, subtraction, abstraction.

aflmælir 1. wattmeter, **2**. dynamometer; *synonyms* (*n*) dynameter, (*v*) bathometer, galvanometer, heliometer, interferometer.

aflögun 1. strain; *synonyms* (*n*) stress, breed, effort, (*v*) filter, screen; *antonym* (*v*) relax, **2**. distortion; *synonyms* (*n*) aberration, contortion, deformation, misrepresentation, (*adj*) deformity, **3**. deformity; *synonyms* (*n*) defect, disfigurement, malformation, blemish, disfiguration, **4**. deformation; *synonyms* (*n*) strain, distortion, buckle, twist, bend, **5**. dislocation; *synonyms* (*n*) breakdown, interruption, confusion, disruption, luxation.

aflrænn dynamical; *synonyms* (*adj*) dynamic, active.

aflróf spectrum; *synonyms* (*n*) range, gamut, (*v*) anamorphosis, distortion, illusion.

aflskiljun centrifugation; *synonym* (*n*) centrifuging.

aflstýritæki controller; *synonyms* (*n*) administrator, superintendent, accountant, comptroller, control.

aflþörf demand; *synonyms* (*n*) claim, request, (*v*) ask, command, need; *antonym* (*v*) supply.

aflvaxinn athletic; *synonyms* (*adj*) muscular, brawny, gymnastic, robust, strong.

aflvél 1. motor; *synonyms* (*n*) engine, automobile, machine, car, (*v*) drive, **2**. engine; *synonyms* (*n*) locomotive, contrivance, implement, instrument, mechanism.

aflvöxtur athletic; *synonyms* (*adj*) muscular, brawny, gymnastic, robust, strong.

aflyfirfærsla transmission; *synonyms* (*n*) circulation, conveyance, contagion, transfer, broadcast.

aflýsa cancel; *synonyms* (*v*) annul, abrogate, erase, expunge, (*adj*) abolish; *antonym* (*v*) validate.

aflýsing cancellation; *synonyms* (*n*) annulment, abolition, cancel, negation, recall.

afmá obliterate; *synonyms* (*v*) annihilate, erase, efface, eradicate, expunge.

afmæli birthday; *synonyms* (*n*) bicentennial, celebration, bicentenary, bissextile, centenary.

afmælisdagur 1. birthdate, **2**. birthday; *synonyms* (*n*) bicentennial, celebration, bicentenary, bissextile, centenary.

afmagna neutralize; *synonyms* (*v*) counteract, cancel, counterbalance, countervail, neutralise.

afmarka localize; *synonyms* (*v*) lay, localise, place, post, locate.

afmarkaður discrete; *synonyms* (*adj*) separate, distinct, different, detached, diverse.

afmenga decontaminate; *synonyms* (*v*) clean, cleanse, disinfect, purify, sterilize; *antonym* (*v*) contaminate.

afmengun decontamination; *synonyms* (*n*) purification, cleansing, sanitization, distillation, refinement.

afmögnun neutralization; *synonyms* (*n*) neutralisation, counteraction, nullification, annulment, chagrin.

afmörkun 1. trap; *synonyms* (*n*) snare, net, ambush, (*v*) catch, entrap, **2**. cutoff; *synonyms* (*n*) crosscut, shortcut, break, interruption, stop, **3**. demarcation; *synonyms* (*n*) boundary, definition, line, border, partition.

afmótari demodulator; *synonyms* (*n*) detector, demod, sensor.

afmótun demodulation; *synonym* (*n*) detection.

afmyndun 1. skewness; *synonym* (*n*) lopsidedness, **2**. deformation; *synonyms* (*n*) contortion, strain, distortion, buckle, twist, **3**. hypertrophy; *synonym* (*n*) tympany.

afnæma desensitize; *synonyms* (*v*) blunt, desensitise, numb, deaden, drug.

afnæming desensitization; *synonym* (*n*) desensitisation.

afnám 1. removal; *synonyms* (*n*) transfer, dismissal, elimination, exclusion, expulsion; *antonyms* (*n*) addition, insertion, retention, **2**. abolition; *synonyms* (*n*) abolishment, annulment, destruction, ending, annihilation; *antonym* (*n*) reinstatement, **3**. abrogation; *synonyms* (*n*) abolition, repeal, cancellation, desertion, **4**. abolishment, **5**. elimination; *synonyms* (*n*) discharge, excretion, deletion, ejection, (*v*) removal; *antonym* (*n*) establishment.

afnámssinni abolitionist; *synonyms* (*n*) emancipationist, (*adj*) radical.

afneitun 1. abjuration; *synonyms* (*n*) renunciation, withdrawal, abdication, denial, disavowal, **2**. denial; *synonyms* (*n*) negation, abnegation, repulse, no, abjuration; *antonyms* (*n*) acceptance, affirmation, declaration, admission, confession.

afnema 1. abrogate; *synonyms* (*v*) abolish, repeal, rescind, (*adj*) annul, nullify, **2**. abolish; *synonyms* (*v*) abrogate, revoke, cancel, end, eradicate; *antonym* (*v*) establish.

afnotagreiðsla royalty; *synonyms* (*n*) regality, kingship, nobility, loyalty, command.

afoxa reduce; *synonyms* (*v*) lower, pare, abbreviate, curtail, (*adj*) abridge; *antonyms* (*v*) increase, bolster, expand, enlarge, exacerbate.

afoxaður reduced; *synonyms* (*adj*) decreased, abridged, curtailed, miniature, cheap; *antonyms* (*adj*) expensive, complete.

afoxun reduction; *synonyms* (*n*) contraction, decrease, decrement, diminution, rebate; *antonyms* (*n*) increase, growth, intensification, strengthening, expansion.

afræningi predator; *synonyms* (*n*) marauder, vulture, piranha, destroyer, scavenger.

afrakstur 1. return; *synonyms* (*n*) yield, pay, recompense, refund, (*v*) recur; *antonyms* (*n*) departure, abolition, confiscation, recovery, (*v*) keep, **2.** yield; *synonyms* (*n*) produce, return, (*v*) surrender, allow, concede; *antonyms* (*v*) resist, persevere, **3.** harvest; *synonyms* (*n*) crop, fruit, (*v*) gain, gather, glean.

afrán predation; *synonym* (*n*) depredation.

afrek achievement; *synonyms* (*n*) accomplishment, performance, completion, deed, execution; *antonym* (*n*) failure.

afreka achieve; *synonyms* (*v*) accomplish, reach, complete, do, effect; *antonym* (*v*) lose.

afrennsli runoff; *synonyms* (*n*) overflow, overspill, excess, flood, grounds.

afrennslisgat drain; *synonyms* (*n*) ditch, culvert, (*v*) deplete, waste, (*adj*) cloaca; *antonym* (*v*) bolster.

afrennslishraði runoff; *synonyms* (*n*) overflow, overspill, excess, flood, grounds.

afrennslisop drain; *synonyms* (*n*) ditch, culvert, (*v*) deplete, waste, (*adj*) cloaca; *antonym* (*v*) bolster.

afrétting truing; *synonyms* (*n*) dressing, trueing.

afréttur reduced; *synonyms* (*adj*) decreased, abridged, curtailed, miniature, cheap; *antonyms* (*adj*) expensive, complete.

afriða rectify; *synonyms* (*v*) amend, correct, improve, better, adjust.

afriðilhylki tank; *synonyms* (*n*) cistern, reservoir, container, cooler, belly.

afriðill 1. rectifier; *synonym* (*n*) rectificator, **2.** converter; *synonyms* (*n*) convertor, adapter, changer, apostle, missionary.

afriðun rectification; *synonyms* (*n*) correction, amendment, improvement, redress, revision.

afrit 1. replica; *synonyms* (*n*) facsimile, imitation, copy, duplicate, reproduction; *antonyms* (*n*) original, (*adj*) genuine, **2.** duplicate; *synonyms* (*adj*) dual, matching, (*v*) double, twin, (*n*) counterpart, **3.** copy; *synonyms* (*v*) counterfeit, imitate, ape, model, pattern, **4.** backup; *synonyms* (*n*) backing, substitute, surrogate, (*adj*) alternate, spare.

afrita copy; *synonyms* (*n*) imitation, (*v*) counterfeit, imitate, ape, duplicate; *antonym* (*n*) original.

afritun replication; *synonyms* (*n*) rejoinder, repetition, reproduction, replica, answer.

afruglari decoder; *synonym* (*n*) decipherer.

afsakið sorry; *synonyms* (*adj*) pathetic, contrite, paltry, penitent, piteous; *antonym* (*adj*) unrepentant.

afsal 1. waiver; *synonyms* (*n*) release, discharge, renunciation, dismissal, acquittance, **2.** conveyance; *synonyms* (*n*) transport, transfer, vehicle, delivery, (*v*) carriage.

afsalsbréf conveyance; *synonyms* (*n*) transport, transfer, vehicle, delivery, (*v*) carriage.

afseglun demagnetisation; *synonym* (*n*) demagnetization.

afsegulmögnun demagnetisation; *synonym* (*n*) demagnetization.

afsíðis apart; *synonyms* (*adv*) aside, (*adj*) aloof, alone, distant, separate.

afsjálfgun depersonalization; *synonyms* (*n*) depersonalisation, reification.

afskauta depolarize; *synonym* (*v*) depolarise.

afskautun depolarization; *synonym* (*n*) depolarisation.

afskiljun centrifugation; *synonym* (*n*) centrifuging.

afskilyrðing extinction; *synonyms* (*n*) destruction, extermination, end, expiration, (*v*) death; *antonyms* (*n*) survival, preservation.

afskipti intervention; *synonyms* (*n*) intercession, interference, intermediation, (*adj*) mediation, interposition.

afskræming distortion; *synonyms* (*n*) aberration, contortion, deformation, misrepresentation, (*adj*) deformity.

afskráning decoding; *synonyms* (*n*) decipherment, decryption, translation.

afskrifa 1. scratch; *synonyms* (*n*) score, mark, (*v*) graze, notch, rub, **2.** depreciate; *synonyms* (*v*) debase, belittle, decry, deprecate, detract; *antonym* (*v*) appreciate, **3.** amortize; *synonyms* (*v*) amortise, destroy.

afskrift 1. depreciation; *synonyms* (*n*) abatement, detraction, disparagement, derogation, deterioration, **2.** depletion; *synonyms* (*n*) consumption, expenditure, loss, (*adj*) flaccidity, vacancy, **3.** amortization; *synonyms* (*n*) amortisation, payment.

afskurðarflötur chamfer; *synonyms* (*n*) cant, fluting, (*v*) bevel, chase, furrow.

afskurður abscission; *synonyms* (*n*) abscision, apocope, (*v*) rescission, recision.

afsláttarmiði coupon; *synonyms* (*n*) voucher, certificate, order, ticket, debenture.

afsláttur 1. rebate; *synonyms* (*n*) discount, rabbet, deduction, (*v*) refund, abate, **2.** discount; *synonyms* (*n*) rebate, allowance, (*v*) reduce, disregard, ignore; *antonym* (*v*) increase, **3.**

allowance; *synonyms* (*n*) allotment, admission, quota, tolerance, maintenance.

afslöppun 1. relaxation; *synonyms* (*n*) ease, diversion, amusement, pastime, entertainment, **2**. quietude; *synonyms* (*n*) quiet, calmness, quietness, peace, composure.

afsögn resignation; *synonyms* (*n*) capitulation, endurance, patience, renunciation, surrender.

afsönnun falsification; *synonyms* (*n*) fake, falsehood, distortion, deceit, deception.

afsprengi progeny; *synonyms* (*n*) issue, posterity, breed, child, (*v*) offspring.

afstaða 1. attitude; *synonyms* (*n*) position, aspect, posture, behavior, mind, **2**. position; *synonyms* (*n*) place, lay, (*v*) grade, fix, locate, **3**. stance; *synonyms* (*n*) attitude, carriage, manner, pose, bearing, **4**. relation; *synonyms* (*n*) connection, account, narration, recital, affinity, **5**. sentiment; *synonyms* (*n*) idea, emotion, feeling, notion, judgement.

afstæði relativity; *synonyms* (*n*) relationship, perspective, relativeness.

afstæðiskenning relativity; *synonyms* (*n*) relationship, perspective, relativeness.

afstæður relative; *synonyms* (*adj*) related, comparative, proportionate, (*n*) relation, (*v*) kinsman; *antonym* (*adj*) absolute.

afstemming reconciliation; *synonyms* (*n*) accommodation, adjustment, agreement, rapprochement, (*v*) concord.

afsteypa 1. casting; *synonyms* (*n*) cast, molding, pouring, air, appearence, **2**. impression; *synonyms* (*n*) belief, conception, feeling, idea, imprint.

afstöðumælir micrometer; *synonyms* (*n*) micron, megameter, megametre, (*v*) nanometer, centimeter.

afsýra reduce; *synonyms* (*v*) lower, pare, abbreviate, curtail, (*adj*) abridge; *antonyms* (*v*) increase, bolster, expand, enlarge, exacerbate.

afsýrður reduced; *synonyms* (*adj*) decreased, abridged, curtailed, miniature, cheap; *antonyms* (*adj*) expensive, complete.

afsýring reduction; *synonyms* (*n*) contraction, decrease, decrement, diminution, rebate; *antonyms* (*n*) increase, growth, intensification, strengthening, expansion.

afsýrir reductant; *synonym* (*n*) reducer.

aftaka execute; *synonyms* (*v*) do, achieve, complete, perform, accomplish.

aftanívagn trailer; *synonyms* (*n*) caravan, leader, ad, advertisement, announcement.

aftekt denudation; *synonyms* (*n*) exposure, baring, husking, stripping, (*adj*) nudation.

aftenging detachment; *synonyms* (*n*) division, separation, dissociation, corps, indifference; *antonyms* (*n*) involvement, attachment, bias, interest.

aftengja disconnect; *synonyms* (*v*) detach, abstract, disengage, divide, separate; *antonyms* (*v*) connect, attach.

aftengjanlegur detachable; *synonyms* (*adj*) movable, removable, divisible, distinguishable, isolatable; *antonym* (*adj*) inseparable.

aftengsl decoupling; *synonym* (*n*) uncoupling.

afþakka 1. reject; *synonyms* (*v*) refuse, decline, deny, disapprove, (*n*) cull; *antonyms* (*v*) accept, approve, choose, select, acknowledge, **2**. shun; *synonyms* (*v*) avoid, evade, escape, elude, (*adj*) eschew, **3**. dismiss; *synonyms* (*v*) discharge, cashier, cast, disband, discard; *antonyms* (*v*) hire, employ.

afþjappa expand; *synonyms* (*v*) amplify, enlarge, balloon, broaden, develop; *antonyms* (*v*) contract, shorten, abbreviate, decrease, deflate.

afþreying recreation; *synonyms* (*n*) amusement, entertainment, distraction, pastime, play.

aftöppun drain; *synonyms* (*n*) ditch, culvert, (*v*) deplete, waste, (*adj*) cloaca; *antonym* (*v*) bolster.

aftur aft; *synonyms* (*adv*) abaft, astern, behind, after, (*n*) back; *antonym* (*adv*) fore.

afturá astern; *synonyms* (*adv*) abaft, aft, after, (*adj*) backward, back; *antonym* (*adv*) fore.

afturábak reverse; *synonyms* (*adj*) opposite, (*v*) annul, repeal, rescind, (*n*) contrary; *antonym* (*n*) front.

afturbati 1. recovery; *synonyms* (*n*) rally, convalescence, improvement, reclamation, rescue; *antonyms* (*n*) decline, loss, return, **2**. convalescence; *synonyms* (*n*) recovery, recuperation, upturn, illness, progress.

afturbolur abdomen; *synonyms* (*n*) belly, stomach, venter, gut, breadbasket.

afturendi tail; *synonyms* (*n*) rear, shadow, (*v*) follow, pursue, track; *antonyms* (*v*) head, front.

afturhaldssamur reactionary; *synonyms* (*adj*) diehard, (*n*) conservative, reactionist, (*v*) antagonistic, conflicting; *antonyms* (*adj*) liberal, (*n*) activist, progressive, radical.

afturhaldsseggur reactionary; *synonyms* (*adj*) diehard, (*n*) conservative, reactionist, (*v*) antagonistic, conflicting; *antonyms* (*adj*) liberal, (*n*) activist, progressive, radical.

afturhalli rake; *synonyms* (*n*) profligate, (*v*) tilt, hoe, harrow, (*adj*) comb.

afturhluti tail; *synonyms* (*n*) rear, shadow, (*v*) follow, pursue, track; *antonyms* (*v*) head, front.

afturhvarf reversion; *synonyms* (*n*) atavism, relapse, reverse, lapse, regress.

afturhvarfsþörf nostalgia; *synonyms* (*n*) homesickness, longing, wistfulness, craving, hunger.

afturhverfur retrogressive; *synonyms* (*adj*) regressive, retrograde, declining, deteriorating, failing.

afturkalla 1. undo; *synonyms* (*v*) loosen, annul, open, cancel, disentangle; *antonyms* (*v*) fasten, attach, close, do, wrap, **2.** cancel; *synonyms* (*v*) abrogate, erase, expunge, invalidate, (*adj*) abolish; *antonym* (*v*) validate.

afturkast 1. recoil; *synonyms* (*n*) reaction, (*v*) bounce, kick, rebound, bound, **2.** rebound; *synonyms* (*n*) backlash, (*v*) recoil, glance, ricochet, rally.

afturkippur recession; *synonyms* (*n*) decline, depression, fall, niche, recess.

afturköllun 1. undo; *synonyms* (*v*) loosen, annul, open, cancel, disentangle; *antonyms* (*v*) fasten, attach, close, do, wrap, **2.** withdrawal; *synonyms* (*n*) removal, retirement, retreat, secession, departure.

afturkræfur reversible; *synonyms* (*adj*) changeable, bilateral, abrogable, repealable.

afturkvæmur reversible; *synonyms* (*adj*) changeable, bilateral, abrogable, repealable.

afturundan astern; *synonyms* (*adv*) abaft, aft, after, (*adj*) backward, back; *antonym* (*adv*) fore.

afturverkandi retroactive; *synonyms* (*adj*) retrospective, introspective, reflex, (*v*) antagonistic, conflicting.

afturverkun feedback; *synonyms* (*n*) reply, response, reaction, repercussion, (*v*) answer.

afturvirkni feedback; *synonyms* (*n*) reply, response, reaction, repercussion, (*v*) answer.

afturvirkur 1. retrograde; *synonyms* (*v*) recede, retreat, retire, decline, (*adj*) backward, **2.** retroactive; *synonyms* (*adj*) retrospective, introspective, reflex, (*v*) antagonistic, conflicting.

afurð 1. product; *synonyms* (*n*) fruit, output, merchandise, proceeds, (*v*) produce, **2.** output; *synonyms* (*n*) crop, harvest, turnout, yield, (*v*) outcome.

afurðir output; *synonyms* (*n*) crop, harvest, turnout, yield, (*v*) outcome.

afvatna detoxify; *synonym* (*v*) detoxicate.

afvaxta discount; *synonyms* (*n*) deduction, rebate, (*v*) reduce, disregard, ignore; *antonym* (*v*) increase.

afvik anomaly; *synonyms* (*n*) abnormality, aberration, anomalousness, deviation, abnormity.

afvötnun dehydration; *synonyms* (*n*) evaporation, desiccation, drought, dryness, dewatering; *antonym* (*n*) wetness.

afvöxtun discounting; *synonym* (*n*) capitalization.

agða 1. trematode; *synonyms* (*n*) fluke, flue, **2.** fluke; *synonyms* (*n*) chance, luck, trematode, accident, coincidence.

agi discipline; *synonyms* (*v*) control, castigate, chastise, train, chasten.

agn lure; *synonyms* (*n*) allure, bait, (*v*) decoy, entice, bribe.

agnakerfi system; *synonyms* (*n*) method, arrangement, network, organization, plan.

agnhald barb; *synonyms* (*n*) point, arrow, jag, gibe, prickle.

agnúði aerosol; *synonyms* (*n*) spray, atomizer, vaporizer, can.

agnúi barb; *synonyms* (*n*) point, arrow, jag, gibe, prickle.

agúrka cucumber; *synonyms* (*n*) cuke, dollar.

aĵo things; *synonyms* (*n*) gear, stuff, belongings, equipment, garb.

aka 1. taxi; *synonyms* (*n*) cab, hack, taxicab, automobile, cabriolet, **2.** pass; *synonyms* (*v*) flow, deliver, give, (*adj*) go, run; *antonym* (*v*) fail.

akcesora 1. accessory; *synonyms* (*adj*) accessary, (*n*) accomplice, abettor, adjunct, (*v*) ancillary, **2.** accessories; *synonyms* (*n*) fittings, equipment, accompaniments, garnishes, possession.

akcesraĵo accessories; *synonyms* (*n*) fittings, equipment, accompaniments, garnishes, possession.

akiro 1. assets; *synonyms* (*n*) property, belongings, capital, funds, means, **2.** asset; *synonyms* (*n*) advantage, strength, benefit, forte, purchase; *antonyms* (*n*) liability, vice.

akkeri anchor; *synonyms* (*n*) mainstay, (*v*) tie, fasten, secure, (*adj*) refuge.

akkerisrauf hawse; *synonyms* (*n*) hawsehole, hawsepipe.

akkerisvinda 1. windlass; *synonyms* (*n*) winch, hoist, stowce, (*v*) crane, derrick, **2.** capstan; *synonyms* (*n*) cathead, (*v*) windlass.

akstur drive; *synonyms* (*n*) ride, force, campaign, (*v*) push, actuate; *antonyms* (*n*) apathy, inertia.

aksturseiginleikar ride; *synonyms* (*n*) outing, run, lift, (*v*) drive, (*adj*) bestride.

akto records; *synonyms* (*n*) archive, documents, minutes, proceedings, certification.

akurhænsn partridge; *synonyms* (*n*) bobwhite, tinamou.

akurhafri oat; *synonyms* (*n*) ait, eyot.

ala 1. alanine, **2.** labour; *synonyms* (*n*) effort, exertion, (*v*) grind, labor, travail.

alabastur alabaster; *synonyms* (*adj*) alabastrine, chalk, ivory, lily, milk.

albatrosi albatross; *synonyms* (*n*) hindrance, burden, load, weight, debt.

albíni albino; *synonyms* (*n*) blonde, (*v*) blinkard.
albínismi albinism; *synonym* (*n*) albinoism.
albínói albino; *synonyms* (*n*) blonde, (*v*) blinkard.
albúmín 1. albumen; *synonyms* (*n*) albumin, (*adj*) glair, cream, milk, gluten, **2**. albumin; *synonyms* (*n*) albumen, ovalbumin.
alda 1. tide; *synonyms* (*n*) current, flow, stream, course, (*v*) wave, **2**. wave; *synonyms* (*n*) billow, gesture, (*v*) brandish, flap, flutter.
aldabil eon; *synonyms* (*n*) aeon, age, period, era, time.
aldauði extinction; *synonyms* (*n*) destruction, extermination, end, expiration, (*v*) death; *antonyms* (*n*) survival, preservation.
aldin fruit; *synonyms* (*n*) effect, crop, outgrowth, product, (*v*) result.
aldinkjöt 1. pulp; *synonyms* (*n*) flesh, puree, (*v*) mash, grind, squash, **2**. purgative; *synonyms* (*adj*) cathartic, evacuant, (*n*) aperient, physic, (*v*) detergent.
aldinmauk 1. jelly; *synonyms* (*n*) gel, conserve, jam, gelatin, (*v*) jellify, **2**. jam; *synonyms* (*n*) crush, crowd, fix, (*v*) block, cram; *antonym* (*v*) free.
aldinsykur fructose; *synonyms* (*n*) levulose, laevulose.
aldur age; *synonyms* (*n*) period, aeon, day, era, time.
aldursákvörðun dating; *synonym* (*n*) invitation.
aldursgreining dating; *synonym* (*n*) invitation.
aldurshópur cohort; *synonyms* (*n*) group, associate, colleague, friend, follower.
aleinn 1. unaccompanied; *synonyms* (*adj*) lone, solitary, (*adv*) alone, only, solo; *antonym* (*adj*) accompanied, **2**. sole; *synonyms* (*adj*) single, singular, one, exclusive, (*n*) bottom, **3**. single; *synonyms* (*adj*) celibate, odd, particular, distinct, individual; *antonyms* (*adj*) married, double, multiple, **4**. solitary; *synonyms* (*adj*) lonesome, forlorn, lonely, (*n*) hermit, recluse, **5**. alone; *synonyms* (*adv*) solely, apart, entirely, exclusively, individually; *antonym* (*adv*) together.
alfa alpha; *synonyms* (*n*) start, origin, beginning, initial, dawn.
alfalfagras alfalfa; *synonyms* (*n*) lucern, alfilaria, banyan, lamp.
algengi prevalence; *synonyms* (*n*) preponderance, domination, advantage, ascendency, ascendancy.
alger 1. absolute; *synonyms* (*adj*) downright, peremptory, total, unconditional, categorical; *antonyms* (*adj*) partial, qualified, **2**. total; *synonyms* (*adj*) aggregate, complete, (*n*) whole, amount, (*v*) count; *antonym* (*adj*) incomplete, **3**. dead; *synonyms* (*adj*) dull, lifeless, cold, defunct, inanimate; *antonyms* (*adj*) alive, animate, (*n*) living.

algerlega absolutely; *synonyms* (*adv*) surely, utterly, categorically, (*int*) positively, certainly; *antonyms* (*adv*) partially, doubtfully, partly.
algilda generalize; *synonyms* (*v*) generalise, universalize, popularize, extrapolate, derive; *antonym* (*v*) specify.
algildi universal; *synonyms* (*adj*) general, ecumenical, global, common, international; *antonyms* (*adj*) local, specific.
algilding generalization; *synonyms* (*n*) generality, generalisation, induction, idea, abstraction; *antonym* (*n*) detail.
algildishyggja absolutism; *synonyms* (*n*) dictatorship, despotism, tyranny, absoluteness.
algildiskenning absolutism; *synonyms* (*n*) dictatorship, despotism, tyranny, absoluteness.
algildur 1. universal; *synonyms* (*adj*) general, ecumenical, global, common, international; *antonyms* (*adj*) local, specific, **2**. absolute; *synonyms* (*adj*) downright, peremptory, total, unconditional, categorical; *antonyms* (*adj*) partial, qualified.
algjör complete; *synonyms* (*adj*) perfect, absolute, (*v*) accomplish, achieve, close; *antonyms* (*adj*) incomplete, partial, unfinished, abridged, (*v*) neglect.
algóritmi algorithm; *synonyms* (*n*) algorism, discovery, (*v*) dactylonomy, rhabdology.
algrím algorithm; *synonyms* (*n*) algorism, discovery, (*v*) dactylonomy, rhabdology.
alhæfa generalize; *synonyms* (*v*) generalise, universalize, popularize, extrapolate, derive; *antonym* (*v*) specify.
alhæfing 1. generalisation; *synonyms* (*n*) generalization, abstract, abstractedness, abstraction, conveyance, **2**. generalization; *synonyms* (*n*) generality, generalisation, induction, idea, dialectics; *antonym* (*n*) detail.
alhæfur 1. universal; *synonyms* (*adj*) general, ecumenical, global, common, international; *antonyms* (*adj*) local, specific, **2**. general; *synonyms* (*adj*) comprehensive, national, universal, (*v*) customary, frequent; *antonyms* (*adj*) individual, narrow, (*n*) particular.
alháll smooth; *synonyms* (*adj*) easy, calm, level, oily, (*v*) quiet; *antonyms* (*adj*) rough, uneven, abrasive, coarse, crumpled.
alheimur 1. universe; *synonyms* (*n*) nature, creation, world, cosmos, population, **2**. cosmos; *synonyms* (*n*) universe, macrocosm, space.
alhliða 1. universal; *synonyms* (*adj*) general, ecumenical, global, common, international; *antonyms* (*adj*) local, specific, **2**. comprehensive; *synonyms* (*adj*) capacious, broad, extensive,

inclusive, complete; *antonyms* *(adj)* narrow, partial, noncomprehensive, restricted.

aligæs goose; *synonyms* *(n)* cuckoo, fathead, goof, fool, jackass.

aliönd duck; *synonyms* *(v)* dip, douse, plunge, dodge, circumvent.

aljafna identity; *synonyms* *(n)* identicalness, unity, individuality, personality, sameness.

alkalí 1. alkaline; *synonyms* *(adj)* alkalic, alkalizate, caustic, salty, acrid; *antonyms* *(adj)* acidic, amphoteric, 2. alkali; *synonyms* *(n)* base, salt, brine, *(adj)* alkaline, *(v)* apozem.

alkalískur 1. basic; *synonyms* *(adj)* first, cardinal, initial, primary, *(n)* essential; *antonyms* *(adj)* secondary, complex, extra, minor, 2. alkaline; *synonyms* *(adj)* alkalic, alkalizate, caustic, salty, acrid; *antonyms* *(adj)* acidic, amphoteric.

alkan paraffin; *synonyms* *(n)* alkane, spermaceti, *(v)* wax, *(adj)* unreactivity.

alkóhól alcohol; *synonyms* *(n)* drink, juice, intoxicant, drinkable, *(v)* alcoholism.

alkóhólismi alcoholism; *synonyms* *(n)* dipsomania, drunkenness, potomania, boozing, *(v)* alcohol.

alkóhólisti alcoholic; *synonyms* *(adj)* strong, *(n)* drunk, boozer, dipsomaniac, lush; *antonym* *(adj)* soft.

alkvæður universal; *synonyms* *(adj)* general, ecumenical, global, common, international; *antonyms* *(adj)* local, specific.

allegóríkur 1. allegorical; *synonyms* *(adj)* allegoric, figurative, metaphorical, symbolic, parabolic; *antonym* *(adj)* literal, 2. allegoric; *synonym* *(adj)* allegorical.

allsherjaratkvæðagreiðsla referendum; *synonyms* *(n)* vote, ballot, election, poll, initiative.

allsherjarfundur plenum; *synonyms* *(n)* fullness, substantiality, substantialness.

allt all; *synonyms* *(adv)* whole, purely, *(adj)* universal, each, every; *antonyms* *(pron)* none, *(det)* some.

alltaf 1. permanently; *synonyms* *(adv)* forever, constantly, lastingly, continuously, abidingly; *antonyms* *(adv)* temporarily, briefly, 2. perpetually; *synonyms* *(adv)* always, eternally, ever, everlastingly, continually, 3. always; *synonyms* *(adv)* whenever, unceasingly, consistently, *(adj)* still, eternal; *antonyms* *(adv)* never, erratically, 4. invariably; *synonyms* *(adv)* incessantly, uniformly, ceaselessly, endlessly, *(adj)* unfailingly, 5. forever; *synonyms* *(adv)* evermore, interminably, permanently, *(n)* eternity, *(adj)* permanent.

allur all; *synonyms* *(adv)* whole, purely, *(adj)* universal, each, every; *antonyms* *(pron)* none, *(det)* some.

almanak calendar; *synonyms* *(n)* almanac, agenda, schedule, diary, *(v)* list.

almenningsgarður park; *synonyms* *(n)* garden, common, *(v)* deposit, locate, place.

almenningsvagn 1. bus; *synonyms* *(n)* automobile, autobus, car, coach, vehicle, 2. omnibus; *synonyms* *(n)* bus, charabanc, motorbus, collection, anthology.

almenningur public; *synonyms* *(adj)* common, national, overt, civic, *(n)* folk; *antonyms* *(adj)* private, confidential, personal.

almennt general; *synonyms* *(adj)* common, comprehensive, national, *(v)* customary, frequent; *antonyms* *(adj)* specific, individual, narrow, *(n)* particular.

almennur 1. public; *synonyms* *(adj)* common, national, overt, civic, *(n)* folk; *antonyms* *(adj)* private, confidential, personal, 2. universal; *synonyms* *(adj)* general, ecumenical, global, international, worldwide; *antonyms* *(adj)* local, specific, 3. general; *synonyms* *(adj)* comprehensive, universal, *(n)* chief, *(v)* customary, frequent; *antonyms* *(adj)* individual, narrow, *(n)* particular, 4. generic; *synonyms* *(adj)* ordinary, basic, cognate, economy, unadorned.

almiðill multimedia; *synonym* *(n)* disc.

almiðlun multimedia; *synonym* *(n)* disc.

almynd hologram; *synonym* *(n)* holograph.

almyrkvun totality; *synonyms* *(n)* aggregate, entirety, sum, total, whole.

alnet internet; *synonyms* *(n)* cyberspace, internetwork.

alpherbejo alp; *synonyms* *(n)* peak, mountain, bullfinch.

alræði 1. autarchy; *synonyms* *(n)* autarky, autocracy, freedom, independence, liberty, 2. autocracy; *synonyms* *(n)* absolutism, dictatorship, despotism, tyranny, autarchy; *antonym* *(n)* democracy.

alræðishyggja totalitarian; *synonyms* *(adj)* authoritarian, dictatorial, autocratic, despotic, *(n)* autocrat; *antonym* *(adj)* liberal.

alræðissinni absolutist; *synonyms* *(n)* authoritarian, dictator, *(adj)* absolutistic, absolute, arbitrary.

alræðisstjórn 1. absolutism; *synonyms* *(n)* dictatorship, despotism, tyranny, absoluteness, 2. autarchy; *synonyms* *(n)* autarky, autocracy, freedom, independence, liberty, 3. autocracy; *synonyms* *(n)* absolutism, autarchy, autonomy, oppression; *antonym* *(n)* democracy.

alræðisvald sovereignty; *synonyms* *(n)* kingdom, reign, empire, autonomy, dominion.

alrófsmælir bolometer; *synonym* *(n)* barretter.

alsamsettur complete; *synonyms* *(adj)* perfect, absolute, *(v)* accomplish, achieve, close; *antonyms* *(adj)* incomplete, partial, unfinished, abridged, *(v)* neglect.

alsamur identical; *synonyms (adj)* equal, corresponding, uniform, consistent, *(v)* same; *antonyms (adj)* different, incompatible, inconsistent.

alsjálfur absolute; *synonyms (adj)* downright, peremptory, total, unconditional, categorical; *antonyms (adj)* partial, qualified.

alsjálfvirkur automatic; *synonyms (adj)* instinctive, involuntary, automated, mechanical, reflex; *antonyms (adj)* manual, deliberate, voluntary.

alskuggi umbra; *synonyms (n)* shadow, shade, soul, spirit.

alskýja overcast; *synonyms (adj)* cloudy, dark, dim, dull, *(n)* cloud; *antonyms (adj)* bright, sunny.

alskýjað overcast; *synonyms (adj)* cloudy, dark, dim, dull, *(n)* cloud; *antonyms (adj)* bright, sunny.

alskýjaður overcast; *synonyms (adj)* cloudy, dark, dim, dull, *(n)* cloud; *antonyms (adj)* bright, sunny.

altækur 1. universal; *synonyms (adj)* general, ecumenical, global, common, international; *antonyms (adj)* local, specific, **2**. absolute; *synonyms (adj)* downright, peremptory, total, unconditional, categorical; *antonyms (adj)* partial, qualified, **3**. global; *synonyms (adj)* overall, cosmopolitan, universal, worldwide, comprehensive; *antonym (adj)* national.

Alþjóðaheilbrigðismálastofnunin who; *synonyms (pron)* one, *(adj)* which, what.

alþjóðahyggja internationalism; *synonym (n)* internationality.

alþjóðarækni internationalism; *synonym (n)* internationality.

alþjóðlegur 1. universal; *synonyms (adj)* general, ecumenical, global, common, international; *antonyms (adj)* local, specific, **2**. cosmopolitan; *synonyms (adj)* universal, sophisticated, *(n)* cosmopolite; *antonym (adj)* provincial, **3**. international; *synonyms (adj)* worldwide, intercontinental, external, away, broad; *antonyms (adj)* national, insular, **4**. global; *synonyms (adj)* overall, cosmopolitan, comprehensive, earthly, total.

alþýða democracy; *synonyms (n)* commonwealth, commonalty, nation, capitalism, country; *antonyms (n)* despotism, dictatorship, totalitarianism, autocracy, tyranny.

altrödd 1. alto; *synonyms (n)* contralto, countertenor, *(adj)* falsetto, soprano, tenor, **2**. contralto; *synonyms (n)* contratenor, *(adj)* alto.

alúmíníum aluminium; *synonym (n)* aluminum.

alvarlegur 1. serious; *synonyms (adj)* grave, heavy, sedate, austere, *(v)* important; *antonyms (adj)* frivolous, lighthearted, cheerful, flippant,

humorous, **2**. solemn; *synonyms (adj)* serious, earnest, devout, formal, *(v)* sober, **3**. staid; *synonyms (adj)* solemn, calm, quiet, demure, composed, **4**. sober; *synonyms (adj)* sane, moderate, modest, abstemious, dull; *antonym (adj)* intoxicated, **5**. earnest; *synonyms (adj)* eager, ardent, diligent, heartfelt, *(n)* guarantee; *antonyms (adj)* halfhearted, uncertain.

alveldi autarchy; *synonyms (n)* autarky, autocracy, freedom, independence, liberty.

amaba 1. ameba; *synonym (n)* amoeba, **2**. amoeba; *synonyms (n)* ameba, *(adj)* spineless.

amba 1. ameba; *synonym (n)* amoeba, **2**. amoeba; *synonyms (n)* ameba, *(adj)* spineless.

ameríkín americium; *synonym (adj)* am.

ameríkíum americium; *synonym (adj)* am.

amín amine; *synonym (n)* aminoalkane.

amma grandmother; *synonyms (n)* gran, grandma, granny, crone, grandam.

amöbulegur ameboid; *synonym (adj)* amoeboid.

amper 1. amp; *synonyms (n)* ampere, a, amplifier, loudspeaker, speaker, **2**. ampere; *synonyms (n)* amp, angstrom, axerophthol.

ampermælir 1. ammeter, **2**. galvanometer; *synonyms (n)* rheometer, *(v)* bathometer, dynamometer, goniometer, heliometer.

ananas pineapple; *synonyms (n)* ananas, pine, *(v)* chowder, chupatty, clam.

ananasjurt pineapple; *synonyms (n)* ananas, pine, *(v)* chowder, chupatty, clam.

anda breathe; *synonyms (v)* blow, exhale, live, subsist, *(n)* respire.

andagift inspiration; *synonyms (n)* afflatus, infusion, breath, encouragement, *(v)* illumination.

andardráttur 1. breath; *synonyms (n)* spirit, wind, air, inspiration, puff, **2**. respiration; *synonyms (n)* breathing, aspiration, delay, exercising, pause, **3**. aspiration; *synonyms (n)* aim, ambition, longing, ambitiousness, *(v)* desire.

andarteppa asthma; *synonym (n)* anhelation.

andarteppuhósti pertussis; *synonyms (adj)* necrosis, phthisis, pneumonia, psora, pyaemia.

andast die; *synonyms (v)* decease, dead, death, depart, *(n)* dice.

andfélagslegur antisocial; *synonyms (adj)* unfriendly, asocial, misanthropic, cold, hostile; *antonym (adj)* law-abiding.

andheiti antonym; *synonyms (n)* opposite, counterterm, negation, *(v)* compellation, description.

andhverfa 1. reverse; *synonyms (adj)* opposite, *(v)* annul, repeal, rescind, *(n)* contrary; *antonym (n)* front, **2**. anticline, **3**. inverse; *synonyms (adj)* converse, (*n*) contrast, reciprocal, antithesis, (*v*) reverse.

andhverfur inverse; *synonyms* (*adj*) contrary, converse, (*n*) opposite, contrast, (*v*) reverse.

andi 1. spirit; *synonyms* (*n*) apparition, courage, ghost, life, mood; *antonyms* (*n*) lethargy, body, **2.** breath; *synonyms* (*n*) spirit, wind, air, inspiration, puff.

andkafahósti pertussis; *synonyms* (*adj*) necrosis, phthisis, pneumonia, psora, pyaemia.

andkvistur antinode; *synonym* (*n*) loop.

andlag object; *synonyms* (*n*) design, aim, cause, end, (*v*) except; *antonym* (*v*) agree.

andlát death; *synonyms* (*n*) demise, end, expiration, close, exit; *antonyms* (*n*) birth, existence, delivery.

andlegur mental; *synonyms* (*adj*) intellectual, ideal, psychic, subjective, insane; *antonyms* (*adj*) physical, bodily.

andlíf antibiosis; *synonym* (*n*) amensalism.

andlífi antibiosis; *synonym* (*n*) amensalism.

andlit face; *synonyms* (*n*) look, aspect, countenance, (*v*) confront, (*adj*) front; *antonyms* (*v*) avoid, back.

andlitsfall physiognomy; *synonyms* (*n*) countenance, face, kisser, mug, phiz.

andlitsroði flush; *synonyms* (*n*) bloom, (*v*) blush, glow, (*adj*) flat, affluent.

andlitssvipur aspect; *synonyms* (*n*) appearance, look, surface, bearing, expression.

andlyf antagonist; *synonyms* (*n*) opponent, adversary, enemy, foe, rival; *antonym* (*n*) friend.

andmæli protest; *synonyms* (*n*) demonstration, objection, (*v*) dissent, assert, complain; *antonym* (*v*) support.

andnauð dyspnea; *synonyms* (*n*) dyspnoea, anhelation.

andóf 1. reactance, **2.** resistance; *synonyms* (*n*) opposition, endurance, friction, immunity, impedance; *antonyms* (*n*) smoothness, agreement, obedience, susceptibility.

andop spiracle; *synonyms* (*n*) larynx, tonsils, windpipe, (*v*) stigma, brand.

andoxunarefni antioxidant; *synonym* (*n*) antioxygen.

andrá moment; *synonyms* (*n*) importance, consequence, flash, instant, jiffy.

andrafögn positron; *synonyms* (*n*) antielectron, electricity.

andrúmsloft 1. air; *synonyms* (*n*) tune, appearance, manner, (*v*) ventilate, broadcast, **2.** atmosphere; *synonyms* (*n*) air, ambience, ambiance, aura, environment.

andsælis anticlockwise; *synonyms* (*adj*) contraclockwise, (*adv*) counterclockwise; *antonym* (*adv*) clockwise.

andspyrna rebellion; *synonyms* (*n*) insurrection, mutiny, revolt, disobedience, uprising.

andstaða 1. antagonism; *synonyms* (*n*) animosity, enmity, resistance, aggression, antithesis; *antonym* (*n*) friendliness, **2.** opposition; *synonyms* (*n*) contrast, conflict, contrary, contrariety, antagonism; *antonym* (*n*) consent.

Andstæ opposition; *synonyms* (*n*) contrast, conflict, antithesis, contrary, contrariety; *antonym* (*n*) consent.

andstæða 1. reverse; *synonyms* (*adj*) opposite, (*v*) annul, repeal, rescind, (*n*) contrary; *antonym* (*n*) front, **2.** antinomy; *synonyms* (*n*) opposition, (*adj*) despotism, outlawry, violence, **3.** contrast; *synonyms* (*n*) contrariety, antithesis, comparison, distinction, (*v*) differ; *antonym* (*n*) similarity, **4.** opposition; *synonyms* (*n*) contrast, conflict, antagonism, enemy, hostility; *antonym* (*n*) consent, **5.** inverse; *synonyms* (*adj*) converse, (*n*) reciprocal, (*v*) reverse.

andstæði contrast; *synonyms* (*n*) contrariety, antithesis, comparison, distinction, (*v*) differ; *antonym* (*n*) similarity.

andstæður 1. refractory; *synonyms* (*adj*) intractable, disobedient, obstinate, perverse, recalcitrant, **2.** antagonistic; *synonyms* (*adj*) hostile, counter, averse, conflicting, (*v*) adverse; *antonym* (*adj*) friendly, **3.** adverse; *synonyms* (*adj*) contrary, unfavorable, harmful, untoward, adversary; *antonym* (*adj*) favorable, **4.** alien; *synonyms* (*adj*) foreign, strange, unknown, (*n*) foreigner, (*v*) alienate; *antonyms* (*adj*) familiar, (*n*) native, citizen, **5.** contrary; *synonyms* (*adj*) opposite, contradictory, reverse, alien, cross.

andstyggð 1. atrocity; *synonyms* (*n*) enormity, brutality, abomination, atrociousness, (*adj*) outrage, **2.** abomination; *synonyms* (*n*) abhorrence, disgust, atrocity, detestation, execration.

andstyggilegur 1. abominable; *synonyms* (*adj*) hateful, abhorrent, odious, awful, detestable; *antonym* (*adj*) pleasant, **2.** awful; *synonyms* (*adj*) abominable, appalling, awesome, dreadful, fearful; *antonyms* (*adj*) excellent, great, marvelous, wonderful, lovely, **3.** abhorrent; *synonyms* (*adj*) offensive, repulsive, repugnant, horrible, (*v*) execrable, **4.** obnoxious; *synonyms* (*adj*) objectionable, disagreeable, distasteful, liable, (*n*) unpleasant, **5.** loathsome; *synonyms* (*adj*) disgusting, foul, hideous, revolting, despicable.

andsvar response; *synonyms* (*n*) answer, reaction, reception, (*v*) reply, rejoinder.

andþrengsli dyspnea; *synonyms* (*n*) dyspnoea, anhelation.

andvægi counterweight; *synonyms* (*n*)
counterbalance, counterpoise, weight, (*v*) balance,
poise.

andvarpa groan; *synonyms* (*n*) grumble, cry, (*v*)
moan, murmur, howl.

andverkandi antagonistic; *synonyms* (*adj*) hostile,
counter, averse, conflicting, (*v*) adverse; *antonym*
(*adj*) friendly.

andverkun antagonism; *synonyms* (*n*) animosity,
enmity, resistance, aggression, antithesis; *antonym*
(*n*) friendliness.

andvirkni 1. counteraction; *synonyms* (*n*)
neutralization, opposition, reaction, remedy,
resistance, **2.** antagonism; *synonyms* (*n*)
animosity, enmity, aggression, antithesis, aversion;
antonym (*n*) friendliness.

andvökur insomnia; *synonyms* (*n*) sleeplessness,
restlessness, indisposition, insomnolence,
restiveness.

aneksa accessories; *synonyms* (*n*) fittings,
equipment, accompaniments, garnishes,
possession.

angalýja 1. ameba; *synonym* (*n*) amoeba, **2.**
amoeba; *synonyms* (*n*) ameba, (*adj*) spineless.

angan odour; *synonyms* (*n*) fragrance, flavour,
aroma, smell, odor.

angandi aromatic; *synonyms* (*adj*) fragrant, spicy,
balmy, odorous, perfumed; *antonyms* (*adj*) smelly,
unscented, odorless.

angaskot budding; *synonyms* (*adj*) young,
blossoming, emergent, green, juvenile.

angíótensín angiotensin; *synonyms* (*n*) hypertensin,
angiotonin.

angist agony; *synonyms* (*n*) anguish, torture, distress,
misery, suffering.

anilín aniline; *synonyms* (*n*) phenylamine,
aminobenzine, crystalline, kyanol.

anker 1. rotor; *synonyms* (*n*) rotator, stator, **2.**
armature; *synonyms* (*n*) armament, armaments,
skeleton, frame, framework.

ankeri anchor; *synonyms* (*n*) mainstay, (*v*) tie, fasten,
secure, (*adj*) refuge.

annar 1. other; *synonyms* (*adj*) additional, another,
different, extra, further; *antonym* (*adj*) same, **2.**
second; *synonyms* (*n*) instant, moment, flash, jiffy,
(*v*) back; *antonym* (*adj*) first, **3.** different;
synonyms (*adj*) assorted, dissimilar, unusual,
various, alien; *antonyms* (*adj*) similar,
corresponding, equal, identical, like, **4.** else;
synonyms (*adv*) besides, also, moreover, (*adj*) more,
other.

annast support; *synonyms* (*n*) help, stand, aid, keep,
(*v*) assist; *antonyms* (*n*) hindrance, (*v*) oppose,
neglect, undermine, abandon.

annattó annatto; *synonyms* (*n*) minium, realgar.

annmarki 1. fault; *synonyms* (*n*) defect, blemish,
error, failing, (*v*) deficiency; *antonyms* (*n*) merit,
strength, **2.** flaw; *synonyms* (*n*) crevice, fault,
chink, (*adj*) blot, (*v*) crack.

annögl cuticle; *synonyms* (*n*) epidermis, shell,
carapace, case, casing.

annóna cherimoya; *synonym* (*n*) cherimolla.

anóða anode; *synonym* (*n*) zincode.

anorakkur anorak; *synonyms* (*n*) jacket, parka,
windbreaker, windcheater.

antaŭa forwards; *synonyms* (*adv*) ahead, forward,
forth, onward, onwards.

antaŭaĵo antecedent; *synonyms* (*adj*) anterior, (*n*)
ancestor, precedent, forerunner, precursor;
antonyms (*adj*) subsequent, (*n*) descendant,
successor.

antaŭen forwards; *synonyms* (*adv*) ahead, forward,
forth, onward, onwards.

antecedentoj 1. record; *synonyms* (*n*) register, list,
account, (*v*) chronicle, file, **2.** records; *synonyms*
(*n*) archive, documents, minutes, proceedings,
certification.

apalegur simian; *synonyms* (*adj*) apelike, simial, (*n*)
monkey.

api 1. ape; *synonyms* (*n*) anthropoid, (*v*) mimic, mock,
copy, echo, **2.** monkey; *synonyms* (*n*) ape, imp,
primate, (*v*) tinker, meddle.

apótek pharmacy; *synonyms* (*n*) drugstore,
pharmaceutics, dispensatory, medicine, fermacy.

appelsína orange; *synonyms* (*adj*) amber, (*n*)
orangeness, lemon, etc, lime.

apríkósa apricot; *synonyms* (*n*) peach, abricock,
orange, beauty, dish.

ar aerosol; *synonyms* (*n*) spray, atomizer, vaporizer,
can.

arða 1. tubercle; *synonyms* (*n*) nodule, tuberosity,
tuber, distinction, eminence, **2.** particle; *synonyms*
(*n*) molecule, grain, speck, bit, (*adj*) atom.

arðbær economic; *synonyms* (*adj*) commercial,
financial, profitable, efficient, economical.

arðhleðsla payload; *synonyms* (*n*) freight, cargo,
load, consignment, lading.

arðmiði coupon; *synonyms* (*n*) voucher, certificate,
order, ticket, debenture.

arðræna exploit; *synonyms* (*v*) act, (*n*) deed,
achievement, feat, accomplishment.

arðrán exploitation; *synonyms* (*n*) abuse,
development, misuse, employment, operation.

arðsemi profitability; *synonyms* (*n*) profitableness,
abundance, expediency, productivity, success.

arður 1. return; *synonyms* (*n*) yield, pay,
recompense, refund, (*v*) recur; *antonyms* (*n*)
departure, abolition, confiscation, recovery, (*v*)

keep, **2**. yield; *synonyms* (*n*) produce, return, (*v*)
surrender, allow, concede; *antonyms* (*v*) resist,
persevere, **3**. dividend; *synonyms* (*n*) allotment,
bonus, gain, division, (*v*) share.

arfbætandi eugenic; *synonym* (*adj*) genetic.

arfbætur eugenics; *synonym* (*n*) heredity.

arfberi 1. carrier; *synonyms* (*n*) bearer, messenger,
courier, mailman, porter, **2**. gene; *synonyms* (*n*)
chromosome, cistron.

arfgengi 1. heredity; *synonyms* (*n*) ancestry, lineage,
telegony, line, descent, **2**. heritability.

arfgengur hereditary; *synonyms* (*adj*) genetic,
ancestral, familial, heritable, inborn.

arfgjafi donor; *synonyms* (*n*) contributor, giver,
donator, presenter, (*v*) feoffer; *antonyms* (*n*)
receiver, recipient.

arfhreinn homozygous; *synonym* (*adj*) homozygotic.

arfleifð inheritance; *synonyms* (*n*) heritage, heredity,
heirloom, legacy, dowry.

arfskapaður 1. inherent; *synonyms* (*adj*) congenital,
inborn, inbred, intrinsic, essential; *antonym* (*adj*)
superficial, **2**. innate; *synonyms* (*adj*) inherent,
indigenous, instinctive, natural, (*v*) born; *antonym*
(*adj*) learned.

arfskemmandi dysgenic; *synonym* (*adj*) cacogenic.

arfspillandi dysgenic; *synonym* (*adj*) cacogenic.

arfstofn gene; *synonyms* (*n*) chromosome, cistron.

arfþegi recipient; *synonyms* (*n*) beneficiary, receiver,
inheritor, legatee, (*adj*) receptive; *antonym* (*n*)
sender.

arfur inheritance; *synonyms* (*n*) heritage, heredity,
heirloom, legacy, dowry.

arhivo archives; *synonyms* (*n*) archive, record,
records, annals, proceedings.

arkitekt architect; *synonyms* (*n*) creator, designer,
founder, inventor, maker; *antonym* (*n*) destroyer.

armabúnaður linkage; *synonyms* (*n*) link, bond,
connection, association, coupling.

armaturo braces; *synonyms* (*n*) brace, suspenders,
bitstock, ribs, bracing.

armband bracelet; *synonyms* (*n*) bangle, annulus,
circlet, hoop, necklace.

armi arms; *synonyms* (*n*) arm, armament, weaponry,
shield, ordnance.

armur 1. arm; *synonyms* (*n*) branch, wing, bay,
department, (*v*) equip; *antonym* (*v*) disarm, **2**. link;
synonyms (*n*) connection, join, joint, (*v*) combine,
tie; *antonym* (*v*) separate, **3**. lever; *synonyms* (*n*)
knob, (*v*) pry, raise, jimmy, prize.

arómatískur aromatic; *synonyms* (*adj*) fragrant,
spicy, balmy, odorous, perfumed; *antonyms* (*adj*)
smelly, unscented, odorless.

arsen 1. arsenic; *synonym* (*n*) as, **2**. as; *synonyms*
(*conj*) qua, because, (*prep*) during, like, (*n*) arsenic.

arsenik arsenic; *synonym* (*n*) as.

arta acne; *synonyms* (*n*) pimple, whelk, papule, ridge,
wale.

artiskokkur 1. artichoke; *synonym* (*n*) cardoon, **2**.
cardoon; *synonym* (*n*) artichoke.

asatíðir menorrhagia; *synonyms* (*n*)
hypermenorrhea, metrorrhagia.

asbest asbestos; *synonyms* (*n*) asbestus, (*adj*) fireproof.

asetat acetate; *synonym* (*n*) ethanoate.

aseton acetone; *synonym* (*n*) propanone.

asetón acetone; *synonym* (*n*) propanone.

asetýlen acetylene; *synonyms* (*n*) alkyne, ethyne,
ethine.

asetýlkólínseytandi cholinergic; *synonym* (*n*)
cholinomimetic.

asfalt asphalt; *synonyms* (*n*) bitumen, asphaltus, (*v*)
tar, (*adj*) tarmac, flags.

aska 1. ashes; *synonyms* (*n*) dust, cinder, cinders,
remains, clay, **2**. ash; *synonyms* (*n*) jasmine, lilac,
privet, (*v*) scoriae, (*adj*) gray, **3**. cinders; *synonyms*
(*n*) ash, powder, (*adj*) ashes, mother, precipitate.

askgró ascospore; *synonym* (*n*) spore.

askur 1. ascus; *synonym* (*n*) asci, **2**. ash; *synonyms*
(*n*) jasmine, lilac, (*v*) cinder, scoriae, (*adj*) gray.

asma asthma; *synonym* (*n*) anhelation.

asn asparagine; *synonym* (*n*) altheine.

asni 1. ass; *synonyms* (*n*) donkey, arse, anus, bottom,
bum, **2**. donkey; *synonyms* (*n*) burro, ass, fool,
idiot, moke.

asparagín asparagine; *synonym* (*n*) altheine.

astat astatine; *synonym* (*n*) at.

astma asthma; *synonym* (*n*) anhelation.

astmi asthma; *synonym* (*n*) anhelation.

ata soil; *synonyms* (*n*) ground, dirt, (*v*) smudge, blot,
contaminate; *antonym* (*v*) clean.

atburðarás scenario; *synonyms* (*n*) plot, continuity,
chronicle, design, forecast.

atburðarit script; *synonyms* (*n*) calligraphy, hand,
book, handwriting, copy.

atburðasvið 1. setting; *synonyms* (*n*) frame, scene,
adjustment, scenery, backdrop, **2**. stage;
synonyms (*n*) grade, phase, floor, degree, level.

atburður 1. achievement; *synonyms* (*n*)
accomplishment, performance, completion, deed,
execution; *antonym* (*n*) failure, **2**. occurrence;
synonyms (*n*) case, event, occasion, accident, (*v*)
incident, **3**. event; *synonyms* (*n*) affair,
consequence, effect, occurrence, circumstance, **4**.
incident; *synonyms* (*n*) fact, adventure, episode,
experience, happening.

atferði 1. behaviour; *synonyms* (*n*) behavior,
conduct, demeanor, demeanour, deportment, **2**.
behavior; *synonyms* (*n*) bearing, act, behaviour,
carriage, manner.

atferli 1. behaviour; *synonyms* (*n*) behavior, conduct, demeanor, demeanour, deportment, **2**. behavior; *synonyms* (*n*) bearing, act, behaviour, carriage, manner.

atferlisfræði ethology; *synonym* (*n*) ethics.

atferlishamla barrier; *synonyms* (*n*) barricade, bar, bulwark, dam, handicap.

atferliskveikja motive; *synonyms* (*n*) cause, ground, account, impulse, incentive.

atferlisstefna 1. behaviourism; *synonym* (*n*) behaviorism, **2**. behaviorism; *synonym* (*n*) behaviourism.

atferlisvaki motive; *synonyms* (*n*) cause, ground, account, impulse, incentive.

atgervi endowment; *synonyms* (*n*) ability, talent, capacity, (*v*) donation, gift.

athafnamaður entrepreneur; *synonyms* (*n*) contractor, enterpriser, businessperson, tycoon, manufacturer.

athafnasvæði premises; *synonyms* (*n*) grounds, facts, lemma, terms, principle.

athafsnemi 1. vigour; *synonyms* (*n*) force, energy, vigor, vim, push, **2**. activity; *synonyms* (*n*) action, activeness, exercise, liveliness, play; *antonyms* (*n*) inactivity, inaction, inactiveness.

athöfn 1. action; *synonyms* (*n*) act, accomplishment, activity, agency, (*v*) achievement; *antonyms* (*n*) inaction, inactivity, **2**. activity; *synonyms* (*n*) action, activeness, exercise, liveliness, play; *antonym* (*n*) inactiveness, **3**. act; *synonyms* (*n*) move, (*v*) behave, deed, go, perform; *antonym* (*v*) refrain.

athuga 1. check; *synonyms* (*v*) bridle, stop, (*n*) control, arrest, curb, **2**. observe; *synonyms* (*v*) celebrate, comment, notice, commemorate, mind; *antonyms* (*v*) ignore, feel.

athugandi observer; *synonyms* (*n*) beholder, bystander, spectator, witness, eyewitness.

athugasemd 1. remark; *synonyms* (*v*) comment, notice, note, observe, mention, **2**. reminder; *synonyms* (*n*) memento, hint, memorandum, memorial, prompt, **3**. reply; *synonyms* (*n*) answer, echo, return, rejoinder, (*v*) respond; *antonym* (*v*) question, **4**. comment; *synonyms* (*n*) annotation, commentary, (*v*) annotate, remark, gloss, **5**. objection; *synonyms* (*n*) dissent, protest, complaint, exception, grievance.

athugasemdafrestur deadline; *synonyms* (*n*) limit, end, aim, goal, target.

athugun 1. review; *synonyms* (*n*) examination, critique, (*v*) check, survey, criticize, **2**. examination; *synonyms* (*n*) audit, exam, search, test, consideration, **3**. investigation; *synonyms* (*n*) research, analysis, inquest, inquiry, inspection, **4**.

observation; *synonyms* (*n*) comment, observance, remark, attention, (*v*) note.

athygli attention; *synonyms* (*n*) mind, aid, alertness, care, consideration; *antonyms* (*n*) inattention, neglect.

athyglisrof distraction; *synonyms* (*n*) amusement, desperation, beguilement, confusion, disturbance; *antonym* (*n*) fascination.

athyglisvakning arousal; *synonyms* (*n*) awakening, stimulation, inspiration, foreplay, rousing.

atkvæðagreiðsla voting; *synonyms* (*n*) vote, ballot, balloting, poll, election.

atkvæðaseðill 1. vote; *synonyms* (*n*) ballot, election, poll, suffrage, (*v*) voice, **2**. ballot; *synonyms* (*n*) vote, choice, plebiscite, balloting, (*v*) ticket.

atkvæðatalning poll; *synonyms* (*n*) election, head, ballot, vote, (*v*) canvass.

atkvæði vote; *synonyms* (*n*) ballot, election, poll, suffrage, (*v*) voice.

atkvæðisréttur vote; *synonyms* (*n*) ballot, election, poll, suffrage, (*v*) voice.

atlag impulse; *synonyms* (*n*) impetus, pulse, urge, drive, force.

atlaga attack; *synonyms* (*n*) incursion, thrust, (*v*) assault, assail, attempt; *antonyms* (*n*) defense, (*v*) defend, protect, retreat.

atóm atom; *synonyms* (*n*) jot, grain, molecule, particle, speck.

atriði 1. scene; *synonyms* (*n*) aspect, view, background, display, (*v*) prospect, **2**. topic; *synonyms* (*n*) matter, question, subject, theme, affair, **3**. documentary; *synonyms* (*n*) docudrama, infotainment, (*adj*) documental, **4**. item; *synonyms* (*n*) piece, detail, article, entry, object, **5**. event; *synonyms* (*n*) case, consequence, effect, occurrence, circumstance.

atríum atrium; *synonyms* (*n*) hall, vestibule, cavity, court, foyer.

atrópín atropine; *synonym* (*n*) daturine.

atvik 1. episode; *synonyms* (*n*) affair, chapter, event, incident, occurrence, **2**. event; *synonyms* (*n*) case, consequence, effect, circumstance, contingency.

atviksbreyting modification; *synonyms* (*n*) alteration, change, adaptation, variation, adjustment.

atvinna 1. vocation; *synonyms* (*n*) calling, profession, occupation, business, (*v*) employment, **2**. occupation; *synonyms* (*n*) occupancy, craft, job, place, affair; *antonym* (*n*) surrender, **3**. employment; *synonyms* (*n*) trade, use, (*v*) application, employ, (*adj*) work; *antonym* (*n*) unemployment.

atvinnuframi career; *synonyms* (*n*) calling, race, (*adj*) job, (*v*) course, dash.

atvinnugrein industry; *synonyms* (*n*) business, application, diligence, effort, industriousness.

atvinnuleysi 1. unemployment; *synonyms* (*n*) idleness, depression, leisure, recession, redundancy; *antonym* (*n*) employment, **2**. underemployment.

atvinnulíf economy; *synonyms* (*n*) frugality, parsimony, saving, thrift, conservation; *antonym* (*n*) extravagance.

atvinnurekandi employer; *synonyms* (*n*) boss, master, businessperson, patron, capitalist; *antonym* (*n*) employee.

atvinnuvegur industry; *synonyms* (*n*) business, application, diligence, effort, industriousness.

auðfræði economics; *synonyms* (*n*) finance, economy, commerce, money, backing.

auðgun enrichment; *synonyms* (*n*) decoration, embellishment, reinforcement, augmentation, improvement.

auðhringur cartel; *synonyms* (*n*) syndicate, trust, combine, compromise, ring.

auðjöfur capitalist; *synonyms* (*adj*) capitalistic, (*n*) financier, banker, businessman, businessperson; *antonym* (*adj*) collective.

auðkenna 1. highlight; *synonyms* (*v*) emphasize, accentuate, spotlight, underline, accent, **2**. identify; *synonyms* (*v*) distinguish, detect, discover, name, ascertain.

auðkenni 1. symptom; *synonyms* (*n*) sign, indication, evidence, mark, note, **2**. criterion; *synonyms* (*n*) benchmark, measure, norm, test, canon, **3**. identification; *synonyms* (*n*) designation, finding, id, identity, naming.

auðkenning identification; *synonyms* (*n*) designation, finding, id, identity, mark.

auðlegð wealth; *synonyms* (*n*) riches, abundance, affluence, (*v*) money, (*adj*) plenty; *antonyms* (*n*) poverty, penury, scarcity.

auðlind resource; *synonyms* (*n*) expedient, imagination, (*v*) recourse, resort, refuge.

auðmagn capital; *synonyms* (*n*) principal, city, stock, (*adj*) main, primary.

auðmótaður plastic; *synonyms* (*adj*) flexible, ductile, elastic, malleable, (*v*) limber.

auðmýing 1. abjection; *synonyms* (*n*) abasement, degradation, (*adj*) laxity, shuffling, trimming, **2**. abasement; *synonyms* (*n*) abjection, humiliation, depression, deterioration, disgrace, **3**. humiliation; *synonyms* (*n*) chagrin, shame, comedown, discredit, dishonor; *antonym* (*n*) honor.

auðmýkja 1. abase; *synonyms* (*v*) degrade, humble, debase, humiliate, (*n*) disgrace, **2**. humiliate; *synonyms* (*v*) abase, demean, insult, mortify, (*n*) dishonor; *antonym* (*v*) respect.

auðn 1. wilderness; *synonyms* (*n*) desert, wild, wasteland, solitude, (*v*) waste, **2**. desert; *synonyms* (*v*) abandon, escape, defect, (*adj*) barren, desolate; *antonyms* (*n*) bog, (*v*) stay.

auðskilinn 1. transparent; *synonyms* (*adj*) diaphanous, lucid, obvious, plain, (*n*) clear; *antonyms* (*adj*) opaque, solid, **2**. lucid; *synonyms* (*adj*) intelligible, transparent, coherent, limpid, distinct; *antonyms* (*adj*) muddled, unintelligible.

auður 1. wealth; *synonyms* (*n*) riches, abundance, affluence, (*v*) money, (*adj*) plenty; *antonyms* (*n*) poverty, penury, scarcity, **2**. empty; *synonyms* (*adj*) discharge, hollow, destitute, (*v*) drain, clear; *antonyms* (*adj*) full, crowded, meaningful, packed, brimming.

auðvaldssinni capitalist; *synonyms* (*adj*) capitalistic, (*n*) financier, banker, businessman, businessperson; *antonym* (*adj*) collective.

auðvaldsskipulag capitalism; *synonyms* (*n*) democracy, commercialism, competition, entrepreneurship, industrialism; *antonyms* (*n*) collectivism, communism, socialism.

auðveldleiki facility; *synonyms* (*n*) ability, dexterity, adroitness, ease, readiness.

auðveldun facilitation; *synonyms* (*n*) assistance, enhancement.

auga eye; *synonyms* (*v*) behold, see, view, gaze, stare.

augabolti eyeball; *synonym* (*n*) eye.

augabrún eyebrow; *synonyms* (*n*) brow, hair, supercilium, hilltop.

augabrúnahár eyebrow; *synonyms* (*n*) brow, hair, supercilium, hilltop.

augasteinn lens; *synonyms* (*n*) meniscus, (*v*) glass, barometer, especially, glaze.

augljós 1. transparent; *synonyms* (*adj*) diaphanous, lucid, obvious, plain, (*n*) clear; *antonyms* (*adj*) opaque, solid, **2**. explicit; *synonyms* (*adj*) distinct, unmistakable, broad, definite, direct; *antonyms* (*adj*) vague, tacit, understood, unspoken, implicit.

auglýsing 1. commercial; *synonyms* (*adj*) business, mercantile, merchant, (*n*) advertisement, ad; *antonyms* (*adj*) charitable, noncommercial, **2**. announcement; *synonyms* (*n*) annunciation, notice, declaration, communication, proclamation.

augnakarl acetabulum; *synonym* (*n*) acetable.

augnalok eyelid; *synonyms* (*n*) lid, chapeau, palpebra, hat.

augnangur conjunctivitis; *synonym* (*n*) pinkeye.

augnasíld shad; *synonyms* (*n*) herring, anchovies, etc, herrings, sardines.

augndíll stigma; *synonyms* (*n*) spot, blot, brand, stain, blemish.

augngler 1. ocular; *synonyms* (*adj*) visual, optical, ophthalmic, visible, (*n*) eyepiece, **2**. eyepiece; *synonyms* (*n*) ocular, barrel, platform, window.

augnhár 1. cilium; *synonyms* (*n*) eyelash, lash, capillament, hair, pili, **2**. lash; *synonyms* (*v*) whip, beat, flog, chastise, bind.

augnknöttur eyeball; *synonyms* (*n*) orb, (*v*) eye, watch, glance, glimpse.

augnkvef conjunctivitis; *synonym* (*n*) pinkeye.

augnlinsa ocular; *synonyms* (*adj*) visual, optical, ophthalmic, visible, (*n*) eyepiece.

augnsnúningur version; *synonyms* (*n*) reading, translation, construction, interpretation, rendering.

augntin nystagmus; *synonyms* (*n*) blearedness, hemeralopia.

augntinun nystagmus; *synonyms* (*n*) blearedness, hemeralopia.

augntótt orbit; *synonyms* (*n*) circle, cycle, field, orb, area.

augnvindingur torsion; *synonyms* (*n*) contortion, torque, tortuosity, crookedness, deformation.

augsær macroscopic; *synonyms* (*adj*) macroscopical, large, big, bombastic, declamatory.

auka 1. increment; *synonyms* (*n*) addition, gain, increase, accession, boost, **2**. increase; *synonyms* (*v*) advance, accrue, extend, grow, (*adj*) augment; *antonyms* (*n*) reduction, contraction, (*v*) decrease, reduce, diminish, **3**. extra; *synonyms* (*adj*) additional, (*adv*) more, (*n*) supplement, accessory, excess; *antonyms* (*adj*) basic, less, (*n*) lack.

aukabiðdagaþóknun demurrage; *synonym* (*n*) demorage.

aukabreyta parameter; *synonyms* (*n*) argument, guideline, limit, directive, modulus.

aukabúnaður accessories; *synonyms* (*n*) fittings, equipment, accompaniments, garnishes, possession.

aukaefni additive; *synonyms* (*adj*) cumulative, (*n*) addition, adjuvant, admixture, supplement.

aukagjald premium; *synonyms* (*n*) bonus, agio, bounty, payment, extra; *antonym* (*adj*) inferior.

aukahringur epicycle; *synonym* (*n*) epicycloid.

aukalegur redundant; *synonyms* (*adj*) excessive, extra, needless, superfluous, excess; *antonym* (*adj*) necessary.

aukamerking connotation; *synonyms* (*n*) intension, implication, meaning, overtone, consequence.

aukapúls extra; *synonyms* (*adj*) additional, (*adv*) more, (*n*) supplement, accessory, excess; *antonyms* (*adj*) basic, less, (*n*) lack.

aukasól parhelion; *synonyms* (*n*) sundog, parhelium.

aukast increase; *synonyms* (*n*) gain, (*v*) advance, accrue, extend, (*adj*) augment; *antonyms* (*n*)

reduction, contraction, (*v*) decrease, reduce, diminish.

aukatæki accessories; *synonyms* (*n*) fittings, equipment, accompaniments, garnishes, possession.

aukaþóknun 1. premium; *synonyms* (*n*) bonus, agio, bounty, payment, extra; *antonym* (*adj*) inferior, **2**. bonus; *synonyms* (*n*) award, compensation, premium, dividend, gift; *antonym* (*n*) disadvantage.

aukefni additive; *synonyms* (*adj*) cumulative, (*n*) addition, adjuvant, admixture, supplement.

auki 1. appendage; *synonyms* (*n*) addition, accessory, adjunct, appendix, increment, **2**. increment; *synonyms* (*n*) gain, increase, accession, boost, accretion, **3**. neoplasm; *synonyms* (*n*) tumor, tumour, bombast.

aukning 1. augmentation; *synonyms* (*n*) addition, enlargement, aggrandizement, extension, (*v*) increase; *antonym* (*n*) contraction, **2**. increment; *synonyms* (*n*) gain, accession, boost, accretion, development, **3**. growth; *synonyms* (*n*) augmentation, evolution, germination, accumulation, advance; *antonyms* (*n*) decrease, reduction, weakening, decline.

aumur tender; *synonyms* (*adj*) affectionate, painful, (*v*) proffer, (*n*) offer, bid; *antonyms* (*adj*) tough, hard, hardhearted, rubbery, rough.

aur mud; *synonyms* (*n*) dirt, filth, grime, (*adj*) clay, (*v*) mire.

aurbreð mudguard; *synonym* (*n*) splashguard.

aurbretti 1. fender; *synonyms* (*n*) wing, cushion, guard, cowcatcher, (*v*) buffer, **2**. mudguard; *synonym* (*n*) splashguard.

aurburður load; *synonyms* (*n*) charge, cargo, freight, (*v*) burden, fill; *antonym* (*v*) unload.

aurhlíf mudguard; *synonym* (*n*) splashguard.

aurriði trout; *synonyms* (*n*) anchovies, herring, sardines, shad, smelts.

avanulo 1. forwards; *synonyms* (*adv*) ahead, forward, forth, onward, onwards, **2**. forward; *synonyms* (*adj*) bold, audacious, (*v*) advance, expedite, (*phr*) dispatch; *antonyms* (*adv*) backward, (*adj*) shy, posterior.

averaĝa 1. mean; *synonyms* (*v*) intend, design, (*adj*) middle, (*n*) average, contemptible; *antonyms* (*adj*) generous, kind, **2**. means; *synonyms* (*n*) expedient, agency, instrument, assets, capital.

avókadó avocado; *synonyms* (*n*) aguacate, (*v*) atole, banana, barbecue, beefsteak.

ax spike; *synonyms* (*n*) pin, point, barb, ear, (*v*) impale.

Á

á 1. river; *synonyms* (n) creek, flow, current, (v) brook, stream, **2**. at; *synonyms* (prep) in, a, (adv) on, along, (prf) all, **3**. by; *synonyms* (prep) beside, at, of, about, (adv, prep) alongside, **4**. over; *synonyms* (adv) beyond, across, (prep) above, during, (adj) finished, **5**. on; *synonyms* (prep) concerning, by, into, (adj) forward, aboard; *antonym* (adv) off.

áætla 1. plan; *synonyms* (n) aim, map, figure, chart, (v) design, **2**. calculate; *synonyms* (v) count, estimate, account, add, appraise, **3**. approximate; *synonyms* (adj) approximative, near, rough, (v) approach, approaching; *antonyms* (v) exact, precise, **4**. assess; *synonyms* (v) evaluate, appreciate, value, gauge, mark, **5**. estimate; *synonyms* (n) calculation, (v) compute, consider, esteem, guess; *antonym* (v) calculate.

áætlanagerð planning; *synonyms* (n) preparation, calculation, organization, programming, plan.

áætlun 1. project; *synonyms* (n) design, device, (v) plan, hurl, contrive, **2**. strategy; *synonyms* (n) dodge, scheme, strategics, game, (v) tactics, **3**. plan; *synonyms* (n) aim, map, figure, chart, (v) devise, **4**. scheme; *synonyms* (n) contrivance, arrangement, (v) plot, intrigue, conspire, **5**. schedule; *synonyms* (n) list, agenda, catalog, program, (v) register.

áætlunarbifreið coach; *synonyms* (n) trainer, tutor, instructor, teacher, (adj) prime.

áætlunargerð planning; *synonyms* (n) preparation, calculation, organization, programming, plan.

áætlunarleið run; *synonyms* (v) flow, rule, (n) pass, campaign, (adj) stream.

áætlunarskip liner; *synonyms* (n) lining, boat, airliner, craft, ship.

áætlunartala estimator; *synonyms* (n) calculator, appraiser, computer, inspector, figurer.

áalíking atavism; *synonyms* (n) reversion, return, throwback, atavist, backsliding.

áavísi atavism; *synonyms* (n) reversion, return, throwback, atavist, backsliding.

ábati 1. profit; *synonyms* (n) gain, benefit, account, good, (adj) advantage; *antonym* (n) lose, **2**. benefit; *synonyms* (v) aid, assist, profit, avail, help; *antonyms* (n) disadvantage, drawback, loss, (v) harm.

ábeking endorsement; *synonyms* (n) approbation, corroboration, confirmation, sanction, approval.

ábekja endorse; *synonyms* (v) defend, approve, back, certify, confirm; *antonyms* (v) disapprove, oppose.

ábending 1. reminder; *synonyms* (n) memento, note, hint, memorandum, memorial, **2**. indication; *synonyms* (n) clue, evidence, index, designation, direction.

áberandi 1. striking; *synonyms* (adj) impressive, dramatic, outstanding, salient, spectacular; *antonyms* (adj) ugly, ordinary, unimpressive, **2**. prominent; *synonyms* (adj) eminent, notable, noted, great, (v) conspicuous; *antonyms* (adj) inconspicuous, unknown, minor.

ábúandi occupant; *synonyms* (n) inhabitant, resident, tenant, denizen, dweller; *antonym* (n) landlord.

ábúð occupancy; *synonyms* (n) habitation, occupation, inhabitancy, employment, ownership.

ábúðartími lease; *synonyms* (v) hire, rent, charter, let, contract.

áburður 1. fertilizer; *synonyms* (n) dung, compost, manure, muck, droppings, **2**. paste; *synonyms* (n) glue, dough, (v) cement, gum, bond, **3**. liniment; *synonyms* (n) embrocation, ointment, cream, balm, salve.

ábyrgð 1. warranty; *synonyms* (n) guarantee, guaranty, security, warrant, assurance, **2**. responsibility; *synonyms* (n) accountability, duty, care, charge, affair, **3**. security; *synonyms* (n) pledge, protection, safety, hostage, insurance; *antonym* (n) danger, **4**. collateral; *synonyms* (adj) secondary, indirect, oblique, (n) warranty, mortgage, **5**. accountability; *synonyms* (n) blame, liability, fault, obligation, burden.

ábyrgðaraðili principal; *synonyms* (adj) master, cardinal, capital, (n) chief, head; *antonym* (adj) minor.

ábyrgðarmaður security; *synonyms* (n) pledge, protection, safety, hostage, insurance; *antonym* (n) danger.

ábyrgðarskil accountability; *synonyms* (n) blame, liability, fault, duty, obligation.

ábyrgðarskírteini guarantee; *synonyms* (n) bail, assure, guaranty, warranty, assurance.

ábyrgðarskylda accountability; *synonyms* (n) blame, liability, fault, duty, obligation.

ábyrgni accountability; *synonyms* (n) blame, liability, fault, duty, obligation.

ábyrgur 1. responsible; *synonyms* (adj) accountable, reliable, dependable, (v) answerable, liable; *antonyms* (adj) irresponsible, innocent, **2**. liable; *synonyms* (adj) amenable, apt, disposed, exposed, inclined; *antonym* (adj) exempt.

áfall 1. trauma; *synonyms* (n) injury, hurt, wound, shock, harm, **2**. shock; *synonyms* (n) blow, daze, impact, collision, (v) jar; *antonym* (v) comfort, **3**.

concussion; *synonyms* (*n*) clash, crash, jolt, percussion, occursion, **4**. attack; *synonyms* (*n*) incursion, thrust, (*v*) assault, assail, attempt; *antonyms* (*n*) defense, (*v*) defend, protect, retreat.

áfangastaður destination; *synonyms* (*n*) goal, address, haven, doom, destiny.

áfangi 1. stage; *synonyms* (*n*) grade, phase, floor, degree, level, **2**. course; *synonyms* (*n*) stream, flow, bearing, career, (*v*) run, **3**. leg; *synonyms* (*n*) stage, blackleg, branch, peg, post, **4**. event; *synonyms* (*n*) affair, case, consequence, effect, occurrence, **5**. milestone; *synonyms* (*n*) milepost, landmark, event, age, happening.

áfengi alcohol; *synonyms* (*n*) drink, juice, intoxicant, drinkable, (*v*) alcoholism.

áfengissjúklingur alcoholic; *synonyms* (*adj*) strong, (*n*) drunk, boozer, dipsomaniac, lush; *antonym* (*adj*) soft.

áfengissýki alcoholism; *synonyms* (*n*) dipsomania, drunkenness, potomania, boozing, (*v*) alcohol.

áferð 1. texture; *synonyms* (*n*) structure, grain, fabric, constitution, (*v*) finish, **2**. finish; *synonyms* (*v*) end, complete, achieve, (*n*) close, consummate; *antonyms* (*v*) start, begin, continue, (*n*) beginning.

áform scheme; *synonyms* (*n*) contrivance, dodge, (*v*) plan, plot, design.

áforma contemplate; *synonyms* (*v*) consider, cogitate, meditate, muse, speculate.

áfram 1. ahead; *synonyms* (*adv*) before, beforehand, formerly, forward, (*adj*) front; *antonyms* (*adv*) behind, late, **2**. forward; *synonyms* (*adv*) onward, (*adj*) bold, audacious, (*v*) advance, (*phr*) dispatch; *antonyms* (*adv*) backward, (*adj*) shy, posterior.

áframhald restart; *synonyms* (*v*) resume, continue, recommence, renew, (*n*) reboot.

áfrýjun 1. review; *synonyms* (*n*) examination, critique, (*v*) check, survey, criticize, **2**. appeal; *synonyms* (*n*) plea, address, (*v*) charm, request, sue; *antonyms* (*n*) unpleasantness, (*v*) repel.

áfylling refuelling; *synonym* (*n*) fuelling.

áfyllingartrekt funnel; *synonyms* (*n*) chimney, flue, (*v*) channel, move, pipe.

ágeislun 1. insolation; *synonyms* (*n*) siriasis, sunstroke, heliotherapy, **2**. irradiation; *synonyms* (*n*) radiotherapy, beam, radiation, actinotherapy, light.

ágeislunarmagn irradiation; *synonyms* (*n*) radiotherapy, beam, radiation, actinotherapy, light.

ágeislunarstyrkur irradiance; *synonyms* (*n*) irradiation, brilliancy, illumination, intensity, irradiancy.

ágengur 1. progressive; *synonyms* (*adj*) advanced, forward, gradual, active, (*n*) liberal; *antonyms* (*adj*) old-fashioned, traditional, (*n*) conservative, **2**.

invasive; *synonyms* (*adj*) incursive, aggressive, encroaching, invading, hostile.

ágiskun conjecture; *synonyms* (*n*) guess, supposition, assumption, (*v*) suppose, estimate; *antonym* (*n*) fact.

ágóði 1. profit; *synonyms* (*n*) gain, benefit, account, good, (*adj*) advantage; *antonym* (*v*) lose, **2**. earnings; *synonyms* (*n*) profit, salary, income, pay, profits, **3**. gain; *synonyms* (*v*) acquire, derive, attain, catch, (*n*) earnings; *antonym* (*n*) loss.

ágræðsla 1. transplantation; *synonyms* (*n*) transplant, relocation, resettlement, graft, (*v*) transmission, **2**. anchoring; *synonyms* (*n*) anchorage, mooring, gripping, **3**. graft; *synonyms* (*n*) scion, corruption, bribery, bud, (*v*) toil.

ágreiningur 1. dissent; *synonyms* (*n*) disagreement, discord, dissension, difference, (*v*) differ; *antonyms* (*n*) agreement, (*v*) agree, assent, **2**. disagreement; *synonyms* (*n*) discrepancy, conflict, dispute, dissidence, argument; *antonyms* (*n*) accord, harmony, **3**. discord; *synonyms* (*n*) division, variance, clash, contention, (*v*) disagree; *antonym* (*n*) unity, **4**. dissension; *synonyms* (*n*) dissonance, faction, friction, misunderstanding, breach, **5**. conflict; *synonyms* (*n*) combat, fight, battle, contest, encounter; *antonym* (*n*) peace.

ágrip 1. summary; *synonyms* (*n*) abstract, compendium, abridgment, (*adj*) brief, compendious, **2**. abstract; *synonyms* (*adj*) theoretical, (*v*) abridge, (*n*) synopsis, abridgement, digest; *antonym* (*adj*) concrete.

áhætta 1. hazard; *synonyms* (*n*) chance, risk, venture, danger, (*v*) endanger; *antonym* (*n*) safety, **2**. risk; *synonyms* (*n*) hazard, peril, gamble, jeopardy, adventure; *antonym* (*v*) protect, **3**. venture; *synonyms* (*n*) attempt, speculation, enterprise, (*v*) stake, (*adj*) dare.

áhættufyrirtæki venture; *synonyms* (*n*) hazard, (*v*) risk, chance, stake, peril.

áhættuvægi leverage; *synonyms* (*n*) lever, advantage, influence, leveraging, purchase.

áhættuvörn hedge; *synonyms* (*n*) fence, (*v*) dodge, fudge, elude, evade.

áhald instrument; *synonyms* (*n*) channel, deed, agency, apparatus, appliance.

áheit donation; *synonyms* (*n*) contribution, gift, benefaction, present, award.

áhersla stress; *synonyms* (*n*) accent, emphasis, pressure, (*v*) strain, emphasize.

áhersluatviksorð intensifier; *synonym* (*n*) intensive.

áheyrnarfulltrúi observer; *synonyms* (*n*) beholder, bystander, spectator, witness, eyewitness.

áheyrnarfundur hearing; *synonyms* (*n*) audition, earshot, ear, trial, (*adj*) audience; *antonym* (*adj*) deaf.

áhleðsla accretion; *synonyms* (*n*) increment, accumulation, increase, augmentation, accession.

áhöfn 1. crew; *synonyms* (*n*) company, cluster, band, bunch, gang, **2.** complement; *synonyms* (*n*) supplement, accessory, adjunct, balance, extra.

áhrif 1. authority; *synonyms* (*n*) ascendancy, command, sanction, administration, authorization, **2.** effect; *synonyms* (*n*) consequence, (*v*) accomplish, achieve, create, cause; *antonym* (*n*) reason, **3.** impact; *synonyms* (*n*) hit, shock, blow, clash, collision, **4.** influence; *synonyms* (*n*) force, authority, control, (*v*) affect, determine, **5.** intensity; *synonyms* (*n*) forcefulness, depth, volume, fierceness, (*adj*) strength; *antonyms* (*n*) dullness, indifference, weakness.

áhrifamáttur force; *synonyms* (*n*) energy, strength, agency, (*v*) drive, coerce; *antonyms* (*n*) weakness, persuasion.

áhrifaríkur effective; *synonyms* (*adj*) beneficial, practical, (*n*) competent, capable, able; *antonyms* (*adj*) ineffective, useless, weak, inoperative.

áhrifasvæði sphere; *synonyms* (*n*) region, range, area, domain, province.

áhrifasvið sphere; *synonyms* (*n*) region, range, area, domain, province.

áhrifavald authority; *synonyms* (*n*) ascendancy, command, sanction, administration, authorization.

áhrifsbreyting analogy; *synonyms* (*n*) semblance, agreement, correspondence, parity, resemblance; *antonym* (*n*) dissimilarity.

áhugahvöt motive; *synonyms* (*n*) cause, ground, account, impulse, incentive.

áhugalaus tepid; *synonyms* (*adj*) lukewarm, warm, mild, cool, indifferent.

áhugamaður amateur; *synonyms* (*adj*) amateurish, inexpert, unskilled, (*n*) novice, beginner; *antonyms* (*adj*) practiced, (*n*) professional, expert.

áhugi interest; *synonyms* (*n*) concern, advantage, affair, (*v*) engage, care; *antonyms* (*n*) indifference, apathy, (*v*) bore.

ákæra 1. complaint; *synonyms* (*n*) accusation, ailment, charge, affection, disease, **2.** accusation; *synonyms* (*n*) accusal, blame, complaint, allegation, condemnation, **3.** charge; *synonyms* (*n*) burden, care, command, commission, (*v*) accuse; *antonyms* (*v*) request, absolve, retreat, **4.** indictment; *synonyms* (*n*) lawsuit, attack.

ákærandi accuser; *synonyms* (*n*) complainant, informer, plaintiff, accusant, delator.

ákærði 1. defendant; *synonyms* (*n*) accused, litigant, party, plaintiff, prisoner, **2.** accused; *synonyms* (*n*) panel, perpetrator.

ákefð intensity; *synonyms* (*n*) force, forcefulness, depth, volume, (*adj*) strength; *antonyms* (*n*) dullness, indifference, weakness.

ákjósanlegur optimal; *synonyms* (*adj*) optimum, best, finest, ideal, superb.

ákoma accumulation; *synonyms* (*n*) store, stock, accretion, mass, accrual; *antonym* (*n*) shortage.

ákominn acquired; *synonyms* (*v*) acquiring, (*adj*) acquisite, acquisitive, derivative, extrinsic.

ákvæði 1. statute; *synonyms* (*n*) law, ordinance, rule, constitution, decree, **2.** provision; *synonyms* (*n*) arrangement, condition, clause, (*v*) preparation, feed; *antonym* (*n*) lack, **3.** stipulation; *synonyms* (*n*) provision, covenant, proviso, compact, promise, **4.** dependency; *synonyms* (*n*) dependence, addiction, colony, dependance, (*adj*) contingency, **5.** clause; *synonyms* (*n*) article, paragraph, rider, section, (*v*) passage.

ákvæðisvextir coupon; *synonyms* (*n*) voucher, certificate, order, ticket, debenture.

ákvarða 1. establish; *synonyms* (*v*) confirm, erect, prove, appoint, base; *antonyms* (*v*) disprove, abolish, terminate, **2.** evaluate; *synonyms* (*v*) appraise, assess, calculate, gauge, estimate.

ákvarðandi determinant; *synonyms* (*n*) clincher, determiner, (*adj*) crucial, determinative, conclusive.

ákveða 1. determinant; *synonyms* (*n*) clincher, determiner, (*adj*) crucial, determinative, conclusive, **2.** establish; *synonyms* (*v*) confirm, erect, prove, appoint, base; *antonyms* (*v*) disprove, abolish, terminate, **3.** nominate; *synonyms* (*v*) name, constitute, establish, (*n*) designate, call.

ákvörðun 1. determination; *synonyms* (*n*) decision, conclusion, definition, resolution, (*v*) award; *antonyms* (*n*) indecision, weakness, compliance, indecisiveness, **2.** decision; *synonyms* (*n*) determination, sentence, verdict, arbitration, (*v*) judgment.

ákvörðunarstaður destination; *synonyms* (*n*) goal, address, haven, doom, destiny.

ál 1. aluminium; *synonym* (*n*) aluminum, **2.** aluminum; *synonym* (*n*) aluminium.

álag 1. stress; *synonyms* (*n*) accent, emphasis, pressure, (*v*) strain, emphasize, **2.** tax; *synonyms* (*n*) charge, duty, burden, (*v*) assess, task, **3.** spread; *synonyms* (*v*) scatter, reach, disperse, expand, extend; *antonym* (*adj*) concentrated, **4.** strain; *synonyms* (*n*) stress, breed, effort, (*v*) filter, screen; *antonym* (*v*) relax, **5.** surcharge; *synonyms* (*v*) overcharge, overload, drench, fleece, gazump.

álaga 1. charge; *synonyms* (*n*) accusation, burden, care, (*v*) accuse, blame; *antonyms* (*v*) request, absolve, retreat, **2.** levy; *synonyms* (*n*) tax, duty, assessment, (*v*) charge, impose.

álagning 1. margin; *synonyms* (*n*) edge, brink, boundary, hem, (*v*) border; *antonym* (*n*) center, **2.** markup.

álagslaus unloaded; *synonyms* (*adj*) unobstructed, untrammeled, unfraught; *antonym* (*adj*) loaded.

álagsrofi switch; *synonyms* (*n*) cane, (*v*) exchange, change, shift, substitute.

álengd elongation; *synonyms* (*n*) extension, expansion, length, production, annex.

álestur 1. sample; *synonyms* (*n*) example, instance, specimen, model, pattern, **2.** reading; *synonyms* (*n*) recital, learning, construction, interpretation, (*v*) read.

álft swan; *synonyms* (*n*) cygnet, (*v*) ramble, roam, rove, wander.

álfur wizard; *synonyms* (*n*) magician, necromancer, sorcerer, conjuror, (*adj*) adept.

álit 1. opinion; *synonyms* (*n*) judgment, feeling, notion, idea, belief, **2.** report; *synonyms* (*n*) description, gossip, notice, (*v*) account, describe; *antonym* (*n*) fact, **3.** sentiment; *synonyms* (*n*) emotion, mind, judgement, opinion, persuasion, **4.** viewpoint; *synonyms* (*n*) angle, outlook, perspective, position, slant, **5.** stand; *synonyms* (*v*) endure, stall, (*n*) attitude, booth, rack; *antonyms* (*v*) sit, lie.

álitafundur hearing; *synonyms* (*n*) audition, earshot, ear, trial, (*adj*) audience; *antonym* (*adj*) deaf.

álitaþing hearing; *synonyms* (*n*) audition, earshot, ear, trial, (*adj*) audience; *antonym* (*adj*) deaf.

álitsgerð report; *synonyms* (*n*) description, gossip, notice, (*v*) account, describe; *antonym* (*n*) fact.

áll eel; *synonyms* (*n*) yeel, (*v*) labyrinth, maze, serpent.

álma ramus; *synonym* (*n*) ramification.

álögur duties; *synonyms* (*n*) avocation, diversion, pursuits.

áloxíð alumina; *synonyms* (*n*) alumine, (*adj*) argil.

álun proliferation; *synonyms* (*n*) growth, propagation, spread, reproduction, upsurge.

ályktun 1. resolution; *synonyms* (*n*) decision, determination, answer, conclusion, firmness; *antonym* (*n*) indecisiveness, **2.** recommendation; *synonyms* (*n*) praise, commendation, advice, counsel, suggestion, **3.** assumption; *synonyms* (*n*) presumption, supposition, hypothesis, premise, adoption, **4.** deduction; *synonyms* (*n*) allowance, discount, abatement, decrease, rebate; *antonym* (*n*) addition, **5.** conclusion; *synonyms* (*n*) closure, close, end, result, cessation; *antonyms* (*n*) beginning, start, opening, preface.

áminning reminder; *synonyms* (*n*) memento, note, hint, memorandum, memorial.

ánægður 1. satisfied; *synonyms* (*adj*) contented, happy, content, full, pleased; *antonyms* (*adj*) unhappy, frustrated, **2.** pleased; *synonyms* (*adj*) delighted, glad, elated, gratified, joyful; *antonyms* (*adj*) displeased, angry, annoyed, worried, **3.** contented; *synonyms* (*adj*) comfortable, cheerful, quiet, calm, complacent; *antonyms* (*adj*) dissatisfied, discontented, **4.** content; *synonyms* (*n*) capacity, contentment, matter, meaning, (*v*) appease; *antonyms* (*adj*) tormented, rebellious, (*v*) discontent, upset, **5.** gratified; *synonyms* (*adj*) grateful, thankful.

ánægjulegur homy; *synonyms* (*adj*) homelike, homely, homey, plain.

áorkan action; *synonyms* (*n*) act, accomplishment, activity, agency, (*v*) achievement; *antonyms* (*n*) inaction, inactivity.

ár year; *synonyms* (*n*) twelvemonth, day, age, time, yr.

ára halo; *synonyms* (*n*) aureole, aura, glory, halation, ring.

árangursríkur 1. real; *synonyms* (*adj*) genuine, material, physical, true, (*v*) actual; *antonyms* (*adj*) unreal, imaginary, apparent, artificial, (*v*) pretend, **2.** actual; *synonyms* (*adj*) real, absolute, factual, authentic, existent; *antonyms* (*adj*) false, hypothetical, supposed, **3.** effective; *synonyms* (*adj*) beneficial, practical, (*n*) competent, capable, able; *antonyms* (*adj*) ineffective, useless, weak, inoperative.

árás attack; *synonyms* (*n*) incursion, thrust, (*v*) assault, assail, attempt; *antonyms* (*n*) defense, (*v*) defend, protect, retreat.

árásargirni aggression; *synonyms* (*n*) hostility, incursion, offensive, onset, onslaught; *antonym* (*n*) friendliness.

árásargjarn aggressive; *synonyms* (*adj*) belligerent, active, energetic, enterprising, hostile; *antonyms* (*adj*) peaceful, friendly, peaceable, passive, peace-loving.

árásarhvöt aggression; *synonyms* (*n*) hostility, incursion, offensive, onset, onslaught; *antonym* (*n*) friendliness.

áraþollur thole; *synonyms* (*n*) oarlock, rowlock, tholepin, bear, endure.

árátta 1. compulsion; *synonyms* (*n*) coercion, force, constraint, enforcement, pressure, **2.** mania; *synonyms* (*n*) craze, delirium, (*adj*) frenzy, insanity, lunacy.

áraun 1. strain; *synonyms* (*n*) stress, breed, effort, (*v*) filter, screen; *antonym* (*v*) relax, **2.** load; *synonyms* (*n*) charge, cargo, freight, (*v*) burden, fill; *antonym* (*v*) unload.

árbreiða lake; *synonyms* (*n*) loch, pond, pool, puddle, carmine.

árbugða meander; *synonyms* (*n*) turn, (*v*) wind, bend, curve, wander.

áreiðanlegur 1. reliable; *synonyms* (*adj*) good, firm, honest, authentic, (*v*) trustworthy; *antonyms* (*adj*) unreliable, fallacious, inconsistent, **2.** dependable; *synonyms* (*adj*) reliable, steady, authoritative, credible, certain; *antonyms* (*adj*) changeable, irresponsible, undependable, **3**. safe; *synonyms* (*adj*) secure, cautious, dependable, harmless, (*n*) closet; *antonyms* (*adj*) dangerous, unsafe, hurt, risky, unprotected, **4**. trustworthy; *synonyms* (*adj*) trusty, safe, true, faithful, sound; *antonyms* (*adj*) dubious, suspect, untrustworthy, **5**. responsible; *synonyms* (*adj*) accountable, amenable, culpable, (*v*) answerable, liable; *antonym* (*adj*) innocent.

áreiðanleiki 1. reliability; *synonyms* (*n*) dependability, dependableness, fidelity, loyalty, responsibility; *antonyms* (*n*) unreliability, dishonesty, fallibility, lateness, **2**. accuracy; *synonyms* (*n*) precision, truth, exactitude, exactness, reliability; *antonyms* (*n*) inaccuracy, vagueness, imprecision.

áreita stimulate; *synonyms* (*v*) excite, incite, arouse, encourage, (*adj*) quicken; *antonym* (*v*) defuse.

áreitaval selectivity; *synonym* (*n*) specificity.

áreiti stimulus; *synonyms* (*n*) incentive, encouragement, provocation, spur, motivation.

áreiting stimulation; *synonyms* (*n*) excitation, incentive, arousal, encouragement, excitement.

áreitni aggression; *synonyms* (*n*) hostility, incursion, offensive, onset, onslaught; *antonym* (*n*) friendliness.

árekstur 1. crash; *synonyms* (*n*) clash, collision, smash, (*v*) bang, collapse, **2**. blow; *synonyms* (*n*) beat, blast, knock, (*v*) puff, (*adj*) gasp; *antonyms* (*v*) calm, save, **3**. collision; *synonyms* (*n*) clashing, conflict, crash, hit, accident, **4**. impact; *synonyms* (*n*) shock, blow, force, (*v*) affect, contact.

áreynsla strain; *synonyms* (*n*) stress, breed, effort, (*v*) filter, screen; *antonym* (*v*) relax.

árfarvegur bed; *synonyms* (*n*) couch, layer, base, basis, berth.

árframburður silt; *synonyms* (*n*) sediment, deposit, (*adj*) mire, mud, alluvium.

árgreiðsla annuity; *synonyms* (*n*) allowance, pension, rente, revenue, payment.

árhólmar delta; *synonyms* (*n*) chersonese, continent, inlet, mainland, mouth.

áriðill 1. inverter, **2**. oscillator; *synonym* (*n*) exciter.

áritun 1. rating; *synonyms* (*n*) assessment, mark, evaluation, appraisal, estimate, **2**. endorsement; *synonyms* (*n*) approbation, corroboration, confirmation, sanction, approval.

árlegur annual; *synonyms* (*adj*) yearly, annuary, (*n*) almanac, yearbook, ephemeris.

ármót 1. confluence; *synonyms* (*n*) concourse, meeting, concurrence, junction, assembly; *antonym* (*n*) divergence, **2**. junction; *synonyms* (*n*) confluence, joint, connection, interchange, articulation.

ármynni 1. mouth (munnur); *synonyms* (*n*) jaw, lip, aperture, lips, (*v*) grimace, **2**. estuary; *synonyms* (*n*) bay, inlet, mouth, bight, cove.

áróður propaganda; *synonyms* (*n*) promotion, information, publicity, advertisement, (*v*) propagandism.

árós estuary; *synonyms* (*n*) bay, inlet, mouth, bight, cove.

árset alluvium; *synonyms* (*n*) alluvion, deposit, flood, inundation, (*adj*) slime.

ársfjórðungur quarter; *synonyms* (*n*) area, part, district, division, (*v*) place.

árstíð season; *synonyms* (*prep*) period, (*v*) flavor, mature, (*adj*) harden, habituate.

árupptök 1. headwaters, **2**. head; *synonyms* (*n*) chief, captain, front, point, boss; *antonyms* (*n*) end, subordinate, (*v*) follow.

árvakur vigilant; *synonyms* (*adj*) alert, attentive, observant, watchful, cautious; *antonym* (*adj*) inattentive.

árvekni vigilance; *synonyms* (*n*) care, alertness, caution, attention, prudence; *antonym* (*n*) carelessness.

ás 1. axis; *synonyms* (*n*) axle, pivot, hinge, center, hub, **2**. axle; *synonyms* (*n*) axis, bobbin, beam, pin, stalk, **3**. spindle; *synonyms* (*n*) mandrel, arbor, mandril, bolt, arbour, **4**. shaft; *synonyms* (*n*) arrow, handle, pit, dart, pillar, **5**. ridge; *synonyms* (*n*) crest, ledge, bank, hill, shelf.

ásælni affinity; *synonyms* (*n*) sympathy, analogy, alliance, bond, kindred.

ásæta epiphyte; *synonyms* (*n*) aerophyte, superplant.

ásaka 1. allege; *synonyms* (*v*) affirm, maintain, plead, say, (*n*) advance; *antonym* (*v*) deny, **2**. charge; *synonyms* (*n*) accusation, burden, care, (*v*) accuse, blame; *antonyms* (*v*) request, absolve, retreat, **3**. accuse; *synonyms* (*v*) impeach, charge, incriminate, arraign, criminate.

ásetningsatferli action; *synonyms* (*n*) act, accomplishment, activity, agency, (*v*) achievement; *antonyms* (*n*) inaction, inactivity.

ásfrálægur abaxial; *synonyms* (*adj*) abaxile, dorsal.

áshorn anomaly; *synonyms* (*n*) abnormality, aberration, anomalousness, deviation, abnormity.

áskapaður congenital; *synonyms* (*adj*) innate, inborn, inherent, natural, indigenous.

áskrifandi subscriber; *synonyms* (*n*) contributor, donor, reader, endorser, ratifier.

áskrift subscription; *synonyms* (*n*) contribution, donation, offering, (*v*) allowance, subsidy.

áskyn awareness; *synonyms* (*n*) consciousness, appreciation, knowledge, perception, sensation; *antonym* (*n*) ignorance.

áslægur axial; *synonyms* (*adj*) axile, central, focal, umbilical, azygous.

ásökun 1. charge; *synonyms* (*n*) accusation, burden, care, (*v*) accuse, blame; *antonyms* (*v*) request, absolve, retreat, **2**. accusal, **3**. allegation; *synonyms* (*n*) statement, plea, allegement, (*v*) charge, affirmation, **4**. complaint; *synonyms* (*n*) ailment, affection, disease, disorder, ill, **5**. blame; *synonyms* (*v*) arraign, censure, reprimand, reproach, (*n*) attack; *antonyms* (*v*) pardon, praise.

ássnið intercept; *synonyms* (*v*) arrest, block, break, check, waylay.

ást 1. love; *synonyms* (*n*) desire, affection, dear, (*v*) cherish, enjoy; *antonyms* (*n*) abhorrence, hatred, (*v*) hate, dislike, abhor, **2**. affection; *synonyms* (*n*) affect, charity, attachment, fondness, affectionateness.

ástæða reason; *synonyms* (*n*) mind, account, intellect, occasion, (*v*) cause.

ástalyf aphrodisiac; *synonyms* (*adj*) amorous, aphrodisiacal, erotic, sexy, venereal.

ástand 1. state; *synonyms* (*n*) nation, position, say, country, (*v*) declare; *antonyms* (*v*) deny, (*adj*) private, **2**. status; *synonyms* (*n*) rank, situation, caste, (*adj*) place, standing, **3**. condition; *synonyms* (*n*) circumstance, provision, status, attitude, (*v*) aspect.

ástandsbreyting transition; *synonyms* (*n*) change, passage, transit, alteration, changeover.

ástandslýsing scenario; *synonyms* (*n*) plot, continuity, chronicle, design, forecast.

ástaræði erotomania; *synonym* (*n*) eroticomania.

ásþétti seal; *synonyms* (*n*) mark, stamp, cachet, (*v*) plug, bar; *antonyms* (*v*) open, unseal.

Ástralíusvertingi aborigine; *synonyms* (*n*) aboriginal, native, cannibal, citizen, inhabitant.

ástúð affection; *synonyms* (*n*) affect, charity, attachment, fondness, affectionateness; *antonym* (*n*) hatred.

ástunga puncture; *synonyms* (*n*) prick, cut, hole, (*v*) bore, drill; *antonym* (*v*) inflate.

ásvelging aspiration; *synonyms* (*n*) aim, ambition, longing, ambitiousness, (*v*) desire.

ásvelta precession; *synonyms* (*n*) precedence, antecedence, antecedency, anteriority, precedency.

ásýnd 1. projection; *synonyms* (*n*) bulge, hump, jut, prominence, protuberance, **2**. phase; *synonyms* (*n*)

aspect, stage, facet, chapter, grade, **3**. state; *synonyms* (*n*) nation, position, say, country, (*v*) declare; *antonyms* (*v*) deny, (*adj*) private, **4**. aspect; *synonyms* (*n*) appearance, look, surface, bearing, expression, **5**. facies.

át 1. predation; *synonym* (*n*) depredation, **2**. corrosion; *synonyms* (*n*) erosion, corroding, decay, deterioration, canker, **3**. ingestion; *synonyms* (*n*) consumption, absorption, intake, drinking, eating.

áta 1. corrosion; *synonyms* (*n*) erosion, corroding, decay, deterioration, canker, **2**. krill.

átak 1. action; *synonyms* (*n*) act, accomplishment, activity, agency, (*v*) achievement; *antonyms* (*n*) inaction, inactivity, **2**. exertion; *synonyms* (*n*) effort, application, exercise, attempt, endeavor, **3**. force; *synonyms* (*n*) energy, strength, (*v*) drive, coerce, pressure; *antonyms* (*n*) weakness, persuasion.

átaksmælir dynamometer; *synonyms* (*n*) dynameter, (*v*) bathometer, galvanometer, heliometer, interferometer.

átelja 1. rebuke; *synonyms* (*n*) blame, rebuff, (*v*) censure, reprimand, chide; *antonyms* (*v*) praise, commend, compliment, **2**. upbraid; *synonyms* (*v*) reproach, rebuke, scold, condemn, berate, **3**. reprove; *synonyms* (*v*) admonish, lecture, accuse, castigate, criticize, **4**. scold; *synonyms* (*v*) abuse, rail, grouch, grumble, (*n*) nag, **5**. reprimand; *synonyms* (*n*) admonition, chastisement, reproof, castigation, (*v*) chastise.

átfrekur voracious; *synonyms* (*adj*) greedy, gluttonous, hungry, rapacious, ravenous.

átfrumnakerfi res; *synonyms* (*n*) resolution, point.

áþreifanlegur tactile; *synonyms* (*adj*) tangible, haptic, tactual, palpable, evident.

átköst bulimia; *synonyms* (*n*) phagedena, bulimy.

átök conflict; *synonyms* (*n*) clash, combat, fight, battle, contention; *antonyms* (*n*) agreement, accord, harmony, peace, (*v*) agree.

átölur 1. reprimand; *synonyms* (*n*) blame, (*v*) rebuke, censure, chide, lecture; *antonyms* (*v*) praise, commend, **2**. reproach; *synonyms* (*n*) charge, abuse, disgrace, (*v*) accuse, reprimand, **3**. rebuke; *synonyms* (*n*) rebuff, reproach, admonition, (*v*) berate, castigate; *antonym* (*v*) compliment, **4**. criticism; *synonyms* (*n*) critique, commentary, review, animadversion, attack; *antonyms* (*n*) approval, admiration.

átt 1. bearing; *synonyms* (*n*) carriage, demeanor, appearance, approach, aspect, **2**. direction; *synonyms* (*n*) administration, conduct, bearing, command, course.

átta eight; *synonyms* (*n*) eighter, eleven, ace, jack, king.

áttarhorn azimuth; *synonym* (*v*) rhumb.

áttastrik point; *synonyms* (*n*) place, grade, peak, nib, (*v*) head.

áttatíu eighty; *synonym* (*n*) fourscore.

áttavísun compass; *synonyms* (*n*) range, scope, area, circle, (*v*) round.

áttavitaskekkja deviation; *synonyms* (*n*) aberration, change, deflection, difference, diversion; *antonym* (*n*) normality.

áttaviti compass; *synonyms* (*n*) range, scope, area, circle, (*v*) round.

átthagabönd localism; *synonyms* (*n*) provincialism, sectionalism, dialect, regionalism, barbarism.

átthyrndur octagonal; *synonyms* (*adj*) octangular, octogonal.

átthyrningur octagon; *synonyms* (*n*) heptagon, hexagon, oxygon, pentagon, polygon.

átthyrnt octagonal; *synonyms* (*adj*) octangular, octogonal.

áttstig octet; *synonyms* (*n*) octette, eight, eighter, eightsome, octad.

áttun orientation; *synonyms* (*n*) bearing, direction, adjustment, course, introduction.

áttund octet; *synonyms* (*n*) octette, eight, eighter, eightsome, octad.

átudrep gangrene; *synonyms* (*n*) mortification, necrosis, (*v*) chagrin, (*adj*) corruption, caries.

átumein cancer; *synonyms* (*n*) canker, tumor, growth, blight, corruption.

átvilla pica; *synonyms* (*n*) em, geophagia, geophagy, magpies, mut.

áunninn acquired; *synonyms* (*v*) acquiring, (*adj*) acquisite, acquisitive, derivative, extrinsic.

ávala dome; *synonyms* (*n*) cupola, arch, roof, cover, bean.

ávali 1. curvature; *synonyms* (*n*) bend, curve, arch, bow, crook, **2**. convexity; *synonyms* (*n*) bulge, convexness, convexedness, hump, roundness.

ávallt 1. permanently; *synonyms* (*adv*) forever, constantly, lastingly, continuously, abidingly; *antonyms* (*adv*) temporarily, briefly, **2**. perpetually; *synonyms* (*adv*) always, eternally, ever, everlastingly, continually, **3**. always; *synonyms* (*adv*) whenever, unceasingly, consistently, (*adj*) still, eternal; *antonyms* (*adv*) never, erratically, **4**. ever; *synonyms* (*adv*) e'er, perpetually, **5**. invariably; *synonyms* (*adv*) incessantly, uniformly, ceaselessly, endlessly, (*adj*) unfailingly.

ávalur 1. round; *synonyms* (*adv*) about, (*adj*) circular, (*n*) circle, bout, ring; *antonyms* (*adj*) slim, sharp, **2**. convex; *synonyms* (*adj*) bulging, gibbous, biconvex, hunched, (*n*) crescent; *antonym* (*adj*) concave.

ávanabinding addiction; *synonyms* (*n*) dependence, dependency, devotion, habit, enslavement.

ávanaefni dope; *synonyms* (*n*) dolt, boob, booby, ass, (*v*) drug.

ávanasýki addiction; *synonyms* (*n*) dependence, dependency, devotion, habit, enslavement.

ávani habituation; *synonyms* (*n*) adaptation, addiction, accustomedness, assuefaction, conditioning.

ávaxtasykur fructose; *synonyms* (*n*) levulose, laevulose.

áveita irrigation; *synonyms* (*v*) affusion, humectation, immersion, infiltration, spargefaction.

áverki 1. trauma; *synonyms* (*n*) injury, hurt, wound, shock, harm, **2**. injury; *synonyms* (*n*) disadvantage, disservice, grievance, damage, detriment; *antonyms* (*n*) ability, reparation, **3**. insult; *synonyms* (*n*) dishonor, abuse, affront, contumely, (*v*) flout; *antonyms* (*v*) compliment, praise.

ávinningur benefit; *synonyms* (*n*) advantage, (*v*) aid, assist, profit, avail; *antonyms* (*n*) disadvantage, drawback, loss, (*v*) harm.

ávirkur effective; *synonyms* (*adj*) beneficial, practical, (*n*) competent, capable, able; *antonyms* (*adj*) ineffective, useless, weak, inoperative.

ávísun 1. voucher; *synonyms* (*n*) certificate, coupon, receipt, ticket, warrant, **2**. check; *synonyms* (*v*) bridle, stop, (*n*) control, arrest, curb.

ávöxtun yield; *synonyms* (*n*) produce, return, (*v*) surrender, allow, concede; *antonyms* (*v*) resist, persevere.

ávöxtur fruit; *synonyms* (*n*) effect, crop, outgrowth, product, (*v*) result.

Æ

æð 1. vessel; *synonyms* (*n*) ship, boat, container, craft, duct, **2**. vein; *synonyms* (*n*) streak, vena, (*adj*) humor, mood, strip, **3**. nerve; *synonyms* (*n*) audacity, cheek, impertinence, boldness, brass; *antonym* (*n*) cowardice.

æðaband ligature; *synonyms* (*n*) binder, ligament, (*v*) bond, tie, knot.

æðahnútur varix; *synonyms* (*n*) varicosity, varices.

æðarsláttur pulse; *synonyms* (*n*) beat, impulse, pulsation, (*v*) pulsate, throb.

æðasamdráttur vasoconstriction; *synonym* (*n*) angiohypertonia.

æðasegamyndun thrombosis; *synonym* (*n*) apoplexy.

æðasegi thrombus; *synonym* (*n*) clot.

æðasetning venation; *synonym* (*v*) venery.

æðaskipan venation; *synonym* (*v*) venery.

æðaskurður venesection; *synonyms* (*n*) bloodletting, phlebotomy, bleeding.

æðasláttur pulse; *synonyms* (*n*) beat, impulse, pulsation, (*v*) pulsate, throb.

æðaþrenging vasoconstriction; *synonym* (*n*) angiohypertonia.

æðavíkkandi vasodilator; *synonym* (*n*) vasodilative.

æðavíkkari vasodilator; *synonym* (*n*) vasodilative.

æðhnoðri glomerulus; *synonym* (*n*) glomerule.

æði 1. so; *synonyms* (*adv*) accordingly, as, consequently, hence, (*pron*) that, **2.** personality; *synonyms* (*n*) individuality, person, celebrity, character, identity; *antonym* (*n*) nobody, **3.** very; *synonyms* (*adv*) extremely, greatly, highly, (*adj*) much, identical; *antonyms* (*adv*) abysmally, slightly, somewhat, **4.** quite; *synonyms* (*adv*) altogether, absolutely, all, completely, entirely, **5.** really; *synonyms* (*adv*) actually, honestly, genuinely, certainly, (*adj*) indeed.

æðisgerðir psychokinesis; *synonym* (*n*) telekinesis.

æðstur sovereign; *synonyms* (*adj*) independent, autonomous, (*n*) monarch, ruler, king; *antonym* (*adj*) dependent.

æfi life; *synonyms* (*n*) animation, energy, spirit, activity, being; *antonym* (*n*) lethargy.

æfing 1. training; *synonyms* (*n*) education, instruction, breeding, practice, preparation, **2.** practice; *synonyms* (*n*) exercise, fashion, convention, (*v*) custom, drill; *antonym* (*n*) performance, **3.** exercise; *synonyms* (*n*) employment, application, (*v*) apply, employ, use.

æfinlegur 1. perpetual; *synonyms* (*adj*) permanent, incessant, ceaseless, constant, continual; *antonyms* (*adj*) temporary, intermittent, **2.** eternal; *synonyms* (*adj*) endless, perpetual, everlasting, lasting, aeonian; *antonyms* (*adj*) mortal, short-lived, finite, **3.** everlasting; *synonyms* (*adj*) eternal, immortal, deathless, ageless, continuous.

æfisaga biography; *synonyms* (*n*) autobiography, history, life, memoirs, memoir.

æki rig; *synonyms* (*n*) array, outfit, (*v*) dress, apparel, attire.

æla vomit; *synonyms* (*v*) spew, heave, puke, cast, disgorge.

æluböggull pellet; *synonyms* (*n*) shot, granule, bead, (*v*) ball, (*adj*) spherule.

ær manic; *synonyms* (*adj*) frenzied, frantic, wild, crazy, demented; *antonym* (*adj*) calm.

ærumeiðing 1. slander; *synonyms* (*n*) insult, scandal, (*v*) libel, defame, (*adj*) abuse; *antonym* (*v*) praise, **2.**
insult; *synonyms* (*n*) dishonor, affront, contumely, disgrace, (*v*) flout; *antonym* (*v*) compliment.

æsing agitation; *synonyms* (*n*) disturbance, excitement, tumult, commotion, convulsion; *antonyms* (*n*) calmness, calm, serenity.

æska 1. youth; *synonyms* (*n*) boy, juvenile, lad, young, (*adj*) adolescent; *antonyms* (*n*) adulthood, adult, ripeness, **2.** adolescence; *synonyms* (*n*) immaturity, boyhood, juvenility, puberty, youth.

æstæður stationary; *synonyms* (*adj*) immovable, fixed, motionless, immobile, static; *antonym* (*adj*) moving.

æstur agitated; *synonyms* (*adj*) restless, excited, nervous, restive, tumultuous; *antonyms* (*adj*) calm, composed, lethargic.

æta 1. corrode; *synonyms* (*v*) canker, consume, eat, gnaw, erode, **2.** etch; *synonyms* (*v*) engrave, carve, cut, inscribe, bite.

ætandi corrosive; *synonyms* (*adj*) caustic, acid, acrid, erosive, biting.

æti medium; *synonyms* (*adj*) intermediate, (*n*) average, mediocre, mean, atmosphere.

ætíð 1. perpetually; *synonyms* (*adv*) forever, always, constantly, eternally, ever, **2.** permanently; *synonyms* (*adv*) lastingly, continuously, abidingly, enduringly, fatally; *antonyms* (*adv*) temporarily, briefly, **3.** always; *synonyms* (*adv*) whenever, unceasingly, consistently, (*adj*) still, eternal; *antonyms* (*adv*) never, erratically, **4.** forever; *synonyms* (*adv*) everlastingly, evermore, continually, (*n*) eternity, (*adj*) permanent, **5.** invariably; *synonyms* (*adv*) incessantly, uniformly, ceaselessly, endlessly, (*adj*) unfailingly.

ætiefni 1. corrosive; *synonyms* (*adj*) caustic, acid, acrid, erosive, biting, **2.** caustic; *synonyms* (*adj*) bitter, acrimonious, sharp, acerbic, (*v*) acute; *antonyms* (*adj*) mild, gentle.

ætimynd etching; *synonyms* (*n*) engraving, print, impression, drawing, silhouette.

æting 1. corrosion; *synonyms* (*n*) erosion, corroding, decay, deterioration, canker, **2.** etching; *synonyms* (*n*) engraving, print, impression, drawing, silhouette.

ætisveppur mushroom; *synonyms* (*n*) fungus, parvenu, upstart, (*v*) expand, spread; *antonym* (*v*) decrease.

ætiþistill 1. cardoon; *synonym* (*n*) artichoke, **2.** artichoke; *synonym* (*n*) cardoon.

ætla 1. plan; *synonyms* (*n*) aim, map, figure, chart, (*v*) design, **2.** propose; *synonyms* (*v*) offer, bid, nominate, plan, (*n*) advance; *antonym* (*v*) withdraw, **3.** intend; *synonyms* (*v*) destine, mean, determine, contemplate, denote, **4.** mean; *synonyms* (*v*) intend, imply, (adj) middle, (n) average, contemptible; *antonyms* (adj) generous, kind.

ætlun assumption; *synonyms* (n) presumption, supposition, hypothesis, premise, adoption.

ætt 1. family; *synonyms* (n) descent, household, name, (adj) home, ancestry, **2**. tribe; *synonyms* (n) family, clan, house, folk, kin, **3**. race; *synonyms* (n) kind, dash, (v) course, run, (adj) lineage.

ættarskrá pedigree; *synonyms* (n) descent, lineage, extraction, ancestry, breed.

ættartafla pedigree; *synonyms* (n) descent, lineage, extraction, ancestry, breed.

ættartala pedigree; *synonyms* (n) descent, lineage, extraction, ancestry, breed.

ættbálkur tribe; *synonyms* (n) family, clan, house, folk, kin.

ættfeðrastjórn patriarchy; *synonyms* (n) patriarchate, patriarchship.

ættflokkur tribe; *synonyms* (n) family, clan, house, folk, kin.

ættgengi heredity; *synonyms* (n) ancestry, lineage, telegony, line, descent.

ættgengisfræði genetics; *synonyms* (n) heredity, inheritance, anatomy, botany, evolution.

ættgengur hereditary; *synonyms* (adj) genetic, ancestral, familial, heritable, inborn.

ættjörð country; *synonyms* (n) state, nation, home, land, area; *antonyms* (n) city, (adj) urban.

ættkvísl genus; *synonyms* (n) class, description, kind, sort, breed.

ættleggur lineage; *synonyms* (n) breed, descent, family, pedigree, extraction.

ættleiða adopt; *synonyms* (v) accept, admit, affiliate, assume, borrow; *antonym* (v) reject.

ættleiðing adoption; *synonyms* (n) acceptance, espousal, assumption, borrowing, (adj) conversion.

æviskeið lifetime; *synonyms* (n) age, life, lifespan, day, decade.

ævistarf career; *synonyms* (n) calling, race, (adj) job, (v) course, dash.

æxli 1. tumor; *synonyms* (n) swelling, tumour, growth, neoplasm, (adj) cancer, **2**. neoplasm; *synonyms* (n) tumor, bombast.

æxliknappur bud; *synonyms* (n) bloom, blossom, flower, (v) graft, shoot.

æxlismyndun neoplasia; *synonym* (n) neoplasty.

æxlun 1. reproduction; *synonyms* (n) replica, propagation, duplicate, breeding, (adj) fake; *antonym* (adj) genuine, **2**. procreation; *synonyms* (n) generation, reproduction, birth, (adj) multiplication, (v) epigenesis.

B

bað 1. bathroom; *synonyms* (n) bath, lavatory, can, lav, privy, **2**. bath; *synonyms* (n) wash, bathroom, tank, bathtub, (v) bathe.

baðmull cotton; *synonyms* (n) thread, yarn, cord, fiber, string.

baðströnd beach; *synonyms* (n) bank, coast, foreshore, shore, strand.

báðumegin bilateral; *synonyms* (adj) mutual, joint, (v) bicephalous, bicipital, bidental; *antonyms* (adj) unilateral, multilateral.

bæjarfélag 1. community; *synonyms* (n) association, public, agreement, commune, (adj) communal; *antonym* (adj) private, **2**. municipality; *synonyms* (n) city, town, metropolis, shrievalty, area.

bæjargöng passage; *synonyms* (n) aisle, course, channel, corridor, gangway.

bæjarhlað yard; *synonyms* (n) court, courtyard, garden, backyard, grounds.

bæjarþil gable; *synonyms* (n) gavel, cable, coping, toll, tribute.

bæki buckwheat; *synonyms* (n) grain, branks, cereal, maize, millet.

bækigrjón buckwheat; *synonyms* (n) grain, branks, cereal, maize, millet.

bæklaður deformed; *synonyms* (adj) crooked, bent, distorted, malformed, misshapen.

bæklingur leaflet; *synonyms* (n) brochure, leaf, booklet, pamphlet, circular.

bæklun deformity; *synonyms* (n) deformation, defect, disfigurement, malformation, blemish.

bæklunarlækningar orthopedics; *synonyms* (n) orthopaedics, orthopedy, orthopraxy.

bæla repress; *synonyms* (v) curb, control, crush, inhibit, quash.

bældur 1. repressed; *synonyms* (adj) subdued, inhibited, composed, forgotten, inner, **2**. depressed; *synonyms* (adj) concave, low, blue, dejected, dispirited; *antonyms* (adj) cheerful, happy, convex.

bæling 1. repression; *synonyms* (n) constraint, restraint, coercion, confinement, check; *antonyms* (n) democracy, expression, **2**. suppression; *synonyms* (n) inhibition, repression, crushing, quelling, stifling; *antonyms* (n) freedom, emancipation.

bælir 1. repressor; *synonym* (n) represser, **2**. suppressor; *synonym* (n) suppresser, **3**. inhibitor; *synonym* (n) stabilizer.

bæn 1. plea; *synonyms* (*n*) defense, justification, answer, apology, appeal, **2**. request; *synonyms* (*n*) petition, bid, (*v*) demand, ask, invite; *antonyms* (*v*) command, order, **3**. prayer; *synonyms* (*n*) invocation, entreaty, plea, orison, request, **4**. petition; *synonyms* (*n*) application, (*v*) desire, beg, claim, crave, **5**. appeal; *synonyms* (*n*) address, attraction, (*v*) charm, sue, attract; *antonyms* (*n*) unpleasantness, (*v*) repel.

bænaskrá petition; *synonyms* (*n*) appeal, (*v*) demand, ask, request, desire.

bær 1. town; *synonyms* (*n*) city, borough, township, (*adj*) municipal, urban, **2**. municipality; *synonyms* (*n*) town, metropolis, shrievalty, commune, area.

bæri parity; *synonyms* (*n*) par, equality, resemblance, balance, equivalence; *antonym* (*n*) inequality.

bæs dip; *synonyms* (*n*) plunge, (*v*) duck, bathe, drop, fall; *antonyms* (*n*) hump, mountain.

bæta 1. repair; *synonyms* (*v*) remedy, mend, patch, redress, correct; *antonym* (*v*) break, **2**. improve; *synonyms* (*v*) advance, heal, emend, help, ameliorate; *antonyms* (*v*) worsen, deteriorate, regress, spoil, **3**. patch; *synonyms* (*n*) darn, fleck, plot, (*v*) piece, botch.

bætandi remedial; *synonyms* (*adj*) curative, healing, therapeutic, corrective, medicinal.

bæti byte; *synonyms* (*v*) bit, doubleword, paragraph, segment, word.

bætur compensation; *synonyms* (*n*) amends, recompense, allowance, indemnification, (*v*) wage.

baggi bale; *synonyms* (*n*) load, package, calamity, cargo, (*v*) bundle.

bak back; *synonyms* (*n*) rear, (*adj*) assist, (*v*) support, advocate, endorse; *antonyms* (*n*) face, (*v*) front, oppose, advance.

baka bake; *synonyms* (*v*) burn, broil, cook, fire, fry.

bakari baker; *synonyms* (*n*) cook, chef, doughboy.

bakarí bakery; *synonyms* (*n*) bakehouse, bakeshop, confectionery, grocery, supermarket.

bakborði port; *synonyms* (*n*) harbor, haven, asylum, carriage, (*adj*) larboard; *antonym* (*n*) starboard.

bakborðshorn quarter; *synonyms* (*n*) area, part, district, division, (*v*) place.

bakflæði reflux; *synonyms* (*n*) ebb, refluence, (*v*) decrement, indraught, reflex.

bakflug 1. reentry, **2**. flyback; *synonym* (*n*) retrace.

bakgrunnur 1. background; *synonyms* (*n*) backdrop, groundwork, setting, basis, context, **2**. context; *synonyms* (*n*) circumstance, environment, surroundings, background, atmosphere.

bakhjarl 1. sponsor; *synonyms* (*n*) backer, benefactor, patron, (*v*) patronize, support, **2**.

fulcrum; *synonyms* (*n*) pivot, hinge, bearing, crux, bracket.

bakhverfur retrogressive; *synonyms* (*adj*) regressive, retrograde, declining, deteriorating, failing.

bakka 1. reverse; *synonyms* (*adj*) opposite, (*v*) annul, repeal, rescind, (*n*) contrary; *antonym* (*n*) front, **2**. backspace; *synonym* (*n*) backspacing.

bakkastokkar shipway; *synonyms* (*n*) slipway, ways, way.

bakkgír reverse; *synonyms* (*adj*) opposite, (*v*) annul, repeal, rescind, (*n*) contrary; *antonym* (*n*) front.

bakki 1. tray; *synonyms* (*n*) plate, dish, basket, bassinet, case, **2**. whaleback.

bakkviknun backfire; *synonyms* (*n*) backburn, (*v*) backlash, miscarry, fail, recoil.

baklægur dorsal; *synonyms* (*adj*) abaxial, posterior, abaxile, notal, (*n*) dosser.

bakland hinterland; *synonyms* (*n*) backwoods, country, boondocks, vicinity, bush.

bakögn electron; *synonyms* (*n*) electricity, molecule, negatron, amber.

bakpoki 1. rucksack; *synonyms* (*n*) backpack, bag, haversack, knapsack, pack, **2**. backpack; *synonyms* (*n*) rucksack, packsack, (*v*) hike.

bakrás regression; *synonyms* (*n*) regress, lapse, setback, degeneration, deterioration.

bakrauf anus; *synonyms* (*n*) arse, arsehole, asshole, bum, bastard.

bakskaut cathode; *synonym* (*n*) platinode.

bakskot backfire; *synonyms* (*n*) backburn, (*v*) backlash, miscarry, fail, recoil.

bakslag 1. recoil; *synonyms* (*n*) reaction, (*v*) bounce, kick, rebound, bound, **2**. relapse; *synonyms* (*n*) lapse, recidivism, (*v*) regress, decline, backslide; *antonyms* (*n*) improvement, (*v*) improve, **3**. backfire; *synonyms* (*n*) backburn, (*v*) backlash, miscarry, fail, recoil, **4**. backlash; *synonyms* (*n*) repercussion, effect, resentment, (*v*) backfire, boomerang.

baksmala disassemble; *synonyms* (*v*) dismantle, decompose, analyse, dismember, detach; *antonym* (*v*) assemble.

bakstæður final; *synonyms* (*adj*) conclusive, decisive, definite, extreme, latter; *antonyms* (*adj*) first, opening, preliminary.

baksveifla flyback; *synonym* (*n*) retrace.

baksveip flyback; *synonym* (*n*) retrace.

baksvið background; *synonyms* (*n*) backdrop, groundwork, setting, basis, context.

baktería bacterium; *synonyms* (*n*) bacteria, microbe, rabbit, (*adj*) virus.

bakteríuæta phage; *synonym* (*n*) bacteriophage.

bakteríueyðandi 1. antibacterial; *synonyms* (*adj*) antiseptic, sterile, clean, (*n*) bactericide, bacteriacide, **2**. bactericidal; *synonyms* *(adj)* disinfectant, germicidal.

bakteríueyðir bactericide; *synonyms* *(n)* antiseptic, germicide, bacteriacide, disinfectant, antibacterial.

bakteríufræði bacteriology; *synonyms* *(n)* microbiology, virology, mycology.

bakteríuhár pilus; *synonyms* *(n)* hair, capillament, cilia, cilium, fuzz.

bakteríukólónía colony; *synonyms* *(n)* settlement, community, plantation, dependency, village.

bakteríulaus aseptic; *synonyms* *(adj)* sterile, antiseptic, clean, healthy, hygienic.

bakteríuleysi asepsis; *synonyms* *(n)* antisepsis, sterileness, sterility, infertility.

bakteríur bacteria; *synonyms* *(n)* germ, bacterium, microbe, bug, *(adj)* virus.

bakteríuskæður antibacterial; *synonyms* *(adj)* antiseptic, sterile, clean, *(n)* bactericide, bacteriacide.

bakteríuþyrping colony; *synonyms* *(n)* settlement, community, plantation, dependency, village.

bakteríuveira 1. phage; *synonym* *(n)* bacteriophage, **2**. bacteriophage; *synonym* *(n)* phage.

baktrygging hedge; *synonyms* *(n)* fence, *(v)* dodge, fudge, elude, evade.

bakvöðvi dorsal; *synonyms* *(adj)* abaxial, posterior, abaxile, notal, *(v)* dosser.

bálför cremation; *synonyms* *(n)* burning, incineration, burial, finances, *(v)* concremation.

bálkur block; *synonyms* *(n)* bar, barricade, pad, *(v)* arrest, stop; *antonyms* *(v)* free, unblock, open.

ballansera counterbalance; *synonyms* *(v)* compensate, counteract, counterpoise, *(n)* balance, counterweight.

ballest ballast; *synonyms* *(n)* weight, ballasting, *(adj)* aplomb, *(v)* stabilize, load.

ballett ballet; *synonyms* *(n)* choreography, afterpiece, burlesque, burletta, comedietta.

balli bale; *synonyms* *(n)* load, package, calamity, cargo, *(v)* bundle.

balsamínutré balsam; *synonyms* *(n)* balm, unguent, cordial, ptisan, theriac.

bálstofa crematory; *synonym* *(n)* crematorium.

bambus bamboo; *synonyms* *(n)* cane, stick, *(adj)* wicker, rush, woven.

bambusreyr bamboo; *synonyms* *(n)* cane, stick, *(adj)* wicker, rush, woven.

banakringla atlas; *synonyms* *(n)* telamon, chart, book, plan, *(adj)* superman.

bananaávöxtur banana; *synonyms* *(n)* comedian, comic, *(v)* atole, avocado, barbecue.

banani banana; *synonyms* *(n)* comedian, comic, *(v)* atole, avocado, barbecue.

band 1. clamp; *synonyms* *(n)* clinch, brace, *(v)* cramp, clench, *(adj)* clasp, **2**. ligament; *synonyms* *(n)* tie, bond, band, knot, sinew.

bandalag 1. union; *synonyms* *(n)* coalition, connection, junction, association, combination; *antonyms* *(n)* separation, divergence, **2**. coalition; *synonyms* *(n)* alliance, league, union, affiliation, alignment; *antonym* *(n)* nonalignment, **3**. alliance; *synonyms* *(n)* affinity, confederacy, alinement, merger, organization, **4**. federation; *synonyms* *(n)* confederation, commonwealth, consolidation, society.

bandalagsríki confederate; *synonyms* *(adj)* allied, *(n)* accomplice, ally, accessory, *(v)* associate.

bandamaður confederate; *synonyms* *(adj)* allied, *(n)* accomplice, ally, accessory, *(v)* associate.

bandmynd video; *synonyms* *(n)* television, picture, film, movie, *(v)* tape.

bandormur taenia; *synonyms* *(n)* tenia, fillet, filet, lemniscus, stopping.

bandstrik hyphen; *synonyms* *(n)* dash, copula, intermedium, line, *(v)* hyphenate.

bandvefsreifar fascia; *synonyms* *(n)* cincture, band, facia, fillet, aponeurosis.

bank knock; *synonyms* *(v)* hit, blow, bump, *(n)* rap, bang; *antonym* *(v)* praise.

bankahólf safe; *synonyms* *(adj)* secure, reliable, cautious, dependable, *(n)* closet; *antonyms* *(adj)* dangerous, unsafe, hurt, risky, unprotected.

bankaleynd confidentiality; *synonyms* *(n)* discretion, intimacy, privacy, secrecy, mystery.

bankaseðill bill; *synonyms* *(n)* account, beak, advertisement, *(v)* placard, advertise.

banki 1. bank; *synonyms* *(n)* dam, coast, slope, *(v)* embankment, gradient; *antonym* *(v)* withdraw, **2**. reservoir; *synonyms* *(n)* cistern, fountain, well, lake, store.

banko 1. bank; *synonyms* *(n)* dam, coast, slope, *(v)* embankment, gradient; *antonym* *(v)* withdraw, **2**. banks; *synonym* *(n)* breast.

bann blockade; *synonyms* *(v)* bar, barricade, block, beleaguer, besiege.

banna inhibit; *synonyms* *(v)* ban, hamper, check, curb, encumber.

banndómur taboo; *synonyms* *(adj)* forbidden, banned, prohibited, *(n)* tabu, *(v)* ban; *antonym* *(adj)* acceptable.

bannhelgi taboo; *synonyms* *(adj)* forbidden, banned, prohibited, *(n)* tabu, *(v)* ban; *antonym* *(adj)* acceptable.

bannorð taboo; *synonyms* *(adj)* forbidden, banned, prohibited, *(n)* tabu, *(v)* ban; *antonym* *(adj)* acceptable.

bannsetning grounding; *synonyms* (*n*) earthing, basis, training, foundation, stranding.

banvænn 1. toxic; *synonyms* (*adj*) poisonous, noxious, venomous, deadly, harmful; *antonyms* (*adj*) harmless, nontoxic, **2**. lethal; *synonyms* (*adj*) fatal, deathly, mortal, murderous, pernicious.

bára wave; *synonyms* (*n*) billow, gesture, (*v*) brandish, flap, flutter.

barako 1. barracks; *synonyms* (*n*) billet, casern, battalion, bivouac, dormitory, **2**. barrack; *synonyms* (*n*) barracks, (*v*) jeer, cheer, gibe, scoff.

barátta conflict; *synonyms* (*n*) clash, combat, fight, battle, contention; *antonyms* (*n*) agreement, accord, harmony, peace, (*v*) agree.

barbitúrat barbiturate; *synonym* (*n*) sedative.

barbitúrsýrulyf barbiturate; *synonym* (*n*) sedative.

barð fin; *synonyms* (*n*) spline, feather, fins, flipper, flippers.

barðaháfur monkfish; *synonyms* (*n*) angler, goosefish, anglerfish, allmouth, angelfish.

barín barium; *synonym* (*n*) ab.

baríum barium; *synonym* (*n*) ab.

barkakvísl bronchus; *synonym* (*n*) bronchi.

barkakýli larynx; *synonyms* (*n*) spiracle, tonsils, windpipe.

barkaopshljóð laryngeal; *synonym* (*adj*) laryngean.

barkapípa bronchus; *synonym* (*n*) bronchi.

barkarenna airway; *synonym* (*n*) airline.

barkarnám decortication; *synonyms* (*adj*) depilation, desquamation, excoriation, (*n*) excortication.

barkarspell decortication; *synonyms* (*adj*) depilation, desquamation, excoriation, (*n*) excortication.

barkarstýfa decorticate; *synonyms* (*v*) peel, pare, strip, scalp, excorticate.

barkarstýfður decorticate; *synonyms* (*v*) peel, pare, strip, scalp, excorticate.

barkfletta decortication; *synonyms* (*adj*) depilation, desquamation, excoriation, (*n*) excortication.

barkhúð cortex; *synonyms* (*n*) bark, crust, peel, rind, pallium.

barki 1. windpipe; *synonyms* (*n*) trachea, larynx, tonsils, throttle, thrapple, **2**. trachea; *synonyms* (*n*) windpipe, throat, weasand, chimney, flue.

barksteri corticosteroid; *synonyms* (*n*) corticoid, adrenocorticosteroid.

barn 1. child; *synonyms* (*n*) baby, boy, babe, bairn, brat; *antonym* (*n*) adult, **2**. infant; *synonyms* (*n*) child, minor, nursling, kid, (*adj*) juvenile, **3**. youngster; *synonyms* (*n*) lad, urchin, toddler, adolescent, youth, **4**. bairn; *synonyms* (*n*) infant, pickaninny, **5**. kid; *synonyms* (*n*) youngster, (*v*) joke, jest, banter, chaff.

barnaat meconium; *synonym* (*n*) opium.

barnabik meconium; *synonym* (*n*) opium.

barnaheimili 1. nursery; *synonyms* (*n*) kindergarten, greenhouse, cradle, seminary, nest, **2**. kindergarten; *synonyms* (*n*) nursery, reformatory, playgroup, crèche.

barnahópur brood; *synonyms* (*n*) breed, issue, offspring, (*v*) hatch, sulk.

barnalækningar pediatrics; *synonym* (*n*) paediatrics.

barnalæknir pediatrician; *synonyms* (*n*) paediatrician, pediatrist.

barnalegur infantile; *synonyms* (*adj*) childish, immature, infant, babyish, infantine; *antonym* (*adj*) mature.

barnamosamýri bog; *synonyms* (*n*) marsh, morass, swamp, marish, mire; *antonym* (*n*) desert.

barnasorta meconium; *synonym* (*n*) opium.

barnavagn 1. pram; *synonyms* (*n*) perambulator, carriage, pushchair, stroller, cart, **2**. perambulator; *synonyms* (*n*) pram, ambulator, coach, handcart, (*v*) pedometer.

barnfóstra nurse; *synonyms* (*v*) nourish, attend, cherish, entertain, foster.

barnsburður parturition; *synonyms* (*n*) birth, childbirth, confinement, delivery, labor.

barnshöfn pregnancy; *synonyms* (*n*) gravidity, gestation, fertility, (*adj*) procreation, propagation.

barnslegur infantile; *synonyms* (*adj*) childish, immature, infant, babyish, infantine; *antonym* (*adj*) mature.

barnsmorð infanticide; *synonyms* (*n*) immolation, mactation, (*v*) fratricide, uxoricide, vaticide.

barnsmorðingi infanticide; *synonyms* (*n*) immolation, mactation, (*v*) fratricide, uxoricide, vaticide.

barrakúda barracuda; *synonym* (*n*) sennet.

barri 1. slab; *synonyms* (*n*) hunk, chunk, bar, (*adj*) table, plate, **2**. bass; *synonyms* (*adj*) deep, low, resonant, (*n*) basso, (*adv*) accompaniment.

barrlind yew; *synonyms* (*n*) yam, zinnia, (*v*) yaw.

barsíli capelin; *synonyms* (*n*) caplin, capelan, capling.

barsmíðar battery; *synonyms* (*n*) troop, army, barrage, company, collection.

báruskel cockle; *synonyms* (*v*) crease, pucker, ruffle, rumple, fold.

báruskeljar cockle; *synonyms* (*v*) crease, pucker, ruffle, rumple, fold.

basafruma basophil; *synonym* (*n*) basophile.

basi 1. base; *synonyms* (*n*) foundation, (*adj*) bottom, abject, mean, dishonorable; *antonyms* (*n*) summit, top, (*adj*) noble, **2**. caustic; *synonyms* (*adj*) biting, acrid, bitter, acrimonious, sharp; *antonyms* (adj) mild, gentle.

basíða basidium; *synonym* (n) promycelium.

basilíka basil; *synonyms* (n) basan, sheepskin, parsley, rosemary, sage.

basilíkum basil; *synonyms* (n) basan, sheepskin, parsley, rosemary, sage.

basill basil; *synonyms* (n) basan, sheepskin, parsley, rosemary, sage.

basískur 1. alkaline; *synonyms* (adj) alkalic, alkalizate, caustic, salty, acrid; *antonyms* (adj) acidic, amphoteric, **2**. basic; *synonyms* (adj) first, cardinal, initial, primary, (n) essential; *antonyms* (adj) secondary, complex, extra, minor.

bastarður 1. chimera; *synonyms* (n) chimaera, dream, fantasy, figment, illusion; *antonym* (n) reality, **2**. hybrid; *synonyms* (adj) crossbred, (n) crossbreed, cross, mixture, (v) composite.

bataskeið convalescence; *synonyms* (n) recovery, recuperation, upturn, illness, progress.

bati healing; *synonyms* (n) cure, convalescence, recuperation, therapy, (adj) curative; *antonym* (adj) injurious.

bátlaga 1. scaphoid; *synonyms* (adj) navicular, cymbiform, (v) uncate, scutate, **2**. navicular; *synonyms* (adj) scaphoid, (v) lobiform, lunate, peltate, remiform.

batna recover; *synonyms* (v) reclaim, recuperate, regain, retrieve, convalesce; *antonyms* (v) deteriorate, lose.

bátsmaður boatswain; *synonyms* (n) bosun, bos'n, cockswain, boson, skua.

bátur boat; *synonyms* (n) yacht, scull, craft, dinghy, ship.

bauganet graticule; *synonyms* (n) reticle, reticule, grating.

baugaskán psoriasis; *synonyms* (n) itch, leucoplakia.

baugmyndun halation; *synonyms* (n) halo, irradiation.

baugur 1. ring; *synonyms* (n) encircle, band, (v) circle, call, peal, **2**. circle; *synonyms* (n) round, association, compass, ring, field, **3**. halo; *synonyms* (n) aureole, aura, glory, halation, corona.

bauja buoy; *synonyms* (v) prop, encourage, bolster, cheer, (adj) float.

baukur capsule; *synonyms* (n) abridgement, lozenge, condensation, pill, (v) encapsulate.

baula clip; *synonyms* (n) clasp, blow, (v) nip, snip, trim; *antonym* (v) lengthen.

baulfiskur croaker; *synonyms* (n) doctor, (v) growler, grumbler, malcontent, dissenter.

baunarlaga 1. pisiform, **2**. sesamoid; *synonym* (adj) sesamoidal.

báxít bauxite; *synonym* (n) beauxite.

bazo grounds; *synonyms* (n) cause, dregs, ground, reason, account.

beð beet; *synonym* (n) beetroot.

bedet bed; *synonyms* (n) couch, layer, base, basis, berth.

beðmi cellulose; *synonyms* (n) fiber, bran, (adj) plastic.

beður bed; *synonyms* (n) couch, layer, base, basis, berth.

beiðni 1. request; *synonyms* (n) petition, bid, (v) demand, ask, invite; *antonyms* (v) command, order, **2**. requisition; *synonyms* (n) claim, (v) request, commandeer, call, require, **3**. claim; *synonyms* (n) charge, allegation, privilege, (v) assert, exact; *antonyms* (v) deny, disclaim, forfeit.

bein 1. bone; *synonyms* (n) os, ivory, (v) cartilage, swot, gristle, **2**. os; *synonyms* (n) bone, osmium, opening, osar, entrance.

beina 1. route; *synonyms* (n) course, path, road, direction, passage, **2**. allocate; *synonyms* (v) divide, apportion, set, place, allot.

beinæta osteoclast; *synonyms* (n) myeloplax, osteophage.

beinafræði osteology; *synonyms* (n) organography, splanchnology, osteography, osteotomy, skeleton.

beinagrind skeleton; *synonyms* (n) carcass, frame, framework, sketch, bones.

beinátfruma osteoclast; *synonyms* (n) myeloplax, osteophage.

beinbris callus; *synonyms* (n) callosity, bump, lump.

beinbrjótur osteoclast; *synonyms* (n) myeloplax, osteophage.

beinbrot fracture; *synonyms* (n) break, breach, (v) crack, rupture, burst.

beinbrotsbrak crepitation; *synonyms* (n) crackle, crackling, crackleware, (v) decrepitation.

beinbrotsrétting reduction; *synonyms* (n) contraction, decrease, decrement, diminution, rebate; *antonyms* (n) increase, growth, intensification, strengthening, expansion.

beind vector; *synonyms* (n) direction, bearing, course, sender, transmitter.

beinfræði osteology; *synonyms* (n) organography, splanchnology, osteography, osteotomy, skeleton.

beinfruma osteocyte; *synonym* (n) osteoblast.

beingerð ossification; *synonyms* (n) conformity, abidance, accord, accordance, compliance.

beinihluti baffle; *synonyms* (v) discomfit, astonish, bewilder, confound, foil; *antonym* (v) enlighten.

beining 1. routing; *synonyms* (n) route, conquest, dispatching, navigation, steering, **2**. deflection; *synonyms* (n) deviation, bend, deflexion, variation, bending.

beinir base; *synonyms* (n) foundation, (adj) bottom, abject, mean, dishonorable; *antonyms* (n) summit, top, (adj) noble.

beinispóla concentrator; *synonym* (n) multiplexer.

beinkímfruma osteoblast; *synonyms* (n) osteoplast, osteocyte.

beinkröm rickets; *synonym* (n) rachitis.

beinkvilli osteopathy; *synonyms* (n) allopathy, heteropathy, homeopathy.

beinlaus boneless; *synonyms* (adj) gutless, cowardly, pathetic, sad, spiritless.

beinlínuröðun alignment; *synonyms* (n) alliance, alinement, arrangement, coalition, organization.

beinmergur marrow; *synonyms* (n) essence, heart, kernel, pith, (adj) gist.

beinmóðir osteoblast; *synonyms* (n) osteoplast, osteocyte.

beinmyndun ossification; *synonyms* (n) conformity, abidance, accord, accordance, compliance.

beinmyndunarfruma osteoblast; *synonyms* (n) osteoplast, osteocyte.

beinn 1. straight; *synonyms* (adj) erect, honest, even, flat, (v) direct; *antonyms* (adv) indirectly, (adj) curly, curved, diluted, winding, 2. erect; *synonyms* (v) build, elevate, raise, construct, (adj) upright; *antonym* (adj) horizontal, 3. explicit; *synonyms* (adj) clear, distinct, unmistakable, broad, definite; *antonyms* (adj) vague, tacit, understood, unspoken, implicit.

beinörshnútur callus; *synonyms* (n) callosity, bump, lump.

beinstilling collimation; *synonyms* (v) aim, dip, tack.

beinstillir collimator; *synonym* (n) effuser.

beint 1. straight; *synonyms* (adj) erect, honest, even, flat, (v) direct; *antonyms* (adv) indirectly, (adj) curly, curved, diluted, winding, 2. steady; *synonyms* (adj) firm, secure, constant, (v) steadfast, calm; *antonyms* (adj) unsteady, shaky, wobbly, intermittent, unreliable.

beinungur cement; *synonyms* (n) glue, adhesive, gum, (v) fasten, fix.

beinútvöxtur apophysis; *synonyms* (n) process, elbow, knob, tooth, bulb.

beinvefur bone (bein); *synonyms* (n) os, ivory, (v) cartilage, swot, gristle.

beiskja tartness; *synonyms* (n) acidity, sourness, acrimony, acerbity, sharpness.

beiskur 1. sour; *synonyms* (adj) morose, sharp, acid, bitter, (n) harsh; *antonyms* (adj) sweet, kindly, 2. tart; *synonyms* (n) pie, pastry, (adj) pungent, sour, keen, 3. acerbic; *synonyms* (adj) acerb, caustic, acrid, astringent, incisive; *antonyms* (adj) mild, gentle, 4. acrid; *synonyms* (adj) acerbic, corrosive,

hot, acrimonious, biting, 5. acid; *synonyms* (adj) acidic, cutting, pointed, sarcastic, (v) tart.

beit pasture; *synonyms* (n) grass, meadow, feed, (v) graze, browse.

beita 1. bait; *synonyms* (n) bribe, decoy, (v) badger, tease, harass, 2. apply; *synonyms* (v) dedicate, devote, employ, ask, (n) give, 3. employ; *synonyms* (v) apply, use, consume, engage, exercise; *antonyms* (v) fire, dismiss.

beitiland 1. pasture; *synonyms* (n) grass, meadow, feed, (v) graze, browse, 2. grassland; *synonyms* (n) field, pasture, plain, prairie, lawn.

beitilyng heather; *synonyms* (n) heath, ling, broom, burbot, cusk.

beiting 1. application; *synonyms* (n) plea, appeal, appliance, concentration, demand, 2. crab; *synonyms* (n) cancer, grouch, (v) gripe, beef, bellyache.

beitiskip cruiser; *synonyms* (n) yacht, destroyer, flagship, liner, philanderer.

beitning baiting; *synonym* (n) chumming.

beittur 1. sharp; *synonyms* (adj) acute, bitter, intelligent, acid, (n) keen; *antonyms* (adj) blunt, dull, mild, gentle, rounded, 2. poignant; *synonyms* (adj) cutting, harsh, moving, (v) acrid, biting, 3. acute; *synonyms* (adj) sharp, incisive, intense, penetrating, critical; *antonym* (adj) obtuse, 4. acrimonious; *synonyms* (adj) sour, caustic, sarcastic, virulent, (v) pungent, 5. acerbic; *synonyms* (adj) acerb, astringent, tart, acrimonious, mordant.

beitusmokkur squid; *synonyms* (n) calamary, calamari, sleevefish.

bekkjardeild class; *synonyms* (n) category, group, (v) sort, place, rank.

bekksögn class; *synonyms* (n) category, group, (v) sort, place, rank.

bekkur 1. pew; *synonyms* (n) bench, booth, stall, pen, sheepfold, 2. bench; *synonyms* (n) settle, chair, court, terrace, workbench.

belgávöxtur pulse; *synonyms* (n) beat, impulse, pulsation, (v) pulsate, throb.

belgbólga bursitis; *synonym* (n) hygroma.

belghýði follicle; *synonyms* (n) cavity, dent, dimple, dint, lacuna.

belgjurt pulse; *synonyms* (n) beat, impulse, pulsation, (v) pulsate, throb.

belgkirtill follicle; *synonyms* (n) cavity, dent, dimple, dint, lacuna.

belgmein bursitis; *synonym* (n) hygroma.

belgur 1. pod; *synonyms* (n) capsule, hull, case, husk, (v) shell, 2. belly; *synonyms* (n) abdomen, stomach, inside, bowels, (v) balloon, 3. capsule; *synonyms* (n) abridgement, lozenge, condensation, pill, (v) encapsulate, **4**. cyst; *synonyms* (*n*) vesicle, blister, tumor, pod, utricle.

belti 1. belt; *synonyms* (*n*) ribbon, area, strap, (*v*) band, hit, **2**. zone; *synonyms* (*n*) district, region, section, belt, locality, **3**. zona; *synonyms* (*n*) zone, layer.

beltun zonation; *synonym* (*n*) banding.

bendill 1. pointer; *synonyms* (*n*) hint, clue, hand, needle, point, **2**. cursor; *synonyms* (*n*) indicator, pointer, arrow.

bending 1. signal; *synonyms* (*n*) sign, gesture, indication, presage, (*v*) omen, **2**. cue; *synonyms* (*n*) prompt, clue, tip, clew, (*v*) hint.

bendir pointer; *synonyms* (*n*) hint, clue, hand, needle, point.

bendistál reinforcement; *synonyms* (*n*) brace, fortification, backing, consolidation, support.

bensen benzene; *synonyms* (*n*) benzol, benzine, phene, carcinogenic.

bensín 1. petrol; *synonyms* (*n*) gasoline, gas, gasolene, petroleum, oil, **2**. gas; *synonyms* (*n*) petrol, air, fumes, accelerator, flatulence, **3**. gasoline; *synonyms* (*n*) fuel, distillate, naphtha, flatulency, kerosene.

bensíndæla primer; *synonyms* (*n*) manual, fuse, fuze, ground, grammar.

bensíngjöf accelerator; *synonyms* (*n*) catalyst, gas, throttle, gun, promotor.

bensli seizing; *synonyms* (*adj*) catching, (*n*) grasping, seizure, prehension, taking.

bensól 1. benzene; *synonyms* (*n*) benzol, benzine, phene, carcinogenic, **2**. benzole.

ber berry; *synonyms* (*n*) fruit, drupe, drupelet, haw, hillock.

bera support; *synonyms* (*n*) help, stand, aid, keep, (*v*) assist; *antonyms* (*n*) hindrance, (*v*) oppose, neglect, undermine, abandon.

berfrymingar mycoplasma; *synonym* (*n*) mycoplasm.

berg rock; *synonyms* (*n*) boulder, calculus, (*v*) jar, (*adj*) pebble, stone.

bergamía bergamot; *synonyms* (*n*) civet, potpourri, pulvil, burgamot.

bergamóappelsína bergamot; *synonyms* (*n*) civet, potpourri, pulvil, burgamot.

bergamótappelsína bergamot; *synonyms* (*n*) civet, potpourri, pulvil, burgamot.

bergbrestur joint; *synonyms* (*n*) articulation, hinge, join, seam, (*v*) articulate; *antonyms* (*adj*) individual, unilateral, private, separate.

bergeitill stocks; *synonyms* (*n*) pillory, bilboes, securities, calls, options.

berggangur dyke; *synonyms* (*n*) dam, ditch, channel, (*v*) dike, (*adj*) lesbian.

berggrunnur 1. bedrock; *synonyms* (*n*) basis, basics, foundation, base, bed, **2**. rock; *synonyms* (*n*) boulder, calculus, (*v*) jar, (*adj*) pebble, stone.

berghlaup slump; *synonyms* (*n*) depression, decline, (*v*) drop, fall, sag; *antonyms* (*n*) upturn, (*v*) rise.

bergkleyfni cleavage; *synonyms* (*n*) cleft, rift, rip, rupture, (*v*) section.

bergkvika magma; *synonyms* (*n*) medley, melange, mess, miscellany, pasticcio.

bergmál echo; *synonyms* (*n*) answer, (*v*) repeat, reproduce, resound, reverberate.

bergminta oregano; *synonyms* (*n*) marjoram, cinnamon, mace, nutmeg, cloves.

bergmynta oregano; *synonyms* (*n*) marjoram, cinnamon, mace, nutmeg, cloves.

bergsprunga fracture; *synonyms* (*n*) break, breach, (*v*) crack, rupture, burst.

bergtegund rock; *synonyms* (*n*) boulder, calculus, (*v*) jar, (*adj*) pebble, stone.

beri carrier; *synonyms* (*n*) bearer, messenger, courier, mailman, porter.

berkill tubercle; *synonyms* (*n*) nodule, tuberosity, tuber, distinction, eminence.

berkja bronchus; *synonym* (*n*) bronchi.

berkjuasma asthma; *synonym* (*n*) anhelation.

bernska childhood; *synonyms* (*n*) babyhood, boyhood, immaturity, infancy, puerility; *antonym* (*n*) adulthood.

berserksgangur amok; *synonyms* (*adv*) amuck, murderously, (*adj*) berserk, demoniac, demoniacal.

berskjaldaður vulnerable; *synonyms* (*adj*) weak, exposed, sensitive, susceptible, tender; *antonyms* (*adj*) safe, impervious, invincible, invulnerable, unassailable.

berskjöldun exposure; *synonyms* (*n*) display, exposition, detection, peril, (*v*) disclosure.

bersýnilegur overt; *synonyms* (*adj*) blatant, open, obvious, apparent, clear; *antonyms* (*adj*) camouflaged, concealed, covert, indirect.

beryllín beryllium; *synonyms* (*n*) be, glucinium.

beryllíum beryllium; *synonyms* (*n*) be, glucinium.

besta maximize; *synonyms* (*v*) increase, maximise, intensify, improve, inflate; *antonym* (*v*) minimize.

bestun optimization; *synonyms* (*n*) optimisation, increase.

bestur 1. best; *synonyms* (*adj*) better, superior, supreme, (*v*) beat, (*n*) top; *antonym* (*n*) worst, **2**. optimal; *synonyms* (*adj*) optimum, best, finest, ideal, superb.

betri better; *synonyms* (*v*) amend, improve, best, mend, recover; *antonyms* (*adj*) lesser, (*adv*) worse, (*n*) inferior, (*v*) worsen.

beyging 1. reflection; *synonyms* (*n*) consideration, contemplation, observation, cogitation, deliberation, **2**. flexion; *synonyms* (*n*) bend, flection, flexure, bending, inflection, **3**. inflection; *synonyms* (*n*) accent, inflexion, flexion, intonation, modulation.

beygingardæmi paradigm; *synonyms* (*n*) example, exemplar, epitome, model, archetype.

beygir flexor; *synonym* (*n*) flector.

beygivöðvi flexor; *synonym* (*n*) flector.

beygja 1. swing; *synonyms* (*v*) sway, fluctuate, oscillate, dangle, hang, **2**. turn; *synonyms* (*n*) bend, curve, roll, coil, go, **3**. bend; *synonyms* (*n*) bow, arch, arc, (*v*) turn, crouch; *antonyms* (*v*) straighten, square, **4**. diffraction; *synonyms* (*n*) deflection, deviation, inflection, **5**. deflection; *synonyms* (*n*) deflexion, variation, bending, digression, diversion.

beygjanlegur flexible; *synonyms* (*adj*) elastic, adaptable, pliable, yielding, lissome; *antonyms* (*adj*) inflexible, rigid, fixed, obstinate, stiff.

beygla 1. dent; *synonyms* (*n*) hollow, nick, recess, (*v*) notch, indent; *antonym* (*v*) increase, **2**. depression; *synonyms* (*n*) basin, cavity, dejection, decline, dent; *antonyms* (*n*) cheerfulness, happiness, boom, elation, encouragement, **3**. kink; *synonyms* (*n*) curl, twist, knot, curve, defect.

beyglaður depressed; *synonyms* (*adj*) concave, low, blue, dejected, dispirited; *antonyms* (*adj*) cheerful, happy, convex.

beyglun buckling; *synonyms* (*n*) warping, capitulation, collapse, embossing, pickling.

beygur 1. trepidation; *synonyms* (*n*) agitation, alarm, apprehension, fear, tremor, **2**. anxiety; *synonyms* (*n*) care, disquiet, solicitude, trouble, anguish; *antonyms* (*n*) calmness, bravery, calm, confidence.

bið 1. delay; *synonyms* (*n*) pause, arrest, deferment, (*v*) defer, check; *antonyms* (*n*) punctuality, decisiveness, (*v*) rush, advance, **2**. dwell; *synonyms* (*v*) abide, inhabit, reside, bide, live, **3**. latency; *synonyms* (*n*) suspension, abeyance, intermission, interruption, latence.

biða ampulla; *synonym* (*n*) flask.

biðdagar demurrage; *synonym* (*n*) demorage.

biðfæra spool; *synonyms* (*n*) bobbin, reel, roll, cylinder, tube.

biðgjald demurrage; *synonym* (*n*) demorage.

biðja 1. request; *synonyms* (*n*) petition, bid, (*v*) demand, ask, invite; *antonyms* (*v*) command, order, **2**. seek; *synonyms* (*v*) search, attempt, endeavor, hunt, look, **3**. beg; *synonyms* (*v*) adjure, appeal, entreat, implore, cadge, **4**. ask; *synonyms* (*v*) inquire, request, beg, interrogate, question; *antonym* (*v*) answer, **5**. bid; *synonyms* (*n*) offer, tender, (*v*) call, beseech, charge.

biðlari client; *synonyms* (*n*) buyer, customer, patron, guest, purchaser.

biðlisti queue; *synonyms* (*n*) cue, rank, row, string, (*v*) line.

biðminni buffer; *synonyms* (*n*) safeguard, pad, protection, bumper, (*v*) cushion.

biðröð queue; *synonyms* (*n*) cue, rank, row, string, (*v*) line.

biðstakkur stack; *synonyms* (*n*) pile, accumulation, mound, rick, (*v*) heap.

biðtími latency; *synonyms* (*n*) suspension, abeyance, intermission, interruption, latence.

biðvista buffer; *synonyms* (*n*) safeguard, pad, protection, bumper, (*v*) cushion.

bifhærður ciliated; *synonyms* (*adj*) ciliate, filamentous, hirsute, cilial, ciliary.

bifhár cilium; *synonyms* (*n*) eyelash, lash, capillament, hair, pili.

bifháraskúfur cirrus; *synonyms* (*n*) woolpack, cirrhus, stratus, cumulus.

bifrar castor; *synonyms* (*n*) beaver, caster, roller, tile, wimple.

bifreið 1. automobile; *synonyms* (*n*) auto, car, bus, machine, vehicle, **2**. car; *synonyms* (*n*) automobile, carriage, coach, truck, tramcar, **3**. auto; *synonyms* (*n*) motorcar, limousine, **4**. limousine; *synonyms* (*n*) limo, clunker, coupe, flivver, jalopy.

bifreiðarstjóri 1. driver; *synonyms* (*n*) coachman, postboy, club, chaser, commuter, **2**. chauffeur; *synonyms* (*n*) driver, engineer, hackman, syce, truckman.

bifur beaver; *synonyms* (*n*) castor, stovepipe, topper, caster, (*adj*) irrepressible.

bifvélavirki mechanic; *synonyms* (*n*) craftsman, artificer, artisan, journeyman, machinist.

bik 1. pitch; *synonyms* (*n*) degree, dip, (*v*) fling, cast, chuck, **2**. asphalt; *synonyms* (*n*) bitumen, asphaltus, (*v*) tar, (*adj*) tarmac, flags.

bikar 1. thimble; *synonyms* (*n*) dipper, ladle, shovel, spatula, spoon, **2**. calyx; *synonyms* (*n*) cancelli, utricle, capsule, cyst, pod, **3**. beaker; *synonyms* (*n*) goblet, mug, bail, canakin, container.

bíkarbónat bicarbonate; *synonym* (*n*) supercarbonate.

bikarglas beaker; *synonyms* (*n*) goblet, mug, bail, canakin, container.

Bikarinn crater; *synonyms* (*n*) hollow, cavity, hole, pit, (*adj*) well.

bil 1. separation; *synonyms* (*n*) detachment, disjunction, disunion, division, partition; *antonyms* (*n*) amalgamation, closeness, connection, marriage, unification, **2**. space; *synonyms* (*n*) length, gap, opening, period, place, **3**. play; *synonyms* (*v*) act, pastime, enact, (*n*) frolic, game; *antonym* (*v*) work,

4. diastasis, **5**. band; *synonyms* (*n*) cluster, party, set, swathe, (*v*) ring.

bila fail; *synonyms* (*v*) abort, collapse, fade, cease, (*adj*) decline; *antonyms* (*v*) succeed, triumph.

bilanagreining 1. troubleshooting; *synonym* (*n*) troubleshoot, **2**. diagnosis; *synonyms* (*n*) diagnosing, distinction, identification, examination, diorism.

bílavog weighbridge; *synonyms* (*adj*) balance, beam, scale, steelyard.

bilfrjáls aperiodic; *synonym* (*adj*) nonperiodic.

bílírúbín bilirubin; *synonyms* (*n*) cholochrome, cholophaein, haematoidin, hematoidin.

biljafn periodic; *synonyms* (*adj*) intermittent, regular, periodical, recurrent, frequent.

bilkvæmi periodicity; *synonyms* (*n*) cyclicity, frequency, rhythm, cycle, periodicalness.

bilkvæmur periodic; *synonyms* (*adj*) intermittent, regular, periodical, recurrent, frequent.

bíll 1. automobile; *synonyms* (*n*) auto, car, bus, machine, vehicle, **2**. car; *synonyms* (*n*) automobile, carriage, coach, truck, tramcar, **3**. auto; *synonyms* (*n*) motorcar, limousine.

bílslys accident; *synonyms* (*n*) chance, casualty, coincidence, crash, fortune.

bílstjóri 1. chauffeur; *synonyms* (*n*) driver, engineer, hackman, syce, truckman, **2**. driver; *synonyms* (*n*) coachman, postboy, club, chaser, commuter.

bilun 1. trouble; *synonyms* (*n*) distress, bother, pain, (*v*) inconvenience, annoy; *antonyms* (*v*) calm, please, **2**. problem; *synonyms* (*n*) conundrum, difficulty, trouble, knot, enigma, **3**. breakdown; *synonyms* (*n*) collapse, fault, analysis, failure, ruin, **4**. fault; *synonyms* (*n*) defect, blemish, error, failing, (*v*) deficiency; *antonyms* (*n*) merit, strength, **5**. failure; *synonyms* (*n*) bankruptcy, breakdown, decline, debacle, defeat; *antonyms* (*n*) success, achievement, hit, winner, victory.

binda 1. tie; *synonyms* (*n*) band, (*v*) link, bond, attach, bind; *antonyms* (*v*) disconnect, untie, undo, **2**. attach; *synonyms* (*v*) add, adhere, append, affix, associate; *antonyms* (*v*) detach, separate, unfasten, **3**. bind; *synonyms* (*v*) tie, bandage, bundle, combine, fasten; *antonyms* (*v*) release, unbind, **4**. moor; *synonyms* (*n*) marsh, (*v*) anchor, berth, dock, secure.

bindefni binder; *synonyms* (*n*) ligature, bookbinder, cement, obligation, assurance.

bindin complex; *synonyms* (*adj*) composite, complicate, abstruse, difficult, elaborate; *antonyms* (*adj*) simple, basic, straightforward, clear, plain.

bindindi abstinence; *synonyms* (*n*) abstemiousness, abstention, forbearance, temperance, chastity; *antonym* (*n*) indulgence.

binding 1. bond; *synonyms* (*n*) association, tie, alliance, deed, (*v*) bind, **2**. fixation; *synonyms* (*n*) obsession, fetish, fixing, mania, complex.

bindingshólf frame; *synonyms* (*n*) design, border, (*v*) form, construct, fabricate.

bindistyrkur avidity; *synonyms* (*n*) avarice, greed, eagerness, greediness, ardor.

bindítími duration; *synonyms* (*n*) length, continuation, continuance, period, standing.

bióða invite; *synonyms* (*v*) draw, allure, bid, call, tempt.

birdo bird; *synonyms* (*n*) birdie, chick, fowl, girl, wench.

Birgðahaugur stockpile; *synonyms* (*n*) reserve, heap, (*v*) stock, hoard, store.

birgðasali supplier; *synonyms* (*n*) provider, vendor, contractor, dealer, benefactor.

Birgðastöð storage; *synonyms* (*n*) conservation, depot, memory, preservation, retention.

birgðatalning stocktaking; *synonyms* (*n*) inventory, inventorying, armory, armoury, checking.

birgðir 1. supplies; *synonyms* (*n*) food, provisions, stores, (*v*) equipment, outfit, **2**. provisions; *synonyms* (*n*) commissariat, provender, supplies, victuals, fare, **3**. supply; *synonyms* (*n*) provision, (*v*) furnish, stock, afford, fill, **4**. stock; *synonyms* (*n*) breed, lineage, store, goods, (*adj*) regular, **5**. storage; *synonyms* (*n*) conservation, depot, memory, preservation, retention.

birgir supplier; *synonyms* (*n*) provider, vendor, contractor, dealer, benefactor.

birgja supply; *synonyms* (*n*) provision, (*v*) furnish, stock, afford, fill.

birta 1. disclose; *synonyms* (*v*) betray, declare, impart, detect, (*adj*) confess; *antonyms* (*v*) conceal, secrete, **2**. brightness; *synonyms* (*n*) flash, clarity, illumination, light, luminance; *antonyms* (*n*) dullness, cloudiness, darkness, dimness, murkiness, **3**. brilliance; *synonyms* (*n*) blaze, grandeur, splendor, brightness, genius, **4**. magnitude; *synonyms* (*n*) extent, bulk, consequence, amount, dimension; *antonym* (*n*) triviality, **5**. illumination; *synonyms* (*n*) clarification, illuminance, elucidation, explanation, (*adj*) irradiation.

birtast present; *synonyms* (*adj*) grant, confer, (*n*) gift, donation, (*v*) bestow; *antonyms* (*adj*) missing, (*n*) past, future, (*v*) withdraw, (*adv*) absent.

birting 1. representation; *synonyms* (*n*) image, performance, depiction, picture, presentation, **2**. display; *synonyms* (*n*) array, (*v*) exhibit, show, disclose, parade; *antonym* (*v*) conceal, **3**. notification; *synonyms* (*n*) notice, advice, information, declaration, note, **4**. penetrance; *synonym* (*n*) penetrancy.

birtingarupplausn resolution; *synonyms* (*n*) decision, determination, answer, conclusion, firmness; *antonym* (*n*) indecisiveness.

birtuskil contrast; *synonyms* (*n*) contrariety, antithesis, comparison, distinction, (*v*) differ; *antonym* (*n*) similarity.

birtustig 1. brightness; *synonyms* (*n*) flash, clarity, illumination, light, luminance; *antonyms* (*n*) dullness, cloudiness, darkness, dimness, murkiness, **2**. magnitude; *synonyms* (*n*) extent, bulk, consequence, amount, dimension; *antonym* (*n*) triviality, **3**. luminosity; *synonyms* (*n*) brightness, glow, brilliance, radiance, brilliancy.

bísamrotta muskrat; *synonyms* (*n*) musquash, champak, horehound, mint, olibanum.

biskup bishop; *synonyms* (*n*) archbishop, primate, clergyman, (*v*) wassail, cup.

bíta 1. bite; *synonyms* (*v*) sting, nip, chew, cut, pinch, **2**. maul; *synonyms* (*v*) mall, mangle, beat, buffet, (*adj*) bruise.

bithagi pasture; *synonyms* (*n*) grass, meadow, feed, (*v*) graze, browse.

biti 1. bit; *synonyms* (*n*) crumb, morsel, piece, (*v*) curb, scrap, **2**. bolus; *synonyms* (*n*) ball, bole, dose, (*v*) sippet, sop, **3**. beam; *synonyms* (*n*) blaze, glow, ray, (*v*) glare, (*adj*) shine, **4**. member; *synonyms* (*n*) limb, part, supporter, extremity, phallus, **5**. girder; *synonyms* (*n*) beam, bar, joist, plank, rafter.

bitkrókur mandible; *synonyms* (*n*) jawbone, jowl, bill, mandibula, (*v*) jaws.

bitlaus dull; *synonyms* (*adj*) dim, blunt, dense, dreary, sluggish; *antonyms* (*adj*) bright, lively, sharp, exciting, interesting.

bixín annatto; *synonyms* (*n*) minium, realgar.

bjagaður biased; *synonyms* (*adj*) partial, partisan, slanted, unfair, skewed; *antonyms* (*adj*) fair, fair-minded, neutral, unbiased, just.

bjagast warp; *synonyms* (*n*) twist, buckle, distortion, (*v*) bend, distort; *antonym* (*v*) straighten.

bjagi bias; *synonyms* (*n*) penchant, drift, (*v*) prejudice, bent, (*adj*) partiality; *antonyms* (*n*) impartiality, neutrality, fairness.

bjálki 1. beam; *synonyms* (*n*) blaze, glow, ray, (*v*) glare, (*adj*) shine, **2**. girder; *synonyms* (*n*) beam, bar, joist, plank, rafter.

bjarg 1. rock; *synonyms* (*n*) boulder, calculus, (*v*) jar, (*adj*) pebble, stone, **2**. boulder; *synonyms* (*n*) bowlder, rock, (*adj*) ball, globe, sphere.

bjarga rescue; *synonyms* (*n*) deliverance, release, (*v*) deliver, extricate, ransom; *antonyms* (*n*) involvement, loss, (*v*) abandon.

bjargræðisvegur industry; *synonyms* (*n*) business, application, diligence, effort, industriousness.

bjarnarber blackberry; *synonyms* (*v*) blancmange, bloater, bouilli, bouillon, breadfruit.

bjärndýr bear; *synonyms* (*v*) carry, accept, abide, acquit, stand.

bjartáll eel; *synonyms* (*n*) yeel, (*v*) labyrinth, maze, serpent.

bjartur bright; *synonyms* (*adj*) clear, alive, apt, intelligent, vivid; *antonyms* (*adj*) dull, cloudy, dark, dim, dreary.

bjögun 1. warping; *synonyms* (*n*) warp, warpage, beaming, buckle, deflection, **2**. strain; *synonyms* (*n*) stress, breed, effort, (*v*) filter, screen; *antonym* (*v*) relax, **3**. skewness; *synonym* (*n*) lopsidedness, **4**. distortion; *synonyms* (*n*) aberration, contortion, deformation, misrepresentation, (*adj*) deformity, **5**. deformation; *synonyms* (*n*) strain, distortion, twist, bend, crookedness.

bjögunarhlaup margin; *synonyms* (*n*) edge, brink, boundary, hem, (*v*) border; *antonym* (*n*) center.

bjór 1. ale; *synonyms* (*n*) beer, eale, (*v*) stingo, liqueur, spirits, **2**. pediment; *synonyms* (*n*) architrave, capital, cornice, epistyle, frieze.

bjórar castor; *synonyms* (*n*) beaver, caster, roller, tile, wimple.

björg thimble; *synonyms* (*n*) dipper, ladle, shovel, spatula, spoon.

björgun salvage; *synonyms* (*v*) rescue, recover, save, deliver, (*n*) delivery; *antonyms* (*v*) lose, (*n*) loss.

björgunarlaun salvage; *synonyms* (*v*) rescue, recover, save, deliver, (*n*) delivery; *antonyms* (*v*) lose, (*n*) loss.

björn bear; *synonyms* (*v*) carry, accept, abide, acquit, stand.

bjúgaldin banana; *synonyms* (*n*) comedian, comic, (*v*) atole, avocado, barbecue.

bjúgborð meniscus; *synonyms* (*n*) crescent, lens, curve, sunglass.

bjúgflötur meniscus; *synonyms* (*n*) crescent, lens, curve, sunglass.

bjúglinsa meniscus; *synonyms* (*n*) crescent, lens, curve, sunglass.

bjúglopi edema; *synonyms* (*n*) dropsy, hydrops, oedema.

bjúgskekkja astigmatism; *synonyms* (*n*) astigmia, blindness.

bjúgur 1. edema; *synonyms* (*n*) dropsy, hydrops, oedema, **2**. oedema; *synonym* (*n*) edema.

bláæð vein; *synonyms* (*n*) streak, vena, (*adj*) humor, mood, strip.

bláæðaskúlk varix; *synonyms* (*n*) varicosity, varices.

bláæðavæðing venation; *synonym* (*v*) venery.

blað 1. leaf; *synonyms* (*n*) blade, page, foliage, folio, (*v*) sheet, **2.** vane; *synonyms* (*n*) beacon, cairn, fan, flagstaff, (*adj*) weathercock, **3.** blade; *synonyms* (*n*) vane, beau, knife, brand, foil, **4.** lobe; *synonyms* (*n*) division, flap, limb, member, arm, **5.** lamella; *synonyms* (*n*) lamina, gill, branchia, lamel.

blaðbeðja chard; *synonyms* (*n*) boundary, shard, division, plant.

blaðdilja dill; *synonyms* (*n*) anise, caraway, carrot, celery, (*adj*) calm.

blaðeyra auricle; *synonyms* (*n*) ear, pinna, heart, capitulum, (*v*) lug.

blaðflatarhlutfall solidity; *synonyms* (*n*) consistency, density, firmness, compactness, rigidity; *antonym* (*n*) brittleness.

blaðgræna chlorophyll; *synonyms* (*n*) chlorophyl, fecula.

blaðhvirfing rosette; *synonyms* (*n*) knot, star, patera.

blaðka 1. blade; *synonyms* (*n*) vane, beau, knife, brand, foil, **2.** diaphragm; *synonyms* (*n*) membrane, midriff, partition, pessary, septum, **3.** membrane; *synonyms* (*n*) diaphragm, film, skin, coat, covering.

blaðkló claw; *synonyms* (*n*) chela, hook, nipper, (*v*) clutch, lacerate.

blaðmyndað coronal; *synonyms* (*adj*) coronary, (*n*) chaplet, crown, garland, wreath.

blaðra 1. talk; *synonyms* (*v*) gossip, converse, lecture, chatter, (*n*) discourse, **2.** vesicle; *synonyms* (*n*) blister, cyst, envelope, capsule, (*adj*) drop, **3.** chatter; *synonyms* (*n*) prattle, (*v*) babble, chat, jabber, cackle, **4.** bulla; *synonym* (*n*) bleb, **5.** cyst; *synonyms* (*n*) vesicle, tumor, pod, utricle, carbuncle.

blaðsellerí celery; *synonyms* (*n*) anise, caraway, carrot, dill.

blaðsíða page; *synonyms* (*n*) attendant, footboy, usher, note, pageboy.

blaðsilla celery; *synonyms* (*n*) anise, caraway, carrot, dill.

blaðskiptur lobate; *synonyms* (*adj*) lobed, lobated, palmated, palmiped.

blaðstæði node; *synonyms* (*n*) knob, connection, joint, knot, nodosity.

blaðþorn spine; *synonyms* (*n*) backbone, thorn, point, prickle, quill.

blæðari bleeder; *synonyms* (*n*) haemophiliac, hemophiliac, bleed, haemophile, hemophile.

blæðing hemorrhage; *synonyms* (*v*) bleed, (*n*) bleeding, haemorrhage, disease, injury.

blæðingarstöðvun hemostasis; *synonyms* (*n*) hemostasia, haemostasia, haemostasis.

blæja canopy; *synonyms* (*n*) awning, cover, screen, shade, ceiling.

blæjubíll cabriolet; *synonyms* (*n*) cab, droshki, drosky, growler, hansom.

blær hue; *synonyms* (*n*) color, complexion, cast, (*v*) colour, tinge.

blæsing ablation; *synonyms* (*n*) excision, extirpation, sublation, (*v*) abduction, abreption.

blæti fetish; *synonyms* (*n*) fetich, charm, fixation, idol, juju.

blætisdýrkun fetishism; *synonyms* (*n*) fetichism, fetish, zoolatry, (*adj*) fetishistic.

bláhaus wolffish; *synonyms* (*n*) catfish, lancetfish, mudcat.

bláhrani roller; *synonyms* (*n*) roll, cylinder, billow, curler, wave.

blaka tab; *synonyms* (*n*) bill, check, account, invoice, flap.

blakhljóð flap; *synonyms* (*n*) fuss, slap, (*v*) flop, beat, wave.

blakkur black (svartur); *synonyms* (*adj*) dark, sable, blackamoor, bleak, darkie; *antonym* (*n*) white.

blanda 1. combination; *synonyms* (*n*) alliance, blend, union, association, coalition; *antonyms* (*n*) separation, (*adj*) simple, **2.** diffuse; *synonyms* (*v*) circulate, disperse, disseminate, spread, broadcast, **3.** compound; *synonyms* (*n*) complex, mix, amalgam, (*v*) alloy, (*adj*) composite, **4.** mixture; *synonyms* (*n*) concoction, assortment, hodgepodge, jumble, medley, **5.** mix; *synonyms* (*n*) mixture, (*v*) intermingle, mingle, combine, compound; *antonym* (*v*) separate.

blandaður composite; *synonyms* (*n*) complex, amalgam, blend, mix, (*v*) compound.

blandanlegur miscible; *synonym* (*adj*) mixable.

blandari mixer; *synonyms* (*n*) blender, social, agitator, churn, sociable.

blár blue; *synonyms* (*adj*) azure, depressed, down, gloomy, low.

blása blow; *synonyms* (*n*) bang, beat, blast, knock, (*adj*) gasp; *antonyms* (*v*) calm, save.

blásari 1. blower; *synonyms* (*n*) bellows, fan, blast, cetacean, feeder, **2.** fan; *synonyms* (*n*) admirer, buff, devotee, enthusiast, (*v*) air; *antonym* (*n*) detractor.

blástur blast; *synonyms* (*n*) bang, slam, (*v*) attack, (*adj*) discharge, explosion.

blauthljóð liquid; *synonyms* (*adj*) flowing, fluent, fluid, juicy, limpid; *antonyms* (*adj*) firm, (*n*) solid, gaseous.

blautur wet; *synonyms* (*adj*) damp, humid, (*v*) moisten, water, dampen; *antonyms* (*adj*) dehydrated, parched, (*v*) dry.

bleðill 1. lobe; *synonyms* (*n*) division, flap, limb, member, arm, **2.** lobule; *synonyms* (*n*) lobe, lobelet, bough, branch, bush.

bleiklax humpback; *synonyms* (*n*) crookback, kyphosis, hump, hunchback.

bleikur pink; *synonyms* (*adj*) flower, (*n*) red, crimson, rose, (*v*) knock.

blekfiskar cuttlefish; *synonyms* (*n*) cuttle, sound, knife, noise, octopuses.

blendingsmál pidgin; *synonym* (*n*) slang.

blendingur 1. chimera; *synonyms* (*n*) chimaera, dream, fantasy, figment, illusion; *antonym* (*n*) reality, **2.** hybrid; *synonyms* (*adj*) crossbred, (*n*) crossbreed, cross, mixture, (*v*) composite.

blendinn heterologous; *synonyms* (*adj*) heterologic, heterological, different.

bless 1. adieu; *synonyms* (*n*) farewell, goodbye, valediction, leave, adios, **2.** bye; *synonyms* (*n*) adieu, cheerio, arrivederci, pass, (*adj*) delitescent, **3.** farewell; *synonyms* (*n*) parting, departure, separation, **4.** goodbye; *synonyms* (*int*) ciao, (*n*) bye, exit.

blettabryngedda billfish; *synonyms* (*n*) garfish, gar, garpike, needlefish, saury.

blettagreining chromatography; *synonyms* (*n*) chromatism, chromatology.

blettahreistur psoriasis; *synonyms* (*n*) itch, leucoplakia.

blettaskán psoriasis; *synonyms* (*n*) itch, leucoplakia.

blettkjarni umbra; *synonyms* (*n*) shadow, shade, soul, spirit.

blettkragi penumbra; *synonyms* (*n*) shade, shadow, eclipse, (*adj*) umbra.

blettmiðja umbra; *synonyms* (*n*) shadow, shade, soul, spirit.

blettóttur punctate; *synonym* (*adj*) speckled.

blettpróf blot; *synonyms* (*n*) blemish, spot, smudge, (*v*) stain, mark.

blettur 1. stain; *synonyms* (*n*) spot, blemish, blot, (*v*) color, dye, **2.** spot; *synonyms* (*n*) place, speck, stain, dot, (*v*) soil, **3.** macula; *synonyms* (*n*) freckle, mole, sunspot, macule.

bleyja nappy; *synonyms* (*n*) diaper, napkin, corned, (*v*) frothy, (*adj*) downy.

bleyta dampen; *synonyms* (*v*) deaden, muffle, depress, dishearten, (*n*) damp; *antonym* (*v*) stimulate.

blíða beauty; *synonyms* (*n*) splendor, attractiveness, beaut, charm, loveliness; *antonym* (*n*) ugliness.

blik 1. scintillation; *synonyms* (*n*) flash, glisten, glitter, sparkle, fire, **2.** corona; *synonyms* (*n*) crown, radiance, halo, aureole, necklace, **3.** flicker; *synonyms* (*n*) flare, glimmer, (*v*) flutter, waver, blaze.

blika cirrostratus; *synonym* (*n*) cumulostratus.

blikk 1. plate; *synonyms* (*n*) dish, leaf, (*v*) gild, sheet, cover, **2.** blinking; *synonyms* (*adj*) bally, (*n*) winking, shimmer, blink, wink; *antonym* (*adj*) constant.

blikka blink; *synonyms* (*v*) wink, flash, twinkle, flicker, (*n*) blinking.

blikkdós 1. tin; *synonyms* (*n*) can, canister, container, (*v*) pot, preserve, **2.** can; *synonyms* (*v*) tin, dismiss, (*n*) bathroom, behind, buttocks; *antonym* (*v*) hire.

blikkræma shim; *synonyms* (*n*) wedge, liner, filling.

bliksjá stroboscope; *synonym* (*n*) strobe.

blikufjaðrir cirrus; *synonyms* (*n*) woolpack, cirrhus, stratus, cumulus.

blikutrefjar cirrus; *synonyms* (*n*) woolpack, cirrhus, stratus, cumulus.

blinda blindness; *synonyms* (*n*) cecity, darkness, sightlessness, ablepsy, ignorance.

blindband recess; *synonyms* (*n*) corner, break, holiday, intermission, niche.

blindhríð blizzard; *synonyms* (*n*) snowstorm, storm, tempest, snowfall, gale.

blindsvæði occlusion; *synonyms* (*n*) closure, block, blockage, stoppage, obstruction.

blinduflekkur scotoma; *synonym* (*n*) scotomy.

blindur blind; *synonyms* (*v*) bedazzle, (*n*) screen, curtain, shutter, awning; *antonym* (*adj*) sighted.

blístrandi sibilant; *synonyms* (*adj*) hissing, fricative, sibilatory, sibilous, spirant.

blísturshljóð sibilant; *synonyms* (*adj*) hissing, fricative, sibilatory, sibilous, spirant.

blóð blood; *synonyms* (*n*) ancestry, birth, gore, descent, family.

blóðbönd consanguinity; *synonyms* (*n*) blood, cognation, kindred, relation, kin.

blóðeitrun 1. septicemia; *synonym* (*n*) septicaemia, **2.** sepsis; *synonyms* (*adj*) infection, pollution, septicity, taint.

blóðflaga platelet; *synonym* (*n*) thrombocyte.

blóðfrumnamyndun hematopoiesis; *synonyms* (*n*) haemopoiesis, hematosis, hemopoiesis, haematogenesis, haematopoiesis.

blóðfrumumyndun hematopoiesis; *synonyms* (*n*) haemopoiesis, hematosis, hemopoiesis, haematogenesis, haematopoiesis.

blóðga bleed; *synonyms* (*v*) ooze, phlebotomize, run, (*n*) bleeding, ache.

blóðgjöf transfusion; *synonyms* (*n*) infusion, mixture, spread.

blóðhlaup ecchymosis; *synonyms* (*n*) effusion, exhalation, extravasation, extrusion, exudation.

blóðhreinsun clearance; *synonyms* (*n*) clearing, clearage, disposal, headroom, settlement; *antonyms* (*n*) blockage, retention.

blóðilda ventilate; *synonyms* (*v*) air, fan, vent, discuss, aerate.

blóðkornamyndun hematopoiesis; *synonyms* (*n*) haemopoiesis, hematosis, hemopoiesis, haematogenesis, haematopoiesis.

blóðkýli furuncle; *synonyms* (*n*) boil, abscess, blister, caruncle, corn.

blóðlaus anemic; *synonyms* (*adj*) anaemic, weak, colorless, insipid, frail.

blóðleysi anemia; *synonym* (*n*) anaemia.

blóðlýsa leukemia; *synonyms* (*n*) leukaemia, (*adj*) cancer, carcinoma, malignancy, tumor.

blóðmítill tick; *synonyms* (*n*) beat, credit, score, (*v*) mark, check.

blóðnasir 1. nosebleed; *synonyms* (*n*) epistaxis, hemorrhage, bleed, 2. epistaxis; *synonym* (*n*) nosebleed.

blóðögusótt schistosomiasis; *synonyms* (*n*) bilharziasis, bilharzia.

blóðögðuveiki schistosomiasis; *synonyms* (*n*) bilharziasis, bilharzia.

blóðrásaskil watershed; *synonyms* (*n*) divide, landmark, basin, border, distinction.

blóðrauðaleysandi hemolytic; *synonym* (*adj*) haemolytic.

blóðrauðalos hemolysis; *synonyms* (*n*) haemolysis, haematolysis, hematolysis.

blóðrauðamiga hemoglobinuria; *synonym* (*n*) haemoglobinuria.

blóðrauði hemoglobin; *synonyms* (*n*) haemoglobin, oxyhemoglobin, blood, hematocrystallin.

blóðrek 1. embolism; *synonyms* (*n*) embolus, clot, intercalation, 2. embolus; *synonym* (*n*) blockade.

blóðreki embolus; *synonyms* (*n*) clot, blockade.

blóðreksstífla embolism; *synonyms* (*n*) embolus, clot, intercalation.

blóðrennslisstöðvun hemostasis; *synonyms* (*n*) hemostasia, haemostasia, haemostasis.

blöðrulaga vesicular; *synonyms* (*adj*) vesiculate, cystic, vascular, ventricular, bladdery.

blöðrulyf vesicant; *synonyms* (*n*) vesicatory, epispastic, eyewater.

blöðrungur vesicle; *synonyms* (*n*) blister, cyst, envelope, capsule, (*adj*) drop.

blöðrustjórn continence; *synonyms* (*n*) abstinence, temperance, chastity, celibacy, continency.

blóðsegi thrombus; *synonym* (*n*) clot.

blóðsermi serum; *synonyms* (*n*) juice, antitoxin, (*adj*) lymph, humor, sap.

blóðsifjar consanguinity; *synonyms* (*n*) blood, cognation, kindred, relation, kin.

blóðsjúkdómafræði hematology; *synonyms* (*n*) haematology, hemology.

blóðskortur anemia; *synonym* (*n*) anaemia.

blóðskyldleiki consanguinity; *synonyms* (*n*) blood, cognation, kindred, relation, kin.

blóðstemmandi styptic; *synonyms* (*adj*) hemostatic, restringent, anastaltic, binding, (*n*) astringent.

blóðstorkuheftir anticoagulant; *synonym* (*n*) decoagulant.

blóðstreymi circulation; *synonyms* (*n*) dissemination, diffusion, distribution, currency, delivery.

blóðsýking sepsis; *synonyms* (*adj*) infection, pollution, septicity, taint.

blóðsýring acidosis; *synonym* (*n*) indigestion.

blóðtappi clot; *synonyms* (*v*) clod, curdle, cake, clabber, clog; *antonym* (*v*) liquefy.

blóðþurrð ischemia; *synonym* (*n*) ischaemia.

blóðvatn serum; *synonyms* (*n*) juice, antitoxin, (*adj*) lymph, humor, sap.

blóðvökvi plasma; *synonyms* (*n*) plasm, onyx, blood, flesh.

blokk block; *synonyms* (*n*) bar, barricade, pad, (*v*) arrest, stop; *antonyms* (*v*) free, unblock, open.

blökk tackle; *synonyms* (*v*) handle, harness, (*n*) gear, equipment, rigging; *antonym* (*v*) avoid.

blokkarflötur deck; *synonyms* (*v*) adorn, beautify, clothe, embellish, floor.

blokki antagonist; *synonyms* (*n*) opponent, adversary, enemy, foe, rival; *antonym* (*n*) friend.

blom 1. bloom; *synonyms* (*n*) blush, bud, (*adj*) blossom, flower, blow; *antonyms* (*v*) wither, shrivel, 2. flower; *synonyms* (*n*) bouquet, cream, efflorescence, (*v*) bloom, (*adj*) prime.

blóm flower; *synonyms* (*n*) bouquet, (*v*) bloom, blossom, blow, (*adj*) prime.

blómbikar calyx; *synonyms* (*n*) cancelli, utricle, capsule, cyst, pod.

blómbotn 1. receptacle; *synonyms* (*n*) container, box, case, can, pocket, 2. torus; *synonyms* (*n*) tore, toroid, thalamus, breast, mamma, 3. thalamus.

blómhnoða glomerulus; *synonym* (*n*) glomerule.

blómi 1. yolk; *synonyms* (*n*) deutoplasm, suint, vitellus, 2. bloom; *synonyms* (*n*) blush, bud, (*adj*) blossom, flower, blow; *antonyms* (*v*) wither, shrivel.

blómkál cauliflower; *synonyms* (*n*) broccoli, colliflower.

blómkróna corolla; *synonym* (*n*) corol.

blómleggur pedicel; *synonyms* (*n*) pedicle, stalk, pedicule, stem.

blómskipunarleggur peduncle; *synonyms* (*n*) stem, (*v*) pedicel, pedicle.

blómskipunarstöngull rachis; *synonyms* (*n*) back, backbone, spine, anchor, backrest.

blómstrandi florid; *synonyms* (*adj*) flamboyant, ornate, aureate, fancy, flowery.

blöndun 1. dubbing; *synonyms* (*n*) daubing, copy, **2.** inclusion; *synonyms* (*n*) comprehension, implication, incorporation, addition, embodiment; *antonyms* (*n*) exclusion, exception, **3.** mixing; *synonyms* (*n*) blending, mix, admixture, commixture, mixture.

blöndunarstig mixer; *synonyms* (*n*) blender, social, agitator, churn, sociable.

blöndungur 1. carburetor; *synonym* (*n*) carburettor, **2.** carburettor; *synonym* (*n*) carburetor.

blóraböggull scapegoat; *synonyms* (*n*) hostage, target, (*v*) dummy, shift, stopgap.

blossi burst; *synonyms* (*v*) break, crack, blast, (*adj*) split, explode; *antonym* (*v*) implode.

blótgripur fetish; *synonyms* (*n*) fetich, charm, fixation, idol, juju.

blý lead; *synonyms* (*v*) head, guide, conduct, contribute, direct; *antonym* (*v*) follow.

blýantur pencil; *synonyms* (*n*) pen, beam, (*v*) brush, draw, design.

blýeitrun saturnism; *synonym* (*n*) plumbism.

blys rocket; *synonyms* (*n*) missile, bomb, (*v*) soar, rise, skyrocket; *antonyms* (*v*) plummet, dawdle.

bobbingur bobbin; *synonyms* (*n*) spool, coil, reel, arbor, spindle.

boð 1. impulse; *synonyms* (*n*) impetus, pulse, urge, drive, force, **2.** offer; *synonyms* (*v*) give, bestow, put, (*n*) bid, proposal; *antonyms* (*v*) withdraw, refuse, **3.** message; *synonyms* (*n*) communication, meaning, information, errand, letter, **4.** invitation; *synonyms* (*n*) call, bidding, temptation, lure, (*v*) invite.

boðbreytir transducer; *synonyms* (*n*) sensor, transductor.

boddí body; *synonyms* (*n*) cadaver, corpse, matter, organization, carcass; *antonym* (*n*) spirit.

boddíhlutir bodywork; *synonyms* (*n*) armature, carcass, frame, framework, hulk.

boðefni 1. transmitter; *synonyms* (*n*) sender, aerial, mast, purveyor, source, **2.** neurotransmitter.

boðfall fading; *synonyms* (*adj*) dying, disappearing, paling, (*n*) attenuation, bleaching; *antonym* (*n*) appearance.

boðkenna program; *synonyms* (*n*) agenda, plan, broadcast, design, (*v*) schedule.

boðrit program; *synonyms* (*n*) agenda, plan, broadcast, design, (*v*) schedule.

boðrita program; *synonyms* (*n*) agenda, plan, broadcast, design, (*v*) schedule.

boðritari programmer; *synonym* (*n*) coder.

boðritun programming; *synonyms* (*n*) programing, scheduling, program, indoctrination, instruction.

boðsal communication; *synonyms* (*n*) announcement, commerce, communicating, contact, conversation.

boðsenda relay; *synonyms* (*n*) relief, spell, (*v*) broadcast, pass, transmit.

boðsending relay; *synonyms* (*n*) relief, spell, (*v*) broadcast, pass, transmit.

boðskipti communication; *synonyms* (*n*) announcement, commerce, communicating, contact, conversation.

böðulslosti sadism; *synonyms* (*n*) cruelty, brutality, aggression, atrocity, (*adj*) sapphism.

böffer buffer; *synonyms* (*n*) safeguard, pad, protection, bumper, (*v*) cushion.

bogaeining radian; *synonym* (*n*) rad.

bogagöng arcade; *synonyms* (*n*) arch, colonnade, piazza, portico, arc.

bogamælieining radian; *synonym* (*n*) rad.

bogamálseining radian; *synonym* (*n*) rad.

bogamínúta minute; *synonyms* (*n*) instant, flash, jiffy, note, (*adj*) little; *antonyms* (*adj*) enormous, huge, big, gigantic.

bogarið arcade; *synonyms* (*n*) arch, colonnade, piazza, portico, arc.

bogasekúnda second; *synonyms* (*n*) instant, moment, flash, jiffy, (*v*) back; *antonym* (*adj*) first.

bogfall misfire; *synonyms* (*n*) flop, dud, (*v*) fail, miscarry, fizzle.

böggull 1. parcel; *synonyms* (*n*) lot, bale, pack, bundle, (*v*) portion, **2.** bundle; *synonyms* (*n*) cluster, pile, sheaf, (*v*) bunch, clump, **3.** pack; *synonyms* (*n*) mob, bevy, company, (*v*) crowd, compress; *antonym* (*v*) unpack, **4.** package; *synonyms* (*n*) packaging, packet, parcel, (*v*) box, wrap; *antonym* (*v*) unwrap.

böggur bug; *synonyms* (*n*) beetle, (*v*) annoy, badger, pester, bother.

bogi 1. arch; *synonyms* (*n*) arc, acute, bend, (*v*) curve, bow; *antonym* (*v*) straightness, **2.** arc; *synonyms* (*n*) arch, crescent, curvature, spark, sweep.

boglína curve; *synonyms* (*n*) bend, crook, bow, (*v*) curl, turn.

bognun 1. diffraction; *synonyms* (*n*) deflection, deviation, inflection, **2.** deflection; *synonyms* (*n*) bend, deflexion, variation, bending, digression.

bogtenntur crenate; *synonyms* (*adj*) crenated, scalloped.

boguggi bowfin; *synonyms* (*n*) dogfish, grindle.

bógur bow; *synonyms* (*n*) arc, curve, (*v*) bend, arch, stoop.

bogviður yew; *synonyms* (*n*) yam, zinnia, (*v*) yaw.

bók book; *synonyms* (*n*) bible, (*v*) order, reserve, apply, inscribe.

bóka 1. record; *synonyms (n)* register, list, account, *(v)* chronicle, file, **2.** register; *synonyms (n)* record, inventory, note, catalogue, *(v)* enroll.

bókarauki appendix; *synonyms (n)* addition, adjunct, addendum, annex, *(v)* supplement.

bókari 1. bookkeeper; *synonyms (n)* accountant, actuary, amanuensis, auditor, babu, **2.** accountant; *synonyms (n)* teller, cashier, controller, almoner, liquidator.

bókasafn library; *synonyms (n)* bibliotheca, annals, archive, bibliotheke, den.

bókfærsla bookkeeping; *synonyms (n)* reckoning, clerking, *(adj)* clerical, office, secretarial.

bókhald 1. bookkeeping; *synonyms (n)* reckoning, clerking, *(adj)* clerical, office, secretarial, **2.** accounting; *synonyms (n)* bookkeeping, account, accountancy, chronicle, explanation.

bókhaldsreikningur account; *synonyms (n)* bill, narrative, reckoning, regard, *(v)* report.

bókhveiti buckwheat; *synonyms (n)* grain, branks, cereal, maize, millet.

bókhveitigrjón buckwheat; *synonyms (n)* grain, branks, cereal, maize, millet.

bókstafareikningur algebra; *synonyms (v)* fluxions, geometry, analysis, arithmetic.

bókstafur letter; *synonyms (n)* epistle, mail, character, communication, dispatch.

bókun 1. protocol; *synonyms (n)* etiquette, manners, ceremony, bill, formality, **2.** reservation; *synonyms (n)* reserve, limitation, booking, condition, qualification; *antonym (n)* certainty, **3.** registration; *synonyms (n)* enrollment, registering, enrolment, entering, entry, **4.** minutes; *synonyms (n)* proceedings, record, transactions, records, journal, **5.** memorandum; *synonyms (n)* memo, note, memorial, letter, memoranda.

bóla 1. vesicle; *synonyms (n)* blister, cyst, envelope, capsule, *(adj)* drop, **2.** bubble; *synonyms (v)* boil, babble, foam, burble, effervesce, **3.** blister; *synonyms (n)* bleb, bubble, bulla, *(v)* scorch, burn, **4.** latent; *synonyms (adj)* covert, potential, secret, dormant, hidden; *antonym (adj)* active.

bólfesta 1. implantation; *synonyms (n)* implant, insertion, nidation, graft, introduction, **2.** nidation; *synonym (n)* implantation.

bolfiskur whitefish; *synonyms (n)* anchovies, herring, sardines, shad, smelts.

bólga inflammation; *synonyms (n)* inflaming, swelling, burning, firing, *(v)* ignition.

bólgnun intumescence; *synonyms (n)* bulge, swelling, tumefaction, dropsy, tumor.

bólguholdgun granulation; *synonyms (n)* aggregation, *(adj)* attenuation, comminution, levigation, multure.

bolli 1. cup; *synonyms (n)* chalice, basin, trophy, destiny, fate, **2.** cups; *synonyms (n)* dishes, dishware, plates, tableware, saucers.

bólómælir bolometer; *synonym (n)* barretter.

bölró resignation; *synonyms (n)* capitulation, endurance, patience, renunciation, surrender.

bólstraský cumulus; *synonyms (n)* heap, mound, pile, stratus, woolpack.

bólstrun padding; *synonyms (n)* pad, cushioning, filling, wadding, *(adj)* cushion.

bólstur puff; *synonyms (n)* gasp, whiff, *(v)* pant, blow, boast.

bólsturský cumulus; *synonyms (n)* heap, mound, pile, stratus, woolpack.

bolti 1. screw; *synonyms (n)* fuck, *(v)* cheat, fasten, *(adj)* bolt, nail, **2.** bolt; *synonyms (n)* arrow, dash, *(v)* bar, abscond, gobble; *antonyms (v)* nibble, unbolt, unlock, **3.** ball; *synonyms (n)* bulb, globe, shot, shell, bead.

bóluefni vaccine; *synonyms (n)* vaccination, immunization, inoculation, *(adj)* animal, bovine.

bolur 1. skirt; *synonyms (n)* border, edge, brim, *(v)* fringe, circumvent, **2.** shaft; *synonyms (n)* arrow, handle, axis, beam, pit, **3.** body; *synonyms (n)* cadaver, corpse, matter, organization, carcass; *antonym (n)* spirit.

bólusetning 1. vaccination; *synonyms (n)* inoculation, immunization, prevention, shot, injection, **2.** immunization; *synonyms (n)* immunisation, vaccine, jab.

bólusótt 1. variola; *synonyms (n)* smallpox, *(adj)* scabies, scarlatina, scrofula, seasickness, **2.** smallpox; *synonym (n)* variola.

bölva 1. swear; *synonyms (v)* affirm, assert, assure, curse, declare, **2.** curse; *synonyms (n)* bane, anathema, blasphemy, *(v)* beshrew, blight, **3.** blaspheme; *synonyms (v)* desecrate, profane, swear, cuss, damn, **4.** cuss; *synonyms (n)* malediction, blighter, chap, expletive, *(v)* blaspheme.

bóma 1. spar; *synonyms (n)* beam, mast, *(v)* quarrel, box, fight, **2.** boom; *synonyms (n)* bang, roar, *(v)* blast, blare, flourish; *antonyms (n)* depression, *(v)* collapse, decline.

bómull cotton; *synonyms (n)* thread, yarn, cord, fiber, string.

bón wax; *synonyms (n)* increase, *(v)* grow, become, rise, mount.

bönd attachment; *synonyms (n)* affection, appendix, accessory, addition, adherence; *antonym (n)* detachment.

bóndabær farm; *synonyms (n)* property, grange, dairy, *(v)* cultivate, raise.

bóndi farmer; *synonyms* (*n*) countryman, agriculturist, rustic, husbandman, granger.

bónus bonus; *synonyms* (*n*) award, compensation, premium, dividend, (*adj*) extra; *antonym* (*n*) disadvantage.

bónuskerfi incentive; *synonyms* (*n*) encouragement, impetus, cause, goad, impulse; *antonyms* (*n*) deterrent, disincentive, constraint.

bor drill; *synonyms* (*n*) exercise, discipline, practice, auger, (*v*) bore.

bór 1. boron; *synonyms* (*n*) bacilli, bacillus, barn, bel, **2**. b; *synonyms* (*n*) boron, hark, look, (*v*) d, e.

bora 1. drill; *synonyms* (*n*) exercise, discipline, practice, auger, (*v*) bore, **2**. crypt; *synonyms* (*n*) vault, tomb, mausoleum, cellar, sepulcher, **3**. bore; *synonyms* (*v*) dig, bother, tire, annoy, (*n*) caliber; *antonyms* (*v*) interest, excite, fascinate.

borald unit; *synonyms* (*n*) troop, element, group, squad, (*adj*) one.

borast penetrate; *synonyms* (*v*) bore, imbue, fathom, infiltrate, permeate.

bórax borax; *synonym* (*adj*) shoddy.

borð 1. plank; *synonyms* (*n*) board, beam, timber, girder, panel, **2**. ullage; *synonym* (*n*) wantage, **3**. table; *synonyms* (*n*) chart, schedule, stand, list, (*v*) defer, **4**. board; *synonyms* (*n*) council, bench, meal, table, office; *antonym* (*v*) disembark, **5**. deal; *synonyms* (*n*) bargain, buy, agreement, (*v*) administer, allot; *antonym* (*n*) purchase.

börð wing; *synonyms* (*n*) annex, arm, fender, limb, (*v*) fly.

borða eat; *synonyms* (*v*) devour, consume, bite, dine, munch.

borðganga boarding; *synonyms* (*n*) embarkation, embarkment, escalade, lodging, livery.

borði 1. strap; *synonyms* (*n*) belt, leash, strop, (*v*) lash, whip, **2**. band; *synonyms* (*n*) cluster, party, set, swathe, (*v*) ring, **3**. lining; *synonyms* (*n*) facing, liner, inside, cladding, padding.

bordo banks; *synonym* (*n*) breast.

borg 1. town; *synonyms* (*n*) city, borough, township, (*adj*) municipal, urban, **2**. city; *synonyms* (*n*) town, burgh, metropolis, municipality, (*adj*) civic; *antonym* (*adj*) rural, **3**. municipality; *synonyms* (*n*) shrievalty, commune, area, capital, region.

borgaraskilningur citizenship; *synonyms* (*n*) nationality, freedom.

borgarastétt bourgeoisie; *synonym* (*n*) class.

borgaravitund citizenship; *synonyms* (*n*) nationality, freedom.

borgarbúar town; *synonyms* (*n*) city, borough, township, (*adj*) municipal, urban.

borgarbúi citizen; *synonyms* (*n*) civilian, denizen, inhabitant, national, resident; *antonym* (*n*) foreigner.

borgari citizen; *synonyms* (*n*) civilian, denizen, inhabitant, national, resident; *antonym* (*n*) foreigner.

borgarís iceberg; *synonyms* (*n*) berg, (*adj*) dispassionate.

borgarísjaki iceberg; *synonyms* (*n*) berg, (*adj*) dispassionate.

borgarísmoli growler; *synonyms* (*n*) grouch, cab, cabriolet, car, (*v*) grumbler.

borgarstjórn municipality; *synonyms* (*n*) city, town, metropolis, shrievalty, commune.

borgmyndun urbanization; *synonym* (*n*) urbanisation.

borgun pay; *synonyms* (*v*) compensate, compensation, liquidate, (*n*) recompense, wage; *antonym* (*v*) owe.

borhola well; *synonyms* (*adv*) right, easily, thoroughly, (*adj*) healthy, (*n*) fountain; *antonyms* (*adv*) ill, badly, poorly, (*adj*) sick, unwell.

börkur 1. bark; *synonyms* (*n*) snarl, yelp, (*v*) yap, skin, cry; *antonyms* (*v*) mutter, whisper, **2**. cork; *synonyms* (*n*) bung, stopper, (*v*) plug, cap, stop, **3**. cortex; *synonyms* (*n*) bark, crust, peel, rind, pallium, **4**. peel; *synonyms* (*n*) hide, (*v*) hull, flake, flay, pare.

borun 1. drilling; *synonyms* (*n*) boring, drill, exercise, discipline, education, **2**. boring; *synonyms* (*adj*) dull, tedious, tiresome, annoying, (*n*) drilling; *antonyms* (*adj*) exciting, fascinating, interesting, gripping, original.

borvídd bore; *synonyms* (*v*) dig, bother, tire, annoy, (*n*) caliber; *antonyms* (*v*) interest, excite, fascinate.

bót patch; *synonyms* (*n*) darn, fleck, mend, plot, (*v*) piece.

bótakrafa claim; *synonyms* (*n*) call, charge, allegation, (*v*) demand, ask; *antonyms* (*v*) deny, disclaim, forfeit.

bótaþegi beneficiary; *synonyms* (*n*) heir, inheritor, receiver, recipient, successor; *antonym* (*n*) donor.

botn bottom; *synonyms* (*n*) base, basis, backside, bed, behind; *antonyms* (*n*) top, pinnacle, (*adj*) highest.

botneðja sludge; *synonyms* (*n*) mud, ooze, slime, (*adj*) silt, mire.

botnefja sludge; *synonyms* (*n*) mud, ooze, slime, (*adj*) silt, mire.

botnfall 1. shedding; *synonyms* (*n*) fluffing, peeling, effusion, desquamation, emission; *antonym* (*adj*) smooth, **2**. precipitate; *synonyms* (*n*) deposit, (*adj*) hasty, headlong, impetuous, sudden, **3**. sediment; *synonyms* (*n*) deposition, lees, dregs, grounds, substance, **4**. deposit; *synonyms* (*n*) charge, (*v*) bank, commit, store, fix; *antonym* (*v*) withdraw.

botnfelling 1. precipitation; *synonyms* (*n*) hurry, rain, precipitancy, downfall, haste, **2**. sedimentation; *synonyms* (*n*) deposit, sediment, settling, alluviation, deposition.

botnlag sediment; *synonyms* (*n*) deposit, deposition, lees, dregs, grounds.

botnlangabólga appendicitis; *synonym* (*adj*) ague.

botnlanganám appendectomy; *synonym* (*n*) appendicectomy.

botnlangaskurður appendectomy; *synonym* (*n*) appendicectomy.

botnlangatota appendix; *synonyms* (*n*) addition, adjunct, addendum, annex, (*v*) supplement.

botnlangi appendix; *synonyms* (*n*) addition, adjunct, addendum, annex, (*v*) supplement.

botnleðja 1. silt; *synonyms* (*n*) sediment, deposit, (*adj*) mire, mud, alluvium, **2**. sludge; *synonyms* (*n*) ooze, slime, muck, (*adj*) silt, quagmire.

botnsætinn 1. sedentary; *synonyms* (*adj*) inactive, lazy, sluggish, domestic, (*v*) untraveled; *antonym* (*adj*) active, **2**. sessile; *synonyms* (*adj*) attached, affiliated, committed, connected, stalkless.

botnsetja sink; *synonyms* (*n*) sag, (*v*) decline, dip, droop, fall; *antonyms* (*v*) rise, float.

botnskál sump; *synonyms* (*n*) bog, cesspit, cesspool, sink, swamp.

botnstallur step; *synonyms* (*n*) degree, measure, stage, walk, (*v*) pace.

botnstykki transducer; *synonyms* (*n*) sensor, transductor.

botntala beauty; *synonyms* (*n*) splendor, attractiveness, beaut, charm, loveliness; *antonym* (*n*) ugliness.

botnvarpa trawl; *synonyms* (*n*) dragnet, (*v*) angle, fish, tow, haul.

bráð 1. flux; *synonyms* (*n*) current, (*v*) flow, dissolve, thaw, course, **2**. melt; *synonyms* (*v*) fuse, deliquesce, run, vanish, (*adj*) liquefy; *antonyms* (*v*) freeze, cool, solidify.

bráðabirgða 1. temporary; *synonyms* (*adj*) ephemeral, passing, temporal, acting, momentary; *antonyms* (*adj*) permanent, continuous, enduring, eternal, everlasting, **2**. provisional; *synonyms* (*adj*) conditional, makeshift, tentative, probationary, interim; *antonym* (*adj*) definite.

bráðafár plague; *synonyms* (*v*) bother, harass, molest, worry, afflict.

bráðaofnæmi anaphylaxis; *synonym* (*n*) anaphylaxy.

bráðavandi crisis; *synonyms* (*n*) exigency, conjuncture, difficulty, emergency, juncture.

bráðger precocious; *synonyms* (*adj*) forward, advanced, early, pert, premature.

bráðlyndur choleric; *synonyms* (*adj*) angry, irascible, passionate, peppery, cantankerous.

bráðna 1. thaw; *synonyms* (*n*) melting, (*v*) melt, dissolve, fuse, liquefy; *antonyms* (*v*) freeze, cool, **2**. melt; *synonyms* (*v*) deliquesce, run, thaw, vanish, coalesce; *antonym* (*v*) solidify.

bráðnun 1. melting; *synonyms* (*adj*) liquescent, (*n*) fusion, melt, thawing, dissolution, **2**. fusion; *synonyms* (*n*) amalgamation, coalition, alliance, coalescence, combination; *antonym* (*n*) separation.

bráðþroska precocious; *synonyms* (*adj*) forward, advanced, early, pert, premature.

bráðþroski precocity; *synonyms* (*n*) precociousness, forwardness, intelligence, advancement, (*adj*) prematurity.

bráður 1. acute; *synonyms* (*adj*) sharp, incisive, intense, keen, penetrating; *antonyms* (*adj*) dull, obtuse, **2**. sharp; *synonyms* (*adj*) acute, bitter, intelligent, acid, acrid; *antonyms* (*adj*) blunt, mild, gentle, rounded, sweet, **3**. stark; *synonyms* (*adj*) austere, bare, bleak, desolate, mere.

bræða 1. smelt; *synonyms* (*v*) fuse, melt, temper, anneal, heat, **2**. dissolve; *synonyms* (*v*) disappear, disperse, dissipate, disband, evaporate; *antonyms* (*v*) appear, harden, solidify, **3**. melt; *synonyms* (*v*) dissolve, deliquesce, run, thaw, (*adj*) liquefy; *antonyms* (*v*) freeze, cool, **4**. fuse; *synonyms* (*v*) combine, amalgamate, blend, coalesce, compound; *antonym* (*v*) separate, **5**. found; *synonyms* (*v*) erect, establish, base, build, form; *antonym* (*adj*) misplaced.

bræðanlegur fusible; *synonyms* (*adj*) liquid, (*v*) cast, founded, fusil.

bræði rage; *synonyms* (*n*) fury, wrath, anger, (*v*) fume, bluster.

bræðivar fuse; *synonyms* (*v*) combine, amalgamate, blend, melt, coalesce; *antonym* (*v*) separate.

bræðsla 1. fusion; *synonyms* (*n*) amalgamation, coalition, alliance, coalescence, combination; *antonym* (*n*) separation, **2**. melting; *synonyms* (*adj*) liquescent, (*n*) fusion, melt, thawing, dissolution.

bræðsluofn furnace; *synonyms* (*n*) heater, hearth, oven, stove, chimney.

bragð 1. taste; *synonyms* (*n*) bit, flavor, (*v*) relish, savor, sample; *antonyms* (*n*) dislike, tastelessness, **2**. gambit; *synonyms* (*n*) maneuver, ploy, ruse, artifice, strategy.

bragðkjarni essence; *synonyms* (*n*) core, entity, aroma, being, crux.

bragðskyn 1. gustation; *synonyms* (*n*) taste, degustation, discernment, tasting, appreciation, **2**.

gustatory; *synonyms* (*adj*) gustative, gustable, gustatorial, sensory.

bragfræði metrics; *synonyms* (*n*) prosody, inflection.

braggi barrack; *synonyms* (*n*) barracks, (*v*) jeer, cheer, gibe, scoff.

brak 1. debris; *synonyms* (*n*) detritus, junk, refuse, rubbish, trash, **2**. fragment; *synonyms* (*n*) fraction, crumb, (*v*) bit, chip, scrap.

braka 1. crackle; *synonyms* (*n*) crackling, crepitation, (*v*) crack, crepitate, crunch, **2**. arms; *synonyms* (*n*) arm, armament, weaponry, shield, ordnance.

brakapogilo arms; *synonyms* (*n*) arm, armament, weaponry, shield, ordnance.

brakki barrack; *synonyms* (*n*) barracks, (*v*) jeer, cheer, gibe, scoff.

brako 1. arms; *synonyms* (*n*) arm, armament, weaponry, shield, ordnance, **2**. arm; *synonyms* (*n*) branch, wing, bay, department, (*v*) equip; *antonym* (*v*) disarm.

brandur gangrene; *synonyms* (*n*) mortification, necrosis, (*v*) chagrin, (*adj*) corruption, caries.

brasa braze; *synonyms* (*v*) stick, temper, harden.

brask speculation; *synonyms* (*n*) hypothesis, guess, reflection, venture, guesswork.

brasmálmur solder; *synonyms* (*n*) glue, paste, (*v*) cement, join, fuse.

brattur steep; *synonyms* (*adj*) high, abrupt, excessive, (*v*) douse, immerse; *antonyms* (*adj*) gentle, gradual.

brauð 1. bread; *synonyms* (*n*) living, livelihood, cash, maintenance, currency, **2**. loaf; *synonyms* (*v*) dawdle, lounge, laze, linger, loiter.

brauðsnúður sandwich; *synonym* (*v*) interlard.

braut 1. runway; *synonyms* (*n*) track, airfield, airport, channel, tarmac, **2**. tract; *synonyms* (*n*) area, essay, expanse, pamphlet, region, **3**. trajectory; *synonyms* (*n*) course, orbit, line, flight, path, **4**. band; *synonyms* (*n*) cluster, party, set, swathe, (*v*) ring, **5**. bar; *synonyms* (*n*) barricade, band, (*v*) ban, block, bolt; *antonyms* (*v*) permit, allow.

brautamót fillet; *synonyms* (*n*) band, strip, cincture, list, (*v*) filet.

brautarhalli inclination; *synonyms* (*n*) disposition, desire, bent, fancy, affection; *antonyms* (*n*) disinclination, reluctance.

brautarhorn anomaly; *synonyms* (*n*) abnormality, aberration, anomalousness, deviation, abnormity.

brautarhringur orb; *synonyms* (*n*) ball, globe, sphere, cycle, circle.

brautarjaðar shoulder; *synonyms* (*n*) elbow, (*v*) bear, carry, push, hold.

brautarsnerting touchdown; *synonyms* (*n*) goal, point, (*v*) land.

brautarteinn rail; *synonyms* (*n*) bar, balustrade, handrail, railing, (*v*) inveigh.

brautryðjandi entrepreneur; *synonyms* (*n*) contractor, enterpriser, businessperson, tycoon, manufacturer.

bréf letter; *synonyms* (*n*) epistle, mail, character, communication, dispatch.

bréfasími 1. fax; *synonyms* (*n*) autotype, (*v*) facsimile, telefax, **2**. facsimile; *synonyms* (*n*) duplicate, copy, model, replica, (*v*) fax; *antonym* (*n*) original.

bréfsími telefax; *synonyms* (*v*) facsimile, fax.

breidd 1. width; *synonyms* (*n*) breadth, extent, latitude, length, size; *antonym* (*n*) thinness, **2**. latitude; *synonyms* (*n*) freedom, room, scope, expanse, compass, **3**. parallel; *synonyms* (*adj*) equivalent, even, (*n*) equal, (*v*) compare, match; *antonyms* (*adj*) conflicting, dissimilar, (*n*) perpendicular, skew.

breiddarbaugur 1. parallel; *synonyms* (*adj*) equivalent, even, (*n*) equal, (*v*) compare, match; *antonyms* (*adj*) conflicting, dissimilar, (*n*) perpendicular, skew, **2**. latitude; *synonyms* (*n*) breadth, freedom, room, scope, expanse.

breiddargráða latitude; *synonyms* (*n*) breadth, freedom, room, scope, expanse.

breiðstræti avenue; *synonyms* (*n*) channel, approach, passage, path, road.

breiður wide; *synonyms* (*adj*) broad, spacious, roomy, comprehensive, extensive; *antonyms* (*adj*) narrow, thin, restricted.

brekán blanket; *synonyms* (*n*) bedding, (*v*) cloak, cover, (*adj*) sweeping, overall.

bremsa brake; *synonyms* (*n*) bracken, bit, curb, (*v*) halt, retard; *antonym* (*v*) accelerate.

bremsukjálki shoe; *synonyms* (*n*) boot, horseshoe, skid, clog, splint.

bremsuklemma caliper; *synonyms* (*n*) thickness, calipers, callipers, (*v*) calliper, measure.

bremsuskór shoe; *synonyms* (*n*) boot, horseshoe, skid, clog, splint.

brengla scramble; *synonyms* (*n*) bustle, (*v*) clamber, climb, struggle, (*adj*) hurry.

brenna burn; *synonyms* (*v*) bite, glow, blaze, incinerate, (*n*) fire; *antonym* (*v*) dawdle.

brennandi caustic; *synonyms* (*adj*) biting, acrid, bitter, acrimonious, sharp; *antonyms* (*adj*) mild, gentle.

brennari burner; *synonyms* (*n*) wick, fluxer.

brenni fuel; *synonyms* (*n*) firewood, combustible, firing, (*v*) fire, arouse.

brenniferill caustic; *synonyms* (*adj*) biting, acrid, bitter, acrimonious, sharp; *antonyms* (*adj*) mild, gentle.

brenniflötur caustic; *synonyms* (*adj*) biting, acrid, bitter, acrimonious, sharp; *antonyms* (*adj*) mild, gentle.

brennipunktur focus; *synonyms* (*n*) centering, (*v*) center, concentrate, converge, aim.

brennir burner; *synonyms* (*n*) wick, fluxer.

brennisteinn 1. sulfur; *synonyms* (*n*) s, mho, sec, second, (*v*) sulphur, 2. sulphur; *synonyms* (*n*) quebrith, siemens, south, (*v*) brimstone, sulfur, 3. s; *synonyms* (*n*) arcsecond, bit, confederacy, dalliance, endorsement, 4. brimstone.

brennisteinsinnihald sulphur; *synonyms* (*n*) s, mho, quebrith, (*v*) brimstone, sulfur.

brennisteinsmeðferð vulcanization; *synonyms* (*n*) vulcanisation, cure, curing.

brennivídd focus; *synonyms* (*n*) centering, (*v*) center, concentrate, converge, aim.

brennsla combustion; *synonyms* (*n*) burning, fire, burn, blaze, conflagration.

brennslugas gas; *synonyms* (*n*) gasoline, petrol, air, fumes, accelerator.

brestur 1. rupture; *synonyms* (*n*) fracture, burst, rift, (*v*) break, crack; *antonym* (*n*) repair, 2. joint; *synonyms* (*n*) articulation, hinge, join, seam, (*v*) articulate; *antonyms* (*adj*) individual, unilateral, private, separate, 3. fracture; *synonyms* (*n*) breach, cleft, fissure, (*v*) rupture, bust.

bretti wing; *synonyms* (*n*) annex, arm, fender, limb, (*v*) fly.

breyta 1. variable; *synonyms* (*adj*) unstable, changeable, fickle, inconstant, capricious; *antonyms* (*adj*) constant, fixed, invariable, regular, set, 2. convert; *synonyms* (*v*) alter, change, adapt, reform, commute, 3. characterisation; *synonyms* (*n*) characterization, delineation, depiction, picture, depicting, 4. modify; *synonyms* (*v*) qualify, limit, adjust, amend, assuage.

breytandi differential; *synonyms* (*adj*) integral, (*n*) derivative, difference, distinction, fluxion.

breytilegur 1. variable; *synonyms* (*adj*) unstable, changeable, fickle, inconstant, capricious; *antonyms* (*adj*) constant, fixed, invariable, regular, set, 2. adjustable; *synonyms* (*adj*) adaptable, flexible, movable, variable, alterable, 3. dynamic; *synonyms* (*adj*) active, aggressive, dynamical, energetic, forceful; *antonyms* (*adj*) dull, static.

breytileiki 1. variation; *synonyms* (*n*) alteration, change, difference, divergence, mutation; *antonym* (*n*) similarity, 2. variance; *synonyms* (*n*) disagreement, discrepancy, dissension, division, deviation, 3. variability; *synonyms* (*n*) changeability, variableness, instability, variance, variation, 4. instability; *synonyms* (*n*) fickleness,

fluctuation, flightiness, unreliability, (*adj*) fugacity; *antonyms* (*n*) stability, calm.

breyting 1. variation; *synonyms* (*n*) alteration, change, difference, divergence, mutation; *antonym* (*n*) similarity, 2. transition; *synonyms* (*n*) passage, transit, changeover, conversion, modulation, 3. revision; *synonyms* (*n*) modification, amendment, review, revisal, revise, 4. change; *synonyms* (*n*) shift, barter, variation, (*v*) exchange, alter; *antonyms* (*v*) stay, leave, idle, maintain, 5. mutation; *synonyms* (*n*) freak, innovation, mutant, vicissitude, metamorphosis.

breytingar modernization; *synonyms* (*n*) modernisation, innovation, renovation, alteration, change.

breytingaskeið climacteric; *synonyms* (*adj*) critical, anility, decrepitude, superannuation, (*n*) menopause.

breytir 1. transducer; *synonyms* (*n*) sensor, transductor, 2. translator; *synonyms* (*n*) interpreter, transcriber, adapter, arranger, representative, 3. converter; *synonyms* (*n*) convertor, changer, apostle, missionary.

breytistærð variable; *synonyms* (*adj*) unstable, changeable, fickle, inconstant, capricious; *antonyms* (*adj*) constant, fixed, invariable, regular, set.

breytistykki adapter; *synonyms* (*n*) adaptor, spider, attachment, arranger, transcriber.

breytiviðnám potentiometer; *synonyms* (*n*) pot, batch, can, cannabis, commode.

brigðull transitory; *synonyms* (*adj*) passing, transient, brief, fleeting, momentary; *antonym* (*adj*) permanent.

brík land; *synonyms* (*n*) ground, country, soil, (*v*) disembark, debark; *antonym* (*adj*) aquatic.

briljantur brilliant; *synonyms* (*adj*) bright, splendid, glorious, illustrious, intelligent; *antonyms* (*adj*) dull, dim, awful, dark.

brim surf; *synonyms* (*n*) breakers, foam, breaker, spray, (*v*) browse.

brimalda surge; *synonyms* (*v*) billow, flood, rise, rush, stream.

brímavaki oestrogen; *synonym* (*n*) estrogen.

brimbrjótur 1. pier; *synonyms* (*n*) dock, wharf, jetty, pillar, quay, 2. breakwater; *synonyms* (*n*) bulwark, groyne, mole, seawall, groin.

brimvarnargarður breakwater; *synonyms* (*n*) bulwark, groyne, jetty, mole, seawall.

bringa 1. breast; *synonyms* (*n*) bosom, boob, chest, knocker, (*v*) front, 2. thorax; *synonyms* (*n*) pectus, bust, bureau, dresser, 3. chest; *synonyms* (*n*) box, case, casket, chamber, crate.

bringubein breastbone; *synonym* (*n*) sternum.

brislingur sprat; *synonym* (n) brisling.

brjálæði insanity; *synonyms* (n) derangement, frenzy, aberration, delirium, (adj) craziness; *antonym* (n) sanity.

brjósk cartilage; *synonyms* (n) gristle, bone.

brjóskvefur cartilage; *synonyms* (n) gristle, bone.

brjóst 1. breast; *synonyms* (n) bosom, boob, chest, knocker, (v) front, 2. thorax; *synonyms* (n) pectus, bust, bureau, dresser, 3. collar; *synonyms* (n) arrest, choker, (v) catch, apprehend, capture, 4. chest; *synonyms* (n) box, case, casket, chamber, crate, 5. bosom; *synonyms* (n) breast, heart, interior, embrace, (v) hug.

brjóstbarn baby; *synonyms* (n) babe, child, (v) coddle, indulge, (adj) infant; *antonym* (adj) giant.

brjóstbein breastbone; *synonym* (n) sternum.

brjóstgrind thorax; *synonyms* (n) chest, pectus, bosom, bust, bureau.

brjósthimnubólga pleurisy; *synonym* (n) pleuritis.

brjósthol thorax; *synonyms* (n) chest, pectus, bosom, bust, bureau.

brjóstkassi chest; *synonyms* (n) bosom, bust, box, bureau, case.

brjóstletraður superscript; *synonyms* (n) superior, master, superordinate, superscription; *antonym* (n) subscript.

brjóstletur superscript; *synonyms* (n) superior, master, superordinate, superscription; *antonym* (n) subscript.

brjóstsviði heartburn; *synonyms* (n) envy, pyrosis, indigestion, (adj) heaves, hemorrhoids.

brjóstvísir superscript; *synonyms* (n) superior, master, superordinate, superscription; *antonym* (n) subscript.

brjóta 1. break; *synonyms* (v) split, crack, burst, (n) breach, fracture; *antonyms* (v) repair, obey, honor, mend, (n) continuation, 2. bead; *synonyms* (n) drop, astragal, beading, pearl, (v) beautify, 3. fold; *synonyms* (n) crease, bend, (v) crinkle, collapse, crumple.

broddgöltur hedgehog; *synonyms* (n) porcupine, urchin, echinus, (adj) beard, thistle.

broddmjólk colostrum; *synonyms* (n) foremilk, biestings.

broddur 1. quill; *synonyms* (n) barb, feather, pen, pinion, prick, 2. pike; *synonyms* (n) point, (adj) peak, crest, arete, bluff, 3. spike; *synonyms* (n) pin, ear, (v) impale, pierce, nail, 4. apex; *synonyms* (n) top, vertex, acme, crown, apices; *antonyms* (n) base, nadir, 5. colostrum; *synonyms* (n) foremilk, biestings.

bróðir 1. brother; *synonyms* (n) fellow, pal, associate, buddy, chum; *antonym* (n) sister, 2. friar;

synonyms (n) monk, conventual, abbot, cenobite, palmer.

bróðurdóttir niece; *synonyms* (n) nephew, aunt, uncle.

bróðurflekkur sibling; *synonyms* (n) sib, relation, relative, cognate, kin.

bróðursonur nephew; *synonyms* (n) aunt, uncle.

brókarsótt nymphomania; *synonyms* (n) andromania, uteromania.

brokkál broccoli; *synonym* (n) cauliflower.

brokkoli broccoli; *synonym* (n) cauliflower.

brokkólí broccoli; *synonym* (n) cauliflower.

bróm bromine; *synonym* (n) brome.

brómber blackberry; *synonyms* (v) blancmange, bloater, bouilli, bouillon, breadfruit.

bros smile; *synonyms* (n) grin, grinning, (v) beam, laugh, chuckle; *antonym* (v) frown.

brosa smile; *synonyms* (n) grin, grinning, (v) beam, laugh, chuckle; *antonym* (v) frown.

brostinn ruptured; *synonyms* (adj) burst, broken, busted, cleft, torn.

brot 1. refraction; *synonyms* (n) bending, deflection, deflexion, (v) obliquation, (adj) reflection, 2. violation; *synonyms* (n) rape, assault, breach, infraction, infringement, 3. vertex; *synonyms* (n) top, apex, crown, peak, summit, 4. crime; *synonyms* (n) offense, blame, guilt, injustice, transgression, 5. fracture; *synonyms* (n) break, cleft, (v) crack, rupture, burst.

brotamælir vernier; *synonym* (n) nonius.

brothættur fragile; *synonyms* (adj) dainty, delicate, frail, breakable, brittle; *antonyms* (adj) strong, unbreakable, substantial, sturdy, permanent.

brotlenda crash; *synonyms* (n) clash, collision, smash, (v) bang, collapse.

brotlending crash; *synonyms* (n) clash, collision, smash, (v) bang, collapse.

brotmark boundary; *synonyms* (n) border, bound, limit, edge, area.

brotna 1. wreck; *synonyms* (n) shipwreck, (v) ruin, smash, damage, spoil; *antonym* (v) conserve, 2. burst; *synonyms* (v) break, crack, blast, (adj) split, explode; *antonym* (v) implode.

brotpunktur 1. vertex; *synonyms* (n) top, apex, crown, peak, summit, 2. pole; *synonyms* (n) perch, bar, picket, post, rod.

brotsjór surge; *synonyms* (v) billow, flood, rise, rush, stream.

brottfall 1. syncope; *synonyms* (n) swoon, faint, syncopation, fainting, deliquium, 2. deletion; *synonyms* (n) cancellation, cut, annulment, elimination, omission; *antonym* (n) addition, 3. deficiency; *synonyms* (n) defect, dearth, want, absence, *(adj)* blemish; **antonyms** *(n)* excess, sufficiency.

brottflug departure; **synonyms** *(n)* death, exit, leave, *(v)* decease, demise; **antonyms** *(n)* arrival, appearance.

brottflutningur 1. emigration; **synonyms** *(n)* departure, exodus, migration, demigration, *(v)* intermigration, 2. evacuation; **synonyms** *(n)* elimination, emptying, excretion, *(v)* discharge, emission.

brottför departure; **synonyms** *(n)* death, exit, leave, *(v)* decease, demise; **antonyms** *(n)* arrival, appearance.

brottnám 1. resection; **synonym** *(v)* section, 2. removal; **synonyms** *(n)* transfer, dismissal, elimination, exclusion, expulsion; **antonyms** *(n)* addition, insertion, retention, 3. ablation; **synonyms** *(n)* excision, extirpation, sublation, *(v)* abduction, abreption, 4. elimination; **synonyms** *(n)* cancellation, discharge, excretion, annihilation, *(v)* removal; **antonym** *(n)* establishment.

brottnámshvarf elimination; **synonyms** *(n)* cancellation, discharge, excretion, annihilation, *(v)* removal; **antonyms** *(n)* addition, establishment.

brottrekstur dismissal; **synonyms** *(n)* discharge, conge, denial, dismission, expulsion.

brottrennsli drainage; **synonyms** *(n)* drain, drive, emanation, *(adj)* arefaction, dephlegmation.

brottskurður 1. abscission; **synonyms** *(n)* abscision, apocope, *(v)* rescission, recision, 2. excision; **synonyms** *(n)* ablation, extirpation, deletion, elimination, *(v)* abscission.

brottvísun exclusion; **synonyms** *(n)* exception, banishment, elimination, debarment, expulsion; **antonyms** *(n)* inclusion, addition, entitlement.

brotvik refraction; **synonyms** *(n)* bending, deflection, deflexion, *(v)* obliquation, *(adj)* reflection.

brú 1. bridge; **synonyms** *(n)* span, viaduct, pontoon, tie, *(v)* stretch, 2. pons.

brúa bridge; **synonyms** *(n)* span, viaduct, pontoon, tie, *(v)* stretch.

brúða puppet; **synonyms** *(n)* doll, pawn, creature, instrument, marionette.

brúðfruma gamete; **synonyms** *(n)* erythroblast, gametangium, invagination, gonocyte.

brúðgumi bridegroom; **synonyms** *(n)* groom, husband, helpmate, hostler, *(v)* bride.

brúðkaup 1. wedding; **synonyms** *(n)* marriage, matrimony, nuptial, nuptials, *(adj)* bridal; **antonym** *(n)* divorce, 2. marriage; **synonyms** *(n)* wedding, espousal, union, wedlock, *(v)* match; **antonym** *(n)* separation.

brúður bride; **synonyms** *(n)* wife, mate, woman, helpmate.

brúka 1. use; **synonyms** *(n)* custom, practice, *(v)* exercise, employ, *(adj)* usage; **antonym** *(v)* conserve, 2. employ; **synonyms** *(v)* apply, use, consume, engage, exploit; **antonyms** *(v)* fire, dismiss.

brum bud; **synonyms** *(n)* bloom, blossom, flower, *(v)* graft, shoot.

brúmm hum; **synonyms** *(n)* humming, *(v)* buzz, croon, drone, murmur.

brún 1. rim; **synonyms** *(n)* border, edge, margin, brim, brink, 2. ridge; **synonyms** *(n)* crest, ledge, bank, hill, shelf, 3. border; **synonyms** *(n)* extremity, fringe, bed, *(v)* verge, abut; **antonyms** *(n)* middle, *(v)* center, 4. edge; **synonyms** *(n)* boundary, blade, advantage, *(v)* bound, hem, 5. margin; **synonyms** *(n)* limit, circumference, perimeter, skirt, allowance.

brunasár burn; **synonyms** *(v)* bite, glow, blaze, incinerate, *(n)* fire; **antonym** *(v)* dawdle.

brúngrani wolffish; **synonyms** *(n)* catfish, lancetfish, mudcat.

bruni 1. burn; **synonyms** *(v)* bite, glow, blaze, incinerate, *(n)* fire; **antonym** *(v)* dawdle, 2. combustion; **synonyms** *(n)* burning, burn, conflagration, *(v)* ambustion.

brúnkol lignite; **synonyms** *(n)* browncoal, charcoal.

brúnn brown; **synonyms** *(adj)* chocolate, swarthy, *(n)* brunette, brownness, *(v)* sear; **antonym** *(adj)* pale.

brunnur 1. well; **synonyms** *(adv)* right, easily, thoroughly, *(adj)* healthy, *(n)* fountain; **antonyms** *(adv)* ill, badly, poorly, *(adj)* sick, unwell, 2. spring; **synonyms** *(n)* jump, leap, bound, *(v)* hop, caper, 3. source; **synonyms** *(n)* origin, root, cause, commencement, beginning, 4. fount; **synonyms** *(n)* font, well, source, spring, type, 5. fountain; **synonyms** *(n)* fount, jet, derivation, spout, squirt.

brúsi canister; **synonyms** *(n)* can, container, cannister, case, tin.

brutaro stocks; **synonyms** *(n)* pillory, bilboes, securities, calls, options.

brutoj stocks; **synonyms** *(n)* pillory, bilboes, securities, calls, options.

brúttó gross; **synonyms** *(adj)* crass, coarse, big, boorish, *(n)* aggregate; **antonyms** *(adj)* attractive, *(v)* net.

brúun interpolation; **synonyms** *(n)* interjection, interposition, interspersion, *(v)* addition, approximation.

bryggja 1. pier; **synonyms** *(n)* dock, wharf, jetty, pillar, quay, 2. wharf; **synonyms** *(n)* harbor, pier, port, waterfront, *(v)* berth, 3. quay; **synonyms** *(n)* embankment, basin, 4. platform; **synonyms** *(n)* dais, floor, rostrum, stage, stand, 5. jetty; **synonyms** *(n)* groyne, breakwater, bulwark, mole, jutty.

bryggjun extrapolation; *synonym* (*n*) projection.
bryggjupláss pier; *synonyms* (*n*) dock, wharf, jetty, pillar, quay.
bryggjupolli bollard; *synonym* (*n*) bitt.
brýna 1. whet; *synonyms* (*v*) sharpen, excite, grind, quicken, stimulate, **2**. sharpen; *synonyms* (*v*) focus, edge, hone, intensify, point; *antonym* (*v*) cloud.
brýni 1. whetstone; *synonyms* (*n*) rub, caoutchouc, chance, failing, (*adj*) grindstone, **2**. hone; *synonyms* (*v*) sharpen, perfect, whet, refine, (*adj*) sharpener.
brynja 1. shielding; *synonyms* (*n*) shadowing, (*adj*) protective, covering, protecting, caring, **2**. armour; *synonym* (*v*) armor.
brýnn essential; *synonyms* (*adj*) necessary, crucial, important, inherent, requisite; *antonyms* (*adj*) minor, secondary, (*n*) inessential, optional, option.
brýnól strop; *synonyms* (*n*) strap, (*v*) whet, sharpen, (*adj*) hone, aculeate.
brýnsla sharpening; *synonyms* (*n*) acumination, aggravation, dressing, filing, (*adj*) abrasive.
brynvörn armour; *synonym* (*v*) armor.
bryti 1. purser; *synonyms* (*n*) cashier, bursar, **2**. steward; *synonyms* (*n*) custodian, keeper, waiter, warden, attendant.
bú 1. property; *synonyms* (*n*) characteristic, capital, peculiarity, feature, (*adj*) attribute, **2**. ranch; *synonyms* (*n*) estate, spread, merestead, (*v*) farm, (*adj*) agricultural, **3**. body; *synonyms* (*n*) cadaver, corpse, matter, organization, carcass; *antonym* (*n*) spirit, **4**. estate; *synonyms* (*n*) condition, land, demesne, order, rank, **5**. follicle; *synonyms* (*n*) cavity, dent, dimple, dint, lacuna.
búa 1. reside; *synonyms* (*v*) inhabit, exist, live, occupy, (*adj*) dwell, **2**. dwell; *synonyms* (*v*) abide, reside, bide, stay, lodge, **3**. live; *synonyms* (*v*) subsist, be, (*adj*) alive, active, animate; *antonyms* (*adj*) dead, inanimate, **4**. equip; *synonyms* (*v*) appoint, clothe, furnish, accommodate, dress.
búamalurt mugwort; *synonyms* (*n*) motherwort, tarragon.
búð shop; *synonyms* (*n*) business, store, factory, plant, (*v*) betray.
buddubólga bursitis; *synonym* (*n*) hygroma.
búfé livestock; *synonyms* (*n*) stock, ancestry, blood, bloodline, breed.
búferlaflutningar migration; *synonyms* (*n*) exodus, movement, journey, (*v*) flit, flitting.
búferlaflutningur immigration; *synonyms* (*n*) migration, colonization, entrance, (*v*) emigration, intermigration.
buffall buffalo; *synonyms* (*n*) bison, yak, zebu, (*v*) cow, bully.

búffer buffer; *synonyms* (*n*) safeguard, pad, protection, bumper, (*v*) cushion.
búgarður 1. property; *synonyms* (*n*) characteristic, capital, peculiarity, feature, (*adj*) attribute, **2**. ranch; *synonyms* (*n*) estate, spread, merestead, (*v*) farm, (*adj*) agricultural, **3**. estate; *synonyms* (*n*) condition, land, demesne, order, rank, **4**. farm; *synonyms* (*n*) property, grange, dairy, (*v*) cultivate, raise.
bugða 1. camber; *synonyms* (*n*) bank, arc, bow, (*v*) arch, bend, **2**. curvature; *synonyms* (*n*) curve, crook, curvity, shape, twist, **3**. meander; *synonyms* (*n*) turn, amble, (*v*) wind, wander, ramble, **4**. flare; *synonyms* (*n*) flash, blaze, (*v*) burn, flame, burst.
bugpunktur antinode; *synonym* (*n*) loop.
bugspjót bowsprit; *synonym* (*n*) bow.
bugur 1. antinode; *synonym* (*n*) loop, **2**. bend; *synonyms* (*n*) bow, arch, arc, (*v*) curve, turn; *antonyms* (*v*) straighten, square.
bújörð land; *synonyms* (*n*) ground, country, soil, (*v*) disembark, debark; *antonym* (*adj*) aquatic.
búkhlaup diarrhea; *synonyms* (*n*) diarrhoea, lax, looseness.
búkhreinsandi purgative; *synonyms* (*adj*) cathartic, evacuant, (*n*) aperient, physic, (*v*) detergent.
búkhreinsilyf purgative; *synonyms* (*adj*) cathartic, evacuant, (*n*) aperient, physic, (*v*) detergent.
búkhreinsun purgation; *synonyms* (*n*) catharsis, purification, abreaction, katharsis, purge.
búkki boss; *synonyms* (*n*) chief, governor, head, (*v*) administer, govern.
búkur belly; *synonyms* (*n*) abdomen, stomach, inside, bowels, (*v*) balloon.
bulla 1. ram; *synonyms* (*v*) beat, cram, crash, drive, jam, **2**. piston; *synonyms* (*n*) plunger, diver, speculator.
búmalurt mugwort; *synonyms* (*n*) motherwort, tarragon.
buna 1. beam; *synonyms* (*n*) blaze, glow, ray, (*v*) glare, (*adj*) shine, **2**. jet; *synonyms* (*n*) squirt, fountain, flow, (*v*) gush, spurt.
BÚNADUR equipment; *synonyms* (*n*) material, apparatus, facility, gear, (*v*) furniture.
búnaður 1. device; *synonyms* (*n*) contrivance, apparatus, appliance, artifice, emblem, **2**. facilities; *synonym* (*n*) equipment, **3**. gear; *synonyms* (*n*) outfit, tackle, device, dress, baggage, **4**. equipment; *synonyms* (*n*) material, facility, gear, furnishings, (*v*) furniture.
bundinn latent; *synonyms* (*adj*) covert, potential, secret, dormant, hidden; *antonym* (*adj*) active.
bunga 1. prominence; *synonyms* (*n*) eminence, hump, importance, protuberance, height; *antonym* (*n*) obscurity, **2**. bulge; *synonyms* (*n*) prominence,

swelling, bilge, (v) belly, bag, **3**. camber; *synonyms* (n) bank, arc, bow, (v) arch, bend.

bungun buckling; *synonyms* (n) warping, capitulation, collapse, embossing, pickling.

bunguvik camber; *synonyms* (n) bank, arc, bow, (v) arch, bend.

bunki batch; *synonyms* (n) band, lot, body, battery, charge.

búnt bundle; *synonyms* (n) cluster, pile, (v) bunch, pack, clump.

búpeningur livestock; *synonyms* (n) stock, ancestry, blood, bloodline, breed.

búr 1. cage; *synonyms* (n) jail, pen, hutch, cell, (v) confine; *antonym* (v) free, **2**. pantry; *synonyms* (n) larder, buttery, store, basement, kitchen.

burðarbiti beam; *synonyms* (n) blaze, glow, ray, (v) glare, (adj) shine.

burðarefni vehicle; *synonyms* (n) medium, instrument, means, automobile, channel.

burðargeta capacity; *synonyms* (n) capability, aptitude, capacitance, function, (adj) ability; *antonyms* (n) inability, incapability.

burðargler slide; *synonyms* (n) glide, chute, (v) drop, slip, fall.

burðarmagn tonnage; *synonyms* (n) tunnage, shipping, cargo, fleet, (adj) capacity.

burðarþolsfræði statics; *synonyms* (n) static, (v) dynamics.

burðarvír messenger; *synonyms* (n) envoy, emissary, harbinger, runner, (v) herald.

burður 1. convection; *synonyms* (n) transfer, (adj) thermal, **2**. birth; *synonyms* (n) beginning, ancestry, descent, extraction, (v) delivery; *antonym* (n) death, **3**. advection.

búrhvalur cachalot; *synonyms* (adj) elephant, hippopotamus, leviathan, porpoise, whale.

burís borax; *synonym* (adj) shoddy.

búrót mugwort; *synonym* (n) motherwort, tarragon.

burstakol brush; *synonyms* (n) brushwood, (v) broom, graze, sweep, touch.

bursti brush; *synonyms* (n) brushwood, (v) broom, graze, sweep, touch.

búseta population; *synonyms* (n) inhabitants, people, nation, community, group.

bústaður 1. residence; *synonyms* (n) abode, dwelling, home, house, accommodation, **2**. domicile; *synonyms* (n) residence, address, lodging, place, (v) lodge, **3**. abode; *synonyms* (n) domicile, abidance, habitat, habitation, (v) bode, **4**. dwelling; *synonyms* (n) apartment, housing, mansion, tenement, (adj) dwell, **5**. habitat; *synonyms* (n) environment, territory, granger.

bústjóri administrator; *synonyms* (n) executive, director, manager, boss, officer.

búsvæði habitat; *synonyms* (n) dwelling, abode, residence, environment, home.

búta quantize; *synonym* (v) quantise.

bútan butane; *synonyms* (n) propane, hydrogen.

bútasaumur quilting; *synonyms* (n) quilt, embroidery.

bútun segmentation; *synonyms* (n) division, cleavage, partition, partitioning, sectionalization.

bútur 1. segment; *synonyms* (n) division, paragraph, bit, (v) section, part, **2**. chord; *synonyms* (n) cord, harmony, (v) accord, harmonise, harmonize, **3**. component; *synonyms* (n) constituent, factor, ingredient, detail, element.

bútýl butyl; *synonym* (n) tetryl.

býfluga bee; *synonyms* (n) honeybee, ant, termite, caprice, (adj) barbecue.

býflugnabóndi apiarist; *synonyms* (n) beekeeper, apiculturist, (v) apiarian.

býflugnabú beehive; *synonyms* (n) apiary, hive, skep, (v) alveary, aviary.

bygg barley; *synonyms* (n) barleycorn, bere.

byggð 1. population; *synonyms* (n) inhabitants, people, nation, community, group, **2**. community; *synonyms* (n) association, public, agreement, commune, (adj) communal; *antonym* (adj) private.

bygging 1. construction; *synonyms* (n) building, fabrication, formation, structure, assembly; *antonym* (n) destruction, **2**. structure; *synonyms* (n) form, arrangement, edifice, shape, constitution, **3**. building; *synonyms* (n) architecture, establishment, construction, fabric, house, **4**. edifice.

byggingajöfur client; *synonyms* (n) buyer, customer, patron, guest, purchaser.

byggingareining subunit; *synonym* (n) protomer.

byggingarlag structure; *synonyms* (n) form, building, arrangement, edifice, shape.

byggja 1. build; *synonyms* (v) make, erect, establish, (n) form, shape; *antonyms* (v) demolish, destroy, **2**. construct; *synonyms* (v) build, compose, fabricate, arrange, (n) concept.

bylgja 1. tide; *synonyms* (n) current, flow, stream, course, (v) wave, **2**. wave; *synonyms* (n) billow, gesture, (v) brandish, flap, flutter.

bylgjubeyging diffraction; *synonyms* (n) deflection, deviation, inflection.

bylgjubeygja diffraction; *synonyms* (n) deflection, deviation, inflection.

bylgjubrot refraction; *synonyms* (n) bending, deflection, deflexion, (v) obliquation, (adj) reflection.

bylgjuform waveform; *synonym* (*n*) waveshape.

bylgjuhjúpur envelope; *synonyms* (*n*) container, pack, (*v*) cover, covering, cloak.

bylgjuhreyfing undulation; *synonyms* (*n*) wave, fluctuation, impulse, oscillation, (*v*) flutter.

bylgjuhreyfingar peristalsis; *synonym* (*n*) vermiculation.

bylgjuleiðari waveguide; *synonym* (*n*) helix.

bylgjulengd wavelength; *synonym* (*n*) insight.

bylgjulögun waveform; *synonym* (*n*) waveshape.

bylgjumót envelope; *synonyms* (*n*) container, pack, (*v*) cover, covering, cloak.

bylgjusveipur eddy; *synonyms* (*n*) spin, twirl, vortex, (*v*) whirl, purl.

bylgjuvíxl interference; *synonyms* (*n*) disturbance, hindrance, handicap, block, (*v*) collision.

bylta transpose; *synonyms* (*v*) exchange, change, shift, transfer, transplant.

bylting revolution; *synonyms* (*n*) change, gyration, insurrection, mutiny, (*v*) circuit.

byrða bunker; *synonyms* (*n*) bin, dugout, trap, ambuscade, ambush.

byrði 1. tax; *synonyms* (*n*) charge, duty, burden, (*v*) assess, task, 2. liability; *synonyms* (*n*) debt, obligation, trust, blame, commitment; *antonym* (*n*) asset.

byrðingur bow; *synonyms* (*n*) arc, curve, (*v*) bend, arch, stoop.

býretta burette; *synonyms* (*n*) buret, jar.

byrging 1. suppression; *synonyms* (*n*) inhibition, repression, crushing, quelling, restraint; *antonyms* (*n*) freedom, emancipation, 2. blanking.

byrgir suppressor; *synonym* (*n*) suppresser.

byrja 1. start; *synonyms* (*v*) begin, originate, commence, (*n*) jump, onset; *antonyms* (*v*) end, finish, stop, conclude, (*n*) conclusion, 2. commence; *synonyms* (*v*) start, open, embark, initiate, arise, 3. begin; *synonyms* (*v*) become, enter, rise, create, dawn, 4. introduce; *synonyms* (*v*) insert, interject, inject, acquaint, advance.

byrjun 1. start; *synonyms* (*v*) begin, originate, commence, (*n*) jump, onset; *antonyms* (*v*) end, finish, stop, conclude, (*n*) conclusion, 2. commencement; *synonyms* (*n*) beginning, opening, origin, start, birth, 3. commence; *synonyms* (*v*) open, embark, initiate, arise, enter, 4. beginning; *synonyms* (*n*) cause, commencement, derivation, dawn, (*adj*) original; *antonyms* (*n*) finale, demise, ending, 5. opening; *synonyms* (*n*) gap, mouth, aperture, break, cleft; *antonyms* (*n*) closing, exit, (*adj*) final.

bývax beeswax; *synonyms* (*n*) business, employment, livelihood, occupation, (*adj*) wax.

C

celi means; *synonyms* (*n*) expedient, agency, instrument, assets, capital.

Celsíusstig centigrade; *synonym* (*adj*) hundred.

cindro 1. ash; *synonyms* (*n*) jasmine, lilac, (*v*) cinder, scoriae, (*adj*) gray, 2. ashes; *synonyms* (*n*) dust, cinders, remains, clay, embers.

cindrokolora ashes; *synonyms* (*n*) dust, cinder, cinders, remains, clay.

cirkonstanco 1. circumstances; *synonyms* (*n*) condition, position, situation, state, case, 2. circumstance; *synonyms* (*n*) affair, accident, chance, event, incident.

D

dá 1. torpor; *synonyms* (*n*) lethargy, inactivity, lassitude, inertia, apathy, 2. coma; *synonyms* (*n*) trance, dream, stupor, sleep, (*v*) doze.

dægrastytting recreation; *synonyms* (*n*) amusement, entertainment, distraction, pastime, play.

dæla pump; *synonyms* (*n*) heart, pumps, ticker, (*v*) interrogate, draw.

dæld 1. pit; *synonyms* (*n*) cavity, dent, hole, depression, (*adj*) hollow, 2. dent; *synonyms* (*n*) nick, recess, blemish, (*v*) notch, indent; *antonym* (*v*) increase, 3. basin; *synonyms* (*n*) bowl, pot, dock, tank, washbasin, 4. depression; *synonyms* (*n*) basin, dejection, decline, dip, impression; *antonyms* (*n*) cheerfulness, happiness, boom, elation, encouragement.

dælda dent; *synonyms* (*n*) hollow, nick, recess, (*v*) notch, indent; *antonym* (*v*) increase.

dæma 1. rule; *synonyms* (*n*) govern, order, decree, (*v*) command, control, 2. judge; *synonyms* (*v*) consider, estimate, evaluate, think, believe.

dæmasafn corpus; *synonyms* (*n*) body, substance, material, matter, principal.

dæmi 1. sample; *synonyms* (*n*) example, instance, specimen, model, pattern, 2. problem; *synonyms* (*n*) bother, conundrum, difficulty, trouble, knot, 3. case; *synonyms* (*n*) box, bin, cover, jacket, shell, 4. example; *synonyms* (*n*) case, exemplar, illustration, lead, sample, 5. instance; *synonyms* (*n*) time, affair, chance, (*v*) exemplify, illustrate.

dæmigerður typical; *synonyms* (*adj*) characteristic, regular, classic, (*v*) normal, representative;

antonyms (*adj*) atypical, unusual, uncharacteristic, unconventional.

dagatal calendar; *synonyms* (*n*) almanac, agenda, schedule, diary, (*v*) list.

dagblað 1. daily; *synonyms* (*adj*) journal, diurnal, everyday, regular, (*n*) newspaper, **2**. newspaper; *synonyms* (*n*) gazette, magazine, paper, news, periodical, **3**. journal; *synonyms* (*n*) diary, book, ephemeris, chronicle, (*adj*) daybook.

dagbók 1. calendar; *synonyms* (*n*) almanac, agenda, schedule, diary, (*v*) list, **2**. journal; *synonyms* (*n*) book, magazine, newspaper, periodical, (*adj*) daybook.

dagdraumur daydream; *synonyms* (*n*) dream, fantasy, reverie, (*v*) fantasize, fancy; *antonym* (*n*) reality.

dagdreymi daydream; *synonyms* (*n*) dream, fantasy, reverie, (*v*) fantasize, fancy; *antonym* (*n*) reality.

daggarstigsmælir hygrometer; *synonym* (*adj*) hygrometry.

daglegur diurnal; *synonyms* (*adj*) daily, journal, diary, ephemeral, daybook.

dagmaður sweeper; *synonyms* (*n*) broom, sweep, janitor, brush, mop.

dagrétta update; *synonyms* (*n*) updating, (*v*) inform, modernize, renovate, revise.

dagrétting update; *synonyms* (*n*) updating, (*v*) inform, modernize, renovate, revise.

dagsetning date; *synonyms* (*n*) age, appointment, assignation, engagement, (*v*) escort.

dagskrá agenda; *synonyms* (*n*) schedule, agendum, diary, docket, plan.

dagur day; *synonyms* (*n*) light, daylight, generation, age, daytime; *antonyms* (*n*) nighttime, night.

daktíli dactyl; *synonyms* (*n*) digit, spondee, trochee, figure, fingerbreadth.

dáleiðing hypnotism; *synonyms* (*n*) mesmerism, magnetism, hint, suggestion, (*v*) pandiculation.

dáleiðsla hypnosis; *synonyms* (*n*) anesthetic, stupor.

dáleiðslufræði hypnotism; *synonyms* (*n*) mesmerism, magnetism, hint, suggestion, (*v*) pandiculation.

dálkahlaupa tabulate; *synonyms* (*v*) file, organize, tabularize, list, catalogue.

dálkur 1. column; *synonyms* (*n*) pillar, procession, row, stanchion, file, **2**. field; *synonyms* (*n*) arena, area, battlefield, domain, ground, **3**. group; *synonyms* (*n*) bunch, brigade, collection, crowd, flock.

dallur tub; *synonyms* (*n*) bath, bathtub, cask, vat, basin.

dalur 1. valley; *synonyms* (*n*) ravine, dale, gully, vale, hollow; *antonym* (*n*) mount, **2**. vale; *synonyms* (*n*) valley, bottom, gorge, basin, cave; *antonym* (*n*) hill,

3. dell; *synonyms* (*n*) dingle, clearing, **4**. dale; *synonyms* (*n*) glen, abyss, cocoon, cavern, cove, **5**. dingle; *synonyms* (*n*) dell, bent, bower, brush, (*v*) chime.

damdisko checkers; *synonyms* (*n*) draughts, dominos, solitaire, chessboard.

dampeco checkers; *synonyms* (*n*) draughts, dominos, solitaire, chessboard.

dánarbú estate; *synonyms* (*n*) condition, land, demesne, order, rank.

dánartala mortality; *synonyms* (*n*) fatality, death, flesh, humanity, mankind; *antonym* (*n*) immortality.

dánartíðni mortality; *synonyms* (*n*) fatality, death, flesh, humanity, mankind; *antonym* (*n*) immortality.

dans 1. saltation; *synonyms* (*n*) jump, bound, leap, spring, hop, **2**. dance; *synonyms* (*v*) caper, bop, cavort, play, shake.

dansa dance; *synonyms* (*v*) bound, caper, hop, bop, cavort.

danssjónleikur ballet; *synonyms* (*n*) choreography, afterpiece, burlesque, burletta, comedietta.

dapur 1. sad; *synonyms* (*adj*) dreary, dismal, distressing, gloomy, miserable; *antonyms* (*adj*) happy, cheerful, joyful, brave, cheery, **2**. somber; *synonyms* (*adj*) dark, dim, drab, dull, grave; *antonym* (*adj*) bright, **3**. sullen; *synonyms* (*adj*) morose, gruff, cross, glum, grim, **4**. sorrowful; *synonyms* (*adj*) melancholy, doleful, lugubrious, rueful, sad; *antonyms* (*adj*) content, successful, **5**. dismal; *synonyms* (*adj*) cheerless, dejected, depressing, desolate, disconsolate.

dáraaldin durian; *synonym* (*n*) durion.

dástjarfasjúklingur cataleptic; *synonyms* (*adj*) comatose, insensible, lifeless.

dástjarfi catalepsy; *synonyms* (*adj*) fixity, immobility.

dástjarfur cataleptic; *synonyms* (*adj*) comatose, insensible, lifeless.

dáþoli hypnotic; *synonyms* (*adj*) magnetic, mesmeric, narcotic, sleepy, (*n*) soporific.

dátími downtime; *synonyms* (*n*) break, cessation, delay, (*adj*) broken, disrepair.

dauðadá 1. coma; *synonyms* (*n*) lethargy, trance, dream, stupor, sleep, **2**. asphyxia; *synonyms* (*n*) suffocation, asphyxy, (*adj*) cholera.

dauðhreinsa sterilize; *synonyms* (*v*) neuter, castrate, disinfect, sterilise, (*adj*) emasculate; *antonym* (*v*) contaminate.

dauðhreinsaður sterile; *synonyms* (*adj*) infertile, barren, fruitless, effete, (*v*) abortive; *antonyms* (*adj*) fertile, unhygienic.

dauðhreinsun sterilization; *synonym* (*n*) sterilisation.

dauði death; *synonyms* (n) demise, end, expiration, close, exit; *antonyms* (n) birth, existence, delivery.

dauðlegur mortal; *synonyms* (adj) deadly, fatal, human, lethal, (n) individual; *antonyms* (adj) eternal, (n) immortal.

dauðleiki mortality; *synonyms* (n) fatality, death, flesh, humanity, mankind; *antonym* (n) immortality.

dauður 1. dead; *synonyms* (adj) dull, lifeless, cold, defunct, inanimate; *antonyms* (adj) alive, animate, (n) living, 2. late; *synonyms* (adj) former, dead, deceased, (adv) dilatory, fresh; *antonyms* (adj) ahead, (adv) early, punctually, promptly, punctual.

daufdumbur 1. dumb; *synonyms* (adj) mute, dense, dim, dull, silent, 2. mute; *synonyms* (adj) dumb, quiet, (v) muffle, dampen, deaden; *antonym* (adj) talkative.

dauffruma neutrophil; *synonyms* (n) neutrophile, (adj) neutrophilic.

daufgerður phlegmatic; *synonyms* (adj) impassive, indifferent, listless, phlegmatical, stolid.

daufkyrningur neutrophil; *synonyms* (n) neutrophile, (adj) neutrophilic.

daufur 1. depressed; *synonyms* (adj) concave, low, blue, dejected, dispirited; *antonyms* (adj) cheerful, happy, convex, 2. obscure; *synonyms* (adj) cloudy, dim, dark, gloomy, ambiguous; *antonyms* (adj) clear, noticeable, simple, obvious, (v) clarify.

dávaldur hypnotist; *synonyms* (n) mesmerist, hypnotiser, hypnotizer.

db decibel; *synonym* (n) db.

deig paste; *synonyms* (n) glue, dough, (v) cement, gum, bond.

deigla crucible; *synonyms* (n) pot, retort, calabash, matrix, pix.

deila 1. share; *synonyms* (n) piece, portion, (v) participate, allot, apportion; *antonym* (v) control, 2. conflict; *synonyms* (n) clash, combat, fight, battle, contention; *antonyms* (n) agreement, accord, harmony, peace, (v) agree.

deild 1. taxon, 2. quotient; *synonyms* (n) proportion, factor, ratio, share, fraction, 3. unit; *synonyms* (n) troop, element, group, squad, (adj) one, 4. section; *synonyms* (n) division, part, portion, compartment, percentage, 5. cell; *synonyms* (n) cage, jail, cadre, hole, cave.

deilda differentiate; *synonyms* (v) characterize, distinguish, discriminate, separate, tell; *antonym* (v) integrate.

deildarsérfræðingur adviser; *synonyms* (n) advisor, consultant, counselor, counsel, guide.

deildaskipta partition; *synonyms* (n) division, part, wall, distribution, (v) divide.

deildi differential; *synonyms* (adj) integral, (n) derivative, difference, distinction, fluxion.

deildun differentiation; *synonyms* (n) difference, distinction, contrast, demarcation, discrimination.

deildur lobate; *synonyms* (adj) lobed, lobated, palmated, palmiped.

deilibil spacing; *synonyms* (n) space, headway, composition, deviation, diastema.

deilibox hub; *synonyms* (n) center, focus, heart, core, nucleus.

deilikorn centriole; *synonym* (n) center.

deiling 1. division; *synonyms* (n) department, disagreement, allotment, branch, break; *antonyms* (n) closeness, convergence, estimation, unification, 2. segmentation; *synonyms* (n) division, cleavage, partition, partitioning, sectionalization.

deilir 1. distributor; *synonyms* (n) distributer, spreader, middleman, allocator, feeder, 2. delimiter.

deilitegund subspecies; *synonyms* (n) race, airstream, backwash, breed, form.

deiltegund subspecies; *synonyms* (n) race, airstream, backwash, breed, form.

deilur conflict; *synonyms* (n) clash, combat, fight, battle, contention; *antonyms* (n) agreement, accord, harmony, peace, (v) agree.

dekk 1. tire; *synonyms* (v) bore, fatigue, exhaust, fag, (n) jade; *antonym* (v) refresh, 2. deck; *synonyms* (v) adorn, beautify, clothe, embellish, floor.

deklari rules; *synonyms* (n) regulations, etiquette, policy, system, convention.

dekra spoil; *synonyms* (v) plunder, corrupt, impair, rot, (n) ruin; *antonyms* (v) enhance, improve, conserve.

dekraður spoiled; *synonyms* (adj) decayed, bad, rotten, stale, coddled; *antonyms* (adj) first-rate, pure.

demba 1. shower; *synonyms* (n) rain, (v) pour, bathe, hail, sprinkle, 2. dump; *synonyms* (v) discard, ditch, abandon, drop, empty; *antonym* (v) keep.

dembing dump; *synonyms* (v) discard, ditch, abandon, drop, empty; *antonym* (v) keep.

demókrati democrat; *synonyms* (n) commoner, plebeian, proletaire, proletary, republican.

dempari damper; *synonyms* (n) check, discouragement, cooler, silencer, constraint.

dempir buffer; *synonyms* (n) safeguard, pad, protection, bumper, (v) cushion.

dento 1. tooth; *synonyms* (n) palate, grain, nap, saw, (adj) nib, 2. teeth; *synonyms* (v) arrastra, fangs, file, grater, gristmill.

depill point; *synonyms* (n) place, grade, peak, nib, (v) head.

depl blink; *synonyms* (v) wink, flash, twinkle, flicker, (n) blinking.

depla blink; *synonyms* (v) wink, flash, twinkle, flicker, (n) blinking.

deplaháfur dogfish; *synonyms* (n) bowfin, grindle.

deplahverfa 1. windowpane; *synonyms* (n) pane, window, casement, porthole, skylight, **2.** brill.

deplasíld alewife; *synonym* (n) gaspereau.

deplaskata blonde; *synonyms* (adj) blond, fair, (n) towheaded, buff, girl; *antonym* (n) brunet.

deplóttur punctate; *synonym* (adj) speckled.

depra depression; *synonyms* (n) basin, cavity, dejection, decline, dent; *antonyms* (n) cheerfulness, happiness, boom, elation, encouragement.

desibel decibel; *synonym* (n) db.

desíbel 1. decibel; *synonym* (n) db, **2.** bel; *synonyms* (n) bacilli, bacillus, barn, boron.

detali details; *synonyms* (n) data, particulars, facts, contents, (adj) minutiae.

detalo 1. detail; *synonyms* (n) report, point, (v) describe, enumerate, relate; *antonym* (n) generalization, **2.** details; *synonyms* (n) data, particulars, facts, contents, (adj) minutiae.

dextrósi dextrose; *synonyms* (n) dextroglucose, sweetener.

deyfa 1. damp; *synonyms* (adj) moist, muggy, (v) break, check, (n) wet; *antonyms* (adj) dry, (n) dryness, **2.** dim; *synonyms* (adj) dark, obscure, cloudy, (v) blur, darken; *antonyms* (adj) bright, brilliant, intelligent, (v) clear, brighten, **3.** attenuate; *synonyms* (v) assuage, dilute, reduce, (adj) tenuous, fine; *antonym* (v) intensify, **4.** dampen; *synonyms* (v) deaden, muffle, depress, dishearten, (n) damp; *antonym* (v) stimulate, **5.** extinguish; *synonyms* (v) destroy, exterminate, quench, annihilate, douse; *antonyms* (v) light, ignite.

deyfandi anesthetic; *synonyms* (adj) anesthesia, soporific, hypnotic, (n) anaesthetic, narcotic.

deyfð drowsiness; *synonyms* (n) sleepiness, somnolence, dullness, lethargy, doziness.

deyfður 1. anesthetic; *synonyms* (adj) anesthesia, soporific, hypnotic, (n) anaesthetic, narcotic, **2.** flat; *synonyms* (adj) dull, bland, even, plain, (n) apartment; *antonyms* (adj) exciting, high-pitched, bumpy.

deyfiliður 1. attenuator, **2.** pad; *synonyms* (n) cushion, apartment, (v) line, inflate, expand.

deyfilyf 1. anesthetic; *synonyms* (adj) anesthesia, soporific, hypnotic, (n) anaesthetic, narcotic, **2.** narcotic; *synonyms* (adj) anodyne, (n) opiate, drug, sedative, stupefacient.

deyfilyfjafíkill narcotic; *synonyms* (adj) soporific, anodyne, (n) opiate, hypnotic, drug.

deyfing 1. suppression; *synonyms* (n) inhibition, repression, crushing, quelling, restraint; *antonyms* (n) freedom, emancipation, **2.** cushion; *synonyms* (n) pad, (v) buffer, bolster, insulate, protect, **3.** analgesia, **4.** anaesthesia; *synonyms* (n) anesthesia, stupor, anaesthesis, (adj) palsy, paralysis, **5.** anesthesia; *synonyms* (n) anaesthesia, asleep, insentience, unconsciousness.

deyfingarlyf anesthetic; *synonyms* (adj) anesthesia, soporific, hypnotic, (n) anaesthetic, narcotic.

deyfir 1. suppressor; *synonym* (n) suppresser, **2.** damper; *synonyms* (n) check, discouragement, cooler, silencer, constraint, **3.** attenuator.

deyja die; *synonyms* (v) decease, dead, death, depart, (n) dice.

diffra differentiate; *synonyms* (v) characterize, distinguish, discriminate, separate, tell; *antonym* (v) integrate.

diffrun differentiation; *synonyms* (n) difference, distinction, contrast, demarcation, discrimination.

diffur differential; *synonyms* (adj) integral, (n) derivative, difference, distinction, fluxion.

dígitalis digitalis; *synonyms* (n) foxglove, digitalin.

digull crucible; *synonyms* (n) pot, retort, calabash, matrix, pix.

digur obese; *synonyms* (adj) fat, corpulent, gross, fleshy, heavy; *antonym* (adj) slim.

dílaroði roseola; *synonyms* (n) anthesis, blizzard, bloom, blossom, blossoming.

dilja dill; *synonyms* (n) anise, caraway, carrot, celery, (adj) calm.

dilkur cell; *synonyms* (n) cage, jail, cadre, hole, cave.

díll 1. spot; *synonyms* (n) blot, place, speck, (v) blemish, soil, **2.** pixel; *synonym* (n) pel, **3.** macula; *synonyms* (n) freckle, mole, sunspot, macule.

dilla dill; *synonyms* (n) anise, caraway, carrot, celery, (adj) calm.

dílspor line; *synonyms* (n) cord, file, house, breed, course.

dimmur dim; *synonyms* (adj) dark, obscure, cloudy, (v) blur, darken; *antonyms* (adj) bright, brilliant, intelligent, (v) clear, brighten.

dindill 1. tail; *synonyms* (n) rear, shadow, (v) follow, pursue, track; *antonyms* (v) lead, front, **2.** outlier, **3.** overshoot; *synonyms* (v) overrun, jump.

dingull 1. pendulum; *synonyms* (n) dial, gnomon, horologe, pendant, (n) flap, **2.** hypophysis; *synonyms* (n) pituitary, cataract.

diplómat diplomat; *synonyms* (n) diplomatist, envoy, ambassador, intermediary, minister.

direkto 1. directions; *synonyms* (n) advice, briefing, commands, orders, will, **2.** direction; *synonyms*

(n) administration, conduct, bearing, command, course.

dísa nozzle; *synonyms* (n) nose, beak, hooter, jet, muzzle.

diskahemlaklafi caliper; *synonyms* (n) thickness, calipers, callipers, (v) calliper, measure.

disklingur diskette; *synonym* (n) floppy.

disko records; *synonyms* (n) archive, documents, minutes, proceedings, certification.

diskur 1. plate; *synonyms* (n) dish, leaf, (v) gild, sheet, cover, 2. disk; *synonyms* (n) disc, discus, dial, circle, diskette, 3. disc; *synonyms* (n) disk, record, platter, round, book.

djöfull devil; *synonyms* (n) demon, fiend, ghost, daemon, deuce.

djúphafsbotn abyss; *synonyms* (n) abysm, chasm, deep, gorge, gulf.

djúprista draught; *synonyms* (n) draft, potion, dose, potation, (v) design.

djúpur 1. profound; *synonyms* (adj) deep, abstruse, intense, heavy, bottomless; *antonyms* (adj) superficial, shallow, trivial, 2. deep; *synonyms* (adj) thick, profound, absorbed, broad, dark; *antonyms* (adj) high, high-pitched, light, soft, weak.

doði weakfish; *synonym* (n) squeteague.

dofna fade; *synonyms* (v) disappear, decline, dissolve, evaporate, (adj) vanish; *antonyms* (v) grow, increase, strengthen.

dofnun 1. attenuation; *synonyms* (n) decrease, reduction, (v) emaciation, tabes, consumption; *antonym* (n) growth, 2. fade; *synonyms* (v) disappear, decline, dissolve, evaporate, (adj) vanish; *antonyms* (v) grow, increase, strengthen, 3. extinction; *synonyms* (n) destruction, extermination, end, expiration, (v) death; *antonyms* (n) survival, preservation.

dögg 1. dew; *synonyms* (n) condensation, mist, freshness, humidity, moisture, 2. condensate; *synonyms* (n) abridgement, abridgment, capsule, compression, (v) condense.

dökkna macula; *synonyms* (n) freckle, mole, sunspot, blemish, macule.

dokumento 1. papers; *synonyms* (n) credentials, document, documents, identification, covenant, 2. paper; *synonyms* (n) article, newspaper, discourse, newsprint, certificate.

dómari judge; *synonyms* (v) consider, estimate, evaluate, think, believe.

dómglöp paranoia; *synonyms* (n) insanity, (adj) schizophrenia.

dómnefnd 1. jury; *synonyms* (n) board, panel, adjudicators, group, team, 2. panel; *synonyms* (n) jury, defendant, committee, plank, (v) empanel.

dómsaga jurisdiction; *synonyms* (n) power, authority, dominion, district, judicature.

dómssalur court; *synonyms* (n) forum, bar, close, (v) woo, attract; *antonyms* (v) avoid, shun.

dómstig instance; *synonyms* (n) example, case, exemplar, time, (v) exemplify.

dómstóll court; *synonyms* (n) forum, bar, close, (v) woo, attract; *antonyms* (v) avoid, shun.

dómsvald jurisdiction; *synonyms* (n) power, authority, dominion, district, judicature.

dómur court; *synonyms* (n) forum, bar, close, (v) woo, attract; *antonyms* (v) avoid, shun.

doppa 1. periwinkle; *synonyms* (n) winkle, spinster, zinnia, 2. caruncle; *synonyms* (n) crest, sarcoma, caruncula, growth, papula, 3. papilla; *synonyms* (n) wart, boob, knocker.

dór 1. arbor; *synonyms* (n) bower, mandrel, axle, spindle, arbour, 2. mandrel; *synonyms* (n) arbor, hinge, bobbin, mandril, core.

doría dory; *synonyms* (n) ark, broadhorn, bully, dinghy, droger.

dormandi dormant; *synonyms* (adj) asleep, inactive, torpid, inert, smoldering; *antonym* (adj) active.

dós 1. tin; *synonyms* (n) can, canister, container, (v) pot, preserve, 2. can; *synonyms* (v) tin, dismiss, (n) bathroom, behind, buttocks; *antonym* (v) hire.

dóttir daughter; *synonyms* (n) girl, child, son, lass, descendant.

dótturfélag subsidiary; *synonyms* (adj) auxiliary, subservient, ancillary, secondary, (v) accessory.

dótturfyrirtæki subsidiary; *synonyms* (adj) auxiliary, subservient, ancillary, secondary, (v) accessory.

dótturhnöttur secondary; *synonyms* (adj) inferior, lower, minor, subordinate, ancillary; *antonyms* (adj) basic, main, central, chief, direct.

drægi 1. range; *synonyms* (v) line, arrange, order, rank, roam, 2. reach; *synonyms* (v) range, overtake, obtain, achieve, (n) fetch.

drafli casein; *synonyms* (n) paracasein, (v) crassamentum.

drag fossa; *synonyms* (n) cavity, fovea, pit, colliery, endocarp.

draga 1. pull; *synonyms* (v) drag, draw, draught, pluck, attract; *antonyms* (v) push, repel, 2. contract; *synonyms* (n) compact, charter, (v) covenant, bargain, (adj) abridge; *antonyms* (v) expand, widen, stretch, 3. drag; *synonyms* (v) haul, puff, trail, (n) pull, bother, 4. absorb; *synonyms* (v) consume, drink, engross, imbibe, assimilate; *antonyms* (v) bore, emit.

dragakraftur drag; *synonyms* (v) attract, haul, draw, puff, (n) pull; *antonym* (v) push.

dragi drag; *synonyms* (*v*) attract, haul, draw, puff, (*n*) pull; *antonym* (*v*) push.

dragkló 1. puller; *synonyms* (*n*) dragger, anchor, tugger, trawler, 2. extractor; *synonyms* (*n*) centrifuge, exhauster, separator, plunger, (*v*) pliers.

dragkraftur pull; *synonyms* (*v*) drag, draw, draught, pluck, attract; *antonyms* (*v*) push, repel.

draglöð die; *synonyms* (*v*) decease, dead, death, depart, (*n*) dice.

dragreipi fall; *synonyms* (*v*) decline, dip, decrease, descend, (*n*) drop; *antonyms* (*v*) rise, increase, ascend, climb, (*n*) ascent.

dragspil accordion; *synonym* (*adj*) plicate.

dragþvinga extractor; *synonyms* (*n*) centrifuge, exhauster, separator, plunger, (*v*) pliers.

dramb arrogance; *synonyms* (*n*) haughtiness, disdain, conceit, presumption, vanity; *antonyms* (*n*) humility, modesty.

drap 1. murder; *synonyms* (*n*) carnage, homicide, slaughter, (*v*) massacre, butcher, 2. homicide; *synonyms* (*n*) assassination, murder, butchery, manslaughter, murderer.

dráttarbraut slip; *synonyms* (*n*) lapse, fault, (*v*) fall, slide, (*adj*) blunder; *antonym* (*v*) improve.

dráttarskífa sheave; *synonyms* (*n*) sheaf, bundle, roller, bullwheel.

dráttarspil winch; *synonyms* (*n*) crank, windlass, (*v*) capstan, derrick, wince.

dráttur 1. drawing; *synonyms* (*n*) draft, drafting, delineation, picture, plan, 2. demurrage; *synonym* (*n*) demorage.

draugur ghost; *synonyms* (*n*) apparition, shade, spirit, soul, (*v*) specter.

draumórar fantasy; *synonyms* (*n*) dream, fancy, illusion, delusion, mirage; *antonyms* (*n*) reality, (*adj*) real.

draumur dream; *synonyms* (*n*) daydream, aspiration, ambition, vision, desire; *antonym* (*n*) reality.

dreggjar 1. residue; *synonyms* (*n*) remainder, remnant, balance, rest, leftover, 2. tailing; *synonyms* (*n*) shadowing, following, tail, abridgment, cobwebbing, 3. sediment; *synonyms* (*n*) deposit, deposition, lees, dregs, grounds.

dregill taenia; *synonyms* (*n*) tenia, fillet, filet, lemniscus, stopping.

dreif 1. scatter; *synonyms* (*v*) disperse, dispel, disseminate, distribute, (*n*) spread; *antonym* (*v*) gather, 2. spread; *synonyms* (*v*) scatter, reach, expand, extend, broadcast; *antonym* (*adj*) concentrated.

dreifa 1. suspension; *synonyms* (*n*) delay, interruption, abeyance, break, intermission, 2. spread; *synonyms* (*v*) scatter, reach, disperse, expand, extend; *antonym* (*adj*) concentrated, 3.

diffuse; *synonyms* (*v*) circulate, disseminate, spread, broadcast, propagate.

dreifari diffuser; *synonyms* (*n*) diffusor, distributor, scatterer.

dreifast diffuse; *synonyms* (*v*) circulate, disperse, disseminate, spread, broadcast.

dreifbær extensive; *synonyms* (*adj*) big, comprehensive, ample, broad, commodious; *antonyms* (*adj*) narrow, restricted, small, limited, minor.

dreifbýli hinterland; *synonyms* (*n*) backwoods, country, boondocks, vicinity, bush.

dreifður 1. sporadic; *synonyms* (*adj*) intermittent, rare, occasional, sparse, infrequent; *antonyms* (*adj*) continuous, constant, nonstop, frequent, regular, 2. diffuse; *synonyms* (*v*) circulate, disperse, disseminate, spread, broadcast.

dreifiblað handout; *synonyms* (*n*) brochure, pamphlet, flyer, leaflet, release.

dreifibréf circular; *synonyms* (*adj*) round, annular, circinate, (*n*) advertisement, bill; *antonym* (*adj*) square.

dreififall distribution; *synonyms* (*n*) diffusion, dispensation, delivery, deal, (*v*) dissemination; *antonym* (*n*) concentration.

dreififelli distribution; *synonyms* (*n*) diffusion, dispensation, delivery, deal, (*v*) dissemination; *antonym* (*n*) concentration.

dreifikerfi grid; *synonyms* (*n*) gridiron, grating, lattice, mesh, netting.

dreifilausn suspension; *synonyms* (*n*) delay, interruption, abeyance, break, intermission.

dreifing 1. scattering; *synonyms* (*n*) diffusion, dispersal, dissipation, dispersion, distribution, 2. propagation; *synonyms* (*n*) generation, dissemination, extension, multiplication, circulation, 3. dispersion; *synonyms* (*n*) spread, scattering, 4. diffusion; *synonyms* (*n*) expansion, propagation, spreading, 5. discharge; *synonyms* (*n*) release, dismissal, (*v*) acquit, clear, absolve; *antonyms* (*v*) capture, hire.

dreifingaraðili distributor; *synonyms* (*n*) distributer, spreader, middleman, allocator, feeder.

dreifir diffuser; *synonyms* (*n*) diffusor, distributor, scatterer.

dreifiskjal handout; *synonyms* (*n*) brochure, pamphlet, flyer, leaflet, release.

dreifistýring decentralization; *synonyms* (*n*) decentralisation, delegation, transfer, transference.

dreifisvið range; *synonyms* (*v*) line, arrange, order, rank, roam.

dreifkjörnungur prokaryote; *synonym* (*n*) procaryote.

dreifni 1. variance; *synonyms* (*n*) difference, disagreement, discrepancy, dissension, division, **2**. diffusion; *synonyms* (*n*) dissemination, dispersion, dispersal, distribution, spread, **3**. dispersion; *synonyms* (*n*) diffusion, dissipation, circulation, scattering.

drekajurt tarragon; *synonyms* (*n*) estragon, mugwort, sagebrush.

drekamalurt tarragon; *synonyms* (*n*) estragon, mugwort, sagebrush.

drekka 1. drink; *synonyms* (*n*) beverage, alcohol, brew, (*v*) draught, booze, **2**. eat; *synonyms* (*v*) devour, consume, bite, dine, munch.

drengur 1. boy; *synonyms* (*n*) lad, fellow, kid, male, man, **2**. lad; *synonyms* (*n*) boy, blighter, chap, cub, cuss.

drep 1. mortification; *synonyms* (*n*) humiliation, chagrin, embarrassment, gangrene, shame, **2**. necrosis; *synonyms* (*n*) mortification, death, (*adj*) pertussis, phthisis, pneumonia.

drepa kill; *synonyms* (*v*) assassinate, destroy, erase, annihilate, eliminate.

drepsótt 1. pestilence; *synonyms* (*n*) plague, pest, epidemic, blight, (*adj*) murrain, **2**. plague; *synonyms* (*v*) bother, harass, molest, worry, afflict.

drepvefur slough; *synonyms* (*n*) bog, marsh, fen, quagmire, morass.

drer cataract; *synonyms* (*n*) cascade, waterfall, deluge, falls, torrent.

dreypa drip; *synonyms* (*n*) dribble, trickle, leak, leakage, (*v*) drop.

dreypari pipette; *synonyms* (*n*) pipet, beaker, flask, carboy, syringe.

dreypilyf infusion; *synonyms* (*n*) extract, infuse, influx, dash, (*v*) injection.

dreyping drip; *synonyms* (*n*) dribble, trickle, leak, leakage, (*v*) drop.

dreyrasýki hemophilia; *synonym* (*n*) haemophilia.

drif 1. propulsion; *synonyms* (*n*) actuation, momentum, push, thrust, power, **2**. drive; *synonyms* (*n*) ride, force, campaign, (*v*) actuate, chase; *antonyms* (*n*) apathy, inertia.

drífa shower; *synonyms* (*n*) rain, (*v*) pour, bathe, hail, sprinkle.

drifborð rotary; *synonyms* (*adj*) revolving, rotatory, rotating, rotative, (*n*) circle.

drifefni propellant; *synonyms* (*n*) propellent, fuel, explosive, (*adj*) propelling, propulsive.

drifhlutfall gearing; *synonyms* (*n*) gear, affairs, behavior, caravan, clothing.

drifhögg drive; *synonyms* (*n*) ride, force, campaign, (*v*) push, actuate; *antonyms* (*n*) apathy, inertia.

drifhús housing; *synonyms* (*n*) habitation, casing, dwelling, lodging, abode; *antonym* (*adj*) business.

drifrás driver; *synonyms* (*n*) coachman, postboy, club, chaser, commuter.

drifrit driver; *synonyms* (*n*) coachman, postboy, club, chaser, commuter.

drjúpa 1. trickle; *synonyms* (*n*) drip, distill, (*v*) drop, dribble, percolate; *antonyms* (*n*) throng, (*v*) gush, **2**. drip; *synonyms* (*n*) trickle, leak, leakage, (*v*) seep, weep, **3**. dribble; *synonyms* (*v*) drool, drivel, slobber, flow, ooze.

dröfnuskata rocker; *synonyms* (*n*) cradle, player, bend.

drög outline; *synonyms* (*n*) sketch, design, (*v*) draft, line, form.

droll lag; *synonyms* (*n*) backwardness, (*v*) dawdle, delay, linger, dally.

drómedari dromedary; *synonyms* (*n*) camel, elephant, llama.

dröngull cylinder; *synonyms* (*n*) barrel, roll, pipe, tube, column.

dropalausn emulsion; *synonyms* (*n*) balm, cream, emulsification, liquid, (*adj*) soup.

dropar dew; *synonyms* (*n*) condensation, mist, freshness, humidity, moisture.

dropi 1. drop; *synonyms* (*v*) fall, decrease, deposit, (*n*) decline, collapse; *antonyms* (*v*) rise, increase, lift, (*n*) growth, **2**. droplet; *synonyms* (*n*) drop, dot, bit, (*adj*) globule, grain.

drotning queen; *synonyms* (*n*) empress, king, lady, sovereign, monarch.

drottin king; *synonyms* (*n*) emperor, mogul, sovereign, chief, baron.

drottnari sovereign; *synonyms* (*adj*) independent, autonomous, (*n*) monarch, ruler, king; *antonym* (*adj*) dependent.

Drottning queen; *synonyms* (*n*) empress, king, lady, sovereign, monarch.

drottnun 1. dominance; *synonyms* (*n*) ascendancy, authority, control, domination, supremacy; *antonym* (*n*) inferiority, **2**. domination; *synonyms* (*n*) command, ascendency, dominance, dominion, mastery.

drottnunargirni dominance; *synonyms* (*n*) ascendancy, authority, control, domination, supremacy; *antonym* (*n*) inferiority.

drullusokkur plunger; *synonyms* (*n*) piston, diver, needle, speculator, frogman.

drunur rumble; *synonyms* (*n*) boom, roll, roar, (*v*) murmur, growl.

drusla 1. scrap; *synonyms* (*n*) fight, morsel, brawl, remnant, (*adj*) fragment; *antonym* (*v*) keep, **2**. rag; *synonyms* (*n*) newspaper, (*v*) banter, bedevil, tease, (*adj*) shred.

drykkfeldniköst dipsomania; *synonyms* (*n*) alcoholism, kleptomania, oenomania, potomania, (*v*) oinomania.

drykkjarbrunnur well; *synonyms* (*adv*) right, easily, thoroughly, (*adj*) healthy, (*n*) fountain; *antonyms* (*adv*) ill, badly, poorly, (*adj*) sick, unwell.

drykkjusjúklingur alcoholic; *synonyms* (*adj*) strong, (*n*) drunk, boozer, dipsomaniac, lush; *antonym* (*adj*) soft.

drykkjusýki alcoholism; *synonyms* (*n*) dipsomania, drunkenness, potomania, boozing, (*v*) alcohol.

drýsill 1. puck; *synonyms* (*n*) fairy, imp, 2. cursor; *synonyms* (*n*) indicator, pointer, needle, arrow, hand.

dúan fluctuation; *synonyms* (*n*) variation, vicissitude, wavering, deviation, hesitation.

duaranga accessories; *synonyms* (*n*) fittings, equipment, accompaniments, garnishes, possession.

dúfa pigeon; *synonyms* (*n*) gull, gudgeon, cully, (*v*) dupe, bilk.

dufl buoy; *synonyms* (*v*) prop, encourage, bolster, cheer, (*adj*) float.

duft powder; *synonyms* (*n*) dust, gunpowder, (*v*) grind, crush, pound.

duftherða cement; *synonyms* (*n*) glue, adhesive, gum, (*v*) fasten, fix.

duftlyf powder; *synonyms* (*n*) dust, gunpowder, (*v*) grind, crush, pound.

dugur potency; *synonyms* (*n*) force, might, effectiveness, efficacy, ability.

dúi buffer; *synonyms* (*n*) safeguard, pad, protection, bumper, (*v*) cushion.

dúklakk dope; *synonyms* (*n*) dolt, boob, booby, ass, (*v*) drug.

dúkstyrking doping; *synonyms* (*n*) swabbing, doctoring, activating.

dúkur fabric; *synonyms* (*n*) building, cloth, composition, frame, (*v*) edifice.

dul latency; *synonyms* (*n*) suspension, abeyance, intermission, interruption, latence.

duld complex; *synonyms* (*adj*) composite, complicate, abstruse, difficult, elaborate; *antonyms* (*adj*) simple, basic, straightforward, clear, plain.

dulinn 1. latent; *synonyms* (*adj*) covert, potential, secret, dormant, hidden; *antonym* (*adj*) active, 2. occult; *synonyms* (*v*) mystic, (*adj*) obscure, cryptic, mysterious, cryptical.

dulnefni pseudonym; *synonyms* (*n*) alias, anonym, name, disguise, title.

dulsálarfræði parapsychology; *synonym* (*n*) telepathy.

dulskyggni clairvoyance; *synonyms* (*n*) foresight, intuition, electrobiology, telepathy, feeling.

dulvitaður unconscious; *synonyms* (*adj*) involuntary, unaware, ignorant, subconscious, unwitting; *antonyms* (*adj*) conscious, awake, deliberate.

dulvitund unconscious; *synonyms* (*adj*) involuntary, unaware, ignorant, subconscious, unwitting; *antonyms* (*adj*) conscious, awake, deliberate.

dumbur 1. dumb; *synonyms* (*adj*) mute, dense, dim, dull, silent, 2. mute; *synonyms* (*adj*) dumb, quiet, (*v*) muffle, dampen, deaden; *antonym* (*adj*) talkative.

dumpning dumping; *synonyms* (*n*) disposal, discarding, clearance, jettisoning, removal.

dúnfjöður plumule; *synonyms* (*n*) acrospire, sprit, feather, plumula, gemmule.

dúnhærður pubescent; *synonyms* (*adj*) adolescent, juvenile, downy, hairy, puberulent; *antonym* (*n*) adult.

dúnkraftur jack; *synonyms* (*n*) knave, flag, jackass, mariner, ace.

durianávöxtur durian; *synonym* (*n*) durion.

dvalartími dwell; *synonyms* (*v*) abide, inhabit, reside, bide, live.

dvali 1. torpor; *synonyms* (*n*) lethargy, inactivity, lassitude, inertia, apathy, 2. trance; *synonyms* (*n*) reverie, coma, fascination, daze, (*adj*) ecstasy, 3. latency; *synonyms* (*n*) suspension, abeyance, intermission, interruption, latence.

dvaltími dwell; *synonyms* (*v*) abide, inhabit, reside, bide, live.

dvalvefja damper; *synonyms* (*n*) check, discouragement, cooler, silencer, constraint.

dvergbítur 1. zucchini; *synonym* (*n*) courgette, 2. courgette; *synonym* (*n*) zucchini.

dverggalangal galangal; *synonyms* (*n*) galanga, galingale.

dvergkráka jackdaw; *synonyms* (*n*) daw, crow, caddow, chough, jay.

dvergur dwarf; *synonyms* (*n*) elf, fairy, gnome, (*adj*) little, midget; *antonym* (*n*) giant.

dvergvaxinn dwarf; *synonyms* (*n*) elf, fairy, gnome, (*adj*) little, midget; *antonym* (*n*) giant.

dvergvöxtur dwarfism; *synonym* (*n*) nanism.

dvína 1. regress; *synonyms* (*v*) recede, lapse, revert, relapse, degenerate; *antonyms* (*v*) improve, progress, 2. lapse; *synonyms* (*n*) fall, (*v*) decline, expire, drop, elapse.

dvínandi regressive; *synonyms* (*adj*) reactionary, retrogressive, returning, backward, (*v*) resilient.

dvöl 1. stay; *synonyms* (*v*) remain, reside, rest, prop, stop; *antonyms* (*v*) leave, change, abscond, depart, 2. dwell; *synonyms* (*v*) abide, inhabit, bide, live, stay.

dýfa immerse; *synonyms* (v) dip, douse, plunge, absorb, drench.

dýfilögur dip; *synonyms* (n) plunge, (v) duck, bathe, drop, fall; *antonyms* (n) hump, mountain.

dýfing immersion; *synonyms* (n) dip, absorption, ducking, concentration, submergence.

dylja mask; *synonyms* (n) cover, conceal, (v) cloak, disguise, hide; *antonym* (v) disclose.

dyljun masking; *synonyms* (n) cover, covering, concealment, mask, screening.

dýna 1. mattress; *synonyms* (n) bedding, bed, 2. pad; *synonyms* (n) cushion, apartment, (v) line, inflate, expand.

dýnamór generator; *synonyms* (n) author, creator, founder, boiler, originator.

dýpi depth; *synonyms* (n) abyss, deepness, profoundness, intensity, profundity.

dýpka dredge; *synonyms* (v) drag, sprinkle, deepen, dust, (n) dredger.

dýpkunarprammi dredger; *synonym* (v) dredge.

dýpkunarskip dredger; *synonym* (v) dredge.

dýpt depth; *synonyms* (n) abyss, deepness, profoundness, intensity, profundity.

dýptarmæling sounding; *synonyms* (adj) audible, looking, hollow, (n) investigation, depth.

dýptarsýn perspective; *synonyms* (n) attitude, aspect, angle, outlook, prospect.

dyr door; *synonyms* (n) gate, threshold, access, doorway, entrance; *antonym* (n) exit.

dýr 1. animal; *synonyms* (n) brute, creature, beast, (adj) bodily, carnal, 2. pricey; *synonyms* (adj) dear, expensive, costly, pricy, beloved; *antonym* (adj) cheap, 3. dear; *synonyms* (adj) close, lovely, precious, (n) darling, love; *antonym* (adj) worthless, 4. costly; *synonyms* (adj) valuable, extravagant, high, luxurious, pricey, 5. expensive; *synonyms* (adj) sumptuous, lavish, overpriced, exclusive, fine; *antonyms* (adj) inexpensive, reasonable.

dyrafaldur architrave; *synonyms* (n) capital, cornice, entablature, frieze, pediment.

dýrafarsótt epizootic; *synonyms* (adj) epidemic, endemic, catching, pandemic, (n) epizooty.

dýrafélag colony; *synonyms* (n) settlement, community, plantation, dependency, village.

dýrafræði zoology; *synonyms* (n) zoonomy, zootomy, anatomy.

dýrahringur zodiac; *synonyms* (n) baldric, band, belt, constellation, girth.

dýrahringurinn zodiac; *synonyms* (n) baldric, band, belt, constellation, girth.

dýralæknir 1. veterinary; *synonyms* (n) vet, veterinarian, veteran, 2. vet; *synonyms* (n) veterinary, (v) inspect, examine, vaquero.

dýramjölvi glycogen; *synonym* (n) glucogen.

dýraríki fauna; *synonyms* (n) animal, beast, brute, creature, puppet.

dýrasambú colony; *synonyms* (n) settlement, community, plantation, dependency, village.

dýrasjúkdómur ringworm; *synonyms* (n) tinea, (adj) necrosis, pertussis, phthisis, pneumonia.

dýrasterkja glycogen; *synonym* (n) glucogen.

dýrseðli bestiality; *synonyms* (n) cruelty, violence, zooerastia, zooerasty.

Ð

Ðflugur strong; *synonyms* (adj) intense, powerful, able, deep, firm; *antonyms* (adj) weak, bland, delicate, faint, feeble.

E

eðalmalurt wormwood; *synonyms* (n) absinth, gall.

eðalvagn limousine; *synonyms* (n) limo, automobile, car, clunker, coupe.

edik vinegar; *synonyms* (n) verjuice, acetum, brine.

eðja sludge; *synonyms* (n) mud, ooze, slime, (adj) silt, mire.

eðjufiskur bowfin; *synonyms* (n) dogfish, grindle.

eðli 1. quality; *synonyms* (n) nature, character, characteristic, class, condition; *antonym* (adj) shoddy, 2. nature; *synonyms* (n) disposition, essence, creation, quality, (adj) kind, 3. essence; *synonyms* (n) core, entity, aroma, being, crux.

eðlilegt normal; *synonyms* (adj) regular, common, conventional, customary, general; *antonyms* (adj) abnormal, unusual, creepy, eccentric, extraordinary.

eðlilegur normal; *synonyms* (adj) regular, common, conventional, customary, general; *antonyms* (adj) abnormal, unusual, creepy, eccentric, extraordinary.

eðlisávísun instinct; *synonyms* (n) intuition, impulse, aptitude, urge, gift.

eðlisbreyting denaturation; *synonym* (n) denaturing.

eðlisbundinn intensive; *synonyms* (adj) intense, concentrated, thorough, exhaustive, (n) intensifier; *antonym* (adj) extensive.

eðlisfræðilegur physical; *synonyms* (adj) material, bodily, actual, corporeal, tangible; *antonyms* (adj) spiritual, mental, intangible.

eðlisgerð constitution; *synonyms* (*n*) composition, code, makeup, organization, temperament.

eðlishvöt instinct; *synonyms* (*n*) intuition, impulse, aptitude, urge, gift.

eðlislægur 1. specific; *synonyms* (*adj*) individual, special, concrete, exact, (*n*) particular; *antonyms* (*adj*) universal, vague, (*n*) general, **2.** constitutional; *synonyms* (*adj*) congenital, essential, inherent, intrinsic, legal; *antonym* (*adj*) unconstitutional, **3.** essential; *synonyms* (*adj*) necessary, crucial, important, requisite, constituent; *antonyms* (*adj*) minor, secondary, (*n*) inessential, optional, option, **4.** intrinsic; *synonyms* (*adj*) immanent, inborn, internal, constitutional, integral; *antonym* (*adj*) extrinsic.

eðlisleiðni conductivity; *synonyms* (*n*) conduction, conductibility, energy.

eðlislíking homology; *synonyms* (*n*) affinity, equality, analogy, relation.

eðlislíkur cognate; *synonyms* (*adj*) akin, alike, allied, related, like.

eðlismassi density; *synonyms* (*n*) compactness, consistency, concentration, denseness, stupidity; *antonym* (*n*) looseness.

eðlissvipting denaturation; *synonym* (*n*) denaturing.

eðlisþyngd density; *synonyms* (*n*) compactness, consistency, concentration, denseness, stupidity; *antonym* (*n*) looseness.

eðlisviðnám resistivity; *synonyms* (*n*) resistance, impedance, immunity, opposition, underground.

eðlisvís instinctive; *synonyms* (*adj*) automatic, inborn, inherent, innate, (*v*) involuntary; *antonyms* (*adj*) voluntary, learned.

eðlisvísan instinct; *synonyms* (*n*) intuition, impulse, aptitude, urge, gift.

eðlisvísir anlage; *synonym* (*n*) primordium.

eðun disjunction; *synonyms* (*n*) disconnection, dissociation, disjuncture, disunion, separation.

ef if; *synonyms* (*conj*) provided, although, providing, whether, (*n*) but.

efa 1. question; *synonyms* (*n*) inquiry, (*v*) doubt, query, distrust, inquire; *antonyms* (*n*) certainty, (*v*) answer, **2.** doubt; *synonyms* (*n*) disbelief, misgiving, question, dispute, (*v*) suspicion; *antonyms* (*n*) confidence, conclusiveness, (*v*) trust.

efi doubt; *synonyms* (*n*) disbelief, misgiving, question, (*v*) distrust, query; *antonyms* (*n*) certainty, confidence, conclusiveness, (*v*) trust.

efiki works; *synonyms* (*n*) factory, plant, workings, mill, manufactory.

efla 1. reinforce; *synonyms* (*v*) bolster, intensify, enhance, buttress, consolidate; *antonym* (*v*) weaken, **2.** strengthen; *synonyms* (*v*) confirm, corroborate, brace, encourage, fortify; *antonym* (*v*) undermine, **3.** promote; *synonyms* (*v*) advance, help, aid, advertise, (*adv*) further; *antonyms* (*v*) demote, discourage, **4.** amplify; *synonyms* (*v*) aggrandize, enlarge, exaggerate, expand, extend; *antonyms* (*v*) reduce, understate.

efli dynamics; *synonyms* (*n*) kinetics, motion, (*v*) statics.

efling 1. strengthening; *synonyms* (*n*) concentration, fortification, consolidation, reenforcement, (*adj*) fortifying; *antonym* (*n*) reduction, **2.** recruitment; *synonyms* (*n*) employment, enrollment, enlisting, mobilization, **3.** potentiation; *synonym* (*n*) potentialization, **4.** promotion; *synonyms* (*n*) furtherance, advance, advancement, advertising, boost; *antonyms* (*n*) demotion, neglect, **5.** consolidation; *synonyms* (*n*) amalgamation, unification, combination, union, condensation.

eflinn dynamic; *synonyms* (*adj*) active, aggressive, dynamical, energetic, forceful; *antonyms* (*adj*) dull, static.

eflir booster; *synonyms* (*n*) admirer, friend, patron, promoter, protagonist.

efnablanda mixture; *synonyms* (*n*) mix, alloy, concoction, assortment, blend.

efnabreyting reaction; *synonyms* (*n*) answer, response, backlash, reply, effect.

efnaferli pathway; *synonyms* (*n*) passage, footpath, lane, path, road.

efnaformúla formula; *synonyms* (*n*) form, law, convention, expression, formality.

efnafræði chemistry; *synonyms* (*n*) alchemy, attraction, charm, (*adj*) acyclic, botany.

efnagreining analysis; *synonyms* (*n*) anatomy, breakdown, decomposition, inquiry, inspection; *antonym* (*n*) synthesis.

efnahagshrun panic; *synonyms* (*n*) alarm, dismay, horror, scare, (*adj*) consternation; *antonym* (*n*) composure.

efnahagskerfi economy; *synonyms* (*n*) frugality, parsimony, saving, thrift, conservation; *antonym* (*n*) extravagance.

efnahagslægð recession; *synonyms* (*n*) decline, depression, fall, niche, recess.

efnahagslegur economic; *synonyms* (*adj*) commercial, financial, profitable, efficient, economical.

efnahagslíf economy; *synonyms* (*n*) frugality, parsimony, saving, thrift, conservation; *antonym* (*n*) extravagance.

efnahagsmál economics; *synonyms* (*n*) finance, economy, commerce, money, backing.

efnahagsþrengingar austerity; *synonyms* (*n*) rigor, acerbity, asceticism, hardship, (*adj*) stringency.

efnahagur economy; *synonyms* (n) frugality, parsimony, saving, thrift, conservation; *antonym* (n) extravagance.

efnahemill inhibitor; *synonym* (n) stabilizer.

efnahópur radical; *synonyms* (adj) extremist, basic, exhaustive, extreme, revolutionary; *antonyms* (adj) conventional, old-fashioned, (n) moderate, conservative, traditionalist.

efnahvarf reaction; *synonyms* (n) answer, response, backlash, reply, effect.

efnahvarfi catalyst; *synonyms* (n) accelerator, goad, incentive, stimulus, spur.

efnahvati 1. reactor; *synonym* (n) stator, **2.** catalyst; *synonyms* (n) accelerator, goad, incentive, stimulus, spur, **3.** activator; *synonym* (n) inducer.

efnalitsjá colorimeter; *synonyms* (n) tintometer, colourimeter.

efnarafmagn galvanism; *synonyms* (n) electricity, infection, inspiration, piquancy, provocation.

efnasamband 1. compound; *synonyms* (n) blend, complex, mix, (v) alloy, (adj) composite; *antonym* (adj) simple, **2.** chemical; *synonyms* (adj) chemic, alchemical, alkaline, plastic, (n) ammunition.

efnasamtenging synthesis; *synonyms* (n) combination, fusion, compound, incorporation, mixture; *antonym* (n) separation.

efnaskipti metabolism; *synonyms* (n) metamorphosis, metastasis, transformation, conversion, life.

efnasmíð synthesis; *synonyms* (n) combination, fusion, compound, incorporation, mixture; *antonym* (n) separation.

efnasmíði synthesis; *synonyms* (n) combination, fusion, compound, incorporation, mixture; *antonym* (n) separation.

efnastyrkur concentration; *synonyms* (n) absorption, concentrate, application, attention, engrossment; *antonym* (n) distraction.

efnatengi bond; *synonyms* (n) association, tie, alliance, deed, (v) bind.

efnavísir indicator; *synonyms* (n) gauge, index, indication, arrow, indicant.

efnaviti indicator; *synonyms* (n) gauge, index, indication, arrow, indicant.

efnhvarfi catalyst; *synonyms* (n) accelerator, goad, incentive, stimulus, spur.

efni 1. substance; *synonyms* (n) essence, body, import, material, matter; *antonym* (n) triviality, **2.** topic; *synonyms* (n) question, subject, theme, affair, issue, **3.** documentary; *synonyms* (n) docudrama, infotainment, (adj) documental, **4.** chemical; *synonyms* (adj) chemic, alchemical, alkaline, plastic, (n) ammunition, **5.** anlage; *synonym* (n) primordium.

efnisfærsla feed; *synonyms* (v) eat, dine, nurture, (n) aliment, food; *antonym* (v) starve.

efnisgrein paragraph; *synonyms* (n) article, item, section, chapter, (v) clause.

efnishyggja materialism; *synonyms* (n) acquisitiveness, anabaptism, avarice, corporealism, covetousness; *antonym* (n) generosity.

efnismagn mass; *synonyms* (n) bulk, heap, crowd, cluster, (v) flock.

efnismikill copious; *synonyms* (adj) abundant, ample, bountiful, affluent, plentiful; *antonyms* (adj) scarce, meager, small, sparse.

efnismolun catabolism; *synonyms* (n) dissimilation, katabolism, anabolism, metabolism, disassimilation.

efnisögn particle; *synonyms* (n) molecule, grain, speck, bit, (adj) atom.

efnisskrá 1. program; *synonyms* (n) agenda, plan, broadcast, design, (v) schedule, **2.** register; *synonyms* (n) record, list, inventory, (v) file, enroll, **3.** directory; *synonyms* (n) catalogue, handbook, roll, catalog, guide, **4.** catalogue; *synonyms* (n) bill, (v) register, sort, **5.** catalog; *synonyms* (n) directory, index, (v) classify, detail, enumerate.

efnisstofn radical; *synonyms* (adj) extremist, basic, exhaustive, extreme, revolutionary; *antonyms* (adj) conventional, old-fashioned, (n) moderate, conservative, traditionalist.

efnisþáttur 1. principle; *synonyms* (n) origin, fundamental, method, rule, cause, **2.** ingredient; *synonyms* (n) constituent, component, element, factor, part.

efnisþykkni concentrate; *synonyms* (v) compress, centre, compact, condense, (adj) centralize; *antonym* (v) disperse.

efnisvísir descriptor; *synonyms* (n) anatomy, bod, build, cast, chassis.

efnisyfirlit directory; *synonyms* (n) catalogue, file, list, record, handbook.

efniviður material; *synonyms* (n) body, cloth, (adj) bodily, corporal, corporeal.

efri 1. superior; *synonyms* (adj) senior, dominant, better, exceptional, predominant; *antonyms* (adj) humble, worse, poor, (n) inferior, subordinate, **2.** dorsal; *synonyms* (adj) abaxial, posterior, abaxile, notal, (n) dosser.

efstur top; *synonyms* (n) crown, peak, acme, apex, (v) best; *antonyms* (adj) worst, (n) bottom, base, nadir.

eftir 1. after; *synonyms* (adv) later, beyond, next, subsequently, (adj) back, **2.** as; *synonyms* (conj) qua, because, (prep) during, like, (n) arsenic, **3.** by; *synonyms* (prep) beside, at, of, about, (adv, prep) alongside, **4.** along; *synonyms* (adv) ahead, forward, lengthwise, on, (prf) by; *antonym* (adv) across, **5**. at; *synonyms* (*prep*) in, a, (*n*) astatine, (*adv*) along, (*prf*) all.

eftirbrennari 1. air; *synonyms* (*n*) tune, appearance, manner, (*v*) ventilate, broadcast, **2**. afterburner; *synonym* (*n*) reheat.

eftirbrennir afterburner; *synonym* (*n*) reheat.

eftirburður afterbirth; *synonyms* (*n*) glean, cleaning.

eftirdropi dribble; *synonyms* (*n*) trickle, (*v*) drip, drool, drop, drivel.

eftirgefanlegur elastic; *synonyms* (*adj*) flexible, buoyant, ductile, limber, pliable; *antonyms* (*adj*) rigid, stiff, inflexible, inelastic.

eftirgjöf 1. remission; *synonyms* (*n*) forgiveness, relief, ease, condonation, (*v*) pardon, **2**. concession; *synonyms* (*n*) admission, compliance, allowance, compromise, discount.

eftirhrif aftereffect; *synonyms* (*n*) consequence, effect, result, sequel, corollary.

eftirlaun pension; *synonyms* (*n*) allowance, annuity, payment, stipend, endowment.

eftirlaunaskeið retirement; *synonyms* (*n*) retreat, resignation, departure, privacy, seclusion.

eftirlíking 1. replica; *synonyms* (*n*) facsimile, imitation, copy, duplicate, reproduction; *antonyms* (*n*) original, (*adj*) genuine, **2**. simulation; *synonyms* (*n*) affectation, pretense, pretence, modelling, pretension, **3**. dummy; *synonyms* (*adj*) sham, spurious, (*n*) counterfeit, model, puppet, **4**. imitation; *synonyms* (*n*) dummy, forgery, (*adj*) fake, bogus, false; *antonym* (*adj*) real.

eftirlit 1. supervision; *synonyms* (*n*) oversight, charge, control, direction, (*v*) inspection, **2**. control; *synonyms* (*n*) rule, authority, (*v*) command, check, curb; *antonyms* (*n*) freedom, weakness, (*v*) intensify, share, **3**. check; *synonyms* (*v*) bridle, stop, block, limit, (*n*) arrest, **4**. monitoring; *synonym* (*n*) observation, **5**. inspection; *synonyms* (*n*) examination, review, surveillance, exploration, inquiry.

eftirlitsmaður 1. supervisor; *synonyms* (*n*) superintendent, director, overseer, boss, chief, **2**. inspector; *synonyms* (*n*) examiner, supervisor, auditor, controller, investigator.

eftirlitsskjár monitor; *synonyms* (*v*) check, regulate, control, eavesdrop, (*n*) admonisher.

eftirlitssveit patrol; *synonyms* (*n*) beat, protection, patrolman, (*v*) watch, guard.

eftirljóm 1. persistence; *synonyms* (*n*) perseverance, continuity, endurance, constancy, stubbornness; *antonym* (*n*) compliance, **2**. afterglow; *synonyms* (*n*) twilight, glimmering, glow, light, luminosity.

eftirljómi persistence; *synonyms* (*n*) perseverance, continuity, endurance, constancy, stubbornness; *antonym* (*n*) compliance.

eftirlýsing paint; *synonyms* (*v*) color, dye, daub, coat, decorate.

eftirmatur 1. sweet; *synonyms* (*adj*) beloved, delicious, fresh, lovely, mellow; *antonyms* (*adj*) sour, acid, bitter, discordant, acidic, **2**. pudding; *synonyms* (*n*) pud, sweet, (*adj*) butter, clay, curd.

eftirmynd replica; *synonyms* (*n*) facsimile, imitation, copy, duplicate, reproduction; *antonyms* (*n*) original, (*adj*) genuine.

eftirmynda replicate; *synonyms* (*v*) duplicate, double, reduplicate, repeat, copy.

eftirmyndun 1. replication; *synonyms* (*n*) rejoinder, repetition, reproduction, replica, answer, **2**. modeling; *synonyms* (*n*) modelling, molding, moulding, model, art, **3**. modelling; *synonyms* (*n*) modeling, border, casting, example, exemplar.

eftirnafn surname; *synonyms* (*n*) cognomen, name, sobriquet, soubriquet, (*v*) patronymic.

eftirskin afterglow; *synonyms* (*n*) twilight, glimmering, glow, light, luminosity.

eftirskjálfti aftershock; *synonyms* (*n*) impact, shock.

eftirsókn affinity; *synonyms* (*n*) sympathy, analogy, alliance, bond, kindred.

eftirspurn demand; *synonyms* (*n*) claim, request, (*v*) ask, command, need; *antonym* (*v*) supply.

eftirstöðvar balance; *synonyms* (*n*) poise, symmetry, (*v*) counterbalance, adjust, offset; *antonyms* (*n*) imbalance, (*v*) unbalance.

eftirsveiflur ringing; *synonyms* (*n*) buzz, peal, resonance, (*adj*) resonant, reverberant.

eftirtekja yield; *synonyms* (*n*) produce, return, (*v*) surrender, allow, concede; *antonyms* (*v*) resist, persevere.

eftirvagn trailer; *synonyms* (*n*) caravan, leader, ad, advertisement, announcement.

egg 1. verge; *synonyms* (*n*) boundary, brink, limit, (*v*) border, edge, **2**. rim; *synonyms* (*n*) margin, brim, verge, lip, (*v*) skirt, **3**. brim; *synonyms* (*n*) hem, periphery, rim, perimeter, mouth, **4**. brink; *synonyms* (*n*) shore, threshold, fringe, **5**. border; *synonyms* (*n*) extremity, bed, (*v*) abut, adjoin, surround; *antonyms* (*n*) middle, (*v*) center.

eggbólstur cumulus; *synonyms* (*n*) heap, mound, pile, stratus, woolpack.

eggbú 1. follicle; *synonyms* (*n*) cavity, dent, dimple, dint, lacuna, **2**. ovule; *synonyms* (*n*) ellipse, oval, gemmule, germ, ovulum.

eggbúsegg ovule; *synonyms* (*n*) ellipse, oval, gemmule, germ, ovulum.

eggbússtig oestrus; *synonyms* (*n*) heat, estrus, rut, arousal, groove.

eggfruma ovum; *synonyms* (*n*) egg, ovule, ova, germ, metaplasm.

egghjúpur integument; *synonyms* (*n*) cover, film, coat, skin, tegument.

eggjahvíta 1. protein; *synonyms* (*n*) cytoplasm, (*adj*) albumen, gluten, glair, cream, **2.** albumen; *synonyms* (*n*) albumin, ovalbumin, (*adj*) milk, starch.

eggjakerfi ovary; *synonyms* (*n*) metaplasm, ontogeny, ovum, oxidation, phylogeny.

eggjarauða yolk; *synonyms* (*n*) deutoplasm, suint, vitellus.

eggjastokkur ovary; *synonyms* (*n*) metaplasm, ontogeny, ovum, oxidation, phylogeny.

eggjun excitation; *synonyms* (*n*) excitement, stimulus, agitation, encouragement, feeling.

egglaga 1. oval; *synonyms* (*adj*) elliptical, elliptic, ovate, oviform, (*n*) ellipse, **2.** ovoid; *synonyms* (*adj*) oval, prolate, ovoidal, (*n*) briquette, **3.** oviform; *synonyms* (*adj*) ovoid, (*n*) adjust, arrange, beauty, bench.

eggleg ovary; *synonyms* (*n*) metaplasm, ontogeny, ovum, oxidation, phylogeny.

eggvarp 1. ovulation, **2.** oviposition; *synonyms* (*n*) ovipositing, laying.

eiði 1. isthmus; *synonyms* (*n*) bridge, oasis, (*adj*) strait, neck, wasp, **2.** neck (háls); *synonyms* (*n*) throat, cervix, neckline, (*v*) pet, (*adj*) stricture.

eiga 1. possess; *synonyms* (*v*) have, hold, occupy, wield, (*adj*) own, **2.** own; *synonyms* (*v*) acknowledge, admit, concede, allow, grant.

eigandi owner; *synonyms* (*n*) master, proprietor, possessor, holder, landholder; *antonym* (*n*) tenant.

eigin 1. personal; *synonyms* (*adj*) individual, own, particular, human, intimate; *antonyms* (*adj*) public, general, **2.** proper; *synonyms* (*adj*) appropriate, correct, due, decent, fit; *antonyms* (*adj*) improper, inappropriate, unseemly, wrong, rude, **3.** very; *synonyms* (*adv*) extremely, greatly, highly, (*adj*) much, identical; *antonyms* (*adv*) abysmally, slightly, somewhat, **4.** own; *synonyms* (*v*) acknowledge, admit, have, concede, allow.

eigind 1. quality; *synonyms* (*n*) nature, character, characteristic, class, condition; *antonym* (*adj*) shoddy, **2.** attribute; *synonyms* (*n*) assign, quality, emblem, feature, (*v*) ascribe.

eigindarvídd dimension; *synonyms* (*n*) degree, breadth, bulk, magnitude, size.

eigindi attribute; *synonyms* (*n*) assign, quality, characteristic, emblem, (*v*) ascribe.

eiginkona 1. wife; *synonyms* (*n*) matron, missis, partner, spouse, consort; *antonym* (*n*) husband, **2.** spouse; *synonyms* (*n*) wife, man, mate, match, companion, **3.** mate; *synonyms* (*n*) associate, compeer, fellow, (*v*) equal, (*adj*) comrade.

eiginleiki 1. quality; *synonyms* (*n*) nature, character, characteristic, class, condition; *antonym* (*adj*) shoddy, **2.** property; *synonyms* (*n*) capital, peculiarity, feature, belongings, (*adj*) attribute, **3.** attribute; *synonyms* (*n*) assign, quality, emblem, (*v*) ascribe, (*adj*) property, **4.** trait; *synonyms* (*n*) lineament, idiosyncrasy, mark, (*adj*) trick, (*v*) stroke, **5.** characteristic; *synonyms* (*adj*) distinctive, individual, typical, (*n*) badge, sign; *antonyms* (*adj*) uncharacteristic, common.

eiginmaður 1. husband; *synonyms* (*n*) consort, wife, hubby, (*v*) conserve, economize, **2.** spouse; *synonyms* (*n*) husband, partner, man, mate, match, **3.** mate; *synonyms* (*n*) companion, associate, compeer, (*v*) equal, (*adj*) comrade.

eign 1. property; *synonyms* (*n*) characteristic, capital, peculiarity, feature, (*adj*) attribute, **2.** possession; *synonyms* (*n*) occupancy, occupation, ownership, keeping, (*v*) acquisition, **3.** asset; *synonyms* (*n*) advantage, strength, benefit, forte, purchase; *antonyms* (*n*) liability, vice, **4.** ownership; *synonyms* (*n*) control, proprietorship, possession, (*adj*) property, claim, **5.** holding; *synonyms* (*n*) estate, belongings, hold, capture, interest.

eigna attribute; *synonyms* (*n*) assign, quality, characteristic, emblem, (*v*) ascribe.

eignahalli insolvency; *synonyms* (*n*) bankruptcy, ruin, poverty, hardship, impoverishment; *antonym* (*n*) solvency.

eignaliðir assets; *synonyms* (*n*) property, belongings, capital, funds, means.

eignanám confiscation; *synonyms* (*n*) seizure, appropriation, arrogation, premunire, (*v*) sequestration; *antonyms* (*n*) restoration, return.

eignaraðild holding; *synonyms* (*n*) estate, belongings, hold, keeping, claim.

eignaréttur title; *synonyms* (*n*) call, designation, caption, (*v*) name, style.

eignarhald 1. holdings; *synonyms* (*n*) property, assets, estate, means, resources, **2.** ownership; *synonyms* (*n*) control, proprietorship, occupancy, possession, (*adj*) claim.

eignarleiga leasing; *synonyms* (*n*) hire, rent, rental, charter, chartering.

eignarnám expropriation; *synonyms* (*n*) dispossession, deprivation, appropriation, (*v*) seizure, abreption.

eignarréttur title; *synonyms* (*n*) call, designation, caption, (*v*) name, style.

eignasafn portfolio; *synonyms* (*n*) briefcase, album, file, bandolier, budget.

eignast occupancy; *synonyms* (*n*) habitation, occupation, inhabitancy, employment, ownership.

eignastétt bourgeoisie; *synonym* (*n*) class.

eignastéttarmaður bourgeois; *synonyms* (*adj*) conservative, (*n*) capitalist, burgess, capitals, caps.

eignaupptaka confiscation; *synonyms* (*n*) seizure, appropriation, arrogation, premunire, (*v*) sequestration; *antonyms* (*n*) restoration, return.

eignavarsla safeguarding; *synonyms* (*adj*) defensive, protective, (*n*) protection, conservation, preservation.

eignfæra capitalize; *synonyms* (*v*) capitalise, gain, profit, fund, use.

eignfærsla capitalization; *synonyms* (*n*) capitalisation, discounting, use.

eignir 1. assets; *synonyms* (*n*) property, belongings, capital, funds, means, **2.** property; *synonyms* (*n*) characteristic, peculiarity, feature, character, (*adj*) attribute, **3.** substance; *synonyms* (*n*) essence, body, import, material, matter; *antonym* (*n*) triviality, **4.** properties, **5.** resources; *synonyms* (*n*) assets, finances, money, substance, wherewithal.

eilífðargreiðslur perpetuity; *synonyms* (*n*) eternity, immortality, sempiternity, infinity, endlessness.

eiming distillation; *synonyms* (*n*) distillate, distillment, brew, purification, refinement.

eimingarflaska retort; *synonyms* (*n*) reply, answer, return, rejoinder, (*v*) respond.

eimingarsúla column; *synonyms* (*n*) pillar, procession, row, stanchion, file.

eimir 1. vaporizer; *synonym* (*n*) spray, **2.** evaporator; *synonym* (*n*) boiler, **3.** emitter; *synonym* (*n*) transmitter.

eimreið locomotive; *synonyms* (*n*) engine, conductor, (*adj*) locomotor, mobile, (*v*) train.

eimsvali condenser; *synonyms* (*n*) capacitor, capacitance, capacity, plugger.

eimþéttir condenser; *synonyms* (*n*) capacitor, capacitance, capacity, plugger.

eimun distillation; *synonyms* (*n*) distillate, distillment, brew, purification, refinement.

eimur 1. vapour; *synonyms* (*n*) vapor, evaporation, gas, vaporisation, vaporization, **2.** steam; *synonyms* (*n*) mist, fog, (*v*) reek, evaporate, exhale, **3.** vapor; *synonyms* (*n*) cloud, haze, steam, vapour, (*v*) bluster, **4.** fume; *synonyms* (*n*) smoke, foam, (*v*) chafe, rage, (*adj*) boil, **5.** exhalation; *synonyms* (*n*) breath, emanation, expiration, emission, fumes.

ein one; *synonyms* (*pron*) any, (*n*) anybody, (*adj*) certain, individual, lone.

einær annual; *synonyms* (*adj*) yearly, annuary, (*n*) almanac, yearbook, ephemeris.

einangra 1. segregate; *synonyms* (*v*) isolate, detach, discriminate, divide, (*adj*) detached, **2.** isolate; *synonyms* (*v*) insulate, maroon, sequester, abstract, dissociate.

einangrað insulated; *synonyms* (*adj*) cloistered, (*prep*) separated, unconnected.

einangrari 1. separator; *synonyms* (*n*) centrifuge, extractor, classifier, arrester, partition, **2.** dielectric; *synonyms* (*n*) insulator, nonconductor, **3.** isolator, **4.** insulator; *synonyms* (*n*) dielectric, insulation, diehard, pad, traditionalist.

einangri insulator; *synonyms* (*n*) dielectric, nonconductor, insulation, diehard, pad.

einangrun 1. abstraction; *synonyms* (*n*) abstract, abstractedness, reverie, engrossment, extraction; *antonyms* (*n*) addition, attentiveness, **2.** insularity; *synonyms* (*n*) insularism, insulation, detachment, prejudice, bigotry, **3.** insulation; *synonyms* (*n*) insularity, insulating, insulant, lining, isolation, **4.** isolation; *synonyms* (*n*) alienation, estrangement, privacy, dissociation, loneliness; *antonyms* (*n*) closeness, companionship.

einangrunarefni insulation; *synonyms* (*n*) insularity, insulating, detachment, insulant, lining.

einangrunarhrun breakdown; *synonyms* (*n*) collapse, fault, analysis, failure, ruin.

einangrunarlag dielectric; *synonyms* (*n*) insulator, nonconductor.

einangur 1. insulated; *synonyms* (*adj*) cloistered, (*prep*) separated, unconnected, **2.** insulator; *synonyms* (*n*) dielectric, nonconductor, insulation, diehard, pad, **3.** isolate; *synonyms* (*v*) insulate, detach, divide, maroon, sequester.

einbeita concentrate; *synonyms* (*v*) compress, centre, compact, condense, (*adj*) centralize; *antonym* (*v*) disperse.

einbeiting 1. concentration; *synonyms* (*n*) absorption, concentrate, application, attention, engrossment; *antonym* (*n*) distraction, **2.** focusing; *synonyms* (*n*) centering, concentration, focus, focussing, focalisation.

einbúi stack; *synonyms* (*n*) pile, accumulation, mound, rick, (*v*) heap.

eind particle; *synonyms* (*n*) molecule, grain, speck, bit, (*adj*) atom.

eindagi deadline; *synonyms* (*n*) limit, end, aim, goal, target.

eindahraðall accelerator; *synonyms* (*n*) catalyst, gas, throttle, gun, promotor.

einelta intercept; *synonyms* (*v*) arrest, block, break, check, waylay.

einelti interception; *synonyms* (*n*) interruption, interclusion.

einfalda reduce; *synonyms* (*v*) lower, pare, abbreviate, curtail, (*adj*) abridge; *antonyms* (*v*) increase, bolster, expand, enlarge, exacerbate.

einfaldur 1. simple; *synonyms* (*adj*) plain, homely, pure, elementary, (*v*) clear; *antonyms* (*adj*) complex, complicated, compound, elaborate, difficult, **2**. single; *synonyms* (*adj*) only, celibate, one, odd, particular; *antonyms* (*adj*) married, double, multiple.

einföldun 1. simplification; *synonyms* (*n*) reduction, clarification, decrease, diminution, generalization; *antonym* (*n*) detail, **2**. abstraction; *synonyms* (*n*) abstract, abstractedness, reverie, engrossment, extraction; *antonyms* (*n*) addition, attentiveness.

einfruma unicellular; *synonym* (*adj*) unicelled.

eingengur irreversible; *synonyms* (*adj*) irreparable, unchangeable, (*v*) irrevocable, irretrievable, indefeasible; *antonym* (*adj*) reversible.

eingerð homogeneity; *synonyms* (*n*) homogeneousness, affinity, alliance, consistency, unity.

eingerður 1. homogeneous; *synonyms* (*adj*) uniform, consistent, kindred, homogenous, similar; *antonyms* (*adj*) diverse, varied, inconsistent, **2**. homogeneity; *synonyms* (*n*) homogeneousness, affinity, alliance, consistency, unity.

eingetnaður parthenogenesis; *synonyms* (*v*) abiogenesis, biogenesis, digenesis, dysmerogenesis, eumerogenesis.

eingildur 1. univalent; *synonyms* (*adj*) monovalent, (*adv*) monatomic, **2**. monovalent; *synonym* (*adj*) univalent.

einhleypur single; *synonyms* (*adj*) only, celibate, one, odd, particular; *antonyms* (*adj*) married, double, multiple.

einhliða unilateral; *synonyms* (*adj*) biased, coloured, lopsided, nonreversible, slanted; *antonyms* (*adj*) bilateral, joint, two-sided.

einhliðmælt unilateral; *synonyms* (*adj*) biased, coloured, lopsided, nonreversible, slanted; *antonyms* (*adj*) bilateral, joint, two-sided.

einhverfur irreversible; *synonyms* (*adj*) irreparable, unchangeable, (*v*) irrevocable, irretrievable, indefeasible; *antonym* (*adj*) reversible.

einindi entity; *synonyms* (*n*) being, existence, object, thing, whole.

eining 1. unit; *synonyms* (*n*) troop, element, group, squad, (*adj*) one, **2**. consensus; *synonyms* (*n*) concord, accord, agreement, harmony, unanimity; *antonym* (*n*) inequality, **3**. item; *synonyms* (*n*) piece, detail, article, entry, object, **4**. exponent; *synonyms* (*n*) advocate, champion, power, proponent, protagonist, **5**. module; *synonyms* (*n*) faculty, part, paradigm, subarray, bay.

einingarhluti subunit; *synonym* (*n*) protomer.

einkaleyfi 1. monopoly; *synonyms* (*n*) impropriation, limitation, retention, business, cartel, **2**. patent; *synonyms* (*adj*) obvious, overt, apparent, evident, manifest; *antonym* (*adj*) unclear.

einkaleyfisþóknun royalty; *synonyms* (*n*) regality, kingship, nobility, loyalty, command.

einkaréttargreiðsla royalty; *synonyms* (*n*) regality, kingship, nobility, loyalty, command.

einkaréttur 1. prerogative; *synonyms* (*n*) franchise, privilege, claim, power, immunity, **2**. franchise; *synonyms* (*n*) exemption, liberty, freedom, suffrage, vote, **3**. monopoly; *synonyms* (*n*) impropriation, limitation, retention, business, cartel.

einkasala monopoly; *synonyms* (*n*) impropriation, limitation, retention, business, cartel.

einkasátt negotiation; *synonyms* (*n*) mediation, bargain, parley, transaction, arbitration.

einkasöluleyfi franchise; *synonyms* (*n*) exemption, liberty, freedom, immunity, privilege.

einkaumboð franchise; *synonyms* (*n*) exemption, liberty, freedom, immunity, privilege.

einkennaferna tetrad; *synonyms* (*n*) four, quaternity, quaternion, foursome, quadruplet.

einkennaflækja complex; *synonyms* (*adj*) composite, complicate, abstruse, difficult, elaborate; *antonyms* (*adj*) simple, basic, straightforward, clear, plain.

einkennaflóki complex; *synonyms* (*adj*) composite, complicate, abstruse, difficult, elaborate; *antonyms* (*adj*) simple, basic, straightforward, clear, plain.

einkennagreining diagnosis; *synonyms* (*n*) diagnosing, distinction, identification, examination, diorism.

einkennamynstur syndrome; *synonyms* (*n*) ailment, complaint, complex, sickness, disorder.

einkennandi 1. characteristic; *synonyms* (*adj*) distinctive, individual, (*n*) badge, attribute, sign; *antonyms* (*adj*) uncharacteristic, common, **2**. diagnostic; *synonyms* (*adj*) characteristic, peculiar, (*n*) criterion, (*v*) demonstrative, diacritical.

einkenni 1. symptom; *synonyms* (*n*) sign, indication, evidence, mark, note, **2**. trait; *synonyms* (*n*) characteristic, peculiarity, attribute, quality, (*v*) feature, **3**. character; *synonyms* (*n*) kind, nature, part, role, type.

einkennisbúningur uniform; *synonyms* (*adj*) regular, even, constant, steady, equal; *antonyms* (*adj*) varied, assorted, inconsistent, unequal.

einkunn attribute; *synonyms* (*n*) assign, quality, characteristic, emblem, (*v*) ascribe.

einkunnagjöf rating; *synonyms* (*n*) assessment, mark, evaluation, appraisal, estimate.

einkynja 1. unisexual, **2**. dioecious; *synonyms* (*adj*) dioecian, dioicous.

einleiki identity; *synonyms* (*n*) identicalness, unity, individuality, personality, sameness.

einleitur 1. homogeneous; *synonyms* (*adj*) uniform, consistent, kindred, homogenous, similar;

antonyms (*adj*) diverse, varied, inconsistent, **2.** homoscedastic.

einlendur endemic; *synonyms* (*adj*) autochthonous, indigenous, native, aboriginal, (*n*) epidemic.

einlitna haploid; *synonyms* (*adj*) monoploid, haploidic.

einlitnungur haploid; *synonyms* (*adj*) monoploid, haploidic.

einlitur 1. monochromatic; *synonyms* (*adj*) monochrome, homochromatic, monochromic, monochromous, **2.** isochromatic.

einmana 1. solitary; *synonyms* (*adj*) lonesome, forlorn, alone, lone, lonely, **2.** single; *synonyms* (*adj*) only, celibate, one, odd, particular; *antonyms* (*adj*) married, double, multiple, **3.** sole; *synonyms* (*adj*) single, singular, exclusive, individual, (*n*) bottom, **4.** unaccompanied; *synonyms* (*adj*) solitary, unescorted, detached, (*adv*) solo, entirely; *antonym* (*adj*) accompanied, **5.** alone; *synonyms* (*adv*) solely, apart, exclusively, individually, separately; *antonym* (*adv*) together.

einn 1. one; *synonyms* (*pron*) any, (*n*) anybody, (*adj*) certain, individual, lone, **2.** single; *synonyms* (*adj*) only, celibate, one, odd, particular; *antonyms* (*adj*) married, double, multiple, **3.** unaccompanied; *synonyms* (*adj*) solitary, unescorted, detached, (*adv*) alone, solo; *antonym* (*adj*) accompanied, **4.** sole; *synonyms* (*adj*) single, singular, exclusive, (*n*) bottom, base, **5.** solitary; *synonyms* (*adj*) lonesome, forlorn, lonely, (*n*) hermit, recluse.

einnig 1. too; *synonyms* (*adv*) also, likewise, besides, excessively, over, **2.** also; *synonyms* (*adv*) too, moreover, more, (*conj*) and, furthermore, **3.** likewise; *synonyms* (*adv*) alike, further, equally, similarly, (*adj*) even.

einoka unitary; *synonyms* (*adj*) single, one, sole, solitary, united.

einokun monopoly; *synonyms* (*n*) impropriation, limitation, retention, business, cartel.

einokunaraðstaða monopoly; *synonyms* (*n*) impropriation, limitation, retention, business, cartel.

einokunarhringur 1. trust; *synonyms* (*n*) charge, confidence, credit, faith, (*v*) believe; *antonyms* (*v*) distrust, doubt, disbelieve, mistrust, **2.** cartel; *synonyms* (*n*) syndicate, trust, combine, compromise, ring.

einræði dictatorship; *synonyms* (*n*) absolutism, autocracy, despotism, tyranny, authoritarianism; *antonym* (*n*) democracy.

einræðisherra dictator; *synonyms* (*n*) authoritarian, governor, head, oppressor, potentate.

einræðisstjórn absolutism; *synonyms* (*n*) dictatorship, despotism, tyranny, absoluteness.

einræðisvald 1. sovereignty; *synonyms* (*n*) kingdom, reign, empire, autonomy, dominion, **2.** dictatorship; *synonyms* (*n*) absolutism, autocracy, despotism, tyranny, authoritarianism; *antonym* (*n*) democracy.

einrækt clone; *synonyms* (*n*) copy, duplicate, clon, (*v*) reproduce, replicate.

einrækta clone; *synonyms* (*n*) copy, duplicate, clon, (*v*) reproduce, replicate.

eins equal; *synonyms* (*adj*) agree, comparable, (*v*) match, compare, correspond; *antonyms* (*adj*) unequal, different, repressive, disproportionate, (*v*) differ.

einsamall solitary; *synonyms* (*adj*) lonesome, forlorn, alone, lone, lonely.

einsátta isotropic; *synonym* (*adj*) isotropous.

einsheiti homonym; *synonym* (*adj*) homonymy.

einskauta unipolar; *synonym* (*adj*) homeopolar.

einslaga isomorphic; *synonyms* (*adj*) isomorphous, isostructural.

einsleitni homogeneity; *synonyms* (*n*) homogeneousness, affinity, alliance, consistency, unity.

einsleitur 1. homogeneous; *synonyms* (*adj*) uniform, consistent, kindred, homogenous, similar; *antonyms* (*adj*) diverse, varied, inconsistent, **2.** homologous; *synonyms* (*adj*) analogous, homogeneous, like, equivalent, equal.

einslögun 1. similarity; *synonyms* (*n*) correspondence, likeness, parallelism, kinship, parallel; *antonyms* (*n*) dissimilarity, difference, **2.** isomorphism.

einsmóta isomorphic; *synonyms* (*adj*) isomorphous, isostructural.

einsömun individuation; *synonyms* (*n*) individualization, individuality, definition, identity, individualisation.

einstæðingur 1. widow; *synonyms* (*n*) relict, (*adj*) additional, (*v*) bereave, **2.** orphan; *synonyms* (*n*) waif, caterpillar, cocoon, nymph, (*adj*) orphaned.

einstæður 1. single; *synonyms* (*adj*) only, celibate, one, odd, particular; *antonyms* (*adj*) married, double, multiple, **2.** univalent; *synonyms* (*adj*) monovalent, (*adv*) monatomic, **3.** individual; *synonyms* (*adj*) distinct, single, different, (*n*) human, creature; *antonyms* (*adj*) joint, combined, common, communal, (*n*) collective.

einstaklingshyggja individualism; *synonyms* (*n*) individuality, uniqueness, identity, autonomy, complexion.

einstaklingsmyndun ontogeny; *synonyms* (*n*) ontogenesis, development, growing, growth, maturation.

einstaklingsþroskun ontogenesis; *synonyms* (*n*) ontogeny, development, growing, growth, maturation.

einstaklingsþróun 1. anthropogenesis; *synonym* (*n*) anthropogeny, **2.** ontogenesis; *synonyms* (*n*) ontogeny, development, growing, growth, maturation.

einstaklingur individual; *synonyms* (*adj*) distinct, particular, single, (*n*) human, creature; *antonyms* (*adj*) joint, combined, common, communal, (*n*) collective.

einstakur special; *synonyms* (*adj*) particular, especial, individual, limited, rare; *antonym* (*adj*) ordinary.

einsteinín einsteinium; *synonyms* (*n*) e, east, tocopherol.

einsteiníum einsteinium; *synonyms* (*n*) e, east, tocopherol.

eintak specimen; *synonyms* (*n*) exemplar, sample, example, instance, copy.

einvaldsríki monarchy; *synonyms* (*n*) kingdom, empire, autocracy, realm, domain.

einvaldur sovereign; *synonyms* (*adj*) independent, autonomous, (*n*) monarch, ruler, king; *antonym* (*adj*) dependent.

einveldi 1. absolutism; *synonyms* (*n*) dictatorship, despotism, tyranny, absoluteness, **2.** autocracy; *synonyms* (*n*) absolutism, autarchy, autonomy, oppression; *antonym* (*n*) democracy, **3.** monarchy; *synonyms* (*n*) kingdom, empire, autocracy, realm, domain.

einveldissinni absolutist; *synonyms* (*n*) authoritarian, dictator, (*adj*) absolutistic, absolute, arbitrary.

einveldisstjórn autocracy; *synonyms* (*n*) absolutism, dictatorship, despotism, tyranny, autarchy; *antonym* (*n*) democracy.

einveldsríki monarchy; *synonyms* (*n*) kingdom, empire, autocracy, realm, domain.

einyrki amp; *synonyms* (*n*) ampere, a, amplifier, loudspeaker, speaker.

eir copper; *synonyms* (*n*) bronze, bull, cop, fuzz, gold.

eirgræna verdigris; *synonyms* (*n*) aerugo, verditer, (*adj*) emerald, green.

eisa 1. plasma; *synonyms* (*n*) plasm, onyx, blood, flesh, **2.** ether; *synonyms* (*n*) aether, (*adj*) air, flatus, fume, reek.

eista testis; *synonyms* (*n*) testicle, ball, ballock, bollock, egg.

eistu testis; *synonyms* (*n*) testicle, ball, ballock, bollock, egg.

eitilæxli lymphoma; *synonym* (*n*) lymphadenoma.

eitilbú follicle; *synonyms* (*n*) cavity, dent, dimple, dint, lacuna.

eitilfrumukrabbamein lymphoma; *synonym* (*n*) lymphadenoma.

eitlaæxli lymphoma; *synonym* (*n*) lymphadenoma.

eitraður 1. toxic; *synonyms* (*adj*) poisonous, noxious, venomous, deadly, harmful; *antonyms* (*adj*) harmless, nontoxic, **2.** poisonous; *synonyms* (*adj*) toxic, mortal, malicious, fatal, baneful, **3.** toxicant; *synonyms* (*n*) poison, intoxicant, (*adj*) virulent, vicious, **4.** noxious; *synonyms* (*adj*) detrimental, injurious, deleterious, evil, bad; *antonyms* (*adj*) innocuous, pleasant.

eitrun 1. poisoning; *synonyms* (*n*) contamination, defoedation, discoloration, oxidation, (*adj*) infectious, **2.** intoxication; *synonyms* (*n*) drunkenness, inebriation, inebriety, poisoning, tipsiness.

eitt one; *synonyms* (*pron*) any, (*n*) anybody, (*adj*) certain, individual, lone.

eitur 1. poison; *synonyms* (*n*) bane, (*v*) infect, contaminate, envenom, defile; *antonym* (*n*) antidote, **2.** toxicant; *synonyms* (*n*) poison, (*adj*) poisonous, toxic, venomous, virulent, **3.** toxin; *synonyms* (*n*) venom, contaminant, impurity, pollutant, toxine.

eiturefni toxin; *synonyms* (*n*) poison, venom, contaminant, impurity, pollutant.

eiturlyfjaneytandi narcotic; *synonyms* (*adj*) soporific, anodyne, (*n*) opiate, hypnotic, drug.

eitursveipur hemlock; *synonyms* (*n*) henbane, nightshade.

eiturúðun fumigation; *synonym* (*n*) steaming.

eiturvirkni toxicity; *synonym* (*n*) perniciousness.

ekill chauffeur; *synonyms* (*n*) driver, engineer, hackman, syce, truckman.

ekkert 1. not; *synonyms* (*adv*) no, nay, nor, nowise, never, **2.** nil; *synonyms* (*n*) zero, cipher, naught, nothing, aught, **3.** nay; *synonyms* (*n*) denial, negative, vote, (*v*) refuse, **4.** no; *synonyms* (*n*) refusal, rejection, number, nix, (*adj*) none.

ekki 1. not; *synonyms* (*adv*) no, nay, nor, nowise, never, **2.** nay; *synonyms* (*n*) denial, negative, vote, (*v*) refuse, **3.** no; *synonyms* (*n*) refusal, rejection, (*adj*) zero, naught, none.

ekkill widower; *synonyms* (*n*) widow, widowman.

ekkja widow; *synonyms* (*n*) relict, (*adj*) additional, (*v*) bereave.

ekla dearth; *synonyms* (*n*) absence, famine, shortage, want, deficiency; *antonyms* (*n*) abundance, excess.

ekra acre; *synonyms* (*n*) acreage, grounds, manor, plot.

ekspedi forwards; *synonyms* (*adv*) ahead, forward, forth, onward, onwards.

ekta genuine; *synonyms* *(adj)* actual, authentic, sincere, true, unsophisticated; *antonyms* *(adj)* bogus, fake, insincere, affected, artificial.

eldast ageing; *synonyms* *(n)* aging, maturing, ripening, senescence, curing.

eldfimur 1. inflammable; *synonyms* *(adj)* combustible, flammable, burnable, ignitable, quick-tempered, **2**. flammable; *synonyms* *(adj)* inflammable, ignitible, arson, explosive.

eldfjall volcano; *synonyms* *(n)* maelstrom, mountain, vent, blowhole, *(adj)* earthquake.

eldfjallaaska ash; *synonyms* *(n)* jasmine, lilac, *(v)* cinder, scoriae, *(adj)* gray.

eldfjallafræði volcanology; *synonym* *(n)* vulcanology.

eldflaug rocket; *synonyms* *(n)* missile, bomb, *(v)* soar, rise, skyrocket; *antonyms* *(v)* plummet, dawdle.

eldgígur crater; *synonyms* *(n)* hollow, cavity, hole, pit, *(adj)* well.

eldgos eruption; *synonyms* *(n)* blast, burst, outbreak, rash, *(adj)* detonation.

eldherða temper; *synonyms* *(n)* mood, character, disposition, *(v)* moderate, soften; *antonyms* *(v)* intensify, upset.

eldhnöttur fireball; *synonyms* *(n)* bolide, cartouche, *(adj)* active, ambitious, capable.

eldhólf hearth; *synonyms* *(n)* fireplace, fire, fireside, chimney, furnace.

eldhús 1. kitchen; *synonyms* *(n)* cookroom, basement, offices, pantry, scullery, **2**. galley; *synonyms* *(n)* caboose, cookhouse, galleyfoist, proof, slice.

eldi culture; *synonyms* *(n)* civilization, breeding, cultivation, acculturation, education.

elding lightning; *synonyms* *(n)* bolt, levin, bolter, dart, *(adj)* wind.

eldkeila cone; *synonyms* *(n)* strobile, pyramid, roll, conoid, pinnacle.

eldkúla fireball; *synonyms* *(n)* bolide, cartouche, *(adj)* active, ambitious, capable.

eldsmíða forge; *synonyms* *(v)* counterfeit, falsify, devise, fabricate, fake.

eldsmíðað forged; *synonyms* *(adj)* counterfeit, false, bogus, fake, phony; *antonym* *(adj)* genuine.

eldsmíði forging; *synonyms* *(n)* manufacturing, origin.

eldsmíðisgripur forging; *synonyms* *(n)* manufacturing, origin.

eldsmiðja forge; *synonyms* *(v)* counterfeit, falsify, devise, fabricate, fake.

eldsneyti 1. propellant; *synonyms* *(n)* propellent, fuel, explosive, *(adj)* propelling, propulsive, **2**. fuel; *synonyms* *(n)* firewood, combustible, firing, *(v)* fire, arouse.

eldsneytiseyðsla consumption; *synonyms* *(n)* expenditure, decline, use, expense, diminution.

eldsneytisgjafi throttle; *synonyms* *(v)* choke, strangle, asphyxiate, smother, strangulate.

eldsneytisgjöf accelerator; *synonyms* *(n)* catalyst, gas, throttle, gun, promotor.

eldsneytisnotkun consumption; *synonyms* *(n)* expenditure, decline, use, expense, diminution.

eldsneytistaka refuelling; *synonym* *(n)* fuelling.

eldspýta match; *synonyms* *(n)* equal, *(v)* agree, mate, meet, parallel; *antonyms* *(v)* clash, contradict.

eldstöð volcano; *synonyms* *(n)* maelstrom, mountain, vent, blowhole, *(adj)* earthquake.

eldur fire; *synonyms* *(n)* discharge, *(v)* excite, eject, blaze, dismiss; *antonym* *(v)* hire.

eldvarnarþil firewall; *synonym* *(n)* baffle.

elektróna electron; *synonyms* *(n)* electricity, molecule, negatron, amber.

elemento 1. elements; *synonyms* *(n)* alphabet, rudiments, grammar, outlines, contents, **2**. element; *synonyms* *(n)* component, constituent, ingredient, factor, substance.

ellefu eleven; *synonyms* *(n)* eight, team.

elli 1. senescence; *synonyms* *(n)* ageing, aging, agedness, decay, *(adj)* senility, **2**. senility; *synonyms* *(n)* dotage, age, infirmity, caducity, decline.

elliær senile; *synonyms* *(adj)* old, doddering, gaga, geriatric, elderly.

ellifjarsýni presbyopia; *synonyms* *(n)* myopia, presbytia, presbytism, blindness, presbyopy.

ellihrörnun senility; *synonyms* *(n)* dotage, age, infirmity, caducity, decline.

ellihrumur senile; *synonyms* *(adj)* old, doddering, gaga, geriatric, elderly.

ellilækningar geriatrics; *synonyms* *(n)* gerontology, *(adj)* nostology.

ellilífeyrir pension; *synonyms* *(n)* allowance, annuity, payment, stipend, endowment.

ellisjón presbyopia; *synonyms* *(n)* myopia, presbytia, presbytism, blindness, presbyopy.

ellisjúkdómafræði geriatrics; *synonyms* *(n)* gerontology, *(adj)* nostology.

elliskeið senescence; *synonyms* *(n)* ageing, aging, agedness, decay, *(adj)* senility.

elna deteriorate; *synonyms* *(v)* degenerate, degrade, decline, spoil, worsen; *antonyms* *(v)* improve, convalesce, recover.

elnun exacerbation; *synonyms* *(n)* aggravation, exasperation, resentment, provocation, *(adj)* malignity.

elri alder; *synonym* *(adj)* aller.

elrir alder; *synonym* *(adj)* aller.

elska 1. love; *synonyms* (*n*) desire, affection, dear, (*v*) cherish, enjoy; *antonyms* (*n*) abhorrence, hatred, (*v*) hate, dislike, abhor, **2**. cherish; *synonyms* (*v*) appreciate, entertain, foster, hug, nurture.

elskulegur 1. alluring; *synonyms* (*adj*) attractive, charming, enticing, seductive, tempting; *antonym* (*adj*) repellent, **2**. disarming; *synonyms* (*adj*) ingratiating, captivating, conciliatory, deferential, (*n*) disarmament; *antonym* (*n*) arming, **3**. charming; *synonyms* (*adj*) amiable, beautiful, delightful, enchanting, lovely; *antonyms* (*adj*) unappealing, unpleasant, **4**. lovely; *synonyms* (*adj*) fine, handsome, lovable, alluring, adorable; *antonyms* (*adj*) hideous, terrible, ugly, unattractive.

elspezo expenses; *synonyms* (*n*) expenditure, charge, costs, fee, spending.

elta 1. trail; *synonyms* (*n*) track, trace, (*v*) haul, drag, hunt, **2**. pursue; *synonyms* (*v*) chase, follow, dog, prosecute, course, **3**. chase; *synonyms* (*n*) game, search, (*v*) pursue, expel, stalk.

eltihalli caster; *synonyms* (*n*) castor, cruet, wheel, founder, author.

eltihjól caster; *synonyms* (*n*) castor, cruet, wheel, founder, author.

eltihorn caster; *synonyms* (*n*) castor, cruet, wheel, founder, author.

elting tracking; *synonyms* (*n*) pursuit, trailing, rutting, trajectography.

em pica; *synonyms* (*n*) em, geophagia, geophagy, magpies, mut.

embætti 1. post; *synonyms* (*n*) place, function, office, position, (*v*) mail, **2**. office; *synonyms* (*n*) charge, agency, duty, commission, appointment.

embættisbók registry; *synonyms* (*n*) register, record, schedule, (*v*) registration, enrollment.

embættislegur official; *synonyms* (*adj*) formal, (*n*) officer, minister, bureaucrat, (*v*) authoritative; *antonyms* (*adj*) unofficial, private, illegal, informal.

embættismaður 1. officer; *synonyms* (*n*) captain, administrator, commander, bureaucrat, executive, **2**. official; *synonyms* (*adj*) formal, (*n*) officer, minister, functionary, (*v*) authoritative; *antonyms* (*adj*) unofficial, private, illegal, informal.

embættismannakerfi bureaucracy; *synonyms* (*n*) bureaucratism, apparatus, cabinet, fascism, formalities.

embættismannastétt officialdom; *synonyms* (*n*) bureaucracy, administration, government, organization.

embættismenn officialdom; *synonyms* (*n*) bureaucracy, administration, government, organization.

empíriskur empirical; *synonyms* (*adj*) empiric, experimental, observational, observed, (*v*) tentative; *antonym* (*adj*) theoretical.

en 1. but; *synonyms* (*conj*) while, (*adv*) alone, only, though, barely, **2**. as; *synonyms* (*conj*) qua, because, (*prep*) during, like, (*n*) arsenic.

enarhivigi 1. archives; *synonyms* (*n*) archive, record, records, annals, proceedings, **2**. archive; *synonyms* (*n*) scroll, archives, paper, return, catalogue.

enarkivigi archives; *synonyms* (*n*) archive, record, records, annals, proceedings.

enbankigi banks; *synonym* (*n*) breast.

endahólkur termination; *synonyms* (*n*) ending, close, end, conclusion, result; *antonym* (*n*) start.

endalok catastrophe; *synonyms* (*n*) calamity, disaster, adversity, cataclysm, tragedy.

endamúffa termination; *synonyms* (*n*) ending, close, end, conclusion, result; *antonym* (*n*) start.

endanlegur ultimate; *synonyms* (*adj*) last, conclusive, final, end, supreme; *antonyms* (*adj*) opening, first.

endastæður terminal; *synonyms* (*adj*) final, last, definitive, (*n*) depot, end.

endastig climax; *synonyms* (*n*) apex, top, acme, culmination, (*v*) peak; *antonym* (*v*) dip.

Endatafl ending; *synonyms* (*n*) conclusion, end, close, closure, closing; *antonyms* (*n*) start, beginning, middle.

endaþarmsop anus; *synonyms* (*n*) arse, arsehole, asshole, bum, bastard.

endaþarmsstíll suppository; *synonyms* (*n*) medicine, bolus, dose, draught, drip.

endaþrýstingur thrust; *synonyms* (*v*) jab, (*n*) push, poke, drive, stab; *antonym* (*v*) pull.

endi 1. termination; *synonyms* (*n*) ending, close, end, conclusion, result; *antonym* (*n*) start, **2**. apex; *synonyms* (*n*) peak, top, vertex, acme, crown; *antonyms* (*n*) base, nadir.

ending 1. durability; *synonyms* (*n*) strength, continuity, durableness, longevity, stamina; *antonym* (*n*) frailty, **2**. life; *synonyms* (*n*) animation, energy, spirit, activity, being; *antonym* (*n*) lethargy.

endingargóður durable; *synonyms* (*adj*) constant, lasting, stable, permanent, enduring; *antonyms* (*adj*) fragile, weak, flimsy, lightweight.

endingartími 1. life; *synonyms* (*n*) animation, energy, spirit, activity, being; *antonym* (*n*) lethargy, **2**. longevity; *synonyms* (*n*) life, endurance, permanence, continuance, seniority.

endir conclusion; *synonyms* (*n*) closure, close, end, result, cessation; *antonyms* (*n*) beginning, start, opening, preface.

endívusalat endive; *synonyms* (*n*) escarole, witloof.

endurbæta improve; *synonyms* (*v*) advance, heal, emend, help, ameliorate; *antonyms* (*v*) worsen, deteriorate, regress, spoil.

endurbætur modernization; *synonyms* (*n*) modernisation, innovation, renovation, alteration, change.

endurbót improvement; *synonyms* (*n*) advancement, amelioration, betterment, correction, amendment; *antonyms* (*n*) decline, deterioration, downgrade.

endurbygging 1. reconditioning, **2**. reconstruction; *synonyms* (*n*) restoration, reconstitution, repair, reestablishment, rehabilitation.

endurbyggja 1. reconstruct; *synonyms* (*v*) rebuild, alter, restore, build, mend, **2**. recondition; *synonyms* (*v*) overhaul, fix, refurbish, renovate, repair, **3**. restore; *synonyms* (*v*) refresh, reinstate, renew, rehabilitate, rejuvenate; *antonym* (*v*) keep, **4**. overhaul; *synonyms* (*n*) inspection, (*v*) check, modernize, overtake, pass.

endureiming rectification; *synonyms* (*n*) correction, amendment, improvement, redress, revision.

endurfylla refill; *synonyms* (*v*) replenish, (*n*) cartridge, replacement, filling, recharge; *antonym* (*v*) deplete.

Endurfylling dump; *synonyms* (*v*) discard, ditch, abandon, drop, empty; *antonym* (*v*) keep.

endurgera reconstruct; *synonyms* (*v*) rebuild, alter, restore, build, mend.

endurgerð 1. restoration; *synonyms* (*n*) restitution, reinstatement, renewal, renovation, restore; *antonyms* (*n*) confiscation, reduction, **2**. reconstruction; *synonyms* (*n*) restoration, reconstitution, repair, reestablishment, rehabilitation, **3**. annealing; *synonym* (*n*) tempering.

endurgerving reconstruction; *synonyms* (*n*) restoration, reconstitution, repair, reestablishment, rehabilitation.

endurgjalda reciprocate; *synonyms* (*v*) exchange, repay, interchange, return, bandy.

endurgjöf feedback; *synonyms* (*n*) reply, response, reaction, repercussion, (*v*) answer.

endurgreiða 1. refund; *synonyms* (*n*) payment, (*v*) repay, reimburse, compensate, pay, **2**. reimburse; *synonyms* (*v*) recompense, recoup, refund, remunerate, replace, **3**. repay; *synonyms* (*v*) reward, render, redeem, requite, return.

endurgreiðsla 1. refund; *synonyms* (*n*) payment, (*v*) repay, reimburse, compensate, pay, **2**. repayment; *synonyms* (*n*) recompense, refund, compensation, remuneration, (*v*) quittance, **3**.

reimbursement; *synonyms* (*n*) repayment, indemnity, amends, damages, return.

endurhæfing rehabilitation; *synonyms* (*n*) reclamation, reinstatement, renewal, repair, replacement.

endurheimt 1. restore; *synonyms* (*v*) mend, refresh, reinstate, renew, (*adj*) repair; *antonym* (*v*) keep, **2**. retrieval; *synonyms* (*n*) recovery, reclamation, redress, recuperation, (*v*) revendication; *antonym* (*n*) loss, **3**. recombination.

endurheimta 1. retrieve; *synonyms* (*v*) recover, regain, reclaim, recoup, rescue; *antonym* (*v*) lose, **2**. recover; *synonyms* (*v*) recuperate, retrieve, convalesce, find, heal; *antonym* (*v*) deteriorate, **3**. restore; *synonyms* (*v*) mend, refresh, reinstate, renew, (*adj*) repair; *antonym* (*v*) keep.

endurhringrás recirculation; *synonym* (*n*) recycling.

endurhvarf regression; *synonyms* (*n*) regress, lapse, setback, degeneration, deterioration.

endurkalla recall; *synonyms* (*v*) retrieve, countermand, recognize, (*n*) anamnesis, memory; *antonym* (*v*) forget.

endurkast 1. rebound; *synonyms* (*n*) bound, kick, (*v*) bounce, recoil, glance, **2**. reflection; *synonyms* (*n*) consideration, contemplation, observation, cogitation, deliberation, **3**. echo; *synonyms* (*n*) answer, (*v*) repeat, reproduce, resound, reverberate.

endurkasta 1. rebound; *synonyms* (*n*) bound, kick, (*v*) bounce, recoil, glance, **2**. reflect; *synonyms* (*v*) deliberate, ponder, cogitate, consider, contemplate.

endurkastari reflector; *synonyms* (*n*) mirror, repeller, lieberkuhn, chromatoscope, refractor.

endurkastshlutfall reflectance; *synonym* (*n*) reflectivity.

endurkastsskaut reflector; *synonyms* (*n*) mirror, repeller, lieberkuhn, chromatoscope, refractor.

endurkoma 1. reentry, **2**. recurrence; *synonyms* (*n*) iteration, repetition, return, frequency, comeback; *antonym* (*n*) disappearance.

endurkröfuréttur recourse; *synonyms* (*n*) resort, refuge, expedient, resource, (*v*) appeal.

endurkvæmur recursive; *synonyms* (*v*) iterative, harping, monotonous, unvaried.

endurlífgun resuscitation; *synonyms* (*n*) revival, reviction, anabiosis.

endurmat 1. revaluation; *synonyms* (*n*) reappraisal, reassessment, revalorization, brushup, critique, **2**. revision; *synonyms* (*n*) alteration, change, modification, amendment, review.

endurmeta revalue; *synonyms* (*v*) appreciate, apprise, apprize, devalue, value.

endurminni anamnesis; *synonyms* (*n*) remembrance, memory, recall, recollection, commemoration.

endurmóta restructure; *synonyms* (v) rearrange, reconstitute, reconstruct, reform, reorganize.

endurmótun restructuring; *synonyms* (n) reorganization, improvement, reform, renovation, alteration.

endurmyndandi regenerative; *synonyms* (adj) cultural, healing, incarnative.

endurmyndast regenerate; *synonyms* (v) renew, reform, restore, revive, (n) convert.

endurmyndun 1. regeneration; *synonyms* (n) revival, rebirth, sanctification, renaissance, resurgence, **2**. restitution; *synonyms* (n) recovery, reparation, restoration, return, recompense; *antonym* (n) abolition.

endurnota reuse; *synonyms* (v) recycle, rehash, reprocess, salvage.

endurnotkun reuse; *synonyms* (v) recycle, rehash, reprocess, salvage.

endurnýja 1. update; *synonyms* (n) updating, (v) inform, modernize, renovate, revise, **2**. renew; *synonyms* (v) regenerate, refresh, rejuvenate, restore, refurbish, **3**. replace; *synonyms* (v) change, exchange, substitute, supersede, supplant, **4**. modify; *synonyms* (v) alter, qualify, adapt, limit, adjust.

endurnýjandi regenerative; *synonyms* (adj) cultural, healing, incarnative.

endurnýjanlegur 1. regenerative; *synonyms* (adj) cultural, healing, incarnative, **2**. renewable.

endurnýjast regenerate; *synonyms* (v) renew, reform, restore, revive, (n) convert.

endurnýjun 1. replacement; *synonyms* (n) exchange, substitute, alternate, deputy, renewal, **2**. reconditioning, **3**. renewal; *synonyms* (n) renaissance, revival, rebirth, reclamation, rehabilitation, **4**. regeneration; *synonyms* (n) sanctification, resurgence, revitalization, (adj) adoption, beatification.

endurnýta 1. reuse; *synonyms* (v) recycle, rehash, reprocess, salvage, **2**. recycle; *synonym* (v) reuse.

endurnýun 1. reconditioning, **2**. renewal; *synonyms* (n) renaissance, revival, rebirth, reclamation, rehabilitation.

endurómur echo; *synonyms* (n) answer, (v) repeat, reproduce, resound, reverberate.

endurræsa restart; *synonyms* (v) resume, continue, recommence, renew, (n) reboot.

endurræsing restart; *synonyms* (v) resume, continue, recommence, renew, (n) reboot.

endurreisn restoration; *synonyms* (n) restitution, reinstatement, renewal, renovation, restore; *antonyms* (n) confiscation, reduction.

endurrétta recover; *synonyms* (v) reclaim, recuperate, regain, retrieve, convalesce; *antonyms* (v) deteriorate, lose.

endurrétting recovery; *synonyms* (n) rally, convalescence, improvement, reclamation, rescue; *antonyms* (n) decline, loss, return.

endurrita restore; *synonyms* (v) mend, refresh, reinstate, renew, (adj) repair; *antonym* (v) keep.

endursemja 1. reconstruct; *synonyms* (v) rebuild, alter, restore, build, mend, **2**. reconstruction; *synonyms* (n) restoration, reconstitution, repair, reestablishment, rehabilitation.

endursetning reset; *synonyms* (v) readjust, transplant, readapt, (n) regripping.

endurskin 1. reflex; *synonyms* (v) reflection, (adj) automatic, involuntary, instinctive, unconscious, **2**. reflection; *synonyms* (n) consideration, contemplation, observation, cogitation, deliberation, **3**. albedo, **4**. glare; *synonyms* (n) blaze, brilliance, (v) beam, flame, flash; *antonym* (v) smile.

endurskinsstuðull reflectance; *synonym* (n) reflectivity.

endurskipulagning 1. restructuring; *synonyms* (n) reorganization, improvement, reform, renovation, alteration, **2**. reorganization; *synonyms* (n) reorganisation, conversion, posting, redeployment, redistribution.

endurskoða 1. update; *synonyms* (n) updating, (v) inform, modernize, renovate, revise, **2**. audit; *synonyms* (n) survey, examination, (v) check, balance, inspect.

endurskoðandi 1. accountant; *synonyms* (n) auditor, teller, cashier, controller, almoner, **2**. auditor; *synonyms* (n) accountant, hearer, listener, bookkeeper, attendant.

endurskoðun 1. revision; *synonyms* (n) alteration, change, modification, amendment, review, **2**. review; *synonyms* (n) examination, critique, (v) check, survey, criticize, **3**. auditing, **4**. audit; *synonyms* (v) balance, inspect, examine, prove, scrutinize.

endursköpun recreation; *synonyms* (n) amusement, entertainment, distraction, pastime, play.

endursmíð restoration; *synonyms* (n) restitution, reinstatement, renewal, renovation, restore; *antonyms* (n) confiscation, reduction.

endursögn paraphrase; *synonyms* (n) translation, paraphrasis, (v) interpret, rephrase, reword.

endurstilla 1. readjust; *synonyms* (v) adapt, adjust, regulate, reset, (adj) dress, **2**. reset; *synonyms* (v) readjust, transplant, readapt, (n) regripping.

endurstilling 1. readjustment; *synonyms* (n) adjustment, accommodation, equilibration, alteration, adaptation, **2**. reset; *synonyms* (*v*) readjust, transplant, readapt, (*n*) regripping.

endurtaka replicate; *synonyms* (*v*) duplicate, double, reduplicate, repeat, copy.

endurtakanleiki reproducibility; *synonym* (*n*) duplicability.

endurteiknari refresh; *synonyms* (*v*) freshen, air, enliven, invigorate, update.

endurtekning 1. replication; *synonyms* (*n*) rejoinder, repetition, reproduction, replica, answer, **2**. replicate; *synonyms* (*v*) duplicate, double, reduplicate, repeat, copy, **3**. repetition; *synonyms* (*n*) gemination, iteration, recurrence, reiteration, replication.

enduruppbygging reconstitution; *synonyms* (*n*) reestablishment, rehabilitation, reinstatement, replacement.

endurvaki repeater; *synonyms* (*n*) recidivist, criminal, revolver, (*v*) floater, keener.

endurvarp 1. reflection; *synonyms* (*n*) consideration, contemplation, observation, cogitation, deliberation, **2**. trace; *synonyms* (*n*) line, shadow, spot, clue, (*v*) track, **3**. echo; *synonyms* (*n*) answer, (*v*) repeat, reproduce, resound, reverberate, **4**. blip; *synonyms* (*n*) pip, breakdown, bug, error, (*v*) slap, **5**. emissivity.

endurvarpa reflect; *synonyms* (*v*) deliberate, ponder, cogitate, consider, contemplate.

endurvarpsflötur reflector; *synonyms* (*n*) mirror, repeller, lieberkuhn, chromatoscope, refractor.

endurvarpsskaut reflector; *synonyms* (*n*) mirror, repeller, lieberkuhn, chromatoscope, refractor.

endurvarpsstuðull reflectance; *synonym* (*n*) reflectivity.

endurvinna recycle; *synonyms* (*v*) reuse, salvage, reprocess.

endurvinnsla 1. recycling; *synonym* (*n*) recirculation, **2**. recycle; *synonyms* (*v*) reuse, salvage, reprocess.

endurvöxtur regeneration; *synonyms* (*n*) revival, rebirth, sanctification, renaissance, resurgence.

engill angel; *synonyms* (*n*) seraph, backer, benefactor, messenger, (*v*) sponsor; *antonym* (*n*) fiend.

enging peristalsis; *synonym* (*n*) vermiculation.

engispretta 1. locust; *synonyms* (*v*) losel, squanderer, **2**. grasshopper; *synonyms* (*n*) hopper, chamois, frog, goat, grounder.

ensím enzyme; *synonyms* (*n*) catalyst, solution.

ensímhvarfefni substrate; *synonyms* (*n*) substratum, ground, feedstock.

enskribi records; *synonyms* (*n*) archive, documents, minutes, proceedings, certification.

enskribo records; *synonyms* (*n*) archive, documents, minutes, proceedings, certification.

eósínfíkinn eosinophil; *synonym* (*n*) eosinophile.

eósíntækur eosinophil; *synonym* (*n*) eosinophile.

epli apple; *synonyms* (*n*) city, world, (*v*) ball, (*adj*) green.

erfð heredity; *synonyms* (*n*) ancestry, lineage, telegony, line, descent.

erfðafræði genetics; *synonyms* (*n*) heredity, inheritance, anatomy, botany, evolution.

erfðamark marker; *synonyms* (*n*) brand, mark, label, token, pointer.

erfðaskrá will; *synonyms* (*v*) bequeath, (*n*) volition, command, desire, inclination.

erfðastétt caste; *synonyms* (*n*) order, class, rank, sort, (*adj*) degree.

erfðavísir gene; *synonyms* (*n*) chromosome, cistron.

erfðir 1. heredity; *synonyms* (*n*) ancestry, lineage, telegony, line, descent, **2**. inheritance; *synonyms* (*n*) heritage, heredity, heirloom, legacy, dowry.

erfður inherited; *synonyms* (*adj*) hereditary, inborn, familial, genetic, ancestral.

erfiða lug; *synonyms* (*v*) draw, haul, drag, pull, (*n*) ear.

erfiði severity; *synonyms* (*n*) cruelty, austerity, harshness, rigor, asperity; *antonyms* (*n*) gentleness, leniency, clemency, flexibility, pleasantness.

erfiður refractory; *synonyms* (*adj*) intractable, disobedient, obstinate, perverse, recalcitrant.

erindreki messenger; *synonyms* (*n*) envoy, emissary, harbinger, runner, (*v*) herald.

erlendur 1. alien; *synonyms* (*adj*) foreign, strange, unknown, (*n*) foreigner, (*v*) alienate; *antonyms* (*adj*) familiar, (*n*) native, citizen, **2**. offshore, **3**. foreign; *synonyms* (*adj*) alien, extraneous, extrinsic, exotic, exterior; *antonyms* (*adj*) domestic, internal, **4**. overseas; *synonyms* (*adj*) across, away, (*adv*) abroad, oversea, afield.

ermi sleeve; *synonyms* (*n*) arm, case, liner, cover, cuff.

ero elements; *synonyms* (*n*) alphabet, rudiments, grammar, outlines, contents.

erta 1. stimulate; *synonyms* (*v*) excite, incite, arouse, encourage, (*adj*) quicken; *antonym* (*v*) defuse, **2**. irritate; *synonyms* (*v*) chafe, fret, gall, incense, harass; *antonyms* (*v*) soothe, pacify, please.

ertandl irritant; *synonyms* (*n*) nuisance, bother, annoyance, pest, irritation.

ertanleiki 1. excitability; *synonyms* (*n*) reactivity, irritability, impetuosity, vehemence, biliousness, **2**. irritability; *synonyms* (*n*) excitability, irascibility, choler, petulance, temper.

erting 1. stimulation; *synonyms* (*n*) excitation, incentive, arousal, encouragement, excitement, **2**. irritation; *synonyms* (*n*) aggravation, exasperation, anger, annoyance, displeasure; *antonym* (n) pleasure.

ertingarefni irritant; *synonyms* (n) nuisance, bother, annoyance, pest, irritation.

ertingarlyf irritant; *synonyms* (n) nuisance, bother, annoyance, pest, irritation.

ertir stimulus; *synonyms* (n) incentive, encouragement, provocation, spur, motivation.

ertiroði flare; *synonyms* (n) flash, blaze, (v) burn, flame, burst.

esdragon tarragon; *synonyms* (n) estragon, mugwort, sagebrush.

espa 1. activate; *synonyms* (v) actuate, start, trigger, aerate, animate, **2**. irritate; *synonyms* (v) chafe, fret, gall, incense, harass; *antonyms* (v) soothe, pacify, please.

espir activator; *synonym* (n) inducer.

espun activation; *synonyms* (n) activating, start, initiation, launch, awakening.

estragon tarragon; *synonyms* (n) estragon, mugwort, sagebrush.

estrógen 1. oestrogen; *synonym* (n) estrogen, **2**. estrogen; *synonym* (n) oestrogen.

eta minutes; *synonyms* (n) proceedings, record, transactions, records, journal.

etanól ethanol; *synonyms* (n) alcohol, gas, gasohol, gasoline, juice.

eter ether; *synonyms* (n) aether, (adj) air, flatus, fume, reek.

etiko 1. ethic; *synonyms* (n) ethics, principle, tradition, virtue, **2**. ethics; *synonyms* (n) morality, morals, conscience, behavior, philosophy.

etri ethcr; *synonyms* (n) aether, (adj) air, flatus, fume, reek.

etýlen ethylene; *synonym* (n) ethene.

evropín europium; *synonym* (n) eu.

evrópín europium; *synonym* (n) eu.

evrópíum europium; *synonym* (n) eu.

evrópuaskur ash; *synonyms* (n) jasmine, lilac, (v) cinder, scoriae, (adj) gray.

exi axe; *synonyms* (n) knife, (v) ax, chop, abort, destroy.

eyða 1. plaque; *synonyms* (n) plate, brass, medal, administration, award, **2**. spend; *synonyms* (v) consume, exhaust, expend, squander, blow; *antonyms* (v) save, conserve, **3**. vacancy; *synonyms* (n) emptiness, blank, vacuity, opening, void, **4**. blank; *synonyms* (adj) bare, empty, unfilled, clean, (n) space; *antonyms* (adj) animated, full, expressive, **5**. consume; *synonyms* (v) absorb, spend, dissipate, use, waste; *antonym* (v) abstain.

eyðast 1. decay; *synonyms* (n) decline, decomposition, (v) rot, decompose, blight; *antonym*

(n) growth, **2**. cancel; *synonyms* (v) annul, abrogate, erase, expunge, (adj) abolish; *antonym* (v) validate.

eyðileggja 1. ravage; *synonyms* (v) damage, devastate, demolish, desolate, destroy, **2**. harry; *synonyms* (v) badger, molest, plague, disturb, (adj) harass.

eyðileggjandi destructive; *synonyms* (adj) baneful, deadly, hurtful, malign, baleful; *antonyms* (adj) harmless, constructive, creative.

eyðimerkurvin oasis; *synonyms* (n) haven, isthmus, harbor, harbour, seaport.

eyðimörk desert; *synonyms* (v) abandon, escape, defect, (adj) waste, barren; *antonyms* (n) bog, (v) stay.

eyðing 1. dissipation; *synonyms* (n) debauchery, diffusion, dissolution, waste, dissemination, **2**. depletion; *synonyms* (n) consumption, expenditure, loss, (adj) flaccidity, vacancy, **3**. delete; *synonyms* (v) cancel, erase, clear, expunge, raze; *antonyms* (v) insert, record, **4**. deletion; *synonyms* (n) cancellation, cut, annulment, elimination, omission; *antonym* (n) addition, **5**. annihilation; *synonyms* (n) abolition, extinction, death, destruction, extermination; *antonym* (n) construction.

eyðingarhamur delete; *synonyms* (v) cancel, erase, clear, expunge, raze; *antonyms* (v) insert, record.

eyðsla 1. waste; *synonyms* (n) desert, (adj) spoil, desolate, (v) consume, exhaust; *antonyms* (v) conserve, save, **2**. consumption; *synonyms* (n) expenditure, decline, use, expense, diminution.

eyðublað 1. schedule; *synonyms* (n) list, agenda, catalog, program, (v) register, **2**. outline; *synonyms* (n) sketch, design, (v) draft, line, form, **3**. form; *synonyms* (n) figure, arrange, (v) cast, make, fashion.

eyðustafur blank; *synonyms* (adj) bare, empty, unfilled, clean, (n) space; *antonyms* (adj) animated, full, expressive.

eyðuveila vacancy; *synonyms* (n) emptiness, blank, vacuity, opening, void.

eyja island; *synonyms* (n) reef, (v) isle, insulate, isolate, segregate.

eymslalaus indolent; *synonyms* (adj) idle, inactive, lazy, slothful, sluggish; *antonyms* (adj) energetic, active.

eyra 1. ear; *synonyms* (n) auricle, handle, hearing, lug, spike, **2**. pinna; *synonyms* (n) ear, capitulum, feather, pinnule, **3**. auricle; *synonyms* (n) pinna, heart, **4**. lug; *synonyms* (v) draw, haul, drag, pull, carry.

eyri spit; *synonyms* (n) broach, saliva, (v) drizzle, impale, expectorate.

eyrnalokkur earring; *synonyms* (*n*) eardrop, earlet, jewelry.
eyrnamergur cerumen; *synonym* (*n*) earwax.
eyrnamerking earmarking; *synonym* (*n*) appropriation.
eyrnatól earphone; *synonyms* (*n*) earpiece, headphone, phone, earplug, sound.
eyrnavala otolith; *synonyms* (*n*) otoconite, otolite.
eyrnavölur otolith; *synonyms* (*n*) otoconite, otolite.

É

éta 1. eat; *synonyms* (*v*) devour, consume, bite, dine, munch, **2.** feed; *synonyms* (*v*) eat, nurture, browse, (*n*) aliment, food; *antonym* (*v*) starve.

F

fá 1. receive; *synonyms* (*v*) accept, admit, get, assume, adopt, **2.** derive; *synonyms* (*v*) deduce, stem, come, deduct, draw, **3.** get; *synonyms* (*v*) acquire, gain, attain, become, catch; *antonyms* (*v*) lose, give, leave, **4.** have; *synonyms* (*v*) contain, bear, carry, hold, possess.
faðir father; *synonyms* (*n*) begetter, dad, sire, (*v*) beget, engender; *antonym* (*n*) mother.
faðma 1. embrace; *synonyms* (*v*) comprise, clasp, hug, admit, adopt; *antonym* (*v*) reject, **2.** hug; *synonyms* (*n*) embrace, hold, clinch, (*v*) cuddle, squeeze.
fæða 1. supply; *synonyms* (*n*) provision, (*v*) furnish, stock, afford, fill, **2.** aliment; *synonyms* (*n*) food, nutriment, sustenance, alimentation, diet, **3.** labour; *synonyms* (*n*) effort, exertion, (*v*) grind, labor, travail, **4.** feed; *synonyms* (*v*) eat, dine, nurture, browse, (*n*) aliment; *antonym* (*v*) starve.
fæði diet; *synonyms* (*n*) congress, convocation, council, convention, nurture; *antonyms* (*v*) binge, (*adj*) fattening.
fæðing 1. birth; *synonyms* (*n*) beginning, ancestry, descent, extraction, (*v*) delivery; *antonym* (*n*) death, **2.** parturition; *synonyms* (*n*) birth, childbirth, confinement, labor, childbed.
fæðingafræði obstetrics; *synonyms* (*n*) midwifery, tocology, (*v*) delivery, accouchement, birth.
fæðingarblettur 1. birthmark; *synonyms* (*n*) blotch, mole, nevus, blemish, defect, **2.** nevus; *synonym* (*n*) birthmark, **3.** mole; *synonyms* (*n*) breakwater, jetty, freckle, bulwark, groyne.

fæðingarfræði obstetrics; *synonyms* (*n*) midwifery, tocology, (*v*) delivery, accouchement, birth.
fæðingarhríðir labor; *synonyms* (*n*) drudgery, effort, endeavor, exertion, (*v*) toil; *antonym* (*v*) rest.
fæðingarstaður cradle; *synonyms* (*n*) bed, cot, birthplace, nursery, berth.
fæðingi native; *synonyms* (*adj*) inborn, inherent, innate, (*n*) aboriginal, autochthon; *antonyms* (*adj*) foreign, learned, (*n*) stranger, immigrant, imported.
fæðir feeder; *synonyms* (*n*) eater, affluent, feed, filler, tributary.
fæðisuppskrift dietary; *synonyms* (*adj*) dietetic, alimentary, dietetical, (*n*) diet, dietetics.
fæðuinntaka ingestion; *synonyms* (*n*) consumption, absorption, intake, drinking, eating.
fægiefni abrasive; *synonyms* (*adj*) rough, harsh, caustic, (*n*) abradant, abrader; *antonym* (*adj*) smooth.
fægja polish; *synonyms* (*n*) finish, gloss, burnish, (*v*) furbish, glaze.
fæla repellent; *synonyms* (*adj*) nasty, offensive, hateful, disgusting, (*v*) odious; *antonyms* (*adj*) alluring, appealing, attractive, charming, pleasant.
fælandi repellent; *synonyms* (*adj*) nasty, offensive, hateful, disgusting, (*v*) odious; *antonyms* (*adj*) alluring, appealing, attractive, charming, pleasant.
fæll file; *synonyms* (*n*) archive, document, list, procession, (*v*) order.
fælni 1. phobia; *synonyms* (*n*) fear, neurosis, dread, complex, obsession, **2.** aversion; *synonyms* (*n*) antipathy, distaste, abhorrence, disgust, (*v*) abomination; *antonyms* (*n*) liking, attraction, love.
færa 1. record; *synonyms* (*n*) register, list, account, (*v*) chronicle, file, **2.** enter; *synonyms* (*v*) enlist, embark, enroll, book, record; *antonyms* (*v*) leave, depart, delete, exit.
færanlegur 1. portable; *synonyms* (*adj*) mobile, movable, portative, light, convenient; *antonym* (*adj*) fixed, **2.** mobile; *synonyms* (*adj*) changeable, fluid, unsettled, mercurial, expressive; *antonyms* (*adj*) immobile, impassive, motionless.
færanleiki mobility; *synonyms* (*n*) movableness, motion, movement, (*adj*) versatility.
færiband conveyor; *synonyms* (*n*) conveyer, transporter, transport, pipe.
færiboð polling; *synonyms* (*n*) ballot, election.
færibreyta parameter; *synonyms* (*n*) argument, guideline, limit, directive, modulus.
færni 1. capability; *synonyms* (*n*) capacity, ability, aptitude, capableness, competence; *antonyms* (*n*) inability, failure, incapability, **2.** facility; *synonyms* (*n*) dexterity, adroitness, ease, readiness, artifice.

færsla 1. transplantation; *synonyms* (*n*) transplant, relocation, resettlement, graft, (*v*) transmission, **2**. shift; *synonyms* (*n*) interchange, turn, (*v*) change, exchange, remove, **3**. record; *synonyms* (*n*) register, list, account, (*v*) chronicle, file, **4**. transformation; *synonyms* (*n*) conversion, alteration, metamorphosis, shift, mutation, **5**. transposition; *synonyms* (*n*) permutation, replacement, reversal, substitution, transposal.

færsluval selection; *synonyms* (*n*) election, choice, option, alternative, extract.

fáfnisgras tarragon; *synonyms* (*n*) estragon, mugwort, sagebrush.

fag 1. profession; *synonyms* (*n*) confession, declaration, employment, occupation, affirmation, **2**. vocation; *synonyms* (*n*) calling, profession, business, career, job, **3**. discipline; *synonyms* (*v*) control, castigate, chastise, train, chasten.

faga 1. phage; *synonym* (*n*) bacteriophage, **2**. bacteriophage; *synonym* (*n*) phage.

fágaður gloss; *synonyms* (*n*) burnish, annotation, (*v*) glaze, comment, annotate; *antonym* (*n*) dullness.

fagkunnátta skill; *synonyms* (*n*) artifice, ability, capability, (*adj*) dexterity, craft; *antonyms* (*n*) clumsiness, inability, incompetence.

fagmál jargon; *synonyms* (*n*) dialect, gibberish, idiom, slang, vernacular.

fagorð term; *synonyms* (*n*) name, expression, period, style, (*v*) call.

fagrikeppur reticulum; *synonym* (*n*) net.

fágun burnishing; *synonyms* (*n*) bronzing, searing, buffing.

fagur 1. pretty; *synonyms* (*adj*) beautiful, fair, graceful, lovely, (*n*) nice; *antonym* (*adj*) ugly, **2**. beautiful; *synonyms* (*adj*) attractive, good-looking, bright, beauteous, fine; *antonym* (*adj*) unattractive, **3**. fair; *synonyms* (*adj*) equitable, clear, average, dispassionate, (*adv*) clean; *antonyms* (*adj*) unfair, biased, dark, exceptional, unjust, **4**. fine; *synonyms* (*adj*) delicate, agreeable, dainty, brave, capital; *antonyms* (*adj*) poor, thick, coarse, substantial, unsatisfactory, **5**. lovely; *synonyms* (*adj*) charming, delightful, enchanting, handsome, lovable; *antonyms* (*adj*) hideous, terrible, unpleasant.

fagurlim box; *synonyms* (*n*) basket, cage, chest, (*v*) cuff, buffet; *antonym* (*v*) unbox.

fagurlitleiki chroma; *synonyms* (*n*) saturation, hue, color, intensity, paint.

fagurt fair; *synonyms* (*adj*) equitable, clear, beautiful, average, (*v*) bright; *antonyms* (*adj*) unfair, biased, dark, exceptional, unjust.

fáir few; *synonyms* (*adj*) infrequent, rare, scarce, occasional, sporadic; *antonyms* (*n*) plenty, (*adj*) many, countless, innumerable, various.

faktúra invoice; *synonyms* (*n*) bill, account, list, reckoning, (*v*) charge.

falda nest; *synonyms* (*n*) den, lair, hole, (*adj*) brood, hive.

faldur 1. skirt; *synonyms* (*n*) border, edge, brim, (*v*) fringe, circumvent, **2**. architrave; *synonyms* (*n*) capital, cornice, entablature, frieze, pediment.

fálki 1. falcon; *synonyms* (*n*) freebooter, mosstrooper, thug, harpy, shark, **2**. gyrfalcon; *synonym* (*n*) gerfalcon.

fall 1. function; *synonyms* (*n*) position, office, place, (*v*) act, exercise, **2**. sink; *synonyms* (*n*) sag, (*v*) decline, dip, droop, fall; *antonyms* (*v*) rise, float, **3**. drop; *synonyms* (*v*) decrease, deposit, dribble, abandon, (*n*) collapse; *antonyms* (*v*) increase, lift, (*n*) growth, **4**. case; *synonyms* (*n*) box, example, bin, cover, jacket, **5**. descent; *synonyms* (*n*) ancestry, birth, blood, declension, declination; *antonyms* (*n*) ascent, improvement.

falla fall; *synonyms* (*v*) decline, dip, decrease, descend, (*n*) drop; *antonyms* (*v*) rise, increase, ascend, climb, (*n*) ascent.

fallandi gradient; *synonyms* (*n*) grade, slope, pitch, (*v*) acclivity, ascent.

fallbeyging inflection; *synonyms* (*n*) accent, flection, inflexion, bending, flexion.

fallegur 1. pretty; *synonyms* (*adj*) beautiful, fair, graceful, lovely, (*n*) nice; *antonym* (*adj*) ugly, **2**. beautiful; *synonyms* (*adj*) attractive, good-looking, bright, beauteous, fine; *antonym* (*adj*) unattractive, **3**. fine; *synonyms* (*adj*) delicate, agreeable, dainty, brave, capital; *antonyms* (*adj*) poor, thick, coarse, substantial, unsatisfactory, **4**. lovely; *synonyms* (*adj*) charming, delightful, enchanting, handsome, lovable; *antonyms* (*adj*) hideous, terrible, unpleasant, **5**. fair; *synonyms* (*adj*) equitable, clear, average, dispassionate, (*adv*) clean; *antonyms* (*adj*) unfair, biased, dark, exceptional, unjust.

Fallinn flag; *synonyms* (*n*) banner, colors, (*v*) decline, (*adj*) droop, fade.

fallkeraröð cascade; *synonyms* (*n*) waterfall, torrent, (*v*) fall, gush, stream; *antonyms* (*v*) trickle, dribble.

fallrit graph; *synonyms* (*n*) figure, diagram, plan, drawing, (*v*) chart.

fallvatn stream; *synonyms* (*n*) flow, brook, (*v*) flood, (*prep*) current, course; *antonym* (*v*) trickle.

fálmari antenna; *synonyms* (*n*) aerial, feeler, advance, finger, forefinger.

fals fraud; *synonyms* (*n*) cheat, deceit, duplicity, counterfeit, deception; *antonym* (*n*) honesty.

falsa 1. forge; *synonyms* (*v*) counterfeit, falsify, devise, fabricate, fake, **2**. fold; *synonyms* (*n*) crease, bend, (*v*) crinkle, collapse, crumple.

falskur 1. spurious; *synonyms* (*adj*) counterfeit, sham, fake, (*n*) bastard, (*adv*) false; *antonym* (*syn*) genuine, **2**. fictitious; *synonyms* (*adj*) bogus, assumed, fictional, artificial, fabricated; *antonym* (*adj*) real.

falur socket; *synonyms* (*n*) cavity, alveolus, sleeve, hollow, pocket.

fána fauna; *synonyms* (*n*) animal, beast, brute, creature, puppet.

fanargeisli barb; *synonyms* (*n*) point, arrow, jag, gibe, prickle.

fangelsi prison; *synonyms* (*n*) jail, calaboose, confinement, lockup, penitentiary.

fáni 1. standard; *synonyms* (*adj*) model, (*n*) degree, measure, average, criterion; *antonyms* (*adj*) unusual, unconventional, special, **2**. flag; *synonyms* (*n*) banner, colors, (*v*) decline, (*adj*) droop, fade.

fansa stow; *synonyms* (*v*) pack, cram, charge, house, load.

far 1. impression; *synonyms* (*n*) belief, conception, feeling, idea, imprint, **2**. migration; *synonyms* (*n*) exodus, movement, journey, (*v*) flit, flitting.

fara 1. depart; *synonyms* (*v*) quit, deviate, go, decease, die; *antonyms* (*v*) stay, arrive, enter, come, **2**. leave; *synonyms* (*v*) depart, forsake, abandon, desert, (*n*) furlough; *antonyms* (*v*) remain, approach, change, **3**. exceed; *synonyms* (*v*) beat, pass, surpass, outdo, (*adj*) better.

faralda surge; *synonyms* (*v*) billow, flood, rise, rush, stream.

faraldur epidemic; *synonyms* (*n*) outbreak, plague, (*adj*) contagious, infectious, catching; *antonym* (*adj*) endemic.

farangur baggage; *synonyms* (*n*) luggage, bag, bags, equipment, gear.

farangursgeymla trunk; *synonyms* (*n*) stem, boot, torso, body, bole.

farangursgeymsla 1. trunk; *synonyms* (*n*) stem, boot, torso, body, bole, **2**. boot; *synonyms* (*n*) kick, trunk, bang, charge, gain.

fáránlegur 1. absurd; *synonyms* (*adj*) foolish, preposterous, ridiculous, unreasonable, irrational; *antonym* (*adj*) sensible, **2**. nonsensical; *synonyms* (*adj*) meaningless, absurd, ludicrous, pointless, silly.

fararstjóri guide; *synonyms* (*n*) escort, directory, (*v*) direct, conduct, govern; *antonym* (*v*) follow.

farbraut trajectory; *synonyms* (*n*) track, course, orbit, line, flight.

farbreyta parameter; *synonyms* (*n*) argument, guideline, limit, directive, modulus.

farðþegafjöldi traffic; *synonyms* (*n*) dealings, commerce, (*v*) exchange, trade, deal.

fareind ion; *synonym* (*n*) molecule.

fareindaleysing ionization; *synonym* (*n*) ionisation.

fargjald fare; *synonyms* (*n*) diet, aliment, food, board, (*v*) do.

farmaður seafarer; *synonyms* (*n*) mariner, gob, sailor, seaman, navigator.

farmaur tick; *synonyms* (*n*) beat, credit, score, (*v*) mark, check.

farmflutingur haulage; *synonyms* (*n*) traction, transport, draw, haul, (*v*) towage.

farmiði ticket; *synonyms* (*n*) pass, card, label, certificate, ballot.

farmskírteini 1. copy; *synonyms* (*n*) imitation, (*v*) counterfeit, imitate, ape, duplicate; *antonym* (*n*) original, **2**. original; *synonyms* (*adj*) first, authentic, native, new, primary; *antonyms* (*adj*) commonplace, banal, copied, corny, (*n*) copy.

farmþungi payload; *synonyms* (*n*) freight, cargo, load, consignment, lading.

farmur 1. cargo; *synonyms* (*n*) burden, loading, freight, wares, (*adj*) load, **2**. freight; *synonyms* (*n*) cargo, lading, consignment, freightage, (*v*) carry, **3**. payload; *synonym* (*n*) shipment.

farnaðarsaga anamnesis; *synonyms* (*n*) remembrance, memory, recall, recollection, commemoration.

farsæld welfare; *synonyms* (*n*) prosperity, benefit, good, happiness, health.

farseðill ticket; *synonyms* (*n*) pass, card, label, certificate, ballot.

farskráning reservation; *synonyms* (*n*) reserve, limitation, booking, condition, qualification; *antonym* (*n*) certainty.

farsótt 1. pestilence; *synonyms* (*n*) plague, pest, epidemic, blight, (*adj*) murrain, **2**. pest; *synonyms* (*n*) bane, bore, nuisance, bother, annoyance, **3**. epidemic; *synonyms* (*n*) outbreak, (*adj*) contagious, infectious, catching, rife; *antonym* (*adj*) endemic.

farþegamiðstöð terminal; *synonyms* (*adj*) final, last, definitive, (*n*) depot, end.

farþegarými cabin; *synonyms* (*n*) booth, hut, chamber, cot, lodge.

farþegi 1. passenger; *synonyms* (*n*) traveler, wayfarer, itinerant, rider, voyager, **2**. fare; *synonyms* (*n*) diet, aliment, food, board, (*v*) do, **3**. occupant; *synonyms* (*n*) inhabitant, resident, tenant, denizen, dweller; *antonym* (*n*) landlord.

farvegur channel; *synonyms* (*n*) canal, conduit, groove, (*v*) carry, conduct.

fárviðri hurricane; *synonyms* (*n*) gale, storm, tempest, cyclone, squall.

fasi 1. phase; *synonyms* (*n*) aspect, stage, facet, chapter, grade, **2**. state; *synonyms* (*n*) nation, position, say, country, (*v*) declare; *antonyms* (*v*) deny, (*adj*) private.

fásinna absurdity; *synonyms* (*n*) foolishness, nonsense, absurdness, silliness, meaninglessness; *antonym* (*n*) sense.

fasismi fascism; *synonyms* (*n*) dictatorship, despotism, oppression, totalitarianism, tyranny; *antonym* (*n*) democracy.

fáskiptni detachment; *synonyms* (*n*) division, separation, dissociation, corps, indifference; *antonyms* (*n*) involvement, attachment, bias, interest.

fasta fast; *synonyms* (*adj*) dissolute, firm, agile, debauched, (*adv*) soon; *antonyms* (*adj*) sluggish, (*adv*) slow, slowly, (*v*) gorge, (*n*) binge.

fastafulltrúi permanent; *synonyms* (*adj*) durable, lasting, fixed, (*v*) constant, continuous; *antonyms* (*adj*) fleeting, temporary, brief, impermanent, provisional.

fastakostnaður overhead; *synonyms* (*adv*) above, aloft, over, up, (*n*) expense.

fastanefnd 1. committee; *synonyms* (*n*) board, council, commission, consignee, trustee, **2**. mission; *synonyms* (*n*) delegation, deputation, job, assignment, charge.

fastastjarna star (stjarna); *synonyms* (*n*) asterisk, celebrity, ace, principal, headliner; *antonym* (*n*) nobody.

fastatala constant; *synonyms* (*adj*) ceaseless, incessant, perpetual, steady, continual; *antonyms* (*adj*) changeable, intermittent, irregular, sporadic, variable.

fastbúandi sedentary; *synonyms* (*adj*) inactive, lazy, sluggish, domestic, (*v*) untraveled; *antonym* (*adj*) active.

fastefni solid; *synonyms* (*adj*) firm, dense, compact, consistent, hard; *antonyms* (*adj*) soft, unreliable, loose, gaseous, (*n*) liquid.

fasteignasali broker; *synonyms* (*n*) mediator, agent, go-between, factor, middleman.

fasteignaveð mortgage; *synonyms* (*n*) gage, (*v*) bond, pawn, pledge, impawn.

fastheldinn conservative; *synonyms* (*adj*) moderate, bourgeois, conventional, cautious, reactionary; *antonyms* (*adj*) activist, wide-ranging, (*n*) liberal, radical.

fasti 1. constant; *synonyms* (*adj*) ceaseless, incessant, perpetual, steady, continual; *antonyms* (*adj*) changeable, intermittent, irregular, sporadic, variable, **2**. parameter; *synonyms* (*n*) argument, guideline, limit, directive, modulus.

fastmerki 1. benchmark; *synonyms* (*n*) criterion, measure, gauge, norm, landmark, **2**. monument; *synonyms* (*n*) memorial, headstone, column, record, tombstone.

fastur 1. stable; *synonyms* (*adj*) firm, permanent, reliable, constant, durable; *antonyms* (*adj*) unstable, shaky, wobbly, dangerous, precarious, **2**. solid; *synonyms* (*adj*) dense, compact, consistent, hard, (*v*) close; *antonyms* (*adj*) soft, unreliable, loose, gaseous, (*n*) liquid, **3**. sedentary; *synonyms* (*adj*) inactive, lazy, sluggish, domestic, (*v*) untraveled; *antonym* (*adj*) active, **4**. constant; *synonyms* (*adj*) ceaseless, incessant, perpetual, steady, continual; *antonyms* (*adj*) changeable, intermittent, irregular, sporadic, variable, **5**. fast; *synonyms* (*adj*) dissolute, agile, debauched, fixed, (*adv*) soon; *antonyms* (*adv*) slow, slowly, leisurely, (*v*) gorge, (*n*) binge.

fastyrðing assertion; *synonyms* (*n*) affirmation, argument, statement, claim, allegation.

fat 1. barrel; *synonyms* (*n*) drum, roll, vessel, barrelful, cask, **2**. fad; *synonyms* (*n*) caprice, craze, rage, fancy, crotchet.

fátækt poverty; *synonyms* (*n*) lack, distress, (*v*) destitution, need, penury; *antonyms* (*n*) wealth, riches.

fátækur 1. poor; *synonyms* (*adj*) bad, low, miserable, paltry, (*v*) meager; *antonyms* (*adj*) rich, wealthy, excellent, first-rate, privileged, **2**. miserable; *synonyms* (*adj*) mean, poor, abject, (*v*) forlorn, wretched; *antonyms* (*adj*) happy, cheerful, generous, **3**. impoverished; *synonyms* (*adj*) destitute, broke, indigent, needy, penniless; *antonym* (*adj*) well-off.

fataskiptahneigð transvestism; *synonym* (*n*) transvestitism.

fatlaður handicapped; *synonyms* (*adj*) disabled, crippled, lame, incapacitated, underprivileged.

fatli sling; *synonyms* (*n*) cast, (*v*) catapult, pitch, fling, (*adj*) hang.

fatra frustrate; *synonyms* (*v*) baffle, counteract, disappoint, fail, foil; *antonym* (*v*) encourage.

fatur frustration; *synonyms* (*n*) failure, defeat, disappointment, letdown, vexation.

fáviti imbecile; *synonyms* (*adj*) foolish, idiotic, (*n*) fool, idiot, moron.

fax facsimile; *synonyms* (*n*) duplicate, copy, autotype, model, (*v*) fax; *antonym* (*n*) original.

faxi fax; *synonyms* (*n*) autotype, (*v*) facsimile, telefax.

fé 1. money; *synonyms* (*n*) capital, coin, currency, funds, means, **2**. livestock; *synonyms* (*n*) stock, ancestry, blood, bloodline, breed.

feðraveldi patriarchy; *synonyms* (*n*) patriarchate, patriarchship.

fegrandi cosmetic; *synonyms* (*n*) cosmetics, cerate, cream, lotion, paint.

fegrun idealization; *synonyms* (*n*) idealisation, glorification, adulation, glory, idolization.

fegrunarefni cosmetic; *synonyms* (*n*) cosmetics, cerate, cream, lotion, paint.

fegurð beauty; *synonyms* (*n*) splendor, attractiveness, beaut, charm, loveliness; *antonym* (*n*) ugliness.

féhirðir treasurer; *synonyms* (*n*) cashier, banker, financier, fiscal, guardian.

feilkveiking misfire; *synonyms* (*n*) flop, dud, (*v*) fail, miscarry, fizzle.

feiminn 1. shy; *synonyms* (*adj*) diffident, fearful, timid, abashed, (*v*) fling; *antonyms* (*adj*) brash, bold, confident, demonstrative, forward, **2**. abashed; *synonyms* (*adj*) bashful, discomfited, mortified, ashamed, confused; *antonym* (*adj*) brazen.

feiti grease; *synonyms* (*n*) fat, bribe, butter, (*v*) oil, boodle.

feitlagni adiposity; *synonyms* (*n*) adiposeness, adiposis, fatness, fattiness, weight.

feitletra boldface; *synonym* (*n*) bold.

feitletraður boldface; *synonym* (*n*) bold.

feitletur bold; *synonyms* (*adj*) adventurous, audacious, manly, resolute, arrogant; *antonyms* (*adj*) cowardly, timid, modest.

feitur 1. bold; *synonyms* (*adj*) adventurous, audacious, manly, resolute, arrogant; *antonyms* (*adj*) cowardly, timid, modest, **2**. fat; *synonyms* (*adj*) stout, corpulent, dense, thick, (*n*) avoirdupois; *antonyms* (*adj*) thin, slim, skinny, slender.

fela mask; *synonyms* (*n*) cover, conceal, (*v*) cloak, disguise, hide; *antonym* (*v*) disclose.

félag 1. corporation; *synonyms* (*n*) association, belly, business, company, concern, **2**. association; *synonyms* (*n*) affiliation, alliance, connection, assembly, affinity, **3**. district; *synonyms* (*n*) area, quarter, region, community, neighborhood, **4**. company; *synonyms* (*n*) companionship, society, band, cohort, collection; *antonym* (*n*) solitude, **5**. organization; *synonyms* (*n*) order, establishment, administration, arrangement, formation.

félagi 1. associate; *synonyms* (*v*) affiliate, connect, (*n*) ally, assistant, companion; *antonyms* (*v*) avoid, dissociate, distance, (*adj*) chief, (*n*) stranger, **2**. member; *synonyms* (*n*) limb, part, supporter, extremity, phallus.

félagsfræði sociology; *synonym* (*n*) anthropology.

félagsgjöld dues; *synonyms* (*n*) duty, tax, obligation, assessment, sess.

félagshyggja socialism; *synonyms* (*n*) communism, collectivism, communalism; *antonym* (*n*) capitalism.

félagslegur social; *synonyms* (*adj*) gregarious, national, companionable, friendly, (*n*) sociable.

félagsmaður member; *synonyms* (*n*) limb, part, supporter, extremity, phallus.

félagsmótun socialization; *synonyms* (*n*) socialisation, socializing, acculturation, assimilation, culture.

félagsstaða 1. status; *synonyms* (*n*) position, rank, situation, (*adj*) place, standing, **2**. caste; *synonyms* (*n*) order, class, sort, (*adj*) degree, baccalaureate.

felga 1. rim; *synonyms* (*n*) border, edge, margin, brim, brink, **2**. wheel; *synonyms* (*n*) circle, cycle, (*v*) roll, revolve, turn.

fell 1. mount; *synonyms* (*v*) ascend, rise, climb, board, arise; *antonyms* (*v*) descend, drop, (*n*) valley, **2**. fascia; *synonyms* (*n*) cincture, band, facia, fillet, aponeurosis.

fella fold; *synonyms* (*n*) crease, bend, (*v*) crinkle, collapse, crumple.

felli functional; *synonyms* (*adj*) practical, effective, handy, operational, operative; *antonyms* (*adj*) nonfunctional, useless.

fellibylur 1. typhoon; *synonyms* (*n*) hurricane, tempest, gale, cyclone, storm, **2**. cyclone; *synonyms* (*n*) tornado, whirlwind, **3**. hurricane; *synonyms* (*n*) squall, twister.

felling 1. precipitation; *synonyms* (*n*) hurry, rain, precipitancy, downfall, haste, **2**. convolution; *synonyms* (*n*) coil, gyrus, twine, complexity, swirl, **3**. folding; *synonyms* (*n*) fold, bend, crease, flexure, breakdown, **4**. fold; *synonyms* (*v*) crinkle, collapse, crumple, double, lap.

fellir 1. precipitant; *synonyms* (*adj*) hurried, hasty, precipitous, headlong, abrupt, **2**. depressor; *synonyms* (*n*) hypotensor, oppressor.

felmtur alarm; *synonyms* (*n*) dismay, alert, consternation, (*v*) awe, scare; *antonyms* (*v*) calm, comfort.

fen 1. phenylalanine, **2**. mire; *synonyms* (*n*) bog, filth, marsh, dirt, (*adj*) mud.

fenging conception; *synonyms* (*n*) notion, concept, idea, creation, thought; *antonym* (*n*) misconception.

fengrani wolffish; *synonyms* (*n*) catfish, lancetfish, mudcat.

fennika fennel; *synonyms* (*n*) cinnamon, cloves, finocchio, mace, nutmeg.

fenníka fennel; *synonyms* (*n*) cinnamon, cloves, finocchio, mace, nutmeg.

fennikka fennel; *synonyms* (*n*) cinnamon, cloves, finocchio, mace, nutmeg.

fennill fennel; *synonyms* (*n*) cinnamon, cloves, finocchio, mace, nutmeg.

ferð 1. trip; *synonyms* (*n*) excursion, expedition, (*v*) journey, slip, stumble; *antonym* (*v*) fix, **2**. speed;

synonyms (n) race, (v) hasten, hurry, quicken, run; antonym (n) slowness, **3**. voyage; synonyms (n) cruise, tour, trip, (v) travel, sail.

ferðalag trip; synonyms (n) excursion, expedition, (v) journey, slip, stumble; antonym (v) fix.

ferðalög 1. trip; synonyms (n) excursion, expedition, (v) journey, slip, stumble; antonym (v) fix, **2**. journey; synonyms (n) jaunt, passage, (v) go, travel, cruise.

ferðamál tourism; synonym (n) touristry.

ferðamannastraumur tourism; synonym (n) touristry.

ferðaþjónusta tourism; synonym (n) touristry.

ferðaútvegur tourism; synonym (n) touristry.

ferfætlingur 1. quadruped; synonyms (adj) quadrupedal, (n) beast, biped, creature, **2**. tetrapod.

fergildur tetravalent; synonyms (adj) quadrivalent, tetratomic.

ferging compression; synonyms (n) compaction, condensation, pressure, compressing, concentration.

ferhyrndur 1. quadrilateral; synonyms (adj) quadrangular, multilateral, (n) quadrangle, quad, tetragon, **2**. tetragonal; synonyms (adj) tetrad, quadratic, square.

ferhyrningur 1. quadrangle; synonyms (n) quad, courtyard, court, tetragon, quadrilateral, **2**. quadrilateral; synonyms (adj) quadrangular, multilateral, bilateral, (n) quadrangle, rectangle, **3**. block; synonyms (n) bar, barricade, pad, (v) arrest, stop; antonyms (v) free, unblock, open.

ferilhnik perturbation; synonyms (n) disturbance, commotion, agitation, fuss, (v) trepidation.

ferilhorn anomaly; synonyms (n) abnormality, aberration, anomalousness, deviation, abnormity.

ferill 1. trail; synonyms (n) track, trace, (v) haul, drag, hunt, **2**. track; synonyms (n) course, path, (v) trail, tail, chase, **3**. trajectory; synonyms (n) orbit, line, flight, curve, (v) passage, **4**. curve; synonyms (n) bend, crook, bow, (v) curl, turn, **5**. arc; synonyms (n) arch, crescent, curvature, spark, sweep.

ferilskráning plot; synonyms (n) conspiracy, plan, lot, (v) intrigue, cabal.

ferilveila dislocation; synonyms (n) breakdown, interruption, confusion, disruption, luxation.

ferja 1. carrier; synonyms (n) bearer, messenger, courier, mailman, porter, **2**. ferryboat; synonyms (n) ferry, ship, ferrying.

ferjald transducer; synonyms (n) sensor, transductor.

ferjustuðull sensitivity; synonyms (n) sensibility, feeling, sensation, sense, sensitiveness; antonym (n) insensitivity.

ferkantur square; synonyms (adj) right, even, rectangular, (n) area, (v) settle.

ferli 1. procedure; synonyms (n) process, formula, practice, routine, fashion, **2**. routing; synonyms (n) route, conquest, dispatching, navigation, steering, **3**. process; synonyms (n) operation, proceeding, method, procedure, (v) action, **4**. loop; synonyms (n) coil, ring, (v) curve, bend, circle.

ferlishemill inhibitor; synonym (n) stabilizer.

ferma load; synonyms (n) charge, cargo, freight, (v) burden, fill; antonym (v) unload.

fermdur laden; synonyms (v) lade, (adj) fraught, burdened, full, loaded; antonym (adj) empty.

ferming 1. transshipment, **2**. confirmation; synonyms (n) affirmation, approval, corroboration, ratification, sanction; antonym (n) contradiction.

ferna tetrad; synonyms (n) four, quaternity, quaternion, foursome, quadruplet.

ferningslaga square; synonyms (adj) right, even, rectangular, (n) area, (v) settle.

ferningstala square; synonyms (adj) right, even, rectangular, (n) area, (v) settle.

ferningur square; synonyms (adj) right, even, rectangular, (n) area, (v) settle.

fernis varnish; synonyms (n) coat, lacquer, paint, (v) gloss, color.

ferskleiki currency; synonyms (n) cash, money, coin, circulation, vogue.

ferskur fresh; synonyms (adj) bracing, brisk, clean, novel, (adv) new; antonyms (adj) old, stale, decayed, exhausted, hot.

ferstrendur quadrate; synonyms (n) square, adjust, fit, (v) suit, coincide.

fertala square; synonyms (adj) right, even, rectangular, (n) area, (v) settle.

fervik variance; synonyms (n) difference, disagreement, discrepancy, dissension, division.

festa 1. stability; synonyms (n) constancy, durability, firmness, permanence, poise; antonym (n) instability, **2**. stick; synonyms (n) bar, (v) adhere, stab, attach, cling, **3**. shackle; synonyms (v) fetter, chain, bind, hobble, (n) hamper, **4**. clip; synonyms (n) clasp, blow, (v) nip, snip, trim; antonym (v) lengthen, **5**. constraint; synonyms (n) coercion, compulsion, force, restraint, confinement; antonym (n) incentive.

festarauga thimble; synonyms (n) dipper, ladle, shovel, spatula, spoon.

festarhæll 1. bollard; synonym (n) bitt, **2**. bitt; synonyms (n) bollard, bitts.

festarkorn mitochondrion; synonym (n) chondriosome.

festast 1. stick; *synonyms* (n) bar, (v) adhere, stab, attach, cling, **2**. bind; *synonyms* (v) tie, bandage, bundle, combine, (n) band; *antonyms* (v) untie, release, unbind, **3**. freeze; *synonyms* (n) frost, (v) congeal, chill, arrest, cool; *antonyms* (v) melt, thaw, boil.

festibúnaður 1. clamping; *synonym* (n) grip, **2**. holdfast; *synonyms* (n) fastener, clamp, fastening, lock, grasp, **3**. fixture; *synonyms* (n) appointment, fixing, attachment, match, (adj) establishment.

festiefni fixative; *synonyms* (n) adhesive, cement, glue.

festiflötur 1. wart; *synonyms* (n) verruca, bulge, growth, tit, swelling, **2**. pad; *synonyms* (n) cushion, apartment, (v) line, inflate, expand.

festing 1. bracket; *synonyms* (n) brace, prop, rack, (v) link, couple, **2**. attachment; *synonyms* (n) affection, appendix, accessory, addition, adherence; *antonym* (n) detachment, **3**. holder; *synonyms* (n) bearer, case, possessor, stand, container, **4**. insertion; *synonyms* (n) inset, enclosure, introduction, intromission, interpolation; *antonym* (n) removal, **5**. fixation; *synonyms* (n) obsession, fetish, fixing, mania, complex.

festiólar harness; *synonyms* (n) gear, rein, tether, (v) hitch, (adj) strap.

festipatrona chuck; *synonyms* (v) cast, fling, ditch, pitch, throw.

festipatróna chuck; *synonyms* (v) cast, fling, ditch, pitch, throw.

festiþræðir pili; *synonyms* (n) cilia, hair, capillament, (adj) fimbriae, villi.

festivökvi fixative; *synonyms* (n) adhesive, cement, glue.

fet foot (fótur); *synonyms* (n) bottom, base, feet, foundation, (v) hoof; *antonym* (n) top.

fetill sling; *synonyms* (n) cast, (v) catapult, pitch, fling, (adj) hang.

feyra 1. detritus; *synonyms* (n) rubble, (adj) debris, trash, magistery, scobs, **2**. litter; *synonyms* (n) brood, bedding, stretcher, (v) clutter, (adj) jumble.

fiðla fiddle; *synonyms* (n) violin, (v) con, cheat, tamper, diddle.

fidrildi butterfly; *synonyms* (n) chameleon, (adj) peacock, (v) bray, coquet, coquette.

fiðrildislirfa caterpillar; *synonyms* (n) cat, larva, worm, maggot, cocoon.

fiðrildisplástur butterfly; *synonyms* (n) chameleon, (adj) peacock, (v) bray, coquet, coquette.

fihelpanto accessories; *synonyms* (n) fittings, equipment, accompaniments, garnishes, possession.

fíkja fig; *synonyms* (n) figure, anatomy, (adj) pin, straw, rush.

fíkn addiction; *synonyms* (n) dependence, dependency, devotion, habit, enslavement.

fíkni affinity; *synonyms* (n) sympathy, analogy, alliance, bond, kindred.

fíkniávani addiction; *synonyms* (n) dependence, dependency, devotion, habit, enslavement.

fíkniefni 1. stimulant; *synonyms* (n) incentive, provocative, excitant, goad, impetus, **2**. dope; *synonyms* (n) dolt, boob, booby, ass, (v) drug.

fílabein ivory; *synonyms* (n) bone, tusk, dentin, elephant, (adj) chalk.

filio arms; *synonyms* (n) arm, armament, weaponry, shield, ordnance.

fíll elephant; *synonyms* (n) camel, dromedary, giant, (adj) behemoth, cachalot.

filma film; *synonyms* (n) membrane, coating, cloud, cinema, (v) mist.

filmo movie; *synonyms* (n) film, flick, pic, picture, show.

fimbulfamb confabulation; *synonyms* (n) colloquy, chat, confab, conversation, converse.

fimlegur acrobatic; *synonyms* (adj) athletic, gymnastic, energetic, flexible, lithe.

fimleikar acrobatics; *synonyms* (n) aerobatics, tumbling, stunting.

fimm five; *synonyms* (n) cinque, quint, quintuplet, fin, (adj) quinary.

fimmhyrningur pentagon; *synonyms* (n) pentangle, polygon.

fimmtíu fifty; *synonyms* (n) l, lambert, liter, litre.

fíngerður smooth; *synonyms* (adj) easy, calm, level, oily, (v) quiet; *antonyms* (adj) rough, uneven, abrasive, coarse, crumpled.

fingrafar fingerprint; *synonyms* (n) fingermark, impression, description, footprint, voiceprint.

fingravettlingar gloves; *synonyms* (n) glove, belt, handbag, ornament, scarf.

fingur 1. finger; *synonyms* (n) digit, dactyl, (v) feel, handle, touch, **2**. digit; *synonyms* (n) figure, cipher, finger, number, integer.

fingurbjargarblóm digitalis; *synonyms* (n) foxglove, digitalin.

fingurgómsbólga felon; *synonyms* (n) criminal, convict, crook, culprit, malefactor.

fingurlegur digital; *synonyms* (adj) numeric, (n) computer.

fingurnögl fingernail; *synonym* (n) claw.

finkull fennel; *synonyms* (n) cinnamon, cloves, finocchio, mace, nutmeg.

finn fine; *synonyms* (adj) delicate, agreeable, dainty, brave, capital; *antonyms* (adj) poor, thick, coarse, substantial, unsatisfactory.

finna 1. strike; *synonyms* (n) knock, assault, (v) bang, beat, hit, **2**. evaluate; *synonyms* (v) appraise, assess, calculate, gauge, estimate, **3**. locate; *synonyms* (v) base, lay, discover, find, (n) place, **4**. find; *synonyms* (v) catch, detect, encounter, (n) detection, disclosure; *antonyms* (v) lose, misplace.

fínpússa finish; *synonyms* (v) end, complete, achieve, (n) close, consummate; *antonyms* (v) start, begin, continue, (n) beginning.

fínrenna relieve; *synonyms* (v) assuage, comfort, ease, allay, (n) alleviate; *antonyms* (v) worsen, burden.

fínrennsli relieving; *synonyms* (adj) applicable, comforting, pertinent, relevant, (n) encouragement.

fínsléttun finish; *synonyms* (v) end, complete, achieve, (n) close, consummate; *antonyms* (v) start, begin, continue, (n) beginning.

fínstilla 1. adjust; *synonyms* (v) temper, accommodate, adapt, align, acclimatize, **2**. calibrate; *synonyms* (v) adjust, regulate, gauge, graduate, measure.

fínstilling trimming; *synonyms* (n) trim, adornment, decoration, dressing, ornament.

fínvinna finish; *synonyms* (v) end, complete, achieve, (n) close, consummate; *antonyms* (v) start, begin, continue, (n) beginning.

firð metric; *synonyms* (adj) metrical, measured, calculated, careful, deliberate.

firma firm; *synonyms* (adj) constant, hard, stable, close, compact; *antonyms* (adj) irresolute, soft, weak, hesitant, limp.

firmamerki logo; *synonyms* (n) emblem, logotype, sign, mark, badge.

firring alienation; *synonyms* (n) estrangement, abalienation, disaffection, dislike, separation.

físibelgur blower; *synonyms* (n) bellows, fan, blast, cetacean, feeder.

fiska fish (fiskur); *synonyms* (n) bird, (v) angle, seek, hunt, pursue.

fiskabúr aquarium; *synonyms* (n) vivarium, (v) fishery.

fiskeldi aquaculture; *synonym* (n) aquiculture.

fiskflak fillet; *synonyms* (n) band, strip, cincture, list, (v) filet.

fiskigarður barrier; *synonyms* (n) barricade, bar, bulwark, dam, handicap.

fiskimaður fisherman; *synonyms* (n) angler, fisher, piscator, (v) sportsman, huntsman.

fiskirækt aquaculture; *synonym* (n) aquiculture.

fiskmóttaka pound; *synonyms* (v) beat, pen, bang, crush, flap.

fiskur fish; *synonyms* (n) bird, (v) angle, seek, hunt, pursue.

fiskúrgangur offal; *synonyms* (n) garbage, litter, waste, junk, leavings.

fit web; *synonyms* (n) mesh, network, tissue, lattice, (v) net.

fita fat; *synonyms* (adj) stout, corpulent, dense, thick, (n) avoirdupois; *antonyms* (adj) thin, slim, skinny, slender.

fitja feature; *synonyms* (n) article, aspect, character, characteristic, detail.

fitjaður webbed; *synonyms* (adj) lacy, netlike, netted, keld, lacelike.

fitjuflokkur category; *synonyms* (n) class, denomination, division, kind, type.

fittni fitness; *synonyms* (n) ability, adequacy, appropriateness, aptness, capability; *antonyms* (n) unsuitability, inability, unfitness.

fituborinn fat; *synonyms* (adj) stout, corpulent, dense, thick, (n) avoirdupois; *antonyms* (adj) thin, slim, skinny, slender.

fituefni lipid; *synonyms* (n) lipide, lipoid.

fituhrörnun atherosclerosis; *synonym* (adj) arteriosclerosis.

fitungar lipid; *synonyms* (n) lipide, lipoid.

fitusækni adiposity; *synonyms* (n) adiposeness, adiposis, fatness, fattiness, weight.

fituútfelling plaque; *synonyms* (n) plate, brass, medal, administration, award.

fituvætir detergent; *synonyms* (adj) detersive, cleansing, (n) abluent, cleanser, (v) lotion.

fjaðra 1. rebound; *synonyms* (n) bound, kick, (v) bounce, recoil, glance, **2**. wormwood; *synonyms* (n) absinth, gall.

fjaðrafellir moulting; *synonyms* (adj) pulled, (n) moult, ecdysis, molt, molting.

fjaðrandi elastic; *synonyms* (adj) flexible, buoyant, ductile, limber, pliable; *antonyms* (adj) rigid, stiff, inflexible, inelastic.

fjaðrarblað spring; *synonyms* (n) jump, leap, bound, (v) hop, caper.

fjaður elasticity; *synonyms* (n) bounce, spring, flexibility, pliability, suppleness.

fjaðurbrúun spline; *synonyms* (n) feather, slat, fin, conclusion, end.

fjaðurmagn 1. resilience; *synonyms* (n) elasticity, spring, stamina, bounce, flexibility; *antonym* (n) pessimism, **2**. elasticity; *synonyms* (n) pliability, suppleness, tone, renitency, tonicity.

fjaðurmagnaður elastic; *synonyms* (adj) flexible, buoyant, ductile, limber, pliable; *antonyms* (adj) rigid, stiff, inflexible, inelastic.

fjær distal; *synonyms* (adj) remote, telescopic.

fjall 1. mountain; *synonyms* (n) mount, heap, height, mass, (v) mound; *antonym* (n) dip, **2**. mount;

synonyms (v) ascend, rise, climb, board, arise; *antonyms* (v) descend, drop, (n) valley.

fjallaferð 1. trek; *synonyms* (n) tour, (v) journey, travel, tramp, expedition, **2**. hike; *synonyms* (n) walk, raise, rise, advance, (v) boost.

fjallarakki 1. ranger; *synonyms* (n) commando, keeper, rover, custodian, custos, **2**. rover; *synonyms* (n) nomad, wanderer, rambler, ranger, roamer.

fjallshryggur ridge; *synonyms* (n) crest, ledge, bank, hill, shelf.

fjandsamlegur hostile; *synonyms* (adj) unfriendly, aggressive, contrary, adverse, belligerent; *antonyms* (adj) friendly, soothing, warm.

fjandsamur hostile; *synonyms* (adj) unfriendly, aggressive, contrary, adverse, belligerent; *antonyms* (adj) friendly, soothing, warm.

fjara 1. beach; *synonyms* (n) bank, coast, foreshore, shore, strand, **2**. shore; *synonyms* (n) prop, beach, edge, land, buttress; *antonym* (n) interior, **3**. ebb; *synonyms* (n) wane, (v) dwindle, abate, decline, decrease; *antonym* (v) tide.

fjárdráttur embezzlement; *synonyms* (n) defalcation, peculation, misappropriation, theft, stealing.

fjárfesting 1. capitalization; *synonyms* (n) capitalisation, discounting, use, **2**. investment; *synonyms* (n) investing, investiture, clothing, siege, finance.

fjárfestir investor; *synonyms* (n) banker, capitalist, financier, speculator, backer.

fjárgjöf endowment; *synonyms* (n) ability, talent, capacity, (v) donation, gift.

fjargler objective; *synonyms* (adj) dispassionate, (n) aim, mark, goal, object; *antonyms* (adj) biased, subjective.

fjárhæð amount; *synonyms* (n) number, quantity, aggregate, measure, sum.

fjárhagsáætlun budget; *synonyms* (n) plan, sack, (v) calculate, compute, (adj) cheap.

fjárhagsáætlunargerð budgeting; *synonyms* (n) appropriation, (adj) financial.

fjárhagshlið economics; *synonyms* (n) finance, economy, commerce, money, backing.

fjárhagslegur 1. financial; *synonyms* (adj) fiscal, economic, monetary, pecuniary, commercial, **2**. monetary; *synonyms* (adj) financial, numismatical, sumptuary, budgetary, capital.

fjárhagsrammi budget; *synonyms* (n) plan, sack, (v) calculate, compute, (adj) cheap.

fjárhagsskuldbinding liability; *synonyms* (n) debt, duty, obligation, trust, blame; *antonym* (n) asset.

fjárhagsstaða finances; *synonyms* (n) assets, money, funds, resources, capital.

fjárhagur finances; *synonyms* (n) assets, money, funds, resources, capital.

fjárhaldsmaður trustee; *synonyms* (n) fiduciary, guardian, regent, consignee, keeper.

fjarhrif psychokinesis; *synonym* (n) telekinesis.

fjárkúgun blackmail; *synonyms* (n) threat, bribe, extortion, (v) threaten, extort.

fjarlægð 1. distance; *synonyms* (n) remove, space, way, gap, (adj) length; *antonyms* (n) nearness, proximity, closeness, intimacy, (v) associate, **2**. detachment; *synonyms* (n) division, separation, dissociation, corps, indifference; *antonyms* (n) involvement, attachment, bias, interest, **3**. offset; *synonyms* (v) counteract, balance, neutralize, cancel, (n) counterbalance.

fjarlægðarmörk reach; *synonyms* (v) range, overtake, obtain, achieve, (n) fetch.

fjarlægja 1. strip; *synonyms* (v) deprive, despoil, divest, peel, plunder; *antonyms* (v) dress, decorate, **2**. evacuate; *synonyms* (v) deplete, void, discharge, quit, (adj) empty.

fjarlægur 1. remote; *synonyms* (adj) distant, aloof, detached, inaccessible, outside; *antonyms* (adj) near, nearby, accessible, **2**. distal; *synonyms* (adj) remote, telescopic, **3**. low; *synonyms* (adj) contemptible, abject, humble, ignoble, (adv) gentle; *antonyms* (adj) cheerful, happy, high-pitched, loud, (n) high.

fjárlagafrumvarp budget; *synonyms* (n) plan, sack, (v) calculate, compute, (adj) cheap.

fjárlagagerð budgeting; *synonyms* (n) appropriation, (adj) financial.

fjárlög 1. budget; *synonyms* (n) plan, sack, (v) calculate, compute, (adj) cheap, **2**. estimates.

fjármagn 1. capital; *synonyms* (n) principal, city, stock, (adj) main, primary, **2**. equity; *synonyms* (n) fairness, honesty, candor, (adj) justice, integrity; *antonym* (n) unfairness.

fjármagna 1. finance; *synonyms* (n) funding, support, (v) back, fund, sponsor, **2**. fund; *synonyms* (n) stock, store, capital, (v) hoard, bankroll.

fjármagnseigandi capitalist; *synonyms* (adj) capitalistic, (n) financier, banker, businessman, businessperson; *antonym* (adj) collective.

fjármagnskerfi capitalism; *synonyms* (n) democracy, commercialism, competition, entrepreneurship, industrialism; *antonyms* (n) collectivism, communism, socialism.

fjármál 1. financing; *synonyms* (n) funding, capital, backing, credit, investment, **2**. finance; *synonyms* (n) support, (v) back, fund, sponsor, bankroll.

fjármálalegur fiscal; *synonyms* (adj) financial, monetary, pecuniary, crumenal, economic.

fjármálaráðuneyti treasury; *synonyms* (*n*) exchequer, storehouse, thesaurus, anthology, bank.

fjármálastjóri controller; *synonyms* (*n*) administrator, superintendent, accountant, comptroller, control.

fjarmiðlun telecommunication; *synonym* (*n*) communication.

fjármögnun 1. capitalization; *synonyms* (*n*) capitalisation, discounting, use, **2**. financing; *synonyms* (*n*) funding, capital, backing, credit, investment, **3**. funding; *synonyms* (*n*) financing, support, appropriation, accompaniment, backup.

fjármögnunarleiga 1. lease; *synonyms* (*v*) hire, rent, charter, let, contract, **2**. leasing; *synonyms* (*n*) rental, chartering.

fjármunaleiga rental; *synonyms* (*n*) hire, lease, letting, renting, apartment.

fjármunir 1. resource; *synonyms* (*n*) expedient, imagination, (*v*) recourse, resort, refuge, **2**. resources; *synonyms* (*n*) means, property, capital, assets, finances, **3**. capital; *synonyms* (*n*) principal, city, stock, (*adj*) main, primary.

fjárnám 1. attachment; *synonyms* (*n*) affection, appendix, accessory, addition, adherence; *antonym* (*n*) detachment, **2**. execution; *synonyms* (*n*) performance, accomplishment, achievement, effect, enforcement.

fjáröflun revenue; *synonyms* (*n*) income, receipts, proceeds, profit, earnings.

fjárreiðustjóri treasurer; *synonyms* (*n*) cashier, banker, financier, fiscal, guardian.

fjárrenta interest; *synonyms* (*n*) concern, advantage, affair, (*v*) engage, care; *antonyms* (*n*) indifference, apathy, (*v*) bore.

fjarri distal; *synonyms* (*adj*) remote, telescopic.

fjarriti 1. teleprinter; *synonyms* (*n*) teletypewriter, telex, **2**. teletypewriter; *synonym* (*n*) teleprinter.

fjarskiptafræði telecommunication; *synonym* (*n*) communication.

fjarskiptaleið link; *synonyms* (*n*) connection, join, joint, (*v*) combine, tie; *antonym* (*v*) separate.

fjarskiptarás channel; *synonyms* (*n*) canal, conduit, groove, (*v*) carry, conduct.

fjarskiptatækni telecommunication; *synonym* (*n*) communication.

fjarskiptatruflanir static; *synonyms* (*adj*) immobile, inactive, motionless, inert, still; *antonym* (*adj*) moving.

fjarskipti 1. telecommunications; *synonym* (*n*) communications, **2**. telecommunication; *synonym* (*n*) communication, **3**. radio; *synonyms* (*n*) wireless, broadcasting, radiotelegram, (*v*) broadcast, transmit.

fjarskynjun telepathy; *synonyms* (*n*) clairvoyance, insight, mind-reading, parapsychology, premonition.

fjarstæða 1. rubbish; *synonyms* (*n*) refuse, garbage, litter, nonsense, trash; *antonym* (*n*) sense, **2**. absurdity; *synonyms* (*n*) foolishness, absurdness, silliness, meaninglessness, nonsensicality, **3**. nonsense; *synonyms* (*n*) gibberish, absurdity, balderdash, baloney, drivel.

fjárstyrkur allowance; *synonyms* (*n*) allotment, admission, discount, quota, tolerance.

fjársvik fraud; *synonyms* (*n*) cheat, deceit, duplicity, counterfeit, deception; *antonym* (*n*) honesty.

fjarsýni 1. hyperopia; *synonyms* (*n*) farsightedness, hypermetropia, hypermetropy, longsightedness, **2**. hypermetropia; *synonyms* (*n*) hyperopia, sagacity, shrewdness.

fjartengdur remote; *synonyms* (*adj*) distant, aloof, detached, inaccessible, outside; *antonyms* (*adj*) near, nearby, accessible.

fjárveiting 1. allocation; *synonyms* (*n*) allotment, portion, allowance, quota, share, **2**. budget; *synonyms* (*n*) plan, sack, (*v*) calculate, compute, (*adj*) cheap, **3**. appropriation; *synonyms* (*n*) adoption, seizure, annexation, embezzlement, assumption, **4**. grant; *synonyms* (*v*) give, allow, award, bestow, admit; *antonyms* (*v*) deny, reject.

fjarvera absence; *synonyms* (*n*) absenteeism, dearth, default, deficiency, lack; *antonyms* (*n*) presence, attendance.

fjarvídd perspective; *synonyms* (*n*) attitude, aspect, angle, outlook, prospect.

fjarvíddaráhrif perspective; *synonyms* (*n*) attitude, aspect, angle, outlook, prospect.

fjarvísi telepathy; *synonyms* (*n*) clairvoyance, insight, mind-reading, parapsychology, premonition.

fjarvist absence; *synonyms* (*n*) absenteeism, dearth, default, deficiency, lack; *antonyms* (*n*) presence, attendance.

fjarvistir absenteeism; *synonyms* (*n*) absence, nonresidence, defection, desertion, malingering.

fjárvörslumaður trustee; *synonyms* (*n*) fiduciary, guardian, regent, consignee, keeper.

fjöðrun 1. suspension; *synonyms* (*n*) delay, interruption, abeyance, break, intermission, **2**. elasticity; *synonyms* (*n*) bounce, spring, flexibility, pliability, suppleness.

fjöður 1. feather; *synonyms* (*n*) pen, pinion, plume, (*v*) fringe, cover, **2**. tongue; *synonyms* (*n*) language, dialect, idiom, lingua, speech, **3**. spring; *synonyms* (*n*) jump, leap, bound, (*v*) hop, caper.

fjöðurstafur 1. quill; *synonyms* (*n*) barb, feather, pen, pinion, prick, **2**. rachis; *synonyms* (*n*) back, backbone, spine, anchor, backrest.

fjögur four; *synonyms* (*n*) quaternity, foursome, quadruplet, quaternary, quaternion.

fjöl deal; *synonyms* (*n*) bargain, buy, agreement, (*v*) administer, allot; *antonym* (*n*) purchase.

fjölbinding overloading; *synonyms* (*n*) overload, congestion, overcrowding, overfilling, overcapacity.

fjölboð multiplex; *synonyms* (*adj*) manifold, multiple, complex, multifarious, multifold.

fjölbreytilegur polymorphic; *synonyms* (*adj*) polymorphous, pleomorphic.

fjölbreytileiki diversity; *synonyms* (*n*) variety, dissimilarity, disparity, variation, difference.

fjölbreytinn polymorphic; *synonyms* (*adj*) polymorphous, pleomorphic.

fjölbreytni 1. polymorphism; *synonyms* (*n*) pleomorphism, metaplasm, ontogeny, ovary, ovum, **2**. pluralism, **3**. diversity; *synonyms* (*n*) variety, dissimilarity, disparity, variation, difference.

fjölbrigðni polymorphism; *synonyms* (*n*) pleomorphism, metaplasm, ontogeny, ovary, ovum.

fjöldahlutfall abundance; *synonyms* (*n*) wealth, amplitude, exuberance, plenitude, (*adj*) plenty; *antonyms* (*n*) dearth, scarcity, aridity, insufficiency, lack.

fjöldi 1. frequency; *synonyms* (*n*) frequence, incidence, commonness, prevalence, constancy, **2**. number; *synonyms* (*n*) count, amount, (*v*) calculate, aggregate, enumerate.

fjölfingrun polydactyly; *synonym* (*n*) hyperdactyly.

fjölgena polygenic; *synonym* (*adj*) polygenetic.

fjölgervi allotropy; *synonym* (*n*) allotropism.

fjölgreinafyrirtæki conglomerate; *synonyms* (*n*) composite, group, complex, (*v*) accumulate, amass.

fjölgreinarekstur conglomerate; *synonyms* (*n*) composite, group, complex, (*v*) accumulate, amass.

fjölgun proliferation; *synonyms* (*n*) growth, propagation, spread, reproduction, upsurge.

fjölhæfur versatile; *synonyms* (*adj*) changeable, adaptable, variable, various, mobile.

fjöllendur pandemic; *synonyms* (*adj*) epidemic, rife, (*n*) endemic, plague, pandemia.

fjölliðun polymerization; *synonym* (*n*) polymerisation.

fjöllita polychromatic; *synonyms* (*adj*) polychromic, polychrome, motley, iridescent, (*v*) dichromatic.

fjöllitna polyploid; *synonym* (*adj*) hyperdiploid.

fjöllitnungur polyploid; *synonym* (*adj*) hyperdiploid.

fjölmæli insult; *synonyms* (*n*) dishonor, abuse, affront, contumely, (*v*) flout; *antonyms* (*v*) compliment, praise.

fjölmiðlar media; *synonyms* (*n*) medium, medial, communications, middle.

fjölmóta polymorphic; *synonyms* (*adj*) polymorphous, pleomorphic.

fjölmótun polymorphism; *synonyms* (*n*) pleomorphism, metaplasm, ontogeny, ovary, ovum.

fjölrásari multiplexer; *synonyms* (*n*) combiner, concentrator.

fjölrásun 1. multiplex; *synonyms* (*adj*) manifold, multiple, complex, multifarious, multifold, **2**. multiplexing.

fjölskylda family; *synonyms* (*n*) descent, household, name, (*adj*) home, ancestry.

fjölstig term; *synonyms* (*n*) name, expression, period, style, (*v*) call.

fjöltáun polydactyly; *synonym* (*n*) hyperdactyly.

fjöltenging multiple; *synonyms* (*adj*) manifold, many, complex, diverse, populous; *antonym* (*adj*) simple.

fjöltengja multiple; *synonyms* (*adj*) manifold, many, complex, diverse, populous; *antonym* (*adj*) simple.

fjölþætta diversify; *synonyms* (*v*) alter, change, vary, differ, modulate; *antonym* (*v*) specialize.

fjölþættur multilateral; *synonyms* (*adj*) quadrilateral, trilateral, multifaceted, multifarious, rectangular.

fjólublár violet; *synonyms* (*adj*) purple, mauve, empurpled, lavender, lilac.

fjölvi macro; *synonyms* (*adj*) comprehensive, inclusive, international, (*n*) macroinstruction, macrocommand.

fjör vitality; *synonyms* (*n*) energy, life, animation, vigor, liveliness; *antonyms* (*n*) lethargy, apathy.

fjórar four; *synonyms* (*n*) quaternity, foursome, quadruplet, quaternary, quaternion.

fjórðastigs quaternary; *synonyms* (*adj*) quaternate, (*n*) four, foursome, quadruplet, quaternion.

fjórðungsbogi quadrant; *synonyms* (*n*) quarter, sextant.

fjórðungsgeiri quadrant; *synonyms* (*n*) quarter, sextant.

fjórðungskortblöð quadrangle; *synonyms* (*n*) quad, courtyard, court, tetragon, quadrilateral.

fjórðungsmælir quadrant; *synonyms* (*n*) quarter, sextant.

fjórðungur 1. quadrant; *synonyms* (*n*) quarter, sextant, **2**. quarter; *synonyms* (*n*) area, part, district, division, (*v*) place.

fjörður 1. bight; *synonyms* (*n*) bay, inlet, cove, gulf, loop, **2**. cove; *synonyms* (*n*) cave, harbor, recess, glen, fjord, **3**. bay; *synonyms* (*n*) alcove, bark, cry,

(v) yap, roar, **4**. creek; *synonyms* (n) brook, stream, river, rivulet, (v) burn.

fjórgildur tetravalent; *synonyms* (adj) quadrivalent, tetratomic.

fjörgun quickening; *synonyms* (adj) bracing, (n) acceleration, hurrying, hastening, speedup.

fjórhliða 1. tetragonal; *synonyms* (adj) tetrad, quadrangular, quadratic, square, **2**. quadrilateral; *synonyms* (adj) multilateral, bilateral, (n) quadrangle, quad, tetragon.

fjórhliðungur quadrilateral; *synonyms* (adj) quadrangular, multilateral, (n) quadrangle, quad, tetragon.

fjórir four; *synonyms* (n) quaternity, foursome, quadruplet, quaternary, quaternion.

fjörmikill dynamic; *synonyms* (adj) active, aggressive, dynamical, energetic, forceful; *antonyms* (adj) dull, static.

fjörudoppa periwinkle; *synonyms* (n) winkle, spinster, zinnia.

fjörugrös carragheen; *synonyms* (n) carrageen, carageen.

fjörutíu forty; *synonyms* (n) forties, (adj) twoscore.

flæð fluid; *synonyms* (adj) liquid, flowing, unsettled, changeable, smooth; *antonym* (n) solid.

flæði 1. diffusion; *synonyms* (n) dissemination, dispersion, dispersal, distribution, spread, **2**. flux; *synonyms* (n) current, (v) flow, dissolve, thaw, course, **3**. osmosis; *synonym* (n) absorption, **4**. flow; *synonyms* (n) flood, discharge, (v) stream, flux, jet.

flæðiengi marsh; *synonyms* (n) bog, fen, quagmire, marish, morass.

flæðiland marsh; *synonyms* (n) bog, fen, quagmire, marish, morass.

flæðisstjórnun logistics; *synonym* (n) reasoning.

flæðistærð flow; *synonyms* (n) flood, current, discharge, (v) stream, course.

flæðitafla matrix; *synonyms* (n) die, alembic, caldron, crucible, groundmass.

flækja plexus; *synonyms* (n) mesh, rete, network, (v) net, skein.

flaga 1. scale; *synonyms* (n) flake, gamut, (v) ascend, climb, (adj) balance; *antonym* (v) descend, **2**. chip; *synonyms* (n) splinter, bit, chipping, (v) crack, cut, **3**. lamella; *synonyms* (n) lamina, gill, branchia, lamel.

flagna peel; *synonyms* (n) skin, hide, (v) hull, bark, flake.

flái bevel; *synonyms* (n) cant, inclination, chamfer, (v) slope, incline.

flak 1. wreck; *synonyms* (n) shipwreck, (v) ruin, smash, damage, spoil; *antonym* (v) conserve, **2**.

fillet; *synonyms* (n) band, strip, cincture, list, (v) filet.

flaka fillet; *synonyms* (n) band, strip, cincture, list, (v) filet.

flákagat doughnut; *synonyms* (n) donut, sinker, annulus, anulus, (v) cracker.

fláki polygon; *synonym* (n) square.

flakk 1. diffusion; *synonyms* (n) dissemination, dispersion, dispersal, distribution, spread, **2**. migration; *synonyms* (n) exodus, movement, journey, (v) flit, flitting.

flakkandi wandering; *synonyms* (adj) itinerant, nomadic, stray, erratic, (n) roving.

flangi flange; *synonyms* (n) brim, edge, lip, brink, border.

fláning exfoliation; *synonyms* (n) scale, lamination, plate, scurf, shell.

flankafero accessories; *synonyms* (n) fittings, equipment, accompaniments, garnishes, possession.

flans flange; *synonyms* (n) brim, edge, lip, brink, border.

flapi flap; *synonyms* (n) fuss, slap, (v) flop, beat, wave.

flasa 1. scurf; *synonyms* (n) dandruff, scale, scruff, dartre, exfoliation, **2**. seborrhea; *synonym* (n) stearrhea.

flaska 1. bottle; *synonyms* (n) container, flask, jug, jar, (v) preserve, **2**. ampulla, **3**. glass; *synonyms* (n) pane, bottle, drink, bowl, cup.

flaskafláki sliver; *synonyms* (n) splinter, shred, fragment, bit, (v) chip.

flaski sliver; *synonyms* (n) splinter, shred, fragment, bit, (v) chip.

flatarfjórðungur quadrant; *synonyms* (n) quarter, sextant.

flatarmál area; *synonyms* (n) place, region, size, width, expanse.

flatarmálseigind area; *synonyms* (n) place, region, size, width, expanse.

flatarmálsfræði geometry; *synonyms* (v) algebra, analysis, arithmetic, hypsometry, stereometry.

flatbytna flatboat; *synonyms* (n) barge, lighter, dugout, galiot, hoy.

flati platform; *synonyms* (n) dais, floor, rostrum, stage, stand.

flatspegill flat; *synonyms* (adj) dull, bland, even, plain, (n) apartment; *antonyms* (adj) exciting, high-pitched, bumpy.

flatur 1. prone; *synonyms* (adj) liable, apt, disposed, inclined, flat; *antonym* (adj) upright, **2**. flat; *synonyms* (adj) dull, bland, even, plain, (n) apartment; *antonyms* (adj) exciting, high-pitched, bumpy.

flaumrænn 1. analogue; *synonyms* (n) analog, parallel, counterpart, match, duplicate, **2.** analog; *synonyms* (n) analogue, computer, mate, (adj) additive, linear.

flaumur flux; *synonyms* (n) current, (v) flow, dissolve, thaw, course.

flaut 1. beep; *synonyms* (n) toot, sound, (v) hoot, tootle, blast, **2.** blast; *synonyms* (n) bang, slam, (v) attack, (adj) discharge, explosion.

flauta 1. flute; *synonyms* (n) wineglass, fluting, furrow, groove, (v) channel, **2.** beep; *synonyms* (n) toot, sound, (v) hoot, tootle, blast, **3.** blast; *synonyms* (n) bang, slam, (v) attack, (adj) discharge, explosion, **4.** horn; *synonyms* (n) hooter, cornet, klaxon, alarm, trumpet.

fleiðrubólga pleurisy; *synonym* (n) pleuritis.

fleiður 1. ulcer; *synonyms* (n) boil, (v) canker, fester, (adj) sore, cancer, **2.** abrasion; *synonyms* (n) attrition, excoriation, erosion, friction, (v) detrition; *antonym* (n) smoothness, **3.** erosion; *synonyms* (n) abrasion, corrosion, corroding, eroding, wear.

fleki 1. raft; *synonyms* (n) float, deal, flock, heap, lot, **2.** plate; *synonyms* (n) dish, leaf, (v) gild, sheet, cover, **3.** slab; *synonyms* (n) hunk, chunk, bar, (adj) table, plate, **4.** panel; *synonyms* (n) board, jury, defendant, committee, (v) empanel.

flekkblæðing ecchymosis; *synonyms* (n) effusion, exhalation, extravasation, extrusion, exudation.

flekkjaháfur wolffish; *synonyms* (n) catfish, lancetfish, mudcat.

flekklaus stainless; *synonyms* (adj) pure, spotless, chaste, clean, faultless.

flekkun spotting; *synonyms* (n) detection, staining, catching, espial, maculation.

flensa 1. influenza; *synonyms* (n) grippe, flu, plague, bug, (adj) grip, **2.** grippe; *synonym* (n) influenza, **3.** flu; *synonyms* (n) disease, sickness, infection, virus.

flesk pork; *synonyms* (n) porc, beef, chicken, ham, lamb.

flétta 1. plexus; *synonyms* (n) mesh, rete, network, (v) net, skein, **2.** combination; *synonyms* (n) alliance, blend, union, association, coalition; *antonyms* (n) separation, (adj) simple, **3.** braid; *synonyms* (n) plait, (adj) k[u]it, string, embroider, lace; *antonym* (v) unbraid, **4.** lichen; *synonym* (n) mold.

fléttari multiplexer; *synonyms* (n) combiner, concentrator.

fléttun 1. splicing; *synonyms* (n) splice, reinforcing, sticking, **2.** convolution; *synonyms* (n) coil, gyrus, twine, complexity, swirl, **3.** linkage; *synonyms* (n) link, bond, connection, association, coupling, **4.** multiplexing, **5.** multiplex; *synonyms* (adj) manifold, multiple, complex, multifarious, multifold.

fleygbein cuneiform; *synonyms* (adj) cuneate, arrowheaded, (v) runic, hieroglyphical, (n) cuniform.

fleygbogaflötur paraboloid; *synonyms* (v) parabolic, sinusoid.

fleygbogi parabola; *synonym* (n) curve.

fleygdrep 1. infarction; *synonyms* (n) infarct, constipation, **2.** infarct; *synonyms* (n) infarction, blockade.

fleygflötur paraboloid; *synonyms* (v) parabolic, sinusoid.

fleygja 1. reject; *synonyms* (v) refuse, decline, deny, disapprove, (n) cull; *antonyms* (v) accept, approve, choose, select, acknowledge, **2.** dump; *synonyms* (v) discard, ditch, abandon, drop, empty; *antonym* (v) keep.

fleygjárn wedge; *synonyms* (n) chock, (v) squeeze, compress, jam, pack.

fleyglaga sphenoid; *synonym* (adj) sphenoidal.

fleygur 1. wedge; *synonyms* (n) chock, (v) squeeze, compress, jam, pack, **2.** insert; *synonyms* (v) embed, enter, put, enclose, interject; *antonyms* (v) remove, erase.

fleyta 1. emulsify; *synonyms* (v) beat, blend, mash, soften, **2.** float; *synonyms* (n) buoy, (v) drift, swim, blow, hover; *antonym* (v) sink.

fleyti emulsion; *synonyms* (n) balm, cream, emulsification, liquid, (adj) soup.

fleytihæfni buoyancy; *synonyms* (n) airiness, animation, buoyance, cheerfulness, levity; *antonym* (n) heaviness.

fleyting flotation; *synonyms* (n) floatation, support.

flipi 1. lobe; *synonyms* (n) division, flap, limb, member, arm, **2.** flap; *synonyms* (n) fuss, slap, (v) flop, beat, wave.

flís 1. tile; *synonyms* (n) bonnet, castor, ceiling, roof, (v) cover, **2.** chip; *synonyms* (n) splinter, bit, flake, chipping, (v) crack.

flisar fragment; *synonyms* (n) fraction, crumb, (v) bit, chip, scrap.

fljóta float; *synonyms* (n) buoy, (v) drift, swim, blow, hover; *antonym* (v) sink.

fljótakrabbi crayfish; *synonyms* (n) crawfish, crawdad, crawdaddy, crabs, ecrevisse.

fljótandi 1. afloat; *synonyms* (adj) buoyant, floating, current, (adv) adrift, (v) afoot, **2.** fluid; *synonyms* (adj) liquid, flowing, unsettled, changeable, smooth; *antonym* (n) solid, **3.** liquid; *synonyms* (adj) fluent, fluid, juicy, limpid, (n) liquor; *antonyms* (adj) firm, (n) gaseous, **4.** floating; *synonyms* (adj) drifting, aimless, loose, (adv) afloat.

fljótanleiki viscosity; *synonyms* (n) consistency, ropiness, viscousness, cohesiveness, (adj) viscidity.

fljótsbreiða lake; *synonyms* (*n*) loch, pond, pool, puddle, carmine.

fljótur fast; *synonyms* (*adj*) dissolute, firm, agile, debauched, (*adv*) soon; *antonyms* (*adj*) sluggish, (*adv*) slow, slowly, (*v*) gorge, (*n*) binge.

fljúga fly; *synonyms* (*v*) escape, dash, drive, (*adj*) break, flit.

fló flea; *synonyms* (*n*) chamois, frog, goat, grasshopper, (*adj*) louse.

flóð 1. tide; *synonyms* (*n*) current, flow, stream, course, (*v*) wave, **2.** cascade; *synonyms* (*n*) waterfall, torrent, deluge, (*v*) fall, gush; *antonyms* (*v*) trickle, dribble, **3.** flux; *synonyms* (*n*) tide, flood, (*v*) dissolve, thaw, fuse, **4.** flood; *synonyms* (*n*) pour, (*v*) drench, inundate, glut, drown; *antonyms* (*n*) drought, shortage.

flóðgarður dyke; *synonyms* (*n*) dam, ditch, channel, (*v*) dike, (*adj*) lesbian.

flóðgátt lock; *synonyms* (*v*) bolt, bar, close, latch, engage; *antonyms* (*v*) unlock, open.

flóðlýsing floodlight; *synonyms* (*n*) spotlight, flood, floodlighting, alluvion, deluge.

flóðlýsingarkastari floodlight; *synonyms* (*n*) spotlight, flood, floodlighting, alluvion, deluge.

flóðlýsingarlampi floodlight; *synonyms* (*n*) spotlight, flood, floodlighting, alluvion, deluge.

flog 1. seizure; *synonyms* (*n*) arrest, capture, confiscation, seizing, apprehension; *antonyms* (*n*) release, return, **2.** epilepsy; *synonyms* (*n*) convulsion, (*v*) bustle, fits, fuss, hubbub.

flogaveiki epilepsy; *synonyms* (*n*) convulsion, (*v*) bustle, fits, fuss, hubbub.

flogaveikilyf antiepileptic; *synonym* (*n*) anticonvulsant.

flogaveikisjúklingur epileptic; *synonym* (*adj*) epileptical.

flogaveikur epileptic; *synonym* (*adj*) epileptical.

flogboði aura; *synonyms* (*n*) air, atmosphere, halo, nimbus, feel.

flogleysandi antiepileptic; *synonym* (*n*) anticonvulsant.

flögnun 1. peeling; *synonyms* (*adj*) flaking, (*n*) peel, desquamation, shelling, hull; *antonym* (*adj*) smooth, **2.** exfoliation; *synonyms* (*n*) scale, lamination, plate, scurf, shell.

flói 1. bay; *synonyms* (*n*) alcove, bark, recess, (*v*) yap, roar, **2.** creek; *synonyms* (*n*) brook, cove, bay, inlet, stream, **3.** cove; *synonyms* (*n*) cave, harbor, glen, fjord, oriel, **4.** bight; *synonyms* (*n*) gulf, loop, fiord, curve, gulph, **5.** inlet; *synonyms* (*n*) entry, entrance, arm, mouth, outlet.

flóki 1. complex; *synonyms* (*adj*) composite, complicate, abstruse, difficult, elaborate; *antonyms* (*adj*) simple, basic, straightforward, clear, plain, **2.** felt; *synonyms* (*v*) mat, snarl, tangle, (*adj*) perceived, sensed.

flókinn complex; *synonyms* (*adj*) composite, complicate, abstruse, difficult, elaborate; *antonyms* (*adj*) simple, basic, straightforward, clear, plain.

flokka sort; *synonyms* (*n*) kind, type, assortment, (*v*) class, group.

flokksformaður chairman; *synonyms* (*n*) chair, chairperson, chairwoman, director, president.

flokksmeðlimur 1. scout; *synonyms* (*n*) guide, lookout, spy, pathfinder, (*v*) explore, **2.** guide; *synonyms* (*n*) escort, directory, (*v*) direct, conduct, govern; *antonym* (*v*) follow.

flokksþing convention; *synonyms* (*n*) conference, congress, meeting, contract, assembly.

flökkuhópur migration; *synonyms* (*n*) exodus, movement, journey, (*v*) flit, flitting.

flokkun 1. rate; *synonyms* (*n*) price, worth, (*v*) assess, estimate, evaluate, **2.** classification; *synonyms* (*n*) arrangement, categorization, class, grading, assortment; *antonym* (*n*) declassification, **3.** categorization; *synonyms* (*n*) categorisation, classification, taxonomy, sorting, breakdown, **4.** grade; *synonyms* (*n*) place, rank, degree, order, (*v*) level.

flokkunarbreyta attribute; *synonyms* (*n*) assign, quality, characteristic, emblem, (*v*) ascribe.

flokkunarfræði 1. taxonomy; *synonyms* (*n*) classification, categorization, (*v*) assortment, allotment, apportionment, **2.** systematics.

flokkunarkerfi nomenclature; *synonyms* (*n*) terminology, language, classification, lyric, (*v*) name.

flokkunarvél grader; *synonyms* (*n*) backhoe, bulldozer, tractor, caterpillar, motorgrader.

flokkur 1. series; *synonyms* (*n*) chain, rank, collection, cycle, (*v*) course, **2.** category; *synonyms* (*n*) class, denomination, division, kind, type, **3.** class; *synonyms* (*n*) category, group, (*v*) sort, place, categorize, **4.** group; *synonyms* (*n*) bunch, brigade, crowd, flock, gang, **5.** party; *synonyms* (*n*) band, company, assembly, association, crew.

flökt 1. volatility; *synonyms* (*n*) fickleness, instability, flightiness, buoyancy, capriciousness, **2.** variability; *synonyms* (*n*) changeability, variableness, variance, variation, flux, **3.** drift; *synonyms* (*n*) stream, current, course, (*v*) aim, blow, **4.** jitter; *synonyms* (*n*) flicker, (*v*) fidget, quiver, tremble, shudder, **5.** flutter; *synonyms* (*n*) bustle, flap, (*v*) beat, flit, (*adj*) flurry.

flökta flutter; *synonyms* (*n*) bustle, flap, (*v*) flicker, beat, (*adj*) flurry.

flökurleiki nausea; *synonyms* (*n*) disgust, sickness, queasiness, (*v*) aversion, loathing; *antonym* (*n*) attraction.

flóra flora; *synonyms* (*n*) vegetation, plant, plants, verdure, foliage.

flöskuháls bottleneck; *synonyms* (*n*) congestion, constriction, jam, snag, (*v*) hinder.

flot 1. supernatant; *synonyms* (*adj*) buoyant, (*v*) incumbent, overlying, superincumbent, **2.** float; *synonyms* (*n*) buoy, (*v*) drift, swim, blow, hover; *antonym* (*v*) sink.

flotaforingi admiral; *synonyms* (*n*) admiralty, administration.

floteiginleiki buoyancy; *synonyms* (*n*) airiness, animation, buoyance, cheerfulness, levity; *antonym* (*n*) heaviness.

flothæfni buoyancy; *synonyms* (*n*) airiness, animation, buoyance, cheerfulness, levity; *antonym* (*n*) heaviness.

flotholt float; *synonyms* (*n*) buoy, (*v*) drift, swim, blow, hover; *antonym* (*v*) sink.

flothylki 1. sponson, **2.** pontoon; *synonyms* (*n*) float, bridge, footbridge, limber, raft, **3.** float; *synonyms* (*n*) buoy, (*v*) drift, swim, blow, hover; *antonym* (*v*) sink.

floti 1. navy; *synonyms* (*n*) fleet, armada, flotilla, blue, army, **2.** fleet; *synonyms* (*adj*) swift, fast, expeditious, agile, quick.

flotkraftur buoyancy; *synonyms* (*n*) airiness, animation, buoyance, cheerfulness, levity; *antonym* (*n*) heaviness.

flotmælir hydrometer; *synonym* (*n*) gravimeter.

flotþol buoyancy; *synonyms* (*n*) airiness, animation, buoyance, cheerfulness, levity; *antonym* (*n*) heaviness.

flötur 1. plane; *synonyms* (*n*) airplane, face, (*adj*) level, even, flat, **2.** surface; *synonyms* (*n*) outside, superficies, (*v*) appear, emerge, (*adj*) exterior; *antonyms* (*n*) core, inside, interior, middle, **3.** tier; *synonyms* (*n*) layer, row, floor, (*adj*) line, rank, **4.** area; *synonyms* (*n*) place, region, size, width, expanse, **5.** facet; *synonyms* (*n*) aspect, side, surface, part, plane.

flotvog hydrometer; *synonym* (*n*) gravimeter.

flug flight; *synonyms* (*n*) escape, herd, flying, run, avolation.

fluga fly; *synonyms* (*v*) escape, dash, drive, (*adj*) break, flit.

flúga fly; *synonyms* (*v*) escape, dash, drive, (*adj*) break, flit.

flugbann grounding; *synonyms* (*n*) earthing, basis, training, foundation, stranding.

flugbragð manoeuvre; *synonyms* (*v*) maneuver, control, direct, go, guide.

flugbraut runway; *synonyms* (*n*) track, airfield, airport, channel, tarmac.

flugdrægi range; *synonyms* (*v*) line, arrange, order, rank, roam.

flugdreki kite; *synonyms* (*n*) parachute, airplane, epistle, former, letter.

flugeldar fireworks; *synonyms* (*n*) bonfire, dispute, exhibition, explosive, noise.

flugfarþegi passenger; *synonyms* (*n*) traveler, wayfarer, itinerant, rider, voyager.

flugfélag airline; *synonym* (*n*) airway.

flugferð flight; *synonyms* (*n*) escape, herd, flying, run, avolation.

flugfragt freight; *synonyms* (*n*) cargo, load, burden, lading, (*v*) carry.

fluggeta performance; *synonyms* (*n*) act, discharge, achievement, execution, (*v*) action; *antonyms* (*n*) omission, practice.

flughæð altitude; *synonyms* (*n*) elevation, height, level, distance, eminence.

flughamur configuration; *synonyms* (*n*) form, arrangement, conformation, shape, organization.

flughlað apron; *synonyms* (*n*) forestage, proscenium, skirt, pall, pontificals.

flughöfn airport; *synonyms* (*n*) aerodrome, airdrome, runway, airstrip, depot.

flugleið 1. route; *synonyms* (*n*) course, path, road, direction, passage, **2.** airline; *synonym* (*n*) airway.

fluglipurð manoeuvrability; *synonyms* (*n*) maneuverability, drivability.

flugmaður pilot; *synonyms* (*n*) guide, leader, aviator, (*v*) manage, lead.

flugrekandi operator; *synonyms* (*n*) driver, hustler, manipulator, agent, doer.

flugskeyti missile; *synonyms* (*n*) bullet, shot, projectile, rocket, bolt.

flugskipti transfer; *synonyms* (*n*) conveyance, (*v*) convey, carry, change, remove; *antonyms* (*v*) hold, keep.

flugstöð airport; *synonyms* (*n*) aerodrome, airdrome, runway, airstrip, depot.

flugþjónn steward; *synonyms* (*n*) custodian, keeper, waiter, warden, attendant.

flugþol endurance; *synonyms* (*n*) durability, stamina, sufferance, tolerance, courage.

flugvallarmerking marking; *synonyms* (*n*) mark, earmark, brand, crisscross, marker.

flugvallarvirkt facilitation; *synonyms* (*n*) assistance, enhancement.

flugvél 1. plane; *synonyms* (*n*) airplane, face, (*adj*) level, even, flat, **2.** aircraft; *synonyms* (*n*) airliner, craft, plane, vessel, airship, **3**. airplane; *synonyms* (*n*) aeroplane, jet, seaplane, (*v*) automobile, bus, **4**. aeroplane; *synonym* (*n*) sheet.

flugvélarbrak wreck; *synonyms* (*n*) shipwreck, (*v*) ruin, smash, damage, spoil; *antonym* (*v*) conserve.

flugvélarflak wreck; *synonyms* (*n*) shipwreck, (*v*) ruin, smash, damage, spoil; *antonym* (*v*) conserve.

flugvöllur **1**. airport; *synonyms* (*n*) aerodrome, airdrome, runway, airstrip, depot, **2**. airfield; *synonyms* (*n*) airport, field, area, arena, bailiwick, **3**. aerodrome, **4**. airdrome; *synonym* (*n*) airfield.

flundra flounder; *synonyms* (*v*) falter, stumble, flop, (*adj*) blunder, boggle.

flúor fluorine; *synonyms* (*n*) f, phthor.

flúr fluorine; *synonyms* (*n*) f, phthor.

flúra megrim; *synonyms* (*n*) hemicrania, freak, migraine, humor.

flúrgeislun fluorescence; *synonyms* (*n*) phosphorescence, epipolism.

flúrljóm fluorescence; *synonyms* (*n*) phosphorescence, epipolism.

flúrljómandi fluorescent; *synonyms* (*adj*) light, phosphorescent, effulgent, phosphoric.

flúrljómun fluorescence; *synonyms* (*n*) phosphorescence, epipolism.

flúrskíma fluorescence; *synonyms* (*n*) phosphorescence, epipolism.

flúrskímandi fluorescent; *synonyms* (*adj*) light, phosphorescent, effulgent, phosphoric.

flúrskin fluorescence; *synonyms* (*n*) phosphorescence, epipolism.

flus peel; *synonyms* (*n*) skin, hide, (*v*) hull, bark, flake.

flutningafræði **1**. shipping; *synonyms* (*n*) freight, transport, conveyance, transportation, moving, **2**. logistics; *synonym* (*n*) reasoning.

flutningaprammi flatboat; *synonyms* (*n*) barge, lighter, dugout, galiot, hoy.

flutningar **1**. transport; *synonyms* (*v*) transfer, transmit, bear, carry, delight; *antonyms* (*v*) disenchant, remain, **2**. transportation; *synonyms* (*n*) deportation, banishment, exile, (*v*) transport, conveyance.

flutningaskip freighter; *synonyms* (*n*) bottom, merchantman, charterer, arse, ass.

flutningastarfsemi transportation; *synonyms* (*n*) deportation, banishment, exile, (*v*) transport, conveyance.

flutningur **1**. transplantation; *synonyms* (*n*) transplant, relocation, resettlement, graft, (*v*) transmission, **2**. transportation; *synonyms* (*n*) deportation, banishment, exile, (*v*) transport, conveyance, **3**. transport; *synonyms* (*v*) transfer, transmit, bear, carry, delight; *antonyms* (*v*) disenchant, remain, **4**. propagation; *synonyms* (*n*)

distribution, diffusion, generation, dissemination, extension, **5**. transit; *synonyms* (*n*) journey, passage, travel, movement, transportation.

flútt flush; *synonyms* (*n*) bloom, (*v*) blush, glow, (*adj*) flat, affluent.

flysjun exfoliation; *synonyms* (*n*) scale, lamination, plate, scurf, shell.

flýta expedite; *synonyms* (*v*) accelerate, dispatch, advance, hasten, assist.

flýtiminni cache; *synonyms* (*n*) depository, reserve, (*v*) hoard, store, bury.

flýting advance; *synonyms* (*n*) progress, (*v*) further, proceed, promote, (*phr*) accelerate; *antonyms* (*n*) deterioration, (*v*) retreat, recede, delay, demote.

flýtivista cache; *synonyms* (*n*) depository, reserve, (*v*) hoard, store, bury.

flýtivísun shortcut; *synonyms* (*n*) crosscut, cutoff, method, path.

flytja **1**. transfer; *synonyms* (*n*) conveyance, (*v*) convey, carry, change, remove; *antonyms* (*v*) hold, keep, **2**. present; *synonyms* (*adj*) grant, confer, (*n*) gift, donation, (*v*) bestow; *antonyms* (*adj*) missing, (*n*) past, future, (*v*) withdraw, (*adv*) absent, **3**. transport; *synonyms* (*v*) transfer, transmit, bear, delight, enrapture; *antonyms* (*v*) disenchant, remain, **4**. move; *synonyms* (*v*) act, affect, excite, go, (*n*) motion; *antonym* (*v*) stay.

flytjanlegur portable; *synonyms* (*adj*) mobile, movable, portative, light, convenient; *antonym* (*adj*) fixed.

flytjanleiki **1**. portability; *synonym* (*n*) portableness, **2**. transferability, **3**. mobility; *synonyms* (*n*) movableness, motion, movement, (*adj*) versatility.

fóarn gizzard; *synonyms* (*n*) stomach, craw, crop, maw, paunch.

fóðra feed; *synonyms* (*v*) eat, dine, nurture, (*n*) aliment, food; *antonym* (*v*) starve.

fóðring **1**. sleeve; *synonyms* (*n*) arm, case, liner, cover, cuff, **2**. bush; *synonyms* (*n*) shrub, bushing, wild, chaparral, hedge, **3**. casing; *synonyms* (*n*) shell, box, jacket, skin, boxing, **4**. bushing; *synonyms* (*n*) bush, mount, filling, **5**. liner; *synonyms* (*n*) lining, boat, airliner, craft, ship.

fóður **1**. aliment; *synonyms* (*n*) food, nutriment, sustenance, alimentation, diet, **2**. lining; *synonyms* (*n*) facing, liner, inside, cladding, padding, **3**. liner; *synonyms* (*n*) lining, boat, airliner, craft, ship.

föðurbróðir uncle; *synonym* (*n*) pawnbroker.

fóðurkál kale; *synonyms* (*n*) borecole, bread, cabbage, chou, dough.

föðurland country; *synonyms* (*n*) state, nation, home, land, area; *antonyms* (*n*) city, (*adj*) urban.

föðurlandsást patriotism; *synonyms* (*n*) nationalism, nationality, loyalty, nation, xenophobia.

föðurlandsvinur patriot; *synonyms* (*n*) nationalist, flag-waver, partisan, patrioteer, scoutmaster; *antonym* (*n*) traitor.

föðurlegur paternal; *synonyms* (*adj*) fatherly, agnate, parental, maternal, agnatic.

fóðurnæpa turnip; *synonym* (*n*) clock.

fóðurrepja rape; *synonyms* (*n*) assault, violation, colza, (*v*) outrage, pillage.

fóðurrófa rape; *synonyms* (*n*) assault, violation, colza, (*v*) outrage, pillage.

fóðurrör casing; *synonyms* (*n*) case, shell, box, jacket, skin.

föðursystir aunt; *synonyms* (*n*) auntie, aunty, uncle, nephew, niece.

fógeti magistrate; *synonyms* (*n*) judge, justice, jurist, official, provost.

fok deflation; *synonyms* (*n*) depression, reduction, depreciation, contraction, comedown; *antonym* (*n*) inflation.

fokjarðvegur loess; *synonyms* (*n*) clay, dust.

fokka jib; *synonyms* (*n*) boom, (*v*) balk, baulk, gybe, jibe.

fokmold loess; *synonyms* (*n*) clay, dust.

fókspóla concentrator; *synonym* (*n*) multiplexer.

fókun focusing; *synonyms* (*n*) centering, concentration, focus, focussing, focalisation.

fold 1. terrain; *synonyms* (*n*) ground, field, land, country, area, 2. earth; *synonyms* (*n*) dirt, world, dust, clay, lair.

földun 1. convolution; *synonyms* (*n*) coil, gyrus, twine, complexity, swirl, 2. folding; *synonyms* (*n*) fold, bend, crease, flexure, breakdown.

fólginn implicit; *synonyms* (*adj*) silent, tacit, understood, undeclared, unsaid; *antonyms* (*adj*) explicit, direct.

fólksfækkun depopulation; *synonyms* (*n*) desolation, vastation, destitution, devastation, (*adj*) desertion.

fólksfjöldi population; *synonyms* (*n*) inhabitants, people, nation, community, group.

fólksflutningar 1. transportation; *synonyms* (*n*) deportation, banishment, exile, (*v*) transport, conveyance, 2. migration; *synonyms* (*n*) exodus, movement, journey, (*v*) flit, flitting.

fólksrými cabin; *synonyms* (*n*) booth, hut, chamber, cot, lodge.

fólksþurrð depopulation; *synonyms* (*n*) desolation, vastation, destitution, devastation, (*adj*) desertion.

fölnun chlorosis; *synonyms* (*n*) greensickness, (*adj*) chorea, cynanche, dartre.

fölsun falsification; *synonyms* (*n*) fake, falsehood, distortion, deceit, deception.

fölvasýki chlorosis; *synonyms* (*n*) greensickness, (*adj*) chorea, cynanche, dartre.

fón phone; *synonyms* (*n*) earpiece, earphone, headphone, (*v*) telephone, call.

fön 1. rib; *synonyms* (*n*) ridge, (*v*) joke, tease, guy, mock, 2. barb; *synonyms* (*n*) point, arrow, jag, gibe, prickle, 3. fin; *synonyms* (*n*) spline, feather, fins, flipper, flippers.

föngun acquisition; *synonyms* (*n*) purchase, accomplishment, acquirement, attainment, achievement.

fönun fanning; *synonym* (*v*) blowing.

fóra file; *synonyms* (*n*) archive, document, list, procession, (*v*) order.

forboði notice; *synonyms* (*n*) advertisement, attention, (*v*) note, look, attend; *antonyms* (*v*) disregard, ignore.

forða save; *synonyms* (*v*) deliver, economize, rescue, conserve, (*prep*) except; *antonyms* (*v*) spend, squander, waste.

forðabúr reservoir; *synonyms* (*n*) cistern, fountain, well, lake, store.

fordæmi paradigm; *synonyms* (*n*) example, exemplar, epitome, model, archetype.

forði resource; *synonyms* (*n*) expedient, imagination, (*v*) recourse, resort, refuge.

forðun avoidance; *synonyms* (*n*) abstinence, escape, evasion, forbearance, cancellation.

foreind proton; *synonym* (*n*) electricity.

foreldrafjarvera absenteeism; *synonyms* (*n*) absence, nonresidence, defection, desertion, malingering.

foreldrar parents; *synonym* (*n*) ancestors.

forensím 1. proenzyme; *synonym* (*n*) zymogen, 2. zymogen; *synonym* (*n*) proenzyme.

forgangsréttur priority; *synonyms* (*n*) precedence, antecedence, antecedency, anteriority, precedency.

forgangur 1. priority; *synonyms* (*n*) precedence, antecedence, antecedency, anteriority, precedency, 2. precedence; *synonyms* (*n*) lead, advantage, priority, pas, preference.

forgarður vestibule; *synonyms* (*n*) hall, lobby, foyer, antechamber, hallway.

forgeislald director; *synonyms* (*n*) commander, manager, administrator, boss, (*v*) conductor.

forgjöf priming; *synonyms* (*n*) primer, undercoat, background, basis, briefing.

forgrunnur foreground; *synonyms* (*n*) forefront, front, (*v*) highlight, spotlight.

forhleðsla priming; *synonyms* (*n*) primer, undercoat, background, basis, briefing.

forhólf atrium; *synonyms* (*n*) hall, vestibule, cavity, court, foyer.

forhúð prepuce; *synonym* (*n*) foreskin.

forhúðarstýfing circumcision; *synonym* (*n*) posthetomy.

foringi master; *synonyms* (*n*) captain, instructor, (*v*) conquer, control, (*adj*) chief.

forjaxl premolar; *synonyms* (*n*) bicuspid, (*adj*) praemolar.

forkaupsréttur preemption; *synonyms* (*n*) option, (*adj*) preemptor.

forklíniskur preclinical; *synonym* (*adj*) presymptomatic.

form 1. relief; *synonyms* (*n*) comfort, aid, consolation, ease, (*v*) assistance, **2**. shape; *synonyms* (*n*) cast, mold, (*v*) form, fashion, model, **3**. format; *synonyms* (*n*) size, formatting, shape, (*v*) set, arrange, **4**. morphology; *synonyms* (*n*) accidence, anatomy, geomorphology, taxonomy, botany.

forma mold; *synonyms* (*n*) cast, matrix, (*v*) model, form, fashion.

formaður 1. president; *synonyms* (*n*) chairman, chief, chair, chairperson, chairwoman, **2**. chairman; *synonyms* (*n*) director, president, administrator, administration, gig.

formaldehýð methanal; *synonym* (*n*) formaldehyde.

formalín formalin; *synonyms* (*n*) formol, formaldehyde.

formaukning epigenesis; *synonyms* (*v*) procreation, progeneration, propagation, fertilization, gemination.

formdeild category; *synonyms* (*n*) class, denomination, division, kind, type.

formendasveiging transition; *synonyms* (*n*) change, passage, transit, alteration, changeover.

formengi domain; *synonyms* (*n*) country, department, realm, area, kingdom; *antonym* (*n*) range.

formerki sign; *synonyms* (*n*) signal, indication, mark, motion, (*v*) gesture.

formfræði morphology; *synonyms* (*n*) accidence, anatomy, geomorphology, taxonomy, botany.

formgerð structure; *synonyms* (*n*) form, building, arrangement, edifice, shape.

formgerðarflokkun typology; *synonym* (*n*) typing.

formgildur authentic; *synonyms* (*adj*) actual, genuine, accurate, real, right; *antonyms* (*adj*) bogus, fake, unrealistic.

formlaus amorphous; *synonyms* (*adj*) shapeless, formless, unformed, amphibious, epicene; *antonyms* (*adj*) distinct, defined.

formlegur technical; *synonyms* (*adj*) technological, industrial, shipshape, technic, complex.

formmyndun epigenesis; *synonyms* (*v*) procreation, progeneration, propagation, fertilization, gemination.

formrammi former; *synonyms* (*adv*) before, (*adj*) antecedent, anterior, bygone, earlier; *antonym* (*adj*) future.

formsatriði detail; *synonyms* (*n*) report, point, (*v*) describe, enumerate, relate; *antonym* (*n*) generalization.

formúla formula; *synonyms* (*n*) form, law, convention, expression, formality.

formun forming; *synonyms* (*n*) formation, shaping, form, organization, construction.

Fórna sacrifice; *synonyms* (*n*) immolation, (*v*) offering, oblation, forfeit, immolate.

fornæmi predisposition; *synonyms* (*n*) bent, bias, leaning, inclination, predilection; *antonym* (*n*) impartiality.

fórnfýsi altruism; *synonyms* (*n*) selflessness, benevolence, charity, unselfishness, generosity; *antonyms* (*n*) self-interest, selfishness.

fornmenntastefna humanism; *synonyms* (*n*) humanitarianism, culture.

fornmynd archetype; *synonyms* (*n*) original, pattern, prototype, epitome, ideal.

fornveðurfræði paleoclimatology; *synonym* (*n*) palaeoclimatology.

fornyrði archaism; *synonyms* (*n*) archaicism, medievalism, antiquity, obsoletism, relic.

forögn proton; *synonym* (*n*) electricity.

forráð hegemony; *synonyms* (*n*) power, domination, jurisdiction, leadership, reign.

forræði 1. authority; *synonyms* (*n*) ascendancy, command, sanction, administration, authorization, **2**. hegemony; *synonyms* (*n*) power, domination, jurisdiction, leadership, reign.

forréttindi privilege; *synonyms* (*n*) charter, immunity, liberty, prerogative, freedom.

forrit 1. program; *synonyms* (*n*) agenda, plan, broadcast, design, (*v*) schedule, **2**. map; *synonyms* (*n*) graph, plat, diagram, (*v*) chart, plot.

forrita program; *synonyms* (*n*) agenda, plan, broadcast, design, (*v*) schedule.

forritari programmer; *synonym* (*n*) coder.

forritseining module; *synonyms* (*n*) faculty, part, paradigm, subarray, bay.

forritun programming; *synonyms* (*n*) programing, scheduling, program, indoctrination, instruction.

forröð leader; *synonyms* (*n*) chief, guide, boss, captain, director; *antonyms* (*n*) follower, straggler.

forsalur hall; *synonyms* (*n*) corridor, foyer, lobby, mansion, vestibule.

forsenda 1. premise; *synonyms* (*n*) assumption, hypothesis, (*v*) premiss, introduce, postulate, **2**. postulate; *synonyms* (*v*) demand, assume, premise, (*n*) axiom, posit, **3**. presupposition;

synonyms (*n*) supposition, presumption, condition, postulation, guess, **4**. assumption; *synonyms* (*n*) adoption, arrogance, acceptance, belief, conclusion, **5**. criterion; *synonyms* (*n*) benchmark, measure, norm, test, canon.

forseti 1. president; *synonyms* (*n*) chairman, chief, chair, chairperson, chairwoman, **2**. chairman; *synonyms* (*n*) director, president, administrator, administration, gig, **3**. moderator; *synonyms* (*n*) mediator, arbitrator, intermediary, negotiator, umpire.

forsjálni 1. prudence; *synonyms* (*n*) foresight, care, caution, economy, (*adj*) discretion; *antonyms* (*n*) foolishness, generosity, imprudence, profligacy, **2**. precaution; *synonyms* (*n*) forethought, prevention, anticipation, circumspection, protection, **3**. foresight; *synonyms* (*n*) prevision, forecast, prospicience, calculation, (*v*) expectation.

forskaut anode; *synonym* (*n*) zincode.

forskeyti prefix; *synonyms* (*n*) preamble, foreword, prelude, (*v*) preface, attach.

forskilyrði presupposition; *synonyms* (*n*) assumption, hypothesis, supposition, presumption, premise.

forskoða preview; *synonyms* (*n*) prevue, trailer, viewing, foretaste, sample.

forskot lead; *synonyms* (*v*) head, guide, conduct, contribute, direct; *antonym* (*v*) follow.

forskrift script; *synonyms* (*n*) calligraphy, hand, book, handwriting, copy.

forskriftar normative; *synonym* (*adj*) prescriptive.

forsmíð prototype; *synonyms* (*n*) model, archetype, epitome, example, exemplar.

forsnið 1. formatting; *synonym* (*n*) format, **2**. format; *synonyms* (*n*) form, size, formatting, (*v*) set, arrange.

forsníða format; *synonyms* (*n*) form, size, formatting, (*v*) set, arrange.

forsögn 1. prognosis; *synonyms* (*n*) forecast, prediction, prospect, outlook, vaticination, **2**. prediction; *synonyms* (*n*) divination, forecasting, foresight, announcement, anticipation.

forspenna 1. preload, **2**. bias; *synonyms* (*n*) penchant, drift, (*v*) prejudice, bent, (*adj*) partiality; *antonyms* (*n*) impartiality, neutrality, fairness.

forsprengja detonator; *synonyms* (*n*) cap, explosive, capital, ceiling, chapiter.

forstillimerki preamble; *synonyms* (*n*) introduction, prelude, foreword, preface, overture.

forstillt preset; *synonyms* (*n*) presetting, (*adj*) predetermined, set, automated, automatic; *antonyms* (*adj*) manual, variable.

forstjóri president; *synonyms* (*n*) chairman, chief, chair, chairperson, chairwoman.

forstöðumaður 1. administrator; *synonyms* (*n*) executive, director, manager, boss, officer, **2**. director; *synonyms* (*n*) commander, administrator, chief, superintendent, (*v*) conductor.

forsýn preview; *synonyms* (*n*) prevue, trailer, viewing, foretaste, sample.

fortakslaus implicit; *synonyms* (*adj*) silent, tacit, understood, undeclared, unsaid; *antonyms* (*adj*) explicit, direct.

fortölur persuasion; *synonyms* (*n*) belief, opinion, faith, inducement, (*adj*) conviction; *antonyms* (*n*) force, pressure.

föruhnöttur planet; *synonyms* (*n*) globe, satellite, world, sphere, orbiter.

forvarnastarf preventive; *synonyms* (*adj*) prophylactic, preventative, defensive, (*n*) contraceptive, deterrent; *antonym* (*adj*) encouraging.

forvaxtareikningur discounting; *synonym* (*n*) capitalization.

forveri 1. precursor; *synonyms* (*n*) forerunner, harbinger, herald, antecedent, messenger; *antonyms* (*n*) descendant, successor, **2**. progenitor; *synonyms* (*n*) predecessor, ancestor, father, ascendant, forefather.

forverndarstarf preventive; *synonyms* (*adj*) prophylactic, preventative, defensive, (*n*) contraceptive, deterrent; *antonym* (*adj*) encouraging.

forvextir discount; *synonyms* (*n*) deduction, rebate, (*v*) reduce, disregard, ignore; *antonym* (*v*) increase.

forvígismaður protagonist; *synonyms* (*n*) hero, booster, champion, exponent, supporter.

forviska precognition; *synonyms* (*n*) clairvoyance, foreknowledge, perception, prenotion, presentiment.

forvörn 1. safeguarding; *synonyms* (*adj*) defensive, protective, (*n*) protection, conservation, preservation, **2**. prophylaxis; *synonym* (*n*) synteresis.

forysta hegemony; *synonyms* (*n*) power, domination, jurisdiction, leadership, reign.

fosfat phosphate; *synonym* (*n*) orthophosphate.

fosfór 1. phosphorus; *synonyms* (*n*) phosphor, daystar, **2**. phosphor; *synonyms* (*n*) phosphorus, phosphide, scintillator.

fosfórljóm phosphorescence; *synonyms* (*n*) flash, glow, light, shimmer.

fósfórljóm phosphorescence; *synonyms* (*n*) flash, glow, light, shimmer.

fosfórljómun phosphorescence; *synonyms* (*n*) flash, glow, light, shimmer.

fosfórskíma phosphorescence; *synonyms* (*n*) flash, glow, light, shimmer.

fósfórskin phosphorescence; *synonyms* (*n*) flash, glow, light, shimmer.

fosilo spade; *synonyms* (*n*) coon, nigger, (*v*) dig, grub, delve.

foss 1. waterfall; *synonyms* (*n*) cascade, cataract, falls, force, coerce, **2**. cascade; *synonyms* (*n*) waterfall, torrent, (*v*) fall, gush, stream; *antonyms* (*v*) trickle, dribble.

fóstrun nurture; *synonyms* (*v*) foster, cherish, grow, (*n*) education, breeding; *antonym* (*v*) neglect.

fóstur 1. foetus; *synonyms* (*n*) fetus, kitten, pup, **2**. fetus; *synonym* (*n*) foetus, **3**. nurture; *synonyms* (*v*) foster, cherish, grow, (*n*) education, breeding; *antonym* (*v*) neglect, **4**. embryo; *synonyms* (*n*) germ, bud, origin, nucleus, seed.

fóstureyðing abortion; *synonyms* (*n*) miscarriage, failure, fiasco, abortive, aborsement.

fósturfræði embryology; *synonym* (*n*) anatomy.

fósturfylgja afterbirth; *synonyms* (*n*) glean, cleaning.

fósturhár lanugo; *synonym* (*n*) fuzz.

fósturlát 1. abortion; *synonyms* (*n*) miscarriage, failure, fiasco, abortive, aborsement, **2**. failure; *synonyms* (*n*) bankruptcy, failing, breakdown, decline, deficiency; *antonyms* (*n*) success, achievement, hit, winner, victory, **3**. miscarriage; *synonyms* (*n*) abortion, flop, defeat, disappointment.

fósturlífsvaki progesterone; *synonym* (*n*) progestin.

fósturnesti yolk; *synonyms* (*n*) deutoplasm, suint, vitellus.

fósturþroskun development; *synonyms* (*n*) evolution, course, growth, improvement, increase; *antonyms* (*n*) deterioration, decline, neglect, decrease.

fósturvísir embryo; *synonyms* (*n*) germ, bud, origin, nucleus, seed.

fösun 1. phasing; *synonym* (*n*) synchronization, **2**. chamfering; *synonym* (*n*) bevelling, **3**. bevel; *synonyms* (*n*) cant, inclination, chamfer, (*v*) slope, incline.

fótabúnaður footwear; *synonyms* (*n*) footgear, boot.

fótalaus apodal; *synonyms* (*n*) apod, apode, (*adj*) apodous, apodan.

fótfesta holdfast; *synonyms* (*n*) fastener, clamp, fastening, lock, grasp.

fótgangandi pedestrian; *synonyms* (*n*) walker, (*adj*) commonplace, humdrum, ordinary, banal.

fótleggur leg; *synonyms* (*n*) stage, blackleg, branch, peg, post.

fótliður acetabulum; *synonym* (*n*) acetable.

fötlun 1. disability; *synonyms* (*n*) handicap, inability, disablement, disqualification, drawback, **2**. handicap; *synonyms* (*n*) balk, hurdle, barrier, (*v*) block, hamper; *antonyms* (*v*) advantage, benefit.

fótónunemi photocell; *synonyms* (*n*) photodiode, photomultiplier.

fótsnyrting podiatry; *synonym* (*n*) chiropody.

fótstólpi spur; *synonyms* (*n*) inducement, incentive, impulse, (*v*) goad, incite.

fótur 1. foot; *synonyms* (*n*) bottom, base, feet, foundation, (*v*) hoof; *antonym* (*n*) top, **2**. spur; *synonyms* (*n*) inducement, incentive, impulse, (*v*) goad, incite, **3**. mounting; *synonyms* (*n*) mount, ascent, climb, frame, (*adj*) climbing, **4**. paw; *synonyms* (*n*) hand, finger, (*v*) feel, claw, handle, **5**. feet; *synonyms* (*n*) fete, (*v*) legs, pegs, pins, trotters.

fráblástur aspiration; *synonyms* (*n*) aim, ambition, longing, ambitiousness, (*v*) desire.

frábrigði 1. abnormality; *synonyms* (*n*) aberration, anomaly, abnormalcy, deviation, eccentricity; *antonym* (*n*) normality, **2**. anomaly; *synonyms* (*n*) abnormality, anomalousness, abnormity, peculiarity, exception, **3**. exception; *synonyms* (*n*) exclusion, objection, exemption, immunity, privilege; *antonym* (*n*) inclusion.

frábrigðilegur 1. anomalous; *synonyms* (*adj*) abnormal, irregular, aberrant, atypical, deviant; *antonym* (*adj*) normal, **2**. atypical; *synonyms* (*adj*) anomalous, odd, unusual, extraordinary, uncommon; *antonyms* (*adj*) typical, model, ordinary.

frábrugðinn exceptional; *synonyms* (*adj*) special, abnormal, excellent, extraordinary, particular; *antonyms* (*adj*) common, mediocre, ordinary, average, normal.

frádrægur negative; *synonyms* (*adj*) minus, (*v*) gainsay, veto, deny, disavow; *antonyms* (*adj*) positive, optimistic, assenting, (*n*) affirmative.

frádrag decrement; *synonyms* (*n*) decrease, cut, deduction, defalcation, defect.

frádráttarbær deductible; *synonyms* (*adj*) consequential, deducible, rebatable, (*n*) excess.

frádráttarhæfur deductible; *synonyms* (*adj*) consequential, deducible, rebatable, (*n*) excess.

frádráttarmerki minus; *synonyms* (*n*) negative, (*v*) bereft, (*adj*) minor, less, lacking; *antonym* (*prep*) plus.

frádráttur 1. subtraction; *synonyms* (*n*) deduction, minus, withdrawal, addition, discount, **2**. deduction; *synonyms* (*n*) allowance, conclusion, abatement, decrease, rebate, **3**. allowance; *synonyms* (*n*) allotment, admission, quota, tolerance, maintenance.

fræ 1. seed; *synonyms* (*n*) germ, issue, posterity, root, (*v*) inseminate, **2**. semen; *synonyms* (*n*) seed, cum, ejaculate, source, birth.

fræbelgur pod; *synonyms* (*n*) capsule, hull, case, husk, (*v*) shell.

fræðasvið theory; *synonyms* (*n*) supposition, assumption, conjecture, guess, hypothesis; *antonym* (*n*) fact.

fræði theory; *synonyms* (*n*) supposition, assumption, conjecture, guess, hypothesis; *antonym* (*n*) fact.

fræðiheiti term; *synonyms* (*n*) name, expression, period, style, (*v*) call.

fræðikenning theory; *synonyms* (*n*) supposition, assumption, conjecture, guess, hypothesis; *antonym* (*n*) fact.

fræðilegur theoretical; *synonyms* (*adj*) hypothetical, abstract, speculative, theoretic, ideal; *antonyms* (*adj*) practical, concrete, real, scientific.

fræfill stamen; *synonyms* (*n*) backbone, stamina, thrum, thread, vigor.

fræhvíta 1. aleurone, 2. albumen; *synonyms* (*n*) albumin, (*adj*) glair, cream, milk, gluten, 3. endosperm.

fræll stamen; *synonyms* (*n*) backbone, stamina, thrum, thread, vigor.

fræloðna coma; *synonyms* (*n*) lethargy, trance, dream, stupor, sleep.

fræmyndun seeding; *synonyms* (*n*) sowing, farming, plantlet, salting, spiking.

frænafli hilum; *synonym* (*n*) hilus.

frændfólk 1. relatives; *synonyms* (*n*) family, relations, kin, kindred, kinsfolk, 2. relations; *synonyms* (*n*) dealings, connections, people, contact, folks, 3. kin; *synonyms* (*n*) folk, house, clan, gender, stock.

frændi 1. relation; *synonyms* (*n*) connection, account, narration, recital, affinity, 2. relative; *synonyms* (*adj*) related, comparative, proportionate, (*n*) relation, (*v*) kinsman; *antonym* (*adj*) absolute, 3. cousin; *synonyms* (*n*) nephew, friend, companion, allied, 4. kinsman; *synonyms* (*n*) relative, kindred, brother, (*v*) ally, auxiliary.

frændsemi relation; *synonyms* (*n*) connection, account, narration, recital, affinity.

fræni stigma; *synonyms* (*n*) spot, blot, brand, stain, blemish.

frænka cousin; *synonyms* (*n*) nephew, friend, companion, allied.

fræsa mill; *synonyms* (*n*) grind, factory, grinder, manufactory, (*v*) crush.

fræsæti placenta; *synonyms* (*n*) secundines, sporophore.

fræsing milling; *synonyms* (*adj*) shuffling, (*n*) mill, grinding, fulling, routing.

fræskurn integument; *synonyms* (*n*) cover, film, coat, skin, tegument.

fræsun milling; *synonyms* (*adj*) shuffling, (*n*) mill, grinding, fulling, routing.

fræva pistil; *synonyms* (*n*) gynoecium, epistle.

frævill stamen; *synonyms* (*n*) backbone, stamina, thrum, thread, vigor.

frævísir ovule; *synonyms* (*n*) ellipse, oval, gemmule, germ, ovulum.

frævísishimna integument; *synonyms* (*n*) cover, film, coat, skin, tegument.

fráfæra abduct; *synonyms* (*v*) kidnap, snatch, abduce, ravish, crimp; *antonym* (*v*) release.

fráfærandi efferent; *synonyms* (*adj*) centrifugal, motorial.

fráfærir abductor; *synonyms* (*n*) crook, kidnapper, snatcher, badger, contrabandist.

fráfærsla abduction; *synonyms* (*n*) rape, capture, seizure, ravishment, (*v*) ablation; *antonym* (*n*) release.

frágangsmeðhöndlun finishing; *synonyms* (*adj*) ending, closing, last, (*n*) finish, completion.

frágangsvinna finish; *synonyms* (*v*) end, complete, achieve, (*n*) close, consummate; *antonyms* (*v*) start, begin, continue, (*n*) beginning.

frágangur finish; *synonyms* (*v*) end, complete, achieve, (*n*) close, consummate; *antonyms* (*v*) start, begin, continue, (*n*) beginning.

fragt freight; *synonyms* (*n*) cargo, load, burden, lading, (*v*) carry.

fragtvél freighter; *synonyms* (*n*) bottom, merchantman, charterer, arse, ass.

fráhalli divergence; *synonyms* (*n*) discrepancy, difference, disagreement, dissimilarity, variance; *antonyms* (*n*) convergence, meeting, agreement, amalgamation.

fráhallur divergent; *synonyms* (*adj*) different, differing, dissimilar, distinct, conflicting; *antonyms* (*adj*) similar, convergent.

fráhrinding repulsion; *synonyms* (*n*) repugnance, revulsion, antipathy, aversion, disgust; *antonyms* (*n*) attraction, charm.

fráhrindingarkraftur repulsion; *synonyms* (*n*) repugnance, revulsion, antipathy, aversion, disgust; *antonyms* (*n*) attraction, charm.

fráhvarf 1. recession; *synonyms* (*n*) decline, depression, fall, niche, recess, 2. abstinence; *synonyms* (*n*) abstemiousness, abstention, forbearance, temperance, chastity; *antonym* (*n*) indulgence.

fráhverfa divergence; *synonyms* (*n*) discrepancy, difference, disagreement, dissimilarity, variance; *antonyms* (*n*) convergence, meeting, agreement, amalgamation.

fráhverfur 1. abaxial; *synonyms* (*adj*) abaxile, dorsal, 2. divergent; *synonyms* (*adj*) different, differing, dissimilar, distinct, conflicting; *antonyms* (*adj*) similar, convergent.

frákennilegur atypical; *synonyms* (*adj*) abnormal, anomalous, irregular, aberrant, odd; *antonyms* (*adj*) typical, normal, model, ordinary.

fráklipping shielding; *synonyms* (*n*) shadowing, (*adj*) protective, covering, protecting, caring.

frakseno ashes; *synonyms* (*n*) dust, cinder, cinders, remains, clay.

frálægur efferent; *synonyms* (*adj*) centrifugal, motorial.

frálag output; *synonyms* (*n*) crop, harvest, turnout, yield, (*v*) outcome.

fráleiðsla abduction; *synonyms* (*n*) rape, capture, seizure, ravishment, (*v*) ablation; *antonym* (*n*) release.

frálifun catabolism; *synonyms* (*n*) dissimilation, katabolism, anabolism, metabolism, disassimilation.

frálíking dissimilation; *synonyms* (*n*) catabolism, act, katabolism.

fram 1. pass; *synonyms* (*v*) flow, deliver, give, (*adj*) go, run; *antonym* (*v*) fail, **2.** front; *synonyms* (*adj*) head, (*n*) countenance, forefront, (*v*) face, confront; *antonyms* (*n*) rear, end, (*v*) back, **3.** forward; *synonyms* (*adv*) onward, (*adj*) bold, audacious, (*v*) advance, (*phr*) dispatch; *antonyms* (*adv*) backward, (*adj*) shy, posterior.

framan 1. front; *synonyms* (*adj*) head, (*n*) countenance, forefront, (*v*) face, confront; *antonyms* (*n*) rear, end, (*v*) back, **2.** frontal; *synonyms* (*adj*) front, anterior, fore, forward, (*n*) facade.

framandi 1. alien; *synonyms* (*adj*) foreign, strange, unknown, (*n*) foreigner, (*v*) alienate; *antonyms* (*adj*) familiar, (*n*) native, citizen, **2.** allochthonous, **3.** adventitious; *synonyms* (*adj*) accidental, casual, random, additional, adventive.

framátt forward; *synonyms* (*adv*) onward, (*adj*) bold, audacious, (*v*) advance, (*phr*) dispatch; *antonyms* (*adv*) backward, (*adj*) shy, posterior.

frambjóðandi candidate; *synonyms* (*n*) applicant, aspirant, contestant, contender, hopeful.

framboð 1. supply; *synonyms* (*n*) provision, (*v*) furnish, stock, afford, fill, **2.** supplies; *synonyms* (*n*) food, provisions, stores, (*v*) equipment, outfit.

frambolur thorax; *synonyms* (*n*) chest, pectus, bosom, bust, bureau.

framburðarmállýska accent; *synonyms* (*n*) stress, dialect, emphasis, (*v*) emphasize, emphasise.

framburður 1. articulation; *synonyms* (*n*) enunciation, joint, juncture, accent, diction, **2.** deposition; *synonyms* (*n*) deposit, affidavit, declaration, dethronement, (*v*) deposal, **3.** load; *synonyms* (*n*) charge, cargo, freight, (*v*) burden, fill; *antonym* (*v*) unload.

framdráttur extraction; *synonyms* (*n*) descent, ancestry, birth, origin, family; *antonym* (*n*) insertion.

framdrif propulsion; *synonyms* (*n*) actuation, momentum, push, thrust, power.

framdrift propulsion; *synonyms* (*n*) actuation, momentum, push, thrust, power.

framfærlsueyrir maintenance; *synonyms* (*n*) livelihood, alimony, care, keep, living; *antonym* (*n*) end.

framfærsla drainage; *synonyms* (*n*) drain, drive, emanation, (*adj*) arefaction, dephlegmation.

framfærslufé maintenance; *synonyms* (*n*) livelihood, alimony, care, keep, living; *antonym* (*n*) end.

framfærslumeðlag maintenance; *synonyms* (*n*) livelihood, alimony, care, keep, living; *antonym* (*n*) end.

framfall prolapse; *synonyms* (*n*) prolapsus, descent, prolapsion, (*v*) descend, protrude.

framfarasinnaður 1. progressive; *synonyms* (*adj*) advanced, forward, gradual, active, (*n*) liberal; *antonyms* (*adj*) old-fashioned, traditional, (*n*) conservative, **2.** liberal; *synonyms* (*adj*) generous, bountiful, free, handsome, abundant; *antonyms* (*adj*) strict, oppressive, totalitarian, intolerant.

framferð transmission; *synonyms* (*n*) circulation, conveyance, contagion, transfer, broadcast.

framferðarhlutfall transmittance; *synonyms* (*n*) transmission, transmittal, contagion, infection, passage.

framför 1. progress; *synonyms* (*n*) headway, improvement, furtherance, (*v*) advance, proceed; *antonyms* (*n*) decline, deterioration, (*v*) regress, **2.** development; *synonyms* (*n*) evolution, course, growth, increase, progress; *antonyms* (*n*) neglect, decrease.

framfylgja enforce; *synonyms* (*v*) coerce, compel, constrain, apply, (*n*) force.

framgangsmáti procedure; *synonyms* (*n*) process, formula, practice, routine, fashion.

framgír advance; *synonyms* (*n*) progress, (*v*) further, proceed, promote, (*phr*) accelerate; *antonyms* (*n*) deterioration, (*v*) retreat, recede, delay, demote.

framgómur palate; *synonyms* (*n*) gusto, liking, relish, taste, tooth.

framhald restart; *synonyms* (*v*) resume, continue, recommence, renew, (*n*) reboot.

framheili prosencephalon; *synonym* (*n*) forebrain.

framhjá pass; *synonyms* (*v*) flow, deliver, give, (*adj*) go, run; *antonym* (*v*) fail.

framhjáhlaup bypass; *synonyms* (*n*) detour, diversion, (*v*) avoid, circumvent, evade.

framhjátenging jumper; *synonyms* (*n*) sweater, blackguard, bounder, cad, dog.

framhlaup slump; *synonyms* (*n*) depression, decline, (*v*) drop, fall, sag; *antonyms* (*n*) upturn, (*v*) rise.

framhlið face; *synonyms* (*n*) look, aspect, countenance, (*v*) confront, (*adj*) front; *antonyms* (*v*) avoid, back.

framhluti anterior; *synonyms* (*adj*) antecedent, prior, fore, former, forward; *antonym* (*adj*) posterior.

framígrip interruption; *synonyms* (*n*) cessation, break, disruption, halt, hindrance.

framjaxl premolar; *synonyms* (*n*) bicuspid, (*adj*) praemolar.

framkalla 1. develop; *synonyms* (*v*) advance, amplify, educate, expand, grow; *antonyms* (*v*) decrease, erupt, neglect, regress, 2. induce; *synonyms* (*v*) attract, generate, cause, tempt, impel.

framknúning propulsion; *synonyms* (*n*) actuation, momentum, push, thrust, power.

framkoma 1. deportment; *synonyms* (*n*) behavior, bearing, conduct, demeanor, (*v*) carriage, 2. conduct; *synonyms* (*n*) administration, manage, (*v*) act, bring, direct, 3. behaviour; *synonyms* (*n*) demeanour, deportment, doings.

framkvæma 1. implement; *synonyms* (*v*) execute, fulfil, (*n*) tool, apparatus, utensil, 2. enforce; *synonyms* (*v*) coerce, compel, constrain, apply, (*n*) force, 3. execute; *synonyms* (*v*) do, achieve, complete, perform, accomplish.

framkvæmd 1. implementation; *synonyms* (*n*) execution, fulfillment, enforcement, accomplishment, effectuation, 2. praxis; *synonyms* (*n*) practice, accidence, grammar, punctuation, custom, 3. transaction; *synonyms* (*n*) deal, business, dealing, dealings, proceeding; *antonym* (*n*) purchase, 4. administration; *synonyms* (*n*) management, direction, organization, running, power, 5. performance; *synonyms* (*n*) act, discharge, achievement, observance, (*v*) action; *antonym* (*n*) omission.

framkvæmdaaðili operator; *synonyms* (*n*) driver, hustler, manipulator, agent, doer.

framkvæmdastjóri 1. director; *synonyms* (*n*) commander, manager, administrator, boss, (*v*) conductor, 2. manager; *synonyms* (*n*) director, coach, executive, head, leader; *antonym* (*n*) underling.

framkvæmdastjórnin commission; *synonyms* (*n*) board, mission, delegation, job, (*v*) assign.

framlægt anterior; *synonyms* (*adj*) antecedent, prior, fore, former, forward; *antonym* (*adj*) posterior.

framlægur anterior; *synonyms* (*adj*) antecedent, prior, fore, former, forward; *antonym* (*adj*) posterior.

framlag contribution; *synonyms* (*n*) allowance, donation, gift, offering, share.

framlagsloforð subscription; *synonyms* (*n*) contribution, donation, offering, (*v*) allowance, subsidy.

framlegð yield; *synonyms* (*n*) produce, return, (*v*) surrender, allow, concede; *antonyms* (*v*) resist, persevere.

framleiðandi 1. producer; *synonyms* (*n*) director, creator, manufacturer, author, maker, 2. manufacturer; *synonyms* (*n*) builder, artificer, shaper, producer, artist.

framleiðinn productive; *synonyms* (*adj*) fertile, fruitful, plentiful, fat, generative; *antonyms* (*adj*) unproductive, barren, unprofitable.

framleiðni productivity; *synonyms* (*n*) efficiency, fertility, fruitfulness, productiveness, abundance; *antonym* (*n*) fruitlessness.

framleiðsla 1. production; *synonyms* (*n*) output, generation, product, manufacturing, performance, 2. product; *synonyms* (*n*) fruit, merchandise, proceeds, outgrowth, (*v*) produce, 3. manufacture; *synonyms* (*n*) construction, fabrication, formation, (*v*) construct, make, 4. manufacturing; *synonyms* (*adj*) industrial, (*n*) production, business, engineering, trade, 5. output; *synonyms* (*n*) crop, harvest, turnout, yield, (*v*) outcome.

framleiðslugeta 1. productivity; *synonyms* (*n*) efficiency, fertility, fruitfulness, productiveness, abundance; *antonym* (*n*) fruitlessness, 2. capacity; *synonyms* (*n*) capability, aptitude, capacitance, function, (*adj*) ability; *antonyms* (*n*) inability, incapability.

framleiðslugrein industry; *synonyms* (*n*) business, application, diligence, effort, industriousness.

framleiðsluréttur franchise; *synonyms* (*n*) exemption, liberty, freedom, immunity, privilege.

framleiðsluþáttur resource; *synonyms* (*n*) expedient, imagination, (*v*) recourse, resort, refuge.

framleiðsluvara 1. product; *synonyms* (*n*) fruit, output, merchandise, proceeds, (*v*) produce, 2. output; *synonyms* (*n*) crop, harvest, turnout, yield, (*v*) outcome.

framlenging 1. renewal; *synonyms* (*n*) renaissance, revival, rebirth, reclamation, rehabilitation, 2. extension; *synonyms* (*n*) continuation, augmentation, enlargement, expansion, addition; *antonyms* (*n*) limitation, contraction, limit, 3. elongation; *synonyms* (*n*) extension, length, production, annex, annexe.

framlengja prolong; *synonyms* (*v*) continue, extend, delay, protract, elongate; *antonyms* (*v*) shorten, stop.

frammæltur front; *synonyms* (*adj*) head, (*n*) countenance, forefront, (*v*) face, confront; *antonyms* (*n*) rear, end, (*v*) back.

frammistaða achievement; *synonyms* (*n*) accomplishment, performance, completion, deed, execution; *antonym* (*n*) failure.

frammistöðuviðmið benchmark; *synonyms* (*n*) criterion, measure, gauge, norm, landmark.

Framræsla drainage; *synonyms* (*n*) drain, drive, emanation, (*adj*) arefaction, dephlegmation.

framrás progression; *synonyms* (*n*) advance, progress, headway, improvement, (*v*) advancement.

framreikningur extrapolation; *synonym* (*n*) projection.

framrúða 1. windscreen; *synonym* (*n*) windshield, 2. windshield; *synonym* (*n*) windscreen.

framsækinn progressive; *synonyms* (*adj*) advanced, forward, gradual, active, (*n*) liberal; *antonyms* (*adj*) old-fashioned, traditional, (*n*) conservative.

framsal 1. propagation; *synonyms* (*n*) distribution, diffusion, generation, dissemination, extension, 2. delegation; *synonyms* (*n*) commission, delegacy, deputation, delegating, devolution, 3. endorsement; *synonyms* (*n*) approbation, corroboration, confirmation, sanction, approval.

framselja 1. transfer; *synonyms* (*n*) conveyance, (*v*) convey, carry, change, remove; *antonyms* (*v*) hold, keep, 2. endorse; *synonyms* (*v*) defend, approve, back, certify, confirm; *antonyms* (*v*) disapprove, oppose.

framseljanlegur 1. transferable; *synonyms* (*adj*) movable, negotiable, assignable, conveyable, moveable, 2. negotiable; *synonyms* (*adj*) alienable, passable, transferable, liquid, transferrable.

framsenda forward; *synonyms* (*adv*) onward, (*adj*) bold, audacious, (*v*) advance, (*phr*) dispatch; *antonyms* (*adv*) backward, (*adj*) shy, posterior.

framsetning 1. presentation; *synonyms* (*n*) donation, exhibition, demonstration, display, introduction, 2. representation; *synonyms* (*n*) image, performance, depiction, picture, presentation, 3. format; *synonyms* (*n*) form, size, formatting, (*v*) set, arrange.

framskögun protrusion; *synonyms* (*n*) projection, bulge, prominence, protuberance, bump.

framsókn precession; *synonyms* (*n*) precedence, antecedence, antecedency, anteriority, precedency.

framstæður initial; *synonyms* (*adj*) beginning, first, elementary, incipient, foremost.

framtak 1. initiative; *synonyms* (*n*) enterprise, gumption, (*adj*) initial, inaugural, initiatory, 2. enterprise; *synonyms* (*n*) business, company, concern, endeavor, activity.

framtaksleysi inertia; *synonyms* (*n*) inactivity, idleness, lethargy, inaction, apathy; *antonym* (*n*) momentum.

framþróun 1. development; *synonyms* (*n*) evolution, course, growth, improvement, increase; *antonyms* (*n*) deterioration, decline, neglect, decrease, 2. evolution; *synonyms* (*n*) development, expansion, movement, process, progress.

framtíðarspá forecast; *synonyms* (*v*) presage, anticipate, augur, calculate, portend.

framtíðarsýn scenario; *synonyms* (*n*) plot, continuity, chronicle, design, forecast.

framundan ahead; *synonyms* (*adv*) before, beforehand, formerly, forward, (*adj*) front; *antonyms* (*adv*) behind, late.

framvinda 1. succession; *synonyms* (*n*) sequence, round, run, series, chain, 2. progress; *synonyms* (*n*) headway, improvement, furtherance, (*v*) advance, proceed; *antonyms* (*v*) decline, deterioration, (*v*) regress, 3. progression; *synonyms* (*n*) progress, course, development, evolution, (*v*) advancement.

frárás outlet; *synonyms* (*n*) shop, market, egress, exit, opening.

frárennsli drain; *synonyms* (*n*) ditch, culvert, (*v*) deplete, waste, (*adj*) cloaca; *antonym* (*v*) bolster.

frárennslisop drain; *synonyms* (*n*) ditch, culvert, (*v*) deplete, waste, (*adj*) cloaca; *antonym* (*v*) bolster.

fráskilinn divorced; *synonyms* (*adj*) separate, single, (*adv*) apart.

frásog absorption; *synonyms* (*n*) assimilation, attention, concentration, inhalation, engrossment.

frásögn storyline; *synonyms* (*n*) plot, drift, gist, sequence, theme.

frátakanlegt detachable; *synonyms* (*adj*) movable, removable, divisible, distinguishable, isolatable; *antonym* (*adj*) inseparable.

frátenging releasing; *synonyms* (*adj*) cathartic, evacuant, psychotherapeutic, purgative, (*n*) acquittal.

frátengja 1. disengage; *synonyms* (*v*) detach, discharge, disentangle, (*adj*) clear, disembarrass; *antonyms* (*v*) fasten, engage, 2. disconnect; *synonyms* (*v*) abstract, disengage, divide, separate, deactivate; *antonyms* (*v*) connect, attach.

frauð foam; *synonyms* (*n*) froth, spume, (*v*) boil, bubble, effervesce.

frávarp projection; *synonyms* (*n*) bulge, hump, jut, prominence, protuberance.

fráveita drainage; *synonyms* (*n*) drain, drive, emanation, (*adj*) arefaction, dephlegmation.

frávik 1. aberration; *synonyms* (*n*) aberrance, aberrancy, abnormality, deviation, diversion, 2.

deviate; *synonyms* (v) depart, deflect, stray, vary, (adj) deviant; *antonym* (v) conform, **3**. residual; *synonyms* (adj) remaining, leftover, (n) remnant, residue, balance, **4**. variance; *synonyms* (n) difference, disagreement, discrepancy, dissension, division, **5**. deflection; *synonyms* (n) bend, deflexion, variation, bending, digression.

frávilla aberration; *synonyms* (n) aberrance, aberrancy, abnormality, deviation, diversion.

frávísun refusal; *synonyms* (n) declination, denial, negative, no, rebuff; *antonym* (n) permission.

freðinn frozen; *synonyms* (adj) cold, frosty, arctic, frigid, glacial; *antonyms* (adj) hot, moving.

freðmýri tundra; *synonyms* (n) plain, waste, (adj) north.

freisting temptation; *synonyms* (n) enticement, lure, attraction, bait, allurement; *antonym* (n) repulsion.

frekna lentigo; *synonyms* (n) freckle, blemish, lenticel, lenticula, freckles.

frelsa liberate; *synonyms* (v) discharge, emancipate, clear, extricate, deliver; *antonyms* (v) confine, enslave.

frelsi freedom; *synonyms* (n) exemption, autonomy, deliverance, discharge, (adj) franchise; *antonyms* (n) imprisonment, restriction, captivity, dependence, restraint.

frelsissvipting imprisonment; *synonyms* (n) captivity, custody, confinement, incarceration, durance; *antonyms* (n) freedom, release.

fremdardýr primates; *synonym* (n) squirarchy.

fremra primary; *synonyms* (adj) chief, basic, elementary, essential, (n) paramount; *antonym* (adj) secondary.

fremstur extreme; *synonyms* (adj) deep, excessive, enormous, immoderate, (n) edge; *antonyms* (adj) middle, reasonable, (n) mild, moderate, slight.

fresta 1. adjourn; *synonyms* (v) postpone, defer, delay, dissolve, procrastinate, **2**. delay; *synonyms* (n) pause, arrest, deferment, wait, (v) check; *antonyms* (n) punctuality, decisiveness, (v) rush, advance.

frestun 1. respite; *synonyms* (n) reprieve, pause, repose, break, intermission, **2**. suspension; *synonyms* (n) delay, interruption, abeyance, recess, respite, **3**. delay; *synonyms* (n) arrest, deferment, wait, (v) defer, check; *antonyms* (n) punctuality, decisiveness, (v) rush, advance.

frestur 1. respite; *synonyms* (n) reprieve, pause, repose, break, intermission, **2**. deadline; *synonyms* (n) limit, end, aim, goal, target.

tretur flatus, *synonyms* (n) breath, fart, wind, (adj) gas, air.

freyða foam; *synonyms* (n) froth, spume, (v) boil, bubble, effervesce.

freyjublóm aconite; *synonyms* (n) belladonna, hellebore, hemlock, henbane, nightshade.

frí leave; *synonyms* (v) depart, forsake, go, abandon, desert; *antonyms* (v) arrive, enter, stay, remain, approach.

friðarhugsjón pacifism; *synonyms* (n) passivism, peace.

friðarstefna pacifism; *synonyms* (n) passivism, peace.

friðarstillir conciliator; *synonyms* (n) peacemaker, mediator, arbitrator, intermediary, negotiator.

friðdómari magistrate; *synonyms* (n) judge, justice, jurist, official, provost.

friðhelgi 1. privacy; *synonyms* (n) seclusion, secrecy, confidentiality, darkness, privateness, **2**. immunity; *synonyms* (n) exemption, freedom, franchise, dispensation, privilege; *antonym* (n) vulnerability, **3**. integrity; *synonyms* (n) honesty, probity, completeness, fairness, (adj) candor; *antonyms* (n) dishonesty, wickedness.

fríðindi immunity; *synonyms* (n) exemption, freedom, franchise, dispensation, privilege; *antonym* (n) vulnerability.

friðkauparstefna appeasement; *synonyms* (n) conciliation, pacification, reconciliation, relief, indulgence.

friðland reserve; *synonyms* (n) backup, (v) keep, save, book, maintain; *antonyms* (n) openness, friendliness, informality, warmth.

friðþæging appeasement; *synonyms* (n) conciliation, pacification, reconciliation, relief, indulgence.

friðun 1. protection; *synonyms* (n) defense, care, conservation, cover, (v) guard; *antonym* (n) destruction, **2**. preservation; *synonyms* (n) maintenance, keeping, protection, custody, upkeep; *antonyms* (n) extinction, release.

friður peace; *synonyms* (n) calm, harmony, serenity, hush, (adj) quiet; *antonyms* (n) noise, chaos, conflict, uproar, commotion.

frígangur play; *synonyms* (v) act, pastime, enact, (n) frolic, game; *antonym* (v) work.

fríhæð clearance; *synonyms* (n) clearing, clearage, disposal, headroom, settlement; *antonyms* (n) blockage, retention.

fríhjól freewheel; *synonyms* (v) drift, coast, blow, cast, cruise.

fríholt fender; *synonyms* (n) wing, cushion, guard, cowcatcher, (v) buffer.

frímerki stamp; *synonyms* (n) mark, seal, brand, (v) imprint, print.

frístund leisure; *synonyms* (n) ease, idleness, convenience, vacation, (adj) idle; *antonym* (n) work.

frítími leisure; *synonyms* (n) ease, idleness, convenience, vacation, (adj) idle; *antonym* (n) work.

frjálslyndi liberalism; *synonyms* (*n*) autonomy, tolerance, permissiveness, progressiveness, (*adj*) liberality; *antonym* (*n*) narrow-mindedness.

frjálslyndisstefna liberalism; *synonyms* (*n*) autonomy, tolerance, permissiveness, progressiveness, (*adj*) liberality; *antonym* (*n*) narrow-mindedness.

frjálslyndur liberal; *synonyms* (*adj*) generous, bountiful, free, handsome, abundant; *antonyms* (*adj*) strict, oppressive, totalitarian, intolerant, (*n*) conservative.

frjálsræði latitude; *synonyms* (*n*) breadth, freedom, room, scope, expanse.

frjó 1. spermatozoon; *synonyms* (*n*) sperm, metaplasm, ontogeny, ovary, ovum, **2.** pollen; *synonym* (*n*) farina, **3.** sperm; *synonyms* (*n*) seed, semen, spermatozoon, germ, birth.

frjófruma 1. spermatozoon; *synonyms* (*n*) sperm, metaplasm, ontogeny, ovary, ovum, **2.** sperm; *synonyms* (*n*) seed, semen, spermatozoon, germ, birth.

frjóhnappshelmingur theca; *synonyms* (*n*) sheath, case, casing, sac, vagina.

frjókorn pollen; *synonym* (*n*) farina.

frjómáttur fecundity; *synonyms* (*n*) fertility, fruitfulness, productivity, richness, productiveness.

frjómóðurfruma spermatocyte; *synonyms* (*n*) spermatoblast, spermoblast.

frjór fertile; *synonyms* (*adj*) productive, fat, fecund, abundant, affluent; *antonyms* (*adj*) infertile, sterile.

frjósa freeze; *synonyms* (*n*) frost, (*v*) congeal, chill, arrest, cool; *antonyms* (*v*) melt, thaw, boil.

frjósamur fertile; *synonyms* (*adj*) productive, fat, fecund, abundant, affluent; *antonyms* (*adj*) infertile, sterile.

frjósemi 1. productivity; *synonyms* (*n*) efficiency, fertility, fruitfulness, productiveness, abundance; *antonym* (*n*) fruitlessness, **2.** fecundity; *synonyms* (*n*) productivity, richness, birthrate, lushness, (*adj*) uberty, **3.** fertility; *synonyms* (*n*) fecundity, affluence, natality, plenty, prolificacy; *antonyms* (*n*) sterility, infertility.

frjóvgaður fertile; *synonyms* (*adj*) productive, fat, fecund, abundant, affluent; *antonyms* (*adj*) infertile, sterile.

frjóvgun fertilization; *synonyms* (*n*) fecundation, fertilisation, dressing, impregnation, (*v*) gemination.

fróa relieve; *synonyms* (*v*) assuage, comfort, ease, allay, (*n*) alleviate; *antonyms* (*v*) worsen, burden.

fróð information; *synonyms* (*n*) advice, communication, data, evidence, note.

froða foam; *synonyms* (*n*) froth, spume, (*v*) boil, bubble, effervesce.

frosinn frozen; *synonyms* (*adj*) cold, frosty, arctic, frigid, glacial; *antonyms* (*adj*) hot, moving.

froskdýr amphibia; *synonyms* (*n*) caecilians, frogs, newts, salamanders, toads.

froskur frog; *synonyms* (*n*) frogs, toad, aigulet, anuran, batrachian.

frostkafli freeze; *synonyms* (*n*) frost, (*v*) congeal, chill, arrest, cool; *antonyms* (*v*) melt, thaw, boil.

frostþurrkun lyophilization; *synonym* (*n*) lyophilisation.

frú 1. lady; *synonyms* (*n*) dame, gentlewoman, female, ma'am, matron; *antonym* (*n*) man, **2.** madam; *synonyms* (*n*) lady, wife, signora, bird, chick, **3.** missis; *synonym* (*n*) missus, **4.** mistress; *synonyms* (*n*) concubine, inamorata, madame, lover, missis.

frúktósi 1. fructose; *synonyms* (*n*) levulose, laevulose, **2.** levulose; *synonym* (*n*) fructose.

fruma cell; *synonyms* (*n*) cage, jail, cadre, hole, cave.

frumbernska infancy; *synonyms* (*n*) babyhood, childhood, cradle, beginning, birth.

frumbernskur infantile; *synonyms* (*adj*) childish, immature, infant, babyish, infantine; *antonym* (*adj*) mature.

frumbjarga autotrophic; *synonym* (*adj*) autophytic.

frumbreyta argument; *synonyms* (*n*) controversy, debate, matter, proof, reason; *antonyms* (*n*) agreement, harmony.

frumbyggi 1. aboriginal; *synonyms* (*adj*) native, original, early, autochthonous, (*n*) aborigine; *antonym* (*adj*) nonnative, **2.** aborigine; *synonyms* (*n*) aboriginal, cannibal, citizen, inhabitant, **3.** autochthon; *synonym* (*n*) indigene, **4.** native; *synonyms* (*adj*) inborn, inherent, innate, natural, (*n*) autochthon; *antonyms* (*adj*) foreign, learned, (*n*) stranger, immigrant, imported, **5.** indigenous; *synonyms* (*adj*) domestic, endemic, vernacular, congenital, autochthonal.

frumdeild somite; *synonyms* (*n*) metamere, segment, portion, section, somatome.

frumdýr 1. protozoon; *synonym* (*n*) protozoan, **2.** protozoa; *synonyms* (*n*) amoebas, foraminifers, metaplasm, ontogeny, ovary.

frumefnabreyting transmutation; *synonyms* (*n*) conversion, transformation, alteration, change, metamorphosis.

frumefni element; *synonyms* (*n*) component, constituent, ingredient, factor, substance.

frumeind atom; *synonyms* (*n*) jot, grain, molecule, particle, speck.

frumeintak prototype; *synonyms* (*n*) model, archetype, epitome, example, exemplar.

frumflokkun categorization; *synonyms* (*n*) categorisation, classification, taxonomy, sorting, arrangement.

frumflokkur category; *synonyms* (*n*) class, denomination, division, kind, type.

frumfóstur embryo; *synonyms* (*n*) germ, bud, origin, nucleus, seed.

frumgerð 1. prototype; *synonyms* (*n*) model, archetype, epitome, example, exemplar, **2**. archetype; *synonyms* (*n*) original, pattern, prototype, ideal, paradigm.

frumgilda initialize; *synonyms* (*v*) initialise, format, arrange.

frumgildi argument; *synonyms* (*n*) controversy, debate, matter, proof, reason; *antonyms* (*n*) agreement, harmony.

frumhæfa postulate; *synonyms* (*v*) demand, assume, (*n*) assumption, axiom, posit.

frumhæfing 1. postulate; *synonyms* (*v*) demand, assume, (*n*) assumption, axiom, posit, **2**. assumption; *synonyms* (*n*) presumption, supposition, hypothesis, premise, adoption.

frumherji pioneer; *synonyms* (*n*) forerunner, guide, colonist, (*v*) initiate, institute.

frumhlutur symbol; *synonyms* (*n*) sign, emblem, number, badge, mark.

fruminnlag hypoblast; *synonyms* (*n*) endoblast, endoderm, entoderm, entoblast.

frumkönnun reconnaissance; *synonyms* (*n*) exploration, examination, investigation, speculation, (*v*) reconnoitering.

Frumkvæði initiative; *synonyms* (*n*) enterprise, gumption, (*adj*) initial, inaugural, initiatory.

frumkvæðisréttur initiative; *synonyms* (*n*) enterprise, gumption, (*adj*) initial, inaugural, initiatory.

frumkvöðull entrepreneur; *synonyms* (*n*) contractor, enterpriser, businessperson, tycoon, manufacturer.

frumlag subject; *synonyms* (*n*) matter, citizen, affair, (*adj*) liable, exposed; *antonym* (*adj*) liberated.

frumlagi subject; *synonyms* (*n*) matter, citizen, affair, (*adj*) liable, exposed; *antonym* (*adj*) liberated.

frumliður somite; *synonyms* (*n*) metamere, segment, portion, section, somatome.

frummynd 1. prototype; *synonyms* (*n*) model, archetype, epitome, example, exemplar, **2**. master; *synonyms* (*n*) captain, instructor, (*v*) conquer, control, (*adj*) chief.

frumregla axiom; *synonyms* (*n*) aphorism, adage, maxim, apothegm, principle.

frumsenda axiom; *synonyms* (*n*) aphorism, adage, maxim, apothegm, principle.

frumsetning axiom; *synonyms* (*n*) aphorism, adage, maxim, apothegm, principle.

frumsjálf id; *synonyms* (*n*) identification, ego, papers, authorization, (*adj*) intradermal.

frumskjal protocol; *synonyms* (*n*) etiquette, manners, ceremony, bill, formality.

frumskógur jungle; *synonyms* (*n*) bush, forest, maze, tangle, snarl.

frumsmíð prototype; *synonyms* (*n*) model, archetype, epitome, example, exemplar.

frumsögn category; *synonyms* (*n*) class, denomination, division, kind, type.

frumstæður primitive; *synonyms* (*adj*) primeval, primary, antediluvian, archaic, crude; *antonym* (*adj*) modern.

frumstærð argument; *synonyms* (*n*) controversy, debate, matter, proof, reason; *antonyms* (*n*) agreement, harmony.

frumstig positive; *synonyms* (*adj*) absolute, certain, affirmative, confident, (*n*) actual; *antonyms* (*adj*) negative, derogatory, uncertain, unsure, pessimistic.

frumstilla initialize; *synonyms* (*v*) initialise, format, arrange.

frumtala prime; *synonyms* (*adj*) main, chief, first, head, (*n*) best; *antonym* (*adj*) minor.

frumþáttur component; *synonyms* (*n*) constituent, factor, ingredient, part, detail.

frumtryggjandi insurer; *synonyms* (*n*) underwriter, ensurer, insurancer.

frumubálkur series; *synonyms* (*n*) chain, rank, collection, cycle, (*v*) course.

frumubörkur cortex; *synonyms* (*n*) bark, crust, peel, rind, pallium.

frumufar migration; *synonyms* (*n*) exodus, movement, journey, (*v*) flit, flitting.

frumufræði cytology; *synonyms* (*n*) anatomy, botany.

frumuhlaup cytosol; *synonym* (*n*) cytoplasma.

frumuhýði pellicle; *synonyms* (*n*) film, coat, skin, shagreen, peel.

frumukrans rosette; *synonyms* (*n*) knot, star, patera.

frumuöndun respiration; *synonyms* (*n*) breathing, aspiration, inspiration, delay, exercising.

frumuræktun culture; *synonyms* (*n*) civilization, breeding, cultivation, acculturation, education.

frumutenging coupling; *synonyms* (*n*) union, coupler, clutch, conjugation, connection.

frumvarp proposal; *synonyms* (*n*) motion, advice, proposition, suggestion, offer.

frumvefur parenchyma; *synonyms* (*n*) substance, body, compages, element, matter.

frumvera protist; *synonym* (*n*) protistan.

frygð libido; *synonyms* (*n*) lust, desire.

frygðarauki aphrodisiac; *synonyms* (*adj*) amorous, aphrodisiacal, erotic, sexy, venereal.

frygðarlyf aphrodisiac; *synonyms* (*adj*) amorous, aphrodisiacal, erotic, sexy, venereal.

frymi 1. protoplasm; *synonyms* (*n*) plasma, matter, proplasm, body, cytoblastema, **2**. element; *synonyms* (*n*) component, constituent, ingredient, factor, substance.

frymisbóla vacuole; *synonyms* (*n*) cell, metaplasm, ontogeny, ovary, ovum.

frymisgrisjuhít cistern; *synonyms* (*n*) tank, container, reservoir, boiler, cisterna.

frymisvökvi cytosol; *synonym* (*n*) cytoplasma.

frysta freeze; *synonyms* (*n*) frost, (*v*) congeal, chill, arrest, cool; *antonyms* (*v*) melt, thaw, boil.

frysting 1. refrigeration; *synonyms* (*n*) cooling, infrigidation, cold, preservation, refrigerium, **2**. freezing; *synonyms* (*adj*) icy, arctic, chilly, frosty, (*n*) freeze; *antonyms* (*adj*) boiling, hot, sweltering, red-hot, warm.

frystur frozen; *synonyms* (*adj*) cold, frosty, arctic, frigid, glacial; *antonyms* (*adj*) hot, moving.

fúga joint; *synonyms* (*n*) articulation, hinge, join, seam, (*v*) articulate; *antonyms* (*adj*) individual, unilateral, private, separate.

fugl bird; *synonyms* (*n*) birdie, chick, fowl, girl, wench.

fuglasótt psittacosis; *synonym* (*n*) ornithosis.

fuglsnef beak; *synonyms* (*n*) bill, nose, snout, prow, bow.

fúkalyf antibiotic; *synonyms* (*n*) analgesic, antifungal, antiviral, carminative, (*adj*) antiseptic.

fúkkalyf antibiotic; *synonyms* (*n*) analgesic, antifungal, antiviral, carminative, (*adj*) antiseptic.

fúll 1. dismal; *synonyms* (*adj*) cheerless, dark, dejected, depressing, desolate; *antonyms* (*adj*) cheerful, bright, happy, **2**. foul; *synonyms* (*adj*) base, disgusting, filthy, (*v*) dirty, corrupt; *antonyms* (*adj*) pleasant, fair, (*v*) clean, pure.

fullbúa implement; *synonyms* (*v*) execute, fulfil, (*n*) tool, apparatus, utensil.

fullgerður complete; *synonyms* (*adj*) perfect, absolute, (*v*) accomplish, achieve, close; *antonyms* (*adj*) incomplete, partial, unfinished, abridged, (*v*) neglect.

fullgert completed; *synonyms* (*adj*) complete, done, accomplished, finished, (*adv*) over.

fullgilda ratify; *synonyms* (*v*) approve, confirm, corroborate, acknowledge, authorize.

fullgilding ratification; *synonyms* (*n*) approval, confirmation, endorsement, sanction, affirmation.

fullkomið complete; *synonyms* (*adj*) perfect, absolute, (*v*) accomplish, achieve, close; *antonyms* (*adj*) incomplete, partial, unfinished, abridged, (*v*) neglect.

fullkominn complete; *synonyms* (*adj*) perfect, absolute, (*v*) accomplish, achieve, close; *antonyms* (*adj*) incomplete, partial, unfinished, abridged, (*v*) neglect.

fullkomleiki completeness; *synonyms* (*n*) entirety, fullness, thoroughness, entireness, unity.

fullkomnunarárátta perfectionism; *synonyms* (*n*) care, diligence, strictness, thoroughness, exactness.

fullnæging 1. climax; *synonyms* (*n*) apex, top, acme, culmination, (*v*) peak; *antonym* (*v*) dip, **2**. gratification; *synonyms* (*n*) contentment, delight, content, enjoyment, pleasure; *antonym* (*n*) dissatisfaction.

fullnusta 1. ratification; *synonyms* (*n*) approval, confirmation, endorsement, sanction, affirmation, **2**. commit; *synonyms* (*v*) commend, assign, charge, consign, apply.

fullnýta deplete; *synonyms* (*v*) consume, exhaust, drain, sap, finish; *antonym* (*v*) refill.

fullnýting depletion; *synonyms* (*n*) consumption, expenditure, loss, (*adj*) flaccidity, vacancy.

fullorðinn 1. adult; *synonyms* (*adj*) big, full-grown, mature, elder, (*n*) grownup; *antonyms* (*adj*) immature, (*n*) adolescent, child, juvenile, teenager, **2**. mature; *synonyms* (*adj*) ripe, (*v*) grow, ripen, develop, age; *antonyms* (*adj*) childish, naive, unripe, young, sophomoric.

fullstækka maximize; *synonyms* (*v*) increase, maximise, intensify, improve, inflate; *antonym* (*v*) minimize.

fullsterkur concentrated; *synonyms* (*adj*) strong, intense, compact, condensed, deep; *antonyms* (*adj*) dispersed, weak, uncondensed, unsaturated.

fullþroski maturity; *synonyms* (*n*) ripeness, adulthood, matureness, perfection, majority; *antonyms* (*n*) childhood, youth, immaturity.

fulltíða adult; *synonyms* (*adj*) big, full-grown, mature, elder, (*n*) grownup; *antonyms* (*adj*) immature, (*n*) adolescent, child, juvenile, teenager.

fulltrúahópur representation; *synonyms* (*n*) image, performance, depiction, picture, presentation.

fulltrúi 1. secretary; *synonyms* (*n*) clerk, escritoire, minister, desk, (*v*) amanuensis, **2**. representative; *synonyms* (*n*) agent, delegate, deputy, envoy, proxy, **3**. representation; *synonyms* (*n*) image, performance, depiction, picture, presentation, **4**. deputy; *synonyms* (*n*) surrogate, alternate, substitute, ambassador, assistant, **5**. associate; *synonyms* (*v*) affiliate, connect, (*n*) ally, companion, fellow; *antonyms* (*v*) avoid, dissociate, distance, (*adj*) chief, (*n*) stranger.

fullur full; *synonyms* (*adj*) complete, absolute, abundant, broad, (*n*) entire; *antonyms* (*adj*) empty, lacking, starving, hungry, sketchy.

fullvaldur sovereign; *synonyms (adj)* independent, autonomous, *(n)* monarch, ruler, king; *antonym (adj)* dependent.

fullveðja adult; *synonyms (adj)* big, full-grown, mature, elder, *(n)* grownup; *antonyms (adj)* immature, *(n)* adolescent, child, juvenile, teenager.

fullveldi 1. sovereignty; *synonyms (n)* kingdom, reign, empire, autonomy, dominion, **2.** sovereign; *synonyms (adj)* independent, autonomous, *(n)* monarch, ruler, king; *antonym (adj)* dependent.

fullvissa 1. assure; *synonyms (v)* guarantee, certify, secure, affirm, *(n)* warrant, **2.** assurance; *synonyms (n)* confidence, belief, pledge, affiance, certitude; *antonym (n)* insecurity.

fullyrðing 1. statement; *synonyms (n)* account, declaration, affirmation, announcement, communication; *antonym (n)* denial, **2.** proposition; *synonyms (n)* offer, overture, bid, motion, proposal.

fundamento elements; *synonyms (n)* alphabet, rudiments, grammar, outlines, contents.

fundarbók journal; *synonyms (n)* diary, book, magazine, newspaper, *(adj)* daybook.

fundargerð minutes; *synonyms (n)* proceedings, record, transactions, records, journal.

fundarstjóri 1. chairman; *synonyms (n)* chair, chairperson, chairwoman, director, president, **2.** moderator; *synonyms (n)* chairman, mediator, arbitrator, intermediary, negotiator.

fundo grounds; *synonyms (n)* cause, dregs, ground, reason, account.

fundur 1. meeting; *synonyms (n)* confluence, convention, gathering, concourse, assembly; *antonym (n)* divergence, **2.** session; *synonyms (n)* meeting, seance, sitting, conference, bout, **3.** assembly; *synonyms (n)* collection, congregation, fabrication, multitude, *(v)* assemblage, **4.** congress; *synonyms (n)* convocation, council, intercourse, association, synod, **5.** conference; *synonyms (n)* colloquy, consultation, interview, negotiation, talk.

funkcii works; *synonyms (n)* factory, plant, workings, mill, manufactory.

funkciigi works; *synonyms (n)* factory, plant, workings, mill, manufactory.

fura 1. pine; *synonyms (v)* languish, long, ache, droop, flag, **2.** fir; *synonym (adj)* green.

furða 1. surprise; *synonyms (n)* fright, *(v)* astound, alarm, amaze, astonish, **2.** wonder; *synonyms (n)* marvel, prodigy, admiration, amazement, astonishment, **3.** astonishment; *synonyms (n)* wonder, surprise, wonderment, confusion, consternation, **4.** amazement; *synonym (n)* stupor.

fúsleiki readiness; *synonyms (n)* facility, alacrity, ease, dexterity, *(v)* preparedness.

fýlasótt psittacosis; *synonym (n)* ornithosis.

fylgdarfrumur glia; *synonym (n)* neuroglia.

fylgibúnaður accessories; *synonyms (n)* fittings, equipment, accompaniments, garnishes, possession.

fylgihlutir accessories; *synonyms (n)* fittings, equipment, accompaniments, garnishes, possession.

fylgihnöttur 1. satellite; *synonyms (n)* follower, moon, planet, attendant, orbiter, **2.** secondary; *synonyms (adj)* inferior, lower, minor, subordinate, ancillary; *antonyms (adj)* basic, main, central, chief, direct.

fylgihnúður satellite; *synonyms (n)* follower, moon, planet, attendant, orbiter.

fylgiorð particle; *synonyms (n)* molecule, grain, speck, bit, *(adj)* atom.

fylgirit enclosure; *synonyms (n)* coop, cage, barrier, enclosing, pen.

fylgiskjal 1. voucher; *synonyms (n)* certificate, coupon, receipt, ticket, warrant, **2.** schedule; *synonyms (n)* list, agenda, catalog, program, *(v)* register, **3.** verification; *synonyms (n)* confirmation, check, proof, substantiation, authentication, **4.** annex; *synonyms (n)* affix, addition, *(v)* add, affiliate, adjoin, **5.** enclosure; *synonyms (n)* coop, cage, barrier, enclosing, pen.

fylgistjarna secondary; *synonyms (adj)* inferior, lower, minor, subordinate, ancillary; *antonyms (adj)* basic, main, central, chief, direct.

fylgitungl satellite; *synonyms (n)* follower, moon, planet, attendant, orbiter.

fylgja 1. trail; *synonyms (n)* track, trace, *(v)* haul, drag, hunt, **2.** placenta; *synonyms (n)* secundines, sporophore, **3.** accompany; *synonyms (v)* attend, follow, associate, companion, *(n)* escort.

fylgni 1. correlation; *synonyms (n)* association, connection, relationship, bond, correspondence, **2.** tracking; *synonyms (n)* pursuit, trailing, rutting, trajectography.

fylki 1. province; *synonyms (n)* country, district, field, county, *(v)* department, **2.** array; *synonyms (n)* arrangement, line, *(v)* attire, dress, adorn; *antonym (v)* disarray, **3.** matrix; *synonyms (n)* die, alembic, caldron, crucible, groundmass.

fylking 1. phylum; *synonyms (n)* division, branch, **2.** array; *synonyms (n)* arrangement, line, *(v)* attire, dress, adorn; *antonym (v)* disarray.

fylkisstjóri governor; *synonyms (n)* director, chief, manager, regulator, administrator.

fylla 1. fill; *synonyms (v)* block, clog, charge, line, stuff; *antonyms (v)* empty, free, **2.** permeate;

synonyms (v) penetrate, infiltrate, diffuse, fill, imbue, **3**. fillet; *synonyms* (n) band, strip, cincture, list, (v) filet, **4**. imbue; *synonyms* (v) color, infuse, permeate, saturate, steep.

fylli filler; *synonyms* (n) feeder, fill, filling, stuffing, complement.

fylliliður complement; *synonyms* (n) supplement, accessory, adjunct, balance, extra.

fyllimengi complement; *synonyms* (n) supplement, accessory, adjunct, balance, extra.

fylling 1. complementarity, **2**. complement; *synonyms* (n) supplement, accessory, adjunct, balance, extra, **3**. fill; *synonyms* (v) block, clog, charge, line, stuff; *antonyms* (v) empty, free, **4**. filler; *synonyms* (n) feeder, fill, filling, stuffing, complement, **5**. padding; *synonyms* (n) pad, cushioning, wadding, (v) wad, (adj) cushion.

fyllir filler; *synonyms* (n) feeder, fill, filling, stuffing, complement.

fyllitala complement; *synonyms* (n) supplement, accessory, adjunct, balance, extra.

fyrir 1. through; *synonyms* (adv) by, (adj) finished, done, direct, straight, **2**. at; *synonyms* (prep) in, a, (adv) on, along, (prf) all, **3**. before; *synonyms* (prep) fore, (adv) above, ahead, afore, (adj) preceding; *antonyms* (prep) later, behind, after, afterward, **4**. for; *synonyms* (prep) because, per, during, (adv) against, as.

fyrirbæri phenomenon; *synonyms* (n) event, appearance, marvel, miracle, incident.

fyrirbinding 1. ligation; *synonyms* (n) link, (v) astriction, attachment, compagination, vincture, **2**. ligature; *synonyms* (n) binder, ligament, (v) bond, tie, knot.

fyrirboði notice; *synonyms* (n) advertisement, attention, (v) note, look, attend; *antonyms* (v) disregard, ignore.

fyrirbrigði phenomenon; *synonyms* (n) event, appearance, marvel, miracle, incident.

fyrirbyggjandi preventive; *synonyms* (adj) prophylactic, preventative, defensive, (n) contraceptive, deterrent; *antonym* (adj) encouraging.

fyrirferð bulk; *synonyms* (n) mass, size, amount, majority, volume; *antonym* (n) minority.

fyrirferðaraukning tumor; *synonyms* (n) swelling, tumour, growth, neoplasm, (adj) cancer.

fyrirferðarlítill compact; *synonyms* (adj) close, (n) agreement, arrangement, contract, (v) compress; *antonyms* (adj) loose, sprawling, bulky, sparse.

fyrirframgreiddur prepaid; *synonym* (adj) postpaid.

fyrirframgreiðsla 1. advance; *synonyms* (n) progress, (v) further, proceed, promote, (phr) accelerate; *antonyms* (n) deterioration, (v) retreat,

recede, delay, demote, **2**. imprest; *synonym* (v) loan.

fyrirframgreitt prepaid; *synonym* (adj) postpaid.

fyrirgefa 1. remit; *synonyms* (v) excuse, relax, acquit, defer, dispatch, **2**. absolve; *synonyms* (v) justify, exculpate, exonerate, forgive, free; *antonyms* (v) convict, blame, condemn, **3**. acquit; *synonyms* (v) absolve, release, clear, discharge, pardon, **4**. forgive; *synonyms* (v) condone, remit, overlook, **5**. pardon; *synonyms* (n) amnesty, forgiveness, (v) spare, absolution, acquittal.

fyrirgefðu sorry; *synonyms* (adj) pathetic, contrite, paltry, penitent, piteous; *antonym* (adj) unrepentant.

fyrirgefning 1. forgiveness; *synonyms* (n) amnesty, mercy, pardon, clemency, kindness, **2**. pardon; *synonyms* (n) forgiveness, (v) absolve, condone, excuse, forgive; *antonym* (v) blame.

fyrirgreiðsla facilitation; *synonyms* (n) assistance, enhancement.

fyrirgreiðslufé bribe; *synonyms* (n) bait, bribery, reward, (v) corrupt, fix.

fyrirhyggja prudence; *synonyms* (n) foresight, care, caution, economy, (adj) discretion; *antonyms* (n) foolishness, generosity, imprudence, profligacy.

fyrirkomulag 1. arrangement; *synonyms* (n) agreement, order, settlement, adjustment, array, **2**. layout; *synonyms* (n) arrangement, composition, design, plan, outline, **3**. organization; *synonyms* (n) establishment, administration, formation, association, constitution.

fyrirmæli 1. directive; *synonyms* (n) decree, direction, edict, (adj) directing, directional, **2**. command; *synonyms* (n) control, (v) charge, order, rule, call; *antonym* (v) request, **3**. order; *synonyms* (n) command, dictate, array, rank, (v) direct; *antonyms* (n) anarchy, chaos, confusion, mayhem, (v) disorder, **4**. injunction; *synonyms* (n) behest, bidding, commandment, enjoining, enjoinment, **5**. instructions; *synonyms* (n) injunction, orders, guide, will, formula.

fyrirmunun exclusion; *synonyms* (n) exception, banishment, elimination, debarment, expulsion; *antonyms* (n) inclusion, addition, entitlement.

fyrirmynd 1. prototype; *synonyms* (n) model, archetype, epitome, example, exemplar, **2**. template; *synonyms* (n) pattern, templet, guide, guidebook, pathfinder, **3**. norm; *synonyms* (n) average, mean, measure, mode, criterion, **4**. pattern; *synonyms* (n) design, fashion, form, mold, (v) mould, **5**. model; *synonyms* (n) image, dummy, figure, (v) copy, imitate; *antonym* (adj) atypical.

fyrirskipa order; *synonyms* (*n*) command, decree, dictate, array, (*v*) direct; *antonyms* (*n*) anarchy, chaos, confusion, (*v*) disorder, request.

fyrirskipaður mandatory; *synonyms* (*adj*) compulsory, obligatory, required, necessary, (*n*) mandatary; *antonym* (*adj*) optional.

fyrirskipun order; *synonyms* (*n*) command, decree, dictate, array, (*v*) direct; *antonyms* (*n*) anarchy, chaos, confusion, (*v*) disorder, request.

fyrirsögn 1. title; *synonyms* (*n*) call, designation, caption, (*v*) name, style, 2. heading; *synonyms* (*n*) bearing, drift, head, title, course.

fyrirspurn 1. question; *synonyms* (*n*) inquiry, (*v*) doubt, query, distrust, inquire; *antonyms* (*n*) certainty, (*v*) answer, 2. query; *synonyms* (*n*) question, interrogative, (*v*) interrogate, ask, examine, 3. inquiry; *synonyms* (*n*) examination, enquiry, investigation, exploration, (*v*) search.

fyrirspurnaþing hearing; *synonyms* (*n*) audition, earshot, ear, trial, (*adj*) audience; *antonym* (*adj*) deaf.

fyrirstaða obstruction; *synonyms* (*n*) obstacle, hindrance, interruption, bar, (*v*) impediment.

fyrirsvar representation; *synonyms* (*n*) image, performance, depiction, picture, presentation.

fyrirtæki 1. concern; *synonyms* (*n*) business, affair, (*v*) worry, affect, care; *antonym* (*v*) unconcern, 2. business; *synonyms* (*n*) employment, matter, subject, calling, concern; *antonyms* (*adj*) charitable, housing, 3. company; *synonyms* (*n*) companionship, society, association, band, cohort; *antonym* (*n*) solitude, 4. enterprise; *synonyms* (*n*) company, endeavor, activity, adventure, energy, 5. establishment; *synonyms* (*n*) constitution, institution, creation, enactment, formation; *antonyms* (*n*) elimination, end.

fyrirtækjahringur 1. trust; *synonyms* (*n*) charge, confidence, credit, faith, (*v*) believe; *antonyms* (*v*) distrust, doubt, disbelieve, mistrust, 2. ring; *synonyms* (*n*) encircle, band, (*v*) circle, call, peal.

fyrirtækjasamsteypa conglomerate; *synonyms* (*n*) composite, group, complex, (*v*) accumulate, amass.

fyrirtækjasamteypa trust; *synonyms* (*n*) charge, confidence, credit, faith, (*v*) believe; *antonyms* (*v*) distrust, doubt, disbelieve, mistrust.

fyrirvari 1. qualification; *synonyms* (*n*) condition, capability, competence, fitness, limitation, 2. reservation; *synonyms* (*n*) reserve, booking, qualification, modesty, exception; *antonym* (*n*) certainty, 3. clause; *synonyms* (*n*) article, paragraph, provision, rider, (*v*) passage.

fyrna depreciate; *synonyms* (*v*) debase, belittle, decry, deprecate, detract; *antonym* (*v*) appreciate.

fyrning 1. amortization; *synonyms* (*n*) amortisation, payment, 2. depletion; *synonyms* (*n*)

consumption, expenditure, loss, (*adj*) flaccidity, vacancy, 3. depreciation; *synonyms* (*n*) abatement, detraction, disparagement, derogation, deterioration, 4. limitation; *synonyms* (*n*) circumscription, limit, restraint, restriction, check; *antonym* (*n*) extension.

fyrra primary; *synonyms* (*adj*) chief, basic, elementary, essential, (*n*) paramount; *antonym* (*adj*) secondary.

fyrst first; *synonyms* (*adv*) foremost, before, (*adj*) best, beginning, chief; *antonyms* (*adj*) last, final, (*n*) end.

fyrtinn splenetic; *synonyms* (*adj*) fretful, peevish, prickly, angry, (*n*) morose.

fystur first; *synonyms* (*adv*) foremost, before, (*adj*) best, beginning, chief; *antonyms* (*adj*) last, final, (*n*) end.

G

g gram; *synonyms* (*n*) gm, gramme, g, (*adj*) kilogram, microgram.

gabba spoof; *synonyms* (*n*) hoax, mockery, (*v*) parody, burlesque, joke.

gaddur 1. spicule; *synonyms* (*n*) spiculum, tooth, (*adj*) point, spike, spine, 2. fluorosis.

gæðaflokkur grade; *synonyms* (*n*) class, place, rank, degree, (*v*) level.

gæðamat commission; *synonyms* (*n*) board, mission, delegation, job, (*v*) assign.

gæði quality; *synonyms* (*n*) nature, character, characteristic, class, condition; *antonym* (*adj*) shoddy.

gæfur tame; *synonyms* (*adj*) docile, meek, (*v*) dull, break, subdue; *antonyms* (*adj*) exciting, wild.

gægjuhneigð voyeurism; *synonym* (*n*) scopophilia.

gær yesterday; *synonyms* (*n*) past, history, bygone, (*adj*) passé, stale; *antonym* (*n*) tomorrow.

gæs goose; *synonyms* (*n*) cuckoo, fathead, goof, fool, jackass.

gæsagammur vulture; *synonyms* (*n*) predator, bloodsucker, (*adj*) bashaw, despot, disciplinarian.

gæsajurt chamomile; *synonym* (*n*) camomile.

gæsla supervision; *synonyms* (*n*) oversight, charge, control, direction, (*v*) inspection.

gæslumaður moderator; *synonyms* (*n*) chairman, mediator, arbitrator, intermediary, negotiator.

gætinn conservative; *synonyms* (*adj*) moderate, bourgeois, conventional, cautious, reactionary; *antonyms* (*adj*) activist, wide-ranging, (*n*) liberal, radical.

gætni 1. prudence; *synonyms* (*n*) foresight, care, caution, economy, (*adj*) discretion; *antonyms* (*n*) foolishness, generosity, imprudence, profligacy, **2**. precaution; *synonyms* (*n*) forethought, prevention, anticipation, circumspection, protection, **3**. discretion; *synonyms* (*n*) delicacy, prudence, diplomacy, calculation, discernment; *antonym* (*n*) recklessness, **4**. foresight; *synonyms* (*n*) prevision, forecast, prospicience, foreknowledge, (*v*) expectation.

gáfa talent; *synonyms* (*n*) gift, genius, ability, aptitude, capacity; *antonym* (*n*) inability.

gaffall fork; *synonyms* (*n*) crotch, branch, bifurcation, branching, (*v*) diverge.

gafl 1. cover; *synonyms* (*v*) coat, conceal, top, bury, (*n*) blind; *antonyms* (*v*) reveal, expose, uncover, **2**. end; *synonyms* (*n*) close, aim, (*v*) cease, complete, finish; *antonyms* (*n*) beginning, maintenance, opening, (*v*) start, begin, **3**. gable; *synonyms* (*n*) gavel, cable, coping, toll, tribute.

gaflbrík pediment; *synonyms* (*n*) architrave, capital, cornice, epistyle, frieze.

gaflflötur tympanum; *synonyms* (*n*) eardrum, kettle, kettledrum, timpani, tympani.

gaflhlað pediment; *synonyms* (*n*) architrave, capital, cornice, epistyle, frieze.

gaflhlaðsþríhyrningur pediment; *synonyms* (*n*) architrave, capital, cornice, epistyle, frieze.

gaflhyrna pediment; *synonyms* (*n*) architrave, capital, cornice, epistyle, frieze.

gáfur endowment; *synonyms* (*n*) ability, talent, capacity, (*v*) donation, gift.

gagn 1. utility; *synonyms* (*n*) use, usefulness, service, value, avail, **2**. benefit; *synonyms* (*n*) advantage, gain, (*v*) aid, assist, profit; *antonyms* (*n*) disadvantage, drawback, loss, (*v*) harm.

gagna benefit; *synonyms* (*n*) advantage, (*v*) aid, assist, profit, avail; *antonyms* (*n*) disadvantage, drawback, loss, (*v*) harm.

gagnabraut bus; *synonyms* (*n*) automobile, autobus, car, coach, vehicle.

gagnademba dump; *synonyms* (*v*) discard, ditch, abandon, drop, empty; *antonym* (*v*) keep.

gagnaðgerð countermeasure; *synonyms* (*n*) remedy, antidote, cure.

gagnagrunnur database; *synonyms* (*n*) chart, directory, folder, profile, (*v*) file.

gagnahjúpun encapsulation; *synonyms* (*n*) packaging, entrapment.

gagnainnsetning editing; *synonyms* (*n*) correction, edition, redaction, cutting, control.

gagnalag overlay; *synonyms* (*n*) coat, sheathing, (*v*) cover, overlap, veneer.

gagnalind source; *synonyms* (*n*) origin, root, cause, commencement, beginning.

gagnamengun contamination; *synonyms* (*n*) contagion, pollution, contaminant, infection, dirtying; *antonym* (*n*) decontamination.

gagnasafn 1. database; *synonyms* (*n*) chart, directory, folder, profile, (*v*) file, **2**. file; *synonyms* (*n*) archive, document, list, procession, (*v*) order.

gagnasamskipti dialogue; *synonyms* (*n*) talk, colloquy, conversation, interlocution, interview.

gagnasetning editing; *synonyms* (*n*) correction, edition, redaction, cutting, control.

gagnaskrá file; *synonyms* (*n*) archive, document, list, procession, (*v*) order.

gagnasnið format; *synonyms* (*n*) form, size, formatting, (*v*) set, arrange.

gagnauga temple; *synonyms* (*n*) church, tabernacle, shrine, brow, synagogue.

gagnaviðbætur patch; *synonyms* (*n*) darn, fleck, mend, plot, (*v*) piece.

gagnger radical; *synonyms* (*adj*) extremist, basic, exhaustive, extreme, revolutionary; *antonyms* (*adj*) conventional, old-fashioned, (*n*) moderate, conservative, traditionalist.

gagngert 1. radically; *synonyms* (*adv*) essentially, fundamentally, basically, absolutely, purely, **2**. thoroughly; *synonyms* (*adv*) completely, entirely, fully, carefully, deeply; *antonyms* (*adv*) carelessly, superficially.

gagnhverfur reversible; *synonyms* (*adj*) changeable, bilateral, abrogable, repealable.

gagnkvæði antinomy; *synonyms* (*n*) opposition, (*adj*) despotism, outlawry, violence.

gagnkvæmni 1. reciprocity; *synonyms* (*n*) correlation, reciprocality, alternation, exchange, interplay, **2**. complementarity.

gagnkvæmur 1. reciprocal; *synonyms* (*adj*) mutual, common, inverse, complementary, interchangeable, **2**. bilateral; *synonyms* (*adj*) joint, (*v*) bicephalous, bicipital, bidental, bifold; *antonyms* (*adj*) unilateral, multilateral, **3**. mutual; *synonyms* (*adj*) reciprocal, communal, bilateral, collective, public; *antonyms* (*adj*) individual, one-sided, private.

gagnmiðlun multimedia; *synonym* (*n*) disc.

gagnráðstöfun countermeasure; *synonyms* (*n*) remedy, antidote, cure.

gagnrýninn critical; *synonyms* (*adj*) acute, decisive, delicate, important, pressing; *antonyms* (*adj*) complimentary, trivial, positive, flattering, insignificant.

gagnsæi transparency; *synonyms* (*n*) transparence, clarity, clearness, slide, pellucidness.

gagnsæismælir densitometer; *synonym* (*n*) densimeter.

gagnsær transparent; *synonyms (adj)* diaphanous, lucid, obvious, plain, *(n)* clear; *antonyms (adj)* opaque, solid.

gagnseglun demagnetisation; *synonym (n)* demagnetization.

gagnsemishyggja 1. pragmatism; *synonyms (n)* practicality, convenience, expediency, naturalism, pride, **2**. utilitarianism.

Gagnsókn counterattack; *synonyms (n)* countermove, opposition, *(v)* counterstrike, oppose, rally.

gagnstaða opposition; *synonyms (n)* contrast, conflict, antithesis, contrary, contrariety; *antonym (n)* consent.

gagnstæða 1. reverse; *synonyms (adj)* opposite, *(v)* annul, repeal, rescind, *(n)* contrary; *antonym (n)* front, **2**. opposition; *synonyms (n)* contrast, conflict, antithesis, contrariety, antagonism; *antonym (n)* consent, **3**. inverse; *synonyms (adj)* converse, *(n)* reciprocal, *(v)* reverse.

gagnstæður 1. reverse; *synonyms (adj)* opposite, *(v)* annul, repeal, rescind, *(n)* contrary; *antonym (n)* front, **2**. reciprocal; *synonyms (adj)* mutual, common, inverse, complementary, interchangeable, **3**. antipodal; *synonyms (adj)* antipodean, converse, subcontrary, contradictory, counter, **4**. counter; *synonyms (n)* buffet, bench, reverse, *(v)* reply, contradict, **5**. inverse; *synonyms (n)* contrast, reciprocal, antithesis.

gagntak reaction; *synonyms (n)* answer, response, backlash, reply, effect.

gagntekning immersion; *synonyms (n)* dip, absorption, ducking, concentration, submergence.

gagnúð transference; *synonyms (n)* transfer, conveyance, transport, delivery, transmission.

gagnvegur geodesic; *synonyms (adj)* geodetic, geodesical, geodetical.

gagnverkandi 1. reactive; *synonyms (adj)* sensitive, responsive, receptive, approachable, hasty, **2**. reciprocal; *synonyms (adj)* mutual, common, inverse, complementary, interchangeable.

gagnverkun 1. reciprocity; *synonyms (n)* correlation, reciprocality, alternation, exchange, interplay, **2**. antagonism; *synonyms (n)* animosity, enmity, resistance, aggression, antithesis; *antonym (n)* friendliness, **3**. interaction; *synonyms (n)* contact, communication, mutuality, affairs, associations.

gagnvirkni 1. reciprocity; *synonyms (n)* correlation, reciprocality, alternation, exchange, interplay, **2**. interoperability, **3**. interaction; *synonyms (n)* contact, communication, mutuality, affairs, associations.

gagnvirkun reaction; *synonyms (n)* answer, response, backlash, reply, effect.

gagnvirkur 1. reciprocal; *synonyms (adj)* mutual, common, inverse, complementary, interchangeable, **2**. antagonistic; *synonyms (adj)* hostile, counter, averse, conflicting, *(v)* adverse; *antonym (adj)* friendly, **3**. interactive; *synonyms (adj)* interactional, synergistic, synergetic.

galaktósi galactose; *synonym (n)* lactose.

galangarót galangal; *synonyms (n)* galanga, galingale.

galari gallery; *synonyms (n)* balcony, audience, drift, veranda, circle.

gálaus negligent; *synonyms (adj)* careless, heedless, neglectful, forgetful, inattentive; *antonyms (adj)* attentive, strict.

galdranorn witch; *synonyms (n)* hag, pythoness, *(v)* enchant, bewitch, charm.

galeiða galley; *synonyms (n)* caboose, cookhouse, galleyfoist, proof, slice.

gáleysi negligence; *synonyms (n)* neglect, carelessness, disregard, inattention, indifference; *antonym (n)* attention.

gálgi gantry; *synonyms (n)* gauntry, stand, derrick, hoist, winch.

gall bile; *synonyms (n)* anger, gall, ebullition, ferment, fume.

gallabuxur jeans; *synonyms (n)* pants, chinos, khakis, slacks, dungarees.

gallaður 1. adverse; *synonyms (adj)* contrary, unfavorable, harmful, hostile, untoward; *antonym (adj)* favorable, **2**. detrimental; *synonyms (adj)* deleterious, adverse, damaging, injurious, hurtful; *antonyms (adj)* helpful, advantageous, harmless.

gallepli gall; *synonyms (n)* anger, bitterness, *(v)* annoy, chafe, fret.

gallerí gallery; *synonyms (n)* balcony, audience, drift, veranda, circle.

gallharður adamantine; *synonyms (adj)* adamant, hard, inexorable, intransigent, strong.

galli 1. trouble; *synonyms (n)* distress, bother, pain, *(v)* inconvenience, annoy; *antonyms (v)* calm, please, **2**. disadvantage; *synonyms (n)* deprivation, limitation, loss, damage, detriment; *antonyms (n)* benefit, bonus, value, *(v)* advantage, **3**. defect; *synonyms (n)* fault, blemish, blot, flaw, shortcoming, **4**. drawback; *synonyms (n)* disadvantage, catch, defect, hitch, snag, **5**. failure; *synonyms (n)* bankruptcy, failing, breakdown, decline, deficiency; *antonyms (n)* success, achievement, hit, winner, victory.

gallrauði bilirubin; *synonyms (n)* cholochrome, cholophaein, haematoidin, hematoidin.

galva galvanize; *synonyms (v)* electrify, galvanise, stimulate, encourage, fire.

galvanhúða galvanize; *synonyms* (*v*) electrify, galvanise, stimulate, encourage, fire.

galvanhúðun galvanization; *synonyms* (*n*) zincing, galvanisation, exhilaration, zincification.

galvanílækning galvanism; *synonyms* (*n*) electricity, infection, inspiration, piquancy, provocation.

galvanímælir galvanometer; *synonyms* (*n*) rheometer, (*v*) bathometer, dynamometer, goniometer, heliometer.

galvanímælitæki galvanometer; *synonyms* (*n*) rheometer, (*v*) bathometer, dynamometer, goniometer, heliometer.

galvínmælir galvanometer; *synonyms* (*n*) rheometer, (*v*) bathometer, dynamometer, goniometer, heliometer.

gamall 1. old; *synonyms* (*adj*) antiquated, obsolete, ancient, former, aged; *antonyms* (*adj*) new, young, modern, fresh, latest, **2.** venerable; *synonyms* (*adj*) old, reverend, estimable, respectable, distinguished.

gammaglóbúlínekla agammaglobulinemia; *synonym* (*n*) hypogammaglobulinemia.

gammur vulture; *synonyms* (*n*) predator, bloodsucker, (*adj*) bashaw, despot, disciplinarian.

gámur container; *synonyms* (*n*) box, jar, package, basket, carton.

gandálfur wizard; *synonyms* (*n*) magician, necromancer, sorcerer, conjuror, (*adj*) adept.

ganga 1. walk; *synonyms* (*v*) ramble, course, hike, (*n*) step, gait, **2.** migration; *synonyms* (*n*) exodus, movement, journey, (*v*) flit, flitting.

gangandi ambulatory; *synonyms* (*adj*) ambulant, mobile, vagrant, itinerant, movable.

gangbrú catwalk; *synonyms* (*n*) walkway, bridge, alley, balcony, boardwalk.

gangfræði kinematics; *synonyms* (*n*) phoronomics, cinematics.

ganghraðastig gear; *synonyms* (*n*) equipment, outfit, tackle, apparatus, device.

gangmál heat; *synonyms* (*n*) glow, (*v*) bake, burn, (*adj*) fever, excitement; *antonyms* (*n*) cold, chill, (*v*) cool.

gangráður 1. regulator; *synonyms* (*n*) governor, controller, director, organizer, control, **2.** governor; *synonyms* (*n*) chief, manager, regulator, administrator, ruler, **3.** pacemaker; *synonyms* (*n*) pacer, pacesetter, leader, innovator, modernizer.

gangriti logger; *synonym* (*n*) recorder.

gangsetja 1. prime; *synonyms* (*adj*) main, chief, first, head, (*n*) best; *antonym* (*adj*) minor, **2.** start; *synonyms* (*v*) begin, originate, commence, (*n*) jump, onset; *antonyms* (*v*) end, finish, stop, conclude, (*n*) conclusion.

gangsetning starting; *synonyms* (*n*) start, commencement, (*adj*) opening, initial, (*prep*) beginning.

gangstillir regulator; *synonyms* (*n*) governor, controller, director, organizer, control.

gangsvalir gallery; *synonyms* (*n*) balcony, audience, drift, veranda, circle.

gangtruflun 1. misfire; *synonyms* (*n*) flop, dud, (*v*) fail, miscarry, fizzle, **2.** malfunction; *synonyms* (*n*) breakdown, bug, trouble, defect, stoppage.

gangur 1. running; *synonyms* (*v*) active, (*adj*) flowing, operative, (*n*) course, motion, **2.** dyke; *synonyms* (*n*) dam, ditch, channel, (*v*) dike, (*adj*) lesbian, **3.** dike; *synonyms* (*n*) dyke, trench, bank, gutter, (*v*) bar, **4.** channel; *synonyms* (*n*) canal, conduit, groove, (*v*) carry, conduct, **5.** corridor; *synonyms* (*n*) aisle, hall, lobby, hallway, (*v*) passage.

gangverk mechanism; *synonyms* (*n*) apparatus, machinery, appliance, contrivance, device.

gangvirki mechanism; *synonyms* (*n*) apparatus, machinery, appliance, contrivance, device.

gangviss dependable; *synonyms* (*adj*) reliable, steady, trustworthy, authoritative, credible; *antonyms* (*adj*) unreliable, changeable, irresponsible, undependable.

gára 1. ripple; *synonyms* (*n*) wave, (*v*) bubble, murmur, gurgle, purl, **2.** knurl; *synonyms* (*n*) knob, lump, swelling, hump, knur.

garðahlynur 1. sycamore; *synonyms* (*n*) lacewood, platan, sycamine, **2.** maple.

garðajarðarber strawberry; *synonym* (*n*) blonde.

garðakál cabbage; *synonyms* (*n*) kale, (*v*) pilfer, filch, crib, nim.

garðalind lime; *synonyms* (*n*) birdlime, basswood, calx, lemon, cement.

garðkál cabbage; *synonyms* (*n*) kale, (*v*) pilfer, filch, crib, nim.

garðnellíka carnation; *synonyms* (*n*) crimson, gillyflower, pink, red, scarlet.

garðrækt horticulture; *synonyms* (*n*) gardening, agriculture, botany, cultivation, gardenship.

garður 1. garden; *synonyms* (*n*) field, bed, orchard, grounds, (*v*) farm, **2.** barrier; *synonyms* (*n*) barricade, bar, bulwark, dam, handicap, **3.** park; *synonyms* (*n*) garden, common, (*v*) deposit, locate, place.

garðyrkja horticulture; *synonyms* (*n*) gardening, agriculture, botany, cultivation, gardenship.

garðyrkjufræði horticulture; *synonyms* (*n*) gardening, agriculture, botany, cultivation, gardenship.

gári flute; *synonyms* (*n*) wineglass, fluting, furrow, groove, (*v*) channel.

garnarteppa obturation; *synonym* (*n*) filling.

garnavindur flatus; *synonyms* (*n*) breath, fart, wind, (*adj*) gas, air.

garnir intestine; *synonyms* (*n*) bowel, gut, catgut, (*adj*) domestic, internal.

gárur ripple; *synonyms* (*n*) wave, (*v*) bubble, murmur, gurgle, purl.

gaseyðing degassing; *synonyms* (*n*) degasing, scavenging.

gasgríma respirator; *synonyms* (*n*) inhalator, ventilator, gasmask, inhaler.

gashylki reservoir; *synonyms* (*n*) cistern, fountain, well, lake, store.

gaskenndur gaseous; *synonyms* (*adj*) volatile, airy, gasiform, ethereal, invisible.

gasmyndun gassing; *synonyms* (*n*) execution, boasting.

gat 1. puncture; *synonyms* (*n*) prick, cut, hole, (*v*) bore, drill; *antonym* (*v*) inflate, 2. perforation; *synonyms* (*n*) puncture, aperture, opening, pit, apertion, 3. hole; *synonyms* (*n*) cavity, crack, den, pocket, (*adj*) gap.

gata 1. street; *synonyms* (*n*) road, avenue, highway, way, route, 2. punch; *synonyms* (*n*) jab, drill, (*v*) poke, hit, prick, 3. road; *synonyms* (*n*) course, passage, track, line, (*v*) path, 4. perforate; *synonyms* (*v*) penetrate, bore, cut, pierce, puncture.

gáta check; *synonyms* (*v*) bridle, stop, (*n*) control, arrest, curb.

gataður perforated; *synonyms* (*adj*) perforate, pierced, punctured, penetrated, entered.

gatari 1. stamp; *synonyms* (*n*) mark, seal, brand, (*v*) imprint, print, 2. punch; *synonyms* (*n*) jab, drill, (*v*) poke, hit, prick, 3. perforator; *synonyms* (*n*) gun, awl, bodkin, borer, bradawl.

gátfáni flag; *synonyms* (*n*) banner, colors, (*v*) decline, (*adj*) droop, fade.

gatfláki 1. torus; *synonyms* (*n*) tore, toroid, thalamus, breast, mamma, 2. hole; *synonyms* (*n*) cavity, aperture, crack, den, (*adj*) gap, 3. island; *synonyms* (*n*) reef, (*v*) isle, insulate, isolate, segregate.

gáti guide; *synonyms* (*n*) escort, directory, (*v*) direct, conduct, govern; *antonym* (*v*) follow.

gatnamót intersection; *synonyms* (*n*) cross, crossroads, crossing, crossroad, intersect.

gátt 1. atrium; *synonyms* (*n*) hall, vestibule, cavity, court, foyer, 2. gate; *synonyms* (*n*) entrance, door, entry, mouth, doorway, 3. gateway; *synonyms* (*n*) gate, opening, cellarway, driveway.

gáttarstífla sluice; *synonyms* (*n*) floodgate, lock, penstock, channel, (*v*) flush.

gaukull 1. glomerule, 2. glomerulus; *synonym* (*n*) glomerule.

gaukur cuckoo; *synonyms* (*n*) fathead, goof, goose, jackass, nut.

gaumfáni flag; *synonyms* (*n*) banner, colors, (*v*) decline, (*adj*) droop, fade.

gaumtæki monitor; *synonyms* (*v*) check, regulate, control, eavesdrop, (*n*) admonisher.

gaumun monitoring; *synonym* (*n*) observation.

gaupa lynx; *synonyms* (*n*) catamount, cat, cougar, painter, panther.

gazeto papers; *synonyms* (*n*) credentials, document, documents, identification, covenant.

geavo grandparent; *synonyms* (*n*) ancestor, antecedent, forerunner, precursor, predecessor.

geð affect; *synonyms* (*v*) touch, move, act, fake, feign.

geðblær 1. affect; *synonyms* (*v*) touch, move, act, fake, feign, 2. mood; *synonyms* (*n*) humor, atmosphere, climate, disposition, air.

geðbrigði emotion; *synonyms* (*n*) affection, love, feeling, passion, sensation; *antonym* (*n*) intelligence.

geðbrigðinn emotional; *synonyms* (*adj*) dramatic, affecting, affective, effusive, moving; *antonyms* (*adj*) impassive, unemotional, unflappable.

geðdeyfð 1. depression; *synonyms* (*n*) basin, cavity, dejection, decline, dent; *antonyms* (*n*) cheerfulness, happiness, boom, elation, encouragement, 2. neurasthenia; *synonyms* (*n*) neurosis, nerves, nervousness.

geðhæð mania; *synonyms* (*n*) craze, delirium, (*adj*) frenzy, insanity, lunacy.

geðheill sane; *synonyms* (*adj*) reasonable, lucid, rational, judicious, right; *antonyms* (*adj*) crazy, unbalanced, insane.

geðhnútur complex; *synonyms* (*adj*) composite, complicate, abstruse, difficult, elaborate; *antonyms* (*adj*) simple, basic, straightforward, clear, plain.

geðhreinsun catharsis; *synonyms* (*n*) abreaction, katharsis, purge, purification, expurgation.

geðhrif affection; *synonyms* (*n*) affect, charity, attachment, fondness, affectionateness; *antonym* (*n*) hatred.

geðklofa schizophrenic; *synonyms* (*adj*) schizoid, hebephrenic, insane.

geðklofasjúklingur schizophrenic; *synonyms* (*adj*) schizoid, hebephrenic, insane.

geðklofi schizophrenia; *synonym* (*adj*) paranoia.

geðlægð 1. depression; *synonyms* (*n*) basin, cavity, dejection, decline, dent; *antonyms* (*n*) cheerfulness, happiness, boom, elation, encouragement, 2. melancholia; *synonyms* (*n*) depression, melancholy, gloom, gloominess, (*adj*) mumps.

geðlæknir psychiatrist, *synonyms* (*n*) analyst, shrink, headhunter, psychoanalyst, counselor.

geðlæknisfræði psychiatry; *synonyms* (*n*) psychiatria, psychoanalysis, psychopathology.

geðlausn abreaction; *synonyms* (*n*) catharsis, purgation, katharsis.

geðrænn 1. affective; *synonyms* (*adj*) affectional, emotive, intense, moving, deep, **2**. emotional; *synonyms* (*adj*) dramatic, affecting, affective, effusive, passionate; *antonyms* (*adj*) impassive, unemotional, unflappable.

geðrættur psychogenic; *synonym* (*adj*) psychic.

geðrof 1. psychosis; *synonyms* (*n*) insanity, lunacy, fixation, madness, neurosis; *antonym* (*n*) sanity, **2**. schizophrenia; *synonym* (*adj*) paranoia.

geðshræring emotion; *synonyms* (*n*) affection, love, feeling, passion, sensation; *antonym* (*n*) intelligence.

geðsjúkdómafræði psychiatry; *synonyms* (*n*) psychiatria, psychoanalysis, psychopathology.

geðsjúkdómalæknir psychiatrist; *synonyms* (*n*) analyst, shrink, headhunter, psychoanalyst, counselor.

geðsjúklingur psychotic; *synonyms* (*adj*) insane, demented, mad, (*n*) lunatic, psycho.

geðsmunir affect; *synonyms* (*v*) touch, move, act, fake, feign.

geðstirður splenetic; *synonyms* (*adj*) fretful, peevish, prickly, angry, (*n*) morose.

geðstjarfi catatonia; *synonym* (*n*) gloom.

geðþótti discretion; *synonyms* (*n*) caution, circumspection, delicacy, prudence, diplomacy; *antonym* (*n*) recklessness.

geðvefrænn psychosomatic; *synonyms* (*adj*) emotional, mental, psychological.

geðveiki psychosis; *synonyms* (*n*) insanity, lunacy, fixation, madness, neurosis; *antonym* (*n*) sanity.

geðveikur psychotic; *synonyms* (*adj*) insane, demented, mad, (*n*) lunatic, psycho.

geðvilla psychopathy; *synonyms* (*n*) lunacy, insanity, neurosis.

geðvillingur psychopath; *synonyms* (*n*) maniac, lunatic, madperson, sociopath, nutcase.

geðvonska irritation; *synonyms* (*n*) aggravation, exasperation, anger, annoyance, displeasure; *antonym* (*n*) pleasure.

gefa 1. give; *synonyms* (*v*) allow, bestow, extend, accord, commit; *antonyms* (*v*) withdraw, take, withhold, **2**. provide; *synonyms* (*v*) give, contribute, furnish, offer, accommodate, **3**. accord; *synonyms* (*n*) agreement, assent, (*v*) agree, concord, consent; *antonyms* (*n*) disagreement, discord, strife, (*v*) conflict, **4**. administer; *synonyms* (*v*) manage, dispense, distribute, deal, operate, **5**. impart; *synonyms* (*v*) announce, communicate, convey, disclose, confer.

gefrata siblings; *synonyms* (*n*) sibs, family.

gefrato 1. siblings; *synonyms* (*n*) sibs, family, **2**. sibling; *synonyms* (*n*) sib, relation, relative, cognate, kin.

gegn versus; *synonyms* (*prep*) anti, about, concerning, (*adv*) against, counter.

gegnbleyta soak; *synonyms* (*v*) dip, drench, saturate, immerse, permeate; *antonym* (*v*) dry.

gegndræpi permeability; *synonyms* (*n*) perviousness, permeableness.

gegndræpur permeable; *synonyms* (*adj*) pervious, porous, absorbent, spongy, gritty; *antonyms* (*adj*) impermeable, resistant, waterproof, water-resistant, watertight.

gegnfær permeable; *synonyms* (*adj*) pervious, porous, absorbent, spongy, gritty; *antonyms* (*adj*) impermeable, resistant, waterproof, water-resistant, watertight.

gegnfararhlutfall transmittance; *synonyms* (*n*) transmission, transmittal, contagion, infection, passage.

gegnflæði 1. penetration; *synonyms* (*n*) insight, acuteness, (*v*) intelligence, discernment, (*adj*) acumen, **2**. osmosis; *synonym* (*n*) absorption.

gegnför transmission; *synonyms* (*n*) circulation, conveyance, contagion, transfer, broadcast.

gegnheill 1. solid; *synonyms* (*adj*) firm, dense, compact, consistent, hard; *antonyms* (*adj*) soft, unreliable, loose, gaseous, (*n*) liquid, **2**. massive; *synonyms* (*adj*) bulky, large, gigantic, huge, big; *antonyms* (*adj*) tiny, small, insignificant, miniature.

gegnhlaup puncture; *synonyms* (*n*) prick, cut, hole, (*v*) bore, drill; *antonym* (*v*) inflate.

gegnhlutun diffusion; *synonyms* (*n*) dissemination, dispersion, dispersal, distribution, spread.

gegnsær 1. transparent; *synonyms* (*adj*) diaphanous, lucid, obvious, plain, (*n*) clear; *antonyms* (*adj*) opaque, solid, **2**. hyaline; *synonyms* (*n*) hyalin, (*adj*) glassy, crystalline, hyaloid, limpid.

gegnsíun filtration; *synonyms* (*n*) percolation, filtering.

gegnskin transmission; *synonyms* (*n*) circulation, conveyance, contagion, transfer, broadcast.

gegntak bushing; *synonyms* (*n*) bush, mount, filling.

gegnþrenging penetration; *synonyms* (*n*) insight, acuteness, (*v*) intelligence, discernment, (*adj*) acumen.

gegnum via; *synonyms* (*prep*) by, with, toward, (*adv*) through, using.

gegnumflutningur transit; *synonyms* (*n*) journey, passage, conveyance, travel, movement.

gegnumlýsing radiography; *synonyms* (*n*) skiagraphy, sciagraphy.

gegnumumferð tandem; *synonyms* (*n*) bicycle, buggy, cycle, dogcart, random.

gegnumvæta soak; *synonyms* (*v*) dip, drench, saturate, immerse, permeate; *antonym* (*v*) dry.

gegnvæta soak; *synonyms* (*v*) dip, drench, saturate, immerse, permeate; *antonym* (*v*) dry.

gegnvæting imbibition; *synonyms* (*n*) imbibing, drinking, boozing, crapulence, drink.

geiga yaw; *synonyms* (*n*) swerve, (*v*) gape, turn, bend, gawk.

geil 1. meatus, **2.** gap; *synonyms* (*n*) break, cleft, crack, crevice, (*v*) breach.

geimfari astronaut; *synonyms* (*n*) cosmonaut, spaceman, astro, moonman, pilot.

geimferðafræði astronautics; *synonyms* (*n*) aeronautics, rocketry, orbiting.

geimlíffræði 1. astrobiology; *synonym* (*n*) exobiology, **2.** exobiology; *synonym* (*n*) astrobiology.

geimsiglingafræði astronautics; *synonyms* (*n*) aeronautics, rocketry, orbiting.

geimský nebula; *synonyms* (*n*) cloud, fog, nebulosity, cloudiness, film.

geimþoka nebula; *synonyms* (*n*) cloud, fog, nebulosity, cloudiness, film.

geimur space; *synonyms* (*n*) length, gap, opening, period, place.

geiraskipting segmentation; *synonyms* (*n*) division, cleavage, partition, partitioning, sectionalization.

geiraskiptur segmental; *synonyms* (*adj*) metameric, segmented.

geiraskurður lobotomy; *synonyms* (*n*) leukotomy, leucotomy.

geiri 1. segment; *synonyms* (*n*) division, paragraph, bit, (*v*) section, part, **2.** slice; *synonyms* (*n*) share, chip, (*v*) cut, slash, carve, **3.** section; *synonyms* (*n*) portion, compartment, percentage, piece, (*v*) segment, **4.** sector; *synonyms* (*n*) department, area, branch, district, region, **5.** lobe; *synonyms* (*n*) flap, limb, member, arm, bough.

geirlaukur garlic; *synonyms* (*n*) ail, caviare, pickle, onion, (*adj*) fungus.

geirnagli dovetail; *synonyms* (*v*) anastomose, fit, mesh, (*adj*) mortise, enchase.

geirnefur skipper; *synonyms* (*n*) captain, commander, master, head, leader.

geirnegla dovetail; *synonyms* (*v*) anastomose, fit, mesh, (*adj*) mortise, enchase.

geirnegling dovetail; *synonyms* (*v*) anastomose, fit, mesh, (*adj*) mortise, enchase.

geirvarta 1. nipple; *synonyms* (*n*) mammilla, teat, breast, dug, mamilla, **2.** mamilla; *synonyms* (*n*) nipple, pap, tit, boob, bosom.

geisl 1. radiation; *synonyms* (*n*) emanation, emission, irradiation, (*v*) radioactivity, (*adj*) radiance, **2.** radian; *synonym* (*n*) rad.

geisla radiate; *synonyms* (*v*) gleam, beam, glow, glitter, shine.

geislabaugar halation; *synonyms* (*n*) halo, irradiation.

geislabaugur halo; *synonyms* (*n*) aureole, aura, glory, halation, ring.

geislabeinir collimator; *synonym* (*n*) effuser.

geisladeyfinn opaque; *synonyms* (*adj*) cloudy, dense, dull, muddy, obscure; *antonyms* (*adj*) clear, transparent, see-through.

geisladeyfni opacity; *synonyms* (*n*) obscurity, opaqueness, cloudiness, murkiness, opaque; *antonym* (*n*) clearness.

geisladreif scatter; *synonyms* (*v*) disperse, dispel, disseminate, distribute, (*n*) spread; *antonym* (*v*) gather.

geislagjafi radiator; *synonyms* (*n*) heater, stove, furnace, warmer.

geislaharka hardness; *synonyms* (*n*) firmness, austerity, asperity, callousness, difficulty; *antonym* (*n*) softness.

geislakerfi aster; *synonym* (*n*) starwort.

geislalægur radial; *synonyms* (*adj*) angelic, centrifugal, spiral, stellate, radiated.

geislalækningar radiology; *synonyms* (*n*) analysis, biopsy, radioscopy, urinalysis.

geislalæknisfræði radiology; *synonyms* (*n*) analysis, biopsy, radioscopy, urinalysis.

geislaloft emanation; *synonyms* (*n*) discharge, emission, effluvium, effusion, effluence.

geislamælir dosimeter; *synonym* (*n*) dosemeter.

geislameðferð radiotherapy; *synonyms* (*n*) irradiation, actinotherapy, radiation.

geislandi 1. radiant; *synonyms* (*adj*) bright, brilliant, beaming, beamy, (*v*) glittering; *antonym* (*adj*) dull, **2.** radial; *synonyms* (*adj*) angelic, centrifugal, spiral, stellate, radiated.

geislaónæmismæling radioimmunoassay; *synonym* (*n*) ria.

geislaorkumælir radiometer; *synonyms* (*n*) actinometer, eriometer, lucimeter, photometer, (*v*) bathometer.

geislapunktur radiant; *synonyms* (*adj*) bright, brilliant, beaming, beamy, (*v*) glittering; *antonym* (*adj*) dull.

geislar aster; *synonym* (*n*) starwort.

geislari radiator; *synonyms* (*n*) heater, stove, furnace, warmer.

geislaskammtamælir dosimeter; *synonym* (*n*) dosemeter.

geislaskammtur 1. dose; *synonyms* (*n*) potion, dosage, draught, medicine, (*v*) drug, **2.** exposure; *synonyms* (*n*) display, exposition, detection, peril, (*v*) disclosure.

geislastengur wishbone; *synonyms* (n) sudarium, triskelion, veronica, boom.

geislastyrkur intensity; *synonyms* (n) force, forcefulness, depth, volume, (adj) strength; *antonyms* (n) dullness, indifference, weakness.

geislavirkni radioactivity; *synonyms* (n) activity, radiation, action, activeness, electricity.

geisli 1. radius; *synonyms* (n) length, semidiameter, spoke, range, compass, 2. ray; *synonyms* (n) beam, light, flash, glow, gleam, 3. beam; *synonyms* (n) blaze, ray, timber, (v) glare, (adj) shine, 4. wireless; *synonyms* (n) radio, radiocommunication, tuner, (v) radiotelephone, intercom, 5. radio; *synonyms* (n) wireless, broadcasting, radiotelegram, (v) broadcast, transmit.

geislóttur centric; *synonyms* (adj) central, centrical.

geislun 1. radiation; *synonyms* (n) emanation, emission, irradiation, (v) radioactivity, (adj) radiance, 2. irradiation; *synonyms* (n) radiotherapy, beam, radiation, actinotherapy, light.

geislunarafl luminosity; *synonyms* (n) brightness, light, illumination, glow, brilliance; *antonym* (n) dullness.

geislunarfræði radiology; *synonyms* (n) analysis, biopsy, radioscopy, urinalysis.

geislunarljómi radiance; *synonyms* (n) gleam, glow, glory, brilliance, brilliancy; *antonym* (n) dullness.

geislunarmælir radiometer; *synonyms* (n) actinometer, eriometer, lucimeter, photometer, (v) bathometer.

geislunarmagn exposure; *synonyms* (n) display, exposition, detection, peril, (v) disclosure.

geislunarmynd radiograph; *synonyms* (n) radiogram, x-ray, shadowgraph, skiagram, skiagraph.

geit goat; *synonyms* (n) butt, lecher, satyr, chamois, fornicator.

gelatín gelatin; *synonyms* (n) gelatine, jelly, mastic, ropy, glutenous.

gelda castrate; *synonyms* (v) emasculate, alter, geld, desexualize, (n) eunuch.

geldæxlun 1. apomixis, 2. parthenogenesis; *synonyms* (v) abiogenesis, biogenesis, digenesis, dysmerogenesis, eumerogenesis.

gelding castration; *synonyms* (n) emasculation, eviration, bowdlerisation, bowdlerization, expurgation.

geldingahnappur thrift; *synonyms* (n) economy, frugality, parsimony, husbandry, prosperity; *antonyms* (n) extravagance, generosity.

geldingur castrate; *synonyms* (v) emasculate, alter, geld, desexualize, (n) eunuch.

geldögn neutron; *synonym* (n) electricity.

geldur sterile; *synonyms* (adj) infertile, barren, fruitless, effete, (v) abortive; *antonyms* (adj) fertile, unhygienic.

gelgjubólur acne; *synonyms* (n) pimple, whelk, papule, ridge, wale.

gelgjuskeið adolescence; *synonyms* (n) immaturity, boyhood, juvenility, puberty, youth.

gelgjuþrymlar acne; *synonyms* (n) pimple, whelk, papule, ridge, wale.

gellir loudspeaker; *synonyms* (n) speaker, amplifier, amp, talker, utterer.

gelsykra agar; *synonym* (n) isinglass.

gelt bark; *synonyms* (n) snarl, yelp, (v) yap, skin, cry; *antonyms* (v) mutter, whisper.

gemsa chamois; *synonyms* (n) shammy, chammy, flea, frog, goat.

gen gene; *synonyms* (n) chromosome, cistron.

genaferja vector; *synonyms* (n) direction, bearing, course, sender, transmitter.

genasæti locus; *synonyms* (n) locale, position, spot, place, venue.

genasamsæta allele; *synonym* (n) allelomorph.

genaturnun conversion; *synonyms* (n) alteration, change, changeover, adaptation, exchange.

genayfirfærsla translocation; *synonyms* (n) shift, interchange.

gengd mechanism; *synonyms* (n) apparatus, machinery, appliance, contrivance, device.

gengi 1. team; *synonyms* (n) crew, company, gang, squad, (v) pair, 2. success; *synonyms* (n) conquest, achievement, hit, prosperity, passing; *antonyms* (n) failure, flop, debacle, defeat, disappointment.

gengisauki premium; *synonyms* (n) bonus, agio, bounty, payment, extra; *antonym* (adj) inferior.

gengisfelling devaluation; *synonyms* (n) depression, deterioration.

gengishækkun 1. revaluation; *synonyms* (n) reappraisal, reassessment, revalorization, brushup, critique, 2. appreciation; *synonyms* (n) admiration, acknowledgment, approval, awareness, (v) sense; *antonym* (n) depreciation.

gengislækkun 1. depreciation; *synonyms* (n) abatement, detraction, disparagement, derogation, deterioration, 2. devaluation; *synonym* (n) depression.

gengismunur agio; *synonyms* (n) premium, agiotage, percentage, drawback, poundage.

gengisris appreciation; *synonyms* (n) admiration, acknowledgment, approval, awareness, (v) sense; *antonym* (n) depreciation.

gengissig depreciation; *synonyms* (n) abatement, detraction, disparagement, derogation, deterioration.

gengjudeiling pitch; *synonyms* (*n*) degree, dip, (*v*) fling, cast, chuck.

gengjur thread; *synonyms* (*n*) string, line, yarn, (*v*) file, range.

genmögnun amplification; *synonyms* (*n*) augmentation, addition, expansion, extension, gain; *antonym* (*n*) reduction.

gensæti locus; *synonyms* (*n*) locale, position, spot, place, venue.

genset locus; *synonyms* (*n*) locale, position, spot, place, venue.

gento stocks; *synonyms* (*n*) pillory, bilboes, securities, calls, options.

gepatro 1. parent; *synonyms* (*n*) mother, origin, (*v*) father, foster, rear; *antonym* (*n*) child, 2. parents; *synonym* (*n*) ancestors.

ger yeast; *synonyms* (*n*) barm, leaven, foam, froth, (*adj*) ferment.

gera 1. do; *synonyms* (*v*) act, cheat, commit, accomplish, complete; *antonyms* (*v*) neglect, unmake, 2. reach; *synonyms* (*v*) range, overtake, obtain, achieve, (*n*) fetch, 3. render; *synonyms* (*v*) afford, interpret, explain, furnish, give, 4. act; *synonyms* (*n*) accomplishment, action, (*v*) achievement, behave, deed; *antonym* (*v*) refrain, 5. commit; *synonyms* (*v*) commend, assign, charge, consign, apply.

gerandefni agonist; *synonyms* (*n*) protagonist, admirer, booster, champion, friend.

gerandi 1. actuator, 2. agent; *synonyms* (*n*) agency, broker, deputy, medium, (*v*) actor, 3. actor; *synonyms* (*n*) doer, player, agent, comedian, (*v*) performer.

gerandvöðvi agonist; *synonyms* (*n*) protagonist, admirer, booster, champion, friend.

gerð 1. structure; *synonyms* (*n*) form, building, arrangement, edifice, shape, 2. style; *synonyms* (*n*) fashion, name, (*v*) call, entitle, (*adj*) manner, 3. type; *synonyms* (*n*) pattern, character, kind, nature, (*adj*) model, 4. version; *synonyms* (*n*) reading, translation, construction, interpretation, rendering, 5. design; *synonyms* (*n*) aim, purpose, scheme, conception, (*v*) plan; *antonym* (*n*) chance.

gerðabók 1. minutes; *synonyms* (*n*) proceedings, record, transactions, records, journal, 2. journal; *synonyms* (*n*) diary, book, magazine, newspaper, (*adj*) daybook.

gerðaflokkun typology; *synonym* (*n*) typing.

gerðafræði typology; *synonym* (*n*) typing.

gerðardómari arbitrator; *synonyms* (*n*) arbiter, mediator, referee, judge, umpire.

gerðardómsmaður arbitrator; *synonyms* (*n*) arbiter, mediator, referee, judge, umpire.

gerðardómsmeðferð arbitration; *synonyms* (*n*) arbitrament, mediation, decision, intervention, judgment.

gerðardómur arbitration; *synonyms* (*n*) arbitrament, mediation, decision, intervention, judgment.

gerðarlýsing schema; *synonyms* (*n*) outline, plan, chart, graph, scheme.

gerðarmaður 1. arbitrator; *synonyms* (*n*) arbiter, mediator, referee, judge, umpire, 2. moderator; *synonyms* (*n*) chairman, arbitrator, intermediary, negotiator, diplomat.

gerði 1. wall; *synonyms* (*n*) partition, bar, barrier, bulwark, (*v*) fence, 2. fence; *synonyms* (*n*) enclosure, hurdle, pale, (*v*) hedge, wall.

gerefti case; *synonyms* (*n*) box, example, bin, cover, jacket.

gerendaskrá cast; *synonyms* (*v*) hurl, throw, form, shed, stamp.

gereyðing extinction; *synonyms* (*n*) destruction, extermination, end, expiration, (*v*) death; *antonyms* (*n*) survival, preservation.

gereyðingarblekking nihilism; *synonyms* (*n*) anarchy, atheism, disbelief, abnegation, (*adj*) nihility.

gerhvati 1. ferment; *synonyms* (*n*) agitation, excitement, barm, (*v*) effervesce, (*adj*) pother, 2. enzyme; *synonyms* (*n*) catalyst, solution.

geri operator; *synonyms* (*n*) driver, hustler, manipulator, agent, doer.

gerilæta phage; *synonym* (*n*) bacteriophage.

gerilhár pilus; *synonyms* (*n*) hair, capillament, cilia, cilium, fuzz.

gerill bacterium; *synonyms* (*n*) bacteria, microbe, rabbit, (*adj*) virus.

gerilsneyðing pasteurization; *synonyms* (*n*) pasteurisation, pasteurism.

gerilveira 1. phage; *synonym* (*n*) bacteriophage, 2. bacteriophage; *synonym* (*n*) phage.

gerja ferment; *synonyms* (*n*) agitation, excitement, barm, (*v*) effervesce, (*adj*) pother.

gerjast ferment; *synonyms* (*n*) agitation, excitement, barm, (*v*) effervesce, (*adj*) pother.

gerjun fermentation; *synonyms* (*n*) ferment, agitation, excitement, effervescence, fermenting.

gerlabani bactericide; *synonyms* (*n*) antiseptic, germicide, bacteriacide, disinfectant, antibacterial.

gerlaeyðandi bactericidal; *synonyms* (*adj*) disinfectant, germicidal, antiseptic.

gerlafræði bacteriology; *synonyms* (*n*) microbiology, virology, mycology.

gerlaleysi sterility; *synonyms* (*n*) infertility, barrenness, impotence, infecundity, antisepsis; *antonym* (*n*) fertility.

gerlar bacteria; *synonyms* (n) germ, bacterium, microbe, bug, (adj) virus.

gerlaþyrping colony; *synonyms* (n) settlement, community, plantation, dependency, village.

gerningur instrument; *synonyms* (n) channel, deed, agency, apparatus, appliance.

gersveppur 1. saccharomyces, 2. yeast; *synonyms* (n) barm, leaven, foam, froth, (adj) ferment.

gervending reversion; *synonyms* (n) atavism, relapse, reverse, lapse, regress.

gervi figure; *synonyms* (n) form, appearance, character, (v) design, cast.

gerviefni 1. polymer, 2. plastic; *synonyms* (adj) flexible, ductile, elastic, malleable, (v) limber.

gervigúmmí neoprene; *synonym* (n) plastic.

gervihnöttur satellite; *synonyms* (n) follower, moon, planet, attendant, orbiter.

gervikló peg; *synonyms* (n) bolt, pin, hook, dowel, leg.

gerviliffæri prosthesis; *synonym* (n) prothesis.

gerving synthesis; *synonyms* (n) combination, fusion, compound, incorporation, mixture; *antonym* (n) separation.

gervingur artifact; *synonyms* (n) artefact, creation, handicraft, product, antique.

gerviómur echo; *synonyms* (n) answer, (v) repeat, reproduce, resound, reverberate.

gervitungl satellite; *synonyms* (n) follower, moon, planet, attendant, orbiter.

gervitvíkynja androgynous; *synonyms* (adj) asexual, genderless, neuter, neutral, sexless.

gesims moulding; *synonyms* (n) molding, modeling, mold, mould, cast.

gestur 1. sojourner; *synonyms* (n) guest, householder, incumbent, inmate, lodger, 2. guest; *synonyms* (n) stranger, caller, alien, customer, visitor.

geta 1. qualifications; *synonyms* (n) competence, capacity, terms, ability, credentials, 2. skill; *synonyms* (n) artifice, capability, knack, (adj) dexterity, craft; *antonyms* (n) clumsiness, inability, incompetence, 3. capability; *synonyms* (n) aptitude, capableness, faculty, gift, potency; *antonyms* (n) failure, incapability.

getgáta conjecture; *synonyms* (n) guess, supposition, assumption, (v) suppose, estimate; *antonym* (n) fact.

getnaðarfæri genitalia; *synonyms* (n) genitals, privates, crotch, fork.

getnaðarverja 1. preservative; *synonyms* (adj) preservatory, protective, conservative, (n) preserver, antiseptic, 2. contraceptive; *synonyms* (adj) prophylactic, antifertility, cautionary, (n) preventive, preventative.

getnaður 1. conception; *synonyms* (n) notion, concept, idea, creation, thought; *antonym* (n) misconception, 2. impregnation; *synonyms* (n) fecundation, fertilization, conception, fertilisation, permeation.

getuleysi impotence; *synonyms* (n) disability, inability, weakness, feebleness, debility.

geyma 1. preserve; *synonyms* (v) maintain, keep, defend, (n) conserve, jam; *antonym* (v) destroy, 2. store; *synonyms* (n) hoard, shop, market, (v) stock, accumulate, 3. carry; *synonyms* (v) bear, bring, convey, conduct, take, 4. archive; *synonyms* (n) record, scroll, archives, records, paper, 5. park; *synonyms* (n) garden, common, (v) deposit, locate, place.

geymabakki tray; *synonyms* (n) plate, dish, basket, bassinet, case.

geymasýra acid; *synonyms* (adj) acerbic, acidic, bitter, caustic, sharp; *antonym* (adj) sweet.

geymd 1. storage; *synonyms* (n) conservation, depot, memory, preservation, retention, 2. conservation; *synonyms* (n) maintenance, upkeep, keep, custody, protection; *antonym* (n) destruction, 3. carry; *synonyms* (v) bear, bring, convey, conduct, take.

geyming storing; *synonyms* (n) warehousing, harvest.

geyminn conservative; *synonyms* (adj) moderate, bourgeois, conventional, cautious, reactionary; *antonyms* (adj) activist, wide-ranging, (n) liberal, radical.

geymir 1. reservoir; *synonyms* (n) cistern, fountain, well, lake, store, 2. receiver; *synonyms* (n) recipient, beneficiary, cashier, earpiece, headset; *antonym* (n) donor, 3. tank; *synonyms* (n) reservoir, container, cooler, belly, boiler.

geymiskassi case; *synonyms* (n) box, example, bin, cover, jacket.

geymsla 1. storage; *synonyms* (n) conservation, depot, memory, preservation, retention, 2. stowage; *synonyms* (n) stowing, storeroom, shipment, cargo, contents, 3. preservation; *synonyms* (n) maintenance, keeping, protection, custody, upkeep; *antonyms* (n) destruction, extinction, release, 4. store; *synonyms* (n) hoard, shop, market, (v) stock, accumulate, 5. memory; *synonyms* (n) memento, recall, recollection, remembrance, reminiscence.

geymsluefni preservative; *synonyms* (adj) preservatory, protective, conservative, (n) preserver, antiseptic.

geymslufé deposit; *synonyms* (n) charge, (v) bank, commit, store, fix; *antonym* (v) withdraw.

geymsluhýsill reservoir; *synonyms* (n) cistern, fountain, well, lake, store.

giftast 1. wed; *synonyms* (*v*) espouse, marry, tie, join, conjoin; *antonym* (*v*) divorce, **2.** marry; *synonyms* (*v*) link, splice, unite, wive, (*n*) wed.

giftur married; *synonyms* (*adj*) marital, wedded, conjugal, matrimonial, connubial; *antonyms* (*adj*) single, unmarried.

gigt rheumatism; *synonyms* (*v*) gout, cephalalgia, earache, lumbago, neuralgia.

gígtappi neck (háls); *synonyms* (*n*) throat, cervix, neckline, (*v*) pet, (*adj*) stricture.

gigtarsjúklingur rheumatic; *synonyms* (*adj*) arthritic, rheumatoid, creaky, arthrodynic, creaking.

gígur crater; *synonyms* (*n*) hollow, cavity, hole, pit, (*adj*) well.

gikkur trigger; *synonyms* (*v*) activate, initiate, spark, start, incite.

gil ravine; *synonyms* (*n*) gorge, canyon, chasm, dell, (*v*) gap.

gildandi 1. approved; *synonyms* (*adj*) accepted, certified, sanctioned, allowed, authorized; *antonyms* (*adj*) informal, unofficial, **2.** current; *synonyms* (*adj*) common, contemporary, (*n*) flow, stream, (*prep*) course; *antonyms* (*adj*) obsolete, past, old, old-fashioned, previous.

gildi 1. value; *synonyms* (*n*) merit, cost, appraise, (*v*) price, appreciate; *antonyms* (*n*) disadvantage, futility, uselessness, insignificance, **2.** validity; *synonyms* (*n*) force, truth, authority, legitimacy, soundness, **3.** valence; *synonyms* (*n*) valency, atomicity, quantivalence, equivalence, (*v*) unsaturation, **4.** valency; *synonym* (*n*) valence.

gilding 1. validation; *synonyms* (*n*) confirmation, proof, substantiation, verification, establishment, **2.** assignment; *synonyms* (*n*) allocation, allotment, appointment, assigning, mission.

gildisákvörðun evaluation; *synonyms* (*n*) appraisal, assessment, estimation, judgment, mark.

gildisdagur currency; *synonyms* (*n*) cash, money, coin, circulation, vogue.

gildislækkun debasement; *synonyms* (*n*) abasement, corruption, adulteration, degradation, (*adj*) abjection; *antonym* (*n*) purification.

gildislok expiration; *synonyms* (*n*) ending, conclusion, end, finish, breath.

gildisskömmtun quantization; *synonym* (*n*) quantisation.

gildissvið scope; *synonyms* (*n*) range, reach, domain, purview, room.

gildistala valence; *synonyms* (*n*) valency, atomicity, quantivalence, equivalence, (*v*) unsaturation.

gildleiki thickness; *synonyms* (*n*) density, consistency, width, layer, heaviness.

Gildra trap; *synonyms* (*n*) snare, net, ambush, (*v*) catch, entrap.

gildur 1. valid; *synonyms* (*adj*) legal, sound, right, genuine, solid; *antonyms* (*adj*) unacceptable, invalid, annulled, bogus, illogical, **2.** effective; *synonyms* (*adj*) beneficial, practical, (*n*) competent, capable, able; *antonyms* (*adj*) ineffective, useless, weak, inoperative.

gimi bud; *synonyms* (*n*) bloom, blossom, flower, (*v*) graft, shoot.

gingkó ginkgo; *synonym* (*n*) gingko.

ginvarta palate; *synonyms* (*n*) gusto, liking, relish, taste, tooth.

gips gypsum; *synonym* (*n*) plaster.

gír gear; *synonyms* (*n*) equipment, outfit, tackle, apparatus, device.

girða fence; *synonyms* (*n*) enclosure, barrier, hurdle, (*v*) hedge, wall.

girði fence; *synonyms* (*n*) enclosure, barrier, hurdle, (*v*) hedge, wall.

girðifaldur skirt; *synonyms* (*n*) border, edge, brim, (*v*) fringe, circumvent.

girðilag film; *synonyms* (*n*) membrane, coating, cloud, cinema, (*v*) mist.

gírhlutfall gearing; *synonyms* (*n*) gear, affairs, behavior, caravan, clothing.

gíring gearing; *synonyms* (*n*) gear, affairs, behavior, caravan, clothing.

gírkassi 1. transmission; *synonyms* (*n*) circulation, conveyance, contagion, transfer, broadcast, **2.** gearbox; *synonym* (*n*) transmission, **3.** gear; *synonyms* (*n*) equipment, outfit, tackle, apparatus, device, **4.** gearing; *synonyms* (*n*) gear, affairs, behavior, caravan, clothing.

gírskipting gearshift; *synonyms* (*n*) gearstick, joystick, shifter, wheel, pedals.

gírstöng gearshift; *synonyms* (*n*) gearstick, joystick, shifter, wheel, pedals.

gisinn lax; *synonyms* (*adj*) slack, careless, flaccid, loose, (*v*) frail; *antonyms* (*adj*) strict, careful, severe.

gisti register; *synonyms* (*n*) record, list, inventory, (*v*) file, enroll.

gistihús hotel; *synonyms* (*n*) lodge, house, inn, tavern, spa.

gistilíf commensalism; *synonym* (*n*) synoecy.

gistilífi commensalism; *synonym* (*n*) synoecy.

gjá 1. precipice; *synonyms* (*n*) cliff, steep, verge, clef, crevice, **2.** abyss; *synonyms* (*n*) abysm, chasm, deep, gorge, gulf, **3.** chasm; *synonyms* (*n*) abyss, breach, gap, hiatus, ravine, **4.** gulf; *synonyms* (*n*) bay, cove, inlet, pit, rift, **5.** fissure; *synonyms* (*n*) crack, break, cleft, cranny, chap; *antonym* (*n*) repair.

gjafafé grant; *synonyms* (*v*) give, allow, award, bestow, admit; *antonyms* (*v*) deny, reject.

gjafaforsenda assumption; *synonyms* (*n*) presumption, supposition, hypothesis, premise, adoption.

gjafari dealer; *synonyms* (*n*) merchant, trader, monger, seller, vendor; *antonym* (*n*) user.

gjafi 1. source; *synonyms* (*n*) origin, root, cause, commencement, beginning, **2**. donor; *synonyms* (*n*) contributor, giver, donator, presenter, (*v*) feoffer; *antonyms* (*n*) receiver, recipient, **3**. generator; *synonyms* (*n*) author, creator, founder, boiler, originator.

gjafmildi 1. unselfishness; *synonyms* (*n*) altruism, generosity, generousness, kindness, care; *antonym* (*n*) selfishness, **2**. generosity; *synonyms* (*n*) charity, benevolence, bounty, liberality, (*adj*) beneficence; *antonyms* (*n*) stinginess, greed, meanness, thrift.

gjald 1. price; *synonyms* (*n*) cost, worth, charge, (*v*) appraise, estimate, **2**. agio; *synonyms* (*n*) premium, agiotage, percentage, drawback, poundage, **3**. duty; *synonyms* (*n*) business, function, commitment, assignment, chore, **4**. levy; *synonyms* (*n*) tax, duty, assessment, (*v*) impose, raise.

gjaldeyrir currency; *synonyms* (*n*) cash, money, coin, circulation, vogue.

gjaldfær solvent; *synonyms* (*n*) resolvent, dissolvent, solution, menstruum, answer; *antonyms* (*adj*) bankrupt, broke.

gjaldfæra charge; *synonyms* (*n*) accusation, burden, care, (*v*) accuse, blame; *antonyms* (*v*) request, absolve, retreat.

gjaldfærni solvency; *synonym* (*n*) solvability.

gjaldfærsla charge; *synonyms* (*n*) accusation, burden, care, (*v*) accuse, blame; *antonyms* (*v*) request, absolve, retreat.

gjaldfærsluhæfur chargeable; *synonyms* (*adj*) liable, guilty, amenable, indictable, responsible; *antonym* (*adj*) exempt.

gjaldfalla mature; *synonyms* (*adj*) ripe, (*v*) grow, ripen, develop, age; *antonyms* (*adj*) childish, naive, unripe, young, (*v*) immature.

gjaldfallinn 1. due; *synonyms* (*adj*) appropriate, (*adv*) right, (*v*) owing, (*n*) debt, duty; *antonyms* (*adj*) paid, undue, **2**. overdue; *synonyms* (*adj*) belated, late, back, due, (*adv*) behind; *antonym* (*adj*) early.

gjaldfrestur credit; *synonyms* (*n*) credence, appreciation, belief, (*v*) believe, accredit; *antonyms* (*n*) cash, (*v*) debit, discredit.

gjaldhæfi solvency; *synonym* (*n*) solvability.

gjaldhæfur solvent; *synonyms* (*n*) resolvent, dissolvent, solution, menstruum, answer; *antonyms* (*adj*) bankrupt, broke.

gjaldkeri 1. treasurer; *synonyms* (*n*) cashier, banker, financier, fiscal, guardian, **2**. cashier; *synonyms* (*n*) accountant, (*v*) depose, discard, reject, discharge.

gjaldkræfur due; *synonyms* (*adj*) appropriate, (*adv*) right, (*v*) owing, (*n*) debt, duty; *antonyms* (*adj*) paid, undue.

gjaldlagning charging; *synonyms* (*n*) decree, blocking.

gjaldmiðill currency; *synonyms* (*n*) cash, money, coin, circulation, vogue.

gjaldskrá tariff; *synonyms* (*n*) duty, charge, excise, custom, tax.

gjaldskyldur chargeable; *synonyms* (*adj*) liable, guilty, amenable, indictable, responsible; *antonym* (*adj*) exempt.

gjaldþol solidity; *synonyms* (*n*) consistency, density, firmness, compactness, rigidity; *antonym* (*n*) brittleness.

gjaldþrot 1. receivership, **2**. bankruptcy; *synonyms* (*n*) failure, insolvency, smash, ruin, indebtedness, **3**. liquidation; *synonyms* (*n*) settlement, bankruptcy, destruction, elimination, extermination, **4**. insolvency; *synonyms* (*n*) poverty, hardship, impoverishment, need, nonsolvency; *antonym* (*n*) solvency.

gjaldþrota bankrupt; *synonyms* (*adj*) insolvent, broke, destitute, (*v*) ruin, break; *antonyms* (*adj*) solvent, rich.

Gjall slag; *synonyms* (*n*) cinder, clinker, dross, scoria, scum.

gjöf 1. donation; *synonyms* (*n*) contribution, gift, benefaction, present, award, **2**. present; *synonyms* (*adj*) grant, confer, (*n*) donation, (*v*) bestow, display; *antonyms* (*adj*) missing, (*n*) past, future, (*v*) withdraw, (*adv*) absent, **3**. administration; *synonyms* (*n*) management, direction, organization, running, power, **4**. gift; *synonyms* (*n*) faculty, flair, (*adj*) endowment, ability, talent; *antonym* (*n*) inability.

gjöld 1. expenditure; *synonyms* (*n*) charge, cost, disbursement, consumption, expense; *antonyms* (*n*) income, savings, **2**. expenses; *synonyms* (*n*) expenditure, costs, fee, spending, overheads.

gjörð 1. strap; *synonyms* (*n*) belt, leash, strop, (*v*) lash, whip, **2**. band; *synonyms* (*n*) cluster, party, set, swathe, (*v*) ring.

gjörhreinsa sanitize; *synonyms* (*v*) disinfect, sterilize, clean, cleanse, purify; *antonym* (*v*) contaminate.

gjörvi processor; *synonyms* (*n*) mainframe, butcher, computer, laptop, notebook.

gjóska ash; *synonyms* (*n*) jasmine, lilac, (*v*) cinder, scoriae, (*adj*) gray.

glaðlyndur 1. cheerful; *synonyms* (*adj*) buoyant, breezy, blithe, bright, carefree; *antonyms* (*adj*) depressed, gloomy, sad, unhappy, dejected, **2.** merry; *synonyms* (*adj*) gay, joyful, lively, cheerful, (*n*) convivial, **3.** gay; *synonyms* (*adj*) festive, gaudy, airy, brave, (*n*) homosexual.

glaðsinna sanguine; *synonyms* (*adj*) hopeful, ruddy, optimistic, red, bloody.

glaður 1. cheerful; *synonyms* (*adj*) buoyant, breezy, blithe, bright, carefree; *antonyms* (*adj*) depressed, gloomy, sad, unhappy, dejected, **2.** happy; *synonyms* (*adj*) fortunate, felicitous, contented, gay, (*n*) auspicious; *antonyms* (*adj*) miserable, sorrowful, **3.** lighthearted; *synonyms* (*adj*) blithesome, cheerful, playful, jovial, gleeful; *antonym* (*adj*) serious, **4.** merry; *synonyms* (*adj*) joyful, lively, glad, jolly, (*n*) convivial, **5.** lively; *synonyms* (*adj*) brisk, active, agile, energetic, keen; *antonyms* (*adj*) dull, inactive, lethargic, listless, lifeless.

glæpur 1. crime; *synonyms* (*n*) offense, blame, guilt, injustice, transgression, **2.** offence; *synonyms* (*n*) infraction, infringement, misdemeanor, misdemeanour, assault.

glær 1. vitreous; *synonyms* (*adj*) glassy, calculous, clear, concrete, crystalline, **2.** translucent; *synonyms* (*adj*) diaphanous, lucid, transparent, semitransparent, limpid; *antonyms* (*adj*) opaque, thick, **3.** hyaline; *synonyms* (*n*) hyalin, (*adj*) hyaloid, transpicuous, vitreous.

glæra 1. varnish; *synonyms* (*n*) coat, lacquer, paint, (*v*) gloss, color, **2.** cornea; *synonyms* (*n*) white, iris, pupil, retina, **3.** acetate; *synonym* (*n*) ethanoate, **4.** overhead; *synonyms* (*adv*) above, aloft, over, up, (*n*) expense.

glærfrymi cytosol; *synonym* (*n*) cytoplasma.

glærulakk varnish; *synonyms* (*n*) coat, lacquer, paint, (*v*) gloss, color.

glærumóða nebula; *synonyms* (*n*) cloud, fog, nebulosity, cloudiness, film.

glæruvagl walleye; *synonym* (*n*) exotropia.

glærvefur hyaline; *synonyms* (*n*) hyalin, (*adj*) clear, glassy, crystalline, hyaloid.

glamra 1. rattle; *synonyms* (*n*) roll, jangle, jingle, click, (*v*) clatter, **2.** chatter; *synonyms* (*n*) prattle, (*v*) babble, chat, gossip, jabber.

glamur chatter; *synonyms* (*n*) prattle, (*v*) babble, chat, gossip, jabber.

glans glaze; *synonyms* (*n*) shine, coating, sheen, (*v*) burnish, glass.

glapdæminn paranoid; *synonyms* (*adj*) absorbed, engrossed, fanatical, hooked, (*n*) paranoiac.

glas 1. glass; *synonyms* (*n*) pane, bottle, drink, bowl, cup, **2.** glasses; *synonyms* (*n*) spectacles, eyeglasses, specs, bifocals, monocle.

glaso 1. glass; *synonyms* (*n*) pane, bottle, drink, bowl, cup, **2.** glasses; *synonyms* (*n*) spectacles, eyeglasses, specs, bifocals, monocle.

gleði joy; *synonyms* (*n*) delight, enjoyment, elation, gladness, (*v*) exult; *antonyms* (*n*) misery, sorrow, sadness, disaster, grief.

gleiðbogamynstur pattern; *synonyms* (*n*) model, design, fashion, form, mold.

gleiðboganet lattice; *synonyms* (*n*) grill, fretwork, grid, grille, net.

gler glass; *synonyms* (*n*) pane, bottle, drink, bowl, cup.

gleráll eel; *synonyms* (*n*) yeel, (*v*) labyrinth, maze, serpent.

gleraugu 1. spectacles; *synonyms* (*n*) eyeglasses, glasses, specs, bifocals, monocle, **2.** glasses; *synonym* (*n*) spectacles, **3.** goggles; *synonym* (*n*) barnacles.

glerharður chilled; *synonyms* (*adj*) cold, frozen, freezing, cool, refrigerated.

glerkenndur vitreous; *synonyms* (*adj*) glassy, calculous, clear, concrete, crystalline.

glerungur 1. glaze; *synonyms* (*n*) shine, coating, sheen, (*v*) burnish, glass, **2.** enamel; *synonyms* (*v*) coat, glaze, varnish, lacker, lacquer.

gleypa 1. absorb; *synonyms* (*v*) consume, drink, engross, imbibe, assimilate; *antonyms* (*v*) bore, emit, **2.** preoccupy; *synonyms* (*v*) occupy, engage, absorb, enthrall, exercise, **3.** engross; *synonyms* (*v*) copy, captivate, engulf, fascinate, (*adj*) immerse, **4.** engage; *synonyms* (*v*) contract, attract, book, employ, betroth; *antonyms* (*v*) fire, disengage.

gleypifruma 1. scavenger; *synonyms* (*n*) magpie, hunter, packrat, predator, quencher, **2.** macrophage.

gleyping absorption; *synonyms* (*n*) assimilation, attention, concentration, inhalation, engrossment.

gleypinn 1. absorbent; *synonyms* (*adj*) absorptive, penetrable, porous, thirsty, (*n*) sorbent; *antonym* (*adj*) impermeable, **2.** absorbing; *synonyms* (*v*) exciting, (*adj*) interesting, engrossing, fascinating, charming.

gleypir collector; *synonyms* (*n*) accumulator, receiver, gatherer, caporal, choregus.

gleypni 1. permeability; *synonyms* (*n*) perviousness, permeableness, **2.** absorption; *synonyms* (*n*) assimilation, attention, concentration, inhalation, engrossment, **3.** absorptivity, **4.** absorptance.

gleypur porous; *synonyms* (*adj*) permeable, leaky, poriferous, holey, open; *antonym* (*adj*) impermeable.

gliðnun 1. dilation; *synonyms* (*n*) dilatation, expansion, swelling, growth, spread, **2.** divergence; *synonyms* (*n*) discrepancy, difference, disagreement, dissimilarity, variance; *antonyms* (*n*) convergence, meeting, agreement, amalgamation, **3**. dispersion; *synonyms* (*n*) diffusion, dispersal, dissipation, distribution, circulation.

glimmer mica; *synonyms* (*n*) isinglass, nacre, glimmer, glist.

glitrandi brilliant; *synonyms* (*adj*) bright, splendid, glorious, illustrious, intelligent; *antonyms* (*adj*) dull, dim, awful, dark.

gljáandi bright; *synonyms* (*adj*) clear, alive, apt, intelligent, vivid; *antonyms* (*adj*) dull, cloudy, dark, dim, dreary.

gljáhúð enamel; *synonyms* (*v*) coat, glaze, varnish, lacker, lacquer.

gljái 1. gloss; *synonyms* (*n*) burnish, annotation, (*v*) glaze, comment, annotate; *antonym* (*n*) dullness, **2**. glaze; *synonyms* (*n*) shine, coating, sheen, enamel, (*v*) glass.

gljákol anthracite; *synonyms* (*n*) culm, carbon, charcoal, coke, coal.

gljálakk shellac; *synonyms* (*n*) lac, (*v*) varnish, clobber, lick, overpower.

gljásteinn mica; *synonyms* (*n*) isinglass, nacre, glimmer, glist.

gljúfur ravine; *synonyms* (*n*) gorge, canyon, chasm, dell, (*v*) gap.

gljúpefni sponge; *synonyms* (*n*) parasite, (*v*) mop, cadge, scrounge, bum.

gljúpleiki 1. porosity; *synonyms* (*n*) porousness, poriness, **2**. permeability; *synonyms* (*n*) perviousness, permeableness.

gljúpur 1. porous; *synonyms* (*adj*) permeable, leaky, poriferous, holey, open; *antonym* (*adj*) impermeable, **2**. cellular; *synonyms* (*adj*) locular, multilocular, polygastric, cellulated, cystic.

gló incandescence; *synonyms* (*n*) glow, glowing, heat, fire, radiance.

glóbrystingur robin; *synonym* (*n*) redbreast.

glóð incandescence; *synonyms* (*n*) glow, glowing, heat, fire, radiance.

glóða anneal; *synonyms* (*v*) temper, harden, season, toughen, (*n*) annealing.

glóðald heater; *synonyms* (*n*) brasier, warmer, bullet, fastball, calefactor.

glóðarker pumpkin; *synonyms* (*n*) head, pumpion, punkin, pompion.

glóðarþráður filament; *synonyms* (*n*) fiber, strand, yarn, fibril, hair.

glompa bunker; *synonyms* (*n*) bin, dugout, trap, ambuscade, ambush.

glópera bulb; *synonyms* (*n*) knob, lightbulb, corm, nodule, (*adj*) globule.

gloppa lacuna; *synonyms* (*n*) gap, blank, hiatus, dent, cavity.

glóþráður filament; *synonyms* (*n*) fiber, strand, yarn, fibril, hair.

glóvír filament; *synonyms* (*n*) fiber, strand, yarn, fibril, hair.

glufa 1. cleft; *synonyms* (*adj*) split, (*n*) break, cleavage, crevice, fissure, **2**. lacuna; *synonyms* (*n*) gap, blank, hiatus, dent, cavity, **3**. fissure; *synonyms* (*n*) crack, chasm, cleft, cranny, breach; *antonym* (*n*) repair.

gluggafaldur case; *synonyms* (*n*) box, example, bin, cover, jacket.

gluggajaðar border; *synonyms* (*n*) margin, brink, extremity, (*v*) edge, verge; *antonyms* (*n*) middle, (*v*) center.

gluggakarmur 1. case; *synonyms* (*n*) box, example, bin, cover, jacket, **2**. border; *synonyms* (*n*) margin, brink, extremity, (*v*) edge, verge; *antonyms* (*n*) middle, (*v*) center.

gluggareitur tile; *synonyms* (*n*) bonnet, castor, ceiling, roof, (*v*) cover.

gluggi window; *synonyms* (*n*) casement, porthole, pane, gap, embrasure.

glúkósi 1. dextrose; *synonyms* (*n*) dextroglucose, sweetener, **2**. glucose; *synonyms* (*n*) caramel, damson.

glundroði chaos; *synonyms* (*n*) anarchy, bedlam, clutter, disarray, disorder; *antonyms* (*n*) order, peace, orderliness, regulation.

glúten gluten; *synonyms* (*adj*) protein, glair, milk, mucilage, gelatin.

gluteo 1. buttocks; *synonyms* (*n*) backside, bottom, arse, ass, bum, **2**. buttock; *synonyms* (*n*) croup, rump, tail, dorsum, loin.

glý glycine; *synonym* (*n*) glycocoll.

glýja glare; *synonyms* (*n*) blaze, brilliance, (*v*) beam, flame, flash; *antonym* (*v*) smile.

glýkógen glycogen; *synonym* (*n*) glucogen.

glýkógenmyndun glycogenesis; *synonyms* (*n*) glucogenesis, glycogeny.

glýserín glycerin; *synonyms* (*n*) glycerol, glycerine.

glýseról 1. glycerol; *synonyms* (*n*) glycerin, glycerine, **2**. glycerine; *synonyms* (*n*) glycerol, (*v*) grease, oil.

glysín glycine; *synonym* (*n*) glycocoll.

glýsín glycine; *synonym* (*n*) glycocoll.

glysserín glycerine; *synonyms* (*n*) glycerin, glycerol, (*v*) grease, oil.

gnægð 1. richness; *synonyms* (*n*) affluence, fertility, opulence, (*adj*) abundance, riches; *antonym* (*n*) emptiness, **2**. plenty; *synonyms* (*n*) copiousness, many, much, plenteousness, (*adj*) enough; *antonyms* (*n*) few, (*adj*) insufficient, **3**. abundance;

synonyms (*n*) wealth, amplitude, exuberance, plenitude, (*adj*) plenty; *antonyms* (*n*) dearth, scarcity, aridity, insufficiency, lack.

gnótt abundance; *synonyms* (*n*) wealth, amplitude, exuberance, plenitude, (*adj*) plenty; *antonyms* (*n*) dearth, scarcity, aridity, insufficiency, lack.

goðadrottning carnation; *synonyms* (*n*) crimson, gillyflower, pink, red, scarlet.

góðæri boom; *synonyms* (*n*) bang, roar, (*v*) blast, blare, flourish; *antonyms* (*n*) depression, (*v*) collapse, decline.

góðgerðarstarfsemi charity; *synonyms* (*n*) bounty, dole, favor, aid, (*v*) almsgiving; *antonyms* (*n*) miserliness, intolerance.

góðkynja benign; *synonyms* (*adj*) benevolent, kind, nice, affable, amiable; *antonym* (*adj*) harmful.

góðkynjaður benign; *synonyms* (*adj*) benevolent, kind, nice, affable, amiable; *antonym* (*adj*) harmful.

góðkynjun eugenics; *synonym* (*n*) heredity.

goðsögn myth; *synonyms* (*n*) fable, legend, story, tale, allegory.

góður 1. good; *synonyms* (*adj*) able, benefit, delicious, right, (*n*) benign; *antonyms* (*adj*) disobedient, poor, wicked, (*n*) evil, bad, **2**. fine; *synonyms* (*adj*) delicate, agreeable, dainty, brave, capital; *antonyms* (*adj*) thick, coarse, substantial, unsatisfactory, wide, **3**. nice; *synonyms* (*adj*) beautiful, fastidious, fine, good, kind; *antonyms* (*adj*) unpleasant, horrible, **4**. okay; *synonyms* (*n*) approval, (*v*) approve, sanction, consent, endorse; *antonym* (*v*) forbid.

göfga sublimate; *synonyms* (*v*) purify, rarefy, distill, purge, (*adj*) refined.

göfgun sublimation; *synonyms* (*n*) condensation, inhibition, paragon.

goggur 1. rostrum; *synonyms* (*n*) ambo, podium, pulpit, beak, dais, **2**. beak; *synonyms* (*n*) bill, nose, snout, prow, bow.

gögn 1. statistics; *synonyms* (*n*) data, census, score, information, list, **2**. data; *synonyms* (*n*) facts, details, evidence, fact, figures, **3**. document; *synonyms* (*n*) charter, deed, credentials, (*v*) record, file, **4**. documentation; *synonyms* (*n*) proof, certificate, certification, corroboration, credential, **5**. information; *synonyms* (*n*) advice, communication, note, enlightenment, report.

gola breeze; *synonyms* (*n*) breath, air, gust, blow, (*v*) move.

gólari howler; *synonyms* (*n*) blunder, mistake, gaffe, error, slip.

gólf floor; *synonyms* (*n*) bed, level, base, layer, bottom; *antonym* (*n*) top.

gólfábreiða 1. rug; *synonyms* (*n*) blanket, carpet, carpeting, mat, coverlet, **2**. mat; *synonyms* (*n*) matte, (*adj*) dull, flat, (*v*) entangle, felt.

gólfræsi gully; *synonyms* (*n*) channel, dike, conduit, gorge, canyon.

gólfteppi 1. rug; *synonyms* (*n*) blanket, carpet, carpeting, mat, coverlet, **2**. mat; *synonyms* (*n*) matte, (*adj*) dull, flat, (*v*) entangle, felt.

golþorskur angler; *synonyms* (*n*) goosefish, monkfish, allmouth, angelfish, anglerfish.

gómur palate; *synonyms* (*n*) gusto, liking, relish, taste, tooth.

göndull rotor; *synonyms* (*n*) rotator, stator.

göng 1. stove; *synonyms* (*n*) range, furnace, heater, ambit, chain, **2**. canal; *synonyms* (*n*) aqueduct, channel, conduit, duct, sound, **3**. duct; *synonyms* (*n*) canal, drain, vessel, ditch, outlet, **4**. channel; *synonyms* (*n*) groove, line, (*v*) carry, conduct, convey, **5**. passage; *synonyms* (*n*) aisle, course, corridor, gangway, hall.

göngumaður pedestrian; *synonyms* (*n*) walker, (*adj*) commonplace, humdrum, ordinary, banal.

gormferill helix; *synonyms* (*n*) coil, spiral, whorl, curl, volute.

gormflug spiral; *synonyms* (*n*) coil, helix, (*adj*) helical, (*v*) curl, loop.

gormlaga 1. acyclic; *synonyms* (*adj*) botany, chemistry, **2**. helical; *synonyms* (*adj*) spiral, turbinate, volute, whorled, (*v*) coiled.

gormlagaður helical; *synonyms* (*adj*) spiral, turbinate, volute, whorled, (*v*) coiled.

gormleggur strut; *synonyms* (*n*) buttress, brace, (*v*) prance, stalk, swagger.

gormlína helix; *synonyms* (*n*) coil, spiral, whorl, curl, volute.

gormraðaður acyclic; *synonyms* (*adj*) botany, chemistry.

gormsýkill spirillum; *synonym* (*n*) spirilla.

gormur 1. spiral; *synonyms* (*n*) coil, helix, (*adj*) helical, (*v*) curl, loop, **2**. spring; *synonyms* (*n*) jump, leap, bound, (*v*) hop, caper, **3**. helix; *synonyms* (*n*) spiral, whorl, volute, curve, (*v*) buckle.

görn 1. intestine; *synonyms* (*n*) bowel, gut, catgut, (*adj*) domestic, internal, **2**. gut; *synonyms* (*n*) belly, abdomen, (*v*) eviscerate, pillage, ransack.

gorta 1. bravado; *synonyms* (*n*) boast, bluster, braggadocio, bluff, bragging; *antonym* (*n*) cowardice, **2**. brag; *synonyms* (*v*) pride, blow, gasconade, (*n*) vaunt, boasting, **3**. boast; *synonyms* (*v*) brag, crow, rodomontade, exult, (*n*) arrogance.

gortari 1. braggart; *synonyms* (*n*) boaster, blowhard, braggadocio, bragger, (*v*) magniloquent, **2**. bragger; *synonyms* (*n*) braggart, vaunter, bighead,

3. boaster; *synonyms* (*n*) bouncer, swaggerer, huff, pretension, rage.

gos eruption; *synonyms* (*n*) blast, burst, outbreak, rash, (*adj*) detonation.

gosaska ash; *synonyms* (*n*) jasmine, lilac, (*v*) cinder, scoriae, (*adj*) gray.

gossúla spout; *synonyms* (*n*) jet, nozzle, (*v*) gush, spurt, spirt.

Gösun gasification; *synonym* (*n*) vaporation.

got brood; *synonyms* (*n*) breed, issue, offspring, (*v*) hatch, sulk.

gotrauf cloaca; *synonyms* (*n*) drain, sewer, culvert, ditch, gully.

götun **1**. fenestration, **2**. perforation; *synonyms* (*n*) hole, puncture, aperture, opening, pit.

götunartæki punch; *synonyms* (*n*) jab, drill, (*v*) poke, hit, prick.

götureitur block; *synonyms* (*n*) bar, barricade, pad, (*v*) arrest, stop; *antonyms* (*v*) free, unblock, open.

grábuska mugwort; *synonyms* (*n*) motherwort, tarragon.

gráð **1**. ripple; *synonyms* (*n*) wave, (*v*) bubble, murmur, gurgle, purl, **2**. burr; *synonyms* (*n*) flash, (*v*) bur, clank, clink, jangle.

gráða **1**. burr; *synonyms* (*n*) flash, (*v*) bur, clank, clink, jangle, **2**. degree; *synonyms* (*n*) class, extent, condition, level, order.

grádreifir neutral; *synonyms* (*adj*) disinterested, impartial, indifferent, dispassionate, (*n*) neuter; *antonyms* (*adj*) biased, aromatic, colorful.

gráðubogi protractor; *synonym* (*n*) protracter.

gráðuhreinsun **1**. trimming; *synonyms* (*n*) trim, adornment, decoration, dressing, ornament, **2**. burring; *synonym* (*n*) plunging.

gráður burr; *synonyms* (*n*) flash, (*v*) bur, clank, clink, jangle.

gráðuskipting graduation; *synonyms* (*n*) commencement, gradation, (*adj*) adaption, adjustment, (*v*) allotment.

græða cure; *synonyms* (*n*) remedy, antidote, medicine, (*v*) correct, help.

græðandi remedial; *synonyms* (*adj*) curative, healing, therapeutic, corrective, medicinal.

græðgi bulimia; *synonyms* (*n*) phagedena, bulimy.

græði graft; *synonyms* (*n*) scion, corruption, bribery, (*v*) transplant, toil.

græðlingur **1**. cutting; *synonyms* (*adj*) sharp, biting, keen, acute, bitter; *antonyms* (*adj*) blunt, mild, (*n*) extension, freedom, **2**. graft; *synonyms* (*n*) scion, corruption, bribery, (*v*) transplant, toil.

græðsla healing; *synonyms* (*n*) cure, convalescence, recuperation, therapy, (*adj*) curative; *antonym* (*adj*) injurious.

grænaldin avocado; *synonyms* (*n*) aguacate, (*v*) atole, banana, barbecue, beefsteak.

grænflekkur scup; *synonyms* (*n*) porgy, scuppaug, swing.

grænn green; *synonyms* (*adj*) fresh, callow, immature, emerald, jealous; *antonym* (*adj*) experienced.

grænsíld alewife; *synonym* (*n*) gaspereau.

grænt green (grænn); *synonyms* (*adj*) fresh, callow, immature, emerald, jealous; *antonym* (*adj*) experienced.

grænukorn chloroplast; *synonym* (*n*) chloroplastid.

graf graph; *synonyms* (*n*) figure, diagram, plan, drawing, (*v*) chart.

grafa **1**. dig; *synonyms* (*v*) jab, delve, prod, burrow, (*n*) poke; *antonym* (*n*) compliment, **2**. fester; *synonyms* (*v*) rot, boil, ferment, decay, (*adj*) rankle, **3**. etch; *synonyms* (*v*) engrave, carve, cut, inscribe, bite.

grafhvelfing crypt; *synonyms* (*n*) vault, tomb, mausoleum, cellar, sepulcher.

grafískur graphic; *synonyms* (*adj*) vivid, descriptive, (*n*) picture, diagram, (*v*) pictorial.

grafít graphite; *synonym* (*n*) plumbago.

graftarbóla pustule; *synonyms* (*n*) pimple, boil, blister, acne, carbuncle.

graftarbólga abscess; *synonyms* (*n*) blister, boil, gathering, (*adj*) sore, ulcer.

graftarkýli **1**. abscess; *synonyms* (*n*) blister, boil, gathering, (*adj*) sore, ulcer, **2**. furuncle; *synonyms* (*n*) abscess, caruncle, corn, eruption, growth.

graftarmyndandi pyogenic; *synonym* (*adj*) pyogenous.

graftarmyndun suppuration; *synonyms* (*n*) pus, purulence, matter, maturation, purulency.

graftarsótt sepsis; *synonyms* (*adj*) infection, pollution, septicity, taint.

graftarþrymlar acne; *synonyms* (*n*) pimple, whelk, papule, ridge, wale.

gráháfur tope; *synonyms* (*n*) tumulus, grove, (*v*) booze, drink, (*adj*) tipple.

gramm **1**. gramme; *synonyms* (*n*) gram, gm, g, chiliad, gee, **2**. gram; *synonyms* (*n*) gramme, gigabyte, (*adj*) kilogram, microgram, milligram.

grámun grey; *synonyms* (*adj*) dim, dull, greyish, (*n*) grayness, (*v*) gray.

granaldin pineapple; *synonyms* (*n*) ananas, pine, (*v*) chowder, chupatty, clam.

grandari bridle; *synonyms* (*n*) bit, curb, arrest, (*v*) check, inhibit.

grandi isthmus; *synonyms* (*n*) bridge, oasis, (*adj*) strait, neck, wasp.

granít granite; *synonyms* (*adj*) stone, crag, crystal, flint, fossil.

grannfrumur glia; *synonym* (*n*) neuroglia.

granni neighbour; *synonyms* (*n*) neighbor, (*adj*) neighboring, neighbouring.

grannskoðun overhaul; *synonyms* (*n*) inspection, (*v*) repair, check, modernize, overtake.

grannsvæðakennsl contiguity; *synonyms* (*n*) adjacency, contact, contiguousness, proximity, neighborhood.

grár 1. grey; *synonyms* (*adj*) dim, dull, greyish, (*n*) grayness, (*v*) gray, **2.** gray; *synonyms* (*adj*) bleak, gloomy, grizzled, (*n*) grizzle, (*v*) grey; *antonym* (*adj*) bright.

gras 1. grass; *synonyms* (*n*) cannabis, forage, (*v*) betray, denounce, (*adj*) pot, **2.** herb; *synonyms* (*n*) plant, seasoning, flavoring, flower, (*v*) bunch.

grasæta herbivore; *synonyms* (*n*) phytophagan, herbivorous.

grasafræði botany; *synonyms* (*n*) phytology, anatomy, (*adj*) acyclic, cyclic, chemistry.

grasalækningar eclecticism; *synonyms* (*n*) electicism, excerption, gleaning, selection.

grasbítur herbivore; *synonyms* (*n*) phytophagan, herbivorous.

grasker squash; *synonyms* (*v*) crush, mash, quell, compress, press.

graslendi grassland; *synonyms* (*n*) field, meadow, pasture, plain, prairie.

grásleppa lump; *synonyms* (*n*) heap, chunk, knot, block, (*v*) clot.

gráta 1. weep; *synonyms* (*v*) cry, wail, bawl, blubber, lament; *antonym* (*v*) laugh, **2.** cry; *synonyms* (*n*) shout, bark, scream, yell, (*v*) call; *antonym* (*v*) whisper.

grátviður cypress; *synonyms* (*adj*) mourning, weeds, willow.

grei gray; *synonyms* (*adj*) dull, bleak, dim, (*n*) grizzle, (*v*) grey; *antonym* (*adj*) bright.

greiðsla 1. remuneration; *synonyms* (*n*) compensation, pay, recompense, earnings, reward, **2.** settlement; *synonyms* (*n*) decision, accommodation, colony, hamlet, payment, **3.** payment; *synonyms* (*n*) bonus, charge, cost, defrayal, expense; *antonym* (*n*) non-payment, **4.** pay; *synonyms* (*v*) compensate, liquidate, (*n*) wage, fee, salary; *antonym* (*v*) owe.

greiðslufær liquid; *synonyms* (*adj*) flowing, fluent, fluid, juicy, limpid; *antonyms* (*adj*) firm, (*n*) solid, gaseous.

greiðslufall default; *synonyms* (*n*) deficit, delinquency, omission, oversight, (*v*) fail; *antonym* (*n*) payment.

greiðsluflæði liquidity; *synonyms* (*n*) fluidity, fluidness, liquid, liquidness, fluency.

greiðslufrestun moratorium; *synonyms* (*n*) delay, suspension, deferment, respite, economy.

greiðslufrestur credit; *synonyms* (*n*) credence, appreciation, belief, (*v*) believe, accredit; *antonyms* (*n*) cash, (*v*) debit, discredit.

greiðslugeta 1. solidity; *synonyms* (*n*) consistency, density, firmness, compactness, rigidity; *antonym* (*n*) brittleness, **2.** liquidity; *synonyms* (*n*) fluidity, fluidness, liquid, liquidness, fluency.

greiðsluhæfi liquidity; *synonyms* (*n*) fluidity, fluidness, liquid, liquidness, fluency.

greiðslukort card; *synonyms* (*n*) bill, board, ticket, label, carte.

greiðslumiðlun clearing; *synonyms* (*n*) clarification, glade, clearance, dell, lot.

greiðslusending remittance; *synonyms* (*n*) payment, remission, allowance, remitment, remittal.

greiðslustöðvun moratorium; *synonyms* (*n*) delay, suspension, deferment, respite, economy.

greiðsluþol liquidity; *synonyms* (*n*) fluidity, fluidness, liquid, liquidness, fluency.

greiðsluþrot insolvency; *synonyms* (*n*) bankruptcy, ruin, poverty, hardship, impoverishment; *antonym* (*n*) solvency.

greifi 1. earl; *synonyms* (*n*) thane, viscount, chief, **2.** count; *synonyms* (*n*) number, calculation, (*v*) calculate, compute, tally.

greifingi badger; *synonyms* (*v*) pester, annoy, tease, bother, harass.

grein 1. branch; *synonyms* (*n*) arm, jump, wing, affiliate, (*v*) fork, **2.** bough; *synonyms* (*n*) branch, limb, member, ramage, tigella, **3.** manifold; *synonyms* (*adj*) multiple, diverse, different, (*v*) duplicate, copy, **4.** paragraph; *synonyms* (*n*) article, item, section, chapter, (*v*) clause.

greina 1. detect; *synonyms* (*v*) catch, discover, find, ascertain, discern, **2.** distinguish; *synonyms* (*v*) discriminate, describe, know, perceive, descry; *antonym* (*v*) confuse, **3.** analyse; *synonyms* (*v*) analyze, canvass, dissect, examine, study.

greinandi 1. analyst; *synonyms* (*n*) psychoanalyst, analyzer, expert, psychiatrist, examiner, **2.** diagnostic; *synonyms* (*adj*) characteristic, individual, (*n*) criterion, (*v*) demonstrative, diacritical.

greinargerð memorandum; *synonyms* (*n*) memo, note, memorial, entry, letter.

greinarmerki punctuation; *synonyms* (*n*) accidence, grammar, praxis, interpunction, pointing.

greinarmerkjasetning punctuation; *synonyms* (*n*) accidence, grammar, praxis, interpunction, pointing.

greind intelligence; *synonyms* (*n*) information, cleverness, intellect, news, tidings; *antonyms* (*n*) stupidity, emotion.

greindur arborescent; *synonyms* (*adj*) arboreous, arborary, arborical, dendroid, arboreal.

greinilína branch; *synonyms* (*n*) arm, jump, wing, affiliate, (*v*) fork.

greinimark 1. threshold; *synonyms* (*n*) brink, limen, beginning, doorsill, doorstep, 2. criterion; *synonyms* (*n*) benchmark, measure, norm, test, canon.

greinimörk threshold; *synonyms* (*n*) brink, limen, beginning, doorsill, doorstep.

greining 1. resolution; *synonyms* (*n*) decision, determination, answer, conclusion, firmness; *antonym* (*n*) indecisiveness, 2. differentiation; *synonyms* (*n*) difference, distinction, contrast, demarcation, discrimination, 3. assay; *synonyms* (*n*) examination, (*v*) test, try, attempt, experiment, 4. analysis; *synonyms* (*n*) anatomy, breakdown, decomposition, inquiry, inspection; *antonym* (*n*) synthesis, 5. diagnosis; *synonyms* (*n*) diagnosing, identification, diorism, recognition, definition.

greiningaráætlun regimen; *synonyms* (*n*) regime, diet, government, treatment, cure.

greiningarhæfni resolution; *synonyms* (*n*) decision, determination, answer, conclusion, firmness; *antonym* (*n*) indecisiveness.

greiningartæki analyzer; *synonyms* (*n*) analyser, critic, scanner.

greinir 1. probe; *synonyms* (*n*) investigation, (*v*) examine, examination, explore, inspect, 2. analyzer; *synonyms* (*n*) analyser, critic, scanner, 3. analyser; *synonyms* (*n*) analyzer, analyse, 4. analyst; *synonyms* (*n*) psychoanalyst, expert, psychiatrist, examiner, commentator, 5. article; *synonyms* (*n*) section, object, thing, chapter, clause.

greinisía analyser; *synonyms* (*n*) analyzer, analyse.

greiniviðbragð discrimination; *synonyms* (*n*) discernment, difference, differentiation, distinction, (*v*) judgment; *antonym* (*n*) tolerance.

greinóttur 1. ramose; *synonyms* (*adj*) ramous, branched, bifurcate, biramous, branching, 2. arborescent; *synonyms* (*adj*) arboreous, arborary, arborical, dendroid, arboreal.

greinrör manifold; *synonyms* (*adj*) multiple, diverse, different, (*v*) duplicate, copy.

grekti case; *synonyms* (*n*) box, example, bin, cover, jacket.

gremjast resent; *synonyms* (*v*) dislike, begrudge, envy, grudge, antagonize.

greni spruce; *synonyms* (*v*) tidy, (*adj*) smart, dapper, neat, jaunty; *antonym* (*adj*) scruffy.

grennast reduce; *synonyms* (*v*) lower, pare, abbreviate, curtail, (*adj*) abridge; *antonyms* (*v*) increase, bolster, expand, enlarge, exacerbate.

grenndun building; *synonyms* (*n*) architecture, establishment, construction, fabric, (*v*) edifice.

grettistak erratic; *synonyms* (*adj*) capricious, changeable, eccentric, irregular, freakish; *antonyms* (*adj*) consistent, constant, certain, dependable, predictable.

grey dog; *synonyms* (*n*) cur, andiron, (*v*) chase, hound, beset.

greyping 1. relieving; *synonyms* (*adj*) applicable, comforting, pertinent, relevant, (*n*) encouragement, 2. incrustation; *synonyms* (*n*) crust, encrustation, scale, obduction, superposition, 3. imprinting.

griðastaður asylum; *synonyms* (*n*) refuge, sanctuary, shelter, haven, home.

griðungur bull; *synonyms* (*n*) bullshit, bunk, hogwash, rot, (*adj*) blunder.

gríma mask; *synonyms* (*n*) cover, conceal, (*v*) cloak, disguise, hide; *antonym* (*v*) disclose.

grimmd 1. abhorrence; *synonyms* (*n*) abomination, antipathy, detestation, hatred, odium; *antonym* (*n*) love, 2. abomination; *synonyms* (*n*) abhorrence, disgust, atrocity, execration, hate, 3. atrocity; *synonyms* (*n*) enormity, brutality, atrociousness, barbarism, (*adj*) outrage, 4. horror; *synonyms* (*n*) awe, dismay, fear, alarm, (*adj*) dread; *antonym* (*n*) pleasantness.

grind 1. rack; *synonyms* (*n*) manger, wrack, (*v*) torture, excruciate, torment, 2. schema; *synonyms* (*n*) outline, plan, chart, graph, scheme, 3. arrack; *synonym* (*n*) arak, 4. cage; *synonyms* (*n*) jail, pen, hutch, cell, (*v*) confine; *antonym* (*v*) free, 5. lattice; *synonyms* (*n*) grill, fretwork, grid, grille, net.

grindarhol pelvis; *synonyms* (*n*) hip, belly, coxa, rosehip.

grindarskaut grid; *synonyms* (*n*) gridiron, grating, lattice, mesh, netting.

grindarvirki framework; *synonyms* (*n*) frame, fabric, framing, chassis, form.

grindverk 1. railing; *synonyms* (*n*) bar, balustrade, rail, barrier, banister, 2. balustrade; *synonyms* (*n*) paling, fence, bannister, handrail, pale, 3. parapet; *synonyms* (*n*) breastwork, bulwark, fortification, bastion, battlement.

grip 1. traction; *synonyms* (*n*) grip, friction, draught, bag, (*v*) tug, 2. capture; *synonyms* (*v*) catch, take, apprehend, (*n*) arrest, seizure; *antonyms* (*v*) release, surrender, 3. catch; *synonyms* (*v*) capture, hook, get, (*n*) haul, hitch, 4. handle; *synonyms* (*v*) administer, conduct, feel, wield, (*n*) clutch.

grípa grab; *synonyms* (*v*) capture, get, snatch, (*n*) arrest, catch.

gripkló clutch; *synonyms* (*n*) clasp, (*v*) grip, clench, clinch, grab.

gripkrani grab; *synonyms* (*v*) capture, get, snatch, (*n*) arrest, catch.

gripla 1. acronym; *synonyms* (*n*) contraction, ellipsis, **2**. dendrite; *synonym* (*n*) arborization.

griplæsing lock; *synonyms* (*v*) bolt, bar, close, latch, engage; *antonyms* (*v*) unlock, open.

gripluþráður dendrite; *synonym* (*n*) arborization.

gripmál calipers; *synonyms* (*n*) caliper, callipers, calliper, (*v*) compass, measure.

gripskófla grab; *synonyms* (*v*) capture, get, snatch, (*n*) arrest, catch.

griptöng pincers; *synonyms* (*v*) forceps, tongs, clutches.

grisja gauze; *synonyms* (*n*) film, bandage, blind, curtain, mantle.

grisjun 1. pruning; *synonym* (*n*) leavings, **2**. thinning; *synonyms* (*n*) cutting, attrition, carving, clipping, contraction.

grisjuþófi compress; *synonyms* (*v*) abridge, compact, press, squeeze, condense; *antonym* (*v*) loosen.

grjótskriða talus; *synonyms* (*n*) astragalus, slope, scree, anklebone, astragal.

gró spore; *synonyms* (*n*) ascospore, sporule, (*adj*) bran, farina, flour.

gróandi vegetation; *synonyms* (*n*) flora, growth, plants, foliage, quietism.

grobbari 1. boaster; *synonyms* (*n*) blowhard, braggart, bragger, vaunter, bouncer, **2**. braggart; *synonyms* (*n*) boaster, braggadocio, (*v*) magniloquent, (*adj*) braggy, crowing, **3**. bragger; *synonym* (*n*) bighead.

gróði 1. profit; *synonyms* (*n*) gain, benefit, account, good, (*adj*) advantage; *antonym* (*v*) lose, **2**. earnings; *synonyms* (*n*) profit, salary, income, pay, profits.

gróðrarhópur colony; *synonyms* (*n*) settlement, community, plantation, dependency, village.

gróður 1. vegetation; *synonyms* (*n*) flora, growth, plants, foliage, quietism, **2**. fruit; *synonyms* (*n*) effect, crop, outgrowth, product, (*v*) result.

gróðuráburður fertilizer; *synonyms* (*n*) dung, compost, manure, muck, droppings.

gróðurbeltun zonation; *synonym* (*n*) banding.

gróðurflokkur classification; *synonyms* (*n*) arrangement, categorization, class, grading, assortment; *antonym* (*n*) declassification.

gróðurfylki alliance; *synonyms* (*n*) connection, league, affinity, association, combination; *antonym* (*n*) nonalignment.

gróðurhúsanellíka carnation; *synonyms* (*n*) crimson, gillyflower, pink, red, scarlet.

gróðurmold 1. topsoil, **2**. humus; *synonyms* (*n*) hummus, compost, hommos, hoummos, humous.

gróðurríki flora; *synonyms* (*n*) vegetation, plant, plants, verdure, foliage.

gróðursnauður barren; *synonyms* (*adj*) infertile, sterile, deserted, abortive, (*v*) bare; *antonyms* (*adj*) fertile, lush, productive.

gróðursveit association; *synonyms* (*n*) affiliation, alliance, connection, assembly, affinity.

gróðurtilbrigði variant; *synonyms* (*n*) variation, version, (*adj*) different, divergent, changeable.

gróf 1. fossa; *synonyms* (*n*) cavity, fovea, pit, colliery, endocarp, **2**. groove; *synonyms* (*n*) furrow, rut, chamfer, (*v*) channel, flute.

gróferna tetrad; *synonyms* (*n*) four, quaternity, quaternion, foursome, quadruplet.

grófleiki pitch; *synonyms* (*n*) degree, dip, (*v*) fling, cast, chuck.

grófsía strainer; *synonyms* (*n*) filter, sieve, stretcher, colature, mesh.

gróft rough; *synonyms* (*adj*) coarse, hard, harsh, raw, crude; *antonyms* (*adj*) gentle, smooth, polished, precise, refined.

grófþeyta suspension; *synonyms* (*n*) delay, interruption, abeyance, break, intermission.

gröftur pus; *synonyms* (*n*) matter, purulence, suppuration, festering, ichor.

grófur 1. rough; *synonyms* (*adj*) coarse, hard, harsh, raw, crude; *antonyms* (*adj*) gentle, smooth, polished, precise, refined, **2**. uneven; *synonyms* (*adj*) rough, unequal, irregular, jagged, erratic; *antonyms* (*adj*) even, straight, equal, symmetrical.

gróhirsla sporangium; *synonym* (*n*) sporocarp.

grókólfur basidium; *synonym* (*n*) promycelium.

grókylfa basidium; *synonym* (*n*) promycelium.

grómagn fecundity; *synonyms* (*n*) fertility, fruitfulness, productivity, richness, productiveness.

grómyndun sporulation; *synonym* (*n*) monogenesis.

gróning union; *synonyms* (*n*) coalition, connection, junction, association, combination; *antonyms* (*n*) separation, divergence.

grop porosity; *synonyms* (*n*) porousness, poriness.

gróp 1. recess; *synonyms* (*n*) corner, break, holiday, intermission, niche, **2**. groove; *synonyms* (*n*) furrow, rut, chamfer, (*v*) channel, flute.

gropa 1. pore; *synonyms* (*n*) interstice, stoma, aorta, artery, (*v*) center, **2**. porosity; *synonyms* (*n*) porousness, poriness.

grophlutfall porosity; *synonyms* (*n*) porousness, poriness.

gropinn 1. permeable; *synonyms* (*adj*) pervious, porous, absorbent, spongy, gritty; *antonyms* (*adj*) impermeable, resistant, waterproof, water-resistant, watertight, **2**. porous; *synonyms* (*adj*) permeable, leaky, poriferous, holey, open, **3.** cellular; *synonyms* (adj) locular, multilocular, polygastric, cellulated, cystic.

groppa permeability; *synonyms* (n) perviousness, permeableness.

grósekkur ascus; *synonym* (n) asci.

gróskumikill luxuriant; *synonyms* (adj) lush, abundant, lavish, exuberant, thick; *antonym* (adj) barren.

gróstilkur basidium; *synonym* (n) promycelium.

grot detritus; *synonyms* (n) rubble, (adj) debris, trash, magistery, scobs.

grotnun decomposition; *synonyms* (n) decay, rot, disintegration, dissolution, putrefaction.

grugg turbidity; *synonyms* (n) turbidness, haze, obscurity, haziness.

grugglausn suspension; *synonyms* (n) delay, interruption, abeyance, break, intermission.

gruggugur 1. turbid; *synonyms* (adj) muddy, thick, murky, opaque, cloudy, **2.** cloudy; *synonyms* (adj) dull, gloomy, nebulous, dark, foggy; *antonyms* (adj) clear, bright, cloudless, sunny.

gruggun turbidity; *synonyms* (n) turbidness, haze, obscurity, haziness.

gruna 1. suspect; *synonyms* (v) doubt, distrust, mistrust, suppose, conjecture; *antonyms* (v) trust, (adj) trustworthy, **2.** assume; *synonyms* (v) affect, accept, adopt, appropriate, arrogate.

grund ground; *synonyms* (n) base, cause, land, floor, (v) bottom; *antonym* (n) ceiling.

grundo 1. grounds; *synonyms* (n) cause, dregs, ground, reason, account, **2.** ground; *synonyms* (n) base, land, floor, (v) bottom, found; *antonym* (n) ceiling.

grundvallarregla axiom; *synonyms* (n) aphorism, adage, maxim, apothegm, principle.

grundvöllur foundation; *synonyms* (n) base, basis, bottom, creation, establishment; *antonym* (n) top.

grunn bank; *synonyms* (n) dam, coast, slope, (v) embankment, gradient; *antonym* (v) withdraw.

grunnflötur base; *synonyms* (n) foundation, (adj) bottom, abject, mean, dishonorable; *antonyms* (n) summit, top, (adj) noble.

grunnfrymi matrix; *synonyms* (n) die, alembic, caldron, crucible, groundmass.

grunnfylki group; *synonyms* (n) bunch, brigade, collection, crowd, flock.

grunngerð infrastructure; *synonyms* (n) base, foundation, basis, groundwork, substructure.

grunnkerfi infrastructure; *synonyms* (n) base, foundation, basis, groundwork, substructure.

grunnlægur superficial; *synonyms* (adj) cursory, shallow, external, sketchy, slight; *antonyms* (adj) deep, innate, real, thorough, profound.

grunnlína 1. base; *synonyms* (n) foundation, (adj) bottom, abject, mean, dishonorable; *antonyms* (n) summit, top, (adj) noble, **2.** baseline.

grunnljómi background; *synonyms* (n) backdrop, groundwork, setting, basis, context.

grunnmála prime; *synonyms* (adj) main, chief, first, head, (n) best; *antonym* (adj) minor.

grunnmálning primer; *synonyms* (n) manual, fuse, fuze, ground, grammar.

grunnmálun priming; *synonyms* (n) primer, undercoat, background, basis, briefing.

grunnmerking signification; *synonyms* (n) import, meaning, purport, intent, (v) sense.

grunnpúlstíðni background; *synonyms* (n) backdrop, groundwork, setting, basis, context.

grunnpunktur triplet; *synonyms* (n) three, triad, tercet, threesome, trio.

grunnregla principle; *synonyms* (n) origin, fundamental, method, rule, cause.

grunnsæri abrasion; *synonyms* (n) attrition, excoriation, erosion, friction, (v) detrition; *antonym* (n) smoothness.

grunntala 1. radix; *synonyms* (n) base, basis, root, foundation, groundwork, **2.** base; *synonyms* (adj) bottom, abject, mean, dishonorable, (v) ground; *antonyms* (n) summit, top, (adj) noble.

grunnungur tench; *synonyms* (n) dace, roach, rudd.

grunnur 1. shallow; *synonyms* (adj) shoal, superficial, low, cursory, petty; *antonyms* (adj) deep, bottomless, **2.** superficial; *synonyms* (adj) shallow, external, sketchy, slight, apparent; *antonyms* (adj) innate, real, thorough, profound, inner, **3.** baseline, **4.** basis; *synonyms* (n) base, foundation, gist, bed, beginning, **5.** foundation; *synonyms* (n) basis, bottom, creation, establishment, foot; *antonym* (n) top.

grunnvefur 1. stroma; *synonym* (n) stromata, **2.** parenchyma; *synonyms* (n) substance, body, compages, element, matter.

grunur feeling; *synonyms* (n) affection, feel, passion, emotion, atmosphere; *antonyms* (n) numbness, indifference.

grúpa group; *synonyms* (n) bunch, brigade, collection, crowd, flock.

grynning shallow; *synonyms* (adj) shoal, superficial, low, cursory, petty; *antonyms* (adj) deep, bottomless.

gubba vomit; *synonyms* (v) spew, heave, puke, cast, disgorge.

guð 1. deity; *synonyms* (*n*) godhead, godhood, godship, idol, (*adj*) divinity, **2.** divinity; *synonyms* (*n*) deity, theology, divineness, immortal, spirit.

guðlax opah; *synonyms* (*n*) moonfish, dollarfish, horsefish, horsehead.

guðveldi theocracy; *synonyms* (*n*) thearchy, democracy, oligarchy, demagogy, dinarchy.

gufa 1. steam; *synonyms* (*n*) mist, fog, (*v*) reek, evaporate, exhale, **2.** vapour; *synonyms* (*n*) vapor, evaporation, gas, vaporisation, vaporization, **3.** vapor; *synonyms* (*n*) cloud, haze, steam, vapour, (*v*) bluster, **4.** fume; *synonyms* (*n*) smoke, foam, (*v*) chafe, rage, (*adj*) boil.

gufuhvolf atmosphere; *synonyms* (*n*) air, ambience, ambiance, aura, environment.

gufuketill boiler; *synonyms* (*n*) kettle, furnace, heater, banality, evaporator.

gufumyndun vaporization; *synonyms* (*n*) evaporation, vapor, vaporisation, volatilization, condensation.

gufusæfir autoclave; *synonyms* (*n*) steriliser, sterilizer, (*v*) sterilize.

gula 1. yolk; *synonyms* (*n*) deutoplasm, suint, vitellus, **2.** jaundice; *synonyms* (*n*) icterus, acerbity, acrimony, bitterness, (*v*) prejudice.

gulaldin lemon; *synonyms* (*n*) automobile, gamboge, auto, buff, bum.

guláll eel; *synonyms* (*n*) yeel, (*v*) labyrinth, maze, serpent.

gulbúshormón progesterone; *synonym* (*n*) progestin.

gulbúsvaki progesterone; *synonym* (*n*) progestin.

gulgrani bullhead; *synonyms* (*n*) catfish, beetlehead, lubber, (*adj*) obdurate.

gull 1. gold; *synonyms* (*n*) money, (*adj*) aureate, gilded, gilt, golden, **2.** golden; *synonyms* (*adj*) fortunate, auspicious, gold, lucky, advantageous.

gúll intumescence; *synonyms* (*n*) bulge, swelling, tumefaction, dropsy, tumor.

gullaldintré mangosteen; *synonyms* (*v*) chowder, chupatty, clam, compote, damper.

gulleitur xanthous; *synonyms* (*adj*) xanthic, yellow, chicken, chickenhearted, jaundiced.

gullmakríll dolphin; *synonyms* (*n*) dolphinfish, mahimahi, trident, pale.

gulnun chlorosis; *synonyms* (*n*) greensickness, (*adj*) chorea, cynanche, dartre.

gúlpur 1. sinus; *synonyms* (*n*) cavity, fistula, pit, indentation, dent, **2.** aneurysm, **3.** bulge; *synonyms* (*n*) prominence, protuberance, swelling, (*v*) belly, bag.

gulrófa rutabaga; *synonym* (*n*) kohlrabi.

gulrót carrot; *synonyms* (*n*) inducement, reward, incentive, lure, prize.

guluforði yolk; *synonyms* (*n*) deutoplasm, suint, vitellus.

gulur 1. yellow; *synonyms* (*adj*) jaundiced, amber, chicken, chickenhearted, (*adv*) cowardly, **2.** xanthic; *synonym* (*adj*) xanthogenic, **3.** xanthous; *synonyms* (*adj*) xanthic, yellow, scandalmongering, sensationalistic, yellowish, **4.** amber; *synonyms* (*n*) succinite, electrum, brown, electron, gold.

gulusótt jaundice; *synonyms* (*n*) icterus, acerbity, acrimony, bitterness, (*v*) prejudice.

gúmmí rubber; *synonyms* (*n*) caoutchouc, condom, eraser, galosh, overshoe.

gúmmíhamar mallet; *synonyms* (*n*) hammer, maul, club, mall, beetle.

gúmmíkragi grommet; *synonyms* (*n*) eyelet, grummet, cringle, child, loop.

gúmmísuða vulcanization; *synonyms* (*n*) vulcanisation, cure, curing.

gúmmítékki bouncer; *synonyms* (*n*) bounce, bluster, guard, rebound.

gúrka cucumber; *synonyms* (*n*) cuke, dollar.

gustur gust; *synonyms* (*n*) burst, eruption, flurry, blast, blow.

gusuhvellur crepitation; *synonyms* (*n*) crackle, crackling, crackleware, (*v*) decrepitation.

gusuvörn crepitation; *synonyms* (*n*) crackle, crackling, crackleware, (*v*) decrepitation.

gvatsekvi 1. tail; *synonyms* (*n*) rear, shadow, (*v*) follow, pursue, track; *antonyms* (*v*) head, front, **2.** tails; *synonyms* (*n*) tailcoat, tail, waste, coat.

gvöndargrös carragheen; *synonyms* (*n*) carrageen, carageen.

gy gray; *synonyms* (*adj*) dull, bleak, dim, (*n*) grizzle, (*v*) grey; *antonym* (*adj*) bright.

gyðingahof synagogue; *synonyms* (*n*) tabernacle, temple, church.

gyðingaprestur rabbi; *synonyms* (*n*) clergyman, priest, chaplain, master, rebbe.

gyðja goddess; *synonyms* (*n*) deity, divinity, beauty, (*adj*) angel, darling.

gyllinæð hemorrhoid; *synonyms* (*n*) haemorrhoid, piles, dozens, gobs, heaps.

Ĝ

ĝemela 1. twins; *synonyms* (*n*) pair, couple, brace, cheeks, deuce, **2.** twin; *synonyms* (*n*) match, counterpart, mate, (*v*) double, duplicate.

ĝemelo twins; *synonyms* (*n*) pair, couple, brace, cheeks, deuce.

H

H hydrogen; *synonyms* (*n*) butane, diacetylmorphine, heroin, horse, hydrogenium.

hábakur abacus; *synonyms* (*n*) aback, (*v*) logometer, slipstick, tallies.

hábaugur meridian; *synonyms* (*n*) culmination, longitude, zenith, acme, apex.

hádegisbaugur meridian; *synonyms* (*n*) culmination, longitude, zenith, acme, apex.

háðhvörf irony; *synonyms* (*n*) sarcasm, ridicule, banter, humor, (*adj*) satire; *antonym* (*n*) exaggeration.

háðsádeila 1. sarcasm; *synonyms* (*n*) irony, gibe, bitterness, (*adj*) ridicule, satire, **2**. satire; *synonyms* (*n*) sarcasm, caricature, lampoon, mockery, parody, **3**. irony; *synonyms* (*n*) banter, humor, raillery, derision, quiz; *antonym* (*n*) exaggeration.

háður 1. dependent; *synonyms* (*adj*) subject, subordinate, contingent, (*n*) dependant, charge; *antonyms* (*adj*) independent, self-governing, self-sufficient, **2**. endogenous; *synonyms* (*adj*) interior, exogenous, endogen, endogenetic, entogenous.

hæð 1. altitude; *synonyms* (*n*) elevation, height, level, distance, eminence, **2**. anticyclone; *synonyms* (*n*) blast, cyclone, gale, gust, hurricane, **3**. antinode; *synonym* (*n*) loop, **4**. height; *synonyms* (*n*) acme, apex, altitude, crest, culmination; *antonym* (*n*) shortness, **5**. level; *synonyms* (*n*) grade, (*adj*) even, equal, (*v*) flat, flatten; *antonyms* (*adj*) inclined, slanting, angled, (*v*) uneven, build.

hæðarhryggur 1. wedge; *synonyms* (*n*) chock, (*v*) squeeze, compress, jam, pack, **2**. ridge; *synonyms* (*n*) crest, ledge, bank, hill, shelf.

hæðarlína contour; *synonyms* (*n*) form, outline, profile, shape, configuration.

hæðarmunur relief; *synonyms* (*n*) comfort, aid, consolation, ease, (*v*) assistance.

hæðarstilling 1. leveling; *synonyms* (*n*) grading, levelling, demolishing, equalisation, equalization, **2**. levelling; *synonyms* (*n*) leveling, evening, flow.

hæðarstýri elevator; *synonyms* (*n*) lift, crane, rise, (*v*) dumbwaiter, escalator.

hæði 1. dependency; *synonyms* (*n*) dependence, addiction, colony, dependance, (*adj*) contingency, **2**. dependence; *synonyms* (*n*) belief, confidence, reliance, dependency, faith; *antonyms* (*n*) independence, self-government, self-sufficiency.

hæðni irony; *synonyms* (*n*) sarcasm, ridicule, banter, humor, (*adj*) satire; *antonym* (*n*) exaggeration.

hæfa 1. generalize; *synonyms* (*v*) generalise, universalize, popularize, extrapolate, derive; *antonym* (*v*) specify, **2**. fit; *synonyms* (*v*) agree, accommodate, meet, suit, (*adj*) decorous; *antonyms* (*adj*) unfit, inappropriate, unwell.

hæfi 1. qualifications; *synonyms* (*n*) competence, capacity, terms, ability, credentials, **2**. qualification; *synonyms* (*n*) condition, capability, fitness, limitation, preparation, **3**. competence; *synonyms* (*n*) adequacy, efficiency, sufficiency, aptitude, (*adj*) proficiency; *antonyms* (*n*) incompetence, inability, **4**. fitness; *synonyms* (*n*) appropriateness, aptness, propriety, correspondence, competency; *antonyms* (*n*) unsuitability, unfitness.

hæfilegur 1. suitable; *synonyms* (*adj*) appropriate, fit, good, apt, proper; *antonyms* (*adj*) inappropriate, unsuitable, wrong, improper, **2**. adequate; *synonyms* (*adj*) sufficient, acceptable, enough, right, condign; *antonyms* (*adj*) inadequate, insufficient, unsatisfactory.

hæfileikar 1. performance; *synonyms* (*n*) act, discharge, achievement, execution, (*v*) action; *antonyms* (*n*) omission, practice, **2**. endowment; *synonyms* (*n*) ability, talent, capacity, (*v*) donation, gift.

hæfileiki aptitude; *synonyms* (*n*) ability, capability, skill, aptness, capacity; *antonyms* (*n*) inability, inaptitude.

hæfing 1. training; *synonyms* (*n*) education, instruction, breeding, practice, preparation, **2**. conditioning; *synonyms* (*n*) training, chilling, cooking, drill, equalizing, **3**. generalisation; *synonyms* (*n*) generalization, abstract, abstractedness, abstraction, conveyance.

hæfni 1. potency; *synonyms* (*n*) force, might, effectiveness, efficacy, ability, **2**. skill; *synonyms* (*n*) artifice, capability, capacity, (*adj*) dexterity, craft; *antonyms* (*n*) clumsiness, inability, incompetence, **3**. qualification; *synonyms* (*n*) condition, competence, fitness, limitation, preparation, **4**. competence; *synonyms* (*n*) adequacy, efficiency, sufficiency, aptitude, (*adj*) proficiency, **5**. ability; *synonyms* (*n*) hand, cleverness, faculty, power, talent; *antonym* (*n*) injury.

hæfnismat rating; *synonyms* (*n*) assessment, mark, evaluation, appraisal, estimate.

hæfur 1. competent; *synonyms* (*adj*) able, capable, adequate, clever, effective; *antonyms* (*adj*) incompetent, useless, inept, **2**. fit; *synonyms* (*v*) agree, accommodate, meet, suit, (*adj*) decorous; *antonyms* (*adj*) unfit, inappropriate, unwell.

hægagangur idling; *synonyms* (*adj*) trifling, (*n*) idleness, loafing, dalliance, faineance.

hægðaaukandi aperient; *synonyms* (n) cathartic, physic, purgative, deobstruent, (adj) aperitive.

hægðalosandi laxative; *synonyms* (adj) aperient, deobstruent, chalybeate, depurative, (v) dentifrice.

hægðalyf 1. aperient; *synonyms* (n) cathartic, physic, purgative, deobstruent, (adj) aperitive, **2.** laxative; *synonyms* (adj) aperient, chalybeate, depurative, roborant, (v) dentifrice.

hægðir 1. stool; *synonyms* (n) chair, seat, bench, dejection, faeces, **2.** defecation; *synonyms* (n) evacuation, settling, abolition, laxation, (v) purification, **3.** feces; *synonyms* (n) dregs, ordure, stool, filth, can.

hægfara 1. slow; *synonyms* (adj) dull, late, easy, sluggish, (v) slack; *antonyms* (adj) fast, intelligent, rapid, bright, (v) accelerate, **2.** indolent; *synonyms* (adj) idle, inactive, lazy, slothful, careless; *antonyms* (adj) energetic, active, **3.** moderate; *synonyms* (adj) temperate, abstemious, middling, mild, (v) calm; *antonyms* (adj) extreme, immoderate, radical, (v) increase, intensify.

hæging 1. retardation; *synonyms* (n) delay, impediment, retard, deceleration, lag, **2.** deceleration; *synonyms* (n) retardation, slowdown, backwardness, slowing, slowness.

hægir 1. retarder; *synonym* (n) restrainer, **2.** moderator; *synonyms* (n) chairman, mediator, arbitrator, intermediary, negotiator.

hæglyndur phlegmatic; *synonyms* (adj) impassive, indifferent, listless, phlegmatical, stolid.

hægri right; *synonyms* (adj) correct, appropriate, due, just, proper; *antonyms* (adj) inappropriate, unjustified, immoral, (n) left, (v) wrong.

hægur slow; *synonyms* (adj) dull, late, easy, sluggish, (v) slack; *antonyms* (adj) fast, intelligent, rapid, bright, (v) accelerate.

hægvöxtur lag; *synonyms* (n) backwardness, (v) dawdle, delay, linger, dally.

hækka 1. promote; *synonyms* (v) advance, encourage, help, aid, (adv) further; *antonyms* (v) demote, discourage, **2.** raise; *synonyms* (v) boost, lift, erect, hoist, increase; *antonym* (v) lower.

hækkun elevation; *synonyms* (n) altitude, height, ascent, exaltation, highness.

hæli asylum; *synonyms* (n) refuge, sanctuary, shelter, haven, home.

hæll 1. stop; *synonyms* (n) halt, hold, stay, check, end; *antonyms* (v) continue, start, begin, encourage, permit, **2.** shoulder; *synonyms* (n) elbow, back, (v) bear, carry, push, **3.** spur; *synonyms* (n) inducement, incentive, impulse, (v) goad, incite, **4.** anchor; *synonyms* (n) mainstay, (v) tie, fasten, secure, (adj) refuge, **5.** heel; *synonyms* (n) blackguard, counter, dog, cad, (v) list.

hælsvæði heel; *synonyms* (n) blackguard, counter, dog, cad, (v) list.

hænd dependency; *synonyms* (n) dependence, addiction, colony, dependance, (adj) contingency.

hænsn chicken; *synonyms* (n) chick, cock, coward, fowl, hen.

hænsnakorn corn; *synonyms* (n) maize, clavus, cereals, callus, wheat.

hærður pilose; *synonyms* (adj) hairy, pilous, pileous, fleecy, pilary.

hæringur capelin; *synonyms* (n) caplin, capelan, capling.

Hætinn critical; *synonyms* (adj) acute, decisive, delicate, important, pressing; *antonyms* (adj) complimentary, trivial, positive, flattering, insignificant.

hætta 1. peril; *synonyms* (n) hazard, danger, jeopardy, menace, (v) endanger; *antonym* (n) safety, **2.** hazard; *synonyms* (n) chance, risk, venture, peril, (v) adventure, **3.** risk; *synonyms* (n) gamble, bet, (v) wager, dare, imperil; *antonym* (v) protect, **4.** danger; *synonyms* (n) threat, trouble, precariousness, slipperiness, difficulty; *antonym* (n) security, **5.** jeopardy; *synonyms* (n) exposure, insecurity.

hættuástand emergency; *synonyms* (n) crisis, contingency, exigency, accident, (adj) extra.

hættuboð alarm; *synonyms* (n) dismay, alert, consternation, (v) awe, scare; *antonyms* (v) calm, comfort.

hættulaus innocuous; *synonyms* (adj) harmless, innocent, inoffensive, safe, innoxious.

hættulegur 1. pernicious; *synonyms* (adj) detrimental, evil, bad, fatal, injurious, **2.** hazardous; *synonyms* (adj) dangerous, risky, perilous, unsafe, (n) daring; *antonym* (adj) safe.

hættumat exposure; *synonyms* (n) display, exposition, detection, peril, (v) disclosure.

hættumerki alarm; *synonyms* (n) dismay, alert, consternation, (v) awe, scare; *antonyms* (v) calm, comfort.

haf 1. sea; *synonyms* (n) ocean, water, (adj) marine, maritime, array, **2.** span; *synonyms* (n) length, space, distance, bridge, couple, **3.** ocean; *synonyms* (n) sea, deep, brine, waves, multitude.

hafa have; *synonyms* (v) contain, gain, bear, carry, get.

hafáll conger; *synonym* (n) congeree.

hafdjúp abyss; *synonyms* (n) abysm, chasm, deep, gorge, gulf.

haffær navigable; *synonyms* (adj) passable, open, sailable, voyageable, crossable.

haffærni navigability; *synonym* (n) navigableness.

haffært seaworthy; *synonyms* (adj) oceangoing, sea, seagoing, maritime, (v) snug.

háflóð tide; *synonyms* (n) current, flow, stream, course, (v) wave.

hafna 1. refuse; *synonyms* (v) deny, reject, decline, (n) garbage, trash; *antonym* (v) accept, **2**. reject; *synonyms* (v) refuse, disapprove, discard, dismiss, (n) cull; *antonyms* (v) approve, choose, select, acknowledge, grant, **3**. dump; *synonyms* (v) ditch, abandon, drop, empty, tip; *antonym* (v) keep, **4**. explode; *synonyms* (v) erupt, detonate, crack, discharge, (n) burst; *antonym* (v) implode.

hafnarbakki quay; *synonyms* (n) dock, wharf, jetty, pier, embankment.

hafnargarður 1. pier; *synonyms* (n) dock, wharf, jetty, pillar, quay, **2**. breakwater; *synonyms* (n) bulwark, groyne, mole, seawall, groin.

hafnargjaldagreiðsla clearance; *synonyms* (n) clearing, clearage, disposal, headroom, settlement; *antonyms* (n) blockage, retention.

hafnarvog weighbridge; *synonyms* (adj) balance, beam, scale, steelyard.

hafnbann 1. blockade; *synonyms* (v) bar, barricade, block, beleaguer, besiege, **2**. embargo; *synonyms* (n) ban, prohibition, sanction, veto, inhibition.

hafnsaga pilotage; *synonyms* (n) piloting, steerage, navigation, leadership, lodemanage.

hafnsögugjald pilotage; *synonyms* (n) piloting, steerage, navigation, leadership, lodemanage.

hafnsögumaður pilot; *synonyms* (n) guide, leader, aviator, (v) manage, lead.

hafri oat; *synonyms* (n) ait, eyot.

hafsbotn abyss; *synonyms* (n) abysm, chasm, deep, gorge, gulf.

hafsvæði waters; *synonym* (n) boot.

haft constriction; *synonyms* (n) contraction, bottleneck, choke, impediment, reduction.

háfur dogfish; *synonyms* (n) bowfin, grindle.

hagamús mouse; *synonyms* (n) track, trail, hunt, (v) sneak, creep.

hagfræði economics; *synonyms* (n) finance, economy, commerce, money, backing.

hagfræðilegur economic; *synonyms* (adj) commercial, financial, profitable, efficient, economical.

hagi pasture; *synonyms* (n) grass, meadow, feed, (v) graze, browse.

hágildi 1. mode; *synonyms* (n) means, fashion, manner, method, form, **2**. maximum; *synonyms* (adj) extreme, maximal, top, greatest, highest; *antonyms* (adj) least, (n) minimum.

hagkerfi economy; *synonyms* (n) frugality, parsimony, saving, thrift, conservation; *antonym* (n) extravagance.

hagkvæmni efficiency; *synonyms* (n) capability, effectiveness, ability, efficacy, effect; *antonyms* (n) inefficiency, incompetence, largeness.

hagkvæmur 1. efficient; *synonyms* (adj) effectual, competent, effective, able, capable; *antonyms* (adj) incompetent, inefficient, **2**. economic; *synonyms* (adj) commercial, financial, profitable, efficient, economical.

hagl 1. hail; *synonyms* (n) greet, (v) address, cry, acclaim, applaud, **2**. pellet; *synonyms* (n) shot, granule, bead, (v) ball, (adj) spherule.

háglansslípun burnishing; *synonyms* (n) bronzing, searing, buffing.

haglél hail; *synonyms* (n) greet, (v) address, cry, acclaim, applaud.

haglendi 1. pasture; *synonyms* (n) grass, meadow, feed, (v) graze, browse, **2**. grassland; *synonyms* (n) field, pasture, plain, prairie, lawn.

hagnaður 1. profit; *synonyms* (n) gain, benefit, account, good, (adj) advantage; *antonym* (v) lose, **2**. revenue; *synonyms* (n) income, receipts, proceeds, profit, earnings, **3**. earnings; *synonyms* (n) salary, pay, profits, revenue, wage, **4**. gain; *synonyms* (v) acquire, derive, attain, catch, earn; *antonym* (n) loss.

hagnýta 1. exploit; *synonyms* (v) act, (n) deed, achievement, feat, accomplishment, **2**. implement; *synonyms* (v) execute, fulfil, (n) tool, apparatus, utensil.

hagnýting 1. exploitation; *synonyms* (n) abuse, development, misuse, employment, operation, **2**. implementation; *synonyms* (n) execution, fulfillment, enforcement, accomplishment, effectuation.

hagnýttur applied; *synonyms* (adj) practical, useful, concrete, activated, adjusted; *antonym* (adj) theoretical.

hagnýtur functional; *synonyms* (adj) practical, effective, handy, operational, operative; *antonyms* (adj) nonfunctional, useless.

hagræði accommodation; *synonyms* (n) adjustment, compromise, loan, lodging, (v) advance.

hagræðing rationalization; *synonyms* (n) explanation, rationalisation, justification, account, defense.

hagrænn economic; *synonyms* (adj) commercial, financial, profitable, efficient, economical.

hagsæld prosperity; *synonyms* (n) affluence, success, wealth, flourish, (adv) happiness; *antonym* (n) poverty.

hagsmunaskipting apportionment; *synonyms* (n) allotment, allocation, distribution, apportioning, deal.

hagsmunir interest; *synonyms* (*n*) concern, advantage, affair, (*v*) engage, care; *antonyms* (*n*) indifference, apathy, (*v*) bore.

hagstæðastur optimal; *synonyms* (*adj*) optimum, best, finest, ideal, superb.

hagstæður 1. advantageous; *synonyms* (*adj*) expedient, favorable, auspicious, useful, beneficial; *antonym* (*adj*) useless, **2**. economic; *synonyms* (*adj*) commercial, financial, profitable, efficient, economical, **3**. optimal; *synonyms* (*adj*) optimum, best, finest, ideal, superb.

hagsýni economy; *synonyms* (*n*) frugality, parsimony, saving, thrift, conservation; *antonym* (*n*) extravagance.

hagsýnn economic; *synonyms* (*adj*) commercial, financial, profitable, efficient, economical.

hagsýsla fiscal; *synonyms* (*adj*) financial, monetary, pecuniary, crumenal, economic.

hagtölur statistics; *synonyms* (*n*) data, census, score, information, list.

hagur 1. state; *synonyms* (*n*) nation, position, say, country, (*v*) declare; *antonyms* (*v*) deny, (*adj*) private, **2**. status; *synonyms* (*n*) rank, situation, caste, (*adj*) place, standing, **3**. benefit; *synonyms* (*n*) advantage, (*v*) aid, assist, profit, avail; *antonyms* (*n*) disadvantage, drawback, loss, (*v*) harm, **4**. interest; *synonyms* (*n*) concern, affair, account, (*v*) engage, care; *antonyms* (*n*) indifference, apathy, (*v*) bore.

háhella abacus; *synonyms* (*n*) aback, (*v*) logometer, slipstick, tallies.

hak 1. tang; *synonyms* (*n*) flavor, smell, relish, savor, odor, **2**. notch; *synonyms* (*n*) cut, gap, mark, (*v*) dent, hack, **3**. pawl; *synonyms* (*n*) detent, ratchet, click, dog, andiron.

haka chin; *synonyms* (*n*) talk, jaw, jawbone, rap, (*v*) speak.

hákarl shark; *synonyms* (*n*) cheat, fraud, swindler, charlatan, crook.

hal haul; *synonyms* (*n*) freight, (*v*) draw, drag, pull, tow; *antonym* (*v*) push.

halabrestur rattle; *synonyms* (*n*) roll, jangle, jingle, click, (*v*) clatter.

haladzi 1. fume; *synonyms* (*n*) smoke, foam, (*v*) chafe, rage, (*adj*) boil, **2**. fumes; *synonyms* (*n*) fume, gas, exhaust, smog, vapor.

haladzo fumes; *synonyms* (*n*) fume, gas, exhaust, smog, vapor.

halamyndun tailing; *synonyms* (*n*) shadowing, following, tail, abridgment, cobwebbing.

halaskekkja coma; *synonyms* (*n*) lethargy, trance, dream, stupor, sleep.

halastjarna 1. comet; *synonym* (*n*) iris, **2**. coma; *synonyms* (*n*) lethargy, trance, dream, stupor, sleep.

hald 1. detention; *synonyms* (*n*) delay, arrest, custody, confinement, apprehension; *antonyms* (*n*) freedom, release, **2**. clamping; *synonym* (*n*) grip, **3**. holding; *synonyms* (*n*) estate, belongings, hold, keeping, claim, **4**. handle; *synonyms* (*v*) administer, conduct, feel, wield, (*n*) clutch, **5**. hold; *synonyms* (*v*) keep, detain, endure, adhere, (*n*) grasp.

halda 1. hold; *synonyms* (*v*) keep, detain, endure, (*n*) grasp, grip; *antonym* (*v*) release, **2**. suppose; *synonyms* (*v*) believe, guess, infer, assume, conjecture, **3**. think; *synonyms* (*v*) consider, reckon, estimate, hold, imagine; *antonym* (*v*) forget, **4**. presume; *synonyms* (*v*) dare, expect, think, esteem, conclude, **5**. surmise; *synonyms* (*v*) suppose, presume, suspect, (*n*) hypothesis, supposition.

haldari 1. retainer; *synonyms* (*n*) servant, attendant, follower, consideration, dependent, **2**. holder; *synonyms* (*n*) bearer, case, possessor, stand, container, **3**. jig; *synonyms* (*n*) jigger, strathspey, (*v*) dance, hop, skip.

haldbær sustainable; *synonyms* (*adj*) bearable, endurable, tolerable, livable.

haldfesta holdfast; *synonyms* (*n*) fastener, clamp, fastening, lock, grasp.

haldrás clamp; *synonyms* (*n*) clinch, brace, (*v*) cramp, clench, (*adj*) clasp.

haldsmaður occupant; *synonyms* (*n*) inhabitant, resident, tenant, denizen, dweller; *antonym* (*n*) landlord.

haldspennusvið regulation; *synonyms* (*n*) rule, adjustment, law, order, (*adj*) control; *antonym* (*n*) chaos.

haldsréttur lien; *synonyms* (*n*) gage, bond, mortgage, pledge, plight.

haldvilla delusion; *synonyms* (*n*) illusion, hallucination, deception, cheat, chimera; *antonyms* (*n*) reality, comprehension.

háleistur sock; *synonyms* (*n*) hit, hose, (*v*) smash, knock, smack.

hálendi highland; *synonyms* (*n*) plateau, upland, eminence, table, hill; *antonym* (*n*) lowland.

hálfdvali 1. stupefaction; *synonyms* (*n*) stupor, astonishment, daze, amazement, shock, **2**. stupor; *synonyms* (*n*) lethargy, stupefaction, coma, insensibility, sluggishness.

hálfeyðimörk bush; *synonyms* (*n*) shrub, bushing, wild, chaparral, hedge.

hálfgagnsær 1. translucent; *synonyms* (*adj*) clear, diaphanous, lucid, transparent, semitransparent; *antonyms* (*adj*) opaque, thick, **2**. opaque; *synonyms* (*adj*) cloudy, dense, dull, muddy, obscure; *antonym* (*adj*) see-through.

hálfglær translucent; *synonyms* (adj) clear, diaphanous, lucid, transparent, semitransparent; *antonyms* (adj) opaque, thick.

hálfhnöttur hemisphere; *synonyms* (n) area, realm, region, sphere, ground.

hálfhvel hemisphere; *synonyms* (n) area, realm, region, sphere, ground.

hálfkúla hemisphere; *synonyms* (n) area, realm, region, sphere, ground.

hálfmálmur metalloid; *synonyms* (n) nonmetal, (adj) metalloidal, acid, negative.

hálfmáni crescent; *synonyms* (n) arc, arcade, arch, bow, carve.

hálfmeðvitaður subconscious; *synonyms* (adj) unconscious, psychological, hidden, (n) mind, psyche; *antonyms* (adj) superficial, conscious.

hálfmeðvitund subconscious; *synonyms* (adj) unconscious, psychological, hidden, (n) mind, psyche; *antonyms* (adj) superficial, conscious.

hálfrið alternation; *synonyms* (n) interchange, variation, vicissitude, alternateness, alternativeness.

hálfsamsíðungur 1. trapezoid; *synonyms* (adj) trapeziform, trapezohedral, trapezoidal, trapezial, 2. trapezium.

hálfsárslegur biannual; *synonyms* (adj) biyearly, semiannual.

hálfsérhljóð glide; *synonyms* (v) slide, coast, float, flow, fly; *antonym* (v) struggle.

hálfsjálfvirkur semiautomatic; *synonym* (adj) autoloading.

hálfskuggi penumbra; *synonyms* (n) shade, shadow, eclipse, (adj) umbra.

hálfsmíðaður blank; *synonyms* (adj) bare, empty, unfilled, clean, (n) space; *antonyms* (adj) animated, full, expressive.

hálfstaða dichotomy; *synonyms* (n) subdichotomy, duality.

hálfur half; *synonyms* (n) mediety, halve, piece, (adj) moiety, part; *antonyms* (n) whole, all.

hálfviti moron; *synonyms* (n) idiot, cretin, imbecile, fool, dumbbell.

hali tail; *synonyms* (n) rear, shadow, (v) follow, pursue, track; *antonyms* (v) head, front.

háll smooth; *synonyms* (adj) easy, calm, level, oily, (v) quiet; *antonyms* (adj) rough, uneven, abrasive, coarse, crumpled.

halla 1. tip; *synonyms* (n) top, hint, (v) incline, tilt, dump, 2. bank; *synonyms* (n) dam, coast, slope, (v) embankment, gradient; *antonym* (v) withdraw.

hallahorn rake; *synonyms* (n) profligate, (v) tilt, hoe, harrow, (adj) comb.

hallamæla level; *synonyms* (n) grade, (adj) even, equal, (v) flat, flatten; *antonyms* (adj) inclined, slanting, angled, (v) uneven, build.

hallamælir 1. inclinometer; *synonym* (n) clinometer, 2. level; *synonyms* (n) grade, (adj) even, equal, (v) flat, flatten; *antonyms* (adj) inclined, slanting, angled, (v) uneven, build.

hallamál level; *synonyms* (n) grade, (adj) even, equal, (v) flat, flatten; *antonyms* (adj) inclined, slanting, angled, (v) uneven, build.

hallandi oblique; *synonyms* (adj) indirect, circuitous, devious, lateral, collateral; *antonyms* (adj) direct, level.

hallar descent; *synonyms* (n) ancestry, decline, birth, fall, blood; *antonyms* (n) ascent, improvement.

hallast 1. tip; *synonyms* (n) top, hint, (v) incline, tilt, dump, 2. incline; *synonyms* (n) slope, bias, (v) cant, bend, dispose.

hallastefna 1. aspect; *synonyms* (n) appearance, look, surface, bearing, expression, 2. exposure; *synonyms* (n) display, exposition, detection, peril, (v) disclosure.

hallatala slope; *synonyms* (n) incline, declivity, (v) pitch, slant, cant.

halli 1. slope; *synonyms* (n) incline, declivity, (v) pitch, slant, cant, 2. ramp; *synonyms* (n) inclination, grade, (v) bound, climb, rage, 3. tilt; *synonyms* (n) slope, list, (v) lean, careen, rock; *antonyms* (v) straighten, surrender, 4. rake; *synonyms* (n) profligate, (v) tilt, hoe, harrow, (adj) comb, 5. bevel; *synonym* (n) chamfer.

halló hello; *synonyms* (n) greeting, hi, howdy, hullo, (v) hail.

háloftaathugun sounding; *synonyms* (adj) audible, looking, hollow, (n) investigation, depth.

háls 1. neck; *synonyms* (n) throat, cervix, neckline, (v) pet, (adj) stricture, 2. cervix; *synonym* (n) neck.

hálsband necklace; *synonyms* (n) choker, collar, chaplet, necklet, corona.

hálsklútur neckerchief; *synonyms* (n) handkerchief, kerchief, neckcloth.

hamar 1. hammer; *synonyms* (n) pound, (v) strike, bang, beat, knock, 2. rock; *synonyms* (n) boulder, calculus, (v) jar, (adj) pebble, stone, 3. malleus; *synonyms* (n) hammer, cock, gavel, hammering, plectrum.

hámark 1. summit; *synonyms* (n) acme, apex, peak, pinnacle, crown; *antonyms* (n) base, nadir, 2. maximum; *synonyms* (adj) extreme, maximal, top, greatest, highest; *antonyms* (adj) least, (n) minimum, 3. peak; *synonyms* (n) crest, maximum, climax, head, height; *antonym* (n) trough, 4. max; *synonyms* (n) goop, majority, preponderance, soap, (adj) most.

hámarka maximize; *synonyms* (*v*) increase, maximise, intensify, improve, inflate; *antonym* (*v*) minimize.

hámarksflughæð ceiling; *synonyms* (*n*) cap, limit, maximum, limitation, roof; *antonym* (*n*) ground.

hambrigði conversion; *synonyms* (*n*) alteration, change, changeover, adaptation, exchange.

hamingja happiness; *synonyms* (*n*) delight, enjoyment, blessedness, bliss, cheerfulness; *antonyms* (*n*) unhappiness, sadness, despair, grief, misery.

hamingjusamur 1. fortunate; *synonyms* (*adj*) favorable, auspicious, lucky, advantageous, blessed; *antonyms* (*adj*) unfortunate, unlucky, **2**. happy; *synonyms* (*adj*) fortunate, felicitous, contented, gay, buoyant; *antonyms* (*adj*) unhappy, sad, dejected, depressed, miserable.

hamla 1. restraint; *synonyms* (*n*) bridle, constraint, control, hindrance, (*v*) check; *antonyms* (*n*) excess, abandon, decadence, incentive, **2**. retard; *synonyms* (*v*) delay, hinder, arrest, detain, impede; *antonym* (*v*) accelerate, **3**. restrict; *synonyms* (*v*) limit, restrain, circumscribe, confine, constrain, **4**. constraint; *synonyms* (*n*) coercion, compulsion, force, restraint, confinement, **5**. damp; *synonyms* (*adj*) moist, muggy, (*v*) break, chill, (*n*) wet; *antonyms* (*adj*) dry, (*n*) dryness.

hamlandi inhibitory; *synonyms* (*adj*) inhibiting, repressive, repressing.

hamlari retarder; *synonym* (*n*) restrainer.

hamning containment; *synonyms* (*n*) control, repression, restriction.

hámörkun optimization; *synonyms* (*n*) optimisation, increase.

hampjurt hemp; *synonyms* (*n*) cannabis, dope, ganja, grass, (*adj*) marijuana.

hampþétta caulk; *synonyms* (*v*) calk, splice, bar, close, stanch.

hampur hemp; *synonyms* (*n*) cannabis, dope, ganja, grass, (*adj*) marijuana.

hamra ram; *synonyms* (*v*) beat, cram, crash, drive, jam.

hamrar cliff; *synonyms* (*n*) bluff, precipice, hill, mountain, promontory.

hamskipti 1. ecdysis; *synonyms* (*n*) moult, exuviation, moulting, molt, molting, **2**. moulting; *synonyms* (*adj*) pulled, pilled, plucked, (*n*) ecdysis.

hamskipting metamorphosis; *synonyms* (*n*) alteration, metabolism, change, conversion, transformation.

hamsleysi amok; *synonyms* (*adv*) amuck, murderously, (*adj*) berserk, demoniac, demoniacal.

hamstola manic; *synonyms* (*adj*) frenzied, frantic, wild, crazy, demented; *antonym* (*adj*) calm.

hamur 1. phase; *synonyms* (*n*) aspect, stage, facet, chapter, grade, **2**. state; *synonyms* (*n*) nation, position, say, country, (*v*) declare; *antonyms* (*v*) deny, (*adj*) private, **3**. setup; *synonyms* (*n*) apparatus, arrangement, setting, system, scheme, **4**. mode; *synonyms* (*n*) means, fashion, manner, method, form, **5**. facies.

handahófskenndur arbitrary; *synonyms* (*adj*) absolute, capricious, dictatorial, optional, erratic.

handahófskennt random; *synonyms* (*adj*) accidental, aimless, irregular, (*n*) haphazard, chance; *antonym* (*adj*) systematic.

handarkriki 1. axilla; *synonym* (*n*) armpit, **2**. armpit; *synonym* (*n*) axilla.

handbær 1. portable; *synonyms* (*adj*) mobile, movable, portative, light, convenient; *antonym* (*adj*) fixed, **2**. liquid; *synonyms* (*adj*) flowing, fluent, fluid, juicy, limpid; *antonyms* (*adj*) firm, (*n*) solid, gaseous.

handbók manual; *synonyms* (*n*) handbook, guide, guidebook, brochure, primer; *antonyms* (*adj*) automatic, mechanized.

handbor gimlet; *synonyms* (*n*) auger, borer, drill, wimble, chisel.

handbragð workmanship; *synonyms* (*n*) craft, handicraft, craftsmanship, skill, artistry.

handfang 1. grip; *synonyms* (*n*) clasp, clutch, (*v*) grasp, hold, catch; *antonyms* (*v*) bore, release, **2**. handle; *synonyms* (*v*) administer, conduct, feel, wield, (*n*) grip.

handfjöllun manipulation; *synonyms* (*n*) handling, management, treatment, use, control.

handfjötlun manipulation; *synonyms* (*n*) handling, management, treatment, use, control.

handhöfn holdings; *synonyms* (*n*) property, assets, estate, means, resources.

handhverfa isomer; *synonym* (*n*) isomeride.

handiðn handicraft; *synonyms* (*n*) craft, handcraft, handiwork, mystery, handwork.

handknúið manual; *synonyms* (*n*) handbook, guide, guidebook, brochure, primer; *antonyms* (*adj*) automatic, mechanized.

handlæknir surgeon; *synonyms* (*n*) doctor, physician, sawbones, chirurgeon.

handlæknisaðgerð operation; *synonyms* (*n*) execution, movement, act, agency, effect.

handlæknisfræði surgery; *synonyms* (*n*) operation, chirurgery, act, functioning, or.

handlag maneuver; *synonyms* (*v*) manoeuvre, guide, (*n*) artifice, ruse, scheme.

handleggur arm; *synonyms* (*n*) branch, wing, bay, department, (*v*) equip; *antonym* (*v*) disarm.

handsveif crank; *synonyms* (*n*) crackpot, grouch, handle, nut, (*adj*) cranky.

handtaka arrest; *synonyms* (*n*) stop, check, halt, (*v*) capture, catch; *antonyms* (*v*) release, discharge.

handveð collateral; *synonyms* (*adj*) secondary, (*n*) warranty, guarantee, mortgage, guaranty.

handvirkt manual; *synonyms* (*n*) handbook, guide, guidebook, brochure, primer; *antonyms* (*adj*) automatic, mechanized.

handvirkur manual; *synonyms* (*n*) handbook, guide, guidebook, brochure, primer; *antonyms* (*adj*) automatic, mechanized.

hang dependency; *synonyms* (*n*) dependence, addiction, colony, dependance, (*adj*) contingency.

hanga 1. droop; *synonyms* (*v*) bend, decline, dangle, wilt, (*n*) sag, 2. hover; *synonyms* (*v*) float, fly, hang, hesitate, brood, 3. hang; *synonyms* (*v*) depend, drape, append, (*n*) suspend, delay.

hangandi 1. suspended; *synonyms* (*adj*) hanging, pendent, dormant, pendulous, abeyant, 2. dependent; *synonyms* (*adj*) subject, subordinate, contingent, (*n*) dependant, charge; *antonyms* (*adj*) independent, self-governing, self-sufficient.

hani tap; *synonyms* (*n*) pat, dab, hit, (*v*) knock, rap.

hann he; *synonyms* (*pron*) cestui, (*n*) male, man, helium.

hanna design; *synonyms* (*n*) aim, purpose, scheme, conception, (*v*) plan; *antonym* (*n*) chance.

hanskar gloves; *synonyms* (*n*) glove, belt, handbag, ornament, scarf.

hanski glove; *synonyms* (*n*) gloves, mitt, sleeve, wristband, (*v*) catch.

happ success; *synonyms* (*n*) conquest, achievement, hit, prosperity, passing; *antonyms* (*n*) failure, flop, debacle, defeat, disappointment.

hápunktur 1. zenith; *synonyms* (*n*) apex, peak, top, acme, climax; *antonyms* (*n*) nadir, base, 2. acme; *synonyms* (*n*) crown, pinnacle, height, summit, vertex, 3. highlight; *synonyms* (*v*) emphasize, accentuate, spotlight, underline, accent.

hár 1. hair; *synonyms* (*n*) fuzz, coat, down, fleece, fur, 2. tall; *synonyms* (*adj*) lofty, elevated, high, exalted, big; *antonyms* (*adj*) short, low, small, 3. pilus; *synonyms* (*n*) hair, capillament, cilia, cilium, hairbreadth, 4. high; *synonyms* (*adj*) eminent, great, expensive, distinguished, tall; *antonyms* (*adj*) deep, sober, 5. lofty; *synonyms* (*adj*) arrogant, grand, haughty, gallant, majestic; *antonym* (*adj*) lowly.

háræð capillary; *synonyms* (*adj*) capilliform, hairlike, (*n*) artery, vein, aorta.

hararo 1. hairs, 2. hair (hár); *synonyms* (*n*) fuzz, coat, down, fleece, fur.

hárauður florid; *synonyms* (*adj*) flamboyant, ornate, aureate, fancy, flowery.

hárbelgur follicle; *synonyms* (*n*) cavity, dent, dimple, dint, lacuna.

harðgúmmí ebonite; *synonym* (*n*) vulcanite.

harðkol anthracite; *synonyms* (*n*) culm, carbon, charcoal, coke, coal.

harðlóða braze; *synonyms* (*v*) stick, temper, harden.

harðmálmur carbide; *synonym* (*n*) carbonide.

harðna solidify; *synonyms* (*v*) congeal, set, condense, concrete, freeze; *antonyms* (*v*) soften, liquefy.

harðstál carbide; *synonym* (*n*) carbonide.

harður 1. sclerous; *synonym* (*adj*) indurated, 2. hard; *synonyms* (*adj*) austere, bad, difficult, grave, (*adv*) firm; *antonyms* (*adj*) easy, soft, kind, (*adv*) gently, lightly.

hárfellir moulting; *synonyms* (*adj*) pulled, (*n*) moult, ecdysis, molt, molting.

hárfínn capillary; *synonyms* (*adj*) capilliform, hairlike, (*n*) artery, vein, aorta.

hark noise; *synonyms* (*n*) clatter, clamor, hubbub, racket, sound; *antonyms* (*n*) silence, quiet.

harka hardness; *synonyms* (*n*) firmness, austerity, asperity, callousness, difficulty; *antonym* (*n*) softness.

harkalegur drastic; *synonyms* (*adj*) severe, desperate, extreme, sweeping, ultra.

harmabót balm; *synonyms* (*n*) ointment, salve, unguent, incense, aroma.

harmóníka accordion; *synonym* (*adj*) plicate.

harmónískur harmonic; *synonyms* (*adj*) harmonious, consonant, harmonical, sympathetic, concordant.

harpeis resin; *synonyms* (*n*) gum, rosin, colophany.

harpeisar resin; *synonyms* (*n*) gum, rosin, colophany.

hárpest sycosis; *synonym* (*n*) mentagra.

hárpípa capillary; *synonyms* (*adj*) capilliform, hairlike, (*n*) artery, vein, aorta.

harpixar resin; *synonyms* (*n*) gum, rosin, colophany.

hártap baldness; *synonyms* (*n*) hairlessness, nakedness, austerity, bluntness, emptiness; *antonym* (*n*) hairiness.

háseti 1. seaman; *synonyms* (*n*) mariner, seafarer, gob, sailor, tar, 2. sailor; *synonyms* (*n*) seaman, bluejacket, boatman, boater, crewman, 3. seafarer; *synonyms* (*n*) navigator, jack, hole, maw, pitch, 4. mariner; *synonyms* (*n*) merman, trap, yap.

hásing housing; *synonyms* (*n*) habitation, casing, dwelling, lodging, abode; *antonym* (*adj*) business.

háskalegur hazardous; *synonyms* (*adj*) dangerous, risky, perilous, unsafe, (*n*) daring; *antonym* (*adj*) safe.

háski hazard; *synonyms* (*n*) chance, risk, venture, danger, (*v*) endanger; *antonym* (*n*) safety.

háskólaráð senate; *synonyms* (*n*) council, legislature, parliament, congress, assembly.

háskóli 1. university; *synonyms* (*n*) school, academy, academe, (*adj*) college, academic, **2.** college; *synonyms* (*n*) faculty, association, institute, society, institution.

háslétta plateau; *synonyms* (*n*) plain, table, tableland, elevation, stage.

háspennukefli coil; *synonyms* (*n*) spiral, roll, loop, (*v*) curl, circle; *antonym* (*v*) uncoil.

háspennuútslag tracking; *synonyms* (*n*) pursuit, trailing, rutting, trajectography.

hass cannabis; *synonyms* (*n*) pot, ganja, grass, marijuana, weed.

hassjurt marijuana; *synonyms* (*n*) cannabis, ganja, grass, hemp, marihuana.

hástæður superscript; *synonyms* (*n*) superior, master, superordinate, superscription; *antonym* (*n*) subscript.

hástafa capitalize; *synonyms* (*v*) capitalise, gain, profit, fund, use.

hástafaritun capitalization; *synonyms* (*n*) capitalisation, discounting, use.

hástig 1. acme; *synonyms* (*n*) apex, crown, peak, pinnacle, top; *antonym* (*n*) nadir, **2.** climax; *synonyms* (*n*) acme, culmination, orgasm, zenith, (*v*) culminate; *antonym* (*v*) dip.

hata hate; *synonyms* (*v*) abhor, detest, (*n*) dislike, enmity, abhorrence; *antonyms* (*v*) love, like, adore.

hátalari loudspeaker; *synonyms* (*n*) speaker, amplifier, amp, talker, utterer.

háþrýstisvæði anticyclone; *synonyms* (*n*) blast, cyclone, gale, gust, hurricane.

hátign majesty; *synonyms* (*n*) glory, grandeur, dignity, loftiness, splendor.

hátindur summit; *synonyms* (*n*) acme, apex, peak, pinnacle, crown; *antonyms* (*n*) base, nadir.

háttbundið periodic; *synonyms* (*adj*) intermittent, regular, periodical, recurrent, frequent.

háttbundinn metrical; *synonyms* (*adj*) metric, measured, cadenced, calculated, careful.

hátternisfræði ethology; *synonym* (*n*) ethics.

hattur 1. pileus; *synonyms* (*n*) cap, capital, ceiling, chapter, crownwork, **2.** hat; *synonyms* (*n*) chapeau, lid, sou'wester, bonus, eyelid.

háttur 1. procedure; *synonyms* (*n*) process, formula, practice, routine, fashion, **2.** channel; *synonyms* (*n*) canal, conduit, groove, (*v*) carry, conduct, **3.** mood; *synonyms* (*n*) humor, atmosphere, climate, disposition, air, **4.** mode; *synonyms* (*n*) means, manner, method, form, way.

háttvís diplomat; *synonyms* (*n*) diplomatist, envoy, ambassador, intermediary, minister.

hatur 1. hate; *synonyms* (*v*) abhor, detest, (*n*) dislike, enmity, abhorrence; *antonyms* (*v*) love, like, adore, **2.** hatred; *synonyms* (*n*) detestation, antipathy, aversion, disgust, (*v*) hate; *antonyms* (*n*) adoration, liking.

haukur hawk; *synonyms* (*n*) eagle, (*v*) peddle, cough, expectorate, huckster.

haull rupture; *synonyms* (*n*) fracture, burst, rift, (*v*) break, crack; *antonym* (*n*) repair.

haulrétting reduction; *synonyms* (*n*) contraction, decrease, decrement, diminution, rebate; *antonyms* (*n*) increase, growth, intensification, strengthening, expansion.

haus 1. header; *synonyms* (*n*) caption, heading, lintel, title, (*v*) dive, **2.** heading; *synonyms* (*n*) bearing, drift, head, course, direction.

hausa head; *synonyms* (*n*) chief, captain, front, point, boss; *antonyms* (*n*) end, subordinate, (*v*) follow.

hausamót fontanelle; *synonym* (*n*) fontanel.

hausbor perforator; *synonyms* (*n*) gun, awl, bodkin, borer, bradawl.

hauskúpa 1. skull; *synonyms* (*n*) pate, noddle, head, noggin, shell, **2.** cranium; *synonyms* (*n*) skull, braincase, brainpan, pericranium, cerebrum.

haust 1. fall; *synonyms* (*v*) decline, dip, decrease, descend, (*n*) drop; *antonyms* (*v*) rise, increase, ascend, climb, (*n*) ascent, **2.** autumn; *synonyms* (*n*) fall, declivity, descent, downfall, harvest.

hausun heading; *synonyms* (*n*) caption, bearing, drift, head, title.

hávaði noise; *synonyms* (*n*) clatter, clamor, hubbub, racket, sound; *antonyms* (*n*) silence, quiet.

háværð loudness; *synonyms* (*n*) garishness, gaudiness, brashness, tastelessness, noisiness.

hávísir superscript; *synonyms* (*n*) superior, master, superordinate, superscription; *antonym* (*n*) subscript.

hefð usage; *synonyms* (*n*) habit, practice, employment, (*v*) use, (*adj*) custom.

hefðbundinn classic; *synonyms* (*adj*) classical, model, archetypal, exemplary, ideal; *antonym* (*n*) second-rate.

hefill plane; *synonyms* (*n*) airplane, face, (*adj*) level, even, flat.

hefja 1. raise; *synonyms* (*v*) boost, lift, erect, hoist, (*n*) advance; *antonym* (*v*) lower, **2.** lever; *synonyms* (*n*) knob, (*v*) pry, raise, jimmy, prize, **3.** elevate; *synonyms* (*v*) exalt, cheer, dignify, promote, rear; *antonym* (*v*) demote, **4.** hoist; *synonyms* (*n*) elevator, (*v*) elevate, haul, heave, uphold, **5.** lift; *synonyms* (*v*) rise, filch, hike, airlift, pilfer.

hefla plane; *synonyms* (*n*) airplane, face, (*adj*) level, even, flat.

hefta 1. staple; *synonyms (n)* pin, material, *(v)* nail, *(adj)* basic, fundamental, **2**. restrict; *synonyms (v)* limit, restrain, circumscribe, confine, constrain, **3**. constraint; *synonyms (n)* coercion, compulsion, force, restraint, confinement; *antonym (n)* incentive, **4**. frustrate; *synonyms (v)* baffle, counteract, disappoint, fail, foil; *antonym (v)* encourage.

hefti 1. staple; *synonyms (n)* pin, material, *(v)* nail, *(adj)* basic, fundamental, **2**. leaflet; *synonyms (n)* brochure, leaf, booklet, pamphlet, circular.

hefting frustration; *synonyms (n)* failure, defeat, disappointment, letdown, vexation.

heftur centric; *synonyms (adj)* central, centrical.

hegðun 1. behavior; *synonyms (n)* bearing, act, behaviour, carriage, conduct, **2**. behaviour; *synonyms (n)* behavior, demeanor, demeanour, deportment, doings, **3**. conduct; *synonyms (n)* administration, manage, *(v)* bring, direct, administer, **4**. deportment; *synonyms (n)* attitude, manner, comportment, air, manners.

hegðunarmynstur norm; *synonyms (n)* average, mean, measure, mode, criterion.

hegðunarreglur norm; *synonyms (n)* average, mean, measure, mode, criterion.

hegning 1. punishment; *synonyms (n)* discipline, correction, penalty, penance, chastisement, **2**. penalty; *synonyms (n)* mulct, fine, forfeit, forfeiture, *(v)* condemnation.

hégómaskapur vanity; *synonyms (n)* conceit, arrogance, egotism, emptiness, pride; *antonyms (n)* modesty, selflessness.

hégómi vanity; *synonyms (n)* conceit, arrogance, egotism, emptiness, pride; *antonyms (n)* modesty, selflessness.

hegri heron; *synonyms (n)* bomber, champion, fighter, grinder, hero.

heiðar heathland; *synonym (n)* heath.

heiðarlegur 1. upright; *synonyms (adj)* perpendicular, straight, erect, vertical, fair; *antonyms (adj)* disreputable, prone, upturned, degenerate, hanging, **2**. honourable; *synonyms (adj)* honest, estimable, honorable, good, ethical, **3**. honest; *synonyms (adj)* genuine, equitable, sincere, artless, candid; *antonyms (adj)* dishonest, corrupt, guarded, lying, misleading, **4**. forthright; *synonyms (adj)* blunt, direct, frank, outspoken, truthful.

heiðblár blue (blár); *synonyms (adj)* azure, depressed, down, gloomy, low.

heiðhvolf stratosphere; *synonym (n)* air.

heiði heath; *synonyms (n)* heather, heathland, prairie, steppe, waste.

heiðursmerkjaveiting decoration; *synonyms (n)* adornment, award, garnish, medal, ornament.

heigull chicken; *synonyms (n)* chick, cock, coward, fowl, hen.

heilaáfall apoplexy; *synonyms (n)* stroke, *(adj)* palsy, paralysis, collapse, deliquium.

heilablóðfall 1. stroke; *synonyms (n)* touch, beat, caress, *(v)* buffet, *(adj)* blow, **2**. apoplexy; *synonyms (n)* stroke, *(adj)* palsy, paralysis, collapse, deliquium.

heilabólga encephalitis; *synonyms (n)* cephalitis, phrenitis.

heilabörkur cortex; *synonyms (n)* bark, crust, peel, rind, pallium.

heiladingull hypophysis; *synonyms (n)* pituitary, cataract.

heilafelling convolution; *synonyms (n)* coil, gyrus, twine, complexity, swirl.

heilaferli cerebration; *synonyms (n)* cogitation, thought, intellection, mentation, thinking.

heilagur 1. sacred; *synonyms (adj)* hallowed, holy, consecrated, dedicated, divine; *antonyms (adj)* secular, profane, **2**. holy; *synonyms (adj)* devout, godly, heavenly, religious, blessed.

heilahol ventricle; *synonyms (n)* paunch, stomach, venter, heart.

heilahristingur concussion; *synonyms (n)* blow, clash, collision, shock, impact.

heilakúpa cranium; *synonyms (n)* skull, braincase, brainpan, head, noddle.

heilaleysi anencephaly; *synonym (n)* anencephalia.

heilalínurit electroencephalogram; *synonyms (n)* encephalogram, pneumoencephalogram.

heilarafrit electroencephalogram; *synonyms (n)* encephalogram, pneumoencephalogram.

heilarit electroencephalogram; *synonyms (n)* encephalogram, pneumoencephalogram.

heilaskúm arachnoid; *synonyms (n)* arachnid, *(adj)* arachnidian, arachnoidal, araneose, spiderlike.

heilaslag apoplexy; *synonyms (n)* stroke, *(adj)* palsy, paralysis, collapse, deliquium.

heilaþvottur brainwashing; *synonyms (n)* education, encoding, indoctrination, persuasion, programming.

heilbrigði health; *synonyms (n)* condition, fitness, welfare, pledge, strength.

heilbrigðisreglur regimen; *synonyms (n)* regime, diet, government, treatment, cure.

heild 1. total; *synonyms (adj)* aggregate, complete, *(n)* whole, amount, *(v)* count; *antonyms (adj)* partial, incomplete, qualified, **2**. totality; *synonyms (n)* entirety, sum, total, completeness, entireness, **3**. completeness; *synonyms (n)* fullness, thoroughness, unity, plenitude, perfection, **4**.

aggregate; *synonyms* (n) agglomerate, complex, pile, (v) accumulate, cluster; *antonyms* (n) individual, part, **5**. entity; *synonyms* (n) being, existence, object, thing, article.

heilda integrate; *synonyms* (v) incorporate, blend, combine, consolidate, fuse; *antonyms* (v) separate, exclude, segregate.

heildarbreytileiki variation; *synonyms* (n) alteration, change, difference, divergence, mutation; *antonym* (n) similarity.

heildari integrator; *synonym* (n) planimeter.

heildarkerfi system; *synonyms* (n) method, arrangement, network, organization, plan.

helldarneysla intake; *synonyms* (n) absorption, consumption, ingestion, drinking, eating.

heildartala total; *synonyms* (adj) aggregate, complete, (n) whole, amount, (v) count; *antonyms* (adj) partial, incomplete, qualified.

heildartíðni turnover; *synonyms* (n) overturn, revolution, sales, upset, pastry.

heildarupphæð aggregate; *synonyms* (n) total, agglomerate, whole, (v) accumulate, cluster; *antonyms* (n) individual, part.

heildi integral; *synonyms* (adj) complete, entire, inherent, full, (n) whole.

heildsær macroscopic; *synonyms* (adj) macroscopical, large, big, bombastic, declamatory.

heildsala wholesale; *synonyms* (adj) sweeping, extensive, indiscriminate, broad, (adv) entirely; *antonyms* (adj) partial, (v) retail.

heildsali wholesaler; *synonyms* (n) merchant, jobber, middleman, broker, contact; *antonym* (n) buyer.

heildun integration; *synonyms* (n) amalgamation, consolidation, embodiment, integrating, merger; *antonym* (n) segregation.

heildverslun wholesale; *synonyms* (adj) sweeping, extensive, indiscriminate, broad, (adv) entirely; *antonyms* (adj) partial, (v) retail.

heilfeldi multiple; *synonyms* (adj) manifold, many, complex, diverse, populous; *antonym* (adj) simple.

heilfeldissveiflur harmonics; *synonyms* (n) harmony, overtones.

heili 1. brain; *synonyms* (n) mastermind, genius, head, mind, reason, **2**. cerebrum; *synonyms* (n) brain, pate, cranium, sconce, noddle.

heilkenni syndrome; *synonyms* (n) ailment, complaint, complex, sickness, disorder.

heilkjörnungur 1. eukaryote; *synonym* (n) eucaryote, **2**. eucaryote; *synonym* (n) eukaryote.

heill 1. integral; *synonyms* (adj) complete, entire, inherent, full, (n) whole, **2**. solid; *synonyms* (adj) firm, dense, compact, consistent, hard; *antonyms* (adj) soft, unreliable, loose, gaseous, (n) liquid, **3**. stark; *synonyms* (adj) austere, bare, bleak, desolate,

mere, **4**. whole; *synonyms* (adj) total, all, integral, aggregate, (n) sum; *antonyms* (adj) incomplete, broken, imperfect, partial, (n) part, **5**. thorough; *synonyms* (adj) absolute, exhaustive, good, profound, careful; *antonyms* (adj) superficial, careless, sketchy, slack.

heillandi 1. seductive; *synonyms* (adj) attractive, alluring, enticing, tempting, seducing, **2**. alluring; *synonyms* (adj) charming, seductive, beguiling, enchanting, glamorous; *antonym* (adj) repellent, **3**. bewitching; *synonyms* (adj) fascinating, captivating, engaging, enthralling, entrancing, **4**. attractive; *synonyms* (adj) amiable, appealing, good-looking, adorable, delightful; *antonyms* (adj) unattractive, ugly, unappealing, disgusting, revolting, **5**. appealing; *synonyms* (adj) absorbing, inviting, prepossessing, likable, magnetic.

heilleiki integrity; *synonyms* (n) honesty, probity, completeness, fairness, (adj) candor; *antonyms* (n) dishonesty, wickedness.

heillyndi integrity; *synonyms* (n) honesty, probity, completeness, fairness, (adj) candor; *antonyms* (n) dishonesty, wickedness.

heilmynd hologram; *synonym* (n) holograph.

heilnæmur 1. salutary; *synonyms* (adj) beneficial, salubrious, good, healthful, healthy, **2**. salubrious; *synonyms* (adj) wholesome, hygienic, salutary, invigorating.

heilsa 1. salute; *synonyms* (n) greeting, salutation, bow, (v) greet, hail, **2**. health; *synonyms* (n) condition, fitness, welfare, pledge, strength, **3**. hail; *synonyms* (n) call, (v) address, cry, acclaim, applaud, **4**. hello; *synonyms* (n) hi, howdy, hullo, welcome, **5**. greet; *synonyms* (v) accost, acknowledge, salute, bid, (n) receive.

heilsufar health; *synonyms* (n) condition, fitness, welfare, pledge, strength.

heilsufræði hygiene; *synonyms* (n) hygienics, sanitation, regimen, salutariness, spotlessness.

heilsugæslustöð clinic; *synonyms* (n) infirmary, hospital, workshop, clinique, (v) clinical.

heilsugestur client; *synonyms* (n) buyer, customer, patron, guest, purchaser.

heilsuspillandi morbid; *synonyms* (adj) diseased, ghoulish, gruesome, macabre, (v) sickly.

heilsutæpur unhealthy; *synonyms* (adj) morbid, harmful, insanitary, sickly, ailing; *antonyms* (adj) healthy, fit, hygienic.

heilsuveðurfræði climatology; *synonym* (n) meteorology.

heilsuveill unhealthy; *synonyms* (adj) morbid, harmful, insanitary, sickly, ailing; *antonyms* (adj) healthy, fit, hygienic.

heiltala integer; *synonyms* (n) digit, figure, cipher, number, numeral.

heilun healing; *synonyms* (n) cure, convalescence, recuperation, therapy, (adj) curative; *antonym* (adj) injurious.

heim home; *synonyms* (n) fireside, abode, domicile, house, base.

heimafenginn autogenous; *synonyms* (adj) autogenic, autogeneal, interior, autogenetic.

heimaland country; *synonyms* (n) state, nation, home, land, area; *antonyms* (n) city, (adj) urban.

heimamaður native; *synonyms* (adj) inborn, inherent, innate, (n) aboriginal, autochthon; *antonyms* (adj) foreign, learned, (n) stranger, immigrant, imported.

heimboð invitation; *synonyms* (n) call, bidding, temptation, lure, (v) invite.

heimila 1. sanction; *synonyms* (n) warrant, assent, (v) approve, permit, countenance; *antonyms* (v) ban, forbid, **2.** authorize; *synonyms* (v) empower, assign, certify, commission, delegate, **3.** grant; *synonyms* (v) give, allow, award, bestow, admit; *antonyms* (v) deny, reject.

heimild 1. proxy; *synonyms* (n) attorney, agent, deputy, alternate, (v) substitute, **2.** source; *synonyms* (n) origin, root, cause, commencement, beginning, **3.** authority; *synonyms* (n) ascendancy, command, sanction, administration, authorization, **4.** authorization; *synonyms* (n) authority, approval, license, permission, authorisation.

heimildir data; *synonyms* (n) information, facts, details, evidence, fact.

heimili 1. residence; *synonyms* (n) abode, dwelling, home, house, accommodation, **2.** venue; *synonyms* (n) locale, place, site, locus, location, **3.** domicile; *synonyms* (n) residence, address, lodging, habitat, (v) lodge, **4.** household; *synonyms* (n) folk, (adj) family, domestic, common, (v) ordinary.

heimilisfang 1. address; *synonyms* (n) accost, lecture, abode, discourse, (v) greet; *antonym* (v) ignore, **2.** domicile; *synonyms* (n) dwelling, home, residence, house, (v) lodge, **3.** location; *synonyms* (n) localization, orientation, position, berth, emplacement.

heimilisfólk household; *synonyms* (adj) family, home, house, domestic, (v) ordinary.

heimilun authorization; *synonyms* (n) authority, sanction, approval, license, permission.

heimkynni habitat; *synonyms* (n) dwelling, abode, residence, environment, home.

heimsálfa continent; *synonyms* (adj) chaste, celibate, abstemious, pure, temperate; *antonym* (adj) incontinent.

heimsborgaralegur cosmopolitan; *synonyms* (adj) international, universal, sophisticated, global, (n) cosmopolite; *antonym* (adj) provincial.

heimsborgari 1. cosmopolite; *synonyms* (n) cosmopolitan, communist, citizen, philanthropist, socialist, **2.** cosmopolitan; *synonyms* (adj) international, universal, sophisticated, global, (n) cosmopolite; *antonym* (adj) provincial.

heimsfaraldur pandemic; *synonyms* (adj) epidemic, rife, (n) endemic, plague, pandemia.

heimsfarsótt pandemic; *synonyms* (adj) epidemic, rife, (n) endemic, plague, pandemia.

heimsfræði cosmology; *synonyms* (n) cosmogony, cosmogeny.

heimskautaljós aurora; *synonyms* (n) dawn, daybreak, morning, sunrise, prime.

heimsmynd 1. system; *synonyms* (n) method, arrangement, network, organization, plan, **2.** cosmology; *synonyms* (n) cosmogony, cosmogeny.

heimsmyndarfræði cosmology; *synonyms* (n) cosmogony, cosmogeny.

heimsmyndunarfræði cosmogony; *synonyms* (n) cosmology, cosmogeny, cosmography.

heimt retrieval; *synonyms* (n) recovery, reclamation, redress, recuperation, (v) revendication; *antonym* (n) loss.

heimta retrieve; *synonyms* (v) recover, regain, reclaim, recoup, rescue; *antonym* (v) lose.

heimur world; *synonyms* (n) cosmos, nature, universe, creation, public.

heinarbrýni hone; *synonyms* (v) sharpen, perfect, whet, refine, (adj) sharpener.

heini hone; *synonyms* (v) sharpen, perfect, whet, refine, (adj) sharpener.

heiti 1. term; *synonyms* (n) name, expression, period, style, (v) call, **2.** title; *synonyms* (n) designation, caption, claim, designate, (v) term.

heitleiðir thermistor; *synonym* (n) thermocouple.

heittempraður subtropical; *synonyms* (adj) semitropical, subtropic, semitropic.

heitur warm; *synonyms* (adj) hot, affectionate, tender, ardent, cordial; *antonyms* (adj) aloof, cold, unfriendly, reserved, (v) cool.

heldur 1. preferably; *synonyms* (adv) rather, sooner, earlier, instead, (adj) before, **2.** rather; *synonyms* (adv) quite, enough, fairly, pretty, moderately; *antonym* (adv) extremely, **3.** ideally; *synonyms* (adv) perfectly, beautifully, unreally, superlatively, supremely.

helftarblinda hemianopia; *synonym* (n) hemianopsia.

helftarhöfuðverkur hemicrania; *synonyms* (n) migraine, megrim.

helgisaga legend; *synonyms* (*n*) caption, fable, fiction, tale, account.

helín helium; *synonym* (*n*) he.

helíum helium; *synonym* (*n*) he.

hella slab; *synonyms* (*n*) hunk, chunk, bar, (*adj*) table, plate.

helminga bisect; *synonyms* (*v*) cross, cut, dichotomize, divide, halve.

helmingun bisection; *synonyms* (*n*) division, equidistance, half, parting.

helstur principal; *synonyms* (*adj*) master, cardinal, capital, (*n*) chief, head; *antonym* (*adj*) minor.

helti 1. claudication; *synonyms* (*n*) gimp, gameness, gimpiness, (*adj*) footfall, fault, 2. limp; *synonyms* (*adj*) flabby, flaccid, (*n*) hobble, (*v*) halt, hitch; *antonyms* (*adj*) taut, firm, (*n*) energetic.

hélun deposition; *synonyms* (*n*) deposit, affidavit, declaration, dethronement, (*v*) deposal.

helvíti 1. damn; *synonyms* (*v*) condemn, bloody, curse, beshrew, blaspheme; *antonym* (*v*) bless, 2. hell; *synonyms* (*n*) blaze, inferno, netherworld, perdition, underworld; *antonym* (*n*) heaven.

hem cuticle; *synonyms* (*n*) epidermis, shell, carapace, case, casing.

hemilefni moderator; *synonyms* (*n*) chairman, mediator, arbitrator, intermediary, negotiator.

hemill 1. brake; *synonyms* (*n*) bracken, bit, curb, (*v*) halt, retard; *antonym* (*v*) accelerate, 2. inhibitor; *synonym* (*n*) stabilizer.

hemiltaugafruma inhibitor; *synonym* (*n*) stabilizer.

hemiltaugungur inhibitor; *synonym* (*n*) stabilizer.

hemjandi inhibitory; *synonyms* (*adj*) inhibiting, repressive, repressing.

hemla brake; *synonyms* (*n*) bracken, bit, curb, (*v*) halt, retard; *antonym* (*v*) accelerate.

hemlun braking; *synonym* (*n*) trapping.

hemóglóbín hemoglobin; *synonyms* (*n*) haemoglobin, oxyhemoglobin, blood, hematocrystallin.

hemoroido haemorrhoid; *synonyms* (*n*) hemorrhoid, piles, dozens, gobs, heaps.

hendi handedness; *synonyms* (*n*) dominance, laterality, lateralisation, lateralization.

hending 1. random; *synonyms* (*adj*) accidental, aimless, irregular, (*n*) haphazard, chance; *antonym* (*adj*) systematic, 2. variate; *synonyms* (*n*) variant, discrepancy, form, strain, var.

hengi 1. suspension; *synonyms* (*n*) delay, interruption, abeyance, break, intermission, 2. hanger; *synonyms* (*n*) hook, dropper, bolt, dowel, 3. mesentery.

hengilás padlock; *synonyms* (*n*) bolt, lock, bar, holdfast, rail.

henging suspension; *synonyms* (*n*) delay, interruption, abeyance, break, intermission.

hengivagn trailer; *synonyms* (*n*) caravan, leader, ad, advertisement, announcement.

hengja 1. suspend; *synonyms* (*v*) defer, delay, adjourn, hang, interrupt; *antonym* (*v*) continue, 2. cornice; *synonyms* (*n*) frieze, architrave, entablature, epistyle, pediment, 3. hang; *synonyms* (*v*) dangle, depend, drape, float, (*n*) suspend.

hengsli 1. suspension; *synonyms* (*n*) delay, interruption, abeyance, break, intermission, 2. shackle; *synonyms* (*v*) fetter, chain, bind, hobble, (*n*) hamper.

hentugleiki convenience; *synonyms* (*n*) advantage, contrivance, accommodation, opportunity, appliance; *antonym* (*n*) inconvenience.

hentugur expedient; *synonyms* (*adj*) fit, adequate, advisable, (*n*) contrivance, makeshift.

heptan heptane; *synonym* (*n*) septane.

her 1. army; *synonyms* (*n*) legion, troop, host, battery, (*adj*) military, 2. military; *synonyms* (*adj*) martial, militant, warlike, soldierly, (*n*) force; *antonym* (*adj*) civilian, 3. host; *synonyms* (*n*) crowd, army, flock, horde, mob.

hér here; *synonyms* (*adv*) hither, in, (*adj*) present, there, (*pron*) her; *antonym* (*adv*) out.

hérað 1. province; *synonyms* (*n*) country, district, field, county, (*v*) department, 2. region; *synonyms* (*n*) land, area, domain, part, realm, 3. county; *synonyms* (*n*) region, state, shire, mofussil, constituency, 4. district; *synonyms* (*n*) quarter, community, neighborhood, territory, (*adj*) local, 5. parish; *synonyms* (*n*) congregation, province, township, borough, church.

héraðsbúar countryside; *synonyms* (*n*) land, landscape, panorama, (*adj*) country, rustic.

hérasótt tularemia; *synonym* (*n*) tularaemia.

herblástur 1. scare; *synonyms* (*n*) dread, (*v*) alarm, dismay, fright, (*adj*) panic, 2. alarm; *synonyms* (*n*) alert, consternation, (*v*) awe, scare, agitate; *antonyms* (*v*) calm, comfort.

herbragð manoeuvre; *synonyms* (*v*) maneuver, control, direct, go, guide.

herða tighten; *synonyms* (*v*) contract, strain, brace, compress, constrict; *antonyms* (*v*) loosen, relax.

herðakistill humpback; *synonyms* (*n*) crookback, kyphosis, hump, hunchback.

herdeild division; *synonyms* (*n*) department, disagreement, allotment, branch, break; *antonyms* (*n*) closeness, convergence, estimation, unification.

héri hare; *synonyms* (*n*) rabbit, cony, puss, cat, (*adj*) antelope.

herkví blockade; *synonyms* (v) bar, barricade, block, beleaguer, besiege.

herma resonance; *synonyms* (n) vibrancy, reverberation, ringing, sonority, vibration.

hermdarverk terrorism; *synonyms* (n) disorder, murder, nihilism, tyranny, (adj) intimidation.

hermdarverkastarfsemi terrorism; *synonyms* (n) disorder, murder, nihilism, tyranny, (adj) intimidation.

hermifall spline; *synonyms* (n) feather, slat, fin, conclusion, end.

herming 1. simulation; *synonyms* (n) affectation, pretense, imitation, pretence, modelling, **2.** emulation; *synonyms* (n) competition, contention, contest, rivalry, strife, **3.** mimesis; *synonym* (n) mimicry.

hermir 1. simulator, **2.** emulator; *synonyms* (n) competitor, rival, copycat, imitator, antagonist.

hermireikningur simulation; *synonyms* (n) affectation, pretense, imitation, pretence, modelling.

hermueind resonance; *synonyms* (n) vibrancy, reverberation, ringing, sonority, vibration.

hermuhol cavity; *synonyms* (n) cavern, cave, hole, hollow, pocket.

hermun simulation; *synonyms* (n) affectation, pretense, imitation, pretence, modelling.

hernaðaráætlun strategy; *synonyms* (n) dodge, plan, scheme, strategics, (v) tactics.

hernaðarátök conflict; *synonyms* (n) clash, combat, fight, battle, contention; *antonyms* (n) agreement, accord, harmony, peace, (v) agree.

hernám occupation; *synonyms* (n) employment, occupancy, business, craft, calling; *antonym* (n) surrender.

herpandi astringent; *synonyms* (adj) acrid, astrictive, acerb, acerbic, acid.

herpanleiki contractility; *synonyms* (n) irritability, motility, fretfulness, petulance.

herpiefni astringent; *synonyms* (adj) acrid, astrictive, acerb, acerbic, acid.

herping 1. shrinkage; *synonyms* (n) contraction, reduction, decrease, decline, diminution, **2.** contraction; *synonyms* (n) abbreviation, constriction, abridgement, abridgment, condensation; *antonym* (n) expansion, **3.** constriction; *synonyms* (n) bottleneck, choke, impediment, strain, tension.

herpir astringent; *synonyms* (adj) acrid, astrictive, acerb, acerbic, acid.

herra 1. sir; *synonyms* (n) esquire, gentleman, master, man, don, **2.** lord; *synonyms* (n) chief, noble, sir, seignior, almighty, **3.** gentleman; *synonyms* (n)

male, patrician, laureate, squireen, (adj) gentilhomme; *antonym* (n) woman.

herseta occupation; *synonyms* (n) employment, occupancy, business, craft, calling; *antonym* (n) surrender.

hershöfðingi general; *synonyms* (adj) common, comprehensive, national, (v) customary, frequent; *antonyms* (adj) specific, individual, narrow, (n) particular.

herskip warship; *synonym* (n) vessel.

hersla 1. drying; *synonyms* (n) dehydration, curing, desiccation, aeration, airing, **2.** anneal; *synonyms* (v) temper, harden, season, toughen, (n) annealing.

herslismyndun induration; *synonyms* (n) hardening, sclerosis, (adj) petrifaction.

hersluduft powder; *synonyms* (n) dust, gunpowder, (v) grind, crush, pound.

hertogi duke; *synonyms* (n) prince, hand, chief, (v) pass, box.

herts hertz; *synonyms* (n) cycle, oscillation, rhythm, round.

hertur sclerous; *synonym* (adj) indurated.

heslihneta hazelnut; *synonyms* (n) filbert, hazel, cobnut, cob.

heslimús dormouse; *synonym* (v) slumberer.

hestafl horsepower; *synonyms* (n) energy, force, power.

hestaflabremsa dynamometer; *synonyms* (n) dynameter, (v) bathometer, galvanometer, heliometer, interferometer.

hesthús stable; *synonyms* (adj) firm, permanent, reliable, constant, durable; *antonyms* (adj) unstable, shaky, wobbly, dangerous, precarious.

hestur horse; *synonyms* (n) cavalry, mount, buck, heroin, junk.

hetta 1. pileus; *synonyms* (n) cap, capital, ceiling, chapiter, crownwork, **2.** cap; *synonyms* (n) cover, bonnet, lid, base, (v) top, **3.** casing; *synonyms* (n) case, shell, box, jacket, skin, **4.** diaphragm; *synonyms* (n) membrane, midriff, partition, pessary, septum, **5.** cowl; *synonyms* (n) hood, cowling, chock, condition, cow.

hettun capping; *synonyms* (n) capsuling, surfacing.

hettusótt 1. mumps; *synonyms* (adj) blues, dismals, dudgeon, lachrymals, measles, **2.** parotitis; *synonym* (n) parotiditis.

hettuvaki adrenaline; *synonyms* (n) epinephrin, epinephrine.

hey hay; *synonyms* (n) fodder, feed, bunk, food, silage.

heyra hear; *synonyms* (v) attend, discover, apprehend, understand, catch.

heyrn 1. auditory; *synonyms* (adj) acoustic, auditive, audience, audio, aural, **2.** hearing; *synonyms* (n) audition, earshot, ear, trial, consultation; *antonym* (*adj*) deaf.

heyrnardeyfa deafness; *synonym* (*n*) surdity.

heyrnarlaus deaf; *synonyms* (*adj*) earless, blind, indifferent, unhearing, (*v*) deafen; *antonym* (*adj*) hearing.

heyrnarleysi deafness; *synonym* (*n*) surdity.

heyrnarskyn hearing; *synonyms* (*n*) audition, earshot, ear, trial, (*adj*) audience; *antonym* (*adj*) deaf.

heyrsla hearing; *synonyms* (*n*) audition, earshot, ear, trial, (*adj*) audience; *antonym* (*adj*) deaf.

hífa 1. heave; *synonyms* (*v*) cast, fling, chuck, gasp, (*n*) tug, **2**. lift; *synonyms* (*n*) elevator, (*v*) hoist, raise, rise, elevate.

hik 1. bog; *synonyms* (*n*) marsh, morass, swamp, marish, mire; *antonym* (*n*) desert, **2**. indecision; *synonyms* (*n*) doubt, hesitation, irresolution, indecisiveness, (*adj*) suspense; *antonyms* (*n*) decisiveness, determination, resolve.

hike trek; *synonyms* (*n*) tour, (*v*) journey, travel, tramp, expedition.

hikst bog; *synonyms* (*n*) marsh, morass, swamp, marish, mire; *antonym* (*n*) desert.

hiksti 1. hiccup; *synonyms* (*n*) hiccough, anomaly, fault, hitch, (*v*) belch, **2**. hiccough; *synonyms* (*n*) singultus, (*v*) hiccup, yex.

hildir afterbirth; *synonyms* (*n*) glean, cleaning.

hilla shelf; *synonyms* (*n*) ledge, rack, bank, flat, projection.

hillingar mirage; *synonyms* (*n*) hallucination, illusion, delusion, fancy, vision.

himberjasótt yaws; *synonyms* (*n*) frambesia, framboesia.

himinbjarmi skylight; *synonyms* (*n*) fanlight, window, light, casement, day.

himinblár blue (blár); *synonyms* (*adj*) azure, depressed, down, gloomy, low.

himinhnöttur orb; *synonyms* (*n*) ball, globe, sphere, cycle, circle.

himinhvel orb; *synonyms* (*n*) ball, globe, sphere, cycle, circle.

himinhvirfill zenith; *synonyms* (*n*) apex, peak, top, acme, climax; *antonyms* (*n*) nadir, base.

himinljós skylight; *synonyms* (*n*) fanlight, window, light, casement, day.

himinn 1. sky; *synonyms* (*n*) air, heaven, atmosphere, heavens, (*v*) fling, **2**. heaven; *synonyms* (*n*) paradise, bliss, glory, nirvana, sky; *antonym* (*n*) hell.

himinskin skylight; *synonyms* (*n*) fanlight, window, light, casement, day.

himintungl planet; *synonyms* (*n*) globe, satellite, world, sphere, orbiter.

himna 1. diaphragm; *synonyms* (*n*) membrane, midriff, partition, pessary, septum, **2**. acetate; *synonym* (*n*) ethanoate, **3**. film; *synonyms* (*n*) coating, cloud, cinema, coat, (*v*) mist, **4**. membrane; *synonyms* (*n*) diaphragm, film, skin, covering, casing.

himnuflæði osmosis; *synonym* (*n*) absorption.

himnukenndur hyaline; *synonyms* (*n*) hyalin, (*adj*) clear, glassy, crystalline, hyaloid.

himnusíun dialysis; *synonyms* (*n*) debility, division.

himnuskiljun dialysis; *synonyms* (*n*) debility, division.

hindber raspberry; *synonyms* (*n*) hiss, razzing, bird, boo, hoot.

hindra 1. block; *synonyms* (*n*) bar, barricade, pad, (*v*) arrest, stop; *antonyms* (*v*) free, unblock, open, **2**. inhibit; *synonyms* (*v*) ban, hamper, check, curb, encumber, **3**. obstruct; *synonyms* (*v*) block, choke, clog, delay, (*n*) hinder; *antonyms* (*v*) encourage, facilitate.

hindraður blocked; *synonyms* (*adj*) jammed, clogged, locked, barren, blind; *antonyms* (*adj*) successful, free.

hindrandi inhibitory; *synonyms* (*adj*) inhibiting, repressive, repressing.

hindri inhibitor; *synonym* (*n*) stabilizer.

hindrun 1. restraint; *synonyms* (*n*) bridle, constraint, control, hindrance, (*v*) check; *antonyms* (*n*) excess, abandon, decadence, incentive, **2**. suppression; *synonyms* (*n*) inhibition, repression, crushing, quelling, restraint; *antonyms* (*n*) freedom, emancipation, **3**. barrier; *synonyms* (*n*) barricade, bar, bulwark, dam, handicap, **4**. inhibition; *synonyms* (*n*) prohibition, suppression, taboo, ban, arrest, **5**. inhibitor; *synonym* (*n*) stabilizer.

hirða scavenge; *synonyms* (*v*) clean, cleanse, salvage, houseclean, pick.

hirðing 1. service; *synonyms* (*n*) help, aid, assistance, avail, (*v*) overhaul, **2**. attendance; *synonyms* (*n*) presence, attending, audience, turnout, hearing; *antonyms* (*n*) absence, nonattendance.

hirðulaus negligent; *synonyms* (*adj*) careless, heedless, neglectful, forgetful, inattentive; *antonyms* (*adj*) attentive, strict.

hirðuleysi carelessness; *synonyms* (*n*) neglect, negligence, inattention, indifference, nonchalance; *antonyms* (*n*) alertness, attention, care, caution, vigilance.

hirsla receptacle; *synonyms* (*n*) container, box, case, can, pocket.

hissa surprisingly; *synonyms* (*adv*) astonishingly, wonderfully, astoundingly, oddly, (*adj*) amazingly; *antonym* (*adv*) unremarkably.

hít cistern; *synonyms* (*n*) tank, container, reservoir, boiler, cisterna.

hitaaflfræði thermodynamics; *synonyms* (*n*) thermology, thermotics.

hitabóla thermal; *synonyms* (*adj*) caloric, thermic, warm, convection.

hitaeining calorie; *synonym* (*n*) kilocalorie.

hitaflutningur crossover; *synonyms* (*n*) crossing, cross, carrefour, crossbreeding, crossroad.

hitageislunarmælir bolometer; *synonym* (*n*) barretter.

hitahvarf inversion; *synonyms* (*n*) antithesis, reversal, transposition, anastrophe, eversion.

hitakassi incubator; *synonyms* (*n*) brooder, hatcher, couveuse, plotter.

hitalækkandi antipyretic; *synonym* (*n*) febrifuge.

hitaleysing 1. pyrolysis, 2. thermolysis; *synonym* (*n*) pyrolysis.

hitaliði thermostat; *synonym* (*n*) thermoregulator.

hitamælir thermometer; *synonyms* (*v*) bathometer, galvanometer, heliometer, interferometer, odometer.

hitameðferð tempering; *synonyms* (*n*) annealing, hardening, toughening, change, drawing.

hitamótstaða thermistor; *synonym* (*n*) thermocouple.

hitapar thermocouple; *synonym* (*n*) thermistor.

hitarafvaki thermocouple; *synonym* (*n*) thermistor.

hitari heater; *synonyms* (*n*) brasier, warmer, bullet, fastball, calefactor.

hitarit thermogram; *synonym* (*n*) thermograph.

hitariti thermograph; *synonyms* (*n*) thermometrograph, thermogram.

hitasírit thermogram; *synonym* (*n*) thermograph.

hitaskápur incubator; *synonyms* (*n*) brooder, hatcher, couveuse, plotter.

hitaslag 1. siriasis; *synonyms* (*n*) insolation, sunstroke, heliotherapy, 2. heatstroke.

hitasótt fever; *synonyms* (*n*) delirium, feverishness, frenzy, heat, pyrexia.

hitastig temperature; *synonyms* (*n*) fever, heat, warmth, breathing, (*v*) calmness.

hitastillir thermostat; *synonym* (*n*) thermoregulator.

hitastýring thermostat; *synonym* (*n*) thermoregulator.

hitatæki heater; *synonyms* (*n*) brasier, warmer, bullet, fastball, calefactor.

hitatvinn thermocouple; *synonym* (*n*) thermistor.

hitauppstreymi thermal; *synonyms* (*adj*) caloric, thermic, warm, convection.

hitaviðnám thermistor; *synonym* (*n*) thermocouple.

hitavökull thermostat; *synonym* (*n*) thermoregulator.

hiti 1. temperature; *synonyms* (*n*) fever, heat, warmth, breathing, (*v*) calmness, 2. heat; *synonyms* (*n*) glow, fervor, (*v*) bake, burn, (*adj*) excitement; *antonyms* (*n*) cold, chill, (*v*) cool, 3. fever; *synonyms* (*n*) delirium, feverishness, frenzy, pyrexia, febricity.

hitta 1. meet; *synonyms* (*v*) converge, find, assemble, congregate, (*adj*) fit; *antonyms* (*v*) avoid, disperse, diverge, 2. encounter; *synonyms* (*n*) collision, combat, battle, conflict, (*v*) clash; *antonym* (*v*) retreat.

hittni accuracy; *synonyms* (*n*) fidelity, precision, truth, exactitude, exactness; *antonyms* (*n*) inaccuracy, vagueness, imprecision.

hjá at; *synonyms* (*prep*) in, a, (*adv*) on, along, (*prf*) all.

hjaðna 1. resolve; *synonyms* (*v*) determine, decide, (*n*) purpose, determination, decision; *antonyms* (*n*) indecision, weakness, 2. fade; *synonyms* (*v*) disappear, decline, dissolve, evaporate, (*adj*) vanish; *antonyms* (*v*) grow, increase, strengthen.

hjákróna corona; *synonyms* (*n*) crown, radiance, halo, aureole, necklace.

hjal babble; *synonyms* (*n*) drivel, (*v*) murmur, chat, gab, gossip; *antonyms* (*v*) quietness, silence, stillness.

hjálægur adventitious; *synonyms* (*adj*) accidental, casual, random, additional, adventive.

hjáleið bypass; *synonyms* (*n*) detour, diversion, (*v*) avoid, circumvent, evade.

hjalli terrace; *synonyms* (*n*) patio, bench, veranda, porch, balcony.

hjálmur 1. radome, 2. acrosome, 3. blister; *synonyms* (*n*) bleb, boil, bubble, bulla, (*v*) scorch, 4. helm; *synonyms* (*n*) wheel, haft, handle, hilt, (*v*) helmet.

hjálp 1. assistance; *synonyms* (*n*) aid, assist, support, boost, encouragement; *antonym* (*n*) hindrance, 2. aid; *synonyms* (*n*) help, assistance, (*v*) benefit, abet, ease; *antonym* (*v*) hinder, 3. benefit; *synonyms* (*n*) advantage, gain, good, (*v*) profit, avail; *antonyms* (*n*) disadvantage, drawback, loss, (*v*) harm, 4. help; *synonyms* (*v*) facilitate, favor, alleviate, (*n*) assistant, cure; *antonyms* (*v*) worsen, (*n*) detriment, 5. mayday; *synonyms* (*n*) signal, warning.

hjálpa 1. assist; *synonyms* (*v*) aid, support, abet, serve, (*n*) help; *antonym* (*v*) hinder, 2. benefit; *synonyms* (*n*) advantage, gain, (*v*) assist, profit, avail; *antonyms* (*n*) disadvantage, drawback, loss, (*v*) harm, 3. aid; *synonyms* (*n*) assistance, encouragement, (*v*) benefit, ease, facilitate; *antonym* (*n*) hindrance, 4. help; *synonyms* (*v*) favor, alleviate, (*n*) assistant, cure, boost; *antonyms* (*v*) worsen, (*n*) detriment.

hjálpandi adjuvant; *synonyms* (*adj*) auxiliary, accessory, adjunct, ancillary, subsidiary.

hjálparefni 1. adjuvant; *synonyms* (*adj*) auxiliary, accessory, adjunct, ancillary, subsidiary, 2. cofactor.

hjálparkíkir finder; *synonyms* (*n*) viewfinder, discoverer, artificer, spotter, lookout.

hjálparlyf adjuvant; *synonyms* (*adj*) auxiliary, accessory, adjunct, ancillary, subsidiary.

hjálparsetning lemma; *synonyms* (*n*) proposition, premises, principle, terms, glumella.

hjálparsjónauki finder; *synonyms* (*n*) viewfinder, discoverer, artificer, spotter, lookout.

hjámiðja eccentric; *synonyms* (*adj*) bizarre, odd, wacky, abnormal, anomalous; *antonyms* (*adj*) normal, ordinary, (*n*) conformist.

hjárás bypass; *synonyms* (*n*) detour, diversion, (*v*) avoid, circumvent, evade.

hjárása bypass; *synonyms* (*n*) detour, diversion, (*v*) avoid, circumvent, evade.

hjarðhvöt gregariousness; *synonym* (*n*) camaraderie.

hjarni cerebrum; *synonyms* (*n*) brain, pate, cranium, sconce, noddle.

hjarta heart; *synonyms* (*n*) core, center, spirit, affection, (*adj*) gist; *antonym* (*n*) edge.

hjartafró balm; *synonyms* (*n*) ointment, salve, unguent, incense, aroma.

hjartagrófarverkur cardialgia; *synonyms* (*adj*) bronchocele, carditis, endocarditis.

hjartahlé diastole; *synonyms* (*n*) distension, dropsy, intumescence, swelling, tumefaction.

hjartalínurit electrocardiogram; *synonym* (*n*) cardiogram.

hjartanlegur 1. warm; *synonyms* (*adj*) hot, affectionate, tender, ardent, cordial; *antonyms* (*adj*) aloof, cold, unfriendly, reserved, (*v*) cool, 2. cordial; *synonyms* (*adj*) hearty, affable, genial, warm, amiable; *antonyms* (*adj*) hostile, stern, 3. cardiac; *synonyms* (*adj*) cardiacal, stimulant, 4. hearty; *synonyms* (*adj*) heartfelt, healthy, sturdy, cheering, fervent; *antonym* (*adj*) feeble.

hjartarafrit electrocardiogram; *synonym* (*n*) cardiogram.

hjartarit cardiogram; *synonym* (*n*) electrocardiogram.

hjartariti cardiograph; *synonyms* (*n*) electrocardiograph, recapper, snowplow, tenpenny, votograph.

hjartasjúklingur cardiac; *synonyms* (*adj*) cardiacal, stimulant.

hjartaskel cockle; *synonyms* (*v*) crease, pucker, ruffle, rumple, fold.

hjartaslag stroke; *synonyms* (*n*) touch, beat, caress, (*v*) buffet, (*adj*) blow.

hjartsláttarónot palpitation; *synonyms* (*n*) beat, pulse, quiver, (*adj*) tremor, quivering.

hjartsláttarsprettur tachycardia; *synonym* (*n*) tachyrhythmia.

hjásól parhelion; *synonyms* (*n*) sundog, parhelium.

hjástoð complement; *synonyms* (*n*) supplement, accessory, adjunct, balance, extra.

hjástreymi shunt; *synonyms* (*n*) bypass, (*v*) shift, avert, move, remove.

hjátrú superstition; *synonyms* (*n*) myth, fallacy, fanaticism, folklore, lore.

hjáveita bypass; *synonyms* (*n*) detour, diversion, (*v*) avoid, circumvent, evade.

hjöðnun 1. subsidence; *synonyms* (*n*) collapse, ebb, remission, settlement, settling, 2. resolution; *synonyms* (*n*) decision, determination, answer, conclusion, firmness; *antonym* (*n*) indecisiveness.

hjól 1. wheel; *synonyms* (*n*) circle, cycle, (*v*) roll, revolve, turn, 2. reel; *synonyms* (*n*) bobbin, coil, (*v*) lurch, rock, spin.

hjólás axle; *synonyms* (*n*) axis, hinge, pivot, bobbin, beam.

hjólasláttur shimmy; *synonyms* (*n*) chemise, shift, (*v*) shake, dance, wobble.

hjólasporun tracking; *synonyms* (*n*) pursuit, trailing, rutting, trajectography.

hjólbarðastofn carcass; *synonyms* (*n*) body, carcase, frame, cadaver, corpse.

hjólbarði 1. tyre; *synonyms* (*n*) tire, band, baldric, belt, girdle, 2. tire; *synonyms* (*v*) bore, fatigue, exhaust, fag, (*n*) jade; *antonym* (*v*) refresh.

hjólfar track; *synonyms* (*n*) course, path, (*v*) trace, trail, hunt.

hjólferill cycloid; *synonyms* (*n*) roulette, ellipsoid, trochoid, (*adj*) cycloidal.

hjólflötur torus; *synonyms* (*n*) tore, toroid, thalamus, breast, mamma.

hjólhalli camber; *synonyms* (*n*) bank, arc, bow, (*v*) arch, bend.

hjólhlíf 1. spat; *synonyms* (*v*) bicker, (*n*) quarrel, squabble, altercation, tiff, 2. wing; *synonyms* (*n*) annex, arm, fender, limb, (*v*) fly, 3. mudguard; *synonym* (*n*) splashguard, 4. fender; *synonyms* (*n*) wing, cushion, guard, cowcatcher, (*v*) buffer.

hjólhringur rim; *synonyms* (*n*) border, edge, margin, brim, brink.

hjólhús wheelhouse; *synonym* (*n*) pilothouse.

hjólkróna borage; *synonym* (*n*) tailwort.

hjólnöf 1. hub; *synonyms* (*n*) center, focus, heart, core, nucleus, 2. nave; *synonyms* (*n*) chancel, choir, hub, omphalos, transept.

hjólskál wheelhouse; *synonym* (*n*) pilothouse.

hjólspor patch; *synonyms* (n) darn, fleck, mend, plot, (v) piece.

hjón couple; *synonyms* (v) pair, connect, associate, combine, attach; *antonym* (v) uncouple.

hjónaband 1. wedlock; *synonyms* (n) marriage, matrimony, union, wedding, **2.** marriage; *synonyms* (n) espousal, nuptial, wedlock, (adj) bridal, (v) match; *antonyms* (n) divorce, separation, **3.** matrimony; *synonyms* (n) nuptials, alloyage, commixion, intermixture.

hjónaskilnaður divorce; *synonyms* (n) separation, (v) detach, dissociate, disunite, separate; *antonyms* (n) marriage, wedding.

hjör hinge; *synonyms* (n) joint, axis, articulation, axle, (v) pivot.

hjöruliðskross spider; *synonyms* (n) lota, mussuk, schooner, spinner, adapter.

hjúkra nurse; *synonyms* (v) nourish, attend, cherish, entertain, foster.

hjúkrunarfræðingur nurse; *synonyms* (v) nourish, attend, cherish, entertain, foster.

hjúpa encapsulate; *synonyms* (v) condense, capsule, capsulize, recap, recapitulate.

hjúpaldin hip; *synonyms* (n) haunch, coxa, (adj) hep, stylish, chic.

hjúpskekkja coma; *synonyms* (n) lethargy, trance, dream, stupor, sleep.

hjúpun encapsulation; *synonyms* (n) packaging, entrapment.

hjúpur 1. sheath; *synonyms* (n) case, envelope, blanket, scabbard, (v) cover, **2.** coma; *synonyms* (n) lethargy, trance, dream, stupor, sleep, **3.** coat; *synonyms* (n) coating, crust, film, (v) cloak, sheath, **4.** capsule; *synonyms* (n) abridgement, lozenge, condensation, pill, (v) encapsulate, **5.** envelope; *synonyms* (n) container, pack, jacket, vesicle, (v) covering.

hlað 1. yard; *synonyms* (n) court, courtyard, garden, backyard, grounds, **2.** apron; *synonyms* (n) forestage, proscenium, skirt, pall, pontificals.

hlaða 1. stow; *synonyms* (v) pack, cram, charge, house, load, **2.** charge; *synonyms* (n) accusation, burden, care, (v) accuse, blame; *antonyms* (v) request, absolve, retreat, **3.** load; *synonyms* (n) cargo, freight, stack, heap, (v) fill; *antonym* (v) unload.

hlaði 1. pile; *synonyms* (n) heap, stack, mass, congeries, (v) pack, **2.** stack; *synonyms* (n) pile, accumulation, mound, rick, (v) load.

hlaðinn 1. energized; *synonyms* (adj) animated, animate, eager, thrilled, **2.** laden; *synonyms* (v) lade, (adj) fraught, burdened, full, loaded; *antonym* (adj) empty.

hlæja laugh; *synonyms* (n) chuckle, chortle, jest, (v) joke, giggle; *antonym* (v) cry.

hláka thaw; *synonyms* (n) melting, (v) melt, dissolve, fuse, liquefy; *antonyms* (v) freeze, cool.

hlass 1. mass; *synonyms* (n) bulk, heap, crowd, cluster, (v) flock, **2.** epiphysis.

hlaup 1. play; *synonyms* (v) act, pastime, enact, (n) frolic, game; *antonym* (v) work, **2.** clearance; *synonyms* (n) clearing, clearage, disposal, headroom, settlement; *antonyms* (n) blockage, retention, **3.** clot; *synonyms* (v) clod, curdle, cake, clabber, clog; *antonym* (v) liquefy, **4.** backlash; *synonyms* (n) kick, repercussion, reaction, (v) backfire, bounce, **5.** coagulum; *synonyms* (n) clot, (v) curd, stone.

hlaupa coagulate; *synonyms* (v) clot, set, condense, congeal, (n) curdle; *antonym* (v) liquefy.

hlaupabreyta parameter; *synonyms* (n) argument, guideline, limit, directive, modulus.

hlaupari fall; *synonyms* (v) decline, dip, decrease, descend, (n) drop; *antonyms* (v) rise, increase, ascend, climb, (n) ascent.

hlaupkenndur gelatinous; *synonyms* (adj) thick, gluey, glutinous, jellylike, gelatinlike; *antonym* (adj) runny.

hlaupmyndun coagulation; *synonyms* (n) clotting, clot, flocculation, curdling, (adj) concretion.

hlaupskriða slide; *synonyms* (n) glide, chute, (v) drop, slip, fall.

hlaupvídd gauge; *synonyms* (n) criterion, caliber, (v) estimate, measure, calculate.

Hlé 1. break; *synonyms* (v) split, crack, burst, (n) breach, fracture; *antonyms* (v) repair, obey, honor, mend, (n) continuation, **2.** interval; *synonyms* (n) intermission, interruption, break, distance, interlude.

hlébarði 1. leopard; *synonyms* (n) cat, marble, nacre, ocelot, opal, **2.** panther; *synonyms* (n) catamount, cougar, jaguar, leopard, (adj) lion.

hlébil diastole; *synonyms* (n) distension, dropsy, intumescence, swelling, tumefaction.

hléborði leeward; *synonyms* (adv) upwind, (n) lee; *antonym* (n) windward.

hleðsla 1. stowage; *synonyms* (n) stowing, storeroom, shipment, cargo, contents, **2.** accumulation; *synonyms* (n) store, stock, accretion, mass, accrual; *antonym* (n) shortage, **3.** charge; *synonyms* (n) accusation, burden, care, (v) accuse, blame; *antonyms* (v) request, absolve, retreat, **4.** load; *synonyms* (n) charge, freight, stack, heap, (v) fill; *antonym* (v) unload, **5.** loading; *synonyms* (n) load, consignment, lading, encumbrance, filler; *antonym* (n) unloading.

hleðslujöfnun compensation; *synonyms* (*n*) amends, recompense, allowance, indemnification, (*v*) wage.

hleðslutala valency; *synonym* (*n*) valence.

hleifamót chill; *synonyms* (*adj*) cold, bleak, icy, chilly, (*v*) cool; *antonyms* (*n*) warmth, (*v*) heat, warm.

hleifur ingot; *synonyms* (*n*) bullion, bar, block, nugget, copper.

hlekkja shackle; *synonyms* (*v*) fetter, chain, bind, hobble, (*n*) hamper.

hlekkur link; *synonyms* (*n*) connection, join, joint, (*v*) combine, tie; *antonym* (*v*) separate.

hlemmur cover; *synonyms* (*v*) coat, conceal, top, bury, (*n*) blind; *antonyms* (*v*) reveal, expose, uncover.

hleri 1. shutter; *synonyms* (*n*) close, curtain, blind, shut, (*v*) screen, 2. cover; *synonyms* (*v*) coat, conceal, top, bury, (*n*) blanket; *antonyms* (*v*) reveal, expose, uncover, 3. hatch; *synonyms* (*n*) brood, (*v*) breed, contrive, concoct, brew.

hlerun tapping; *synonyms* (*n*) tap, paracentesis, tick, beating, drumbeat.

hleypa coagulate; *synonyms* (*v*) clot, set, condense, congeal, (*n*) curdle; *antonym* (*v*) liquefy.

hleypandi coagulant; *synonym* (*n*) coagulator.

hleyping coagulation; *synonyms* (*n*) clotting, clot, flocculation, curdling, (*adj*) concretion.

hleypir 1. rennin; *synonym* (*n*) chymosin, 2. coagulant; *synonym* (*n*) coagulator.

hlið 1. window; *synonyms* (*n*) casement, porthole, pane, gap, embrasure, 2. side; *synonyms* (*n*) edge, rim, faction, border, brink; *antonym* (*adj*) distant, 3. flank; *synonyms* (*n*) side, wing, lee, (*v*) skirt, (*adj*) cover, 4. hilum; *synonym* (*n*) hilus, 5. gate; *synonyms* (*n*) entrance, door, entry, mouth, doorway.

hliðarbraut bypass; *synonyms* (*n*) detour, diversion, (*v*) avoid, circumvent, evade.

hlíðardrag rise; *synonyms* (*n*) elevation, lift, (*v*) climb, mount, ascend; *antonyms* (*v*) fall, decrease, drop, sink, descend.

hliðargrein 1. shunt; *synonyms* (*n*) bypass, (*v*) shift, avert, move, remove, 2. collateral; *synonyms* (*adj*) secondary, (*n*) warranty, guarantee, mortgage, guaranty.

hliðarhreyfing yaw; *synonyms* (*n*) swerve, (*v*) gape, turn, bend, gawk.

hliðarstýri rudder; *synonyms* (*n*) helm, wheel, guide, tail, controls.

hliðarsveigja deflection; *synonyms* (*n*) deviation, bend, deflexion, variation, bending.

hliðarviðnám shunt; *synonyms* (*n*) bypass, (*v*) shift, avert, move, remove.

hliðhallt sideways; *synonyms* (*adv*) obliquely, laterally, (*adj*) oblique, side, crabwise; *antonyms* (*adj*) direct, level.

hliðlægi laterality; *synonyms* (*n*) dominance, handedness, ascendance, ascendancy, ascendence.

hliðlægt lateral; *synonyms* (*adj*) side, sidelong, collateral, accidental, incidental.

hliðlægur lateral; *synonyms* (*adj*) side, sidelong, collateral, accidental, incidental.

hliðmælt lateral; *synonyms* (*adj*) side, sidelong, collateral, accidental, incidental.

hliðra translate; *synonyms* (*v*) interpret, construe, decipher, transform, explain.

hliðrænn analog; *synonyms* (*n*) analogue, parallel, computer, (*adj*) additive, linear.

hliðranlegur sliding; *synonyms* (*adj*) gliding, down, downhill, (*n*) slipping, skating.

hliðrun 1. slip; *synonyms* (*n*) lapse, fault, (*v*) fall, slide, (*adj*) blunder; *antonym* (*v*) improve, 2. translation; *synonyms* (*n*) displacement, interpretation, rendering, transformation, version, 3. avoidance; *synonyms* (*n*) abstinence, escape, evasion, forbearance, cancellation, 4. parallax, 5. offset; *synonyms* (*v*) counteract, balance, neutralize, cancel, (*n*) counterbalance.

hliðsetning juxtaposition; *synonyms* (*n*) apposition, proximity, contact, contiguity, abuttal.

hliðskipun apposition; *synonyms* (*n*) union, juxtaposition, (*prep*) addition, accompaniment, accord.

hliðstaða 1. analogy; *synonyms* (*n*) semblance, agreement, correspondence, parity, resemblance; *antonym* (*n*) dissimilarity, 2. juxtaposition; *synonyms* (*n*) apposition, proximity, contact, contiguity, abuttal.

hliðstæða 1. correspondence; *synonyms* (*n*) conformity, accord, agreement, communication, connection; *antonyms* (*n*) difference, asymmetry, dissimilarity, 2. analogue; *synonyms* (*n*) analog, parallel, counterpart, match, duplicate.

hliðstæður 1. analogous; *synonyms* (*adj*) alike, similar, akin, analogical, comparable; *antonym* (*adj*) dissimilar, 2. corresponding; *synonyms* (*adj*) congruent, equal, same, commensurate, consonant; *antonym* (*adj*) different, 3. collateral; *synonyms* (*adj*) secondary, (*n*) warranty, guarantee, mortgage, guaranty, 4. lateral; *synonyms* (*adj*) side, sidelong, collateral, accidental, incidental, 5. parallel; *synonyms* (*adj*) equivalent, even, (*n*) analogy, (*v*) compare, match; *antonyms* (*adj*) conflicting, (*n*) perpendicular, skew.

hliðtenging parallel; *synonyms* (*adj*) equivalent, even, (*n*) equal, (*v*) compare, match; *antonyms* (*adj*) conflicting, dissimilar, (*n*) perpendicular, skew.

hlíf 1. screen; *synonyms* (*n*) shade, blind, (*v*) cover, shield, conceal, **2**. screening; *synonyms* (*n*) screen, sieving, concealment, covering, masking, **3**. shade; *synonyms* (*n*) tinge, color, ghost, hue, (*v*) darken; *antonyms* (*n*) light, brightness, **4**. protection; *synonyms* (*n*) defense, care, conservation, custody, (*v*) guard; *antonym* (*n*) destruction, **5**. shield; *synonyms* (*n*) shelter, buffer, (*v*) safeguard, preserve, secure; *antonym* (*v*) expose.

hlífðarbúnaður guard; *synonyms* (*n*) defend, defense, bulwark, care, cover.

hlífðargleraugu goggles; *synonyms* (*n*) glasses, eyeglasses, spectacles, barnacles, specs.

hlífðarplata cover; *synonyms* (*v*) coat, conceal, top, bury, (*n*) blind; *antonyms* (*v*) reveal, expose, uncover.

hlífigrind guard; *synonyms* (*n*) defend, defense, bulwark, care, cover.

hlífispjald baffle; *synonyms* (*v*) discomfit, astonish, bewilder, confound, foil; *antonym* (*v*) enlighten.

hlíta comply; *synonyms* (*v*) agree, accede, assent, acquiesce, consent.

hlítarárátta perfectionism; *synonyms* (*n*) care, diligence, strictness, thoroughness, exactness.

hljóð 1. sound; *synonyms* (*n*) echo, (*v*) ring, chime, (*adj*) reasonable, complete; *antonyms* (*n*) silence, (*adj*) illogical, unsound, confused, **2**. noise; *synonyms* (*n*) clatter, clamor, hubbub, racket, sound; *antonym* (*n*) quiet.

hljóðbein ossicle; *synonyms* (*n*) ossiculum, bonelet.

hljóðdeyfir 1. silencer; *synonym* (*n*) muffler, **2**. muffler; *synonyms* (*n*) silencer, damper, cape, kirtle, plaid.

hljóðeðlisfræðlingur acoustic; *synonyms* (*adj*) acoustical, aural, phonic, (*v*) auditory, auricular.

hljóðfirring dissimilation; *synonyms* (*n*) catabolism, act, katabolism.

hljóðfræði 1. phonetics; *synonyms* (*n*) phonics, (*adj*) phonography, **2**. acoustics.

hljóðfrár supersonic; *synonyms* (*adj*) ultrasonic, speedy, swift, (*n*) jet.

hljóðgildi quality; *synonyms* (*n*) nature, character, characteristic, class, condition; *antonym* (*adj*) shoddy.

hljóðgjafi sounder; *synonym* (*n*) sounds.

hljóðhimna 1. tympanum; *synonyms* (*n*) eardrum, kettle, kettledrum, timpani, tympani, **2**. eardrum; *synonyms* (*n*) tympanum, myringa.

hljóðkútur 1. silencer; *synonym* (*n*) muffler, **2**. muffler; *synonyms* (*n*) silencer, damper, cape, kirtle, plaid.

hljóðlátur silent; *synonyms* (*adj*) motionless, dumb, mute, tacit, (*adv*) quiet; *antonyms* (*adj*) noisy, spoken, loud, talkative, explicit.

hljóðmagn volume; *synonyms* (*n*) bulk, size, book, magnitude, mass; *antonym* (*n*) quietness.

hljóðmerki buzz; *synonyms* (*n*) hum, rumor, hearsay, (*v*) call, drone.

hljóðmögnun amplification; *synonyms* (*n*) augmentation, addition, expansion, extension, gain; *antonym* (*n*) reduction.

hljóðmyndun articulation; *synonyms* (*n*) enunciation, joint, juncture, accent, diction.

hljóðnemi 1. mike; *synonym* (*n*) microphone, **2**. microphone; *synonym* (*n*) mike.

hljóðrænn acoustic; *synonyms* (*adj*) acoustical, aural, phonic, (*v*) auditory, auricular.

hljóðróf spectrum; *synonyms* (*n*) range, gamut, (*v*) anamorphosis, distortion, illusion.

hljóðrófsriti spectrograph; *synonyms* (*n*) spectrogram, spectroscope, prism, spectrometer.

hljóðsetning dubbing; *synonyms* (*n*) daubing, copy.

hljóðsía filter; *synonyms* (*v*) percolate, sieve, drip, leak, filtrate; *antonym* (*v*) contaminate.

hljóðsjá sonar; *synonyms* (*n*) asdic, beacon.

hljóðstyrkur 1. volume; *synonyms* (*n*) bulk, size, book, magnitude, mass; *antonym* (*n*) quietness, **2**. loudness; *synonyms* (*n*) garishness, gaudiness, brashness, tastelessness, noisiness.

hljóðvarp 1. radio; *synonyms* (*n*) wireless, broadcasting, radiotelegram, (*v*) broadcast, transmit, **2**. mutation; *synonyms* (*n*) alteration, change, variation, freak, innovation.

hljóðver studio; *synonyms* (*n*) atelier, cabinet, accommodation, building, bungalow.

hljómblær timbre; *synonyms* (*n*) pitch, quality, tone, character, spirit.

hljómmikill sonorous; *synonyms* (*adj*) loud, resonant, rich, harmonious, round.

hljómplata album; *synonyms* (*n*) record, portfolio, recording, volume, anthology.

hljómspuni improvisation; *synonyms* (*n*) extemporization, impromptu, extemporisation, invention, construction.

hljómsveit orchestra; *synonyms* (*n*) band, minstrelsy, ensemble, group, orchester.

hljómur sound; *synonyms* (*n*) echo, (*v*) ring, chime, (*adj*) reasonable, complete; *antonyms* (*n*) silence, (*adj*) illogical, unsound, confused.

hlot body; *synonyms* (*n*) cadaver, corpse, matter, organization, carcass; *antonym* (*n*) spirit.

hlotnast receive; *synonyms* (*v*) accept, admit, get, assume, adopt.

hlust 1. receiver; *synonyms* (*n*) recipient, beneficiary, cashier, earpiece, headset; *antonym* (*n*) donor, **2**. meatus.

hlustarverkur 1. earache; *synonyms* (*n*) otalgia, (*v*) cephalalgia, gout, lumbago, neuralgia, **2**. otalgia;

synonyms (n) earache, (v) odontalgia, podagra, rheumatism, sciatica.

hlustun auscultation; *synonym* (v) audition.

hlutabréf share; *synonyms* (n) piece, portion, (v) participate, allot, apportion; *antonym* (v) control.

hlutadýrkun fetishism; *synonyms* (n) fetichism, fetish, zoolatry, (adj) fetishistic.

hlutafélag 1. corporation; *synonyms* (n) association, belly, business, company, concern, **2.** limited; *synonyms* (adj) finite, circumscribed, moderate, qualified, special; *antonyms* (adj) boundless, infinite, limitless, open, complete.

hlutafjáreigandi shareholder; *synonyms* (n) participant, shareowner, stockholder, saver, depositor.

hlutafjárloforð subscription; *synonyms* (n) contribution, donation, offering, (v) allowance, subsidy.

hlutasamstæða 1. assembly; *synonyms* (n) gathering, meeting, collection, congregation, (v) assemblage, **2.** cluster; *synonyms* (n) bunch, clump, batch, group, (v) bundle; *antonym* (v) disperse.

hlutavelta 1. raffle; *synonyms* (n) draw, sweepstake, benefit, bet, chance, **2.** lottery; *synonyms* (n) drawing, draft, brag, cassino, connections.

hlutdeild 1. share; *synonyms* (n) piece, portion, (v) participate, allot, apportion; *antonym* (v) control, **2.** participation; *synonyms* (n) involvement, interest, contribution, attendance, complicity.

hlutdeildarfélag affiliate; *synonyms* (n) member, chapter, (v) associate, ally, unite.

hlutdrægni bias; *synonyms* (n) penchant, drift, (v) prejudice, bent, (adj) partiality; *antonyms* (n) impartiality, neutrality, fairness.

hlutdrægur biased; *synonyms* (adj) partial, partisan, slanted, unfair, skewed; *antonyms* (adj) fair, fair-minded, neutral, unbiased, just.

hlutfall 1. ratio; *synonyms* (n) percentage, degree, proportion, measure, scale, **2.** proportion; *synonyms* (n) balance, ratio, portion, slice, dimension, **3.** rate; *synonyms* (n) price, worth, (v) assess, estimate, evaluate, **4.** quotient; *synonyms* (n) factor, share, fraction, dividend, divisor, **5.** ration; *synonyms* (n) allowance, helping, part, (v) allocate, apportion.

hlutfallsbundinn proportional; *synonyms* (adj) proportionate, commensurate, proportionable, relative, balanced.

hlutfallslegur 1. proportional; *synonyms* (adj) proportionate, commensurate, proportionable, relative, balanced, **2.** relative; *synonyms* (adj) related, comparative, (n) relation, brother, (v) kinsman; *antonym* (adj) absolute.

hlutfallstala 1. ratio; *synonyms* (n) percentage, degree, proportion, measure, scale, **2.** index; *synonyms* (n) catalogue, exponent, file, table, (v) list.

hlutgengi capability; *synonyms* (n) capacity, ability, aptitude, capableness, competence; *antonyms* (n) inability, failure, incapability.

hlutgler objective; *synonyms* (adj) dispassionate, (n) aim, mark, goal, object; *antonyms* (adj) biased, subjective.

hluthafi 1. shareholder; *synonyms* (n) participant, shareowner, stockholder, saver, depositor, **2.** stockholder; *synonym* (n) shareholder.

hluthverfur concrete; *synonyms* (adj) actual, positive, (n) cement, (v) coagulate, congeal; *antonyms* (adj) theoretical, intangible, abstract, hypothetical, incidental.

hluthyggja realism; *synonyms* (n) naturalism, reality, authenticity, fidelity, realness; *antonym* (n) idealism.

hluti 1. stratum; *synonyms* (n) layer, bed, level, floor, seam, **2.** segment; *synonyms* (n) division, paragraph, bit, (v) section, part, **3.** section; *synonyms* (n) portion, compartment, percentage, piece, (v) segment, **4.** strata; *synonyms* (n) stratum, course, escarpment, flag, slab, **5.** part; *synonyms* (n) constituent, article, (v) branch, break, disjoin; *antonyms* (n) whole, entirety, (adj) complete.

hlutlægur objective; *synonyms* (adj) dispassionate, (n) aim, mark, goal, object; *antonyms* (adj) biased, subjective.

hlutlag object; *synonyms* (n) design, aim, cause, end, (v) except; *antonym* (v) agree.

hlutlaus 1. neutral; *synonyms* (adj) disinterested, impartial, indifferent, dispassionate, (n) neuter; *antonyms* (adj) biased, aromatic, colorful, **2.** passive; *synonyms* (adj) inactive, apathetic, inert, submissive, lifeless; *antonyms* (adj) active, assertive, spirited, working.

hlutleysa neutralize; *synonyms* (v) counteract, cancel, counterbalance, countervail, neutralise.

hlutleysi independence; *synonyms* (n) autonomy, freedom, liberty, independency, individuality; *antonyms* (n) dependence, childhood.

hlutleysing neutralization; *synonyms* (n) neutralisation, counteraction, nullification, annulment, chagrin.

hlutlinsa objective; *synonyms* (adj) dispassionate, (n) aim, mark, goal, object; *antonyms* (adj) biased, subjective.

hlutmengi subset; *synonyms* (n) set, breed, caste, clan, detachment.

hlutmergð abundance; *synonyms* (n) wealth, amplitude, exuberance, plenitude, (adj) plenty;

antonyms (*n*) dearth, scarcity, aridity, insufficiency, lack.

hlutmynd field; *synonyms* (*n*) arena, area, battlefield, domain, ground.

hlutrænn 1. concrete; *synonyms* (*adj*) actual, positive, (*n*) cement, (*v*) coagulate, congeal; *antonyms* (*adj*) theoretical, intangible, abstract, hypothetical, incidental, **2**. objective; *synonyms* (*adj*) dispassionate, (*n*) aim, mark, goal, object; *antonyms* (*adj*) biased, subjective.

hlutstæður concrete; *synonyms* (*adj*) actual, positive, (*n*) cement, (*v*) coagulate, congeal; *antonyms* (*adj*) theoretical, intangible, abstract, hypothetical, incidental.

hluttekning empathy; *synonyms* (*n*) sympathy, compassion, affiliation, affinity, association.

hlutun 1. segmentation; *synonyms* (*n*) division, cleavage, partition, partitioning, sectionalization, **2**. fragmentation; *synonyms* (*n*) atomisation, atomization, disintegration, fracture, destruction, **3**. fractionation.

hlutur 1. stock; *synonyms* (*n*) breed, lineage, store, goods, (*adj*) regular, **2**. share; *synonyms* (*n*) piece, portion, (*v*) participate, allot, apportion; *antonym* (*v*) control, **3**. piece; *synonyms* (*n*) cut, division, fragment, part, article, **4**. body; *synonyms* (*n*) cadaver, corpse, matter, organization, carcass; *antonym* (*n*) spirit, **5**. object; *synonyms* (*n*) design, aim, cause, end, (*v*) except; *antonym* (*v*) agree.

hlutverk 1. role; *synonyms* (*n*) part, function, position, character, (*v*) office, **2**. mission; *synonyms* (*n*) commission, delegation, deputation, job, assignment.

hlutverkslegur functional; *synonyms* (*adj*) practical, effective, handy, operational, operative; *antonyms* (*adj*) nonfunctional, useless.

hlýðni compliance; *synonyms* (*n*) agreement, approval, observance, accordance, acquiescence; *antonyms* (*n*) disobedience, stubbornness, nonconformity.

hlykkur bend; *synonyms* (*n*) bow, arch, arc, (*v*) curve, turn; *antonyms* (*v*) straighten, square.

hlynur 1. sycamore; *synonyms* (*n*) lacewood, platan, sycamine, **2**. maple.

hlýr warm; *synonyms* (*adj*) hot, affectionate, tender, ardent, cordial; *antonyms* (*adj*) aloof, cold, unfriendly, reserved, (*v*) cool.

hlýtempraður subtropical; *synonyms* (*adj*) semitropical, subtropic, semitropic.

hnakkur saddle; *synonyms* (*n*) saddleback, (*v*) charge, burden, load, encumber.

hnappaborð keyboard; *synonym* (*n*) upright.

hnappþráður filament; *synonyms* (*n*) fiber, strand, yarn, fibril, hair.

hnappur 1. button; *synonyms* (*n*) knop, buckle, (*v*) knob, (*adj*) pin, tie, **2**. key; *synonyms* (*adj*) central, fundamental, basic, cardinal, (*n*) guide.

hnattlaga globular; *synonyms* (*adj*) round, circular, global, globose, spheric.

hnattlaukur onion; *synonyms* (*n*) caviare, pickle, leek, chive.

hnattlíkan globe; *synonyms* (*n*) ball, world, orb, sphere, circle.

hnattrænn global; *synonyms* (*adj*) general, international, overall, cosmopolitan, universal; *antonyms* (*adj*) local, national.

hné 1. knee; *synonyms* (*n*) elbow, genu, scythe, sickle, zigzag, **2**. elbow; *synonyms* (*n*) bend, cubitus, (*v*) poke, jostle, nudge, **3**. node; *synonyms* (*n*) knob, connection, joint, knot, nodosity.

hneigð 1. trend; *synonyms* (*n*) fashion, tendency, fad, inclination, (*v*) style, **2**. bias; *synonyms* (*n*) penchant, drift, (*v*) prejudice, bent, (*adj*) partiality; *antonyms* (*n*) impartiality, neutrality, fairness, **3**. disposition; *synonyms* (*n*) attitude, character, disposal, arrangement, bias.

hnéletraður subscript; *synonyms* (*n*) inferior, (*adj*) deficient, lower, lowly, secondary; *antonym* (*n*) superscript.

hnéletur subscript; *synonyms* (*n*) inferior, (*adj*) deficient, lower, lowly, secondary; *antonym* (*n*) superscript.

hnéliður knee; *synonyms* (*n*) elbow, genu, scythe, sickle, zigzag.

hneppi 1. cluster; *synonyms* (*n*) bunch, clump, batch, group, (*v*) bundle; *antonym* (*v*) disperse, **2**. domain; *synonyms* (*n*) country, department, realm, area, kingdom; *antonym* (*n*) range.

hnerra sneeze; *synonyms* (*v*) arrest, (*n*) sneezing, sternutation.

hnéskel 1. patella; *synonyms* (*n*) kneecap, kneepan, epergne, patera, tazza, **2**. kneecap; *synonym* (*n*) patella.

hneta nut; *synonyms* (*n*) lunatic, crackpot, crank, eccentric, egg.

hnettla coccus; *synonym* (*n*) cocci.

hnévísir subscript; *synonyms* (*n*) inferior, (*adj*) deficient, lower, lowly, secondary; *antonym* (*n*) superscript.

hnífapör cutlery; *synonyms* (*n*) cutter, tableware, (*adj*) blade, penknife, razor.

hnífur 1. knife; *synonyms* (*n*) dagger, tongue, (*v*) stab, (*adj*) blade, cutlery, **2**. knives.

hnig 1. sink; *synonyms* (*n*) sag, (*v*) decline, dip, droop, fall; *antonyms* (*v*) rise, float, **2**. dip; *synonyms* (*n*) plunge, (*v*) duck, bathe, drop, bow; *antonyms* (*n*) hump, mountain.

hnignun 1. devolution; *synonyms* (*n*) degeneration, delegation, degeneracy, decadence, transfer, **2.** involution; *synonyms* (*n*) exponentiation, intricacy, complexity, complication, (*v*) convolution.

hnik 1. variation; *synonyms* (*n*) alteration, change, difference, divergence, mutation; *antonym* (*n*) similarity, **2.** translation; *synonyms* (*n*) displacement, interpretation, rendering, transformation, version, **3.** perturbation; *synonyms* (*n*) disturbance, commotion, agitation, fuss, (*v*) trepidation.

hnikun variation; *synonyms* (*n*) alteration, change, difference, divergence, mutation; *antonym* (*n*) similarity.

hnit coordinate; *synonyms* (*v*) align, adjust, harmonize, regulate, (*adj*) equal.

hnít curve; *synonyms* (*n*) bend, crook, bow, (*v*) curl, turn.

hnita 1. pinpoint; *synonyms* (*v*) locate, find, identify, spot, (*n*) fleck, **2.** plot; *synonyms* (*n*) conspiracy, plan, lot, (*v*) intrigue, cabal, **3.** coordinate; *synonyms* (*v*) align, adjust, harmonize, regulate, (*adj*) equal.

hnitakerfi grid; *synonyms* (*n*) gridiron, grating, lattice, mesh, netting.

hnitarit graph; *synonyms* (*n*) figure, diagram, plan, drawing, (*v*) chart.

hnitklukka chronometer; *synonyms* (*n*) clock, timepiece, watch, metronome.

hnitmiðja origin; *synonyms* (*n*) cause, lineage, base, beginning, birth; *antonym* (*n*) end.

hnitstaða pinpoint; *synonyms* (*v*) locate, find, identify, spot, (*n*) fleck.

hnitun 1. coordination; *synonyms* (*n*) regulation, classification, organization, arrangement, orientation, **2.** encoding; *synonyms* (*n*) encryption, indoctrination, brainwashing, training.

hnjáliður knee; *synonyms* (*n*) elbow, genu, scythe, sickle, zigzag.

hnjótur tubercle; *synonyms* (*n*) nodule, tuberosity, tuber, distinction, eminence.

hnoð rivet; *synonyms* (*n*) bolt, (*v*) concentrate, focus, clinch, (*adj*) nail.

hnoða 1. rivet, *synonyms* (*n*) bolt, (*v*) concentrate, focus, clinch, (*adj*) nail, **2.** upset; *synonyms* (*v*) overturn, agitate, disquiet, (*n*) disorder, trouble; *antonyms* (*v*) calm, please, encourage, soothe, (*adj*) pleased, **3.** glomerulus; *synonym* (*n*) glomerule, **4.** peen; *synonyms* (*v*) confine, inclose, pin, (*n*) pane, piend, **5.** ganglion.

hnoðnagli rivet, *synonyms* (*n*) bolt, (*v*) concentrate, focus, clinch, (*adj*) nail.

hnoðnegla rivet; *synonyms* (*n*) bolt, (*v*) concentrate, focus, clinch, (*adj*) nail.

hnoðnegling riveting; *synonyms* (*adj*) engrossing, fascinating, gripping, absorbing, enthralling; *antonym* (*adj*) boring.

hnoðri 1. glomerule, **2.** globule; *synonyms* (*n*) bead, drip, blob, (*v*) ball, (*adj*) drop, **3.** glomerulus; *synonym* (*n*) glomerule.

hnoðun 1. riveting; *synonyms* (*adj*) engrossing, fascinating, gripping, absorbing, enthralling; *antonym* (*adj*) boring, **2.** peen; *synonyms* (*v*) confine, inclose, pin, (*n*) pane, piend.

hnökri 1. corpuscle; *synonyms* (*n*) atom, corpuscle, (*adj*) molecule, particle, dot, **2.** kink; *synonyms* (*n*) curl, twist, knot, curve, defect, **3.** nodule; *synonyms* (*n*) node, bump, lump, knob, tubercle.

hnökróttur nodular; *synonyms* (*adj*) nodulated, noduled, (*v*) bossed, bossy, embossed.

hnökur judder; *synonyms* (*v*) shake, agitate, didder, excite, (*n*) vibration.

hnöttóttur 1. spherical; *synonyms* (*adj*) round, circular, global, globose, globular, **2.** globose; *synonyms* (*adj*) globous, orbicular, spheric, spherical, globated.

hnöttur 1. ball; *synonyms* (*n*) bulb, globe, shot, shell, bead, **2.** sphere; *synonyms* (*n*) region, range, area, domain, province, **3.** globe; *synonyms* (*n*) ball, world, orb, sphere, circle.

hnotutré walnut; *synonyms* (*v*) chowder, chupatty, clam, compote, damper.

hnotviður walnut; *synonyms* (*v*) chowder, chupatty, clam, compote, damper.

hnúaliður knuckle; *synonyms* (*n*) elbow, knee, scythe, sickle, (*v*) submit.

hnúðlax humpback; *synonyms* (*n*) crookback, kyphosis, hump, hunchback.

hnúðóttur 1. granulomatous, **2.** nodular; *synonyms* (*adj*) nodulated, noduled, (*v*) bossed, bossy, embossed.

hnúður 1. cusp; *synonyms* (*n*) angle, apex, top, point, tip, **2.** nodule; *synonyms* (*n*) node, knot, bump, lump, knob, **3.** node; *synonyms* (*n*) connection, joint, nodosity, nub, swelling.

hnúfa condyle; *synonyms* (*n*) apophysis, elbow, knob, process, tooth.

hnugginn 1. depressed; *synonyms* (*adj*) concave, low, blue, dejected, dispirited; *antonyms* (*adj*) cheerful, happy, convex, **2.** blue (blár); *synonyms* (*adj*) azure, depressed, down, gloomy, cheerless.

hnúi 1. condyle; *synonyms* (*n*) apophysis, elbow, knob, process, tooth, **2.** knuckle; *synonyms* (*n*) knee, scythe, sickle, zigzag, (*v*) submit.

hnúta 1. knot; *synonyms* (*n*) bow, cluster, tie, (*v*) entangle, knit, **2.** node; *synonyms* (*n*) knob, connection, joint, knot, nodosity.

hnútahersli atherosclerosis; *synonym* (*adj*) arteriosclerosis.

hnútamál height; *synonyms* (*n*) acme, apex, altitude, crest, culmination; *antonym* (*n*) shortness.

hnútpunktur node; *synonyms* (*n*) knob, connection, joint, knot, nodosity.

hnútur 1. knot; *synonyms* (*n*) bow, cluster, tie, (*v*) entangle, knit, **2.** node; *synonyms* (*n*) knob, connection, joint, knot, nodosity, **3.** vertex; *synonyms* (*n*) top, apex, crown, peak, summit, **4.** tumor; *synonyms* (*n*) swelling, tumour, growth, neoplasm, (*adj*) cancer, **5.** lump; *synonyms* (*n*) heap, chunk, block, clod, (*v*) clot.

hnykill cerebellum; *synonym* (*n*) brain.

hnykkingar 1. chiropractic, **2.** osteopathy; *synonyms* (*n*) allopathy, heteropathy, homeopathy.

hnykkir osteopath; *synonym* (*n*) osteopathist.

hnykkur 1. shock; *synonyms* (*n*) blow, daze, impact, collision, (*v*) jar; *antonym* (*v*) comfort, **2.** surge; *synonyms* (*v*) billow, flood, rise, rush, stream, **3.** pulse; *synonyms* (*n*) beat, impulse, pulsation, (*v*) pulsate, throb, **4.** spike; *synonyms* (*n*) pin, point, barb, ear, (*v*) impale, **5.** jolt; *synonyms* (*n*) jerk, hustle, (*v*) jog, shake, bump.

hnýta knot; *synonyms* (*n*) bow, cluster, tie, (*v*) entangle, knit.

hof temple; *synonyms* (*n*) church, tabernacle, shrine, brow, synagogue.

höfði promontory; *synonyms* (*n*) cape, headland, mull, ness, point.

hófdýr ungulate; *synonyms* (*adj*) hoofed, hooved, ungulated.

höfn 1. port; *synonyms* (*n*) harbor, haven, asylum, carriage, (*adj*) larboard; *antonym* (*n*) starboard, **2.** harbour; *synonyms* (*v*) entertain, contain, bear, hold, nurse.

höfnun rejection; *synonyms* (*n*) exclusion, dismissal, denial, rebuff, refusal; *antonyms* (*n*) acceptance, approval.

hófsamur 1. conservative; *synonyms* (*adj*) moderate, bourgeois, conventional, cautious, reactionary; *antonyms* (*adj*) activist, wide-ranging, (*n*) liberal, radical, **2.** moderate; *synonyms* (*adj*) temperate, abstemious, middling, mild, (*v*) calm; *antonyms* (*adj*) extreme, immoderate, (*v*) increase, intensify.

hofstöpull pylon; *synonym* (*n*) column.

höft 1. restriction; *synonyms* (*n*) limitation, limit, restraint, curb, (*v*) hindrance; *antonyms* (*n*) freedom, extension, **2.** constraint; *synonyms* (*n*) coercion, compulsion, force, confinement, duress; *antonym* (*n*) incentive.

höfuð head; *synonyms* (*n*) chief, captain, front, point, boss; *antonyms* (*n*) end, subordinate, (*v*) follow.

höfuðafurð staple; *synonyms* (*n*) pin, material, (*v*) nail, (*adj*) basic, fundamental.

höfuðbók ledger; *synonyms* (*n*) journal, book, daybook, account, books.

höfuðborg capital; *synonyms* (*n*) principal, city, stock, (*adj*) main, primary.

höfuðkúpa skull; *synonyms* (*n*) pate, noddle, head, noggin, shell.

höfuðkvef coryza; *synonym* (*n*) rhinitis.

höfuðlagsfræði phrenology; *synonyms* (*n*) organoscopy, pneumatology, craniology.

höfuðlaus acephalous; *synonym* (*adj*) deranged.

höfuðlausn disengagement; *synonyms* (*n*) detachment, disconnection, separation, disentanglement, disjunction.

höfuðlína headline; *synonyms* (*n*) title, caption, heading, (*v*) emphasize, feature.

höfuðmerki brand; *synonyms* (*n*) badge, blade, (*v*) mark, (*adj*) stigma, blot.

höfuðskepna element; *synonyms* (*n*) component, constituent, ingredient, factor, substance.

höfuðsmaður 1. admiral; *synonyms* (*n*) admiralty, administration, **2.** captain; *synonyms* (*n*) chief, head, leader, master, boss.

höfuðsteinn boss; *synonyms* (*n*) chief, governor, head, (*v*) administer, govern.

höfuðstöðvar headquarters; *synonyms* (*n*) seat, base, residence, center, office.

höfuðstóll 1. principal; *synonyms* (*adj*) master, cardinal, capital, (*n*) chief, head; *antonym* (*adj*) minor, **2.** capital; *synonyms* (*n*) principal, city, stock, (*adj*) main, primary, **3.** fund; *synonyms* (*n*) store, bank, (*v*) hoard, bankroll, finance.

höfuðverkur headache; *synonyms* (*n*) cephalalgia, nuisance, pain, bother, vexation.

höfundarlaun royalty; *synonyms* (*n*) regality, kingship, nobility, loyalty, command.

höfundarréttargreiðsla royalty; *synonyms* (*n*) regality, kingship, nobility, loyalty, command.

höfundarréttur copyright; *synonyms* (*n*) monopoly, patent, rights, (*adj*) copyrighted, (*v*) monopolize.

höfundur originator; *synonyms* (*n*) father, creator, author, founder, architect.

högg 1. shock; *synonyms* (*n*) blow, daze, impact, collision, (*v*) jar; *antonym* (*v*) comfort, **2.** pulse; *synonyms* (*n*) beat, impulse, pulsation, (*v*) pulsate, throb, **3.** blow; *synonyms* (*n*) bang, blast, knock, (*v*) puff, (*adj*) gasp; *antonyms* (*v*) calm, save, **4.** dash; *synonyms* (*n*) rush, sprint, (*v*) dart, touch, strike; *antonym* (*n*) lethargy, **5.** impulse; *synonyms* (*n*) impetus, pulse, urge, drive, force.

höggbor jumper; *synonyms* (*n*) sweater, blackguard, bounder, cad, dog.

höggbylgja blast; *synonyms* (*n*) bang, slam, (*v*) attack, (*adj*) discharge, explosion.

höggormur adder; *synonyms* (*n*) viper, snake, summer, nadder, nedder.

höggpúði buffer; *synonyms* (*n*) safeguard, pad, protection, bumper, (*v*) cushion.

höggun tectonics; *synonym* (*n*) architectonics.

höggunarfræði tectonics; *synonym* (*n*) architectonics.

höggvari bumper; *synonyms* (*n*) buffer, cushion, (*v*) fill, load, (*adj*) plentiful.

hógvær 1. unassuming; *synonyms* (*adj*) modest, humble, retiring, unobtrusive, lowly; *antonyms* (*adj*) arrogant, conspicuous, elaborate, 2. simple; *synonyms* (*adj*) plain, homely, pure, elementary, (*v*) clear; *antonyms* (*adj*) complex, complicated, compound, difficult, multiple, 3. unpretentious; *synonyms* (*adj*) quiet, simple, unassuming, unpretending, unostentatious; *antonyms* (*adj*) pretentious, affected, 4. discrete; *synonyms* (*adj*) separate, distinct, different, detached, diverse, 5. modest; *synonyms* (*adj*) bashful, diffident, moderate, gentle, chaste; *antonyms* (*adj*) conceited, pompous, proud, self-important, showy.

hol 1. atrium; *synonyms* (*n*) hall, vestibule, cavity, court, foyer, 2. cavity; *synonyms* (*n*) cavern, cave, hole, hollow, pocket, 3. hall; *synonyms* (*n*) corridor, lobby, mansion, auditorium, anteroom, 4. latent; *synonyms* (*adj*) covert, potential, secret, dormant, hidden; *antonym* (*adj*) active, 5. lumen; *synonym* (*n*) lm.

hola 1. pit; *synonyms* (*n*) cavity, dent, hole, depression, (*adj*) hollow, 2. sinus; *synonyms* (*n*) fistula, pit, indentation, dimple, dint, 3. cavity; *synonyms* (*n*) cavern, cave, pocket, caries, chamber, 4. hole; *synonyms* (*n*) aperture, crack, den, breach, (*adj*) gap.

holbor perforator; *synonyms* (*n*) gun, awl, bodkin, borer, bradawl.

holdfrauð fungus; *synonyms* (*n*) rust, mushroom, growth, fungi, (*adj*) garlic.

holdfúi necrosis; *synonyms* (*n*) mortification, gangrene, death, (*adj*) pertussis, phthisis.

holdhersll induration; *synonyms* (*n*) hardening, sclerosis, (*adj*) petrifaction.

holdmikill obese; *synonyms* (*adj*) fat, corpulent, gross, fleshy, heavy; *antonym* (*adj*) slim.

holdsveiki leprosy; *synonyms* (*n*) measles, lepra, (*adj*) caries, corruption, gangrene.

holdugur fat; *synonyms* (*adj*) stout, corpulent, dense, thick, (*n*) avoirdupois; *antonyms* (*adj*) thin, slim, skinny, slender.

holefni clathrate; *synonyms* (*adj*) cancellate, cancellated, cancellous.

holeind hole; *synonyms* (*n*) cavity, aperture, crack, den, (*adj*) gap.

hólf 1. tray; *synonyms* (*n*) plate, dish, basket, bassinet, case, 2. ventricle; *synonyms* (*n*) paunch, stomach, venter, heart, 3. barrel; *synonyms* (*n*) drum, roll, vessel, barrelful, cask, 4. cell; *synonyms* (*n*) cage, jail, cadre, hole, cave, 5. compartment; *synonyms* (*n*) cell, division, cabin, cubicle, (*v*) apartment.

hólfaplata honeycomb; *synonyms* (*n*) comb, chaser, (*v*) perforate, riddle, (*adj*) alveolate.

hólflaga honeycomb; *synonyms* (*n*) comb, chaser, (*v*) perforate, riddle, (*adj*) alveolate.

holhönd axilla; *synonym* (*n*) armpit.

holhringsrör toroid; *synonyms* (*n*) tore, torus.

hólklaga tubular; *synonyms* (*adj*) cannular, tubulate, fistuliform, piped, tubeform.

hólkur 1. sleeve; *synonyms* (*n*) arm, case, liner, cover, cuff, 2. socket; *synonyms* (*n*) cavity, alveolus, sleeve, hollow, pocket, 3. cylinder; *synonyms* (*n*) barrel, roll, pipe, tube, column, 4. hopper; *synonyms* (*n*) grasshopper, bin, basket, boor, clown, 5. liner; *synonyms* (*n*) lining, boat, airliner, craft, ship.

höll 1. atrium; *synonyms* (*n*) hall, vestibule, cavity, court, foyer, 2. palace; *synonyms* (*n*) castle, mansion, chateau.

holleggur catheter; *synonyms* (*n*) infusion, transfusion.

hollur salubrious; *synonyms* (*adj*) healthy, healthful, wholesome, beneficial, hygienic.

hólmi 1. doughnut; *synonyms* (*n*) donut, sinker, annulus, anulus, (*v*) cracker, 2. island; *synonyms* (*n*) reef, (*v*) isle, insulate, isolate, segregate.

holóttur porous; *synonyms* (*adj*) permeable, leaky, poriferous, holey, open; *antonym* (*adj*) impermeable.

holplata honeycomb; *synonyms* (*n*) comb, chaser, (*v*) perforate, riddle, (*adj*) alveolate.

holrúm 1. well; *synonyms* (*adv*) right, easily, thoroughly, (*adj*) healthy, (*n*) fountain; *antonyms* (*adv*) ill, badly, poorly, (*adj*) sick, unwell, 2. recess; *synonyms* (*n*) corner, break, holiday, intermission, niche, 3. cavity; *synonyms* (*n*) cavern, cave, hole, hollow, pocket, 4. antrum.

holsepi polyp; *synonyms* (*n*) polypus, polype.

holun excavation; *synonyms* (*n*) mine, pit, dig, digging, hole.

holur hollow; *synonyms* (*adj*) blank, concave, empty, (*n*) cavity, hole; *antonyms* (*adj*) convex, (*n*) solid, hump.

hómi homosexual; *synonyms* (*n*) gay, lesbian, homo, dyke, human.

hömluhak ratchet; *synonyms* (*n*) rachet, ratch, wheel, (*adj*) cog, spoke.

hömlun inhibition; *synonyms* (n) check, prohibition, restraint, suppression, taboo.

hömlur 1. restriction; *synonyms* (n) limitation, limit, restraint, curb, (v) hindrance; *antonyms* (n) freedom, extension, **2**. constraint; *synonyms* (n) coercion, compulsion, force, confinement, duress; *antonym* (n) incentive.

hommi homosexual; *synonyms* (n) gay, lesbian, homo, dyke, human.

hönd hand; *synonyms* (n) deal, (v) deliver, give, pass, commit.

höndla deal; *synonyms* (n) bargain, buy, agreement, (v) administer, allot; *antonym* (n) purchase.

höndlari dealer; *synonyms* (n) merchant, trader, monger, seller, vendor; *antonym* (n) user.

hönk complex; *synonyms* (adj) composite, complicate, abstruse, difficult, elaborate; *antonyms* (adj) simple, basic, straightforward, clear, plain.

hönnun design; *synonyms* (n) aim, purpose, scheme, conception, (v) plan; *antonym* (n) chance.

hönnunarlýsing specification; *synonyms* (n) designation, provision, stipulation, particular, condition.

hóp lagoon; *synonyms* (n) lagune, lake, bay, mere, pond.

hopa backspace; *synonym* (n) backspacing.

hópbifreið coach; *synonyms* (n) trainer, tutor, instructor, teacher, (adj) prime.

hópfelling agglutination; *synonyms* (n) conglutination, union, polysynthesis, clumping.

hópmál jargon; *synonyms* (n) dialect, gibberish, idiom, slang, vernacular.

hópmyndun aggregation; *synonyms* (n) accumulation, congregation, heap, lot, (v) assemblage.

hopp hop; *synonyms* (n) jump, leap, bound, (v) dance, gambol.

hoppa jump; *synonyms* (n) leap, bound, bounce, start, caper; *antonyms* (v) decrease, fall.

hópun aggregation; *synonyms* (n) accumulation, congregation, heap, lot, (v) assemblage.

hópur 1. team; *synonyms* (n) crew, company, gang, squad, (v) pair, **2**. tribe; *synonyms* (n) family, clan, house, folk, kin, **3**. population; *synonyms* (n) inhabitants, people, nation, community, group, **4**. category; *synonyms* (n) class, denomination, division, kind, type, **5**. aggregation; *synonyms* (n) accumulation, congregation, heap, lot, (v) assemblage.

hor inanition; *synonyms* (n) emptiness, lethargy, lassitude, (adj) exhaustion, collapse.

hóra 1. whore; *synonyms* (n) prostitute, harlot, trollop, courtesan, strumpet, **2**. hooker; *synonyms* (n) floozie, floozy, hustler, slattern, streetwalker.

hörðnun solidification; *synonyms* (n) hardening, set, consolidation, setting, (adj) solidation.

hordo 1. bands, **2**. band; *synonyms* (n) cluster, party, set, swathe, (v) ring.

horf 1. aspect; *synonyms* (n) appearance, look, surface, bearing, expression, **2**. attitude; *synonyms* (n) position, aspect, posture, behavior, mind.

hörfa regress; *synonyms* (v) recede, lapse, revert, relapse, degenerate; *antonyms* (v) improve, progress.

horfur prognosis; *synonyms* (n) forecast, prediction, prospect, outlook, vaticination.

hörgull dearth; *synonyms* (n) absence, famine, shortage, want, deficiency; *antonyms* (n) abundance, excess.

hörgultímar austerity; *synonyms* (n) rigor, acerbity, asceticism, hardship, (adj) stringency.

hormón hormone; *synonym* (n) contraceptive.

hormóni hormone; *synonym* (n) contraceptive.

horn 1. square; *synonyms* (adj) right, even, rectangular, (n) area, (v) settle, **2**. argument; *synonyms* (n) controversy, debate, matter, proof, reason; *antonyms* (n) agreement, harmony, **3**. angle; *synonyms* (n) hook, incline, (v) slant, lean, tilt, **4**. cusp; *synonyms* (n) angle, apex, top, point, tip, **5**. corner; *synonyms* (n) bend, turn, coign, dilemma, hole.

hornafræði 1. trigonometry; *synonyms* (n) trig, goniometry, **2**. geometry; *synonyms* (v) algebra, analysis, arithmetic, hypsometry, stereometry.

hornalína diagonal; *synonyms* (adj) oblique, aslant, slanting, sloping, (n) bias; *antonym* (adj) level.

hornamælir goniometer; *synonyms* (n) clinometer, graphometer, (v) bathometer, dynamometer, galvanometer.

hornarit polygon; *synonym* (n) square.

hornefni keratin; *synonyms* (n) ceratin, epidermose.

horneining radian; *synonym* (n) rad.

hornfiskur 1. skipper; *synonyms* (n) captain, commander, master, head, leader, **2**. garfish; *synonyms* (n) gar, needlefish, garpike, billfish, girrock.

horngæla garfish; *synonyms* (n) gar, needlefish, garpike, billfish, girrock.

horngerð keratinization; *synonym* (n) keratinisation.

hornhimna cornea; *synonyms* (n) white, iris, pupil, retina.

hornhraðamælir tachometer; *synonyms* (n) tach, (adj) speedometer, odometer, strobe.

hornklofi bracket; *synonyms* (n) brace, prop, rack, (v) link, couple.

hornloftnet horn; *synonyms* (n) hooter, cornet, klaxon, alarm, trumpet.

hornmælir 1. theodolite; *synonyms (n)* altometer, passage, transit, transportation, **2.** goniometer; *synonyms (n)* clinometer, graphometer, *(v)* bathometer, dynamometer, galvanometer.

hornmyndaður angular; *synonyms (adj)* angulate, bony, gaunt, lean, skinny; *antonym (adj)* rounded.

hornmyndun keratinization; *synonym (n)* keratinisation.

hornpunktur vertex; *synonyms (n)* top, apex, crown, peak, summit.

hornréttur 1. perpendicular; *synonyms (adj)* erect, upright, vertical, plumb, steep; *antonym (adj)* horizontal, **2.** rectangular; *synonyms (adj)* orthogonal, oblong, square, rectangled, rectangle, **3.** orthogonal; *synonyms (adj)* rectangular, external, extraneous, foreign, immaterial.

hornsíli stickleback; *synonyms (n)* prickleback, sharpling.

hornskakkur oblique; *synonyms (adj)* indirect, circuitous, devious, lateral, collateral; *antonyms (adj)* direct, level.

hörpudiskur scallop; *synonyms (n)* scollop, cutlet, *(v)* indent, crimp, notch.

Hörpun sizing; *synonyms (n)* size, calibrate, dimensioning, classification, coining.

hörpuskel scallop; *synonyms (n)* scollop, cutlet, *(v)* indent, crimp, notch.

hörsl plaque; *synonyms (n)* plate, brass, medal, administration, award.

hörund integument; *synonyms (n)* cover, film, coat, skin, tegument.

hörundskröm pellagra; *synonym (n)* maidism.

hóruungi 1. widow; *synonyms (n)* relict, *(adj)* additional, *(v)* bereave, **2.** orphan; *synonyms (n)* waif, caterpillar, cocoon, nymph, *(adj)* orphaned.

hosa hose; *synonyms (n)* stocking, pipe, tights, hosepipe, *(v)* water.

hossast jounce; *synonyms (n)* jolt, jar, *(v)* bounce, jog, joggle.

hósta cough; *synonyms (n)* coughing, sneeze, *(v)* choke, convulse, vomit.

hóstameðal expectorant; *synonyms (n)* expectorator, spitter.

hóstastillandi antitussive; *synonyms (n)* analgesic, antiseptic, antiviral, carminative, emetic.

hósti cough; *synonyms (n)* coughing, sneeze, *(v)* choke, convulse, vomit.

Hótun threat; *synonyms (n)* menace, danger, hazard, peril, risk; *antonym (n)* safety.

hraðaaukning acceleration; *synonyms (n)* speed, rapidity, rise, quickening, quickness.

hraðafræði kinetics; *synonym (n)* dynamics.

hraðall accelerator; *synonyms (n)* catalyst, gas, throttle, gun, promotor.

hraðamælir speedometer; *synonyms (adj)* odometer, strobe.

hraðaminnkun deceleration; *synonyms (n)* retardation, slowdown, backwardness, slowing, lag.

hraðaráður governor; *synonyms (n)* director, chief, manager, regulator, administrator.

hraðastjórnun speed; *synonyms (n)* race, *(v)* hasten, hurry, quicken, run; *antonym (n)* slowness.

hraðavektor velocity; *synonyms (n)* speed, celerity, rapidity, *(v)* pace, rate; *antonym (n)* slowness.

hraðavigur velocity; *synonyms (n)* speed, celerity, rapidity, *(v)* pace, rate; *antonym (n)* slowness.

hraðbruni detonation; *synonyms (n)* blast, explosion, burst, bang, *(v)* discharge.

hraði 1. speed; *synonyms (n)* race, *(v)* hasten, hurry, quicken, run; *antonym (n)* slowness, **2.** rate; *synonyms (n)* price, worth, *(v)* assess, estimate, evaluate, **3.** velocity; *synonyms (n)* speed, celerity, rapidity, *(v)* pace, rate, **4.** ratio; *synonyms (n)* percentage, degree, proportion, measure, scale.

Hraðskák blitz; *synonyms (n)* attack, assault, onslaught, bombardment, *(v)* bombard.

hraðskreiður fast; *synonyms (adj)* dissolute, firm, agile, debauched, *(adv)* soon; *antonyms (adj)* sluggish, *(adv)* slow, slowly, *(v)* gorge, *(n)* binge.

hraðtaktur tachycardia; *synonym (n)* tachyrhythmia.

hraður fast; *synonyms (adj)* dissolute, firm, agile, debauched, *(adv)* soon; *antonyms (adj)* sluggish, *(adv)* slow, slowly, *(v)* gorge, *(n)* binge.

hrææta scavenger; *synonyms (n)* magpie, hunter, packrat, predator, quencher.

hræðilegur 1. horrible; *synonyms (adj)* abominable, atrocious, awful, fearful, frightful; *antonyms (adj)* pleasant, wonderful, lovely, nice, **2.** terrible; *synonyms (adj)* dreadful, horrible, horrid, monstrous, appalling, **3.** vile; *synonyms (adj)* foul, contemptible, despicable, *(n)* dirty, *(v)* base; *antonym (adj)* attractive, **4.** dismal; *synonyms (adj)* cheerless, dark, dejected, depressing, desolate; *antonyms (adj)* cheerful, bright, happy, **5.** abysmal; *synonyms (adj)* abyssal, deep, profound, terrible, unfathomable; *antonyms (adj)* excellent, exceptional.

hræðsla 1. fear; *synonyms (n)* apprehension, awe, alarm, *(v)* dread, concern; *antonyms (n)* bravery, confidence, fearlessness, reassurance, **2.** terror; *synonyms (n)* fright, dismay, fear, scare, consternation, **3.** alarm; *synonyms (n)* alert, affright, *(v)* agitate, horrify, panic; *antonyms (v)* calm, comfort, **4.** agony; *synonyms (n)* anguish, torture, distress, misery, suffering, **5.** dread;

synonyms (n) anxiety, foreboding, terror, trepidation, doubt.

hráefni staple; *synonyms* (n) pin, material, (v) nail, (adj) basic, fundamental.

hrægammur scavenger; *synonyms* (n) magpie, hunter, packrat, predator, quencher.

hræking expectoration; *synonyms* (n) spit, spitting, saliva, tongue.

hrækja 1. spit; *synonyms* (n) broach, saliva, (v) drizzle, impale, expectorate, **2**. expectorate; *synonyms* (v) cough, spit, slabber, slaver, slobber.

hræring 1. disturbance; *synonyms* (n) agitation, commotion, disorder, turmoil, (adj) trouble, **2**. movement; *synonyms* (n) motion, move, action, activity, campaign.

hrafn 1. raven; *synonyms* (adj) black, (n) crow, (v) prey, devour, feed, **2**. crow; *synonyms* (v) boast, brag, cackle, chuckle, cry.

hraka deteriorate; *synonyms* (v) degenerate, degrade, decline, spoil, worsen; *antonyms* (v) improve, convalesce, recover.

hráki sputum; *synonyms* (n) phlegm, spit, saliva, belch, dig.

hrakning falsification; *synonyms* (n) fake, falsehood, distortion, deceit, deception.

hráolía petroleum; *synonyms* (n) crude, oil, petrol, alcohol, coal.

hrapa crash; *synonyms* (n) clash, collision, smash, (v) bang, collapse.

hrapsteinn meteor; *synonyms* (n) aerolite, effluvium, emanation, evaporation, exhalation.

hrár 1. uncooked; *synonyms* (adj) raw, unblown, unpolished, tough, unfashioned, **2**. raw; *synonyms* (adj) crude, fresh, immature, bleak, coarse; *antonyms* (adj) refined, cooked, **3**. rough; *synonyms* (adj) hard, harsh, cruel, grating, gross; *antonyms* (adj) gentle, smooth, polished, precise, silky.

hratt 1. rapid; *synonyms* (adj) fast, quick, prompt, swift, agile; *antonyms* (adj) slow, gradual, **2**. speedy; *synonyms* (adj) rapid, fleet, ready, immediate, cursory, **3**. prompt; *synonyms* (adj) nimble, punctual, dexterous, (v) actuate, incite; *antonym* (adj) late, **4**. quick; *synonyms* (adj) bright, active, clever, hasty, intelligent; *antonyms* (adj) leisurely, dull, **5**. swift; *synonyms* (adj) speedy, alert, expeditious, hurried, lively; *antonym* (adj) considered.

hraun lava; *synonyms* (n) rock, (adj) pituite.

hraunbreiða lava; *synonyms* (n) rock, (adj) pituite.

hraunhella lava; *synonyms* (n) rock, (adj) pituite.

hraunkvika lava; *synonyms* (n) rock, (adj) pituite.

hraunleðja lava; *synonyms* (n) rock, (adj) pituite.

hrávara commodity; *synonyms* (n) merchandise, article, product, object, thing.

hreiðrun implantation; *synonyms* (n) implant, insertion, nidation, graft, introduction.

hreiður 1. nest; *synonyms* (n) den, lair, hole, (adj) brood, hive, **2**. den; *synonyms* (n) cavern, burrow, cell, cavity, (v) cave, **3**. nidus; *synonyms* (n) focus, nest, cradle, snuggery, centering, **4**. lair; *synonyms* (n) hideaway, hideout, retreat, (adj) sty.

hreifi wrist; *synonyms* (n) carpus, (v) finger, hand, paw.

hreinhljóma harmonic; *synonyms* (adj) harmonious, consonant, harmonical, sympathetic, concordant.

hreinlæti hygiene; *synonyms* (n) hygienics, sanitation, regimen, salutariness, spotlessness.

hreinn 1. clean; *synonyms* (adj) clear, fair, antiseptic, blank, (v) brush; *antonyms* (adj) filthy, unclean, (v) dirty, soil, contaminate, **2**. pure; *synonyms* (adj) just, absolute, genuine, natural, (n) chaste; *antonyms* (adj) impure, contaminated, diluted, dishonored, tainted, **3**. untainted; *synonyms* (adj) pure, unstained, unsullied, unspotted, innocent, **4**. clear; *synonyms* (adj) clean, certain, (v) bright, acquit, free; *antonyms* (adj) cloudy, opaque, unclear, dark, fuzzy, **5**. net; *synonyms* (n) network, bag, (v) mesh, gain, make; *antonym* (v) gross.

hreinræktun isolation; *synonyms* (n) alienation, estrangement, insulation, privacy, dissociation; *antonyms* (n) closeness, companionship.

hreinsa 1. purify; *synonyms* (v) clean, disinfect, purge, (adj) clear, cleanse; *antonyms* (v) contaminate, pollute, **2**. clean; *synonyms* (adj) fair, antiseptic, blank, pure, (v) brush; *antonyms* (adj) filthy, unclean, muddy, (v) dirty, soil, **3**. refine; *synonyms* (v) cultivate, purify, civilize, elaborate, (adj) clarify, **4**. purge; *synonyms* (n) purgation, purification, (v) expurgate, eradicate, liquidate; *antonym* (v) binge, **5**. scavenge; *synonyms* (v) salvage, houseclean, pick, prowl, relieve.

hreinsari cleaner; *synonyms* (n) cleanser, lifter, custodian, donkeyman.

hreinsiefni 1. cleaner; *synonyms* (n) cleanser, lifter, custodian, donkeyman, **2**. detergent; *synonyms* (adj) detersive, cleansing, (n) abluent, (v) lotion, wash.

hreinskilni honesty; *synonyms* (n) candor, fairness, integrity, justice, candidness; *antonyms* (n) dishonesty, deceit, deception, deviousness, treachery.

hreinsun 1. refining; *synonyms* (n) refinement, purification, cleansing, decontamination, beating, **2**. toilet; *synonyms* (n) bathroom, lavatory, attire, can, dress, **3**. purification; *synonyms* (n) defecation, purge, catharsis, refining, rectification;

antonyms (n) ruining, debasement, **4**. refinery, **5**. purge; *synonyms* (v) cleanse, clean, expurgate, eradicate, clear; *antonym* (v) binge.

hreintóna harmonic; *synonyms* (adj) harmonious, consonant, harmonical, sympathetic, concordant.

hreistraður squamous; *synonyms* (adj) flaky, (v) scaly, cortical, cutaneous, cuticular.

hreisturflaga scale; *synonyms* (n) flake, gamut, (v) ascend, climb, (adj) balance; *antonym* (v) descend.

hreisturglæsir bleak; *synonyms* (adj) austere, bare, barren, cold, dreary; *antonyms* (adj) cheerful, hopeful, lush, mild, sunny.

hrekja explode; *synonyms* (v) erupt, detonate, crack, discharge, (n) burst; *antonym* (v) implode.

hremma trap; *synonyms* (n) snare, net, ambush, (v) catch, entrap.

hremming capture; *synonyms* (v) bag, catch, take, (n) arrest, seizure; *antonyms* (v) release, surrender.

hremmir 1. raider; *synonyms* (n) looter, plunderer, aggressor, robber, intruder, **2**. getter.

hreppapólitík localism; *synonyms* (n) provincialism, sectionalism, dialect, regionalism, barbarism.

hreppsfélag municipality; *synonyms* (n) city, town, metropolis, shrievalty, commune.

hressandi bracing; *synonyms* (adj) fresh, brisk, invigorating, cool, (n) brace.

hreyfanlegur 1. portable; *synonyms* (adj) mobile, movable, portative, light, convenient; *antonym* (adj) fixed, **2**. versatile; *synonyms* (adj) changeable, adaptable, variable, various, fickle, **3**. dynamical; *synonyms* (adj) dynamic, active, **4**. mobile; *synonyms* (adj) fluid, unsettled, mercurial, expressive, lively; *antonyms* (adj) immobile, impassive, motionless.

hreyfanleiki mobility; *synonyms* (n) movableness, motion, movement, (adj) versatility.

hreyfiafl kinematic; *synonym* (adj) cinematical.

hreyfifræði dynamics; *synonyms* (n) kinetics, motion, (v) statics.

hreyfifræðilegur 1. dynamical; *synonyms* (adj) dynamic, active, **2**. kinematic; *synonym* (adj) cinematical.

hreyfiglöp ataxia; *synonyms* (n) chaos, disarray, disorder, ataxy, clutter.

hreyfihömlun disability; *synonyms* (n) handicap, inability, disablement, disqualification, drawback.

hreyfilaukatæki accessories; *synonyms* (n) fittings, equipment, accompaniments, garnishes, possession.

hreyfill 1. motor; *synonyms* (n) engine, automobile, machine, car, (v) drive, **2**. engine; *synonyms* (n) locomotive, contrivance, implement, instrument, mechanism.

hreyfilögmál dynamics; *synonyms* (n) kinetics, motion, (v) statics.

hreyfimagn momentum; *synonyms* (n) impetus, impulse, force, drive, impulsion; *antonym* (n) inertia.

hreyfimörk excursion; *synonyms* (n) digression, drive, expedition, hike, jaunt.

hreyfing 1. transaction; *synonyms* (n) deal, business, dealing, dealings, proceeding; *antonym* (n) purchase, **2**. motion; *synonyms* (n) gesture, action, movement, wave, (v) sign, **3**. movement; *synonyms* (n) motion, move, activity, campaign, crusade.

hreyfingafræði kinematics; *synonyms* (n) phoronomics, cinematics.

hreyfingarfræðilegur kinematic; *synonym* (adj) cinematical.

hreyfingarlaus inert; *synonyms* (adj) idle, dead, dull, inactive, indolent; *antonyms* (adj) moving, active, animate.

hreyfingarleyi akinesis; *synonym* (n) akinesia.

hreyfiskyn 1. kinesthesia; *synonyms* (n) kinaesthesia, kinaesthesis, kinesthesis, kinesthetics, sense, **2**. kinesthesis; *synonyms* (n) kinesthesia, proprioception.

hreyfistol apraxia; *synonym* (n) dyspraxia.

hreyfivirkur motor; *synonyms* (n) engine, automobile, machine, car, (v) drive.

hreysiköttur weasel; *synonyms* (n) informer, (v) equivocate, evade, hedge, confess.

hríð blizzard; *synonyms* (n) snowstorm, storm, tempest, snowfall, gale.

hríðahormón oxytocin; *synonym* (n) ocytocin.

hríðarbylur blizzard; *synonyms* (n) snowstorm, storm, tempest, snowfall, gale.

hrif effect; *synonyms* (n) consequence, (v) accomplish, achieve, create, cause; *antonym* (n) reason.

hrífa rake; *synonyms* (n) profligate, (v) tilt, hoe, harrow, (adj) comb.

hrífandi 1. seductive; *synonyms* (adj) attractive, alluring, enticing, tempting, seducing, **2**. bewitching; *synonyms* (adj) charming, enchanting, fascinating, captivating, engaging, **3**. appealing; *synonyms* (adj) absorbing, adorable, inviting, prepossessing, likable; *antonyms* (adj) unappealing, repellent, disgusting, **4**. attractive; *synonyms* (adj) amiable, appealing, good-looking, delightful, glamorous; *antonyms* (adj) unattractive, ugly, revolting, repulsive, straight, **5**. alluring; *synonyms* (adj) seductive, beguiling, magnetic, desirable, enthralling.

hrifill effector; *synonym* (n) effecter.

hrifnæmi 1. susceptibility; *synonyms* (n) predisposition, sensitivity, impressibility, liability, inclination; *antonym* (n) resistance, **2**. affectivity; *synonyms* (n) emotion, passion, sentiment, **3**. irritability; *synonyms* (n) excitability, irascibility, choler, petulance, temper.

hrifnæmur irritable; *synonyms* (adj) angry, fractious, irascible, edgy, cantankerous; *antonyms* (adj) calm, easygoing, good-humored, good-natured, even-tempered.

hrifnánd exposure; *synonyms* (n) display, exposition, detection, peril, (v) disclosure.

hrifning exaltation; *synonyms* (n) elation, apotheosis, ecstasy, praise, (adj) elevation.

hrifsari raider; *synonyms* (n) looter, plunderer, aggressor, robber, intruder.

hrím rime; *synonyms* (n) frost, hoar, hoarfrost, cleft, (v) rhyme.

hrina burst; *synonyms* (v) break, crack, blast, (adj) split, explode; *antonym* (v) implode.

hringbogi arc; *synonyms* (n) arch, bow, bend, crescent, (v) curve.

hringbraut circuit; *synonyms* (n) beat, (v) circle, tour, trip, journey.

hringekja **1**. roundabout; *synonyms* (adj) circuitous, indirect, oblique, devious, (n) circuit; *antonyms* (adj) direct, straight, **2**. merry-go-round; *synonyms* (n) comedy, diversion, recreation.

hringfari **1**. calipers; *synonyms* (n) caliper, callipers, calliper, (v) compass, measure, **2**. dividers, **3**. circle; *synonyms* (n) round, association, band, ring, field, **4**. compass; *synonyms* (n) range, scope, area, circle, circumference.

hringfeldi torus; *synonyms* (n) tore, toroid, thalamus, breast, mamma.

hringferð circuit; *synonyms* (n) beat, (v) circle, tour, trip, journey.

hringferill **1**. circle; *synonyms* (n) round, association, band, compass, ring, **2**. circumference; *synonyms* (n) circuit, border, boundary, perimeter, brim.

hringgeiri sector; *synonyms* (n) department, area, branch, district, division.

hringiða **1**. turbulence; *synonyms* (n) disorder, tumult, confusion, agitation, commotion; *antonyms* (n) calm, peace, **2**. whirlpool; *synonyms* (n) eddy, vortex, maelstrom, (v) whirl, swirl, **3**. eddy; *synonyms* (n) spin, twirl, gurge, (v) purl, whirlpool.

hringing ringing; *synonyms* (n) buzz, peal, resonance, (adj) resonant, reverberant.

hringjaðar circumference; *synonyms* (n) circuit, border, boundary, perimeter, brim.

hringla rattle; *synonyms* (n) roll, jangle, jingle, click, (v) clatter.

hringlaga **1**. round; *synonyms* (adv) about, (adj) circular, (n) circle, bout, ring; *antonyms* (adj) slim,

sharp, **2**. cyclic; *synonyms* (adj) periodic, cyclical, recurring, regular, repeated; *antonym* (adj) irregular, **3**. annular; *synonyms* (adj) round, annulate, annulated, circinate, rounded, **4**. orbicular; *synonyms* (adj) globular, global, globose, annular, orbiculate.

hringmyndaður annular; *synonyms* (adj) circular, round, annulate, annulated, circinate.

hringnet loop; *synonyms* (n) coil, ring, (v) curve, bend, circle.

hringormur **1**. ringworm; *synonyms* (n) tinea, (adj) necrosis, pertussis, phthisis, pneumonia, **2**. nematode; *synonyms* (n) roundworm, eelworm, ringworm.

hringrás **1**. recirculation; *synonym* (n) recycling, **2**. circulation; *synonyms* (n) dissemination, diffusion, distribution, currency, delivery, **3**. cycle; *synonyms* (n) bicycle, circle, round, (v) bike, motorcycle, **4**. circuit; *synonyms* (n) beat, area, (v) tour, trip, journey.

hringrása circulate; *synonyms* (v) spread, broadcast, circle, disseminate, disperse.

hringrif atoll; *synonyms* (n) ait, isle, islet, breaker, eyot.

hringröksemd tautology; *synonyms* (n) repetition, battology, circumlocution, verbiage, (v) polylogy.

hringskyrfi ringworm; *synonyms* (n) tinea, (adj) necrosis, pertussis, phthisis, pneumonia.

hringsóla circulate; *synonyms* (v) spread, broadcast, circle, disseminate, disperse.

hringspóla toroid; *synonyms* (n) tore, torus.

hringstallur counterbore; *synonym* (n) countersink.

hringstreymi **1**. turbulence; *synonyms* (n) disorder, tumult, confusion, agitation, commotion; *antonyms* (n) calm, peace, **2**. circulation; *synonyms* (n) dissemination, diffusion, distribution, currency, delivery, **3**. convection; *synonyms* (n) transfer, (adj) thermal.

hringtengdur cyclic; *synonyms* (adj) periodic, circular, cyclical, recurring, regular; *antonym* (adj) irregular.

hringþétti gland; *synonyms* (n) secreter, secretor, glandula.

hringur **1**. ring; *synonyms* (n) encircle, band, (v) circle, call, peal, **2**. circle; *synonyms* (n) round, association, compass, ring, field, **3**. round; *synonyms* (adv) about, (adj) circular, (n) bout, beat, circuit; *antonyms* (adj) slim, sharp, **4**. cycle; *synonyms* (n) bicycle, sequence, (v) bike, motorcycle, wheel, **5**. cartel; *synonyms* (n) syndicate, trust, combine, compromise, group.

hringvik eccentricity; *synonyms* (n) oddity, abnormality, idiosyncrasy, oddness, peculiarity; *antonym* (n) normality.

hringvöðvi sphincter; *synonym* (*n*) constrictor.

hrip percolation; *synonyms* (*n*) leakage, seeping, filtration, extravasation, leak.

hrísgrjón rice; *synonyms* (*n*) cereal, (*adj*) meal, bran, farina, flour.

hrísla tree; *synonyms* (*n*) gallows, gibbet, stem, house, tribe.

hrísluskipan tree; *synonyms* (*n*) gallows, gibbet, stem, house, tribe.

hrista jolt; *synonyms* (*n*) jerk, jar, (*v*) jog, shake, bump.

hristing agitation; *synonyms* (*n*) disturbance, excitement, tumult, commotion, convulsion; *antonyms* (*n*) calmness, calm, serenity.

hristingur 1. vibration; *synonyms* (*n*) quiver, shudder, tremor, beat, pulse, **2**. concussion; *synonyms* (*n*) blow, clash, collision, shock, impact.

hrjóstrugur barren; *synonyms* (*adj*) infertile, sterile, deserted, abortive, (*v*) bare; *antonyms* (*adj*) fertile, lush, productive.

hrjúfur 1. poignant; *synonyms* (*adj*) bitter, acute, cutting, (*v*) acrid, biting, **2**. sharp; *synonyms* (*adj*) intelligent, acid, harsh, incisive, (*n*) keen; *antonyms* (*adj*) blunt, dull, mild, gentle, rounded, **3**. rough; *synonyms* (*adj*) coarse, hard, raw, crude, cruel; *antonyms* (*adj*) smooth, polished, precise, refined, silky, **4**. acute; *synonyms* (*adj*) sharp, intense, penetrating, critical, (*v*) high; *antonym* (*adj*) obtuse, **5**. acerbic; *synonyms* (*adj*) acerb, caustic, astringent, tart, acrimonious.

hroði 1. debris; *synonyms* (*n*) detritus, junk, refuse, rubbish, trash, **2**. mud; *synonyms* (*n*) dirt, filth, grime, (*adj*) clay, (*v*) mire.

hröðun acceleration; *synonyms* (*n*) speed, rapidity, rise, quickening, quickness.

hröðunarrafskaut accelerator; *synonyms* (*n*) catalyst, gas, throttle, gun, promotor.

hrogn roe; *synonyms* (*n*) deer, egg, doe, buck, stag.

hrognamál jargon; *synonyms* (*n*) dialect, gibberish, idiom, slang, vernacular.

hrognaseiði capelin; *synonyms* (*n*) caplin, capelan, capling.

hrognasíli capelin; *synonyms* (*n*) caplin, capelan, capling.

hrognkelsi 1. lump; *synonyms* (*n*) heap, chunk, knot, block, (*v*) clot, **2**. lumpfish.

Hróka castle; *synonyms* (*n*) rook, citadel, fortification, fortress, castling.

hroki arrogance; *synonyms* (*n*) haughtiness, disdain, conceit, presumption, vanity; *antonyms* (*n*) humility, modesty.

hrökk 1. transition; *synonyms* (*n*) change, passage, transit, alteration, changeover, **2**. reflex; *synonyms* (*v*) reflection, (*adj*) automatic, involuntary, instinctive, unconscious.

Hrókur rook; *synonyms* (*n*) castle, (*v*) con, defraud, bilk, cheat.

hrollur shiver; *synonyms* (*n*) quiver, (*v*) shake, tremble, quake, shudder.

hrörlegur feeble; *synonyms* (*adj*) delicate, weak, decrepit, (*v*) faint, debilitated; *antonyms* (*adj*) strong, vigorous, hearty, tough.

hrörleiki degeneracy; *synonyms* (*n*) corruption, decadence, depravity, degeneration, decline.

hrörna decay; *synonyms* (*n*) decline, decomposition, (*v*) rot, decompose, blight; *antonym* (*n*) growth.

hrörnandi carious; *synonyms* (*adj*) decayed, rotten, rancid, (*v*) peccant, purulent.

hrörnun 1. decay; *synonyms* (*n*) decline, decomposition, (*v*) rot, decompose, blight; *antonym* (*n*) growth, **2**. disintegration; *synonyms* (*n*) collapse, decay, breakdown, annihilation, breakup, **3**. degeneration; *synonyms* (*n*) corruption, degeneracy, abasement, decadence, degradation; *antonym* (*n*) improvement.

hross horse; *synonyms* (*n*) cavalry, mount, buck, heroin, junk.

hrossaraekja barnacle; *synonyms* (*n*) bernacle, cerriped, cerripede, hanger-on, parasite.

hrúður crust; *synonyms* (*n*) bark, cheekiness, covering, gall, (*v*) coat.

hrúðurkarl barnacle; *synonyms* (*n*) bernacle, cerriped, cerripede, hanger-on, parasite.

hrúðurkenndur crustaceous; *synonym* (*adj*) crustacean.

hrufl abrasion; *synonyms* (*n*) attrition, excoriation, erosion, friction, (*v*) detrition; *antonym* (*n*) smoothness.

hrufur fluting; *synonyms* (*n*) flute, groove, chamfer, furrow, channel.

hrúga 1. colony; *synonyms* (*n*) settlement, community, plantation, dependency, village, **2**. heap; *synonyms* (*n*) pile, stack, accumulation, (*v*) aggregate, bank.

hrúgald 1. agglomerate; *synonyms* (*v*) accumulate, (*n*) conglomerate, aggregate, (*adj*) agglomerated, agglomerative, **2**. conglomerate; *synonyms* (*n*) composite, group, complex, agglomerate, (*v*) amass.

hrun 1. collapse; *synonyms* (*n*) crash, breakdown, fall, (*v*) break, slump, **2**. implosion; *synonym* (*n*) failure.

hrunskriða talus; *synonyms* (*n*) astragalus, slope, scree, anklebone, astragal.

hrútur 1. ram; *synonyms* (*v*) beat, cram, crash, drive, jam, **2**. tup; *synonyms* (*n*) ram, buck, greenback, hob, (*v*) cover.

hryðja squall; *synonyms* (*n*) cry, gust, (*v*) shout, shriek, howl.

hryðjuverk terrorism; *synonyms* (*n*) disorder, murder, nihilism, tyranny, (*adj*) intimidation.

hryðjuverkastarfsemi terrorism; *synonyms* (*n*) disorder, murder, nihilism, tyranny, (*adj*) intimidation.

hryggdýr vertebrate; *synonyms* (*adj*) backboned, (*n*) mammal, vertebral, craniate, animal.

hrygglægur spinal; *synonyms* (*adj*) vertebral, rachidian, (*n*) anesthetic.

hrygglaus invertebrate; *synonyms* (*adj*) spineless, invertebrated, (*n*) animal, coward, weakling.

hryggleysingi invertebrate; *synonyms* (*adj*) spineless, invertebrated, (*n*) animal, coward, weakling.

hryggur 1. ridge; *synonyms* (*n*) crest, ledge, bank, hill, shelf, 2. spine; *synonyms* (*n*) backbone, thorn, point, prickle, quill, 3. back; *synonyms* (*n*) rear, (*adj*) assist, (*v*) support, advocate, endorse; *antonyms* (*n*) face, (*v*) front, oppose, advance, 4. backbone; *synonyms* (*n*) back, guts, strength, bottom, courage.

hrygna spawn; *synonyms* (*v*) engender, generate, (*n*) egg, offspring, breed.

hrylla 1. abhor; *synonyms* (*v*) loathe, detest, hate, abominate, execrate; *antonyms* (*v*) love, adore, 2. detest; *synonyms* (*v*) abhor, despise, dislike, nauseate, 3. abominate, 4. loathe; *synonym* (*v*) disgust.

hryllilegur 1. terrible; *synonyms* (*adj*) atrocious, dreadful, horrible, horrid, monstrous; *antonyms* (*adj*) wonderful, lovely, pleasant, 2. alarmed; *synonyms* (*adj*) afraid, scared, frightened, anxious, apprehensive, 3. dismayed; *synonyms* (*adj*) appalled, aghast, shocked, horrified, startled; *antonym* (*adj*) delighted, 4. abysmal; *synonyms* (*adj*) abyssal, deep, appalling, profound, terrible; *antonyms* (*adj*) excellent, exceptional, 5. abominable; *synonyms* (*adj*) hateful, abhorrent, odious, awful, detestable.

hryllingur horror; *synonyms* (*n*) awe, abomination, abhorrence, dismay, (*adj*) dread; *antonym* (*n*) pleasantness.

hrynja collapse; *synonyms* (*n*) crash, breakdown, fall, (*v*) break, slump.

hrynjandi 1. rhythm; *synonyms* (*n*) measure, cadence, meter, beat, pulse, 2. round; *synonyms* (*adv*) about, (*adj*) circular, (*n*) circle, bout, ring; *antonyms* (*adj*) slim, sharp, 3. cycle; *synonyms* (*n*) bicycle, round, (*v*) bike, motorcycle, wheel.

húð 1. skin; *synonyms* (*n*) peel, hide, coating, (*v*) pare, bark, 2. cuticle; *synonyms* (*n*) epidermis, shell, carapace, case, casing, 3. integument; *synonyms* (*n*) cover, film, coat, skin, tegument.

húða 1. render; *synonyms* (*v*) afford, interpret, explain, furnish, give, 2. encapsulate; *synonyms* (*v*) condense, capsule, capsulize, recap, recapitulate.

húðangur pellagra; *synonym* (*n*) maidism.

húðbeðslyf hypodermic; *synonyms* (*adj*) subcutaneous, hypodermatic, (*n*) hypo, syringe, needle.

húðbeðssprauta hypodermic; *synonyms* (*adj*) subcutaneous, hypodermatic, (*n*) hypo, syringe, needle.

húðbruni scald; *synonyms* (*v*) burn, cook, scorch, boil, (*n*) blister.

húdd bonnet; *synonyms* (*n*) hood, cap, tile, wimple, castor.

húðdrafna macule; *synonyms* (*n*) macula, smudge, mackle, sunspot.

húðkröm pellagra; *synonym* (*n*) maidism.

húðlögur lotion; *synonyms* (*n*) ointment, wash, balm, application, cerate.

húðskæni lichen; *synonym* (*n*) mold.

húðskæningur lichen; *synonym* (*n*) mold.

húðþekja epidermis; *synonyms* (*n*) cuticle, scarfskin, skin, carapace, coat.

húðun encapsulation; *synonyms* (*n*) packaging, entrapment.

hugarburður fantasy; *synonyms* (*n*) dream, fancy, illusion, delusion, mirage; *antonyms* (*n*) reality, (*adj*) real.

hugarfar mentality; *synonyms* (*n*) brain, intelligence, intellect, wit, brainpower.

hugarflug 1. brainstorming, 2. fantasy; *synonyms* (*n*) dream, fancy, illusion, delusion, mirage; *antonyms* (*n*) reality, (*adj*) real.

hugarmisræmi dissonance; *synonyms* (*n*) discord, discrepancy, disharmony, disaccord, disagreement; *antonym* (*n*) harmony.

hugarró sedation; *synonyms* (*n*) drugging, moderation.

hugarstarf cognition; *synonyms* (*n*) knowledge, perception, cognizance, conception, cognoscence.

hugarsýn visualization; *synonyms* (*n*) visualisation, image, fancy, idea, imagination.

hugboð anticipation; *synonyms* (*n*) expectation, forecast, hope, foresight, (*v*) outlook; *antonym* (*n*) despair.

hugbúnaður software; *synonyms* (*n*) bundle, package, packet, parcel, ware.

hugð sentiment; *synonyms* (*n*) idea, emotion, feeling, mind, notion.

hugðarefni interest; *synonyms* (*n*) concern, advantage, affair, (*v*) engage, care; *antonyms* (*n*) indifference, apathy, (*v*) bore.

hugerni mentality; *synonyms* (*n*) brain, intelligence, intellect, wit, brainpower.

hugga 1. comfort; *synonyms* (*n*) solace, ease, consolation, (*v*) allay, assuage; *antonyms* (*n*) discomfort, aggravation, (*v*) alarm, annoy, frighten, **2**. console; *synonyms* (*n*) cabinet, (*v*) comfort, cheer, soothe, quiet.

huggrip apperception; *synonyms* (*n*) comprehension, conception, identification, mind, recognition.

huggun 1. solace; *synonyms* (*n*) comfort, consolation, ease, (*v*) cheer, console, **2**. consolation; *synonyms* (*n*) solace, relief, balm, succor, encouragement, **3**. comfort; *synonyms* (*n*) aid, amenity, (*v*) allay, assuage, alleviate; *antonyms* (*n*) discomfort, aggravation, (*v*) alarm, annoy, frighten.

hughvarf conversion; *synonyms* (*n*) alteration, change, changeover, adaptation, exchange.

hughyggja idealism; *synonyms* (*n*) impracticality, immaterialism, delusion, dream, fantasy; *antonyms* (*n*) realism, reality.

hugjórtur rumination; *synonyms* (*n*) contemplation, reflection, consideration, musing, meditation.

hugkleyfur schizoid; *synonyms* (*adj*) schizophrenic, demented, hebephrenic, lunatic, (*n*) maniac.

huglægi subjectivity; *synonym* (*n*) subjectiveness.

huglægni subjectivity; *synonym* (*n*) subjectiveness.

huglægur subjective; *synonyms* (*adj*) mental, biased, internal, objective, immanent; *antonym* (*adj*) impartial.

huglag subject; *synonyms* (*n*) matter, citizen, affair, (*adj*) liable, exposed; *antonym* (*adj*) liberated.

hugleiða contemplate; *synonyms* (*v*) consider, cogitate, meditate, muse, speculate.

hugleiðsla meditation; *synonyms* (*n*) cogitation, consideration, contemplation, reflection, deliberation.

hugljómun illumination; *synonyms* (*n*) brightness, clarification, illuminance, light, elucidation.

hugmynd 1. project; *synonyms* (*n*) design, device, (*v*) plan, hurl, contrive, **2**. assumption; *synonyms* (*n*) presumption, supposition, hypothesis, premise, adoption, **3**. inspiration; *synonyms* (*n*) afflatus, infusion, breath, encouragement, (*v*) illumination, **4**. image; *synonyms* (*n*) figure, picture, fancy, conception, effigy, **5**. idea; *synonyms* (*n*) belief, concept, meaning, opinion, apprehension.

hugmyndafræði ideology; *synonyms* (*n*) philosophy, belief, theory, opinion, approach.

hugmyndakerfi ideology; *synonyms* (*n*) philosophy, belief, theory, opinion, approach.

hugmyndasaga ideology; *synonyms* (*n*) philosophy, belief, theory, opinion, approach.

hugmyndasmiðja workshop; *synonyms* (*n*) shop, factory, studio, workhouse, atelier.

hugrænn 1. subjective; *synonyms* (*adj*) mental, biased, internal, objective, immanent; *antonym* (*adj*) impartial, **2**. abstract; *synonyms* (*adj*) theoretical, (*v*) abridge, (*n*) synopsis, abridgement, digest; *antonym* (*adj*) concrete, **3**. cognitive; *synonyms* (*adj*) psychological, rational, reasonable.

hugríki fantasy; *synonyms* (*n*) dream, fancy, illusion, delusion, mirage; *antonyms* (*n*) reality, (*adj*) real.

hugrof dissociation; *synonyms* (*n*) disintegration, divorce, disassociation, separation, distancing.

hugrríki fantasy; *synonyms* (*n*) dream, fancy, illusion, delusion, mirage; *antonyms* (*n*) reality, (*adj*) real.

hugsa think; *synonyms* (*v*) consider, believe, reckon, estimate, guess; *antonym* (*v*) forget.

hugsæi intuition; *synonyms* (*n*) feeling, hunch, insight, instinct, notion.

hugsanasamhengi coherence; *synonyms* (*n*) consistency, comprehensibility, agreement, clarity, coherency; *antonym* (*n*) incoherence.

hugsjón ideal; *synonyms* (*adj*) fanciful, perfect, consummate, (*n*) model, paragon.

hugsjónastefna idealism; *synonyms* (*n*) impracticality, immaterialism, delusion, dream, fantasy; *antonyms* (*n*) realism, reality.

hugsjúkur neurotic; *synonyms* (*adj*) nervous, unstable, jittery, disturbed, excitable; *antonym* (*adj*) modern.

hugsmíð construct; *synonyms* (*v*) make, build, compose, erect, fabricate; *antonyms* (*v*) destroy, demolish.

hugstol stupor; *synonyms* (*n*) daze, lethargy, stupefaction, coma, shock.

hugstola stuporous; *synonyms* (*adj*) dazed, foggy, groggy, hazy, logy.

hugsun 1. thought; *synonyms* (*n*) notion, idea, opinion, conception, consideration; *antonym* (*n*) fact, **2**. sentiment; *synonyms* (*n*) emotion, feeling, mind, judgement, judgment, **3**. thinking; *synonyms* (*adj*) intelligent, thoughtful, (*n*) thought, reasoning, intellection.

hugsýki neurosis; *synonyms* (*n*) breakdown, complex, fixation, insanity, neuroticism.

hugsýn imagery; *synonyms* (*n*) imagination, imaging, portraiture, images, (*adj*) image.

hugsýnn intuitive; *synonyms* (*adj*) instinctive, inborn, innate, automatic, impulsive.

hugtak 1. term; *synonyms* (*n*) name, expression, period, style, (*v*) call, **2**. concept; *synonyms* (*n*) conception, notion, belief, idea, theory.

hugtakabók thesaurus; *synonyms* (*n*) glossary, lexicon, treasury, book, list.

hugtakalíkan construct; *synonyms* (v) make, build, compose, erect, fabricate; *antonyms* (v) destroy, demolish.

hugtakamyndun conception; *synonyms* (n) notion, concept, idea, creation, thought; *antonym* (n) misconception.

hugtakasafn thesaurus; *synonyms* (n) glossary, lexicon, treasury, book, list.

hugtenging association; *synonyms* (n) affiliation, alliance, connection, assembly, affinity.

hugtengsl association; *synonyms* (n) affiliation, alliance, connection, assembly, affinity.

hugur mind; *synonyms* (n) intellect, (v) care, look, attend, (adj) heed; *antonym* (v) forget.

hugvíkkandi psychedelic; *synonyms* (adj) colorful, bright, consciousness-expanding, crazy, experimental.

hugvilla delusion; *synonyms* (n) illusion, hallucination, deception, cheat, chimera; *antonyms* (n) reality, comprehension.

hula 1. theca; *synonyms* (n) sheath, case, casing, sac, vagina, 2. sheath; *synonyms* (n) envelope, blanket, scabbard, skin, (v) cover, 3. tegument; *synonyms* (n) integument, cutis, coat, rind, cloth, 4. mask; *synonyms* (n) conceal, veil, (v) cloak, disguise, hide; *antonym* (v) disclose, 5. integument; *synonyms* (n) film, tegument, shell, tunic, outside.

hulinn latent; *synonyms* (adj) covert, potential, secret, dormant, hidden; *antonym* (adj) active.

hulstur 1. cassette; *synonyms* (n) tape, copy, demo, footage, record, 2. case; *synonyms* (n) box, example, bin, cover, jacket.

humall hop; *synonyms* (n) jump, leap, bound, (v) dance, gambol.

húmanismi humanism; *synonyms* (n) humanitarianism, culture.

húmus humus; *synonyms* (n) hummus, compost, hommos, hoummos, humous.

hunang honey; *synonyms* (n) darling, dear, beloved, love, sweetheart.

hundaæði rabies; *synonyms* (n) hydrophobia, madness, lyssa, fury, (adj) mania.

hundabitsæði rabies; *synonyms* (n) hydrophobia, madness, lyssa, fury, (adj) mania.

hundrað hundred; *synonyms* (n) century, cent, centred, lathe, riding.

hundraðshlutamark 1. centile; *synonym* (n) percentile, 2. percentile; *synonym* (n) centile.

hundraðshluti 1. rate; *synonyms* (n) price, worth, (v) assess, estimate, evaluate, 2. percentile; *synonym* (n) centile, 3. percentage; *synonyms* (n) part, share, cut, lot, percent.

hundraðsmark percentile; *synonym* (n) centile.

hundraðstala percentage; *synonyms* (n) part, share, cut, lot, percent.

hundsa 1. disregard; *synonyms* (n) carelessness, contempt, (v) neglect, disdain, discount; *antonyms* (n) respect, (v) notice, regard, 2. override; *synonyms* (v) overrule, trample, annul, overreach, countermand.

hundsspor psoriasis; *synonyms* (n) itch, leucoplakia.

hundur 1. dog; *synonyms* (n) cur, andiron, (v) chase, hound, beset, 2. hound; *synonyms* (n) dog, (v) bloodhound, hunt, badger, course.

hungur 1. starvation; *synonyms* (n) hunger, inanition, famine, famishment, starving, 2. hunger; *synonyms* (n) desire, thirst, appetite, craving, (v) crave; *antonym* (n) moderation.

huppur flank; *synonyms* (n) edge, side, wing, (v) border, skirt.

hurai cheer; *synonyms* (v) encourage, animate, applaud, amuse, comfort; *antonyms* (v) dishearten, depress, (n) sadness.

hurð door; *synonyms* (n) gate, threshold, access, doorway, entrance; *antonym* (n) exit.

hurðarstýring dovetail; *synonyms* (v) anastomose, fit, mesh, (adj) mortise, enchase.

hús 1. shell; *synonyms* (n) peel, rind, bullet, case, (v) bomb, 2. case; *synonyms* (n) box, example, bin, cover, jacket, 3. body; *synonyms* (n) cadaver, corpse, matter, organization, carcass; *antonym* (n) spirit, 4. casing; *synonyms* (n) shell, skin, boxing, holder, coating, 5. nacelle; *synonym* (n) basket.

hùs house; *synonyms* (n) family, home, dwelling, firm, (v) accommodate.

húsasamstæða block; *synonyms* (n) bar, barricade, pad, (v) arrest, stop; *antonyms* (v) free, unblock, open.

húsaþyrping settlement; *synonyms* (n) decision, accommodation, colony, hamlet, payment.

húseign building; *synonyms* (n) architecture, establishment, construction, fabric, (v) edifice.

húsgafl gable; *synonyms* (n) gavel, cable, coping, toll, tribute.

húsleit search; *synonyms* (n) hunt, pursuit, examination, exploration, (v) grope.

húsnæði housing; *synonyms* (n) habitation, casing, dwelling, lodging, abode; *antonym* (adj) business.

húsnúmer number; *synonyms* (n) count, amount, (v) calculate, aggregate, enumerate.

húsrannsókn search; *synonyms* (n) hunt, pursuit, examination, exploration, (v) grope.

hússtyrja beluga; *synonym* (n) hausen.

hústökumaður squatter; *synonyms* (n) settler, homesteader, intruder, nester, resident.

hvað how; *synonyms* *(adv)* whereby, however, whence, nevertheless, nonetheless.

hvaðan whence; *synonyms* *(adv)* wherefrom, because, for, hence, then.

hvalambur spermaceti; *synonyms* *(n)* paraffin, sperm.

hvalsauki spermaceti; *synonyms* *(n)* paraffin, sperm.

hvalskutull harpoon; *synonyms* *(n)* dart, javelin, lance, spear, striker.

hvalspik blubber; *synonyms* *(n)* cry, fat, *(v)* sob, weep, bawl.

hvaltennur ivory; *synonyms* *(n)* bone, tusk, dentin, elephant, *(adj)* chalk.

hvalur whale; *synonyms* *(n)* giant, monster, behemoth, *(v)* thrash, beat.

hvalveiðar whaling; *synonyms* *(adj)* giant, gigantic.

hvapholda flabby; *synonyms* *(adj)* loose, feeble, flaccid, baggy, drooping; *antonyms* *(adj)* firm, slim.

hvar where; *synonyms* *(adv)* there, here, wherever, whither, anywhere.

hvarf 1. reaction; *synonyms* *(n)* answer, response, backlash, reply, effect, **2**. process; *synonyms* *(n)* operation, proceeding, method, procedure, *(v)* action, **3**. bunker; *synonyms* *(n)* bin, dugout, trap, ambuscade, ambush, **4**. immersion; *synonyms* *(n)* dip, absorption, ducking, concentration, submergence.

hvarfafræði kinetics; *synonym* *(n)* dynamics.

hvarfast react; *synonyms* *(v)* answer, respond, act, oppose, recoil; *antonym* *(v)* ignore.

hvarfbaugur tropic; *synonyms* *(adj)* tropical, hot, torrid.

hvarfefni 1. substrate; *synonyms* *(n)* substratum, ground, feedstock, **2**. reactant; *synonym* *(n)* catalyst.

hvarffræði kinetics; *synonym* *(n)* dynamics.

hvarfgjarn reactive; *synonyms* *(adj)* sensitive, responsive, receptive, approachable, hasty.

hvarfhraðafræði kinetics; *synonym* *(n)* dynamics.

hvarfi reactor; *synonym* *(n)* stator.

hvarfl 1. dithering; *synonyms* *(n)* faltering, indecision, *(adj)* wavering, hesitant, indecisive; *antonym* *(n)* decisiveness, **2**. fading; *synonyms* *(adj)* dying, disappearing, paling, *(n)* attenuation, bleaching; *antonym* *(n)* appearance.

hvarftregur inactive; *synonyms* *(adj)* idle, dead, dormant, dull, inert; *antonyms* *(adj)* active, lively, moving.

hvarmur eyelid; *synonyms* *(n)* lid, chapeau, palpebra, hat.

hvass sharp; *synonyms* *(adj)* acute, bitter, intelligent, acid, *(n)* keen; *antonyms* *(adj)* blunt, dull, mild, gentle, rounded.

hvassleiki 1. sharpness; *synonyms* *(n)* acuteness, keenness, severity, asperity, bitterness; *antonym* *(n)* sweetness, **2**. poignancy; *synonyms* *(n)* pathos, acerbity, poignance, acrimony, harshness, **3**. acrimony; *synonyms* *(n)* acridity, gall, pique, tartness, virulence, **4**. acerbity; *synonyms* *(n)* austerity, huff, *(adj)* petulance, **5**. acuity; *synonyms* *(n)* sharpness, acumen, discernment, awareness, *(adj)* acumination.

hvassviðri gale; *synonyms* *(n)* blast, blow, gust, hurricane, squall.

hvatamaður initiator; *synonyms* *(n)* creator, originator, author, founder, father.

hvatberi mitochondrion; *synonym* *(n)* chondriosome.

hvati 1. stimulus; *synonyms* *(n)* incentive, encouragement, provocation, spur, motivation, **2**. catalyst; *synonyms* *(n)* accelerator, goad, stimulus, impulse, **3**. incentive; *synonyms* *(n)* impetus, cause, motive, fillip, inspiration; *antonyms* *(n)* deterrent, disincentive, constraint.

hvatning 1. stimulus; *synonyms* *(n)* incentive, encouragement, provocation, spur, motivation, **2**. prompt; *synonyms* *(adj)* agile, quick, nimble, *(v)* actuate, incite; *antonyms* *(adj)* slow, late, **3**. motivation; *synonyms* *(n)* motive, impulse, cause, reason, impetus, **4**. incentive; *synonyms* *(n)* goad, stimulus, fillip, inspiration, whip; *antonyms* *(n)* deterrent, disincentive, constraint.

hvatvís impulsive; *synonyms* *(adj)* impetuous, capricious, hasty, driving, rash; *antonyms* *(adj)* cautious, considered, predictable.

hveiti wheat; *synonyms* *(n)* corn, clavus, maize, *(adj)* golden.

hvekkskjatti utricle; *synonyms* *(n)* vesicle, calyx, cancelli, capsule, cyst.

hvel 1. shell; *synonyms* *(n)* peel, rind, bullet, case, *(v)* bomb, **2**. sphere; *synonyms* *(n)* region, range, area, domain, province, **3**. dome; *synonyms* *(n)* cupola, arch, roof, cover, bean, **4**. hemisphere; *synonyms* *(n)* realm, sphere, ground, orb, quarter, **5**. orb; *synonyms* *(n)* ball, globe, cycle, circle, circuit.

hvelaheili cerebrum; *synonyms* *(n)* brain, pate, cranium, sconce, noddle.

hvelfdur concave; *synonyms* *(adj)* hollow, cavernous, crescent, biconcave, cupped; *antonyms* *(adj)* convex, curved.

hvelfing concavity; *synonyms* *(n)* concaveness, hollow, dent, basin, hole.

hveljur jellyfish; *synonyms* *(n)* medusan, coward, hydromedusae, *(adj)* apprehensive, frightened.

hvelkápa pallium; *synonyms* *(n)* mantle, pall, cortex, gown, robe.

hvellhetta detonator; *synonyms* (*n*) cap, explosive, capital, ceiling, chapter.

hvellur 1. sharp; *synonyms* (*adj*) acute, bitter, intelligent, acid, (*n*) keen; *antonyms* (*adj*) blunt, dull, mild, gentle, rounded, **2.** snappy; *synonyms* (*adj*) racy, sharp, animated, brisk, crisp, **3.** strident; *synonyms* (*adj*) raucous, loud, blatant, harsh, noisy; *antonyms* (*adj*) soft, quiet, **4.** shrill; *synonyms* (*adj*) piercing, penetrating, (*v*) high, screech, shriek; *antonym* (*adj*) low, **5.** acrid; *synonyms* (*adj*) pungent, acerbic, caustic, acerb, corrosive; *antonym* (*adj*) sweet.

hvenær 1. when; *synonyms* (*adv*) as, once, then, (*conj*) although, while, **2.** as; *synonyms* (*conj*) qua, because, (*prep*) during, like, (*n*) arsenic.

hver who; *synonyms* (*pron*) one, (*adj*) which, what.

hverfa 1. isomer; *synonym* (*n*) isomeride, **2.** invert; *synonyms* (*v*) reverse, change, transpose, capsize, overturn.

hverfandi negligible; *synonyms* (*adj*) inconsequential, insignificant, trifling, marginal, minor; *antonym* (*adj*) significant.

hverfi 1. precinct; *synonyms* (*n*) district, area, region, limit, bound, **2.** district; *synonyms* (*n*) quarter, community, neighborhood, territory, (*adj*) local.

hverfilblásari fan; *synonyms* (*n*) admirer, buff, devotee, enthusiast, (*v*) air; *antonym* (*n*) detractor.

hverfilbylur cyclone; *synonyms* (*n*) hurricane, storm, tempest, tornado, gale.

hverfileggur radius; *synonyms* (*n*) length, semidiameter, spoke, range, compass.

hverfill 1. turbine; *synonyms* (*n*) propeller, screw, **2.** impeller; *synonyms* (*n*) runner, pump.

hverfing inversion; *synonyms* (*n*) antithesis, reversal, transposition, anastrophe, eversion.

hverfisenditilboð polling; *synonyms* (*n*) ballot, election.

hverfisteinn 1. whetstone; *synonyms* (*n*) rub, caoutchouc, chance, failing, (*adj*) grindstone, **2.** grindstone; *synonyms* (*v*) grinder, mill, arrastra, file, grater.

hverflyndur labile; *synonym* (*adj*) unstable.

hverfull transitory; *synonyms* (*adj*) passing, transient, brief, fleeting, momentary; *antonym* (*adj*) permanent.

hverfulleiki volatility; *synonyms* (*n*) fickleness, instability, flightiness, buoyancy, capriciousness.

hvergi nowhere; *synonyms* (*adv*) minus, nowhither, (*adj*) tiresome, average, banal.

hverna cavern; *synonyms* (*n*) cave, hollow, cove, hole, vault.

hvernig 1. how; *synonyms* (*adv*) whereby, however, whence, nevertheless, nonetheless, **2.** as; *synonyms* (*conj*) qua, because, (*prep*) during, like, (*n*)

arsenic, **3.** like; *synonyms* (*v*) corresponding, enjoy, (*adj*) equal, equivalent, alike; *antonyms* (*prep*) unlike, (*v*) dislike, (*adj*) different.

hvert where; *synonyms* (*adv*) there, here, wherever, whither, anywhere.

hvessa 1. sharpen; *synonyms* (*v*) focus, edge, hone, intensify, point; *antonym* (*v*) cloud, **2.** whet; *synonyms* (*v*) sharpen, excite, grind, quicken, stimulate.

hvetja 1. prompt; *synonyms* (*adj*) agile, quick, nimble, (*v*) actuate, incite; *antonyms* (*adj*) slow, late, **2.** catalyze; *synonyms* (*v*) mobilize, catalyse.

hviða 1. beat; *synonyms* (*v*) batter, flap, (*n*) pulse, thump, knock; *antonym* (*v*) lose, **2.** gust; *synonyms* (*n*) burst, eruption, flurry, blast, blow, **3.** fit; *synonyms* (*v*) agree, accommodate, meet, suit, (*adj*) decorous; *antonyms* (*adj*) unfit, inappropriate, unwell.

hvik flutter; *synonyms* (*n*) bustle, flap, (*v*) flicker, beat, (*adj*) flurry.

hviklyndi volatility; *synonyms* (*n*) fickleness, instability, flightiness, buoyancy, capriciousness.

hvikull chaotic; *synonyms* (*adj*) disorderly, confused, disorganized, hectic, messy; *antonyms* (*adj*) neat, orderly, organized.

hvikulleiki chaos; *synonyms* (*n*) anarchy, bedlam, clutter, disarray, disorder; *antonyms* (*n*) order, peace, orderliness, regulation.

hvílandi idle; *synonyms* (*adj*) inactive, indolent, lazy, free, baseless; *antonyms* (*adj*) busy, active, employed, (*v*) change.

hvíldarástand marking; *synonyms* (*n*) mark, earmark, brand, crisscross, marker.

hvíldarland fallow; *synonyms* (*adj*) barren, dormant, uncultivated, yellow, aureate.

hvilft 1. sinus; *synonyms* (*n*) cavity, fistula, pit, indentation, dent, **2.** cirque; *synonyms* (*n*) circle, corrie, cwm.

hvirfilbylur 1. tornado; *synonyms* (*n*) hurricane, storm, tempest, gale, cyclone, **2.** typhoon; *synonyms* (*n*) tornado, squall, whirlwind, **3.** cyclone.

hvirfill 1. vortex; *synonyms* (*n*) eddy, swirl, whirlpool, convolution, maelstrom, **2.** whirl; *synonyms* (*n*) turn, wheel, (*v*) spin, twirl, roll, **3.** eddy; *synonyms* (*n*) vortex, gurge, twist, (*v*) whirl, purl.

hvirfilpunktur zenith; *synonyms* (*n*) apex, peak, top, acme, climax; *antonyms* (*n*) nadir, base.

hvirfilvindur whirlwind; *synonyms* (*n*) hurricane, storm, tornado, twister, gale.

hvirfing whorl; *synonyms* (*n*) curl, coil, spiral, gyre, helix.

hvísla whisper; *synonyms* (*n*) buzz, hum, (*v*) murmur, breathe, mumble; *antonym* (*v*) shout.

hviss hiss; *synonyms* (*n*) buzz, hoot, jeer, (*v*) boo, fizz.

hvíta 1. protein; *synonyms* (*n*) cytoplasm, (*adj*) albumen, gluten, glair, cream, **2**. sclera, **3**. sclerotic; *synonyms* (*adj*) sclerosed, hard, sclerous, hardened, indurated, **4**. albumen; *synonyms* (*n*) albumin, ovalbumin, (*adj*) milk, starch.

hvítagull platinum; *synonyms* (*n*) platina, blonde.

hvítblæði leukemia; *synonyms* (*n*) leukaemia, (*adj*) cancer, carcinoma, malignancy, tumor.

hvítfruma leukocyte; *synonym* (*n*) leucocyte.

hvítfrumnafæð leukopenia; *synonym* (*n*) leucopenia.

hvítfrumnafjölgun leukocytosis; *synonyms* (*n*) leucocytosis, hyperleukocytosis.

hvítfrumnaskortur leukopenia; *synonym* (*n*) leucopenia.

hvítfrumufæð leukopenia; *synonym* (*n*) leucopenia.

hvítingi albino; *synonyms* (*n*) blonde, (*v*) blinkard.

hvítingseðli albinism; *synonym* (*n*) albinoism.

hvítingur albino; *synonyms* (*n*) blonde, (*v*) blinkard.

hvítkál cabbage; *synonyms* (*n*) kale, (*v*) pilfer, filch, crib, nim.

hvítkorn leukocyte; *synonym* (*n*) leucocyte.

hvítkornafæð leukopenia; *synonym* (*n*) leucopenia.

hvítkornafjölgun leukocytosis; *synonyms* (*n*) leucocytosis, hyperleukocytosis.

hvítkornaútstreymi emigration; *synonyms* (*n*) departure, exodus, migration, demigration, (*v*) intermigration.

hvítsveppasýking candidiasis; *synonyms* (*n*) candidosis, moniliasis.

Hvítt white; *synonyms* (*adj*) fair, ashen, blank, clean, (*n*) pale; *antonyms* (*adj*) dark, rosy, (*n*) black.

hvítukljúfur protease; *synonyms* (*n*) proteinase, peptidase.

hvítulíkur albuminoid; *synonym* (*n*) scleroprotein.

hvítur 1. white; *synonyms* (*adj*) fair, ashen, blank, clean, (*n*) pale; *antonyms* (*adj*) dark, rosy, (*n*) black, **2**. blank; *synonyms* (*adj*) bare, empty, unfilled, vacant, (*n*) space; *antonyms* (*adj*) animated, full, expressive.

hvítuskurður lobotomy; *synonyms* (*n*) leukotomy, leucotomy.

hvítviður whitewood; *synonyms* (*n*) tulipwood, abele.

hvolf 1. sphere; *synonyms* (*n*) region, range, area, domain, province, **2**. ventricle; *synonyms* (*n*) paunch, stomach, venter, heart, **3**. dome; *synonyms* (*n*) cupola, arch, roof, cover, bean.

hvolfstóll drum; *synonyms* (*n*) barrel, cask, tympan, (*v*) beat, roll.

hvolfþak dome; *synonyms* (*n*) cupola, arch, roof, cover, bean.

hvoreind neutron; *synonym* (*n*) electricity.

hvörf 1. reaction; *synonyms* (*n*) answer, response, backlash, reply, effect, **2**. process; *synonyms* (*n*) operation, proceeding, method, procedure, (*v*) action.

hvöt 1. drive; *synonyms* (*n*) ride, force, campaign, (*v*) push, actuate; *antonyms* (*n*) apathy, inertia, **2**. incentive; *synonyms* (*n*) encouragement, impetus, cause, goad, impulse; *antonyms* (*n*) deterrent, disincentive, constraint.

hvötun catalysis; *synonyms* (*n*) dissolution, analysis, decomposition, dissection, resolution.

hýði 1. capsule; *synonyms* (*n*) abridgement, lozenge, condensation, pill, (*v*) encapsulate, **2**. peel; *synonyms* (*n*) skin, hide, (*v*) hull, bark, flake.

hýðisaldin capsule; *synonyms* (*n*) abridgement, lozenge, condensation, pill, (*v*) encapsulate.

hýdrat hydrate; *synonym* (*n*) hydroxide.

hýdríð hydride; *synonyms* (*n*) hydroguret, hydruret.

hýdrókortísón cortisol; *synonym* (*n*) hydrocortisone.

hýdrókortísón hydrocortisone; *synonym* (*n*) cortisol.

hýdroxíð hydroxide; *synonym* (*n*) hydrate.

hyggja conception; *synonyms* (*n*) notion, concept, idea, creation, thought; *antonym* (*n*) misconception.

hyldýpi 1. precipice; *synonyms* (*n*) cliff, steep, verge, clef, crevice, **2**. chasm; *synonyms* (*n*) abyss, breach, gap, gulf, hiatus, **3**. abyss; *synonyms* (*n*) abysm, chasm, deep, gorge, ravine, **4**. gulf; *synonyms* (*n*) bay, cove, inlet, pit, rift.

hylja 1. protect; *synonyms* (*v*) defend, keep, cover, preserve, (*n*) guard; *antonyms* (*v*) attack, expose, neglect, risk, **2**. cover; *synonyms* (*v*) coat, conceal, top, bury, (*n*) blind; *antonyms* (*v*) reveal, uncover, **3**. mask; *synonyms* (*v*) veil, camouflage, (*v*) cloak, disguise, hide; *antonym* (*v*) disclose, **4**. obscure; *synonyms* (*adj*) cloudy, dim, dark, gloomy, ambiguous; *antonyms* (*adj*) clear, noticeable, simple, obvious, (*v*) clarify.

hylki 1. receiver; *synonyms* (*n*) recipient, beneficiary, cashier, earpiece, headset; *antonym* (*n*) donor, **2**. tank; *synonyms* (*n*) cistern, reservoir, container, cooler, belly, **3**. canister; *synonyms* (*n*) can, cannister, case, tin, drum, **4**. bulb; *synonyms* (*n*) knob, lightbulb, corm, nodule, (*adj*) globule, **5**. casing; *synonyms* (*n*) shell, box, jacket, skin, boxing.

hylla shelf; *synonyms* (*n*) ledge, rack, bank, flat, projection.

hyrna process; *synonyms* (*n*) operation, proceeding, method, procedure, (*v*) action.

hyrndur angular; *synonyms* (adj) angulate, bony, gaunt, lean, skinny; *antonym* (adj) rounded.

hyrni keratin; *synonyms* (n) ceratin, epidermose.

hyrningur polygon; *synonym* (n) square.

hyrnishúðun keratinization; *synonym* (n) keratinisation.

hyrnismyndun keratinization; *synonym* (n) keratinisation.

hýsill host; *synonyms* (n) crowd, army, flock, horde, mob.

hýsing outsourcing; *synonym* (n) relocation.

I

i 1. a; *synonyms* (n) amp, ampere, angstrom, axerophthol, (adj) cream, **2.** in; *synonyms* (prep) during, between, by, through, (adj) stylish; *antonyms* (prep) out, outside, **3.** on; *synonyms* (prep) at, about, concerning, (adj) forward, (prf) along; *antonym* (adv) off, **4.** inside; *synonyms* (n) interior, middle, (adj) inner, internal, indoor; *antonyms* (n) exterior, (adj) free.

iða 1. squirm; *synonyms* (v) wiggle, wriggle, twist, fidget, writhe, **2.** turbulence; *synonyms* (n) disorder, tumult, confusion, agitation, commotion; *antonyms* (n) calm, peace, **3.** vortex; *synonyms* (n) eddy, swirl, whirlpool, convolution, maelstrom, **4.** whirl; *synonyms* (n) turn, wheel, (v) spin, twirl, roll, **5.** cavitation.

iðgjald premium; *synonyms* (n) bonus, agio, bounty, payment, extra; *antonym* (adj) inferior.

iðja occupation; *synonyms* (n) employment, occupancy, business, craft, calling; *antonym* (n) surrender.

iðjulaus idle; *synonyms* (adj) inactive, indolent, lazy, free, baseless; *antonyms* (adj) busy, active, employed, (v) change.

iðjuver factory; *synonyms* (n) manufactory, mill, plant, business, shop.

iðkun practice; *synonyms* (n) exercise, fashion, convention, (v) custom, drill; *antonym* (n) performance.

iðn trade; *synonyms* (n) deal, business, barter, commerce, (v) change; *antonyms* (n) purchase, (adj) charitable.

iðnaður 1. industry; *synonyms* (n) business, application, diligence, effort, industriousness, **2.** manufacturing; *synonyms* (adj) industrial, (n) output, production, engineering, trade.

iðnbúskapur agribusiness; *synonyms* (n) agriculture, agrobusiness, farming, husbandry.

iðnframleiðsla 1. manufacturing; *synonyms* (adj) industrial, (n) output, production, business, engineering, **2.** manufacture; *synonyms* (n) construction, fabrication, formation, (v) construct, make.

iðngrein 1. trade; *synonyms* (n) deal, business, barter, commerce, (v) change; *antonyms* (n) purchase, (adj) charitable, **2.** industry; *synonyms* (n) application, diligence, effort, industriousness, labor.

iðnnámstími apprenticeship; *synonyms* (n) education, instruction, apprenticeage, apprenticehood, prenticeship.

iðnnemi apprentice; *synonyms* (n) learner, beginner, greenhorn, novice, prentice.

iðnvæðing industrialization; *synonym* (n) industrialisation.

iðrahreyfing peristalsis; *synonym* (n) vermiculation.

iðrakveisa colic; *synonyms* (n) bellyache, mulligrubs, enteralgia, cramp, heartburn.

iðramjólkuræð lacteal; *synonyms* (adj) lacteous, milky, lactean, (n) lactiferous.

iðraskynfæri interoceptor; *synonym* (n) enteroceptor.

iðrast regret; *synonyms* (v) bewail, grieve, bemoan, (n) grief, compunction.

iðraverkir cramp; *synonyms* (n) convulsion, spasm, (v) confine, constrict, restrict.

iðuhitun convection; *synonyms* (n) transfer, (adj) thermal.

iðumyndun turbulence; *synonyms* (n) disorder, tumult, confusion, agitation, commotion; *antonyms* (n) calm, peace.

iður viscera; *synonyms* (n) entrails, bowels, innards, intestines, guts.

iðustraumur eddy; *synonyms* (n) spin, twirl, vortex, (v) whirl, purl.

iðustreymi turbulence; *synonyms* (n) disorder, tumult, confusion, agitation, commotion; *antonyms* (n) calm, peace.

ikta fluke; *synonyms* (n) chance, luck, trematode, accident, coincidence.

il sole; *synonyms* (adj) lone, single, singular, one, (n) bottom.

ildi oxygen; *synonym* (n) o.

iljarsvæði sole; *synonyms* (adj) lone, single, singular, one, (n) bottom.

illgresi weed; *synonyms* (n) grass, marijuana, pot, (v) rake, eliminate.

illgresiseyðir herbicide; *synonym* (n) weedkiller.

illkynja malignant; *synonyms* (adj) malign, malevolent, evil, malicious, malefic.

illkynjaður 1. pernicious; *synonyms* (adj) detrimental, evil, bad, fatal, injurious, **2.**

malignant; *synonyms* (*adj*) malign, malevolent, malicious, malefic, mischievous.

illskeytahríð flame; *synonyms* (*n*) blaze, fire, ardour, (*v*) burn, flash.

illur 1. poor; *synonyms* (*adj*) bad, low, miserable, paltry, (*v*) meager; *antonyms* (*adj*) rich, wealthy, excellent, first-rate, privileged, **2.** bad; *synonyms* (*adj*) evil, adverse, harmful, immoral, (*v*) decayed; *antonyms* (*adj*) fresh, pleasant, well, well-behaved, (*n*) good, **3.** nasty; *synonyms* (*adj*) dirty, loathsome, disgusting, filthy, foul; *antonyms* (*adj*) agreeable, kind, nice, charitable, lovely, **4.** miserable; *synonyms* (*adj*) mean, poor, abject, (*v*) forlorn, wretched; *antonyms* (*adj*) happy, cheerful, generous, **5.** evil; *synonyms* (*adj*) corrupt, criminal, ill, wicked, (*n*) damage; *antonyms* (*adj*) kindhearted, (*n*) goodness, righteousness.

illviðri 1. weather; *synonyms* (*v*) endure, survive, resist, withstand, brave, **2.** storm; *synonyms* (*n*) tempest, attack, (*v*) rage, rush, assault.

ilmandi aromatic; *synonyms* (*adj*) fragrant, spicy, balmy, odorous, perfumed; *antonyms* (*adj*) smelly, unscented, odorless.

ilmappelsína bergamot; *synonyms* (*n*) civet, potpourri, pulvil, burgamot.

ilmefni aromatic; *synonyms* (*adj*) fragrant, spicy, balmy, odorous, perfumed; *antonyms* (*adj*) smelly, unscented, odorless.

ilmjurt aromatic; *synonyms* (*adj*) fragrant, spicy, balmy, odorous, perfumed; *antonyms* (*adj*) smelly, unscented, odorless.

ilmkvoða balsam; *synonyms* (*n*) balm, unguent, cordial, ptisan, theriac.

ilmur odour; *synonyms* (*n*) fragrance, flavour, aroma, smell, odor.

ilmvatn perfume; *synonyms* (*n*) fragrance, aroma, essence, odor, (*v*) scent.

ilpunktur nadir; *synonyms* (*n*) bottom, foot, minimum, zero, root; *antonyms* (*n*) acme, peak, pinnacle, zenith.

indín 1. indium; *synonyms* (*n*) in, inch, **2.** in; *synonyms* (*prep*) during, between, by, through, (*adj*) stylish; *antonyms* (*prep*) out, outside.

indíum indium; *synonyms* (*n*) in, inch.

inflúensa 1. influenza; *synonyms* (*n*) grippe, flu, plague, bug, (*adj*) grip, **2.** flu; *synonyms* (*n*) influenza, disease, sickness, infection, virus, **3.** grippe.

ingredienco elements; *synonyms* (*n*) alphabet, rudiments, grammar, outlines, contents.

inna execute; *synonyms* (*v*) do, achieve, complete, perform, accomplish.

innæxlun inbreeding; *synonyms* (*n*) consanguinity, selfing.

innankönnun exploration; *synonyms* (*n*) examination, search, discovery, expedition, inquiry.

innanrannsókn exploration; *synonyms* (*n*) examination, search, discovery, expedition, inquiry.

innantaka colic; *synonyms* (*n*) bellyache, mulligrubs, enteralgia, cramp, heartburn.

innanþreifing exploration; *synonyms* (*n*) examination, search, discovery, expedition, inquiry.

innanverður 1. internal; *synonyms* (*adj*) interior, domestic, inner, inside, home; *antonyms* (*adj*) external, foreign, **2.** interior; *synonyms* (*adj*) internal, inland, inward, midland, (*n*) center; *antonyms* (*n*) outside, exterior, shore, shoreline.

innátenging intrusion; *synonyms* (*n*) interference, infringement, disturbance, encroachment, incursion.

innbjúgur concave; *synonyms* (*adj*) hollow, cavernous, crescent, biconcave, cupped; *antonyms* (*adj*) convex, curved.

innblæðing apoplexy; *synonyms* (*n*) stroke, (*adj*) palsy, paralysis, collapse, deliquium.

innblástur inspiration; *synonyms* (*n*) afflatus, infusion, breath, encouragement, (*v*) illumination.

innblöndun 1. flash; *synonyms* (*n*) sparkle, blaze, shimmer, (*v*) flicker, twinkle, **2.** entrainment; *synonym* (*n*) induction.

innborgun 1. reimbursement; *synonyms* (*n*) compensation, refund, repayment, indemnity, pay, **2.** deposit; *synonyms* (*n*) charge, (*v*) bank, commit, store, fix; *antonym* (*v*) withdraw.

innbrot penetration; *synonyms* (*n*) insight, acuteness, (*v*) intelligence, discernment, (*adj*) acumen.

innbrotsþjófur burglar; *synonyms* (*n*) robber, thief, cracksman, prowler, plunderer.

innbú furniture; *synonyms* (*n*) equipment, appointments, goods, fitting, (*v*) stuff.

innbyggður structural; *synonyms* (*adj*) organic, tectonic, geomorphologic, geomorphological, morphologic.

innbyrðing ingestion; *synonyms* (*n*) consumption, absorption, intake, drinking, eating.

inndæling injection; *synonyms* (*n*) shot, clyster, enema, inoculation, jab.

inndraganlegur retractable; *synonyms* (*adj*) retractible, removable.

inndráttur 1. retraction; *synonyms* (*n*) cancellation, recantation, abjuration, annulment, (*v*) repudiation, **2.** indention, **3.** indent; *synonyms* (*v*) dent, indenture, cut, impress, (*n*) notch.

inneign credit; *synonyms* (n) credence, appreciation, belief, (v) believe, accredit; *antonyms* (n) cash, (v) debit, discredit.

innfæddur 1. autochthonous; *synonyms* (adj) autochthonal, autochthonic, indigenous, native, endemic, 2. indigenous; *synonyms* (adj) aboriginal, autochthonous, domestic, vernacular, congenital, 3. native; *synonyms* (adj) inborn, inherent, innate, natural, (n) autochthon; *antonyms* (adj) foreign, learned, (n) stranger, immigrant, imported.

innfærsla entry; *synonyms* (n) entrance, admission, article, door, accession; *antonym* (n) exit.

innfar immigration; *synonyms* (n) migration, colonization, entrance, (v) emigration, intermigration.

innfelling 1. insert; *synonyms* (v) embed, enter, put, enclose, interject; *antonyms* (v) remove, erase, 2. embedding; *synonym* (n) bedding.

innferð penetration; *synonyms* (n) insight, acuteness, (v) intelligence, discernment, (adj) acumen.

innflæði 1. inflow; *synonym* (n) influx, 2. influx; *synonyms* (n) inflow, concourse, introduction, invasion, affluence.

innfláki 1. void; *synonyms* (adj) empty, null, (n) hollow, blank, emptiness; *antonyms* (adj) valid, full, (v) validate, 2. hole; *synonyms* (n) cavity, aperture, crack, den, (adj) gap, 3. island; *synonyms* (n) reef, (v) isle, insulate, isolate, segregate.

innflutningsgjald tariff; *synonyms* (n) duty, charge, excise, custom, tax.

innflutningur 1. import; *synonyms* (n) consequence, meaning, sense, effect, (v) matter; *antonym* (v) export, 2. importation; *synonyms* (n) import, entree, importing, admission, admittance.

innflytjandi immigrant; *synonyms* (n) migrant, alien, foreigner, emigrant, newcomer.

innflytjendur immigration; *synonyms* (n) migration, colonization, entrance, (v) emigration, intermigration.

innganga admission; *synonyms* (n) acceptance, access, acknowledgment, confession, admittance; *antonym* (n) denial.

inngangur 1. inlet; *synonyms* (n) bay, cove, entry, gulf, entrance, 2. entry; *synonyms* (n) admission, article, door, accession, access; *antonym* (n) exit.

inngrip 1. intervention; *synonyms* (n) intercession, interference, intermediation, (adj) mediation, interposition, 2. intrusion; *synonyms* (n) infringement, disturbance, encroachment, incursion, inroad.

innheimta 1. collection; *synonyms* (n) accumulation, assembly, assortment, bundle, (v) assemblage, 2.

collect; *synonyms* (v) assemble, accumulate, amass, gather, pick; *antonyms* (v) disperse, distribute.

innherji insider; *synonyms* (n) accessory, accomplice.

innhvarfi introvert; *synonyms* (v) invert, (adj) introverted, inhibited, introspective, introvertive; *antonym* (n) extrovert.

innhvelfing invagination; *synonyms* (n) intussusception, erythroblast, gametangium, gamete, infolding.

innhverfa introversion; *synonyms* (n) eversion, introspection, bashfulness, coyness, infolding; *antonym* (n) boldness.

innhverfing 1. endocytosis, 2. inversion; *synonyms* (n) antithesis, reversal, transposition, anastrophe, eversion, 3. invagination; *synonyms* (n) intussusception, erythroblast, gametangium, gamete, infolding.

innhverfur introvert; *synonyms* (v) invert, (adj) introverted, inhibited, introspective, introvertive; *antonym* (n) extrovert.

inni interior; *synonyms* (adj) inside, inner, internal, inland, inward; *antonyms* (adj) external, (n) outside, exterior, shore, shoreline.

innifalinn included; *synonyms* (adj) numbered, confined, inclosed, integrated, (adv) under.

innihald content; *synonyms* (n) capacity, contentment, (adj) contented, happy, (v) appease; *antonyms* (adj) tormented, unhappy, discontented, dissatisfied, (v) discontent.

innihalda contain; *synonyms* (v) comprise, accommodate, comprehend, curb, include; *antonyms* (v) exclude, express.

innilokun 1. containment; *synonyms* (n) control, repression, restriction, 2. confinement; *synonyms* (n) captivity, childbirth, custody, detention, (v) delivery; *antonyms* (n) freedom, release.

innilokunarstefna containment; *synonyms* (n) control, repression, restriction.

inning execution; *synonyms* (n) performance, accomplishment, achievement, effect, enforcement.

innitaugar wiring; *synonyms* (n) cabling, installation, network, electrics.

innkaup purchase; *synonyms* (n) acquisition, bargain, (v) buy, get, obtain; *antonyms* (n) transaction, (v) sell.

innköllun call; *synonyms* (v) cry, bellow, name, shout, (n) appeal; *antonym* (v) dismiss.

innkoma entry; *synonyms* (n) entrance, admission, article, door, accession; *antonym* (n) exit.

innkomandi incoming; *synonyms* (adj) inward, (n) entrance, entree, entering, entry; *antonyms* (adj) outgoing, outward.

innkýldur impacted; *synonym* (adj) wedged.

innkýling impaction; *synonyms* (*n*) encroachment, impact, impingement.

innlag hypoblast; *synonyms* (*n*) endoblast, endoderm, entoderm, entoblast.

innlagskím hypoblast; *synonyms* (*n*) endoblast, endoderm, entoderm, entoblast.

innlán deposits; *synonyms* (*n*) sediments, diggings.

innlausn 1. realization; *synonyms* (*n*) execution, accomplishment, awareness, comprehension, fulfillment, **2**. redemption; *synonyms* (*n*) ransom, atonement, salvation, discharge, expiation.

innlausnarréttur call; *synonyms* (*v*) cry, bellow, name, shout, (*n*) appeal; *antonym* (*v*) dismiss.

innlegg deposit; *synonyms* (*n*) charge, (*v*) bank, commit, store, fix; *antonym* (*v*) withdraw.

innleggshólkur collet; *synonym* (*n*) ferrule.

innleiða institute; *synonyms* (*v*) establish, found, build, constitute, appoint.

innleiðing institution; *synonyms* (*n*) creation, establishment, institute, formation, asylum.

innleiðsla 1. transposition; *synonyms* (*n*) exchange, permutation, replacement, reversal, substitution, **2**. transfection.

innlendingur autochthon; *synonyms* (*n*) native, indigene, inhabitant.

innlendur 1. domestic; *synonyms* (*adj*) home, tame, civil, familiar, (*n*) homely; *antonyms* (*adj*) foreign, wild, external, **2**. internal; *synonyms* (*adj*) interior, domestic, inner, inside, intimate.

innleysa 1. redeem; *synonyms* (*v*) atone, deliver, recover, recoup, expiate, **2**. retire; *synonyms* (*v*) recede, resign, leave, retreat, withdraw.

innleysanlegur redeemable; *synonyms* (*adj*) cashable, callable, negotiable, (*v*) rescuable, extricable.

innlima 1. annex; *synonyms* (*n*) affix, addition, (*v*) add, affiliate, adjoin, **2**. incorporate; *synonyms* (*v*) comprise, contain, encompass, combine, embody; *antonym* (*v*) exclude.

innlimum incorporation; *synonyms* (*n*) annexation, inclusion, union, amalgamation, consolidation.

innlimun 1. annexation; *synonyms* (*n*) addition, annexion, seizure, takeover, (*v*) annexment, **2**. integration; *synonyms* (*n*) amalgamation, consolidation, embodiment, integrating, merger; *antonym* (*n*) segregation, **3**. incorporation; *synonyms* (*n*) annexation, inclusion, union, absorption, affiliation.

innmúra embed; *synonyms* (*v*) fix, bury, bed, imbed, insert.

innöndun 1. aspiration; *synonyms* (*n*) aim, ambition, longing, ambitiousness, (*v*) desire, **2**. inhalation; *synonyms* (*n*) breath, absorption, drag, gasp,

inhalant, **3**. inspiration; *synonyms* (*n*) afflatus, infusion, encouragement, idea, (*v*) illumination.

innöndunarlyf 1. inhalant; *synonyms* (*adj*) inhaling, (*n*) anesthetic, **2**. inhalation; *synonyms* (*n*) breath, absorption, drag, gasp, inhalant.

innrækt 1. inbreeding; *synonyms* (*n*) consanguinity, selfing, **2**. endogamy; *synonyms* (*n*) inmarriage, intermarriage, exogamy, **3**. homogamy.

innrænn 1. adiabatic, **2**. endogenous; *synonyms* (*adj*) interior, exogenous, endogen, endogenetic, entogenous.

innrás invasion; *synonyms* (*n*) attack, assault, aggression, incursion, inroad; *antonyms* (*n*) retreat, surrender.

innrauður infrared; *synonym* (*n*) red.

innrautt infrared; *synonym* (*n*) red.

innreiknun interpolation; *synonyms* (*n*) interjection, interposition, interspersion, (*v*) addition, approximation.

innrennsli inlet; *synonyms* (*n*) bay, cove, entry, gulf, entrance.

innrennslislyf infusion; *synonyms* (*n*) extract, infuse, influx, dash, (*v*) injection.

innrétta 1. install; *synonyms* (*v*) establish, fix, inaugurate, appoint, erect; *antonym* (*v*) overthrow, **2**. tidy; *synonyms* (*adj*) clean, neat, trim, spruce, (*v*) clear; *antonyms* (*adj*) untidy, disheveled, knotted, **3**. sort; *synonyms* (*n*) kind, type, assortment, (*v*) class, group, **4**. set; *synonyms* (*v*) place, lay, put, locate, (*adj*) fixed; *antonyms* (*v*) soften, liquefy, (*n*) combing, comb-out, (*adj*) variable, **5**. collate; *synonyms* (*v*) contrast, compare, collect, compile, sort.

innrétting 1. arrangement; *synonyms* (*n*) agreement, order, settlement, adjustment, array, **2**. trim; *synonyms* (*adj*) tidy, (*v*) cut, dress, clip, garnish; *antonym* (*adj*) fat, **3**. scheme; *synonyms* (*n*) contrivance, dodge, (*v*) plan, plot, design, **4**. adjustment; *synonyms* (*n*) adaptation, accommodation, alteration, control, fit, **5**. pattern; *synonyms* (*n*) model, fashion, form, mold, (*v*) mould.

innri 1. intrinsic; *synonyms* (*adj*) inherent, immanent, inborn, internal, constitutional; *antonym* (*adj*) extrinsic, **2**. internal; *synonyms* (*adj*) interior, domestic, inner, inside, home; *antonyms* (*adj*) external, foreign, **3**. endogenous; *synonyms* (*adj*) exogenous, endogen, endogenetic, entogenous, primary.

innrita 1. register; *synonyms* (*n*) record, list, inventory, (*v*) file, enroll, **2**. record; *synonyms* (*n*) register, account, book, disk, (*v*) chronicle.

innritun registration; *synonyms* (*n*) enrollment, registering, enrolment, entering, entry.

innroði infrared; *synonym* (*n*) red.

innrúm matrix; *synonyms* (*n*) die, alembic, caldron, crucible, groundmass.

innsækinn afferent; *synonym* (*adj*) sensory.

innsetning substitution; *synonyms* (*n*) replacement, exchange, change, substitute, interchange.

innseytinn endocrine; *synonyms* (*adj*) endocrinal, (*n*) hormone.

innsigla seal; *synonyms* (*n*) mark, stamp, cachet, (*v*) plug, bar; *antonyms* (*v*) open, unseal.

innsigli seal; *synonyms* (*n*) mark, stamp, cachet, (*v*) plug, bar; *antonyms* (*v*) open, unseal.

innskeyti intercalation; *synonyms* (*n*) embolism, interjection, interpolation, intercurrence, interdigitation.

innskeyting intercalation; *synonyms* (*n*) embolism, interjection, interpolation, intercurrence, interdigitation.

innskot 1. intercalation; *synonyms* (*n*) embolism, interjection, interpolation, intercurrence, interdigitation, **2**. insert; *synonyms* (*v*) embed, enter, put, enclose, interject; *antonyms* (*v*) remove, erase, **3**. intrusion; *synonyms* (*n*) interference, infringement, disturbance, encroachment, incursion.

innskotshamur insert; *synonyms* (*v*) embed, enter, put, enclose, interject; *antonyms* (*v*) remove, erase.

innskrið involution; *synonyms* (*n*) exponentiation, intricacy, complexity, complication, (*v*) convolution.

innsláttarform mask; *synonyms* (*n*) cover, conceal, (*v*) cloak, disguise, hide; *antonym* (*v*) disclose.

innsníkill endoparasite; *synonyms* (*n*) entozoon, endozoa, endozoan, entoparasite, entozoa.

innsog choke; *synonyms* (*v*) asphyxiate, block, throttle, stifle, clog; *antonym* (*v*) unclog.

innsókn penetration; *synonyms* (*n*) insight, acuteness, (*v*) intelligence, discernment, (*adj*) acumen.

innsprautun injection; *synonyms* (*n*) shot, clyster, enema, inoculation, jab.

innsprautunarventill nozzle; *synonyms* (*n*) nose, beak, hooter, jet, muzzle.

innspýting injection; *synonyms* (*n*) shot, clyster, enema, inoculation, jab.

innstæður medial; *synonyms* (*adj*) intermediate, average, mean, middle, medium.

innsteypa embed; *synonyms* (*v*) fix, bury, bed, imbed, insert.

innsteyping embedding; *synonym* (*n*) bedding.

innstilling setting; *synonyms* (*n*) frame, scene, adjustment, scenery, backdrop.

innstreymi 1. inflow; *synonym* (*n*) influx, **2**. inlet; *synonyms* (*n*) bay, cove, entry, gulf, entrance.

innstreymisop spiracle; *synonyms* (*n*) larynx, tonsils, windpipe, (*v*) stigma, brand.

innstunga 1. socket; *synonyms* (*n*) cavity, alveolus, sleeve, hollow, pocket, **2**. insertion; *synonyms* (*n*) inset, enclosure, introduction, intromission, interpolation; *antonym* (*n*) removal.

innsýn perspective; *synonyms* (*n*) attitude, aspect, angle, outlook, prospect.

inntak 1. sense; *synonyms* (*n*) intelligence, perception, meaning, (*v*) feel, intellect; *antonyms* (*n*) garbage, ludicrousness, nonsense, stupidity, foolishness, **2**. inlet; *synonyms* (*n*) bay, cove, entry, gulf, entrance, **3**. input; *synonyms* (*n*) contribution, incoming, data, advice, feed, **4**. intake; *synonyms* (*n*) absorption, consumption, ingestion, drinking, eating.

inntaka 1. ingestion; *synonyms* (*n*) consumption, absorption, intake, drinking, eating, **2**. induction; *synonyms* (*n*) inauguration, deduction, initiation, beginning, elicitation.

innþorna shrink; *synonyms* (*v*) dwindle, flinch, recoil, contract, shorten; *antonyms* (*v*) expand, increase, enlarge.

innúðalyf inhalant; *synonyms* (*adj*) inhaling, (*n*) anesthetic.

innvensl endogamy; *synonyms* (*n*) inmarriage, intermarriage, exogamy.

innverminn endothermic; *synonym* (*adj*) endothermal.

innviðir infrastructure; *synonyms* (*n*) base, foundation, basis, groundwork, substructure.

innvirki infrastructure; *synonyms* (*n*) base, foundation, basis, groundwork, substructure.

innvortis internal; *synonyms* (*adj*) interior, domestic, inner, inside, home; *antonyms* (*adj*) external, foreign.

innyflahreinsa eviscerate; *synonyms* (*v*) disembowel, draw, gut, debilitate, withdraw.

innyflanám evisceration; *synonyms* (*n*) disembowelment, exenteration, (*adj*) disemboweling.

innyfli 1. viscera; *synonyms* (*n*) entrails, bowels, innards, intestines, guts, **2**. guts; *synonyms* (*n*) backbone, boldness, bravery, courage, fortitude; *antonym* (*n*) cowardice, **3**. offal; *synonyms* (*n*) garbage, litter, waste, junk, leavings.

intenci means; *synonyms* (*n*) expedient, agency, instrument, assets, capital.

interfasi interphase; *synonyms* (*n*) interface, interkinesis.

interligiteco relations; *synonyms* (*n*) family, dealings, kin, connections, people.

interrilato 1. relations; *synonyms* (*n*) family, dealings, kin, connections, people, **2**. relation; *synonyms* (*n*) connection, account, narration, recital, affinity.

intesto 1. intestine; *synonyms* (*n*) bowel, gut, catgut, (*adj*) domestic, internal, **2**. guts; *synonyms* (*n*) bowels, backbone, boldness, bravery, courage; *antonym* (*n*) cowardice, **3**. magi; *synonyms* (*n*) authority, luminary, oracle, solon, (*adj*) heretical.

inúlín inulin; *synonym* (*n*) alantin.

iu as; *synonyms* (*conj*) qua, because, (*prep*) during, like, (*n*) arsenic.

Í

í in; *synonyms* (*prep*) during, between, by, through, (*adj*) stylish; *antonyms* (*prep*) out, outside.

íæðun venation; *synonym* (*v*) venery.

íbæta dope; *synonyms* (*n*) dolt, boob, booby, ass, (*v*) drug.

íbæting doping; *synonyms* (*n*) swabbing, doctoring, activating.

íbenviður ebony; *synonyms* (*n*) sable, (*adj*) black, ebon, dark, jet.

íbjúgur concave; *synonyms* (*adj*) hollow, cavernous, crescent, biconcave, cupped; *antonyms* (*adj*) convex, curved.

íblendi ingredient; *synonyms* (*n*) constituent, component, element, factor, part.

íblendiefni additive; *synonyms* (*adj*) cumulative, (*n*) addition, adjuvant, admixture, supplement.

íblöndun doping; *synonyms* (*n*) swabbing, doctoring, activating.

íblöndunarefni additive; *synonyms* (*adj*) cumulative, (*n*) addition, adjuvant, admixture, supplement.

íbót impurity; *synonyms* (*n*) contamination, filth, impureness, pollution, defilement.

íbúafjöldi population; *synonyms* (*n*) inhabitants, people, nation, community, group.

íbúar population; *synonyms* (*n*) inhabitants, people, nation, community, group.

íbúatala population; *synonyms* (*n*) inhabitants, people, nation, community, group.

íbúð 1. apartment; *synonyms* (*n*) flat, lodging, residence, chamber, dwelling, **2**. flat; *synonyms* (*adj*) dull, bland, even, plain, (*n*) apartment; *antonyms* (*adj*) exciting, high-pitched, bumpy.

íbúi 1. resident; *synonyms* (*adj*) native, (*n*) inhabitant, occupant, dweller, tenant; *antonyms* (*adj*) migratory, (*n*) landlord, drifter, **2**. occupant; *synonyms* (*n*) resident, denizen, occupier, holder, citizen.

ídæling injection; *synonyms* (*n*) shot, clyster, enema, inoculation, jab.

ídælingarefni injection; *synonyms* (*n*) shot, clyster, enema, inoculation, jab.

íðal ideal; *synonyms* (*adj*) fanciful, perfect, consummate, (*n*) model, paragon.

íðefni chemical; *synonyms* (*adj*) chemic, alchemical, alkaline, plastic, (*n*) ammunition.

íðheiti term; *synonyms* (*n*) name, expression, period, style, (*v*) call.

íðorð term; *synonyms* (*n*) name, expression, period, style, (*v*) call.

íðorðaforði nomenclature; *synonyms* (*n*) terminology, language, classification, lyric, (*v*) name.

ídýfing immersion; *synonyms* (*n*) dip, absorption, ducking, concentration, submergence.

íefni constituent; *synonyms* (*n*) component, ingredient, element, factor, part; *antonyms* (*n*) aggregate, composite, whole.

ífara infiltrate; *synonyms* (*v*) soak, enter, penetrate, permeate, inculcate.

ífarandi invasive; *synonyms* (*adj*) incursive, aggressive, encroaching, invading, hostile.

ífarinn infiltrate; *synonyms* (*v*) soak, enter, penetrate, permeate, inculcate.

ífelling implantation; *synonyms* (*n*) implant, insertion, nidation, graft, introduction.

íferð infiltration; *synonyms* (*n*) invasion, penetration, percolation, (*v*) immersion, humectation.

íflekkur child; *synonyms* (*n*) baby, boy, babe, bairn, brat; *antonym* (*n*) adult.

ígerð abscess; *synonyms* (*n*) blister, boil, gathering, (*adj*) sore, ulcer.

ígræði implant; *synonyms* (*v*) graft, fix, embed, engraft, plant.

ígræðlingur implant; *synonyms* (*v*) graft, fix, embed, engraft, plant.

ígræðsla 1. transplantation; *synonyms* (*n*) transplant, relocation, resettlement, graft, (*v*) transmission, **2**. implantation; *synonyms* (*n*) implant, insertion, nidation, introduction, doctrine.

ígrip interrupt; *synonyms* (*v*) break, disturb, hinder, intermit, (*adj*) discontinue.

ígróinn inherent; *synonyms* (*adj*) congenital, inborn, inbred, intrinsic, essential; *antonym* (*adj*) superficial.

ígulber rambutan; *synonym* (*n*) rambotan.

íhald 1. conservatism; *synonyms* (*n*) maintenance, support, temperance, **2**. holdfast; *synonyms* (*n*) fastener, clamp, fastening, lock, grasp.

íhaldssamur conservative; *synonyms* (*adj*) moderate, bourgeois, conventional, cautious, reactionary; *antonyms* (*adj*) activist, wide-ranging, (*n*) liberal, radical.

íhaldsstefna conservatism; *synonyms* (*n*) maintenance, support, temperance.

íhlutun 1. intervention; *synonyms* (*n*) intercession, interference, intermediation, (*adj*) mediation, interposition, **2**. interference; *synonyms* (*n*) disturbance, hindrance, handicap, block, (*v*) collision.

íhlutunartruflun interference; *synonyms* (*n*) disturbance, hindrance, handicap, block, (*v*) collision.

íhlutur component; *synonyms* (*n*) constituent, factor, ingredient, part, detail.

íhöfn content; *synonyms* (*n*) capacity, contentment, (*adj*) contented, happy, (*v*) appease; *antonyms* (*adj*) tormented, unhappy, discontented, dissatisfied, (*v*) discontent.

íholur concave; *synonyms* (*adj*) hollow, cavernous, crescent, biconcave, cupped; *antonyms* (*adj*) convex, curved.

íhrif impression; *synonyms* (*n*) belief, conception, feeling, idea, imprint.

íhuga contemplate; *synonyms* (*v*) consider, cogitate, meditate, muse, speculate.

íhvelft concavity; *synonyms* (*n*) concaveness, hollow, dent, basin, hole.

íhvolfa concavity; *synonyms* (*n*) concaveness, hollow, dent, basin, hole.

íhvolfur 1. concave; *synonyms* (*adj*) hollow, cavernous, crescent, biconcave, cupped; *antonyms* (*adj*) convex, curved, **2**. convex; *synonyms* (*adj*) bulging, gibbous, biconvex, hunched, (*v*) projecting; *antonym* (*adj*) concave.

íkorni squirrel; *synonyms* (*n*) accumulator, collector, (*adj*) antelope, (*v*) bank, cache.

íkveikja fire; *synonyms* (*n*) discharge, (*v*) excite, eject, blaze, dismiss; *antonym* (*v*) hire.

ílag input; *synonyms* (*n*) contribution, incoming, data, advice, feed.

ílát 1. vessel; *synonyms* (*n*) ship, boat, container, craft, duct, **2**. bowl; *synonyms* (*n*) basin, pot, plate, hollow, stadium, **3**. container; *synonyms* (*n*) box, jar, package, basket, carton, **4**. bin; *synonyms* (*n*) bunker, binful, case, silo, (*v*) store.

íle isoleucine; *synonym* (*n*) ile.

ílending 1. acclimation; *synonyms* (*n*) acclimatization, acclimatisation, adjustment, acclimatement, **2**. acclimatization; *synonyms* (*n*) acclimation, adaptation, acclimatation, orientation, alteration.

ílengd elongation; *synonyms* (*n*) extension, expansion, length, production, annex.

ílifun 1. assimilation; *synonyms* (*n*) absorption, acculturation, incorporation, integration, addition,

2. anabolism; *synonyms* (*n*) catabolism, metabolism.

ílimun incorporation; *synonyms* (*n*) annexation, inclusion, union, amalgamation, consolidation.

ílöngun appetite; *synonyms* (*n*) desire, appetence, appetency, relish, craving; *antonym* (*n*) dislike.

ímynd 1. image; *synonyms* (*n*) figure, picture, fancy, conception, effigy, **2**. figure; *synonyms* (*n*) form, appearance, character, (*v*) design, cast, **3**. imago; *synonym* (*n*) adult, **4**. model; *synonyms* (*n*) fashion, example, image, (*v*) copy, pattern; *antonym* (*adj*) atypical.

ímyndaður virtual; *synonyms* (*adj*) potential, practical, unreal, implicit, comparative; *antonym* (*adj*) genuine.

ímyndun imagination; *synonyms* (*n*) fantasy, fancy, vision, dream, conceit; *antonym* (*n*) reality.

ímyndunarafl imagination; *synonyms* (*n*) fantasy, fancy, vision, dream, conceit; *antonym* (*n*) reality.

ímyndunarveikur hypochondriac; *synonyms* (*adj*) hypochondriacal, afflictive, calamitous, disconsolate, (*n*) atrabilarian.

ís ice; *synonyms* (*n*) frosting, glass, (*v*) frost, cool, refrigerate.

ísæi insight; *synonyms* (*n*) discernment, vision, acumen, penetration, perception.

ísetning installation; *synonyms* (*n*) establishment, induction, facility, inauguration, initiation.

ísfugl 1. kingfisher, **2**. halcyon; *synonyms* (*adj*) calm, peaceful, tranquil, untroubled, quiet.

íshagl hail; *synonyms* (*n*) greet, (*v*) address, cry, acclaim, applaud.

ísing icing; *synonyms* (*n*) freeze, frost, frosting, ice, diamonds.

ísíun penetration; *synonyms* (*n*) insight, acuteness, (*v*) intelligence, discernment, (*adj*) acumen.

ískaldur 1. arctic; *synonyms* (*adj*) freezing, icy, polar, (*v*) glacial, boreal; *antonym* (*adj*) hot, **2**. frigid; *synonyms* (*adj*) cold, chilly, chill, arctic, cool; *antonym* (*adj*) warm.

ískorn sleet; *synonyms* (*n*) precipitation, rain, hail, glaze, moment.

ískrap sludge; *synonyms* (*n*) mud, ooze, slime, (*adj*) silt, mire.

ískuldi frigidity; *synonyms* (*n*) cold, coldness, coolness, chill, iciness.

ískur 1. screech; *synonyms* (*n*) scream, cry, shout, shriek, (*v*) screak, **2**. squeak; *synonyms* (*n*) screech, (*v*) peep, creak, yell, scrape.

ísog 1. absorption; *synonyms* (*n*) assimilation, attention, concentration, inhalation, engrossment, **2**. imbibition; *synonyms* (*n*) imbibing, drinking, boozing, crapulence, drink.

ísólefsín isoleucine; *synonym* (n) ile.
ísóleusín isoleucine; *synonym* (n) ile.
ísólevsín isoleucine; *synonym* (n) ile.
ísómer isomer; *synonym* (n) isomeride.
íspuni confabulation; *synonyms* (n) colloquy, chat, confab, conversation, converse.
ístað stapes; *synonym* (n) stirrup.
ísvari defroster; *synonym* (n) deicer.
ítak easement; *synonyms* (n) ease, alleviation, relief, easing, lullaby.
ítaugun innervation; *synonyms* (n) excitation, excitement, feeling, irritation.
íþrótt sport; *synonyms* (n) frolic, play, jest, pastime, diversion.
íþróttamaður athlete; *synonyms* (n) player, gymnast, acrobat, contestant, jock.
íþróttavöllur 1. stadium; *synonyms* (n) arena, coliseum, bowl, field, gymnasium, 2. arena; *synonyms* (n) ring, battlefield, sphere, theater, amphitheater.
íþyngjandi depressive; *synonyms* (adj) blue, gloomy, oppressive, black, (v) depressing.
ítónun intonation; *synonyms* (n) accent, inflection, tone, expression, timbre.
ítrekaður recurrent; *synonyms* (adj) periodic, recurring, repeated, continual, frequent; *antonym* (adj) occasional.
ítrekun 1. repetition; *synonyms* (n) repeat, gemination, iteration, recurrence, reiteration, 2. reminder; *synonyms* (n) memento, note, hint, memorandum, memorial, 3. iteration; *synonyms* (n) repetition, iterance, run, succession, frequency.
ítroðning tamponade; *synonym* (n) tamponage.
ítroðsla tamponade; *synonym* (n) tamponage.
ítrun iteration; *synonyms* (n) repetition, iterance, reiteration, run, succession.
ívilnun concession; *synonyms* (n) admission, compliance, allowance, compromise, discount.

J

já 1. yes; *synonyms* (int) surely, (adv) ay, yea, certainly, positively, 2. yeah; *synonyms* (int) hurrah, hurray, yippee.
jaðar 1. periphery; *synonyms* (n) perimeter, fringe, border, bound, boundary; *antonym* (n) center, 2. peripheral; *synonyms* (adj) exterior, outer, external, marginal, extraneous; *antonyms* (adj) central, vital, 3. border; *synonyms* (n) margin, brink, extremity, (v) edge, verge; *antonym* (n) middle, 4. boundary; *synonyms* (n) limit, area, end, periphery, barrier, 5. buffer; *synonyms* (n) safeguard, pad, protection, bumper, (v) cushion.
jaðarsvæði periphery; *synonyms* (n) perimeter, fringe, border, bound, boundary; *antonym* (n) center.
jáeind positron; *synonyms* (n) antielectron, electricity.
jafn 1. steady; *synonyms* (adj) firm, even, secure, (v) steadfast, calm; *antonyms* (adj) unsteady, shaky, wobbly, intermittent, unreliable, 2. homogeneous; *synonyms* (adj) uniform, consistent, kindred, homogenous, similar; *antonyms* (adj) diverse, varied, inconsistent, 3. equal; *synonyms* (adj) agree, comparable, (v) match, compare, correspond; *antonyms* (adj) unequal, different, repressive, disproportionate, (v) differ.
jafna 1. unify; *synonyms* (v) combine, integrate, amalgamate, consolidate, merge, 2. round; *synonyms* (adv) about, (adj) circular, (n) circle, bout, ring; *antonyms* (adj) slim, sharp, 3. balance; *synonyms* (n) poise, symmetry, (v) counterbalance, adjust, offset; *antonyms* (n) imbalance, (v) unbalance, 4. compensate; *synonyms* (v) balance, pay, recompense, reimburse, recoup, 5. justify; *synonyms* (v) excuse, explain, absolve, confirm, (n) warrant.
jafnaðarmaður democrat; *synonyms* (n) commoner, plebeian, proletaire, proletary, republican.
jafnaðarstefna socialism; *synonyms* (n) communism, collectivism, communalism; *antonym* (n) capitalism.
jafnalausn buffer; *synonyms* (n) safeguard, pad, protection, bumper, (v) cushion.
jafnari 1. grader; *synonyms* (n) backhoe, bulldozer, tractor, caterpillar, motorgrader, 2. equalizer; *synonyms* (n) equaliser, balance, counterbalance, counterpoise, counterweight.
jafnátta 1. isentropic, 2. isotropic; *synonym* (adj) isotropous.
jafndreifður diffuse; *synonyms* (v) circulate, disperse, disseminate, spread, broadcast.
jafngengi 1. reversibility, 2. parity; *synonyms* (n) par, equality, resemblance, balance, equivalence; *antonym* (n) inequality.
jafngengur reversible; *synonyms* (adj) changeable, bilateral, abrogable, repealable.
jafngildi 1. compatibility; *synonyms* (n) rapport, agreement, accord, harmony, propriety; *antonym* (n) incompatibility, 2. balance; *synonyms* (n) poise, symmetry, (v) counterbalance, adjust, offset; *antonyms* (n) imbalance, (v) unbalance, 3. equivalence; *synonyms* (n) equality, correspondence, parity, balance, (v) equivalent; *antonyms* (n) difference, dissimilarity, 4.

equivalent; *synonyms* (*adj*) equal, comparable, alike, analogous, (*n*) counterpart; *antonyms* (*adj*) unlike, (*n*) different, dissimilar.

jafngildislína 1. contour; *synonyms* (*n*) form, outline, profile, shape, configuration, **2**. isoline; *synonym* (*n*) isogram, **3**. isopleth; *synonym* (*n*) isarithm.

jafngildur 1. compatible; *synonyms* (*adj*) agreeable, congruent, accordant, congenial, (*n*) consistent; *antonym* (*adj*) incompatible, **2**. authentic; *synonyms* (*adj*) actual, genuine, accurate, real, right; *antonyms* (*adj*) bogus, fake, unrealistic, **3**. equivalent; *synonyms* (*adj*) equal, comparable, alike, analogous, (*n*) counterpart; *antonyms* (*adj*) unlike, (*n*) different, dissimilar.

jafngreiðsla annuity; *synonyms* (*n*) allowance, pension, rente, revenue, payment.

jafngreiðsluröð annuity; *synonyms* (*n*) allowance, pension, rente, revenue, payment.

jafnhliða 1. abreast; *synonyms* (*adj*) near, (*adv*) acquainted, off, opposite, (*prep*) against, **2**. equilateral; *synonyms* (*adj*) square, (*n*) lozenge, rhombus, shape.

jafnhverfur reversible; *synonyms* (*adj*) changeable, bilateral, abrogable, repealable.

jafni 1. potentiometer; *synonyms* (*n*) pot, batch, can, cannabis, commode, **2**. buffer; *synonyms* (*n*) safeguard, pad, protection, bumper, (*v*) cushion.

jafningi peer; *synonyms* (*n*) match, peep, mate, noble, (*v*) peek.

jafnkeypisviðskipti clearing; *synonyms* (*n*) clarification, glade, clearance, dell, lot.

Jafnliðun isomerization; *synonym* (*n*) isomerisation.

jafnmjókkandi attenuate; *synonyms* (*v*) assuage, dilute, reduce, (*adj*) tenuous, fine; *antonym* (*v*) intensify.

jafnrétti equality; *synonyms* (*n*) equivalence, balance, identity, parity, evenness; *antonyms* (*n*) inequality, disparity, difference.

jafnréttisstefna egalitarianism; *synonyms* (*n*) equality, democracy, equalitarianism, fairness, impartiality; *antonym* (*n*) inequality.

jafnskauta bipolar; *synonym* (*adj*) amphipathic.

jafnskipting 1. karyokinesis; *synonym* (*n*) mitosis, **2**. mitosis.

jafnstaða inclusion; *synonyms* (*n*) comprehension, implication, incorporation, addition, embodiment; *antonyms* (*n*) exclusion, exception.

Jafntefli draw; *synonyms* (*v*) attract, drag, delineate, pull, depict; *antonyms* (*v*) push, repel.

jafnþrýstiflötur isobar; *synonyms* (*n*) climate, weather.

jafnþrýstilína isobar; *synonyms* (*n*) climate, weather.

jafnþrýstinn isotonic; *synonyms* (*adj*) isosmotic, (*n*) concentual, symphonizing, unisonant.

jafntímalag horizon; *synonyms* (*n*) perspective, prospect, purview, reach, skyline.

Jafnvægi 1. balance; *synonyms* (*n*) poise, symmetry, (*v*) counterbalance, adjust, offset; *antonyms* (*n*) imbalance, (*v*) unbalance, **2**. equivalence; *synonyms* (*n*) equality, correspondence, parity, balance, (*v*) equivalent; *antonyms* (*n*) difference, dissimilarity, **3**. equilibrium; *synonyms* (*n*) counterpoise, equipoise, steadiness, counterweight, par; *antonym* (*n*) disequilibrium.

jafnvægisbúnaður stabilizer; *synonyms* (*n*) ballast, inhibitor, skedge, (*adj*) additive, preservative.

jafnvægisfræði statics; *synonyms* (*n*) static, (*v*) dynamics.

jafnvægiskorn otolith; *synonyms* (*n*) otoconite, otolite.

jafnvægismissir disequilibrium; *synonym* (*n*) instability; *antonym* (*n*) equilibrium.

jafnvægisskortur disequilibrium; *synonym* (*n*) instability; *antonym* (*n*) equilibrium.

jafnvægisstilla 1. balance; *synonyms* (*n*) poise, symmetry, (*v*) counterbalance, adjust, offset; *antonyms* (*n*) imbalance, (*v*) unbalance, **2**. counterbalance; *synonyms* (*v*) compensate, counteract, counterpoise, (*n*) balance, counterweight.

jafnvægur balanced; *synonyms* (*adj*) equal, even, firm, regular, stable; *antonyms* (*adj*) biased, unbalanced, unfair.

jafnvætting equilibration; *synonym* (*n*) readjustment.

jakkakjóll costume; *synonyms* (*n*) attire, clothing, apparel, clothes, dress.

jakobsfiskur whiting; *synonyms* (*n*) whitening, kingfishes.

jákvæður positive; *synonyms* (*adj*) absolute, certain, affirmative, confident, (*n*) actual; *antonyms* (*adj*) negative, derogatory, uncertain, unsure, pessimistic.

jamrótarhnýði yam; *synonyms* (*n*) yew, zinnia, (*v*) eat, speak.

japanspera quince; *synonym* (*n*) melocotoon.

jarðarber strawberry; *synonym* (*n*) blonde.

jarðarbúar earth; *synonyms* (*n*) dirt, world, dust, ground, land.

jarðarhálfhvel hemisphere; *synonyms* (*n*) area, realm, region, sphere, ground.

jarðarkringlan earth; *synonyms* (*n*) dirt, world, dust, ground, land.

jarðaryfirborð ground; *synonyms* (*n*) base, cause, land, floor, (*v*) bottom; *antonym* (*n*) ceiling.

jarðefnaleit prospecting; *synonym* (*n*) exploration.

jarðeign 1. domain; *synonyms* (*n*) country, department, realm, area, kingdom; *antonym* (*n*) range, **2**. land; *synonyms* (*n*) ground, soil, field, (*v*) disembark, debark; *antonym* (*adj*) aquatic, **3**. estate; *synonyms* (*n*) condition, land, demesne, order, rank.

jarðeldafræði volcanology; *synonym* (*n*) vulcanology.

jarðfirð apogee; *synonyms* (*n*) apex, acme, culmination, pinnacle, summit.

jarðfræði geology; *synonyms* (*n*) formation, mineralogy, geoscopy, constitution, establishment.

jarðhnik tectonics; *synonym* (*n*) architectonics.

jarðhniksfræði tectonics; *synonym* (*n*) architectonics.

jarðhrun slump; *synonyms* (*n*) depression, decline, (*v*) drop, fall, sag; *antonyms* (*n*) upturn, (*v*) rise.

jarðhumall yarrow; *synonyms* (*n*) milfoil, sassafras.

jarðlægur 1. prostrate; *synonyms* (*adj*) flat, prone, exhaust, (*v*) fell, level, **2**. procumbent; *synonyms* (*adj*) prostrate, recumbent, decumbent, humifuse, trailing.

jarðlag 1. stratum; *synonyms* (*n*) layer, bed, level, floor, seam, **2**. strata; *synonyms* (*n*) stratum, course, escarpment, flag, slab.

jarðlagaskeið stage; *synonyms* (*n*) grade, phase, floor, degree, level.

jarðlagastrik strike; *synonyms* (*n*) knock, assault, (*v*) bang, beat, hit.

jarðlagatenging correlation; *synonyms* (*n*) association, connection, relationship, bond, correspondence.

jarðlagshalli dip; *synonyms* (*n*) plunge, (*v*) duck, bathe, drop, fall; *antonyms* (*n*) hump, mountain.

jarðmöttull mantle; *synonyms* (*n*) cloak, cape, cover, pall, (*adj*) blush.

jarðnæði land; *synonyms* (*n*) ground, country, soil, (*v*) disembark, debark; *antonym* (*adj*) aquatic.

jarðnánd perigee; *synonyms* (*n*) epigee, epigeum, orbit, perigeum.

jarðneskur terrestrial; *synonyms* (*adj*) earthly, mundane, sublunary, terrene, worldly; *antonym* (*adj*) aquatic.

jarðolía petroleum; *synonyms* (*n*) crude, oil, petrol, alcohol, coal.

jarðpera groundnut; *synonyms* (*n*) goober, peanut, earthnut, truffle.

jarðrækt agriculture; *synonyms* (*n*) farming, agribusiness, agronomy, husbandry, tillage.

jarðræktarfræði agronomy; *synonyms* (*n*) agriculture, farming, tillage, gardening, vintage.

jarðræktunarfræði agronomy; *synonyms* (*n*) agriculture, farming, tillage, gardening, vintage.

jarðsamband 1. earth; *synonyms* (*n*) dirt, world, dust, ground, land, **2**. ground; *synonyms* (*n*) base, cause, floor, (*v*) bottom, found; *antonym* (*n*) ceiling.

jarðskautsleiðari counterpoise; *synonyms* (*n*) counterbalance, balance, poise, equilibrium, (*v*) counterweight.

jarðskjálftamælir seismograph; *synonym* (*n*) sismograph.

jarðskjálftariti seismograph; *synonym* (*n*) sismograph.

jarðskjálfti earthquake; *synonyms* (*n*) quake, shock, tremor, temblor, (*adj*) thunderstorm.

jarðskorpa 1. crust; *synonyms* (*n*) bark, cheekiness, covering, gall, (*v*) coat, **2**. lithosphere; *synonyms* (*n*) geosphere, sial.

jarðskrið slip; *synonyms* (*n*) lapse, fault, (*v*) fall, slide, (*adj*) blunder; *antonym* (*v*) improve.

jarðstöngulhnýði corm; *synonyms* (*n*) cormus, rhizome.

jarðstrengur cable; *synonyms* (*n*) rope, line, cablegram, telegram, (*v*) wire.

jarðtenging earth; *synonyms* (*n*) dirt, world, dust, ground, land.

jarðvegsfræði agrology; *synonym* (*n*) culture.

jarðvegshlaup landslide; *synonyms* (*n*) landslip, avalanche, descent, drop, (*v*) debacle.

jarðvegshrun landslide; *synonyms* (*n*) landslip, avalanche, descent, drop, (*v*) debacle.

jarðvegsjafnari scraper; *synonyms* (*n*) rasper, doctor.

jarðvegsskriða landslide; *synonyms* (*n*) landslip, avalanche, descent, drop, (*v*) debacle.

jarðvegur 1. soil; *synonyms* (*n*) ground, dirt, (*v*) smudge, blot, contaminate; *antonym* (*v*) clean, **2**. ground; *synonyms* (*n*) base, cause, land, floor, (*v*) bottom; *antonym* (*n*) ceiling, **3**. land; *synonyms* (*n*) country, soil, field, (*v*) disembark, debark; *antonym* (*adj*) aquatic.

jarðyrkja agriculture; *synonyms* (*n*) farming, agribusiness, agronomy, husbandry, tillage.

jarðýta bulldozer; *synonyms* (*n*) dozer, hoodlum, hooligan, larrikin, roarer.

járn iron; *synonyms* (*n*) chain, (*v*) firm, flatten, (*adj*) hard, adamant.

járnblandað ferrous; *synonyms* (*adj*) ferric, iron.

járnbraut 1. railway; *synonyms* (*n*) railroad, line, tramway, **2**. railroad; *synonyms* (*n*) railway, (*v*) coerce, dragoon, push, accelerate.

járnbrautarspor rail; *synonyms* (*n*) bar, balustrade, handrail, railing, (*v*) inveigh.

járnbrautarstöð station; *synonyms* (*n*) rank, position, (*v*) place, locate, post.

járnbrautarteinn rail; *synonyms* (*n*) bar, balustrade, handrail, railing, (*v*) inveigh.

járnsmíði forging; *synonyms* (*n*) manufacturing, origin.
járnsmiðja smithy; *synonyms* (*n*) forge, smithery, stithy, anvil, coin.
jaskaður worn; *synonyms* (*adj*) haggard, shabby, tired, ragged, tattered; *antonyms* (*adj*) fresh, new.
jáskaut anode; *synonym* (*n*) zincode.
játa 1. profess; *synonyms* (*v*) assert, declare, feign, affirm, avow, 2. concede; *synonyms* (*v*) allow, acknowledge, admit, accord, agree, 3. acknowledge; *synonyms* (*v*) accept, confess, recognize, own, profess; *antonyms* (*v*) deny, ignore, overlook, reject, 4. confess; *synonyms* (*v*) concede, disclose, divulge, reveal, grant, 5. admit; *synonyms* (*v*) accede, include, permit, take, appreciate; *antonym* (*v*) exclude.
jaxl molar; *synonyms* (*adj*) molal, (*n*) grinder, bomber, hero, hoagie.
jeppi jeep; *synonyms* (*n*) car, landrover, recruit, roadster, truck.
jepplingur jeep; *synonyms* (*n*) car, landrover, recruit, roadster, truck.
joð iodine; *synonyms* (*n*) iodin, ace, one, single, unity.
jóðsótt labor; *synonyms* (*n*) drudgery, effort, endeavor, exertion, (*v*) toil; *antonym* (*v*) rest.
jöfnuður 1. balance; *synonyms* (*n*) poise, symmetry, (*v*) counterbalance, adjust, offset; *antonyms* (*n*) imbalance, (*v*) unbalance, 2. equality; *synonyms* (*n*) equivalence, balance, identity, parity, evenness; *antonyms* (*n*) inequality, disparity, difference.
jöfnun 1. unification; *synonyms* (*n*) union, amalgamation, combination, merger, fusion; *antonyms* (*n*) separation, division, segregation, 2. smoothing; *synonyms* (*adj*) smooth, even, sleek, abrasive, bland, 3. compensation; *synonyms* (*n*) amends, recompense, allowance, indemnification, (*v*) wage, 4. homogenization; *synonym* (*n*) homogenisation, 5. justification; *synonyms* (*n*) apology, defense, account, reason, (*v*) excuse.
jöfnunarspóla choke; *synonyms* (*v*) asphyxiate, block, throttle, stifle, clog; *antonym* (*v*) unclog.
jöfnunartenging equalizer; *synonyms* (*n*) equaliser, balance, counterbalance, counterpoise, counterweight.
jökulalda moraine; *synonym* (*n*) ridge.
jökulgarður moraine; *synonym* (*n*) ridge.
jökulgjá crevasse; *synonyms* (*n*) chasm, crack, ravine, crevice, abyss.
jökulkast calving; *synonym* (*n*) freshening.
jökulker kettle; *synonyms* (*n*) boiler, can, kettledrum, kettleful, timpani.
jökulmelur moraine; *synonym* (*n*) ridge.
jökulruðningur till; *synonyms* (*prep*) until, unto, (*v*) cultivate, plow, hoe.

jökulskál cirque; *synonyms* (*n*) circle, corrie, cwm.
jökulsprunga crevasse; *synonyms* (*n*) chasm, crack, ravine, crevice, abyss.
jökulurð moraine; *synonym* (*n*) ridge.
jón ion; *synonym* (*n*) molecule.
jóna ionize; *synonym* (*v*) ionise.
jónaefni salt; *synonyms* (*adj*) salty, saline, briny, (*v*) cure, pickle.
jónfærsla electrophoresis; *synonyms* (*n*) cataphoresis, ionophoresis.
jónhvolfssylla ledge; *synonyms* (*n*) edge, projection, bulge, board, jetty.
jónun 1. ionization; *synonym* (*n*) ionisation, 2. ionisation; *synonym* (*n*) ionization.
jörð 1. earth; *synonyms* (*n*) dirt, world, dust, ground, land, 2. soil; *synonyms* (*n*) grime, (*v*) smudge, blot, contaminate, dirty; *antonym* (*v*) clean, 3. ground; *synonyms* (*n*) base, cause, floor, (*v*) bottom, found; *antonym* (*n*) ceiling, 4. parcel; *synonyms* (*n*) lot, bale, pack, bundle, (*v*) portion, 5. land; *synonyms* (*n*) country, soil, field, (*v*) disembark, debark; *antonym* (*adj*) aquatic.
Jörðin 1. earth; *synonyms* (*n*) dirt, world, dust, ground, land, 2. globe; *synonyms* (*n*) ball, orb, sphere, circle, eyeball.
jórtur rumination; *synonyms* (*n*) contemplation, reflection, consideration, musing, meditation.
jórturdýr ruminant; *synonyms* (*adj*) ruminal, ruminating.
júðafiskur jewfish; *synonyms* (*n*) groupers, mulloway.
juĝi rules; *synonyms* (*n*) regulations, etiquette, policy, system, convention.
júl joule; *synonym* (*n*) j.
jurt 1. plant; *synonyms* (*n*) manufactory, equipment, (*v*) fix, place, embed, 2. herb; *synonyms* (*n*) plant, seasoning, flavoring, flower, (*v*) bunch.
jurtaæta 1. vegetarian, 2. herbivore; *synonyms* (*n*) phytophagan, herbivorous.
jurtagróður flora; *synonyms* (*n*) vegetation, plant, plants, verdure, foliage.
jurtaríki flora; *synonyms* (*n*) vegetation, plant, plants, verdure, foliage.
jurtaseyði extract; *synonyms* (*n*) excerpt, (*v*) draw, abstract, derive, educe.
jurtir vegetation; *synonyms* (*n*) flora, growth, plants, foliage, quietism.
jútarunni jute; *synonyms* (*n*) hemp, cord, cotton, oakum, packthread.
jútujurt jute; *synonyms* (*n*) hemp, cord, cotton, oakum, packthread.

Ĵ

ĵetkubo dice; *synonyms* (*n*) die, (*v*) cube, cut, chop, bet.

K

kabyssa caboose; *synonyms* (*n*) galley, cabin, camboose, cookhouse, jail.

kaðall 1. rope; *synonyms* (*n*) cable, lasso, lariat, noose, cord, **2**. cable; *synonyms* (*n*) rope, line, cablegram, telegram, (*v*) wire.

kaðalslengd cable; *synonyms* (*n*) rope, line, cablegram, telegram, (*v*) wire.

kadmín cadmium; *synonyms* (*n*) candela, candle, (*adj*) ocher.

kadmíum cadmium; *synonyms* (*n*) candela, candle, (*adj*) ocher.

kæfa 1. quench; *synonyms* (*v*) extinguish, allay, appease, quash, destroy, **2**. smother; *synonyms* (*v*) quench, choke, muffle, stifle, suffocate, **3**. choke; *synonyms* (*v*) asphyxiate, block, throttle, clog, foul; *antonym* (*v*) unclog, **4**. asphyxiate; *synonyms* (*v*) smother, strangle, strangulate, garrote.

kæfing 1. quenching; *synonyms* (*n*) extinction, extinguishing, quench, chilling, cooling, **2**. suffocation; *synonyms* (*n*) asphyxiation, apnoea.

kæla cool; *synonyms* (*adj*) chilly, cold, (*v*) calm, chill, assuage; *antonyms* (*adj*) agitated, hot, excited, (*v*) warm, heat.

kælandi refrigerant; *synonyms* (*adj*) refrigerating, (*n*) refrigerative.

kældur chilled; *synonyms* (*adj*) cold, frozen, freezing, cool, refrigerated.

kælibúnaður refrigerator; *synonym* (*n*) icebox.

kæliefni 1. refrigerant; *synonyms* (*adj*) refrigerating, (*n*) refrigerative, **2**. coolant.

kællmlðlll 1. refrigerant; *synonyms* (*adj*) refrigerating, (*n*) refrigerative, **2**. coolant.

kælimiðilsbeinir guide; *synonyms* (*n*) escort, directory, (*v*) direct, conduct, govern; *antonym* (*v*) follow.

kæling 1. refrigeration; *synonyms* (*n*) cooling, infrigidation, cold, preservation, refrigerium, **2**. cooling; *synonyms* (*adj*) caller, refrigerant, refrigerative, (*n*) chilling, crystallizing.

kæliplata lamella; *synonyms* (*n*) lamina, gill, branchia, lamel.

kælir 1. radiator; *synonyms* (*n*) heater, stove, furnace, warmer, **2**. refrigerator; *synonym* (*n*) icebox, **3**. cooler; *synonyms* (*n*) beverage, penitentiary, prison, jail, answer.

kælirör pipe; *synonyms* (*n*) tube, conduit, channel, duct, (*v*) cry.

kæliskápur refrigerator; *synonym* (*n*) icebox.

kælistokkur pipe; *synonyms* (*n*) tube, conduit, channel, duct, (*v*) cry.

kælivifta fan; *synonyms* (*n*) admirer, buff, devotee, enthusiast, (*v*) air; *antonym* (*n*) detractor.

kæra 1. appeal; *synonyms* (*n*) plea, address, (*v*) charm, request, sue; *antonyms* (*n*) unpleasantness, (*v*) repel, **2**. allege; *synonyms* (*v*) affirm, maintain, plead, say, (*n*) advance; *antonym* (*v*) deny, **3**. charge; *synonyms* (*n*) accusation, burden, care, (*v*) accuse, blame; *antonyms* (*v*) absolve, retreat, **4**. accuse; *synonyms* (*v*) impeach, charge, incriminate, arraign, criminate, **5**. announcement; *synonyms* (*n*) annunciation, notice, advertisement, declaration, communication.

kærleikur 1. affection; *synonyms* (*n*) affect, charity, attachment, fondness, affectionateness; *antonym* (*n*) hatred, **2**. love; *synonyms* (*n*) desire, affection, dear, (*v*) cherish, enjoy; *antonyms* (*n*) abhorrence, aversion, (*v*) hate, dislike, abhor.

kæruleysi carelessness; *synonyms* (*n*) neglect, negligence, inattention, indifference, nonchalance; *antonyms* (*n*) alertness, attention, care, caution, vigilance.

kæruskjal bill; *synonyms* (*n*) account, beak, advertisement, (*v*) placard, advertise.

káeta cabin; *synonyms* (*n*) booth, hut, chamber, cot, lodge.

kafald snow (snjór); *synonyms* (*n*) cocaine, coke, precipitation, (*v*) beguile, overwhelm.

kafaraverkir bends; *synonym* (*n*) aeroembolism.

kafbátur submarine; *synonyms* (*n*) pigboat, sub, bomber, (*adj*) subaqueous, undersea.

kaffær submersible; *synonyms* (*adj*) submergible, impervious, (*n*) submarine.

kaffæra 1. overwhelm; *synonyms* (*v*) defeat, flood, inundate, overcome, overpower, **2**. immerse; *synonyms* (*v*) dip, douse, plunge, absorb, drench.

kaffærður engulfed; *synonyms* (*adj*) beaten, conquered, enveloped, flooded, inundated.

kaffæring 1. submersion; *synonyms* (*n*) submergence, immersion, plunge, (*adj*) draught, soundings, **2**. immersion; *synonyms* (*n*) dip, absorption, ducking, concentration, submersion.

kaffi coffee; *synonyms* (*n*) brown, chocolate, cocoa, beige, tan.

kaffifífill chicory; *synonyms* (*n*) succory, chiccory.

kafhlaup submersion; *synonyms* (*n*) submergence, immersion, plunge, (*adj*) draught, soundings.

kaflahleðsla segmentation; *synonyms* (*n*) division, cleavage, partition, partitioning, sectionalization.

kafli 1. segment; *synonyms* (*n*) division, paragraph, bit, (*v*) section, part, **2**. spell; *synonyms* (*n*) magic, fascination, bout, conjuration, (*v*) charm, **3**. chapter; *synonyms* (*n*) episode, branch, article, convocation, head, **4**. episode; *synonyms* (*n*) affair, chapter, event, incident, occurrence.

kafmæði asthma; *synonym* (*n*) anhelation.

kafna 1. smother; *synonyms* (*v*) quench, choke, muffle, stifle, suffocate, **2**. asphyxiate; *synonyms* (*v*) smother, strangle, throttle, strangulate, garrote.

kafteinn captain; *synonyms* (*n*) chief, head, leader, master, boss.

kajakár paddle; *synonyms* (*n*) blade, oar, (*v*) dabble, dodder, row.

kakó 1. cocoa; *synonyms* (*n*) chocolate, brown, umber, (*v*) tea, coffee, **2**. cacao.

kakóplanta cocoa; *synonyms* (*n*) chocolate, brown, umber, (*v*) tea, coffee.

kal frostbite; *synonyms* (*n*) cryopathy, cold, (*v*) numbness.

kál 1. cabbage; *synonyms* (*n*) kale, (*v*) pilfer, filch, crib, nim, **2**. mustard; *synonym* (*n*) eagerness.

kalda chill; *synonyms* (*adj*) cold, bleak, icy, chilly, (*v*) cool; *antonyms* (*n*) warmth, (*v*) heat, warm.

kaldbleyting maceration; *synonyms* (*n*) emaciation, dilution, fasting, gauntness, shrift.

kaldforma stamp; *synonyms* (*n*) mark, seal, brand, (*v*) imprint, print.

kaldlæti frigidity; *synonyms* (*n*) cold, coldness, coolness, chill, iciness.

kaldlátur frigid; *synonyms* (*adj*) cold, chilly, chill, arctic, cool; *antonym* (*adj*) warm.

kaldur 1. cold; *synonyms* (*adj*) chilly, frigid, aloof, callous, (*n*) chilliness; *antonyms* (*adj*) warm, friendly, hot, burning, (*n*) heat, **2**. bleak; *synonyms* (*adj*) austere, bare, barren, cold, dreary; *antonyms* (*adj*) cheerful, hopeful, lush, mild, sunny, **3**. cool; *synonyms* (*adj*) collected, composed, (*v*) calm, chill, assuage; *antonyms* (*adj*) agitated, excited, enthusiastic, feverish, temperate, **4**. chilly; *synonyms* (*adj*) bleak, cool, unfriendly, algid, freezing.

kálfskjöt veal; *synonyms* (*n*) calf, beef, chicken, ham, lamb.

kálfur calf; *synonyms* (*n*) calfskin, sura, colt, foal, kitten.

kaliforníukoli 1. windowpane; *synonyms* (*n*) pane, window, casement, porthole, skylight, **2**. brill.

kalín 1. potassium; *synonyms* (*n*) kalium, chiliad, g, grand, green, **2**. k; *synonyms* (*n*) m, kilobyte, curtilage, gee, (*adj*) thousand.

kalínítrat saltpetre; *synonyms* (*n*) saltpeter, niter, nitre.

kalísaltpétur saltpetre; *synonyms* (*n*) saltpeter, niter, nitre.

kalíum potassium; *synonyms* (*n*) kalium, chiliad, g, grand, green.

kalíumnítrat 1. saltpetre; *synonyms* (*n*) saltpeter, niter, nitre, **2**. saltpeter; *synonyms* (*n*) saltpetre, anatron, natron, brine.

kalk 1. calcium, **2**. lime; *synonyms* (*n*) birdlime, basswood, calx, lemon, cement.

kalkborinn calcareous; *synonyms* (*adj*) chalky, favillous, calcified.

kalkkenndur calcareous; *synonyms* (*adj*) chalky, favillous, calcified.

kalkkrampi tetany; *synonym* (*n*) tetanilla.

kalkspat calcite; *synonym* (*n*) calcspar.

kalkstjarfi tetany; *synonym* (*n*) tetanilla.

Kalkún turkey; *synonyms* (*n*) dud, failure, bomb, flop, joker.

kall call; *synonyms* (*v*) cry, bellow, name, shout, (*n*) appeal; *antonym* (*v*) dismiss.

kalla 1. summon; *synonyms* (*v*) cite, assemble, convene, demand, ask, **2**. call; *synonyms* (*v*) cry, bellow, name, shout, (*n*) appeal; *antonym* (*v*) dismiss, **3**. hello; *synonyms* (*n*) greeting, hi, howdy, hullo, (*v*) hail.

kalómel calomel; *synonyms* (*n*) agueweed, arnica, benzoin, boneset, catnip.

kaloría calorie; *synonym* (*n*) kilocalorie.

kalsít calcite; *synonym* (*n*) calcspar.

kalsitónín calcitonin; *synonym* (*n*) thyrocalcitonin.

kalsítónín calcitonin; *synonym* (*n*) thyrocalcitonin.

kalsono 1. shorts; *synonyms* (*n*) pants, knickers, drawers, trunks, underwear, **2**. underpants; *synonyms* (*n*) trousers, underclothes, undershirt, undies, **3**. briefs, **4**. knickers; *synonyms* (*n*) bloomers, breeches, knickerbockers, boxers, underdrawers, **5**. pants; *synonyms* (*n*) underpants, short, (*v*) bricks, crap, defecate.

kambabolla cardoon; *synonym* (*n*) artichoke.

kambsbrún style; *synonyms* (*n*) fashion, name, (*v*) call, entitle, (*adj*) manner.

kambur 1. comb; *synonyms* (*n*) cockscomb, (*v*) brush, ransack, search, dress, **2**. ridge; *synonyms* (*n*) crest, ledge, bank, hill, shelf, **3**. cam; *synonyms* (*n*) cleat, wedge, (*adj*) cockeyed, crooked, **4**. lobe; *synonyms* (*n*) division, flap, limb, member, arm, **5**. gnomon; *synonyms* (*n*) dial, horologe, hourglass, pendulum, sundial.

kamfóra camphor; *synonym* (*v*) camphorate.

kamfórutré camphor; *synonym* (v) camphorate.

kampasíld capelin; *synonyms* (n) caplin, capelan, capling.

kámugur sticky; *synonyms* (adj) adhesive, awkward, clammy, muggy, embarrassing; *antonyms* (adj) dry, fresh, easy.

kanaborri perch; *synonyms* (v) roost, light, abide, lodge, (adj) dwell.

kandela candela; *synonyms* (n) candle, cadmium, taper.

kandídat candidate; *synonyms* (n) applicant, aspirant, contestant, contender, hopeful.

kandíssykur sweet; *synonyms* (adj) beloved, delicious, fresh, lovely, mellow; *antonyms* (adj) sour, acid, bitter, discordant, acidic.

kanell cinnamon; *synonyms* (n) beige, (adj) brown, auburn, bay, castaneous.

kanill cinnamon; *synonyms* (n) beige, (adj) brown, auburn, bay, castaneous.

kaniltré cinnamon; *synonyms* (n) beige, (adj) brown, auburn, bay, castaneous.

kanína 1. rabbit; *synonyms* (n) coney, cony, hare, lapin, shuttle, 2. cony; *synonyms* (n) rabbit, cherogril, das, dassie, hyrax, 3. bunny.

kanna 1. can; *synonyms* (v) tin, dismiss, (n) bathroom, behind, buttocks; *antonym* (v) hire, 2. inspect; *synonyms* (v) examine, overhaul, overlook, survey, explore.

kannabis cannabis; *synonyms* (n) pot, ganja, grass, marijuana, weed.

kannabisplanta hemp; *synonyms* (n) cannabis, dope, ganja, grass, (adj) marijuana.

kanni 1. sound; *synonyms* (n) echo, (v) ring, chime, (adj) reasonable, complete; *antonyms* (n) silence, (adj) illogical, unsound, confused, 2. probe; *synonyms* (n) investigation, (v) examine, examination, explore, inspect.

kantalúpmelóna cantaloupe; *synonym* (n) cantaloup.

kantur ridge; *synonyms* (n) crest, ledge, bank, hill, shelf.

kápa 1. sheath; *synonyms* (n) case, envelope, blanket, scabbard, (v) cover, 2. wraparound, 3. mantle; *synonyms* (n) cloak, cape, pall, curtain, (adj) blush, 4. jacket; *synonyms* (n) casing, sheath, covering, coat, skin.

kapall 1. wire; *synonyms* (n) cable, telegram, line, rope, (v) telegraph, 2. cable; *synonyms* (n) cablegram, cord, guy, ribbon, (v) wire.

kapar caper; *synonyms* (n) prank, skip, (v) bound, dance, frolic.

kaper caper; *synonyms* (n) prank, skip, (v) bound, dance, frolic.

kapers caper; *synonyms* (n) prank, skip, (v) bound, dance, frolic.

kapersrunni caper; *synonyms* (n) prank, skip, (v) bound, dance, frolic.

kapítalismi capitalism; *synonyms* (n) democracy, commercialism, competition, entrepreneurship, industrialism; *antonyms* (n) collectivism, communism, socialism.

kapítalisti capitalist; *synonyms* (adj) capitalistic, (n) financier, banker, businessman, businessperson; *antonym* (adj) collective.

kapítlalismi capitalism; *synonyms* (n) democracy, commercialism, competition, entrepreneurship, industrialism; *antonyms* (n) collectivism, communism, socialism.

kapphlaup 1. race; *synonyms* (n) kind, dash, family, (v) course, (n) lineage, 2. breed; *synonyms* (n) race, variety, ancestry, (v) engender, beget.

kappnógur 1. profuse; *synonyms* (adj) abundant, generous, plentiful, liberal, ample; *antonym* (adj) scarce, 2. rich; *synonyms* (adj) copious, fertile, productive, fruitful, full; *antonyms* (adj) poor, broke, destitute, impoverished, light, 3. plentiful; *synonyms* (adj) bountiful, opulent, luxuriant, affluent, lavish; *antonyms* (adj) meager, scanty, sparse, 4. ample; *synonyms* (adj) big, broad, large, considerable, heavy; *antonyms* (adj) inadequate, small, insufficient, 5. copious; *synonyms* (adj) plenteous, rich, much, diffuse, many.

kappreiðabraut 1. track; *synonyms* (n) course, path, (v) trace, trail, hunt, 2. runway; *synonyms* (n) track, airfield, airport, channel, tarmac, 3. course; *synonyms* (n) stream, flow, bearing, career, (v) run.

kappsmál aspiration; *synonyms* (n) aim, ambition, longing, ambitiousness, (v) desire.

kapteinn commander; *synonyms* (n) captain, chief, commandant, leader, head.

kápuvörn serving; *synonyms* (n) portion, helping, service, share, piece.

karbamíð 1. urea; *synonym* (n) carbamide, 2. carbamide; *synonym* (n) urea.

karbíð carbide; *synonym* (n) carbonide.

karbítur carbide; *synonym* (n) carbonide.

karbónýl carbonyl; *synonym* (adj) carbonylic.

karboskorio 1. cinder; *synonyms* (n) scoriae, clinker, charcoal, scoria, scum, 2. cinders; *synonyms* (n) dust, ash, powder, (adj) ashes, mother.

kardimomma cardamom; *synonyms* (n) cardamon, cardamum.

kardimommujurt cardamom; *synonyms* (n) cardamon, cardamum.

karfa 1. pot; *synonyms* (n) caldron, boiler, can, (adj) deal, marijuana, 2. trash; *synonyms* (n) nonsense, rubbish, junk, litter, (v) scrap.

karfi 1. redfish; *synonyms* (n) rosefish, fathead, **2**. carp; *synonyms* (v) complain, criticize, gripe, grumble, quibble; *antonym* (v) praise.

kargi rough; *synonyms* (adj) coarse, hard, harsh, raw, crude; *antonyms* (adj) gentle, smooth, polished, precise, refined.

karl male; *synonyms* (adj) masculine, (n) chap, guy, man, (obj) he; *antonyms* (adj) feminine, (n) female, woman.

karldýr male; *synonyms* (adj) masculine, (n) chap, guy, man, (obj) he; *antonyms* (adj) feminine, (n) female, woman.

karlmaður 1. male; *synonyms* (adj) masculine, (n) chap, guy, man, (obj) he; *antonyms* (adj) feminine, (n) female, woman, **2**. bloke; *synonyms* (n) fellow, geezer, **3**. fellow; *synonyms* (adj) comrade, (n) companion, associate, boy, equal, **4**. guy; *synonyms* (n) lad, cat, bozo, hombre, male, **5**. man (maður); *synonyms* (n) gentleman, person, husband, homo, human.

karlmannlegur virile; *synonyms* (adj) masculine, strong, male, manly, potent; *antonym* (adj) impotent.

karlveldi patriarchy; *synonyms* (n) patriarchate, patriarchship.

karmín carmine; *synonyms* (n) vermilion, cardinal, (adj) red, scarlet, crimson.

karótín carotene; *synonym* (n) carotin.

karri drain; *synonyms* (n) ditch, culvert, (v) deplete, waste, (adj) cloaca; *antonym* (v) bolster.

kartafla potato; *synonyms* (n) murphy, spud, tater, bittersweet, countenance.

kartöflubaun groundnut; *synonyms* (n) goober, peanut, earthnut, truffle.

kasein casein; *synonyms* (n) paracasein, (v) crassamentum.

kasín casein; *synonyms* (n) paracasein, (v) crassamentum.

kassava cassava; *synonyms* (n) manioc, mandioca, casava, gari, manioca.

kassavamjöl cassava; *synonyms* (n) manioc, mandioca, casava, gari, manioca.

kassavarunni cassava; *synonyms* (n) manioc, mandioca, casava, gari, manioca.

kassi 1. casing; *synonyms* (n) case, shell, box, jacket, skin, **2**. bin; *synonyms* (n) bunker, binful, container, silo, (v) store, **3**. case; *synonyms* (n) example, bin, cover, affair, bag, **4**. box; *synonyms* (n) basket, cage, chest, (v) cuff, buffet; *antonym* (v) unbox.

kassía cassia; *synonym* (n) cinnamon.

kassíakanell cassia; *synonym* (n) cinnamon.

kassíukanill cassia; *synonym* (n) cinnamon.

kast 1. seizure; *synonyms* (n) arrest, capture, confiscation, seizing, apprehension; *antonyms* (n) release, return, **2**. warping; *synonyms* (n) warp, warpage, beaming, buckle, deflection, **3**. attack; *synonyms* (n) incursion, thrust, (v) assault, assail, attempt; *antonyms* (n) defense, (v) defend, protect, retreat, **4**. fit; *synonyms* (v) agree, accommodate, meet, suit, (adj) decorous; *antonyms* (adj) unfit, inappropriate, unwell, **5**. epiphysis.

kasta 1. throw; *synonyms* (v) cast, fling, shed, hurl, (n) pitch, **2**. cast; *synonyms* (v) throw, form, stamp, shape, (n) appearance, **3**. shoot; *synonyms* (v) bud, discharge, dart, (n) scion, branch, **4**. toss; *synonyms* (v) agitate, chuck, flip, shake, convulse, **5**. pitch; *synonyms* (n) degree, dip, (v) lurch, tilt, toss.

kasthlutur projectile; *synonyms* (n) missile, bullet, shot, bolt, quoit.

Kastor castor; *synonyms* (n) beaver, caster, roller, tile, wimple.

katóða cathode; *synonym* (n) platinode.

kaup 1. purchase; *synonyms* (n) acquisition, bargain, (v) buy, get, obtain; *antonyms* (n) transaction, (v) sell, **2**. wages; *synonyms* (n) salary, pay, wage, earnings, reward, **3**. buy; *synonyms* (v) acquire, bribe, take, shop, (n) purchase, **4**. acquisition; *synonyms* (n) accomplishment, acquirement, attainment, achievement, conquest, **5**. pay; *synonyms* (v) compensate, compensation, liquidate, (n) recompense, fee; *antonym* (v) owe.

kaupa 1. purchase; *synonyms* (n) acquisition, bargain, (v) buy, get, obtain; *antonyms* (n) transaction, (v) sell, **2**. buy; *synonyms* (v) acquire, bribe, take, shop, (n) purchase.

kaupandi 1. buyer; *synonyms* (n) purchaser, client, customer, consumer, emptor; *antonyms* (n) seller, vendor, **2**. purchaser; *synonyms* (n) buyer, patron, punter, shopper, vendee, **3**. customer; *synonyms* (n) guest, fellow, passenger, person, spender.

kaupauðgiskenning mercantilism; *synonyms* (n) commercialism, commerce, capitalism.

kaupauðgisstefna mercantilism; *synonyms* (n) commercialism, commerce, capitalism.

kaupauðgistefna mercantilism; *synonyms* (n) commercialism, commerce, capitalism.

kaupauki bonus; *synonyms* (n) award, compensation, premium, dividend, (adj) extra; *antonym* (n) disadvantage.

kaupbætir premium; *synonyms* (n) bonus, agio, bounty, payment, extra; *antonym* (adj) inferior.

kaupbann boycott; *synonyms* (n) ban, (v) ostracize, exclude, proscribe, strike; *antonym* (v) patronize.

kaupheimild warrant; *synonyms* (n) guarantee, authority, vouch, (v) permit, license.

kaupleiga 1. lease; *synonyms* (v) hire, rent, charter, let, contract, **2**. leasing; *synonyms* (n) rental, chartering.

kaupleiguíbúð condominium; *synonyms* (n) condo, domicile, habitat, home, house.

kaupréttur call; *synonyms* (v) cry, bellow, name, shout, (n) appeal; *antonym* (v) dismiss.

kaupskaparstefna mercantilism; *synonyms* (n) commercialism, commerce, capitalism.

kaupstaður town; *synonyms* (n) city, borough, township, (adj) municipal, urban.

kauptilboð bid; *synonyms* (n) offer, tender, (v) ask, call, command.

kaupvilnun call; *synonyms* (v) cry, bellow, name, shout, (n) appeal; *antonym* (v) dismiss.

keðja 1. series; *synonyms* (n) chain, rank, collection, cycle, (v) course, **2**. chain; *synonyms* (n) string, network, tether, rope, (v) bind; *antonym* (v) release, **3**. cable; *synonyms* (n) line, cablegram, telegram, cord, (v) wire, **4**. cascade; *synonyms* (n) waterfall, torrent, (v) fall, gush, stream; *antonyms* (v) trickle, dribble, **5**. network; *synonyms* (n) net, grid, mesh, netting, reticulation.

keðjuferill catenary; *synonyms* (n) festoon, curve.

keðjuhnettla streptococcus; *synonyms* (n) strep, streptococci.

keðjukokkur streptococcus; *synonyms* (n) strep, streptococci.

keðjulás shackle; *synonyms* (v) fetter, chain, bind, hobble, (n) hamper.

keðjumögnun cascade; *synonyms* (n) waterfall, torrent, (v) fall, gush, stream; *antonyms* (v) trickle, dribble.

keðjun 1. chaining; *synonym* (n) taping, **2**. condensation; *synonyms* (n) abridgement, digest, abridgment, capsule, compression.

keðjusýkill bacterium; *synonyms* (n) bacteria, microbe, rabbit, (adj) virus.

keðjuverkun cascade; *synonyms* (n) waterfall, torrent, (v) fall, gush, stream; *antonyms* (v) trickle, dribble.

kefli 1. spool; *synonyms* (n) bobbin, reel, roll, cylinder, tube, **2**. roller; *synonyms* (n) billow, curler, wave, wheel, brace, **3**. reel; *synonyms* (n) coil, spool, (v) lurch, rock, spin, **4**. cylinder; *synonyms* (n) barrel, pipe, column, container, (adj) cylindroid.

keila 1. tusk; *synonyms* (n) ivory, (v) detusk, horn, (adj) tooth, nib, **2**. taper; *synonyms* (n) candle, (adj) narrow, (v) point, sharpen, acuminate, **3**. cone; *synonyms* (n) strobile, pyramid, roll, conoid, pinnacle, **4**. cusk; *synonyms* (n) burbot, torsk, broom, eelpout, ling, **5**. conus.

keiluhólkur socket; *synonyms* (n) cavity, alveolus, sleeve, hollow, pocket.

keilulaga 1. conical; *synonyms* (adj) conic, pyramidal, copped, tapering, conelike, **2**. conic; *synonym* (adj) conical.

keiluþekjufruma cone; *synonyms* (n) strobile, pyramid, roll, conoid, pinnacle.

keipur rowlock; *synonyms* (n) oarlock, peg, pin, pivot, thole.

kekkja agglutinate; *synonyms* (v) fuse, join, (adj) agglutinative, polysynthetic.

kekkjast agglutinate; *synonyms* (v) fuse, join, (adj) agglutinative, polysynthetic.

kekkjun agglutination; *synonyms* (n) conglutination, union, polysynthesis, clumping.

kemba 1. screen; *synonyms* (n) shade, blind, (v) cover, shield, conceal, **2**. debug; *synonyms* (v) correct, right, repair, revise, fix.

kembari comber; *synonyms* (n) wave, billow, surge, encumbrance, (v) cumber.

kembirannsókn screening; *synonyms* (n) screen, sieving, concealment, cover, covering.

kenna identify; *synonyms* (v) distinguish, detect, discover, name, ascertain.

kennari teacher; *synonyms* (n) instructor, master, coach, preceptor, educator; *antonym* (n) student.

kennd 1. sensation; *synonyms* (n) impression, emotion, feel, (v) feeling, affection; *antonym* (n) numbness, **2**. feeling; *synonyms* (n) passion, atmosphere, belief, hunch, intuition; *antonym* (n) indifference.

kenni identifier; *synonym* (n) qualifier.

kennidæmi paradigm; *synonyms* (n) example, exemplar, epitome, model, archetype.

kenniefni tracer; *synonyms* (n) marker, sensor.

kennilegur theoretical; *synonyms* (adj) hypothetical, abstract, speculative, theoretic, ideal; *antonyms* (adj) practical, concrete, real, scientific.

kennileitaflug pilotage; *synonyms* (n) piloting, steerage, navigation, leadership, lodemanage.

kennileiti landmark; *synonyms* (n) milestone, merestone, boundary, milepost, seamark.

kennilína characteristic; *synonyms* (adj) distinctive, individual, (n) badge, attribute, sign; *antonyms* (adj) uncharacteristic, common.

kennimark logo; *synonyms* (n) emblem, logotype, sign, mark, badge.

kennimerki 1. stigma; *synonyms* (n) spot, blot, brand, stain, blemish, **2**. identifier; *synonym* (n) qualifier.

kenning theory; *synonyms* (n) supposition, assumption, conjecture, guess, hypothesis; *antonym* (n) fact.

kenningakerfi ideology; *synonyms* (*n*) philosophy, belief, theory, opinion, approach.

kennisetning theorem; *synonyms* (*n*) axiom, proposition, formula, principle, thesis.

kennistærð parameter; *synonyms* (*n*) argument, guideline, limit, directive, modulus.

kennitala 1. ratio; *synonyms* (*n*) percentage, degree, proportion, measure, scale, 2. characteristic; *synonyms* (*adj*) distinctive, individual, (*n*) badge, attribute, sign; *antonyms* (*adj*) uncharacteristic, common.

kenniþekja identity; *synonyms* (*n*) identicalness, unity, individuality, personality, sameness.

kenniviðnám resistivity; *synonyms* (*n*) resistance, impedance, immunity, opposition, underground.

kennsl 1. recognition; *synonyms* (*n*) acknowledgment, appreciation, identification, perception, cognizance, 2. identification; *synonyms* (*n*) designation, finding, id, identity, mark.

kennsla teaching; *synonyms* (*n*) education, instruction, indoctrination, doctrine, pedagogy.

kennslubók reader; *synonyms* (*n*) lecturer, professor, lector, proofreader, reviewer.

kepalaukur onion; *synonyms* (*n*) caviare, pickle, leek, chive.

keppni competition; *synonyms* (*n*) contest, rivalry, bout, competitor, contention; *antonym* (*n*) cooperation.

keppur 1. struma; *synonyms* (*n*) goiter, goitre, scrofula, (*adj*) scabies, scarlatina, 2. reticulum; *synonym* (*n*) net.

ker 1. skip; *synonyms* (*n*) jump, bound, hop, (*v*) leap, dance, 2. tub; *synonyms* (*n*) bath, bathtub, cask, vat, basin, 3. pot; *synonyms* (*n*) caldron, boiler, can, (*adj*) deal, marijuana, 4. jar; *synonyms* (*n*) jangle, blow, crock, (*v*) jolt, clash.

keraröð net; *synonyms* (*n*) network, (*v*) mesh, clear, gain, make; *antonym* (*v*) gross.

keratín keratin; *synonyms* (*n*) ceratin, epidermose.

kerbyrði shell; *synonyms* (*n*) peel, rind, bullet, case, (*v*) bomb.

kerfasafn directory; *synonyms* (*n*) catalogue, file, list, record, handbook.

kerfi 1. system; *synonyms* (*n*) method, arrangement, network, organization, plan, 2. plant; *synonyms* (*n*) manufactory, equipment, (*v*) fix, place, embed, 3. network; *synonyms* (*n*) net, grid, mesh, netting, reticulation.

kerfisbundið routine; *synonyms* (*n*) round, (*adj*) everyday, ordinary, regular, common; *antonym* (*adj*) unusual.

kerfisbundinn systematic; *synonyms* (*adj*) methodical, orderly, regular, tidy, neat; *antonym* (*adj*) unsystematic.

kerfislægur structural; *synonyms* (*adj*) organic, tectonic, geomorphologic, geomorphological, morphologic.

keri drain; *synonyms* (*n*) ditch, culvert, (*v*) deplete, waste, (*adj*) cloaca; *antonym* (*v*) bolster.

kerra car; *synonyms* (*n*) automobile, auto, carriage, coach, truck.

kerti candela; *synonyms* (*n*) candle, cadmium, taper.

ketill boiler; *synonyms* (*n*) kettle, furnace, heater, banality, evaporator.

ketónmiga ketonuria; *synonyms* (*n*) acetonuria, ketoaciduria.

keyra operate; *synonyms* (*v*) act, function, run, direct, employ.

kialo grounds; *synonyms* (*n*) cause, dregs, ground, reason, account.

kíghósti pertussis; *synonyms* (*adj*) necrosis, phthisis, pneumonia, psora, pyaemia.

kikhósti pertussis; *synonyms* (*adj*) necrosis, phthisis, pneumonia, psora, pyaemia.

kíkir 1. telescope; *synonyms* (*n*) scope, ambit, background, compass, (*v*) condense, 2. binocular; *synonyms* (*n*) binoculars, spyglass.

kílfesta key; *synonyms* (*adj*) central, fundamental, basic, cardinal, (*n*) guide.

kíll 1. wedge; *synonyms* (*n*) chock, (*v*) squeeze, compress, jam, pack, 2. key; *synonyms* (*adj*) central, fundamental, basic, cardinal, (*n*) guide.

kílókaloría kilocalorie; *synonym* (*n*) calorie.

kílómetri 1. kilometre; *synonyms* (*n*) kilometer, klick, km, 2. kilometer; *synonyms* (*n*) kilometre, (*v*) centimeter, cm, meter, micrometer.

kílóvatt kilowatt; *synonym* (*n*) kw.

kílówatt kilowatt; *synonym* (*n*) kw.

kím 1. germ; *synonyms* (*n*) bug, beginning, bud, kernel, microbe, 2. embryo; *synonyms* (*n*) germ, origin, nucleus, seed, conceptus.

kímblöðrudiskur blastoderm; *synonym* (*n*) blastodisc.

kímblöðruveggur blastoderm; *synonym* (*n*) blastodisc.

kímfruma gamete; *synonyms* (*n*) erythroblast, gametangium, invagination, gonocyte.

kímmiðja follicle; *synonyms* (*n*) cavity, dent, dimple, dint, lacuna.

kímstöð follicle; *synonyms* (*n*) cavity, dent, dimple, dint, lacuna.

kínakartafla yam; *synonyms* (*n*) yew, zinnia, (*v*) eat, speak.

Reference: Webster's Online Dictionary (www.websters-online-dictionary.org)

kínín 1. quinine; *synonyms* (*n*) quinquina, abuse, quinia, **2.** kinin; *synonym* (*n*) cytokinin.

kíníntré quinine; *synonyms* (*n*) quinquina, abuse, quinia.

kink pitch; *synonyms* (*n*) degree, dip, (*v*) fling, cast, chuck.

kinka pitch; *synonyms* (*n*) degree, dip, (*v*) fling, cast, chuck.

kinn cheek; *synonyms* (*n*) audacity, boldness, brass, face, impertinence; *antonym* (*n*) respect.

kinnroði blush; *synonyms* (*n*) flush, bloom, color, red, (*v*) glow; *antonym* (*n*) pallor.

kinnungur prow; *synonyms* (*n*) bow, fore, stem, beak, nose.

kippstýring inching; *synonyms* (*n*) jogging, jog.

kippur 1. jerk; *synonyms* (*v*) jolt, jump, shake, yank, jar, **2.** impulse; *synonyms* (*n*) impetus, pulse, urge, drive, force.

Kirkja church; *synonyms* (*n*) cathedral, temple, denomination, meetinghouse, minster.

kirkjubygging church; *synonyms* (*n*) cathedral, temple, denomination, meetinghouse, minster.

kirkjupallur gallery; *synonyms* (*n*) balcony, audience, drift, veranda, circle.

kirkjuskip nave; *synonyms* (*n*) chancel, choir, hub, omphalos, transept.

kirkjusvalir gallery; *synonyms* (*n*) balcony, audience, drift, veranda, circle.

kirni 1. nuclide, **2.** extract; *synonyms* (*n*) excerpt, (*v*) draw, abstract, derive, educe, **3.** nucleotide.

kirtilblaðra 1. acinus; *synonym* (*n*) grapestone, **2.** alveolus; *synonyms* (*n*) follicle, lacuna, cavity, dent, dimple, **3.** follicle; *synonyms* (*n*) dint, pit, sinus, cell, conceptacle.

kirtilhol crypt; *synonyms* (*n*) vault, tomb, mausoleum, cellar, sepulcher.

kirtill gland; *synonyms* (*n*) secreter, secretor, glandula.

kirtillíkur adenoid; *synonyms* (*adj*) adeniform, lymphoid.

kirtilsafi secretion; *synonyms* (*n*) exudation, discharge, emission, exhalation, extrusion.

kirtilvaki hormone; *synonym* (*n*) contraceptive.

kísilflaga 1. chip; *synonyms* (*n*) splinter, bit, flake, chipping, (*v*) crack, **2.** microchip; *synonyms* (*n*) chip, microprocessor, check, crisp, fleck.

kisilgúr diatomite; *synonym* (*n*) kieselguhr.

kísill silicon; *synonyms* (*n*) silicium, si, ti.

kísilsýrusteinn quartz; *synonyms* (*n*) crystal, lechatelierite, (*adj*) flint, crag, fossil.

kista 1. box; *synonyms* (*n*) basket, cage, chest, (*v*) cuff, buffet; *antonym* (*v*) unbox, **2.** chest; *synonyms* (*n*) bosom, bust, box, bureau, case.

kítín chitin; *synonym* (*n*) elytrin.

kítta putty; *synonyms* (*n*) cement, paste, glue, lute, mastic.

kítti putty; *synonyms* (*n*) cement, paste, glue, lute, mastic.

kíttisspaði spatula; *synonyms* (*n*) slice, shovel, trowel, tablespoon, thimble.

kívíflétta kiwi; *synonym* (*n*) apteryx.

kjaftagelgja angler; *synonyms* (*n*) goosefish, monkfish, allmouth, angelfish, anglerfish.

kjaftstærð gap; *synonyms* (*n*) break, cleft, crack, crevice, (*v*) breach.

kjaftur jaw; *synonyms* (*v*) chatter, gossip, chat, gab, jabber.

kjálkahyrna angular; *synonyms* (*adj*) angulate, bony, gaunt, lean, skinny; *antonym* (*adj*) rounded.

kjálki 1. mandible; *synonyms* (*n*) jawbone, jowl, bill, mandibula, (*v*) jaws, **2.** jaw; *synonyms* (*v*) chatter, gossip, chat, gab, jabber.

kjalsog bilge; *synonyms* (*n*) bull, rubbish, protrusion, (*v*) bulge, (*adj*) hold.

kjalvídd gutter; *synonyms* (*n*) channel, groove, ditch, drain, trough.

kjammi jaw; *synonyms* (*v*) chatter, gossip, chat, gab, jabber.

kjarakaup bargain; *synonyms* (*n*) contract, agreement, covenant, deal, (*adj*) cheap; *antonym* (*n*) rip-off.

kjarkur guts; *synonyms* (*n*) bowels, backbone, boldness, bravery, courage; *antonym* (*n*) cowardice.

kjarnablóðkorn normoblast; *synonym* (*n*) erythroblast.

kjarnafrymi nucleoplasm; *synonyms* (*n*) karyoplasm, karyoplasma.

kjarnakorn nucleolus; *synonyms* (*n*) nucleole, endoplastule, nucleus.

kjarnakvik karyokinesis; *synonym* (*n*) mitosis.

kjarnaofn 1. pile; *synonyms* (*n*) heap, stack, mass, congeries, (*v*) pack, **2.** reactor; *synonym* (*n*) stator.

kjarnasafi nucleoplasm; *synonyms* (*n*) karyoplasm, karyoplasma.

kjarnasamruni fusion; *synonyms* (*n*) amalgamation, coalition, alliance, coalescence, combination; *antonym* (*n*) separation.

kjarnaskipting 1. karyokinesis; *synonym* (*n*) mitosis, **2.** mitosis.

kjarni 1. nucleus; *synonyms* (*n*) core, heart, kernel, center, essence, **2.** topic; *synonyms* (*n*) matter, question, subject, theme, affair, **3.** umbra; *synonyms* (*n*) shadow, shade, soul, spirit, **4.** substance; *synonyms* (*n*) body, import, material, meaning, significance; *antonym* (*n*) triviality, **5.**

core; *synonyms* (*n*) bosom, gist, marrow, quintessence, stone; *antonym* (*adj*) minor.

kjarnkleyfur fissile; *synonyms* (*adj*) fissionable, brash, brittle, breakable, fragile.

kjarnskipting karyokinesis; *synonym* (*n*) mitosis.

kjarnviður 1. duramen; *synonym* (*n*) heartwood, 2. heartwood; *synonym* (*n*) duramen.

kjarr 1. scrub; *synonyms* (*n*) brush, bush, (*v*) scour, scratch, scrape, 2. copse; *synonyms* (*n*) coppice, brake, brushwood, forest, grove.

kjarrmæra oregano; *synonyms* (*n*) marjoram, cinnamon, mace, nutmeg, cloves.

kjarrminta oregano; *synonyms* (*n*) marjoram, cinnamon, mace, nutmeg, cloves.

kjölfar wake; *synonyms* (*v*) awaken, awake, rouse, stir, (*n*) train; *antonym* (*v*) sleep.

kjölfarssog slipstream; *synonyms* (*n*) airstream, backwash, race, aftermath, laundry.

kjölfesta ballast; *synonyms* (*n*) weight, ballasting, (*adj*) aplomb, (*v*) stabilize, load.

kjölur 1. carina, 2. keel; *synonyms* (*n*) bottom, carina, foot, hoof, (*v*) careen.

kjölvatn bilge; *synonyms* (*n*) bull, rubbish, protrusion, (*v*) bulge, (*adj*) hold.

kjör state; *synonyms* (*n*) nation, position, say, country, (*v*) declare; *antonyms* (*v*) deny, (*adj*) private.

kjörbýli habitat; *synonyms* (*n*) dwelling, abode, residence, environment, home.

kjördæmi constituency; *synonyms* (*n*) ward, electorate, clientele, district, area.

kjörfrjáls facultative; *synonyms* (*adj*) optional, elective, discretionary.

kjörgildi optimum; *synonyms* (*adj*) best, optimal, superlative, all-out, (*n*) acme.

kjörhæfni selectivity; *synonym* (*n*) specificity.

kjörhópur elite; *synonyms* (*n*) cream, best, pick, prime, (*adj*) flower.

kjörlendi habitat; *synonyms* (*n*) dwelling, abode, residence, environment, home.

kjörnari punch; *synonyms* (*n*) jab, drill, (*v*) poke, hit, prick.

kjörnungur 1. eukaryote; *synonym* (*n*) eucaryote, 2. eucaryote; *synonym* (*n*) eukaryote.

kjörseðill ballot; *synonyms* (*n*) poll, vote, election, choice, plebiscite.

kjörstaða optimum; *synonyms* (*adj*) best, optimal, superlative, all-out, (*n*) acme.

kjörstilling 1. resource; *synonyms* (*n*) expedient, imagination, (*v*) recourse, resort, refuge, 2. preference; *synonyms* (*n*) choice, inclination, liking, option, predilection.

kjörvís selective; *synonyms* (*adj*) select, particular, discriminating, elective, exclusive.

kjörvísi selectivity; *synonym* (*n*) specificity.

kjósa constitute; *synonyms* (*v*) compose, form, make, commission, appoint.

kjósandi 1. voter; *synonyms* (*n*) elector, citizen, inhabitant, national, resident, 2. constituent; *synonyms* (*n*) component, ingredient, element, factor, part; *antonyms* (*n*) aggregate, composite, whole.

kjöt 1. meat; *synonyms* (*n*) flesh, core, essence, food, gist, 2. flesh; *synonyms* (*n*) brawn, mortality, beef, (*adj*) carnality, concupiscence.

kláði itch; *synonyms* (*n*) desire, urge, impulse, (*v*) irritate, tickle.

klæðaföll menstruation; *synonyms* (*n*) menses, catamenia, flow, period, current.

klæði 1. skin; *synonyms* (*n*) peel, hide, coating, (*v*) pare, bark, 2. fabric; *synonyms* (*n*) building, cloth, composition, frame, (*v*) edifice.

klæðing skin; *synonyms* (*n*) peel, hide, coating, (*v*) pare, bark.

klæðning 1. trim; *synonyms* (*adj*) tidy, (*v*) cut, dress, clip, garnish; *antonym* (*adj*) fat, 2. skin; *synonyms* (*n*) peel, hide, coating, (*v*) pare, bark, 3. lining; *synonyms* (*n*) facing, liner, inside, cladding, padding, 4. lagging; *synonyms* (*n*) insulation, cover, (*adj*) slow, lazy, slack.

klæðskiptahneigð transvestism; *synonym* (*n*) transvestitism.

klafi 1. saddle; *synonyms* (*n*) saddleback, (*v*) charge, burden, load, encumber, 2. yoke; *synonyms* (*n*) pair, (*v*) couple, link, connect, (*adj*) brace, 3. cap; *synonyms* (*n*) cover, bonnet, lid, capital, (*v*) top.

klak incubation; *synonyms* (*n*) gestation, brooding, incubiture, incumbition, (*v*) batching.

klakkur process; *synonyms* (*n*) operation, proceeding, method, procedure, (*v*) action.

klakskápur incubator; *synonyms* (*n*) brooder, hatcher, couveuse, plotter.

klasaður agglomerate; *synonyms* (*v*) accumulate, (*n*) conglomerate, aggregate, (*adj*) agglomerated, agglomerative.

klasagerill staphylococcus; *synonyms* (*n*) staph, staphylococci.

klasahnettla staphylococcus; *synonyms* (*n*) staph, staphylococci.

klasahús cluster; *synonyms* (*n*) bunch, clump, batch, group, (*v*) bundle; *antonym* (*v*) disperse.

klasakenndur racemose; *synonym* (*adj*) racemous.

klasakokkur staphylococcus; *synonyms* (*n*) staph, staphylococci.

klasaleitur racemose; *synonym* (*adj*) racemous.

klasi 1. class; *synonyms* (*n*) category, group, (*v*) sort, place, rank, **2**. cluster; *synonyms* (*n*) bunch, clump, batch, (*v*) bundle, huddle; *antonym* (*v*) disperse.

klassískur classic; *synonyms* (*adj*) classical, model, archetypal, exemplary, ideal; *antonym* (*n*) second-rate.

klásúla provision; *synonyms* (*n*) arrangement, condition, clause, (*v*) preparation, feed; *antonym* (*n*) lack.

klaufjárn crowbar; *synonyms* (*n*) crow, pry, ringer, (*v*) brag.

klausa 1. provision; *synonyms* (*n*) arrangement, condition, clause, (*v*) preparation, feed; *antonym* (*n*) lack, **2**. clause; *synonyms* (*n*) article, paragraph, provision, rider, (*v*) passage.

klefi 1. pod; *synonyms* (*n*) capsule, hull, case, husk, (*v*) shell, **2**. cabin; *synonyms* (*n*) booth, hut, chamber, cot, lodge, **3**. cell; *synonyms* (*n*) cage, jail, cadre, hole, cave.

kleggi body; *synonyms* (*n*) cadaver, corpse, matter, organization, carcass; *antonym* (*n*) spirit.

klemma 1. terminal; *synonyms* (*adj*) final, last, definitive, (*n*) depot, end, **2**. clamp; *synonyms* (*n*) clinch, brace, (*v*) cramp, clench, (*adj*) clasp, **3**. clip; *synonyms* (*n*) blow, buckle, (*v*) nip, snip, trim; *antonym* (*v*) lengthen, **4**. impaction; *synonyms* (*n*) encroachment, impact, impingement, **5**. fixture; *synonyms* (*n*) appointment, fixing, attachment, match, (*adj*) establishment.

klemmdur impacted; *synonym* (*adj*) wedged.

klemmijárn clamp; *synonyms* (*n*) clinch, brace, (*v*) cramp, clench, (*adj*) clasp.

klerkaveldi theocracy; *synonyms* (*n*) thearchy, democracy, oligarchy, demagogy, dinarchy.

klerkdómur ministry; *synonyms* (*n*) cabinet, government, clergy, ministration, administration.

klettaveggur cliff; *synonyms* (*n*) bluff, precipice, hill, mountain, promontory.

klettur rock; *synonyms* (*n*) boulder, calculus, (*v*) jar, (*adj*) pebble, stone.

kleyfhuga schizophrenic; *synonyms* (*adj*) schizoid, hebephrenic, insane.

kleyfhugasýki schizophrenia; *synonym* (*adj*) paranoia.

kleyfhugi schizoid; *synonyms* (*adj*) schizophrenic, demented, hebephrenic, lunatic, (*n*) maniac.

kleyfni cleavage; *synonyms* (*n*) cleft, rift, rip, rupture, (*v*) section.

kleyfur 1. reducible, **2**. fissile; *synonyms* (*adj*) fissionable, brash, brittle, breakable, fragile.

kliður 1. babble; *synonyms* (*n*) drivel, (*v*) murmur, chat, gab, gossip; *antonyms* (*v*) quietness, silence, stillness, **2**. noise; *synonyms* (*n*) clatter, clamor, hubbub, racket, sound; *antonym* (*n*) quiet.

klif cliff; *synonyms* (*n*) bluff, precipice, hill, mountain, promontory.

klifra climb; *synonyms* (*v*) ascend, arise, clamber, (*n*) rise, mount; *antonyms* (*v*) descend, drop.

klifun 1. repetition; *synonyms* (*n*) repeat, gemination, iteration, recurrence, reiteration, **2**. tautology; *synonyms* (*n*) repetition, battology, circumlocution, verbiage, (*v*) polylogy.

klifur climb; *synonyms* (*v*) ascend, arise, clamber, (*n*) rise, mount; *antonyms* (*v*) descend, drop.

klifurjurt vine; *synonyms* (*n*) climber, creeper, bush, flower, plant.

klígja nausea; *synonyms* (*n*) disgust, sickness, queasiness, (*v*) aversion, loathing; *antonym* (*n*) attraction.

klíník clinic; *synonyms* (*n*) infirmary, hospital, workshop, clinique, (*v*) clinical.

klínískur clinical; *synonyms* (*adj*) neutral, antiseptic, emotionless, scientific.

klinka latch; *synonyms* (*n*) catch, hasp, (*v*) bar, bolt, lock.

klinkulæsing latching; *synonyms* (*n*) latch, crossbow, lace, lasket, snare.

klippa 1. shear; *synonyms* (*v*) clip, cut, fleece, lop, pare, **2**. cut; *synonyms* (*v*) carve, chop, (*n*) notch, slice, cutting; *antonyms* (*v*) increase, lengthen, (*n*) addition, extension, **3**. clip; *synonyms* (*n*) clasp, blow, (*v*) nip, snip, trim.

klipping 1. cut; *synonyms* (*v*) carve, chop, clip, (*n*) notch, slice; *antonyms* (*v*) increase, lengthen, (*n*) addition, extension, **2**. clipping; *synonyms* (*n*) trimming, cutting, snip, trim, (*adj*) hair, **3**. clip; *synonyms* (*n*) clasp, blow, buckle, (*v*) nip, crop.

klippir clipper; *synonyms* (*n*) clippers, cutter, limiter, foist, hoy.

klippkraftur shear; *synonyms* (*v*) clip, cut, fleece, lop, pare.

klippur shears; *synonyms* (*n*) shear, (*adj*) scissors, cutters.

klístraður viscid; *synonyms* (*adj*) sticky, gluey, glutinous, viscous, adhesive.

klístrun aggregation; *synonyms* (*n*) accumulation, congregation, heap, lot, (*v*) assemblage.

kljúfa divide; *synonyms* (*v*) cut, distribute, part, dissociate, (*n*) break; *antonyms* (*v*) unite, join.

kljúfanlegur 1. reducible, **2**. fissile; *synonyms* (*adj*) fissionable, brash, brittle, breakable, fragile.

kló 1. plug; *synonyms* (*n*) hype, stopper, bung, (*v*) advertise, block, **2**. clutch; *synonyms* (*n*) clasp, (*v*) grip, clench, clinch, grab, **3**. claw; *synonyms* (*n*) chela, hook, nipper, (*v*) clutch, lacerate.

klóarkúpling clutch; *synonyms* (*n*) clasp, (*v*) grip, clench, clinch, grab.

klofajárn wishbone; *synonyms* (*n*) sudarium, triskelion, veronica, boom.

klofi clevis; *synonyms* (*n*) yoke, shackle, clavel, fetter, gyve.

klofið split; *synonyms* (*v*) crack, cut, fracture, (*n*) break, rip; *antonyms* (*v*) join, unite, merge.

klofinn cleft; *synonyms* (*adj*) split, (*n*) break, cleavage, crevice, fissure.

klofning dissociation; *synonyms* (*n*) disintegration, divorce, disassociation, separation, distancing.

Klofningsgösun cracking; *synonyms* (*adj*) bully, corking, (*n*) breaking, crack, break; *antonym* (*adj*) smooth.

klofningsþáttur cleavage; *synonyms* (*n*) cleft, rift, rip, rupture, (*v*) section.

klofningur 1. dichotomy; *synonyms* (*n*) subdichotomy, duality, 2. cracking; *synonyms* (*adj*) bully, corking, (*n*) breaking, crack, break; *antonym* (*adj*) smooth, 3. cleavage; *synonyms* (*n*) cleft, rift, rip, rupture, (*v*) section.

klofnun 1. scission, 2. segmentation; *synonyms* (*n*) division, cleavage, partition, partitioning, sectionalization, 3. dissociation; *synonyms* (*n*) disintegration, divorce, disassociation, separation, distancing, 4. cleavage; *synonyms* (*n*) cleft, rift, rip, rupture, (*v*) section, 5. dichotomy; *synonyms* (*n*) subdichotomy, duality.

klofnunarskeið cleavage; *synonyms* (*n*) cleft, rift, rip, rupture, (*v*) section.

klofspyrna wishbone; *synonyms* (*n*) sudarium, triskelion, veronica, boom.

klón clone; *synonyms* (*n*) copy, duplicate, clon, (*v*) reproduce, replicate.

klóna clone; *synonyms* (*n*) copy, duplicate, clon, (*v*) reproduce, replicate.

klónn clone; *synonyms* (*n*) copy, duplicate, clon, (*v*) reproduce, replicate.

klöpp rock; *synonyms* (*n*) boulder, calculus, (*v*) jar, (*adj*) pebble, stone.

klór chlorine; *synonyms* (*n*) centiliter, centilitre.

klóra scratch; *synonyms* (*n*) score, mark, (*v*) graze, notch, rub.

klórflúrkolefni chlorofluorocarbon; *synonym* (*n*) fluorocarbon.

klóríð chloride; *synonyms* (*n*) muriate, oxymuriate.

klóróform chloroform; *synonyms* (*n*) trichloromethane, (*v*) deaden, (*adj*) ether, opium.

klórófýl chlorophyll; *synonyms* (*n*) chlorophyl, fecula.

klósamband chelate; *synonym* (*adj*) chelated.

klósigar cirrus; *synonyms* (*n*) woolpack, cirrhus, stratus, cumulus.

klossi pad; *synonyms* (*n*) cushion, apartment, (*v*) line, inflate, expand.

Klukka 1. clock; *synonyms* (*n*) alarm, chronograph, (*v*) time, measure, stopwatch, 2. globe; *synonyms* (*n*) ball, world, orb, sphere, circle.

klukknahljómur chime; *synonyms* (*n*) bell, melody, (*v*) buzz, clang, go.

klukkuskífa dial; *synonyms* (*n*) face, control, gnomon, hourglass, (*v*) telephone.

klukkustillir regulator; *synonyms* (*n*) governor, controller, director, organizer, control.

klukkustund hour; *synonyms* (*n*) epoch, time, hr, moment, nonce.

klukkutími hour; *synonyms* (*n*) epoch, time, hr, moment, nonce.

klumba bulb; *synonyms* (*n*) knob, lightbulb, corm, nodule, (*adj*) globule.

kluss hawse; *synonyms* (*n*) hawsehole, hawsepipe.

knappskot budding; *synonyms* (*adj*) young, blossoming, emergent, green, juvenile.

knappur bud; *synonyms* (*n*) bloom, blossom, flower, (*v*) graft, shoot.

knastur cam; *synonyms* (*n*) cleat, wedge, (*adj*) cockeyed, crooked.

knattgerill coccus; *synonym* (*n*) cocci.

knattspyrna football; *synonyms* (*n*) soccer, hockey, note, baseball, basketball.

knattsýkill coccus; *synonym* (*n*) cocci.

kné knee; *synonyms* (*n*) elbow, genu, scythe, sickle, zigzag.

knekti bracket; *synonyms* (*n*) brace, prop, rack, (*v*) link, couple.

knippi 1. bundle; *synonyms* (*n*) cluster, pile, (*v*) bunch, pack, clump, 2. harness; *synonyms* (*n*) gear, rein, tether, (*v*) hitch, (*adj*) strap, 3. fascicle; *synonyms* (*n*) fasciculus, fascicule, gavel, hattock, stook, 4. group; *synonyms* (*n*) brigade, collection, crowd, flock, gang.

kný thrust; *synonyms* (*v*) jab, (*n*) push, poke, drive, stab; *antonym* (*v*) pull.

knýing propulsion; *synonyms* (*n*) actuation, momentum, push, thrust, power.

knýr thrust; *synonyms* (*v*) jab, (*n*) push, poke, drive, stab; *antonym* (*v*) pull.

kóbalt cobalt; *synonyms* (*n*) blue, (*adj*) cyanogen, azure, smalt, ultramarine.

kóbolt cobalt; *synonyms* (*n*) blue, (*adj*) cyanogen, azure, smalt, ultramarine.

kóða 1. code; *synonyms* (*n*) cipher, charter, law, act, (*v*) cypher, 2. encode; *synonyms* (*v*) code, encipher, encrypt, autograph, calculate.

kódeín codeine; *synonym* (*n*) codeia.

kóði code; *synonyms* (*n*) cipher, charter, law, act, (*v*) cypher.

kódín codeine; *synonym* (*n*) codeia.

kóðun encoding; *synonyms* (*n*) encryption, indoctrination, brainwashing, training.

kóðunarregla code; *synonyms* (*n*) cipher, charter, law, act, (*v*) cypher.

kofi hut; *synonyms* (*n*) cabin, cot, booth, hovel, cottage.

köfnun 1. suffocation; *synonyms* (*n*) asphyxiation, apnoea, **2.** asphyxia; *synonyms* (*n*) suffocation, stupor, asphyxy, (*adj*) cholera, **3.** apnea.

köfnunarefni 1. nitrogen; *synonyms* (*n*) n, newton, normality, north, **2.** azote; *synonyms* (*n*) blacksnake, bullwhack, chicote, kurbash, quirt, **3.** n; *synonyms* (*n*) esteem, estimate, nitrogen, secretary, wages.

Köggull briquette; *synonyms* (*n*) briquet, ovoid.

kögraður fimbriate; *synonyms* (*adj*) fimbriated, fimbricate, fringed, (*v*) fringe, hem.

koja berth; *synonyms* (*n*) bed, bunk, dock, place, (*v*) wharf.

kok 1. pharynx; *synonym* (*n*) throat, **2.** throttle; *synonyms* (*v*) choke, strangle, asphyxiate, smother, strangulate.

kóka coca; *synonym* (*n*) cuca.

kókaín cocaine; *synonyms* (*n*) cocain, coke, snow, blow, carbon.

kókarunni coca; *synonym* (*n*) cuca.

kokeitla adenoid; *synonyms* (*adj*) adeniform, lymphoid.

kokkur 1. coccus; *synonym* (*n*) cocci, **2.** cook; *synonyms* (*n*) chef, (*v*) boil, bake, brew, make.

kökkur 1. agglutinate; *synonyms* (*v*) fuse, join, (*adj*) agglutinative, polysynthetic, **2.** clot; *synonyms* (*v*) clod, curdle, cake, clabber, clog; *antonym* (*v*) liquefy, **3.** coagulum; *synonyms* (*n*) clot, (*v*) curd, stone, **4.** lump; *synonyms* (*n*) heap, chunk, knot, block, hunk.

kókó 1. cacao, **2.** cocoa; *synonyms* (*n*) chocolate, brown, umber, (*v*) tea, coffee.

kókoshneta coconut; *synonyms* (*n*) coco, cocoanut, head.

kókóshneta coconut; *synonyms* (*n*) coco, cocoanut, head.

kokrenna airway; *synonym* (*n*) airline.

koks coke; *synonyms* (*n*) carbon, cocain, cocaine, snow, coal.

kol 1. coal; *synonyms* (*n*) ember, culm, (*v*) char, blacken, (*adj*) black, **2.** brush; *synonyms* (*n*) brushwood, (*v*) broom, graze, sweep, touch.

kola collier; *synonyms* (*n*) pitman, lighter, slaver, whaler.

kolahljóðnemi microphone; *synonym* (*n*) mike.

kolamylsnuköggull briquette; *synonyms* (*n*) briquet, ovoid.

kolbrandur gangrene; *synonyms* (*n*) mortification, necrosis, (*v*) chagrin, (*adj*) corruption, caries.

köldusótt fever; *synonyms* (*n*) delirium, feverishness, frenzy, heat, pyrexia.

kolefni 1. carbon; *synonyms* (*n*) coke, coal, anthracite, carbonado, (*v*) copy, **2.** c; *synonyms* (*n*) cocaine, graphite, hundred, blow, capacitance.

kólesteról cholesterol; *synonym* (*n*) cholesterin.

kólfur 1. plunger; *synonyms* (*n*) piston, diver, needle, speculator, frogman, **2.** piston; *synonym* (*n*) plunger, **3.** basidium; *synonym* (*n*) promycelium, **4.** pendulum; *synonyms* (*n*) dial, gnomon, horologe, pendant, (*v*) flap.

kolhýdrat carbohydrate; *synonyms* (*n*) saccharide, sugar.

kólínergur cholinergic; *synonym* (*n*) cholinomimetic.

kolkrabbi 1. squid; *synonyms* (*n*) calamary, calamari, sleevefish, **2.** octopus; *synonyms* (*n*) devilfish, alacran, alligator, crocodile, mosquito.

kollar cap; *synonyms* (*n*) cover, bonnet, lid, capital, (*v*) top.

kollektor collector; *synonyms* (*n*) accumulator, receiver, gatherer, caporal, choregus.

köllun vocation; *synonyms* (*n*) calling, profession, occupation, business, (*v*) employment.

kollur 1. condyle; *synonyms* (*n*) apophysis, elbow, knob, process, tooth, **2.** capitulum; *synonyms* (*n*) top, head, poll, auricle, brain.

kólónía colony; *synonyms* (*n*) settlement, community, plantation, dependency, village.

koltvísýringsaukning hypercapnia; *synonym* (*n*) hypercarbia.

koltvísýringshækkun hypercapnia; *synonym* (*n*) hypercarbia.

kólumbíum niobium; *synonyms* (*n*) catnap, nazism.

kolun carbonization; *synonyms* (*n*) carbonisation, charring.

kolvatn carbohydrate; *synonyms* (*n*) saccharide, sugar.

kolvatnsefni hydrocarbon; *synonyms* (*n*) carbohydride, hydrocarbonate.

kolvetni 1. carbohydrate; *synonyms* (*n*) saccharide, sugar, **2.** hydrocarbon; *synonyms* (*n*) carbohydride, hydrocarbonate, **3.** heptane; *synonym* (*n*) septane.

kolvetnisgas acetylene; *synonyms* (*n*) alkyne, ethyne, ethine.

kólvirkur cholinergic; *synonym* (*n*) cholinomimetic.

koma 1. come; *synonyms* (*v*) approach, become, aggregate, appear, arise; *antonyms* (*v*) go, leave, **2.**

arrive; *synonyms* (v) come, mature, attain, fall, land; *antonym* (v) depart, **3**. get; *synonyms* (v) acquire, gain, catch, earn, buy; *antonyms* (v) lose, give.

komma point; *synonyms* (n) place, grade, peak, nib, (v) head.

kommúna collective; *synonyms* (adj) aggregate, general, joint, common, cumulative; *antonyms* (adj) capitalist, distributive, private.

kommúnismi communism; *synonyms* (n) collectivism, socialism, phalansterianism, communalism, dictatorship; *antonym* (n) capitalism.

kommúnisti communist; *synonyms* (adj) communistic, carbonaro, frondeur, (n) commie, cosmopolite.

kompás compass; *synonyms* (n) range, scope, area, circle, (v) round.

kompásskekkja deviation; *synonyms* (n) aberration, change, deflection, difference, diversion; *antonym* (n) normality.

kompásstrik point; *synonyms* (n) place, grade, peak, nib, (v) head.

komplement complement; *synonyms* (n) supplement, accessory, adjunct, balance, extra.

komplico accessories; *synonyms* (n) fittings, equipment, accompaniments, garnishes, possession.

kompressa compress; *synonyms* (v) abridge, compact, press, squeeze, condense; *antonym* (v) loosen.

kon gene; *synonyms* (n) chromosome, cistron.

kona 1. woman; *synonyms* (n) wife, girl, maid, (obj) female, she; *antonyms* (n) man, gentleman, **2**. female; *synonyms* (adj) distaff, feminine, pistillate, (n) lady, woman; *antonyms* (adj) masculine, (n) male, **3**. spouse; *synonyms* (n) consort, husband, partner, mate, match, **4**. wife; *synonyms* (n) matron, missis, spouse, helpmate, mistress, **5**. dame; *synonyms* (n) gentlewoman, ma'am, skirt, wench, bird.

konduki wages; *synonyms* (n) salary, pay, wage, earnings, reward.

konfekt sweet; *synonyms* (adj) beloved, delicious, fresh, lovely, mellow; *antonyms* (adj) sour, acid, bitter, discordant, acidic.

kóngasalat tarragon; *synonyms* (n) estragon, mugwort, sagebrush.

köngull cone; *synonyms* (n) strobile, pyramid, roll, conoid, pinnacle.

konguló spider; *synonyms* (n) lota, mussuk, schooner, spinner, adapter.

kónguló spider; *synonyms* (n) lota, mussuk, schooner, spinner, adapter.

Kóngur king; *synonyms* (n) emperor, mogul, sovereign, chief, baron.

köngur spider; *synonyms* (n) lota, mussuk, schooner, spinner, adapter.

kónn 1. taper; *synonyms* (n) candle, (adj) narrow, (v) point, sharpen, acuminate, **2**. cone; *synonyms* (n) strobile, pyramid, roll, conoid, pinnacle.

könnun 1. research; *synonyms* (n) exploration, inquiry, search, examination, (v) check, **2**. review; *synonyms* (n) critique, inspection, retrospect, (v) survey, criticize, **3**. sounding; *synonyms* (adj) audible, looking, hollow, (n) investigation, depth, **4**. survey; *synonyms* (n) poll, review, (v) study, measure, view; *antonym* (v) neglect, **5**. preparation; *synonyms* (n) arrangement, concoction, provision, readiness, training.

könnunarleiðangur exploration; *synonyms* (n) examination, search, discovery, expedition, inquiry.

konsistigaĵo elements; *synonyms* (n) alphabet, rudiments, grammar, outlines, contents.

konsúll consul; *synonyms* (n) archon, diplomat, chancellor, internuncio, legate.

kontraŭanto opossum; *synonyms* (n) possum, pedimane, phalanger.

kontraŭulo 1. opossum; *synonyms* (n) possum, pedimane, phalanger, **2**. opponent; *synonyms* (n) enemy, antagonist, adversary, competitor, foe; *antonyms* (n) ally, supporter, follower.

kontrolisto 1. checker; *synonyms* (n) examiner, counter, (v) check, chequer, (adj) variegate, **2**. checkers; *synonyms* (n) draughts, dominos, solitaire, chessboard.

konungdæmi 1. realm; *synonyms* (n) kingdom, area, country, domain, field, **2**. monarchy; *synonyms* (n) empire, autocracy, realm, crown, department.

konungdómur kingdom; *synonyms* (n) country, domain, realm, dominion, empire.

Konungsdæmið monarchy; *synonyms* (n) kingdom, empire, autocracy, realm, domain.

konungsríki 1. realm; *synonyms* (n) kingdom, area, country, domain, field, **2**. monarchy; *synonyms* (n) empire, autocracy, realm, crown, department, **3**. kingdom; *synonyms* (n) dominion, state, nation, territory, land.

konungssonur prince; *synonyms* (n) monarch, potentate, duke, sovereign, king.

konungsveldi kingdom; *synonyms* (n) country, domain, realm, dominion, empire.

Konungsveldið monarchy; *synonyms* (n) kingdom, empire, autocracy, realm, domain.

konungur king; *synonyms* (n) emperor, mogul, sovereign, chief, baron.

kopar copper; *synonyms* (*n*) bronze, bull, cop, fuzz, gold.

kóraldýr corals; *synonyms* (*n*) hydras, jellyfishes, polyps.

kórallar corals; *synonyms* (*n*) hydras, jellyfishes, polyps.

kóralrif atoll; *synonyms* (*n*) ait, isle, islet, breaker, eyot.

körfukál 1. artichoke; *synonym* (*n*) cardoon, **2**. cardoon; *synonym* (*n*) artichoke.

körfuknattleikur basketball; *synonyms* (*n*) baseball, football, hockey, soccer, hoops.

kórgöng ambulatory; *synonyms* (*adj*) ambulant, mobile, vagrant, itinerant, movable.

kóríander coriander; *synonym* (*n*) cilantro.

kóríandrajurt coriander; *synonym* (*n*) cilantro.

kóríandri coriander; *synonym* (*n*) cilantro.

kóríandur coriander; *synonym* (*n*) cilantro.

kork cork; *synonyms* (*n*) bung, stopper, (*v*) plug, cap, stop.

korkudvergur cretin; *synonyms* (*n*) idiot, moron, fool, imbecile, changeling.

korkur cork; *synonyms* (*n*) bung, stopper, (*v*) plug, cap, stop.

korkvefur cork; *synonyms* (*n*) bung, stopper, (*v*) plug, cap, stop.

korn 1. grain; *synonyms* (*n*) corn, crumb, bit, berry, cereal, **2**. granule; *synonyms* (*n*) grain, (*adj*) scruple, dash, drop, droplet.

kornabarn infant; *synonyms* (*n*) baby, babe, child, minor, (*adj*) juvenile.

kornáferð granulation; *synonyms* (*n*) aggregation, (*adj*) attenuation, comminution, levigation, multure.

kornamyndun granulation; *synonyms* (*n*) aggregation, (*adj*) attenuation, comminution, levigation, multure.

kornhæna quail; *synonyms* (*v*) flinch, cower, cringe, funk, quake.

kornóttur granular; *synonyms* (*adj*) grainy, gritty, chondritic, coarse, granulated.

kóróna corona; *synonyms* (*n*) crown, radiance, halo, aureole, necklace.

kort 1. map; *synonyms* (*n*) design, graph, plat, (*v*) chart, plan, **2**. plat; *synonyms* (*v*) plait, plot, braid, diagram, mat, **3**. scheme; *synonyms* (*n*) contrivance, dodge, arrangement, (*v*) intrigue, devise, **4**. chart; *synonyms* (*n*) table, graphic, (*v*) map, sketch, draw, **5**. diagram; *synonyms* (*n*) figure, drawing, illustration, outline, picture.

kortabók atlas; *synonyms* (*n*) telamon, chart, book, plan, (*adj*) superman.

kortagerð 1. cartography; *synonyms* (*n*) mapmaking, ichnography, **2**. mapping; *synonyms*

(*n*) map, correspondence, agreement, balance, commensurateness.

kortaritun plotting; *synonyms* (*n*) plot, machinations, evaluation, (*adj*) deep, faithless.

kortavörpun projection; *synonyms* (*n*) bulge, hump, jut, prominence, protuberance.

kortblaðsflötur face; *synonyms* (*n*) look, aspect, countenance, (*v*) confront, (*adj*) front; *antonyms* (*v*) avoid, back.

kortisól cortisol; *synonym* (*n*) hydrocortisone.

kortlagning mapping; *synonyms* (*n*) map, correspondence, agreement, balance, commensurateness.

kortleggja 1. chart; *synonyms* (*n*) plan, plot, (*v*) map, graph, sketch, **2**. map; *synonyms* (*n*) design, plat, diagram, mapping, (*v*) chart.

kortsetja plot; *synonyms* (*n*) conspiracy, plan, lot, (*v*) intrigue, cabal.

kortsetning plot; *synonyms* (*n*) conspiracy, plan, lot, (*v*) intrigue, cabal.

kortsýn view; *synonyms* (*n*) look, sight, judgment, opinion, (*v*) regard.

kös heap; *synonyms* (*n*) pile, stack, accumulation, (*v*) aggregate, bank.

kósínus cosine; *synonyms* (*n*) cos, romaine.

kosning vote; *synonyms* (*n*) ballot, election, poll, suffrage, (*v*) voice.

kosningaréttur 1. vote; *synonyms* (*n*) ballot, election, poll, suffrage, (*v*) voice, **2**. franchise; *synonyms* (*n*) exemption, liberty, freedom, immunity, privilege.

kosningarréttur ballot; *synonyms* (*n*) poll, vote, election, choice, plebiscite.

koss kiss; *synonyms* (*n*) buss, brush, (*v*) caress, embrace, osculate.

kosta 1. sponsor; *synonyms* (*n*) backer, benefactor, patron, (*v*) patronize, support, **2**. cost; *synonyms* (*n*) price, charge, amount, expense, toll.

kostandi sponsor; *synonyms* (*n*) backer, benefactor, patron, (*v*) patronize, support.

kostnaðaráætlun 1. quotation; *synonyms* (*n*) citation, extract, mention, excerpt, passage, **2**. budget; *synonyms* (*n*) plan, sack, (*v*) calculate, compute, (*adj*) cheap.

kostnaður 1. price; *synonyms* (*n*) cost, worth, charge, (*v*) appraise, estimate, **2**. cost; *synonyms* (*n*) price, amount, expense, toll, (*v*) be, **3**. expenditure; *synonyms* (*n*) disbursement, consumption, outlay, exhaustion, outgo; *antonyms* (*n*) income, savings.

kostoj 1. expenses; *synonyms* (*n*) expenditure, charge, costs, fee, spending, **2**. expense; *synonyms* (*n*) cost, disbursement, price, outlay, amount.

kostur 1. edge; *synonyms* (*n*) boundary, margin, verge, (*v*) border, bound; *antonyms* (*n*) center, (*v*) middle, **2**. advantage; *synonyms* (*n*) behalf, privilege, profit, account, (*v*) benefit; *antonyms* (*n*) drawback, detriment, difficulty, (*v*) disadvantage, **3**. benefit; *synonyms* (*n*) advantage, gain, (*v*) aid, assist, avail; *antonyms* (*n*) loss, (*v*) harm, **4**. option; *synonyms* (*n*) choice, election, alternative, preference, possibility; *antonyms* (*n*) essential, necessity, obligation.

kóta encode; *synonyms* (*v*) cipher, code, cypher, encipher, encrypt.

kótangens cotangent; *synonym* (*n*) cotan.

kotbóndi peasant; *synonyms* (*n*) boor, farmer, churl, bucolic, countryman.

kóti 1. code; *synonyms* (*n*) cipher, charter, law, act, (*v*) cypher, **2**. height; *synonyms* (*n*) acme, apex, altitude, crest, culmination; *antonym* (*n*) shortness.

köttur 1. cat; *synonyms* (*n*) caterpillar, guy, lynx, bozo, (*v*) disgorge, **2**. pussy; *synonyms* (*n*) cat, puss, cunt, kitty, (*adj*) purulent, **3**. puss; *synonyms* (*n*) kitten, pussy, pussycat, countenance, feline, **4**. fib; *synonyms* (*n*) lie, fable, falsehood, story, tale; *antonym* (*n*) truth.

kótun coding; *synonyms* (*n*) cryptography, encoding, programming, cryptanalysis, cryptanalytics.

kox coke; *synonyms* (*n*) carbon, cocain, cocaine, snow, coal.

krabbalíkur cancerous; *synonyms* (*adj*) malignant, cancriform, destructive.

krabbamein 1. carcinoma; *synonyms* (*n*) cancer, tumor, epithelioma, (*adj*) leukemia, malignancy, **2**. cancer; *synonyms* (*n*) canker, growth, blight, corruption, (*adj*) sting.

krabbameinsvaldandi 1. carcinogenic; *synonyms* (*adj*) deadly, (*n*) benzene, benzine, benzol, **2**. oncogenic.

krabbavaldandi carcinogenic; *synonyms* (*adj*) deadly, (*n*) benzene, benzine, benzol.

krabbi 1. crab; *synonyms* (*n*) cancer, grouch, (*v*) gripe, beef, bellyache, **2**. cancer; *synonyms* (*n*) canker, tumor, growth, blight, corruption.

Krabbinn cancer; *synonyms* (*n*) canker, tumor, growth, blight, corruption.

krækja link; *synonyms* (*n*) connection, join, joint, (*v*) combine, tie; *antonym* (*v*) separate.

krafa 1. requirement; *synonyms* (*n*) need, necessity, demand, essential, obligation; *antonym* (*n*) option, **2**. demand; *synonyms* (*n*) claim, request, (*v*) ask, command, require; *antonym* (*n*) supply, **3**. claim; *synonyms* (*n*) call, charge, allegation, (*v*) assert, exact; *antonyms* (*v*) deny, disclaim, forfeit.

kraftapar couple; *synonyms* (*v*) pair, connect, associate, combine, attach; *antonym* (*v*) uncouple.

kraftfræði mechanics; *synonyms* (*n*) mechanism, workings, procedure.

kraftmælir 1. dynamometer; *synonyms* (*n*) dynameter, (*v*) bathometer, galvanometer, heliometer, interferometer, **2**. ergometer; *synonym* (*n*) dynamometer.

kraftmikill dynamic; *synonyms* (*adj*) active, aggressive, dynamical, energetic, forceful; *antonyms* (*adj*) dull, static.

kraftrænn mechanical; *synonyms* (*adj*) automatic, instinctive, unthinking, automated, (*v*) involuntary; *antonym* (*adj*) manual.

kraftur 1. force; *synonyms* (*n*) energy, strength, agency, (*v*) drive, coerce; *antonyms* (*n*) weakness, persuasion, **2**. vigour; *synonyms* (*n*) force, vigor, vim, push, **3**. strength; *synonyms* (*n*) power, firmness, intensity, endurance, (*v*) might; *antonyms* (*n*) frailty, flaw, shortcoming, **4**. activity; *synonyms* (*n*) action, activeness, exercise, liveliness, play; *antonyms* (*n*) inactivity, inaction, inactiveness.

kraftvægi 1. torque; *synonyms* (*n*) torsion, broach, contortion, crookedness, pin, **2**. moment; *synonyms* (*n*) importance, consequence, flash, instant, jiffy.

kraftvirkur mechanical; *synonyms* (*adj*) automatic, instinctive, unthinking, automated, (*v*) involuntary; *antonym* (*adj*) manual.

kragi 1. collar; *synonyms* (*n*) arrest, choker, (*v*) catch, apprehend, capture, **2**. bulge; *synonyms* (*n*) prominence, protuberance, swelling, (*v*) belly, bag, **3**. boss; *synonyms* (*n*) chief, governor, head, (*v*) administer, govern, **4**. annulus; *synonyms* (*n*) ring, circle, hoop, armlet, anulus, **5**. limb; *synonyms* (*n*) arm, bough, branch, member, extremity.

kráka crow; *synonyms* (*v*) boast, brag, cackle, chuckle, cry.

kramning crush; *synonyms* (*n*) squeeze, (*v*) beat, break, compress, conquer.

krampaeyðandi antispasmodic; *synonyms* (*adj*) antispastic, (*n*) antidote, antifebrile, antipoison, (*v*) laudanum.

krampakast fit; *synonyms* (*v*) agree, accommodate, meet, suit, (*adj*) decorous; *antonyms* (*adj*) unfit, inappropriate, unwell.

krampakenndur spasmodic; *synonyms* (*adj*) fitful, convulsive, spastic, intermittent, broken.

krampakynjaður spastic; *synonyms* (*adj*) convulsive, spasmodic, fitful, paroxysmal, broken.

krampaleysandi anticonvulsant; *synonym* (*n*) antiepileptic.

krampaleysir anticonvulsant; *synonym* (*n*) antiepileptic.

krampalosandi antispasmodic; *synonyms* (adj) antispastic, (n) antidote, antifebrile, antipoison, (v) laudanum.

krampalyf antispasmodic; *synonyms* (adj) antispastic, (n) antidote, antifebrile, antipoison, (v) laudanum.

krampi 1. spasm; *synonyms* (n) seizure, fit, cramp, outburst, attack, 2. braces; *synonyms* (n) brace, suspenders, bitstock, ribs, bracing, 3. convulsion; *synonyms* (n) spasm, paroxysm, commotion, disturbance, shake.

krampo braces; *synonyms* (n) brace, suspenders, bitstock, ribs, bracing.

krani 1. tap; *synonyms* (n) pat, dab, hit, (v) knock, rap, 2. stopcock; *synonyms* (n) cock, cork, plug, bung, turncock, 3. cock; *synonyms* (n) rooster, chicken, stack, fowl, hammer, 4. derrick; *synonyms* (n) hoist, oilrig, (v) crane, winch, windlass, 5. faucet; *synonyms* (n) tap, valve, bar, fosset, taproom.

kraparigning sleet; *synonyms* (n) precipitation, rain, hail, glaze, moment.

krappi 1. curvature; *synonyms* (n) bend, curve, arch, bow, crook, 2. brace; *synonyms* (n) couple, duo, pair, (v) clamp, invigorate; *antonym* (v) weaken, 3. bracket; *synonyms* (n) brace, prop, rack, stand, (v) link.

krappur 1. narrow; *synonyms* (adj) close, limited, (v) confined, contract, limit; *antonyms* (adj) wide, broad, comprehensive, extensive, (v) widen, 2. sharp; *synonyms* (adj) acute, bitter, intelligent, acid, (n) keen; *antonyms* (adj) blunt, dull, mild, gentle, rounded.

krásjurt herb; *synonyms* (n) plant, seasoning, flavoring, flower, (v) bunch.

kreddufastur doctrinaire; *synonyms* (adj) dogmatic, (v) pedant, (n) doctrinarian, bigot, dogmatist; *antonyms* (adj) flexible, (n) dilettante.

kreddukenndur doctrinaire; *synonyms* (adj) dogmatic, (v) pedant, (n) doctrinarian, bigot, dogmatist; *antonyms* (adj) flexible, (n) dilettante.

kredduþræll doctrinaire; *synonyms* (adj) dogmatic, (v) pedant, (n) doctrinarian, bigot, dogmatist; *antonyms* (adj) flexible, (n) dilettante.

kredlt credit; *synonyms* (n) credence, appreciation, belief, (v) believe, accredit; *antonyms* (n) cash, (v) debit, discredit.

krefjast 1. demand; *synonyms* (n) claim, request, (v) ask, command, need; *antonym* (v) supply, 2. claim; *synonyms* (n) call, charge, allegation, (v) demand, assert; *antonyms* (v) deny, disclaim, forfeit.

krem paste; *synonyms* (n) glue, dough, (v) cement, gum, bond.

kremja crush; *synonyms* (n) squeeze, (v) beat, break, compress, conquer.

kreppa 1. depression; *synonyms* (n) basin, cavity, dejection, decline, dent; *antonyms* (n) cheerfulness, happiness, boom, elation, encouragement, 2. crisis; *synonyms* (n) exigency, conjuncture, difficulty, emergency, juncture, 3. contracture, 4. panic; *synonyms* (n) alarm, dismay, horror, scare, (adj) consternation; *antonym* (n) composure.

kretíndvergur cretin; *synonyms* (n) idiot, moron, fool, imbecile, changeling.

kringdur round; *synonyms* (adv) about, (adj) circular, (n) circle, bout, ring; *antonyms* (adj) slim, sharp.

kringing rounding; *synonyms* (n) bruting, labializing, service, (adj) roundish.

kringla disc; *synonyms* (n) circle, disk, record, platter, round.

kringlóttur 1. round; *synonyms* (adv) about, (adj) circular, (n) circle, bout, ring; *antonyms* (adj) slim, sharp, 2. orbicular; *synonyms* (adj) round, globular, global, globose, annular.

kripplun buckling; *synonyms* (n) warping, capitulation, collapse, embossing, pickling.

kristalgler crystal; *synonyms* (n) glass, quartz, (adj) clear, bright, pebble.

kristall crystal; *synonyms* (n) glass, quartz, (adj) clear, bright, pebble.

kristallast crystallize; *synonyms* (v) clear, crystalize, crystallise, effloresce, (adj) candy.

kristallskenndur crystalline; *synonyms* (adj) clear, limpid, crystal, lucid, transparent.

kristallsmyndun crystallization; *synonyms* (n) crystallisation, crystal, crystallizing, condensation, (adj) precipitation.

kristallur crystal; *synonyms* (n) glass, quartz, (adj) clear, bright, pebble.

kró bifurcation; *synonyms* (n) fork, forking, furcation, divergence, split.

kröftugur dynamic; *synonyms* (adj) active, aggressive, dynamical, energetic, forceful; *antonyms* (adj) dull, static.

kröfuhafi creditor; *synonyms* (n) debtee, lienor.

kröfukaup factoring; *synonyms* (n) factorisation, factorization.

kröfuskipti clearing; *synonyms* (n) clarification, glade, clearance, dell, lot.

krókhár barb; *synonyms* (n) point, arrow, jag, gibe, prickle.

króklaga hamate; *synonyms* (adj) hamous, hamated, hamular, hooklike, (v) hamiform.

krókódíll crocodile; *synonyms* (n) alligator, alacran, mosquito, octopus.

krókstjaki hook; *synonyms* (n) clasp, crook, claw, (v) catch, bend.

krókur 1. hook; *synonyms* (*n*) clasp, crook, claw, (*v*) catch, bend, **2**. hitch; *synonyms* (*n*) hindrance, limp, arrest, (*v*) fasten, attach; *antonym* (*v*) unhitch.

krókyddur hamate; *synonyms* (*adj*) hamous, hamated, hamular, hooklike, (*v*) hamiform.

króm 1. chromium; *synonym* (*n*) chrome, **2**. chrome; *synonyms* (*n*) yellow, (*v*) plate.

kröm 1. cachexia; *synonyms* (*n*) cachexy, atrophy, (*adj*) decrepitude, adynamy, asthenia, **2**. marasmus; *synonyms* (*adj*) cachexia, (*v*) collapse, tabes, attenuation, blight.

króma chrome; *synonyms* (*n*) yellow, (*v*) plate.

króna 1. crown; *synonyms* (*n*) top, apex, cover, crest, (*v*) cap, **2**. corolla; *synonym* (*n*) corol.

kroppur body; *synonyms* (*n*) cadaver, corpse, matter, organization, carcass; *antonym* (*n*) spirit.

kross 1. spider; *synonyms* (*n*) lota, mussuk, schooner, spinner, adapter, **2**. cross; *synonyms* (*v*) intersect, baffle, (*adj*) crabbed, crabby, angry; *antonyms* (*v*) uncross, (*adj*) calm, good-tempered.

krossbrú chiasma; *synonyms* (*n*) chiasm, commissure, decussation, chiasmata.

krossfiskar starfish; *synonyms* (*n*) asteridian, crossfish, stellerid.

krossfiskur 1. starfish; *synonyms* (*n*) asteridian, crossfish, stellerid, **2**. asteroid; *synonym* (*n*) planetoid.

krossgagnstæður decussate; *synonyms* (*v*) cross, intersect, cloth, cut, (*adj*) intersectant.

krossgáta crossword; *synonyms* (*n*) conundrum, puzzle, enigma, jigsaw, mystery.

krosslaga crucial; *synonyms* (*adj*) decisive, important, critical, essential, (*v*) categorical; *antonyms* (*adj*) trivial, unimportant, insignificant.

krossliður sacrum; *synonym* (*n*) rump.

krosspunktur node; *synonyms* (*n*) knob, connection, joint, knot, nodosity.

krosstengsl chiasma; *synonyms* (*n*) chiasm, commissure, decussation, chiasmata.

krossviður plywood; *synonym* (*n*) plyboard.

krufning autopsy; *synonyms* (*n*) necropsy, postmortem, dissection, division, espionage.

krumpa 1. shrink; *synonyms* (*v*) dwindle, flinch, recoil, contract, shorten; *antonyms* (*v*) expand, increase, enlarge, **2**. crush; *synonyms* (*n*) squeeze, (*v*) beat, break, compress, conquer.

krumpast shrink; *synonyms* (*v*) dwindle, flinch, recoil, contract, shorten; *antonyms* (*v*) expand, increase, enlarge.

krumpsprunga flaw; *synonyms* (*n*) defect, blemish, crevice, fault, (*adj*) blot; *antonym* (*n*) strength.

krumpun shrinkage; *synonyms* (*n*) contraction, reduction, decrease, decline, diminution.

krúnpassi calipers; *synonyms* (*n*) caliper, callipers, calliper, (*v*) compass, measure.

krusa tack; *synonyms* (*n*) nail, pin, (*v*) affix, baste, attach.

kruss tack; *synonyms* (*n*) nail, pin, (*v*) affix, baste, attach.

krussa tack; *synonyms* (*n*) nail, pin, (*v*) affix, baste, attach.

kryddjurt herb; *synonyms* (*n*) plant, seasoning, flavoring, flower, (*v*) bunch.

krypplingur hunchback; *synonyms* (*n*) crookback, humpback, hump, (*adj*) humpbacked, hunchbacked.

krypplun buckling; *synonyms* (*n*) warping, capitulation, collapse, embossing, pickling.

kryppugildi mode; *synonyms* (*n*) means, fashion, manner, method, form.

kúabóla vaccinia; *synonyms* (*n*) cowpox, vaccina, vaccine.

kúabóluefni vaccine; *synonyms* (*n*) vaccination, immunization, inoculation, (*adj*) animal, bovine.

kúabólusetning vaccination; *synonyms* (*n*) inoculation, immunization, prevention, shot, injection.

kúabóluveira vaccinia; *synonyms* (*n*) cowpox, vaccina, vaccine.

kubbur chip; *synonyms* (*n*) splinter, bit, flake, chipping, (*v*) crack.

kúbein crowbar; *synonyms* (*n*) crow, pry, ringer, (*v*) brag.

kuðungsferill spiral; *synonyms* (*n*) coil, helix, (*adj*) helical, (*v*) curl, loop.

kúla 1. ball; *synonyms* (*n*) bulb, globe, shot, shell, bead, **2**. sphere; *synonyms* (*n*) region, range, area, domain, province, **3**. pellet; *synonyms* (*n*) granule, missile, (*v*) ball, (*adj*) spherule, bullet, **4**. orb; *synonyms* (*n*) sphere, cycle, circle, circuit, eyeball.

kulborði windward; *synonyms* (*adj*) airy, boisterous, empty, (*adv*) downwind, (*n*) upwind; *antonym* (*n*) leeward.

kulborðsmegin windward; *synonyms* (*adj*) airy, boisterous, empty, (*adv*) downwind, (*n*) upwind; *antonym* (*n*) leeward.

kuldahrollur chill; *synonyms* (*adj*) cold, bleak, icy, chilly, (*v*) cool; *antonyms* (*n*) warmth, (*v*) heat, warm.

kuldakast freeze; *synonyms* (*n*) frost, (*v*) congeal, chill, arrest, cool; *antonyms* (*v*) melt, thaw, boil.

kuldi cold; *synonyms* (*adj*) chilly, frigid, aloof, callous, (*n*) chilliness; *antonyms* (*adj*) warm, friendly, hot, burning, (*n*) heat.

kulnun burnout; *synonyms* (*n*) exhaustion, fatigue, (*v*) blowout, disintegration, meltdown.

kúlomb coulomb; *synonyms* (*n*) carbon, centred, century, cocain, cocaine.

kultivi works; *synonyms* (*n*) factory, plant, workings, mill, manufactory.

kúlubaktería coccus; *synonym* (*n*) cocci.

kúluflötur sphere; *synonyms* (*n*) region, range, area, domain, province.

kúlufrávik flattening; *synonyms* (*n*) crushing, annihilation, destruction, devastation, ellipticity.

kúlugerill coccus; *synonym* (*n*) cocci.

kúlulaga 1. spherical; *synonyms* (*adj*) round, circular, global, globose, globular, **2**. spheroid; *synonyms* (*n*) sphere, (*v*) ball, **3**. globular; *synonyms* (*adj*) spheric, spherical, orbicular, rotund, rounded.

kúlulíki spheroid; *synonyms* (*n*) sphere, (*adj*) circular, round, (*v*) ball.

kúlupenni pen; *synonyms* (*n*) corral, cage, ballpoint, (*v*) enclose, confine.

kúluskel sphere; *synonyms* (*n*) region, range, area, domain, province.

kúluþoka globule; *synonyms* (*n*) bead, drip, blob, (*v*) ball, (*adj*) drop.

kúmen caraway; *synonyms* (*n*) anise, carrot, celery, dill.

kuml token; *synonyms* (*n*) mark, memento, souvenir, note, keepsake.

kunkulpa accessories; *synonyms* (*n*) fittings, equipment, accompaniments, garnishes, possession.

kunkulpulo accessories; *synonyms* (*n*) fittings, equipment, accompaniments, garnishes, possession.

kunnátta achievement; *synonyms* (*n*) accomplishment, performance, completion, deed, execution; *antonym* (*n*) failure.

kunningi acquaintance; *synonyms* (*n*) connection, familiarity, friend, acquaintanceship, (*v*) knowledge; *antonyms* (*n*) ignorance, stranger.

kúpa sphere; *synonyms* (*n*) region, range, area, domain, province.

kúpling 1. coupling; *synonyms* (*n*) union, coupler, clutch, conjugation, connection, **2**. clutch; *synonyms* (*n*) clasp, (*v*) grip, clench, clinch, grab.

kúpni convexity; *synonyms* (*n*) bulge, convexness, convexedness, hump, roundness.

kúptur convex; *synonyms* (*adj*) bulging, gibbous, biconvex, hunched, (*n*) crescent; *antonym* (*adj*) concave.

kúpull 1. dome; *synonyms* (*n*) cupola, arch, roof, cover, bean, **2**. globe; *synonyms* (*n*) ball, world, orb, sphere, circle.

kuraĝiĝi braces; *synonyms* (*n*) brace, suspenders, bitstock, ribs, bracing.

kúrbítur 1. squash; *synonyms* (*v*) crush, mash, quell, compress, press, **2**. zucchini; *synonym* (*n*) courgette, **3**. courgette; *synonym* (*n*) zucchini.

kúrín curium; *synonyms* (*n*) cm, centimeter, centimetre.

kúríum curium; *synonyms* (*n*) cm, centimeter, centimetre.

kurteis 1. polite; *synonyms* (*adj*) courteous, cultured, civil, courtly, genteel; *antonyms* (*adj*) impolite, rude, bad-mannered, discourteous, boorish, **2**. courteous; *synonyms* (*adj*) polite, affable, attentive, chivalrous, decorous; *antonym* (*adj*) insulting.

kúrva curve; *synonyms* (*n*) bend, crook, bow, (*n*) curl, turn.

kutimo 1. custom; *synonyms* (*n*) tradition, habit, convention, practice, usage, **2**. customs; *synonyms* (*n*) custom, duty, impost, civilization, mores.

kvaðaskipti swap; *synonyms* (*v*) exchange, change, switch, trade, (*n*) barter.

kvaðning prompt; *synonyms* (*adj*) agile, quick, nimble, (*v*) actuate, incite; *antonyms* (*adj*) slow, late.

kvaðrant quadrant; *synonyms* (*n*) quarter, sextant.

kvaðrantur quadrant; *synonyms* (*n*) quarter, sextant.

kvaðrat square; *synonyms* (*adj*) right, even, rectangular, (*n*) area, (*v*) settle.

kvæði poem; *synonyms* (*n*) song, rhyme, verse, ballad, composition.

kvalalosti sadism; *synonyms* (*n*) cruelty, brutality, aggression, atrocity, (*adj*) sapphism.

kvalastillandi analgesic; *synonyms* (*n*) sedative, anesthetic, painkiller, (*adj*) anodyne, analgetic.

kvanti quantum; *synonyms* (*n*) amount, measure, magnitude, quantity, mass.

kvarða calibrate; *synonyms* (*v*) adjust, regulate, gauge, graduate, measure.

kvarðabreyting scaling; *synonyms* (*n*) ascent, flaking, furring, grading, scale.

kvarðaeining division; *synonyms* (*n*) department, disagreement, allotment, branch, break; *antonyms* (*n*) closeness, convergence, estimation, unification.

kvarði 1. scale; *synonyms* (*n*) flake, gamut, (*v*) ascend, climb, (*adj*) balance; *antonym* (*v*) descend, **2**. dial; *synonyms* (*n*) face, control, gnomon, hourglass, (*v*) telephone, **3**. gauge; *synonyms* (*n*) criterion, caliber, (*v*) estimate, measure, calculate.

kvarnir otolith; *synonyms* (*n*) otoconite, otolite.

kvaronjaro quarters; *synonyms* (*n*) dwelling, abode, domicile, lodging, residence.

kvarono quarters; *synonyms* (*n*) dwelling, abode, domicile, lodging, residence.

kvars 1. quartz; *synonyms* (*n*) crystal, lechatelierite, (*adj*) flint, crag, fossil, **2**. crystal; *synonyms* (*n*) glass, quartz, (*adj*) clear, bright, pebble.

kvartalo 1. quarter; *synonyms* (*n*) area, part, district, division, (*v*) place, **2.** quarters; *synonyms* (*n*) dwelling, abode, domicile, lodging, residence.

kvarter quaternary; *synonyms* (*adj*) quaternate, (*n*) four, foursome, quadruplet, quaternion.

kvartertímabil quaternary; *synonyms* (*adj*) quaternate, (*n*) four, foursome, quadruplet, quaternion.

kvartil 1. quarter; *synonyms* (*n*) area, part, district, division, (*v*) place, **2.** phase; *synonyms* (*n*) aspect, stage, facet, chapter, grade.

kvartmílubíll 1. rail; *synonyms* (*n*) bar, balustrade, handrail, railing, (*v*) inveigh, **2.** slingshot; *synonyms* (*n*) catapult, sling, arbalest, arbalist, ballista.

kvartmílugjöf drag; *synonyms* (*v*) attract, haul, draw, puff, (*n*) pull; *antonym* (*v*) push.

kvarts quartz; *synonyms* (*n*) crystal, lechatelierite, (*adj*) flint, crag, fossil.

kvashósti croup; *synonyms* (*n*) rump, croupe, hindquarters, tail, dorsum.

kveða quince; *synonym* (*n*) melocotoon.

kveði quince; *synonym* (*n*) melocotoon.

kveðja prompt; *synonyms* (*adj*) agile, quick, nimble, (*v*) actuate, incite; *antonyms* (*adj*) slow, late.

kvef cold; *synonyms* (*adj*) chilly, frigid, aloof, callous, (*n*) chilliness; *antonyms* (*adj*) warm, friendly, hot, burning, (*n*) heat.

kvefpest influenza; *synonyms* (*n*) grippe, flu, plague, bug, (*adj*) grip.

kvefslím phlegm; *synonyms* (*n*) apathy, impassiveness, impassivity, indifference, lethargy.

kveikibank 1. ping; *synonyms* (*n*) chink, ring, chime, jingle, (*v*) knock, **2.** pinking; *synonyms* (*n*) ping, pinging, **3.** detonation; *synonyms* (*n*) blast, explosion, burst, bang, (*v*) discharge.

kveiking 1. welding; *synonyms* (*n*) fusion, assembly, synthesis, **2.** brazing, **3.** firing; *synonyms* (*adj*) combustible, (*n*) discharge, dismissal, fire, combustion, **4.** ignition; *synonyms* (*n*) firing, burning, inflammation, kindling, lighting.

kveikir igniter; *synonyms* (*n*) ignitor, lighter, barge, brightness, flatboat.

kveikja 1. trigger; *synonyms* (*v*) activate, initiate, spark, start, incite, **2.** distributor; *synonyms* (*n*) distributer, spreader, middleman, allocator, feeder, **3.** fire; *synonyms* (*n*) discharge, (*v*) excite, eject, blaze, dismiss; *antonym* (*v*) hire, **4.** light; *synonyms* (*adj*) fair, clear, (*v*) fire, kindle, inflame; *antonyms* (*n*) dark, darkness, gloom, shade, (*alt sp*) heavy, **5.** ignition; *synonyms* (*n*) firing, burning, combustion, inflammation, kindling.

kveikjari igniter; *synonyms* (*n*) ignitor, lighter, barge, brightness, flatboat.

kveikur wick; *synonyms* (*n*) taper, candle, wich.

kveisa colic; *synonyms* (*n*) bellyache, mulligrubs, enteralgia, cramp, heartburn.

kvellislekja neurasthenia; *synonyms* (*n*) neurosis, nerves, nervousness.

kvendýr female; *synonyms* (*adj*) distaff, feminine, (*n*) lady, woman, girl; *antonyms* (*adj*) masculine, (*n*) male, man.

kvenhormón estrogen; *synonym* (*n*) oestrogen.

kvenkyn feminine; *synonyms* (*adj*) female, womanly, maidenly, pistillate, wifely; *antonyms* (*adj*) masculine, male.

kvenlegur feminine; *synonyms* (*adj*) female, womanly, maidenly, pistillate, wifely; *antonyms* (*adj*) masculine, male.

kvenmaður 1. woman; *synonyms* (*n*) wife, girl, maid, (*obj*) female, she; *antonyms* (*n*) man, gentleman, **2.** broad; *synonyms* (*adj*) wide, ample, comprehensive, extensive, general; *antonyms* (*adj*) narrow, specific, thin, **3.** dame; *synonyms* (*n*) lady, gentlewoman, ma'am, matron, skirt, **4.** female; *synonyms* (*adj*) distaff, feminine, pistillate, (*n*) woman; *antonyms* (*adj*) masculine, (*n*) male, **5.** lady; *synonyms* (*n*) dame, noble, (*v*) squaw.

kvensjúkdómafræði gynecology; *synonyms* (*n*) gynaecology, dentistry, midwifery, obstetrics.

kvertertímabil quaternary; *synonyms* (*adj*) quaternate, (*n*) four, foursome, quadruplet, quaternion.

kvíðakennd 1. apprehension; *synonyms* (*n*) alarm, comprehension, dread, arrest, (*adj*) anxiety; *antonyms* (*n*) reassurance, release, confidence, calmness, **2.** anxiety; *synonyms* (*n*) care, disquiet, fear, solicitude, trouble; *antonyms* (*n*) bravery, calm.

kviðdómur jury; *synonyms* (*n*) board, panel, adjudicators, group, team.

kvíði anxiety; *synonyms* (*n*) alarm, care, disquiet, fear, solicitude; *antonyms* (*n*) calmness, bravery, calm, confidence.

kviðlægur ventral; *synonyms* (*adj*) abdominal, adaxial, front, forward, intestinal.

kviðskjöldur sternum; *synonyms* (*n*) breastbone, sternite.

kviðslit rupture; *synonyms* (*n*) fracture, burst, rift, (*v*) break, crack; *antonym* (*n*) repair.

kviðuggalaus apodal; *synonyms* (*n*) apod, apode, (*adj*) apodous, apodan.

kviður 1. belly; *synonyms* (*n*) abdomen, stomach, inside, bowels, (*v*) balloon, **2.** abdomen; *synonyms* (*n*) belly, venter, gut, breadbasket, guts, **3.** tummy; *synonyms* (*n*) corporation, pot, potbelly, tum, **4.** gut; *synonyms* (*n*) bowel, (*v*) eviscerate, pillage, ransack, despoil, **5.** jury;

synonyms (*n*) board, panel, adjudicators, group, team.

kvika 1. pulp; *synonyms* (*n*) flesh, puree, (*v*) mash, grind, squash, **2**. turbulence; *synonyms* (*n*) disorder, tumult, confusion, agitation, commotion; *antonyms* (*n*) calm, peace, **3**. dynamics; *synonyms* (*n*) kinetics, motion, (*v*) statics, **4**. magma; *synonyms* (*n*) medley, melange, mess, miscellany, pasticcio.

kvikasilfur quicksilver; *synonyms* (*n*) hydrargyrum, (*adj*) fickle, mercurial, arrow, chameleon.

kvikasilfursklóríð calomel; *synonyms* (*n*) agueweed, arnica, benzoin, boneset, catnip.

kvikasilfursmelmi amalgam; *synonyms* (*n*) alloy, mix, compound, mixture, blend.

kvikband video; *synonyms* (*n*) television, picture, film, movie, (*v*) tape.

kvikefni fluid; *synonyms* (*adj*) liquid, flowing, unsettled, changeable, smooth; *antonym* (*n*) solid.

kvikskurður vivisection; *synonyms* (*n*) dissection, division, (*v*) martyrdom, (*adj*) torture.

kvikur dynamic; *synonyms* (*adj*) active, aggressive, dynamical, energetic, forceful; *antonyms* (*adj*) dull, static.

kvilli malady; *synonyms* (*n*) disease, illness, ailment, (*adj*) disorder, complaint.

kvísl 1. branch; *synonyms* (*n*) arm, jump, wing, affiliate, (*v*) fork, **2**. ramus; *synonym* (*n*) ramification, **3**. bough; *synonyms* (*n*) branch, limb, member, ramage, tigella.

kvíslóttur ramose; *synonyms* (*adj*) ramous, branched, bifurcate, biramous, branching.

kvíslun bifurcation; *synonyms* (*n*) fork, forking, furcation, divergence, split.

kvistur 1. twig; *synonyms* (*n*) branch, sprig, bough, limb, shoot, **2**. sprig; *synonyms* (*n*) offshoot, scion, spray, twig, staff, **3**. knot; *synonyms* (*n*) bow, cluster, tie, (*v*) entangle, knit, **4**. node; *synonyms* (*n*) knob, connection, joint, knot, nodosity.

kvittun 1. voucher; *synonyms* (*n*) certificate, coupon, receipt, ticket, warrant, **2**. receipt; *synonyms* (*n*) reception, acceptance, acknowledgment, acquittance, (*v*) acknowledge; *antonym* (*n*) dispatch.

kvíun incubation; *synonyms* (*n*) gestation, brooding, incubature, incumbition, (*v*) batching.

kvöð 1. duty; *synonyms* (*n*) business, function, commitment, assignment, charge, **2**. easement; *synonyms* (*n*) ease, alleviation, relief, easing, lullaby, **3**. commitment; *synonyms* (*n*) dedication, allegiance, appointment, committal, devotion, **4**. obligation; *synonyms* (*n*) debt, bond, duty, liability, burden; *antonym* (*n*) option.

kvoða 1. resin; *synonyms* (*n*) gum, rosin, colophany, **2**. sol; *synonyms* (*n*) so, soh, gold, sou, **3**. gel; *synonyms* (*v*) thicken, clot, coagulate, congeal, set.

kvoðulausn colloid; *synonyms* (*adj*) colloidal, gelatinous.

kvöðull releaser; *synonym* (*n*) abandonee.

kvoðutré sapodilla; *synonyms* (*n*) sapota, zapotilla.

kvöl ache; *synonyms* (*n*) hunger, pain, twinge, (*v*) hurt, long; *antonym* (*n*) pleasure.

kvöld evening; *synonyms* (*n*) even, dusk, dark, eve, eventide; *antonyms* (*n*) dawn, daybreak.

kvörðun 1. scaling; *synonyms* (*n*) ascent, flaking, furring, grading, scale, **2**. calibration, *synonyms* (*n*) gauging, standardization, gradation, measurement, standardisation.

kvörn mill; *synonyms* (*n*) grind, factory, grinder, manufactory, (*v*) crush.

kvörtun protest; *synonyms* (*n*) demonstration, objection, (*v*) dissent, assert, complain; *antonym* (*v*) support.

kvos excavation; *synonyms* (*n*) mine, pit, dig, digging, hole.

kvóti 1. quota; *synonyms* (*n*) portion, proportion, share, contingent, allowance, **2**. quotient; *synonyms* (*n*) factor, ratio, fraction, dividend, divisor.

kW kilowatt; *synonym* (*n*) kw.

kýlapest pest; *synonyms* (*n*) bane, bore, blight, nuisance, plague.

kylfa mallet; *synonyms* (*n*) hammer, maul, club, mall, beetle.

kýli 1. boil; *synonyms* (*v*) seethe, bubble, churn, simmer, (*n*) abscess; *antonym* (*v*) freeze, **2**. furuncle; *synonyms* (*n*) boil, blister, caruncle, corn, eruption.

kyn 1. sex; *synonyms* (*n*) gender, intercourse, copulation, coitus, (*adj*) sexual, **2**. gender; *synonyms* (*n*) sex, sexuality, kind, femininity, (*v*) copulate, **3**. race; *synonyms* (*n*) dash, family, (*v*) course, run, (*adj*) lineage.

kynæði erotomania; *synonym* (*n*) eroticomania.

kynæxlun breeding; *synonyms* (*n*) education, generation, manners, nurture, reproduction.

kynbætur 1. breeding; *synonyms* (*n*) education, generation, manners, nurture, reproduction, **2**. eugenics; *synonym* (*n*) heredity.

kynblandaður hybrid; *synonyms* (*adj*) crossbred, (*n*) crossbreed, cross, mixture, (*v*) composite.

kynblendingur 1. bastard; *synonyms* (*adj*) illegitimate, spurious, fake, misbegotten, phony; *antonym* (*n*) legitimate, **2**. cross; *synonyms* (*v*) intersect, baffle, (*adj*) crabbed, crabby, angry; *antonyms* (*v*) uncross, (*adj*) calm, good-tempered, **3**.

hybrid; *synonyms* *(adj)* crossbred, *(n)* crossbreed, cross, mixture, *(v)* composite.

kynblöndun 1. cross; *synonyms* *(v)* intersect, baffle, *(adj)* crabbed, crabby, angry; *antonyms* *(v)* uncross, *(adj)* calm, good-tempered, **2.** hybridization; *synonyms* *(n)* hybridisation, cross, crossing, crossbreeding, carrefour.

kynbótafræði eugenics; *synonym* *(n)* heredity.

kynbótarækt breeding; *synonyms* *(n)* education, generation, manners, nurture, reproduction.

kynbótastefna eugenics; *synonym* *(n)* heredity.

kyndiklefi stokehold; *synonyms* *(n)* stokehole, fireroom.

kyndikorn mitochondrion; *synonym* *(n)* chondriosome.

kyndill 1. torch; *synonyms* *(n)* flashlight, brand, light, blowlamp, blowtorch, **2.** flashlight; *synonyms* *(n)* torch, spotlight, **3.** flare; *synonyms* *(n)* flash, blaze, *(v)* burn, flame, burst.

kynding firing; *synonyms* *(adj)* combustible, *(n)* discharge, dismissal, fire, combustion.

kyndirúm stokehold; *synonyms* *(n)* stokehole, fireroom.

kynfæri 1. genitalia; *synonyms* *(n)* genitals, privates, crotch, fork, **2.** genitals; *synonym* *(n)* genitalia.

kynferði 1. sexuality; *synonyms* *(n)* sex, gender, **2.** sex; *synonyms* *(n)* intercourse, copulation, coitus, sexuality, *(adj)* sexual.

kynferðislegur 1. sexual; *synonyms* *(adj)* sensual, sexy, erotic, intimate, amphigonic, **2.** generative; *synonyms* *(adj)* fertile, procreative, productive, fruitful, prolific.

kynfruma gamete; *synonyms* *(n)* erythroblast, gametangium, invagination, gonocyte.

kynging 1. swallowing; *synonyms* *(n)* deglutition, consumption, *(adj)* absorbent, absorbing, absorptive, **2.** deglutition; *synonyms* *(n)* swallow, *(v)* epulation, manducation, mastication, rumination.

kyngingartregða dysphagia; *synonym* *(n)* dysphagy.

kynhneigð sexuality; *synonyms* *(n)* sex, gender.

kynhvarfi homosexual; *synonyms* *(n)* gay, lesbian, homo, dyke, human.

kynhvarfur homosexual; *synonyms* *(n)* gay, lesbian, homo, dyke, human.

kynhvörf homosexuality; *synonyms* *(n)* gayness, homoeroticism, homosexualism, bisexuality.

kynjalyf panacea; *synonyms* *(n)* catholicon, nostrum, cure, gesture, panpharmacon.

kynkaldur frigid; *synonyms* *(adj)* cold, chilly, chill, arctic, cool; *antonym* *(adj)* warm.

kynkuldi frigidity; *synonyms* *(n)* cold, coldness, coolness, chill, iciness.

kynkvísl 1. race; *synonyms* *(n)* kind, dash, family, *(v)* course, *(adj)* lineage, **2.** tribe; *synonyms* *(n)* clan, house, folk, kin, kindred.

kynlaus asexual; *synonyms* *(adj)* agamous, nonsexual, genderless, esexual, androgynous.

kynlif sex; *synonyms* *(n)* gender, intercourse, copulation, coitus, *(adj)* sexual.

kynlöngun erotism; *synonyms* *(n)* eroticism, amativeness, amorousness, enamoredness, sexiness.

kynna 1. present; *synonyms* *(adj)* grant, confer, *(n)* gift, donation, *(v)* bestow; *antonyms* *(adj)* missing, *(n)* past, future, *(v)* withdraw, *(adv)* absent, **2.** reenact; *synonyms* *(v)* enact, model, ordain, assume, copy, **3.** tender; *synonyms* *(adj)* affectionate, painful, *(v)* proffer, *(n)* offer, bid; *antonyms* *(adj)* tough, hard, hardhearted, rubbery, rough, **4.** render; *synonyms* *(v)* afford, interpret, explain, furnish, give, **5.** play; *synonyms* *(v)* act, pastime, exercise, *(n)* frolic, game; *antonym* *(v)* work.

kynnæmur erogenous; *synonym* *(adj)* erotic.

kynnautn 1. eroticism; *synonyms* *(n)* amorousness, erotism, amativeness, lust, enamoredness, **2.** erotism; *synonyms* *(n)* eroticism, sexiness.

kynning 1. presentation; *synonyms* *(n)* donation, exhibition, demonstration, display, introduction, **2.** demonstration; *synonyms* *(n)* parade, proof, argument, manifestation, presentation, **3.** information; *synonyms* *(n)* advice, communication, data, evidence, note.

kynningarbæklingur 1. prospectus; *synonyms* *(n)* program, programme, catalogue, plan, syllabus, **2.** brochure; *synonyms* *(n)* booklet, leaflet, pamphlet, folder, handout.

kynningareintak model; *synonyms* *(n)* form, fashion, example, *(v)* copy, pattern; *antonym* *(adj)* atypical.

kynningarrit brochure; *synonyms* *(n)* booklet, leaflet, pamphlet, folder, handout.

kynningarskjal prospectus; *synonyms* *(n)* program, programme, catalogue, plan, syllabus.

kynningarspóla trailer; *synonyms* *(n)* caravan, leader, ad, advertisement, announcement.

kynningarstarf promotion; *synonyms* *(n)* furtherance, advance, advancement, advertising, boost; *antonyms* *(n)* demotion, neglect.

kynorkuaukandi aphrodisiac; *synonyms* *(adj)* amorous, aphrodisiacal, erotic, sexy, venereal.

kynorkulyf aphrodisiac; *synonyms* *(adj)* amorous, aphrodisiacal, erotic, sexy, venereal.

kynslóð generation; *synonyms* *(n)* age, creation, epoch, era, genesis.

kynslóðartími generation; *synonyms* *(n)* age, creation, epoch, era, genesis.

kynstofn race; *synonyms* (*n*) kind, dash, family, (*v*) course, (*adj*) lineage.

kynþáttaaðskilnaður apartheid; *synonyms* (*n*) prejudice, racism.

kynþáttaaðskilnarstefna apartheid; *synonyms* (*n*) prejudice, racism.

kynþáttafordómar racism; *synonyms* (*n*) racialism, prejudice, bigotry, chauvinism, fascism.

kynþáttahatur racism; *synonyms* (*n*) racialism, prejudice, bigotry, chauvinism, fascism.

kynþáttahroki racism; *synonyms* (*n*) racialism, prejudice, bigotry, chauvinism, fascism.

kynþáttaraðskilnaðarstefna apartheid; *synonyms* (*n*) prejudice, racism.

kynþáttarembingur racism; *synonyms* (*n*) racialism, prejudice, bigotry, chauvinism, fascism.

kynþáttastefna racism; *synonyms* (*n*) racialism, prejudice, bigotry, chauvinism, fascism.

kynþáttur 1. race; *synonyms* (*n*) kind, dash, family, (*v*) course, (*adj*) lineage, 2. tribe; *synonyms* (*n*) clan, house, folk, kin, kindred, 3. stock; *synonyms* (*n*) breed, store, goods, ancestry, (*adj*) regular, 4. clan; *synonyms* (*n*) tribe, race, stock, genus, company, 5. people; *synonyms* (*n*) nation, community, multitude, (*v*) inhabit, occupy.

kynþóttafórdomar racism; *synonyms* (*n*) racialism, prejudice, bigotry, chauvinism, fascism.

kynþroska 1. pubescent; *synonyms* (*adj*) adolescent, juvenile, downy, hairy, puberulent; *antonym* (*n*) adult, 2. imago.

kynþroskaaldur puberty; *synonyms* (*n*) youth, pubescence, cradle, nursery, pucelage.

kynþroskaskeið puberty; *synonyms* (*n*) youth, pubescence, cradle, nursery, pucelage.

kynþroski 1. puberty; *synonyms* (*n*) youth, pubescence, cradle, nursery, pucelage, 2. pubescence; *synonyms* (*n*) puberty, adolescence, down, fertility, prime.

kyntigla gynandromorph; *synonyms* (*n*) androgyne, epicine, hermaphrodite, intersex.

kynvilla homosexuality; *synonyms* (*n*) gayness, homoeroticism, homosexualism, bisexuality.

kynvilltur homosexual; *synonyms* (*n*) gay, lesbian, homo, dyke, human.

kynvís heterosexual; *synonyms* (*n*) straight, straightaway.

kynvísl heterosexuality; *synonyms* (*n*) heterosexualism, directness, straightness.

kýr 1. cattle; *synonyms* (*n*) beast, cows, stock, kine, livestock, 2. cow; *synonyms* (*v*) bully, intimidate, awe, browbeat, daunt.

kýrauga 1. sidelight, 2. porthole; *synonyms* (*n*) port, embrasure, loophole, skylight, window.

kyrking strangulation; *synonyms* (*n*) choking, strangling, throttling, execution, (*v*) suffocation.

kyrkingur 1. dystrophy, 2. cretinism; *synonym* (*n*) idiocy, 3. atrophy; *synonyms* (*n*) decay, (*v*) attenuation, emaciation, tabes, waste.

kyrkivöxtur cretinism; *synonym* (*n*) idiocy.

kyrkja choke; *synonyms* (*v*) asphyxiate, block, throttle, stifle, clog; *antonym* (*v*) unclog.

kyrningahrap agranulocytosis; *synonyms* (*n*) agranulosis, granulocytopenia.

kyrpa dwarf; *synonyms* (*n*) elf, fairy, gnome, (*adj*) little, midget; *antonym* (*n*) giant.

kyrr stabile; *synonyms* (*adj*) immovable, immoveable, constant, static, equable.

kyrrabelti doldrums; *synonyms* (*n*) boredom, stagnancy, stagnation, (*adj*) blues, dumps; *antonym* (*n*) happiness.

kyrrabeltið doldrums; *synonyms* (*n*) boredom, stagnancy, stagnation, (*adj*) blues, dumps; *antonym* (*n*) happiness.

Kyrrahaf pacific; *synonyms* (*adj*) calm, conciliatory, gentle, mild, moderate.

kyrrahafsþorskur dogfish; *synonyms* (*n*) bowfin, grindle.

kyrrðarstund taps; *synonyms* (*n*) decease, demise.

kyrrilyf tranquilizer; *synonyms* (*n*) sedative, tranquillizer, tranquilliser, ataractic, (*v*) lullaby.

kyrrsetning 1. sequestration; *synonyms* (*n*) segregation, separation, damages, deodand, escheat, 2. arrest; *synonyms* (*n*) stop, check, halt, (*v*) capture, catch; *antonyms* (*v*) release, discharge, 3. attachment; *synonyms* (*n*) affection, appendix, accessory, addition, adherence; *antonym* (*n*) detachment, 4. detention; *synonyms* (*n*) delay, arrest, custody, confinement, apprehension; *antonym* (*n*) freedom, 5. embargo; *synonyms* (*n*) ban, prohibition, sanction, veto, inhibition.

kyrrstaða 1. rest; *synonyms* (*n*) remnant, repose, balance, pause, (*adj*) remainder; *antonym* (*v*) work, 2. stagnation; *synonyms* (*n*) doldrums, recession, depression, stagnancy, slump, 3. stasis; *synonym* (*n*) poise.

kyrrstæður 1. sedentary; *synonyms* (*adj*) inactive, lazy, sluggish, domestic, (*v*) untraveled; *antonym* (*adj*) active, 2. static; *synonyms* (*adj*) immobile, motionless, inert, still, stagnant; *antonym* (*adj*) moving, 3. standstill; *synonyms* (*n*) deadlock, impasse, stalemate, cessation, halt.

kyssa kiss; *synonyms* (*n*) buss, brush, (*v*) caress, embrace, osculate.

L

l aerobic; *synonyms* (*adj*) aerophilic, aerophilous.

laborenspezo wages; *synonyms* (*n*) salary, pay, wage, earnings, reward.

labori works; *synonyms* (*n*) factory, plant, workings, mill, manufactory.

laboro works; *synonyms* (*n*) factory, plant, workings, mill, manufactory.

laborpago wages; *synonyms* (*n*) salary, pay, wage, earnings, reward.

láð 1. earth; *synonyms* (*n*) dirt, world, dust, ground, land, **2.** land; *synonyms* (*n*) country, soil, field, (*v*) disembark, debark; *antonym* (*adj*) aquatic.

ládeyða plateau; *synonyms* (*n*) plain, table, tableland, elevation, stage.

lægð 1. pit; *synonyms* (*n*) cavity, dent, hole, depression, (*adj*) hollow, **2.** trough; *synonyms* (*n*) trench, channel, chute, gutter, manger; *antonym* (*n*) peak, **3.** dish; *synonyms* (*n*) bowl, beauty, disk, plate, platter, **4.** cyclone; *synonyms* (*n*) hurricane, storm, tempest, tornado, gale, **5.** basin; *synonyms* (*n*) pot, dock, tank, washbasin, washbowl.

lægðardrag trough; *synonyms* (*n*) trench, channel, chute, gutter, manger; *antonym* (*n*) peak.

lægðarsvæði depression; *synonyms* (*n*) basin, cavity, dejection, decline, dent; *antonyms* (*n*) cheerfulness, happiness, boom, elation, encouragement.

læging masking; *synonyms* (*n*) cover, covering, concealment, mask, screening.

lægri lower; *synonyms* (*adj*) debase, (*v*) degrade, diminish, frown, (*n*) depress; *antonyms* (*v*) increase, raise.

lækka 1. reduce; *synonyms* (*v*) lower, pare, abbreviate, curtail, (*adj*) abridge; *antonyms* (*v*) increase, bolster, expand, enlarge, exacerbate, **2.** decrease; *synonyms* (*n*) decline, cut, (*v*) abate, lessen, diminish; *antonyms* (*n*) growth, extension, (*v*) rise, grow, intensify, **3.** decline; *synonyms* (*n*) decay, (*v*) wane, drop, reject, fall; *antonyms* (*n*) improvement, recovery, development, (*v*) accept, flourish.

lækkar descent; *synonyms* (*n*) ancestry, decline, birth, fall, blood; *antonyms* (*n*) ascent, improvement.

lækkun 1. depression; *synonyms* (*n*) basin, cavity, dejection, decline, dent; *antonyms* (*n*) cheerfulness, happiness, boom, elation, encouragement, **2.** descent; *synonyms* (*n*) ancestry, birth, fall, blood, declension; *antonyms* (*n*) ascent, improvement, **3.**

abatement; *synonyms* (*n*) remission, rebate, deduction, discount, (*v*) reduction.

lækna cure; *synonyms* (*n*) remedy, antidote, medicine, (*v*) correct, help.

læknahús clinic; *synonyms* (*n*) infirmary, hospital, workshop, clinique, (*v*) clinical.

læknamiðstöð clinic; *synonyms* (*n*) infirmary, hospital, workshop, clinique, (*v*) clinical.

læknamóttaka surgery; *synonyms* (*n*) operation, chirurgery, act, functioning, or.

læknandi therapeutic; *synonyms* (*adj*) curative, remedial, healing, medicinal, therapeutical.

lækning 1. therapy; *synonyms* (*n*) cure, medication, remedy, treatment, healing, **2.** cure; *synonyms* (*n*) antidote, medicine, (*v*) correct, help, treat, **3.** healing; *synonyms* (*n*) convalescence, recuperation, therapy, (*adj*) curative, beneficial; *antonym* (*adj*) injurious.

lækningajurt herb; *synonyms* (*n*) plant, seasoning, flavoring, flower, (*v*) bunch.

lækningamaður therapist; *synonyms* (*n*) healer, analyst, nurse, psychiatrist, psychoanalyst.

lækningastarfsemi practice; *synonyms* (*n*) exercise, fashion, convention, (*v*) custom, drill; *antonym* (*n*) performance.

lækningastofa 1. surgery; *synonyms* (*n*) operation, chirurgery, act, functioning, or, **2.** clinic; *synonyms* (*n*) infirmary, hospital, workshop, clinique, (*v*) clinical.

læknir 1. doctor; *synonyms* (*n*) physician, doc, (*v*) cure, adulterate, attend; *antonym* (*v*) break, **2.** physician; *synonyms* (*n*) doctor, medico, medicine, healer, cathartic, **3.** clinician.

læknisdómur remedy; *synonyms* (*n*) cure, redress, medicine, (*v*) heal, help.

læknisfræði 1. medicine; *synonyms* (*n*) cure, drug, medicament, medication, (*v*) medicate, **2.** pharmaceutical; *synonyms* (*adj*) pharmaceutic, (*n*) medicine, physic, remedy, galenicals, **3.** drug; *synonyms* (*n*) anesthetic, prescription, (*v*) dose, potion, (*adj*) chaff, **4.** medication; *synonyms* (*n*) treatment, therapy, sedative.

læknisfræðilegur medical; *synonyms* (*adj*) aesculapian, medicinal, medic, (*n*) checkup, examination.

lækur 1. stream; *synonyms* (*n*) flow, brook, (*v*) flood, (*prep*) current, course; *antonym* (*v*) trickle, **2.** spring; *synonyms* (*n*) jump, leap, bound, (*v*) hop, caper, **3.** brook; *synonyms* (*n*) creek, (*v*) bear, abide, endure, digest.

læma lime; *synonyms* (*n*) birdlime, basswood, calx, lemon, cement.

læmutré lime; *synonyms* (*n*) birdlime, basswood, calx, lemon, cement.

læra learn; *synonyms* (*v*) discover, get, know, find, ascertain.

lærdómur learning; *synonyms* (*n*) erudition, acquisition, education, enlightenment, (*v*) knowledge.

læring learning; *synonyms* (*n*) erudition, acquisition, education, enlightenment, (*v*) knowledge.

lærkriki groin; *synonyms* (*n*) groyne, ankle, breakwater, bulwark, elbow.

lærlingsstaða apprenticeship; *synonyms* (*n*) education, instruction, apprenticeage, apprenticehood, prenticeship.

lærlingur apprentice; *synonyms* (*n*) learner, beginner, greenhorn, novice, prentice.

læsa lock; *synonyms* (*v*) bolt, bar, close, latch, engage; *antonyms* (*v*) unlock, open.

læsast interlock; *synonyms* (*v*) engage, interlace, mesh, entwine, connect.

læsi literacy; *synonyms* (*n*) education, scholarship, enlightenment, erudition, articulacy; *antonym* (*n*) illiteracy.

læsibúnaður lock; *synonyms* (*v*) bolt, bar, close, latch, engage; *antonyms* (*v*) unlock, open.

læsing lockout; *synonyms* (*n*) exclusion, stoppage.

lævirki lark; *synonyms* (*n*) escapade, frolic, joke, fun, (*v*) romp.

lag 1. stratum; *synonyms* (*n*) layer, bed, level, floor, seam, 2. bed; *synonyms* (*n*) couch, base, basis, berth, bottom, 3. layer; *synonyms* (*n*) coat, course, coating, cover, film, 4. sheet; *synonyms* (*n*) board, leaf, canvas, paper, blanket, 5. ply; *synonyms* (*n*) fold, (*v*) feed, handle, run, incline.

laga 1. straighten; *synonyms* (*v*) tidy, unbend, neaten, extend, dress; *antonyms* (*v*) bend, deform, 2. fix; *synonyms* (*v*) establish, assign, determine, (*n*) bind, (*adj*) ascertain; *antonyms* (*v*) break, unfasten, 3. improve; *synonyms* (*v*) advance, heal, emend, help, ameliorate; *antonyms* (*v*) worsen, deteriorate, regress, spoil.

lagaboð statute; *synonyms* (*n*) law, ordinance, rule, constitution, decree.

lagabreyting amendment; *synonyms* (*n*) alteration, betterment, correction, redress, improvement.

lagalegur statutory; *synonyms* (*adj*) legal, lawful, legitimate, statutable, constitutional.

lagamót 1. horizon; *synonyms* (*n*) perspective, prospect, purview, reach, skyline, 2. interface; *synonyms* (*n*) link, port, boundary, junction, (*v*) contact.

lagasetning legislation; *synonyms* (*n*) lawmaking, legislating, law, conduct, government.

lagatúlkun construction; *synonyms* (*n*) building, fabrication, formation, structure, assembly; *antonym* (*n*) destruction.

lagdeiling stratification; *synonyms* (*n*) bedding, lamination.

lager 1. stock; *synonyms* (*n*) breed, lineage, store, goods, (*adj*) regular, 2. bearing; *synonyms* (*n*) carriage, demeanor, appearance, approach, aspect.

lagfæra 1. rectify; *synonyms* (*v*) amend, correct, improve, better, adjust, 2. repair; *synonyms* (*v*) remedy, mend, patch, redress, cure; *antonym* (*v*) break, 3. mend; *synonyms* (*v*) repair, doctor, heal, restore, (*n*) fix.

lagfæring 1. rectification; *synonyms* (*n*) correction, amendment, improvement, redress, revision, 2. repair; *synonyms* (*v*) remedy, mend, patch, correct, cure; *antonym* (*v*) break, 3. improvement; *synonyms* (*n*) advancement, amelioration, betterment, development, repair; *antonyms* (*n*) decline, deterioration, downgrade.

laggangur sill; *synonyms* (*n*) doorsill, ledge, threshold, rung, step.

lággildi minimum; *synonyms* (*adj*) minimal, least, smallest, hint, trace; *antonyms* (*n*) maximum, most.

lágmark minimum; *synonyms* (*adj*) minimal, least, smallest, hint, trace; *antonyms* (*n*) maximum, most.

lágmarka minimize; *synonyms* (*v*) belittle, disparage, diminish, decrease, derogate; *antonyms* (*v*) exaggerate, maximize.

lágmarks nominal; *synonyms* (*adj*) titular, formal, token, minimal, (*v*) cognominal; *antonym* (*adj*) real.

lagskipt laminated; *synonyms* (*adj*) laminate, laminiferous, tabular, coated, covered.

lagskipta stratify; *synonym* (*v*) plate.

lagskipting 1. stratification; *synonyms* (*n*) bedding, lamination, 2. apposition; *synonyms* (*n*) union, juxtaposition, (*prep*) addition, accompaniment, accord.

lagskiptur 1. stratified; *synonyms* (*adj*) bedded, graded, ranked, stratiform, graveled, 2. laminar; *synonyms* (*adj*) laminal, laminary, 3. laminated; *synonyms* (*adj*) laminate, laminiferous, tabular, coated, covered.

lágský stratus; *synonyms* (*n*) cirrus, cumulus, woolpack.

lágstæður subscript; *synonyms* (*n*) inferior, (*adj*) deficient, lower, lowly, secondary; *antonym* (*n*) superscript.

lágstafa lowercase; *synonyms* (*adj*) belittled, brief, diminished, fiddling, footling.

lagsverð rapier; *synonyms* (*n*) sword, blade, brand, foil, glaive.

lágur low; *synonyms* (*adj*) contemptible, abject, humble, ignoble, (*adv*) gentle; *antonyms* (*adj*) cheerful, happy, high-pitched, loud, (*n*) high.

lágvísir subscript; *synonyms* (*n*) inferior, (*adj*) deficient, lower, lowly, secondary; *antonym* (*n*) superscript.

láhnit abscissa; *synonym* (*n*) absciss.

laki 1. psalterium; *synonym* (*n*) omasum, **2**. omasum; *synonym* (*n*) psalterium.

lakk 1. shellac; *synonyms* (*n*) lac, (*v*) varnish, clobber, lick, overpower, **2**. varnish; *synonyms* (*n*) coat, lacquer, paint, (*v*) gloss, color.

lakkmúslitur litmus; *synonyms* (*n*) lacmus, (*adj*) turnsole, heliotrope.

laktat lactate; *synonyms* (*v*) nurse, suck, suckle, breastfeed, absorb.

laktósi lactose; *synonym* (*n*) galactose.

lakur inferior; *synonyms* (*adj*) bad, secondary, subordinate, humble, poor; *antonyms* (*adj*) better, choice, excellent, first-rate, (*n*) superior.

lami paralytic; *synonyms* (*adj*) palsied, paralytical, paralyzed, (*n*) invalid, (*v*) withered.

lampi 1. lamp; *synonyms* (*n*) light, look, beacon, (*v*) behold, regard, **2**. tube; *synonyms* (*n*) pipe, conduit, duct, subway, hose, **3**. valve; *synonyms* (*n*) lock, sluice, door, gauge, monitor.

lán 1. credit; *synonyms* (*n*) credence, appreciation, belief, (*v*) believe, accredit; *antonyms* (*n*) cash, (*v*) debit, discredit, **2**. borrowing; *synonyms* (*n*) adoption, loan, pledging, acceptance, acceptation, **3**. loan; *synonyms* (*n*) credit, loanword, (*v*) advance, lend, trust; *antonym* (*v*) borrow.

lánardrottinn creditor; *synonyms* (*n*) debtee, lienor.

land 1. country; *synonyms* (*n*) state, nation, home, land, area; *antonyms* (*n*) city, (*adj*) urban, **2**. state; *synonyms* (*n*) position, say, country, (*v*) declare, expound; *antonyms* (*v*) deny, (*adj*) private, **3**. premises; *synonyms* (*n*) grounds, facts, lemma, terms, principle, **4**. soil; *synonyms* (*n*) ground, dirt, (*v*) smudge, blot, contaminate; *antonym* (*v*) clean, **5**. earth; *synonyms* (*n*) world, dust, clay, lair, creation.

landa land; *synonyms* (*n*) ground, country, soil, (*v*) disembark, debark; *antonym* (*adj*) aquatic.

landabréf map; *synonyms* (*n*) design, graph, plat, (*v*) chart, plan.

landafræði geography; *synonyms* (*n*) topography, geographics, backcloth, backdrop, background.

landakort 1. chart; *synonyms* (*n*) plan, plot, (*v*) map, graph, sketch, **2**. map; *synonyms* (*n*) design, plat, diagram, mapping, (*v*) chart.

landakortabók atlas; *synonyms* (*n*) telamon, chart, book, plan, (*adj*) superman.

landamærahéruð frontier; *synonyms* (*n*) border, boundary, edge, line, bound.

landamæri 1. boundary; *synonyms* (*n*) border, bound, limit, edge, area, **2**. border; *synonyms* (*n*) margin, brink, extremity, fringe, (*v*) verge; *antonyms* (*n*) middle, (*v*) center, **3**. frontier; *synonyms* (*n*) boundary, line, perimeter, stint, (*adj*) terminal.

landamerki 1. boundary; *synonyms* (*n*) border, bound, limit, edge, area, **2**. landmark; *synonyms* (*n*) milestone, merestone, boundary, milepost, seamark.

landamerkjalýsing delineation; *synonyms* (*n*) portrayal, description, picture, definition, depiction.

landamerkjamæling demarcation; *synonyms* (*n*) boundary, definition, line, border, partition.

landamerkjauppdráttur plat; *synonyms* (*n*) chart, (*v*) plait, plot, braid, diagram.

landareign 1. premises; *synonyms* (*n*) grounds, facts, lemma, terms, principle, **2**. domain; *synonyms* (*n*) country, department, realm, area, kingdom; *antonym* (*n*) range, **3**. parcel; *synonyms* (*n*) lot, bale, pack, bundle, (*v*) portion, **4**. land; *synonyms* (*n*) ground, soil, field, (*v*) disembark, debark; *antonym* (*adj*) aquatic, **5**. estate; *synonyms* (*n*) condition, land, demesne, order, rank.

landauki reclamation; *synonyms* (*n*) claim, reclaim, recovery, reformation, retrieval.

landbrú isthmus; *synonyms* (*n*) bridge, oasis, (*adj*) strait, neck, wasp.

landbúnaðarverkamaður peasant; *synonyms* (*n*) boor, farmer, churl, bucolic, countryman.

landbúnaðarviðskipti agribusiness; *synonyms* (*n*) agriculture, agrobusiness, farming, husbandry.

landbúnaður agriculture; *synonyms* (*n*) farming, agribusiness, agronomy, husbandry, tillage.

landeyjar delta; *synonyms* (*n*) chersonese, continent, inlet, mainland, mouth.

landfarsótt epidemic; *synonyms* (*n*) outbreak, plague, (*adj*) contagious, infectious, catching; *antonym* (*adj*) endemic.

landflótti emigration; *synonyms* (*n*) departure, exodus, migration, demigration, (*v*) intermigration.

landflutningur haulage; *synonyms* (*n*) traction, transport, draw, haul, (*v*) towage.

landfræðilegur geographical; *synonyms* (*adj*) geographic, biological, ecological, environmental, local.

landgangur 1. finger; *synonyms* (*n*) digit, dactyl, (*v*) feel, handle, touch, **2**. gangway; *synonyms* (*n*) aisle, gangboard, gangplank, walkway, footbridge.

landgöngubryggja pier; *synonyms* (*n*) dock, wharf, jetty, pillar, quay.

landgönguliði mariner; *synonyms* (*n*) gob, sailor, seafarer, seaman, tar.

landhæð elevation; *synonyms* (*n*) altitude, height, ascent, exaltation, highness.

landkönnun exploration; *synonyms* (*n*) examination, search, discovery, expedition, inquiry.

landlægur endemic; *synonyms* (*adj*) autochthonous, indigenous, native, aboriginal, (*n*) epidemic.

landmæling 1. surveying; *synonyms* (*adj*) observant, (*n*) investigation, topography, **2.** geodesy; *synonym* (*v*) geodetics.

landmælingafræði geodesy; *synonym* (*v*) geodetics.

landmælingakort survey; *synonyms* (*n*) poll, review, (*v*) study, measure, view; *antonym* (*v*) neglect.

landmælingamaður surveyor; *synonyms* (*n*) inspector, assessor, visitor, engineer, husband.

landmælingar 1. survey; *synonyms* (*n*) poll, review, (*v*) study, measure, view; *antonym* (*v*) neglect, **2.** geodesy; *synonym* (*v*) geodetics.

landmótunarfræði geomorphology; *synonym* (*n*) morphology.

landnám settlement; *synonyms* (*n*) decision, accommodation, colony, hamlet, payment.

landnemi pioneer; *synonyms* (*n*) forerunner, guide, colonist, (*v*) initiate, institute.

landris uplift; *synonyms* (*n*) lift, upheaval, (*v*) elate, elevate, raise.

landsig subsidence; *synonyms* (*n*) collapse, ebb, remission, settlement, settling.

landskjálfti earthquake; *synonyms* (*n*) quake, shock, tremor, temblor, (*adj*) thunderstorm.

landslag 1. landscape; *synonyms* (*n*) outlook, scene, scenery, sight, (*v*) prospect, **2.** topography; *synonyms* (*n*) terrain, backcloth, backdrop, background, countryside, **3.** relief; *synonyms* (*n*) comfort, aid, consolation, ease, (*v*) assistance, **4.** country; *synonyms* (*n*) state, nation, home, land, area; *antonyms* (*n*) city, (*adj*) urban, **5.** morphology; *synonyms* (*n*) accidence, anatomy, geomorphology, taxonomy, botany.

landslagsútlínur topography; *synonyms* (*n*) terrain, backcloth, backdrop, background, countryside.

landsmenn country; *synonyms* (*n*) state, nation, home, land, area; *antonyms* (*n*) city, (*adj*) urban.

landssvæði district; *synonyms* (*n*) area, quarter, region, community, neighborhood.

landstjóri governor; *synonyms* (*n*) director, chief, manager, regulator, administrator.

landsuppdráttur map, *synonyms* (*n*) design, graph, plat, (*v*) chart, plan.

landsvæði 1. terrain; *synonyms* (*n*) ground, field, land, country, area, **2.** territory; *synonyms* (*n*) district, dominion, region, state, domain, **3.** land; *synonyms* (*n*) soil, kingdom, (*v*) disembark, debark, alight; *antonym* (*adj*) aquatic.

landsvala swallow; *synonyms* (*v*) eat, bolt, gulp, consume, (*n*) drink; *antonym* (*v*) regurgitate.

landsýn landfall; *synonym* (*n*) approaches.

landtaka landfall; *synonym* (*n*) approaches.

landvætti monument; *synonyms* (*n*) memorial, headstone, column, record, tombstone.

landvistarleyfi asylum; *synonyms* (*n*) refuge, sanctuary, shelter, haven, home.

langa ling; *synonyms* (*n*) heather, burbot, broom, cusk, eelpout.

langær persistent; *synonyms* (*adj*) durable, constant, continual, insistent, lasting; *antonyms* (*adj*) contained, occasional.

langband rail; *synonyms* (*n*) bar, balustrade, handrail, railing, (*v*) inveigh.

langeldur hearth; *synonyms* (*n*) fireplace, fire, fireside, chimney, furnace.

langferðabifreið coach; *synonyms* (*n*) trainer, tutor, instructor, teacher, (*adj*) prime.

langhlið hypotenuse; *synonym* (*n*) hypothenuse.

langlenda overshoot; *synonyms* (*v*) overrun, jump.

langliður tibia; *synonyms* (*n*) shin, shinbone.

langlífi longevity; *synonyms* (*n*) life, endurance, permanence, continuance, seniority.

langljómun phosphorescence; *synonyms* (*n*) flash, glow, light, shimmer.

langlúra witch; *synonyms* (*n*) hag, pythoness, (*v*) enchant, bewitch, charm.

langrauf spline; *synonyms* (*n*) feather, slat, fin, conclusion, end.

langsetill stretcher; *synonyms* (*n*) litter, cot, bed, berth, brancard.

langsnið landscape; *synonyms* (*n*) outlook, scene, scenery, sight, (*v*) prospect.

langsýni hypermetropia; *synonyms* (*n*) farsightedness, hyperopia, hypermetropy, longsightedness, sagacity.

langt far; *synonyms* (*adv*) wide, off, widely, (*adj*) distant, aloof; *antonyms* (*adv*) close, briefly, (*adj*) near.

langtímaleiga leasing; *synonyms* (*n*) hire, rent, rental, charter, chartering.

langtímaþróun trend; *synonyms* (*n*) fashion, tendency, fad, inclination, (*v*) style.

langtímaverðbréf investments; *synonyms* (*n*) assets, capital, cash, funds, money.

langur 1. long; *synonyms* (*v*) aspire, desire, hanker, languish, (*n*) extensive; *antonyms* (*adj*) short, brief, **2.** lengthy; *synonyms* (*adj*) extended, long, protracted, wordy, copious.

langvinnur chronic; *synonyms* (*adj*) confirmed, habitual, inveterate, constant, accustomed; *antonym* (*adj*) temporary.

langyddur acuminate; *synonyms* (*adj*) pointed, acute, sharp, (*v*) sharpen.

lánshæfi credit; *synonyms* (*n*) credence, appreciation, belief, (*v*) believe, accredit; *antonyms* (*n*) cash, (*v*) debit, discredit.

lánstraust credit; *synonyms* (*n*) credence, appreciation, belief, (*v*) believe, accredit; *antonyms* (*n*) cash, (*v*) debit, discredit.

lántaka borrowing; *synonyms* (*n*) adoption, loan, pledging, acceptance, acceptation.

lántakandi borrower; *synonym* (*n*) beggar.

lantan lanthanum; *synonym* (*n*) lah.

lantaníð lanthanide; *synonyms* (*n*) lanthanoid, lanthanon.

lanþan lanthanum; *synonym* (*n*) lah.

lanþaníð lanthanide; *synonyms* (*n*) lanthanoid, lanthanon.

lánveitandi 1. creditor; *synonyms* (*n*) debtee, lienor, **2.** lender; *synonyms* (*n*) creditor, loaner, mortgagee.

láréttur horizontal; *synonyms* (*adj*) even, flat, level, plane, straight; *antonym* (*adj*) vertical.

lárpera avocado; *synonyms* (*n*) aguacate, (*v*) atole, banana, barbecue, beefsteak.

lás 1. lock; *synonyms* (*v*) bolt, bar, close, latch, engage; *antonyms* (*v*) unlock, open, **2.** latch; *synonyms* (*n*) catch, hasp, clasp, hook, (*v*) lock.

lása clip; *synonyms* (*n*) clasp, blow, (*v*) nip, snip, trim; *antonym* (*v*) lengthen.

lasburða faint; *synonyms* (*adj*) collapse, dim, dizzy, feeble, indistinct; *antonyms* (*adj*) distinct, strong, clear, obvious, considerable.

lásfleygur cotter; *synonyms* (*n*) cottier, key, cottager, wedge, keynote.

láshlekkur shackle; *synonyms* (*v*) fetter, chain, bind, hobble, (*n*) hamper.

laska damage; *synonyms* (*n*) blemish, injury, (*v*) harm, hurt, abuse; *antonyms* (*n*) service, (*v*) conserve, enhance, repair, bolster.

laskaður damaged; *synonyms* (*adj*) faulty, unsound, defective, broken, dilapidated; *antonym* (*adj*) undamaged.

lasleiki malaise; *synonyms* (*n*) disquietude, disquiet, unrest, unease, (*v*) discomfort.

lastahneigð perversion; *synonyms* (*n*) distortion, misrepresentation, corruption, falsification, depravity.

lástefna bearing; *synonyms* (*n*) carriage, demeanor, appearance, approach, aspect.

látast simulate; *synonyms* (*v*) mimic, dissemble, mock, affect, feign.

lati inhibitor; *synonym* (*n*) stabilizer.

látlaus constant; *synonyms* (*adj*) ceaseless, incessant, perpetual, steady, continual; *antonyms* (*adj*) changeable, intermittent, irregular, sporadic, variable.

latning inhibition; *synonyms* (*n*) check, prohibition, restraint, suppression, taboo.

látún brass; *synonyms* (*n*) boldness, face, cheek, nerve, (*v*) audacity.

latur 1. slack; *synonyms* (*adj*) loose, lax, idle, indolent, negligent; *antonyms* (*adj*) tight, strict, taut, thorough, **2.** lazy; *synonyms* (*adj*) inert, drowsy, inactive, shiftless, dull; *antonyms* (*adj*) energetic, diligent, active, **3.** idle; *synonyms* (*adj*) lazy, free, baseless, frivolous, fruitless; *antonyms* (*adj*) busy, employed, (*v*) change.

lauf 1. leaf; *synonyms* (*n*) blade, page, foliage, folio, (*v*) sheet, **2.** sheet; *synonyms* (*n*) board, layer, leaf, canvas, film.

laufblað leaf; *synonyms* (*n*) blade, page, foliage, folio, (*v*) sheet.

lauffall abscission; *synonyms* (*n*) abscision, apocope, (*v*) rescission, recision.

lauffelling 1. defoliation; *synonym* (*n*) devastation, **2.** abscission; *synonyms* (*n*) abscision, apocope, (*v*) rescission, recision.

lauffeyra litter; *synonyms* (*n*) brood, bedding, stretcher, (*v*) clutter, (*adj*) jumble.

laufgræna chlorophyll; *synonyms* (*n*) chlorophyl, fecula.

laufþak canopy; *synonyms* (*n*) awning, cover, screen, shade, ceiling.

laufþekja canopy; *synonyms* (*n*) awning, cover, screen, shade, ceiling.

laugardagur sabbath; *synonyms* (*n*) recess, vacation, sabbat.

laukknappur bulb; *synonyms* (*n*) knob, lightbulb, corm, nodule, (*adj*) globule.

laukur 1. onion; *synonyms* (*n*) caviare, pickle, leek, chive, **2.** bulb; *synonyms* (*n*) knob, lightbulb, corm, nodule, (*adj*) globule, **3.** corm; *synonyms* (*n*) cormus, rhizome.

laun 1. salary; *synonyms* (*n*) wage, pay, allowance, earnings, fee, **2.** remuneration; *synonyms* (*n*) compensation, recompense, reward, payment, salary, **3.** wages; *synonyms* (*n*) stipend, hire, income, payoff, **4.** pay; *synonyms* (*v*) compensate, liquidate, yield, afford, clear; *antonym* (*v*) owe, **5.** wage; *synonyms* (*n*) remuneration, (*v*) fight, engage, prosecute, pursue.

launaauki bonus; *synonyms* (*n*) award, compensation, premium, dividend, (*adj*) extra; *antonym* (*n*) disadvantage.

launagjöld payroll; *synonyms* (*n*) paysheet, expense, salary.

launaskrá payroll; *synonyms* (*n*) paysheet, expense, salary.

launþegar labor; *synonyms* (*n*) drudgery, effort, endeavor, exertion, (*v*) toil; *antonym* (*v*) rest.

launþegi 1. labour; *synonyms* (*n*) effort, exertion, (*v*) grind, labor, travail, 2. employee; *synonyms* (*n*) clerk, laborer, hand, worker, apprentice; *antonym* (*n*) employer.

laupur frame; *synonyms* (*n*) design, border, (*v*) form, construct, fabricate.

laus 1. removable; *synonyms* (*adj*) detachable, obliterable, movable, amovable, dispensable; *antonym* (*adj*) fixed, 2. free; *synonyms* (*adj*) loose, (*v*) clear, exempt, liberate, discharge; *antonyms* (*adj*) bound, restricted, compelled, confined, imprisoned.

lausabeinsmyndun sequestration; *synonyms* (*n*) segregation, separation, damages, deodand, escheat.

lausafjárstaða liquidity; *synonyms* (*n*) fluidity, fluidness, liquid, liquidness, fluency.

lausafregn grapevine; *synonyms* (*n*) grape, vine, gossip, buzz, hearsay.

lausagangur 1. idle; *synonyms* (*adj*) inactive, indolent, lazy, free, baseless; *antonyms* (*adj*) busy, active, employed, (*v*) change, 2. idling; *synonyms* (*adj*) trifling, (*n*) idleness, loafing, dalliance, faineance.

lausagrjót debris; *synonyms* (*n*) detritus, junk, refuse, rubbish, trash.

lausaleiksbarn bastard; *synonyms* (*adj*) illegitimate, spurious, fake, misbegotten, phony; *antonym* (*n*) legitimate.

lausamaður freelance; *synonyms* (*n*) independent, mugwump, (*adj*) irregular, temporary.

lausastigi ladder; *synonyms* (*n*) scale, run, steps, washboard, (*v*) bleed.

lausataug 1. cord; *synonyms* (*n*) band, string, bond, tie, twine, 2. flexible; *synonyms* (*adj*) elastic, adaptable, pliable, yielding, lissome; *antonyms* (*adj*) inflexible, rigid, fixed, obstinate, stiff.

lausheldni incontinence; *synonyms* (*n*) incontinency, dissoluteness, debauchery, unchastity, (*adj*) intrigue.

lausn 1. resolution; *synonyms* (*n*) decision, determination, answer, conclusion, firmness; *antonym* (*n*) indecisiveness, 2. solution; *synonyms* (*n*) dissolution, resolution, settlement, resolve, explanation, 3. release; *synonyms* (*n*) discharge, (*v*) exempt, free, liberate, (*adj*) disengage; *antonyms* (*n*) imprisonment, abduction, (*v*) capture, confine, imprison, 4. disengagement; *synonyms* (*n*) detachment, disconnection, separation, disentanglement, disjunction.

lausnarbeiðni resignation; *synonyms* (*n*) capitulation, endurance, patience, renunciation, surrender.

lausnargjald ransom; *synonyms* (*n*) rescue, blackmail, (*v*) deliver, redeem, repurchase.

laust 1. bulk; *synonyms* (*n*) mass, size, amount, majority, volume; *antonym* (*n*) minority, 2. aweigh; *synonyms* (*adj*) atrip.

lax salmon; *synonyms* (*n*) orange, red.

laxaborri bass; *synonyms* (*adj*) deep, low, resonant, (*n*) basso, (*adv*) accompaniment.

laxaseiði 1. smolt, 2. parr; *synonym* (*n*) par.

leðja 1. sludge; *synonyms* (*n*) mud, ooze, slime, (*adj*) silt, mire, 2. mud; *synonyms* (*n*) dirt, filth, grime, (*adj*) clay, (*v*) muck.

leður 1. leather; *synonyms* (*n*) fur, fleece, skin, buckskin, fell, 2. dermis; *synonyms* (*n*) derma, corium, cutis, (*v*) derm, 3. corium; *synonym* (*n*) dermis.

leðurblaka bat; *synonyms* (*n*) club, rapidity, (*v*) hit, beat, blink.

leðurhúð 1. dermis; *synonyms* (*n*) derma, corium, cutis, skin, (*v*) derm, 2. corium; *synonym* (*n*) dermis.

leg 1. uterus; *synonym* (*n*) womb, 2. womb; *synonyms* (*n*) uterus, belly, bowels, chitterings, cradle, 3. bearing; *synonyms* (*n*) carriage, demeanor, appearance, approach, aspect, 4. locus; *synonyms* (*n*) locale, position, spot, place, venue.

lega 1. situation; *synonyms* (*n*) place, employment, position, post, job, 2. site; *synonyms* (*n*) locate, location, point, room, (*v*) set, 3. bearing; *synonyms* (*n*) carriage, demeanor, appearance, approach, aspect, 4. attitude; *synonyms* (*n*) posture, behavior, mind, notion, air, 5. location; *synonyms* (*n*) localization, orientation, berth, emplacement, fix.

legástunga amniocentesis; *synonym* (*n*) amnio.

leggangaskolun douche; *synonyms* (*n*) shower, bath, (*v*) affusion, irrigation, flush.

legghlíf spat; *synonyms* (*v*) bicker, (*n*) quarrel, squabble, altercation, tiff.

leggja 1. put; *synonyms* (*v*) place, fix, lay, position, (*n*) deposit, 2. set; *synonyms* (*v*) put, locate, regulate, (*n*) class, (*adj*) fixed; *antonyms* (*v*) soften, liquefy, (*n*) combing, comb-out, (*adj*) variable, 3. place; *synonyms* (*n*) domicile, (*v*) post, arrange, rank, station; *antonym* (*v*) remove, 4. lay; *synonyms* (*v*) set, install, (*adj*) secular, (*n*) ballad, pitch, 5. park; *synonyms* (*n*) garden, common, green, parkland, arena.

leggjarhöfuð condyle; *synonyms* (*n*) apophysis, elbow, knob, process, tooth.

leggur 1. leg; *synonyms* (*n*) stage, blackleg, branch, peg, post, **2.** shank; *synonyms* (*n*) handle, haft, hilt, cannon, shaft, **3.** strut; *synonyms* (*n*) buttress, brace, (*v*) prance, stalk, swagger, **4.** shaft; *synonyms* (*n*) arrow, axis, beam, pit, dart, **5.** stern; *synonyms* (*adj*) harsh, rigid, severe, rigorous, austere; *antonym* (*adj*) cordial.

legháls cervix; *synonym* (*n*) neck.

leghetta diaphragm; *synonyms* (*n*) membrane, midriff, partition, pessary, septum.

legkaka placenta; *synonyms* (*n*) secundines, sporophore.

legoddur pivot; *synonyms* (*n*) axle, axis, pin, hub, (*v*) revolve.

legstunga amniocentesis; *synonym* (*n*) amnio.

legubakki bush; *synonyms* (*n*) shrub, bushing, wild, chaparral, hedge.

legufeiti grease; *synonyms* (*n*) fat, bribe, butter, (*v*) oil, boodle.

leguhringur race; *synonyms* (*n*) kind, dash, family, (*v*) course, (*adj*) lineage.

leguhús casing; *synonyms* (*n*) case, shell, box, jacket, skin.

legupláss berth; *synonyms* (*n*) bed, bunk, dock, place, (*v*) wharf.

legurými berth; *synonyms* (*n*) bed, bunk, dock, place, (*v*) wharf.

legutími downtime; *synonyms* (*n*) break, cessation, delay, (*adj*) broken, disrepair.

leguvölur journal; *synonyms* (*n*) diary, book, magazine, newspaper, (*adj*) daybook.

legvatn waters; *synonym* (*n*) boot.

legvatnsástunga amniocentesis; *synonym* (*n*) amnio.

leið 1. routing; *synonyms* (*n*) route, conquest, dispatching, navigation, steering, **2.** route; *synonyms* (*n*) course, path, road, direction, passage, **3.** path; *synonyms* (*n*) way, highway, line, orbit, track.

leiðamót 1. hub; *synonyms* (*n*) center, focus, heart, core, nucleus, **2.** intersection; *synonyms* (*n*) cross, crossroads, crossing, crossroad, intersect.

leiðari 1. conductor; *synonyms* (*n*) leader, chief, director, (*v*) guard, guide; *antonym* (*n*) insulator, **2.** connector; *synonyms* (*n*) connective, connecter, connection, coupling, conjunction, **3.** leader; *synonyms* (*n*) boss, captain, head, chieftain, commander; *antonyms* (*n*) follower, straggler.

leiðarlag horizon; *synonyms* (*n*) perspective, prospect, purview, reach, skyline.

leiðarmark landmark; *synonyms* (*n*) milestone, merestone, boundary, milepost, seamark.

leiðarval routing; *synonyms* (*n*) route, conquest, dispatching, navigation, steering.

leiðarvísir instruction; *synonyms* (*n*) charge, command, advice, counsel, direction.

leiðaval vine; *synonyms* (*n*) climber, creeper, bush, flower, plant.

leiðbeina guide; *synonyms* (*n*) escort, directory, (*v*) direct, conduct, govern; *antonym* (*v*) follow.

leiðbeinandi 1. supervisor; *synonyms* (*n*) superintendent, director, overseer, boss, chief, **2.** heuristic; *synonym* (*adj*) inquiring.

leiðbeining 1. instruction; *synonyms* (*n*) charge, command, advice, counsel, direction, **2.** guidance; *synonyms* (*n*) government, control, administration, lead, (*v*) conduct, **3.** guideline; *synonyms* (*n*) directive, rule, principle, parameter, gauge.

leiðbeiningar 1. directory; *synonyms* (*n*) catalogue, file, list, record, handbook, **2.** instructions; *synonyms* (*n*) direction, injunction, charge, orders, guide.

leiðing 1. conduction; *synonyms* (*n*) guidance, conductivity, convection, leadership, contagion, **2.** implication; *synonyms* (*n*) allusion, hint, significance, consequence, deduction.

leiðir conductor; *synonyms* (*n*) leader, chief, director, (*v*) guard, guide; *antonym* (*n*) insulator.

leiðni 1. transmissivity, **2.** conduction; *synonyms* (*n*) guidance, conductivity, convection, leadership, contagion, **3.** conductance, **4.** conductivity; *synonyms* (*n*) conduction, conductibility, energy.

leiðniátt forward; *synonyms* (*adv*) onward, (*adj*) bold, audacious, (*v*) advance, (*phr*) dispatch; *antonyms* (*adv*) backward, (*adj*) shy, posterior.

leiðrétta 1. rectify; *synonyms* (*v*) amend, correct, improve, better, adjust, **2.** correct; *synonyms* (*adj*) right, accurate, appropriate, (*v*) castigate, chastise; *antonyms* (*adj*) incorrect, false, faulty, inappropriate, (*v*) wrong, **3.** reform; *synonyms* (*v*) change, rectify, modify, transform, ameliorate, **4.** update; *synonyms* (*n*) updating, (*v*) inform, modernize, renovate, revise, **5.** calibrate; *synonyms* (*v*) regulate, gauge, graduate, measure, (*n*) sizing.

leiðrétting 1. rectification; *synonyms* (*n*) correction, amendment, improvement, redress, revision, **2.** adjustment; *synonyms* (*n*) adaptation, accommodation, alteration, control, fit, **3.** correction; *synonyms* (*n*) adjustment, castigation, chastisement, discipline, modification; *antonym* (*n*) fabrication, **4.** amendment; *synonyms* (*n*) betterment, transformation, change, conversion, mend.

leiðsaga navigation; *synonyms* (*n*) guidance, sailing, steering, seafaring, shipping.

leiðsagnarregla heuristic; *synonym* (*adj*) inquiring.

leiðsla 1. trance; *synonyms* (n) reverie, coma, fascination, daze, (adj) ecstasy, **2.** reverie; *synonyms* (n) daydream, dream, fantasy, revery, (adj) preoccupation, **3.** wire; *synonyms* (n) cable, telegram, line, rope, (v) telegraph, **4.** cable; *synonyms* (n) cablegram, cord, guy, ribbon, (v) wire, **5.** lead; *synonyms* (v) head, guide, conduct, contribute, direct; *antonym* (v) follow.

leiðslukerfi loom; *synonyms* (v) appear, threaten, emerge, lower, menace.

leiðsluknippi harness; *synonyms* (n) gear, rein, tether, (v) hitch, (adj) strap.

leiðsögn 1. guidance; *synonyms* (n) direction, government, control, advice, (v) conduct, **2.** navigation; *synonyms* (n) guidance, sailing, steering, seafaring, shipping.

leiðsögumaður 1. navigator; *synonyms* (n) pilot, mariner, sailor, aviator, aeroplanist, **2.** guide; *synonyms* (n) escort, directory, (v) direct, conduct, govern; *antonym* (v) follow.

leif 1. residual; *synonyms* (adj) remaining, leftover, (n) remnant, residue, balance, **2.** vestige; *synonyms* (n) trace, remains, track, relic, shadow, **3.** residue; *synonyms* (n) remainder, rest, end, remnants, (adj) residual.

leifar 1. pickling; *synonyms* (n) buckling, preservation, **2.** residue; *synonyms* (n) remainder, remnant, balance, rest, leftover.

leifð residual; *synonyms* (adj) remaining, leftover, (n) remnant, residue, balance.

leiftandi 1. poignant; *synonyms* (adj) bitter, acute, cutting, (v) acrid, biting, **2.** sharp; *synonyms* (adj) intelligent, acid, harsh, incisive, (n) keen; *antonyms* (adj) blunt, dull, mild, gentle, rounded, **3.** acute; *synonyms* (adj) sharp, intense, penetrating, critical, (v) high; *antonym* (adj) obtuse, **4.** acerbic; *synonyms* (adj) acerb, caustic, astringent, tart, acrimonious, **5.** acrimonious; *synonyms* (adj) sour, sarcastic, virulent, acerbic, (v) pungent.

leifturljós strobe; *synonyms* (n) stroboscope, (adj) odometer, speedometer, tachometer.

leiga 1. rental; *synonyms* (n) hire, lease, letting, renting, apartment, **2.** rent; *synonyms* (n) breach, cleft, fissure, let, crevice, **3.** charter; *synonyms* (n) permit, authority, code, (v) rent, engage, **4.** lease; *synonyms* (n) leasing, rental, (v) charter, contract, demise.

leigja 1. rent; *synonyms* (n) breach, cleft, fissure, lease, (v) hire, **2.** lease; *synonyms* (v) rent, charter, let, contract, demise, **3.** hire; *synonyms* (n) wage, employment, (v) employ, engage, enlist; *antonym* (v) dismiss, **4.** let; *synonyms* (v) allow, admit, leave, permit, have; *antonyms* (v) forbid, prevent.

leigjandi 1. tenant; *synonyms* (n) inhabitant, lodger, occupant, resident, holder; *antonyms* (n) landlord, proprietor, **2.** renter; *synonyms* (n) tenant, underlessee, distributor, guest, (v) finedraw.

leigubíll 1. taxi; *synonyms* (n) cab, hack, taxicab, automobile, cabriolet, **2.** cab; *synonyms* (n) taxi, car, fly, droshki, drosky.

leiguflug charter; *synonyms* (n) hire, permit, authority, (v) let, rent.

leiguflugssamningur charter; *synonyms* (n) hire, permit, authority, (v) let, rent.

leigugjald rent; *synonyms* (n) breach, cleft, fissure, lease, (v) hire.

leigugreiðsla rent; *synonyms* (n) breach, cleft, fissure, lease, (v) hire.

leigusali lessor; *synonyms* (n) creditor, landlord, lender, mortgagee.

leigusamnigur lease; *synonyms* (v) hire, rent, charter, let, contract.

leigusamningur lease; *synonyms* (v) hire, rent, charter, let, contract.

leiguskip 1. tramp; *synonyms* (n) hike, bum, hobo, (v) trudge, walk; *antonym* (v) loyalist, **2.** charter; *synonyms* (n) hire, permit, authority, (v) let, rent.

leigutaka charter; *synonyms* (n) hire, permit, authority, (v) let, rent.

leigutaki 1. charterer, **2.** lessee; *synonyms* (n) leaseholder, lodger, renter, tenant, occupant; *antonym* (n) landlord.

leigutekjur 1. rental; *synonyms* (n) hire, lease, letting, renting, apartment, **2.** rent; *synonyms* (n) breach, cleft, fissure, let, crevice.

leigutími lease; *synonyms* (v) hire, rent, charter, let, contract.

leika 1. play; *synonyms* (v) act, pastime, enact, (n) frolic, game; *antonym* (v) work, **2.** act; *synonyms* (n) accomplishment, action, (v) achievement, behave, deed; *antonym* (v) refrain, **3.** perform; *synonyms* (v) execute, accomplish, do, fulfill, achieve; *antonym* (v) neglect.

leikáætlun strategy; *synonyms* (n) dodge, plan, scheme, strategics, (v) tactics.

leikandi atlas; *synonyms* (n) telamon, chart, book, plan, (adj) superman.

leikari 1. actor; *synonyms* (n) doer, player, agent, comedian, (v) performer, **2.** performer; *synonyms* (n) actor, musician, artiste, conjurer, juggler.

leikfang plaything; *synonyms* (n) toy, trifle, amusement, knickknack, sport.

leikfimi gymnastics; *synonyms* (n) aerobatics, bars, body-building, horse, (v) gladiatorship.

leikhús playhouse; *synonyms* (n) theater, theatre, arena, auditorium, toyhouse.

leikhverfing dramatization; *synonyms* (*n*) dramatisation, performance, enactment, production.

leikkona actress; *synonyms* (*n*) actor, player, artist, entertainer, musician.

leikmaður amateur; *synonyms* (*adj*) amateurish, inexpert, unskilled, (*n*) novice, beginner; *antonyms* (*adj*) practiced, (*n*) professional, expert.

leikni 1. technique; *synonyms* (*n*) approach, means, method, skill, fashion, 2. skill; *synonyms* (*n*) artifice, ability, capability, (*adj*) dexterity, craft; *antonyms* (*n*) clumsiness, inability, incompetence.

Leikur 1. move; *synonyms* (*v*) act, affect, carry, excite, go; *antonym* (*v*) stay, 2. play; *synonyms* (*v*) pastime, enact, exercise, (*n*) frolic, game; *antonym* (*v*) work.

leir clay; *synonyms* (*n*) soil, remains, pottery, dirt, (*adj*) earthen.

leirgedda bowfin; *synonyms* (*n*) dogfish, grindle.

leirslabbi bream; *synonym* (*v*) broom.

leit 1. prospecting; *synonym* (*n*) exploration, 2. search; *synonyms* (*n*) hunt, pursuit, examination, inquire, (*v*) grope, 3. hunting; *synonyms* (*n*) chase, search, cycling, lagging, (*v*) battue, 4. finding; *synonyms* (*n*) decision, detection, determination, discovery, judgment.

leita search; *synonyms* (*n*) hunt, pursuit, examination, exploration, (*v*) grope.

leitaraðferð heuristic; *synonym* (*adj*) inquiring.

leitarhamur search; *synonyms* (*n*) hunt, pursuit, examination, exploration, (*v*) grope.

leitarmaður trailer; *synonyms* (*n*) caravan, leader, ad, advertisement, announcement.

leitarnám heuristic; *synonym* (*adj*) inquiring.

leitarsjónauki finder; *synonyms* (*n*) viewfinder, discoverer, artificer, spotter, lookout.

leitni 1. trend; *synonyms* (*n*) fashion, tendency, fad, inclination, (*v*) style, 2. tropism.

leka 1. trickle; *synonyms* (*n*) drip, distill, (*v*) drop, dribble, percolate; *antonyms* (*n*) throng, (*v*) gush, 2. leak; *synonyms* (*n*) leakage, crevice, breach, disclosure, (*v*) reveal.

lekandi gonorrhea; *synonyms* (*n*) clap, gonorrhoea, bang, blennorrhea, (*adj*) gallstone.

leki 1. drip; *synonyms* (*n*) dribble, trickle, leak, leakage, (*v*) drop, 2. escape; *synonyms* (*v*) elude, break, dodge, avoid, evade; *antonyms* (*v*) capture, return, 3. leak; *synonyms* (*n*) crevice, breach, disclosure, (*v*) reveal, release, 4. leakage; *synonyms* (*n*) escape, outpouring, outflow, seepage, extravasation.

lekinn permeable; *synonyms* (*adj*) pervious, porous, absorbent, spongy, gritty; *antonyms* (*adj*)

impermeable, resistant, waterproof, water-resistant, watertight.

lekt permeability; *synonyms* (*n*) perviousness, permeableness.

lekur permeable; *synonyms* (*adj*) pervious, porous, absorbent, spongy, gritty; *antonyms* (*adj*) impermeable, resistant, waterproof, water-resistant, watertight.

lélegur inferior; *synonyms* (*adj*) bad, secondary, subordinate, humble, poor; *antonyms* (*adj*) better, choice, excellent, first-rate, (*n*) superior.

lémögnun collapse; *synonyms* (*n*) crash, breakdown, fall, (*v*) break, slump.

lén domain; *synonyms* (*n*) country, department, realm, area, kingdom; *antonym* (*n*) range.

lend croup; *synonyms* (*n*) rump, croupe, hindquarters, tail, dorsum.

lenda land; *synonyms* (*n*) ground, country, soil, (*v*) disembark, debark; *antonym* (*adj*) aquatic.

lendagigt lumbago; *synonyms* (*v*) backache, (*v*) sciatica, cephalalgia, earache, gout.

lending landing; *synonyms* (*n*) land, dock, touchdown, floor, platform.

lengd 1. length; *synonyms* (*n*) extent, distance, range, duration, compass; *antonyms* (*n*) briefness, shortness, width, 2. duration; *synonyms* (*n*) length, continuation, continuance, period, standing, 3. longitude; *synonyms* (*n*) meridian, place, 4. magnitude; *synonyms* (*n*) bulk, consequence, amount, dimension, mass; *antonym* (*n*) triviality, 5. norm; *synonyms* (*n*) average, mean, measure, mode, criterion.

lengdarbaugur 1. meridian; *synonyms* (*n*) culmination, longitude, zenith, acme, apex, 2. longitude; *synonyms* (*n*) length, meridian, place.

lengdargráða longitude; *synonyms* (*n*) length, meridian, place.

lenging 1. dilation; *synonyms* (*n*) dilatation, expansion, swelling, growth, spread, 2. elongation; *synonyms* (*n*) extension, length, production, annex, annexe.

lengja prolong; *synonyms* (*v*) continue, extend, delay, protract, elongate; *antonyms* (*v*) shorten, stop.

lénsskipulag feudalism; *synonyms* (*n*) feodality, slavery.

lénsveldi feudalism; *synonyms* (*n*) feodality, slavery.

leppur alias; *synonyms* (*n*) name, pseudonym, nickname, soubriquet, title.

lesa read; *synonyms* (*v*) interpret, construe, decipher, gather, indicate.

lesandi reader; *synonyms* (*n*) lecturer, professor, lector, proofreader, reviewer.

lesba lesbian; *synonyms* (*adj*) gay, sapphic, dykey, (*n*) homosexual, tribade.

lesbía lesbian; *synonyms* (*adj*) gay, sapphic, dykey, (*n*) homosexual, tribade.

lesefni reading; *synonyms* (*n*) recital, learning, construction, interpretation, (*v*) read.

lesmál text; *synonyms* (*n*) copy, matter, script, theme, subject.

lespa lesbian; *synonyms* (*adj*) gay, sapphic, dykey, (*n*) homosexual, tribade.

lespískur lesbian; *synonyms* (*adj*) gay, sapphic, dykey, (*n*) homosexual, tribade.

lest 1. train; *synonyms* (*v*) aim, coach, direct, educate, exercise, **2.** hold; *synonyms* (*v*) keep, detain, endure, (*n*) grasp, grip; *antonym* (*v*) release.

lestaður loaded; *synonyms* (*adj*) laden, full, burdened, flush, moneyed; *antonym* (*adj*) poor.

lestarbelgur belly; *synonyms* (*n*) abdomen, stomach, inside, bowels, (*v*) balloon.

lestarhluti compartment; *synonyms* (*n*) cell, division, cabin, cubicle, (*v*) apartment.

lestarlúga hatch; *synonyms* (*n*) brood, (*v*) breed, contrive, concoct, brew.

lestarop hatch; *synonyms* (*n*) brood, (*v*) breed, contrive, concoct, brew.

lestarými stowage; *synonyms* (*n*) stowing, storeroom, shipment, cargo, contents.

lestun loading; *synonyms* (*n*) cargo, freight, load, burden, consignment; *antonym* (*n*) unloading.

lestunarstjóri stevedore; *synonyms* (*n*) docker, loader, longshoreman, lumper, dockhand.

lestur reading; *synonyms* (*n*) recital, learning, construction, interpretation, (*v*) read.

letjandi inhibitory; *synonyms* (*adj*) inhibiting, repressive, repressing.

létta lift; *synonyms* (*n*) elevator, (*v*) hoist, raise, rise, elevate.

léttasótt labor; *synonyms* (*n*) drudgery, effort, endeavor, exertion, (*v*) toil; *antonym* (*v*) rest.

léttfljótandi fluid; *synonyms* (*adj*) liquid, flowing, unsettled, changeable, smooth; *antonym* (*n*) solid.

léttir 1. relief; *synonyms* (*n*) comfort, aid, consolation, ease, (*v*) assistance, **2.** remission; *synonyms* (*n*) forgiveness, relief, condonation, absolution, (*v*) pardon, **3.** levator.

léttlyndur sanguine; *synonyms* (*adj*) hopeful, ruddy, optimistic, red, bloody.

léttur light; *synonyms* (*adj*) fair, clear, (*v*) fire, kindle, inflame; *antonyms* (*n*) dark, darkness, gloom, shade, (*alt sp*) heavy.

letur font; *synonyms* (*n*) fount, fountain, type, baptistery, print.

leturborð keyboard; *synonym* (*n*) upright.

leturbrigði style; *synonyms* (*n*) fashion, name, (*v*) call, entitle, (*adj*) manner.

leturgerð font; *synonyms* (*n*) fount, fountain, type, baptistery, print.

leturprentun letterpress; *synonym* (*n*) print.

leyfa sanction; *synonyms* (*n*) warrant, assent, (*v*) approve, permit, countenance; *antonyms* (*v*) ban, forbid.

leyfi 1. permit; *synonyms* (*v*) allow, give, license, (*n*) consent, (*adj*) grant; *antonyms* (*v*) forbid, ban, prevent, prohibit, stop, **2.** concession; *synonyms* (*n*) admission, compliance, allowance, compromise, discount, **3.** license; *synonyms* (*n*) permit, freedom, liberty, permission, (*v*) charter, **4.** leave; *synonyms* (*v*) depart, forsake, go, abandon, desert; *antonyms* (*v*) arrive, enter, stay, remain, approach, **5.** licence; *synonyms* (*v*) certify, endorse, evidence, attest, demonstrate.

leyfiheimild sanction; *synonyms* (*n*) warrant, assent, (*v*) approve, permit, countenance; *antonyms* (*v*) ban, forbid.

leyfisbréf permit; *synonyms* (*v*) allow, give, license, (*n*) consent, (*adj*) grant; *antonyms* (*v*) forbid, ban, prevent, prohibit, stop.

leyfishafi subscriber; *synonyms* (*n*) contributor, donor, reader, endorser, ratifier.

leyfisveiting licensing; *synonym* (*n*) licensure.

leynd 1. confidentiality; *synonyms* (*n*) discretion, intimacy, privacy, secrecy, mystery, **2.** latency; *synonyms* (*n*) suspension, abeyance, intermission, interruption, latence.

leyndur latent; *synonyms* (*adj*) covert, potential, secret, dormant, hidden; *antonym* (*adj*) active.

leynimakk collusion; *synonyms* (*n*) connivance, complicity, intrigue, plot, circumvention.

leyniorð password; *synonyms* (*n*) countersign, catchword, parole, watchword, (*v*) key.

leysa 1. release; *synonyms* (*n*) discharge, (*v*) exempt, free, liberate, (*adj*) disengage; *antonyms* (*n*) imprisonment, abduction, (*v*) capture, confine, imprison, **2.** liberate; *synonyms* (*v*) emancipate, clear, extricate, deliver, release; *antonym* (*v*) enslave, **3.** expand; *synonyms* (*v*) amplify, enlarge, balloon, broaden, develop; *antonyms* (*v*) contract, shorten, abbreviate, decrease, deflate.

leysanlegur soluble; *synonyms* (*adj*) dissolvable, alkaline, cheerful, free, hence.

leysiefni solvent; *synonyms* (*n*) resolvent, dissolvent, solution, menstruum, answer; *antonyms* (*adj*) bankrupt, broke.

leysiensím lysozyme; *synonym* (*n*) muramidase.

leysigeisli laser; *synonym* (*n*) beam.

leysing 1. solution; *synonyms* (*n*) dissolution, resolution, answer, settlement, resolve, **2.** clearing; *synonyms* (*n*) clarification, glade, clearance, dell, lot, **3.** ablation; *synonyms* (*n*) excision, extirpation, sublation, (v) abduction, abreption, **4**. lysis, **5**. emission; *synonyms* (n) discharge, emanation, effusion, ejection, venting.

leysinn soluble; *synonyms* (adj) dissolvable, alkaline, cheerful, free, hence.

leysir 1. solvent; *synonyms* (n) resolvent, dissolvent, solution, menstruum, answer; *antonyms* (adj) bankrupt, broke, **2**. laser; *synonym* (n) beam.

leysitæki laser; *synonym* (n) beam.

leysni solubility; *synonym* (n) dissolvability.

libro book; *synonyms* (n) bible, (v) order, reserve, apply, inscribe.

lið team; *synonyms* (n) crew, company, gang, squad, (v) pair.

liða expand; *synonyms* (v) amplify, enlarge, balloon, broaden, develop; *antonyms* (v) contract, shorten, abbreviate, decrease, deflate.

liðaður articulate; *synonyms* (v) pronounce, speak, utter, vocalize, voice; *antonyms* (adj) incoherent, (v) inarticulate.

liðamót 1. articulation; *synonyms* (n) enunciation, joint, juncture, accent, diction, **2**. joint; *synonyms* (n) articulation, hinge, join, seam, (v) articulate; *antonyms* (adj) individual, unilateral, private, separate.

liðband ligament; *synonyms* (n) tie, bond, band, knot, sinew.

liðbólgusjúklingur arthritic; *synonyms* (adj) rheumatic, aching, creaky, painful, palsied.

liðbrak crepitation; *synonyms* (n) crackle, crackling, crackleware, (v) decrepitation.

liðdýr arthropod; *synonyms* (n) crustacean, amphibian, bird, condylopod, fish.

liðfætla arthropod; *synonyms* (n) crustacean, amphibian, bird, condylopod, fish.

liðfall ellipsis; *synonyms* (n) eclipsis, abbreviation, contraction, acronym, (v) elision.

liðhlaup 1. dislocation; *synonyms* (n) breakdown, interruption, confusion, disruption, luxation, **2**. luxation; *synonyms* (n) dislocation, exarticulation.

liðhlaupsaðgerð reduction; *synonyms* (n) contraction, decrease, decrement, diminution, rebate; *antonyms* (n) increase, growth, intensification, strengthening, expansion.

liði 1. relay; *synonyms* (n) relief, spell, (v) broadcast, pass, transmit, **2**. actuator.

liðka mobilize; *synonyms* (v) circulate, marshal, gather, mobilise, rally; *antonym* (v) demobilize.

liðkun mobilization; *synonyms* (n) mobilisation, draft, militarisation, militarization, muster.

liðmarr crepitation; *synonyms* (n) crackle, crackling, crackleware, (v) decrepitation.

liðrétting reduction; *synonyms* (n) contraction, decrease, decrement, diminution, rebate; *antonyms*

(n) increase, growth, intensification, strengthening, expansion.

liðsforingi officer; *synonyms* (n) captain, administrator, commander, bureaucrat, executive.

liðskipting segmentation; *synonyms* (n) division, cleavage, partition, partitioning, sectionalization.

liðskiptur 1. segmental; *synonyms* (adj) metameric, segmented, **2**. articulate; *synonyms* (v) pronounce, speak, utter, vocalize, voice; *antonyms* (adj) incoherent, (v) inarticulate, **3**. articulated; *synonyms* (adj) articulate, jointed, voiced, expressed, spoken.

liðskönnun muster; *synonyms* (v) assemble, congregate, gather, collect, (n) levy.

liðtognun distortion; *synonyms* (n) aberration, contortion, deformation, misrepresentation, (adj) deformity.

liðun 1. segmentation; *synonyms* (n) division, cleavage, partition, partitioning, sectionalization, **2**. polymerization; *synonym* (n) polymerisation, **3**. metamerism, **4**. expansion; *synonyms* (n) amplification, enlargement, development, (v) extension, augmentation; *antonyms* (n) contraction, decrease, reduction, abbreviation.

liður 1. treatment; *synonyms* (n) cure, conduct, handling, management, manipulation, **2**. pivot; *synonyms* (n) axle, axis, pin, hub, (v) revolve, **3**. phrase; *synonyms* (n) expression, idiom, (v) express, formulate, couch, **4**. shackle; *synonyms* (v) fetter, chain, bind, hobble, (n) hamper, **5**. segment; *synonyms* (n) division, paragraph, bit, (v) section, part.

liðvinding distortion; *synonyms* (n) aberration, contortion, deformation, misrepresentation, (adj) deformity.

líf 1. life; *synonyms* (n) animation, energy, spirit, activity, being; *antonym* (n) lethargy, **2**. live; *synonyms* (v) exist, inhabit, reside, subsist, (adj) alive; *antonyms* (adj) dead, inanimate.

lifa live; *synonyms* (v) exist, inhabit, reside, subsist, (adj) alive; *antonyms* (adj) dead, inanimate.

lifandi 1. alive; *synonyms* (adj) active, live, living, sensible, vivacious; *antonyms* (adj) dead, deceased, inanimate, **2**. organic; *synonyms* (adj) constitutional, natural, constitutive, fundamental, constituent; *antonym* (adj) refined.

lífbrotgjarn biodegradable; *synonyms* (adj) ecological, environmental, green, recyclable.

lífeðlisfræði physiology; *synonyms* (n) anatomy, bionomy, botany.

lífeðlisfræðilegur physiological; *synonym* (adj) physiologic.

lífefnamyndun biosynthesis; *synonyms* (n) biogenesis, biogeny.

lífefnasmíð biosynthesis; *synonyms* (*n*) biogenesis, biogeny.

lífefnasundrun catabolism; *synonyms* (*n*) dissimilation, katabolism, anabolism, metabolism, disassimilation.

lífefnatækni biotechnology; *synonyms* (*n*) bioengineering, ergonomics, biotech.

lífeyrir pension; *synonyms* (*n*) allowance, annuity, payment, stipend, endowment.

lífeyrisgreiðsla annuity; *synonyms* (*n*) allowance, pension, rente, revenue, payment.

líffæraauki hypertrophy; *synonym* (*n*) tympany.

líffærafræði anatomy; *synonyms* (*n*) frame, morphology, physiology, body, chassis.

líffæri organ; *synonyms* (*n*) instrument, member, limb, agency, harmonium.

líffærisbilun insufficiency; *synonyms* (*n*) imperfection, inadequacy, deficit, deficiency, shortage; *antonyms* (*n*) adequacy, abundance, sufficiency.

líffærisleif 1. rudiment; *synonyms* (*n*) basis, fundamental, germ, egg, embryo, **2**. vestige; *synonyms* (*n*) trace, remains, track, relic, shadow.

líffæristæming evisceration; *synonyms* (*n*) disembowelment, exenteration, (*adj*) disemboweling.

líffærisvísir rudiment; *synonyms* (*n*) basis, fundamental, germ, egg, embryo.

líffélag community; *synonyms* (*n*) association, public, agreement, commune, (*adj*) communal; *antonym* (*adj*) private.

líffræði biology; *synonyms* (*n*) physiology, anatomy, biota.

líffræðilegur biological; *synonyms* (*adj*) biologic, organic, environmental, natal, natural.

lífgun 1. vivification; *synonyms* (*n*) animation, invigoration, aliveness, awakening, brio, **2**. animation; *synonyms* (*n*) life, liveliness, vitality, activity, dash; *antonym* (*n*) lethargy.

lífheimur biosphere; *synonyms* (*n*) habitat, ecosphere.

lífheldni survival; *synonyms* (*n*) existence, relic, life, endurance, selection; *antonym* (*n*) extinction.

lífhvatl enzyme; *synonyms* (*n*) catalyst, solution.

lífhverfur biodegradable; *synonyms* (*adj*) ecological, environmental, green, recyclable.

lífhvolf biosphere; *synonyms* (*n*) habitat, ecosphere.

lífkviknun biogenesis; *synonyms* (*v*) digenesis, dysmerogenesis, eumerogenesis, heterogenesis, homogenesis.

líflengd life, *synonyms* (*n*) animation, energy, spirit, activity, being; *antonym* (*n*) lethargy.

lífljómi phosphorescence; *synonyms* (*n*) flash, glow, light, shimmer.

lífmælingar 1. biostatistics, **2**. biometry; *synonym* (*n*) biometrics.

lífmyndun biogenesis; *synonyms* (*v*) digenesis, dysmerogenesis, eumerogenesis, heterogenesis, homogenesis.

lífræðilegur biological; *synonyms* (*adj*) biologic, organic, environmental, natal, natural.

lífrænn 1. biotic; *synonym* (*adj*) organic, **2**. organic; *synonyms* (*adj*) constitutional, natural, constitutive, fundamental, constituent; *antonym* (*adj*) refined.

lifraræxli hepatoma; *synonym* (*n*) hepatocarcinoma.

lifrarfrumukrabbamein hepatoma; *synonym* (*n*) hepatocarcinoma.

lífríki 1. ecosystem; *synonyms* (*n*) complex, nature, **2**. biota; *synonym* (*n*) biology.

lifrun coagulation; *synonyms* (*n*) clotting, clot, flocculation, curdling, (*adj*) concretion.

lífsbjörg subsistence; *synonyms* (*n*) being, existence, life, entity, maintenance.

lífsfjör vitality; *synonyms* (*n*) energy, life, animation, vigor, liveliness; *antonyms* (*n*) lethargy, apathy.

lífsfrjór fertile; *synonyms* (*adj*) productive, fat, fecund, abundant, affluent; *antonyms* (*adj*) infertile, sterile.

lífshvöt libido; *synonyms* (*n*) lust, desire.

lífsmáti lifestyle; *synonyms* (*n*) life, behavior, circumstances, culture, living.

lífsnauðsynlegur essential; *synonyms* (*adj*) necessary, crucial, important, inherent, requisite; *antonyms* (*adj*) minor, secondary, (*n*) inessential, optional, option.

lífsorka vitality; *synonyms* (*n*) energy, life, animation, vigor, liveliness; *antonyms* (*n*) lethargy, apathy.

lífsprakur biodegradable; *synonyms* (*adj*) ecological, environmental, green, recyclable.

lífsstíll lifestyle; *synonyms* (*n*) life, behavior, circumstances, culture, living.

lífsþægindagræðgi materialism; *synonyms* (*n*) acquisitiveness, anabaptism, avarice, corporealism, covetousness; *antonym* (*n*) generosity.

lífsþróttur vitality; *synonyms* (*n*) energy, life, animation, vigor, liveliness; *antonyms* (*n*) lethargy, apathy.

lífsviðurværi subsistence; *synonyms* (*n*) being, existence, life, entity, maintenance.

lífsýki diarrhea; *synonyms* (*n*) diarrhoea, lax, looseness.

líftækni 1. biotechnology; *synonyms* (*n*) bioengineering, ergonomics, biotech, **2**. bioengineering; *synonym* (*n*) biotechnology.

líftölfræði 1. biostatistics, **2**. biometrics, **3**. biometry; *synonym* (*n*) biometrics.

lifun survival; *synonyms* (*n*) existence, relic, life, endurance, selection; *antonym* (*n*) extinction.

lifur liver; *synonyms* (*n*) denizen, resident.

lífvæni viability; *synonyms* (*n*) life, vitality, profitability, practicability, achievability.

lífvænleiki viability; *synonyms* (*n*) life, vitality, profitability, practicability, achievability.

lífvænn viable; *synonyms* (*adj*) feasible, practicable, possible, workable, practical; *antonym* (*adj*) impossible.

lífvera organism; *synonyms* (*n*) being, organization, constitution, animal, life.

lífverkfræði bioengineering; *synonyms* (*n*) biotechnology, ergonomics.

lífvirkur biological; *synonyms* (*adj*) biologic, organic, environmental, natal, natural.

lígasi ligase; *synonym* (*n*) synthetase.

liggja 1. recline; *synonyms* (*v*) lie, lean, loll, lounge, repose, 2. lie; *synonyms* (*v*) consist, (*n*) fabrication, falsehood, falsity, fib; *antonyms* (*v*) stand, (*n*) truth.

lignín lignin; *synonyms* (*n*) lignone, lignose, sclerogen, xylogen.

lík cadaver; *synonyms* (*n*) corpse, body, carcass, remains, skeleton.

líka 1. too; *synonyms* (*adv*) also, likewise, besides, excessively, over, 2. also; *synonyms* (*adv*) too, moreover, more, (*conj*) and, furthermore, 3. likewise; *synonyms* (*adv*) alike, further, equally, similarly, (*adj*) even.

líkami 1. body; *synonyms* (*n*) cadaver, corpse, matter, organization, carcass; *antonym* (*n*) spirit, 2. soma; *synonyms* (*n*) bod, haoma, anatomy, build, cast, 3. solid; *synonyms* (*adj*) firm, dense, compact, consistent, hard; *antonyms* (*adj*) soft, unreliable, loose, gaseous, (*n*) liquid.

líkamlegur 1. physical; *synonyms* (*adj*) material, bodily, actual, corporeal, tangible; *antonyms* (*adj*) spiritual, mental, intangible, 2. somatic; *synonyms* (*adj*) physical, corporal, carnal, bodied, (*adv*) fleshly, 3. organic; *synonyms* (*adj*) constitutional, natural, constitutive, fundamental, constituent; *antonym* (*adj*) refined.

líkamsæfingar gymnastics; *synonyms* (*n*) aerobatics, bars, body-building, horse, (*v*) gladiatorship.

líkamsburður posture; *synonyms* (*n*) position, attitude, pose, condition, (*v*) place.

líkamsbygging constitution; *synonyms* (*n*) composition, code, makeup, organization, temperament.

líkamsfræði morphology; *synonyms* (*n*) accidence, anatomy, geomorphology, taxonomy, botany.

líkamshiti temperature; *synonyms* (*n*) fever, heat, warmth, breathing, (*v*) calmness.

líkan model; *synonyms* (*n*) form, fashion, example, (*v*) copy, pattern; *antonym* (*adj*) atypical.

líkanagerð modelling; *synonyms* (*n*) modeling, model, molding, moulding, border.

líkbrennsla cremation; *synonyms* (*n*) burning, incineration, burial, finances, (*v*) concremation.

líkbrennsluofn crematory; *synonym* (*n*) crematorium.

líkhár lanugo; *synonym* (*n*) fuzz.

liki substitute; *synonyms* (*adj*) replacement, alternative, (*n*) deputy, (*v*) alternate, shift.

líkindasvæði orbital; *synonyms* (*adj*) orbiter, periodic.

líkindi probability; *synonyms* (*n*) chance, likelihood, odds, possibility, likeliness.

líking 1. similarity; *synonyms* (*n*) correspondence, likeness, parallelism, kinship, parallel; *antonyms* (*n*) dissimilarity, difference, 2. similitude; *synonyms* (*n*) resemblance, semblance, similarity, comparison, image, 3. simulation; *synonyms* (*n*) affectation, pretense, imitation, pretence, modelling, 4. resemblance; *synonyms* (*n*) affinity, conformity, appearance, analogy, representation, 5. image; *synonyms* (*n*) figure, picture, fancy, conception, effigy.

líkingalæti symbolism; *synonyms* (*n*) symbolization, allegory, charactery, suggestion, symbolic.

líkjast resemble; *synonyms* (*v*) imitate, seem, compare, correspond, agree.

líklegur 1. liable; *synonyms* (*adj*) amenable, accountable, answerable, apt, disposed; *antonym* (*adj*) exempt, 2. incident; *synonyms* (*n*) event, fact, adventure, case, circumstance.

líkn palliation; *synonyms* (*n*) mitigation, alleviation, easement, extenuation, plea.

líknarbelgur amnion; *synonym* (*n*) amnios.

líknardauði euthanasia; *synonyms* (*n*) death, (*v*) sacrifice.

líknardráp euthanasia; *synonyms* (*n*) death, (*v*) sacrifice.

líkneski imagery; *synonyms* (*n*) imagination, imaging, portraiture, images, (*adj*) image.

líkskoðun autopsy; *synonyms* (*n*) necropsy, postmortem, dissection, division, espionage.

líkskurður dissection; *synonyms* (*n*) analysis, anatomy, autopsy, breakdown, cut.

líkþrá leprosy; *synonyms* (*n*) measles, lepra, (*adj*) caries, corruption, gangrene.

líkur 1. probability; *synonyms* (*n*) chance, likelihood, odds, possibility, likeliness, 2. even; *synonyms* (*adj*) direct, equal, constant, (*v*) level, balance; *antonyms* (*adj*) uneven, inconsistent, irregular, jagged, unequal, 3. odds; *synonyms* (*n*) advantage, probability, chances, (*v*) difference, dissension, 4. level; *synonyms* (*n*) grade, (*adj*) even, (*v*) flat, flatten, floor; *antonyms* *(adj)* inclined, slanting, angled, *(v)* build, raise, **5**. equal; *synonyms* *(adj)* agree, comparable, *(v)* match, compare, correspond; *antonyms* *(adj)* different, repressive, disproportionate, unlike, *(v)* differ.

lím 1. glue; *synonyms* *(n)* adhesive, *(v)* cement, adhere, affix, fasten, **2**. cement; *synonyms* *(n)* glue, gum, paste, *(v)* fix, join.

líma 1. glue; *synonyms* *(n)* adhesive, *(v)* cement, adhere, affix, fasten, **2**. paste; *synonyms* *(n)* glue, dough, plaster, *(v)* gum, bond, **3**. stick; *synonyms* *(n)* bar, *(v)* stab, attach, cling, fix, **4**. cement; *synonyms* *(n)* paste, size, *(v)* join, stick, bind, **5**. adhere; *synonyms* *(v)* cohere, abide, accede, cleave, *(adj)* agree.

límast adhere; *synonyms* *(v)* cohere, abide, accede, attach, bond.

límband tape; *synonyms* *(n)* band, ribbon, strip, *(v)* record, videotape.

límefni shellac; *synonyms* *(n)* lac, *(v)* varnish, clobber, lick, overpower.

limgerði 1. windbreak; *synonyms* *(n)* hedge, shelterbelt, **2**. hedge; *synonyms* *(n)* fence, *(v)* dodge, fudge, elude, evade.

límhlaup gelatin; *synonyms* *(n)* gelatine, jelly, mastic, ropy, glutenous.

límhylki capsule; *synonyms* *(n)* abridgement, lozenge, condensation, pill, *(v)* encapsulate.

líming 1. bond; *synonyms* *(n)* association, tie, alliance, deed, *(v)* bind, **2**. ligation; *synonyms* *(n)* link, *(v)* astriction, attachment, compagination, vincture, **3**. paste; *synonyms* *(n)* glue, dough, *(v)* cement, gum, bond.

límingasíun dialysis; *synonyms* *(n)* debility, division.

líminn viscid; *synonyms* *(adj)* sticky, gluey, glutinous, viscous, adhesive.

límir ligase; *synonym* *(n)* synthetase.

límkenndur sticky; *synonyms* *(adj)* adhesive, awkward, clammy, muggy, embarrassing; *antonyms* *(adj)* dry, fresh, easy.

límmiði sticker; *synonyms* *(n)* label, ticket, pricker, prickle, spine.

límóna lime; *synonyms* *(n)* birdlime, basswood, calx, lemon, cement.

límonía lemon; *synonyms* *(n)* automobile, gamboge, auto, buff, bum.

limstaða erection; *synonyms* *(n)* building, edifice, assembly, construction, structure.

limur limb; *synonyms* *(n)* arm, bough, branch, member, extremity.

lina relieve; *synonyms* *(v)* assuage, comfort, ease, allay, *(n)* alleviate; *antonyms* *(v)* worsen, burden.

lína 1. row; *synonyms* *(n)* altercation, line, *(v)* quarrel, brawl, fight; *antonyms* *(n)* agreement, *(v)* agree, **2**.

tuple, **3**. circuit; *synonyms* *(n)* beat, *(v)* circle, tour, trip, journey, **4**. cable; *synonyms* *(n)* rope, cablegram, telegram, cord, *(v)* wire, **5**. arc; *synonyms* *(n)* arch, bow, bend, crescent, *(v)* curve.

lind 1. well; *synonyms* *(adv)* right, easily, thoroughly, *(adj)* healthy, *(n)* fountain; *antonyms* *(adv)* ill, badly, poorly, *(adj)* sick, unwell, **2**. spring; *synonyms* *(n)* jump, leap, bound, *(v)* hop, caper, **3**. reservoir; *synonyms* *(n)* cistern, well, lake, store, bank, **4**. source; *synonyms* *(n)* origin, root, cause, commencement, beginning, **5**. lime; *synonyms* *(n)* birdlime, basswood, calx, lemon, cement.

lindarblettur fontanelle; *synonym* *(n)* fontanel.

linditré lime; *synonyms* *(n)* birdlime, basswood, calx, lemon, cement.

lindiviður lime; *synonyms* *(n)* birdlime, basswood, calx, lemon, cement.

linsa 1. lens; *synonyms* *(n)* meniscus, *(v)* glass, barometer, especially, glaze, **2**. lentil.

linsufrekna lentigo; *synonyms* *(n)* freckle, blemish, lenticel, lenticula, freckles.

linsulaga lenticular; *synonyms* *(adj)* lentiform, biconvex, phacoid.

linsusjónauki refractor; *synonyms* *(n)* telescope, reflector, chromatoscope, divaricator.

linsuskekkja aberration; *synonyms* *(n)* aberrance, aberrancy, abnormality, deviation, diversion.

linsuvilla aberration; *synonyms* *(n)* aberrance, aberrancy, abnormality, deviation, diversion.

línþófi compress; *synonyms* *(v)* abridge, compact, press, squeeze, condense; *antonym* *(v)* loosen.

línubútur 1. segment; *synonyms* *(n)* division, paragraph, bit, *(v)* section, part, **2**. chord; *synonyms* *(n)* cord, harmony, *(v)* accord, harmonise, harmonize.

línuhlaupsbjögun pairing; *synonyms* *(n)* coupling, mating, conjugation, union, matching.

línulaga linear; *synonyms* *(adj)* lineal, rectilinear, running, additive, analog.

línulegur linear; *synonyms* *(adj)* lineal, rectilinear, running, additive, analog.

linun remission; *synonyms* *(n)* forgiveness, relief, ease, condonation, *(v)* pardon.

linur flaccid; *synonyms* *(adj)* flabby, limp, lax, loose, slack; *antonyms* *(adj)* firm, stiff.

línurit 1. scheme; *synonyms* *(n)* contrivance, dodge, *(v)* plan, plot, design, **2**. chart; *synonyms* *(n)* table, graphic, *(v)* map, graph, sketch, **3**. diagram; *synonyms* *(n)* chart, figure, drawing, illustration, outline, **4**. figure; *synonyms* *(n)* form, appearance, character, *(v)* cast, count, **5**. graph; *synonym* *(n)* diagram.

línuröðun alignment; *synonyms* *(n)* alliance, alinement, arrangement, coalition, organization.

línusamdragi concentrator; *synonym* (*n*)
multiplexer.

línustrik segment; *synonyms* (*n*) division, paragraph,
bit, (*v*) section, part.

línutvennd doublet; *synonyms* (*n*) couple, jerkin,
pair, waistcoat, barbe.

línuval selection; *synonyms* (*n*) election, choice,
option, alternative, extract.

lípíð lipid; *synonyms* (*n*) lipide, lipoid.

lipurð manoeuvrability; *synonyms* (*n*)
maneuverability, drivability.

lirfa larva; *synonyms* (*n*) grub, caterpillar, chicken,
pullet, whelp.

lirfugleypir pope; *synonyms* (*n*) pontiff, cardinal, (*adj*)
church, gospel, scripture.

list art; *synonyms* (*n*) know-how, skill, talent, trick,
artistry.

lista list; *synonyms* (*n*) catalog, catalogue, file,
inclination, index.

listbær gallery; *synonyms* (*n*) balcony, audience,
drift, veranda, circle.

listhús gallery; *synonyms* (*n*) balcony, audience, drift,
veranda, circle.

listi 1. schedule; *synonyms* (*n*) list, agenda, catalog,
program, (*v*) register, 2. strip; *synonyms* (*v*)
deprive, despoil, divest, peel, plunder; *antonyms*
(*v*) dress, decorate, 3. list; *synonyms* (*n*) catalogue,
file, inclination, index, (*v*) lean.

listskrubba gallery; *synonyms* (*n*) balcony, audience,
drift, veranda, circle.

liststöð gallery; *synonyms* (*n*) balcony, audience,
drift, veranda, circle.

listval gallery; *synonyms* (*n*) balcony, audience, drift,
veranda, circle.

listvör gallery; *synonyms* (*n*) balcony, audience, drift,
veranda, circle.

lita 1. dye; *synonyms* (*n*) color, tint, hue, stain, (*v*)
tinge, 2. iris; *synonyms* (*n*) diaphragm, flag, pupil,
rainbow, comet.

litarefni 1. pigment; *synonyms* (*n*) color, paint,
coloring, colorant, (*v*) dye, 2. dye; *synonyms* (*n*)
tint, hue, stain, dyestuff, (*v*) tinge.

litarleysi albinism; *synonym* (*n*) albinoism.

litbaugur corona; *synonyms* (*n*) crown, radiance,
halo, aureole, necklace.

litblær 1. tone; *synonyms* (*n*) character, note, accent,
air, (*v*) color, 2. chroma; *synonyms* (*n*) saturation,
hue, intensity, paint, tint, 3. hue; *synonyms* (*n*)
complexion, cast, chromaticity, (*v*) colour, tinge.

litfestir fixative; *synonyms* (*n*) adhesive, cement,
glue.

litfléttun dithering; *synonyms* (*n*) faltering,
indecision, (*adj*) wavering, hesitant, indecisive;
antonym (*n*) decisiveness.

litgildi chroma; *synonyms* (*n*) saturation, hue, color,
intensity, paint.

litgleipinn chromatic; *synonyms* (*adj*) colorful,
chromatical, (*n*) enharmonic, diatonic, (*v*) prismatic.

lithimna iris; *synonyms* (*n*) diaphragm, flag, pupil,
rainbow, comet.

lithvolf chromosphere; *synonyms* (*n*)
chromatosphere, photosphere.

lítið few; *synonyms* (*adj*) infrequent, rare, scarce,
occasional, sporadic; *antonyms* (*n*) plenty, (*adj*)
many, countless, innumerable, various.

lítill 1. small; *synonyms* (*adj*) little, minute, narrow,
fine, inadequate; *antonyms* (*adj*) bulky, colossal,
considerable, (*syn*) big, large, 2. little; *synonyms*
(*adj*) small, diminutive, insignificant, brief, petty;
antonyms (*adj*) enormous, important.

litillækkun 1. abjection; *synonyms* (*n*) abasement,
degradation, (*adj*) laxity, shuffling, trimming, 2.
abasement; *synonyms* (*n*) abjection, humiliation,
depression, deterioration, disgrace, 3.
humiliation; *synonyms* (*n*) chagrin, shame,
comedown, discredit, dishonor; *antonym* (*n*) honor.

lítilræði mite; *synonyms* (*n*) bit, speck, atom, crumb,
hint.

litkaaldin litchi; *synonyms* (*n*) lichee, lychee, lichi,
leechee, litchee.

litkaber litchi; *synonyms* (*n*) lichee, lychee, lichi,
leechee, litchee.

litkaplóma litchi; *synonyms* (*n*) lichee, lychee, lichi,
leechee, litchee.

litkjarni karyosome; *synonym* (*n*) nucleosome.

litlaus 1. achromatic; *synonyms* (*adj*) colorless, white,
neutral, aplanatic, snowy, 2. dull; *synonyms* (*adj*)
dim, blunt, dense, dreary, sluggish; *antonyms* (*adj*)
bright, lively, sharp, exciting, interesting.

litleysi achromasia; *synonyms* (*n*) lividity, lividness,
luridness, paleness, pallidness.

litmælir colorimeter; *synonyms* (*n*) tintometer,
colourimeter.

litni 1. chromatin, 2. hue; *synonyms* (*n*) color,
complexion, cast, (*v*) colour, tinge.

litningapar bivalent; *synonyms* (*adj*) divalent,
double, doubled, dual, duple.

litningapörun synapsis; *synonym* (*n*) synapse.

litningayfirfærsla translocation; *synonyms* (*n*) shift,
interchange.

litningsspeni satellite; *synonyms* (*n*) follower, moon,
planet, attendant, orbiter.

litningsþráðaferna bivalent; *synonyms* (*adj*)
divalent, double, doubled, dual, duple.

litningur chromosome; *synonyms* (*n*) antherozoid, bioplasm, biotaxy, dysmeromorph, gene.

lítri liter; *synonyms* (*n*) litre, l, fifty, lambert.

litritun chromatography; *synonyms* (*n*) chromatism, chromatology.

litróf spectrum; *synonyms* (*n*) range, gamut, (*v*) anamorphosis, distortion, illusion.

litrófsfræði spectroscopy; *synonyms* (*n*) chromatics, spectrometry.

litrófsgreining spectroscopy; *synonyms* (*n*) chromatics, spectrometry.

litrófsljósmælir spectrophotometer; *synonym* (*n*) photospectrometer.

litrófsmælir 1. spectrophotometer; *synonym* (*n*) photospectrometer, 2. spectrometer; *synonyms* (*n*) spectroscope, prism, spectrograph, monochrometer.

litrófsmynd spectrogram; *synonym* (*n*) spectrograph.

litrófsrannsókn spectroscopy; *synonyms* (*n*) chromatics, spectrometry.

litrófsrit spectrogram; *synonym* (*n*) spectrograph.

litrófsriti spectrograph; *synonyms* (*n*) spectrogram, spectroscope, prism, spectrometer.

litrófssamfella continuum; *synonyms* (*n*) continuity, range, band, field, gamut.

litrófssjá spectroscope; *synonyms* (*n*) abdominoscope, gastroscope, helioscope, polariscope, polemoscope.

litrófsþáttur band; *synonyms* (*n*) cluster, party, set, swathe, (*v*) ring.

litsjá 1. spectroscope; *synonyms* (*n*) abdominoscope, gastroscope, helioscope, polariscope, polemoscope, 2. spectrometer; *synonyms* (*n*) spectroscope, prism, spectrograph, monochrometer.

litskiljun chromatography; *synonyms* (*n*) chromatism, chromatology.

litsterkur chromatic; *synonyms* (*adj*) colorful, chromatical, (*n*) enharmonic, diatonic, (*v*) prismatic.

litstilling chroma; *synonyms* (*n*) saturation, hue, color, intensity, paint.

litstökun quantization; *synonym* (*n*) quantisation.

litukrampi miosis; *synonyms* (*n*) meiosis, litotes, myosis.

litun stain; *synonyms* (*n*) spot, blemish, blot, (*v*) color, dye.

litunarefni dye; *synonyms* (*n*) color, tint, hue, stain, (*v*) tinge.

litur 1. dye; *synonyms* (*n*) color, tint, hue, stain, (*v*) tinge, 2. colour; *synonyms* (*n*) coloration, coloring, colouring, (*v*) discolor, discolour, 3. stain; *synonyms* (*n*) spot, blemish, blot, (*v*) dye, tarnish, 4. color; *synonyms* (*n*) blush, colour, (*v*) flush, paint, redden; *antonym* (*n*) colorlessness.

litvilla dichromatism; *synonyms* (*n*) dichromacy, dichromasy, dichromatopsia.

litvilltur dichromatic; *synonyms* (*v*) polychromatic, (*adj*) bicolour, bichrome, bicolor, bicolored.

litvísir indicator; *synonyms* (*n*) gauge, index, indication, arrow, indicant.

ljóm luminescence; *synonyms* (*n*) glow, radiance, glowing, freshness, gleam.

ljómandi brilliant; *synonyms* (*adj*) bright, splendid, glorious, illustrious, intelligent; *antonyms* (*adj*) dull, dim, awful, dark.

ljómefni phosphor; *synonyms* (*n*) phosphorus, phosphide, scintillator.

ljómeitur poison; *synonyms* (*n*) bane, (*v*) infect, contaminate, envenom, defile; *antonym* (*n*) antidote.

ljómi luminance; *synonyms* (*n*) brightness, illumination, light, luminosity, lighting.

ljómstækkun irradiation; *synonyms* (*n*) radiotherapy, beam, radiation, actinotherapy, light.

ljómun 1. photoluminescence, 2. luminescence; *synonyms* (*n*) glow, radiance, glowing, freshness, gleam, 3. highlight; *synonyms* (*v*) emphasize, accentuate, spotlight, underline, accent.

ljón lion; *synonyms* (*n*) celebrity, cat, curiosity, (*adj*) hero, worthy.

ljóni liner; *synonyms* (*n*) lining, boat, airliner, craft, ship.

ljóri skylight; *synonyms* (*n*) fanlight, window, light, casement, day.

ljörvi laser; *synonym* (*n*) beam.

ljós light; *synonyms* (*adj*) fair, clear, (*v*) fire, kindle, inflame; *antonyms* (*n*) dark, darkness, gloom, shade, (*alt sp*) heavy.

ljósafl luminosity; *synonyms* (*n*) brightness, light, illumination, glow, brilliance; *antonym* (*n*) dullness.

ljósálfur 1. brownie; *synonyms* (*n*) fairy, elf, goblin, imp, pixie, 2. cub; *synonyms* (*n*) child, whelp, youngster, greenhorn, lad.

ljósapera bulb; *synonyms* (*n*) knob, lightbulb, corm, nodule, (*adj*) globule.

ljósaskipti twilight; *synonyms* (*n*) dusk, nightfall, night, evening, gloaming; *antonyms* (*n*) dawn, daybreak.

ljósband video; *synonyms* (*n*) television, picture, film, movie, (*v*) tape.

ljósbaugur halo; *synonyms* (*n*) aureole, aura, glory, halation, ring.

ljósbeyging diffraction; *synonyms* (*n*) deflection, deviation, inflection.

ljósbogi arc; *synonyms* (*n*) arch, bow, bend, crescent, (*v*) curve.

ljósbrjótur refractor; *synonyms* (*n*) telescope, reflector, chromatoscope, divaricator.

ljósbrot refraction; *synonyms* (*n*) bending, deflection, deflexion, (*v*) obliquation, (*adj*) reflection.

ljósbrotsmælir refractometer; *synonyms* (*v*) bathometer, galvanometer, heliometer, interferometer, odometer.

ljósbrotsvik refraction; *synonyms* (*n*) bending, deflection, deflexion, (*v*) obliquation, (*adj*) reflection.

ljósdepill blip; *synonyms* (*n*) pip, breakdown, bug, error, (*v*) slap.

ljósdeyfinn opaque; *synonyms* (*adj*) cloudy, dense, dull, muddy, obscure; *antonyms* (*adj*) clear, transparent, see-through.

ljósdeyfitala opacity; *synonyms* (*n*) obscurity, opaqueness, cloudiness, murkiness, opaque; *antonym* (*n*) clearness.

ljósdeyfni opacity; *synonyms* (*n*) obscurity, opaqueness, cloudiness, murkiness, opaque; *antonym* (*n*) clearness.

ljósdreifing scattering; *synonyms* (*n*) diffusion, dispersal, dissipation, dispersion, distribution.

ljóseðlisfræði optics; *synonyms* (*n*) vision, photology, orbs, sight.

ljósfræði optics; *synonyms* (*n*) vision, photology, orbs, sight.

ljósfræðilegur optical; *synonyms* (*adj*) optic, visual, ocular, opthalmic, eye.

ljósgeisli 1. ray; *synonyms* (*n*) beam, light, flash, glow, gleam, 2. beam; *synonyms* (*n*) blaze, ray, timber, (*v*) glare, (*adj*) shine.

ljósgreiða grating; *synonyms* (*adj*) rough, harsh, hoarse, strident, discordant; *antonyms* (*adj*) soft, pleasing.

ljóshlíf shade; *synonyms* (*n*) screen, tinge, color, ghost, (*v*) darken; *antonyms* (*n*) light, brightness.

ljóshylki bulb; *synonyms* (*n*) knob, lightbulb, corm, nodule, (*adj*) globule.

ljóskastari 1. spotlight; *synonyms* (*n*) limelight, spot, (*v*) highlight, light, focus, 2. projector; *synonyms* (*n*) schemer, searchlight, planner, intriguer, (*v*) promoter.

ljósker 1. lamp; *synonyms* (*n*) light, look, beacon, (*v*) behold, regard, 2. lantern; *synonyms* (*n*) lamp, dormer, buat, cupola, lanthorn.

ljósleiðninemi photocell; *synonyms* (*n*) photodiode, photomultiplier.

ljósleitni 1. phototropism, 2. heliotropism; *synonym* (*n*) phototropism.

ljósleysir laser; *synonym* (*n*) beam.

ljósmælifræði photometry; *synonym* (*adj*) photology.

ljósmæling photometry; *synonym* (*adj*) photology.

ljósmælingar photometry; *synonym* (*adj*) photology.

ljósmælir photometer; *synonyms* (*n*) lucimeter, radiometer.

ljósmóðir midwife; *synonyms* (*n*) accoucheuse, accoucheur, oculist, howdy, (*v*) midwive.

ljósmynd 1. snapshot; *synonyms* (*n*) photograph, picture, photo, shot, snap, 2. snap; *synonyms* (*v*) crack, bite, break, fracture, nip, 3. photograph; *synonyms* (*n*) image, likeness, portrait, print, (*v*) film, 4. photo; *synonyms* (*n*) pic, exposure.

ljósnæmi speed; *synonyms* (*n*) race, (*v*) hasten, hurry, quicken, run; *antonym* (*n*) slowness.

ljósnæmishlutfall luminosity; *synonyms* (*n*) brightness, light, illumination, glow, brilliance; *antonym* (*n*) dullness.

ljósnemi 1. photocell; *synonyms* (*n*) photodiode, photomultiplier, 2. photoreceptor.

ljósop 1. pupil; *synonyms* (*n*) follower, learner, student, scholar, apprentice, 2. aperture; *synonyms* (*n*) hole, breach, opening, puncture, slit.

ljósopsþrenging miosis; *synonyms* (*n*) meiosis, litotes, myosis.

ljósopsþynna diaphragm; *synonyms* (*n*) membrane, midriff, partition, pessary, septum.

ljósröfunarnemi photocell; *synonyms* (*n*) photodiode, photomultiplier.

ljóssella photocell; *synonyms* (*n*) photodiode, photomultiplier.

ljóssía filter; *synonyms* (*v*) percolate, sieve, drip, leak, filtrate; *antonym* (*v*) contaminate.

ljósspennunemi photocell; *synonyms* (*n*) photodiode, photomultiplier.

ljósstefnuvik aberration; *synonyms* (*n*) aberrance, aberrancy, abnormality, deviation, diversion.

ljósstyrkur intensity; *synonyms* (*n*) force, forcefulness, depth, volume, (*adj*) strength; *antonyms* (*n*) dullness, indifference, weakness.

ljósþéttir condenser; *synonyms* (*n*) capacitor, capacitance, capacity, plugger.

ljósturn lantern; *synonyms* (*n*) lamp, beacon, light, dormer, buat.

ljósvaki ether; *synonyms* (*n*) aether, (*adj*) air, flatus, fume, reek.

ljósvik aberration; *synonyms* (*n*) aberrance, aberrancy, abnormality, deviation, diversion.

ljósvilla aberration; *synonyms* (*n*) aberrance, aberrancy, abnormality, deviation, diversion.

ljósvísir spot; *synonyms* (*n*) blot, place, speck, (*v*) blemish, soil.

ljótur 1. ugly; *synonyms* (*adj*) nasty, disagreeable, forbidding, frightful, gruesome; *antonyms* (*adj*) beautiful, attractive, good-looking, flowing, ornamental, 2. nasty; *synonyms* (*adj*) dirty, loathsome, disgusting, filthy, foul; *antonyms* (*adj*) agreeable, kind, pleasant, nice, charitable.

ljúga 1. lie; *synonyms* (v) consist, (n) fabrication, falsehood, falsity, fib; *antonyms* (v) stand, (n) truth, 2. fib; *synonyms* (n) lie, fable, story, tale, (v) fabricate.

ló pubescence; *synonyms* (n) puberty, adolescence, down, fertility, prime.

lóð 1. plat; *synonyms* (n) chart, (v) plait, plot, braid, diagram, 2. weight; *synonyms* (n) load, burden, charge, consequence, heaviness; *antonym* (n) triviality, 3. site; *synonyms* (n) place, position, locate, (v) post, set, 4. parcel; *synonyms* (n) lot, bale, pack, bundle, (v) portion, 5. location; *synonyms* (n) localization, orientation, berth, emplacement, fix.

löð 1. valence; *synonyms* (n) valency, atomicity, quantivalence, equivalence, (v) unsaturation, 2. die; *synonyms* (v) decease, dead, death, depart, (n) dice.

lóða solder; *synonyms* (n) glue, paste, (v) cement, join, fuse.

lóðhnit ordinate; *synonyms* (v) coordinate, adjust, align, aline, array.

loðinn 1. villous; *synonyms* (adj) bushy, hispid, villose, hairy, nappy, 2. hirsute; *synonyms* (adj) bearded, shaggy, ciliated, filamentous, fimbriated.

loðka capelin; *synonyms* (n) caplin, capelan, capling.

lóðlína 1. vertical; *synonyms* (adj) upright, perpendicular, straight, erect, sheer; *antonyms* (adj) horizontal, prone, 2. perpendicular; *synonyms* (adj) vertical, plumb, steep, normal, orthogonal.

lóðmálmur solder; *synonyms* (n) glue, paste, (v) cement, join, fuse.

loðna 1. pubescence; *synonyms* (n) puberty, adolescence, down, fertility, prime, 2. capelin; *synonyms* (n) caplin, capelan, capling.

lóðning 1. sounding; *synonyms* (adj) audible, looking, hollow, (n) investigation, depth, 2. trace; *synonyms* (n) line, shadow, spot, clue, (v) track.

lóðrétt vertical; *synonyms* (adj) upright, perpendicular, straight, erect, sheer; *antonyms* (adj) horizontal, prone.

lóðréttur 1. vertical; *synonyms* (adj) upright, perpendicular, straight, erect, sheer; *antonyms* (adj) horizontal, prone, 2. perpendicular; *synonyms* (adj) vertical, plumb, steep, normal, orthogonal.

lóðs pilot; *synonyms* (n) guide, leader, aviator, (v) manage, lead.

loðsíld capelin; *synonyms* (n) caplin, capelan, capling.

loðsíli capelin; *synonyms* (n) caplin, capelan, capling.

lóðstreymi convection; *synonyms* (n) transfer, (adj) thermal.

lóðtin solder; *synonyms* (n) glue, paste, (v) cement, join, fuse.

lóðun 1. welding; *synonyms* (n) fusion, assembly, synthesis, 2. soldering; *synonyms* (n) bonding, brazing, (v) sticking.

löður foam; *synonyms* (n) froth, spume, (v) boil, bubble, effervesce.

lofa promise; *synonyms* (v) pledge, covenant, guarantee, contract, vow.

lófalægur palmar; *synonyms* (adj) thenar, chief, palmary, palmy, preeminent.

lófatak acclamation; *synonyms* (n) acclaim, applause, ovation, plaudit, praise.

lófi palm; *synonyms* (n) decoration, medal, prize, (v) hand, filch.

loforð 1. promise; *synonyms* (v) pledge, covenant, guarantee, contract, vow, 2. affirmation; *synonyms* (n) assertion, statement, affirmance, admission, allegation; *antonym* (n) denial, 3. assurance; *synonyms* (n) confidence, belief, affiance, certitude, conviction; *antonym* (n) insecurity.

loft 1. air; *synonyms* (n) tune, appearance, manner, (v) ventilate, broadcast, 2. atmosphere; *synonyms* (n) air, ambience, ambiance, aura, environment, 3. ambience; *synonyms* (n) atmosphere, feel, climate, setting, medium, 4. gas; *synonyms* (n) gasoline, petrol, fumes, accelerator, flatulence.

loftæð trachea; *synonyms* (n) windpipe, throat, weasand, chimney, flue.

loftæðaop spiracle; *synonyms* (n) larynx, tonsils, windpipe, (v) stigma, brand.

loftaflfræði 1. pneumatics; *synonyms* (n) aerometry, (adj) pneumatostatics, 2. aerodynamics; *synonyms* (n) aeromechanics, aviation, (adj) aerostatics, anemography.

loftauga stoma; *synonyms* (n) pore, aperture, hole, stomate.

loftbóla bubble; *synonyms* (n) blister, (v) boil, babble, foam, burble.

loftbólurek aeroembolism; *synonym* (n) bends.

loftborinn airborne; *synonyms* (adj) flying, aerial, soaring.

loftbraut airway; *synonym* (n) airline.

loftfæla anaerobe; *synonyms* (n) aerobe, microbe, archaebacteria, halophile, methanogen.

loftfælinn anaerobic; *synonym* (adj) anaerobiotic.

loftfíkinn aerobic; *synonyms* (adj) aerophilic, aerophilous.

loftfimleikamaður acrobat; *synonyms* (n) tumbler, clown, charlatan, harlequin, mountebank.

loftfirrður anaerobic; *synonym* (adj) anaerobiotic.

loftfræði aerodynamics; *synonyms* (n) aeromechanics, aviation, (adj) aerostatics, anemography.

loftfylltur pneumatic; *synonyms (adj)* aerial, airy, aeronautic, aerostatical, pneumatical.

loftgat vent; *synonyms (n)* outlet, exit, discharge, opening, *(v)* air.

lofthádur aerobic; *synonyms (adj)* aerophilic, aerophilous.

lofthjúpur atmosphere; *synonyms (n)* air, ambience, ambiance, aura, environment.

lofthreyfifræði aerodynamics; *synonyms (n)* aeromechanics, aviation, *(adj)* aerostatics, anemography.

loftinntak scoop; *synonyms (n)* ladle, spade, *(v)* draw, dig, excavate.

loftkenndur gaseous; *synonyms (adj)* volatile, airy, gasiform, ethereal, invisible.

loftknúið pneumatic; *synonyms (adj)* aerial, airy, aeronautic, acrostatical, pneumatical.

loftknúinn pneumatic; *synonyms (adj)* aerial, airy, aeronautic, aerostatical, pneumatical.

loftkveikjandi pyrophoric; *synonym (adj)* pyrophorous.

loftlagsbelti zone; *synonyms (n)* area, district, region, section, belt.

loftlagsfræði climatology; *synonym (n)* meteorology.

loftlína airline; *synonym (n)* airway.

loftnet 1. antenna; *synonyms (n)* aerial, feeler, advance, finger, forefinger, 2. aerial; *synonyms (adj)* airy, aery, ethereal, unreal, *(n)* antenna.

loftop vent; *synonyms (n)* outlet, exit, discharge, opening, *(v)* air.

loftpoki aerostat; *synonyms (n)* aeronaut, balloonist.

loftpressa compressor; *synonym (n)* supercharger.

loftpúðaskip hovercraft; *synonyms (n)* catamaran, hydroplane, caravel, carvel, coracle.

loftræsing ventilation; *synonyms (n)* airing, exploitation, discussion, deliberation, air.

loftræsta ventilate; *synonyms (v)* air, fan, vent, discuss, aerate.

loftræsting ventilation; *synonyms (n)* airing, exploitation, discussion, deliberation, air.

loftræstitæki ventilator; *synonyms (n)* fan, vent, *(v)* bellows, blowpipe, lungs.

loftsækinn aerobic; *synonyms (adj)* aerophilic, aerophilous.

loftskeytatækni radio; *synonyms (n)* wireless, broadcasting, radiotelegram, *(v)* broadcast, transmit.

loftskipting ventilation; *synonyms (n)* airing, exploitation, discussion, deliberation, air.

loftskolun injection; *synonyms (n)* shot, clyster, enema, inoculation, jab.

loftskrúfa propeller; *synonyms (n)* screw, fan, turbine, extortioner, niggard.

loftslag climate; *synonyms (n)* atmosphere, clime, ambience, latitude, environment.

loftslagsfræði climatology; *synonym (n)* meteorology.

loftsog suction; *synonyms (n)* suck, sucking, aspiration, absorption, draft.

loftsteinn 1. fireball; *synonyms (n)* bolide, cartouche, *(adj)* active, ambitious, capable, 2. meteorite; *synonyms (n)* aerolite, uranolite, meteorolite, 3. meteor; *synonyms (n)* effluvium, emanation, evaporation, exhalation, meteoroid.

loftsteinsslóð train; *synonyms (v)* aim, coach, direct, educate, exercise.

loftstraumfræði aerodynamics; *synonyms (n)* aeromechanics, aviation, *(adj)* aerostatics, anemography.

loftstraumur draught; *synonyms (n)* draft, potion, dose, potation, *(v)* design.

loftsveipir turbulence; *synonyms (n)* disorder, tumult, confusion, agitation, commotion; *antonyms (n)* calm, peace.

lofttæmi vacuum; *synonyms (n)* emptiness, void, vacancy, vacuity, gap.

lofttegund gas; *synonyms (n)* gasoline, petrol, air, fumes, accelerator.

loftþrýstitækni pneumatics; *synonyms (n)* aerometry, *(adj)* pneumatostatics.

loftþurfi aerobic; *synonyms (adj)* aerophilic, aerophilous.

loftþyngd atmosphere; *synonyms (n)* air, ambience, ambiance, aura, environment.

lofttómshreinsun degassing; *synonyms (n)* degasing, scavenging.

loftúði aerosol; *synonyms (n)* spray, atomizer, vaporizer, can.

Loftun ventilation; *synonyms (n)* airing, exploitation, discussion, deliberation, air.

loftunarop vent; *synonyms (n)* outlet, exit, discharge, opening, *(v)* air.

loftvera aerobe; *synonyms (n)* microbe, anaerobe, archaebacteria, halophile, methanogen.

loftvog barometer; *synonyms (n)* baroscope, aeroscope, eudiometer, gauge, *(v)* glass.

lög 1. law; *synonyms (n)* rule, canon, decree, act, edict, 2. act; *synonyms (n)* accomplishment, action, *(v)* achievement, behave, deed; *antonym (v)* refrain, 3. statute; *synonyms (n)* law, ordinance, constitution, charter, enactment, 4. rule; *synonyms (v)* govern, order, dominion, *(v)* command, control, 5. rules; *synonyms (n)* regulations, etiquette, policy, system, convention.

lögaðili corporation; *synonyms (n)* association, belly, business, company, concern.

lögákveðinn statutory; *synonyms* *(adj)* legal, lawful, legitimate, statutable, constitutional.

lógaritmi logarithm; *synonyms* *(n)* log, exponent, index, backlog, *(adj)* numeric.

lögbær competent; *synonyms* *(adj)* able, capable, adequate, clever, effective; *antonyms* *(adj)* incompetent, useless, inept.

lögbann injunction; *synonyms* *(n)* behest, charge, command, dictate, bidding.

lögboðinn 1. statutory; *synonyms* *(adj)* legal, lawful, legitimate, statutable, constitutional, **2.** compulsory; *synonyms* *(adj)* obligatory, required, binding, involuntary, mandatory; *antonyms* *(adj)* optional, voluntary, **3.** mandatory; *synonyms* *(adj)* compulsory, necessary, imperative, requisite, *(n)* mandatary.

lögbundinn 1. statutory; *synonyms* *(adj)* legal, lawful, legitimate, statutable, constitutional, **2.** constitutional; *synonyms* *(adj)* congenital, essential, inherent, intrinsic, organic; *antonym* *(adj)* unconstitutional.

lögfræði law; *synonyms* *(n)* rule, canon, decree, act, edict.

lögfræðilegur legal; *synonyms* *(adj)* lawful, sound, valid, juridical, *(v)* allowable; *antonyms* *(adj)* illegal, unlawful, bogus.

lögfræðingur attorney; *synonyms* *(n)* advocate, lawyer, agent, counsel, counselor.

löggæzla police; *synonyms* *(n)* constabulary, law, *(v)* control, guard, watch.

löggæzlulið police; *synonyms* *(n)* constabulary, law, *(v)* control, guard, watch.

löggengur deterministic; *synonym* *(adj)* determinist.

löggilda 1. validate; *synonyms* *(v)* corroborate, substantiate, confirm, sustain, ratify; *antonyms* *(v)* invalidate, cancel, nullify, overturn, **2.** ratify; *synonyms* *(v)* approve, acknowledge, authorize, endorse, sanction, **3.** accredit; *synonyms* *(v)* credit, ascribe, assign, attribute, certify, **4.** authorize; *synonyms* *(v)* empower, commission, delegate, license, pass.

löggilding authorization; *synonyms* *(n)* authority, sanction, approval, license, permission.

löggiltur statutory, *synonyms* *(adj)* legal, lawful, legitimate, statutable, constitutional.

löggjöf legislation; *synonyms* *(n)* lawmaking, legislating, law, conduct, government.

löghald sequestration; *synonyms* *(n)* segregation, separation, damages, deodand, escheat.

lögheimili domicile; *synonyms* *(n)* abode, dwelling, home, residence, house.

löghyggja determinism; *synonym* *(n)* fatalism.

logi flame; *synonyms* *(n)* blaze, fire, ardour, *(v)* burn, flash.

löglegur 1. lawful; *synonyms* *(adj)* legitimate, legal, just, rightful, *(n)* allowable; *antonyms* *(adj)* illegal, unlawful, **2.** legal; *synonyms* *(adj)* lawful, sound, valid, juridical, constitutional; *antonym* *(adj)* bogus.

lögleiðing transposition; *synonyms* *(n)* exchange, permutation, replacement, reversal, substitution.

lögmaður 1. attorney; *synonyms* *(n)* advocate, lawyer, agent, counsel, counselor, **2.** counsel; *synonyms* *(n)* caution, *(v)* advice, advise, consult, admonish, **3.** lawyer; *synonyms* *(n)* attorney, representative, advisor, leguleian, beagle.

lögmæltur statutory; *synonyms* *(adj)* legal, lawful, legitimate, statutable, constitutional.

lögmæti validity; *synonyms* *(n)* force, truth, authority, legitimacy, soundness.

lögmætur 1. legal; *synonyms* *(adj)* lawful, sound, valid, juridical, *(v)* allowable; *antonyms* *(adj)* illegal, unlawful, bogus, **2.** legitimate; *synonyms* *(adj)* legal, authentic, genuine, just, *(v)* legalize; *antonyms* *(adj)* banned, informal, illegitimate, invalid.

lögmál 1. principle; *synonyms* *(n)* origin, fundamental, method, rule, cause, **2.** law; *synonyms* *(n)* canon, decree, act, edict, regulation.

logn calm; *synonyms* *(adj)* quiet, *(v)* assuage, appease, cool, still; *antonyms* *(adj)* agitated, angry, nervous, *(v)* agitate, *(n)* agitation.

lögn duct; *synonyms* *(n)* channel, conduit, canal, drain, aqueduct.

lögpersóna corporation; *synonyms* *(n)* association, belly, business, company, concern.

lögræðisaldur majority; *synonyms* *(n)* bulk, age, plurality, body, mass; *antonym* *(n)* minority.

lögregluðjónn 1. policeman; *synonyms* *(n)* cop, officer, detective, watchman, *(adj)* patrolman, **2.** copper; *synonyms* *(n)* bronze, bull, fuzz, gold, pig, **3.** cop; *synonyms* *(n)* bust, *(v)* catch, apprehend, arrest, collar, **4.** constable; *synonyms* *(n)* policeman, alderman, burgomaster, portreeve, alguazil, **5.** officer; *synonyms* *(n)* captain, administrator, commander, bureaucrat, executive.

lögreglumaður 1. policeman; *synonyms* *(n)* cop, officer, detective, watchman, *(adj)* patrolman, **2.** copper; *synonyms* *(n)* bronze, bull, fuzz, gold, pig, **3.** constable; *synonyms* *(n)* policeman, alderman, burgomaster, portreeve, alguazil, **4.** cop; *synonyms* *(n)* bust, *(v)* catch, apprehend, arrest, collar, **5.** officer; *synonyms* *(n)* captain, administrator, commander, bureaucrat, executive.

lögreglustjóri commissioner; *synonyms* *(n)* commissary, delegate, agent, executive, official.

lögregluþjónn 1. bobby; *synonyms* *(n)* clod, dolt, **2.** officer; *synonyms* *(n)* captain, administrator, commander, bureaucrat, executive, **3.** peeler;

synonyms (n) stripper, ecdysiast, (adj) cop, fuzz, zarp.

logri logarithm; synonyms (n) log, exponent, index, backlog, (adj) numeric.

lógrími logarithm; synonyms (n) log, exponent, index, backlog, (adj) numeric.

lögsaga jurisdiction; synonyms (n) power, authority, dominion, district, judicature.

lögsagnarumdæmi jurisdiction; synonyms (n) power, authority, dominion, district, judicature.

logsjóða weld; synonyms (v) join, solder, bond, cement, fasten.

lögskilnaður divorce; synonyms (n) separation, (v) detach, dissociate, disunite, separate; antonyms (n) marriage, wedding.

lögskipa constitute; synonyms (v) compose, form, make, commission, appoint.

lögskipaður 1. statutory; synonyms (adj) legal, lawful, legitimate, statutable, constitutional, **2.** mandatory; synonyms (adj) compulsory, obligatory, required, necessary, (n) mandatary; antonym (adj) optional, **3.** legal; synonyms (adj) sound, valid, juridical, judicial, (v) allowable; antonyms (adj) illegal, unlawful, bogus.

lögskýring construction; synonyms (n) building, fabrication, formation, structure, assembly; antonym (n) destruction.

lögstétt estate; synonyms (n) condition, land, demesne, order, rank.

logsuða welding; synonyms (n) fusion, assembly, synthesis.

logsuðugas acetylene; synonyms (n) alkyne, ethyne, ethine.

logsuðulampi torch; synonyms (n) flashlight, brand, light, blowlamp, blowtorch.

lögtak 1. distraint; synonyms (n) distress, hurt, suffering, **2.** distress; synonyms (n) agony, anguish, pain, (v) afflict, torment; antonyms (v) comfort, please, **3.** execution; synonyms (n) performance, accomplishment, achievement, effect, enforcement.

lögun 1. profile; synonyms (n) contour, outline, form, figure, shape, **2.** shape; synonyms (n) cast, mold, (v) fashion, model, mould, **3.** liquefaction; synonyms (n) dissolution, fusion, condensation, melting, solvolysis, **4.** form; synonyms (n) design, arrange, ceremony, (v) make, build, **5.** morphology; synonyms (n) accidence, anatomy, geomorphology, taxonomy, botany.

lögur 1. fluid; synonyms (adj) liquid, flowing, unsettled, changeable, smooth; antonym (n) solid, **2.** liquid; synonyms (adj) fluent, fluid, juicy, limpid, (n) liquor; antonyms (adj) firm, (n) gaseous.

lóhærður pubescent; synonyms (adj) adolescent, juvenile, downy, hairy, puberulent; antonym (n) adult.

lok 1. cover; synonyms (v) coat, conceal, top, bury, (n) blind; antonyms (v) reveal, expose, uncover, **2.** lid; synonyms (n) cover, chapeau, eyelid, hat, closure, **3.** wrapper; synonyms (n) jacket, wrap, cloak, covering, housecoat, **4.** conclusion; synonyms (n) close, end, result, cessation, (v) closing; antonyms (n) beginning, start, opening, preface, **5.** cap; synonyms (n) bonnet, lid, capital, base, (v) beat.

loka 1. valve; synonyms (n) lock, sluice, door, gauge, monitor, **2.** close; synonyms (adj) near, adjacent, nearby, accurate, (n) end; antonyms (adj) distant, airy, fresh, (v) open, start, **3.** block; synonyms (n) bar, barricade, pad, (v) arrest, stop; antonyms (v) free, unblock, **4.** latch; synonyms (n) catch, hasp, clasp, hook, (v) bolt.

lokaður 1. closed; synonyms (v) close, (adj) blind, blocked, finished, shut; antonym (adj) open, **2.** blind; synonyms (v) bedazzle, (n) screen, curtain, shutter, awning; antonym (adj) sighted.

lokari shutter; synonyms (n) close, curtain, blind, shut, (v) screen.

lokasteinn keystone; synonyms (n) keynote, basis, foundation, headstone, key.

lokhljóð stop; synonyms (n) halt, hold, stay, check, end; antonyms (v) continue, start, begin, encourage, permit.

loki 1. terminator; synonyms (n) eradicator, exterminator, **2.** valve; synonyms (n) lock, sluice, door, gauge, monitor.

lokið completed; synonyms (adj) complete, done, accomplished, finished, (adv) over.

lökkun lacquering; synonym (n) varnishing.

loktákn terminator; synonyms (n) eradicator, exterminator.

lokuhrúður vegetation; synonyms (n) flora, growth, plants, foliage, quietism.

lokun 1. closure; synonyms (n) closing, close, blockade, blockage, closedown; antonym (n) inauguration, **2.** obturation; synonym (n) filling, **3.** occlusion; synonyms (n) closure, block, stoppage, obstruction, plug, **4.** obliteration; synonyms (n) annihilation, eradication, abolition, (v) erasure, (adj) extirpation.

lokunarventill stop; synonyms (n) halt, hold, stay, check, end; antonyms (v) continue, start, begin, encourage, permit.

lokuvöðvi sphincter; synonym (n) constrictor.

löm hinge; synonyms (n) joint, axis, articulation, axle, (v) pivot.

lömun 1. palsy; *synonyms* (*n*) paralysis, (*v*) cripple, paralyze, (*adj*) consumption, decline, **2**. paralysis; *synonyms* (*n*) palsy, disability, depression, (*adj*) sideration, syncope.

lömunarveiki 1. poliomyelitis; *synonym* (*n*) polio, **2**. polio; *synonyms* (*n*) poliomyelitis, (*adj*) measles, mumps.

lón lagoon; *synonyms* (*n*) lagune, lake, bay, mere, pond.

löndun landing; *synonyms* (*n*) land, dock, touchdown, floor, platform.

longanber longan; *synonyms* (*n*) longanberry, lungen, lungan.

lopi edema; *synonyms* (*n*) dropsy, hydrops, oedema.

lorno 1. binocular; *synonyms* (*n*) binoculars, spyglass, **2**. binoculars; *synonym* (*n*) binocular.

los ablation; *synonyms* (*n*) excision, extirpation, sublation, (*v*) abduction, abreption.

losa 1. release; *synonyms* (*n*) discharge, (*v*) exempt, free, liberate, (*adj*) disengage; *antonyms* (*n*) imprisonment, abduction, (*v*) capture, confine, imprison, **2**. mobilize; *synonyms* (*v*) circulate, marshal, gather, mobilise, rally; *antonym* (*v*) demobilize.

löskun 1. trauma; *synonyms* (*n*) injury, hurt, wound, shock, harm, **2**. lesion; *synonyms* (*n*) abrasion, scrape, scratch, abscess, canker.

löss loess; *synonyms* (*n*) clay, dust.

lost shock; *synonyms* (*n*) blow, daze, impact, collision, (*v*) jar; *antonym* (*v*) comfort.

lostaböðull sadist; *synonym* (*n*) brute.

lostakælandi anaphrodisiac; *synonyms* (*adj*) antaphrodisiac, (*v*) antiorgastic.

lostakælir anaphrodisiac; *synonyms* (*adj*) antaphrodisiac, (*v*) antiorgastic.

lostakvalari sadist; *synonym* (*n*) brute.

lostavekjandi aphrodisiac; *synonyms* (*adj*) amorous, aphrodisiacal, erotic, sexy, venereal.

losun 1. stripping; *synonyms* (*n*) baring, husking, denudation, scrubbing, discovery, **2**. discharge; *synonyms* (*n*) release, dismissal, (*v*) acquit, clear, absolve; *antonyms* (*v*) capture, hire, **3**. dumping; *synonyms* (*n*) disposal, discarding, clearance, jettisoning, removal, **4**. detachment; *synonyms* (*n*) division, separation, dissociation, corps, indifference; *antonyms* (*n*) involvement, attachment, bias, interest, **5**. clearing; *synonyms* (*n*) clarification, glade, dell, lot, aisle.

losunaróhapp episode; *synonyms* (*n*) affair, chapter, event, incident, occurrence.

lot dip; *synonyms* (*n*) plunge, (*v*) duck, bathe, drop, fall; *antonyms* (*n*) hump, mountain.

lota 1. turn; *synonyms* (*n*) bend, curve, roll, coil, go, **2**. session; *synonyms* (*n*) meeting, seance, sitting,

conference, bout, **3**. series; *synonyms* (*n*) chain, rank, collection, cycle, (*v*) course, **4**. cycle; *synonyms* (*n*) bicycle, circle, round, (*v*) bike, motorcycle, **5**. batch; *synonyms* (*n*) band, lot, body, battery, charge.

lotilo dice; *synonyms* (*n*) die, (*v*) cube, cut, chop, bet.

lotubundinn periodic; *synonyms* (*adj*) intermittent, regular, periodical, recurrent, frequent.

lotukvæmur cyclic; *synonyms* (*adj*) periodic, circular, cyclical, recurring, regular; *antonym* (*adj*) irregular.

lotulaus aperiodic; *synonym* (*adj*) nonperiodic.

lotun cutoff; *synonyms* (*n*) crosscut, shortcut, break, interruption, stop.

lotutími period; *synonyms* (*n*) age, dot, epoch, era, point.

lotutíminn periodic; *synonyms* (*adj*) intermittent, regular, periodical, recurrent, frequent.

lúða halibut; *synonym* (*n*) holibut.

lúga hatch; *synonyms* (*n*) brood, (*v*) breed, contrive, concoct, brew.

lúgugatsábreiða tarpaulin; *synonyms* (*n*) tarp, counterpane, cover, coverlet, quilt.

lúkning closure; *synonyms* (*n*) closing, close, blockade, blockage, closedown; *antonym* (*n*) inauguration.

lukt lamp; *synonyms* (*n*) light, look, beacon, (*v*) behold, regard.

lúmen lumen; *synonym* (*n*) lm.

lummari butterfish; *synonym* (*n*) stromateid.

lundarfar temperament; *synonyms* (*n*) temper, character, disposition, nature, constitution.

lundaseiði whiting; *synonyms* (*n*) whitening, kingfishes.

lundur grove; *synonyms* (*n*) copse, forest, coppice, orchard, thicket.

lungnablaðra alveolus; *synonyms* (*n*) follicle, lacuna, cavity, dent, dimple.

lungnablöðruseyti surfactant; *synonym* (*n*) bedwetter.

lungnabólga pneumonia; *synonyms* (*adj*) necrosis, pertussis, phthisis, psora, pyaemia.

lungnapípa bronchus; *synonym* (*n*) bronchi.

lunning rail; *synonyms* (*n*) bar, balustrade, handrail, railing, (*v*) inveigh.

lús 1. louse; *synonyms* (*n*) worm, insect, cad, miscreant, (*adj*) vermin, **2**. bug; *synonyms* (*n*) beetle, (*v*) annoy, badger, pester, bother.

lúsaegg nit; *synonyms* (*n*) louse, bug, tick, mite.

lúserna alfalfa; *synonyms* (*n*) lucern, alfilaria, banyan, lamp.

lútarsalt alkali; *synonyms* (*n*) base, salt, brine, (*adj*) alkaline, (*v*) caustic.

lútesín lutetium; *synonym* (*n*) lutecium.

lútetín lutetium; *synonym* (*n*) lutecium.

lútetíum lutetium; *synonym* (n) lutecium.

lútfíkill basophil; *synonym* (n) basophile.

lútkenndur basic; *synonyms* (adj) first, cardinal, initial, primary, (n) essential; *antonyms* (adj) secondary, complex, extra, minor.

lútur base; *synonyms* (n) foundation, (adj) bottom, abject, mean, dishonorable; *antonyms* (n) summit, top, (adj) noble.

lúx lux; *synonyms* (n) lx, sixty, (v) luxate.

lýðnet internet; *synonyms* (n) cyberspace, internetwork.

lýðræði democracy; *synonyms* (n) commonwealth, commonalty, nation, capitalism, country; *antonyms* (n) despotism, dictatorship, totalitarianism, autocracy, tyranny.

lýðræðisríki democracy; *synonyms* (n) commonwealth, commonalty, nation, capitalism, country; *antonyms* (n) despotism, dictatorship, totalitarianism, autocracy, tyranny.

lýðræðissinni democrat; *synonyms* (n) commoner, plebeian, proletaire, proletary, republican.

lýðræðisstjórn democracy; *synonyms* (n) commonwealth, commonalty, nation, capitalism, country; *antonyms* (n) despotism, dictatorship, totalitarianism, autocracy, tyranny.

lýðveldi republic; *synonyms* (n) commonwealth, democracy, state, nation, country.

lýðveldissinni republican; *synonyms* (n) commoner, democrat, plebeian, roturier.

lyf 1. medicine; *synonyms* (n) cure, drug, medicament, medication, (v) medicate, 2. pharmaceutical; *synonyms* (adj) pharmaceutic, (n) medicine, physic, remedy, galenicals, 3. drug; *synonyms* (n) anesthetic, prescription, (v) dose, potion, (adj) chaff.

lyfjablanda mixture; *synonyms* (n) mix, alloy, concoction, assortment, blend.

lyfjabúð 1. pharmacy; *synonyms* (n) drugstore, pharmaceutics, dispensatory, medicine, fermacy, 2. dispensary; *synonym* (n) booth, 3. drugstore; *synonyms* (n) pharmacy, bookstore, market, store, tobacconists.

lyfjadæla syringe; *synonyms* (n) douche, beaker, flask, needle, (v) hydrant.

lyfjaduft powder; *synonyms* (n) dust, gunpowder, (v) grind, crush, pound.

lyfjaforskrift formula; *synonyms* (n) form, law, convention, expression, formality.

lyfjafræði pharmacology; *synonym* (n) pharmacy.

lyfjagjöf dosage; *synonyms* (n) dose, amount, quantity, capsule, drug.

lyfjaglas glass; *synonyms* (n) pane, bottle, drink, bowl, cup.

lyfjahylki capsule; *synonyms* (n) abridgement, lozenge, condensation, pill, (v) encapsulate.

lyfjameðferð 1. chemotherapy, 2. medication; *synonyms* (n) cure, medicine, drug, medicament, treatment.

lyfjamisnotkun habituation; *synonyms* (n) adaptation, addiction, accustomedness, assuefaction, conditioning.

lyfjaseyði extract; *synonyms* (n) excerpt, (v) draw, abstract, derive, educe.

lyfjaþol habituation; *synonyms* (n) adaptation, addiction, accustomedness, assuefaction, conditioning.

lyfjaþykkni extract; *synonyms* (n) excerpt, (v) draw, abstract, derive, educe.

lyflæknisfræði medicine; *synonyms* (n) cure, drug, medicament, medication, (v) medicate.

lyflæknisfræðilegur medical; *synonyms* (adj) aesculapian, medicinal, medic, (n) checkup, examination.

lyfleysa placebo; *synonyms* (n) bracer, cure, gesture, panacea, (v) blarney.

lyfta 1. lift; *synonyms* (n) elevator, (v) hoist, raise, rise, elevate, 2. hoist; *synonyms* (n) boost, (v) haul, heave, lift, erect, 3. raise; *synonyms* (v) increase, build, enhance, foster, (n) advance; *antonym* (v) lower, 4. heave; *synonyms* (v) cast, fling, chuck, gasp, (n) tug, 5. elevate; *synonyms* (v) exalt, cheer, dignify, promote, rear; *antonym* (v) demote.

lyftiarmur boom; *synonyms* (n) bang, roar, (v) blast, blare, flourish; *antonyms* (n) depression, (v) collapse, decline.

lyftibúnaður hoist; *synonyms* (n) boost, (v) elevate, haul, heave, lift.

lyftijárn elevator; *synonyms* (n) lift, crane, rise, (v) dumbwaiter, escalator.

lyftikraftur lift; *synonyms* (n) elevator, (v) hoist, raise, rise, elevate.

lyftikrani 1. derrick; *synonyms* (n) hoist, oilrig, (v) crane, winch, windlass, 2. crane; *synonyms* (n) pulley, ankle, elevator, (v) extend, stretch.

lyfting 1. rise; *synonyms* (n) elevation, lift, (v) climb, mount, ascend; *antonyms* (v) fall, decrease, drop, sink, descend, 2. suspension; *synonyms* (n) delay, interruption, abeyance, break, intermission.

lyftispillir spoiler; *synonyms* (n) depredator, looter, pillager, plunderer, raider.

lyftistöng lever; *synonyms* (n) knob, (v) pry, raise, jimmy, prize.

lygi 1. lie; *synonyms* (v) consist, (n) fabrication, falsehood, falsity, fib; *antonyms* (v) stand, (n) truth, 2. falsehood; *synonyms* (n) fable, deceit, deception, lie, untruth; *antonyms* (n) fact, honesty.

lykill 1. key; *synonyms* *(adj)* central, fundamental, basic, cardinal, *(n)* guide, **2.** primer; *synonyms* *(n)* manual, fuse, fuze, ground, grammar, **3.** wrench; *synonyms* *(n)* spanner, *(v)* sprain, pull, jerk, strain, **4.** code; *synonyms* *(n)* cipher, charter, law, act, *(v)* cypher.

lykilorð password; *synonyms* *(n)* countersign, catchword, parole, watchword, *(v)* key.

lykja 1. ampulla; *synonym* *(n)* flask, **2.** cycle; *synonyms* *(n)* bicycle, circle, round, *(v)* bike, motorcycle.

lykkja 1. contour; *synonyms* *(n)* form, outline, profile, shape, configuration, **2.** loop; *synonyms* *(n)* coil, ring, *(v)* curve, bend, circle, **3.** jumper; *synonyms* *(n)* sweater, blackguard, bounder, cad, dog, **4.** lobe; *synonyms* *(n)* division, flap, limb, member, arm.

lyklaborð keyboard; *synonym* *(n)* upright.

lykt 1. smell; *synonyms* *(n)* odor, fragrance, *(v)* reek, nose, perfume, **2.** odour; *synonyms* *(n)* flavour, aroma, smell, scent, flavor.

lykta smell; *synonyms* *(n)* odor, fragrance, *(v)* reek, nose, perfume.

lyktarskyn 1. olfaction; *synonyms* *(n)* smell, aroma, feel, feeling, flavor, **2.** olfactory; *synonyms* *(adj)* olfactive, odorous, sensory.

lykteyðandi deodorant; *synonyms* *(adj)* odorless, *(n)* deodorization, cleanser.

lykteyðir deodorant; *synonyms* *(adj)* odorless, *(n)* deodorization, cleanser.

lympa malaise; *synonyms* *(n)* disquietude, disquiet, unrest, unease, *(v)* discomfort.

lyndi mood; *synonyms* *(n)* humor, atmosphere, climate, disposition, air.

lyng broom; *synonyms* *(n)* besom, brush, *(v)* sweep, filter, rake.

lyngheiði 1. heath; *synonyms* *(n)* heather, heathland, prairie, steppe, waste, **2.** moor; *synonyms* *(n)* marsh, *(v)* anchor, berth, fasten, tie.

lyngmói heath; *synonyms* *(n)* heather, heathland, prairie, steppe, waste.

lýsa 1. whiting; *synonyms* *(n)* whitening, kingfishes, **2.** photon.

lýsi brightness, *synonyms* *(n)* flash, clarity, illumination, light, luminance; *antonyms* *(n)* dullness, cloudiness, darkness, dimness, murkiness.

lýsing 1. rendering; *synonyms* *(n)* interpretation, reading, rendition, translation, representation, **2.** schema; *synonyms* *(n)* outline, plan, chart, graph, scheme, **3.** representation; *synonyms* *(n)* image, performance, depiction, picture, presentation, **4.** light; *synonyms* *(adj)* fair, clear, *(v)* fire, kindle, inflame; *antonyms* *(n)* dark, darkness, gloom,

shade, *(alt sp)* heavy, **5.** lighting; *synonyms* *(n)* illumination, light, firing, ignition, kindling.

lýsingarmagn exposure; *synonyms* *(n)* display, exposition, detection, peril, *(v)* disclosure.

lýsingur descriptor; *synonyms* *(n)* anatomy, bod, build, cast, chassis.

lýsiorð descriptor; *synonyms* *(n)* anatomy, bod, build, cast, chassis.

lýsir descriptor; *synonyms* *(n)* anatomy, bod, build, cast, chassis.

lýsitala statistic; *synonyms* *(n)* fact, guide, marker, number, sign.

lýsitölufall statistic; *synonyms* *(n)* fact, guide, marker, number, sign.

lystarleysi anorexia; *synonyms* *(adj)* inappetency, anorexy.

lystiskúta yacht; *synonyms* *(n)* boat, vessel, ship, craft, dinghy.

lýti 1. stigma; *synonyms* *(n)* spot, blot, brand, stain, blemish, **2.** flaw; *synonyms* *(n)* defect, crevice, fault, chink, *(v)* crack; *antonym* *(n)* strength.

M

maðkur worm; *synonyms* *(v)* squirm, wriggle, twist, helix, *(adj)* insect.

maður 1. man; *synonyms* *(n)* fellow, gentleman, guy, person, husband; *antonym* *(n)* woman, **2.** person; *synonyms* *(n)* human, individual, man, being, body; *antonym* *(n)* automaton, **3.** spouse; *synonyms* *(n)* consort, partner, wife, mate, match, **4.** personage; *synonyms* *(n)* celebrity, notable, personality, figure, character, **5.** piece; *synonyms* *(n)* cut, division, fragment, part, article.

mæða modality; *synonyms* *(n)* mode, mood, manner, schesis, fashion.

mæddur depressed; *synonyms* *(adj)* concave, low, blue, dejected, dispirited; *antonyms* *(adj)* cheerful, happy, convex.

mæði dyspnea; *synonyms* *(n)* dyspnoea, anhelation.

mægðir affinity; *synonyms* *(n)* sympathy, analogy, alliance, bond, kindred.

mæla 1. quantify; *synonyms* *(v)* measure, gauge, evaluate, assess, determine, **2.** detect; *synonyms* *(v)* catch, discover, find, ascertain, discern, **3.** assay; *synonyms* *(n)* examination, *(v)* test, try, attempt, experiment, **4.** observe; *synonyms* *(v)* celebrate, comment, notice, commemorate, mind; *antonyms* *(n)* ignore, feel, **5.** gauge; *synonyms* *(n)* criterion, caliber, gage, *(v)* estimate, calculate.

mælaborð 1. dashboard; *synonyms* (*n*) splashboard, splasher, bank, sprayboard, washboard, **2**. panel; *synonyms* (*n*) board, jury, defendant, committee, (*v*) empanel, **3**. fascia; *synonyms* (*n*) cincture, band, facia, fillet, aponeurosis.

mælahús binnacle; *synonym* (*n*) bittacle.

mælandi speaker; *synonyms* (*n*) loudspeaker, narrator, orator, president, spokesman.

mælanlegur quantitative; *synonyms* (*adj*) some, measurable, quantitive, wholesale.

mældur empirical; *synonyms* (*adj*) empiric, experimental, observational, observed, (*v*) tentative; *antonym* (*adj*) theoretical.

mæli voice; *synonyms* (*n*) speech, (*v*) enunciate, express, pronounce, say.

mæliblað plat; *synonyms* (*n*) chart, (*v*) plait, plot, braid, diagram.

mælibrú bridge; *synonyms* (*n*) span, viaduct, pontoon, tie, (*v*) stretch.

mælieining 1. unit; *synonyms* (*n*) troop, element, group, squad, (*adj*) one, **2**. measure; *synonyms* (*n*) amount, criterion, extent, beat, benchmark.

mæligreina assay; *synonyms* (*n*) examination, (*v*) test, try, attempt, experiment.

mæligreining assay; *synonyms* (*n*) examination, (*v*) test, try, attempt, experiment.

mælihlutfall rate; *synonyms* (*n*) price, worth, (*v*) assess, estimate, evaluate.

mælikerfi measurement; *synonyms* (*n*) dimension, gauge, magnitude, measure, proportion.

mælikvarði 1. scale; *synonyms* (*n*) flake, gamut, (*v*) ascend, climb, (*adj*) balance; *antonym* (*v*) descend, **2**. standard; *synonyms* (*adj*) model, (*n*) degree, measure, average, criterion; *antonyms* (*adj*) unusual, unconventional, special, **3**. criterion; *synonyms* (*n*) benchmark, norm, test, canon, mark.

mæling 1. survey; *synonyms* (*n*) poll, review, (*v*) study, measure, view; *antonym* (*v*) neglect, **2**. assay; *synonyms* (*n*) examination, (*v*) test, try, attempt, experiment, **3**. determination; *synonyms* (*n*) decision, conclusion, definition, resolution, (*v*) award; *antonyms* (*n*) indecision, weakness, compliance, indecisiveness, **4**. measurement; *synonyms* (*n*) dimension, gauge, magnitude, proportion, observation, **5**. observation; *synonyms* (*n*) comment, observance, remark, attention, inspection.

mælingar measurement; *synonyms* (*n*) dimension, gauge, magnitude, measure, proportion.

mælipípa 1. pipette; *synonyms* (*n*) pipet, beaker, flask, carboy, syringe, **2**. burette; *synonyms* (*n*) buret, jar.

mælir 1. instrument; *synonyms* (*n*) channel, deed, agency, apparatus, appliance, **2**. meter; *synonyms*

(*n*) gauge, measure, metre, beat, counter, **3**. gauge; *synonyms* (*n*) criterion, caliber, gage, (*v*) estimate, calculate.

mælisálestur reading; *synonyms* (*n*) recital, learning, construction, interpretation, (*v*) read.

mælistaðall standard; *synonyms* (*adj*) model, (*n*) degree, measure, average, criterion; *antonyms* (*adj*) unusual, unconventional, special.

mælistærð parameter; *synonyms* (*n*) argument, guideline, limit, directive, modulus.

mælisvið range; *synonyms* (*v*) line, arrange, order, rank, roam.

mælitæki 1. indicator; *synonyms* (*n*) gauge, index, indication, arrow, indicant, **2**. instrument; *synonyms* (*n*) channel, deed, agency, apparatus, appliance, **3**. gauge; *synonyms* (*n*) criterion, caliber, (*v*) estimate, measure, calculate.

mælitækjavæðing instrumentation; *synonyms* (*n*) orchestration, arrangement, instrumentality, channel, means.

mælitækni instrumentation; *synonyms* (*n*) orchestration, arrangement, instrumentality, channel, means.

mælitöng calipers; *synonyms* (*n*) caliper, callipers, calliper, (*v*) compass, measure.

mælivídd 1. span; *synonyms* (*n*) length, space, distance, bridge, couple, **2**. dimension; *synonyms* (*n*) degree, breadth, bulk, magnitude, size.

mæna monitor; *synonyms* (*v*) check, regulate, control, eavesdrop, (*n*) admonisher.

mænir monitor; *synonyms* (*v*) check, regulate, control, eavesdrop, (*n*) admonisher.

mænugránabólga poliomyelitis; *synonym* (*n*) polio.

mænusótt 1. polio; *synonyms* (*n*) poliomyelitis, (*adj*) measles, mumps, **2**. poliomyelitis; *synonym* (*n*) polio.

mænuveiki 1. poliomyelitis; *synonym* (*n*) polio, **2**. polio; *synonyms* (*n*) poliomyelitis, (*adj*) measles, mumps.

mæri boundary; *synonyms* (*n*) border, bound, limit, edge, area.

mæs corn; *synonyms* (*n*) maize, clavus, cereals, callus, wheat.

mæta 1. meet; *synonyms* (*v*) converge, find, assemble, congregate, (*adj*) fit; *antonyms* (*v*) avoid, disperse, diverge, **2**. encounter; *synonyms* (*n*) collision, combat, battle, conflict, (*v*) clash; *antonym* (*v*) retreat.

mætingar attendance; *synonyms* (*n*) presence, attending, audience, turnout, hearing; *antonyms* (*n*) absence, nonattendance.

mætti 1. potential; *synonyms* (*adj*) likely, possible, (*n*) capability, potency, ability, **2**. potency; *synonyms* (*n*) force, might, effectiveness, efficacy, energy.

máfuglar lari; *synonyms* (*n*) gulls, skimmers, terns.

máfur gull; *synonyms* (*n*) dupe, fool, (*v*) cheat, deceive, beguile.

magasin rack; *synonyms* (*n*) manger, wrack, (*v*) torture, excruciate, torment.

magaverkur gastralgia; *synonyms* (*n*) stomachache, bellyache.

magi 1. stomach; *synonyms* (*v*) accept, brook, abide, bear, (*adj*) digest, 2. belly; *synonyms* (*n*) abdomen, stomach, inside, bowels, (*v*) balloon, 3. tummy; *synonyms* (*n*) belly, breadbasket, corporation, pot, potbelly, 4. abdomen; *synonyms* (*n*) venter, gut, guts, intestines, middle, 5. gut; *synonyms* (*n*) bowel, (*v*) eviscerate, pillage, ransack, despoil.

magn 1. quantity; *synonyms* (*n*) amount, extent, measure, multitude, quantum, 2. volume; *synonyms* (*n*) bulk, size, book, magnitude, mass; *antonym* (*n*) quietness, 3. quantitative; *synonyms* (*adj*) some, measurable, quantitive, wholesale, 4. concentration; *synonyms* (*n*) absorption, concentrate, application, attention, engrossment; *antonym* (*n*) distraction, 5. amplitude; *synonyms* (*n*) breadth, latitude, width, expanse, fullness.

magna 1. amplify; *synonyms* (*v*) aggrandize, enlarge, exaggerate, expand, extend; *antonyms* (*v*) reduce, understate, 2. excite; *synonyms* (*v*) animate, arouse, disturb, enliven, agitate; *antonyms* (*v*) calm, pacify, bore.

magnaður intensive; *synonyms* (*adj*) intense, concentrated, thorough, exhaustive, (*n*) intensifier; *antonym* (*adj*) extensive.

magnákvörðun quantification; *synonym* (*n*) measurement.

magnari 1. repeater; *synonyms* (*n*) recidivist, criminal, revolver, (*v*) floater, keener, 2. amplifier.

magnbundinn 1. quantitative; *synonyms* (*adj*) some, measurable, quantitive, wholesale, 2. extensive; *synonyms* (*adj*) big, comprehensive, ample, broad, commodious; *antonyms* (*adj*) narrow, restricted, small, limited, minor.

magnesín magnesium; *synonyms* (*n*) mg, chalk, milligram.

magnesíum magnesium; *synonyms* (*n*) mg, chalk, milligram.

magnfesta quantify; *synonyms* (*v*) measure, gauge, evaluate, assess, determine.

magnfesting quantification; *synonym* (*n*) measurement.

magngreina quantify; *synonyms* (*v*) measure, gauge, evaluate, assess, determine.

magnhæfa quantify; *synonyms* (*v*) measure, gauge, evaluate, assess, determine.

magnhæfing quantification; *synonym* (*n*) measurement.

magni complement; *synonyms* (*n*) supplement, accessory, adjunct, balance, extra.

magnín magnesium; *synonyms* (*n*) mg, chalk, milligram.

magníum magnesium; *synonyms* (*n*) mg, chalk, milligram.

magnmæling quantification; *synonym* (*n*) measurement.

magnsetja quantification; *synonym* (*n*) measurement.

magnstol fatigue; *synonyms* (*n*) exhaustion, tiredness, weariness, (*v*) exhaust, tire; *antonyms* (*n*) energy, (*v*) refresh.

Maí may; *synonyms* (*v*) can, could, get, might, acquire.

maímánuður may; *synonyms* (*v*) can, could, get, might, acquire.

maís 1. corn; *synonyms* (*n*) maize, clavus, cereals, callus, wheat, 2. maize; *synonyms* (*n*) corn, cereal, gamboge, lemon, grain.

maísíld shad; *synonyms* (*n*) herring, anchovies, etc, herrings, sardines.

maískorn corn; *synonyms* (*n*) maize, clavus, cereals, callus, wheat.

makríll mackerel; *synonyms* (*n*) bass, muskelunge, sailfish, sardine, trout.

makstur unction; *synonyms* (*n*) inunction, balm, ointment, salve, unguent.

makzelo 1. jaws; *synonyms* (*n*) mouth, jaw, lips, (*v*) mazard, gob, 2. jaw; *synonyms* (*v*) chatter, gossip, chat, gab, jabber.

mál 1. speech; *synonyms* (*n*) address, delivery, expression, lecture, conversation, 2. dimension; *synonyms* (*n*) degree, breadth, bulk, magnitude, size, 3. matter; *synonyms* (*n*) event, affair, business, concern, issue, 4. language; *synonyms* (*n*) dialect, speech, diction, idiom, lingo, 5. measure; *synonyms* (*n*) amount, criterion, extent, beat, benchmark.

mala 1. mill; *synonyms* (*n*) grind, factory, grinder, manufactory, (*v*) crush, 2. grind; *synonyms* (*v*) labor, toil, comminute, crunch, drudge.

mála 1. paint; *synonyms* (*v*) color, dye, daub, coat, decorate, 2. coat; *synonyms* (*n*) cover, coating, (*v*) cloak, sheath, blanket.

málaflutningsmaður 1. attorney; *synonyms* (*n*) advocate, lawyer, agent, counsel, counselor, 2. lawyer; *synonyms* (*n*) attorney, representative, advisor, leguleian, beagle.

málaleitan request; *synonyms* (*n*) petition, bid, (*v*) demand, ask, invite; *antonyms* (*v*) command, order.

málamiðlari conciliator; *synonyms* (*n*) peacemaker, mediator, arbitrator, intermediary, negotiator.

málamiðlun 1. compromise; *synonyms* (*n*) agreement, arrangement, bargain, accommodation, (*v*) compound; *antonym* (*v*) dispute, **2.** accommodation; *synonyms* (*n*) adjustment, compromise, loan, lodging, (*v*) advance, **3.** mediation; *synonyms* (*n*) arbitration, intercession, intervention, agency, intermediation, **4.** intervention; *synonyms* (*n*) interference, intervene, hindrance, (*adj*) mediation, interposition.

málamiðlunarsamkomulag compromise; *synonyms* (*n*) agreement, arrangement, bargain, accommodation, (*v*) compound; *antonym* (*v*) dispute.

malarás esker; *synonyms* (*n*) eskar, hill, ridge, eschar.

málari painter; *synonyms* (*n*) artist, limner, cable, catamount, cougar.

malarsandur gravel; *synonyms* (*v*) bedevil, get, nonplus, rag, (*adj*) bother.

málbein hyoid; *synonym* (*adj*) hypsiloid.

málbeiting performance; *synonyms* (*n*) act, discharge, achievement, execution, (*v*) action; *antonyms* (*n*) omission, practice.

malbik asphalt; *synonyms* (*n*) bitumen, asphaltus, (*v*) tar, (*adj*) tarmac, flags.

málboð message; *synonyms* (*n*) communication, meaning, information, errand, letter.

málefni subject; *synonyms* (*n*) matter, citizen, affair, (*adj*) liable, exposed; *antonym* (*adj*) liberated.

málefniskeðja thread; *synonyms* (*n*) string, line, yarn, (*v*) file, range.

málfærslumaður 1. solicitor; *synonyms* (*n*) lawyer, advocate, counsel, attorney, petitioner, **2.** attorney; *synonyms* (*n*) agent, counselor, factor, solicitor, representative, **3.** barrister; *synonym* (*n*) adviser, **4.** advocate; *synonyms* (*n*) backer, champion, sponsor, (*v*) recommend, support; *antonyms* (*n*) detractor, skeptic, (*v*) oppose, **5.** counsel; *synonyms* (*n*) caution, (*v*) advice, advise, consult, admonish.

málflutningsmaður counsel; *synonyms* (*n*) caution, (*n*) advice, advise, consult, admonish.

málflutningur representation; *synonyms* (*n*) image, performance, depiction, picture, presentation.

málflytjandi lawyer; *synonyms* (*n*) advocate, attorney, agent, representative, advisor.

málfræði 1. syntax; *synonyms* (*n*) grammar, accidence, syntaxis, organism, **2.** grammar; *synonyms* (*n*) rudiments, elements, praxis, punctuation, (*v*) initiation.

málfræðilegur grammatical; *synonym* (*adj*) grammatic.

málfyrning archaism; *synonyms* (*n*) archaicism, medievalism, antiquity, obsoletism, relic.

málgögn data; *synonyms* (*n*) information, facts, details, evidence, fact.

málhæfni competence; *synonyms* (*n*) capacity, adequacy, ability, capability, (*adj*) proficiency; *antonyms* (*n*) incompetence, inability.

málhljóð phone; *synonyms* (*n*) earpiece, earphone, headphone, (*v*) telephone, call.

málhreimur accent; *synonyms* (*n*) stress, dialect, emphasis, (*v*) emphasize, emphasise.

málkunnátta competence; *synonyms* (*n*) capacity, adequacy, ability, capability, (*adj*) proficiency; *antonyms* (*n*) incompetence, inability.

mállaus 1. dumb; *synonyms* (*adj*) mute, dense, dim, dull, silent, **2.** mute; *synonyms* (*adj*) dumb, quiet, (*v*) muffle, dampen, deaden; *antonym* (*adj*) talkative.

mállýska dialect; *synonyms* (*n*) idiom, language, speech, accent, lingo.

mállýskubundinn dialectal; *synonyms* (*adj*) vernacular, colloquial.

málmblanda alloy; *synonyms* (*n*) admixture, amalgam, (*v*) adulterate, devalue, (*adj*) sophisticate.

málmblendi alloy; *synonyms* (*n*) admixture, amalgam, (*v*) adulterate, devalue, (*adj*) sophisticate.

málmbróðir metalloid; *synonyms* (*n*) nonmetal, (*adj*) metalloidal, acid, negative.

málmerki mark; *synonyms* (*n*) brand, evidence, score, (*v*) blemish, (*adj*) notice.

málmgjall slag; *synonyms* (*n*) cinder, clinker, dross, scoria, scum.

málmgrýti ore; *synonyms* (*n*) timber, rock, wood, clemency, favor.

málmhleifur ingot; *synonyms* (*n*) bullion, bar, block, nugget, copper.

málmhringsamband chelate; *synonym* (*adj*) chelated.

málmleysingi nonmetal; *synonyms* (*n*) metalloid, (*adj*) nonmetallic.

málmsteypa casting; *synonyms* (*n*) cast, molding, pouring, air, appearence.

málmsuða 1. weld; *synonyms* (*v*) join, solder, bond, cement, fasten, **2.** welding; *synonyms* (*n*) fusion, assembly, synthesis.

málmþreyta fatigue; *synonyms* (*n*) exhaustion, tiredness, weariness, (*v*) exhaust, tire; *antonyms* (*n*) energy, (*v*) refresh.

málmþynna shim; *synonyms* (*n*) wedge, liner, filling.

málmungur metalloid; *synonyms* (*n*) nonmetal, (*adj*) metalloidal, acid, negative.

málmur metal; *synonyms* (*n*) ore, admixture, aggregate, alloy, clemency.

málmvír wire; *synonyms* (*n*) cable, telegram, line, rope, (*v*) telegraph.

málning paint; *synonyms* (v) color, dye, daub, coat, decorate.

malnobla means; *synonyms* (n) expedient, agency, instrument, assets, capital.

málnotkun usage; *synonyms* (n) habit, practice, employment, (v) use, (adj) custom.

málraun rating; *synonyms* (n) assessment, mark, evaluation, appraisal, estimate.

málsaðili party; *synonyms* (n) gang, band, company, assembly, association.

málsatvik fact; *synonyms* (n) event, incident, detail, deed, particular; *antonyms* (n) guesswork, rumor, conjecture, fallacy, falsehood.

málsgrein 1. sentence; *synonyms* (n) judgment, finding, decision, (v) condemn, convict, **2**. paragraph; *synonyms* (n) article, item, section, chapter, (v) clause.

málskipan syntax; *synonyms* (n) grammar, accidence, syntaxis, organism.

málskostnaður expenses; *synonyms* (n) expenditure, charge, costs, fee, spending.

málskot 1. review; *synonyms* (n) examination, critique, (v) check, survey, criticize, **2**. appeal; *synonyms* (n) plea, address, (v) charm, request, sue; *antonyms* (n) unpleasantness, (v) repel.

málsmeðferð procedure; *synonyms* (n) process, formula, practice, routine, fashion.

málsskjal petition; *synonyms* (n) appeal, (v) demand, ask, request, desire.

málsskjöl 1. dossier; *synonyms* (n) file, information, folder, data, papers, **2**. document; *synonyms* (n) charter, deed, credentials, (v) record, list.

málsskot appeal; *synonyms* (n) plea, address, (v) charm, request, sue; *antonyms* (n) unpleasantness, (v) repel.

málstærð norm; *synonyms* (n) average, mean, measure, mode, criterion.

málstærðir rating; *synonyms* (n) assessment, mark, evaluation, appraisal, estimate.

málstola aphasic; *synonyms* (adj) mute, speechless.

málstoli aphasic; *synonyms* (adj) mute, speechless.

málsvari protagonist; *synonyms* (n) hero, booster, champion, exponent, supporter.

máltákn sign; *synonyms* (n) signal, indication, mark, motion, (v) gesture.

málþing 1. symposium; *synonyms* (n) conference, discussion, regale, dialogue, meeting, **2**. forum; *synonyms* (n) agora, assembly, court, pulpit, square.

máltilfinning intuition; *synonyms* (n) feeling, hunch, insight, instinct, notion.

málun painting; *synonyms* (n) picture, portrait, likeness, depiction, icon.

malurt 1. wormwood; *synonyms* (n) absinth, gall, **2**. mugwort; *synonyms* (n) motherwort, tarragon.

malurtarbrennivín absinth; *synonym* (n) absinthe.

málvenja usage; *synonyms* (n) habit, practice, employment, (v) use, (adj) custom.

málverk 1. picture; *synonyms* (n) photograph, effigy, paint, (v) image, describe, **2**. painting; *synonyms* (n) picture, portrait, likeness, depiction, icon.

málvik tolerance; *synonyms* (n) endurance, allowance, indulgence, leniency, patience; *antonyms* (n) intolerance, narrow-mindedness, bigotry, chauvinism, extremism.

málvísindi linguistics; *synonyms* (n) glossology, philology, glossary, glottology.

mánaðarlega monthly; *synonyms* (adj) menstrual, mensal, (n) magazine, periodical, journal.

mánasigð crescent; *synonyms* (n) arc, arcade, arch, bow, carve.

mangan manganese; *synonym* (n) manganium.

mangó 1. mangosteen; *synonyms* (v) chowder, chupatty, clam, compote, damper, **2**. mango; *synonyms* (v) fish, frumenty, grapes, lettuce, mangosteen.

mangóávöxtur mango; *synonyms* (v) chowder, chupatty, clam, compote, damper.

mangostan mangosteen; *synonyms* (v) chowder, chupatty, clam, compote, damper.

mangóstan mangosteen; *synonyms* (v) chowder, chupatty, clam, compote, damper.

mangóstantré mangosteen; *synonyms* (v) chowder, chupatty, clam, compote, damper.

máni meniscus; *synonyms* (n) crescent, lens, curve, sunglass.

máninn moon (tungl); *synonyms* (n) lunation, moonlight, moonshine, satellite, (v) daydream.

manjók cassava; *synonyms* (n) manioc, mandioca, casava, gari, manioca.

manjokrunni cassava; *synonyms* (n) manioc, mandioca, casava, gari, manioca.

mannafli 1. workforce; *synonyms* (n) manpower, personnel, employees, hands, men, **2**. manpower; *synonyms* (n) workforce, custody.

mannakynbætur eugenics; *synonym* (n) heredity.

mannbætur eugenics; *synonym* (n) heredity.

mannblendni gregariousness; *synonym* (n) camaraderie.

manndauði lethality; *synonyms* (n) deadliness, fatality, mortality.

manneskja man (maður); *synonyms* (n) fellow, gentleman, guy, person, husband; *antonym* (n) woman.

mannfélag society; *synonyms* (n) club, institution, public, association, community.

mannfjöldi population; *synonyms* (n) inhabitants, people, nation, community, group.

mannflokkur race; *synonyms* (n) kind, dash, family, (v) course, (adj) lineage.

mannfræði anthropology; *synonyms* (n) anthroposophy, entomology, helminthology, herpetology, ichthyology.

manngerð type; *synonyms* (n) pattern, character, kind, nature, (adj) model.

manngerðaflokkun typology; *synonym* (n) typing.

manngerðafræði typology; *synonym* (n) typing.

manngerður anthropogenic; *synonym* (adj) anthropogenetic.

manngervastefna anthropomorphism; *synonyms* (n) theanthropism, anthropomorphitism, (adj) anthropomorphitic.

manngerving anthropomorphism; *synonyms* (n) theanthropism, anthropomorphitism, (adj) anthropomorphitic.

mannhatur misanthropy; *synonyms* (n) demonophobia, gynephobia, misanthropia.

mannheimar earth; *synonyms* (n) dirt, world, dust, ground, land.

mannhyggja humanism; *synonyms* (n) humanitarianism, culture.

mannkyn mankind; *synonyms* (n) man, humanity, humankind, world, humans.

mannlaus deserted; *synonyms* (adj) abandoned, desert, solitary, bleak, (v) forlorn; *antonyms* (adj) inhabited, occupied, packed.

mannlegur human; *synonyms* (n) mortal, man, person, homo, (adv) fleshly.

mannlíkur anthropoid; *synonyms* (adj) manlike, anthropoidal, human, apelike, (n) ape.

mannmótað anthropogenic; *synonym* (adj) anthropogenetic.

mannmótaður anthropogenic; *synonym* (adj) anthropogenetic.

mannop porthole; *synonyms* (n) port, embrasure, loophole, skylight, window.

manntal census; *synonyms* (n) list, returns, cense, (v) poll, recapitulation.

mannþróun anthropogenesis; *synonym* (n) anthropogeny.

mannþyrping crowd; *synonyms* (n) huddle, swarm, collection, (v) bunch, flock; *antonym* (v) disperse.

mannúðarstefna humanism; *synonyms* (n) humanitarianism, culture.

mannvera man (maður); *synonyms* (n) fellow, gentleman, guy, person, husband; *antonym* (n) woman.

mannvirðing status; *synonyms* (n) position, rank, situation, (adj) place, standing.

mannvirki 1. culture; *synonyms* (n) civilization, breeding, cultivation, acculturation, education, **2.** facilities; *synonym* (n) equipment.

mánuður month; *synonyms* (n) moon, day, hour, minute, quarter.

mappa folder; *synonyms* (n) brochure, file, book, booklet, case.

mar 1. bruise; *synonyms* (n) blow, contusion, (v) crush, hurt, wound, **2.** hematoma; *synonym* (n) haematoma.

mara incubus; *synonyms* (n) nightmare, demon, load, weight, onus.

marantarót arrowroot; *synonym* (n) achira.

marflatur prostrate; *synonyms* (adj) flat, prone, exhaust, (v) fell, level.

margbreytilegur polymorphic; *synonyms* (adj) polymorphous, pleomorphic.

margfaldari multiplier; *synonyms* (n) multiplicator, multiplicand, multiple.

margfaldur multiple; *synonyms* (adj) manifold, many, complex, diverse, populous; *antonym* (adj) simple.

margfeldi 1. product; *synonyms* (n) fruit, output, merchandise, proceeds, (v) produce, **2.** multiple; *synonyms* (adj) manifold, many, complex, diverse, populous; *antonym* (adj) simple.

margfeldni degeneracy; *synonyms* (n) corruption, decadence, depravity, degeneration, decline.

margföldun 1. multiplication; *synonyms* (n) growth, augmentation, generation, increase, addition; *antonym* (n) estimation, **2.** proliferation; *synonyms* (n) propagation, spread, reproduction, upsurge, breeding.

marghliða multilateral; *synonyms* (adj) quadrilateral, trilateral, multifaceted, multifarious, rectangular.

marghyrningur polygon; *synonym* (n) square.

margir many; *synonyms* (adj) manifold, abundant, countless, frequent, (n) number; *antonym* (n) few.

marglaga laminated; *synonyms* (adj) laminate, laminiferous, tabular, coated, covered.

margleitni polymorphism; *synonyms* (n) pleomorphism, metaplasm, ontogeny, ovary, ovum.

margleitur polymorphic; *synonyms* (adj) polymorphous, pleomorphic.

marglytta jellyfish; *synonyms* (n) medusan, coward, hydromedusae, (adj) apprehensive, frightened.

marglyttur jellyfish; *synonyms* (n) medusan, coward, hydromedusae, (adj) apprehensive, frightened.

margmiðlun 1. hypermedia, **2.** multimedia; *synonym* (n) disc.

margræðni ambiguity; *synonyms* (n) equivocation, doubt, uncertainty, unclearness, equivocalness; *antonyms* (n) clearness, precision, unambiguity.

margræður ambiguous; *synonyms* (adj) equivocal, indistinct, indeterminate, uncertain, (v) vague; *antonyms* (adj) clear, definite, unambiguous, unequivocal.

margþættur multiplex; *synonyms* (adj) manifold, multiple, complex, multifarious, multifold.

margúll hematoma; *synonym* (n) haematoma.

maríúana marijuana; *synonyms* (n) cannabis, ganja, grass, hemp, marihuana.

mark 1. target; *synonyms* (n) butt, goal, (v) aim, point, purpose, **2**. stigma; *synonyms* (n) spot, blot, brand, stain, blemish, **3**. point; *synonyms* (n) place, grade, peak, nib, (v) head, **4**. degree; *synonyms* (n) class, extent, condition, level, order, **5**. limit; *synonyms* (n) bound, boundary, (v) border, restrict, circumscribe; *antonyms* (n) center, extension, minimum, (v) broaden, extend.

marka locate; *synonyms* (v) base, lay, discover, find, (n) place.

markaðsfærsla marketing; *synonyms* (n) sale, commerce, merchandising, selling, distribution.

markaðsfræði marketing; *synonyms* (n) sale, commerce, merchandising, selling, distribution.

markaðshæfur marketable; *synonyms* (adj) commercial, merchantable, salable, saleable, vendible.

markaðskerfi capitalism; *synonyms* (n) democracy, commercialism, competition, entrepreneurship, industrialism; *antonyms* (n) collectivism, communism, socialism.

markaðssamtök cartel; *synonyms* (n) syndicate, trust, combine, compromise, ring.

markaðssetja market; *synonyms* (n) fair, shop, bazaar, marketplace, (v) demand.

markaðssetning 1. sale; *synonyms* (n) fair, disposal, demand, market, vend, **2**. marketing; *synonyms* (n) sale, commerce, merchandising, selling, distribution.

markaður market; *synonyms* (n) fair, shop, bazaar, marketplace, (v) demand.

markari marker; *synonyms* (n) brand, mark, label, token, pointer.

markgildi 1. threshold; *synonyms* (n) brink, limen, beginning, doorsill, doorstep, **2**. limit; *synonyms* (n) bound, boundary, (v) border, restrict, (prep) extent; *antonyms* (n) center, extension, minimum, (v) broaden, extend.

marki marker; *synonyms* (n) brand, mark, label, token, pointer.

markmið 1. purpose; *synonyms* (n) aim, plan, design, mind, (v) intention, **2**. objective; *synonyms*

(adj) dispassionate, fair, (n) mark, goal, object; *antonyms* (adj) biased, subjective, **3**. goal; *synonyms* (n) butt, destination, end, purpose, basket.

markmiðshugsjón entelechy; *synonym* (n) actuality.

markstikla anchor; *synonyms* (n) mainstay, (v) tie, fasten, secure, (adj) refuge.

marktækni significance; *synonyms* (n) import, sense, connotation, consequence, meaning; *antonyms* (n) insignificance, triviality.

marktækur significant; *synonyms* (adj) important, material, momentous, grave, (v) considerable; *antonyms* (adj) insignificant, minor, unimportant, small, trivial.

marktekt significance; *synonyms* (n) import, sense, connotation, consequence, meaning; *antonyms* (n) insignificance, triviality.

markvirkni effectiveness; *synonyms* (n) efficacy, effect, strength, result, powerfulness; *antonyms* (n) uselessness, inefficiency, ineffectiveness.

marr squeak; *synonyms* (n) cry, screech, (v) shriek, scream, peep.

Mars march; *synonyms* (n) walk, hike, parade, demonstration, (v) journey.

marsmánuður march; *synonyms* (n) walk, hike, parade, demonstration, (v) journey.

marz march; *synonyms* (n) walk, hike, parade, demonstration, (v) journey.

masa 1. talk; *synonyms* (v) gossip, converse, lecture, chatter, (n) discourse, **2**. chatter; *synonyms* (n) prattle, (v) babble, chat, jabber, cackle, **3**. chat; *synonyms* (n) talk, chitchat, conversation, causerie, (v) chaffer; *antonym* (v) listen, **4**. gossip; *synonyms* (n) rumor, gab, chatterbox, comment, (v) natter; *antonym* (n) fact.

massi mass; *synonyms* (n) bulk, heap, crowd, cluster, (v) flock.

mastfruma mastocyte; *synonym* (n) labrocyte.

mastur 1. pole; *synonyms* (n) perch, bar, picket, post, rod, **2**. pylon; *synonym* (n) column, **3**. tower; *synonyms* (v) soar, ascend, rise, arise, (adj) pillar, **4**. mast; *synonyms* (n) tower, aerial, prop, stick, support.

mastursfótur foot (fótur); *synonyms* (n) bottom, base, feet, foundation, (v) hoof; *antonym* (n) top.

mat 1. estimate; *synonyms* (n) calculation, (v) compute, consider, count, esteem; *antonym* (v) calculate, **2**. valuation; *synonyms* (n) estimation, appraisal, evaluation, estimate, appraisement, **3**. assessment; *synonyms* (n) judgment, review, valuation, appreciation, duty, **4**. appraisal; *synonyms* (n) assessment, value, examination, assay, check, **5**. estimating; *synonym* (n) computation.

mát 1. template; *synonyms* (n) pattern, templet, guide, guidebook, pathfinder, **2.** mate; *synonyms* (n) match, companion, partner, (v) equal, (adj) comrade, **3.** gauge; *synonyms* (n) criterion, caliber, (v) estimate, measure, calculate, **4.** jig; *synonyms* (n) jigger, strathspey, (v) dance, hop, skip, **5.** module; *synonyms* (n) faculty, part, paradigm, subarray, bay.

mata feed; *synonyms* (v) eat, dine, nurture, (n) aliment, food; *antonym* (v) starve.

mataræði diet; *synonyms* (n) congress, convocation, council, convention, nurture; *antonyms* (v) binge, (adj) fattening.

matarbúr pantry; *synonyms* (n) larder, buttery, store, basement, kitchen.

matarlaukur onion; *synonyms* (n) caviare, pickle, leek, chive.

matarlyst appetite; *synonyms* (n) desire, appetence, appetency, relish, craving; *antonym* (n) dislike.

matarsalt salt; *synonyms* (adj) salty, saline, briny, (v) cure, pickle.

matarskammtur dietary; *synonyms* (adj) dietetic, alimentary, dietetical, (n) diet, dietetics.

materia 1. material; *synonyms* (n) body, cloth, (adj) bodily, corporal, corporeal, **2.** materials; *synonyms* (n) data, goods, resources, order, provisions.

materiala materials; *synonyms* (n) data, goods, resources, order, provisions.

materialo materials; *synonyms* (n) data, goods, resources, order, provisions.

matgráðugur voracious; *synonyms* (adj) greedy, gluttonous, hungry, rapacious, ravenous.

matgræðgi 1. bulimia; *synonyms* (n) phagedena, bulimy, **2.** hyperphagia.

máti mode; *synonyms* (n) means, fashion, manner, method, form.

matlaukur onion; *synonyms* (n) caviare, pickle, leek, chive.

matseðill menu; *synonyms* (n) fare, bill, card, carte, list.

matsgjörð valuation; *synonyms* (n) estimation, appraisal, evaluation, estimate, appraisement.

matshækkun appreciation; *synonyms* (n) admiration, acknowledgment, approval, awareness, (v) sense; *antonym* (v) depreciation.

matsveinn cook; *synonyms* (n) chef, (v) boil, bake, brew, make.

máttagur 1. vigorous; *synonyms* (adj) robust, strong, energetic, hardy, lively; *antonyms* (adj) feeble, lethargic, weak, dull, unenergetic, **2.** strong; *synonyms* (adj) intense, powerful, able, deep, firm; *antonyms* (adj) bland, delicate, faint, frail, mild, **3.** tough; *synonyms* (adj) hard, difficult, tenacious,

arduous, (n) bully; *antonyms* (adj) tender, easy, flimsy, soft, lightweight, **4.** forceful; *synonyms* (adj) assertive, cogent, dynamic, effective, emphatic; *antonym* (adj) unconvincing.

máttfarinn feeble; *synonyms* (adj) delicate, weak, decrepit, (v) faint, debilitated; *antonyms* (adj) strong, vigorous, hearty, tough.

máttleysi asthenia; *synonyms* (n) abirritation, (adj) cachexia, cachexy, sprain, strain.

máttlítill 1. faint; *synonyms* (adj) collapse, dim, dizzy, feeble, indistinct; *antonyms* (adj) distinct, strong, clear, obvious, considerable, **2.** flabby; *synonyms* (adj) loose, flaccid, baggy, drooping, limp; *antonyms* (adj) firm, slim.

máttstol fatigue; *synonyms* (n) exhaustion, tiredness, weariness, (v) exhaust, tire; *antonyms* (n) energy, (v) refresh.

mattur 1. dull; *synonyms* (adj) dim, blunt, dense, dreary, sluggish; *antonyms* (adj) bright, lively, sharp, exciting, interesting, **2.** opaque; *synonyms* (adj) cloudy, dull, muddy, obscure, hazy; *antonyms* (adj) clear, transparent, see-through.

mátun 1. fit; *synonyms* (v) agree, accommodate, meet, suit, (adj) decorous; *antonyms* (adj) unfit, inappropriate, unwell, **2.** matching; *synonyms* (adj) equal, corresponding, duplicate, like, twin; *antonyms* (adj) different, incompatible.

matur 1. meal; *synonyms* (n) food, feed, flour, repast, banquet, **2.** food; *synonyms* (n) board, edible, fare, aliment, diet.

mauk 1. chyme, **2.** detritus; *synonyms* (n) rubble, (adj) debris, trash, magistery, scobs.

maur 1. ant; *synonyms* (n) emmet, pismire, aerial, bee, (adj) anti, **2.** pismire; *synonym* (n) ant, **3.** emmet; *synonyms* (adj) animalcule, entozoon, fly, gnat, maggot.

maurakláði scabies; *synonyms* (n) itch, itchiness, itching, (adj) scarlatina, scrofula.

með 1. with; *synonyms* (prep) by, for, (adv) on, beside, (adj) including, **2.** webbed; *synonyms* (adj) lacy, netlike, netted, keld, lacelike.

meðal 1. remedy; *synonyms* (n) cure, redress, medicine, (v) heal, help, **2.** medicine; *synonyms* (n) drug, medicament, medication, physic, (v) medicate.

meðalævi lifetime; *synonyms* (n) age, life, lifespan, day, decade.

meðalafl demand; *synonyms* (n) claim, request, (v) ask, command, need; *antonym* (v) supply.

meðaldæmi norm; *synonyms* (n) average, mean, measure, mode, criterion.

meðalganga mediation; *synonyms* (n) arbitration, intercession, intervention, agency, intermediation.

meðalgildi 1. expectation; *synonyms* (n) anticipation, expectancy, belief, hope, prospect; *antonym* (n) despair, **2.** mean; *synonyms* (v) intend, design, (adj) middle, (n) average, contemptible; *antonyms* (adj) generous, kind.

meðalgildisréttur unbiased; *synonyms* (adj) fair, impartial, indifferent, neutral, just; *antonyms* (adj) biased, prejudiced.

meðalgildisskakkur biased; *synonyms* (adj) partial, partisan, slanted, unfair, skewed; *antonyms* (adj) fair, fair-minded, neutral, unbiased, just.

meðaltal 1. average; *synonyms* (adj) mean, median, fair, common, medium; *antonyms* (adj) exceptional, extraordinary, abnormal, (v) maximum, minimum, **2.** mean; *synonyms* (v) intend, design, (adj) middle, (n) average, contemptible; *antonyms* (adj) generous, kind.

meðaltölugildisfrávik mad; *synonyms* (adj) frantic, frenzied, demented, foolish, (n) furious; *antonyms* (adj) sane, calm, sensible.

meðan 1. whereas; *synonyms* (conj) though, while, (adv) although, when, (prep) because, **2.** while; *synonyms* (conj) as, whereas, (n) spell, time, period, **3.** through; *synonyms* (adv) by, (adj) finished, done, direct, straight, **4.** during; *synonyms* (prep) within, on, for, of, pending, **5.** at; *synonyms* (prep) in, a, (n) astatine, (adv) along, (prf) all.

meðaumkun 1. sympathy; *synonyms* (n) compassion, pity, benevolence, commiseration, feeling; *antonyms* (n) indifference, cruelty, **2.** pity; *synonyms* (n) mercy, condolence, (v) commiserate, compassionate, sympathize; *antonym* (n) blame, **3.** compassion; *synonyms* (n) clemency, charity, sympathy, forgiveness, (adj) kindness, **4.** mercy; *synonyms* (n) favor, grace, humanity, leniency, pardon.

meðeigandi partner; *synonyms* (n) consort, copartner, accomplice, associate, companion.

meðfæddur 1. congenital; *synonyms* (adj) innate, inborn, inherent, natural, indigenous, **2.** inherent; *synonyms* (adj) congenital, inbred, intrinsic, essential, immanent; *antonym* (adj) superficial.

meðfærilegur 1. tractable; *synonyms* (adj) amenable, docile, obedient, pliable, (v) flexible, *antonyms* (adj) disobedient, intractable, **2.** manageable; *synonyms* (adj) easy, malleable, ductile, handy, (v) governable; *antonyms* (adj) unwieldy, awkward, unbearable, uncontrollable, unmanageable.

meðferð 1. treatment; *synonyms* (n) cure, conduct, handling, management, manipulation, **2.** therapy; *synonyms* (n) medication, remedy, treatment, healing, analysis.

meðferðaraðili therapist; *synonyms* (n) healer, analyst, nurse, psychiatrist, psychoanalyst.

meðferðaráform regimen; *synonyms* (n) regime, diet, government, treatment, cure.

meðferðarheldni compliance; *synonyms* (n) agreement, approval, observance, accordance, acquiescence; *antonyms* (n) disobedience, stubbornness, nonconformity.

meðferðarreglur procedure; *synonyms* (n) process, formula, practice, routine, fashion.

meðferðarvantrú nihilism; *synonyms* (n) anarchy, atheism, disbelief, abnegation, (adj) nihility.

meðför implication; *synonyms* (n) allusion, hint, significance, consequence, deduction.

meðganga 1. gestation; *synonyms* (n) pregnancy, ferry, behavior, (v) incubation, sitting, **2.** incubation; *synonyms* (n) gestation, brooding, incubiture, incumbition, (v) batching.

meðgönguhormón progesterone; *synonym* (n) progestin.

meðgöngutími gestation; *synonyms* (n) pregnancy, ferry, behavior, (v) incubation, sitting.

meðhöndla handle; *synonyms* (v) administer, conduct, feel, wield, (n) grip.

meðhöndlun 1. treatment; *synonyms* (n) cure, conduct, handling, management, manipulation, **2.** process; *synonyms* (n) operation, proceeding, method, procedure, (v) action.

meðlimur member; *synonyms* (n) limb, part, supporter, extremity, phallus.

meðmæli recommendation; *synonyms* (n) praise, commendation, advice, counsel, suggestion.

meðsog entrainment; *synonym* (n) induction.

meðsveiflun resonance; *synonyms* (n) vibrancy, reverberation, ringing, sonority, vibration.

meðtalinn included; *synonyms* (adj) numbered, confined, inclosed, integrated, (adv) under.

meðundirrita initial; *synonyms* (adj) beginning, first, elementary, incipient, foremost.

meðvirkur reactive; *synonyms* (adj) sensitive, responsive, receptive, approachable, hasty.

meðvitandi conscious; *synonyms* (adj) aware, alive, calculated, cognizant, deliberate; *antonyms* (adj) unconscious, unaware, ignorant.

meðvitund consciousness; *synonyms* (n) awareness, feeling, sense, conscience, cognizance; *antonym* (n) unconsciousness.

meðvitundarlaus unconscious; *synonyms* (adj) involuntary, unaware, ignorant, subconscious, unwitting; *antonyms* (adj) conscious, awake, deliberate.

megind quantity; *synonyms* (n) amount, extent, measure, multitude, quantum.

megindlegur 1. quantitative; *synonyms* (adj) some, measurable, quantitive, wholesale, **2.** quantity;

synonyms (n) amount, extent, measure, multitude, quantum.

meginhluti bulk; **synonyms** (n) mass, size, amount, majority, volume; **antonym** (n) minority.

meginland continent; **synonyms** (adj) chaste, celibate, abstemious, pure, temperate; **antonym** (adj) incontinent.

meginlandsskjöldur shield; **synonyms** (n) screen, shelter, (v) cover, guard, safeguard; **antonym** (v) expose.

meginregla principle; **synonyms** (n) origin, fundamental, method, rule, cause.

meginstjarna primary; **synonyms** (adj) chief, basic, elementary, essential, (n) paramount; **antonym** (adj) secondary.

meginstofn axis; **synonyms** (n) axle, pivot, hinge, center, hub.

meginstöngull axis; **synonyms** (n) axle, pivot, hinge, center, hub.

megintölva mainframe; **synonyms** (n) computer, processor, management, laptop, notebook.

megn 1. concentrated; **synonyms** (adj) strong, intense, compact, condensed, deep; **antonyms** (adj) dispersed, weak, uncondensed, unsaturated, 2. intensive; **synonyms** (adj) concentrated, thorough, exhaustive, augmentative, (n) intensifier; **antonym** (adj) extensive.

mehanikisto 1. mechanic; **synonyms** (n) craftsman, artificer, artisan, journeyman, machinist, 2. mechanics; **synonyms** (n) mechanism, workings, procedure.

meiðsli 1. trauma; **synonyms** (n) injury, hurt, wound, shock, harm, 2. injury; **synonyms** (n) disadvantage, disservice, grievance, damage, detriment; **antonyms** (n) ability, reparation.

meiðyrði slander; **synonyms** (n) insult, scandal, (v) libel, defame, (adj) abuse; **antonym** (v) praise.

mein disease; **synonyms** (n) ailment, condition, illness, sickness, complaint.

meinafræði pathology; **synonym** (n) botany.

meinafræðilegur pathologic; **synonyms** (adj) morbid, pathological, diseased, ghoulish.

meinaleit screening; **synonyms** (n) screen, sieving, concealment, cover, covering.

meindýr vermin; **synonyms** (n) bug, varmint, trash, fly, insect.

meinlætamunaður masochism; **synonyms** (n) cruelty, algophilia.

meinlaus innocuous; **synonyms** (adj) harmless, innocent, inoffensive, safe, innoxious.

meinlíf antibiosis; **synonym** (n) amensalism.

meinrek metastasis; **synonyms** (n) metabolism, anastrophy, parenthesis, synchysis, tmesis.

meinsáð metastasis; **synonyms** (n) metabolism, anastrophy, parenthesis, synchysis, tmesis.

meinvaldandi pathogenic; **synonyms** (adj) infective, morbific, infectious, pathogenetic.

meinvaldur pathogen; **synonyms** (n) germ, microbe.

meinvarp metastasis; **synonyms** (n) metabolism, anastrophy, parenthesis, synchysis, tmesis.

meinvirkni virulence; **synonyms** (n) rancor, acerbity, animosity, (adj) acrimony, venom.

meinvirkur 1. virulent; **synonyms** (adj) bitter, caustic, deadly, malicious, lethal, 2. pathogenic; **synonyms** (adj) infective, morbific, infectious, pathogenetic.

meiósa meiosis; **synonyms** (n) litotes, miosis, diminution, myosis.

meiri major; **synonyms** (adj) chief, key, large, main, superior; **antonyms** (adj) minor, unimportant, lesser, petty, slight.

meiriháttar major; **synonyms** (adj) chief, key, large, main, superior; **antonyms** (adj) minor, unimportant, lesser, petty, slight.

meirihluti 1. bulk; **synonyms** (n) mass, size, amount, majority, volume; **antonym** (n) minority, 2. majority; **synonyms** (n) bulk, age, plurality, body, maturity.

meis magazine; **synonyms** (n) journal, cartridge, newspaper, periodical, book.

meisa tit; **synonyms** (n) nipple, teat, mammilla, pap, boob.

Meistari master; **synonyms** (n) captain, instructor, (v) conquer, control, (adj) chief.

meitill chisel; **synonyms** (v) carve, cheat, cut, shape, beguile.

mekantílismi mercantilism; **synonyms** (n) commercialism, commerce, capitalism.

méla silt; **synonyms** (n) sediment, deposit, (adj) mire, mud, alluvium.

mellifolia yarrow; **synonyms** (n) milfoil, sassafras.

melmi alloy; **synonyms** (n) admixture, amalgam, (v) adulterate, devalue, (adj) sophisticate.

melmingur metalloid; **synonyms** (n) nonmetal, (adj) metalloidal, acid, negative.

melóna 1. cantaloupe; **synonym** (n) cantaloup, 2. melon; **synonyms** (n) dividend, cantaloupes, cucumbers, earnings, income.

melónuplanta cantaloupe; **synonym** (n) cantaloup.

melónutré papaya; **synonyms** (n) papaia, papaw, pawpaw.

melting 1. digestion; **synonyms** (n) absorption, (v) concoction, analysis, classification, clustering, 2. assimilation; **synonyms** (n) acculturation, incorporation, integration, addition, amalgamation.

meltingarörvandi digestive; *synonyms* (*adj*) peptic, concoctive, (*n*) tonic.

meltingarvegur gut; *synonyms* (*n*) belly, abdomen, bowel, (*v*) eviscerate, pillage.

membra membrane; *synonyms* (*n*) diaphragm, film, skin, coat, covering.

memuaro papers; *synonyms* (*n*) credentials, document, documents, identification, covenant.

mendelefin mendelevium; *synonyms* (*n*) mv, doc, doctor, medico, millivolt.

mendelevín mendelevium; *synonyms* (*n*) mv, doc, doctor, medico, millivolt.

mendelevíum mendelevium; *synonyms* (*n*) mv, doc, doctor, medico, millivolt.

menga contaminate; *synonyms* (*v*) pollute, infect, taint, adulterate, befoul; *antonyms* (*v*) cleanse, purify, clean, sterilize.

mengaður foul; *synonyms* (*adj*) base, disgusting, filthy, (*v*) dirty, corrupt; *antonyms* (*adj*) pleasant, fair, (*v*) clean, pure.

mengari polluter; *synonym* (*n*) defiler.

mengi 1. set; *synonyms* (*v*) fix, place, lay, put, (*n*) class; *antonyms* (*v*) soften, liquefy, (*n*) combing, comb-out, (*adj*) variable, 2. category; *synonyms* (*n*) denomination, division, kind, type, variety.

mengill polluter; *synonym* (*n*) defiler.

mengun 1. pollution; *synonyms* (*n*) contamination, filth, infection, befoulment, (*adj*) defilement, 2. contamination; *synonyms* (*n*) contagion, pollution, contaminant, dirtying, corruption; *antonym* (*n*) decontamination, 3. doping; *synonyms* (*n*) swabbing, doctoring, activating, 4. impurity; *synonyms* (*n*) impureness, dirt, dross, foulness, indecency.

mengunarefni pollutant; *synonyms* (*n*) poison, impurity, toxin, venom.

mengunarský smog; *synonyms* (*n*) fog, mist, haze, vapor, fumes.

mengunarvaldar pollutant; *synonyms* (*n*) poison, impurity, toxin, venom.

mengunarvaldur 1. pollutant; *synonyms* (*n*) poison, impurity, toxin, venom, 2. contaminant; *synonyms* (*n*) pollutant, contamination, pollution, taint.

menn 1. man (maður); *synonyms* (*n*) fellow, gentleman, guy, person, husband; *antonym* (*n*) woman, 2. homo; *synonyms* (*n*) gay, homosexual, human, man, somebody.

menning 1. civilization; *synonyms* (*n*) culture, refinement, civilisation, cultivation, (*adj*) civility, 2. culture; *synonyms* (*n*) civilization, breeding, acculturation, education, learning.

menningaraðlögun 1. assimilation; *synonyms* (*n*) absorption, acculturation, incorporation,

integration, addition, 2. acculturation; *synonyms* (*n*) assimilation, civilization, culture, socialisation, socialization.

menningarblöndun acculturation; *synonyms* (*n*) assimilation, civilization, culture, absorption, socialisation.

menningarhættir culture; *synonyms* (*n*) civilization, breeding, cultivation, acculturation, education.

menningarnám acculturation; *synonyms* (*n*) assimilation, civilization, culture, absorption, socialisation.

menntun 1. qualification; *synonyms* (*n*) condition, capability, competence, fitness, limitation, 2. education; *synonyms* (*n*) training, discipline, instruction, teaching, breeding.

menntunarbót enrichment; *synonyms* (*n*) decoration, embellishment, reinforcement, augmentation, improvement.

ment art; *synonyms* (*n*) know-how, skill, talent, trick, artistry.

mentur mint; *synonyms* (*n*) fortune, heap, pile, (*v*) coin, invent.

mergja marrow; *synonyms* (*n*) essence, heart, kernel, pith, (*adj*) gist.

mergur 1. pith; *synonyms* (*n*) marrow, essence, core, heart, (*adj*) gist, 2. pulp; *synonyms* (*n*) flesh, puree, (*v*) mash, grind, squash, 3. stroma; *synonym* (*n*) stromata, 4. marrow; *synonyms* (*n*) kernel, pith, quintessence, substance, backbone, 5. medulla; *synonyms* (*n*) bulb, lightbulb, myelin, myeline.

mergvaki adrenaline; *synonyms* (*n*) epinephrin, epinephrine.

merja bruise; *synonyms* (*n*) blow, contusion, (*v*) crush, hurt, wound.

merkantílismi mercantilism; *synonyms* (*n*) commercialism, commerce, capitalism.

merki 1. tic; *synonyms* (*n*) twitching, spasm, jerk, quiver, (*v*) twitch, 2. tag; *synonyms* (*n*) tail, (*v*) label, dog, mark, name, 3. pylon; *synonym* (*n*) column, 4. symbol; *synonyms* (*n*) sign, emblem, number, badge, stamp, 5. sign; *synonyms* (*n*) signal, indication, motion, portent, (*v*) gesture.

merkiefni tracer; *synonyms* (*n*) marker, sensor.

merkigen marker; *synonyms* (*n*) brand, mark, label, token, pointer.

merkiljós signal; *synonyms* (*n*) sign, gesture, indication, presage, (*v*) omen.

merkimiði label; *synonyms* (*n*) name, brand, tag, (*v*) mark, call.

merking 1. definition; *synonyms* (*n*) description, account, explanation, interpretation, limitation; *antonym* (*n*) bagginess, 2. marking; *synonyms* (*n*) mark, earmark, brand, crisscross, marker, 3.

meaning; *synonyms* (n) import, gist, implication, intent, design.

merkingarauki connotation; *synonyms* (n) intension, implication, meaning, overtone, consequence.

merkingarblær connotation; *synonyms* (n) intension, implication, meaning, overtone, consequence.

merkingarháttur modality; *synonyms* (n) mode, mood, manner, schesis, fashion.

merkingarkjarni 1. sense; *synonyms* (n) intelligence, perception, meaning, (v) feel, intellect; *antonyms* (n) garbage, ludicrousness, nonsense, stupidity, foolishness, **2.** denotation; *synonyms* (n) sense, indication, character, reference, extension.

merkingarlaus anomalous; *synonyms* (adj) abnormal, irregular, aberrant, atypical, deviant; *antonym* (adj) normal.

merkingarleysa anomaly; *synonyms* (n) abnormality, aberration, anomalousness, deviation, abnormity.

merkingarskipti metonymy; *synonyms* (n) metaphor, synecdoche, metonym.

merkipunktur seed; *synonyms* (n) germ, issue, posterity, root, (v) inseminate.

merkiskjöldur escutcheon; *synonyms* (n) scutcheon, shield, arms, escocheon.

merkispjald tag; *synonyms* (n) tail, (v) label, dog, mark, name.

merkisspjald badge; *synonyms* (n) emblem, insignia, mark, sign, medal.

merkja 1. represent; *synonyms* (v) depict, portray, act, be, (adj) express, **2.** signify; *synonyms* (v) imply, intend, mark, (n) mean, import, **3.** denote; *synonyms* (v) indicate, point, name, (n) declare, betoken, **4.** label; *synonyms* (n) brand, tag, title, (v) call, classify, **5.** mean; *synonyms* (v) design, (adj) middle, (n) average, contemptible, low; *antonyms* (adj) generous, kind.

merkjablöndun crosstalk; *synonym* (n) diaphony.

merkjabreytir transducer; *synonyms* (n) sensor, transductor.

merkjaforskeyti prefix; *synonyms* (n) preamble, foreword, prelude, (v) preface, attach.

merkjaviðskeyti suffix; *synonyms* (n) affix, ending, sequel, (v) postfix, annex.

merski marsh; *synonyms* (n) bog, fen, quagmire, marish, morass.

mesóna meson; *synonyms* (n) mesotron, ventrimeson.

messi mess; *synonyms* (n) clutter, jumble, muddle, confusion, (v) botch; *antonym* (n) order.

messing brass; *synonyms* (n) boldness, face, cheek, nerve, (v) audacity.

met methionine; *synonym* (n) met.

meta 1. quantify; *synonyms* (v) measure, gauge, evaluate, assess, determine, **2.** appraise; *synonyms* (v) value, estimate, rate, calculate, consider, **3.** assess; *synonyms* (v) appraise, appreciate, mark, review, tax, **4.** adjust; *synonyms* (v) temper, accommodate, adapt, align, acclimatize, **5.** estimate; *synonyms* (n) calculation, (v) compute, count, esteem, guess.

metakerfi hierarchy; *synonyms* (n) order, rank, class, apparatus, executive.

metanól methanol; *synonyms* (n) alcohol, ethanol, gas, gasohol, gasoline.

metaskiptur hierarchic; *synonyms* (adj) hierarchal, hierarchical.

meþíónín methionine; *synonym* (n) met.

metill estimator; *synonyms* (n) calculator, appraiser, computer, inspector, figurer.

metíónín methionine; *synonym* (n) met.

metri 1. metre; *synonyms* (n) meter, measure, beat, rhythm, m, **2.** meter; *synonyms* (n) gauge, metre, counter, measurement, time.

mettaður saturated; *synonyms* (adj) drenched, sodden, wet, concentrated, soaked; *antonym* (adj) dry.

mettun 1. satiation; *synonyms* (n) repletion, fullness, satiety, cloyment, disgust, **2.** saturation; *synonyms* (n) chroma, satiation, impregnation, glut, intensity.

meyfæðing parthenogenesis; *synonyms* (v) abiogenesis, biogenesis, digenesis, dysmerogenesis, eumerogenesis.

meyjafölvi chlorosis; *synonyms* (n) greensickness, (adj) chorea, cynanche, dartre.

meza means; *synonyms* (n) expedient, agency, instrument, assets, capital.

meznombra means; *synonyms* (n) expedient, agency, instrument, assets, capital.

mezo means; *synonyms* (n) expedient, agency, instrument, assets, capital.

mið 1. tic; *synonyms* (n) twitching, spasm, jerk, quiver, (v) twitch, **2.** landmark; *synonyms* (n) milestone, merestone, boundary, milepost, seamark.

miða reckon; *synonyms* (v) deem, count, enumerate, estimate, judge.

miðbær town; *synonyms* (n) city, borough, township, (adj) municipal, urban.

miðbaugsbreidd declination; *synonyms* (n) declension, descent, decay, decline, refusal.

miðbaugur equator; *synonyms* (n) circle, colures, midriff, orbit, round.

miðbik center; *synonyms* (n) centre, middle, core, heart, (v) focus; *antonyms* (n) edge, periphery, border.

Miðborð center; *synonyms* (n) centre, middle, core, heart, (v) focus; *antonyms* (n) edge, periphery, border.

miðborg town; *synonyms* (n) city, borough, township, (adj) municipal, urban.

miðdepill center; *synonyms* (n) centre, middle, core, heart, (v) focus; *antonyms* (n) edge, periphery, border.

miðeind meson; *synonyms* (n) mesotron, ventrimeson.

miðfælinn centrifugal; *synonyms* (adj) efferent, motor, (n) reel, (v) divergent, radiant; *antonym* (adj) centripetal.

miðflótta centrifugal; *synonyms* (adj) efferent, motor, (n) reel, (v) divergent, radiant; *antonym* (adj) centripetal.

miðfrálægur eccentric; *synonyms* (adj) bizarre, odd, wacky, abnormal, anomalous; *antonyms* (adj) normal, ordinary, (n) conformist.

miðgildi median; *synonyms* (adj) middle, medial, mesial, (n) mean, average.

miðheili midbrain; *synonym* (n) mesencephalon.

miðhluti barrel; *synonyms* (n) drum, roll, vessel, barrelful, cask.

miði label; *synonyms* (n) name, brand, tag, (v) mark, call.

miðill 1. modulator, **2.** medium; *synonyms* (adj) intermediate, (n) average, mediocre, mean, atmosphere, **3.** media; *synonyms* (n) medium, medial, communications, middle.

miðja 1. center; *synonyms* (n) centre, middle, core, heart, (v) focus; *antonyms* (n) edge, periphery, border, **2.** centre; *synonyms* (n) midpoint, (v) center, centralize, concentrate.

miðjarðarlína equator; *synonyms* (n) circle, colures, midriff, orbit, round.

miðjumaður moderate; *synonyms* (adj) temperate, abstemious, middling, mild, (v) calm; *antonyms* (adj) extreme, immoderate, radical, (v) increase, intensify.

miðjunarstig compactness; *synonyms* (n) density, denseness, closeness, firmness, (v) compression.

miðjustilla center; *synonyms* (n) centre, middle, core, heart, (v) focus; *antonyms* (n) edge, periphery, border.

miðla deal; *synonyms* (n) bargain, buy, agreement, (v) administer, allot; *antonym* (n) purchase.

miðlægur 1. central; *synonyms* (adj) basic, capital, cardinal, fundamental, chief; *antonyms* (adj) peripheral, minor, regional, tangential, **2.** mesial; *synonyms* (adj) medial, middle, inclosed, inherent,

interior, **3.** medial; *synonyms* (adj) intermediate, average, mean, medium, median.

miðlari 1. server; *synonyms* (n) host, waiter, attendant, emcee, horde, **2.** broker; *synonyms* (n) mediator, agent, go-between, factor, middleman, **3.** dealer; *synonyms* (n) merchant, trader, monger, seller, vendor; *antonym* (n) user, **4.** intermediary; *synonyms* (adj) intermediate, (n) broker, arbiter, arbitrator, medium, **5.** mediator; *synonyms* (n) intermediary, intercessor, intermediator, peacemaker, diplomat; *antonym* (n) troublemaker.

miðleitinn centripetal; *synonyms* (adj) afferent, acropetal, receptive, sensory, unifying.

miðlun 1. communication; *synonyms* (n) announcement, commerce, communicating, contact, conversation, **2.** brokerage; *synonyms* (n) commission, brokage, freightage, wharfage, tax, **3.** mediation; *synonyms* (n) arbitration, intercession, intervention, agency, intermediation.

miðmark median; *synonyms* (adj) middle, medial, mesial, (n) mean, average.

miðögn 1. centriole; *synonym* (n) center, **2.** meson; *synonyms* (n) mesotron, ventrimeson.

miðpunktur 1. center; *synonyms* (n) centre, middle, core, heart, (v) focus; *antonyms* (n) edge, periphery, border, **2.** centroid.

miðskakkur eccentric; *synonyms* (adj) bizarre, odd, wacky, abnormal, anomalous; *antonyms* (adj) normal, ordinary, (n) conformist.

miðskekkja eccentricity; *synonyms* (n) oddity, abnormality, idiosyncrasy, oddness, peculiarity; *antonym* (n) normality.

miðskip nave; *synonyms* (n) chancel, choir, hub, omphalos, transept.

miðskipan concentration; *synonyms* (n) absorption, concentrate, application, attention, engrossment; *antonym* (n) distraction.

miðstétt bourgeoisie; *synonym* (n) class.

miðstéttarmaður bourgeois; *synonyms* (adj) conservative, (n) capitalist, burgess, capitals, caps.

miðstöð 1. center; *synonyms* (n) centre, middle, core, heart, (v) focus; *antonyms* (n) edge, periphery, border, **2.** heater; *synonyms* (n) brazier, warmer, bullet, fastball, calefactor, **3.** exchange; *synonyms* (n) commutation, swap, (v) change, barter, interchange, **4.** forum; *synonyms* (n) agora, assembly, court, pulpit, square.

miðstöðvarketill furnace; *synonyms* (n) heater, hearth, oven, stove, chimney.

miðstöðvarofn radiator; *synonyms* (n) heater, stove, furnace, warmer.

miðstrengur diameter; *synonyms* (n) caliber, width, diam, radius, breadth.

miðstýring 1. centralism, **2.** centralization; *synonyms* (*n*) centralisation, concentration, absorption, amalgamation, blending.

miðsvæði center; *synonyms* (*n*) centre, middle, core, heart, (*v*) focus; *antonyms* (*n*) edge, periphery, border.

miðtækur normative; *synonym* (*adj*) prescriptive.

miðtala median; *synonyms* (*adj*) middle, medial, mesial, (*n*) mean, average.

miðtaugakerfishrörnun degeneration; *synonyms* (*n*) decay, corruption, decline, degeneracy, abasement; *antonyms* (*n*) improvement, growth.

miðun bearing; *synonyms* (*n*) carriage, demeanor, appearance, approach, aspect.

miðvik eccentricity; *synonyms* (*n*) oddity, abnormality, idiosyncrasy, oddness, peculiarity; *antonym* (*n*) normality.

mikill 1. substantial; *synonyms* (*adj*) actual, solid, firm, real, strong; *antonyms* (*adj*) insignificant, insubstantial, small, ethereal, fine, **2.** big; *synonyms* (*adj*) ample, major, heavy, important, (*adv*) large; *antonyms* (*adj*) little, puny, (*syn*) tiny, **3.** large; *synonyms* (*adj*) big, extensive, generous, broad, bulky; *antonym* (*adj*) cramped, **4.** great; *synonyms* (*adj*) eminent, famous, gigantic, distinguished, extreme; *antonyms* (*adj*) awful, mild, **5.** major; *synonyms* (*adj*) chief, key, main, superior, considerable; *antonyms* (*adj*) minor, unimportant, lesser, petty, slight.

mikilleiki intensity; *synonyms* (*n*) force, forcefulness, depth, volume, (*adj*) strength; *antonyms* (*n*) dullness, indifference, weakness.

mikilmennskuæði megalomania; *synonym* (*n*) egoism.

mikilvægur 1. significant; *synonyms* (*adj*) important, material, momentous, grave, (*v*) considerable; *antonyms* (*adj*) insignificant, minor, unimportant, small, trivial, **2.** material; *synonyms* (*n*) body, cloth, (*adj*) bodily, corporal, corporeal.

míkrókvarði micrometer; *synonyms* (*n*) micron, megameter, megametre, (*v*) nanometer, centimeter.

míkrómælir micrometer; *synonyms* (*n*) micron, megameter, megametre, (*v*) nanometer, centimeter.

míkrómál micrometer; *synonyms* (*n*) micron, megameter, megametre, (*v*) nanometer, centimeter.

míkrómetri micrometer; *synonyms* (*n*) micron, megameter, megametre, (*v*) nanometer, centimeter.

míkron 1. micrometer; *synonyms* (*n*) micron, megameter, megametre, (*v*) nanometer, centimeter, **2.** micron; *synonyms* (*n*) micrometer, torr, (*v*) cm, kilometer, km.

míkróskrúfa micrometer; *synonyms* (*n*) micron, megameter, megametre, (*v*) nanometer, centimeter.

míkróskrúfa micrometer; *synonyms* (*n*) micron, megameter, megametre, (*v*) nanometer, centimeter.

míla mile; *synonyms* (*n*) knot, burl, (*v*) cubit, ell, fathom.

mildandi remedial; *synonyms* (*adj*) curative, healing, therapeutic, corrective, medicinal.

millibil interval; *synonyms* (*n*) intermission, interruption, break, distance, interlude.

milliefni intermediate; *synonyms* (*adj*) average, medium, mean, mediate, (*n*) intermediary.

millifærsla transfer; *synonyms* (*n*) conveyance, (*v*) convey, carry, change, remove; *antonyms* (*v*) hold, keep.

millifasi interphase; *synonyms* (*n*) interface, interkinesis.

milliganga 1. interposition; *synonyms* (*n*) interference, interpolation, intervention, (*adj*) intercession, mediation, **2.** mediation; *synonyms* (*n*) arbitration, agency, intermediation, interposition, propitiation.

milligátt gateway; *synonyms* (*n*) door, entrance, gate, doorway, entry.

milligöngumaður intermediary; *synonyms* (*n*) broker, arbiter, agent, arbitrator, go-between.

millihaldari adapter; *synonyms* (*n*) adaptor, spider, attachment, arranger, transcriber.

milliheili diencephalon; *synonyms* (*n*) interbrain, betweenbrain, thalmencephalon.

milliheyrsla crosstalk; *synonym* (*n*) diaphony.

millihimna diaphragm; *synonyms* (*n*) membrane, midriff, partition, pessary, septum.

millikyn 1. intersexuality, **2.** intersex; *synonyms* (*n*) hermaphrodite, intersexuality, androgyne, epicine, gynandromorph.

millikynjungur intersex; *synonyms* (*n*) hermaphrodite, intersexuality, androgyne, epicine, gynandromorph.

millilægur 1. interstitial; *synonyms* (*v*) intermediate, intervening, intercalary, intercurrent, interjacent, **2.** intermediate; *synonyms* (*adj*) average, medium, mean, mediate, (*n*) intermediary.

millilæsing 1. interlocking; *synonyms* (*adj*) interlacing, interlinking, (*n*) interlock, meshing, engagement, **2.** interlock; *synonyms* (*v*) engage, interlace, mesh, entwine, connect.

millilegg 1. shim; *synonyms* (*n*) wedge, liner, filling, **2.** bead; *synonyms* (*n*) drop, astragal, beading, pearl, (*v*) beautify.

millilidur 1. intermediary; *synonyms* (*n*) broker, arbiter, agent, arbitrator, go-between, **2.** intermediate; *synonyms* (*adj*) average, medium, mean, mediate, (*n*) intermediary, **3.** mediator; *synonyms* (*n*) intercessor, intermediator, peacemaker, diplomat, negotiator; *antonym* (*n*) troublemaker.

millimagnari repeater; *synonyms* (*n*) recidivist, criminal, revolver, (*v*) floater, keener.

millimetri millimeter; *synonyms* (*n*) millimetre, (*v*) micrometer, micron, millimicron, nanometer.

millímetri millimeter; *synonyms* (*n*) millimetre, (*v*) micrometer, micron, millimicron, nanometer.

millímíkron nanometer; *synonyms* (*n*) micromillimeter, micromillimetre, millimicron, nanometre, (*v*) centimeter.

millinetagátt gateway; *synonyms* (*n*) door, entrance, gate, doorway, entry.

milliplata shim; *synonyms* (*n*) wedge, liner, filling.

millirifjaverkur pleurodynia; *synonyms* (*n*) costalgia, pleuralgia.

milliríkjasamningur 1. treaty; *synonyms* (*n*) agreement, convention, protocol, accord, concord, **2**. pact; *synonyms* (*n*) contract, bargain, bond, deal, alliance.

milliríkjasáttmáli pact; *synonyms* (*n*) accord, agreement, contract, bargain, bond.

milliskorageiri internode; *synonyms* (*n*) phalanx, phalanstery, segment.

millistig interphase; *synonyms* (*n*) interface, interkinesis.

millistykki 1. adapter; *synonyms* (*n*) adaptor, spider, attachment, arranger, transcriber, **2**. adaptor; *synonyms* (*n*) adapter, receiver.

millitenging jumper; *synonyms* (*n*) sweater, blackguard, bounder, cad, dog.

millitengsl interconnection; *synonyms* (*n*) interconnectedness, link, joint, correlation, relationship.

milliverkun interaction; *synonyms* (*n*) interplay, contact, correlation, communication, mutuality.

milljarður billion; *synonym* (*v*) milliard.

milljón million; *synonyms* (*n*) meg, myriad, heap, mint.

milta 1. spleen; *synonyms* (*n*) anger, spite, resentment, rage, bitterness, **2**. lien; *synonyms* (*n*) gage, bond, mortgage, pledge, plight.

milti 1. spleen; *synonyms* (*n*) anger, spite, resentment, rage, bitterness, **2**. lien; *synonyms* (*n*) gage, bond, mortgage, pledge, plight.

miltisbrandsdrep anthrax; *synonyms* (*n*) carbuncle, (*adj*) bighead.

miltisbrandur anthrax; *synonyms* (*n*) carbuncle, (*adj*) bighead.

miltissjúkur splenetic; *synonyms* (*adj*) fretful, peevish, prickly, angry, (*n*) morose.

minn mine; *synonyms* (*n*) dig, excavation, (*v*) excavate, sap, burrow.

minni 1. memory; *synonyms* (*n*) memento, recall, recollection, remembrance, reminiscence, **2**. store; *synonyms* (*n*) hoard, shop, market, (*v*) stock, accumulate.

minniháttar 1. secondary; *synonyms* (*adj*) inferior, lower, minor, subordinate, ancillary; *antonyms* (*adj*) basic, main, central, chief, direct, **2**. minor; *synonyms* (*adj*) little, insignificant, junior, lesser, (*n*) child; *antonyms* (*adj*) major, important, significant, fundamental, leading.

minnihlutaálit protest; *synonyms* (*n*) demonstration, objection, (*v*) dissent, assert, complain; *antonym* (*v*) support.

minnihluti minority; *synonyms* (*n*) nonage, infancy, adolescence, inferiority, (*adj*) few.

minning reminiscence; *synonyms* (*n*) remembrance, memory, recall, recollection, anamnesis.

minninhlutahópur minority; *synonyms* (*n*) nonage, infancy, adolescence, inferiority, (*adj*) few.

minnisatriði memorandum; *synonyms* (*n*) memo, note, memorial, entry, letter.

minnisblað memorandum; *synonyms* (*n*) memo, note, memorial, entry, letter.

minnisblöð memorandum; *synonyms* (*n*) memo, note, memorial, entry, letter.

minnisbót reminiscence; *synonyms* (*n*) remembrance, memory, recall, recollection, anamnesis.

minnisefling mnemonics; *synonym* (*n*) mnemotechny.

minnisgeymd retention; *synonyms* (*n*) memory, detention, holding, keeping, possession; *antonym* (*n*) removal.

minnisgluggi window; *synonyms* (*n*) casement, porthole, pane, gap, embrasure.

minnisgrein memorandum; *synonyms* (*n*) memo, note, memorial, entry, letter.

minnisheimt recollection; *synonyms* (*n*) memory, recall, reminiscence, anamnesis, (*v*) mind.

minnishjálp mnemonics; *synonym* (*n*) mnemotechny.

minnishylki cartridge; *synonyms* (*n*) bullet, cassette, cartouch, ammunition, magazine.

minnisleysi amnesia; *synonyms* (*n*) forgetfulness, oblivion, blackout, brownout, dimout.

minnistækni mnemonics; *synonym* (*n*) mnemotechny.

minnistap fugue; *synonyms* (*n*) notturno, serenade, flight, forgetfulness, quodlibet.

minnka 1. shrink; *synonyms* (*v*) dwindle, flinch, recoil, contract, shorten, *antonyms* (*v*) expand, increase, enlarge, **2**. reduce; *synonyms* (*v*) lower, pare, abbreviate, curtail, (*adj*) abridge; *antonyms* (*v*) bolster, exacerbate, intensify, **3**. decrease;

synonyms (n) decline, cut, (v) abate, lessen, diminish; **antonyms** (n) growth, extension, (v) rise, grow, **4**. decrement; **synonyms** (n) decrease, deduction, defalcation, defect, discount.

minnkun 1. reduction; **synonyms** (n) contraction, decrease, decrement, diminution, rebate; **antonyms** (n) increase, growth, intensification, strengthening, expansion, **2**. decrement; **synonyms** (n) cut, deduction, defalcation, defect, discount.

minnstur minimal; **synonyms** (adj) minimum, least, minute, insignificant, marginal; **antonym** (adj) maximal.

mintur mint; **synonyms** (n) fortune, heap, pile, (v) coin, invent.

mínus 1. minus; **synonyms** (n) negative, (v) bereft, (adj) minor, less, lacking; **antonym** (prep) plus, **2**. negative; **synonyms** (adj) minus, (v) gainsay, veto, deny, disavow; **antonyms** (adj) positive, optimistic, assenting, (n) affirmative.

mínusmerki minus; **synonyms** (n) negative, (v) bereft, (adj) minor, less, lacking; **antonym** (prep) plus.

mínusskaut cathode; **synonym** (n) platinode.

mínustenging minus; **synonyms** (n) negative, (v) bereft, (adj) minor, less, lacking; **antonym** (prep) plus.

mínúta minute; **synonyms** (n) instant, flash, jiffy, note, (adj) little; **antonyms** (adj) enormous, huge, big, gigantic.

minuto 1. minutes; **synonyms** (n) proceedings, record, transactions, records, journal, **2**. minute; **synonyms** (n) instant, flash, jiffy, note, (adj) little; **antonyms** (adj) enormous, huge, big, gigantic.

mínútumerki prime; **synonyms** (adj) main, chief, first, head, (n) best; **antonym** (adj) minor.

misátta anisotropic; **synonyms** (adj) anisotrope, anisotropous.

misáttun 1. anisotropy, **2**. disorientation; **synonyms** (n) confusion, awkwardness, bafflement, bewilderment, embarrassment.

misbeiting abuse; **synonyms** (n) affront, misuse, harm, (v) insult, mistreat; **antonyms** (v) praise, respect.

misgengi 1. slip; **synonyms** (n) lapse, fault, (v) fall, slide, (adj) blunder; **antonym** (v) improve, **2**. inequality; **synonyms** (n) disparity, difference, disproportion, dissimilitude, (adj) odds; **antonyms** (n) equality, justice, parity, **3**. fault; **synonyms** (n) defect, blemish, error, failing, (v) deficiency; **antonyms** (n) merit, strength.

misgengisfleygur wedge; **synonyms** (n) chock, (v) squeeze, compress, jam, pack.

misgengishreyfing faulting; **synonym** (n) faultage.

misgerður discordant; **synonyms** (adj) contrary, conflicting, dissonant, discrepant, disharmonious;

antonyms (adj) harmonious, musical, pleasant-sounding, melodic.

mishæfing maladjustment; **synonym** (n) neurosis.

mishljómur dissonance; **synonyms** (n) discord, discrepancy, disharmony, disaccord, disagreement; **antonym** (n) harmony.

mishverfa asymmetry; **synonyms** (n) irregularity, dissymmetry, imbalance, skewness, disproportion; **antonym** (n) symmetry.

mishverfur asymmetric; **synonyms** (adj) asymmetrical, unbalanced, crooked, (v) unsymmetric, irregular.

miskveiking misfire; **synonyms** (n) flop, dud, (v) fail, miscarry, fizzle.

miskveikja misfire; **synonyms** (n) flop, dud, (v) fail, miscarry, fizzle.

mislægi 1. unconformity; **synonyms** (n) anomaly, variation, **2**. discordance; **synonyms** (n) discord, nonconformity, discrepancy, difference, disagreement.

mislangur unequal; **synonyms** (adj) dissimilar, different, unlike, inadequate, lopsided; **antonyms** (adj) equal, even.

misleitur 1. heterogenous; **synonyms** (adj) heterogeneous, heterogene, heterogenetic, **2**. heterologous; **synonyms** (adj) heterologic, heterological, different, **3**. heterogeneous; **synonyms** (adj) dissimilar, assorted, miscellaneous, heterogenous, (v) diverse; **antonym** (adj) homogeneous.

mislingar 1. rubeola; **synonyms** (n) measles, morbilli, (adj) necrosis, pertussis, phthisis, **2**. measles; **synonyms** (n) rubeola, (adj) mumps, polio.

mismunadrif differential; **synonyms** (adj) integral, (n) derivative, difference, distinction, fluxion.

mismunun discrimination; **synonyms** (n) discernment, difference, differentiation, distinction, (v) judgment; **antonym** (n) tolerance.

mismunur 1. variance; **synonyms** (n) difference, disagreement, discrepancy, dissension, division, **2**. difference; **synonyms** (n) conflict, deviation, change, contention, controversy; **antonyms** (n) correspondence, resemblance, sameness, similarity, agreement.

misnotkun abuse; **synonyms** (n) affront, misuse, harm, (v) insult, mistreat; **antonyms** (v) praise, respect.

mispörun mismatch; **synonyms** (v) disparity, clash, jar, (adj) differ, ablude.

misræmi 1. discrepancy; **synonyms** (n) difference, deviation, disagreement, departure, divergence; **antonym** (n) consistency, **2**. dissonance; **synonyms** (n) discord, discrepancy, disharmony, disaccord, dissension; **antonym** (n) harmony, **3**.

discordance; *synonyms* (n) nonconformity, contrariety, dissonance.

misrétti discrimination; *synonyms* (n) discernment, difference, differentiation, distinction, (v) judgment; *antonym* (n) tolerance.

missa misfire; *synonyms* (n) flop, dud, (v) fail, miscarry, fizzle.

missætti 1. disagreement; *synonyms* (n) difference, discrepancy, conflict, discord, dispute; *antonyms* (n) agreement, accord, harmony, **2.** dissension; *synonyms* (n) contention, disagreement, variance, dissonance, division, **3.** discord; *synonyms* (n) dissension, clash, split, (v) disagree, dissent; *antonym* (n) unity, **4.** dissent; *synonyms* (n) protest, objection, (v) differ, object, contradict; *antonyms* (v) agree, assent.

misseravindur monsoon; *synonyms* (n) cyclone, downpour, harmattan, hurricane, storm.

misserislegur biannual; *synonyms* (adj) biyearly, semiannual.

misserisvindar monsoon; *synonyms* (n) cyclone, downpour, harmattan, hurricane, storm.

misstilling mismatch; *synonyms* (v) disparity, clash, jar, (adj) differ, ablude.

misþátta heterogeneous; *synonyms* (adj) dissimilar, different, assorted, miscellaneous, (v) diverse; *antonym* (adj) homogeneous.

mistök 1. error; *synonyms* (n) deviation, blunder, fault, mistake, wrong; *antonym* (n) correctness, **2.** mistake; *synonyms* (n) defect, error, failure, (v) err, misapprehend, **3.** aberration; *synonyms* (n) aberrance, aberrancy, abnormality, diversion, frenzy, **4.** fail; *synonyms* (v) abort, collapse, fade, cease, (adj) decline; *antonyms* (v) succeed, triumph, **5.** fault; *synonyms* (n) blemish, failing, blame, blot, (v) deficiency; *antonyms* (n) merit, strength.

mistur 1. haze; *synonyms* (n) fog, cloud, blur, confusion, (v) mist, **2.** mist; *synonyms* (n) haze, vapor, (v) befog, cover, obscure, **3.** fog; *synonyms* (n) brume, (v) confuse, dim, becloud, darken.

misvægi 1. skewness; *synonym* (n) lopsidedness, **2.** unbalance; *synonyms* (v) derange, craze, (n) imbalance, derangement, insanity; *antonym* (v) balance, **3.** disequilibrium; *synonym* (n) instability; *antonym* (n) equilibrium, **4.** conation; *synonyms* (n) volition, velleity, design, intent, will, **5.** imbalance; *synonyms* (n) asymmetry, disproportion, disparity, inequality, unbalance.

misvísandi magnetic; *synonyms* (adj) attractive, charismatic, fascinating, inviting, magnetized.

misvísun 1. variation; *synonyms* (n) alteration, change, difference, divergence, mutation; *antonym* (n) similarity, **2.** deviation; *synonyms* (n) aberration, deflection, diversion, variation,

abnormality; *antonym* (n) normality, **3.** declination; *synonyms* (n) declension, descent, decay, decline, refusal.

mítósa 1. mitosis, **2.** karyokinesis; *synonym* (n) mitosis.

mitti waist; *synonyms* (n) waistline, shank, middle, (adj) neck, stricture.

mjaðmagrind pelvis; *synonyms* (n) hip, belly, coxa, rosehip.

mjaðmarskál acetabulum; *synonym* (n) acetable.

mjaðmarsvæði hip; *synonyms* (n) haunch, coxa, (adj) hep, stylish, chic.

mjak inching; *synonyms* (n) jogging, jog.

mjaltavaki oxytocin; *synonym* (n) ocytocin.

mjódd isthmus; *synonyms* (n) bridge, oasis, (adj) strait, neck, wasp.

mjöðm hip; *synonyms* (n) haunch, coxa, (adj) hep, stylish, chic.

mjög 1. so; *synonyms* (adv) accordingly, as, consequently, hence, (pron) that, **2.** really; *synonyms* (adv) actually, honestly, absolutely, genuinely, certainly, **3.** very; *synonyms* (adv) extremely, greatly, highly, (adj) much, identical; *antonyms* (adv) abysmally, slightly, somewhat, **4.** well; *synonyms* (adv) right, easily, thoroughly, (adj) healthy, (n) fountain; *antonyms* (adv) ill, badly, poorly, (adj) sick, unwell, **5.** quite; *synonyms* (adv) altogether, all, completely, entirely, fully.

mjókka narrow; *synonyms* (adj) close, limited, (v) confined, contract, limit; *antonyms* (adj) wide, broad, comprehensive, extensive, (v) widen.

mjöl 1. flour; *synonyms* (v) powder, (adj) meal, bran, paddy, rice, **2.** meal; *synonyms* (n) food, feed, flour, repast, banquet.

mjólk milk; *synonyms* (v) exploit, squeeze, drain, tap, (adj) albumen.

mjólka 1. milk; *synonyms* (v) exploit, squeeze, drain, tap, (adj) albumen, **2.** lactate; *synonyms* (v) nurse, suck, suckle, breastfeed, absorb.

mjólkurhormón prolactin; *synonym* (n) luteotropin.

mjólkurkenndur lacteal; *synonyms* (adj) lacteous, milky, lactean, (n) lactiferous.

mjólkurmyndun lactation; *synonyms* (n) suckling, nurseling, nursling.

mjólkurmyndunarvaki prolactin; *synonym* (n) luteotropin.

mjólkursafi latex; *synonyms* (n) rubber, whalebone, paint.

mjólkursteinn alabaster; *synonyms* (adj) alabastrine, chalk, ivory, lily, milk.

mjólkursykur lactose; *synonym* (n) galactose.

mjölrót arrowroot; *synonym* (n) achira.

mjölvakenndur amyloid; *synonyms* (adj) amylaceous, amyloidal, starchlike.

mjölvi starch; *synonyms* (*n*) amylum, vitality, (*v*) stiffen, (*adj*) stiff, glair.

mjór 1. thin; *synonyms* (*adj*) flimsy, gaunt, lean, light, (*v*) slender; *antonyms* (*adj*) thick, fat, concentrated, chubby, plump, **2.** slim; *synonyms* (*adj*) narrow, slight, thin, remote, fine; *antonyms* (*adj*) heavy, hefty, stocky, wide, **3.** slender; *synonyms* (*adj*) little, lithe, delicate, faint, feeble, **4.** gaunt; *synonyms* (*adj*) emaciated, bleak, cadaverous, desolate, bony, **5.** lean; *synonyms* (*v*) incline, bend, list, slant, (*n*) tilt.

mjósi ling; *synonyms* (*n*) heather, burbot, broom, cusk, eelpout.

mjúkhærður pilose; *synonyms* (*adj*) hairy, pilous, pileous, fleecy, pilary.

mjúkhljóð liquid; *synonyms* (*adj*) flowing, fluent, fluid, juicy, limpid; *antonyms* (*adj*) firm, (*n*) solid, gaseous.

mjúkt soft; *synonyms* (*adj*) gentle, easy, light, limp, balmy; *antonyms* (*adj*) hard, firm, harsh, loud, hoarse.

mjúkur 1. soft; *synonyms* (*adj*) gentle, easy, light, limp, balmy; *antonyms* (*adj*) hard, firm, harsh, loud, hoarse, **2.** bland; *synonyms* (*adj*) benign, flat, insipid, mild, moderate; *antonyms* (*adj*) tasty, exciting, spicy, strong, explicit, **3.** flaccid; *synonyms* (*adj*) flabby, lax, loose, slack, soft; *antonym* (*adj*) stiff, **4.** gentle; *synonyms* (*adj*) clement, calm, friendly, affable, kind; *antonyms* (*adj*) caustic, cruel, fierce, violent, rough, **5.** mild; *synonyms* (*adj*) kindly, gracious, lenient, docile, humble; *antonyms* (*adj*) intense, extreme, pungent, severe, sharp.

móar heath; *synonyms* (*n*) heather, heathland, prairie, steppe, waste.

módel pattern; *synonyms* (*n*) model, design, fashion, form, mold.

móðga 1. wrong; *synonyms* (*adj*) harm, evil, false, ill, (*n*) damage; *antonyms* (*adj*) correct, good, proper, (*adv*) correctly, (*v*) right, **2.** abuse; *synonyms* (*n*) affront, misuse, (*v*) insult, mistreat, injure; *antonyms* (*v*) praise, respect, **3.** insult; *synonyms* (*n*) dishonor, abuse, contumely, disgrace, (*v*) flout; *antonym* (*v*) compliment, **4.** hurt; *synonyms* (*v*) pain, wound, afflict, (*n*) detriment, ache; *antonyms* (*v*) encourage, (*adj*) uninjured, unhurt, **5.** offend; *synonyms* (*v*) irritate, contravene, disgust, infringe, anger; *antonym* (*v*) please.

móðgun 1. insult; *synonyms* (*n*) dishonor, abuse, affront, contumely, (*v*) flout; *antonyms* (*v*) compliment, praise, **2.** abuse; *synonyms* (*n*) misuse, harm, (*v*) insult, mistreat, injure; *antonym* (*v*) respect, **3.** affront; *synonyms* (*n*) outrage, slight, disgrace, (*v*) face, offend, **4.** offence; *synonyms* (*n*)

guilt, infraction, infringement, misdemeanor, misdemeanour, **5.** injury; *synonyms* (*n*) disadvantage, disservice, grievance, damage, detriment; *antonyms* (*n*) ability, reparation.

móðir mother; *synonyms* (*n*) mamma, (*v*) father, beget, engender, generate.

móðurbróðir uncle; *synonym* (*n*) pawnbroker.

móðurhnöttur primary; *synonyms* (*adj*) chief, basic, elementary, essential, (*n*) paramount; *antonym* (*adj*) secondary.

móðurlegur maternal; *synonyms* (*adj*) motherly, parental, paternal, agnate, agnatic.

móðurmerki brand; *synonyms* (*n*) badge, blade, (*v*) mark, (*adj*) stigma, blot.

móðurstjarna primary; *synonyms* (*adj*) chief, basic, elementary, essential, (*n*) paramount; *antonym* (*adj*) secondary.

móðursýki hysteria; *synonyms* (*n*) hysterics, delirium, frenzy, madness, craze.

móðursystir aunt; *synonyms* (*n*) auntie, aunty, uncle, nephew, niece.

mögnuður complement; *synonyms* (*n*) supplement, accessory, adjunct, balance, extra.

mögnun 1. amplification; *synonyms* (*n*) augmentation, addition, expansion, extension, gain; *antonym* (*n*) reduction, **2.** gain; *synonyms* (*v*) acquire, benefit, derive, (*n*) profit, earnings; *antonyms* (*v*) lose, (*n*) loss.

mögnunarstuðull gain; *synonyms* (*v*) acquire, benefit, derive, (*n*) profit, earnings; *antonyms* (*v*) lose, (*n*) loss.

mögulegur potential; *synonyms* (*adj*) likely, possible, (*n*) capability, potency, ability.

möguleiki potential; *synonyms* (*adj*) likely, possible, (*n*) capability, potency, ability.

mók torpor; *synonyms* (*n*) lethargy, inactivity, lassitude, inertia, apathy.

mökkur cloud; *synonyms* (*n*) mist, (*v*) fog, becloud, obscure, befog; *antonym* (*v*) sharpen.

mókol lignite; *synonyms* (*n*) browncoal, charcoal.

mól 1. mole; *synonyms* (*n*) breakwater, jetty, freckle, bulwark, groyne, **2.** mol; *synonyms* (*n*) mole, counterspy, groin, seawall.

möl gravel; *synonyms* (*v*) bedevil, get, nonplus, rag, (*adj*) bother.

molar pickling; *synonyms* (*n*) buckling, preservation.

mold 1. topsoil, **2.** clay; *synonyms* (*n*) soil, remains, pottery, dirt, (*adj*) earthen, **3.** ground; *synonyms* (*n*) base, cause, land, floor, (*v*) bottom; *antonym* (*n*) ceiling.

moldarefni humus; *synonyms* (*n*) hummus, compost, hommos, hoummos, humous.

moldarkökkur clod; *synonyms* (*n*) chunk, ball, glebe, lump, oaf.

moldun compost; *synonyms* (*n*) compound, dung, composite, (*v*) fertilize, (*adj*) manure.

moldvarpa mole; *synonyms* (*n*) breakwater, jetty, freckle, bulwark, groyne.

mólendi heath; *synonyms* (*n*) heather, heathland, prairie, steppe, waste.

mólikúl molecule; *synonyms* (*n*) atom, corpuscle, grain, iota, jot.

mólin molar; *synonyms* (*adj*) molal, (*n*) grinder, bomber, hero, hoagie.

mollulegt close; *synonyms* (*adj*) near, adjacent, nearby, accurate, (*n*) end; *antonyms* (*adj*) distant, airy, fresh, (*v*) open, start.

mólmassi mole; *synonyms* (*n*) breakwater, jetty, freckle, bulwark, groyne.

molnun disintegration; *synonyms* (*n*) collapse, decay, decomposition, breakdown, annihilation.

molta compost; *synonyms* (*n*) compound, dung, composite, (*v*) fertilize, (*adj*) manure.

moltugryfja compost; *synonyms* (*n*) compound, dung, composite, (*v*) fertilize, (*adj*) manure.

moltukassi compost; *synonyms* (*n*) compound, dung, composite, (*v*) fertilize, (*adj*) manure.

möndulhalli obliquity; *synonyms* (*n*) crookedness, dishonesty, inclination, slope, asynclitism.

möndull 1. arbor; *synonyms* (*n*) bower, mandrel, axle, spindle, arbour, **2.** axis; *synonyms* (*n*) pivot, hinge, center, hub, stem.

möndullægur axial; *synonyms* (*adj*) axile, central, focal, umbilical, azygous.

möndulvelta precession; *synonyms* (*n*) precedence, antecedence, antecedency, anteriority, precedency.

mongólítagervi mongolism; *synonym* (*n*) mongolianism.

mongólóíðaháttur mongolism; *synonym* (*n*) mongolianism.

monsún monsoon; *synonyms* (*n*) cyclone, downpour, harmattan, hurricane, storm.

monsúntími monsoon; *synonyms* (*n*) cyclone, downpour, harmattan, hurricane, storm.

monsúnvindur monsoon; *synonyms* (*n*) cyclone, downpour, harmattan, hurricane, storm.

montprik 1. braggart; *synonyms* (*n*) boaster, blowhard, braggadocio, bragger, (*v*) magniloquent, **2.** boaster; *synonyms* (*n*) braggart, vaunter, bouncer, swaggerer, huff, **3.** bragger; *synonym* (*n*) bighead.

mor turbidity; *synonyms* (*n*) turbidness, haze, obscurity, haziness.

Mór peat; *synonyms* (*n*) turf, bog, pel.

morala 1. moral; *synonyms* (*adj*) ethical, decent, good, honest, (*n*) lesson; *antonyms* (*adj*) immoral,

bad, unwholesome, **2.** morals; *synonyms* (*n*) morality, ethics, behavior, honor, principles.

moralaĵo morals; *synonyms* (*n*) morality, ethics, behavior, honor, principles.

moralinstruo morals; *synonyms* (*n*) morality, ethics, behavior, honor, principles.

mórauður brown; *synonyms* (*adj*) chocolate, swarthy, (*n*) brunette, brownness, (*v*) sear; *antonym* (*adj*) pale.

morð 1. homicide; *synonyms* (*n*) assassination, murder, carnage, butchery, manslaughter, **2.** murder; *synonyms* (*n*) homicide, slaughter, (*v*) massacre, butcher, kill.

mórena moraine; *synonym* (*n*) ridge.

morgun morning; *synonyms* (*n*) dawn, daybreak, sunrise, daylight, forenoon; *antonym* (*n*) dusk.

morgunberkja cherimoya; *synonym* (*n*) cherimolla.

mörk 1. boundary; *synonyms* (*n*) border, bound, limit, edge, area, **2.** border; *synonyms* (*n*) margin, brink, extremity, fringe, (*v*) verge; *antonyms* (*n*) middle, (*v*) center, **3.** limit; *synonyms* (*n*) boundary, (*v*) restrict, circumscribe, confine, (*prep*) extent; *antonyms* (*n*) extension, minimum, (*v*) broaden, extend, **4.** margin; *synonyms* (*n*) hem, brim, bank, circumference, perimeter.

morkna 1. putrefy; *synonyms* (*v*) decay, rot, decompose, fester, corrupt, **2.** rot; *synonyms* (*n*) corruption, drivel, (*v*) canker, disintegrate, molder.

mörkun 1. imprinting, **2.** marking; *synonyms* (*n*) mark, earmark, brand, crisscross, marker, **3.** modification; *synonyms* (*n*) alteration, change, adaptation, variation, adjustment.

moro customs; *synonyms* (*n*) custom, duty, impost, civilization, mores.

mortél mortar; *synonyms* (*n*) howitzer, plaster, birdlime, cannon, (*v*) cement.

morti 1. dice; *synonyms* (*n*) die, (*v*) cube, cut, chop, bet, **2.** die; *synonyms* (*v*) decease, dead, death, depart, (*n*) dice.

morugur turbid; *synonyms* (*adj*) muddy, thick, murky, opaque, cloudy.

mósaík mosaic; *synonyms* (*n*) tesserae, strigae, (*adj*) tessellated, heterogeneous, (*v*) plaid.

móskugur opaque; *synonyms* (*adj*) cloudy, dense, dull, muddy, obscure; *antonyms* (*adj*) clear, transparent, see-through.

moskusmelóna cantaloupe; *synonym* (*n*) cantaloup.

moskusrotta muskrat; *synonyms* (*n*) musquash, champak, horehound, mint, olibanum.

möskvi mesh; *synonyms* (*n*) interlock, network, entanglement, (*v*) engage, lock.

Mót 1. tournament; *synonyms* (*n*) tilt, competition, contest, tourney, (*v*) action, **2.** style; *synonyms* (*n*) fashion, name, (*v*) call, entitle, (*adj*) manner, **3.** template; *synonyms* (*n*) pattern, templet, guide, guidebook, pathfinder, **4**. anastomosis; *synonyms* (n) inosculation, (v) communication, concatenation, mortise, infibulation, **5**. commissure; *synonyms* (v) articulation, joint, juncture, gore, gusset.

móta 1. mold; *synonyms* (n) cast, matrix, (v) model, form, fashion, **2**. modulate; *synonyms* (v) moderate, modify, change, inflect, qualify, **3**. forge; *synonyms* (v) counterfeit, falsify, devise, fabricate, fake.

mótandi formative; *synonyms* (adj) creative, inchoative, (v) genetic, genial, genital.

mótbára objection; *synonyms* (n) dissent, protest, complaint, exception, grievance.

mótefnaskortur agammaglobulinemia; *synonym* (n) hypogammaglobulinemia.

mótefnaþurrð agammaglobulinemia; *synonym* (n) hypogammaglobulinemia.

mótefni 1. antibody; *synonyms* (n) antitoxin, germ, ab, **2**. immunoglobulin.

móteitur 1. antidote; *synonyms* (n) cure, counterpoison, remedy, antifebrile, antipoison; *antonym* (n) poison, **2**. antitoxin; *synonyms* (n) antidote, medicine, antibiotic, antiseptic, antiserum.

móthald stop; *synonyms* (n) halt, hold, stay, check, end; *antonyms* (v) continue, start, begin, encourage, permit.

móti counter; *synonyms* (n) buffet, bench, reverse, (v) reply, (adj) converse.

motivo grounds; *synonyms* (n) cause, dregs, ground, reason, account.

mótlyf antagonist; *synonyms* (n) opponent, adversary, enemy, foe, rival; *antonym* (n) friend.

mótmæli 1. protest; *synonyms* (n) demonstration, objection, (v) dissent, assert, complain; *antonym* (v) support, **2**. demonstration; *synonyms* (n) parade, proof, argument, display, manifestation, **3**. objection; *synonyms* (n) protest, complaint, exception, grievance, gripe.

mótor motor; *synonyms* (n) engine, automobile, machine, car, (v) drive.

mótreikna offset; *synonyms* (v) counteract, balance, neutralize, cancel, (n) counterbalance.

mótsermi antiserum; *synonym* (n) antitoxin.

mótsetning 1. antithesis; *synonyms* (n) antagonism, contrast, foil, opposite, contrariety, **2**. contradistinction; *synonyms* (n) distinction, opposition, antithesis, variation, **3**. contrast; *synonyms* (n) comparison, difference, (v) differ, conflict, oppose; *antonym* (n) similarity, **4**. opposition; *synonyms* (n) contrary, enemy, hostility, opponent, competition; *antonym* (n) consent.

mótsögn paradox; *synonyms* (n) incongruity, ambiguity, inconsistency, puzzle, catch-22.

Motspíspil counterplay; *synonyms* (n) counterattack, countermove, revenge.

mótstaða 1. resistance; *synonyms* (n) opposition, endurance, friction, immunity, impedance; *antonyms* (n) smoothness, agreement, obedience, susceptibility, **2**. resistor; *synonyms* (n) resistance, resistivity, underground, **3**. impedance; *synonyms* (n) clog, hindrance, interference.

mótstæður 1. alien; *synonyms* (adj) foreign, strange, unknown, (n) foreigner, (v) alienate; *antonyms* (adj) familiar, (n) native, citizen, **2**. contrary; *synonyms* (adj) opposite, contradictory, adverse, conflicting, reverse, **3**. adverse; *synonyms* (adj) contrary, unfavorable, harmful, hostile, untoward; *antonym* (adj) favorable, **4**. opposite; *synonyms* (adj) diametric, different, opposing, (adv) counter, (n) opponent; *antonym* (adj) similar.

mótsvarandi complementary; *synonyms* (adj) complemental, additional, auxiliary, supplementary, reciprocal.

motta mat; *synonyms* (n) matte, (adj) dull, flat, (v) entangle, felt.

móttækilegur 1. susceptible; *synonyms* (adj) impressionable, receptive, responsive, sensitive, subject; *antonyms* (adj) resistant, unsusceptible, **2**. accessible; *synonyms* (adj) approachable, available, open, convenient, amenable; *antonyms* (adj) inaccessible, out-of-the-way, unavailable, **3**. headwind.

móttakandi receiver; *synonyms* (n) recipient, beneficiary, cashier, earpiece, headset; *antonym* (n) donor.

móttakari receiver; *synonyms* (n) recipient, beneficiary, cashier, earpiece, headset; *antonym* (n) donor.

mótþrói rebellion; *synonyms* (n) insurrection, mutiny, revolt, disobedience, uprising.

móttökuhæfni competence; *synonyms* (n) capacity, adequacy, ability, capability, (adj) proficiency; *antonyms* (n) incompetence, inability.

möttull 1. jacket; *synonyms* (n) casing, sheath, case, cover, covering, **2**. mantle; *synonyms* (n) cloak, cape, pall, blanket, (adj) blush.

mótun 1. shaping; *synonyms* (n) formation, defining, (adj) forming, formative, **2**. stamping; *synonyms* (n) marking, impression, blocking, coin, coining, **3**. modulation; *synonyms* (n) accent, intonation, inflection, transition, passage, **4**. forming; *synonyms* (n) shaping, form, organization, construction, conformation.

mötun 1. delivery; *synonyms* (n) childbirth, birth, consignment, discharge, rescue; *antonyms* (n) death, dispatch, **2.** feed; *synonyms* (*v*) eat, dine, nurture, (*n*) aliment, food; *antonym* (*v*) starve.

mótunarverkfæri 1. die; *synonyms* (*v*) decease, dead, death, depart, (*n*) dice, **2.** former; *synonyms* (*adv*) before, (*adj*) antecedent, anterior, bygone, earlier; *antonym* (*adj*) future.

mötuneyti mess; *synonyms* (*n*) clutter, jumble, muddle, confusion, (*v*) botch; *antonym* (*n*) order.

mótvægi 1. counterpoise; *synonyms* (*n*) counterbalance, balance, poise, equilibrium, (*v*) counterweight, **2.** counterweight; *synonyms* (*n*) counterpoise, weight, ballast, correspondence, (*v*) counterpose, **3.** counterbalance; *synonyms* (*v*) compensate, counteract, countervail, neutralize, cover.

mótvægisaðgerð countermeasure; *synonyms* (*n*) remedy, antidote, cure.

mótverkun antagonism; *synonyms* (*n*) animosity, enmity, resistance, aggression, antithesis; *antonym* (*n*) friendliness.

mótvigt counterbalance; *synonyms* (*v*) compensate, counteract, counterpoise, (*n*) balance, counterweight.

mótvirkur antagonistic; *synonyms* (*adj*) hostile, counter, averse, conflicting, (*v*) adverse; *antonym* (*adj*) friendly.

múffa 1. socket; *synonyms* (*n*) cavity, alveolus, sleeve, hollow, pocket, **2.** collar; *synonyms* (*n*) arrest, choker, (*v*) catch, apprehend, capture.

múgur 1. rabble; *synonyms* (*n*) mob, crowd, masses, trash, herd, **2.** crowd; *synonyms* (*n*) huddle, swarm, collection, (*v*) bunch, flock; *antonym* (*v*) disperse.

muldur murmur; *synonyms* (*n*) mutter, (*v*) buzz, grumble, hum, mumble.

mulinn comminute; *synonyms* (*v*) bray, crush, grind, powder, mash.

múll mole; *synonyms* (*n*) breakwater, jetty, freckle, bulwark, groyne.

munaðarhyggja sensualism; *synonyms* (*n*) sensationalism, sensuality, carnalism, lust, carnality.

munaður luxury; *synonyms* (*adj*) delicacy, (*n*) comfort, extravagance, lavishness, luxuriousness; *antonyms* (*n*) essential, paucity.

mundur endowment; *synonyms* (*n*) ability, talent, capacity, (*v*) donation, gift.

munnbiti bolus; *synonyms* (*n*) ball, bole, (*v*) morsel, sippet, sop.

munnhol gullet; *synonyms* (*n*) esophagus, gorge, mouth, muzzle, oesophagus.

munni 1. aperture; *synonyms* (*n*) hole, breach, opening, puncture, slit, **2.** mouth (munnur); *synonyms* (*n*) jaw, lip, aperture, lips, (*v*) grimace.

munnþurka napkin; *synonyms* (*n*) diaper, cloth, handkerchief, serviette, nappy.

munnur 1. mouth; *synonyms* (*n*) jaw, lip, aperture, lips, (*v*) grimace, **2.** stoma; *synonyms* (*n*) pore, hole, stomate, **3.** os; *synonyms* (*n*) bone, osmium, opening, ivory, osar.

munnvatn saliva; *synonyms* (*n*) spit, spittle, sputum, slabber, belch.

munnvatnsmyndun salivation; *synonyms* (*n*) ptyalism, jellyfish, slobber, slabber.

munnvatnsrennsli salivation; *synonyms* (*n*) ptyalism, jellyfish, slobber, slabber.

munúð climax; *synonyms* (*n*) apex, top, acme, culmination, (*v*) peak; *antonym* (*v*) dip.

munuðvíma orgasm; *synonyms* (*n*) climax, coming, advent, approach, approaching.

munúðvíma orgasm; *synonyms* (*n*) climax, coming, advent, approach, approaching.

munur difference; *synonyms* (*n*) conflict, deviation, change, contention, controversy; *antonyms* (*n*) correspondence, resemblance, sameness, similarity, agreement.

múrbrún moulding; *synonyms* (*n*) molding, modeling, mold, mould, cast.

murkrampo 1. brace; *synonyms* (*n*) couple, duo, pair, (*v*) clamp, invigorate; *antonym* (*v*) weaken, **2.** braces; *synonyms* (*n*) brace, suspenders, bitstock, ribs, bracing.

múrmeldýr marmot; *synonyms* (*v*) dormouse, slumberer.

murpapero papers; *synonyms* (*n*) credentials, document, documents, identification, covenant.

murr 1. hum; *synonyms* (*n*) humming, (*v*) buzz, croon, drone, murmur, **2.** murmur; *synonyms* (*n*) mutter, (*v*) grumble, hum, mumble, whisper.

múrsteinn 1. piece; *synonyms* (*n*) cut, division, fragment, part, article, **2.** brick; *synonyms* (*n*) block, lump, brown, (*adj*) trump, concrete, **3.** cake; *synonyms* (*n*) bar, pastry, (*v*) harden, (*adj*) clot, fix.

mús mouse; *synonyms* (*n*) track, trail, hunt, (*v*) sneak, creep.

músháfur tope; *synonyms* (*n*) tumulus, grove, (*v*) booze, drink, (*adj*) tipple.

mustarðar mustard; *synonym* (*n*) eagerness.

musterishneta ginkgo; *synonym* (*n*) gingko.

musteristré ginkgo; *synonym* (*n*) gingko.

músvákur buzzard; *synonyms* (*n*) calf, chicken, colt, doodle, dullard.

múta bribe; *synonyms* (*n*) bait, bribery, reward, (*v*) corrupt, fix.

mútufé bribe; *synonyms* (*n*) bait, bribery, reward, (*v*) corrupt, fix.

mútur bribe; *synonyms* (*n*) bait, bribery, reward, (*v*) corrupt, fix.

mý mosquito; *synonyms* (*n*) fly, alacran, alligator, crocodile, mugger.

mýelín myelin; *synonyms* (*n*) medulla, bulb, myeline.

mýfluga mosquito; *synonyms* (*n*) fly, alacran, alligator, crocodile, mugger.

mygla 1. mold; *synonyms* (*n*) cast, matrix, (*v*) model, form, fashion, **2.** mycelium.

myglusveppur mold; *synonyms* (*n*) cast, matrix, (*v*) model, form, fashion.

mýking cushion; *synonyms* (*n*) pad, (*v*) buffer, bolster, insulate, protect.

mýkjandi emollient; *synonyms* (*adj*) demulcent, lenitive, (*n*) balm, lenient, cream.

mýkt flexibility; *synonyms* (*n*) pliability, spring, adaptability, elasticity, suppleness; *antonyms* (*n*) inflexibility, obstinacy, rigidity, stubbornness, severity.

myldi humus; *synonyms* (*n*) hummus, compost, hommos, hoummos, humous.

mýli myelin; *synonyms* (*n*) medulla, bulb, myeline.

mýlishimna neurolemma; *synonym* (*n*) neurilemma.

mylja 1. comminute; *synonyms* (*v*) bray, crush, grind, powder, mash, **2.** grind; *synonyms* (*v*) labor, toil, comminute, crunch, drudge.

mylker mortar; *synonyms* (*n*) howitzer, plaster, birdlime, cannon, (*v*) cement.

mylking lactation; *synonyms* (*n*) suckling, nurseling, nursling.

mylla 1. chopper; *synonyms* (*n*) ax, helicopter, cleaver, whirlybird, chop, **2.** mill; *synonyms* (*n*) grind, factory, grinder, manufactory, (*v*) crush.

mynd 1. voice; *synonyms* (*n*) speech, (*v*) enunciate, express, pronounce, say, **2.** range; *synonyms* (*v*) line, arrange, order, rank, roam, **3.** scheme; *synonyms* (*n*) contrivance, dodge, (*v*) plan, plot, design, **4.** plot; *synonyms* (*n*) conspiracy, lot, (*v*) intrigue, cabal, plat, **5.** picture; *synonyms* (*n*) photograph, effigy, paint, (*v*) image, describe.

mynda 1. constitute; *synonyms* (*v*) compose, form, make, commission, appoint, **2.** form; *synonyms* (*n*) figure, design, arrange, (*v*) cast, fashion.

myndandi formative; *synonyms* (*adj*) creative, inchoative, (*v*) genetic, genial, genital.

myndband video; *synonyms* (*n*) television, picture, film, movie, (*v*) tape.

myndbirting visualization; *synonyms* (*n*) visualisation, image, fancy, idea, imagination.

myndbreyting 1. metamorphism, **2.** metamorphosis; *synonyms* (*n*) alteration, metabolism, change, conversion, transformation.

myndbrigði 1. allomorph, **2.** isomer; *synonym* (*n*) isomeride.

myndefni product; *synonyms* (*n*) fruit, output, merchandise, proceeds, (*v*) produce.

myndeind pixel; *synonym* (*n*) pel.

myndeining pixel; *synonym* (*n*) pel.

myndfærsla imaging; *synonyms* (*n*) imagery, imagination, imaginativeness, tomography, resource.

myndfall transform; *synonyms* (*v*) change, alter, convert, metamorphose, modify.

myndfóstur fetus; *synonym* (*n*) foetus.

myndgagnasafn library; *synonyms* (*n*) bibliotheca, annals, archive, bibliotheke, den.

myndhermig imaging; *synonyms* (*n*) imagery, imagination, imaginativeness, tomography, resource.

myndhöndlun imaging; *synonyms* (*n*) imagery, imagination, imaginativeness, tomography, resource.

myndhús gallery; *synonyms* (*n*) balcony, audience, drift, veranda, circle.

myndhverfing metaphor; *synonyms* (*n*) allegory, analogy, parable, trope, fable.

myndhvörf metaphor; *synonyms* (*n*) allegory, analogy, parable, trope, fable.

myndlaus amorphous; *synonyms* (*adj*) shapeless, formless, unformed, amphibious, epicene; *antonyms* (*adj*) distinct, defined.

myndleif afterimage; *synonyms* (*n*) aftersensation, sight.

myndlífgun animation; *synonyms* (*n*) life, liveliness, vitality, activity, dash; *antonym* (*n*) lethargy.

myndlíking metaphor; *synonyms* (*n*) allegory, analogy, parable, trope, fable.

myndlína trace; *synonyms* (*n*) line, shadow, spot, clue, (*v*) track.

myndlykill decoder; *synonym* (*n*) decipherer.

myndmál imagery; *synonyms* (*n*) imagination, imaging, portraiture, images, (*adj*) image.

myndmengi range; *synonyms* (*v*) line, arrange, order, rank, roam.

myndrænn 1. graphical; *synonyms* (*adj*) graphic, lifelike, **2.** graphic; *synonyms* (*adj*) vivid, descriptive, (*n*) picture, diagram, (*v*) pictorial.

myndrit 1. diagram; *synonyms* (*n*) design, chart, sketch, figure, (*adj*) plan, **2.** graph; *synonyms* (*n*) diagram, drawing, illustration, map, table.

myndriti facsimile; *synonyms* (*n*) duplicate, copy, autotype, model, (*v*) fax; *antonym* (*n*) original.

myndsetning rendering; *synonyms* (*n*) interpretation, reading, rendition, translation, representation.

myndsími telefax; *synonyms* (*v*) facsimile, fax.

myndsjá video; *synonyms* (*n*) television, picture, film, movie, (*v*) tape.

myndskæni film; *synonyms* (*n*) membrane, coating, cloud, cinema, (*v*) mist.

myndskekkja aberration; *synonyms* (*n*) aberrance, aberrancy, abnormality, deviation, diversion.

myndskjálfti jitter; *synonyms* (*n*) flicker, (*v*) fidget, quiver, tremble, shudder.

myndskot snap; *synonyms* (*v*) crack, bite, break, fracture, (*n*) photograph.

myndstilling focusing; *synonyms* (*n*) centering, concentration, focus, focussing, focalisation.

myndsvið scene; *synonyms* (*n*) aspect, view, background, display, (*v*) prospect.

myndtákn icon; *synonyms* (*n*) effigy, image, picture, figure, likeness.

myndugleiki authority; *synonyms* (*n*) ascendancy, command, sanction, administration, authorization.

myndun 1. production; *synonyms* (*n*) output, generation, product, manufacturing, performance, **2**. formation; *synonyms* (*n*) constitution, creation, establishment, construction, genesis; *antonym* (*n*) destruction, **3**. genesis; *synonyms* (*n*) beginning, ancestry, birth, origin, descent; *antonym* (*n*) end.

myndunarfræði morphology; *synonyms* (*n*) accidence, anatomy, geomorphology, taxonomy, botany.

myndvarp video; *synonyms* (*n*) television, picture, film, movie, (*v*) tape.

mynni 1. peristome, **2**. stoma; *synonyms* (*n*) pore, aperture, hole, stomate, **3**. mouth (munnur); *synonyms* (*n*) jaw, lip, lips, (*v*) grimace, articulate.

mynstrasafn epoch; *synonyms* (*n*) age, era, date, day, period.

mynstrun masking; *synonyms* (*n*) cover, covering, concealment, mask, screening.

mynstur 1. trace; *synonyms* (*n*) line, shadow, spot, clue, (*v*) track, **2**. master; *synonyms* (*n*) captain, instructor, (*v*) conquer, control, (*adj*) chief, **3**. pattern; *synonyms* (*n*) model, design, fashion, form, mold.

mynsturfar signature; *synonyms* (*n*) autograph, mark, endorsement, earmark, (*v*) sign.

myntslátta 1. coinage; *synonyms* (*n*) coin, currency, money, coining, coins, **2**. coining; *synonyms* (*n*) forgery, stamping.

myntur mint; *synonyms* (*n*) fortune, heap, pile, (*v*) coin, invent.

mýóglóbín myoglobin; *synonym* (*n*) mb.

mýrarfen mire; *synonyms* (*n*) bog, filth, marsh, dirt, (*adj*) mud.

mýrarköldukast ague; *synonyms* (*n*) acute, (*adj*) appendicitis.

mýri 1. marsh; *synonyms* (*n*) bog, fen, quagmire, marish, morass, **2**. mire; *synonyms* (*n*) filth, marsh, dirt, (*v*) involve, (*adj*) mud.

myrkur 1. dark; *synonyms* (*adj*) black, dismal, cheerless, dim, (*n*) cloudy; *antonyms* (*adj*) bright,

sunny, fair, (*n*) light, day, **2**. darkness; *synonyms* (*n*) dark, night, shade, shadow, blindness; *antonyms* (*n*) brightness, lightness, **3**. murk; *synonyms* (*n*) darkness, fog, murkiness, (*adj*) gloom, obscurity, **4**. obscurity; *synonyms* (*n*) dimness, obscureness, haze, oblivion, abstruseness; *antonym* (*n*) clarity, **5**. obscure; *synonyms* (*adj*) gloomy, ambiguous, concealed, darken, hidden; *antonyms* (*adj*) clear, noticeable, simple, obvious, (*v*) clarify.

myrkvablossi occult; *synonyms* (*v*) mystic, (*adj*) hidden, obscure, cryptic, mysterious.

myrkvastig magnitude; *synonyms* (*n*) extent, bulk, consequence, amount, dimension; *antonym* (*n*) triviality.

myrkvi 1. eclipse; *synonyms* (*n*) disappearance, (*v*) darken, cloud, outdo, overshadow, **2**. occultation; *synonyms* (*n*) eclipse, evanescence, concealment, eclipsing, (*adj*) adumbration.

mýrlendi 1. bog; *synonyms* (*n*) marsh, morass, swamp, marish, mire; *antonym* (*n*) desert, **2**. moor; *synonyms* (*v*) anchor, berth, fasten, tie, dock, **3**. mire; *synonyms* (*n*) bog, filth, dirt, quagmire, (*adj*) mud.

N

nabbi papilla; *synonyms* (*n*) wart, boob, knocker.

nábítur pyrosis; *synonyms* (*n*) heartburn, (*adj*) necrosis, pertussis, phthisis, pneumonia.

náðarvald charisma; *synonyms* (*n*) allure, charm, fascination, magnetism, appeal.

naðra asp; *synonyms* (*n*) aspick, rattlesnake, aspen, cobra, serpent.

náðun amnesty; *synonyms* (*n*) pardon, absolution, forgiveness, remission, (*v*) forgive; *antonym* (*n*) blame.

nægilegur 1. sufficient; *synonyms* (*adj*) adequate, enough, satisfactory, commensurate, competent; *antonyms* (*adj*) inadequate, insufficient, **2**. adequate; *synonyms* (*adj*) sufficient, acceptable, right, condign, effectual; *antonym* (*adj*) unsatisfactory, **3**. enough; *synonyms* (*adv*) rather, plenty, (*n*) adequacy, fill, (*adj*) ample.

nægjanleiki sufficiency; *synonyms* (*n*) adequacy, enough, fill, abundance, (*adj*) plenty; *antonym* (*n*) insufficiency.

næma 1. prime; *synonyms* (*adj*) main, chief, first, head, (*v*) best; *antonym* (*adj*) minor, **2**. sensitize; *synonyms* (*v*) sensitise, sensibilize, sensify, irritate.

næmi 1. sensitivity; *synonyms* (*n*) sensibility, feeling, sensation, sense, sensitiveness; *antonym* (*n*) insensitivity, **2**. elasticity; *synonyms* (*n*) bounce, spring, flexibility, pliability, suppleness, **3**. excitability; *synonyms* (*n*) reactivity, irritability, impetuosity, vehemence, biliousness.

næming sensitization; *synonyms* (*n*) sensitisation, sensitising, sensitizing.

næmir sensitizer; *synonym* (*n*) sensitiser.

næmisaukning facilitation; *synonyms* (*n*) assistance, enhancement.

næmisstuðull sensitivity; *synonyms* (*n*) sensibility, feeling, sensation, sense, sensitiveness; *antonym* (*n*) insensitivity.

næmleikastuðull sensitivity; *synonyms* (*n*) sensibility, feeling, sensation, sense, sensitiveness; *antonym* (*n*) insensitivity.

næmleiki sensibility; *synonyms* (*n*) emotion, consciousness, (*adj*) feeling, (*v*) sensation, appreciation.

næmni 1. sensitivity; *synonyms* (*n*) sensibility, feeling, sensation, sense, sensitiveness; *antonym* (*n*) insensitivity, **2**. affinity; *synonyms* (*n*) sympathy, analogy, alliance, bond, kindred.

næmur 1. susceptible; *synonyms* (*adj*) impressionable, receptive, responsive, sensitive, subject; *antonyms* (*adj*) resistant, unsusceptible, **2**. sensitive; *synonyms* (*adj*) delicate, excitable, sensible, sore, tender; *antonyms* (*adj*) insensitive, numb, hardhearted, tactless, thick-skinned, **3**. elastic; *synonyms* (*adj*) flexible, buoyant, ductile, limber, pliable; *antonyms* (*adj*) rigid, stiff, inflexible, inelastic, **4**. infective; *synonyms* (*adj*) infectious, catching, virulent, morbific, pathogenic.

næpa turnip; *synonym* (*n*) clock.

næpukál turnip; *synonym* (*n*) clock.

nær 1. practically; *synonyms* (*adv*) almost, nearly, virtually, about, much; *antonyms* (*adv*) theoretically, unrealistically, **2**. virtually; *synonyms* (*adv*) literally, most, (*adj*) near, practically, nigh, **3**. almost; *synonyms* (*adv*) approximately, just, around, roughly, (*adj*) approaching; *antonym* (*adv*) barely, **4**. near; *synonyms* (*prep*) by, (*adv*) close, (*adj*) adjoining, (*v*) familiar, approximate; *antonym* (*adj*) distant, **5**. nearly; *synonyms* (*adv*) closely, intimately, dear, halfway, (*adj*) thereabouts.

nærandi 1. nutrient; *synonyms* (*adj*) alimentary, nourishing, nutritious, nutritive, (*n*) food, **2**. nutritive; *synonyms* (*adj*) nutrient, alimental, wholesome.

nærbuxur knickers; *synonyms* (*n*) bloomers, breeches, drawers, knickerbockers, trousers.

næring 1. aliment; *synonyms* (*n*) food, nutriment, sustenance, alimentation, diet, **2**. nutrient; *synonyms* (*adj*) alimentary, nourishing, nutritious,

nutritive, alimental, **3**. nutriment; *synonyms* (*n*) aliment, nourishment, fare, nutrient, nutrition.

næringarefni nutrient; *synonyms* (*adj*) alimentary, nourishing, nutritious, nutritive, (*n*) food.

næringarferli nutrition; *synonyms* (*n*) nourishment, alimentation, food, nutriment, sustenance.

næringarfræði nutrition; *synonyms* (*n*) nourishment, alimentation, food, nutriment, sustenance.

næringarskortur malnutrition; *synonyms* (*n*) undernourishment, starvation.

nærkona midwife; *synonyms* (*n*) accoucheuse, accoucheur, oculist, howdy, (*v*) midwive.

nærlægur proximal; *synonyms* (*adj*) near, proximate, immediate.

nærliggjandi proximal; *synonyms* (*adj*) near, proximate, immediate.

nærri 1. proximal; *synonyms* (*adj*) near, proximate, immediate, **2**. proximate; *synonyms* (*adj*) close, next, approximate, direct, proximal.

nærsifjar inbreeding; *synonyms* (*n*) consanguinity, selfing.

nærsýni myopia; *synonyms* (*n*) nearsightedness, shortsightedness, myopy, presbyopia, blindness.

nærtækastur proximate; *synonyms* (*adj*) near, close, immediate, next, approximate.

næstum 1. practically; *synonyms* (*adv*) almost, nearly, virtually, about, much; *antonyms* (*adv*) theoretically, unrealistically, **2**. virtually; *synonyms* (*adv*) literally, most, (*adj*) near, practically, nigh, **3**. almost; *synonyms* (*adv*) approximately, just, around, roughly, (*adj*) approaching; *antonym* (*adv*) barely, **4**. nearly; *synonyms* (*adv*) close, closely, intimately, dear, (*adj*) thereabouts.

næstur proximate; *synonyms* (*adj*) near, close, immediate, next, approximate.

næturgali nightingale; *synonyms* (*n*) thrush, etc, nighthawk, singer.

nafar mole; *synonyms* (*n*) breakwater, jetty, freckle, bulwark, groyne.

nafarhlíf spinner; *synonyms* (*n*) spinster, goatsucker, spinneret.

nafli 1. navel; *synonyms* (*n*) bellybutton, center, umbilicus, nave, omphalos, **2**. tip; *synonyms* (*n*) top, hint, (*v*) incline, tilt, dump, **3**. hilum; *synonym* (*n*) hilus.

nafn 1. name; *synonyms* (*n*) call, title, (*v*) appoint, baptize, describe, **2**. term; *synonyms* (*n*) name, expression, period, style, (*v*) designate, **3**. appellation; *synonyms* (*n*) designation, denomination, nickname, appellative, epithet, **4**. denomination; *synonyms* (*n*) appellation, cognomen, class, communion, sect.

nafnakall muster; *synonyms* (*v*) assemble, congregate, gather, collect, (*n*) levy.

nafnakerfi nomenclature; *synonyms* (*n*) terminology, language, classification, lyric, (*v*) name.

nafnauki extension; *synonyms* (*n*) continuation, augmentation, enlargement, expansion, addition; *antonyms* (*n*) limitation, contraction, limit.

nafnfræði taxonomy; *synonyms* (*n*) classification, categorization, (*v*) assortment, allotment, apportionment.

nafngildi nominal; *synonyms* (*adj*) titular, formal, token, minimal, (*v*) cognominal; *antonym* (*adj*) real.

nafnhvörf metonymy; *synonyms* (*n*) metaphor, synecdoche, metonym.

nafnmerki logo; *synonyms* (*n*) emblem, logotype, sign, mark, badge.

nafnorð noun; *synonyms* (*v*) expression, term.

nafnvextir coupon; *synonyms* (*n*) voucher, certificate, order, ticket, debenture.

nafnyrði nominal; *synonyms* (*adj*) titular, formal, token, minimal, (*v*) cognominal; *antonym* (*adj*) real.

nagandi rodent; *synonyms* (*n*) gnawer, (*v*) biting, corroding.

nagdýr rodent; *synonyms* (*n*) gnawer, (*v*) biting, corroding.

naglbítur nippers; *synonyms* (*v*) forceps, pincers, tongs, clutches, vice.

nagli 1. nail; *synonyms* (*n*) arrest, (*v*) catch, apprehend, collar, (*adj*) tack, **2.** pin; *synonyms* (*n*) needle, nail, clip, (*v*) clasp, fix, **3.** spike; *synonyms* (*n*) pin, point, barb, ear, (*v*) impale, **4.** fingernail; *synonym* (*n*) claw.

nagltöng nippers; *synonyms* (*v*) forceps, pincers, tongs, clutches, vice.

náhvalur narwhal; *synonyms* (*n*) narwal, narwhale.

náinn 1. personal; *synonyms* (*adj*) individual, own, particular, human, intimate; *antonyms* (*adj*) public, general, **2.** close; *synonyms* (*adj*) near, adjacent, nearby, accurate, (*n*) end; *antonyms* (*adj*) distant, airy, fresh, (*v*) open, start, **3.** deep; *synonyms* (*adj*) thick, profound, absorbed, abstruse, (*v*) intense; *antonyms* (*adj*) shallow, superficial, high, high-pitched, light, **4.** innermost; *synonyms* (*adj*) inmost, inward, inner, interior, (*n*) inside; *antonym* (*adj*) furthest, **5.** intimate; *synonyms* (*adj*) close, (*v*) express, allude, hint, (*n*) familiar.

nakinn naked; *synonyms* (*adj*) bald, bare, exposed, nude, open; *antonyms* (*adj*) covered, concealed.

nákvæmlega 1. regularly; *synonyms* (*adv*) often, generally, always, customarily, frequently; *antonyms* (*adv*) inconsistently, unusually, constantly, **2.** sharp; *synonyms* (*adj*) acute, bitter, intelligent, acid, (*n*) keen; *antonyms* (*adj*) blunt, dull,

mild, gentle, rounded, **3.** promptly; *synonyms* (*adv*) immediately, forthwith, directly, exactly, instantly; *antonyms* (*adv*) later, slowly, late, **4.** punctually; *synonyms* (*adv*) duly, promptly, precisely, sharp, **5.** exactly; *synonyms* (*adv*) correctly, right, truly, absolutely, just; *antonyms* (*adv*) approximately, inaccurately, (*prep*) about.

nákvæmni 1. precision; *synonyms* (*n*) accuracy, correctness, exactness, accurateness, (*adj*) precise; *antonyms* (*n*) inaccuracy, vagueness, ambiguity, imprecision, **2.** accuracy; *synonyms* (*n*) fidelity, precision, truth, exactitude, reliability, **3.** promptness; *synonyms* (*n*) haste, agility, celerity, promptitude, readiness; *antonyms* (*n*) lateness, slowness, sluggishness, **4.** punctuality; *synonyms* (*n*) promptness, steadiness, punctualness, expedition, (*adj*) rigor; *antonym* (*n*) tardiness, **5.** definition; *synonyms* (*n*) description, account, explanation, interpretation, limitation; *antonym* (*n*) bagginess.

nákvæmur 1. punctual; *synonyms* (*adj*) correct, accurate, exact, prompt, punctilious; *antonym* (*adj*) late, **2.** prompt; *synonyms* (*adj*) agile, quick, nimble, (*v*) actuate, incite; *antonym* (*adj*) slow, **3.** regular; *synonyms* (*adj*) normal, orderly, steady, (*n*) fixed, constant; *antonyms* (*adj*) irregular, erratic, inconsistent, unusual, variable, **4.** timely; *synonyms* (*adj*) opportune, convenient, punctual, appropriate, (*v*) seasonable; *antonyms* (*adj*) untimely, inopportune, **5.** specific; *synonyms* (*adj*) individual, special, concrete, peculiar, (*n*) particular; *antonyms* (*adj*) universal, vague, (*n*) general.

nál 1. spicule; *synonyms* (*n*) spiculum, tooth, (*adj*) point, spike, spine, **2.** jet; *synonyms* (*n*) squirt, fountain, flow, (*v*) gush, spurt.

náladofi tingle; *synonyms* (*n*) thrill, (*v*) itch, prickle, tickle, smart.

nálægð 1. proximity; *synonyms* (*n*) nearness, neighborhood, propinquity, vicinity, contiguity; *antonym* (*n*) distance, **2.** involvement; *synonyms* (*n*) entanglement, concern, interest, implication, inclusion; *antonym* (*n*) disconnection.

nálægja approximate; *synonyms* (*adj*) approximative, near, rough, (*v*) approach, approaching; *antonyms* (*v*) exact, precise.

nálægur 1. approximate; *synonyms* (*adj*) approximative, near, rough, (*v*) approach, approaching; *antonyms* (*v*) exact, precise, **2.** closed; *synonyms* (*v*) close, (*adj*) blind, blocked, finished, shut; *antonym* (*adj*) open, **3.** adjacent; *synonyms* (*adj*) abutting, adjoining, contiguous, conterminous, nearby; *antonym* (*adj*) distant, **4.** near; *synonyms* (*prep*) about, by, (*adv*) almost, (*v*) familiar, approximate.

nálarstunga acupuncture; *synonyms* (*n*) acupuncturation, (*v*) penetration, empalement, pertusion, puncture.

nálastunga acupuncture; *synonyms* (*n*) acupuncturation, (*v*) penetration, empalement, pertusion, puncture.

nálastungulækningar acupuncture; *synonyms* (*n*) acupuncturation, (*v*) penetration, empalement, pertusion, puncture.

nálga approximate; *synonyms* (*adj*) approximative, near, rough, (*v*) approach, approaching; *antonyms* (*v*) exact, precise.

nálgast 1. approach; *synonyms* (*n*) access, entry, (*v*) advance, accost, address; *antonym* (*v*) leave, **2.** approximate; *synonyms* (*adj*) approximative, near, rough, (*v*) approach, approaching; *antonyms* (*v*) exact, precise.

nálgun 1. approximation; *synonyms* (*n*) approach, guess, affinity, estimate, (*v*) estimation, **2.** approach; *synonyms* (*n*) access, entry, (*v*) advance, accost, address; *antonym* (*v*) leave.

nállaga acicular; *synonyms* (*adj*) acerate, acerose, pointed, needlelike, aciculated.

nálormur nematode; *synonyms* (*n*) roundworm, eelworm, ringworm, tinea.

nálstunga acupuncture; *synonyms* (*n*) acupuncturation, (*v*) penetration, empalement, pertusion, puncture.

nám 1. recovery; *synonyms* (*n*) rally, convalescence, improvement, reclamation, rescue; *antonyms* (*n*) decline, loss, return, **2.** mining; *synonyms* (*n*) excavation, minelaying, digging, extraction, dig, **3.** learning; *synonyms* (*n*) erudition, acquisition, education, enlightenment, (*v*) knowledge.

náma 1. reservoir; *synonyms* (*n*) cistern, fountain, well, lake, store, **2.** mine; *synonyms* (*n*) dig, excavation, (*v*) excavate, sap, burrow.

námsgrein discipline; *synonyms* (*v*) control, castigate, chastise, train, chasten.

námskeið course; *synonyms* (*n*) stream, flow, bearing, career, (*v*) run.

námugröftur mining; *synonyms* (*n*) excavation, minelaying, digging, extraction, dig.

námunda round; *synonyms* (*adv*) about, (*adj*) circular, (*n*) circle, bout, ring; *antonyms* (*adj*) slim, sharp.

námundun approximation; *synonyms* (*n*) approach, guess, affinity, estimate, (*v*) estimation.

námuvinnsla mining; *synonyms* (*n*) excavation, minelaying, digging, extraction, dig.

nánd 1. proximity; *synonyms* (*n*) nearness, neighborhood, propinquity, vicinity, contiguity; *antonym* (*n*) distance, **2.** contiguity; *synonyms* (*n*) adjacency, contact, contiguousness, proximity, confinity.

nándarmælir micrometer; *synonyms* (*n*) micron, megameter, megametre, (*v*) nanometer, centimeter.

nándhrif exposure; *synonyms* (*n*) display, exposition, detection, peril, (*v*) disclosure.

nanómetri nanometer; *synonyms* (*n*) micromillimeter, micromillimetre, millimicron, nanometre, (*v*) centimeter.

nár cadaver; *synonyms* (*n*) corpse, body, carcass, remains, skeleton.

nári groin; *synonyms* (*n*) groyne, ankle, breakwater, bulwark, elbow.

nasaop nostrils; *synonym* (*n*) nose.

nashyrningur rhino; *synonyms* (*n*) rhinoceros, salt, (*adj*) nostalgic.

nasir nostrils; *synonym* (*n*) nose.

natríumklóríð salt; *synonyms* (*adj*) salty, saline, briny, (*v*) cure, pickle.

náttblinda hemeralopia; *synonyms* (*n*) blearedness, nystagmus.

náttfall dew; *synonyms* (*n*) condensation, mist, freshness, humidity, moisture.

náttföt pyjamas; *synonyms* (*n*) pajamas, jammies.

nátthús binnacle; *synonym* (*n*) bittacle.

náttúra nature; *synonyms* (*n*) character, disposition, class, essence, (*adj*) kind.

náttúran nature; *synonyms* (*n*) character, disposition, class, essence, (*adj*) kind.

náttúrubundinn natural; *synonyms* (*adj*) inherent, innate, artless, instinctive, unaffected; *antonyms* (*adj*) artificial, affected, cultivated, false, refined.

náttúruhamfarir catastrophe; *synonyms* (*n*) calamity, disaster, adversity, cataclysm, tragedy.

náttúrulegur natural; *synonyms* (*adj*) inherent, innate, artless, instinctive, unaffected; *antonyms* (*adj*) artificial, affected, cultivated, false, refined.

náttúrulíf wildlife; *synonym* (*n*) life.

náttúruvætti monument; *synonyms* (*n*) memorial, headstone, column, record, tombstone.

náttúruvernd conservation; *synonyms* (*n*) maintenance, preservation, upkeep, keep, custody; *antonym* (*n*) destruction.

nauðasamningar composition; *synonyms* (*n*) arrangement, constitution, construction, texture, alloy.

nauðasamningur composition; *synonyms* (*n*) arrangement, constitution, construction, texture, alloy.

nauðbeita feather; *synonyms* (*n*) pen, pinion, plume, (*v*) fringe, cover.

nauðbundinn obligate; *synonyms* (*v*) force, bind, compel, oblige, (*adj*) bound.

nauðgengur deterministic; *synonym* (*adj*) determinist.

nauðgun rape; *synonyms* (*n*) assault, violation, colza, (*v*) outrage, pillage.

nauðhyggja determinism; *synonym* (*n*) fatalism.

nauðsynlegur obligatory; *synonyms* (*adj*) necessary, compulsory, imperative, binding, inevitable; *antonyms* (*adj*) optional, voluntary.

nauðþurftir subsistence; *synonyms* (*n*) being, existence, life, entity, maintenance.

nauðugur involuntary; *synonyms* (*adj*) automatic, instinctive, forced, mechanical, unconscious; *antonyms* (*adj*) deliberate, voluntary, intentional.

nauðung compulsion; *synonyms* (*n*) coercion, force, constraint, enforcement, pressure.

nauðungarsamningur composition; *synonyms* (*n*) arrangement, constitution, construction, texture, alloy.

nauður compulsion; *synonyms* (*n*) coercion, force, constraint, enforcement, pressure.

naut 1. cattle; *synonyms* (*n*) beast, cows, stock, kine, livestock, **2.** bull; *synonyms* (*n*) bullshit, bunk, hogwash, rot, (*adj*) blunder.

nautabauti beefsteak; *synonyms* (*v*) atole, avocado, banana, barbecue.

nautakjöt beef; *synonyms* (*n*) gripe, grumble, moan, grouse, (*v*) complain.

nautgripaklafi stanchion; *synonyms* (*n*) prop, brace, stake, buttress, pillar.

nautnalyf stimulant; *synonyms* (*n*) incentive, provocative, excitant, goad, impetus.

nautpeningur cow; *synonyms* (*v*) bully, intimidate, awe, browbeat, daunt.

neĉefa accessories; *synonyms* (*n*) fittings, equipment, accompaniments, garnishes, possession.

neðan below; *synonyms* (*adv*) beneath, under, (*prep*) underneath, (*adj*) low, after; *antonyms* (*prep*) above, over.

neðanjarðarlest 1. underground; *synonyms* (*adj*) clandestine, secret, covert, hidden, undercover, **2.** subway; *synonyms* (*n*) metro, underground, tube, tunnel, underpass, **3.** metro; *synonyms* (*n*) subway, pipe, resistance, tubing.

neðanmarka subliminal; *synonyms* (*adj*) unconscious, mental, hidden, intuitive, (*n*) subconscious.

neðansjávar submarine; *synonyms* (*n*) pigboat, sub, bomber, (*adj*) subaqueous, undersea.

neðri 1. inferior; *synonyms* (*adj*) bad, secondary, subordinate, humble, poor; *antonyms* (*adj*) better, choice, excellent, first-rate, (*n*) superior, **2.** lower; *synonyms* (*adj*) debase, (*v*) degrade, diminish, frown, (*n*) depress; *antonyms* (*v*) increase, raise.

nef 1. nose; *synonyms* (*n*) beak, hooter, nozzle, proboscis, (*v*) pry, **2.** shoulder; *synonyms* (*n*) elbow, (*v*) bear, carry, push, hold, **3.** beak; *synonyms* (*n*) bill, nose, snout, prow, bow.

nefeitla adenoid; *synonyms* (*adj*) adeniform, lymphoid.

nefhljóð nasal; *synonyms* (*adj*) rhinal, adenoidal, bony, (*v*) guttural, inarticulate.

nefkveðið nasal; *synonyms* (*adj*) rhinal, adenoidal, bony, (*v*) guttural, inarticulate.

nefkvef 1. rhinitis; *synonyms* (*n*) coryza, cold, **2.** coryza; *synonym* (*n*) rhinitis.

neflægur nasal; *synonyms* (*adj*) rhinal, adenoidal, bony, (*v*) guttural, inarticulate.

nefna 1. term; *synonyms* (*n*) name, expression, period, style, (*v*) call, **2.** designate; *synonyms* (*v*) denominate, allocate, appoint, assign, note, **3.** dub; *synonyms* (*v*) designate, christen, entitle, baptize, nickname, **4.** call; *synonyms* (*v*) cry, bellow, shout, bid, (*n*) appeal; *antonym* (*v*) dismiss, **5.** label; *synonyms* (*n*) brand, tag, title, (*v*) mark, classify.

nefnari denominator; *synonyms* (*n*) number, numerator.

nefnd 1. board; *synonyms* (*n*) council, bench, meal, panel, table; *antonym* (*v*) disembark, **2.** committee; *synonyms* (*n*) board, commission, consignee, trustee, cabinet, **3.** commission; *synonyms* (*n*) mission, delegation, job, mandate, (*v*) assign.

nefndarmaður commissioner; *synonyms* (*n*) commissary, delegate, agent, executive, official.

nefni identifier; *synonym* (*n*) qualifier.

nefslímubólga rhinitis; *synonyms* (*n*) coryza, cold.

nefstefna heading; *synonyms* (*n*) caption, bearing, drift, head, title.

neftróna neutron; *synonym* (*n*) electricity.

negla 1. stopper; *synonyms* (*n*) plug, stopple, (*v*) stop, block, clog, **2.** fix; *synonyms* (*v*) establish, assign, determine, (*n*) bind, (*adj*) ascertain; *antonyms* (*v*) break, unfasten.

negling 1. fixation; *synonyms* (*n*) obsession, fetish, fixing, mania, complex, **2.** latching; *synonyms* (*n*) latch, crossbow, lace, lasket, snare.

negravaĵo accessories; *synonyms* (*n*) fittings, equipment, accompaniments, garnishes, possession.

neikvæði negativism; *synonyms* (*n*) negativity, electronegativity, negativeness, opposition.

neikvæður 1. negative; *synonyms* (*adj*) minus, (*v*) gainsay, veto, deny, disavow; *antonyms* (*adj*) positive, optimistic, assenting, (*n*) affirmative, **2.** minus; *synonyms* (*n*) negative, (*v*) bereft, (*adj*) minor, less, lacking; *antonym* (*prep*) plus.

neikvætt negative; *synonyms* (*adj*) minus, (*v*) gainsay, veto, deny, disavow; *antonyms* (*adj*) positive, optimistic, assenting, (*n*) affirmative.

neind neutron; *synonym* (*n*) electricity.

neiskaut cathode; *synonym* (*n*) platinode.

neistabank 1. ping; *synonyms* (*n*) chink, ring, chime, jingle, (*v*) knock, **2**. detonation; *synonyms* (*n*) blast, explosion, burst, bang, (*v*) discharge.

neistadreifir distributor; *synonyms* (*n*) distributer, spreader, middleman, allocator, feeder.

neistahlaup spark; *synonyms* (*n*) flicker, (*v*) flash, sparkle, gleam, glint.

neistatruflanir static; *synonyms* (*adj*) immobile, inactive, motionless, inert, still; *antonym* (*adj*) moving.

neisti spark; *synonyms* (*n*) flicker, (*v*) flash, sparkle, gleam, glint.

neita 1. refuse; *synonyms* (*v*) deny, reject, decline, (*n*) garbage, trash; *antonym* (*v*) accept, **2**. reject; *synonyms* (*v*) refuse, disapprove, discard, dismiss, (*n*) cull; *antonyms* (*v*) approve, choose, select, acknowledge, grant, **3**. abnegate; *synonyms* (*v*) disown, disclaim, relinquish, renounce, abdicate, **4**. deny; *synonyms* (*v*) contradict, controvert, disavow, rebuff, abnegate; *antonyms* (*v*) admit, affirm, claim, declare, agree, **5**. decline; *synonyms* (*n*) decay, (*v*) wane, drop, fall, abate; *antonyms* (*n*) improvement, recovery, development, (*v*) increase, rise.

neitun negation; *synonyms* (*n*) denial, contradiction, negate, opposition, disavowal; *antonym* (*n*) acceptance.

neitunarorð negative; *synonyms* (*adj*) minus, (*v*) gainsay, veto, deny, disavow; *antonyms* (*adj*) positive, optimistic, assenting, (*n*) affirmative.

neitunarvald veto; *synonyms* (*n*) bar, (*v*) ban, disallow, forbid, prohibit; *antonyms* (*n*) approval, permission, (*v*) approve, permit, sanction.

nema 1. but; *synonyms* (*conj*) while, (*adv*) alone, only, though, barely, **2**. detect; *synonyms* (*v*) catch, discover, find, ascertain, discern.

nemandi pupil; *synonyms* (*n*) follower, learner, student, scholar, apprentice.

nemi 1. probe; *synonyms* (*n*) investigation, (*v*) examine, examination, explore, inspect, **2**. receptor, **3**. sensor; *synonyms* (*n*) detector, antenna, demodulator, tracer, (*adj*) sensory, **4**. receiver; *synonyms* (*n*) recipient, beneficiary, cashier, earpiece, headset; *antonym* (*n*) donor, **5**. counter; *synonyms* (*n*) buffet, bench, reverse, (*v*) reply, (*adj*) converse.

nerti vulnerability; *synonyms* (*n*) exposure, weakness, danger, vulnerableness, defenselessness; *antonym* (*n*) invulnerability.

nes peninsula; *synonyms* (*n*) chersonese, cape, promontory, continent, mainland.

nesjamennska insularity; *synonyms* (*n*) insularism, insulation, detachment, prejudice, bigotry.

net 1. screen; *synonyms* (*n*) shade, blind, (*v*) cover, shield, conceal, **2**. network; *synonyms* (*n*) net, grid, mesh, netting, reticulation, **3**. grid; *synonyms* (*n*) gridiron, grating, lattice, network, web, **4**. matrix; *synonyms* (*n*) die, alembic, caldron, crucible, groundmass.

netheimar cyberspace; *synonym* (*n*) net.

nethimna retina; *synonym* (*n*) white.

nethimnugróf fovea; *synonym* (*n*) foveola.

Netið 1. reticulum; *synonym* (*n*) net, **2**. internet; *synonyms* (*n*) cyberspace, internetwork.

netkerfi network; *synonyms* (*n*) net, grid, mesh, netting, reticulation.

netkort grid; *synonyms* (*n*) gridiron, grating, lattice, mesh, netting.

netlykkja lobe; *synonyms* (*n*) division, flap, limb, member, arm.

netskoðari navigator; *synonyms* (*n*) pilot, mariner, sailor, aviator, aeroplanist.

nettó net; *synonyms* (*n*) network, (*v*) mesh, clear, gain, make; *antonym* (*v*) gross.

netvörn firewall; *synonym* (*n*) baffle.

nevtróna neutron; *synonym* (*n*) electricity.

neyð emergency; *synonyms* (*n*) crisis, contingency, exigency, accident, (*adj*) extra.

neyða 1. require; *synonyms* (*v*) need, charge, crave, ask, claim, **2**. constrain; *synonyms* (*v*) coerce, compel, confine, drive, force; *antonym* (*v*) liberate, **3**. compel; *synonyms* (*v*) cause, command, constrain, enforce, make, **4**. mandate; *synonyms* (*n*) injunction, authority, behest, bidding, instruction, **5**. necessitate; *synonyms* (*v*) entail, involve, imply, demand, take.

neyðarástand emergency; *synonyms* (*n*) crisis, contingency, exigency, accident, (*adj*) extra.

neyðartilfelli emergency; *synonyms* (*n*) crisis, contingency, exigency, accident, (*adj*) extra.

neyðartilvik emergency; *synonyms* (*n*) crisis, contingency, exigency, accident, (*adj*) extra.

neysla 1. consumption; *synonyms* (*n*) expenditure, decline, use, expense, diminution, **2**. ingestion; *synonyms* (*n*) consumption, absorption, intake, drinking, eating.

neyta consume; *synonyms* (*v*) absorb, exhaust, spend, dissipate, use; *antonyms* (*v*) save, abstain.

neytandi consumer; *synonyms* (*n*) buyer, client, customer, patron, purchaser; *antonym* (*n*) seller.

nibba spine; *synonyms* (*n*) backbone, thorn, point, prickle, quill.

nibbulegur spinal; *synonyms* (*adj*) vertebral, rachidian, (*n*) anesthetic.

niðurbældur depressed; *synonyms* (adj) concave, low, blue, dejected, dispirited; *antonyms* (adj) cheerful, happy, convex.

niðurbrot 1. decomposition; *synonyms* (n) decay, rot, disintegration, dissolution, putrefaction, **2**. degradation; *synonyms* (n) abasement, fall, degeneracy, corruption, abjection.

niðurdrepandi depressive; *synonyms* (adj) blue, gloomy, oppressive, black, (v) depressing.

niðurfærir depressor; *synonyms* (n) hypotensor, oppressor.

niðurfærsla reduction; *synonyms* (n) contraction, decrease, decrement, diminution, rebate; *antonyms* (n) increase, growth, intensification, strengthening, expansion.

niðurfall drain; *synonyms* (n) ditch, culvert, (v) deplete, waste, (adj) cloaca; *antonym* (v) bolster.

niðurfallssýki epilepsy; *synonyms* (n) convulsion, (v) bustle, fits, fuss, hubbub.

niðurfelling suspension; *synonyms* (n) delay, interruption, abeyance, break, intermission.

niðurgangur diarrhea; *synonyms* (n) diarrhoea, lax, looseness.

niðurgreiðsla subsidy; *synonyms* (n) grant, aid, allowance, backing, support.

niðurlægja 1. decrease; *synonyms* (n) decline, cut, (v) abate, lessen, abridge; *antonyms* (n) growth, (v) increase, rise, grow, intensify, **2**. abase; *synonyms* (v) degrade, humble, debase, humiliate, (n) disgrace, **3**. abate; *synonyms* (v) subside, allay, bate, diminish, fade, **4**. lower; *synonyms* (v) frown, dip, abase, descend, (n) depress; *antonym* (v) raise.

niðurrif degradation; *synonyms* (n) abasement, fall, degeneracy, corruption, abjection.

niðurröðun 1. disposal; *synonyms* (n) disposition, administration, distribution, organization, sale, **2**. classification; *synonyms* (n) arrangement, categorization, class, grading, assortment; *antonym* (n) declassification.

niðursetning installation; *synonyms* (n) establishment, induction, facility, inauguration, initiation.

niðurseyðing condensation; *synonyms* (n) abridgement, digest, abridgment, capsule, compression.

niðurskipan classification; *synonyms* (n) arrangement, categorization, class, grading, assortment; *antonym* (n) declassification.

niðurskurður cut; *synonyms* (v) carve, chop, clip, (n) notch, slice; *antonyms* (v) increase, lengthen, (n) addition, extension.

niðurstaða 1. result; *synonyms* (n) consequence, fruit, issue, outcome, (v) ensue; *antonym* (v) cause, **2**. conclusion; *synonyms* (n) closure, close, end,

result, cessation; *antonyms* (n) beginning, start, opening, preface.

niðurstreymi subsidence; *synonyms* (n) collapse, ebb, remission, settlement, settling.

niðurstreymisstrókur chimney; *synonyms* (n) stack, flue, shaft, smokestack, vent.

niðursuða canning; *synonyms* (n) cladding, preservation.

nifteind neutron; *synonym* (n) electricity.

nikkel nickel; *synonyms* (n) moss, pile, quarter, rock, (v) plate.

nikkelhúða nickel; *synonyms* (n) moss, pile, quarter, rock, (v) plate.

nikull nickel; *synonyms* (n) moss, pile, quarter, rock, (v) plate.

nióbín niobium; *synonyms* (n) catnap, nazism.

níóbín niobium; *synonyms* (n) catnap, nazism.

níóbíum niobium; *synonyms* (n) catnap, nazism.

nippill nipple; *synonyms* (n) mammilla, teat, breast, dug, mamilla.

nítratmyndun nitrification; *synonym* (n) nitration.

nítrít nitrite; *synonym* (n) azotite.

nítrun nitrification; *synonym* (n) nitration.

nitur nitrogen; *synonyms* (n) n, newton, normality, north.

nítur nitrogen; *synonyms* (n) n, newton, normality, north.

níu nine; *synonyms* (n) niner, club, ennead, ace, cabaret.

níundarkvarði vernier; *synonym* (n) nonius.

níutíu ninety; *synonym* (n) xc.

njálgsýking oxyuriasis; *synonym* (n) enterobiasis.

njótandi beneficiary; *synonyms* (n) heir, inheritor, receiver, recipient, successor; *antonym* (n) donor.

njúton newton; *synonyms* (n) n, nitrogen, normality, north.

nóbelín nobelium; *synonym* (n) no.

nóbelíum nobelium; *synonym* (n) no.

nöf 1. spider; *synonyms* (n) lota, mussuk, schooner, spinner, adapter, **2**. boss; *synonyms* (n) chief, governor, head, (v) administer, govern, **3**. hub; *synonyms* (n) center, focus, heart, core, nucleus, **4**. nave; *synonyms* (n) chancel, choir, hub, omphalos, transept.

nóg 1. quite; *synonyms* (adv) altogether, absolutely, all, completely, entirely; *antonym* (adv) extremely, **2**. pretty; *synonyms* (adj) beautiful, fair, graceful, lovely, (n) nice; *antonym* (adj) ugly, **3**. rather; *synonyms* (adv) quite, enough, fairly, pretty, moderately, **4**. sufficiently; *synonyms* (adv) amply, fully, adequately, richly, abundantly; *antonym* (adv) insufficiently, **5**. enough; *synonyms* (n) adequacy, (adj) ample, sufficient, adequate, competent; *antonym* (adj) inadequate.

nögl 1. claw; *synonyms* (*n*) chela, hook, nipper, (*v*) clutch, lacerate, **2.** fingernail; *synonym* (*n*) claw, **3.** nail; *synonyms* (*n*) arrest, (*v*) catch, apprehend, collar, (*adj*) tack.

nógur adequate; *synonyms* (*adj*) sufficient, acceptable, enough, right, condign; *antonyms* (*adj*) inadequate, insufficient, unsatisfactory.

nokkuð some; *synonyms* (*adv*) nearly, rather, somewhat, about, (*adj*) few.

noradrenalín noradrenaline; *synonym* (*n*) norepinephrine.

norðlægur 1. boreal; *synonyms* (*adj*) northern, north, circumboreal, (*v*) hyemal, brumal, **2.** northern; *synonyms* (*adj*) northerly, boreal, arctic, hyperborean, frigid.

norðurljós aurora; *synonyms* (*n*) dawn, daybreak, morning, sunrise, prime.

Norðurpóll arctic; *synonyms* (*adj*) freezing, icy, polar, (*v*) glacial, boreal; *antonym* (*adj*) hot.

norma normalise; *synonyms* (*v*) normalize, renormalise, renormalize.

not 1. usage; *synonyms* (*n*) habit, practice, employment, (*v*) use, (*adj*) custom, **2.** utility; *synonyms* (*n*) usefulness, service, value, avail, purpose.

nót slot; *synonyms* (*n*) groove, place, notch, gap, (*v*) slit.

nota 1. employ; *synonyms* (*v*) apply, use, consume, engage, exercise; *antonyms* (*v*) fire, dismiss, **2.** use; *synonyms* (*n*) custom, practice, benefit, (*v*) employ, (*adj*) usage; *antonym* (*v*) conserve, **3.** utilize; *synonyms* (*v*) exert, utilise, take, harness, (*n*) exploit, **4.** deploy; *synonyms* (*v*) dilate, stretch, dispel, maneuver, marshal, **5.** apply; *synonyms* (*v*) dedicate, devote, ask, resort, (*n*) give.

notaður worn; *synonyms* (*adj*) haggard, shabby, tired, ragged, tattered; *antonyms* (*adj*) fresh, new.

notagildi utility; *synonyms* (*n*) use, usefulness, service, value, avail.

notahyggja pragmatism; *synonyms* (*n*) practicality, convenience, expediency, naturalism, pride.

notalegur homy; *synonyms* (*adj*) homelike, homely, homey, plain.

notandi 1. user; *synonyms* (*n*) consumer, buyer, exploiter, addict, customer; *antonym* (*n*) dealer, **2.** consumer; *synonyms* (*n*) client, patron, purchaser, shopper, (*adj*) capitalist; *antonym* (*n*) seller.

notendaskrá directory; *synonyms* (*n*) catalogue, file, list, record, handbook.

notendaviðmót view; *synonyms* (*n*) look, sight, judgment, opinion, (*v*) regard.

notfrjáls public; *synonyms* (*adj*) common, national, overt, civic, (*n*) folk; *antonyms* (*adj*) private, confidential, personal.

nothæfur 1. utility; *synonyms* (*n*) use, usefulness, service, value, avail, **2.** suitable; *synonyms* (*adj*) appropriate, fit, good, apt, proper; *antonyms* (*adj*) inappropriate, unsuitable, wrong, improper, **3.** functional; *synonyms* (*adj*) practical, effective, handy, operational, operative; *antonyms* (*adj*) nonfunctional, useless.

notkun 1. utility; *synonyms* (*n*) use, usefulness, service, value, avail, **2.** service; *synonyms* (*n*) help, aid, assistance, employment, (*v*) overhaul, **3.** usage; *synonyms* (*n*) habit, practice, method, convention, (*adj*) custom, **4.** consumption; *synonyms* (*n*) expenditure, decline, expense, diminution, exhaustion, **5.** application; *synonyms* (*n*) plea, appeal, appliance, concentration, demand.

notkunarréttur franchise; *synonyms* (*n*) exemption, liberty, freedom, immunity, privilege.

nótt 1. night; *synonyms* (*n*) dark, evening, dusk, darkness, (*adj*) nocturnal; *antonyms* (*adj*) day, light, **2.** nighttime; *synonyms* (*n*) night, iniquity, nightertale, shadow, (*adj*) nightly.

nú now; *synonyms* (*adv*) forthwith, here, immediately, currently, (*adj*) current; *antonyms* (*adv*) later, soon.

núa chafe; *synonyms* (*v*) rub, annoy, gall, grate, (*adj*) fret.

núast chafe; *synonyms* (*v*) rub, annoy, gall, grate, (*adj*) fret.

nudd attrition; *synonyms* (*n*) friction, abrasion, contrition, corrosion, detrition.

nudda rub; *synonyms* (*v*) fray, grate, gall, chafe, (*n*) check.

núðlur macaroni; *synonyms* (*n*) coxcomb, fop, beau, exquisite, dude.

núgildandi 1. topical; *synonyms* (*adj*) current, contemporary, new, topic, (*n*) local, **2.** present; *synonyms* (*adj*) grant, confer, (*n*) gift, donation, (*v*) bestow; *antonyms* (*adj*) missing, (*n*) past, future, (*v*) withdraw, (*adv*) absent, **3.** contemporary; *synonyms* (*adj*) contemporaneous, modern, present, recent, (*n*) coeval; *antonyms* (*adj*) old, old-fashioned, **4.** current; *synonyms* (*adj*) common, fashionable, (*n*) flow, stream, (*prep*) course; *antonyms* (*adj*) obsolete, previous.

nukso 1. nuts; *synonyms* (*adj*) crazy, insane, balmy, crackers, nutty; *antonyms* (*adj*) sane, sensible, **2.** nut; *synonyms* (*n*) lunatic, crackpot, crank, eccentric, egg.

núll 1. zero; *synonyms* (*n*) nil, nothing, nobody, cipher, naught, **2.** nil; *synonyms* (*n*) zero, aught, cypher, nihil, zilch, **3.** neutral; *synonyms* (*adj*) disinterested, impartial, indifferent, dispassionate, (*n*) neuter; *antonyms* (*adj*) biased, aromatic, colorful, **4.** nought; *synonyms* (*adj*) no, (*n*) nix, null, nada.

núllstöð 1. root; *synonyms* (*n*) base, foundation, origin, basis, (*v*) establish, **2.** zero; *synonyms* (*n*) nil, nothing, nobody, cipher, naught.

núllsvið swing; *synonyms* (*v*) sway, fluctuate, oscillate, dangle, hang.

númer number; *synonyms* (*n*) count, amount, (*v*) calculate, aggregate, enumerate.

núna now; *synonyms* (*adv*) forthwith, here, immediately, currently, (*adj*) current; *antonyms* (*adv*) later, soon.

núningskraftur friction; *synonyms* (*n*) discord, abrasion, attrition, dispute, rub.

núningslaus smooth; *synonyms* (*adj*) easy, calm, level, oily, (*v*) quiet; *antonyms* (*adj*) rough, uneven, abrasive, coarse, crumpled.

núningsmótstaða friction; *synonyms* (*n*) discord, abrasion, attrition, dispute, rub.

núningsviðnám friction; *synonyms* (*n*) discord, abrasion, attrition, dispute, rub.

núningur 1. chafing; *synonyms* (*n*) friction, abrasion, rubbing, resistance, (*adj*) impatient, **2.** friction; *synonyms* (*n*) discord, attrition, dispute, rub, disagreement.

núrétta update; *synonyms* (*n*) updating, (*v*) inform, modernize, renovate, revise.

núrétting update; *synonyms* (*n*) updating, (*v*) inform, modernize, renovate, revise.

nurta papilla; *synonyms* (*n*) wart, boob, knocker.

nútíð present; *synonyms* (*adj*) grant, confer, (*n*) gift, donation, (*v*) bestow; *antonyms* (*adj*) missing, (*n*) past, future, (*v*) withdraw, (*adv*) absent.

nútímalegur 1. topical; *synonyms* (*adj*) current, contemporary, new, topic, (*n*) local, **2.** present; *synonyms* (*adj*) grant, confer, (*n*) gift, donation, (*v*) bestow; *antonyms* (*adj*) missing, (*n*) past, future, (*v*) withdraw, (*adv*) absent, **3.** contemporary; *synonyms* (*adj*) contemporaneous, modern, present, recent, (*n*) coeval; *antonyms* (*adj*) old, old-fashioned, **4.** current; *synonyms* (*adj*) common, fashionable, (*n*) flow, stream, (*prep*) course; *antonyms* (*adj*) obsolete, previous.

nútímavæðing modernization; *synonyms* (*n*) modernisation, innovation, renovation, alteration, change.

nútími recent; *synonyms* (*adj*) late, modern, new, novel, latest; *antonym* (*adj*) old.

núverandi 1. topical; *synonyms* (*adj*) current, contemporary, new, topic, (*n*) local, **2.** present; *synonyms* (*adj*) grant, confer, (*n*) gift, donation, (*v*) bestow; *antonyms* (*adj*) missing, (*n*) past, future, (*v*) withdraw, (*adv*) absent, **3.** contemporary; *synonyms* (*adj*) contemporaneous, modern, present, recent, (*n*) coeval; *antonyms* (*adj*) old, old-fashioned, **4.** current; *synonyms* (*adj*) common, fashionable,

(*n*) flow, stream, (*prep*) course; *antonyms* (*adj*) obsolete, previous.

núvirðing discounting; *synonym* (*n*) capitalization.

nýbreytni innovation; *synonyms* (*n*) change, alteration, invention, mutation, novelty.

nýburakassi incubator; *synonyms* (*n*) brooder, hatcher, couveuse, plotter.

nýbyggð settlement; *synonyms* (*n*) decision, accommodation, colony, hamlet, payment.

nýfæddur newborn; *synonyms* (*adj*) infant, (*n*) babe, baby, neonate, child.

nýgengi incidence; *synonyms* (*n*) occurrence, commonness, incidency, pervasiveness, attack.

nýglæða refresh; *synonyms* (*v*) freshen, air, enliven, invigorate, update.

nýglæðing refresh; *synonyms* (*v*) freshen, air, enliven, invigorate, update.

nýjun propagation; *synonyms* (*n*) distribution, diffusion, generation, dissemination, extension.

nýjung innovation; *synonyms* (*n*) change, alteration, invention, mutation, novelty.

nýlenda 1. colony; *synonyms* (*n*) settlement, community, plantation, dependency, village, **2.** settlement; *synonyms* (*n*) decision, accommodation, colony, hamlet, payment.

nýliðun recruitment; *synonyms* (*n*) employment, enrollment, enlisting, mobilization.

nýmæli innovation; *synonyms* (*n*) change, alteration, invention, mutation, novelty.

nýmyndun synthesis; *synonyms* (*n*) combination, fusion, compound, incorporation, mixture; *antonym* (*n*) separation.

nýpa hip; *synonyms* (*n*) haunch, coxa, (*adj*) hep, stylish, chic.

nýr 1. new; *synonyms* (*adj*) green, modern, novel, original, (*adv*) fresh; *antonyms* (*adj*) old, familiar, outgoing, second-hand, traditional, **2.** novel; *synonyms* (*adj*) (*n*) new, curious, different, unprecedented.

nýra kidney; *synonyms* (*n*) class, variety, feather, kind, nature.

nýráðning recruitment; *synonyms* (*n*) employment, enrollment, enlisting, mobilization.

nýrakvilli nephropathy; *synonym* (*n*) nephrosis.

nýrapípnaskemmd nephrosis; *synonym* (*n*) nephropathy.

nýrilmergvaki adrenaline; *synonyms* (*n*) epinephrin, epinephrine.

nýskipan restructuring; *synonyms* (*n*) reorganization, improvement, reform, renovation, alteration.

nýsköpun 1. modernization; *synonyms* (*n*) modernisation, innovation, renovation, alteration, change, **2**. innovation; *synonyms* (*n*) invention, mutation, novelty, variation, creation.

nýskráning recruitment; *synonyms* (*n*) employment, enrollment, enlisting, mobilization.

nýsmíð synthesis; *synonyms* (*n*) combination, fusion, compound, incorporation, mixture; *antonym* (*n*) separation.

nýta 1. utilize; *synonyms* (*v*) employ, use, apply, exert, (*n*) exploit, **2**. deploy; *synonyms* (*v*) dilate, stretch, dispel, maneuver, marshal, **3**. apply; *synonyms* (*v*) dedicate, devote, ask, consume, (*n*) give, **4**. exploit; *synonyms* (*v*) act, (*n*) deed, achievement, feat, accomplishment.

nýting 1. utilization; *synonyms* (*n*) use, application, employment, exercise, utilisation, **2**. efficiency; *synonyms* (*n*) capability, effectiveness, ability, efficacy, effect; *antonyms* (*n*) inefficiency, incompetence, largeness, **3**. exploitation; *synonyms* (*n*) abuse, development, misuse, operation, using.

nýtinn 1. efficient; *synonyms* (*adj*) effectual, competent, effective, able, capable; *antonyms* (*adj*) incompetent, inefficient, **2**. economic; *synonyms* (*adj*) commercial, financial, profitable, efficient, economical.

nýtir user; *synonyms* (*n*) consumer, buyer, exploiter, addict, customer; *antonym* (*n*) dealer.

nytjagróður fruit; *synonyms* (*n*) effect, crop, outgrowth, product, (*v*) result.

nytjahyggja utilitarianism; *synonym* (*n*) expediency.

nytjar 1. service; *synonyms* (*n*) help, aid, assistance, avail, (*v*) overhaul, **2**. utility; *synonyms* (*n*) use, usefulness, service, value, purpose.

nytjastefna 1. utilitarianism; *synonym* (*n*) expediency, **2**. functionalism.

nýtni efficiency; *synonyms* (*n*) capability, effectiveness, ability, efficacy, effect; *antonyms* (*n*) inefficiency, incompetence, largeness.

nytsemi utility; *synonyms* (*n*) use, usefulness, service, value, avail.

nytsemishyggja utilitarianism; *synonym* (*n*) expediency.

nýuppfinning innovation; *synonyms* (*n*) change, alteration, invention, mutation, novelty.

nýyrði neologism; *synonyms* (*n*) neology, coinage, jargon, mintage, neologianism.

O

objekto 1. things; *synonyms* (*n*) gear, stuff, belongings, equipment, garb, **2**. thing; *synonyms* (*n*) matter, affair, event, object, occurrence.

oddbaugóttur elliptic; *synonyms* (*adj*) elliptical, oval, ovate, oviform, ovoid.

odddreginn acuminate; *synonyms* (*adj*) pointed, acute, sharp, (*v*) sharpen.

oddhvass 1. acuminate; *synonyms* (*adj*) pointed, acute, sharp, (*v*) sharpen, **2**. acute; *synonyms* (*adj*) incisive, intense, keen, penetrating, critical; *antonyms* (*adj*) dull, obtuse.

oddi spit; *synonyms* (*n*) broach, saliva, (*v*) drizzle, impale, expectorate.

oddpunktur vertex; *synonyms* (*n*) top, apex, crown, peak, summit.

oddur 1. point; *synonyms* (*n*) place, grade, peak, nib, (*v*) head, **2**. apex; *synonyms* (*n*) top, vertex, acme, crown, apices; *antonyms* (*n*) base, nadir.

of 1. too; *synonyms* (*adv*) also, likewise, besides, excessively, over, **2**. overly; *synonyms* (*adv*) too, extremely, unduly, disproportionately, (*adj*) careless.

ofanfall fallout; *synonyms* (*n*) effect, consequence, consequences, outcome, repercussion.

ofanjarðar aerial; *synonyms* (*adj*) airy, aery, ethereal, unreal, (*n*) antenna.

ofanvarp projection; *synonyms* (*n*) bulge, hump, jut, prominence, protuberance.

ofanvörpun projection; *synonyms* (*n*) bulge, hump, jut, prominence, protuberance.

ofauki redundancy; *synonyms* (*n*) excess, redundance, diffuseness, verbiage, (*v*) pleonasm; *antonym* (*n*) employment.

ofaukið redundant; *synonyms* (*adj*) excessive, extra, needless, superfluous, excess; *antonym* (*adj*) necessary.

ofbætur overcompensation; *synonym* (*n*) recompense.

ofbirta glare; *synonyms* (*n*) blaze, brilliance, (*v*) beam, flame, flash; *antonym* (*v*) smile.

ofdrykkjumaður alcoholic; *synonyms* (*adj*) strong, (*n*) drunk, boozer, dipsomaniac, lush; *antonym* (*adj*) soft.

offita 1. adiposity; *synonyms* (*n*) adiposeness, adiposis, fatness, fattiness, weight, **2**. obesity; *synonyms* (*n*) fleshiness, corpulency, fat, chubbiness, (*adj*) corpulence; *antonym* (*n*) slenderness.

offramleiðsla overproduction; *synonyms* (*n*)
depression, overflow, overrun.

offylli engorgement; *synonyms* (*n*) load, sickener,
surfeit, bulge, bump.

offylling flooding; *synonyms* (*n*) flood, overflow,
cataclysm, (*adj*) overflowing, bloated.

ofgnótt 1. surplus; *synonyms* (*adj*) extra, (*n*) excess,
remainder, balance, overabundance; *antonyms* (*n*)
necessary, lack, shortage, scarcity, **2.** excess;
synonyms (*n*) surplus, dissipation, extravagance,
plethora, abundance; *antonyms* (*n*) restraint,
moderation, dearth, shortfall.

ofhlaða overload; *synonyms* (*n*) overburden, (*v*)
burden, overcharge, encumber, oppress.

ofhleðsla overload; *synonyms* (*n*) overburden, (*v*)
burden, overcharge, encumber, oppress.

ofhvörf hyperbole; *synonyms* (*n*) exaggeration,
amplification, overstatement, magnification, strain;
antonym (*n*) understatement.

ofkæling 1. chill; *synonyms* (*adj*) cold, bleak, icy,
chilly, (*v*) cool; *antonyms* (*n*) warmth, (*v*) heat,
warm, **2.** hypothermia; *synonym* (*n*) hypothermy.

oflæti mania; *synonyms* (*n*) craze, delirium, (*adj*)
frenzy, insanity, lunacy.

ofloðna hirsutism; *synonym* (*n*) hirsuteness.

ofn 1. radiator; *synonyms* (*n*) heater, stove, furnace,
warmer, **2.** stove; *synonyms* (*n*) range, ambit,
chain, compass, grasp, **3.** furnace; *synonyms* (*n*)
hearth, oven, chimney, **4.** oven; *synonyms* (*n*) kiln,
boiler.

ofnæmi allergy; *synonyms* (*n*) antipathy, aversion.

ofnautn abuse; *synonyms* (*n*) affront, misuse, harm,
(*v*) insult, mistreat; *antonyms* (*v*) praise, respect.

ofraun overload; *synonyms* (*n*) overburden, (*v*)
burden, overcharge, encumber, oppress.

ofreisa stall; *synonyms* (*n*) booth, bench, barn, carrel,
compartment.

ofris stall; *synonyms* (*n*) booth, bench, barn, carrel,
compartment.

ofrísa stall; *synonyms* (*n*) booth, bench, barn, carrel,
compartment.

ofsagleði exaltation; *synonyms* (*n*) elation,
apotheosis, ecstasy, praise, (*adj*) elevation.

ofsahræðsla panic; *synonyms* (*n*) alarm, dismay,
horror, scare, (*adj*) consternation; *antonym* (*n*)
composure.

ofsakláði 1. urticaria; *synonyms* (*n*) hives, urtication,
2. hives; *synonyms* (*n*) rash, urticaria,
inflammation, irritation, itchiness.

ofsalegur fierce; *synonyms* (*adj*) bitter, violent, acute,
cruel, ferocious; *antonyms* (*adj*) gentle, mild.

ofskynjun hallucination; *synonyms* (*n*) illusion,
dream, apparition, vision, (*adj*) delusion.

ofstækkun hypertrophy; *synonym* (*n*) tympany.

ofstæling hypertonia; *synonyms* (*n*) hypertonicity,
hypertonus.

oft 1. regularly; *synonyms* (*adv*) often, generally,
always, customarily, frequently; *antonyms* (*adv*)
inconsistently, unusually, constantly, **2.**
commonly; *synonyms* (*adv*) normally, ordinarily,
usually, currently, habitually; *antonyms* (*adv*)
rarely, uncommonly, **3.** often; *synonyms* (*adv*) oft,
much, oftentimes, ofttimes, repeatedly; *antonym*
(*adv*) seldom, **4.** oftentimes, **5.** frequently;
synonyms (*adv*) commonly, continually, hourly,
mostly, regularly; *antonym* (*adv*) infrequently.

ofurálag 1. overstress; *synonyms* (*v*) exaggerate,
magnify, overemphasize, overstate,
overemphasise, **2.** overload; *synonyms* (*n*)
overburden, (*v*) burden, overcharge, encumber,
oppress.

ofurhiti hyperthermia; *synonym* (*n*) hyperthermy.

ofurkvöl hyperalgesia; *synonym* (*n*) hyperalgia.

ofurmagni squid; *synonyms* (*n*) calamary, calamari,
sleevefish.

ofurnæmi hypersensitivity; *synonyms* (*n*)
hypersensibility, reaction, sensitivity, antipathy,
aversion.

ofursætur saccharine; *synonyms* (*adj*) sweet, syrupy,
sugary, treacly, cloying.

ofursársaukanæmi hyperalgesia; *synonym* (*n*)
hyperalgia.

ofurslef salivation; *synonyms* (*n*) ptyalism, jellyfish,
slobber, slabber.

ofurtölva supercomputer; *synonyms* (*n*) computer,
mainframe, processor, laptop, notebook.

ofvaxinn luxuriant; *synonyms* (*adj*) lush, abundant,
lavish, exuberant, thick; *antonym* (*adj*) barren.

ofvirkur hyperactive; *synonyms* (*adj*) frantic,
overactive, furious, harried, hysterical.

ofvöxtur 1. vegetation; *synonyms* (*n*) flora, growth,
plants, foliage, quietism, **2.** hypertrophy;
synonym (*n*) tympany.

og and; *synonyms* (*conj*) with, (*adv*) also, (*prep*) plus,
including, (*adj*) more.

ogun conjunction; *synonyms* (*n*) combination,
association, coincidence, concurrence, coalition.

ok yoke; *synonyms* (*n*) pair, (*v*) couple, link, connect,
(*adj*) brace.

okfruma zygote; *synonyms* (*n*) metaplasm, ontogeny,
ovary, ovum, oxidation.

oki 1. yoke; *synonyms* (*n*) pair, (*v*) couple, link,
connect, (*adj*) brace, **2.** cleat; *synonyms* (*n*) wedge,
batten, cam, finger.

okþráðlufasi zygotene; *synonym* (*n*) synaptene.

okun conjugation; *synonyms* (*n*) junction, union,
coupling, declension, (*v*) conjunction.

okur usury; *synonyms* (*v*) usance, accustom, application, custom, employ.

okurlán usury; *synonyms* (*v*) usance, accustom, application, custom, employ.

okurvextir usury; *synonyms* (*v*) usance, accustom, application, custom, employ.

olía 1. oil; *synonyms* (*n*) petroleum, fat, ointment, (*v*) lubricate, anoint, **2.** lube.

olífa olive; *synonyms* (*adj*) glaucous, green, (*n*) cherry, drupe, elderberry.

olíubiða sump; *synonyms* (*n*) bog, cesspit, cesspool, sink, swamp.

olíuborinn fat; *synonyms* (*adj*) stout, corpulent, dense, thick, (*n*) avoirdupois; *antonyms* (*adj*) thin, slim, skinny, slender.

olíugeymir bunker; *synonyms* (*n*) bin, dugout, trap, ambuscade, ambush.

olíugjöf accelerator; *synonyms* (*n*) catalyst, gas, throttle, gun, promotor.

olíugöng gallery; *synonyms* (*n*) balcony, audience, drift, veranda, circle.

olíupanna sump; *synonyms* (*n*) bog, cesspit, cesspool, sink, swamp.

olíurepja rape; *synonyms* (*n*) assault, violation, colza, (*v*) outrage, pillage.

Olíuskip tanker; *synonyms* (*n*) oiler, fighter.

olnbogi elbow; *synonyms* (*n*) bend, cubitus, (*v*) poke, jostle, nudge.

op 1. stoma; *synonyms* (*n*) pore, aperture, hole, stomate, **2.** pore; *synonyms* (*n*) interstice, stoma, aorta, artery, (*v*) center, **3.** port; *synonyms* (*n*) harbor, haven, asylum, carriage, (*adj*) larboard; *antonym* (*n*) starboard, **4.** aperture; *synonyms* (*n*) breach, opening, puncture, slit, cleft, **5.** gap; *synonyms* (*n*) break, crack, crevice, fissure, chasm.

opbreidd aperture; *synonyms* (*n*) hole, breach, opening, puncture, slit.

opinber 1. public; *synonyms* (*adj*) common, national, overt, civic, (*n*) folk; *antonyms* (*adj*) private, confidential, personal, **2.** overt; *synonyms* (*adj*) blatant, open, obvious, apparent, clear; *antonyms* (*adj*) camouflaged, concealed, covert, indirect, **3.** official; *synonyms* (*adj*) formal, (*n*) officer, minister, bureaucrat, (*v*) authoritative; *antonyms* (*adj*) unofficial, illegal, informal.

opinn 1. patent; *synonyms* (*adj*) obvious, overt, apparent, evident, manifest; *antonym* (*adj*) unclear, **2.** open; *synonyms* (*adj*) frank, artless, exposed, (*n*) candid, clear; *antonyms* (*adj*) devious, secretive, concealed, (*v*) shut, (*tr v*) close, **3.** lax; *synonyms* (*adj*) slack, careless, flaccid, loose, (*v*) frail; *antonyms* (*adj*) strict, careful, severe.

opna 1. open; *synonyms* (*adj*) frank, obvious, artless, (*n*) candid, clear; *antonyms* (*adj*) devious, secretive, concealed, (*v*) shut, (*tr v*) close, **2.** clear; *synonyms* (*adj*) clean, certain, (*v*) bright, acquit, absolute; *antonyms* (*adj*) cloudy, opaque, unclear, dark, fuzzy, **3.** outcrop; *synonyms* (*n*) outcropping, cape, crest, edge, headland; *antonym* (*n*) depression.

opnun 1. dehiscence; *synonyms* (*n*) pandiculation, patefaction, hiation, oscitancy, yawning, **2.** opening; *synonyms* (*n*) gap, mouth, aperture, break, beginning; *antonyms* (*n*) end, closing, exit, finale, (*adj*) final.

oponanto opossum; *synonyms* (*n*) possum, pedimane, phalanger.

opþvermál aperture; *synonyms* (*n*) hole, breach, opening, puncture, slit.

opvídd aperture; *synonyms* (*n*) hole, breach, opening, puncture, slit.

orð word; *synonyms* (*n*) promise, news, tidings, advice, (*v*) formulate.

orða decoration; *synonyms* (*n*) adornment, award, garnish, medal, ornament.

ordabóg dictionary; *synonyms* (*n*) lexicon, wordbook, book, language, list.

orðabók 1. vocabulary; *synonyms* (*n*) dictionary, lexicon, wordbook, words, language, **2.** dictionary; *synonyms* (*n*) book, list, onomasticon, reference.

orðaklipping clipping; *synonyms* (*n*) clip, trimming, cutting, snip, trim.

orðasafn 1. dictionary; *synonyms* (*n*) lexicon, wordbook, book, language, list, **2.** lexicon; *synonyms* (*n*) dictionary, vocabulary, glossary, context, jargon.

orðaskrín thesaurus; *synonyms* (*n*) glossary, lexicon, treasury, book, list.

orðastæða collocation; *synonyms* (*n*) collection, classification, junction, apposition, juxtaposition.

orðastýfing clipping; *synonyms* (*n*) clip, trimming, cutting, snip, trim.

orðhlutafræði morphology; *synonyms* (*n*) accidence, anatomy, geomorphology, taxonomy, botany.

orðmerki logo; *synonyms* (*n*) emblem, logotype, sign, mark, badge.

orðmyndunaratferli neologism; *synonyms* (*n*) neology, coinage, jargon, mintage, neologianism.

orðrómur grapevine; *synonyms* (*n*) grape, vine, gossip, buzz, hearsay.

orðsending 1. communication; *synonyms* (*n*) announcement, commerce, communicating, contact, conversation, **2.** memorandum; *synonyms* (*n*) memo, note, memorial, entry, letter.

orðsifjafræði etymology; *synonyms* (*n*) derivation, (*v*) absorb, acquisition, attainment, engross.

orðstöðulykill concordance; *synonyms* (*n*) accord, agreement, concord, accordance, concert.

orgel organ; *synonyms* (*n*) instrument, member, limb, agency, harmonium.

orka energy; *synonyms* (*n*) animation, dash, force, life, spirit; *antonyms* (*n*) lethargy, apathy, exhaustion, tiredness, weakness.

orkubreytir transducer; *synonyms* (*n*) sensor, transductor.

orkugæfur 1. exoergic, 2. exothermic; *synonym* (*adj*) exothermal.

orkugjafi fuel; *synonyms* (*n*) firewood, combustible, firing, (*v*) fire, arouse.

orkukorn mitochondrion; *synonym* (*n*) chondriosome.

orkukræfur endothermic; *synonym* (*adj*) endothermal.

orkuleysing neutralization; *synonyms* (*n*) neutralisation, counteraction, nullification, annulment, chagrin.

orkunýting efficiency; *synonyms* (*n*) capability, effectiveness, ability, efficacy, effect; *antonyms* (*n*) inefficiency, incompetence, largeness.

orkutap dissipation; *synonyms* (*n*) debauchery, diffusion, dissolution, waste, dissemination.

ormaeyðandi anthelmintic; *synonyms* (*adj*) helminthic, anthelminthic, antiscolic, parasiticidal, (*n*) vermifuge.

ormalegur vermicular; *synonyms* (*adj*) vermiculated, molluscous, vermiculate, vermiform.

ormalyf 1. vermifuge; *synonyms* (*n*) anthelmintic, helminthic, anthelminthic, helminthagogue, 2. vermicide, 3. anthelmintic; *synonyms* (*adj*) antiscolic, parasiticidal, vermifugal, (*n*) vermifuge.

ormlaga 1. vermiform; *synonyms* (*v*) serpent, (*adj*) helminthoid, lumbriciform, vermicular, wormlike, 2. vermicular; *synonyms* (*adj*) vermiculated, molluscous, vermiculate, vermiform.

ormur 1. worm; *synonyms* (*v*) squirm, wriggle, twist, helix, (*adj*) insect, 2. snake; *synonyms* (*n*) ophidian, serpent, (*n*) meander, wind, coil, 3. serpent; *synonyms* (*n*) snake, viper, reptile, bassoon, contrafagotto, 4. mole; *synonyms* (*n*) breakwater, jetty, freckle, bulwark, groyne.

orniþín ornithine; *synonym* (*n*) ornithin.

ornitín ornithine; *synonym* (*n*) ornithin.

orsaka 1. provoke; *synonyms* (*v*) excite, incite, defy, offend, anger; *antonyms* (*v*) calm, mollify, please, soothe, 2. pose; *synonyms* (*v*) attitudinize, masquerade, (*n*) attitude, position, affectation, 3. cause; *synonyms* (*n*) case, action, (*v*) make, breed,

do; *antonym* (*n*) consequence, 4. activate; *synonyms* (*v*) actuate, start, trigger, aerate, animate.

orsakaflétta nexus; *synonyms* (*n*) link, bond, connection, concatenation, connexion.

orsakafræði etiology; *synonyms* (*n*) aetiology, attribution, rationale, anatomy, (*adj*) nosology.

orsakalögmál causality; *synonym* (*n*) origin.

orsakasamband causality; *synonym* (*n*) origin.

orsakasamhengi causality; *synonym* (*n*) origin.

orsakatrú determinism; *synonym* (*n*) fatalism.

orsakavaldur agent; *synonyms* (*n*) agency, broker, deputy, medium, (*v*) actor.

orsök 1. reason; *synonyms* (*n*) mind, account, intellect, occasion, (*v*) cause, 2. cause; *synonyms* (*n*) case, action, (*v*) make, breed, do; *antonym* (*n*) consequence.

osmín osmium; *synonyms* (*n*) os, bone.

osmósa osmosis; *synonym* (*n*) absorption.

osmósuflæði osmosis; *synonym* (*n*) absorption.

ostefni casein; *synonyms* (*n*) paracasein, (*v*) crassamentum.

osteopati osteopath; *synonym* (*n*) osteopathist.

ostur cheese; *synonyms* (*n*) cheeseflower, exaggeration, cake, (*v*) misrepresent.

oxa oxidize; *synonyms* (*v*) oxidise, rust, oxidate, oxygenize, corrode.

oxast oxidize; *synonyms* (*v*) oxidise, rust, oxidate, oxygenize, corrode.

oxíð oxide; *synonym* (*n*) oxid.

oxun oxidation; *synonyms* (*n*) calcination, rust, oxygenation, oxidization, corrosion.

oxytósín oxytocin; *synonym* (*n*) ocytocin.

Ó

óaðgætinn inadvertent; *synonyms* (*adj*) accidental, careless, heedless, casual, chance; *antonyms* (*adj*) intentional, deliberate.

óaðskiljanlegur integral; *synonyms* (*adj*) complete, entire, inherent, full, (*n*) whole.

óætisfíkn pica; *synonyms* (*n*) em, geophagia, geophagy, magpies, mut.

óafturkallanlegur irreversible; *synonyms* (*adj*) irreparable, unchangeable, (*v*) irrevocable, irretrievable, indefeasible; *antonym* (*adj*) reversible.

óafturkvæmur irreversible; *synonyms* (*adj*) irreparable, unchangeable, (*v*) irrevocable, irretrievable, indefeasible; *antonym* (*adj*) reversible.

óafturrækur irreversible; *synonyms* (*adj*) irreparable, unchangeable, (*v*) irrevocable, irretrievable, indefeasible; *antonym* (*adj*) reversible.

óákveðni indecision; *synonyms* (*n*) doubt, hesitation, irresolution, indecisiveness, (*adj*) suspense; *antonyms* (*n*) decisiveness, determination, resolve.

óánægður 1. discontented; *synonyms* (*adj*) discontent, disaffected, disgruntled, displeased, (*v*) querulous; *antonyms* (*adj*) contented, pleased, happy, satisfied, **2.** disgruntled; *synonyms* (*adj*) discontented, dissatisfied, disappointed, grumpy, unsatisfied, **3.** displeased; *synonyms* (*v*) pained, (*adj*) angry, annoyed, irritated, peeved, **4.** dissatisfied; *synonyms* (*adj*) malcontent, complaining; *antonym* (*adj*) content.

óáreiðanlegur 1. untrustworthy; *synonyms* (*adj*) unreliable, unfaithful, treacherous, faithless, slippery; *antonyms* (*adj*) trustworthy, reliable, dependable, faithful, honest, **2.** unreliable; *synonyms* (*adj*) irresponsible, uncertain, undependable, precarious, dubious; *antonyms* (*adj*) consistent, constant, **3.** dodgy; *synonyms* (*adj*) crafty, dicey, chancy, cunning, unsafe, **4.** dicey; *synonyms* (*adj*) risky, dangerous, dodgy, hazardous, perilous; *antonym* (*adj*) safe.

óbærileiki intolerance; *synonyms* (*n*) bigotry, impatience, discrimination, fanaticism, bias; *antonyms* (*n*) tolerance, lenience, broadmindedness.

óbeinn implicit; *synonyms* (*adj*) silent, tacit, understood, undeclared, unsaid; *antonyms* (*adj*) explicit, direct.

óbeit 1. aversion; *synonyms* (*n*) antipathy, distaste, abhorrence, disgust, (*v*) abomination; *antonyms* (*n*) liking, attraction, love, **2.** abomination; *synonyms* (*n*) atrocity, detestation, execration, hate, hatred, **3.** atrocity; *synonyms* (*n*) enormity, brutality, atrociousness, barbarism, (*adj*) outrage.

óbilkvæmur aperiodic; *synonym* (*adj*) nonperiodic.

óbjagaður unbiased; *synonyms* (*adj*) fair, impartial, indifferent, neutral, just; *antonyms* (*adj*) biased, prejudiced.

óblandaður concentrated; *synonyms* (*adj*) strong, intense, compact, condensed, deep; *antonyms* (*adj*) dispersed, weak, uncondensed, unsaturated.

óblandanlegur immiscible; *synonyms* (*adj*) nonadhesive, unmixable; *antonym* (*adj*) miscible.

óbókfærður unrecorded; *synonyms* (*adj*) live, bouncy, hot, lively, (*v*) unregistered; *antonym* (*adj*) recorded.

óbókfært unrecorded; *synonyms* (*adj*) live, bouncy, hot, lively, (*v*) unregistered; *antonym* (*adj*) recorded.

óbrennanlegur incombustible; *synonyms* (*adj*) fireproof, noncombustible, asbestine, apyrous, asbestic; *antonym* (*adj*) combustible.

óbreyta invariant; *synonyms* (*adj*) changeless, constant, steady, unvarying, firm.

óbreytanlegur 1. invariable; *synonyms* (*adj*) constant, fixed, consistent, even, immutable; *antonym* (*adj*) variable, **2.** irreversible; *synonyms* (*adj*) irreparable, unchangeable, (*v*) irrevocable, irretrievable, indefeasible; *antonym* (*adj*) reversible.

óbreytilegur invariant; *synonyms* (*adj*) changeless, constant, steady, unvarying, firm.

óbreytinn invariant; *synonyms* (*adj*) changeless, constant, steady, unvarying, firm.

óburður mole; *synonyms* (*n*) breakwater, jetty, freckle, bulwark, groyne.

óbyggð 1. wilderness; *synonyms* (*n*) desert, wild, wasteland, solitude, (*v*) waste, **2.** desert; *synonyms* (*v*) abandon, escape, defect, (*adj*) barren, desolate; *antonyms* (*n*) bog, (*v*) stay.

ódæðismaður felon; *synonyms* (*n*) criminal, convict, crook, culprit, malefactor.

óðal 1. territory; *synonyms* (*n*) district, dominion, area, field, land, **2.** domain; *synonyms* (*n*) country, department, realm, kingdom, arena; *antonym* (*n*) range.

óðjurt hemlock; *synonyms* (*n*) henbane, nightshade.

ódugur impotence; *synonyms* (*n*) disability, inability, weakness, feebleness, debility.

óður 1. rabid; *synonyms* (*adj*) furious, fanatical, mad, fanatic, (*v*) fierce, **2.** mad; *synonyms* (*adj*) frantic, frenzied, demented, foolish, insane; *antonyms* (*adj*) sane, calm, sensible, **3.** manic; *synonyms* (*adj*) wild, crazy, delirious, frenetic, maniacal.

óeðlilegur abnormal; *synonyms* (*adj*) aberrant, anomalous, atypical, irregular, monstrous; *antonyms* (*adj*) normal, typical, usual.

óekta dummy; *synonyms* (*adj*) sham, spurious, (*n*) counterfeit, model, puppet.

óeldfimur incombustible; *synonyms* (*adj*) fireproof, noncombustible, asbestine, apyrous, asbestic; *antonym* (*adj*) combustible.

óendanlegt infinity; *synonyms* (*n*) eternity, infinite, boundlessness, immensity, infiniteness.

óendanlegur infinite; *synonyms* (*adj*) absolute, boundless, countless, endless, eternal; *antonyms* (*adj*) finite, limited, restricted.

óendanleiki infinity; *synonyms* (*n*) eternity, infinite, boundlessness, immensity, infiniteness.

ófalsaður authentic; *synonyms* (*adj*) actual, genuine, accurate, real, right; *antonyms* (*adj*) bogus, fake, unrealistic.

ófarir catastrophe; *synonyms* (*n*) calamity, disaster, adversity, cataclysm, tragedy.

ófeiti inanition; *synonyms* (*n*) emptiness, lethargy, lassitude, (*adj*) exhaustion, collapse.

ófélagslegur asocial; *synonyms* (*adj*) antisocial, thoughtless.

ófjaðrandi inelastic; *synonyms* (adj) stiff, rigid, inflexible, unyielding, firm; *antonym* (adj) elastic.

ófjósemi infertility; *synonyms* (n) sterility, dysgenesis, incompatibility, unproductiveness, antisepsis; *antonyms* (n) fertility, fruitfulness.

óformlegur informal; *synonyms* (adj) colloquial, familiar, casual, easy, free; *antonyms* (adj) formal, authorized, official.

ófreskigáfa psi; *synonym* (n) j.

ófriður 1. war; *synonyms* (n) combat, battle, fight, warfare, conflict; *antonyms* (n) peace, (v) ceasefire, **2.** warfare; *synonyms* (n) war, contest, fighting, action, hostility.

ófrjór 1. sterile; *synonyms* (adj) infertile, barren, fruitless, effete, (v) abortive; *antonyms* (adj) fertile, unhygienic, **2.** barren; *synonyms* (adj) sterile, deserted, arid, dry, (v) bare; *antonyms* (adj) lush, productive.

ófrjósamur sterile; *synonyms* (adj) infertile, barren, fruitless, effete, (v) abortive; *antonyms* (adj) fertile, unhygienic.

ófrjósemi 1. sterility; *synonyms* (n) infertility, barrenness, impotence, infecundity, antisepsis; *antonym* (n) fertility, **2.** poverty; *synonyms* (n) lack, distress, (v) destitution, need, penury; *antonyms* (n) wealth, riches, **3.** infertility; *synonyms* (n) sterility, dysgenesis, incompatibility, unproductiveness, asepsis; *antonym* (n) fruitfulness.

ófrumbjarga heterotrophic; *synonyms* (adj) holozoic, heterotroph.

ófullburða abortive; *synonyms* (adj) fruitless, futile, stillborn, unsuccessful, useless; *antonym* (adj) successful.

ófullkominn incomplete; *synonyms* (adj) defective, deficient, faulty, imperfect, inadequate; *antonyms* (adj) complete, finished, whole.

ófullnægjandi 1. deficient; *synonyms* (adj) defective, inadequate, wanting, imperfect, scanty; *antonyms* (adj) adequate, sufficient, **2.** incomplete; *synonyms* (adj) deficient, faulty, halfway, lacking, short; *antonyms* (adj) complete, finished, whole.

ófyrirséð contingency; *synonyms* (n) accident, chance, eventuality, possibility, circumstance.

ógætni carelessness; *synonyms* (n) neglect, negligence, inattention, indifference, nonchalance; *antonyms* (n) alertness, attention, care, caution, vigilance.

ógagnhverfur irreversible; *synonyms* (adj) irreparable, unchangeable, (v) irrevocable, irretrievable, indefeasible; *antonym* (adj) reversible.

ógagnsæi opacity; *synonyms* (n) obscurity, opaqueness, cloudiness, murkiness, opaque; *antonym* (n) clearness.

ógagnsær opaque; *synonyms* (adj) cloudy, dense, dull, muddy, obscure; *antonyms* (adj) clear, transparent, see-through.

ógegnsæi opacity; *synonyms* (n) obscurity, opaqueness, cloudiness, murkiness, opaque; *antonym* (n) clearness.

ógegnsær opaque; *synonyms* (adj) cloudy, dense, dull, muddy, obscure; *antonyms* (adj) clear, transparent, see-through.

ógiftur 1. unmarried; *synonyms* (adj) single, unwedded, sole, alone, individual; *antonyms* (adj) married, attached, marital, **2.** single; *synonyms* (adj) only, celibate, one, odd, particular; *antonyms* (adj) double, multiple.

ógilda 1. undo; *synonyms* (v) loosen, annul, open, cancel, disentangle; *antonyms* (v) fasten, attach, close, do, wrap, **2.** annul; *synonyms* (v) abrogate, abolish, repeal, rescind, (adj) nullify; *antonym* (v) validate, **3.** cancel; *synonyms* (v) erase, expunge, invalidate, remit, revoke, **4.** extinguish; *synonyms* (v) destroy, exterminate, quench, annihilate, douse; *antonyms* (v) light, ignite.

ógilding 1. undoing; *synonyms* (n) downfall, ruin, destruction, loss, curse, **2.** undo; *synonyms* (v) loosen, annul, open, cancel, disentangle; *antonyms* (v) fasten, attach, close, do, wrap, **3.** abolition; *synonyms* (n) abolishment, annulment, ending, annihilation, cancellation; *antonym* (n) reinstatement, **4.** abolishment; *synonym* (n) abolition, **5.** abrogation; *synonyms* (n) repeal, desertion.

ógiltur void; *synonyms* (adj) empty, null, (n) hollow, blank, emptiness; *antonyms* (adj) valid, full, (v) validate.

ógjaldfær insolvent; *synonyms* (n) bankrupt, (adj) broke, destitute, impoverished, penniless; *antonym* (adj) solvent.

ógjaldfærni insolvency; *synonyms* (n) bankruptcy, ruin, poverty, hardship, impoverishment; *antonym* (n) solvency.

ógleði nausea; *synonyms* (n) disgust, sickness, queasiness, (v) aversion, loathing; *antonym* (n) attraction.

ógn terror; *synonyms* (n) alarm, dread, fright, awe, dismay.

ógnarstjórn terrorism; *synonyms* (n) disorder, murder, nihilism, tyranny, (adj) intimidation.

ógnarverk terrorism; *synonyms* (n) disorder, murder, nihilism, tyranny, (adj) intimidation.

ógnvekjandi alarming; *synonyms* (adj) frightful, scary, awful, formidable, shocking; *antonyms* (adj) reassuring, soothing.

ógreindur simple; *synonyms* (*adj*) plain, homely, pure, elementary, (*v*) clear; *antonyms* (*adj*) complex, complicated, compound, elaborate, difficult.

ógrynni mass; *synonyms* (*n*) bulk, heap, crowd, cluster, (*v*) flock.

óháður 1. autonomous; *synonyms* (*adj*) independent, sovereign, autonomic, free, separate; *antonym* (*adj*) dependent, **2.** independent; *synonyms* (*adj*) autonomous, substantive, impartial, nonpartisan, (*n*) freelance; *antonym* (*adj*) simultaneous, **3.** objective; *synonyms* (*adj*) dispassionate, (*n*) aim, mark, goal, object; *antonyms* (*adj*) biased, subjective.

óhæði independence; *synonyms* (*n*) autonomy, freedom, liberty, independency, individuality; *antonyms* (*n*) dependence, childhood.

óhæfi incompetence; *synonyms* (*n*) incapacity, inability, inaptitude, disqualification, inadequacy; *antonyms* (*n*) competence, efficiency.

óhamingjusamur 1. sad; *synonyms* (*adj*) dreary, dismal, distressing, gloomy, miserable; *antonyms* (*adj*) happy, cheerful, joyful, brave, cheery, **2.** unhappy; *synonyms* (*adj*) unfortunate, depressed, melancholy, sad, disconsolate; *antonyms* (*adj*) pleased, satisfied.

óhapp 1. accident; *synonyms* (*n*) chance, casualty, coincidence, crash, fortune, **2.** mishap; *synonyms* (*n*) accident, adversity, misfortune, calamity, disaster, **3.** failure; *synonyms* (*n*) bankruptcy, failing, breakdown, decline, deficiency; *antonyms* (*n*) success, achievement, hit, winner, victory.

óháttbundið aperiodic; *synonym* (*adj*) nonperiodic.

óheiðarlegur 1. underhand; *synonyms* (*adj*) surreptitious, stealthy, furtive, clandestine, sly, **2.** crooked; *synonyms* (*adj*) bent, awry, corrupt, irregular, askew; *antonyms* (*adj*) straight, honest, even, principled, **3.** dishonest; *synonyms* (*adj*) crooked, deceitful, crafty, fraudulent, underhand; *antonyms* (*adj*) truthful, sincere, aboveboard, sporting, **4.** deceitful; *synonyms* (*adj*) dishonest, false, insincere, artful, (*adv*) counterfeit; *antonyms* (*adj*) straightforward, genuine, trustworthy.

óheimilt unauthorized; *synonyms* (*adj*) illegal, illicit, unauthorised, illegitimate, wildcat; *antonyms* (*adj*) authorized, official.

óheppinn unfortunate; *synonyms* (*adj*) inauspicious, poor, sad, bad, disastrous; *antonyms* (*adj*) fortunate, lucky.

óhlaðinn 1. unloaded; *synonyms* (*adj*) unobstructed, untrammeled, unfraught; *antonym* (*adj*) loaded, **2.** neutral; *synonyms* (*adj*) disinterested, impartial, indifferent, dispassionate, (*n*) neuter; *antonyms* (*adj*) biased, aromatic, colorful.

óhlutbundinn abstract; *synonyms* (*adj*) theoretical, (*v*) abridge, (*n*) synopsis, abridgement, digest; *antonym* (*adj*) concrete.

óhlutdrægur unbiased; *synonyms* (*adj*) fair, impartial, indifferent, neutral, just; *antonyms* (*adj*) biased, prejudiced.

óhlutstæður abstract; *synonyms* (*adj*) theoretical, (*v*) abridge, (*n*) synopsis, abridgement, digest; *antonym* (*adj*) concrete.

óhollur morbid; *synonyms* (*adj*) diseased, ghoulish, gruesome, macabre, (*v*) sickly.

óhraustlegur unhealthy; *synonyms* (*adj*) morbid, harmful, insanitary, sickly, ailing; *antonyms* (*adj*) healthy, fit, hygienic.

óhreinindi impurity; *synonyms* (*n*) contamination, filth, impureness, pollution, defilement.

óhreinka 1. soil; *synonyms* (*n*) ground, dirt, (*v*) smudge, blot, contaminate; *antonym* (*v*) clean, **2.** contaminate; *synonyms* (*v*) pollute, infect, taint, adulterate, befoul; *antonyms* (*v*) cleanse, purify, sterilize.

óhreinkun 1. pollution; *synonyms* (*n*) contamination, filth, infection, befoulment, (*adj*) defilement, **2.** contamination; *synonyms* (*n*) contagion, pollution, contaminant, dirtying, corruption; *antonym* (*n*) decontamination, **3.** doping; *synonyms* (*n*) swabbing, doctoring, activating.

óhvarfgjarn 1. stabile; *synonyms* (*adj*) immovable, immoveable, constant, static, equable, **2.** inactive; *synonyms* (*adj*) idle, dead, dormant, dull, inert; *antonyms* (*adj*) active, lively, moving.

óhverfanlegur irreversible; *synonyms* (*adj*) irreparable, unchangeable, (*v*) irrevocable, irretrievable, indefeasible; *antonym* (*adj*) reversible.

óhverfur irreversible; *synonyms* (*adj*) irreparable, unchangeable, (*v*) irrevocable, irretrievable, indefeasible; *antonym* (*adj*) reversible.

ójafn 1. uneven; *synonyms* (*adj*) rough, unequal, irregular, jagged, erratic; *antonyms* (*adj*) even, smooth, straight, equal, symmetrical, **2.** unequal; *synonyms* (*adj*) dissimilar, different, unlike, inadequate, lopsided.

ójafna inequality; *synonyms* (*n*) disparity, difference, disproportion, dissimilitude, (*adj*) odds; *antonyms* (*n*) equality, justice, parity.

ójafnt rough; *synonyms* (*adj*) coarse, hard, harsh, raw, crude; *antonyms* (*adj*) gentle, smooth, polished, precise, refined.

ójafnvægi 1. unbalance; *synonyms* (*v*) derange, craze, (*n*) imbalance, derangement, insanity; *antonym* (*v*) balance, **2.** imbalance; *synonyms* (*n*) asymmetry, disproportion, disparity, inequality, unbalance.

ójöfnuður inequality; *synonyms* (*n*) disparity, difference, disproportion, dissimilitude, (*adj*) odds; *antonyms* (*n*) equality, justice, parity.

ókristallaður amorphous; *synonyms* (*adj*) shapeless, formless, unformed, amphibious, epicene; *antonyms* (*adj*) distinct, defined.

ókurteis 1. vulgar; *synonyms* (*adj*) coarse, rude, uncouth, common, low; *antonyms* (*adj*) refined, sophisticated, tasteful, polite, **2**. rude; *synonyms* (*adj*) gross, rough, impudent, blunt, (*n*) abrupt; *antonyms* (*adj*) respectful, chivalrous, courteous, civil, decent, **3**. impolite; *synonyms* (*adj*) discourteous, gruff, brusque, churlish, disrespectful.

ókyrrð turbulence; *synonyms* (*n*) disorder, tumult, confusion, agitation, commotion; *antonyms* (*n*) calm, peace.

ólæsi illiteracy; *synonyms* (*n*) ignorance, illiterature; *antonym* (*n*) literacy.

ólag malfunction; *synonyms* (*n*) breakdown, bug, trouble, defect, stoppage.

ólaskaður undamaged; *synonyms* (*adj*) intact, whole, entire, safe, sound; *antonyms* (*adj*) hurt, damaged.

ólekur impermeable; *synonyms* (*adj*) impenetrable, impervious, close, rainproof, tight; *antonyms* (*adj*) permeable, absorbent.

óleysanlegur insoluble; *synonyms* (*adj*) indissoluble, inextricable, insolvable, irresoluble, firm; *antonym* (*adj*) soluble.

ólga turbulence; *synonyms* (*n*) disorder, tumult, confusion, agitation, commotion; *antonyms* (*n*) calm, peace.

ólífa olive; *synonyms* (*adj*) glaucous, green, (*n*) cherry, drupe, elderberry.

ólífrænn 1. abiotic, **2**. inorganic; *synonyms* (*adj*) lifeless, dead, inorganical, inorganized, inert.

ólíkur different; *synonyms* (*adj*) another, assorted, dissimilar, unusual, various; *antonyms* (*adj*) similar, corresponding, equal, identical, like.

ólita achromatic; *synonyms* (*adj*) colorless, white, neutral, aplanatic, snowy.

óljós 1. faint; *synonyms* (*adj*) collapse, dim, dizzy, feeble, indistinct; *antonyms* (*adj*) distinct, strong, clear, obvious, considerable, **2**. obscure; *synonyms* (*adj*) cloudy, dark, gloomy, ambiguous, concealed; *antonyms* (*adj*) noticeable, simple, mainstream, (*v*) clarify, **3**. implicit; *synonyms* (*adj*) silent, tacit, understood, undeclared, unsaid; *antonyms* (*adj*) explicit, direct.

ólöglegur illegal; *synonyms* (*adj*) criminal, forbidden, prohibited, unauthorized, unlawful; *antonyms* (*adj*) legal, lawful, honest, legitimate, official.

ólögmætur illegal; *synonyms* (*adj*) criminal, forbidden, prohibited, unauthorized, unlawful;

antonyms (*adj*) legal, lawful, honest, legitimate, official.

ólotubundinn aperiodic; *synonym* (*adj*) nonperiodic.

ómeðvitaður vegetative; *synonyms* (*adj*) vegetal, vegetational, fertile, vegetive, (*v*) vegetating.

ómega omega; *synonyms* (*n*) last, conclusion, ending, finale, finis.

ómegin syncope; *synonyms* (*n*) swoon, faint, syncopation, fainting, deliquium.

ómerkilegur inferior; *synonyms* (*adj*) bad, secondary, subordinate, humble, poor; *antonyms* (*adj*) better, choice, excellent, first-rate, (*n*) superior.

ómettaður unsaturated; *synonym* (*adj*) diluted; *antonym* (*adj*) saturated.

óminni amnesia; *synonyms* (*n*) forgetfulness, oblivion, blackout, brownout, dimout.

ómissandi 1. integral; *synonyms* (*adj*) complete, entire, inherent, full, (*n*) whole, **2**. essential; *synonyms* (*adj*) necessary, crucial, important, requisite, constituent; *antonyms* (*adj*) minor, secondary, (*n*) inessential, optional, option.

ómótaður amorphous; *synonyms* (*adj*) shapeless, formless, unformed, amphibious, epicene; *antonyms* (*adj*) distinct, defined.

ómsjá sonar; *synonyms* (*n*) asdic, beacon.

ómskoðun sonar; *synonyms* (*n*) asdic, beacon.

ómun reverberation; *synonyms* (*n*) repercussion, echo, reflection, rebound, (*v*) reflexion.

ómur 1. resonance; *synonyms* (*n*) vibrancy, reverberation, ringing, sonority, vibration, **2**. reverberation; *synonyms* (*n*) repercussion, echo, reflection, rebound, (*v*) reflexion.

ónæma desensitize; *synonyms* (*v*) blunt, desensitise, numb, deaden, drug.

ónæmi 1. resistance; *synonyms* (*n*) opposition, endurance, friction, immunity, impedance; *antonyms* (*n*) smoothness, agreement, obedience, susceptibility, **2**. immunity; *synonyms* (*n*) exemption, freedom, franchise, dispensation, privilege; *antonym* (*n*) vulnerability.

ónæming 1. vaccination; *synonyms* (*n*) inoculation, immunization, prevention, shot, injection, **2**. desensitization; *synonym* (*n*) desensitisation, **3**. immunization; *synonyms* (*n*) immunisation, vaccine, jab.

ónæmingarefni vaccine; *synonyms* (*n*) vaccination, immunization, inoculation, (*adj*) animal, bovine.

ónæmingargeta antigenicity; *synonyms* (*n*) immunogenicity, potency.

ónæmisaðgerð immunization; *synonyms* (*n*) immunisation, inoculation, shot, vaccine, prevention.

ónæmisbæling immunosuppression; *synonym* (*n*) immunodepression.

ónæmisblóðvatn antiserum; *synonym* (n) antitoxin.

ónæmisfræðingur immunologist; *synonym* (n) serologist.

ónæmisglæðir adjuvant; *synonyms* (adj) auxiliary, accessory, adjunct, ancillary, subsidiary.

ónæmissermi antiserum; *synonym* (n) antitoxin.

ónæmissetja inoculate; *synonyms* (v) infuse, imbue, immunize, impregnate, instill.

ónæmissetning inoculation; *synonyms* (n) injection, immunization, vaccination, (v) indoctrination, inculcation.

ónæmur 1. resistant; *synonyms* (adj) immune, impervious, durable, tough, (v) resistive; *antonyms* (adj) fragile, permeable, submissive, agreeable, 2. inelastic; *synonyms* (adj) stiff, rigid, inflexible, unyielding, firm; *antonym* (adj) elastic, 3. immune; *synonyms* (adj) exempt, free, resistant, sacred, secure.

óneyti impotence; *synonyms* (n) disability, inability, weakness, feebleness, debility.

ónógur inferior; *synonyms* (adj) bad, secondary, subordinate, humble, poor; *antonyms* (adj) better, choice, excellent, first-rate, (n) superior.

ónotakennd dysphoria; *synonyms* (n) fidget, sadness, dissatisfaction, restlessness, uneasiness.

óráð delirium; *synonyms* (n) frenzy, craze, insanity, mania, (adj) fury.

óráðinn neutral; *synonyms* (adj) disinterested, impartial, indifferent, dispassionate, (n) neuter; *antonyms* (adj) biased, aromatic, colorful.

óræður irrational; *synonyms* (adj) foolish, absurd, inconsistent, silly, blind; *antonyms* (adj) rational, logical.

óreganó oregano; *synonyms* (n) marjoram, cinnamon, mace, nutmeg, cloves.

óregla 1. disorder; *synonyms* (n) ailment, complaint, clutter, (v) derange, disarray; *antonyms* (n) orderliness, calm, peace, (v) order, 2. anomaly; *synonyms* (n) abnormality, aberration, anomalousness, deviation, abnormity.

óregluhreyfing ataxia; *synonyms* (n) chaos, disarray, disorder, ataxy, clutter.

óreglulegur 1. asymmetric; *synonyms* (adj) asymmetrical, unbalanced, crooked, (v) unsymmetric, irregular, 2. erratic; *synonyms* (adj) capricious, changeable, eccentric, freakish, broken; *antonyms* (adj) consistent, constant, certain, dependable, predictable, 3. irregular; *synonyms* (adj) abnormal, atypical, anomalous, erratic, desultory; *antonyms* (adj) regular, even, normal, smooth, symmetrical.

óreiða 1. derangement; *synonyms* (n) delirium, disorder, disturbance, insanity, lunacy, 2. disorder; *synonyms* (n) ailment, complaint, clutter,

(v) derange, disarray; *antonyms* (n) orderliness, calm, peace, (v) order, 3. entropy; *synonyms* (n) chaos, data, information, randomness, haphazardness.

óreiðustig entropy; *synonyms* (n) chaos, data, information, randomness, haphazardness.

órigan oregano; *synonyms* (n) marjoram, cinnamon, mace, nutmeg, cloves.

óriganó oregano; *synonyms* (n) marjoram, cinnamon, mace, nutmeg, cloves.

órökrænn irrational; *synonyms* (adj) foolish, absurd, inconsistent, silly, blind; *antonyms* (adj) rational, logical.

órósemi agitation; *synonyms* (n) disturbance, excitement, tumult, commotion, convulsion; *antonyms* (n) calmness, calm, serenity.

ós mouth (munnur); *synonyms* (n) jaw, lip, aperture, lips, (v) grimace.

ósamfellanleiki incompatibility; *synonyms* (n) incongruity, inconsistency, disagreement, repugnance, antipathy; *antonym* (n) compatibility.

ósamhverfa asymmetry; *synonyms* (n) irregularity, dissymmetry, imbalance, skewness, disproportion; *antonym* (n) symmetry.

ósamhverfur asymmetric; *synonyms* (adj) asymmetrical, unbalanced, crooked, (v) unsymmetric, irregular.

ósamkynja heterogenous; *synonyms* (adj) heterogeneous, heterogene, heterogenetic.

ósamlægi nonconformity; *synonyms* (n) dissent, disagreement, unorthodoxy, inconformity, difference; *antonyms* (n) normality, conformity.

ósamleitinn divergent; *synonyms* (adj) different, differing, dissimilar, distinct, conflicting; *antonyms* (adj) similar, convergent.

ósamleitni divergence; *synonyms* (n) discrepancy, difference, disagreement, dissimilarity, variance; *antonyms* (n) convergence, meeting, agreement, amalgamation.

ósamloka 1. asymmetrical; *synonyms* (adj) asymmetric, unbalanced, cockeyed, crooked, irregular; *antonyms* (adj) symmetrical, equal, regular, 2. asymmetric; *synonyms* (adj) asymmetrical, disproportionate, (v) unsymmetric, askew, awry.

ósammiðja eccentric; *synonyms* (adj) bizarre, odd, wacky, abnormal, anomalous; *antonyms* (adj) normal, ordinary, (n) conformist.

ósamræmi 1. discordance; *synonyms* (n) discord, nonconformity, discrepancy, difference, disagreement, 2. nonconformity; *synonyms* (n) dissent, unorthodoxy, inconformity, eccentricity, heresy; *antonyms* (n) normality, conformity.

ósamræmur discordant; *synonyms* (*adj*) contrary, conflicting, dissonant, discrepant, disharmonious; *antonyms* (*adj*) harmonious, musical, pleasant-sounding, melodic.

ósamrýmanlegur incompatible; *synonyms* (*adj*) contradictory, conflicting, discordant, discrepant, inappropriate; *antonyms* (*adj*) compatible, consistent, identical, matching.

ósamrýmanleiki incompatibility; *synonyms* (*n*) incongruity, inconsistency, disagreement, repugnance, antipathy; *antonym* (*n*) compatibility.

ósamstæður heterologous; *synonyms* (*adj*) heterologic, heterological, different.

ósamþykkt unauthorized; *synonyms* (*adj*) illegal, illicit, unauthorised, illegitimate, wildcat; *antonyms* (*adj*) authorized, official.

ósannur 1. untrue; *synonyms* (*adj*) false, erroneous, unfaithful, disloyal, incorrect; *antonyms* (*adj*) faithful, true, factual, valid, 2. fictitious; *synonyms* (*adj*) bogus, assumed, counterfeit, fictional, artificial; *antonym* (*adj*) real, 3. false; *synonyms* (*adj*) bastard, untrue, deceitful, dishonest, deceptive; *antonyms* (*adj*) correct, genuine, natural, truthful, honest.

ósérplægni altruism; *synonyms* (*n*) selflessness, benevolence, charity, unselfishness, generosity; *antonyms* (*n*) self-interest, selfishness.

óseyrar delta; *synonyms* (*n*) chersonese, continent, inlet, mainland, mouth.

óseyri delta; *synonyms* (*n*) chersonese, continent, inlet, mainland, mouth.

óshólmar delta; *synonyms* (*n*) chersonese, continent, inlet, mainland, mouth.

ósjálfráður 1. vegetative; *synonyms* (*adj*) vegetal, vegetational, fertile, vegetive, (*v*) vegetating, 2. autonomic; *synonym* (*adj*) free, 3. involuntary; *synonyms* (*adj*) automatic, instinctive, forced, mechanical, unconscious; *antonyms* (*adj*) deliberate, voluntary, intentional.

ósjálfstæði 1. dependence; *synonyms* (*n*) belief, confidence, reliance, addiction, dependance; *antonyms* (*n*) independence, self-government, self-sufficiency, 2. dependency; *synonyms* (*n*) dependence, colony, relationship, settlement, (*adj*) contingency.

ósjálfstæður dependent; *synonyms* (*adj*) subject, subordinate, contingent, (*n*) dependant, charge; *antonyms* (*adj*) independent, self-governing, self-sufficient.

ósk 1. wish; *synonyms* (*v*) desire, hope, like, (*n*) want, (*adv*) will; *antonyms* (*v*) dislike, hate, 2. want; *synonyms* (*v*) need, (*n*) lack, poverty, wish, deficiency, 3. desire; *synonyms* (*n*) ambition, aspiration, (*v*) fancy, aspire, seek; *antonyms* (*n*) aversion, reality.

óska 1. wish; *synonyms* (*v*) desire, hope, like, (*n*) want, (*adv*) will; *antonyms* (*v*) dislike, hate, 2. desire; *synonyms* (*n*) ambition, aspiration, wish, (*v*) fancy, aspire; *antonyms* (*n*) aversion, reality.

óskaðlegur innocuous; *synonyms* (*adj*) harmless, innocent, inoffensive, safe, innoxious.

óskapnaður chaos; *synonyms* (*n*) anarchy, bedlam, clutter, disarray, disorder; *antonyms* (*n*) order, peace, orderliness, regulation.

óskemmdur undamaged; *synonyms* (*adj*) intact, whole, entire, safe, sound; *antonyms* (*adj*) hurt, damaged.

óskilgreindur unspecified; *synonyms* (*adj*) undefined, anonymous, indeterminate, unidentified, indefinite; *antonym* (*adj*) specified.

óskiptur 1. unitary; *synonyms* (*adj*) single, one, sole, solitary, united, 2. integral; *synonyms* (*adj*) complete, entire, inherent, full, (*n*) whole.

óskipulagður informal; *synonyms* (*adj*) colloquial, familiar, casual, easy, free; *antonyms* (*adj*) formal, authorized, official.

óskyldraæxlun 1. outbreeding, 2. exogamy; *synonyms* (*n*) intermarriage, endogamy, inmarriage.

óskynjanlegur insensible; *synonyms* (*adj*) callous, imperceptible, numb, unconscious, unfeeling; *antonym* (*adj*) sensible.

óskýr faint; *synonyms* (*adj*) collapse, dim, dizzy, feeble, indistinct; *antonyms* (*adj*) distinct, strong, clear, obvious, considerable.

ósléttur 1. rough; *synonyms* (*adj*) coarse, hard, harsh, raw, crude; *antonyms* (*adj*) gentle, smooth, polished, precise, refined, 2. uneven; *synonyms* (*adj*) rough, unequal, irregular, jagged, erratic; *antonyms* (*adj*) even, straight, equal, symmetrical.

óslitinn continuous; *synonyms* (*adj*) constant, continual, ceaseless, endless, perpetual; *antonyms* (*adj*) intermittent, temporary, discontinuous, sporadic.

óson ozone; *synonym* (*n*) air.

óstarfhæfur idle; *synonyms* (*adj*) inactive, indolent, lazy, free, baseless; *antonyms* (*adj*) busy, active, employed, (*v*) change.

óstjórn 1. anarchism; *synonyms* (*n*) anarchy, disorder, chaos, lawlessness, riot, 2. anarchy; *synonyms* (*n*) muddle, confusion, pandemonium, bedlam, disarray; *antonym* (*n*) order.

óstöðugleiki 1. volatility; *synonyms* (*n*) fickleness, instability, flightiness, buoyancy, capriciousness, 2. instability; *synonyms* (*n*) fluctuation, unreliability, flux, changeability, (*adj*) fugacity; *antonyms* (*n*) stability, calm, 3. lability; 4. fluctuation; *synonyms* (*n*) variation, vicissitude, wavering, deviation, hesitation.

óstöðugt unsettled; *synonyms* (*adj*) uncertain, changeable, doubtful, undecided, unfixed; *antonyms* (*adj*) settled, confident, definite.

óstöðugur 1. unstable; *synonyms* (*adj*) changeable, precarious, insecure, shaky, unsettled; *antonyms* (*adj*) stable, steady, constant, **2.** erratic; *synonyms* (*adj*) capricious, eccentric, irregular, freakish, broken; *antonyms* (*adj*) consistent, certain, dependable, predictable, regular, **3.** labile; *synonym* (*adj*) unstable.

ósvífinn 1. rude; *synonyms* (*adj*) gross, rough, impudent, blunt, coarse; *antonyms* (*adj*) polite, respectful, chivalrous, courteous, refined, **2.** brazen; *synonyms* (*adj*) audacious, barefaced, brassy, insolent, blatant; *antonyms* (*adj*) shy, abashed, **3.** impertinent; *synonyms* (*adj*) fresh, pert, saucy, forward, brash; *antonym* (*adj*) well-behaved.

ósvikinn 1. authentic; *synonyms* (*adj*) actual, genuine, accurate, real, right; *antonyms* (*adj*) bogus, fake, unrealistic, **2.** genuine; *synonyms* (*adj*) authentic, sincere, true, unsophisticated, candid; *antonyms* (*adj*) insincere, affected, artificial, dishonest, false.

ótær cloudy; *synonyms* (*adj*) dull, gloomy, murky, nebulous, opaque; *antonyms* (*adj*) clear, bright, cloudless, sunny.

óteyginn inelastic; *synonyms* (*adj*) stiff, rigid, inflexible, unyielding, firm; *antonym* (*adj*) elastic.

óþægilegur 1. unpleasant; *synonyms* (*adj*) disagreeable, harsh, nasty, obnoxious, offensive; *antonyms* (*adj*) pleasant, agreeable, delightful, attractive, comfortable, **2.** unpalatable; *synonyms* (*adj*) distasteful, unpleasant, unsavory, insipid, unappetizing; *antonym* (*adj*) palatable, **3.** repellent; *synonyms* (*adj*) hateful, disgusting, foul, loathsome, (*v*) odious; *antonyms* (*adj*) alluring, appealing, charming, **4.** distasteful; *synonyms* (*adj*) unwelcome, ugly, revolting, undesirable, dirty; *antonym* (*adj*) tasteful, **5.** bleak; *synonyms* (*adj*) austere, bare, barren, cold, dreary; *antonyms* (*adj*) cheerful, hopeful, lush, mild, sunny.

óþéttur permeable; *synonyms* (*adj*) pervious, porous, absorbent, spongy, gritty; *antonyms* (*adj*) impermeable, resistant, waterproof, water-resistant, watertight.

óþjáll refractory; *synonyms* (*adj*) intractable, disobedient, obstinate, perverse, recalcitrant.

óþol intolerance; *synonyms* (*n*) bigotry, impatience, discrimination, fanaticism, bias; *antonyms* (*n*) tolerance, lenience, broadmindedness.

óþolinmóður impatient; *synonyms* (*adj*) eager, hasty, anxious, petulant, fidgety; *antonyms* (*adj*) patient, enduring.

óþroskaður immature; *synonyms* (*adj*) adolescent, green, childish, crude, raw; *antonyms* (*adj*) mature, adult, developed, full-grown, grown-up.

ótilgreindur unspecified; *synonyms* (*adj*) undefined, anonymous, indeterminate, unidentified, indefinite; *antonym* (*adj*) specified.

ótiltekinn arbitrary; *synonyms* (*adj*) absolute, capricious, dictatorial, optional, erratic.

ótímabær premature; *synonyms* (*adj*) early, precocious, untimely, immature, forward.

ótraustur 1. unreliable; *synonyms* (*adj*) irresponsible, treacherous, uncertain, undependable, precarious; *antonyms* (*adj*) reliable, consistent, dependable, honest, constant, **2.** untrustworthy; *synonyms* (*adj*) unreliable, unfaithful, faithless, slippery, deceitful; *antonyms* (*adj*) trustworthy, faithful, **3.** dodgy; *synonyms* (*adj*) crafty, dicey, chancy, cunning, unsafe, **4.** dicey; *synonyms* (*adj*) risky, dangerous, dodgy, hazardous, perilous; *antonym* (*adj*) safe, **5.** labile; *synonym* (*adj*) unstable.

óttast fear; *synonyms* (*n*) apprehension, awe, alarm, (*v*) dread, concern; *antonyms* (*n*) bravery, confidence, fearlessness, reassurance.

ótti 1. alarm; *synonyms* (*n*) dismay, alert, consternation, (*v*) awe, scare; *antonyms* (*v*) calm, comfort, **2.** fear; *synonyms* (*n*) apprehension, alarm, doubt, (*v*) dread, concern; *antonyms* (*n*) bravery, confidence, fearlessness, reassurance.

óunninn rough; *synonyms* (*adj*) coarse, hard, harsh, raw, crude; *antonyms* (*adj*) gentle, smooth, polished, precise, refined.

óuppleysanlegur insoluble; *synonyms* (*adj*) indissoluble, inextricable, insolvable, irresoluble, firm; *antonym* (*adj*) soluble.

óvænn 1. sullen; *synonyms* (*adj*) morose, gloomy, gruff, cross, dark; *antonym* (*adj*) cheerful, **2.** surly; *synonyms* (*adj*) grumpy, sullen, peevish, (*n*) harsh, rude, **3.** unkind; *synonyms* (*adj*) cruel, unfeeling, heartless, inconsiderate, pitiless; *antonym* (*adj*) kind, **4.** rough; *synonyms* (*adj*) coarse, hard, raw, crude, grating; *antonyms* (*adj*) gentle, smooth, polished, precise, refined, **5.** unpleasant; *synonyms* (*adj*) disagreeable, nasty, obnoxious, offensive, ugly; *antonyms* (*adj*) pleasant, agreeable, delightful, attractive, comfortable.

óværa infestation; *synonyms* (*n*) plague, blight, (*adj*) infection, molestation, pollution.

óværð perturbation; *synonyms* (*n*) disturbance, commotion, agitation, fuss, (*v*) trepidation.

óværi irritation; *synonyms* (*n*) aggravation, exasperation, anger, annoyance, displeasure; *antonym* (*n*) pleasure.

óvanlegur abnormal; *synonyms* (adj) aberrant, anomalous, atypical, irregular, monstrous; *antonyms* (adj) normal, typical, usual.

óvarinn open; *synonyms* (adj) frank, obvious, artless, (n) candid, clear; *antonyms* (adj) devious, secretive, concealed, (v) shut, (tr v) close.

óveður 1. storm; *synonyms* (n) tempest, attack, (v) rage, rush, assault, 2. weather; *synonyms* (v) endure, survive, resist, withstand, brave.

óviðkomandi unauthorized; *synonyms* (adj) illegal, illicit, unauthorised, illegitimate, wildcat; *antonyms* (adj) authorized, official.

óviðkunnanlegur 1. unpleasant; *synonyms* (adj) disagreeable, harsh, nasty, obnoxious, offensive; *antonyms* (adj) pleasant, agreeable, delightful, attractive, comfortable, 2. uncongenial; *synonyms* (adj) incompatible, unfriendly, hostile, cold, incongenial; *antonym* (adj) congenial, 3. cold; *synonyms* (adj) chilly, frigid, aloof, callous, (n) chilliness; *antonyms* (adj) warm, friendly, hot, burning, (n) heat, 4. nasty; *synonyms* (adj) dirty, loathsome, disgusting, filthy, foul; *antonyms* (adj) kind, nice, charitable, lovely.

óvilhallur unbiased; *synonyms* (adj) fair, impartial, indifferent, neutral, just; *antonyms* (adj) biased, prejudiced.

óviljaverk error; *synonyms* (n) deviation, blunder, fault, mistake, wrong; *antonym* (n) correctness.

óvingjarnlegur 1. sullen; *synonyms* (adj) morose, gloomy, gruff, cross, dark; *antonym* (adj) cheerful, 2. rough; *synonyms* (adj) coarse, hard, harsh, raw, crude; *antonyms* (adj) gentle, smooth, polished, precise, refined, 3. unkind; *synonyms* (adj) cruel, unfeeling, heartless, inconsiderate, pitiless; *antonym* (adj) kind, 4. sour; *synonyms* (adj) sharp, acid, bitter, rancid, severe; *antonyms* (adj) sweet, kindly, 5. surly; *synonyms* (adj) grumpy, sullen, peevish, crusty, (n) rude.

óvinur 1. adversary; *synonyms* (n) opponent, antagonist, enemy, foe, competitor; *antonym* (n) ally, 2. foe; *synonyms* (n) adversary, opposition, assailant, foeman, rival, 3. enemy; *synonyms* (n) hostile, challenger, contender; *antonyms* (n) friend, supporter.

óvinveittur hostile; *synonyms* (adj) unfriendly, aggressive, contrary, adverse, belligerent; *antonyms* (adj) friendly, soothing, warm.

óvirkur 1. silent; *synonyms* (adj) motionless, dumb, mute, tacit, (adv) quiet; *antonyms* (adj) noisy, spoken, loud, talkative, explicit, 2. quiescent; *synonyms* (adj) dormant, inactive, calm, passive, inert; *antonym* (adj) active, 3. dormant; *synonyms* (adj) asleep, torpid, smoldering, inoperative, suspended, 4. neutral; *synonyms* (adj)

disinterested, impartial, indifferent, dispassionate, (n) neuter; *antonyms* (adj) biased, aromatic, colorful, 5. inactive; *synonyms* (adj) idle, dead, dull, slow, sluggish; *antonyms* (adj) lively, moving.

óvís 1. undoubted; *synonyms* (adj) certain, undisputed, unquestionable, indisputable, undeniable, 2. unquestionable; *synonyms* (adj) incontrovertible, sure, incontestable, indubitable, irrefutable; *antonyms* (adj) questionable, dubious, uncertain, 3. unmistakable; *synonyms* (adj) clear, obvious, evident, plain, (v) unequivocal, 4. definite; *synonyms* (adj) accurate, absolute, categorical, conclusive, concrete; *antonyms* (adj) imprecise, unclear, vague, doubtful, undefined, 5. outright; *synonyms* (adj) complete, entire, straight, altogether, (adv) completely.

óvissa 1. uncertainty; *synonyms* (n) doubt, doubtfulness, distrust, indecision, suspicion; *antonyms* (n) certainty, confidence, decisiveness, clarity, 2. error; *synonyms* (n) deviation, blunder, fault, mistake, wrong; *antonym* (n) correctness.

Ö

öfgafullur extreme; *synonyms* (adj) deep, excessive, enormous, immoderate, (n) edge; *antonyms* (adj) middle, reasonable, (n) mild, moderate, slight.

öfgakenndur extreme; *synonyms* (adj) deep, excessive, enormous, immoderate, (n) edge; *antonyms* (adj) middle, reasonable, (n) mild, moderate, slight.

öfugkjafta megrim; *synonyms* (n) hemicrania, freak, migraine, humor.

öfugstreymi regurgitation; *synonyms* (n) vomit, backwater, disgorgement, (v) reflux, eddy.

öfugt retrograde; *synonyms* (v) recede, retreat, retire, decline, (adj) backward.

öfugþróun devolution; *synonyms* (n) degeneration, delegation, degeneracy, decadence, transfer.

öfuguggaháttur degeneracy; *synonyms* (n) corruption, decadence, depravity, degeneration, decline.

öfugur 1. inverse; *synonyms* (adj) contrary, converse, (n) opposite, contrast, (v) reverse, 2. inverted; *synonyms* (adj) inverse, upside-down, anatropous, backward, overturned; *antonym* (adj) upright.

öfund envy; *synonyms* (n) desire, enviousness, resentment, (v) begrudge, covet.

öfunda envy; *synonyms* (n) desire, enviousness, resentment, (v) begrudge, covet.

öfundarfullur envious; *synonyms* (adj) covetous, jealous, invidious, jaundiced, malicious.

öfundsjúkur jealous; *synonyms* *(adj)* covetous, distrustful, envious, suspicious, resentful.

ögðulirfa redia; *synonyms* *(n)* nurse, sporosac.

öggur gudgeon; *synonyms* *(n)* dupe, gull, goby, axle, victim.

ögn 1. corpuscle; *synonyms* *(n)* atom, corpuscule, *(adj)* molecule, particle, dot, **2**. granule; *synonyms* *(n)* grain, crumb, *(adj)* scruple, dash, drop, **3**. particle; *synonyms* *(n)* speck, bit, fragment, iota, jot.

ökklabein talus; *synonyms* *(n)* astragalus, slope, scree, anklebone, astragal.

ökli ankle; *synonyms* *(n)* knuckle, crane, crotch, crutch, fluke.

ökumaður 1. driver; *synonyms* *(n)* coachman, postboy, club, chaser, commuter, **2**. chauffeur; *synonyms* *(n)* driver, engineer, hackman, syce, truckman.

ökuslóði track; *synonyms* *(n)* course, path, *(v)* trace, trail, hunt.

ökutæki vehicle; *synonyms* *(n)* medium, instrument, means, automobile, channel.

öl 1. beer; *synonyms* *(n)* cocktail, *(v)* wine, stingo, liqueur, spirits, **2**. ale; *synonyms* *(n)* beer, eale.

öld 1. century; *synonyms* *(n)* age, centenary, hundred, centred, millennium, **2**. age; *synonyms* *(n)* period, aeon, day, era, time, **3**. centennial; *synonyms* *(n)* anniversary, centurial, bicentenary, birthday, *(v)* secular, **4**. era; *synonyms* *(n)* epoch, date, cycle, style.

öldrun 1. senescence; *synonyms* *(n)* ageing, aging, agedness, decay, *(adj)* senility, **2**. ageing; *synonyms* *(n)* maturing, ripening, senescence, curing, souring.

öldrunarfræði gerontology; *synonym* *(n)* geriatrics.

öldrunarlækningar geriatrics; *synonyms* *(n)* gerontology, *(adj)* nostology.

öldubeygja diffraction; *synonyms* *(n)* deflection, deviation, inflection.

öldubrjótur breakwater; *synonyms* *(n)* bulwark, groyne, jetty, mole, seawall.

öldubrot refraction; *synonyms* *(n)* bending, deflection, deflexion, *(v)* obliquation, *(adj)* reflection.

öldudalur trough; *synonyms* *(n)* trench, channel, chute, gutter, manger; *antonym* *(n)* peak.

ölduhreyfing fluctuation; *synonyms* *(n)* variation, vicissitude, wavering, deviation, hesitation.

öldukambur ridge; *synonyms* *(n)* crest, ledge, bank, hill, shelf.

ölduleiðir waveguide; *synonym* *(n)* helix.

öldulengd wavelength; *synonym* *(n)* insight.

öldungadeild senate; *synonyms* *(n)* council, legislature, parliament, congress, assembly.

öldungadeildin senate; *synonyms* *(n)* council, legislature, parliament, congress, assembly.

öldungaráð senate; *synonyms* *(n)* council, legislature, parliament, congress, assembly.

öldustokkur waveguide; *synonym* *(n)* helix.

ölduvíxl interference; *synonyms* *(n)* disturbance, hindrance, handicap, block, *(v)* collision.

ölgleymi blackout; *synonyms* *(n)* faint, brownout, darkness, dimout, amnesia.

ölur alder; *synonym* *(adj)* aller.

ölvaður 1. drunken; *synonyms* *(adj)* drunk, boozy, sottish, intoxicated, tight, **2**. drunk; *synonyms* *(adj)* tipsy, wet, inebriated, *(n)* inebriate, drunkard; *antonym* *(adj)* sober, **3**. intoxicated; *synonyms* *(adj)* drunken, elated.

ölvandi intoxicant; *synonyms* *(adj)* heady, *(n)* alcohol, inebriant, drink, liquor.

ölvíma intoxication; *synonyms* *(n)* drunkenness, inebriation, inebriety, poisoning, tipsiness.

ölvun intoxication; *synonyms* *(n)* drunkenness, inebriation, inebriety, poisoning, tipsiness.

ömbulegur ameboid; *synonym* *(adj)* amoeboid.

önd 1. duck; *synonyms* *(v)* dip, douse, plunge, dodge, circumvent, **2**. vestibule; *synonyms* *(n)* hall, lobby, foyer, antechamber, hallway, **3**. spirit; *synonyms* *(n)* apparition, courage, ghost, life, mood; *antonyms* *(n)* lethargy, body, **4**. breath; *synonyms* *(n)* spirit, wind, air, inspiration, puff.

öndun 1. respiration; *synonyms* *(n)* breathing, aspiration, inspiration, delay, exercising, **2**. ventilation; *synonyms* *(n)* airing, exploitation, discussion, deliberation, air.

öndunarefnaflutningur respiration; *synonyms* *(n)* breathing, aspiration, inspiration, delay, exercising.

öndunarfæraslím phlegm; *synonyms* *(n)* apathy, impassiveness, impassivity, indifference, lethargy.

öndunargríma inhaler; *synonyms* *(n)* inhalator, respirator.

öndunarop vent; *synonyms* *(n)* outlet, exit, discharge, opening, *(v)* air.

öndunarvél respirator; *synonyms* *(n)* inhalator, ventilator, gasmask, inhaler.

öng 1. congestion; *synonyms* *(n)* blockage, engorgement, overcrowding, aggregation, crowding; *antonym* *(n)* emptiness, **2**. angina; *synonyms* *(v)* gripe, headache, heartburn, twinge, twitch, **3**. degeneracy; *synonyms* *(n)* corruption, decadence, depravity, degeneration, decline.

öngstig degeneracy; *synonyms* *(n)* corruption, decadence, depravity, degeneration, decline.

öngull hook; *synonyms* *(n)* clasp, crook, claw, *(v)* catch, bend.

öngvit syncope; *synonyms* *(n)* swoon, faint, syncopation, fainting, deliquium.

önnur second; *synonyms* *(n)* instant, moment, flash, jiffy, *(v)* back; *antonym* *(adj)* first.

ör 1. scar; *synonyms* (*n*) mark, cicatrix, blemish, seam, cicatrice, **2**. arrow; *synonyms* (*n*) pointer, barb, bolt, dart, missile.

öræfi 1. wilderness; *synonyms* (*n*) desert, wild, wasteland, solitude, (*v*) waste, **2**. desert; *synonyms* (*v*) abandon, escape, defect, (*adj*) barren, desolate; *antonyms* (*n*) bog, (*v*) stay.

örbirgð poverty; *synonyms* (*n*) lack, distress, (*v*) destitution, need, penury; *antonyms* (*n*) wealth, riches.

örbylgja microwave; *synonyms* (*v*) cook, atomise, atomize, fix, nuke.

ördeyðuskeið plateau; *synonyms* (*n*) plain, table, tableland, elevation, stage.

öreigalýður proletariat; *synonyms* (*n*) labor, labour, mob, masses, trash.

öreigar proletariat; *synonyms* (*n*) labor, labour, mob, masses, trash.

öreigastétt proletariat; *synonyms* (*n*) labor, labour, mob, masses, trash.

örfitja fragment; *synonyms* (*n*) fraction, crumb, (*v*) bit, chip, scrap.

örgjörvi microprocessor; *synonyms* (*n*) chip, microchip.

örhljóð ultrasound; *synonyms* (*n*) sonography, ultrasonography.

örhljóðs ultrasonic; *synonyms* (*adj*) supersonic, speedy.

örkvarði micrometer; *synonyms* (*n*) micron, megameter, megametre, (*v*) nanometer, centimeter.

örlæti 1. unselfishness; *synonyms* (*n*) altruism, generosity, generousness, kindness, care; *antonym* (*n*) selfishness, **2**. generosity; *synonyms* (*n*) charity, benevolence, bounty, liberality, (*adj*) beneficence; *antonyms* (*n*) stinginess, greed, meanness, thrift.

örlítill minimal; *synonyms* (*adj*) minimum, least, minute, insignificant, marginal; *antonym* (*adj*) maximal.

örmagna prostrate; *synonyms* (*adj*) flat, prone, exhaust, (*v*) fell, level.

örmagnast prostrate; *synonyms* (*adj*) flat, prone, exhaust, (*v*) fell, level.

örmagni squid; *synonyms* (*n*) calamary, calamari, sleevefish.

örmögnun 1. depletion; *synonyms* (*n*) consumption, expenditure, loss, (*adj*) flaccidity, vacancy, **2**. exhaustion; *synonyms* (*n*) fatigue, enervation, lassitude, tiredness, (*adj*) collapse; *antonym* (*n*) energy

örn eagle; *synonyms* (*n*) colors, labarum, oriflamb, oriflamme, aviator.

örorka 1. disability; *synonyms* (*n*) handicap, inability, disablement, disqualification, drawback,

2. handicap; *synonyms* (*n*) balk, hurdle, barrier, (*v*) block, hamper; *antonyms* (*v*) advantage, benefit.

örsmæð infinitesimal; *synonyms* (*adj*) minute, microscopic, insignificant, tiny, little; *antonym* (*adj*) gigantic.

örsmæðareikningur calculus; *synonyms* (*n*) concretion, stone, calculi, tartar, (*v*) calculation.

örsmár infinitesimal; *synonyms* (*adj*) minute, microscopic, insignificant, tiny, little; *antonym* (*adj*) gigantic.

örstak fragment; *synonyms* (*n*) fraction, crumb, (*v*) bit, chip, scrap.

örsvif colloid; *synonyms* (*adj*) colloidal, gelatinous.

örþeyta colloid; *synonyms* (*adj*) colloidal, gelatinous.

örtölva microcomputer; *synonym* (*n*) computer.

örtölvuflaga microchip; *synonyms* (*n*) chip, microprocessor, bit, check, chipping.

öruggur safe; *synonyms* (*adj*) secure, reliable, cautious, dependable, (*n*) closet; *antonyms* (*adj*) dangerous, unsafe, hurt, risky, unprotected.

örva 1. stir; *synonyms* (*v*) arouse, budge, move, (*n*) movement, (*adj*) bustle, **2**. promote; *synonyms* (*v*) advance, encourage, help, aid, (*adv*) further; *antonyms* (*v*) demote, discourage, **3**. stimulate; *synonyms* (*v*) excite, incite, enliven, inspire, (*adj*) quicken; *antonym* (*v*) defuse, **4**. activate; *synonyms* (*v*) actuate, start, trigger, aerate, animate, **5**. excite; *synonyms* (*v*) disturb, agitate, energize, awaken, electrify; *antonyms* (*v*) calm, pacify, bore.

örvæntingarfullur 1. desperate; *synonyms* (*adj*) hopeless, despairing, dire, critical, (*v*) forlorn; *antonym* (*adj*) hopeful, **2**. hopeless; *synonyms* (*adj*) despondent, incurable, disconsolate, abject, desperate; *antonyms* (*adj*) cheerful, competent, promising.

örvandi 1. stimulant; *synonyms* (*n*) incentive, provocative, excitant, goad, impetus, **2**. analeptic; *synonyms* (*n*) stimulant, (*adj*) tonic, therapeutic, corroborant, chirurgical, **3**. excitant; *synonyms* (*adj*) excitative, excitatory, (*n*) excitive, impulse, spur.

örvari activator; *synonym* (*n*) inducer.

örvarrót arrowroot; *synonym* (*n*) achira.

örvera 1. microorganism; *synonyms* (*n*) microbe, germ, bug, bacteria, virus, **2**. germ; *synonyms* (*n*) beginning, bud, kernel, egg, nucleus, **3**. microbe; *synonyms* (*n*) pathogen, amphibian, arthropod, bird, crustacean.

örverueyðandi antimicrobial; *synonyms* (*n*) antimicrobic, disinfectant, germicide.

örverufræði microbiology; *synonyms* (*n*) bacteriology, mycology, virology.

örverugróður flora; *synonyms* (*n*) vegetation, plant, plants, verdure, foliage.

örveruræktun culture; *synonyms* (*n*) civilization, breeding, cultivation, acculturation, education.

örvhendur sinistral; *synonyms* (*adj*) left, sinistrorsal, sinistrorse, absurd, perverse.

örvi inducer; *synonyms* (*n*) persuader, activator.

örviti idiot; *synonyms* (*n*) fool, dolt, dunce, dimwit, moron.

örvun 1. stimulus; *synonyms* (*n*) incentive, encouragement, provocation, spur, motivation, **2.** stimulation; *synonyms* (*n*) excitation, arousal, excitement, goad, inspiration, **3.** activation; *synonyms* (*n*) activating, start, initiation, launch, awakening, **4.** arousal; *synonyms* (*n*) stimulation, foreplay, rousing, estrus, input, **5.** motivation; *synonyms* (*n*) motive, impulse, cause, reason, impetus.

öryggi 1. security; *synonyms* (*n*) pledge, protection, safety, hostage, insurance; *antonym* (*n*) danger, **2.** fuse; *synonyms* (*v*) combine, amalgamate, blend, melt, coalesce; *antonym* (*v*) separate.

öryggisafrit backup; *synonyms* (*n*) backing, substitute, surrogate, (*adj*) alternate, spare.

öryggismál security; *synonyms* (*n*) pledge, protection, safety, hostage, insurance; *antonym* (*n*) danger.

öryggisráðstöfun safeguard; *synonyms* (*v*) preserve, ensure, (*n*) guard, protection, shield.

öskjubaugur ellipse; *synonyms* (*n*) ellipsis, oval, ovule, curve, orbit.

östrógen oestrogen; *synonym* (*n*) estrogen.

öxi axe; *synonyms* (*n*) knife, (*v*) ax, chop, abort, destroy.

öxl shoulder; *synonyms* (*n*) elbow, (*v*) bear, carry, push, hold.

öxulkragi dog; *synonyms* (*n*) cur, andiron, (*v*) chase, hound, beset.

öxull 1. axle; *synonyms* (*n*) axis, hinge, pivot, bobbin, beam, **2.** axis; *synonyms* (*n*) axle, center, hub, spindle, stem, **3.** spindle; *synonyms* (*n*) mandrel, arbor, mandril, bolt, arbour, **4.** shaft; *synonyms* (*n*) arrow, handle, pit, dart, pillar, **5.** mandrel; *synonym* (*n*) core.

P

paðreimur stadium; *synonyms* (*n*) arena, coliseum, bowl, field, gymnasium.

pækill 1. pickle; *synonyms* (*n*) fix, jam, mess, hole, (*v*) cure, **2.** brine; *synonyms* (*n*) deep, ocean, salt, sea, (*v*) pickle.

páfagaukasótt psittacosis; *synonym* (*n*) ornithosis.

páfagaukaveiki psittacosis; *synonym* (*n*) ornithosis.

páfagaukur parrot; *synonyms* (*n*) poll, popinjay, (*v*) echo, mimic, ape.

páfugl peacock; *synonyms* (*n*) iris, fop, (*v*) strut, swagger, (*adj*) green.

pakkhús warehouse; *synonyms* (*n*) store, storehouse, godown, depository, (*v*) magazine.

pakki 1. packet; *synonyms* (*n*) package, bundle, bale, container, parcel, **2.** parcel; *synonyms* (*n*) lot, pack, division, (*v*) portion, distribute, **3.** package; *synonyms* (*n*) packaging, packet, carton, (*v*) box, wrap; *antonym* (*v*) unwrap.

pakkning 1. packing; *synonyms* (*n*) boxing, pack, pad, wadding, backpacking, **2.** gasket.

pall 1. latch; *synonyms* (*n*) catch, hasp, (*v*) bar, bolt, lock, **2.** pawl; *synonyms* (*n*) detent, ratchet, click, dog, andiron.

palladín palladium; *synonym* (*n*) safeguard.

palladíum palladium; *synonym* (*n*) safeguard.

pallborð panel; *synonyms* (*n*) board, jury, defendant, committee, (*v*) empanel.

pallur 1. platform; *synonyms* (*n*) dais, floor, rostrum, stage, stand, **2.** mounting; *synonyms* (*n*) mount, ascent, climb, frame, (*adj*) climbing, **3.** pallet; *synonyms* (*n*) palette, bed, berth, stillage, shakedown.

pálmi palm; *synonyms* (*n*) decoration, medal, prize, (*v*) hand, filch.

Pálsskata skate; *synonyms* (*v*) glide, skim, slip, coast, slide.

panill panel; *synonyms* (*n*) board, jury, defendant, committee, (*v*) empanel.

panna 1. sump; *synonyms* (*n*) bog, cesspit, cesspool, sink, swamp, **2.** pan; *synonyms* (*n*) dish, knock, rap, panning, (*v*) slam.

panta order; *synonyms* (*n*) command, decree, dictate, array, (*v*) direct; *antonyms* (*n*) anarchy, chaos, confusion, (*v*) disorder, request.

papaja papaya; *synonyms* (*n*) papaia, papaw, pawpaw.

papava papaw; *synonyms* (*n*) pawpaw, papaia.

papero papers; *synonyms* (*n*) credentials, document, documents, identification, covenant.

pappi cardboard; *synonyms* (*n*) card, (*adj*) flimsy, paper, ponderous, unlifelike.

pappír 1. paper; *synonyms* (*n*) document, article, newspaper, discourse, newsprint, **2.** instrument; *synonyms* (*n*) channel, deed, agency, apparatus, appliance.

paprikuduft paprika; *synonyms* (*n*) pimento, pimiento.

par 1. couple; *synonyms* (*v*) pair, connect, associate, combine, attach; *antonym* (*v*) uncouple, **2.** pair; *synonyms* (*n*) match, brace, duet, duo, (*v*) couple.

para match; *synonyms* (*n*) equal, (*v*) agree, mate, meet, parallel; *antonyms* (*v*) clash, contradict.

paraffín paraffin; *synonyms* (*n*) alkane, spermaceti, (*v*) wax, (*adj*) unreactivity.

pardusdýr panther; *synonyms* (*n*) catamount, cougar, jaguar, leopard, (*adj*) lion.

parencino 1. relatives; *synonyms* (*n*) family, relations, kin, kindred, kinsfolk, 2. relative; *synonyms* (*adj*) related, comparative, proportionate, (*n*) relation, (*v*) kinsman; *antonym* (*adj*) absolute.

parenco 1. relations; *synonyms* (*n*) family, dealings, kin, connections, people, 2. relatives; *synonyms* (*n*) relations, kindred, kinsfolk, relationship, affinity.

partur part; *synonyms* (*n*) constituent, piece, (*v*) branch, break, disjoin; *antonyms* (*n*) whole, entirety, (*adj*) complete.

paŝi 1. step; *synonyms* (*n*) degree, measure, stage, walk, (*v*) pace, 2. steps; *synonyms* (*n*) staircase, stairs, stairway, scale, way.

paŝo steps; *synonyms* (*n*) staircase, stairs, stairway, scale, way.

passa fit; *synonyms* (*v*) agree, accommodate, meet, suit, (*adj*) decorous; *antonyms* (*adj*) unfit, inappropriate, unwell.

patrico dice; *synonyms* (*n*) die, (*v*) cube, cut, chop, bet.

patróna 1. collet; *synonym* (*n*) ferrule, 2. chuck; *synonyms* (*v*) cast, fling, ditch, pitch, throw.

patrónukjaftur jaw; *synonyms* (*v*) chatter, gossip, chat, gab, jabber.

Patt stalemate; *synonyms* (*n*) deadlock, impasse, standstill, (*adj*) checkmate, nonplus.

Peð pawn; *synonyms* (*n*) pledge, bail, hostage, instrument, (*v*) hock.

pektín pectin; *synonym* (*n*) preserves.

pendill pendulum; *synonyms* (*n*) dial, gnomon, horologe, pendant, (*v*) flap.

pendla hunt; *synonyms* (*n*) search, (*v*) chase, course, follow, hound.

pendull pendulum; *synonyms* (*n*) dial, gnomon, horologe, pendant, (*v*) flap.

pendúll pendulum; *synonyms* (*n*) dial, gnomon, horologe, pendant, (*v*) flap.

peningalegur monetary; *synonyms* (*adj*) financial, pecuniary, commercial, economic, numismatical.

peningar money; *synonyms* (*n*) capital, coin, currency, funds, means.

peningasending remittance; *synonyms* (*n*) payment, remission, allowance, remitment, remittal.

peningaskápur safe; *synonyms* (*adj*) secure, reliable, cautious, dependable, (*n*) closet; *antonyms* (*adj*) dangerous, unsafe, hurt, risky, unprotected.

peningur money; *synonyms* (*n*) capital, coin, currency, funds, means.

pensill brush; *synonyms* (*n*) brushwood, (*v*) broom, graze, sweep, touch.

peptíð peptide; *synonym* (*n*) polypeptide.

pera 1. bulb; *synonyms* (*n*) knob, lightbulb, corm, nodule, (*adj*) globule, 2. pear, 3. lamp; *synonyms* (*n*) light, look, beacon, (*v*) behold, regard.

persóna 1. person; *synonyms* (*n*) fellow, human, individual, man, being; *antonym* (*n*) automaton, 2. persona; *synonyms* (*n*) character, role, part, appearance, image, 3. personage; *synonyms* (*n*) person, celebrity, notable, personality, figure.

persono 1. person; *synonyms* (*n*) fellow, human, individual, man, being; *antonym* (*n*) automaton, 2. persons; *synonyms* (*n*) people, public, society, world, folks.

persónugerð personality; *synonyms* (*n*) individuality, person, celebrity, character, identity; *antonym* (*n*) nobody.

persónukenni identity; *synonyms* (*n*) identicalness, unity, individuality, personality, sameness.

persónuleikarof dissociation; *synonyms* (*n*) disintegration, divorce, disassociation, separation, distancing.

persónuleiki 1. personality; *synonyms* (*n*) individuality, person, celebrity, character, identity; *antonym* (*n*) nobody, 2. character; *synonyms* (*n*) kind, nature, note, part, quality, 3. nature; *synonyms* (*n*) disposition, class, essence, creation, breed.

persónuskilríki credential; *synonyms* (*n*) certificate, certification, diploma, credentials, authority.

persónutöfrar charisma; *synonyms* (*n*) allure, charm, fascination, magnetism, appeal.

perubróðir quince; *synonym* (*n*) melocotoon.

perustæði socket; *synonym* (*n*) cavity, alveolus, sleeve, hollow, pocket.

pétursfiskur dory; *synonyms* (*n*) ark, broadhorn, bully, dinghy, droger.

peysa 1. sweater; *synonym* (*n*) perspirer, 2. pullover; *synonyms* (*n*) sweater, slipover, turtleneck, 3. jumper; *synonyms* (*n*) blackguard, bounder, cad, dog, heel.

pí pi; *synonyms* (*v*) pie, muddle, (*n*) operative, shamus, sherlock.

piezorör piezometer; *synonym* (*n*) standpipe.

pílári spoke; *synonyms* (*n*) bar, radius, rung, clog, line.

pilla 1. pill; *synonyms* (*n*) capsule, lozenge, tablet, (*v*) ball, (*adj*) pellet, 2. peel; *synonyms* (*n*) skin, hide, (*v*) hull, bark, flake.

pillun peeling; *synonyms* (*adj*) flaking, (*n*) peel, desquamation, shelling, hull; *antonym* (*adj*) smooth.

pils skirt; *synonyms* (*n*) border, edge, brim, (*v*) fringe, circumvent.

piltur 1. boy; *synonyms* (n) lad, fellow, kid, male, man, **2.** lad; *synonyms* (n) boy, blighter, chap, cub, cuss.

pína lug; *synonyms* (v) draw, haul, drag, pull, (n) ear.

pinnbolti stud; *synonyms* (n) boss, rivet, (v) knob, button, dot.

pinni 1. pivot; *synonyms* (n) axle, axis, pin, hub, (v) revolve, **2.** pin; *synonyms* (n) needle, nail, (v) tack, clasp, fix, **3.** peg; *synonyms* (n) bolt, hook, dowel, leg, nog.

pinnjón pinion; *synonyms* (n) feather, pennon, (v) fetter, bind, (adj) tie.

pinsetta forceps; *synonyms* (n) pincette, (v) tongs, clutches, corkscrew, extractor.

pípa 1. pipe; *synonyms* (n) tube, conduit, channel, duct, (v) cry, **2.** waterspout; *synonyms* (n) cloudburst, deluge, downpour, soaker, torrent, **3.** tube; *synonyms* (n) pipe, subway, hose, cylinder, metro, **4.** conduit; *synonyms* (n) canal, aqueduct, drain, watercourse, culvert, **5.** lamp; *synonyms* (n) light, look, beacon, (v) behold, regard.

pipar pepper; *synonyms* (n) capsicum, peppercorn, (v) pelt, bombard, sprinkle.

piparminta peppermint; *synonyms* (n) bilsted, marri.

piparmynta peppermint; *synonyms* (n) bilsted, marri.

pípetta pipette; *synonyms* (n) pipet, beaker, flask, carboy, syringe.

pípla tubule; *synonym* (n) vessel.

pípuhné knee; *synonyms* (n) elbow, genu, scythe, sickle, zigzag.

pípulaga tubular; *synonyms* (adj) cannular, tubulate, fistuliform, piped, tubeform.

pípulögn piping; *synonyms* (adj) high, shrill, (n) pipage, pipe, line.

pípusetning intubation; *synonyms* (n) cannulation, cannulization, canulation, canulization.

pípusmokkur union; *synonyms* (n) coalition, connection, junction, association, combination; *antonyms* (n) separation, divergence.

pípustúka union; *synonyms* (n) coalition, connection, junction, association, combination; *antonyms* (n) separation, divergence.

píramídi pyramid; *synonyms* (n) pile, mass, heap, congeries, (adj) spire.

píramíði pyramid; *synonyms* (n) pile, mass, heap, congeries, (adj) spire.

píramíti pyramid; *synonyms* (n) pile, mass, heap, congeries, (adj) spire.

píslarvottur martyr; *synonyms* (n) sufferer, victim, prey, (v) martyrize, persecute.

pittur pit; *synonyms* (n) cavity, dent, hole, depression, (adj) hollow.

plægja 1. plough; *synonyms* (v) plow, hoe, delve, dibble, dig, **2.** dredge; *synonyms* (v) drag, sprinkle, deepen, dust, (n) dredger.

plága 1. pestilence; *synonyms* (n) plague, pest, epidemic, blight, (adj) murrain, **2.** plague; *synonyms* (v) bother, harass, molest, worry, afflict, **3.** pest; *synonyms* (n) bane, bore, nuisance, annoyance, gadfly.

plana plane; *synonyms* (n) airplane, face, (adj) level, even, flat.

pláneta planet; *synonyms* (n) globe, satellite, world, sphere, orbiter.

plánetuhjól satellite; *synonyms* (n) follower, moon, planet, attendant, orbiter.

planki plank; *synonyms* (n) board, beam, timber, girder, panel.

planrennsli facing; *synonyms* (n) face, revetment, cladding, coating, (prep) opposite.

planta plant; *synonyms* (n) manufactory, equipment, (v) fix, place, embed.

plantekra plantation; *synonyms* (n) estate, orchard, farm, planting, settlement.

plasmi plasma; *synonyms* (n) plasm, onyx, blood, flesh.

pláss 1. place; *synonyms* (n) position, (v) post, arrange, fix, lay; *antonym* (v) remove, **2.** space; *synonyms* (n) length, gap, opening, period, place.

plast plastic; *synonyms* (adj) flexible, ductile, elastic, malleable, (v) limber.

plastefni plastic; *synonyms* (adj) flexible, ductile, elastic, malleable, (v) limber.

plastíð plastid; *synonym* (n) cell.

plástra strap; *synonyms* (n) belt, leash, strop, (v) lash, whip.

plástur 1. strap; *synonyms* (n) belt, leash, strop, (v) lash, whip, **2.** plaster; *synonyms* (n) mortar, cement, (v) coat, daub, stucco.

plata 1. slab; *synonyms* (n) hunk, chunk, bar, (adj) table, plate, **2.** separator; *synonyms* (n) centrifuge, extractor, classifier, arrester, partition, **3.** plate; *synonyms* (n) dish, leaf, (v) gild, sheet, cover, **4.** sheet; *synonyms* (n) board, layer, canvas, film, paper, **5.** cover; *synonyms* (v) coat, conceal, top, bury, (n) blind; *antonyms* (v) reveal, expose, uncover.

platína platinum; *synonyms* (n) platina, blonde.

plestinn plastic; *synonyms* (adj) flexible, ductile, elastic, malleable, (v) limber.

plógur dredge; *synonyms* (v) drag, sprinkle, deepen, dust, (n) dredger.

plöntulandafræði phytogeography; *synonym (n)* botany.

plöntuör callus; *synonyms (n)* callosity, bump, lump.

plöntur vegetation; *synonyms (n)* flora, growth, plants, foliage, quietism.

plönturíki flora; *synonyms (n)* vegetation, plant, plants, verdure, foliage.

plöntusamfélag association; *synonyms (n)* affiliation, alliance, connection, assembly, affinity.

plönun facing; *synonyms (n)* face, revetment, cladding, coating, *(prep)* opposite.

plötuklippur shears; *synonyms (n)* shear, *(adj)* scissors, cutters.

plötuknippi group; *synonyms (n)* bunch, brigade, collection, crowd, flock.

plötupar couple; *synonyms (v)* pair, connect, associate, combine, attach; *antonym (v)* uncouple.

plötupressun stamping; *synonyms (n)* marking, impression, blocking, coin, coining.

plötutvennd couple; *synonyms (v)* pair, connect, associate, combine, attach; *antonym (v)* uncouple.

plús 1. plus; *synonyms (prep)* besides, *(n)* extra, advantage, addition, *(adv)* more; *antonyms (prep)* minus, *(n)* disadvantage, **2.** positive; *synonyms (adj)* absolute, certain, affirmative, confident, *(n)* actual; *antonyms (adj)* negative, derogatory, uncertain, unsure, pessimistic.

plúsmerki plus; *synonyms (prep)* besides, *(n)* extra, advantage, addition, *(adv)* more; *antonyms (prep)* minus, *(n)* disadvantage.

plússkaut anode; *synonym (n)* zincode.

plúton plutonium; *synonyms (v)* radiation, radioactivity, tritium, uranium, radium.

plútón plutonium; *synonyms (v)* radiation, radioactivity, tritium, uranium, radium.

plútóníum plutonium; *synonyms (v)* radiation, radioactivity, tritium, uranium, radium.

po as; *synonyms (conj)* qua, because, *(prep)* during, like, *(n)* arsenic.

pokabyssa messenger; *synonyms (n)* envoy, emissary, harbinger, runner, *(v)* herald.

pokastrigi burlap; *synonyms (n)* gunny, hessian, muslin, toile.

poki 1. sack; *synonyms (v)* pillage, bag, plunder, discharge, dismiss; *antonym (v)* hire, **2.** sac; *synonyms (n)* pocket, pouch, poke, sack, blister, **3.** pocket; *synonyms (n)* cavity, *(v)* take, appropriate, steal, lift, **4.** bunt; *synonyms (n)* carom, *(v)* butt, jab, abut, adjoin, **5.** bag; *synonyms (n)* package, briefcase, purse, *(v)* bulge, capture.

pökkun 1. packing; *synonyms (n)* boxing, pack, pad, wadding, backpacking, **2.** packaging; *synonyms (n)* packing, wrap, covering, wrapping, baling.

pökkur puck; *synonyms (n)* fairy, imp.

pólaður polar; *synonyms (adj)* arctic, diametric, opposite, cold, freezing.

pólera polish; *synonyms (n)* finish, gloss, burnish, *(v)* furbish, glaze.

pólering burnishing; *synonyms (n)* bronzing, searing, buffing.

pólitík politics; *synonyms (n)* government, diplomacy, policy, governance, authorities.

póll pole; *synonyms (n)* perch, bar, picket, post, rod.

póllægur polar; *synonyms (adj)* arctic, diametric, opposite, cold, freezing.

polli 1. bollard; *synonym (n)* bitt, **2.** bitt; *synonyms (n)* bollard, bitts.

pollur pit; *synonyms (n)* cavity, dent, hole, depression, *(adj)* hollow.

pólriða nutation; *synonym (n)* circumnutation.

pólstefna polarity; *synonyms (n)* antagonism, augury, house, mansion, mark.

pólstilltur equatorial; *synonym (adj)* tropical.

pólun 1. polarization; *synonyms (n)* polarisation, bias, divergence, discord, division, **2.** polarity; *synonyms (n)* antagonism, augury, house, mansion, mark.

pólunarmælir polarimeter; *synonym (n)* polariscope.

pólvelta precession; *synonyms (n)* precedence, antecedence, antecedency, anteriority, precedency.

pönnun panning; *synonyms (n)* pan, criticism.

pöntun order; *synonyms (n)* command, decree, dictate, array, *(v)* direct; *antonyms (n)* anarchy, chaos, confusion, *(v)* disorder, request.

por as; *synonyms (conj)* qua, because, *(prep)* during, like, *(n)* arsenic.

port hilus; *synonym (n)* hilum.

pörun 1. synapsis; *synonym (n)* synapse, **2.** matching; *synonyms (adj)* equal, corresponding, duplicate, like, twin; *antonyms (adj)* different, incompatible, **3.** pairing; *synonyms (n)* coupling, mating, conjugation, union, matching.

posi 1. sacculus; *synonym (n)* saccule, **2.** saccule; *synonyms (n)* sac, sacculus, pocket, bag, pouch.

pósitífismi positivism; *synonyms (n)* positivity, certainty, anabaptism, deism, externalism.

pósitróna positron; *synonyms (n)* antielectron, electricity.

postaĵo tails; *synonyms (n)* tailcoat, tail, waste, coat.

póstþegi recipient; *synonyms (n)* beneficiary, receiver, inheritor, legatee, *(adj)* receptive; *antonym (n)* sender.

postulín porcelain; *synonyms (n)* collectibles, figurines, *(v)* ceramics, crockery, pottery.

póstur 1. post; *synonyms (n)* place, function, office, position, *(v)* mail, **2.** mail; *synonyms (n)* armor, *(v)* post, send, remit, habergeon.

postvango buttocks; *synonyms* (*n*) backside, bottom, arse, ass, bum.

præma prime; *synonyms* (*adj*) main, chief, first, head, (*n*) best; *antonym* (*adj*) minor.

prammi hopper; *synonyms* (*n*) grasshopper, bin, basket, boor, clown.

prentari printer; *synonyms* (*n*) pressman, typographer, correspondent, newspaperman, newspaperwoman.

prentmál letterpress; *synonym* (*n*) print.

preskribo 1. regulation; *synonyms* (*n*) rule, adjustment, law, order, (*adj*) control; *antonym* (*n*) chaos, 2. regulations; *synonyms* (*n*) policy, system, convention.

pressa 1. press; *synonyms* (*v*) crush, crowd, force, squeeze, pack, 2. ram; *synonyms* (*v*) beat, cram, crash, drive, jam, 3. compression; *synonyms* (*n*) compaction, condensation, pressure, compressing, concentration, 4. crush; *synonyms* (*n*) press, (*v*) break, compress, conquer, crunch, 5. express; *synonyms* (*v*) exhibit, articulate, convey, (*adj*) explicit, direct; *antonyms* (*v*) suppress, hide, (*adj*) slow, vague.

pressumót die; *synonyms* (*v*) decease, dead, death, depart, (*n*) dice.

pressun 1. coining; *synonyms* (*n*) forgery, stamping, 2. embossing; *synonyms* (*n*) adornment, beautification, buckling, decoration, embroidery, 3. expression; *synonyms* (*n*) diction, phrase, voice, appearance, aspect; *antonym* (*n*) repression.

prestaveldi theocracy; *synonyms* (*n*) thearchy, democracy, oligarchy, demagogy, dinarchy.

prestur priest; *synonyms* (*n*) clergyman, minister, ecclesiastic, churchman, (*adj*) divine.

prímatar primates; *synonym* (*n*) squirarchy.

prisma prism; *synonyms* (*n*) pyramid, spectroscope, spectrograph, spectrometer.

próf 1. test; *synonyms* (*n*) trial, audition, (*v*) assay, essay, examine, 2. assay; *synonyms* (*n*) examination, (*v*) test, try, attempt, experiment.

prófa 1. prove; *synonyms* (*v*) demonstrate, attest, confirm, manifest, establish; *antonym* (*v*) disprove, 2. test; *synonyms* (*n*) trial, audition, (*v*) assay, essay, examine, 3. check; *synonyms* (*v*) bridle, stop, (*n*) control, arrest, curb, 4. examine; *synonyms* (*v*) audit, consider, overhaul, try, check.

prófdómari moderator; *synonyms* (*n*) chairman, mediator, arbitrator, intermediary, negotiator.

prófefni 1. test; *synonyms* (*n*) trial, audition, (*v*) assay, essay, examine, 2. reagent; *synonyms* (*n*) crucible, touchstone, chemical.

prófkjör primary; *synonyms* (*adj*) chief, basic, elementary, essential, (*n*) paramount; *antonym* (*adj*) secondary.

prófseinkunn mark; *synonyms* (*n*) brand, evidence, score, (*v*) blemish, (*adj*) notice.

prófskírteini mark; *synonyms* (*n*) brand, evidence, score, (*v*) blemish, (*adj*) notice.

prófun 1. test; *synonyms* (*n*) trial, audition, (*v*) assay, essay, examine, 2. trial; *synonyms* (*n*) test, examination, experiment, affliction, hardship, 3. assay; *synonyms* (*v*) try, attempt, seek, survey, appraise, 4. examination; *synonyms* (*n*) audit, check, exam, search, consideration.

prófunarefni reagent; *synonyms* (*n*) crucible, touchstone, chemical.

prófviðbragð reaction; *synonyms* (*n*) answer, response, backlash, reply, effect.

prógesterón progesterone; *synonym* (*n*) progestin.

prólaktín prolactin; *synonym* (*n*) luteotropin.

prósent percentile; *synonym* (*n*) centile.

prósenta percentage; *synonyms* (*n*) part, share, cut, lot, percent.

protaktín protactinium; *synonyms* (*n*) protoactinium, pa.

prótaktín protactinium; *synonyms* (*n*) protoactinium, pa.

próteasi protease; *synonyms* (*n*) proteinase, peptidase.

prótein protein; *synonyms* (*n*) cytoplasm, (*adj*) albumen, gluten, glair, cream.

prótín 1. protium, 2. protein; *synonyms* (*n*) cytoplasm, (*adj*) albumen, gluten, glair, cream.

prótíninnkljúfur endopeptidase; *synonym* (*n*) proteinase.

prótínkljúfur protease; *synonyms* (*n*) proteinase, peptidase.

prótóna proton; *synonym* (*n*) electricity.

provizo stocks; *synonyms* (*n*) pillory, bilboes, securities, calls, options.

prufuleiðsla jumper; *synonyms* (*n*) sweater, blackguard, bounder, cad, dog.

psí psi; *synonym* (*n*) j.

psóríasis psoriasis; *synonyms* (*n*) itch, leucoplakia.

púði 1. cushion; *synonyms* (*n*) pad, (*v*) buffer, bolster, insulate, protect, 2. pad; *synonyms* (*n*) cushion, apartment, (*v*) line, inflate, expand.

púður powder; *synonyms* (*n*) dust, gunpowder, (*v*) grind, crush, pound.

púls pulse; *synonyms* (*n*) beat, impulse, pulsation, (*v*) pulsate, throb.

púlsafjöldi count; *synonyms* (*n*) number, calculation, (*v*) calculate, compute, tally.

púlshvarf failure; *synonyms* (*n*) bankruptcy, failing, breakdown, decline, deficiency; *antonyms* (*n*) success, achievement, hit, winner, victory.

púlskveikjari ignitor; *synonyms* (*n*) igniter, barge, brightness, flatboat, hoy.

púlsræsir ignitor; *synonyms* (*n*) igniter, barge, brightness, flatboat, hoy.

pund pound; *synonyms* (*v*) beat, pen, bang, crush, flap.

punktasíld alewife; *synonym* (*n*) gaspereau.

punktljós spotlight; *synonyms* (*n*) limelight, spot, (*v*) highlight, light, focus.

punktur 1. point; *synonyms* (*n*) place, grade, peak, nib, (*v*) head, **2**. nadir; *synonyms* (*n*) bottom, foot, minimum, zero, root; *antonyms* (*n*) acme, pinnacle, zenith.

púpa 1. pupa; *synonyms* (*n*) cocoon, nymph, caterpillar, nympha, orphan, **2**. chrysalis; *synonyms* (*n*) larva, chicken, cub, fry, pullet.

pussa 1. pussy; *synonyms* (*n*) cat, puss, cunt, kitty, (*adj*) purulent, **2**. cunt; *synonyms* (*n*) bitch, pussy, slit, snatch, twat.

pússa 1. polish; *synonyms* (*n*) finish, gloss, burnish, (*v*) furbish, glaze, **2**. clean; *synonyms* (*adj*) clear, fair, antiseptic, blank, (*v*) brush; *antonyms* (*adj*) filthy, unclean, (*v*) dirty, soil, contaminate.

puti 1. digit; *synonyms* (*n*) figure, cipher, dactyl, finger, number, **2**. finger; *synonyms* (*n*) digit, (*v*) feel, handle, touch, hand.

pylsa sausage; *synonyms* (*n*) frankfurter, blimp, pudding, intestine.

pýramídi pyramid; *synonyms* (*n*) pile, mass, heap, congeries, (*adj*) spire.

pýramíti pyramid; *synonyms* (*n*) pile, mass, heap, congeries, (*adj*) spire.

R

rabbi asp; *synonyms* (*n*) aspick, rattlesnake, aspen, cobra, serpent.

rabbíni rabbi; *synonyms* (*n*) clergyman, priest, chaplain, master, rebbe.

ráð 1. chamber; *synonyms* (*n*) bedroom, hall, bedchamber, cavity, cell, **2**. counsel; *synonyms* (*n*) caution, (*v*) advice, advise, consult, admonish, **3**. advice; *synonyms* (*n*) admonition, counsel, warning, exhortation, instruction, **4** director; *synonyms* (*n*) commander, manager, administrator, boss, (*v*) conductor, **5**. council; *synonyms* (*n*) assembly, board, congress, consultation, convention.

raða 1. sort; *synonyms* (*n*) kind, type, assortment, (*v*) class, group, **2**. file; *synonyms* (*n*) archive, document, list, procession, (*v*) order.

ráða 1. counsel; *synonyms* (*n*) caution, (*v*) advice, advise, consult, admonish, **2**. advise; *synonyms* (*v*) acquaint, inform, propose, recommend, suggest; *antonym* (*v*) oppose, **3**. evaluate; *synonyms* (*v*) appraise, assess, calculate, gauge, estimate, **4**. employ; *synonyms* (*v*) apply, use, consume, engage, exercise; *antonyms* (*v*) fire, dismiss.

ráðaleitun consultation; *synonyms* (*n*) advice, conference, interview, negotiation, counsel.

ráðataka acquisition; *synonyms* (*n*) purchase, accomplishment, acquirement, attainment, achievement.

raðbrigði 1. recombinant, **2**. isomer; *synonym* (*n*) isomeride.

raðbrögð isomerization; *synonym* (*n*) isomerisation.

raðbundinn serial; *synonyms* (*adj*) sequential, consecutive, recurrent, sequent, (*n*) periodical.

raddarmissir aphonia; *synonyms* (*n*) aphony, voicelessness.

ráðdeild thrift; *synonyms* (*n*) economy, frugality, parsimony, husbandry, prosperity; *antonyms* (*n*) extravagance, generosity.

raddleysi aphonia; *synonyms* (*n*) aphony, voicelessness.

raddlömun aphonia; *synonyms* (*n*) aphony, voicelessness.

raddstol aphonia; *synonyms* (*n*) aphony, voicelessness.

raðflétta permutation; *synonyms* (*n*) change, commutation, exchange, modification, transposition.

ráðgefandi advisory; *synonyms* (*adj*) consultative, instructive, consultatory, hortative, admonitory.

raðgildi rank; *synonyms* (*n*) range, place, (*v*) arrange, order, class; *antonym* (*adj*) fresh.

ráðgjafi 1. consultant; *synonyms* (*n*) advisor, adviser, expert, authority, specialist, **2**. adviser; *synonyms* (*n*) consultant, counselor, counsel, guide, prompter, **3**. coach; *synonyms* (*n*) trainer, tutor, instructor, teacher, (*adj*) prime.

ráðgjöf 1. consultation; *synonyms* (*n*) advice, conference, interview, negotiation, counsel, **2**. counseling; *synonyms* (*n*) counselling, advocate, assistance, charge, (*adj*) advisory.

raðgreiðsla installment; *synonyms* (*n*) episode, installation, deposit, installing, instalment.

ráðherra 1. secretary; *synonyms* (*n*) clerk, escritoire, minister, desk, (*v*) amanuensis, **2**. minister; *synonyms* (*n*) pastor, envoy, priest, deputy, divine.

ráðherraembætti 1. portfolio; *synonyms* (*n*) briefcase, album, file, bandolier, budget, **2**. ministry; *synonyms* (*n*) cabinet, government, clergy, ministration, administration.

radíani radian; *synonym* (*n*) rad.

radín radium; *synonyms* (*v*) plutonium, radiation, radioactivity, radon, tritium.

radíum radium; *synonyms* (*v*) plutonium, radiation, radioactivity, radon, tritium.

radíus radius; *synonyms* (*n*) length, semidiameter, spoke, range, compass.

ráðkænska policy; *synonyms* (*n*) course, plan, approach, insurance, tactics.

ráðlegur expedient; *synonyms* (*adj*) fit, adequate, advisable, (*n*) contrivance, makeshift.

raðmögnun cascade; *synonyms* (*n*) waterfall, torrent, (*v*) fall, gush, stream; *antonyms* (*v*) trickle, dribble.

ráðning 1. recruitment; *synonyms* (*n*) employment, enrollment, enlisting, mobilization, **2.** evaluation; *synonyms* (*n*) appraisal, assessment, estimation, judgment, mark, **3.** engagement; *synonyms* (*n*) combat, battle, appointment, commitment, conflict, **4.** employment; *synonyms* (*n*) business, (*v*) application, employ, calling, (*adj*) work; *antonym* (*n*) unemployment.

ráðningarsamningur indenture; *synonyms* (*n*) bond, indent, agreement, contract, covenant.

ráðningarstarfsemi recruitment; *synonyms* (*n*) employment, enrollment, enlisting, mobilization.

ráðningartenging linkage; *synonyms* (*n*) link, bond, connection, association, coupling.

ráðstafa allocate; *synonyms* (*v*) divide, apportion, set, place, allot.

ráðstefna 1. convention; *synonyms* (*n*) conference, congress, meeting, contract, assembly, **2.** congress; *synonyms* (*n*) convention, convocation, council, intercourse, congregation, **3.** conference; *synonyms* (*n*) colloquy, consultation, interview, negotiation, talk.

ráðstöfun 1. provision; *synonyms* (*n*) arrangement, condition, clause, (*v*) preparation, feed; *antonym* (*n*) lack, **2.** arrangement; *synonyms* (*n*) agreement, order, settlement, adjustment, array, **3.** appropriation; *synonyms* (*n*) allotment, adoption, seizure, annexation, embezzlement, **4.** allocation; *synonyms* (*n*) portion, allowance, quota, share, grant, **5.** disposal; *synonyms* (*n*) disposition, administration, distribution, organization, sale.

ráðstöfunarvald optional; *synonyms* (*adj*) discretionary, arbitrary, voluntary, nonobligatory, unrestricted; *antonyms* (*adj*) obligatory, compulsory, required, essential, necessary.

raðtala rank; *synonyms* (*n*) range, place, (*v*) arrange, order, class; *antonym* (*adj*) fresh.

raðtenging series; *synonyms* (*n*) chain, rank, collection, cycle, (*v*) course.

ráðunautur 1. consultant; *synonyms* (*n*) advisor, adviser, expert, authority, specialist, **2.** adviser;

synonyms (*n*) consultant, counselor, counsel, guide, prompter.

ráðuneyti 1. cabinet; *synonyms* (*n*) case, closet, locker, press, cupboard, **2.** department; *synonyms* (*n*) bureau, compartment, area, agency, class, **3.** ministry; *synonyms* (*n*) cabinet, government, clergy, ministration, administration.

ráðvendni honesty; *synonyms* (*n*) candor, fairness, integrity, justice, candidness; *antonyms* (*n*) dishonesty, deceit, deception, deviousness, treachery.

ræða speech; *synonyms* (*n*) address, delivery, expression, lecture, conversation.

ræði rowlock; *synonyms* (*n*) oarlock, peg, pin, pivot, thole.

ræðismaður consul; *synonyms* (*n*) archon, diplomat, chancellor, internuncio, legate.

ræðismannsbústaður consulate; *synonyms* (*n*) consulship, administration.

ræðismannsskrifstofa consulate; *synonyms* (*n*) consulship, administration.

ræðumaður speaker; *synonyms* (*n*) loudspeaker, narrator, orator, president, spokesman.

ræður rational; *synonyms* (*adj*) intellectual, reasonable, intelligent, judicious, logical; *antonyms* (*adj*) irrational, illogical, anxious.

rækja prawn; *synonyms* (*n*) shrimp, peewee, runt.

rækt 1. culture; *synonyms* (*n*) civilization, breeding, cultivation, acculturation, education, **2.** breeding; *synonyms* (*n*) generation, manners, nurture, reproduction, upbringing.

rækta culture; *synonyms* (*n*) civilization, breeding, cultivation, acculturation, education.

ræktun 1. breeding; *synonyms* (*n*) education, generation, manners, nurture, reproduction, **2.** culture; *synonyms* (*n*) civilization, breeding, cultivation, acculturation, learning.

ræktunarfræði agronomy; *synonyms* (*n*) agriculture, farming, tillage, gardening, vintage.

ræma 1. tape; *synonyms* (*n*) band, ribbon, strip, (*v*) record, videotape, **2.** corridor; *synonyms* (*n*) aisle, hall, lobby, hallway, (*v*) passage.

rænuleysi absence; *synonyms* (*n*) absenteeism, dearth, default, deficiency, lack; *antonyms* (*n*) presence, attendance.

ræpa diarrhea; *synonyms* (*n*) diarrhoea, lax, looseness.

ræsa 1. start; *synonyms* (*v*) begin, originate, commence, (*n*) jump, onset; *antonyms* (*v*) end, finish, stop, conclude, (*n*) conclusion, **2.** trigger; *synonyms* (*v*) activate, initiate, spark, start, incite, **3.** boot; *synonyms* (*n*) kick, trunk, bang, charge, gain.

ræsimætti starting; *synonyms* (*n*) start, commencement, (*adj*) opening, initial, (*prep*) beginning.

ræsimerki trigger; *synonyms* (*v*) activate, initiate, spark, start, incite.

ræsing 1. start; *synonyms* (*v*) begin, originate, commence, (*n*) jump, onset; *antonyms* (*v*) end, finish, stop, conclude, (*n*) conclusion, **2.** starting; *synonyms* (*n*) start, commencement, (*adj*) opening, initial, (*prep*) beginning, **3.** activation; *synonyms* (*n*) activating, initiation, launch, awakening, creation, **4.** boot; *synonyms* (*n*) kick, trunk, bang, charge, gain.

ræsir 1. starter; *synonyms* (*n*) appetizer, beginner, crank, dispatcher, entrant, **2.** trigger; *synonyms* (*v*) activate, initiate, spark, start, incite, **3.** activator; *synonym* (*n*) inducer.

raf amber; *synonyms* (*n*) succinite, yellow, electrum, brown, electron.

rafaldsmynd radiograph; *synonyms* (*n*) radiogram, x-ray, shadowgraph, skiagram, skiagraph.

rafali generator; *synonyms* (*n*) author, creator, founder, boiler, originator.

rafall 1. dynamo, **2.** generator; *synonyms* (*n*) author, creator, founder, boiler, originator.

rafberi carrier; *synonyms* (*n*) bearer, messenger, courier, mailman, porter.

rafbrynja shielding; *synonyms* (*n*) shadowing, (*adj*) protective, covering, protecting, caring.

rafbúnaður 1. armature; *synonyms* (*n*) armament, armaments, skeleton, frame, framework, **2.** equipment; *synonyms* (*n*) material, apparatus, facility, gear, (*v*) furniture.

rafdeyðing electrocution; *synonyms* (*n*) burning, burn, combustion, execution, (*v*) scarpines.

rafdráttur 1. iontophoresis, **2.** electrophoresis; *synonyms* (*n*) cataphoresis, ionophoresis.

rafeind electron; *synonyms* (*n*) electricity, molecule, negatron, amber.

rafeindadrægur electronegative; *synonyms* (*adj*) damaging, disconfirming, negative, minus.

rafeindagæfur electropositive; *synonyms* (*adj*) cocksure, confirming, positive, favorable, incontrovertible.

rafeindahola hole; *synonyms* (*n*) cavity, aperture, crack, den, (*adj*) gap.

rafeindajákvæður electropositive; *synonyms* (*adj*) cocksure, confirming, positive, favorable, incontrovertible.

rafeindaneikvæður electronegative; *synonyms* (*adj*) damaging, disconfirming, negative, minus.

rafeindarstökk transition; *synonyms* (*n*) change, passage, transit, alteration, changeover.

rafeindastýrður electronic; *synonyms* (*adj*) automated, automatic.

rafeindatæknilegur electronic; *synonyms* (*adj*) automated, automatic.

rafeindavæddur electronic; *synonyms* (*adj*) automated, automatic.

raferti excitability; *synonyms* (*n*) reactivity, irritability, impetuosity, vehemence, biliousness.

rafertimörk threshold; *synonyms* (*n*) brink, limen, beginning, doorsill, doorstep.

rafgas plasma; *synonyms* (*n*) plasm, onyx, blood, flesh.

rafgeymamælir hydrometer; *synonym* (*n*) gravimeter.

rafgeymir 1. accumulator; *synonyms* (*n*) collector, gatherer, store, saver, aggregator, **2.** battery; *synonyms* (*n*) troop, army, barrage, company, collection.

rafgjafi donor; *synonyms* (*n*) contributor, giver, donator, presenter, (*v*) feoffer; *antonyms* (*n*) receiver, recipient.

rafhlað 1. battery; *synonyms* (*n*) troop, army, barrage, company, collection, **2.** cell; *synonyms* (*n*) cage, jail, cadre, hole, cave.

rafhlaða battery; *synonyms* (*n*) troop, army, barrage, company, collection.

rafhleðsla 1. charge; *synonyms* (*n*) accusation, burden, care, (*v*) accuse, blame; *antonyms* (*v*) request, absolve, retreat, **2.** capacitance; *synonyms* (*n*) capacity, capability, capacitor, condenser.

rafhlöðueining cell; *synonyms* (*n*) cage, jail, cadre, hole, cave.

rafhúða galvanize; *synonyms* (*v*) electrify, galvanise, stimulate, encourage, fire.

rafi ion; *synonym* (*n*) molecule.

rafker cell; *synonyms* (*n*) cage, jail, cadre, hole, cave.

rafknúið electric; *synonyms* (*adj*) exciting, electrical, galvanic, emotional, (*v*) mercurial.

raflækning electrotherapy; *synonym* (*n*) electrotherapeutics.

rafleiðsla circuit; *synonyms* (*n*) beat, (*v*) circle, tour, trip, journey.

rafleiðslukerfi harness; *synonyms* (*n*) gear, rein, tether, (*v*) hitch, (*adj*) strap.

rafliði relay; *synonyms* (*n*) relief, spell, (*v*) broadcast, pass, transmit.

rafloki rectifier; *synonym* (*n*) rectificator.

rafmagn electricity; *synonyms* (*adj*) light, lightning, electromagnetism, magnetism, voltaism.

rafmagnsfræði electricity; *synonyms* (*adj*) light, lightning, electromagnetism, magnetism, voltaism.

rafmagnskapall cable; *synonyms* (*n*) rope, line, cablegram, telegram, (*v*) wire.

rafmagnskló plug; *synonyms* (*n*) hype, stopper, bung, (*v*) advertise, block.

rafmagnspúls trigger; *synonyms* (*v*) activate, initiate, spark, start, incite.

rafmagnstafla switchboard; *synonyms* (*n*) patchboard, plugboard.

rafmagnstengill plug; *synonyms* (*n*) hype, stopper, bung, (*v*) advertise, block.

rafmagnsvír wire; *synonyms* (*n*) cable, telegram, line, rope, (*v*) telegraph.

rafmeðferð electrotherapy; *synonym* (*n*) electrotherapeutics.

rafmerki pulse; *synonyms* (*n*) beat, impulse, pulsation, (*v*) pulsate, throb.

rafmögnun electrification; *synonyms* (*n*) electrization, exhilaration.

rafnæmi sensitivity; *synonyms* (*n*) sensibility, feeling, sensation, sense, sensitiveness; *antonym* (*n*) insensitivity.

rafneisti 1. spark; *synonyms* (*n*) flicker, (*v*) flash, sparkle, gleam, glint, **2**. arc; *synonyms* (*n*) arch, bow, bend, crescent, (*v*) curve.

rafnemi electrode; *synonym* (*n*) rheophore.

rafögn electron; *synonyms* (*n*) electricity, molecule, negatron, amber.

raforka electricity; *synonyms* (*adj*) light, lightning, electromagnetism, magnetism, voltaism.

rafpóll electrode; *synonym* (*n*) rheophore.

rafrás circuit; *synonyms* (*n*) beat, (*v*) circle, tour, trip, journey.

rafreiknir computer; *synonyms* (*n*) calculator, mainframe, machine, reckoner, laptop.

rafrýmd capacitance; *synonyms* (*n*) capacity, capability, capacitor, condenser.

rafsamband contact; *synonyms* (*n*) touch, connection, collision, communication, (*v*) call.

rafsegulafl electromagnetism; *synonyms* (*n*) electromagnetics, (*adj*) electricity, galvanism, gravity, magnetism.

rafsegulbylgja signal; *synonyms* (*n*) sign, gesture, indication, presage, (*v*) omen.

rafsegulfræði 1. electromagnetism; *synonyms* (*n*) electromagnetics, (*adj*) electricity, galvanism, gravity, magnetism, **2**. electrodynamics.

rafsegulmagn electromagnetism; *synonyms* (*n*) electromagnetics, (*adj*) electricity, galvanism, gravity, magnetism.

rafsegulmögnun excitation; *synonyms* (*n*) excitement, stimulus, agitation, encouragement, feeling.

rafsegulspönun inductance; *synonyms* (*n*) inductor, induction, elicitation, evocation, generalisation.

rafsía filter; *synonyms* (*v*) percolate, sieve, drip, leak, filtrate; *antonym* (*v*) contaminate.

rafsjóða weld; *synonyms* (*v*) join, solder, bond, cement, fasten.

rafskaut electrode; *synonym* (*n*) rheophore.

rafskautun polarization; *synonyms* (*n*) polarisation, bias, divergence, discord, division.

rafspenna 1. tension; *synonyms* (*n*) tenseness, pressure, strain, nervousness, stress; *antonyms* (*n*) calmness, looseness, **2**. voltage; *synonyms* (*n*) potential, emf, energy, power, current.

rafspóla coil; *synonyms* (*n*) spiral, roll, loop, (*v*) curl, circle; *antonym* (*v*) uncoil.

rafstraumsmælir galvanometer; *synonyms* (*n*) rheometer, (*v*) bathometer, dynamometer, goniometer, heliometer.

rafstraumur 1. electricity; *synonyms* (*adj*) light, lightning, electromagnetism, magnetism, voltaism, **2**. current; *synonyms* (*adj*) common, contemporary, (*n*) flow, stream, (*prep*) course; *antonyms* (*adj*) obsolete, past, old, old-fashioned, previous.

rafsvari dielectric; *synonyms* (*n*) insulator, nonconductor.

raftæknilegur electronic; *synonyms* (*adj*) automated, automatic.

raftaugakerfi network; *synonyms* (*n*) net, grid, mesh, netting, reticulation.

raftaugarhlíf shield; *synonyms* (*n*) screen, shelter, (*v*) cover, guard, safeguard; *antonym* (*v*) expose.

raftengi contact; *synonyms* (*n*) touch, connection, collision, communication, (*v*) call.

raftenging contact; *synonyms* (*n*) touch, connection, collision, communication, (*v*) call.

rafþegi acceptor; *synonyms* (*n*) accepter, respecter.

rafþéttir 1. capacitor; *synonyms* (*n*) condenser, capacitance, capacity, **2**. condenser; *synonyms* (*n*) capacitor, plugger.

raftur rafter; *synonyms* (*n*) beam, balk, girder, raftsman, timber.

rafvæðing electrification; *synonyms* (*n*) electrization, exhilaration.

raggeit chicken; *synonyms* (*n*) chick, cock, coward, fowl, hen.

ragú 1. stew; *synonyms* (*v*) boil, cook, fret, simmer, (*adj*) brothel, **2**. ragout; *synonyms* (*v*) stew, hash, rechauffe, releve, remove.

rák 1. band; *synonyms* (*n*) cluster, party, set, swathe, (*v*) ring, **2**. fringe; *synonyms* (*n*) brim, brink, edge, boundary, (*v*) border.

raka rake; *synonyms* (*n*) profligate, (*v*) tilt, hoe, harrow, (*adj*) comb.

rakadrægur 1. absorbent; *synonyms* (*adj*) absorptive, penetrable, porous, thirsty, (*n*) sorbent; *antonym* (*adj*) impermeable, **2**. desiccant; *synonyms* (*adj*) dry, drying, (*n*) drier, dryer.

rakadráttur desiccation; *synonyms* (n) dehydration, drought, evaporation, dryness, (adj) exsiccation.

rakagleypir desiccator; *synonym* (n) exsiccator.

rakamælir 1. psychrometer, 2. hygrometer; *synonym* (adj) hygrometry.

rakamagn humidity; *synonyms* (n) damp, dampness, moisture, wet, wetness; *antonym* (n) dryness.

rakariti hygrograph; *synonym* (n) hygrogram.

rakasíriti hygrograph; *synonym* (n) hygrogram.

rakastig humidity; *synonyms* (n) damp, dampness, moisture, wet, wetness; *antonym* (n) dryness.

rakaþétting condensation; *synonyms* (n) abridgement, digest, abridgment, capsule, compression.

rakhnífur razor; *synonyms* (n) rasour, (adj) blade, knife, cutlery, penknife.

raki 1. damp; *synonyms* (adj) moist, muggy, (v) break, check, (n) wet; *antonyms* (adj) dry, (n) dryness, 2. humidity; *synonyms* (n) damp, dampness, moisture, wetness, humidness, 3. moisture; *synonyms* (n) humidity, moistness, vapor.

rakleið geodesic; *synonyms* (adj) geodetic, geodesical, geodetical.

rakning tracing; *synonyms* (n) drawing, trace, copy, design, model.

rakningur trace; *synonyms* (n) line, shadow, spot, clue, (v) track.

rákóttur 1. striate; *synonym* (v) streak, 2. striated; *synonyms* (adj) striate, streaked, (v) ribbed, sulcated, veined.

rakur 1. wet; *synonyms* (adj) damp, humid, (v) moisten, water, dampen; *antonyms* (adj) dehydrated, parched, (v) dry, 2. damp; *synonyms* (adj) moist, muggy, (v) break, check, (n) wet; *antonym* (n) dryness, 3. humid; *synonyms* (adj) dank, sultry, clammy, oppressive, soggy; *antonym* (adj) fresh, 4. moist; *synonyms* (adj) dampish, wettish, juicy, sodden, sticky.

rakvél razor; *synonyms* (n) rasour, (adj) blade, knife, cutlery, penknife.

rammi 1. box; *synonyms* (n) basket, cage, chest, (v) cuff, buffet; *antonym* (v) unbox, 2. bezel; *synonyms* (n) crown, flange, 3. frame; *synonyms* (n) design, border, (v) form, construct, fabricate, 4. framework; *synonyms* (n) frame, fabric, framing, chassis, shell.

ramo bough; *synonyms* (n) branch, arm, limb, member, ramage.

rampi ramp; *synonyms* (n) incline, inclination, slant, (v) bound, climb.

rampur ramp; *synonyms* (n) incline, inclination, slant, (v) bound, climb.

rán larceny; *synonyms* (n) theft, embezzlement, robbery, stealing, burglary.

randaborri rock; *synonyms* (n) boulder, calculus, (v) jar, (adj) pebble, stone.

randbyggð 1. suburbia; *synonyms* (n) suburb, outskirts, 2. block; *synonyms* (n) bar, barricade, pad, (v) arrest, stop; *antonyms* (v) free, unblock, open.

randbygging block; *synonyms* (n) bar, barricade, pad, (v) arrest, stop; *antonyms* (v) free, unblock, open.

randhærður ciliated; *synonyms* (adj) ciliate, filamentous, hirsute, cilial, ciliary.

randhár cilium; *synonyms* (n) eyelash, lash, capillament, hair, pili.

randstæður marginal; *synonyms* (adj) borderline, border, peripheral, edge, fringe.

rándýr 1. predator; *synonyms* (n) marauder, vulture, piranha, destroyer, scavenger, 2. carnivore.

rangeygð strabismus; *synonyms* (n) squint, strabism.

ranggeislunarhorn squint; *synonyms* (n) glance, look, (v) leer, (adj) askant, sidelong.

ranghorn squint; *synonyms* (n) glance, look, (v) leer, (adj) askant, sidelong.

rangsælis 1. upstream; *synonyms* (adj) difficult, (adv) upriver, 2. counterclockwise; *synonyms* (adv) anticlockwise, (adj) contraclockwise; *antonym* (adv) clockwise, 3. back; *synonyms* (n) rear, (adj) assist, (v) support, advocate, endorse; *antonyms* (n) face, (v) front, oppose, advance, 4. anticlockwise; *synonym* (adv) counterclockwise.

rangtúlkun falsification; *synonyms* (n) fake, falsehood, distortion, deceit, deception.

Rangur wrong; *synonyms* (adj) harm, evil, false, ill, (n) damage; *antonyms* (adj) correct, good, proper, (adv) correctly, (v) right.

rani spur; *synonyms* (n) inducement, incentive, impulse, (v) goad, incite.

ránlíf predation; *synonym* (n) depredation.

rannsaka 1. research; *synonyms* (n) exploration, inquiry, search, examination, (v) check, 2. test; *synonyms* (n) trial, audition, (v) assay, essay, examine, 3. probe; *synonyms* (n) investigation, (v) explore, inspect, fathom, investigate, 4. examine; *synonyms* (v) audit, consider, overhaul, try, control.

rannsókn 1. investigation; *synonyms* (n) examination, research, analysis, inquest, inquiry, 2. survey; *synonyms* (n) poll, review, (v) study, measure, view; *antonym* (v) neglect, 3. research; *synonyms* (n) exploration, search, investigation, (v) check, explore, 4. examination; *synonyms* (n) audit, exam, test, consideration, (adj) examen, 5. inquiry; *synonyms* (n) enquiry, hearing, query, question, trial.

rannsóknaráætlun regimen; *synonyms* (*n*) regime, diet, government, treatment, cure.

rannsóknarefni material; *synonyms* (*n*) body, cloth, (*adj*) bodily, corporal, corporeal.

rannsóknarstofa laboratory; *synonyms* (*n*) lab, factory, course, (*adj*) experimental, alembic.

rannsóknarþýði cohort; *synonyms* (*n*) group, associate, colleague, friend, follower.

rannsóknastofa laboratory; *synonyms* (*n*) lab, factory, course, (*adj*) experimental, alembic.

rannsóknir 1. research; *synonyms* (*n*) exploration, inquiry, search, examination, (*v*) check, **2.** exploration; *synonyms* (*n*) discovery, expedition, investigation, probe, quest.

ráp browse; *synonyms* (*v*) graze, crop, scan, skim, (*n*) browsing; *antonym* (*v*) study.

rápa 1. browse; *synonyms* (*v*) graze, crop, scan, skim, (*n*) browsing; *antonym* (*v*) study, **2.** navigate; *synonyms* (*v*) cruise, guide, sail, fly, pilot.

rápforrit 1. browser, **2.** navigator; *synonyms* (*n*) pilot, mariner, sailor, aviator, aeroplanist.

raporto 1. records; *synonyms* (*n*) archive, documents, minutes, proceedings, certification, **2.** papers; *synonyms* (*n*) credentials, document, identification, covenant, deed.

rár spar; *synonyms* (*n*) beam, mast, (*v*) quarrel, box, fight.

rás 1. track; *synonyms* (*n*) course, path, (*v*) trace, trail, hunt, **2.** suppressor; *synonym* (*n*) suppresser, **3.** train; *synonyms* (*v*) aim, coach, direct, educate, exercise, **4.** duct; *synonyms* (*n*) channel, conduit, canal, drain, aqueduct, **5.** channel; *synonyms* (*n*) groove, duct, (*n*) carry, conduct, convey.

rása 1. purge; *synonyms* (*v*) cleanse, clean, expurgate, eradicate, clear; *antonym* (*v*) binge, **2.** swing; *synonyms* (*v*) sway, fluctuate, oscillate, dangle, hang.

rásaður cyclic; *synonyms* (*adj*) periodic, circular, cyclical, recurring, regular; *antonym* (*adj*) irregular.

rásaskiptir distributor; *synonyms* (*n*) distributer, spreader, middleman, allocator, feeder.

rásasmit crosstalk; *synonym* (*n*) diaphony.

rasi race; *synonyms* (*n*) kind, dash, family, (*v*) course, (*adj*) lineage.

ráskerðingur stockfish; *synonym* (*n*) titling.

raspa 1. rasp; *synonyms* (*v*) grate, scrape, abrade, chafe, file, **2.** grate; *synonyms* (*v*) creak, grind, fret, gall, gnash.

raspur rasp; *synonyms* (*v*) grate, scrape, abrade, chafe, file.

rass 1. bottom; *synonyms* (*n*) base, basis, backside, bed, behind; *antonyms* (*n*) top, pinnacle, (*adj*) highest, **2.** buttocks; *synonyms* (*n*) bottom, arse,

ass, bum, butt, **3.** backside; *synonyms* (*n*) back, rear, reverse, buttocks, can; *antonym* (*n*) front, **4.** behind; *synonyms* (*prep*) after, abaft, (*adv*) backward, backwards, late; *antonyms* (*adv*) ahead, early, fore.

rasskinnar buttocks; *synonyms* (*n*) backside, bottom, arse, ass, bum.

ratsjá radar; *synonyms* (*n*) radiolocation, beacon, monitor.

ratsjártækni radar; *synonyms* (*n*) radiolocation, beacon, monitor.

rauða yolk; *synonyms* (*n*) deutoplasm, suint, vitellus.

rauðaleysandi hemolytic; *synonym* (*adj*) haemolytic.

rauðalos hemolysis; *synonyms* (*n*) haemolysis, haematolysis, hematolysis.

rauðauga roach; *synonyms* (*n*) cockroach, dace, circle, roofy, rope.

rauðbeða beetroot; *synonym* (*n*) beet.

rauðbeðja beetroot; *synonym* (*n*) beet.

rauðber cowberry; *synonyms* (*n*) foxberry, lingberry, lingenberry, lingonberry.

rauðberjalyng cowberry; *synonyms* (*n*) foxberry, lingberry, lingenberry, lingonberry.

rauðelri alder; *synonym* (*adj*) aller.

rauðfrumuforveri erythroblast; *synonyms* (*n*) gametangium, gamete, invagination, normoblast.

rauðgulur orange; *synonyms* (*adj*) amber, (*n*) orangeness, lemon, etc, lime.

rauðhundar rubella; *synonym* (*n*) rubeola.

rauðkornamóðir erythroblast; *synonyms* (*n*) gametangium, gamete, invagination, normoblast.

rauðkornarjúfandi hemolytic; *synonym* (*adj*) haemolytic.

rauðkornarof hemolysis; *synonyms* (*n*) haemolysis, haematolysis, hematolysis.

rauðkornskímfruma erythroblast; *synonyms* (*n*) gametangium, gamete, invagination, normoblast.

rauðmagi lump; *synonyms* (*n*) heap, chunk, knot, block, (*v*) clot.

rauðolur alder; *synonym* (*adj*) aller.

rauðrófa beetroot; *synonym* (*n*) beet.

rauðspretta plaice; *synonyms* (*n*) flounder, tonguefishes.

rauður red; *synonyms* (*adj*) crimson, flushed, carmine, glowing, rosy.

rauf 1. rifle; *synonyms* (*n*) gun, (*v*) pillage, plunder, despoil, loot, **2.** slot; *synonyms* (*n*) groove, place, notch, gap, (*v*) slit, **3.** score; *synonyms* (*n*) mark, bill, count, scratch, line, **4.** stoma; *synonyms* (*n*) pore, aperture, hole, stomate, **5.** cloaca; *synonyms* (*n*) drain, sewer, culvert, ditch, gully.

raufa perforate; *synonyms* (*v*) penetrate, bore, drill, cut, pierce.

raufagler grating; *synonyms* (*adj*) rough, harsh, hoarse, strident, discordant; *antonyms* (*adj*) soft, pleasing.

raufaræðahnútur hemorrhoid; *synonyms* (*n*) haemorrhoid, piles, dozens, gobs, heaps.

raufarhleri shutter; *synonyms* (*n*) close, curtain, blind, shut, (*v*) screen.

raufun perforation; *synonyms* (*n*) hole, puncture, aperture, opening, pit.

raufungur slat; *synonyms* (*n*) board, plank, spline, amount, stick.

raungildi absolute; *synonyms* (*adj*) downright, peremptory, total, unconditional, categorical; *antonyms* (*adj*) partial, qualified.

raungildur real; *synonyms* (*adj*) genuine, material, physical, true, (*v*) actual; *antonyms* (*adj*) unreal, imaginary, apparent, artificial, (*v*) pretend.

raunhorn radian; *synonym* (*n*) rad.

raunhyggja 1. realism; *synonyms* (*n*) naturalism, reality, authenticity, fidelity, realness; *antonym* (*n*) idealism, 2. positivism; *synonyms* (*n*) positivity, certainty, anabaptism, deism, externalism, 3. empiricism; *synonyms* (*n*) quackery, charlatanism, charlatanry, discovery, experience.

raunhyggjuaðferð empiricism; *synonyms* (*n*) quackery, charlatanism, charlatanry, discovery, experience.

raunlægur physical; *synonyms* (*adj*) material, bodily, actual, corporeal, tangible; *antonyms* (*adj*) spiritual, mental, intangible.

raunsæi 1. realism; *synonyms* (*n*) naturalism, reality, authenticity, fidelity, realness; *antonym* (*n*) idealism, 2. pragmatism; *synonyms* (*n*) practicality, convenience, expediency, pride, realism.

raunsæishyggja realism; *synonyms* (*n*) naturalism, reality, authenticity, fidelity, realness; *antonym* (*n*) idealism.

raunsæismaður realist; *synonym* (*n*) real; *antonyms* (*n*) romantic, theorist, visionary.

raunsæisstefna realism; *synonyms* (*n*) naturalism, reality, authenticity, fidelity, realness; *antonym* (*n*) idealism.

raunsær realistic; *synonyms* (*adj*) naturalistic, graphic, lifelike, practical, pragmatic; *antonym* (*adj*) unrealistic.

raunspeki positivism; *synonyms* (*n*) positivity, certainty, anabaptism, deism, externalism.

raunverulegur 1. real; *synonyms* (*adj*) genuine, material, physical, true, (*v*) actual; *antonyms* (*adj*) unreal, imaginary, apparent, artificial, (*v*) pretend, 2. practical; *synonyms* (*adj*) operative, practicable, efficient, feasible, functional; *antonyms* (*adj*) impractical, theoretical, unrealistic, useless,

impossible, 3. realistic; *synonyms* (*adj*) naturalistic, graphic, lifelike, practical, pragmatic, 4. actual; *synonyms* (*adj*) real, absolute, factual, authentic, existent; *antonyms* (*adj*) false, hypothetical, supposed, 5. objective; *synonyms* (*adj*) dispassionate, (*n*) aim, mark, goal, object; *antonyms* (*adj*) biased, subjective.

raunveruleiki reality; *synonyms* (*n*) fact, existence, actuality, certainty, realism; *antonyms* (*n*) fantasy, delusion, dream, imagination, vision.

raunviðnám 1. resistivity; *synonyms* (*n*) resistance, impedance, immunity, opposition, underground, 2. resistance; *synonyms* (*n*) endurance, friction, obstacle, (*v*) rebellion, interference; *antonyms* (*n*) smoothness, agreement, obedience, susceptibility.

raunvirða deflate; *synonyms* (*v*) collapse, lower, depress, contract, reduce; *antonyms* (*v*) inflate, swell.

raunvirði volume; *synonyms* (*n*) bulk, size, book, magnitude, mass; *antonym* (*n*) quietness.

raunvís empirical; *synonyms* (*adj*) empiric, experimental, observational, observed, (*v*) tentative; *antonym* (*adj*) theoretical.

raunvísindalegur empirical; *synonyms* (*adj*) empiric, experimental, observational, observed, (*v*) tentative; *antonym* (*adj*) theoretical.

raunvísindi science; *synonyms* (*n*) learning, lore, knowledge, literature, (*adj*) art.

rausnarskapur 1. unselfishness; *synonyms* (*n*) altruism, generosity, generousness, kindness, care; *antonym* (*n*) selfishness, 2. generosity; *synonyms* (*n*) charity, benevolence, bounty, liberality, (*adj*) beneficence; *antonyms* (*n*) stinginess, greed, meanness, thrift.

reagens reagent; *synonyms* (*n*) crucible, touchstone, chemical.

reðurfylld erection; *synonyms* (*n*) building, edifice, assembly, construction, structure.

reðurspenna erection; *synonyms* (*n*) building, edifice, assembly, construction, structure.

reðurstaða erection; *synonyms* (*n*) building, edifice, assembly, construction, structure.

reðurstýfing emasculation; *synonyms* (*n*) castration, (*adj*) orchotomy, orchiotomy.

refasmári alfalfa; *synonyms* (*n*) lucern, alfilaria, banyan, lamp.

referaðo papers; *synonyms* (*n*) credentials, document, documents, identification, covenant.

reformur 1. tinea; *synonyms* (*n*) ringworm, roundworm, nematode, 2. ringworm; *synonyms* (*n*) tinea, (*adj*) necrosis, pertussis, phthisis, pneumonia.

refsiaðgerð sanction; *synonyms* (*n*) warrant, assent, (*v*) approve, permit, countenance; *antonyms* (*v*) ban, forbid.

refsiákvæði sanction; *synonyms* (*n*) warrant, assent, (*v*) approve, permit, countenance; *antonyms* (*v*) ban, forbid.

refsing 1. punishment; *synonyms* (*n*) discipline, correction, penalty, penance, chastisement, **2.** penalty; *synonyms* (*n*) mulct, fine, forfeit, forfeiture, (*v*) condemnation.

refsivist imprisonment; *synonyms* (*n*) captivity, custody, confinement, incarceration, durance; *antonyms* (*n*) freedom, release.

refur fox; *synonyms* (*n*) dodger, (*v*) confound, confuse, fob, bewilder.

regado 1. rules; *synonyms* (*n*) regulations, etiquette, policy, system, convention, **2.** regulations.

regi 1. rule; *synonyms* (*n*) govern, order, decree, (*v*) command, control, **2.** rules; *synonyms* (*n*) regulations, etiquette, policy, system, convention.

registri records; *synonyms* (*n*) archive, documents, minutes, proceedings, certification.

registro records; *synonyms* (*n*) archive, documents, minutes, proceedings, certification.

regla 1. rule; *synonyms* (*n*) govern, order, decree, (*v*) command, control, **2.** regulations; *synonyms* (*n*) policy, system, convention, **3.** principle; *synonyms* (*n*) origin, fundamental, method, rule, cause, **4.** constitution; *synonyms* (*n*) composition, code, makeup, organization, temperament, **5.** directive; *synonyms* (*n*) direction, edict, instruction, (*adj*) directing, directional.

reglaus arid; *synonyms* (*adj*) dry, dull, barren, boring, (*v*) monotonous; *antonyms* (*adj*) wet, verdant.

reglubundið routine; *synonyms* (*n*) round, (*adj*) everyday, ordinary, regular, common; *antonym* (*adj*) unusual.

reglugerð 1. regulation; *synonyms* (*n*) rule, adjustment, law, order, (*adj*) control; *antonym* (*n*) chaos, **2.** regulations; *synonyms* (*n*) policy, system, convention, **3.** circular; *synonyms* (*adj*) round, annular, circinate, (*n*) advertisement, bill; *antonym* (*adj*) square, **4.** directive; *synonyms* (*n*) decree, direction, edict, (*adj*) directing, directional.

reglugerðir regulations; *synonyms* (*n*) policy, system, convention.

reglun regulation; *synonyms* (*n*) rule, adjustment, law, order, (*adj*) control; *antonym* (*n*) chaos.

reglur regulations; *synonyms* (*n*) policy, system, convention.

reglustika 1. ruler; *synonyms* (*n*) master, governor, monarch, (*adj*) rule, regent, **2.** rule; *synonyms* (*n*) govern, order, decree, (*v*) command, control.

regluveldi bureaucracy; *synonyms* (*n*) bureaucratism, apparatus, cabinet, fascism, formalities.

regn rain; *synonyms* (*n*) precipitation, (*v*) pour, stream, hail, precipitate.

regna rain; *synonyms* (*n*) precipitation, (*v*) pour, stream, hail, precipitate.

regnbogahimna iris; *synonyms* (*n*) diaphragm, flag, pupil, rainbow, comet.

regnbogi rainbow; *synonyms* (*n*) iris, tulip, sunbow, chimera, (*adj*) colorful.

regnfrakki raincoat; *synonyms* (*n*) mackintosh, waterproof, coat, slicker, oilskin.

regnský 1. nimbus; *synonyms* (*n*) halo, glory, aureole, aura, (*v*) flush, **2.** nimbostratus.

regnþykkni 1. nimbus; *synonyms* (*n*) halo, glory, aureole, aura, (*v*) flush, **2.** nimbostratus.

reguligo regulations; *synonyms* (*n*) policy, system, convention.

regulo 1. regulations; *synonyms* (*n*) policy, system, convention, **2.** rules; *synonyms* (*n*) regulations, etiquette.

reið 1. vehicle; *synonyms* (*n*) medium, instrument, means, automobile, channel, **2.** transportation; *synonyms* (*n*) deportation, banishment, exile, (*v*) transport, conveyance, **3.** transport; *synonyms* (*v*) transfer, transmit, bear, carry, delight; *antonyms* (*v*) disenchant, remain.

reiða availability; *synonyms* (*n*) accessibility, handiness, approachability, availableness, opening.

reiðhjól 1. bicycle; *synonyms* (*n*) machine, (*v*) bike, wheel, cycle, pedal, **2.** cycle; *synonyms* (*n*) bicycle, circle, round, ring, (*v*) motorcycle, **3.** bike; *synonym* (*n*) motorbike.

reiði 1. rig; *synonyms* (*n*) array, outfit, (*v*) dress, apparel, attire, **2.** anger; *synonyms* (*n*) displeasure, fury, rage, (*v*) enrage, incense; *antonyms* (*n*) pleasure, (*v*) please, placate, pacify, calm, **3.** ire; *synonyms* (*n*) indignation, anger, wrath, choler, resentment.

reiðubúinn 1. ready; *synonyms* (*adj*) fit, prompt, quick, (*v*) prepare, (*n*) available; *antonyms* (*adj*) unprepared, unwilling, **2.** willing; *synonyms* (*adj*) agreeable, disposed, ready, spontaneous, voluntary; *antonym* (*adj*) reluctant, **3.** obliging; *synonyms* (*v*) complaisant, (*adj*) accommodating, affable, amiable, gentle; *antonyms* (*adj*) unhelpful, uncooperative.

reiðufé cash; *synonyms* (*n*) ready, bread, capital, change, funds; *antonym* (*n*) credit.

reiðufjárgeta liquidity; *synonyms* (*n*) fluidity, fluidness, liquid, liquidness, fluency.

reiðufjárhæfni liquidity; *synonyms* (*n*) fluidity, fluidness, liquid, liquidness, fluency.

reiður 1. wild; *synonyms* (*adj*) desert, waste, fierce, boisterous, violent; *antonyms* (*adj*) calm, orderly, domestic, manageable, sane, **2.** angry; *synonyms* (*adj*) furious, incensed, provoked, irate, raging; *antonyms* (*adj*) pleased, gentle, **3.** cross; *synonyms* (*v*) intersect, baffle, (*adj*) crabbed, crabby, angry; *antonyms* (*v*) uncross, (*adj*) good-tempered, **4.** heated; *synonyms* (*adj*) burning, ardent, excited, hot, passionate.

reik wobble; *synonyms* (*v*) totter, rock, sway, lurch, (*n*) shake.

reikifrumnaútstreymi emigration; *synonyms* (*n*) departure, exodus, migration, demigration, (*v*) intermigration.

reikistjarna planet; *synonyms* (*n*) globe, satellite, world, sphere, orbiter.

reikna 1. calculate; *synonyms* (*v*) count, estimate, account, add, appraise, **2.** reckon; *synonyms* (*v*) deem, enumerate, judge, hold, calculate, **3.** tally; *synonyms* (*n*) check, (*v*) correspond, agree, fit, number, **4.** account; *synonyms* (*n*) bill, narrative, reckoning, regard, (*v*) report, **5.** count; *synonyms* (*n*) calculation, computation, (*v*) compute, tally, cipher.

reikniaðferð algorithm; *synonyms* (*n*) algorism, discovery, (*v*) dactylonomy, rhabdology.

reiknigrind abacus; *synonyms* (*n*) aback, (*v*) logometer, slipstick, tallies.

reiknihending statistic; *synonyms* (*n*) fact, guide, marker, number, sign.

reikningsfærslugreinargerð accounting; *synonyms* (*adj*) clerical, office, (*n*) bookkeeping, account, accountancy.

reikningshald 1. accounting; *synonyms* (*adj*) clerical, office, (*n*) bookkeeping, account, accountancy, **2.** bookkeeping; *synonyms* (*n*) reckoning, clerking, (*adj*) secretarial, **3.** accountancy; *synonym* (*n*) accounting.

reikningsyfirlit statement; *synonyms* (*n*) account, declaration, affirmation, announcement, communication; *antonym* (*n*) denial.

reikningur 1. account; *synonyms* (*n*) bill, narrative, reckoning, regard, (*v*) report, **2.** bill; *synonyms* (*n*) account, beak, advertisement, (*v*) placard, advertise, **3.** invoice; *synonyms* (*n*) list, tab, receipt, score, (*v*) charge, **4.** arithmetic; *synonyms* (*adj*) arithmetical, (*n*) calculation, computation, (*v*) fluxions, geometry, **5.** calculation; *synonyms* (*n*) analysis, arithmetic, deliberation, discretion, estimate; *antonym* (*n*) estimation.

reiknir calculator; *synonyms* (*n*) computer, estimator, reckoner, (*v*) counter, arithmetician.

reiknirit algorithm; *synonyms* (*n*) algorism, discovery, (*v*) dactylonomy, rhabdology.

reiknisögn algorithm; *synonyms* (*n*) algorism, discovery, (*v*) dactylonomy, rhabdology.

reiknivél calculator; *synonyms* (*n*) computer, estimator, reckoner, (*v*) counter, arithmetician.

reiknivísi calculus; *synonyms* (*n*) concretion, stone, calculi, tartar, (*v*) calculation.

reikull erratic; *synonyms* (*adj*) capricious, changeable, eccentric, irregular, freakish; *antonyms* (*adj*) consistent, constant, certain, dependable, predictable.

reim 1. belt; *synonyms* (*n*) ribbon, area, strap, (*v*) band, hit, **2.** lace; *synonyms* (*v*) braid, enlace, entwine, interlace, bind.

reimhjól pulley; *synonyms* (*n*) block, crane, windlass, winch, wheel.

reimskífa pulley; *synonyms* (*n*) block, crane, windlass, winch, wheel.

rein lane; *synonyms* (*n*) course, alley, road, aisle, avenue.

reipi 1. rope; *synonyms* (*n*) cable, lasso, lariat, noose, cord, **2.** lashing; *synonyms* (*n*) beating, drubbing, flagellation, flogging, trouncing.

reisa 1. rotate; *synonyms* (*v*) revolve, reel, roll, alternate, gyrate, **2.** raise; *synonyms* (*v*) boost, lift, erect, hoist, (*n*) advance; *antonym* (*v*) lower, **3.** elevate; *synonyms* (*v*) raise, exalt, cheer, dignify, promote; *antonym* (*v*) demote, **4.** heave; *synonyms* (*v*) cast, fling, chuck, gasp, (*n*) tug, **5.** hoist; *synonyms* (*n*) elevator, (*v*) elevate, haul, heave, rear.

reising 1. rotation; *synonyms* (*n*) revolution, gyration, roll, round, turn, **2.** erection; *synonyms* (*n*) building, edifice, assembly, construction, structure.

reita stimulate; *synonyms* (*v*) excite, incite, arouse, encourage, (*adj*) quicken; *antonym* (*v*) defuse.

reitabretti tablet; *synonyms* (*n*) pad, slab, table, lozenge, pill.

reiti stimulus; *synonyms* (*n*) incentive, encouragement, provocation, spur, motivation.

reiting stimulation; *synonyms* (*n*) excitation, incentive, arousal, encouragement, excitement.

reitur 1. tile; *synonyms* (*n*) bonnet, castor, ceiling, roof, (*v*) cover, **2.** plot; *synonyms* (*n*) conspiracy, plan, lot, (*v*) intrigue, cabal, **3.** square; *synonyms* (*adj*) right, even, rectangular, (*n*) area, (*v*) settle, **4.** beet; *synonym* (*n*) beetroot, **5.** areola; *synonyms* (*n*) armlet, bracelet, hoop, roundlet, areolation.

rek 1. drift; *synonyms* (*n*) stream, current, course, (*v*) aim, blow, **2.** migration; *synonyms* (*n*) exodus, movement, journey, (*v*) flit, flitting.

reka 1. pierce; *synonyms* (*v*) impale, cut, perforate, bore, (*n*) prick, **2.** drift; *synonyms* (*n*) stream, current, course, (*v*) aim, blow, **3.** dismiss;

synonyms (v) discharge, cashier, cast, disband, discard; *antonyms* (v) hire, employ, **4**. operate; *synonyms* (v) act, function, run, direct, go.

rekill 1. catkin; *synonym* (n) ament, **2**. driver; *synonyms* (n) coachman, postboy, club, chaser, commuter.

rekja trace; *synonyms* (n) line, shadow, spot, clue, (v) track.

rekki fitness; *synonyms* (n) ability, adequacy, appropriateness, aptness, capability; *antonyms* (n) unsuitability, inability, unfitness.

rekkur rack; *synonyms* (n) manger, wrack, (v) torture, excruciate, torment.

rekkverk rail; *synonyms* (n) bar, balustrade, handrail, railing, (v) inveigh.

rekorda records; *synonyms* (n) archive, documents, minutes, proceedings, certification.

rekordo records; *synonyms* (n) archive, documents, minutes, proceedings, certification.

rekstraráætlun budget; *synonyms* (n) plan, sack, (v) calculate, compute, (adj) cheap.

rekstrarafkoma performance; *synonyms* (n) act, discharge, achievement, execution, (v) action; *antonyms* (n) omission, practice.

rekstrareind establishment; *synonyms* (n) business, company, constitution, institution, concern; *antonyms* (n) elimination, end.

rekstrareining establishment; *synonyms* (n) business, company, constitution, institution, concern; *antonyms* (n) elimination, end.

rekstrarhagkvæmni economy; *synonyms* (n) frugality, parsimony, saving, thrift, conservation; *antonym* (n) extravagance.

rekstrarkostnaður overhead; *synonyms* (adv) above, aloft, over, up, (n) expense.

rekstrarvörubirgðir supplies; *synonyms* (n) food, provisions, stores, (v) equipment, outfit.

rekstur 1. duty; *synonyms* (n) business, function, commitment, assignment, charge, **2**. operation; *synonyms* (n) execution, movement, act, agency, effect.

relativa relatives; *synonyms* (n) family, relations, kin, kindred, kinsfolk.

remma concentration; *synonyms* (n) absorption, concentrate, application, attention, engrossment; *antonym* (n) distraction.

remmujurt wormwood; *synonyms* (n) absinth, gall.

rengi blubber; *synonyms* (n) cry, fat, (v) sob, weep, bawl.

renín 1. rhenium; *synonym* (n) ray, **2**. renin.

reníum rhenium; *synonym* (n) ray.

renna 1. run; *synonyms* (v) flow, rule, (n) pass, campaign, (adj) stream, **2**. slide; *synonyms* (n) glide, chute, (v) drop, slip, fall, **3**. turn; *synonyms*

(n) bend, curve, roll, coil, go, **4**. zoom; *synonyms* (v) soar, zip, race, surge, whiz, **5**. coast; *synonyms* (n) bank, beach, seaside, shore, (v) slide; *antonym* (n) interior.

rennibekkur lathe; *synonyms* (n) machine, tool, engine, hundred, implement.

rennibraut 1. shipway; *synonyms* (n) slipway, ways, way, **2**. slide; *synonyms* (n) glide, chute, (v) drop, slip, fall.

rennifljúga glide; *synonyms* (v) slide, coast, float, flow, fly; *antonym* (v) struggle.

renniflug glide; *synonyms* (v) slide, coast, float, flow, fly; *antonym* (v) struggle.

rennilás zipper; *synonyms* (n) zip, fastening, tie, aught, buckle.

rennimál calipers; *synonyms* (n) caliper, callipers, calliper, (v) compass, measure.

rennipípa pipette; *synonyms* (n) pipet, beaker, flask, carboy, syringe.

rennivölur mandrel; *synonyms* (n) arbor, spindle, axle, hinge, bobbin.

rennsli 1. skid; *synonyms* (n) shoe, sideslip, (v) slip, slide, glide, **2**. discharge; *synonyms* (n) release, dismissal, (v) acquit, clear, absolve; *antonyms* (v) capture, hire, **3**. flow; *synonyms* (n) flood, current, discharge, (v) stream, course.

rennslisauga jet; *synonyms* (n) squirt, fountain, flow, (v) gush, spurt.

rennslismagn discharge; *synonyms* (n) release, dismissal, (v) acquit, clear, absolve; *antonyms* (v) capture, hire.

rennslisop orifice; *synonyms* (n) mouth, opening, gap, hole, aperture.

rennslisstöðvun stasis; *synonyms* (n) balance, poise.

renta rent; *synonyms* (n) breach, cleft, fissure, lease, (v) hire.

rénun decrement; *synonyms* (n) decrease, cut, deduction, defalcation, defect.

repja rape; *synonyms* (n) assault, violation, colza, (v) outrage, pillage.

resín resin; *synonyms* (n) gum, rosin, colophany.

rétt correct; *synonyms* (adj) right, accurate, (v) adjust, amend, castigate; *antonyms* (adj) incorrect, false, faulty, inappropriate, (v) wrong.

rétta 1. rectify; *synonyms* (v) amend, correct, improve, better, adjust, **2**. straighten; *synonyms* (v) tidy, unbend, neaten, extend, dress; *antonyms* (v) bend, deform.

réttarhald trial; *synonyms* (n) test, examination, experiment, affliction, essay.

réttarhlé recess; *synonyms* (n) corner, break, holiday, intermission, niche.

réttarregla instrument; *synonyms* (*n*) channel, deed, agency, apparatus, appliance.

réttarsalur court; *synonyms* (*n*) forum, bar, close, (*v*) woo, attract; *antonyms* (*v*) avoid, shun.

réttarstaða constitution; *synonyms* (*n*) composition, code, makeup, organization, temperament.

rétthafi beneficiary; *synonyms* (*n*) heir, inheritor, receiver, recipient, successor; *antonym* (*n*) donor.

rétthverfing supination; *synonym* (*adj*) accubation.

rétthyrndur 1. rectangular; *synonyms* (*adj*) orthogonal, oblong, square, rectangled, rectangle, 2. orthogonal; *synonyms* (*adj*) rectangular, external, extraneous, foreign, immaterial.

rétthyrningur rectangle; *synonyms* (*n*) quadrangle, tetragon, tetract, cube, rhombus.

réttihæfni extensibility; *synonyms* (*n*) extensibleness, flexibility, (*adj*) extendibility.

réttindi competence; *synonyms* (*n*) capacity, adequacy, ability, capability, (*adj*) proficiency; *antonyms* (*n*) incompetence, inability.

rétting 1. rectification; *synonyms* (*n*) correction, amendment, improvement, redress, revision, 2. taxis; *synonyms* (*v*) allotment, apportionment, assortment, taxonomy, 3. straightening, 4. correction; *synonyms* (*n*) adjustment, alteration, castigation, chastisement, discipline; *antonym* (*n*) fabrication, 5. finishing; *synonyms* (*adj*) ending, closing, last, (*n*) finish, completion.

réttlæti equity; *synonyms* (*n*) fairness, honesty, candor, (*adj*) justice, integrity; *antonym* (*n*) unfairness.

réttlæting 1. rationalization; *synonyms* (*n*) explanation, rationalisation, justification, account, defense, 2. justification; *synonyms* (*n*) apology, reason, defence, cause, (*v*) excuse.

réttlætng rationalization; *synonyms* (*n*) explanation, rationalisation, justification, account, defense.

réttlátur equitable; *synonyms* (*adj*) fair, impartial, just, correct, even-handed; *antonym* (*adj*) inequitable.

réttmæti validity; *synonyms* (*n*) force, truth, authority, legitimacy, soundness.

réttmæting validation; *synonyms* (*n*) confirmation, proof, substantiation, verification, establishment.

réttmætur 1. valid; *synonyms* (*adj*) legal, sound, right, genuine, solid; *antonyms* (*adj*) unacceptable, invalid, annulled, bogus, illogical, 2. legitimate; *synonyms* (*adj*) authentic, lawful, just, orthodox, (*v*) legalize; *antonyms* (*adj*) banned, illegal, informal, unlawful, illegitimate.

réttsælis 1. clockwise; *synonym* (*adj*) right; *antonym* (*adv*) counterclockwise, 2. downstream; *synonyms* (*adv*) downriver, (*adj*) later.

réttur 1. privilege; *synonyms* (*n*) charter, immunity, liberty, prerogative, freedom, 2. true; *synonyms* (*adj*) real, actual, faithful, right, (*n*) genuine; *antonyms* (*adj*) false, bogus, inaccurate, untrue, 3. right; *synonyms* (*adj*) correct, appropriate, due, just, proper; *antonyms* (*adj*) inappropriate, unjustified, immoral, (*n*) left, (*v*) wrong, 4. straight; *synonyms* (*adj*) erect, honest, even, flat, (*v*) direct; *antonyms* (*adv*) indirectly, (*adj*) curly, curved, diluted, winding, 5. correct; *synonyms* (*adj*) accurate, (*v*) adjust, amend, castigate, chastise; *antonyms* (*adj*) incorrect, faulty, mistaken, improper, (*v*) spoil.

réttvísandi true; *synonyms* (*adj*) real, actual, faithful, right, (*n*) genuine; *antonyms* (*adj*) false, bogus, inaccurate, untrue.

reykelsi frankincense; *synonyms* (*n*) olibanum, incense, musk, thus, balm.

reykelsistré frankincense; *synonyms* (*n*) olibanum, incense, musk, thus, balm.

reykháfur 1. stack; *synonyms* (*n*) pile, accumulation, mound, rick, (*v*) heap, 2. chimney; *synonyms* (*n*) stack, flue, shaft, smokestack, vent, 3. funnel; *synonyms* (*n*) chimney, tunnel, (*v*) channel, move, pipe.

reykja smoke; *synonyms* (*n*) fumes, (*v*) fume, reek, fumigate, puff.

reykjarmóða smog; *synonyms* (*n*) fog, mist, haze, vapor, fumes.

Reykþoka smog; *synonyms* (*n*) fog, mist, haze, vapor, fumes.

reykur 1. smoke; *synonyms* (*n*) fumes, (*v*) fume, reek, fumigate, puff, 2. fume; *synonyms* (*n*) smoke, foam, (*v*) chafe, rage, (*adj*) boil.

reynd praxis; *synonyms* (*n*) practice, accidence, grammar, punctuation, custom.

reyndartvístirni binary; *synonyms* (*adj*) dual, twin, double, numeric, (*n*) duality.

reynsla experience; *synonyms* (*n*) event, (*v*) encounter, endure, suffer, (*adj*) see; *antonym* (*n*) inexperience.

reynslustefna empiricism; *synonyms* (*n*) quackery, charlatanism, charlatanry, discovery, experience.

reynsluvísindalegur empirical; *synonyms* (*adj*) empiric, experimental, observational, observed, (*v*) tentative; *antonym* (*adj*) theoretical.

reyring strangulation; *synonyms* (*n*) choking, strangling, throttling, execution, (*v*) suffocation.

reyrsykur sucrose; *synonyms* (*n*) saccharose, saccharobiose.

rið 1. rail; *synonyms* (*n*) bar, balustrade, handrail, railing, (*v*) inveigh, 2. cycle; *synonyms* (*n*) bicycle, circle, round, (*v*) bike, motorcycle, 3. hertz;

synonyms (n) cycle, oscillation, rhythm, **4**. period; *synonyms* (n) age, dot, epoch, era, point.

riða 1. scrapie; *synonyms* (adj) glanders, mange, **2**. tremor; *synonyms* (n) quiver, shiver, shudder, agitation, (v) quake.

riðari chopper; *synonyms* (n) ax, helicopter, cleaver, whirlybird, chop.

Riddari knight; *synonyms* (n) cavalier, horseman, horse, chevalier, (v) dub.

riðstraumsviðnám impedance; *synonyms* (n) resistance, clog, friction, hindrance, immunity.

riðtími period; *synonyms* (n) age, dot, epoch, era, point.

riðuveiki scrapie; *synonyms* (adj) glanders, mange.

rif 1. reef; *synonyms* (n) ledge, rock, ait, eyot, isle, **2**. rib; *synonyms* (n) ridge, (v) joke, tease, guy, mock.

rifa 1. reef; *synonyms* (n) ledge, rock, ait, eyot, isle, **2**. rupture; *synonyms* (n) fracture, burst, rift, (v) break, crack; *antonym* (n) repair, **3**. crevice; *synonyms* (n) cleft, chink, cranny, chap, fissure, **4**. crack; *synonyms* (v) crevice, split, breach, snap, clap; *antonym* (v) mend.

rífa tear; *synonyms* (n) split, rupture, (v) break, rip, crack.

rífast 1. quarrel; *synonyms* (n) brawl, feud, altercation, (v) dispute, fight; *antonyms* (n) agreement, (v) agree, **2**. squabble; *synonyms* (n) quarrel, bicker, scrap, contention, (v) row, **3**. wrangle; *synonyms* (n) squabble, tiff, (v) debate, argue, contest.

rifbein rib; *synonyms* (n) ridge, (v) joke, tease, guy, mock.

riffla 1. rib; *synonyms* (n) ridge, (v) joke, tease, guy, mock, **2**. rifle; *synonyms* (n) gun, (v) pillage, plunder, despoil, loot, **3**. knurl; *synonyms* (n) knob, lump, swelling, hump, knur, **4**. flute; *synonyms* (n) wineglass, fluting, furrow, groove, (v) channel.

rifflar fluting; *synonyms* (n) flute, groove, chamfer, furrow, channel.

rifflur fluting; *synonyms* (n) flute, groove, chamfer, furrow, channel.

rifgataður perforated; *synonyms* (adj) perforate, pierced, punctured, penetrated, entered.

rifna burst; *synonyms* (v) break, crack, blast, (adj) split, explode; *antonym* (v) implode.

rifnun rupture; *synonyms* (n) fracture, burst, rift, (v) break, crack; *antonym* (n) repair.

rifrildi 1. quarrel; *synonyms* (n) brawl, feud, altercation, (v) dispute, fight; *antonyms* (n) agreement, (v) agree, **2**. scrap; *synonyms* (n) morsel, remnant, bit, chip, (adj) fragment; *antonym* (v) keep, **3**. squabble; *synonyms* (n) quarrel,

bicker, scrap, contention, (v) row, **4**. row; *synonyms* (n) line, file, rank, squabble, wrangle, **5**. wrangle; *synonyms* (n) tiff, (v) debate, argue, contest, bickering.

rígbinda lash; *synonyms* (v) whip, beat, flog, chastise, bind.

rigna rain; *synonyms* (n) precipitation, (v) pour, stream, hail, precipitate.

rigning rain; *synonyms* (n) precipitation, (v) pour, stream, hail, precipitate.

rigningarskúr shower; *synonyms* (n) rain, (v) pour, bathe, hail, sprinkle.

ríki 1. realm; *synonyms* (n) kingdom, area, country, domain, field, **2**. kingdom; *synonyms* (n) realm, dominion, empire, state, nation, **3**. state; *synonyms* (n) position, say, (v) declare, expound, express; *antonyms* (v) deny, (adj) private, **4**. dominance; *synonyms* (n) ascendancy, authority, control, domination, supremacy; *antonym* (n) inferiority, **5**. domain; *synonyms* (n) department, arena, land, province, ambit; *antonym* (n) range.

ríkisafsögn abdication; *synonyms* (n) resignation, abandonment, renunciation, retirement, surrender.

ríkisár reign; *synonyms* (n) dominance, control, (v) rule, command, govern.

ríkisborgararéttur 1. citizenship; *synonyms* (n) nationality, freedom, **2**. nationality; *synonyms* (n) nation, nationalism, patriotism, people, civism.

ríkisborgari 1. citizen; *synonyms* (n) civilian, denizen, inhabitant, national, resident; *antonym* (n) foreigner, **2**. national; *synonyms* (adj) internal, domestic, home, civil, (n) citizen; *antonyms* (adj) international, foreign, local, private.

ríkiserindreki diplomat; *synonyms* (n) diplomatist, envoy, ambassador, intermediary, minister.

ríkisfang 1. citizenship; *synonyms* (n) nationality, freedom, **2**. nationality; *synonyms* (n) nation, nationalism, patriotism, people, civism, **3**. national; *synonyms* (adj) internal, domestic, home, civil, (n) citizen; *antonyms* (adj) international, foreign, local, private, (n) foreigner.

ríkissjóður treasury; *synonyms* (n) exchequer, storehouse, thesaurus, anthology, bank.

ríkisstjóri governor; *synonyms* (n) director, chief, manager, regulator, administrator.

ríkisstjórn 1. government; *synonyms* (n) administration, authority, control, direction, (adj) empire, **2**. cabinet; *synonyms* (n) case, closet, locker, press, cupboard, **3**. administration; *synonyms* (n) management, organization, running, power, execution.

ríkistekjur revenue; *synonyms* (n) income, receipts, proceeds, profit, earnings.

ríkisvald government; *synonyms* (*n*) administration, authority, control, direction, (*adj*) empire.

ríkja reign; *synonyms* (*n*) dominance, control, (*v*) rule, command, govern.

ríkjabandalag alliance; *synonyms* (*n*) connection, league, affinity, association, combination; *antonym* (*n*) nonalignment.

ríkjandi 1. sovereign; *synonyms* (*adj*) independent, autonomous, (*n*) monarch, ruler, king; *antonym* (*adj*) dependent, **2.** prevailing; *synonyms* (*adj*) predominant, dominant, prevalent, rife, common; *antonym* (*adj*) minor, **3.** dominant; *synonyms* (*adj*) commanding, influential, leading, overriding, paramount; *antonyms* (*adj*) submissive, subordinate.

ríkjasamband 1. union; *synonyms* (*n*) coalition, connection, junction, association, combination; *antonyms* (*n*) separation, divergence, **2.** commonwealth; *synonyms* (*n*) commonweal, country, nation, state, province, **3.** federation; *synonyms* (*n*) alliance, confederacy, confederation, league, organization.

ríkjasamningur treaty; *synonyms* (*n*) agreement, convention, protocol, accord, concord.

rikkur jerk; *synonyms* (*v*) jolt, jump, shake, yank, jar.

rikordo records; *synonyms* (*n*) archive, documents, minutes, proceedings, certification.

ríkulegur 1. copious; *synonyms* (*adj*) abundant, ample, bountiful, affluent, plentiful; *antonyms* (*adj*) scarce, meager, small, sparse, **2.** plentiful; *synonyms* (*adj*) fertile, opulent, copious, fruitful, full; *antonym* (*adj*) scanty, **3.** rich; *synonyms* (*adj*) productive, deep, fat, luxurious, prolific; *antonyms* (*adj*) poor, broke, destitute, impoverished, light, **4.** profuse; *synonyms* (*adj*) generous, liberal, bounteous, exuberant, lavish, **5.** abundant; *synonyms* (*adj*) lush, luxuriant, thick, plenty, rich.

ríkur 1. wealthy; *synonyms* (*adj*) rich, moneyed, affluent, flush, opulent; *antonyms* (*adj*) poor, impoverished, **2.** rich; *synonyms* (*adj*) abundant, copious, fertile, productive, fruitful; *antonyms* (*adj*) broke, destitute, light, **3.** affluent; *synonyms* (*adj*) wealthy, exuberant, prosperous, fat, (*n*) tributary.

ríla 1. spline; *synonyms* (*n*) feather, slat, fin, conclusion, end, **2.** flute; *synonyms* (*n*) wineglass, fluting, furrow, groove, (*v*) channel.

rllato relations; *synonyms* (*n*) family, dealings, kin, connections, people.

rílur fluting; *synonyms* (*n*) flute, groove, chamfer, furrow, channel.

rim rail; *synonyms* (*n*) bar, balustrade, handrail, railing, (*v*) inveigh.

rimill 1. rail; *synonyms* (*n*) bar, balustrade, handrail, railing, (*v*) inveigh, **2.** spoke; *synonyms* (*n*) radius, rung, clog, line, rule.

rimlagirðing 1. railing; *synonyms* (*n*) bar, balustrade, rail, barrier, banister, **2.** balustrade; *synonyms* (*n*) paling, fence, bannister, handrail, pale, **3.** parapet; *synonyms* (*n*) breastwork, bulwark, fortification, bastion, battlement.

rimlagrind grate; *synonyms* (*v*) chafe, creak, grind, abrade, scrape.

ringlun confusion; *synonyms* (*n*) bewilderment, chaos, commotion, disarray, agitation; *antonyms* (*n*) clarity, order.

ringulfar chaos; *synonyms* (*n*) anarchy, bedlam, clutter, disarray, disorder; *antonyms* (*n*) order, peace, orderliness, regulation.

ringulreið chaos; *synonyms* (*n*) anarchy, bedlam, clutter, disarray, disorder; *antonyms* (*n*) order, peace, orderliness, regulation.

ris climax; *synonyms* (*n*) apex, top, acme, culmination, (*v*) peak; *antonym* (*v*) dip.

risaborri 1. barramundi; *synonym* (*n*) barramunda, **2.** lungfish.

risagrasker pumpkin; *synonyms* (*n*) head, pumpion, punkin, pompion.

risasameind macromolecule; *synonym* (*n*) supermolecule.

risastjarna giant; *synonyms* (*adj*) colossal, gargantuan, gigantic, jumbo, (*n*) monster; *antonyms* (*adj*) small, tiny, miniature.

risavöxtur 1. gigantism; *synonyms* (*n*) giantism, overgrowth, **2.** giantism; *synonym* (*n*) gigantism.

risgengi thrust; *synonyms* (*v*) jab, (*n*) push, poke, drive, stab; *antonym* (*v*) pull.

risi giant; *synonyms* (*adj*) colossal, gargantuan, gigantic, jumbo, (*n*) monster; *antonyms* (*adj*) small, tiny, miniature.

rismynd relief; *synonyms* (*n*) comfort, aid, consolation, ease, (*v*) assistance.

rispa 1. scratch; *synonyms* (*n*) score, mark, (*v*) graze, notch, rub, **2.** score; *synonyms* (*n*) bill, count, scratch, line, (*v*) cut.

rispun scarification; *synonym* (*n*) cut.

riss 1. sketch; *synonyms* (*n*) plan, drawing, outline, (*v*) design, paint, **2.** draft; *synonyms* (*n*) bill, conscription, sketch, (*v*) draught, blueprint; *antonym* (*v*) discharge.

rissa 1. scratch; *synonyms* (*n*) score, mark, (*v*) graze, notch, rub, **2.** scribe; *synonyms* (*n*) author, amanuensis, clerk, copyist, (*v*) writer.

rissmynd scheme; *synonyms* (*n*) contrivance, dodge, (*v*) plan, plot, design.

rissnál scriber; *synonyms* (*n*) scribe, copyist, penman, scribbler, scrivener.

rist grid; *synonyms* (*n*) gridiron, grating, lattice, mesh, netting.

rista 1. draw; *synonyms* (*v*) attract, drag, delineate, pull, depict; *antonyms* (*v*) push, repel, 2. etch; *synonyms* (*v*) engrave, carve, cut, inscribe, bite, 3. incision; *synonyms* (*n*) dent, gash, groove, (*v*) slit, crack.

ristarhleri louver; *synonyms* (*n*) fin, cinque, fins, five, fivesome.

ristill 1. shingles; *synonym* (*n*) zoster, 2. zoster; *synonym* (*n*) shingles, 3. colon; *synonyms* (*n*) bowel, (*v*) period, semicolon, comma.

risting incision; *synonyms* (*n*) cut, dent, gash, groove, (*v*) slit.

rit record; *synonyms* (*n*) register, list, account, (*v*) chronicle, file.

rita 1. type; *synonyms* (*n*) pattern, character, kind, nature, (*adj*) model, 2. write; *synonyms* (*v*) compose, indite, pen, correspond, compile, 3. kittiwake.

ritari 1. secretary; *synonyms* (*n*) clerk, escritoire, minister, desk, (*v*) amanuensis, 2. registrar; *synonyms* (*n*) recorder, register, enroll, registrary, schedule, 3. official; *synonyms* (*adj*) formal, (*n*) officer, bureaucrat, executive, (*v*) authoritative; *antonyms* (*adj*) unofficial, private, illegal, informal.

ritblý pencil; *synonyms* (*n*) pen, beam, (*v*) brush, draw, design.

ritferjald cutter; *synonyms* (*n*) carver, cutlery, knife, pinnace, (*adj*) billhook.

rithállur notation; *synonyms* (*n*) annotation, memo, note, memorandum, register.

ritill editor; *synonyms* (*n*) redactor, writer, editioner, journalist, press.

ritla edit; *synonyms* (*v*) delete, compile, cut, redact, (*n*) editing.

ritrýna referee; *synonyms* (*n*) arbiter, arbitrator, (*v*) judge, arbitrate, mediate.

ritrýnir referee; *synonyms* (*n*) arbiter, arbitrator, (*v*) judge, arbitrate, mediate.

ritsetja edit; *synonyms* (*v*) delete, compile, cut, redact, (*n*) editing.

ritsetning editing; *synonyms* (*n*) correction, edition, redaction, cutting, control.

ritsímakerfi telegraphy; *synonyms* (*n*) telegraph, freemasonry.

ritsími telegraphy; *synonyms* (*n*) telegraph, freemasonry.

ritskoðun censorship; *synonyms* (*n*) censoring, ban, silence, blackout, control.

ritstol agraphia; *synonyms* (*n*) anorthography, logagraphia.

ritstýra edit; *synonyms* (*v*) delete, compile, cut, redact, (*n*) editing.

rittákn character; *synonyms* (*n*) kind, nature, note, part, quality.

ritun notation; *synonyms* (*n*) annotation, memo, note, memorandum, register.

ritunarkerfi notation; *synonyms* (*n*) annotation, memo, note, memorandum, register.

ritvél typewriter; *synonyms* (*n*) typist, (*v*) stenographer.

ritvinna edit; *synonyms* (*v*) delete, compile, cut, redact, (*n*) editing.

rjúfa 1. disengage; *synonyms* (*v*) detach, discharge, disentangle, (*adj*) clear, disembarrass; *antonyms* (*v*) fasten, engage, 2. break; *synonyms* (*v*) split, crack, burst, (*n*) breach, fracture; *antonyms* (*v*) repair, obey, honor, mend, (*n*) continuation, 3. block; *synonyms* (*n*) bar, barricade, pad, (*v*) arrest, stop; *antonyms* (*v*) free, unblock, open, 4. disconnect; *synonyms* (*v*) abstract, disengage, divide, separate, deactivate; *antonyms* (*v*) connect, attach, 5. interrupt; *synonyms* (*v*) break, disturb, hinder, intermit, (*adj*) discontinue.

ró 1. quietness; *synonyms* (*n*) peace, quiet, serenity, calm, calmness; *antonyms* (*n*) harshness, volume, 2. nut; *synonyms* (*n*) lunatic, crackpot, crank, eccentric, egg.

róa row; *synonyms* (*n*) altercation, line, (*v*) quarrel, brawl, fight; *antonyms* (*n*) agreement, (*v*) agree.

róandi 1. sedative; *synonyms* (*adj*) ataractic, ataraxic, (*n*) narcotic, depressant, downer, 2. ataractic; *synonyms* (*adj*) sedative, tranquilizing, (*n*) tranquillizer, tranquilizer, tranquilliser.

Róari moderator; *synonyms* (*n*) chairman, mediator, arbitrator, intermediary, negotiator.

róarlyf tranquilizer; *synonyms* (*n*) sedative, tranquillizer, tranquilliser, ataractic, (*v*) lullaby.

róbóti robot; *synonyms* (*n*) automaton, machine, golem, zombie, labor.

roð 1. skin; *synonyms* (*n*) peel, hide, coating, (*v*) pare, bark, 2. leather; *synonyms* (*n*) fur, fleece, skin, buckskin, fell.

röð 1. rank; *synonyms* (*n*) range, place, (*v*) arrange, order, class; *antonym* (*adj*) fresh, 2. row; *synonyms* (*n*) altercation, line, (*v*) quarrel, brawl, fight; *antonyms* (*n*) agreement, (*v*) agree, 3. sequence; *synonyms* (*n*) series, succession, course, arrangement, chain, 4. line; *synonyms* (*n*) cord, file, house, breed, family, 5. run; *synonyms* (*v*) flow, rule, (*n*) pass, campaign, (*adj*) stream.

roðafræ annatto; *synonyms* (*n*) minium, realgar.

roðagægir roach; *synonyms* (*n*) cockroach, dace, circle, roofy, rope.

roðarunnaaldin quince; *synonym* (*n*) melocotoon.

roðarunnaepli quince; *synonym* (*n*) melocotoon.

roðarunni quince; *synonym* (*n*) melocotoon.

rödd voice; *synonyms* (*n*) speech, (*v*) enunciate, express, pronounce, say.

röddun voicing; *synonyms* (*n*) articulation, expression, speech.

roðfletta skin; *synonyms* (*n*) peel, hide, coating, (*v*) pare, bark.

roðna blush; *synonyms* (*n*) flush, bloom, color, red, (*v*) glow; *antonym* (*n*) pallor.

róðrarspaði paddle; *synonyms* (*n*) blade, oar, (*v*) dabble, dodder, row.

röðun 1. rank; *synonyms* (*n*) range, place, (*v*) arrange, order, class; *antonym* (*adj*) fresh, 2. sequencing, 3. setup; *synonyms* (*n*) apparatus, arrangement, setting, system, scheme, 4. permutation; *synonyms* (*n*) change, commutation, exchange, modification, transposition, 5. configuration; *synonyms* (*n*) form, conformation, shape, organization, outline.

röðunarmat rating; *synonyms* (*n*) assessment, mark, evaluation, appraisal, estimate.

rof 1. rupture; *synonyms* (*n*) fracture, burst, rift, (*v*) break, crack; *antonym* (*n*) repair, 2. violation; *synonyms* (*n*) rape, assault, breach, infraction, infringement, 3. denudation; *synonyms* (*n*) exposure, baring, husking, stripping, (*adj*) nudation, 4. break; *synonyms* (*v*) split, (*n*) pause, rupture, stop, collapse; *antonyms* (*v*) obey, honor, mend, (*n*) continuation, 5. block; *synonyms* (*n*) bar, barricade, pad, (*v*) arrest, hinder; *antonyms* (*v*) free, unblock, open.

róf spectrum; *synonyms* (*n*) range, gamut, (*v*) anamorphosis, distortion, illusion.

rófa tail; *synonyms* (*n*) rear, shadow, (*v*) follow, pursue, track; *antonyms* (*v*) head, front.

rofatafla switchboard; *synonyms* (*n*) patchboard, plugboard.

rófgreining spectroscopy; *synonyms* (*n*) chromatics, spectrometry.

rófgreinir spectrometer; *synonyms* (*n*) spectroscope, prism, spectrograph, monochrometer.

rofi 1. switch; *synonyms* (*n*) cane, (*v*) exchange, change, shift, substitute, 2. interrupter; *synonym* (*n*) intruder.

rofinn ruptured; *synonyms* (*adj*) burst, broken, busted, cleft, torn.

róflegur spectral; *synonyms* (*adj*) ghostly, apparitional, phantasmal, ghostlike, unearthly.

róflínuriti spectrograph; *synonyms* (*n*) spectrogram, spectroscope, prism, spectrometer.

rófljósmælir spectrophotometer; *synonym* (*n*) photospectrometer.

rófmynd spectrogram; *synonym* (*n*) spectrograph.

rófrænn spectral; *synonyms* (*adj*) ghostly, apparitional, phantasmal, ghostlike, unearthly.

rófrit spectrogram; *synonym* (*n*) spectrograph.

rófriti spectrograph; *synonyms* (*n*) spectrogram, spectroscope, prism, spectrometer.

rófsjá 1. spectrometer; *synonyms* (*n*) spectroscope, prism, spectrograph, monochrometer, 2. spectroscope; *synonyms* (*n*) abdominoscope, gastroscope, helioscope, polariscope, polemoscope.

rófukál chard; *synonyms* (*n*) boundary, shard, division, plant.

röfun ionization; *synonym* (*n*) ionisation.

rok storm; *synonyms* (*n*) tempest, attack, (*v*) rage, rush, assault.

roka 1. squall; *synonyms* (*n*) cry, gust, (*v*) shout, shriek, howl, 2. surge; *synonyms* (*v*) billow, flood, rise, rush, stream.

rökfærsla rationalization; *synonyms* (*n*) explanation, rationalisation, justification, account, defense.

rokgirni volatility; *synonyms* (*n*) fickleness, instability, flightiness, buoyancy, capriciousness.

rokgjarn volatile; *synonyms* (*adj*) changeable, erratic, frivolous, unstable, (*v*) fickle; *antonym* (*adj*) stable.

rökhlið gate; *synonyms* (*n*) entrance, door, entry, mouth, doorway.

rökhugsun reasoning; *synonyms* (*n*) inference, argumentation, deduction, argument, (*adj*) rational.

rökhyggja rationalism; *synonyms* (*n*) freethinking, philosophy, classicism, (*adj*) antichristianity, infidelity.

rökkur 1. twilight; *synonyms* (*n*) dusk, nightfall, night, evening, gloaming; *antonyms* (*n*) dawn, daybreak, 2. dusk; *synonyms* (*n*) dark, twilight, darkness, gloom, shade; *antonyms* (*n*) sunrise, light.

rökleiðing implication; *synonyms* (*n*) allusion, hint, significance, consequence, deduction.

rökleiðsla 1. reasoning; *synonyms* (*n*) inference, argumentation, deduction, argument, (*adj*) rational, 2. argumentation; *synonyms* (*n*) debate, discussion, disputation, dispute, reasoning, 3. derivation; *synonyms* (*n*) ancestry, origin, birth, cause, derivative.

rökliður argument; *synonyms* (*n*) controversy, debate, matter, proof, reason; *antonyms* (*n*) agreement, harmony.

rökréttur rational; *synonyms* (*adj*) intellectual, reasonable, intelligent, judicious, logical; *antonyms* (*adj*) irrational, illogical, anxious.

röksemd argument; *synonyms* (*n*) controversy, debate, matter, proof, reason; *antonyms* (*n*) agreement, harmony.

röksemdafærsla argument; *synonyms* (*n*) controversy, debate, matter, proof, reason; *antonyms* (*n*) agreement, harmony.

rökstuðningur justification; *synonyms* (*n*) apology, defense, account, reason, (*v*) excuse.

rökþróun dialectic; *synonyms* (*n*) debate, (*adj*) polemical, dialectical, (*v*) argumentative, controversial.

rökþróunarkenning dialectic; *synonyms* (*n*) debate, (*adj*) polemical, dialectical, (*v*) argumentative, controversial.

rökyrðing predicate; *synonyms* (*v*) affirm, assert, allege, base, connote.

róla 1. swing; *synonyms* (*v*) sway, fluctuate, oscillate, dangle, hang, **2.** reciprocate; *synonyms* (*v*) exchange, repay, interchange, return, bandy.

rólfær ambulatory; *synonyms* (*adj*) ambulant, mobile, vagrant, itinerant, movable.

rólyndur phlegmatic; *synonyms* (*adj*) impassive, indifferent, listless, phlegmatical, stolid.

römmun trap; *synonyms* (*n*) snare, net, ambush, (*v*) catch, entrap.

rómur voice; *synonyms* (*n*) speech, (*v*) enunciate, express, pronounce, say.

rönd 1. periphery; *synonyms* (*n*) perimeter, fringe, border, bound, boundary; *antonym* (*n*) center, **2.** limb; *synonyms* (*n*) arm, bough, branch, member, extremity, **3.** margin; *synonyms* (*n*) edge, brink, hem, brim, limit.

rondo quarters; *synonyms* (*n*) dwelling, abode, domicile, lodging, residence.

röng rib; *synonyms* (*n*) ridge, (*v*) joke, tease, guy, mock.

röntgenmynd radiograph; *synonyms* (*n*) radiogram, x-ray, shadowgraph, skiagram, skiagraph.

röntgenmynda radiograph; *synonyms* (*n*) radiogram, x-ray, shadowgraph, skiagram, skiagraph.

röntgenmyndun radiography; *synonyms* (*n*) skiagraphy, sciagraphy.

ropa belch; *synonyms* (*n*) belching, eructation, (*v*) burp, vomit, eruct.

rör 1. tube; *synonyms* (*n*) pipe, conduit, duct, subway, hose, **2.** waterspout; *synonyms* (*n*) cloudburst, deluge, downpour, soaker, torrent, **3.** pipe; *synonyms* (*n*) tube, channel, flue, passage, (*v*) cry, **4.** conduit; *synonyms* (*n*) canal, aqueduct, drain, watercourse, culvert.

röragrein manifold; *synonyms* (*adj*) multiple, diverse, different, (*v*) duplicate, copy.

röralögn piping; *synonyms* (*adj*) high, shrill, (*n*) pipage, pipe, line.

rörbeygja elbow; *synonyms* (*n*) bend, cubitus, (*v*) poke, jostle, nudge.

rörlaga tubular; *synonyms* (*adj*) cannular, tubulate, fistuliform, piped, tubeform.

rórmaður helmsman; *synonyms* (*n*) pilot, steerer, steersman, wheelman, decoy.

rós rose; *synonyms* (*v*) flush, redden, (*adj*) pink, rosaceous, roseate.

rosabaugur halo; *synonyms* (*n*) aureole, aura, glory, halation, ring.

rósaldin hip; *synonyms* (*n*) haunch, coxa, (*adj*) hep, stylish, chic.

rósaraldin hip; *synonyms* (*n*) haunch, coxa, (*adj*) hep, stylish, chic.

röskun 1. disorder; *synonyms* (*n*) ailment, complaint, clutter, (*v*) derange, disarray; *antonyms* (*n*) orderliness, calm, peace, (*v*) order, **2.** disturbance; *synonyms* (*n*) agitation, commotion, disorder, turmoil, (*adj*) trouble.

rostungstennur ivory; *synonyms* (*n*) bone, tusk, dentin, elephant, (*adj*) chalk.

rostungur walrus; *synonyms* (*n*) seahorse, waltron, (*adj*) lumbering.

rót 1. root; *synonyms* (*n*) base, foundation, origin, basis, (*v*) establish, **2.** radix; *synonyms* (*n*) root, groundwork, radical, fundament, foot, **3.** radical; *synonyms* (*adj*) extremist, basic, exhaustive, extreme, revolutionary; *antonyms* (*adj*) conventional, old-fashioned, (*n*) moderate, conservative, traditionalist, **4.** stem; *synonyms* (*n*) bow, branch, shank, (*v*) originate, block.

rótarhnúður corm; *synonyms* (*n*) cormus, rhizome.

rótarskot sucker; *synonyms* (*n*) dupe, fool, sap, jay, lollipop.

rótarstærð radical; *synonyms* (*adj*) extremist, basic, exhaustive, extreme, revolutionary; *antonyms* (*adj*) conventional, old-fashioned, (*n*) moderate, conservative, traditionalist.

róteind proton; *synonym* (*n*) electricity.

rotinn putrid; *synonyms* (*adj*) foul, fetid, malodorous, rotten, corrupt; *antonym* (*adj*) fresh.

rotna 1. decay; *synonyms* (*n*) decline, decomposition, (*v*) rot, decompose, blight; *antonym* (*n*) growth, **2.** decompose; *synonyms* (*v*) decay, crumble, analyse, analyze, disintegrate.

rotnandi carious; *synonyms* (*adj*) decayed, rotten, rancid, (*v*) peccant, purulent.

rotnun 1. putrefaction; *synonyms* (*n*) decay, rot, corruption, decomposition, putridity, **2.** decay; *synonyms* (*n*) decline, ebb, (*v*) decompose, blight, rust; *antonym* (*n*) growth.

rotta rat; *synonyms* (*n*) grass, informer, apostate, (*v*) blackleg, denounce.

róttæklingur radical; *synonyms* (*adj*) extremist, basic, exhaustive, extreme, revolutionary; *antonyms* (*adj*) conventional, old-fashioned, (n) moderate, conservative, traditionalist.

róttækur 1. radical; *synonyms* (adj) extremist, basic, exhaustive, extreme, revolutionary; *antonyms* (adj) conventional, old-fashioned, (n) moderate, conservative, traditionalist, **2.** extreme; *synonyms* (adj) deep, excessive, enormous, immoderate, (n) edge; *antonyms* (adj) middle, reasonable, near, (n) mild, slight.

rotþró compost; *synonyms* (n) compound, dung, composite, (v) fertilize, (adj) manure.

rotvarnarefni preservative; *synonyms* (adj) preservatory, protective, conservative, (n) preserver, antiseptic.

róun sedation; *synonyms* (n) drugging, moderation.

rúða pane; *synonyms* (n) window, paneling, panelling, board, leaf.

rugl delirium; *synonyms* (n) frenzy, craze, insanity, mania, (adj) fury.

rugla scramble; *synonyms* (n) bustle, (v) clamber, climb, struggle, (adj) hurry.

ruglingur derangement; *synonyms* (n) delirium, disorder, disturbance, insanity, lunacy.

rúlla 1. roll; *synonyms* (n) list, (v) coil, reel, curl, enfold, **2.** roller; *synonyms* (n) roll, cylinder, billow, curler, wave.

rúllukefli roller; *synonyms* (n) roll, cylinder, billow, curler, wave.

rúm 1. bed; *synonyms* (n) couch, layer, base, basis, berth, **2.** space; *synonyms* (n) length, gap, opening, period, place.

rúma accommodate; *synonyms* (v) adapt, adjust, fit, oblige, (adj) suit; *antonym* (v) evict.

rúmfræði geometry; *synonyms* (v) algebra, analysis, arithmetic, hypsometry, stereometry.

rúmfræðiteikning construct; *synonyms* (v) make, build, compose, erect, fabricate; *antonyms* (v) destroy, demolish.

rúmgóður 1. wide; *synonyms* (adj) broad, spacious, roomy, comprehensive, extensive; *antonyms* (adj) narrow, thin, restricted, **2.** spacious; *synonyms* (adj) large, ample, wide, capacious, commodious; *antonym* (adj) cramped, **3.** vast; *synonyms* (adj) huge, immense, boundless, colossal, enormous; *antonyms* (adj) limited, small, tiny, **4.** capacious; *synonyms* (adj) big, vast, expansive, voluminous, **5.** commodious; *synonyms* (adj) comfortable, useful, (v) convenient, easy.

rúmhlutur solid; *synonyms* (adj) firm, dense, compact, consistent, hard; *antonyms* (adj) soft, unreliable, loose, gaseous, (n) liquid.

rúmhornseining steradian; *synonym* (n) strontium.

rúmi secondary; *synonyms* (adj) inferior, lower, minor, subordinate, ancillary; *antonyms* (adj) basic, main, central, chief, direct.

rúmmál volume; *synonyms* (n) bulk, size, book, magnitude, mass; *antonym* (n) quietness.

rúmmynd solid; *synonyms* (adj) firm, dense, compact, consistent, hard; *antonyms* (adj) soft, unreliable, loose, gaseous, (n) liquid.

rúmsýn perspective; *synonyms* (n) attitude, aspect, angle, outlook, prospect.

rúmtak 1. volume; *synonyms* (n) bulk, size, book, magnitude, mass; *antonym* (n) quietness, **2.** capacity; *synonyms* (n) capability, aptitude, capacitance, function, (adj) ability; *antonyms* (n) inability, incapability.

rúmtala volume; *synonyms* (n) bulk, size, book, magnitude, mass; *antonym* (n) quietness.

rumungur asp; *synonyms* (n) aspick, rattlesnake, aspen, cobra, serpent.

rúmvídd dimension; *synonyms* (n) degree, breadth, bulk, magnitude, size.

runa 1. sequence; *synonyms* (n) order, series, succession, course, arrangement, **2.** batch; *synonyms* (n) band, lot, body, battery, charge.

runnar copse; *synonyms* (n) brush, coppice, brake, brushwood, forest.

runnasteppa bush; *synonyms* (n) shrub, bushing, wild, chaparral, hedge.

runni bush; *synonyms* (n) shrub, bushing, wild, chaparral, hedge.

runubundinn sequential; *synonyms* (adj) consequent, consecutive, sequent, serial, successive.

rusl 1. waste; *synonyms* (n) desert, (adj) spoil, desolate, (v) consume, exhaust; *antonyms* (v) conserve, save, **2.** scrap; *synonyms* (n) fight, morsel, brawl, remnant, (adj) fragment; *antonym* (v) keep, **3.** dump; *synonyms* (v) discard, ditch, abandon, drop, empty.

ruslahaugar dump; *synonyms* (v) discard, ditch, abandon, drop, empty; *antonym* (v) keep.

rústrauður ferruginous; *synonyms* (adj) ferrugineous, martial.

rúta coach; *synonyms* (n) trainer, tutor, instructor, teacher, (adj) prime.

rútur roach; *synonyms* (n) cockroach, dace, circle, roofy, rope.

rúturunni rue; *synonyms* (n) regret, (v) deplore, mourn, bewail, lament.

ryð rust; *synonyms* (n) decay, corrosion, (v) corrode, eat, (adj) rusty.

ryðfrír 1. stainless; *synonyms* (adj) pure, spotless, chaste, clean, faultless, **2.** rustproof; *synonym* (adj) rustproofed.

ryðfrítt rustproof; *synonym* (*adj*) rustproofed.
ryðga 1. rust; *synonyms* (*n*) decay, corrosion, (*v*)
    corrode, eat, (*adj*) rusty, **2.** corrode; *synonyms* (*v*)
    canker, consume, gnaw, erode, fret.
ryðgun corrosion; *synonyms* (*n*) erosion, corroding,
    decay, deterioration, canker.
ryðrauður ferruginous; *synonyms* (*adj*)
    ferrugineous, martial.
ryðsveppur rust; *synonyms* (*n*) decay, corrosion, (*v*)
    corrode, eat, (*adj*) rusty.
ryk dust; *synonyms* (*n*) powder, dirt, (*v*) clean,
    sprinkle, spray.
rykkjakrampi convulsion; *synonyms* (*n*) spasm, fit,
    paroxysm, commotion, disturbance.
rykkur 1. shock; *synonyms* (*n*) blow, daze, impact,
    collision, (*v*) jar; *antonym* (*v*) comfort, **2.** jolt;
    synonyms (*n*) jerk, hustle, (*v*) jog, shake, bump.
rýma 1. broach; *synonyms* (*v*) mention, utter, (*n*)
    brooch, propose, advance, **2.** evacuate; *synonyms*
    (*v*) deplete, void, discharge, quit, (*adj*) empty.
rýmað ream; *synonyms* (*n*) quire, (*v*) widen, broaden,
    cheat, bore.
rýmari 1. reamer; *synonyms* (*n*) juicer, drinker,
    imbiber, toper, **2.** broach; *synonyms* (*v*) mention,
    utter, (*n*) brooch, propose, advance.
rýmd 1. replacement; *synonyms* (*n*) exchange,
    substitute, alternate, deputy, renewal, **2.** storage;
    synonyms (*n*) conservation, depot, memory,
    preservation, retention, **3.** capacitance; *synonyms*
    (*n*) capacity, capability, capacitor, condenser, **4.**
    capacity; *synonyms* (*n*) aptitude, capacitance,
    function, intelligence, (*adj*) ability; *antonyms* (*n*)
    inability, incapability.
rými 1. space; *synonyms* (*n*) length, gap, opening,
    period, place, **2.** room; *synonyms* (*n*) chamber,
    latitude, occasion, apartment, (*v*) board, **3.**
    volume; *synonyms* (*n*) bulk, size, book,
    magnitude, mass; *antonym* (*n*) quietness, **4.**
    compartment; *synonyms* (*n*) cell, division, cabin,
    cubicle, (*v*) partition, **5.** capacity; *synonyms* (*n*)
    capability, aptitude, capacitance, function, (*adj*)
    ability; *antonyms* (*n*) inability, incapability.
rýming 1. ream; *synonyms* (*n*) quire, (*v*) widen,
    broaden, cheat, bore, **2.** broach; *synonyms* (*v*)
    mention, utter, (*n*) brooch, propose, advance, **3.**
    evacuation; *synonyms* (*n*) elimination, emptying,
    departure, (*v*) discharge, emission.
rýmir 1. reamer; *synonyms* (*n*) juicer, drinker,
    imbiber, toper, **2.** spacer, **3.** capacitor; *synonyms*
    (*n*) condenser, capacitance, capacity.
rýmka extend; *synonyms* (*v*) expand, enlarge,
    amplify, broaden, dilate; *antonyms* (*v*) withdraw,
    shorten, limit, narrow, shrink.

rýmunardór drift; *synonyms* (*n*) stream, current,
    course, (*v*) aim, blow.
rýna referee; *synonyms* (*n*) arbiter, arbitrator, (*v*)
    judge, arbitrate, mediate.
rýrð poverty; *synonyms* (*n*) lack, distress, (*v*)
    destitution, need, penury; *antonyms* (*n*) wealth,
    riches.
rýrður reduced; *synonyms* (*adj*) decreased, abridged,
    curtailed, miniature, cheap; *antonyms* (*adj*)
    expensive, complete.
rýriskipting 1. reduction; *synonyms* (*n*) contraction,
    decrease, decrement, diminution, rebate; *antonyms*
    (*n*) increase, growth, intensification, strengthening,
    expansion, **2.** meiosis; *synonyms* (*n*) litotes,
    miosis, myosis.
rýrna 1. shrink; *synonyms* (*v*) dwindle, flinch, recoil,
    contract, shorten; *antonyms* (*v*) expand, increase,
    enlarge, **2.** waste; *synonyms* (*n*) desert, (*adj*) spoil,
    desolate, (*v*) consume, exhaust; *antonyms* (*v*)
    conserve, save, **3.** atrophy; *synonyms* (*n*) decay, (*v*)
    attenuation, emaciation, tabes, waste.
rýrnun 1. decrement; *synonyms* (*n*) decrease, cut,
    deduction, defalcation, defect, **2.** depletion;
    synonyms (*n*) consumption, expenditure, loss, (*adj*)
    flaccidity, vacancy, **3.** degeneration; *synonyms*
    (*n*) decay, corruption, decline, degeneracy,
    abasement; *antonyms* (*n*) improvement, growth, **4.**
    deterioration; *synonyms* (*n*) degradation, failure,
    damage, debasement, (*v*) depravation; *antonym* (*n*)
    development, **5.** atrophy; *synonyms* (*v*)
    attenuation, emaciation, tabes, waste, wither.
rytmi 1. rhythm; *synonyms* (*n*) measure, cadence,
    meter, beat, pulse, **2.** round; *synonyms* (*adv*) about,
    (*adj*) circular, (*n*) circle, bout, ring; *antonyms* (*adj*)
    slim, sharp, **3.** cycle; *synonyms* (*n*) bicycle, round,
    (*v*) bike, motorcycle, wheel.

S

sá inoculate; *synonyms* (*v*) infuse, imbue, immunize,
    impregnate, instill.
saaga 1. tale; *synonyms* (*n*) story, account, narrative,
    fable, fib, **2.** story; *synonyms* (*n*) layer, history,
    narration, recital, report; *antonym* (*n*) truth.
sablobenko banks; *synonym* (*n*) breast.
sáð 1. sperm; *synonyms* (*n*) seed, semen,
    spermatozoon, germ, birth, **2.** inoculum;
    synonym (*n*) inoculant.
sáðfall 1. pollution; *synonyms* (*n*) contamination,
    filth, infection, befoulment, (*adj*) defilement, **2.**

ejaculation; *synonyms* (*n*) exclamation, cry, emission, interjection, vociferation.

sáðfruma 1. spermatozoon; *synonyms* (*n*) sperm, metaplasm, ontogeny, ovary, ovum, **2**. spermatocyte; *synonyms* (*n*) spermatoblast, spermoblast, **3**. sperm; *synonyms* (*n*) seed, semen, spermatozoon, germ, birth.

sáðfrumnadeyðir spermicide; *synonym* (*n*) spermatocide.

sáðfrumnaeyðir spermicide; *synonym* (*n*) spermatocide.

sáðfrumuvísir spermatocyte; *synonyms* (*n*) spermatoblast, spermoblast.

sáðkorn seed; *synonyms* (*n*) germ, issue, posterity, root, (*v*) inseminate.

sáðkristallur seed; *synonyms* (*n*) germ, issue, posterity, root, (*v*) inseminate.

sáðlát ejaculation; *synonyms* (*n*) exclamation, cry, emission, interjection, vociferation.

sáðlaukur onion; *synonyms* (*n*) caviare, pickle, leek, chive.

sáðmein metastasis; *synonyms* (*n*) metabolism, anastrophy, parenthesis, synchysis, tmesis.

sáðmóðurfruma spermatocyte; *synonyms* (*n*) spermatoblast, spermoblast.

saðning satiation; *synonyms* (*n*) repletion, fullness, satiety, cloyment, disgust.

sáðræsing emission; *synonyms* (*n*) discharge, emanation, effusion, ejection, venting.

sæbrattur steep; *synonyms* (*adj*) high, abrupt, excessive, (*v*) douse, immerse; *antonyms* (*adj*) gentle, gradual.

sæði 1. seed; *synonyms* (*n*) germ, issue, posterity, root, (*v*) inseminate, **2**. semen; *synonyms* (*n*) seed, cum, ejaculate, source, birth.

sæðing insemination; *synonym* (*n*) conception.

sæðisfruma 1. spermatozoon; *synonyms* (*n*) sperm, metaplasm, ontogeny, ovary, ovum, **2**. sperm; *synonyms* (*n*) seed, semen, spermatozoon, germ, birth.

sæðisfrumuvísir spermatocyte; *synonyms* (*n*) spermatoblast, spermoblast.

sæfa autoclave; *synonyms* (*n*) steriliser, sterilizer, (*v*) sterilize.

sæfari mariner; *synonyms* (*n*) gob, sailor, seafarer, seaman, tar.

sæfiflar corals; *synonyms* (*n*) hydras, jellyfishes, polyps.

sækja retrieve; *synonyms* (*v*) recover, regain, reclaim, recoup, rescue; *antonym* (*v*) lose.

sækjandi plaintiff; *synonyms* (*n*) complainant, accuser, prosecutor, pursuer, applicant.

sækni 1. taxis; *synonyms* (*v*) allotment, apportionment, assortment, taxonomy, **2**. affinity;

synonyms (*n*) sympathy, analogy, alliance, bond, kindred.

sæl happy; *synonyms* (*adj*) fortunate, felicitous, contented, gay, (*n*) auspicious; *antonyms* (*adj*) unhappy, sad, dejected, depressed, miserable.

sældarhyggja hedonism; *synonyms* (*n*) hedonics, sensuality, indulgence, decadence, enjoyment; *antonym* (*n*) self-denial.

sældarvilla euphoria; *synonyms* (*n*) elation, ecstasy, jubilation, delight, happiness; *antonym* (*n*) dysphoria.

sæll 1. hello; *synonyms* (*n*) greeting, hi, howdy, hullo, (*v*) hail, **2**. hi; *synonyms* (*int*) ciao, (*n*) hello.

sæluhús refuge; *synonyms* (*n*) protection, asylum, sanctuary, resort, (*v*) recourse.

sæmandi appropriate; *synonyms* (*adj*) pertinent, proper, true, (*v*) annex, allocate; *antonyms* (*adj*) inappropriate, unsuitable, unrelated, untimely, (*v*) surrender.

sængurlega confinement; *synonyms* (*n*) captivity, childbirth, custody, detention, (*v*) delivery; *antonyms* (*n*) freedom, release.

særa 1. chip; *synonyms* (*n*) splinter, bit, flake, chipping, (*v*) crack, **2**. bruise; *synonyms* (*n*) blow, contusion, (*v*) crush, hurt, wound.

særanlegur vulnerable; *synonyms* (*adj*) weak, exposed, sensitive, susceptible, tender; *antonyms* (*adj*) safe, impervious, invincible, invulnerable, unassailable.

særanleiki vulnerability; *synonyms* (*n*) exposure, weakness, danger, vulnerableness, defenselessness; *antonym* (*n*) invulnerability.

særður 1. wounded; *synonyms* (*adj*) hurt, bruised, bloody, (*n*) casualty, maimed; *antonym* (*adj*) composed, **2**. injured; *synonyms* (*adj*) aggrieved, broken, wounded, affected, damaged; *antonym* (*adj*) unharmed.

særi 1. ulcer; *synonyms* (*n*) boil, (*v*) canker, fester, (*adj*) sore, cancer, **2**. wound; *synonyms* (*n*) bruise, harm, pain, (*v*) hurt, cut.

sæstjarna 1. starfish; *synonyms* (*n*) asteridian, crossfish, stellerid, **2**. asteroid; *synonym* (*n*) planetoid.

sæta saccharify; *synonym* (*v*) sugar.

sætaldintré mangosteen; *synonyms* (*v*) chowder, chupatty, clam, compote, damper.

sæti 1. rank; *synonyms* (*n*) range, place, (*v*) arrange, order, class; *antonym* (*adj*) fresh, **2**. seat; *synonyms* (*n*) bench, base, backside, (*v*) locate, put, **3**. place; *synonyms* (*n*) position, (*v*) post, fix, lay, rank; *antonym* (*v*) remove, **4**. saddle; *synonyms* (*n*) saddleback, (*v*) charge, burden, load, encumber, **5**. socket; *synonyms* (*n*) cavity, alveolus, sleeve, hollow, pocket.

sætistala rank; *synonyms* (*n*) range, place, (*v*) arrange, order, class; *antonym* (*adj*) fresh.

sætta adjust; *synonyms* (*v*) temper, accommodate, adapt, align, acclimatize.

sættir reconciliation; *synonyms* (*n*) accommodation, adjustment, agreement, rapprochement, (*v*) concord.

sætur 1. valuable; *synonyms* (*adj*) costly, estimable, precious, beneficial, expensive; *antonyms* (*adj*) worthless, useless, 2. precious; *synonyms* (*adj*) dear, beloved, cherished, valuable, invaluable, 3. dear; *synonyms* (*adj*) close, lovely, near, (*n*) darling, love; *antonym* (*adj*) cheap, 4. cherished; *synonyms* (*adj*) loved, treasured, intimate, prized, valued, 5. beloved; *synonyms* (*adj*) favorite, pet, (*n*) dearest, honey, sweetheart.

sæúr chronometer; *synonyms* (*n*) clock, timepiece, watch, metronome.

safabóla vacuole; *synonyms* (*n*) cell, metaplasm, ontogeny, ovary, ovum.

safamikill succulent; *synonyms* (*adj*) juicy, lush, fleshy, luscious, sappy; *antonym* (*adj*) dry.

saffismi lesbianism; *synonyms* (*n*) sapphism, homosexuality, gayness, bisexuality.

safi 1. extract; *synonyms* (*n*) excerpt, (*v*) draw, abstract, derive, educe, 2. juice; *synonyms* (*n*) extract, water, blood, gravy, (*adj*) humor.

safn library; *synonyms* (*n*) bibliotheca, annals, archive, bibliotheke, den.

safna 1. store; *synonyms* (*n*) hoard, shop, market, (*v*) stock, accumulate, 2. stack; *synonyms* (*n*) pile, accumulation, mound, rick, (*v*) heap, 3. accumulate; *synonyms* (*v*) amass, collect, gather, store, accrue; *antonyms* (*v*) disperse, distribute, dwindle, 4. collect; *synonyms* (*v*) assemble, pick, acquire, aggregate, cluster, 5. heap; *synonyms* (*n*) stack, collection, group, lot, (*v*) bank.

safnari 1. accumulator; *synonyms* (*n*) collector, gatherer, store, saver, aggregator, 2. collector; *synonyms* (*n*) accumulator, receiver, caporal, choregus, commissioner.

safngrein manifold; *synonyms* (*adj*) multiple, diverse, different, (*v*) duplicate, copy.

safnhaugamold compost; *synonyms* (*n*) compound, dung, composite, (*v*) fertilize, (*adj*) manure.

safnhaugur compost; *synonyms* (*n*) compound, dung, composite, (*v*) fertilize, (*adj*) manure.

safnplanta accumulator; *synonyms* (*n*) collector, gatherer, store, saver, aggregator.

safnstútur nozzle; *synonyms* (*n*) nose, beak, hooter, jet, muzzle.

safnvista archive; *synonyms* (*n*) record, scroll, archives, records, paper.

safnvöllur hub; *synonyms* (*n*) center, focus, heart, core, nucleus.

safnvörður librarian; *synonyms* (*n*) bibliothec, bibliothecary.

safnvörsluforrit librarian; *synonyms* (*n*) bibliothec, bibliothecary.

saga 1. tale; *synonyms* (*n*) story, account, narrative, fable, fib, 2. story; *synonyms* (*n*) layer, history, narration, recital, report; *antonym* (*n*) truth, 3. account; *synonyms* (*n*) bill, reckoning, regard, score, tale, 4. narrative; *synonyms* (*n*) anecdote, chronicle, legend, relation, yarn, 5. history; *synonyms* (*n*) annals, background, record, explanation, yesteryear; *antonym* (*n*) present.

sagnarögn particle; *synonyms* (*n*) molecule, grain, speck, bit, (*adj*) atom.

sagnorð verb; *synonym* (*n*) vocable.

sagtenning serration; *synonyms* (*n*) notch, nick, serrations, serrature, groove.

sagtenntur serrated; *synonyms* (*adj*) jagged, notched, serrate, toothed, aduncous; *antonym* (*adj*) smooth.

sakarforræði optional; *synonyms* (*adj*) discretionary, arbitrary, voluntary, nonobligatory, unrestricted; *antonyms* (*adj*) obligatory, compulsory, required, essential, necessary.

sakaruppgjöf immunity; *synonyms* (*n*) exemption, freedom, franchise, dispensation, privilege; *antonym* (*n*) vulnerability.

sakborningur 1. defendant; *synonyms* (*n*) accused, litigant, party, plaintiff, prisoner, 2. accused; *synonyms* (*n*) panel, perpetrator.

sakka 1. sinker; *synonyms* (*n*) weight, doughnut, donut, annulus, anulus, 2. plumb; *synonyms* (*v*) fathom, (*adj*) perpendicular, vertical, upright, erect, 3. ballast; *synonyms* (*n*) ballasting, counterbalance, (*adj*) aplomb, (*v*) stabilize, load.

sakkarín saccharin; *synonyms* (*n*) aspartame, benzosulfimide, cyclamate.

saklaus 1. blameless; *synonyms* (*adj*) irreproachable, faultless, perfect, guiltless, inculpable; *antonym* (*adj*) guilty, 2. innocent; *synonyms* (*adj*) harmless, chaste, artless, clear, ingenuous; *antonyms* (*adj*) culpable, responsible, wary, wicked, 3. guiltless; *synonyms* (*adj*) blameless, innocent, clean, stainless, unsullied.

sako bag; *synonyms* (*n*) pocket, pouch, package, briefcase, purse.

sál psyche; *synonyms* (*n*) brain, mind, ego, spirit, intellect.

sala 1. sale; *synonyms* (*n*) fair, disposal, demand, market, vend, 2. sales; *synonyms* (*n*) business, trade, (*adj*) commercial, 3. business; *synonyms* (*n*) employment, matter, subject, affair, calling; *antonyms* (*adj*) charitable, housing.

salajro 1. wages; *synonyms* (*n*) salary, pay, wage, earnings, reward, **2.** wage; *synonyms* (*n*) fee, payment, income, allowance, (*v*) fight.

sálarfræði psychology; *synonyms* (*n*) psychics, mentality, animastic, metaphysics, ontology.

sálarlífeðlisfræði psychophysiology; *synonym* (*n*) neuropsychology.

salatfífill endive; *synonyms* (*n*) escarole, witloof.

salatþistill cardoon; *synonym* (*n*) artichoke.

sáld 1. sieve; *synonyms* (*n*) screen, (*v*) filter, riddle, sift, strain, **2.** strainer; *synonyms* (*n*) sieve, stretcher, colature, mesh.

sáldvefur bast; *synonym* (*n*) phloem.

salerni 1. convenience; *synonyms* (*n*) advantage, contrivance, accommodation, opportunity, appliance; *antonym* (*n*) inconvenience, **2.** lavatory; *synonyms* (*n*) bathroom, can, toilet, commode, lav.

sálfræði psychology; *synonyms* (*n*) psychics, mentality, animastic, metaphysics, ontology.

sálfræðingur psychologist; *synonym* (*n*) psychologue.

sálgreining psychoanalysis; *synonyms* (*n*) analysis, psychotherapy, cure, healing, rehabilitation.

sálgreinir psychoanalyst; *synonyms* (*n*) analyst, psychiatrist, therapist, consultant, counselor.

sali dealer; *synonyms* (*n*) merchant, trader, monger, seller, vendor; *antonym* (*n*) user.

sálkönnuður psychoanalyst; *synonyms* (*n*) analyst, psychiatrist, therapist, consultant, counselor.

sálkönnunarkenning psychoanalysis; *synonyms* (*n*) analysis, psychotherapy, cure, healing, rehabilitation.

sállækning psychotherapy; *synonyms* (*n*) psychotherapeutics, analysis, psychoanalysis, psychiatry, cure.

salli detritus; *synonyms* (*n*) rubble, (*adj*) debris, trash, magistery, scobs.

sálrænn psychogenic; *synonym* (*adj*) psychic.

sálsýkisfræði psychopathology; *synonym* (*n*) psychiatry.

salt acetate; *synonym* (*n*) ethanoate.

saltpétur 1. saltpetre; *synonyms* (*n*) saltpeter, niter, nitre, **2.** saltpeter; *synonyms* (*n*) saltpetre, anatron, natron, brine.

saltsýrusalt chloride; *synonyms* (*n*) muriate, oxymuriate.

saltur saline; *synonyms* (*adj*) salty, salt, brackish, piquant, salary.

saltvatn saline; *synonyms* (*adj*) salty, salt, brackish, piquant, salary.

salur hall; *synonyms* (*n*) corridor, foyer, lobby, mansion, vestibule.

samæxla 1. cross; *synonyms* (*v*) intersect, baffle, (*adj*) crabbed, crabby, angry; *antonyms* (*v*) uncross, (*adj*) calm, good-tempered, **2.** crossbreed; *synonyms* (*n*) cross, hybrid, (*v*) hybridize, interbreed, (*adj*) hinny.

samæxlun cross; *synonyms* (*v*) intersect, baffle, (*adj*) crabbed, crabby, angry; *antonyms* (*v*) uncross, (*adj*) calm, good-tempered.

saman 1. together; *synonyms* (*adv*) jointly, conjointly, simultaneously, collectively, (*adj*) united; *antonyms* (*adv*) individually, separately, independently, (*adj*) separate, **2.** jointly; *synonyms* (*adv*) together, unitedly, mutually.

samanbuðartafla nomogram; *synonyms* (*n*) nomograph, abacus.

samanburðarfall contrast; *synonyms* (*n*) contrariety, antithesis, comparison, distinction, (*v*) differ; *antonym* (*n*) similarity.

samanburðarhæfi comparability; *synonyms* (*n*) comparison, compare, correspondence, equivalence, resemblance.

samanburðarhæfni comparability; *synonyms* (*n*) comparison, compare, correspondence, equivalence, resemblance.

samanburður comparison; *synonyms* (*n*) analogy, compare, likeness, resemblance, comparing; *antonym* (*n*) dissimilarity.

samanfellanlegur collapsible; *synonyms* (*adj*) collapsable, foldable.

samanhalli convergence; *synonyms* (*n*) confluence, meeting, concentration, concourse, convergency; *antonyms* (*n*) divergence, division.

samanlagt 1. total; *synonyms* (*adj*) aggregate, complete, (*n*) whole, amount, (*v*) count; *antonyms* (*adj*) partial, incomplete, qualified, **2.** aggregate; *synonyms* (*n*) total, agglomerate, complex, (*v*) accumulate, cluster; *antonyms* (*n*) individual, part.

samansig collapse; *synonyms* (*n*) crash, breakdown, fall, (*v*) break, slump.

samantekt 1. superposition; *synonyms* (*n*) incrustation, superimposition, **2.** summary; *synonyms* (*n*) abstract, compendium, abridgment, (*adj*) brief, compendious, **3.** combination; *synonyms* (*n*) alliance, blend, union, association, coalition; *antonyms* (*n*) separation, (*adj*) simple.

samása coaxial; *synonym* (*adj*) coaxal.

sambærilegur 1. comparable; *synonyms* (*adj*) analogous, corresponding, like, alike, commensurate; *antonyms* (*adj*) different, dissimilar, incomparable, **2.** analogous; *synonyms* (*adj*) similar, akin, analogical, comparable, equivalent.

samband 1. contact; *synonyms* (*n*) touch, connection, collision, communication, (*v*) call, **2.** rapport; *synonyms* (*n*) harmony, accord, affinity, compatibility, relationship, **3.** relation; *synonyms*

(n) account, narration, recital, association, description, **4**. union; *synonyms* (n) coalition, junction, combination, league, merger; *antonyms* (n) separation, divergence, **5**. relationship; *synonyms* (n) relation, affiliation, ratio, consanguinity, correlation.

sambandsríki federation; *synonyms* (n) alliance, association, coalition, confederacy, combination.

sambeining 1. collimation; *synonyms* (v) aim, dip, tack, **2**. focusing; *synonyms* (n) centering, concentration, focus, focussing, focalisation.

sambland conglomerate; *synonyms* (n) composite, group, complex, (v) accumulate, amass.

sambræðsla freezing; *synonyms* (adj) cold, icy, arctic, chilly, (n) freeze; *antonyms* (adj) boiling, hot, sweltering, red-hot, warm.

sambreyskingur conglomerate; *synonyms* (n) composite, group, complex, (v) accumulate, amass.

sambryskja symphysis; *synonyms* (n) amphiarthrosis, (v) infibulation, inosculation, confluence.

sambú colony; *synonyms* (n) settlement, community, plantation, dependency, village.

sambúð cohabitation; *synonyms* (n) bed, coverture.

samburar litter; *synonyms* (n) brood, bedding, stretcher, (v) clutter, (adj) jumble.

sambyggt integral; *synonyms* (adj) complete, entire, inherent, full, (n) whole.

sambýli collective; *synonyms* (adj) aggregate, general, joint, common, cumulative; *antonyms* (adj) capitalist, distributive, private.

sambýlismaður companion; *synonyms* (n) colleague, buddy, mate, peer, (adj) associate; *antonym* (n) enemy.

samdráttarástand 1. tone; *synonyms* (n) character, note, accent, air, (v) color, **2**. tonus; *synonyms* (n) tone, tonicity, feel, feeling, flavor.

samdráttargeta contractility; *synonyms* (n) irritability, motility, fretfulness, petulance.

samdráttarhæfni contractility; *synonyms* (n) irritability, motility, fretfulness, petulance.

samdráttarskeið recession; *synonyms* (n) decline, depression, fall, niche, recess.

samdráttarsmellur snap; *synonyms* (v) crack, bite, break, fracture, (n) photograph.

samdráttur 1. retraction; *synonyms* (n) cancellation, recantation, abjuration, annulment, (v) repudiation, **2**. shrinkage; *synonyms* (n) contraction, reduction, decrease, decline, diminution, **3**. contraction; *synonyms* (n) abbreviation, constriction, abridgement, abridgment, condensation; *antonym* (n) expansion.

samdrykkja symposium; *synonyms* (n) conference, discussion, regale, dialogue, meeting.

samefling synergism; *synonyms* (n) synergy, cooperation.

samefni compound; *synonyms* (n) blend, complex, mix, (v) alloy, (adj) composite; *antonym* (adj) simple.

sameiginlegur 1. single; *synonyms* (adj) only, celibate, one, odd, particular; *antonyms* (adj) married, double, multiple, **2**. common; *synonyms* (adj) ordinary, coarse, cheap, mutual, usual; *antonyms* (adj) individual, uncommon, rare, unusual, characteristic, **3**. concerted; *synonyms* (adj) combined, joint, cooperative, united, unanimous, **4**. communal; *synonyms* (adj) common, civic, public, social, national; *antonym* (adj) private, **5**. mutual; *synonyms* (adj) reciprocal, communal, bilateral, collective, alternate; *antonyms* (adj) unilateral, one-sided.

sameign community; *synonyms* (n) association, public, agreement, commune, (adj) communal; *antonym* (adj) private.

sameignarfélag partnership; *synonyms* (n) company, corporation, alliance, association, copartnership.

sameignarsinni communist; *synonyms* (adj) communistic, carbonaro, frondeur, (n) commie, cosmopolite.

sameignarskipan communism; *synonyms* (n) collectivism, socialism, phalansterianism, communalism, dictatorship; *antonym* (n) capitalism.

sameignarstefna 1. socialism; *synonyms* (n) communism, collectivism, communalism; *antonym* (n) capitalism, **2**. collectivism; *synonyms* (n) sovietism, socialism, **3**. communism; *synonyms* (n) phalansterianism, dictatorship, (v) statism.

sameina 1. unify; *synonyms* (v) combine, integrate, amalgamate, consolidate, merge, **2**. associate; *synonyms* (v) affiliate, connect, (n) ally, assistant, companion; *antonyms* (v) avoid, dissociate, distance, (adj) chief, (n) stranger, **3**. dissolve; *synonyms* (v) disappear, disperse, dissipate, disband, evaporate; *antonyms* (v) appear, harden, solidify, **4**. consolidate; *synonyms* (v) compact, fuse, coagulate, coalesce, concentrate, **5**. integrate; *synonyms* (v) incorporate, blend, embody, unify, unite; *antonyms* (v) separate, exclude, segregate.

sameinaður joint; *synonyms* (n) articulation, hinge, join, seam, (v) articulate; *antonyms* (adj) individual, unilateral, private, separate.

sameinast 1. unify; *synonyms* (v) combine, integrate, amalgamate, consolidate, merge, **2**. consolidate; *synonyms* (v) compact, fuse, coagulate, coalesce, concentrate, **3**. fuse; *synonyms* (v) blend, melt, compound, dissolve, mix; *antonym* (v) separate.

sameind molecule; *synonyms* (*n*) atom, corpuscle, grain, iota, jot.

sameindastofn radical; *synonyms* (*adj*) extremist, basic, exhaustive, extreme, revolutionary; *antonyms* (*adj*) conventional, old-fashioned, (*n*) moderate, conservative, traditionalist.

sameindasundrun dissociation; *synonyms* (*n*) disintegration, divorce, disassociation, separation, distancing.

sameining 1. recombination, **2.** union; *synonyms* (*n*) coalition, connection, junction, association, combination; *antonyms* (*n*) separation, divergence, **3.** unification; *synonyms* (*n*) union, amalgamation, merger, fusion, synthesis; *antonyms* (*n*) division, segregation, **4.** consolidation; *synonyms* (*n*) unification, fortification, condensation, joinder, integration, **5.** coalition; *synonyms* (*n*) alliance, league, affiliation, alignment, alinement; *antonym* (*n*) nonalignment.

samfærsla 1. registration; *synonyms* (*n*) enrollment, registering, enrolment, entering, entry, **2.** apposition; *synonyms* (*n*) union, juxtaposition, (*prep*) addition, accompaniment, accord.

samfall collapse; *synonyms* (*n*) crash, breakdown, fall, (*v*) break, slump.

samfallandi complementary; *synonyms* (*adj*) complemental, additional, auxiliary, supplementary, reciprocal.

samfallstími overlap; *synonyms* (*n*) lap, intersection, (*v*) fold, cross, concur.

samfarablossi orgasm; *synonyms* (*n*) climax, coming, advent, approach, approaching.

samfas synchronism; *synonyms* (*n*) synchrony, synchronization, synchronizing, synchroneity, synchronicity.

samfasa 1. synchronism; *synonyms* (*n*) synchrony, synchronization, synchronizing, synchroneity, synchronicity, **2.** synchronous; *synonyms* (*adj*) simultaneous, synchronal, concurrent, synchronic, coincident, **3.** coherent; *synonyms* (*adj*) logical, rational, consistent, lucid, tenacious; *antonyms* (*adj*) incoherent, illogical, confused, disjointed, rambling.

samfasari synchronizer; *synonyms* (*n*) synchroniser, synchroscope, synchronoscope.

samfélag 1. society; *synonyms* (*n*) club, institution, public, association, community, **2.** community; *synonyms* (*n*) agreement, commune, nation, (*adj*) communal, neighborhood; *antonym* (*adj*) private.

samfélagsvitund citizenship; *synonyms* (*n*) nationality, freedom.

samfella 1. confluence; *synonyms* (*n*) concourse, meeting, concurrence, junction, assembly; *antonym* (*n*) divergence, **2.** coherence; *synonyms* (*n*) consistency, comprehensibility, agreement, clarity,

coherency; *antonym* (*n*) incoherence, **3.** continuum; *synonyms* (*n*) continuity, range, band, field, gamut, **4.** continuity; *synonyms* (*n*) continuation, coherence, continuance, duration, persistence; *antonym* (*n*) discontinuity.

samfellanlegur collapsible; *synonyms* (*adj*) collapsable, foldable.

samfelldni 1. continuity; *synonyms* (*n*) continuation, coherence, continuance, duration, persistence; *antonym* (*n*) discontinuity, **2.** homogeneity; *synonyms* (*n*) homogeneousness, affinity, alliance, consistency, unity.

samfelldur 1. seamless; *synonyms* (*adj*) faultless, flawless, textbook, unlined, unseamed, **2.** analog; *synonyms* (*n*) analogue, parallel, computer, (*adj*) additive, linear, **3.** coherent; *synonyms* (*adj*) logical, rational, consistent, lucid, tenacious; *antonyms* (*adj*) incoherent, illogical, confused, disjointed, rambling, **4.** continuous; *synonyms* (*adj*) constant, continual, ceaseless, endless, perpetual; *antonyms* (*adj*) intermittent, temporary, discontinuous, sporadic.

samfelling overlay; *synonyms* (*n*) coat, sheathing, (*v*) cover, overlap, veneer.

samferð sympathy; *synonyms* (*n*) compassion, pity, benevolence, commiseration, feeling; *antonyms* (*n*) indifference, cruelty.

samfesta cohesion; *synonyms* (*n*) coherency, continuity, coherence, consistency, cohesiveness.

samfestingur overall; *synonyms* (*adj*) entire, total, whole, (*n*) smock, boilersuit.

samflæði confluence; *synonyms* (*n*) concourse, meeting, concurrence, junction, assembly; *antonym* (*n*) divergence.

samfösun 1. synchronizing; *synonyms* (*n*) synchronization, synchronisation, synchronising, synchronism, synchroneity, **2.** synchronization; *synonyms* (*n*) coordination, synchronizing, synchrony, synchronicity, harmonization, **3.** coherence; *synonyms* (*n*) consistency, comprehensibility, agreement, clarity, coherency; *antonym* (*n*) incoherence.

samfrysting congelation; *synonyms* (*n*) coagulation, congealment, chilling, cold, coldness.

samgangur 1. anastomosis; *synonyms* (*n*) inosculation, (*v*) communication, concatenation, mortise, infibulation, **2.** interconnection; *synonyms* (*n*) interconnectedness, link, joint, correlation, relationship.

samgengi synchronism; *synonyms* (*n*) synchrony, synchronization, synchronizing, synchroneity, synchronicity.

samgepatrido siblings; *synonyms* (*n*) sibs, family.

samgerð configuration; *synonyms* (*n*) form, arrangement, conformation, shape, organization.

samgildi degeneracy; *synonyms* (*n*) corruption, decadence, depravity, degeneration, decline.

samgöngukerfi transportation; *synonyms* (*n*) deportation, banishment, exile, (*v*) transport, conveyance.

samgöngur transportation; *synonyms* (*n*) deportation, banishment, exile, (*v*) transport, conveyance.

samgötun anastomosis; *synonyms* (*n*) inosculation, (*v*) communication, concatenation, mortise, infibulation.

samgróning 1. symphysis; *synonyms* (*n*) amphiarthrosis, (*v*) infibulation, inosculation, confluence, **2**. adhesion; *synonyms* (*n*) adherence, bond, stickiness, adhesiveness, attachment.

samgróningur adhesion; *synonyms* (*n*) adherence, bond, stickiness, adhesiveness, attachment.

samhæði interdependence; *synonyms* (*n*) correlation, mutuality, interdependency, dependence, (*adj*) link.

samhæfa coordinate; *synonyms* (*v*) align, adjust, harmonize, regulate, (*adj*) equal.

samhæfi 1. comparability; *synonyms* (*n*) comparison, compare, correspondence, equivalence, resemblance, **2**. compatibility; *synonyms* (*n*) rapport, agreement, accord, harmony, propriety; *antonym* (*n*) incompatibility.

samhæfing 1. synchronization; *synonyms* (*n*) synchronisation, coordination, synchronism, synchronizing, synchrony, **2**. adjustment; *synonyms* (*n*) adaptation, accommodation, alteration, control, fit, **3**. coordination; *synonyms* (*n*) regulation, classification, organization, arrangement, orientation, **4**. harmonization; *synonyms* (*n*) harmonisation, management, **5**. liaison; *synonyms* (*n*) connection, amour, affair, bond, intrigue.

samhæfni compatibility; *synonyms* (*n*) rapport, agreement, accord, harmony, propriety; *antonym* (*n*) incompatibility.

samhæfur compatible; *synonyms* (*adj*) agreeable, congruent, accordant, congenial, (*n*) consistent; *antonym* (*adj*) incompatible.

samhangandi coherent; *synonyms* (*adj*) logical, rational, consistent, lucid, tenacious; *antonyms* (*adj*) incoherent, illogical, confused, disjointed, rambling.

samheildun inclusion; *synonyms* (*n*) comprehension, implication, incorporation, addition, embodiment; *antonyms* (*n*) exclusion, exception.

samheitaorðabók thesaurus; *synonyms* (*n*) glossary, lexicon, treasury, book, list.

samheiti synonym; *synonyms* (*n*) definition, equivalence.

samheldinn coherent; *synonyms* (*adj*) logical, rational, consistent, lucid, tenacious; *antonyms* (*adj*) incoherent, illogical, confused, disjointed, rambling.

samheldni 1. coherence; *synonyms* (*n*) consistency, comprehensibility, agreement, clarity, coherency; *antonym* (*n*) incoherence, **2**. cohesion; *synonyms* (*n*) continuity, coherence, cohesiveness, unity, grasp.

samhengi 1. context; *synonyms* (*n*) circumstance, environment, setting, surroundings, background, **2**. continuity; *synonyms* (*n*) continuation, coherence, continuance, duration, persistence; *antonym* (*n*) discontinuity, **3**. coherence; *synonyms* (*n*) consistency, comprehensibility, agreement, clarity, coherency; *antonym* (*n*) incoherence, **4**. cohesion; *synonyms* (*n*) continuity, cohesiveness, unity, grasp, grip.

samhjálp 1. symbiosis; *synonyms* (*n*) mutualism, cooperation, life, union, **2**. mutualism; *synonym* (*n*) symbiosis.

samhlekkjun chaining; *synonym* (*n*) taping.

samhliða 1. adjacent; *synonyms* (*adj*) abutting, adjoining, close, contiguous, (*adv*) near; *antonym* (*adj*) distant, **2**. abreast; *synonyms* (*adj*) arow, (*adv*) acquainted, off, opposite, (*prep*) against, **3**. collateral; *synonyms* (*adj*) secondary, (*n*) warranty, guarantee, mortgage, guaranty, **4**. parallel; *synonyms* (*adj*) equivalent, even, (*n*) equal, (*v*) compare, match; *antonyms* (*adj*) conflicting, dissimilar, (*n*) perpendicular, skew.

samhljóða 1. unanimity; *synonyms* (*n*) accord, concord, harmony, agreement, consensus, **2**. consensus; *synonyms* (*n*) unanimity, unity, equality, classlessness, (*adj*) unanimous; *antonym* (*n*) inequality.

samhljóman chime; *synonyms* (*n*) bell, melody, (*v*) buzz, clang, go.

samhljómun resonance; *synonyms* (*n*) vibrancy, reverberation, ringing, sonority, vibration.

samhljómur 1. agreement; *synonyms* (*n*) accord, acquiescence, concord, accordance, coincidence; *antonyms* (*n*) disagreement, argument, conflict, discord, rejection, **2**. concord; *synonyms* (*n*) agreement, concert, harmony, peace, union, **3**. accord; *synonyms* (*n*) assent, (*v*) agree, consent, give, bestow; *antonym* (*n*) strife, **4**. concurrence; *synonyms* (*n*) approval, compliance, concourse, combination, confluence, **5**. accordance; *synonyms* (*n*) concordance, conformity, unison.

samhorf symmetry; *synonyms* (*n*) balance, proportion, order, correspondence, equilibrium; *antonyms* (*n*) asymmetry, disproportion, irregularity.

samhraða synchronize; *synonyms* (*v*) sync,
synchronise, adjust, contemporize, coincide.

samhröðun synchronization; *synonyms* (*n*)
synchronisation, coordination, synchronism,
synchronizing, synchrony.

samhrúgaður conglomerate; *synonyms* (*n*)
composite, group, complex, (*v*) accumulate, amass.

samhrúgun agglomeration; *synonyms* (*n*)
accumulation, bunch, lump, agglutination,
collection.

samhverfa 1. syncline, **2.** symmetry; *synonyms* (*n*)
balance, proportion, order, correspondence,
equilibrium; *antonyms* (*n*) asymmetry,
disproportion, irregularity, **3.** convergence;
synonyms (*n*) confluence, meeting, concentration,
concourse, convergency; *antonyms* (*n*) divergence,
division.

samhverfing convergence; *synonyms* (*n*) confluence,
meeting, concentration, concourse, convergency;
antonyms (*n*) divergence, division.

samhverfur 1. symmetric; *synonyms* (*adj*)
symmetrical, proportionate, harmonious, **2.**
symmetrical; *synonyms* (*adj*) symmetric, balanced,
shapely, methodical, regular; *antonyms* (*adj*)
asymmetrical, irregular.

samingsaðili contractor; *synonyms* (*n*) builder,
entrepreneur, party, undertaker, affirmer.

samkennd empathy; *synonyms* (*n*) sympathy,
compassion, affiliation, affinity, association.

samkeppni 1. competition; *synonyms* (*n*) contest,
rivalry, bout, competitor, contention; *antonym* (*n*)
cooperation, **2.** contention; *synonyms* (*n*)
competition, argument, argumentation, battle,
conflict; *antonym* (*n*) harmony.

samkeppnishæfi competitiveness; *synonyms* (*n*)
battle, bout, combat, fight, conflict.

samkeppnishæfni competitiveness; *synonyms* (*n*)
battle, bout, combat, fight, conflict.

samkjörnungur 1. eucaryote; *synonym* (*n*)
eukaryote, **2.** eukaryote; *synonym* (*n*) eucaryote.

samkoma assembly; *synonyms* (*n*) gathering,
meeting, collection, congregation, (*v*) assemblage.

samkomulag 1. agreement; *synonyms* (*n*) accord,
acquiescence, concord, accordance, coincidence;
antonyms (*n*) disagreement, argument, conflict,
discord, rejection, **2.** accord; *synonyms* (*n*)
agreement, assent, (*v*) agree, consent, give;
antonym (*n*) strife, **3.** stipulation; *synonyms* (*n*)
condition, provision, covenant, proviso, compact,
4. settlement; *synonyms* (*n*) decision,
accommodation, colony, hamlet, payment, **5.**
reconciliation; *synonyms* (*n*) adjustment,
rapprochement, appeasement, harmony, (*v*) peace.

samkræking interlocking; *synonyms* (*adj*)
interlacing, interlinking, (*n*) interlock, meshing,
engagement.

samkunda assembly; *synonyms* (*n*) gathering,
meeting, collection, congregation, (*v*) assemblage.

samkvæmni 1. consistency; *synonyms* (*n*)
consistence, agreement, body, coherence,
consonance; *antonyms* (*n*) inconsistency,
discrepancy, **2.** concordance; *synonyms* (*n*)
accord, concord, accordance, concert, harmony, **3.**
integrity; *synonyms* (*n*) honesty, probity,
completeness, fairness, (*adj*) candor; *antonyms* (*n*)
dishonesty, wickedness.

samkvæmt 1. at; *synonyms* (*prep*) in, a, (*adv*) on, along,
(*prf*) all, **2.** as; *synonyms* (*conj*) qua, because, (*prep*)
during, like, (*n*) arsenic, **3.** along; *synonyms* (*adv*)
ahead, forward, lengthwise, (*prep*) beside, (*prf*) by;
antonym (*adv*) across, **4.** by; *synonyms* (*prep*) at, of,
about, (*adv*) aside, (*adv, prep*) alongside, **5.**
following; *synonyms* (*adj*) consequent, next,
ensuing, subsequent, consecutive; *antonym* (*adj*)
preceding.

samkynhneigð homosexuality; *synonyms* (*n*)
gayness, homoeroticism, homosexualism,
bisexuality.

samkynhneigður homosexual; *synonyms* (*n*) gay,
lesbian, homo, dyke, human.

samkynja 1. bisexual; *synonyms* (*adj*) epicene,
adelomorphous, monoclinous, bisexuous,
ambidextrous, **2.** homogeneous; *synonyms* (*adj*)
uniform, consistent, kindred, homogenous, similar;
antonyms (*adj*) diverse, varied, inconsistent.

samkynjungur hermaphrodite; *synonyms* (*n*)
androgyne, intersex, (*adj*) bisexual, androgynous,
hermaphroditic.

samkynmök homosexuality; *synonyms* (*n*) gayness,
homoeroticism, homosexualism, bisexuality.

samlægi concordance; *synonyms* (*n*) accord,
agreement, concord, accordance, concert.

samlægur 1. contiguous; *synonyms* (*adj*) adjacent,
adjoining, close, abutting, conterminous; *antonym*
(*adj*) distant, **2.** adjacent; *synonyms* (*adj*)
contiguous, nearby, neighboring, next, (*adv*) near.

samlæta relate; *synonyms* (*v*) connect, narrate,
recount, associate, link.

samlæti relation; *synonyms* (*n*) connection, account,
narration, recital, affinity.

samlaga 1. assimilate; *synonyms* (*v*) absorb,
compare, imbibe, incorporate, comprehend, **2.**
integrate; *synonyms* (*v*) blend, combine,
consolidate, fuse, amalgamate; *antonyms* (*v*)
separate, exclude, segregate.

samlagast 1. assimilate; *synonyms* (*v*) absorb,
compare, imbibe, incorporate, comprehend, **2.**

integrate; *synonyms* (*v*) blend, combine,
consolidate, fuse, amalgamate; *antonyms* (*v*)
separate, exclude, segregate.
samlagning 1. addition; *synonyms* (*n*) accession,
accessory, addendum, extension, (*prep*)
accumulation; *antonyms* (*n*) subtraction, removal,
estimation, **2**. superposition; *synonyms* (*n*)
incrustation, superimposition.
samlagningarmerki plus; *synonyms* (*prep*) besides,
(*n*) extra, advantage, addition, (*adv*) more; *antonyms*
(*prep*) minus, (*n*) disadvantage.
samlegð synergy; *synonyms* (*n*) synergism,
cooperation, additivity, concert.
samlegðaráhrif synergy; *synonyms* (*n*) synergism,
cooperation, additivity, concert.
samleggjandi additive; *synonyms* (*adj*) cumulative,
(*n*) addition, adjuvant, admixture, supplement.
samleggjari adder; *synonyms* (*n*) viper, snake,
summer, nadder, nedder.
samleiðni admittance; *synonyms* (*n*) admission,
access, accession, introduction, entrance.
samleiðsla shunt; *synonyms* (*n*) bypass, (*v*) shift,
avert, move, remove.
samleitinn convergent; *synonyms* (*adj*) concurrent,
converging, (*v*) confluent.
samleitni 1. concordance; *synonyms* (*n*) accord,
agreement, concord, accordance, concert, **2**.
concrescence; *synonym* (*n*) growth, **3**. allotropy;
synonym (*n*) allotropism, **4**. convergence;
synonyms (*n*) confluence, meeting, concentration,
concourse, convergency; *antonyms* (*n*) divergence,
division.
samleitur homogeneous; *synonyms* (*adj*) uniform,
consistent, kindred, homogenous, similar;
antonyms (*adj*) diverse, varied, inconsistent.
samliðast interfere; *synonyms* (*v*) intercede, obstruct,
disturb, conflict, (*n*) interpose.
samliðumælir interferometer; *synonyms* (*v*)
bathometer, galvanometer, heliometer,
dynamometer, goniometer.
samliðun interference; *synonyms* (*n*) disturbance,
hindrance, handicap, block, (*v*) collision.
samlíf symbiosis; *synonyms* (*n*) mutualism,
cooperation, life, union.
samlífi symbiosis; *synonyms* (*n*) mutualism,
cooperation, life, union.
samliggjandi 1. contiguous; *synonyms* (*adj*)
adjacent, adjoining, close, abutting, conterminous;
antonym (*adj*) distant, **2**. adjacent; *synonyms* (*adj*)
contiguous, nearby, neighboring, next, (*adv*) near.
samloðandi 1. coherent; *synonyms* (*adj*) logical,
rational, consistent, lucid, tenacious; *antonyms* (*adj*)
incoherent, illogical, confused, disjointed,

rambling, **2**. cohesive; *synonyms* (*adj*) adhesive,
united, amalgamated, caring, (*v*) coherent.
samloðun 1. adhesion; *synonyms* (*n*) adherence,
bond, stickiness, adhesiveness, attachment, **2**.
cohesion; *synonyms* (*n*) coherency, continuity,
coherence, consistency, cohesiveness.
samlögun 1. assimilation; *synonyms* (*n*) absorption,
acculturation, incorporation, integration, addition,
2. integration; *synonyms* (*n*) amalgamation,
consolidation, embodiment, integrating, merger;
antonym (*n*) segregation.
samloka symmetrical; *synonyms* (*adj*) harmonious,
symmetric, balanced, shapely, methodical;
antonyms (*adj*) asymmetrical, irregular.
samlokukjarni core; *synonyms* (*n*) bosom, center,
essence, gist, heart; *antonym* (*adj*) minor.
sammengi union; *synonyms* (*n*) coalition, connection,
junction, association, combination; *antonyms* (*n*)
separation, divergence.
sammiðja 1. axial; *synonyms* (*adj*) axile, central, focal,
umbilical, azygous, **2**. concentric; *synonyms* (*adj*)
concentrical, homocentric, unrelieved, axial, **3**.
coaxial; *synonym* (*adj*) coaxal.
sammynning anastomosis; *synonyms* (*n*)
inosculation, (*v*) communication, concatenation,
mortise, infibulation.
samnefni 1. alias; *synonyms* (*n*) name, pseudonym,
nickname, soubriquet, title, **2**. synonym;
synonyms (*n*) definition, equivalence.
samninganefnd delegation; *synonyms* (*n*)
commission, delegacy, deputation, delegating,
devolution.
samningaumleitanir negotiation; *synonyms* (*n*)
mediation, bargain, parley, transaction, arbitration.
samningaviðræður 1. conference; *synonyms* (*n*)
assembly, colloquy, meeting, council, consultation,
2. negotiation; *synonyms* (*n*) mediation, bargain,
parley, transaction, arbitration.
samningsaðili contractor; *synonyms* (*n*) builder,
entrepreneur, party, undertaker, affirmer.
samningsumleitanir negotiation; *synonyms* (*n*)
mediation, bargain, parley, transaction, arbitration.
samningsumleitun negotiation; *synonyms* (*n*)
mediation, bargain, parley, transaction, arbitration.
samningsviðræður negotiation; *synonyms* (*n*)
mediation, bargain, parley, transaction, arbitration.
samningur 1. agreement; *synonyms* (*n*) accord,
acquiescence, concord, accordance, coincidence;
antonyms (*n*) disagreement, argument, conflict,
discord, rejection, **2**. settlement; *synonyms* (*n*)
decision, accommodation, colony, hamlet,
payment, **3**. concurrence; *synonyms* (*n*) assent,
agreement, approval, consent, compliance, **4**.
contract; *synonyms* (*n*) compact, charter, (*v*)

covenant, bargain, (adj) abridge; antonyms (v)
expand, widen, stretch, 5. consonance; synonyms
(n) conformity, concert, consistency, compatibility,
harmony.

samnýta share; synonyms (n) piece, portion, (v)
participate, allot, apportion; antonym (v) control.

samnýtanlegur compatible; synonyms (adj)
agreeable, congruent, accordant, congenial, (n)
consistent; antonym (adj) incompatible.

samoka conjugate; synonyms (v) join, couple, (adj)
united, conjugated, coupled.

samokun conjugation; synonyms (n) junction, union,
coupling, declension, (v) conjunction.

samop anastomosis; synonyms (n) inosculation, (v)
communication, concatenation, mortise,
infibulation.

samráð 1. consultation; synonyms (n) advice,
conference, interview, negotiation, counsel, 2.
collusion; synonyms (n) connivance, complicity,
intrigue, plot, circumvention.

Samræður dialogue; synonyms (n) talk, colloquy,
conversation, interlocution, interview.

samræma 1. unify; synonyms (v) combine, integrate,
amalgamate, consolidate, merge, 2. coordinate;
synonyms (v) align, adjust, harmonize, regulate,
(adj) equal, 3. approximate; synonyms (adj)
approximative, near, rough, (v) approach,
approaching; antonyms (v) exact, precise.

samræmanlegur compatible; synonyms (adj)
agreeable, congruent, accordant, congenial, (n)
consistent; antonym (adj) incompatible.

samræmdur unitary; synonyms (adj) single, one,
sole, solitary, united.

samræmi 1. agreement; synonyms (n) accord,
acquiescence, concord, accordance, coincidence;
antonyms (n) disagreement, argument, conflict,
discord, rejection, 2. accord; synonyms (n)
agreement, assent, (v) agree, consent, give;
antonym (n) strife, 3. consonance; synonyms (n)
conformity, concert, consistency, compatibility,
harmony, 4. consistency; synonyms (n)
consistence, body, coherence, consonance,
congruence; antonyms (n) inconsistency,
discrepancy, 5. accordance; synonyms (n)
concordance, unison.

samræming 1. unification; synonyms (n) union,
amalgamation, combination, merger, fusion;
antonyms (n) separation, division, segregation, 2.
alignment; synonyms (n) alliance, alinement,
arrangement, coalition, organization, 3.
approximation; synonyms (n) approach, guess,
affinity, estimate, (v) estimation, 4. coordination;
synonyms (n) regulation, classification, orientation,
running, scheme, 5. harmonization; synonyms
(n) harmonisation, management.

samrennsli confluence; synonyms (n) concourse,
meeting, concurrence, junction, assembly; antonym
(n) divergence.

samrit 1. strainer; synonyms (n) filter, sieve,
stretcher, colature, mesh, 2. duplicate; synonyms
(adj) dual, (v) copy, double, twin, (n) counterpart;
antonym (n) original.

samröðun 1. assortment; synonyms (n) miscellany,
range, set, variety, categorization, 2. assembly;
synonyms (n) gathering, meeting, collection,
congregation, (v) assemblage.

samruni 1. recombination, 2. union; synonyms (n)
coalition, connection, junction, association,
combination; antonyms (n) separation, divergence,
3. amalgamation; synonyms (n) amalgam,
merger, synthesis, alliance, blend; antonym (n)
expulsion, 4. coalescence; synonyms (n)
unification, amalgamation, concretion,
conglutination, embodiment, 5. fusion; synonyms
(n) coalescence, union, compound, mixture, alloy.

samrunninn confluent; synonyms (adj) concurrent,
blending, merging, mingling, (v) convergent.

samrýmanlegur compatible; synonyms (adj)
agreeable, congruent, accordant, congenial, (n)
consistent; antonym (adj) incompatible.

samsækni affinity; synonyms (n) sympathy, analogy,
alliance, bond, kindred.

samsæri plot; synonyms (n) conspiracy, plan, lot, (v)
intrigue, cabal.

samsærisfélagi confederate; synonyms (adj) allied,
(n) accomplice, ally, accessory, (v) associate.

samsæta 1. isotope, 2. allele; synonym (n)
allelomorph.

samsætuberi carrier; synonyms (n) bearer,
messenger, courier, mailman, porter.

samsætuensím 1. isoenzyme, 2. isozyme;
synonym (n) isoenzyme.

samsafn 1. aggregation; synonyms (n) accumulation,
congregation, heap, lot, (v) assemblage, 2.
aggregate; synonyms (n) total, agglomerate,
whole, (v) accumulate, cluster; antonyms (n)
individual, part, 3. assortment; synonyms (n)
miscellany, range, set, variety, categorization.

samsama identify; synonyms (v) distinguish, detect,
discover, name, ascertain.

samsemd identity; synonyms (n) identicalness, unity,
individuality, personality, sameness.

samsetning 1. synthesis; synonyms (n) combination,
fusion, compound, incorporation, mixture;
antonym (n) separation, 2. composition;
synonyms (n) arrangement, constitution,
construction, texture, alloy, 3. assembly;
synonyms (n) gathering, meeting, collection,
congregation, (v) assemblage, 4. assembling;

synonyms (*n*) assembly, collecting, compilation, aggregation, accumulation, **5**. mosaic; *synonyms* (*n*) tesserae, strigae, (*adj*) tessellated, heterogeneous, (*v*) plaid.

samsetningur 1. composite; *synonyms* (*n*) complex, amalgam, blend, mix, (*v*) compound, **2**. combination; *synonyms* (*n*) alliance, union, association, coalition, league; *antonyms* (*n*) separation, (*adj*) simple.

samsettur 1. composite; *synonyms* (*n*) complex, amalgam, blend, mix, (*v*) compound, **2**. compound; *synonyms* (*n*) combination, (*v*) alloy, amalgamate, combine, (*adj*) composite; *antonym* (*adj*) simple, **3**. complex; *synonyms* (*adj*) complicate, abstruse, difficult, elaborate, intricate; *antonyms* (*adj*) basic, straightforward, clear, plain.

samsíða 1. abreast; *synonyms* (*adj*) near, (*adv*) acquainted, off, opposite, (*prep*) against, **2**. parallel; *synonyms* (*adj*) equivalent, even, (*n*) equal, (*v*) compare, match; *antonyms* (*adj*) conflicting, dissimilar, (*n*) perpendicular, skew.

samsíðungur parallelogram; *synonyms* (*n*) rectangle, rhomb, diamond, oblong, quadrangle.

samskeyti 1. seam; *synonyms* (*n*) joint, layer, bed, furrow, (*v*) crinkle, **2**. boundary; *synonyms* (*n*) border, bound, limit, edge, area, **3**. interface; *synonyms* (*n*) link, port, boundary, junction, (*v*) contact, **4**. junction; *synonyms* (*n*) confluence, connection, meeting, interchange, articulation, **5**. joint; *synonyms* (*adj*) collective, (*n*) hinge, join, seam, (*v*) articulate; *antonyms* (*adj*) individual, unilateral, private, separate.

samskeyting splicing; *synonyms* (*n*) splice, reinforcing, sticking.

samskil occlusion; *synonyms* (*n*) closure, block, blockage, stoppage, obstruction.

samskipan configuration; *synonyms* (*n*) form, arrangement, conformation, shape, organization.

samskiptaaðferð protocol; *synonyms* (*n*) etiquette, manners, ceremony, bill, formality.

samskiptabann boycott; *synonyms* (*n*) ban, (*v*) ostracize, exclude, proscribe, strike; *antonym* (*v*) patronize.

samskiptalýsing primitive; *synonyms* (*adj*) primeval, primary, antediluvian, archaic, crude; *antonym* (*adj*) modern.

samskiptamáti protocol; *synonyms* (*n*) etiquette, manners, ceremony, bill, formality.

samskiptareglur protocol; *synonyms* (*n*) etiquette, manners, ceremony, bill, formality.

samskiptarit chart; *synonyms* (*n*) plan, plot, (*v*) map, graph, sketch.

samskipti 1. communication; *synonyms* (*n*) announcement, commerce, communicating,

contact, conversation, **2**. interaction; *synonyms* (*n*) interplay, correlation, communication, mutuality, affairs.

samskonar identical; *synonyms* (*adj*) equal, corresponding, uniform, consistent, (*v*) same; *antonyms* (*adj*) different, incompatible, inconsistent.

samsláttur jounce; *synonyms* (*n*) jolt, jar, (*v*) bounce, jog, joggle.

samslíping lapping; *synonyms* (*n*) lap, overlapping, imbrication, facetting, wash.

samslípun 1. honing, **2**. lapping; *synonyms* (*n*) lap, overlapping, imbrication, facetting, wash.

samsnið conformity; *synonyms* (*n*) accord, agreement, compliance, concord, accordance; *antonyms* (*n*) disobedience, nonconformity.

samsniða conform; *synonyms* (*v*) accommodate, adapt, adjust, agree, accord; *antonyms* (*v*) deviate, differ.

samsníða conform; *synonyms* (*v*) accommodate, adapt, adjust, agree, accord; *antonyms* (*v*) deviate, differ.

samsöfnun 1. concentration; *synonyms* (*n*) absorption, concentrate, application, attention, engrossment; *antonym* (*n*) distraction, **2**. aggregation; *synonyms* (*n*) accumulation, congregation, heap, lot, (*v*) assemblage, **3**. compilation; *synonyms* (*n*) collection, anthology, compiling, digest, miscellany, **4**. assembly; *synonyms* (*n*) gathering, meeting, convention, fabrication, multitude.

samsömun identification; *synonyms* (*n*) designation, finding, id, identity, mark.

samspil interaction; *synonyms* (*n*) interplay, contact, correlation, communication, mutuality.

samstaða 1. unanimity; *synonyms* (*n*) accord, concord, harmony, agreement, consensus, **2**. consensus; *synonyms* (*n*) unanimity, unity, equality, classlessness, (*adj*) unanimous; *antonym* (*n*) inequality, **3**. coupling; *synonyms* (*n*) union, coupler, clutch, conjugation, connection, **4**. conjunction; *synonyms* (*n*) combination, association, coincidence, concurrence, coalition.

Samstæð united; *synonyms* (*adj*) joined, joint, combined, cooperative, connected; *antonyms* (*adj*) individual, separate, divided.

samstæða 1. unit; *synonyms* (*n*) troop, element, group, squad, (*adj*) one, **2**. set; *synonyms* (*v*) fix, place, lay, put, (*n*) class; *antonyms* (*v*) soften, liquefy, (*n*) combing, comb-out, (*adj*) variable, **3**. combination; *synonyms* (*n*) alliance, blend, union, association, coalition; *antonyms* (*n*) separation, (*adj*) simple, **4**. consolidation; *synonyms* (*n*) amalgamation, unification, combination, fortification, condensation, **5**. complex; *synonyms* (adj) composite, complicate, abstruse, difficult, elaborate; *antonyms* (adj) basic, straightforward, clear, plain.

samstæður homologous; *synonyms* (adj) analogous, homogeneous, like, equivalent, equal.

samstarf 1. cooperation; *synonyms* (n) concurrence, aid, assistance, association, teamwork, *antonyms* (n) stubbornness, competition, confrontation, rivalry, **2.** liaison; *synonyms* (n) connection, amour, affair, bond, intrigue, **3.** interaction; *synonyms* (n) interplay, contact, correlation, communication, mutuality.

samstarfandi synergist; *synonym* (n) catalyst.

samstarfsmaður 1. associate; *synonyms* (v) affiliate, connect, (n) ally, assistant, companion; *antonyms* (v) avoid, dissociate, distance, (adj) chief, (n) stranger, **2.** colleague; *synonyms* (n) associate, buddy, collaborator, friend, partner.

samstarfspáttur factor; *synonyms* (n) agent, component, broker, divisor, (adj) constituent.

samsteypa 1. coalition; *synonyms* (n) alliance, association, combination, league, union; *antonym* (n) nonalignment, **2.** consortium; *synonyms* (n) syndicate, cartel, organization, pool, federation, **3.** aggregation; *synonyms* (n) accumulation, congregation, heap, lot, (v) assemblage, **4.** alliance; *synonyms* (n) connection, affinity, confederacy, affiliation, alignment, **5.** merger; *synonyms* (n) amalgamation, fusion, unification, coalition, consolidation.

samstig 1. coherence; *synonyms* (n) consistency, comprehensibility, agreement, clarity, coherency; *antonym* (n) incoherence, **2.** pacing; *synonyms* (n) pace, tempo.

samstilla 1. synchronize; *synonyms* (v) sync, synchronise, adjust, contemporize, coincide, **2.** coordinate; *synonyms* (v) align, harmonize, regulate, organize, (adj) equal, **3.** match; *synonyms* (v) agree, mate, meet, parallel, accord; *antonyms* (v) clash, contradict.

samstilling 1. tune; *synonyms* (n) melody, song, strain, air, (v) adjust, **2.** synchronization; *synonyms* (n) synchronisation, coordination, synchronism, synchronizing, synchrony, **3.** synchronous; *synonyms* (adj) simultaneous, synchronal, concurrent, synchronic, coincident, **4.** alignment; *synonyms* (n) alliance, alinement, arrangement, coalition, organization, **5.** focusing; *synonyms* (n) centering, concentration, focus, focussing, focalisation.

samstilltur synchronous; *synonyms* (adj) simultaneous, synchronal, concurrent, synchronic, coincident.

samstjórn condominium; *synonyms* (n) condo, domicile, habitat, home, house.

samstofna cognate; *synonyms* (adj) akin, alike, allied, related, like.

samstunda synchronous; *synonyms* (adj) simultaneous, synchronal, concurrent, synchronic, coincident.

samstundis instantaneous; *synonyms* (adj) instant, immediate, prompt, precipitate, sudden; *antonym* (adj) consecutive.

samsvar echo; *synonyms* (n) answer, (v) repeat, reproduce, resound, reverberate.

samsvarandi 1. corresponding; *synonyms* (adj) congruent, comparable, equal, same, similar; *antonym* (adj) different, **2.** analogous; *synonyms* (adj) alike, akin, analogical, corresponding, equivalent; *antonym* (adj) dissimilar, **3.** equivalent; *synonyms* (adj) analogous, even, identical, (n) counterpart, (v) consideration; *antonym* (adj) unlike, **4.** homologous; *synonyms* (adj) homogeneous, like, homogenous.

samsveiflun 1. resonance; *synonyms* (n) vibrancy, reverberation, ringing, sonority, vibration, **2.** coherence; *synonyms* (n) consistency, comprehensibility, agreement, clarity, coherency; *antonym* (n) incoherence.

samsvörun 1. concordance; *synonyms* (n) accord, agreement, concord, accordance, concert, **2.** correspondence; *synonyms* (n) conformity, communication, connection, coincidence, affinity; *antonyms* (n) difference, asymmetry, dissimilarity, **3.** analogy; *synonyms* (n) semblance, correspondence, parity, resemblance, similarity, **4.** homology; *synonyms* (n) equality, analogy, relation.

samtak 1. synergy; *synonyms* (n) synergism, cooperation, additivity, concert, **2.** combination; *synonyms* (n) alliance, blend, union, association, coalition; *antonyms* (n) separation, (adj) simple.

samtaka coherent; *synonyms* (adj) logical, rational, consistent, lucid, tenacious; *antonyms* (adj) incoherent, illogical, confused, disjointed, rambling.

samtal conversation; *synonyms* (n) chat, conference, talk, colloquy, communication.

samtala 1. total; *synonyms* (adj) aggregate, complete, (n) whole, amount, (v) count; *antonyms* (adj) partial, incomplete, qualified, **2.** sum; *synonyms* (n) total, quantity, entirety, (v) figure, number.

samtekt combination; *synonyms* (n) alliance, blend, union, association, coalition; *antonyms* (n) separation, (adj) simple.

samtengdur 1. synthetic; *synonyms* (adj) artificial, ersatz, false, simulated, synthetical; *antonyms* (adj)

natural, genuine, real, **2**. interactive; *synonyms*
(*adj*) interactional, mutual, synergistic, synergetic.
samtengi interface; *synonyms* (*n*) link, port,
boundary, junction, (*v*) contact.
samtengiafl cohesion; *synonyms* (*n*) coherency,
continuity, coherence, consistency, cohesiveness.
samtenging 1. recombination, **2**. synthesis;
synonyms (*n*) combination, fusion, compound,
incorporation, mixture; *antonym* (*n*) separation, **3**.
union; *synonyms* (*n*) coalition, connection,
junction, association, league; *antonym* (*n*)
divergence, **4**. conjunction; *synonyms* (*n*)
coincidence, concurrence, alliance, confluence, (*v*)
joinder, **5**. connection; *synonyms* (*n*) bond,
communication, attachment, concatenation, joint;
antonym (*n*) disconnection.
samþætta integrate; *synonyms* (*v*) incorporate,
blend, combine, consolidate, fuse; *antonyms* (*v*)
separate, exclude, segregate.
samþætti homogeneity; *synonyms* (*n*)
homogeneousness, affinity, alliance, consistency,
unity.
samþætting 1. annealing; *synonym* (*n*) tempering, **2**.
integration; *synonyms* (*n*) amalgamation,
consolidation, embodiment, integrating, merger;
antonym (*n*) segregation.
samþátta homogeneous; *synonyms* (*adj*) uniform,
consistent, kindred, homogenous, similar;
antonyms (*adj*) diverse, varied, inconsistent.
samþáttun confounding; *synonyms* (*adj*) confusing,
amazing, astounding, conflicting, (*n*) confusion.
samþjappaður compact; *synonyms* (*adj*) close, (*n*)
agreement, arrangement, contract, (*v*) compress;
antonyms (*adj*) loose, sprawling, bulky, sparse.
samþjappari compressor; *synonym* (*n*)
supercharger.
samþjöppun 1. compression; *synonyms* (*n*)
compaction, condensation, pressure, compressing,
concentration, **2**. compactness; *synonyms* (*n*)
density, denseness, closeness, firmness, (*v*)
compression, **3**. concentration; *synonyms* (*n*)
absorption, concentrate, application, attention,
engrossment; *antonym* (*n*) distraction, **4**.
compaction; *synonyms* (*n*) calculus, coalescence,
coalescency, coalition, concretion.
samþrýstingur compaction; *synonyms* (*n*)
compressing, compression, calculus, coalescence,
coalescency.
samþýðanlegur compatible; *synonyms* (*adj*)
agreeable, congruent, accordant, congenial, (*n*)
consistent; *antonym* (*adj*) incompatible.
samþýðing adaptation; *synonyms* (*n*)
accommodation, adjustment, alteration, version,
reworking.

samþykki 1. consent; *synonyms* (*n*) accord,
acquiescence, (*v*) assent, agree, approve; *antonyms*
(*n*) opposition, refusal, (*v*) disagree, refuse, veto, **2**.
certificate; *synonyms* (*n*) bond, diploma,
certification, credential, (*v*) certify, **3**. approval;
synonyms (*n*) acceptance, applause, approbation,
acclaim, agreement; *antonyms* (*n*) disapproval,
rejection, condemnation, scorn, criticism.
samþykkja 1. accept; *synonyms* (*v*) receive,
acknowledge, admit, take, recognize; *antonyms* (*v*)
refuse, reject, deny, snub, oppose, **2**. take;
synonyms (*v*) get, hold, adopt, (*n*) seize, (*phr*) accept;
antonyms (*v*) give, abstain, add, lose, **3**. receive;
synonyms (*v*) assume, bear, have, obtain, welcome,
4. agree; *synonyms* (*v*) accord, acquiesce, adjust,
accede, bargain; *antonyms* (*v*) disagree, differ,
argue, object, refute, **5**. adopt; *synonyms* (*v*)
affiliate, borrow, espouse, pass, acquire.
samþykkjandi acceptor; *synonyms* (*n*) accepter,
respecter.
samþykkt 1. statute; *synonyms* (*n*) law, ordinance,
rule, constitution, decree, **2**. resolution; *synonyms*
(*n*) decision, determination, answer, conclusion,
firmness; *antonym* (*n*) indecisiveness, **3**.
constitution; *synonyms* (*n*) composition, code,
makeup, organization, temperament, **4**.
convention; *synonyms* (*n*) conference, congress,
meeting, contract, assembly, **5**. approval;
synonyms (*n*) acceptance, applause, approbation,
acclaim, agreement; *antonyms* (*n*) disapproval,
rejection, condemnation, scorn, criticism.
samþykktur approved; *synonyms* (*adj*) accepted,
certified, sanctioned, allowed, authorized;
antonyms (*adj*) informal, unofficial.
samþyrping aggregation; *synonyms* (*n*)
accumulation, congregation, heap, lot, (*v*)
assemblage.
samtíma 1. synchronous; *synonyms* (*adj*)
simultaneous, synchronal, concurrent, synchronic,
coincident, **2**. simultaneous; *synonyms* (*adj*)
coincidental, synchronous, contemporary,
coinciding, cooccurring; *antonyms* (*adj*)
independent, separate.
samtímahugtak simultaneity; *synonyms* (*n*)
simultaneousness, overlapping.
samtími simultaneity; *synonyms* (*n*)
simultaneousness, overlapping.
samtímis 1. simultaneous; *synonyms* (*adj*)
coincident, concurrent, coincidental, synchronous,
contemporary; *antonyms* (*adj*) independent,
separate, **2**. synchronous; *synonyms* (*adj*)
simultaneous, synchronal, synchronic,
synchronical, concomitant.

samtímissending duplex; *synonyms* (*adj*) double, dual, duplicate, (*n*) moderator.

samtímistal duplex; *synonyms* (*adj*) double, dual, duplicate, (*n*) moderator.

samtök 1. union; *synonyms* (*n*) coalition, connection, junction, association, combination; *antonyms* (*n*) separation, divergence, **2.** association; *synonyms* (*n*) affiliation, alliance, assembly, affinity, company, **3.** organization; *synonyms* (*n*) order, establishment, administration, arrangement, formation, **4.** institution; *synonyms* (*n*) creation, institute, asylum, founding, academy, **5.** federation; *synonyms* (*n*) confederacy, confederation, league, organization, union.

samtvinnun 1. interdependence; *synonyms* (*n*) correlation, mutuality, interdependency, dependence, (*adj*) link, **2.** integration; *synonyms* (*n*) amalgamation, consolidation, embodiment, integrating, merger; *antonym* (*n*) segregation.

samúð sympathy; *synonyms* (*n*) compassion, pity, benevolence, commiseration, feeling; *antonyms* (*n*) indifference, cruelty.

samundinn agglomerate; *synonyms* (*v*) accumulate, (*n*) conglomerate, aggregate, (*adj*) agglomerated, agglomerative.

samur same; *synonyms* (*adj*) alike, identical, corresponding, equal, like; *antonym* (*adj*) different.

samvalinn match; *synonyms* (*n*) equal, (*v*) agree, mate, meet, parallel; *antonyms* (*v*) clash, contradict.

samvaxa accrete; *synonyms* (*v*) add, adhere.

samvaxinn 1. concrete; *synonyms* (*adj*) actual, positive, (*n*) cement, (*v*) coagulate, congeal; *antonyms* (*adj*) theoretical, intangible, abstract, hypothetical, incidental, **2.** confluent; *synonyms* (*adj*) concurrent, blending, merging, mingling, (*v*) convergent.

samveita shunt; *synonyms* (*n*) bypass, (*v*) shift, avert, move, remove.

samveldi commonwealth; *synonyms* (*n*) commonweal, country, nation, state, province.

samverkan interaction; *synonyms* (*n*) interplay, contact, correlation, communication, mutuality.

samverkun 1. synergism; *synonyms* (*n*) synergy, cooperation, **2.** synergy; *synonyms* (*n*) synergism, additivity, concert, **3.** interaction; *synonyms* (*n*) interplay, contact, correlation, communication, mutuality.

samviðnám impedance; *synonyms* (*n*) resistance, clog, friction, hindrance, immunity.

samvinna cooperation; *synonyms* (*n*) concurrence, aid, assistance, association, teamwork; *antonyms* (*n*) stubbornness, competition, confrontation, rivalry.

samvirkni 1. synergy; *synonyms* (*n*) synergism, cooperation, additivity, concert, **2.** transaction; *synonyms* (*n*) deal, business, dealing, dealings, proceeding; *antonym* (*n*) purchase.

samvirkur synergistic; *synonyms* (*adj*) synergetic, interactive, concomitant, interactional, (*n*) coactive.

samviska conscience; *synonyms* (*n*) shame, scruple, principles, (*adj*) abandoned, (*v*) absolve.

samvísun convergence; *synonyms* (*n*) confluence, meeting, concentration, concourse, convergency; *antonyms* (*n*) divergence, division.

samvöxtur 1. symphysis; *synonyms* (*n*) amphiarthrosis, (*v*) infibulation, inosculation, confluence, **2.** accretion; *synonyms* (*n*) increment, accumulation, increase, augmentation, accession, **3.** coalescence; *synonyms* (*n*) synthesis, unification, amalgamation, coalition, concretion, **4.** concrescence; *synonym* (*n*) growth.

samyrkja synergy; *synonyms* (*n*) synergism, cooperation, additivity, concert.

samyrkjubú collective; *synonyms* (*adj*) aggregate, general, joint, common, cumulative; *antonyms* (*adj*) capitalist, distributive, private.

sandalda dune; *synonyms* (*n*) down, bank, hill, hump, mound.

sandauðn desert; *synonyms* (*v*) abandon, escape, defect, (*adj*) waste, barren; *antonyms* (*n*) bog, (*v*) stay.

sandborinn arenaceous; *synonyms* (*adj*) sandy, friable, arenarious, arenose, dusty.

sandbylur blizzard; *synonyms* (*n*) snowstorm, storm, tempest, snowfall, gale.

sandeðla lizard; *synonyms* (*n*) loafer, purse.

sandfláki sandbank; *synonyms* (*n*) bank, reef, hill, mound, ridge.

sandgrynning shoal; *synonyms* (*n*) shallow, school, shelf, swarm, multitude.

sandhóll dune; *synonyms* (*n*) down, bank, hill, hump, mound.

sandhverfa turbot; *synonyms* (*n*) flounder, plaice, sole, tonguefishes.

sandkoli dab; *synonyms* (*n*) pat, adept, bit, tap, (*v*) dot.

sandmaðkur lugworm; *synonyms* (*n*) lobworm, lug, lugsail.

sandpappír abrasive; *synonyms* (*adj*) rough, harsh, caustic, (*n*) abradant, abrader; *antonym* (*adj*) smooth.

sandrif 1. sandbank; *synonyms* (*n*) bank, reef, hill, mound, ridge, **2.** bar; *synonyms* (*n*) barricade, band, (*v*) ban, block, bolt; *antonyms* (*v*) permit, allow.

sandskel gaper; *synonyms* (*n*) bystander, mirror, spectator.

sandsteinn sandstone; *synonyms* (*n*) brickwork, granite, mineral, stone, stonework.

sandur sand; *synonyms* (*n*) grit, guts, dust, beach, (*adj*) powder.

sáning 1. seeding; *synonyms* (*n*) sowing, farming, plantlet, salting, spiking, **2.** inoculation; *synonyms* (*n*) injection, immunization, vaccination, (*v*) indoctrination, inculcation.

sanna 1. verify; *synonyms* (*v*) ascertain, confirm, corroborate, check, (*n*) substantiate; *antonym* (*v*) disprove, **2.** prove; *synonyms* (*v*) demonstrate, attest, manifest, establish, evidence.

sannfæra 1. persuade; *synonyms* (*v*) convince, inveigle, allure, assure, cajole; *antonyms* (*v*) discourage, dissuade, **2.** convince; *synonyms* (*v*) persuade, convert, sway, convict, (*adj*) satisfy.

sannfærður 1. convincing; *synonyms* (*adj*) conclusive, cogent, compelling, forceful, persuasive; *antonym* (*adj*) unconvincing, **2.** compelling; *synonyms* (*adj*) captivating, effective, forcible, commanding, powerful; *antonyms* (*adj*) weak, boring.

sannfæring 1. conviction; *synonyms* (*n*) assurance, belief, certainty, condemnation, confidence; *antonym* (*n*) uncertainty, **2.** creed; *synonyms* (*n*) conviction, gospel, religion, credo, faith, **3.** belief; *synonyms* (*n*) assumption, doctrine, feeling, idea, impression; *antonyms* (*n*) disbelief, unbelief.

sanngirni equity; *synonyms* (*n*) fairness, honesty, candor, (*adj*) justice, integrity; *antonym* (*n*) unfairness.

sanngjarn 1. equitable; *synonyms* (*adj*) fair, impartial, just, correct, even-handed; *antonym* (*adj*) inequitable, **2.** moderate; *synonyms* (*adj*) temperate, abstemious, middling, mild, (*v*) calm; *antonyms* (*adj*) extreme, immoderate, radical, (*v*) increase, intensify.

sanngreining identification; *synonyms* (*n*) designation, finding, id, identity, mark.

sannleikur 1. truth; *synonyms* (*n*) exactness, reality, actuality, sincerity, correctness; *antonyms* (*n*) untruth, dishonesty, fabrication, falsehood, fiction, **2.** reality; *synonyms* (*n*) fact, existence, certainty, realism, being; *antonyms* (*n*) fantasy, delusion, dream, imagination, vision.

sannprófa verify; *synonyms* (*v*) ascertain, confirm, corroborate, check, (*n*) substantiate; *antonym* (*v*) disprove.

sannprófun verification; *synonyms* (*n*) confirmation, check, proof, substantiation, authentication.

sannreyna ascertain; *synonyms* (*v*) see, check, determine, discover, establish.

sannur 1. real; *synonyms* (*adj*) genuine, material, physical, true, (*v*) actual; *antonyms* (*adj*) unreal, imaginary, apparent, artificial, (*v*) pretend, **2.** true; *synonyms* (*adj*) real, faithful, right, even, accurate; *antonyms* (*adj*) false, bogus, inaccurate, untrue, **3.** authority; *synonyms* (*n*) ascendancy, command, sanction, administration, authorization, **4.** apparent; *synonyms* (*adj*) manifest, discernible, patent, plain, (*adv*) visible; *antonyms* (*adj*) unclear, mysterious, obscure, **5.** authentic; *synonyms* (*adj*) straight, believable, trustworthy, valid, (*v*) authoritative; *antonyms* (*adj*) fake, unrealistic.

sanþófýll xanthophyll; *synonyms* (*n*) xanthophyl, lutein.

sápa soap; *synonyms* (*v*) lather, bribe, grease, oil, wheedle.

sapódilla sapodilla; *synonyms* (*n*) sapota, zapotilla.

sapódillaplóma sapodilla; *synonyms* (*n*) sapota, zapotilla.

sapódillatré sapodilla; *synonyms* (*n*) sapota, zapotilla.

sápuefni detergent; *synonyms* (*adj*) detersive, cleansing, (*n*) abluent, cleanser, (*v*) lotion.

sar savory; *synonyms* (*adj*) dainty, palatable, spicy, fragrant, appetizing.

sár 1. wound; *synonyms* (*n*) bruise, harm, pain, (*v*) hurt, cut, **2.** ulcer; *synonyms* (*n*) boil, (*v*) canker, fester, (*adj*) sore, cancer, **3.** lesion; *synonyms* (*n*) injury, wound, abrasion, scrape, scratch, **4.** injury; *synonyms* (*n*) disadvantage, disservice, grievance, damage, detriment; *antonyms* (*n*) ability, reparation.

sárabindi bandage; *synonyms* (*n*) band, swathe, (*v*) bind, wrap, (*adj*) truss.

sárakörtur granulation; *synonyms* (*n*) aggregation, (*adj*) attenuation, comminution, levigation, multure.

sáraléreft gauze; *synonyms* (*n*) film, bandage, blind, curtain, mantle.

sárasótt 1. syphilis; *synonyms* (*n*) pox, syph, siphilis, venereal, **2.** lues.

sardína pilchard; *synonyms* (*n*) sardine, sard, sardius.

sarkmein sarcoma; *synonyms* (*n*) growth, tumor, disease, malignancy, melanoma.

sárlokun closure; *synonyms* (*n*) closing, close, blockade, blockage, closedown; *antonym* (*n*) inauguration.

sarpur 1. crop; *synonyms* (*n*) fruit, harvest, (*v*) browse, graze, (*adj*) clip, **2.** economizer; *synonym* (*n*) economiser.

sársaukalaus indolent; *synonyms* (*adj*) idle, inactive, lazy, slothful, sluggish; *antonyms* (*adj*) energetic, active.

sársauki pain; *synonyms* (*n*) distress, ache, bother, (*v*) hurt, afflict; *antonym* (*n*) pleasure.

satíra 1. sarcasm; *synonyms* (n) irony, gibe, bitterness, (adj) ridicule, satire, **2**. satire; *synonyms* (n) sarcasm, caricature, lampoon, mockery, parody, **3**. irony; *synonyms* (n) banter, humor, raillery, derision, quiz; *antonym* (n) exaggeration.

sátt 1. reconciliation; *synonyms* (n) accommodation, adjustment, agreement, rapprochement, (v) concord, **2**. conciliation; *synonyms* (n) mediation, appeasement, peace, pacification, placation; *antonym* (n) provocation.

sáttamaður conciliator; *synonyms* (n) peacemaker, mediator, arbitrator, intermediary, negotiator.

sáttargerð 1. settlement; *synonyms* (n) decision, accommodation, colony, hamlet, payment, **2**. agreement; *synonyms* (n) accord, acquiescence, concord, accordance, coincidence; *antonyms* (n) disagreement, argument, conflict, discord, rejection.

sáttasemjari conciliator; *synonyms* (n) peacemaker, mediator, arbitrator, intermediary, negotiator.

sáttaumleitun 1. conciliation; *synonyms* (n) mediation, appeasement, peace, pacification, placation; *antonym* (n) provocation, **2**. interposition; *synonyms* (n) interference, interpolation, intervention, insertion, (adj) intercession, **3**. mediation; *synonyms* (n) arbitration, agency, intermediation, interposition, propitiation.

sáttmáli 1. treaty; *synonyms* (n) agreement, convention, protocol, accord, concord, **2**. covenant; *synonyms* (n) contract, compact, bond, arrangement, (v) bargain, **3**. convention; *synonyms* (n) conference, congress, meeting, assembly, convocation, **4**. bond; *synonyms* (n) association, tie, alliance, deed, (v) bind, **5**. agreement; *synonyms* (n) acquiescence, accordance, coincidence, acceptance, appointment; *antonyms* (n) disagreement, argument, conflict, discord, rejection.

sátur 1. stator; *synonyms* (n) reactor, rotor, **2**. reactor; *synonym* (n) stator.

sauðkind sheep; *synonyms* (n) mutton, goat, cattle, follower, stock.

sauður sheep; *synonyms* (n) mutton, goat, cattle, follower, stock.

sauma 1. suture; *synonyms* (n) joint, seam, (v) commissure, juncture, articulation, **2**. sew; *synonyms* (v) patch, knit, mend, stitch, tack.

saumlaus seamless; *synonyms* (adj) faultless, flawless, textbook, unlined, unseamed.

saumlaust seamless; *synonyms* (adj) faultless, flawless, textbook, unlined, unseamed.

saumur 1. suture; *synonyms* (n) joint, seam, (v) commissure, juncture, articulation, **2**. seam; *synonyms* (n) layer, bed, furrow, line, (v) crinkle.

saur 1. stool; *synonyms* (n) chair, seat, bench, dejection, faeces, **2**. faeces; *synonyms* (n) dung, excrement, feces, ordure, stool, **3**. feces; *synonyms* (n) dregs, filth, can, commode, crapper.

saurfræði scatology; *synonym* (n) obscenity.

saurgun contamination; *synonyms* (n) contagion, pollution, contaminant, infection, dirtying; *antonym* (n) decontamination.

saurhneigð scatology; *synonym* (n) obscenity.

saurindi 1. waste; *synonyms* (n) desert, (adj) spoil, desolate, (v) consume, exhaust; *antonyms* (v) conserve, save, **2**. excrement; *synonyms* (n) dejection, faeces, dirt, evacuation, dung.

saurlát defecation; *synonyms* (n) evacuation, settling, abolition, laxation, (v) purification.

saurteppa impaction; *synonyms* (n) encroachment, impact, impingement.

savanni savanna; *synonyms* (n) steppe, basin, desert, pampas, wold.

saxari chopper; *synonyms* (n) ax, helicopter, cleaver, whirlybird, chop.

sebrahestur zebra; *synonym* (n) referee.

sefandi neuroleptic; *synonym* (n) antipsychotic.

sefasýki hysteria; *synonyms* (n) hysterics, delirium, frenzy, madness, craze.

sefjandi suggestive; *synonyms* (adj) indicative, expressive, obscene, spicy, bawdy.

sefjun suggestion; *synonyms* (n) hint, advice, intimation, proposal, allusion.

sefnæmur suggestible; *synonyms* (adj) impressionable, receptive, susceptible, amenable, biddable.

sefun appeasement; *synonyms* (n) conciliation, pacification, reconciliation, relief, indulgence.

segamyndun thrombosis; *synonym* (n) apoplexy.

segavarnarefni anticoagulant; *synonym* (n) decoagulant.

segavarnarlyf anticoagulant; *synonym* (n) decoagulant.

segð 1. utterance; *synonyms* (n) declaration, expression, pronunciation, speech, exclamation, **2**. expression; *synonyms* (n) diction, phrase, voice, appearance, aspect; *antonym* (n) repression.

segi thrombus; *synonym* (n) clot.

segja 1. say; *synonyms* (v) remark, articulate, express, pronounce, (n) declare, **2**. recount; *synonyms* (v) narrate, tell, recite, relate, describe, **3**. relate; *synonyms* (v) connect, recount, associate, link, appertain, **4**. state; *synonyms* (n) nation, position, say, country, (v) expound; *antonyms* (v) deny, (adj) private, **5**. tell; *synonyms* (v) divulge, impart, reveal, (n) disclose, count; *antonym* (v) request.

segl 1. velum; *synonyms* (n) veil, conceal, cover, curtain, disguise, **2**. sail; *synonyms* (n) float, voyage, (v) cruise, navigate, run.

seglanlegur magnetic; *synonyms* (adj) attractive, charismatic, fascinating, inviting, magnetized.

seglgarn twine; *synonyms* (n) coil, string, (v) wind, entwine, lace; *antonym* (v) untwist.

seglskip clipper; *synonyms* (n) clippers, cutter, limiter, foist, hoy.

segulafl magnetism; *synonyms* (n) allure, attraction, charisma, charm, fascination.

segulband tape; *synonyms* (n) band, ribbon, strip, (v) record, videotape.

segulbandsspóla cassette; *synonyms* (n) tape, copy, demo, footage, record.

segulfræði magnetism; *synonyms* (n) allure, attraction, charisma, charm, fascination.

segulkraftlínur flux; *synonyms* (n) current, (v) flow, dissolve, thaw, course.

segulkraftlínustraumur flux; *synonyms* (n) current, (v) flow, dissolve, thaw, course.

segull magnet; *synonyms* (n) attraction, lodestone, magnetic, prestige, seduction.

segullægð bay; *synonyms* (n) alcove, bark, recess, (v) yap, roar.

segulleiðni permeability; *synonyms* (n) perviousness, permeableness.

segulleif remanence; *synonym* (adj) remanency.

segulleifð remanence; *synonym* (adj) remanency.

segulljós aurora; *synonyms* (n) dawn, daybreak, morning, sunrise, prime.

segulmælir magnetometer; *synonym* (n) gaussmeter.

segulmagn magnetism; *synonyms* (n) allure, attraction, charisma, charm, fascination.

segulmagnaður magnetic; *synonyms* (adj) attractive, charismatic, fascinating, inviting, magnetized.

segulmagnsvél exciter; *synonyms* (n) agitator, incendiary, oscillator.

segulmögnun 1. magnetization; *synonym* (n) magnetisation, **2**. excitation; *synonyms* (n) excitement, stimulus, agitation, encouragement, feeling.

segulmögnunarkerfi exciter; *synonyms* (n) agitator, incendiary, oscillator.

segulmögnunarvél exciter; *synonyms* (n) agitator, incendiary, oscillator.

segulnagli swivel; *synonyms* (n) hinge, (v) pivot, turn, rotate, roll.

segulpóll pole; *synonyms* (n) perch, bar, picket, post, rod.

segulrofi 1. relay; *synonyms* (n) relief, spell, (v) broadcast, pass, transmit, **2**. contactor.

segulskekkja 1. variation; *synonyms* (n) alteration, change, difference, divergence, mutation; *antonym* (n) similarity, **2**. deviation; *synonyms* (n) aberration, deflection, diversion, variation, abnormality; *antonym* (n) normality, **3**. declination; *synonyms* (n) declension, descent, decay, decline, refusal.

segulstál magnet; *synonyms* (n) attraction, lodestone, magnetic, prestige, seduction.

segulstefna polarity; *synonyms* (n) antagonism, augury, house, mansion, mark.

segulstuðull permeability; *synonyms* (n) perviousness, permeableness.

segulsviðsmælir magnetometer; *synonym* (n) gaussmeter.

segulsvörunarstuðull permeability; *synonyms* (n) perviousness, permeableness.

segulvaki exciter; *synonyms* (n) agitator, incendiary, oscillator.

segulviðnám reluctance; *synonyms* (n) disinclination, aversion, hesitation, indisposition, distaste; *antonym* (n) inclination.

segulviðtak susceptibility; *synonyms* (n) predisposition, sensitivity, impressibility, liability, inclination; *antonym* (n) resistance.

seigfljótandi 1. viscid; *synonyms* (adj) sticky, gluey, glutinous, viscous, adhesive, **2**. thick; *synonyms* (adj) dense, compact, stupid, crowded, dull; *antonyms* (adj) thin, intelligent, bright, sparse, clever, **3**. viscous; *synonyms* (adj) thick, gummy, gooey, (v) tenacious, (n) viscid.

seighersla tempering; *synonyms* (n) annealing, hardening, toughening, change, drawing.

seigja 1. viscosity; *synonyms* (n) consistency, ropiness, viscousness, cohesiveness, (adj) viscidity, **2**. consistence; *synonyms* (n) body, torso, trunk, (adj) spissitude, constipation.

seigjumælir viscometer; *synonym* (n) viscosimeter.

seigla 1. viscosity; *synonyms* (n) consistency, ropiness, viscousness, cohesiveness, (adj) viscidity, **2**. persistence; *synonyms* (n) perseverance, continuity, endurance, constancy, stubbornness; *antonym* (n) compliance, **3**. tenacity; *synonyms* (n) determination, persistence, resolution, doggedness, persistency.

seigur viscous; *synonyms* (adj) sticky, thick, gluey, glutinous, gummy.

seilarmiðlag chordamesoderm; *synonym* (n) chordomesoderm.

seiling 1. reach; *synonyms* (v) range, overtake, obtain, achieve, (n) fetch, **2**. range; *synonyms* (v) line, arrange, order, rank, roam.

seinka 1. retard; *synonyms* (*v*) delay, check, hinder, arrest, detain; *antonym* (*v*) accelerate, **2.** delay; *synonyms* (*n*) pause, deferment, wait, (*v*) defer, postpone; *antonyms* (*n*) punctuality, decisiveness, (*v*) rush, advance, **3.** delete; *synonyms* (*v*) cancel, erase, clear, expunge, raze; *antonyms* (*v*) insert, record.

selnkun 1. retardation; *synonyms* (*n*) delay, impediment, retard, deceleration, lag, **2.** delay; *synonyms* (*n*) pause, arrest, deferment, (*v*) defer, check; *antonyms* (*n*) punctuality, decisiveness, (*v*) rush, advance, **3.** lag; *synonyms* (*n*) backwardness, (*v*) dawdle, linger, dally, drag.

seinn 1. slow; *synonyms* (*adj*) dull, late, easy, sluggish, (*v*) slack; *antonyms* (*adj*) fast, intelligent, rapid, bright, (*v*) accelerate, **2.** indolent; *synonyms* (*adj*) idle, inactive, lazy, slothful, careless; *antonyms* (*adj*) energetic, active.

seinþroski retardation; *synonyms* (*n*) delay, impediment, retard, deceleration, lag.

sekans secant; *synonyms* (*v*) crossbarred, cruciate, palmiped, (*n*) s, sec.

sekkgró ascospore; *synonym* (*n*) spore.

sekt fine; *synonyms* (*adj*) delicate, agreeable, dainty, brave, capital; *antonyms* (*adj*) poor, thick, coarse, substantial, unsatisfactory.

sektor sector; *synonyms* (*n*) department, area, branch, district, division.

sekúnda second; *synonyms* (*n*) instant, moment, flash, jiffy, (*v*) back; *antonym* (*adj*) first.

selen selenium; *synonym* (*n*) southeast.

selením selenium; *synonym* (*n*) southeast.

selir seals; *synonyms* (*n*) key, talisman, signet, walruses.

selja 1. sell; *synonyms* (*v*) peddle, deal, handle, betray, give; *antonym* (*v*) buy, **2.** vend; *synonyms* (*v*) sell, hawk, huckster, monger, trade.

seljandi 1. vendor; *synonyms* (*n*) seller, dealer, vender, merchant, trafficker; *antonym* (*n*) buyer, **2.** seller; *synonyms* (*n*) vendor, trader; *antonym* (*n*) purchaser.

seljanlegur 1. saleable; *synonyms* (*adj*) salable, commercial, profitable, viable, (*adv*) saleably, **2.** marketable; *synonyms* (*adj*) merchantable, saleable, vendible, interchangeable, wanted.

sella cell; *synonyms* (*n*) cage, jail, cadre, hole, cave.

séllakk shellac; *synonyms* (*n*) lac, (*v*) varnish, clobber, lick, overpower.

sellulósi cellulose; *synonyms* (*n*) fiber, bran, (*adj*) plastic.

selspik blubber; *synonyms* (*n*) cry, fat, (*v*) sob, weep, bawl.

selta salinity; *synonyms* (*n*) salt, saltiness, brininess, salineness.

selur seal; *synonyms* (*n*) mark, stamp, cachet, (*v*) plug, bar; *antonyms* (*v*) open, unseal.

selveiðiskip sealer; *synonym* (*n*) sealant.

semja 1. prepare; *synonyms* (*v*) arrange, fix, form, plan, dress, **2.** bargain; *synonyms* (*n*) contract, agreement, covenant, deal, (*adj*) cheap; *antonym* (*n*) rip-off.

senda 1. transmit; *synonyms* (*v*) pass, communicate, convey, carry, send, **2.** submit; *synonyms* (*v*) comply, obey, acquiesce, present, resign; *antonyms* (*v*) withdraw, resist, **3.** send; *synonyms* (*v*) despatch, deliver, dispatch, forward, give, **4.** remit; *synonyms* (*v*) excuse, relax, acquit, defer, forgive, **5.** forward; *synonyms* (*adv*) onward, (*adj*) bold, audacious, (*v*) advance, expedite; *antonyms* (*adv*) backward, (*adj*) shy, posterior.

sendandi originator; *synonyms* (*n*) father, creator, author, founder, architect.

sendibifreið van; *synonyms* (*n*) caravan, vehicle, front, truck, vanguard.

sendibíll van; *synonyms* (*n*) caravan, vehicle, front, truck, vanguard.

sendiboði messenger; *synonyms* (*n*) envoy, emissary, harbinger, runner, (*v*) herald.

sendibréf letter; *synonyms* (*n*) epistle, mail, character, communication, dispatch.

sendiferðabíll van; *synonyms* (*n*) caravan, vehicle, front, truck, vanguard.

sendifulltrúi diplomat; *synonyms* (*n*) diplomatist, envoy, ambassador, intermediary, minister.

sendiherra 1. ambassador; *synonyms* (*n*) agent, delegate, emissary, envoy, messenger, **2.** minister; *synonyms* (*n*) pastor, priest, deputy, divine, ambassador, **3.** envoy; *synonyms* (*n*) diplomat, minister, courier, representative, envoi.

sendiherrabústaður embassy; *synonyms* (*n*) deputation, legation, delegation, mission, commission.

sendimaður minister; *synonyms* (*n*) pastor, envoy, priest, deputy, divine.

sendinefnd 1. delegation; *synonyms* (*n*) commission, delegacy, deputation, delegating, devolution, **2.** embassy; *synonyms* (*n*) legation, delegation, mission, errand, cable, **3.** mission; *synonyms* (*n*) job, assignment, charge, duty, goal.

sending 1. submission; *synonyms* (*n*) compliance, obedience, acquiescence, bid, (*adj*) resignation, **2.** transmission; *synonyms* (*n*) circulation, conveyance, contagion, transfer, broadcast, **3.** delivery; *synonyms* (*n*) childbirth, birth, consignment, discharge, rescue; *antonyms* (*n*) death, dispatch, **4.** emission; *synonyms* (*n*) emanation, effusion, ejection, venting, vent.

sendir transmitter; *synonyms* (*n*) sender, aerial, mast, purveyor, source.

sendiráð embassy; *synonyms* (*n*) deputation, legation, delegation, mission, commission.

sendiráðsstarfsmaður diplomat; *synonyms* (*n*) diplomatist, envoy, ambassador, intermediary, minister.

senditæki transmitter; *synonyms* (*n*) sender, aerial, mast, purveyor, source.

seng bed; *synonyms* (*n*) couch, layer, base, basis, berth.

sengen bed; *synonyms* (*n*) couch, layer, base, basis, berth.

senintestigi 1. gut; *synonyms* (*n*) belly, abdomen, bowel, (*v*) eviscerate, pillage, 2. guts; *synonyms* (*n*) bowels, backbone, boldness, bravery, courage; *antonym* (*n*) cowardice.

sennilegur 1. probable; *synonyms* (*adj*) credible, likely, plausible, possible, potential; *antonyms* (*adj*) unlikely, improbable, 2. likely; *synonyms* (*adj*) believable, probable, expected, conceivable, (*adv*) possibly.

sennileiki 1. probability; *synonyms* (*n*) chance, likelihood, odds, possibility, likeliness, 2. likelihood; *synonyms* (*n*) probability, eventuality, expectation, prospect, expectancy; *antonyms* (*n*) unlikelihood, improbability.

sent 1. cent; *synonyms* (*n*) penny, centime, (*adj*) mill, picayune, pistareen, 2. penny; *synonyms* (*n*) cent, change, groat, money, doit.

sentimetri centimetre; *synonyms* (*n*) centimeter, cm, curium.

sepi 1. polyp; *synonyms* (*n*) polypus, polype, 2. caruncle; *synonyms* (*n*) crest, sarcoma, caruncula, growth, papula.

sérbýlinn dioecious; *synonyms* (*adj*) dioecian, dioicous.

séreigind idiosyncrasy; *synonyms* (*n*) characteristic, eccentricity, individuality, mannerism, foible.

séreignarskipan capitalism; *synonyms* (*n*) democracy, commercialism, competition, entrepreneurship, industrialism; *antonyms* (*n*) collectivism, communism, socialism.

sérfæði diet; *synonyms* (*n*) congress, convocation, council, convention, nurture; *antonyms* (*v*) binge, (*adj*) fattening.

sérfræðingur 1. specialist; *synonyms* (*adj*) expert, specialized, (*n*) authority, professional, connoisseur; *antonym* (*n*) amateur, 2. consultant; *synonyms* (*n*) advisor, adviser, specialist, analyst, psychoanalyst.

sérfræðistarf profession; *synonyms* (*n*) confession, declaration, employment, occupation, affirmation.

sérgrein field; *synonyms* (*n*) arena, area, battlefield, domain, ground.

sérgreina qualify; *synonyms* (*v*) modify, prepare, moderate, capacitate, characterize; *antonym* (*v*) disqualify.

sérgreindur specific; *synonyms* (*adj*) individual, special, concrete, exact, (*n*) particular; *antonyms* (*adj*) universal, vague, (*n*) general.

sérgreining differentiation; *synonyms* (*n*) difference, distinction, contrast, demarcation, discrimination.

sérhæfing 1. specialization; *synonyms* (*n*) specialisation, differentiation, specialism, speciality, specialty, 2. differentiation; *synonyms* (*n*) difference, distinction, contrast, demarcation, discrimination.

sérhæfni specificity; *synonym* (*n*) selectivity.

sérkennandi characteristic; *synonyms* (*adj*) distinctive, individual, (*n*) badge, attribute, sign; *antonyms* (*adj*) uncharacteristic, common.

sérkenni 1. property; *synonyms* (*n*) characteristic, capital, peculiarity, feature, (*adj*) attribute, 2. character; *synonyms* (*n*) kind, nature, note, part, quality, 3. characteristic; *synonyms* (*adj*) distinctive, individual, typical, (*n*) badge, sign; *antonyms* (*adj*) uncharacteristic, common, 4. feature; *synonyms* (*n*) article, aspect, character, detail, lineament.

sérkennilegur 1. characteristic; *synonyms* (*adj*) distinctive, individual, (*n*) badge, attribute, sign; *antonyms* (*adj*) uncharacteristic, common, 2. individual; *synonyms* (*adj*) distinct, particular, single, (*n*) human, creature; *antonyms* (*adj*) joint, combined, communal, general, (*n*) collective.

sérkennileiki 1. characteristic; *synonyms* (*adj*) distinctive, individual, (*n*) badge, attribute, sign; *antonyms* (*adj*) uncharacteristic, common, 2. idiosyncrasy; *synonyms* (*n*) characteristic, eccentricity, individuality, mannerism, foible.

sérlegur specific; *synonyms* (*adj*) individual, special, concrete, exact, (*n*) particular; *antonyms* (*adj*) universal, vague, (*n*) general.

sérleyfi 1. concession; *synonyms* (*n*) admission, compliance, allowance, compromise, discount, 2. franchise; *synonyms* (*n*) exemption, liberty, freedom, immunity, privilege.

sérleyfisgjald royalty; *synonyms* (*n*) regality, kingship, nobility, loyalty, command.

sérmál jargon; *synonyms* (*n*) dialect, gibberish, idiom, slang, vernacular.

sermi serum; *synonyms* (*n*) juice, antitoxin, (*adj*) lymph, humor, sap.

serótónín serotonin; *synonym* (*n*) hydroxytryptamine.

sérréttindi 1. privilege; *synonyms* (*n*) charter, immunity, liberty, prerogative, freedom, 2. immunity; *synonyms* (*n*) exemption, franchise, dispensation, privilege, exception; *antonym* (*n*) vulnerability.

sérrímóla cherimoya; *synonym* (*n*) cherimolla.

sérstaða singularity; *synonyms* (*n*) oddity, peculiarity, individuality, eccentricity, idiosyncrasy.

sérstæða singularity; *synonyms* (*n*) oddity, peculiarity, individuality, eccentricity, idiosyncrasy.

sérstæði identity; *synonyms* (*n*) identicalness, unity, individuality, personality, sameness.

sérstæður exceptional; *synonyms* (*adj*) special, abnormal, excellent, extraordinary, particular; *antonyms* (*adj*) common, mediocre, ordinary, average, normal.

sérstaklegur 1. special; *synonyms* (*adj*) particular, especial, individual, limited, rare; *antonym* (*adj*) ordinary, **2.** particular; *synonyms* (*adj*) special, fastidious, careful, definite, (*n*) detail; *antonyms* (*adj*) careless, easy, vague, (*n*) general.

sérstakt specific; *synonyms* (*adj*) individual, special, concrete, exact, (*n*) particular; *antonyms* (*adj*) universal, vague, (*n*) general.

sérstakur 1. specific; *synonyms* (*adj*) individual, special, concrete, exact, (*n*) particular; *antonyms* (*adj*) universal, vague, (*n*) general, **2.** special; *synonyms* (*adj*) especial, limited, rare, different, distinguished; *antonym* (*adj*) ordinary.

sérstöðupunktur singularity; *synonyms* (*n*) oddity, peculiarity, individuality, eccentricity, idiosyncrasy.

sérsvæða 1. zone; *synonyms* (*n*) area, district, region, section, belt, **2.** allopatric.

sérsvæði zone; *synonyms* (*n*) area, district, region, section, belt.

sértæki specificity; *synonym* (*n*) selectivity.

sértækur 1. specific; *synonyms* (*adj*) individual, special, concrete, exact, (*n*) particular; *antonyms* (*adj*) universal, vague, (*n*) general, **2.** abstract; *synonyms* (*adj*) theoretical, (*v*) abridge, (*n*) synopsis, abridgement, digest.

sértak abstract; *synonyms* (*adj*) theoretical, (*v*) abridge, (*n*) synopsis, abridgement, digest; *antonym* (*adj*) concrete.

sértaka abstract; *synonyms* (*adj*) theoretical, (*v*) abridge, (*n*) synopsis, abridgement, digest; *antonym* (*adj*) concrete.

sértekinn 1. concrete; *synonyms* (*adj*) actual, positive, (*n*) cement, (*v*) coagulate, congeal; *antonyms* (*adj*) theoretical, intangible, abstract, hypothetical, incidental, **2.** abstract; *synonyms* (*v*) abridge, (*n*) synopsis, abridgement, digest, epitome; *antonym* (*adj*) concrete.

sértekning abstraction; *synonyms* (*n*) abstract, abstractedness, reverie, engrossment, extraction; *antonyms* (*n*) addition, attentiveness.

sérvefur parenchyma; *synonyms* (*n*) substance, body, compages, element, matter.

sérvirkni specificity; *synonym* (*n*) selectivity.

sérvitringur eccentric; *synonyms* (*adj*) bizarre, odd, wacky, abnormal, anomalous; *antonyms* (*adj*) normal, ordinary, (*n*) conformist.

sérvitur eccentric; *synonyms* (*adj*) bizarre, odd, wacky, abnormal, anomalous; *antonyms* (*adj*) normal, ordinary, (*n*) conformist.

sesín 1. caesium; *synonym* (*n*) cesium, **2.** cesium; *synonym* (*n*) caesium.

sess niche; *synonyms* (*n*) corner, alcove, hole, bay, recess.

sessa cushion; *synonyms* (*n*) pad, (*v*) buffer, bolster, insulate, protect.

set 1. sediment; *synonyms* (*n*) deposit, deposition, lees, dregs, grounds, **2.** site; *synonyms* (*n*) place, position, locate, (*v*) post, set, **3.** locus; *synonyms* (*n*) locale, spot, venue, point, orbit.

seta session; *synonyms* (*n*) meeting, seance, sitting, conference, bout.

sethraðagreining washing; *synonyms* (*n*) laundry, wash, laundering, lavation, cleaning.

setja 1. put; *synonyms* (*v*) place, fix, lay, position, (*n*) deposit, **2.** set; *synonyms* (*v*) put, locate, regulate, (*n*) class, (*adj*) fixed; *antonyms* (*v*) soften, liquefy, (*n*) combing, comb-out, (*adj*) variable, **3.** place; *synonyms* (*n*) domicile, (*v*) post, arrange, rank, station; *antonym* (*v*) remove, **4.** lay; *synonyms* (*v*) set, install, (*adj*) secular, (*n*) ballad, pitch.

setlag sediment; *synonyms* (*n*) deposit, deposition, lees, dregs, grounds.

setmyndun 1. sedimentation; *synonyms* (*n*) deposit, sediment, settling, alluviation, deposition, **2.** deposition; *synonyms* (*n*) affidavit, declaration, dethronement, evidence, (*v*) deposal.

setning 1. proposition; *synonyms* (*n*) offer, overture, bid, motion, proposal, **2.** statement; *synonyms* (*n*) account, declaration, affirmation, announcement, communication; *antonym* (*n*) denial, **3.** sentence; *synonyms* (*n*) judgment, finding, decision, (*v*) condemn, convict, **4.** theorem; *synonyms* (*n*) axiom, proposition, formula, principle, thesis, **5.** clause; *synonyms* (*n*) article, paragraph, provision, rider, (*v*) passage.

setningafræði syntax; *synonyms* (*n*) grammar, accidence, syntaxis, organism.

setningarfræði syntax; *synonyms* (*n*) grammar, accidence, syntaxis, organism.

setningarliður phrase; *synonyms* (*n*) expression, idiom, (*v*) express, formulate, couch.

sett set; *synonyms* (v) fix, place, lay, put, (n) class; *antonyms* (v) soften, liquefy, (n) combing, combout, (adj) variable.

settaugarbólga sciatica; *synonyms* (v) lumbago, cephalalgia, earache, gout, neuralgia.

setur setting; *synonyms* (n) frame, scene, adjustment, scenery, backdrop.

sex six; *synonyms* (n) sise, sixer, hexad, sestet, sextet.

sexhyrningur hexagon; *synonyms* (n) octagon, oxygon, pentagon, polygon, sexangle.

sexkantur hexagon; *synonyms* (n) octagon, oxygon, pentagon, polygon, sexangle.

sextánskur hexadecimal; *synonym* (adj) hex.

sextantur sextant; *synonym* (n) quadrant.

sextíu sixty; *synonyms* (adj) lx, threescore, (n) lux.

sextungur sextant; *synonym* (n) quadrant.

seyði extract; *synonyms* (n) excerpt, (v) draw, abstract, derive, educe.

seymi suture; *synonyms* (n) joint, seam, (v) commissure, juncture, articulation.

seyra sludge; *synonyms* (n) mud, ooze, slime, (adj) silt, mire.

seyti 1. secretion; *synonyms* (n) exudation, discharge, emission, exhalation, extrusion, **2.** juice; *synonyms* (n) extract, water, blood, gravy, (adj) humor.

seyting secretion; *synonyms* (n) exudation, discharge, emission, exhalation, extrusion.

seytl 1. weeping; *synonyms* (v) lament, wailing, (n) lamentation, (adj) crying, tearful, **2.** seepage; *synonyms* (n) leak, flow, ooze, oozing, percolation, **3.** percolation; *synonyms* (n) leakage, seeping, filtration, extravasation, perspiration.

seytla trickle; *synonyms* (n) drip, distill, (v) drop, dribble, percolate; *antonyms* (n) throng, (v) gush.

sía 1. sieve; *synonyms* (n) screen, (v) filter, riddle, sift, strain, **2.** filter; *synonyms* (v) percolate, sieve, drip, leak, filtrate; *antonym* (v) contaminate, **3.** filtrate; *synonyms* (n) deposit, dregs, (v) deform, distort, dribble.

síbeygjukrampar spasticity; *synonym* (n) spasmodism.

síbrotamaður recidivist; *synonyms* (n) backslider, repeater, (v) blackleg, crawfish, mugwump.

síða 1. side; *synonyms* (n) edge, rim, faction, border, brink; *antonym* (adj) distant, **2.** aspect; *synonyms* (n) appearance, look, surface, bearing, expression, **3.** page; *synonyms* (n) attendant, footboy, usher, note, pageboy, **4.** flank; *synonyms* (n) side, wing, lee, (v) skirt, (adj) cover.

síðareglur protocol; *synonyms* (n) etiquette, manners, ceremony, bill, formality.

síðbirting epigenesis; *synonyms* (v) procreation, progeneration, propagation, fertilization, gemination.

síðblinda psychopathy; *synonyms* (n) lunacy, insanity, neurosis.

síðblindingi psychopath; *synonyms* (n) maniac, lunatic, madperson, sociopath, nutcase.

síðfágun civilization; *synonyms* (n) culture, refinement, civilisation, cultivation, (adj) civility.

síðfræði ethics; *synonyms* (n) morality, morals, conscience, behavior, philosophy.

síðgát censorship; *synonyms* (n) censoring, ban, silence, blackout, control.

síðir mores; *synonyms* (n) custom, tradition, civilization, morality, etiquette.

síðkominn delayed; *synonyms* (adj) belated, late, tardy, protracted, (adv) behind; *antonyms* (adj) brief, early.

síðmenning civilization; *synonyms* (n) culture, refinement, civilisation, cultivation, (adj) civility.

síðmynd afterimage; *synonyms* (n) aftersensation, sight.

síðuhaus header; *synonyms* (n) caption, heading, lintel, title, (v) dive.

síður 1. usage; *synonyms* (n) habit, practice, employment, (v) use, (adj) custom, **2.** custom; *synonyms* (n) tradition, convention, usage, (v) accustom, (adj) bespoke.

sidvango buttocks; *synonyms* (n) backside, bottom, arse, ass, bum.

síðvarsla censorship; *synonyms* (n) censoring, ban, silence, blackout, control.

síðvenja convention; *synonyms* (n) conference, congress, meeting, contract, assembly.

síendurtekinn recurring; *synonyms* (adj) recurrent, frequent, intermittent, cyclic, periodic; *antonym* (adj) unique.

sífella perpetuity; *synonyms* (n) eternity, immortality, sempiternity, infinity, endlessness.

sífelldur constant; *synonyms* (adj) ceaseless, incessant, perpetual, steady, continual; *antonyms* (adj) changeable, intermittent, irregular, sporadic, variable.

sífill syphilis; *synonyms* (n) pox, syph, siphilis, venereal.

sifjar kinship; *synonyms* (n) consanguinity, affinity, connection, kin, relation.

sifjaspell incest; *synonyms* (n) fornication, adultery, idolatry.

sig 1. prolapse; *synonyms* (n) prolapsus, descent, prolapsion, (v) descend, protrude, **2.** sag; *synonyms* (n) decline, dip, (v) droop, flag, (adj) swag; *antonym* (v) rise, **3.** subsidence; *synonyms* (n) collapse, ebb, remission, settlement, settling, **4.** descent; *synonyms* (n) ancestry, birth, fall, blood, declension; *antonyms* (n) ascent, improvement, **5.**

hypostasis; *synonyms* (*n*) substantiality, epistasis, body, person, element.

síga 1. sag; *synonyms* (*n*) decline, dip, (*v*) droop, flag, (*adj*) swag; *antonym* (*v*) rise, **2.** prolapse; *synonyms* (*n*) prolapsus, descent, prolapsion, (*v*) descend, protrude.

sigð crescent; *synonyms* (*n*) arc, arcade, arch, bow, carve.

sigdalur 1. trough; *synonyms* (*n*) trench, channel, chute, gutter, manger; *antonym* (*n*) peak, **2.** graben.

sigðlaga falciform; *synonym* (*adj*) falcate.

sigg 1. callosity; *synonyms* (*n*) callus, (*adj*) durity, inflexibility, temper, **2.** callus; *synonyms* (*n*) callosity, bump, lump.

sígildur classic; *synonyms* (*adj*) classical, model, archetypal, exemplary, ideal; *antonym* (*n*) second-rate.

sigla 1. sail; *synonyms* (*n*) float, voyage, (*v*) cruise, navigate, run, **2.** steam; *synonyms* (*n*) mist, fog, (*v*) reek, evaporate, exhale, **3.** navigate; *synonyms* (*v*) guide, sail, fly, pilot, cross, **4.** mast; *synonyms* (*n*) post, column, tower, aerial, prop.

síglæðari refresh; *synonyms* (*v*) freshen, air, enliven, invigorate, update.

sigling voyage; *synonyms* (*n*) cruise, tour, (*v*) journey, travel, sail.

siglingafræði navigation; *synonyms* (*n*) guidance, sailing, steering, seafaring, shipping.

siglingaleið track; *synonyms* (*n*) course, path, (*v*) trace, trail, hunt.

siglingar 1. shipping; *synonyms* (*n*) freight, transport, conveyance, transportation, moving, **2.** trade; *synonyms* (*n*) deal, business, barter, commerce, (*v*) change; *antonyms* (*n*) purchase, (*adj*) charitable, **3.** navigation; *synonyms* (*n*) guidance, sailing, steering, seafaring, shipping.

siglur spar; *synonyms* (*n*) beam, mast, (*v*) quarrel, box, fight.

siglutré mast; *synonyms* (*n*) post, column, tower, aerial, prop.

signifi means; *synonyms* (*n*) expedient, agency, instrument, assets, capital.

sígóð fennel; *synonyms* (*n*) cinnamon, cloves, finocchio, mace, nutmeg.

sígreiðslur perpetuity; *synonyms* (*n*) eternity, immortality, sempiternity, infinity, endlessness.

sigti 1. sieve; *synonyms* (*n*) screen, (*v*) filter, riddle, sift, strain, **2.** strainer; *synonyms* (*n*) sieve, stretcher, colature, mesh.

sigurkufl caul; *synonym* (*n*) veil.

sigurnagli swivel; *synonyms* (*n*) hinge, (*v*) pivot, turn, rotate, roll.

Síka psyche; *synonyms* (*n*) brain, mind, ego, spirit, intellect.

síkomusjúklingur recidivist; *synonyms* (*n*) backslider, repeater, (*v*) blackleg, crawfish, mugwump.

síkoría chicory; *synonyms* (*n*) succory, chiccory.

síld herring; *synonyms* (*n*) anchovies, sardines, smelts, tarpon, trout.

silfur silver; *synonyms* (*adj*) silvery, argent, (*n*) money, gold, (*v*) plate.

silfurgægir dace; *synonyms* (*n*) dare, rudd, tench.

silfurkóngur tarpon; *synonyms* (*n*) anchovies, herring, sardines, shad, smelts.

silfurloðna smelt; *synonyms* (*v*) fuse, melt, temper, anneal, heat.

silfurskjaddi alewife; *synonym* (*n*) gaspereau.

síling percolation; *synonyms* (*n*) leakage, seeping, filtration, extravasation, leak.

silisíum silicon; *synonyms* (*n*) silicium, si, ti.

silki silk; *synonyms* (*adj*) silky, down, velure, velvet.

síll drift; *synonyms* (*n*) stream, current, course, (*v*) aim, blow.

síls sill; *synonyms* (*n*) doorsill, ledge, threshold, rung, step.

silungur trout; *synonyms* (*n*) anchovies, herring, sardines, shad, smelts.

síma 1. wire; *synonyms* (*n*) cable, telegram, line, rope, (*v*) telegraph, **2.** telegraph; *synonyms* (*n*) telegraphy, (*v*) wire, broadcast, electrify, forecast.

símabréf fax; *synonyms* (*n*) autotype, (*v*) facsimile, telefax.

símaliður internode; *synonyms* (*n*) phalanx, phalanstery, segment.

símarka strobe; *synonyms* (*n*) stroboscope, (*adj*) odometer, speedometer, tachometer.

símasamskipti telecommunications; *synonym* (*n*) communications.

símbréf fax; *synonyms* (*n*) autotype, (*v*) facsimile, telefax.

símfax fax; *synonyms* (*n*) autotype, (*v*) facsimile, telefax.

sími 1. ticker; *synonyms* (*n*) heart, pump, watch, clock, affection, **2.** phone; *synonyms* (*n*) earpiece, earphone, headphone, (*v*) telephone, call, **3.** telegraph; *synonyms* (*n*) telegram, telegraphy, (*v*) cable, wire, broadcast, **4.** telephone; *synonyms* (*n*) telephony, (*v*) phone, ring, telegraph, **5.** wire; *synonyms* (*n*) line, rope, cord, string, (*v*) electrify.

símogen zymogen; *synonym* (*n*) proenzyme.

símógen zymogen; *synonym* (*n*) proenzyme.

símrit telefax; *synonyms* (*v*) facsimile, fax.

símriti telefax; *synonyms* (*v*) facsimile, fax.

símsenda fax; *synonyms* (*n*) autotype, (*v*) facsimile, telefax.

símsending telefax; *synonyms* (v) facsimile, fax.

símskeyti telegram; *synonyms* (n) wire, news, report, flash, radiogram.

símstöð exchange; *synonyms* (n) commutation, swap, (v) change, barter, interchange.

sin 1. sinew; *synonyms* (n) brawn, tendon, nerve, force, (adj) muscle, **2**. tendon; *synonyms* (n) sinew, cord, bond, tendril.

sina litter; *synonyms* (n) brood, bedding, stretcher, (v) clutter, (adj) jumble.

sinadráttur cramp; *synonyms* (n) convulsion, spasm, (v) confine, constrict, restrict.

sinarbólga tendinitis; *synonym* (n) tendonitis.

sindra sinter; *synonym* (n) incrustation.

sindrun sinter; *synonym* (n) incrustation.

sindur 1. scintillation; *synonyms* (n) flash, glisten, glitter, sparkle, fire, **2**. slag; *synonyms* (n) cinder, clinker, dross, scoria, scum.

sink zinc; *synonym* (n) spelter.

sinna involvement; *synonyms* (n) entanglement, concern, interest, implication, inclusion; *antonym* (n) disconnection.

sinnep mustard; *synonym* (n) eagerness.

sinnepsjurtir mustard; *synonym* (n) eagerness.

sinnuleysi 1. torpor; *synonyms* (n) lethargy, inactivity, lassitude, inertia, apathy, **2**. apathy; *synonyms* (n) indifference, emotionlessness, lukewarmness, passiveness, passivity; *antonyms* (n) enthusiasm, energy, keenness, drive, eagerness.

sinnustig involvement; *synonyms* (n) entanglement, concern, interest, implication, inclusion; *antonym* (n) disconnection.

sínus sine; *synonyms* (n) sin, hell, sinfulness, sinning, wickedness.

sírena siren; *synonyms* (n) enchantress, alarm, syren, temptress, (adj) fascinating.

sírita monitor; *synonyms* (v) check, regulate, control, eavesdrop, (n) admonisher.

síritandi recording; *synonyms* (n) record, album, transcription, scan, (adj) registering.

síriti 1. recorder; *synonyms* (n) clerk, registrar, register, reporter, enroll, **2**. polygraph, **3**. monitor; *synonyms* (v) check, regulate, control, eavesdrop, (n) admonisher, **4**. logger; *synonym* (n) recorder.

síritun recording; *synonyms* (n) record, album, transcription, scan, (adj) registering.

sirkill 1. dividers, **2**. calipers; *synonyms* (n) caliper, callipers, calliper, (v) compass, measure.

sísanna tautology; *synonyms* (n) repetition, battology, circumlocution, verbiage, (v) polylogy.

sísegull magnet; *synonyms* (n) attraction, lodestone, magnetic, prestige, seduction.

sísjá monitor; *synonyms* (v) check, regulate, control, eavesdrop, (n) admonisher.

sístæður 1. static; *synonyms* (adj) immobile, inactive, motionless, inert, still; *antonym* (adj) moving, **2**. stationary; *synonyms* (adj) immovable, fixed, static, unmoving, sedentary.

síþreyta asthenia; *synonyms* (n) abirritation, (adj) cachexia, cachexy, sprain, strain.

sitja sit; *synonyms* (v) model, pose, rest, ride, place; *antonyms* (v) stand, rise.

sitjandi buttocks; *synonyms* (n) backside, bottom, arse, ass, bum.

sítróna lemon; *synonyms* (n) automobile, gamboge, auto, buff, bum.

sítrónumelissa balm; *synonyms* (n) ointment, salve, unguent, incense, aroma.

sítrónutré lemon; *synonyms* (n) automobile, gamboge, auto, buff, bum.

síun 1. smoothing; *synonyms* (adj) smooth, even, sleek, abrasive, bland, **2**. filtering; *synonyms* (n) filtration, straining, refinement, **3**. filtration; *synonyms* (n) percolation, filtering.

síuvökvi filtrate; *synonyms* (n) deposit, (v) filter, percolate, strain, deform.

sívaka monitor; *synonyms* (v) check, regulate, control, eavesdrop, (n) admonisher.

sívaki monitor; *synonyms* (v) check, regulate, control, eavesdrop, (n) admonisher.

sívalningslaga centric; *synonyms* (adj) central, centrical.

sívalningur cylinder; *synonyms* (n) barrel, roll, pipe, tube, column.

sívalur round; *synonyms* (adv) about, (adj) circular, (n) circle, bout, ring; *antonyms* (adj) slim, sharp.

sjá 1. see; *synonyms* (v) look, feel, discover, (adj) observe, perceive, **2**. video; *synonyms* (n) television, picture, film, movie, (v) tape, **3**. sight; *synonyms* (n) vision, glimpse, prospect, (v) aim, spot, **4**. scope; *synonyms* (n) range, reach, domain, purview, room, **5**. display; *synonyms* (n) array, (v) exhibit, show, disclose, parade; *antonym* (v) conceal.

sjáaldur pupil; *synonyms* (n) follower, learner, student, scholar, apprentice.

sjáaldursjurt belladonna; *synonyms* (n) henbane, hellebore, hemlock, nightshade, bittersweet.

sjáaldursrönd areola; *synonyms* (n) armlet, bracelet, hoop, roundlet, areolation.

sjáanlegur visible; *synonyms* (adj) obvious, perceptible, conspicuous, apparent, evident; *antonyms* (adj) invisible, imperceptible.

sjáfsákvörðunarréttur autonomy; *synonyms* (n) independence, freedom, autocracy, liberty, sovereignty; *antonym* (n) dependence.

sjaldan 1. rarely; *synonyms* (*adv*) seldom, infrequently, hardly, uncommonly, unusually; *antonyms* (*adv*) frequently, often, usually, **2.** seldom; *synonyms* (*adv*) rarely, occasionally, scarcely, (*adj*) scarce, rare.

sjaldgæfur 1. rare; *synonyms* (*adj*) extraordinary, uncommon, exceptional, infrequent, precious, *antonyms* (*adj*) common, frequent, ordinary, **2.** precious; *synonyms* (*adj*) dear, beloved, cherished, costly, valuable; *antonym* (*adj*) worthless, **3.** uncommon; *synonyms* (*adj*) rare, odd, peculiar, scarce, singular; *antonym* (*adj*) typical.

sjálf 1. self; *synonyms* (*n*) ego, person, being, individual, (*adj*) same, **2.** ego; *synonyms* (*n*) self, egotism, pride, arrogance, character.

sjálfbær sustainable; *synonyms* (*adj*) bearable, endurable, tolerable, livable.

sjálfbirgur autotrophic; *synonym* (*adj*) autophytic.

sjálfgefið default; *synonyms* (*n*) deficit, delinquency, omission, oversight, (*v*) fail; *antonym* (*n*) payment.

sjálfgefinn default; *synonyms* (*n*) deficit, delinquency, omission, oversight, (*v*) fail; *antonym* (*n*) payment.

sjálfgengi automatism; *synonyms* (*n*) involuntariness, unwillingness.

sjálfhverfur 1. reflexive; *synonyms* (*adj*) reflex, reciprocal, reflective, automatic, involuntary, **2.** autistic.

sjálfi robot; *synonyms* (*n*) automaton, machine, golem, zombie, labor.

sjálfkrafa spontaneous; *synonyms* (*adj*) gratuitous, automatic, instinctive, natural, (*v*) voluntary; *antonyms* (*adj*) planned, forced, prearranged, prepared.

sjálfkvæmni consistence; *synonyms* (*n*) body, consistency, torso, (*adj*) spissitude, constipation.

sjálfkvæmur spontaneous; *synonyms* (*adj*) gratuitous, automatic, instinctive, natural, (*v*) voluntary; *antonyms* (*adj*) planned, forced, prearranged, prepared.

sjálfkveiking detonation; *synonyms* (*n*) blast, explosion, burst, bang, (*v*) discharge.

sjálfkveiktur autogenous; *synonyms* (*adj*) autogenic, autogeneal, interior, autogenetic.

sjálflægur egocentric; *synonyms* (*adj*) egotistic, selfish, egoistical, egotistical, (*n*) egoist; *antonym* (*adj*) altruistic.

sjálfmyndaður autogenous; *synonyms* (*adj*) autogenic, autogeneal, interior, autogenetic.

sjálfráða autonomous; *synonyms* (*adj*) independent, sovereign, autonomic, free, separate; *antonym* (*adj*) dependent.

sjálfráður 1. voluntary; *synonyms* (*adj*) spontaneous, optional, deliberate, gratuitous, intentional;

antonyms (*adj*) involuntary, compulsory, forced, instinctive, **2.** autonomic; *synonym* (*adj*) free.

sjálfræði autonomy; *synonyms* (*n*) independence, freedom, autocracy, liberty, sovereignty; *antonym* (*n*) dependence.

sjálfröðun auto; *synonyms* (*n*) automobile, car, machine, motorcar, limousine.

sjálfsafneitun abnegation; *synonyms* (*n*) denial, negation, renunciation, refusal, abstinence.

sjálfsálit self-esteem; *synonyms* (*n*) confidence, dignity, morale, narcissism, self-content.

sjálfsást narcissism; *synonyms* (*n*) conceit, egotism, narcism, egoism, vanity; *antonym* (*n*) humility.

sjálfsforræði autonomy; *synonyms* (*n*) independence, freedom, autocracy, liberty, sovereignty; *antonym* (*n*) dependence.

sjálfsfrævandi autogamous; *synonym* (*adj*) autogamic.

sjálfsfrjóvgandi autogamous; *synonym* (*adj*) autogamic.

sjálfsfróun masturbation; *synonyms* (*n*) onanism, delusion, wanking.

sjálfskapaður autogenous; *synonyms* (*adj*) autogenic, autogeneal, interior, autogenetic.

sjálfskilningur insight; *synonyms* (*n*) discernment, vision, acumen, penetration, perception.

sjálfskviknun abiogenesis; *synonyms* (*n*) autogenesis, (*v*) digenesis, dysmerogenesis, eumerogenesis, homogenesis.

sjálfsmyndaður autogenous; *synonyms* (*adj*) autogenic, autogeneal, interior, autogenetic.

sjálfsmyndun autogenesis; *synonyms* (*n*) abiogenesis, autogeny.

sjálfspíslahvöt masochism; *synonyms* (*n*) cruelty, algophilia.

sjálfsprottinn spontaneous; *synonyms* (*adj*) gratuitous, automatic, instinctive, natural, (*v*) voluntary; *antonyms* (*adj*) planned, forced, prearranged, prepared.

sjálfssefjun autosuggestion; *synonym* (*n*) suggestion.

sjálfssemd identity; *synonyms* (*n*) identicalness, unity, individuality, personality, sameness.

sjálfsskoðun introspection; *synonyms* (*n*) rumination, discernment, insight, look, (*v*) study.

sjálfssömun identity; *synonyms* (*n*) identicalness, unity, individuality, personality, sameness.

sjálfsstjórn 1. sovereignty; *synonyms* (*n*) kingdom, reign, empire, autonomy, dominion, **2.** autonomy; *synonyms* (*n*) independence, freedom, autocracy, liberty, sovereignty; *antonym* (*n*) dependence, **3.** autarchy; *synonym* (*n*) autarky.

sjálfsstjórnarríki autonomy; *synonyms* (n) independence, freedom, autocracy, liberty, sovereignty; *antonym* (n) dependence.

sjálfsstjórnarumdæmi autonomy; *synonyms* (n) independence, freedom, autocracy, liberty, sovereignty; *antonym* (n) dependence.

sjálfstæði 1. autonomy; *synonyms* (n) independence, freedom, autocracy, liberty, sovereignty; *antonym* (n) dependence, **2.** independence; *synonyms* (n) autonomy, independency, individuality, latitude, detachment; *antonym* (n) childhood.

sjálfstæðishreyfing nationalism; *synonyms* (n) chauvinism, patriotism, loyalty, partisanship, xenophobia.

sjálfstæðisstefna nationalism; *synonyms* (n) chauvinism, patriotism, loyalty, partisanship, xenophobia.

sjálfstæður 1. autonomic; *synonym* (adj) free, **2.** autonomous; *synonyms* (adj) independent, sovereign, autonomic, separate; *antonym* (adj) dependent, **3.** independent; *synonyms* (adj) autonomous, substantive, impartial, nonpartisan, (n) freelance; *antonym* (adj) simultaneous, **4.** objective; *synonyms* (adj) dispassionate, (n) aim, mark, goal, object; *antonyms* (adj) biased, subjective.

sjálfsþurftarbúskapur autarky; *synonyms* (n) autarchy, autocracy.

sjálfsþurftir subsistence; *synonyms* (n) being, existence, life, entity, maintenance.

sjálfstjórnarsvæði sovereignty; *synonyms* (n) kingdom, reign, empire, autonomy, dominion.

sjálfstraust confidence; *synonyms* (n) assurance, trust, belief, certainty, certitude; *antonyms* (n) insecurity, uncertainty, doubt, nervousness, anxiety.

sjálfstýribúnaður servo; *synonyms* (n) servomechanism, servosystem, (adj) servomechanical.

sjálfstýrikerfi servomechanism; *synonyms* (n) servo, servosystem.

sjálfstýring 1. servomechanism; *synonyms* (n) servo, servosystem, **2.** autopilot.

sjálfstýriverk servomechanism; *synonyms* (n) servo, servosystem.

sjálftamiðja epicentre; *synonym* (n) epicenter.

sjálfun 1. autogamy, **2.** fork; *synonyms* (n) crotch, branch, bifurcation, branching, (v) diverge.

sjálfur self; *synonyms* (n) ego, person, being, individual, (adj) same.

sjálfvakinn idiopathic; *synonyms* (adj) idiopathic, essential, existent, idiopathical, indispensable.

sjálfval default; *synonyms* (n) deficit, delinquency, omission, oversight, (v) fail; *antonym* (n) payment.

sjálfvirkjun automation; *synonyms* (n) mechanization, automatization, mechanisation, computerization.

sjálfvirkni 1. automation; *synonyms* (n) mechanization, automatization, mechanisation, computerization, **2.** automatism; *synonyms* (n) involuntariness, unwillingness.

sjálfvirkniaðgerð automation; *synonyms* (n) mechanization, automatization, mechanisation, computerization.

sjálfvirkur 1. autonomic; *synonym* (adj) free, **2.** automatic; *synonyms* (adj) instinctive, involuntary, automated, mechanical, reflex; *antonyms* (adj) manual, deliberate, voluntary, **3.** auto; *synonyms* (n) automobile, car, machine, motorcar, limousine.

sjalottulaukur shallot; *synonym* (n) eschalot.

sjáumst 1. bye; *synonyms* (n) adieu, adios, cheerio, arrivederci, (adj) delitescent, **2.** goodbye; *synonyms* (int) ciao, (n) bye, farewell, valediction, (adj) parting.

sjávarfall tide; *synonyms* (n) current, flow, stream, course, (v) wave.

sjávarföll tide; *synonyms* (n) current, flow, stream, course, (v) wave.

sjávargróður seaweed; *synonyms* (n) seaware, heed, reit, ware, sedge.

sjávarhamar cliff; *synonyms* (n) bluff, precipice, hill, mountain, promontory.

sjávarströnd coast; *synonyms* (n) bank, beach, seaside, shore, (v) glide; *antonym* (n) interior.

sjáver gallery; *synonyms* (n) balcony, audience, drift, veranda, circle.

sjö seven; *synonyms* (n) heptad, septet, ace, eight, jack.

sjóbirtingur trout; *synonyms* (n) anchovies, herring, sardines, shad, smelts.

sjóða 1. boil; *synonyms* (v) seethe, bubble, churn, simmer, (n) abscess; *antonym* (v) freeze, **2.** weld; *synonyms* (v) join, solder, bond, cement, fasten, **3.** cook; *synonyms* (n) chef, (v) boil, bake, brew, make.

sjóður fund; *synonyms* (n) stock, store, capital, (v) hoard, bankroll.

sjófær seaworthy; *synonyms* (adj) oceangoing, sea, seagoing, maritime, (v) snug.

sjófarandi seafarer; *synonyms* (n) mariner, gob, sailor, seaman, navigator.

sjóferð passage; *synonyms* (n) aisle, course, channel, corridor, gangway.

sjóflutningar shipping; *synonyms* (n) freight, transport, conveyance, transportation, moving.

sjóher navy; *synonyms* (n) fleet, armada, flotilla, blue, army.

sjókort chart; *synonyms* (n) plan, plot, (v) map, graph, sketch.

sjólag sea; *synonyms* (n) ocean, water, (adj) marine, maritime, array.

sjóleið seaway; *synonyms* (n) heaving, ocean.

sjóliðsforingi commander; *synonyms* (n) captain, chief, commandant, leader, head.

sjómaður fisherman; *synonyms* (n) angler, fisher, piscator, (v) sportsman, huntsman.

sjómælingar hydrography; *synonym* (n) drainage.

sjómerki beacon; *synonyms* (n) cairn, flare, buoy, light, (v) guide.

sjón 1. vision; *synonyms* (n) sight, view, dream, daydream, (v) fancy; *antonym* (n) reality, **2.** sight; *synonyms* (n) vision, glimpse, prospect, (v) aim, spot, **3.** visual; *synonyms* (adj) visible, graphic, ocular, optic, optical.

sjóna retina; *synonym* (n) white.

sjónarhorn 1. perspective; *synonyms* (n) attitude, aspect, angle, outlook, prospect, **2.** view; *synonyms* (n) look, sight, judgment, opinion, (v) regard.

sjónarmið 1. perspective; *synonyms* (n) attitude, aspect, angle, outlook, prospect, **2.** angle; *synonyms* (n) hook, incline, (v) slant, lean, tilt, **3.** aspect; *synonyms* (n) appearance, look, surface, bearing, expression.

sjónarrönd horizon; *synonyms* (n) perspective, prospect, purview, reach, skyline.

sjónaukastæði mounting; *synonyms* (n) mount, ascent, climb, frame, (adj) climbing.

sjónauki 1. telescope; *synonyms* (n) scope, ambit, background, compass, (v) condense, **2.** binocular; *synonyms* (n) binoculars, spyglass.

sjónbaugur horizon; *synonyms* (n) perspective, prospect, purview, reach, skyline.

sjónbeiting fixation; *synonyms* (n) obsession, fetish, fixing, mania, complex.

sjóndeildarhringur horizon; *synonyms* (n) perspective, prospect, purview, reach, skyline.

sjónfesting fixation; *synonyms* (n) obsession, fetish, fixing, mania, complex.

sjónfræði optics; *synonyms* (n) vision, photology, orbs, sight.

sjónfylgd tracking; *synonyms* (n) pursuit, trailing, rutting, trajectography.

sjóngler lens; *synonyms* (n) meniscus, (v) glass, barometer, especially, glaze.

sjóngögn video; *synonyms* (n) television, picture, film, movie, (v) tape.

sjóngróf fovea; *synonym* (n) foveola.

sjónhimna retina; *synonym* (n) white.

sjónhorf perspective; *synonyms* (n) attitude, aspect, angle, outlook, prospect.

sjónlag refraction; *synonyms* (n) bending, deflection, deflexion, (v) obliquation, (adj) reflection.

sjónlagsmælir refractometer; *synonyms* (v) bathometer, galvanometer, heliometer, interferometer, odometer.

sjónlagsrétting refraction; *synonyms* (n) bending, deflection, deflexion, (v) obliquation, (adj) reflection.

sjónleiðsaga pilotage; *synonyms* (n) piloting, steerage, navigation, leadership, lodemanage.

sjónleysi blindness; *synonyms* (n) cecity, darkness, sightlessness, ablepsy, ignorance.

sjónlína course; *synonyms* (n) stream, flow, bearing, career, (v) run.

sjónmyrkvi blackout; *synonyms* (n) faint, brownout, darkness, dimout, amnesia.

sjónnæmismælir photometer; *synonyms* (n) lucimeter, radiometer.

sjónskekkja astigmatism; *synonyms* (n) astigmia, blindness.

sjónstilling accommodation; *synonyms* (n) adjustment, compromise, loan, lodging, (v) advance.

sjónsviðseyða scotoma; *synonym* (n) scotomy.

sjónsviðsmælir perimeter; *synonyms* (n) border, boundary, edge, margin, circumference; *antonyms* (n) center, middle.

sjóntæki display; *synonyms* (n) array, (v) exhibit, show, disclose, parade; *antonym* (v) conceal.

sjóntemprun accommodation; *synonyms* (n) adjustment, compromise, loan, lodging, (v) advance.

sjóntenging fusion; *synonyms* (n) amalgamation, coalition, alliance, coalescence, combination; *antonym* (n) separation.

sjónugróf fovea; *synonym* (n) foveola.

sjónukeila cone; *synonyms* (n) strobile, pyramid, roll, conoid, pinnacle.

sjónustafur rod; *synonyms* (n) bar, baton, perch, shaft, (v) stick.

sjónvarp television; *synonyms* (n) tube, telly, video, telecasting, box.

sjór sea; *synonyms* (n) ocean, water, (adj) marine, maritime, array.

sjóræningi pirate; *synonyms* (n) buccaneer, corsair, bandit, freebooter, (v) hijack.

sjóræningjaskip pirate; *synonyms* (n) buccaneer, corsair, bandit, freebooter, (v) hijack.

sjórán 1. piracy; *synonyms* (n) plagiarism, buccaneering, robbery, freebooting, (v) privateering, **2.** pirate; *synonyms* (n) buccaneer, corsair, bandit, freebooter, (v) hijack.

sjórnsýsla government; *synonyms* (n) administration, authority, control, direction, (adj) empire.

Sjóskáti guide; *synonyms* (n) escort, directory, (v) direct, conduct, govern; *antonym* (v) follow.

sjötnun decrement; *synonyms* (*n*) decrease, cut, deduction, defalcation, defect.

sjöttungsmælir sextant; *synonym* (*n*) quadrant.

sjóurriði trout; *synonyms* (*n*) anchovies, herring, sardines, shad, smelts.

sjóveiki seasickness; *synonyms* (*n*) naupathia, nausea, loathing, qualm, (*adj*) scabies.

sjúga suck; *synonyms* (*v*) draw, drink, imbibe, nurse, absorb.

sjúkdómafræði 1. etiology; *synonyms* (*n*) aetiology, attribution, rationale, anatomy, (*adj*) nosology, **2**. pathology; *synonym* (*n*) botany.

sjúkdómsástand morbidity; *synonyms* (*n*) morbidness, deathrate, mortality, gloom, (*adj*) morbosity.

sjúkdómseinkenni symptom; *synonyms* (*n*) sign, indication, evidence, mark, note.

sjúkdómsgreining diagnosis; *synonyms* (*n*) diagnosing, distinction, identification, examination, diorism.

sjúkdómsherming simulation; *synonyms* (*n*) affectation, pretense, imitation, pretence, modelling.

sjúkdómshlé remission; *synonyms* (*n*) forgiveness, relief, ease, condonation, (*v*) pardon.

sjúkdómshreiður focus; *synonyms* (*n*) centering, (*v*) center, concentrate, converge, aim.

sjúkdómsmynd syndrome; *synonyms* (*n*) ailment, complaint, complex, sickness, disorder.

sjúkdómsorsakir etiology; *synonyms* (*n*) aetiology, attribution, rationale, anatomy, (*adj*) nosology.

sjúkdómsvaldandi pathogenic; *synonyms* (*adj*) infective, morbific, infectious, pathogenetic.

sjúkdómsvaldur pathogen; *synonyms* (*n*) germ, microbe.

sjúkdómsvörn prophylaxis; *synonym* (*n*) synteresis.

sjúkdómur 1. sickness; *synonyms* (*n*) illness, indisposition, complaint, (*v*) disease, disorder, **2**. disease; *synonyms* (*n*) ailment, condition, sickness, infirmity, affection.

sjúklegur 1. morbid; *synonyms* (*adj*) diseased, ghoulish, gruesome, macabre, (*v*) sickly, **2**. pathological; *synonyms* (*adj*) pathologic, morbid, **3**. pathologic; *synonym* (*adj*) pathological.

sjúkleiki 1. disorder; *synonyms* (*n*) ailment, complaint, clutter, (*v*) derange, disarray; *antonyms* (*n*) orderliness, calm, peace, (*v*) order, **2**. illness; *synonyms* (*n*) disease, sickness, disorder, distemper, malady.

sjúklingur patient; *synonyms* (*adj*) invalid, forbearing, passive, calm, enduring; *antonym* (*adj*) impatient.

sjúkrabíll ambulance; *synonyms* (*n*) brancard, crate, hurdle, litter, stretcher.

sjúkrabörur 1. stretcher; *synonyms* (*n*) litter, cot, bed, berth, brancard, **2**. litter; *synonyms* (*n*) brood, bedding, stretcher, (*v*) clutter, (*adj*) jumble.

sjúkradeild ward; *synonyms* (*n*) guard, charge, custody, protection, (*v*) shelter.

sjúkrafæði diet; *synonyms* (*n*) congress, convocation, council, convention, nurture; *antonyms* (*v*) binge, (*adj*) fattening.

sjúkrahlutfall morbidity; *synonyms* (*n*) morbidness, deathrate, mortality, gloom, (*adj*) morbosity.

sjúkrahús hospital; *synonyms* (*n*) infirmary, home, institution, sanitarium, sickroom.

sjúkrasaga anamnesis; *synonyms* (*n*) remembrance, memory, recall, recollection, commemoration.

sjúkur 1. sick; *synonyms* (*adj*) ill, queasy, ailing, indisposed, poorly; *antonyms* (*adj*) well, healthy, **2**. unwell; *synonyms* (*adj*) sick, sickly, unhealthy, bad, seedy; *antonym* (*adj*) fit, **3**. ailing; *synonyms* (*adj*) unwell, invalid, diseased, feeble, (*n*) illness, **4**. ill; *synonyms* (*adv*) badly, (*n*) evil, harm, complaint, hurt.

skábraut ramp; *synonyms* (*n*) incline, inclination, slant, (*v*) bound, climb.

skábrún bevel; *synonyms* (*n*) cant, inclination, chamfer, (*v*) slope, incline.

skaða damage; *synonyms* (*n*) blemish, injury, (*v*) harm, hurt, abuse; *antonyms* (*n*) service, (*v*) conserve, enhance, repair, bolster.

skaðabætur 1. compensation; *synonyms* (*n*) amends, recompense, allowance, indemnification, (*v*) wage, **2**. damages; *synonyms* (*n*) compensation, reparation, indemnity, redress, reimbursement, **3**. indemnity; *synonyms* (*n*) damages, pay, restitution, excuse, exoneration, **4**. penalty; *synonyms* (*n*) mulct, fine, forfeit, forfeiture, (*v*) condemnation.

skaðabótaskylda liability; *synonyms* (*n*) debt, duty, obligation, trust, blame; *antonym* (*n*) asset.

skaði loss; *synonyms* (*n*) hurt, damage, defeat, detriment, injury; *antonyms* (*n*) appearance, retrieval, victory, gaining, income.

skaðlegur destructive; *synonyms* (*adj*) baneful, deadly, hurtful, malign, baleful; *antonyms* (*adj*) harmless, constructive, creative.

skaðleysi indemnity; *synonyms* (*n*) amends, compensation, damages, indemnification, pay.

skaðsamur destructive; *synonyms* (*adj*) baneful, deadly, hurtful, malign, baleful; *antonyms* (*adj*) harmless, constructive, creative.

skaðvænn noxious; *synonyms* (*adj*) detrimental, injurious, deleterious, harmful, deadly; *antonyms* (*adj*) harmless, innocuous, pleasant.

skaðvaldur pest; *synonyms* (*n*) bane, bore, blight, nuisance, plague.

skæður pernicious; *synonyms (adj)* detrimental, evil, bad, fatal, injurious.

skækja 1. whore; *synonyms (n)* prostitute, harlot, trollop, courtesan, strumpet, **2.** hooker; *synonyms (n)* floozie, floozy, hustler, slattern, streetwalker.

skæni 1. pellicle; *synonyms (n)* film, coat, skin, shagreen, peel, **2.** film; *synonyms (n)* membrane, coating, cloud, cinema, *(v)* mist.

skær bright; *synonyms (adj)* clear, alive, apt, intelligent, vivid; *antonyms (adj)* dull, cloudy, dark, dim, dreary.

skærð magnitude; *synonyms (n)* extent, bulk, consequence, amount, dimension; *antonym (n)* triviality.

skæri shears; *synonyms (n)* shear, *(adj)* scissors, cutters.

skærleiki 1. brightness; *synonyms (n)* flash, clarity, illumination, light, luminance; *antonyms (n)* dullness, cloudiness, darkness, dimness, murkiness, **2.** luminosity; *synonyms (n)* brightness, glow, brilliance, radiance, brilliancy.

skærlitaður chromatic; *synonyms (adj)* colorful, chromatical, *(n)* enharmonic, diatonic, *(v)* prismatic.

skaf attrition; *synonyms (n)* friction, abrasion, contrition, corrosion, detrition.

skafa 1. scrape; *synonyms (v)* scratch, graze, rub, pare, rake, **2.** scraper; *synonyms (n)* rasper, doctor, **3.** chafe; *synonyms (v)* annoy, gall, grate, irritate, *(adj)* fret.

skáflötur diagonal; *synonyms (adj)* oblique, aslant, slanting, sloping, *(n)* bias; *antonym (adj)* level.

skaft shaft; *synonyms (n)* arrow, handle, axis, beam, pit.

skagi peninsula; *synonyms (n)* chersonese, cape, promontory, continent, mainland.

skái 1. skew; *synonyms (v)* slope, incline, tilt, *(adj)* oblique, skewed, **2.** bevel; *synonyms (n)* cant, inclination, chamfer, *(v)* slant, **3.** obliquity; *synonyms (n)* crookedness, dishonesty, asynclitism, deceptiveness, grade.

skak concussion; *synonyms (n)* blow, clash, collision, shock, impact.

skák 1. tract; *synonyms (n)* area, essay, expanse, pamphlet, region, **2.** check; *synonyms (v)* bridle, stop, *(n)* control, arrest, curb.

skaka 1. jolt; *synonyms (n)* jerk, jar, *(v)* jog, shake, bump, **2.** jig; *synonyms (n)* jigger, strathspey, *(v)* dance, hop, skip.

skakkalaus unbiased; *synonyms (adj)* fair, impartial, indifferent, neutral, just; *antonyms (adj)* biased, prejudiced.

skakki 1. skew; *synonyms (v)* slope, incline, tilt, *(adj)* oblique, skewed, **2.** skewness; *synonym (n)* lopsidedness, **3.** bias; *synonyms (n)* penchant,

drift, *(v)* prejudice, bent, *(adj)* partiality; *antonyms (n)* impartiality, neutrality, fairness.

skakkur 1. skew; *synonyms (v)* slope, incline, tilt, *(adj)* oblique, skewed, **2.** biased; *synonyms (adj)* partial, partisan, slanted, unfair, coloured; *antonyms (adj)* fair, fair-minded, neutral, unbiased, just, **3.** oblique; *synonyms (adj)* indirect, circuitous, devious, lateral, collateral; *antonyms (adj)* direct, level.

skál 1. washbowl; *synonyms (n)* basin, washbasin, handbasin, lavabo, lavatory, **2.** drum; *synonyms (n)* barrel, cask, tympan, *(v)* beat, roll, **3.** bowl; *synonyms (n)* pot, plate, container, hollow, stadium, **4.** basin; *synonyms (n)* bowl, depression, dock, tank, washbowl, **5.** dish; *synonyms (n)* beauty, disk, platter, saucer, dishful.

skala scale; *synonyms (n)* flake, gamut, *(v)* ascend, climb, *(adj)* balance; *antonym (v)* descend.

skáld poet; *synonyms (n)* bard, author, maker, lyricist, muse.

skáldun scald; *synonyms (v)* burn, cook, scorch, boil, *(n)* blister.

skáletur italics; *synonyms (n)* justification, linotype, logotype, sublineation, underlining.

skálhveljur jellyfish; *synonyms (n)* medusan, coward, hydromedusae, *(adj)* apprehensive, frightened.

skali scale; *synonyms (n)* flake, gamut, *(v)* ascend, climb, *(adj)* balance; *antonym (v)* descend.

skáli 1. hut; *synonyms (n)* cabin, cot, booth, hovel, cottage, **2.** hall; *synonyms (n)* corridor, foyer, lobby, mansion, vestibule.

Skálína diagonal; *synonyms (adj)* oblique, aslant, slanting, sloping, *(n)* bias; *antonym (adj)* level.

skalo scale; *synonyms (n)* flake, gamut, *(v)* ascend, climb, *(adj)* balance; *antonym (v)* descend.

skalotlaukur shallot; *synonym (n)* eschalot.

skalottlaukur shallot; *synonym (n)* eschalot.

skamma 1. revile; *synonyms (v)* insult, abuse, rail, *(n)* malign, *(adj)* profane, **2.** curse; *synonyms (n)* bane, anathema, blasphemy, *(v)* beshrew, blight, **3.** abuse; *synonyms (n)* affront, misuse, harm, *(v)* mistreat, injure; *antonyms (v)* praise, respect, **4.** offend; *synonyms (v)* irritate, contravene, disgust, infringe, anger; *antonym (v)* please, **5.** insult; *synonyms (n)* dishonor, contumely, disgrace, indignity, *(v)* flout; *antonym (v)* compliment.

skammær deciduous; *synonyms (adj)* caducous, transient, short-lived, *(v)* labent, undermined.

skammaryrði invective; *synonyms (n)* abuse, insult, contumely, denunciation, diatribe.

skammleiðsla jumper; *synonyms (n)* sweater, blackguard, bounder, cad, dog.

skammljómun fluorescence; *synonyms* (*n*) phosphorescence, epipolism.

skammstöfun abbreviation; *synonyms* (*n*) abridgement, abridgment, contraction, abstraction, summary; *antonym* (*n*) expansion.

skammta quantize; *synonym* (*v*) quantise.

skammtamælir dosimeter; *synonym* (*n*) dosemeter.

skammtapípa pipette; *synonyms* (*n*) pipet, beaker, flask, carboy, syringe.

skammtari hopper; *synonyms* (*n*) grasshopper, bin, basket, boor, clown.

Skammtþéttni dose; *synonyms* (*n*) potion, dosage, draught, medicine, (*v*) drug.

skammtur 1. share; *synonyms* (*n*) piece, portion, (*v*) participate, allot, apportion; *antonym* (*v*) control, **2**. quantity; *synonyms* (*n*) amount, extent, measure, multitude, quantum, **3**. quantum; *synonyms* (*n*) magnitude, quantity, mass, measurement, sum, **4**. dose; *synonyms* (*n*) potion, dosage, draught, medicine, (*v*) drug, **5**. dosage; *synonyms* (*n*) dose, capsule, lozenge, pill.

skammvinnur 1. transient; *synonyms* (*adj*) brief, fleeting, passing, temporary, transitory; *antonyms* (*adj*) permanent, enduring, **2**. ephemeral; *synonyms* (*adj*) transient, momentary, cursory, evanescent, fugacious; *antonym* (*adj*) lasting.

skammyrði acronym; *synonyms* (*n*) contraction, ellipsis.

skán 1. scale; *synonyms* (*n*) flake, gamut, (*v*) ascend, climb, (*adj*) balance; *antonym* (*v*) descend, **2**. epistasis; *synonyms* (*n*) epistasy, hypostasis.

skann scanning; *synonym* (*n*) sweep.

skanna scan; *synonyms* (*n*) examination, inspection, (*v*) survey, inspect, rake.

skanni scanner; *synonym* (*n*) analyzer.

skansgluggi oriel; *synonyms* (*n*) corner, cove, crypt, niche, nook.

skap 1. temper; *synonyms* (*n*) mood, character, disposition, (*v*) moderate, soften; *antonyms* (*v*) intensify, upset, **2**. humour; *synonyms* (*n*) temper, wit, witticism, biliousness, (*v*) humor, **3**. mood; *synonyms* (*n*) atmosphere, climate, air, attitude, feeling.

skapahárastaða escutcheon; *synonyms* (*n*) scutcheon, shield, arms, escocheon.

skapalon 1. template; *synonyms* (*n*) pattern, templet, guide, guidebook, pathfinder, **2**. jig; *synonyms* (*n*) jigger, strathspey, (*v*) dance, hop, skip.

skapferli temperament; *synonyms* (*n*) temper, character, disposition, nature, constitution.

skapgerð character; *synonyms* (*n*) kind, nature, note, part, quality.

skaphöfn character; *synonyms* (*n*) kind, nature, note, part, quality.

skapkenni character; *synonyms* (*n*) kind, nature, note, part, quality.

skapstyggð irritability; *synonyms* (*n*) excitability, irascibility, choler, petulance, temper.

skapstyggur irritable; *synonyms* (*adj*) angry, fractious, irascible, edgy, cantankerous; *antonyms* (*adj*) calm, easygoing, good-humored, good-natured, even-tempered.

skápur 1. wardrobe; *synonyms* (*n*) closet, clothing, costume, cupboard, garb, **2**. cabinet; *synonyms* (*n*) case, locker, press, chamber, console.

skara 1. imbricate; *synonyms* (*v*) overlap, lap, (*adj*) imbricated, imbricative, **2**. intersect; *synonyms* (*v*) cross, cut, divide, meet, bisect, **3**. overlap; *synonyms* (*n*) intersection, overlay, (*v*) fold, concur, match.

skaraður imbricate; *synonyms* (*v*) overlap, lap, (*adj*) imbricated, imbricative.

skarð 1. chip; *synonyms* (*n*) splinter, bit, flake, chipping, (*v*) crack, **2**. gap; *synonyms* (*n*) break, cleft, crevice, fissure, (*v*) breach.

skarkoli plaice; *synonyms* (*n*) flounder, tonguefishes.

skarlatssótt scarlatina; *synonyms* (*adj*) scabies, scrofula, seasickness, struma, syntexis.

skarpa 1. sharpen; *synonyms* (*v*) focus, edge, hone, intensify, point; *antonym* (*v*) cloud, **2**. whet; *synonyms* (*v*) sharpen, excite, grind, quicken, stimulate.

skarpskyggni 1. poignancy; *synonyms* (*n*) pathos, acerbity, poignance, acrimony, keenness, **2**. sharpness; *synonyms* (*n*) acuteness, severity, asperity, bitterness, acumen; *antonym* (*n*) sweetness, **3**. acrimony; *synonyms* (*n*) acridity, gall, harshness, pique, tartness, **4**. acerbity; *synonyms* (*n*) austerity, huff, (*adj*) petulance, **5**. acuity; *synonyms* (*n*) sharpness, discernment, awareness, insight, (*adj*) acumination.

skarpur 1. sharp; *synonyms* (*adj*) acute, bitter, intelligent, acid, (*n*) keen; *antonyms* (*adj*) blunt, dull, mild, gentle, rounded, **2**. acute; *synonyms* (*adj*) sharp, incisive, intense, penetrating, critical; *antonym* (*adj*) obtuse, **3**. poignant; *synonyms* (*adj*) cutting, harsh, moving, (*v*) acrid, biting, **4**. acrid; *synonyms* (*adj*) pungent, acerbic, caustic, acerb, corrosive; *antonym* (*adj*) sweet, **5**. acerbic; *synonyms* (*adj*) astringent, tart, acrimonious, mordant, severe.

skásetning pitch; *synonyms* (*n*) degree, dip, (*v*) fling, cast, chuck.

skásettur 1. diagonal; *synonyms* (*adj*) oblique, aslant, slanting, sloping, (*n*) bias; *antonym* (*adj*) level, **2**. oblique; *synonyms* (*adj*) indirect, circuitous, devious, lateral, collateral; *antonym* (*adj*) direct.

skásneiða chamfer; *synonyms* (*n*) cant, fluting, (*v*) bevel, chase, furrow.

skásnið chamfer; *synonyms* (*n*) cant, fluting, (*v*) bevel, chase, furrow.

skata skate; *synonyms* (*v*) glide, skim, slip, coast, slide.

skátaflokkur patrol; *synonyms* (*n*) beat, protection, patrolman, (*v*) watch, guard.

skátamót camp; *synonyms* (*n*) bivouac, encampment, faction, base, barracks.

skátastarf 1. scouting; *synonyms* (*adj*) disdainful, (*n*) reconnoitering, inspection, patrol, investigation, **2.** guiding; *synonyms* (*adj*) directing, directive, leading, controlling, directional.

skattálagning assessment; *synonyms* (*n*) appraisal, estimate, estimation, evaluation, judgment.

skattalegur fiscal; *synonyms* (*adj*) financial, monetary, pecuniary, crumenal, economic.

skattlagning taxation; *synonyms* (*n*) tax, revenue, assessment, gross, receipts.

skattleggja tax; *synonyms* (*n*) charge, duty, burden, (*v*) assess, task.

skattskyldur taxable; *synonyms* (*adj*) nonexempt, declarable.

skattskylt taxable; *synonyms* (*adj*) nonexempt, declarable.

skattur 1. tax; *synonyms* (*n*) charge, duty, burden, (*v*) assess, task, **2.** toll; *synonyms* (*n*) fee, price, tax, (*v*) ring, chime, **3.** taxation; *synonyms* (*n*) revenue, assessment, gross, receipts, accusation, **4.** levy; *synonyms* (*n*) impost, (*v*) impose, raise, inflict, collect.

skaut 1. pole; *synonyms* (*n*) perch, bar, picket, post, rod, **2.** electrode; *synonym* (*n*) rheophore.

skautaðZur polar; *synonyms* (*adj*) arctic, diametric, opposite, cold, freezing.

skautari polarizer; *synonyms* (*n*) illuminator, reticle.

skautnæmi dichroism; *synonyms* (*n*) colors, trichroism.

skautplata plate; *synonyms* (*n*) dish, leaf, (*v*) gild, sheet, cover.

skautsjá polariscope; *synonyms* (*n*) polarimeter, abdominoscope, gastroscope, helioscope, polemoscope.

skautstefna polarity; *synonyms* (*n*) antagonism, augury, house, mansion, mark.

skautun 1. polarity; *synonyms* (*n*) antagonism, augury, house, mansion, mark, **2.** polarization; *synonyms* (*n*) polarisation, bias, divergence, discord, division.

skautunarefni polarizer; *synonyms* (*n*) illuminator, reticle.

skautunarmælir polarimeter; *synonym* (*n*) polariscope.

skautunarsía polarizer; *synonyms* (*n*) illuminator, reticle.

skávik skew; *synonyms* (*v*) slope, incline, tilt, (*adj*) oblique, skewed.

skefill excavator; *synonyms* (*n*) digger, shovel, miner, sapper, archaeologist.

skegg beard; *synonyms* (*n*) awn, hair, (*v*) dare, defy, (*adj*) brave.

skeggur bib; *synonyms* (*n*) brat, (*v*) tipple, (*adj*) besot, booze, bouse.

skeið 1. vagina, **2.** stadium; *synonyms* (*n*) arena, coliseum, bowl, field, gymnasium, **3.** sheath; *synonyms* (*n*) case, envelope, blanket, scabbard, (*v*) cover, **4.** spoon; *synonyms* (*n*) ladle, spoonful, shovel, (*v*) scoop, smooch, **5.** age; *synonyms* (*n*) period, aeon, day, era, time.

skeiðvöllur 1. runway; *synonyms* (*n*) track, airfield, airport, channel, tarmac, **2.** track; *synonyms* (*n*) course, path, (*v*) trace, trail, hunt, **3.** course; *synonyms* (*n*) stream, flow, bearing, career, (*v*) run.

skeif skewness; *synonym* (*n*) lopsidedness.

skeina abrasion; *synonyms* (*n*) attrition, excoriation, erosion, friction, (*v*) detrition; *antonym* (*n*) smoothness.

skekinn agitated; *synonyms* (*adj*) restless, excited, nervous, restive, tumultuous; *antonyms* (*adj*) calm, composed, lethargic.

skekking 1. skewness; *synonym* (*n*) lopsidedness, **2.** deformation; *synonyms* (*n*) contortion, strain, distortion, buckle, twist, **3.** dislocation; *synonyms* (*n*) breakdown, interruption, confusion, disruption, luxation.

skekkja 1. error; *synonyms* (*n*) deviation, blunder, fault, mistake, wrong; *antonym* (*n*) correctness, **2.** set; *synonyms* (*v*) fix, place, lay, put, (*n*) class; *antonyms* (*v*) soften, liquefy, (*n*) combing, comb-out, (*adj*) variable, **3.** deform; *synonyms* (*v*) distort, deface, bend, contort, disfigure; *antonym* (*v*) straighten, **4.** deviation; *synonyms* (*n*) aberration, change, deflection, difference, diversion; *antonym* (*n*) normality.

skel 1. shell; *synonyms* (*n*) peel, rind, bullet, case, (*v*) bomb, **2.** crust; *synonyms* (*n*) bark, cheekiness, covering, gall, (*v*) coat.

skelfletting peeling; *synonyms* (*adj*) flaking, (*n*) peel, desquamation, shelling, hull; *antonym* (*adj*) smooth.

skella plaque; *synonyms* (*n*) plate, brass, medal, administration, award.

skellihljóð flap; *synonyms* (*n*) fuss, slap, (*v*) flop, beat, wave.

skellur 1. shock; *synonyms* (*n*) blow, daze, impact, collision, (*v*) jar; *antonym* (*v*) comfort, **2.** concussion; *synonyms* (*n*) clash, shock, crash, jolt, percussion, **3**. blow; *synonyms* (*n*) bang, beat, blast, knock, (*adj*) gasp; *antonyms* (*v*) calm, save.

skelveggur facing; *synonyms* (*n*) face, revetment, cladding, coating, (*prep*) opposite.

skema 1. schema; *synonyms* (*n*) outline, plan, chart, graph, scheme, **2**. scheme; *synonyms* (*n*) contrivance, dodge, (*v*) plot, design, intrigue.

skemmd 1. damage; *synonyms* (*n*) blemish, injury, (*v*) harm, hurt, abuse; *antonyms* (*n*) service, (*v*) conserve, enhance, repair, bolster, **2**. flaw; *synonyms* (*n*) defect, crevice, fault, chink, (*adj*) blot; *antonym* (*n*) strength, **3**. lesion; *synonyms* (*n*) wound, abrasion, scrape, scratch, abscess.

skemmdir injury; *synonyms* (*n*) disadvantage, disservice, harm, grievance, damage; *antonyms* (*n*) ability, reparation.

skemmdur damaged; *synonyms* (*adj*) faulty, unsound, defective, broken, dilapidated; *antonym* (*adj*) undamaged.

skemmtigarður park; *synonyms* (*n*) garden, common, (*v*) deposit, locate, place.

skepnuskapur bestiality; *synonyms* (*n*) cruelty, violence, zooerastia, zooerasty.

skera 1. cut; *synonyms* (*v*) carve, chop, clip, (*n*) notch, slice; *antonyms* (*v*) increase, lengthen, (*n*) addition, extension, **2**. shear; *synonyms* (*v*) cut, fleece, lop, pare, prune, **3**. mill; *synonyms* (*n*) grind, factory, grinder, manufactory, (*v*) crush, **4**. etch; *synonyms* (*n*) etching, (*v*) engrave, inscribe, bite, grave.

skerandi 1. strident; *synonyms* (*adj*) raucous, loud, blatant, harsh, noisy; *antonyms* (*adj*) soft, quiet, **2**. snappy; *synonyms* (*adj*) racy, sharp, animated, brisk, crisp, **3**. sharp; *synonyms* (*adj*) acute, bitter, intelligent, acid, (*n*) keen; *antonyms* (*adj*) blunt, dull, mild, gentle, rounded, **4**. shrill; *synonyms* (*adj*) piercing, penetrating, (*v*) high, screech, shriek; *antonym* (*adj*) low, **5**. acrimonious; *synonyms* (*adj*) sour, biting, caustic, (*v*) acrid, pungent.

skerast 1. decussate; *synonyms* (*v*) cross, intersect, cloth, cut, (*adj*) intersectant, **2**. intersect; *synonyms* (*v*) divide, meet, bisect, traverse, intertwine.

skerðing 1. restriction; *synonyms* (*n*) limitation, limit, restraint, curb, (*v*) hindrance; *antonyms* (*n*) freedom, extension, **2**. sinus; *synonyms* (*n*) cavity, fistula, pit, indentation, dent, **3**. reduction; *synonyms* (*n*) contraction, decrease, decrement, diminution, rebate; *antonyms* (*n*) increase, growth, intensification, strengthening, expansion, **4**. clipping; *synonyms* (*n*) clip, trimming, cutting, snip, trim, **5**. depletion; *synonyms* (*n*) consumption, expenditure, loss, (*adj*) flaccidity, vacancy.

skerfur 1. share; *synonyms* (*n*) piece, portion, (*v*) participate, allot, apportion; *antonym* (*v*) control, **2**.

contribution; *synonyms* (*n*) allowance, donation, gift, offering, share.

skeri cutter; *synonyms* (*n*) carver, cutlery, knife, pinnace, (*adj*) billhook.

skering cut; *synonyms* (*v*) carve, chop, clip, (*n*) notch, slice; *antonyms* (*v*) increase, lengthen, (*n*) addition, extension.

skerjasteinbítur butterfish; *synonym* (*n*) stromateid.

skerming shielding; *synonyms* (*n*) shadowing, (*adj*) protective, covering, protecting, caring.

skermir screen; *synonyms* (*n*) shade, blind, (*v*) cover, shield, conceal.

skermun shielding; *synonyms* (*n*) shadowing, (*adj*) protective, covering, protecting, caring.

skermur 1. screen; *synonyms* (*n*) shade, blind, (*v*) cover, shield, conceal, **2**. shade; *synonyms* (*n*) screen, tinge, color, ghost, (*v*) darken; *antonyms* (*n*) light, brightness.

skerpa 1. whet; *synonyms* (*v*) sharpen, excite, grind, quicken, stimulate, **2**. sharpen; *synonyms* (*v*) focus, edge, hone, intensify, point; *antonym* (*v*) cloud, **3**. definition; *synonyms* (*n*) description, account, explanation, interpretation, limitation; *antonym* (*n*) bagginess, **4**. acuity; *synonyms* (*n*) sharpness, acumen, acuteness, discernment, keenness, **5**. contrast; *synonyms* (*n*) contrariety, antithesis, comparison, distinction, (*v*) differ; *antonym* (*n*) similarity.

skerping sharpening; *synonyms* (*n*) acumination, aggravation, dressing, filing, (*adj*) abrasive.

skertur reduced; *synonyms* (*adj*) decreased, abridged, curtailed, miniature, cheap; *antonyms* (*adj*) expensive, complete.

skeyta append; *synonyms* (*v*) adjoin, add, affix, annex, attach.

skeytaheimt retrieval; *synonyms* (*n*) recovery, reclamation, redress, recuperation, (*v*) revendication; *antonym* (*n*) loss.

skeyti 1. projectile; *synonyms* (*n*) missile, bullet, shot, bolt, quoit, **2**. message; *synonyms* (*n*) communication, meaning, information, errand, letter, **3**. missile; *synonyms* (*n*) projectile, rocket, bomb, explosive, ammunition, **4**. intersection; *synonyms* (*n*) cross, crossroads, crossing, crossroad, intersect.

skeyting registration; *synonyms* (*n*) enrollment, registering, enrolment, entering, entry.

skeytingarmerki tic; *synonyms* (*n*) twitching, spasm, jerk, quiver, (*v*) twitch.

skeytismerking label; *synonyms* (*n*) name, brand, tag, (*v*) mark, call.

skíði ski; *synonym* (*n*) skis.

skíðisfótur pedestal; *synonyms* (*n*) base, bottom, foot, groundwork, basis.

skífa 1. washer; *synonyms* (*n*) potcher, bandage, breaker, cloth, clout, **2.** dial; *synonyms* (*n*) face, control, gnomon, hourglass, (*v*) telephone, **3.** disk; *synonyms* (*n*) disc, discus, dial, circle, diskette, **4.** disc; *synonyms* (*n*) disk, record, platter, round, book, **5.** diskette; *synonym* (*n*) floppy.

skifting partition; *synonyms* (*n*) division, part, wall, distribution, (*v*) divide.

skífumiðja grommet; *synonyms* (*n*) eyelet, grummet, cringle, child, loop.

skiki parcel; *synonyms* (*n*) lot, bale, pack, bundle, (*v*) portion.

skil 1. break; *synonyms* (*v*) split, crack, burst, (*n*) breach, fracture; *antonyms* (*v*) repair, obey, honor, mend, (*n*) continuation, **2.** delivery; *synonyms* (*n*) childbirth, birth, consignment, discharge, rescue; *antonyms* (*n*) death, dispatch, **3.** interface; *synonyms* (*n*) link, port, boundary, junction, (*v*) contact, **4.** front; *synonyms* (*adj*) head, (*n*) countenance, forefront, (*v*) face, confront; *antonyms* (*n*) rear, end, (*v*) back, **5.** performance; *synonyms* (*n*) act, achievement, execution, fulfillment, (*v*) action; *antonyms* (*n*) omission, practice.

skilaboð message; *synonyms* (*n*) communication, meaning, information, errand, letter.

skilaflutningur transmittal; *synonyms* (*n*) transmission, transmitting, transfer, allowance, consignment.

skilaskylda accountability; *synonyms* (*n*) blame, liability, fault, duty, obligation.

skilbinding dependence; *synonyms* (*n*) belief, confidence, reliance, addiction, dependance; *antonyms* (*n*) independence, self-government, self-sufficiency.

skildagatíð conditional; *synonyms* (*adj*) contingent, dependent, qualified, hypothetical, guarded; *antonym* (*adj*) unconditional.

skilflötur 1. interface; *synonyms* (*n*) link, port, boundary, junction, (*v*) contact, **2.** front; *synonyms* (*adj*) head, (*n*) countenance, forefront, (*v*) face, confront; *antonyms* (*n*) rear, end, (*v*) back.

skilgreina 1. qualify; *synonyms* (*v*) modify, prepare, moderate, capacitate, characterize; *antonym* (*v*) disqualify, **2.** identify; *synonyms* (*v*) distinguish, detect, discover, name, ascertain.

skilgreining 1. specification; *synonyms* (*n*) designation, provision, stipulation, particular, condition, **2.** definition; *synonyms* (*n*) description, account, explanation, interpretation, limitation; *antonym* (*n*) bagginess, **3.** declaration; *synonyms* (*n*) announcement, affirmation, assertion, allegation, avowal; *antonym* (*n*) denial, **4.** identification; *synonyms* (*n*) finding, id, identity, mark, naming.

skili separator; *synonyms* (*n*) centrifuge, extractor, classifier, arrester, partition.

skilinn cognitive; *synonyms* (*adj*) psychological, rational, reasonable.

skilja 1. realize; *synonyms* (*v*) fulfill, achieve, perform, discover, attain, **2.** purify; *synonyms* (*v*) clean, disinfect, purge, (*adj*) clear, cleanse; *antonyms* (*v*) contaminate, pollute, **3.** understand; *synonyms* (*v*) interpret, recognize, catch, hear, learn; *antonyms* (*v*) misinterpret, misconstrue, misunderstand, **4.** separator; *synonyms* (*n*) centrifuge, extractor, classifier, arrester, partition, **5.** see; *synonyms* (*v*) look, feel, appreciate, (*adj*) observe, perceive.

skiljun 1. purification; *synonyms* (*n*) defecation, purge, refinement, catharsis, refining; *antonyms* (*n*) ruining, debasement, **2.** centrifugation; *synonym* (*n*) centrifuging.

skillag separator; *synonyms* (*n*) centrifuge, extractor, classifier, arrester, partition.

skilmálar terms; *synonyms* (*n*) condition, conditions, provision, stipulation, cost.

skilmerkilegur explicit; *synonyms* (*adj*) clear, distinct, unmistakable, broad, definite; *antonyms* (*adj*) vague, tacit, understood, unspoken, implicit.

skilnaður 1. segregation; *synonyms* (*n*) dissociation, separation, elimination, discrimination, (*v*) detachment; *antonyms* (*n*) integration, inclusion, **2.** dispersion; *synonyms* (*n*) diffusion, dispersal, dissipation, distribution, circulation, **3.** divorce; *synonyms* (*v*) detach, dissociate, disunite, separate, divide; *antonyms* (*n*) marriage, wedding.

skilning 1. chromatography; *synonyms* (*n*) chromatism, chromatology, **2.** centrifugation; *synonym* (*n*) centrifuging.

skilningarvit 1. sense; *synonyms* (*n*) intelligence, perception, meaning, (*v*) feel, intellect; *antonyms* (*n*) garbage, ludicrousness, nonsense, stupidity, foolishness, **2.** modality; *synonyms* (*n*) mode, mood, manner, schesis, fashion.

skilningur 1. comprehension; *synonyms* (*n*) apprehension, conception, grasp, inclusion, intelligence; *antonyms* (*n*) misunderstanding, incomprehension, **2.** apprehension; *synonyms* (*n*) alarm, comprehension, dread, arrest, (*adj*) anxiety; *antonyms* (*n*) reassurance, release, confidence, calmness, **3.** realization; *synonyms* (*n*) execution, accomplishment, awareness, fulfillment, implementation, **4.** sense; *synonyms* (*n*) perception, meaning, (*v*) feel, intellect, mind; *antonyms* (*n*) garbage, ludicrousness, nonsense, stupidity, foolishness, **5.** notion; *synonyms* (*n*) feeling, belief, idea, impression, (*v*) judgment.

skiloroðsbinding suspension; *synonyms* (n) delay, interruption, abeyance, break, intermission.

skiloroðsbundinn conditional; *synonyms* (adj) contingent, dependent, qualified, hypothetical, guarded; *antonym* (adj) unconditional.

skilríki 1. credentials; *synonyms* (n) certification, certificate, credential, papers, document, **2.** document; *synonyms* (n) charter, deed, credentials, (v) record, file, **3.** documentation; *synonyms* (n) proof, corroboration, evidence.

skilrúm 1. separator; *synonyms* (n) centrifuge, extractor, classifier, arrester, partition, **2.** divider; *synonyms* (n) screen, bunton, wall, barrier, division, **3.** bulkhead, **4.** baffle; *synonyms* (v) discomfit, astonish, bewilder, confound, foil; *antonym* (v) enlighten, **5.** partition; *synonyms* (n) part, distribution, divider, split, (v) divide.

skiltákn separator; *synonyms* (n) centrifuge, extractor, classifier, arrester, partition.

skilti sign; *synonyms* (n) signal, indication, mark, motion, (v) gesture.

skilveggur partition; *synonyms* (n) division, part, wall, distribution, (v) divide.

skilviður separator; *synonyms* (n) centrifuge, extractor, classifier, arrester, partition.

skilvinda 1. separator; *synonyms* (n) centrifuge, extractor, classifier, arrester, partition, **2.** centrifuge; *synonyms* (n) separator, ultracentrifuge, (v) centrifugate.

skilvirkni efficiency; *synonyms* (n) capability, effectiveness, ability, efficacy, effect; *antonyms* (n) inefficiency, incompetence, largeness.

skilvirkur 1. effective; *synonyms* (adj) beneficial, practical, (n) competent, capable, able; *antonyms* (adj) ineffective, useless, weak, inoperative, **2.** efficient; *synonyms* (adj) effectual, effective, valid, efficacious, (v) clever; *antonyms* (adj) incompetent, inefficient.

skilvit cognition; *synonyms* (n) knowledge, perception, cognizance, conception, cognoscence.

skilvitlegur cognitive; *synonyms* (adj) psychological, rational, reasonable.

skilyrða condition; *synonyms* (n) circumstance, position, provision, status, (v) aspect.

skilyrði 1. constraint; *synonyms* (n) coercion, compulsion, force, restraint, confinement; *antonym* (n) incentive, **2.** qualification; *synonyms* (n) condition, capability, competence, fitness, limitation, **3.** provision; *synonyms* (n) arrangement, clause, proviso, (v) preparation, feed; *antonym* (n) lack, **4.** reservation; *synonyms* (n) reserve, booking, qualification, modesty, exception; *antonym* (n) certainty, **5.** clause; *synonyms* (n) article, paragraph, provision, rider, (v) passage.

skilyrðing conditioning; *synonyms* (n) training, chilling, cooking, drill, equalizing.

skilyrðislaus 1. absolute; *synonyms* (adj) downright, peremptory, total, unconditional, categorical; *antonyms* (adj) partial, qualified, **2.** implicit; *synonyms* (adj) silent, tacit, understood, undeclared, unsaid; *antonyms* (adj) explicit, direct.

skilyrtur 1. conditional; *synonyms* (adj) contingent, dependent, qualified, hypothetical, guarded; *antonym* (adj) unconditional, **2.** conditioned; *synonyms* (adj) finite, involuntary, learned, ripe, tough.

skim scan; *synonyms* (n) examination, inspection, (v) survey, inspect, rake.

skima scan; *synonyms* (n) examination, inspection, (v) survey, inspect, rake.

skíma luminescence; *synonyms* (n) glow, radiance, glowing, freshness, gleam.

skimari scanner; *synonym* (n) analyzer.

skimrás multiplexer; *synonyms* (n) combiner, concentrator.

skimun 1. screening; *synonyms* (n) screen, sieving, concealment, cover, covering, **2.** scanning; *synonym* (n) sweep.

skin 1. luminescence; *synonyms* (n) glow, radiance, glowing, freshness, gleam, **2.** luminance; *synonyms* (n) brightness, illumination, light, luminosity, lighting.

skinefni phosphor; *synonyms* (n) phosphorus, phosphide, scintillator.

skinfótur pseudopodium; *synonyms* (n) pseudopod, lobopodium.

skinhreyfisjá stroboscope; *synonym* (n) strobe.

Skinn 1. skin; *synonyms* (n) peel, hide, coating, (v) pare, bark, **2.** leather; *synonyms* (n) fur, fleece, skin, buckskin, fell.

skinna plate; *synonyms* (n) dish, leaf, (v) gild, sheet, cover.

skinnflagningur exfoliation; *synonyms* (n) scale, lamination, plate, scurf, shell.

skip 1. ship; *synonyms* (n) boat, ferry, (v) dispatch, send, forward, **2.** nave; *synonyms* (n) chancel, choir, hub, omphalos, transept, **3.** liner; *synonyms* (n) lining, airliner, craft, ship, steamboat.

skipa 1. command; *synonyms* (n) control, (v) charge, order, rule, call; *antonym* (v) request, **2.** constitute; *synonyms* (v) compose, form, make, commission, appoint, **3.** order; *synonyms* (n) command, decree, dictate, array, (v) direct; *antonyms* (n) anarchy, chaos, confusion, mayhem, (v) disorder.

skipaferðir service; *synonyms* (n) help, aid, assistance, avail, (v) overhaul.

skipalægi roadstead; *synonyms* (*n*) anchorage, roads, road, harbor, port.

skipan 1. structure; *synonyms* (*n*) form, building, arrangement, edifice, shape, **2**. order; *synonyms* (*n*) command, decree, dictate, array, (*v*) direct; *antonyms* (*n*) anarchy, chaos, confusion, (*v*) disorder, request.

skipanabretti tablet; *synonyms* (*n*) pad, slab, table, lozenge, pill.

skipaskurður canal; *synonyms* (*n*) aqueduct, channel, conduit, duct, sound.

skipastigi lock; *synonyms* (*v*) bolt, bar, close, latch, engage; *antonyms* (*v*) unlock, open.

skipbrot loss; *synonyms* (*n*) hurt, damage, defeat, detriment, injury; *antonyms* (*n*) appearance, retrieval, victory, gaining, income.

skipgengi navigability; *synonym* (*n*) navigableness.

skipgengur navigable; *synonyms* (*adj*) passable, open, sailable, voyageable, crossable.

skipherra commander; *synonyms* (*n*) captain, chief, commandant, leader, head.

skipreiki loss; *synonyms* (*n*) hurt, damage, defeat, detriment, injury; *antonyms* (*n*) appearance, retrieval, victory, gaining, income.

skipsbátur 1. dinghy; *synonyms* (*n*) boat, rowboat, dingey, cruiser, dingy, **2**. launch; *synonyms* (*v*) initiate, begin, dart, found, fire; *antonym* (*v*) end.

skipsbógur bow; *synonyms* (*n*) arc, curve, (*v*) bend, arch, stoop.

skipsflak shipwreck; *synonyms* (*n*) wreck, hulk, (*v*) ruin, defeat, (*adj*) sink.

skipsklukka chronometer; *synonyms* (*n*) clock, timepiece, watch, metronome.

skipssíða wing; *synonyms* (*n*) annex, arm, fender, limb, (*v*) fly.

skipsskrokkur hull; *synonyms* (*n*) crust, shell, hulk, husk, (*v*) skin.

skipsskrúfa propeller; *synonyms* (*n*) screw, fan, turbine, extortioner, niggard.

skipstjóri 1. skipper; *synonyms* (*n*) captain, commander, master, head, leader, **2**. commander; *synonyms* (*n*) chief, commandant, governor, chieftain, conductor, **3**. captain; *synonyms* (*n*) boss, commodore, guide, (*v*) govern, manage.

skipstjórn navigation; *synonyms* (*n*) guidance, sailing, steering, seafaring, shipping.

skipstjórnarmaður navigator; *synonyms* (*n*) pilot, mariner, sailor, aviator, aeroplanist.

skipta 1. toggle; *synonyms* (*n*) pin, button, clasp, clip, closure, **2**. allocate; *synonyms* (*v*) divide, apportion, set, place, allot, **3**. divide; *synonyms* (*v*) cut, distribute, part, dissociate, (*n*) break; *antonyms* (*v*) unite, join, **4**. change; *synonyms* (*n*) shift,

alteration, barter, (*v*) exchange, alter; *antonyms* (*v*) stay, leave, idle, maintain.

Skiptamunur exchange; *synonyms* (*n*) commutation, swap, (*v*) change, barter, interchange.

skiptaráðandi administrator; *synonyms* (*n*) executive, director, manager, boss, officer.

skipti 1. substitution; *synonyms* (*n*) replacement, exchange, change, substitute, interchange, **2**. shift; *synonyms* (*n*) turn, (*v*) remove, quibble, alter, budge, **3**. swap; *synonyms* (*v*) switch, trade, shift, deal, (*n*) barter, **4**. separation; *synonyms* (*n*) detachment, disjunction, disunion, division, partition; *antonyms* (*n*) amalgamation, closeness, connection, marriage, unification, **5**. change; *synonyms* (*n*) alteration, modification, variation, (*v*) adapt, alternate; *antonyms* (*v*) stay, leave, idle, maintain.

skiptiborð switchboard; *synonyms* (*n*) patchboard, plugboard.

skiptiefnahvarf substitution; *synonyms* (*n*) replacement, exchange, change, substitute, interchange.

skiptihæfi interchangeability; *synonyms* (*n*) exchangeability, fungibility, interchangeableness, equivalence.

skiptihvarf substitution; *synonyms* (*n*) replacement, exchange, change, substitute, interchange.

skiptimynt change; *synonyms* (*n*) shift, alteration, barter, (*v*) exchange, alter; *antonyms* (*v*) stay, leave, idle, maintain.

skipting 1. segmentation; *synonyms* (*n*) division, cleavage, partition, partitioning, sectionalization, **2**. stratification; *synonyms* (*n*) bedding, lamination, **3**. scission, **4**. septation, **5**. allocation; *synonyms* (*n*) allotment, portion, allowance, quota, share.

skiptisending simplex; *synonym* (*adj*) elementary.

skiptital simplex; *synonym* (*adj*) elementary.

skiptivara substitute; *synonyms* (*adj*) replacement, alternative, (*n*) deputy, (*v*) alternate, shift.

skipulag 1. planning; *synonyms* (*n*) preparation, calculation, organization, programming, plan, **2**. arrangement; *synonyms* (*n*) agreement, order, settlement, adjustment, array, **3**. organization; *synonyms* (*n*) establishment, administration, arrangement, formation, association.

skipulagning 1. planning; *synonyms* (*n*) preparation, calculation, organization, programming, plan, **2**. normalization; *synonyms* (*n*) normalisation, standardization, calibration, regularisation, regularization.

skipulagsbók organizer; *synonyms* (*n*) arranger, organiser, administrator, manager, founder.

skipulagsbreyting reorganization; *synonyms* (*n*) reorganisation, reform, conversion, renovation, improvement.

skipulagsgerð infrastructure; *synonyms* (*n*) base, foundation, basis, groundwork, substructure.

skipulagsheild organization; *synonyms* (*n*) order, establishment, administration, arrangement, formation.

skipulagssnilli strategy; *synonyms* (*n*) dodge, plan, scheme, strategics, (*v*) tactics.

skipulagsuppdráttur plat; *synonyms* (*n*) chart, (*v*) plait, plot, braid, diagram.

skipun 1. constitution; *synonyms* (*n*) composition, code, makeup, organization, temperament, **2**. appointment; *synonyms* (*n*) assignment, date, designation, engagement, fitting, **3**. command; *synonyms* (*n*) control, (*v*) charge, order, rule, call; *antonym* (*v*) request, **4**. instruction; *synonyms* (*n*) command, advice, counsel, direction, education, **5**. order; *synonyms* (*n*) decree, dictate, array, rank, (*v*) direct; *antonyms* (*n*) anarchy, chaos, confusion, mayhem, (*v*) disorder.

skíra refine; *synonyms* (*v*) cultivate, clear, purify, (*adj*) clarify, purge.

skírðarlögur pickle; *synonyms* (*n*) fix, jam, mess, hole, (*v*) cure.

skírnarnafn forename; *synonyms* (*n*) handle, moniker, nickname, surname, (*v*) prenominate.

skírteini 1. certificate; *synonyms* (*n*) bond, diploma, certification, credential, (*v*) certify, **2**. record; *synonyms* (*n*) register, list, account, (*v*) chronicle, file, **3**. diploma; *synonyms* (*n*) certificate, sheepskin, brevet, warrant, authority, **4**. bill; *synonyms* (*n*) beak, advertisement, card, (*v*) placard, advertise, **5**. deed; *synonyms* (*n*) accomplishment, achievement, act, feat, behavior.

skírteinisútgáfa certification; *synonyms* (*n*) authentication, certificate, verification, accreditation, corroboration.

skissa 1. scheme; *synonyms* (*n*) contrivance, dodge, (*v*) plan, plot, design, **2**. sketch; *synonyms* (*n*) drawing, outline, (*v*) paint, draft, draw, **3**. draft; *synonyms* (*n*) bill, conscription, sketch, (*v*) draught, blueprint; *antonym* (*v*) discharge.

skítugur dirty; *synonyms* (*adj*) foul, dirt, (*v*) muddy, corrupt, soil; *antonyms* (*adj*) hygienic, pure, spotless, immaculate, (*v*) clean.

skjáborð desktop; *synonyms* (*n*) background, backcloth, backdrop, ground, scope.

skjáhopp swap; *synonyms* (*v*) exchange, change, switch, trade, (*n*) barter.

skjal 1. document; *synonyms* (*n*) charter, deed, credentials, (*v*) record, file, **2**. instrument;

synonyms (*n*) channel, agency, apparatus, appliance, document.

skjala 1. archive; *synonyms* (*n*) record, scroll, archives, records, paper, **2**. document; *synonyms* (*n*) charter, deed, credentials, (*v*) file, list.

skjalahald documentation; *synonyms* (*n*) proof, record, certificate, certification, corroboration.

skjalamappa portfolio; *synonyms* (*n*) briefcase, album, file, bandolier, budget.

skjalasafn archive; *synonyms* (*n*) record, scroll, archives, records, paper.

skjalataska 1. briefcase; *synonyms* (*n*) bag, case, suitcase, baggage, dispatch, **2**. portfolio; *synonyms* (*n*) briefcase, album, file, bandolier, budget.

skjalavistun filing; *synonyms* (*n*) arrangement, friction, order, sharpening.

skjalbúa document; *synonyms* (*n*) charter, deed, credentials, (*v*) record, file.

skjalbúnaður documentation; *synonyms* (*n*) proof, record, certificate, certification, corroboration.

skjaldbaka turtle; *synonyms* (*n*) turkle, (*adj*) game, venison, (*v*) capsize.

skjaldkirtilsauki goitre; *synonyms* (*n*) goiter, struma, scrofula.

skjaldkirtilshormón thyroxine; *synonyms* (*n*) thyroxin, liothyronine, terabyte, tonne, triiodothyronine.

skjaldkyrkingsdvergur cretin; *synonyms* (*n*) idiot, moron, fool, imbecile, changeling.

skjaldlaga thyroid; *synonyms* (*adj*) thyroidal, thyroideal.

skjaldvakaeitrun hyperthyroidism; *synonym* (*n*) thyrotoxicosis.

skjálftamælir seismograph; *synonym* (*n*) sismograph.

skjálftamiðja epicentre; *synonym* (*n*) epicenter.

skjálftanemi geophone; *synonyms* (*n*) sismograph, jug.

skjálfti 1. tremor; *synonyms* (*n*) quiver, shiver, shudder, agitation, (*v*) quake, **2**. shiver; *synonyms* (*n*) fragment, (*v*) shake, tremble, palpitate, shatter, **3**. shimmy; *synonyms* (*n*) chemise, shift, vibration, (*v*) dance, wobble, **4**. earthquake; *synonyms* (*n*) shock, tremor, temblor, (*adj*) thunderstorm, volcano.

skjálgi 1. squint; *synonyms* (*n*) glance, look, (*v*) leer, (*adj*) askant, sidelong, **2**. strabismus; *synonyms* (*n*) squint, strabism, **3**. topknot.

skjálgur strabismus; *synonyms* (*n*) squint, strabism.

skjámynd display; *synonyms* (*n*) array, (*v*) exhibit, show, disclose, parade; *antonym* (*v*) conceal.

skjár 1. window; *synonyms* (*n*) casement, porthole, pane, gap, embrasure, **2**. screen; *synonyms* (*n*) shade, blind, (*v*) cover, shield, conceal, **3**. scope;

synonyms (*n*) range, reach, domain, purview, room, **4**. display; *synonyms* (*n*) array, (*v*) exhibit, show, disclose, parade.

skjátæki display; *synonyms* (*n*) array, (*v*) exhibit, show, disclose, parade; *antonym* (*v*) conceal.

skjatti 1. utricle; *synonyms* (*n*) vesicle, calyx, cancelli, capsule, cyst, **2**. saccule; *synonyms* (*n*) sac, sacculus, pocket, bag, pouch, **3**. sacculus; *synonym* (*n*) saccule.

skjóða 1. utricle; *synonyms* (*n*) vesicle, calyx, cancelli, capsule, cyst, **2**. sacculus; *synonym* (*n*) saccule.

skjögur wobble; *synonyms* (*v*) totter, rock, sway, lurch, (*n*) shake.

skjól 1. screen; *synonyms* (*n*) shade, blind, (*v*) cover, shield, conceal, **2**. screening; *synonyms* (*n*) screen, sieving, concealment, covering, masking, **3**. asylum; *synonyms* (*n*) refuge, sanctuary, shelter, haven, home.

skjöl 1. documentation; *synonyms* (*n*) proof, record, certificate, certification, corroboration, **2**. document; *synonyms* (*n*) charter, deed, credentials, (*v*) file, list.

skjólbelti windbreak; *synonyms* (*n*) hedge, shelterbelt.

skjólborði leeward; *synonyms* (*adv*) upwind, (*n*) lee; *antonym* (*n*) windward.

skjöldur 1. shield; *synonyms* (*n*) screen, shelter, (*v*) cover, guard, safeguard; *antonym* (*v*) expose, **2**. carapace; *synonyms* (*n*) shell, skin, carapax, (*v*) apron, buffer.

skjólgarður windbreak; *synonyms* (*n*) hedge, shelterbelt.

skjóllag lagging; *synonyms* (*n*) insulation, cover, (*adj*) slow, lazy, slack.

skjólstæðingur client; *synonyms* (*n*) buyer, customer, patron, guest, purchaser.

skjólveggur windbreak; *synonyms* (*n*) hedge, shelterbelt.

skjór magpie; *synonyms* (*n*) jay, pie, chatterbox, gossip, (*v*) parrot.

skoða 1. probe; *synonyms* (*n*) investigation, (*v*) examine, examination, explore, inspect, **2**. browse; *synonyms* (*v*) graze, crop, scan, skim, (*n*) browsing; *antonym* (*v*) study, **3**. check; *synonyms* (*v*) bridle, stop, (*n*) control, arrest, curb, **4**. observe; *synonyms* (*v*) celebrate, comment, notice, commemorate, mind; *antonyms* (*v*) ignore, feel, **5**. examine; *synonyms* (*v*) assay, audit, consider, overhaul, try.

skoðanahópur persuasion; *synonyms* (*n*) belief, opinion, faith, inducement, (*adj*) conviction; *antonyms* (*n*) force, pressure.

skoðanaskipti dialogue; *synonyms* (*n*) talk, colloquy, conversation, interlocution, interview.

skoðari 1. browser, **2**. observer; *synonyms* (*n*) beholder, bystander, spectator, witness, eyewitness.

sköddun injury; *synonyms* (*n*) disadvantage, disservice, harm, grievance, damage; *antonyms* (*n*) ability, reparation.

skoðun 1. opinion; *synonyms* (*n*) judgment, feeling, notion, idea, belief, **2**. stand; *synonyms* (*v*) endure, stall, (*n*) attitude, booth, rack; *antonyms* (*v*) sit, lie, **3**. sentiment; *synonyms* (*n*) emotion, mind, judgement, opinion, persuasion, **4**. persuasion; *synonyms* (*n*) faith, inducement, creed, exhortation, (*adj*) conviction; *antonyms* (*n*) force, pressure, **5**. survey; *synonyms* (*n*) poll, review, (*v*) study, measure, view; *antonym* (*v*) neglect.

skoðunarmaður surveyor; *synonyms* (*n*) inspector, assessor, visitor, engineer, husband.

skóf lichen; *synonym* (*n*) mold.

skófatnaður footwear; *synonyms* (*n*) footgear, boot.

skófla spade; *synonyms* (*n*) coon, nigger, (*v*) dig, grub, delve.

skófluhjól impeller; *synonyms* (*n*) runner, pump.

sköflungur 1. shinbone; *synonyms* (*n*) shin, tibia, **2**. shin; *synonyms* (*n*) shinbone, (*v*) clamber, scramble, shinny, abrade, **3**. tibia.

skógarhöggsmaður 1. woodcutter; *synonyms* (*n*) woodman, cultivator, farmer, forester, hunter, **2**. woodsman; *synonym* (*n*) woodworker, **3**. logger; *synonym* (*n*) recorder.

skógarköttur wildcat; *synonyms* (*n*) beast, brute, savage, animal, (*adj*) unauthorized.

skógrækt 1. afforestation, **2**. forestry; *synonyms* (*n*) sylviculture, arboriculture.

skögun 1. projection; *synonyms* (*n*) bulge, hump, jut, prominence, protuberance, **2**. overhang; *synonyms* (*n*) projection, (*v*) beetle, hang, project, protrude.

skógur 1. forest; *synonyms* (*n*) timber, jungle, woodland, timberland, (*v*) afforest, **2**. wood; *synonyms* (*n*) forest, woods, tree, lumber, coppice, **3**. timber; *synonyms* (*n*) wood, beam, plank, girder, rafter, **4**. timberland; *synonyms* (*n*) backwoods, quality, timbre, tone, **5**. woodland; *synonyms* (*n*) bush, (*v*) bound, cause, dart, emerge.

skola 1. irrigate; *synonyms* (*n*) water, dilute, dip, drink, (*adj*) dabble, **2**. flush; *synonyms* (*n*) bloom, (*v*) blush, glow, (*adj*) flat, affluent.

skólastjóri principal; *synonyms* (*adj*) master, cardinal, capital, (*n*) chief, head; *antonym* (*adj*) minor.

skóli school; *synonyms* (*n*) academy, class, (*v*) educate, instruct, train.

skollahrákar jellyfish; *synonyms* (*n*) medusan, coward, hydromedusae, (*adj*) apprehensive, frightened.

skollaskyrpur jellyfish; *synonyms* (*n*) medusan, coward, hydromedusae, (*adj*) apprehensive, frightened.

skolp sewage; *synonyms* (*n*) sewerage, sullage, dirt, filth, cloaca.

skólp sewage; *synonyms* (*n*) sewerage, sullage, dirt, filth, cloaca.

skólpræsi sewer; *synonyms* (*n*) cloaca, channel, ditch, gully, (*adj*) drain.

skolun 1. purge; *synonyms* (*v*) cleanse, clean, expurgate, eradicate, clear; *antonym* (*v*) binge, **2.** circulation; *synonyms* (*n*) dissemination, diffusion, distribution, currency, delivery, **3.** irrigation; *synonyms* (*v*) affusion, humectation, immersion, infiltration, spargefaction.

skölun scaling; *synonyms* (*n*) ascent, flaking, furring, grading, scale.

skömmtun dosage; *synonyms* (*n*) dose, amount, quantity, capsule, drug.

skömmtunarmiði coupon; *synonyms* (*n*) voucher, certificate, order, ticket, debenture.

skönnun scanning; *synonym* (*n*) sweep.

skopparakringla top; *synonyms* (*n*) crown, peak, acme, apex, (*v*) best; *antonyms* (*adj*) worst, (*n*) bottom, base, nadir.

skopstæling spoof; *synonyms* (*n*) hoax, mockery, (*v*) parody, burlesque, joke.

sköpulagsfræði morphology; *synonyms* (*n*) accidence, anatomy, geomorphology, taxonomy, botany.

sköpun genesis; *synonyms* (*n*) beginning, ancestry, birth, origin, descent; *antonym* (*n*) end.

sköpunargáfa creativity; *synonyms* (*n*) creativeness, invention, originality, cleverness, imagination; *antonym* (*n*) literalism.

skor 1. cohort; *synonyms* (*n*) group, associate, colleague, friend, follower, **2.** department; *synonyms* (*n*) bureau, compartment, area, agency, class.

skora 1. score; *synonyms* (*n*) mark, bill, count, scratch, (*v*) notch, **2.** notch; *synonyms* (*n*) cut, gap, (*v*) dent, hack, indent, **3.** flute; *synonyms* (*n*) wineglass, fluting, furrow, groove, (*v*) channel.

skorða 1. constraint; *synonyms* (*n*) coercion, compulsion, force, restraint, confinement; *antonym* (*n*) incentive, **2.** fix; *synonyms* (*v*) establish, assign, determine, (*n*) bind, (*adj*) ascertain; *antonyms* (*v*) break, unfasten.

skorðaður fast; *synonyms* (*adj*) dissolute, firm, agile, debauched, (*adv*) soon; *antonyms* (*adj*) sluggish, (*adv*) slow, slowly, (*v*) gorge, (*n*) binge.

skörðóttur serrated; *synonyms* (*adj*) jagged, notched, serrate, toothed, aduncous; *antonym* (*adj*) smooth.

skorðun 1. constraint; *synonyms* (*n*) coercion, compulsion, force, restraint, confinement; *antonym* (*n*) incentive, **2.** fixation; *synonyms* (*n*) obsession, fetish, fixing, mania, complex.

skorður dunnage; *synonym* (*n*) fardage.

skordýrafræði entomology; *synonyms* (*n*) insectology, anthropology, mastology, oryctology, paleontology.

skorinn 1. truncated; *synonyms* (*adj*) abbreviated, shortened, cut, docked, garbled, **2.** slot; *synonyms* (*n*) groove, place, notch, gap, (*v*) slit.

skorpa crust; *synonyms* (*n*) bark, cheekiness, covering, gall, (*v*) coat.

skorpukenndur crustaceous; *synonym* (*adj*) crustacean.

skorpumyndun incrustation; *synonyms* (*n*) crust, encrustation, scale, obduction, superposition.

skorsteinn chimney; *synonyms* (*n*) stack, flue, shaft, smokestack, vent.

skortítur hemiptera; *synonyms* (*n*) bedbugs, hemipteroid.

skortur 1. shortage; *synonyms* (*n*) dearth, defect, deficiency, lack, paucity; *antonyms* (*n*) abundance, excess, overabundance, surplus, affluence, **2.** deficiency; *synonyms* (*n*) want, absence, deficit, failing, (*adj*) blemish; *antonym* (*n*) sufficiency, **3.** dearth; *synonyms* (*n*) famine, shortage, scarcity, inadequacy, insufficiency.

skoruhjól 1. sheave; *synonyms* (*n*) sheaf, bundle, roller, bullwheel, **2.** pulley; *synonyms* (*n*) block, crane, windlass, winch, wheel.

skörun 1. confusion; *synonyms* (*n*) bewilderment, chaos, commotion, disarray, agitation; *antonyms* (*n*) clarity, order, **2.** intersect; *synonyms* (*v*) cross, cut, divide, meet, bisect, **3.** intersection; *synonyms* (*n*) crossroads, crossing, crossroad, intersect, crossway, **4.** overlapping; *synonyms* (*n*) lapping, overlap, imbrication, lap, duplication, **5.** overlap; *synonyms* (*n*) intersection, overlay, (*v*) fold, concur, match.

skörungur rake; *synonyms* (*n*) profligate, (*v*) tilt, hoe, harrow, (*adj*) comb.

skorur fluting; *synonyms* (*n*) flute, groove, chamfer, furrow, channel.

skot 1. recess; *synonyms* (*n*) corner, break, holiday, intermission, niche, **2.** projectile; *synonyms* (*n*) missile, bullet, shot, bolt, quoit.

skotlengd range; *synonyms* (*v*) line, arrange, order, rank, roam.

skotmál 1. range; *synonyms* (*v*) line, arrange, order, rank, roam, **2.** reach; *synonyms* (*v*) range, overtake, obtain, achieve, (*n*) fetch.

skotmark target; *synonyms* (*n*) butt, goal, (*v*) aim, point, purpose.

skotra pan; *synonyms* (*n*) dish, knock, rap, panning, (*v*) slam.

skotrun panning; *synonyms* (*n*) pan, criticism.

skotskífa target; *synonyms* (*n*) butt, goal, (*v*) aim, point, purpose.

skott 1. tail; *synonyms* (*n*) rear, shadow, (*v*) follow, pursue, track; *antonyms* (*v*) head, front, **2.** trunk; *synonyms* (*n*) stem, boot, torso, body, bole, **3.** boot; *synonyms* (*n*) kick, trunk, bang, charge, gain.

sköttun taxation; *synonyms* (*n*) tax, revenue, assessment, gross, receipts.

skötuselur angler; *synonyms* (*n*) goosefish, monkfish, allmouth, angelfish, anglerfish.

skozur scotch; *synonyms* (*v*) bilk, chock, cross, foil, frustrate.

skrá 1. directory; *synonyms* (*n*) catalogue, file, list, record, handbook, **2.** list; *synonyms* (*n*) catalog, inclination, index, schedule, (*v*) lean, **3.** record; *synonyms* (*n*) register, account, book, disk, (*v*) chronicle, **4.** register; *synonyms* (*n*) inventory, note, (*v*) enroll, enter, indicate, **5.** schedule; *synonyms* (*n*) agenda, program, calendar, table, roll.

skrækskaði jay; *synonyms* (*n*) chough, crow, (*v*) magpie, parrot, poll.

skrækur 1. snappy; *synonyms* (*adj*) racy, sharp, animated, brisk, crisp, **2.** sharp; *synonyms* (*adj*) acute, bitter, intelligent, acid, (*n*) keen; *antonyms* (*adj*) blunt, dull, mild, gentle, rounded, **3.** shrill; *synonyms* (*adj*) piercing, penetrating, (*v*) high, screech, shriek; *antonyms* (*adj*) soft, low, **4.** strident; *synonyms* (*adj*) raucous, loud, blatant, harsh, noisy; *antonym* (*adj*) quiet, **5.** acrimonious; *synonyms* (*adj*) sour, biting, caustic, (*v*) acrid, pungent.

skrælnaður arid; *synonyms* (*adj*) dry, dull, barren, boring, (*v*) monotonous; *antonyms* (*adj*) wet, verdant.

skrall ratchet; *synonyms* (*n*) rachet, ratch, wheel, (*adj*) cog, spoke.

skráma abrasion; *synonyms* (*n*) attrition, excoriation, erosion, friction, (*v*) detrition; *antonym* (*n*) smoothness.

skráning 1. recognition; *synonyms* (*n*) acknowledgment, appreciation, identification, perception, cognizance, **2.** recording; *synonyms* (*n*) record, album, transcription, scan, (*adj*) registering, **3.** recruitment; *synonyms* (*n*) employment, enrollment, enlisting, mobilization, **4.** record; *synonyms* (*n*) register, list, account, (*v*) chronicle, file, **5.** registration; *synonyms* (*n*) enrolment, entering, entry, registry, adjustment.

skráningarform mask; *synonyms* (*n*) cover, conceal, (*v*) cloak, disguise, hide; *antonym* (*v*) disclose.

skráningarskírteini registration; *synonyms* (*n*) enrollment, registering, enrolment, entering, entry.

skráningartæki recorder; *synonyms* (*n*) clerk, registrar, register, reporter, enroll.

skrapa scrape; *synonyms* (*v*) scratch, graze, rub, pare, rake.

skrásetja 1. record; *synonyms* (*n*) register, list, account, (*v*) chronicle, file, **2.** register; *synonyms* (*n*) record, inventory, note, catalogue, (*v*) enroll, **3.** file; *synonyms* (*n*) archive, document, procession, rank, (*v*) order.

skrásetjari registrar; *synonyms* (*n*) recorder, clerk, register, enroll, registrary.

skrásetning 1. registry; *synonyms* (*n*) register, record, schedule, (*v*) registration, enrollment, **2.** registration; *synonyms* (*n*) registering, enrolment, entering, entry, registry.

skraut decoration; *synonyms* (*n*) adornment, award, garnish, medal, ornament.

skrauthvörf euphemism; *synonyms* (*n*) circumlocution, delicacy, (*adj*) euphemistic, euphonious, euphuism.

skrautlisti moulding; *synonyms* (*n*) molding, modeling, mold, mould, cast.

skref 1. web; *synonyms* (*n*) mesh, network, tissue, lattice, (*v*) net, **2.** step; *synonyms* (*n*) degree, measure, stage, walk, (*v*) pace, **3.** move; *synonyms* (*v*) act, affect, carry, excite, go; *antonym* (*v*) stay.

skreið stockfish; *synonym* (*n*) titling.

skreppa 1. ratchet; *synonyms* (*n*) rachet, ratch, wheel, (*adj*) cog, spoke, **2.** catch; *synonyms* (*v*) arrest, capture, hook, apprehend, get; *antonym* (*v*) release, **3.** pawl; *synonyms* (*n*) detent, ratchet, click, dog, andiron.

skreyta trim; *synonyms* (*adj*) tidy, (*v*) cut, dress, clip, garnish; *antonym* (*adj*) fat.

skreyting decoration; *synonyms* (*n*) adornment, award, garnish, medal, ornament.

skrið 1. skid; *synonyms* (*n*) shoe, sideslip, (*v*) slip, slide, glide, **2.** drift; *synonyms* (*n*) stream, current, course, (*v*) aim, blow, **3.** drag; *synonyms* (*v*) attract, haul, draw, puff, (*n*) pull; *antonym* (*v*) push, **4.** creep; *synonyms* (*v*) crawl, grovel, sneak, steal, (*n*) crawling.

skriða 1. talus; *synonyms* (*n*) astragalus, slope, scree, anklebone, astragal, **2.** slide; *synonyms* (*n*) glide, chute, (*v*) drop, slip, fall, **3.** cascade; *synonyms* (*n*) waterfall, torrent, deluge, (*v*) gush, stream; *antonyms* (*v*) trickle, dribble, **4.** avalanche; *synonyms* (*n*) landslide, cascade, plenty, barrage, (*v*) debacle, **5.** landslide; *synonyms* (*n*) landslip, avalanche, descent, flood, rush.

skríða creep; *synonyms* (v) crawl, grovel, sneak, steal, (n) crawling.

skriðbelti caterpillar; *synonyms* (n) cat, larva, worm, maggot, cocoon.

skriðdreki tank; *synonyms* (n) cistern, reservoir, container, cooler, belly.

skriðhljóð glide; *synonyms* (v) slide, coast, float, flow, fly; *antonym* (v) struggle.

skriðþungi 1. momentum; *synonyms* (n) impetus, impulse, force, drive, impulsion; *antonym* (n) inertia, **2.** impetus; *synonyms* (n) power, goad, incentive, momentum, (v) energy.

skriðufall 1. slide; *synonyms* (n) glide, chute, (v) drop, slip, fall, **2.** landslide; *synonyms* (n) landslip, avalanche, descent, flood, (v) debacle.

skriðuhlaup 1. slide; *synonyms* (n) glide, chute, (v) drop, slip, fall, **2.** landslide; *synonyms* (n) landslip, avalanche, descent, flood, (v) debacle.

skriður impetus; *synonyms* (n) impulse, drive, force, impulsion, power.

skrifa write; *synonyms* (v) compose, indite, pen, correspond, compile.

skrifari 1. recorder; *synonyms* (n) clerk, registrar, register, reporter, enroll, **2.** polygraph.

skrifborð 1. desktop; *synonyms* (n) background, backcloth, backdrop, ground, scope, **2.** bureau; *synonyms* (n) agency, office, authority, chest, department.

skriffinnska bureaucracy; *synonyms* (n) bureaucratism, apparatus, cabinet, fascism, formalities.

skrifræði bureaucracy; *synonyms* (n) bureaucratism, apparatus, cabinet, fascism, formalities.

skrifstofa 1. secretariat; *synonyms* (n) bureau, department, secretariate, cutchery, **2.** department; *synonyms* (n) compartment, area, agency, class, faculty, **3.** division; *synonyms* (n) disagreement, allotment, branch, break, (adj) constituent; *antonyms* (n) closeness, convergence, estimation, unification, **4.** office; *synonyms* (n) charge, duty, function, position, commission.

Skrifstofan bureau; *synonyms* (n) agency, office, authority, chest, department.

skrifstofumaður clerk; *synonyms* (n) writer, transcriber, accountant, (v) amanuensis, secretary.

skrifstofustjóri director; *synonyms* (n) commander, manager, administrator, boss, (v) conductor.

skrifstofustúlka clerk; *synonyms* (n) writer, transcriber, accountant, (v) amanuensis, secretary.

skrifstofuveldi bureaucracy; *synonyms* (n) bureaucratism, apparatus, cabinet, fascism, formalities.

skrifstol agraphia; *synonyms* (n) anorthography, logographia.

skrik 1. skid; *synonyms* (n) shoe, sideslip, (v) slip, slide, glide, **2.** drift; *synonyms* (n) stream, current, course, (v) aim, blow.

skrika slip; *synonyms* (n) lapse, fault, (v) fall, slide, (adj) blunder; *antonym* (v) improve.

skrikun slip; *synonyms* (n) lapse, fault, (v) fall, slide, (adj) blunder; *antonym* (v) improve.

skríll rabble; *synonyms* (n) mob, crowd, masses, trash, herd.

skrín box; *synonyms* (n) basket, cage, chest, (v) cuff, buffet; *antonym* (v) unbox.

skrokklanga ling; *synonyms* (n) heather, burbot, broom, cusk, eelpout.

skrokkur hull; *synonyms* (n) crust, shell, hulk, husk, (v) skin.

skrökva 1. fib; *synonyms* (n) lie, fable, falsehood, story, tale; *antonym* (n) truth, **2.** lie; *synonyms* (v) consist, (n) fabrication, falsity, fib, fiction; *antonym* (v) stand.

skrölt 1. rattle; *synonyms* (n) roll, jangle, jingle, click, (v) clatter, **2.** chatter; *synonyms* (n) prattle, (v) babble, chat, gossip, jabber.

skrölta 1. rattle; *synonyms* (n) roll, jangle, jingle, click, (v) clatter, **2.** snap; *synonyms* (v) crack, bite, break, fracture, (n) photograph, **3.** click; *synonyms* (n) catch, chink, (v) clack, snap, chatter, **4.** clap; *synonyms* (v) blast, acclaim, (n) bang, boom, applause; *antonym* (v) boo, **5.** chatter; *synonyms* (n) prattle, (v) babble, chat, gossip, jabber.

skröltormur rattlesnake; *synonyms* (n) rattler, serpent, asp, cobra.

skróp absenteeism; *synonyms* (n) absence, nonresidence, defection, desertion, malingering.

skruðningur rumble; *synonyms* (n) boom, roll, roar, (v) murmur, growl.

skrúfa 1. screw; *synonyms* (n) fuck, (v) cheat, fasten, (adj) bolt, nail, **2.** propeller; *synonyms* (n) screw, fan, turbine, extortioner, niggard.

skrúfgangur thread; *synonyms* (n) string, line, yarn, (v) file, range.

skrúfhólkur bushing; *synonyms* (n) bush, mount, filling.

skrúfjárn screwdriver; *synonym* (n) turnscrew.

skrúflína helix; *synonyms* (n) coil, spiral, whorl, curl, volute.

skrúflykill 1. spanner; *synonyms* (n) wrench, pull, twist, **2.** wrench; *synonyms* (n) spanner, turn, (v) sprain, jerk, strain.

skrúfmál micrometer; *synonyms* (n) micron, megameter, megametre, (v) nanometer, centimeter.

skrúfstykki vice; *synonyms* (adj) defect, fault, imperfection, (n) blemish, corruption; *antonym* (n) asset.

skrúfþvinga cramp; *synonyms* (*n*) convulsion, spasm, (*v*) confine, constrict, restrict.

skrúfugangur thread; *synonyms* (*n*) string, line, yarn, (*v*) file, range.

skrúfugraftarverkfæri chaser; *synonyms* (*n*) carver, pursuer, figuriste, modeler, statuary.

skrúfuhringur nozzle; *synonyms* (*n*) nose, beak, hooter, jet, muzzle.

skrúfukraftur wrench; *synonyms* (*n*) spanner, (*v*) sprain, pull, jerk, strain.

skrúfulengd reach; *synonyms* (*v*) range, overtake, obtain, achieve, (*n*) fetch.

skrúfulína helix; *synonyms* (*n*) coil, spiral, whorl, curl, volute.

skrúfumótun chase; *synonyms* (*n*) game, (*v*) hunt, pursue, expel, follow.

skrúfuröst slipstream; *synonyms* (*n*) airstream, backwash, race, aftermath, laundry.

skrúfuskeri chaser; *synonyms* (*n*) carver, pursuer, figuriste, modeler, statuary.

skrugga thunder; *synonyms* (*n*) boom, bang, roll, (*v*) roar, (*adj*) peal.

skruma 1. boast; *synonyms* (*v*) bluster, vaunt, blow, brag, crow, **2**. brag; *synonyms* (*v*) boast, pride, gasconade, (*n*) boasting, bounce.

skrun 1. scroll; *synonyms* (*n*) coil, roll, curl, curlicue, (*v*) list, **2**. scrolling.

skruna scroll; *synonyms* (*n*) coil, roll, curl, curlicue, (*v*) list.

skrunskoðun browsing; *synonyms* (*n*) browse, bruting, navigating.

skrýfing transposition; *synonyms* (*n*) exchange, permutation, replacement, reversal, substitution.

skrykkur saltation; *synonyms* (*n*) jump, bound, leap, spring, hop.

skrýtinn 1. strange; *synonyms* (*adj*) extraneous, foreign, peculiar, abnormal, curious; *antonyms* (*adj*) normal, ordinary, familiar, typical, **2**. weird; *synonyms* (*adj*) strange, supernatural, uncanny, unearthly, bizarre; *antonym* (*adj*) real, **3**. eccentric; *synonyms* (*adj*) odd, wacky, anomalous, crazy, (*n*) character; *antonym* (*n*) conformist, **4**. curious; *synonyms* (*adj*) funny, interested, unusual, extraordinary, inquiring; *antonym* (*adj*) incurious, **5**. odd; *synonyms* (*adj*) grotesque, exceptional, droll, eccentric, singular; *antonym* (*adj*) even.

skúfa 1. push; *synonyms* (*n*) press, thrust, (*v*) drive, impel, crowd; *antonyms* (*v*) pull, drag, haul, **2**. shear; *synonyms* (*v*) clip, cut, fleece, lop, pare.

skúfast shear; *synonyms* (*v*) clip, cut, fleece, lop, parc.

skúffa 1. drawer; *synonyms* (*n*) draftsman, draughtsman, till, commode, engraver, **2**. bin; *synonyms* (*n*) bunker, binful, box, case, container.

skúfun push; *synonyms* (*n*) press, thrust, (*v*) drive, impel, crowd; *antonyms* (*v*) pull, drag, haul.

skúfur 1. puff; *synonyms* (*n*) gasp, whiff, (*v*) pant, blow, boast, **2**. radiation; *synonyms* (*n*) emanation, emission, irradiation, (*v*) radioactivity, (*adj*) radiance, **3**. cirrus; *synonyms* (*n*) woolpack, cirrlus, stratus, cumulus, **4**. coelacanth.

skuggafölvi etiolation; *synonyms* (*adj*) albification, (*n*) feebleness.

skuggamyndun shading; *synonyms* (*n*) blending, shadowing, eclipse, nuance, adumbration.

skuggaskil terminator; *synonyms* (*n*) eradicator, exterminator.

skuggavöxtur etiolation; *synonyms* (*adj*) albification, (*n*) feebleness.

skuggi 1. shade; *synonyms* (*n*) screen, tinge, color, ghost, (*v*) darken; *antonyms* (*n*) light, brightness, **2**. shadow; *synonyms* (*n*) shade, tail, trace, darkness, (*v*) eclipse, **3**. contrast; *synonyms* (*n*) contrariety, antithesis, comparison, distinction, (*v*) differ; *antonym* (*n*) similarity.

skuggsæi symmetry; *synonyms* (*n*) balance, proportion, order, correspondence, equilibrium; *antonyms* (*n*) asymmetry, disproportion, irregularity.

skuggsær symmetrical; *synonyms* (*adj*) harmonious, symmetric, balanced, shapely, methodical; *antonyms* (*adj*) asymmetrical, irregular.

skuld 1. debt; *synonyms* (*n*) debit, score, due, liability, obligation, **2**. liability; *synonyms* (*n*) debt, duty, trust, blame, commitment; *antonym* (*n*) asset, **3**. obligation; *synonyms* (*n*) bond, charge, burden, necessity, need; *antonym* (*n*) option.

skuldabréf 1. debenture; *synonyms* (*n*) bond, coupon, hypothecation, pawn, pignoration, **2**. bond; *synonyms* (*n*) association, tie, alliance, deed, (*v*) bind.

skuldalúkning settlement; *synonyms* (*n*) decision, accommodation, colony, hamlet, payment.

skuldari debtor; *synonyms* (*n*) bankrupt, debitor, levanter, stag, welsher.

skuldbinding 1. commitment; *synonyms* (*n*) dedication, charge, allegiance, appointment, committal, **2**. obligation; *synonyms* (*n*) debt, bond, commitment, duty, liability; *antonym* (*n*) option.

skuldbindingar liabilities; *synonyms* (*n*) acquit, assets, expenditure, equities.

skuldir liabilities; *synonyms* (*n*) acquit, assets, expenditure, equities.

skuldsetning 1. gearing; *synonyms* (*n*) gear, affairs, behavior, caravan, clothing, **2**. leverage; *synonyms* (*n*) lever, advantage, influence, leveraging, purchase.

skuldunautur debtor; *synonyms* (*n*) bankrupt, debitor, levanter, stag, welsher.

skulpti works; *synonyms* (*n*) factory, plant, workings, mill, manufactory.

skúm arachnoid; *synonyms* (*n*) arachnid, (*adj*) arachnidian, arachnoidal, araneose, spiderlike.

skúmhærður arachnoid; *synonyms* (*n*) arachnid, (*adj*) arachnidian, arachnoidal, araneose, spiderlike.

skúr 1. shed; *synonyms* (*v*) cast, discard, drop, moult, (*n*) hut, **2.** shower; *synonyms* (*n*) rain, (*v*) pour, bathe, hail, sprinkle, **3.** penthouse; *synonyms* (*n*) apartment, canopy, pentice, (*adj*) leaning, overhanging.

skúraflákar cumulonimbus; *synonym* (*n*) thundercloud.

skúraský cumulonimbus; *synonym* (*n*) thundercloud.

skurðaðgerð operation; *synonyms* (*n*) execution, movement, act, agency, effect.

skurðarlínur bias; *synonyms* (*n*) penchant, drift, (*v*) prejudice, bent, (*adj*) partiality; *antonyms* (*n*) impartiality, neutrality, fairness.

skurðarpunktur intersection; *synonyms* (*n*) cross, crossroads, crossing, crossroad, intersect.

skurðlæknir surgeon; *synonyms* (*n*) doctor, physician, sawbones, chirurgeon.

skurðlæknisfræði surgery; *synonyms* (*n*) operation, chirurgery, act, functioning, or.

skurðpunktur 1. intercept; *synonyms* (*v*) arrest, block, break, check, waylay, **2.** intersection; *synonyms* (*n*) cross, crossroads, crossing, crossroad, intersect.

skurðsvæði field; *synonyms* (*n*) arena, area, battlefield, domain, ground.

skurður 1. cut; *synonyms* (*v*) carve, chop, clip, (*n*) notch, slice; *antonyms* (*v*) increase, lengthen, (*n*) addition, extension, **2.** pitch; *synonyms* (*n*) degree, dip, (*v*) fling, cast, chuck, **3.** undercut; *synonyms* (*v*) challenge, (*n*) cut, tenderloin, cutting, deletion, **4.** plane; *synonyms* (*n*) airplane, face, (*adj*) level, even, flat, **5.** section; *synonyms* (*n*) division, part, portion, compartment, percentage.

skurn 1. crust; *synonyms* (*n*) bark, cheekiness, covering, gall, (*v*) coat, **2.** cuticle; *synonyms* (*n*) epidermis, shell, carapace, case, casing, **3.** peel; *synonyms* (*n*) skin, hide, (*v*) hull, flake, flay.

skutpallur poop; *synonyms* (*n*) crap, nincompoop, ninny, shit, stern.

skutull harpoon; *synonyms* (*n*) dart, javelin, lance, spear, striker.

skutur stern; *synonyms* (*adj*) harsh, rigid, severe, rigorous, austere; *antonym* (*adj*) cordial.

skvass 1. squash; *synonyms* (*v*) crush, mash, quell, compress, press, **2.** courgette; *synonym* (*n*) zucchini.

ský cloud; *synonyms* (*n*) mist, (*v*) fog, becloud, obscure, befog; *antonym* (*v*) sharpen.

skygging 1. shade; *synonyms* (*n*) screen, tinge, color, ghost, (*v*) darken; *antonyms* (*n*) light, brightness, **2.** shading; *synonyms* (*n*) blending, shadowing, eclipse, nuance, adumbration, **3.** interposition; *synonyms* (*n*) interference, interpolation, intervention, (*adj*) intercession, mediation, **4.** masking; *synonyms* (*n*) cover, covering, concealment, mask, screening.

skyggja shadow; *synonyms* (*n*) shade, ghost, tail, trace, (*v*) eclipse.

skyggna slide; *synonyms* (*n*) glide, chute, (*v*) drop, slip, fall.

skyggni visibility; *synonyms* (*n*) visibleness, conspicuousness, apparition, (*v*) sight, view.

skyggnir scanner; *synonym* (*n*) analyzer.

skýjablika cirrostratus; *synonym* (*n*) cumulostratus.

skýjabólstur cumulus; *synonyms* (*n*) heap, mound, pile, stratus, woolpack.

skýjaður cloudy; *synonyms* (*adj*) dull, gloomy, murky, nebulous, opaque; *antonyms* (*adj*) clear, bright, cloudless, sunny.

skýjahetta pileus; *synonyms* (*n*) cap, capital, ceiling, chapiter, crownwork.

skýjaþekjuhæð ceiling; *synonyms* (*n*) cap, limit, maximum, limitation, roof; *antonym* (*n*) ground.

skýla deflector; *synonyms* (*n*) shield, cowl.

skylda 1. commitment; *synonyms* (*n*) dedication, charge, allegiance, appointment, committal, **2.** duty; *synonyms* (*n*) business, function, commitment, assignment, chore, **3.** obligation; *synonyms* (*n*) debt, bond, duty, liability, burden; *antonym* (*n*) option.

skyldleiki 1. relation; *synonyms* (*n*) connection, account, narration, recital, affinity, **2.** consanguinity; *synonyms* (*n*) blood, cognation, kindred, relation, kin.

skyldraæxlun 1. inbreeding; *synonyms* (*n*) consanguinity, selfing, **2.** endogamy; *synonyms* (*n*) inmarriage, intermarriage, exogamy.

skyldubundinn compulsory; *synonyms* (*adj*) obligatory, required, binding, involuntary, mandatory; *antonyms* (*adj*) optional, voluntary.

skyldugur 1. compulsory; *synonyms* (*adj*) obligatory, required, binding, involuntary, mandatory; *antonyms* (*adj*) optional, voluntary, **2.** liable; *synonyms* (*adj*) amenable, accountable, answerable, apt, disposed; *antonym* (*adj*) exempt, **3.** mandatory; *synonyms* (*adj*) compulsory, necessary, imperative, requisite, (*n*) mandatary.

skylduögun conditioning; *synonyms* (*n*) training, chilling, cooking, drill, equalizing.

skyldur 1. cognate; *synonyms* (*adj*) akin, alike, allied, related, like, **2.** obligatory; *synonyms* (*adj*) necessary, compulsory, imperative, binding, inevitable; *antonyms* (*adj*) optional, voluntary.

skýli 1. shed; *synonyms* (*v*) cast, discard, drop, moult, (*n*) hut, **2.** refuge; *synonyms* (*n*) protection, asylum, sanctuary, resort, (*v*) recourse, **3.** penthouse; *synonyms* (*n*) apartment, canopy, pentice, (*adj*) leaning, overhanging.

skýling screening; *synonyms* (*n*) screen, sieving, concealment, cover, covering.

skylmingasverð rapier; *synonyms* (*n*) sword, blade, brand, foil, glaive.

skyn sense; *synonyms* (*n*) intelligence, perception, meaning, (*v*) feel, intellect; *antonyms* (*n*) garbage, ludicrousness, nonsense, stupidity, foolishness.

skyndi instant; *synonyms* (*adj*) immediate, present, exigent, (*n*) moment, flash; *antonyms* (*adj*) gradual, long-term.

skyndiæði amok; *synonyms* (*adv*) amuck, murderously, (*adj*) berserk, demoniac, demoniacal.

skyndibreyting transient; *synonyms* (*adj*) brief, fleeting, passing, temporary, transitory; *antonyms* (*adj*) permanent, enduring.

skyndihvöt impulse; *synonyms* (*n*) impetus, pulse, urge, drive, force.

skyndilega 1. suddenly; *synonyms* (*adv*) abruptly, short, sudden, presto, dead; *antonyms* (*adv*) gradually, increasingly, predictably, slowly, **2.** rudely; *synonyms* (*adv*) discourteously, coarsely, crudely, impolitely, roughly; *antonyms* (*adv*) politely, graciously, respectfully, **3.** shortly; *synonyms* (*adv*) presently, briefly, soon, immediately, concisely, **4.** sharply; *synonyms* (*adv*) sharp, severely, piercingly, acutely, (*adj*) harshly; *antonyms* (*adv*) gently, stupidly, kindly, **5.** abruptly; *synonyms* (*adv*) suddenly, precipitously, bluntly, brusquely, curtly; *antonym* (*adv*) civilly.

skyndilegur 1. sharp; *synonyms* (*adj*) acute, bitter, intelligent, acid, (*n*) keen; *antonyms* (*adj*) blunt, dull, mild, gentle, rounded, **2.** sudden; *synonyms* (*adj*) abrupt, hasty, precipitous, quick, rash; *antonyms* (*adj*) gradual, considered, **3.** rude; *synonyms* (*adj*) gross, rough, impudent, coarse, bold; *antonyms* (*adj*) polite, respectful, chivalrous, courteous, refined, **4.** sheer; *synonyms* (*adj*) absolute, pure, mere, (*n*) complete, perfect; *antonym* (*adj*) thick, **5.** short; *synonyms* (*adj*) brief, concise, scarce, brusque, close; *antonyms* (*adj*) long, tall, high, lengthy.

skyndiminni cache; *synonyms* (*n*) depository, reserve, (*v*) hoard, store, bury.

skyndivista cache; *synonyms* (*n*) depository, reserve, (*v*) hoard, store, bury.

skynfæri sensorium; *synonym* (*n*) sensory.

skynform modality; *synonyms* (*n*) mode, mood, manner, schesis, fashion.

skynhrif sensation; *synonyms* (*n*) impression, emotion, feel, (*v*) feeling, affection; *antonym* (*n*) numbness.

skynja 1. sense; *synonyms* (*n*) intelligence, perception, meaning, (*v*) feel, intellect; *antonyms* (*n*) garbage, ludicrousness, nonsense, stupidity, foolishness, **2.** distinguish; *synonyms* (*v*) discern, discriminate, describe, know, perceive; *antonym* (*v*) confuse, **3.** detect; *synonyms* (*v*) catch, discover, find, ascertain, notice.

skynjanlegur sensible; *synonyms* (*adj*) reasonable, aware, judicious, perceptible, prudent; *antonyms* (*adj*) foolish, absurd, crazy, idiotic, imprudent.

skynjari 1. transmitter; *synonyms* (*n*) sender, aerial, mast, purveyor, source, **2.** sensor; *synonyms* (*n*) detector, antenna, demodulator, tracer, (*adj*) sensory, **3.** detector; *synonyms* (*n*) sensor, detecter, selector, **4.** analyser; *synonyms* (*n*) analyzer, analyse.

skynjun 1. sensation; *synonyms* (*n*) impression, emotion, feel, (*v*) feeling, affection; *antonym* (*n*) numbness, **2.** sense; *synonyms* (*n*) intelligence, perception, meaning, (*v*) intellect, mind; *antonyms* (*n*) garbage, ludicrousness, nonsense, stupidity, foolishness, **3.** sensory; *synonyms* (*adj*) sensorial, sensational, sensitive, sensuous, (*n*) sensorium, **4.** detection; *synonyms* (*n*) discovery, demodulation, detecting, uncovering, unearthing, **5.** perception; *synonyms* (*n*) apprehension, conception, idea, notion, discernment.

skynnæmur perceptive; *synonyms* (*adj*) discerning, alert, acute, astute, keen; *antonym* (*adj*) dull.

skynsamlegur rational; *synonyms* (*adj*) intellectual, reasonable, intelligent, judicious, logical; *antonyms* (*adj*) irrational, illogical, anxious.

skynsamur 1. rational; *synonyms* (*adj*) intellectual, reasonable, intelligent, judicious, logical; *antonyms* (*adj*) irrational, illogical, anxious, **2.** reasonable; *synonyms* (*adj*) just, moderate, rational, fair, legitimate; *antonyms* (*adj*) unreasonable, expensive, unfair, unsatisfactory, inadequate.

skynsemi 1. precaution; *synonyms* (*n*) forethought, foresight, care, discretion, prevention, **2.** prudence; *synonyms* (*n*) caution, economy, frugality, circumspection, deliberation; *antonyms* (*n*) foolishness, generosity, imprudence, profligacy, **3.** reason; *synonyms* (*n*) mind, account, intellect, occasion, (*v*) cause, **4.** foresight; *synonyms* (*n*) anticipation, prevision, forecast, prospicience, (v) expectation.

skynsemishyggja rationalism; *synonyms* (n) freethinking, philosophy, classicism, (adj) antichristianity, infidelity.

skynsemisstefna rationalism; *synonyms* (n) freethinking, philosophy, classicism, (adj) antichristianity, infidelity.

skynsvipta desensitize; *synonyms* (v) blunt, desensitise, numb, deaden, drug.

skyntak percept; *synonyms* (n) perception, sensing.

skyntúlkun perception; *synonyms* (n) apprehension, conception, idea, notion, discernment.

skynvilla 1. illusion; *synonyms* (n) delusion, hallucination, fantasy, apparition, deception; *antonym* (n) reality, 2. hallucination; *synonyms* (n) illusion, dream, vision, phantom, aberration.

skýr 1. lucid; *synonyms* (adj) clear, intelligible, transparent, coherent, limpid; *antonyms* (adj) muddled, opaque, unintelligible, 2. explicit; *synonyms* (adj) distinct, unmistakable, broad, definite, direct; *antonyms* (adj) vague, tacit, understood, unspoken, implicit, 3. straightforward; *synonyms* (adj) straight, open, square, candid, honest; *antonyms* (adj) complicated, difficult, complex, deceitful, tricky, 4. plain; *synonyms* (adj) ordinary, comprehensible, apparent, downright, (n) flat; *antonyms* (adj) elaborate, fancy, unclear, mottled, multicolored, 5. distinct; *synonyms* (adj) articulate, different, discrete, distinctive, palpable; *antonyms* (adj) indistinct, similar, inaudible, shapeless.

skyrbjúgur 1. scorbutus; *synonym* (n) scurvy, 2. scurvy; *synonyms* (adj) contemptible, miserable, paltry, abject, (v) base.

skýrgreining definition; *synonyms* (n) description, account, explanation, interpretation, limitation; *antonym* (n) bagginess.

skýring 1. caption; *synonyms* (n) legend, title, subtitle, dedication, (v) capture, 2. account; *synonyms* (n) bill, narrative, reckoning, regard, (v) report, 3. clarification; *synonyms* (n) illustration, clearing, elucidation, illumination, fining, 4. note; *synonyms* (n) comment, mention, remark, (v) notice, mind; *antonym* (v) ignore, 5. exposition; *synonyms* (n) display, exhibition, explanation, show, clarification.

skýringar 1. disclosure; *synonyms* (n) discovery, exposure, revelation, declaration, confession, 2. analyse; *synonyms* (v) analyze, canvass, dissect, examine, study, 3. legend; *synonyms* (n) caption, fable, fiction, tale, account.

skýringarmynd 1. schema; *synonyms* (n) outline, plan, chart, graph, scheme, 2. diagram; *synonyms*

(n) design, sketch, figure, drawing, illustration, 3. figure; *synonyms* (n) form, appearance, character, (v) cast, count.

skýringarteikning diagram; *synonyms* (n) design, chart, sketch, figure, (adj) plan.

skýringartexti legend; *synonyms* (n) caption, fable, fiction, tale, account.

skýrleiki 1. articulation; *synonyms* (n) enunciation, joint, juncture, accent, diction, 2. definition; *synonyms* (n) description, account, explanation, interpretation, limitation; *antonym* (n) bagginess.

skýrsla 1. report; *synonyms* (n) description, gossip, notice, (v) account, describe; *antonym* (n) fact, 2. statement; *synonyms* (n) declaration, affirmation, announcement, communication, instruction; *antonym* (n) denial, 3. announcement; *synonyms* (n) annunciation, advertisement, proclamation, promulgation, pronouncement, 4. communication; *synonyms* (n) commerce, communicating, contact, conversation, discourse, 5. bill; *synonyms* (n) beak, card, invoice, (v) placard, advertise.

skýrslugjöf hearing; *synonyms* (n) audition, earshot, ear, trial, (adj) audience; *antonym* (adj) deaf.

skyrta shirt; *synonym* (n) shirtwaist.

skýstrokkur 1. waterspout; *synonyms* (n) cloudburst, deluge, downpour, soaker, torrent, 2. tornado; *synonyms* (n) hurricane, storm, tempest, gale, cyclone.

skýstrókur tornado; *synonyms* (n) hurricane, storm, tempest, gale, cyclone.

slá 1. beat; *synonyms* (v) batter, flap, (n) pulse, thump, knock; *antonym* (v) lose, 2. hit; *synonyms* (v) strike, (n) bang, smash, touch, chance; *antonyms* (n) failure, flop, 3. strike; *synonyms* (n) assault, clap, (v) beat, hit, impress.

sladdi wolffish; *synonyms* (n) catfish, lancetfish, mudcat.

slæða slide; *synonyms* (n) glide, chute, (v) drop, slip, fall.

slægja 1. gut; *synonyms* (n) belly, abdomen, bowel, (v) eviscerate, pillage, 2. eviscerate; *synonyms* (v) disembowel, draw, gut, debilitate, withdraw.

slæmur 1. bad; *synonyms* (adj) evil, adverse, harmful, immoral, (v) decayed; *antonyms* (adj) fresh, pleasant, well, well-behaved, (n) good, 2. poor; *synonyms* (adj) bad, low, miserable, paltry, (v) meager; *antonyms* (adj) rich, wealthy, excellent, first-rate, privileged, 3. nasty; *synonyms* (adj) dirty, loathsome, disgusting, filthy, foul; *antonyms* (adj) agreeable, kind, nice, charitable, lovely, 4. miserable; *synonyms* (adj) mean, poor, abject, (v) forlorn, wretched; *antonyms* (adj) happy, cheerful, generous, 5. evil; *synonyms* (adj) corrupt, criminal, ill, wicked, (n) damage; *antonyms* (adj) kindhearted, (n) goodness, righteousness.

slævilyf sedative; *synonyms* (adj) ataractic, ataraxic, (n) narcotic, depressant, downer.

slag 1. play; *synonyms* (v) act, pastime, enact, (n) frolic, game; *antonym* (v) work, **2.** stroke; *synonyms* (n) touch, beat, caress, (v) buffet, (adj) blow, **3.** strike; *synonyms* (n) knock, assault, clap, (v) bang, hit, **4.** systole, **5.** pulse; *synonyms* (n) impulse, pulsation, heartbeat, (v) pulsate, throb.

slagæð artery; *synonyms* (n) vein, corridor, road, thoroughfare, aisle.

slagæðlingur arteriole; *synonym* (n) arteriola.

slagbor jumper; *synonyms* (n) sweater, blackguard, bounder, cad, dog.

slaglengd stroke; *synonyms* (n) touch, beat, caress, (v) buffet, (adj) blow.

slagrými displacement; *synonyms* (n) deposition, transfer, movement, shift, motion.

slagsíða 1. tilt; *synonyms* (n) slope, (v) incline, lean, pitch, slant; *antonyms* (v) straighten, surrender, **2.** loll; *synonyms* (v) droop, loaf, sprawl, drop, lounge, **3.** list; *synonyms* (n) catalog, catalogue, file, inclination, index.

slagsmál 1. scuffle; *synonyms* (n) brawl, scrap, (v) tussle, fight, grapple, **2.** struggle; *synonyms* (n) contest, battle, combat, conflict, strain; *antonyms* (v) flourish, glide, **3.** clash; *synonyms* (n) bang, brush, clang, (v) jar, impact; *antonyms* (n) agreement, (v) agree, **4.** combat; *synonyms* (n) encounter, action, fighting, fray, (v) clash, **5.** battle; *synonyms* (n) struggle, war, scuffle, warfare, (v) quarrel.

slaka relax; *synonyms* (v) loose, abate, give, lounge, (n) loosen; *antonyms* (v) tighten, tense.

slakandi relaxant; *synonyms* (n) relaxative, (v) hypnotic, lullaby, sedative, tranquilizer.

slaki 1. slack; *synonyms* (adj) loose, lax, idle, indolent, negligent; *antonyms* (adj) tight, strict, taut, thorough, **2.** sag; *synonyms* (n) decline, dip, (v) droop, flag, (adj) swag; *antonym* (v) rise.

slakna 1. settle; *synonyms* (v) fix, place, clarify, establish, pay, **2.** relax; *synonyms* (v) loose, abate, give, lounge, (n) loosen; *antonyms* (v) tighten, tense, **3.** sag; *synonyms* (n) decline, dip, (v) droop, flag, (adj) swag; *antonym* (v) rise.

slakur 1. hypotonic, **2.** lax; *synonyms* (adj) slack, careless, flaccid, loose, (v) frail; *antonyms* (adj) strict, careful, severe, **3.** limp; *synonyms* (adj) flabby, flexible, (n) hobble, (v) halt, hitch; *antonyms* (adj) taut, firm, (n) energetic, **4.** flaccid; *synonyms* (adj) limp, lax, soft, weak, baggy; *antonym* (adj) stiff.

slanga 1. tube; *synonyms* (n) pipe, conduit, duct, subway, hose, **2.** snake; *synonyms* (n) ophidian,

serpent, (v) meander, wind, twist, **3.** hose; *synonyms* (n) stocking, tights, hosepipe, hosiery, (v) water.

slangur slang; *synonyms* (n) jargon, lingo, cant, argot, vernacular.

slappur flabby; *synonyms* (adj) loose, feeble, flaccid, baggy, drooping; *antonyms* (adj) firm, slim.

slást 1. strive; *synonyms* (v) endeavor, labor, attempt, contend, contest, **2.** struggle; *synonyms* (n) battle, combat, conflict, strain, (v) fight; *antonyms* (v) flourish, glide, **3.** contend; *synonyms* (v) assert, compete, wrestle, argue, (n) allege, **4.** fight; *synonyms* (v) quarrel, feud, (n) dispute, engagement, (adj) brawl; *antonyms* (v) agree, retreat, withdrawal.

sláttarhljóð tap; *synonyms* (n) pat, dab, hit, (v) knock, rap.

sláttarmót die; *synonyms* (v) decease, dead, death, depart, (n) dice.

sláttarónot palpitation; *synonyms* (n) beat, pulse, quiver, (adj) tremor, quivering.

sláttur 1. throb; *synonyms* (v) beat, quiver, ache, pulsate, pulse, **2.** pulsation; *synonyms* (n) pounding, impulse, heartbeat, throb, tremor, **3.** dash; *synonyms* (n) rush, sprint, (v) dart, touch, strike; *antonym* (n) lethargy, **4.** beat; *synonyms* (v) batter, flap, (n) thump, knock, round; *antonym* (v) lose, **5.** flutter; *synonyms* (v) bustle, (v) flicker, flit, flitter, (adj) flurry.

slaufa 1. loop; *synonyms* (n) coil, ring, (v) curve, bend, circle, **2.** line; *synonyms* (n) cord, file, house, breed, course, **3.** jumper; *synonyms* (n) sweater, blackguard, bounder, cad, dog.

sleðabraut link; *synonyms* (n) connection, join, joint, (v) combine, tie; *antonym* (v) separate.

sleði 1. slider; *synonyms* (n) slide, skidder, (adj) slidder, **2.** sledge; *synonyms* (n) sled, maul, sleigh, toboggan, (v) sledgehammer, **3.** carriage; *synonyms* (n) attitude, transport, behavior, conveyance, (v) bearing.

slef salivation; *synonyms* (n) ptyalism, jellyfish, slobber, slabber.

slefun salivation; *synonyms* (n) ptyalism, jellyfish, slobber, slabber.

sleggja maul; *synonyms* (v) mall, mangle, beat, buffet, (adj) bruise.

slegill ventricle; *synonyms* (n) paunch, stomach, venter, heart.

sleif scoop; *synonyms* (n) ladle, spade, (v) draw, dig, excavate.

sleipur smooth; *synonyms* (adj) easy, calm, level, oily, (v) quiet; *antonyms* (adj) rough, uneven, abrasive, coarse, crumpled.

sleita slip; *synonyms* (n) lapse, fault, (v) fall, slide, (adj) blunder; *antonym* (v) improve.

slekja hypotonia; *synonyms* (n) hypotonus, hypotonicity.

slembifundur serendipity; *synonyms* (n) destiny, luck.

slen asthenia; *synonyms* (n) abirritation, (adj) cachexia, cachexy, sprain, strain.

sleppa 1. release; *synonyms* (n) discharge, (v) exempt, free, liberate, (adj) disengage; *antonyms* (n) imprisonment, abduction, (v) capture, confine, imprison, **2**. pass; *synonyms* (v) flow, deliver, give, (adj) go, run; *antonym* (v) fail.

slétta 1. plane; *synonyms* (n) airplane, face, (adj) level, even, flat, **2**. plateau; *synonyms* (n) plain, table, tableland, elevation, stage, **3**. plain; *synonyms* (adj) ordinary, comprehensible, intelligible, apparent, clear; *antonyms* (adj) elaborate, fancy, unclear, mottled, multicolored, **4**. mare; *synonyms* (n) bitch, doe, hen, horse, jennet.

sléttháfur tope; *synonyms* (n) tumulus, grove, (v) booze, drink, (adj) tipple.

slétthverfa 1. windowpane; *synonyms* (n) pane, window, casement, porthole, skylight, **2**. brill.

sléttun 1. smoothing; *synonyms* (adj) smooth, even, sleek, abrasive, bland, **2**. burnishing; *synonyms* (n) bronzing, searing, buffing.

sléttur 1. smooth; *synonyms* (adj) easy, calm, level, oily, (v) quiet; *antonyms* (adj) rough, uneven, abrasive, coarse, crumpled, **2**. plane; *synonyms* (n) airplane, face, (adj) even, flat, horizontal, **3**. plain; *synonyms* (adj) ordinary, comprehensible, intelligible, apparent, clear; *antonyms* (adj) elaborate, fancy, unclear, mottled, multicolored.

slíðrun invagination; *synonyms* (n) intussusception, erythroblast, gametangium, gamete, infolding.

slíður 1. vagina, **2**. sheath; *synonyms* (n) case, envelope, blanket, scabbard, (v) cover.

slíf 1. sleeve; *synonyms* (n) arm, case, liner, cover, cuff, **2**. liner; *synonyms* (n) lining, boat, airliner, craft, ship.

sligandi exhaustive; *synonyms* (adj) complete, comprehensive, detailed, profound, thorough.

slím mucus; *synonym* (adj) goo.

slíma 1. mucosa, **2**. mucus; *synonym* (adj) goo.

slímdýr 1. amoeba; *synonyms* (n) ameba, (adj) spineless, **2**. ameba; *synonym* (n) amoeba.

slímhjúpur capsule; *synonyms* (n) abridgement, lozenge, condensation, pill, (v) encapsulate.

slímkenndur mucoid; *synonym* (adj) mucoidal.

slímlíki mucoid; *synonym* (adj) mucoidal.

slímlosandi expectorant; *synonyms* (n) expectorator, spitter.

slingur ataxia; *synonyms* (n) chaos, disarray, disorder, ataxy, clutter.

slípa 1. polish; *synonyms* (n) finish, gloss, burnish, (v) furbish, glaze, **2**. grind; *synonyms* (v) labor, toil, comminute, crunch, drudge.

slípiduft abrasive; *synonyms* (adj) rough, harsh, caustic, (n) abradant, abrader; *antonym* (adj) smooth.

slípisteinn 1. grindstone; *synonyms* (v) grinder, mill, arrastra, file, grater, **2**. hone; *synonyms* (v) sharpen, perfect, whet, refine, (adj) sharpener.

slippur shipyard; *synonyms* (n) barnyard, cowyard, inclosure, yard.

slípun 1. honing, **2**. grinding; *synonyms* (v) cutting, (adj) grating, (n) attrition, abrasion, friction, **3**. leveling; *synonyms* (n) grading, levelling, demolishing, equalisation, equalization.

sliskja catwalk; *synonyms* (n) walkway, bridge, alley, balcony, boardwalk.

slit 1. shedding; *synonyms* (n) fluffing, peeling, effusion, desquamation, emission; *antonym* (adj) smooth, **2**. wear; *synonyms* (v) dress, endure, (n) clothing, apparel, attire; *antonym* (v) refresh, **3**. attrition; *synonyms* (n) friction, abrasion, contrition, corrosion, detrition, **4**. deterioration; *synonyms* (n) decline, degradation, decay, failure, (adj) degeneracy; *antonyms* (n) improvement, development, growth, **5**. friction; *synonyms* (n) discord, attrition, dispute, rub, disagreement.

slíta tear; *synonyms* (n) split, rupture, (v) break, rip, crack.

slitinn 1. worn; *synonyms* (adj) haggard, shabby, tired, ragged, tattered; *antonyms* (adj) fresh, new, **2**. discrete; *synonyms* (adj) separate, distinct, different, detached, diverse.

slitna wear; *synonyms* (v) dress, endure, (n) clothing, apparel, attire; *antonym* (v) refresh.

slitrótt intermittent; *synonyms* (adj) broken, occasional, sporadic, discontinuous, fitful; *antonyms* (adj) continuous, constant, continual, repeated.

slitróttur 1. spasmodic; *synonyms* (adj) fitful, convulsive, spastic, intermittent, broken, **2**. intermittent; *synonyms* (adj) occasional, sporadic, discontinuous, irregular, periodic; *antonyms* (adj) continuous, constant, continual, repeated.

slitþol wear; *synonyms* (v) dress, endure, (n) clothing, apparel, attire; *antonym* (v) refresh.

slitþolinn durable; *synonyms* (adj) constant, lasting, stable, permanent, enduring; *antonyms* (adj) fragile, weak, flimsy, lightweight.

sliturbergmál break; *synonyms* (v) split, crack, burst, (n) breach, fracture; *antonyms* (v) repair, obey, honor, mend, (n) continuation.

sljóleiki torpor; *synonyms* (n) lethargy, inactivity, lassitude, inertia, apathy.

sljór torpid; *synonyms* (adj) inactive, inert, sluggish, dull, indolent; *antonym* (adj) active.

slóð 1. trail; *synonyms* (n) track, trace, (v) haul, drag, hunt, **2.** trace; *synonyms* (n) line, shadow, spot, clue, dash, **3.** track; *synonyms* (n) course, path, (v) trail, tail, chase, **4.** path; *synonyms* (n) direction, way, highway, orbit, (v) passage.

slóði leader; *synonyms* (n) chief, guide, boss, captain, director; *antonyms* (n) follower, straggler.

slóg offal; *synonyms* (n) garbage, litter, waste, junk, leavings.

slögun beat; *synonyms* (v) batter, flap, (n) pulse, thump, knock; *antonym* (v) lose.

slokknun extinction; *synonyms* (n) destruction, extermination, end, expiration, (v) death; *antonyms* (n) survival, preservation.

slökkva 1. quench; *synonyms* (v) extinguish, allay, appease, quash, destroy, **2.** extinguish; *synonyms* (v) exterminate, quench, annihilate, douse, eradicate; *antonyms* (v) light, ignite.

slökun 1. relaxation; *synonyms* (n) ease, diversion, amusement, pastime, entertainment, **2.** modification; *synonyms* (n) alteration, change, adaptation, variation, adjustment.

slöngvari ejector; *synonyms* (n) knockout, eductor, ouster, ousting, pusher.

slöppun sag; *synonyms* (n) decline, dip, (v) droop, flag, (adj) swag; *antonym* (v) rise.

slúðra 1. slander; *synonyms* (n) insult, scandal, (v) libel, defame, (adj) abuse; *antonym* (v) praise, **2.** vilify; *synonyms* (v) malign, slander, disparage, revile, (adj) asperse; *antonym* (v) compliment, **3.** defame; *synonyms* (v) vilify, calumniate, denigrate, smear, (n) disgrace, **4.** libel; *synonyms* (n) aspersion, defamation, denigration, (v) lampoon, slur, **5.** malign; *synonyms* (adj) malicious, malevolent, evil, harmful, (v) badmouth.

slúður 1. scandal; *synonyms* (n) disgrace, dishonor, gossip, outrage, discredit; *antonym* (n) honor, **2.** slander; *synonyms* (n) insult, scandal, (v) libel, defame, (adj) abuse; *antonym* (v) praise, **3.** defamation; *synonyms* (n) aspersion, calumny, slander, vilification, backbiting, **4.** libel; *synonyms* (n) defamation, denigration, (v) denigrate, asperse, calumniate.

slússa 1. sluice; *synonyms* (n) floodgate, lock, penstock, channel, (v) flush, **2.** lock; *synonyms* (v) bolt, bar, close, latch, engage; *antonyms* (v) unlock, open.

slúti overhang; *synonyms* (n) projection, (v) beetle, jut, hang, project.

slydda sleet; *synonyms* (n) precipitation, rain, hail, glaze, moment.

slys 1. accident; *synonyms* (n) chance, casualty, coincidence, crash, fortune, **2.** mishap; *synonyms* (n) accident, adversity, misfortune, calamity, disaster.

smábarn baby; *synonyms* (n) babe, child, (v) coddle, indulge, (adj) infant; *antonym* (adj) giant.

smábein ossicle; *synonyms* (n) ossiculum, bonelet.

smáber acinus; *synonym* (n) grapestone.

smáblað 1. pinna; *synonyms* (n) auricle, ear, capitulum, feather, pinnule, **2.** leaflet; *synonyms* (n) brochure, leaf, booklet, pamphlet, circular.

smábóndi peasant; *synonyms* (n) boor, farmer, churl, bucolic, countryman.

smádropi 1. droplet; *synonyms* (n) drop, dot, bit, (adj) globule, grain, **2.** globule; *synonyms* (n) bead, drip, blob, droplet, (v) ball.

smæð element; *synonyms* (n) component, constituent, ingredient, factor, substance.

smækkaður reduced; *synonyms* (adj) decreased, abridged, curtailed, miniature, cheap; *antonyms* (adj) expensive, complete.

smæstur minimal; *synonyms* (adj) minimum, least, minute, insignificant, marginal; *antonym* (adj) maximal.

smágötóttur clathrate; *synonyms* (adj) cancellate, cancelled, cancellous.

smágreiðslusjóður imprest; *synonym* (v) loan.

smáhnúður tubercle; *synonyms* (n) nodule, tuberosity, tuber, distinction, eminence.

smakka 1. taste; *synonyms* (n) bit, flavor, (v) relish, savor, sample; *antonyms* (n) dislike, tastelessness, **2.** savour; *synonyms* (v) taste, enjoy, (n) flavour, sapidity, gusto, **3.** liking; *synonyms* (n) inclination, fancy, appetite, fondness, affection; *antonym* (n) aversion, **4.** flavour; *synonyms* (n) aroma, smell, feel, feeling, savour.

smala assemble; *synonyms* (v) amass, accumulate, aggregate, convene, gather; *antonyms* (v) dismantle, disperse, disband, disassemble.

smámagni squid; *synonyms* (n) calamary, calamari, sleevefish.

smámaur mite; *synonyms* (n) bit, speck, atom, crumb, hint.

smápilla pellet; *synonyms* (n) shot, granule, bead, (v) ball, (adj) spherule.

smár 1. small; *synonyms* (adj) little, minute, narrow, fine, inadequate; *antonyms* (adj) bulky, colossal, considerable, (syn) big, large, **2.** compact; *synonyms* (adj) close, (n) agreement, arrangement, contract, (v) compress; *antonyms* (adj) loose, sprawling, sparse, **3.** little; *synonyms* (adj) small, diminutive, insignificant, brief, petty; *antonyms* (*adj*) enormous, important.

smárit prospectus; *synonyms* (*n*) program, programme, catalogue, plan, syllabus.

smásær microscopic; *synonyms* (*adj*) infinitesimal, minute, little, atomic, tiny; *antonym* (*adj*) enormous.

smásali retailer; *synonyms* (*n*) merchant, dealer, seller, shopman, vendor; *antonym* (*n*) buyer.

smáseiði parr; *synonym* (*n*) par.

smásjárkvarði micrometer; *synonyms* (*n*) micron, megameter, megametre, (*v*) nanometer, centimeter.

smásjármynd 1. photomicrograph; *synonym* (*n*) micrograph, **2.** micrograph.

smástirni asteroid; *synonym* (*n*) planetoid.

smávægilegur negligible; *synonyms* (*adj*) inconsequential, insignificant, trifling, marginal, minor; *antonym* (*adj*) significant.

smáverugróður culture; *synonyms* (*n*) civilization, breeding, cultivation, acculturation, education.

smekkur taste; *synonyms* (*n*) bit, flavor, (*v*) relish, savor, sample; *antonyms* (*n*) dislike, tastelessness.

smella 1. snap; *synonyms* (*v*) crack, bite, break, fracture, (*n*) photograph, **2.** click; *synonyms* (*n*) catch, chink, (*v*) clack, snap, chatter.

smellur 1. snap; *synonyms* (*v*) crack, bite, break, fracture, (*n*) photograph, **2.** click; *synonyms* (*n*) catch, chink, (*v*) clack, snap, chatter, **3.** dash; *synonyms* (*n*) rush, sprint, (*v*) dart, touch, strike; *antonym* (*n*) lethargy.

smeragður emerald; *synonyms* (*n*) beryl, (*adj*) green, malachite, verdigris, awkward.

smergel emery; *synonyms* (*n*) emeril, (*adj*) steel.

smergill emery; *synonyms* (*n*) emeril, (*adj*) steel.

smeyging invagination; *synonyms* (*n*) intussusception, erythroblast, gametangium, gamete, infolding.

smíð 1. workmanship; *synonyms* (*n*) craft, handicraft, craftsmanship, skill, artistry, **2.** construct; *synonyms* (*v*) make, build, compose, erect, fabricate; *antonyms* (*v*) destroy, demolish.

smíða 1. construct; *synonyms* (*v*) make, build, compose, erect, fabricate; *antonyms* (*v*) destroy, demolish, **2.** build; *synonyms* (*v*) establish, raise, (*n*) form, shape, frame.

smíðaður synthetic; *synonyms* (*adj*) artificial, ersatz, false, simulated, synthetical; *antonyms* (*adj*) natural, genuine, real.

smíðaefni material; *synonyms* (*n*) body, cloth, (*adj*) bodily, corporal, corporeal.

smíðavirki structure; *synonyms* (*n*) form, building, arrangement, edifice, shape.

smíði construction; *synonyms* (*n*) building, fabrication, formation, structure, assembly; *antonym* (*n*) destruction.

smiðja 1. smithy; *synonyms* (*n*) forge, smithery, stithy, anvil, coin, **2.** workshop; *synonyms* (*n*) shop, factory, studio, workhouse, atelier, **3.** forge; *synonyms* (*v*) counterfeit, falsify, devise, fabricate, fake.

smiðjubelgur blower; *synonyms* (*n*) bellows, fan, blast, cetacean, feeder.

smígur bevel; *synonyms* (*n*) cant, inclination, chamfer, (*v*) slope, incline.

smit 1. spillover; *synonyms* (*n*) overflow, **2.** contact; *synonyms* (*n*) touch, connection, collision, communication, (*v*) call, **3.** contagion; *synonyms* (*n*) infection, plague, contamination, disease, taint, **4.** infection; *synonyms* (*n*) contagion, corruption, septicity, illness, (*adj*) pollution.

smita infect; *synonyms* (*v*) taint, contaminate, corrupt, affect, inspire; *antonyms* (*v*) disinfect, purify.

smitaður infectious; *synonyms* (*adj*) contagious, catching, communicable, pestiferous, epidemic.

smitáhrif spillover; *synonym* (*n*) overflow.

smitandi 1. infectious; *synonyms* (*adj*) contagious, catching, communicable, pestiferous, epidemic, **2.** infective; *synonyms* (*adj*) infectious, virulent, morbific, pathogenic, poisonous.

smitberi 1. vector; *synonyms* (*n*) direction, bearing, course, sender, transmitter, **2.** carrier; *synonyms* (*n*) bearer, messenger, courier, mailman, porter.

smiteyðing disinfection; *synonym* (*n*) purification.

smitgát asepsis; *synonyms* (*n*) antisepsis, sterileness, sterility, infertility.

smithæfni virulence; *synonyms* (*n*) rancor, acerbity, animosity, (*adj*) acrimony, venom.

smitlaus aseptic; *synonyms* (*adj*) sterile, antiseptic, clean, healthy, hygienic.

smitsæfa sterilize; *synonyms* (*v*) neuter, castrate, disinfect, sterilise, (*adj*) emasculate; *antonym* (*v*) contaminate.

smitsæfður sterile; *synonyms* (*adj*) infertile, barren, fruitless, effete, (*v*) abortive; *antonyms* (*adj*) fertile, unhygienic.

smitsæfing sterilization; *synonym* (*n*) sterilisation.

smitun 1. contamination; *synonyms* (*n*) contagion, pollution, contaminant, infection, dirtying; *antonym* (*n*) decontamination, **2.** infection; *synonyms* (*n*) disease, contamination, taint, corruption, septicity.

smitvarnarefni antiseptic; *synonyms* (*adj*) clean, sterile, germicidal, unpolluted, (*n*) disinfectant; *antonym* (*adj*) septic.

smitvörn antisepsis; *synonyms* (*n*) asepsis, sterileness, sterility, infertility.

smjör butter; *synonyms* (*n*) fat, (*v*) blarney, gloze, slaver, (*adj*) dough.

smjörfiskur butterfish; *synonym* (*n*) stromateid.

smjúga penetrate; *synonyms* (*v*) bore, imbue, fathom, infiltrate, permeate.

smokkfiskur squid; *synonyms* (*n*) calamary, calamari, sleevefish.

smokkur 1. rubber; *synonyms* (*n*) caoutchouc, condom, eraser, galosh, overshoe, **2.** squid; *synonyms* (*n*) calamary, calamari, sleevefish, **3.** condom; *synonyms* (*n*) prophylactic, rubber, preventative, preventive, arctic.

smokra manoeuvre; *synonyms* (*v*) maneuver, control, direct, go, guide.

smurefni 1. lubricator; *synonyms* (*n*) lubricant, oiler, **2.** lubricant; *synonyms* (*n*) lubricator, fat, oil, (*adj*) oily, **3.** lube; *synonyms* (*v*) anoint, lubricate.

smurfeiti lubricant; *synonyms* (*n*) lubricator, fat, oil, (*adj*) oily.

smurgryfja pit; *synonyms* (*n*) cavity, dent, hole, depression, (*adj*) hollow.

smurkoppur 1. grease; *synonyms* (*n*) fat, bribe, butter, (*v*) oil, boodle, **2.** lubricator; *synonyms* (*n*) lubricant, oiler.

smurning lubrication; *synonyms* (*n*) lubrification, (*adj*) lubricity.

smurningur lubrication; *synonyms* (*n*) lubrification, (*adj*) lubricity.

smurnippill lubricator; *synonyms* (*n*) lubricant, oiler.

smurtittur sweeper; *synonyms* (*n*) broom, sweep, janitor, brush, mop.

smyrja 1. oil; *synonyms* (*n*) petroleum, fat, ointment, (*v*) lubricate, anoint, **2.** lubricate; *synonyms* (*v*) bribe, grease, lube, buy, fix.

smyrjari oiler; *synonym* (*n*) tanker.

smyrsl 1. salve; *synonyms* (*v*) relieve, salvage, (*n*) cream, ointment, balm, **2.** balsam; *synonyms* (*n*) unguent, cordial, ptisan, theriac, liniment.

snælda 1. spindle; *synonyms* (*n*) axle, mandrel, pivot, arbor, axis, **2.** cassette; *synonyms* (*n*) tape, copy, demo, footage, record.

snældulaga fusiform; *synonyms* (*adj*) digitated, snaggy.

snæri cord; *synonyms* (*n*) band, string, bond, tie, twine.

snákur 1. snake; *synonyms* (*n*) ophidian, serpent, (*v*) meander, wind, twist, **2.** worm; *synonyms* (*v*) squirm, wriggle, helix, spiral, (*adj*) insect.

snapa scavenge; *synonyms* (*v*) clean, cleanse, salvage, houseclean, pick.

snapi scavenger; *synonyms* (*n*) magpie, hunter, packrat, predator, quencher.

snara transform; *synonyms* (*v*) change, alter, convert, metamorphose, modify.

snaralur 1. reamer; *synonyms* (*n*) juicer, drinker, imbiber, toper, **2.** broach; *synonyms* (*v*) mention, utter, (*n*) brooch, propose, advance.

snarkolla spinner; *synonyms* (*n*) spinster, goatsucker, spinneret.

snarpur acute; *synonyms* (*adj*) sharp, incisive, intense, keen, penetrating; *antonyms* (*adj*) dull, obtuse.

snarsnúa whirl; *synonyms* (*n*) turn, (*v*) spin, twirl, eddy, roll.

snarsnúningur whirl; *synonyms* (*n*) turn, (*v*) spin, twirl, eddy, roll.

snarstefjun improvisation; *synonyms* (*n*) extemporization, impromptu, extemporisation, invention, construction.

snasar snooks; *synonyms* (*n*) bourgeois, cockney, epicier, robalos.

snati gopher; *synonyms* (*n*) goffer, courier, gauffer, spermophile, victim.

snefill trace; *synonyms* (*n*) line, shadow, spot, clue, (*v*) track.

sneið 1. slice; *synonyms* (*n*) share, part, section, (*v*) cut, slash, **2.** segment; *synonyms* (*n*) division, paragraph, bit, (*v*) divide, partition, **3.** section; *synonyms* (*n*) portion, compartment, percentage, piece, (*v*) segment, **4.** slab; *synonyms* (*n*) hunk, chunk, bar, (*adj*) table, plate.

sneiða 1. slice; *synonyms* (*n*) share, part, section, (*v*) cut, slash, **2.** slab; *synonyms* (*n*) hunk, chunk, bar, (*adj*) table, plate, **3.** section; *synonyms* (*n*) division, portion, compartment, percentage, piece.

sneiðing 1. section; *synonyms* (*n*) division, part, portion, compartment, percentage, **2.** profile; *synonyms* (*n*) contour, outline, form, figure, shape.

sneiðmyndagerð tomography; *synonyms* (*n*) imaging, imagery, imagination.

sneiðmyndataka 1. tomography; *synonyms* (*n*) imaging, imagery, imagination, **2.** stratigraphy.

snekkja yacht; *synonyms* (*n*) boat, vessel, ship, craft, dinghy.

snemma early; *synonyms* (*adj*) initial, first, primitive, prompt, (*adv*) betimes; *antonyms* (*adj*) delayed, last-minute, slow, (*adv*) late.

snemmþroska precocious; *synonyms* (*adj*) forward, advanced, early, pert, premature.

snemmvaxinn precocious; *synonyms* (*adj*) forward, advanced, early, pert, premature.

snepill 1. cusp; *synonyms* (*n*) angle, apex, top, point, tip, **2.** lobule; *synonyms* (*n*) lobe, limb, lobelet, member, arm.

snerill knob; *synonyms* (*n*) button, handle, bump, grip, (*adj*) bulb.

snerpir booster; *synonyms* (*n*) admirer, friend, patron, promoter, protagonist.

snerpivél booster; *synonyms* (*n*) admirer, friend, patron, promoter, protagonist.

snerta 1. touch; *synonyms* (*n*) feel, (*v*) affect, contact, hit, border, **2**. contact; *synonyms* (*n*) touch, connection, collision, communication, (*v*) call.

snertiflötur interface; *synonyms* (*n*) link, port, boundary, junction, (*v*) contact.

snertilína tangent; *synonyms* (*n*) aside, burn, departure, digression, grade.

snertill tangent; *synonyms* (*n*) aside, burn, departure, digression, grade.

snerting 1. touch; *synonyms* (*n*) feel, (*v*) affect, contact, hit, border, **2**. contact; *synonyms* (*n*) touch, connection, collision, communication, (*v*) call.

snertipunktur interface; *synonyms* (*n*) link, port, boundary, junction, (*v*) contact.

snertiskyn tactile; *synonyms* (*adj*) tangible, haptic, tactual, palpable, evident.

snertispennunemi thermocouple; *synonym* (*n*) thermistor.

snertivarinn protected; *synonyms* (*adj*) secure, immune, saved, secured, sheltered.

snertusafn bank; *synonyms* (*n*) dam, coast, slope, (*v*) embankment, gradient; *antonym* (*v*) withdraw.

snið 1. profile; *synonyms* (*n*) contour, outline, form, figure, shape, **2**. section; *synonyms* (*n*) division, part, portion, compartment, percentage, **3**. plane; *synonyms* (*n*) airplane, face, (*adj*) level, even, flat, **4**. shape; *synonyms* (*n*) cast, mold, (*v*) fashion, model, mould, **5**. transect; *synonym* (*v*) cut.

sníða 1. slice; *synonyms* (*n*) share, part, section, (*v*) cut, slash, **2**. cut; *synonyms* (*v*) carve, chop, clip, (*n*) notch, slice; *antonyms* (*v*) increase, lengthen, (*n*) addition, extension, **3**. format; *synonyms* (*n*) form, size, formatting, (*v*) set, arrange.

sniðbrún bevel; *synonyms* (*n*) cant, inclination, chamfer, (*v*) slope, incline.

sniði shear; *synonyms* (*v*) clip, cut, fleece, lop, pare.

sniðill 1. secant; *synonyms* (*v*) crossbarred, cruciate, palmiped, (*n*) s, sec, **2**. chord; *synonyms* (*n*) cord, harmony, (*v*) accord, harmonise, harmonize.

sniðmát 1. template; *synonyms* (*n*) pattern, templet, guide, guidebook, pathfinder, **2**. jig; *synonyms* (*n*) jigger, strathspey, (*v*) dance, hop, skip.

sniðmengi intersection; *synonyms* (*n*) cross, crossroads, crossing, crossroad, intersect.

sniðmótun formatting; *synonym* (*n*) format.

sniðrit profile; *synonyms* (*n*) contour, outline, form, figure, shape.

sniðsetning editing; *synonyms* (*n*) correction, edition, redaction, cutting, control.

sniðskera chamfer; *synonyms* (*n*) cant, fluting, (*v*) bevel, chase, furrow.

sniðskurður chamfering; *synonym* (*n*) bevelling.

snigilkrappi console; *synonyms* (*n*) cabinet, (*v*) comfort, cheer, solace, soothe.

snigill 1. spiral; *synonyms* (*n*) coil, helix, (*adj*) helical, (*v*) curl, loop, **2**. worm; *synonyms* (*v*) squirm, wriggle, twist, spiral, (*adj*) insect, **3**. cochlea, **4**. helix; *synonyms* (*n*) whorl, volute, curve, (*v*) buckle.

sníkiálag burden; *synonyms* (*n*) load, anxiety, (*v*) bother, weight, burthen; *antonyms* (*v*) relieve, unburden.

sníkill parasite; *synonyms* (*n*) leech, sponge, freeloader, sponger, sycophant; *antonym* (*n*) host.

sníkjudýr parasite; *synonyms* (*n*) leech, sponge, freeloader, sponger, sycophant; *antonym* (*n*) host.

sníkjulíf parasitism; *synonym* (*n*) parasitization.

sníkjulífi parasitism; *synonym* (*n*) parasitization.

sníkjuvera parasite; *synonyms* (*n*) leech, sponge, freeloader, sponger, sycophant; *antonym* (*n*) host.

snilligáfa genius; *synonyms* (*n*) capacity, ability, flair, faculty, (*adj*) endowment; *antonym* (*n*) stupidity.

snillingur genius; *synonyms* (*n*) capacity, ability, flair, faculty, (*adj*) endowment; *antonym* (*n*) stupidity.

snitta thread; *synonyms* (*n*) string, line, yarn, (*v*) file, range.

snittappi tap; *synonyms* (*n*) pat, dab, hit, (*v*) knock, rap.

snittbakki die; *synonyms* (*v*) decease, dead, death, depart, (*n*) dice.

snitti die; *synonyms* (*v*) decease, dead, death, depart, (*n*) dice.

snitttappi tap; *synonyms* (*n*) pat, dab, hit, (*v*) knock, rap.

snjádurmús shrew; *synonyms* (*n*) scold, shrewmouse, harridan, termagant, dragon.

snjáldra shrew; *synonyms* (*n*) scold, shrewmouse, harridan, termagant, dragon.

snjóflóð avalanche; *synonyms* (*n*) landslide, deluge, cascade, plenty, (*v*) debacle.

snjókoma snow (snjór); *synonyms* (*n*) cocaine, coke, precipitation, (*v*) beguile, overwhelm.

snjóplógur snowplow; *synonyms* (*n*) snowplough, cardiograph, recapper, tenpenny, votograph.

snjór snow; *synonyms* (*n*) cocaine, coke, precipitation, (*v*) beguile, overwhelm.

snjóskriða avalanche; *synonyms* (*n*) landslide, deluge, cascade, plenty, (*v*) debacle.

snöggkæla quench; *synonyms* (*v*) extinguish, allay, appease, quash, destroy.

snögglosa jettison; *synonyms* (v) discard, ditch, scrap, dump, chuck; *antonym* (v) keep.

snöggur 1. sudden; *synonyms* (adj) abrupt, hasty, precipitous, quick, rash; *antonyms* (adj) gradual, considered, **2.** dramatic; *synonyms* (adj) spectacular, theatrical, impressive, scenic, exciting; *antonym* (adj) undramatic, **3.** abrupt; *synonyms* (adj) sudden, brusque, sharp, steep, (n) bold; *antonyms* (adj) civil, gentle, gracious, rambling, **4.** naked; *synonyms* (adj) bald, bare, exposed, nude, open; *antonyms* (adj) covered, concealed.

snörun transformation; *synonyms* (n) conversion, alteration, metamorphosis, change, shift.

snúa 1. turn; *synonyms* (n) bend, curve, roll, coil, go, **2.** rotate; *synonyms* (v) revolve, reel, alternate, gyrate, spin, **3.** revolve; *synonyms* (v) consider, deliberate, meditate, ponder, circle, **4.** swing; *synonyms* (v) sway, fluctuate, oscillate, dangle, hang, **5.** crank; *synonyms* (n) crackpot, grouch, handle, nut, (adj) cranky.

snúast 1. veer; *synonyms* (v) turn, shift, swerve, deviate, curve, **2.** revolve; *synonyms* (v) reel, consider, deliberate, meditate, (n) gyrate, **3.** swing; *synonyms* (v) sway, fluctuate, oscillate, dangle, hang, **4.** rotate; *synonyms* (v) revolve, roll, alternate, spin, swing.

snuða slip; *synonyms* (n) lapse, fault, (v) fall, slide, (adj) blunder; *antonym* (v) improve.

snúða gyroscope; *synonym* (n) gyro.

snúðáttaviti gyrocompass; *synonym* (n) gyro.

snúðkúla orb; *synonyms* (n) ball, globe, sphere, cycle, circle.

snúðleiðir twist; *synonyms* (n) twine, (v) turn, bend, distort, curl; *antonyms* (v) straighten, untwist.

snúðsjá stroboscope; *synonym* (n) strobe.

snúðstjarna spider; *synonyms* (n) lota, mussuk, schooner, spinner, adapter.

snúðteinn pivot; *synonyms* (n) axle, axis, pin, hub, (v) revolve.

snúður 1. rotor; *synonyms* (n) rotator, stator, **2.** top; *synonyms* (n) crown, peak, acme, apex, (v) best; *antonyms* (adj) worst, (n) bottom, base, nadir, **3.** armature; *synonyms* (n) armament, armaments, skeleton, frame, framework, **4.** gyroscope; *synonym* (n) gyro.

snúðvala spheroid; *synonyms* (n) sphere, (adj) circular, round, (v) ball.

snúðvísir gyroscope; *synonym* (n) gyro.

snúðviti gyrocompass; *synonym* (n) gyro.

snúningsás 1. shaft; *synonyms* (n) arrow, handle, axis, beam, pit, **2.** axis; *synonyms* (n) axle, pivot, hinge, center, hub.

snúningsátak torque; *synonyms* (n) torsion, broach, contortion, crookedness, pin.

snúningshraðamælir tachometer; *synonyms* (n) tach, (adj) speedometer, odometer, strobe.

snúningsmælir tachometer; *synonyms* (n) tach, (adj) speedometer, odometer, strobe.

snúningsmætti torque; *synonyms* (n) torsion, broach, contortion, crookedness, pin.

snúningsmiðjuoddur centre; *synonyms* (n) core, middle, (v) center, centralize, concentrate.

snúningssjá stroboscope; *synonym* (n) strobe.

snúningstala periodicity; *synonyms* (n) cyclicity, frequency, rhythm, cycle, periodicalness.

snúningsþvermál swing; *synonyms* (v) sway, fluctuate, oscillate, dangle, hang.

snúningsvægi 1. torque; *synonyms* (n) torsion, broach, contortion, crookedness, pin, **2.** moment; *synonyms* (n) importance, consequence, flash, instant, jiffy.

snúningur 1. revolution; *synonyms* (n) change, gyration, insurrection, mutiny, (v) circuit, **2.** rotation; *synonyms* (n) revolution, roll, round, turn, circulation, **3.** transposition; *synonyms* (n) exchange, permutation, replacement, reversal, substitution, **4.** spin; *synonyms* (n) twirl, whirl, (v) revolve, twist, run, **5.** torsion; *synonyms* (n) contortion, torque, tortuosity, crookedness, deformation.

snúninsmætti moment; *synonyms* (n) importance, consequence, flash, instant, jiffy.

snúra line; *synonyms* (n) cord, file, house, breed, course.

snurða kink; *synonyms* (n) curl, twist, knot, curve, defect.

snyrta 1. round; *synonyms* (adv) about, (adj) circular, (n) circle, bout, ring; *antonyms* (adj) slim, sharp, **2.** trim; *synonyms* (adj) tidy, (v) cut, dress, clip, garnish; *antonym* (adj) fat.

snyrting 1. pruning; *synonym* (n) leavings, **2.** trimming; *synonyms* (n) trim, adornment, decoration, dressing, ornament, **3.** rounding; *synonyms* (n) bruting, labializing, service, (adj) roundish.

snytti thread; *synonyms* (n) string, line, yarn, (v) file, range.

sódómska 1. sodomy; *synonyms* (n) buggery, pederasty, **2.** bestiality; *synonyms* (n) cruelty, violence, zooerastia, zooerasty.

sódómusaurlifnaður bestiality; *synonyms* (n) cruelty, violence, zooerastia, zooerasty.

söðull col; *synonyms* (n) gap, break, crack, disruption, interruption.

söðulsvæði col; *synonyms* (n) gap, break, crack, disruption, interruption.

sofa sleep; *synonyms* (n) nap, doze, (v) rest, repose, catnap.

sófl broom; *synonyms* (*n*) besom, brush, (*v*) sweep, filter, rake.

söfnuður parish; *synonyms* (*n*) district, community, congregation, region, province.

söfnun 1. compilation; *synonyms* (*n*) collection, anthology, compiling, digest, miscellany, **2.** collection; *synonyms* (*n*) accumulation, assembly, assortment, bundle, (*v*) assemblage, **3.** accumulation; *synonyms* (*n*) store, stock, accretion, mass, accrual; *antonym* (*n*) shortage.

söfnunarfé subscription; *synonyms* (*n*) contribution, donation, offering, (*v*) allowance, subsidy.

sog suction; *synonyms* (*n*) suck, sucking, aspiration, absorption, draft.

sög saw; *synonyms* (*n*) adage, byword, proverb, dictum, maxim.

soga aspirate; *synonyms* (*v*) accentuate, articulate, deliver, mouth, enunciate.

sogabarnaveiki croup; *synonyms* (*n*) rump, croupe, hindquarters, tail, dorsum.

sogæð lymphatic; *synonyms* (*adj*) aqueous, hydrous, torpid, listless, aquatic.

sogæðavökvi lymph; *synonyms* (*n*) crystal, glass, (*adj*) rheum, sanies, serosity.

sogahósti pertussis; *synonyms* (*adj*) necrosis, phthisis, pneumonia, psora, pyaemia.

sogari siphon; *synonyms* (*n*) cloaca, culvert, (*v*) drain, syphon, draw.

soggúlar suckers; *synonyms* (*n*) carp, loaches.

sogkarpar suckers; *synonyms* (*n*) carp, loaches.

sogkraftur vacuum; *synonyms* (*n*) emptiness, void, vacancy, vacuity, gap.

sogpípa syphon; *synonym* (*v*) siphon.

sograni acetabulum; *synonym* (*n*) acetable.

sogskál 1. sucker; *synonyms* (*n*) dupe, fool, sap, jay, lollipop, **2.** acetabulum; *synonym* (*n*) acetable.

sogtrantar suckers; *synonyms* (*n*) carp, loaches.

sogun suction; *synonyms* (*n*) suck, sucking, aspiration, absorption, draft.

sök liability; *synonyms* (*n*) debt, duty, obligation, trust, blame; *antonym* (*n*) asset.

sökk sedimentation; *synonyms* (*n*) deposit, sediment, settling, alluviation, deposition.

sökkull 1. shell; *synonyms* (*n*) peel, rind, bullet, case, (*v*) bomb, **2.** base; *synonyms* (*n*) foundation, (*adj*) bottom, abject, mean, dishonorable; *antonyms* (*n*) summit, top, (*adj*) noble, **3.** foundation; *synonyms* (*n*) base, basis, creation, establishment, foot.

sokkur sock; *synonyms* (*n*) hit, hose, (*v*) smash, knock, smack.

sökkva 1. sink; *synonyms* (*n*) sag, (*v*) decline, dip, droop, fall; *antonyms* (*v*) rise, float, **2.** immerse;

synonyms (*v*) douse, plunge, absorb, drench, drown.

Sókn 1. attack; *synonyms* (*n*) incursion, thrust, (*v*) assault, assail, attempt; *antonyms* (*n*) defense, (*v*) defend, protect, retreat, **2.** retrieval; *synonyms* (*n*) recovery, reclamation, redress, recuperation, (*v*) revendication; *antonym* (*n*) loss.

sóknarnefnd vestry; *synonyms* (*n*) sacristy, aisle, chancel, chapter, choir.

sóknarpunktur apex; *synonyms* (*n*) peak, top, vertex, acme, crown; *antonyms* (*n*) base, nadir.

sól 1. sun; *synonyms* (*n*) light, sunlight, (*adj*) star, (*v*) bask, sunbathe, **2.** sol; *synonyms* (*n*) so, soh, gold, sou.

sólaldin papaya; *synonyms* (*n*) papaia, papaw, pawpaw.

sólaldintré papaya; *synonyms* (*n*) papaia, papaw, pawpaw.

sólar solar; *synonyms* (*adj*) astral, astronomical, astrophysical, cosmological, lunar.

sólarhringur day; *synonyms* (*n*) light, daylight, generation, age, daytime; *antonyms* (*n*) nighttime, night.

sólarsinnis clockwise; *synonym* (*adj*) right; *antonym* (*adv*) counterclockwise.

sólbaugur ecliptic; *synonyms* (*n*) colures, orbit, circle, equator.

sólblettur sunspot; *synonyms* (*n*) macula, macule.

sólblossi flare; *synonyms* (*n*) flash, blaze, (*v*) burn, flame, burst.

sólborri opah; *synonyms* (*n*) moonfish, dollarfish, horsefish, horsehead.

sólbraut ecliptic; *synonyms* (*n*) colures, orbit, circle, equator.

sólbroddur spicule; *synonyms* (*n*) spiculum, tooth, (*adj*) point, spike, spine.

sólbruni sunburn; *synonyms* (*n*) burn, tan, suntan, burning, (*v*) bite.

sóldíll pore; *synonyms* (*n*) interstice, stoma, aorta, artery, (*v*) center.

sólflekkur plage; *synonyms* (*n*) country, region.

sólgeislun insolation; *synonyms* (*n*) siriasis, sunstroke, heliotherapy.

sólgos flare; *synonyms* (*n*) flash, blaze, (*v*) burn, flame, burst.

sólhlíf shading; *synonyms* (*n*) blending, shadowing, eclipse, nuance, adumbration.

sólhorf 1. configuration; *synonyms* (*n*) form, arrangement, conformation, shape, organization, **2.** aspect; *synonyms* (*n*) appearance, look, surface, bearing, expression.

sólhvarfapunktur solstice; *synonym* (*n*) height.

sólhvörf solstice; *synonym* (*n*) height.

sólkorn granule; *synonyms* (*n*) grain, crumb, (*adj*) scruple, dash, drop.

sólmark apex; *synonyms* (*n*) peak, top, vertex, acme, crown; *antonyms* (*n*) base, nadir.

sólmið apex; *synonyms* (*n*) peak, top, vertex, acme, crown; *antonyms* (*n*) base, nadir.

sólnál spicule; *synonyms* (*n*) spiculum, tooth, (*adj*) point, spike, spine.

sólnánd perihelion; *synonym* (*n*) perihelium.

sólreitur granule; *synonyms* (*n*) grain, crumb, (*adj*) scruple, dash, drop.

sólselja dill; *synonyms* (*n*) anise, caraway, carrot, celery, (*adj*) calm.

sólskinslækning heliotherapy; *synonyms* (*n*) insolation, siriasis, sunstroke.

sólsproti gnomon; *synonyms* (*n*) dial, horologe, hourglass, pendulum, sundial.

sólstingur 1. sunstroke; *synonyms* (*n*) insolation, siriasis, dryness, heliotherapy, thirst, **2**. siriasis; *synonym* (*n*) sunstroke, **3**. insolation.

sólstjarna star (stjarna); *synonyms* (*n*) asterisk, celebrity, ace, principal, headliner; *antonym* (*n*) nobody.

sólstöðupunktur solstice; *synonym* (*n*) height.

sólstöðor solstice; *synonym* (*n*) height.

sólstrókur prominence; *synonyms* (*n*) eminence, hump, importance, protuberance, height; *antonym* (*n*) obscurity.

sólþræðlingur fibril; *synonyms* (*n*) fiber, fibrilla, filament, chain, strand.

sóltjald awning; *synonyms* (*n*) sunshade, screen, blind, canopy, cover.

sóltoppur spicule; *synonyms* (*n*) spiculum, tooth, (*adj*) point, spike, spine.

sölubúð shop; *synonyms* (*n*) business, store, factory, plant, (*v*) betray.

söluhæfur 1. saleable; *synonyms* (*adj*) salable, commercial, profitable, viable, (*adv*) saleably, **2**. marketable; *synonyms* (*adj*) merchantable, saleable, vendible, interchangeable, wanted.

sólúr sundial; *synonyms* (*n*) dial, clock.

söluréttur put; *synonyms* (*v*) place, fix, lay, position, (*n*) deposit.

sölutryggja underwrite; *synonyms* (*v*) guarantee, insure, subscribe, cover, indemnify.

sölutryggjandi underwriter; *synonyms* (*n*) insurer, sponsor, attorney, backer, bailiff.

söluvara merchandise; *synonyms* (*n*) cargo, freight, commodity, (*v*) market, (*adj*) commodities.

söluvarningur merchandise; *synonyms* (*n*) cargo, freight, commodity, (*v*) market, (*adj*) commodities.

söluvilnun put; *synonyms* (*v*) place, fix, lay, position, (*n*) deposit.

sólýra granule; *synonyms* (*n*) grain, crumb, (*adj*) scruple, dash, drop.

sólýringur granulation; *synonyms* (*n*) aggregation, (*adj*) attenuation, comminution, levigation, multure.

sönnuður authority; *synonyms* (*n*) ascendancy, command, sanction, administration, authorization.

sönnun 1. proof; *synonyms* (*n*) confirmation, demonstration, probation, argument, authentication, **2**. verification; *synonyms* (*n*) check, proof, substantiation, corroboration, evidence, **3**. evidence; *synonyms* (*n*) mark, data, (*v*) display, demonstrate, attest.

sönnunargagn 1. proof; *synonyms* (*n*) confirmation, demonstration, probation, argument, authentication, **2**. evidence; *synonyms* (*n*) mark, proof, data, (*v*) display, demonstrate.

sonur son; *synonyms* (*n*) offspring, boy, lad, child, descendant.

sópa sweep; *synonyms* (*n*) compass, expanse, range, (*v*) brush, rake.

sópur broom; *synonyms* (*n*) besom, brush, (*v*) sweep, filter, rake.

sori 1. slag; *synonyms* (*n*) cinder, clinker, dross, scoria, scum, **2**. impurity; *synonyms* (*n*) contamination, filth, impureness, pollution, defilement.

sóri psoriasis; *synonyms* (*n*) itch, leucoplakia.

sorp 1. scrap; *synonyms* (*n*) fight, morsel, brawl, remnant, (*adj*) fragment; *antonym* (*v*) keep, **2**. waste; *synonyms* (*n*) desert, (*adj*) spoil, desolate, (*v*) consume, exhaust; *antonyms* (*v*) conserve, save, **3**. trash; *synonyms* (*n*) nonsense, rubbish, junk, litter, (*v*) scrap.

sorphaugar dump; *synonyms* (*v*) discard, ditch, abandon, drop, empty; *antonym* (*v*) keep.

sorphaugur dump; *synonyms* (*v*) discard, ditch, abandon, drop, empty; *antonym* (*v*) keep.

sorti melanosis; *synonym* (*n*) melanism.

sortnun melanosis; *synonym* (*n*) melanism.

sortuæxli melanoma; *synonyms* (*n*) growth, malignancy, tumor, disease, sarcoma.

sortumiga alkaptonuria; *synonym* (*n*) alcaptonuria.

sósíalismi socialism; *synonyms* (*n*) communism, collectivism, communalism; *antonym* (*n*) capitalism.

sót 1. soot; *synonyms* (*n*) smut, grime, lampblack, (*adj*) smoke, ink, **2**. carbon; *synonyms* (*n*) coke, coal, anthracite, carbonado, (*v*) copy.

sóta soot; *synonyms* (*n*) smut, grime, lampblack, (*adj*) smoke, ink.

sótaður brand; *synonyms* (*n*) badge, blade, (*v*) mark, (*adj*) stigma, blot.

sótlag deposit; *synonyms* (*n*) charge, (*v*) bank, commit, store, fix; *antonym* (*v*) withdraw.

sóttarfar morbidity; *synonyms* (*n*) morbidness, deathrate, mortality, gloom, (*adj*) morbosity.

sóttarhlé remission; *synonyms* (*n*) forgiveness, relief, ease, condonation, (*v*) pardon.

sóttbrigði crisis; *synonyms* (*n*) exigency, conjuncture, difficulty, emergency, juncture.

sótthiti fever; *synonyms* (*n*) delirium, feverishness, frenzy, heat, pyrexia.

sótthræðsla hypochondria; *synonyms* (*n*) hypochondriasis, hypo.

sótthreinsun disinfection; *synonym* (*n*) purification.

sótthreinsunarefni bactericide; *synonyms* (*n*) antiseptic, germicide, bacteriacide, disinfectant, antibacterial.

sótthvörf crisis; *synonyms* (*n*) exigency, conjuncture, difficulty, emergency, juncture.

sóttkví quarantine; *synonyms* (*n*) detention, seclusion, (*v*) isolate, segregate, seal.

sóttkvíun isolation; *synonyms* (*n*) alienation, estrangement, insulation, privacy, dissociation; *antonyms* (*n*) closeness, companionship.

sóttnæmi susceptibility; *synonyms* (*n*) predisposition, sensitivity, impressibility, liability, inclination; *antonym* (*n*) resistance.

sóttnæmur susceptible; *synonyms* (*adj*) impressionable, receptive, responsive, sensitive, subject; *antonyms* (*adj*) resistant, unsusceptible.

sóttsýki hypochondria; *synonyms* (*n*) hypochondriasis, hypo.

sóttvarnandi antiseptic; *synonyms* (*adj*) clean, sterile, germicidal, unpolluted, (*n*) disinfectant; *antonym* (*adj*) septic.

sóttvarnarlyf 1. antiseptic; *synonyms* (*adj*) clean, sterile, germicidal, unpolluted, (*n*) disinfectant; *antonym* (*adj*) septic, **2.** antisepsis; *synonyms* (*n*) asepsis, sterileness, sterility, infertility.

sóttvörn antisepsis; *synonyms* (*n*) asepsis, sterileness, sterility, infertility.

sóun waste; *synonyms* (*n*) desert, (*adj*) spoil, desolate, (*v*) consume, exhaust; *antonyms* (*v*) conserve, save.

spá 1. prediction; *synonyms* (*n*) divination, forecast, forecasting, foresight, announcement, **2.** prognosis; *synonyms* (*n*) prediction, prospect, outlook, vaticination, calculation, **3.** forecast; *synonyms* (*v*) presage, anticipate, augur, calculate, portend.

spaðabátur hydrofoil; *synonyms* (*n*) hydroplane, enhancer, foil, hydrovane, seaplane.

spaðastyrja paddlefish; *synonyms* (*n*) duckbill, platypus.

spaði 1. vane; *synonyms* (*n*) blade, beacon, cairn, fan, (*adj*) weathercock, **2.** spatula; *synonyms* (*n*) slice, shovel, trowel, tablespoon, thimble.

spádómur prediction; *synonyms* (*n*) divination, forecast, forecasting, foresight, announcement.

spælkross spider; *synonyms* (*n*) lota, mussuk, schooner, spinner, adapter.

spæll spoke; *synonyms* (*n*) bar, radius, rung, clog, line.

spæringur psoriasis; *synonyms* (*n*) itch, leucoplakia.

spæta woodpecker; *synonyms* (*n*) pecker, beak, bill, cock, nib.

spákaupmennska speculation; *synonyms* (*n*) hypothesis, guess, reflection, venture, guesswork.

spakur tame; *synonyms* (*adj*) docile, meek, (*v*) dull, break, subdue; *antonyms* (*adj*) exciting, wild.

span 1. induction; *synonyms* (*n*) inauguration, deduction, initiation, beginning, elicitation, **2.** excitation; *synonyms* (*n*) excitement, stimulus, agitation, encouragement, feeling.

spana induce; *synonyms* (*v*) attract, generate, cause, tempt, impel.

spanald inductor; *synonyms* (*n*) inductance, induction.

spanali armature; *synonyms* (*n*) armament, armaments, skeleton, frame, framework.

spankveiking welding; *synonyms* (*n*) fusion, assembly, synthesis.

spanlóðun welding; *synonyms* (*n*) fusion, assembly, synthesis.

spanna span; *synonyms* (*n*) length, space, distance, bridge, couple.

spanrafmagn induction; *synonyms* (*n*) inauguration, deduction, initiation, beginning, elicitation.

spansgræna verdigris; *synonyms* (*n*) aerugo, verditer, (*adj*) emerald, green.

spanskgræna verdigris; *synonyms* (*n*) aerugo, verditer, (*adj*) emerald, green.

spanskreyrspálmi rattan; *synonyms* (*n*) ratan, cane, bamboo, wicker.

spanspóla inductor; *synonyms* (*n*) inductance, induction.

spanstuðull inductance; *synonyms* (*n*) inductor, induction, elicitation, evocation, generalisation.

spansuða welding; *synonyms* (*n*) fusion, assembly, synthesis.

sparifé saving; *synonyms* (*n*) economy, conservation, (*adj*) economical, frugal, thrifty; *antonym* (*n*) extravagance.

sparnaður 1. saving; *synonyms* (*n*) economy, conservation, (*adj*) economical, frugal, thrifty; *antonym* (*n*) extravagance, **2.** economy; *synonyms* (*n*) frugality, parsimony, saving, thrift, efficiency.

sparsemi 1. thrift; *synonyms* (*n*) economy, frugality, parsimony, husbandry, prosperity; *antonyms* (*n*) extravagance, generosity, **2**. economy; *synonyms* (*n*) saving, thrift, conservation, efficiency, prudence.

spartl putty; *synonyms* (*n*) cement, paste, glue, lute, mastic.

spartla putty; *synonyms* (*n*) cement, paste, glue, lute, mastic.

spáskekkja residual; *synonyms* (*adj*) remaining, leftover, (*n*) remnant, residue, balance.

spasmi spasm; *synonyms* (*n*) seizure, fit, cramp, outburst, attack.

spássía margin; *synonyms* (*n*) edge, brink, boundary, hem, (*v*) border; *antonym* (*n*) center.

spastískur spastic; *synonyms* (*adj*) convulsive, spasmodic, fitful, paroxysmal, broken.

spegilfesting spider; *synonyms* (*n*) lota, mussuk, schooner, spinner, adapter.

spegill **1**. mirror; *synonyms* (*n*) echo, (*v*) glass, imitate, copy, reflect, **2**. reflector; *synonyms* (*n*) mirror, repeller, lieberkuhn, chromatoscope, refractor.

spegilsjónauki reflector; *synonyms* (*n*) mirror, repeller, lieberkuhn, chromatoscope, refractor.

spegilskekkja aberration; *synonyms* (*n*) aberrance, aberrancy, abnormality, deviation, diversion.

spegilvilla aberration; *synonyms* (*n*) aberrance, aberrancy, abnormality, deviation, diversion.

spegilvirkur reflexive; *synonyms* (*adj*) reflex, reciprocal, reflective, automatic, involuntary.

spegla **1**. reflect; *synonyms* (*v*) deliberate, ponder, cogitate, consider, contemplate, **2**. mirror; *synonyms* (*n*) echo, (*v*) glass, imitate, copy, reflect.

speglun **1**. reflection; *synonyms* (*n*) consideration, contemplation, observation, cogitation, deliberation, **2**. reversal; *synonyms* (*n*) reverse, setback, retrogression, regression, annulment, **3**. mirroring; *synonym* (*n*) imitation, **4**. inversion; *synonyms* (*n*) antithesis, reversal, transposition, anastrophe, eversion.

speglunartala parity; *synonyms* (*n*) par, equality, resemblance, balance, equivalence; *antonym* (*n*) inequality.

spektaklo **1**. spectacle; *synonyms* (*n*) display, pageant, scene, sight, (*v*) show; *antonym* (*n*) modesty, **2**. spectacles; *synonyms* (*n*) eyeglasses, glasses, specs, bifocals, monocle.

speldi **1**. flap; *synonyms* (*n*) fuss, slap, (*v*) flop, beat, wave, **2**. epiglottis.

spelka brace; *synonyms* (*n*) couple, duo, pair, (*v*) clamp, invigorate; *antonym* (*v*) weaken.

spendýr mammal; *synonyms* (*n*) vertebrate, mollusk, reptile, shellfish, worm.

spenna **1**. stress; *synonyms* (*n*) accent, emphasis, pressure, (*v*) strain, emphasize, **2**. tension; *synonyms* (*n*) tenseness, nervousness, stress, tautness, tensity; *antonyms* (*n*) calmness, looseness,

3. strap; *synonyms* (*n*) belt, leash, strop, (*v*) lash, whip, **4**. voltage; *synonyms* (*n*) potential, emf, energy, power, current, **5**. potential; *synonyms* (*adj*) likely, possible, (*n*) capability, potency, ability.

spennihólkur collet; *synonym* (*n*) ferrule.

spennir **1**. tensor, **2**. transformer; *synonym* (*n*) transducer.

spennitöng pliers; *synonyms* (*v*) pincers, forceps, nippers, tongs, clutches.

spennitreyja straitjacket; *synonyms* (*n*) straightjacket, restraint.

spenntur rigid; *synonyms* (*adj*) harsh, fixed, hard, inflexible, stiff; *antonyms* (*adj*) flexible, elastic, soft.

spennubreytir transformer; *synonym* (*n*) transducer.

spennubroddur spike; *synonyms* (*n*) pin, point, barb, ear, (*v*) impale.

spennufallsmunur regulation; *synonyms* (*n*) rule, adjustment, law, order, (*adj*) control; *antonym* (*n*) chaos.

spennugildi potential; *synonyms* (*adj*) likely, possible, (*n*) capability, potency, ability.

spennuhnykkur **1**. spike; *synonyms* (*n*) pin, point, barb, ear, (*v*) impale, **2**. surge; *synonyms* (*v*) billow, flood, rise, rush, stream.

spennujafnari regulator; *synonyms* (*n*) governor, controller, director, organizer, control.

spennujöfnun regulation; *synonyms* (*n*) rule, adjustment, law, order, (*adj*) control; *antonym* (*n*) chaos.

spennumælir **1**. voltmeter, **2**. tonometer; *synonym* (*n*) ophthalmotonometer, **3**. electrometer.

spennumunur voltage; *synonyms* (*n*) potential, emf, energy, power, current.

spennustillir regulator; *synonyms* (*n*) governor, controller, director, organizer, control.

spergilkál broccoli; *synonym* (*n*) cauliflower.

sperra rafter; *synonyms* (*n*) beam, balk, girder, raftsman, timber.

spik **1**. blubber; *synonyms* (*n*) cry, fat, (*v*) sob, weep, bawl, **2**. fat; *synonyms* (*adj*) stout, corpulent, dense, thick, (*n*) avoirdupois; *antonyms* (*adj*) thin, slim, skinny, slender.

spíkur spike; *synonyms* (*n*) pin, point, barb, ear, (*v*) impale.

spil **1**. winch; *synonyms* (*n*) crank, windlass, (*v*) capstan, derrick, wince, **2**. windlass; *synonyms* (*n*) winch, hoist, stowce, windas, (*v*) crane.

spilda **1**. plat; *synonyms* (*n*) chart, (*v*) plait, plot, braid, diagram, **2**. tract; *synonyms* (*n*) area, essay, expanse, pamphlet, region.

spilla **1**. spill; *synonyms* (*v*) fall, shed, drop, empty, (*n*) overflow, **2**. contaminate; *synonyms* (*v*) pollute,

infect, taint, adulterate, befoul; *antonyms* (v)
cleanse, purify, clean, sterilize, **3**. impair;
synonyms (v) blemish, damage, mar, degrade,
corrupt.

spilliefnaflæði loading; *synonyms* (n) cargo, freight,
load, burden, consignment; *antonym* (n) unloading.

spilling corruption; *synonyms* (n) contamination,
depravity, adulteration, pollution, bribery;
antonyms (n) purification, decency, honesty,
incorruptness.

spilltur contaminated; *synonyms* (adj) dirty, impure,
infected, unclean, (v) poisoned; *antonym* (adj) pure.

spindilbolti kingpin; *synonyms* (n) headpin,
kingbolt, bigwig, leader, authority.

spindill 1. spindle; *synonyms* (n) axle, mandrel,
pivot, arbor, axis, **2**. knuckle; *synonyms* (n) elbow,
knee, scythe, sickle, (v) submit.

spirito 1. spirit; *synonyms* (n) apparition, courage,
ghost, life, mood; *antonyms* (n) lethargy, body, **2**.
spirits; *synonyms* (n) liquor, alcohol, booze,
humor, (adj) cheer.

spíritus spirit; *synonyms* (n) apparition, courage,
ghost, life, mood; *antonyms* (n) lethargy, body.

spírun germination; *synonyms* (n) growth,
sprouting, (v) fertilization, gemination, heterogamy.

spíss 1. injector, **2**. nozzle; *synonyms* (n) nose, beak,
hooter, jet, muzzle.

spjald 1. vane; *synonyms* (n) blade, beacon, cairn, fan,
(adj) weathercock, **2**. trap; *synonyms* (n) snare, net,
ambush, (v) catch, entrap, **3**. baffle; *synonyms* (v)
discomfit, astonish, bewilder, confound, foil;
antonym (v) enlighten, **4**. adapter; *synonyms* (n)
adaptor, spider, attachment, arranger, transcriber,
5. flap; *synonyms* (n) fuss, slap, (v) flop, beat, wave.

spjaldbein sacrum; *synonym* (n) rump.

spjaldhryggur sacrum; *synonym* (n) rump.

spjaldliðir sacrum; *synonym* (n) rump.

spjall chat; *synonyms* (n) gossip, talk, chatter,
chitchat, (v) converse; *antonym* (v) listen.

spjalla 1. talk; *synonyms* (v) gossip, converse, lecture,
chatter, (n) discourse, **2**. speak; *synonyms* (v)
express, pronounce, articulate, deliver, say.

spjallrás chat; *synonyms* (n) gossip, talk, chatter,
chitchat, (v) converse; *antonym* (v) listen.

splæsa splice; *synonyms* (n) joint, (v) link, conjoin,
join, (adj) tie.

splæsifall spline; *synonyms* (n) feather, slat, fin,
conclusion, end.

splæsing 1. quilting; *synonyms* (n) quilt, embroidery,
2. splicing; *synonyms* (n) splice, reinforcing,
sticking.

splitti cotter; *synonyms* (n) cottier, key, cottager,
wedge, keynote.

spóla 1. winding; *synonyms* (adj) tortuous, indirect,
twisting, (n) twist, wind; *antonyms* (adj) straight,
direct, **2**. solenoid, **3**. spindle; *synonyms* (n) axle,
mandrel, pivot, arbor, axis, **4**. reel; *synonyms* (n)
bobbin, coil, roll, (v) lurch, rock, **5**. coil; *synonyms*
(n) spiral, loop, (v) curl, circle, round; *antonym* (v)
uncoil.

spólulaga fusiform; *synonyms* (adj) digitated, snaggy.

spónaplata fibreboard; *synonym* (n) fiberboard.

spónarhorn rake; *synonyms* (n) profligate, (v) tilt,
hoe, harrow, (adj) comb.

spöng jumper; *synonyms* (n) sweater, blackguard,
bounder, cad, dog.

spónlögn veneer; *synonyms* (n) face, facade, facing,
coating, (v) varnish.

spónn chip; *synonyms* (n) splinter, bit, flake,
chipping, (v) crack.

spönn 1. range; *synonyms* (v) line, arrange, order,
rank, roam, **2**. span; *synonyms* (n) length, space,
distance, bridge, couple.

spönnuður generator; *synonyms* (n) author, creator,
founder, boiler, originator.

spönnun range; *synonyms* (v) line, arrange, order,
rank, roam.

spons 1. tap; *synonyms* (n) pat, dab, hit, (v) knock, rap,
2. bung; *synonyms* (n) cork, (v) plug, stop, cap,
block.

sponsgat bung; *synonyms* (n) cork, (v) plug, stop, cap,
block.

spönun loading; *synonyms* (n) cargo, freight, load,
burden, consignment; *antonym* (n) unloading.

spor 1. slot; *synonyms* (n) groove, place, notch, gap,
(v) slit, **2**. trace; *synonyms* (n) line, shadow, spot,
clue, (v) track, **3**. groove; *synonyms* (n) furrow, rut,
chamfer, (v) channel, flute, **4**. hollow; *synonyms*
(adj) blank, concave, empty, (n) cavity, hole;
antonyms (adj) convex, (n) solid, hump, **5**. line;
synonyms (n) cord, file, house, breed, course.

sporbaugóttur ellipsoid; *synonyms* (adj) spheroid,
ellipsoidal, spheroidal.

sporbaugsflötur ellipsoid; *synonyms* (adj) spheroid,
ellipsoidal, spheroidal.

sporbaugur ellipse; *synonyms* (n) ellipsis, oval,
ovule, curve, orbit.

sporður tail; *synonyms* (n) rear, shadow, (v) follow,
pursue, track; *antonyms* (v) head, front.

sporefni tracer; *synonyms* (n) marker, sensor.

sporhundur trailer; *synonyms* (n) caravan, leader, ad,
advertisement, announcement.

spori spur; *synonyms* (n) inducement, incentive,
impulse, (v) goad, incite.

sporjárn chisel; *synonyms* (v) carve, cheat, cut, shape,
beguile.

sporöskjulaga elliptic; *synonyms* (*adj*) elliptical, oval, ovate, oviform, ovoid.

sporvala ellipsoid; *synonyms* (*adj*) spheroid, ellipsoidal, spheroidal.

sporvídd 1. track; *synonyms* (*n*) course, path, (*v*) trace, trail, hunt, **2.** gauge; *synonyms* (*n*) criterion, caliber, (*v*) estimate, measure, calculate.

sporvöluflötur ellipsoid; *synonyms* (*adj*) spheroid, ellipsoidal, spheroidal.

spotti edge; *synonyms* (*n*) boundary, margin, verge, (*v*) border, bound; *antonyms* (*n*) center, (*v*) middle.

sprang surfing; *synonyms* (*n*) surfboarding, surfriding.

spranga surf; *synonyms* (*n*) breakers, foam, breaker, spray, (*v*) browse.

sprauta 1. syringe; *synonyms* (*n*) douche, beaker, flask, needle, (*v*) hydrant, **2.** spray; *synonyms* (*n*) jet, mist, froth, aerosol, atomizer.

sprengiefni explosive; *synonyms* (*adj*) volatile, combustible, unstable, (*n*) bomb, (*v*) convulsive; *antonym* (*adj*) stable.

sprengikúla bomb; *synonyms* (*n*) grenade, (*v*) blast, bombard, fail, flop.

sprenging 1. detonation; *synonyms* (*n*) blast, explosion, burst, bang, (*v*) discharge, **2.** blast; *synonyms* (*n*) slam, (*v*) attack, blare, blight, bomb, **3.** explosion; *synonyms* (*n*) boom, detonation, eruption, fulmination, outbreak.

sprengja 1. blow; *synonyms* (*n*) bang, beat, blast, knock, (*adj*) gasp; *antonyms* (*v*) calm, save, **2.** bomb; *synonyms* (*n*) grenade, shell, (*v*) bombard, fail, flop, **3.** explode; *synonyms* (*v*) erupt, detonate, crack, discharge, (*n*) burst; *antonym* (*v*) implode.

sprettfiskur butterfish; *synonym* (*n*) stromateid.

springa 1. puncture; *synonyms* (*n*) prick, cut, hole, (*v*) bore, drill; *antonym* (*v*) inflate, **2.** burst; *synonyms* (*v*) break, crack, blast, (*adj*) split, explode; *antonym* (*v*) implode, **3.** explode; *synonyms* (*v*) erupt, detonate, discharge, fulminate, (*n*) burst.

springur spring; *synonyms* (*n*) jump, leap, bound, (*v*) hop, caper.

spritt spirit; *synonyms* (*n*) apparition, courage, ghost, life, mood; *antonyms* (*n*) lethargy, body.

sprossi bar; *synonyms* (*n*) barricade, band, (*v*) ban, block, bolt; *antonyms* (*v*) permit, allow.

sproti 1. shoot; *synonyms* (*v*) bud, discharge, dart, (*n*) scion, branch, **2.** bar; *synonyms* (*n*) barricade, band, (*v*) ban, block, bolt; *antonyms* (*v*) permit, allow, **3.** gnomon; *synonyms* (*n*) dial, horologe, hourglass, pendulum, sundial.

sprunga 1. rupture; *synonyms* (*n*) fracture, burst, rift, (*v*) break, crack; *antonym* (*n*) repair, **2.** crack;

synonyms (*n*) cleft, fissure, (*v*) chink, crevice, split; *antonym* (*v*) mend, **3.** crevice; *synonyms* (*n*) cranny, chap, gap, hole, interstice, **4.** joint; *synonyms* (*n*) articulation, hinge, join, seam, (*v*) articulate; *antonyms* (*adj*) individual, unilateral, private, separate, **5.** fracture; *synonyms* (*n*) breach, breaking, (*v*) rupture, bust, smash.

spúla flush; *synonyms* (*n*) bloom, (*v*) blush, glow, (*adj*) flat, affluent.

spunamælir spinner; *synonyms* (*n*) spinster, goatsucker, spinneret.

spuni 1. spin; *synonyms* (*n*) turn, twirl, whirl, (*v*) revolve, twist, **2.** improvisation; *synonyms* (*n*) extemporization, impromptu, extemporisation, invention, construction.

spurn query; *synonyms* (*n*) question, doubt, inquiry, (*v*) inquire, interrogate; *antonym* (*v*) answer.

spurning 1. question; *synonyms* (*n*) inquiry, (*v*) doubt, query, distrust, inquire; *antonyms* (*n*) certainty, (*v*) answer, **2.** point; *synonyms* (*n*) place, grade, peak, nib, (*v*) head, **3.** issue; *synonyms* (*n*) aftermath, egress, (*v*) flow, emanate, arise, **4.** enquiry; *synonyms* (*n*) question, research, doubtfulness, dubiousness, motion, **5.** inquiry; *synonyms* (*n*) examination, enquiry, investigation, exploration, (*v*) search.

spurningaeyðublað questionnaire; *synonyms* (*n*) form, document, enclosure, examination, paper.

spurningalisti questionnaire; *synonyms* (*n*) form, document, enclosure, examination, paper.

spurningaskrá questionnaire; *synonyms* (*n*) form, document, enclosure, examination, paper.

spýja vomit; *synonyms* (*v*) spew, heave, puke, cast, disgorge.

spyrða associate; *synonyms* (*v*) affiliate, connect, (*n*) ally, assistant, companion; *antonyms* (*v*) avoid, dissociate, distance, (*adj*) chief, (*n*) stranger.

spyrðing association; *synonyms* (*n*) affiliation, alliance, connection, assembly, affinity.

spyrja 1. ask; *synonyms* (*v*) inquire, request, appeal, beg, demand; *antonym* (*v*) answer, **2.** enquire; *synonyms* (*v*) ask, investigate, query, question, wonder.

spyrna 1. thrust; *synonyms* (*v*) jab, (*n*) push, poke, drive, stab; *antonym* (*v*) pull, **2.** traction; *synonyms* (*n*) grip, friction, draught, bag, (*v*) tug, **3.** wishbone; *synonyms* (*n*) sudarium, triskelion, veronica, boom.

Staða 1. position; *synonyms* (*n*) place, lay, (*v*) grade, fix, locate, **2.** role; *synonyms* (*n*) part, function, position, character, (*v*) office, **3.** place; *synonyms* (*n*) domicile, (*v*) post, arrange, rank, station; *antonym* (*v*) remove, **4.** status; *synonyms* (*n*) situation, caste, condition, order, (*adj*) standing, **5.**

post; *synonyms* (*n*) pillar, stake, attitude, (*v*) mail, base.

staðall 1. standard; *synonyms* (*adj*) model, (*n*) degree, measure, average, criterion; *antonyms* (*adj*) unusual, unconventional, special, **2.** norm; *synonyms* (*n*) mean, mode, median, gauge, par, **3.** master; *synonyms* (*n*) captain, instructor, (*v*) conquer, control, (*adj*) chief.

staðalloftþyngd atmosphere; *synonyms* (*n*) air, ambience, ambiance, aura, environment.

staðalmynd stereotype; *synonyms* (*n*) engrave, stereo, cliché, (*v*) pigeonhole, stamp.

staðalýsing topography; *synonyms* (*n*) terrain, backcloth, backdrop, background, countryside.

staðarákvörðun 1. position; *synonyms* (*n*) place, lay, (*v*) grade, fix, locate, **2.** positioning; *synonyms* (*n*) emplacement, locating, location, placement, position, **3.** fix; *synonyms* (*v*) establish, assign, determine, (*n*) bind, (*adj*) ascertain; *antonyms* (*v*) break, unfasten.

staðarhnit fix; *synonyms* (*v*) establish, assign, determine, (*n*) bind, (*adj*) ascertain; *antonyms* (*v*) break, unfasten.

staðarval location; *synonyms* (*n*) localization, orientation, position, berth, emplacement.

staðbinda 1. localize; *synonyms* (*v*) lay, localise, place, post, locate, **2.** focalize; *synonyms* (*v*) focus, center, concentrate, localize, centre.

staðbinding localization; *synonyms* (*n*) localisation, location, fix, emplacement, fixing.

staðbundinn 1. sedentary; *synonyms* (*adj*) inactive, lazy, sluggish, domestic, (*v*) untraveled; *antonym* (*adj*) active, **2.** topical; *synonyms* (*adj*) current, contemporary, new, topic, (*n*) local, **3.** regional; *synonyms* (*adj*) district, parochial, sectional, neighborhood, topical; *antonym* (*adj*) central, **4.** localized; *synonyms* (*adj*) localised, thick, **5.** local; *synonyms* (*adj*) native, home, indigenous, municipal, (*n*) resident; *antonyms* (*adj*) national, foreign, universal, worldwide.

staðfærsla localization; *synonyms* (*n*) localisation, location, fix, emplacement, fixing.

staðfastur stable; *synonyms* (*adj*) firm, permanent, reliable, constant, durable; *antonyms* (*adj*) unstable, shaky, wobbly, dangerous, precarious.

staðfélag community; *synonyms* (*n*) association, public, agreement, commune, (*adj*) communal; *antonym* (*adj*) private.

staðfesta 1. ratify; *synonyms* (*v*) approve, confirm, corroborate, acknowledge, authorize, **2.** sanction; *synonyms* (*n*) warrant, assent, (*v*) permit, countenance, allow; *antonyms* (*v*) ban, forbid, **3.** verify; *synonyms* (*v*) ascertain, check, establish, prove, (*n*) substantiate; *antonym* (*v*) disprove, **4.**

validate; *synonyms* (*v*) sustain, ratify, affirm, pass, support; *antonyms* (*v*) invalidate, cancel, nullify, overturn, **5.** accept; *synonyms* (*v*) receive, admit, take, recognize, abide; *antonyms* (*v*) refuse, reject, deny, snub, oppose.

staðfesting 1. ratification; *synonyms* (*n*) approval, confirmation, endorsement, sanction, affirmation, **2.** validation; *synonyms* (*n*) proof, substantiation, verification, establishment, justification, **3.** verification; *synonyms* (*n*) check, authentication, corroboration, evidence, testimony, **4.** approval; *synonyms* (*n*) acceptance, applause, approbation, acclaim, agreement; *antonyms* (*n*) disapproval, rejection, condemnation, scorn, criticism, **5.** confirmation; *synonyms* (*n*) ratification, demonstration, averment, visa, acknowledgment; *antonym* (*n*) contradiction.

staðfræði 1. topography; *synonyms* (*n*) terrain, backcloth, backdrop, background, countryside, **2.** chorology.

staðganga substitution; *synonyms* (*n*) replacement, exchange, change, substitute, interchange.

staðgengill 1. replacement; *synonyms* (*n*) exchange, substitute, alternate, deputy, renewal, **2.** substitute; *synonyms* (*adj*) replacement, alternative, (*v*) shift, change, replace.

staðgengur representative; *synonyms* (*n*) agent, delegate, deputy, envoy, proxy.

staðgönguefni substitute; *synonyms* (*adj*) replacement, alternative, (*n*) deputy, (*v*) alternate, shift.

staðgönguvara substitute; *synonyms* (*adj*) replacement, alternative, (*n*) deputy, (*v*) alternate, shift.

staðgreiðsla payment; *synonyms* (*n*) pay, compensation, bonus, charge, cost; *antonym* (*n*) non-payment.

staðgreina localize; *synonyms* (*v*) lay, localise, place, post, locate.

staðgreining localization; *synonyms* (*n*) localisation, location, fix, emplacement, fixing.

staðhæfa 1. state; *synonyms* (*n*) nation, position, say, country, (*v*) declare; *antonyms* (*v*) deny, (*adj*) private, **2.** allege; *synonyms* (*v*) affirm, maintain, plead, argue, (*n*) advance, **3.** assert; *synonyms* (*v*) allege, claim, aver, avow, insist, **4.** claim; *synonyms* (*n*) call, charge, allegation, (*v*) demand, ask; *antonyms* (*v*) disclaim, forfeit.

staðhæfing 1. assertion; *synonyms* (*n*) affirmation, argument, statement, claim, allegation, **2.** statement; *synonyms* (*n*) account, declaration, announcement, communication, instruction; *antonym* (*n*) denial, **3.** claim; *synonyms* (*n*) call, charge, (*v*) demand, ask, assert; *antonyms* (*v*) deny, disclaim, forfeit, **4**. allegation; *synonyms* (*n*) accusation, plea, allegement, assertion, indictment, **5**. contention; *synonyms* (*n*) competition, argumentation, battle, conflict, controversy; *antonym* (*n*) harmony.

staðkvæmni substitution; *synonyms* (*n*) replacement, exchange, change, substitute, interchange.

staðla 1. standardize; *synonyms* (*v*) normalize, regulate, order, standardise, adjust, **2**. normalize; *synonyms* (*v*) normalise, standardize, anneal, control, legalize, **3**. normalise; *synonyms* (*v*) renormalise, renormalize.

staðlandi normative; *synonym* (*adj*) prescriptive.

staðmarka localize; *synonyms* (*v*) lay, localise, place, post, locate.

staðmarkaður localized; *synonyms* (*adj*) localised, sectional, thick.

staðning locomotion; *synonyms* (*n*) motion, movement, travel, motivity, (*v*) clip.

staðrétta justify; *synonyms* (*v*) excuse, explain, absolve, confirm, (*n*) warrant.

staðreyna 1. ascertain; *synonyms* (*v*) see, check, determine, discover, establish, **2**. observe; *synonyms* (*v*) celebrate, comment, notice, commemorate, mind; *antonyms* (*v*) ignore, feel.

staðreynd 1. proof; *synonyms* (*n*) confirmation, demonstration, probation, argument, authentication, **2**. fact; *synonyms* (*n*) event, incident, detail, deed, particular; *antonyms* (*n*) guesswork, rumor, conjecture, fallacy, falsehood.

staðreyndahyggja positivism; *synonyms* (*n*) positivity, certainty, anabaptism, deism, externalism.

staðsetja 1. locate; *synonyms* (*v*) base, lay, discover, find, (*n*) place, **2**. localize; *synonyms* (*v*) localise, post, locate, set, situate.

staðsetning 1. situation; *synonyms* (*n*) place, employment, position, post, job, **2**. position; *synonyms* (*n*) lay, (*v*) grade, fix, locate, arrange, **3**. site; *synonyms* (*n*) location, point, room, seat, (*v*) set, **4**. location; *synonyms* (*n*) localization, orientation, berth, emplacement, lieu, **5**. localization; *synonyms* (*n*) localisation, fixing, hole, jam, locating.

staðsetningarviti locator; *synonym* (*n*) locater.

staðtengdur local; *synonyms* (*adj*) native, sectional, topical, home, (*n*) resident; *antonyms* (*adj*) national, foreign, universal, worldwide.

staðtölur statistics; *synonyms* (*n*) data, census, score, information, list.

staður 1. position; *synonyms* (*n*) place, lay, (*v*) grade, fix, locate, **2**. situation; *synonyms* (*n*) employment, position, post, job, matter, **3**. venue; *synonyms* (*n*)

locale, site, locus, location, seat, **4**. place; *synonyms* (*n*) domicile, (*v*) arrange, rank, station, deposit; *antonym* (*v*) remove, **5**. town; *synonyms* (*n*) city, borough, township, (*adj*) municipal, urban.

staðvær local; *synonyms* (*adj*) native, sectional, topical, home, (*n*) resident; *antonyms* (*adj*) national, foreign, universal, worldwide.

staðvindur monsoon; *synonyms* (*n*) cyclone, downpour, harmattan, hurricane, storm.

staðvísir marker; *synonyms* (*n*) brand, mark, label, token, pointer.

stæða expression; *synonyms* (*n*) diction, phrase, voice, appearance, aspect; *antonym* (*n*) repression.

stæði 1. socket; *synonyms* (*n*) cavity, alveolus, sleeve, hollow, pocket, **2**. site; *synonyms* (*n*) place, position, locate, (*v*) post, set.

stæður stationary; *synonyms* (*adj*) immovable, fixed, motionless, immobile, static; *antonym* (*adj*) moving.

stækka 1. extend; *synonyms* (*v*) expand, enlarge, amplify, broaden, dilate; *antonyms* (*v*) withdraw, shorten, limit, narrow, shrink, **2**. enlarge; *synonyms* (*v*) aggrandize, augment, distend, elaborate, increase; *antonyms* (*v*) reduce, contract, decrease, **3**. expand; *synonyms* (*v*) balloon, develop, extend, inflate, swell; *antonyms* (*v*) abbreviate, deflate, summarize.

stækkun 1. stretch; *synonyms* (*n*) extent, (*v*) extend, reach, strain, elongate; *antonym* (*v*) shorten, **2**. augmentation; *synonyms* (*n*) addition, enlargement, aggrandizement, extension, (*v*) increase; *antonym* (*n*) contraction, **3**. extension; *synonyms* (*n*) continuation, augmentation, expansion, annex, elongation; *antonyms* (*n*) limitation, limit, **4**. expansion; *synonyms* (*n*) amplification, development, dilatation, dilation, elaboration; *antonyms* (*n*) decrease, reduction, abbreviation, **5**. magnification; *synonyms* (*n*) exaggeration, exaltation, hyperbole.

stækkunarhæfni extensibility; *synonyms* (*n*) extensibleness, flexibility, (*adj*) extendibility.

stæling imitation; *synonyms* (*n*) counterfeit, dummy, sham, (*adj*) fake, bogus; *antonyms* (*n*) original, (*adj*) genuine, real.

stælingarlyf tonic; *synonyms* (*n*) stimulant, (*adj*) bracing, brisk, fresh, invigorating.

stæll elastic; *synonyms* (*adj*) flexible, buoyant, ductile, limber, pliable; *antonyms* (*adj*) rigid, stiff, inflexible, inelastic.

stælni elasticity; *synonyms* (*n*) bounce, spring, flexibility, pliability, suppleness.

stærð 1. dimension; *synonyms* (*n*) degree, breadth, bulk, magnitude, size, **2**. bulk; *synonyms* (*adj*) mass, amount, majority, volume, capacity; *antonym* (*n*) minority, **3**. size; *synonyms* (*n*) measure, dimension, dimensions, extent, (v) gauge; *antonyms* (n) length, slenderness, **4**. scope; *synonyms* (n) range, reach, domain, purview, room, **5**. scale; *synonyms* (n) flake, gamut, (v) ascend, climb, (adj) balance; *antonym* (v) descend.

stærða grade; *synonyms* (n) class, place, rank, degree, (v) level.

stærðarhlutfall scale; *synonyms* (n) flake, gamut, (v) ascend, climb, (adj) balance; *antonym* (v) descend.

stærðfræði mathematics; *synonyms* (n) math, arithmetic, maths, mathesis, sums.

stærðfræðigreining 1. analysis; *synonyms* (n) anatomy, breakdown, decomposition, inquiry, inspection; *antonym* (n) synthesis, **2**. calculus; *synonyms* (n) concretion, stone, calculi, tartar, (v) calculation.

stærðtákn expression; *synonyms* (n) diction, phrase, voice, appearance, aspect; *antonym* (n) repression.

stærir dilator; *synonyms* (n) dilatator, dilater.

stærisýki megalomania; *synonym* (n) egoism.

stærivöðvi dilator; *synonyms* (n) dilatator, dilater.

stærri major; *synonyms* (adj) chief, key, large, main, superior; *antonyms* (adj) minor, unimportant, lesser, petty, slight.

stafa spell; *synonyms* (n) magic, fascination, bout, conjuration, (v) charm.

stafagerð font; *synonyms* (n) fount, fountain, type, baptistery, print.

stafanákvæmni precision; *synonyms* (n) accuracy, correctness, exactness, accurateness, (adj) precise; *antonyms* (n) inaccuracy, vagueness, ambiguity, imprecision.

stafbaktería 1. rod; *synonyms* (n) bar, baton, perch, shaft, (v) stick, **2**. bacillus; *synonyms* (n) bacilli, bug, microbe, barn, bel.

staffruma rod; *synonyms* (n) bar, baton, perch, shaft, (v) stick.

staffylli filler; *synonyms* (n) feeder, fill, filling, stuffing, complement.

staffylling padding; *synonyms* (n) pad, cushioning, filling, wadding, (adj) cushion.

stafgerill 1. rod; *synonyms* (n) bar, baton, perch, shaft, (v) stick, **2**. bacillus; *synonyms* (n) bacilli, bug, microbe, barn, bel.

stafgólf bay; *synonyms* (n) alcove, bark, recess, (v) yap, roar.

stafla 1. stow; *synonyms* (v) pack, cram, charge, house, load, **2**. stack; *synonyms* (n) pile, accumulation, mound, rick, (v) heap, **3**. cascade; *synonyms* (n) waterfall, torrent, (v) fall, gush, stream; *antonyms* (v) trickle, dribble.

staflaga bacillary; *synonyms* (adj) bacillar, baccilar, bacilliform, baculiform, rodlike.

stafli 1. stack; *synonyms* (n) pile, accumulation, mound, rick, (v) heap, **2**. cascade; *synonyms* (n) waterfall, torrent, (v) fall, gush, stream; *antonyms* (v) trickle, dribble.

stafnhalli trim; *synonyms* (adj) tidy, (v) cut, dress, clip, garnish; *antonym* (adj) fat.

stafnrið prostyle; *synonym* (adj) pseudoprostyle.

stafnriðshof prostyle; *synonym* (adj) pseudoprostyle.

stafrænn digital; *synonyms* (adj) numeric, (n) computer.

stafróf 1. rudiments; *synonyms* (n) basics, fundamentals, grammar, abecedary, primer, **2**. basics; *synonyms* (n) rudiments, bedrock, foundation, resources, structure, **3**. alphabet; *synonyms* (n) letter, elements, rudiment, outlines, **4**. fundamentals; *synonyms* (n) essentials, essence, groundwork, handbook, practicalities, **5**. elements; *synonyms* (n) alphabet, contents, principia.

stafsía mask; *synonyms* (n) cover, conceal, (v) cloak, disguise, hide; *antonym* (v) disclose.

stafþekjufruma rod; *synonyms* (n) bar, baton, perch, shaft, (v) stick.

stafur 1. stick; *synonyms* (n) bar, (v) adhere, stab, attach, cling, **2**. rod; *synonyms* (n) baton, perch, shaft, whip, (v) stick, **3**. pillar; *synonyms* (n) column, brace, mainstay, obelisk, post, **4**. character; *synonyms* (n) kind, nature, note, part, quality, **5**. letter; *synonyms* (n) epistle, mail, character, communication, dispatch.

stag 1. strut; *synonyms* (n) buttress, brace, (v) prance, stalk, swagger, **2**. stay; *synonyms* (v) remain, reside, rest, prop, stop; *antonyms* (v) leave, change, abscond, depart.

staga patch; *synonyms* (n) darn, fleck, mend, plot, (v) piece.

stagfesta anchor; *synonyms* (n) mainstay, (v) tie, fasten, secure, (adj) refuge.

stagherðir turnbuckle; *synonym* (n) tourniquet.

stagvenda tack; *synonyms* (n) nail, pin, (v) affix, baste, attach.

stagvending tack; *synonyms* (n) nail, pin, (v) affix, baste, attach.

stajo braces; *synonyms* (n) brace, suspenders, bitstock, ribs, bracing.

stak 1. item; *synonyms* (n) piece, detail, article, entry, object, **2**. element; *synonyms* (n) component, constituent, ingredient, factor, substance.

stakaskil transition; *synonyms* (n) change, passage, transit, alteration, changeover.

staklitningur univalent; *synonyms* (adj) monovalent, (adv) monatomic.

stakmótun individualization; *synonym* (*n*) individuation.

stakrænn discrete; *synonyms* (*adj*) separate, distinct, different, detached, diverse.

staksettur discrete; *synonyms* (*adj*) separate, distinct, different, detached, diverse.

stakstæður 1. sporadic; *synonyms* (*adj*) intermittent, rare, occasional, sparse, infrequent; *antonyms* (*adj*) continuous, constant, nonstop, frequent, regular, **2**. alternate; *synonyms* (*v*) reciprocate, (*n*) substitute, alternative, surrogate, standby; *antonym* (*n*) original, **3**. discrete; *synonyms* (*adj*) separate, distinct, different, detached, diverse.

Stakt isolated; *synonyms* (*adj*) detached, apart, deserted, separate, distant; *antonym* (*adj*) inhabited.

staktrjáaslétta savanna; *synonyms* (*n*) steppe, basin, desert, pampas, wold.

stakur 1. single; *synonyms* (*adj*) only, celibate, one, odd, particular; *antonyms* (*adj*) married, double, multiple, **2**. sporadic; *synonyms* (*adj*) intermittent, rare, occasional, sparse, infrequent; *antonyms* (*adj*) continuous, constant, nonstop, frequent, regular, **3**. solitary; *synonyms* (*adj*) lonesome, forlorn, alone, lone, lonely, **4**. discrete; *synonyms* (*adj*) separate, distinct, different, detached, diverse.

stál 1. steel; *synonyms* (*n*) harden, blade, brand, (*adj*) iron, (*v*) nerve, **2**. tool; *synonyms* (*n*) instrument, implement, machine, puppet, pawn.

stallbakur 1. sedan; *synonyms* (*n*) saloon, automobile, car, auto, limousine, **2**. saloon; *synonyms* (*n*) bar, pub, barroom, pothouse, inn.

stallur pedestal; *synonyms* (*n*) base, bottom, foot, groundwork, basis.

stáltunna drum; *synonyms* (*n*) barrel, cask, tympan, (*v*) beat, roll.

stam stammer; *synonyms* (*v*) stutter, falter, hesitate, bumble, stumble.

stama stammer; *synonyms* (*v*) stutter, falter, hesitate, bumble, stumble.

standa stand; *synonyms* (*v*) endure, stall, (*n*) attitude, booth, rack; *antonyms* (*v*) sit, lie.

standliður axis; *synonyms* (*n*) axle, pivot, hinge, center, hub.

standsetja refit; *synonyms* (*v*) mend, repair, renovate, equip, fix.

standur 1. pillar; *synonyms* (*n*) column, brace, mainstay, obelisk, post, **2**. rack; *synonyms* (*n*) manger, wrack, (*v*) torture, excruciate, torment, **3**. stand; *synonyms* (*v*) endure, stall, (*n*) attitude, booth, rack; *antonyms* (*v*) sit, lie, **4**. arrack; *synonym* (*n*) arak, **5**. frame; *synonyms* (*n*) design, border, (*v*) form, construct, fabricate.

stanga ram; *synonyms* (*v*) beat, cram, crash, drive, jam.

stangveiðimaður angler; *synonyms* (*n*) goosefish, monkfish, allmouth, angelfish, anglerfish.

stans 1. stamp; *synonyms* (*n*) mark, seal, brand, (*v*) imprint, print, **2**. punch; *synonyms* (*n*) jab, drill, (*v*) poke, hit, prick, **3**. standstill; *synonyms* (*n*) deadlock, impasse, stalemate, cessation, halt, **4**. die; *synonyms* (*v*) decease, dead, death, depart, (*n*) dice.

stansa 1. stamp; *synonyms* (*n*) mark, seal, brand, (*v*) imprint, print, **2**. punch; *synonyms* (*n*) jab, drill, (*v*) poke, hit, prick.

stansaður stamping; *synonyms* (*n*) marking, impression, blocking, coin, coining.

stanslaus constant; *synonyms* (*adj*) ceaseless, incessant, perpetual, steady, continual; *antonyms* (*adj*) changeable, intermittent, irregular, sporadic, variable.

stapp tramp; *synonyms* (*n*) hike, bum, hobo, (*v*) trudge, walk; *antonym* (*v*) loyalist.

star cataract; *synonyms* (*n*) cascade, waterfall, deluge, falls, torrent.

starblinda cataract; *synonyms* (*n*) cascade, waterfall, deluge, falls, torrent.

starf 1. vocation; *synonyms* (*n*) calling, profession, occupation, business, (*v*) employment, **2**. post; *synonyms* (*n*) place, function, office, position, (*v*) mail, **3**. action; *synonyms* (*n*) act, accomplishment, activity, agency, (*v*) achievement; *antonyms* (*n*) inaction, inactivity, **4**. function; *synonyms* (*n*) role, service, (*v*) exercise, run, serve, **5**. employment; *synonyms* (*n*) trade, use, (*v*) application, employ, (*adj*) work; *antonym* (*n*) unemployment.

starfa 1. work; *synonyms* (*n*) exercise, business, (*v*) labor, operate, toil; *antonyms* (*v*) idle, malfunction, **2**. function; *synonyms* (*n*) position, office, place, role, (*v*) act.

starfandi 1. active; *synonyms* (*adj*) energetic, alert, busy, diligent, effective; *antonyms* (*adj*) dormant, inactive, sluggish, idle, latent, **2**. functional; *synonyms* (*adj*) practical, handy, operational, operative, working; *antonyms* (*adj*) nonfunctional, useless.

starfrænn functional; *synonyms* (*adj*) practical, effective, handy, operational, operative; *antonyms* (*adj*) nonfunctional, useless.

starfsástand marking; *synonyms* (*n*) mark, earmark, brand, crisscross, marker.

starfsbilun 1. insufficiency; *synonyms* (*n*) imperfection, inadequacy, deficit, deficiency, shortage; *antonyms* (*n*) adequacy, abundance, sufficiency, **2**. malfunction; *synonyms* (*n*) breakdown, bug, trouble, defect, stoppage.

starfsbróðir colleague; *synonyms* (*n*) associate, buddy, assistant, collaborator, friend.

starfsemi 1. action; *synonyms* (*n*) act, accomplishment, activity, agency, (*v*) achievement; *antonyms* (*n*) inaction, inactivity, **2**. activity; *synonyms* (*n*) action, activeness, exercise, liveliness, play; *antonym* (*n*) inactiveness, **3**. operation; *synonyms* (*n*) execution, movement, effect, business, management, **4**. function; *synonyms* (*n*) position, office, place, role, (*v*) run.

starfsfé capital; *synonyms* (*n*) principal, city, stock, (*adj*) main, primary.

starfsferill career; *synonyms* (*n*) calling, race, (*adj*) job, (*v*) course, dash.

starfsfólk 1. staff; *synonyms* (*n*) cane, club, post, employees, (*v*) crutch, **2**. personnel; *synonyms* (*n*) staff, workers, workforce, force, troops.

starfsframi career; *synonyms* (*n*) calling, race, (*adj*) job, (*v*) course, dash.

starfsgalli deficit; *synonyms* (*n*) deficiency, failure, shortage, dearth, (*adj*) defect; *antonym* (*n*) excess.

starfsglöp apraxia; *synonym* (*n*) dyspraxia.

starfsgrein 1. profession; *synonyms* (*n*) confession, declaration, employment, occupation, affirmation, **2**. trade; *synonyms* (*n*) deal, business, barter, commerce, (*v*) change; *antonyms* (*n*) purchase, (*adj*) charitable, **3**. vocation; *synonyms* (*n*) calling, profession, career, job, trade, **4**. occupation; *synonyms* (*n*) occupancy, craft, place, affair, conquest; *antonym* (*n*) surrender.

starfsgreining differentiation; *synonyms* (*n*) difference, distinction, contrast, demarcation, discrimination.

starfshættir procedure; *synonyms* (*n*) process, formula, practice, routine, fashion.

starfsháttur function; *synonyms* (*n*) position, office, place, (*v*) act, exercise.

starfshópur team; *synonyms* (*n*) crew, company, gang, squad, (*v*) pair.

starfslið 1. workforce; *synonyms* (*n*) manpower, personnel, employees, hands, men, **2**. staff; *synonyms* (*n*) cane, club, post, faculty, (*v*) crutch, **3**. personnel; *synonyms* (*n*) staff, workers, workforce, force, troops.

starfslok retirement; *synonyms* (*n*) retreat, resignation, departure, privacy, seclusion.

starfsmaður 1. worker; *synonyms* (*n*) employee, hand, proletarian, workman, actor, **2**. official; *synonyms* (*adj*) formal, (*n*) officer, minister, bureaucrat, (*v*) authoritative; *antonyms* (*adj*) unofficial, private, illegal, informal, **3**. employee; *synonyms* (*n*) clerk, laborer, worker, apprentice, assistant; *antonym* (*n*) employer, **4**. officer;

synonyms (*n*) captain, administrator, commander, executive, officeholder.

starfsmenn staff; *synonyms* (*n*) cane, club, post, employees, (*v*) crutch.

starfsmögnun 1. synergism; *synonyms* (*n*) synergy, cooperation, **2**. synergy; *synonyms* (*n*) synergism, additivity, concert.

starfsreglur regulations; *synonyms* (*n*) policy, system, convention.

starfsröskun malfunction; *synonyms* (*n*) breakdown, bug, trouble, defect, stoppage.

starfsstétt profession; *synonyms* (*n*) confession, declaration, employment, occupation, affirmation.

starfsstöð establishment; *synonyms* (*n*) business, company, constitution, institution, concern; *antonyms* (*n*) elimination, end.

starfsstuðull factor; *synonyms* (*n*) agent, component, broker, divisor, (*adj*) constituent.

starfssvæði premises; *synonyms* (*n*) grounds, facts, lemma, terms, principle.

starfsþjálfun practice; *synonyms* (*n*) exercise, fashion, convention, (*v*) custom, drill; *antonym* (*n*) performance.

starfsþreyta burnout; *synonyms* (*n*) exhaustion, fatigue, (*v*) blowout, disintegration, meltdown.

starfstruflun dysfunction; *synonyms* (*n*) disfunction, attack, malfunction.

starfsvefur parenchyma; *synonyms* (*n*) substance, body, compages, element, matter.

stari starling; *synonyms* (*n*) sterling, (*adj*) earthquake, loud.

starta start; *synonyms* (*v*) begin, originate, commence, (*n*) jump, onset; *antonyms* (*v*) end, finish, stop, conclude, (*n*) conclusion.

startari starter; *synonyms* (*n*) appetizer, beginner, crank, dispatcher, entrant.

staumlína streamline; *synonyms* (*v*) simplify, centralize, order, reorganize, shape.

staur pole; *synonyms* (*n*) perch, bar, picket, post, rod.

staurliður ankylosis; *synonyms* (*n*) anchylosis, (*adj*) aplomb, solidity, immobility, soundness.

stautur 1. ejector; *synonyms* (*n*) knockout, eductor, ouster, ousting, pusher, **2**. finger; *synonyms* (*n*) digit, dactyl, (*v*) feel, handle, touch.

steðji 1. anvil; *synonyms* (*n*) incus, stithy, fulciment, prop, stand, **2**. incus; *synonyms* (*n*) anvil, stithe.

stef 1. theme; *synonyms* (*n*) matter, motif, subject, base, composition, **2**. routine; *synonyms* (*n*) round, (*adj*) everyday, ordinary, regular, common; *antonym* (*adj*) unusual.

stefja 1. procedure; *synonyms* (*n*) process, formula, practice, routine, fashion, **2**. subroutine; *synonyms* (*n*) procedure, subprogram, function, act, bit.

stefna 1. summon; *synonyms* (*v*) cite, assemble, convene, demand, ask, 2. policy; *synonyms* (*n*) course, plan, approach, insurance, tactics, 3. vector; *synonyms* (*n*) direction, bearing, sender, transmitter, vehicle, 4. trend; *synonyms* (*n*) fashion, tendency, fad, inclination, (*v*) style, 5. strategy; *synonyms* (*n*) dodge, scheme, strategics, game, design.

stefnandi plaintiff; *synonyms* (*n*) complainant, accuser, prosecutor, pursuer, applicant.

stefndi defendant; *synonyms* (*n*) accused, litigant, party, plaintiff, prisoner.

stefni stem; *synonyms* (*n*) root, bow, branch, (*v*) originate, block.

stefnir prow; *synonyms* (*n*) bow, fore, stem, beak, nose.

stefnubreyting 1. tack; *synonyms* (*n*) nail, pin, (*v*) affix, baste, attach, 2. manoeuvre; *synonyms* (*v*) maneuver, control, direct, go, guide.

stefnufesta commitment; *synonyms* (*n*) dedication, charge, allegiance, appointment, committal.

stefnufrávik deflection; *synonyms* (*n*) deviation, bend, deflexion, variation, bending.

stefnugeiri lobe; *synonyms* (*n*) division, flap, limb, member, arm.

stefnugeisli radial; *synonyms* (*adj*) angelic, centrifugal, spiral, stellate, radiated.

stefnuháður anisotropic; *synonyms* (*adj*) anisotrope, anisotropous.

stefnuhneigður anisotropic; *synonyms* (*adj*) anisotrope, anisotropous.

stefnuhorn 1. argument; *synonyms* (*n*) controversy, debate, matter, proof, reason; *antonyms* (*n*) agreement, harmony, 2. azimuth; *synonym* (*v*) rhumb.

stefnumælir goniometer; *synonyms* (*n*) clinometer, graphometer, (*v*) bathometer, dynamometer, galvanometer.

stefnumál policy; *synonyms* (*n*) course, plan, approach, insurance, tactics.

stefnumörkun strategy; *synonyms* (*n*) dodge, plan, scheme, strategics, (*v*) tactics.

stefnumótun strategy; *synonyms* (*n*) dodge, plan, scheme, strategics, (*v*) tactics.

stefnusnauður isotropic; *synonym* (*adj*) isotropous.

stefnusneyða isotropy; *synonyms* (*n*) isotropism, symmetry.

stefnuvirkni directivity; *synonym* (*n*) directionality.

stegla stereotype; *synonyms* (*n*) engrave, stereo, cliché, (*v*) pigeonhole, stamp.

steglingur stereotype; *synonyms* (*n*) engrave, stereo, cliché, (*v*) pigeonhole, stamp.

stego braces; *synonyms* (*n*) brace, suspenders, bitstock, ribs, bracing.

steik roast; *synonyms* (*n*) ridicule, (*v*) broil, burn, bake, grill.

stein stone; *synonyms* (*n*) jewel, rock, calculus, gem, (*v*) pit.

steinaldin drupe; *synonyms* (*n*) cherry, berry, fruit.

steinber drupe; *synonyms* (*n*) cherry, berry, fruit.

steinbítsbarn wolffish; *synonyms* (*n*) catfish, lancetfish, mudcat.

steinbítsgóna wolffish; *synonyms* (*n*) catfish, lancetfish, mudcat.

steinbítur 1. wolffish; *synonyms* (*n*) catfish, lancetfish, mudcat, 2. catfish; *synonyms* (*n*) wolffish, goujon.

steinbrýni 1. whetstone; *synonyms* (*n*) rub, caoutchouc, chance, failing, (*adj*) grindstone, 2. grindstone; *synonyms* (*v*) grinder, mill, arrastra, file, grater.

steind mineral; *synonyms* (*adj*) inanimate, (*n*) rock, petroleum, granite, limestone.

steinefnahnútur tophus; *synonyms* (*n*) calculus, chalkstone, dragon, tartar, tofus.

steinefni mineral; *synonyms* (*adj*) inanimate, (*n*) rock, petroleum, granite, limestone.

steingeit ibex; *synonym* (*n*) steinbok.

steingervingur fossil; *synonyms* (*n*) fogey, fogy, dodo, (*adj*) flint, obsolete.

steinhvel lithosphere; *synonyms* (*n*) geosphere, sial.

steinhvolf lithosphere; *synonyms* (*n*) geosphere, sial.

steinkvörn concretion; *synonyms* (*n*) coagulation, coalescence, compression, union, calculus.

steinmyndun concretion; *synonyms* (*n*) coagulation, coalescence, compression, union, calculus.

steinn 1. stone; *synonyms* (*n*) jewel, rock, calculus, gem, (*v*) pit, 2. calculus; *synonyms* (*n*) concretion, stone, calculi, tartar, (*v*) calculation, 3. concretion; *synonyms* (*n*) coagulation, coalescence, compression, union, compaction.

steinolía kerosene; *synonyms* (*n*) petroleum, kerosine, oil, petrol, (*v*) gasoline.

steinsmuga diarrhea; *synonyms* (*n*) diarrhoea, lax, looseness.

steinsteypa concrete; *synonyms* (*adj*) actual, positive, (*n*) cement, (*v*) coagulate, congeal; *antonyms* (*adj*) theoretical, intangible, abstract, hypothetical, incidental.

steintegund mineral; *synonyms* (*adj*) inanimate, (*n*) rock, petroleum, granite, limestone.

steinungur cement; *synonyms* (*n*) glue, adhesive, gum, (*v*) fasten, fix.

stekja monad; *synonyms* (*n*) monas, (*adj*) animalcule, shrimp, worm.

stél tail; *synonyms* (*n*) rear, shadow, (*v*) follow, pursue, track; *antonyms* (*v*) head, front.

stela 1. purloin; *synonyms* (*v*) filch, pilfer, pinch, steal, abstract, **2**. steal; *synonyms* (*v*) lift, purloin, creep, misappropriate, (*n*) bargain, **3**. abstract; *synonyms* (*adj*) theoretical, (*v*) abridge, (*n*) synopsis, abridgement, digest; *antonym* (*adj*) concrete, **4**. nick; *synonyms* (*n*) notch, mark, cut, chip, (*v*) dent.

stelling 1. position; *synonyms* (*n*) place, lay, (*v*) grade, fix, locate, **2**. configuration; *synonyms* (*n*) form, arrangement, conformation, shape, organization.

stelpa 1. wench; *synonyms* (*n*) girl, quean, slut, strumpet, (*v*) drab, **2**. gal; *synonyms* (*n*) gallon, woman, congius, female, lady, **3**. lass; *synonyms* (*n*) lassie, harlot, nymph, youngster, schoolgirl, **4**. girl; *synonyms* (*n*) damsel, daughter, fille, lass, maid.

stelsýki kleptomania; *synonyms* (*n*) cleptomania, dipsomania, (*v*) rapacity, thievishness.

stemma caulk; *synonyms* (*v*) calk, splice, bar, close, stanch.

stemmir barrier; *synonyms* (*n*) barricade, bar, bulwark, dam, handicap.

stemmistál chisel; *synonyms* (*v*) carve, cheat, cut, shape, beguile.

steradíani steradian; *synonym* (*n*) strontium.

steri steroid; *synonym* (*adj*) steroidal.

sterkja starch; *synonyms* (*n*) amylum, vitality, (*v*) stiffen, (*adj*) stiff, glair.

sterkjulíki amyloid; *synonyms* (*adj*) amylaceous, amyloidal, starchlike.

sterkjurót arrowroot; *synonym* (*n*) achira.

sterkur 1. solid; *synonyms* (*adj*) firm, dense, compact, consistent, hard; *antonyms* (*adj*) soft, unreliable, loose, gaseous, (*n*) liquid, **2**. vigorous; *synonyms* (*adj*) robust, strong, energetic, hardy, lively; *antonyms* (*adj*) feeble, lethargic, weak, dull, unenergetic, **3**. tough; *synonyms* (*adj*) difficult, tenacious, arduous, laborious, (*n*) bully; *antonyms* (*adj*) tender, easy, flimsy, lightweight, simple, **4**. strong; *synonyms* (*adj*) intense, powerful, able, deep, stable; *antonyms* (*adj*) bland, delicate, faint, frail, mild, **5**. concentrated; *synonyms* (*adj*) condensed, heavy, solid, intensive, intent; *antonyms* (*adj*) dispersed, uncondensed, unsaturated.

stermót stereotype; *synonyms* (*n*) engrave, stereo, cliché, (*v*) pigeonhole, stamp.

steróíð steroid; *synonym* (*adj*) steroidal.

stétt 1. place; *synonyms* (*n*) position, (*v*) post, arrange, fix, lay; *antonym* (*v*) remove, **2**. class; *synonyms* (*n*) category, group, (*v*) sort, place, rank, **3**. caste; *synonyms* (*n*) order, class, variety, (*adj*) degree, baccalaureate, **4**. estate; *synonyms* (*n*) condition, land, demesne, domain, acres.

stéttakerfi caste; *synonyms* (*n*) order, class, rank, sort, (*adj*) degree.

stéttarstaða caste; *synonyms* (*n*) order, class, rank, sort, (*adj*) degree.

stéttskipting stratification; *synonyms* (*n*) bedding, lamination.

steypa 1. cast; *synonyms* (*v*) hurl, throw, form, shed, stamp, **2**. fix; *synonyms* (*v*) establish, assign, determine, (*n*) bind, (*adj*) ascertain; *antonyms* (*v*) break, unfasten, **3**. found; *synonyms* (*v*) erect, base, build, constitute, construct; *antonym* (*adj*) misplaced, **4**. mold; *synonyms* (*n*) cast, matrix, frame, (*v*) model, fashion.

steypibað 1. shower; *synonyms* (*n*) rain, (*v*) pour, bathe, hail, sprinkle, **2**. douche; *synonyms* (*n*) shower, bath, (*v*) affusion, irrigation, flush.

steyping embedding; *synonym* (*n*) bedding.

steypumót 1. casting; *synonyms* (*n*) cast, molding, pouring, air, appearence, **2**. mold; *synonyms* (*n*) matrix, frame, (*v*) model, form, fashion, **3**. mould; *synonyms* (*n*) mildew, (*v*) mold, make, forge, knead.

steypumótun casting; *synonyms* (*n*) cast, molding, pouring, air, appearence.

steypustyrktarjárn reinforcement; *synonyms* (*n*) brace, fortification, backing, consolidation, support.

steytill mortar; *synonyms* (*n*) howitzer, plaster, birdlime, cannon, (*v*) cement.

steyting contention; *synonyms* (*n*) competition, argument, argumentation, battle, conflict; *antonym* (*n*) harmony.

steytir stop; *synonyms* (*n*) halt, hold, stay, check, end; *antonyms* (*v*) continue, start, begin, encourage, permit.

Stía bunker; *synonyms* (*n*) bin, dugout, trap, ambuscade, ambush.

stífa brace; *synonyms* (*n*) couple, duo, pair, (*v*) clamp, invigorate; *antonym* (*v*) weaken.

stífkrampi tetanus; *synonyms* (*n*) lockjaw, (*adj*) scabies, scarlatina, scrofula, seasickness.

stífla 1. skate; *synonyms* (*v*) glide, skim, slip, coast, slide, **2**. stuff; *synonyms* (*n*) material, (*v*) cram, fill, jam, pack; *antonym* (*v*) unstuff, **3**. dam; *synonyms* (*n*) barrage, barricade, dike, dyke, (*v*) block, **4**. block; *synonyms* (*n*) bar, pad, (*v*) arrest, stop, hinder; *antonyms* (*v*) free, unblock, open.

stíflíður ankylosis; *synonyms* (*n*) anchylosis, (*adj*) aplomb, solidity, immobility, soundness.

stíflisskata skate; *synonyms* (*v*) glide, skim, slip, coast, slide.

stífludrep infarct; *synonyms* (*n*) infarction, blockade.

stíflufleygsmyndun infarction; *synonyms* (*n*) infarct, constipation.

stífluﬂeygun infarction; *synonyms* (*n*) infarct, constipation.

stífluﬂeygur infarct; *synonyms* (*n*) infarction, blockade.

stíﬂugarður 1. dam; *synonyms* (*n*) barrage, barricade, dike, dyke, (*v*) block, **2.** dyke; *synonyms* (*n*) dam, ditch, channel, gutter, (*adj*) lesbian.

stiflun 1. obstruction; *synonyms* (*n*) obstacle, hindrance, interruption, bar, (*v*) impediment, **2.** occlusion; *synonyms* (*n*) closure, block, blockage, stoppage, obstruction.

stífna freeze; *synonyms* (*n*) frost, (*v*) congeal, chill, arrest, cool; *antonyms* (*v*) melt, thaw, boil.

stífni rigidity; *synonyms* (*n*) austerity, firmness, inflexibility, hardness, rigor; *antonyms* (*n*) flexibility, malleability, pliability, softness.

stífur rigid; *synonyms* (*adj*) harsh, fixed, hard, inflexible, stiff; *antonyms* (*adj*) flexible, elastic, soft.

stig 1. step; *synonyms* (*n*) degree, measure, stage, walk, (*v*) pace, **2.** stage; *synonyms* (*n*) grade, phase, floor, level, period, **3.** score; *synonyms* (*n*) mark, bill, count, scratch, (*v*) notch, **4.** rate; *synonyms* (*n*) price, worth, (*v*) assess, estimate, evaluate, **5.** degree; *synonyms* (*n*) class, extent, condition, order, place.

stiga grade; *synonyms* (*n*) class, place, rank, degree, (*v*) level.

stíga 1. wheel; *synonyms* (*n*) circle, cycle, (*v*) roll, revolve, turn, **2.** cycle; *synonyms* (*n*) bicycle, round, (*v*) bike, motorcycle, wheel, **3.** bicycle; *synonyms* (*n*) machine, vehicle, coach, (*v*) pedal, drive, **4.** climb; *synonyms* (*v*) ascend, arise, clamber, (*n*) rise, mount; *antonyms* (*v*) descend, drop, **5.** pedal; *synonyms* (*n*) treadle, bar, handle, knob, (*adj*) pedalian.

stigbæta upgrade; *synonyms* (*v*) advance, boost, enhance, elevate, (*n*) raise; *antonyms* (*v*) demote, downgrade.

stigbót upgrade; *synonyms* (*v*) advance, boost, enhance, elevate, (*n*) raise; *antonyms* (*v*) demote, downgrade.

stigbreyting comparison; *synonyms* (*n*) analogy, compare, likeness, resemblance, comparing; *antonym* (*n*) dissimilarity.

stigflokkun staging; *synonyms* (*n*) production, scaffolding, scaffold, presentation, stage.

stiggreining 1. staging; *synonyms* (*n*) production, scaffolding, scaffold, presentation, stage, **2.** hierarchy; *synonyms* (*n*) order, rank, class, apparatus, executive.

stighækkandi progressive; *synonyms* (*adj*) advanced, forward, gradual, active, (*n*) liberal; *antonyms* (*adj*) old-fashioned, traditional, (*n*) conservative.

stigi ladder; *synonyms* (*n*) scale, run, steps, washboard, (*v*) bleed.

stiglækkandi regressive; *synonyms* (*adj*) reactionary, retrogressive, returning, backward, (*v*) resilient.

stigsetning staging; *synonyms* (*n*) production, scaffolding, scaffold, presentation, stage.

stigskipt hierarchical; *synonyms* (*adj*) hierarchal, hierarchic, archiepiscopal.

stigskipting 1. graduation; *synonyms* (*n*) commencement, gradation, (*adj*) adaption, adjustment, (*v*) allotment, **2.** hierarchy; *synonyms* (*n*) order, rank, class, apparatus, executive.

stigskiptur 1. hierarchic; *synonyms* (*adj*) hierarchal, hierarchical, **2.** hierarchical; *synonyms* (*adj*) hierarchic, archiepiscopal.

stigskipun hierarchy; *synonyms* (*n*) order, rank, class, apparatus, executive.

stigull gradient; *synonyms* (*n*) grade, slope, pitch, (*v*) acclivity, ascent.

stigun staging; *synonyms* (*n*) production, scaffolding, scaffold, presentation, stage.

stígvél boot; *synonyms* (*n*) kick, trunk, bang, charge, gain.

stigveldi hierarchy; *synonyms* (*n*) order, rank, class, apparatus, executive.

stigveldun hierarchy; *synonyms* (*n*) order, rank, class, apparatus, executive.

stigverkandi progressive; *synonyms* (*adj*) advanced, forward, gradual, active, (*n*) liberal; *antonyms* (*adj*) old-fashioned, traditional, (*n*) conservative.

stigvöxtur hierarchy; *synonyms* (*n*) order, rank, class, apparatus, executive.

stika ruler; *synonyms* (*n*) master, governor, monarch, (*adj*) rule, regent.

stiki parameter; *synonyms* (*n*) argument, guideline, limit, directive, modulus.

stikill pedicel; *synonyms* (*n*) pedicle, stalk, pedicule, stem.

stikla 1. trailer; *synonyms* (*n*) caravan, leader, ad, advertisement, announcement, **2.** link; *synonyms* (*n*) connection, join, joint, (*v*) combine, tie; *antonym* (*v*) separate.

stílabók notebook; *synonyms* (*n*) book, laptop, pad, album, computer.

stilklaus sessile; *synonyms* (*adj*) attached, affiliated, committed, connected, stalkless.

stilkselja celery; *synonyms* (*n*) anise, caraway, carrot, dill.

stilksellerí celery; *synonyms* (*n*) anise, caraway, carrot, dill.

stilkur 1. rachis; *synonyms* (*n*) back, backbone, spine, anchor, backrest, **2.** stem; *synonyms* (*n*) root, bow, branch, (*v*) originate, block.

still style; *synonyms* (*n*) fashion, name, (*v*) call, entitle, (*adj*) manner.

stilla 1. regulate; *synonyms* (*v*) adjust, arrange, manage, control, direct, **2.** reign; *synonyms* (*n*) dominance, (*v*) rule, command, govern, dominate, **3.** set; *synonyms* (*v*) fix, place, lay, put, (*n*) class; *antonyms* (*v*) soften, liquefy, (*n*) combing, combout, (*adj*) variable, **4.** restrain; *synonyms* (*v*) bridle, confine, curb, hold, rein, **5.** tune; *synonyms* (*n*) melody, song, strain, air, (*v*) regulate.

stillanlegur adjustable; *synonyms* (*adj*) adaptable, flexible, movable, variable, changeable; *antonym* (*adj*) fixed.

stilli regulator; *synonyms* (*n*) governor, controller, director, organizer, control.

stillibreyta parameter; *synonyms* (*n*) argument, guideline, limit, directive, modulus.

stilligen operator; *synonyms* (*n*) driver, hustler, manipulator, agent, doer.

stilligildi setting; *synonyms* (*n*) frame, scene, adjustment, scenery, backdrop.

stilling 1. rigging; *synonyms* (*n*) gear, rig, tackle, apparatus, outfit, **2.** setting; *synonyms* (*n*) frame, scene, adjustment, scenery, backdrop, **3.** adjustment; *synonyms* (*n*) adaptation, accommodation, alteration, control, fit, **4.** alignment; *synonyms* (*n*) alliance, alinement, arrangement, coalition, organization.

stillingar adjustment; *synonyms* (*n*) adaptation, accommodation, alteration, control, fit.

stillir 1. regulator; *synonyms* (*n*) governor, controller, director, organizer, control, **2.** adjuster; *synonyms* (*n*) adjustor, dresser, **3.** operator; *synonyms* (*n*) driver, hustler, manipulator, agent, doer, **4.** organizer; *synonyms* (*n*) arranger, organiser, administrator, manager, founder, **5.** modulator.

stillisvæði operator; *synonyms* (*n*) driver, hustler, manipulator, agent, doer.

stíma steam; *synonyms* (*n*) mist, fog, (*v*) reek, evaporate, exhale.

stimpill 1. piston; *synonyms* (*n*) plunger, diver, speculator, **2.** stereotype; *synonyms* (*n*) engrave, stereo, cliché, (*v*) pigeonhole, stamp.

stinga pierce; *synonyms* (*v*) impale, cut, perforate, bore, (*n*) prick.

stinnhvolf lithosphere; *synonyms* (*n*) geosphere, sial.

stirðleiki rigidity; *synonyms* (*n*) austerity, firmness, inflexibility, hardness, rigor; *antonyms* (*n*) flexibility, malleability, pliability, softness.

stirðnun 1. rigidity; *synonyms* (*n*) austerity, firmness, inflexibility, hardness, rigor; *antonyms* (*n*) flexibility, malleability, pliability, softness, **2.** catalepsy; *synonyms* (*adj*) fixity, immobility.

stirður 1. rigid; *synonyms* (*adj*) harsh, fixed, hard, inflexible, stiff; *antonyms* (*adj*) flexible, elastic, soft, **2.** stiff; *synonyms* (*adj*) rigid, difficult, formal, (*n*) stark, cadaver; *antonyms* (*adj*) relaxed, floppy, supple, free, pliable.

stirfinn rigid; *synonyms* (*adj*) harsh, fixed, hard, inflexible, stiff; *antonyms* (*adj*) flexible, elastic, soft.

stjak shift; *synonyms* (*n*) interchange, turn, (*v*) change, exchange, remove.

stjaka shift; *synonyms* (*n*) interchange, turn, (*v*) change, exchange, remove.

stjarfi tetanus; *synonyms* (*n*) lockjaw, (*adj*) scabies, scarlatina, scrofula, seasickness.

stjarfur rigid; *synonyms* (*adj*) harsh, fixed, hard, inflexible, stiff; *antonyms* (*adj*) flexible, elastic, soft.

stjarki tetany; *synonym* (*n*) tetanilla.

stjarna star; *synonyms* (*n*) asterisk, celebrity, ace, principal, headliner; *antonym* (*n*) nobody.

stjarnfræði astronomy; *synonyms* (*n*) astrology, uranology.

stjarnfræðingur astronomer; *synonyms* (*n*) astrologer, stargazer, uranologist.

stjarnlaga stellate; *synonyms* (*adj*) stellar, radial, starry, sparkling, stellary.

stjarnvísindi astronomy; *synonyms* (*n*) astrology, uranology.

stjórn 1. administration; *synonyms* (*n*) management, direction, organization, running, power, **2.** government; *synonyms* (*n*) administration, authority, control, command, (*adj*) empire, **3.** regimen; *synonyms* (*n*) regime, diet, government, treatment, cure, **4.** steerage; *synonyms* (*n*) guidance, steering, regulation, **5.** reign; *synonyms* (*n*) dominance, dominion, (*v*) rule, govern, dominate.

stjórna 1. regulate; *synonyms* (*v*) adjust, arrange, manage, control, direct, **2.** reign; *synonyms* (*n*) dominance, (*v*) rule, command, govern, dominate, **3.** supervise; *synonyms* (*v*) administer, superintend, check, monitor, oversee, **4.** control; *synonyms* (*n*) authority, care, (*v*) curb, bridle, conduct; *antonyms* (*n*) freedom, weakness, (*v*) intensify, share, **5.** operate; *synonyms* (*v*) act, function, run, employ, go.

stjórnandi 1. controller; *synonyms* (*n*) administrator, superintendent, accountant, comptroller, control, **2.** administrator; *synonyms* (*n*) executive, director, manager, boss, officer, **3.** operator; *synonyms* (*n*) driver, hustler, manipulator, agent, doer, **4.** master; *synonyms* (*n*) captain, instructor, (*v*) conquer, command, (*adj*) chief, **5.** entrepreneur; *synonyms* (*n*) contractor, enterpriser, businessperson, tycoon, manufacturer.

stjórnardeild secretariat; *synonyms* (n) bureau, department, secretariate, cutcherry.

stjórnarerindreki diplomat; *synonyms* (n) diplomatist, envoy, ambassador, intermediary, minister.

stjórnarfar regime; *synonyms* (n) administration, government, dynasty, management, regimen.

stjórnarfarslegur administrative; *synonyms* (adj) departmental, official, managerial, authoritative, (v) executive.

stjórnarformaður chairman; *synonyms* (n) chair, chairperson, chairwoman, director, president.

stjórnarfyrirkomulag regime; *synonyms* (n) administration, government, dynasty, management, regimen.

stjórnarmaður director; *synonyms* (n) commander, manager, administrator, boss, (v) conductor.

stjórnarnefnd board; *synonyms* (n) council, bench, meal, panel, table; *antonym* (v) disembark.

stjórnarnefndarmaður commissioner; *synonyms* (n) commissary, delegate, agent, executive, official.

stjórnarráðsfulltrúi secretary; *synonyms* (n) clerk, escritoire, minister, desk, (v) amanuensis.

stjórnarskrá constitution; *synonyms* (n) composition, code, makeup, organization, temperament.

stjórnarskrárbundinn constitutional; *synonyms* (adj) congenital, essential, inherent, intrinsic, legal; *antonym* (adj) unconstitutional.

stjórnarskrárlegur constitutional; *synonyms* (adj) congenital, essential, inherent, intrinsic, legal; *antonym* (adj) unconstitutional.

stjórnarskrifstofa secretariat; *synonyms* (n) bureau, department, secretariate, cutcherry.

stjórnarstefna policy; *synonyms* (n) course, plan, approach, insurance, tactics.

stjórnarstofnun administration; *synonyms* (n) management, direction, organization, running, power.

stjórnborð 1. console; *synonyms* (n) cabinet, (v) comfort, cheer, solace, soothe, 2. panel; *synonyms* (n) board, jury, defendant, committee, (v) empanel.

stjórnborði starboard; *synonyms* (n) dexter, offside, (adj) right, proper, correct.

stjórnborðshorn quarter; *synonyms* (n) area, part, district, division, (v) place.

stjórnbretti dial; *synonyms* (n) face, control, gnomon, hourglass, (v) telephone.

stjórnendur administration; *synonyms* (n) management, direction, organization, running, power.

stjórnfræði politics; *synonyms* (n) government, diplomacy, policy, governance, authorities.

stjórnhæfi controllability; *synonym* (n) controllableness.

stjórnhæfni manoeuvrability; *synonyms* (n) maneuverability, drivability.

stjórnkænska policy; *synonyms* (n) course, plan, approach, insurance, tactics.

stjórnleysi 1. anarchism; *synonyms* (n) anarchy, disorder, chaos, lawlessness, riot, 2. anarchy; *synonyms* (n) muddle, confusion, pandemonium, bedlam, disarray; *antonym* (n) order.

stjórnleysisstefna anarchism; *synonyms* (n) anarchy, disorder, chaos, lawlessness, riot.

stjórnlög constitution; *synonyms* (n) composition, code, makeup, organization, temperament.

stjórnmál politics; *synonyms* (n) government, diplomacy, policy, governance, authorities.

stjórnmálaflokkur party; *synonyms* (n) gang, band, company, assembly, association.

stjórnmálafræði politics; *synonyms* (n) government, diplomacy, policy, governance, authorities.

stjórnmálaskoðun politics; *synonyms* (n) government, diplomacy, policy, governance, authorities.

stjórnskipulag constitution; *synonyms* (n) composition, code, makeup, organization, temperament.

stjórnskipulegur constitutional; *synonyms* (adj) congenital, essential, inherent, intrinsic, legal; *antonym* (adj) unconstitutional.

stjórnskipun constitution; *synonyms* (n) composition, code, makeup, organization, temperament.

stjórnsýsla administration; *synonyms* (n) management, direction, organization, running, power.

stjórnsýsluskrifstofa administration; *synonyms* (n) management, direction, organization, running, power.

stjórnsýslustofnun administration; *synonyms* (n) management, direction, organization, running, power.

stjórnsýsluumdæmi parish; *synonyms* (n) district, community, congregation, region, province.

stjórntæki 1. control; *synonyms* (n) rule, authority, (v) command, check, curb; *antonyms* (n) freedom, weakness, (v) intensify, share, 2. instrument; *synonyms* (n) channel, deed, agency, apparatus, appliance.

stjórntök manoeuvre; *synonyms* (v) maneuver, control, direct, go, guide.

stjörnualmanak ephemeris; *synonyms* (n) almanac, calendar, ledger, log, magazine.

stjörnuathugunarstöð observatory; *synonyms* (n) lookout, picket, scout, sentinel, sentry.

stjörnubreidd declination; *synonyms* (*n*) declension, descent, decay, decline, refusal.

stjörnubyggð population; *synonyms* (*n*) inhabitants, people, nation, community, group.

stjörnufélag association; *synonyms* (*n*) affiliation, alliance, connection, assembly, affinity.

stjörnufífill aster; *synonym* (*n*) starwort.

stjörnufræði astronomy; *synonyms* (*n*) astrology, uranology.

stjörnufræðingur astronomer; *synonyms* (*n*) astrologer, stargazer, uranologist.

stjörnugírshjól satellite; *synonyms* (*n*) follower, moon, planet, attendant, orbiter.

stjörnuhæð altitude; *synonyms* (*n*) elevation, height, level, distance, eminence.

stjörnuhæðarmælir astrolabe; *synonyms* (*n*) meteoroscope, planisphere.

stjörnuháfur tope; *synonyms* (*n*) tumulus, grove, (*v*) booze, drink, (*adj*) tipple.

stjörnuhnitatafla ephemeris; *synonyms* (*n*) almanac, calendar, ledger, log, magazine.

stjörnuhrap meteor; *synonyms* (*n*) aerolite, effluvium, emanation, evaporation, exhalation.

stjörnulaga stellate; *synonyms* (*adj*) stellar, radial, starry, sparkling, stellary.

stjörnulíffræði astrobiology; *synonym* (*n*) exobiology.

stjórnum operation; *synonyms* (*n*) execution, movement, act, agency, effect.

stjörnumát horoscope; *synonyms* (*n*) nativity, figure, appearance, birth, destiny.

stjörnumerki 1. sign; *synonyms* (*n*) signal, indication, mark, motion, (*v*) gesture, 2. constellation; *synonyms* (*n*) configuration, asterism, group, (*adj*) galaxy, star.

stjörnumyrkvi occultation; *synonyms* (*n*) eclipse, disappearance, evanescence, concealment, (*adj*) adumbration.

stjórnun 1. regulation; *synonyms* (*n*) rule, adjustment, law, order, (*adj*) control; *antonym* (*n*) chaos, 2. directory; *synonyms* (*n*) catalogue, file, list, record, handbook, 3. adjustment; *synonyms* (*n*) adaptation, accommodation, alteration, fit, settlement, 4. control; *synonyms* (*n*) authority, (*v*) command, check, curb, bridle; *antonyms* (*n*) freedom, weakness, (*v*) intensify, share, 5. administration; *synonyms* (*n*) management, direction, organization, running, power.

stjórnunarkeðja cascade; *synonyms* (*n*) waterfall, torrent, (*v*) fall, gush, stream; *antonyms* (*v*) trickle, dribble.

stjörnusjá telescope; *synonyms* (*n*) scope, ambit, background, compass, (*v*) condense.

stjörnuskífa astrolabe; *synonyms* (*n*) meteoroscope, planisphere.

stjörnuskoðandi observer; *synonyms* (*n*) beholder, bystander, spectator, witness, eyewitness.

stjörnuspáfræði astrology; *synonyms* (*n*) astronomy, genethlialogy, magic, starcraft.

stjörnuspeki astrology; *synonyms* (*n*) astronomy, genethlialogy, magic, starcraft.

stjörnustöð observatory; *synonyms* (*n*) lookout, picket, scout, sentinel, sentry.

stjörnuþoka galaxy; *synonyms* (*n*) constellation, beetleweed, bevy, (*adj*) array, army.

stjörnuþyrping cluster; *synonyms* (*n*) bunch, clump, batch, group, (*v*) bundle; *antonym* (*v*) disperse.

stjörnuturn observatory; *synonyms* (*n*) lookout, picket, scout, sentinel, sentry.

stjórnvísindi politics; *synonyms* (*n*) government, diplomacy, policy, governance, authorities.

stjórnviska politics; *synonyms* (*n*) government, diplomacy, policy, governance, authorities.

stjórnvöld administration; *synonyms* (*n*) management, direction, organization, running, power.

stjórnvölur joystick; *synonyms* (*n*) stick, wheel, gearshift, pedals, reins.

stoð 1. pillar; *synonyms* (*n*) column, brace, mainstay, obelisk, post, 2. stay; *synonyms* (*v*) remain, reside, rest, prop, stop; *antonyms* (*v*) leave, change, abscond, depart, 3. strut; *synonyms* (*n*) buttress, (*v*) prance, stalk, swagger, parade, 4. support; *synonyms* (*n*) help, stand, aid, keep, (*v*) assist; *antonyms* (*n*) hindrance, (*v*) oppose, neglect, undermine, abandon, 5. column; *synonyms* (*n*) pillar, procession, row, stanchion, file.

stöð 1. stop; *synonyms* (*n*) halt, hold, stay, check, end; *antonyms* (*v*) continue, start, begin, encourage, permit, 2. cell; *synonyms* (*n*) cage, jail, cadre, hole, cave, 3. center; *synonyms* (*n*) centre, middle, core, heart, (*v*) focus; *antonyms* (*n*) edge, periphery, border.

stoðband ligament; *synonyms* (*n*) tie, bond, band, knot, sinew.

stoðeind radical; *synonyms* (*adj*) extremist, basic, exhaustive, extreme, revolutionary; *antonyms* (*adj*) conventional, old-fashioned, (*n*) moderate, conservative, traditionalist.

stoðfótur outrigger; *synonyms* (*n*) boom, bar, heel, lap, rod.

stoðgrind skeleton; *synonyms* (*n*) carcass, frame, framework, sketch, bones.

stöðlun standardization; *synonyms* (*n*) standardisation, calibration, normalisation, normalization, adjustment.

stöðlunar normative; *synonym* (*adj*) prescriptive.

stöðnun 1. stagnation; *synonyms* (*n*) doldrums, recession, depression, stagnancy, slump, **2.** fixation; *synonyms* (*n*) obsession, fetish, fixing, mania, complex.

stöðufræði statics; *synonyms* (*n*) static, (*v*) dynamics.

stöðugleiki 1. stability; *synonyms* (*n*) constancy, durability, firmness, permanence, poise; *antonym* (*n*) instability, **2.** constancy; *synonyms* (*n*) stability, allegiance, devotion, faithfulness, fidelity; *antonym* (*n*) inconstancy.

stöðugur 1. steady; *synonyms* (*adj*) firm, even, secure, (*v*) steadfast, calm; *antonyms* (*adj*) unsteady, shaky, wobbly, intermittent, unreliable, **2.** stable; *synonyms* (*adj*) permanent, reliable, constant, durable, fast; *antonyms* (*adj*) unstable, dangerous, precarious, rickety, volatile, **3.** stationary; *synonyms* (*adj*) immovable, fixed, motionless, immobile, static; *antonym* (*adj*) moving, **4.** permanent; *synonyms* (*adj*) lasting, eternal, everlasting, perennial, (*v*) continuous; *antonyms* (*adj*) fleeting, temporary, brief, impermanent, provisional, **5.** static; *synonyms* (*adj*) inactive, inert, still, stagnant, (*n*) atmospherics.

stöðuhækkun promotion; *synonyms* (*n*) furtherance, advance, advancement, advertising, boost; *antonyms* (*n*) demotion, neglect.

stöðuhorn cut; *synonyms* (*v*) carve, chop, clip, (*n*) notch, slice; *antonyms* (*v*) increase, lengthen, (*n*) addition, extension.

stöðuskipti transition; *synonyms* (*n*) change, passage, transit, alteration, changeover.

stöðustærð stock; *synonyms* (*n*) breed, lineage, store, goods, (*adj*) regular.

stöðusteinn otolith; *synonyms* (*n*) otoconite, otolite.

stöðuvatn lake; *synonyms* (*n*) loch, pond, pool, puddle, carmine.

stöðuveifa flag; *synonyms* (*n*) banner, colors, (*v*) decline, (*adj*) droop, fade.

stöðuvísir flag; *synonyms* (*n*) banner, colors, (*v*) decline, (*adj*) droop, fade.

stöðva 1. stop; *synonyms* (*n*) halt, hold, stay, check, end; *antonyms* (*v*) continue, start, begin, encourage, permit, **2.** arrest; *synonyms* (*n*) stop, apprehension, custody, (*v*) capture, catch; *antonyms* (*v*) release, discharge, **3.** jam; *synonyms* (*n*) crush, crowd, fix, (*v*) block, cram; *antonym* (*v*) free.

stöðvapar pair; *synonyms* (*n*) match, brace, duet, duo, (*v*) couple.

stöðvast stall; *synonyms* (*n*) booth, bench, barn, carrel, compartment.

stöðvun 1. truncation; *synonyms* (*n*) shortness, abruptness, brusqueness, curtness, gruffness, **2.** suppression; *synonyms* (*n*) inhibition, repression, crushing, quelling, restraint; *antonyms* (*n*) freedom, emancipation, **3.** arrest; *synonyms* (*n*) stop, check, halt, (*v*) capture, catch; *antonyms* (*v*) release, discharge, **4.** interruption; *synonyms* (*n*) cessation, break, disruption, hindrance, (*v*) impediment.

stöðvunarstefna containment; *synonyms* (*n*) control, repression, restriction.

stöðvunartími downtime; *synonyms* (*n*) break, cessation, delay, (*adj*) broken, disrepair.

stofa lounge; *synonyms* (*n*) couch, (*v*) loiter, loll, loaf, recline.

stofn 1. trunk; *synonyms* (*n*) stem, boot, torso, body, bole, **2.** variety; *synonyms* (*n*) kind, sort, species, change, (*adj*) class; *antonym* (*n*) uniformity, **3.** strain; *synonyms* (*n*) stress, breed, effort, (*v*) filter, screen; *antonym* (*v*) relax, **4.** stem; *synonyms* (*n*) root, bow, branch, (*v*) originate, block, **5.** population; *synonyms* (*n*) inhabitants, people, nation, community, group.

stofna 1. constitute; *synonyms* (*v*) compose, form, make, commission, appoint, **2.** establish; *synonyms* (*v*) confirm, erect, prove, base, build; *antonyms* (*v*) disprove, abolish, terminate.

stofneind primitive; *synonyms* (*adj*) primeval, primary, antediluvian, archaic, crude; *antonym* (*adj*) modern.

stofnfall primitive; *synonyms* (*adj*) primeval, primary, antediluvian, archaic, crude; *antonym* (*adj*) modern.

stofngrein manifold; *synonyms* (*adj*) multiple, diverse, different, (*v*) duplicate, copy.

stofnhluti 1. phrase; *synonyms* (*n*) expression, idiom, (*v*) express, formulate, couch, **2.** constituent; *synonyms* (*n*) component, ingredient, element, factor, part; *antonyms* (*n*) aggregate, composite, whole.

stofnlögn main; *synonyms* (*adj*) chief, grand, great, head, leading; *antonyms* (*adj*) minor, auxiliary, secondary, supplementary.

stofnrænn generic; *synonyms* (*adj*) general, common, universal, ordinary, basic.

stofnsamþykkt statute; *synonyms* (*n*) law, ordinance, rule, constitution, decree.

stofnsetja 1. institute; *synonyms* (*v*) establish, found, build, constitute, appoint, **2.** establish; *synonyms* (*v*) confirm, erect, prove, base, demonstrate; *antonyms* (*v*) disprove, abolish, terminate.

stofnsetning establishment; *synonyms* (*n*) business, company, constitution, institution, concern; *antonyms* (*n*) elimination, end.

stofnskot 1. sucker; *synonyms* (*n*) dupe, fool, sap, jay, lollipop, **2.** tiller; *synonyms* (*n*) cultivator, helm, till, handle, rudder.

stofnskrá charter; *synonyms* (*n*) hire, permit, authority, (*v*) let, rent.

stofnstæður radical; *synonyms* (*adj*) extremist, basic, exhaustive, extreme, revolutionary; *antonyms* (*adj*) conventional, old-fashioned, (*n*) moderate, conservative, traditionalist.

stofnstærð stock; *synonyms* (*n*) breed, lineage, store, goods, (*adj*) regular.

stofntala 1. radix; *synonyms* (*n*) base, basis, root, foundation, groundwork, 2. base; *synonyms* (*adj*) bottom, abject, mean, dishonorable, (*v*) ground; *antonyms* (*n*) summit, top, (*adj*) noble.

stofnteinungur tiller; *synonyms* (*n*) cultivator, helm, till, handle, rudder.

stofnun 1. agency; *synonyms* (*n*) bureau, office, authority, (*v*) action, act, 2. foundation; *synonyms* (*n*) base, basis, bottom, creation, establishment; *antonym* (*n*) top, 3. establishment; *synonyms* (*n*) business, company, constitution, institution, concern; *antonyms* (*n*) elimination, end, 4. institute; *synonyms* (*v*) establish, found, build, constitute, appoint, 5. institution; *synonyms* (*n*) institute, formation, asylum, founding, academy.

stofuananas pineapple; *synonyms* (*n*) ananas, pine, (*v*) chowder, chupatty, clam.

stoki stocks; *synonyms* (*n*) pillory, bilboes, securities, calls, options.

stökk 1. transition; *synonyms* (*n*) change, passage, transit, alteration, changeover, 2. transposition; *synonyms* (*n*) exchange, permutation, replacement, reversal, substitution, 3. saltation; *synonyms* (*n*) jump, bound, leap, spring, hop, 4. jump; *synonyms* (*v*) dive, hurdle, (*n*) bounce, start, caper; *antonyms* (*v*) decrease, fall.

stökkbreyting mutation; *synonyms* (*n*) alteration, change, variation, freak, innovation.

stökkbreyttur mutant; *synonyms* (*adj*) abnormal, (*n*) freak, mutation, monster, sport.

stökkbrigði mutant; *synonyms* (*adj*) abnormal, (*n*) freak, mutation, monster, sport.

stokkönd mallard; *synonym* (*adj*) drake.

stokkur 1. sinus; *synonyms* (*n*) cavity, fistula, pit, indentation, dent, 2. video; *synonyms* (*n*) television, picture, film, movie, (*v*) tape, 3. channel; *synonyms* (*n*) canal, conduit, groove, (*v*) carry, conduct, 4. console; *synonyms* (*n*) cabinet, (*v*) comfort, cheer, solace, soothe.

stökkur 1. short; *synonyms* (*adj*) brief, concise, scarce, brusque, close; *antonyms* (*adj*) long, tall, high, lengthy, 2. fragile; *synonyms* (*adj*) dainty, delicate, frail, breakable, brittle; *antonyms* (*adj*) strong, unbreakable, substantial, sturdy, permanent.

stökkva jump; *synonyms* (*n*) leap, bound, bounce, start, caper; *antonyms* (*v*) decrease, fall.

stoko 1. stock; *synonyms* (*n*) breed, lineage, store, goods, (*adj*) regular, 2. stocks; *synonyms* (*n*) pillory, bilboes, securities, calls, options.

stóll 1. seat; *synonyms* (*n*) place, bench, base, (*v*) locate, put, 2. chair; *synonyms* (*n*) chairman, chairperson, president, throne, (*v*) moderate.

stólpi pole; *synonyms* (*n*) perch, bar, picket, post, rod.

stöng 1. rod; *synonyms* (*n*) bar, baton, perch, shaft, (*v*) stick, 2. bar; *synonyms* (*n*) barricade, band, (*v*) ban, block, bolt; *antonyms* (*v*) permit, allow, 3. lever; *synonyms* (*n*) knob, (*v*) pry, raise, jimmy, prize.

stöngull stem; *synonyms* (*n*) root, bow, branch, (*v*) originate, block.

stöngulliðamót node; *synonyms* (*n*) knob, connection, joint, knot, nodosity.

stöngulliður internode; *synonyms* (*n*) phalanx, phalanstery, segment.

stönsun 1. coining; *synonyms* (*n*) forgery, stamping, 2. embossing; *synonyms* (*n*) adornment, beautification, buckling, decoration, embroidery.

stopp standstill; *synonyms* (*n*) deadlock, impasse, stalemate, cessation, halt.

stoppistöð stop; *synonyms* (*n*) halt, hold, stay, check, end; *antonyms* (*v*) continue, start, begin, encourage, permit.

stöpull pylon; *synonym* (*n*) column.

stór 1. big; *synonyms* (*adj*) ample, major, heavy, important, (*adv*) large; *antonyms* (*adj*) little, puny, (*adv*) small, (*syn*) tiny, 2. substantial; *synonyms* (*adj*) actual, solid, firm, real, strong; *antonyms* (*adj*) insignificant, insubstantial, ethereal, fine, worthless, 3. large; *synonyms* (*adj*) big, extensive, generous, broad, bulky; *antonym* (*adj*) cramped, 4. grand; *synonyms* (*adj*) excellent, gorgeous, dignified, (*n*) glorious, noble; *antonyms* (*adj*) unimpressive, humble, modest, 5. major; *synonyms* (*adj*) chief, key, main, superior, considerable; *antonyms* (*adj*) minor, unimportant, lesser, petty, slight.

stórabóla smallpox; *synonym* (*n*) variola.

stórbær city; *synonyms* (*n*) town, borough, burgh, (*adj*) municipal, civic; *antonym* (*adj*) rural.

stórbóndi 1. rancher; *synonyms* (*n*) farmer, countryman, 2. farmer; *synonyms* (*n*) agriculturist, rustic, husbandman, granger, sodbuster.

stórbýli 1. ranch; *synonyms* (*n*) estate, spread, merestead, (*v*) farm, (*adj*) agricultural, 2. property; *synonyms* (*n*) characteristic, capital, peculiarity, feature, (*adj*) attribute, 3. estate; *synonyms* (*n*) condition, land, demesne, order, rank, 4. farm; *synonyms* (*n*) property, grange, dairy, (*v*) cultivate, raise.

stórgalangal galangal; *synonyms* (*n*) galanga, galingale.

stórgró megaspore; *synonym* (*n*) macrospore.

stórheili cerebrum; *synonyms* (*n*) brain, pate, cranium, sconce, noddle.

stórhesli filbert; *synonyms* (*n*) hazelnut, cob, cobnut.

stórheslihneta filbert; *synonyms* (*n*) hazelnut, cob, cobnut.

stórhríð blizzard; *synonyms* (*n*) snowstorm, storm, tempest, snowfall, gale.

stórhveljur jellyfish; *synonyms* (*n*) medusan, coward, hydromedusae, (*adj*) apprehensive, frightened.

storka solid; *synonyms* (*adj*) firm, dense, compact, consistent, hard; *antonyms* (*adj*) soft, unreliable, loose, gaseous, (*n*) liquid.

stórkaupmaður wholesaler; *synonyms* (*n*) merchant, jobber, middleman, broker, contact; *antonym* (*n*) buyer.

stórkjafta megrim; *synonyms* (*n*) hemicrania, freak, migraine, humor.

storkna coagulate; *synonyms* (*v*) clot, set, condense, congeal, (*n*) curdle; *antonym* (*v*) liquefy.

storknun 1. solidification; *synonyms* (*n*) hardening, set, consolidation, setting, (*adj*) solidation, 2. setting; *synonyms* (*n*) frame, scene, adjustment, scenery, backdrop, 3. coagulation; *synonyms* (*n*) clotting, clot, flocculation, curdling, (*adj*) concretion.

storkuvari anticoagulant; *synonym* (*n*) decoagulant.

stórmaur tick; *synonyms* (*n*) beat, credit, score, (*v*) mark, check.

stórmennskubrjálun megalomania; *synonym* (*n*) egoism.

stormsveipur cyclone; *synonyms* (*n*) hurricane, storm, tempest, tornado, gale.

stormur 1. tempest; *synonyms* (*n*) storm, gale, hurricane, gust, squall, 2. storm; *synonyms* (*n*) tempest, attack, (*v*) rage, rush, assault, 3. gale; *synonyms* (*n*) blast, blow, blizzard, thunderstorm, wind.

stórnetja caul; *synonym* (*n*) veil.

stórsær macroscopic; *synonyms* (*adj*) macroscopical, large, big, bombastic, declamatory.

stórsameind macromolecule; *synonym* (*n*) supermolecule.

stórslys 1. disaster; *synonyms* (*n*) calamity, catastrophe, accident, adversity, blow; *antonyms* (*n*) success, blessing, joy, 2. catastrophe; *synonyms* (*n*) disaster, cataclysm, tragedy, misfortune, bale.

stórtölva mainframe; *synonyms* (*n*) computer, processor, management, laptop, notebook.

strætisvagn 1. bus; *synonyms* (*n*) automobile, autobus, car, coach, vehicle, 2. omnibus; *synonyms* (*n*) bus, charabanc, motorbus, collection, anthology.

strákur 1. boy; *synonyms* (*n*) lad, fellow, kid, male, man, 2. lad; *synonyms* (*n*) boy, blighter, chap, cub, cuss.

strammi stroma; *synonym* (*n*) stromata.

strand 1. stranding; *synonym* (*n*) grounding, 2. grounding; *synonyms* (*n*) earthing, basis, training, foundation, stranding.

strandblaðka chard; *synonyms* (*n*) boundary, shard, division, plant.

strandlengja coastline; *synonyms* (*n*) coast, seaside, seaside, shore, shoreline.

strandlón lagoon; *synonyms* (*n*) lagune, lake, bay, mere, pond.

strangleiki severity; *synonyms* (*n*) cruelty, austerity, harshness, rigor, asperity; *antonyms* (*n*) gentleness, leniency, clemency, flexibility, pleasantness.

straujárn iron; *synonyms* (*n*) chain, (*v*) firm, flatten, (*adj*) hard, adamant.

straumbreytir 1. convertor; *synonyms* (*n*) converter, transformer, 2. converter; *synonyms* (*n*) convertor, adapter, changer, apostle, missionary.

straumbroddur spike; *synonyms* (*n*) pin, point, barb, ear, (*v*) impale.

straumburður convection; *synonyms* (*n*) transfer, (*adj*) thermal.

straumefni fluid; *synonyms* (*adj*) liquid, flowing, unsettled, changeable, smooth; *antonym* (*n*) solid.

straumfesta ballast; *synonyms* (*n*) weight, ballasting, (*adj*) aplomb, (*v*) stabilize, load.

straumfræði hydrodynamics; *synonyms* (*n*) hydrokinetics, (*adj*) hydrology, hydrostatics.

straumfræðilegur hydrodynamic; *synonym* (*adj*) hydrodynamical.

straumgægir rudd; *synonyms* (*n*) dace, roach, tench.

straumhaft ballast; *synonyms* (*n*) weight, ballasting, (*adj*) aplomb, (*v*) stabilize, load.

straumhlaup commutation; *synonyms* (*n*) substitution, exchange, composition, intermutation, commuting.

straumhnykkur surge; *synonyms* (*v*) billow, flood, rise, rush, stream.

straumhvirfill eddy; *synonyms* (*n*) spin, twirl, vortex, (*v*) whirl, purl.

straumiða eddy; *synonyms* (*n*) spin, twirl, vortex, (*v*) whirl, purl.

straumlalli minnow; *synonyms* (*adj*) animalcule, emmet, fly, gnat, insect.

straumleki leakage; *synonyms* (*n*) escape, leak, outpouring, outflow, seepage.

straumlína 1. streamline; *synonyms* (*v*) simplify, centralize, order, reorganize, shape, 2. curvature; *synonyms* (*n*) bend, curve, arch, bow, crook.

straumlínulagaður streamline; *synonyms* (*v*) simplify, centralize, order, reorganize, shape.

straumlykkja loop; *synonyms* (n) coil, ring, (v) curve, bend, circle.

straummælir 1. ammeter, **2**. galvanometer; *synonyms* (n) rheometer, (v) bathometer, dynamometer, goniometer, heliometer.

straumrás circuit; *synonyms* (n) beat, (v) circle, tour, trip, journey.

straumrof open; *synonyms* (adj) frank, obvious, artless, (n) candid, clear; *antonyms* (adj) devious, secretive, concealed, (v) shut, (tr v) close.

straumrofi 1. switch; *synonyms* (n) cane, (v) exchange, change, shift, substitute, **2**. interrupter; *synonym* (n) intruder.

straumskipting commutation; *synonyms* (n) substitution, exchange, composition, intermutation, commuting.

straumskiptir 1. switch; *synonyms* (n) cane, (v) exchange, change, shift, substitute, **2**. commutator; *synonyms* (n) break, electrepeter.

straumstærð flow; *synonyms* (n) flood, current, discharge, (v) stream, course.

straumstefna polarity; *synonyms* (n) antagonism, augury, house, mansion, mark.

straumstillir regulator; *synonyms* (n) governor, controller, director, organizer, control.

straumsveifla signal; *synonyms* (n) sign, gesture, indication, presage, (v) omen.

straumsveipur vortex; *synonyms* (n) eddy, swirl, whirlpool, convolution, maelstrom.

straumur 1. tide; *synonyms* (n) current, flow, stream, course, (v) wave, **2**. stream; *synonyms* (n) brook, river, run, (v) flood, crowd; *antonym* (v) trickle, **3**. current; *synonyms* (adj) common, contemporary, fashionable, instant, actual; *antonyms* (adj) obsolete, past, old, old-fashioned, previous, **4**. jet; *synonyms* (n) squirt, fountain, (v) gush, spurt, fly.

straumvatn stream; *synonyms* (n) flow, brook, (v) flood, (prep) current, course; *antonym* (v) trickle.

straumvatnaset alluvium; *synonyms* (n) alluvion, deposit, flood, inundation, (adj) slime.

straumvatnsset alluvium; *synonyms* (n) alluvion, deposit, flood, inundation, (adj) slime.

straumvending commutation; *synonyms* (n) substitution, exchange, composition, intermutation, commuting.

straumvendir commutator; *synonyms* (n) break, electrepeter.

streita stress; *synonyms* (n) accent, emphasis, pressure, (v) strain, emphasize.

strekking 1. tension; *synonyms* (n) tenseness, pressure, strain, nervousness, stress; *antonyms* (n) calmness, looseness, **2**. dilation; *synonyms* (n) dilatation, expansion, swelling, growth, spread.

strekkingarró turnbuckle; *synonym* (n) tourniquet.

strekkja stretch; *synonyms* (n) extent, (v) extend, reach, strain, elongate; *antonym* (v) shorten.

strekktur tense; *synonyms* (adj) strained, edgy, nervous, taut, (v) overwrought; *antonyms* (adj) relaxed, calm, comfortable, tranquil, loose.

strendingur prism; *synonyms* (n) pyramid, spectroscope, spectrograph, spectrometer.

strendur angular; *synonyms* (adj) angulate, bony, gaunt, lean, skinny; *antonym* (adj) rounded.

strengiró turnbuckle; *synonym* (n) tourniquet.

strengskór lug; *synonyms* (v) draw, haul, drag, pull, (n) ear.

strengur 1. vein; *synonyms* (n) streak, vena, (adj) humor, mood, strip, **2**. string; *synonyms* (n) chain, file, row, strand, (adj) line, **3**. cord; *synonyms* (n) band, string, bond, tie, twine, **4**. cable; *synonyms* (n) rope, cablegram, telegram, cord, (v) wire, **5**. chord; *synonyms* (n) harmony, (v) accord, harmonise, harmonize, (adj) subtense.

streymi flow; *synonyms* (n) flood, current, discharge, (v) stream, course.

streymisslit separation; *synonyms* (n) detachment, disjunction, disunion, division, partition; *antonyms* (n) amalgamation, closeness, connection, marriage, unification.

stríð conflict; *synonyms* (n) clash, combat, fight, battle, contention; *antonyms* (n) agreement, accord, harmony, peace, (v) agree.

stríðsæsingamaður warmonger; *synonyms* (n) militarist, soldier, mercenary.

strigi burlap; *synonyms* (n) gunny, hessian, muslin, toile.

strik 1. strike; *synonyms* (n) knock, assault, (v) bang, beat, hit, **2**. segment; *synonyms* (n) division, paragraph, bit, (v) section, part, **3**. dash; *synonyms* (n) rush, sprint, (v) dart, touch, strike; *antonym* (n) lethargy.

strika 1. scribe; *synonyms* (n) author, amanuensis, clerk, copyist, (v) writer, **2**. scratch; *synonyms* (n) score, mark, (v) graze, notch, rub.

striklaga linear; *synonyms* (adj) lineal, rectilinear, running, additive, analog.

strikstefna strike; *synonyms* (n) knock, assault, (v) bang, beat, hit.

strikun hatch; *synonyms* (n) brood, (v) breed, contrive, concoct, brew.

strípilögur strip; *synonyms* (v) deprive, despoil, divest, peel, plunder; *antonyms* (v) dress, decorate.

strípun stripping; *synonyms* (n) baring, husking, denudation, scrubbing, discovery.

strjáll discrete; *synonyms* (adj) separate, distinct, different, detached, diverse.

strjúka desert; *synonyms* (v) abandon, escape, defect, (adj) waste, barren; *antonyms* (n) bog, (v) stay.

strok 1. smear; *synonyms* (n) blot, smudge, (v) slur, libel, (adj) daub, **2**. swab; *synonyms* (v) mop, clean, swob, wipe, (adj) sponge, **3**. escape; *synonyms* (v) elude, break, dodge, avoid, (n) leak; *antonyms* (v) capture, return.

stroka sweep; *synonyms* (n) compass, expanse, range, (v) brush, rake.

strokka displacement; *synonyms* (n) deposition, transfer, movement, shift, motion.

strokkaröð bank; *synonyms* (n) dam, coast, slope, (v) embankment, gradient; *antonym* (v) withdraw.

strokkstykki block; *synonyms* (n) bar, barricade, pad, (v) arrest, stop; *antonyms* (v) free, unblock, open.

strokkþvermál bore; *synonyms* (v) dig, bother, tire, annoy, (n) caliber; *antonyms* (v) interest, excite, fascinate.

strokkur 1. barrel; *synonyms* (n) drum, roll, vessel, barrelful, cask, **2**. cylinder; *synonyms* (n) barrel, pipe, tube, column, container.

strókur jet; *synonyms* (n) squirt, fountain, flow, (v) gush, spurt.

strönd 1. coast; *synonyms* (n) bank, beach, seaside, shore, (v) glide; *antonym* (n) interior, **2**. seaside; *synonyms* (n) coast, seaboard, seashore, coastline, (adj) seacoast, **3**. shore; *synonyms* (n) prop, edge, land, buttress, stay, **4**. seaboard; *synonym* (n) shoreline, **5**. coastline; *synonym* (n) sand.

strontín strontium; *synonym* (n) steradian.

strontíum strontium; *synonym* (n) steradian.

strópa strobe; *synonyms* (n) stroboscope, (adj) odometer, speedometer, tachometer.

strútur ostrich; *synonyms* (adj) antelope, chickaree, chipmunk, courser, doe.

strýta 1. pyramid; *synonyms* (n) pile, mass, heap, congeries, (adj) spire, **2**. taper; *synonyms* (n) candle, (adj) narrow, (v) point, sharpen, acuminate, **3**. conus.

stúa stow; *synonyms* (v) pack, cram, charge, house, load.

stuð impulse; *synonyms* (n) impetus, pulse, urge, drive, force.

stuðari bumper; *synonyms* (n) buffer, cushion, (v) fill, load, (adj) plentiful.

Stúdera study; *synonyms* (v) consider, examine, review, learn, research.

stúdíó studio; *synonyms* (n) atelier, cabinet, accommodation, building, bungalow.

stuðlunarsprunga joint; *synonyms* (n) articulation, hinge, join, seam, (v) articulate; *antonyms* (adj) individual, unilateral, private, separate.

stuðningsafrit backup; *synonyms* (n) backing, substitute, surrogate, (adj) alternate, spare.

stuðningsmaður 1. adherent; *synonyms* (n) disciple, follower, believer, devotee, fan, **2**. constituency; *synonyms* (n) ward, electorate, clientele, district, area, **3**. adept; *synonyms* (adj) expert, skillful, able, accomplished, (n) proficient; *antonyms* (adj) clumsy, incompetent, inept, **4**. acolyte; *synonym* (n) acolyth.

stuðningsörk handout; *synonyms* (n) brochure, pamphlet, flyer, leaflet, release.

stuðningur 1. stay; *synonyms* (v) remain, reside, rest, prop, stop; *antonyms* (v) leave, change, abscond, depart, **2**. support; *synonyms* (n) help, stand, aid, keep, (v) assist; *antonyms* (n) hindrance, (v) oppose, neglect, undermine, abandon, **3**. approval; *synonyms* (n) acceptance, applause, approbation, acclaim, agreement; *antonyms* (n) disapproval, rejection, condemnation, scorn, criticism, **4**. endorsement; *synonyms* (n) corroboration, confirmation, sanction, approval, authorization.

stuðull 1. coefficient; *synonyms* (n) accessory, multiple, (adj) concomitant, cooperative, cooperating, **2**. column; *synonyms* (n) pillar, procession, row, stanchion, file, **3**. multiplier; *synonyms* (n) multiplicator, multiplicand, **4**. onset; *synonyms* (n) incursion, charge, aggression, assault, (v) attack, **5**. index; *synonyms* (n) catalogue, exponent, table, catalog, (v) list.

stúfsett butt; *synonyms* (n) push, extremity, stump, grip, (v) bunt.

stúfsettur butt; *synonyms* (n) push, extremity, stump, grip, (v) bunt.

stúfur stub; *synonyms* (n) butt, counterfoil, end, ticket, (v) stump.

stúlka 1. wench; *synonyms* (n) girl, quean, slut, strumpet, (v) drab, **2**. lass; *synonyms* (n) lassie, woman, harlot, nymph, youngster, **3**. girl; *synonyms* (n) damsel, lady, daughter, fille, lass, **4**. gal; *synonyms* (n) gallon, congius, female.

stuna groan; *synonyms* (n) grumble, cry, (v) moan, murmur, howl.

stund 1. hour; *synonyms* (n) epoch, time, hr, moment, nonce, **2**. time; *synonyms* (n) hour, period, duration, era, measure; *antonym* (n) death.

stundvís punctual; *synonyms* (adj) correct, accurate, exact, prompt, punctilious; *antonym* (adj) late.

stundvíslega sharp; *synonyms* (adj) acute, bitter, intelligent, acid, (n) keen; *antonyms* (adj) blunt, dull, mild, gentle, rounded.

stunga 1. puncture; *synonyms* (n) prick, cut, hole, (v) bore, drill; *antonym* (v) inflate, **2**. port; *synonyms* (n) harbor, haven, asylum, carriage, (adj) larboard; *antonym* (n) starboard, **3**. injection; *synonyms* (n) shot, clyster, enema, inoculation, jab.

stungutengi plug; *synonyms* (*n*) hype, stopper, bung, (*v*) advertise, block.

stungutengill jack; *synonyms* (*n*) knave, flag, jackass, mariner, ace.

stunguveita infusion; *synonyms* (*n*) extract, infuse, influx, dash, (*v*) injection.

stúrinn depressed; *synonyms* (*adj*) concave, low, blue, dejected, dispirited; *antonyms* (*adj*) cheerful, happy, convex.

sturlun 1. psychosis; *synonyms* (*n*) insanity, lunacy, fixation, madness, neurosis; *antonym* (*n*) sanity, **2**. derangement; *synonyms* (*n*) delirium, disorder, disturbance, aberration, jumble.

sturttæming dumping; *synonyms* (*n*) disposal, discarding, clearance, jettisoning, removal.

stuttfrumuvefur parenchyma; *synonyms* (*n*) substance, body, compages, element, matter.

stuttur short; *synonyms* (*adj*) brief, concise, scarce, brusque, close; *antonyms* (*adj*) long, tall, high, lengthy.

stútur 1. spout; *synonyms* (*n*) jet, nozzle, (*v*) gush, spurt, spirt, **2**. nozzle; *synonyms* (*n*) nose, beak, hooter, muzzle, snout, **3**. neck (háls); *synonyms* (*n*) throat, cervix, neckline, (*v*) pet, (*adj*) stricture.

styðja 1. sustain; *synonyms* (*v*) support, bear, carry, keep, continue, **2**. support; *synonyms* (*n*) help, stand, aid, (*v*) assist, prop; *antonyms* (*n*) hindrance, (*v*) oppose, neglect, undermine, abandon, **3**. endorse; *synonyms* (*v*) defend, approve, back, certify, confirm; *antonym* (*v*) disapprove.

stýfa 1. resect; *synonyms* (*v*) excise, eviscerate, **2**. truncate; *synonyms* (*v*) curtail, cut, abridge, shorten, clip; *antonym* (*v*) lengthen.

stýfður truncated; *synonyms* (*adj*) abbreviated, shortened, cut, docked, garbled.

stýfing 1. resection; *synonym* (*v*) section, **2**. pruning; *synonym* (*n*) leavings, **3**. truncation; *synonyms* (*n*) shortness, abruptness, brusqueness, curtness, gruffness.

stygglyndi irritability; *synonyms* (*n*) excitability, irascibility, choler, petulance, temper.

stygglyndur irritable; *synonyms* (*adj*) angry, fractious, irascible, edgy, cantankerous; *antonyms* (*adj*) calm, easygoing, good-humored, good-natured, even-tempered.

styggur irritable; *synonyms* (*adj*) angry, fractious, irascible, edgy, cantankerous; *antonyms* (*adj*) calm, easygoing, good-humored, good-natured, even-tempered.

stykki piece; *synonyms* (*n*) cut, division, fragment, part, article.

stynja groan; *synonyms* (*n*) grumble, cry, (*v*) moan, murmur, howl.

stýra 1. regulate; *synonyms* (*v*) adjust, arrange, manage, control, direct, **2**. control; *synonyms* (*n*) rule, authority, (*v*) command, check, curb; *antonyms* (*n*) freedom, weakness, (*v*) intensify, share, **3**. navigate; *synonyms* (*v*) cruise, guide, sail, fly, pilot.

stýranlegur navigable; *synonyms* (*adj*) passable, open, sailable, voyageable, crossable.

stýranleiki controllability; *synonym* (*n*) controllableness.

stýri 1. rudder; *synonyms* (*n*) helm, wheel, guide, tail, controls, **2**. helm; *synonyms* (*n*) haft, handle, hilt, rudder, (*v*) helmet.

stýriarmur throttle; *synonyms* (*v*) choke, strangle, asphyxiate, smother, strangulate.

stýridór arbor; *synonyms* (*n*) bower, mandrel, axle, spindle, arbour.

stýrifetill throttle; *synonyms* (*v*) choke, strangle, asphyxiate, smother, strangulate.

stýrihandfang throttle; *synonyms* (*v*) choke, strangle, asphyxiate, smother, strangulate.

stýriháttur mode; *synonyms* (*n*) means, fashion, manner, method, form.

stýrikeila pilot; *synonyms* (*n*) guide, leader, aviator, (*v*) manage, lead.

stýrikerfi system; *synonyms* (*n*) method, arrangement, network, organization, plan.

stýrikraftur entelechy; *synonym* (*n*) actuality.

stýrill promoter; *synonyms* (*n*) backer, advocate, booster, sponsor, patron.

stýrinef key; *synonyms* (*adj*) central, fundamental, basic, cardinal, (*n*) guide.

stýring 1. steering; *synonyms* (*n*) direction, guidance, management, steerage, navigation, **2**. regulation; *synonyms* (*n*) rule, adjustment, law, order, (*adj*) control; *antonym* (*n*) chaos, **3**. directive; *synonyms* (*n*) decree, edict, instruction, (*adj*) directing, directional, **4**. control; *synonyms* (*n*) authority, (*v*) command, check, curb, bridle; *antonyms* (*n*) freedom, weakness, (*v*) intensify, share, **5**. guide; *synonyms* (*n*) escort, directory, (*v*) direct, conduct, govern; *antonym* (*v*) follow.

stýringardór arbor; *synonyms* (*n*) bower, mandrel, axle, spindle, arbour.

stýripinni joystick; *synonyms* (*n*) stick, wheel, gearshift, pedals, reins.

stýrisameind effector; *synonym* (*n*) effecter.

stýrisblað rudder; *synonyms* (*n*) helm, wheel, guide, tail, controls.

stýrisbúnaður steering; *synonyms* (*n*) direction, guidance, management, steerage, navigation.

stýrishjól helm; *synonyms* (*n*) wheel, haft, handle, hilt, (*v*) helmet.

stýrishús 1. wheelhouse; *synonym* (n) pilothouse, **2**. cab; *synonyms* (n) cabriolet, taxi, taxicab, car, fly.

stýriskambur stabilizer; *synonyms* (n) ballast, inhibitor, skedge, (adj) additive, preservative.

stýriskaut gate; *synonyms* (n) entrance, door, entry, mouth, doorway.

stýrismaður helmsman; *synonyms* (n) pilot, steerer, steersman, wheelman, decoy.

stýrisskjálfti shimmy; *synonyms* (n) chemise, shift, (v) shake, dance, wobble.

stýrissveif tiller; *synonyms* (n) cultivator, helm, till, handle, rudder.

stýristautur joystick; *synonyms* (n) stick, wheel, gearshift, pedals, reins.

stýristöng joystick; *synonyms* (n) stick, wheel, gearshift, pedals, reins.

stýrisvæði promoter; *synonyms* (n) backer, advocate, booster, sponsor, patron.

stýrisvölur kingpin; *synonyms* (n) headpin, kingbolt, bigwig, leader, authority.

stýritækni automation; *synonyms* (n) mechanization, automatization, mechanisation, computerization.

stýritappi pilot; *synonyms* (n) guide, leader, aviator, (v) manage, lead.

stýriþræll servomechanism; *synonyms* (n) servo, servosystem.

styrking 1. web; *synonyms* (n) mesh, network, tissue, lattice, (v) net, **2**. reinforcement; *synonyms* (n) brace, fortification, backing, consolidation, support, **3**. rib; *synonyms* (n) ridge, (v) joke, tease, guy, mock, **4**. bracing; *synonyms* (adj) fresh, brisk, invigorating, cool, enlivening, **5**. bulkhead.

styrkingarbrún bead; *synonyms* (n) drop, astragal, beading, pearl, (v) beautify.

styrkingarfjöður rib; *synonyms* (n) ridge, (v) joke, tease, guy, mock.

styrkingarkantur bead; *synonyms* (n) drop, astragal, beading, pearl, (v) beautify.

styrkja 1. reinforce; *synonyms* (v) bolster, intensify, enhance, buttress, consolidate; *antonym* (v) weaken, **2**. strengthen; *synonyms* (v) confirm, corroborate, brace, encourage, fortify; *antonym* (v) undermine, **3**. promote; *synonyms* (v) advance, help, aid, advertise, (adv) further; *antonyms* (v) demote, discourage.

styrkjandi bracing; *synonyms* (adj) fresh, brisk, invigorating, cool, (n) brace.

styrkleiki intensity; *synonyms* (n) force, forcefulness, depth, volume, (adj) strength; *antonyms* (n) dullness, indifference, weakness.

styrkt concentration; *synonyms* (n) absorption, concentrate, application, attention, engrossment; *antonym* (n) distraction.

styrktarsjóður endowment; *synonyms* (n) ability, talent, capacity, (v) donation, gift.

styrktarvaf reinforcement; *synonyms* (n) brace, fortification, backing, consolidation, support.

styrkþegi beneficiary; *synonyms* (n) heir, inheritor, receiver, recipient, successor; *antonym* (n) donor.

styrkur 1. power; *synonyms* (n) force, ability, potency, (v) influence, might; *antonyms* (n) powerlessness, helplessness, weakness, **2**. strength; *synonyms* (n) power, energy, firmness, intensity, vigor; *antonyms* (n) frailty, flaw, shortcoming, **3**. subsidy; *synonyms* (n) grant, aid, allowance, backing, support, **4**. volume; *synonyms* (n) bulk, size, book, magnitude, mass; *antonym* (n) quietness, **5**. benefit; *synonyms* (n) advantage, gain, (v) assist, profit, avail; *antonyms* (n) disadvantage, drawback, loss, (v) harm.

stytta 1. upset; *synonyms* (v) overturn, agitate, disquiet, (n) disorder, trouble; *antonyms* (v) calm, please, encourage, soothe, (adj) pleased, **2**. reduce; *synonyms* (v) lower, pare, abbreviate, curtail, (adj) abridge; *antonyms* (v) increase, bolster, expand, enlarge, exacerbate, **3**. cancel; *synonyms* (v) annul, abrogate, erase, expunge, (adj) abolish; *antonym* (v) validate.

stytting 1. truncate; *synonyms* (v) curtail, cut, abridge, shorten, clip; *antonym* (v) lengthen, **2**. abbreviation; *synonyms* (n) abridgement, abridgment, contraction, abstraction, summary; *antonym* (n) expansion.

súblimat sublimate; *synonyms* (v) purify, rarefy, distill, purge, (adj) refined.

suð 1. buzz; *synonyms* (n) hum, rumor, hearsay, (v) call, drone, **2**. noise; *synonyms* (n) clatter, clamor, hubbub, racket, sound; *antonyms* (n) silence, quiet.

suða 1. welding; *synonyms* (n) fusion, assembly, synthesis, **2**. weld; *synonyms* (v) join, solder, bond, cement, fasten, **3**. boiling; *synonyms* (adj) hot, effervescent, heated, burning, scalding; *antonyms* (adj) cold, freezing, **4**. boil; *synonyms* (v) seethe, bubble, churn, simmer, (n) abscess; *antonym* (v) freeze, **5**. gassing; *synonyms* (n) execution, boasting.

suðugleraugu goggles; *synonyms* (n) glasses, eyeglasses, spectacles, barnacles, specs.

suður south; *synonyms* (n) southland, confederacy, s, confederation, conspiracy.

Suðurpóll antarctic; *synonyms* (adj) austral, southern, glacial.

súgur draught; *synonyms* (n) draft, potion, dose, potation, (v) design.

súkkulaði chocolate; *synonyms* (n) brown, bonbon, cocoa, coffee, (adj) brunette.

súkrósi sucrose; *synonyms* (*n*) saccharose, saccharobiose.

súla 1. pillar; *synonyms* (*n*) column, brace, mainstay, obelisk, post, **2.** bar; *synonyms* (*n*) barricade, band, (*v*) ban, block, bolt; *antonyms* (*v*) permit, allow, **3.** column; *synonyms* (*n*) pillar, procession, row, stanchion, file, **4.** crus; *synonym* (*n*) crura.

súld drizzle; *synonyms* (*v*) mizzle, rain, mist, spray, drip; *antonym* (*v*) pour.

súlfat sulfate; *synonym* (*n*) sulphate.

sullast spill; *synonyms* (*v*) fall, shed, drop, empty, (*n*) overflow.

súlnaás architrave; *synonyms* (*n*) capital, cornice, entablature, frieze, pediment.

súlnagöng colonnade; *synonyms* (*n*) arcade, circus, arcades, column, crescent.

súlnaregla order; *synonyms* (*n*) command, decree, dictate, array, (*v*) direct; *antonyms* (*n*) anarchy, chaos, confusion, (*v*) disorder, request.

súlnarið colonnade; *synonyms* (*n*) arcade, circus, arcades, column, crescent.

sultur hunger; *synonyms* (*n*) desire, thirst, appetite, craving, (*v*) crave; *antonym* (*n*) moderation.

súluhöfuð capital; *synonyms* (*n*) principal, city, stock, (*adj*) main, primary.

súluskaft shaft; *synonyms* (*n*) arrow, handle, axis, beam, pit.

súma zoom; *synonyms* (*v*) soar, zip, race, surge, whiz.

sumar summer; *synonyms* (*n*) summertime, beam, joist, lintel, rafter.

sumardá aestivation; *synonyms* (*n*) estivation, prefloration, preflowering.

sumardvali aestivation; *synonyms* (*n*) estivation, prefloration, preflowering.

sumarflundra flounder; *synonyms* (*v*) falter, stumble, flop, (*adj*) blunder, boggle.

sumargrænn deciduous; *synonyms* (*adj*) caducous, transient, short-lived, (*v*) labent, undermined.

sumir some; *synonyms* (*adv*) nearly, rather, somewhat, about, (*adj*) few.

summa sum; *synonyms* (*n*) total, quantity, (*v*) amount, aggregate, figure.

summuáhrif summation; *synonyms* (*n*) addition, sum, computation, reckoning, summary.

summun summation; *synonyms* (*n*) addition, sum, computation, reckoning, summary.

sund 1. strait; *synonyms* (*n*) inlet, need, pass, pinch, (*adj*) narrow, **2.** channel; *synonyms* (*n*) canal, conduit, groove, (*v*) carry, conduct, **3.** narrows; *synonyms* (*n*) bay, fairway.

sundl dizziness; *synonyms* (*n*) vertigo, giddiness, swimming, faint, (*v*) scotomy.

sundra 1. decompose; *synonyms* (*v*) decay, crumble, rot, analyse, analyze, **2.** disassemble; *synonyms* (*v*) dismantle, decompose, dismember, detach, break; *antonym* (*v*) assemble.

sundrun 1. vaporization; *synonyms* (*n*) evaporation, vapor, vaporisation, volatilization, condensation, **2.** disintegration; *synonyms* (*n*) collapse, decay, decomposition, breakdown, annihilation, **3.** decay; *synonyms* (*n*) decline, ebb, (*v*) rot, decompose, blight; *antonym* (*n*) growth, **4.** atomization; *synonyms* (*n*) atomisation, spraying, fragmentation, nebulization, **5.** lysis.

sundrunarferli catabolism; *synonyms* (*n*) dissimilation, katabolism, anabolism, metabolism, disassimilation.

sundur 1. apart; *synonyms* (*adv*) aside, (*adj*) aloof, alone, distant, separate, **2.** extract; *synonyms* (*n*) excerpt, (*v*) draw, abstract, derive, educe.

sundurdraganlegur telescopic; *synonyms* (*adj*) remote, distant, sliding, telescopical.

sundurdráttur distraction; *synonyms* (*n*) amusement, desperation, beguilement, confusion, disturbance; *antonym* (*n*) fascination.

sundurdregin telescope; *synonyms* (*n*) scope, ambit, background, compass, (*v*) condense.

sundurgreina resolve; *synonyms* (*v*) determine, decide, (*n*) purpose, determination, decision; *antonyms* (*n*) indecision, weakness.

sundurgreining 1. resolution; *synonyms* (*n*) decision, determination, answer, conclusion, firmness; *antonym* (*n*) indecisiveness, **2.** disjunction; *synonyms* (*n*) disconnection, dissociation, disjuncture, disunion, separation, **3.** discrimination; *synonyms* (*n*) discernment, difference, differentiation, distinction, (*v*) judgment; *antonym* (*n*) tolerance, **4.** analysis; *synonyms* (*n*) anatomy, breakdown, decomposition, inquiry, inspection; *antonym* (*n*) synthesis.

sundurgreinir discriminator; *synonym* (*n*) differentiator.

sundurhvarf divergence; *synonyms* (*n*) discrepancy, difference, disagreement, dissimilarity, variance; *antonyms* (*n*) convergence, meeting, agreement, amalgamation.

sundurhverfur divergent; *synonyms* (*adj*) different, differing, dissimilar, distinct, conflicting; *antonyms* (*adj*) similar, convergent.

sundurlægur disjoint; *synonyms* (*v*) dislocate, disarticulate, disjoin, separate, dismember.

sundurlaus discrete; *synonyms* (*adj*) separate, distinct, different, detached, diverse.

sundurlausn dissolution; *synonyms* (*n*) decay, breakup, decomposition, abolition, cancellation.

sundurleitinn divergent; *synonyms* *(adj)* different, differing, dissimilar, distinct, conflicting; *antonyms* *(adj)* similar, convergent.

sundurleitni divergence; *synonyms* *(n)* discrepancy, difference, disagreement, dissimilarity, variance; *antonyms* *(n)* convergence, meeting, agreement, amalgamation.

sundurleitun divergence; *synonyms* *(n)* discrepancy, difference, disagreement, dissimilarity, variance; *antonyms* *(n)* convergence, meeting, agreement, amalgamation.

sundurleitur heterogeneous; *synonyms* *(adj)* dissimilar, different, assorted, miscellaneous, *(v)* diverse; *antonym* *(adj)* homogeneous.

sundurleysing decomposition; *synonyms* *(n)* decay, rot, disintegration, dissolution, putrefaction.

sundurliða itemize; *synonyms* *(v)* list, enumerate, detail, specify, itemise.

sundurliðun 1. specification; *synonyms* *(n)* designation, provision, stipulation, particular, condition, 2. decomposition; *synonyms* *(n)* decay, rot, disintegration, dissolution, putrefaction.

sundurskiptur fragmented; *synonyms* *(adj)* broken, crumbled, disconnected, disjointed, disunited.

sundursláttur rebound; *synonyms* *(n)* bound, kick, *(v)* bounce, recoil, glance.

sundurtæta lacerate; *synonyms* *(v)* rip, cut, gash, slash, mangle.

sundurtæting laceration; *synonyms* *(n)* rip, cut, gash, injury, tear.

sundurvísandi divergent; *synonyms* *(adj)* different, differing, dissimilar, distinct, conflicting; *antonyms* *(adj)* similar, convergent.

sundurvísun divergence; *synonyms* *(n)* discrepancy, difference, disagreement, dissimilarity, variance; *antonyms* *(n)* convergence, meeting, agreement, amalgamation.

súr 1. acid; *synonyms* *(adj)* acerbic, acidic, bitter, caustic, sharp; *antonym* *(adj)* sweet, 2. sour; *synonyms* *(adj)* morose, acid, rancid, severe, *(n)* harsh; *antonym* *(adj)* kindly, 3. tart; *synonyms* *(n)* pie, pastry, *(adj)* pungent, sour, keen, 4. acidic; *synonyms* *(adj)* acidulent, acidulous, corrosive, astringent, 5. acetous; *synonyms* *(adj)* acetose, vinegary, currish, peevish.

súrál alumina; *synonyms* *(n)* alumine, *(adj)* argil.

súraldin lime; *synonyms* *(n)* birdlime, basswood, calx, lemon, cement.

súraldintré lime; *synonyms* *(n)* birdlime, basswood, calx, lemon, cement.

súrefni oxygen; *synonym* *(n)* o.

súrefniskassi incubator; *synonyms* *(n)* brooder, hatcher, couveuse, plotter.

súrhey silage; *synonyms* *(n)* ensilage, food, hay.

súrna 1. sour; *synonyms* *(adj)* morose, sharp, acid, bitter, *(n)* harsh; *antonyms* *(adj)* sweet, kindly, 2. acidify; *synonyms* *(v)* acetify, sour, acidulate, turn, *(n)* curdle.

súrnun acidification; *synonyms* *(n)* souring, acidizing

surpapera papers; *synonyms* *(n)* credentials, document, documents, identification, covenant.

surtarbrandur lignite; *synonyms* *(n)* browncoal, charcoal.

sút dejection; *synonyms* *(n)* depression, discouragement, gloom, sadness, despair; *antonyms* *(n)* happiness, cheerfulness.

svæða zone; *synonyms* *(n)* area, district, region, section, belt.

svæðalýsing topography; *synonyms* *(n)* terrain, backcloth, backdrop, background, countryside.

svæðavæðing localism; *synonyms* *(n)* provincialism, sectionalism, dialect, regionalism, barbarism.

svæði 1. precinct; *synonyms* *(n)* district, area, region, limit, bound, 2. range; *synonyms* *(v)* line, arrange, order, rank, roam, 3. region; *synonyms* *(n)* land, country, field, domain, part, 4. territory; *synonyms* *(n)* dominion, state, kingdom, province, realm, 5. tract; *synonyms* *(n)* essay, expanse, pamphlet, dissertation, extent.

svæðisbundinn 1. regional; *synonyms* *(adj)* district, local, parochial, sectional, neighborhood; *antonym* *(adj)* central, 2. areal.

svæðislýsing topography; *synonyms* *(n)* terrain, backcloth, backdrop, background, countryside.

svæðisnúmer code; *synonyms* *(n)* cipher, charter, law, act, *(v)* cypher.

svæðisrammi boundary; *synonyms* *(n)* border, bound, limit, edge, area.

svæðisskipting sector; *synonyms* *(n)* department, area, branch, district, division.

svæfa occlude; *synonyms* *(v)* block, close, obstruct, barricade, jam.

svæfandi 1. anesthetic; *synonyms* *(adj)* anesthesia, soporific, hypnotic, *(n)* anaesthetic, narcotic, 2. hypnotic; *synonyms* *(adj)* magnetic, mesmeric, sleepy, mesmerizing, *(n)* sedative.

svæfður anesthetic; *synonyms* *(adj)* anesthesia, soporific, hypnotic, *(n)* anaesthetic, narcotic.

svæfing 1. anesthesia; *synonyms* *(n)* anaesthesia, asleep, insentience, stupor, unconsciousness, 2. anaesthesia; *synonyms* *(n)* anesthesia, anaesthesis, *(adj)* palsy, paralysis, paraesthesia.

svæfingalyf narcotic; *synonyms* *(adj)* soporific, anodyne, *(n)* opiate, hypnotic, drug.

svæfingarlyf 1. anaesthetic; *synonyms* *(n)* anesthetic, *(v)* hypnotic, lullaby, relaxant, sedative,

2. anesthetic; *synonyms* (*adj*) anesthesia, soporific, bloodless, (*n*) anaesthetic, narcotic.

svæling fumigation; *synonym* (*n*) steaming.

svaf damping; *synonyms* (*n*) attenuation, wetting, dampening.

svala swallow; *synonyms* (*v*) eat, bolt, gulp, consume, (*n*) drink; *antonym* (*v*) regurgitate.

svalir balcony; *synonyms* (*n*) loggia, porch, veranda, arch, terrace.

svalur cool; *synonyms* (*adj*) chilly, cold, (*v*) calm, chill, assuage; *antonyms* (*adj*) agitated, hot, excited, (*v*) warm, heat.

svampkenndur spongy; *synonyms* (*adj*) porous, soft, absorbent, fungous, soggy; *antonyms* (*adj*) firm, hard, impermeable.

svampur sponge; *synonyms* (*n*) parasite, (*v*) mop, cadge, scrounge, bum.

svangur hungry; *synonyms* (*adj*) avid, eager, esurient, famished, (*v*) craving; *antonyms* (*adj*) full, sated, satiated.

svansa yaw; *synonyms* (*n*) swerve, (*v*) gape, turn, bend, gawk.

svanur swan; *synonyms* (*n*) cygnet, (*v*) ramble, roam, rove, wander.

svar 1. reply; *synonyms* (*n*) answer, echo, return, rejoinder, (*v*) respond; *antonym* (*v*) question, **2.** response; *synonyms* (*n*) reaction, reception, retort, effect, (*v*) reply, **3.** answer; *synonyms* (*n*) solution, (*v*) counter, resolve, serve, acknowledge; *antonym* (*v*) ask.

svara 1. reply; *synonyms* (*n*) answer, echo, return, rejoinder, (*v*) respond; *antonym* (*v*) question, **2.** respond; *synonyms* (*v*) reply, counter, rejoin, react, (*adj*) correspond; *antonym* (*v*) ignore, **3.** react; *synonyms* (*v*) act, oppose, recoil, behave, retort, **4.** answer; *synonyms* (*n*) solution, (*v*) resolve, serve, acknowledge, agree; *antonym* (*v*) ask.

svarandi respondent; *synonyms* (*n*) defendant, answerer, accused, responder, (*adj*) responsive.

svarbúinn responsive; *synonyms* (*adj*) sensitive, amenable, receptive, susceptible, agreeable.

svarðarhneta groundnut; *synonyms* (*n*) goober, peanut, earthnut, truffle.

svardeyfing extinction; *synonyms* (*n*) destruction, extermination, end, expiration, (*v*) death; *antonyms* (*n*) survival, preservation.

svarf abrasion; *synonyms* (*n*) attrition, excoriation, erosion, friction, (*v*) detrition; *antonym* (*n*) smoothness.

svari effector; *synonym* (*n*) effecter.

svart black (svartur); *synonyms* (*adj*) dark, sable, blackamoor, bleak, darkie; *antonym* (*n*) white.

svarthyrna anglerfish; *synonyms* (*n*) goosefish, allmouth, angler, angelfish, lotte.

svartidauði 1. plague; *synonyms* (*v*) bother, harass, molest, worry, afflict, **2.** pestilence; *synonyms* (*n*) plague, pest, epidemic, blight, (*adj*) murrain.

svartlyfting pedestal; *synonyms* (*n*) base, bottom, foot, groundwork, basis.

svartþröstur blackbird; *synonyms* (*n*) merle, ousel, ouzel, merl.

svartur black; *synonyms* (*adj*) dark, sable, blackamoor, bleak, darkie; *antonym* (*n*) white.

svartviður ebony; *synonyms* (*n*) sable, (*adj*) black, ebon, dark, jet.

svarviðbrögð respondent; *synonyms* (*n*) defendant, answerer, accused, responder, (*adj*) responsive.

svefn sleep; *synonyms* (*n*) nap, doze, (*v*) rest, repose, catnap.

svefndá sopor; *synonym* (*n*) stupor.

svefnganga somnambulism; *synonyms* (*n*) noctambulism, noctambulation, sleepwalking, somnambulation.

svefngengill somnambulist; *synonyms* (*n*) noctambulist, sleepwalker, hypnobate, somnambulator, somnambule.

svefnhöfgi 1. drowsiness; *synonyms* (*n*) sleepiness, somnolence, dullness, lethargy, doziness, **2.** lethargy; *synonyms* (*n*) drowsiness, indifference, apathy, inactivity, fatigue; *antonyms* (*n*) energy, liveliness, verve, vitality, nimbleness.

svefnhöfugur hypnagogic; *synonyms* (*adj*) somniferous, soporific, hypnogogic, somnific, soporiferous.

svefnleysi insomnia; *synonyms* (*n*) sleeplessness, restlessness, indisposition, insomnolence, restiveness.

sveif 1. radius; *synonyms* (*n*) length, semidiameter, spoke, range, compass, **2.** crank; *synonyms* (*n*) crackpot, grouch, handle, nut, (*adj*) cranky.

sveifarlægur radial; *synonyms* (*adj*) angelic, centrifugal, spiral, stellate, radiated.

sveifarlengd throw; *synonyms* (*v*) cast, fling, shed, hurl, (*n*) pitch.

sveifill oscillator; *synonym* (*n*) exciter.

sveifla 1. cycle; *synonyms* (*n*) bicycle, circle, round, (*v*) bike, motorcycle, **2.** swing; *synonyms* (*v*) sway, fluctuate, oscillate, dangle, hang, **3.** sweep; *synonyms* (*n*) compass, expanse, range, (*v*) brush, rake, **4.** surge; *synonyms* (*v*) billow, flood, rise, rush, stream, **5.** round; *synonyms* (*adv*) about, (*adj*) circular, (*n*) bout, ring, beat; *antonyms* (*adj*) slim, sharp.

sveiflast 1. swing; *synonyms* (*v*) sway, fluctuate, oscillate, dangle, hang, **2.** oscillate; *synonyms* (*v*) swing, vibrate, hesitate, wag, alternate.

sveiflugjafi oscillator; *synonym* (*n*) exciter.

sveifluhæð amplitude; *synonyms* (*n*) breadth, latitude, magnitude, width, mass.

sveifluháttur mode; *synonyms* (*n*) means, fashion, manner, method, form.

sveifluhreyfing oscillation; *synonyms* (*n*) beat, pulse, swing, vibration, quiver.

sveiflukenndur volatile; *synonyms* (*adj*) changeable, erratic, frivolous, unstable, (*v*) fickle; *antonym* (*adj*) stable.

sveiflunemi geophone; *synonyms* (*n*) sismograph, jug.

sveiflur fluctuation; *synonyms* (*n*) variation, vicissitude, wavering, deviation, hesitation.

sveiflusjá oscilloscope; *synonyms* (*n*) scope, ambit, background, compass, orbit.

sveiflustærð amplitude; *synonyms* (*n*) breadth, latitude, magnitude, width, mass.

sveiflutími period; *synonyms* (*n*) age, dot, epoch, era, point.

sveifluvaki oscillator; *synonym* (*n*) exciter.

sveifluvídd amplitude; *synonyms* (*n*) breadth, latitude, magnitude, width, mass.

sveifluvik displacement; *synonyms* (*n*) deposition, transfer, movement, shift, motion.

sveiging reflection; *synonyms* (*n*) consideration, contemplation, observation, cogitation, deliberation.

sveigja 1. winding; *synonyms* (*adj*) tortuous, indirect, twisting, (*n*) twist, wind; *antonyms* (*adj*) straight, direct, 2. reflect; *synonyms* (*v*) deliberate, ponder, cogitate, consider, contemplate, 3. curve; *synonyms* (*n*) bend, crook, bow, (*v*) curl, turn, 4. deflection; *synonyms* (*n*) deviation, deflexion, variation, bending, digression, 5. deflect; *synonyms* (*v*) avert, deviate, divert, parry, swerve.

sveigjanlegur 1. elastic; *synonyms* (*adj*) flexible, buoyant, ductile, limber, pliable; *antonyms* (*adj*) rigid, stiff, inflexible, inelastic, 2. flexible; *synonyms* (*adj*) elastic, adaptable, yielding, lissome, pliant; *antonyms* (*adj*) fixed, obstinate, stubborn.

sveigjanleiki flexibility; *synonyms* (*n*) pliability, spring, adaptability, elasticity, suppleness; *antonyms* (*n*) inflexibility, obstinacy, rigidity, stubbornness, severity.

sveim diffusion; *synonyms* (*n*) dissemination, dispersion, dispersal, distribution, spread.

sveima diffuse; *synonyms* (*v*) circulate, disperse, disseminate, spread, broadcast.

sveimandi wandering; *synonyms* (*adj*) itinerant, nomadic, stray, erratic, (*n*) roving.

sveinmök pederasty; *synonym* (*n*) paederasty.

sveip sweep; *synonyms* (*n*) compass, expanse, range, (*v*) brush, rake.

sveipur 1. whorl; *synonyms* (*n*) curl, coil, spiral, gyre, helix, 2. vortex; *synonyms* (*n*) eddy, swirl, whirlpool, convolution, maelstrom, 3. transient; *synonyms* (*adj*) brief, fleeting, passing, temporary, transitory; *antonyms* (*adj*) permanent, enduring, 4. eddy; *synonyms* (*n*) spin, twirl, vortex, (*v*) whirl, purl, 5. cyclone; *synonyms* (*n*) hurricane, storm, tempest, tornado, gale.

sveit 1. troop; *synonyms* (*n*) company, group, corps, band, crowd, 2. district; *synonyms* (*n*) area, quarter, region, community, neighborhood, 3. countryside; *synonyms* (*n*) land, landscape, panorama, (*adj*) country, rustic, 4. country; *synonyms* (*n*) state, nation, home, commonwealth, kingdom; *antonyms* (*n*) city, (*adj*) urban, 5. group; *synonyms* (*n*) bunch, brigade, collection, flock, gang.

sveitafólk countryside; *synonyms* (*n*) land, landscape, panorama, (*adj*) country, rustic.

sveitahérað countryside; *synonyms* (*n*) land, landscape, panorama, (*adj*) country, rustic.

sveitarfélag 1. municipality; *synonyms* (*n*) city, town, metropolis, shrievalty, commune, 2. community; *synonyms* (*n*) association, public, agreement, nation, (*adj*) communal; *antonym* (*adj*) private.

sveitarstjórn council; *synonyms* (*n*) assembly, board, congress, consultation, convention.

sveitasetur estate; *synonyms* (*n*) condition, land, demesne, order, rank.

svelgrás sink; *synonyms* (*n*) sag, (*v*) decline, dip, droop, fall; *antonyms* (*v*) rise, float.

svelgur 1. sink; *synonyms* (*n*) sag, (*v*) decline, dip, droop, fall; *antonyms* (*v*) rise, float, 2. whirlpool; *synonyms* (*n*) eddy, vortex, maelstrom, (*v*) whirl, swirl.

svengd hunger; *synonyms* (*n*) desire, thirst, appetite, craving, (*v*) crave; *antonym* (*n*) moderation.

sveppadeyðandi fungicidal; *synonym* (*adj*) antifungal.

sveppadeyðir fungicide; *synonyms* (*n*) antifungal, antimycotic.

sveppaeyðandi antifungal; *synonyms* (*n*) antimycotic, fungicide, analgesic, antibiotic, carminative.

sveppafræði mycology; *synonyms* (*n*) fungology, herborization, bacteriology, dendrology, microbiology.

sveppalyf antifungal; *synonyms* (*n*) antimycotic, fungicide, analgesic, antibiotic, carminative.

sveppasýktur fungous; *synonyms* (*adj*) fungal, fungoid.

sveppdeyðandi fungicidal; *synonym* (*adj*) antifungal.

sveppeyðandi fungicidal; *synonym* (*adj*) antifungal.

sveppeyðir fungicide; *synonyms* (*n*) antifungal, antimycotic.

svepphattur pileus; *synonyms* (*n*) cap, capital, ceiling, chapiter, crownwork.

sveppir fungi; *synonyms* (*n*) bacteria, lichens.

sveppur 1. fungus; *synonyms* (*n*) rust, mushroom, growth, fungi, (*adj*) garlic, 2. fungi; *synonyms* (*n*) bacteria, lichens.

sverðfiskur 1. swordfish, 2. broadbill; *synonyms* (*n*) bluebill, boatbill, scaup, shoveler, shoveller.

sverðlaga xiphoid; *synonyms* (*adj*) setarious, spinuliferous, subulate, tetrahedral, xiphoidian.

sverfing attrition; *synonyms* (*n*) friction, abrasion, contrition, corrosion, detrition.

svið 1. scope; *synonyms* (*n*) range, reach, domain, purview, room, 2. realm; *synonyms* (*n*) kingdom, area, country, field, region, 3. range; *synonyms* (*v*) line, arrange, order, rank, roam, 4. stage; *synonyms* (*n*) grade, phase, floor, degree, level, 5. department; *synonyms* (*n*) bureau, compartment, agency, class, faculty.

sviðsatriði scene; *synonyms* (*n*) aspect, view, background, display, (*v*) prospect.

sviðsetning staging; *synonyms* (*n*) production, scaffolding, scaffold, presentation, stage.

sviðsmynd scenario; *synonyms* (*n*) plot, continuity, chronicle, design, forecast.

svif glide; *synonyms* (*v*) slide, coast, float, flow, fly; *antonym* (*v*) struggle.

svífa glide; *synonyms* (*v*) slide, coast, float, flow, fly; *antonym* (*v*) struggle.

svifbiti cantilever; *synonyms* (*n*) arm, beam, modillion, brace, extension.

svifefnablanda suspension; *synonyms* (*n*) delay, interruption, abeyance, break, intermission.

svifefnasíun dialysis; *synonyms* (*n*) debility, division.

sviflausn suspension; *synonyms* (*n*) delay, interruption, abeyance, break, intermission.

svifnökkvi hovercraft; *synonyms* (*n*) catamaran, hydroplane, caravel, carvel, coracle.

svig deflection; *synonyms* (*n*) deviation, bend, deflexion, variation, bending.

svigar parenthesis; *synonyms* (*n*) aside, bracket, digression, interlude, anastrophe.

svigi 1. bracket; *synonyms* (*n*) brace, prop, rack, (*v*) link, couple, 2. parenthesis; *synonyms* (*n*) aside, bracket, digression, interlude, anastrophe.

svigna deflect; *synonyms* (*v*) bend, avert, deviate, divert, parry.

svigrúm 1. latitude; *synonyms* (*n*) breadth, freedom, room, scope, expanse, 2. orbital; *synonyms* (*adj*) orbitar, periodic.

svik 1. swindle; *synonyms* (*n*) cheat, imposture, (*v*) con, defraud, do, 2. scam; *synonyms* (*n*) cozenage, deception, fiddle, fraud, (*v*) swindle, 3. duplicity; *synonyms* (*n*) deceit, dishonesty, artifice, craft, betrayal; *antonym* (*n*) honesty, 4. deceit; *synonyms* (*n*) guile, falsehood, pretense, ruse, (*adj*) cunning; *antonym* (*n*) sincerity.

svíkja 1. trick; *synonyms* (*n*) deceit, deception, (*v*) swindle, cheat, deceive, 2. deceive; *synonyms* (*v*) betray, bamboozle, circumvent, dupe, pretend, 3. con; *synonyms* (*v*) trick, bunco, defraud, hoax, bilk; *antonym* (*n*) pro, 4. delude; *synonyms* (*v*) beguile, cozen, fool, mislead, cajole, 5. cheat; *synonyms* (*v*) fake, (*n*) con, fraud, impostor, sham.

svimi 1. vertigo; *synonyms* (*n*) dizziness, giddiness, lightheadedness, swimming, bewilderment, 2. dizziness; *synonyms* (*n*) vertigo, faint, flightiness, lightheartedness, (*v*) scotomy.

svín 1. pig; *synonyms* (*n*) hog, boar, bull, cop, copper, 2. swine; *synonyms* (*n*) pig, beast, barrow, brute, bully, 3. hog; *synonyms* (*n*) glutton, porker, swine, grunter, (*adj*) cormorant, 4. porker.

svínslæri ham; *synonyms* (*n*) gammon, village, actor, dorp, (*v*) act.

svipa 1. lash; *synonyms* (*v*) whip, beat, flog, chastise, bind, 2. whip; *synonyms* (*v*) scourge, lash, strap, flagellate, goad, 3. flagellum; *synonyms* (*n*) bane, curse, nemesis, terror, threat.

svipall transient; *synonyms* (*adj*) brief, fleeting, passing, temporary, transitory; *antonyms* (*adj*) permanent, enduring.

svipbrigðafræði physiognomy; *synonyms* (*n*) countenance, face, kisser, mug, phiz.

svipkenni feature; *synonyms* (*n*) article, aspect, character, characteristic, detail.

svipkennni feature; *synonyms* (*n*) article, aspect, character, characteristic, detail.

svipmót similarity; *synonyms* (*n*) correspondence, likeness, parallelism, kinship, parallel; *antonyms* (*n*) dissimilarity, difference.

svipta deprive; *synonyms* (*v*) strip, bereave, divest, abridge, despoil; *antonym* (*v*) enrich.

svipting 1. suspension; *synonyms* (*n*) delay, interruption, abeyance, break, intermission, 2. cancellation; *synonyms* (*n*) annulment, abolition, cancel, negation, recall, 3. deprivation; *synonyms* (*n*) bereavement, privation, cost, loss, need.

svipukrabbi crawfish; *synonyms* (*n*) crayfish, crawdad, crawdaddy, (*v*) blackleg, crawl.

svipull 1. transient; *synonyms* (*adj*) brief, fleeting, passing, temporary, transitory; *antonyms* (*adj*) permanent, enduring, 2. transitory; *synonyms* (*adj*) transient, momentary, ephemeral, temporal, fugacious.

svipur physiognomy; *synonyms* (*n*) countenance, face, kisser, mug, phiz.

sviputrekt reservoir; *synonyms* (*n*) cistern, fountain, well, lake, store.

svitaaukandi diaphoretic; *synonyms* (*adj*) sudorific, diaphoretical.

svitalyf 1. diaphoretic; *synonyms* (*adj*) sudorific, diaphoretical, **2.** antiperspirant.

svitalyktareyðir deodorant; *synonyms* (*adj*) odorless, (*n*) deodorization, cleanser.

sviti 1. sweat; *synonyms* (*n*) labor, perspiration, (*v*) work, perspire, toil, **2.** perspiration; *synonyms* (*n*) sweat, diaphoresis, hidrosis, sudor, sweating.

svitna sweat; *synonyms* (*n*) labor, perspiration, (*v*) work, perspire, toil.

svitnun 1. sudation; *synonyms* (*n*) hidrosis, perspiration, diaphoresis, sweating, sudor, **2.** hidrosis; *synonym* (*n*) sudation.

svörður peat; *synonyms* (*n*) turf, bog, pet.

svörfun 1. abrasion; *synonyms* (*n*) attrition, excoriation, erosion, friction, (*v*) detrition; *antonym* (*n*) smoothness, **2.** erosion; *synonyms* (*n*) abrasion, corrosion, corroding, eroding, wear.

svörun 1. response; *synonyms* (*n*) answer, reaction, reception, (*v*) reply, rejoinder, **2.** reaction; *synonyms* (*n*) response, backlash, effect, repercussion, retort, **3.** feedback; *synonym* (*v*) respond.

svunta 1. skirt; *synonyms* (*n*) border, edge, brim, (*v*) fringe, circumvent, **2.** apron; *synonyms* (*n*) forestage, proscenium, skirt, pall, pontificals.

sýanókóbalamín cyanocobalamin; *synonym* (*n*) cobalamin.

sýfilis syphilis; *synonyms* (*n*) pox, syph, siphilis, venereal.

sýfílis syphilis; *synonyms* (*n*) pox, syph, siphilis, venereal.

syfja drowsiness; *synonyms* (*n*) sleepiness, somnolence, dullness, lethargy, doziness.

sýki disease; *synonyms* (*n*) ailment, condition, illness, sickness, complaint.

sýkilæta neutrophil; *synonyms* (*n*) neutrophile, (*adj*) neutrophilic.

sýkill 1. contagion; *synonyms* (*n*) infection, plague, contamination, disease, taint, **2.** pathogen; *synonyms* (*n*) germ, microbe.

sýkilvirkur pathogenic; *synonyms* (*adj*) infective, morbific, infectious, pathogenetic.

sýking infection; *synonyms* (*n*) contagion, disease, contamination, taint, (*adj*) pollution.

sýkingarhreiður nidus; *synonyms* (*n*) focus, nest, cradle, snuggery, centering.

sýkingarmáttur virulence; *synonyms* (*n*) rancor, acerbity, animosity, (*adj*) acrimony, venom.

sýkingatala morbidity; *synonyms* (*n*) morbidness, deathrate, mortality, gloom, (*adj*) morbosity.

sýkingatíðni morbidity; *synonyms* (*n*) morbidness, deathrate, mortality, gloom, (*adj*) morbosity.

sýkinn infectious; *synonyms* (*adj*) contagious, catching, communicable, pestiferous, epidemic.

sýkjandi pathogenic; *synonyms* (*adj*) infective, morbific, infectious, pathogenetic.

sýklaáreiti challenge; *synonyms* (*n*) question, defiance, (*v*) defy, dare, brave; *antonym* (*v*) obey.

sýkladrepandi bactericidal; *synonyms* (*adj*) disinfectant, germicidal, antiseptic.

sýklaeyðandi antiseptic; *synonyms* (*adj*) clean, sterile, germicidal, unpolluted, (*n*) disinfectant; *antonym* (*adj*) septic.

sýklaeyðir bactericide; *synonyms* (*n*) antiseptic, germicide, bacteriacide, disinfectant, antibacterial.

sýklalyf antibiotic; *synonyms* (*n*) analgesic, antifungal, antiviral, carminative, (*adj*) antiseptic.

sýklaögrun challenge; *synonyms* (*n*) question, defiance, (*v*) defy, dare, brave; *antonym* (*v*) obey.

sýklavörn asepsis; *synonyms* (*n*) antisepsis, sterileness, sterility, infertility.

sýkna 1. acquit; *synonyms* (*v*) absolve, exculpate, exonerate, release, clear; *antonym* (*v*) convict, **2.** absolve; *synonyms* (*v*) excuse, justify, acquit, forgive, free; *antonyms* (*v*) blame, condemn.

sykra 1. sugar; *synonyms* (*n*) honey, darling, carbohydrate, saccharide, (*adj*) dear, **2.** saccharify; *synonym* (*v*) sugar, **3.** carbohydrate.

sykrungur carbohydrate; *synonyms* (*n*) saccharide, sugar.

sykur 1. sugar; *synonyms* (*n*) honey, darling, carbohydrate, saccharide, (*adj*) dear, **2.** saccharum, **3.** sucrose; *synonyms* (*n*) saccharose, saccharobiose, **4.** saccharose; *synonym* (*n*) sucrose.

sykurmelóna cantaloupe; *synonym* (*n*) cantaloup.

sykursjúkur diabetic; *synonym* (*adj*) diabetical.

sykursmælir saccharimeter; *synonym* (*n*) saccharometer.

sykursýkissjúklingur diabetic; *synonym* (*adj*) diabetical.

sýlen xylene; *synonym* (*n*) xylol.

sylla plateau; *synonyms* (*n*) plain, table, tableland, elevation, stage.

syllusnigill console; *synonyms* (*n*) cabinet, (*v*) comfort, cheer, solace, soothe.

sýlól xylene; *synonym* (*n*) xylol.

sylti silt; *synonyms* (*n*) sediment, deposit, (*adj*) mire, mud, alluvium.

sýn 1. view; *synonyms* (*n*) look, sight, judgment, opinion, (*v*) regard, **2.** vision; *synonyms* (*n*) view, dream, daydream, imagination, (v) fancy; *antonym* (n) reality.

sýna 1. display; *synonyms* (n) array, (v) exhibit, show, disclose, parade; *antonym* (v) conceal, **2.** disclose; *synonyms* (v) betray, declare, impart, detect, (adj) confess; *antonym* (v) secrete.

sýnataka sampling; *synonyms* (n) sample, example, case, poll, taste.

sýnd 1. view; *synonyms* (n) look, sight, judgment, opinion, (v) regard, **2.** penetrance; *synonym* (n) penetrancy.

synda swim; *synonyms* (v) float, hover, drift, (n) dip, (adj) rise.

syndafyrirgefning 1. absolution; *synonyms* (n) pardon, remission, exemption, exoneration, (v) excuse; *antonym* (n) blame, **2.** acquittal; *synonyms* (n) absolution, discharge, acquitment, acquittance, justification; *antonym* (n) conviction.

sýndarfærsla 1. parallel; *synonyms* (adj) equivalent, even, (n) equal, (v) compare, match; *antonyms* (adj) conflicting, dissimilar, (n) perpendicular, skew, **2.** parallax.

sýndarfótur pseudopodium; *synonyms* (n) pseudopod, lobopodium.

sýndarhliðrun 1. parallel; *synonyms* (adj) equivalent, even, (n) equal, (v) compare, match; *antonyms* (adj) conflicting, dissimilar, (n) perpendicular, skew, **2.** parallax.

sýndarleiðni admittance; *synonyms* (n) admission, access, accession, introduction, entrance.

sýndarviðnám impedance; *synonyms* (n) resistance, clog, friction, hindrance, immunity.

syngja sing; *synonyms* (v) chant, hymn, chirp, hum, drone.

sýni 1. specimen; *synonyms* (n) exemplar, sample, example, instance, copy, **2.** sample; *synonyms* (n) specimen, model, pattern, (v) taste, try.

sýnihneigð exhibitionism; *synonyms* (n) immodesty, ostentation.

sýnikennsla demonstration; *synonyms* (n) parade, proof, argument, display, manifestation.

sýnilegur 1. visible; *synonyms* (adj) obvious, perceptible, conspicuous, apparent, evident; *antonyms* (adj) invisible, imperceptible, **2.** patent; *synonyms* (adj) overt, manifest, clear, open, palpable; *antonym* (adj) unclear.

sýning 1. display; *synonyms* (n) array, (v) exhibit, show, disclose, parade; *antonym* (v) conceal, **2.** demonstration; *synonyms* (n) proof, argument, display, manifestation, presentation.

sýnisgler slide; *synonyms* (n) glide, chute, (v) drop, slip, fall.

sýnishorn 1. sample; *synonyms* (n) example, instance, specimen, model, pattern, **2.** specimen;

synonyms (n) exemplar, sample, copy, person, illustration.

sýnistaka sampling; *synonyms* (n) sample, example, case, poll, taste.

synjun 1. rejection; *synonyms* (n) exclusion, dismissal, denial, rebuff, refusal; *antonyms* (n) acceptance, approval, **2.** refusal; *synonyms* (n) declination, negative, no, rejection, ban; *antonym* (n) permission.

synjunarvald veto; *synonyms* (n) bar, (v) ban, disallow, forbid, prohibit; *antonyms* (n) approval, permission, (v) approve, permit, sanction.

sýprus cypress; *synonyms* (adj) mourning, weeds, willow.

sýprusviður cypress; *synonyms* (adj) mourning, weeds, willow.

sýra acid; *synonyms* (adj) acerbic, acidic, bitter, caustic, sharp; *antonym* (adj) sweet.

sýri oxide; *synonym* (n) oxid.

sýring 1. acidification; *synonyms* (n) souring, acidizing, **2.** oxidation; *synonyms* (n) calcination, rust, oxygenation, oxidization, corrosion.

sýringareitrun acidosis; *synonym* (n) indigestion.

syrja 1. precipitate; *synonyms* (n) deposit, (adj) hasty, headlong, impetuous, sudden, **2.** sediment; *synonyms* (n) deposition, lees, dregs, grounds, substance.

syrjun precipitation; *synonyms* (n) hurry, rain, precipitancy, downfall, haste.

syrpa 1. member; *synonyms* (n) limb, part, supporter, extremity, phallus, **2.** formation; *synonyms* (n) constitution, creation, establishment, construction, genesis; *antonym* (n) destruction.

sýruaukning acidification; *synonyms* (n) souring, acidizing.

sýrublanda pickle; *synonyms* (n) fix, jam, mess, hole, (v) cure.

sýrudrómi antacid; *synonyms* (adj) alkaline, metallic, (n) antiacid, alkalizer, alkaliser.

sýrueyðir antacid; *synonyms* (adj) alkaline, metallic, (n) antiacid, alkalizer, alkaliser.

sýrufíkill acidophil; *synonym* (n) acidophile.

sýrufruma eosinophil; *synonym* (n) eosinophile.

sýrukær acidophilic; *synonyms* (adj) acidophilous, aciduric.

sýrumyndun acidification; *synonyms* (n) souring, acidizing.

sýrusækinn acidophilic; *synonyms* (adj) acidophilous, aciduric.

sýrusólginn acidophilic; *synonyms* (adj) acidophilous, aciduric.

sýruþvo pickle; *synonyms* (n) fix, jam, mess, hole, (v) cure.

sýruþvottur pickling; *synonyms* (*n*) buckling, preservation.

sýsl edit; *synonyms* (*v*) delete, compile, cut, redact, (*n*) editing.

sýsla 1. county; *synonyms* (*n*) region, state, area, district, shire, 2. parish; *synonyms* (*n*) community, congregation, province, township, borough.

sýslari driver; *synonyms* (*n*) coachman, postboy, club, chaser, commuter.

sýslumaður magistrate; *synonyms* (*n*) judge, justice, jurist, official, provost.

systir sister; *synonyms* (*n*) nun, nurse, brother, mate, twin.

systkin 1. sibling; *synonyms* (*n*) sib, relation, relative, cognate, kin, 2. siblings; *synonyms* (*n*) sibs, family, 3. sibs; *synonym* (*n*) siblings.

systurdóttir niece; *synonyms* (*n*) nephew, aunt, uncle.

systurefni isomer; *synonym* (*n*) isomeride.

systurfélag affiliate; *synonyms* (*n*) member, chapter, (*v*) associate, ally, unite.

systurkjarni isomer; *synonym* (*n*) isomeride.

systursonur nephew; *synonyms* (*n*) aunt, uncle.

systurtegund isomer; *synonym* (*n*) isomeride.

Ŝ

ŝraŭbingo nuts; *synonyms* (*adj*) crazy, insane, balmy, crackers, nutty; *antonyms* (*adj*) sane, sensible.

ŝtelsekvi tails; *synonyms* (*n*) tailcoat, tail, waste, coat.

ŝtofo materials; *synonyms* (*n*) data, goods, resources, order, provisions.

ŝtupo 1. stair; *synonyms* (*n*) step, degree, footstep, staircase, stairway, 2. stairs; *synonyms* (*n*) stair, steps, 3. steps; *synonyms* (*n*) stairs, scale, way, formula, guidelines.

T

tá 1. toe; *synonyms* (*n*) digit, extremity, foot, bottom, (*adj*) toed, 2. digit; *synonyms* (*n*) figure, cipher, dactyl, finger, number.

tæki 1. unit; *synonyms* (*n*) troop, element, group, squad, (*adj*) one, 2. tool; *synonyms* (*n*) instrument, implement, machine, puppet, pawn, 3. apparatus; *synonyms* (*n*) appliance, device, plant, tackle, equipment, 4. device; *synonyms* (*n*) contrivance, apparatus, artifice, emblem,

contraption, 5. machine; *synonyms* (*n*) car, auto, automobile, gadget, organization.

tækjabeiting instrumentation; *synonyms* (*n*) orchestration, arrangement, instrumentality, channel, means.

tækjabúnaður 1. apparatus; *synonyms* (*n*) appliance, device, implement, instrument, plant, 2. equipment; *synonyms* (*n*) material, apparatus, facility, gear, (*v*) furniture, 3. instrumentation; *synonyms* (*n*) orchestration, arrangement, instrumentality, channel, means.

tækjakostur equipment; *synonyms* (*n*) material, apparatus, facility, gear, (*v*) furniture.

tækjastilling calibration; *synonyms* (*n*) gauging, scale, standardization, gradation, measurement.

tækni 1. technique; *synonyms* (*n*) approach, means, method, skill, fashion, 2. technology; *synonyms* (*n*) engineering, apparatus, competence, equipment, (*adj*) technicality.

tækniaðferð technology; *synonyms* (*n*) engineering, apparatus, competence, equipment, (*adj*) technicality.

tækniaðferðir technology; *synonyms* (*n*) engineering, apparatus, competence, equipment, (*adj*) technicality.

tæknibeiting technique; *synonyms* (*n*) approach, means, method, skill, fashion.

tæknifræði technology; *synonyms* (*n*) engineering, apparatus, competence, equipment, (*adj*) technicality.

tæknifræðilegur technological; *synonyms* (*adj*) technical, technologic, technicological, industrial, mechanical.

tæknifrjóvgun insemination; *synonym* (*n*) conception.

tæknilegur technical; *synonyms* (*adj*) technological, industrial, shipshape, technic, complex.

tæknilýsing specification; *synonyms* (*n*) designation, provision, stipulation, particular, condition.

tæma 1. drain; *synonyms* (*n*) ditch, culvert, (*v*) deplete, waste, (*adj*) cloaca; *antonym* (*v*) bolster, 2. evacuate; *synonyms* (*v*) void, discharge, quit, clear, (*adj*) empty.

tæmandi exhaustive; *synonyms* (*adj*) complete, comprehensive, detailed, profound, thorough.

tæming 1. depletion; *synonyms* (*n*) consumption, expenditure, loss, (*adj*) flaccidity, vacancy, 2. evacuation; *synonyms* (*n*) elimination, emptying, departure, (*v*) discharge, emission.

tær clear; *synonyms* (*adj*) clean, certain, (*v*) bright, acquit, absolute; *antonyms* (*adj*) cloudy, opaque, unclear, dark, fuzzy.

tæra 1. seize; *synonyms* (*v*) capture, catch, grab, arrest, apprehend; *antonym* (*v*) release, **2.** corrode; *synonyms* (*v*) canker, consume, eat, gnaw, erode.

tærandi corrosive; *synonyms* (*adj*) caustic, acid, acrid, erosive, biting.

tærast 1. waste; *synonyms* (*n*) desert, (*adj*) spoil, desolate, (*v*) consume, exhaust; *antonyms* (*v*) conserve, save, **2.** corrode; *synonyms* (*v*) canker, eat, gnaw, erode, fret.

tæring 1. rust; *synonyms* (*n*) decay, corrosion, (*v*) corrode, eat, (*adj*) rusty, **2.** tabes, **3.** corrosion; *synonyms* (*n*) erosion, corroding, deterioration, canker, rot, **4.** erosion; *synonyms* (*n*) attrition, abrasion, eroding, friction, wear, **5.** oxidation; *synonyms* (*n*) calcination, rust, oxygenation, oxidization, oxidizement.

tærinn corrosive; *synonyms* (*adj*) caustic, acid, acrid, erosive, biting.

tærisýra caustic; *synonyms* (*adj*) biting, acrid, bitter, acrimonious, sharp; *antonyms* (*adj*) mild, gentle.

tafarlaus instantaneous; *synonyms* (*adj*) instant, immediate, prompt, precipitate, sudden; *antonym* (*adj*) consecutive.

tafinn delayed; *synonyms* (*adj*) belated, late, tardy, protracted, (*adv*) behind; *antonyms* (*adj*) brief, early.

tafla 1. relation; *synonyms* (*n*) connection, account, narration, recital, affinity, **2.** table; *synonyms* (*n*) board, chart, schedule, stand, (*v*) defer, **3.** schedule; *synonyms* (*n*) list, agenda, catalog, program, (*v*) register, **4.** switchboard; *synonyms* (*n*) patchboard, plugboard, **5.** puck; *synonyms* (*n*) fairy, imp.

tag 1. taxon, **2.** type; *synonyms* (*n*) pattern, character, kind, nature, (*adj*) model.

tagaður typed; *synonym* (*adj*) typewritten.

tagl tail; *synonyms* (*n*) rear, shadow, (*v*) follow, pursue, track; *antonyms* (*v*) head, front.

tagmynd picture; *synonyms* (*n*) photograph, effigy, paint, (*v*) image, describe.

tagskiptur typed; *synonym* (*adj*) typewritten.

tak 1. pleurodynia; *synonyms* (*n*) costalgia, pleuralgia, **2.** grip; *synonyms* (*n*) clasp, clutch, (*v*) grasp, hold, catch; *antonyms* (*v*) bore, release.

taka 1. seizure; *synonyms* (*n*) arrest, capture, confiscation, seizing, apprehension; *antonyms* (*n*) release, return, **2.** arrest; *synonyms* (*n*) stop, check, halt, custody, (*v*) catch; *antonym* (*v*) discharge.

takki 1. button; *synonyms* (*n*) knop, buckle, (*v*) knob, (*adj*) pin, tie, **2.** knob; *synonyms* (*n*) button, handle, bump, grip, (*adj*) bulb.

takmark 1. limit; *synonyms* (*n*) bound, boundary, (*v*) border, restrict, (*prep*) extent; *antonyms* (*n*) center, extension, minimum, (*v*) broaden, extend, **2.** goal; *synonyms* (*n*) aim, butt, design, destination, end.

takmarka restrict; *synonyms* (*v*) limit, restrain, circumscribe, confine, constrain.

takmarkaður limited; *synonyms* (*adj*) finite, circumscribed, moderate, qualified, special; *antonyms* (*adj*) boundless, infinite, limitless, open, complete.

takmarkalaus infinite; *synonyms* (*adj*) absolute, boundless, countless, endless, eternal; *antonyms* (*adj*) finite, limited, restricted.

takmarkandi restrictive; *synonyms* (*adj*) prohibitive, restraining, exclusive, restricted, (*v*) limitary; *antonym* (*adj*) encouraging.

takmarkanir 1. restriction; *synonyms* (*n*) limitation, limit, restraint, curb, (*v*) hindrance; *antonyms* (*n*) freedom, extension, **2.** limitation; *synonyms* (*n*) circumscription, restriction, check, constraint, control.

takmarkari limiter; *synonyms* (*n*) clipper, clippers.

takmörk 1. boundary; *synonyms* (*n*) border, bound, limit, edge, area, **2.** limit; *synonyms* (*n*) boundary, (*v*) restrict, circumscribe, confine, (*prep*) extent; *antonyms* (*n*) center, extension, minimum, (*v*) broaden, extend.

takmörkun 1. restriction; *synonyms* (*n*) limitation, limit, restraint, curb, (*v*) hindrance; *antonyms* (*n*) freedom, extension, **2.** demarcation; *synonyms* (*n*) boundary, definition, line, border, partition, **3.** constraint; *synonyms* (*n*) coercion, compulsion, force, confinement, duress; *antonym* (*n*) incentive, **4.** limitation; *synonyms* (*n*) circumscription, restriction, check, constraint, control, **5.** limit; *synonyms* (*n*) bound, (*v*) restrict, circumscribe, confine, (*prep*) extent; *antonyms* (*n*) center, minimum, (*v*) broaden, extend.

tákn 1. signal; *synonyms* (*n*) sign, gesture, indication, presage, (*v*) omen, **2.** symbol; *synonyms* (*n*) emblem, number, badge, mark, stamp, **3.** icon; *synonyms* (*n*) effigy, image, picture, figure, likeness.

tákna 1. code; *synonyms* (*n*) cipher, charter, law, act, (*v*) cypher, **2.** encode; *synonyms* (*v*) code, encipher, encrypt, autograph, calculate.

taknagrind abacus; *synonyms* (*n*) aback, (*v*) logometer, slipstick, tallies.

táknaraðarbútur exon; *synonym* (*n*) exempt.

táknaskýring reference; *synonyms* (*n*) citation, mention, quotation, quote, allusion.

táknfræði semiotics; *synonyms* (*n*) semiology, semeiology, semeiotics, symptomatology.

tákngjafi signifier; *synonyms* (*n*) anatomy, bod, build, cast, chassis.

táknkerfi 1. symbolism; *synonyms* (*n*) symbolization, allegory, charactery, suggestion, symbolic, **2**. notation; *synonyms* (*n*) annotation, memo, note, memorandum, register.

táknmál 1. code; *synonyms* (*n*) cipher, charter, law, act, (*v*) cypher, **2**. notation; *synonyms* (*n*) annotation, memo, note, memorandum, register.

táknmerking significance; *synonyms* (*n*) import, sense, connotation, consequence, meaning; *antonyms* (*n*) insignificance, triviality.

táknmynd 1. symbol; *synonyms* (*n*) sign, emblem, number, badge, mark, **2**. icon; *synonyms* (*n*) effigy, image, picture, figure, likeness.

táknröð exon; *synonym* (*n*) exempt.

táknróf code; *synonyms* (*n*) cipher, charter, law, act, (*v*) cypher.

táknsaga allegory; *synonyms* (*n*) fable, parable, apologue, emblem, (*adj*) simile.

táknsetning coding; *synonyms* (*n*) cryptography, encoding, programming, cryptanalysis, cryptanalytics.

táknsögulegur 1. allegoric; *synonym* (*adj*) allegorical, **2**. allegorical; *synonyms* (*adj*) allegoric, figurative, metaphorical, symbolic, parabolic; *antonym* (*adj*) literal.

táknun 1. symbolization; *synonyms* (*n*) symbol, symbolism, allegory, meaning, art, **2**. notation; *synonyms* (*n*) annotation, memo, note, memorandum, register.

taktbundinn periodic; *synonyms* (*adj*) intermittent, regular, periodical, recurrent, frequent.

taktiko 1. tactics; *synonyms* (*n*) tactic, plan, method, system, scheme, **2**. tactic; *synonyms* (*n*) maneuver, manoeuvre, means, strategy, approach.

taktræsir focus; *synonyms* (*n*) centering, (*v*) center, concentrate, converge, aim.

taktur 1. rhythm; *synonyms* (*n*) measure, cadence, meter, beat, pulse, **2**. round; *synonyms* (*adv*) about, (*adj*) circular, (*n*) circle, bout, ring; *antonyms* (*adj*) slim, sharp, **3**. cycle; *synonyms* (*n*) bicycle, round, (*v*) bike, motorcycle, wheel.

tal 1. speech; *synonyms* (*n*) address, delivery, expression, lecture, conversation, **2**. term; *synonyms* (*n*) name, period, style, title, (*v*) call.

tala 1. number; *synonyms* (*n*) count, amount, (*v*) calculate, aggregate, enumerate, **2**. speak; *synonyms* (*v*) express, converse, pronounce, articulate, deliver, **3**. puck; *synonyms* (*n*) fairy, imp, **4**. scalar, **5**. talk; *synonyms* (*v*) gossip, lecture, chatter, address, (*n*) discourse.

taldós microphone; *synonym* (*n*) mike.

talfælni phonophobia; *synonym* (*n*) acousticophobia.

talía tackle; *synonyms* (*v*) handle, harness, (*n*) gear, equipment, rigging; *antonym* (*v*) avoid.

talk talc; *synonym* (*n*) talcum.

tálkn 1. branchia; *synonyms* (*n*) gill, lamella, leech, sweetheart, wattle, **2**. gill; *synonyms* (*n*) branchia, (*v*) rivulet, gullet, (*adj*) adze, ax.

tálknahol atrium; *synonyms* (*n*) hall, vestibule, cavity, court, foyer.

tálknalok operculum; *synonyms* (*n*) lid, top, covercle, door, opercle.

talkúm talc; *synonym* (*n*) talcum.

tálma obstruct; *synonyms* (*v*) bar, block, check, (*n*) hinder, barricade; *antonyms* (*v*) encourage, facilitate, free.

tálmandi inhibitory; *synonyms* (*adj*) inhibiting, repressive, repressing.

tálmi 1. block; *synonyms* (*n*) bar, barricade, pad, (*v*) arrest, stop; *antonyms* (*v*) free, unblock, open, **2**. barrier; *synonyms* (*n*) bulwark, dam, handicap, hurdle, obstruction, **3**. obstruction; *synonyms* (*n*) obstacle, hindrance, interruption, (*v*) impediment, check, **4**. inhibitor; *synonym* (*n*) stabilizer.

tálmun 1. blanking, **2**. barrier; *synonyms* (*n*) barricade, bar, bulwark, dam, handicap, **3**. inhibition; *synonyms* (*n*) check, prohibition, restraint, suppression, taboo.

talnagrind abacus; *synonyms* (*n*) aback, (*v*) logometer, slipstick, tallies.

talning census; *synonyms* (*n*) list, returns, cense, (*v*) poll, recapitulation.

talningarpúls count; *synonyms* (*n*) number, calculation, (*v*) calculate, compute, tally.

talsímakerfi telephony; *synonyms* (*n*) telephone, phone.

talsími 1. telephone; *synonyms* (*n*) telephony, (*v*) call, phone, ring, telegraph, **2**. phone; *synonyms* (*n*) earpiece, earphone, headphone, receiver, (*v*) telephone, **3**. telephony.

taminn tame; *synonyms* (*adj*) docile, meek, (*v*) dull, break, subdue; *antonyms* (*adj*) exciting, wild.

tangens tangent; *synonyms* (*n*) aside, burn, departure, digression, grade.

tangerína tangerine; *synonym* (*n*) orange.

tangi spit; *synonyms* (*n*) broach, saliva, (*v*) drizzle, impale, expectorate.

tankbíll tanker; *synonyms* (*n*) oiler, fighter.

Tankskip tanker; *synonyms* (*n*) oiler, fighter.

tankur tank; *synonyms* (*n*) cistern, reservoir, container, cooler, belly.

tannaslit abrasion; *synonyms* (*n*) attrition, excoriation, erosion, friction, (*v*) detrition; *antonym* (*n*) smoothness.

tannatilfærsla drift; *synonyms* (*n*) stream, current, course, (*v*) aim, blow.

tannbergsmæltur alveolar; *synonyms* (*adj*) alveolary, honeycombed.

tannbogi quadrant; *synonyms* (*n*) quarter, sextant.

tanndráttur extraction; *synonyms* (*n*) descent, ancestry, birth, origin, family; *antonym* (*n*) insertion.

tannfræði odontology; *synonym* (*n*) dentistry.

tannfylling cement; *synonyms* (*n*) glue, adhesive, gum, (*v*) fasten, fix.

tanngerð dentition; *synonyms* (*n*) teething, teeth, odontiasis, dentilation.

tannhjól 1. cogwheel; *synonyms* (*n*) gear, appurtenances, paraphernalia, 2. gear; *synonyms* (*n*) equipment, outfit, tackle, apparatus, device.

tannhjólagrip mesh; *synonyms* (*n*) interlock, network, entanglement, (*v*) engage, lock.

tannhjólakerfi gear; *synonyms* (*n*) equipment, outfit, tackle, apparatus, device.

tannhjólasamstæða gear; *synonyms* (*n*) equipment, outfit, tackle, apparatus, device.

tannhjólasett gearing; *synonyms* (*n*) gear, affairs, behavior, caravan, clothing.

tannhjólatenging gearing; *synonyms* (*n*) gear, affairs, behavior, caravan, clothing.

tannhola alveolus; *synonyms* (*n*) follicle, lacuna, cavity, dent, dimple.

tannhold gum; *synonyms* (*n*) gingiva, paste, mucilage, (*v*) glue, cement.

tannholubor excavator; *synonyms* (*n*) digger, shovel, miner, sapper, archaeologist.

tannkoma 1. dentition; *synonyms* (*n*) teething, teeth, odontiasis, dentilation, 2. eruption; *synonyms* (*n*) blast, burst, outbreak, rash, (*adj*) detonation.

tannlím cement; *synonyms* (*n*) glue, adhesive, gum, (*v*) fasten, fix.

tannloðna smelt; *synonyms* (*v*) fuse, melt, temper, anneal, heat.

tannrót root; *synonyms* (*n*) base, foundation, origin, basis, (*v*) establish.

tannsetning dentition; *synonyms* (*n*) teething, teeth, odontiasis, dentilation.

tannsíld sprat; *synonym* (*n*) brisling.

tannskorpa cement; *synonyms* (*n*) glue, adhesive, gum, (*v*) fasten, fix.

tannstangargír rack; *synonyms* (*n*) manger, wrack, (*v*) torture, excruciate, torment.

tannsteinn tartar; *synonyms* (*adj*) dandruff, brabbler, (*n*) calculus, dragon, concretion.

tannsýkla plaque; *synonyms* (*n*) plate, brass, medal, administration, award.

tanntaka 1. teething; *synonyms* (*n*) dentition, teeth, odontiasis, 2. dentition; *synonyms* (*n*) teething, dentilation.

tannteppa retention; *synonyms* (*n*) memory, detention, holding, keeping, possession; *antonym* (*n*) removal.

tap 1. deficit; *synonyms* (*n*) deficiency, failure, shortage, dearth, (*adj*) defect; *antonym* (*n*) excess, 2. claim; *synonyms* (*n*) call, charge, allegation, (*v*) demand, ask; *antonyms* (*v*) deny, disclaim, forfeit, 3. degeneration; *synonyms* (*n*) decay, corruption, decline, degeneracy, abasement; *antonyms* (*n*) improvement, growth, 4. losses; *synonyms* (*n*) losings, dead, fatalities, toll, wounded, 5. loss; *synonyms* (*n*) hurt, damage, defeat, detriment, injury; *antonyms* (*n*) appearance, retrieval, victory, gaining, income.

táp vitality; *synonyms* (*n*) energy, life, animation, vigor, liveliness; *antonyms* (*n*) lethargy, apathy.

tapeti papers; *synonyms* (*n*) credentials, document, documents, identification, covenant.

tapíókamjöl cassava; *synonyms* (*n*) manioc, mandioca, casava, gari, manioca.

tápmikill dynamic; *synonyms* (*adj*) active, aggressive, dynamical, energetic, forceful; *antonyms* (*adj*) dull, static.

tappasnittun tapping; *synonyms* (*n*) tap, paracentesis, tick, beating, drumbeat.

tappi 1. tampon; *synonyms* (*n*) plug, closure, dabber, 2. plug; *synonyms* (*n*) hype, stopper, bung, (*v*) advertise, block, 3. stopper; *synonyms* (*n*) stopple, top, (*v*) stop, clog, obstruct.

tár tear; *synonyms* (*n*) split, rupture, (*v*) break, rip, crack.

tárabólga conjunctivitis; *synonym* (*n*) pinkeye.

tarfur bull; *synonyms* (*n*) bullshit, bunk, hogwash, rot, (*adj*) blunder.

targa target; *synonyms* (*n*) butt, goal, (*v*) aim, point, purpose.

tarpúnn tarpon; *synonyms* (*n*) anchovies, herring, sardines, shad, smelts.

tárubólga conjunctivitis; *synonym* (*n*) pinkeye.

taska 1. sack; *synonyms* (*v*) pillage, bag, plunder, discharge, dismiss; *antonym* (*v*) hire, 2. bag; *synonyms* (*n*) pocket, pouch, package, briefcase, purse, 3. case; *synonyms* (*n*) box, example, bin, cover, jacket.

táta turtle; *synonyms* (*n*) turkle, (*adj*) game, venison, (*v*) capsize.

taug 1. nerve; *synonyms* (*n*) audacity, cheek, impertinence, boldness, brass; *antonym* (*n*) cowardice, 2. string; *synonyms* (*n*) chain, file, row, strand, (*adj*) line, 3. rope; *synonyms* (*n*) cable, lasso, lariat, noose, cord, 4. cord; *synonyms* (*n*) band, string, bond, tie, twine, 5. line; *synonyms* (*n*) house, breed, course, family, lineage.

taugaboð impulse; *synonyms* (*n*) impetus, pulse, urge, drive, force.

taugabraut pathway; *synonyms* (*n*) passage, footpath, lane, path, road.

taugafræði neurology; *synonyms* (*n*) myology, organography, osteology, splanchnology.

taugafruma neuron; *synonym* (*n*) myelencephalon.

taugahvot neuralgia; *synonyms* (*n*) neuralgy, (*v*) cephalalgia, earache, gout, lumbago.

taugaóstyrkur nervous; *synonyms* (*adj*) anxious, excitable, tense, cowardly, afraid; *antonyms* (*adj*) calm, brave, relaxed.

taugapína neuralgia; *synonyms* (*n*) neuralgy, (*v*) cephalalgia, earache, gout, lumbago.

taugarenna moulding; *synonyms* (*n*) molding, modeling, mold, mould, cast.

taugarfruma neuron; *synonym* (*n*) myelencephalon.

taugarinntak bush; *synonyms* (*n*) shrub, bushing, wild, chaparral, hedge.

taugarnám enervation; *synonyms* (*n*) debility, debilitation, enfeeblement, exhaustion, (*adj*) languor.

taugarslíður neurolemma; *synonym* (*n*) neurilemma.

taugasími axon; *synonym* (*n*) axone.

taugasjúkdómafræði neurology; *synonyms* (*n*) myology, organography, osteology, splanchnology.

taugaskipan innervation; *synonyms* (*n*) excitation, excitement, feeling, irritation.

taugaskipun innervation; *synonyms* (*n*) excitation, excitement, feeling, irritation.

taugaslíður 1. myelin; *synonyms* (*n*) medulla, bulb, myeline, **2.** neurilemma; *synonym* (*n*) neurolemma.

taugatrefja 1. neurofibril, **2.** fibril; *synonyms* (*n*) fiber, fibrilla, filament, chain, strand.

taugatróð glia; *synonym* (*n*) neuroglia.

taugaveiklun neurosis; *synonyms* (*n*) breakdown, complex, fixation, insanity, neuroticism.

taugungur neuron; *synonym* (*n*) myelencephalon.

taumleysi abandonment; *synonyms* (*n*) renunciation, resignation, desertion, neglect, (*v*) abandon.

te tea; *synonyms* (*n*) reception, meal, (*v*) chocolate, cocoa, coffee.

tefja retard; *synonyms* (*v*) delay, check, hinder, arrest, detain; *antonym* (*v*) accelerate.

tegra integrate; *synonyms* (*v*) incorporate, blend, combine, consolidate, fuse; *antonyms* (*v*) separate, exclude, segregate.

tegrun integration; *synonyms* (*n*) amalgamation, consolidation, embodiment, integrating, merger; *antonym* (*n*) segregation.

tegund 1. type; *synonyms* (*n*) pattern, character, kind, nature, (*adj*) model, **2.** species; *synonyms* (*n*) sort, breed, class, genus, appearance, **3.** category; *synonyms* (*n*) denomination, division, type, variety, form.

tegundablendingur hybrid; *synonyms* (*adj*) crossbred, (*n*) crossbreed, cross, mixture, (*v*) composite.

tegundardæmi type; *synonyms* (*n*) pattern, character, kind, nature, (*adj*) model.

tegundareinkenni character; *synonyms* (*n*) kind, nature, note, part, quality.

tegundargreining identification; *synonyms* (*n*) designation, finding, id, identity, mark.

tegundarhópur strain; *synonyms* (*n*) stress, breed, effort, (*v*) filter, screen; *antonym* (*v*) relax.

tegundarþróun 1. phylogenesis; *synonyms* (*n*) phylogeny, evolution, development, **2.** phylogeny; *synonyms* (*n*) phylogenesis, metaplasm, ontogeny, ovary, ovum, **3.** anthropogenesis; *synonym* (*n*) anthropogeny.

tegur integral; *synonyms* (*adj*) complete, entire, inherent, full, (*n*) whole.

teikn 1. sign; *synonyms* (*n*) signal, indication, mark, motion, (*v*) gesture, **2.** logo; *synonyms* (*n*) emblem, logotype, sign, badge, symbol, **3.** icon; *synonyms* (*n*) effigy, image, picture, figure, likeness.

teikna plot; *synonyms* (*n*) conspiracy, plan, lot, (*v*) intrigue, cabal.

teiknari plotter; *synonyms* (*n*) conspirator, machinator, schemer, designer, coconspirator.

teiknilag level; *synonyms* (*n*) grade, (*adj*) even, equal, (*v*) flat, flatten; *antonyms* (*adj*) inclined, slanting, angled, (*v*) uneven, build.

teikning 1. plot; *synonyms* (*n*) conspiracy, plan, lot, (*v*) intrigue, cabal, **2.** plan; *synonyms* (*n*) aim, map, figure, chart, (*v*) design, **3.** drawing; *synonyms* (*n*) draft, drafting, delineation, picture, cartoon.

teiknivél plotter; *synonyms* (*n*) conspirator, machinator, schemer, designer, coconspirator.

teiknun 1. design; *synonyms* (*n*) aim, purpose, scheme, conception, (*v*) plan; *antonym* (*n*) chance, **2.** graphics; *synonyms* (*n*) drawing, art, artwork, artistry, scan.

teinn rail; *synonyms* (*n*) bar, balustrade, handrail, railing, (*v*) inveigh.

teinungur sucker; *synonyms* (*n*) dupe, fool, sap, jay, lollipop.

teistufiskur butterfish; *synonym* (*n*) stromateid.

tekjuafgangur 1. profit; *synonyms* (*n*) gain, benefit, account, good, (*adj*) advantage; *antonym* (*v*) lose, **2.** surplus; *synonyms* (*adj*) extra, (*n*) excess, remainder, balance, overabundance; *antonyms* (*n*) necessary, lack, shortage, scarcity, **3.** earnings; *synonyms* (*n*) profit, salary, income, pay, profits.

tekjuliður revenue; *synonyms* (*n*) income, receipts, proceeds, profit, earnings.

tekjulind revenue; *synonyms* (*n*) income, receipts, proceeds, profit, earnings.

tekjur 1. revenue; *synonyms* (*n*) income, receipts, proceeds, profit, earnings, **2.** rent; *synonyms* (*n*) breach, cleft, fissure, lease, (*v*) hire, **3.** income; *synonyms* (*n*) revenue, gain, means, pay, return; *antonym* (*n*) loss.

tekjurafrakstur revenue; *synonyms* (*n*) income, receipts, proceeds, profit, earnings.

tékki 1. cheque; *synonyms* (*n*) draft, arrest, assay, bridle, (*v*) check, **2.** check; *synonyms* (*v*) stop, block, limit, (*n*) control, curb.

tektóník tectonics; *synonym* (*n*) architectonics.

telja count; *synonyms* (*n*) number, calculation, (*v*) calculate, compute, tally.

teljari 1. scaler, **2.** counter; *synonyms* (*n*) buffet, bench, reverse, (*v*) reply, (*adj*) converse, **3.** numerator; *synonym* (*n*) number.

tellúr tellurium; *synonyms* (*n*) si, ti.

tema theme; *synonyms* (*n*) matter, motif, subject, base, composition.

tempra 1. condition; *synonyms* (*n*) circumstance, position, provision, status, (*v*) aspect, **2.** modulate; *synonyms* (*v*) moderate, modify, change, inflect, qualify.

temprun 1. regulation; *synonyms* (*n*) rule, adjustment, law, order, (*adj*) control; *antonym* (*n*) chaos, **2.** homeostasis.

tenajlo pincers; *synonyms* (*v*) forceps, tongs, clutches.

tendra ignite; *synonyms* (*v*) light, kindle, arouse, enkindle, fire; *antonym* (*v*) extinguish.

tengdur conjugate; *synonyms* (*v*) join, couple, (*adj*) united, conjugated, coupled.

tengi 1. port; *synonyms* (*n*) harbor, haven, asylum, carriage, (*adj*) larboard; *antonym* (*n*) starboard, **2.** terminal; *synonyms* (*adj*) final, last, definitive, (*n*) depot, end, **3.** bond; *synonyms* (*n*) association, tie, alliance, deed, (*v*) bind, **4.** coupling; *synonyms* (*n*) union, coupler, clutch, conjugation, connection, **5.** contactor.

tengiæxlun conjugation; *synonyms* (*n*) junction, union, coupling, declension, (*v*) conjunction.

tengibogi fillet; *synonyms* (*n*) band, strip, cincture, list, (*v*) filet.

tengibraut 1. bus; *synonyms* (*n*) automobile, autobus, car, coach, vehicle, **2.** highway; *synonyms* (*n*) road, highroad, way, course, path.

tengibúnaður 1. terminal; *synonyms* (*adj*) final, last, definitive, (*n*) depot, end, **2.** port; *synonyms* (*n*) harbor, haven, asylum, carriage, (*adj*) larboard; *antonym* (*n*) starboard, **3.** interface; *synonyms* (*n*) link, port, boundary, junction, (*v*) contact.

tengidós box; *synonyms* (*n*) basket, cage, chest, (*v*) cuff, buffet; *antonym* (*v*) unbox.

tengiensím ligase; *synonym* (*n*) synthetase.

tengiflötur tier; *synonyms* (*n*) layer, row, floor, (*adj*) line, rank.

tengihólkur collar; *synonyms* (*n*) arrest, choker, (*v*) catch, apprehend, capture.

tengiklemma terminal; *synonyms* (*adj*) final, last, definitive, (*n*) depot, end.

tengikragi flange; *synonyms* (*n*) brim, edge, lip, brink, border.

tengildi adapter; *synonyms* (*n*) adaptor, spider, attachment, arranger, transcriber.

tengiliður associate; *synonyms* (*v*) affiliate, connect, (*n*) ally, assistant, companion; *antonyms* (*v*) avoid, dissociate, distance, (*adj*) chief, (*n*) stranger.

tengilína trunk; *synonyms* (*n*) stem, boot, torso, body, bole.

tengilkvísl plug; *synonyms* (*n*) hype, stopper, bung, (*v*) advertise, block.

tengill 1. terminal; *synonyms* (*adj*) final, last, definitive, (*n*) depot, end, **2.** plug; *synonyms* (*n*) hype, stopper, bung, (*v*) advertise, block, **3.** socket; *synonyms* (*n*) cavity, alveolus, sleeve, hollow, pocket, **4.** connector; *synonyms* (*n*) connective, connecter, connection, coupling, conjunction, **5.** ligand.

tenging 1. coupling; *synonyms* (*n*) union, coupler, clutch, conjugation, connection, **2.** synthesis; *synonyms* (*n*) combination, fusion, compound, incorporation, mixture; *antonym* (*n*) separation, **3.** bond; *synonyms* (*n*) association, tie, alliance, deed, (*v*) bind, **4.** conjugation; *synonyms* (*n*) junction, coupling, declension, inflection, (*v*) conjunction, **5.** contact; *synonyms* (*n*) touch, collision, communication, link, (*v*) call.

tenginn associative; *synonyms* (*adj*) associatory, clannish, concomitant.

tengipunktur 1. terminal; *synonyms* (*adj*) final, last, definitive, (*n*) depot, end, **2.** vertex; *synonyms* (*n*) top, apex, crown, peak, summit.

tengir ligase; *synonym* (*n*) synthetase.

tengiröð series; *synonyms* (*n*) chain, rank, collection, cycle, (*v*) course.

tengispjald adapter; *synonyms* (*n*) adaptor, spider, attachment, arranger, transcriber.

tengistétt coupling; *synonyms* (*n*) union, coupler, clutch, conjugation, connection.

tengistig connectivity; *synonym* (*n*) connectability.

tengiþráður lead; *synonyms* (*v*) head, guide, conduct, contribute, direct; *antonym* (*v*) follow.

tengivagn 1. trailer; *synonyms* (*n*) caravan, leader, ad, advertisement, announcement, **2.** tandem; *synonyms* (*n*) bicycle, buggy, cycle, dogcart, random.

tengja 1. splice; *synonyms* (*n*) joint, (*v*) link, conjoin, join, (*adj*) tie, **2.** relate; *synonyms* (*v*) connect, narrate, recount, associate, tell, **3.** connect; *synonyms* (*v*) bind, attach, bond, annex, combine; *antonyms* (*v*) disconnect, separate, **4.** bridge; *synonyms* (*n*) span, viaduct, pontoon, crossing, (*v*) stretch, **5.** clutch; *synonyms* (*n*) clasp, (*v*) grip, clench, clinch, grab.

tengjanleiki connectivity; *synonym* (*n*) connectability.

tengjast 1. relate; *synonyms* (*v*) connect, narrate, recount, associate, link, **2.** fuse; *synonyms* (*v*) combine, amalgamate, blend, melt, coalesce; *antonym* (*v*) separate.

tengni connectivity; *synonym* (*n*) connectability.

tengsl 1. relationship; *synonyms* (*n*) affinity, relation, affiliation, association, connection, **2.** association; *synonyms* (*n*) alliance, assembly, company, fellowship, link, **3.** affiliation; *synonyms* (*n*) coalition, relationship, filiation, partnership, bond, **4.** coupling; *synonyms* (*n*) union, coupler, clutch, conjugation, yoke, **5.** commissure; *synonyms* (*v*) articulation, joint, juncture, gore, gusset.

tengslafasi coupling; *synonyms* (*n*) union, coupler, clutch, conjugation, connection.

tengslalíkur contingency; *synonyms* (*n*) accident, chance, eventuality, possibility, circumstance.

tengslarit chart; *synonyms* (*n*) plan, plot, (*v*) map, graph, sketch.

tengsli 1. coupling; *synonyms* (*n*) union, coupler, clutch, conjugation, connection, **2.** clutch; *synonyms* (*n*) clasp, (*v*) grip, clench, clinch, grab.

tengslkragi coupling; *synonyms* (*n*) union, coupler, clutch, conjugation, connection.

tengt mesh; *synonyms* (*n*) interlock, network, entanglement, (*v*) engage, lock.

tengur tongs; *synonyms* (*n*) lifter, poker, trivet, jaws, (*v*) clutches.

teningslaga cubic; *synonyms* (*adj*) solid, compact, dense, firm, genuine.

teningur cube; *synonyms* (*n*) block, rhomboid, blockage, blocking, (*v*) dice.

tenna indent; *synonyms* (*v*) dent, indenture, cut, impress, (*n*) notch.

tenning serration; *synonyms* (*n*) notch, nick, serrations, serrature, groove.

tennur teeth; *synonyms* (*v*) arrastra, fangs, file, grater, gristmill.

teppa 1. retention; *synonyms* (*n*) memory, detention, holding, keeping, possession; *antonym* (*n*) removal, **2.** congestion; *synonyms* (*n*) blockage, engorgement, overcrowding, aggregation, crowding; *antonym* (*n*) emptiness, **3.** obstruct;

synonyms (*v*) bar, block, check, (*n*) hinder, barricade; *antonyms* (*v*) encourage, facilitate, free.

tepping 1. tamponade; *synonym* (*n*) tamponage, **2.** obstruction; *synonyms* (*n*) obstacle, hindrance, interruption, bar, (*v*) impediment.

tepptur impacted; *synonym* (*adj*) wedged.

tereno grounds; *synonyms* (*n*) cause, dregs, ground, reason, account.

terkonekti grounds; *synonyms* (*n*) cause, dregs, ground, reason, account.

termistor thermistor; *synonym* (*n*) thermocouple.

tero grounds; *synonyms* (*n*) cause, dregs, ground, reason, account.

terpentína turpentine; *synonym* (*n*) turps.

tersurfaco grounds; *synonyms* (*n*) cause, dregs, ground, reason, account.

tertíer tertiary; *synonyms* (*adj*) third, cretaceous, quaternary, tertial.

tertíertímabil tertiary; *synonyms* (*adj*) third, cretaceous, quaternary, tertial.

terunni tea; *synonyms* (*n*) reception, meal, (*v*) chocolate, cocoa, coffee.

textajöfnun justification; *synonyms* (*n*) apology, defense, account, reason, (*v*) excuse.

textaröðun alignment; *synonyms* (*n*) alliance, alinement, arrangement, coalition, organization.

textasafn corpus; *synonyms* (*n*) body, substance, material, matter, principal.

textastilling alignment; *synonyms* (*n*) alliance, alinement, arrangement, coalition, organization.

texti 1. text; *synonyms* (*n*) copy, matter, script, theme, subject, **2.** legend; *synonyms* (*n*) caption, fable, fiction, tale, account.

teyging 1. warping; *synonyms* (*n*) warp, warpage, beaming, buckle, deflection, **2.** dilation; *synonyms* (*n*) dilatation, expansion, swelling, growth, spread, **3.** extension; *synonyms* (*n*) continuation, augmentation, enlargement, addition, increase; *antonyms* (*n*) limitation, contraction, limit.

teyginn elastic; *synonyms* (*adj*) flexible, buoyant, ductile, limber, pliable; *antonyms* (*adj*) rigid, stiff, inflexible, inelastic.

teygja 1. stretch; *synonyms* (*n*) extent, (*v*) extend, reach, strain, elongate; *antonym* (*v*) shorten, **2.** elongation; *synonyms* (*n*) extension, expansion, length, production, annex.

teygjanlegt ductile; *synonyms* (*adj*) elastic, flexible, malleable, pliable, supple.

teygjanlegur 1. tensile; *synonyms* (*adj*) elastic, flexible, ductile, malleable, pliable, **2.** ductile; *synonyms* (*adj*) supple, tensile, yielding, limp, plastic, **3.** elastic; *synonyms* (*adj*) buoyant, limber, pliant, resilient, soft; *antonyms* (*adj*) rigid, stiff, inflexible, inelastic.

teygjudýr 1. ameba; *synonym* (*n*) amoeba, **2.** amoeba; *synonyms* (*n*) ameba, (*adj*) spineless.

teygni elasticity; *synonyms* (*n*) bounce, spring, flexibility, pliability, suppleness.

teymi team; *synonyms* (*n*) crew, company, gang, squad, (*v*) pair.

tíbrá 1. scintillation; *synonyms* (*n*) flash, glisten, glitter, sparkle, fire, **2.** mirage; *synonyms* (*n*) hallucination, illusion, delusion, fancy, vision.

tíð 1. time; *synonyms* (*n*) hour, moment, period, duration, epoch; *antonym* (*n*) death, **2.** tense; *synonyms* (*adj*) strained, edgy, nervous, taut, (*v*) overwrought; *antonyms* (*adj*) relaxed, calm, comfortable, tranquil, loose, **3.** while; *synonyms* (*conj*) as, whereas, although, (*n*) spell, time, **4.** period; *synonyms* (*n*) age, dot, era, point, generation.

tíðahvörf 1. climacteric; *synonyms* (*adj*) critical, anility, decrepitude, superannuation, (*n*) menopause, **2.** menopause; *synonym* (*n*) climacteric.

tíðalok menopause; *synonym* (*n*) climacteric.

tíðbeyging conjugation; *synonyms* (*n*) junction, union, coupling, declension, (*v*) conjunction.

tídd frequency; *synonyms* (*n*) frequence, incidence, commonness, prevalence, constancy.

tíðir 1. terms; *synonyms* (*n*) condition, conditions, provision, stipulation, cost, **2.** menstruation; *synonyms* (*n*) menses, catamenia, flow, period, current.

tíðni frequency; *synonyms* (*n*) frequence, incidence, commonness, prevalence, constancy.

tíðniafmótari discriminator; *synonym* (*n*) differentiator.

tíðnibil 1. bandwidth, **2.** band; *synonyms* (*n*) cluster, party, set, swathe, (*v*) ring.

tíðnisindur scintillation; *synonyms* (*n*) flash, glisten, glitter, sparkle, fire.

tíðniskerpa selectivity; *synonym* (*n*) specificity.

tíðnistilla tune; *synonyms* (*n*) melody, song, strain, air, (*v*) adjust.

tigla 1. tile; *synonyms* (*n*) bonnet, castor, ceiling, roof, (*v*) cover, **2.** mosaic; *synonyms* (*n*) tesserae, strigae, (*adj*) tessellated, heterogeneous, (*v*) plaid.

tign majesty; *synonyms* (*n*) glory, grandeur, dignity, loftiness, splendor.

tignun idealization; *synonyms* (*n*) idealisation, glorification, adulation, glory, idolization.

tigull 1. rhombus; *synonyms* (*n*) rhomb, diamond, lozenge, parallelogram, oblong, **2.** tile; *synonyms* (*n*) bonnet, castor, ceiling, roof, (*v*) cover.

tígull rhombus; *synonyms* (*n*) rhomb, diamond, lozenge, parallelogram, oblong.

tígulsteinn brick; *synonyms* (*n*) block, lump, brown, (*adj*) trump, concrete.

til 1. to; *synonyms* (*prep*) at, by, in, (*prf*) on, (*v*) till, **2.** for; *synonyms* (*prep*) because, behind, per, (*adv*) against, as.

tilboð 1. proposal; *synonyms* (*n*) motion, advice, proposition, suggestion, offer, **2.** tender; *synonyms* (*adj*) affectionate, painful, loving, (*v*) proffer, (*n*) bid; *antonyms* (*adj*) tough, hard, hardhearted, rubbery, rough, **3.** bid; *synonyms* (*n*) tender, attempt, (*v*) ask, call, command, **4.** offer; *synonyms* (*v*) give, bestow, put, advance, (*n*) proposal; *antonyms* (*v*) withdraw, refuse.

tilbrigði 1. variation; *synonyms* (*n*) alteration, change, difference, divergence, mutation; *antonym* (*n*) similarity, **2.** variant; *synonyms* (*n*) variation, version, (*adj*) different, divergent, changeable, **3.** form; *synonyms* (*n*) figure, design, (*v*) cast, make, fashion.

tilbúinn 1. standby; *synonyms* (*adj*) extra, (*n*) reserve, deputy, substitute, understudy, **2.** synthetic; *synonyms* (*adj*) artificial, ersatz, false, simulated, synthetical; *antonyms* (*adj*) natural, genuine, real.

tilbúnaður set; *synonyms* (*v*) fix, place, lay, put, (*n*) class; *antonyms* (*v*) soften, liquefy, (*n*) combing, comb-out, (*adj*) variable.

tilefni 1. time; *synonyms* (*n*) hour, moment, period, duration, epoch; *antonym* (*n*) death, **2.** reason; *synonyms* (*n*) mind, account, intellect, occasion, (*v*) cause, **3.** chance; *synonyms* (*n*) hazard, fortune, (*adj*) accidental, (*v*) gamble, adventure; *antonyms* (*n*) predictability, (*adj*) deliberate, intentional, (*v*) design, plan, **4.** instance; *synonyms* (*n*) example, case, exemplar, time, (*v*) exemplify, **5.** opportunity; *synonyms* (*n*) chance, opening, luck, crack, event.

tileinkun acquisition; *synonyms* (*n*) purchase, accomplishment, acquirement, attainment, achievement.

tilfæring manipulation; *synonyms* (*n*) handling, management, treatment, use, control.

tilfærsla 1. transfer; *synonyms* (*n*) conveyance, (*v*) convey, carry, change, remove; *antonyms* (*v*) hold, keep, **2.** translocation; *synonyms* (*n*) shift, interchange, **3.** shift; *synonyms* (*n*) turn, (*v*) exchange, quibble, alter, budge, **4.** transposition; *synonyms* (*n*) permutation, replacement, reversal, substitution, transposal, **5.** displacement; *synonyms* (*n*) deposition, transfer, movement, motion, translation.

tilfallandi accidental; *synonyms* (*adj*) casual, fortuitous, adventitious, chance, incidental; *antonyms* (*adj*) intentional, deliberate.

tilfang resource; *synonyms* (*n*) expedient, imagination, (*v*) recourse, resort, refuge.

tilfangaþrot starvation; *synonyms* (*n*) hunger, inanition, famine, famishment, starving.

tilfelli case; *synonyms* (*n*) box, example, bin, cover, jacket.

tilfinning 1. sensation; *synonyms* (*n*) impression, emotion, feel, (*v*) feeling, affection; *antonym* (*n*) numbness, **2**. sense; *synonyms* (*n*) intelligence, perception, meaning, (*v*) intellect, mind; *antonyms* (*n*) garbage, ludicrousness, nonsense, stupidity, foolishness, **3**. feeling; *synonyms* (*n*) passion, atmosphere, belief, hunch, intuition; *antonym* (*n*) indifference, **4**. emotion; *synonyms* (*n*) love, sensation, heart, agitation, commotion.

tilfinningaleysi anesthesia; *synonyms* (*n*) anaesthesia, asleep, insentience, stupor, unconsciousness.

tilfinninganæmur susceptible; *synonyms* (*adj*) impressionable, receptive, responsive, sensitive, subject; *antonyms* (*adj*) resistant, unsusceptible.

tilfinningaofsi intoxication; *synonyms* (*n*) drunkenness, inebriation, inebriety, poisoning, tipsiness.

tilfinningarleysi anesthesia; *synonyms* (*n*) anaesthesia, asleep, insentience, stupor, unconsciousness.

tilfinningasamurlegur 1. touching; *synonyms* (*v*) affecting, (*adj*) moving, poignant, pathetic, pitiful, **2**. affecting; *synonyms* (*adj*) touching, emotional, emotive, stirring, heartbreaking, **3**. moving; *synonyms* (*adj*) active, exciting, impressive, mobile, (*n*) movement; *antonyms* (*adj*) motionless, still, depressing, stationary, unemotional, **4**. emotional; *synonyms* (*adj*) dramatic, affective, effusive, passionate, sensational; *antonyms* (*adj*) impassive, unflappable.

tilgangur 1. purpose; *synonyms* (*n*) aim, plan, design, mind, (*v*) intention, **2**. mission; *synonyms* (*n*) commission, delegation, deputation, job, assignment, **3**. goal; *synonyms* (*n*) butt, destination, end, purpose, basket.

tilgáta 1. conjecture; *synonyms* (*n*) guess, supposition, assumption, (*v*) suppose, estimate; *antonym* (*n*) fact, **2**. hypothesis; *synonyms* (*n*) conjecture, theory, speculation, belief, condition.

tilgátuhús replica; *synonyms* (*n*) facsimile, imitation, copy, duplicate, reproduction; *antonyms* (*n*) original, (*adj*) genuine.

tilgreina disclose; *synonyms* (*v*) betray, declare, impart, detect, (*adj*) confess; *antonyms* (*v*) conceal, secrete.

tilhliðrun modification; *synonyms* (*n*) alteration, change, adaptation, variation, adjustment.

tilhneigð predisposition; *synonyms* (*n*) bent, bias, leaning, inclination, predilection; *antonym* (*n*) impartiality.

tilhneiging trend; *synonyms* (*n*) fashion, tendency, fad, inclination, (*v*) style.

tilhögun 1. procedure; *synonyms* (*n*) process, formula, practice, routine, fashion, **2**. arrangement; *synonyms* (*n*) agreement, order, settlement, adjustment, array.

tilhvatning motivation; *synonyms* (*n*) motive, impulse, cause, incentive, reason.

tilhvöt motive; *synonyms* (*n*) cause, ground, account, impulse, incentive.

tilkenningarleysi anaesthesia; *synonyms* (*n*) anesthesia, stupor, anaesthesis, (*adj*) palsy, paralysis.

tilkoma inclusion; *synonyms* (*n*) comprehension, implication, incorporation, addition, embodiment; *antonyms* (*n*) exclusion, exception.

tilkynning 1. serving; *synonyms* (*n*) portion, helping, service, share, piece, **2**. report; *synonyms* (*n*) description, gossip, notice, (*v*) account, describe; *antonym* (*n*) fact, **3**. announcement; *synonyms* (*n*) annunciation, advertisement, declaration, communication, proclamation, **4**. communication; *synonyms* (*n*) announcement, commerce, communicating, contact, conversation, **5**. notification; *synonyms* (*n*) advice, information, note, intelligence, warning.

tillæti plasticity; *synonyms* (*n*) flexibility, malleability, elasticity, give, adaptability.

tillag appropriation; *synonyms* (*n*) allotment, adoption, seizure, annexation, embezzlement.

tillaga 1. proposal; *synonyms* (*n*) motion, advice, proposition, suggestion, offer, **2**. recommendation; *synonyms* (*n*) praise, commendation, counsel, advocacy, reference.

tillátur plastic; *synonyms* (*adj*) flexible, ductile, elastic, malleable, (*v*) limber.

tillbúinn 1. through; *synonyms* (*adv*) by, (*adj*) finished, done, direct, straight, **2**. ready; *synonyms* (*adj*) fit, prompt, quick, (*v*) prepare, (*n*) available; *antonyms* (*adj*) unprepared, unwilling, **3**. finished; *synonyms* (*adj*) complete, completed, ended, perfect, consummate; *antonyms* (*adj*) unfinished, incomplete, remaining, rough.

tillífgun anabolism; *synonyms* (*n*) catabolism, metabolism.

tillífun 1. synthesis; *synonyms* (*n*) combination, fusion, compound, incorporation, mixture; *antonym* (*n*) separation, **2**. biosynthesis; *synonyms* (*n*) biogenesis, biogeny, **3**. assimilation; *synonyms* (*n*) absorption, acculturation, integration, addition, amalgamation, **4**. anabolism; *synonyms* (*n*) catabolism, metabolism.

tillíking assimilation; *synonyms* (*n*) absorption, acculturation, incorporation, integration, addition.

tilmæli 1. request; *synonyms* (*n*) petition, bid, (*v*) demand, ask, invite; *antonyms* (*v*) command, order, **2**. recommendation; *synonyms* (*n*) praise, commendation, advice, counsel, suggestion, **3**. claim; *synonyms* (*n*) call, charge, allegation, (*v*) assert, exact; *antonyms* (*v*) deny, disclaim, forfeit.

tilnefna 1. assign; *synonyms* (*v*) allot, apportion, delegate, allow, apply, **2**. nominate; *synonyms* (*v*) appoint, name, constitute, (*n*) designate, call.

tilnefning appointment; *synonyms* (*n*) assignment, date, designation, engagement, fitting.

tilraun 1. trial; *synonyms* (*n*) test, examination, experiment, affliction, essay, **2**. test; *synonyms* (*n*) trial, audition, (*v*) assay, examine, prove, **3**. experiment; *synonyms* (*n*) attempt, tentative, try, taste, (*v*) venture.

tilraunadýr subject; *synonyms* (*n*) matter, citizen, affair, (*adj*) liable, exposed; *antonym* (*adj*) liberated.

tilraunalegur experimental; *synonyms* (*adj*) empirical, tentative, scientific, observational, pilot.

tilraunaliður treatment; *synonyms* (*n*) cure, conduct, handling, management, manipulation.

tilraunamaður subject; *synonyms* (*n*) matter, citizen, affair, (*adj*) liable, exposed; *antonym* (*adj*) liberated.

tilraunastofa laboratory; *synonyms* (*n*) lab, factory, course, (*adj*) experimental, alembic.

tilraunaviðfang subject; *synonyms* (*n*) matter, citizen, affair, (*adj*) liable, exposed; *antonym* (*adj*) liberated.

tilreiða edit; *synonyms* (*v*) delete, compile, cut, redact, (*n*) editing.

Tilreiðsla preparation; *synonyms* (*n*) arrangement, concoction, provision, readiness, training.

tilskipaður mandatory; *synonyms* (*adj*) compulsory, obligatory, required, necessary, (*n*) mandatary; *antonym* (*adj*) optional.

tilskipun 1. regulation; *synonyms* (*n*) rule, adjustment, law, order, (*adj*) control; *antonym* (*n*) chaos, **2**. directive; *synonyms* (*n*) decree, direction, edict, (*adj*) directing, directional, **3**. constitution; *synonyms* (*n*) composition, code, makeup, organization, temperament.

tilslökun 1. waiver; *synonyms* (*n*) release, discharge, renunciation, dismissal, acquittance, **2**. concession; *synonyms* (*n*) admission, compliance, allowance, compromise, discount.

tilsvarandi corresponding; *synonyms* (*adj*) congruent, comparable, equal, same, similar; *antonym* (*adj*) different.

tiltækileiki availability; *synonyms* (*n*) accessibility, handiness, approachability, availableness, opening.

tiltækt availability; *synonyms* (*n*) accessibility, handiness, approachability, availableness, opening.

tiltækur 1. quiescent; *synonyms* (*adj*) dormant, inactive, calm, passive, inert; *antonym* (*adj*) active, **2**. available; *synonyms* (*adj*) accessible, free, possible, attainable, (*adv*) present; *antonyms* (*adj*) unavailable, occupied, suppressed, concealed, engaged.

tiltekið specific; *synonyms* (*adj*) individual, special, concrete, exact, (*n*) particular; *antonyms* (*adj*) universal, vague, (*n*) general.

tiltekinn specific; *synonyms* (*adj*) individual, special, concrete, exact, (*n*) particular; *antonyms* (*adj*) universal, vague, (*n*) general.

tiltölulegur relative; *synonyms* (*adj*) related, comparative, proportionate, (*n*) relation, (*v*) kinsman; *antonym* (*adj*) absolute.

tilvarp project; *synonyms* (*n*) design, device, (*v*) plan, hurl, contrive.

tilvik 1. event; *synonyms* (*n*) affair, case, consequence, effect, occurrence, **2**. instance; *synonyms* (*n*) example, exemplar, time, (*v*) exemplify, illustrate, **3**. incident; *synonyms* (*n*) event, fact, adventure, circumstance, episode.

tilviljunarkenndur 1. random; *synonyms* (*adj*) accidental, aimless, irregular, (*n*) haphazard, chance; *antonym* (*adj*) systematic, **2**. stray; *synonyms* (*v*) roam, digress, ramble, range, wander, **3**. temporary; *synonyms* (*adj*) ephemeral, passing, temporal, acting, momentary; *antonyms* (*adj*) permanent, continuous, enduring, eternal, everlasting, **4**. stochastic; *synonyms* (*adj*) hypothetical, conjectural, stochastical, **5**. chance; *synonyms* (*n*) hazard, fortune, opportunity, (*v*) gamble, adventure; *antonyms* (*n*) predictability, (*adj*) deliberate, intentional, (*v*) design, plan.

tilvísanleiki visibility; *synonyms* (*n*) visibleness, conspicuousness, apparition, (*v*) sight, view.

tilvísun 1. reference; *synonyms* (*n*) citation, mention, quotation, quote, allusion, **2**. referral.

tilvitnun quotation; *synonyms* (*n*) citation, extract, mention, excerpt, passage.

tilvitund awareness; *synonyms* (*n*) consciousness, appreciation, knowledge, perception, sensation; *antonym* (*n*) ignorance.

tíma secondary; *synonyms* (*adj*) inferior, lower, minor, subordinate, ancillary; *antonyms* (*adj*) basic, main, central, chief, direct.

tímaáætlun schedule; *synonyms* (*n*) list, agenda, catalog, program, (*v*) register.

tímabil 1. term; *synonyms* (*n*) name, expression, period, style, (*v*) call, **2**. spell; *synonyms* (*n*) magic, fascination, bout, conjuration, (v) charm, **3**. time; *synonyms* (n) hour, moment, duration, epoch, era; *antonym* (n) death, **4**. stadium; *synonyms* (n) arena, coliseum, bowl, field, gymnasium, **5**. age; *synonyms* (n) aeon, day, time, cycle, (v) mature.

tímabundið temporary; *synonyms* (adj) ephemeral, passing, temporal, acting, momentary; *antonyms* (adj) permanent, continuous, enduring, eternal, everlasting.

tímabundin 1. suspension; *synonyms* (n) delay, interruption, abeyance, break, intermission, **2**. temporal; *synonyms* (adj) worldly, secular, earthly, profane, carnal.

tímabundinn 1. temporary; *synonyms* (adj) ephemeral, passing, temporal, acting, momentary; *antonyms* (adj) permanent, continuous, enduring, eternal, everlasting, **2**. provisional; *synonyms* (adj) conditional, makeshift, tentative, probationary, interim; *antonym* (adj) definite, **3**. periodical; *synonyms* (n) journal, magazine, newspaper, (adj) periodic, intermittent.

tímaferli history; *synonyms* (n) account, chronicle, story, annals, background; *antonym* (n) present.

tímaflötur horizon; *synonyms* (n) perspective, prospect, purview, reach, skyline.

tímagisti timer; *synonyms* (n) timepiece, timekeeper, clock, regulator, watch.

tímalengd 1. time; *synonyms* (n) hour, moment, period, duration, epoch; *antonym* (n) death, **2**. duration; *synonyms* (n) length, continuation, continuance, standing, stretch.

tímamörk deadline; *synonyms* (n) limit, end, aim, goal, target.

timamunur lag; *synonyms* (n) backwardness, (v) dawdle, delay, linger, dally.

tímamunur lag; *synonyms* (n) backwardness, (v) dawdle, delay, linger, dally.

tímapunktur instant; *synonyms* (adj) immediate, present, exigent, (n) moment, flash; *antonyms* (adj) gradual, long-term.

tímarit 1. periodical; *synonyms* (n) journal, magazine, newspaper, (adj) periodic, intermittent, **2**. review; *synonyms* (n) examination, critique, (v) check, survey, criticize, **3**. magazine; *synonyms* (n) cartridge, periodical, book, clip, entrepot, **4**. journal; *synonyms* (n) diary, ephemeris, chronicle, (adj) daybook, daily, **5**. organ; *synonyms* (n) instrument, member, limb, agency, harmonium.

tímasetja schedule; *synonyms* (n) list, agenda, catalog, program, (v) register.

tímasetning timing, *synonyms* (n) timekeeping, running.

tímaskeið age; *synonyms* (n) period, aeon, day, era, time.

tímastilling timing; *synonyms* (n) timekeeping, running.

tímastýring timer; *synonyms* (n) timepiece, timekeeper, clock, regulator, watch.

tímatafla schedule; *synonyms* (n) list, agenda, catalog, program, (v) register.

tímatal calendar; *synonyms* (n) almanac, agenda, schedule, diary, (v) list.

tímatengdur dynamic; *synonyms* (adj) active, aggressive, dynamical, energetic, forceful; *antonyms* (adj) dull, static.

tímatöf lag; *synonyms* (n) backwardness, (v) dawdle, delay, linger, dally.

timburfleki raft; *synonyms* (n) float, deal, flock, heap, lot.

tímgun 1. propagation; *synonyms* (n) distribution, diffusion, generation, dissemination, extension, **2**. reproduction; *synonyms* (n) replica, propagation, duplicate, breeding, (adj) fake; *antonym* (adj) genuine.

tími 1. time; *synonyms* (n) hour, moment, period, duration, epoch; *antonym* (n) death, **2**. hour; *synonyms* (n) time, hr, nonce, crisis, day, **3**. while; *synonyms* (conj) as, whereas, although, (n) spell, (prep) during, **4**. term; *synonyms* (n) name, expression, style, title, (v) call, **5**. duration; *synonyms* (n) length, continuation, continuance, standing, stretch.

tina tin; *synonyms* (n) can, canister, container, (v) pot, preserve.

tindaknurri piper; *synonyms* (n) bagpiper, fiddler, fifer, harper, trumpeter.

tindatala mode; *synonyms* (n) means, fashion, manner, method, form.

tindur 1. pin; *synonyms* (n) needle, nail, (v) tack, clasp, fix, **2**. peak; *synonyms* (n) crest, maximum, top, acme, apex; *antonyms* (n) nadir, base, trough.

tinhúða tin; *synonyms* (n) can, canister, container, (v) pot, preserve.

tinlóðun soldering; *synonyms* (n) bonding, brazing, (v) sticking.

tinnuviður ebony; *synonyms* (n) sable, (adj) black, ebon, dark, jet.

tippun dump; *synonyms* (v) discard, ditch, abandon, drop, empty; *antonym* (v) keep.

tirkesto 1. drawer; *synonyms* (n) draftsman, draughtsman, till, commode, engraver, **2**. drawers; *synonyms* (n) knickers, pants, shorts, tights, bloomers.

tisja tissue; *synonyms* (n) texture, web, lump, heap, (adj) mass.

tissjú tissue; *synonyms* (n) texture, web, lump, heap, (adj) mass.

titan titanium; *synonyms* (n) ti, si.

títan titanium; *synonyms* (*n*) ti, si.

títer titer; *synonym* (*n*) titre.

titill 1. title; *synonyms* (*n*) call, designation, caption, (*v*) name, style, **2**. heading; *synonyms* (*n*) bearing, drift, head, title, course.

titra 1. swing; *synonyms* (*v*) sway, fluctuate, oscillate, dangle, hang, **2**. oscillate; *synonyms* (*v*) swing, vibrate, hesitate, wag, alternate.

títri 1. titer; *synonym* (*n*) titre, **2**. titre; *synonym* (*n*) titer.

titringur 1. vibration; *synonyms* (*n*) quiver, shudder, tremor, beat, pulse, **2**. shimmy; *synonyms* (*n*) chemise, shift, (*v*) shake, dance, wobble, **3**. tremor; *synonyms* (*n*) shiver, agitation, convulsion, (*v*) quake, flutter, **4**. oscillation; *synonyms* (*n*) swing, vibration, vacillation, variation, impulse, **5**. fibrillation.

tittlingur penis; *synonyms* (*n*) member, phallus, appendage, extremity.

tittur peg; *synonyms* (*n*) bolt, pin, hook, dowel, leg.

tíu ten; *synonyms* (*n*) tenner, decade, ace, break, (*adj*) perfect.

tíundarmark decile; *synonym* (*n*) decil.

tjá express; *synonyms* (*v*) exhibit, articulate, convey, (*adj*) explicit, direct; *antonyms* (*v*) suppress, hide, (*adj*) slow, vague.

tjakkur jack; *synonyms* (*n*) knave, flag, jackass, mariner, ace.

tjald 1. screen; *synonyms* (*n*) shade, blind, (*v*) cover, shield, conceal, **2**. tent; *synonyms* (*n*) awning, camp, canopy, barracks, (*v*) bivouac.

tjaldhiminn 1. tarpaulin; *synonyms* (*n*) tarp, counterpane, cover, coverlet, quilt, **2**. canvas; *synonyms* (*n*) picture, duck, sail, (*v*) canvass, painting.

tjaldþak 1. canopy; *synonyms* (*n*) awning, cover, screen, shade, ceiling, **2**. awning; *synonyms* (*n*) sunshade, blind, canopy, marquee, sunblind.

tjáning expression; *synonyms* (*n*) diction, phrase, voice, appearance, aspect; *antonym* (*n*) repression.

tjáningarröð exon; *synonym* (*n*) exempt.

tjáningarstig penetrance; *synonym* (*n*) penetrancy.

tjara tar; *synonyms* (*n*) pitch, seaman, bitumen, mariner, seafarer.

tjáröð exon; *synonym* (*n*) exempt.

tjáskipti communication; *synonyms* (*n*) announcement, commerce, communicating, contact, conversation.

tjón 1. damage; *synonyms* (*n*) blemish, injury, (*v*) harm, hurt, abuse; *antonyms* (*n*) service, (*v*) conserve, enhance, repair, bolster, **2**. claim; *synonyms* (*n*) call, charge, allegation, (*v*) demand, ask; *antonyms* (*v*) deny, disclaim, forfeit, **3**. loss; *synonyms* (*n*) damage, defeat, detriment, deficit,

deprivation; *antonyms* (*n*) appearance, retrieval, victory, gaining, income, **4**. losses; *synonyms* (*n*) losings, dead, fatalities, toll, wounded.

tjónnæmi vulnerability; *synonyms* (*n*) exposure, weakness, danger, vulnerableness, defenselessness; *antonym* (*n*) invulnerability.

tjörn lake; *synonyms* (*n*) loch, pond, pool, puddle, carmine.

töf 1. retardation; *synonyms* (*n*) delay, impediment, retard, deceleration, lag, **2**. demurrage; *synonym* (*n*) demorage, **3**. delay; *synonyms* (*n*) pause, arrest, deferment, (*v*) defer, check; *antonyms* (*n*) punctuality, decisiveness, (*v*) rush, advance, **4**. lag; *synonyms* (*n*) backwardness, (*v*) dawdle, linger, dally, drag, **5**. latency; *synonyms* (*n*) suspension, abeyance, intermission, interruption, latence.

tófa fox; *synonyms* (*n*) dodger, (*v*) confound, confuse, fob, bewilder.

töflureiknir spreadsheet; *synonyms* (*n*) chart, diagram, graph, catalog, database.

töflusýn view; *synonyms* (*n*) look, sight, judgment, opinion, (*v*) regard.

töflutenging join; *synonyms* (*v*) connect, unite, associate, combine, link; *antonyms* (*v*) detach, secede, separate, split, undo.

tog 1. traction; *synonyms* (*n*) grip, friction, draught, bag, (*v*) tug, **2**. tension; *synonyms* (*n*) tenseness, pressure, strain, nervousness, stress; *antonyms* (*n*) calmness, looseness, **3**. drag; *synonyms* (*v*) attract, haul, draw, puff, (*n*) pull; *antonym* (*v*) push, **4**. haul; *synonyms* (*n*) freight, (*v*) drag, tow, carry, cart.

toga 1. pull; *synonyms* (*v*) drag, draw, draught, pluck, attract; *antonyms* (*v*) push, repel, **2**. haul; *synonyms* (*n*) freight, (*v*) pull, tow, carry, cart.

togari trawler; *synonyms* (*n*) dragger, puller, tugger.

toggálgi gantry; *synonyms* (*n*) gauntry, stand, derrick, hoist, winch.

togkraftur 1. tension; *synonyms* (*n*) tenseness, pressure, strain, nervousness, stress; *antonyms* (*n*) calmness, looseness, **2**. pull; *synonyms* (*v*) drag, draw, draught, pluck, attract; *antonyms* (*v*) push, repel.

tognun 1. strain; *synonyms* (*n*) stress, breed, effort, (*v*) filter, screen; *antonym* (*v*) relax, **2**. sprain; *synonyms* (*n*) strain, (*v*) wrench, rick, twist, pull, **3**. dilation; *synonyms* (*n*) dilatation, expansion, swelling, growth, spread.

togsprunga fissure; *synonyms* (*n*) crack, crevice, break, chasm, cleft; *antonym* (*n*) repair.

togstreita conflict; *synonyms* (*n*) clash, combat, fight, battle, contention; *antonyms* (*n*) agreement, accord, harmony, peace, (*v*) agree.

togun traction; *synonyms* (n) grip, friction, draught, bag, (v) tug.

togveiðar trawling; *synonym* (n) boating.

tóki token; *synonyms* (n) mark, memento, souvenir, note, keepsake.

tökutími speed; *synonyms* (n) race, (v) hasten, hurry, quicken, run; *antonym* (n) slowness.

tól 1. tool; *synonyms* (n) instrument, implement, machine, puppet, pawn, **2.** device; *synonyms* (n) contrivance, apparatus, appliance, artifice, emblem.

tólf twelve; *synonym* (n) dozen.

tólffótungur caterpillar; *synonyms* (n) cat, larva, worm, maggot, cocoon.

tölfræði 1. statistics; *synonyms* (n) data, census, score, information, list, **2.** statistic; *synonyms* (n) fact, guide, marker, number, sign.

tölfræðilegar statistics; *synonyms* (n) data, census, score, information, list.

tölfræðilegur 1. statistical; *synonyms* (adj) statistic, algebraic, arithmetical, analytic, random, **2.** statistic; *synonyms* (n) fact, guide, marker, number, sign.

tollaákvæði duty; *synonyms* (n) business, function, commitment, assignment, charge.

tollafgreiða clear; *synonyms* (adj) clean, certain, (v) bright, acquit, absolute; *antonyms* (adj) cloudy, opaque, unclear, dark, fuzzy.

tollar dues; *synonyms* (n) duty, tax, obligation, assessment, sess.

tollfríðindi remission; *synonyms* (n) forgiveness, relief, ease, condonation, (v) pardon.

tollgæsla customs; *synonyms* (n) custom, duty, impost, civilization, mores.

tollgæsluvöllur gateway; *synonyms* (n) door, entrance, gate, doorway, entry.

tollskrá tariff; *synonyms* (n) duty, charge, excise, custom, tax.

tollur 1. customs; *synonyms* (n) custom, duty, impost, civilization, mores, **2.** tariff; *synonyms* (n) charge, excise, tax, assessment, price, **3.** duty; *synonyms* (n) business, function, commitment, assignment, chore.

tölubúa quantify; *synonyms* (n) measure, gauge, evaluate, assess, determine.

tölulegur numerical; *synonyms* (adj) numeric, numeral, mathematical, arithmetical, consecutive.

töluorð numeral; *synonyms* (n) number, figure, character, digit, (adj) numeric.

tölusamræmi agreement; *synonyms* (n) accord, acquiescence, concord, accordance, coincidence; *antonyms* (n) disagreement, argument, conflict, discord, rejection.

tölustafur digit; *synonyms* (n) figure, cipher, dactyl, finger, number.

tölutákn 1. digit; *synonyms* (n) figure, cipher, dactyl, finger, number, **2.** numeral; *synonyms* (n) character, digit, amount, (adj) numeric, numerical.

tölva computer; *synonyms* (n) calculator, mainframe, machine, reckoner, laptop.

tölvari operator; *synonyms* (n) driver, hustler, manipulator, agent, doer.

tölvubúnaður hardware; *synonyms* (n) ironmongery, ironware, gun, armament, medal.

tölvugarpur hacker; *synonyms* (n) hack, drudge, cab, cyberpunk, jade.

tölvurefur hacker; *synonyms* (n) hack, drudge, cab, cyberpunk, jade.

tölvuskeyti message; *synonyms* (n) communication, meaning, information, errand, letter.

tölvustafur byte; *synonyms* (v) bit, doubleword, paragraph, segment, word.

tölvuþrjótur hacker; *synonyms* (n) hack, drudge, cab, cyberpunk, jade.

tölvutilfang resource; *synonyms* (n) expedient, imagination, (v) recourse, resort, refuge.

tölvutorg forum; *synonyms* (n) agora, assembly, court, pulpit, square.

tölvuvæða computerize; *synonyms* (v) computerise, cybernate, mechanize.

tölvuvæðing computerization; *synonyms* (n) automation, mechanization, cybernation.

tóm 1. vacuum; *synonyms* (n) emptiness, void, vacancy, vacuity, gap, **2.** cavitation.

tómarúm vacuum; *synonyms* (n) emptiness, void, vacancy, vacuity, gap.

tómati tomato; *synonyms* (n) cranberry, female, girl, prostitute, woman.

tómbóla 1. raffle; *synonyms* (n) draw, sweepstake, benefit, bet, chance, **2.** lottery; *synonyms* (n) drawing, draft, brag, cassino, connections.

tomma inch; *synonyms* (n) in, (v) edge, crawl, creep, ease.

tómstund leisure; *synonyms* (n) ease, idleness, convenience, vacation, (adj) idle; *antonym* (n) work.

tómstundaiðja recreation; *synonyms* (n) amusement, entertainment, distraction, pastime, play.

tómstundargaman recreation; *synonyms* (n) amusement, entertainment, distraction, pastime, play.

tómstundir leisure; *synonyms* (n) ease, idleness, convenience, vacation, (adj) idle; *antonym* (n) work.

tómur 1. empty; *synonyms* (adj) discharge, hollow, destitute, (v) drain, clear; *antonyms* (adj) full, crowded, meaningful, packed, brimming, **2.** void; *synonyms* (adj) empty, null, vacant, (n) blank, emptiness; *antonyms* (adj) valid, (v) validate, **3.** bare; *synonyms* (adj) naked, austere, bald, stark, (v) show; *antonyms* (adj) covered, cultivated, ornate, concealed, (v) cover, **4**. hollow; *synonyms* (adj) concave, false, (n) cavity, hole, (v) excavate; *antonyms* (adj) convex, (n) solid, hump.

tondilo scissors; *synonyms* (n) clippers, shears, (adj) cutters.

tónfall intonation; *synonyms* (n) accent, inflection, tone, expression, timbre.

töng 1. tongs; *synonyms* (n) lifter, poker, trivet, jaws, (v) clutches, **2**. pliers; *synonyms* (v) pincers, forceps, nippers, tongs, corkscrew, **3**. nippers; *synonym* (v) vice, **4**. forceps; *synonyms* (n) pincette, (v) extractor.

tónhæð pitch; *synonyms* (n) degree, dip, (v) fling, cast, chuck.

tónlist music; *synonyms* (n) harmony, melody, chorus, musical, composition.

tonn 1. tonne; *synonyms* (n) liothyronine, terabyte, thyroxin, thyroxine, triiodothyronine, **2**. ton; *synonyms* (n) fashion, style, amount, (adj) load, arroba.

tónn tone; *synonyms* (n) character, note, accent, air, (v) color.

tönn 1. tooth; *synonyms* (n) palate, grain, nap, saw, (adj) nib, **2**. teeth; *synonyms* (v) arrastra, fangs, file, grater, gristmill, **3**. cog; *synonyms* (n) sprocket, coble, cockleshell, kedge, (v) collogue.

tónstigi scale; *synonyms* (n) flake, gamut, (v) ascend, climb, (adj) balance; *antonym* (v) descend.

töp losses; *synonyms* (n) losings, dead, fatalities, toll, wounded.

topplægur apical; *synonyms* (adj) top, apicular, sharp, uppermost.

topptala 1. top; *synonyms* (n) crown, peak, acme, apex, (v) best; *antonyms* (adj) worst, (n) bottom, base, nadir, **2**. truth; *synonyms* (n) exactness, reality, actuality, sincerity, correctness; *antonyms* (n) untruth, dishonesty, fabrication, falsehood, fiction.

toppur 1. tuft; *synonyms* (n) bunch, cluster, crest, wisp, feather, **2**. spike; *synonyms* (n) pin, point, barb, ear, (v) impale, **3**. roof; *synonyms* (n) crown, ceiling, housing, (v) top, cover, **4**. point; *synonyms* (n) place, grade, peak, nib, (v) head, **5**. top; *synonyms* (adj) maximum, (n) acme, apex, (v) best, cap; *antonyms* (adj) worst, (n) bottom, base, nadir.

torfa shoal; *synonyms* (n) shallow, school, shelf, swarm, multitude.

torleiði 1. rough; *synonyms* (adj) coarse, hard, harsh, raw, crude; *antonyms* (adj) gentle, smooth, polished, precise, refined, **2**. dielectric; *synonyms* (n) insulator, nonconductor.

torleiðiefni dielectric; *synonyms* (n) insulator, nonconductor.

torleiðisfærsla displacement; *synonyms* (n) deposition, transfer, movement, shift, motion.

torræður 1. transcendental; *synonyms* (adj) transcendent, preternatural, supernatural, nonnatural, otherworldly, **2**. obscure; *synonyms* (adj) cloudy, dim, dark, gloomy, ambiguous; *antonyms* (adj) clear, noticeable, simple, obvious, (v) clarify.

tortryggnisýki paranoia; *synonyms* (n) insanity, (adj) schizophrenia.

tos stutter; *synonyms* (n) stammer, (v) falter, hesitate, stumble, bumble.

tosa stutter; *synonyms* (n) stammer, (v) falter, hesitate, stumble, bumble.

tota 1. tip; *synonyms* (n) top, hint, (v) incline, tilt, dump, **2**. papilla; *synonyms* (n) wart, boob, knocker.

traktaĵo papers; *synonyms* (n) credentials, document, documents, identification, covenant.

trana crane; *synonyms* (n) hoist, pulley, winch, (v) extend, stretch.

trans trance; *synonyms* (n) reverie, coma, fascination, daze, (adj) ecstasy.

trapisa 1. trapezium, **2**. trapezoid; *synonyms* (adj) trapeziform, trapezohedral, trapezoidal, trapezial.

tratato drawers; *synonyms* (n) knickers, pants, shorts, tights, bloomers.

traust 1. trust; *synonyms* (n) charge, confidence, credit, faith, (v) believe; *antonyms* (v) distrust, doubt, disbelieve, mistrust, **2**. confidence; *synonyms* (n) assurance, trust, belief, certainty, certitude; *antonyms* (n) insecurity, uncertainty, nervousness, anxiety, diffidence, **3**. faith; *synonyms* (n) conviction, credence, creed, cult, allegiance; *antonym* (n) unbelief.

traustur 1. dependable; *synonyms* (adj) reliable, steady, trustworthy, authoritative, credible; *antonyms* (adj) unreliable, changeable, irresponsible, undependable, **2**. responsible; *synonyms* (adj) accountable, dependable, amenable, (v) answerable, liable; *antonym* (adj) innocent, **3**. rigid; *synonyms* (adj) harsh, fixed, hard, inflexible, stiff; *antonyms* (adj) flexible, elastic, soft, **4**. stable; *synonyms* (adj) firm, permanent, constant, durable, fast; *antonyms* (adj) unstable, shaky, wobbly, dangerous, precarious, **5**. trustworthy; *synonyms* (adj) honest, trusty, safe, true, faithful; *antonyms* (adj) dubious, suspect, untrustworthy.

tré 1. tree; *synonyms* (n) gallows, gibbet, stem, house, tribe, **2**. wood; *synonyms* (n) forest, timber, woods, tree, lumber, **3**. timber; *synonyms* (n) wood, beam, plank, girder, rafter.

tréefni lignin; *synonyms* (n) lignone, lignose, sclerogen, xylogen.

trefill 1. scarf; *synonyms* (*n*) handkerchief, stole, cravat, shawl, stock, **2.** muffler; *synonyms* (*n*) silencer, damper, cape, kirtle, plaid.

trefja 1. bast; *synonym* (*n*) phloem, **2.** fibre; *synonyms* (*n*) fiber, character, case, eccentric, grapheme, **3.** fiber; *synonyms* (*n*) fibre, filament, strand, bristle, cord, **4.** fibril; *synonyms* (*n*) fibrilla, chain, filum, string.

trefjablanda composite; *synonyms* (*n*) complex, amalgam, blend, mix, (*v*) compound.

trefjaefni 1. fibrin, **2.** fiber; *synonyms* (*n*) fibre, filament, strand, character, bristle.

trefjalíkur fibrous; *synonyms* (*adj*) stringy, tough, ropy, brawny, fibry; *antonym* (*adj*) tender.

trefjaplata fibreboard; *synonym* (*n*) fiberboard.

trefjar fiber; *synonyms* (*n*) fibre, filament, strand, character, bristle.

trefjóttur fibrous; *synonyms* (*adj*) stringy, tough, ropy, brawny, fibry; *antonym* (*adj*) tender.

trefjungur filament; *synonyms* (*n*) fiber, strand, yarn, fibril, hair.

tregða 1. rigidity; *synonyms* (*n*) austerity, firmness, inflexibility, hardness, rigor; *antonyms* (*n*) flexibility, malleability, pliability, softness, **2.** inertia; *synonyms* (*n*) inactivity, idleness, lethargy, inaction, apathy; *antonym* (*n*) momentum, **3.** lag; *synonyms* (*n*) backwardness, (*v*) dawdle, delay, linger, dally.

tregðuskeið lag; *synonyms* (*n*) backwardness, (*v*) dawdle, delay, linger, dally.

tregur inert; *synonyms* (*adj*) idle, dead, dull, inactive, indolent; *antonyms* (*adj*) moving, active, animate.

trekt 1. funnel; *synonyms* (*n*) chimney, flue, (*v*) channel, move, pipe, **2.** horn; *synonyms* (*n*) hooter, cornet, klaxon, alarm, trumpet.

trenaþo tails; *synonyms* (*n*) tailcoat, tail, waste, coat.

tréni 1. cellulose; *synonyms* (*n*) fiber, bran, (*adj*) plastic, **2.** lignin; *synonyms* (*n*) lignone, lignose, sclerogen, xylogen.

tréspíri methanol; *synonyms* (*n*) alcohol, ethanol, gas, gasohol, gasoline.

tréspíritus methanol; *synonyms* (*n*) alcohol, ethanol, gas, gasohol, gasoline.

trimestro quarters; *synonyms* (*n*) dwelling, abode, domicile, lodging, residence.

trissa 1. pulley; *synonyms* (*n*) block, crane, windlass, winch, wheel, **2.** sheave; *synonyms* (*n*) sheaf, bundle, roller, bullwheel.

trítill 1. transistor, **2.** toddler; *synonyms* (*n*) baby, child, infant, tot, bambino.

trjábörkur bark; *synonyms* (*n*) snarl, yelp, (*v*) yap, skin, cry; *antonyms* (*v*) mutter, whisper.

trjábýll arboreal; *synonyms* (*adj*) arborary, arboreous, dendriform, arboraceous, arborescent.

trjákróna crown; *synonyms* (*n*) top, apex, cover, crest, (*v*) cap.

trjákynjaður arboraceous; *synonyms* (*adj*) arboreous, woody, woodsy, arboresque, arboriform.

trjáviður wood; *synonyms* (*n*) forest, timber, woods, tree, lumber.

trjóna rostrum; *synonyms* (*n*) ambo, podium, pulpit, beak, dais.

troð avenue; *synonyms* (*n*) channel, approach, passage, path, road.

tróð 1. tampon; *synonyms* (*n*) plug, closure, dabber, **2.** dunnage; *synonym* (*n*) fardage.

troða thrust; *synonyms* (*v*) jab, (*n*) push, poke, drive, stab; *antonym* (*v*) pull.

troðningur congestion; *synonyms* (*n*) blockage, engorgement, overcrowding, aggregation, crowding; *antonym* (*n*) emptiness.

troðsla packing; *synonyms* (*n*) boxing, pack, pad, wadding, backpacking.

trog trough; *synonyms* (*n*) trench, channel, chute, gutter, manger; *antonym* (*n*) peak.

troll trawl; *synonyms* (*n*) dragnet, (*v*) angle, fish, tow, haul.

tröllagrasker pumpkin; *synonyms* (*n*) head, pumpion, punkin, pompion.

tröllepli cantaloupe; *synonym* (*n*) cantaloup.

trollgarn twine; *synonyms* (*n*) coil, string, (*v*) wind, entwine, lace; *antonym* (*v*) untwist.

tröllvöxtur gigantism; *synonyms* (*n*) giantism, overgrowth.

tromla drum; *synonyms* (*n*) barrel, cask, tympan, (*v*) beat, roll.

tromma drum; *synonyms* (*n*) barrel, cask, tympan, (*v*) beat, roll.

trompet tuba; *synonym* (*n*) sousaphone.

trossa shackle; *synonyms* (*v*) fetter, chain, bind, hobble, (*n*) hamper.

trú 1. tenet; *synonyms* (*n*) principle, belief, doctrine, dogma, creed, **2.** religion; *synonyms* (*n*) piety, faith, cult, denomination, sect, **3.** belief; *synonyms* (*n*) assumption, confidence, feeling, idea, impression; *antonyms* (*n*) disbelief, unbelief, **4.** creed; *synonyms* (*n*) conviction, gospel, religion, credo, persuasion.

trúa 1. believe; *synonyms* (*v*) think, accredit, assume, conceive, (*n*) belief; *antonyms* (*v*) disbelieve, distrust, **2.** deem; *synonyms* (*v*) believe, consider, count, hold, feel, **3.** accredit; *synonyms* (*v*) credit, authorize, ascribe, assign, attribute, **4.** account; *synonyms* (*n*) bill, narrative, reckoning, regard, (*v*) report.

trúaður religious; *synonyms* (*adj*) pious, devout, divine, sacred, (*n*) monk; *antonym* (*adj*) secular.

trudema forwards; *synonyms* (adv) ahead, forward, forth, onward, onwards.

trufla arrest; *synonyms* (n) stop, check, halt, (v) capture, catch; *antonyms* (v) release, discharge.

truflanagreining troubleshooting; *synonym* (n) troubleshoot.

truflanakæfir suppressor; *synonym* (n) suppresser.

truflun 1. perturbation; *synonyms* (n) disturbance, commotion, agitation, fuss, (v) trepidation, **2.** disturbance; *synonyms* (n) disorder, turmoil, brawl, derangement, (adj) trouble, **3.** distraction; *synonyms* (n) amusement, desperation, beguilement, confusion, diversion; *antonym* (n) fascination, **4.** disorder; *synonyms* (n) ailment, complaint, clutter, (v) derange, disarray; *antonyms* (n) orderliness, calm, peace, (v) order, **5.** interference; *synonyms* (n) hindrance, handicap, block, blocking, (v) collision.

trúlofun 1. engagement; *synonyms* (n) combat, battle, appointment, commitment, conflict, **2.** betrothal; *synonyms* (n) engagement, troth, affiance, betrothment, espousal.

trúnaðarbréf credentials; *synonyms* (n) certification, certificate, credential, papers, document.

trúnaðarkvöð confidentiality; *synonyms* (n) discretion, intimacy, privacy, secrecy, mystery.

trúnaðarmaður secretary; *synonyms* (n) clerk, escritoire, minister, desk, (v) amanuensis.

trúnaðarmál confidential; *synonyms* (adj) close, classified, private, secret, clandestine; *antonym* (adj) public.

trúnaðarsamband confidentiality; *synonyms* (n) discretion, intimacy, privacy, secrecy, mystery.

trúnaðarstaðfesting accreditation; *synonyms* (n) credentials, warrant.

trúnaðarstig confidentiality; *synonyms* (n) discretion, intimacy, privacy, secrecy, mystery.

trúnaður confidentiality; *synonyms* (n) discretion, intimacy, privacy, secrecy, mystery.

trý tryptophan; *synonym* (n) tryptophane.

tryggð truth; *synonyms* (n) exactness, reality, actuality, sincerity, correctness; *antonyms* (n) untruth, dishonesty, fabrication, falsehood, fiction.

trygging 1. security; *synonyms* (n) pledge, protection, safety, hostage, insurance; *antonym* (n) danger, **2.** collateral; *synonyms* (adj) secondary, (n) warranty, guarantee, mortgage, guaranty, **3.** insurance; *synonyms* (n) assurance, indemnity, coverage, policy, security, **4.** guarantee; *synonyms* (n) bail, assure, warrant, (v) certify, promise, **5.** margin; *synonyms* (n) edge, brink, boundary, hem, (v) border; *antonym* (n) center.

tryggingafræðingur actuary; *synonyms* (n) accountant, statistician, bookkeeper, auditor.

tryggingasali insurer; *synonyms* (n) underwriter, ensurer, insurancer.

tryggingatilkynning declaration; *synonyms* (n) announcement, affirmation, assertion, allegation, avowal; *antonym* (n) denial.

tryggja 1. underwrite; *synonyms* (v) guarantee, insure, subscribe, cover, indemnify, **2.** assure; *synonyms* (v) certify, secure, affirm, ascertain, (n) warrant, **3.** insure; *synonyms* (v) assure, ensure, underwrite, control, verify.

tryggjandi 1. underwriter; *synonyms* (n) insurer, sponsor, attorney, backer, bailiff, **2.** insurer; *synonyms* (n) underwriter, ensurer, insurancer.

trylltur fierce; *synonyms* (adj) bitter, violent, acute, cruel, ferocious; *antonyms* (adj) gentle, mild.

trýptófan tryptophan; *synonym* (n) tryptophane.

túða nozzle; *synonyms* (n) nose, beak, hooter, jet, muzzle.

tugakomma point; *synonyms* (n) place, grade, peak, nib, (v) head.

tugastafur decimal; *synonyms* (adj) denary, aliquot, complementary, decuple, figurate.

tugga bolus; *synonyms* (n) ball, bole, (v) morsel, sippet, sop.

tugur decimal; *synonyms* (adj) denary, aliquot, complementary, decuple, figurate.

túlípanviður whitewood; *synonyms* (n) tulipwood, abele.

túlka 1. interpret; *synonyms* (v) clarify, construe, elucidate, illustrate, read, **2.** construe; *synonyms* (v) interpret, expound, define, explain, illuminate.

túlkun 1. interpretation; *synonyms* (n) version, construction, explanation, exposition, clarification, **2.** implementation; *synonyms* (n) execution, fulfillment, enforcement, accomplishment, effectuation.

túlkur interpreter; *synonyms* (n) dragoman, commentator, explainer, exponent, translator.

túndra tundra; *synonyms* (n) plain, waste, (adj) north.

tundurdufl mine; *synonyms* (n) dig, excavation, (v) excavate, sap, burrow.

túnfiskur tuna; *synonyms* (n) tunny, bass, basses, fellow, (adj) handsome.

tunga 1. tongue; *synonyms* (n) language, dialect, idiom, lingua, speech, **2.** projection; *synonyms* (n) bulge, hump, jut, prominence, protuberance, **3.** language; *synonyms* (n) expression, diction, lingo, tongue, conversation.

tungl 1. moon; *synonyms* (n) lunation, moonlight, moonshine, satellite, (v) daydream, **2.** satellite; *synonyms* (n) follower, moon, planet, attendant, orbiter.

tunglfiskur 1. opah; *synonyms* (*n*) moonfish, dollarfish, horsefish, horsehead, **2.** moonfish; *synonym* (*n*) opah.

tunglfjórðungur quarter; *synonyms* (*n*) area, part, district, division, (*v*) place.

tunglflói sinus; *synonyms* (*n*) cavity, fistula, pit, indentation, dent.

tunglhaf mare; *synonyms* (*n*) bitch, doe, hen, horse, jennet.

tunglið moon (tungl); *synonyms* (*n*) lunation, moonlight, moonshine, satellite, (*v*) daydream.

tunglmánuður month; *synonyms* (*n*) moon, day, hour, minute, quarter.

tunglseinkun retardation; *synonyms* (*n*) delay, impediment, retard, deceleration, lag.

tunglsprunga cleft; *synonyms* (*adj*) split, (*n*) break, cleavage, crevice, fissure.

tunglvik libration; *synonym* (*n*) vibration.

tungubein hyoid; *synonym* (*adj*) hypsiloid.

tungubroddshljóð apical; *synonyms* (*adj*) top, apicular, sharp, uppermost.

tungumál language; *synonyms* (*n*) dialect, expression, speech, diction, idiom.

tunna 1. drum; *synonyms* (*n*) barrel, cask, tympan, (*v*) beat, roll, **2.** barrel; *synonyms* (*n*) drum, vessel, barrelful, container, vase.

tunnukrani tap; *synonyms* (*n*) pat, dab, hit, (*v*) knock, rap.

túradrykkja dipsomania; *synonyms* (*n*) alcoholism, kleptomania, oenomania, potomania, (*v*) oinomania.

túrbína turbine; *synonyms* (*n*) propeller, screw.

turn 1. pylon; *synonym* (*n*) column, **2.** tower; *synonyms* (*v*) soar, ascend, rise, arise, (*adj*) pillar.

turnun conversion; *synonyms* (*n*) alteration, change, changeover, adaptation, exchange.

turnvirki keep; *synonyms* (*v*) hold, preserve, retain, defend, continue; *antonyms* (*v*) dump, lose.

tuska 1. rag; *synonyms* (*n*) newspaper, (*v*) banter, bedevil, tease, (*adj*) shred, **2.** scrap; *synonyms* (*n*) fight, morsel, brawl, remnant, (*adj*) fragment; *antonym* (*v*) keep.

tútinn turgid; *synonyms* (*adj*) bombastic, swollen, inflated, (*prep*) pompous, (*v*) bloated.

tútnaður turgid; *synonyms* (*adj*) bombastic, swollen, inflated, (*prep*) pompous, (*v*) bloated.

tútnun inflation; *synonyms* (*n*) expansion, dilatation, increase, rise, boom; *antonyms* (*n*) deflation, depression.

tuttuga twenty; *synonym* (*adj*) twice.

tvær two; *synonyms* (*n*) deuce, pair, binary, demon, devil.

tveggja two; *synonyms* (*n*) deuce, pair, binary, demon, devil.

tveir 1. two; *synonyms* (*n*) deuce, pair, binary, demon, devil, **2.** couple; *synonyms* (*n*) brace, (*v*) connect, associate, combine, attach; *antonym* (*v*) uncouple.

tvenna 1. couple; *synonyms* (*v*) pair, connect, associate, combine, attach; *antonym* (*v*) uncouple, **2.** dimer, **3.** pair; *synonyms* (*n*) match, brace, duet, duo, (*v*) couple.

tvenndargen allele; *synonym* (*n*) allelomorph.

tvennun synapsis; *synonym* (*n*) synapse.

tví twin; *synonyms* (*n*) match, counterpart, mate, (*v*) double, duplicate.

tvíær biennial; *synonyms* (*adj*) biannual, biyearly, semiannual, (*v*) triennial, (*n*) perennial.

tvíár biennial; *synonyms* (*adj*) biannual, biyearly, semiannual, (*v*) triennial, (*n*) perennial.

tvíátta ambivalent; *synonyms* (*adj*) uncertain, ambiguous, equivocal, unsure, vague.

tvíáttasending duplex; *synonyms* (*adj*) double, dual, duplicate, (*n*) moderator.

tvíaugna binocular; *synonyms* (*n*) binoculars, spyglass.

tvíbentur ambivalent; *synonyms* (*adj*) uncertain, ambiguous, equivocal, unsure, vague.

tvíburi twin; *synonyms* (*n*) match, counterpart, mate, (*v*) double, duplicate.

tvíbýlinn dioecious; *synonyms* (*adj*) dioecian, dioicous.

tvífætla biped; *synonyms* (*adj*) bipedal, (*n*) human, quadruped.

tvífætlingur biped; *synonyms* (*adj*) bipedal, (*n*) human, quadruped.

tvífald duplicate; *synonyms* (*adj*) dual, (*v*) copy, double, twin, (*n*) counterpart; *antonym* (*n*) original.

tvífalda duplicate; *synonyms* (*adj*) dual, (*v*) copy, double, twin, (*n*) counterpart; *antonym* (*n*) original.

tvíflokkun dichotomy; *synonyms* (*n*) subdichotomy, duality.

tvígildi bivalent; *synonyms* (*adj*) divalent, double, doubled, dual, duple.

tvígildur 1. divalent; *synonyms* (*adj*) bivalent, diacid, double, **2.** binary; *synonyms* (*adj*) dual, twin, numeric, (*n*) duality, two, **3.** bivalent; *synonyms* (*adj*) divalent, doubled, duple, forked, (*v*) dyad.

tvíglerungur doublet; *synonyms* (*n*) couple, jerkin, pair, waistcoat, barbe.

tvígreining dichotomy; *synonyms* (*n*) subdichotomy, duality.

tvíhliða bilateral; *synonyms* (*adj*) mutual, joint, (*v*) bicephalous, bicipital, bidental; *antonyms* (*adj*) unilateral, multilateral.

tvíhliðmælt bilateral; *synonyms* (*adj*) mutual, joint, (*v*) bicephalous, bicipital, bidental; *antonyms* (*adj*) unilateral, multilateral.

tvíhorfsþróun dialectic; *synonyms* (n) debate, (adj) polemical, dialectical, (v) argumentative, controversial.

tvíhvolfur biconcave; *synonyms* (adj) concave, amphicoelous.

tvíhyggja dualism; *synonyms* (n) duality, duplicity, bitheism, ditheism.

tvíklofinn bifid; *synonyms* (adj) bifidate, forked, (v) bipartite, biconjugate, bicuspid.

tvíklofnun 1. dichotomy; *synonyms* (n) subdichotomy, duality, 2. bifurcation; *synonyms* (n) fork, forking, furcation, divergence, split.

tvíkynhneigð bisexuality; *synonyms* (n) androgyny, hermaphroditism, homosexuality, lesbianism, hermaphrodism.

tvíkynhneigður bisexual; *synonyms* (adj) epicene, adelomorphous, monoclinous, bisexuous, ambidextrous.

tvíkynja 1. androgynous; *synonyms* (adj) asexual, genderless, neuter, neutral, sexless, 2. bisexual; *synonyms* (adj) epicene, adelomorphous, monoclinous, bisexuous, ambidextrous, 3. hermaphroditic; *synonyms* (adj) hermaphrodite, androgynal.

tvíkynjun bisexuality; *synonyms* (n) androgyny, hermaphroditism, homosexuality, lesbianism, hermaphrodism.

tvíkynjungur hermaphrodite; *synonyms* (n) androgyne, intersex, (adj) bisexual, androgynous, hermaphroditic.

tvíliða 1. binomial; *synonyms* (adj) binary, binominal, 2. dimer.

tvílitni dichroism; *synonyms* (n) colors, trichroism.

tvílitur dichromatic; *synonyms* (v) polychromatic, (adj) bicolour, bichrome, bicolor, bicolored.

tvílræði indecision; *synonyms* (n) doubt, hesitation, irresolution, indecisiveness, (adj) suspense; *antonyms* (n) decisiveness, determination, resolve.

tvímálma bimetal; *synonyms* (adj) bimetallic, bimetallistic.

tvímálmur bimetal; *synonyms* (adj) bimetallic, bimetallistic.

tvínafn binomial; *synonyms* (adj) binary, binominal.

tvinn 1. thermocouple; *synonym* (n) thermistor, 2. couple; *synonyms* (v) pair, connect, associate, combine, attach; *antonym* (v) uncouple.

tvinna merge; *synonyms* (v) amalgamate, blend, combine, melt, coalesce; *antonyms* (v) separate, split.

tvinnhlaði thermopile; *synonyms* (n) thermobattery, thermoscope.

tvinnleiðni admittance; *synonyms* (n) admission, access, accession, introduction, entrance.

tvinnviðmnám impedance; *synonyms* (n) resistance, clog, friction, hindrance, immunity.

tvinnviðnám impedance; *synonyms* (n) resistance, clog, friction, hindrance, immunity.

Tvípeð doubled; *synonyms* (adj) double, twofold, bivalent, reduplicate, duple.

tvípunktur colon; *synonyms* (n) bowel, (v) period, semicolon, comma.

tvíræðni 1. alias; *synonyms* (n) name, pseudonym, nickname, soubriquet, title, 2. ambiguity; *synonyms* (n) equivocation, doubt, uncertainty, unclearness, equivocalness; *antonyms* (n) clearness, precision, unambiguity.

tvíræður ambiguous; *synonyms* (adj) equivocal, indistinct, indeterminate, uncertain, (v) vague; *antonyms* (adj) clear, definite, unambiguous, unequivocal.

tvírit duplicate; *synonyms* (adj) dual, (v) copy, double, twin, (n) counterpart; *antonym* (n) original.

tvísæi diplopia; *synonym* (n) diplopy.

tvísær binocular; *synonyms* (n) binoculars, spyglass.

tvískauta bipolar; *synonym* (adj) amphipathic.

tvískipting dichotomy; *synonyms* (n) subdichotomy, duality.

tvískiptur 1. binary; *synonyms* (adj) dual, twin, double, numeric, (n) duality, 2. dual; *synonyms* (adj) duplex, duple, twofold, doubled, bivalent; *antonyms* (adj) individual, single.

tvístig doublet; *synonyms* (n) couple, jerkin, pair, waistcoat, barbe.

tvístirni binary; *synonyms* (adj) dual, twin, double, numeric, (n) duality.

tvístra diffuse; *synonyms* (v) circulate, disperse, disseminate, spread, broadcast.

tvístraður fragmented; *synonyms* (adj) broken, crumbled, disconnected, disjointed, disunited.

tvístringur fragmentation; *synonyms* (n) atomisation, atomization, disintegration, fracture, destruction.

tvístrun 1. scattering; *synonyms* (n) diffusion, dispersal, dissipation, dispersion, distribution, 2. dispersion; *synonyms* (n) circulation, dissemination, spread, scattering, 3. fragmentation; *synonyms* (n) atomisation, atomization, disintegration, fracture, destruction.

tvistur 1. cotton; *synonyms* (n) thread, yarn, cord, fiber, string, 2. diode.

tvístur 1. dispersion; *synonyms* (n) diffusion, dispersal, dissipation, distribution, circulation, 2. fragmentation; *synonyms* (n) atomisation, atomization, disintegration, fracture, destruction.

tvísýni diplopia; *synonym* (n) diplopy.

tvísýnn critical; *synonyms* (adj) acute, decisive, delicate, important, pressing; *antonyms* (adj) complimentary, trivial, positive, flattering, insignificant.

tvítak duplicate; *synonyms* (*adj*) dual, (*v*) copy, double, twin, (*n*) counterpart; *antonym* (*n*) original.

tvítala dual; *synonyms* (*adj*) double, duplex, duple, twin, twofold; *antonyms* (*adj*) individual, single.

tvítekning reduplication; *synonyms* (*n*) doubling, replica, anadiplosis, (*v*) duplication, repetition.

tvíþættur dual; *synonyms* (*adj*) double, duplex, duple, twin, twofold; *antonyms* (*adj*) individual, single.

tvíþátta duplex; *synonyms* (*adj*) double, dual, duplicate, (*n*) moderator.

tvíþáttungur duplex; *synonyms* (*adj*) double, dual, duplicate, (*n*) moderator.

tvítuggning rumination; *synonyms* (*n*) contemplation, reflection, consideration, musing, meditation.

tvítyngdur bilingual; *synonym* (*adj*) bilinguar.

tvítyngi bilingualism; *synonym* (*n*) diglottism.

tvíundatölustafur bit; *synonyms* (*n*) crumb, morsel, piece, (*v*) curb, scrap.

tvíveðrungur ambivalence; *synonyms* (*n*) ambivalency, uncertainty.

tvíveldi square; *synonyms* (*adj*) right, even, rectangular, (*n*) area, (*v*) settle.

tvíveldisfrávik variance; *synonyms* (*n*) difference, disagreement, discrepancy, dissension, division.

tvö two; *synonyms* (*n*) deuce, pair, binary, demon, devil.

tvöfaldur 1. duplex; *synonyms* (*adj*) double, dual, duplicate, (*n*) moderator, 2. double; *synonyms* (*adj*) duple, (*v*) fold, reduplicate, bend, (*n*) twin; *antonym* (*n*) single, 3. dual; *synonyms* (*adj*) duplex, twofold, doubled, bivalent, combined; *antonym* (*adj*) individual, 4. binary; *synonyms* (*adj*) numeric, (*n*) duality, two.

tvöföldun 1. reduplication; *synonyms* (*n*) doubling, replica, anadiplosis, (*v*) duplication, repetition, 2. duplication; *synonyms* (*n*) duplicate, copy, imitation, gemination, replication.

tyggigúmmítré sapodilla; *synonyms* (*n*) sapota, zapotilla.

tygging mastication; *synonyms* (*n*) chew, chewing, (*v*) deglutition, epulation, gulp.

tygjun mobilization; *synonyms* (*n*) mobilisation, draft, militarisation, militarization, muster.

tylgi steroid; *synonym* (*adj*) steroidal.

týmídín thymidine; *synonym* (*n*) deoxythymidine.

tyrkjakorn corn; *synonyms* (*n*) maize, clavus, cereals, callus, wheat.

týtuber cowberry; *synonyms* (*n*) foxberry, lingberry, lingenberry, lingonberry.

Þ

þá then; *synonyms* (*adv*) so, accordingly, afterward, again, (*conj*) therefore.

þægilegur 1. pleasant; *synonyms* (*adj*) bright, acceptable, agreeable, amiable, charming; *antonyms* (*adj*) unpleasant, disagreeable, disgusting, foul, gruesome, 2. agreeable; *synonyms* (*adj*) accordant, pleasant, pleasing, nice, affable; *antonyms* (*adj*) discordant, nasty, unwilling, aggressive, resistant, 3. congenial; *synonyms* (*adj*) concordant, compatible, delightful, genial, (*v*) consonant; *antonyms* (*adj*) uncongenial, unfriendly, 4. enjoyable; *synonyms* (*adj*) delectable, amusing, delicious, gratifying, lovely, 5. nice; *synonyms* (*adj*) beautiful, dainty, fastidious, fine, good; *antonym* (*adj*) horrible.

þægindi convenience; *synonyms* (*n*) advantage, contrivance, accommodation, opportunity, appliance; *antonym* (*n*) inconvenience.

þagmælska discretion; *synonyms* (*n*) caution, circumspection, delicacy, prudence, diplomacy; *antonym* (*n*) recklessness.

þagnarskylda confidentiality; *synonyms* (*n*) discretion, intimacy, privacy, secrecy, mystery.

þak 1. roof; *synonyms* (*n*) crown, ceiling, housing, (*v*) top, cover, 2. top; *synonyms* (*n*) peak, acme, apex, (*v*) best, cap; *antonyms* (*adj*) worst, (*n*) bottom, base, nadir, 3. cap; *synonyms* (*n*) bonnet, lid, capital, crest, (*v*) beat, 4. ceiling; *synonyms* (*n*) limit, maximum, limitation, roof, thatch; *antonym* (*n*) ground.

þakka 1. receive; *synonyms* (*v*) accept, admit, get, assume, adopt, 2. thank; *synonyms* (*v*) acknowledge, bless, remercy, kiss, praise, 3. take; *synonyms* (*v*) hold, bear, carry, (*n*) seize, (*phr*) receive; *antonyms* (*v*) give, refuse, abstain, add, lose, 4. accept; *synonyms* (*v*) take, recognize, abide, accede, acquiesce; *antonyms* (*v*) reject, deny, snub, oppose, renounce.

þakklátur 1. thankful; *synonyms* (*adj*) grateful, indebted, contented, pleased, gratified; *antonyms* (*adj*) ungrateful, worried, 2. grateful; *synonyms* (*adj*) thankful, agreeable, appreciative, beholden, (*n*) welcome.

þaklag overburden; *synonyms* (*v*) drive, overcharge, load, (*n*) overload, (*adj*) overwork.

þakrenna gutter; *synonyms* (*n*) channel, groove, ditch, drain, trough.

þaksperra rafter; *synonyms* (*n*) beam, balk, girder, raftsman, timber.

þan 1. tone; *synonyms* (*n*) character, note, accent, air, (*v*) color, **2.** strain; *synonyms* (*n*) stress, breed, effort, (*v*) filter, screen; *antonym* (*v*) relax, **3.** diastole; *synonyms* (*n*) distension, dropsy, intumescence, swelling, tumefaction.

þanbil diastole; *synonyms* (*n*) distension, dropsy, intumescence, swelling, tumefaction.

þang 1. seaweed; *synonyms* (*n*) seaware, heed, reit, ware, sedge, **2.** tang; *synonyms* (*n*) flavor, smell, relish, savor, odor.

þangað 1. thither; *synonyms* (*adv*) there, hither, whither, (*adj*) further, remoter, **2.** there; *synonyms* (*adv*) here, thither, present, thereat, (*adj*) adept, **3.** yonder; *synonyms* (*adv*) beyond, abroad, farther, (*adj*) yon, distant.

þanhæfni extensibility; *synonyms* (*n*) extensibleness, flexibility, (*adj*) extendibility.

þani expander; *synonym* (*n*) expandor.

þanið tense; *synonyms* (*adj*) strained, edgy, nervous, taut, (*v*) overwrought; *antonyms* (*adj*) relaxed, calm, comfortable, tranquil, loose.

þanþol elasticity; *synonyms* (*n*) bounce, spring, flexibility, pliability, suppleness.

þanþolinn ductile; *synonyms* (*adj*) elastic, flexible, malleable, pliable, supple.

þar 1. there; *synonyms* (*adv*) here, thither, present, thereat, (*adj*) adept, **2.** yonder; *synonyms* (*adv*) beyond, abroad, farther, (*adj*) yon, distant.

þari seaweed; *synonyms* (*n*) seaware, heed, reit, ware, sedge.

þarmar intestine; *synonyms* (*n*) bowel, gut, catgut, (*adj*) domestic, internal.

þarmastjórn continence; *synonyms* (*n*) abstinence, temperance, chastity, celibacy, continency.

þarmur 1. intestine; *synonyms* (*n*) bowel, gut, catgut, (*adj*) domestic, internal, **2.** gut; *synonyms* (*n*) belly, abdomen, (*v*) eviscerate, pillage, ransack.

þáttapörun hybridization; *synonyms* (*n*) hybridisation, cross, crossing, crossbreeding, carrefour.

þáttatenging 1. annealing; *synonym* (*n*) tempering, **2.** hybridization; *synonyms* (*n*) hybridisation, cross, crossing, crossbreeding, carrefour.

þátttaka 1. participation; *synonyms* (*n*) involvement, interest, contribution, attendance, complicity, **2.** involvement; *synonyms* (*n*) entanglement, concern, implication, inclusion, connection; *antonym* (*n*) disconnection.

þátttakandi protagonist; *synonyms* (*n*) hero, booster, champion, exponent, supporter.

þáttun 1. factoring; *synonyms* (*n*) factorisation, factorization, **2.** fractionation.

þáttur 1. factor; *synonyms* (*n*) agent, component, broker, divisor, (*adj*) constituent, **2.** strand;

synonyms (*n*) coast, shore, rope, (*v*) beach, maroon, **3.** wire; *synonyms* (*n*) cable, telegram, line, (*v*) telegraph, electrify, **4.** record; *synonyms* (*n*) register, list, account, (*v*) chronicle, file, **5.** vector; *synonyms* (*n*) direction, bearing, course, sender, transmitter.

þáverandi 1. former; *synonyms* (*adv*) before, (*adj*) antecedent, anterior, bygone, earlier; *antonym* (*adj*) future, **2.** existing; *synonyms* (*adj*) actual, alive, current, existent, (*v*) being; *antonym* (*adj*) lost.

þefskyn olfaction; *synonyms* (*n*) smell, aroma, feel, feeling, flavor.

þefur 1. smell; *synonyms* (*n*) odor, fragrance, (*v*) reek, nose, perfume, **2.** odour; *synonyms* (*n*) flavour, aroma, smell, scent, flavor.

þegi 1. recipient; *synonyms* (*n*) beneficiary, receiver, inheritor, legatee, (*adj*) receptive; *antonym* (*n*) sender, **2.** host; *synonyms* (*n*) crowd, army, flock, horde, mob.

þegjandi tacit; *synonyms* (*adj*) silent, implicit, understood, implied, undeclared; *antonyms* (*adj*) explicit, spoken.

þegn 1. citizen; *synonyms* (*n*) civilian, denizen, inhabitant, national, resident; *antonym* (*n*) foreigner, **2.** national; *synonyms* (*adj*) internal, domestic, home, civil, (*n*) citizen; *antonyms* (*adj*) international, foreign, local, private.

þegnskapur citizenship; *synonyms* (*n*) nationality, freedom.

þekja 1. cover; *synonyms* (*v*) coat, conceal, top, bury, (*n*) blind; *antonyms* (*v*) reveal, expose, uncover, **2.** protect; *synonyms* (*v*) defend, keep, cover, preserve, (*n*) guard; *antonyms* (*v*) attack, neglect, risk, **3.** coverage; *synonyms* (*n*) area, scope, span, extent, insurance, **4.** hood; *synonyms* (*n*) cap, bonnet, cowl, hat, coif, **5.** overlay; *synonyms* (*n*) sheathing, overlayer, (*v*) overlap, veneer, spread.

þekjubil gap; *synonyms* (*n*) break, cleft, crack, crevice, (*v*) breach.

þekjuhúð epidermis; *synonyms* (*n*) cuticle, scarfskin, skin, carapace, coat.

þekjustig coverage; *synonyms* (*n*) area, scope, span, extent, insurance.

þekjuvefskrabbamein carcinoma; *synonyms* (*n*) cancer, tumor, epithelioma, (*adj*) leukemia, malignancy.

þekjuvefur epithelium; *synonyms* (*n*) ecderon, ecteron.

þekkingargrind schema; *synonyms* (*n*) outline, plan, chart, graph, scheme.

þekkingarsvið discipline; *synonyms* (*v*) control, castigate, chastise, train, chasten.

þekkja 1. recognise; *synonyms* (*v*) admit, acknowledge, identify, know, accredit, **2.** know;

synonyms (*v*) discern, comprehend, can, distinguish, have.

þema theme; *synonyms* (*n*) matter, motif, subject, base, composition.

þenja expand; *synonyms* (*v*) amplify, enlarge, balloon, broaden, develop; *antonyms* (*v*) contract, shorten, abbreviate, decrease, deflate.

þenjari expander; *synonym* (*n*) expandor.

þensla 1. tension; *synonyms* (*n*) tenseness, pressure, strain, nervousness, stress; *antonyms* (*n*) calmness, looseness, 2. dilation; *synonyms* (*n*) dilatation, expansion, swelling, growth, spread, 3. expansion; *synonyms* (*n*) amplification, enlargement, development, (*v*) extension, augmentation; *antonyms* (*n*) contraction, decrease, reduction, abbreviation.

þér thou; *synonyms* (*n*) chiliad, g, grand, m, curtilage.

þermimök sodomy; *synonyms* (*n*) buggery, pederasty.

þerna 1. worker; *synonyms* (*n*) employee, hand, proletarian, workman, actor, 2. auxiliary; *synonyms* (*adj*) ancillary, subsidiary, (*n*) assistant, accessory, adjunct; *antonym* (*adj*) main.

þerrir desiccant; *synonyms* (*adj*) dry, drying, (*n*) drier, dryer.

þétta 1. seal; *synonyms* (*n*) mark, stamp, cachet, (*v*) plug, bar; *antonyms* (*v*) open, unseal, 2. tighten; *synonyms* (*v*) contract, strain, brace, compress, constrict; *antonyms* (*v*) loosen, relax, 3. condensate; *synonyms* (*n*) condensation, abridgement, abridgment, capsule, compression, 4. caulk; *synonyms* (*v*) calk, splice, close, stanch, staunch, 5. pack; *synonyms* (*n*) bundle, mob, bevy, bunch, (*v*) crowd; *antonym* (*n*) unpack.

þéttbær intensive; *synonyms* (*adj*) intense, concentrated, thorough, exhaustive, (*n*) intensifier; *antonym* (*adj*) extensive.

þéttbýli town; *synonyms* (*n*) city, borough, township, (*adj*) municipal, urban.

þéttbýlismyndun 1. urbanization; *synonym* (*n*) urbanisation, 2. nucleation.

þétti 1. seal; *synonyms* (*n*) mark, stamp, cachet, (*v*) plug, bar; *antonyms* (*v*) open, unseal, 2. condensate; *synonyms* (*n*) condensation, abridgement, abridgment, capsule, compression, 3. packing; *synonyms* (*n*) boxing, pack, pad, wadding, backpacking, 4. gasket.

þéttiefni 1. sealer; *synonym* (*n*) sealant, 2. shellac; *synonyms* (*n*) lac, (*v*) varnish, clobber, lick, overpower.

þéttihringur gland; *synonyms* (*n*) secreter, secretor, glandula.

þéttihvarf condensation; *synonyms* (*n*) abridgement, digest, abridgment, capsule, compression.

þéttikragi gland; *synonyms* (*n*) secreter, secretor, glandula.

þéttilinsa condenser; *synonyms* (*n*) capacitor, capacitance, capacity, plugger.

þétting 1. sealing; *synonyms* (*n*) packing, cementation, fixing, leakproofing, waterproofing, 2. compaction; *synonyms* (*n*) compressing, compression, calculus, coalescence, coalescency, 3. condensation; *synonyms* (*n*) abridgement, digest, abridgment, capsule, contraction, 4. concentration; *synonyms* (*n*) absorption, concentrate, application, attention, engrossment; *antonym* (*n*) distraction, 5. liquefaction; *synonyms* (*n*) dissolution, fusion, condensation, melting, solvolysis.

þéttir 1. seal; *synonyms* (*n*) mark, stamp, cachet, (*v*) plug, bar; *antonyms* (*v*) open, unseal, 2. condenser; *synonyms* (*n*) capacitor, capacitance, capacity, plugger, 3. capacitor; *synonym* (*n*) condenser.

þéttispegill condenser; *synonyms* (*n*) capacitor, capacitance, capacity, plugger.

þéttivatn condensate; *synonyms* (*n*) condensation, abridgement, abridgment, capsule, compression.

þéttleikamælir densitometer; *synonym* (*n*) densimeter.

þéttleiki 1. consistency; *synonyms* (*n*) consistence, agreement, body, coherence, consonance; *antonyms* (*n*) inconsistency, discrepancy, 2. density; *synonyms* (*n*) compactness, consistency, concentration, denseness, stupidity; *antonym* (*n*) looseness, 3. compactness; *synonyms* (*n*) density, closeness, firmness, solidity, (*v*) compression, 4. consistence; *synonyms* (*n*) torso, trunk, (*adj*) spissitude, constipation, 5. intensity; *synonyms* (*n*) force, forcefulness, depth, volume, (*adj*) strength; *antonyms* (*n*) dullness, indifference, weakness.

þéttni 1. concentration; *synonyms* (*n*) absorption, concentrate, application, attention, engrossment; *antonym* (*n*) distraction, 2. density; *synonyms* (*n*) compactness, consistency, concentration, denseness, stupidity; *antonym* (*n*) looseness.

þéttun condensation; *synonyms* (*n*) abridgement, digest, abridgment, capsule, compression.

þéttur 1. solid; *synonyms* (*adj*) firm, dense, compact, consistent, hard; *antonyms* (*adj*) soft, unreliable, loose, gaseous, (*n*) liquid, 2. compact; *synonyms* (*adj*) close, (*n*) agreement, arrangement, contract, (*v*) compress; *antonyms* (*adj*) sprawling, bulky, sparse, 3. impermeable; *synonyms* (*adj*) impenetrable, impervious, rainproof, tight, waterproof; *antonyms* (*adj*) permeable, absorbent.

þeyta 1. emulsify; *synonyms* (*v*) beat, blend, mash, soften, **2.** emulsion; *synonyms* (*n*) balm, cream, emulsification, liquid, (*adj*) soup.

þeytihjól impeller; *synonyms* (*n*) runner, pump.

þeytingur whirl; *synonyms* (*n*) turn, (*v*) spin, twirl, eddy, roll.

þeytivinda centrifuge; *synonyms* (*n*) separator, ultracentrifuge, extractor, (*v*) centrifugate.

þeytulausn emulsion; *synonyms* (*n*) balm, cream, emulsification, liquid, (*adj*) soup.

þíamín thiamine; *synonyms* (*n*) thiamin, aneurin.

þíða 1. thaw; *synonyms* (*n*) melting, (*v*) melt, dissolve, fuse, liquefy; *antonyms* (*v*) freeze, cool, **2.** defrost; *synonyms* (*v*) thaw, soften, **3.** melt; *synonyms* (*v*) deliquesce, run, vanish, coalesce, combine; *antonym* (*v*) solidify.

þíðingarbúnaður defroster; *synonym* (*n*) deicer.

þiðna 1. thaw; *synonyms* (*n*) melting, (*v*) melt, dissolve, fuse, liquefy; *antonyms* (*v*) freeze, cool, **2.** melt; *synonyms* (*v*) deliquesce, run, thaw, vanish, coalesce; *antonym* (*v*) solidify.

þiður capercaillie; *synonym* (*n*) capercailzie.

þiggjandi receiver; *synonyms* (*n*) recipient, beneficiary, cashier, earpiece, headset; *antonym* (*n*) donor.

þil 1. wall; *synonyms* (*n*) partition, bar, barrier, bulwark, (*v*) fence, **2.** panel; *synonyms* (*n*) board, jury, defendant, committee, (*v*) empanel.

þilfar deck; *synonyms* (*v*) adorn, beautify, clothe, embellish, floor.

þilfarspláss steerage; *synonyms* (*n*) direction, guidance, steering, regulation.

þilfarspolli bitt; *synonyms* (*n*) bollard, bitts.

þilfarsvinda capstan; *synonyms* (*n*) cathead, (*v*) crane, windlass, derrick.

þiljuljóri skylight; *synonyms* (*n*) fanlight, window, light, casement, day.

þind 1. diaphragm; *synonyms* (*n*) membrane, midriff, partition, pessary, septum, **2.** membrane; *synonyms* (*n*) diaphragm, film, skin, coat, covering.

þing 1. parliament; *synonyms* (*n*) congress, council, diet, assembly, legislature, **2.** congress; *synonyms* (*n*) convention, convocation, conference, intercourse, meeting, **3.** assembly; *synonyms* (*n*) gathering, collection, congregation, fabrication, (*v*) assemblage, **4.** conference; *synonyms* (*n*) colloquy, consultation, interview, negotiation, talk, **5.** convention; *synonyms* (*n*) contract, custom, tradition, agreement, bargain.

þingbundinn constitutional; *synonyms* (*adj*) congenital, essential, inherent, intrinsic, legal; *antonym* (*adj*) unconstitutional.

þingdeild chamber; *synonyms* (*n*) bedroom, hall, bedchamber, cavity, cell.

þinglýsa register; *synonyms* (*n*) record, list, inventory, (*v*) file, enroll.

þinglýsing registration; *synonyms* (*n*) enrollment, registering, enrolment, entering, entry.

þingmaður parliamentarian; *synonym* (*adj*) legislative.

þingnefnd committee; *synonyms* (*n*) board, council, commission, consignee, trustee.

þingsæti seat; *synonyms* (*n*) place, bench, base, (*v*) locate, put.

þingsalur chamber; *synonyms* (*n*) bedroom, hall, bedchamber, cavity, cell.

þingsenda post; *synonyms* (*n*) place, function, office, position, (*v*) mail.

þinur 1. fir; *synonym* (*adj*) green, **2.** tensor.

þjalakoli megrim; *synonyms* (*n*) hemicrania, freak, migraine, humor.

þjálfa train; *synonyms* (*v*) aim, coach, direct, educate, exercise.

þjálfun training; *synonyms* (*n*) education, instruction, breeding, practice, preparation.

þjáll 1. plastic; *synonyms* (*adj*) flexible, ductile, elastic, malleable, (*v*) limber, **2.** smooth; *synonyms* (*adj*) easy, calm, level, oily, (*v*) quiet; *antonyms* (*adj*) rough, uneven, abrasive, coarse, crumpled.

þjappa 1. ram; *synonyms* (*v*) beat, cram, crash, drive, jam, **2.** compressor; *synonym* (*v*) supercharger, **3.** compress; *synonyms* (*v*) abridge, compact, press, squeeze, condense; *antonym* (*v*) loosen, **4.** pack; *synonyms* (*n*) bundle, mob, bevy, bunch, (*v*) crowd; *antonym* (*v*) unpack.

þjappaður compact; *synonyms* (*adj*) close, (*n*) agreement, arrangement, contract, (*v*) compress; *antonyms* (*adj*) loose, sprawling, bulky, sparse.

þjappi 1. concentrator; *synonym* (*n*) multiplexer, **2.** compressor; *synonym* (*n*) supercharger.

þjarki robot; *synonyms* (*n*) automaton, machine, golem, zombie, labor.

þjó buttocks; *synonyms* (*n*) backside, bottom, arse, ass, bum.

þjóð 1. nation; *synonyms* (*n*) state, country, kingdom, commonwealth, community, **2.** country; *synonyms* (*n*) nation, home, land, area, place; *antonyms* (*n*) city, (*adj*) urban, **3.** folk; *synonyms* (*n*) family, people, clan, kin, kindred, **4.** nationality; *synonyms* (*n*) nationalism, patriotism, civism, race, folk, **5.** people; *synonyms* (*n*) multitude, populace, (*v*) inhabit, occupy, reside.

þjóðabandalag alliance; *synonyms* (*n*) connection, league, affinity, association, combination; *antonym* (*n*) nonalignment.

þjóðarafkoma economics; *synonyms* (*n*) finance, economy, commerce, money, backing.

þjóðaratkvæðagreiðsla referendum; *synonyms* (*n*) vote, ballot, election, poll, initiative.

þjóðarauður resource; *synonyms* (*n*) expedient, imagination, (*v*) recourse, resort, refuge.

þjóðarbúskapur economy; *synonyms* (*n*) frugality, parsimony, saving, thrift, conservation; *antonym* (*n*) extravagance.

þjóðarmorð genocide; *synonym* (*n*) massacre.

þjóðerni 1. nationality; *synonyms* (*n*) nation, nationalism, patriotism, people, civism, 2. citizenship; *synonyms* (*n*) nationality, freedom.

þjóðerniseinkenni ethnicity; *synonyms* (*n*) background, civilization, mores, society, traditions.

þjóðernislegur 1. ethnic; *synonyms* (*adj*) national, ethnical, heathen, pagan, cultural, 2. national; *synonyms* (*adj*) internal, domestic, home, civil, (*n*) citizen; *antonyms* (*adj*) international, foreign, local, private, (*n*) foreigner.

þjóðernisrembingur nationalism; *synonyms* (*n*) chauvinism, patriotism, loyalty, partisanship, xenophobia.

þjóðernisstefna nationalism; *synonyms* (*n*) chauvinism, patriotism, loyalty, partisanship, xenophobia.

þjóðfélag 1. society; *synonyms* (*n*) club, institution, public, association, community, 2. commonwealth; *synonyms* (*n*) commonweal, country, nation, state, province.

þjóðfélagshópur class; *synonyms* (*n*) category, group, (*v*) sort, place, rank.

þjóðfélagslegur social; *synonyms* (*adj*) gregarious, national, companionable, friendly, (*n*) sociable.

þjóðfélagsstéttir estate; *synonyms* (*n*) condition, land, demesne, order, rank.

þjóðfélagsstofnun institution; *synonyms* (*n*) creation, establishment, institute, formation, asylum.

þjóðfræði 1. ethnography; *synonym* (*n*) ethnology, 2. ethnology; *synonym* (*n*) culture.

þjóðgarður 1. park; *synonyms* (*n*) garden, common, (*v*) deposit, locate, place, 2. monument; *synonyms* (*n*) memorial, headstone, column, record, tombstone.

þjóðháttafræði ethnology; *synonym* (*n*) culture.

þjóðháttarfræði ethnology; *synonym* (*n*) culture.

þjóðhöfðingi sovereign; *synonyms* (*adj*) independent, autonomous, (*n*) monarch, ruler, king; *antonym* (*adj*) dependent.

þjóðland 1. country; *synonyms* (*n*) state, nation, home, land, area; *antonyms* (*n*) city, (*adj*) urban, 2. nation; *synonyms* (*n*) country, kingdom, commonwealth, community, people.

þjóðlegur 1. ethnic; *synonyms* (*adj*) national, ethnical, heathen, pagan, cultural, 2. national; *synonyms* (*adj*) internal, domestic, home, civil, (*n*) citizen; *antonyms* (*adj*) international, foreign, local, private, (*n*) foreigner.

þjóðlýsing ethnography; *synonym* (*n*) ethnology.

þjóðmegunarfræði economics; *synonyms* (*n*) finance, economy, commerce, money, backing.

þjóðmenning culture; *synonyms* (*n*) civilization, breeding, cultivation, acculturation, education.

þjóðnýting nationalization; *synonym* (*n*) nationalisation.

þjóðræknisstefna nationalism; *synonyms* (*n*) chauvinism, patriotism, loyalty, partisanship, xenophobia.

þjóðríki nation; *synonyms* (*n*) state, country, kingdom, commonwealth, community.

þjóðtunga language; *synonyms* (*n*) dialect, expression, speech, diction, idiom.

þjófnaður larceny; *synonyms* (*n*) theft, embezzlement, robbery, stealing, burglary.

þjófur thief; *synonyms* (*n*) robber, burglar, bandit, pirate, plunderer.

þjóhnappar buttocks; *synonyms* (*n*) backside, bottom, arse, ass, bum.

þjöl file; *synonyms* (*n*) archive, document, list, procession, (*v*) order.

þjónn 1. server; *synonyms* (*n*) host, waiter, attendant, emcee, horde, 2. servant; *synonyms* (*n*) domestic, boy, employee, retainer, follower, 3. waiter; *synonyms* (*n*) server, salver, servant, tray, bridegroom, 4. attendant; *synonyms* (*adj*) accompanying, (*n*) companion, assistant, escort, subordinate.

þjónusta 1. services; *synonyms* (*n*) facilities, amenities, commencement, liturgy, military, 2. service; *synonyms* (*n*) help, aid, assistance, avail, (*v*) overhaul.

þjónustuhæfni serviceability; *synonyms* (*n*) utility, use, convenience, kindness, service.

þjónustuleiga leasing; *synonyms* (*n*) hire, rent, rental, charter, chartering.

þjónustustjóri purser; *synonyms* (*n*) cashier, bursar.

þjónustuþegi client; *synonyms* (*n*) buyer, customer, patron, guest, purchaser.

þjöppubakslag surge; *synonyms* (*v*) billow, flood, rise, rush, stream.

þjöppun 1. condensation; *synonyms* (*n*) abridgement, digest, abridgment, capsule, compression, 2. compression; *synonyms* (*n*) compaction, condensation, pressure, compressing, concentration, 3. packing; *synonyms* (*n*) boxing, pack, pad, wadding, backpacking.

þjöppunarstig compactness; *synonyms* (*n*) density, denseness, closeness, firmness, (*v*) compression.

þjótak sciatica; *synonyms* (*v*) lumbago, cephalalgia, earache, gout, neuralgia.

þó 1. still; *synonyms* (*adv*) however, (*adj*) calm, (*v*) quiet, assuage, compose; *antonyms* (*adj*) moving, effervescent, fizzy, windy, (*n*) noisy, **2.** yet; *synonyms* (*adv*) but, notwithstanding, (*conj*) nevertheless, (*n*) already, (*v*) still, **3.** but; *synonyms* (*conj*) while, (*adv*) alone, only, though, barely, **4.** however; *synonyms* (*adv*) although, anyway, yet, how, (*conj*) albeit, **5.** nevertheless; *synonyms* (*adv*) anyhow, even, nonetheless, regardless, (*conj*) howbeit.

þófi 1. buffer; *synonyms* (*n*) safeguard, pad, protection, bumper, (*v*) cushion, **2.** disk; *synonyms* (*n*) disc, discus, dial, circle, diskette, **3.** pad; *synonyms* (*n*) apartment, (*v*) line, inflate, expand, bolster.

þögull 1. silent; *synonyms* (*adj*) motionless, dumb, mute, tacit, (*adv*) quiet; *antonyms* (*adj*) noisy, spoken, loud, talkative, explicit, **2.** mute; *synonyms* (*adj*) silent, (*v*) muffle, dampen, deaden, dull.

þoka 1. fog; *synonyms* (*n*) cloud, haze, (*v*) mist, confuse, blur, **2.** mist; *synonyms* (*n*) fog, vapor, (*v*) befog, cover, obscure.

þökk 1. thanks; *synonyms* (*n*) acknowledgment, appreciation, gratitude, blessing, grace, **2.** gratitude; *synonyms* (*n*) thanks, feeling, anger, benediction, conviction; *antonym* (*n*) ingratitude.

þóknun 1. remuneration; *synonyms* (*n*) compensation, pay, recompense, earnings, reward, **2.** retainer; *synonyms* (*n*) servant, attendant, follower, consideration, dependent, **3.** compensation; *synonyms* (*n*) amends, allowance, indemnification, price, (*v*) wage, **4.** commission; *synonyms* (*n*) board, mission, delegation, job, (*v*) assign, **5.** agio; *synonyms* (*n*) premium, agiotage, percentage, drawback, poundage.

þokumóða 1. haze; *synonyms* (*n*) fog, cloud, blur, confusion, (*v*) mist, **2.** mist; *synonyms* (*n*) haze, vapor, (*v*) befog, cover, obscure.

þokuský stratus; *synonyms* (*n*) cirrus, cumulus, woolpack.

þol 1. resistance; *synonyms* (*n*) opposition, endurance, friction, immunity, impedance; *antonyms* (*n*) smoothness, agreement, obedience, susceptibility, **2.** tenacity; *synonyms* (*n*) perseverance, determination, persistence, resolution, doggedness; *antonym* (*n*) compliance, **3.** tolerance; *synonyms* (*n*) allowance, indulgence, leniency, patience, lenience; *antonyms* (*n*) intolerance, narrow-mindedness, bigotry,

chauvinism, extremism, **4.** immunity; *synonyms* (*n*) exemption, freedom, franchise, dispensation, privilege; *antonym* (*n*) vulnerability, **5.** endurance; *synonyms* (*n*) durability, stamina, sufferance, tolerance, courage.

þola 1. sustain; *synonyms* (*v*) support, bear, carry, keep, continue, **2.** tolerate; *synonyms* (*v*) suffer, endure, let, permit, (*adj*) accept, **3.** suffer; *synonyms* (*v*) encounter, abide, brook, experience, (*adj*) allow, **4.** stand; *synonyms* (*v*) stall, undergo, (*n*) attitude, booth, rack; *antonyms* (*v*) sit, lie, **5.** permit; *synonyms* (*v*) give, license, admit, (*n*) consent, (*adj*) grant; *antonyms* (*v*) forbid, ban, prevent, prohibit, stop.

þolandi 1. operand; *synonym* (*n*) faciend, **2.** patient; *synonyms* (*adj*) invalid, forbearing, passive, calm, enduring; *antonym* (*adj*) impatient.

þolfall accusative; *synonyms* (*adj*) accusatory, accusing, accusive, objective, nonsubjective.

þolhjúpur cyst; *synonyms* (*n*) vesicle, blister, capsule, tumor, pod.

þoli operand; *synonym* (*n*) faciend.

þolinmæði patience; *synonyms* (*n*) endurance, forbearance, fortitude, longanimity, (*v*) moderation; *antonym* (*n*) impatience.

þolinmóður 1. stud; *synonyms* (*n*) boss, rivet, (*v*) knob, button, dot, **2.** pivot; *synonyms* (*n*) axle, axis, pin, hub, (*v*) revolve, **3.** patient; *synonyms* (*adj*) invalid, forbearing, passive, calm, enduring; *antonym* (*adj*) impatient.

þolinn 1. resistant; *synonyms* (*adj*) immune, impervious, durable, tough, (*v*) resistive; *antonyms* (*adj*) fragile, permeable, submissive, agreeable, **2.** fast; *synonyms* (*adj*) dissolute, firm, agile, debauched, (*adv*) soon; *antonyms* (*adj*) sluggish, (*adv*) slow, slowly, (*v*) gorge, (*n*) binge.

þöll hemlock; *synonyms* (*n*) henbane, nightshade.

þollur thole; *synonyms* (*n*) oarlock, rowlock, tholepin, bear, endure.

þolmörk tolerance; *synonyms* (*n*) endurance, allowance, indulgence, leniency, patience; *antonyms* (*n*) intolerance, narrow-mindedness, bigotry, chauvinism, extremism.

þolmyndarsetning passive; *synonyms* (*adj*) inactive, apathetic, inert, submissive, indifferent; *antonyms* (*adj*) active, assertive, spirited, working.

þolvik tolerance; *synonyms* (*n*) endurance, allowance, indulgence, leniency, patience; *antonyms* (*n*) intolerance, narrow-mindedness, bigotry, chauvinism, extremism.

þora 1. venture; *synonyms* (*n*) hazard, (*v*) risk, chance, stake, peril, **2.** dare; *synonyms* (*v*) defy, brave, (*n*) challenge, venture, adventure.

þörf 1. requirement; *synonyms* (*n*) need, necessity, demand, essential, obligation; *antonym* (*n*) option, 2. demand; *synonyms* (*n*) claim, request, (*v*) ask, command, require; *antonym* (*v*) supply, 3. need; *synonyms* (*v*) lack, (*n*) want, desire, deficiency, must; *antonym* (*n*) wealth.

þorp 1. village; *synonyms* (*n*) hamlet, city, community, neighborhood, settlement, 2. settlement; *synonyms* (*n*) decision, accommodation, colony, payment, arrangement.

þorpsbúar village; *synonyms* (*n*) hamlet, city, community, neighborhood, settlement.

þorskhryggur backbone; *synonyms* (*n*) back, guts, strength, bottom, courage.

þorskur 1. cod; *synonyms* (*n*) codfish, (*v*) befool, dupe, fool, gull, 2. codfish; *synonym* (*n*) cod.

þorsti thirst; *synonyms* (*n*) desire, hunger, lust, longing, appetite.

þörungar algae; *synonym* (*n*) alga.

þota jet; *synonyms* (*n*) squirt, fountain, flow, (*v*) gush, spurt.

þótt 1. though; *synonyms* (*conj*) nevertheless, notwithstanding, still, (*adj*) although, however, 2. although; *synonyms* (*conj*) albeit, whereas, (*adv*) though, even, 3. however; *synonyms* (*adv*) but, anyway, yet, how, nonetheless.

þrá 1. yearning; *synonyms* (*n*) longing, aspiration, craving, hankering, thirst, 2. yearn; *synonyms* (*v*) long, languish, pine, wish, ache, 3. ache; *synonyms* (*n*) hunger, pain, twinge, (*v*) hurt, itch; *antonym* (*n*) pleasure, 4. longing; *synonyms* (*n*) desire, nostalgia, (*adj*) eager, wistful, yearning, 5. hankering; *synonyms* (*n*) eagerness, yen, appetite, urge.

þráarhindri antioxidant; *synonym* (*n*) antioxygen.

þráavari antioxidant; *synonym* (*n*) antioxygen.

þráavarnarefni antioxidant; *synonym* (*n*) antioxygen.

þráðla 1. fibril; *synonyms* (*n*) fiber, fibrilla, filament, chain, strand, 2. filament; *synonyms* (*n*) yarn, fibril, hair, cobweb, line.

þráðlaga filiform; *synonyms* (*adj*) filamentous, threadlike, thready, filaceous, filamentiferous.

þráðlaus wireless; *synonyms* (*n*) radio, radiocommunication, tuner, (*v*) radiotelephone, intercom.

þráðormur 1. filaria; *synonyms* (*n*) alfilaria, alfileria, clocks, filaree, 2. nematode; *synonyms* (*n*) roundworm, eelworm, ringworm, tinea.

þráður 1. pilus; *synonyms* (*n*) hair, capillament, cilia, cilium, fuzz, 2. thread; *synonyms* (*n*) string, line, yarn, (*v*) file, range, 3. cord; *synonyms* (*n*) band, bond, tie, twine, tape, 4. cable; *synonyms* (*n*) rope, cablegram, telegram, cord, (*v*) wire, 5. fiber;

synonyms (*n*) fibre, filament, strand, character, bristle.

þræðlingur fibril; *synonyms* (*n*) fiber, fibrilla, filament, chain, strand.

þræll servomechanism; *synonyms* (*n*) servo, servosystem.

þræsinn rancid; *synonyms* (*adj*) bad, putrid, high, musty, rank; *antonym* (*adj*) fresh.

þráhyggja obsession; *synonyms* (*n*) compulsion, fixation, complex, mania, neurosis.

þrálátur chronic; *synonyms* (*adj*) confirmed, habitual, inveterate, constant, accustomed; *antonym* (*adj*) temporary.

þránaður rancid; *synonyms* (*adj*) bad, putrid, high, musty, rank; *antonym* (*adj*) fresh.

þrár rancid; *synonyms* (*adj*) bad, putrid, high, musty, rank; *antonym* (*adj*) fresh.

þráttarhyggja dialectic; *synonyms* (*n*) debate, (*adj*) polemical, dialectical, (*v*) argumentative, controversial.

þraut problem; *synonyms* (*n*) bother, conundrum, difficulty, trouble, knot.

þrautastillandi anodyne; *synonyms* (*adj*) opiate, sedative, (*n*) analgesic, paregoric, (*v*) balm.

þrávirkni persistence; *synonyms* (*n*) perseverance, continuity, endurance, constancy, stubbornness; *antonym* (*n*) compliance.

þreifanlegur palpable; *synonyms* (*adj*) manifest, obvious, tangible, evident, apparent; *antonyms* (*adj*) imaginary, intangible.

þreifari 1. probe; *synonyms* (*n*) investigation, (*v*) examine, examination, explore, inspect, 2. antenna; *synonyms* (*n*) aerial, feeler, advance, finger, forefinger.

þreifiþráður barb; *synonyms* (*n*) point, arrow, jag, gibe, prickle.

þreifun heuristic; *synonym* (*adj*) inquiring.

þreklyf energizer; *synonyms* (*n*) stimulant, animator, boost, energiser, vitaliser.

þrekþurrð burnout; *synonyms* (*n*) exhaustion, fatigue, (*v*) blowout, disintegration, meltdown.

þrenging 1. throttle; *synonyms* (*v*) choke, strangle, asphyxiate, smother, strangulate, 2. restriction; *synonyms* (*n*) limitation, limit, restraint, curb, (*v*) hindrance; *antonyms* (*n*) freedom, extension, 3. shrinkage; *synonyms* (*n*) contraction, reduction, decrease, decline, diminution, 4. choke; *synonyms* (*v*) block, throttle, stifle, clog, foul; *antonym* (*v*) unclog.

þrengir sphincter; *synonym* (*n*) constrictor.

þrengivöðvi sphincter; *synonym* (*n*) constrictor.

þrengja 1. restrict; *synonyms* (*v*) limit, restrain, circumscribe, confine, constrain, 2. shrink;

synonyms (v) dwindle, flinch, recoil, contract, shorten; **antonyms** (v) expand, increase, enlarge.

þrengjast narrow; **synonyms** (adj) close, limited, (v) confined, contract, limit; **antonyms** (adj) wide, broad, comprehensive, extensive, (v) widen.

þrenna triplet; **synonyms** (n) three, triad, tercet, threesome, trio.

þrennd triplet; **synonyms** (n) three, triad, tercet, threesome, trio.

þrep 1. step; **synonyms** (n) degree, measure, stage, walk, (v) pace, **2.** stage; **synonyms** (n) grade, phase, floor, level, period, **3.** web; **synonyms** (n) mesh, network, tissue, lattice, (v) net, **4.** order; **synonyms** (n) command, decree, dictate, array, (v) direct; **antonyms** (n) anarchy, chaos, confusion, (v) disorder, request, **5.** interval; **synonyms** (n) intermission, interruption, break, distance, interlude.

þrepaverkun cascade; **synonyms** (n) waterfall, torrent, (v) fall, gush, stream; **antonyms** (v) trickle, dribble.

þrepskiptur fractional; **synonyms** (adj) incomplete, fragmentary, aliquot, complementary, divisible.

þrepun induction; **synonyms** (n) inauguration, deduction, initiation, beginning, elicitation.

þrepúttak tapping; **synonyms** (n) tap, paracentesis, tick, beating, drumbeat.

þrepveldi hierarchy; **synonyms** (n) order, rank, class, apparatus, executive.

þreykur smog; **synonyms** (n) fog, mist, haze, vapor, fumes.

þreyta fatigue; **synonyms** (n) exhaustion, tiredness, weariness, (v) exhaust, tire; **antonyms** (n) energy, (v) refresh.

þreytast fatigue; **synonyms** (n) exhaustion, tiredness, weariness, (v) exhaust, tire; **antonyms** (n) energy, (v) refresh.

þríburi triplet; **synonyms** (n) three, triad, tercet, threesome, trio.

þriðja third; **synonyms** (n) second, three, inquiry, (adj) tertiary, (adv) thirdly.

þriðji third; **synonyms** (n) second, three, inquiry, (adj) tertiary, (adv) thirdly.

þrif cleaning; **synonyms** (n) cleansing, purge, purification, clearing, cleanup.

þrígildur trivalent; **synonym** (adj) triatomic.

þríhyrna triangle; **synonyms** (n) trigon, trilateral, reed, trident, triennium.

þríhyrningur triangle; **synonyms** (n) trigon, trilateral, reed, trident, triennium.

þríhyrnunet tin; **synonyms** (n) can, canister, container, (v) pot, preserve.

þrír three; **synonyms** (n) leash, triplet, tercet, ternary, ternion.

þrístig triplet; **synonyms** (n) three, triad, tercet, threesome, trio.

þrístrendingur prism; **synonyms** (n) pyramid, spectroscope, spectrograph, spectrometer.

þríveldi cube; **synonyms** (n) block, rhomboid, blockage, blocking, (v) dice.

þrívetni tritium; **synonyms** (v) radiation, radioactivity, plutonium, radium, radon.

þrívídd perspective; **synonyms** (n) attitude, aspect, angle, outlook, prospect.

þrívíður solid; **synonyms** (adj) firm, dense, compact, consistent, hard; **antonyms** (adj) soft, unreliable, loose, gaseous, (n) liquid.

þrjátíu thirty; **synonyms** (n) xxx, termination, dash, (adj) thretty.

þró sump; **synonyms** (n) bog, cesspit, cesspool, sink, swamp.

þróa 1. develop; **synonyms** (v) advance, amplify, educate, expand, grow; **antonyms** (v) decrease, erupt, neglect, regress, **2.** evolve; **synonyms** (v) develop, derive, change, educe, build.

þróast progress; **synonyms** (n) headway, improvement, furtherance, (v) advance, proceed; **antonyms** (n) decline, deterioration, (v) regress.

þröm threshold; **synonyms** (n) brink, limen, beginning, doorsill, doorstep.

þrombóplastín thromboplastin; **synonym** (n) thrombokinase.

þröng congestion; **synonyms** (n) blockage, engorgement, overcrowding, aggregation, crowding; **antonym** (n) emptiness.

þröngsýni insularity; **synonyms** (n) insularism, insulation, detachment, prejudice, bigotry.

þröngur 1. narrow; **synonyms** (adj) close, limited, (v) confined, contract, limit; **antonyms** (adj) wide, broad, comprehensive, extensive, (v) widen, **2.** close; **synonyms** (adj) near, adjacent, nearby, accurate, (n) end; **antonyms** (adj) distant, airy, fresh, (v) open, start, **3.** cramped; **synonyms** (adj) cramp, constrained, contracted, crowded, narrow; **antonyms** (adj) roomy, spacious.

þroska develop; **synonyms** (v) advance, amplify, educate, expand, grow; **antonyms** (v) decrease, erupt, neglect, regress.

þroski 1. development; **synonyms** (n) evolution, course, growth, improvement, increase; **antonyms** (n) deterioration, decline, neglect, decrease, **2.** maturity; **synonyms** (n) ripeness, adulthood, matureness, perfection, majority; **antonyms** (n) childhood, youth, immaturity.

þröskuldsgildi threshold; **synonyms** (n) brink, limen, beginning, doorsill, doorstep.

þröskuldur 1. threshold; *synonyms* (*n*) brink, limen, beginning, doorsill, doorstep, 2. sill; *synonyms* (*n*) ledge, threshold, rung, step, round, 3. discriminator; *synonym* (*n*) differentiator, 4. barrier; *synonyms* (*n*) barricade, bar, bulwark, dam, handicap.

þroskun 1. development; *synonyms* (*n*) evolution, course, growth, improvement, increase; *antonyms* (*n*) deterioration, decline, neglect, decrease, 2. maturation; *synonyms* (*n*) development, ripening, ageing, maturement, growing, 3. ontogenesis; *synonyms* (*n*) ontogeny, maturation, developing, emergence, exploitation.

þroskunarsaga ontogenesis; *synonyms* (*n*) ontogeny, development, growing, growth, maturation.

þroskunarstöðvun abort; *synonyms* (*v*) expel, fail, terminate, cancel, (*n*) miscarry.

þrot deprivation; *synonyms* (*n*) bereavement, privation, cost, loss, need.

þroti inflammation; *synonyms* (*n*) inflaming, swelling, burning, firing, (*v*) ignition.

þróttur 1. vigour; *synonyms* (*n*) force, energy, vigor, vim, push, 2. activity; *synonyms* (*n*) action, activeness, exercise, liveliness, play; *antonyms* (*n*) inactivity, inaction, inactiveness.

Þroun development; *synonyms* (*n*) evolution, course, growth, improvement, increase; *antonyms* (*n*) deterioration, decline, neglect, decrease.

þróun 1. development; *synonyms* (*n*) evolution, course, growth, improvement, increase; *antonyms* (*n*) deterioration, decline, neglect, decrease, 2. evolution; *synonyms* (*n*) development, expansion, movement, process, progress.

þróunaraðstoð aid; *synonyms* (*n*) assist, help, assistance, (*v*) support, benefit; *antonyms* (*n*) hindrance, (*v*) hinder.

þróunarferill 1. process; *synonyms* (*n*) operation, proceeding, method, procedure, (*v*) action, 2. phylogeny; *synonyms* (*n*) phylogenesis, evolution, development, metaplasm, ontogeny.

þróunarferli cycle; *synonyms* (*n*) bicycle, circle, round, (*v*) bike, motorcycle.

þrúgun suppression; *synonyms* (*n*) inhibition, repression, crushing, quelling, restraint; *antonyms* (*n*) freedom, emancipation.

þrúgusykur 1. dextrose; *synonyms* (*n*) dextroglucose, sweetener, 2. glucose; *synonyms* (*n*) caramel, damson.

þruma thunder; *synonyms* (*n*) boom, bang, roll, (*v*) roar, (*adj*) peal.

þrumuský cumulonimbus; *synonym* (*n*) thundercloud.

þrumuveður thunderstorm; *synonyms* (*n*) storm, tempest, blizzard, cloudburst, (*adj*) earthquake.

þruska 1. thrush; *synonyms* (*n*) nightingale, philomel, prunella, prunello, sprew, 2. candidiasis; *synonyms* (*n*) candidosis, moniliasis.

þrútinn turgid; *synonyms* (*adj*) bombastic, swollen, inflated, (*prep*) pompous, (*v*) bloated.

þrútnun intumescence; *synonyms* (*n*) bulge, swelling, tumefaction, dropsy, tumor.

þrykk blot; *synonyms* (*n*) blemish, spot, smudge, (*v*) stain, mark.

þrykking stamping; *synonyms* (*n*) marking, impression, blocking, coin, coining.

þrykkja 1. stamp; *synonyms* (*n*) mark, seal, brand, (*v*) imprint, print, 2. blot; *synonyms* (*n*) blemish, spot, smudge, blotch, (*v*) stain.

þrykktur forged; *synonyms* (*adj*) counterfeit, false, bogus, fake, phony; *antonym* (*adj*) genuine.

þrýsta 1. push; *synonyms* (*n*) press, thrust, (*v*) drive, impel, crowd; *antonyms* (*v*) pull, drag, haul, 2. press; *synonyms* (*v*) crush, force, squeeze, pack, coerce.

þrýstifágun burnishing; *synonyms* (*n*) bronzing, searing, buffing.

þrýstifall depression; *synonyms* (*n*) basin, cavity, dejection, decline, dent; *antonyms* (*n*) cheerfulness, happiness, boom, elation, encouragement.

þrýstigeymir accumulator; *synonyms* (*n*) collector, gatherer, store, saver, aggregator.

þrýstiketill autoclave; *synonyms* (*n*) steriliser, sterilizer, (*v*) sterilize.

þrýstikraftur thrust; *synonyms* (*v*) jab, (*n*) push, poke, drive, stab; *antonym* (*v*) pull.

þrýstikragi shoulder; *synonyms* (*n*) elbow, (*v*) bear, carry, push, hold.

þrýstilína isobar; *synonyms* (*n*) climate, weather.

þrýstiloft propellant; *synonyms* (*n*) propellent, fuel, explosive, (*adj*) propelling, propulsive.

þrýstimælir 1. piezometer; *synonym* (*n*) standpipe, 2. manometer.

þrýstingslína isobar; *synonyms* (*n*) climate, weather.

þrýstingur 1. pressure; *synonyms* (*n*) force, compulsion, (*v*) drive, press, coerce; *antonym* (*n*) persuasion, 2. compression; *synonyms* (*n*) compaction, condensation, pressure, compressing, concentration.

þrýstiriti barograph; *synonym* (*n*) barogram.

þrýstisjóða autoclave; *synonyms* (*n*) steriliser, sterilizer, (*v*) sterilize.

þrýstistoð strut; *synonyms* (*n*) buttress, brace, (*v*) prance, stalk, swagger.

þrýstivatnspípa penstock; *synonyms* (*n*) floodgate, sluice, penchute, pentrough, sluicegate.

þú thou; *synonyms* (*n*) chiliad, g, grand, m, curtilage.

þúfa 1. tuft; *synonyms* (n) bunch, cluster, crest, wisp, feather, 2. hummock; *synonyms* (n) hill, hillock, knoll, mound, hammock.

þula code; *synonyms* (n) cipher, charter, law, act, (v) cypher.

þumbaldaháttur negativism; *synonyms* (n) negativity, electronegativity, negativeness, opposition.

þumlungur inch; *synonyms* (n) in, (v) edge, crawl, creep, ease.

þungaður pregnant; *synonyms* (adj) pithy, significant, fraught, enceinte, expectant.

þungbúinn cloudy; *synonyms* (adj) dull, gloomy, murky, nebulous, opaque; *antonyms* (adj) clear, bright, cloudless, sunny.

þungefni metal; *synonyms* (n) ore, admixture, aggregate, alloy, clemency.

þunglyndi melancholy; *synonyms* (adj) dreary, depressed, dejected, (n) gloom, depression; *antonyms* (adj) cheerful, happy, (n) happiness.

þunglyndur 1. depressed; *synonyms* (adj) concave, low, blue, dejected, dispirited; *antonyms* (adj) cheerful, happy, convex, 2. melancholic; *synonyms* (adj) sad, gloomy, melancholy, (n) melancholiac, (v) lachrymose.

þungsteinn tungsten; *synonyms* (n) wolfram, w, watt, west.

þungt heavy; *synonyms* (adj) dull, deep, dark, dense, fat; *antonyms* (adj) light, easy, slim, thin, slight.

þungun 1. pregnancy; *synonyms* (n) gravidity, gestation, fertility, (adj) procreation, propagation, 2. gestation; *synonyms* (n) pregnancy, ferry, behavior, (v) incubation, sitting.

þungur 1. heavy; *synonyms* (adj) dull, deep, dark, dense, fat; *antonyms* (adj) light, easy, slim, thin, slight, 2. tough; *synonyms* (adj) hard, difficult, tenacious, strong, arduous; *antonyms* (adj) tender, weak, flimsy, soft, feeble, 3. difficult; *synonyms* (adj) awkward, demanding, burdensome, complicated, delicate; *antonyms* (adj) simple, straightforward, good-natured, rewarding, clear, 4. burdensome; *synonyms* (adj) heavy, weighty, cumbrous, cumbersome, (v) onerous, 5. onerous; *synonyms* (adj) laborious, tough, formidable, oppressive, taxing.

þunnildi wing; *synonyms* (n) annex, arm, fender, limb, (v) fly.

þunnlífi diarrhea; *synonyms* (n) diarrhoea, lax, looseness.

þunnur 1. thin; *synonyms* (adj) flimsy, gaunt, lean, light, (v) slender; *antonyms* (adj) thick, fat, concentrated, chubby, plump, 2. slender; *synonyms* (adj) narrow, little, thin, fine, lithe; *antonyms* (adj) stocky, wide, 3. gaunt; *synonyms*

(adj) emaciated, bleak, cadaverous, desolate, bony, 4. lean; *synonyms* (v) incline, bend, list, slant, (n) tilt, 5. light; *synonyms* (adj) fair, clear, (v) fire, kindle, inflame; *antonyms* (n) dark, darkness, gloom, shade, (alt sp) heavy.

þurka wipe; *synonyms* (v) rub, clean, mop, towel, (adj) sponge.

þurr 1. dry; *synonyms* (adj) thirsty, arid, barren, boring, (v) dehydrate; *antonyms* (adj) wet, damp, moist, saturated, soaked, 2. arid; *synonyms* (adj) dry, dull, parched, sterile, (v) monotonous; *antonym* (adj) verdant.

þurramistur haze; *synonyms* (n) fog, cloud, blur, confusion, (v) mist.

þurraustur exhaustion; *synonyms* (n) fatigue, consumption, enervation, lassitude, tiredness; *antonym* (n) energy.

þurrð 1. deficit; *synonyms* (n) deficiency, failure, shortage, dearth, (adj) defect; *antonym* (n) excess, 2. dearth; *synonyms* (n) absence, famine, want, lack, paucity; *antonym* (n) abundance.

þurrgufun sublimation; *synonyms* (n) condensation, inhibition, paragon.

þurrka 1. wiper, 2. dry; *synonyms* (adj) thirsty, arid, barren, boring, (v) dehydrate; *antonyms* (adj) wet, damp, moist, saturated, soaked.

þurrkandi desiccant; *synonyms* (adj) dry, drying, (n) drier, dryer.

þurrkar drought; *synonyms* (n) famine, parchedness, absence, dryness, (adj) aridity; *antonym* (n) wetness.

þurrkaskur desiccator; *synonym* (n) exsiccator.

þurrkefni desiccant; *synonyms* (adj) dry, drying, (n) drier, dryer.

þurrkskál desiccator; *synonym* (n) exsiccator.

Þurrkun 1. dehydration; *synonyms* (n) evaporation, desiccation, drought, dryness, dewatering; *antonym* (n) wetness, 2. drying; *synonyms* (adj) burning, (n) dehydration, curing, aeration, airing, 3. drainage; *synonyms* (n) drain, drive, emanation, (adj) arefaction, dephlegmation, 4. desiccation; *synonyms* (n) aridity, aridness, waterlessness, parchedness, (adj) exsiccation.

þurrkur drought; *synonyms* (n) famine, parchedness, absence, dryness, (adj) aridity; *antonym* (n) wetness.

þurrlitarefni pigment; *synonyms* (n) color, paint, coloring, colorant, (v) dye.

þurrviðrasamur arid; *synonyms* (adj) dry, dull, barren, boring, (v) monotonous; *antonyms* (adj) wet, verdant.

þursabit lumbago; *synonyms* (n) backache, (v) sciatica, cephalalgia, earache, gout.

þursaviður peppermint; *synonyms* (n) bilsted, marri.

þvag urine; *synonyms* (n) piss, pee, water, piddle, emiction.

þvagaukandi diuretic; *synonyms* (adj) uretic, diuretical, emictory, urinative, urinary.

þvagefni 1. urea; *synonym* (n) carbamide, 2. carbamide; *synonym* (n) urea.

þvageitrun uremia; *synonyms* (n) uraemia, azotaemia, azotemia.

þvagfærafræði urology; *synonyms* (n) ourology, uronology.

þvagleggur catheter; *synonyms* (n) infusion, transfusion.

þvagleysi anuria; *synonym* (n) anuresis.

þvagræsilyf diuretic; *synonyms* (adj) uretic, diuretical, emictory, urinative, urinary.

þvagsandur gravel; *synonyms* (v) bedevil, get, nonplus, rag, (adj) bother.

þvagsýrugigtarhnútur tophus; *synonyms* (n) calculus, chalkstone, dragon, tartar, tofus.

þvagsýrugigtarsteinn tophus; *synonyms* (n) calculus, chalkstone, dragon, tartar, tofus.

þvagþurrð 1. anuria; *synonym* (n) anuresis, 2. oliguria.

þvalur moist; *synonyms* (adj) humid, damp, wet, clammy, dank; *antonym* (adj) dry.

þveiti excretion; *synonyms* (n) discharge, elimination, evacuation, excrement, excreta.

þver orthogonal; *synonyms* (adj) rectangular, square, external, extraneous, foreign.

þverá branch; *synonyms* (n) arm, jump, wing, affiliate, (v) fork.

þverbiti 1. transom; *synonyms* (n) crosspiece, lintel, beam, skylight, traverse, 2. beam; *synonyms* (n) blaze, glow, ray, (v) glare, (adj) shine, 3. architrave; *synonyms* (n) capital, cornice, entablature, frieze, pediment.

þverganga 1. transit; *synonyms* (n) journey, passage, conveyance, travel, movement, 2. culmination; *synonyms* (n) acme, apex, apogee, climax, crest; *antonym* (n) beginning.

þverill normal; *synonyms* (adj) regular, common, conventional, customary, general; *antonyms* (adj) abnormal, unusual, creepy, eccentric, extraordinary.

þverlægur transversal; *synonyms* (adj) cross, transverse, crossing, crosswise, thwartwise.

þverlami paraplegic; *synonyms* (adj) disabled, paralytic.

þverlína normal; *synonyms* (adj) regular, common, conventional, customary, general; *antonyms* (adj) abnormal, unusual, creepy, eccentric, extraordinary.

þvermál diameter; *synonyms* (n) caliber, width, diam, radius, breadth.

þveröngull gorge; *synonyms* (v) devour, glut, cram, fill, gobble; *antonyms* (n) hill, (v) nibble, fast.

þverra lapse; *synonyms* (n) fall, (v) relapse, decline, expire, drop.

þverrif rib; *synonyms* (n) ridge, (v) joke, tease, guy, mock.

þversetill header; *synonyms* (n) caption, heading, lintel, title, (v) dive.

þverskera transect; *synonym* (v) cut.

þverskurðarmynd profile; *synonyms* (n) contour, outline, form, figure, shape.

þversnið 1. transverse; *synonyms* (adj) transversal, cross, crosswise, oblique, crossing, 2. transect; *synonym* (v) cut.

þversögn paradox; *synonyms* (n) incongruity, ambiguity, inconsistency, puzzle, catch-22.

þverstaða quadrature; *synonyms* (n) quadruplet, quadrifoil, quadriform, (adj) quadrate, square.

þverstæða paradox; *synonyms* (n) incongruity, ambiguity, inconsistency, puzzle, catch-22.

þverstæður 1. transverse; *synonyms* (adj) transversal, cross, crosswise, oblique, crossing, 2. perpendicular; *synonyms* (adj) erect, upright, vertical, plumb, steep; *antonym* (adj) horizontal, 3. orthogonal; *synonyms* (adj) rectangular, square, external, extraneous, foreign.

þverstag transom; *synonyms* (n) crosspiece, lintel, beam, skylight, traverse.

þverstrengur commissure; *synonyms* (v) articulation, joint, juncture, gore, gusset.

þverstýfður truncate; *synonyms* (v) curtail, cut, abridge, shorten, clip; *antonym* (v) lengthen.

þversum 1. transverse; *synonyms* (adj) transversal, cross, crosswise, oblique, crossing, 2. cross; *synonyms* (v) intersect, baffle, (adj) crabbed, crabby, angry; *antonyms* (v) uncross, (adj) calm, good-tempered.

þvertré cleat; *synonyms* (n) wedge, batten, cam, finger.

því 1. therefore; *synonyms* (adv) consequently, accordingly, hence, so, thence, 2. so; *synonyms* (adv) as, thus, indeed, (pron) that, (adj) likewise, 3. thus; *synonyms* (adv) therefore, then, ergo, thusly, 4. hence; *synonyms* (adv) away, because, for, whence.

þvinga 1. press; *synonyms* (v) crush, crowd, force, squeeze, pack, 2. require; *synonyms* (v) need, charge, crave, ask, claim, 3. compel; *synonyms* (v) coerce, cause, command, constrain, enforce, 4. clamp; *synonyms* (n) clinch, brace, (v) cramp, clench, (adj) clasp, 5. constrain; *synonyms* (v)

compel, confine, drive, make, bind; *antonym* (v)
liberate.

þvingunarvistun detention; *synonyms* (n) delay,
arrest, custody, confinement, apprehension;
antonyms (n) freedom, release.

þviti briquette; *synonyms* (n) briquet, ovoid.

þvo 1. wash; *synonyms* (v) rinse, paint, bathe, (n)
soak, ablution; *antonym* (v) dirty, **2**. rinse;
synonyms (n) wash, clean, (v) cleanse, flush, gargle,
3. launder; *synonyms* (v) scour, fence, (adj) lave.

þvogl jargon; *synonyms* (n) dialect, gibberish, idiom,
slang, vernacular.

þvottabjörn raccoon; *synonym* (n) racoon.

þvottaefni detergent; *synonyms* (adj) detersive,
cleansing, (n) abluent, cleanser, (v) lotion.

þvottatæki washer; *synonyms* (n) potcher, bandage,
breaker, cloth, clout.

þybba fender; *synonyms* (n) wing, cushion, guard,
cowcatcher, (v) buffer.

þýða 1. translate; *synonyms* (v) interpret, construe,
decipher, transform, explain, **2**. signify; *synonyms*
(v) imply, intend, mark, (n) mean, import, **3**.
represent; *synonyms* (v) depict, portray, act, be,
(adj) express, **4**. construe; *synonyms* (v) read,
expound, define, illuminate, infer, **5**. denote;
synonyms (v) indicate, point, name, (n) declare,
betoken.

þýðandi 1. translator; *synonyms* (n) interpreter,
transcriber, adapter, arranger, representative, **2**.
compiler; *synonyms* (n) bookmaker, compilator,
encyclopedist, encyclopaedist.

þýði population; *synonyms* (n) inhabitants, people,
nation, community, group.

þýðing 1. version; *synonyms* (n) reading, translation,
construction, interpretation, rendering, **2**.
translation; *synonyms* (n) displacement,
transformation, version, rendition, paraphrase, **3**.
compilation; *synonyms* (n) collection, anthology,
compiling, digest, miscellany, **4**. gloss; *synonyms*
(n) burnish, annotation, (v) glaze, comment,
annotate; *antonym* (n) dullness.

þýðingarjafngildi equivalence; *synonyms* (n)
equality, correspondence, parity, balance, (v)
equivalent; *antonyms* (n) difference, dissimilarity.

þýðistölur parameter; *synonyms* (n) argument,
guideline, limit, directive, modulus.

þykja 1. think; *synonyms* (v) consider, believe,
reckon, estimate, guess; *antonym* (v) forget, **2**.
seem; *synonyms* (v) look, appear, feel, expect,
beseem, **3**. appear; *synonyms* (v) occur, rise, seem,
sound, emerge; *antonyms* (v) disappear, vanish, **4**.
look; *synonyms* (n) face, gaze, appearance, aspect,
air.

þykjast 1. pretend; *synonyms* (v) assume, feign,
dissimulate, counterfeit, (adj) sham; *antonyms* (v)
real, (adj) genuine, natural, **2**. simulate; *synonyms*
(v) mimic, dissemble, mock, affect, pretend, **3**.
feign; *synonyms* (v) fake, simulate, deceive, act,
fabricate.

þykkfljótandi thick; *synonyms* (adj) dense, compact,
stupid, crowded, dull; *antonyms* (adj) thin,
intelligent, bright, sparse, clever.

þykkt 1. viscosity; *synonyms* (n) consistency,
ropiness, viscousness, cohesiveness, (adj) viscidity,
2. thickness; *synonyms* (n) density, width, layer,
heaviness, body, **3**. pregnancy; *synonyms* (n)
gravidity, gestation, fertility, (adj) procreation,
propagation, **4**. consistence; *synonyms* (n) torso,
trunk, (adj) spissitude, constipation, **5**. heavy;
synonyms (adj) dull, deep, dark, dense, fat;
antonyms (adj) light, easy, slim, thin, slight.

þykkur 1. thick; *synonyms* (adj) dense, compact,
stupid, crowded, dull; *antonyms* (adj) thin,
intelligent, bright, sparse, clever, **2**. heavy;
synonyms (adj) deep, dark, fat, full, grave;
antonyms (adj) light, easy, slim, slight, gentle.

þýlundaður 1. subservient; *synonyms* (adj)
submissive, subordinate, obsequious, accessory,
obedient; *antonym* (adj) domineering, **2**.
submissive; *synonyms* (adj) humble, meek,
passive, dutiful, compliant; *antonyms* (adj)
assertive, resistant, disobedient, (adv) bossily, **3**.
slavish; *synonyms* (adj) servile, fawning, menial,
cringing, abject, **4**. servile; *synonyms* (adj) base,
ignoble, slavish, (n) mean, low.

þyngd 1. weight; *synonyms* (n) load, burden, charge,
consequence, heaviness; *antonym* (n) triviality, **2**.
gravity; *synonyms* (n) earnestness, solemnity,
graveness, gravitation, seriousness; *antonyms* (n)
flippancy, insignificance, lightheartedness.

þyngdarafl 1. gravitation; *synonyms* (n) attraction,
gravity, graveness, habit, soberness, **2**. gravity;
synonyms (n) earnestness, solemnity, gravitation,
seriousness, significance; *antonyms* (n) flippancy,
insignificance, lightheartedness.

þyngdaráhrif gravitation; *synonyms* (n) attraction,
gravity, graveness, habit, soberness.

þyngdarhlutfall abundance; *synonyms* (n) wealth,
amplitude, exuberance, plenitude, (adj) plenty;
antonyms (n) dearth, scarcity, aridity, insufficiency,
lack.

þyngdarhröðun g; *synonyms* (n) chiliad, gigabyte, m,
curtilage, gee.

þyngdarverkun gravitation; *synonyms* (n)
attraction, gravity, graveness, habit, soberness.

þynna 1. dilute; *synonyms* (v) cut, adulterate, thin,
(adj) diluted, watery, **2**. sheet; *synonyms* (n) board,

layer, leaf, canvas, film, **3**. weaken; *synonyms* (*v*) dilute, enfeeble, lessen, attenuate, (*adj*) reduce; *antonyms* (*v*) strengthen, bolster, grow, **4**. film; *synonyms* (*n*) membrane, coating, cloud, cinema, (*v*) mist, **5**. lamella; *synonyms* (*n*) lamina, gill, branchia, lamel.

þynning 1. thinning; *synonyms* (*n*) cutting, attrition, carving, clipping, contraction, **2**. rarefaction; *synonyms* (*n*) aggrandizement, development, dilation, growth, increment, **3**. dilution; *synonyms* (*n*) lotion, maceration, blending, concentration, dip.

þynningarefni diluent; *synonyms* (*adj*) balneal, humectant, (*n*) attenuant, thinner, dilutant.

þynningur dilution; *synonyms* (*n*) lotion, maceration, blending, concentration, dip.

þynnir thinner; *synonyms* (*n*) diluent, dilutant, reducer.

þynntur dilute; *synonyms* (*v*) cut, adulterate, thin, (*adj*) diluted, watery.

þyrill 1. rotor; *synonyms* (*n*) rotator, stator, **2**. corona; *synonyms* (*n*) crown, radiance, halo, aureole, necklace.

þyrla helicopter; *synonyms* (*n*) chopper, whirlybird, eggbeater, airliner, airplane.

þyrlast whirl; *synonyms* (*n*) turn, (*v*) spin, twirl, eddy, roll.

þyrnir spine; *synonyms* (*n*) backbone, thorn, point, prickle, quill.

þýroxín thyroxine; *synonyms* (*n*) thyroxin, liothyronine, terabyte, tonne, triiodothyronine.

þyrpa 1. aggregate; *synonyms* (*n*) total, agglomerate, whole, (*v*) accumulate, cluster; *antonyms* (*n*) individual, part, **2**. cluster; *synonyms* (*n*) bunch, clump, batch, group, (*v*) bundle; *antonym* (*v*) disperse.

þyrping 1. aggregate; *synonyms* (*n*) total, agglomerate, whole, (*v*) accumulate, cluster; *antonyms* (*n*) individual, part, **2**. aggregation; *synonyms* (*n*) accumulation, congregation, heap, lot, (*v*) assemblage, **3**. cluster; *synonyms* (*n*) bunch, clump, batch, group, (*v*) bundle; *antonym* (*v*) disperse, **4**. colony; *synonyms* (*n*) settlement, community, plantation, dependency, village.

þys noise; *synonyms* (*n*) clatter, clamor, hubbub, racket, sound; *antonyms* (*n*) silence, quiet.

þysja zoom; *synonyms* (*v*) soar, zip, race, surge, whiz.

U

ufsi saithe; *synonym* (*n*) sillock.

uggi fin; *synonyms* (*n*) spline, feather, fins, flipper, flippers.

uggur trepidation; *synonyms* (*n*) agitation, alarm, apprehension, fear, tremor.

ugla owl; *synonyms* (*n*) hooter, booby, dolt, looby, nizy.

ull wool; *synonyms* (*n*) fleece, fur, coat, hair, woolen.

ullarrábreiða blanket; *synonyms* (*n*) bedding, (*v*) cloak, cover, (*adj*) sweeping, overall.

ullinseyra auricle; *synonyms* (*n*) ear, pinna, heart, capitulum, (*v*) lug.

ulo persons; *synonyms* (*n*) people, public, society, world, folks.

um 1. via; *synonyms* (*prep*) by, with, toward, (*adv*) through, using, **2**. about; *synonyms* (*adv*) around, approximately, almost, nearly, most; *antonyms* (*prep*) exactly, precisely, **3**. by; *synonyms* (*prep*) beside, at, of, about, (*adv*, *prep*) alongside, **4**. over; *synonyms* (*adv*) beyond, across, (*prep*) above, during, (*adj*) finished, **5**. for; *synonyms* (*prep*) because, behind, per, (*adv*) against, as.

umbjóðandi 1. consignor; *synonyms* (*n*) consigner, shipper, **2**. client; *synonyms* (*n*) buyer, customer, patron, guest, purchaser.

umboð 1. proxy; *synonyms* (*n*) attorney, agent, deputy, alternate, (*v*) substitute, **2**. seat; *synonyms* (*n*) place, bench, base, (*v*) locate, put, **3**. commission; *synonyms* (*n*) board, mission, delegation, job, (*v*) assign, **4**. authority; *synonyms* (*n*) ascendancy, command, sanction, administration, authorization, **5**. agency; *synonyms* (*n*) bureau, office, authority, (*v*) action, act.

umboðsaðili agent; *synonyms* (*n*) agency, broker, deputy, medium, (*v*) actor.

umboðslaun 1. royalty; *synonyms* (*n*) regality, kingship, nobility, loyalty, command, **2**. commission; *synonyms* (*n*) board, mission, delegation, job, (*v*) assign, **3**. agio; *synonyms* (*n*) premium, agiotage, percentage, drawback, poundage.

umboðsmaður 1. representative; *synonyms* (*n*) agent, delegate, deputy, envoy, proxy, **2**. consignee; *synonyms* (*n*) depositary, nominee, bearer, consignatary, factor, **3**. dealer; *synonyms* (*n*) merchant, trader, monger, seller, vendor; *antonym* (*n*) user, **4**. agent; *synonyms* (*n*) agency, broker, medium, instrument, (*v*) actor.

umboðsskrifstofa agency; *synonyms* (*n*) bureau, office, authority, (*v*) action, act.

umboðsviðskipti consignment; *synonyms* (*n*) cargo, commission, commitment, freight, load.

umbót relieve; *synonyms* (*v*) assuage, comfort, ease, allay, (*n*) alleviate; *antonyms* (*v*) worsen, burden.

umbreyta 1. turn; *synonyms* (*n*) bend, curve, roll, coil, go, **2.** shift; *synonyms* (*n*) interchange, turn, (*v*) change, exchange, remove, **3.** revise; *synonyms* (*v*) edit, amend, emend, alter, (*n*) review, **4.** convert; *synonyms* (*v*) adapt, reform, commute, invert, modify, **5.** alter; *synonyms* (*v*) move, adjust, affect, castrate, convert; *antonym* (*v*) maintain.

umbreyting 1. transformation; *synonyms* (*n*) conversion, alteration, metamorphosis, change, shift, **2.** transduction, **3.** conversion; *synonyms* (*n*) changeover, adaptation, exchange, transformation, (*adj*) salvation, **4.** adaptation; *synonyms* (*n*) accommodation, adjustment, version, reworking, adaption, **5.** modification; *synonyms* (*n*) variation, limitation, deviation, qualification, amendment.

umbreytir 1. transducer; *synonyms* (*n*) sensor, transductor, **2.** converter; *synonyms* (*n*) convertor, adapter, changer, apostle, missionary.

umbrot 1. convulsion; *synonyms* (*n*) spasm, fit, paroxysm, commotion, disturbance, **2.** layout; *synonyms* (*n*) arrangement, composition, design, plan, array.

umbrotakrampi convulsion; *synonyms* (*n*) spasm, fit, paroxysm, commotion, disturbance.

umbúðir 1. bandage; *synonyms* (*n*) band, swathe, (*v*) bind, wrap, (*adj*) truss, **2.** dressing; *synonyms* (*n*) bandage, bandaging, binding, fertilization, stuffing, **3.** packaging; *synonyms* (*n*) packing, covering, wrapping, baling, advancement.

umbun 1. premium; *synonyms* (*n*) bonus, agio, bounty, payment, extra; *antonym* (*adj*) inferior, **2.** reward; *synonyms* (*n*) pay, return, guerdon, (*v*) recompense, compensation; *antonym* (*v*) punish, **3.** retainer; *synonyms* (*n*) servant, attendant, follower, consideration, dependent.

umbuna 1. reward; *synonyms* (*n*) pay, return, guerdon, (*v*) recompense, compensation; *antonym* (*v*) punish, **2.** compensate; *synonyms* (*v*) balance, reimburse, counterbalance, recoup, remunerate.

umburðarbréf circular; *synonyms* (*adj*) round, annular, circinate, (*n*) advertisement, bill; *antonym* (*adj*) square.

umburðarlaus intolerant; *synonyms* (*adj*) impatient, bigoted, illiberal, dogmatic, racist; *antonyms* (*adj*) tolerant, broadminded, liberal.

umburðarlyndur 1. tolerant; *synonyms* (*adj*) indulgent, liberal, patient, broad, lenient; *antonyms*

(*adj*) intolerant, narrow-minded, strict, impatient, **2.** forbearing; *synonyms* (*adj*) clement, tolerant, easy, charitable, permissive, **3.** liberal; *synonyms* (*adj*) generous, bountiful, free, handsome, abundant; *antonyms* (*adj*) oppressive, totalitarian, (*n*) conservative.

umdæmi 1. precinct; *synonyms* (*n*) district, area, region, limit, bound, **2.** region; *synonyms* (*n*) land, country, field, domain, part, **3.** district; *synonyms* (*n*) quarter, community, neighborhood, territory, (*adj*) local, **4.** domain; *synonyms* (*n*) department, realm, kingdom, arena, province; *antonym* (*n*) range, **5.** jurisdiction; *synonyms* (*n*) power, authority, dominion, judicature, influence.

umfang 1. scope; *synonyms* (*n*) range, reach, domain, purview, room, **2.** coverage; *synonyms* (*n*) area, scope, span, extent, insurance.

umfar cycle; *synonyms* (*n*) bicycle, circle, round, (*v*) bike, motorcycle.

Umferð 1. round; *synonyms* (*adv*) about, (*adj*) circular, (*n*) circle, bout, ring; *antonyms* (*adj*) slim, sharp, **2.** traffic; *synonyms* (*n*) dealings, commerce, (*v*) exchange, trade, deal, **3.** revolution; *synonyms* (*n*) change, gyration, insurrection, mutiny, (*v*) circuit, **4.** circulation; *synonyms* (*n*) dissemination, diffusion, distribution, currency, delivery, **5.** cycle; *synonyms* (*n*) bicycle, round, (*v*) bike, motorcycle, wheel.

umferðaræð artery; *synonyms* (*n*) vein, corridor, road, thoroughfare, aisle.

umferðarbeining routing; *synonyms* (*n*) route, conquest, dispatching, navigation, steering.

umferðarheildi circulation; *synonyms* (*n*) dissemination, diffusion, distribution, currency, delivery.

umferðartegur circulation; *synonyms* (*n*) dissemination, diffusion, distribution, currency, delivery.

umferðarþungi traffic; *synonyms* (*n*) dealings, commerce, (*v*) exchange, trade, deal.

umferðartími period; *synonyms* (*n*) age, dot, epoch, era, point.

umferill periphery; *synonyms* (*n*) perimeter, fringe, border, bound, boundary; *antonym* (*n*) center.

umfjöllunaraðilji instance; *synonyms* (*n*) example, case, exemplar, time, (*v*) exemplify.

umflutningur transit; *synonyms* (*n*) journey, passage, conveyance, travel, movement.

umforma convert; *synonyms* (*v*) alter, change, adapt, reform, commute.

umfram excess; *synonyms* (*adj*) extra, (*n*) surplus, dissipation, extravagance, plethora; *antonyms* (*n*) lack, shortage, restraint, moderation, dearth.

umframbirgðir surplus; *synonyms* *(adj)* extra, *(n)* excess, remainder, balance, overabundance; *antonyms* *(n)* necessary, lack, shortage, scarcity.

umframmagn surplus; *synonyms* *(adj)* extra, *(n)* excess, remainder, balance, overabundance; *antonyms* *(n)* necessary, lack, shortage, scarcity.

umframur redundant; *synonyms* *(adj)* excessive, extra, needless, superfluous, excess; *antonym* *(adj)* necessary.

umfremd redundancy; *synonyms* *(n)* excess, redundance, diffuseness, verbiage, *(v)* pleonasm; *antonym* *(n)* employment.

umfremi redundancy; *synonyms* *(n)* excess, redundance, diffuseness, verbiage, *(v)* pleonasm; *antonym* *(n)* employment.

umfrymi cytoplasm; *synonyms* *(n)* cytoplasma, protein, protoplasm.

umgangast 1. interrelate; *synonyms* *(v)* associate, connect, relate, complicate, concern, **2.** interact; *synonyms* *(v)* communicate, correlate, cooperate, bridge, contact.

umgjörð 1. shroud; *synonyms* *(n)* screen, cover, cloak, conceal, *(v)* hide, **2.** corona; *synonyms* *(n)* crown, radiance, halo, aureole, necklace, **3.** circumference; *synonyms* *(n)* circuit, border, boundary, perimeter, brim, **4.** envelope; *synonyms* *(n)* container, pack, case, jacket, *(v)* covering, **5.** perimeter; *synonyms* *(n)* edge, margin, circumference, limit, bound; *antonyms* *(n)* center, middle.

umhorf milieu; *synonyms* *(n)* environment, medium, background, climate, surroundings.

umhverfa 1. reciprocal; *synonyms* *(adj)* mutual, common, inverse, complementary, interchangeable, **2.** transpose; *synonyms* *(v)* exchange, change, shift, transfer, transplant, **3.** inverse; *synonyms* *(adj)* contrary, converse, *(n)* opposite, contrast, *(v)* reverse, **4.** inversion; *synonyms* *(n)* antithesis, reversal, transposition, anastrophe, eversion.

umhverfður inverted; *synonyms* *(adj)* inverse, upside-down, anatropous, backward, overturned; *antonym* *(adj)* upright.

umhverfi 1. environment; *synonyms* *(n)* circumstance, background, habitat, atmosphere, context, **2.** medium; *synonyms* *(adj)* intermediate, fair, *(n)* average, mediocre, mean.

umhverfing inversion; *synonyms* *(n)* antithesis, reversal, transposition, anastrophe, eversion.

umhverfis ambient; *synonyms* *(adj)* circumfused, investing, *(n)* ambience, medium.

umhverfisaðlögun acclimatization; *synonyms* *(n)* acclimation, acclimatisation, adjustment, adaptation, acclimatation.

umhverfishyggja environmentalism; *synonyms* *(n)* ecology, conservationism.

umhverfiskerfi ecosystem; *synonyms* *(n)* complex, nature.

umhverfislöghyggja environmentalism; *synonyms* *(n)* ecology, conservationism.

umhverfisverndarsinni environmentalist; *synonyms* *(n)* conservationist, ecologist, biologist, naturalist, preservationist.

umhverfur 1. reversible; *synonyms* *(adj)* changeable, bilateral, abrogable, repealable, **2.** inverse; *synonyms* *(adj)* contrary, converse, *(n)* opposite, contrast, *(v)* reverse.

umhyggja care; *synonyms* *(n)* attention, bother, caution, *(v)* anxiety, charge; *antonyms* *(n)* carelessness, recklessness, rashness, *(v)* neglect, disregard.

umlukinn engulfed; *synonyms* *(adj)* beaten, conquered, enveloped, flooded, inundated.

umlukt closed; *synonyms* *(v)* close, *(adj)* blind, blocked, finished, shut; *antonym* *(adj)* open.

umlykjandi 1. ambient; *synonyms* *(adj)* circumfused, investing, *(n)* ambience, medium, **2.** circumferential; *synonyms* *(adj)* circuitous, encircling, encompassing, *(n)* bypass, *(v)* suburban.

umlýsa reverse; *synonyms* *(adj)* opposite, *(v)* annul, repeal, rescind, *(n)* contrary; *antonym* *(n)* front.

ummæli comment; *synonyms* *(n)* annotation, commentary, *(v)* annotate, remark, gloss.

ummál 1. circumference; *synonyms* *(n)* circuit, border, boundary, perimeter, brim, **2.** perimeter; *synonyms* *(n)* edge, margin, circumference, limit, bound; *antonyms* *(n)* center, middle.

ummerki trace; *synonyms* *(n)* line, shadow, spot, clue, *(v)* track.

ummóta restructure; *synonyms* *(v)* rearrange, reconstitute, reconstruct, reform, reorganize.

ummótun restructuring; *synonyms* *(n)* reorganization, improvement, reform, renovation, alteration.

ummynd transform; *synonyms* *(v)* change, alter, convert, metamorphose, modify.

ummynda transform; *synonyms* *(v)* change, alter, convert, metamorphose, modify.

ummyndun 1. transformation; *synonyms* *(n)* conversion, alteration, metamorphosis, change, shift, **2.** transition; *synonyms* *(n)* passage, transit, changeover, modulation, **3.** alteration; *synonyms* *(n)* adaptation, adjustment, revision, amendment, deviation.

umönnun care; *synonyms* *(n)* attention, bother, caution, *(v)* anxiety, charge; *antonyms* *(n)* carelessness, recklessness, rashness, *(v)* neglect, disregard.

umorða paraphrase; *synonyms* (*n*) translation, paraphrasis, (*v*) interpret, rephrase, reword.

umpóla depolarize; *synonym* (*v*) depolarise.

umráð occupancy; *synonyms* (*n*) habitation, occupation, inhabitancy, employment, ownership.

umráðasvæði realm; *synonyms* (*n*) kingdom, area, country, domain, field.

umræðuefni topic; *synonyms* (*n*) matter, question, subject, theme, affair.

umræðufundur conference; *synonyms* (*n*) assembly, colloquy, meeting, council, consultation.

umræður dialogue; *synonyms* (*n*) talk, colloquy, conversation, interlocution, interview.

umreikningur conversion; *synonyms* (*n*) alteration, change, changeover, adaptation, exchange.

umriðill 1. converter; *synonyms* (*n*) convertor, adapter, changer, apostle, missionary, **2.** convertor; *synonyms* (*n*) converter, transformer.

umritun transcription; *synonyms* (*n*) transcript, recording, copy, arrangement, record.

umröðun 1. rearrangement; *synonyms* (*n*) realignment, relocation, shift, transposition, redeployment, **2.** transposition; *synonyms* (*n*) exchange, permutation, replacement, reversal, substitution, **3.** permutation; *synonyms* (*n*) change, commutation, modification, alteration, mutation.

umröðunarhvarf rearrangement; *synonyms* (*n*) realignment, relocation, shift, transposition, redeployment.

umsækjandi candidate; *synonyms* (*n*) applicant, aspirant, contestant, contender, hopeful.

umsemjanlegur negotiable; *synonyms* (*adj*) alienable, assignable, passable, transferable, conveyable.

umsetning turnover; *synonyms* (*n*) overturn, revolution, sales, upset, pastry.

umsjárhópur practice; *synonyms* (*n*) exercise, fashion, convention, (*v*) custom, drill; *antonym* (*n*) performance.

umsjón 1. supervision; *synonyms* (*n*) oversight, charge, control, direction, (*v*) inspection, **2.** surveillance; *synonyms* (*n*) supervision, vigilance, watch, observation, scrutiny; *antonym* (*n*) neglect, **3.** administration; *synonyms* (*n*) management, organization, running, power, execution, **4.** attendance; *synonyms* (*n*) presence, attending, audience, turnout, hearing; *antonyms* (*n*) absence, nonattendance.

umsjónarmaður 1. supervisor; *synonyms* (*n*) superintendent, director, overseer, boss, chief, **2.** administrator; *synonyms* (*n*) executive, manager, officer, official, supervisor.

umskautun reversal; *synonyms* (*n*) reverse, setback, retrogression, regression, annulment.

umskipa restructure; *synonyms* (*v*) rearrange, reconstitute, reconstruct, reform, reorganize.

umskiptanlegt interchangeable; *synonyms* (*adj*) convertible, commutative, exchangeable, identical, reciprocal.

umskiptanlegur removable; *synonyms* (*adj*) detachable, obliterable, movable, amovable, dispensable; *antonym* (*adj*) fixed.

umskiptanleiki interchangeability; *synonyms* (*n*) exchangeability, fungibility, interchangeableness, equivalence.

umskipti 1. reversal; *synonyms* (*n*) reverse, setback, retrogression, regression, annulment, **2.** transformation; *synonyms* (*n*) conversion, alteration, metamorphosis, change, shift, **3.** transition; *synonyms* (*n*) passage, transit, changeover, modulation, **4.** alteration; *synonyms* (*n*) adaptation, adjustment, revision, amendment, deviation.

umskipting 1. replace; *synonyms* (*v*) change, exchange, substitute, supersede, supplant, **2.** commutation; *synonyms* (*n*) substitution, composition, intermutation, commuting, compromise.

umskiptingarhamur replace; *synonyms* (*v*) change, exchange, substitute, supersede, supplant.

umskipun 1. transshipment, **2.** transhipment; *synonym* (*n*) transshipment.

umskrá convert; *synonyms* (*v*) alter, change, adapt, reform, commute.

umskurður circumcision; *synonym* (*n*) posthetomy.

umskurn circumcision; *synonym* (*n*) posthetomy.

umslag envelope; *synonyms* (*n*) container, pack, (*v*) cover, covering, cloak.

umsnúinn inverted; *synonyms* (*adj*) inverse, upside-down, anatropous, backward, overturned; *antonym* (*adj*) upright.

umsnúningur 1. reversal; *synonyms* (*n*) reverse, setback, retrogression, regression, annulment, **2.** inversion; *synonyms* (*n*) antithesis, reversal, transposition, anastrophe, eversion.

umsögn predicate; *synonyms* (*v*) affirm, assert, allege, base, connote.

umsókn 1. request; *synonyms* (*n*) petition, bid, (*v*) demand, ask, invite; *antonyms* (*v*) command, order, **2.** application; *synonyms* (*n*) plea, appeal, appliance, concentration, diligence.

umsvif business; *synonyms* (*n*) employment, matter, subject, affair, calling; *antonyms* (*adj*) charitable, housing.

umtákna encode; *synonyms* (*v*) cipher, code, cypher, encipher, encrypt.

umtáknun encoding; *synonyms* (*n*) encryption, indoctrination, brainwashing, training.

umvarpa transform; *synonyms* (*v*) change, alter, convert, metamorphose, modify.

umvörpun transformation; *synonyms* (*n*) conversion, alteration, metamorphosis, change, shift.

undanfaraeinkenni prodrome; *synonyms* (*n*) forerunner, pioneer, prodroma, prodromus, vancourier.

undanfari precursor; *synonyms* (*n*) forerunner, harbinger, herald, antecedent, messenger; *antonyms* (*n*) descendant, successor.

undanhald recession; *synonyms* (*n*) decline, depression, fall, niche, recess.

undanlátslaus rigid; *synonyms* (*adj*) harsh, fixed, hard, inflexible, stiff; *antonyms* (*adj*) flexible, elastic, soft.

undanskilinn implicit; *synonyms* (*adj*) silent, tacit, understood, undeclared, unsaid; *antonyms* (*adj*) explicit, direct.

undanskilja exempt; *synonyms* (*v*) absolve, excuse, discharge, free, dispense; *antonyms* (*adj*) chargeable, liable, (*v*) nonexempt.

undantekning 1. exceptional; *synonyms* (*adj*) special, abnormal, excellent, extraordinary, particular; *antonyms* (*adj*) common, mediocre, ordinary, average, normal, **2.** exception; *synonyms* (*n*) exclusion, objection, exemption, anomaly, immunity; *antonym* (*n*) inclusion.

undanþága 1. waiver; *synonyms* (*n*) release, discharge, renunciation, dismissal, acquittance, **2.** immunity; *synonyms* (*n*) exemption, freedom, franchise, dispensation, privilege; *antonym* (*n*) vulnerability, **3.** exemption; *synonyms* (*n*) acquittal, immunity, exception, impunity, liberty; *antonym* (*n*) liability.

undanþeginn exempt; *synonyms* (*v*) absolve, excuse, discharge, free, dispense; *antonyms* (*adj*) chargeable, liable, (*v*) nonexempt.

undanþiggja exempt; *synonyms* (*v*) absolve, excuse, discharge, free, dispense; *antonyms* (*adj*) chargeable, liable, (*v*) nonexempt.

undarlegur 1. remarkable; *synonyms* (*adj*) exceptional, extraordinary, notable, noteworthy, odd; *antonyms* (*adj*) ordinary, insignificant, unremarkable, **2.** noteworthy; *synonyms* (*adj*) important, eminent, remarkable, significant, considerable, **3.** noticeable; *synonyms* (*adj*) conspicuous, apparent, discernible, evident, marked; *antonyms* (*adj*) imperceptible, obscure, inconspicuous, hidden, unobtrusive, **4.** notable; *synonyms* (*adj*) distinguished, celebrated, illustrious, famous, (*n*) celebrity.

undir below; *synonyms* (*adv*) beneath, under, (*prep*) underneath, (*adj*) low, after; *antonyms* (*prep*) above, over.

undiralda swell; *synonyms* (*v*) surge, enlarge, expand, heave, increase; *antonyms* (*v*) decrease, deflate, desiccate.

undirbjóða dump; *synonyms* (*v*) discard, ditch, abandon, drop, empty; *antonym* (*v*) keep.

undirboð dumping; *synonyms* (*n*) disposal, discarding, clearance, jettisoning, removal.

undirbúa 1. prepare; *synonyms* (*v*) arrange, fix, form, plan, dress, **2.** adopt; *synonyms* (*v*) accept, admit, affiliate, assume, borrow; *antonym* (*v*) reject.

undirbúningur preparation; *synonyms* (*n*) arrangement, concoction, provision, readiness, training.

undirbygging frame; *synonyms* (*n*) design, border, (*v*) form, construct, fabricate.

undireining subunit; *synonym* (*n*) protomer.

undirflokkur subclass; *synonym* (*n*) order.

undirfylki company; *synonyms* (*n*) companionship, society, association, band, business; *antonym* (*n*) solitude.

undirgefni 1. subordination; *synonyms* (*n*) dependence, dependency, domination, control, hyponymy, **2.** submission; *synonyms* (*n*) compliance, obedience, acquiescence, bid, (*adj*) resignation.

undirhluti exponent; *synonyms* (*n*) advocate, champion, power, proponent, protagonist.

undirkæling supercooling; *synonym* (*n*) undercooling.

undirklasi subclass; *synonym* (*n*) order.

undirlag 1. substratum; *synonyms* (*n*) substrate, bed, groundwork, matter, (*adj*) substance, **2.** carcass; *synonyms* (*n*) body, carcase, frame, cadaver, corpse.

undirlyfta 1. tappet, **2.** lifter; *synonyms* (*n*) thief, weightlifter, cleaner, tongs, hoist.

undirlyftuarmur lifter; *synonyms* (*n*) thief, weightlifter, cleaner, tongs, hoist.

undirlyftutappi 1. tappet, **2.** lifter; *synonyms* (*n*) thief, weightlifter, cleaner, tongs, hoist.

undirmeðvitund subconscious; *synonyms* (*adj*) unconscious, psychological, hidden, (*n*) mind, psyche; *antonyms* (*adj*) superficial, conscious.

undirritun signature; *synonyms* (*n*) autograph, mark, endorsement, earmark, (*v*) sign.

undirrót agent; *synonyms* (*n*) agency, broker, deputy, medium, (*v*) actor.

undirsætinn superior; *synonyms* (*adj*) senior, dominant, better, exceptional, predominant; *antonyms* (*adj*) humble, worse, poor, (*n*) inferior, subordinate.

undirsetning 1. subordination; *synonyms* (*n*) dependence, dependency, domination, control, hyponymy, **2.** hypostasis; *synonyms* (*n*) substantiality, epistasis, body, person, element.

undirsinka countersink; *synonyms* (*v*) adjust, arrange, coif, coiffe, (*n*) counterbore.

undirskilinn 1. tacit; *synonyms* (*adj*) silent, implicit, understood, implied, undeclared; *antonyms* (*adj*) explicit, spoken, **2.** implicit; *synonyms* (*adj*) tacit, unsaid, inherent, unquestioning, virtual; *antonym* (*adj*) direct.

undirskipan subordination; *synonyms* (*n*) dependence, dependency, domination, control, hyponymy.

undirskrifa sign; *synonyms* (*n*) signal, indication, mark, motion, (*v*) gesture.

undirskrift 1. signature; *synonyms* (*n*) autograph, mark, endorsement, earmark, (*v*) sign, **2.** autograph; *synonyms* (*n*) autography, name, (*v*) signature, endorse, subscribe.

undirstaða 1. support; *synonyms* (*n*) help, stand, aid, keep, (*v*) assist; *antonyms* (*n*) hindrance, (*v*) oppose, neglect, undermine, abandon, **2.** base; *synonyms* (*n*) foundation, (*adj*) bottom, abject, mean, dishonorable; *antonyms* (*n*) summit, top, (*adj*) noble, **3.** bed; *synonyms* (*n*) couch, layer, base, basis, berth, **4.** hypostasis; *synonyms* (*n*) substantiality, epistasis, body, person, element, **5.** foundation; *synonyms* (*n*) creation, establishment, foot, institution, principle.

undirstæði hypostasis; *synonyms* (*n*) substantiality, epistasis, body, person, element.

undirstæðni hypostasis; *synonyms* (*n*) substantiality, epistasis, body, person, element.

undirstærð undersize; *synonyms* (*adj*) undersized, diminutive, (*n*) throughs.

undirstöðuafurð staple; *synonyms* (*n*) pin, material, (*v*) nail, (*adj*) basic, fundamental.

undirstöðuatriði 1. principle; *synonyms* (*n*) origin, fundamental, method, rule, cause, **2.** fundamental; *synonyms* (*adj*) central, essential, basic, (*n*) base, basis; *antonyms* (*adj*) minor, (*n*) secondary.

undirstöðuefni substrate; *synonyms* (*n*) substratum, ground, feedstock.

undirstöðuvara staple; *synonyms* (*n*) pin, material, (*v*) nail, (*adj*) basic, fundamental.

undirstrik underscore; *synonyms* (*v*) emphasize, stress, accent, accentuate, (*n*) underline.

undirstrika underline; *synonyms* (*v*) emphasize, stress, accent, accentuate, punctuate.

undirsvæði module; *synonyms* (*n*) faculty, part, paradigm, subarray, bay.

undirtegund subspecies; *synonyms* (*n*) race, airstream, backwash, breed, form.

undirþrýstingur vacuum; *synonyms* (*n*) emptiness, void, vacancy, vacuity, gap.

undirvagn chassis; *synonyms* (*n*) body, anatomy, flesh, frame, figure.

undralyf panacea; *synonyms* (*n*) catholicon, nostrum, cure, gesture, panpharmacon.

undrandi surprisingly; *synonyms* (*adv*) astonishingly, wonderfully, astoundingly, oddly, (*adj*) amazingly; *antonym* (*adv*) unremarkably.

undrast 1. wonder; *synonyms* (*n*) marvel, prodigy, admiration, amazement, astonishment, **2.** marvel; *synonyms* (*n*) wonder, curiosity, phenomenon, miracle, (*v*) admire.

undrun 1. surprise; *synonyms* (*n*) fright, (*v*) astound, alarm, amaze, astonish, **2.** wonder; *synonyms* (*n*) marvel, prodigy, admiration, amazement, astonishment, **3.** amazement; *synonyms* (*n*) surprise, wonder, consternation, stupor, **4.** astonishment; *synonyms* (*n*) wonderment, confusion, awe.

ungahópur brood; *synonyms* (*n*) breed, issue, offspring, (*v*) hatch, sulk.

ungbarn 1. baby; *synonyms* (*n*) babe, child, (*v*) coddle, indulge, (*adj*) infant; *antonym* (*adj*) giant, **2.** infant; *synonyms* (*n*) baby, minor, nursling, kid, (*adj*) juvenile.

ungbarnakveisa colic; *synonyms* (*n*) bellyache, mulligrubs, enteralgia, cramp, heartburn.

ungdómur 1. youth; *synonyms* (*n*) boy, juvenile, lad, young, (*adj*) adolescent; *antonyms* (*n*) adulthood, adult, ripeness, **2.** youngster; *synonyms* (*n*) child, kid, urchin, toddler, youth, **3.** juvenile; *synonyms* (*adj*) childish, immature, puerile, youthful, babyish.

ungfóstur embryo; *synonyms* (*n*) germ, bud, origin, nucleus, seed.

unglingsár adolescence; *synonyms* (*n*) immaturity, boyhood, juvenility, puberty, youth.

ungplanta plant; *synonyms* (*n*) manufactory, equipment, (*v*) fix, place, embed.

ungur 1. young; *synonyms* (*adj*) green, juvenile, immature, (*n*) offspring, progeny; *antonyms* (*adj*) old, mature, adult, (*n*) aged, **2.** juvenile; *synonyms* (*adj*) childish, puerile, young, youthful, (*n*) adolescent.

unnusta bride; *synonyms* (*n*) wife, mate, woman, helpmate.

unz 1. till; *synonyms* (*prep*) until, unto, (*v*) cultivate, plow, hoe, **2.** pending; *synonyms* (*prep*) during, (*adj*) forthcoming, undecided, unresolved, (*n*) abeyance; *antonym* (*adj*) distant.

upp upward; *synonyms* (*adj*) up, overhead, rising, (*adv*) upwardly, upwards; *antonym* (*adj*) descending.

upparmur arm; *synonyms* (*n*) branch, wing, bay, department, (*v*) equip; *antonym* (*v*) disarm.

uppáskrift certificate; *synonyms* (*n*) bond, diploma, certification, credential, (*v*) certify.

uppboð auction; *synonyms* (*n*) bidding, vendue, angle, (*v*) auctioneer, sale.

uppbót 1. substitute; *synonyms* (*adj*) replacement, alternative, (*n*) deputy, (*v*) alternate, shift, **2.** substitution; *synonyms* (*n*) exchange, change, substitute, interchange, permutation, **3.** complementation; *synonym* (*n*) complementing.

uppbygging 1. structure; *synonyms* (*n*) form, building, arrangement, edifice, shape, **2.** development; *synonyms* (*n*) evolution, course, growth, improvement, increase; *antonyms* (*n*) deterioration, decline, neglect, decrease, **3.** infrastructure; *synonyms* (*n*) base, foundation, basis, groundwork, substructure.

uppdráttarsýki cachexia; *synonyms* (*n*) cachexy, atrophy, (*adj*) decrepitude, adynamy, asthenia.

uppdráttur 1. plan; *synonyms* (*n*) aim, map, figure, chart, (*v*) design, **2.** survey; *synonyms* (*n*) poll, review, (*v*) study, measure, view; *antonym* (*v*) neglect, **3.** drawing; *synonyms* (*n*) draft, drafting, delineation, picture, plan, **4.** design; *synonyms* (*n*) purpose, scheme, conception, drawing, arrangement; *antonym* (*n*) chance, **5.** diagram; *synonyms* (*n*) sketch, graph, illustration, outline, plat.

uppdrif buoyancy; *synonyms* (*n*) airiness, animation, buoyance, cheerfulness, levity; *antonym* (*n*) heaviness.

uppeldi education; *synonyms* (*n*) training, discipline, instruction, teaching, breeding.

uppfæra update; *synonyms* (*n*) updating, (*v*) inform, modernize, renovate, revise.

uppfærsla 1. transaction; *synonyms* (*n*) deal, business, dealing, dealings, proceeding; *antonym* (*n*) purchase, **2.** promotion; *synonyms* (*n*) furtherance, advance, advancement, advertising, boost; *antonyms* (*n*) demotion, neglect.

uppfærsluaðgerð transaction; *synonyms* (*n*) deal, business, dealing, dealings, proceeding; *antonym* (*n*) purchase.

uppfinning invention; *synonyms* (*n*) contrivance, conception, fabrication, creation, fiction.

uppflettimynd lemma; *synonyms* (*n*) proposition, premises, principle, terms, glumella.

uppflutningur upload; *synonym* (*n*) uploading.

uppfylla comply; *synonyms* (*v*) agree, accede, assent, acquiesce, consent.

uppfylling compliance; *synonyms* (*n*) agreement, approval, observance, accordance, acquiescence; *antonyms* (*n*) disobedience, stubbornness, nonconformity.

uppgangstími boom; *synonyms* (*n*) bang, roar, (*v*) blast, blare, flourish; *antonyms* (*n*) depression, (*v*) collapse, decline.

uppgangur 1. sputum; *synonyms* (*n*) phlegm, spit, saliva, belch, dig, **2.** boom; *synonyms* (*n*) bang, roar, (*v*) blast, blare, flourish; *antonyms* (*n*) depression, (*v*) collapse, decline, **3.** expansion; *synonyms* (*n*) amplification, enlargement, development, (*v*) extension, augmentation; *antonyms* (*n*) contraction, decrease, reduction, abbreviation.

uppgefast collapse; *synonyms* (*n*) crash, breakdown, fall, (*v*) break, slump.

uppgerð simulation; *synonyms* (*n*) affectation, pretense, imitation, pretence, modelling.

uppgjör settlement; *synonyms* (*n*) decision, accommodation, colony, hamlet, payment.

uppgómur velum; *synonyms* (*n*) veil, conceal, cover, curtain, disguise.

uppgötva detect; *synonyms* (*v*) catch, discover, find, ascertain, discern.

uppgötvun detection; *synonyms* (*n*) discovery, demodulation, detecting, uncovering, unearthing.

uppgröftur excavation; *synonyms* (*n*) mine, pit, dig, digging, hole.

uppgufun 1. vaporization; *synonyms* (*n*) evaporation, vapor, vaporisation, volatilization, condensation, **2.** gassing; *synonyms* (*n*) execution, boasting, **3.** evaporation; *synonyms* (*n*) vaporization, dehydration, disappearance, desiccation, vaporation; *antonym* (*n*) appearance.

upphaf 1. commence; *synonyms* (*v*) begin, start, open, embark, initiate; *antonyms* (*v*) end, finish, stop, **2.** onset; *synonyms* (*n*) incursion, charge, aggression, assault, (*v*) attack, **3.** initial; *synonyms* (*adj*) beginning, first, elementary, incipient, foremost, **4.** genesis; *synonyms* (*n*) ancestry, birth, origin, descent, cause.

upphaflegur initial; *synonyms* (*adj*) beginning, first, elementary, incipient, foremost.

upphafsefni initiator; *synonyms* (*n*) creator, originator, author, founder, father.

upphafsmaður initiator; *synonyms* (*n*) creator, originator, author, founder, father.

upphafspunktur origin; *synonyms* (*n*) cause, lineage, base, beginning, birth; *antonym* (*n*) end.

upphafsstafaheiti acronym; *synonyms* (*n*) contraction, ellipsis.

upphafsstafanafn acronym; *synonyms* (*n*) contraction, ellipsis.

upphafsstafaorð acronym; *synonyms* (n) contraction, ellipsis.

upphafsstafur initial; *synonyms* (adj) beginning, first, elementary, incipient, foremost.

upphandleggur arm; *synonyms* (n) branch, wing, bay, department, (v) equip; *antonym* (v) disarm.

upphefja extinguish; *synonyms* (v) destroy, exterminate, quench, annihilate, douse; *antonyms* (v) light, ignite.

upphengja suspension; *synonyms* (n) delay, interruption, abeyance, break, intermission.

upphengjulager hanger; *synonyms* (n) hook, dropper, bolt, dowel.

upphleyptur 1. relief; *synonyms* (n) comfort, aid, consolation, ease, (v) assistance, 2. embossed; *synonyms* (adj) bossed, raised, brocaded, bossy, prominent.

upphrifning ecstasy; *synonyms* (n) delight, rapture, bliss, joy, (v) transport; *antonyms* (n) misery, desolation, gloom.

uppíloft supine; *synonyms* (adj) lazy, idle, listless, slothful, languid.

uppistaða stroma; *synonym* (n) stromata.

uppistöðuefni matrix; *synonyms* (n) die, alembic, caldron, crucible, groundmass.

uppistöðulón dam; *synonyms* (n) barrage, barricade, dike, dyke, (v) block.

uppistöðuvefur stroma; *synonym* (n) stromata.

uppkall call; *synonyms* (v) cry, bellow, name, shout, (n) appeal; *antonym* (v) dismiss.

uppkallsleitari finder; *synonyms* (n) viewfinder, discoverer, artificer, spotter, lookout.

uppkast 1. protocol; *synonyms* (n) etiquette, manners, ceremony, bill, formality, 2. draft; *synonyms* (n) conscription, sketch, (v) draught, outline, design; *antonym* (v) discharge, 3. outline; *synonyms* (n) edge, abstract, (v) draft, line, form.

uppköst vomiting; *synonyms* (n) emesis, vomit, disgorgement, nausea, puking.

upplægi exposure; *synonyms* (n) display, exposition, detection, peril, (v) disclosure.

upplag anlage; *synonym* (n) primordium.

uppland 1. inland; *synonyms* (adj) domestic, interior, internal, inner, inside, 2. hinterland; *synonyms* (n) backwoods, country, boondocks, vicinity, bush.

upplausn 1. resolution; *synonyms* (n) decision, determination, answer, conclusion, firmness; *antonym* (n) indecisiveness, 2. solution; *synonyms* (n) dissolution, resolution, settlement, resolve, explanation, 3. definition; *synonyms* (n) description, account, interpretation, limitation, definiteness; *antonym* (n) bagginess.

upplausnarefni solvent; *synonyms* (n) resolvent, dissolvent, solution, menstruum, answer; *antonyms* (adj) bankrupt, broke.

uppleysandi solvent; *synonyms* (n) resolvent, dissolvent, solution, menstruum, answer; *antonyms* (adj) bankrupt, broke.

uppleysing dissolution; *synonyms* (n) decay, breakup, decomposition, abolition, cancellation.

uppljómun highlight; *synonyms* (v) emphasize, accentuate, spotlight, underline, accent.

uppljóstrun 1. denunciation; *synonyms* (n) condemnation, accusation, curse, criticism, denouncement, 2. disclosure; *synonyms* (n) discovery, exposure, revelation, declaration, confession.

upplyfting recreation; *synonyms* (n) amusement, entertainment, distraction, pastime, play.

upplýsingar 1. data; *synonyms* (n) information, facts, details, evidence, fact, 2. detail; *synonyms* (n) report, point, (v) describe, enumerate, relate; *antonym* (n) generalization, 3. disclosure; *synonyms* (n) discovery, exposure, revelation, declaration, confession, 4. information; *synonyms* (n) advice, communication, data, note, enlightenment.

upplýsingaskjal documentation; *synonyms* (n) proof, record, certificate, certification, corroboration.

uppmæltur back; *synonyms* (n) rear, (adj) assist, (v) support, advocate, endorse; *antonyms* (n) face, (v) front, oppose, advance.

uppnefni alias; *synonyms* (n) name, pseudonym, nickname, soubriquet, title.

uppörvun incentive; *synonyms* (n) encouragement, impetus, cause, goad, impulse; *antonyms* (n) deterrent, disincentive, constraint.

uppreisn 1. revolution; *synonyms* (n) change, gyration, insurrection, mutiny, (v) circuit, 2. rebellion; *synonyms* (n) revolt, disobedience, uprising, defiance, outbreak, 3. mutiny; *synonyms* (n) revolution, rising, (v) rebellion, rebel, rise.

upprétting rectification; *synonyms* (n) correction, amendment, improvement, redress, revision.

uppréttur 1. upright; *synonyms* (adj) perpendicular, straight, erect, vertical, fair; *antonyms* (adj) disreputable, prone, upturned, degenerate, hanging, 2. erect; *synonyms* (v) build, elevate, raise, construct, (adj) upright; *antonym* (adj) horizontal.

upprifinn agitated; *synonyms* (adj) restless, excited, nervous, restive, tumultuous; *antonyms* (adj) calm, composed, lethargic.

upprifjun 1. recall; *synonyms* (*v*) retrieve, countermand, recognize, (*n*) anamnesis, memory; *antonym* (*v*) forget, **2.** anamnesis; *synonyms* (*n*) remembrance, recall, recollection, commemoration, memorial.

upprunaferli source; *synonyms* (*n*) origin, root, cause, commencement, beginning.

upprunafræði cosmogony; *synonyms* (*n*) cosmology, cosmogeny, cosmography.

upprunalegur 1. primary; *synonyms* (*adj*) chief, basic, elementary, essential, (*n*) paramount; *antonym* (*adj*) secondary, **2.** authentic; *synonyms* (*adj*) actual, genuine, accurate, real, right; *antonyms* (*adj*) bogus, fake, unrealistic, **3.** aboriginal; *synonyms* (*adj*) native, original, early, autochthonous, (*n*) aborigine; *antonym* (*adj*) nonnative, **4.** autochthonous; *synonyms* (*adj*) autochthonal, autochthonic, indigenous, endemic, endemical, **5.** native; *synonyms* (*adj*) inborn, inherent, innate, (*n*) aboriginal, autochthon; *antonyms* (*adj*) foreign, learned, (*n*) stranger, immigrant, imported.

uppruni 1. origin; *synonyms* (*n*) cause, lineage, base, beginning, birth; *antonym* (*n*) end, **2.** lineage; *synonyms* (*n*) breed, descent, family, pedigree, extraction, **3.** genesis; *synonyms* (*n*) ancestry, origin, commencement, generation, creation.

uppsafnað aggregate; *synonyms* (*n*) total, agglomerate, whole, (*v*) accumulate, cluster; *antonyms* (*n*) individual, part.

uppsala 1. vomiting; *synonyms* (*n*) emesis, vomit, disgorgement, nausea, puking, **2.** vomit; *synonyms* (*v*) spew, heave, puke, cast, disgorge.

uppsetning 1. setup; *synonyms* (*n*) apparatus, arrangement, setting, system, scheme, **2.** arrangement; *synonyms* (*n*) agreement, order, settlement, adjustment, array, **3.** erection; *synonyms* (*n*) building, edifice, assembly, construction, structure, **4.** installation; *synonyms* (*n*) establishment, induction, facility, inauguration, initiation.

uppskera 1. crop; *synonyms* (*n*) fruit, harvest, (*v*) browse, graze, (*adj*) clip, **2.** harvest; *synonyms* (*n*) crop, (*v*) gain, gather, glean, amass.

Uppskipti change; *synonyms* (*n*) shift, alteration, barter, (*v*) exchange, alter; *antonyms* (*v*) stay, leave, idle, maintain.

uppsöfnun accumulation; *synonyms* (*n*) store, stock, accretion, mass, accrual; *antonym* (*n*) shortage.

uppsog 1. resorption; *synonyms* (*n*) reabsorption, traction, **2** absorption; *synonyms* (*n*) assimilation, attention, concentration, inhalation, engrossment.

uppsögn 1. resignation; *synonyms* (*n*) capitulation, endurance, patience, renunciation, surrender, **2.**

termination; *synonyms* (*n*) ending, close, end, conclusion, result; *antonym* (*n*) start, **3.** cancellation; *synonyms* (*n*) annulment, abolition, cancel, negation, recall, **4.** denunciation; *synonyms* (*n*) condemnation, accusation, curse, criticism, denouncement, **5.** dismissal; *synonyms* (*n*) discharge, conge, denial, dismission, expulsion.

uppsölulyf 1. antiemetic; *synonym* (*n*) antinauseant, **2.** emetic; *synonyms* (*adj*) vomitory, (*n*) vomit, antiseptic, vomitive, disgorgement.

uppsölustillandi antiemetic; *synonym* (*n*) antinauseant.

uppspretta 1. well; *synonyms* (*adv*) right, easily, thoroughly, (*adj*) healthy, (*n*) fountain; *antonyms* (*adv*) ill, badly, poorly, (*adj*) sick, unwell, **2.** source; *synonyms* (*n*) origin, root, cause, commencement, beginning.

uppspuni fabrication; *synonyms* (*n*) construction, fable, fiction, assembly, (*v*) invention; *antonyms* (*n*) truth, honesty, correction, dismantling, fact.

uppstilling arrangement; *synonyms* (*n*) agreement, order, settlement, adjustment, array.

uppsveifla boom; *synonyms* (*n*) bang, roar, (*v*) blast, blare, flourish; *antonyms* (*n*) depression, (*v*) collapse, decline.

upptaka 1. transposition; *synonyms* (*n*) exchange, permutation, replacement, reversal, substitution, **2.** seizing; *synonyms* (*adj*) catching, (*n*) grasping, seizure, prehension, taking, **3.** absorption; *synonyms* (*n*) assimilation, attention, concentration, inhalation, engrossment, **4.** adoption; *synonyms* (*n*) acceptance, espousal, assumption, borrowing, (*adj*) conversion, **5.** intake; *synonyms* (*n*) absorption, consumption, ingestion, drinking, eating.

upptekinn busy; *synonyms* (*adj*) active, brisk, assiduous, engaged, occupied; *antonyms* (*adj*) idle, free, inactive.

upptekning recurrence; *synonyms* (*n*) iteration, repetition, return, frequency, comeback; *antonym* (*n*) disappearance.

upptekt seizure; *synonyms* (*n*) arrest, capture, confiscation, seizing, apprehension; *antonyms* (*n*) release, return.

uppþemba flatulence; *synonyms* (*n*) flatulency, gas, turgidity, wind, windiness.

uppþornun desiccation; *synonyms* (*n*) dehydration, drought, evaporation, dryness, (*adj*) exsiccation.

uppþot 1. scare; *synonyms* (*n*) dread, (*v*) alarm, dismay, fright, (*adj*) panic, **2.** alarm; *synonyms* (*n*) alert, consternation, (*v*) awe, scare, agitate; *antonyms* (*v*) calm, comfort.

upptíningur pickling; *synonyms* (*n*) buckling, preservation.

upptök 1. spring; *synonyms* (*n*) jump, leap, bound, (*v*) hop, caper, **2.** source; *synonyms* (*n*) origin, root, cause, commencement, beginning.

upptökusalur studio; *synonyms* (*n*) atelier, cabinet, accommodation, building, bungalow.

uppvella regurgitation; *synonyms* (*n*) vomit, backwater, disgorgement, (*v*) reflux, eddy.

urðarmáni fireball; *synonyms* (*n*) bolide, cartouche, (*adj*) active, ambitious, capable.

urg rumble; *synonyms* (*n*) boom, roll, roar, (*v*) murmur, growl.

urpt 1. brood; *synonyms* (*n*) breed, issue, offspring, (*v*) hatch, sulk, **2.** litter; *synonyms* (*n*) brood, bedding, stretcher, (*v*) clutter, (*adj*) jumble.

urrari growler; *synonyms* (*n*) grouch, cab, cabriolet, car, (*v*) grumbler.

urri growler; *synonyms* (*n*) grouch, cab, cabriolet, car, (*v*) grumbler.

urriði trout; *synonyms* (*n*) anchovies, herring, sardines, shad, smelts.

urt herb; *synonyms* (*n*) plant, seasoning, flavoring, flower, (*v*) bunch.

utan 1. abroad; *synonyms* (*adv*) away, afield, forth, (*adj*) overseas, out, **2.** outside; *synonyms* (*adj*) external, outdoor, foreign, (*adv*) outdoors, (*n*) exterior; *antonyms* (*prep*) inside, in, (*adj*) indoor, internal, (*adv*) indoors, **3.** out; *synonyms* (*adv*) off, forward, beyond, (*v*) reveal, (*adj*) extinct.

utanaðkomandi 1. adventitious; *synonyms* (*adj*) accidental, casual, random, additional, adventive, **2.** exogenous; *synonyms* (*adj*) endogenous, exogenetic, extogenous, secondary, **3.** outside; *synonyms* (*adj*) external, out, outdoor, (*adv*) outdoors, (*n*) exterior; *antonyms* (*prep*) inside, in, (*adj*) indoor, internal, (*adv*) indoors.

utanæðablæðing extravasation; *synonyms* (*n*) effusion, exhalation, leakage, oozing, percolation.

utankaup outsourcing; *synonym* (*n*) relocation.

utanlands 1. abroad; *synonyms* (*adv*) away, afield, forth, (*adj*) overseas, out, **2.** offshore; *synonym* (*adj*) foreign, **3.** overseas; *synonyms* (*adj*) across, distant, transpacific, (*adv*) abroad, oversea.

utanmál circumference; *synonyms* (*n*) circuit, border, boundary, perimeter, brim.

utanríkisstefna policy; *synonyms* (*n*) course, plan, approach, insurance, tactics.

utanverður 1. outside; *synonyms* (*adj*) external, out, outdoor, (*adv*) outdoors, (*n*) exterior; *antonyms* (*prep*) inside, in, (*adj*) indoor, internal, (*adv*) indoors, **2.** external; *synonyms* (*adj*) outside, extraneous, extrinsic, outward, foreign; *antonyms* (*adj*) inner, interior, domestic, inmost.

uxi ox; *synonyms* (*n*) cattle, kine, capon, stot, oaf.

Ú

úða 1. sprinkle; *synonyms* (*v*) scatter, drizzle, splash, moisten, cast, **2.** spray; *synonyms* (*n*) jet, mist, froth, aerosol, atomizer.

úðabað douche; *synonyms* (*n*) shower, bath, (*v*) affusion, irrigation, flush.

úðari nozzle; *synonyms* (*n*) nose, beak, hooter, jet, muzzle.

úðastútur nozzle; *synonyms* (*n*) nose, beak, hooter, jet, muzzle.

úðatæki inhaler; *synonyms* (*n*) inhalator, respirator.

úði 1. spray; *synonyms* (*n*) jet, mist, froth, aerosol, atomizer, **2.** drizzle; *synonyms* (*n*) rainfall, (*v*) mizzle, rain, spray, drip; *antonym* (*v*) pour, **3.** mist; *synonyms* (*n*) fog, cloud, (*v*) blur, befog, cover.

úðun atomization; *synonyms* (*n*) atomisation, spraying, decomposition, fragmentation, nebulization.

úldinn putrid; *synonyms* (*adj*) foul, fetid, malodorous, rotten, corrupt; *antonym* (*adj*) fresh.

úlfaldi camel; *synonyms* (*n*) beige, elephant, llama, (*adj*) fawn, buff.

úlfur wolf; *synonyms* (*n*) philanderer, beast, (*v*) devour, gobble, gorge.

úllinseyra auricle; *synonyms* (*n*) ear, pinna, heart, capitulum, (*v*) lug.

úlnliður wrist; *synonyms* (*n*) carpus, (*v*) finger, hand, paw.

úlundseyra auricle; *synonyms* (*n*) ear, pinna, heart, capitulum, (*v*) lug.

únsa ounce; *synonyms* (*n*) iota, atom, crumb, modicum, (*adj*) grain.

úr 1. watch; *synonyms* (*v*) observe, clock, (*n*) guard, view, sentinel, **2.** clock; *synonyms* (*n*) alarm, chronograph, (*v*) time, measure, stopwatch, **3.** lymph; *synonyms* (*n*) crystal, glass, (*adj*) rheum, sanies, serosity.

úrættun degeneracy; *synonyms* (*n*) corruption, decadence, depravity, degeneration, decline.

úran uranium; *synonyms* (*v*) radiation, radioactivity, tritium, plutonium, radium.

úraníum uranium; *synonyms* (*v*) radiation, radioactivity, tritium, plutonium, radium.

úrbræðsla 1. seizure; *synonyms* (*n*) arrest, capture, confiscation, seizing, apprehension; *antonyms* (*n*) release, return, **2.** freezing; *synonyms* (*adj*) cold, icy, arctic, chilly, (*n*) freeze; *antonyms* (*adj*) boiling, hot, sweltering, red-hot, warm.

úrdráttur extraction; *synonyms* (*n*) descent, ancestry, birth, origin, family; *antonym* (*n*) insertion.

úrefni derivative; *synonyms* (*adj*) derived, (*n*) derivate, derivation, differential, offshoot; *antonym* (*n*) original.

úrelt obsolete; *synonyms* (*adj*) antiquated, dead, ancient, antique, archaic; *antonyms* (*adj*) current, contemporary, modern.

úreltur obsolete; *synonyms* (*adj*) antiquated, dead, ancient, antique, archaic; *antonyms* (*adj*) current, contemporary, modern.

úrfall fallout; *synonyms* (*n*) effect, consequence, consequences, outcome, repercussion.

úrfelling 1. deficiency; *synonyms* (*n*) defect, dearth, want, absence, (*adj*) blemish; *antonyms* (*n*) excess, sufficiency, **2.** deletion; *synonyms* (*n*) cancellation, cut, annulment, elimination, omission; *antonym* (*n*) addition, **3.** misfire; *synonyms* (*n*) flop, dud, (*v*) fail, miscarry, fizzle.

úrgangsefni excretion; *synonyms* (*n*) discharge, elimination, evacuation, excrement, excreta.

úrgangshaugur stockpile; *synonyms* (*n*) reserve, heap, (*v*) stock, hoard, store.

úrgangslosun excretion; *synonyms* (*n*) discharge, elimination, evacuation, excrement, excreta.

úrgangur 1. waste; *synonyms* (*n*) desert, (*adj*) spoil, desolate, (*v*) consume, exhaust; *antonyms* (*v*) conserve, save, **2.** scrap; *synonyms* (*n*) fight, morsel, brawl, remnant, (*adj*) fragment; *antonym* (*v*) keep.

úrhluta extract; *synonyms* (*n*) excerpt, (*v*) draw, abstract, derive, educe.

úrhlutun extraction; *synonyms* (*n*) descent, ancestry, birth, origin, family; *antonym* (*n*) insertion.

úrkoma precipitation; *synonyms* (*n*) hurry, rain, precipitancy, downfall, haste.

úrkomusafnmælir totalizer; *synonyms* (*n*) totalizator, totalisator, totaliser.

úrkomuskortur drought; *synonyms* (*n*) famine, parchedness, absence, dryness, (*adj*) aridity; *antonym* (*n*) wetness.

úrkomuský nimbus; *synonyms* (*n*) halo, glory, aureole, aura, (*v*) flush.

úrkomusnauður arid; *synonyms* (*adj*) dry, dull, barren, boring, (*v*) monotonous; *antonyms* (*adj*) wet, verdant.

úrkynjun degeneration; *synonyms* (*n*) decay, corruption, decline, degeneracy, abasement; *antonyms* (*n*) improvement, growth.

úrlausn solution; *synonyms* (*n*) dissolution, resolution, answer, settlement, resolve.

úrlausnarefni problem; *synonyms* (*n*) bother, conundrum, difficulty, trouble, knot.

úrnám resection; *synonym* (*v*) section.

úrræði 1. strategy; *synonyms* (*n*) dodge, plan, scheme, strategics, (*v*) tactics, **2.** expedient; *synonyms* (*adj*) fit, adequate, advisable, (*n*) contrivance, makeshift.

úrrek 1. punch; *synonyms* (*n*) jab, drill, (*v*) poke, hit, prick, **2.** mandrel; *synonyms* (*n*) arbor, spindle, axle, hinge, bobbin.

úrskurða 1. rule; *synonyms* (*n*) govern, order, decree, (*v*) command, control, **2.** hold; *synonyms* (*v*) keep, detain, endure, (*n*) grasp, grip; *antonym* (*v*) release.

úrskurður 1. arbitration; *synonyms* (*n*) arbitrament, mediation, decision, intervention, judgment, **2.** decision; *synonyms* (*n*) conclusion, determination, resolution, sentence, verdict.

úrslitaatriði determinant; *synonyms* (*n*) clincher, determiner, (*adj*) crucial, determinative, conclusive.

úrsnari countersink; *synonyms* (*v*) adjust, arrange, coif, coiffe, (*n*) counterbore.

úrsnörun 1. undercut; *synonyms* (*v*) challenge, (*n*) cut, tenderloin, cutting, deletion, **2.** recess; *synonyms* (*n*) corner, break, holiday, intermission, niche, **3.** counterbore; *synonym* (*n*) countersink.

úrsögn withdrawal; *synonyms* (*n*) removal, retirement, retreat, secession, departure.

úrtak 1. sample; *synonyms* (*n*) example, instance, specimen, model, pattern, **2.** slot; *synonyms* (*n*) groove, place, notch, gap, (*v*) slit, **3.** recess; *synonyms* (*n*) corner, break, holiday, intermission, niche, **4.** notch; *synonyms* (*n*) cut, mark, (*v*) dent, hack, indent.

úrtaka sampling; *synonyms* (*n*) sample, example, case, poll, taste.

úrtekinn slot; *synonyms* (*n*) groove, place, notch, gap, (*v*) slit.

úrval 1. selection; *synonyms* (*n*) election, choice, option, alternative, extract, **2.** assortment; *synonyms* (*n*) miscellany, range, set, variety, categorization, **3.** elite; *synonyms* (*n*) cream, best, pick, prime, (*adj*) flower.

úrvalsstefna eclecticism; *synonyms* (*n*) electicism, exception, gleaning, selection.

úrvötnun dehydration; *synonyms* (*n*) evaporation, desiccation, drought, dryness, dewatering; *antonym* (*n*) wetness.

út 1. peripheral; *synonyms* (*adj*) exterior, outer, external, marginal, extraneous; *antonyms* (*adj*) central, vital, **2.** forth; *synonyms* (*adv*) along, away, forward, ahead, onward, **3.** out; *synonyms* (*adv*) off, beyond, (*v*) reveal, (*adj*) extinct, outside; *antonyms* (*adv*) in, (*prep*) inside.

útæð artery; *synonyms* (n) vein, corridor, road, thoroughfare, aisle.

útæxlun 1. outbreeding, 2. exogamy; *synonyms* (n) intermarriage, endogamy, inmarriage.

útblámi ultraviolet; *synonyms* (adj) purple, violet.

útblár ultraviolet; *synonyms* (adj) purple, violet.

útblástur 1. outlet; *synonyms* (n) shop, market, egress, exit, opening, 2. emission; *synonyms* (n) discharge, emanation, effusion, ejection, venting, 3. exhaust; *synonyms* (v) consume, drain, spend, empty, tire; *antonyms* (v) conserve, refresh, invigorate.

útblástursgas exhaust; *synonyms* (v) consume, drain, spend, empty, tire; *antonyms* (v) conserve, refresh, invigorate.

útboð 1. tender; *synonyms* (adj) affectionate, painful, (v) proffer, (n) offer, bid; *antonyms* (adj) tough, hard, hardhearted, rubbery, rough, 2. bid; *synonyms* (n) tender, attempt, (v) ask, call, command.

útboðslýsing prospectus; *synonyms* (n) program, programme, catalogue, plan, syllabus.

útboðssamningur contract; *synonyms* (n) compact, charter, (v) covenant, bargain, (adj) abridge; *antonyms* (v) expand, widen, stretch.

útborg suburb; *synonyms* (n) outskirts, suburbia, community, neighborhood, environs.

útborun 1. bore; *synonyms* (v) dig, bother, tire, annoy, (n) caliber; *antonyms* (v) interest, excite, fascinate, 2. boring; *synonyms* (adj) dull, tedious, tiresome, annoying, (n) drilling; *antonyms* (adj) exciting, fascinating, interesting, gripping, original.

útbreiðsla 1. propagation; *synonyms* (n) distribution, diffusion, generation, dissemination, extension, 2. diffusion; *synonyms* (n) dispersion, dispersal, spread, circulation, dissipation, 3. distribution; *synonyms* (n) dispensation, delivery, deal, allotment, apportionment; *antonym* (n) concentration, 4. circulation; *synonyms* (n) currency, gyration, revolution, rotation, round.

útbreiðslustarf promotion; *synonyms* (n) furtherance, advance, advancement, advertising, boost; *antonyms* (n) demotion, neglect.

útbrot rash; *synonyms* (adj) foolhardy, imprudent, heedless, (n) hasty, eruption; *antonyms* (adj) cautious, careful, sensible, considered, deliberate.

útbruni burnout; *synonyms* (n) exhaustion, fatigue, (v) blowout, disintegration, meltdown.

útbúa 1. establish; *synonyms* (v) confirm, erect, prove, appoint, base; *antonyms* (v) disprove, abolish, terminate, 2. equip; *synonyms* (v) clothe, furnish, accommodate, dress, accoutre.

útbúnaður 1. equipment; *synonyms* (n) material, apparatus, facility, gear, (v) furniture, 2. outfit;

synonyms (n) dress, garb, kit, apparel, (v) equipment.

útburður eviction; *synonyms* (n) dispossession, expulsion, ejection, exclusion, deportation.

útdauði extinction; *synonyms* (n) destruction, extermination, end, expiration, (v) death; *antonyms* (n) survival, preservation.

útdindill overshoot; *synonyms* (v) overrun, jump.

útdráttarrúlla roller; *synonyms* (n) roll, cylinder, billow, curler, wave.

útdráttarvalti roller; *synonyms* (n) roll, cylinder, billow, curler, wave.

útdráttur 1. summary; *synonyms* (n) abstract, compendium, abridgment, (adj) brief, compendious, 2. abstract; *synonyms* (adj) theoretical, (v) abridge, (n) synopsis, abridgement, digest; *antonym* (adj) concrete, 3. abstraction; *synonyms* (n) abstractedness, reverie, engrossment, extraction, removal; *antonyms* (n) addition, attentiveness, 4. extraction; *synonyms* (n) descent, ancestry, birth, origin, family; *antonym* (n) insertion, 5. extract; *synonyms* (n) excerpt, (v) draw, derive, educe, elicit.

úteyra 1. pinna; *synonyms* (n) auricle, ear, capitulum, feather, pinnule, 2. auricle; *synonyms* (n) pinna, heart, spike, (v) lug.

útfærsla extraction; *synonyms* (n) descent, ancestry, birth, origin, family; *antonym* (n) insertion.

útfall 1. precipitate; *synonyms* (n) deposit, (adj) hasty, headlong, impetuous, sudden, 2. ebb; *synonyms* (n) wane, (v) dwindle, abate, decline, decrease; *antonym* (v) tide.

útfarandi outgoing; *synonyms* (adj) friendly, expansive, forthcoming, gregarious, demonstrative; *antonyms* (adj) inward, next, reserved, incoming, introverted.

útfelling 1. precipitation; *synonyms* (n) hurry, rain, precipitancy, downfall, haste, 2. deposit; *synonyms* (n) charge, (v) bank, commit, store, fix; *antonym* (v) withdraw, 3. gum; *synonyms* (n) gingiva, paste, mucilage, (v) glue, cement.

útferð exudation; *synonyms* (n) sweating, exhalation, sweat, transudation, exudate.

útfjólublár ultraviolet; *synonyms* (adj) purple, violet.

útflæði effusion; *synonyms* (n) effluence, efflux, ejection, emanation, emission.

útflutningur export; *synonyms* (n) exportation, business, (v) import, trade, smuggle.

útflygsun coagulation; *synonyms* (n) clotting, clot, flocculation, curdling, (adj) concretion.

útflytjandi emigrant; *synonyms* (n) immigrant, expatriate, emigre, emigree, migrant.

útfrymi 1. cortex; *synonyms* (n) bark, crust, peel, rind, pallium, 2. ectoplasm; *synonyms* (n) ectosarc, cell, psychoplasm.

útgáfa 1. publication; *synonyms* (*n*) announcement, book, issue, newspaper, periodical, **2.** version; *synonyms* (*n*) reading, translation, construction, interpretation, rendering, **3.** edition; *synonyms* (*n*) version, print, circulation, copy, number, **4.** flotation; *synonyms* (*n*) floatation, support, **5.** issue; *synonyms* (*n*) aftermath, egress, (*v*) flow, emanate, arise.

útgáfudagur currency; *synonyms* (*n*) cash, money, coin, circulation, vogue.

útgangur 1. exit; *synonyms* (*n*) departure, door, egress, (*v*) depart, go; *antonyms* (*n*) arrival, entry, (*v*) enter, **2.** outlet; *synonyms* (*n*) shop, market, exit, opening, store.

útgeislun emission; *synonyms* (*n*) discharge, emanation, effusion, ejection, venting.

útgiskun extrapolation; *synonym* (*n*) projection.

útgjöld expenditure; *synonyms* (*n*) charge, cost, disbursement, consumption, expense; *antonyms* (*n*) income, savings.

útgufun 1. transpiration; *synonyms* (*n*) development, occurrence, **2.** expiration; *synonyms* (*n*) ending, conclusion, end, finish, breath.

úthelling effusion; *synonyms* (*n*) effluence, efflux, ejection, emanation, emission.

úthenda handout; *synonyms* (*n*) brochure, pamphlet, flyer, leaflet, release.

úthjúpur adventitia; *synonym* (*n*) tunic.

úthljóð ultrasound; *synonyms* (*n*) sonography, ultrasonography.

úthluta 1. assign; *synonyms* (*v*) allot, apportion, delegate, allow, apply, **2.** allocate; *synonyms* (*v*) divide, set, place, assign, award.

úthlutun allocation; *synonyms* (*n*) allotment, portion, allowance, quota, share.

úthverfa extroversion; *synonyms* (*n*) extraversion, sociability, unreservedness, companionability, conviviality.

úthverfi 1. suburb; *synonyms* (*n*) outskirts, suburbia, community, neighborhood, environs, **2.** suburbia; *synonym* (*n*) suburb.

úthverfing eversion; *synonyms* (*n*) everting, inversion, introversion, retroversion, reversion.

úthverfur 1. extrovert; *synonyms* (*adj*) extroverted, outgoing, extraverted, extravertive, (*n*) extravert; *antonym* (*n*) introvert, **2.** inverted; *synonyms* (*adj*) inverse, upside-down, anatropous, backward, overturned; *antonym* (*adj*) upright.

úthýsing outsourcing; *synonym* (*n*) relocation.

úti 1. out; *synonyms* (*adv*) off, forward, beyond, (*v*) reveal, (*adj*) away; *antonyms* (*adv*) in, (*prep*) inside, **2.** outside; *synonyms* (*adj*) external, out, outdoor, (*adv*) outdoors, (*n*) exterior; *antonyms* (*adj*) indoor,

internal, (*adv*) indoors, **3.** abroad; *synonyms* (*adv*) afield, forth, farther, further, (*adj*) overseas.

útibú branch; *synonyms* (*n*) arm, jump, wing, affiliate, (*v*) fork.

útiloka exclude; *synonyms* (*v*) banish, bar, eject, except, expel; *antonyms* (*v*) include, incorporate, admit, comprise, permit.

útilokun exclusion; *synonyms* (*n*) exception, banishment, elimination, debarment, expulsion; *antonyms* (*n*) inclusion, addition, entitlement.

útistandandi due; *synonyms* (*adj*) appropriate, (*adv*) right, (*v*) owing, (*n*) debt, duty; *antonyms* (*adj*) paid, undue.

útivistarsvæði park; *synonyms* (*n*) garden, common, (*v*) deposit, locate, place.

útjaðar 1. periphery; *synonyms* (*n*) perimeter, fringe, border, bound, boundary; *antonym* (*n*) center, **2.** extremity; *synonyms* (*n*) end, extreme, member, close, appendage; *antonym* (*n*) middle.

útjöfnun 1. neutralization; *synonyms* (*n*) neutralisation, counteraction, nullification, annulment, chagrin, **2.** levelling; *synonyms* (*n*) leveling, equalization, evening, flow.

útkast ejection; *synonyms* (*n*) exclusion, expulsion, ejectment, discharge, eviction; *antonym* (*n*) addition.

útkastarahringur ejector; *synonyms* (*n*) knockout, eductor, ouster, ousting, pusher.

útkastarastautur ejector; *synonyms* (*n*) knockout, eductor, ouster, ousting, pusher.

útkastari ejector; *synonyms* (*n*) knockout, eductor, ouster, ousting, pusher.

útkoma 1. result; *synonyms* (*n*) consequence, fruit, issue, outcome, (*v*) ensue; *antonym* (*v*) cause, **2.** output; *synonyms* (*n*) crop, harvest, turnout, yield, outturn.

útkulnun burnout; *synonyms* (*n*) exhaustion, fatigue, (*v*) blowout, disintegration, meltdown.

útlag ectoderm; *synonyms* (*n*) ectoblast, coat, exoderm.

útlán 1. credit; *synonyms* (*n*) credence, appreciation, belief, (*v*) believe, accredit; *antonyms* (*n*) cash, (*v*) debit, discredit, **2.** loan; *synonyms* (*n*) credit, loanword, (*v*) advance, lend, trust; *antonym* (*v*) borrow.

útleiðsla 1. deduction; *synonyms* (*n*) allowance, conclusion, discount, abatement, decrease; *antonym* (*n*) addition, **2.** derivation; *synonyms* (*n*) ancestry, origin, birth, cause, derivative.

útlelga rental; *synonyms* (*n*) hire, lease, letting, renting, apartment.

útlendingur 1. alien; *synonyms* (*adj*) foreign, strange, unknown, (*n*) foreigner, (*v*) alienate; *antonyms* (*adj*) familiar, (n) native, citizen, **2**. foreigner; *synonyms* (n) alien, stranger, outlander, outsider, barbarian.

útlendur 1. alien; *synonyms* (adj) foreign, strange, unknown, (n) foreigner, (v) alienate; *antonyms* (adj) familiar, (n) native, citizen, **2**. offshore, **3**. foreign; *synonyms* (adj) alien, extraneous, extrinsic, exotic, exterior; *antonyms* (adj) domestic, internal, **4**. overseas; *synonyms* (adj) across, away, (adv) abroad, oversea, afield.

útlimur 1. appendage; *synonyms* (n) addition, accessory, adjunct, appendix, increment, **2**. limb; *synonyms* (n) arm, bough, branch, member, extremity, **3**. extremity; *synonyms* (n) end, extreme, boundary, bound, close; *antonym* (n) middle.

útlína 1. edge; *synonyms* (n) boundary, margin, verge, (v) border, bound; *antonyms* (n) center, (v) middle, **2**. contour; *synonyms* (n) form, outline, profile, shape, configuration, **3**. outline; *synonyms* (n) sketch, design, edge, (v) draft, line.

útlínur 1. profile; *synonyms* (n) contour, outline, form, figure, shape, **2**. contour; *synonyms* (n) profile, configuration, line, silhouette, circuit.

útlista 1. elucidate; *synonyms* (v) clarify, enlighten, explain, expound, illuminate; *antonyms* (v) confuse, obfuscate, **2**. explain; *synonyms* (v) comment, elucidate, interpret, account, decipher.

útlistun specification; *synonyms* (n) designation, provision, stipulation, particular, condition.

útlit style; *synonyms* (n) fashion, name, (v) call, entitle, (adj) manner.

útlitsfræði morphology; *synonyms* (n) accidence, anatomy, geomorphology, taxonomy, botany.

útlitsmynd projection; *synonyms* (n) bulge, hump, jut, prominence, protuberance.

útloftun ventilation; *synonyms* (n) airing, exploitation, discussion, deliberation, air.

útmægðir exogamy; *synonyms* (n) intermarriage, endogamy, inmarriage.

útmörk periphery; *synonyms* (n) perimeter, fringe, border, bound, boundary; *antonym* (n) center.

útnefna constitute; *synonyms* (v) compose, form, make, commission, appoint.

útnefning 1. constitution; *synonyms* (n) composition, code, makeup, organization, temperament, **2**. appointment; *synonyms* (n) assignment, date, designation, engagement, fitting.

útöndun 1. expiration; *synonyms* (n) ending, conclusion, end, finish, breath, **2**. exhalation; *synonyms* (n) emanation, expiration, emission, fumes, vapor.

útprent printout; *synonym* (n) blowback.

útrænn exogenous; *synonyms* (adj) endogenous, exogenetic, extogenous, secondary.

útrás 1. vent; *synonyms* (n) outlet, exit, discharge, opening, (v) air, **2**. outfall; *synonyms* (n) overfall, quarrel.

útreikningur calculation; *synonyms* (n) reckoning, account, analysis, arithmetic, computation; *antonym* (n) estimation.

útrekstur exclusion; *synonyms* (n) exception, banishment, elimination, debarment, expulsion; *antonyms* (n) inclusion, addition, entitlement.

útrennsli outlet; *synonyms* (n) shop, market, egress, exit, opening.

útrennslisop outlet; *synonyms* (n) shop, market, egress, exit, opening.

útröð exon; *synonym* (n) exempt.

útrýming extinction; *synonyms* (n) destruction, extermination, end, expiration, (v) death; *antonyms* (n) survival, preservation.

útsæði seed; *synonyms* (n) germ, issue, posterity, root, (v) inseminate.

útsækinn efferent; *synonyms* (adj) centrifugal, motorial.

útsala sale; *synonyms* (n) fair, disposal, demand, market, vend.

útsending 1. transmission; *synonyms* (n) circulation, conveyance, contagion, transfer, broadcast, **2**. emission; *synonyms* (n) discharge, emanation, effusion, ejection, venting.

útsetning representation; *synonyms* (n) image, performance, depiction, picture, presentation.

útskjár repeater; *synonyms* (n) recidivist, criminal, revolver, (v) floater, keener.

útskolun leaching; *synonyms* (n) leach, lixiviation, bleeding, leak, leakage.

útskot 1. protrusion; *synonyms* (n) projection, bulge, prominence, protuberance, bump, **2**. oriel; *synonyms* (n) corner, cove, crypt, niche, nook.

útskotsgluggi oriel; *synonyms* (n) corner, cove, crypt, niche, nook.

útskrið skid; *synonyms* (n) shoe, sideslip, (v) slip, slide, glide.

útskrift printout; *synonym* (n) blowback.

útskúfun exclusion; *synonyms* (n) exception, banishment, elimination, debarment, expulsion; *antonyms* (n) inclusion, addition, entitlement.

útskýra 1. elucidate; *synonyms* (v) clarify, enlighten, explain, expound, illuminate; *antonyms* (v) confuse, obfuscate, **2**. explain; *synonyms* (v) comment, elucidate, interpret, account, decipher.

útslag 1. amplitude; *synonyms* (n) breadth, latitude, magnitude, width, mass, **2**. deflection; *synonyms* (n) deviation, bend, deflexion, variation, bending.

útsláttarflækja complex; *synonyms* (*adj*) composite, complicate, abstruse, difficult, elaborate; *antonyms* (*adj*) simple, basic, straightforward, clear, plain.

útsláttur 1. release; *synonyms* (*n*) discharge, (*v*) exempt, free, liberate, (*adj*) disengage; *antonyms* (*n*) imprisonment, abduction, (*v*) capture, confine, imprison, **2.** eruption; *synonyms* (*n*) blast, burst, outbreak, rash, (*adj*) detonation, **3.** opening; *synonyms* (*n*) gap, mouth, aperture, break, beginning; *antonyms* (*n*) end, closing, exit, finale, (*adj*) final.

útsníkill ectoparasite; *synonyms* (*n*) ectozoa, ectozoon, epizoa, epizoon, ectozoan.

útsog aspiration; *synonyms* (*n*) aim, ambition, longing, ambitiousness, (*v*) desire.

útstæður 1. spreading; *synonyms* (*n*) diffusion, dissemination, propagation, dispersion, circulation, **2.** patent; *synonyms* (*adj*) obvious, overt, apparent, evident, manifest; *antonym* (*adj*) unclear.

útstandandi protrusion; *synonyms* (*n*) projection, bulge, prominence, protuberance, bump.

útstöð terminal; *synonyms* (*adj*) final, last, definitive, (*n*) depot, end.

útstreymi 1. effusion; *synonyms* (*n*) effluence, efflux, ejection, emanation, emission, **2.** emanation; *synonyms* (*n*) discharge, effluvium, effusion, excretion, exhalation, **3.** outflow; *synonyms* (*n*) escape, leak, leakage, flow, gush, **4.** emission; *synonyms* (*n*) venting, vent, dismission.

útstrikun deletion; *synonyms* (*n*) cancellation, cut, annulment, elimination, omission; *antonym* (*n*) addition.

útsveim effusion; *synonyms* (*n*) effluence, efflux, ejection, emanation, emission.

útsýn view; *synonyms* (*n*) look, sight, judgment, opinion, (*v*) regard.

útsýnisgreining exposure; *synonyms* (*n*) display, exposition, detection, peril, (*v*) disclosure.

útsynningsklakkar cumulonimbus; *synonym* (*n*) thundercloud.

úttak 1. termination; *synonyms* (*n*) ending, close, end, conclusion, result; *antonym* (*n*) start, **2.** terminal; *synonyms* (*adj*) final, last, definitive, endmost, (*n*) depot, **3.** tapping; *synonyms* (*n*) tap, paracentesis, tick, beating, drumbeat, **4.** tap; *synonyms* (*n*) pat, dab, hit, (*v*) knock, rap, **5.** socket; *synonyms* (*n*) cavity, alveolus, sleeve, hollow, pocket.

úttekt 1. withdrawal; *synonyms* (*n*) removal, retirement, retreat, secession, departure, **2.** review; *synonyms* (*n*) examination, critique, (*v*) check, survey, criticize, **3.** assessment; *synonyms* (*n*) appraisal, estimate, estimation, evaluation, judgment.

úttektarseðill voucher; *synonyms* (*n*) certificate, coupon, receipt, ticket, warrant.

útþekja epithelium; *synonyms* (*n*) ecderon, ecteron.

útþensla 1. dilation; *synonyms* (*n*) dilatation, expansion, swelling, growth, spread, **2.** intumescence; *synonyms* (*n*) bulge, tumefaction, dropsy, tumor, intumescency, **3.** expansion; *synonyms* (*n*) amplification, enlargement, development, (*v*) extension, augmentation; *antonyms* (*n*) contraction, decrease, reduction, abbreviation.

útþensluaðgerð dilatation; *synonyms* (*n*) dilation, expansion, distension, extension, subtilization.

útþot eruption; *synonyms* (*n*) blast, burst, outbreak, rash, (*adj*) detonation.

útþrýsting expression; *synonyms* (*n*) diction, phrase, voice, appearance, aspect; *antonym* (*n*) repression.

útþynning dilution; *synonyms* (*n*) lotion, maceration, blending, concentration, dip.

útúrkrókur excursion; *synonyms* (*n*) digression, drive, expedition, hike, jaunt.

útvær external; *synonyms* (*adj*) exterior, outside, extraneous, extrinsic, outward; *antonyms* (*adj*) inner, interior, internal, domestic, inmost.

útvarp 1. radio; *synonyms* (*n*) wireless, broadcasting, radiotelegram, (*v*) broadcast, transmit, **2.** radius; *synonyms* (*n*) length, semidiameter, spoke, range, compass, **3.** wireless; *synonyms* (*n*) radio, radiocommunication, tuner, (*v*) radiotelephone, intercom, **4.** ray; *synonyms* (*n*) beam, light, flash, glow, gleam, **5.** broadcast; *synonyms* (*v*) air, announce, circulate, disperse, (*n*) spread.

útvarpslampi 1. valve; *synonyms* (*n*) lock, sluice, door, gauge, monitor, **2.** tube; *synonyms* (*n*) pipe, conduit, duct, subway, hose.

útvarpstæki radio; *synonyms* (*n*) wireless, broadcasting, radiotelegram, (*v*) broadcast, transmit.

útvarpstækni radio; *synonyms* (*n*) wireless, broadcasting, radiotelegram, (*v*) broadcast, transmit.

útvarpsviðtæki radio; *synonyms* (*n*) wireless, broadcasting, radiotelegram, (*v*) broadcast, transmit.

útvega 1. provide; *synonyms* (*v*) give, contribute, furnish, offer, accommodate, **2.** supply; *synonyms* (*n*) provision, (*v*) stock, afford, fill, store.

útvegun provision; *synonyms* (*n*) arrangement, condition, clause, (*v*) preparation, feed; *antonym* (*n*) lack.

útverminn exothermic; *synonym* (*adj*) exothermal.

útvíkka extend; *synonyms* (*v*) expand, enlarge, amplify, broaden, dilate; *antonyms* (*v*) withdraw, shorten, limit, narrow, shrink.

útvíkkun 1. dilatation; *synonyms* (*n*) dilation, expansion, distension, extension, subtilization, **2.** extension; *synonyms* (*n*) continuation, augmentation, enlargement, addition, increase; *antonyms* (*n*) limitation, contraction, limit.

útvistun outsourcing; *synonym* (*n*) relocation.

útvöxtur apophysis; *synonyms* (*n*) process, elbow, knob, tooth, bulb.

V

vá 1. risk; *synonyms* (*n*) hazard, peril, chance, danger, gamble; *antonyms* (*n*) safety, (*v*) protect, **2.** hazard; *synonyms* (*n*) risk, venture, fortune, (*v*) endanger, adventure.

váboði alarm; *synonyms* (*n*) dismay, alert, consternation, (*v*) awe, scare; *antonyms* (*v*) calm, comfort.

vægi 1. weight; *synonyms* (*n*) load, burden, charge, consequence, heaviness; *antonym* (*n*) triviality, **2.** moment; *synonyms* (*n*) importance, flash, instant, jiffy, minute, **3.** torque; *synonyms* (*n*) torsion, broach, contortion, crookedness, pin.

vægisteinn pivot; *synonyms* (*n*) axle, axis, pin, hub, (*v*) revolve.

vændir expectations; *synonyms* (*n*) prospect, outlook, potential, opportunity.

vængbarð flap; *synonyms* (*n*) fuss, slap, (*v*) flop, beat, wave.

vængbiti spar; *synonyms* (*n*) beam, mast, (*v*) quarrel, box, fight.

vængbrík fence; *synonyms* (*n*) enclosure, barrier, hurdle, (*v*) hedge, wall.

vængendaskögun overhang; *synonyms* (*n*) projection, (*v*) beetle, jut, hang, project.

vænghaf span; *synonyms* (*n*) length, space, distance, bridge, couple.

vængildi aerofoil; *synonyms* (*n*) airfoil, surface, open.

vænglaga alar; *synonyms* (*adj*) alary, aliform, axillary, (*n*) daminozide.

vænglína chord; *synonyms* (*n*) cord, harmony, (*v*) accord, harmonise, harmonize.

vængmyndaður alar; *synonyms* (*adj*) alary, aliform, axillary, (*n*) daminozide.

vængrif rib; *synonyms* (*n*) ridge, (*v*) joke, tease, guy, mock.

vængskekkja coma; *synonyms* (*n*) lethargy, trance, dream, stupor, sleep.

vængskrið slip; *synonyms* (*n*) lapse, fault, (*v*) fall, slide, (*adj*) blunder; *antonym* (*v*) improve.

vængur wing; *synonyms* (*n*) annex, arm, fender, limb, (*v*) fly.

vænisjúkur paranoid; *synonyms* (*adj*) absorbed, engrossed, fanatical, hooked, (*n*) paranoiac.

vænisýki paranoia; *synonyms* (*n*) insanity, (*adj*) schizophrenia.

vænn 1. affable; *synonyms* (*adj*) cordial, amiable, civil, courteous, friendly; *antonyms* (*adj*) disagreeable, hostile, reserved, **2.** kind; *synonyms* (*n*) form, helpful, sort, benign, brand; *antonyms* (*adj*) unkind, callous, cruel, hardhearted, mean, **3.** kindly; *synonyms* (*adj*) kind, genial, gentle, affable, (*n*) benevolent; *antonyms* (*adv*) unkindly, harshly, callously, cruelly, nastily, **4.** friendly; *synonyms* (*adj*) favorable, affectionate, amicable, companionable, convivial; *antonyms* (*adj*) unfriendly, aggressive, aloof, distant, formal.

vænta 1. wait; *synonyms* (*v*) expect, anticipate, (*n*) delay, pause, hold, **2.** abide; *synonyms* (*v*) endure, bide, bear, brook, (*n*) stand, **3.** await; *synonyms* (*v*) abide, tarry, wait, attend, look, **4.** expect; *synonyms* (*v*) assume, believe, demand, understand, await.

væntigildi expectation; *synonyms* (*n*) anticipation, expectancy, belief, hope, prospect; *antonym* (*n*) despair.

vænting expectation; *synonyms* (*n*) anticipation, expectancy, belief, hope, prospect; *antonym* (*n*) despair.

væntingar expectations; *synonyms* (*n*) prospect, outlook, potential, opportunity.

vætl 1. seepage; *synonyms* (*n*) leak, flow, ooze, oozing, percolation, **2.** weeping; *synonyms* (*v*) lament, wailing, (*n*) lamentation, (*adj*) crying, tearful.

vætla exude; *synonyms* (*v*) emit, excrete, ooze, secrete, sweat.

vætukarsi watercress; *synonym* (*adj*) cresson.

vaf 1. winding; *synonyms* (*adj*) tortuous, indirect, twisting, (*n*) twist, wind; *antonyms* (*adj*) straight, direct, **2.** turn; *synonyms* (*n*) bend, curve, roll, coil, go.

vafalaust 1. unquestionably; *synonyms* (*adv*) certainly, undoubtedly, definitely, decidedly, (*adj*) doubtless; *antonym* (*adv*) questionably, **2.** undoubtedly; *synonyms* (*adv*) surely, indubitably, positively, clearly, unquestionably, **3.** unmistakably; *synonyms* (*adv*) manifestly, apparently, evidently, remarkably, signally, **4.** decidedly; *synonyms* (*adv*) absolutely, unequivocally, emphatically, very.

vafningar turn; *synonyms* (*n*) bend, curve, roll, coil, go.

vafningsjurt vine; *synonyms* (n) climber, creeper, bush, flower, plant.

vafningur 1. winding; *synonyms* (adj) tortuous, indirect, twisting, (n) twist, wind; *antonyms* (adj) straight, direct, **2**. spiral; *synonyms* (n) coil, helix, (adj) helical, (v) curl, loop, **3**. coil; *synonyms* (n) spiral, roll, reel, (v) circle, round; *antonym* (v) uncoil.

vag hunting; *synonyms* (n) hunt, chase, pursuit, search, (v) battue.

vagn 1. carriage; *synonyms* (n) attitude, transport, behavior, conveyance, (v) bearing, **2**. van; *synonyms* (n) caravan, vehicle, front, truck, vanguard, **3**. truck; *synonyms* (n) traffic, car, cart, (v) exchange, barter, **4**. vehicle; *synonyms* (n) medium, instrument, means, automobile, channel, **5**. waggon; *synonyms* (n) wagon, dipper, plough.

váhrif exposure; *synonyms* (n) display, exposition, detection, peril, (v) disclosure.

vakahæfni antigenicity; *synonyms* (n) immunogenicity, potency.

vaki 1. antigen, **2**. generator; *synonyms* (n) author, creator, founder, boiler, originator, **3**. hormone; *synonym* (n) contraceptive, **4**. inducer; *synonyms* (n) persuader, activator.

vakning 1. recovery; *synonyms* (n) rally, convalescence, improvement, reclamation, rescue; *antonyms* (n) decline, loss, return, **2**. activation; *synonyms* (n) activating, start, initiation, launch, awakening, **3**. induction; *synonyms* (n) inauguration, deduction, beginning, elicitation, inductance.

vakt 1. shift; *synonyms* (n) interchange, turn, (v) change, exchange, remove, **2**. spell; *synonyms* (n) magic, fascination, bout, conjuration, (v) charm.

vakta monitor; *synonyms* (v) check, regulate, control, eavesdrop, (n) admonisher.

vaktari monitor; *synonyms* (v) check, regulate, control, eavesdrop, (n) admonisher.

vakúm vacuum; *synonyms* (n) emptiness, void, vacancy, vacuity, gap.

val 1. option; *synonyms* (n) choice, election, alternative, preference, possibility; *antonyms* (n) essential, necessity, obligation, **2**. valine, **3**. selection; *synonyms* (n) option, extract, quotation, assortment, pick, **4**. selecting; *synonyms* (adj) selective, eclectic, elective, electoral, (n) selection, **5**. election; *synonyms* (n) ballot, poll, volition, vote, doom.

vala 1. puck; *synonyms* (n) fairy, imp, **2**. talus; *synonyms* (n) astragalus, slope, scree, anklebone, astragal.

valblað menu; *synonyms* (n) fare, bill, card, carte, list.

valbundinn 1. selective; *synonyms* (adj) select, particular, discriminating, elective, exclusive, **2**. facultative; *synonyms* (adj) optional, discretionary.

vald 1. power; *synonyms* (n) force, ability, potency, (v) influence, might; *antonyms* (n) powerlessness, helplessness, weakness, **2**. authority; *synonyms* (n) ascendancy, command, sanction, administration, authorization.

valdaaðili authority; *synonyms* (n) ascendancy, command, sanction, administration, authorization.

valdbærni authority; *synonyms* (n) ascendancy, command, sanction, administration, authorization.

valdbeiting discrimination; *synonyms* (n) discernment, difference, differentiation, distinction, (v) judgment; *antonym* (n) tolerance.

valddreifing 1. devolution; *synonyms* (n) degeneration, delegation, degeneracy, decadence, transfer, **2**. decentralization; *synonyms* (n) decentralisation, transference.

valdframsal delegation; *synonyms* (n) commission, delegacy, deputation, delegating, devolution.

valdmörk competence; *synonyms* (n) capacity, adequacy, ability, capability, (adj) proficiency; *antonyms* (n) incompetence, inability.

valdsvið 1. competence; *synonyms* (n) capacity, adequacy, ability, capability, (adj) proficiency; *antonyms* (n) incompetence, inability, **2**. domain; *synonyms* (n) country, department, realm, area, kingdom; *antonym* (n) range.

valfrelsi option; *synonyms* (n) choice, election, alternative, preference, possibility; *antonyms* (n) essential, necessity, obligation.

valfrjáls 1. optional; *synonyms* (adj) discretionary, arbitrary, voluntary, nonobligatory, unrestricted; *antonyms* (adj) obligatory, compulsory, required, essential, necessary, **2**. facultative; *synonyms* (adj) optional, elective.

valfrjálst optional; *synonyms* (adj) discretionary, arbitrary, voluntary, nonobligatory, unrestricted; *antonyms* (adj) obligatory, compulsory, required, essential, necessary.

valhneta walnut; *synonyms* (v) chowder, chupatty, clam, compote, damper.

valhnot walnut; *synonyms* (v) chowder, chupatty, clam, compote, damper.

vali selector; *synonyms* (n) chooser, detector, picker.

valkostur option; *synonyms* (n) choice, election, alternative, preference, possibility; *antonyms* (n) essential, necessity, obligation.

valkvæður optional; *synonyms* (adj) discretionary, arbitrary, voluntary, nonobligatory, unrestricted; *antonyms* (adj) obligatory, compulsory, required, essential, necessary.

vallarmarki marker; *synonyms* (n) brand, mark, label, token, pointer.

vallhumall yarrow; *synonyms* (n) milfoil, sassafras.

valllendi grassland; *synonyms* (n) field, meadow, pasture, plain, prairie.

valmynd menu; *synonyms* (n) fare, bill, card, carte, list.

valoraĵo assets; *synonyms* (n) property, belongings, capital, funds, means.

valréttur option; *synonyms* (n) choice, election, alternative, preference, possibility; *antonyms* (n) essential, necessity, obligation.

vals roller; *synonyms* (n) roll, cylinder, billow, curler, wave.

valsa mill; *synonyms* (n) grind, factory, grinder, manufactory, (v) crush.

valseðill menu; *synonyms* (n) fare, bill, card, carte, list.

valskífa dial; *synonyms* (n) face, control, gnomon, hourglass, (v) telephone.

valtari roller; *synonyms* (n) roll, cylinder, billow, curler, wave.

valþekja cover; *synonyms* (v) coat, conceal, top, bury, (n) blind; *antonyms* (v) reveal, expose, uncover.

valtur unstable; *synonyms* (adj) changeable, precarious, insecure, shaky, unsettled; *antonyms* (adj) stable, steady, constant.

valur falcon; *synonyms* (n) freebooter, mosstrooper, thug, harpy, shark.

valvísi selectivity; *synonym* (n) specificity.

vana 1. sterilize; *synonyms* (v) neuter, castrate, disinfect, sterilise, (adj) emasculate; *antonym* (v) contaminate, **2.** castrate; *synonyms* (v) alter, geld, desexualize, sterilize, (n) eunuch.

vanabinding fixation; *synonyms* (n) obsession, fetish, fixing, mania, complex.

vanadín vanadium; *synonyms* (n) cinque, fin, five, fivesome, pentad.

vanadíum vanadium; *synonyms* (n) cinque, fin, five, fivesome, pentad.

Vandamál problem; *synonyms* (n) bother, conundrum, difficulty, trouble, knot.

vandi problem; *synonyms* (n) bother, conundrum, difficulty, trouble, knot.

vandur 1. tough; *synonyms* (adj) hard, difficult, tenacious, strong, arduous; *antonyms* (adj) tender, easy, weak, flimsy, soft, **2.** difficult; *synonyms* (adj) awkward, demanding, burdensome, complicated, delicate; *antonyms* (adj) simple, straightforward, good-natured, rewarding, clear, **3.** hard; *synonyms* (adj) austere, bad, grave, severe, (adv) firm; *antonyms* (adj) kind, merciful, soggy, (adv) gently, lightly, **4.** inconvenient; *synonyms* (adj) annoying, disadvantageous, inopportune,

bothersome, troublesome; *antonym* (adj) convenient.

vanefnd default; *synonyms* (n) deficit, delinquency, omission, oversight, (v) fail; *antonym* (n) payment.

vanfrjósemi infertility; *synonyms* (n) sterility, dysgenesis, incompatibility, unproductiveness, antisepsis; *antonyms* (n) fertility, fruitfulness.

vangakirtilsbólga parotitis; *synonym* (n) parotiditis.

vangi cheek; *synonyms* (n) audacity, boldness, brass, face, impertinence; *antonym* (n) respect.

vangur scene; *synonyms* (n) aspect, view, background, display, (v) prospect.

vanhæfi 1. challenge; *synonyms* (n) question, defiance, (v) defy, dare, brave; *antonym* (v) obey, **2.** incompetence; *synonyms* (n) incapacity, inability, inaptitude, disqualification, inadequacy; *antonyms* (n) competence, efficiency.

vanheill morbid; *synonyms* (adj) diseased, ghoulish, gruesome, macabre, (v) sickly.

vani 1. habit; *synonyms* (n) custom, clothing, attire, character, convention, **2.** way; *synonyms* (n) course, method, path, passage, road, **3.** practice; *synonyms* (n) exercise, fashion, discipline, experience, (v) drill; *antonym* (n) performance, **4.** custom; *synonyms* (n) tradition, habit, practice, usage, use, **5.** fashion; *synonyms* (n) cut, mode, craze, (v) form, construct.

vannæring malnutrition; *synonyms* (n) undernourishment, starvation.

vanögn neutron; *synonym* (n) electricity.

vanræksla 1. negligence; *synonyms* (n) neglect, carelessness, disregard, inattention, indifference; *antonym* (n) attention, **2.** omission; *synonyms* (n) failure, error, exclusion, fault, ellipsis; *antonyms* (n) inclusion, adherence.

vanskapaður deformed; *synonyms* (adj) crooked, bent, distorted, malformed, misshapen.

vanskapanafræði teratology; *synonyms* (v) bombast, magniloquence, rodomontade, vaporing, (adj) declamation.

vanskil default; *synonyms* (n) deficit, delinquency, omission, oversight, (v) fail; *antonym* (n) payment.

vansköpun malformation; *synonyms* (n) deformity, freak, distortion, disfigurement, abnormality.

vanskráning 1. understatement; *synonyms* (n) dryness, irony, wryness, sarcasm; *antonym* (n) exaggeration, **2.** omission; *synonyms* (n) failure, error, exclusion, fault, ellipsis; *antonyms* (n) inclusion, adherence.

vanþakklátur 1. ungrateful; *synonyms* (adj) thankless, unmindful, unappreciative, unthankful, unnatural; *antonyms* (adj) grateful, thankful, **2.** unthankful; *synonyms* (adj) ungrateful, disagreeable, unacceptable, unappreciated,

ungratifying, **3**. thankless; *synonyms* (*adj*)
unrewarding, boring, distasteful, fruitless,
ingrateful.

vanþroska 1. subnormal; *synonyms* (*adj*) backward,
defective, poor, retarded, subordinate, **2**. abortive;
synonyms (*adj*) fruitless, futile, stillborn,
unsuccessful, useless; *antonym* (*adj*) successful.

vanþróun lagging; *synonyms* (*n*) insulation, cover,
(*adj*) slow, lazy, slack.

vantraust 1. suspicion; *synonyms* (*n*) apprehension,
distrust, mistrust, inkling, (*v*) doubt; *antonyms* (*n*)
trust, certainty, **2**. mistrust; *synonyms* (*n*)
suspicion, misgiving, disbelief, (*v*) suspect,
disbelieve.

vantreysta 1. suspect; *synonyms* (*v*) doubt, distrust,
mistrust, suppose, conjecture; *antonyms* (*v*) trust,
(*adj*) trustworthy, **2**. distrust; *synonyms* (*n*)
suspicion, misgiving, disbelief, (*v*) disbelieve,
discredit; *antonyms* (*n*) confidence, faith, (*v*)
believe, **3**. mistrust; *synonyms* (*n*) apprehension,
wariness, hesitation, (*v*) suspect, query.

vanvirkni 1. dysfunction; *synonyms* (*n*) disfunction,
attack, malfunction, **2**. anergy.

vanviti moron; *synonyms* (*n*) idiot, cretin, imbecile,
fool, dumbbell.

var fusc; *synonyms* (*v*) combine, amalgamate, blend,
melt, coalesce; *antonym* (*v*) separate.

vara 1. warn; *synonyms* (*v*) admonish, advise,
caution, counsel, inform, **2**. commodity;
synonyms (*n*) merchandise, article, product, object,
thing, **3**. caution; *synonyms* (*n*) advice,
carefulness, precaution, vigilance, (*v*) care;
antonyms (*n*) recklessness, carelessness, rashness.

varaafrit backup; *synonyms* (*n*) backing, substitute,
surrogate, (*adj*) alternate, spare.

varabirgðir stockpile; *synonyms* (*n*) reserve, heap,
(*v*) stock, hoard, store.

varafiskar wrasses; *synonym* (*n*) hogfishes.

varaforði reserve; *synonyms* (*n*) backup, (*v*) keep,
save, book, maintain; *antonyms* (*n*) openness,
friendliness, informality, warmth.

varahljóð labial; *synonyms* (*n*) liquid, mute.

varamaður 1. substitute; *synonyms* (*adj*)
replacement, alternative, (*n*) deputy, (*v*) alternate,
shift, **2**. deputy; *synonyms* (*n*) agent, surrogate,
delegate, substitute, ambassador, **3**. alternate;
synonyms (*v*) reciprocate, change, fluctuate,
interchange, (*n*) standby; *antonym* (*n*) original.

varamæltur labial; *synonyms* (*n*) liquid, mute.

varandi duration; *synonyms* (*n*) length, continuation,
continuance, period, standing.

varanleiki persistence; *synonyms* (*n*) perseverance,
continuity, endurance, constancy, stubbornness;
antonym (*n*) compliance.

varasjóður reserve; *synonyms* (*n*) backup, (*v*) keep,
save, book, maintain; *antonyms* (*n*) openness,
friendliness, informality, warmth.

varða 1. protect; *synonyms* (*v*) defend, keep, cover,
preserve, (*n*) guard; *antonyms* (*v*) attack, expose,
neglect, risk, **2**. defend; *synonyms* (*v*) assert,
justify, protect, advocate, champion; *antonym* (*v*)
prosecute, **3**. cover; *synonyms* (*v*) coat, conceal,
top, bury, (*n*) blind; *antonyms* (*v*) reveal, uncover,
4. milestone; *synonyms* (*n*) milepost, landmark,
event, age, happening.

varðveisla 1. preservation; *synonyms* (*n*)
conservation, maintenance, keeping, protection,
custody; *antonyms* (*n*) destruction, extinction,
release, **2**. conservation; *synonyms* (*n*)
preservation, upkeep, keep.

varðveisluefni stabilizer; *synonyms* (*n*) ballast,
inhibitor, skedge, (*adj*) additive, preservative.

varðveita 1. preserve; *synonyms* (*v*) maintain, keep,
defend, (*n*) conserve, jam; *antonym* (*v*) destroy, **2**.
conserve; *synonyms* (*v*) economize, embalm,
husband, (*n*) preserve, conserves; *antonyms* (*v*)
spend, use, waste, expend, damage.

varfærinn conservative; *synonyms* (*adj*) moderate,
bourgeois, conventional, cautious, reactionary;
antonyms (*adj*) activist, wide-ranging, (*n*) liberal,
radical.

varfærni prudence; *synonyms* (*n*) foresight, care,
caution, economy, (*adj*) discretion; *antonyms* (*n*)
foolishness, generosity, imprudence, profligacy.

varfærnisregla conservatism; *synonyms* (*n*)
maintenance, support, temperance.

vargur wolf; *synonyms* (*n*) philanderer, beast, (*v*)
devour, gobble, gorge.

varhugaverður critical; *synonyms* (*adj*) acute,
decisive, delicate, important, pressing; *antonyms*
(*adj*) complimentary, trivial, positive, flattering,
insignificant.

Varijanta variation; *synonyms* (*n*) alteration, change,
difference, divergence, mutation; *antonym* (*n*)
similarity.

varinn protected; *synonyms* (*adj*) secure, immune,
saved, secured, sheltered.

varkárnisregla conservatism; *synonyms* (*n*)
maintenance, support, temperance.

varmaaflfræði thermodynamics; *synonyms* (*n*)
thermology, thermotics.

varmaaflfræðilegur thermodynamic; *synonym*
(*adj*) thermodynamical.

varmaburður convection; *synonyms* (*n*) transfer,
(*adj*) thermal.

varmadrægur endothermic; *synonym* (*adj*)
endothermal.

varmaeining calorie; *synonym* (*n*) kilocalorie.

varmaflutningur convection; *synonyms* (*n*) transfer, (*adj*) thermal.

varmafræði thermodynamics; *synonyms* (*n*) thermology, thermotics.

varmafræðilegur thermodynamic; *synonym* (*adj*) thermodynamical.

varmagæfur exothermic; *synonym* (*adj*) exothermal.

varmagleypinn endothermic; *synonym* (*adj*) endothermal.

varmahitamælir bolometer; *synonym* (*n*) barretter.

varmaiða convection; *synonyms* (*n*) transfer, (*adj*) thermal.

varmamælir calorimeter; *synonym* (*n*) pyrometer.

varmaskiptamælir calorimeter; *synonym* (*n*) pyrometer.

varmasundrun thermolysis; *synonym* (*n*) pyrolysis.

varmi heat; *synonyms* (*n*) glow, (*v*) bake, burn, (*adj*) fever, excitement; *antonyms* (*n*) cold, chill, (*v*) cool.

varmur warm; *synonyms* (*adj*) hot, affectionate, tender, ardent, cordial; *antonyms* (*adj*) aloof, cold, unfriendly, reserved, (*v*) cool.

varna obstruct; *synonyms* (*v*) bar, block, check, (*n*) hinder, barricade; *antonyms* (*v*) encourage, facilitate, free.

varnaraðili defendant; *synonyms* (*n*) accused, litigant, party, plaintiff, prisoner.

varnarbúnaður armature; *synonyms* (*n*) armament, armaments, skeleton, frame, framework.

varnarleysi vulnerability; *synonyms* (*n*) exposure, weakness, danger, vulnerableness, defenselessness; *antonym* (*n*) invulnerability.

varningur 1. goods; *synonyms* (*n*) cargo, freight, belongings, commodity, merchandise, **2.** merchandise; *synonyms* (*n*) goods, product, (*v*) market, deal, (*adj*) commodities.

varp oviposition; *synonyms* (*n*) ovipositing, laying.

varpa 1. throw; *synonyms* (*v*) cast, fling, shed, hurl, (*n*) pitch, **2.** project; *synonyms* (*n*) design, device, (*v*) plan, contrive, jut, **3.** trawl; *synonyms* (*n*) dragnet, (*v*) angle, fish, tow, haul.

varphópur clutch; *synonyms* (*n*) clasp, (*v*) grip, clench, clinch, grab.

varsla containment; *synonyms* (*n*) control, repression, restriction.

varta 1. verruca; *synonyms* (*n*) wart, blob, papule, **2.** wart; *synonyms* (*n*) verruca, bulge, growth, tit, swelling, **3.** caruncle; *synonyms* (*n*) crest, sarcoma, caruncula, papula, pimple, **4.** mamilla; *synonyms* (*n*) mammilla, nipple, pap, teat, boob, **5.** papilla; *synonym* (*n*) knocker.

vartari bass; *synonyms* (*adj*) deep, low, resonant, (*n*) basso, (*adv*) accompaniment.

varúð 1. precaution; *synonyms* (*n*) forethought, foresight, care, discretion, prevention, **2.** caution; *synonyms* (*n*) advice, carefulness, precaution, vigilance, wariness; *antonyms* (*n*) recklessness, carelessness, rashness.

varúðarráðstöfun precaution; *synonyms* (*n*) forethought, foresight, care, discretion, prevention.

vasaljós torch; *synonyms* (*n*) flashlight, brand, light, blowlamp, blowtorch.

vásetning compromise; *synonyms* (*n*) agreement, arrangement, bargain, accommodation, (*v*) compound; *antonym* (*v*) dispute.

vasi 1. pocket; *synonyms* (*n*) cavity, pouch, (*v*) bag, take, appropriate, **2.** stove; *synonyms* (*n*) range, furnace, heater, ambit, chain.

vaskur sink; *synonyms* (*n*) sag, (*v*) decline, dip, droop, fall; *antonyms* (*v*) rise, float.

vatn 1. water; *synonyms* (*n*) urine, (*v*) irrigate, moisten, wet, soak, **2.** lake; *synonyms* (*n*) loch, pond, pool, puddle, carmine, **3.** river; *synonyms* (*n*) creek, flow, current, (*v*) brook, stream, **4.** loch; *synonyms* (*n*) bay, lake, inlet, plash, slab, **5.** mere; *synonyms* (*adj*) bare, entire, pure, simple, (*n*) downright.

vatna 1. water (vatn); *synonyms* (*n*) urine, (*v*) irrigate, moisten, wet, soak, **2.** aquatic; *synonyms* (*adj*) marine, nautical, aqueous, oceanic, watery; *antonym* (*adj*) terrestrial.

vatnableikja trout; *synonyms* (*n*) anchovies, herring, sardines, shad, smelts.

vatnaborri perch; *synonyms* (*v*) roost, light, abide, lodge, (*adj*) dwell.

vatnaður hydrated; *synonym* (*adj*) hydrous.

vatnaflekkur 1. burbot; *synonyms* (*n*) eelpout, ling, broom, cusk, lota, **2.** ling; *synonyms* (*n*) heather, burbot, pout, torsk.

vatnafræði hydrology; *synonym* (*adj*) hydrostatics.

vatnakarpi carp; *synonyms* (*v*) complain, criticize, gripe, grumble, quibble; *antonym* (*v*) praise.

vatnakrabbi crayfish; *synonyms* (*n*) crawfish, crawdad, crawdaddy, crabs, ecrevisse.

vatnaloðna smelt; *synonyms* (*v*) fuse, melt, temper, anneal, heat.

vatnamælingar hydrography; *synonym* (*n*) drainage.

vatnaskeggi barbel; *synonyms* (*n*) advance, antenna, approach, barble, feeler.

vatnaskeggur barbel; *synonyms* (*n*) advance, antenna, approach, barble, feeler.

vatnaskil watershed; *synonyms* (*n*) divide, landmark, basin, border, distinction.

vatnastúfa vole; *synonym* (*n*) fieldmouse.

vatnasvið watershed; *synonyms* (*n*) divide, landmark, basin, border, distinction.

vatnaurriði trout; *synonyms* (*n*) anchovies, herring, sardines, shad, smelts.

vatnavængildi hydrofoil; *synonyms* (*n*) hydroplane, enhancer, foil, hydrovane, seaplane.

vatns aquatic; *synonyms* (*adj*) marine, nautical, aqueous, oceanic, watery; *antonym* (*adj*) terrestrial.

vatnsblanda emulsify; *synonyms* (*v*) beat, blend, mash, soften.

vatnsblöndun emulsion; *synonyms* (*n*) balm, cream, emulsification, liquid, (*adj*) soup.

vatnsból well; *synonyms* (*adv*) right, easily, thoroughly, (*adj*) healthy, (*n*) fountain; *antonyms* (*adv*) ill, badly, poorly, (*adj*) sick, unwell.

vatnsbraut channel; *synonyms* (*n*) canal, conduit, groove, (*v*) carry, conduct.

vatnsbretti sill; *synonyms* (*n*) doorsill, ledge, threshold, rung, step.

vatnsdælustöð waterworks; *synonyms* (*n*) aqueduct, tear.

vatnsefni 1. hydrogen; *synonyms* (*n*) butane, diacetylmorphine, heroin, horse, hydrogenium, 2. h; *synonyms* (*n*) asshole, bastard, buck, bull, bullshit.

vatnselgur flood; *synonyms* (*n*) deluge, pour, (*v*) drench, flow, inundate; *antonyms* (*n*) drought, shortage, (*v*) trickle.

vatnsfælinn hydrophobic; *synonyms* (*adj*) aquaphobic, rabid.

vatnsfælni hydrophobia; *synonyms* (*n*) rabies, lyssa, madness, fury, hydrophoby.

vatnsfall stream; *synonyms* (*n*) flow, brook, (*v*) flood, (*prep*) current, course; *antonym* (*v*) trickle.

vatnsfirrtur anhydrous; *synonyms* (*adj*) dry, arid.

vatnsflæmi flood; *synonyms* (*n*) deluge, pour, (*v*) drench, flow, inundate; *antonyms* (*n*) drought, shortage, (*v*) trickle.

vatnsfræði hydrology; *synonym* (*adj*) hydrostatics.

vatnsfrír anhydrous; *synonyms* (*adj*) dry, arid.

vatnsfrítt anhydrous; *synonyms* (*adj*) dry, arid.

vatnsgufa steam; *synonyms* (*n*) mist, fog, (*v*) reek, evaporate, exhale.

vatnshaldinn hydrated; *synonym* (*adj*) hydrous.

vatnsheldur waterproof; *synonyms* (*adj*) rainproof, impervious, waterproofed, (*n*) mackintosh, raincoat; *antonym* (*adj*) permeable.

vatnshöfði hydrocephalus; *synonyms* (*n*) hydrocephaly, hydrophthalmus.

vatnshöfðun hydrocephalus; *synonyms* (*n*) hydrocephaly, hydrophthalmus.

vatnshöfuð hydrocephalus; *synonyms* (*n*) hydrocephaly, hydrophthalmus.

vatnshræðsla hydrophobia; *synonyms* (*n*) rabies, lyssa, madness, fury, hydrophoby.

vatnskassi radiator; *synonyms* (*n*) heater, stove, furnace, warmer.

vatnsklær cirrus; *synonyms* (*n*) woolpack, cirrhus, stratus, cumulus.

vatnskrani 1. tap; *synonyms* (*n*) pat, dab, hit, (*v*) knock, rap, 2. cock; *synonyms* (*n*) rooster, chicken, stack, fowl, hammer.

vatnslás thermostat; *synonym* (*n*) thermoregulator.

vatnsleiðinn permeable; *synonyms* (*adj*) pervious, porous, absorbent, spongy, gritty; *antonyms* (*adj*) impermeable, resistant, waterproof, water-resistant, watertight.

vatnsleiðsla aqueduct; *synonyms* (*n*) adit, canal, channel, conduit, duct.

vatnsósa waterlogged; *synonyms* (*adj*) soggy, sodden, damp, (*v*) crumbling, ramshackle; *antonym* (*adj*) dry.

vatnspýtingur salivation; *synonyms* (*n*) ptyalism, jellyfish, slobber, slabber.

vatnsrænn aquatic; *synonyms* (*adj*) marine, nautical, aqueous, oceanic, watery; *antonym* (*adj*) terrestrial.

vatnsrás 1. baffle; *synonyms* (*v*) discomfit, astonish, bewilder, confound, foil; *antonym* (*v*) enlighten, 2. aqueduct; *synonyms* (*n*) adit, canal, channel, conduit, duct.

vatnsrýmd storage; *synonyms* (*n*) conservation, depot, memory, preservation, retention.

vatnsskolun washing; *synonyms* (*n*) laundry, wash, laundering, lavation, cleaning.

vatnssósa waterlogged; *synonyms* (*adj*) soggy, sodden, damp, (*v*) crumbling, ramshackle; *antonym* (*adj*) dry.

vatnsstrokkur waterspout; *synonyms* (*n*) cloudburst, deluge, downpour, soaker, torrent.

vatnssúla spout; *synonyms* (*n*) jet, nozzle, (*v*) gush, spurt, spirt.

vatnsþétt waterproof; *synonyms* (*adj*) rainproof, impervious, waterproofed, (*n*) mackintosh, raincoat; *antonym* (*adj*) permeable.

vatnsþéttur 1. watertight; *synonyms* (*adj*) unassailable, waterproof, tight, firm, impregnable; *antonyms* (*adj*) permeable, indefensible, 2. waterproof; *synonyms* (*adj*) rainproof, impervious, waterproofed, (*n*) mackintosh, raincoat.

vatnsþolið waterproof; *synonyms* (*adj*) rainproof, impervious, waterproofed, (*n*) mackintosh, raincoat; *antonym* (*adj*) permeable.

vatnsþró cistern; *synonyms* (*n*) tank, container, reservoir, boiler, cisterna.

vatnsveita waterworks; *synonyms* (*n*) aqueduct, tear.

vatnsveitubrú aqueduct; *synonyms* (*n*) adit, canal, channel, conduit, duct.

vatnsveitustokkur aqueduct; *synonyms* (*n*) adit, canal, channel, conduit, duct.

vátrygging insurance; *synonyms* (*n*) assurance, guarantee, indemnity, coverage, policy.

vátryggingariðgjald premium; *synonyms* (*n*) bonus, agio, bounty, payment, extra; *antonym* (*adj*) inferior.

vátryggingarskírteini policy; *synonyms* (*n*) course, plan, approach, insurance, tactics.

vátryggja 1. underwrite; *synonyms* (*v*) guarantee, insure, subscribe, cover, indemnify, **2.** insure; *synonyms* (*v*) assure, secure, ensure, underwrite, ascertain.

vátryggjandi 1. underwriter; *synonyms* (*n*) insurer, sponsor, attorney, backer, bailiff, **2.** insurer; *synonyms* (*n*) underwriter, ensurer, insurancer.

vatt watt; *synonyms* (*n*) tungsten, w, west, wolfram.

vax 1. wax; *synonyms* (*n*) increase, (*v*) grow, become, rise, mount, **2.** paraffin; *synonyms* (*n*) alkane, spermaceti, (*v*) wax, (*adj*) unreactivity.

vaxa 1. wax; *synonyms* (*n*) increase, (*v*) grow, become, rise, mount, **2.** accrue; *synonyms* (*v*) accumulate, collect, fall, result, yield, **3.** grow; *synonyms* (*v*) advance, augment, develop, enlarge, expand; *antonyms* (*v*) decrease, weaken, shrink.

vaxandi 1. progressive; *synonyms* (*adj*) advanced, forward, gradual, active, (*n*) liberal; *antonyms* (*adj*) old-fashioned, traditional, (*n*) conservative, **2.** crescent; *synonyms* (*n*) arc, arcade, arch, bow, carve.

vaxtaálag margin; *synonyms* (*n*) edge, brink, boundary, hem, (*v*) border; *antonym* (*n*) center.

vaxtabréf bond; *synonyms* (*n*) association, tie, alliance, deed, (*v*) bind.

vaxtagjöld interest; *synonyms* (*n*) concern, advantage, affair, (*v*) engage, care; *antonyms* (*n*) indifference, apathy, (*v*) bore.

vaxtahámark cap; *synonyms* (*n*) cover, bonnet, lid, capital, (*v*) top.

vaxtakragi collar; *synonyms* (*n*) arrest, choker, (*v*) catch, apprehend, capture.

vaxtaþak cap; *synonyms* (*n*) cover, bonnet, lid, capital, (*v*) top.

vébönd 1. domain; *synonyms* (*n*) country, department, realm, area, kingdom; *antonym* (*n*) range, **2.** association; *synonyms* (*n*) affiliation, alliance, connection, assembly, affinity.

veð 1. collateral; *synonyms* (*adj*) secondary, (*n*) warranty, guarantee, mortgage, guaranty, **2.** mortgage; *synonyms* (*n*) gage, (*v*) bond, pawn, pledge, impawn.

veðja 1. wager; *synonyms* (*n*) bet, stake, venture, (*v*) hazard, risk, **2.** bet; *synonyms* (*v*) gamble, play, lay, (*n*) wager, stakes.

veðrahvolf troposphere; *synonyms* (*n*) air, atmosphere.

veðrátta climate; *synonyms* (*n*) atmosphere, clime, ambience, latitude, environment.

veðrun 1. weathering; *synonym* (*n*) ageing, **2.** ageing; *synonyms* (*n*) aging, maturing, ripening, senescence, curing.

veðsetja mortgage; *synonyms* (*n*) gage, (*v*) bond, pawn, pledge, impawn.

veður 1. weather; *synonyms* (*v*) endure, survive, resist, withstand, brave, **2.** wind; *synonyms* (*v*) coil, twist, curl, meander, turn.

veðurathugunarmaður observer; *synonyms* (*n*) beholder, bystander, spectator, witness, eyewitness.

veðurfar 1. weather; *synonyms* (*v*) endure, survive, resist, withstand, brave, **2.** climate; *synonyms* (*n*) atmosphere, clime, ambience, latitude, environment.

veðurfarsfræði climatology; *synonym* (*n*) meteorology.

veðurfarslegur climatic; *synonyms* (*adj*) climatical, climatal, crucial.

veðurfarssaga paleoclimatology; *synonym* (*n*) palaeoclimatology.

veðurfyrirbæri meteor; *synonyms* (*n*) aerolite, effluvium, emanation, evaporation, exhalation.

veðurlag climate; *synonyms* (*n*) atmosphere, clime, ambience, latitude, environment.

veðurspá forecast; *synonyms* (*v*) presage, anticipate, augur, calculate, portend.

veðurspjall briefing; *synonyms* (*n*) instruction, announcement, communication, direction, instructions.

vefenging challenge; *synonyms* (*n*) question, defiance, (*v*) defy, dare, brave; *antonym* (*v*) obey.

vefeyðandi caustic; *synonyms* (*adj*) biting, acrid, bitter, acrimonious, sharp; *antonyms* (*adj*) mild, gentle.

vefeyðir caustic; *synonyms* (*adj*) biting, acrid, bitter, acrimonious, sharp; *antonyms* (*adj*) mild, gentle.

veffetill sling; *synonyms* (*n*) cast, (*v*) catapult, pitch, fling, (*adj*) hang.

vefja 1. winding; *synonyms* (*adj*) tortuous, indirect, twisting, (*n*) twist, wind; *antonyms* (*adj*) straight, direct, **2.** spiral; *synonyms* (*n*) coil, helix, (*adj*) helical, (*v*) curl, loop.

vefjaflátning dissection; *synonyms* (*n*) analysis, anatomy, autopsy, breakdown, cut.

vefjafræði histology; *synonyms* (*n*) anatomy, histiology.

vefjagula xanthophyll; *synonyms* (*n*) xanthophyl, lutein.

vefjahrúður vegetation; *synonyms* (*n*) flora, growth, plants, foliage, quietism.

vefjamarr crepitation; *synonyms* (*n*) crackle, crackling, crackleware, (*v*) decrepitation.

vefjaöndun respiration; *synonyms* (*n*) breathing, aspiration, inspiration, delay, exercising.

vefjasýni biopsy; *synonyms* (*n*) analysis, radiology, examination, urinalysis.

veflíkur webbed; *synonyms* (*adj*) lacy, netlike, netted, keld, lacelike.

vefnaður 1. web; *synonyms* (*n*) mesh, network, tissue, lattice, (*v*) net, **2.** fabric; *synonyms* (*n*) building, cloth, composition, frame, (*v*) edifice.

vefrænn organic; *synonyms* (*adj*) constitutional, natural, constitutive, fundamental, constituent; *antonym* (*adj*) refined.

vefskemmd lesion; *synonyms* (*n*) injury, wound, abrasion, scrape, scratch.

vefsprang surfing; *synonyms* (*n*) surfboarding, surfriding.

vefsteyping fixation; *synonyms* (*n*) obsession, fetish, fixing, mania, complex.

vefsýni biopsy; *synonyms* (*n*) analysis, radiology, examination, urinalysis.

vefsýnitaka biopsy; *synonyms* (*n*) analysis, radiology, examination, urinalysis.

vefur 1. tissue; *synonyms* (*n*) texture, web, lump, heap, (*adj*) mass, **2.** web; *synonyms* (*n*) mesh, network, tissue, lattice, (*v*) net.

vegabréf passport; *synonyms* (*n*) pass, permit, protection, identification, safeguard.

vegalengd run; *synonyms* (*v*) flow, rule, (*n*) pass, campaign, (*adj*) stream.

vegalengdarmælir odometer; *synonyms* (*n*) hodometer, mileometer, milometer, (*v*) bathometer, galvanometer.

vegamót 1. intersection; *synonyms* (*n*) cross, crossroads, crossing, crossroad, intersect, **2.** junction; *synonyms* (*n*) confluence, joint, connection, meeting, interchange.

veganlegur quantitative; *synonyms* (*adj*) some, measurable, quantitive, wholesale.

vegartilfinning ride; *synonyms* (*n*) outing, run, lift, (*v*) drive, (*adj*) bestride.

veggbrún moulding; *synonyms* (*n*) molding, modeling, mold, mould, cast.

vegghetta weathering; *synonym* (*n*) ageing.

veggjahvilft niche; *synonyms* (*n*) corner, alcove, hole, bay, recess.

veggkróna moulding; *synonyms* (*n*) molding, modeling, mold, mould, cast.

veggleysingi protoplast; *synonym* (*n*) energid.

veggrif pier; *synonyms* (*n*) dock, wharf, jetty, pillar, quay.

veggskot niche; *synonyms* (*n*) corner, alcove, hole, bay, recess.

veggtafla blackboard; *synonym* (*n*) chalkboard.

veggur wall; *synonyms* (*n*) partition, bar, barrier, bulwark, (*v*) fence.

veghefill grader; *synonyms* (*n*) backhoe, bulldozer, tractor, caterpillar, motorgrader.

vegmælir 1. log; *synonyms* (*n*) journal, record, block, diary, timber, **2.** odometer; *synonyms* (*n*) hodometer, mileometer, milometer, (*v*) bathometer, galvanometer.

vegur 1. road; *synonyms* (*n*) course, passage, track, way, (*v*) path, **2.** passage; *synonyms* (*n*) aisle, channel, corridor, gangway, hall, **3.** route; *synonyms* (*n*) road, direction, avenue, circuit, (*v*) direct, **4.** way; *synonyms* (*n*) method, route, custom, form, manner, **5.** course; *synonyms* (*n*) stream, flow, bearing, career, (*v*) run.

veiða 1. angle; *synonyms* (*n*) hook, incline, (*v*) slant, lean, tilt, **2.** catch; *synonyms* (*v*) arrest, capture, apprehend, get, (*n*) haul; *antonym* (*v*) release, **3.** hunt; *synonyms* (*n*) search, (*v*) chase, course, follow, hound, **4.** fish (fiskur); *synonyms* (*n*) bird, (*v*) angle, seek, hunt, pursue.

veiðar 1. fishery; *synonyms* (*n*) fishing, piscary, piscation, (*v*) aquarium, **2.** hunting; *synonyms* (*n*) hunt, chase, pursuit, search, (*v*) battue.

veiði 1. catch; *synonyms* (*v*) arrest, capture, hook, apprehend, get; *antonym* (*v*) release, **2.** fishing; *synonyms* (*n*) fishery, (*adj*) halieutic, (*v*) angling, coursing, hawking.

veiðistöðvun moratorium; *synonyms* (*n*) delay, suspension, deferment, respite, economy.

veiðiþjófur poacher; *synonyms* (*n*) thief, lurcher, glutton, gormandizer, smuggler.

veifa flag; *synonyms* (*n*) banner, colors, (*v*) decline, (*adj*) droop, fade.

veifill chopper; *synonyms* (*n*) ax, helicopter, cleaver, whirlybird, chop.

veikindi sickness; *synonyms* (*n*) illness, indisposition, complaint, (*v*) disease, disorder.

veiking 1. weakening; *synonyms* (*n*) exhaustion, decline, (*adj*) fading, enervating, enfeebling; *antonym* (*n*) growth, **2.** attenuation; *synonyms* (*n*) decrease, reduction, (*v*) emaciation, tabes, consumption.

veikja attenuate; *synonyms* (*v*) assuage, dilute, reduce, (*adj*) tenuous, fine; *antonym* (*v*) intensify.

veikjast impair; *synonyms* (*v*) blemish, damage, mar, degrade, corrupt.

veikstraumsmælir galvanometer; *synonyms* (*n*) rheometer, (*v*) bathometer, dynamometer, goniometer, heliometer.

veikur 1. sick; *synonyms* (*adj*) ill, queasy, ailing, indisposed, poorly; *antonyms* (*adj*) well, healthy, **2.** weak; *synonyms* (*adj*) feeble, frail, faint, flat, flimsy; *antonyms* (*adj*) strong, brave, concentrated, firm, safe, **3.** unwell; *synonyms* (*adj*) sick, sickly, unhealthy, bad, seedy; *antonym* (*adj*) fit, **4.** ailing; *synonyms* (*adj*) unwell, invalid, diseased, infirm, (*n*) illness, **5.** ill; *synonyms* (*adv*) badly, (*n*) evil, harm, complaint, hurt.

veila 1. vulnerability; *synonyms* (*n*) exposure, weakness, danger, vulnerableness, defenselessness; *antonym* (*n*) invulnerability, **2.** defect; *synonyms* (*n*) fault, blemish, blot, flaw, shortcoming, **3.** flaw; *synonyms* (*n*) defect, crevice, chink, demerit, (*v*) crack; *antonym* (*n*) strength.

veira virus; *synonyms* (*n*) bug, infection, germ, poison, venom.

veirubinding lysogeny; *synonym* (*n*) lysogenicity.

veirueyðandi antiviral; *synonyms* (*n*) analgesic, antibiotic, antiinflammatory, antiseptic, antitussive.

veirufræði virology; *synonyms* (*n*) microbiology, bacteriology, mycology.

veiruhamlandi antiviral; *synonyms* (*n*) analgesic, antibiotic, antiinflammatory, antiseptic, antitussive.

veiruhjúpur capsid; *synonym* (*n*) mirid.

veiruhylki capsid; *synonym* (*n*) mirid.

veirungur viroid; *synonym* (*n*) virusoid.

veiruskurn capsid; *synonym* (*n*) mirid.

veising excretion; *synonyms* (*n*) discharge, elimination, evacuation, excrement, excreta.

veisla 1. celebration; *synonyms* (*n*) gala, anniversary, commemoration, fair, (*adj*) dedication; *antonym* (*n*) lament, **2.** festivity; *synonyms* (*n*) feast, celebration, festival, joy, conviviality, **3.** feast; *synonyms* (*n*) banquet, dinner, entertainment, (*v*) junket, fete; *antonym* (*v*) fast, **4.** festival; *synonyms* (*n*) carnival, festivity, holiday, fête, fiesta, **5.** party; *synonyms* (*n*) gang, band, company, assembly, association.

veita 1. utility; *synonyms* (*n*) use, usefulness, service, value, avail, **2.** appropriate; *synonyms* (*adj*) pertinent, proper, true, (*v*) annex, allocate; *antonyms* (*adj*) inappropriate, unsuitable, unrelated, untimely, (*v*) surrender, **3.** allocate; *synonyms* (*v*) divide, apportion, set, place, allot, **4.** accreditation; *synonyms* (*n*) credentials, warrant, **5.** grant; *synonyms* (*v*) give, allow, award, bestow, admit; *antonyms* (*v*) deny, reject.

veitilína feeder; *synonyms* (*n*) eater, affluent, feed, filler, tributary.

veiting administration; *synonyms* (*n*) management, direction, organization, running, power.

veitingahús restaurant; *synonyms* (*n*) cafeteria, canteen, bistro, coffeehouse, buffet.

veititaug feeder; *synonyms* (*n*) eater, affluent, feed, filler, tributary.

veitukerfi network; *synonyms* (*n*) net, grid, mesh, netting, reticulation.

veitur facilities; *synonym* (*n*) equipment.

vekja 1. activate; *synonyms* (*v*) actuate, start, trigger, aerate, animate, **2.** induce; *synonyms* (*v*) attract, generate, cause, tempt, impel.

vektor vector; *synonyms* (*n*) direction, bearing, course, sender, transmitter.

vel 1. well; *synonyms* (*adv*) right, easily, thoroughly, (*adj*) healthy, (*n*) fountain; *antonyms* (*adv*) ill, badly, poorly, (*adj*) sick, unwell, **2.** fine; *synonyms* (*adj*) delicate, agreeable, dainty, brave, capital; *antonyms* (*adj*) poor, thick, coarse, substantial, unsatisfactory, **3.** okay; *synonyms* (*adv*) fine, (*adj*) good, (*v*) approve, sanction, consent; *antonym* (*v*) forbid.

vél 1. machine; *synonyms* (*n*) instrument, apparatus, device, implement, car, **2.** engine; *synonyms* (*n*) locomotive, machine, contrivance, mechanism, organ, **3.** mechanism; *synonyms* (*n*) machinery, appliance, action, mechanics, agency.

vélakostur plant; *synonyms* (*n*) manufactory, equipment, (*v*) fix, place, embed.

vélamaður mechanic; *synonyms* (*n*) craftsman, artificer, artisan, journeyman, machinist.

vélar machinery; *synonyms* (*n*) apparatus, machine, enginery, equipment, plant.

vélarbilun breakdown; *synonyms* (*n*) collapse, fault, analysis, failure, ruin.

vélarblokk block; *synonyms* (*n*) bar, barricade, pad, (*v*) arrest, stop; *antonyms* (*v*) free, unblock, open.

vélarhlíf 1. skirt; *synonyms* (*n*) border, edge, brim, (*v*) fringe, circumvent, **2.** shield; *synonyms* (*n*) screen, shelter, (*v*) cover, guard, safeguard; *antonym* (*v*) expose, **3.** bonnet; *synonyms* (*n*) hood, cap, tile, wimple, castor, **4.** cowl; *synonyms* (*n*) bonnet, cowling, chock, condition, cow, **5.** hood; *synonyms* (*n*) cowl, hat, coif, headdress, hoodlum.

vélbúnaður 1. apparatus; *synonyms* (*n*) appliance, device, implement, instrument, plant, **2.** machinery; *synonyms* (*n*) apparatus, machine, enginery, equipment, gear, **3.** hardware; *synonyms* (*n*) ironmongery, ironware, gun, armament, medal.

veldi 1. power; *synonyms* (*n*) force, ability, potency, (*v*) influence, might; *antonyms* (*n*) powerlessness, helplessness, weakness, **2.** domain; *synonyms* (*n*) country, department, realm, area, kingdom;

antonym (n) range, 3. majesty; synonyms (n) glory, grandeur, dignity, loftiness, splendor.

veldishnöttur globe; synonyms (n) ball, world, orb, sphere, circle.

veldisvísir exponent; synonyms (n) advocate, champion, power, proponent, protagonist.

velferð welfare; synonyms (n) prosperity, benefit, good, happiness, health.

vélflauta siren; synonyms (n) enchantress, alarm, syren, temptress, (adj) fascinating.

vélfræði engineering; synonyms (n) mechanism, technology, architecture, business, (adj) manufacturing.

vélfræðilegur mechanical; synonyms (adj) automatic, instinctive, unthinking, automated, (v) involuntary; antonym (adj) manual.

vélgengi mechanism; synonyms (n) apparatus, machinery, appliance, contrivance, device.

velgengni prosperity; synonyms (n) affluence, success, wealth, flourish, (adv) happiness; antonym (n) poverty.

vélgerving synthesis; synonyms (n) combination, fusion, compound, incorporation, mixture; antonym (n) separation.

velgja nausea; synonyms (n) disgust, sickness, queasiness, (v) aversion, loathing; antonym (n) attraction.

vélhyggja mechanism; synonyms (n) apparatus, machinery, appliance, contrivance, device.

vélinda esophagus; synonyms (n) gorge, gullet, oesophagus, throat, defile.

vélindi gullet; synonyms (n) esophagus, gorge, mouth, muzzle, oesophagus.

velja 1. select; synonyms (v) pick, extract, adopt, choose, (adj) choice; antonym (v) reject, 2. nominate; synonyms (v) appoint, name, constitute, (n) designate, call.

veljari selector; synonyms (n) chooser, detector, picker.

vélknúinn 1. automotive, 2. motorization; synonym (n) motorisation.

velli secretion; synonyms (n) exudation, discharge, emission, exhalation, extrusion.

vellíðan euphoria; synonyms (n) elation, ecstasy, jubilation, delight, happiness; antonym (n) dysphoria.

velmegun 1. prosperity; synonyms (n) affluence, success, wealth, flourish, (adv) happiness; antonym (n) poverty, 2. welfare; synonyms (n) prosperity, benefit, good, health, advantage.

vélmenni robot; synonyms (n) automaton, machine, golem, zombie, labor.

vélrænn mechanical; synonyms (adj) automatic, instinctive, unthinking, automated, (v) involuntary; antonym (adj) manual.

vélrænt mechanical; synonyms (adj) automatic, instinctive, unthinking, automated, (v) involuntary; antonym (adj) manual.

vélsmiður mechanic; synonyms (n) craftsman, artificer, artisan, journeyman, machinist.

vélstjóri 1. engineer; synonyms (n) architect, (v) devise, conduct, contrive, direct, 2. mechanic; synonyms (n) craftsman, artificer, artisan, journeyman, machinist.

velta 1. roll; synonyms (n) list, (v) coil, reel, curl, enfold, 2. turnover; synonyms (n) overturn, revolution, sales, upset, pastry, 3. rolling; synonyms (adj) resounding, rolled, (n) roll, peal, curling.

vélþræll robot; synonyms (n) automaton, machine, golem, zombie, labor.

veltiás fulcrum; synonyms (n) pivot, hinge, bearing, crux, support.

veltingur 1. rolling; synonyms (adj) resounding, rolled, (n) roll, peal, curling, 2. yaw; synonyms (n) swerve, (v) gape, turn, bend, gawk.

veltuhraði velocity; synonyms (n) speed, celerity, rapidity, (v) pace, rate; antonym (n) slowness.

vélvæðing 1. motorization; synonym (n) motorisation, 2. mechanization; synonyms (n) automation, mechanisation, computerization.

vélvinna machine; synonyms (n) instrument, apparatus, device, implement, car.

vélvirki mechanic; synonyms (n) craftsman, artificer, artisan, journeyman, machinist.

vélvirkur mechanical; synonyms (adj) automatic, instinctive, unthinking, automated, (v) involuntary; antonym (adj) manual.

vémynd icon; synonyms (n) effigy, image, picture, figure, likeness.

vending 1. reversal; synonyms (n) reverse, setback, retrogression, regression, annulment, 2. version; synonyms (n) reading, translation, construction, interpretation, rendering.

venja 1. usage; synonyms (n) habit, practice, employment, (v) use, (adj) custom, 2. practice; synonyms (n) exercise, fashion, convention, discipline, (v) drill; antonym (n) performance, 3. convention; synonyms (n) conference, congress, meeting, contract, assembly, 4. custom; synonyms (n) tradition, usage, impost, (v) accustom, (adj) bespoke, 5. habit; synonyms (n) clothing, attire, character, dress, garb.

venjubundið 1. routine; synonyms (n) round, (adj) everyday, ordinary, regular, common; antonym (adj) unusual, 2. conventional; synonyms (adj) formal, orthodox, accepted, customary, (v) commonplace; *antonyms* (adj) unconventional, radical, relaxed, original, rebellious.

venjulegt conventional; *synonyms* (adj) formal, orthodox, accepted, common, (v) commonplace; *antonyms* (adj) unconventional, radical, relaxed, unusual, original.

venjulegur 1. standard; *synonyms* (adj) model, (n) degree, measure, average, criterion; *antonyms* (adj) unusual, unconventional, special, **2.** usual; *synonyms* (adj) common, ordinary, accustomed, habitual, (n) customary; *antonyms* (adj) abnormal, extraordinary, **3.** customary; *synonyms* (adj) conventional, usual, commonplace, traditional, everyday, **4.** accustomed; *synonyms* (adj) familiar, normal, wonted, natural, habituated; *antonym* (adj) unaccustomed, **5.** conventional; *synonyms* (adj) formal, orthodox, accepted, conservative, decorous; *antonyms* (adj) radical, relaxed, original, rebellious, unorthodox.

vensl 1. relation; *synonyms* (n) connection, account, narration, recital, affinity, **2.** relationship; *synonyms* (n) relation, affiliation, association, ratio, consanguinity.

vensla relate; *synonyms* (v) connect, narrate, recount, associate, link.

venslarit nomogram; *synonyms* (n) nomograph, abacus.

ventill valve; *synonyms* (n) lock, sluice, door, gauge, monitor.

ventilsplitti keeper; *synonyms* (n) custodian, curator, guardian, guard, warden.

ventlastjórnun timing; *synonyms* (n) timekeeping, running.

ventro guts; *synonyms* (n) bowels, backbone, boldness, bravery, courage; *antonym* (n) cowardice.

venusvagn aconite; *synonyms* (n) belladonna, hellebore, hemlock, henbane, nightshade.

vera be; *synonyms* (v) exist, live, act, consist, constitute.

veraldarhyggja materialism; *synonyms* (n) acquisitiveness, anabaptism, avarice, corporealism, covetousness; *antonym* (n) generosity.

veraldarvefur web; *synonyms* (n) mesh, network, tissue, lattice, (v) net.

veraldlegur secular; *synonyms* (adj) profane, lay, worldly, earthly, laic; *antonyms* (adj) holy, religious, spiritual.

verð 1. price; *synonyms* (n) cost, worth, charge, (v) appraise, estimate, **2.** value; *synonyms* (n) merit, (v) price, appreciate, assess, esteem; *antonyms* (n) disadvantage, futility, uselessness, insignificance, **3.** worth; *synonyms* (n) value, virtue, importance, excellence, dignity; *antonym* (n) worthlessness.

verða 1. become; *synonyms* (v) be, grow, suit, arise, get, **2.** grow; *synonyms* (v) advance, augment, develop, enlarge, expand; *antonyms* (v) decrease, weaken, shrink, **3.** happen; *synonyms* (v) befall, chance, come, fall, (n) betide, **4.** get; *synonyms* (v) acquire, gain, attain, become, catch; *antonyms* (v) lose, give, leave.

verðbóla bubble; *synonyms* (n) blister, (v) boil, babble, foam, burble.

verðbólga 1. boom; *synonyms* (n) bang, roar, (v) blast, blare, flourish; *antonyms* (n) depression, (v) collapse, decline, **2.** inflation; *synonyms* (n) expansion, dilatation, increase, rise, boom; *antonym* (n) deflation.

verðbréf security; *synonyms* (n) pledge, protection, safety, hostage, insurance; *antonym* (n) danger.

verðbréfamiðlari stockbroker; *synonyms* (n) broker, agent, financier, dealer, negotiator.

verðbréfamiðlun brokerage; *synonyms* (n) commission, brokage, freightage, wharfage, tax.

verðbréfasafn portfolio; *synonyms* (n) briefcase, album, file, bandolier, budget.

verðbréfasali 1. stockbroker; *synonyms* (n) broker, agent, financier, dealer, negotiator, **2.** broker; *synonyms* (n) mediator, go-between, factor, middleman, attorney.

verðbréfaskipti conversion; *synonyms* (n) alteration, change, changeover, adaptation, exchange.

verðbreytingarfærsla revaluation; *synonyms* (n) reappraisal, reassessment, revalorization, brushup, critique.

verðfall decline; *synonyms* (n) decay, (v) wane, drop, reject, fall; *antonyms* (n) improvement, recovery, (v) increase, rise, accept.

verðgildi value; *synonyms* (n) merit, cost, appraise, (v) price, appreciate; *antonyms* (n) disadvantage, futility, uselessness, insignificance.

verðgildishækkun appreciation; *synonyms* (n) admiration, acknowledgment, approval, awareness, (v) sense; *antonym* (n) depreciation.

verðhjöðnun deflation; *synonyms* (n) depression, reduction, depreciation, contraction, comedown; *antonym* (n) inflation.

verðhrun deflation; *synonyms* (n) depression, reduction, depreciation, contraction, comedown; *antonym* (n) inflation.

verði ft; *synonyms* (n) foot, base, foundation, fundament, groundwork.

verðlækkun 1. deflation; *synonyms* (n) depression, reduction, depreciation, contraction, comedown; *antonym* (n) inflation, **2.** markdown; *synonyms* (n) discount, bargain.

verðlagning pricing; *synonyms* (n) appraisal, costing.

verðleggja price; *synonyms* (*n*) cost, worth, charge, (*v*) appraise, estimate.

verðleikar qualification; *synonyms* (*n*) condition, capability, competence, fitness, limitation.

verðmæti value; *synonyms* (*n*) merit, cost, appraise, (*v*) price, appreciate; *antonyms* (*n*) disadvantage, futility, uselessness, insignificance.

verðrýrnun 1. debasement; *synonyms* (*n*) abasement, corruption, adulteration, degradation, (*adj*) abjection; *antonym* (*n*) purification, **2.** depreciation; *synonyms* (*n*) abatement, detraction, disparagement, derogation, deterioration.

verðsamtök cartel; *synonyms* (*n*) syndicate, trust, combine, compromise, ring.

verðskrá tariff; *synonyms* (*n*) duty, charge, excise, custom, tax.

verðþensla inflation; *synonyms* (*n*) expansion, dilatation, increase, rise, boom; *antonyms* (*n*) deflation, depression.

verður 1. worthwhile; *synonyms* (*adj*) profitable, useful, valuable, beneficial, gainful; *antonyms* (*adj*) pointless, wasted, worthless, **2.** worthy; *synonyms* (*adj*) noble, estimable, good, meritorious, respectable; *antonym* (*adj*) unworthy, **3.** deserving; *synonyms* (*adj*) admirable, creditable, commendable, fit, (*n*) worthy; *antonym* (*adj*) undeserving.

vergirni nymphomania; *synonyms* (*n*) andromania, uteromania.

vergur gross; *synonyms* (*adj*) crass, coarse, big, boorish, (*n*) aggregate; *antonyms* (*adj*) attractive, (*v*) net.

verja 1. spend; *synonyms* (*v*) consume, exhaust, expend, squander, blow; *antonyms* (*v*) save, conserve, **2.** appropriate; *synonyms* (*adj*) pertinent, proper, true, (*v*) annex, allocate; *antonyms* (*adj*) inappropriate, unsuitable, unrelated, untimely, (*v*) surrender, **3.** lock; *synonyms* (*v*) bolt, bar, close, latch, engage; *antonyms* (*v*) unlock, open.

verk 1. work; *synonyms* (*n*) exercise, business, (*v*) labor, operate, toil; *antonyms* (*v*) idle, malfunction, **2.** task; *synonyms* (*n*) job, assignment, charge, commission, (*v*) tax, **3.** transaction; *synonyms* (*n*) deal, dealing, dealings, proceeding, trade; *antonym* (*n*) purchase, **4.** commission; *synonyms* (*n*) board, mission, delegation, mandate, (*v*) assign, **5.** job; *synonyms* (*n*) chore, employment, position, work, career.

verka 1. work; *synonyms* (*n*) exercise, business, (*v*) labor, operate, toil; *antonyms* (*v*) idle, malfunction, **2.** labour; *synonyms* (*n*) effort, exertion, childbed, (*v*) grind, travail.

verkalýðsfélag union; *synonyms* (*n*) coalition, connection, junction, association, combination; *antonyms* (*n*) separation, divergence.

verkalýður 1. proletariat; *synonyms* (*n*) labor, labour, mob, masses, trash, **2.** labor; *synonyms* (*n*) drudgery, effort, endeavor, exertion, (*v*) toil; *antonym* (*v*) rest.

verkamaður 1. worker; *synonyms* (*n*) employee, hand, proletarian, workman, actor, **2.** workman; *synonyms* (*n*) worker, mechanic, artificer, carpenter, drudge, **3.** hand (hönd); *synonyms* (*n*) deal, (*v*) deliver, give, pass, commit, **4.** operative; *synonyms* (*adj*) effective, functional, (*n*) labourer, efficient, spy; *antonym* (*adj*) inoperative, **5.** labourer; *synonyms* (*n*) laborer, jack, floorman.

verkaskrá agenda; *synonyms* (*n*) schedule, agendum, diary, docket, plan.

verkbann 1. boycott; *synonyms* (*n*) ban, (*v*) ostracize, exclude, proscribe, strike; *antonym* (*v*) patronize, **2.** lockout; *synonyms* (*n*) exclusion, stoppage.

verkefni 1. problem; *synonyms* (*n*) bother, conundrum, difficulty, trouble, knot, **2.** project; *synonyms* (*n*) design, device, (*v*) plan, hurl, contrive, **3.** commission; *synonyms* (*n*) board, mission, delegation, job, (*v*) assign, **4.** material, *synonyms* (*n*) body, cloth, (*adj*) bodily, corporal, corporeal.

verkeining task; *synonyms* (*n*) job, assignment, charge, (*v*) tax, exercise.

verkfæri 1. tool; *synonyms* (*n*) instrument, implement, machine, puppet, pawn, **2.** apparatus; *synonyms* (*n*) appliance, device, plant, tackle, equipment, **3.** instrument; *synonyms* (*n*) channel, deed, agency, apparatus, document, **4.** implement; *synonyms* (*v*) execute, fulfil, accomplish, (*n*) tool, utensil.

verkfall strike; *synonyms* (*n*) knock, assault, (*v*) bang, beat, hit.

verkfræðingur engineer; *synonyms* (*n*) architect, (*v*) devise, conduct, contrive, direct.

verkfræðistörf engineering; *synonyms* (*n*) mechanism, technology, architecture, business, (*adj*) manufacturing.

verkframkvæmd construction; *synonyms* (*n*) building, fabrication, formation, structure, assembly; *antonym* (*n*) destruction.

verkgangur procedure; *synonyms* (*n*) process, formula, practice, routine, fashion.

verkgeta praxis; *synonyms* (*n*) practice, accidence, grammar, punctuation, custom.

verkhús laboratory; *synonyms* (*n*) lab, factory, course, (*adj*) experimental, alembic.

verkjalyf anodyne; *synonyms* (*adj*) opiate, sedative, (*n*) analgesic, paregoric, (*v*) balm.

verklag 1. technique; *synonyms (n)* approach, means, method, skill, fashion, **2.** procedure; *synonyms (n)* process, formula, practice, routine, custom.

verklagsregla discipline; *synonyms (v)* control, castigate, chastise, train, chasten.

verklagsreglur procedure; *synonyms (n)* process, formula, practice, routine, fashion.

verklýsing 1. protocol; *synonyms (n)* etiquette, manners, ceremony, bill, formality, **2.** specification; *synonyms (n)* designation, provision, stipulation, particular, condition.

verknaður action; *synonyms (n)* act, accomplishment, activity, agency, *(v)* achievement; *antonyms (n)* inaction, inactivity.

verko 1. work; *synonyms (n)* exercise, business, *(v)* labor, operate, toil; *antonyms (v)* idle, malfunction, **2.** works; *synonyms (n)* factory, plant, workings, mill, manufactory.

verkröðun 1. scheduling; *synonyms (n)* programming, planning, arrangement, development, preparation, **2.** dispatching; *synonyms (n)* disposal, murder, dropping, routing.

verksamningur contract; *synonyms (n)* compact, charter, *(v)* covenant, bargain, *(adj)* abridge; *antonyms (v)* expand, widen, stretch.

verkskömmtun assignment; *synonyms (n)* allocation, allotment, appointment, assigning, mission.

verksmiðja 1. plant; *synonyms (n)* manufactory, equipment, *(v)* fix, place, embed, **2.** mill; *synonyms (n)* grind, factory, grinder, machine, *(v)* crush, **3.** factory; *synonyms (n)* mill, plant, business, shop, works.

verksmiðjuvinna manufacturing; *synonyms (adj)* industrial, *(n)* output, production, business, engineering.

verkstæði workshop; *synonyms (n)* shop, factory, studio, workhouse, atelier.

verkstjóri foreman; *synonyms (n)* boss, chief, gaffer, supervisor, leader.

verkstjórn supervision; *synonyms (n)* oversight, charge, control, direction, *(v)* inspection.

verkstofa workshop; *synonyms (n)* shop, factory, studio, workhouse, atelier.

verkstol apraxia; *synonym (n)* dyspraxia.

verktaki 1. contractor; *synonyms (n)* builder, entrepreneur, party, undertaker, affirmer, **2.** builder; *synonyms (n)* architect, constructor, founder, artificer, creator.

verkþáttur 1. task; *synonyms (n)* job, assignment, charge, *(v)* tax, exercise, **2.** activity; *synonyms (n)* action, activeness, liveliness, play, agency; *antonyms (n)* inactivity, inaction, inactiveness.

verkun 1. processing; *synonyms (n)* working, refinement, developing, manufacture, dispensation, **2.** action; *synonyms (n)* act, accomplishment, activity, agency, *(v)* achievement; *antonyms (n)* inaction, inactivity, **3.** effect; *synonyms (n)* consequence, *(v)* accomplish, achieve, create, cause; *antonym (n)* reason.

verkur 1. ache; *synonyms (n)* hunger, pain, twinge, *(v)* hurt, long; *antonym (n)* pleasure, **2.** pain; *synonyms (n)* distress, ache, bother, ill, *(v)* afflict, **3.** soreness; *synonyms (n)* discomfort, tenderness, irritation, pique, *(v)* sore, **4.** distress; *synonyms (n)* agony, anguish, trouble, *(v)* torment, concern; *antonyms (v)* comfort, please.

verkvangur platform; *synonyms (n)* dais, floor, rostrum, stage, stand.

verma calorie; *synonym (n)* kilocalorie.

vermandi calefacient; *synonyms (adj)* warming, heating.

vermibreyta entropy; *synonyms (n)* chaos, data, information, randomness, haphazardness.

vermilyf calefacient; *synonyms (adj)* warming, heating.

vernd 1. protection; *synonyms (n)* defense, care, conservation, cover, *(v)* guard; *antonym (n)* destruction, **2.** conservation; *synonyms (n)* maintenance, preservation, upkeep, keep, custody, **3.** immunity; *synonyms (n)* exemption, freedom, franchise, dispensation, privilege; *antonym (n)* vulnerability.

vernda conserve; *synonyms (v)* economize, embalm, husband, *(n)* preserve, conserves; *antonyms (v)* spend, use, waste, expend, damage.

verndaður protected; *synonyms (adj)* secure, immune, saved, secured, sheltered.

verndarríki protectorate; *synonyms (n)* protectorship, colony, empire, kingdom, principality.

verndarsvæði protectorate; *synonyms (n)* protectorship, colony, empire, kingdom, principality.

verndun 1. protection; *synonyms (n)* defense, care, conservation, cover, *(v)* guard; *antonym (n)* destruction, **2.** conservation; *synonyms (n)* maintenance, preservation, upkeep, keep, custody.

verndunarefni preservative; *synonyms (adj)* preservatory, protective, conservative, *(n)* preserver, antiseptic.

veröld world; *synonyms (n)* cosmos, nature, universe, creation, public.

verpast warp; *synonyms (n)* twist, buckle, distortion, *(v)* bend, distort; *antonym (v)* straighten.

verping warping; *synonyms (n)* warp, warpage, beaming, buckle, deflection.

verpingur warping; *synonyms* (*n*) warp, warpage, beaming, buckle, deflection.

verri worse; *synonyms* (*adj*) inferior, worser, impaired, junior, lesser; *antonyms* (*adj*) better, improved, healthier.

versla deal; *synonyms* (*n*) bargain, buy, agreement, (*v*) administer, allot; *antonym* (*n*) purchase.

verslanamiðstöð mall; *synonyms* (*n*) center, hammer, plaza, promenade, walk.

verslun 1. shop; *synonyms* (*n*) business, store, factory, plant, (*v*) betray, **2**. trade; *synonyms* (*n*) deal, barter, commerce, (*v*) change, exchange; *antonyms* (*n*) purchase, (*adj*) charitable, **3**. commerce; *synonyms* (*n*) connection, dealings, intercourse, association, (*v*) trade, **4**. market; *synonyms* (*n*) fair, shop, bazaar, marketplace, (*v*) demand.

verslunarhús shop; *synonyms* (*n*) business, store, factory, plant, (*v*) betray.

verslunarvara commodity; *synonyms* (*n*) merchandise, article, product, object, thing.

versna deteriorate; *synonyms* (*v*) degenerate, degrade, decline, spoil, worsen; *antonyms* (*v*) improve, convalesce, recover.

verstur worst; *synonyms* (*v*) whip, defeat, trounce, best, rout; *antonym* (*adj*) highest.

verufræði ontology; *synonyms* (*n*) metaphysics, philosophy, psychology.

verulegur material; *synonyms* (*n*) body, cloth, (*adj*) bodily, corporal, corporeal.

veruleiki reality; *synonyms* (*n*) fact, existence, actuality, certainty, realism; *antonyms* (*n*) fantasy, delusion, dream, imagination, vision.

vervo spirits; *synonyms* (*n*) liquor, alcohol, booze, humor, (*adj*) cheer.

verzlun 1. trade; *synonyms* (*n*) deal, business, barter, commerce, (*v*) change; *antonyms* (*n*) purchase, (*adj*) charitable, **2**. transaction; *synonyms* (*n*) dealing, dealings, proceeding, trade, concern, **3**. deal; *synonyms* (*n*) bargain, buy, agreement, (*v*) administer, allot, **4**. business; *synonyms* (*n*) employment, matter, subject, affair, calling; *antonym* (*adj*) housing, **5**. commerce; *synonyms* (*n*) exchange, connection, intercourse, association, communication.

vesla weasel; *synonyms* (*n*) informer, (*v*) equivocate, evade, hedge, confess.

vésögn myth; *synonyms* (*n*) fable, legend, story, tale, allegory.

vespa scooter; *synonyms* (*n*) iceboat, icebreaker, scoter.

vessaæð lymphatic; *synonyms* (*adj*) aqueous, hydrous, torpid, listless, aquatic.

vessabjúgur lymphedema; *synonym* (*n*) lymphoedema.

vessagrotnun maceration; *synonyms* (*n*) emaciation, dilution, fasting, gauntness, shrift.

vessaþurrð dehydration; *synonyms* (*n*) evaporation, desiccation, drought, dryness, dewatering; *antonym* (*n*) wetness.

vessavökvi plasma; *synonyms* (*n*) plasm, onyx, blood, flesh.

vessi lymph; *synonyms* (*n*) crystal, glass, (*adj*) rheum, sanies, serosity.

vestur 1. west; *synonyms* (*n*) occident, w, tungsten, watt, (*v*) south, **2**. westward; *synonyms* (*adv*) west, westwards, (*adj*) westerly, westbound, western, **3**. westwards; *synonym* (*adv*) westward.

vetni 1. hydrogen; *synonyms* (*n*) butane, diacetylmorphine, heroin, horse, hydrogenium, **2**. h; *synonyms* (*n*) asshole, bastard, buck, bull, bullshit.

vetniskol hydrocarbon; *synonyms* (*n*) carbohydride, hydrocarbonate.

vetniskolefni hydrocarbon; *synonyms* (*n*) carbohydride, hydrocarbonate.

vetrarbraut galaxy; *synonyms* (*n*) constellation, beetleweed, bevy, (*adj*) array, army.

Vetrarbrautin galaxy; *synonyms* (*n*) constellation, beetleweed, bevy, (*adj*) array, army.

vetrardvali hibernation; *synonyms* (*n*) sleep, overwintering, (*v*) coma, dream, nap.

vetrarlegur winter; *synonyms* (*n*) wintertime, season, chill, frost, (*v*) hibernate.

vetrarsalat endive; *synonyms* (*n*) escarole, witloof.

vettvangur 1. place; *synonyms* (*n*) position, (*v*) post, arrange, fix, lay; *antonym* (*v*) remove, **2**. realm; *synonyms* (*n*) kingdom, area, country, domain, field, **3**. venue; *synonyms* (*n*) locale, place, site, locus, location, **4**. domain; *synonyms* (*n*) department, realm, arena, land, province; *antonym* (*n*) range, **5**. context; *synonyms* (*n*) circumstance, environment, setting, surroundings, background.

vetur winter; *synonyms* (*n*) wintertime, season, chill, frost, (*v*) hibernate.

vextir interest; *synonyms* (*n*) concern, advantage, affair, (*v*) engage, care; *antonyms* (*n*) indifference, apathy, (*v*) bore.

við 1. thou; *synonyms* (*n*) chiliad, g, grand, m, curtilage, **2**. with; *synonyms* (*prep*) by, for, (*adv*) on, beside, (*adj*) including.

víða video; *synonyms* (*n*) television, picture, film, movie, (*v*) tape.

viðaræð trachea; *synonyms* (*n*) windpipe, throat, weasand, chimney, flue.

viðarkenndur woody; *synonyms* (*adj*) wooded, arboreous, ligneous, wooden, arboraceous.

viðarkol 1. charcoal; *synonyms* (*n*) coal, fusain, (*v*) carbon, coke, (*adj*) soot, **2.** coal; *synonyms* (*n*) ember, culm, (*v*) char, blacken, (*adj*) black.

viðarkolahylki canister; *synonyms* (*n*) can, container, cannister, case, tin.

viðarkvoða resin; *synonyms* (*n*) gum, rosin, colophany.

viðarlögn veneer; *synonyms* (*n*) face, facade, facing, coating, (*v*) varnish.

viðarspónn veneer; *synonyms* (*n*) face, facade, facing, coating, (*v*) varnish.

víðátta manifold; *synonyms* (*adj*) multiple, diverse, different, (*v*) duplicate, copy.

viðauki 1. appendix; *synonyms* (*n*) addition, adjunct, addendum, annex, (*v*) supplement, **2.** addition; *synonyms* (*n*) accession, accessory, extension, increase, (*prep*) accumulation; *antonyms* (*n*) subtraction, removal, estimation, **3.** complement; *synonyms* (*n*) balance, extra, counterpart, foil, (*v*) enhance, **4.** allowance; *synonyms* (*n*) allotment, admission, discount, quota, tolerance, **5.** annex; *synonyms* (*n*) affix, annexe, (*v*) add, affiliate, adjoin.

viðbætinn additive; *synonyms* (*adj*) cumulative, (*n*) addition, adjuvant, admixture, supplement.

viðbætir 1. appendix; *synonyms* (*n*) addition, adjunct, addendum, annex, (*v*) supplement, **2.** complement; *synonyms* (*n*) accessory, balance, extra, counterpart, foil.

viðbein clavicle; *synonym* (*n*) collarbone.

viðbjóðslegur 1. vile; *synonyms* (*adj*) foul, contemptible, despicable, (*n*) dirty, (*v*) base; *antonyms* (*adj*) pleasant, attractive, **2.** dismal; *synonyms* (*adj*) cheerless, dark, dejected, depressing, desolate; *antonyms* (*adj*) cheerful, bright, happy, **3.** dreary; *synonyms* (*adj*) drab, dull, dismal, drear, gloomy; *antonym* (*adj*) interesting, **4.** detestable; *synonyms* (*adj*) abominable, abhorrent, hateful, damnable, (*v*) cursed, **5.** hideous; *synonyms* (*adj*) awful, dreadful, frightful, fearful, ghastly; *antonym* (*adj*) lovely.

viðbjóður 1. atrocity; *synonyms* (*n*) enormity, brutality, abomination, atrociousness, (*adj*) outrage, **2.** abhorrence; *synonyms* (*n*) antipathy, detestation, hatred, odium, aversion; *antonym* (*n*) love, **3.** abomination; *synonyms* (*n*) abhorrence, disgust, atrocity, execration, hate, **4.** horror; *synonyms* (*n*) awe, dismay, fear, alarm, (*adj*) dread; *antonym* (*n*) pleasantness.

viðbót 1. allowance; *synonyms* (*n*) allotment, admission, discount, quota, tolerance, **2.** addition; *synonyms* (*n*) accession, accessory, addendum, extension, (*prep*) accumulation; *antonyms* (*n*) subtraction, removal, estimation, **3.** complement;

synonyms (*n*) supplement, adjunct, balance, extra, addition, **4.** mantissa, **5.** increment; *synonyms* (*n*) gain, increase, boost, accretion, development.

viðbótarbúnaður attachment; *synonyms* (*n*) affection, appendix, accessory, addition, adherence; *antonym* (*n*) detachment.

viðbótargjald surcharge; *synonyms* (*v*) overcharge, overload, drench, fleece, gazump.

viðbótargreiðsla charge; *synonyms* (*n*) accusation, burden, care, (*v*) accuse, blame; *antonyms* (*v*) request, absolve, retreat.

viðbótarvöxtur apposition; *synonyms* (*n*) union, juxtaposition, (*prep*) addition, accompaniment, accord.

viðbragð 1. reaction; *synonyms* (*n*) answer, response, backlash, reply, effect, **2.** response; *synonyms* (*n*) reaction, reception, echo, retort, (*v*) rejoinder, **3.** reflex; *synonyms* (*v*) reflection, (*adj*) automatic, involuntary, instinctive, unconscious, **4.** breakaway; *synonyms* (*adj*) separatist, fissiparous, **5.** acceleration; *synonyms* (*n*) speed, rapidity, rise, quickening, quickness.

viðbragðafjör erethism; *synonym* (*n*) orgasm.

viðbragðafræði reflexology; *synonyms* (*n*) kneading, manipulation, massage, rub, rubdown.

viðbragðahyggja reflexology; *synonyms* (*n*) kneading, manipulation, massage, rub, rubdown.

viðbragðshæfni reactivity; *synonyms* (*n*) excitability, responsiveness, sensitivity.

viðbragðsmerki cue; *synonyms* (*n*) prompt, clue, tip, clew, (*v*) hint.

viðbrögð 1. response; *synonyms* (*n*) answer, reaction, reception, (*v*) reply, rejoinder, **2.** feedback; *synonyms* (*n*) response, repercussion, retort, (*v*) respond.

viðbúinn standby; *synonyms* (*adj*) extra, (*n*) reserve, deputy, substitute, understudy.

viðbygging annex; *synonyms* (*n*) affix, addition, (*v*) add, affiliate, adjoin.

vídd 1. width; *synonyms* (*n*) breadth, extent, latitude, length, size; *antonym* (*n*) thinness, **2.** dimension; *synonyms* (*n*) degree, bulk, magnitude, attribute, proportion, **3.** calibre; *synonyms* (*n*) caliber, bore, quality, aegir, dullard, **4.** caliber; *synonyms* (*n*) calibre, diameter, amplitude, class, status.

víddarmælir caliper; *synonyms* (*n*) thickness, calipers, callipers, (*v*) calliper, measure.

víddartala dimension; *synonyms* (*n*) degree, breadth, bulk, magnitude, size.

viðeigandi 1. suitable; *synonyms* (*adj*) appropriate, fit, good, apt, proper; *antonyms* (*adj*) inappropriate, unsuitable, wrong, improper, **2.** appropriate; *synonyms* (*adj*) pertinent, true, (*v*) annex, allocate, adopt; *antonyms* (*adj*) unrelated, untimely, (*v*) surrender, **3**. fit; *synonyms* (*v*) agree, accommodate, meet, suit, (*adj*) decorous; *antonyms* (*adj*) unfit, unwell.

viðeiganleiki application; *synonyms* (*n*) plea, appeal, appliance, concentration, demand.

viðeign application; *synonyms* (*n*) plea, appeal, appliance, concentration, demand.

vídeó video; *synonyms* (*n*) television, picture, film, movie, (*v*) tape.

viðfang 1. subject; *synonyms* (*n*) matter, citizen, affair, (*adj*) liable, exposed; *antonym* (*adj*) liberated, **2**. application; *synonyms* (*n*) plea, appeal, appliance, concentration, demand, **3**. object; *synonyms* (*n*) design, aim, cause, end, (*v*) except; *antonym* (*v*) agree.

viðfangsefni 1. subject; *synonyms* (*n*) matter, citizen, affair, (*adj*) liable, exposed; *antonym* (*adj*) liberated, **2**. problem; *synonyms* (*n*) bother, conundrum, difficulty, trouble, knot, **3**. occupation; *synonyms* (*n*) employment, occupancy, business, craft, calling; *antonym* (*n*) surrender.

víðfeðmur global; *synonyms* (*adj*) general, international, overall, cosmopolitan, universal; *antonyms* (*adj*) local, national.

viðgangur dynamic; *synonyms* (*adj*) active, aggressive, dynamical, energetic, forceful; *antonyms* (*adj*) dull, static.

viðgerð 1. repair; *synonyms* (*v*) remedy, mend, patch, redress, correct; *antonym* (*v*) break, **2**. refit; *synonyms* (*n*) renovation, (*v*) repair, renovate, equip, fix.

viðgerðamaður mechanic; *synonyms* (*n*) craftsman, artificer, artisan, journeyman, machinist.

viðgerðarmaður mechanic; *synonyms* (*n*) craftsman, artificer, artisan, journeyman, machinist.

viðgerðir service; *synonyms* (*n*) help, aid, assistance, avail, (*v*) overhaul.

viðgjöf feedback; *synonyms* (*n*) reply, response, reaction, repercussion, (*v*) answer.

viðhald 1. repair; *synonyms* (*v*) remedy, mend, patch, redress, correct; *antonym* (*v*) break, **2**. upkeep; *synonyms* (*n*) maintenance, support, care, conservation, keep, **3**. maintenance; *synonyms* (*n*) livelihood, alimony, living, sustenance, charge; *antonym* (*n*) end.

viðhalda maintain; *synonyms* (*v*) continue, justify, affirm, allege, assert; *antonyms* (*v*) deny, change.

viðhaldsbær sustainable; *synonyms* (*adj*) bearable, endurable, tolerable, livable.

viðhengi attachment; *synonyms* (*n*) affection, appendix, accessory, addition, adherence; *antonym* (*n*) detachment.

viðhorf attitude; *synonyms* (*n*) position, aspect, posture, behavior, mind.

viðhverfa view; *synonyms* (*n*) look, sight, judgment, opinion, (*v*) regard.

viðkoma proliferation; *synonyms* (*n*) growth, propagation, spread, reproduction, upsurge.

viðkomugeta resilience; *synonyms* (*n*) elasticity, spring, stamina, bounce, flexibility; *antonym* (*n*) pessimism.

viðkunnanlegur 1. sympathetic; *synonyms* (*adj*) kind, compassionate, kindly, congenial, tender; *antonyms* (*adj*) unsympathetic, hardhearted, unfeeling, **2**. sensitive; *synonyms* (*adj*) delicate, excitable, sensible, sore, painful; *antonyms* (*adj*) insensitive, numb, tactless, thick-skinned, **3**. approachable; *synonyms* (*adj*) accessible, affable, receptive, gracious, amenable; *antonyms* (*adj*) unapproachable, aloof, distant, **4**. congenial; *synonyms* (*adj*) agreeable, concordant, compatible, delightful, (*v*) consonant; *antonyms* (*adj*) disagreeable, uncongenial, unfriendly, **5**. likable; *synonyms* (*adj*) likeable, pleasant, pleasing, amiable, engaging.

viðkvæði feedback; *synonyms* (*n*) reply, response, reaction, repercussion, (*v*) answer.

viðkvæmni 1. sensibility; *synonyms* (*n*) emotion, consciousness, (*adj*) feeling, (*v*) sensation, appreciation, **2**. irritability; *synonyms* (*n*) excitability, irascibility, choler, petulance, temper, **3**. excitability; *synonyms* (*n*) reactivity, irritability, impetuosity, vehemence, biliousness.

viðkvæmur 1. sensible; *synonyms* (*adj*) reasonable, aware, judicious, perceptible, prudent; *antonyms* (*adj*) foolish, absurd, crazy, idiotic, imprudent, **2**. sensitive; *synonyms* (*adj*) delicate, excitable, sensible, sore, tender; *antonyms* (*adj*) insensitive, numb, hardhearted, tactless, thick-skinned, **3**. fragile; *synonyms* (*adj*) dainty, frail, breakable, brittle, flimsy; *antonyms* (*adj*) strong, unbreakable, substantial, sturdy, permanent, **4**. irritable; *synonyms* (*adj*) angry, fractious, irascible, edgy, cantankerous; *antonyms* (*adj*) calm, easygoing, good-humored, good-natured, even-tempered.

viðlægur positive; *synonyms* (*adj*) absolute, certain, affirmative, confident, (*n*) actual; *antonyms* (*adj*) negative, derogatory, uncertain, unsure, pessimistic.

viðlegð superposition; *synonyms* (*n*) incrustation, superimposition.

viðlegukantur quay; *synonyms* (*n*) dock, wharf, jetty, pier, embankment.

viðlegutími downtime; *synonyms* (*n*) break, cessation, delay, (*adj*) broken, disrepair.

viðloða adhesive; *synonyms* (*adj*) tacky, clingy, gummy, (*n*) cement, glue; *antonym* (*adj*) nonadhesive.

viðloðandi adherent; *synonyms* (*n*) disciple, follower, believer, devotee, fan.

viðloðnun adhesion; *synonyms* (*n*) adherence, bond, stickiness, adhesiveness, attachment.

viðloðun adhesion; *synonyms* (*n*) adherence, bond, stickiness, adhesiveness, attachment.

viðmælandi addressee; *synonyms* (*n*) receiver, beneficiary, heir, inhabitant, occupant.

viðmið 1. control; *synonyms* (*n*) rule, authority, (*v*) command, check, curb; *antonyms* (*n*) freedom, weakness, (*v*) intensify, share, 2. reference; *synonyms* (*n*) citation, mention, quotation, quote, allusion, 3. system; *synonyms* (*n*) method, arrangement, network, organization, plan, 4. benchmark; *synonyms* (*n*) criterion, measure, gauge, norm, landmark, 5. datum; *synonyms* (*n*) data, fact, note.

viðmiðshæð datum; *synonyms* (*n*) data, fact, note.

viðmiðun 1. reference; *synonyms* (*n*) citation, mention, quotation, quote, allusion, 2. criterion; *synonyms* (*n*) benchmark, measure, norm, test, canon, 3. guideline; *synonyms* (*n*) directive, rule, principle, parameter, gauge, 4. norm; *synonyms* (*n*) average, mean, mode, criterion, model.

viðmiðunarhæð datum; *synonyms* (*n*) data, fact, note.

viðmiðunarkerfi system; *synonyms* (*n*) method, arrangement, network, organization, plan.

viðmiðunarmerki 1. tic; *synonyms* (*n*) twitching, spasm, jerk, quiver, (*v*) twitch, 2. benchmark; *synonyms* (*n*) criterion, measure, gauge, norm, landmark.

viðmiðunarmörk threshold; *synonyms* (*n*) brink, limen, beginning, doorsill, doorstep.

viðmiðunarregla guideline; *synonyms* (*n*) directive, rule, principle, parameter, gauge.

viðmiðunartími epoch; *synonyms* (*n*) age, era, date, day, period.

viðmót interface; *synonyms* (*n*) link, port, boundary, junction, (*v*) contact.

viðnæmi reactivity; *synonyms* (*n*) excitability, responsiveness, sensitivity.

viðnám 1. resistance; *synonyms* (*n*) opposition, endurance, friction, immunity, impedance; *antonyms* (*n*) smoothness, agreement, obedience, susceptibility, 2. resistor; *synonyms* (*n*) resistance, resistivity, underground, 3. drag; *synonyms* (*v*) attract, haul, draw, puff, (*n*) pull; *antonym* (*v*) push, 4. friction; *synonyms* (*n*) discord, abrasion, attrition, dispute, rub, 5. impedance; *synonyms* (*n*) clog, hindrance, interference.

viðnámskveikir ignitor; *synonyms* (*n*) igniter, barge, brightness, flatboat, hoy.

viðnámsstefna containment; *synonyms* (*n*) control, repression, restriction.

viðnámstæki resistor; *synonyms* (*n*) resistance, opposition, impedance, resistivity, immunity.

viðra ventilate; *synonyms* (*v*) air, fan, vent, discuss, aerate.

viðræðufundur consultation; *synonyms* (*n*) advice, conference, interview, negotiation, counsel.

viðræður consultation; *synonyms* (*n*) advice, conference, interview, negotiation, counsel.

viðrétting recovery; *synonyms* (*n*) rally, convalescence, improvement, reclamation, rescue; *antonyms* (*n*) decline, loss, return.

viðrini intersex; *synonyms* (*n*) hermaphrodite, intersexuality, androgyne, epicine, gynandromorph.

viðsjá 1. video; *synonyms* (*n*) television, picture, film, movie, (*v*) tape, 2. stereoscope.

viðskeyti suffix; *synonyms* (*n*) affix, ending, sequel, (*v*) postfix, annex.

viðskeyting append; *synonyms* (*v*) adjoin, add, affix, annex, attach.

viðskeytingarhamur append; *synonyms* (*v*) adjoin, add, affix, annex, attach.

viðskil exit; *synonyms* (*n*) departure, door, egress, (*v*) depart, go; *antonyms* (*n*) arrival, entry, (*v*) enter.

viðskilnaður death; *synonyms* (*n*) demise, end, expiration, close, exit; *antonyms* (*n*) birth, existence, delivery.

viðskiptabann 1. boycott; *synonyms* (*n*) ban, (*v*) ostracize, exclude, proscribe, strike; *antonym* (*v*) patronize, 2. embargo; *synonyms* (*n*) prohibition, sanction, veto, inhibition, injunction.

viðskiptabréf instrument; *synonyms* (*n*) channel, deed, agency, apparatus, appliance.

viðskiptaeinangrun boycott; *synonyms* (*n*) ban, (*v*) ostracize, exclude, proscribe, strike; *antonym* (*v*) patronize.

viðskiptakröfur receivables; *synonym* (*n*) advances.

viðskiptamaður customer; *synonyms* (*n*) consumer, buyer, patron, client, guest; *antonym* (*n*) seller.

viðskiptavelta turnover; *synonyms* (*n*) overturn, revolution, sales, upset, pastry.

viðskiptavenja practice; *synonyms* (*n*) exercise, fashion, convention, (*v*) custom, drill; *antonym* (*n*) performance.

viðskiptavild goodwill; *synonyms* (*n*) friendship, friendliness, amity, grace, kindness; *antonyms* (*n*) hostility, malice.

viðskiptavinur 1. client; *synonyms* (*n*) buyer, customer, patron, guest, purchaser, 2. consumer; *synonyms* (*n*) client, shopper, (*adj*) capitalist, consumerist, entrepreneurial; *antonym* (*n*) seller, 3.

customer; *synonyms* (*n*) consumer, fellow, passenger, person, spender.

viðskipti 1. trade; *synonyms* (*n*) deal, business, barter, commerce, (*v*) change; *antonyms* (*n*) purchase, (*adj*) charitable, **2**. transaction; *synonyms* (*n*) dealing, dealings, proceeding, trade, concern, **3**. business; *synonyms* (*n*) employment, matter, subject, affair, calling; *antonym* (*adj*) housing, **4**. commerce; *synonyms* (*n*) exchange, connection, intercourse, association, communication.

viðsmjör olive; *synonyms* (*adj*) glaucous, green, (*n*) cherry, drupe, elderberry.

viðsnúinn inverse; *synonyms* (*adj*) contrary, converse, (*n*) opposite, contrast, (*v*) reverse.

viðsnúningur 1. reversal; *synonyms* (*n*) reverse, setback, retrogression, regression, annulment, **2**. reversion; *synonyms* (*n*) atavism, relapse, lapse, regress, return.

viðspyrna 1. stud; *synonyms* (*n*) boss, rivet, (*v*) knob, button, dot, **2**. stop; *synonyms* (*n*) halt, hold, stay, check, end; *antonyms* (*v*) continue, start, begin, encourage, permit.

viðstaddur present; *synonyms* (*adj*) grant, confer, (*n*) gift, donation, (*v*) bestow; *antonyms* (*adj*) missing, (*n*) past, future, (*v*) withdraw, (*adv*) absent.

víðsýnn liberal; *synonyms* (*adj*) generous, bountiful, free, handsome, abundant; *antonyms* (*adj*) strict, oppressive, totalitarian, intolerant, (*n*) conservative.

viðtæki 1. receiver; *synonyms* (*n*) recipient, beneficiary, cashier, earpiece, headset; *antonym* (*n*) donor, **2**. radio; *synonyms* (*n*) wireless, broadcasting, radiotelegram, (*v*) broadcast, transmit.

víðtækur global; *synonyms* (*adj*) general, international, overall, cosmopolitan, universal; *antonyms* (*adj*) local, national.

viðtak 1. susceptibility; *synonyms* (*n*) predisposition, sensitivity, impressibility, liability, inclination; *antonym* (*n*) resistance, **2**. antenna; *synonyms* (*n*) aerial, feeler, advance, finger, forefinger.

viðtaka receipt; *synonyms* (*n*) reception, acceptance, acknowledgment, acquittance, (*v*) acknowledge; *antonym* (*n*) dispatch.

viðtakandi 1. recipient; *synonyms* (*n*) beneficiary, receiver, inheritor, legatee, (*adj*) receptive; *antonym* (*n*) sender, **2**. receiver; *synonyms* (*n*) recipient, cashier, earpiece, headset, liquidator; *antonym* (*n*) donor, **3**. acceptor; *synonyms* (*n*) accepter, respecter, **4**. consignee; *synonyms* (*n*) depositary, nominee, agent, bearer, consignatary, **5**. addressee; *synonyms* (*n*) heir, inhabitant, occupant, tenant.

viðtakar audience; *synonyms* (*n*) hearing, interview, attendance, house, (*v*) auditory.

viðtaki 1. receptor, **2**. sink; *synonyms* (*n*) sag, (*v*) decline, dip, droop, fall; *antonyms* (*v*) rise, float, **3**. receiver; *synonyms* (*n*) recipient, beneficiary, cashier, earpiece, headset; *antonym* (*n*) donor, **4**. audience; *synonyms* (*n*) hearing, interview, attendance, house, (*v*) auditory.

viðtökuskoðun acceptance; *synonyms* (*n*) acceptation, acknowledgment, adoption, recognition, accession; *antonyms* (*n*) rejection, refutation, dispatch.

viðtökuval selecting; *synonyms* (*adj*) selective, eclectic, elective, electoral, (*n*) selection.

Viður wood; *synonyms* (*n*) forest, timber, woods, tree, lumber.

víður 1. spacious; *synonyms* (*adj*) roomy, broad, extensive, large, ample; *antonyms* (*adj*) cramped, narrow, **2**. vast; *synonyms* (*adj*) huge, immense, spacious, boundless, colossal; *antonyms* (*adj*) limited, small, tiny, **3**. wide; *synonyms* (*adj*) comprehensive, vast, capacious, expanded, extended; *antonyms* (*adj*) thin, restricted, **4**. capacious; *synonyms* (*adj*) big, commodious, expansive, voluminous, wide, **5**. broad; *synonyms* (*adj*) general, sweeping, free, blanket, (*n*) female; *antonym* (*adj*) specific.

viðurkenna 1. validate; *synonyms* (*v*) corroborate, substantiate, confirm, sustain, ratify; *antonyms* (*v*) invalidate, cancel, nullify, overturn, **2**. recognise; *synonyms* (*v*) admit, acknowledge, identify, know, accredit, **3**. sanction; *synonyms* (*n*) warrant, assent, (*v*) approve, permit, countenance; *antonyms* (*v*) ban, forbid, **4**. approve; *synonyms* (*v*) sanction, adopt, accept, allow, agree; *antonyms* (*v*) reject, censure, condemn, disapprove, veto, **5**. concede; *synonyms* (*v*) accord, cede, confess, yield, submit.

viðurkenndur approved; *synonyms* (*adj*) accepted, certified, sanctioned, allowed, authorized; *antonyms* (*adj*) informal, unofficial.

viðurkenning 1. status; *synonyms* (*n*) position, rank, situation, (*adj*) place, standing, **2**. validation; *synonyms* (*n*) confirmation, proof, substantiation, verification, establishment, **3**. recognition; *synonyms* (*n*) acknowledgment, appreciation, identification, perception, cognizance, **4**. approval; *synonyms* (*n*) acceptance, applause, approbation, acclaim, agreement; *antonyms* (*n*) disapproval, rejection, condemnation, scorn, criticism.

viðurlag apposition; *synonyms* (*n*) union, juxtaposition, (*prep*) addition, accompaniment, accord.

viðurlög 1. sanction; *synonyms* (n) warrant, assent, (v) approve, permit, countenance; *antonyms* (v) ban, forbid, **2**. penalty; *synonyms* (n) mulct, fine, forfeit, forfeiture, (v) condemnation.

viðvær global; *synonyms* (adj) general, international, overall, cosmopolitan, universal; *antonyms* (adj) local, national.

viðvani habituation; *synonyms* (n) adaptation, addiction, accustomedness, assuefaction, conditioning.

viðvaningur 1. amateur; *synonyms* (adj) amateurish, inexpert, unskilled, (n) novice, beginner; *antonyms* (adj) practiced, (n) professional, expert, **2**. apprentice; *synonyms* (n) learner, greenhorn, prentice, student, trainee.

viðvarandi prevailing; *synonyms* (adj) predominant, dominant, prevalent, rife, common; *antonym* (adj) minor.

viðvarp broadcast; *synonyms* (v) air, announce, circulate, disperse, (n) spread.

viðvörum caution; *synonyms* (n) advice, carefulness, precaution, vigilance, (v) care; *antonyms* (n) recklessness, carelessness, rashness.

viðvörun alarm; *synonyms* (n) dismay, alert, consternation, (v) awe, scare; *antonyms* (v) calm, comfort.

vifta 1. ventilator; *synonyms* (n) fan, vent, (v) bellows, blowpipe, lungs, **2**. fan; *synonyms* (n) admirer, buff, devotee, enthusiast, (v) air; *antonym* (n) detractor.

vígahnöttur 1. fireball; *synonyms* (n) bolide, cartouche, (adj) active, ambitious, capable, **2**. meteor; *synonyms* (n) aerolite, effluvium, emanation, evaporation, exhalation.

vigleco spirits; *synonyms* (n) liquor, alcohol, booze, humor, (adj) cheer.

vigt weight; *synonyms* (n) load, burden, charge, consequence, heaviness; *antonym* (n) triviality.

vigur vector; *synonyms* (n) direction, bearing, course, sender, transmitter.

vígur virulent; *synonyms* (adj) bitter, caustic, deadly, malicious, lethal.

vik 1. shift; *synonyms* (n) interchange, turn, (v) change, exchange, remove, **2**. deviation; *synonyms* (n) aberration, deflection, difference, diversion, variation; *antonym* (n) normality.

vík 1. bight; *synonyms* (n) bay, inlet, cove, gulf, loop, **2**. cove; *synonyms* (n) cave, harbor, recess, glen, fjord, **3**. bay; *synonyms* (n) alcove, bark, cry, (v) yap, roar, **4**. creek; *synonyms* (n) brook, stream, river, rivulet, (v) burn, **5**. inlet; *synonyms* (n) entry, entrance, arm, mouth, outlet.

vika week; *synonyms* (n) hebdomad, day, hour, minute, second.

víkja 1. suspend; *synonyms* (v) defer, delay, adjourn, hang, interrupt; *antonym* (v) continue, **2**. aberrate; *synonyms* (v) deviate, diverge, digress, wander, **3**. deviate; *synonyms* (v) depart, deflect, stray, vary, (adj) deviant; *antonym* (v) conform.

víkjandi recessive; *synonyms* (adj) recessionary, retiring, shy, unsociable, receding.

víkka 1. spread; *synonyms* (v) scatter, reach, disperse, expand, extend; *antonym* (adj) concentrated, **2**. extend; *synonyms* (v) enlarge, amplify, broaden, dilate, widen; *antonyms* (v) withdraw, shorten, limit, narrow, shrink.

víkkari 1. reamer; *synonyms* (n) juicer, drinker, imbiber, toper, **2**. dilator; *synonyms* (n) dilatator, dilater.

víkkun 1. spread; *synonyms* (v) scatter, reach, disperse, expand, extend; *antonym* (adj) concentrated, **2**. dilation; *synonyms* (n) dilatation, expansion, swelling, growth, spread, **3**. bore; *synonyms* (v) dig, bother, tire, annoy, (n) caliber; *antonyms* (v) interest, excite, fascinate, **4**. dilatation; *synonyms* (n) dilation, distension, extension, subtilization, delay.

vikmörk 1. tolerance; *synonyms* (n) endurance, allowance, indulgence, leniency, patience; *antonyms* (n) intolerance, narrow-mindedness, bigotry, chauvinism, extremism, **2**. margin; *synonyms* (n) edge, brink, boundary, hem, (v) border; *antonym* (n) center.

vikur pumice; *synonyms* (v) scour, buff.

vild 1. preference; *synonyms* (n) choice, inclination, liking, option, predilection, **2**. affiliation; *synonyms* (n) association, alliance, coalition, connection, relationship.

vilhalli bias; *synonyms* (n) penchant, drift, (v) prejudice, bent, (adj) partiality; *antonyms* (n) impartiality, neutrality, fairness.

vilhallur biased; *synonyms* (adj) partial, partisan, slanted, unfair, skewed; *antonyms* (adj) fair, fair-minded, neutral, unbiased, just.

vilja 1. want; *synonyms* (v) need, desire, (n) lack, poverty, wish; *antonyms* (v) dislike, hate, **2**. wish; *synonyms* (v) hope, like, aspiration, (n) want, (adv) will.

viljabeiting conation; *synonyms* (n) volition, velleity, design, intent, will.

viljadoði abulia; *synonym* (n) aboulia.

viljafrjáls voluntary; *synonyms* (adj) spontaneous, optional, deliberate, gratuitous, intentional; *antonyms* (adj) involuntary, compulsory, forced, instinctive.

viljalaus vegetative; *synonyms* (adj) vegetal, vegetational, fertile, vegetive, (v) vegetating.

viljastol abulia; *synonym* (n) aboulia.

viljastýrður voluntary; *synonyms* (*adj*) spontaneous, optional, deliberate, gratuitous, intentional; *antonyms* (*adj*) involuntary, compulsory, forced, instinctive.

vilji 1. will; *synonyms* (*v*) bequeath, (*n*) volition, command, desire, inclination, **2.** wish; *synonyms* (*v*) hope, like, (*n*) want, need, (*adv*) will; *antonyms* (*v*) dislike, hate, **3.** volition; *synonyms* (*n*) choice, option, testament, (*v*) purpose, **4.** willingness; *synonyms* (*n*) readiness, alacrity, obedience, promptness, appetite; *antonym* (*n*) unwillingness.

villa 1. bug; *synonyms* (*n*) beetle, (*v*) annoy, badger, pester, bother, **2.** aberration; *synonyms* (*n*) aberrance, aberrancy, abnormality, deviation, diversion, **3.** error; *synonyms* (*n*) blunder, fault, mistake, wrong, delusion; *antonym* (*n*) correctness.

villikál cabbage; *synonyms* (*n*) kale, (*v*) pilfer, filch, crib, nim.

villiköttur wildcat; *synonyms* (*n*) beast, brute, savage, animal, (*adj*) unauthorized.

villisproti sucker; *synonyms* (*n*) dupe, fool, sap, jay, lollipop.

vilnun option; *synonyms* (*n*) choice, election, alternative, preference, possibility; *antonyms* (*n*) essential, necessity, obligation.

vilsa 1. exudate; *synonyms* (*n*) gum, effusion, (*v*) excrete, expel, exude, **2.** exude; *synonyms* (*v*) emit, ooze, secrete, sweat, exudate.

vilsun exudation; *synonyms* (*n*) sweating, exhalation, sweat, transudation, exudate.

víma intoxication; *synonyms* (*n*) drunkenness, inebriation, inebriety, poisoning, tipsiness.

vímugjafi intoxicant; *synonyms* (*adj*) heady, (*n*) alcohol, inebriant, drink, liquor.

vin 1. wine; *synonyms* (*n*) vintage, vino, (*v*) entertain, (*adj*) lavender, lilac, **2.** oasis; *synonyms* (*n*) haven, isthmus, harbor, harbour, seaport.

vínandi alcohol; *synonyms* (*n*) drink, juice, intoxicant, drinkable, (*v*) alcoholism.

vinátta friendship; *synonyms* (*n*) fellowship, association, affection, familiarity, amity; *antonyms* (*n*) enmity, hostility.

vínberjasykur dextrose; *synonyms* (*n*) dextroglucose, sweetener.

vinda 1. winch; *synonyms* (*n*) crank, windlass, (*v*) capstan, derrick, wince, **2.** windlass; *synonyms* (*n*) winch, hoist, stowce, windas, (*v*) crane, **3.** wind; *synonyms* (*v*) coil, twist, curl, meander, turn.

vindalda sea; *synonyms* (*n*) ocean, water, (*adj*) marine, maritime, array.

vindátt windward; *synonyms* (*adj*) airy, boisterous, empty, (*adv*) downwind, (*n*) upwind; *antonym* (*n*) leeward.

vindborði windward; *synonyms* (*adj*) airy, boisterous, empty, (*adv*) downwind, (*n*) upwind; *antonym* (*n*) leeward.

vindborðsmegin windward; *synonyms* (*adj*) airy, boisterous, empty, (*adv*) downwind, (*n*) upwind; *antonym* (*n*) leeward.

vindborinn 1. aeolian; *synonyms* (*adj*) aerial, (*n*) eolian, **2.** airborne; *synonyms* (*adj*) flying, soaring.

vindgangur flatulence; *synonyms* (*n*) flatulency, gas, turgidity, wind, windiness.

vindgarður squall; *synonyms* (*n*) cry, gust, (*v*) shout, shriek, howl.

vindhviða 1. squall; *synonyms* (*n*) cry, gust, (*v*) shout, shriek, howl, **2.** gust; *synonyms* (*n*) burst, eruption, flurry, blast, blow.

vindingur 1. squirm; *synonyms* (*v*) wiggle, wriggle, twist, fidget, writhe, **2.** winding; *synonyms* (*adj*) tortuous, indirect, twisting, crooked, (*n*) wind; *antonyms* (*adj*) straight, direct, **3.** warping; *synonyms* (*n*) warp, warpage, beaming, buckle, deflection, **4.** torsion; *synonyms* (*n*) contortion, torque, tortuosity, crookedness, deformation, **5.** gyration; *synonyms* (*n*) revolution, roll, rotation, twirl, circulation.

vindkljúfur spoiler; *synonyms* (*n*) depredator, looter, pillager, plunderer, raider.

vindmælir anemometer; *synonym* (*adj*) anemoscope.

vindmylla windmill; *synonyms* (*n*) whirligig, aerogenerator, screw, fan, pinwheel.

vindriti anemograph; *synonyms* (*n*) anemometrograph, anemogram.

vindrof deflation; *synonyms* (*n*) depression, reduction, depreciation, contraction, comedown; *antonym* (*n*) inflation.

vindsveipur 1. squall; *synonyms* (*n*) cry, gust, (*v*) shout, shriek, howl, **2.** cyclone; *synonyms* (*n*) hurricane, storm, tempest, tornado, gale.

vindþembingur flatulence; *synonyms* (*n*) flatulency, gas, turgidity, wind, windiness.

vindur 1. wind; *synonyms* (*v*) coil, twist, curl, meander, turn, **2.** flatus; *synonyms* (*n*) breath, fart, wind, (*adj*) gas, air.

vingjarnlegur 1. affable; *synonyms* (*adj*) cordial, amiable, civil, courteous, friendly; *antonyms* (*adj*) disagreeable, hostile, reserved, **2.** friendly; *synonyms* (*adj*) favorable, affectionate, amicable, benevolent, companionable; *antonyms* (*adj*) unfriendly, aggressive, aloof, distant, formal, **3.** kindly; *synonyms* (*adj*) kind, benign, genial, gentle, affable; *antonyms* (*adv*) unkindly, harshly, callously, cruelly, nastily, **4.** kind; *synonyms* (*n*) form, helpful, sort, brand, breed; *antonyms* (*adj*) unkind, callous, cruel, hardhearted, mean.

vingl instability; *synonyms* (*n*) fickleness, fluctuation, flightiness, unreliability, (*adj*) fugacity; *antonyms* (*n*) stability, calm.

vinglaður faint; *synonyms* (*adj*) collapse, dim, dizzy, feeble, indistinct; *antonyms* (*adj*) distinct, strong, clear, obvious, considerable.

vinkona 1. friend; *synonyms* (*n*) fellow, acquaintance, (*adj*) associate, companion, comrade; *antonyms* (*n*) enemy, foe, stranger, rival, 2. girlfriend; *synonyms* (*n*) girl, lover, mistress, sweetheart, woman.

vínlandskarfi rosefish; *synonym* (*n*) redfish.

vinna 1. work; *synonyms* (*n*) exercise, business, (*v*) labor, operate, toil; *antonyms* (*v*) idle, malfunction, 2. service; *synonyms* (*n*) help, aid, assistance, avail, (*v*) overhaul, 3. occupation; *synonyms* (*n*) employment, occupancy, craft, calling, job; *antonym* (*n*) surrender, 4. labor; *synonyms* (*n*) drudgery, effort, endeavor, exertion, travail; *antonym* (*v*) rest, 5. labour; *synonyms* (*n*) childbed, confinement, (*v*) grind, drive, drudge.

vinnanlegur workable; *synonyms* (*adj*) feasible, possible, practicable, viable, practical; *antonym* (*adj*) impossible.

vinningshlutfall odds; *synonyms* (*n*) advantage, chance, likelihood, possibility, (*v*) difference.

vinningslíkur odds; *synonyms* (*n*) advantage, chance, likelihood, possibility, (*v*) difference.

vinningur 1. profit; *synonyms* (*n*) gain, benefit, account, good, (*adj*) advantage; *antonym* (*v*) lose, 2. benefit; *synonyms* (*v*) aid, assist, profit, avail, help; *antonyms* (*n*) disadvantage, drawback, loss, (*v*) harm, 3. advantage; *synonyms* (*n*) behalf, privilege, expediency, lead, preponderance; *antonyms* (*n*) detriment, difficulty, 4. gain; *synonyms* (*v*) acquire, derive, attain, catch, (*n*) earnings.

vinnsla 1. processing; *synonyms* (*n*) working, refinement, developing, manufacture, dispensation, 2. preparation; *synonyms* (*n*) arrangement, concoction, provision, readiness, training, 3. performance; *synonyms* (*n*) act, discharge, achievement, execution, (*v*) action; *antonyms* (*n*) omission, practice.

vinnsluminni ram; *synonyms* (*v*) beat, cram, crash, drive, jam.

vinnsluslit abort; *synonyms* (*v*) expel, fail, terminate, cancel, (*n*) miscarry.

vinnslustig presentation; *synonyms* (*n*) donation, exhibition, demonstration, display, introduction.

vinnsluverk microprocessor; *synonyms* (*n*) chip, microchip.

vinnuafl labor; *synonyms* (*n*) drudgery, effort, endeavor, exertion, (*v*) toil; *antonym* (*v*) rest.

vinnuaflsnotkun employment; *synonyms* (*n*) business, (*v*) application, employ, calling, (*adj*) work; *antonym* (*n*) unemployment.

vinnuborð desktop; *synonyms* (*n*) background, backcloth, backdrop, ground, scope.

vinnudagur workday; *synonym* (*adj*) mundane.

vinnudýr worker; *synonyms* (*n*) employee, hand, proletarian, workman, actor.

vinnuferill operation; *synonyms* (*n*) execution, movement, act, agency, effect.

vinnufundur workshop; *synonyms* (*n*) shop, factory, studio, workhouse, atelier.

vinnuhollustufræði ergonomics; *synonyms* (*n*) bioengineering, biotechnology.

vinnuhringur cycle; *synonyms* (*n*) bicycle, circle, round, (*v*) bike, motorcycle.

vinnulaun wages; *synonyms* (*n*) salary, pay, wage, earnings, reward.

vinnulota spell; *synonyms* (*n*) magic, fascination, bout, conjuration, (*v*) charm.

vinnumaur worker; *synonyms* (*n*) employee, hand, proletarian, workman, actor.

vinnuregla discipline; *synonyms* (*v*) control, castigate, chastise, train, chasten.

vinnusloppur overall; *synonyms* (*adj*) entire, total, whole, (*n*) smock, boilersuit.

vinnustöð workstation; *synonyms* (*n*) computer, laptop, mainframe, notebook, office.

vinnustofa laboratory; *synonyms* (*n*) lab, factory, course, (*adj*) experimental, alembic.

vinnuveitandi employer; *synonyms* (*n*) boss, master, businessperson, patron, capitalist; *antonym* (*n*) employee.

vinnuvistfræði ergonomics; *synonyms* (*n*) bioengineering, biotechnology.

vinsa scope; *synonyms* (*n*) range, reach, domain, purview, room.

vinsamlegur 1. warm; *synonyms* (*adj*) hot, affectionate, tender, ardent, cordial; *antonyms* (*adj*) aloof, cold, unfriendly, reserved, (*v*) cool, 2. cordial; *synonyms* (*adj*) hearty, affable, genial, warm, amiable; *antonyms* (*adj*) hostile, stern, 3. friendly; *synonyms* (*adj*) favorable, amicable, benevolent, companionable, convivial; *antonyms* (*adj*) aggressive, disagreeable, distant, formal, bad-tempered.

vínsteinn tartar; *synonyms* (*adj*) dandruff, brabbler, (*n*) calculus, dragon, concretion.

vinstri 1. left; *synonyms* (*adj*) gone, absent, odd, port, remaining; *antonym* (*n*) right, 2. sinistral; *synonyms* (*adj*) left, sinistrorsal, sinistrorse, absurd, perverse.

vinstur abomasum; *synonym* (*n*) abomasus.

vinsun screening; *synonyms* (*n*) screen, sieving, concealment, cover, covering.

vinur 1. friend; *synonyms* (*n*) fellow, acquaintance, (*adj*) associate, companion, comrade; *antonyms* (*n*) enemy, foe, stranger, rival, **2**. mate; *synonyms* (*n*) match, partner, compeer, consort, (*v*) equal.

vír 1. wire; *synonyms* (*n*) cable, telegram, line, rope, (*v*) telegraph, **2**. cable; *synonyms* (*n*) cablegram, cord, guy, ribbon, (*v*) wire.

virða 1. respect; *synonyms* (*n*) honor, esteem, homage, (*v*) regard, observe; *antonyms* (*n*) cheek, insolence, (*v*) disrespect, scorn, despise, **2**. appraise; *synonyms* (*v*) evaluate, value, assess, estimate, measure, **3**. evaluate; *synonyms* (*v*) appraise, calculate, gauge, grade, rank.

virði 1. value; *synonyms* (*n*) merit, cost, appraise, (*v*) price, appreciate; *antonyms* (*n*) disadvantage, futility, uselessness, insignificance, **2**. worth; *synonyms* (*n*) value, virtue, importance, excellence, dignity; *antonym* (*n*) worthlessness.

virðing 1. self-respect; *synonyms* (*n*) pride, self-esteem, dignity, face, honesty, **2**. valuation; *synonyms* (*n*) estimation, appraisal, evaluation, estimate, appraisement, **3**. self-esteem; *synonyms* (*n*) confidence, morale, narcissism, self-content, worth, **4**. appraisal; *synonyms* (*n*) assessment, review, valuation, value, examination, **5**. goodwill; *synonyms* (*n*) friendship, friendliness, amity, grace, kindness; *antonyms* (*n*) hostility, malice.

virðingaröð hierarchy; *synonyms* (*n*) order, rank, class, apparatus, executive.

virðisrýrnun 1. depreciation; *synonyms* (*n*) abatement, detraction, disparagement, derogation, deterioration, **2**. impairment; *synonyms* (*n*) damage, harm, disability, hurt, (*adj*) detriment.

virðuleiki 1. self-esteem; *synonyms* (*n*) confidence, dignity, morale, narcissism, self-content, **2**. self-respect; *synonyms* (*n*) pride, self-esteem, face, honesty.

virka function; *synonyms* (*n*) position, office, place, (*v*) act, exercise.

virki 1. operator; *synonyms* (*n*) driver, hustler, manipulator, agent, doer, **2**. equipment; *synonyms* (*n*) material, apparatus, facility, gear, (*v*) furniture.

virking activation; *synonyms* (*n*) activating, start, initiation, launch, awakening.

virkir 1. activator; *synonym* (*n*) inducer, **2**. operator; *synonyms* (*n*) driver, hustler, manipulator, agent, doer.

virkisgarður rampart; *synonyms* (*n*) bulwark, fortification, wall, earthwork, (*v*) battlement.

virkja 1. activate; *synonyms* (*v*) actuate, start, trigger, aerate, animate, **2**. engage; *synonyms* (*v*) contract, attract, book, employ, absorb; *antonyms* (*v*) fire, disengage, **3**. harness; *synonyms* (*n*) gear, rein, tether, (*v*) hitch, (*adj*) strap, **4**. induce; *synonyms* (*v*) generate, cause, tempt, impel, bring.

virkjun activation; *synonyms* (*n*) activating, start, initiation, launch, awakening.

virkni 1. activity; *synonyms* (*n*) action, activeness, exercise, liveliness, play; *antonyms* (*n*) inactivity, inaction, inactiveness, **2**. vigour; *synonyms* (*n*) force, energy, vigor, vim, push, **3**. reactivity; *synonyms* (*n*) excitability, responsiveness, sensitivity, **4**. action; *synonyms* (*n*) act, accomplishment, activity, agency, (*v*) achievement, **5**. creativity; *synonyms* (*n*) creativeness, invention, originality, cleverness, imagination; *antonym* (*n*) literalism.

virknisaukning potentiation; *synonym* (*n*) potentialization.

virkur 1. active; *synonyms* (*adj*) energetic, alert, busy, diligent, effective; *antonyms* (*adj*) dormant, inactive, sluggish, idle, latent, **2**. radioactive, **3**. dynamic; *synonyms* (*adj*) active, aggressive, dynamical, forceful, powerful; *antonyms* (*adj*) dull, static, **4**. effective; *synonyms* (*adj*) beneficial, practical, (*n*) competent, capable, able; *antonyms* (*adj*) ineffective, useless, weak, inoperative, **5**. functional; *synonyms* (*adj*) handy, operational, operative, working, serviceable; *antonym* (*adj*) nonfunctional.

vírus virus; *synonyms* (*n*) bug, infection, germ, poison, venom.

vís 1. sure; *synonyms* (*adj*) certain, reliable, secure, safe, (*v*) steady; *antonyms* (*adj*) doubtful, uncertain, unsure, hesitant, **2**. certain; *synonyms* (*adj*) actual, definite, sure, absolute, assured; *antonym* (*adj*) questionable.

vísbending 1. cue; *synonyms* (*n*) prompt, clue, tip, clew, (*v*) hint, **2**. evidence; *synonyms* (*n*) confirmation, mark, proof, (*v*) display, demonstrate, **3**. indication; *synonyms* (*n*) evidence, index, designation, direction, forerunner, **4**. indicator; *synonyms* (*n*) gauge, indication, arrow, indicant, pointer.

vísbendir indicator; *synonyms* (*n*) gauge, index, indication, arrow, indicant.

vísifingur index; *synonyms* (*n*) catalogue, exponent, file, table, (*v*) list.

vísindagrein 1. science; *synonyms* (*n*) learning, lore, knowledge, literature, (*adj*) art, **2**. discipline; *synonyms* (*v*) control, castigate, chastise, train, chasten.

vísindi science; *synonyms* (*n*) learning, lore, knowledge, literature, (*adj*) art.

vísir 1. indicator; *synonyms* (*n*) gauge, index, indication, arrow, indicant, **2.** index; *synonyms* (*n*) catalogue, exponent, file, table, (*v*) list, **3.** pointer; *synonyms* (*n*) hint, clue, hand, needle, point, **4.** primer; *synonyms* (*n*) manual, fuse, fuze, ground, grammar, **5.** amplitude; *synonyms* (*n*) breadth, latitude, magnitude, width, mass.

vísitala 1. quotient; *synonyms* (*n*) proportion, factor, ratio, share, fraction, **2.** index; *synonyms* (*n*) catalogue, exponent, file, table, (*v*) list.

vísitölubinda index; *synonyms* (*n*) catalogue, exponent, file, table, (*v*) list.

viska intelligence; *synonyms* (*n*) information, cleverness, intellect, news, tidings; *antonyms* (*n*) stupidity, emotion.

visna atrophy; *synonyms* (*n*) decay, (*v*) attenuation, emaciation, tabes, waste.

visnun 1. tabes, **2.** atrophy; *synonyms* (*n*) decay, (*v*) attenuation, emaciation, tabes, waste, **3.** involution; *synonyms* (*n*) exponentiation, intricacy, complexity, complication, (*v*) convolution.

vissulegur 1. sure; *synonyms* (*adj*) certain, reliable, secure, safe, (*v*) steady; *antonyms* (*adj*) doubtful, uncertain, unsure, hesitant, **2.** certain; *synonyms* (*adj*) actual, definite, sure, absolute, assured; *antonym* (*adj*) questionable.

vissustefna positivism; *synonyms* (*n*) positivity, certainty, anabaptism, deism, externalism.

vist 1. habitat; *synonyms* (*n*) dwelling, abode, residence, environment, home, **2.** niche; *synonyms* (*n*) corner, alcove, hole, bay, recess.

vista save; *synonyms* (*v*) deliver, economize, rescue, conserve, (*prep*) except; *antonyms* (*v*) spend, squander, waste.

vistarfirring disorientation; *synonyms* (*n*) confusion, awkwardness, bafflement, bewilderment, embarrassment.

vistarverur accommodation; *synonyms* (*n*) adjustment, compromise, loan, lodging, (*v*) advance.

vistfang address; *synonyms* (*n*) accost, lecture, abode, discourse, (*v*) greet; *antonym* (*v*) ignore.

vistfastur resident; *synonyms* (*adj*) native, (*n*) inhabitant, occupant, dweller, tenant; *antonyms* (*adj*) migratory, (*n*) landlord, drifter.

vistfengja address; *synonyms* (*n*) accost, lecture, abode, discourse, (*v*) greet; *antonym* (*v*) ignore.

vistfræði ecology; *synonyms* (*n*) bionomics, botany, conservationism, network, system.

vistfræðilegur ecological; *synonyms* (*adj*) ecologic, environmental, bionomic, bionomical, biological.

visthverfur biodegradable; *synonyms* (*adj*) ecological, environmental, green, recyclable.

vistir provisions; *synonyms* (*n*) food, commissariat, provender, supplies, victuals.

vistkerfi ecosystem; *synonyms* (*n*) complex, nature.

vistmerki label; *synonyms* (*n*) name, brand, tag, (*v*) mark, call.

vistrænn ecological; *synonyms* (*adj*) ecologic, environmental, bionomic, bionomical, biological.

vistþýða compile; *synonyms* (*v*) accumulate, amass, build, collect, assemble.

vistþýðandi compiler; *synonyms* (*n*) bookmaker, compilator, encyclopedist, encyclopaedist.

vistþýðing compilation; *synonyms* (*n*) collection, anthology, compiling, digest, miscellany.

vistun 1. save; *synonyms* (*v*) deliver, economize, rescue, conserve, (*prep*) except; *antonyms* (*v*) spend, squander, waste, **2.** admission; *synonyms* (*n*) acceptance, access, acknowledgment, confession, admittance; *antonym* (*n*) denial, **3.** outsourcing; *synonym* (*n*) relocation.

vistunarhamur save; *synonyms* (*v*) deliver, economize, rescue, conserve, (*prep*) except; *antonyms* (*v*) spend, squander, waste.

vísun 1. reference; *synonyms* (*n*) citation, mention, quotation, quote, allusion, **2.** indication; *synonyms* (*n*) clue, evidence, index, designation, direction.

vísunarsvið visibility; *synonyms* (*n*) visibleness, conspicuousness, apparition, (*v*) sight, view.

vit 1. intelligence; *synonyms* (*n*) information, cleverness, intellect, news, tidings; *antonyms* (*n*) stupidity, emotion, **2.** gnosis; *synonym* (*n*) gnosia.

vita know; *synonyms* (*v*) discern, comprehend, can, distinguish, have.

vitahús lighthouse; *synonyms* (*n*) beacon, light, pharos, faro.

vitfirring insanity; *synonyms* (*n*) derangement, frenzy, aberration, delirium, (*adj*) craziness; *antonym* (*n*) sanity.

vitglöp dementia; *synonyms* (*n*) insanity, lunacy, mania, delirium, demency.

viti 1. lighthouse; *synonyms* (*n*) beacon, light, pharos, faro, **2.** beacon; *synonyms* (*n*) cairn, flare, buoy, lighthouse, (*v*) guide.

vitlaus 1. strange; *synonyms* (*adj*) extraneous, foreign, peculiar, abnormal, curious; *antonyms* (*adj*) normal, ordinary, familiar, typical, **2.** weird; *synonyms* (*adj*) strange, supernatural, uncanny, unearthly, bizarre; *antonym* (*adj*) real, **3.** eccentric; *synonyms* (*adj*) odd, wacky, anomalous, crazy, (*n*) character; *antonym* (*n*) conformist, **4.** curious; *synonyms* (*adj*) funny, interested, unusual, extraordinary, inquiring; *antonym* (*adj*) incurious, **5.** odd; *synonyms* (*adj*) grotesque, exceptional, droll, eccentric, singular; *antonym* (*adj*) even.

vitmynd idea; *synonyms* (*n*) belief, concept, meaning, opinion, apprehension.

vitnaleiðsla hearing; *synonyms* (*n*) audition, earshot, ear, trial, (*adj*) audience; *antonym* (*adj*) deaf.

vitnaleiðslur hearing; *synonyms* (*n*) audition, earshot, ear, trial, (*adj*) audience; *antonym* (*adj*) deaf.

vitneskja information; *synonyms* (*n*) advice, communication, data, evidence, note.

vitorðsmaður confederate; *synonyms* (*adj*) allied, (*n*) accomplice, ally, accessory, (*v*) associate.

vitra glasses; *synonyms* (*n*) spectacles, eyeglasses, specs, bifocals, monocle.

vitrænn cognitive; *synonyms* (*adj*) psychological, rational, reasonable.

vitro glasses; *synonyms* (*n*) spectacles, eyeglasses, specs, bifocals, monocle.

vitsmunalegur intellectual; *synonyms* (*adj*) cerebral, mental, rational, (*n*) intellect, brain.

vitsmunaskerðing dementia; *synonyms* (*n*) insanity, lunacy, mania, delirium, demency.

vitsmunir 1. cognition; *synonyms* (*n*) knowledge, perception, cognizance, conception, cognoscence, 2. intellect; *synonyms* (*n*) brain, mind, intelligence, brains, head.

vitund consciousness; *synonyms* (*n*) awareness, feeling, sense, conscience, cognizance; *antonym* (*n*) unconsciousness.

víxill 1. commutator; *synonyms* (*n*) break, electrepeter, 2. acceptance; *synonyms* (*n*) acceptation, acknowledgment, adoption, recognition, accession; *antonyms* (*n*) rejection, refutation, dispatch, 3. draft; *synonyms* (*n*) bill, conscription, (*v*) draught, outline, design; *antonym* (*v*) discharge.

víxl 1. substitution; *synonyms* (*n*) replacement, exchange, change, substitute, interchange, 2. alternation; *synonyms* (*n*) variation, vicissitude, alternateness, alternativeness, reciprocity, 3. interference; *synonyms* (*n*) disturbance, hindrance, handicap, block, (*v*) collision.

víxla 1. swap; *synonyms* (*v*) exchange, change, switch, trade, (*n*) barter, 2. toggle; *synonyms* (*n*) pin, button, clasp, clip, closure, 3. commute; *synonyms* (*v*) transform, alter, convert, permute, transpose.

víxlanlegur interchangeable; *synonyms* (*adj*) convertible, commutative, exchangeable, identical, reciprocal.

víxlarák fringe; *synonyms* (*n*) brim, brink, edge, boundary, (*v*) border.

víxlast 1. commute; *synonyms* (*v*) change, barter, exchange, transform, alter, 2. decussate; *synonyms* (*v*) cross, intersect, cloth, cut, (*adj*)

intersectant, 3. interfere; *synonyms* (*v*) intercede, obstruct, disturb, conflict, (*n*) interpose.

víxlhrif interference; *synonyms* (*n*) disturbance, hindrance, handicap, block, (*v*) collision.

víxlmælir interferometer; *synonyms* (*v*) bathometer, galvanometer, heliometer, dynamometer, goniometer.

víxlstaða repulsion; *synonyms* (*n*) repugnance, revulsion, antipathy, aversion, disgust; *antonyms* (*n*) attraction, charm.

víxlun 1. transposition; *synonyms* (*n*) exchange, permutation, replacement, reversal, substitution, 2. crossover; *synonyms* (*n*) crossing, cross, carrefour, crossbreeding, crossroad, 3. cross; *synonyms* (*v*) intersect, baffle, (*adj*) crabbed, crabby, angry; *antonyms* (*v*) uncross, (*adj*) calm, good-tempered, 4. exchange; *synonyms* (*n*) commutation, swap, (*v*) change, barter, interchange.

víxlunarmælir interferometer; *synonyms* (*v*) bathometer, galvanometer, heliometer, dynamometer, goniometer.

víxlverka interact; *synonyms* (*v*) communicate, associate, correlate, cooperate, bridge.

víxlverkandi interactive; *synonyms* (*adj*) interactional, mutual, synergistic, synergetic.

víxlverkun 1. interaction; *synonyms* (*n*) interplay, contact, correlation, communication, mutuality, 2. interference; *synonyms* (*n*) disturbance, hindrance, handicap, block, (*v*) collision.

víxlvirkur interactive; *synonyms* (*adj*) interactional, mutual, synergistic, synergetic.

vöðvafesta insertion; *synonyms* (*n*) inset, enclosure, introduction, intromission, interpolation; *antonym* (*n*) removal.

vöðvaglóbín myoglobin; *synonym* (*n*) mb.

vöðvahald insertion; *synonyms* (*n*) inset, enclosure, introduction, intromission, interpolation; *antonym* (*n*) removal.

vöðvahlaup cramp; *synonyms* (*n*) convulsion, spasm, (*v*) confine, constrict, restrict.

vöðvakvik tic; *synonyms* (*n*) twitching, spasm, jerk, quiver, (*v*) twitch.

vöðvamikill muscular; *synonyms* (*adj*) athletic, brawny, strong, burly, hefty; *antonyms* (*adj*) puny, slight.

vöðvarauði myoglobin; *synonym* (*n*) mb.

vöðvaspenna 1. tonus; *synonyms* (*n*) tone, tonicity, feel, feeling, flavor, 2. tone; *synonyms* (*n*) character, note, accent, air, (*v*) color.

vöðvastifni rigidity; *synonyms* (*n*) austerity, firmness, inflexibility, hardness, rigor; *antonyms* (*n*) flexibility, malleability, pliability, softness.

vöðvaþráðla myofibril; *synonyms* (*n*) myofibrilla, sarcostyle.

vöðvatrefja myofibril; *synonyms* (*n*) myofibrilla, sarcostyle.

vöðvaupphaf origin; *synonyms* (*n*) cause, lineage, base, beginning, birth; *antonym* (*n*) end.

vöðvaviðbragð jerk; *synonyms* (*v*) jolt, jump, shake, yank, jar.

vöðvi muscle; *synonyms* (*n*) brawn, potency, sinew, might, power.

vöf turn; *synonyms* (*n*) bend, curve, roll, coil, go.

vog 1. weight; *synonyms* (*n*) load, burden, charge, consequence, heaviness; *antonym* (*n*) triviality, **2.** scale; *synonyms* (*n*) flake, gamut, (*v*) ascend, climb, (*adj*) balance; *antonym* (*v*) descend, **3.** balance; *synonyms* (*n*) poise, symmetry, (*v*) counterbalance, adjust, offset; *antonyms* (*n*) imbalance, (*v*) unbalance.

vogarafl leverage; *synonyms* (*n*) lever, advantage, influence, leveraging, purchase.

vogararmur lever; *synonyms* (*n*) knob, (*v*) pry, raise, jimmy, prize.

vogarás fulcrum; *synonyms* (*n*) pivot, hinge, bearing, crux, support.

vogarskál balance; *synonyms* (*n*) poise, symmetry, (*v*) counterbalance, adjust, offset; *antonyms* (*n*) imbalance, (*v*) unbalance.

vogarstöng lever; *synonyms* (*n*) knob, (*v*) pry, raise, jimmy, prize.

vögguljóð 1. berceuse; *synonyms* (*n*) lullaby, cradlesong, **2.** cradlesong; *synonym* (*n*) berceuse, **3.** lullaby; *synonyms* (*n*) alleviation, easement, mitigation, (*v*) lull, sedative.

vögguvísa 1. berceuse; *synonyms* (*n*) lullaby, cradlesong, **2.** cradlesong; *synonym* (*n*) berceuse, **3.** lullaby; *synonyms* (*n*) alleviation, easement, mitigation, (*v*) lull, sedative.

vogris stye; *synonyms* (*n*) hordeolum, sty, pigsty, pigpen.

vogtala weight; *synonyms* (*n*) load, burden, charge, consequence, heaviness; *antonym* (*n*) triviality.

vogun 1. venture; *synonyms* (*n*) hazard, (*v*) risk, chance, stake, peril, **2.** risk; *synonyms* (*n*) danger, gamble, jeopardy, adventure, bet; *antonyms* (*n*) safety, (*v*) protect, **3.** leverage; *synonyms* (*n*) lever, advantage, influence, leveraging, purchase.

vogur 1. pus; *synonyms* (*n*) matter, purulence, suppuration, festering, ichor, **2.** estuary; *synonyms* (*n*) bay, inlet, mouth, bight, cove, **3.** inlet; *synonyms* (*n*) entry, gulf, entrance, arm, outlet.

voka hover; *synonyms* (*v*) float, fly, hang, hesitate, brood.

vöknun recovery; *synonyms* (*n*) rally, convalescence, improvement, reclamation, rescue; *antonyms* (*n*) decline, loss, return.

vöktun 1. supervision; *synonyms* (*n*) oversight, charge, control, direction, (*v*) inspection, **2.** monitoring; *synonym* (*n*) observation.

vökuvitund wakefulness; *synonyms* (*n*) sleeplessness, insomnia, vigilance, (*v*) vigil, watch; *antonym* (*n*) sleepiness.

vökva 1. irrigate; *synonyms* (*v*) water, dilute, dip, drink, (*adj*) dabble, **2.** water (vatn); *synonyms* (*n*) urine, (*v*) irrigate, moisten, wet, soak.

vökvaaflfræði 1. hydrodynamics; *synonyms* (*n*) hydrokinetics, (*adj*) hydrology, hydrostatics, **2.** hydrodynamic; *synonym* (*adj*) hydrodynamical.

vökvaaflfræðilegur hydrodynamic; *synonym* (*adj*) hydrodynamical.

vökvablanda emulsion; *synonyms* (*n*) balm, cream, emulsification, liquid, (*adj*) soup.

vökvagerð liquefaction; *synonyms* (*n*) dissolution, fusion, condensation, melting, solvolysis.

vökvageymir reservoir; *synonyms* (*n*) cistern, fountain, well, lake, store.

vökvahreyfifræði 1. hydraulics, **2.** hydrodynamic; *synonym* (*adj*) hydrodynamical.

vökvakúpull meniscus; *synonyms* (*n*) crescent, lens, curve, sunglass.

vökvakyrrstaða hydrostatics; *synonym* (*adj*) hydrology.

vökvamyndun liquefaction; *synonyms* (*n*) dissolution, fusion, condensation, melting, solvolysis.

vökvasókn congestion; *synonyms* (*n*) blockage, engorgement, overcrowding, aggregation, crowding; *antonym* (*n*) emptiness.

vökvastöðufræði 1. hydrostatics; *synonym* (*adj*) hydrology, **2.** hydraulics.

vökvastraumfræði hydrodynamics; *synonyms* (*n*) hydrokinetics, (*adj*) hydrology, hydrostatics.

vökvasuga siphon; *synonyms* (*n*) cloaca, culvert, (*v*) drain, syphon, draw.

vökvatæma bleed; *synonyms* (*v*) ooze, phlebotomize, run, (*n*) bleeding, ache.

vökvaþrútnun imbibition; *synonyms* (*n*) imbibing, drinking, boozing, crapulence, drink.

vökvi 1. liquid; *synonyms* (*adj*) flowing, fluent, fluid, juicy, limpid; *antonyms* (*adj*) firm, (*n*) solid, gaseous, **2.** fluid; *synonyms* (*adj*) liquid, unsettled, changeable, smooth, mobile.

vökvun 1. irrigation; *synonyms* (*v*) affusion, humectation, immersion, infiltration, spargefaction, **2.** hydration.

volfram tungsten; *synonyms* (*n*) wolfram, w, watt, west.

volgur 1. tepid; *synonyms* (adj) lukewarm, warm, mild, cool, indifferent, **2**. lukewarm; *synonyms* (adj) tepid, cold, listless, halfhearted, unenthusiastic; *antonym* (adj) enthusiastic.

völlur field; *synonyms* (n) arena, area, battlefield, domain, ground.

voltamælir voltameter; *synonym* (n) coulometer.

völuberg conglomerate; *synonyms* (n) composite, group, complex, (v) accumulate, amass.

völundarhús 1. maze; *synonyms* (n) labyrinth, tangle, snarl, web, complication, **2**. labyrinth; *synonyms* (n) maze, confusion, network, (v) eel.

völur 1. stud; *synonyms* (n) boss, rivet, (v) knob, button, dot, **2**. spindle; *synonyms* (n) axle, mandrel, pivot, arbor, axis.

völvuauga belladonna; *synonyms* (n) henbane, hellebore, hemlock, nightshade, bittersweet.

von 1. hope; *synonyms* (v) trust, (n) aspiration, belief, desire, expectation; *antonyms* (v) despair, (n) reality, **2**. advertency; *synonym* (n) advertence, **3**. advertence; *synonyms* (n) advertency, reference, **4**. attention; *synonyms* (n) mind, aid, alertness, care, consideration; *antonyms* (n) inattention, neglect, **5**. acuity; *synonyms* (n) sharpness, acumen, acuteness, discernment, keenness.

vona hope; *synonyms* (v) trust, (n) aspiration, belief, desire, expectation; *antonyms* (v) despair, (n) reality.

vonbrigði 1. disappointment; *synonyms* (n) defeat, anticlimax, comedown, failure, frustration; *antonyms* (n) success, satisfaction, boost, **2**. bummer; *synonyms* (n) disappointment, adversity, beggar, (adj) appalling, bad, **3**. disillusionment; *synonyms* (n) disenchantment, disillusion, letdown, apathy, discontent, **4**. frustration; *synonyms* (n) vexation, setback, check, disillusionment, anger.

vondur 1. bad; *synonyms* (adj) evil, adverse, harmful, immoral, (v) decayed; *antonyms* (adj) fresh, pleasant, well, well-behaved, (n) good, **2**. poor; *synonyms* (adj) bad, low, miserable, paltry, (v) meager; *antonyms* (adj) rich, wealthy, excellent, first-rate, privileged, **3**. miserable; *synonyms* (adj) mean, poor, abject, (v) forlorn, wretched; *antonyms* (adj) happy, cheerful, generous, **4**. evil; *synonyms* (adj) corrupt, criminal, ill, wicked, (n) damage; *antonyms* (adj) kindhearted, (n) goodness, righteousness, **5**. nasty; *synonyms* (adj) dirty, loathsome, disgusting, filthy, foul; *antonyms* (adj) agreeable, kind, nice, charitable, lovely.

vongildi expectation; *synonyms* (n) anticipation, expectancy, belief, hope, prospect; *antonym* (n) despair.

vöntun absence; *synonyms* (n) absenteeism, dearth, default, deficiency, lack; *antonyms* (n) presence, attendance.

vönun 1. sterilization; *synonym* (n) sterilisation, **2**. castration; *synonyms* (n) emasculation, eviration, bowdlerisation, bowdlerization, expurgation.

vopn weapon; *synonyms* (n) gun, arm, missile, artillery, blade.

vor 1. spring; *synonyms* (n) jump, leap, bound, (v) hop, caper, **2**. springtime; *synonyms* (n) spring, prime, springtide, bounce, fountain.

vör lip; *synonyms* (n) border, brim, cheek, edge, impertinence.

vörður guard; *synonyms* (n) defend, defense, bulwark, care, cover.

vorkenna pity; *synonyms* (n) compassion, commiseration, mercy, (v) commiserate, compassionate; *antonym* (n) blame.

vörn 1. protection; *synonyms* (n) defense, care, conservation, cover, (v) guard; *antonym* (n) destruction, **2**. protective; *synonyms* (adj) defensive, preventive, caring, maternal, (adv) fatherly, **3**. restraint; *synonyms* (n) bridle, constraint, control, hindrance, (v) check; *antonyms* (n) excess, abandon, decadence, incentive, **4**. defense; *synonyms* (n) apology, defence, excuse, fortification, justification; *antonyms* (n) attack, criticism, offense, **5**. defence; *synonyms* (n) vindication, denial, abnegation, demurrer, refutation.

vörpun 1. projection; *synonyms* (n) bulge, hump, jut, prominence, protuberance, **2**. transformation; *synonyms* (n) conversion, alteration, metamorphosis, change, shift, **3**. mapping; *synonyms* (n) map, correspondence, agreement, balance, commensurateness, **4**. map; *synonyms* (n) design, graph, plat, (v) chart, plan.

vorsíld capelin; *synonyms* (n) caplin, capelan, capling.

vorsíli capelin; *synonyms* (n) caplin, capelan, capling.

vortími 1. springtime; *synonyms* (n) spring, prime, springtide, bounce, bound, **2**. spring; *synonyms* (n) jump, leap, fountain, (v) hop, caper.

vörtubaugur areola; *synonyms* (n) armlet, bracelet, hoop, roundlet, areolation.

vörtuber longan; *synonyms* (n) longanberry, lungen, lungan.

vörtuberjatré longan; *synonyms* (n) longanberry, lungen, lungan.

vöruafbrigði brand; *synonyms* (n) badge, blade, (v) mark, (adj) stigma, blot.

vörubifreið truck; *synonyms* (n) traffic, car, cart, (v) exchange, barter.

vörubíll 1. truck; *synonyms* (*n*) traffic, car, cart, (*v*) exchange, barter, **2.** lorry; *synonyms* (*n*) dray, camion, truck, waggon, wagon.

vörublanda unit; *synonyms* (*n*) troop, element, group, squad, (*adj*) one.

vörublendi unit; *synonyms* (*n*) troop, element, group, squad, (*adj*) one.

vörubretti pallet; *synonyms* (*n*) palette, bed, berth, stillage, shakedown.

vöruferilsstjórn logistics; *synonym* (*n*) reasoning.

vöruferlisstjórnun logistics; *synonym* (*n*) reasoning.

vöruflutningaprammi barge; *synonyms* (*n*) lighter, boat, craft, flatboat, hoy.

vöruflutningar transportation; *synonyms* (*n*) deportation, banishment, exile, (*v*) transport, conveyance.

vöruflutningaskip freighter; *synonyms* (*n*) bottom, merchantman, charterer, arse, ass.

vöruflutningavél freighter; *synonyms* (*n*) bottom, merchantman, charterer, arse, ass.

vöruflytjandi shipper; *synonyms* (*n*) sender, carrier, carter, hauler, merchant.

vörugeymsla warehouse; *synonyms* (*n*) store, storehouse, godown, depository, (*v*) magazine.

vöruhús warehouse; *synonyms* (*n*) store, storehouse, godown, depository, (*v*) magazine.

vörulisti catalog; *synonyms* (*n*) list, (*v*) catalogue, record, file, classify.

vörumengi unit; *synonyms* (*n*) troop, element, group, squad, (*adj*) one.

vörumerki 1. trademark; *synonyms* (*n*) brand, earmark, hallmark, mark, label, **2.** brand; *synonyms* (*n*) badge, blade, class, (*adj*) stigma, blot.

vörumóttakandi consignee; *synonyms* (*n*) depositary, nominee, agent, bearer, consignatary.

vörur 1. cargo; *synonyms* (*n*) burden, loading, freight, wares, (*adj*) load, **2.** goods; *synonyms* (*n*) cargo, belongings, commodity, merchandise, product.

vörureikningar invoice; *synonyms* (*n*) bill, account, list, reckoning, (*v*) charge.

vörureikningur bill; *synonyms* (*n*) account, beak, advertisement, (*v*) placard, advertise.

vörusendandi consignor; *synonyms* (*n*) consigner, shipper.

vörusending consignment; *synonyms* (*n*) cargo, commission, commitment, freight, load.

vöruskipti 1. barter; *synonyms* (*n*) trade, commutation, swap, (*v*) exchange, bargain, **2.** exchange; *synonyms* (*v*) change, barter, interchange, commute, counterchange.

vörustjórnun logistics; *synonym* (*n*) reasoning.

vörutegund brand; *synonyms* (*n*) badge, blade, (*v*) mark, (*adj*) stigma, blot.

vöruvagn truck; *synonyms* (*n*) traffic, car, cart, (*v*) exchange, barter.

vosto tails; *synonyms* (*n*) tailcoat, tail, waste, coat.

vothey silage; *synonyms* (*n*) ensilage, food, hay.

votlendi 1. wetland; *synonyms* (*n*) marsh, bog, swamp, fen, marshland, **2.** marsh; *synonyms* (*n*) quagmire, marish, morass, mire, swampland.

vottorð certificate; *synonyms* (*n*) bond, diploma, certification, credential, (*v*) certify.

vottun certification; *synonyms* (*n*) authentication, certificate, verification, accreditation, corroboration.

votur wet; *synonyms* (*adj*) damp, humid, (*v*) moisten, water, dampen; *antonyms* (*adj*) dehydrated, parched, (*v*) dry.

vöxtur 1. growth; *synonyms* (*n*) development, accretion, augmentation, evolution, gain; *antonyms* (*n*) decrease, reduction, weakening, decline, **2.** accretion; *synonyms* (*n*) increment, accumulation, increase, accession, addition, **3.** accession; *synonyms* (*n*) acceptance, access, acquisition, agreement, arrival, **4.** increment; *synonyms* (*n*) boost, growth, extra, aggrandizement, enlargement.

W

wolfram tungsten; *synonyms* (*n*) wolfram, w, watt, west.

X

xýlen xylene; *synonym* (*n*) xylol.

Y

yddur acute; *synonyms* (*adj*) sharp, incisive, intense, keen, penetrating; *antonyms* (*adj*) dull, obtuse.

yfir 1. above; *synonyms* (*prep*) on, (*adv*) over, beyond, aloft, (*adj*) preceding; *antonym* (*prep*) below, **2.** beyond; *synonyms* (*prep*) above, (*adv*) further, without, besides, (*adj*) across; *antonym* (*prep*) within, **3.** over; *synonyms* (*adv*) more, by, (*prep*) during, (*n*) overs, (*adj*) finished.

yfirálag 1. overstress; *synonyms* (*v*) exaggerate, magnify, overemphasize, overstate, overemphasise, **2.** overload; *synonyms* (*n*) overburden, *(v)* burden, overcharge, encumber, oppress.

yfirborð 1. surface; *synonyms (n)* level, face, *(v)* appear, emerge, *(adj)* exterior; *antonyms (n)* core, inside, interior, middle, **2**. face; *synonyms (n)* look, aspect, countenance, *(v)* confront, *(adj)* front; *antonyms (v)* avoid, back.

yfirborðsbatn runoff; *synonyms (n)* overflow, overspill, excess, flood, grounds.

yfirborðsflötur area; *synonyms (n)* place, region, size, width, expanse.

yfirborðshæð level; *synonyms (n)* grade, *(adj)* even, equal, *(v)* flat, flatten; *antonyms (adj)* inclined, slanting, angled, *(v)* uneven, build.

yfirbragð style; *synonyms (n)* fashion, name, *(v)* call, entitle, *(adj)* manner.

yfirbreiðsla tarpaulin; *synonyms (n)* tarp, counterpane, cover, coverlet, quilt.

yfirbygging 1. superstructure; *synonyms (n)* building, edifice, pavement, superstruction, **2**. body; *synonyms (n)* cadaver, corpse, matter, organization, carcass; *antonym (n)* spirit, **3**. hull; *synonyms (n)* crust, shell, hulk, husk, *(v)* skin, **4**. overhead; *synonyms (adv)* above, aloft, over, up, *(n)* expense.

yfirbyggingarhlutir bodywork; *synonyms (n)* armature, carcass, frame, framework, hulk.

yfirbyggingarvinna bodywork; *synonyms (n)* armature, carcass, frame, framework, hulk.

yfirdráttur overdraft; *synonyms (n)* bankruptcy, ratching.

yfirfæra transpose; *synonyms (v)* exchange, change, shift, transfer, transplant.

yfirfæranlegur transferable; *synonyms (adj)* movable, negotiable, assignable, conveyable, moveable.

yfirfærsla 1. transfer; *synonyms (n)* conveyance, *(v)* convey, carry, change, remove; *antonyms (v)* hold, keep, **2**. translation; *synonyms (n)* displacement, interpretation, rendering, transformation, version, **3**. translocation; *synonyms (n)* shift, interchange, **4**. generalization; *synonyms (n)* generality, generalisation, induction, idea, abstraction; *antonym (n)* detail.

yfirfall overflow; *synonyms (n)* flood, deluge, inundation, excess, *(v)* inundate.

yfirfallsrör overflow; *synonyms (n)* flood, deluge, inundation, excess, *(v)* inundate.

yfirfara 1. review; *synonyms (n)* examination, critique, *(v)* check, survey, criticize, **2**. inspect; *synonyms (v)* examine, overhaul, overlook, explore, inquire, **3**. examine; *synonyms (v)* assay, audit, consider, try, control.

yfirferð sweep; *synonyms (n)* compass, expanse, range, *(v)* brush, rake.

yfirflæði 1. spillover; *synonym (n)* overflow, **2**. overflow; *synonyms (n)* flood, deluge, inundation, excess, *(v)* inundate.

yfirfylling flooding; *synonyms (n)* flood, overflow, cataclysm, *(adj)* overflowing, bloated.

yfirgefa 1. desert; *synonyms (v)* abandon, escape, defect, *(adj)* waste, barren; *antonyms (n)* bog, *(v)* stay, **2**. quit; *synonyms (v)* leave, go, discharge, drop, part; *antonym (v)* continue, **3**. abandon; *synonyms (v)* quit, relinquish, renounce, resign, vacate; *antonyms (v)* keep, support, maintain, *(n)* restraint, **4**. abdicate; *synonyms (v)* cede, desert, forgo, forsake, yield, **5**. drop; *synonyms (v)* fall, decrease, deposit, *(n)* decline, collapse; *antonyms (v)* rise, increase, lift, *(n)* growth.

yfirgefinn 1. abandoned; *synonyms (adj)* forlorn, immoral, deserted, empty, profligate; *antonyms (adj)* restrained, inhabited, orderly, overcrowded, **2**. deserted; *synonyms (adj)* abandoned, desert, solitary, bleak, derelict; *antonyms (adj)* occupied, packed, **3**. immoral; *synonyms (adj)* wicked, bad, evil, corrupt, depraved; *antonyms (adj)* moral, decent, honest, ethical, good, **4**. nasty; *synonyms (adj)* dirty, loathsome, disgusting, filthy, foul; *antonyms (adj)* agreeable, kind, pleasant, nice, charitable.

yfirgengi premium; *synonyms (n)* bonus, agio, bounty, payment, extra; *antonym (adj)* inferior.

yfirgír overdrive; *synonym (v)* overuse.

yfirgripsmikill comprehensive; *synonyms (adj)* capacious, broad, extensive, inclusive, complete; *antonyms (adj)* narrow, partial, noncomprehensive, restricted.

yfirhala overhaul; *synonyms (n)* inspection, *(v)* repair, check, modernize, overtake.

yfirhalning overhauling; *synonyms (n)* overhaul, revision.

yfirheyrsla hearing; *synonyms (n)* audition, earshot, ear, trial, *(adj)* audience; *antonym (adj)* deaf.

yfirhitun superheating; *synonym (n)* overheating.

yfirhlaup skip; *synonyms (n)* jump, bound, hop, *(v)* leap, dance.

yfirhljóð ultrasound; *synonyms (n)* sonography, ultrasonography.

yfirhúð 1. cuticle; *synonyms (n)* epidermis, shell, carapace, case, casing, **2**. epidermis; *synonyms (n)* cuticle, scarfskin, skin, coat, pelt.

yfirlið syncope; *synonyms (n)* swoon, faint, syncopation, fainting, deliquium.

yfirlit 1. statement; *synonyms (n)* account, declaration, affirmation, announcement, communication; *antonym (n)* denial, **2**. summary;

synonyms (n) abstract, compendium, abridgment, (adj) brief, compendious, **3**. view; **synonyms** (n) look, sight, judgment, opinion, (v) regard, **4**. schema; **synonyms** (n) outline, plan, chart, graph, scheme, **5**. abstract; **synonyms** (adj) theoretical, (v) abridge, (n) synopsis, abridgement, digest; **antonym** (adj) concrete.

yfirlög overlay; **synonyms** (n) coat, sheathing, (v) cover, overlap, veneer.

yfirlýsing 1. statement; **synonyms** (n) account, declaration, affirmation, announcement, communication; **antonym** (n) denial, **2**. declaration; **synonyms** (n) assertion, allegation, avowal, claim, expression.

yfirmaður 1. supervisor; **synonyms** (n) superintendent, director, overseer, boss, chief, **2**. superior; **synonyms** (adj) senior, dominant, better, exceptional, predominant; **antonyms** (adj) humble, worse, poor, (n) inferior, subordinate, **3**. master; **synonyms** (n) captain, instructor, (v) conquer, control, command, **4**. officer; **synonyms** (n) administrator, commander, bureaucrat, executive, officeholder, **5**. executive; **synonyms** (n) manager, administration, (adj) administrative, managerial, (v) authoritative.

yfirmál interference; **synonyms** (n) disturbance, hindrance, handicap, block, (v) collision.

yfirráð 1. sovereignty; **synonyms** (n) kingdom, reign, empire, autonomy, dominion, **2**. control; **synonyms** (n) rule, authority, (v) command, check, curb; **antonyms** (n) freedom, weakness, (v) intensify, share, **3**. dominance; **synonyms** (n) ascendancy, control, domination, supremacy, advantage; **antonym** (n) inferiority, **4**. domination; **synonyms** (n) ascendency, dominance, mastery, power, superiority, **5**. authority; **synonyms** (n) sanction, administration, authorization, hold, judge.

yfirráðaréttur sovereignty; **synonyms** (n) kingdom, reign, empire, autonomy, dominion.

yfirráðasvæði 1. territory; **synonyms** (n) district, dominion, area, field, land, **2**. dependency; **synonyms** (n) dependence, addiction, colony, dependance, (adj) contingency.

yfirráðasvið domain; **synonyms** (n) country, department, realm, area, kingdom; **antonym** (n) range.

yfirrita overwrite; **synonym** (n) overwriting.

yfirsætinn inferior; **synonyms** (adj) bad, secondary, subordinate, humble, poor; **antonyms** (adj) better, choice, excellent, first-rate, (n) superior.

yfirsetning epistasis; **synonyms** (n) epistasy, hypostasis.

yfirsetukona midwife; **synonyms** (n) accoucheuse, accoucheur, oculist, howdy, (v) midwive.

yfirsjálf superego; **synonyms** (n) conscience, scruple.

yfirsjón omission; **synonyms** (n) failure, error, exclusion, fault, ellipsis; **antonyms** (n) inclusion, adherence.

yfirskegg moustache; **synonyms** (n) hair, mustache, (adj) beard, whisker, brush.

yfirskilvitlegur transcendental; **synonyms** (adj) transcendent, preternatural, supernatural, nonnatural, otherworldly.

yfirskot overshoot; **synonyms** (v) overrun, jump.

yfirstaða epistasis; **synonyms** (n) epistasy, hypostasis.

yfirstæði epistasis; **synonyms** (n) epistasy, hypostasis.

yfirstæðni epistasis; **synonyms** (n) epistasy, hypostasis.

yfirstærð oversize; **synonyms** (adj) outsize, oversized, big, huge, outsized.

yfirstétt elite; **synonyms** (n) cream, best, pick, prime, (adj) flower.

yfirstór oversize; **synonyms** (adj) outsize, oversized, big, huge, outsized.

yfirstýring overloading; **synonyms** (n) overload, congestion, overcrowding, overfilling, overcapacity.

yfirsveiflur harmonics; **synonyms** (n) harmony, overtones.

yfirtaka 1. usurp; **synonyms** (v) assume, appropriate, arrogate, seize, commandeer, **2**. acquisition; **synonyms** (n) purchase, accomplishment, acquirement, attainment, achievement, **3**. overpower; **synonyms** (v) overcome, defeat, overwhelm, conquer, crush.

yfirtónn 1. overtone; **synonyms** (n) implication, connotation, suggestion, undertone, allusion; **antonym** (n) hint, **2**. harmonic; **synonyms** (adj) harmonious, consonant, harmonical, sympathetic, concordant.

yfirvald 1. authority; **synonyms** (n) ascendancy, command, sanction, administration, authorization, **2**. magistrate; **synonyms** (n) judge, justice, jurist, official, provost.

yfirvararskegg moustache; **synonyms** (n) hair, mustache, (adj) beard, whisker, brush.

yfirverð premium; **synonyms** (n) bonus, agio, bounty, payment, extra; **antonym** (adj) inferior.

yfirvofandi imminent; **synonyms** (adj) impending, close, coming, forthcoming, approaching; **antonym** (adj) far-off.

yfrráðasvæði realm; **synonyms** (n) kingdom, area, country, domain, field.

ylfingur 1. brownie; *synonyms* (*n*) fairy, elf, goblin, imp, pixie, **2.** cub; *synonyms* (*n*) child, whelp, youngster, greenhorn, lad.

yrðing 1. predicate; *synonyms* (*v*) affirm, assert, allege, base, connote, **2.** statement; *synonyms* (*n*) account, declaration, affirmation, announcement, communication; *antonym* (*n*) denial, **3.** proposition; *synonyms* (*n*) offer, overture, bid, motion, proposal.

yrtur verbal; *synonyms* (*adj*) spoken, oral, literal, unwritten, vocal; *antonym* (*adj*) written.

ystur extreme; *synonyms* (*adj*) deep, excessive, enormous, immoderate, (*n*) edge; *antonyms* (*adj*) middle, reasonable, (*n*) mild, moderate, slight.

ytri 1. external; *synonyms* (*adj*) exterior, outside, extraneous, extrinsic, outward; *antonyms* (*adj*) inner, interior, internal, domestic, inmost, **2.** extrinsic; *synonyms* (*adj*) external, exotic, alien, foreign, outer; *antonym* (*adj*) intrinsic.

yttrín 1. yttrium, **2.** y; *synonyms* (*n*) yttrium, wye.

ýring atomization; *synonyms* (*n*) atomisation, spraying, decomposition, fragmentation, nebulization.

ýristútur jet; *synonyms* (*n*) squirt, fountain, flow, (*v*) gush, spurt.

ýrubað douche; *synonyms* (*n*) shower, bath, (*v*) affusion, irrigation, flush.

ýrulausn emulsion; *synonyms* (*n*) balm, cream, emulsification, liquid, (*adj*) soup.

ýta 1. push; *synonyms* (*n*) press, thrust, (*v*) drive, impel, crowd; *antonyms* (*v*) pull, drag, haul, **2.** thrust; *synonyms* (*v*) jab, force, (*n*) push, poke, stab.

ýviður yew; *synonyms* (*n*) yam, zinnia, (*v*) yaw.

Z

zink zinc (sink); *synonym* (*n*) spelter.

Ý

ýfa knurl; *synonyms* (*n*) knob, lump, swelling, hump, knur.

ýfing knurl; *synonyms* (*n*) knob, lump, swelling, hump, knur.

ýfinn irritable; *synonyms* (*adj*) angry, fractious, irascible, edgy, cantankerous; *antonyms* (*adj*) calm, easygoing, good-humored, good-natured, even-tempered.

ýgi aggression; *synonyms* (*n*) hostility, incursion, offensive, onset, onslaught; *antonym* (*n*) friendliness.

ýgur aggressive; *synonyms* (*adj*) belligerent, active, energetic, enterprising, hostile; *antonyms* (*adj*) peaceful, friendly, peaceable, passive, peace-loving.

ýkjur hyperbole; *synonyms* (*n*) exaggeration, amplification, overstatement, magnification, strain; *antonym* (*n*) understatement.

ýlda putrefaction; *synonyms* (*n*) decay, rot, corruption, decomposition, putridity.

ýldudrep gangrene; *synonyms* (*n*) mortification, necrosis, (*v*) chagrin, (*adj*) corruption, caries.

ýmislegt special; *synonyms* (*adj*) particular, especial, individual, limited, rare; *antonym* (*adj*) ordinary.

ýr yew; *synonyms* (*n*) yam, zinnia, (*v*) yaw.

ýra 1. sprinkle; *synonyms* (*v*) scatter, drizzle, splash, moisten, cast, **2.** emulsion; *synonyms* (*n*) balm, cream, emulsification, liquid, (*adj*) soup.

Index of English Subjects to Icelandic Subjects

A

a *see* 1. i, 2. að.
abacus *see* 1. reiknigrind, 2. abakus, 3. hábakur, 4. háhella, 5. taknagrind.
abandon *see* yfirgefa.
abandoned *see* yfirgefinn.
abandonment *see* taumleysi.
abase *see* 1. niðurlægja, 2. auðmýkja.
abasement *see* 1. auðmýing, 2. litillækkun.
abashed *see* feiminn.
abate *see* niðurlægja.
abatement *see* lækkun.
abaxial *see* 1. fráhverfur, 2. ásfrálægur.
abbreviation *see* 1. skammstöfun, 2. stytting.
abdicate *see* yfirgefa.
abdication *see* ríkisafsögn.
abdomen *see* 1. kviður, 2. afturbolur, 3. magi.
abduct *see* fráfæra.
abduction *see* 1. fráleiðsla, 2. fráfærsla.
abductor *see* fráfærir.
abeam *see* þvert.
aberrate *see* víkja.
aberration *see* 1. frávik, 2. mistök, 3. villa, 4. spegilvilla, 5. spegilskekkja.
abhor *see* hrylla.
abhorrence *see* 1. viðbjóður, 2. grimmd.
abhorrent *see* 1. andstyggilegur, 2. hryllilegur.
abide *see* 1. þola, 2. vænta.
ability *see* hæfni.
abiogenesis *see* sjálfskviknun.
abiotic *see* 1. ólífrænn, 2. líflaus, 3. lífvana.
abjection *see* 1. litillækkun, 2. auðmýing.
abjuration *see* afneitun.
ablation *see* 1. blæsing, 2. brottnám, 3. leysing, 4. los.
ablative *see* svitafall.
abnegate *see* neita.
abnegation *see* sjálfsafneitun.
abnormal *see* 1. afbrigðilegur, 2. óeðlilegur, 3. óvanlegur.
abnormality *see* 1. afbrigðileiki, 2. frábrigði, 3. afbrigði.
abode *see* bústaður.
abolish *see* afnema.

abolishment *see* 1. ógilding, 2. afnám.
abolition *see* 1. afnám, 2. ógilding.
abolitionist *see* afnámssinni.
abomasum *see* vinstur.
abominable *see* 1. hryllilegur, 2. andstyggilegur.
abominate *see* hrylla.
abomination *see* 1. grimmd, 2. óbeit, 3. viðbjóður, 4. andstyggð.
aboriginal *see* 1. frumbyggi, 2. upprunalegur.
aborigine *see* 1. Ástralíusvertingi, 2. frumbyggi.
abort *see* 1. þroskunarstöðvun, 2. vinnsluslit.
abortion *see* 1. fósturlát, 2. fóstureyðing.
abortionist *see* fóstureyðir.
abortive *see* 1. ófullburða, 2. vanþroska.
about *see* um.
above *see* yfir.
abrasion *see* 1. fleiður, 2. tannaslit, 3. svörfun, 4. svarf, 5. skráma.
abrasive *see* 1. hvellur, 2. skrækur, 3. slípiduft, 4. fægiefni, 5. skerandi.
abreaction *see* geðlausn.
abreast *see* 1. jafnhliða, 2. samhliða, 3. samsíða.
abroad *see* 1. utanlands, 2. úti, 3. utan.
abrogate *see* afnema.
abrogation *see* 1. afnám, 2. ógilding.
abrupt *see* 1. skyndilegur, 2. snöggur.
abruptly *see* skyndilega.
abscess *see* 1. ígerð, 2. graftarkýli, 3. graftarbólga.
abscissa *see* láhnit.
abscission *see* 1. affall, 2. afskurður, 3. brottskurður, 4. lauffall, 5. lauffelling.
absence *see* 1. fjarvist, 2. rænuleysi, 3. fjarvera, 4. vöntun.
absenteeism *see* 1. fjarvistir, 2. foreldrafjarvera, 3. skróp.
absinth *see* malurtarbrennivín.
absolute *see* 1. alger, 2. skilyrðislaus, 3. raungildi, 4. algildur, 5. alsjálfur.
absolutely *see* algerlega.
absolution *see* 1. aflausn, 2. syndafyrirgefning.
absolutism *see* 1. alræðisstjórn, 2. einræðisstjórn, 3. einveldi, 4. algildishyggja, 5. algildiskenning.
absolutist *see* 1. alræðissinni, 2. einveldissinni.
absolve *see* 1. fyrirgefa, 2. sýkna.
absorb *see* 1. gleypa, 2. draga.
absorbent *see* 1. gleypinn, 2. rakadrægur.
absorbing *see* gleypinn.
absorptance *see* 1. ísogstala, 2. gleypnitala, 3. gleypni, 4. ísogshlutfall, 5. ísogshæfni.
absorption *see* 1. gleyping, 2. ísog, 3. frásog, 4. gleypni, 5. uppsog.
absorptivity *see* 1. ísogshæfni, 2. ljósþéttni, 3. gleypni.
abstinence *see* 1. fráhvarf, 2. bindindi.

abstract *see* 1. óhlutstæður, 2. afhverfur, 3. yfirlit, 4. útdráttur, 5. stela.

abstraction *see* 1. einföldun, 2. sértekning, 3. einangrun, 4. afhverfing, 5. útdráttur.

absurd *see* fáránlegur.

absurdity *see* 1. fásinna, 2. fjarstæða.

abulia *see* 1. viljadoði, 2. viljastol.

abundance *see* 1. tjöldahlutfall, 2. þyngdarhlutfall, 3. hlutmergð, 4. gnægð, 5. gnótt.

abundant *see* 1. kappnógur, 2. ríkulegur.

abuse *see* 1. misbeiting, 2. misnotkun, 3. móðga, 4. móðgun, 5. ofnautn.

abysmal *see* 1. hræðilegur, 2. hryllilegur.

abyss *see* 1. djúphafsbotn, 2. hyldýpi, 3. hafsbotn, 4. gjá, 5. hafdjúp.

acacia *see* 1. akasía, 2. akasíutré.

acceleration *see* 1. hröðun, 2. hraðaaukning, 3. viðbragð.

accelerator *see* 1. eindahraðall, 2. olíugjöf, 3. hröðunarrafskaut, 4. eldsneytisgjöf, 5. bensíngjöf.

accent *see* 1. framburðarmállýska, 2. málhreimur.

accept *see* 1. samþykkja, 2. staðfesta, 3. þakka.

acceptance *see* 1. viðtökuskoðun, 2. víxill.

acceptor *see* 1. rafþegi, 2. samþykkjandi, 3. viðtakandi.

access *see* 1. aðgangur, 2. aðkomuleið.

accessibility *see* 1. aðgengi, 2. aðgengileiki.

accessible *see* 1. aðgengilegur, 2. móttækilegur.

accession *see* vöxtur.

accessories *see* 1. fíhelpanto, 2. neĉefa, 3. kunkulpulo, 4. kunkulpa, 5. komplico.

accessory *see* akcesora.

accident *see* 1. slys, 2. óhapp, 3. bílslys.

accidental *see* 1. tilfallandi, 2. tilviljunarkenndur.

acclamation *see* lófatak.

acclimation *see* ílending.

acclimatization *see* 1. umhverfisaðlögun, 2. ílending.

accommodate *see* 1. rúma, 2. aðlagast.

accommodation *see* 1. aðlögun, 2. vistarverur, 3. aðhæfing, 4. hagræði, 5. málamiðlun.

accompany *see* fylgja.

accord *see* 1. samkomulag, 2. samhljómur, 3. samningur, 4. samræmi, 5. samþykkja.

accordance *see* 1. samningur, 2. samræmi, 3. samhljómur, 4. samkomulag.

accordion *see* 1. dragspil, 2. harmoníka.

account *see* 1. reikningur, 2. skýring, 3. trúa, 4. saga, 5. reikna.

accountability *see* 1. ábyrgðarskil, 2. ábyrgðarskylda, 3. ábyrgni, 4. skilaskylda, 5. ábyrgð.

accountancy *see* reikningshald.

accountant *see* 1. bókari, 2. endurskoðandi.

accounting *see* 1. bókhald, 2. reikningshald, 3. reikningsfærslugreinargerð.

accredit *see* 1. löggilda, 2. trúa.

accreditation *see* 1. trúnaðarstaðfesting, 2. veita.

accrete *see* samvaxa.

accretion *see* 1. áhleðsla, 2. samvöxtur, 3. aðsóp, 4. vöxtur.

accrue *see* vaxa.

acculturation *see* 1. aðlifun, 2. menningaraðlögun, 3. menningarblöndun, 4. menningarnám.

accumulate *see* safna.

accumulation *see* 1. söfnun, 2. uppsöfnun, 3. ákoma, 4. hleðsla.

accumulator *see* 1. rafgeymir, 2. safnari, 3. safnplanta, 4. þrýstigeymir.

accuracy *see* 1. nákvæmni, 2. áreiðanleiki, 3. hittni.

accurate *see* nákvæmur.

accusal *see* ásökun.

accusation *see* 1. ákæra, 2. ásökun.

accusative *see* þolfall.

accuse *see* 1. ásaka, 2. kæra.

accused *see* 1. ákærði, 2. sakborningur.

accuser *see* ákærandi.

accustomed *see* venjulegur.

acephalous *see* höfuðlaus.

acerbic *see* 1. skarpur, 2. beiskur, 3. beittur, 4. hrjúfur, 5. leiftandi.

acerbity *see* 1. hvassleiki, 2. skarpskyggni.

acetabulum *see* 1. augnakarl, 2. fótliður, 3. mjaðmarskál, 4. sograni, 5. sogskál.

acetate *see* 1. salt, 2. asetat, 3. glæra, 4. himna.

acetone *see* 1. aseton, 2. asetón.

acetous *see* súr.

acetyl *see* asetýl.

acetylcholine *see* 1. asetýlkólín, 2. asetílkólín.

acetylene *see* 1. kolvetnisgas, 2. logsuðugas, 3. asetýlen.

ache *see* 1. verkur, 2. kvöl, 3. þrá.

achieve *see* afreka.

achievement *see* 1. kunnátta, 2. frammistaða, 3. atburður, 4. afrek.

achromasia *see* litleysi.

achromatic *see* 1. litlaus, 2. ólita.

acicular *see* nállaga.

acid *see* 1. súr, 2. sýra, 3. geymasýra, 4. beiskur.

acidic *see* súr.

acidification *see* 1. súrnun, 2. sýring, 3. sýruaukning, 4. sýrumyndun.

acidify *see* súrna.

acidophil *see* sýrufíkill.

acidophilic *see* 1. sýrusækinn, 2. sýrusólginn, 3. sýrukær.

acidosis *see* 1. sýringareitrun, 2. blóðsýring.

acinus *see* 1. kirtilblaðra, 2. smáber.

acknowledge *see* játa.

acme see 1. hápunktur, 2. hástig.
acne see 1. arta, 2. graftarþrymlar, 3. gelgjubólur, 4. gelgjuþrymlar.
acolyte see stuðningsmaður.
aconite see 1. freyjublóm, 2. venusvagn.
acoustic see 1. hljóðeðlisfræðlingur, 2. hljóðrænn.
acoustics see 1. hljóðeðlisfræði, 2. hljómburður, 3. hljóðfræði.
acquaintance see kunningi.
acquired see 1. ákominn, 2. áunninn.
acquisition see 1. tileinkun, 2. yfirtaka, 3. ráðataka, 4. kaup, 5. föngun.
acquit see 1. sýkna, 2. fyrirgefa.
acquittal see 1. aflausn, 2. syndafyrirgefning.
acre see ekra.
acrid see 1. leiftandi, 2. skarpur, 3. skerandi, 4. hrjúfur, 5. skrækur.
acrimonious see 1. skarpur, 2. skerandi, 3. leiftandi, 4. hvellur, 5. hrjúfur.
acrimony see 1. hvassleiki, 2. skarpskyggni.
acrobat see loftfimleikamaður.
acrobatic see fimlegur.
acrobatics see fimleikar.
acrocentric see 1. endaheftur, 2. endheftur.
acronym see 1. skammyrði, 2. upphafsstafaorð, 3. gripla, 4. upphafsstafanafn, 5. upphafsstafaheiti.
acrosome see 1. hjálmur, 2. sáðfrumuhjálmur.
act see 1. lög, 2. skírteini, 3. þáttur, 4. leika, 5. gera.
actinium see 1. aktín, 2. aktíníum.
actinomycosis see 1. ígulmygla, 2. geislagerlakvilli, 3. ígulgerlabólga.
action see 1 virkni, 2. verkun, 3. starf, 4. verknaður, 5. starfsemi.
activate see 1. vekja, 2. virkja, 3. örva, 4. orsaka, 5. espa.
activation see 1. virkjun, 2. örvun, 3. ræsing, 4. vakning, 5. virking.
activator see 1. virkir, 2. ræsir, 3. örvari, 4. efnahvati, 5. espir.
active see 1. virkur, 2. starfandi.
activity see 1. virkni, 2. athafsnemi, 3. athöfn, 4. kraftur, 5. starfsemi.
actomyosin see aktómýósín.
actor see 1. leikari, 2. gerandi.
actress see leikkona.
actual see 1. árangursríkur, 2. raunverulegur.
actuary see tryggingafræðingur.
actuator see 1. liði, 2. átakshluti, 3. gerandi, 4. hreyfiliði, 5. hreyfir.
acuity see 1. von, 2. skerpa, 3. hvassleiki, 4. skarpskyggni.
acuminate see 1. langyddur, 2. odddreginn, 3. oddhvass.

acupuncture see 1. nálstunga, 2. nálastungulækningar, 3. nálastunga, 4. nálarstunga.
acute see 1. bráður, 2. skarpur, 3. snarpur, 4. beittur, 5. yddur.
acyclic see 1. gormraðaður, 2. gormlaga.
adamantine see gallharður.
adapt see 1. aðlaga, 2. aðlagast.
adaptability see 1. aðlögunarhæfileiki, 2. aðlögunarhæfni.
adaptation see 1. aðlögun, 2. samþýðing, 3. umbreyting, 4. aðhæfing.
adapter see 1. breytistykki, 2. millihaldari, 3. millistykki, 4. spjald, 5. tengildi.
adaption see aðlögun.
adaptor see millistykki.
adder see 1. höggormur, 2. samleggjari.
addiction see 1. fíkn, 2. ávanasýki, 3. fíkníávani, 4. ávanabinding.
addition see 1. samlagning, 2. viðauki, 3. viðbót.
additive see 1. íblöndunarefni, 2. samleggjandi, 3. viðbætinn, 4. aukaefni, 5. aukefni.
address see 1. heimilisfang, 2. vistfang, 3. vistfengja.
addressee see 1. viðtakandi, 2. viðmælandi.
adduction see aðfærsla.
adductor see aðfærir.
adenine see adenín.
adenitis see kirtilbólga.
adenocarcinoma see 1. kirtilkrabbamein, 2. kirtilkrabbi.
adenoid see 1. nefeitla, 2. kokeitla, 3. kirtillíkur.
adenoma see kirtilæxli.
adept see stuðningsmaður.
adequate see 1. hæfilegur, 2. nægilegur, 3. nógur.
adhere see 1. límast, 2. líma.
adherent see 1. stuðningsmaður, 2. viðloðandi.
adhesion see 1. samgróningur, 2. samgróning, 3. samloðun, 4. viðloðnun, 5. viðloðun.
adhesive see viðloða.
adiabatic see 1. adíabatískur, 2. óverminn, 3. innrænn.
adieu see bless.
adiposity see 1. feitlagni, 2. fitusækni, 3. offita.
adjacent see 1. nálægur, 2. samliggjandi, 3. samhliða, 4. aðliggjandi, 5. aðlægur.
adjourn see fresta.
adjunct see viðauki.
adjust see 1. aðlaga, 2. meta, 3. sætta, 4. stilla, 5. fínstilla.
adjustable see 1. breytilegur, 2. stillanlegur.
adjuster see stillir.
adjustment see 1. aðlögun, 2. stillingar, 3. stjórnun, 4. stilling, 5. aðhæfing.

adjuvant see 1. hjálpandi, 2. ónæmisglæðir, 3. hjálparlyf, 4. hjálparefni.
administer see gefa.
administration see 1. stjórn, 2. stjórnsýsluskrifstofa, 3. veiting, 4. stjórnvöld, 5. stjórnun.
administrative see stjórnarfarslegur
administrator see 1. bústjóri, 2. forstöðumaður, 3. skiptaráðandi, 4. stjórnandi, 5. umsjónarmaður.
admiral see 1. aðmíráll, 2. höfuðsmaður, 3. flotaforingi.
admission see 1. aðgangur, 2. innganga, 3. vistun.
admit see 1. játa, 2. viðurkenna.
admittance see 1. sýndarleiðni, 2. tvinnleiðni, 3. samleiðni.
adolescence see 1. gelgjuskeið, 2. unglingsár, 3. æska.
adopt see 1. ættleiða, 2. samþykkja, 3. undirbúa.
adoption see 1. samþykkt, 2. upptaka, 3. ættleiðing.
adrenal see nýrlægur.
adrenaline see 1. adrenalín, 2. hettuvaki, 3. mergvaki, 4. nýrilmergvaki.
adrenergic see 1. aðrenvirkur, 2. adrenergur, 3. adrenvirkur.
adsorbent see aðseygur.
adsorption see 1. aðsog, 2. ásog, 3. aðloðun.
adult see 1. fullorðinn, 2. fulltíða, 3. fullveðja.
advance see 1. fyrirframgreiðsla, 2. flýting, 3. framgír.
advantage see 1. vinningur, 2. kostur.
advantageous see hagstæður.
advection see 1. aðstreymi, 2. burður, 3. láburður, 4. meðburður.
adventitia see úthjúpur.
adventitious see 1. aðkominn, 2. utanaðkomandi, 3. tilviljunarkenndur, 4. framandi, 5. hjálægur.
adversary see óvinur.
adverse see 1. andstæður, 2. gallaður, 3. mótstæður.
advertence see von.
advertency see von.
advice see ráð.
advise see ráða.
adviser see 1. deildarsérfræðingur, 2. ráðgjafi, 3. ráðunautur.
advisory see ráðgefandi.
advocate see málfærslumaður.
aeolian see vindborinn.
aerial see 1. loftnet, 2. ofanjarðar.
aerobe see loftvera.
aerobic see 1. l, 2. loftfíkinn, 3. lofthádur, 4. loftsækinn, 5. loftþurfi.
aerobiology see loftlíffræði.
aerobiosis see loftlíf.
aerodrome see flugvöllur.

aerodynamics see 1. loftfræði, 2. lofthreyfifræði, 3. loftstraumfræði, 4. loftaflfræði.
aeroembolism see loftbólurek.
aerofoil see vængildi.
aeroplane see flugvél.
aerosol see 1. agnúði, 2. ar, 3. loftúði.
aerostat see loftpoki.
aestivation see 1. sumardá, 2. sumardvali.
affable see 1. vænn, 2. vingjarnlegur.
affect see 1. geðsmunir, 2. geðblær, 3. geð.
affecting see tilfinningasamurlegur.
affection see 1. ást, 2. ástúð, 3. geðhrif, 4. kærleikur.
affective see geðrænn.
affectivity see hrifnæmi.
afferent see 1. aðfærandi, 2. innsækinn, 3. aðlægur, 4. aðliggjandi.
affiliate see 1. hlutdeildarfélag, 2. systurfélag.
affiliation see 1. tengsl, 2. vild.
affinity see 1. fíkni, 2. samsækni, 3. sækni, 4. næmni, 5. eftirsókn.
affirmation see 1. loforð, 2. staðfesting.
affluent see ríkur.
afforestation see 1 skógrœkt, 2. skóggræðsla.
affront see móðgun.
aflatoxin see aflatoxín.
afloat see fljótandi.
aft see aftur.
after see eftir.
afterbirth see 1. eftirburður, 2. fósturfylgja, 3. hildir.
afterburner see 1. eftirbrennir, 2. eftirbrennari.
aftereffect see eftirhrif.
afterglow see 1. eftirljóm, 2. eftirskin.
afterimage see 1. myndleif, 2. síðmynd.
aftershock see eftirskjálfti.
agammaglobulinemia see 1. mótefnaþurrð, 2. gammaglóbúlínekla, 3. mótefnaskortur.
agar see gelsykra.
age see 1. aldur, 2. öld, 3. skeið, 4. tímabil, 5. tímaskeið.
ageing see 1. veðrun, 2. eldast, 3. öldrun.
agency see 1. umboðsskrifstofa, 2. umboð, 3. stofnun.
agenda see 1. dagskrá, 2. verkaskrá.
agent see 1. umboðsaðili, 2. umboðsmaður, 3. orsakavaldur, 4. gerandi, 5. fulltrúi.
agglomerate see 1. hrúgald, 2. klasaður, 3. samundinn.
agglomeration see samhrúgun.
agglutinate see 1. kökkur, 2. kekkja, 3. kekkjast.
agglutination see 1. hópfelling, 2. kekkjun.
agglutinin see 1. hópfellir, 2. kekkir, 3. kekkjunarmótefni, 4. kekkjunarvaldur.

aggregate *see* 1. heildarupphæð, 2. uppsafnað, 3. þyrping, 4. þyrpa, 5. samanlagt.
aggregation *see* 1. klístrun, 2. samþyrping, 3. samsteypa, 4. þyrping, 5. hópur.
aggression *see* 1. ýgi, 2. árásargirni, 3. árásarhvöt, 4. áreitni.
aggressive *see* 1. árásargjarn, 2. ýgur.
agio *see* 1. gengismunur, 2. gjald, 3. laun, 4. þóknun, 5. umboðslaun.
agitated *see* 1. skekinn, 2. upprifinn, 3. æstur.
agitation *see* 1. æsing, 2. hristing, 3. órósemi.
agnosia *see* 1. ókynni, 2. túlkunarstol.
agonist *see* 1. gerandefni, 2. gerandvöðvi.
agony *see* 1. angist, 2. hræðsla.
agoraphobia *see* 1. víðáttufælni, 2. torgageigur.
agranulocytosis *see* kyrningahrap.
agraphia *see* 1. ritstol, 2. skrifstol.
agree *see* samþykkja.
agreeable *see* þægilegur.
agreement *see* 1. samræmi, 2. samningur, 3. samkomulag, 4. sáttargerð, 5. samhljómur.
agribusiness *see* 1. iðnbúskapur, 2. landbúnaðarviðskipti.
agriculture *see* 1. landbúnaður, 2. jarðrækt, 3. jarðyrkja.
agrology *see* jarðvegsfræði.
agronomy *see* 1. jarðræktarfræði, 2. jarðræktunarfræði, 3. ræktunarfræði.
ague *see* mýrarköldukast.
ahead *see* 1. áfram, 2. framundan.
aid *see* 1. hjálp, 2. þróunaraðstoð, 3. hjálpa.
ailing *see* 1. sjúkur, 2. veikur.
air *see* 1. loft, 2. andrúmsloft, 3. eftirbrennari.
airborne *see* 1. loftborinn, 2. vindborinn.
aircraft *see* flugvél.
airdrome *see* flugvöllur.
airfield *see* flugvöllur.
airline *see* 1. flugfélag, 2. flugleið, 3. loftlína.
airplane *see* flugvél.
airport *see* 1. flugvöllur, 2. flughöfn, 3. flugstöð.
airway *see* 1. loftbraut, 2. kokrenna, 3. barkarenna.
akinesis *see* hreyfingarleysi.
alabaster *see* 1. alabastur, 2. mjólkursteinn.
alanine *see* 1. ala, 2. alanín.
alar *see* 1. vængmyndaður, 2. vænglaga.
alarm *see* 1. viðvörun, 2. váboði, 3. uppþot, 4. ótti, 5. hræðsla.
alarmed *see* hryllilegur.
alarming *see* ógnvekjandi.
albatross *see* albatrosi.
albedo *see* 1. endurskin, 2. endurskinshæfni, 3. endurskinshlutfall, 4. hvítbörkur, 5. innbörkur.
albescent *see* 1. hvítnaður, 2. hvítleitur.
albinism *see* 1. litarleysi, 2. albínismi, 3. hvítingseðli.

albino *see* 1. albínói, 2. hvítingi, 3. albíni, 4. hvítingur.
album *see* hljómplata.
albumen *see* 1. hvíta, 2. fræhvíta, 3. albúmín, 4. eggjahvíta.
albumin *see* albúmín.
albuminoid *see* hvítulíkur.
alcohol *see* 1. alkóhól, 2. áfengi, 3. vínandi.
alcoholic *see* 1. áfengissjúklingur, 2. ofdrykkjumaður, 3. alkóhólisti, 4. drykkjusjúklingur.
alcoholism *see* 1. alkóhólismi, 2. áfengissýki, 3. drykkjusýki.
aldehyde *see* aldehýð.
alder *see* 1. rauðölur, 2. rauðelri, 3. elrir, 4. elri, 5. ölur.
aldosterone *see* aldósterón.
ale *see* 1. bjór, 2. öl.
aleurone *see* 1. fræhvíta, 2. fræhvítuhjúpur.
alewife *see* 1. grænsíld, 2. punktasíld, 3. deplasíld, 4. silfurskjaddi.
alexia *see* 1. lesblinda, 2. lesstol.
alfalfa *see* 1. alfalfagras, 2. lúserna, 3. refasmári.
algae *see* þörungar.
algebra *see* bókstafareikningur.
algorithm *see* 1. reiknisögn, 2. reiknirit, 3. algóritmi, 4. algrím, 5. reikniaðferð.
alias *see* 1. samnefni, 2. leppur, 3. tvíræðni, 4. uppnefni.
alien *see* 1. erlendur, 2. útlendur, 3. útlendingur, 4. framandi, 5. andstæður.
alienation *see* 1. aðskilnaðarkennd, 2. firring.
alignment *see* 1. stilling, 2. afstaða, 3. textaröðun, 4. textstilling, 5. samstilling.
aliment *see* 1. fæða, 2. fóður, 3. næring.
aliphatic *see* alifatískur.
alive *see* lifandi.
alkali *see* 1. alkalí, 2. lútarsalt.
alkaline *see* 1. alkalí, 2. alkalískur, 3. basískur.
alkalosis *see* 1. blóðlýting, 2. líkamslútun, 3. líkamsbösun.
alkaptonuria *see* sortumiga.
all *see* 1. allt, 2. allur.
allantoin *see* allantóin.
allegation *see* 1. ásökun, 2. staðhæfing.
allege *see* 1. ásaka, 2. kæra, 3. staðhæfa.
allegoric *see* 1. allegóríkur, 2. táknsögulegur.
allegorical *see* 1. allegóríkur, 2. táknsögulegur.
allegory *see* táknsaga.
allele *see* 1. tvenndargen, 2. samsæta, 3. genasamsæta.
allergen *see* 1. ofnæmisvaldur, 2. ofnæmisvaki.
allergy *see* ofnæmi.
alliance *see* 1. samsteypa, 2. þjóðabandalag, 3. samband, 4. ríkjabandalag, 5. gróðurfylki.

allocate *see* 1. ráðstafa, 2. skipta, 3. úthluta, 4. veita, 5. beina.
allocation *see* 1. úthlutun, 2. fjárveiting, 3. ráðstöfun, 4. skipting.
allochthonous *see* 1. framandi, 2. aðfluttur.
allogeneic *see* ósamgena.
allogenic *see* ósamgena.
allomorph *see* myndbrigði.
allopatric *see* 1. mislendur, 2. sérlendur, 3. sérsvæða.
allotropy *see* 1. fjölgervi, 2. samleitni.
allotype *see* samsætugerð.
allowance *see* 1. afsláttur, 2. álag, 3. fjárstyrkur, 4. frádráttur, 5. viðauki.
alloy *see* 1. málmblanda, 2. málmblendi, 3. melmi.
alluring *see* 1. elskulegur, 2. heillandi, 3. hrífandi.
alluvium *see* 1. árset, 2. straumvatnaset, 3. straumvatnsset.
almond *see* mandla.
almost *see* 1. nær, 2. næstum.
alone *see* 1. einmana, 2. einn, 3. aleinn.
along *see* 1. eftir, 2. samkvæmt.
alp *see* alpherbejo.
alpha *see* alfa.
alphabet *see* stafróf.
also *see* 1 einnig, 2. líka.
altazimuth *see* lóðstilltur.
alter *see* umbreyta.
alteration *see* 1. ummyndun, 2. umskipti.
altercation *see* rifrildi.
alternate *see* 1. stakstæður, 2. varamaður.
alternation *see* 1. víxl, 2. hálfrið.
alternator *see* 1. riðstraumsrafali, 2. riðstraumsrafall.
although *see* þótt.
altimeter *see* hæðarmælir.
altitude *see* 1. flughæð, 2. hæð, 3. stjörnuhæð.
alto *see* altrödd.
altocumulus *see* 1. netjuský, 2. röggvarský, 3. netjuþykkni, 4. dröfnuský, 5. gluggaþykkni.
altostratus *see* gráblika.
altruism *see* 1. fórnfýsi, 2. ósérplægni.
alumina *see* 1. súrál, 2. áloxíð.
aluminium *see* 1. ál, 2. alúmíníum.
aluminum *see* ál.
alveolar *see* tannbergsmæltur.
alveolus *see* 1. kirtilblaðra, 2. lungnablaðra, 3 tannhola.
always *see* 1. ætíð, 2. ávallt, 3. alltaf.
amalgam *see* kvikasilfursmelmi.
amalgamation *see* 1. sameining, 2. samruni.
amateur *see* 1. áhugamaður, 2. leikmaður, 3. viðvaningur.
amazement *see* 1. furða, 2. undrun.
ambassador *see* sendiherra.

amber *see* 1. raf, 2. gulur.
ambience *see* loft.
ambient *see* 1. umhverfis, 2. umlykjandi.
ambiguity *see* 1. margræðni, 2. tvíræðni.
ambiguous *see* 1. margræður, 2. tvíræður.
ambivalence *see* tvíveðrungur.
ambivalent *see* 1. tvíátta, 2. tvíbentur.
ambulance *see* sjúkrabíll.
ambulatory *see* 1. gangandi, 2. kórgöng, 3. rólfær.
ameba *see* 1. amaba, 2. teygjudýr, 3. slímdýr, 4. amba, 5. angalýja.
ameboid *see* 1. amöbulegur, 2. ömbulegur.
amend *see* umbreyta.
amendment *see* 1. lagabreyting, 2. leiðrétting.
americium *see* 1. ameríkín, 2. ameríkíum.
amide *see* amíð.
amine *see* amín.
ammeter *see* 1. ampermælir, 2. straummælir.
amnesia *see* 1. minnisleysi, 2. óminni.
amnesty *see* náðun.
amniocentesis *see* 1. legástunga, 2. legstunga, 3. legvatnsástunga.
amnion *see* líknarbelgur.
amoeba *see* 1. amaba, 2. amba, 3. angalýja, 4. slímdýr, 5. teygjudýr.
amok *see* 1. skyndiæði, 2. hamsleysi, 3. berserksgangur.
amorphous *see* 1. myndlaus, 2. ókristallaður, 3. ómótaður, 4. formlaus.
amortization *see* 1. afborgun, 2. afskrift, 3. fyrning.
amortize *see* afskrifa.
amount *see* fjárhæð.
amp *see* 1. einyrki, 2. amper, 3. adenosíneinfosfat, 4. AEF.
amperage *see* straumstyrkur.
ampere *see* amper.
amphibia *see* froskdýr.
ample *see* 1. ríkulegur, 2. kappnógur.
amplification *see* 1. mögnun, 2. genmögnun, 3. hljóðmögnun.
amplifier *see* 1. magnari, 2. mögnunarlampi.
amplify *see* 1. efla, 2. magna.
amplitude *see* 1. sveiflustærð, 2. vísir, 3. sveifluvídd, 4. sveifluhæð, 5. magn.
ampulla *see* 1. biða, 2. flaska, 3. lykja.
amputation *see* aflimun.
amylase *see* 1. mjölvakljúfur, 2. amýlasi.
amyloid *see* 1. sterkjulíki, 2. mjölvakenndur.
amylopectin *see* amýlópektín.
amylose *see* amýlósi.
anabolic *see* vefaukandi.
anabolism *see* 1. tillífun, 2. aðlífun, 3. ílífun, 4. tillífgun.
anaerobe *see* loftfæla.
anaerobic *see* 1. loftfirrður, 2. loftfælinn.

anaesthesia *see* 1. deyfing, 2. svæfing, 3. tilkenningarleysi.
anaesthetic *see* svæfingarlyf.
analeptic *see* örvandi.
analgesia *see* 1. sársaukaleysi, 2. verkjadeyfing, 3. deyfing, 4. dofi.
analgesic *see* kvalastillandi.
analog *see* 1. flaumrænn, 2. hliðrænn, 3. samfelldur.
analogous *see* 1. samsvarandi, 2. hliðstæður, 3. sambærilegur.
analogue *see* 1. flaumrænn, 2. hliðstæða.
analogy *see* 1. áhrifsbreyting, 2. hliðstaða, 3. samsvörun.
analyse *see* 1. greina, 2. Skýringar.
analyser *see* 1. skynjari, 2. greinisía, 3. greinir.
analysis *see* 1. greining, 2. stærðfræðigreining, 3. sundurgreining, 4. efnagreining.
analyst *see* 1. greinandi, 2. greinir.
analyzer *see* 1. greinir, 2. greiningartæki.
anamnesis *see* 1. upprifjun, 2. sjúkrasaga, 3. endurminni, 4. farnaðarsaga.
anaphase *see* 1. aðskilnaðarstig, 2. anafasi, 3. síðfasi.
anaphrodisiac *see* 1. lostakælir, 2. lostakælandi.
anaphylactic *see* næmisaukandi.
anaphylatoxin *see* 1. óþolseitur, 2. bólgumiðill.
anaphylaxis *see* bráðaofnæmi.
anarchism *see* 1. stjórnleysisstefna, 2. óstjórn, 3. stjórnleysi.
anarchy *see* 1. stjórnleysi, 2. óstjórn.
anastomosis *see* 1. samop, 2. sammynning, 3. samgötun, 4. mót, 5. samgangur.
anatomy *see* líffærafræði
anatoxin *see* afeitur.
anchor *see* 1. akkeri, 2. ankeri, 3. stagfesta, 4. markstikla, 5. hæll.
anchoring *see* ágræðsla.
anchovy *see* 1. ansjósa, 2. ansjósur.
and *see* og.
androgen *see* 1. andrógen, 2. karlhormón.
androgynous *see* 1. gervitvíkynja, 2. tvíkynja.
anemia *see* 1. blóðskortur, 2. blóðleysi.
anemic *see* blóðlaus.
anemograph *see* vindriti.
anemometer *see* vindmælir.
anencephaly *see* heilaleysi.
anergy *see* 1. vanvirkni, 2. óvirkni, 3. næmisleysi.
anesthesia *see* 1. svæfing, 2. tilfinningaleysi, 3. tilfinningarleysi, 4. deyfing.
anesthetic *see* 1. deyfingarlyf, 2. svæfingarlyf, 3. svæfandi, 4. deyfilyf, 5. deyfður.
aneuploidy *see* 1. mislitnun, 2. ójafnlitnun.
aneurysm *see* 1. gúlpur, 2. slagæðargúlpur.
angel *see* engill.
anger *see* reiði.

angina *see* öng.
angiology *see* æðafræði.
angiotensin *see* angíótensín.
angle *see* 1. horn, 2. sjónarmið, 3. veiða.
angler *see* 1. skötuselur, 2. stangveiðimaður, 3. kjaftagelgja, 4. golþorskur.
anglerfish *see* svarthyrna.
angry *see* reiður.
angstrom *see* aangström.
anguish *see* hræðsla.
angular *see* 1. hyrndur, 2. strendur, 3. hornmyndaður, 4. kjálkahyrna.
anhydride *see* 1. anhýdríð, 2. þurrefni.
anhydrous *see* 1. vatnsfirrtur, 2. vatnsfrír, 3. vatnsfrítt.
aniline *see* anilín.
animal *see* dýr.
animation *see* 1. lífgun, 2. myndlífgun.
anion *see* 1. anjón, 2. neirafi, 3. neijón, 4. mínusjón, 5. forjón.
anisotropic *see* 1. misátta, 2. stefnuháður, 3. stefnuhneigður.
anisotropy *see* 1. misáttun, 2. stefnuhneigð.
ankle *see* ökli.
ankylosis *see* 1. staurliður, 2. stífliður.
anlage *see* 1. eðlisvísir, 2. efni, 3. upplag, 4. vísir.
annatto *see* 1. annattó, 2. bixín, 3. roðafræ.
anneal *see* 1. glóða, 2. hersla.
annealing *see* 1. afdráttur, 2. endurgerð, 3. samþætting, 4. þáttatenging.
annex *see* 1. viðbygging, 2. viðauki, 3. innlima, 4. fylgiskjal.
annexation *see* 1. sameining, 2. innlimun.
annihilation *see* eyðing.
announcement *see* 1. skýrsla, 2. tilkynning, 3. kæra, 4. auglýsing.
annual *see* 1. einær, 2. árlegur.
annuity *see* 1. árgreiðsla, 2. jafngreiðsla, 3. jafngreiðsluröð, 4. lífeyrisgreiðsla.
annul *see* ógilda.
annular *see* 1. hringlaga, 2. hringmyndaður.
annulus *see* 1. kragi, 2. liður.
anode *see* 1. anóða, 2. forskaut, 3. jáskaut, 4. plússkaut.
anodyne *see* 1. þrautastillandi, 2. verkjalyf.
anomalous *see* 1. frábrigðilegur, 2. merkingarlaus, 3. afbrigðilegur.
anomaly *see* 1. ferilhorn, 2. merkingarleysa, 3. óregla, 4. frávik, 5. frábrigði.
anomia *see* 1. nafnstol, 2. nefnistol.
anopheles *see* 1. malaríumý, 2. mýraköldumý.
anorak *see* anorakkur.
anorexia *see* lystarleysi.
anorexiant *see* 1. lystarslævir, 2. lystarslævandi.
anoxemia *see* blóðildisskortur.

anoxia see 1. súrefnisskortur, 2. ildisþurrð, 3. vanilding, 4. vefildisþurrð.
answer see 1. svar, 2. svara.
ant see maur.
antacid see 1. sýrudrómi, 2. sýrueyðir.
antagonism see 1. andstaða, 2. andverkun, 3. andvirkni, 4. gagnverkun, 5. mótverkun
antagonist see 1. mótlyf, 2. andlyf, 3. blokki.
antagonistic see 1. mótvirkur, 2. gagnvirkur, 3. andstæður, 4. andverkandi.
antarctic see Suðurpóll.
antecedent see antaŭajo.
antenna see 1. viðtak, 2. fálmari, 3. loftnet, 4. þreifari.
anterior see 1. framlægur, 2. framlægt, 3. framhluti.
anterograde see 1. framflutningur, 2. framvirkur, 3. framvísandi.
anthelmintic see 1. ormaeyðandi, 2. ormalyf.
anther see 1. frjóknappur, 2. frjóhnappur.
anthracite see 1. gljákol, 2. harðkol.
anthraquinone see 1. antrakínón, 2. svepparauði.
anthrax see 1. miltisbrandur, 2. miltisbrandsdrep.
anthropogenesis see 1. einstaklingsþróun, 2. mannþróun, 3. tegundarþróun.
anthropogenic see 1. mannmótaður, 2. manngerður, 3. mannmótað.
anthropoid see mannlíkur.
anthropology see mannfræði.
anthropometry see 1. mannfræðimælingar, 2. mannmælingafræði, 3. mannslíkamafræði.
anthropomorphism see 1. manngerving, 2. manngervastefna.
antiarrhythmic see 1. sláttarglapastillandi, 2. sláttarglapastillir.
antibacterial see 1. bakteríueyðandi, 2. bakteríuskæður.
antibiosis see 1. andlíf, 2. andlífi, 3. meinlíf.
antibiotic see 1. sýklalyf, 2. fúkkalyf, 3. fúkalyf.
antibody see mótefni.
anticipation see hugboð.
anticline see 1. andhverfa, 2. antiklína.
anticlockwise see 1. andsælis, 2. rangsælis.
anticoagulant see 1. segavarnarefni, 2. segavarnarlyf, 3. blóðstorkuheftir, 4. storkuvari.
anticodon see andtákni.
anticonvulsant see 1. krampaleysandi, 2. krampaleysir.
anticyclone see 1. hæð, 2. háþrýstisvæði.
antidepressant see 1. geðdeyfðarlyf, 2. geðlægðarlyf, 3. geðdeyfðarleysandi, 4. þunglyndislyf.
antidiabetic see 1. sykursýkileysandi, 2. sykursýkislyf.
antidiuretic see þvagtemprandi.
antidote see móteitur.

antiemetic see 1. uppsölulyf, 2. uppsölustillandi.
antiepileptic see 1. flogaveikilyf, 2. flogleysandi.
antifungal see 1. sveppalyf, 2. sveppaeyðandi.
antigen see 1. mótefnavaki, 2. mótefnisvaki, 3. ónæmisvaki, 4. vaki.
antigenicity see 1. ónæmingargeta, 2. vakahæfni.
antihemorrhagic see 1. blæðingarlyf, 2. blæðingarstöðvandi.
antihistamine see andhistamín.
antihormone see 1. andvaki, 2. móthormón.
antihypertensive see 1. háþrýstingslyf, 2. þrýstingslækkandi.
antimatter see andefni.
antimicrobial see örverueyðandi.
antimony see antímon.
antinode see 1. hæð, 2. bugur, 3. andkvistur, 4. bugpunktur.
antinomy see 1. andstæða, 2. gagnkvæði.
antioxidant see 1. þráavarnarefni, 2. andoxunarefni, 3. þráarhindri, 4. þráavari.
antiparallel see 1. mótsamsíða, 2. andsamsíða.
antiparticle see andeind.
antiperspirant see 1. svitalyf, 2. svitastemmandi.
antiphlogistic see 1. bólgueyðandi, 2. bólgueyðir.
antipodal see gagnstæður.
antipruritic see kláðastillandi.
antipyretic see hitalækkandi.
anti-semitism see gyðingahatur.
antisepsis see 1. smitvörn, 2. sóttvarnarlyf, 3. sóttvörn.
antiseptic see 1. sýklaeyðandi, 2. smitvarnarefni, 3. sóttvarnandi, 4. sóttvarnarlyf.
antiserum see 1. ónæmissermi, 2. ónæmisblóðvatn, 3. mótsermi.
antisocial see andfélagslegur.
antispasmodic see 1. krampaeyðandi, 2. krampalosandi, 3. krampalyf.
antithesis see mótsetning.
antithrombin see andþrombín.
antitoxic see eitureyðandi.
antitoxin see móteitur.
antitussive see hóstastillandi.
antiviral see 1. veirueyðandi, 2. veiruhamlandi.
antonym see andheiti.
antrum see 1. eggbúsblaðra, 2. hellir, 3. holrúm.
anuria see 1. þvagleysi, 2. þvagþurrð.
anus see 1. endaþarmsop, 2. bakrauf.
anvil see steðji.
anxiety see 1. kvíði, 2. beygur, 3. kvíðakennd.
apart see 1. sundur, 2. afsíðis.
apartheid see 1. kynþáttaraðskilnaðarstefna, 2. kynþáttaaðskilnaður, 3. kynþáttaaðskilnarstefna.
apartment see íbúð.
apathy see sinnuleysi.
ape see api.

aperient see 1. hægðaaukandi, 2. hægðalyf.
aperiodic see 1. lotulaus, 2. ólotubundinn, 3.
bilfrjáls, 4. óháttbundið, 5. óbilkvæmur.
aperture see 1. opvídd, 2. ljósop, 3. munni, 4. op, 5.
opbreidd.
apex see 1. toppur, 2. sólmið, 3. sólmark, 4.
sóknarpunktur, 5. oddur.
aphasia see 1. málstol, 2. orðdeyfa, 3. ómæli, 4.
málleysi, 5. máltruflun.
aphasic see 1. málstola, 2. málstoli.
aphelion see sólfirð.
aphonia see 1. raddlömun, 2. raddstol, 3. raddleysi,
4. raddarmissir.
aphrodisiac see 1. frygðarauki, 2. frygðarlyf, 3.
kynorkuaukandi, 4. kynorkulyf, 5. lostavekjandi.
apiarist see býflugnabóndi.
apical see 1. tungubroddshljóð, 2. topplægur.
aplasia see 1. frumubrestur, 2. vanþroskun.
apnea see 1. köfnun, 2. öndunarstöðvun.
apodal see 1. fótalaus, 2. kviðuggalaus.
apogee see jarðfirð.
apomixis see geldæxlun.
apophysis see 1. útvöxtur, 2. beinútvöxtur.
apoplexy see 1. innblæðing, 2. heilaslag, 3.
heilaáfall, 4. heilablóðfall.
apoptosis see 1. feigðarferli, 2. sjálfdrep.
appalling see 1. hryllilegur, 2. hræðilegur.
apparatus see 1. verkfæri, 2. vélbúnaður, 3.
tækjabúnaður, 4. tæki.
apparent see sannur.
appeal see 1. málskot, 2. málsskot, 3. kæra, 4. biðja,
5. bæn.
appealing see 1. hrífandi, 2. heillandi.
appear see þykja.
appeasement see 1. friðkauparstefna, 2. friðþæging,
3. sefun.
appellation see nafn.
append see 1. skeyta, 2. viðskeytingarhamur, 3.
viðskeyting.
appendage see 1. auki, 2. útlimur.
appendectomy see 1. botnlanganám, 2.
botnlangaskurður.
appendicitis see botnlangabólga.
appendix see 1. botnlangi, 2. viðauki, 3.
botnlangatota, 4. bókarauki, 5. viðbætir.
apperception see huggrip.
appetite see 1. ílöngun, 2. matarlyst.
apple see epli.
application see 1. beiting, 2. viðfang, 3. viðeign, 4.
viðeiganleiki, 5. bæn.
applied see hagnýttur.
apply see 1. nýta, 2. beita, 3. biðja, 4. nota.
appointment see 1. útnefning, 2. tilnefning, 3.
setning, 4. skipun.

apportionment see 1. hagsmunaskipting, 2.
skipting.
apposition see 1. samfærsla, 2. viðbótarvöxtur, 3.
hliðskipun, 4. viðurlag, 5. lagskipting.
appraisal see 1. mat, 2. virðing.
appraise see 1. meta, 2. virða.
appreciate see skilja.
appreciation see 1. gengishækkun, 2.
verðgildishækkun, 3. gengisris, 4. matshækkun.
apprehend see skilja.
apprehension see 1. skilningur, 2. kvíðakennd.
apprentice see 1. iðnnemi, 2. lærlingur, 3.
viðvaningur.
apprenticeship see 1. iðnnámstími, 2.
lærlingsstaða.
approach see 1. aðflug, 2. nálgast, 3. nálgun.
approachable see viðkunnanlegur.
appropriate see 1. sæmandi, 2. veita, 3. verja, 4.
viðeigandi.
appropriation see 1. fjárveiting, 2. ráðstöfun, 3.
tillag.
approval see 1. samþykki, 2. samþykkt, 3.
staðfesting, 4. stuðningur, 5. viðurkenning.
approve see 1. viðurkenna, 2. samþykkja.
approved see 1. viðurkenndur, 2. samþykktur, 3.
gildandi.
approximate see 1. áætla, 2. nálægja, 3. nálægur, 4.
nálga, 5. nálgast.
approximation see 1. námundun, 2. samræming, 3.
áætlun, 4. nálgun.
apraxia see 1. hreyfistol, 2. starfsglöp, 3. verkstol.
apricot see apríkósa.
apron see 1. svunta, 2. flughlað, 3. hlað.
aptitude see hæfileiki.
aquaculture see 1. fiskirækt, 2. fiskeldi.
aquaplane see fleytast.
aquarium see fiskabúr.
aquatic see 1. vatna, 2. vatns, 3. vatnsrænn.
aqueduct see 1. vatnsveitubrú, 2. vatnsveitustokkur,
3. vatnsleiðsla, 4. vatnsrás.
aquifer see 1. grunnvatnsgeymir, 2. vatnsberi, 3.
veitir.
arachnoid see 1. heilaskúm, 2. skúm, 3.
skúmhærður.
arbitrage see 1. högnun, 2. verðmunarviðskipti, 3.
misvirðiskaup.
arbitrary see 1. handahófskenndur, 2. ótiltekinn.
arbitration see 1. gerð, 2. gerðardómsmeðferð, 3.
gerðardómur, 4. úrskurður.
arbitrator see 1. gerðardómari, 2.
gerðardómsmaður, 3. gerðarmaður.
arbor see 1. ás, 2. dór, 3. möndull, 4. stýridór, 5.
stýringardór.
arboraceous see trjákynjaður.
arboreal see trjábýll.

arborescent *see* 1. greindur, 2. greinóttur.
arc *see* 1. bogi, 2. ferill, 3. hringbogi, 4. lína, 5. ljósbogi.
arcade *see* 1. bogarið, 2. bogagöng.
arch *see* bogi.
archaism *see* 1. málfyrning, 2. fornyrði.
archetype *see* 1. fornmynd, 2. frumgerð.
archipelago *see* 1. eyjaklasi, 2. eyjahaf.
architect *see* arkitekt.
architrave *see* 1. súlnaás, 2. faldur, 3. dyrafaldur, 4. þverbiti.
archive *see* 1. enarhivigi, 2. geyma, 3. safnvista, 4. skjala, 5. skjalasafn.
archives *see* 1. enarhivigi, 2. enarkivigi, 3. arhivo.
arctic *see* 1. Norðurpóll, 2. ískaldur.
area *see* 1. flatarmál, 2. flatarmálseigind, 3. flötur, 4. svæði, 5. yfirborðsflötur.
areal *see* svæðisbundinn.
areflexia *see* viðbragðaleysi.
arena *see* íþróttavöllur.
arenaceous *see* sandborinn.
areola *see* 1. reitur, 2. sjáaldursrönd, 3. vörtubaugur.
arginine *see* 1. arg, 2. arginín.
argument *see* 1. frumgildi, 2. stefnuhorn, 3. röksemdafærsla, 4. röksemd, 5. rökliður
argumentation *see* rökleiðsla.
arid *see* 1. skrælnaður, 2. úrkomusnauður, 3. þurr, 4. reglaus, 5. þurrviðrasamur.
arithmetic *see* reikningur.
arm *see* 1. armur, 2. handleggur, 3. brako, 4. upparmur, 5. upphandleggur.
armature *see* 1. anker, 2. varnarbúnaður, 3. spanali, 4. rafbúnaður, 5. snúður.
armour *see* 1. brynja, 2. brynvörn, 3. styrking.
armpit *see* handarkriki.
arms *see* 1. armi, 2. filio, 3. brako, 4. brakapogilo, 5. braka.
army *see* her.
aromatic *see* 1. ilmjurt, 2. angandi, 3. arómatískur, 4. ilmandi, 5. ilmefni.
arousal *see* 1. athyglisvakning, 2. örvun.
arrack *see* 1. grind, 2. standur.
arrange *see* innrétta.
arrangement *see* 1. innrétting, 2. uppstilling, 3. uppsetning, 4. tilhögun, 5. samkomulag.
array *see* 1. fylki, 2. fylking, 3. röðun.
arrest *see* 1. kyrrsetning, 2. trufla, 3. taka, 4. stöðva, 5. handtaka.
arrhythmia *see* 1. hjartsláttaróregla, 2. hjartsláttartruflun, 3. sláttarglöp.
arrive *see* koma.
arrogance *see* 1. dramb, 2. hroki.
arrow *see* 1. ör, 2. vísir.
arrowroot *see* 1. marantarót, 2. mjölrót, 3. örvarrót, 4. sterkjurót.

arsenic *see* 1. arsen, 2. arsenik.
art *see* 1. list, 2. ment.
arteriography *see* 1. slagæðamyndataka, 2. slagæðamyndun.
arteriole *see* slagæðlingur.
arteritis *see* 1 slagæðabólga, 2. slagæðarbólga.
artery *see* 1. útæð, 2. umferðaræð, 3. slagæð.
arthritic *see* liðbólgusjúklingur.
arthritis *see* 1. iktsýki, 2. liðagigt, 3. liðbólga.
arthroplasty *see* 1. liðskipti, 2. liðsköpun.
arthropod *see* 1. liðdýr, 2. liðfætla.
arthroscopy *see* liðspeglun.
artichoke *see* 1. körfukál, 2. ætiþistill, 3. artiskokkur.
article *see* greinir.
articulate *see* 1. liðaður, 2. liðskiptur.
articulated *see* liðskiptur.
articulation *see* 1. framburður, 2. skýrleiki, 3. liður, 4. liðamót, 5. hljóðmyndun.
artifact *see* gervingur.
as *see* 1. hvernig, 2. samkvæmt, 3. por, 4. iu, 5. hvenær.
asbestos *see* asbest.
asbestosis *see* 1. asbestreitrun, 2. asbestveiki.
ascarid *see* 1. spólormur, 2. spóluormur, 3. iðraþráðormur.
ascertain *see* 1. sannreyna, 2. staðreyna.
ascospore *see* 1. askgró, 2. sekkgró.
ascus *see* 1. askur, 2. grósekkur.
asepsis *see* 1. bakteríuleysi, 2. smitgát, 3. sýklavörn.
aseptic *see* 1. bakteríulaus, 2. smitlaus.
asexual *see* kynlaus.
ash *see* 1. aska, 2. gjóska, 3. evrópuaskur, 4. gosaska, 5. cindro.
ashes *see* 1. aska, 2. cindro, 3. cindrokolora, 4. frakseno.
ask *see* 1. spyrja, 2. biðja.
asocial *see* ófélagslegur.
asp *see* 1. rabbi, 2. rumungur, 3. naðra.
asparagine *see* 1. asn, 2. asparagín.
aspect *see* 1. hallastefna, 2. sjónarmið, 3. sólhorf, 4. horf, 5. andlitssvipur.
aspen *see* 1. blæösp, 2. espitré, 3. ösp.
asphalt *see* 1. malbik, 2. asfalt, 3. bik.
asphyxia *see* 1. köfnun, 2. dauðadá.
asphyxiate *see* 1. kæfa, 2. kafna.
aspirate *see* soga.
aspiration *see* 1. fráblástur, 2. útsog, 3. innöndun, 4. andardráttur, 5. kappsmál.
ass *see* asni.
assay *see* 1. mæligreining, 2. prófun, 3. mæling, 4. mæligreina, 5. mæla.
assemble *see* smala.
assembler *see* smali.
assembling *see* samsetning.

assembly see 1. samkunda, 2. samstæða, 3. samsöfnun, 4. þing, 5. samkoma.
assert see staðhæfa.
assertion see 1. staðhæfing, 2. fastyrðing.
assess see 1. meta, 2. áætla.
assessment see 1. úttekt, 2. mat, 3. skattálagning.
asset see 1. akiro, 2. eign.
assets see 1. eignir, 2. akiro, 3. eignaliðir, 4. valorajo.
assign see 1. tilnefna, 2. úthluta.
assignment see 1. verkskömmtun, 2. gilding.
assimilate see 1. samlaga, 2. samlagast.
assimilation see 1. menningaraðlögun, 2. tillíking, 3. samlögun, 4. melting, 5. ílifun.
assist see 1. hjálpa, 2. aðstoða.
assistance see 1. aðstoð, 2. hjálp.
associate see 1. spyrða, 2. tengja, 3. tengiliður, 4. sameina, 5. félagi.
association see 1. plöntusamfélag, 2. vébönd, 3. tengsl, 4. tenging, 5. stjörnufélag.
associative see tenginn.
assortment see 1. úrval, 2. samsafn, 3. samröðun.
assume see 1. gruna, 2. halda.
assumption see 1. frumhæfing, 2. gjafaforsenda, 3. forsenda, 4. ályktun, 5. ætlun.
assurance see 1. fullvissa, 2. loforð.
assure see 1. fullvissa, 2. tryggja.
astatine see astat.
aster see 1. geislakerfi, 2. stjörnufífill, 3. geislar.
astern see 1. afturá, 2. afturundan.
asteroid see 1. krossfiskur, 2. sæstjarna, 3. smástirni
asthenia see 1. síþreyta, 2. slen, 3. máttleysi.
asthenosphere see 1. seighvolf, 2. linhvolf.
asthma see 1. kafmæði, 2. andarteppa, 3. asma, 4. astma, 5. astmi.
astigmatism see 1. sjónskekkja, 2. bjúgskekkja.
astonishment see 1. furða, 2. undrun.
astringent see 1. herpandi, 2. herpiefni, 3. herpir.
astrobiology see 1. stjörnulíffræði, 2. geimlíffræði.
astrocyte see stjarnfruma.
astrolabe see 1. stjörnuskífa, 2. stjörnuhæðarmælir.
astrology see 1. stjörnuspáfræði, 2. stjörnuspeki.
astrometry see 1. stjarnmælingafræði, 2. stjörnuhnitafræði.
astronaut see geimfari.
astronautics see 1. geimsiglingafræði, 2. geimferðafræði.
astronomer see 1. stjörnufræðingur, 2. stjarnfræðingur.
astronomy see 1. stjörnufræði, 2. stjarnfræði, 3. stjarnvísindi.
astrophysics see stjarneðlisfræði.
asylum see 1. landvistarleyfi, 2. skjól, 3. hæli, 4. griðastaður.

asymmetric see 1. óreglulegur, 2. ósamhverfur, 3. ósamloka, 4. mishverfur.
asymmetrical see ósamloka.
asymmetry see 1. mishverfa, 2. ósamhverfa.
asymptote see 1. ósnertill, 2. aðfella.
asymptotic see aðfelldur.
asynchronous see 1. ósamfasa, 2. ósamhæfður, 3. ósamstilltur.
at see 1. hjá, 2. meðan, 3. fyrir, 4. eftir, 5. að.
ataractic see róandi.
atavism see 1. áalíking, 2. áavísi.
ataxia see 1. hreyfiglöp, 2. óregluhreyfing, 3. slingur.
atelectasis see lungnahrun.
atherosclerosis see 1. fituhrörnun, 2. hnútahersli.
athlete see íþróttamaður.
athletic see 1. aflvaxinn, 2. aflvöxtur.
atlas see 1. leikandi, 2. banakringla, 3. kortabók, 4. landakortabók.
atmosphere see 1. loft, 2. staðalloftþyngd, 3. loftþyngd, 4. lofthjúpur, 5. andrúmsloft.
atoll see 1. hringrif, 2. kóralrif.
atom see 1. frumeind, 2. atóm.
atomization see 1. úðun, 2. ýring, 3. sundrun.
atopy see 1. bráðaofnæmishneigð, 2. ofnæmistilhneiging.
atrium see 1. gátt, 2. tálknahol, 3. hol, 4. forhólf, 5. atríum.
atrocity see 1. andstyggð, 2. grimmd, 3. óbeit, 4. viðbjóður.
atrophy see 1. visnun, 2. visna, 3. rýrna, 4. kyrkingur, 5. rýrnun.
atropine see atrópín.
attach see binda.
attachment see 1. viðbótarbúnaður, 2. viðhengi, 3. kyrrsetning, 4. fjárnám, 5. festing.
attack see 1. sókn, 2. árás, 3. atlaga, 4. kast, 5. áfall.
attendance see 1. hirðing, 2. mætingar, 3. umsjón.
attendant see þjónn.
attention see 1. von, 2. athygli.
attenuate see 1. deyfa, 2. jafnmjókkandi, 3. veikja.
attenuation see 1. deyfing, 2. dofnun, 3. veiking.
attenuator see 1. deyfir, 2. deyfiliður.
attitude see 1. afstaða, 2. lega, 3. staða, 4. viðhorf, 5. horf.
attorney see 1. málfærslumaður, 2. lögfræðingur, 3. lögmaður, 4. málaflutningsmaður.
attraction see 1. aðdráttur, 2. aðdráttarafl, 3. aðdráttarkraftur.
attractive see 1. heillandi, 2. hrífandi.
attribute see 1. flokkunarbreyta, 2. eiginleiki, 3. einkunn, 4. eigna, 5. eigindi.
attrition see 1. skaf, 2. slit, 3. sverfing, 4. nudd.
attune see aðlagast.
atypical see 1. frábrigðilegur, 2. frákennilegur.

auction see uppboð.
audience see 1. viðtakar, 2. viðtaki.
audiometer see heyrnarmælir.
audit see 1. endurskoða, 2. endurskoðun.
auditing see endurskoðun.
auditor see endurskoðandi.
auditory see heyrn.
augmentation see 1. stækkun, 2. aukning.
aunt see 1. föðursystir, 2. móðursystir.
aura see flogboði.
auricle see 1. úteyra, 2. blaðeyra, 3. eyra (ear), 4. ullinseyra, 5. úllinseyra.
aurora see 1. segulljós, 2. norðurljós, 3. heimskautaljós.
auscultation see hlustun.
austerity see 1. efnahagsþrengingar, 2. hörgultímar.
autarchy see 1. alræði, 2. alræðisstjórn, 3. alveldi, 4. sjálfsstjórn.
autarky see sjálfsþurftarbúskapur.
authentic see 1. jafngildur, 2. upprunalegur, 3. sannur, 4. réttur, 5. ófalsaður.
authority see 1. umboð, 2. áhrif, 3. yfirráð, 4. yfirvald, 5. valdbærni.
authorization see 1. heimild, 2. heimilun, 3. löggilding.
authorize see 1. heimila, 2. löggilda.
autism see 1. einhverfa, 2. sjálfhverfa.
autistic see sjálfhverfur.
auto see 1. bifreið, 2. bíll, 3. sjálfröðun, 4. sjálfvirkur.
autoantibody see sjálfsmótefni.
autoantigen see 1. sjálfsofnæmisvaki, 2. sjálfsvaki.
autochthon see 1. frumbyggi, 2. innlendingur.
autochthonous see 1. upprunalegur, 2. innfæddur.
autoclave see 1. gufusæfir, 2. sæfa, 3. þrýstiketill, 4. þrýstisjóða.
autocorrelation see eiginfylgni.
autocracy see 1. einveldisstjórn, 2. einveldi, 3. alræði, 4. alræðisstjórn.
autogamous see 1. sjálfsfrævandi, 2. sjálfsfrjóvgandi.
autogamy see 1. sjálfsæxlun, 2. sjálfsfrjóvgun, 3. sjálfun.
autogenesis see sjálfsmyndun.
autogenous see 1. sjálfmyndaður, 2. sjálfskapaður, 3. sjálfmyndaður, 4. heimafenginn, 5. sjálfkveiktur.
autograft see sjálfsgræðlingur.
autograph see undirskrift.
autohypnosis see sjálfsdáleiðsla.
autoimmunity see 1. sjálfsnæmi, 2. sjálfsónæmi, 3. sjálfsofnæmi.
autolysis see 1. sjálfsrof, 2. sjálfeyðing, 3. sjálfleysing, 4. sjálfrot, 5. sjálfseyðing.
automatic see 1. alsjálfvirkur, 2. sjálfvirkur.

automation see 1. sjálfvirkjun, 2. sjálfvirkni, 3. sjálfvirkniaðgerð, 4. stýritækni.
automatism see 1. sjálfgengi, 2. sjálfvirkni.
automobile see 1. bifreið, 2. bíll.
automotive see vélknúinn.
autonomic see 1. ósjálfráður, 2. sjálfráður, 3. sjálfstæður, 4. sjálfvirkur.
autonomous see 1. óháður, 2. sjálfstæður, 3. sjálfráða.
autonomy see 1. sjálfstæði, 2. sjálfsstjórnarumdæmi, 3. sjálfsstjórnarríki, 4. sjálfsstjórn, 5. sjálfsforræði.
autopilot see sjálfstýring.
autopsy see 1. líkskoðun, 2. krufning.
autoregression see sjálfverfur.
autosome see 1. frílitningur, 2. líkfrumulitningur, 3. sjálfflitningur.
autosuggestion see sjálfssefjun.
autotrophic see 1. frumbjarga, 2. sjálfbirgur.
autumn see haust.
auxiliary see þerna.
availability see 1. tiltækt, 2. tiltækileiki, 3. aðgengileiki, 4. reiða.
available see 1. aðgengilegur, 2. tiltækur.
avalanche see 1. snjóflóð, 2. snjóskriða, 3. skriða.
avenue see 1. troð, 2. breiðstræti.
average see meðaltal.
aversion see 1. fælni, 2. óbeit.
avidity see bindistyrkur.
avocado see 1. lárpera, 2. avókadó, 3. grænaldin.
avoidance see 1. forðun, 2. hliðrun.
await see vænta.
awareness see 1. áskyn, 2. tilvitund.
aweigh see laust.
awful see 1. andstyggilegur, 2. hræðilegur, 3. hryllilegur.
awning see 1. sóltjald, 2. tjaldþak.
axe see 1. öxi, 2. exi.
axial see 1. áslægur, 2. möndullægur, 3. sammiðja.
axilla see 1. holhönd, 2. handarkriki.
axiom see 1. grundvallarregla, 2. frumsenda, 3. frumsetning, 4. frumregla.
axis see 1. öxull, 2. ás, 3. standliður, 4. snúningsás, 5. meginstöngull.
axle see 1. ás, 2. öxull, 3. hjólás.
axon see 1. sími, 2. taugasími.
azimuth see 1. stefnuhorn, 2. áttarhorn.
azote see köfnunarefni.

B

b see bór.
babble see 1. hjal, 2. kliður.

baby *see* 1. brjóstbarn, 2. smábarn, 3. ungbarn.
bacillary *see* staflaga.
bacillus *see* 1. stafbaktería, 2. stafgerill.
bacitracin *see* basítrasín.
back *see* 1. bak, 2. hryggur, 3. rangsælis, 4. uppmæltur.
backbone *see* 1. hryggur, 2. þorskhryggur.
backfire *see* 1. bakslag, 2. bakkviknun, 3. bakskot.
background *see* 1. grunnpúlstíðni, 2. grunnljómi, 3. bakgrunnur, 4. baksvið.
backlash *see* 1. bakslag, 2. hlaup, 3. slag.
backpack *see* bakpoki.
backside *see* rass.
backspace *see* 1. hopa, 2. bakka.
backup *see* 1. afrit, 2. öryggisafrit, 3. stuðningsafrit, 4. varaafrit.
bacteria *see* 1. bakteríur, 2. gerlar.
bactericidal *see* 1. bakteríueyðandi, 2. gerlaeyðandi, 3. sýkladrepandi.
bactericide *see* 1. bakteríueyðir, 2. gerlabani, 3. sótthreinsunarefni, 4. sýklaeyðir.
bacteriology *see* 1. bakteríufræði, 2. gerlafræði, gerilveira.
bacteriophage *see* 1. bakteríuveira, 2. faga, 3. gerilveira.
bacteriostasis *see* 1. bakteríuhefting, 2. bakteríustöðvun.
bacteriostatic *see* 1. bakteríuheftandi, 2. bakteríuhemjandi, 3. bakteríustöðvandi, 4. gerilheftandi, 5. gerlahemjandi.
bacterium *see* 1. baktería, 2. gerill, 3. keðjusýkill.
bad *see* 1. vondur, 2. slæmur, 3. illur.
badge *see* merkisspjald.
badger *see* greifingi.
baffle *see* 1. beinihluti, 2. vatnsrás, 3. spjald, 4. hlíf, 5. hlífispjald.
bag *see* 1. poki, 2. sako, 3. taska.
baggage *see* farangur.
bairn *see* barn.
bait *see* beita.
baiting *see* beitning.
bake *see* baka.
baker *see* bakari.
bakery *see* bakarí.
balance *see* 1. Jafnvægi, 2. vog, 3. vogarskál, 4. jafnvægisstilla, 5. jafna.
balanced *see* jafnvægur.
balcony *see* svalir.
baldness *see* hártap.
bale *see* 1. balli, 2. baggi.
ball *see* 1. kúla, 2. hnöttur, 3. bolti.
ballast *see* 1. ballest, 2. kjölfesta, 3. sakka, 4. straumfesta, 5. straumhaft.
ballet *see* 1. ballett, 2. danssjónleikur.
ballot *see* 1. kosningarréttur, 2. atkvæðaseðill, 3. kjörseðill.

balm *see* 1. harmabót, 2. hjartafró, 3. sítrónumelissa.
balsam *see* 1. balsamínutré, 2. ilmkvoða, 3. smyrsl.
balustrade *see* 1. grindverk, 2. rimlagirðing.
bamboo *see* 1. bambusreyr, 2. bambus.
banana *see* 1. bananaávöxtur, 2. banani, 3. bjúgaldin.
band *see* 1. litrófsþáttur, 2. bil, 3. rák, 4. tíðnibil, 5. gjörð.
bandage *see* 1. umbúðir, 2. sárabindi.
bands *see* 1. bando, 2. bendo, 3. ĉirkaŭligo, 4. fanfaro, 5. hordo.
bandwidth *see* 1. borðabreidd, 2. tíðnibil, 3. bandvídd, 4. bandbreidd, 5. tíðnissvið.
bank *see* 1. banki, 2. snertusafn, 3. strokkaröð, 4. halli, 5. halla.
bankrupt *see* gjaldþrota.
bankruptcy *see* gjaldþrot.
banks *see* 1. banko, 2. bordo, 3. enbankigi, 4. sablobenko.
baobab *see* apabrauðstré.
bar *see* 1. stöng, 2. sproti, 3. súla, 4. sandrif, 5. braut.
barb *see* 1. krókhár, 2. þreifiþráður, 3. fön, 4. fanargeisli, 5. agnúi.
barbel *see* 1. vatnaskeggur, 2. vatnaskeggi.
barbiturate *see* 1. barbitúrat, 2. barbitúrsýrulyf.
bare *see* tómur.
bargain *see* 1. semja, 2. kjarakaup, 3. samkomulag.
barge *see* vöruflutningaprammi.
barium *see* 1. barín, 2. baríum.
bark *see* 1. börkur, 2. gelt, 3. trjábörkur.
barley *see* bygg.
barnacle *see* 1. hrúðurkarl, 2. hrossaríkja.
barograph *see* þrýstiriti.
barometer *see* loftvog.
barrack *see* 1. barako, 2. braggi, 3. brakki.
barracks *see* barako.
barracuda *see* barrakúda.
barramundi *see* risaborri.
barrel *see* 1. hólf, 2. tunna, 3. strokkur, 4. fat, 5. miðhluti.
barren *see* 1. gróðursnauður, 2. hrjóstrugur, 3. ófrjór.
barrette *see* 1. ljósastika, 2. stuttslá.
barrier *see* 1. garður, 2. þröskuldur, 3. tálmun, 4. tálmi, 5. hindrun.
barrister *see* málfærslumaður.
barter *see* vöruskipti.
base *see* 1. lútur, 2. basi, 3. stofntala, 4. undirstaða, 5. sökkull.
baseband *see* grunnband.
baseline *see* 1. grunnlína, 2. grunnur, 3. grunnviðmiðun, 4. mállína.
basic *see* 1. alkalískur, 2. basískur, 3. lútkenndur.
basics *see* stafróf.

basidium see 1. grókólfur, 2. kólfur, 3. grókylfa, 4. basíða, 5. gróstilkur.
basil see 1. basilíka, 2. basilíkum, 3. basill.
basin see 1. skál, 2. dæld, 3. lægð.
basis see grunnur.
basketball see körfuknattleikur.
basophil see 1. basafruma, 2. lútfíkill.
basophilia see 1. lútsækni, 2. rauðkornablettun.
bass see 1. barri, 2. laxaborri, 3. vartari.
bast see 1. sáldvefur, 2. trefja.
bastard see 1. lausaleiksbarn, 2. kynblendingur.
bat see leðurblaka.
batch see 1. bunki, 2. lota, 3. runa.
bath see bað.
bathroom see bað.
battery see 1. rafgeymir, 2. samstæða, 3. rafhlaða, 4. barsmíðar, 5. rafhlað.
battle see slagsmál.
baud see bot.
bauxite see báxít.
bay see 1. flói, 2. vík, 3. stafgólf, 4. segullægð, 5. fjörður.
be see vera.
beach see 1. fjara, 2. baðströnd, 3. strönd.
beacon see 1. sjómerki, 2. viti.
bead see 1. styrkingarbrún, 2. styrkingarkantur, 3. millilegg, 4. brjóta.
beak see 1. goggur, 2. nef (nose), 3. fuglsnef.
beaker see 1. bikar, 2. bikarglas.
beam see 1. geisli, 2. biti, 3. þverbiti, 4. útvarp, 5. ljósgeisli.
bear see 1. björn, 2. bjärndýr, 3. þola.
beard see skegg.
bearing see 1. stefna, 2. átt, 3. lager, 4. lástefna, 5. leg.
beat see 1. slá, 2. hviða, 3. slag, 4. sláttur, 5. slögun.
beautiful see 1. fagur, 2. fallegur.
beauty see 1. blíða, 2. botntala, 3. fegurð.
beaver see bifur.
become see verða.
bed see 1. rúm, 2. lag, 3. seng, 4. sengen, 5. undirstaða.
bedrock see berggrunnur.
bee see býfluga.
beef see nautakjöt.
beefsteak see nautabauti.
beehive see býflugnabú.
beep see 1. flaut, 2. flauta.
beer see öl.
beeswax see bývax.
beet see 1. beð, 2. reitur
beetroot see 1. rauðbeða, 2. rauðbeðja, 3. rauðrófa.
before see fyrir.
beg see biðja.
begin see byrja.

beginning see byrjun.
behavior see 1. hegðun, 2. atferli, 3. atferði.
behaviorism see atferlisstefna.
behaviour see 1. hegðun, 2. atferði, 3. atferli, 4. framkoma.
behaviourism see atferlisstefna.
behind see rass.
bel see desíbel.
belch see ropa.
belief see 1. sannfæring, 2. trú.
believe see trúa.
belladonna see 1. sjáaldursjurt, 2. völvuauga.
belly see 1. kviður, 2. magi, 3. búkur, 4. lestarbelgur, 5. belgur.
beloved see sætur.
below see 1. neðan, 2. undir.
belt see 1. belti, 2. svæði, 3. reim.
beluga see hússtyrja.
bench see bekkur.
benchmark see 1. fastmerki, 2. frammistöðuviðmið, 3. viðmið, 4. viðmiðunarmerki.
bend see 1. hlykkur, 2. beygja, 3. bugur.
bends see kafaraverkir.
beneficiary see 1. hótaþegi, 2. njótandi, 3. rétthafi, 4. styrkþegi.
benefit see 1. gagna, 2. vinningur, 3. styrkur, 4. kostur, 5. hjálpa.
benign see 1. góðkynja, 2. góðkynjaður.
benzene see 1. bensen, 2. bensól.
benzidine see bensidín.
benzole see bensól.
berceuse see 1. vögguljóð, 2. vögguvísa.
bergamot see 1. ilmappelsína, 2. bergamía, 3. bergamóappelsína, 4. bergamótappelsína.
beriberi see taugakröm.
berkelium see 1. berkelín, 2. berkelíum, 3. berklín, 4. berkel.
berry see ber.
berth see 1. koja, 2. leguplás, 3. legurými.
beryllium see 1. beryllín, 2. beryllíum.
best see bestur.
bestiality see 1. dýrseðli, 2. skepnuskapur, 3. sódómska, 4. sódómusaurlifnaður.
bet see veðja.
betatron see 1. betatrónn, 2. rafagnaslöngvir, 3. betahraðall.
betrothal see trúlofun.
better see betri.
bevel see 1. sniðbrún, 2. flái, 3. fösun, 4. halli, 5. skábrún.
bewitching see 1. heillandi, 2. hrífandi.
beyond see yfir.
bezel see rammi.
biannual see 1. hálfsárslegur, 2. misserislegur.

bias *see* 1. bjagi, 2. hlutdrægni, 3. vilhalli, 4. skurðarlínur, 5. hneigð.
biased *see* 1. bjagaður, 2. hlutdrægur, 3. meðalgildisskakkur, 4. skakkur, 5. vilhallur.
bib *see* skeggur.
bicarbonate *see* bíkarbónat.
biceps *see* tvíhöfði.
biconcave *see* tvíhvolfur.
bicycle *see* 1. reiðhjól, 2. stíga.
bid *see* 1. tilboð, 2. útboð, 3. kauptilboð, 4. biðja, 5. bæn.
biennial *see* 1. tvíár, 2. tvíær.
bifid *see* tvíklofinn.
bifocal *see* tvífeðmur.
bifurcation *see* 1. tvíklofnun, 2. klofnun, 3. kró, 4. kvíslun.
big *see* 1. stór, 2. mikill.
bight *see* 1. fjörður, 2. flói, 3. vík.
bike *see* reiðhjól.
bilateral *see* 1. tvíhliða, 2. tvíhliðmælt, 3. gagnkvæmur, 4. báðumegin.
bilberry *see* 1. aðalbláberjalyng, 2. aðalbláber.
bile *see* gall.
bilge *see* 1. kjalsog, 2. kjölvatn.
bilingual *see* tvítyngdur.
bilingualism *see* tvítyngi.
bilirubin *see* 1. gallrauði, 2. bílírúbín.
biliverdin *see* gallgræna.
bill *see* 1. reikningur, 2. vörureikningur, 3. bankaseðil, 4. kæruskjal, 5. skírteini.
billfish *see* blettabryngedda.
billion *see* milljarður.
bimetal *see* 1. tvímálma, 2. tvímálmur.
bin *see* 1. ílát, 2. kassi, 3. skúffa.
binary *see* 1. tvígildur, 2. tvöfaldur, 3. reyndartvístirni, 4. tvískiptur, 5. tvístirni.
bind *see* 1. binda, 2. festast.
binder *see* bindefni.
binnacle *see* 1. mælahús, 2. nátthús.
binocular *see* 1. kíkir, 2. tvísær, 3. tvíaugna, 4. lorno, 5. sjónauki.
binoculars *see* lorno.
binomial *see* 1. tvíliða, 2. tvínafn.
bioassay *see* 1. lífvirkniprófun, 2. kvikmæling, 3. lífgreining.
biochemistry *see* lífefnafræði.
bioclimatology *see* 1. lífloftslagsfræði, 2. lífveðurfræði.
biodegradable *see* 1. lífbrotgjarn, 2. lífhverfur, 3. lífsprakur, 4. visthverfur.
biodegradation *see* lífsundrun.
biodiversity *see* lífjölbreytni.
bioelectricity *see* 1. lífraf, 2. lífrafmagn.
bioenergetics *see* líforkufræði.
bioengineering *see* 1. líftækni, 2. lífverkfræði.

bioethics *see* lífsiðfræði.
biofeedback *see* 1. lífsvörun, 2. endursvörun, 3. ístjórn.
biogenesis *see* 1. lífmyndun, 2. lífkviknun.
biogeography *see* líflandafræði.
biography *see* æfisaga.
biological *see* 1. líffræðilegur, 2. lífræðilegur, 3. lífvirkur.
biology *see* líffræði.
bioluminescence *see* 1. lífefnaljóm, 2. lífljómun.
biomass *see* 1. lífmagn, 2. lífmassi, 3. lífþyngd, 4. lífefnamagn.
biometrics *see* 1. lífkenni, 2. líftölfræði.
biometry *see* 1. lífmælingar, 2. líftölfræði.
biopsy *see* 1. vefjasýni, 2. vefsýnitaka, 3. vefsýni.
biorhythm *see* 1. lífhrynjandi, 2. lífritmi, 3. líftaktur.
biosphere *see* 1. lífheimur, 2. lífhvolf.
biostatistics *see* 1. lífmælingar, 2. líftölfræði.
biosynthesis *see* 1. tillífun, 2. lífefnamyndun, 3. lífefnasmíð.
biota *see* lífríki.
biotechnology *see* 1. lífefnatækni, 2. líftækni.
biotic *see* lífrænn.
biotin *see* bíótín.
biotope *see* vistgerð.
biotype *see* 1. lífgerð, 2. lífmynd.
biped *see* 1. tvífætla, 2. tvífætlingur.
bipolar *see* 1. jafnskauta, 2. tvískauta.
bird *see* 1. fugl, 2. birdo.
birefringence *see* tvíbrot.
birth *see* 1. burður, 2. fæðing.
birthdate *see* afmælisdagur.
birthday *see* 1. afmæli, 2. afmælisdagur.
birthmark *see* fæðingarblettur.
biscuits *see* tvíbaka.
bisect *see* helminga.
bisection *see* helmingun.
bisexual *see* 1. tvíkynja, 2. tvíkynhneigður, 3. samkynja.
bisexuality *see* 1. tvíkynjun, 2. tvíkynhneigð.
bishop *see* biskup.
bismuth *see* 1. bismút, 2. vismút.
bit *see* 1. biti, 2. tvíundatölustafur.
bite *see* bíta.
bitmap *see* punktafylki.
bitt *see* 1. polli, 2. þilfarspolli, 3. festarhæll.
bivalent *see* 1. litningapar, 2. litningsþráðaferna, 3. tvígildi, 4. tvígildur.
black *see* 1. svartur, 2. svart, 3. blakkur.
blackberry *see* 1. bjarnarber, 2. brómber.
blackbird *see* svartþröstur.
blackboard *see* veggtafla.
blackbody *see* svarthlutur.
blackmail *see* fjárkúgun.

blackout see 1. ölgleymi, 2. sjónmyrkvi.

bladder see blaðra.

blade see 1. blað, 2. blaðka.

blame see 1. ásökun, 2. átelja.

blameless see saklaus.

bland see mjúkur.

blank see 1. hálfsmíðaður, 2. eyðustafur, 3. cyða, 4. hvítur.

blanket see 1. brekán, 2. ullarrábreiða.

blanking see 1. byrging, 2. slökk, 3. tálmun.

blaspheme see bölva.

blast see 1. blástur, 2. sprenging, 3. höggbylgja, 4. flaut, 5. flauta.

blastema see 1. frumustofn, 2. útlimsvísir.

blastoderm see 1. kímblöðrudiskur, 2. kímblöðruveggur.

blastomycosis see sprotamygla.

blastopore see 1. frummunnur, 2. vembilsvör, 3. kímrauf.

blastula see 1. blaðra, 2. blastúla, 3. blöðrufóstur, 4. kímblaðra.

bleak see 1. kaldur, 2. óþægilegur, 3. hreisturglæsir, 4. dapur.

bleed see 1. vökvatæma, 2. blóðga.

bleeder see blæðari.

blind see 1. blindur, 2. hlíf, 3. lokaður.

blindness see 1. sjónleysi, 2. blinda.

blink see 1. depla, 2. depl, 3. blikka.

blinking see blikk.

blip see 1. endurvarp, 2. ljósdepill.

blister see 1. blaðra, 2. bóla, 3. hjálmur.

blitz see Hraðskák.

blizzard see 1. hríð, 2. stórhríð, 3. hríðarbylur, 4. blindhríð, 5. sandbylur.

block see 1. randbygging, 2. götureitur, 3. vélarblokk, 4. tálmi, 5. strokkstykki.

blockade see 1. bann, 2. hafnbann, 3. herkví.

blocked see hindraður.

bloke see 1. karlmaður, 2. maður (man).

blonde see deplaskata.

blood see blóð.

bloom see 1. blómi, 2. blom.

blot see 1. blettpróf, 2. þrykk, 3. þrykkja.

blow see 1. blása, 2. skellur, 3. slag, 4. högg, 5. árekstur.

blower see 1. blásari, 2. físibelgur, 3. smiðjubelgur.

blubber see 1. spik, 2. hvalspik, 3. rengi, 4. selspik

blue see 1. blár, 2. dapur, 3. heiðblár, 4. himinblár, 5. hnugginn.

blueberry see runnabláber.

bluefish see vígablámi.

blunder see Afleikur.

blush see 1. kinnroði, 2. roðna.

board see 1. nefnd, 2. ráð, 3. stjórn, 4. stjórnarnefnd, 5. borð.

boarding see borðganga.

boast see 1. gorta, 2. skruma.

boaster see 1. gortari, 2. montprik, 3. grobbari.

boat see bátur.

boatswain see bátsmaður.

bobbin see bobbingur

bobby see lögregluþjónn.

body see 1. líkami, 2. bú, 3. yfirbygging, 4. kroppur, 5. kleggi.

bodywork see 1. boddíhlutir, 2. yfirbyggingarvinna, 3. yfirbyggingarhlutir.

bog see 1. barnamosamýri, 2. hik, 3. hikst, 4. mýrlendi.

boil see 1. sjóða, 2. suða, 3. kýli.

boiler see 1. gufuketill, 2. ketill.

boiling see suða.

bold see 1. feitletur, 2. feitur.

boldface see 1. feitletra, 2. feitletraður.

bollard see 1. polli, 2. festarhæll, 3. bryggjupolli.

bolometer see 1. bólómælir, 2. hitageislunarmælir, 3. varmahitamælir, 4. alrófsmælir.

bolt see bolti.

bolus see 1. biti, 2. munnbiti, 3. tugga.

bomb see 1. sprengikúla, 2. sprengja.

bond see 1. tenging, 2. vaxtabréf, 3. tengi, 4. skuldabréf, 5. líming.

bone see 1. bein, 2. beinvefur.

boneless see beinlaus.

bonnet see 1. húdd, 2. vélarhlíf.

bonus see 1. bónus, 2. kaupauki, 3. aukaþóknun, 4. launaauki.

book see 1. bók, 2. libro.

bookkeeper see bókari.

bookkeeping see 1. bókfærsla, 2. bókhald, 3. reikningshald.

boom see 1. uppgangstími, 2. verðbólga, 3. uppgangur, 4. lyftiarmur, 5. góðæri.

booster see 1. aflauki, 2. eflir, 3. snerpir, 4. snerpivél.

boot see 1. farangursgeymsla, 2. stígvél, 3. skott, 4. ræsing, 5. ræsa.

bootstrap see 1. ræsiforrit, 2. sjálfþýða.

borage see hjólkróna.

borax see 1. bórax, 2. burís.

border see 1. egg, 2. gluggajaðar, 3. gluggakarmur, 4. jaðar, 5. landamæri.

bore see 1. bora, 2. víkkun, 3. útborun, 4. borvídd, 5. strokkþvermál.

boreal see norðlægur.

boring see 1. borun, 2. útborun.

boron see bór.

borrower see lántakandi.

borrowing see 1. lán, 2. lántaka.

bosom see brjóst.

boss see 1. búkki, 2. höfuðsteinn, 3. kragi, 4. nöf.

botany see grasafræði.
bottle see flaska.
bottleneck see flöskuháls.
bottom see 1. botn, 2. rass.
bough see 1. kvísl, 2. ramo, 3. grein.
boulder see bjarg.
bouncer see gúmmítékki.
boundary see 1. landamæri, 2. svæðisrammi, 3. samskeyti, 4. takmörk, 5. mörk.
bourgeois see 1. eignastéttarmaður, 2. miðstéttarmaður.
bourgeoisie see 1. eignastétt, 2. miðstétt, 3. borgarastétt.
bow see 1. byrðingur, 2. skipsbógur, 3. bógur.
bowfin see 1. boguggi, 2. eðjufiskur, 3. leirgedda.
bowl see 1. skál, 2. ílát.
bowsprit see bugspjót.
box see 1. fagurlim, 2. kassi, 3. kista, 4. rammi, 5. skrín.
boy see 1. drengur, 2. piltur, 3. strákur.
boycott see 1. kaupbann, 2. samskiptabann, 3. verkbann, 4. viðskiptabann, 5. viðskiptaeinangrun.
brace see 1. stífa, 2. spelka, 3. murkrampo, 4. krappi.
bracelet see armband.
braces see 1. stego, 2. armaturo, 3. krampi, 4. krampo, 5. kuraĝiĝi.
bracing see 1. styrkjandi, 2. hressandi, 3. styrking.
bracket see 1. festing, 2. hornklofi, 3. knekti, 4. krappi, 5. svigi.
bradycardia see hægsláttur.
brag see 1. gorta, 2. skruma.
braggart see 1. gortari, 2. grobbari, 3. montprik.
bragger see 1. gortari, 2. grobbari, 3. montprik.
braid see flétta.
brain see heili.
brainstorming see 1. þankaþeyr, 2. þankahríð, 3. hugrenningur, 4. hugmyndaregn, 5. heilabylur.
brainwashing see heilaþvottur.
brake see 1. hemla, 2. bremsa, 3. hemill.
braking see hemlun.
branch see 1. grein, 2. kvísl, 3. deild, 4. greinilína, 5. leggur.
branchia see tálkn.
branchial see branka.
brand see 1. móðurmerki, 2. sótaður, 3. vöruafbrigði, 4. vörumerki, 5. vörutegund.
brass see 1. látún, 2. messing.
bravado see gorta.
braze see 1. brasa, 2. harðlóða.
brazen see ósvífinn.
brazil see Brasilía.
brazing see kveiking.
bread see brauð.
breadth see stærð.

break see 1. Hlé, 2. rjúfa, 3. sliturbergmál, 4. rof, 5. brjóta.
breakaway see viðbragð.
breakdown see 1. bilun, 2. einangrunarhrun, 3. vélarbilun.
breakpoint see 1. rofstaður, 2. gjaldflokkamörk.
breakwater see 1. öldubrjótur, 2. hafnargarður, 3. brimvarnargarður, 4. brimbrjótur.
bream see leirslabbi.
breast see 1. brjóst, 2. bringa.
breastbone see 1. bringubein, 2. brjóstbein.
breath see 1. andardráttur, 2. andi, 3. önd.
breathe see anda.
breccia see 1. brotaberg, 2. gosþursti, 3. þursaberg.
breed see kapphlaup.
breeding see 1. kynæxlun, 2. ræktun, 3. rækt, 4. kynbótarækt, 5. kynbætur.
breeze see gola.
bribe see 1. fyrirgreiðslufé, 2. múta, 3. mútufé, 4. mútur.
brick see 1. tígulsteinn, 2. múrsteinn.
bride see 1. brúður, 2. unnusta.
bridegroom see brúðgumi.
bridge see 1. brú, 2. brúa, 3. mælibrú, 4. tengja.
bridle see grandari.
briefcase see skjalataska.
briefing see 1. veðurspjall, 2. aðflugsgreining.
briefs see kalsono.
bright see 1. bjartur, 2. gljáandi, 3. skær.
brightness see 1. lýsi, 2. skærleiki, 3. birtustig, 4. birta.
brill see 1. deplahverfa, 2. kaliforníukoli, 3. slétthverfa, 4. augnhula.
brilliance see birta.
brilliant see 1. ljómandi, 2. briljantur, 3. glitrandi.
brim see egg.
brimstone see brennisteinn.
brine see pækill.
brink see egg.
briquette see 1. Köggull, 2. kolamylsnuköggull, 3. þviti.
broach see 1. rýming, 2. snaralur, 3. rýmari, 4. rýma.
broad see 1. kvenmaður, 2. rúmgóður, 3. víður, 4. kona.
broadbill see sverðfiskur.
broadcast see 1. útvarp, 2. víðvarp.
broccoli see 1. brokkál, 2. spergilkál, 3. brokkoli, 4. brokkóli.
brochure see 1. kynningarbæklingur, 2. kynningarrit.
broker see 1. fasteignasali, 2. miðlari, 3. verðbréfasali.
brokerage see 1. þóknun, 2. verðbréfamiðlun, 3. miðlun.
bromine see bróm.

bronchitis *see* 1. berkjubólga, 2. berkjukvef, 3. berknakvef, 4. bronkítis, 5. lungnakvef.
bronchoscopy *see* berkjuspeglun.
bronchus *see* 1. berkja, 2. lungnapípa, 3. barkakvísl, 4. barkapípa.
brood *see* 1. barnahópur, 2. got, 3. ungahópur, 4. urpt.
brook *see* 1. lækur, 2. þola.
broom *see* 1. lyng, 2. sófl, 3. sópur.
brother *see* bróðir.
brown *see* 1. brúnn, 2. mórauður.
brownie *see* 1. ljósálfur, 2. ylfingur.
browse *see* 1. skoða, 2. rápa, 3. ráp, 4. skoðun.
browser *see* 1. rápari, 2. rápforrit, 3. skoðari, 4. skoðunarforrit.
browsing *see* skrunskoðun.
brucellosis *see* öldusótt.
bruise *see* 1. mar, 2. merja, 3. særa.
brush *see* 1. burstakol, 2. bursti, 3. kol, 4. pensill.
brutal *see* 1. óvænn, 2. óvingjarnlegur.
bubble *see* 1. verðbóla, 2. bóla, 3. loftbóla.
buckling *see* 1. beyglun, 2. bungun, 3. kripplun, 4. krypplun.
buckwheat *see* 1. bókhveitigrjón, 2. bæki, 3. bækigrjón, 4. bókhveiti.
bud *see* 1. knappur, 2. girni, 3. æxlıknappur, 4. brum.
budding *see* 1. angaskot, 2. knappskot.
budget *see* 1. fjárhagsrammi, 2. rekstraráætlun, 3. kostnaðaráætlun, 4. fjárveiting, 5. fjárhagsáætlun.
budgeting *see* 1. fjárhagsáætlunargerð, 2. fjárlagagerð.
buffalo *see* buffall.
buffer *see* 1. biðvista, 2. jafni, 3. jafnalausn, 4. jaðar, 5. höggpúði.
buffering *see* jaðra.
bug *see* 1. lús, 2. villa, 3. böggur.
build *see* 1. byggja, 2. smíða.
builder *see* verktaki.
building *see* 1. grenndun, 2. húseign, 3. bygging.
bulb *see* 1. pera, 2. hylki, 3. klumba, 4. laukknappur, 5. laukur.
bulge *see* 1. kragi, 2. gúlpur, 3. bunga.
bulimia *see* 1. átköst, 2. græðgi, 3. matgræðgi.
bulk *see* 1. stærð, 2. meirihluti, 3. meginhluti, 4. laust, 5. fyrirferð.
bulkhead *see* 1. lestarþil, 2. milliþilja, 3. skilrúm, 4. styrking, 5. þverþil.
bull *see* 1. tarfur, 2. naut, 3. griðungur.
bulla *see* blaðra.
bulldozer *see* jarðýta.
bullhead *see* gulgranı.
bummer *see* vonbrigði.
bumper *see* 1. höggvari, 2. stuðari.

bumping *see* 1. farsynjun, 2. hnykksuða, 3. höggsuða.
bundle *see* 1. böggull, 2. búnt, 3. knippi.
bung *see* 1. spons, 2. sponsgat.
bunker *see* 1. olíugeymir, 2. hvarf, 3. glompa, 4. byrða, 5. Stía.
bunny *see* kanína.
bunt *see* poki.
buoy *see* 1. bauja, 2. dufl.
buoyancy *see* 1. flothæfni, 2. uppdrif, 3. flotkraftur, 4. floteiginleiki, 5. fleytihæfni.
burbot *see* vatnaflekkur.
burden *see* sníkiálag.
burdensome *see* þungur.
bureau *see* 1. skrifborð, 2. Skrifstofan.
bureaucracy *see* 1. regluveldi, 2. skrifstofuveldi, 3. skriffinnska, 4. embættismannakerfi, 5. skrifræði.
burette *see* 1. býretta, 2. mælipípa.
burglar *see* innbrotsþjófur.
burlap *see* 1. pokastrigi, 2. strigi.
burn *see* 1. brenna, 2. brunasár, 3. bruni.
burner *see* 1. brennir, 2. brennari.
burnishing *see* 1. þrýstifágun, 2. fágun, 3. háglansslípun, 4. pólering, 5. sléttun.
burnout *see* 1. útkulnun, 2. útbruni, 3. kulnun, 4. starfsþreyta, 5. þrekþurrð.
burr *see* 1. gráð, 2. gráða, 3. gráður.
burring *see* gráðuhreinsun.
bursitis *see* 1. belgbólga, 2. belgmein, 3. buddubólga.
burst *see* 1. blossi, 2. brotna, 3. hrina, 4. rifna, 5. springa.
bus *see* 1. strætisvagn, 2. tengibraut, 3. gagnabraut, 4. almenningsvagn, 5. braut.
bush *see* 1. fóðring, 2. hálfeyðimörk, 3. legubakki, 4. runnasteppa, 5. runni.
bushing *see* 1. fóðring, 2. gegntak, 3. skrúfhólkur.
business *see* 1. fyrirtæki, 2. sala, 3. umsvif, 4. verzlun, 5. viðskipti.
busy *see* upptekinn.
but *see* 1. þó, 2. nema, 3. en.
butane *see* bútan.
butt *see* 1. stúfsett, 2. stúfsettur.
butter *see* smjör.
butterfish *see* 1. teistufiskur, 2. lummari, 3. skerjasteinbítur, 4. smjörfiskur, 5. sprettfiskur.
butterfly *see* 1. fidrildi, 2. fiðrildısplástur.
butternut *see* 1. forðahneta, 2. smjörhneta, 3. smjörhnetutré, 4. smjörhnot.
buttock *see* gluteo.
buttocks *see* 1. sidvango, 2. þjó, 3. þjóhnappar, 4. sitjandi, 5. rass.
button *see* 1. hnappur, 2. takki, 3. tala.
butyl *see* bútýl.
buy *see* 1. kaup, 2. kaupa.

buyer *see* kaupandi.
buzz *see* 1. aðvörunarhljóð, 2. hljóðmerki, 3. suð.
buzzard *see* músvákur.
by *see* 1. eftir, 2. samkvæmt, 3. um, 4. á.
bye *see* 1. bless, 2. sjáumst.
bypass *see* 1. hjárása, 2. hjáveita, 3. hjárás, 4. hjáleið, 5. framhjáhlaup.
byte *see* 1. bæti, 2. tölvustafur.

C

c *see* kolefni.
cab *see* 1. leigubíll, 2. stýrishús.
cabbage *see* 1. garðkál, 2. villikál, 3. kál, 4. garðakál, 5. hvítkál.
cabin *see* 1. farþegarými, 2. fólksrými, 3. káeta, 4. klefi.
cabinet *see* 1. ráðuneyti, 2. ríkisstjórn, 3. skápur.
cable *see* 1. rafmagnskapall, 2. vír, 3. þráður, 4. sími, 5. lína.
caboose *see* kabyssa.
cabriolet *see* blæjubíll.
cacao *see* 1. kakótré, 2. kókó, 3. kakó.
cachalot *see* búrhvalur.
cache *see* 1. flýtiminni, 2. flýtivista, 3. skyndiminni, 4. skyndivista.
cachexia *see* 1. kröm, 2. uppdráttarsýki.
cadaver *see* 1. lík, 2. nár.
cadmium *see* 1. kadmín, 2. kadmíum.
caesium *see* sesín.
cage *see* 1. búr, 2. grind.
cake *see* múrsteinn.
calcareous *see* 1. kalkborinn, 2. kalkkenndur.
calcification *see* 1. kölkun, 2. kalkmyndun.
calcite *see* 1. kalkspat, 2. kalsít.
calcitonin *see* 1. kalsitónín, 2. kalsítónín.
calcium *see* 1. kalsín, 2. kalk, 3. kalsíum.
calculate *see* 1. reikna, 2. áætla.
calculation *see* 1. reikningur, 2. útreikningur.
calculator *see* 1. reiknir, 2. reiknivél.
calculus *see* 1. örsmæðareikningur, 2. reiknivísi, 3. stærðfræðigreining, 4. steinn.
caldera *see* 1. sigketill, 2. askja.
calefacient *see* 1. vermandi, 2. vermilyf.
calendar *see* 1. almanak, 2. dagatal, 3. dagbók, 4. tímatal.
calf *see* kálfur.
caliber *see* vídd.
calibrate *see* 1. fínstilla, 2. stilla, 3. leiðrétta, 4. kvarða.
calibration *see* 1. kvörðun, 2. tækjastilling.
calibre *see* 1. eiginleiki, 2. vídd.

californium *see* 1. kalifornín, 2. kalífornín, 3. kaliforníum.
caliper *see* 1. diskahemlaklafi, 2. víddarmælir, 3. bremsuklemma.
calipers *see* 1. sirkill, 2. hringfari, 3. krúnpassi, 4. mælitöng, 5. rennimál.
call *see* 1. kall, 2. kaupvilnun, 3. uppkall, 4. nefna, 5. kaupréttur.
callosity *see* sigg.
callus *see* 1. beinbris, 2. beinörshnútur, 3. plöntuör, 4. sigg.
calm *see* logn.
calomel *see* 1. kalómel, 2. kvikasilfursklóríð.
calorie *see* 1. varmaeining, 2. verma, 3. hitaeining, 4. kaloría.
calorimeter *see* 1. varmamælir, 2. varmaskiptamælir.
calorimetry *see* 1. varmamælifræði, 2. varmamæling, 3. varmamælingar.
calving *see* jökulkast.
calyx *see* 1. bikar, 2. blómbikar.
cam *see* 1. knastur, 2. kambur.
camber *see* 1. bugða, 2. bunga, 3. bunguvik, 4. hjólhalli.
camel *see* úlfaldi.
camp *see* skátamót.
camphor *see* 1. kamfóra, 2. kamfórutré.
camshaft *see* 1. kambás, 2. knastás, 3. stjórnás.
can *see* 1. blikkdós, 2. dós, 3. hylki, 4. kanna.
canal *see* 1. göng, 2. skipaskurður, 3. skurður.
cancel *see* 1. aflýsa, 2. afturkalla, 3. eyða, 4. eyðast, 5. ógilda.
cancellation *see* 1. ógilding, 2. svipting, 3. uppsögn, 4. aflýsing.
cancer *see* 1. átumein, 2. krabbamein, 3. krabbi, 4. Krabbinn.
cancerous *see* krabbalíkur.
candela *see* 1. kandela, 2. kerti.
candidate *see* 1. kandídat, 2. umsækjandi, 3. frambjóðandi.
candidiasis *see* 1. hvítsveppasýking, 2. þruska.
canister *see* 1. viðarkolahylki, 2. brúsi, 3. hylki.
cannabis *see* 1. kannabis, 2. hass.
canning *see* niðursuða.
canopy *see* 1. blæja, 2. laufþak, 3. laufþekja, 4. tjaldþak.
cantaloupe *see* 1. melóna, 2. tröllepli, 3. sykurmelóna, 4. melónuplanta, 5. kantalúpmelóna.
cantilever *see* svifbiti.
canvas *see* tjaldhiminn.
cap *see* 1. þak, 2. vaxtaþak, 3. lok, 4. kollar, 5. klafi.
capability *see* 1. afköst, 2. færni, 3. geta, 4. hlutgengi.
capacious *see* 1. rúmgóður, 2. víður.

capacitance see 1. rafrýmd, 2. rýmd, 3. rafhleðsla.
capacitor see 1. rafþéttir, 2. rýmir, 3. þéttir.
capacity see 1. afköst, 2. rýmd, 3. rými, 4. rúmtak,
  5. afkastageta.
capelin see 1. loðka, 2. vorsíli, 3. vorsíld, 4. loðsíli,
  5. loðna.
caper see 1. kapersrunni, 2. kapar, 3. kaper, 4.
  kapers.
capercaillie see þiður.
capillarity see 1. hárpípuhrif, 2. hárpípukraftur, 3.
  hárpípuverkun, 4. sogpípukraftur.
capillary see 1. háræð, 2. hárfínn, 3. hárpípa.
capital see 1. höfuðborg, 2. auðmagn, 3. súluhöfuð,
  4. starfsfé, 5. höfuðstóll.
capitalism see 1. kapítlalismi, 2. séreignarskipan, 3.
  kapítalismi, 4. fjármagnskerfi, 5.
  auðvaldsskipulag.
capitalist see 1. auðjöfur, 2. auðvaldssinni, 3.
  fjármagnseigandi, 4. kapítalisti.
capitalization see 1. fjárfesting, 2. fjármögnun, 3.
  eignfærsla, 4. hástafaritun.
capitalize see 1. eignfæra, 2. hástafa.
capitulum see kollur.
capping see hettun.
capsid see 1. veiruhjúpur, 2. veiruhylki, 3.
  veiruskurn
capstan see 1. akkerisvinda, 2. þilfarsvinda.
capsule see 1. lyfjahylki, 2. slímhjúpur, 3. límhylki,
  4. hylki, 5. hýðisaldin.
captain see 1. kafteinn, 2. skipstjóri, 3.
  höfuðsmaður.
caption see skýring.
capture see 1. grip, 2. hremming.
car see 1. bifreið, 2. bíll, 3. kerra, 4. vagn.
carapace see skjöldur.
caraway see kúmen.
carbamide see 1. karbamíð, 2. þvagefni.
carbide see 1. karbítur, 2. harðmálmur, 3. harðstál,
  4. karbíð.
carbohydrate see 1. sykrungur, 2. sykra, 3.
  kolvetni, 4. kolhýdrat, 5. kolvatn.
carbon see 1. kolefni, 2. sót.
carbonate see karbónat.
carbonization see kolun.
carbonyl see karbónýl.
carboxylase see karboxýlasi.
carburetor see blöndungur.
carburettor see blöndungur.
carcass see 1. hjólbarðastofn, 2. undirlag.
carcinogen see 1. krabbavaldur, 2.
  krabbameinsvaki, 3. krabbameinsvaldur, 4.
  krabbavaki.
carcinogenesis see 1. krabbameinsmyndun, 2.
  krabbamyndun.

carcinogenic see 1. krabbameinsvaldandi, 2.
  krabbavaldandi.
carcinoma see 1. krabbamein, 2.
  þekjuvefskrabbamein.
card see greiðslukort.
cardamom see 1. kardimomma, 2. kardimommujurt.
cardboard see pappi.
cardiac see 1. hjartasjúklingur, 2. hjartanlegur.
cardialgia see hjartagrófarverkur.
cardiogenic see hjartaupprunninn.
cardiogram see hjartarit.
cardiograph see hjartarit.
cardiology see hjartasjúkdómafræði.
cardoon see 1. artiskokkur, 2. salatþistill, 3.
  kambabolla, 4. ætiþistill, 5. körfukál.
care see 1. umhyggja, 2. umönnun.
career see 1. ævistarf, 2. atvinnuframi, 3. starfsferill,
  4. starfsframi.
carelessness see 1. ógætni, 2. hirðuleysi, 3.
  kæruleysi.
cargo see 1. farmur, 2. vörur.
carina see 1. bringubeinskjölur, 2. kjölur, 3.
  Kjölurinn.
carious see 1. rotnandi, 2. hrörnandi.
carmine see karmín.
carnation see 1. goðadrottning, 2.
  gróðurhúsanellíka, 3. garðnellíka.
carnivore see 1. kjötæta, 2. rándýr, 3. ránplanta.
carotene see karótín.
carp see 1. karfi, 2. vatnakarpi.
carpal see úlnliðs.
carragheen see 1. fjörugrös, 2. gvöndargrös.
carriage see 1. vagn, 2. flutningur, 3. sleði.
carrier see 1. beri, 2. smitberi, 3. samsætuberi, 4.
  ferja, 5. arfberi.
carrot see gulrót.
carry see 1. geyma, 2. geymd.
cartel see 1. markaðssamtök, 2. hringur, 3.
  einokunarhringur, 4. auðhringur, 5. verðsamtök.
cartilage see 1. brjósk, 2. brjóskvefur.
cartography see kortagerð.
cartridge see minnishylki.
caruncle see 1. doppa, 2. sepi, 3. varta.
cascade see 1. skriða, 2. þrepaverkun, 3.
  stjórnunarkeðja, 4. stafla, 5. raðmögnun.
case see 1. geymiskassi, 2. tilfelli, 3. taska, 4. kassi,
  5. hús.
casein see 1. ostefni, 2. kasín, 3. kasein, 4. drafli.
caseous see 1. ostkenndur, 2. berklaystur.
cash see reiðufé.
cashew see kasúhneta.
cashier see gjaldkeri.
casing see 1. föðurrör, 2. leguhús, 3. kassi, 4. hylki,
  5. hús.

cassava *see* 1. manjók, 2. manjokrunni, 3. tapíókamjöl, 4. kassavamjöl, 5. kassava.
cassette *see* 1. hulstur, 2. segulbandsspóla, 3. snælda.
cassia *see* 1. kassía, 2. kassíakanell, 3. kassíukanill.
cast *see* 1. kasta, 2. steypa, 3. gerendaskrá.
caste *see* 1. félagsstaða, 2. stétt, 3. stéttakerfi, 4. stéttarstaða, 5. erfðastétt.
caster *see* 1. eltihorn, 2. eltihalli, 3. eltihjól.
casting *see* 1. steypumótun, 2. steypumót, 3. málmsteypa, 4. afsteypa.
castle *see* Hróka.
castor *see* 1. bifrar, 2. bjórar, 3. Kastor.
castrate *see* 1. vana, 2. gelda, 3. geldingur.
castration *see* 1. vönun, 2. afkynjun, 3. gelding.
cat *see* köttur.
catabolism *see* 1. efnismolun, 2. frálífun, 3. lífefnasundrun, 4. sundrunarferli.
catadromous *see* sjávarsækinn.
catalepsy *see* 1. dástjarfi, 2. stirðnun.
cataleptic *see* 1. dástjarfur, 2. dástjarfasjúklingur.
catalog *see* 1. efnisskrá, 2. skrá, 3. vörulisti.
catalogue *see* 1. efnisskrá, 2. skrá.
catalysis *see* hvötun.
catalyst *see* 1. efnahvarfi, 2. hvati, 3. efnahvati, 4. efnhvarfi.
catalyze *see* hvetja.
cataplexy *see* slekjukast.
cataract *see* 1. drer, 2. star, 3. starblinda.
catastrophe *see* 1. stórslys, 2. endalok, 3. náttúruhamfarir, 4. ófarir.
catatonia *see* geðstjarfi.
catch *see* 1. veiða, 2. veiði, 3. skreppa, 4. skilja, 5. grip.
catecholamine *see* katekólamín.
categorization *see* 1. flokkun, 2. frumflokkun.
categorize *see* innrétta.
category *see* 1. frumflokkur, 2. frumsögn, 3. tegund, 4. mengi, 5. formdeild.
catenary *see* keðjuferill.
caterpillar *see* 1. fiðrildislirfa, 2. skriðbelti, 3. tólffótungur.
catfish *see* steinbítur.
catharsis *see* geðhreinsun.
catheter *see* 1. þvagleggur, 2. holleggur.
cathode *see* 1. bakskaut, 2. katóða, 3. mínusskaut, 4. neiskaut.
cation *see* 1. járafi, 2. katjón, 3. plúsjón, 4. bakjón, 5. jájón.
catkin *see* rekill.
cattle *see* 1. kýr, 2. naut.
catwalk *see* 1. gangbrú, 2. sliskja.
caul *see* 1. sigurkufl, 2. stórnetja.
cauliflower *see* blómkál.
caulk *see* 1. hampþétta, 2. stemma, 3. þétta.

causalgia *see* 1. brunakennd, 2. brunaverkur.
causality *see* 1. orsakasamhengi, 2. orsakasamband, 3. orsakalögmál.
cause *see* 1. orsök, 2. orsaka.
caustic *see* 1. tærisýra, 2. vefeyðandi, 3. brenniflötur, 4. brenniferill, 5. brennandi.
caution *see* 1. vara, 2. varúð, 3. viðvörum.
cavern *see* hverna.
cavitation *see* 1. holmyndun, 2. slagsuða, 3. tóm, 4. iða, 5. eimbólutæring.
cavity *see* 1. hermuhol, 2. hol, 3. hola, 4. holrúm.
ceiling *see* 1. skýjaþekjuhæð, 2. þak, 3. hámarksflughæð.
celebration *see* veisla.
celeriac *see* 1. hnúðselja, 2. hnúðsellerí, 3. hnúðsilla, 4. rótsellerí, 5. sellerírót.
celery *see* 1. blaðsellerí, 2. stilksellerí, 3. stilkselja, 4. blaðsilla.
cell *see* 1. fruma, 2. rafhlað, 3. stöð, 4. sella, 5. rafhlöðueining.
cellular *see* 1. gljúpur, 2. gropinn.
cellulose *see* 1. sellulósi, 2. tréni, 3. beðmi.
cement *see* 1. duftherða, 2. lím, 3. líma, 4. steinungur, 5. tannfylling.
censorship *see* 1. ritskoðun, 2. siðgát, 3. siðvarsla.
census *see* 1. manntal, 2. talning.
cent *see* sent.
centennial *see* öld.
center *see* 1. miðpunktur, 2. Miðborð, 3. stöð, 4. miðsvæði, 5. miðstöð.
centigrade *see* Celsíusstig.
centile *see* hundraðshlutamark.
centimetre *see* sentimetri.
central *see* miðlægur.
centralism *see* 1. miðstýring, 2. miðstýringarstefna.
centralization *see* miðstýring.
centre *see* 1. kjarni, 2. miðja, 3. snúningsmiðjuoddur.
centric *see* 1. heftur, 2. sívalningslaga, 3. geislóttur.
centrifugal *see* 1. miðflótta, 2. miðfælinn.
centrifugation *see* 1. aflskiljun, 2. afskiljun, 3. skiljun, 4. skilning.
centrifuge *see* 1. skilvinda, 2. þeytivinda, 3. skilja.
centriole *see* 1. deilikorn, 2. miðögn.
centripetal *see* miðleitinn.
centroid *see* 1. miðpunktur, 2. þyngdarpunktur.
centromere *see* þráðhaft.
centrosphere *see* 1. deilihnöttur, 2. deilimassi.
century *see* öld.
cerebellum *see* hnykill.
cerebration *see* heilaferli.
cerebrum *see* 1. heili, 2. hjarni, 3. hvelaheili, 4. stórheili.
cerium *see* 1. serín, 2. seríum.
certain *see* 1. vís, 2. vissulegur.

certificate see 1. skírteini, 2. þáttur, 3. uppáskrift, 4. vottorð, 5. samþykki.
certification see 1. skírteinisútgáfa, 2. vottun.
cerumen see eyrnamergur.
cervix see 1. háls (neck), 2. legháls.
cesium see sesín.
chafe see 1. núa, 2. núast, 3. skafa.
chafing see núningur.
chain see keðja.
chaining see 1. keðjun, 2. samhlekkjun.
chair see stóll.
chairman see 1. flokksformaður, 2. stjórnarformaður, 3. fundarstjóri, 4. formaður, 5. forseti.
challenge see 1. sýklaáreiti, 2. sýklaögrun, 3. vanhæfi, 4. vefenging.
chamber see 1. ráð, 2. þingsalur, 3. þingdeild, 4. deild, 5. hólf.
chamfer see 1. afskurðarflötur, 2. skásneiða, 3. skásnið, 4. sniðskera.
chamfering see 1. fösun, 2. sniðskurður.
chamois see gemsa.
chamomile see gæsajurt.
chance see 1. tilefni, 2. tilviljunarkenndur.
change see 1. breyting, 2. umbreyta, 3. Uppskipti, 4. skipting, 5. skipta.
channel see 1. háttur, 2. vatnsbraut, 3. sund, 4. rás, 5. göng.
chaos see 1. ringulreið, 2. glundroði, 3. hvikulleiki, 4. óskapnaður, 5. ringulfar.
chaotic see hvikull.
chapter see kafli.
character see 1. skapgerð, 2. tegundareinkenni, 3. stafur, 4. skaphöfn, 5. sérkenni.
characterisation see breyta.
characteristic see 1. kennilína, 2. sérkennilegur, 3. sérkenni, 4. sérkennileiki, 5. einkennandi.
charcoal see viðarkol.
chard see 1. blaðbeðja, 2. rófukál, 3. strandblaðka.
charge see 1. kæra, 2. rafhleðsla, 3. hleðsla, 4. hlaða, 5. gjaldfærsla.
chargeable see 1. gjaldfærsluhæfur, 2. gjaldskyldur.
charging see gjaldlagning.
charisma see 1. persónutöfrar, 2. náðarvald.
charity see góðgerðarstarfsemi.
charming see elskulegur.
chart see 1. kort, 2. kortleggja, 3. landakort, 4. línurit, 5. samskiptarit.
charter see 1. leiguskip, 2. stofnskrá, 3. leiguflugssamningur, 4. leiguflug, 5. leiga.
charterer see leigutaki.
chase see 1. elta, 2. skrúfumótun.
chaser see 1. skrúfugraftarverkfæri, 2. skrúfuskeri.
chasm see 1. gjá, 2. hyldýpi.
chassis see undirvagn.

chat see 1. blaðra, 2. masa, 3. spjall, 4. spjallrás.
chatter see 1. masa, 2. skrölta, 3. glamur, 4. glamra, 5. blaðra.
chauffeur see 1. bifreiðarstjóri, 2. bílstjóri, 3. ekill, 4. ökumaður.
cheat see svíkja.
check see 1. aðgæta, 2. tékki, 3. skoða, 4. Skák, 5. prófa.
checker see kontrolisto.
checkers see 1. damdisko, 2. kontrolisto, 3. dampeco.
checkpoint see gátstaður.
cheek see 1. kinn, 2. vangi.
cheer see hurai.
cheerful see 1. glaðlyndur, 2. glaður.
cheese see ostur.
chelate see 1. klósamband, 2. málmhringsamband.
chelation see 1. klófesting, 2. klósambandsmyndun, 3. málmhringsmyndun.
chemical see 1. efnasamband, 2. efni, 3. íðefni.
chemiluminescence see 1. efnaljóm, 2. hvarfaljómun, 3. efnaskin, 4. efnaljómi.
chemistry see efnafræði.
chemokinesis see efnakjörleitni.
chemoreceptor see 1. efnanemi, 2. efnaskynjari, 3. efnaviðtaki.
chemosynthesis see efnatillífun.
chemotaxis see 1. efnaans, 2. efnasvörun, 3. efnatog.
chemotherapy see 1. efnalækningar, 2. efnameðferð, 3. lyfjameðferð, 4. lyflækning.
cheque see tékki.
cherimoya see 1. morgunberkja, 2. sérrímóla, 3. annóna.
cherish see elska.
cherished see sætur.
chest see 1. bringa, 2. brjóst, 3. brjóstkassi, 4. kista.
chiasma see 1. krosstengsl, 2. krossbrú.
chicken see 1. raggeit, 2. hænsn, 3. heigull.
chicory see 1. kaffifífill, 2. síkoría.
child see 1. barn, 2. íflekkur.
childhood see bernska.
chill see 1. kalda, 2. kuldahrollur, 3. hleifamót, 4. ofkæling.
chilled see 1. glerharður, 2. kældur.
chilly see kaldur.
chime see 1. klukknahljómur, 2. samhljóman.
chimera see 1. blendingur, 2. bastarður.
chimney see 1. skorsteinn, 2. niðurstreymisstrókur, 3. reykháfur.
chin see haka
chip see 1. spónn, 2. flaga, 3. flís, 4. kísilflaga, 5. kubbur.
chiropractic see 1. hnykkingar, 2. liðfræði.
chisel see 1. meitill, 2. sporjárn, 3. stemmistál.

chitin *see* kítín.
chlamydia *see* 1. möttulbaktería, 2. möttulgerill, 3. klamydía, 4. slíðurbaktería.
chloride *see* 1. klóríð, 2. saltsýrusalt.
chlorine *see* klór.
chlorofluorocarbon *see* klórflúrkolefni.
chloroform *see* klóróform.
chlorophyll *see* 1. klórófýl, 2. laufgræna, 3. blaðgræna.
chloroplast *see* grænukorn.
chlorosis *see* 1. fölnun, 2. fölvasýki, 3. gulnun, 4. meyjafölvi.
chocolate *see* súkkulaði.
choice *see* val.
choke *see* 1. innsog, 2. þrenging, 3. kyrkja, 4. jöfnunarspóla, 5. kæfa.
cholecystectomy *see* gallblöðrunám.
cholera *see* kólera.
choleric *see* bráðlyndur.
cholesterol *see* kólesteról.
cholinergic *see* 1. kólínergur, 2. kólvirkur, 3. asetýlkólínseytandi.
chondroblast *see* brjóskkímfruma.
chondrocalcinosis *see* brjóskkölkun.
chondrocyte *see* brjóskfruma.
chopper *see* 1. mylla, 2. riðari, 3. saxari, 4. veifill.
chord *see* 1. línubútur, 2. vænglína, 3. sniðill, 4. bútur, 5. strengur.
chordamesoderm *see* seilarmiðlag.
choroid *see* 1. æða, 2. æðahimna, 3. æðahýði.
chorology *see* 1. útbreiðslufræði, 2. staðfræði.
chroma *see* 1. litstilling, 2. litgildi, 3. litblær, 4. fagurlitleiki.
chromate *see* 1. krómat, 2. krómsalt.
chromatic *see* 1. litgleipinn, 2. litsterkur, 3. skærlitaður.
chromatid *see* litningsþráður.
chromatin *see* litni.
chromatography *see* 1. litritun, 2. litskiljun, 3. skilning, 4. blettagreining.
chromatometer *see* litskali.
chromatophore *see* litberi.
chrome *see* 1. króma, 2. króm.
chromium *see* króm.
chromosome *see* litningur.
chromosphere *see* lithvolf.
chronic *see* 1. langvinnur, 2. þrálátur.
chronometer *see* 1. hnitklukka, 2. sæúr, 3. skipsklukka.
chrysalis *see* púpa.
chub *see* vatnagægir.
chuck *see* 1. festipatróna, 2. patróna, 3. festipatrona.
church *see* 1. Kirkja, 2. kirkjubygging.
chyle *see* 1. iðrakirni, 2. iðramjólk.

chyme *see* 1. fæðumauk, 2. mauk, 3. iðraþykkni, 4. iðramauk.
chymotrypsin *see* kýmótrypsín.
cicatrization *see* örmyndun.
cichlids *see* síklíðar.
ciliated *see* 1. bifhærður, 2. randhærður.
cilium *see* 1. bifhár, 2. randhár, 3. augnhár.
cinder *see* karboskorio.
cinders *see* 1. aska, 2. karboskorio.
cinnamon *see* 1. kanell, 2. kanill, 3. kaniltré.
circle *see* 1. hringur, 2. hringferill, 3. baugur, 4. hringfari.
circuit *see* 1. rás, 2. hringbraut, 3. straumrás, 4. rafrás, 5. rafleiðsla.
circular *see* 1. reglugerð, 2. umburðarbréf, 3. dreifibréf.
circulate *see* 1. hringrása, 2. hringsóla.
circulation *see* 1. skolun, 2. umferðartegur, 3. útbreiðsla, 4. umferð, 5. hringrás.
circumcision *see* 1. forhúðarstýfing, 2. umskurður, 3. umskurn.
circumference *see* 1. umgjörð, 2. ummál, 3. hringjaðar, 4. hringferill, 5. utanmál.
circumferential *see* umlykjandi.
circumpolar *see* pólhverfur.
circumstance *see* cirkonstanco.
circumstances *see* cirkonstanco.
cirque *see* 1. hvilft, 2. jökulskál.
cirrhosis *see* 1. hersli, 2. skorpulifur, 3. skorpnun, 4. lifrarskorpnun.
cirrocumulus *see* 1. blikuhnoðrar, 2. dröfnuský, 3. maríutása.
cirrostratus *see* 1. blika, 2. skýjablika.
cirrus *see* 1. blikufjaðrir, 2. vatnsklær, 3. skúfur, 4. blikutrefjar, 5. bifháraskúfur.
cisco *see* 1. hvítfiskur, 2. lagarsíld, 3. vatnasíld.
cistern *see* 1. vatnsþró, 2. hít, 3. frymisgrisjuhít.
citizen *see* 1. ríkisborgari, 2. borgari, 3. þegn, 4. borgarbúi.
citizenship *see* 1. ríkisfang, 2. þjóðerni, 3. samfélagsvitund, 4. ríkisborgararéttur, 5. borgaravitund.
citrate *see* sítrat.
city *see* 1. borg, 2. staður, 3. stórbær.
civilization *see* 1. siðfágun, 2. siðmenning, 3. menning.
claim *see* 1. tilmæli, 2. beiðni, 3. tjón, 4. tap, 5. staðhæfing.
clairvoyance *see* dulskyggni.
clamp *see* 1. þvinga, 2. band, 3. festa, 4. halda, 5. haldrás.
clamping *see* 1. festibúnaður, 2. hald.
clan *see* kynþáttur.
clap *see* skrölta.
clarification *see* skýring.

462 English - Icelandic

clarify see þýða.

clash see slagsmál.

class see 1. bekksögn, 2. þjóðfélagshópur, 3. stétt, 4. klasi, 5. bil.

classic see 1. hefðbundinn, 2. klassískur, 3. sígildur.

classification see 1. niðurröðun, 2. niðurskipan, 3. flokkun, 4. gróðurflokkur.

clathrate see 1. smágötóttur, 2. holefni.

claudication see helti.

clause see 1. skilyrði, 2. ákvæði, 3. fyrirvari, 4. klausa, 5. setning.

claustrophobia see 1. innilokunarfælni, 2. öngfælni.

clavicle see viðbein.

claw see 1. blaðkló, 2. kló, 3. nögl.

clay see 1. leir, 2. mold.

clean see 1. hreinsa, 2. hreinn, 3. pússa.

cleaner see 1. hreinsari, 2. hreinsiefni.

cleaning see 1. hreinsun, 2. þrif.

cleanse see hreinsa.

clear see 1. skýr, 2. tær, 3. opna, 4. hreinsa, 5. hreinn.

clearance see 1. bil, 2. blóðhreinsun, 3. fríhæð, 4. hafnargjaldagreiðsla, 5. hlaup.

clearing see 1. greiðslumiðlun, 2. losun, 3. leysing, 4. hreinsun, 5. kröfuskipti.

cleat see 1. oki, 2. þvertré.

cleavage see 1. klofningur, 2. skipting, 3. klofnun, 4. klofningsþáttur, 5. kleyfni.

cleft see 1. glufa, 2. klofinn, 3. tunglsprunga.

clerk see 1. skrifstofumaður, 2. skrifstofustúlka.

clevis see klofi.

click see 1. smellur, 2. smella, 3. skrölta.

client see 1. umbjóðandi, 2. viðskiptavinur, 3. þjónustuþegi, 4. skjólstæðingur, 5. heilsugestur.

cliff see 1. klettaveggur, 2. klif, 3. sjávarhamar, 4. hamrar.

climacteric see 1. tíðahvörf, 2. breytingaskeið.

climate see 1. veðurlag, 2. veðurfar, 3. veðrátta, 4. loftslag.

climatic see veðurfarslegur.

climatology see 1. veðurfarsfræði, 2. heilsuveðurfræði, 3. loftlagsfræði, 4. loftslagsfræði.

climax see 1. endastig, 2. ris, 3. munúð, 4. fullnæging, 5. hástig.

climb see 1. klifra, 2. klifur, 3. stíga.

clinic see 1. lækningastofa, 2. læknamiðstöð, 3. klíník, 4. heilsugæslustöð, 5. læknahús.

clinical see klínískur.

clinician see læknir.

clip see 1. klipping, 2. lása, 3. klippa, 4. klemma, 5. festa.

clipboard see klemmuspjald.

clipper see 1. klippir, 2. seglskip.

clipping see 1. klipping, 2. orðaklipping, 3. orðastýfing, 4. skerðing.

cloaca see 1. rauf, 2. gotrauf.

clock see 1. Klukka, 2. úr.

clockwise see 1. réttsælis, 2. sólarsinnis.

clod see moldarkökkur.

clone see 1. klóna, 2. klónn, 3. klón, 4. einrækta, 5. einrækt.

cloning see 1. einun, 2. klónun, 3. einræktun.

clonus see 1. kippir, 2. klónus, 3. krampakippir.

close see 1. þröngur, 2. náinn, 3. loka, 4. mollulegt.

closed see 1. lokaður, 2. nálægur, 3. umlukt.

closure see 1. lokun, 2. lúkning, 3. sárlokun.

clot see 1. hlaup, 2. kökkur, 3. blóðtappi.

cloud see 1. ský, 2. mökkur.

cloudy see 1. gruggugur, 2. ótær, 3. skýjaður, 4. þungbúinn.

cluster see 1. stjörnuþyrping, 2. þyrping, 3. þyrpa, 4. hlutasamstæða, 5. hneppi.

clutch see 1. tengja, 2. tengsli, 3. kúpling, 4. klóarkúpling, 5. kló.

coach see 1. áætlunarbifreið, 2. hópbifreið, 3. langferðabifreið, 4. ráðgjafi, 5. rúta.

coagulant see 1. hleypandi, 2. hleypir.

coagulate see 1. hlaupa, 2. hleypa, 3. storkna.

coagulation see 1. storknun, 2. útflygsun, 3. lifrun, 4. hleyping, 5. hlaupmyndun.

coagulum see 1. kökkur, 2. hlaup.

coal see 1. kol, 2. viðarkol.

coalescence see 1. samruni, 2. samvöxtur.

coalition see 1. sameining, 2. samsteypa, 3. bandalag, 4. samband.

coast see 1. strönd, 2. renna, 3. sjávarströnd.

coastline see 1. strandlengja, 2. strönd.

coat see 1. lag, 2. mála, 3. hjúpur.

coaxial see 1. sammiðja, 2. samása.

cobalt see 1. kóbolt, 2. kóbalt.

cobia see foringjafiskur.

coca see 1. kóka, 2. kókarunni.

cocaine see kókaín.

coccidiosis see hníslasótt.

coccus see 1. hnettla, 2. knattgerill, 3. knattsýkill, 4. kokkur, 5. kúlubaktería.

cochlea see 1. snigill, 2. kuðungur.

cock see 1. krani, 2. vatnskrani.

cockle see 1. báruskel, 2. báruskeljar, 3. hjartaskel.

cocoa see 1 kakó, 2. kakóplanta, 3. kókó.

coconut see 1. kókóshneta, 2. kókoshneta.

cod see þorskur.

code see 1. svæðisnúmer, 2. þula, 3. táknróf, 4. tákna, 5. skrá.

codeine see 1. kódeín, 2. kódín.

codfish see þorskur.

coding see 1. kótun, 2. táknsetning.

codominant see 1. jafnríkjandi, 2. meðríkjandi.

codon see tákni.
coefficient see 1. stuðull, 2. tala.
coelacanth see 1. skúfuggi, 2. skúfur.
coenzyme see 1. hjálparensím, 2. stoðensím, 3. hjálparhvati, 4. hjáensím, 5. ensímstoð.
cofactor see 1. fylgiþáttur, 2. hjálparefni, 3. hjálparþáttur, 4. hjáþáttur.
coffee see kaffi.
cog see tönn.
cognate see 1. skyldur, 2. samstofna, 3. eðlislíkur.
cognition see 1. hugarstarf, 2. skilvit, 3. vitsmunir.
cognitive see 1. hugrænn, 2. skilinn, 3. skilvitlegur, 4. vitrænn.
cogwheel see tannhjól.
cohabitation see sambúð.
coherence see 1. samfella, 2. samfösun, 3. samheldni, 4. samhengi, 5. samstig.
coherent see 1. samheldinn, 2. samloðandi, 3. samtaka, 4. samhangandi, 5. samfasa.
cohesion see 1. samfesta, 2. samheldni, 3. samhengi, 4. samloðun, 5. samtengiafl.
cohesive see samloðandi.
cohort see 1. aldurshópur, 2. hópur, 3. rannsóknarþýði, 4. skor.
coil see 1. rafspóla, 2. spóla, 3. vafningur, 4. háspennukefli.
coinage see myntslátta.
coining see 1. myntslátta, 2. pressun, 3. stönsun.
coke see 1. koks, 2. kox.
col see 1. söðulsvæði, 2. söðull.
cold see 1. kaldur, 2. kuldi, 3. kvef, 4. óviðkunnanlegur.
colectomy see ristilnám.
colic see 1. iðrakveisa, 2. innantaka, 3. kveisa, 4. ungbarnakveisa.
collagen see 1. kollagen, 2. límgjafi, 3. límfóstri.
collapse see 1. hrun, 2. hrynja, 3. lémögnun, 4. samansig, 5. samfall.
collapsible see 1. samfellanlegur, 2. samanfellanlegur.
collar see 1. kragi, 2. múffa, 3. tengihólkur, 4. vaxtakragi, 5. brjóst.
collate see innrétta.
collateral see 1. samhliða, 2. ábyrgð, 3. trygging, 4. veð, 5. handveð.
colleague see 1. samstarfsmaður, 2. starfsbróðir.
collect see 1. innheimta, 2. safna.
collection see 1. söfnun, 2. innheimta.
collective see 1. samyrkjubú, 2. kommúna, 3. sambýli.
collectivism see sameignarstefna.
collector see 1. gleypir, 2. kollektor, 3. safnari.
college see háskóli.
collet see 1. spennihólkur, 2. patróna, 3. innleggshólkur.

collier see kola.
collimation see 1. beinstilling, 2. sambeining.
collimator see 1. beinstillir, 2. geislabeinir.
collision see árekstur.
collocation see orðastæða.
colloid see 1. örsvif, 2. örþeyta, 3. kvoðulausn.
collusion see 1. leynimakk, 2. samráð.
coloboma see lituglufa.
colon see 1. ristill, 2. tvípunktur.
colonialism see nýlendustefna.
colonnade see 1. súlnagöng, 2. súlnarið.
colony see 1. nýlenda, 2. dýrasambú, 3. þyrping, 4. sambú, 5. kólónía.
color see litur.
colorimeter see 1. efnalitsjá, 2. litmælir.
colorimetry see 1. litgreining, 2. litmælifræði, 3. litmæling, 4. litamæling.
colostrum see 1. broddmjólk, 2. broddur.
colour see litur.
column see 1. súla, 2. stuðull, 3. stoð, 4. dálkur, 5. eimingarsúla.
coma see 1. halastjarna, 2. hjúpur, 3. vængskekkja, 4. hjúpskekkja, 5. fræloðna.
comb see kambur.
combat see slagsmál.
comber see kembari.
combination see 1. samsetningur, 2. samtekt, 3. samstæða, 4. samantekt, 5. flétta.
combustion see 1. brennsla, 2. bruni.
come see koma.
comet see halastjarna.
comfort see 1. huggun, 2. hugga.
command see 1. stilla, 2. skipun, 3. skipa, 4. fyrirmæli.
commander see 1. kapteinn, 2. sjóliðsforingi, 3. skipherra, 4. skipstjóri.
commence see 1. upphaf, 2. byrja, 3. byrjun.
commencement see byrjun.
commensalism see 1. gistilífi, 2. gistilíf.
comment see 1. athugasemd, 2. ummæli.
commerce see 1. verslun, 2. verzlun, 3. viðskipti.
commercial see auglýsing.
comminute see 1. mulinn, 2. mylja.
commission see 1. framkvæmdastjórnin, 2. gæðamat, 3. nefnd, 4. þóknun, 5. umboð.
commissioner see 1. lögreglustjóri, 2. nefndarmaður, 3. stjórnarnefndarmaður.
commissure see 1. mót, 2. tengsl, 3. þverstrengur.
commit see 1. staðfesta, 2. fullnusta, 3. gera.
commitment see 1. stefnufesta, 2. skylda, 3. skuldbinding, 4. kvöð.
committee see 1. fastanefnd, 2. nefnd, 3. þingnefnd.
commodious see 1. rúmgóður, 2. víður.
commodity see 1. hrávara, 2. vara, 3. verslunarvara.
common see 1. sameiginlegur, 2. venjulegur.

commonly *see* oft.
commonplace *see* venjulegur.
commonwealth *see* 1. þjóðfélag, 2. ríkjasamband, 3. samveldi.
communal *see* sameiginlegur.
communication *see* 1. tilkynning, 2. tjáskipti, 3. skýrsla, 4. samskipti, 5. orðsending.
communism *see* 1. sameignarskipan, 2. sameignarstefna, 3. kommúnismi.
communist *see* 1. kommúnisti, 2. sameignarsinni.
community *see* 1. samfélag, 2. sameign, 3. staðfélag, 4. byggð, 5. bæjarfélag.
commutation *see* 1. straumhlaup, 2. straumskipting, 3. straumvending, 4. umskipting.
commutator *see* 1. straumvendir, 2. víxill, 3. straumskiptir.
commute *see* 1. víxlast, 2. víxla.
compact *see* 1. fyrirferðarlítill, 2. samkomulag, 3. samningur, 4. samþjappaður, 5. smár.
compaction *see* 1. samþjöppun, 2. þétting, 3. samþrýstingur.
compactness *see* 1. miðjunarstig, 2. samþjöppun, 3. þéttleiki, 4. þjöppunarstig.
companion *see* sambýlismaður.
company *see* 1. fyrirtæki, 2. undirfylki, 3. félag.
comparability *see* 1. samanburðarhæfni, 2. samhæfi, 3. samanburðarhæfi.
comparable *see* sambærilegur.
comparator *see* 1. samberi, 2. viksjá.
comparison *see* 1. samanburður, 2. stigbreyting.
compartment *see* 1. hólf, 2. lestarhluti, 3. rými.
compass *see* 1. áttaviti, 2. áttavísun, 3. hringfari, 4. kompás.
compassion *see* meðaumkun.
compatibility *see* 1. samhæfni, 2. jafngildi, 3. samhæfi.
compatible *see* 1. samþýðanlegur, 2. samrýmanlegur, 3. samræmanlegur, 4. samnýtanlegur, 5. jafngildur.
compel *see* 1. neyða, 2. þvinga.
compelling *see* sannfærður.
compensate *see* 1. jafna, 2. umbuna.
compensation *see* 1. bætur, 2. hleðslujöfnun, 3. jöfnun, 4. laun, 5. skaðabætur.
compensator *see* 1. þenslujafnari, 2. mótvægismælir.
competence *see* 1. valdsvið, 2. valdmörk, 3. réttindi, 4. móttökuhæfni, 5. málkunnátta.
competent *see* 1. lögbær, 2. hæfur.
competition *see* 1. samkeppni, 2. keppni.
competitiveness *see* 1. samkeppnishæfi, 2. samkeppnishæfni.
compilation *see* 1. samsöfnun, 2. söfnun, 3. þýðing, 4. vistþýðing.
compile *see* 1. vistþýða, 2. þýða.

compiler *see* 1. þýðandi, 2. vistþýðandi.
complaint *see* 1. ákæra, 2. ásökun.
complement *see* 1. magni, 2. viðbætir, 3. viðauki, 4. fyllimengi, 5. mögnuður.
complementarity *see* 1. fyllidarlögmál, 2. gagnkvæmni, 3. fylling, 4. fylld, 5. andstæðulögmál.
complementary *see* 1. mótsvarandi, 2. samfallandi.
complementation *see* uppbót.
complete *see* 1. fullkomið, 2. heill, 3. fullkominn, 4. fullgerður, 5. algjör.
completed *see* 1. fullgert, 2. lokið.
completeness *see* 1. fullkomleiki, 2. heild.
complex *see* 1. geðhnútur, 2. útsláttarflækja, 3. samstæða, 4. samsettur, 5. samband.
compliance *see* 1. meðferðarheldni, 2. uppfylling, 3. hlýðni.
comply *see* 1. uppfylla, 2. hlíta.
component *see* 1. þáttur, 2. liður, 3. íhlutur, 4. bútur, 5. frumþáttur.
composite *see* 1. trefjablanda, 2. blandaður, 3. samsetningur, 4. samsettur.
composition *see* 1. samsetning, 2. nauðungarsamningur, 3. nauðasamningar, 4. nauðasamningur.
compost *see* 1. safnhaugur, 2. moldun, 3. molta, 4. moltugryfja, 5. moltukassi.
compound *see* 1. samsettur, 2. samefni, 3. blanda, 4. efnasamband.
comprehend *see* skilja.
comprehension *see* skilningur.
comprehensive *see* 1. yfirgripsmikill, 2. alhliða.
compress *see* 1. þjappa, 2. línþófi, 3. kompressa, 4. grisjuþófi.
compression *see* 1. ferging, 2. pressa, 3. samþjöppun, 4. þjöppun, 5. þrýstingur.
compressor *see* 1. samþjappari, 2. þjappa, 3. loftpressa, 4. þjappi.
compromise *see* 1. málamiðlun, 2. málamiðlunarsamkomulag, 3. vásetning.
compulsion *see* 1. árátta, 2. nauðung, 3. nauður.
compulsory *see* 1. lögboðinn, 2. skyldugur, 3. skyldubundinn.
compute *see* reikna.
computer *see* 1. tölva, 2. rafreiknir.
computerization *see* tölvuvæðing.
computerize *see* tölvuvæða.
con *see* svíkja.
conation *see* 1. misvægi, 2. viljabeiting.
concave *see* 1. íbjúgur, 2. íholur, 3. íhvolfur, 4. innbjúgur, 5. hvelfdur.
concavity *see* 1. hvelfing, 2. íhvelft, 3. íhvolfa.
concede *see* 1. játa, 2. viðurkenna.
concentrate *see* 1. einbeita, 2. efnisþykkni.

concentrated *see* 1. fullsterkur, 2. megn, 3. óblandaður, 4. sterkur.
concentration *see* 1. magn, 2. þétting, 3. styrkur, 4. styrkt, 5. samþjöppun.
concentrator *see* 1. þjappi, 2. línusamdragi, 3. fókspóla, 4. beinispóla.
concentric *see* sammiðja.
concept *see* 1. álit, 2. hugtak.
conception *see* 1. hugtakamyndun, 2. hyggja, 3. getnaður, 4. fenging.
concern *see* fyrirtæki.
concerted *see* sameiginlegur.
concession *see* 1. eftirgjöf, 2. ívilnun, 3. leyfi, 4. sérleyfi, 5. tilslökun.
conciliation *see* 1. samkomulag, 2. sáttaumleitun, 3. sátt.
conciliator *see* 1. friðarstillir, 2. málamiðlari, 3. sáttamaður, 4. sáttasemjari.
conclusion *see* 1. ályktun, 2. endir, 3. lok, 4. niðurstaða.
concord *see* 1. samhljómur, 2. samkomulag.
concordance *see* 1. samræmi, 2. samsvörun, 3. samleitni, 4. samkvæmni, 5. orðstöðulykill.
concrescence *see* 1. samleitni, 2. samvöxtur.
concrete *see* 1. steinsteypa, 2. sértekinn, 3. samvaxinn, 4. hlutstæður, 5. hlutrænn.
concretion *see* 1. steinmyndun, 2. steinn, 3. steinkvörn.
concurrence *see* 1. samhljómur, 2. samkomulag, 3. samningur, 4. samræmi.
concussion *see* 1. skak, 2. skellur, 3. heilahristingur, 4. áfall, 5. hristingur.
condensate *see* 1. dögg, 2. þétta, 3. þétti, 4. þéttivatn.
condensation *see* 1. keðjun, 2. þjöppun, 3. þéttun, 4. þétting, 5. þéttihvarf.
condenser *see* 1. rafþéttir, 2. þéttir, 3. þéttilinsa, 4. eimþéttir, 5. eimsvali.
condition *see* 1. ástand, 2. skilyrða, 3. skilyrði, 4. tempra.
conditional *see* 1. skilyrtur, 2. skildagatíð, 3. skilorðsbundinn.
conditioned *see* skilyrtur.
conditioning *see* 1. skilyrðing, 2. skylduögun, 3. Hæfing.
condom *see* smokkur.
condominium *see* 1. kaupleiguíbúð, 2. samstjórn.
condone *see* þola.
conduct *see* 1. framkoma, 2. hegðun.
conductance *see* 1. leiðni, 2. raunleiðni.
conduction *see* 1. leiðing, 2. leiðni.
conductivity *see* 1. eðlisleiðni, 2. leiðni.
conductor *see* 1. leiðari, 2. leiðir.
conduit *see* 1. rör, 2. pípa.

condyle *see* 1. leggjarhöfuð, 2. kollur, 3. hnúfa, 4. hnúi.
cone *see* 1. sjónukeila, 2. eldkeila, 3. keila, 4. keiluþekjufruma, 5. köngull.
cones *see* keilur.
confabulation *see* 1. fimbulfamb, 2. íspuni.
confederate *see* 1. bandalagsríki, 2. bandamaður, 3. samsærisfélagi, 4. vitorðsmaður.
conference *see* 1. samningaviðræður, 2. þing, 3. ráðstefna, 4. fundur, 5. umræðufundur.
confess *see* játa.
confidence *see* 1. sjálfstraust, 2. traust.
confidential *see* trúnaðarmál.
confidentiality *see* 1. leynd, 2. trúnaður, 3. trúnaðarstig, 4. trúnaðarsamband, 5. trúnaðarkvöð.
configuration *see* 1. stelling, 2. flughamur, 3. röðun, 4. samgerð, 5. samskipan.
confinement *see* 1. innilokun, 2. sængurlega.
confirmation *see* 1. ferming, 2. staðfesting.
confiscation *see* 1. eignanám, 2. eignaupptaka.
conflict *see* 1. hernaðarátök, 2. ágreiningur, 3. stríð, 4. togstreita, 5. deilur.
confluence *see* 1. ármót, 2. samfella, 3. samflæði, 4. samrennsli.
confluent *see* 1. samrunninn, 2. samvaxinn.
conform *see* 1. samsniða, 2. samsníða.
conformity *see* 1. samræmi, 2. samsnið.
confounding *see* samþáttun.
confusion *see* 1. skörun, 2. ringlun.
congelation *see* samfrysting.
congenial *see* 1. þægilegur, 2. viðkunnanlegur.
congenital *see* 1. áskapaður, 2. meðfæddur.
conger *see* háfáll.
congestion *see* 1. vökvasókn, 2. troðningur, 3. þröng, 4. öng, 5. teppa.
conglomerate *see* 1. sambreyskingur, 2. völuberg, 3. sambland, 4. fyrirtækjasamsteypa, 5. fjölgreinarekstur.
congress *see* 1. fundur, 2. ráðstefna, 3. þing.
conic *see* keilulaga.
conical *see* keilulaga.
conjecture *see* 1. tilgáta, 2. ágiskun, 3. getgáta.
conjugate *see* 1. samoka, 2. tengdur.
conjugation *see* 1. okun, 2. samokun, 3. tengiæxlun, 4. tenging, 5. tíðbeyging.
conjunction *see* 1. ogun, 2. samstaða, 3. samtenging.
conjunctiva *see* 1. augnslímhúð, 2. tára.
conjunctivitis *see* 1. augnangur, 2. augnkvef, 3. tárabólga, 4. tárubólga.
connect *see* tengja.
connection *see* 1. tenging, 2. samband, 3. samtenging.

connectivity see 1. tengistig, 2. tengjanleiki, 3. tengni.
connector see 1. tenging, 2. leiðari, 3. tengill.
connotation see 1. merkingarblær, 2. merkingarauki, 3. aukamerking.
consanguinity see 1. blóðbönd, 2. blóðsifjar, 3. blóðskyldleiki, 4. skyldleiki.
conscience see samviska.
conscious see meðvitandi.
consciousness see 1. meðvitund, 2. vitund.
consensus see 1. samhljóða, 2. samkomulag, 3. samstaða, 4. eining.
consent see samþykki.
conservation see 1. náttúruvernd, 2. verndun, 3. vernd, 4. varðveisla, 5. geymd.
conservatism see 1. íhaldsstefna, 2. varfærnisregla, 3. varkárnisregla, 4. íhald.
conservative see 1. hófsamur, 2. íhaldssamur, 3. geyminn, 4. gætinn, 5. fastheldinn.
conserve see 1. varðveita, 2. vernda.
consignee see 1. umboðsmaður, 2. viðtakandi, 3. vörumóttakandi.
consignment see 1. umboðsviðskipti, 2. vörusending.
consignor see 1. umbjóðandi, 2. vörusendandi.
consistence see 1. seigja, 2. sjálfkvæmni, 3. þéttleiki, 4. þykkt.
consistency see 1. dreifing, 2. samkvæmni, 3. samræmi, 4. þéttleiki.
consol see eilífðarbréf.
consolation see huggun.
console see 1. snigilkrappi, 2. stjórnborð, 3. stokkur, 4. syllusnigill, 5. hugga.
consolidate see 1. sameinast, 2. sameina.
consolidation see 1. styrking, 2. samstæða, 3. sameining, 4. efling.
consonance see 1. samhljómur, 2. samkomulag, 3. samningur, 4. samraemi.
consortium see samsteypa.
constable see 1. lögreglumaður, 2. lögregluðjónn.
constancy see 1. festa, 2. stöðugleiki.
constant see 1. stöðugur, 2. fastatala, 3. fasti, 4. fastur, 5. látlaus.
constellation see stjörnumerki.
constituency see 1. stuðningsmaður, 2. kjördæmi.
constituent see 1. iefni, 2. kjósandi, 3. stofnhluti.
constitute see 1. mynda, 2. útnefna, 3. skipa, 4. lögskipa, 5. kjósa.
constitution see 1. stjórnarskrá, 2. útnefning, 3. tilskipun, 4. stjórnskipun, 5. stjórnskipulag.
constitutional see 1. stjórnarskrárbundinn, 2. þingbundinn, 3. stjórnarskrárlegur, 4. lögbundinn, 5. eðlislægur.
constrain see 1. neyða, 2. þvinga.
constraint see 1. skilyrði, 2. takmörkun, 3. skorðun, 4. skorða, 5. hefta.

constriction see 1. haft, 2. herping.
construct see 1. smíða, 2. hugsmíð, 3. smíð, 4. hugtakalíkan, 5. byggja.
construction see 1. bygging, 2. verkframkvæmd, 3. gerð, 4. lagatúlkun, 5. lögskýring.
construe see 1. túlka, 2. þýða.
consul see 1. konsúll, 2. ræðismaður.
consulate see 1. ræðismannsbústaður, 2. ræðismannsskrifstofa.
consultant see 1. sérfræðingur, 2. ráðgjafi, 3. ráðunautur.
consultation see 1. viðræður, 2. viðræðufundur, 3. samráð, 4. ráðaleitun, 5. ráðgjöf.
consume see 1. eyða, 2. neyta, 3. nota.
consumer see 1. neytandi, 2. viðskiptavinur, 3. Notandi.
consumerism see 1. neysluaukningarstefna, 2. neytendahyggja, 3. neytendavernd, 4. neytendaverndarstefna.
consumption see 1. eyðsla, 2. neysla, 3. eldsneytisnotkun, 4. eldsneytiseyðsla, 5. notkun.
contact see 1. samband, 2. tenging, 3. rafsamband, 4. raftengi, 5. raftenging.
contactor see 1. tengi, 2. segulrofi.
contagion see 1. smit, 2. sýkill.
contain see innihalda.
container see 1. gámur, 2. ílát.
containment see 1. innilokunarstefna, 2. viðnámsstefna, 3. stöðvunarstefna, 4. innilokun, 5. hamning.
contaminant see 1. aðskotaefni, 2. mengunarvaldur.
contaminate see 1. menga, 2. óhreinka, 3. spilla.
contaminated see spilltur.
contamination see 1. smitun, 2. saurgun, 3. gagnamengun, 4. mengun, 5. óhreinkun.
contemplate see 1. áforma, 2. hugleiða, 3. íhuga.
contemporary see 1. núverandi, 2. núgildandi, 3. nútímalegur.
contend see slást.
content see 1. efni, 2. íhöfn, 3. innihald, 4. ánægður.
contented see ánægður.
contention see 1. álit, 2. steyting, 3. staðhæfing, 4. skoðun, 5. samkeppni.
context see 1. aðstæður, 2. bakgrunnur, 3. samhengi, 4. vettvangur.
contiguity see 1. nánd, 2. grannsvæðakennsl.
contiguous see 1. samliggjandi, 2. samlægur, 3. aðlægur, 4. aðliggjandi.
continence see 1. blöðrustjórn, 2. þarmastjórn.
continent see 1. heimsálfa, 2. meginland.
contingency see 1. ófyrirséð, 2. tengslalíkur.
continuity see 1. samfelldni, 2. samhengi, 3. samfella.
continuous see 1. óslitinn, 2. samfelldur.
continuum see 1. litrófssamfella, 2. samfella.

contour see 1. hæðarlína, 2. útlínur, 3. útlína, 4. jafngildislína, 5. lykkja.
contraception see 1. getnaðarvörn, 2. þungunarvörn.
contraceptive see getnaðarverja.
contract see 1. útboðssamningur, 2. verksamningur, 3. draga, 4. samningur.
contractile see 1. samdrægur, 2. samdráttarhæfur.
contractility see 1. herpanleiki, 2. samdráttargeta, 3. samdráttarhæfni.
contraction see 1. herping, 2. samdráttur.
contractor see 1. verktaki, 2. samningsaðili, 3. samingsaðili.
contracture see 1. síherping, 2. kreppa.
contradistinction see mótsetning.
contrail see flugslóði.
contralto see altrödd.
contrary see 1. mótstæður, 2. andstæður.
contrast see 1. samanburðarfall, 2. skuggi, 3. skerpa, 4. birtuskil, 5. andstæða.
contribution see 1. framlag, 2. skerfur.
control see 1. viðmið, 2. stilla, 3. stýring, 4. stýra, 5. stjórnun.
controllability see 1. stjórnhæfi, 2. stýranleiki.
controller see 1. aflstýritæki, 2. fjármálastjóri, 3. stjórnandi.
controversy see rifrildi.
conus see 1. keila, 2. strýta.
convalescence see 1. bataskeið, 2. afturbati.
convection see 1. varmaflutningur, 2. varmaburður, 3. straumburður, 4. lóðstreymi, 5. iðuhitun.
convenience see 1. þægindi, 2. salerni, 3. hentugleiki.
convention see 1. siðvenja, 2. þing, 3. sáttmáli, 4. samþykkt, 5. samningur.
conventional see 1. venjubundið, 2. venjulegt, 3. venjulegur.
convergence see 1. samhverfa, 2. aðhneiging, 3. samvísun, 4. samleitni, 5. samhverfing.
convergent see 1. aðhverfur, 2. samleitinn.
conversation see samtal.
conversion see 1. hughvarf, 2. verðbréfaskipti, 3. umreikningur, 4. turnun, 5. hambrigði.
convert see 1. umskrá, 2. breyta, 3. umbreyta, 4. umforma.
converter see 1. umriðill, 2. umbreytir, 3. afriðill, 4. breytir, 5. straumbreytir.
convertor see 1. straumbreytir, 2. umriðill.
convex see 1. kúptur, 2. ávalur, 3. íhvolfur.
convexity see 1. ávali, 2. kúpni.
conveyance see 1. afsal, 2. afsalsbréf, 3. flutningur.
conveyor see færiband.
conviction see sannfæring.
convince see sannfæra.
convincing see sannfærður.

convolution see 1. felling, 2. fléttun, 3. földun, 4. heilafelling.
convulsion see 1. umbrotakrampi, 2. krampi, 3. rykkjakrampi, 4. umbrot.
cony see kanína.
cook see 1. matsveinn, 2. sjóða, 3. kokkur.
cool see 1. svalur, 2. kæla, 3. kaldur.
coolant see 1. kælimiðill, 2. kælivökvi, 3. kæliefni.
cooler see kælir.
cooling see kæling.
cooperation see 1. samstarf, 2. samvinna.
coordinate see 1. samræma, 2. samstilla, 3. samhæfa, 4. hnita, 5. hnit.
coordination see 1. samhæfing, 2. samræming, 3. hnitun.
cop see 1. lögregluðjónn, 2. lögreglumaður.
copious see 1. ríkulegur, 2. efnismikill, 3. kappnógur.
copper see 1. kopar, 2. eir, 3. lögregluðjónn, 4. lögreglumaður.
coprocessor see samgjörvi.
copse see 1. kjarr, 2. runnar.
copy see 1. afrit, 2. afrita, 3. farmskírteini.
copyright see höfundarréttur.
coracoid see 1. krummahyrna, 2. krummanefsbein.
corals see 1. kóraldýr, 2. kórallar, 3. sæfíflar.
cord see 1. þráður, 2. lausataug, 3. snæri, 4. strengur, 5. taug.
cordial see 1. hjartanlegur, 2. vinsamlegur.
core see 1. kjarni, 2. samlokukjarni.
coriander see 1. kóríander, 2. kóríandrajurt, 3. kóríandri, 4. kóríandur.
corium see 1. leðurhúð, 2. leður.
cork see 1. korkvefur, 2. korkur, 3. börkur, 4. kork.
corm see 1. jarðstöngulhnýði, 2. laukur, 3. rótarhnúður.
corn see 1. maís, 2. maískorn, 3. tyrkjakorn, 4. hænsnakorn, 5. mæs.
cornea see 1. glæra, 2. hornhimna.
corner see Horn.
cornice see hengja.
corolla see 1. blómkróna, 2. króna.
corona see 1. blik, 2. umgjörð, 3. þyrill, 4. litbaugur, 5. hjákróna.
coronal see blaðmyndað.
coronary see hjartaáfall.
corporation see 1. félag, 2. lögpersóna, 3. lögaðili, 4. hlutafélag.
corpus see 1. dæmasafn, 2. textasafn.
corpuscle see 1. hnøkri, 2. ögn.
correct see 1. leiðrétta, 2. rétt, 3. réttur.
correction see 1. rétting, 2. leiðrétting.
correlation see 1. fylgni, 2. jarðlagatenging.
correspondence see 1. hliðstæða, 2. samsvörun.

corresponding see 1. hliðstæður, 2. samsvarandi, 3. tilsvarandi.
corridor see 1. gangur, 2. jaðar, 3. ræma.
corrode see 1. tærast, 2. æta, 3. ryðga, 4. tæra.
corrosion see 1. tæring, 2. ryðgun, 3. áta, 4. æting, 5. át.
corrosive see 1. tærinn, 2. ætandi, 3. ætiefni, 4. tærandi.
corruption see spilling.
cortex see 1. barkhúð, 2. börkur, 3. frumubörkur, 4. heilabörkur, 5. útfrymi.
corticosteroid see barksteri.
cortisol see 1. kortisól, 2. hýdrókortisón.
cortisone see 1. kortisón, 2. kortísón.
coryza see 1. höfuðkvef, 2. nefkvef.
cosine see kósínus.
cosmetic see 1. fegrandi, 2. fegrunarefni.
cosmogony see 1. heimsmyndunarfræði, 2. upprunafræði.
cosmology see 1. heimsfræði, 2. heimsmyndarfræði, 3. heimsmynd.
cosmopolitan see 1. alþjóðlegur, 2. heimsborgaralegur, 3. heimsborgari.
cosmopolite see heimsborgari.
cosmos see alheimur.
cost see 1. kostnaður, 2. kosta.
costly see dýr (animal).
costume see jakkakjóll.
cotangent see kótangens.
cotter see 1. lásfleygur, 2. splitti.
cotton see 1. bómull, 2. baðmull, 3. tvistur.
cotyledon see 1. kímblað, 2. legkökutotur, 3. fósturskúfur.
cough see 1. hósta, 2. hósti.
coulomb see kúlomb.
council see 1. ráð, 2. sveitarstjórn.
counsel see 1. málflutningsmaður, 2. ráð, 3. málfærslumaður, 4. lögmaður, 5. ráða.
counseling see ráðgjöf.
count see 1. telja, 2. greifi, 3. púlsafjöldi, 4. reikna, 5. talningarpúls.
counter see 1. teljari, 2. nemi, 3. gagnstæður, 4. móti.
counteraction see andvirkni.
counterattack see Gagnsókn.
counterbalance see 1. ballansera, 2. jafnvægisstilla, 3. mótvægi, 4. mótvigt.
counterbore see 1. hringstallur, 2. úrsnörun.
counterclockwise see rangsælis.
counterculture see 1. andfélag, 2. andmenning.
countermeasure see 1. gagnaðgerð, 2. gagnráðstöfun, 3. mótvægisaðgerð.
counterplay see Motspíspil.
counterpoise see 1. mótvægi, 2. jarðskautsleiðari.
countershaft see 1. milliás, 2. tromluás.

countersink see 1. undirsinka, 2. úrsnari.
counterweight see 1. andvægi, 2. mótvægi.
country see 1. land, 2. þjóð, 3. sveit, 4. svæði, 5. ríki.
countryside see 1. sveitahérað, 2. sveitafólk, 3. héraðsbúar, 4. sveit.
county see 1. hérað, 2. sýsla.
couple see 1. par, 2. plötutvennd, 3. tvinn, 4. tvenna, 5. tengja.
coupling see 1. tenging, 2. tengsli, 3. tengslafasi, 4. tengsl, 5. tengslkragi.
coupon see 1. arðmiði, 2. nafnvextir, 3. ákvæðisvextir, 4. afsláttarmiði, 5. skömmtunarmiði.
courgette see 1. dvergbítur, 2. kúrbítur, 3. skvass.
course see 1. sjónlína, 2. skeiðvöllur, 3. stefna, 4. vegur, 5. kappreiðabraut.
court see 1. dómssalur, 2. dómstóll, 3. dómur, 4. réttarsalur.
courteous see kurteis.
cousin see 1. frændi, 2. frænka.
covariance see 1. samdreifni, 2. sambreytni, 3. samfylgni, 4. tvíveldissamstæða.
cove see 1. vík, 2. fjörður, 3. flói.
covenant see 1. sáttmáli, 2. samningur.
cover see 1. lok, 2. þekja, 3. hleri, 4. hlíf, 5. hlífðarplata.
coverage see 1. þekja, 2. þekjustig, 3. umfang.
cow see 1. kýr, 2. nautpeningur.
cowberry see 1. rauðber, 2. týtuber, 3. rauðberjalyng.
cowl see 1. hetta, 2. hlíf, 3. vélarhlíf.
crab see 1. beiting, 2. krabbi.
crack see 1. skrölta, 2. sprunga, 3. rifa.
cracking see 1. Klofningur, 2. Klofningsgösun.
crackle see braka.
cradle see fæðingarstaður.
cradlesong see 1. vögguljóð, 2. vögguvísa.
cramp see 1. sinadráttur, 2. skrúfþvinga, 3. iðraverkir, 4. vöðvahlaup.
cramped see þröngur.
crane see 1. lyftikrani, 2. trana.
craniometry see 1. hauskúpumæling, 2. kúpumæling.
cranium see 1. heilakúpa, 2. hauskúpa.
crank see 1. sveif, 2. handsveif, 3. snúa.
crankcase see sveifarhús.
crankshaft see sveifarás.
crash see 1. árekstur, 2. brotlenda, 3. brotlending, 4. hrapa.
crater see 1. gígur, 2. eldgígur, 3. Bikarinn.
crawfish see svipukrabbi.
crayfish see 1. fljótakrabbi, 2. vatnakrabbi.
creativity see 1. sköpunargáfa, 2. virkni.
credential see persónuskilríki.

credentials *see* 1. skilríki, 2. trúnaðarbréf.
credit *see* 1. lánstraust, 2. útlán, 3. lánshæfi, 4. lán,
5. inneign.
creditor *see* 1. kröfuhafi, 2. lánardrottinn, 3.
lánveitandi.
creed *see* 1. sannfæring, 2. trú.
creek *see* 1. fjörður, 2. flói, 3. vík.
creep *see* 1. skrið, 2. skríða.
cremation *see* 1. bálför, 2. líkbrennsla.
crematory *see* 1. bálstofa, 2. líkbrennsluofn.
crenate *see* bogtenntur.
crepitation *see* 1. liðbrak, 2. liðmarr, 3. gusuhvellur,
4. beinbrotsbrak, 5. vefjamarr.
crescent *see* 1. hálfmáni, 2. mánasigð, 3. sigð, 4.
vaxandi.
cretin *see* 1. kretíndvergur, 2.
skjaldkyrkingsdvergur, 3. korkudvergur.
cretinism *see* 1. kyrkivöxtur, 2. kyrkingur.
crevasse *see* 1. jökulgjá, 2. jökulsprunga.
crevice *see* 1. rifa, 2. sprunga.
crew *see* áhöfn.
crime *see* 1. afbrotaiðni, 2. brot, 3. glæpur, 4. afbrot.
crisis *see* 1. bráðavandi, 2. kreppa, 3. sóttbrigði, 4.
sótthvörf.
criterion *see* 1. mælikvarði, 2. viðmið, 3.
greinimark, 4. forsenda, 5. auðkenni.
critical *see* 1. gagnrýninn, 2. Hætinn, 3. tvísýnn, 4.
varhugaverður.
criticism *see* átölur.
croaker *see* baulfiskur.
crocodile *see* krókódíll.
crooked *see* óheiðarlegur.
crop *see* 1. uppskera, 2. sarpur.
cross *see* 1. víxlun, 2. kross, 3. kynblendingur, 4.
kynblöndun, 5. reiður.
crossbreed *see* samæxla.
crossover *see* 1. víxlun, 2. hitaflutningur.
crosstalk *see* 1. merkjablöndun, 2. milliheyrsla, 3.
rásasmit.
crossword *see* krossgáta.
croup *see* 1. sogabarnaveiki, 2. kvashósti, 3. lend.
crow *see* 1. kráka, 2. hrafn.
crowbar *see* 1. klaufjárn, 2. kúbein.
crowd *see* 1. mannþyrping, 2. múgur.
crown *see* 1. króna, 2. trjákróna.
crucial *see* krosslaga.
crucible *see* 1. deigla, 2. digull.
cruiser *see* beitiskip.
crus *see* 1. leggur, 2. súla.
crush *see* 1. kramning, 2. kremja, 3. krumpa, 4.
pressa.
crust *see* 1. skurn, 2. jarðskorpa, 3. hrúður, 4.
skorpa, 5. skel.
crustaceous *see* 1. hrúðurkenndur, 2.
skorpukenndur.

cry *see* gráta.
cryostat *see* 1. frystipottur, 2. kælipottur, 3.
kuldahald.
crypt *see* 1. bora, 2. grafhvelfing, 3. kirtilhol.
cryptococcosis *see* sætumygla.
crystal *see* 1. kristalgler, 2. kristall, 3. kristallur, 4.
kvars.
crystalline *see* kristallskenndur.
crystallization *see* kristallsmyndun.
crystallize *see* kristallast.
crystalloid *see* 1. kristallslegur, 2. kristallslíki.
cub *see* 1. ljósálfur, 2. ylfingur.
cube *see* 1. teningur, 2. þríveldi.
cubic *see* teningslaga.
cuckoo *see* gaukur.
cucumber *see* 1. gúrka, 2. agúrka.
cue *see* 1. vísbending, 2. bending, 3. viðbragðsmerki.
culmination *see* þverganga.
culture *see* 1. eldi, 2. rækt, 3. smáverugróður, 4.
þjóðmenning, 5. ræktun.
cumin *see* 1. kummin, 2. ostakúmen, 3. kúmín, 4.
krosskúmen, 5. broddkúmen.
cumulonimbus *see* 1. skúraský, 2. þrumuský, 3.
útsynningsklakkar, 4. skúraflákar.
cumulus *see* 1. skýjabólstur, 2. bólstraský, 3.
bólstursský, 4. eggbólstur.
cuneiform *see* fleygbein.
cunt *see* pussa.
cup *see* bolli.
cups *see* bolli.
cure *see* 1. græða, 2. lækna, 3. lækning.
curious *see* 1. vitlaus, 2. skrýtinn.
curium *see* 1. kúrín, 2. kúríum.
currency *see* 1 gjaldmiðill, 2. ferskleiki, 3.
gildisdagur, 4. gjaldeyrir, 5. útgáfudagur.
current *see* 1. gildandi, 2. straumur, 3. rafstraumur,
4. núgildandi, 5. nútímalegur.
curse *see* 1. bölva, 2. skamma.
cursor *see* 1. bendill, 2. drýsill.
curvature *see* 1. ávali, 2. bugða, 3. krappi, 4.
straumlína, 5. sveigja.
curve *see* 1. hnít, 2. kúrva, 3. boglína, 4. beygja, 5.
ferill.
cushion *see* 1. deyfing, 2. mýking, 3. púði, 4. sessa.
cusk *see* keila.
cusp *see* 1. snepill, 2. hnúður, 3. horn.
cuss *see* bölva.
custom *see* 1. kutimo, 2. siður, 3. vani, 4. venja.
customary *see* venjulegur.
customer *see* 1. kaupandi, 2. viðskiptavinur, 3.
viðskiptamaður.
customs *see* 1. tollur, 2. kutimo, 3. moro, 4.
tollgæsla.
cut *see* 1. skera, 2. skurður, 3. stöðuhorn, 4. sníða, 5.
skering.

cutback see skerðing.
cuticle see 1. skurn, 2. húð, 3. hem, 4. annögl, 5. yfirhúð.
cutin see 1. kútín, 2. vaxefni.
cutlery see hnífapör.
cutoff see 1. afmörkun, 2. lotun.
cutter see 1. skeri, 2. ritferjald.
cutting see 1. afleggjari, 2. græðlingur.
cuttlefish see blekfiskar.
cyanocobalamin see sýanókóbalamín.
cyanosis see blámi.
cybernetics see 1. kerfisfræði, 2. stýrifræði.
cyberspace see netheimar.
cyclamen see 1. klunguralpafjóla, 2. klungurfjóla, 3. alpafjóla.
cycle see 1. reiðhjól, 2. sveifla, 3. rytmi, 4. hringrás, 5. vinnuhringur.
cyclic see 1. lotukvæmur, 2. hringtengdur, 3. hringlaga, 4. rásaður.
cycloid see hjólferill.
cyclone see 1. sveipur, 2. vindsveipur, 3. stormsveipur, 4. lægð, 5. hvirfilbylur.
cyclotron see 1. hringhraðall, 2. síklótrónn, 3. hlaðeindahraðandi.
cylinder see 1. sívalningur, 2. dröngull, 3. hólkur, 4. kefli, 5. strokkur.
cypress see 1. grátviður, 2. sýprusviður, 3. sýprus.
cyst see 1. belgur, 2. blaðra, 3. þolhjúpur.
cystectomy see 1. blöðrunám, 2. þvagblöðrunám.
cysticercus see bandormslirfa.
cystitis see blöðrubólga.
cystotomy see 1. blöðruskurður, 2. hýðisskurður.
cytochrome see sýtókróm.
cytogenetics see frumuerfðafræði.
cytology see frumufræði.
cytolysis see 1. frumueyðing, 2. frumuleysing.
cytoplasm see umfrymi.
cytosine see 1. sýtosín, 2. sýtósín.
cytosol see 1. frumuhlaup, 2. frymisvökvi, 3. glærfrymi.
cytostatic see 1. frumuhamlandi, 2. frumuhemjandi, 3. frumuskiptahamlandi.
cytotoxic see frumudrepandi.

D

dab see sandkoli.
dace see silfurgægir.
dactyl see daktíli.
daily see dagblað.
dale see dalur.
dam see 1. stífla, 2. stíflugarður, 3. uppistöðulón.
damage see 1. skemmd, 2. tjón, 3. laska, 4. skaða.

damaged see 1. laskaður, 2. skemmdur.
damages see skaðabætur.
dame see 1. kona, 2. kvenmaður.
damn see helvíti.
damp see 1. deyfa, 2. rakur, 3. hamla, 4. raki.
dampen see 1. bleyta, 2. deyfa.
damper see 1. dempari, 2. deyfir, 3. dvalvefja.
damping see 1. svaf, 2. deyfing.
dance see 1. dansa, 2. dans.
danger see hætta.
dare see þora.
dark see 1. dapur, 2. myrkur.
darkness see myrkur.
dash see 1. sláttur, 2. smellur, 3. merki, 4. högg, 5. strik.
dashboard see mælaborð.
dashpot see deyfingarhylki.
data see 1. gögn, 2. heimildir, 3. málgögn, 4. upplýsingar.
database see 1. gagnagrunnur, 2. gagnasafn.
date see dagsetning.
dating see 1. aldursákvörðun, 2. aldursgreining.
datum see 1. viðmið, 2. viðmiðshæð, 3. viðmiðunarhæð.
daughter see dóttir.
davit see 1. davíða, 2. bátsugla.
day see 1. dagur, 2. sólarhringur.
daydream see 1. dagdraumur, 2. dagdreymi.
dazzled see hryllilegur.
dead see 1. alger, 2. dauður.
deadline see 1. tímamörk, 2. frestur, 3. eindagi, 4. athugasemdafrestur.
deaf see heyrnarlaus.
deafness see 1. heyrnardeyfa, 2. heyrnarleysi.
deal see 1. samningur, 2. versla, 3. miðla, 4. höndla, 5. fjöl.
dealer see 1. gjafari, 2. höndlari, 3. miðlari, 4. sali, 5. umboðsmaður.
dear see 1. sætur, 2. dýr (animal).
dearth see 1. þurrð, 2. skortur, 3. hörgull, 4. ekla.
death see 1. dauði, 2. andlát, 3. viðskilnaður.
debasement see 1. gildislækkun, 2. verðrýrnun.
debenture see skuldabréf.
debris see 1. brak, 2. hroði, 3. lausagrjót.
debt see skuld.
debtor see 1. skuldari, 2. skuldunautur.
debug see kemba.
decay see 1. hrörna, 2. rotnun, 3. sundrun, 4. eyðing, 5. eyðast.
deceit see svik.
deceitful see óheiðarlegur.
deceive see svíkja.
deceleration see 1. hæging, 2. hraðaminnkun, 3. afhröðun.

decentralization *see* 1. dreifistýring, 2. valddreifing, 3. dreifing.

decibel *see* 1. desíbel, 2. db, 3. desibel.

decidedly *see* vafalaust.

deciduous *see* 1. skammær, 2. sumargrænn.

decile *see* tíundarmark.

decimal *see* 1. tugastafur, 2. tugur.

decision *see* 1. ákvörðun, 2. úrskurður.

deck *see* 1. þilfar, 2. blokkarflötur, 3. dekk.

declaration *see* 1. yfirlýsing, 2. skilgreining, 3. tryggingatilkynning.

declination *see* 1. miðbaugsbreidd, 2. misvísun, 3. segulskekkja, 4. stjörnubreidd.

decline *see* 1. verðfall, 2. neita, 3. lækka.

decode *see* afkóta.

decoder *see* 1. afkótari, 2. afruglari, 3. myndlykill.

decoding *see* 1. afkóðun, 2. afskráning.

decompose *see* 1. sundra, 2. rotna.

decomposition *see* 1. sundurliðun, 2. sundurleysing, 3. grotnun, 4. niðurbrot.

decontaminate *see* 1. afmenga, 2. hreinsa.

decontamination *see* 1. afmengun, 2. Hreinsun.

decoration *see* 1. orða, 2. skraut, 3. skreyting, 4. heiðursmerkjaveiting.

decorticate *see* 1. barkarstýfa, 2. barkarstýður.

decortication *see* 1. barkarnám, 2. barkarspell, 3. barkfletta.

decoupling *see* 1. aftengsl, 2. afkúpling.

decrease *see* 1. niðurlægja, 2. lækka, 3. minnka.

decrement *see* 1. frádrag, 2. minnka, 3. minnkun, 4. rénun, 5. rýrnun.

decussate *see* 1. krossgagnstæður, 2. víxlast, 3. skerast.

deductible *see* 1. frádráttarbær, 2. frádráttarhæfur.

deduction *see* 1. afleiðsla, 2. ályktun, 3. frádráttur, 4. útleiðsla.

deed *see* 1. skírteini, 2. þáttur.

deem *see* 1. trúa, 2. halda.

deep *see* 1. djúpur, 2. náinn.

defamation *see* slúður.

defame *see* slúðra.

default *see* 1. sjálfgefinn, 2. vanskil, 3. sjálfval, 4. greiðslufall, 5. vanefnd.

defecation *see* 1. hægðir, 2. saurlát.

defect *see* 1. galli, 2. veila.

defence *see* Vörn.

defend *see* varða.

defendant *see* 1. sakborningur, 2. stefndi, 3. varnaraðili, 4. ákærði.

defense *see* vörn.

deferent *see* aðalhringur.

defibrillation *see* hjartastilling.

deficiency *see* 1. brottfall, 2. skortur, 3. úrfelling.

deficient *see* ófullnægjandi.

deficit *see* 1. halli, 2. starfsgalli, 3. tap, 4. þurrð.

definite *see* óvís.

definition *see* 1. merking, 2. upplausn, 3. skýrleiki, 4. skýrgreining, 5. skilgreining.

deflate *see* raunvirða.

deflation *see* 1. verðlækkun, 2. verðhrun, 3. verðhjöðnun, 4. fok, 5. vindrof.

deflect *see* 1. sveigja, 2. svigna.

deflection *see* 1. hliðarsveigja, 2. útslag, 3. svig, 4. stefnufrávik, 5. frávik.

deflector *see* 1. hlíf, 2. skýla.

defoliation *see* lauffelling.

deform *see* 1. skekkja, 2. aflaga.

deformation *see* 1. skekking, 2. bjögun, 3. afmyndun, 4. aflögun.

deformed *see* 1. aflagaður, 2. bæklaður, 3. vanskapaður.

deformity *see* 1. aflögun, 2. bæklun.

defrost *see* 1. affrysta, 2. þíða.

defroster *see* 1. ísvari, 2. þíðingarbúnaður, 3. afísingarbúnaður.

degassing *see* 1. gaseyðing, 2. lofttómshreinsun.

degeneracy *see* 1. öngstig, 2. öng, 3. samgildi, 4. öfuguggaháttur, 5. margfeldni.

degeneration *see* 1. hrörnun, 2. miðtaugakerfishrörnun, 3. rýrnun, 4. tap, 5. úrkynjun.

deglutition *see* kynging.

degradation *see* 1. niðurbrot, 2. niðurrif.

degranulation *see* 1. kornatæming, 2. úrkornun.

degree *see* 1. gráða, 2. mark, 3. stig.

dehiscence *see* opnun.

dehydration *see* 1. afvötnun, 2. vessaþurrð, 3. úrvötnun, 4. Þurrkun.

dehydrogenation *see* vetnissvipting.

deity *see* guð.

dejection *see* sút.

delay *see* 1. seinka, 2. seinkun, 3. frestun, 4. fresta, 5. bið.

delayed *see* 1. síðkominn, 2. tafinn.

delegation *see* 1. framsal, 2. samninganefnd, 3. sendinefnd, 4. valdframsal.

delete *see* 1. eyða, 2. seinka, 3. eyðingarhamur, 4. eyðing.

deletion *see* 1. brottfall, 2. eyðing, 3. úrfelling, 4. útstrikun.

delimiter *see* 1. afmarkari, 2. deilir.

delineation *see* landamerkjalýsing.

delirium *see* 1. rugl, 2. æði, 3. óráð.

delivery *see* 1. afhending, 2. mötun, 3. sending, 4. skil.

dell *see* dalur.

delta *see* 1. landeyjar, 2. óshólmar, 3. árhólmar, 4. óseyri, 5. óseyrar.

deltoid *see* 1. axlarvöðvi, 2. þríhyrndur.

delude *see* svíkja.

delusion see 1. haldvilla, 2. hugvilla.
demagnetisation see 1. afseglun, 2.
afsegulmögnun, 3. gagnseglun.
demand see 1. afl, 2. aflþörf, 3. eftirspurn, 4. krafa,
5. krefjast.
demarcation see 1. afmörkun, 2.
landamerkjamæling, 3. takmörkun.
dementia see 1. vitglöp, 2. vitsmunaskerðing.
democracy see 1. alþýða, 2. lýðræði, 3. lýðræðisríki,
4. lýðræðisstjórn.
democrat see 1. jafnaðarmaður, 2. lýðræðissinni, 3.
demókrati.
demodulation see afmótun.
demodulator see afmótari.
demography see 1. fólksfjöldafræði, 2. lýðfræði, 3.
manntalsfræði, 4. mannvistarfræði, 5. stofnfræði.
demonstration see 1. kynning, 2. sýning, 3.
sýnikennsla, 4. mótmæli.
demurrage see 1. aukabiðdagaþóknun, 2. biðdagar,
3. biðgjald, 4. dráttur, 5. töf.
den see hreiður.
denaturation see 1. eðlisbreyting, 2. eðlissvipting.
dendrite see 1. gripluþráður, 2. gripla.
denervation see 1. aftaugun, 2. taugaskerðing.
denial see afneitun.
denier see 1. afneitari, 2. neitari.
denomination see nafn.
denominator see nefnari.
denotation see 1. aðalmerking, 2. merkingarkjarni.
denote see 1. merkja, 2. þýða.
densitometer see 1. gagnsæismælir, 2.
þéttleikamælir.
density see 1. eðlismassi, 2. eðlisþyngd, 3. þéttleiki,
4. þéttni.
dent see 1. beygla, 2. dæld, 3. dælda.
dentition see 1. tanngerð, 2. tannkoma, 3.
tannsetning, 4. tanntaka.
denudation see 1. aftekt, 2. rof.
denunciation see 1. uppsögn, 2. uppljóstrun.
deny see neita.
deodorant see 1. lykteyðandi, 2. lykteyðir, 3.
svitalyktareyðir.
depart see fara.
department see 1. deild, 2. svið, 3. skrifstofa, 4.
ráðuneyti, 5. skor.
departure see 1. brottflug, 2. brottför.
dependable see 1. traustur, 2. áreiðanlegur, 3.
gangviss.
dependence see 1. skilbinding, 2. hæði, 3.
ósjálfstæði.
dependency see 1. yfirráðasvæði, 2. ákvæði, 3.
hæði, 4. hænd, 5. hang.
dependent see 1. háður, 2. ósjálfstæður, 3.
hangandi.
depersonalization see afsjálfgun.

deplete see fullnýta.
depletion see 1. örmögnun, 2. rýrnun, 3. skerðing,
4. fullnýting, 5. tæming.
deploy see 1. nota, 2. nýta.
depolarization see afskautun.
depolarize see 1. afskauta, 2. umpóla.
depolarizer see afskautunarefni.
depopulation see 1. fólksfækkun, 2. fólksþurrð.
deportment see 1. framkoma, 2. hegðun.
deposit see 1. útfelling, 2. botnfall, 3. geymslufé, 4.
innborgun, 5. innlegg.
deposition see 1. setmyndun, 2. hélun, 3.
framburður.
deposits see innlán.
depreciate see 1. afskrifa, 2. fyrna.
depreciation see 1. afskrift, 2. fyrning, 3.
gengislækkun, 4. gengissig, 5. verðrýrnun.
depressed see 1. þunglyndur, 2. niðurbældur, 3.
mæddur, 4. hnugginn, 5. dapur.
depression see 1. geðlægð, 2. þrýstifall, 3. lækkun,
4. lægðarsvæði, 5. kreppa.
depressive see 1. íþyngjandi, 2. niðurdrepandi.
depressor see 1. fellir, 2. niðurfærir.
deprivation see 1. þrot, 2. svipting.
deprive see svipta.
depth see 1. dýpi, 2. dýpt.
deputy see 1. fulltrúi, 2. varamaður.
derangement see 1. óreiða, 2. ruglingur, 3. sturlun.
derivation see 1. afleiðsla, 2. rökleiðsla, 3. útleiðsla.
derivative see 1. afefni, 2. afleiða, 3. afleiðandi, 4.
afleiddur, 5. úrefni.
derive see fá.
dermatoglyphics see 1. húðlínufræði, 2. húðlínur.
dermatology see húðsjúkdómafræði.
dermatome see 1. húðgeiri, 2. húðhnífur.
dermis see 1. leður, 2. leðurhúð.
derrick see 1. krani, 2. lyftikrani.
descaling see 1. afhreistrun, 2. ryðhreinsun.
descender see 1. lágleggur, 2. lágleggsstafur.
descent see 1. fall, 2. hallar, 3. lækkar, 4. lækkun, 5.
sig.
descriptor see 1. lýsir, 2. lýsiorð, 3. lýsingur, 4.
efnisvísir.
desensitization see 1. ónæming, 2. afnæming.
desensitize see 1. afnæma, 2. ónæma, 3. skynsvipta.
desert see 1. eyðimörk, 2. yfirgefa, 3. strjúka, 4.
sandauðn, 5. óbyggð.
deserted see 1. mannlaus, 2. yfirgefinn.
deserving see verður.
desiccant see 1. þurrkandi, 2. þerrir, 3. rakadrægur,
4. þurrkefni.
desiccation see 1. rakadráttur, 2. þurrkun, 3.
uppþornun.
desiccator see 1. rakagleypir, 2. þurrkaskur, 3.
þurrkskál.

design see 1. hanna, 2. uppdráttur, 3. hönnun, 4. gerð, 5. teiknun.
designate see nefna.
desire see 1. ósk, 2. óska.
desktop see 1. vinnuborð, 2. skjáborð, 3. skrifborð.
desmosome see 1. togtengi, 2. heilfrumutengi, 3. halddepill.
desperate see örvæntingarfullur.
destination see 1. áfangastaður, 2. ákvörðunarstaður.
destructive see 1. eyðileggjandi, 2. skaðlegur, 3. skaðsamur.
detachable see 1. aftengjanlegur, 2. frátakanlegt.
detachment see 1. fáskiptni, 2. fjarlægð, 3. losun, 4. aftenging.
detail see 1. detalo, 2. formsatriði, 3. upplýsingar.
details see 1. detali, 2. detalo.
detect see 1. greina, 2. mæla, 3. nema, 4. skynja, 5. uppgötva.
detection see 1. skynjun, 2. uppgötvun.
detector see 1. nemi, 2. skynjari.
detention see 1. kyrrsetning, 2. þvingunarvistun, 3. hald.
detergent see 1. fituvætir, 2. hreinsiefni, 3. sápuefni, 4. þvottaefni.
deteriorate see 1. hraka, 2. versna, 3. elna.
deterioration see 1. slit, 2. rýrnun.
determinant see 1. afgerandi, 2. ákvarðandi, 3. ákveða, 4. úrslitaatriði.
determination see 1. ákvörðun, 2. mæling.
determinism see 1. löghyggja, 2. nauðhyggja, 3. orsakatrú.
deterministic see 1. löggengur, 2. nauðgengur.
detest see hrylla.
detestable see 1. hræðilegur, 2. viðbjóðslegur.
detonation see 1. hraðbruni, 2. sprenging, 3. sjálfkveiking, 4. kveikibank, 5. neistabank.
detonator see 1. forsprengja, 2. hvellhetta.
detoxification see afeitrun.
detoxify see 1. afeitra, 2. afvatna.
detrimental see gallaður.
detritus see 1. salli, 2. mauk, 3. feyra, 4. grot.
detumescence see 1. bólguhjöðnun, 2. niðurlyppun, 3. þrotahjöðnun.
deuterium see tvívetni.
deuteron see 1. devtróna, 2. tvíeind, 3. þungvetniseind.
devaluation see 1. gengisfelling, 2. gengislækkun.
develop see 1. framkalla, 2. þróa, 3. þroska.
development see 1. framþróun, 2. uppbygging, 3. þróun, 4. þroun, 5. þroski.
deviate see 1. frávik, 2. víkja.
deviation see 1. frávik, 2. vik, 3. skekkja, 4. segulskekkja, 5. misvísun.
device see 1. búnaður, 2. tæki, 3. tól.

devil see djöfull.
devolution see 1. hnignun, 2. öfugþróun, 3. valddreifing.
dew see 1. dögg, 2. dropar, 3. náttfall.
dewberry see 1. daggarber, 2. elgsber.
dextrose see 1. dextrósi, 2. vínberjasykur, 3. glúkósi, 4. þrúgusykur.
diabetes see 1. sykursýki, 2. þvagvaxtarkvilli.
diabetic see 1. sykursjúkur, 2. sykursýkissjúklingur.
diagnosis see 1. sjúkdómsgreining, 2. bilanagreining, 3. einkennagreining, 4. greining.
diagnostic see 1. greinandi, 2. aðgreinandi, 3. einkennandi.
diagonal see 1. Skálína, 2. hornalína, 3. skáflötur, 4. skásettur.
diagram see 1. kort, 2. uppdráttur, 3. skýringarteikning, 4. línurit, 5. myndrit.
dial see 1. valskífa, 2. klukkuskífa, 3. kvarði, 4. skífa, 5. stjórnbretti.
dialect see mállýska.
dialectal see mállýskubundinn.
dialectic see 1. rökþróun, 2. rökþróunarkenning, 3. þráttarhyggja, 4. tvíhorfsþróun.
dialogue see 1. skoðanaskipti, 2. umræður, 3. gagnasamskipti, 4. Samræður.
dialysis see 1. himnusíun, 2. himnuskiljun, 3. límingasíun, 4. svifefnasíun.
dialyzer see 1. svifefnasía, 2. himnuskilja, 3. límingasía, 4. skiljuhimna.
diamagnetism see mótseglun.
diameter see 1. þvermál, 2. miðstrengur.
diapedesis see 1. blóðfrumnafar, 2. hvítfrumuskrið, 3. rauðkornaútstreymi.
diaphoretic see 1. svitaaukandi, 2. svitalyf.
diaphragm see 1. ljósopsþynna, 2. þind, 3. millihimna, 4. leghetta, 5. himna.
diarrhea see 1. búkhlaup, 2. lífsýki, 3. niðurgangur, 4. ræpa, 5. steinsmuga.
diaspore see dreifieining.
diastase see sterkjukljúfur.
diastasis see bil.
diastole see 1. þan, 2. þanbil, 3. hjartahlé, 4. aðfallsfasi, 5. hlébil.
diathermy see 1. gegnhitun, 2. gegnhitunarrafstraumur, 3. gegnhitunartæki, 4. innhitun.
diatomite see kísilgúr.
diatoms see kísilþörungar.
dice see 1. patrico, 2. morti, 3. ĵetkubo, 4. lotilo.
dicey see 1. óáreiðanlegur, 2. ótraustur.
dichotomy see 1. tvíflokkun, 2. tvískipting, 3. tvígreining, 4. klofnun, 5. klofningur.
dichroism see 1. skautnæmi, 2. tvílitni.
dichromatic see 1. litvilltur, 2. tvílitur.
dichromatism see litvilla.

dictator see einræðisherra.

dictatorship see 1. einræði, 2. einræðisvald.

dictionary see 1. ordabóg, 2. orðabók, 3. orðasafn.

die see 1. deyja, 2. pressumót, 3. löð, 4. stans, 5. snitti.

dielectric see 1. torleiði, 2. torleiðiefni, 3. rafsvari, 4. einangrunarlag, 5. einangrari.

diencephalon see milliheili.

diet see 1. fæði, 2. mataræði, 3. sérfæði, 4. sjúkrafæði.

dietary see 1. fæðisuppskrift, 2. matarskammtur.

difference see 1. munur, 2. mismunur.

different see 1. annar, 2. ólíkur.

differential see 1. breytandi, 2. deildi, 3. diffur, 4. mismunadrif.

differentiate see 1. deilda, 2. diffra.

differentiation see 1. deildun, 2. starfsgreining, 3. sérhæfing, 4. sérgreining, 5. diffrun.

difficult see 1. þungur, 2. vandur.

diffraction see 1. ljósbeyging, 2. beygja, 3. öldubeyga, 4. bylgjubeyging, 5. bognun.

diffuse see 1. blanda, 2. dreifa, 3. dreifast, 4. dreifður, 5. jafndreifður.

diffuser see 1. dreifari, 2. dreifir.

diffusion see 1. gegnhlutun, 2. sveim, 3. flakk, 4. dreifni, 5. dreifing.

dig see grafa.

digestion see melting.

digestive see meltingarörvandi.

digit see 1. fingur, 2. tá, 3. tölustafur, 4. puti, 5. tölutákn.

digital see 1. fingurlegur, 2. stafrænn.

digitalis see 1. dígitalis, 2. fingurbjargarblóm.

dihybrid see tvíblendingur.

dike see gangur.

dilatation see 1. víkkun, 2. útvíkkun, 3. útþensluaðgerð.

dilation see 1. víkkun, 2. lenging, 3. strekking, 4. teyging, 5. þensla.

dilator see 1. víkkari, 2. stærir, 3. stærivöðvi.

dill see 1. blaðdilja, 2. dilja, 3. dilla, 4. sólselja.

diluent see þynningarefni.

dilute see 1. þynna, 2. þynntur.

dilution see 1. þynningur, 2. útþynning, 3. þynning.

dim see 1. deyfa, 2. dimmur.

dimension see 1. stærð, 2. víddartala, 3. vídd, 4. mál, 5. mælivídd.

dimer see 1. tvenna, 2. tvennd, 3. tvíliða.

dimorphism see 1. tvíbreytni, 2. tvíbrigðni.

dinghy see skipsbátur.

dingle see dalur.

dIode see 1. díóða, 2. straumbeinir, 3. tvískautalampi, 4. tvískauti, 5. tvistur.

dioecious see 1. tvíbýlinn, 2. einkynja, 3. sérbýlinn.

dip see 1. lot, 2. jarðlagshalli, 3. hnig, 4. halli, 5. bæs.

diploid see 1. tvílitnungur, 2. tvílitna, 3. tvílitningur.

diploidy see tvílitnun.

diploma see 1. skírteini, 2. þáttur.

diplomat see 1. stjórnarerindreki, 2. diplómat, 3. háttvís, 4. ríkiserindreki, 5. sendifulltrúi.

diplopia see 1. tvísæi, 2. tvísýni.

dipole see 1. dípóll, 2. tvipóla, 3. tvípóll, 4. tvískaut.

dipsomania see 1. drykkfeldniköst, 2. túradrykkja.

dipstick see 1. prófstrimill, 2. olíukvarði.

direct see réttur.

direction see 1. direkto, 2. stefna, 3. átt.

directions see direkto.

directive see 1. tilskipun, 2. fyrirmæli, 3. regla, 4. reglugerð, 5. stýring.

directivity see stefnuvirkni.

director see 1. forstöðumaður, 2. framkvæmdastjóri, 3. ráð, 4. skrifstofustjóri, 5. stjórnarmaður.

directory see 1. skrá, 2. notendaskrá, 3. stjórnun, 4. efnisskrá, 5. efnisyfirlit.

dirty see skítugur.

disability see 1. fötlun, 2. hreyfihömlun, 3. örorka.

disaccharide see tvísykra.

disadvantage see galli.

disaggregation see aðgreining.

disagreement see 1. ágreiningur, 2. missætti, 3. rifrildi.

disappointment see vonbrigði.

disarming see elskulegur.

disassemble see 1. baksmala, 2. sundra.

disaster see stórslys.

disc see 1. diskur, 2. kringla, 3. skifa.

discharge see 1. rennsli, 2. rennslismagn, 3. losun, 4. dreifing, 5. afhleðsla.

discharging see afgreiðsla.

discipline see 1. vísindagrein, 2. agi, 3. fag, 4. námsgrein, 5. þekkingarsvið.

disclose see 1. tilgreina, 2. sýna, 3. birta.

disclosure see 1. skýringar, 2. uppljóstrun, 3. upplýsingar.

disconnect see 1. aftengja, 2. frátengja, 3. rjúfa.

discontented see óánægður.

discord see 1. ágreiningur, 2. missætti.

discordance see 1. mislægi, 2. misræmi, 3. ósamræmi.

discordant see 1. misgerður, 2. ósamræmur.

discount see 1. afföll, 2. forvextir, 3. afvaxta, 4. afsláttur.

discounting see 1. afvöxtun, 2. forvaxtareikningur, 3. núvirðing.

discrepancy see misræmi.

discrete see 1. hógvær, 2. sundurlaus, 3. strjáll, 4. stakur, 5. stakstæður.

discretion see 1. þagmælska, 2. geðþótti, 3. gætni.

discrimination see 1. greiniviðbragð, 2. mismunun, 3. misrétti, 4. sundurgreining, 5. valdbeiting.

discriminator see 1. þröskuldur, 2. tíðniafmótari, 3. sundurgreinir.

disease see 1. sjúkdómur, 2. sýki, 3. mein.

disengage see 1. frátengja, 2. rjúfa.

disengagement see 1. höfuðlausn, 2. lausn.

disequilibrium see 1. jafnvægisskortur, 2. misvægi, 3. jafnvægismissir.

disgruntled see óánægður.

dish see 1. lægð, 2. skál.

dishonest see óheiðarlegur.

disillusionment see vonbrigði.

disinfection see 1. smiteyðing, 2. sótthreinsun.

disinflation see verðbólguhjöðnun.

disintegration see 1. sundrun, 2. molnun, 3. eyðing, 4. hrörnun.

disjoint see 1. aðskilinn, 2. sundurlægur.

disjunction see 1. sundurgreining, 2. aðskilnaður, 3. eðun.

disk see 1. þófi, 2. skífa, 3. diskur.

diskette see 1. disklingur, 2. plata, 3. skífa.

dislocation see 1. skekking, 2. tilfærsla, 3. liðhlaup, 4. ferilveila, 5. aflögun.

dismal see 1. fúll, 2. hræðilegur, 3. óþægilegur, 4. viðbjóðslegur, 5. dapur.

dismayed see hryllilegur.

dismiss see 1. reka, 2. afþakka.

dismissal see 1. uppsögn, 2. brottrekstur.

dismissive see skyndilegur.

disorder see 1. óregla, 2. óreiða, 3. röskun, 4. sjúkleiki, 5. truflun.

disorientation see 1. vistarfirring, 2. misáttun.

dispatching see verkröðun.

dispensary see lyfjabúð.

dispersion see 1. dreifing, 2. dreifni, 3. gliðnun, 4. skilnaður, 5. tvístrun.

displacement see 1. sveifluvik, 2. torleiðisfærsla, 3. tilfærsla, 4. slagrými, 5. færsla.

display see 1. sjóntæki, 2. sýning, 3. sýna, 4. skjátæki, 5. skjámynd.

displeased see óánægður.

disposal see 1. ráðstöfun, 2. niðurröðun, 3. losun.

disposition see hneigð.

dispute see rifrildi.

disregard see hundsa.

dissatisfied see óánægður.

dissection see 1. líkskurður, 2. vefjafláning.

dissension see 1. missætti, 2. ágreiningur.

dissent see 1. ágreiningur, 2. missætti.

dissimilation see 1. frálíking, 2. hljóðfirring.

dissipation see 1. dreifing, 2. eyðing, 3. orkutap.

dissociation see 1. klofning, 2. sameindasundrun, 3. persónuleikarof, 4. hugrof, 5. klofnun.

dissolution see 1. sundurlausn, 2. uppleysing.

dissolve see 1. bræða, 2. sameina.

dissonance see 1. mishljómur, 2. misræmi, 3. hugarmisræmi.

distal see 1. fjarlægur, 2. fjarri, 3. fjær.

distance see fjarlægð.

distasteful see óþægilegur.

distillation see 1. eiming, 2. eimun.

distinct see skýr.

distinguish see 1. aðgreina, 2. skynja, 3. greina.

distort see afbaka.

distortion see 1. aflögun, 2. afskræming, 3. bjögun, 4. liðtognun, 5. liðvinding.

distraction see 1. sundurdráttur, 2. truflun, 3. athyglisrof.

distraint see lögtak.

distress see 1. lögtak, 2. verkur.

distribution see 1. útbreiðsla, 2. dreififall, 3. dreififelli, 4. dreifing.

distributor see 1. rásaskiptir, 2. neistadreifir, 3. deilir, 4. dreifingaraðili, 5. kveikja.

district see 1. svæði, 2. sveit, 3. landssvæði, 4. hverfi, 5. hérað.

distrust see vantreysta.

disturbance see 1. hræring, 2. röskun, 3. truflun.

dithering see 1. hvarfl, 2. litfléttun.

diuretic see 1. þvagaukandi, 2. þvagræsilyf.

diurnal see daglegur.

divalent see tvígildur.

divergence see 1. sundurleitni, 2. sundurleitun, 3. sundurhvarf, 4. ósamleitni, 5. gliðnun.

divergent see 1. sundurvísandi, 2. afhverfur, 3. fráhallur, 4. fráhverfur, 5. ósamleitinn.

diversify see fjölþætta.

diversity see 1. fjölbreytileiki, 2. fjölbreytni.

divide see 1. kljúfa, 2. skipta.

dividend see arður.

divider see skilrúm.

dividers see 1. sirkill, 2. hringfari.

divinity see guð.

division see 1. deiling, 2. deild, 3. herdeild, 4. kvarðaeining, 5. skipting.

divorce see 1. skilja, 2. skilnaður, 3. hjónaskilnaður, 4. lögskilnaður.

divorced see fráskilinn.

dizziness see 1. sundl, 2. svimi.

do see gera.

doctor see læknir.

doctrinaire see 1. kreddufastur, 2. kreddukenndur, 3. kredduþræll.

document see 1. skjöl, 2. þáttur, 3. skjalbúa, 4. skjala, 5. skírteini.

documentary see 1. efni, 2. atriði.

documentation see 1. skjalbúnaður, 2. upplýsingaskjal, 3. skjöl, 4. skjalahald, 5. skilríki.

dodgy see 1. óáreiðanlegur, 2. ótraustur.

dog see 1. hundur, 2. grey, 3. öxulkragi.
dogfish see 1. deplaháfur, 2. háfur, 3. kyrrahafsþorskur.
doldrums see 1. kyrrabelti, 2. kyrrabeltið.
dolphin see gullmakríll.
domain see 1. ríki, 2. yfirráðasvið, 3. vettvangur, 4. veldi, 5. vébönd.
dome see 1. hvel, 2. kúpull, 3. ávala, 4. hvolf, 5. hvolfþak.
domestic see innlendur.
domicile see 1. bústaður, 2. heimili, 3. heimilisfang, 4. lögheimili.
dominance see 1. drottnun, 2. yfirráð, 3. drottnunargirni, 4. ríki.
dominant see ríkjandi.
domination see 1. drottnun, 2. yfirráð.
donation see 1. gjöf, 2. áheit.
donkey see asni.
donor see 1. arfgjafi, 2. gjafi, 3. rafgjafi.
door see 1. dyr, 2. hurð.
dope see 1. íbæta, 2. aðskotaefni, 3. ávanaefni, 4. dúklakk, 5. fíkniefni.
doping see 1. óhreinkun, 2. mengun, 3. íblöndun, 4. dúkstyrking, 5. íbæting.
dormant see 1. dormandi, 2. óvirkur.
dormouse see heslimús.
dorsal see 1. efri, 2. bakvöðvi, 3. baklægur.
dory see 1. pétursfiskur, 2. doría.
dosage see 1. lyfjagjöf, 2. skammtur, 3. skömmtun.
dose see 1. skammtur, 2. geislaskammtur, 3. Skammtþéttni.
dosimeter see 1. skammtamælir, 2. geislamælir, 3. geislaskammtamælir.
dosimetry see 1. geislunarmælingar, 2. Skammtamæling, 3. skammtamælingar.
dossier see málsskjöl.
double see tvöfaldur.
doubled see Tvípeð.
doublet see 1. tvístig, 2. tvíglerungur, 3. línutvennd.
doubt see 1. efa, 2. efi.
douche see 1. leggangaskolun, 2. steypibað, 3. úðabað, 4. ýrubað.
doughnut see 1. flákagat, 2. hólmi.
dovetail see 1. geirnegla, 2. geirnegling, 3. hurðarstyring, 4. geirnagli.
download see niðurflutningur.
downstream see réttsælis.
downtime see 1. legutími, 2. stöðvunartími, 3. viðlegutími, 4. dátími.
draft see 1. riss, 2. skissa, 3. uppkast, 4. víxill.
drag see 1. dragi, 2. viðnám, 3. tog, 4. kvartmílugjöf, 5. dragakraftur.
dragonet see skrautglitnir.
drain see 1. afrennslisop, 2. niðurfall, 3. karri, 4. keri, 5. tæma.

drainage see 1. þurrkun, 2. brottrennsli, 3. framfærsla, 4. Framræsla, 5. fráveita.
dramatic see snöggur.
dramatization see leikhverfing.
drastic see harkalegur.
draught see 1. djúprista, 2. loftstraumur, 3. súgur.
draw see 1. Jafntefli, 2. rista.
drawback see galli.
drawer see 1. tirkesto, 2. skúffa.
drawers see 1. tirkesto, 2. tratanto.
drawing see 1. dráttur, 2. teikning, 3. uppdráttur.
dread see hræðsla.
dreadful see 1. hræðilegur, 2. hryllilegur.
dream see draumur.
dreary see 1. dapur, 2. hræðilegur, 3. óþægilegur, 4. viðbjóðslegur.
dredge see 1. dýpka, 2. plægja, 3. plógur.
dredger see 1. dýpkunarprammi, 2. dýpkunarskip.
dressing see 1. umbúðir, 2. aðgerð.
dribble see 1. drjúpa, 2. eftirdropi.
drift see 1. rýmunardór, 2. tannatilfærsla, 3. skrik, 4. síll, 5. reka.
drill see 1. bor, 2. bora.
drilling see borun.
drink see drekka.
drip see 1. dreypa, 2. leki, 3. dreyping, 4. drjúpa.
drive see 1. akstur, 2. drif, 3. drifhögg, 4. hvöt, 5. tengsl.
driver see 1. bílstjóri, 2. sýslari, 3. rekill, 4. ökumaður, 5. drifrás.
drizzle see 1. súld, 2. úði.
dromedary see drómedari.
droop see hanga.
drop see 1. dropi, 2. fall, 3. yfirgefa.
droplet see 1. dropi, 2. smádropi.
drought see 1. úrkomuskortur, 2. þurrkar, 3. þurrkur.
drowsiness see 1. syfja, 2. deyfð, 3. svefnhöfgi.
drug see 1. læknisfræði, 2. lyf.
drugstore see lyfjabúð.
drum see 1. tromma, 2. tromla, 3. tunna, 4. skál, 5. hvolfstóll.
drunk see ölvaður.
drunken see ölvaður.
drupe see 1. steinaldin, 2. steinber.
dry see 1. þurr, 2. þurrka.
drying see 1. hersla, 2. Þurrkun.
dual see 1. tvískiptur, 2. tvítala, 3. tvíþættur, 4. tvöfaldur.
dualism see tvíhyggja.
dub see nefna.
dubbing see 1. blöndun, 2. hljóðsetning.
duck see 1. önd, 2. aliönd.
duct see 1. göng, 2. lögn, 3. rás.

ductile *see* 1. teygjanlegt, 2. teygjanlegur, 3. þanþolinn.
due *see* 1. gjaldkræfur, 2. útistandandi, 3. gjaldfallinn.
dues *see* 1. tollar, 2. félagsgjöld.
duke *see* hertogi.
dull *see* 1. bitlaus, 2. litlaus, 3. mattur.
dulse *see* söl.
dumb *see* 1. daufdumbur, 2. dumbur, 3. mállaus.
dumbfounded *see* hryllilegur.
dummy *see* 1. eftirlíking, 2. óekta.
dump *see* 1. fleygja, 2. undirbjóða, 3. tippun, 4. sorphaugur, 5. sorphaugar.
dumping *see* 1. undirboð, 2. sturttæming, 3. losun, 4. dumpning.
dune *see* 1. sandhóll, 2. sandalda.
dunnage *see* 1. skorður, 2. tróð.
duplex *see* 1. tvíáttasending, 2. tvöfaldur, 3. tvíþátta, 4. samtímistal, 5. samtímissending.
duplicate *see* 1. afrit, 2. samrit, 3. tvífald, 4. tvífalda, 5. tvírit.
duplication *see* tvöföldun.
duplicity *see* svik.
durability *see* ending.
durable *see* 1. endingargóður, 2. slitþolinn.
duramen *see* kjarnviður.
duration *see* 1. tími, 2. varandi, 3. tímalengd, 4. lengd, 5. binditími.
durian *see* 1. durianávöxtur, 2. dáraaldin.
during *see* meðan.
dusk *see* rökkur.
dust *see* ryk.
duties *see* álögur.
duty *see* 1. skylda, 2. tollur, 3. rekstur, 4. kvöð, 5. gjald.
dwarf *see* 1. dvergur, 2. dvergvaxinn, 3. kyrpa.
dwarfism *see* dvergvöxtur.
dwell *see* 1. dvalartími, 2. dvaltími, 3. búa, 4. bið, 5. dvöl.
dwelling *see* bústaður.
dyadic *see* tvennur.
dye *see* 1. litur, 2. lita, 3. litarefni, 4. litunarefni.
dyke *see* 1. berggangur, 2. stíflugarður, 3. gangur, 4. flóðgarður.
dynamic *see* 1. kvikur, 2. virkur, 3. viðgangur, 4. tápmikill, 5. kröftugur.
dynamical *see* 1. aflrænn, 2. hreyfanlegur, 3. hreyfifræðilegur.
dynamics *see* 1. efli, 2. kvika, 3. hreyfilögmál, 4. hreyfifræði.
dynamo *see* 1. rafall, 2. rakstraumsrafali.
dynamometer *see* 1. kraftmælir, 2. afkastamælir, 3. aflmælir, 4. átaksmælir, 5. hestaflabremsa.
dyne *see* 1. dyn, 2. dýn.
dysfunction *see* 1. starfstruflun, 2. vanvirkni.

dysgenic *see* 1. arfskemmandi, 2. arfspillandi.
dysgraphia *see* 1. rithömlun, 2. rittregða.
dyskinesia *see* 1. hreyfibilun, 2. hreyfingatregða.
dyslexia *see* 1. lesblinda, 2. lesröskun, 3. lesstol, 4. lestrarglöp, 5. lestrarörðugleikar.
dysmenorrhea *see* tíðaþrautir.
dysphagia *see* kyngingartregða.
dysphoria *see* ónotakennd.
dysplasia *see* misvöxtur.
dyspnea *see* 1. andnauð, 2. andþrengsli, 3. mæði.
dysprosium *see* 1. dysprósín, 2. dysprósíum.
dystrophy *see* 1. kyrkingur, 2. vaneldi, 3. vöðvavisnun, 4. korka.

E

eagle *see* örn.
ear *see* eyra.
earache *see* hlustarverkur.
eardrum *see* hljóðhimna.
earl *see* greifi.
early *see* snemma.
earmarking *see* eyrnamerking.
earnest *see* alvarlegur.
earnings *see* 1. ágóði, 2. tekjuafgangur, 3. gróði, 4. hagnaður.
earphone *see* eyrnatól.
earring *see* eyrnalokkur.
earth *see* 1. jörð, 2. Jörðin, 3. land, 4. jarðarbúar, 5. láð.
earthquake *see* 1. jarðskjálfti, 2. landskjálfti, 3. skjálfti.
earthshine *see* 1. grámi, 2. jarðskin.
easement *see* 1. ítak, 2. kvöð, 3. réttur.
eat *see* 1. éta, 2. borða, 3. drekka.
ebb *see* 1. útfall, 2. fjara.
ebonite *see* harðgúmmí.
ebony *see* 1. íbenviður, 2. svartviður, 3. tinnuviður.
eccentric *see* 1. sérvitringur, 2. vitlaus, 3. sérvitur, 4. ósammiðja, 5. miðskakkur.
eccentricity *see* 1. hringvik, 2. miðskekkja, 3. miðvik.
ecchymosis *see* 1. blóðhlaup, 2. flekkblæðing.
ecdysis *see* hamskipti.
echo *see* 1. bergmál, 2. gerviómur, 3. samsvar, 4. endurómur, 5. endurkast.
echolalia *see* bergmálstal.
eclecticism *see* 1. grasalækningar, 2. úrvalsstefna.
eclipse *see* myrkvi.
ecliptic *see* 1. sólbraut, 2. sólbaugur.
ecological *see* 1. vistfræðilegur, 2. vistrænn.
ecology *see* vistfræði.

econometrics see 1. hagmælingar, 2. hagrannsóknir, 3. hagtölfræði.

economic see 1. hagrænn, 2. nýtinn, 3. hagsýnn, 4. hagstæður, 5. hagfræðilegur.

economics see 1. auðfræði, 2. efnahagsmál, 3. fjárhagshlið, 4. hagfræði, 5. þjóðarafkoma.

economizer see sarpur.

economy see 1. hagsýni, 2. þjóðarbúskapur, 3. sparsemi, 4. rekstrarhagkvæmni, 5. efnahagur.

ecosystem see 1. vistkerfi, 2. lífríki, 3. umhverfiskerfi.

ecstasy see upphrifning.

ectoderm see útlag.

ectoparasite see útsníkill.

ectopic see 1. staðvilltur, 2. villtur.

ectoplasm see útfrymi.

ectropion see augnloksúthverfing.

eczema see 1. eksem, 2. þrotakláði, 3. þref, 4. exem, 5. eksi.

eddy see 1. straumhvirfill, 2. straumiða, 3. iðustraumur, 4. iða, 5. hvirfill.

edema see 1. bjúglopi, 2. bjúgur, 3. lopi.

edge see 1. spotti, 2. lína, 3. útlína, 4. egg, 5. brún.

edging see egg.

edifice see bygging.

edit see 1. sýsl, 2. tilreiða, 3. ritvinna, 4. ritstýra, 5. ritsetja.

editing see 1. gagnasetning, 2. ritsetning, 3. sniðsetning, 4. gagnainnsetning.

edition see útgáfa.

editor see ritill.

educable see bóknámshæfur.

education see 1. uppeldi, 2. menntun.

eel see 1. áll, 2. gleráll, 3. guláll, 4. bjartáll.

effect see 1. verkun, 2. afl, 3. afleiðing, 4. áhrif, 5. hrif.

effective see 1. virkur, 2. skilvirkur, 3. gildur, 4. ávirkur, 5. árangursríkur.

effectiveness see 1. virkni, 2. markvirkni.

effector see 1. svari, 2. stýrisameind, 3. hrifill.

efferent see 1. fráfærandi, 2. frálægur, 3. útsækinn.

efficiency see 1. nýtni, 2. orkunýting, 3. skilvirkni, 4. nýting, 5. hagkvæmni.

efficient see 1. hagkvæmur, 2. nýtinn, 3. skilvirkur, 4. afkastamikill.

effusion see 1. útsveim, 2. útflæði, 3. úthelling, 4. útstreymi.

egalitarianism see jafnréttisstefna

ego see sjálf.

egocentric see sjálflægur.

eidetic see sjónmunamaður.

eigenvalue see eigingildi.

eigenvector see eiginvigur.

eight see átta.

eighteen see átján.

eighty see áttatíu.

einsteinium see 1. einsteinín, 2. einsteiníum.

ejaculation see 1. sáðfall, 2. sáðlát.

ejection see útkast.

ejector see 1. útkastari, 2. útkastarastautur, 3. stautur, 4. slöngvari, 5. útkastarahringur.

elastic see 1. teyginn, 2. eftirgefanlegur, 3. teygjanlegur, 4. sveigjanlegur, 5. stæll.

elasticity see 1. fjaðurmagn, 2. fjöðrun, 3. næmi, 4. stælni, 5. teygni.

elastin see elastín.

elastomer see gúmmílíki.

elbow see 1. hné, 2. rörbeygja, 3. olnbogi.

election see val.

electric see rafknúið.

electricity see 1. rafmagn, 2. rafmagnsfræði, 3. raforka, 4. rafstraumur.

electrification see 1. rafmögnun, 2. rafvæðing.

electrocardiogram see 1. hjartarafrit, 2. hjartalínurit.

electrochemical see rafefnafræðilegur.

electrochemistry see rafefnafræði.

electrocoagulation see rafhleyping.

electrocution see rafdeyðing.

electrode see 1. rafskaut, 2. skaut, 3. rafnemi, 4. rafpóll.

electrodynamics see 1. rafsegulfræði, 2. rafkraftafræði.

electroencephalogram see 1. heilalínurit, 2. heilarafrit, 3. heilarit.

electrolysis see 1. rafsundrun, 2. rafgreining, 3. rafleysing.

electrolyte see 1. rafvökvi, 2. rafvaki, 3. raflausn, 4. jónefni, 5. rafklofi.

electromagnet see rafsegull.

electromagnetic see 1. rafsegulfræðilegur, 2. rafsegulknúið, 3. rafsegulknúinn.

electromagnetism see 1. rafsegulfræði, 2. rafsegulafl, 3. rafsegulmagn.

electrometer see 1. hleðslumælir, 2. rafhleðslumælir, 3. rafstöðuspennumælir, 4. spennumælir.

electron see 1. rafeind, 2. rafögn, 3. elektróna, 4. bakögn.

electronegative see 1. rafeindaneikvæður, 2. rafeindadrægur.

electronic see 1. rafeindastýrður, 2. rafeindatæknilegur, 3. rafeindavæddur, 4. raftæknilegur.

electronics see 1. rafeindatækni, 2. raftækni, 3. rafeindafræði.

electrophoresis see 1. rafdráttur, 2. jónfærsla.

electroplating see rafhúðun.

electroporation see rafgötun.

electropositive see 1. rafeindagæfur, 2. rafeindajákvæður.

electroscope see rafsjá.
electrostatics see rafstöðufræði.
electrotherapy see 1. raflækning, 2. rafmeðferð.
element see 1. frumefni, 2. frymi, 3. höfuðskepna, 4. smæð, 5. stak.
elements see 1. ero, 2. konsistigajo, 3. stafróf, 4. elemento, 5. fundamento.
elephant see fíll.
elephantiasis see 1. fílablástur, 2. fílaveiki, 3. fílildi.
elevate see 1. reisa, 2. hefja, 3. lyfta.
elevation see 1. landhæð, 2. hæð, 3. hækkun.
elevator see 1. hæðarstýri, 2. lyfta, 3. lyftijárn.
eleven see ellefu.
elimination see 1. afnám, 2. losun, 3. eyðing, 4. brottnámshvarf, 5. brottnám.
elite see 1. kjarni, 2. kjörhópur, 3. úrval, 4. yfirstétt.
ellipse see 1. sporbaugur, 2. öskjubaugur.
ellipsis see liðfall.
ellipsoid see 1. sporbaugsflötur, 2. sporvala, 3. sporvöluflötur, 4. sporbaugóttur.
elliptic see 1. sporöskjulaga, 2. oddbaugóttur.
elongation see 1. teygja, 2. lenging, 3. álengd, 4. framlenging, 5. ílengd.
else see annar.
elucidate see 1. þýða, 2. útlista, 3. útskýra.
emanation see 1. útstreymi, 2. geislaloft.
emasculation see 1. affræflun, 2. reðurstýfing.
embargo see 1. hafnbann, 2. kyrrsetning, 3. viðskiptabann.
embassy see 1. sendiherrabústaður, 2. sendinefnd, 3. sendiráð.
embed see 1. innmúra, 2. innsteypa.
embedding see 1. innfelling, 2. innsteyping, 3. steyping.
embezzlement see fjárdráttur.
embolism see 1. blóðrek, 2. blóðreksstífla.
embolus see 1. blóðreki, 2. blóðrek.
embossed see upphleyptur.
embossing see 1. stönsun, 2. pressun.
embrace see faðma.
embryo see 1. vísir, 2. fóstur, 3. fósturvísir, 4. frumfóstur, 5. kím.
embryology see fósturfræði.
emend see leiðrétta.
emerald see smeragður.
emergency see 1. hættuástand, 2. neyð, 3. neyðarástand, 4. neyðartilfelli, 5. neyðartilvik.
emery see 1. smergill, 2. smergel.
emetic see uppsölulyf.
emigrant see útflytjandi.
emigration see 1. brottflutningur, 2. hvítkornaútstreymi, 3. landflótti, 4. reikifrumnaútstreymi.

emission see 1. Losun, 2. útsending, 3. útstreymi, 4. útgeislun, 5. sáðræsing.
emissivity see 1. eðlisgeislun, 2. endurvarp, 3. geislagleypni.
emitter see eimir.
emmet see maur.
emollient see mýkjandi.
emotion see 1. geðbrigði, 2. geðshræring, 3. tilfinning.
emotional see 1. geðbrigðinn, 2. geðrænn, 3. tilfinningasamurlegur.
empathy see 1. hluttekning, 2. samkennd.
emphysema see 1. lungnaþan, 2. lungnaþemba, 3. vefjaþemba.
empirical see 1. reynsluvísindalegur, 2. empírískur, 3. mældur, 4. raunvís, 5. raunvísindalegur.
empiricism see 1. reynslustefna, 2. raunhyggja, 3. raunhyggjuaðferð.
employ see 1. nota, 2. beita, 3. brúka, 4. ráða.
employee see 1. starfsmaður, 2. launþegi.
employer see 1. vinnuveitandi, 2. atvinnurekandi.
employment see 1. atvinna, 2. ráðning, 3. staða, 4. starf, 5. vinna.
empty see 1. tómur, 2. auður.
empyema see holsígerð.
emulation see herming.
emulator see hermir.
emulsifier see 1. bindiefni, 2. fleytir, 3. þeytiefni, 4. ýruefni.
emulsify see 1. fleyta, 2. þeyta, 3. blanda, 4. vatnsblanda.
emulsion see 1. ýra, 2. ýrulausn, 3. vökvablanda, 4. vatnsblöndun, 5. þeytulausn.
enamel see 1. gljáhúð, 2. glerungur.
enamelled see 1. glerhúðað, 2. glerhúðaður, 3. glerjað, 4. glerjaður.
encapsulate see 1. húða, 2. hjúpa.
encapsulation see 1. húðun, 2. hjúpun, 3. gagnahjúpun.
encephalitis see heilabólga.
enchanting see 1. heillandi, 2. hrífandi.
enclosure see 1. fylgirit, 2. fylgiskjal.
encode see 1. kóta, 2. tákna, 3. kóða, 4. umtákna.
encoding see 1. hnitun, 2. kóðun, 3. umtáknun.
encounter see 1. hitta, 2. mæta.
end see gafl.
endemic see 1. einlendur, 2. landlægur.
ending see Endatafl.
endive see 1. endívusalat, 2. salatfífill, 3. vetrarsalat.
endocrine see innseytinn.
endocrinology see 1. innkirtlafræði, 2. vakafræði, 3. hormónafræði.
endocytosis see 1. innhverfing, 2. innfrumun, 3. innfryming.

endogamy see 1. innrækt, 2. innvensl, 3. skyldraæxlun.

endogenous see 1. innri, 2. háður, 3. innrænn.

endolymph see 1. völundarhússvökvi, 2. innanvessi.

endonuclease see kjarnsýruinnkljúfur.

endoparasite see innsníkill.

endopeptidase see prótíninnkljúfur.

endorse see 1. samþykkja, 2. styðja, 3. framselja, 4. aðhyllast, 5. ábekja.

endorsement see 1. áritun, 2. framsal, 3. stuðningur, 4. ábeking.

endosperm see fræhvíta.

endospore see 1. dvalagró, 2. dvalgró.

endothelium see 1. innþekja, 2. innhjúpur, 3. æðaþel, 4. þel.

endothermic see 1. aðverminn, 2. innverminn, 3. orkukræfur, 4. varmadrægur, 5. varmagleypinn.

endotoxin see inneitur.

endowment see 1. atgervi, 2. styrktarsjóður, 3. mundur, 4. hæfileikar, 5. fjárgjöf.

endurance see 1. flugþol, 2. þol.

endure see þola.

enemy see óvinur.

energized see hlaðinn.

energizer see þreklyf.

energy see orka.

enervation see taugarnám.

enforce see 1. framfylgja, 2. framkvæma.

engage see 1. virkja, 2. gleypa, 3. tengja.

engagement see 1. trúlofun, 2. ráðning.

engine see 1. vél, 2. aflvél, 3. hreyfill.

engineer see 1. vélstjóri, 2. verkfræðingur.

engineering see 1. vélfræði, 2. verkfræðistörf.

engorgement see offylli.

engram see minnisspor.

engross see gleypa.

engulfed see 1. kaffærður, 2. umlukinn.

enjoyable see þægilegur.

enlarge see stækka.

enough see 1. nægilegur, 2. nóg.

enquire see spyrja.

enquiry see spurning.

enrichment see 1. auðgun, 2 menntunarbót, 3. styrking.

entelechy see 1. markmiðshugsjón, 2. stýrikraftur.

enter see færa.

enterovirus see iðraveira.

enterprise see 1. fyrirtæki, 2. framtak.

enthalpy see 1. vermi, 2. varmagildi.

entire see heill.

entitlement see réttur.

entity see 1. heild, 2. stofnun, 3. fyrirtæki, 4. eining, 5. einindi.

entomology see skordýrafræði.

entrainment see 1. innblöndun, 2. meðsog.

entrance see aðgangur.

entrepreneur see 1. stjórnandi, 2. athafnamaður, 3. brautryðjandi, 4. frumkvöðull.

entropy see 1. vermibreyta, 2. óreiðustig, 3. óreiða.

entry see 1. færsla, 2. innfærsla, 3. inngangur, 4. innkoma.

envelope see 1. hjúpur, 2. umslag, 3. hylki, 4. bylgjumót, 5. bylgjuhjúpur.

envious see öfundarfullur.

environment see umhverfi.

environmentalism see 1. umhverfishyggja, 2. umhverfislöghyggja.

environmentalist see umhverfisverndarsinni.

envoy see sendiherra.

envy see 1. öfund, 2. öfunda.

enzyme see 1. ensím, 2. gerhvati, 3. lífhvati.

eon see aldabil.

eosinophil see 1. sýrufruma, 2. eósínfíkinn, 3. eósíntækur.

eosinophilia see 1. eósínfíklafjöld, 2. eósínfíklager.

ephemeral see skammvinnur.

ephemeris see 1. stjörnualmanak, 2. stjörnuhnitatafla.

epicentre see 1. sjálftamiðja, 2. skjálftamiðja.

epicondylitis see 1. ölnargnípubólga, 2. gnípubólga.

epicycle see aukahringur.

epidemic see 1. faraldur, 2. farsótt, 3. landfarsótt.

epidemiology see 1. faraldsfræði, 2. faraldursfræði, 3. farsóttafræði.

epidermis see 1. húðþekja, 2. þekjuhúð, 3. yfirhúð.

epigenesis see 1. formaukning, 2. formmyndun, 3. síðbirting.

epiglottis see 1. barkalok, 2. speldi, 3. barkakýlislok, 4. barkablaðka.

epilepsy see 1. flogaveiki, 2. niðurfallssýki, 3. flog.

epileptic see 1. flogaveikisjúklingur, 2. flogaveikur.

epinephrine see adrenalín.

epiphysis see 1. hlass, 2. liðhöfuð, 3. kast, 4. legghöfuð.

epiphyte see ásæta.

episode see 1. atvik, 2. kafli, 3. losunaróhapp.

epistasis see 1. yfirstæði, 2 yfirstæðni, 3. skán, 4. yfirsetning, 5. yfirstaða.

epistaxis see blóðnasir.

epistemology see þekkingarfræði.

epithelium see 1. þekja, 2. þekjuvefur, 3. útþekja.

epizootic see dýrafarsótt.

epoch see 1. viðmiðunartími, 2. mynstrasafn, 3. tími.

epsilon see epsílon.

equal see 1. eins, 2. jafn, 3. líkur.

equality see 1. jafnrétti, 2. jöfnuður.

equalize see jafna.

equalizer see 1. jöfnunartenging, 2. jafnari.

equation see 1. jafna, 2. líking.
equator see 1. miðbaugur, 2. miðjarðarlína.
equatorial see pólstilltur.
equilateral see jafnhliða.
equilibration see jafnvætting.
equilibrium see jafnvægi.
equinox see 1. jafndægri, 2. jafndægur, 3. jafndægrapunktur.
equip see 1. búa, 2. útbúa.
equipment see 1. tækjabúnaður, 2. útbúnaður, 3. virki, 4. tækjakostur, 5. rafbúnaður.
equitable see 1. sanngjarn, 2. réttlátur.
equity see 1. fjármagn, 2. réttlæti, 3. sanngirni.
equivalence see 1. jafngildi, 2. jafnvægi, 3. þýðingarjafngildi.
equivalent see 1. jafngildi, 2. jafngildur, 3. samsvarandi.
era see öld.
eraser see strokleður.
erbium see 1. erbín, 2. erbíum.
erect see 1. beinn, 2. uppréttur, 3. réttur.
erection see 1. limstaða, 2. reðurfylld, 3. reðurspenna, 4. reðurstaða, 5. reising.
erethism see viðbragðafjör.
ergometer see kraftmælir.
ergonomic see 1. vinnuhollur, 2. vinnuvistfræðilegur.
ergonomics see 1. vinnuhollustufræði, 2. vinnuvistfræði.
ergot see 1. korndrjóli, 2. meldrjóli.
erogenous see kynnæmur.
erosion see 1. fleiður, 2. tæring, 3. svörfun, 4. rof, 5. slit.
eroticism see kynnautn.
erotism see 1. kynlöngun, 2. kynnautn.
erotomania see 1. ástaræði, 2. kynæði.
erratic see 1. óreglulegur, 2. óstöðugur, 3. grettistak, 4. aðkomusteinn, 5. reikull.
error see 1. mistök, 2. skekkja, 3. óviljaverk, 4. óvissa, 5. villa.
eruption see 1. eldgos, 2. útþot, 3. útsláttur, 4. tannkoma, 5. gos.
erysipelas see 1. áma, 2. ámusótt, 3. heimakoma.
erysipeloid see 1. ámla, 2. ámulegur.
erythema see 1. hörundsroði, 2. roðaþot, 3. roði.
erythroblast see 1. rauðfrumuforveri, 2. rauðkornamóðir, 3. rauðkornskímfruma.
erythrocyte see 1. roðafruma, 2. blóðtala, 3. rauðfruma, 4. rauðkorn.
erythropoiesis see rauðkornamyndun.
erythropoietin see rauðkornavaki.
escape see 1. leki, 2. strok.
escutcheon see 1. merkiskjöldur, 2. skapahárastaða.
esker see malarás.
esophagus see vélinda.

essence see 1. bragðkjarni, 2. eðli.
essential see 1. brýnn, 2. eðlislægur, 3. lífsnauðsynlegur, 4. ómissandi.
establish see 1. staðfesta, 2. stofna, 3. stofnsetja, 4. ákveða, 5. ákvarða.
establishment see 1. fyrirtæki, 2. rekstrareind, 3. rekstrareining, 4. starfsstöð, 5. stofnsetning.
estate see 1. bú, 2. sveitasetur, 3. stórbýli, 4. stétt, 5. lögstétt.
estimate see 1. mat, 2. meta, 3. áætlun, 4. áætla.
estimates see 1. fjárlög, 2. matsstærðir.
estimating see mat.
estimation see 1. áætlun, 2. mat.
estimator see 1. metill, 2. áætlunartala.
estrogen see 1. kvenhormón, 2. estrógen.
estuary see 1. árós, 2. ármynni, 3. vík, 4. vogur.
etch see 1. grafa, 2. rista, 3. skera, 4. æta.
etching see 1. ætimynd, 2. æting.
eternal see æfinlegur.
ethanol see etanól.
ether see 1. etri, 2. ljósvaki, 3. eter, 4. eisa.
ethic see etiko.
ethics see 1. etiko, 2. siðfræði.
ethnic see 1. þjóðernislegur, 2. þjóðlegur.
ethnicity see þjóðerniseinkenni.
ethnocentrism see þjóðhverfa.
ethnography see 1. þjóðfræði, 2. þjóðlýsing.
ethnology see 1. þjóðfræði, 2. þjóðháttafræði, 3. þjóðháttarfræði.
ethologist see hátternisfræðingur.
ethology see 1. atferlisfræði, 2. hátternisfræði.
ethylene see etýlen.
etiolation see 1. skuggafölvi, 2. skuggavöxtur.
etiology see 1. sjúkdómafræði, 2 sjúkdómsorsakir, 3. orsakafræði.
etymology see orðsifjafræði.
eucaryote see 1. heilkjörnungur, 2. kjörnungur, 3. samkjörnungur.
euchromatin see dreiflitni.
eugenic see arfbætandi.
eugenics see 1. arfbætur, 2. góðkynjun, 3. kynbætur, 4. kynbótafræði, 5. kynbótastefna.
eukaryote see 1. heilkjörnungur, 2. kjörnungur, 3. samkjörnungur.
euphemism see skrauthvörf.
euphoria see 1. sældarvilla, 2. vellíðan.
euphoriant see 1. kætandi, 2. kætilyf.
euro see evra.
europium see 1. evrópín, 2. evrópíum, 3. evropín.
euthanasia see 1. líknardauði, 2. líknardráp.
evacuate see 1. fjarlægja, 2. rýma, 3. tæma.
evacuation see 1. tæming, 2. brottflutningur, 3. rýming.
evaluate see 1. virða, 2. ráða, 3. meta, 4. ákvarða, 5. finna.

evaluation *see* 1. gildisákvörðun, 2. mat, 3. ráðning.
evaporation *see* uppgufun.
evaporator *see* eimir.
evapotranspiration *see* 1. gufun, 2. gnóttargufun.
even *see* líkur.
evening *see* kvöld.
event *see* 1. mót, 2. tilefni, 3. atvik, 4. atriði, 5. atburður.
ever *see* 1. ætíð, 2. alltaf, 3. ávallt.
everlasting *see* æfinlegur.
eversion *see* úthverfing.
everyday *see* venjulegur.
eviction *see* útburður.
evidence *see* 1. sönnun, 2. vísbending, 3. sönnunargagn.
evil *see* 1. illur, 2. slæmur, 3. vondur.
eviscerate *see* 1. innyflahreinsa, 2. slægja.
evisceration *see* 1. líffæristæming, 2. innyflanám.
evolution *see* 1. framþróun, 2. þróun.
evolve *see* þróa.
exacerbation *see* elnun.
exactitude *see* nákvæmni.
exactly *see* nákvæmlega.
exaltation *see* 1. hrifning, 2. ofsagleði.
examination *see* 1. rannsókn, 2. prófun, 3. athugun.
examine *see* 1. rannsaka, 2. skoða, 3. yfirfara, 4. prófa.
example *see* dæmi.
excavation *see* 1. uppgröftur, 2. holun, 3. kvos.
excavator *see* 1. skefill, 2. tannholubor.
exceed *see* fara.
exception *see* 1. frábrigði, 2. frávik, 3. undantekning.
exceptional *see* 1. frábrugðinn, 2. sérstæður, 3. undantekning.
excess *see* 1. ofgnótt, 2. umfram.
exchange *see* 1. miðstöð, 2. símstöð, 3. Skiptamunur, 4. skipti, 5. víxlun.
exchanger *see* skiptir.
excision *see* brottskurður.
excitability *see* 1. viðkvæmni, 2. raferti, 3. ertanleiki, 4. næmi.
excitant *see* örvandi.
excitation *see* 1. span, 2. eggjun, 3. örvun, 4. rafsegulmögnun, 5. segulmögnun.
excite *see* 1. magna, 2. örva.
exciter *see* 1. segulmagnsvél, 2. segulmögnunarkerfi, 3. segulmögnunarvél, 4. segulvaki.
exclude *see* 1. útiloka, 2. yfirgefa.
exclusion *see* 1. aðskilnaður, 2. útskúfun, 3. útrekstur, 4. útilokun, 5. brottvísun.
excrement *see* saurindi.
excretion *see* 1. veising, 2. þveiti, 3. úrgangsefni, 4. úrgangslosun.

excursion *see* 1. útúrkrókur, 2. hreyfimörk.
excuse *see* fyrirgefa.
execute *see* 1. aftaka, 2. framkvæma, 3. inna.
execution *see* 1. fjárnám, 2. inning, 3. lögtak.
executive *see* 1. stjórnandi, 2. yfirmaður.
exempt *see* 1. undanþeginn, 2. undanþiggja, 3. undanskilja.
exemption *see* undanþága.
exercise *see* æfing.
exergy *see* aðgengisorka.
exertion *see* átak.
exfoliation *see* 1. fláning, 2. skinnflagningur, 3. flysjun, 4. flögnun.
exhalation *see* 1. eimur, 2. útöndun.
exhaust *see* 1. útblástur, 2. útblástursgas.
exhaustion *see* 1. örmögnun, 2. þurraustur.
exhaustive *see* 1. sligandi, 2. tæmandi.
exhibitionism *see* sýnihneigð.
existentialism *see* tilvistarstefna.
existing *see* þáverandi.
exit *see* 1. útgangur, 2. viðskil.
exobiology *see* geimlíffræði.
exocytosis *see* 1. útfryming, 2. útfrumun.
exoenzyme *see* útensím.
exoergic *see* orkugæfur.
exogamy *see* 1. aðkvæni, 2. óskyldraæxlun, 3. útæxlun, 4. útmægðir.
exogenous *see* 1. aðvífandi, 2. utanaðkomandi, 3. útrænn.
exon *see* 1. táknaraðarbútur, 2. útröð, 3. tjáröð, 4. táknröð, 5. tjáningarröð.
exosphere *see* úthvolf.
exothermic *see* 1. orkugæfur, 2. útverminn, 3. varmagæfur.
exotoxin *see* úteitur.
expand *see* 1. þenja, 2. stækka, 3. afþjappa, 4. leysa, 5. liða.
expander *see* 1. þani, 2. þenjari.
expansion *see* 1. þensla, 2. uppgangur, 3. stækkun, 4. liðun, 5. útþensla.
expect *see* vænta.
expectation *see* 1. meðalgildi, 2. vænting, 3. væntigildi, 4. vongildi.
expectations *see* 1. væntingar, 2. vændir.
expectorant *see* 1. slímlosandi, 2. hóstameðal.
expectorate *see* hrækja.
expectoration *see* hræking.
expedient *see* 1. hentugur, 2. ráðlegur, 3. úrræði.
expedite *see* flýta.
expeditious *see* hratt.
expenditure *see* 1. útgjöld, 2. gjöld, 3. kostnaður.
expense *see* kostoj.
expenses *see* 1. elspezo, 2. gjöld, 3. kostoj, 4. málskostnaður.
expensive *see* 1. sætur, 2. dýr (animal).

experience *see* reynsla.
experiment *see* tilraun.
experimental *see* tilraunalegur.
expiration *see* 1. gildislok, 2. útgufun, 3. útöndun.
explain *see* 1. útskýra, 2. þýða, 3. útlista.
explanation *see* skýring.
explicit *see* 1. skýr, 2. beinn, 3. skilmerkilegur, 4. augljós.
explode *see* 1. springa, 2. hafna, 3. hrekja, 4. sprengja.
exploit *see* 1. nýta, 2. hagnýta, 3. arðræna.
exploitation *see* 1. arðrán, 2. hagnýting, 3. nýting.
exploration *see* 1. könnun, 2. rannsóknir, 3. könnunarleiðangur, 4. innanþreifing, 5. innanrannsókn.
explosion *see* sprenging.
explosive *see* sprengiefni.
exponent *see* 1. eining, 2. undirhluti, 3. veldisvísir.
export *see* útflutningur.
exposition *see* skýring.
exposure *see* 1. lýsing, 2. váhrif, 3. útsýnisgreining, 4. upplægi, 5. afhjúpun.
express *see* 1. pressa, 2. tjá.
expression *see* 1. stærðtákn, 2. tjáning, 3. segð, 4. pressun, 5. útþrýsting.
expropriation *see* eignarnám.
extend *see* 1. víkka, 2. rýmka, 3. stækka, 4. stærð, 5. útvíkka.
extensibility *see* 1. þanhæfni, 2. réttihæfni, 3. stækkunarhæfni.
extension *see* 1. útvíkkun, 2. framlenging, 3. nafnauki, 4. rétting, 5. stækkun.
extensive *see* 1. víður, 2. rúmgóður, 3. dreifbær, 4. magnbundinn.
extensor *see* 1. réttir, 2. réttivöðvi.
external *see* 1. utanverður, 2. útvær, 3. ytri.
extinction *see* 1. aldauði, 2. útrýming, 3. útdauði, 4. svardeyfing, 5. slokknun.
extinguish *see* 1. ógilda, 2. slökkva, 3. upphefja, 4. deyfa.
extra *see* 1. auka, 2. aukapúls.
extracellular *see* utanfrumu.
extract *see* 1. kjarni, 2. útdráttur, 3. úrhluta, 4. sundur, 5. seyði.
extraction *see* 1. úrhlutun, 2. útdráttur, 3. tanndráttur, 4. framdráttur, 5. útfærsla.
extractor *see* 1. afdragi, 2. dragkló, 3. dragþvinga.
extrapolation *see* 1. framreikningur, 2. bryggjun, 3. útgiskun.
extrasystole *see* aukaslag.
extravasation *see* utanæðablæðing.
extreme *see* 1. öfgafullur, 2. öfgakenndur, 3. róttækur, 4. ystur, 5. fremstur.
extremity *see* 1. útjaðar, 2. útlimur.
extrinsic *see* 1. aðkomandi, 2. ytri.

extroversion *see* úthverfa.
extrovert *see* úthverfur.
exuberant *see* glaður.
exudate *see* vilsa.
exudation *see* 1. útferð, 2. vilsun.
exude *see* 1. vætla, 2. vilsa.
eye *see* auga.
eyeball *see* augnknöttur.
eyebolt *see* augabolti.
eyebrow *see* 1. augabrúnahár, 2. augabrún.
eyelid *see* 1. augnalok, 2. hvarmur.
eyepiece *see* augngler.

F

fabric *see* 1. vefnaður, 2. dúkur, 3. klæði.
fabrication *see* uppspuni.
face *see* 1. andlit, 2. flötur, 3. framhlið, 4. kortblaðsflötur, 5. yfirborð.
facet *see* 1. flötur, 2. reitur.
facies *see* 1. ásýnd, 2. hamur, 3. gerð, 4. gróðurskiki.
facilitation *see* 1. auðveldun, 2. flugvallarvirkt, 3. fyrirgreiðsla, 4. næmisaukning, 5. örvun.
facilities *see* 1. mannvirki, 2. búnaður, 3. aðstaða, 4. veitur.
facility *see* 1. aðstaða, 2. auðveldleiki, 3. færni, 4. hæfni.
facing *see* 1. skelveggur, 2. planrennsli, 3. plönun.
facsimile *see* 1. myndriti, 2. bréfasími, 3. fax.
fact *see* 1. málsatvik, 2. staðreynd.
factor *see* 1. þáttur, 2. liður, 3. samstarfsþáttur, 4. starfsstuðull, 5. stuðull.
factorial *see* 1. aðfeldi, 2. aðfaldaður, 3. aðfeldisfall, 4. hrópfall, 5. hrópmerktur.
factoring *see* 1. kröfukaup, 2. þáttun.
factory *see* 1. iðjuver, 2. verksmiðja.
facultative *see* 1. valbundinn, 2. valfrjáls, 3. kjörfrjáls.
fad *see* FAT.
fade *see* 1. dofna, 2. dofnun, 3. hjaðna.
fading *see* 1. hvarfl, 2. boðfall.
faeces *see* saur.
fail *see* 1. bila, 2. galli, 3. mistök.
failure *see* 1. púlshvarf, 2. bilun, 3. fósturlát, 4. galli, 5. óhapp.
faint *see* 1. vinglaður, 2. veikur, 3. óskýr, 4. óljós, 5. lasburða.
fair *see* 1. fallegur, 2. fagur, 3. fagurt.
faith *see* traust.
faithful *see* 1. áreiðanlegur, 2. traustur.
falciform *see* sigðlaga.
falcon *see* 1. fálki, 2. valur.

fall see 1. haust, 2. hlaupari, 3. falla, 4. dragreipi.
fallout see 1. úrfall, 2. ofanfall.
fallow see hvíldarland.
false see ósannur.
falsehood see lygi.
falsification see 1. rangtúlkun, 2. afsönnun, 3. fölsun, 4. hrakning.
family see 1. fjölskylda, 2. ætt, 3. hús, 4. kynþáttur.
fan see 1. blásari, 2. hverfilblásari, 3. kælivifta, 4. vifta.
fanning see fönun.
fantasy see 1. draumórar, 2. hugrríki, 3. hugríki, 4. hugarburður, 5. hugarflug.
far see langt.
fare see 1. fargjald, 2. farþegi.
farewell see bless.
farm see 1. bóndabær, 2. stórbýli, 3. búgarður, 4. bú.
farmer see 1. bóndi, 2. stórbóndi.
fascia see 1. bandvefsreifar, 2. fell, 3. mælaborð.
fascicle see knippi.
fasciculation see 1. knippismyndun, 2. vöðvaknippiskipringur, 3. vöðvatitringur.
fascinating see 1. heillandi, 2. hrífandi.
fascism see fasismi.
fashion see vani.
fast see 1. hraður, 2. þolinn, 3. hratt, 4. fljótur, 5. fastur.
fat see 1. fita, 2. olíuborinn, 3. spik, 4. holdugur, 5. fituborinn.
father see faðir.
fatigue see 1. magnstol, 2. málmþreyta, 3. máttstol, 4. þreyta, 5. þreytast.
faucet see krani.
fault see 1. bilun, 2. mistök, 3. misgengi, 4. annmarki, 5. galli.
faulting see misgengishreyfing.
fauna see 1. dýraríki, 2. fána.
fax see 1. símbréf, 2. símfax, 3. símabréf, 4. faxi, 5. bréfasími.
fear see 1. hræðsla, 2. óttast, 3. ótti.
feast see veisla.
feather see 1. fjöður, 2. nauðbeita.
feature see 1. þáttur, 2. svipkennni, 3. fitja, 4. svipkenni, 5. sérkenni.
feces see 1. hægðir, 2. saur.
fecundity see 1. frjómáttur, 2. frjósemi, 3. grómagn.
federation see 1. ríkjasamband, 2. sambandsríki, 3. bandalag, 4. samtök.
fee see þóknun.
feeble see 1. hrörlegur, 2. máttfarinn, 3. veikur.
feed see 1. éta, 2. mata, 3. mötun, 4. gefa, 5. efnisfærsla.
feedback see 1. svörun, 2. viðkvæði, 3. viðbrögð, 4. örvun, 5. endurgjöf.

feeder see 1. aðleiðir, 2. fæðir, 3. veitilína, 4. veititaug.
feeling see 1. kennd, 2. tilfinning, 3. grunur.
feet see fótur (foot).
feign see þykjast.
feijoa see joðber.
fellow see 1. karlmaður, 2. maður (man).
felon see 1. fingurgómsbólga, 2. ódæðismaður.
felt see flóki.
female see 1. kona, 2. kvendýr, 3. kvenmaður.
feminine see 1. kvenkyn, 2. kvenlegur.
feminism see 1. kvenréttindastefna, 2. feminismi, 3. femínismi, 4. kvenfrelsisstefna, 5. kvengerð.
fence see 1. vængbrík, 2. girði, 3. gerði, 4. girða.
fender see 1. aurbretti, 2. fríholt, 3. hjólhlíf, 4. þybba.
fenestration see götun.
fennel see 1. fennika, 2. sígóð, 3. finkull, 4. fennill, 5. fenníka.
ferment see 1. gerhvati, 2. gerja, 3. gerjast.
fermentation see gerjun.
fermium see 1. fermín, 2. fermíum.
ferrite see ferrít.
ferromagnetic see 1. járnseglandi, 2. járnsegulmagnaður.
ferrous see járnblandað.
ferruginous see 1. rústrauður, 2. ryðrauður.
ferryboat see ferja.
fertile see 1. lífsfrjór, 2. frjóvgaður, 3. frjór, 4. frjósamur.
fertility see frjósemi.
fertilization see frjóvgun.
fertilizer see 1. áburður, 2. gróðuráburður.
fester see grafa.
festival see veisla.
festivity see veisla.
fetish see 1. blótgripur, 2. blæti.
fetishism see 1. blætisdýrkun, 2. hlutadýrkun.
fetus see 1. fóstur, 2. myndfóstur.
feudalism see 1. lénsskipulag, 2. lénsveldi.
fever see 1. hitasótt, 2. sótthiti, 3. hiti, 4. köldusótt.
few see 1. fáir, 2. lítið.
fib see 1. köttur (cat), 2. ljúga, 3. skrökva.
fiber see 1. trefjar, 2. þráður, 3. trefja, 4. trefjaefni.
fibre see 1. þráður, 2. trefja.
fibreboard see 1. spónaplata, 2. trefjaplata.
fibril see 1. þræðlingur, 2. trefja, 3. þráðla, 4. taugatrefja, 5. sólþræðlingur.
fibrillation see 1. tif, 2. titringur, 3. vöðvakipringur, 4. flökt.
fibrin see 1. fíbrín, 2. traf, 3. trefjaefni.
fibrinogen see fíbrínógen.
fibrinolysis see 1. storkueyðing, 2. fíbrínleysing, 3. blóðstorkueyðing.
fibroblast see 1. fíbróblast, 2. trefjakímfruma.

fibrocartilage see trefjabrjósk.
fibrous see 1. trefjalíkur, 2. trefjóttur.
fictitious see 1. ósannur, 2. falskur.
fiddle see fiðla.
field see 1. hlutmynd, 2. sérgrein, 3. skurðsvæði, 4. svæði, 5. svið.
fierce see 1. ofsalegur, 2. trylltur.
fiesta see veisla.
fifteen see fimtán.
fifty see fimmtíu.
fig see fíkja.
fight see 1. slagsmál, 2. slást.
figure see 1. gervi, 2. skýringarmynd, 3. reikna, 4. ímynd, 5. ásýnd.
filament see 1. trefjungur, 2. glóðarþráður, 3. glóþráður, 4. glóvír, 5. hnappþráður.
filaria see þráðormur.
filbert see 1. stórheslihneta, 2. stórhesli.
file see 1. raða, 2. þjöl, 3. skrásetja, 4. röð, 5. Lína.
filiform see þráðlaga.
filing see skjalavistun.
fill see 1. fylla, 2. fylling.
filler see 1. fyllir, 2. fylling, 3. fylli, 4. staffylli.
fillet see 1. brautamót, 2. fiskflak, 3. flak, 4. flaka, 5. fylla.
film see 1. filma, 2. þynna, 3. skæni, 4. myndskæni, 5. girðilag.
filter see 1. hljóðsía, 2. ljóssía, 3. rafsía, 4. sía.
filtering see síun.
filtrate see 1. síuvökvi, 2. sía.
filtration see 1. gegnsíun, 2. síun.
fimbriate see kögraður.
fin see 1. barð, 2. fön, 3. uggi.
final see bakstæður.
finance see 1. fjármagna, 2. fjármál.
finances see 1. fjárhagsstaða, 2. fjárhagur.
financial see fjárhagslegur.
financing see 1. fjármál, 2. fjármögnun.
find see finna.
finder see 1. leitarsjónauki, 2. hjálparsjónauki, 3. hjálparkíkir, 4. uppkallsleitari.
finding see leit.
fine see 1. fagur, 2. fallegur, 3. fínn, 4. góður, 5. sekt.
finger see 1. fingur, 2. stautur, 3. landgangur, 4. puti.
fingernail see 1. fingurnögl, 2. nagli, 3. nögl.
fingerprint see fingrafar.
finish see 1. fínpússa, 2. frágangur, 3. frágangsvinna, 4. fínvinna, 5. áferð.
finished see tillbúinn.
finishing see 1. frágangsmeðhöndlun, 2. rétting.
fir see 1. fura, 2. þinur.
fire see 1. eldur, 2. íkveikja, 3. kveikja.

fireball see 1. eldhnöttur, 2. eldkúla, 3. loftsteinn, 4. urðarmáni, 5. vígahnöttur.
firewall see 1. netvörn, 2. eldvarnarþil.
fireworks see flugeldar.
firing see 1. kveiking, 2. kynding.
firm see 1. firma, 2. fyrirtæki.
firmament see festing.
first see 1. fystur, 2. fyrst.
fiscal see 1. skattalegur, 2. fjármálalegur, 3. hagsýsla.
fish see 1. fiskur, 2. fiska, 3. veiða.
fisherman see 1. fiskimaður, 2. sjómaður.
fishery see veiðar.
fishing see veiði.
fissile see 1. kleyfur, 2. kljúfanlegur, 3. kjarnkleyfur.
fission see 1. skipting, 2. kjarnaklofnun, 3. kjarnasundrun, 4. klofnun.
fissure see 1. togsprunga, 2. sprunga, 3. gjá, 4. glufa.
fit see 1. kast, 2. passa, 3. viðeigandi, 4. mátun, 5. krampakast.
fitness see 1. hæfi, 2. hæfni, 3. rekki, 4. fittni.
five see fimm.
fix see 1. aðlagast, 2. steypa, 3. staðarhnit, 4. staðarákvörðun, 5. skorða.
fixation see 1. negling, 2. vanabinding, 3. stöðnun, 4. vefsteyping, 5. skorðun.
fixative see 1. festiefni, 2. festivökvi, 3. litfestir.
fixture see 1. klemma, 2. festibúnaður.
flabby see 1. slappur, 2. hvapholda, 3. máttlítill.
flaccid see 1. linur, 2. mjúkur, 3. slakur.
flag see 1. gaumfáni, 2. stöðuvísir, 3. veifa, 4. merki, 5 fáni.
flagellum see svipa.
flame see 1. illskeytahríð, 2. logi.
flammable see eldfimur.
flange see 1. flangi, 2. tengikragi, 3. flans, 4. kragi.
flank see 1. brún, 2. hlið, 3. huppur, 4. síða.
flap see 1. flipi, 2. vængbarð, 3. spjald, 4. speldi, 5. flapi.
flare see 1. sólgos, 2. bugða, 3. ertiroði, 4. kyndill, 5. sólblossi.
flash see innblöndun.
flashlight see kyndill.
flat see 1. deyfður, 2. flatspegill, 3. flatur, 4. íbúð.
flatboat see 1. flatbytna, 2. flutningaprammi.
flatfish see 1. plattfiskur, 2. flatfiskur.
flattening see kúlufrávik.
flatulence see 1. uppþemba, 2. vindgangur, 3. vindþembingur.
flatus see 1. fretur, 2. garnavindur, 3. vindur.
flavin see flavín.
flavoprotein see flavóprótín.
flavour see smakka.

flaw *see* 1. galli, 2. krumpsprunga, 3. lýti, 4. skemmd, 5. veila.
flea *see* fló.
fleet *see* floti.
flesh *see* kjöt.
flexibility *see* 1. sveigjanleiki, 2. mýkt.
flexible *see* 1. beygjanlegur, 2. lausataug, 3. sveigjanlegur.
flexion *see* beyging.
flexor *see* 1. beygir, 2. beygivöðvi.
flicker *see* 1. blik, 2. flökt.
flight *see* 1. flugferð, 2. flug.
float *see* 1. fljóta, 2. fleyta, 3. flot, 4. flotholt, 5. flothylki.
floating *see* fljótandi.
flood *see* 1. vatnsflæmi, 2. flóð, 3. vatnselgur.
flooding *see* 1. offylling, 2. yfirfylling.
floodlight *see* 1. flóðlýsing, 2. flóðlýsingarkastari, 3. flóðlýsingarlampi.
floodplain *see* flóðslétta.
floor *see* gólf.
flora *see* 1. flóra, 2. plönturíki, 3. örverugróður, 4. jurtaríki, 5. gróðurríki.
florid *see* 1. blómstrandi, 2. hárauður.
flotation *see* 1. fleyting, 2. útgáfa.
flounder *see* 1. sumarflundra, 2. flundra.
flour *see* mjöl.
flow *see* 1. aðfall, 2. flæði, 3. flæðistærð, 4. rennsli, 5. straumstærð.
flowchart *see* 1. flæðirit, 2. leiðarit.
flower *see* 1. blóm, 2. blom.
flu *see* 1. inflúensa, 2. flensa.
fluctuation *see* 1. dúan, 2. flökt, 3. ölduhreyfing, 4. óstöðugleiki, 5. sveiflur.
fluid *see* 1. lögur, 2. vökvi, 3. straumefni, 4. kvikefni, 5. flæð.
fluke *see* 1. agða, 2. ikta.
fluorescence *see* 1. flúrskíma, 2. flúrskin, 3. flúrljómun, 4. flúrljóm, 5. flúrgeislun.
fluorescent *see* 1. flúrljómandi, 2. flúrskímandi.
fluorine *see* 1. flúor, 2. flúr.
fluorosis *see* 1. gaddur, 2. flúreitrun.
flush *see* 1. spúla, 2. skola, 3. flútt, 4. andlitsroði.
flute *see* 1. flauta, 2. ríla, 3. skora, 4. riffla, 5. rauf.
fluting *see* 1. skorur, 2. rifflar, 3. rifflur, 4. rilur, 5. hrufur.
flutter *see* 1. sláttur, 2. hvik, 3. flökta, 4. flökt.
flux *see* 1. segulkraftlínustraumur, 2. bráð, 3. flæði, 4. flaumur, 5. flóð.
fly *see* 1. fluga, 2. flúga, 3. fljúga.
flyback *see* 1. bakflug, 2. baksveifla, 3. baksveip.
flywheel *see* kasthjól.
foam *see* 1. löður, 2. froða, 3. freyða, 4. frauð.
focalize *see* staðbinda.

focus *see* 1. brennipunktur, 2. brennivídd, 3. sjúkdómshreiður, 4. taktræsir.
focusing *see* 1. myndstilling, 2. sambeining, 3. fókun, 4. einbeiting, 5. samstilling.
foe *see* óvinur.
foetus *see* fóstur.
fog *see* 1. þoka, 2. mistur.
fold *see* 1. felling, 2. brjóta, 3. falsa, 4. fella.
folder *see* mappa.
folding *see* 1. felling, 2. földun.
folk *see* þjóð.
follicle *see* 1. eitilbú, 2. kirtilblaðra, 3. kímstöð, 4. hárbelgur, 5. eggbú.
following *see* 1. eftir, 2. samkvæmt.
font *see* 1. stafagerð, 2. letur, 3. leturgerð.
fontanelle *see* 1. lindarblettur, 2. hausamót.
food *see* matur.
fool *see* svíkja.
foot *see* 1. fótur, 2. fet, 3. mastursfótur.
football *see* knattspyrna.
footballer *see* knattspyrnumaður.
footwear *see* 1. fótabúnaður, 2. skófatnaður.
for *see* 1. fyrir, 2. meðan, 3. til, 4. um.
forbearing *see* umburðarlyndur.
force *see* 1. kraftur, 2. styrkur, 3. þvinga, 4. áhrifamáttur, 5. neyða.
forceful *see* 1. máttagur, 2. sterkur.
forceps *see* 1. pinsetta, 2. töng.
forecast *see* 1. spá, 2. veðurspá, 3. framtíðarspá.
forecastle *see* 1. stafnlyfting, 2. lúkar.
foreground *see* forgrunnur.
foreign *see* 1. erlendur, 2. útlendur.
foreigner *see* útlendingur.
foreman *see* verkstjóri.
forename *see* skírnarnafn.
foreshore *see* flæðarmál.
foresight *see* 1. gætni, 2. skynsemi, 3. forsjálni.
forest *see* skógur.
forestry *see* skógrækt.
forever *see* 1. ávallt, 2. ætíð, 3. alltaf.
forge *see* 1. smiðja, 2. móta, 3. falsa, 4. eldsmiðja, 5. afl.
forged *see* 1. eldsmíðað, 2. þrykktur.
forging *see* 1. járnsmíði, 2. eldsmíðisgripur, 3. eldsmíði.
forgive *see* fyrirgefa.
forgiveness *see* fyrirgefning.
fork *see* 1. gaffall, 2. sjálfun.
form *see* 1. mót, 2. mynda, 3. lögun, 4. gera, 5. eyðublað.
formalin *see* formalín.
format *see* 1. sníða, 2. form, 3. forsnið, 4. forsníða, 5. framsetning.
formation *see* 1. syrpa, 2. myndun.
formative *see* 1. mótandi, 2. myndandi.

formatting *see* 1. forsnið, 2. sniðmótun.
former *see* 1. þáverandi, 2. formrammi, 3. mótunarverkfæri.
forming *see* 1. formun, 2. mótun.
formula *see* 1. efnaformúla, 2. formúla, 3. lyfjaforskrift.
forsake *see* yfirgefa.
forth *see* út.
forthright *see* heiðarlegur.
fortuitous *see* tilviljunarkenndur.
fortunate *see* hamingjusamur.
forty *see* fjörutíu.
forum *see* 1. málþing, 2. miðstöð, 3. tölvutorg, 4. vettvangur.
forward *see* 1. framátt, 2. senda, 3. framsenda, 4. fram, 5. avanulo.
forwards *see* 1. antaũa, 2. antaũen, 3. avanulo, 4. ekspedi, 5. trudema.
fossa *see* 1. gróf, 2. skál, 3. drag.
fossil *see* steingervingur.
foul *see* 1. fúll, 2. mengaður.
found *see* 1. bræða, 2. steypa.
foundation *see* 1. sökkull, 2. stofnun, 3. grunnur, 4. grundvöllur, 5. undirstaða.
fount *see* brunnur.
fountain *see* brunnur.
four *see* 1. fjórir, 2. fjögur, 3. fjórar.
fourteen *see* fjórtán.
fovea *see* 1. sjóngróf, 2. sjónugróf, 3. nethimnugróf.
fox *see* 1. refur, 2. tófa.
fractal *see* 1. brotamynd, 2. broti.
fractile *see* hlutsfallsmark.
fraction *see* brot.
fractional *see* þrepskiptur.
fractionation *see* 1. hlutun, 2. þrepræktun, 3. þáttun, 4. þætting, 5. þættun.
fracture *see* 1. beinbrot, 2. bergsprunga, 3. brestur, 4. brot, 5. sprunga.
fragile *see* 1. brothættur, 2. viðkvæmur, 3. stökkur.
fragment *see* 1. brak, 2. brot, 3. flisar, 4. örfitja, 5. örstak.
fragmentation *see* 1. hlutun, 2. tvístur, 3. tvístringur, 4. brot, 5. tvístrun.
fragmented *see* 1. sundurskiptur, 2. tvístraður.
frail *see* veikur.
frame *see* 1. rammi, 2. bindingshólf, 3. undirbygging, 4. standur, 5. hylki.
framework *see* 1. grindarvirki, 2. rammi.
franchise *see* 1. einkaumboð, 2. sérleyfi, 3. notkunarréttur, 4. framleiðsluréttur, 5. einkasöluleyfi.
francium *see* 1. fransín, 2. fransíum.
frankincense *see* 1. reykelsi, 2. reykelsistré.
fraud *see* 1. fals, 2. fjársvik.
fray *see* slagsmál.

free *see* laus.
freedom *see* frelsi.
freelance *see* lausamaður.
freewheel *see* fríhjól.
freeze *see* 1. frjósa, 2. stífna, 3. kuldakast, 4. frostkafli, 5. festast.
freezing *see* 1. frysting, 2. sambræðsla, 3. úrbræðsla.
freight *see* 1. fragt, 2. flugfragt, 3. farmur.
freighter *see* 1. fragtvél, 2. vöruflutningaskip, 3. vöruflutningavél, 4. flutningaskip.
frequency *see* 1. fjöldi, 2. tíðni, 3. tídd.
frequently *see* oft.
fresh *see* ferskur.
freshwater *see* ferskvatn.
friar *see* bróðir.
friction *see* 1. viðnám, 2. núningskraftur, 3. núningsmótstaða, 4. núningsviðnám, 5. núningur.
friend *see* 1. vinur, 2. vinkona.
friendly *see* 1. vænn, 2. vingjarnlegur, 3. vinsamlegur.
friendship *see* vinátta.
fright *see* hræðsla.
frigid *see* 1. kaldlátur, 2. kynkaldur, 3. ískaldur.
frigidity *see* 1. kaldlæti, 2. kynkuldi, 3. ískuldi.
fringe *see* 1. egg, 2. rák, 3. víxlarák.
frog *see* froskur.
front *see* 1. skil, 2. skilflötur, 3. framan, 4. fram, 5. frammæltur.
frontal *see* framan.
frontier *see* 1. landamærahéruð, 2. landamæri.
frostbite *see* kal.
frozen *see* 1. frystur, 2. freðinn, 3. frosinn.
fructose *see* 1. frúktósi, 2. aldinsykur, 3 ávaxtasykur.
fruit *see* 1. ávöxtur, 2. aldin, 3. gróður, 4. nytjagróður.
frustrate *see* 1. hefta, 2. fatra.
frustration *see* 1. vonbrigði, 2. hefting, 3. fatur.
ft *see* verði.
fuel *see* 1. brenni, 2. eldsneyti, 3. orkugjafi.
fugue *see* minnistap.
fulcrum *see* 1. liður, 2. veltiás, 3. bakhjarl, 4. vogarás.
full *see* fullur.
fulmar *see* 1. fýll, 2. múkki.
fume *see* 1. reykur, 2. eimur, 3. gufa, 4. haladzi.
fumes *see* 1. haladzo, 2. haladzi.
fumigation *see* 1. eiturúðun, 2. svæling.
function *see* 1. fall, 2. virka, 3. virkni, 4. starfsháttur, 5. starfsemi.
functional *see* 1. virkur, 2. hagnýtur, 3. hlutverkslegur, 4. nothæfur, 5. starfandi.

functionalism see 1. starfsemishyggja, 2. verkhyggja, 3. virknishyggja, 4. nýtistefna, 5. fünksjónalismi.
fund see 1. fjármagna, 2. höfuðstóll, 3. sjóður.
fundamental see undirstöðuatriði.
fundamentals see stafróf.
funding see fjármögnun.
fungi see 1. sveppir, 2. sveppur.
fungicidal see 1. sveppadeyðandi, 2. sveppdeyðandi, 3. sveppeyðandi.
fungicide see 1. sveppeyðir, 2. sveppadeyðir.
fungous see sveppasýktur.
fungus see 1. sveppur, 2. holdfrauð.
funnel see 1. áfyllingartrekt, 2. reykháfur, 3. trekt.
furnace see 1. ofn, 2. bræðsluofn, 3. miðstöðvarketill.
furniture see innbú.
furuncle see 1. graftarkýli, 2. kýli, 3. blóðkýli.
furunculosis see 1. kýlasótt, 2. kýlasýki.
fuse see 1. tengjast, 2. öryggi, 3. var, 4. bræða, 5. bræðivar.
fusible see bræðanlegur.
fusiform see 1. snældulaga, 2. spólulaga.
fusion see 1. bræðsla, 2. sjóntenging, 3. kjarnasamruni, 4. bráðnun, 5. samruni.

G

g see þyngdarhröðun.
gabbro see gabbró.
gable see 1. bæjarþil, 2. gafl, 3. húsgafl.
gadolinium see 1. gadólín, 2. gadólíníum, 3. gadólín.
gain see 1. hagnaður, 2. mögnun, 3. mögnunarstuðull, 4. vinningur, 5. ágóði.
gal see 1. stelpa, 2. stúlka.
galactose see galaktósi.
galangal see 1. dverggalangal, 2. galangarót, 3. stórgalangal.
galaxy see 1. stjörnuþoka, 2. vetrarbraut, 3. Vetrarbrautin.
galc see 1. hvassviðri, 2. stormur.
gall see gallepli.
gallbladder see gallblaðra.
gallery see 1. listskrubba, 2. sjáver, 3. olíugöng, 4. myndhús, 5. listvör.
galley see 1. eldhús, 2. galeiða.
gallium see 1. gallín, 2. gallíum.
galvanism see 1. efnarafmagn, 2. galvanílækning.
galvanization see galvanhúðun.
galvanize see 1. galva, 2. galvanhúða, 3. rafhúða.

galvanometer see 1. galvínmælir, 2. veikstraumsmælir, 3. rafstraumsmælir, 4. galvanímælitæki, 5. galvanímælir.
gambit see Bragð.
gamete see 1. brúðfruma, 2. kímfruma, 3. kynfruma.
gametocyte see 1. kynfrumumóðir, 2. kynfrumumóðurfruma, 3. forkynfruma.
gametogenesis see kynfrumumyndun.
ganglion see 1. hnoða, 2. sinarhlaupbelgur, 3. taugahnoð, 4. taugahnoða.
gangrene see 1. kolbrandur, 2. ýldudrep, 3. brandur, 4. átudrep.
gangway see landgangur.
gantry see 1. gálgi, 2. toggálgi.
gap see 1. þekjubil, 2. bil, 3. geil, 4. kjaftstærð, 5. op.
gaper see sandskel.
garage see 1. bílaverkstæði, 2. bílskúr.
garden see garður.
garfish see 1. hornfiskur, 2. horngæla.
garlic see geirlaukur.
gas see 1. bensín, 2. brennslugas, 3. loft, 4. lofttegund.
gaseous see 1. gaskenndur, 2. loftkenndur.
gasification see Gösun.
gasket see 1. pakkning, 2. þétti, 3. vélaþétti.
gasoline see bensín.
gassing see 1. gasmyndun, 2. uppgufun, 3. suða.
gastralgia see magaverkur.
gastroenterology see 1. meltingarfærafræði, 2. meltingarsjúkdómafræði.
gastrulation see 1. holfósturmyndun, 2. vembilsmyndun.
gate see 1. hlið, 2. rökhlið, 3. gátt, 4. stýriskaut.
gateway see 1. gátt, 2. milligátt, 3. millinetagátt, 4. tollgæsluvöllur.
gauge see 1. mælitæki, 2. sporvídd, 3. stilla, 4. mát, 5. mæla.
gaunt see 1. dapur, 2. mjór, 3. þunnur.
gauze see 1. grisja, 2. sáraléreft.
gay see 1. glaðlyndur, 2. glaður.
gear see 1. tannhjólakerfi, 2. tannhjólasamstæða, 3. tannhjól, 4. gírkassi, 5. ganghraðastig.
gearbox see gírkassi.
gearing see 1. tannhjólasett, 2. tannhjólatenging, 3. skuldsetning, 4. gírkassi, 5. gíring.
gearshift see 1. gírstöng, 2. gírskipting.
gel see 1. hlaup, 2. kvoða.
gelatin see 1. gelatín, 2. límhlaup.
gelatinous see hlaupkenndur.
gender see kyn.
gene see 1. erfðavísir, 2. gen, 3. arfstofn, 4. arfberi, 5. kon.
general see 1. alhæfur, 2. almennt, 3. almennur, 4. hershöfðingi.

generalisation *see* 1. hæfing, 2. sameining, 3. alhæfing.
generalization *see* 1. alhæfing, 2. yfirfærsla, 3. algilding.
generalize *see* 1. algilda, 2. alhæfa, 3. hæfa.
generation *see* 1. kynslóðartími, 2. framleiðsla, 3. kynslóð.
generative *see* kynferðislegur.
generator *see* 1. gjafi, 2. rafali, 3. rafall, 4. spönnuður, 5. vaki.
generic *see* 1. stofnrænn, 2. almennur, 3. sameiginlegur.
generosity *see* 1. rausnarskapur, 2. gjafmildi, 3. örlæti.
genesis *see* 1. myndun, 2. sköpun, 3. upphaf, 4. uppruni.
genetics *see* 1. erfðafræði, 2. ættgengisfræði.
genitalia *see* 1. getnaðarfæri, 2. kynfæri.
genitals *see* kynfæri.
genius *see* 1. snilligáfa, 2. snillingur.
genocide *see* þjóðarmorð.
genome *see* 1. genamengi, 2. genóm.
genotype *see* 1. erfðafar, 2. erfðagervi, 3. arfgerð.
gentle *see* mjúkur.
gentleman *see* herra.
genuine *see* 1. ekta, 2. ósvikinn, 3. sannur, 4. upprunalegur.
genus *see* ættkvísl.
geochemistry *see* jarðefnafræði.
geodesic *see* 1. gagnvegur, 2. rakleið.
geodesy *see* 1. landmælingafræði, 2. landmælingar, 3. landmæling.
geographical *see* landfræðilegur.
geography *see* landafræði.
geology *see* jarðfræði.
geomagnetism *see* 1. jarðsegulmagn, 2. jarðsegulfræði.
geometry *see* 1. rúmfræði, 2. flatarmálsfræði, 3. hornafræði.
geomorphology *see* landmótunarfræði.
geophone *see* 1. skjálftanemi, 2. sveiflunemi.
geophysics *see* jarðeðlisfræði.
geriatrics *see* 1. öldrunarlækningar, 2. ellilækningar, 3. ellisjúkdómafræði.
germ *see* 1. örvera, 2. kím.
germanium *see* 1. german, 2. germaníum.
germination *see* spírun.
gerontology *see* öldrunarfræði.
gestalt *see* skynheild.
gestation *see* 1. meðgöngutími, 2. þungun, 3. meðganga.
get *see* 1. koma, 2. verða, 3. fá.
getter *see* 1. fangefni, 2. hremmir.
ghastly *see* 1. hræðilegur, 2. viðbjóðslegur.
ghost *see* draugur.

giant *see* 1. risi, 2. risastjarna.
giantism *see* risavöxtur.
gift *see* gjöf.
gigantism *see* 1. risavöxtur, 2. tröllvöxtur.
gill *see* tálkn.
gillnet *see* lagnet.
gimlet *see* handbor.
ginkgo *see* 1. musterishneta, 2. musteristré, 3. gingkó.
girder *see* 1. bjálki, 2. biti.
girl *see* 1. stelpa, 2. stúlka.
girlfriend *see* vinkona.
give *see* gefa.
gizzard *see* fóarn.
glacier *see* 1. skriðjökull, 2. jökull.
glad *see* glaður.
gland *see* 1. hringþétti, 2. kirtill, 3. þéttihringur, 4. þéttikragi.
glare *see* 1. endurskin, 2. glýja, 3. ofbirta.
glass *see* 1. glas, 2. gler, 3. flaska, 4. lyfjaglas, 5. glaso.
glasses *see* 1. glas, 2. glaso, 3. gleraugu, 4. vitra, 5. vitro.
glaucoma *see* gláka.
glaze *see* 1. glans, 2. gljái, 3. glerungur.
glia *see* 1. fylgdarfrumur, 2. grannfrumur, 3. taugatróð.
glide *see* 1. svif, 2. svífa, 3. skriðhljóð, 4. renniflug, 5. rennifljúga.
global *see* 1. alþjóðlegur, 2. heill, 3. hnattrænn, 4. víðfeðmur, 5. víðtækur.
globe *see* 1. klukka, 2. veldishnöttur, 3. kúpull, 4. hnattlíkan, 5. jörðin.
globin *see* glóbín.
globose *see* hnöttóttur.
globular *see* 1. hnattlaga, 2. kúlulaga.
globule *see* 1. kúluþoka, 2. smádropi, 3. hnoðri.
globulin *see* 1. glóbúlín, 2. glóbulín.
glomerule *see* 1. gaukull, 2. hnoðri, 3. nýrahnoðri.
glomerulonephritis *see* 1. nýrnahnoðrabólga, 2. nýrahnoðrabólga.
glomerulus *see* 1. hnoðri, 2. hnoða, 3. æðhnoðri, 4. blómhnoða, 5. gaukull.
gloomy *see* dapur.
gloss *see* 1. fágaður, 2. gljái, 3. þýðing.
glottis *see* 1. raddglufa, 2. raddrauf.
glove *see* hanski.
gloves *see* 1. fingravettlingar, 2. hanskar.
glucagon *see* glúkagon.
glucosamine *see* glúkósamín.
glucose *see* 1. þrúgusykur, 2. glúkósi.
glucoside *see* glúkósíð.
glue *see* 1. lím, 2. líma.
gluten *see* glúten.
glycerin *see* glýserín.

glycerine *see* 1. glýseról, 2. glysserín.
glycerol *see* glýseról.
glycine *see* 1. glý, 2. glysín, 3. glýsín.
glycogen *see* 1. dýramjölvi, 2. dýrasterkja, 3. glýkógen.
glycogenesis *see* glýkógenmyndun.
glycogenolysis *see* 1. glýkógenlosun, 2. glýkógensundrun.
glycolysis *see* 1. sykurrof, 2. sykurleysing, 3. sykrusundrun, 4. sykursundrun.
glycoprotein *see* 1. glýkóprótín, 2. sykruhvíta, 3. sykurhvíta.
glycoside *see* 1. glúkósíð, 2. glýkósíð.
glycosuria *see* sykurmiga.
gnomon *see* 1. kambur, 2. sólsproti, 3. sproti.
gnosis *see* vit.
goal *see* 1. mark, 2. markmið, 3. takmark, 4. tilgangur.
goat *see* geit.
goddess *see* gyðja.
goggles *see* 1. gleraugu, 2. suðugleraugu, 3. hlífðargleraugu.
goitre *see* skjaldkirtilsauki.
gold *see* gull.
golden *see* gull.
gonad *see* kynkirtill.
goniometer *see* 1. stefnumælir, 2. hornamælir, 3. hornmælir.
gonorrhea *see* lekandi.
good *see* góður.
goodbye *see* 1. bless, 2. sjáumst.
goods *see* 1. varningur, 2. vörur.
goodwill *see* 1. álit, 2. viðskiptavild, 3. virðing.
goose *see* 1. gæs, 2. aligæs.
gopher *see* snati.
gorge *see* þveröngull.
goshawk *see* gáshaukur.
gossip *see* 1. blaðra, 2. masa.
govern *see* stilla.
government *see* 1. stjórn, 2. ríkisstjórn, 3. stjórnun, 4. ríkisvald, 5. ríki.
governor *see* 1. ríkisstjóri, 2. fylkisstjóri, 3. gangráður, 4. hraðaráður, 5. landstjóri.
grab *see* 1. halda, 2. gripskófla, 3. gripkrani, 4. grípa.
graben *see* 1. sigdæld, 2. sigdalur.
grade *see* 1. stiga, 2. flokkun, 3. gæðaflokkur, 4. stærða, 5. stig.
grader *see* 1. veghefill, 2. flokkunarvél, 3. jafnari.
gradient *see* 1. fallandi, 2. stigull.
graduation *see* 1. gráðuskipting, 2. stigskipting.
graft *see* 1. græðlingur, 2. græði, 3. ágræðsla.
grain *see* korn.
gram *see* 1. g, 2. gramm.
grammar *see* málfræði.

grammatical *see* málfræðilegur.
gramme *see* gramm.
grand *see* 1. stór, 2. mikill.
grandeur *see* stærð.
grandfather *see* afi.
grandmother *see* amma.
grandparent *see* geavo.
grandson *see* barnabarn.
granite *see* granit.
grant *see* 1. samþykkja, 2. viðurkenna, 3. styrkur, 4. veita, 5. gjafafé.
granular *see* kornóttur.
granulation *see* 1. sárakörtur, 2. sólýringur, 3. kornamyndun, 4. kornáferð, 5. bólguholdgun.
granule *see* 1. ögn, 2. sólkorn, 3. sólreitur, 4. sólýra, 5. korn.
granulocyte *see* 1. kornfruma, 2. kyrningur.
granuloma *see* 1. bólguhnúður, 2. gleypifrumnahnúður, 3. holdgunarhnúður, 4. átfrumuhnúður.
granulomatous *see* hnúðóttur.
grapefruit *see* 1. greip, 2. greipaldin, 3. greipaldintré, 4. tröllaldin, 5. yggli.
grapevine *see* 1. lausafregn, 2. orðrómur.
graph *see* 1. graf, 2. hnitarit, 3. línurit, 4. mynd, 5. myndrit.
graphic *see* 1. grafískur, 2. myndrænn.
graphical *see* myndrænn.
graphics *see* teiknun.
graphite *see* grafít.
grass *see* gras.
grasshopper *see* engispretta.
grassland *see* 1. graslendi, 2. beitiland, 3. haglendi, 4. valllendi.
grate *see* 1. rimlagrind, 2. raspa.
grateful *see* þakklátur.
graticule *see* bauganet.
gratification *see* fullnæging.
gratified *see* ánægður.
grating *see* 1. grind, 2. ljósgreiða, 3. raufagler.
gratitude *see* þökk.
grave *see* alvarlegur.
gravel *see* 1. þvagsandur, 2. möl, 3. malarsandur.
gravitation *see* 1. aðdráttarafl, 2. þyngdarafl, 3. þyngdaráhrif, 4. þyngdarverkun.
gravity *see* 1. þyngd, 2. þyngdarafl.
gray *see* 1. grár, 2. grei, 3. gy.
grayling *see* harri.
grease *see* 1. feiti, 2. legufeiti, 3. smurkoppur.
great *see* 1. mikill, 2. stór.
greatness *see* stærð.
green *see* 1. grænn, 2. grænt.
greet *see* heilsa.
gregariousness *see* 1. hjarðhvöt, 2. mannblendni.
grenadiers *see* langhalar.

grey *see* 1. grár, 2. grámun.
grid *see* 1. dreifikerfi, 2. rist, 3. netkort, 4. net, 5.
  hnitakerfi.
grim *see* dapur.
grind *see* 1. slípa, 2. mala, 3. mylja.
grinding *see* slípun.
grindstone *see* 1. hverfisteinn, 2. slípisteinn, 3.
  steinbrýni.
grip *see* 1. handfang, 2. tak.
grippe *see* 1. flensa, 2. inflúensa.
groan *see* 1. andvarpa, 2. stuna, 3. stynja.
groin *see* 1. lærkriki, 2. nári.
grommet *see* 1. gúmmíkragi, 2. kragi, 3. skífumiðja.
groove *see* 1. gróf, 2. spor, 3. renna, 4. gróp, 5. rás.
gross *see* 1. brúttó, 2. vergur.
ground *see* 1. mold, 2. grund, 3. grundo, 4.
  jarðaryfirborð, 5. jarðsamband.
grounding *see* 1. strand, 2. bannsetning, 3.
  flugbann.
groundnut *see* 1. jarðpera, 2. kartöflubaun, 3.
  svarðarhneta.
grounds *see* 1. tereno, 2. tersurfaco, 3. tero, 4. bazo,
  5. terkonekti.
groundwater *see* 1. jarðvatn, 2. grunnvatn.
group *see* 1. sveit, 2. dálkur, 3. flokkur, 4.
  grunnfylki, 5. grúpa.
grove *see* lundur.
grow *see* 1. verða, 2. vaxa.
growler *see* 1. borgarísmoli, 2. urrari, 3. urri.
growth *see* 1. vöxtur, 2. aukning.
gruesome *see* 1. hræðilegur, 2. hryllilegur, 3.
  andstyggilegur.
gruff *see* 1. óvingjarnlegur, 2. óvænn.
guanine *see* 1. gúanín, 2. gvanín.
guarantee *see* 1. ábyrgð, 2. ábyrgðarskírteini, 3.
  trygging.
guard *see* 1. hlíf, 2. vörður, 3. hlífðarbúnaður, 4.
  hlífigrind.
guava *see* 1. eldaldin, 2. gvava.
gudgeon *see* öggur.
guess *see* halda.
guest *see* gestur.
guidance *see* 1. leiðsögn, 2. leiðbeining.
guide *see* 1. Sjóskáti, 2. leiðsögumaður, 3. leiðbeina,
  4. kælimiðilsbeinir, 5. gáti.
guideline *see* 1. viðmiðunarregla, 2. viðmiðun, 3.
  leiðbeining.
guiding *see* skátastarf.
guiltless *see* saklaus.
gulf *see* 1. gjá, 2. hyldýpi.
gull *see* máfur.
gullet *see* 1. munnhol, 2. vélindi.
gully *see* gólfræsi.
gum *see* 1. tannhold, 2. útfelling.
gust *see* 1. gustur, 2. hviða, 3. vindhviða.

gustation *see* bragðskyn.
gustatory *see* bragðskyn.
gut *see* 1. senintestigi, 2. þarmur, 3. slægja, 4. görn,
  5. kviður.
guts *see* 1. ventro, 2. innyfli, 3. intesto, 4. kjarkur, 5.
  senintestigi.
gutter *see* 1. þakrenna, 2. kjalvídd, 3. renna.
guy *see* 1. karlmaður, 2. maður (man).
guyot *see* neðansjávarfjall.
gymnastics *see* 1. leikfimi, 2. líkamsæfingar.
gynandromorph *see* kyntigla.
gynecology *see* kvensjúkdómafræði.
gypsum *see* gips.
gyration *see* vindingur.
gyrfalcon *see* fálki.
gyrocompass *see* 1. snúðáttaviti, 2. snúðviti.
gyroscope *see* 1. snúða, 2. snúður, 3. snúðvísir.

H

h *see* 1. vatnsefni, 2. vetni.
habit *see* 1. vani, 2. venja. .
habitat *see* 1. búsvæði, 2. kjörbýli, 3. kjörlendi, 4.
  bústaður, 5. vist.
habitual *see* venjulegur.
habituation *see* 1. aðlögun, 2. ávani, 3.
  lyfjamisnotkun, 4. lyfjaþol, 5. viðvani.
hacker *see* 1. tölvugarpur, 2. tölvurefur, 3.
  tölvuþrjótur.
haddock *see* 1. ýsa, 2. gaddmerarýsa, 3. kalýsa, 4.
  kurlýsa, 5. skrokkýsa.
haemorrhoid *see* hemoroido.
hafnium *see* 1. hafnín, 2. hafníum.
hail *see* 1. hagl, 2. haglél, 3. heilsa, 4. íshagl.
hair *see* 1. hár, 2. hararo.
hairs *see* 1. hararo, 2. haro, 3. haroj.
halation *see* 1. baugmyndun, 2. geislabaugar.
halcyon *see* ísfugl.
half *see* hálfur.
halibut *see* lúða.
hall *see* 1. skáli, 2. salur, 3. hol, 4. forsalur.
hallucination *see* 1. skynvilla, 2. ofskynjun.
hallucinogen *see* 1. ofskynjunarefni, 2. sýngæfur,
  3. sýngjafi.
halo *see* 1. geislabaugur, 2. rosabaugur, 3. hjúpur, 4.
  baugur, 5. ára.
halocarbon *see* halógenkolefni.
halogen *see* 1. halógen, 2. halógenefni, 3. halógeni,
  4. söltungur.
ham *see* svínslæri.
hamate *see* 1. króklaga, 2. krókyddur.
hammer *see* hamar.

hamster *see* hamstur.
hand *see* 1. hönd, 2. verkamaður, 3. vísir.
handedness *see* hendi.
handicap *see* 1. örorka, 2. fötlun.
handicapped *see* fatlaður.
handicraft *see* handiðn.
handle *see* 1. grip, 2. hald, 3. handfang, 4. meðhöndla.
handline *see* handfæri.
handout *see* 1. stuðningsörk, 2. úthenda, 3. dreifiblað, 4. dreifiskjal.
handsome *see* 1. fagur, 2. fallegur.
hang *see* 1. hanga, 2. hengja.
hanger *see* 1. festing, 2. hengi, 3. upphengjulager.
hankering *see* þrá.
haploid *see* 1. einlitna, 2. einlitnungur.
haploidy *see* einlitnun.
haplotype *see* setröð.
happen *see* verða.
happiness *see* hamingja.
happy *see* 1. sæl, 2. ánægður, 3. glaður, 4. hamingjusamur.
harbour *see* höfn.
hard *see* 1. harður, 2. þungur, 3. vandur.
hardness *see* 1. geislaharka, 2. harka.
hardware *see* 1. tölvubúnaður, 2. vélbúnaður.
hare *see* héri.
harmonic *see* 1. harmónískur, 2. yfirtónn, 3. hreintóna, 4. hreinhljóma, 5. hreinn.
harmonics *see* 1. heilfeldissveiflur, 2. yfirsveiflur.
harmonization *see* 1. samræming, 2. samhæfing.
harness *see* 1. virkja, 2. rafleiðslukerfi, 3. festiólar, 4. knippi, 5. leiðsluknippi.
harpoon *see* 1. hvalskutull, 2. skutull.
harry *see* eyðileggja.
harsh *see* 1. óvænn, 2. óvingjarnlegur, 3. beiskur.
harshness *see* 1. skarpskyggni, 2. hvassleiki.
harvest *see* 1. afrakstur, 2. uppskera.
hat *see* hattur.
hatch *see* 1. lúga, 2. strikun, 3. lestarlúga, 4. hleri, 5. lestarop.
hate *see* 1. hata, 2. hatur.
hatred *see* hatur.
haul *see* 1. hal, 2. tog, 3. toga.
haulage *see* 1. farmflutingur, 2. landflutningur.
have *see* 1. hafa, 2. fá.
hawk *see* haukur.
hawse *see* 1. akkerisrauf, 2. kluss.
hay *see* hey.
hazard *see* 1. áhætta, 2. hætta, 3. háski, 4. vá.
hazardous *see* 1. háskalegur, 2. hættulegur.
haze *see* 1. mistur, 2. þokumóða, 3. þurramistur.
hazelnut *see* heslihneta.
he *see* hann.

head *see* 1. höfuð, 2. stefna, 3. hausa, 4. árupptök, 5. lok.
headache *see* höfuðverkur.
headed *see* hausaður.
header *see* 1. haus, 2. síðuhaus, 3. þversetill.
heading *see* 1. fyrirsögn, 2. titill, 3. nefstefna, 4. hausun, 5. haus.
headline *see* höfuðlína.
headquarters *see* höfuðstöðvar.
headwaters *see* árupptök.
headwind *see* 1. móttækilegur, 2. mótvindur.
healing *see* 1. lækning, 2. bati, 3. græðsla, 4. heilun.
health *see* 1. heilbrigði, 2. heilsufar, 3. heilsa.
heap *see* 1. hrúga, 2. kös, 3. safna.
hear *see* heyra.
hearing *see* 1. heyrsla, 2. yfirheyrsla, 3. vitnaleiðslur, 4. vitnaleiðsla, 5. skýrslugjöf.
heart *see* hjarta.
heartburn *see* brjóstsviði.
hearth *see* 1. eldhólf, 2. langeldur.
heartwood *see* kjarnviður.
hearty *see* hjartanlegur.
heat *see* 1. varmi, 2. hiti, 3. gangmál.
heated *see* reiður.
heater *see* 1. glóðald, 2. hitari, 3. hitatæki, 4. miðstöð.
heath *see* 1. lyngmói, 2. móar, 3. lyngheiði, 4. heiði, 5. mólendi.
heather *see* beitilyng.
heathland *see* heiðar.
heatstroke *see* hitaslag.
heave *see* 1. reisa, 2. hefja, 3. hífa, 4. lyfta.
heaven *see* himinn.
heavy *see* 1. þungur, 2. sterkur, 3. þungt, 4. þykkt, 5. þykkur.
hedge *see* 1. limgerði, 2. áhættuvörn, 3. baktrygging.
hedgehog *see* broddgöltur.
hedonism *see* sældarhyggja.
heed *see* von.
heel *see* 1. hæll, 2. hælsvæði.
hegemony *see* 1. forráð, 2. forræði, 3. forysta, 4. yfirráð.
height *see* 1. hæð, 2. hnútamál, 3. kóti.
helical *see* 1. gormlaga, 2. gormlagaður.
helicopter *see* þyrla.
heliotherapy *see* sólskinslækning.
heliotropism *see* ljósleitni.
helium *see* 1. helín, 2. helíum.
helix *see* 1. snigill, 2. skrúfulína, 3. skrúflína, 4. gormur, 5. gormferill.
hell *see* helvíti.
hello *see* 1. halló, 2. sæll, 3. kalla, 4. heilsa.
helm *see* 1. stýri, 2. stýrishjól, 3. hjálmur.
helmsman *see* 1. rórmaður, 2. stýrismaður.

help *see* 1. hjálp, 2. hjálpa.
hematology *see* blóðsjúkdómafræði.
hematoma *see* 1. mar, 2. margúll.
hematopoiesis *see* 1. blóðfrumumyndun, 2. blóðkornamyndun, 3. blóðfrumnamyndun.
hemeralopia *see* náttblinda.
hemianopia *see* helftarblinda.
hemicrania *see* helftarhöfuðverkur.
hemiptera *see* skortítur.
hemisphere *see* 1. jarðarhálfhvel, 2. hvel, 3. hálfhnöttur, 4. hálfhvel, 5. hálfkúla.
hemlock *see* 1. eitursveipur, 2. óðjurt, 3. þöll.
hemoglobin *see* 1. blóðrauði, 2. hemóglóbín.
hemoglobinuria *see* blóðrauðamiga.
hemolysis *see* 1. rauðkornarof, 2. blóðrauðalos, 3. rauðalos.
hemolytic *see* 1. blóðrauðaleysandi, 2. rauðaleysandi, 3. rauðkornarjúfandi.
hemophilia *see* dreyrasýki.
hemorrhage *see* blæðing.
hemorrhoid *see* 1. gyllinæð, 2. raufaræðahnútur.
hemostasis *see* 1. blæðingarstöðvun, 2. blóðrennslisstöðvun.
hemp *see* 1. hampjurt, 2. hampur, 3. kannabisplanta.
hence *see* því.
heparin *see* 1. heparín, 2. blóðstorkutálmi.
hepatitis *see* lifrarbólga.
hepatoma *see* 1. lifrarfrumukrabbamein, 2. lifraræxli.
hepatotoxin *see* lifrareitur.
heptane *see* 1. heptan, 2. kolvetni.
herb *see* 1. kryddjurt, 2. urt, 3. lækningajurt, 4. jurt, 5. gras.
herbicide *see* illgresiseyðir.
herbivore *see* 1. grasæta, 2. grasbítur, 3. jurtaæta.
here *see* hér.
hereditary *see* 1. ættgengur, 2. arfgengur.
heredity *see* 1. arfgengi, 2. erfð, 3. erfðir, 4. ættgengi.
heritability *see* 1. arfgengi, 2. arfstuðull, 3. erfi.
hermaphrodite *see* 1. tvíkynjungur, 2. samkynjungur.
hermaphroditic *see* tvíkynja.
heron *see* hegri.
herring *see* síld.
hertz *see* 1. herts, 2. rið, 3. sveifla.
heterochromatin *see* þéttlitni.
heteroduplex *see* misþáttungur.
heterogametic *see* miskynfrumna.
heterogeneous *see* 1. sundurleitur, 2. misleitur, 3. misþátta.
heterogenous *see* 1. aðfenginn, 2. misleitur, 3. ósamkynja.
heterologous *see* 1. ósamstæður, 2. afbrigðilegur, 3. blendinn, 4. misleitur.

heterosexual *see* kynvís.
heterosexuality *see* kynvísi.
heterosis *see* 1. blendingsstyrkur, 2. blendingsþróttur.
heterotrophic *see* ófrumbjarga.
heterozygote *see* arfblendingur.
heterozygous *see* arfblendinn.
heuristic *see* 1. leiðsagnarregla, 2. þreifun, 3. leitaraðferð, 4. leiðbeinandi, 5. leitarnám.
hexadecimal *see* sextánskur.
hexagon *see* 1. sexhyrningur, 2. sexkantur.
hexose *see* hexósi.
hi *see* sæll.
hibernation *see* vetrardvali.
hiccough *see* hiksti.
hiccup *see* hiksti.
hideous *see* 1. hræðilegur, 2. hryllilegur, 3. viðbjóðslegur, 4. andstyggilegur.
hidrosis *see* svitnun.
hierarchic *see* 1. metaskiptur, 2. stigskiptur.
hierarchical *see* 1. stigskiptur, 2. stigskipt.
hierarchy *see* 1. virðingaröð, 2. þrepveldi, 3. stigvöxtur, 4. stigveldun, 5. stigveldi.
high *see* 1. hæð, 2. hár (hair).
highland *see* hálendi.
highlight *see* 1. auðkenna, 2. hápunktur, 3. ljómun, 4. uppljómun.
highway *see* 1. aðalbraut, 2. tengibraut.
hike *see* fjallaferð.
hilum *see* 1. hlið, 2. nafli, 3. frænafli.
hilus *see* port.
hinge *see* 1. hjör, 2. liður, 3. löm.
hinterland *see* 1. bakland, 2. dreifbýli, 3. uppland.
hip *see* 1. hjúpaldin, 2. rósaraldin, 3. rósaldin, 4. mjaðmarsvæði, 5. mjöðm.
hipbone *see* 1. hlaun, 2. mjaðmarbein.
hire *see* leigja.
hirsute *see* loðinn.
hirsutism *see* ofloðna.
hiss *see* hviss.
histamine *see* 1. histamín, 2. lostefni.
histidine *see* 1. his, 2. histidín.
histiocyte *see* 1. traffruma, 2. vefjakorn.
histochemistry *see* vefjaefnafræði.
histogram *see* 1. stuðlarit, 2. súlurit, 3. súlnarit, 4. stöplarit.
histology *see* vefjafræði.
histone *see* 1. histón, 2. histónn.
histopathology *see* 1. vefjameinafræði, 2. vefjaskemmdir.
history *see* 1. tímaferli, 2. saga.
hit *see* 1. slá, 2. slag.
hitch *see* 1. krókur, 2. tenging.
hives *see* ofsakláði.
hog *see* svín.

hoist *see* 1. lyfta, 2. reisa, 3. lyftibúnaður, 4. hefja, 5. krani.
hold *see* 1. halda, 2. hald, 3. lest, 4. úrskurða.
holder *see* 1. festing, 2. haldari.
holdfast *see* 1. fótfesta, 2. haldfesta, 3. festibúnaður, 4. íhald.
holding *see* 1. eign, 2. eignaraðild, 3. hald.
holdings *see* 1. eignarhald, 2. handhöfn.
hole *see* 1. holeind, 2. rafeindahola, 3. innfláki, 4. gat, 5. hola.
holism *see* 1. heildarhyggja, 2. kerfishyggja.
hollow *see* 1. holur, 2. rauf, 3. spor, 4. tómur.
holmium *see* 1. holmín, 2. hólmín, 3. hólmíum.
hologram *see* 1. almynd, 2. heilmynd.
holy *see* heilagur.
home *see* 1. bústaður, 2. heim.
homeostasis *see* 1. temprun, 2. jafnvægishneigð, 3. samvægi.
homicide *see* 1. drap, 2. morð.
homing *see* 1. heimfærsla, 2. heimferð, 3. heimhvarf, 4. heimleiðing, 5. heimun.
homo *see* 1. menn, 2. maður (man).
homogamy *see* 1. jafnvensl, 2. einsblóma, 3. innrækt.
homogeneity *see* 1. eingerð, 2. eingerður, 3. einslcitni, 4. samfelldni, 5. samþætti.
homogeneous *see* 1. samkynja, 2. samþátta, 3. samleitur, 4. einsleitur, 5. eingerður.
homogenization *see* jöfnun.
homologous *see* 1. einsleitur, 2. samstæður, 3. samsvarandi.
homology *see* 1. eðlislíking, 2. samsvörun.
homonym *see* einsheiti.
homoscedastic *see* einleitur.
homosexual *see* 1. kynvilltur, 2. samkynhneigður, 3. kynhvarfur, 4. hommi, 5. hómi.
homosexuality *see* 1. kynhvörf, 2. kynvilla, 3. samkynhneigð, 4. samkynmök.
homozygote *see* arfhreiningi.
homozygous *see* arfhreinn.
homy *see* 1. ánægjulegur, 2. notalegur.
hone *see* 1. heinarbrýni, 2. heini, 3. slípisteinn, 4. brýni.
honest *see* heiðarlegur.
honesty *see* 1. hreinskilni, 2. ráðvendni.
honey *see* hunang.
honeycomb *see* 1. holplata, 2. hólflaga, 3. hólfaplata.
honing *see* 1. brýning, 2. samslípun, 3. slípun.
honourable *see* heiðarlegur.
hood *see* 1. vélarhlíf, 2. lok, 3. þekja.
hook *see* 1. krókur, 2. öngull, 3. krókstjaki.
hooker *see* 1. hóra, 2. skækja.
hop *see* 1. hopp, 2. humall.
hope *see* 1. von, 2. vona.

hopeless *see* örvæntingarfullur.
hopper *see* 1. hólkur, 2. prammi, 3. skammtari.
horizon *see* 1. sjóndeildarhringur, 2. sjónbaugur, 3. sjónarrönd, 4. leiðarlag, 5. lagamót.
horizontal *see* láréttur.
hormone *see* 1. hormón, 2. hormóni, 3. kirtilvaki, 4. vaki.
horn *see* 1. trekt, 2. flauta, 3. hornloftnet.
horoscope *see* stjörnumát.
horrible *see* 1. hræðilegur, 2. hryllilegur, 3. óþægilegur, 4. viðbjóðslegur.
horror *see* 1. grimmd, 2. hryllingur, 3. viðbjóður.
horse *see* 1. hestur, 2. hross.
horsepower *see* hestafl.
horseradish *see* piparrót.
horst *see* rishryggur.
horticulture *see* 1. garðrækt, 2. garðyrkja, 3. garðyrkjufræði.
hose *see* 1. slanga, 2. hosa.
hospital *see* sjúkrahús.
host *see* 1. hýsill, 2. þegi, 3. her.
hostile *see* 1. fjandsamlegur, 2. fjandsamur, 3. óvinveittur.
hotel *see* gistihús.
hound *see* hundur.
hour *see* 1. tími, 2. stund, 3. klukkustund, 4. klukkutími.
house *see* 1. hús, 2. hús.
household *see* 1. heimilisfólk, 2. heimili.
housing *see* 1. húsnæði, 2. hús, 3. hásing, 4. drifhús.
hover *see* 1. hanga, 2. voka.
hovercraft *see* 1. loftpúðaskip, 2. svifnökkvi.
how *see* 1. hvernig, 2. hvað.
however *see* 1. þó, 2. þótt.
howler *see* gólari.
hub *see* 1. hjólnöf, 2. deilibox, 3. leiðamót, 4. nöf, 5. safnvöllur.
hue *see* 1. litni, 2. litblær, 3. blær.
hug *see* faðma.
hull *see* 1. skipsskrokkur, 2. skrokkur, 3. yfirbygging.
hum *see* 1. brúmm, 2. murr.
human *see* 1. mannlegur, 2. maður (man).
humanism *see* 1. mannúðarstefna, 2. mannhyggja, 3. fornmenntastefna, 4. húmanismi.
humid *see* rakur.
humidity *see* 1. rakamagn, 2. rakastig, 3. raki.
humiliate *see* auðmýkja.
humiliation *see* 1. auðmýing, 2. litillækkun.
hummock *see* þúfa.
humour *see* skap.
humpback *see* 1. bleiklax, 2. herðakistill, 3. hnúðlax.
humus *see* 1. moldarefni, 2. myldi, 3. húmus, 4. gróðurmold.

hunchback *see* krypplingur.
hundred *see* hundrað.
hunger *see* 1. sultur, 2. hungur, 3. svengd.
hungry *see* svangur.
hunt *see* 1. pendla, 2. veiða.
hunting *see* 1. leit, 2. vag, 3. veiðar.
hurricane *see* 1. fárviðri, 2. fellibylur.
hurt *see* móðga.
husband *see* 1. eiginmaður, 2. maður (man).
hut *see* 1. skáli, 2. kofi.
hyaline *see* 1. himnukenndur, 2. glærvefur, 3. gegnsær, 4. glær.
hybrid *see* 1. bastarður, 2. blendingur, 3. kynblandaður, 4. kynblendingur, 5. tegundablendingur.
hybridization *see* 1. kynblöndun, 2. þáttatenging, 3. þáttapörun.
hybridoma *see* 1. frumubastarður, 2. frumublendingur.
hydatid *see* blöðruleif.
hydrate *see* hýdrat.
hydrated *see* 1. vatnaður, 2. vatnshaldinn.
hydration *see* 1. vökvun, 2. vötnun.
hydraulic *see* 1. vökvaknúinn, 2. vökvknúinn, 3. vökvaknúið.
hydraulics *see* 1. straumtækni, 2. vökvahreyfifræði, 3. vökvastöðufræði.
hydride *see* hýdríð.
hydrocarbon *see* 1. kolvatnsefni, 2. vetniskolefni, 3. vetniskol, 4. kolvetni.
hydrocele *see* vatnshaull.
hydrocephalus *see* 1. vatnshöfði, 2. vatnshöfðun, 3. vatnshöfuð.
hydrocortisone *see* hýdrókortísón.
hydrodynamic *see* 1. vökvaaflfræði, 2. vökvaaflfræðilegur, 3. straumfræðilegur, 4. vökvahreyfifræði.
hydrodynamics *see* 1. straumfræði, 2. vökvaaflfræði, 3. vökvastraumfræði.
hydrofoil *see* 1. spaðabátur, 2. vatnavængildi.
hydrogen *see* 1. vetni, 2. vatnsefni, 3. H.
hydrography *see* 1. sjómælingar, 2. vatnamælingar.
hydrology *see* 1. vatnafræði, 2. vatnsfræði.
hydrolysis *see* 1. vatnsleysing, 2. vatnsrof, 3. vatsrof.
hydrometer *see* 1. flotmælir, 2. flotvog, 3. rafgeymamælir.
hydrophilic *see* 1. vatnsfíkinn, 2. vatnssækinn.
hydrophobia *see* 1. vatnsfælni, 2. vatnshræðsla.
hydrophobic *see* vatnsfælinn.
hydrophone *see* vatnshljóðmælir.
hydrosphere *see* 1. vatnshvel, 2. vatnshvolf, 3. vatnshjúpur.
hydrostatics *see* 1. vökvakyrrstaða, 2. vökvastöðufræði.

hydroxide *see* hýdroxíð.
hygiene *see* 1. heilsufræði, 2. hreinlæti.
hygrograph *see* 1. rakariti, 2. rakasíriti.
hygrometer *see* 1. daggarstigsmælir, 2. rakamælir.
hygroscopic *see* vökvasæll.
hyoid *see* 1. málbein, 2. tungubein.
hyperactive *see* ofvirkur.
hyperactivity *see* ofvirkni.
hyperalgesia *see* 1. ofurkvöl, 2. ofursársaukanæmi.
hyperbole *see* 1. ýkjur, 2. ofhvörf.
hypercapnia *see* 1. koltvísýringsaukning, 2. koltvísýringshækkun.
hyperlink *see* stikluleggur.
hypermedia *see* 1. margmiðlun, 2. ofurmiðlun, 3. stiklumiðlun, 4. tengimiðlun.
hypermetropia *see* 1. fjarsýni, 2. langsýni.
hyperopia *see* fjarsýni.
hyperphagia *see* matgræðgi.
hypersensitivity *see* ofurnæmi.
hypersomnia *see* svefnsækni.
hypertension *see* 1. háþrýstingur, 2. ofþrýstingur.
hypertext *see* 1. tengitexti, 2. stiklutexti, 3. gjörtexti, 4. fjölvíddartexti, 5. stiklutextakerfi.
hyperthermia *see* ofurhiti.
hyperthyroidism *see* skjaldvakaeitrun.
hypertonia *see* ofstæling.
hypertonic *see* 1. ofstæltur, 2. ofþrýstinn.
hypertrophy *see* 1. líffæraauki, 2. ofstækkun, 3. afmyndun, 4. ofvöxtur.
hyperventilation *see* oföndun.
hypha *see* 1. íma, 2. sveppþráður.
hyphen *see* bandstrik.
hypnagogic *see* svefnhöfugur.
hypnosis *see* dáleiðsla.
hypnotherapy *see* 1. dámeðferð, 2. dálækning, 3. dáleiðslumeðferð.
hypnotic *see* 1. dáþoli, 2. svæfandi.
hypnotism *see* 1. dáleiðing, 2. dáleiðslufræði.
hypnotist *see* dávaldur.
hypoblast *see* 1. fruminnlag, 2. innlag, 3. innlagskím.
hypochondria *see* 1. sóttsýki, 2. sótthræðsla.
hypochondriac *see* ímyndunarveikur.
hypodermic *see* 1. húðbeðssprauta, 2. húðbeðslyf.
hypomania *see* ólmhugur.
hypophysis *see* 1. dingull, 2. heiladingull.
hyposensitization *see* vannæming.
hypospadias *see* 1. neðanrás, 2. innanrás.
hypostasis *see* 1. undirstæðni, 2. undirstæði, 3. sig, 4. undirsetning, 5. undirstaða.
hypotension *see* vanþrýstingur.
hypotensive *see* lágþrýstingsvaldandi.
hypotenuse *see* langhlið.
hypothalamus *see* 1. undirstúka, 2. heiladyngjubotn.

hypothermia see ofkæling.
hypothesis see tilgáta.
hypothyroidism see skjaldvakabrestur.
hypotonia see slekja.
hypotonic see 1. slakur, 2. vanþrýstinn.
hypoxia see vefildisskortur.
hysterectomy see legnám.
hysteresis see 1. segultregða, 2. segulheldni, 3. heldni.
hysteria see 1. sefasýki, 2. móðursýki.

I

ibex see steingeit.
ice see ís.
iceberg see 1. borgarís, 2. borgarísjaki.
icing see ísing.
icon see 1. vémynd, 2. teikn, 3. táknmynd, 4. myndtákn, 5. tákn.
id see frumsjálf.
idea see 1. vitmynd, 2. álit, 3. hugmynd.
ideal see 1. hugsjón, 2. íðal.
idealism see 1. hughyggja, 2. hugsjónastefna.
idealization see 1. fegrun, 2. tignun.
ideally see heldur.
identical see 1. samskonar, 2. alsamur.
identification see 1. tegundargreining, 2. skilgreining, 3. sanngreining, 4. samsömun, 5. kennsl.
identifier see 1. kennimerki, 2. nefni, 3. kenni.
identify see 1. auðkenna, 2. kenna, 3. samsama, 4. skilgreina.
identity see 1. persónukenni, 2. sjálfssömun, 3. sjálfssemd, 4. samsemd, 5. kenniþekja.
ideology see 1. hugmyndafræði, 2. hugmyndakerfi, 3. hugmyndasaga, 4. kenningakerfi.
idiopathic see sjálfvakinn.
idiosyncrasy see 1. séreigind, 2. sérkennileiki.
idiot see örviti.
idle see 1. hvílandi, 2. iðjulaus, 3. latur, 4. lausagangur, 5. óstarfhæfur.
idling see 1. hægagangur, 2. lausagangur.
if see ef.
ignite see 1. kveikja, 2. tendra.
igniter see 1. kveikir, 2. kveikjari.
ignition see 1. kveikja, 2. kveiking.
ignitor see 1. viðnámskveikir, 2. púlsræsir, 3. púlskveikjari, 4. kveikja.
ill see 1. sjúkur, 2. veikur.
illegal see 1. ólöglegur, 2. ólögmætur.
illiteracy see ólæsi.
illness see sjúkleiki.
illuminance see lýsing.

illumination see 1. lýsing, 2. birta, 3. hugljómun.
illusion see skynvilla.
image see 1. hugmynd, 2. ímynd, 3. líking, 4. mynd.
imagery see 1. hugsýn, 2. myndmál, 3. mynd, 4. líkneski.
imagination see 1. ímyndun, 2. ímyndunarafl.
imaging see 1. myndfærsla, 2. myndheimig, 3. myndhöndlun.
imago see 1. kynþroska, 2. ímynd.
imbalance see 1. misvægi, 2. ójafnvægi.
imbecile see fáviti.
imbibition see 1. gegnvæting, 2. ísog, 3. vökvaþrútnun.
imbricate see 1. skara, 2. skaraður.
imbue see fylla.
imitation see 1. stæling, 2. eftirlíking.
immature see óþroskaður.
immerse see 1. dýfa, 2. kaffæra, 3. sökkva.
immersion see 1. hvarf, 2. ídýfing, 3. gagntekning, 4. dýfing, 5. kaffæring.
immigrant see innflytjandi.
immigration see 1. búferlaflutningur, 2. innfar, 3. innflytjendur.
imminent see yfirvofandi.
immiscible see óblandanlegur.
immoral see yfirgefinn.
immune see ónæmur.
immunity see 1. vernd, 2. fríðindi, 3. ónæmi, 4. sakaruppgjöf, 5. sérréttindi.
immunization see 1. ónæmisaðgerð, 2. bólusetning, 3. ónæming.
immunodeficiency see ónæmisbrestur.
immunoelectrophoresis see ónæmisrafdráttur.
immunofluorescence see 1. ónæmisflúrljóm, 2. ónæmisflúrljómun, 3. ónæmisflúrskíma, 4. ónæmisflúrskin.
immunogen see 1. mótefnavaki, 2. ónæmisvaki.
immunogenetics see ónæmiserfðafræði.
immunogenic see 1. ónæmisvaldandi, 2. ónæmisvekjandi.
immunoglobulin see 1. mótefni, 2. ónæmisglóbúlín.
immunologist see ónæmisfræðingur.
immunology see ónæmisfræði.
immunosuppression see ónæmisbæling.
immunotherapy see 1. ónæmingarmeðferð, 2. ónæmisbælingarmeðferð.
impact see 1. áhrif, 2. árekstur, 3. högg, 4. slag.
impacted see 1. innkýldur, 2. klemmdur, 3. tepptur.
impaction see 1. innkýling, 2. klemma, 3. saurteppa.
impair see 1. spilla, 2. veikjast.
impairment see 1. skerðing, 2. virðisrýrnun.
impart see gefa.
impatient see óþolinmóður.

impedance *see* 1. mótstaða, 2. viðnám, 3. tvinnviðnám, 4. tvinnviðmnám, 5. sýndarviðnám.
impeller *see* 1. þeytihjól, 2. hverfill, 3. skófluhjól.
imperialism *see* 1. keisarastjórn, 2. imperíalismi, 3. heimsvaldastefna.
impermeable *see* 1. ólekur, 2. þéttur.
impertinent *see* ósvífinn.
impetus *see* 1. skriðþungi, 2. skriður.
implant *see* 1. ígræði, 2. ígræðlingur.
implantation *see* 1. festing, 2. hreiðrun, 3. ífelling, 4. ígræðsla, 5. bólfesta.
implement *see* 1. innrétta, 2. verkfæri, 3. fullbúa, 4. framkvæma, 5. hagnýta.
implementation *see* 1. framkvæmd, 2. hagnýting, 3. túlkun.
implication *see* 1. rökleiðing, 2. ályktun, 3. leiðing, 4. meðför.
implicit *see* 1. undirskilinn, 2. undanskilinn, 3. skilyrðislaus, 4. óljós, 5. óbeinn.
implosion *see* hrun.
imply *see* 1. merkja, 2. þýða.
impolite *see* ókurteis.
import *see* innflutningur.
importation *see* innflutningur.
impotence *see* 1. getuleysi, 2. ódugur, 3. óneyti.
impoverished *see* fátækur.
impregnation *see* getnaður.
impression *see* 1. áhrif, 2. spor, 3. mót, 4. far, 5. afsteypa.
imprest *see* 1. fyrirframgreiðsla, 2. smágreiðslusjóður.
imprinting *see* 1. greyping, 2. hæning, 3. mörkun.
imprisonment *see* 1. frelsissvipting, 2. refsivist.
improve *see* 1. endurbæta, 2. laga, 3. bæta.
improvement *see* 1. endurbót, 2. lagfæring.
improvisation *see* 1. spuni, 2. hljómspuni, 3. snarstefjun.
impulse *see* 1. taugaboð, 2. stuð, 3. skyndihvöt, 4. kippur, 5. högg.
impulsive *see* hvatvís.
impurity *see* 1. íbót, 2. sori, 3. óhreinindi, 4. mengun.
in *see* 1. í, 2. að, 3. i, 4. indín.
inactive *see* 1. hvarftregur, 2. óhvarfgjarn, 3. óvirkur.
inadvertent *see* óaðgætinn.
inanition *see* 1. hor, 2. ófeiti.
inbreeding *see* 1. innæxlun, 2. innrækt, 3. nærsifjar, 4. skyldraæxlun.
incandescence *see* 1. gló, 2. glóð.
incentive *see* 1. hvöt, 2. kveikja, 3. uppörvun, 4. bónuskerfi, 5. hvati.
incest *see* sifjaspell.
inch *see* 1. þumlungur, 2. tomma.
inching *see* 1. mjak, 2. kippstýring.

incidence *see* nýgengi.
incident *see* 1. atburður, 2. líklegur, 3. tilvik, 4. truflun, 5. aðfallandi.
incinerator *see* brennsluofn.
incision *see* 1. skurður, 2. risting, 3. rista.
inclination *see* 1. brautarhalli, 2. halli.
incline *see* hallast.
inclining *see* aðsveigður.
inclinometer *see* hallamælir.
included *see* 1. meðtalinn, 2. innifalinn.
inclusion *see* 1. tilkoma, 2. skráning, 3. samheildun, 4. jafnstaða, 5. aðlögun.
incombustible *see* 1. óbrennanlegur, 2. óeldfimur.
income *see* tekjur.
incoming *see* innkomandi.
incompatibility *see* 1. ósamfellanleiki, 2. ósamrýmanleiki.
incompatible *see* ósamrýmanlegur.
incompetence *see* 1. óhæfi, 2. vanhæfi.
incomplete *see* 1. ófullkominn, 2. ófullnægjandi.
incompressible *see* óþjappanlegur.
incontinence *see* lausheldni.
inconvenient *see* 1. vandur, 2. þungur.
incorporate *see* innlima.
incorporation *see* 1. ílimun, 2. innlimun, 3. innlimun, 4. sameining, 5. samruni.
increase *see* 1. auka, 2. aukast.
increment *see* 1. auki, 2. aukning, 3. viðbót, 4. vöxtur, 5. auka.
incrustation *see* 1. greyping, 2. skorpumyndun.
incubation *see* 1. klak, 2. kvíun, 3. meðganga.
incubator *see* 1. hitakassi, 2. hitaskápur, 3. klakskápur, 4. nýburakassi, 5. súrefniskassi.
incubus *see* mara.
incus *see* steðji.
indecision *see* 1. tvílræði, 2. óákveðni, 3. hik.
indemnity *see* 1. skaðabætur, 2. skaðleysi, 3. þóknun.
indent *see* 1. inndráttur, 2. tenna.
indention *see* inndráttur.
indenture *see* 1. aðalskuldabréf, 2. ráðningarsamningur.
independence *see* 1. óháði, 2. sjálfstæði, 3. hlutleysi.
independent *see* 1. óháður, 2. sjálfstæður.
index *see* 1. vísir, 2. vísitölubinda, 3. vísitala, 4. stuðull, 5. skrá.
indexation *see* 1. vísitölutenging, 2. verðbætur, 3. verðtrygging, 4. vísitölubinding.
indexing *see* 1. vísasetning, 2. lyklun, 3. skipting.
indication *see* 1. ábending, 2. vísbending, 3. vísun.
indicator *see* 1. vísir, 2. mælitæki, 3. vísbending, 4. vísbendir, 5. efnaviti.
indictment *see* 1. ákæra, 2. ásökun.
indigenous *see* 1. frumbyggi, 2. innfæddur.

indium see 1. indín, 2. indíum.
individual see 1. einstaklingur, 2. einstæður, 3. sérkennilegur.
individualism see einstaklingshyggja.
individualization see stakmótun.
individuation see einsömun.
indolent see 1. eymslalaus, 2. hægfara, 3. sársaukalaus, 4. seinn.
induce see 1. framkalla, 2. virkja, 3. vekja, 4. spana.
inducer see 1. örvi, 2. vaki.
inductance see 1. rafsegulspönun, 2. spanstuðull.
induction see 1. inntaka, 2. vakning, 3. þrepun, 4. span, 5. aðleiðsluaðferð.
inductor see 1. spanald, 2. spanspóla, 3. spóla.
induration see 1. holdhersli, 2. herslismyndun.
industrialization see iðnvæðing.
industry see 1. atvinnugrein, 2. atvinnuvegur, 3. bjargræðisvegur, 4. framleiðslugrein, 5. iðnaður.
inelastic see 1. ónæmur, 2. óteyginn, 3. ófjaðrandi.
inequality see 1. ójafna, 2. ójöfnuður, 3. misgengi.
inert see 1. hreyfingarlaus, 2. tregur.
inertia see 1. aðgerðaleysi, 2. framtaksleysi, 3. tregða.
infancy see frumbernska.
infant see 1. barn, 2. kornabarn, 3. ungbarn.
infanticide see 1. barnsmorð, 2. barnsmorðingi.
infantile see 1. barnalegur, 2. barnslegur, 3. frumbernskur.
infarct see 1. fleygdrep, 2. stífludrep, 3. stíflufleygur.
infarction see 1. fleygdrep, 2. stíflufleygsmyndun, 3. stíflufleygun.
infect see smita.
infection see 1. smit, 2. smitun, 3. sýking.
infectious see 1. smitaður, 2. sýkinn, 3. smitandi.
infective see 1. næmur, 2. smitandi.
inference see ályktun.
inferior see 1. ómerkilegur, 2. ónógur, 3. neðri, 4. lélegur, 5. lakur.
infertility see 1. ófjósemi, 2. ófrjósemi, 3. vanfrjósemi.
infestation see óværa.
infiltrate see 1. ífara, 2. ífarinn.
infiltration see íferð.
infinite see 1. óendanlegur, 2. takmarkalaus.
infinitesimal see 1. örsmæð, 2. örsmár.
infinity see 1. óendanlegt, 2. óendanleiki.
inflammable see eldfimur.
inflammation see 1. bólga, 2. þroti.
inflation see 1. tútnun, 2. verðbólga, 3. verðþensla.
inflationary see 1. verðbólguhvetjandi, 2. verðbólguvaldandi.
inflection see 1. beyging, 2. fallbeyging.
inflow see 1. innflæði, 2. innstreymi.
influence see áhrif.

influenza see 1. flensa, 2. inflúensa, 3. kvefpest.
influx see innflæði.
informal see 1. óformlegur, 2. óskipulagður.
information see 1. upplýsingar, 2. vitneskja, 3. kynning, 4. gögn, 5. fróð.
infrared see 1. innrautt, 2. innroði, 3. innrauður.
infrastructure see 1. uppbygging, 2. grunngerð, 3. grunnkerfi, 4. innviðir, 5. innvirki.
infundibulum see 1. undirstúkusygill, 2. sígill.
infusion see 1. dreypilyf, 2. innrennslislyf, 3. stunguveita.
ingestion see 1. inntaka, 2. neysla, 3. innbyrðing, 4. fæðuinntaka, 5. át.
ingot see 1. málmhleifur, 2. hleifur.
ingredient see 1. efnisþáttur, 2. íblendi.
inhalant see 1. innöndunarlyf, 2. innúðalyf.
inhalation see 1. innöndun, 2. innöndunarlyf.
inhaler see 1. öndunargríma, 2. úðatæki.
inherent see 1. arfskapaður, 2. ígróinn, 3. meðfæddur.
inheritance see 1. arfleifð, 2. arfur, 3. erfðir.
inherited see erfður.
inhibit see 1. hamla, 2. hindra, 3. banna.
inhibition see 1. hömlun, 2. latning, 3. tálmun, 4. hindrun.
inhibitor see 1. hemill, 2. tálmi, 3. lati, 4. hindrun, 5. hindri.
inhibitory see 1. letjandi, 2. tálmandi, 3. hindrandi, 4. hemjandi, 5. hamlandi.
initial see 1. meðundirrita, 2. upphaf, 3. upphaflegur, 4. upphafsstafur, 5. framstæður.
initialize see 1. frumgilda, 2. frumstilla.
initiative see 1. Frumkvæði, 2. frumkvæðisréttur, 3. framtak.
initiator see 1. hvatamaður, 2. upphafsefni, 3. upphafsmaður.
injection see 1. insprautun, 2. stunga, 3. innspýting, 4. inndæling, 5. ídælingarefni.
injector see 1. innsprautunarloki, 2. innsprautunarspíss, 3. spíss.
injunction see 1. skipun, 2. fyrirmæli, 3. kyrrsetning, 4. lögbann.
injured see særður.
injury see 1. meiðsli, 2. móðgun, 3. sár, 4. skemmdir, 5. sköddun.
inland see uppland.
inlet see 1. flói, 2. vogur, 3. vík, 4. inntak, 5. innstreymi.
inmost see náinn.
innate see arfskapaður.
innermost see náinn.
innervation see 1. ítaugun, 2. taugaskipun, 3. taugaskipan.
innings see röð.
innocent see saklaus.

innocuous see 1. hættulaus, 2. meinlaus, 3. óskaðlegur.
innovation see 1. nýmæli, 2. nýsköpun, 3. nýjung, 4. nýbreytni, 5. nýuppfinning.
inoculate see 1. ónæmissetja, 2. sá.
inoculation see 1. ónæmissetning, 2. sáning.
inoculum see sáð.
inorganic see ólífrænn.
input see 1. aðfærsla, 2. inntak, 3. ílag, 4. aðföng.
inquiry see 1. fyrirspurn, 2. rannsókn, 3. spurning.
insanity see 1. brjálæði, 2. vitfirring.
insemination see 1. tæknifrjóvgun, 2. sæðing.
insensible see óskynjanlegur.
insert see 1. innfelling, 2. innskot, 3. innskotshamur, 4. fleygur.
insertion see 1. festing, 2. innstunga, 3. vöðvafesta, 4. vöðvahald.
inside see 1. að, 2. í.
insider see innherji.
insight see 1. ísæi, 2. sjálfskilningur.
insolation see 1. ágeislun, 2. sólgeislun, 3. sólstingur.
insoluble see 1. óuppleysanlegur, 2. óleysanlegur.
insolvency see 1. ógjaldfærni, 2. greiðsluþrot, 3. eignahalli, 4. gjaldþrot.
insolvent see ógjaldfær.
insomnia see 1. andvökur, 2. svefnleysi.
inspect see 1. yfirfara, 2. kanna, 3. skoða.
inspection see 1. skoðun, 2. eftirlit.
inspector see eftirlitsmaður.
inspiration see 1. andagift, 2. hugmynd, 3. innblástur, 4. innöndun.
instability see 1. óstöðugleiki, 2. vingl, 3. flökt, 4. breytileiki.
install see innrétta.
installation see 1. ísetning, 2. niðursetning, 3. uppsetning.
installment see 1. afborgun, 2. raðgreiðsla.
instalment see afborgun.
instance see 1. dæmi, 2. tilvik, 3. umfjöllunaraðilji, 4. stig, 5. dómstig.
instant see 1. skyndi, 2. tímapunktur.
instantaneous see 1. samstundis, 2. tafarlaus.
instinct see 1. eðlisávísun, 2. eðlishvöt, 3. eðlisvísan.
instinctive see eðlisvís.
institute see 1. hefja, 2. innleiða, 3. stofnsetja, 4. stofnun.
institution see 1. stofnun, 2. samtök, 3. innleiðing, 4. þjóðfélagsstofnun.
instruction see 1. leiðarvísir, 2. leiðbeining, 3. skipun.
instructions see 1. fyrirmæli, 2. leiðbeiningar.
instrument see 1. mælir, 2. viðskiptabréf, 3. verkfæri, 4. tæki, 5. stjórntæki.

instrumentation see 1. mælitækjavæðing, 2. tækjabúnaður, 3. tækjabeiting, 4. mælitækni.
insufficiency see 1. líffærisbilun, 2. starfsbilun.
insularity see 1. einangrun, 2. nesjamennska, 3. þröngsýni.
insulated see 1. einangur, 2. einangrað.
insulation see 1. einangrun, 2. einangrunarefni.
insulator see 1. einangrari, 2. einangri, 3. einangur.
insulin see 1. insúlín, 2. eyjavaki.
insult see 1. móðgun, 2. móðga, 3. skamma, 4. fjölmæli, 5. ærumeiðing.
insurance see 1. trygging, 2. vátrygging.
insure see 1. tryggja, 2. vátryggja.
insurer see 1. tryggingasali, 2. tryggjandi, 3. frumtryggjandi, 4. vátryggjandi.
intake see 1. heildarneysla, 2. inntak, 3. Upptaka
integer see heiltala.
integral see 1. heill, 2. ómissandi, 3. óskiptur, 4. tegur, 5. óaðskiljanlegur.
integrate see 1. samþætta, 2. tegra, 3. samlagast, 4. samlaga, 5. sameina.
integration see 1. innlimun, 2. samlögun, 3. samþætting, 4. samtvinnun, 5. tegrun.
integrator see heildari.
integrity see 1. samkvæmni, 2. heillyndi, 3. heilleiki, 4. friðhelgi.
integument see 1. egghjúpur, 2. fræskurn, 3. frævísishimna, 4. hjúpur, 5. hörund.
intellect see vitsmunir.
intellectual see vitsmunalegur.
intelligence see 1. viska, 2. vit, 3. greind.
intend see ætla.
intensifier see áhersluatviksorð.
intensity see 1. styrkleiki, 2. áhrif, 3. styrkur, 4. þéttleiki, 5. mikilleiki.
intensive see 1. eðlisbundinn, 2. magnaður, 3. megn, 4. þéttbær.
interact see 1. umgangast, 2. víxlverka.
interaction see 1. samspil, 2. samstarf, 3. víxlverkun, 4. samverkun, 5. samskipti.
interactive see 1. víxlvirkur, 2. gagnvirkur, 3. samtengdur, 4. víxlverkandi.
intercalation see 1. innskot, 2. innskeyti, 3. innskeyting.
intercept see 1. ássnið, 2. einelta, 3. skurðpunktur.
interception see einelti.
interchangeability see 1. umskiptanleiki, 2. skiptihæfi.
interchangeable see 1. umskiptanlegt, 2. víxlanlegur.
interconnection see 1. millitengsl, 2. samgangur, 3. Samtenging.
interdependence see 1. samhæði, 2. samtvinnun.
interdisciplinary see þverfaglegur.

interest *see* 1. áhugi, 2. vextir, 3. vaxtagjöld, 4. hugðarefni, 5. hagur.
interface *see* 1. snertiflötur, 2. viðmót, 3. tengibúnaður, 4. skilflötur, 5. skil.
interfere *see* 1. samliðast, 2. víxlast.
interference *see* 1. íhlutun, 2. yfirmál, 3. víxlverkun, 4. víxlhrif, 5. víxl.
interferometer *see* 1. víxlunarmælir, 2. víxlmælir, 3. samliðumælir.
interferon *see* 1. trufli, 2. veiruvarnaboði, 3. interferón.
interior *see* 1. innanverður, 2. inni.
interlock *see* 1. læsast, 2. millilæsing.
interlocking *see* 1. samkræking, 2. millilæsing.
intermediary *see* 1. milliliður, 2. miðlari, 3. milligöngumaður.
intermediate *see* 1. milliefni, 2. millilægur, 3. milliliður.
intermittent *see* 1. slitrótt, 2. slitróttur.
internal *see* 1. innanverður, 2. innvortis, 3. innri, 4. innlendur.
international *see* alþjóðlegur.
internationalism *see* 1. alþjóðahyggja, 2. alþjóðarækni.
internet *see* 1. alnet, 2. lýðnet, 3. Netið.
internode *see* 1. milliskoragciri, 2. símaliður, 3. stöngulliður.
interoceptor *see* iðraskynfæri.
interoperability *see* 1. gagnvirkni, 2. samstarfshæfni.
interphase *see* 1. interfasi, 2. millifasi, 3. millistig.
interpolation *see* 1. brúun, 2. innreiknun.
interposition *see* 1. sáttaumleitun, 2. skygging, 3. milliganga.
interpret *see* 1. túlka, 2. þýða.
interpretation *see* túlkun.
interpreter *see* túlkur.
interrelate *see* umgangast.
interrupt *see* 1. rof, 2. ígrip, 3. rjúfa.
interrupter *see* 1. rofi, 2. straumrofi.
interruption *see* 1. framígrip, 2. rof, 3. stöðvun, 4. truflun.
intersect *see* 1. skara, 2. skörun, 3. skerast.
intersection *see* 1. sniðmengi, 2. snið, 3. skurðpunktur, 4. skurðarpunktur, 5. skörun.
intersex *see* 1. millikyn, 2. millikynjungur, 3. viðrini.
intersexuality *see* millikyn.
interstitial *see* millilægur.
interval *see* 1. millibil, 2. skeið, 3. bil, 4. þrep, 5. hlé.
intervention *see* 1. afskipti, 2. íhlutun, 3. inngrip, 4. málamiðlun.
intestine *see* 1. intesto, 2. þarmar, 3. görn, 4. garnir, 5. þarmur.

intimate *see* náinn.
intolerance *see* 1. óbærileiki, 2. óþol.
intolerant *see* umburðarlaus.
intonation *see* 1. ítónun, 2. tónfall.
intoxicant *see* 1. vímugjafi, 2. ölvandi.
intoxicated *see* ölvaður.
intoxication *see* 1. ölvíma, 2. ölvun, 3. tilfinningaofsi, 4. víma, 5. eitrun.
intracellular *see* innanfrumu.
intrinsic *see* 1. innri, 2. eðlislægur.
introduce *see* 1. byrja, 2. kynna.
introjection *see* innvarp.
intron *see* innröð.
introspection *see* sjálfsskoðun.
introversion *see* innhverfa.
introvert *see* 1. innhvarfi, 2. innhverfur.
intrusion *see* 1. innskot, 2. inngrip, 3. innátenging.
intubation *see* pípusetning.
intuition *see* 1. hugsæi, 2. máltilfinning.
intuitive *see* hugsýnn.
intumescence *see* 1. útþensla, 2. bólgnun, 3. gúll, 4. þrútnun.
inulin *see* inúlín.
invagination *see* 1. innhverfing, 2. slíðrun, 3. smeyging, 4. innhvelfing.
invariable *see* óbreytanlegur.
invariably *see* 1. ætíð, 2. alltaf, 3. ávallt.
invariant *see* 1. óbreyta, 2. óbreytinn, 3. óbreytilegur.
invasion *see* innrás.
invasive *see* 1. ágengur, 2. ífarandi.
invective *see* skammaryrði.
invention *see* uppfinning.
inventory *see* 1. birgðir, 2. skrá.
inverse *see* 1. andhverfur, 2. viðsnúinn, 3. umhverfur, 4. umhverfa, 5. öfugur.
inversion *see* 1. umhverfa, 2. hitahvarf, 3. umhverfing, 4. umsnúningur, 5. hverfing.
invert *see* hverfa.
invertebrate *see* 1. hrygglaus, 2. hryggleysingi.
inverted *see* 1. umhverfður, 2. umsnúinn, 3. öfugur, 4. úthverfur.
inverter *see* 1. áriðill, 2. formerkisbreytir, 3. riðill.
investigation *see* 1. rannsókn, 2. athugun, 3. könnun.
investment *see* fjárfesting.
investments *see* langtímaverðbréf.
investor *see* fjárfestir.
invitation *see* 1. boð, 2. heimboð.
invite *see* bjóða.
invoice *see* 1. reikningur, 2. vörureikningar, 3. faktúra.
involuntary *see* 1. ósjálfráður, 2. nauðugur.
involution *see* 1. hnignun, 2. innskrið, 3. rýrnun, 4. visnun.

involvement *see* **1**. sinnustig, **2**. þátttaka, **3**. nálægð, **4**. aðild, **5**. sinna.
iodine *see* joð.
ion *see* **1**. fareind, **2**. jón, **3**. rafi.
ionisation *see* jónun.
ionization *see* **1**. jónun, **2**. röfun, **3**. fareindaleysing.
ionize *see* jóna.
ionosphere *see* **1**. jónhvolf, **2**. rafhvolf.
iontophoresis *see* **1**. fareindalækning, **2**. rafdráttur.
ire *see* reiði.
iridium *see* **1**. iridín, **2**. iridíum.
iris *see* **1**. lithimna, **2**. regnbogahimna, **3**. lita.
iritis *see* **1**. lithimnubólga, **2**. litubólga.
iron *see* **1**. járn, **2**. straujárn.
irony *see* **1**. háðhvörf, **2**. háðsádeila, **3**. hæðni, **4**. satíra.
irradiance *see* ágeislunarstyrkur.
irradiation *see* **1**. ágeislun, **2**. ljómstækkun, **3**. ágeislunarmagn, **4**. geislun.
irrational *see* **1**. óræður, **2**. órökrænn.
irregular *see* óreglulegur.
irreversible *see* **1**. óbreytanlegur, **2**. óhverfanlegur, **3**. einhverfur, **4**. ógagnhverfur, **5**. óhverfur.
irrigate *see* **1**. vökva, **2**. skola.
irrigation *see* **1**. skolun, **2**. vökvun, **3**. áveita.
irritability *see* **1**. hrifnæmi, **2**. skapstyggð, **3**. stygglyndi, **4**. viðkvæmni, **5**. ertanleiki.
irritable *see* **1**. hrifnæmur, **2**. ýfinn, **3**. viðkvæmur, **4**. skapstyggur, **5**. stygglyndur.
irritant *see* **1**. ertandi, **2**. ertingarefni, **3**. ertingarlyf.
irritate *see* **1**. erta, **2**. espa.
irritation *see* **1**. geðvonska, **2**. óværi, **3**. erting.
ischemia *see* blóðþurrð.
isentropic *see* **1**. isentropískur, **2**. jafnátta.
island *see* **1**. eyja, **2**. gatfláki, **3**. hólmi, **4**. innfláki.
isobar *see* **1**. jafnþrýstiflötur, **2**. þrýstingslína, **3**. jafnþrýstilína, **4**. þrýstilína.
isochromatic *see* einlitur.
isochrone *see* jafntímalína.
isoenzyme *see* samsætuensím.
isogonal *see* jafnskekkjulína.
isolate *see* **1**. einangra, **2**. einangur.
isolated *see* Stakt.
isolation *see* **1**. sóttkvíun, **2**. einangrun, **3**. hreinræktun.
isolator *see* **1**. teinrofi, **2**. einangrari, **3**. skilrofi, **4**. stefnudeilir, **5**. stefnudeyfir.
isoleucine *see* **1**. ísólevsín, **2**. ísóleusin, **3**. ísólefsín, **4**. íle.
isoline *see* jafngildislína.
isomer *see* **1**. raðbrigði, **2**. systurtegund, **3**. systurefni, **4**. myndbrigði, **5**. ísómer.
isomerism *see* **1**. hverfni, **2**. systralag.
isomerization *see* **1**. Jafnliðun, **2**. raðbrögð.
isomorphic *see* **1**. einsmóta, **2**. einslaga.

isomorphism *see* **1**. einsmótun, **2**. einslögun.
isopleth *see* jafngildislína.
isostasy *see* **1**. flotajafnvægi, **2**. flotjafnvægi.
isotherm *see* **1**. hitalína, **2**. jafnhitaflötur, **3**. jafnhitalína.
isotonic *see* jafnþrýstinn.
isotope *see* **1**. samsæta, **2**. sáti, **3**. ísótópur.
isotropic *see* **1**. einsátta, **2**. jafnátta, **3**. stefnusnauður.
isotropy *see* stefnusneyða.
isozyme *see* samsætuensím.
issue *see* **1**. spurning, **2**. útgáfa.
isthmus *see* **1**. eiði, **2**. grandi, **3**. landbrú, **4**. mjódd.
italics *see* skáletur.
itch *see* kláði.
item *see* **1**. eining, **2**. hlutur, **3**. atriði, **4**. stak.
itemize *see* sundurliða.
iteration *see* **1**. ítrekun, **2**. ítrun.
ivory *see* **1**. fílabein, **2**. hvaltennur, **3**. rostungstennur.

J

jack *see* **1**. dúnkraftur, **2**. tjakkur, **3**. stungutengill, **4**. lyfta.
jackdaw *see* dvergkráka.
jacket *see* **1**. hlíf, **2**. kápa, **3**. lok, **4**. möttull.
jackknife *see* skerðingaraðferð.
jam *see* **1**. aldinmauk, **2**. festa, **3**. stöðva.
jar *see* ker.
jargon *see* **1**. fagmál, **2**. hópmál, **3**. hrognamál, **4**. sérmál, **5**. þvogl.
jaundice *see* **1**. gula, **2**. gulusótt.
jaw *see* **1**. kjaftur, **2**. kjálki, **3**. kjammi, **4**. makzelo, **5**. patrónukjaftur.
jaws *see* makzelo.
jay *see* skrækskaði.
jealous *see* öfundsjúkur.
jeans *see* gallabuxur.
jeep *see* **1**. jeppi, **2**. jepplingur.
jelly *see* aldinmauk.
jellyfish *see* **1**. skollahrákar, **2**. stórhveljur, **3**. skollaskyrpur, **4**. marglyttur, **5**. marglytta.
jeopardy *see* hætta.
jerk *see* **1**. kippur, **2**. rikkur, **3**. vöðvaviðbragð.
jet *see* **1**. rennslisauga, **2**. ýristútur, **3**. þota, **4**. straumur, **5**. nál.
jettison *see* snögglosa.
jetty *see* bryggja.
jewfish *see* júðafiskur.
jib *see* fokka.

jig *see* 1. skaka, 2. sniðmát, 3. skapalon, 4. mát, 5. haldari.
jitter *see* 1. flökt, 2. myndskjálfti.
job *see* 1. starf, 2. verk.
join *see* 1. samtenging, 2. tengja, 3. töflutenging.
joint *see* 1. sprunga, 2. stuðlunarsprunga, 3. samskeyti, 4. sameinaður, 5. liðamót.
jointly *see* saman.
jolt *see* 1. skaka, 2. hnykkur, 3. hrista, 4. rykkur.
joule *see* júl.
jounce *see* 1. samsláttur, 2. hossast.
journal *see* 1. dagblað, 2. dagbók, 3. fundarbók, 4. gerðabók, 5. leguvölur.
journey *see* ferðalög.
joy *see* gleði.
joyful *see* glaður.
joyous *see* glaður.
joystick *see* 1. stjórnvölur, 2. stýripinni, 3. stýristautur, 4. stýristöng.
judder *see* 1. hnökur, 2. sláttur.
judge *see* 1. dómari, 2. dæma.
juice *see* 1. safi, 2. seyti.
jump *see* 1. hoppa, 2. stökk, 3. stökkva.
jumper *see* 1. peysa, 2. slaufa, 3. slagbor, 4. spöng, 5. prufuleiðsla.
junction *see* 1. samtenging, 2. tenging, 3. samskeyti, 4. mót, 5. ármót.
jungle *see* frumskógur.
jurisdiction *see* 1. dómsaga, 2. dómsvald, 3. lögsaga, 4. lögsagnarumdæmi, 5. umdæmi.
jury *see* 1. kviður, 2. kviðdómur, 3. dómnefnd.
justification *see* 1. réttlæting, 2. rökstuðningur, 3. textajöfnun, 4. jöfnun.
justify *see* 1. jafna, 2. staðrétta.
jute *see* 1. jútujurt, 2. jútarunni.
juvenile *see* 1. ungdómur, 2. ungur.
juxtaposition *see* 1. hliðsetning, 2. hliðstaða.

K

k *see* kalín.
kalc *see* fóðurkál.
kangaroo *see* kengúra.
kaon *see* káeind.
karyokinesis *see* 1. kjarnskipting, 2. kjarnaskipting, 3. kjarnakvik, 4. jafnskipting, 5. mítósa.
karyosome *see* litkjarni.
karyotype *see* 1. kjarnagerð, 2. kjarngerð.
keel *see* kjölur.
keelson *see* 1. kjalsvín, 2. kjalbakki, 3. kjalband.
keen *see* 1. skarpur, 2. leiftandi, 3. beittur, 4. hrjúfur.
keep *see* turnvirki.
keeper *see* ventilsplitti.

keratin *see* 1. keratín, 2. hornefni, 3. hyrni.
keratinization *see* 1. hyrnismyndun, 2. hyrnishúðun, 3. hornmyndun, 4. horngerð.
kernel *see* kjarni.
kerosene *see* steinolía.
kestrel *see* turnfálki.
ketonuria *see* ketónmiga.
kettle *see* jökulker.
key *see* 1. lykill, 2. stýrinef, 3. kílfesta, 4. hnappur, 5. kíll.
keyboard *see* 1. hnappaborð, 2. leturborð, 3. lyklaborð.
keystone *see* lokasteinn.
kid *see* barn.
kidney *see* nýra.
kill *see* drepa.
kilocalorie *see* kílókaloría.
kilometer *see* kílómetri.
kilometre *see* kílómetri.
kilowatt *see* 1. kílóvatt, 2. kílówatt, 3. kW.
kin *see* 1. kynþáttur, 2. frændfólk.
kind *see* 1. vingjarnlegur, 2. kynþáttur, 3. vænn.
kindergarten *see* barnaheimili.
kindly *see* 1. vænn, 2. vingjarnlegur.
kinematic *see* 1. hreyfingarfræðilegur, 2. hreyfiafl, 3. hreyfifræðilegur.
kinematics *see* 1. hreyfingafræði, 2. gangfræði.
kinesthesia *see* hreyfiskyn.
kinesthesis *see* hreyfiskyn.
kinetics *see* 1. hraðafræði, 2. hvarfafræði, 3. hvarffræði, 4. hvarfhraðafræði.
king *see* 1. Kóngur, 2. drottin, 3. konungur.
kingdom *see* 1. ríki, 2. konungdómur, 3. konungsríki, 4. konungsveldi.
kingfisher *see* ísfugl.
kingpin *see* 1. stýrisvölur, 2. spindilbolti.
kinin *see* kínín.
kink *see* 1. beygla, 2. hnökri, 3. snurða.
kinship *see* sifjar.
kinsman *see* frændi.
kiss *see* 1. koss, 2. kyssa.
kitchen *see* eldhús.
kite *see* flugdreki.
kittiwake *see* rita.
kiwi *see* kívíflétta.
kleptomania *see* stelsýki.
klystron *see* 1. klístrónn, 2. klýstróna, 3. örbylgjuvaki.
knee *see* 1. hné, 2. liður, 3. kné, 4. hnjáliður, 5. hnéliður.
kneecap *see* hnéskel.
knickers *see* 1. kalsono, 2. nærbuxur.
knife *see* hnífur.
knight *see* Riddari.
knives *see* hnífur.

knob see 1. snerill, 2. takki.
knock see bank.
knot see 1. hnútur, 2. hnúta, 3. hnýta, 4. kvistur.
know see 1. þekkja, 2. vita.
knuckle see 1. hnúaliður, 2. spindill, 3. hnúi.
knurl see 1. gára, 2. riffla, 3. ýfa, 4. ýfing.
kohlrabi see hnúðkál.
krill see 1. kríli, 2. ljósáta, 3. hvaláta, 4. áta.
kurtosis see 1. ferilris, 2. hnítarris, 3. typping.
kwashiorkor see 1. kvasíorkor, 2. prótínkröm, 3.
  prótínvaneldi.

L

label see 1. merkja, 2. skeytismerking, 3. vistmerki,
  4. merkimiði, 5. merki.
labial see 1. varahljóð, 2. varamæltur.
labile see 1. hverflyndur, 2. óstöðugur, 3. ótraustur.
lability see 1. hverflyndi, 2. óstöðugleiki.
labor see 1. jóðsótt, 2. launþegar, 3. léttasótt, 4.
  verkalýður, 5. vinna.
laboratory see 1. rannsóknarstofa, 2. vinnustofa, 3.
  verkhús, 4. tilraunastofa, 5. rannsóknastofa.
labour see 1. vinna, 2. ala, 3. fæða, 4. launþegi, 5.
  verk.
labourer see verkamaður.
labyrinth see völundarhús.
lace see reim.
lacerate see sundurtæta.
laceration see sundurtæting.
lacquering see lökkun.
lactase see 1. laktasi, 2. mjólkursykurkljúfur.
lactate see 1. laktat, 2. mjólka.
lactation see 1. mjólkurmyndun, 2. mylking.
lacteal see 1. iðramjólkuræð, 2. mjólkurkenndur.
lactose see 1. laktósi, 2. mjólkursykur.
lacuna see 1. gloppa, 2. glufa, 3. eyða.
lad see 1. piltur, 2. strákur, 3. drengur.
ladder see 1. lausastigi, 2. stigi.
laden see 1. fermdur, 2. hlaðinn.
lady see 1. frú, 2. kona, 3. kvenmaður.
lag see 1. tregða, 2. droll, 3. tregðuskeið, 4. töf, 5.
  tímatöf.
lagging see 1. skjóllag, 2. vanþróun, 3. klæðning.
lagoon see 1. hóp, 2. lón, 3. strandlón.
lair see hreiður.
lake see 1. stöðuvatn, 2. vatn (water), 3. árbreiða, 4.
  tjörn, 5. fljótsbreiða.
lamella see 1. blað, 2. flaga, 3. kæliplata, 4. lag, 5.
  þynna.
laminar see lagskiptur.

laminated see 1. lagskiptur, 2. marglaga, 3.
  lagskipt.
lamp see 1. lampi, 2. ljósker, 3. lukt, 4. pera, 5. pípa.
land see 1. lenda, 2. brún, 3. láð, 4. landsvæði, 5.
  landareign.
landfall see 1. landsýn, 2. landtaka.
landing see 1. lending, 2. löndun.
landmark see 1. kennileiti, 2. landamerki, 3.
  leiðarmark, 4. mið.
landscape see 1. landslag, 2. langsnið.
landslide see 1. jarðvegshlaup, 2. jarðvegshrun, 3.
  jarðvegsskriða, 4. skriða, 5. skriðufall.
lane see rein.
language see 1. tungumál, 2. mál, 3. þjóðtunga, 4.
  tunga.
lantern see 1. ljósker, 2. ljósturn.
lanthanide see 1. lantaníð, 2. lanþaníð.
lanthanum see 1. lanþan, 2. lantan.
lanugo see 1. fósturhár, 2. líkhár.
laparotomy see lendaskurður.
lapping see 1. samslíping, 2. samslípun.
lapse see 1. dvína, 2. þverra.
larceny see 1. rán, 2. þjófnaður.
large see 1. mikill, 2. stór.
lari see máfuglar.
lark see lævirki.
larva see lirfa.
laryngeal see barkaopshljóð.
laryngitis see barkakýlisbólga.
larynx see 1. adamsepli, 2. barkakýli.
laser see 1. leysir, 2. ljósleysir, 3. ljörvi, 4.
  leysigeisli, 5. leysitæki.
lash see 1. svipa, 2. augnhár, 3. bil, 4. hlaup, 5.
  rígbinda.
lashing see reipi.
lass see 1. stelpa, 2. stúlka.
latch see 1. lás, 2. loka, 3. pall, 4. klinka.
latching see 1. klinkulæsing, 2. negling.
late see dauður.
latency see 1. dvali, 2. töf, 3. leynd, 4. bið, 5.
  biðtími.
latent see 1. hol, 2. óvirkur, 3. hulinn, 4. dulinn, 5.
  bundinn.
later see eftir.
lateral see 1. hliðstæður, 2. hliðlægt, 3. hliðlægur, 4.
  hliðmælt.
laterality see hliðlægi.
latex see mjólkursafi.
lathe see rennibekkur.
latitude see 1. breidd, 2. breiddarbaugur, 3.
  breiddargráða, 4. frjálsræði, 5. svigrúm.
lattice see 1. gleiðboganet, 2. grind.
laugh see hlæja.
launch see skipsbátur.
launder see 1. hreinsa, 2. þvo.

lava see 1. hraunleðja, 2. hraun, 3. hraunbreiða, 4. hraunhella, 5. hraunkvika.
lavatory see salerni.
law see 1. lög, 2. lögfræði, 3. lögmál, 4. regla.
lawful see löglegur.
lawnmower see sláttuvél.
lawrencium see 1. lárensín, 2. lárensíum.
lawyer see 1. málflytjandi, 2. málfærslumaður, 3. lögmaður, 4. málaflutningsmaður.
lax see 1. gisinn, 2. opinn, 3. slakur.
laxative see 1. hægðalosandi, 2. hægðalyf.
lay see 1. leggja, 2. setja.
layer see lag.
layout see 1. fyrirkomulag, 2. umbrot.
lazy see latur.
leaching see útskolun.
lead see 1. blý, 2. tengiþráður, 3. forskot, 4. leiðsla.
leader see 1. slóði, 2. forröð, 3. leiðari.
leaf see 1. lauf, 2. blað, 3. laufblað.
leaflet see 1. bæklingur, 2. hefti, 3. smáblað.
leak see 1. leka, 2. leki.
leakage see 1. straumleki, 2. leki.
lean see 1. mjór, 2. þunnur.
learn see læra.
learning see 1. lærdómur, 2. læring, 3. nám.
lease see 1. ábúðartími, 2. leigutími, 3. leigusamningur, 4. leigusamnigur, 5. leigja.
leasing see 1. eignarleiga, 2. þjónustuleiga, 3. langtímaleiga, 4. fjármögnunarleiga, 5. kaupleiga.
leather see 1. leður, 2. roð, 3. skinn.
leave see 1. fara, 2. frí, 3. leyfi, 4. yfirgefa.
lecithin see lesiþín.
ledge see jónhvolfssylla.
ledger see höfuðbók.
leeward see 1. hléborði, 2. skjólborði.
left see vinstri.
leg see 1. leggur, 2. áfangi, 3. fótleggur.
legal see 1. lögskipaður, 2. lögmætur, 3. löglegur, 4. lögfræðilegur.
legend see 1. helgisaga, 2. skýringar, 3. skýringartexti, 4. texti.
legislation see 1. löggjöf, 2. lagasetning.
legislature see þing.
legitimate see 1. réttmætur, 2. sannur, 3. lögmætur.
leisure see 1. tómstundir, 2. frístund, 3. frítími, 4. tómstund.
lemma see 1. uppflettimynd, 2. hjálparsetning.
lemon see 1. gulaldin, 2. limonía, 3. sítróna, 4. sítrónutré.
lender see lánveitandi.
length see lengd
lengthy see langur.
lens see 1. sjóngler, 2. augasteinn, 3. linsa.
lenticular see linsulaga.
lentigo see 1. frekna, 2. linsufrekna.

lentil see 1. linsa, 2. linsubaun.
leopard see hlébarði.
leprosy see 1. holdsveiki, 2. líkþrá.
lepton see létteind.
lesbian see 1. lesba, 2. lesbía, 3. lespa, 4. lespískur.
lesbianism see saffismi.
lesion see 1. sár, 2. skemmd, 3. löskun, 4. vefskemmd.
lessee see leigutaki.
lessor see leigusali.
let see leigja.
lethal see banvænn.
lethality see manndauði.
lethargy see svefnhöfgi.
letter see 1. bókstafur, 2. bréf, 3. stafur, 4. sendibréf.
letterpress see 1. leturprentun, 2. prentmál.
leucine see 1. lefsín, 2. leu, 3. leusín, 4. levsín.
leukemia see 1. blóðlýsa, 2. hvítblæði.
leukocyte see 1. hvítkorn, 2. hvítfruma.
leukocytosis see 1. hvítfrumnafjölgun, 2. hvítkornafjölgun.
leukopenia see 1. hvítfrumnafæð, 2. hvítfrumnaskortur, 3. hvítfrumufæð, 4. hvítkornafæð.
leukoplakia see slímuþykkildi
levator see 1. lyftir, 2. léttir.
level see 1. staða, 2. yfirborðshæð, 3. stig, 4. líkur, 5. lag.
leveling see 1. hæðarstilling, 2. slípun.
levelling see 1. hæðarstilling, 2. útjöfnun.
lever see 1. lyfta, 2. armur, 3. lyftistöng, 4. reisa, 5. stöng.
leverage see 1. áhættuvægi, 2. skuldsetning, 3. vogarafl, 4. vogun.
levulose see frúktósi.
levy see 1. skattur, 2. álaga, 3. gjald.
lexeme see les.
lexicon see orðasafn.
liabilities see 1. skuldbindingar, 2. skuldir.
liability see 1. byrði, 2. sök, 3. skuld, 4. skaðabótaskylda, 5. ábyrgð.
liable see 1. ábyrgur, 2. líklegur, 3. skyldugur, 4. traustur.
liaison see 1. samstarf, 2. samhæfing.
libel see 1. slúðra, 2. slúður.
liberal see 1. framfarasinnaður, 2. frjálslyndur, 3. umburðarlyndur, 4. víðsýnn.
liberalism see 1. frjálslyndi, 2. frjálslyndisstefna.
liberate see 1. frelsa, 2. leysa.
libido see 1. lífshvöt, 2. frygð.
librarian see 1. safnvörður, 2. safnvörsluforrit.
library see 1. bókasafn, 2. myndgagnasafn, 3. safn.
libration see tunglvik.
licence see 1. leyfi, 2. skírteini.
license see leyfi.

licensing *see* leyfisveiting.
lichen *see* 1. flétta, 2. húðskæni, 3. húðskæningur, 4. skóf.
lid *see* lok.
lie *see* 1. ljúga, 2. skrökva, 3. lygi, 4. liggja, 5. leggja.
lien *see* 1. haldsréttur, 2. milta, 3. milti.
life *see* 1. endingartími, 2. líf, 3. ending, 4. æfi, 5. líflengd.
lifestyle *see* 1. lífsmáti, 2. lífsstíll.
lifetime *see* 1. æviskeið, 2. meðalævi.
lift *see* 1. lyfta, 2. reisa, 3. lyftikraftur, 4. létta, 5. hefja.
lifter *see* 1. undirlyfta, 2. undirlyftuarmur, 3. undirlyftutappi.
ligament *see* 1. stoðband, 2. strengur, 3. liðhand, 4. band.
ligand *see* 1. tengihópur, 2. tengill, 3. bindill.
ligase *see* 1. lígasi, 2. límir, 3. tengiensím, 4. tengir.
ligation *see* 1. fyrirbinding, 2. tenging, 3. líming.
ligature *see* 1. æðaband, 2. fyrirbinding.
light *see* 1. ljós, 2. þunnur, 3. veikur, 4. lýsing, 5. léttur.
lighthearted *see* glaður.
lighthouse *see* 1. viti, 2. vitahús.
lighting *see* lýsing.
lightning *see* elding.
lignin *see* 1. lignín, 2. tréefni, 3. tréni.
lignite *see* 1. brúnkol, 2. mókol, 3. surtarbrandur.
likable *see* viðkunnanlegur.
like *see* hvernig.
likelihood *see* sennileiki.
likely *see* sennilegur.
likeness *see* líking.
likewise *see* 1. einnig, 2. líka.
liking *see* smakka.
limb *see* 1. útlimur, 2. rönd, 3. limur, 4. jaðar, 5. kragi.
lime *see* 1. læmutré, 2. súraldin, 3. lindiviður, 4. linditré, 5. súraldintré.
limit *see* 1. takmark, 2. takmörk, 3. mörk, 4. markgildi, 5. mark.
limitation *see* 1. fyrning, 2. takmarkanir, 3. takmörkun.
limited *see* 1. hlutafélag, 2. takmarkaður.
limiter *see* takmarkari.
limousine *see* 1. bifreið, 2. eðalvagn.
limp *see* 1. helti, 2. slakur.
line *see* 1. röð, 2. snúra, 3. spor, 4. slaufa, 5. rás.
lineage *see* 1. ættleggur, 2. uppruni.
linear *see* 1. línulaga, 2. línulegur, 3. striklaga.
liner *see* 1. fóðring, 2. ljóni, 3. slíf, 4. skip, 5. fóður.
ling *see* 1. langa, 2. mjósi, 3. skrokklanga, 4. vatnaflekkur.
linguistics *see* málvísindi.

liniment *see* áburður.
lining *see* 1. fóður, 2. klæðning, 3. borði.
link *see* 1. sleðabraut, 2. hlekkur, 3. tengja, 4. tengill, 5. stikla.
linkage *see* 1. tengsl, 2. armabúnaður, 3. fléttun, 4. ráðningartenging, 5. tengi.
linker *see* tengill.
lion *see* ljón.
lip *see* vör.
lipase *see* 1. fitukljúfur, 2. lípasi.
lipid *see* 1. lípíð, 2. fituefni, 3. fitungar.
lipoprotein *see* 1. lípóprótín, 2. fituhvíta, 3. fituprótín.
liquefaction *see* 1. Lögun, 2. þétting, 3. vökvagerð, 4. vökvamyndun.
liquid *see* 1. vökvi, 2. fljótandi, 3. mjúkhljóð, 4. lögur, 5. greiðslufær.
liquidation *see* gjaldþrot.
liquidity *see* 1. greiðsluþol, 2. reiðufjárgeta, 3. lausafjárstaða, 4. greiðslugeta, 5. greiðsluflæði.
list *see* 1. skrá, 2. slagsíða, 3. halli, 4. lista, 5. listi.
litchi *see* 1. litkaplóma, 2. litkaaldin, 3. litkaber.
liter *see* litri.
literacy *see* læsi.
lithium *see* 1. litín, 2. liþín, 3. litíum.
lithosphere *see* 1. steinhvolf, 2. steinhvel, 3. jarðskorpa, 4. stinnhvolf.
litmus *see* lakkmúslitur.
litter *see* 1. feyra, 2. lauffeyra, 3. samburar, 4. sina, 5. sjúkrabörur.
little *see* 1. lítill, 2. smár.
live *see* 1. líf, 2. lifa, 3. virkur, 4. búa.
lively *see* glaður.
liver *see* lifur.
livestock *see* 1. fé, 2. búfé, 3. búpeningur.
lizard *see* sandeðla.
loach *see* spáfiskur.
load *see* 1. hleðsla, 2. álag, 3. áraun, 4. aurburður, 5. ferma.
loaded *see* lestaður.
loading *see* 1. lestun, 2. spilliefnaflæði, 3. spönun, 4. hleðsla.
loaf *see* brauð.
loan *see* 1. lán, 2. útlán.
loathe *see* hrylla.
loathsome *see* 1. andstyggilegur, 2. hryllilegur.
lobate *see* 1. blaðskiptur, 2. deildur.
lobe *see* 1. lykkja, 2. netlykkja, 3. kambur, 4. geiri, 5. flipi.
lobotomy *see* 1. geiraskurður, 2. hvítuskurður.
lobule *see* 1. bleðill, 2. snepill.
local *see* 1. staðbundinn, 2. staðtengdur, 3. staðvær.
localism *see* 1. átthagabönd, 2. svæðavæðing, 3. hreppapólitík.

localization see **1**. staðbinding, **2**. staðfærsla, **3**. staðgreining, **4**. staðsetning.
localize see **1**. staðgreina, **2**. staðmarka, **3**. staðbinda, **4**. afmarka, **5**. staðsetja.
localized see **1**. staðbundinn, **2**. staðmarkaður.
locate see **1**. finna, **2**. marka, **3**. staðsetja.
location see **1**. lega, **2**. staður, **3**. staðsetning, **4**. heimilistang, **5**. loð.
locator see **1**. aðflugshringviti, **2**. staðsetningarviti.
loch see vatn (water).
lock see **1**. lás, **2**. verja, **3**. þvinga, **4**. slússa, **5**. skipastigi.
lockout see **1**. læsing, **2**. verkbann.
locomotion see staðning.
locomotive see eimreið.
locus see **1**. gensæti, **2**. genset, **3**. leg, **4**. set, **5**. staður.
locust see engispretta.
loess see **1**. fokmold, **2**. löss, **3**. fokjarðvegur.
lofty see hár (hair).
log see vegmælir.
logarithm see **1**. lógaritmi, **2**. logri, **3**. lógrími.
logger see **1**. skógarhöggsmaður, **2**. gangriti, **3**. síriti.
logistics see **1**. vörustjórnun, **2**. vöruferlisstjórnun, **3**. flæðisstjórnun, **4**. flutningafræði, **5**. vöruferilsstjórn.
logo see **1**. teikn, **2**. firmamerki, **3**. kennimark, **4**. nafnmerki, **5**. orðmerki.
loll see **1**. halli, **2**. slagsíða.
long see **1**. langur, **2**. þrá.
longan see **1**. longanber, **2**. vörtuber, **3**. vörtuberjatré.
longevity see **1**. langlífi, **2**. endingartími.
longing see þrá.
longitude see **1**. lengdarbaugur, **2**. lengdargráða, **3**. lengd.
longitudinal see langsum.
look see þykja.
loom see leiðslukerfi.
loop see **1**. hringnet, **2**. straumlykkja, **3**. lykkja, **4**. ferli, **5**. slaufa.
loquat see **1**. dúnepli, **2**. japansplóma.
lord see herra.
lorry see vörubíll.
loss see **1**. tjón, **2**. tap, **3**. skipbrot, **4**. skaði, **5**. skipreiki.
losses see **1**. tap, **2**. tjón, **3**. töp.
lotion see húðlögur.
lottery see **1**. hlutavelta, **2**. tombóla.
lotus see lótusblóm.
loudness see **1**. háværð, **2**. hljóðstyrkur.
loudspeaker see **1**. hátalari, **2**. gellir.
lounge see stofa.
louse see lús.
louver see ristarhleri.

love see **1**. ást, **2**. elska, **3**. kærleikur.
lovely see **1**. þægilegur, **2**. sætur, **3**. elskulegur, **4**. fagur, **5**. fallegur.
low see **1**. fjarlægur, **2**. lægð, **3**. lágur.
lower see **1**. niðurlægja, **2**. lægri, **3**. neðri.
lowercase see lágstafa.
lube see **1**. smurefni, **2**. olía.
lubricant see **1**. smurefni, **2**. smurfeiti.
lubricate see smyrja.
lubrication see **1**. smurning, **2**. smurningur.
lubricator see **1**. smurefni, **2**. smurnippill, **3**. smurkoppur.
lucid see **1**. skýr, **2**. auðskilinn.
lues see sárasótt.
lug see **1**. strengskór, **2**. þvinga, **3**. pína, **4**. eyra (ear), **5**. erfiða.
lugubrious see dapur.
lugworm see sandmaðkur.
lukewarm see volgur.
lullaby see **1**. vögguljóð, **2**. vögguvísa.
lumbago see **1**. lendagigt, **2**. þursabit.
lumen see **1**. hol, **2**. lúmen.
luminance see **1**. ljómi, **2**. skin.
luminescence see **1**. ljóm, **2**. ljómun, **3**. skíma, **4**. skin.
luminosity see **1**. geislunarafl, **2**. skærlciki, **3**. ljósafl, **4**. birtustig, **5**. ljósnæmishlutfall.
lump see **1**. grásleppa, **2**. hnútur, **3**. hrognkelsi, **4**. kökkur, **5**. rauðmagi.
lumpfish see hrognkelsi.
lung see lunga.
lungfish see **1**. risaborri, **2**. lungnafiskar.
lupus see Úlfurinn.
lure see agn.
lurid see **1**. beittur, **2**. hrjúfur, **3**. leiftandi, **4**. skarpur.
lutetium see **1**. lútetín, **2**. lútesín, **3**. lútetíum.
lux see lúx.
luxation see liðhlaup.
luxuriant see **1**. gróskumikill, **2**. ofvaxinn.
luxury see munaður.
lymph see **1**. vessi, **2**. sogæðavökvi, **3**. úr.
lymphadenitis see **1**. eitlaþroti, **2**. eitilbólga, **3**. eitlabólga.
lymphadenopathy see **1**. eitilastækkun, **2**. eitlakvilli.
lymphatic see **1**. sogæð, **2**. vessaæð.
lymphedema see vessabjúgur.
lymphocyte see **1**. eitlafruma, **2**. eitlingur, **3**. eitilkorn, **4**. eitilfruma.
lymphoma see **1**. eitilfrumukrabbamein, **2**. eitlaæxli, **3**. eitilæxli.
lynx see gaupa.
lyophilization see frostþurrkun.
lysine see **1**. lýsín, **2**. lýs.

lysis see 1. sundrun, 2. sótthitasig, 3. leysing, 4. rof,
5. samvaxtalosun.
lysogeny see veirubinding.
lysozyme see leysiensím.
lytic see 1. sundrandi, 2. leysandi, 3. rjúfandi.

M

macaroni see núðlur.
maceration see 1. vessagrotnun, 2. kaldbleyting.
machine see 1. vél, 2. renna, 3. tæki, 4. vélvinna.
machined see 1. vélunninn, 2. vélunnið.
machinery see 1. vélbúnaður, 2. vélar.
mackerel see makríll.
macro see fjölvi.
macroeconomics see 1. heildarhagfræði, 2.
þjóðhagfræði.
macroglobulin see 1. risaglóbúlín, 2. stórglóbúlín.
macromolecule see 1. stórsameind, 2. risasameind.
macrophage see 1. vefjakorn, 2. stórháma, 3.
stórátfruma, 4. stóræta, 5. gleypifruma.
macroscopic see 1. stórsær, 2. augsær, 3. heildsær.
macula see 1. dökkna, 2. blettur, 3. díll.
macule see húðdrafna.
mad see 1. meðaltölugildisfrávik, 2. óður.
madam see frú.
magazine see 1. meis, 2. tímarit.
magi see intesto.
magistrate see 1. yfirvald, 2. sýslumaður, 3. fógeti,
4. friðdómari.
magma see 1. bergkvika, 2. kvika.
magnesium see 1. magnín, 2. magnesín, 3.
magníum, 4. magnesíum.
magnet see 1. segulstál, 2. sísegull, 3. segull.
magnetic see 1. misvísandi, 2. seglanlegur, 3.
segulmagnaður.
magnetism see 1. segulmagn, 2. segulafl, 3.
segulfræði.
magnetization see segulmögnun.
magneto see 1. segulkveikja, 2. sísegulrafali, 3.
kveikja.
magnetohydrodynamics see segulstraumfræði.
magnetometer see 1. segulmælir, 2.
segulsviðsmælir.
magnetosphere see segulhvolf.
magnetron see 1. magnetróna, 2. segulsviðsrör, 3.
segulrör, 4. magnetrónn, 5. örbylgjuvaki.
magnification see stækkun.
magnitude see 1. magn, 2. styrkur, 3. stærð, 4.
myrkvastig, 5. lengd.
magpie see skjór.
mail see póstur.
main see 1. aðallögn, 2. stofnlögn.

mainframe see 1. megintölva, 2. stórtölva.
maintain see viðhalda.
maintenance see 1. framfærlsueyrir, 2.
framfærslufé, 3. framfærslumeðlag, 4. viðhald.
maize see maís.
majesty see 1. tign, 2. veldi, 3. hátign.
major see 1. meirihháttar, 2. mikill, 3. stærri, 4. stór,
5. meiri.
majority see 1. lögræðisaldur, 2. meirihluti.
make see 1. gera, 2. gerð, 3. framleiðsla.
malabsorption see 1. vanupptaka, 2. vanfrásog.
maladjustment see 1. aðlögunarörðugleikar, 2.
mishæfing.
malady see kvilli.
malaise see 1. lasleiki, 2. lympa.
male see 1. karlmaður, 2. maður (man), 3. karl, 4.
karldýr.
malformation see vansköpun.
malfunction see 1. bilun, 2. gangtruflun, 3. ólag, 4.
starfsbilun, 5. starfsröskun.
malign see slúðra.
malignant see 1. illkynjaður, 2. illkynja.
mall see verslanamiðstöð.
mallard see stokkönd.
mallet see 1. gúmmíhamar, 2. kylfa.
malleus see hamar.
malnutrition see 1. vannæring, 2. næringarskortur.
maltose see 1. maltósi, 2. maltsykur.
mamilla see 1. geirvarta, 2. varta.
mammal see spendýr.
mammography see 1. brjóstamyndataka, 2.
brjóstmyndataka.
man see 1. maður, 2. manneskja, 3. mannvera, 4.
menn, 5. karlmaður.
manage see stilla.
manageable see meðfærilegur.
management see 1. stjórn, 2. stjórnun, 3. stýring.
manager see 1. framkvæmdastjóri, 2. stjórnandi.
mandate see 1. neyða, 2. þvinga.
mandatory see 1. lögboðinn, 2. lögskipaður, 3.
skyldugur, 4. tilskipaður, 5. fyrirskipaður.
mandible see 1. bitkrókur, 2. kjálki.
mandrel see 1. úrrek, 2. dór, 3. öxull, 4. rennivölur.
maneuver see handlag.
manganese see mangan.
mango see 1. mangó, 2. mangóávöxtur.
mangosteen see 1. mangóstan, 2. mangóstantré, 3.
mangostan, 4. mangó, 5. gullaldintré.
manhole see 1. brunnur, 2. op.
mania see 1. æði, 2. árátta, 3. geðhæð, 4. oflæti.
manic see 1. hamstola, 2. óður, 3. ær.
manifold see 1. greinrör, 2. röragrein, 3. safngrein,
4. stofngrein, 5. víðátta.
manipulation see 1. tilfæring, 2. handfjöllun, 3.
handfjötlun.

mankind see mannkyn.
mannitol see mannitól.
mannose see mannósi.
manoeuvrability see 1. fluglipurð, 2. lipurð, 3. stjórnhæfni.
manoeuvre see 1. flugbragð, 2. tilfærsla, 3. stjórntök, 4. stjórna, 5. herbragð.
manometer see 1. þrýstimælir, 2. þrýstingsmælir.
manpower see mannafli.
mantissa see 1. tölukjarni, 2. viðbót, 3. kjarni.
mantle see 1. hlíf, 2. jarðmöttull, 3. kápa, 4. möttull, 5. hjúpur.
manual see 1. handvirkt, 2. handvirkur, 3. handbók, 4. handknúið.
manufacture see 1. framleiðsla, 2. iðnframleiðsla.
manufacturer see framleiðandi.
manufacturing see 1. verksmiðjuvinna, 2. framleiðsla, 3. iðnaður, 4. iðnframleiðsla.
many see margir.
map see 1. kort, 2. kortleggja, 3. landabréf, 4. landakort, 5. landsuppdráttur.
maple see 1. mösur, 2. hlynur, 3. garðahlynur, 4. ahorntré.
mapping see 1. kortlagning, 2. vörpun, 3. kortagerð.
marasmus see kröm.
march see 1. Mars, 2. marsmánuður, 3. marz.
mare see 1. tunglhaf, 2. slétta.
margin see 1. jaðar, 2. vikmörk, 3. vaxtaálag, 4. rönd, 5. spássía.
marginal see randstæður.
marijuana see 1. hassjurt, 2. maríúana.
mariner see 1. háseti, 2. landgönguliði, 3. sæfari.
mark see 1. málmerki, 2. merki, 3. merkja, 4. prófseinkunn, 5. prófskírteini.
markdown see verðlækkun.
marker see 1. mark, 2. vallarmarki, 3. staðvísir, 4. merkigen, 5. markari.
market see 1. markaðssetja, 2. markaður, 3. verslun.
marketable see 1. seljanlegur, 2. söluhæfur, 3. markaðshæfur.
marketing see 1. markaðsfræði, 2. markaðssetning, 3. markaðsfærsla.
marking see 1. starfsástand, 2. flugvallarmerking, 3. hvíldarástand, 4. merking, 5. mörkun.
markup see 1. verðhækkun, 2. ívaf, 3. álagning.
marmot see múrmeldýr.
marriage see 1. brúðkaup, 2. hjónaband.
married see giftur.
marrow see 1. mergur, 2. beinmergur, 3. mergja.
marry see giftast.
marsh see 1. flæðiengi, 2. flæðiland, 3. merski, 4. mýri, 5. votlendi.
marten see mörður.
martyr see píslarvottur.
marvel see undrast.

maser see 1. örbylgjuleysir, 2. meysir.
mask see 1. skráningarform, 2. stafsía, 3. innsláttarform, 4. hylja, 5. hula.
masking see 1. læging, 2. mynstrun, 3. skygging, 4. dyljun.
masochism see 1. meinlætamunaður, 2. sjálfspíslahvöt.
mass see 1. massi, 2. ógrynni, 3. hlass, 4. efnismagn.
masseur see 1. nuddmaður, 2. nuddtæki, 3. nuddari.
massive see 1. gegnheill, 2. heill.
mast see 1. siglutré, 2. mastur, 3. sigla.
mastectomy see brjóstnám.
master see 1. frummynd, 2. fyrirmynd, 3. Meistari, 4. mynstur, 5. staðall.
mastication see tygging.
mastocyte see mastfruma.
masturbation see sjálfsfróun.
mat see 1. gólfábreiða, 2. gólfteppi, 3. motta.
match see 1. eldspýta, 2. para, 3. samstilla, 4. samvalinn.
matching see 1. mátun, 2. pörun.
mate see 1. eiginmaður, 2. kona, 3. maður (man), 4. Mát, 5. vinur.
material see 1. efniviður, 2. verkefni, 3. verulegur, 4. smíðaefni, 5. materia.
materialism see 1. efnishyggja, 2. lífsþægindagræðgi, 3. veraldarhyggja.
materials see 1. materiala, 2. materialo, 3. materia, 4. ŝtofo.
maternal see móðurlegur.
mathematics see stærðfræði.
matrimony see hjónaband.
matrix see 1. mergur, 2. net, 3. uppistöðuefni, 4. mót, 5. grunnfrymi.
matter see 1. efni, 2. mál.
mattress see dýna.
maturation see þroskun.
mature see 1. fullorðinn, 2. gjaldfalla.
maturity see 1. fullþroski, 2. þroski.
maul see 1. bíta, 2. sleggja.
max see hámark.
maxilla see kinnkjálki.
maximize see 1. besta, 2. hámarka, 3. fullstækka.
maximum see 1. hágildi, 2. hámark.
may see 1. Maí, 2. maímánuður.
mayday see hjálp.
maze see völundarhús.
meal see 1. matur, 2. mjöl.
mean see 1. averaĝa, 2. meðalgildi, 3. meðaltal, 4. merkja, 5. þýða.
meander see 1. árbugða, 2. bugða.
meaning see merking.
meaningful see alvarlegur.
means see 1. signifi, 2. averaĝa, 3. celi, 4. intenci, 5. malnobla.

measles *see* mislingar.
measure *see* 1. aðgerðir, 2. mæla, 3. mælieining, 4. mál, 5. ráðstöfun.
measurement *see* 1. mælikerfi, 2. mæling, 3. mælingar.
measuring *see* mæling.
meat *see* kjöt.
meatus *see* 1. geil, 2. göng, 3. hlust, 4. vegur.
mechanic *see* 1. bifvélavirki, 2. viðgerðarmaður, 3. viðgerðamaður, 4. vélvirki, 5. vélstjóri.
mechanical *see* 1. kraftvirkur, 2. vélvirkur, 3. vélrænt, 4. vélrænn, 5. kraftrænn.
mechanics *see* 1. aflfræði, 2. kraftfræði, 3. mehanikisto.
mechanism *see* 1. gangvirki, 2. vélhyggja, 3. vélgengi, 4. gengd, 5. gangverk.
mechanization *see* vélvæðing.
mechanoreceptor *see* aflnemi.
meconium *see* 1. barnasorta, 2. barnaat, 3. barnabik.
media *see* 1. miðill, 2. fjölmiðlar.
medial *see* 1. innstæður, 2. miðlægur.
median *see* 1. miðgildi, 2. miðmark, 3. miðtala.
mediation *see* 1. meðalganga, 2. sáttaumleitun, 3. miðlun, 4. málamiðlun, 5. milliganga.
mediator *see* 1. miðlari, 2. milliliður.
medical *see* 1. læknisfræðilegur, 2. lyflæknisfræðilegur.
medication *see* 1. læknisfræði, 2. lyfjameðferð.
medicine *see* 1. læknisfræði, 2. lyf, 3. lyflæknisfræði, 4. meðal.
meditation *see* hugleiðsla.
medium *see* 1. æti, 2. efni, 3. miðill, 4. umhverfi.
medulla *see* mergur.
meet *see* 1. hitta, 2. mæta.
meeting *see* fundur.
megalomania *see* 1. mikilmennskuæði, 2. stærisýki, 3. stórmennskubrjálun.
megaspore *see* stórgró.
megrim *see* 1. stórkjafta, 2. þjalakoli, 3. flúra, 4. öfugkjafta.
meiosis *see* 1. meiósa, 2. rýriskipting.
melancholia *see* geðlægð.
melancholic *see* þunglyndur.
melancholy *see* þunglyndi.
melanin *see* 1. sortuefni, 2. sverta, 3. sorta, 4. melanín.
melanocyte *see* 1. sortufruma, 2. litfruma.
melanoma *see* sortuæxli.
melanosis *see* 1. sorti, 2. sortnun.
melatonin *see* melatónín.
melon *see* melóna.
melt *see* 1. bráðna, 2. þiðna, 3. bráð, 4. þíða, 5. bræða.
melting *see* 1. bráðnun, 2. bræðsla.

member *see* 1. félagsmaður, 2. meðlimur, 3. félagi, 4. biti, 5. aðili.
membrane *see* 1. blaðka, 2. himna, 3. membra, 4. þind.
memorandum *see* 1. minnisatriði, 2. orðsending, 3. minnisgrein, 4. minnisblöð, 5. greinargerð.
memory *see* 1. minni, 2. geymsla.
men *see* maður (man).
mend *see* lagfæra.
mendelevium *see* 1. mendelevín, 2. mendelefín, 3. mendelevíum.
meningitis *see* 1. heilahimnubólga, 2. mænuhimnubólga, 3. mengisbólga.
meniscus *see* 1. vökvakúpull, 2. bjúgborð, 3. bjúgflötur, 4. bjúglinsa, 5. máni.
menopause *see* 1. tíðalok, 2. tíðahvörf.
menorrhagia *see* asatíðir.
menstruation *see* 1. klæðaföll, 2. tíðir.
mental *see* andlegur.
mentality *see* 1. hugarfar, 2. hugerni.
menu *see* 1. matseðill, 2. valseðill, 3. valblað, 4. valmynd.
mercantilism *see* 1. merkantílismi, 2. kaupauðgiskenning, 3. kaupauðgisstefna, 4. kaupauðgistefna, 5. kaupskaparstefna.
merchandise *see* 1. söluvara, 2. varningur, 3. söluvarningur.
mercy *see* meðaumkun.
mere *see* vatn (water).
merge *see* 1. sameina, 2. tvinna.
merger *see* 1. samruni, 2. samsteypa.
meridian *see* 1. hábaugur, 2. hádegisbaugur, 3. lengdarbaugur.
merry *see* 1. glaðlyndur, 2. glaður.
merry-go-round *see* hringekja.
mesentery *see* 1. garnahengi, 2. hengi.
mesh *see* 1. tengt, 2. möskvi, 3. tannhjólagrip.
mesial *see* miðlægur.
meson *see* 1. mesóna, 2. miðeind, 3. miðögn.
mesophilic *see* miðlungshitakær.
mesosphere *see* miðhvolf.
mess *see* 1. messi, 2. mötuneyti.
message *see* 1. boð, 2. tölvuskeyti, 3. skilaboð, 4. málboð, 5. skeyti.
messenger *see* 1. burðarvír, 2. erindreki, 3. pokabyssa, 4. sendiboði.
metabolism *see* efnaskipti.
metabolite *see* 1. umbrotsefni, 2. skiptiefni, 3. lífefni.
metal *see* 1. málmur, 2. þungefni.
metalanguage *see* 1. lýsimál, 2. stoðmál.
metalloid *see* 1. málmungur, 2. melmingur, 3. málmbróðir, 4. hálfmálmur.
metallurgy *see* 1. málmfræði, 2. efnisfræði.
metamerism *see* liðun.

metamorphism *see* myndbreyting.
metamorphosis *see* 1. hamskipting, 2.
myndbreyting.
metaphor *see* 1. myndhvörf, 2. myndlíking, 3.
myndhverfing.
metastable *see* hálfstöðugur.
metastasis *see* 1. meinrek, 2. meinsáð, 3. meinvarp,
4. sáðmein.
meteor *see* 1. stjörnuhrap, 2. veðurfyrirbæri, 3.
loftsteinn, 4. hrapsteinn, 5. vígahnöttur.
meteorite *see* loftsteinn.
meteoroid *see* 1. geimgrýti, 2. geimsteinn, 3.
reikisteinn.
meteorologist *see* veðurfræðingur.
meteorology *see* veðurfræði.
meter *see* 1. metri, 2. mælir.
methanal *see* formaldehýð.
methane *see* metan.
methanol *see* 1. metanól, 2. tréspíri, 3. tréspíritus.
methionine *see* 1. met, 2. meþíónín, 3. metíónín.
method *see* aðferð.
methodology *see* 1. aðferð, 2. aðferðafræði.
metonymy *see* 1. merkingarskipti, 2. nafnhvörf.
metre *see* metri.
metric *see* firð.
metrical *see* háttbundinn.
metrics *see* bragfræði.
metro *see* neðanjarðarlest.
mica *see* 1. glimmer, 2. gljásteinn.
microbe *see* örvera.
microbiology *see* örverufræði.
microchip *see* 1. kísilflaga, 2. örtölvuflaga.
microclimate *see* 1. nærveður, 2. nærviðri, 3.
örveður, 4. örviðri.
microcomputer *see* örtölva.
microelectronics *see* 1. dvergrásatækni, 2.
öreindafræði.
microflora *see* 1. smáflóra, 2. örflóra.
micrograph *see* 1. örriti, 2. smásjármynd.
micrometer *see* 1. míkróskrúfa, 2. smásjárkvarði, 3.
skrúfmál, 4. örkvarði, 5. míkrókvarði.
micron *see* míkron.
micronutrient *see* snefilefni.
microorganism *see* örvera.
microphone *see* 1. hljóðnemi, 2. kolahljóðnemi, 3.
taldós.
microprocessor *see* 1. örgjörvi, 2. vinnsluverk.
microscope *see* smásjá.
microscopic *see* smásær.
microtome *see* 1. örskeri, 2. smáskeri, 3. vefjaskeri.
microwave *see* örbylgja
midbrain *see* miðheili.
midship *see* miðsvæðis.
midwife *see* 1. ljósmóðir, 2. nærkona, 3.
yfirsetukona.

migration *see* 1. far, 2. flakk, 3. flökkuhópur, 4.
fólksflutningar, 5. frumufar.
mike *see* hljóðnemi.
mild *see* mjúkur.
mile *see* míla.
milestone *see* 1. áfangi, 2. varða.
milieu *see* umhorf.
military *see* her.
milk *see* 1. mjólk, 2. mjólka.
mill *see* 1. fræsa, 2. verksmiðja, 3. valsa, 4. skera, 5.
mylla.
millibar *see* millíbar.
millimeter *see* 1. millimetri, 2. millímetri.
milling *see* 1. fræsing, 2. fræsun.
million *see* milljón.
mimesis *see* herming.
mind *see* hugur.
mine *see* 1. minn, 2. náma, 3. tundurdufl.
mineral *see* 1. steind, 2. steintegund, 3. steinefni.
mineralization *see* steinefnaútfelling.
mineralocorticoid *see* saltsteri.
minimal *see* 1. minnstur, 2. örlítill, 3. smæstur.
minimize *see* lágmarka.
minimum *see* 1. lágmark, 2. lággildi.
mining *see* 1. námuvinnsla, 2. námugröftur, 3. Nám,
4. losun.
minister *see* 1. sendiherra, 2. ráðherra, 3.
sendimaður.
ministry *see* 1. ráðuneyti, 2. klerkdómur, 3.
ráðherraembætti.
minnow *see* straumlalli.
minor *see* minniháttar.
minority *see* 1. minnihluti, 2. minninhlutahópur.
mint *see* 1. mentur, 2. mintur, 3. myntur.
minus *see* 1. mínusmerki, 2. mínustenging, 3.
frádráttarmerki, 4. neikvæður, 5. mínus.
minute *see* 1. mínúta, 2. bogamínúta, 3. minuto.
minutes *see* 1. fundargerð, 2. gerðabók, 3. eta, 4.
bókun, 5. minuto.
miosis *see* 1. litukrampi, 2. ljósopsþrenging.
mirage *see* 1. hillingar, 2. tíbrá.
mire *see* 1. mýrlendi, 2. fen, 3. mýrarfen, 4. mýri.
mirror *see* 1. spegill, 2. spegla.
mirroring *see* speglun.
misanthropy *see* mannhatur.
miscarriage *see* fósturlát.
miscible *see* blandanlegur.
miserable *see* 1. slæmur, 2. vondur, 3. illur, 4.
fátækur, 5. dapur.
misfire *see* 1. feilkveiking, 2. gangtruflun, 3.
miskveiking, 4. miskveikja, 5. missa.
mishap *see* 1. slys, 2. óhapp.
mislead *see* svíkja.
mismatch *see* 1. mispörun, 2. misstilling.
missile *see* 1. flugskeyti, 2. skeyti.

mission *see* 1. tilgangur, 2. fastanefnd, 3. hlutverk, 4. sendinefnd.

missis *see* frú.

mist *see* 1. þoka, 2. þokumóða, 3. úði, 4. mistur.

mistake *see* mistök.

mistress *see* frú.

mistrust *see* 1. vantraust, 2. vantreysta.

mite *see* 1. lítilræði, 2. smámaur.

mitochondrion *see* 1. hvatberi, 2. festarkorn, 3. kyndikorn, 4. orkukorn.

mitosis *see* 1. frumuskipting, 2. jafnskipting, 3. kjarnaskipting, 4. mítósa.

mix *see* blanda.

mixer *see* 1. blandari, 2. blöndunarstig.

mixing *see* blöndun.

mixture *see* 1. blanda, 2. efnablanda, 3. lyfjablanda.

mnemonics *see* 1. minnisefling, 2. minnishjálp, 3. minnistækni.

mobile *see* 1. færanlegur, 2. hreyfanlegur.

mobility *see* 1. hreyfanleiki, 2. flytjanleiki, 3. færanleiki.

mobilization *see* 1. liðkun, 2. losun, 3. tygjun.

mobilize *see* 1. liðka, 2. losa.

modality *see* 1. merkingarháttur, 2. skilningarvit, 3. skynform, 4. mæða.

mode *see* 1. kryppugildi, 2. máti, 3. stýriháttur, 4. tindatala, 5. hamur.

model *see* 1. fyrirmynd, 2. gerð, 3. ímynd, 4. kynningareintak, 5. líkan.

modeling *see* eftirmyndun.

modelling *see* 1. eftirmyndun, 2. líkanagerð.

modem *see* mótald.

moderate *see* 1. hægfara, 2. hófsamur, 3. miðjumaður, 4. sanngjarn.

moderator *see* 1. hemilefni, 2. forseti, 3. prófdómari, 4. Róari, 5. gerðarmaður.

modernization *see* 1. breytingar, 2. endurbætur, 3. nútímavæðing, 4. nýsköpun.

modest *see* hógvær.

modification *see* 1. umbreyting, 2. tilhliðrun, 3. takmörkun, 4. slökun, 5. mörkun.

modify *see* 1. breyta, 2. endurnýja.

modulate *see* 1. móta, 2. tempra, 3. stilla.

modulation *see* mótun.

modulator *see* 1. miðill, 2. mótari, 3. stillir.

module *see* 1. samstæða, 2. undirsvæði, 3. mát, 4. forritseining, 5. eining.

moist *see* 1. þvalur, 2. rakur.

moisture *see* raki.

mol *see* mól.

molar *see* 1. jaxl, 2. mólin.

mold *see* 1. myglusveppur, 2. steypa, 3. steypumót, 4. móta, 5. forma.

mole *see* 1. moldvarpa, 2. mól, 3. múll, 4. ormur, 5. nafar.

molecule *see* 1. sameind, 2. mólikúl.

molybdenum *see* 1. mólýbden, 2. mólýbdin.

moment *see* 1. vægi, 2. andrá, 3. snúninsmætti, 4. kraftvægi, 5. snúningsvægi.

momentum *see* 1. hreyfimagn, 2. skriðþungi.

monad *see* stekja.

monarchy *see* 1. einvaldsríki, 2. einveldi, 3. einveldsríki, 4. konungdæmi, 5. Konungsdæmið.

monetary *see* 1. fjárhagslegur, 2. peningalegur.

money *see* 1. fé, 2. peningar, 3. peningur.

mongolism *see* 1. mongólítagervi, 2. mongólóíðaháttur.

monism *see* einhyggja.

monitor *see* 1. mænir, 2. vaktari, 3. vakta, 4. sívaki, 5. sívaka.

monitoring *see* 1. vöktun, 2. skráning, 3. gaumun, 4. eftirlit.

monkey *see* api.

monkfish *see* barðaháfur.

monochromatic *see* einlitur.

monocyte *see* 1. einkjörnungur, 2. hnattkjarnaátfruma, 3. smáæta.

monolayer *see* einlag.

monomer *see* einliða.

monopoly *see* 1. einokunaraðstaða, 2. einokun, 3. einkasala, 4. einkaleyfi, 5. einkaréttur.

monosomy *see* 1. einstæða, 2. staklitnun.

monovalent *see* eingildur.

monsoon *see* 1. monsún, 2. staðvindur, 3. monsúntími, 4. misserisvindar, 5. misseravindur.

month *see* 1. mánuður, 2. tunglmánuður.

monthly *see* mánaðarlega.

monument *see* 1. náttúruvætti, 2. þjóðgarður, 3. landvætti, 4. fastmerki.

mood *see* 1. háttur, 2. lyndi, 3. skap, 4. geðblær.

moon *see* 1. tungl, 2. máninn, 3. tunglið.

moonfish *see* tunglfiskur.

moor *see* 1. binda, 2. mýrlendi, 3. lyngheiði.

moraine *see* 1. jökulalda, 2. jökulgarður, 3. jökulmelur, 4. jökulurð, 5. mórena.

moral *see* morala.

morals *see* 1. moralajô, 2. moralinstruo, 3. morala.

moratorium *see* 1. greiðslustöðvun, 2. veiðistöðvun, 3. greiðslufrestun.

morbid *see* 1. vanheill, 2. heilsuspillandi, 3. óhollur, 4. sjúklegur.

morbidity *see* 1. sýkingatíðni, 2. sýkingatala, 3. sjúkdómsástand, 4. sjúkrahlutfall, 5. sóttarfar.

mores *see* siðir.

morning *see* morgun.

moron *see* 1. hálfviti, 2. vanviti.

morpheme *see* myndan.

morphinism *see* 1. morfíneitrun, 2. morfínfíkn.

morphology *see* 1. sköpulagsfræði, 2. útlitsfræði, 3. orðhlutafræði, 4. myndunarfræði, 5. líkamsfræði.

mortal *see* dauðlegur.
mortality *see* 1. afföll, 2. dánartala, 3. dánartíðni, 4. dauðleiki.
mortar *see* 1. mortél, 2. mylker, 3. steytill.
mortgage *see* 1. fasteignaveð, 2. veð, 3. veðsetja.
mortification *see* drep.
mosaic *see* 1. mósaík, 2. samsetning, 3. tigla.
mosquito *see* 1. mý, 2. mýfluga.
most *see* 1. æði, 2. mjög.
mother *see* móðir.
motherboard *see* 1. móðurborð, 2. móðurspjald.
motion *see* 1. gangur, 2. hreyfing.
motivation *see* 1. tilhvatning, 2. hvatning, 3. örvun.
motive *see* 1. tilhvöt, 2. kveikja, 3. atferlisvaki, 4. áhugahvöt, 5. atferliskveikja.
motor *see* 1. aflvél, 2. hreyfill, 3. hreyfivirkur, 4. mótor.
motorization *see* 1. vélknúinn, 2. vélvæðing.
mould *see* 1. steypumót, 2. mót.
moulding *see* 1. veggkróna, 2. gesims, 3. múrbrún, 4. skrautlisti, 5. taugarenna.
moulting *see* 1. hárfellir, 2. fjaðrafellir, 3. hamskipti.
mount *see* 1. fjall, 2. aðlagast, 3. fell, 4. hæð.
mountain *see* fjall.
mounting *see* 1. undirstaða, 2. sjónaukastæði, 3. festing, 4. fótur (foot), 5. pallur.
mouse *see* 1. mús, 2. hagamús.
moustache *see* 1. yfirskegg, 2. yfirvararskegg.
mouth *see* 1. munnur, 2. ós, 3. op, 4. munni, 5. ármynni.
move *see* 1. Leikur, 2. flutningur, 3. flytja, 4. skref.
movement *see* 1. færsla, 2. hreyfing, 3. hræring.
movie *see* filmo.
moving *see* tilfinningasamurlegur.
mrna *see* mRKS.
mucoid *see* 1. slímkenndur, 2. slímlíki.
mucosa *see* 1. slímhimna, 2. slíma.
mucus *see* 1. slím, 2. slíma.
mud *see* 1. aur, 2. hroði, 3. leðja.
mudguard *see* 1. aurbreð, 2. aurbretti, 3. aurhlíf, 4. hjólhlíf.
muffler *see* 1. hljóðdeyfir, 2. trefill, 3. hljóðkútur.
mugwort *see* 1 búamalurt, 2. búmalurt, 3. búrót, 4. grábuska, 5. malurt.
multicellular *see* 1. margfruma, 2. fjölfruma.
multilateral *see* 1. fjölþættur, 2. marghliða.
multimedia *see* 1. almiðill, 2. almiðlun, 3. gagnmiðlun, 4. margmiðlun.
multipartite *see* margskiptur.
multiple *see* 1. heilfeldi, 2. margfaldur, 3. fjöltenging, 4. fjöltengja, 5. margfeldi.
multiplex *see* 1. fjölboð, 2. fjölrásun, 3. fléttun, 4. margþættur.
multiplexer *see* 1. skimrás, 2. fjölrásari, 3. fléttari.

multiplexing *see* 1. fléttun, 2. fjölfléttun, 3. fjölrásun.
multiplication *see* margföldun.
multiplier *see* 1. margfaldari, 2. stuðull.
multiprocessing *see* fjölgjörvavinnsla.
multiprogramming *see* fjölforritavinnsla.
multitasking *see* fjölverkavinnsla.
multivibrator *see* vippa.
mummification *see* 1. skorpnun, 2. skrælnun.
mumps *see* hettusótt.
municipality *see* 1. sveitarfélag, 2. sveit, 3. hreppsfélag, 4. borgarstjórn, 5. borg.
muon *see* 1. mýeind, 2. míeind.
murder *see* 1. drap, 2. morð.
murk *see* myrkur.
murmur *see* 1. muldur, 2. murr.
muscle *see* vöðvi.
muscular *see* vöðvamikill.
mushroom *see* ætisveppur.
music *see* tónlist.
muskrat *see* 1. bísamrotta, 2. moskusrotta.
mustard *see* 1. kál, 2. mustarðar, 3. sinnep, 4. sinnepsjurtir.
muster *see* 1. nafnakall, 2. liðskönnun.
mutagen *see* 1. breytigen, 2. stökkbreytivaldur.
mutagenic *see* stokkbreytandi.
mutant *see* 1. stökkbreyttur, 2. stökkbrigði.
mutation *see* 1. stökkbreyting, 2. breyting, 3. hljóðvarp.
mute *see* 1. þögull, 2. mállaus, 3. dumbur, 4. daufdumbur.
mutiny *see* uppreisn.
mutual *see* 1. gagnkvæmur, 2. sameiginlegur.
mutualism *see* samhjálp.
mycelium *see* 1. sveppflækja, 2. mygla, 3. mýsli.
mycology *see* sveppafræði.
mycoplasma *see* berfrymingar.
mycosis *see* 1. sveppasýking, 2. sveppsýki.
mydriatic *see* 1. ljósopsstærandi, 2. ljósopsstærir.
myelin *see* 1. taugaslíður, 2. mýelín, 3. mýli.
myelitis *see* 1. mergbólga, 2. mænubólga.
myeloblast *see* 1. mergfrumumóðir, 2. merglingskímfruma.
myeloma *see* mergæxli.
myofibril *see* 1. vöðvaþráðla, 2. vöðvatrefja.
myoglobin *see* 1. vöðvaglóbín, 2. vöðvarauði, 3. mýóglóbín.
myopia *see* nærsýni.
myosin *see* mýósín.
myth *see* 1. goðsögn, 2. vésögn.

N

n *see* köfnunarefni.
nacelle *see* 1. hlíf, 2. hús.
nadir *see* 1. ilpunktur, 2. punktur.
nail *see* 1. nagli, 2. nögl.
naked *see* 1. nakinn, 2. snöggur.
name *see* 1. nafn, 2. nefna.
nanometer *see* 1. millímíkron, 2. nanómetri.
napkin *see* munnþurka.
nappy *see* bleyja.
narcissism *see* sjálfsást.
narcotic *see* 1. deyfilyf, 2. deyfilyfjafíkill, 3. eiturlyfjaneytandi, 4. svæfingalyf.
narcotism *see* 1. deyfilyfjaeitrun, 2. deyfilyfjanautn.
narrate *see* segja.
narrative *see* saga.
narrow *see* 1. þröngur, 2. krappur, 3. mjókka, 4. mjór, 5. þrengjast.
narrows *see* sund.
narwhal *see* náhvalur.
nasal *see* 1. nefkveðið, 2. neflægur, 3. nefhljóð.
nasopharynx *see* nefkok.
nasty *see* 1. óviðkunnanlegur, 2. slæmur, 3. yfirgefinn, 4. viðbjóðslegur, 5. hræðilegur.
nation *see* 1. þjóð, 2. land, 3. þjóðland, 4. þjóðríki.
national *see* 1. ríkisborgari, 2. þjóðlegur, 3. þjóðernislegur, 4. ríkisfang, 5. þegn.
nationalism *see* 1. þjóðræknisstefna, 2. sjálfstæðishreyfing, 3. sjálfstæðisstefna, 4. þjóðernisrembingur, 5. þjóðernisstefna.
nationality *see* 1. þjóðerni, 2. þjóð, 3. ríkisfang, 4. ríkisborgararéttur.
nationalization *see* þjóðnýting.
native *see* 1. fæðingi, 2. frumbyggi, 3. heimamaður, 4. innfæddur, 5. upprunalegur.
natural *see* 1. náttúrubundinn, 2. náttúrulegur.
nature *see* 1. eðli, 2. eiginleiki, 3. náttúra, 4. náttúran, 5. persónuleiki.
nausea *see* 1. velgja, 2. ógleði, 3. klígja, 4. flökurleiki.
nave *see* 1. hjólnöf, 2. kirkjuskip, 3. miðskip, 4. nöf, 5. skip.
navel *see* nafli.
navicular *see* bátlaga.
navigability *see* 1. haffærni, 2. skipgengi.
navigable *see* 1. haffær, 2. skipgengur, 3. stýranlegur.
navigate *see* 1. rápa, 2. sigla, 3. stýra.
navigation *see* 1. leiðsaga, 2. skipstjórn, 3. siglingar, 4. siglingafræði, 5. leiðsögn.

navigator *see* 1. leiðsögumaður, 2. netskoðari, 3. rápforrit, 4. skipstjórnarmaður.
navy *see* 1. sjóher, 2. floti.
nay *see* 1. ekkert, 2. ekki.
near *see* 1. nær, 2. nálægur.
nearly *see* 1. nær, 2. næstum.
nebula *see* 1. glærumóða, 2. geimský, 3. geimþoka.
necessitate *see* 1. þvinga, 2. neyða.
neck *see* 1. háls, 2. eiði, 3. gígtappi, 4. stútur.
neckerchief *see* hálsklútur.
necklace *see* hálsband.
necrosis *see* 1. drep, 2. holdfúi.
need *see* þörf.
negation *see* neitun.
negative *see* 1. frádrægur, 2. mínus, 3. neikvæður, 4. neikvætt, 5. neitunarorð.
negativism *see* 1. þumbaldaháttur, 2. neikvæði.
negligence *see* 1. gáleysi, 2. vanræksla.
negligent *see* 1. gálaus, 2. hirðulaus.
negligible *see* 1. hverfandi, 2. smávægilegur.
negotiable *see* 1. framseljanlegur, 2. umsemjanlegur.
negotiation *see* 1. samningaumleitanir, 2. samningur, 3. samningsviðræður, 4. samningsumleitun, 5. samningaviðræður.
neighbour *see* granni.
nematode *see* 1. hringormur, 2. nálormur, 3. þráðormur.
neodymium *see* 1. neodým, 2. neódým.
neolithic *see* nýsteinöld.
neologism *see* 1. nýyrði, 2. orðmyndunaratferli.
neoplasia *see* æxlismyndun.
neoplasm *see* 1. æxli, 2. auki.
neoprene *see* gervigúmmí.
nephew *see* 1. systursonur, 2. bróðursonur.
nephritis *see* 1. nýrabólga, 2. nýrnabólga.
nephropathy *see* nýrakvilli.
nephrosis *see* nýrapípnaskemmd.
neptunium *see* neptún.
nerve *see* 1. taug, 2. æð, 3. strengur.
nervous *see* taugaóstyrkur.
nest *see* 1. hreiður, 2. bú, 3. falda.
net *see* 1. hreinn, 2. keraröð, 3. nettó.
network *see* 1. netkerfi, 2. raftaugakerfi, 3. net, 4. kerfi, 5. keðja.
neuralgia *see* 1. taugahvot, 2. taugapína.
neurasthenia *see* 1. geðdeyfð, 2. kvellislekja.
neurilemma *see* taugaslíður.
neuritis *see* 1. taugarþroti, 2. taugarbólga, 3. taugabólga.
neurofibril *see* taugatrefja.
neurolemma *see* 1. mýlishimna, 2. taugarslíður.
neuroleptic *see* sefandi.
neurology *see* 1. taugafræði, 2. taugasjúkdómafræði.

neuron *see* 1. taugafruma, 2. taugungur, 3. taugarfruma.
neurosis *see* 1. hugsýki, 2. taugaveiklun.
neurotic *see* hugsjúkur.
neurotoxin *see* taugaeitur.
neurotransmitter *see* 1. boðefni, 2. taugaboðefni.
neurotropic *see* 1. taugasækinn, 2. taugasólginn.
neutral *see* 1. grádreifir, 2. óvirkur, 3. óráðinn, 4. hlutlaus, 5. núll.
neutralization *see* 1. afmögnun, 2. hlutleysing, 3. orkuleysing, 4. útjöfnun.
neutralize *see* 1. hlutleysa, 2. afmagna.
neutrino *see* fiseind.
neutron *see* 1. nifteind, 2. vanögn, 3. hvoreind, 4. neftróna, 5. neind.
neutrophil *see* 1. sýkilæta, 2. daufkyrningur, 3. dauffruma.
nevertheless *see* þó.
nevus *see* fæðingarblettur.
new *see* nýr.
newborn *see* nýfæddur.
newspaper *see* 1. tímarit, 2. dagblað.
newton *see* njúton.
nexus *see* orsakaflétta.
niacin *see* 1. níasín, 2. nikótínsýra.
nice *see* 1. góður, 2. þægilegur, 3. viðkunnanlegur.
niche *see* 1. vist, 2. veggskot, 3. veggjahvilft, 4. sess.
nick *see* stela.
nickel *see* 1. nikkel, 2. nikull, 3. nikkelhúða.
nicking *see* rifun.
nidation *see* 1. bólfesta, 2. festing.
nidus *see* 1. hreiður, 2. sýkingarhreiður.
niece *see* 1. systurdóttir, 2. bróðurdóttir.
night *see* nótt.
nightingale *see* næturgali.
nighttime *see* nótt.
nihilism *see* 1. gereyðingarblekking, 2. meðferðarvantrú.
nil *see* 1. núll, 2. ekkert.
nimbostratus *see* 1. regnþykkni, 2. regnský.
nimbus *see* 1. regnský, 2. regnþykkni, 3. úrkomuský.
nine *see* níu.
nineteen *see* nítján.
ninety *see* níutíu.
niobium *see* 1. nióbín, 2. níóbín, 3. níóbíum, 4. kólumbíum.
nippers *see* 1. naglbítur, 2. nagltöng, 3. töng.
nipple *see* 1. geirvarta, 2. nippill.
nit *see* lúsaegg.
nitrate *see* nítrat.
nitrification *see* 1. nítrun, 2. nítratmyndun.
nitrite *see* nítrít.
nitrogen *see* 1. köfnunarefni, 2. nitur, 3. nítur.

no *see* 1. ekkert, 2. ekki.
nobelium *see* 1. nóbelín, 2. nóbelíum.
node *see* 1. hnútur, 2. stöngulliðamót, 3. hné, 4. hnúður, 5. hnúta.
nodular *see* 1. hnúðóttur, 2. hnökróttur.
nodule *see* 1. hnökri, 2. hnúður.
noise *see* 1. hávaði, 2. kliður, 3. truflun, 4. suð, 5. hljóð.
nomadism *see* 1. flakkhneigð, 2. hirðingjahættir, 3. hirðingjalíf, 4. hjarðmennska.
nomenclature *see* 1. íðorðaforði, 2. nafnakerfi, 3. flokkunarkerfi.
nominal *see* 1. nafngildi, 2. nafnyrði, 3. lágmarks.
nominate *see* 1. ákveða, 2. tilnefna, 3. velja.
nomogram *see* 1. venslarit, 2. samanbuðartafla.
nonconformity *see* 1. ósamlægi, 2. ósamræmi.
nonmetal *see* málmleysingi.
nonsense *see* fjarstæða.
nonsensical *see* fáránlegur.
noradrenaline *see* noradrenalín.
norm *see* 1. málstærð, 2. viðmiðun, 3. meðaldæmi, 4. staðall, 5. hegðunarreglur.
normal *see* 1. venjulegur, 2. eðlilegt, 3. eðlilegur, 4. þverill, 5. þverlína.
normalise *see* 1. norma, 2. staðla.
normalization *see* skipulagning.
normalize *see* staðla.
normative *see* 1. forskriftar, 2. miðtækur, 3. staðlandi, 4. stöðlunar.
normoblast *see* kjarnablóðkorn.
northern *see* norðlægur.
nose *see* nef.
nosebleed *see* blóðnasir.
nostalgia *see* afturhvarfsþörf.
nostrils *see* 1. nasaop, 2. nasir.
not *see* 1. ekki, 2. ekkert.
notable *see* undarlegur.
notation *see* 1. ritun, 2. táknun, 3. táknmál, 4. ritunarkerfi, 5. rithättur.
notch *see* 1. hak, 2. rauf, 3. skora, 4. úrtak.
note *see* 1. skýring, 2. athugasemd.
notebook *see* stílabók.
noteworthy *see* undarlegur.
notice *see* 1. forboði, 2. fyrirboði, 3. tilkynning.
noticeable *see* undarlegur.
notification *see* 1. birting, 2. tilkynning.
notion *see* 1. álit, 2. skilningur.
notochord *see* 1. seil, 2. hryggstrengur.
nought *see* núll.
noun *see* nafnorð.
nova *see* 1. nýstirni, 2. skæra.
novel *see* nýr.
now *see* 1. núna, 2. nú.
nowhere *see* hvergi.
noxious *see* 1. eitraður, 2. skaðvænn.

nozzle see 1. túða, 2. úðari, 3. stútur, 4. spíss, 5. skrúfuhringur.
nuclease see 1. kjarnsýrukljúfur, 2. núkleasi.
nucleation see 1. kjarnamyndun, 2. kjörnun, 3. þéttbýlismyndun.
nucleolus see kjarnakorn.
nucleon see 1. kjarneind, 2. kjarnögn, 3. kjarnaögn, 4. kjarnaeind.
nucleoplasm see 1. kjarnafrymi, 2. kjarnasafi.
nucleoprotein see 1. kjarnhvíta, 2. kjarnprótín.
nucleoside see 1. kirnisleif, 2. núkleósíð.
nucleotide see 1. kirni, 2. núkleótíð.
nucleus see kjarni.
nuclide see 1. kirni, 2. kjarnategund.
number see 1. tala, 2. fjöldi, 3. húsnúmer, 4. númer, 5. reikna.
numeral see 1. tölutákn, 2. töluorð.
numerator see teljari.
numerical see tölulegur.
nurse see 1. hjúkrunarfræðingur, 2. barnfóstra, 3. hjúkra.
nursery see barnaheimili.
nurture see 1. aðbúð, 2. fóstrun, 3. fóstur.
nut see 1. hneta, 2. nukso, 3. ró.
nutation see pólriða.
nutrient see 1. nærandi, 2. næring, 3. næringarefni.
nutriment see næring.
nutrition see 1. næringarfræði, 2. næringarferli.
nutritive see nærandi.
nuts see 1. nukso, 2. ŝraŭbingo.
nymphomania see 1. brókarsótt, 2. vergirni.
nystagmus see 1. augntinun, 2. augntin.

O

oasis see 1. eyðimerkurvin, 2. vin.
oat see 1. akurhafri, 2. hafri.
obese see 1. digur, 2. holdmikill.
obesity see offita.
object see 1. viðfang, 2. hlutur, 3. hlutlag, 4. andlag.
objection see 1. mótbára, 2. mótmæli, 3. athugasemd.
objective see 1. hlutrænn, 2. sjálfstæður, 3. raunverulegur, 4. markmið, 5. hlutlinsa.
obligate see nauðbundinn.
obligation see 1. kvöð, 2. skuld, 3. skuldbinding, 4. skylda.
obligatory see 1. nauðsynlegur, 2. skyldur.
oblige see 1. neyða, 2. þvinga.
obliging see reiðubúinn.
oblique see 1. hallandi, 2. hornskakkur, 3. skakkur, 4. skásettur.

obliquity see 1. halli, 2. möndulhalli, 3. skái.
obliterate see 1. afmá, 2. eyða.
obliteration see 1. eyðing, 2. lokun.
obnoxious see 1. andstyggilegur, 2. viðbjóðslegur.
obscure see 1. hylja, 2. torræður, 3. daufur, 4. óljós, 5. myrkur.
obscurity see myrkur.
observation see 1. athugun, 2. mæling, 3. skoðun.
observatory see 1. stjörnustöð, 2. stjörnuturn, 3. stjörnuathugunarstöð.
observe see 1. mæla, 2. skoða, 3. staðreyna, 4. athuga.
observer see 1. veðurathugunarmaður, 2. áheyrnarfulltrúi, 3. athugandi, 4. skoðari, 5. stjörnuskoðandi.
obsession see þráhyggja.
obsolete see 1. úreltur, 2. úrelt.
obstacle see hindrun.
obstetrics see 1. fæðingafræði, 2. fæðingarfræði.
obstruct see 1. varna, 2. hindra, 3. tálma, 4. teppa.
obstruction see 1. tepping, 2. tálmi, 3. stíflun, 4. fyrirstaða, 5. hindrun.
obturation see 1. garnarteppa, 2. lokun.
obturator see gervigómfylla.
obvious see skýr.
occasion see tilefni.
occlude see svæfa.
occlusion see 1. blindsvæði, 2. lokun, 3. samskil, 4. stíflun.
occult see 1. dulinn, 2. myrkvablossi.
occultation see 1. myrkvi, 2. stjörnumyrkvi.
occupancy see 1. ábúð, 2. eignast, 3. umráð.
occupant see 1. ábúandi, 2. farþegi, 3. haldsmaður, 4. íbúi.
occupation see 1. hernám, 2. viðfangsefni, 3. vinna, 4. starfsgrein, 5. herseta.
occurrence see atburður.
ocean see haf.
oceanography see haffræði.
octagon see átthyrningur.
octagonal see 1. átthyrndur, 2. átthyrnt.
octant see áttungur.
octet see 1. áttstig, 2. áttund.
octopus see kolkrabbi.
ocular see 1. augngler, 2. augnlinsa.
odd see 1. vitlaus, 2. skrýtinn.
odds see 1. vinningslíkur, 2. vinningshlutfall, 3. líkur.
odometer see 1. vegalengdarmælir, 2. vegmælir.
odontology see tannfræði.
odour see 1. lykt, 2. þefur, 3. ilmur, 4. angan.
oedema see bjúgur.
oestrogen see 1. brímavaki, 2. estrógen, 3. östrógen.
oestrus see eggbússtig.
offal see 1. slóg, 2. fiskúrgangur, 3. innyfli.

offence *see* 1. móðgun, 2. glæpur.
offend *see* 1. móðga, 2. skamma.
offer *see* 1. boð, 2. kynna, 3. tilboð.
offhand *see* skyndilegur.
offhandedly *see* skyndilega.
office *see* 1. embætti, 2. skrifstofa.
officer *see* 1. starfsmaður, 2. yfirmaður, 3. lögregluþjónn, 4. lögreglumaður, 5. liðsforingi.
official *see* 1. embættislegur, 2. embættismaður, 3. opinber, 4. ritari, 5. starfsmaður.
officialdom *see* 1. embættismannastétt, 2. embættismenn.
offset *see* 1. hliðrun, 2. mótreikna, 3. fjarlægð.
offshore *see* 1. erlendur, 2. utanlands, 3. útlendur.
often *see* oft.
oftentimes *see* oft.
ogive *see* 1. skári, 2. oddbogi, 3. jökulskári, 4. summuferill.
ohm *see* óm.
ohmmeter *see* 1. ohmmælir, 2. viðnámsmælir.
oil *see* 1. olía, 2. smyrja.
oiler *see* smyrjari.
okay *see* 1. góður, 2. vel.
old *see* gamall.
olfaction *see* 1. lyktarskyn, 2. þefskyn.
olfactory *see* lyktarskyn.
oliguria *see* þvagþurrð.
olive *see* 1. viðsmjör, 2. olífa, 3. ólífa.
omasum *see* laki.
omega *see* ómega.
omission *see* 1. vanræksla, 2. vanskráning, 3. yfirsjón.
omit *see* yfirgefa.
omnibus *see* 1. almenningsvagn, 2. strætisvagn.
omnivore *see* alæta.
on *see* 1. i, 2. á, 3. að.
onchocerciasis *see* árblinda.
oncogene *see* æxlisgen.
oncogenic *see* 1. æxlisvaldandi, 2. krabbameinsvaldandi.
oncology *see* æxlafræði.
one *see* 1. einn, 2. eitt, 3. ein, 4. aleinn, 5. einmana.
onerous *see* þungur.
onion *see* 1. laukur, 2. matlaukur, 3. sáðlaukur, 4. matarlaukur, 5. kepalaukur.
only *see* 1. einmana, 2. einn, 3. aleinn.
onset *see* 1. byrjun, 2. stuðull, 3. upphaf.
ontogenesis *see* 1. þroskun, 2. þroskunarsaga, 3. einstaklingsþróun, 4. einstaklingsþroskun.
ontogeny *see* einstaklingsmyndun.
ontology *see* verufræði.
opacity *see* 1. geisladeyfni, 2. ljósdeyfitala, 3. ljósdeyfni, 4. ógagnsæi, 5. ógegnsæi.
opah *see* 1. guðlax, 2. sólborri, 3. tunglfiskur.

opaque *see* 1. geisladeyfinn, 2. hálfgagnsær, 3. ljósdeyfinn, 4. mattur, 5. móskugur.
open *see* 1. opna, 2. óvarinn, 3. straumrof, 4. opinn.
opening *see* 1. Byrjun, 2. op, 3. opnun, 4. rof, 5. útsláttur.
operand *see* 1. þoli, 2. þolandi.
operate *see* 1. vinna, 2. stjórna, 3. stilla, 4. reka, 5. gera.
operation *see* 1. skurðaðgerð, 2. vinnuferill, 3. starfsemi, 4. handlæknisaðgerð, 5. aðgerð.
operative *see* verkamaður.
operator *see* 1. stilligen, 2. virkir, 3. virki, 4. tölvari, 5. stjórnandi.
operculum *see* 1. hetta, 2. lok, 3. tálknalok.
operon *see* genagengi.
opinion *see* 1. álit, 2. skoðun.
opossum *see* 1. kontraŭanto, 2. kontraŭulo, 3. oponanto.
opponent *see* kontraŭulo.
opportunity *see* tilefni.
opposite *see* 1. andstæður, 2. mótstæður.
opposition *see* 1. Andstæ, 2. mótsetning, 3. gagnstæða, 4. andstæða, 5. andstaða.
optical *see* ljósfræðilegur.
optics *see* 1. sjónfræði, 2. ljóseðlisfræði, 3. ljósfræði.
optimal *see* 1. hagstæður, 2. hagstæðastur, 3. ákjósanlegur, 4. bestur.
optimization *see* 1. bestun, 2. hámörkun.
optimum *see* 1. kjörgildi, 2. kjörstaða.
option *see* 1. val, 2. vilnun, 3. valréttur, 4. valfrelsi, 5. kostur.
optional *see* 1. valkvæður, 2. ráðstöfunarvald, 3. sakarforræði, 4. valfrjáls, 5. valfrjálst.
optometry *see* sjónmæling.
orange *see* 1. appelsína, 2. rauðgulur.
orb *see* 1. braut, 2. brautarhringur, 3. himinhnöttur, 4. himinhvel, 5. hvel.
orbicular *see* 1. kringlóttur, 2. hringlaga.
orbit *see* 1. augntótt, 2. braut.
orbital *see* 1. líkindasvæði, 2. svigrúm.
orchestra *see* hljómsveit.
order *see* 1. röðun, 2. súlnaregla, 3. fyrirskipa, 4. stig, 5. þrep.
ordinary *see* venjulegur.
ordinate *see* lóðhnit.
ore *see* málmgrýti.
oregano *see* 1. kjarrmæra, 2. órigan, 3. óriganó, 4. bergmynta, 5. bergminta.
orfe *see* gullgægir.
organ *see* 1. tímarit, 2. líffæri, 3. orgel.
organelle *see* frumulíffæri.
organic *see* 1. lífrænn, 2. líkamlegur, 3. vefrænn, 4. lifandi.
organism *see* lífvera.

organization *see* 1. skipulag, 2. skipulagsheild, 3. stofnun, 4. fyrirkomulag, 5. félag.
organizer *see* 1. skipulagsbók, 2. stillir.
orgasm *see* 1. munuðvíma, 2. munúðvíma, 3. samfarablossi.
oriel *see* 1. útskot, 2. útskotsgluggi, 3. skansgluggi.
orientation *see* 1. stefna, 2. áttun.
orienteering *see* ratleikur.
orifice *see* 1. op, 2. rennslisop.
origin *see* 1. hnitmiðja, 2. upphafspunktur, 3. uppruni, 4. vöðvaupphaf.
original *see* 1. farmskírteini, 2. upprunalegur.
originator *see* 1. höfundur, 2. sendandi.
ormer *see* 1. gliteyra, 2. sæeyra.
ornithine *see* 1. orniþín, 2. ornitín.
orogeny *see* 1. fellingahreyfing, 2. fjallamyndun, 3. fellingafjallamyndun.
orphan *see* 1. hóruungi, 2. einstæðingur.
orthogenesis *see* réttstefnuþróun.
orthogonal *see* 1. þver, 2. hornréttur, 3. rétthyrndur, 4. þverstæður.
orthopedics *see* bæklunarlækningar.
os *see* 1. bein (bone), 2. munnur (mouth).
oscillate *see* 1. snúa, 2. sveiflast, 3. titra.
oscillation *see* 1. sveifla, 2. sveifluhreyfing, 3. titringur.
oscillator *see* 1. sveifill, 2. sveiflugjafi, 3. áriðill, 4. sveifluvaki.
oscillogram *see* sveiflurit.
oscillograph *see* 1. sveiflumynstur, 2. sveifluriti.
oscilloscope *see* sveiflusjá.
osmium *see* osmín.
osmolarity *see* osmósuþéttni.
osmosis *see* 1. gegnflæði, 2. osmósuflæði, 3. osmósa, 4. flæði, 5. himnuflæði.
ossicle *see* 1. hljóðbein, 2. smábein.
ossification *see* 1. beingerð, 2. beinmyndun.
osteoarthritis *see* slitgigt.
osteoblast *see* 1. beinkímfruma, 2. beinmóðir, 3. beinmyndunarfruma.
osteoclast *see* 1. beinæta, 2. beinátfruma, 3. beinbrjótur.
osteocyte *see* beinfruma.
osteology *see* 1. beinafræði, 2. beinfræði.
osteolysis *see* 1. beinhrörnun, 2. beineyðing.
osteonecrosis *see* beindrep.
osteopath *see* 1. hnykkir, 2. osteopati.
osteopathy *see* 1. beinkvilli, 2. hnykkingar.
osteopetrosis *see* beinmergsherðing.
osteoporosis *see* 1. beingisnun, 2. beinþynning.
osteosclerosis *see* beinherðing.
ostrich *see* strútur.
otalgia *see* hlustarverkur.
other *see* annar.

otolith *see* 1. eyrnavala, 2. eyrnavölur, 3. jafnvægiskorn, 4. kvarnir, 5. stöðusteinn.
otter *see* otur.
ounce *see* únsa.
out *see* 1. úti, 2. út, 3. utan.
outbreeding *see* 1. óskyldraæxlun, 2. útæxlun, 3. útrækt.
outcrop *see* opna.
outfall *see* útrás.
outfit *see* útbúnaður.
outflow *see* útstreymi.
outgoing *see* útfarandi.
outlet *see* 1. úttak, 2. útrennslisop, 3. útrennsli, 4. útgangur, 5. frárás.
outlier *see* 1. útsker, 2. dindill, 3. einfari.
outline *see* 1. útlína, 2. uppkast, 3. eyðublað, 4. drög.
output *see* 1. framleiðsla, 2. úttak, 3. framleiðsluvara, 4. frálag, 5. afurðir.
outrigger *see* 1. grind, 2. stoðfótur.
outright *see* 1. óvís, 2. heill.
outside *see* 1. úti, 2. utanverður, 3. utanaðkomandi, 4. utan.
outsourcing *see* 1. hýsing, 2. utankaup, 3. úthýsing, 4. útvistun, 5. vistun.
oval *see* egglaga.
ovary *see* 1. eggjakerfi, 2. eggjastokkur, 3. eggleg.
oven *see* ofn.
over *see* 1. á, 2. meðan, 3. um, 4. yfir.
overall *see* 1. vinnusloppur, 2. samfestingur, 3. heill.
overburden *see* 1. þekja, 2. þaklag.
overcast *see* 1. alskýja, 2. alskýjað, 3. alskýjaður.
overcompensation *see* ofbætur.
overdraft *see* yfirdráttur.
overdrive *see* yfirgír.
overdue *see* gjaldfallinn.
overflow *see* 1. yfirfallsrör, 2. yfirflæði, 3. yfirfall.
overgrazing *see* ofbeit.
overhang *see* 1. skögun, 2. slúti, 3. vængendaskögun.
overhaul *see* 1. grannskoðun, 2. skoða, 3. yfirhala, 4. endurbyggja.
overhauling *see* yfirhalning.
overhead *see* 1. fastakostnaður, 2. glæra, 3. rekstrarkostnaður, 4. yfirbygging.
overlap *see* 1. skara, 2. skörun, 3. samfallstími.
overlapping *see* skörun.
overlay *see* 1. gagnalag, 2. lag, 3. samfelling, 4. þekja, 5. yfirlög.
overload *see* 1. ofhleðsla, 2. yfirálag, 3. ofhlaða, 4. ofraun, 5. ofurálag.
overloading *see* 1. fjölbinding, 2. yfirstýring.
overly *see* of.
overpower *see* yfirtaka.
overproduction *see* offramleiðsla.

override see hundsa.
overseas see 1. útlendur, 2. erlendur, 3. utanlands.
oversee see stilla.
overshoot see 1. dindill, 2. langlenda, 3. útdindill, 4. yfirskot.
oversize see 1. yfirstór, 2. yfirstærð.
overstress see 1. yfirálag, 2. ofurálag.
overt see 1. bersýnilegur, 2. opinber.
overtime see yfirvinna.
overtone see yfirtónn.
overwhelm see kaffæra.
overwrite see yfirrita.
oviduct see 1. eggjagöng, 2. eggjaleiðari, 3. eggrás.
oviform see egglaga.
oviposition see 1. eggvarp, 2. varp.
ovoid see egglaga.
ovulation see 1. egglos, 2. eggvarp.
ovule see 1. frævísir, 2. eggbúsegg, 3. eggbú.
ovum see 1. eggfruma, 2. egg.
owl see ugla.
own see 1. eiga, 2. eigin.
owner see eigandi.
ownership see 1. eignarhald, 2. eign.
ox see uxi.
oxidation see 1. sýring, 2. tæring, 3. oxun.
oxide see 1. oxíð, 2. sýri.
oxidize see 1. oxa, 2. oxast.
oxygen see 1. súrefni, 2. ildi.
oxyhydrogen see hvellgas.
oxytocin see 1. hríðahormón, 2. mjaltavaki, 3. oxytósín.
oxyuriasis see njálgsýking.
ozone see óson.

P

pacemaker see gangráður.
pachytene see sverþráðlufasi.
pacific see Kyrrahaf.
pacifism see 1. friðarhugsjón, 2. friðarstefna.
pacing see samstig.
pack see 1. böggull, 2. þétta, 3. þjappa.
package see 1. böggull, 2. pakki.
packaging see 1. umbúðir, 2. pökkun.
packet see pakki.
packing see 1. pakkning, 2. pökkun, 3. þétti, 4. þjöppun, 5. troðsla.
pact see 1. samkomulag, 2. samningur, 3. milliríkjasáttmáli, 4. milliríkjasamningur, 5. sáttmáli.
pad see 1. deyfiliður, 2. dýna, 3. festiflötur, 4. klossi, 5. púði.

padding see 1. fylling, 2. staffylling, 3. bólstrun.
paddle see 1. kajakár, 2. róðrarspaði.
paddlefish see spaðastyrja.
padlock see hengilás.
page see 1. blaðsíða, 2. síða.
pain see 1. verkur, 2. sársauki.
paint see 1. mála, 2. málning, 3. eftirlýsing.
painter see málari.
painting see 1. málun, 2. málverk.
pair see 1. par, 2. stöðvapar, 3. tvenna.
pairing see 1. línuhlaupsbjögun, 2. pörun.
palace see höll.
palaeolithic see 1. ársteinöld, 2. fornsteinöld.
palate see 1. framgómur, 2. ginvarta, 3. gómur.
paleoclimatology see 1. veðurfarssaga, 2. fornveðurfræði.
palimpsest see 1. skafgígur, 2. uppskafningsminni.
palladium see 1. palladín, 2. palladíum.
pallet see 1. pallur, 2. vörubretti.
palliation see líkn.
pallium see hvelkápa.
palm see 1. pálmi, 2. lófi.
palmar see lófalægur.
palpable see þreifanlegur.
palpitation see 1. hjartsláttarónot, 2. sláttarónot.
palsy see lömun.
pan see 1. panna, 2. skotra.
panacea see 1. kynjalyf, 2. undralyf.
pancreas see 1. bris, 2. briskirtill.
pandemic see 1. heimsfaraldur, 2. heimsfarsótt, 3. fjöllendur.
pane see rúða.
panel see 1. pallborð, 2. þil, 3. stjórnborð, 4. stjórn, 5. vettvangur.
panic see 1. kreppa, 2. ofsahræðsla, 3. efnahagshrun.
panning see 1. skotrun, 2. pönnun.
pannus see tætla.
panther see 1. hlébarði, 2. pardusdýr.
pantry see 1. búr, 2. matarbúr.
pants see kalsono.
papaw see papava.
papaya see 1. melónutré, 2. papaja, 3. sólaldin, 4. sólaldintré.
paper see 1. pappír, 2. dokumento.
papers see 1. memuaro, 2. traktaĵo, 3. tapeti, 4. surpapera, 5. referaĵo.
papilla see 1. doppa, 2. varta, 3. tota, 4. nurta, 5. nabbi.
paprika see paprikuduft.
parabola see fleygbogi.
paraboloid see 1. fleygbogaflötur, 2. fleygflötur.
paradigm see 1. fordæmi, 2. kennidæmi, 3. beygingardæmi, 4. viðmið.
paradox see 1. mótsögn, 2. þversögn, 3. þverstæða.
paraffin see 1. alkan, 2. paraffín, 3. vax.

paragraph see 1. efnisgrein, 2. málsgrein, 3. grein.
parallax see 1. hliðrun, 2. sjónstöðumunur, 3. sýndarfærsla, 4. sýndarhliðrun.
parallel see 1. samsíða, 2. sýndarfærsla, 3. samhliða, 4. hliðtenging, 5. hliðstæður.
parallelogram see samsíðungur.
paralysis see lömun.
paralytic see lami.
paramagnetism see meðseglun.
paramedics see sjúkraliði.
parameter see 1. stiki, 2. kennistærð, 3. stillibreyta, 4. þýðistölur, 5. mælistærð.
paranoia see 1. dómglöp, 2. tortryggnisýki, 3. vænisýki.
paranoid see 1. glapdæminn, 2. vænisjúkur.
parapet see 1. grindverk, 2. rimlagirðing.
paraphimosis see 1. reðurhúfukreppa, 2. augnlokskreppa.
paraphrase see 1. umorða, 2. endursögn.
paraplegic see þverlami.
parapsychology see dulsálarfræði.
parasite see 1. sníkill, 2. sníkjudýr, 3. sníkjuvera.
parasitism see 1. sníkjulífi, 2. sníkjulíf.
parcel see 1. böggull, 2. landareign, 3. lóð, 4. pakki, 5. skiki.
pardon see 1. fyrirgefa, 2. fyrirgefning.
parenchyma see 1. starfsvefur, 2. sérvefur, 3. grunnvefur, 4. frumvefur, 5. stuttfrumuvefur.
parent see gepatro.
parenthesis see 1. svigar, 2. svigi.
parents see 1. foreldrar, 2. gepatro.
paresis see 1. lömunarsnertur, 2. slýni.
parhelion see 1. aukasól, 2. hjásól.
parish see 1. söfnuður, 2. stjórnsýsluumdæmi, 3. sýsla, 4. hérað.
parity see 1. speglunartala, 2. bæri, 3. jafngengi.
park see 1. skemmtigarður, 2. þjóðgarður, 3. útivistarsvæði, 4. geyma, 5. almenningsgarður.
parliament see þing.
parliamentarian see þingmaður.
parotitis see 1. vangakirtilsbólga, 2. hettusótt.
parr see 1. laxaseiði, 2. smáseiði.
parrot see páfagaukur.
part see 1. hluti, 2. hlutur, 3. partur.
parthenogenesis see 1. meyfæðing, 2. eingetnaður, 3. geldæxlun.
participation see 1. hlutdeild, 2. þátttaka.
particle see 1. arða, 2. efnisögn, 3. eind, 4. fylgiorð, 5. ögn.
particular see sérstaklegur.
partition see 1. skipting, 2. skilveggur, 3. skilrúm, 4. skifting, 5. deild.
partner see meðeigandi.
partnership see sameignarfélag.
partridge see akurhænsn.

parturition see 1. fæðing, 2. barnsburður.
party see 1. aðili, 2. flokkur, 3. málsaðili, 4. stjórnmálaflokkur, 5. veisla.
pass see 1. fram, 2. framhjá, 3. aka, 4. sleppa.
passage see 1. vegur, 2. bæjargöng, 3. gangur, 4. göng, 5. rás.
passenger see 1. farþegi, 2. flugfarþegi.
passive see 1. aðfenginn, 2. hlutlaus, 3. óvirkur, 4. þolmyndarsetning.
passover see páskar.
passport see vegabréf.
password see 1. leyniorð, 2. lykilorð, 3. aðgangsorð.
paste see 1. líma, 2. deig, 3. hlaup, 4. krem, 5. líming.
pasteurization see gerilsneyðing.
pasture see 1. hagi, 2. bithagi, 3. beitiland, 4. beit, 5. haglendi.
patch see 1. bæta, 2. bót, 3. gagnaviðbætur, 4. hjólspor, 5. staga.
patella see hnéskel.
patent see 1. útstæður, 2. sýnilegur, 3. einkaleyfi, 4. opinn.
paternal see föðurlegur.
path see 1. braut, 2. leið, 3. slóð, 4. vegur.
pathogen see 1. meinvaldur, 2. sýkill, 3. sjúkdómsvaldur.
pathogenic see 1. meinvaldandi, 2. meinvirkur, 3. sjúkdómsvaldandi, 4. sýkilvirkur, 5. sýkjandi.
pathologic see 1. meinafræðilegur, 2. sjúklegur.
pathological see sjúklegur.
pathology see 1. meinafræði, 2. sjúkdómafræði.
pathway see 1. efnaferli, 2. taugabraut, 3. vegur.
patience see þolinmæði
patient see 1. sjúklingur, 2. þolandi, 3. þolinmóður.
patriarchy see 1. ættfeðrastjórn, 2. karlveldi, 3. feðraveldi.
patriot see föðurlandsvinur.
patriotism see föðurlandsást.
patrol see 1. eftirlitssveit, 2. skátaflokkur.
pattern see 1. módel, 2. mynstur, 3. innrétting, 4. gleiðbogamynstur, 5. fyrirmynd.
paunch see kviður.
paw see fótur (foot).
pawl see 1. hak, 2. pall, 3. skreppa.
pawn see Peð.
pay see 1. laun, 2. borgun, 3. kaup, 4. greiðsla.
payload see 1. arðhleðsla, 2. farmþungi, 3. farmur.
payment see 1. greiðsla, 2. staðgreiðsla.
payroll see 1. launaskrá, 2. launagjöld.
peace see friður.
peacock see páfugl.
peak see 1. hámark, 2. tindur, 3. toppur.
pear see pera.

peasant see 1. smábóndi, 2. kotbóndi, 3. landbúnaðarverkamaður.
peat see 1. svörður, 2. Mór.
pectin see pektín.
peculiar see 1. skrýtinn, 2. vitlaus.
pedal see stíga.
pederasty see sveinmök.
pedestal see 1. stallur, 2. undirstaða, 3. standur, 4. skíðisfótur, 5. svartlyfting.
pedestrian see 1. fótgangandi, 2. göngumaður.
pediatrician see barnalæknir.
pediatrics see barnalækningar.
pedicel see 1. blómleggur, 2. stikill.
pedigree see 1. ættarskrá, 2. ættartafla, 3. ættartala.
pediment see 1. bjór, 2. gaflbrík, 3. gaflhlað, 4. gaflhlaðsþríhyrningur, 5. gaflhyrna.
peduncle see 1. stoð, 2. blómskipunarleggur.
peel see 1. skurn, 2. pilla, 3. hýði, 4. flus, 5. börkur.
peeler see lögregluþjónn.
peeling see 1. skelfletting, 2. flögnun, 3. pillun.
peen see 1. hnoða, 2. hnoðun.
peer see jafningi.
peg see 1. gervikló, 2. hæll, 3. pinni, 4. tittur.
pellagra see 1. húðkröm, 2. hörundskröm, 3. húðangur.
pellet see 1. smápilla, 2. kúla, 3. æluböggull, 4. hagl.
pellicle see 1. frumuhýði, 2. skæni.
pelvis see 1. mjaðmagrind, 2. grindarhol.
pen see kúlupenni.
penalty see 1. hegning, 2. viðurlög, 3. skaðabætur, 4. refsing.
pencil see 1. blýantur, 2. ritblý.
pending see unz.
pendulum see 1. pendull, 2. pendúll, 3. pendill, 4. kólfur, 5. dingull.
peneplain see rofslétta.
penetrance see 1. birting, 2. sýnd, 3. tjáningarstig.
penetrate see 1. borast, 2. smjúga.
penetration see 1. gegnflæði, 2. ísíun, 3. innsókn, 4. gegnþrenging, 5. innbrot.
penicillin see 1. penisillín, 2. pensilín.
peninsula see 1. nes, 2. skagi.
penis see tittlingur.
penny see sent.
pension see 1. eftirlaun, 2. lífeyrir, 3. ellilífeyrir.
penstock see 1. aðrennslisrör, 2. þrýstivatnspípa.
pentagon see fimmhyrningur.
penthouse see 1. skúr, 2. skýli.
pentode see 1. fimmskautalampi, 2. pentóða, 3. fimmskauti.
pentose see pentósi.
penumbra see 1. blettkragi, 2. hálfskuggi.
people see 1. kynþáttur, 2. þjóð.
pepper see pipar.

peppermint see 1. piparminta, 2. piparmynta, 3. þursaviður.
pepsin see pepsín.
peptide see peptíð.
perambulator see barnavagn.
percentage see 1. hundraðshluti, 2. hundraðstala, 3. prósenta.
percentile see 1. hundraðshlutamark, 2. prósent, 3. hundraðshluti, 4. hundraðsmark.
percept see skyntak.
perception see 1. skynjun, 2. skyntúlkun.
perceptive see skynnæmur.
perceptual see skynrænn.
perch see 1. aborri, 2. kanaborri, 3. vatnaborri.
percolation see 1. hrip, 2. seytl, 3. síling.
perfectionism see 1. fullkomnunarárátta, 2. hlítarárátta.
perforate see 1. raufa, 2. gata.
perforated see 1. rifgataður, 2. gataður.
perforation see 1. gat, 2. götun, 3. rauf, 4. raufun.
perforator see 1. hausbor, 2. holbor, 3. gatari.
perform see 1. kynna, 2. leika, 3. gera.
performance see 1. hæfileikar, 2. málbeiting, 3. rekstrarafkoma, 4. vinnsla, 5. hæfni.
performer see leikari.
perfume see ilmvatn.
perigee see jarðnánd.
perihelion see sólnánd.
peril see hætta.
perilymph see utanvessi.
perimeter see 1. jaðar, 2. sjónsviðsmælir, 3. umgjörð, 4. ummál.
period see 1. riðtími, 2. umferð, 3. tími, 4. tímabil, 5. umferðartími.
periodic see 1. lotutíminn, 2. taktbundinn, 3. lotubundinn, 4. háttbundið, 5. bilkvæmur.
periodical see 1. tímarit, 2. tímabundinn.
periodicity see 1. bilkvæmi, 2. snúningstala.
peripheral see 1. jaðar, 2. út.
periphery see 1. jaðarsvæði, 2. útjaðar, 3. útmörk, 4. jaðar, 5. umferill.
peristalsis see 1. bylgjuhreyfingar, 2. enging, 3. iðrahreyfing.
peristome see 1. mynni, 2. opkrans.
peritonitis see 1. lífhimnubólga, 2. skinubólga.
peritrichous see 1. kringhærður, 2. hringhærður.
periwinkle see 1. doppa, 2. fjörudoppa.
permafrost see 1. sífreri, 2. freðjörð.
permanent see 1. stöðugur, 2. fastafulltrúi.
permanently see 1. ávallt, 2. alltaf, 3. ætíð.
permeability see 1. segulstuðull, 2. segulsvörunarstuðull, 3. segulleiðni, 4. lekt, 5. groppa.
permeable see 1. gegnfær, 2. gropinn, 3. lekinn, 4. lekur, 5. óþéttur.

permease *see* gegndræpihvati.
permeate *see* fylla.
permit *see* 1. leyfisbréf, 2. þola, 3. leyfi.
permittivity *see* torleiðnistuðull.
permutation *see* 1. raðflétta, 2. röðun, 3. umröðun.
pernicious *see* 1. illkynjaður, 2. skæður, 3. hættulegur.
perpendicular *see* 1. lóðlína, 2. lóðréttur, 3. þverstæður, 4. hornréttur.
perpetual *see* æfinlegur.
perpetually *see* 1. ávallt, 2. ætíð, 3. alltaf.
perpetuity *see* 1. sígreiðslur, 2. sífella, 3. eilifðargreiðslur.
persistence *see* 1. eftirljóm, 2. eftirljómi, 3. seigla, 4. þrávirkni, 5. varanleiki.
persistent *see* langær.
person *see* 1. persóna, 2. maður (man), 3. persono.
persona *see* persóna.
personage *see* 1. maður (man), 2. persóna.
personal *see* 1. eigin, 2. náinn.
personality *see* 1. persónuleiki, 2. persónugerð, 3. æði.
personnel *see* 1. starfsfólk, 2. starfslið.
persons *see* 1. persono, 2. ulo.
perspective *see* 1. rúmsýn, 2. þrívídd, 3. sjónhorf, 4. sjónarhorn, 5. innsýn.
perspiration *see* sviti.
persuade *see* sannfæra.
persuasion *see* 1. skoðun, 2. fortölur, 3. skoðanahópur.
perturbation *see* 1. truflun, 2. óværð, 3. ferilhnik, 4. hnik.
pertussis *see* 1. andarteppuhósti, 2. andkafahósti, 3. kíghósti, 4. kikhósti, 5. sogahósti.
perversion *see* lastahneigð.
pest *see* 1. skaðvaldur, 2. plága, 3. farsótt, 4. kýlapest.
pesticide *see* 1. plágueyðir, 2. skordýraeitur, 3. varnarefni.
pestilence *see* 1. farsótt, 2. plága, 3. svartidauði, 4. drepsótt.
petition *see* 1. bæn, 2. bænaskrá, 3. málsskjal.
petrol *see* bensín.
petroleum *see* 1. hráolía, 2. jarðolía.
pew *see* bekkur.
ph *see* sýrustig.
phage *see* 1. bakteríuveira, 2. faga, 3. gerilæta, 4. gerilveira, 5. bakteríuæta.
phagocyte *see* átfruma.
phagocytosis *see* 1. agnát, 2. sýklaát, 3. frumuát, 4. agnaát, 5. agnafryming.
pharmaceutical *see* 1. læknisfræði, 2. lyf.
pharmacology *see* lyfjafræði.
pharmacy *see* 1. lyfjabúð, 2. apótek.
pharynx *see* kok.

phase *see* 1. hamur, 2. kvartil, 3. ásýnd, 4. fasi.
phasing *see* fösun.
pheasant *see* fashani.
phenomenology *see* fyrirbærafræði.
phenomenon *see* 1. fyrirbæri, 2. fyrirbrigði.
phenotype *see* 1. svipfar, 2. svipgerð.
phenylalanine *see* 1. fen, 2. fenýlalanín.
phenylketonuria *see* 1. fenílketónúría, 2. fenýlketónmiga.
phlebitis *see* bláæðarbólga.
phlegm *see* 1. kvefslím, 2. öndunarfæraslím.
phlegmatic *see* 1. hæglyndur, 2. rólyndur, 3. daufgerður.
phobia *see* fælni.
phone *see* 1. fón, 2. málhljóð, 3. sími, 4. talsími.
phoneme *see* 1. hljóðungur, 2. fæni, 3. fónem, 4. hljóðan.
phonetics *see* hljóðfræði.
phonophobia *see* talfælni.
phosphatase *see* fosfatasi.
phosphate *see* fosfat.
phospholipid *see* fosfórlípíð.
phosphor *see* 1. fosfór, 2. ljómefni, 3. skinefni.
phosphorescence *see* 1. fósfórljóm, 2. lífljómi, 3. langljómun, 4. fósfórskin, 5. fosfórljómun.
phosphorus *see* fosfór.
phosphorylation *see* fosfórun.
photo *see* ljósmynd.
photocell *see* 1. ljósröfunarnemi, 2. ljósspennunemi, 3. ljóssella, 4. fótónunemi, 5. ljósnemi.
photochemical *see* ljósefnavirkur.
photograph *see* ljósmynd.
photoluminescence *see* 1. fótónuljóm, 2. ljómun, 3. ljóseindaljóm, 4. ljósljómun.
photolysis *see* 1. ljósrof, 2. ljóssundrun.
photometer *see* 1. sjónnæmismælir, 2. ljósmælir.
photometry *see* 1. ljósmælifræði, 2. ljósmæling, 3. ljósmælingar.
photomicrograph *see* smásjármynd.
photon *see* 1. fótóna, 2. lýsa, 3. ljóskammtur, 4. ljósögn, 5. ljóseind.
photoperiod *see* ljóslota.
photoreceptor *see* ljósnemi.
photosensitive *see* ljósnæmur.
photosensitization *see* ljósnæming.
photosphere *see* ljóshvolf.
photosynthesis *see* 1. ljóstillífun, 2. fjörglæðing.
phototherapy *see* 1. ljóslækning, 2. ljósameðferð.
phototropism *see* ljósleitni.
phrase *see* 1. liður, 2. setningarliður, 3. stofnhluti.
phrenology *see* höfuðlagsfræði.
phylogenesis *see* tegundarþróun.
phylogeny *see* 1. tegundarþróun, 2. þróunarferill.
phylum *see* fylking.

physical see 1. eðlisfræðilegur, 2. líkamlegur, 3. raunlægur.
physician see læknir.
physics see eðlisfræði.
physiognomy see 1. svipur, 2. andlitsfall, 3. svipbrigðafræði.
physiological see lífeðlisfræðilegur.
physiology see lífeðlisfræði.
physiotherapist see sjúkraþjálfari.
phytogeography see plöntulandafræði.
phytohormone see plöntuhormón.
phytopathology see plöntusjúkdómafræði.
phytoplankton see 1. jurtasvif, 2. plöntusvif.
pi see pí.
pica see 1. átvilla, 2. em, 3. óætisfíkn.
pickle see 1. sýruþvo, 2. pækill, 3. skírðarlögur, 4. sýrublanda.
pickling see 1. upptíningur, 2. sýruþvottur, 3. leifar, 4. molar.
picture see 1. málverk, 2. mynd, 3. tagmynd.
pidgin see blendingsmál.
piece see 1. Maður (man), 2. múrsteinn, 3. stykki, 4. hlutur.
pier see 1. bryggja, 2. brimbrjótur, 3. bryggjupláss, 4. hafnargarður, 5. landgöngubryggja.
pierce see 1. reka, 2. stinga.
piezometer see 1. þrýstimælir, 2. piezorör.
pig see svín.
pigeon see dúfa.
pigment see 1. litarefni, 2. þurrlitarefni.
pike see broddur.
pilchard see sardína.
pile see 1. hlaði, 2. kjarnaofn.
pileus see 1. hattur, 2. hetta, 3. skýjahetta, 4. svepphattur.
pili see festiþræðir.
pill see pilla.
pillar see 1. súla, 2. stoð, 3. standur, 4. stafur.
pilose see 1. mjúkhærður, 2. hærður.
pilot see 1. stýritappi, 2. flugmaður, 3. hafnsögumaður, 4. lóðs, 5. stýrikeila.
pilotage see 1. sjónleiðsaga, 2. kennileitaflug, 3. hafnsögugjald, 4. hafnsaga.
pilus see 1. bakteríuhár, 2. gerilhár, 3. hár (hair), 4. þráður.
pin see 1. tindur, 2. nagli, 3. pinni.
pincers see 1. griptöng, 2. tenajlo.
pine see fura.
pineapple see 1. ananas, 2. ananasjurt, 3. granaldin, 4. stofuananas.
ping see 1. kveikibank, 2. neistabank.
pinion see 1. aflhjól, 2. pinnjón.
pink see bleikur.
pinking see kveikibank.
pinna see 1. eyra (ear), 2. smáblað, 3. úteyra.

pinpoint see 1. hnita, 2. hnitstaða.
pint see hálfpottur.
pion see píeind.
pioneer see 1. frumherji, 2. landnemi.
pipe see 1. kælirör, 2. kælistokkur, 3. pípa, 4. rör.
piper see tindaknurri.
pipette see 1. dreypari, 2. skammtapípa, 3. rennipípa, 4. pípetta, 5. mælipípa.
piping see 1. pípulögn, 2. röralögn.
piracy see sjórán.
pirate see 1. sjórán, 2. sjóræningi, 3. sjóræningjaskip.
pisiform see baunarlaga.
pismire see maur.
pistil see fræva.
piston see 1. bulla, 2. kólfur, 3. stimpill.
pit see 1. pittur, 2. pollur, 3. hola, 4. dæld, 5. smurgryfja.
pitch see 1. kinka, 2. tónhæð, 3. skásetning, 4. kink, 5. kasta.
pith see mergur.
pity see 1. meðaumkun, 2. vorkenna.
pityriasis see hreisturkvilli.
pivot see 1. pinni, 2. vægisteinn, 3. snúðteinn, 4. legoddur, 5. þolinmóður.
pixel see 1. dill, 2. myndeind, 3. myndeining.
place see 1. pláss, 2. vettvangur, 3. stétt, 4. staður, 5. staða.
placebo see lyfleysa.
placenta see 1. legkaka, 2. fylgja, 3. fræsæti.
placentation see fylgjumyndun.
plage see sólflekkur.
plague see 1. bráðafár, 2. drepsótt, 3. plága, 4. svartidauði.
plaice see 1. skarkoli, 2. rauðspretta.
plain see 1. slétta, 2. skýr, 3. slétta.
plaintiff see 1. sækjandi, 2. stefnandi.
plan see 1. uppdráttur, 2. áætla, 3. áætlun, 4. ætla, 5. teikning.
plane see 1. flugvél, 2. slétta, 3. flötur, 4. sléttur, 5. skurður.
planet see 1. reikistjarna, 2. föruhnöttur, 3. himintungl, 4. pláneta.
planetarium see 1. sólkerfislíkan, 2. stjörnuver, 3. stjörnusalur, 4. himinvarpi, 5. himinsýningarvél.
plank see 1. borð, 2. planki.
planning see 1. skipulag, 2. skipulagning, 3. áætlunargerð, 4. áætlanagerð.
plant see 1. kerfi, 2. planta, 3. ungplanta, 4. vélakostur, 5. verksmiðja.
plantain see mjölbanani.
plantation see plantekra.
plaque see 1. tannsýkla, 2. skella, 3. eyða, 4. fituútfelling, 5. hörsl.

plasma *see* 1. blóðvökvi, 2. eisa, 3. plasmi, 4. rafgas, 5. vessavökvi.
plasmodium *see* 1. mýrakölduvaldur, 2. samfrumungur, 3. mýraköldusýkill.
plaster *see* plástur.
plastic *see* 1. auðmótaður, 2. gerviefni, 3. plast, 4. plastefni, 5. plestinn.
plasticity *see* tillæti.
plastid *see* plastið.
plat *see* 1. landamerkjauppdráttur, 2. lóð, 3. mæliblað, 4. skipulagsuppdráttur, 5. spilda.
plate *see* 1. diskur, 2. fleki, 3. skinna, 4. plata, 5. blikk.
plateau *see* 1. háslétta, 2. ládeyða, 3. ördeyðuskeið, 4. slétta, 5. sylla.
platelet *see* blóðflaga.
platform *see* 1. pallur, 2. verkvangur, 3. bryggja, 4. flati.
platinum *see* 1. platína, 2. hvítagull.
play *see* 1. leika, 2. leikur, 3. kynna, 4. hlaup, 5. frígangur.
playback *see* 1. aflestur, 2. spilun, 3. upprakning.
playhouse *see* leikhús.
plaything *see* leikfang.
plea *see* bæn.
pleasant *see* þægilegur.
pleased *see* ánægður.
plentiful *see* 1. ríkulegur, 2. kappnógur.
plenty *see* gnægð.
plenum *see* allsherjarfundur.
pleura *see* 1. brjósthimna, 2. fleiðra.
pleurisy *see* 1. brjósthimnubólga, 2. fleiðrubólga.
pleurodynia *see* 1. millirifjaverkur, 2. tak.
plexus *see* 1. flétta, 2. flækja.
pliers *see* 1. spennitöng, 2. töng.
ploidy *see* litnun.
plot *see* 1. reitur, 2. teikning, 3. teikna, 4. samsæri, 5. kortsetning.
plotter *see* 1. teiknari, 2. teiknivél.
plotting *see* kortaritun.
plough *see* plægja.
plug *see* 1. rafmagnskló, 2. rafmagnstengill, 3. stungutengi, 4. tappi, 5. tengilkvísl.
plumb *see* sakka.
plumule *see* dúnfjöður.
plunger *see* 1. drullusokkur, 2. kólfur.
pluralism *see* 1. fjölbreytni, 2. fjölbýli, 3. fjölhyggja, 4. fjölræði, 5. margræði.
plus *see* 1. plús, 2. plúsmerki, 3. samlagningarmerki.
plutonium *see* 1. plúton, 2. plútón, 3. plútóníum.
ply *see* lag.
plywood *see* krossviður.
pneumatic *see* 1. loftknúið, 2. loftknúinn, 3. loftfylltur.
pneumatics *see* 1. loftaflfræði, 2. loftþrýstitækni.

pneumonia *see* lungnabólga.
poacher *see* veiðiþjófur.
pocket *see* 1. afhol, 2. poki, 3. vasi.
pod *see* 1. belgur, 2. fræbelgur, 3. klefi.
podiatry *see* fótsnyrting.
poem *see* kvæði.
poet *see* skáld.
poignancy *see* 1. hvassleiki, 2. skarpskyggni.
poignant *see* 1. hrjúfur, 2. leiftandi, 3. skarpur, 4. beittur.
point *see* 1. punktur, 2. tugakomma, 3. spurning, 4. oddur, 5. mark.
pointer *see* 1. bendill, 2. bendir, 3. vísir.
poison *see* 1. eitur, 2. ljómeitur.
poisoning *see* eitrun.
poisonous *see* eitraður.
polar *see* 1. póllægur, 2. skautaður, 3. pólaður.
polarimeter *see* 1. pólunarmælir, 2. skautunarmælir.
polariscope *see* skautsjá.
polarity *see* 1. skautstefna, 2. skautun, 3. segulstefna, 4. pólun, 5. pólstefna.
polarization *see* 1. pólun, 2. rafskautun, 3. skautun.
polarizer *see* 1. skautunarsía, 2. skautari, 3. skautunarefni.
pole *see* 1. skaut, 2. stólpi, 3. staur, 4. póll, 5. brotpunktur.
police *see* 1. löggæzla, 2. löggæzlulið.
policeman *see* 1. lögreglumaður, 2. lögregluðjónn.
policy *see* 1. vátryggingarskírteini, 2. utanríkisstefna, 3. stjórnkænska, 4. stjórnarstefna, 5. stefnumál.
polio *see* 1. lömunarveiki, 2. mænuveiki, 3. mænusótt.
poliomyelitis *see* 1. lömunarveiki, 2. mænugránabólga, 3. mænusótt, 4. mænuveiki.
polish *see* 1. pússa, 2. slípa, 3. pólera, 4. fægja.
polite *see* kurteis.
politics *see* 1. pólitík, 2. stjórnfræði, 3. stjórnmál, 4. stjórnmálafræði, 5. stjórnmálaskoðun.
poll *see* atkvæðatalning.
pollen *see* 1. frjó, 2. frjókorn.
polling *see* 1. færiboð, 2. hverfisenditilboð.
pollutant *see* 1. mengunarefni, 2. mengunarvaldar, 3. mengunarvaldur.
polluter *see* 1. mengill, 2. mengari.
pollution *see* 1. sáðfall, 2. mengun, 3. óhreinkun.
polonium *see* pólon.
polychromatic *see* fjöllita.
polydactyly *see* 1. fjölfingrun, 2. fjöltáun.
polygenic *see* fjölgena.
polygon *see* 1. fláki, 2. marghyrningur, 3. hyrningur, 4. hornarit.
polygraph *see* 1. fleirrit, 2. fleirriti, 3. síriti, 4. skrifari.
polymer *see* 1. gerviefni, 2. fjölliða.

polymerization see 1. fjölliðun, 2. liðun.
polymorphic see 1. fjölbreytilegur, 2. fjölbreytinn,
　3. fjölmóta, 4. margbreytilegur, 5. margleitur.
polymorphism see 1. margleitni, 2. fjölmótun, 3.
　fjölbrigðni, 4. fjölbreytni.
polynomial see 1. margliða, 2. fleirliða.
polyp see 1. holsepi, 2. sepi.
polypeptide see 1. fjölpeðtíð, 2. fjölpeptíð.
polypharmacy see 1. lyfjaofgjöf, 2.
　fjölllyfjameðferð.
polyploid see 1. fjöllitna, 2. fjöllitnungur.
polyploidy see fjöllitnun.
polyuria see ofsamiga.
pons see 1. brú, 2. heilabrú.
pontoon see flothylki.
poop see skutpallur.
poor see 1. illur, 2. slæmur, 3. vondur, 4. fátækur.
pope see lirfugleypir.
poplar see ösp.
population see 1. þýði, 2. fólksfjöldi, 3. íbúafjöldi,
　4. stofn, 5. stjörnubyggð.
porbeagle see hámeri.
porcelain see postulín.
pore see 1. op, 2. sóldíll, 3. gropa.
pork see flesk.
porker see svín.
porosity see 1. gljúpleiki, 2. grop, 3. gropa, 4.
　grophlutfall.
porous see 1. gljúpur, 2. gropinn, 3. gleypur, 4.
　holóttur.
porphyria see 1. porfýría, 2. purpuraveiki.
port see 1. tengibúnaður, 2. bakborði, 3. höfn, 4. op,
　5. stunga.
portability see flytjanleiki.
portable see 1. færanlegur, 2. flytjanlegur, 3.
　handbær, 4. hreyfanlegur.
portfolio see 1. skjalamappa, 2. skjalataska, 3.
　ráðherraembætti, 4. eignasafn, 5. verðbréfasafn.
porthole see 1. kýrauga, 2. mannop.
pose see orsaka.
position see 1. Staða, 2. staður, 3. stelling, 4.
　afstaða, 5. staðarákvörðun.
positioning see staðarákvörðun.
positive see 1. frumstig, 2. jákvæður, 3. plús, 4.
　viðlægur.
positivism see 1. raunhyggja, 2. vissustefna, 3.
　raunspeki, 4. pósitífismi, 5. staðreyndahyggja.
positron see 1. andrafögn, 2. jáeind, 3. pósitróna.
possess see eiga.
possession see eign.
post see 1. starf, 2. staða, 3. póstur, 4. embætti, 5
　þingsenda.
postulate see 1. forsenda, 2. frumhæfa, 3.
　frumhæfing.
posture see líkamsburður.

pot see 1. karfa, 2. ker.
potassium see 1. kalín, 2. kalíum.
potato see kartafla.
potency see 1. dugur, 2. hæfni, 3. mætti.
potential see 1. spennugildi, 2. spenna, 3.
　mögulegur, 4. mætti, 5. möguleiki.
potentiation see 1. virknisaukning, 2. efling
potentiometer see 1. breytiviðnám, 2. jafni.
pound see 1. fiskmóttaka, 2. pund.
poverty see 1. fátækt, 2. rýrð, 3. ófrjósemi, 4.
　örbirgð.
powder see 1. duft, 2. duftlyf, 3. hersluduft, 4.
　lyfjaduft, 5. púður.
power see 1. vald, 2. styrkur, 3. veldi, 4. afl, 5.
　afköst.
poxvirus see bóluveira.
practical see raunverulegur.
practically see 1. nær, 2. næstum.
practice see 1. lækningastarfsemi, 2. viðskiptavenja,
　3. venja, 4. vani, 5. starfsþjálfun.
pragmatics see 1. aðstæðufræði, 2.
　málnotkunarfræði.
pragmatism see 1. raunsæi, 2. gagnsemishyggja, 3.
　notahyggja.
pram see barnavagn.
praseodymium see 1. praseódým, 2. praseodým.
prawn see rækja.
praxis see 1. framkvæmd, 2. reynd, 3. verkgeta.
prayer see bæn.
preamble see 1. aðdragandi, 2. forstillimerki.
precaution see 1. gætni, 2. forsjálni, 3. skynsemi, 4.
　varúð, 5. varúðarráðstöfun.
precedence see forgangur.
precession see 1. möndulvelta, 2. framsókn, 3.
　ásvelta, 4. pólvelta.
precinct see 1. hverfi, 2. svæði, 3. umdæmi.
precious see 1. sætur, 2. sjaldgæfur.
precipice see 1. hyldýpi, 2. gjá.
precipitant see fellir.
precipitate see 1. syrja, 2. útfall, 3. botnfall.
precipitation see 1. botnfelling, 2. felling, 3. syrjun,
　4. úrkoma, 5. útfelling.
precision see 1. nákvæmni, 2. stafanákvæmni.
preclinical see forklínískur.
precocious see 1. bráðger, 2. bráðþroska, 3.
　snemmþroska, 4. snemmvaxinn.
precocity see bráðþroski.
precognition see forviska.
precursor see 1. undanfari, 2. forveri.
predation see 1. ránlíf, 2. afrán, 3. át.
predator see 1. afæta, 2. afræningi, 3. rándýr.
predicate see 1. rökyrðing, 2. umsögn, 3. yrðing.
prediction see 1. forsögn, 2. spá, 3. spádómur.
predisposition see 1. fornæmi, 2. tilhneigð.
preemption see forkaupsréttur.

preferably see heldur.
preference see 1. kjörstilling, 2. vild.
prefix see 1. forskeyti, 2. merkjaforskeyti.
pregnancy see 1. þungun, 2. þykkt, 3. barnshöfn.
pregnant see þungaður.
preheating see forhitun.
preload see 1. forspenna, 2. þvingun.
premature see ótímabær.
premedication see 1. forgjafarlyf, 2. lyfjaforgjöf.
premise see forsenda.
premises see 1. athafnasvæði, 2. land, 3. landareign, 4. starfssvæði.
premium see 1. gengisauki, 2. yfirverð, 3. yfirgengi, 4. vátryggingariðgjald, 5. umbun.
premolar see 1. forjaxl, 2. framjaxl.
preoccupy see gleypa.
prepaid see 1. fyrirframgreiddur, 2. fyrirframgreitt.
preparation see 1. aðfari, 2. könnun, 3. Tilreiðsla, 4. undirbúningur, 5. vinnsla.
prepare see 1. undirbúa, 2. semja.
prepuce see forhúð.
prerogative see einkaréttur.
presbyopia see 1. ellifjarsýni, 2. ellisjón.
present see 1. kynna, 2. núverandi, 3. nútímalegur, 4. nútíð, 5. gjöf.
presentation see 1. aðburður, 2. framsetning, 3. kynning, 4. vinnslustig.
preservation see 1. geymsla, 2. varðveisla, 3. friðun.
preservative see 1. geymsluefni, 2. rotvarnarefni, 3. verndunarefni, 4. getnaðarverja.
preserve see 1. geyma, 2. varðveita.
preset see forstillt.
president see 1. forseti, 2. forstjóri, 3. formaður.
press see 1. þvinga, 2. þrýsta, 3. pressa.
pressure see þrýstingur.
presume see halda.
presupposition see 1. forsenda, 2. forskilyrði.
pretend see þykjast.
pretty see 1. fallegur, 2. nóg, 3. fagur.
prevailing see 1. viðvarandi, 2. ríkjandi.
prevalence see algengi.
preventive see 1. forvarnastarf, 2. forverndarstarf, 3. fyrirbyggjandi.
preview see 1. forsýn, 2. forskoða.
priapism see sístaða.
price see 1. kostnaður, 2. verð, 3. verðleggja, 4. gjald.
pricey see dýr (animal).
pricing see verðlagning.
priest see prestur.
primary see 1. aðal, 2. upprunalegur, 3. prófkjör, 4. móðurstjarna, 5. móðurhnöttur.
primates see 1. fremdardýr, 2. prímatar.

prime see 1. gangsetja, 2. grunnmála, 3. mínútumerki, 4. næma, 5. præma.
primer see 1. lykill, 2. vísir, 3. grunnmálning, 4. bensíndæla.
priming see 1. forhleðsla, 2. grunnmálun, 3. forgjöf.
primitive see 1. frumstæður, 2. samskiptalýsing, 3. stofneind, 4. stofnfall.
prince see konungssonur.
principal see 1. skólastjóri, 2. höfuðstóll, 3. helstur, 4. ábyrgðaraðili.
principle see 1. undirstöðuatriði, 2. efnisþáttur, 3. grunnregla, 4. lögmál, 5. meginregla.
printer see prentari.
printout see 1. útskrift, 2. útprent.
prion see 1. príon, 2. prjón, 3. prótínsýkill.
priority see 1. forgangsréttur, 2. forgangur.
prism see 1. prisma, 2. strendingur, 3. þrístrendingur.
prison see fangelsi.
privacy see friðhelgi.
privatization see einkavæðing.
privilege see 1. sérréttindi, 2. forréttindi, 3. réttur.
probability see 1. líkindi, 2. líkur, 3. sennileiki.
probable see sennilegur.
proband see vísitilvik.
probe see 1. rannsaka, 2. nemi, 3. þreifari, 4. greinir, 5. kanni.
problem see 1. Vandamál, 2. viðfangsefni, 3. vandi, 4. úrlausnarefni, 5. þraut.
procedure see 1. tilhögun, 2. meðferðarreglur, 3. verklagsreglur, 4. verkgangur, 5. stefja.
process see 1. hvarf, 2. þróunarferill, 3. meðhöndlun, 4. klakkur, 5. hvörf.
processing see 1. verkun, 2. vinnsla.
processor see gjörvi.
procreation see æxlun.
procumbent see jarðlægur.
prodrome see undanfaraeinkenni.
producer see framleiðandi.
product see 1. afurð, 2. framleiðsla, 3. framleiðsluvara, 4. margfeldi, 5. myndefni.
production see 1. framleiðsla, 2. myndun.
productive see framleiðinn.
productivity see 1. frjósemi, 2. framleiðni, 3. framleiðslugeta.
proenzyme see forensím.
profess see játa.
profession see 1. fag, 2. sérfræðistarf, 3. starfsgrein, 4. starfsstétt.
profile see 1. þverskurðarmynd, 2. sniðrit, 3. útlínur, 4. sneiðing, 5. lögun.
profit see 1. vinningur, 2. ábati, 3. ágóði, 4. gróði, 5. hagnaður.
profitability see arðsemi.
profound see djúpur.

profuse *see* 1. kappnógur, 2. ríkulegur.
progenitor *see* forveri.
progeny *see* 1. afsprengi, 2. afkomandi, 3. afkomendur, 4. afkvæmi.
progesterone *see* 1. prógesterón, 2. meðgönguhormón, 3. fósturlífsvaki, 4. gulbúshormón, 5. gulbúsvaki.
prognosis *see* 1. forsögn, 2. horfur, 3. spá.
program *see* 1. boðrita, 2. forrita, 3. efnisskrá, 4. boðrit, 5. boðkenna.
programmer *see* 1. boðritari, 2. forritari.
programming *see* 1. boðritun, 2. forritun.
progress *see* 1. framvinda, 2. þróast, 3. framför.
progression *see* 1. framvinda, 2. framrás.
progressive *see* 1. ágengur, 2. framfarasinnaður, 3. framsækinn, 4. stighækkandi, 5. stigverkandi.
project *see* 1. hugmynd, 2. verkefni, 3. tilvarp, 4. áætlun, 5. varpa.
projectile *see* 1. kasthlutur, 2. skeyti, 3. skot.
projection *see* 1. kortavörpun, 2. útlitsmynd, 3. tunga, 4. vörpun, 5. skögun.
projector *see* ljóskastari.
prokaryote *see* dreifkjörnungur.
prolactin *see* 1. prólaktín, 2. mjólkurhormón, 3. mjólkurmyndunarvaki.
prolapse *see* 1. síga, 2. framfall, 3. sig.
proletariat *see* 1. verkalýður, 2. öreigalýður, 3. öreigar, 4. öreigastétt.
proliferation *see* 1. viðkoma, 2. margföldun, 3. álun, 4. fjölgun.
proline *see* 1. pró, 2. prólín.
prolong *see* 1. framlengja, 2. lengja.
promethium *see* 1. prómetín, 2. prómetíum, 3. prómeþín.
prominence *see* 1. sólstrókur, 2. bunga.
prominent *see* áberandi.
promise *see* 1. loforð, 2. lofa.
promontory *see* höfði.
promote *see* 1. örva, 2. styrkja, 3. hækka, 4. efla, 5. kynna.
promoter *see* 1. stýrisvæði, 2. stýrill.
promotion *see* 1. efling, 2. kynningarstarf, 3. stöðuhækkun, 4. uppfærsla, 5. útbreiðslustarf.
prompt *see* 1. hratt, 2. nákvæmur, 3. kveðja, 4. kvaðning, 5. hvatning.
promptly *see* nákvæmlega.
promptness *see* nákvæmni.
pronation *see* ranghverfing.
prone *see* flatur.
pronoun *see* fornafn.
proof *see* 1. staðreynd, 2. sönnunargagn, 3. sönnun.
propaganda *see* áróður.
propagation *see* 1. útbreiðsla, 2. dreifing, 3. flutningur, 4. framsal, 5. nýjun.

propellant *see* 1. þrýstiloft, 2. eldsneyti, 3. aflgjafi, 4. drifefni.
propeller *see* 1. loftskrúfa, 2. skipsskrúfa, 3. skrúfa.
proper *see* eigin.
properties *see* 1. eiginleikar, 2. eignir.
property *see* 1. eign, 2. eiginleiki, 3. bú, 4. búgarður, 5. eignir.
prophage *see* 1. dulveira, 2. forveira.
prophase *see* 1. forstig, 2. prófasi, 3. forfasi.
prophylaxis *see* 1. forvörn, 2. sjúkdómsvörn.
proportion *see* hlutfall.
proportional *see* 1. hlutfallslegur, 2. hlutfallsbundinn.
proposal *see* 1. tillaga, 2. tilboð, 3. frumvarp.
propose *see* ætla.
proposition *see* 1. fullyrðing, 2. setning, 3. yrðing.
propulsion *see* 1. framdrif, 2. knýing, 3. framdrift, 4. drif, 5. framknúning.
prosencephalon *see* framheili.
prospecting *see* 1. jarðefnaleit, 2. leit.
prospector *see* jarðefnaleitaraðili.
prospectus *see* 1. útboðslýsing, 2. smárit, 3. kynningarskjal, 4. kynningarbæklingur.
prosperity *see* 1. velgengni, 2. velmegun, 3. hagsæld.
prostaglandin *see* prostaglandín.
prostatitis *see* 1. blöðruhálskirtilsbólga, 2. hvekkbólga.
prosthesis *see* gervilíffæri.
prostrate *see* 1. örmagnast, 2. örmagna, 3. jarðlægur, 4. marflatur.
prostyle *see* 1. stafnrið, 2. stafnriðshof.
protactinium *see* 1. protaktín, 2. prótaktín.
protagonist *see* 1. málsvari, 2. þátttakandi, 3. aðalhvatamaður, 4. forvígismaður.
protease *see* 1. hvítukljúfur, 2. próteasi, 3. prótínkljúfur.
protect *see* 1. hylja, 2. þekja, 3. varða.
protected *see* 1. snertivarinn, 2. varinn, 3. verndaður.
protection *see* 1. friðun, 2. hlíf, 3. vernd, 4. verndun, 5. vörn.
protectionism *see* 1. verndarstefna, 2. verndartollastefna, 3. tollverndarfyrirkomulag, 4. tollverndarstefna.
protective *see* vörn.
protectorate *see* 1. verndarríki, 2. verndarsvæði.
protein *see* 1. eggjahvíta, 2. hvíta, 3. prótein, 4. prótín.
proteolysis *see* 1. hvítusundrun, 2. prótínsundrun, 3. prótínleysing, 4. prótínrof.
protest *see* 1. aðfinnslur, 2. andmæli, 3. kvörtun, 4. minnihlutaálit, 5. mótmæli.
prothrombin *see* próþrombín.
protist *see* frumvera.

protium see 1. prótín, 2. einvetni.
protocol see 1. samskiptareglur, 2. verklýsing, 3. siðareglur, 4. samskiptamáti, 5. samskiptaaðferð.
proton see 1. foreind, 2. forögn, 3. prótóna, 4. róteind.
protoplasm see frymi.
protoplast see veggleysingi.
prototype see 1. forsmíð, 2. frumeintak, 3. frumgerð, 4. frummynd, 5. frumsmíð.
protozoa see frumdýr.
protozoon see frumdýr.
protractor see gráðubogi.
protrusion see 1. framskögun, 2. útskot, 3. útstandandi.
prove see 1. prófa, 2. sanna.
provide see 1. útvega, 2. afla, 3. geta.
province see 1. fylki, 2. hérað.
provirus see forveira.
provision see 1. ákvæði, 2. klásúla, 3. klausa, 4. ráðstöfun, 5. skilyrði.
provisional see 1. bráðabirgða, 2. tímabundinn.
provisions see 1. vistir, 2. birgðir.
provoke see orsaka.
prow see 1. kinnungur, 2. stefnir.
proximal see 1. nærlægur, 2. nærliggjandi, 3. nærri.
proximate see 1. nærtækastur, 2. næstur, 3. nærri.
proximity see 1. nánd, 2. nálægð.
proxy see 1. heimild, 2. umboð.
prudence see 1. gætni, 2. skynsemi, 3. varfærni, 4. forsjálni, 5. fyrirhyggja.
pruning see 1. grisjun, 2. snyrting, 3. stýfing.
psalterium see laki.
pseudonym see dulnefni.
pseudopodium see 1. skinfótur, 2. sýndarfótur.
psi see 1. ófreskigáfa, 2. psí.
psittacosis see 1. páfagaukasótt, 2. páfagaukaveiki, 3. fýlasótt, 4. fuglasótt.
psoriasis see 1. sóri, 2. baugaskán, 3. spæringur, 4. psóríasis, 5. hundsspor.
psyche see 1. Síka, 2. sál.
psychedelic see hugvíkkandi.
psychiatrist see 1. geðlæknir, 2. geðsjúkdómalæknir.
psychiatry see 1. geðsjúkdómafræði, 2. geðlæknisfræði.
psychoanalysis see 1. sálkönnunarkenning, 2. sálgreining.
psychoanalyst see 1. sálgreinir, 2. sálkönnuður.
psychodrama see geðleikur.
psychogenic see 1. geðrættur, 2. sálrænn.
psychokinesis see 1. æðisgerðir, 2. fjarhrif.
psycholeptic see hugslakandi.
psycholinguistics see málsálarfræði.
psychologist see sálfræðingur.
psychology see 1. sálfræði, 2. sálarfræði.

psychopath see 1. geðvillingur, 2. siðblindingi.
psychopathology see sálsýkisfræði.
psychopathy see 1. geðvilla, 2. siðblinda.
psychopharmacology see geðlyfjunarfræði.
psychophysiology see sálarlífeðlisfræði.
psychosis see 1. geðrof, 2. geðveiki, 3. sturlun.
psychosomatic see geðvefrænn.
psychotherapy see sállækning.
psychotic see 1. geðsjúklingur, 2. geðveikur.
psychrometer see 1. þurrkmælir, 2. rakamælir, 3. loftrakamælir.
ptyalin see 1. sterkjukljúfur, 2. mjölvakljúfur.
puberty see 1. kynþroskaaldur, 2. kynþroskaskeið, 3. kynþroski.
pubescence see 1. kynþroski, 2. ló, 3. loðna.
pubescent see 1. dúnhærður, 2. kynþroska, 3. lóhærður.
public see 1. notfrjáls, 2. opinber, 3. almennur, 4. almenningur.
publication see útgáfa.
puck see 1. vala, 2. drýsill, 3. pökkur, 4. tafla, 5. tala.
pudding see eftirmatur.
puff see 1. skúfur, 2. bólstur.
pull see 1. toga, 2. aðdráttarkraftur, 3. draga, 4. dragkraftur, 5. togkraftur.
puller see 1. afdragi, 2. dragkló, 3. afdráttarþvinga.
pulley see 1. reimhjól, 2. reimskífa, 3. skoruhjól, 4. trissa.
pullover see peysa.
pulp see 1. kvika, 2. mergur, 3. aldinkjöt.
pulsar see 1. tifstjarna, 2. slagstjarna.
pulsation see 1. slag, 2. sláttur.
pulse see 1. æðasláttur, 2. högg, 3. rafmerki, 4. púls, 5. slag.
pumice see vikur.
pump see dæla.
pumpkin see 1. glóðarker, 2. risagrasker, 3. tröllagrasker.
punch see 1. gatari, 2. úrrek, 3. stansa, 4. stans, 5. götunartæki.
punctate see 1. blettóttur, 2. deplóttur.
punctual see 1. nákvæmur, 2. stundvís.
punctuality see nákvæmni.
punctually see nákvæmlega.
punctuation see 1. greinarmerki, 2. greinarmerkjasetning.
puncture see 1. springa, 2. stunga, 3. gat, 4. ástunga, 5. gegnhlaup.
punishment see 1. hegning, 2. refsing.
pupa see púpa.
pupil see 1. nemandi, 2. sjáaldur, 3. ljósop.
puppet see brúða.
purchase see 1. kaup, 2. kaupa, 3. innkaup.
purchaser see kaupandi.

pure *see* hreinn.
purgation *see* búkhreinsun.
purgative *see* 1. búkhreinsilyf, 2. búkhreinsandi, 3. aldinkjöt.
purge *see* 1. hreinsa, 2. hreinsun, 3. rása, 4. skolun.
purification *see* 1. hreinsun, 2. skiljun.
purify *see* 1. hreinsa, 2. skilja.
purine *see* púrín.
purloin *see* stela.
purpose *see* 1. tilgangur, 2. markmið.
purser *see* 1. bryti, 2. þjónustustjóri.
pursue *see* elta.
pus *see* 1. gröftur, 2. vogur.
push *see* 1. ýta, 2. skúfa, 3. skúfun, 4. þrýsta.
puss *see* köttur (cat).
pussy *see* 1. köttur (cat), 2. pussa.
pustule *see* graftarbóla.
put *see* 1. söluréttur, 2. söluvilnun, 3. leggja, 4. setja.
putrefaction *see* 1. rotnun, 2. ýlda.
putrefy *see* morkna.
putrid *see* 1. rotinn, 2. úldinn.
putty *see* 1. kítta, 2. kítti, 3. spartl, 4. spartla.
pyjamas *see* náttföt.
pylon *see* 1. merki, 2. stöpull, 3. mastur, 4. hofstöpull, 5. turn.
pyogenic *see* graftarmyndandi.
pyramid *see* 1. pýramídi, 2. pýramíti, 3. píramíti, 4. píramíði, 5. píramídi.
pyrimidine *see* 1. pyrimídín, 2. pýrimidín, 3. pýrimídín.
pyrolysis *see* 1. hitasundrun, 2. hitaleysing, 3. hitarof.
pyrometer *see* 1. háhitamælir, 2. glómælir, 3. glóðhitamælir.
pyrophoric *see* loftkveikjandi.
pyrosis *see* nábítur.
pyuria *see* graftarmiga.

Q

quadrangle *see* 1. ferhyrningur, 2. fjórðungskortblöð.
quadrant *see* 1. kvaðrantur, 2. tannbogi, 3. kvaðrant, 4. flatarfjórðungur, 5. fjórðungsmælir.
quadrate *see* ferstrendur.
quadrature *see* þverstaða.
quadrilateral *see* 1. fjórhliða, 2. fjórhliðungur, 3. ferhyrningur, 4. ferhyrndur.
quadruped *see* ferfætlingur.
quail *see* kornhæna.
qualification *see* 1. verðleikar, 2. fyrirvari, 3. hæfi, 4. hæfni, 5. menntun.
qualifications *see* 1. hæfi, 2. geta.

qualify *see* 1. sérgreina, 2. skilgreina.
qualitative *see* eigindlegur.
quality *see* 1. eiginleiki, 2. eðli, 3. eigind, 4. gæði, 5. hljóðgildi.
quantification *see* 1. magnmæling, 2. magnsetja, 3. magnfesting, 4. magnákvörðun, 5. magnhæfing.
quantify *see* 1. meta, 2. mæla, 3. tölubúa, 4. magnhæfa, 5. magngreina.
quantitative *see* 1. magn, 2. magnbundinn, 3. megindlegur, 4. veganlegur, 5. mælanlegur.
quantity *see* 1. skammtur, 2. stærð, 3. megind, 4. magn, 5. megindlegur.
quantization *see* 1. gildisskömmtun, 2. litstökun.
quantize *see* 1. búta, 2. skammta.
quantum *see* 1. skammtur, 2. kvanti.
quarantine *see* sóttkví.
quark *see* 1. kvark, 2. kvarki, 3. kvarkur, 4. kvarg.
quarrel *see* 1. rífast, 2. rifrildi.
quarter *see* 1. kvartil, 2. stjórnborðshorn, 3. tunglfjórðungur, 4. kvartalo, 5. fjórðungur.
quarters *see* 1. kvaronjaro, 2. kvarono, 3. kvartalo, 4. rondo, 5. trimestro.
quartile *see* fjórðungsmark.
quartz *see* 1. kvarts, 2. kísilsýrusteinn, 3. kvars.
quasar *see* 1. kvasi, 2. dulstirni.
quaternary *see* 1. fjórðastigs, 2. kvarter, 3. kvartertímabil, 4. kvertertímabil.
quay *see* 1. bryggja, 2. hafnarbakki, 3. viðlegukantur.
queen *see* 1. drotning, 2. Drottning.
quench *see* 1. kæfa, 2. slökkva, 3. snöggkæla.
quenching *see* kæfing.
query *see* 1. fyrirspurn, 2. spurn.
question *see* 1. spurning, 2. efa, 3. fyrirspurn.
questionnaire *see* 1. spurningaeyðublað, 2. spurningalisti, 3. spurningaskrá.
queue *see* 1. biðlisti, 2. biðröð, 3. röð.
quick *see* hratt.
quickening *see* fjörgun.
quicksilver *see* kvikasilfur.
quiescent *see* 1. óvirkur, 2. tiltækur.
quietness *see* ró.
quietude *see* afslöppun.
quill *see* 1. broddur, 2. fjöðurstafur.
quilting *see* 1. bútasaumur, 2. splæsing.
quince *see* 1. japanspera, 2. kveða, 3. kveði, 4. perubróðir, 5. roðarunnaaldin.
quinine *see* 1. kínín, 2. kiníntré.
quinoa *see* 1. inkanjóli, 2. frumbyggjanjóli.
quit *see* yfirgefa.
quota *see* kvóti.
quotation *see* 1. kostnaðaráætlun, 2. tilvitnun.
quote *see* skrá.
quotient *see* 1. vísitala, 2. deild, 3. hlutfall, 4. kvóti.

R

rabbi see 1. rabbíni, 2. gyðingaprestur.
rabbit see kanína.
rabble see 1. múgur, 2. skríll.
rabid see óður.
rabies see 1. hundaæði, 2. hundabitsæði.
raccoon see þvottabjörn.
race see 1. kynþáttur, 2. rasi, 3. leguhringur, 4. kynstofn, 5. kyn.
racemose see 1. klasakenndur, 2. klasaleitur.
rachis see 1. blómskipunarstöngull, 2. stilkur, 3. fjöðurstafur, 4. leggur.
racism see 1. kynþáttahatur, 2. kynþóttafördomar, 3. kynþáttafordómar, 4. kynþáttahroki, 5. kynþáttarembingur.
rack see 1. grind, 2. magasin, 3. rekkur, 4. standur, 5. tannstangargír.
racon see 1. ratsjársvari, 2. ratsjársvarviti.
radar see 1. ratsjá, 2. ratsjártækni.
radial see 1. sveifarlægur, 2. stefnugeisli, 3. geisli, 4. geislalægur, 5. geislandi.
radian see 1. horneining, 2. bogaeining, 3. radíani, 4. raunhorn, 5. geisl.
radiance see geislunarljómi.
radiant see 1. geislandi, 2. geislapunktur.
radiate see geisla.
radiation see 1. geislun, 2. geisl, 3. skúfur.
radiator see 1. vatnskassi, 2. kælir, 3. miðstöðvarofn, 4. geislari, 5. geislagjafi.
radical see 1. róttæklingur, 2. róttækur, 3. gagnger, 4. rót, 5. rótarstærð.
radically see gagngert.
radio see 1. útvarp, 2. fjarskipti, 3. viðtæki, 4. útvarpsviðtæki, 5. útvarpstækni.
radioactive see 1. geislavirkur, 2. virkur.
radioactivity see geislavirkni.
radiograph see 1. röntgenmynda, 2. geislunarmynd, 3. rafaldsmynd, 4. röntgenmynd.
radiography see 1. röntgenmyndun, 2. gegnumlýsing.
radioimmunoassay see geislaónæmismæling.
radioisotope see geislasamsæta.
radiology see 1. geislalækningar, 2. geislalæknisfræði, 3. geislunarfræði.
radiometer see 1. geislaorkumælir, 2. geislunarmælir.
radiometry see 1. geislmælifræði, 2. geislunarmæling.
radiosonde see veðurkanni.
radiotherapy see geislameðferð.
radish see 1. radísa, 2. hreðka.

radium see 1. radín, 2. radíum.
radius see 1. radíus, 2. geisli, 3. hverfileggur, 4. sveif, 5. útvarp.
radix see 1. grunntala, 2. rót, 3. stofntala.
radome see 1. hjálmur, 2. loftnetshlíf.
raffle see 1. hlutavelta, 2. tombóla.
raft see 1. fleki, 2. timburfleki.
rafter see 1. raftur, 2. sperra, 3. þaksperra.
rag see 1. tuska, 2. drusla.
rage see bræði.
ragout see ragú.
raider see 1. hremmir, 2. hrifsari.
rail see 1. langband, 2. teinn, 3. rimill, 4. rim, 5. rið.
railing see 1. grindverk, 2. rimlagirðing.
railroad see járnbraut.
railway see járnbraut.
rain see 1. regn, 2. regna, 3. rigna, 4. rigning.
rainbow see regnbogi.
raincoat see regnfrakki.
rainforest see regnskógur.
raise see 1. hækka, 2. hefja, 3. lyfta, 4. reisa.
rake see 1. hrífa, 2. spónarhorn, 3. skörungur, 4. raka, 5. hallahorn.
ram see 1. hrútur, 2. þjappa, 3. vinnsluminni, 4. stanga, 5. hamra.
rambutan see ígulber.
ramose see 1. greinóttur, 2. kvíslóttur.
ramp see 1. halli, 2. rampi, 3. rampur, 4. skábraut.
rampart see virkisgarður.
ramus see 1. álma, 2. kvísl.
ranch see 1. bú, 2. búgarður, 3. stórbýli.
rancher see stórbóndi.
rancid see 1. þrár, 2. þræsinn, 3. þránaður.
random see 1. tilviljunarkenndur, 2. hending, 3. handahófskennt.
range see 1. seiling, 2. drægi, 3. skotlengd, 4. svið, 5. svæði.
ranger see fjallarakki.
rank see 1. röð, 2. raðgildi, 3. röðun, 4. sæti, 5. sætistala.
ransom see lausnargjald.
rape see 1. repja, 2. olíurepja, 3. fóðurrepja, 4. fóðurrófa, 5. nauðgun.
rapid see hratt.
rapier see 1. lagsverð, 2. skylmingasverð.
rapport see samband.
rare see sjaldgæfur.
rarefaction see þynning.
rarely see sjaldan.
rash see útbrot.
rasp see 1. raspa, 2. raspur.
raspberry see hindber.
raster see 1. línumynstur, 2. rasti.
rat see rotta.
ratchet see 1. hömluhak, 2. skrall, 3. skreppa.

rate see 1. hlutfall, 2. hraði, 3. flokkun, 4.
hundraðshluti, 5. mælihlutfall.
rather see 1. nóg, 2. heldur.
ratification see 1. staðfesting, 2. fullnusta, 3.
fullgilding.
ratify see 1. staðfesta, 2. fullgilda, 3. löggilda.
rating see 1. áritun, 2. einkunnagjöf, 3. hæfnismat,
4. málraun, 5. málstærðir.
ratio see 1. hlutfall, 2. kennitala, 3. hlutfallstala, 4.
hraði.
ration see hlutfall.
rational see 1. skynsamur, 2. rökréttur, 3.
skynsamlegur, 4. ræður.
rationalism see 1. rökhyggja, 2. skynsemishyggja,
3. skynsemisstefna.
rationalization see 1. hagræðing, 2. réttlæting, 3.
réttlætng, 4. rökfærsla.
rattan see spanskreyrspálmi.
rattle see 1. skrölta, 2. halabrestur, 3. glamra, 4.
skrölt, 5. hringla.
rattlesnake see skröltormur.
ravage see eyðileggja.
raven see hrafn.
ravine see 1. gil, 2. gljúfur.
raw see hrár.
ray see 1. geisli, 2. útvarp, 3. ljósgeisli.
razor see 1. rakhnífur, 2. rakvél.
reach see 1. seiling, 2. drægi, 3. skotmál, 4.
skrúfulengd, 5. fjarlægðarmörk.
react see 1. hvarfast, 2. svara.
reactance see 1. andóf, 2. launviðnám, 3.
þverviðnám.
reactant see hvarfefni.
reaction see 1. viðbragð, 2. hvörf, 3. svörun, 4.
hvarf, 5. gagnvirkun.
reactionary see 1. afturhaldssamur, 2.
afturhaldsseggur.
reactive see 1. gagnverkandi, 2. hvarfgjarn, 3.
meðvirkur.
reactivity see 1. viðbragðshæfni, 2. viðnæmi, 3.
Virkni.
reactor see 1. kjarnaofn, 2. sátur, 3. hvarfi, 4.
efnahvati.
read see lesa.
reader see 1. kennslubók, 2. lesandi.
readiness see fúsleiki.
reading see 1. álestur, 2. mælisálestur, 3. lesefni, 4.
aflestur, 5. lestur.
readjust see endurstilla.
readjustment see endurstilling.
ready see 1. reiðubúinn, 2. tillbúinn.
reagent see 1. prófunarefni, 2. reagens, 3. prófefni.
real see 1. raunverulegur, 2. raungildur, 3. sannur, 4.
árangursríkur.

realism see 1. raunsæi, 2. raunsæishyggja, 3.
raunhyggja, 4. hluthyggja, 5. raunsæisstefna.
realist see raunsæismaður.
realistic see 1. raunsær, 2. raunverulegur.
reality see 1. veruleiki, 2. raunveruleiki, 3.
sannleikur.
realization see 1. skilningur, 2. innlausn.
realize see skilja.
really see 1. æði, 2. mjög.
realm see 1. ríki, 2. yfrráðasvæði, 3. vettvangur, 4.
svið, 5. konungsríki.
ream see 1. rýming, 2. rýmað.
reamer see 1. víkkari, 2. snaralur, 3. rýmir, 4.
rýmari.
rearrangement see 1. umröðun, 2. umröðunarhvarf.
reason see 1. orsök, 2. ástæða, 3. skynsemi, 4.
tilefni.
reasonable see skynsamur.
reasoning see 1. rökleiðsla, 2. rökhugsun.
rebate see afsláttur.
rebellion see 1. andspyrna, 2. mótþrói, 3. uppreisn.
rebound see 1. endurkasta, 2. sundursláttur, 3.
fjaðra, 4. endurkast, 5. aflétting.
rebuke see 1. átelja, 2. átölur.
recall see 1. endurkalla, 2. upprifjun.
receipt see 1. kvittun, 2. viðtaka.
receivables see viðskiptakröfur.
receive see 1. hlotnast, 2. samþykkja, 3. þakka, 4. fá.
receiver see 1. geymir, 2. hlust, 3. hylki, 4.
móttakandi, 5. móttakari.
receivership see 1. gjaldþrot, 2. skiptameðferð.
recent see nútími.
receptacle see 1. blómbotn, 2. hirsla.
receptor see 1. nemi, 2. skynnemi, 3. viðtaki.
recess see 1. blindband, 2. gróp, 3. holrúm, 4.
réttarhlé, 5. skot.
recession see 1. afturkippur, 2. undanhald, 3.
samdráttarskeið, 4. efnahagslægð, 5. fráhvarf.
recessive see víkjandi.
recidivist see 1. síbrotamaður, 2. síkomusjúklingur.
recipient see 1. arfþegi, 2. póstþegi, 3. þegi, 4.
viðtakandi.
reciprocal see 1. gagnkvæmur, 2. gagnstæður, 3.
gagnverkandi, 4. gagnvirkur, 5. umhverfa.
reciprocate see 1. endurgjalda, 2. róla.
reciprocity see 1. gagnkvæmni, 2. gagnverkun, 3.
gagnvirkni.
recirculation see 1. endurhringrás, 2. hringrás.
reckon see 1. miða, 2. reikna.
reclamation see landauki.
reclassify see 1. endurflokka, 2. umflokka.
recline see liggja.
recognise see 1. þekkja, 2. viðurkenna.
recognition see 1. kennsl, 2. skráning, 3.
viðurkenning.

recognize see skrá.
recoil see 1. afturkast, 2. bakslag.
recollection see minnisheimt.
recombinant see 1. raðbrigði, 2. endurraðað.
recombination see 1. samtenging, 2. samruni, 3.
    sameining, 4. jónfang, 5. endurheimt.
recommendation see 1. ályktun, 2. tilmæli, 3.
    meðmæli, 4. tillaga.
reconciliation see 1. afstemming, 2. sættir, 3.
    samkomulag, 4. sátt.
recondition see endurbyggja.
reconditioning see 1. endurbygging, 2. endurnýjun,
    3. endurnýun, 4. endurskilyrðing, 5. standsetning.
reconnaissance see frumkönnun.
reconstitution see enduruppbygging.
reconstruct see 1. endursemja, 2. endurgera, 3.
    endurbyggja.
reconstruction see 1. endurbygging, 2. endurgerð,
    3. endurgerving, 4. endursemja.
record see 1. skrá, 2. þáttur, 3. skráning, 4. skírteini,
    5. rit.
recorder see 1. skráningartæki, 2. skrifari, 3. síriti.
recording see 1. síritun, 2. skráning, 3. síritandi.
records see 1. raporto, 2. rekordo, 3. rekorda, 4.
    rikordo, 5. registri.
recount see segja.
recourse see endurkröfuréttur.
recover see 1. batna, 2. endurheimta, 3. endurrétta.
recovery see 1. vakning, 2. viðrétting, 3.
    endurrétting, 4. afturbati, 5. vöknun.
recreation see 1. tómstundargaman, 2. upplyfting, 3.
    tómstundaiðja, 4. endursköpun, 5. dægrastytting.
recruitment see 1. nýliðun, 2. nýráðning, 3.
    nýskráning, 4. ráðning, 5. ráðningarstarfsemi.
rectangle see rétthyrningur.
rectangular see 1. rétthyrndur, 2. hornréttur.
rectification see 1. afbjögun, 2. afriðun, 3.
    endureiming, 4. lagfæring, 5. leiðrétting.
rectifier see 1. afriðill, 2. rafloki.
rectify see 1. leiðrétta, 2. rétta, 3. afriða, 4. lagfæra.
rectum see 1. endaþarmur, 2. endagörn.
recurrence see 1. endurkoma, 2. upptekning.
recurrent see ítrekaður.
recurring see síendurtekinn.
recursive see endurkvæmur.
recycle see 1. endurnýta, 2. endurvinna, 3.
    endurvinnsla.
recycling see endurvinnsla.
red see rauður.
redeem see innleysa.
redeemable see innleysanlegur.
redemption see innlausn.
redfish see karfi.
redia see ögðulirfa.

reduce see 1. stytta, 2. afsýra, 3. einfalda, 4.
    grennast, 5. lækka.
reduced see 1. smækkaður, 2. skertur, 3. rýrður, 4.
    afsýrður, 5. afoxaður.
reducible see 1. afsýranlegur, 2. þættanlegur, 3.
    réttanlegur, 4. kleyfur, 5. kljúfanlegur.
reductant see afsýrir.
reduction see 1. skerðing, 2. afoxun, 3. afsýring, 4.
    beinbrotsrétting, 5. haulrétting.
redundancy see 1. umfremi, 2. umfremd, 3. ofauki.
redundant see 1. aukalegur, 2. ofaukið, 3.
    umframur.
reduplication see 1. tvítekning, 2. tvöföldun.
reeducation see endurmenntun.
reef see 1. rif, 2. rifa.
reel see 1. hjól, 2. kefli, 3. spóla.
reenact see kynna.
reentry see 1. bakflug, 2. endurkoma.
referee see 1. ritrýnir, 2. rýna, 3. ritrýna.
reference see 1. táknaskýring, 2. tilvísun, 3. viðmið,
    4. viðmiðun, 5. vísun.
referendum see 1. þjóðaratkvæðagreiðsla, 2.
    allsherjaratkvæðagreiðsla.
referral see tilvísun.
refill see endurfylla.
refinance see endurfjármagna.
refine see 1. hreinsa, 2. skíra.
refinery see 1. hreinsun, 2. hreinsunarstöð, 3.
    hreinsistöð.
refining see hreinsun.
refit see 1. standsetja, 2. viðgerð.
reflect see 1. endurkasta, 2. sveigja, 3. endurvarpa,
    4. spegla.
reflectance see 1. endurkastshlutfall, 2.
    endurskinsstuðull, 3. endurvarpsstuðull.
reflection see 1. beyging, 2. sveiging, 3. speglun, 4.
    endurvarp, 5. endurkast.
reflector see 1. endurkastari, 2. endurkastsskaut, 3.
    endurvarpsflötur, 4. endurvarpsskaut, 5. spegill.
reflex see 1. endurskin, 2. hrökk, 3. viðbragð.
reflexive see 1. sjálfhverfur, 2. spegilvirkur.
reflexology see 1. viðbragðafræði, 2.
    viðbragðahyggja.
reflux see bakflæði.
reform see leiðrétta.
refraction see 1. brot, 2. brotvik, 3. bylgjubrot, 4.
    ljósbrot, 5. ljósbrotsvik.
refractometer see 1. sjónlagsmælir, 2.
    ljósbrotsmælir.
refractor see 1. linsusjónauki, 2. ljósbrjótur.
refractory see 1. andstæður, 2. erfiður, 3. óþjáll.
refresh see 1. endurteiknari, 2. nýglæða, 3.
    nýglæðing, 4. síglæðari.
refrigerant see 1. kælandi, 2. kæliefni, 3. kælimiðill.
refrigeration see 1. frysting, 2. kæling.

refrigerator *see* 1. kælibúnaður, 2. kæliskápur, 3. kælir.
refuelling *see* 1. áfylling, 2. eldsneytistaka.
refuge *see* 1. sæluhús, 2. skýli.
refund *see* 1. endurgreiða, 2. endurgreiðsla.
refusal *see* 1. frávísun, 2. synjun.
refuse *see* 1. neita, 2. hafna.
regenerate *see* 1. endurmyndast, 2. endurnýjast.
regeneration *see* 1. endurmyndun, 2. endurnýjun, 3. endurvöxtur.
regenerative *see* 1. endurmyndandi, 2. endurnýjandi, 3. endurnýjanlegur.
regime *see* 1. stjórnarfyrirkomulag, 2. stjórn, 3. stjórnarfar.
regimen *see* 1. stjórn, 2. rannsóknaráætlun, 3. meðferðaráform, 4. greiningaráætlun, 5. heilbrigðisreglur.
region *see* 1. umdæmi, 2. hérað, 3. svæði.
regional *see* 1. svæðisbundinn, 2. staðbundinn.
register *see* 1. bóka, 2. efnisskrá, 3. gisti, 4. innrita, 5. skrá.
registrar *see* 1. ritari, 2. skrásetjari.
registration *see* 1. skeyting, 2. þinglýsing, 3. skrásetning, 4. skráning, 5. samfærsla.
registry *see* 1. embættisbók, 2. skrásetning.
regolith *see* 1. jarðvegsþekja, 2. berghula.
regress *see* 1. dvína, 2. hörfa.
regression *see* 1. aðhvarf, 2. aðfella, 3. afflæði, 4. bakrás, 5. endurhvarf.
regressive *see* 1. dvínandi, 2. stiglækkandi.
regret *see* iðrast.
regular *see* nákvæmur.
regularly *see* 1. nákvæmlega, 2. oft.
regulate *see* 1. stilla, 2. stjórna, 3. stýra.
regulation *see* 1. stjórnun, 2. tilskipun, 3. stýring, 4. spennujöfnun, 5. reglun.
regulations *see* 1. regla, 2. starfsreglur, 3. regulo, 4. reguligo, 5. reglur.
regulator *see* 1. stilli, 2. straumstillir, 3. stillir, 4. gangráður, 5. spennujafnari.
regurgitation *see* 1. öfugstreymi, 2. uppvella.
rehabilitation *see* endurhæfing.
reign *see* 1. ríkisár, 2. stjórna, 3. stjórn, 4. ríkja, 5. stilla.
reimburse *see* endurgreiða.
reimbursement *see* 1. endurgreiðsla, 2. innborgun.
reinfection *see* endursmitun.
reinforce *see* 1. efla, 2. styrkja.
reinforcement *see* 1. bendistál, 2. steypustyrktarjárn, 3. styrking, 4. styrktarvaf.
reinsurance *see* endurtrygging.
reject *see* 1. afþakka, 2. neita, 3. fleygja, 4. hafna.
rejection *see* 1. höfnun, 2. synjun.
relapse *see* bakslag.

relate *see* 1. tengjast, 2. vensla, 3. samlæta, 4. segja, 5. tengja.
relation *see* 1. afstaða, 2. frændi, 3. frændsemi, 4. interrilato, 5. samband.
relations *see* 1. interligiteco, 2. rilato, 3. interrilato, 4. frændfólk, 5. parenco.
relationship *see* 1. samband, 2. tengsl, 3. vensl.
relative *see* 1. aðstandendur, 2. afstæður, 3. frændi, 4. hlutfallslegur, 5. parencino.
relatives *see* 1. relativa, 2. parenco, 3. parencino, 4. frændfólk.
relativistic *see* 1. hraðfara, 2. afstæðilegur.
relativity *see* 1. afstæði, 2. afstæðiskenning.
relax *see* 1. slaka, 2. slakna.
relaxant *see* slakandi.
relaxation *see* 1. afslöppun, 2. slökun.
relay *see* 1. rafliði, 2. segulrofi, 3. boðsenda, 4. boðsending, 5. liði.
release *see* 1. útsláttur, 2. lausn, 3. leysa, 4. losa, 5. sleppa.
releaser *see* kvöðull.
releasing *see* 1. frátenging, 2. afhleyping.
reliability *see* áreiðanleiki.
reliable *see* 1. áreiðanlegur, 2. traustur.
relief *see* 1. léttir, 2. landslag, 3. upphleyptur, 4. hæðarmunur, 5. torm.
relieve *see* 1. lina, 2. umbót, 3. fróa, 4. finrenna, 5. aflétta.
relieving *see* 1. greyping, 2. finrennsli.
religion *see* trú.
religious *see* trúaður.
reluctance *see* segulviðnám.
rem *see* svefnblik.
remanence *see* 1. segulleif, 2. segulleifð.
remark *see* athugasemd.
remarkable *see* undarlegur.
remedial *see* 1. bætandi, 2. græðandi, 3. mildandi.
remedy *see* 1. meðal, 2. læknisdómur.
reminder *see* 1. ítrekun, 2. athugasemd, 3. ábending, 4. áminning.
reminiscence *see* 1. minnisbót, 2. minning.
remission *see* 1. sjúkdómshlé, 2. sóttarhlé, 3. tollfríðindi, 4. eftirgjöf, 5. léttir.
remit *see* 1. fyrirgefa, 2. senda.
remittance *see* 1. greiðslusending, 2. peningasending.
remote *see* 1. fjarlægur, 2. fjartengdur.
removable *see* 1. laus, 2. umskiptanlegur.
removal *see* 1. flutningur, 2. afnám, 3. brottnám.
remuneration *see* 1. laun, 2. þóknun, 3. greiðsla.
renaturation *see* 1. eðlisheimt, 2. endurtenging.
render *see* 1. gera, 2. húða, 3. kynna.
rendering *see* 1. lýsing, 2. myndsetning.
renew *see* endurnýja.
renewable *see* 1. endurnær, 2. endurnýjanlegur.

renewal see 1. framlenging, 2. endurnýun, 3. endurnýjun.
reniform see 1. nýrlaga, 2. nýralaga.
renin see renín.
rennin see hleypir.
rent see 1. leigja, 2. afgjald, 3. leiga, 4. leigugjald, 5. leigugreiðsla.
rental see 1. fjármunaleiga, 2. útleiga, 3. leiga, 4. leigutekjur.
renter see leigjandi.
reorganization see 1. endurskipulagning, 2. skipulagsbreyting.
repair see 1. bæta, 2. lagfæra, 3. lagfæring, 4. viðgerð, 5. viðhald.
repay see endurgreiða.
repayment see endurgreiðsla.
repeater see 1. magnari, 2. millimagnari, 3. útskjár, 4. endurvaki.
repellent see 1. fæla, 2. fælandi, 3. óþægilegur.
repetition see 1. endurtekning, 2. ítrekun, 3. klifun.
replace see 1. endurnýja, 2. umskipting, 3. umskiptingarhamur.
replacement see 1. rýmd, 2. staðgengill, 3. endurnýjun, 4. afleysingamaður.
replica see 1. eftirlíking, 2. eftirmynd, 3. tilgátuhús, 4. afrit.
replicate see 1. endurtaka, 2. endurtekning, 3. eftirmynda.
replication see 1. endurtekning, 2. eftirmyndun, 3. afritun.
replicon see eftirmyndunareining.
reply see 1. svara, 2. svar, 3. athugasemd.
repolarization see endurskautun.
report see 1. álitsgerð, 2. skýrsla, 3. tilkynning, 4. álit.
represent see 1. merkja, 2. þýða.
representation see 1. birting, 2. málflutningur, 3. lýsing, 4. fyrirsvar, 5. fulltrúi.
representative see 1. umboðsmaður, 2. fulltrúi, 3. staðgengur.
repress see bæla.
repressed see bældur.
repression see bæling.
repressor see bælir.
reprimand see 1. átelja, 2. átölur.
reproach see 1. átelja, 2. átölur.
reproducibility see endurtakanleiki.
reproduction see 1. æxlun, 2. tímgun.
reprove see átelja.
republic see lýðveldi.
republican see lýðveldissinni.
repulsion see 1. fráhrinding, 2. fráhrindingarkraftur, 3. víxlstaða.
request see 1. bæn, 2. beiðni, 3. biðja, 4. málaleitan, 5. tilmæli.

require see 1. neyða, 2. þvinga.
requirement see 1. þörf, 2. krafa.
requisition see beiðni.
res see átfrumnakerfi.
rescue see bjarga.
research see 1. könnun, 2. rannsaka, 3. rannsókn, 4. rannsóknir.
resect see stýfa.
resection see 1. úrnám, 2. brottnám, 3. stýfing.
resemblance see líking.
resemble see líkjast.
resent see gremjast.
reservation see 1. fyrirvari, 2. farskráning, 3. bókun, 4. skilyrði.
reserve see 1. afgangur, 2. friðland, 3. varaforði, 4. varasjóður.
reservoir see 1. forðabúr, 2. sviputrekt, 3. náma, 4. lind, 5. geymsluhýsill.
reset see 1. endurstilling, 2. endursetning, 3. endurstilla.
reside see búa.
residence see 1. bústaður, 2. aðsetur, 3. heimili.
resident see 1. íbúi, 2. vistfastur.
residual see 1. afgangur, 2. frávik, 3. leif, 4. leifð, 5. spáskekkja.
residue see 1. afgangur, 2. leifar, 3. leif, 4. dreggjar.
resignation see 1. afsögn, 2. bölró, 3. lausnarbeiðni, 4. uppsögn.
resilience see 1. viðkomugeta, 2. fjaðurmagn.
resin see 1. viðarkvoða, 2. resín, 3. kvoða, 4. harpixar, 5. harpeis.
resistance see 1. þol, 2. mótstaða, 3. viðnám, 4. ónæmi, 5. andóf.
resistant see 1. ónæmur, 2. þolinn.
resistivity see 1. raunviðnám, 2. eðlisviðnám, 3. kenniviðnám.
resistor see 1. viðnámstæki, 2. mótstaða, 3. viðnám.
resolution see 1. lausn, 2. sundurgreining, 3. ályktun, 4. samþykkt, 5. upplausn.
resolve see 1. sundurgreina, 2. aðgreina, 3. hjaðna.
resonance see 1. samhljómun, 2. ómur, 3. meðsveiflun, 4. herma, 5. samsveiflun.
resonator see 1. sveiflujafnari, 2. sveifluhermir, 3. hermill, 4. ómhermir.
resorption see uppsog.
resource see 1. auðlind, 2. fjármunir, 3. forði, 4. framleiðsluþáttur, 5. kjörstilling.
resources see 1. eignir, 2. fjármunir.
respect see virða.
respiration see 1. öndun, 2. andardráttur, 3. frumuöndun, 4. öndunarefnaflutningur, 5. vefjaöndun.
respirator see 1. gasgríma, 2. öndunarvél.
respite see 1. frestur, 2. frestun.
respond see svara.

534   English - Icelandic

respondent *see* 1. svarandi, 2. svarviðbrögð.
response *see* 1. svar, 2. viðbrögð, 3. viðbragð, 4.
andsvar, 5. svörun.
responsibility *see* ábyrgð.
responsible *see* 1. ábyrgur, 2. áreiðanlegur, 3.
traustur.
responsive *see* svarbúinn.
rest *see* kyrrstaða.
restart *see* 1. endurræsa, 2. endurræsing, 3.
framhald, 4. áframhald.
restaurant *see* veitingahús.
restitution *see* endurmyndun.
restoration *see* 1. endursmíð, 2. endurgerð, 3.
endurreisn.
restore *see* 1. endurbyggja, 2. endurheimt, 3.
endurheimta, 4. endurrita.
restrain *see* stilla.
restraint *see* 1. hamla, 2. hindrun, 3. vörn.
restrict *see* 1. hamla, 2. hefta, 3. takmarka, 4.
þrengja.
restriction *see* 1. höft, 2. þrenging, 3. takmörkun, 4.
takmarkanir, 5. hömlur.
restrictive *see* 1. aðhaldssamur, 2. takmarkandi.
restructure *see* 1. endurmóta, 2. ummóta, 3.
umskipa.
restructuring *see* 1. ummótun, 2. endurmótun, 3.
endurskipulagning, 4. nýskipan.
result *see* 1. útkoma, 2. niðurstaða, 3. afleiðing.
resuscitation *see* endurlífgun.
retailer *see* smásali.
retainer *see* 1. haldari, 2. þóknun, 3. umbun.
retard *see* 1. hamla, 2. seinka, 3. tefja.
retardation *see* 1. tunglseinkun, 2. hæging, 3.
seinkun, 4. seinþroski, 5. töf.
retarder *see* 1. hægir, 2. hamlari.
retention *see* 1. minnisgeymd, 2. tannteppa, 3.
teppa.
reticulum *see* 1. fagrikeppur, 2. keppur, 3. Netið.
retina *see* 1. nethimna, 2. sjóna, 3. sjónhimna.
retire *see* innleysa.
retirement *see* 1. eftirlaunaskeið, 2. starfslok.
retort *see* eimingarflaska.
retractable *see* inndraganlegur.
retraction *see* 1. inndráttur, 2. samdráttur.
retrieval *see* 1. endurheimt, 2. heimt, 3.
skeytaheimt, 4. sókn.
retrieve *see* 1. endurheimta, 2. heimta, 3. sækja.
retroactive *see* 1. afturverkandi, 2. afturvirkur.
retrograde *see* 1. afturvirkur, 2. öfugt.
retrogressive *see* 1. afturhverfur, 2. bakhverfur.
retrovirus *see* 1. víxlveira, 2. retróveira.
return *see* 1. afrakstur, 2. arður.
reuse *see* 1. endurnýta, 2. endurnota, 3.
endurnotkun.

revaluation *see* 1. verðbreytingarfærsla, 2.
endurmat, 3. gengishækkun.
revalue *see* endurmeta.
revenue *see* 1. tekjulind, 2. fjáröflun, 3. tekjur, 4.
tekjurafrakstur, 5. hagnaður.
reverberation *see* 1. ómun, 2. ómur.
reverie *see* leiðsla.
reversal *see* 1. umskautun, 2. viðsnúningur, 3.
vending, 4. umskipti, 5. speglun.
reverse *see* 1. andstæða, 2. umlýsa, 3. gagnstæður,
4. gagnstæða, 5. bakka.
reversibility *see* 1. afturkvæmni, 2. gagnhvarf, 3.
jafngengi.
reversible *see* 1. afturkræfur, 2. afturkvæmur, 3.
gagnhverfur, 4. jafngengur, 5. jafnhverfur.
reversion *see* 1. afturhvarf, 2. gervending, 3.
viðsnúningur.
review *see* 1. tímarit, 2. úttekt, 3. málskot, 4.
könnun, 5. endurskoðun.
revile *see* skamma.
revise *see* umbreyta.
revision *see* 1. endurskoðun, 2. breyting, 3.
endurmat.
revolution *see* 1. uppreisn, 2. umferð, 3. bylting, 4.
snúningur.
revolve *see* 1. snúa, 2. snúast.
reward *see* 1. umbun, 2. umbuna.
rhenium *see* 1. renín, 2. reníum.
rheology *see* hnigfræði.
rheostat *see* 1. rennimótstaða, 2. renniviðnám, 3.
stillimótstaða, 4. stilliviðnám.
rheumatic *see* gigtarsjúklingur.
rheumatism *see* gigt.
rhinitis *see* 1. nefkvef, 2. nefslímubólga.
rhino *see* nashyrningur.
rhinorrhea *see* nefrennsli.
rhodium *see* 1. ródín, 2. ródíum.
rhombus *see* 1. tígull, 2. tigull.
rhythm *see* 1. taktur, 2. hrynjandi, 3. sveifla, 4.
rytmi.
rhytidome *see* dauðbörkur.
rib *see* 1. styrking, 2. vængrif, 3. þverrif, 4. fön, 5.
styrkingarfjöður.
ribonuclease *see* ríbónúkleasi.
ribose *see* ríbósi.
ribosome *see* 1. netkorn, 2. ríbósóm, 3. rípla.
rice *see* hrísgrjón.
rich *see* 1. kappnógur, 2. ríkur, 3. ríkulegur.
richness *see* gnægð.
rickets *see* beinkröm.
ride *see* 1. aksturseiginleikar, 2. vegartilfinning.
ridge *see* 1. ás, 2. brún, 3. fjallshryggur, 4.
hæðarhryggur, 5. hryggur.
rifle *see* 1. rauf, 2. riffla.
rig *see* 1. reiði, 2. æki.

rigging *see* stilling.
right *see* 1. hægri, 2. réttur.
rigid *see* 1. stirður, 2. undanlátslaus, 3. traustur, 4. stjarfur, 5. stífur.
rigidity *see* 1. stífni, 2. vöðvastífni, 3. tregða, 4. stirðnun, 5. stirðleiki.
rim *see* 1. brún, 2. egg, 3. felga, 4. hjólhringur.
rime *see* hrím.
ring *see* 1. hringur, 2. baugur, 3. fyrirtækjahringur, 4. lag.
ringing *see* 1. eftirsveiflur, 2. hringing.
ringworm *see* 1. hringormur, 2. hringskyrfi, 3. dýrasjúkdómur, 4. reformur.
rinse *see* þvo.
ripple *see* 1. gára, 2. gárur, 3. gráð.
rise *see* 1. lyfting, 2. hlíðardrag.
risk *see* 1. vogun, 2. vá, 3. áhætta, 4. hætta.
river *see* 1. á, 2. vatn (water).
rivet *see* 1. hnoða, 2. hnoðnagli, 3. hnoð, 4. hnoðnegla.
riveting *see* 1. hnoðnegling, 2. hnoðun.
roach *see* 1. rauðauga, 2. roðagægir, 3. rútur.
road *see* 1. vegur, 2. gata.
roadstead *see* skipalægi.
roast *see* steik.
robin *see* glóbrystingur.
robot *see* 1. þjarki, 2. vélmenni, 3. sjálfi, 4. róbóti, 5. vélþræll.
rock *see* 1. hamar, 2. randaborri, 3. klettur, 4. bjarg, 5. bergtegund.
rocker *see* dröfnuskata.
rocket *see* 1. eldflaug, 2. blys.
rod *see* 1. stafþekjufruma, 2. stafur, 3. stöng, 4. staffruma, 5. sjónustafur.
rodent *see* 1. nagandi, 2. nagdýr.
rodenticide *see* 1. nagdýraeyðir, 2. nagdýraeitur.
roe *see* hrogn.
role *see* 1. staða, 2. hlutverk.
roll *see* 1. rúlla, 2. velta.
roller *see* 1. útdráttarvalti, 2. valtari, 3. vals, 4. bláhrani, 5. útdráttarrúlla.
rolling *see* 1. velta, 2. veltingur.
roof *see* 1. þak, 2. toppur.
rook *see* Hrókur.
room *see* rými.
root *see* 1. rót, 2. núllstöð, 3. tannrót.
rope *see* 1. kaðall, 2. reipi, 3. taug.
rose *see* rós.
rosefish *see* vínlandskarfi.
roseola *see* dílaroði.
rosette *see* 1. blaðhvirfing, 2. frumukrans.
rostrum *see* 1. goggur, 2. trjóna.
rot *see* morkna.
rotary *see* drifborð.
rotate *see* 1. snúast, 2. reisa, 3. snúa.

rotation *see* 1. reising, 2. snúningur.
rotor *see* 1. anker, 2. göndull, 3. snúður, 4. þyrill.
rough *see* 1. kargi, 2. torleiði, 3. óvingjarnlegur, 4. óvænn, 5. óunninn.
round *see* 1. hringlaga, 2. kringlóttur, 3. röð, 4. Umferð, 5. taktur.
roundabout *see* hringekja.
rounding *see* 1. kringing, 2. snyrting.
route *see* 1. beina, 2. flugleið, 3. leið, 4. vegur.
routine *see* 1. reglubundið, 2. stef, 3. kerfisbundið, 4. venjubundið.
routing *see* 1. beining, 2. ferli, 3. leið, 4. leiðarval, 5. umferðarbeining.
rover *see* fjallarakki.
row *see* 1. röð, 2. færsla, 3. róa, 4. lína, 5. rifrildi.
rowlock *see* 1. keipur, 2. ræði.
royalty *see* 1. höfundarréttargreiðsla, 2. umboðslaun, 3. sérleyfisgjald, 4. höfundarlaun, 5. einkaréttargreiðsla.
rub *see* nudda.
rubber *see* 1. gúmmí, 2. smokkur.
rubbish *see* fjarstæða.
rubella *see* rauðhundar.
rubeola *see* mislingar.
rubidium *see* 1. rúbidín, 2. rúbidíum.
rucksack *see* bakpoki.
rudd *see* straumgægir.
rudder *see* 1. hliðarstýri, 2. stýri, 3. stýrisblað.
rude *see* 1. ókurteis, 2. ósvífinn, 3. skyndilegur.
rudely *see* skyndilega.
rudiment *see* 1. liffærisleif, 2. liffærisvísir.
rudiments *see* stafróf.
rue *see* rúturunni.
rug *see* 1. gólfábreiða, 2. gólfteppi.
rule *see* 1. reglustika, 2. úrskurða, 3. stilla, 4. regla, 5. regi.
ruler *see* 1. reglustika, 2. stika.
rules *see* 1. regulo, 2. deklari, 3. juĝi, 4. lög, 5. regado.
rumble *see* 1. urg, 2. drunur, 3. skruðningur.
rumen *see* vömb.
ruminant *see* jórturdýr.
rumination *see* 1. hugjórtur, 2. jórtur, 3. tvítuggning.
run *see* 1. áætlunarleið, 2. vegalengd, 3. renna, 4. röð.
running *see* gangur.
runoff *see* 1. yfirborðsbatn, 2. afrennsli, 3. afrennslishraði.
runway *see* 1. skeiðvöllur, 2. kappreiðabraut, 3. braut, 4. flugbraut.
rupture *see* 1. brestur, 2. haull, 3. kviðslit, 4. rifa, 5. rifnun.
ruptured *see* 1. brostinn, 2. rofinn.
rust *see* 1. ryðsveppur, 2. ryðga, 3. ryð, 4. tæring.

rustproof *see* 1. ryðfrír, 2. ryðfrítt.
rutabaga *see* gulrófa.
ruthenium *see* 1. rúten, 2. rúteníum, 3. rúþeníum.

S

s *see* brennisteinn.
sabbath *see* laugardagur.
sac *see* poki.
saccharify *see* 1. sæta, 2. sykra.
saccharimeter *see* sykursmælir.
saccharin *see* sakkarín.
saccharine *see* ofursætur.
saccharomyces *see* gersveppur.
saccharose *see* sykur.
saccharum *see* sykur.
sacculation *see* pokun.
saccule *see* 1. posi, 2. skjatti.
sacculus *see* 1. posi, 2. skjatti, 3. skjóða.
sack *see* 1. poki, 2. taska.
sacred *see* heilagur.
sacrifice *see* Fórna.
sacrum *see* 1. krossliður, 2. spjaldliðir, 3. spjaldhryggur, 4. spjaldbein.
sad *see* 1. dapur, 2. óhamingjusamur.
saddle *see* 1. hnakkur, 2. klafi, 3. sæti.
sadism *see* 1. böðulslosti, 2. kvalalosti.
sadist *see* 1. lostaböðull, 2. lostakvalari.
safe *see* 1. öruggur, 2. peningaskápur, 3. áreiðanlegur, 4. bankahólf.
safeguard *see* öryggisráðstöfun.
safeguarding *see* 1. eignavarsla, 2. forvörn.
safflower *see* 1. safflúr, 2. litunarkollur, 3. litunarþistill.
sag *see* 1. slöppun, 2. slakna, 3. slaki, 4. sig, 5. síga.
sago *see* 1. viðgrjón, 2. pálmagrjón, 3. sagógrjón.
sail *see* 1. segl, 2. sigla.
sailor *see* háseti.
saithe *see* ufsi.
salary *see* laun.
sale *see* 1. markaðssetning, 2. sala, 3. útsala.
saleable *see* 1. seljanlegur, 2. söluhæfur.
sales *see* sala.
saline *see* 1. saltur, 2. saltvatn.
salinity *see* selta.
saliva *see* munnvatn.
salivation *see* 1. slef, 2. vatnspýtingur, 3. slefun, 4. ofurslef, 5. munnvatnsmyndun.
salmon *see* lax.
salmonella *see* bifstafur.
salmonellosis *see* 1. bifstafasýking, 2. salmónellusýki, 3. salmonellusýking.

saloon *see* stallbakur.
salt *see* 1. natríumklóríð, 2. jónaefni, 3. matarsalt.
saltation *see* 1. stökk, 2. skrykkur, 3. dans.
saltpeter *see* 1. kalíumnítrat, 2. saltpétur.
saltpetre *see* 1. kalínítrat, 2. kalísaltpétur, 3. kalíumnítrat, 4. saltpétur.
salubrious *see* 1. heilnæmur, 2. hollur.
salutary *see* heilnæmur.
salute *see* heilsa.
salvage *see* 1. björgun, 2. björgunarlaun.
salve *see* smyrsl.
samarium *see* 1. samarín, 2. samaríum.
same *see* samur.
sample *see* 1. úrtak, 2. dæmi, 3. álestur, 4. sýni, 5. sýnishorn.
sampling *see* 1. sýnataka, 2. sýnistaka, 3. úrtaka.
sanction *see* 1. refsiaðgerð, 2. refsiákvæði, 3. viðurlög, 4. viðurkenna, 5. heimila.
sand *see* sandur.
sandbank *see* 1. sandfláki, 2. sandrif.
sandblast *see* 1. sandblásta, 2. sandblása.
sandstone *see* sandsteinn.
sandwich *see* brauðsnúður.
sane *see* geðheill.
sanguine *see* 1. glaðsinna, 2. léttlyndur.
sanitize *see* 1. hreinsa, 2. gjörhreinsa.
sapodilla *see* 1. tyggigúmmítré, 2. sapódillatré, 3. sapódillaplóma, 4. kvoðutré, 5. sapódilla.
saponification *see* 1. sápumyndun, 2. sápun.
saprophyte *see* 1. rotplanta, 2. rotvera.
sarcasm *see* 1. háðsádeila, 2. satíra.
sarcoma *see* sarkmein.
satellite *see* 1. fylgitungl, 2. tungl (moon), 3. stjörnugírshjól, 4. plánetuhjól, 5. litningsspeni.
satiation *see* 1. mettun, 2. saðning.
satire *see* 1. háðsádeila, 2. satíra.
satisfied *see* ánægður.
saturated *see* mettaður.
saturation *see* mettun.
saturnism *see* blýeitrun.
sausage *see* pylsa.
savanna *see* 1. savanni, 2. staktrjáaslétta.
save *see* 1. vista, 2. vistun, 3. vistunarhamur, 4. forða.
saving *see* 1. sparifé, 2. sparnaður.
savory *see* sar.
savour *see* smakka.
saw *see* sög.
say *see* segja.
scabicide *see* 1. kláðamaursdeyðir, 2. kláðamaurseyðir.
scabies *see* maurakláði.
scalability *see* 1. stigfrelsi, 2. stækkunarleiki, 3. kvarðanleiki.

scalar *see* 1. kverða, 2. stigstærð, 3. tala, 4. tölustærð.
scald *see* 1. húðbruni, 2. skáldun.
scale *see* 1. skalo, 2. vog, 3. tónstigi, 4. stærðarhlutfall, 5. skán.
scaler *see* 1. stiklari, 2. teljari.
scaling *see* 1. kvörðun, 2. skölun, 3. kvarðabreyting.
scallop *see* 1. hörpudiskur, 2. hörpuskel.
scam *see* svik.
scan *see* 1. skim, 2. skima, 3. skanna.
scandal *see* slúður.
scandium *see* 1. skandín, 2. skandíum.
scanner *see* 1. skanni, 2. skimari, 3. skyggnir.
scanning *see* 1. skann, 2. skimun, 3. skönnun.
scapegoat *see* blóraböggull.
scaphoid *see* bátlaga.
scar *see* ör.
scare *see* 1. uppþot, 2. herblástur.
scarf *see* trefill.
scarification *see* rispun.
scarlatina *see* skarlatssótt.
scatology *see* 1. saurfræði, 2. saurhneigð.
scatter *see* 1. dreif, 2. geisladreif.
scattering *see* 1. dreifing, 2. ljósdreifing, 3. tvístrun.
scavenge *see* 1. hirða, 2. hreinsa, 3. snapa.
scavenger *see* 1. gleypifruma, 2. snapi, 3. hrægammur, 4. hrææta.
scenario *see* 1. ástandslýsing, 2. atburðarás, 3. framtíðarsýn, 4. sviðsmynd.
scene *see* 1. atriði, 2. myndsvið, 3. sviðsatriði, 4. vangur.
schedule *see* 1. tafla, 2. tímatafla, 3. tímaáætlun, 4. skrá, 5. fylgiskjal.
scheduling *see* verkröðun.
schema *see* 1. lýsing, 2. yfirlit, 3. þekkingargrind, 4. skema, 5. grind.
scheme *see* 1. innrétting, 2. skissa, 3. skema, 4. rissmynd, 5. mynd.
schistosomiasis *see* 1. blóðögðusótt, 2. blóðögðuveiki.
schizoid *see* 1. hugkleyfur, 2. kleyfhugi.
schizophrenia *see* 1. geðklofi, 2. geðrof, 3. kleyfhugasýki.
schizophrenic *see* 1. kleyfhuga, 2. geðklofa, 3. geðklofasjúklingur.
school *see* skóli.
sciatica *see* 1. þjótak, 2. settaugarbólga.
science *see* 1. vísindi, 2. raunvísindi, 3. vísindagrein.
scintillation *see* 1. blik, 2. sindur, 3. tíbrá, 4. tíðnisindur.
scission *see* 1. klofnun, 2. skipting.
scissors *see* tondilo.
sclera *see* 1. augnhvíta, 2. hvíta.
sclerotic *see* hvíta.
sclerous *see* 1. harður, 2. hertur.

scold *see* átelja.
scolex *see* bandormshaus.
scoop *see* 1. loftinntak, 2. sleif.
scooter *see* vespa.
scope *see* 1. umfang, 2. vinsa, 3. svið, 4. skjár, 5. sjá.
scorbutus *see* skyrbjúgur.
score *see* 1. stig, 2. rauf, 3. rispa, 4. skora.
scotch *see* skozur.
scotoma *see* 1. sjónsviðseyða, 2. blinduflekkur.
scout *see* flokksmeðlimur.
scouting *see* skátastarf.
scramble *see* 1. brengla, 2. rugla.
scrambler *see* 1. klifurplanta, 2. ruglari, 3. brenglari.
scrap *see* 1. rifrildi, 2. rusl, 3. sorp, 4. tuska, 5. úrgangur.
scrape *see* 1. skafa, 2. skrapa.
scraper *see* 1. jarðvegsjafnari, 2. skafa.
scrapie *see* 1. riða, 2. riðuveiki.
scratch *see* 1. klóra, 2. strika, 3. rispa, 4. afskrifa, 5. rissa.
screech *see* ískur.
screen *see* 1. hlíf, 2. kemba, 3. net, 4. skermir, 5. skermur.
screening *see* 1. skimun, 2. vinsun, 3. skjól, 4. meinaleit, 5. kembirannsókn.
screw *see* 1. bolti, 2. skrúfa.
screwdriver *see* skrúfjárn.
scribe *see* 1. rissa, 2. strika.
scriber *see* rissnál.
script *see* 1. atburðarit, 2. forskrift.
scroll *see* 1. skrun, 2. skruna.
scrolling *see* 1. skrun, 2. skrunun.
scrub *see* kjarr.
scuffle *see* slagsmál.
scup *see* grænflekkur.
scurf *see* flasa.
scurvy *see* skyrbjúgur.
sea *see* 1. sjór, 2. haf, 3. vindalda, 4. sjólag.
seaboard *see* strönd.
seafarer *see* 1. háseti, 2. sjófarandi, 3. farmaður.
seafood *see* sjávarréttir.
seal *see* 1. selur, 2. þéttir, 3. þétti, 4. þétta, 5. ásþétti.
sealer *see* 1. selveiðiskip, 2. þéttiefni.
sealing *see* þétting.
seals *see* selir.
seam *see* 1. samskeyti, 2. saumur.
seaman *see* háseti.
seamless *see* 1. saumlaust, 2. samfelldur, 3. saumlaus.
seamount *see* 1. neðansjávareldfjall, 2. neðansjávarfjall.
search *see* 1. húsleit, 2. húsrannsókn, 3. leit, 4. leita, 5. leitarhamur.
searchlight *see* 1. leitarljós, 2. leitarljóskastari.
seasickness *see* sjóveiki.

seaside *see* strönd.
season *see* árstíð.
seat *see* 1. sæti, 2. umboð, 3. þingsæti, 4. stóll.
seaway *see* sjóleið.
seaweed *see* 1. sjávargróður, 2. þang, 3. þari.
seaworthy *see* 1. haffært, 2. sjófær.
seborrhea *see* flasa.
sebum *see* húðfeiti.
secant *see* 1. sekans, 2. sniðill.
second *see* 1. sekúnda, 2. annar, 3. önnur, 4. bogasekúnda.
secondary *see* 1. fylgihnöttur, 2. fylgistjarna, 3. minniháttar, 4. rúmi, 5. tíma.
secretariat *see* 1. skrifstofa, 2. stjórnardeild, 3. stjórnarskrifstofa.
secretary *see* 1. ritari, 2. trúnaðarmaður, 3. fulltrúi, 4. ráðherra, 5. stjórnarráðsfulltrúi.
secretin *see* 1. brisvaki, 2. sekretín.
secretion *see* 1. kirtilsafi, 2. seyti, 3. seyting, 4. velli.
section *see* 1. geiri, 2. snið, 3. sneiðing, 4. sneiða, 5. sneið.
sector *see* 1. geiri, 2. svæðisskipting, 3. hringgeiri, 4. sektor.
secular *see* veraldlegur.
secularization *see* athelgun.
security *see* 1. ábyrgð, 2. ábyrgðarmaður, 3. öryggi, 4. öryggismál, 5. trygging.
sedan *see* stallbakur.
sedation *see* 1. hugarró, 2. róun.
sedative *see* 1. róandi, 2. slævilyf.
sedentary *see* 1. fastbúandi, 2. fastur, 3. kyrrstæður, 4. staðbundinn, 5. botnsætinn.
sediment *see* 1. botnlag, 2. syrja, 3. setlag, 4. dreggjar, 5. botnfall.
sedimentation *see* 1. botnfelling, 2. setmyndun, 3. sökk.
seductive *see* 1. hrífandi, 2. heillandi.
see *see* 1. skilja, 2. sjá.
seed *see* 1. fræ, 2. sæði, 3. merkipunktur, 4. sáðkorn, 5. sáðkristallur.
seeding *see* 1. fræmyndun, 2. sáning.
seek *see* biðja.
seem *see* þykja.
seepage *see* 1. seytl, 2. vætl.
segment *see* 1. línubútur, 2. strik, 3. sneið, 4. línustrik, 5. kafli.
segmental *see* 1. geiraskiptur, 2. liðskiptur.
segmentation *see* 1. klofnun, 2. skipting, 3. liðskipting, 4. kaflahleðsla, 5. geiraskipting.
segregate *see* 1. einangra, 2. aðgreina, 3. aðskilja.
segregation *see* 1. skilnaður, 2. aðskilnaður, 3. aðgreining, 4. aðskilnaðarstefna.
seiche *see* 1. grunnsveifla, 2. seissáhrif.
seismogram *see* skjálftarit.

seismograph *see* 1. skjálftamælir, 2. jarðskjálftariti, 3. jarðskjálftamælir.
seismology *see* 1. jarðskjálftafræði, 2. skjálftafræði.
seize *see* tæra.
seizing *see* 1. bensli, 2. upptaka.
seizure *see* 1. flog, 2. kast, 3. taka, 4. upptekt, 5. úrbræðsla.
seldom *see* sjaldan.
select *see* velja.
selecting *see* 1. val, 2. viðtökuval.
selection *see* 1. línuval, 2. úrval, 3. val, 4. færsluval.
selective *see* 1. kjörvís, 2. valbundinn.
selectivity *see* 1. áreitaval, 2. kjörhæfni, 3. kjörvísi, 4. tíðniskerpa, 5. valvísi.
selector *see* 1. vali, 2. veljari.
selenium *see* 1. selen, 2. seleníum.
selenography *see* tungllandafræði.
selenology *see* tunglfræði.
self *see* 1. sjálf, 2. sjálfur.
self-esteem *see* 1. sjálfsálit, 2. virðing, 3. virðuleiki.
self-respect *see* 1. virðing, 2. virðuleiki.
sell *see* selja.
seller *see* seljandi.
semantics *see* merkingarfræði.
semen *see* 1. sæði, 2. fræ.
semiautomatic *see* hálfsjálfvirkur.
semiconductor *see* 1. hálfleiðari, 2. torleiðari, 3. torleiðir.
semiotics *see* táknfræði.
semipermeable *see* 1. hálfgegndræpur, 2. hálflekur, 3. misgegndræpur.
senate *see* 1. háskólaráð, 2. öldungadeild, 3. öldungadeildin, 4. öldungaráð.
send *see* senda.
senescence *see* 1. öldrun, 2. elliskeið, 3. elli.
senile *see* 1. ellihrumur, 2. elliær.
senility *see* 1. elli, 2. ellihrörnun.
sensation *see* 1. kennd, 2. skynhrif, 3. skynjun, 4. tilfinning.
sense *see* 1. skilningur, 2. tilfinning, 3. skynjun, 4. skyn, 5. skilningarvit.
sensibility *see* 1. næmleiki, 2. viðkvæmni.
sensible *see* 1. skynjanlegur, 2. viðkvæmur.
sensitive *see* 1. næmur, 2. viðkunnanlegur, 3. viðkvæmur.
sensitivity *see* 1. næmleikastuðull, 2. næmni, 3. ferjustuðull, 4. næmi, 5. næmisstuðull.
sensitization *see* næming.
sensitize *see* næma.
sensitizer *see* næmir.
sensor *see* 1. nemi, 2. skynjari.
sensorium *see* skynfæri.
sensory *see* skynjun.
sensualism *see* munaðarhyggja.
sentence *see* 1. málsgrein, 2. setning.

sentiment *see* 1. afstaða, 2. skoðun, 3. hugsun, 4. álit, 5. hugð.
separate *see* 1. aðskilinn, 2. aðskilja.
separation *see* 1. aðgreining, 2. aðskilnaður, 3. bil, 4. skipti, 5. streymisslit.
separatism *see* aðskilnaðarstefna.
separator *see* 1. skilrúm, 2. skilviður, 3. skilvinda, 4. skiltákn, 5. skilja.
sepsis *see* 1. graftarsótt, 2. blóðeitrun, 3. blóðsýking.
septation *see* skipting.
septicemia *see* blóðeitrun.
sequence *see* 1. röð, 2. runa.
sequencing *see* 1. röðun, 2. runun.
sequential *see* runubundinn.
sequestration *see* 1. kyrrsetning, 2. löghald, 3. lausabeinsmyndun.
serendipity *see* slembifundur.
serial *see* raðbundinn.
series *see* 1. lota, 2. tengiröð, 3. raðtenging, 4. keðja, 5. frumubálkur.
serine *see* 1. ser, 2. serín.
serious *see* alvarlegur.
serology *see* 1. sermifræði, 2. sermisfræði, 3. blóðvatnsfræði.
serotonin *see* serótónín.
serpent *see* ormur.
serrated *see* 1. sagtenntur, 2. skörðóttur.
serration *see* 1. sagtenning, 2. tenning.
serum *see* 1. blóðsermi, 2. blóðvatn, 3. sermi.
servant *see* þjónn.
server *see* 1. miðlari, 2. þjónn.
service *see* 1. nytjar, 2. viðgerðir, 3. vinna, 4. notkun, 5. hirðing.
serviceability *see* þjónustuhæfni.
services *see* þjónusta.
servile *see* þýlundaður.
serving *see* 1. kápuvörn, 2. tilkynning.
servo *see* sjálfstýribúnaður.
servomechanism *see* 1. sjálfstýrikerfi, 2. sjálfstýring, 3. sjálfstýriverk, 4. stýriþræll, 5. þræll.
servomotor *see* 1. stýrivél, 2. stýrihreyfill, 3. stöðugjafi.
sesamoid *see* baunarlaga.
sessile *see* 1. botnsætinn, 2. stilklaus.
session *see* 1. fundur, 2. lota, 3. seta.
set *see* 1. skekkja, 2. stilla, 3. sett, 4. setja, 5. mengi.
setting *see* 1. setur, 2. storknun, 3. stilligildi, 4. innstilling, 5. atburðasvið.
settle *see* slakna.
settlement *see* 1. samningur, 2. samkomulag, 3. uppgjör, 4. þorp, 5. skuldalúkning.
setup *see* 1. hamur, 2. röðun, 3. uppsetning.
seven *see* sjö.
seventeen *see* 1. sautján, 2. seytján.

seventy *see* sjötíu.
severity *see* 1. strangleiki, 2. erfiði.
sew *see* sauma.
sewage *see* 1. skólp, 2. skolp.
sewer *see* skólpræsi.
sex *see* 1. kyn, 2. kynferði, 3. kynlíf.
sextant *see* 1. sextantur, 2. sextungur, 3. sjöttungsmælir.
sexual *see* kynferðislegur.
sexuality *see* 1. kynferði, 2. kynhneigð.
shackle *see* 1. láshlekkur, 2. keðjulás, 3. liður, 4. trossa, 5. hengsli.
shad *see* 1. augnasíld, 2. maísíld.
shade *see* 1. skuggi, 2. hlíf, 3. ljóshlíf, 4. skermur, 5. skygging.
shading *see* 1. skuggamyndun, 2. skygging, 3. sólhlíf.
shadow *see* 1. skuggi, 2. skyggja.
shaft *see* 1. súluskaft, 2. bolur, 3. leggur, 4. öxull, 5. skaft.
shallot *see* 1. skalottlaukur, 2. sjalottulaukur, 3. skalotlaukur.
shallow *see* 1. grunnur, 2. grynning.
shank *see* leggur.
shanny *see* fjörufiskur.
shape *see* 1. form, 2. snið, 3. lögun.
shaping *see* mótun.
share *see* 1. skerfur, 2. deila, 3. hlutabréf, 4. hlutdeild, 5. hlutur.
shareholder *see* 1. hlutafjáreigandi, 2. hluthafi.
shark *see* hákarl.
sharp *see* 1. beittur, 2. skarpur, 3. hvellur, 4. skyndilegur, 5. skrækur.
sharpen *see* 1. brýna, 2. hvessa, 3. skarpa, 4. skerpa.
sharpening *see* 1. skerping, 2. brýnsla.
sharply *see* skyndilega.
sharpness *see* 1. skarpskyggni, 2. hvassleiki.
shear *see* 1. klippa, 2. klippkraftur, 3. skera, 4. skúfa, 5. skúfast.
shears *see* 1. klippur, 2. plötuklippur, 3. skæri.
sheath *see* 1. kápa, 2. skeið, 3. hula, 4. hjúpur, 5. slíður.
sheave *see* 1. dráttarskífa, 2. skoruhjól, 3. trissa.
shed *see* 1. skýli, 2. skúr.
shedding *see* 1. botnfall, 2. slit.
sheep *see* 1. sauðkind, 2. sauður.
sheepshead *see* 1. kindarhaus, 2. vatnabaulari.
sheer *see* skyndilegur.
sheet *see* 1. plata, 2. þynna, 3. lag, 4. lauf.
shelf *see* 1. hilla, 2. hylla.
shell *see* 1. skel, 2. sökkull, 3. kerbyrði, 4. hvel, 5. hús.
shellac *see* 1. þéttiefni, 2. lakk, 3. límefni, 4. séllakk, 5. gljálakk.

shield *see* 1. vélarhlíf, 2. skjöldur, 3. raftaugarhlíf, 4. hlíf, 5. meginlandsskjöldur.
shielding *see* 1. brynja, 2. fráklipping, 3. rafbrynja, 4. skerming, 5. skermun.
shift *see* 1. tilfærsla, 2. stjaka, 3. vik, 4. vakt, 5. færsla.
shigellosis *see* blóðsótt.
shim *see* 1. millilegg, 2. milliplata, 3. málmþynna, 4. blikkræma.
shimmy *see* 1. skjálfti, 2. stýrisskjálfti, 3. titringur, 4. hjólasláttur.
shin *see* sköflungur.
shinbone *see* sköflungur.
shingles *see* ristill.
ship *see* skip.
shipper *see* vöruflytjandi.
shipping *see* 1. flutningafræði, 2. siglingar, 3. sjóflutningar.
shipway *see* 1. bakkastokkar, 2. rennibraut.
shipwreck *see* skipsflak.
shipyard *see* slippur.
shirt *see* skyrta.
shiver *see* 1. hrollur, 2. skjálfti.
shoal *see* 1. sandgrynning, 2. torfa.
shock *see* 1. lost, 2. skellur, 3. rykkur, 4. áfall, 5. högg.
shoe *see* 1. bremsukjálki, 2. bremsuskór.
shoot *see* 1. kasta, 2. sproti.
shop *see* 1. búð, 2. sölubúð, 3. verslun, 4. verslunarhús.
shore *see* 1. strönd, 2. fjara.
short *see* 1. stuttur, 2. skyndilegur, 3. stökkur.
shortage *see* skortur.
shortcut *see* flýtivísun.
shortly *see* skyndilega.
shorts *see* kalsono.
shoulder *see* 1. öxl, 2. brautarjaðar, 3. hæll, 4. nef (nose), 5. þrýstikragi.
shower *see* 1. rigningarskúr, 2. skúr, 3. drífa, 4. demba, 5. steypibað.
shrew *see* 1. snjádurmús, 2. snjáldra.
shrill *see* 1. skrækur, 2. hvellur, 3. skerandi.
shrink *see* 1. þrengja, 2. rýrna, 3. minnka, 4. krumpast, 5. innþorna.
shrinkage *see* 1. herping, 2. þrenging, 3. krumpun, 4. samdráttur.
shroud *see* umgjörð.
shun *see* alþakka.
shunt *see* 1. affall, 2. affallssegulmagnaður, 3. hjástreymi, 4. hliðargrein, 5. hliðarviðnám.
shutter *see* 1. raufarhleri, 2. hleri, 3. lokari.
shy *see* feiminn.
sibilant *see* 1. blístrandi, 2. blísturshljóð.
sibling *see* 1. bróðurflekkur, 2. gefrato, 3. systkin.

siblings *see* 1. gefrata, 2. gefrato, 3. samgepatrido, 4. systkin.
sibs *see* systkin.
sick *see* 1. sjúkur, 2. veikur.
sickness *see* 1. veikindi, 2. sjúkdómur.
side *see* 1. síða, 2. hlið.
sidelight *see* 1. hliðarljós, 2. kýrauga.
sidereal *see* 1. stjarnbundinn, 2. stjörnumiðaður.
sideways *see* hliðhallt.
sieve *see* 1. sáld, 2. sía, 3. sigti.
sight *see* 1. sjá, 2. sjón.
sign *see* 1. merki, 2. undirskrifa, 3. teikn, 4. stjörnumerki, 5. skrá.
signal *see* 1. bending, 2. merki, 3. merkiljós, 4. rafsegulbylgja, 5. straumsveifla.
signature *see* 1. undirskrift, 2. mynsturfar, 3. undirritun.
significance *see* 1. marktækni, 2. marktekt, 3. táknmerking.
significant *see* 1. mikilvægur, 2. marktækur.
signification *see* grunnmerking.
signifier *see* tákngjafi.
signify *see* 1. merkja, 2. þýða.
silage *see* 1. súrhey, 2. vothey.
silencer *see* 1. hljóðdeyfir, 2. hljóðkútur.
silent *see* 1. hljóðlátur, 2. óvirkur, 3. þögull.
silica *see* 1. kísiltvíoxíð, 2. kísl.
silicon *see* 1. kísill, 2. silisíum.
silicosis *see* kísillunga.
silk *see* silki.
sill *see* 1. laggangur, 2. síls, 3. þröskuldur, 4. vatnsbretti.
silt *see* 1. árframburður, 2. botnleðja, 3. méla, 4. sylti.
silver *see* silfur.
simian *see* apalegur.
similarity *see* 1. líking, 2. svipmót, 3. einslögun.
similitude *see* líking.
simple *see* 1. einfaldur, 2. hógvær, 3. ógreindur.
simplex *see* 1. skiptisending, 2. skiptital.
simplification *see* einföldun.
simulate *see* 1. látast, 2. þykjast.
simulation *see* 1. sjúkdómsherming, 2. líking, 3. uppgerð, 4. hermireikningur, 5. hermun.
simulator *see* 1. hermir, 2. samlíkir, 3. eftirlíkir.
simultaneity *see* 1. samtímahugtak, 2. samtími.
simultaneous *see* 1. samtíma, 2. samtímis.
sine *see* sínus.
sinew *see* sin.
sing *see* syngja.
single *see* 1. einstæður, 2. einn, 3. einfaldur, 4. stakur, 5. sameiginlegur.
singularity *see* 1. sérstaða, 2. sérstæða, 3. sérstöðupunktur.
sinistral *see* 1. örvhendur, 2. vinstri.

sink *see* 1. svelgur, 2. hnig, 3. viðtaki, 4. vaskur, 5. sökkva.
sinker *see* sakka.
sinter *see* 1. sindra, 2. sindrun.
sinus *see* 1. gúlpur, 2. hola, 3. hvilft, 4. skerðing, 5. stokkur.
siphon *see* 1. vökvasuga, 2. sogari.
sir *see* herra.
siren *see* 1. vélflauta, 2. sírena.
siriasis *see* 1. hitaslag, 2. sólstingur.
sister *see* systir.
sit *see* sitja.
site *see* 1. lega, 2. lóð, 3. set, 4. staðsetning, 5. staður.
situation *see* 1. staðsetning, 2. lega, 3. aðstæður, 4. staður.
six *see* sex.
sixteen *see* sextán.
sixty *see* sextíu.
size *see* stærð.
sizing *see* Hörpun.
skate *see* 1. Pálsskata, 2. stíflisskata, 3. skata, 4. stífla.
skeleton *see* 1. beinagrind, 2. stoðgrind.
sketch *see* 1. riss, 2. skissa.
skew *see* 1. skái, 2. skávik, 3. skakki, 4. skakkur.
skewness *see* 1. skeif, 2. afmyndun, 3. bjögun, 4. misvægi, 5. skakki.
ski *see* skíði.
skid *see* 1. rennsli, 2. skrið, 3. skrik, 4. útskrið.
skill *see* 1. fagkunnátta, 2. leikni, 3. geta, 4. hæfni.
skin *see* 1. húð, 2. roðfletta, 3. Skinn, 4. roð, 5. klæðning.
skip *see* 1. yfirhlaup, 2. ker.
skipper *see* 1. geirnefur, 2. hornfiskur, 3. skipstjóri.
skirt *see* 1. bolur, 2. vélarhlíf, 3. svunta, 4. pils, 5. faldur.
skull *see* 1. höfuðkúpa, 2. hauskúpa.
sky *see* himinn.
skylight *see* 1. himinbjarmi, 2. himinljós, 3. himinskin, 4. ljóri, 5. þiljuljóri.
slab *see* 1. barri, 2. sneiða, 3. sneið, 4. fleki, 5. hella.
slack *see* 1. latur, 2. slaki.
slag *see* 1. Gjall, 2. málmgjall, 3. sindur, 4. sori.
slander *see* 1. ærumeiðing, 2. meiðyrði, 3. slúðra, 4. slúður.
slang *see* slangur.
slat *see* raufungur.
slavish *see* þýlundaður.
sledge *see* sleði.
sleep *see* 1. sofa, 2. svefn.
sleet *see* 1. ískorn, 2. kraparigning, 3. slydda.
sleeve *see* 1. ermi, 2. fóðring, 3. hólkur, 4. slíf.
slender *see* 1. mjór, 2. þunnur.
slice *see* 1. sneiða, 2. sníða, 3. geiri, 4. sneið.

slicer *see* 1. sneiðir, 2. tvígildistakmarkari.
slide *see* 1. slæða, 2. sýnisgler, 3. skyggna, 4. skriðuhlaup, 5. skriðufall.
slider *see* sleði.
sliding *see* hliðranlegur.
slim *see* mjór.
sling *see* 1. fatli, 2. fetill, 3. veffetill.
slinger *see* 1. kasthringur, 2. þeytari.
slingshot *see* kvartmílubíll.
slip *see* 1. skrikun, 2. vængskrið, 3. snuða, 4. sleita, 5. misgengi.
slipstream *see* 1. kjölfarssog, 2. skrúfuröst.
sliver *see* 1. flaskafláki, 2. flaski.
slope *see* 1. hallatala, 2. halli.
slot *see* 1. úrtak, 2. úrtekinn, 3. spor, 4. rauf, 5. nót.
slough *see* drepvefur.
slow *see* 1. hægfara, 2. hægur, 3. seinn.
sludge *see* 1. botnefja, 2. seyra, 3. leðja, 4. ískrap, 5. botnleðja.
sluice *see* 1. gáttarstífla, 2. slússa.
slump *see* 1. framhlaup, 2. jarðhrun, 3. berghlaup.
small *see* 1. lítill, 2. smár.
smallpox *see* 1. bólusótt, 2. stórabóla.
smear *see* strok.
smegma *see* 1. reðurfarði, 2. limfarði.
smell *see* 1. þefur, 2. lykt, 3. lykta.
smelt *see* 1. bræða, 2. silfurloðna, 3. tannloðna, 4. vatnaloðna.
smile *see* 1. bros, 2. brosa.
smithy *see* 1. járnsmiðja, 2. smiðja.
smog *see* 1. mengunarský, 2. reykjarmóða, 3. Reykþoka, 4. þreykur.
smoke *see* 1. reykur, 2. reykja.
smolt *see* 1. laxaseiði, 2. seiði, 3. sjógönguseiði, 4. gönguseiði.
smooth *see* 1. fingerður, 2. sléttur, 3. þjáll, 4. sleipur, 5. alháll.
smoothing *see* 1. jöfnun, 2. síun, 3. sléttun.
smother *see* 1. kæfa, 2. kafna.
snake *see* 1. snákur, 2. ormur, 3. slanga.
snap *see* 1. skrölta, 2. smella, 3. smellur, 4. myndskot, 5. ljósmynd.
snappy *see* 1. hvellur, 2. skerandi, 3. skrækur.
snapshot *see* ljósmynd.
sneeze *see* hnerra.
snooks *see* snasar.
snow *see* 1. snjór, 2. snjókoma, 3. kafald.
snowplow *see* snjóplógur.
so *see* 1. því, 2. æði, 3. mjög.
soak *see* 1. gegnvæta, 2. gegnumvæta, 3. gegnbleyta.
soap *see* sápa.
sober *see* alvarlegur.
social *see* 1. félagslegur, 2. þjóðfélagslegur.
socialism *see* 1. félagshyggja, 2. jafnaðarstefna, 3. sameignarstefna, 4. sósíalismi.

socialization *see* félagsmótun.
society *see* 1. mannfélag, 2. samfélag, 3. þjóðfélag.
sociology *see* félagsfræði.
sociometry *see* félagstengslakönnun.
sock *see* 1. sokkur, 2. háleistur.
socket *see* 1. falur, 2. hólkur, 3. innstunga, 4. keiluhólkur, 5. múffa.
sodium *see* 1. natur, 2. natrín, 3. natríum.
sodomy *see* 1. þermimök, 2. sódómska.
soft *see* 1. mjúkur, 2. mjúkt.
software *see* hugbúnaður.
soil *see* 1. ata, 2. jarðvegur, 3. jörð, 4. land, 5. óhreinka.
sojourner *see* gestur.
sol *see* 1. kvoða, 2. sól (sun).
solace *see* huggun.
solar *see* sólar.
solder *see* 1. lóða, 2. lóðmálmur, 3. lóðtin, 4. brasmálmur.
soldering *see* 1. lóðun, 2. tinlóðun.
sole *see* 1. aleinn, 2. iljarsvæði, 3. il, 4. einmana, 5. einn.
solemn *see* alvarlegur.
solenoid *see* 1. rafsegull, 2. segulspóla, 3. spóla, 4. langspóla, 5. segulliði.
soles *see* tunguflúrur.
solicitor *see* málfærslumaður.
solid *see* 1. þéttur, 2. þrívíður, 3. storka, 4. sterkur, 5. rúmmynd.
solidification *see* 1. hörðnun, 2. storknun.
solidify *see* harðna.
solidity *see* 1. greiðslugeta, 2. blaðflatarhlutfall, 3. gjaldþol.
solitary *see* 1. aleinn, 2. einmana, 3. einn, 4. einsamall, 5. stakur.
solstice *see* 1. sólhvarfapunktur, 2. sólstöður, 3. sólstöðupunktur, 4. sólhvörf.
solubility *see* leysni.
soluble *see* 1. leysanlegur, 2. leysinn.
solution *see* 1. lausn, 2. leysing, 3. upplausn, 4. úrlausn.
solvency *see* 1. gjaldfærni, 2. gjaldhæfi.
solvent *see* 1. leysir, 2. upplausnarefni, 3. gjaldfær, 4. gjaldhæfur, 5. uppleysandi
soma *see* líkami.
somatic *see* líkamlegur.
somatotype *see* líkamsgerð.
somber *see* dapur.
some *see* 1. nokkuð, 2. sumir.
somite *see* 1. frumdeild, 2. frumliður.
somnambulism *see* svefnganga.
somnambulist *see* svefngengill.
son *see* sonur.
sonar *see* 1. ómskoðun, 2. ómsjá, 3. hljóðsjá.
sonogram *see* tónrit.

sonorous *see* hljómmikill.
soot *see* 1. sót, 2. sóta.
sopor *see* svefndá.
soreness *see* verkur.
sorrowful *see* dapur.
sorry *see* 1. afsakið, 2. fyrirgefðu.
sort *see* 1. flokka, 2. innrétta, 3. raða.
sound *see* 1. hljómur, 2. kanni, 3. hljóð.
sounder *see* hljóðgjafi.
sounding *see* 1. dýptarmæling, 2. háloftaathugun, 3. könnun, 4. lóðning.
sour *see* 1. beiskur, 2. óvænn, 3. óvingjarnlegur, 4. súr, 5. súrna.
source *see* 1. heimild, 2. uppspretta, 3. upptök, 4. lind, 5. gagnalind.
south *see* suður.
sovereign *see* 1. einvaldur, 2. þjóðhöfðingi, 3. ríkjandi, 4. fullvaldur, 5. drottnari.
sovereignty *see* 1. fullveldi, 2. sjálfstjórnarsvæði, 3. yfirráðaréttur, 4. yfirráð, 5. einræðisvald.
space *see* 1. rými, 2. bil, 3. geimur, 4. pláss, 5. rúm.
spacer *see* 1. stöðuhólkur, 2. þykktarhólkur, 3. þykktarskífa, 4. rýmir, 5. millileggsskifa.
spacing *see* deilibil.
spacious *see* 1. rúmgóður, 2. víður.
spade *see* 1. skófla, 2. fosilo.
spam *see* amapóstur.
span *see* 1. mælividd, 2. spanna, 3. spönn, 4. vænghaf, 5. haf.
spanner *see* skrúflykill.
spar *see* 1. bóma, 2. vængbiti, 3. rár, 4. siglur.
spark *see* 1. neistahlaup, 2. neisti, 3. rafneisti.
spasm *see* 1. krampi, 2. spasmi.
spasmodic *see* 1. krampakenndur, 2. slitróttur.
spastic *see* 1. krampakynjaður, 2. spastískur.
spasticity *see* síbeygjukrampar.
spat *see* 1. hjólhlíf, 2. legghlíf.
spatula *see* 1. kíttisspaði, 2. spaði.
spawn *see* hrygna.
speak *see* 1. spjalla, 2. tala.
speaker *see* 1. mælandi, 2. ræðumaður.
special *see* 1. sérstakur, 2. ýmislegt, 3. sérstaklegur, 4. einstakur.
specialist *see* sérfræðingur.
specialization *see* sérhæfing.
speciation *see* 1. tegundaklofnun, 2. tegundamyndun.
species *see* tegund.
specific *see* 1. sérstakur, 2. tiltekinn, 3. tiltekið, 4. sértækur, 5. sérstakt.
specification *see* 1. verklýsing, 2. hönnunarlýsing, 3. skilgreining, 4. sundurliðun, 5. tæknilýsing.
specificity *see* 1. sérvirkni, 2. sérhæfni, 3. sértæki.
specimen *see* 1. eintak, 2. sýni, 3. sýnishorn.
spectacle *see* spektaklo.

spectacles *see* 1. spektaklo, 2. gleraugu.
spectral *see* 1. róflegur, 2. rófrænn.
spectrogram *see* 1. litrófsmynd, 2. litrófsrit, 3. rófmynd, 4. rófrit.
spectrograph *see* 1. hljóðrófsriti, 2. rófriti, 3. litrófsriti, 4. róflínuriti.
spectrometer *see* 1. litrófsmælir, 2. litsjá, 3. rófgreinir, 4. rófsjá.
spectrophotometer *see* 1. litrófsljósmælir, 2. litrófsmælir, 3. rófljósmælir.
spectroscope *see* 1. litrófssjá, 2. litsjá, 3. rófsjá.
spectroscopy *see* 1. litrófsfræði, 2. rófgreining, 3. litrófsrannsókn, 4. litrófsgreining.
spectrum *see* 1. aflróf, 2. hljóðróf, 3. litróf, 4. róf.
speculation *see* 1. brask, 2. spákaupmennska.
speech *see* 1. mál, 2. ræða, 3. tal.
speed *see* 1. hraði, 2. ljósnæmi, 3. tökutími, 4. hraðastjórnun, 5. ferð.
speedometer *see* hraðamælir.
speedy *see* hratt.
spell *see* 1. vakt, 2. vinnulota, 3. tímabil, 4. stafa, 5. kafli.
spend *see* 1. verja, 2. eyða.
sperm *see* 1. sæðisfruma, 2. frjó, 3. frjófruma, 4. sáð, 5. sáðfruma.
spermaceti *see* 1. hvalsauki, 2. hvalambur.
spermatheca *see* sáðgeymsla.
spermatocyte *see* 1. frjómóðurfruma, 2. sáðfruma, 3. sáðfrumuvísir, 4. sáðmóðurfruma, 5. sæðisfrumuvísir.
spermatogenesis *see* sæðismyndun.
spermatozoon *see* 1. frjó, 2. frjófruma, 3. sáðfruma, 4. sæðisfruma.
spermicidal *see* sáðdrepandi.
spermicide *see* 1. sáðfrumnadeyðir, 2. sáðfrumnaeyðir.
spermiogenesis *see* 1. sáðþroskun, 2. sæðisþroskun, 3. frjóþroskun.
sphenoid *see* fleyglaga.
sphere *see* 1. áhrifasvæði, 2. áhrifasvið, 3. hnöttur, 4. hvel, 5. hvolf.
spherical *see* 1. hnöttóttur, 2. kúlulaga.
spheroid *see* 1. kúlulaga, 2. kúlulíki, 3. snúðvala.
sphincter *see* 1. þrengivöðvi, 2. hringvöðvi, 3. lokuvöðvi, 4. þrengir.
spicule *see* 1. sólnál, 2. sólbroddur, 3. gaddur, 4. sóltoppur, 5. nál.
spider *see* 1. nöf, 2. spegilfesting, 3. spælkross, 4. snúðstjarna, 5. kross.
spike *see* 1. spennubroddur, 2. spíkur, 3. straumbroddur, 4. spennuhnykkur, 5. hnykkur.
spill *see* 1. spilla, 2. sullast.
spillover *see* 1. smit, 2. smitáhrif, 3. yfirflæði.
spin *see* 1. snúningur, 2. spuni.
spinal *see* 1. hrygglægur, 2. nibbulegur.

spindle *see* 1. öxull, 2. spóla, 3. völur, 4. snælda, 5. ás.
spine *see* 1. blaðþorn, 2. hryggur, 3. nibba, 4. þyrnir.
spinner *see* 1. nafarhlíf, 2. snarkolla, 3. spunamælir.
spiracle *see* 1. andop, 2. innstreymisop, 3. loftæðaop.
spiral *see* 1. snigill, 2. vafningur, 3. gormur, 4. gormflug, 5. vefja.
spirillum *see* gormsýkill.
spirit *see* 1. andi, 2. önd, 3. spirito, 4. spíritus, 5. spritt.
spirits *see* 1. spirito, 2. vervo, 3. vigleco.
spit *see* 1. eyri, 2. tangi, 3. hrækja, 4. oddi.
spleen *see* 1. milta, 2. milti.
splenetic *see* 1. fyrtinn, 2. geðstirður, 3. miltissjúkur.
splice *see* 1. splæsa, 2. tengja.
splicing *see* 1. fléttun, 2. samskeyting, 3. splæsing.
spline *see* 1. ríla, 2. splæsifall, 3. hermifall, 4. fjaðurbrúun, 5. langrauf.
split *see* 1. klofið, 2. aðskilið.
spoil *see* dekra.
spoiled *see* dekraður.
spoiler *see* 1. vindkljúfur, 2. lyftispillir.
spoke *see* 1. spæll, 2. pílári, 3. rimill.
sponge *see* 1. svampur, 2. gljúpefni.
spongy *see* svampkenndur.
sponson *see* 1. flotstúfur, 2. flothylki.
sponsor *see* 1. kostandi, 2. kosta, 3. bakhjarl.
spontaneous *see* 1. sjálfkrafa, 2. sjálfkvæmur, 3. sjálfsprottinn.
spoof *see* 1. gabba, 2. skopstæling.
spool *see* 1. biðfæra, 2. kefli.
spoon *see* skeið.
sporadic *see* 1. dreifður, 2. stakstæður, 3. stakur.
sporangium *see* gróhirsla.
spore *see* gró.
sporophyte *see* gróliður.
sport *see* íþrótt.
sporulation *see* grómyndun.
spot *see* 1. blettur, 2. díll, 3. ljósvísir.
spotlight *see* 1. ljóskastari, 2. punktljós.
spotting *see* flekkun.
spouse *see* 1. maður (man), 2. kona, 3. eiginkona, 4. eiginmaður.
spout *see* 1. gossúla, 2. stútur, 3. vatnssúla.
sprain *see* tognun.
sprat *see* 1. brislingur, 2. tannsíld.
spray *see* 1. sprauta, 2. úða, 3. úði.
spread *see* 1. víkka, 2. víkkun, 3. dreifa, 4. dreif, 5. álag.
spreading *see* útstæður.
spreadsheet *see* töflureiknir.
sprig *see* kvistur.

spring see 1. vor, 2. springur, 3. fjöður, 4. vortími, 5. upptök.
springtime see 1. vor, 2. vortími.
sprinkle see 1. úða, 2. ýra.
spruce see greni.
spur see 1. spori, 2. fótstólpi, 3. fótur (foot), 4. hæll, 5. rani.
spurious see falskur.
sputum see 1. hráki, 2. uppgangur.
squabble see 1. rífast, 2. rifrildi.
squall see 1. vindgarður, 2. vindhviða, 3. roka, 4. hryðja, 5. vindsveipur.
squamous see hreistraður.
square see 1. ferkantur, 2. horn, 3. tvíveldi, 4. Reitur, 5. kvaðrat.
squash see 1. grasker, 2. kúrbítur, 3. skvass.
squatter see hústökumaður.
squeak see 1. ískur, 2. marr.
squid see 1. örmagni, 2. smokkur, 3. smámagni, 4. ofurmagni, 5. kolkrabbi.
squint see 1. ranggeislunarhorn, 2. ranghorn, 3. skjálgi.
squirm see 1. iða, 2. vindingur.
squirrel see íkorni.
stabile see 1. kyrr, 2. óhvarfgjarn.
stability see 1. festa, 2. stöðugleiki.
stabilizer see 1. stýriskambur, 2. varðveisluefni, 3. jafnvægisbúnaður.
stable see 1. hesthús, 2. staðfastur, 3. stöðugur, 4. traustur, 5. fastur.
stack see 1. einbúi, 2. stafli, 3. stafla, 4. safna, 5. hlaði.
stacking see stöflun.
stadium see 1. tímabil, 2. skeið, 3. íþróttavöllur, 4. paðreimur.
staff see 1. starfsfólk, 2. starfslið, 3. starfsmenn.
stage see 1. áfangi, 2. atburðasvið, 3. jarðlagaskeið, 4. stig, 5. svið.
staging see 1. stigun, 2. sviðsetning, 3. stiggreining, 4. stigflokkun, 5. stigsetning.
stagnation see 1. kyrrstaða, 2. stöðnun.
staid see alvarlegur.
stain see 1. litun, 2. litur, 3. blettur.
stainless see 1. ryðfrír, 2 flekklaus.
stair see stupo.
stairs see stupo.
stakeholder see hagsmunaaðili.
stalemate see Patt.
stall see 1. ofreisa, 2. stöðvast, 3. ofris, 4. ofrísa.
stamen see 1. fræfill, 2. fræll, 3. frævill.
stammer see 1. stam, 2. stama.
stamp see 1. þrykkja, 2. frímerki, 3. gatari, 4. kaldforma, 5. stans.
stamping see 1. þrykking, 2. stansaður, 3. plötupressun, 4. mótun.

stance see afstaða.
stanchion see nautgripaklafi.
stand see 1. standa, 2. álit, 3. skoðun, 4. standur, 5. þola.
standard see 1. venjulegur, 2. fáni, 3. mælikvarði, 4. mælistaðall, 5. staðall.
standardization see stöðlun.
standardize see staðla.
standby see 1. tilbúinn, 2. viðbúinn.
standstill see 1. kyrrstæður, 2. stans, 3. stopp.
stapes see ístað.
staphylococcus see 1. klasagerill, 2. klasahnettla, 3. klasakokkur.
staple see 1. hefti, 2. undirstöðuafurð, 3. undirstöðuvara, 4. hefta, 5. aðalframleiðsluvara.
star see 1. stjarna, 2. fastastjarna, 3. sólstjarna.
starboard see stjórnborði.
starch see 1. mjölvi, 2. sterkja.
starfish see 1. krossfiskar, 2. krossfiskur, 3. sæstjarna.
stark see 1. heill, 2. bráður.
starling see stari.
start see 1. byrjun, 2. gangsetja, 3. ræsa, 4. ræsing, 5. starta.
starter see 1. ræsir, 2. startari.
starting see 1. gangsetning, 2. ræsimætti, 3. ræsing.
starvation see 1. hungur, 2. tilfangaþrot.
stasis see 1. kyrrstaða, 2. rennslisstöðvun.
state see 1. ásýnd, 2. fasi, 3. hagur, 4. hamur, 5. kjör.
statement see 1. skýrsla, 2. yrðing, 3. yfirlýsing, 4. staðhæfing, 5. setning.
static see 1. fjarskiptatruflanir, 2. kyrrstæður, 3. neistatruflanir, 4. sístæður, 5. stöðugur.
statics see 1. burðarþolsfræði, 2. jafnvægisfræði, 3. stöðufræði.
station see járnbrautarstöð.
stationary see 1. stöðugur, 2. stæður, 3. sístæður, 4. æstæður.
statistic see 1. lýsitölufall, 2. reiknihending, 3. tölfræði, 4. tölfræðilegur, 5. lýsitala.
statistical see tölfræðilegur.
statistics see 1. tölfræði, 2. gögn, 3. staðtölur, 4. tölfræðilegar, 5. hagtölur.
stator see sátur.
status see 1. mannvirðing, 2. viðurkenning, 3. hagur, 4. félagsstaða, 5. ástand.
statute see 1. stofnsamþykkt, 2. ákvæði, 3. lagaboð, 4. lög, 5. samþykkt.
statutory see 1. lögmæltur, 2. löggiltur, 3. lögbundinn, 4. lögboðinn, 5. lagalegur.
stay see 1. stuðningur, 2. stoð, 3. stag, 4. dvöl.
steady see 1. beint, 2. jafn, 3. stöðugur.
steal see stela.
steam see 1. gufa, 2. eimur, 3. sigla, 4. stíma, 5. vatnsgufa.

steatosis *see* fitukirtlakvilli.

steel *see* stál.

steep *see* 1. sæbrattur, 2. brattur.

steerage *see* 1. stjórn, 2. þilfarspláss.

steering *see* 1. stýring, 2. stýrisbúnaður.

stellate *see* 1. stjarnlaga, 2. stjörnulaga.

stem *see* 1. leggur, 2. rót, 3. stefni, 4. stilkur, 5. stofn.

step *see* 1. botnstallur, 2. þrep, 3. stig, 4. paði, 5. skref.

steps *see* 1. paði, 2. paðo, 3. ðtupo.

steradian *see* 1. rúmhornseining, 2. steradíani.

stereochemistry *see* 1. rúmefnafræði, 2. þrívíddarefnafræði.

stereogram *see* 1. þrívíddarmynd, 2. þrívíddarrit, 3. tvenndarmynd.

stereoscope *see* 1. þrívíddarsjá, 2. víðsjá, 3. þrívíddarmyndasjá, 4. rúmsjá.

stereotype *see* 1. stegla, 2. steglingur, 3. stermót, 4. stimpill, 5. staðalmynd.

stereotypy *see* 1. stegling, 2. stermótun.

sterile *see* 1. geldur, 2. ófrjór, 3. ófrjósamur, 4. smitsæfður, 5. dauðhreinsaður.

sterility *see* 1. ófrjósemi, 2. gerlaleysi.

sterilization *see* 1. vönun, 2. smitsæfing, 3. dauðhreinsun.

sterilize *see* 1. dauðhreinsa, 2. smitsæfa, 3. vana.

stern *see* 1. leggur, 2. skutur.

sternum *see* kviðskjöldur.

steroid *see* 1. steri, 2. steróíð, 3. tylgi.

stethoscope *see* 1. hlustpípa, 2. hlustunarpípa, 3. hlustunartæki.

stevedore *see* lestunarstjóri.

stew *see* ragú.

steward *see* 1. flugþjónn, 2. bryti.

stick *see* 1. festa, 2. festast, 3. líma, 4. stafur.

sticker *see* límmiði.

stickleback *see* hornsíli.

sticky *see* 1. kámugur, 2. límkenndur.

stiff *see* stirður.

stigma *see* 1. augndíll, 2. mark, 3. lýti, 4. kennimerki, 5. fræni.

still *see* þó.

stimulant *see* 1. fíkniefni, 2. nautnalyf, 3. örvandi.

stimulate *see* 1. áreita, 2. erta, 3. örva, 4. reita.

stimulation *see* 1. örvun, 2. reiting, 3. erting, 4. áreiting.

stimulus *see* 1. ertir, 2. hvati, 3. hvatning, 4. örvun, 5. reiti.

stipulation *see* 1. ákvæði, 2. samkomulag.

stir *see* örva.

stochastic *see* tilviljunarkenndur.

stock *see* 1. stofn, 2. stöðustærð, 3. stofnstærð, 4. kynþáttur, 5. lager.

stockbroker *see* 1. verðbréfamiðlari, 2. verðbréfasali.

stockfish *see* 1. ráskerðingur, 2. skreið.

stockholder *see* hluthafi.

stockpile *see* 1. Birgðahaugur, 2. úrgangshaugur, 3. varabirgðir.

stocks *see* 1. brutaro, 2. stoki, 3. provizo, 4. stoko, 5. birgðir.

stocktaking *see* birgðatalning.

stoichiometry *see* 1. efnahlutfallareikningur, 2. hlutfallaefnafræði.

stokehold *see* 1. kyndiklefi, 2. kyndirúm.

stoma *see* 1. munnur (mouth), 2. mynni, 3. op, 4. rauf, 5. loftauga.

stomach *see* magi.

stomatitis *see* 1. munnbólga, 2. munnþroti.

stone *see* 1. steinn, 2. stein.

stool *see* 1. hægðir, 2. saur.

stop *see* 1. lokunarventill, 2. viðspyrna, 3. stoppistöð, 4. stöðva, 5. stöð.

stopcock *see* krani.

stopper *see* 1. negla, 2. tappi.

storage *see* 1. birgðir, 2. geymd, 3. geymsla, 4. rými, 5. vatnsrýmd.

store *see* 1. geyma, 2. safna, 3. geymsla, 4. minni.

stores *see* aðföng.

storing *see* geyming.

stork *see* storkur.

storm *see* 1. stormur, 2. rok, 3. óveður, 4. illviðri.

story *see* 1. saaga, 2. saga.

storyline *see* frásögn.

stove *see* 1. göng, 2. ofn, 3. vasi.

stow *see* 1. fansa, 2. hlaða, 3. stafla, 4. stúa.

stowage *see* 1. hleðsla, 2. lestarými, 3. geymsla.

strabismus *see* 1. skjálgi, 2. skjálgur, 3. rangeygð.

straight *see* 1. beinn, 2. beint, 3. réttur.

straighten *see* 1. laga, 2. rétta.

straightening *see* rétting.

straightforward *see* skýr.

strain *see* 1. stofn, 2. tognun, 3. þan, 4. tegundarhópur, 5. áreynsla.

strainer *see* 1. grófsía, 2. sáld, 3. samrit, 4. sigti.

strait *see* sund.

straitjacket *see* spennitreyja.

strand *see* þáttur.

stranding *see* strand.

strange *see* 1. skrýtinn, 2. vitlaus.

strangulation *see* 1. reyring, 2. kyrking.

strap *see* 1. borði, 2. gjörð, 3. plástra, 4. plástur, 5. spenna.

strata *see* 1. hluti, 2. jarðlag, 3. lag.

strategy *see* 1. stefna, 2. úrræði, 3. stefnumótun, 4. skipulagssnilli, 5. leikáætlun.

stratification *see* 1. lagskipting, 2. skipting, 3. stéttskipting, 4. lagdeiling.

stratified *see* lagskiptur.

stratify *see* lagskipta.

stratigraphy *see* 1. jarðlagafræði, 2. jarðlagaskipan, 3. sneiðmyndataka.

stratosphere *see* heiðhvolf.

stratum *see* 1. lag, 2. hluti, 3. jarðlag.

stratus *see* 1. lágský, 2. þokuský.

strawberry *see* 1. jarðarber, 2. garðajarðarber.

stray *see* tilviljunarkenndur.

stream *see* 1. lækur, 2. fallvatn, 3. straumur, 4. straumvatn, 5. vatnsfall.

streamline *see* 1. straumlínulagaður, 2. staumlína, 3. straumlína.

street *see* gata.

strength *see* 1. kraftur, 2. styrkur.

strengthen *see* 1. efla, 2. styrkja.

strengthening *see* efling.

streptococcus *see* 1. keðjuhnettla, 2. keðjukokkur.

streptokinase *see* streptókínasi.

stress *see* 1. streita, 2. áhersla, 3. álag, 4. spenna.

stressor *see* 1. streitir, 2. streituvaldur.

stretch *see* 1. strekkja, 2. teygja, 3. stækkun.

stretcher *see* 1. langsetill, 2. sjúkrabörur.

striate *see* rákóttur.

striated *see* rákóttur.

strident *see* 1. hvellur, 2. skerandi, 3. skrækur.

strike *see* 1. slag, 2. strikstefna, 3. strik, 4. jarðlagastrik, 5. finna.

striking *see* áberandi.

string *see* 1. strengur, 2. taug.

strip *see* 1. fjarlægja, 2. strípilögur, 3. hreinsa, 4. listi.

stripper *see* afeinangrunartæki.

stripping *see* 1. losun, 2. strípun.

strive *see* slást.

strobe *see* 1. leifturljós, 2. strópa, 3. símarka.

stroboscope *see* 1. bliksjá, 2. skinhreyfisjá, 3. snúðsjá, 4. snúningssjá.

stroke *see* 1. hjartaslag, 2. slag, 3. heilablóðfall, 4. slaglengd.

stroma *see* 1. grunnvefur, 2. mergur, 3. strammi, 4. uppistaða, 5. uppistöðuvefur.

strong *see* 1. Ðflugur, 2. máttagur, 3. sterkur.

strontium *see* 1. strontín, 2. strontíum.

strop *see* brýnól.

structural *see* 1. innbyggður, 2. kerfislægur.

structuralism *see* 1. formgerðarstefna, 2. strúktúralismi.

structure *see* 1. smíðavirki, 2. uppbygging, 3. skipan, 4. formgerð, 5. byggingarlag.

struggle *see* 1. slást, 2. slagsmál.

struma *see* keppur.

strut *see* 1. leggur, 2. þrýstistoð, 3. stag, 4. gormleggur, 5. stoð.

stub *see* stúfur.

stud *see* 1. pinnbolti, 2. þolinmóður, 3. viðspyrna, 4. völur.

studio *see* 1. hljóðver, 2. upptökusalur, 3. stúdíó.

study *see* Stúdera.

stuff *see* stifla.

stupefaction *see* hálfdvali.

stupor *see* 1. hálfdvali, 2. hugstol.

stuporous *see* hugstola.

stutter *see* 1. tos, 2. tosa.

stye *see* vogris.

style *see* 1. mót, 2. yfirbragð, 3. stíll, 4. kambsbrún, 5. gerð.

styptic *see* blóðstemmandi.

subacute *see* 1. hægbráður, 2. meðalbráður.

subclass *see* 1. undirflokkur, 2. undirklasi.

subconscious *see* 1. hálfmeðvitund, 2. undirmeðvitund, 3. hálfmeðvitaður.

subcontractor *see* undirverktaki.

subcortical *see* neðanbarkar.

subculture *see* 1. afræktun, 2. menningarkimi, 3. undirrækt, 4. afrækt, 5. menningarafkimi.

subfamily *see* 1. málaflokkur, 2. undirætt.

subject *see* 1. frumlag, 2. frumlagi, 3. huglag, 4. málefni, 5. tilraunadýr.

subjective *see* 1. huglægur, 2. hugrænn.

subjectivity *see* 1. huglægni, 2. huglægi.

sublimate *see* 1. göfga, 2. súblimat.

sublimation *see* 1. göfgun, 2. þurrgufun.

subliminal *see* neðanmarka.

submarine *see* 1. kafbátur, 2. neðansjávar.

submersible *see* kaffær.

submersion *see* 1. kaffæring, 2. kafhlaup.

submetacentric *see* hjámiðheftur.

submission *see* 1. sending, 2. undirgefni.

submissive *see* þýlundaður.

submit *see* senda.

subnormal *see* vanþroska.

suborder *see* undirættbálkur.

subordination *see* 1. undirgefni, 2. undirsetning, 3. undirskipan.

subroutine *see* stefja.

subsampling *see* deiliúrtaka.

subscriber *see* 1. áskrifandi, 2. leyfishafi.

subscript *see* 1. hnévísir, 2. lágstæður, 3. hnéletraður, 4. lágvísir, 5. hnéletur.

subscription *see* 1. áskrift, 2. framlagsloforð, 3. hlutafjárloforð, 4. söfnunarfé.

subservient *see* þýlundaður.

subset *see* hlutmengi.

subsidence *see* 1. landsig, 2. niðurstreymi, 3. sig, 4. hjöðnun.

subsidiary *see* 1. dótturfélag, 2. dótturfyrirtæki.

subsidy *see* 1. niðurgreiðsla, 2. styrkur.

subsistence *see* 1. afkoma, 2. lífsbjörg, 3. lífsviðurværi, 4. nauðþurftir, 5. sjálfsþurftir.

subspecies *see* 1. undirtegund, 2. deilitegund, 3. deiltegund.
substance *see* 1. kjarni, 2. efni, 3. eignir.
substantial *see* 1. mikill, 2. stór.
substitute *see* 1. staðgönguvara, 2. varamaður, 3. uppbót, 4. líki, 5. staðgönguefni.
substitution *see* 1. innsetning, 2. skipti, 3. skiptiefnahvarf, 4. skiptihvarf, 5. staðganga.
substrate *see* 1. ensímhvarfefni, 2. undirstöðuefni, 3. hvarfefni.
substratum *see* undirlag.
subsystem *see* undirkerfi.
subtotal *see* millisamtala.
subtraction *see* frádráttur.
subtropical *see* 1. heittempraður, 2. hlýtempraður.
subunit *see* 1. byggingareining, 2. einingarhluti, 3. undireining.
suburb *see* 1. útborg, 2. úthverfi.
suburbia *see* 1. úthverfi, 2. randbyggð.
subway *see* neðanjarðarlest.
success *see* 1. happ, 2. gengi.
succession *see* framvinda.
succulent *see* safamikill.
suck *see* sjúga.
sucker *see* 1. rótarskot, 2. sogskál, 3. stofnskot, 4. teinungur, 5. villisproti.
suckers *see* 1. soggúlar, 2. sogkarpar, 3. sogtrantar.
sucrose *see* 1. reyrsykur, 2. sykur, 3. súkrósi.
suction *see* 1. loftsog, 2. sog, 3. sogun.
sudation *see* svitnun.
sudden *see* 1. skyndilegur, 2. snöggur.
suddenly *see* skyndilega.
suffer *see* þola.
sufficiency *see* nægjanleiki.
sufficient *see* nægilegur.
sufficiently *see* nóg.
suffix *see* 1. viðskeyti, 2. merkjaviðskeyti.
suffocation *see* 1. kæfing, 2. köfnun.
sugar *see* 1. sykur, 2. sykra.
suggestibility *see* sefnæmi.
suggestible *see* sefnæmur.
suggestion *see* sefjun.
suggestive *see* sefjandi.
suicide *see* 1. sjálfsmorð, 2. sjálfsbani, 3. sjálfsmorðingi, 4. sjálfsvíg.
suitable *see* 1. viðeigandi, 2. hæfilegur, 3. nothæfur.
sulfate *see* súlfat.
sulfur *see* brennisteinn.
sullen *see* 1. dapur, 2. óvænn, 3. óvingjarnlegur.
sulphur *see* 1. brennisteinn, 2. brennisteinsinnihald.
sum *see* 1. samtala, 2. summa.
summary *see* 1. ágrip, 2. samantekt, 3. útdráttur, 4. yfirlit.
summation *see* 1. summun, 2. summuáhrif.
summer *see* sumar.

summit *see* 1. hátindur, 2. hámark.
summon *see* 1. kalla, 2. stefna.
sump *see* 1. botnskál, 2. olíubiða, 3. olíupanna, 4. panna, 5. þró.
sun *see* sól.
sunburn *see* sólbruni.
sundial *see* sólúr.
sunspot *see* sólblettur.
sunstroke *see* sólstingur.
supercharger *see* forþjappa.
supercomputer *see* ofurtölva.
supercooling *see* undirkæling.
superego *see* yfirsjálf.
superfamily *see* 1. stórfjölskylda, 2. yfirætt.
superficial *see* 1. grunnlægur, 2. grunnur.
superheater *see* yfirhitari.
superheating *see* yfirhitun.
superinfection *see* 1. endursýking, 2. yfirsýking.
superior *see* 1. yfirmaður, 2. efri, 3. undirsætinn.
supernatant *see* flot.
supernova *see* sprengistjarna.
superposition *see* 1. samantekt, 2. samlagning, 3. viðlegð.
supersaturation *see* 1. ofmettun, 2. ofurmettun, 3. yfirmettun.
superscript *see* 1. brjóstvísir, 2. brjóstletraður, 3. brjóstletur, 4. hástæður, 5. hávísir.
supersonic *see* hljóðfrár.
superstition *see* hjátrú.
superstructure *see* yfirbygging.
supervise *see* stjórna.
supervision *see* 1. eftirlit, 2. gæsla, 3. umsjón, 4. verkstjórn, 5. vöktun.
supervisor *see* 1. eftirlitsmaður, 2. yfirmaður, 3. leiðbeinandi, 4. umsjónarmaður.
supination *see* rétthverfing.
supine *see* uppíloft.
supplier *see* 1. birgir, 2. birgðasali.
supplies *see* 1. rekstrarvörubirgðir, 2. framboð, 3. aðdráttir, 4. birgðir.
supply *see* 1. aðfærsla, 2. aðföng, 3. birgðir, 4. birgja, 5. fæða.
support *see* 1. stoð, 2. undirstaða, 3. stuðningur, 4. annast, 5. styðja.
suppose *see* halda.
suppository *see* endaþarmsstíll.
suppression *see* 1. deyfing, 2. þrúgun, 3. hindrun, 4. byrging, 5. bæling.
suppressor *see* 1. bælir, 2. byrgir, 3. deyfir, 4. rás, 5. truflanakæfir.
suppuration *see* graftarmyndun.
supranational *see* yfirþjóðlegur.
surcharge *see* 1. álag, 2. viðbótargjald.
sure *see* 1. vís, 2. vissulegur.
surf *see* 1. brim, 2. spranga.

surface *see* 1. flötur, 2. yfirborð.
surfactant *see* lungnablöðruseyti.
surfing *see* 1. sprang, 2. vefsprang.
surge *see* 1. spennuhnykkur, 2. brimalda, 3. sveifla, 4. þjöppubakslag, 5. straumhnykkur.
surgeon *see* 1. handlæknir, 2. skurðlæknir.
surgery *see* 1 handlæknisfræði, 2. læknamóttaka, 3. lækningastofa, 4. skurðlæknisfræði.
surly *see* 1. óvænn, 2. óvingjarnlegur.
surmise *see* halda.
surname *see* eftirnafn.
surplus *see* 1. ofgnótt, 2. tekjuafgangur, 3. umframbirgðir, 4. umframmagn, 5. afgangur.
surprise *see* 1. furða, 2. undrun.
surprisingly *see* 1. hissa, 2. undrandi.
surveillance *see* umsjón.
survey *see* 1. rannsókn, 2. uppdráttur, 3. mæling, 4. landmælingar, 5. landmælingakort.
surveying *see* landmæling.
surveyor *see* 1. landmælingamaður, 2. skoðunarmaður.
survival *see* 1. lífheldni, 2. lifun, 3. afkoma.
susceptance *see* 1. launviðtak, 2. þverleiðni, 3. launleiðni.
susceptibility *see* 1. viðtak, 2. hrifnæmi, 3. segulviðtak, 4. sóttnæmi.
susceptible *see* 1. sóttnæmur, 2. tilfinninganæmur, 3. móttækilegur, 4. næmur.
suspect *see* 1. gruna, 2. vantreysta.
suspend *see* 1. hengja, 2. víkja.
suspended *see* hangandi.
suspension *see* 1. frestun, 2. niðurfelling, 3. skilorðsbinding, 4. svifefnablanda, 5. sviflausn.
suspicion *see* vantraust.
sustain *see* 1. styðja, 2. þola.
sustainable *see* 1. haldbær, 2. sjálfbær, 3. viðhaldsbær.
suture *see* 1. sauma, 2. saumur, 3. seymi.
swab *see* strok.
swallow *see* 1. svala, 2. landsvala.
swallowing *see* kynging.
swan *see* 1. svanur, 2. álft.
swap *see* 1. skipti, 2. skjáhopp, 3. kvaðaskipti, 4. víxla.
swear *see* bölva.
sweat *see* 1. sviti, 2. svitna.
sweater *see* peysa.
sweep *see* 1. sópa, 2. stroka, 3. sveifla, 4. sveip, 5. yfirferð.
sweeper *see* 1. smurtittur, 2. dagmaður.
sweet *see* 1. konfekt, 2. eftirmatur, 3. kandíssykur.
swell *see* undiralda.
swift *see* hratt.
swim *see* synda.
swindle *see* svik.

swine *see* svín.
swing *see* 1. snúast, 2. sveiflast, 3. titra, 4. sveifla, 5. snúningsþvermál.
switch *see* 1. straumrofi, 2. straumskiptir, 3. rofi, 4. álagsrofi.
switchboard *see* 1. rofatafla, 2. skiptiborð, 3. tafla, 4. rafmagnstafla.
swivel *see* 1. segulnagli, 2. sigurnagli.
swordfish *see* sverðfiskur.
sycamore *see* 1. garðahlynur, 2. hlynur.
sycosis *see* hárpest.
symbiosis *see* 1. samhjálp, 2. samlíf, 3. samlífi.
symbol *see* 1. táknmynd, 2. frumhlutur, 3. merki, 4. tákn.
symbolism *see* 1. líkingalæti, 2. táknkerfi.
symbolization *see* táknun.
symmetric *see* samhverfur.
symmetrical *see* 1. samhverfur, 2. samloka, 3. skuggsær.
symmetry *see* 1. samhverfa, 2. skuggsæi, 3. samhorf.
sympathetic *see* viðkunnanlegur.
sympathy *see* 1. meðaumkun, 2. samferð, 3. samúð.
sympatric *see* 1. samlendur, 2. samsvæða.
symphysis *see* 1. sambryskja, 2. samgróning, 3. samvöxtur.
symposium *see* 1. málþing, 2. samdrykkja.
symptom *see* 1. einkenni, 2. sjúkdómseinkenni, 3. auðkenni.
synagogue *see* gyðingahof.
synapse *see* taugamót.
synapsis *see* 1. litningapörun, 2. pörun, 3. tvennun.
synchronism *see* 1. samfas, 2. samfasa, 3. samgengi.
synchronization *see* 1. samfösun, 2. samhæfing, 3. samhröðun, 4. samstilling.
synchronize *see* 1. samstilla, 2. samhraða.
synchronizer *see* samfasari.
synchronizing *see* samfösun.
synchronous *see* 1. samfasa, 2. samstilling, 3. samstilltur, 4. samstunda, 5. samtíma.
synchrotron *see* 1. samhraðall, 2. sínkrótrónn.
syncline *see* 1. fellingadæld, 2. samhverfa.
syncope *see* 1. ómegin, 2. öngvit, 3. aðsvif, 4. brottfall, 5. yfirlið.
syncytium *see* 1. samfrumungur, 2. samfrymi.
syndrome *see* 1. sjúkdómsmynd, 2. einkennamynstur, 3. heilkenni.
synergism *see* 1. starfsmögnun, 2. samefling, 3. samverkun.
synergist *see* samstarfandi.
synergistic *see* samvirkur.
synergy *see* 1. samverkun, 2. samvirkni, 3. samyrkja, 4. starfsmögnun, 5. samlegðaráhrif.
synonym *see* 1. samheiti, 2. samnefni.

syntax see 1. málfræði, 2. málskipan, 3. setningafræði, 4. setningarfræði.
synthesis see 1. samsetning, 2. vélgerving, 3. tillífun, 4. samtenging, 5. nýsmíð.
synthetic see 1. tilbúinn, 2. samtengdur, 3. smíðaður.
syphilis see 1. sýfilis, 2. sýfilis, 3. sárasótt, 4. sífill.
syphon see sogpípa.
syringe see 1. lyfjadæla, 2. sprauta.
system see 1. stýrikerfi, 2. viðmið, 3. viðmiðunarkerfi, 4. heimsmynd, 5. agnakerfi.
systematic see kerfisbundinn.
systematics see flokkunarfræði.
systemic see 1. fjölkerfa, 2. kerfistengdur, 3. útbreiddur.
systole see 1. slag, 2. slagbil, 3. sýstóla, 4. útfallsfasi.

T

tab see blaka.
tabes see 1. visnun, 2. mænuvisnun, 3. tæring.
table see 1. borð, 2. tafla.
tablet see 1. reitabretti, 2. skipanabretti, 3. tafla.
taboo see 1. banndómur, 2. bannhelgi, 3. bannorð.
tabulate see dálkahlaupa.
tachograph see 1. hraðriti, 2. ökuriti.
tachometer see 1. hornhraðamælir, 2. snúningshraðamælir, 3. snúningsmælir.
tachycardia see 1. hjartsláttarsprettur, 2. hraðtaktur.
tachypnea see 1. hraðöndun, 2. más.
tacit see 1. undirskilinn, 2. þegjandi.
tack see 1. stefnubreyting, 2. stagvending, 3. stagvenda, 4. krussa, 5. krusa.
tackle see 1. blökk, 2. talía.
tactic see taktiko.
tactics see taktiko.
tactile see 1. áþreifanlegur, 2. snertiskyn.
taenia see 1. bandormur, 2. dregill.
taeniasis see 1. bandormakvilli, 2. bandormasýki, 3. bandormasýking.
tag see 1. merki, 2. merkispjald.
taiga see barrskógabelti.
tail see 1. hali, 2. skott, 3. sporður, 4. rófa, 5. afturhluti.
tailing see 1. dreggjar, 2. halamyndun.
tails see 1. gvatsekvi, 2. postaĵo, 3. ŝtelsekvi, 4. trenaĵo, 5. vosto.
take see 1. þakka, 2. samþykkja.
talc see 1. talk, 2. talkúm.
tale see 1. saaga, 2. saga.
talent see gáfa.
talk see 1. blaðra, 2. masa, 3. spjalla, 4. tala.

tall see hár (hair).
tally see reikna.
talus see 1. skriða, 2. ökklabein, 3. hrunskriða, 4. grjótskriða, 5. vala.
tame see 1. gæfur, 2. spakur, 3. taminn.
tampon see 1. tróð, 2. tappi.
tamponade see 1. tepping, 2. ítroðning, 3. ítroðsla.
tandem see 1. gegnumumferð, 2. tengivagn.
tang see 1. þang, 2. hak.
tangent see 1. tangens, 2. snertilína, 3. snertill.
tangerine see tangerína.
tank see 1. afriðilhylki, 2. geymir, 3. hylki, 4. skriðdreki, 5. tankur.
tanker see 1. Olíuskip, 2. tankbíll, 3. Tankskip.
tannin see 1. barksýra, 2. sútunarsýra, 3. tannín.
tantalum see tantal.
tap see 1. krani, 2. úttak, 3. hani, 4. vatnskrani, 5. tunnukrani.
tape see 1. ræma, 2. segulband, 3. límband.
taper see 1. keila, 2. kónn, 3. strýta.
tapioca see tapíókagrjón.
tappet see 1. ventillyfta, 2. undirlyfta, 3. undirlyftutappi.
tapping see 1. hlerun, 2. tappasnittun, 3. þrepúttak, 4. úttak.
taps see kyrrðarstund.
tar see tjara.
target see 1. mark, 2. skotmark, 3. skotskífa, 4. targa.
tariff see 1. gjaldskrá, 2. verðskrá, 3. tollur, 4. tollskrá, 5. innflutningsgjald.
tarpaulin see 1. lúgugatsábreiða, 2. tjaldhiminn, 3. yfirbreiðsla.
tarpon see 1. silfurkóngur, 2. tarpúnn.
tarragon see 1. drekajurt, 2. drekamalurt, 3. esdragon, 4. estragon, 5. fáfnisgras.
tart see 1. súr, 2. beiskur.
tartar see 1. tannsteinn, 2. vínsteinn.
tartness see beiskja.
tartrate see tartrat.
task see 1. verk, 2. verkeining, 3. verkþáttur.
taste see 1. smakka, 2. bragð, 3. smekkur.
tautology see 1. hringröksemd, 2. klifun, 3. sísanna.
tax see 1. skattur, 2. byrði, 3. álag, 4. skattleggja.
taxable see 1. skattskyldur, 2. skattskylt.
taxation see 1. skattlagning, 2. skattur, 3. sköttun.
taxi see 1. aka, 2. leigubíll.
taxis see 1. rétting, 2. sækni.
taxon see 1. kerfiseining, 2. tag, 3. flokkunareining, 4. deild, 5. flokkunarheild.
taxonomy see 1. flokkunarfræði, 2. nafnfræði.
tea see 1. te, 2. terunni.
teacher see kennari.
teaching see kennsla.

team see 1. hópur, 2. lið, 3. starfshópur, 4. teymi, 5. gengi.
tear see 1. tár, 2. rífa, 3. slíta.
technetium see 1. teknetín, 2. teknetíum.
technical see 1. formlegur, 2. tæknilegur.
technique see 1. leikni, 2. tækni, 3. tæknibeiting, 4. verklag
technological see tæknifræðilegur.
technology see 1. tækni, 2. tækniaðferð, 3. tækniaðferðir, 4. tæknifræði.
tectonics see 1. jarðhnik, 2. jarðhniksfræði, 3. höggunarfræði, 4. höggun, 5. tektónik.
teeth see 1. dento, 2. tennur, 3. tönn.
teething see tanntaka.
tegument see hula.
telecommunication see 1. fjarskipti, 2. fjarskiptatækni, 3. fjarmiðlun, 4. fjarskiptafræði.
telecommunications see 1. fjarskipti, 2. símasamskipti.
telecontrol see fjarstýring.
telefax see 1. símsending, 2. símriti, 3. bréfsími, 4. myndsími, 5. símrit.
telegram see símskeyti.
telegraph see 1. síma, 2. sími.
telegraphy see 1. ritsímakerfi, 2. ritsími.
telemetry see 1. fjarmæling, 2. fjarsending.
teleology see 1. markhyggja, 2. markmiðskenning, 3. tilgangshyggja.
telepathy see 1. fjarskynjun, 2. fjarvísi.
telephone see 1. talsími, 2. sími.
telephony see 1. talsímakerfi, 2. talsími.
teleprinter see fjarriti.
teleprocessing see fjarvinnsla.
telescope see 1. kíkir, 2. sjónauki, 3. stjörnusjá, 4. sundurdregin.
telescopic see sundurdraganlegur.
teletypewriter see fjarriti.
television see sjónvarp.
tell see segja.
tellurium see tellúr.
telomere see 1. litningsendi, 2. oddhluti.
telophase see 1. lokafasi, 2. telófasi.
temper see 1. skap, 2. eldherða.
temperament see 1. lundarfar, 2. skapferli.
temperature see 1. hitastig, 2. hiti, 3. líkamshiti.
tempering see 1. hitameðferð, 2. seighersla, 3. afglóðun.
tempest see stormur.
template see 1. fyrirmynd, 2. mát, 3. mót, 4. skapalon, 5. snið.
temple see 1. hof, 2. gagnauga.
temporal see tímabundin.
temporary see 1. tímabundinn, 2. bráðabirgða, 3. tilviljunarkenndur, 4. tímabundið.
temptation see freisting.

ten see tíu.
tenacity see 1. seigla, 2. þol.
tenant see leigjandi.
tench see grunnungur.
tender see 1. aumur, 2. kynna, 3. tilboð, 4. útboð.
tendinitis see sinarbólga.
tendon see sin.
tenet see trú.
tense see 1. þanið, 2. tíð, 3. strekktur.
tensile see teygjanlegur.
tension see 1. togkraftur, 2. rafspenna, 3. spenna, 4. strekking, 5. þensla.
tensor see 1. spennir, 2. þinur.
tent see tjald.
tepid see 1. áhugalaus, 2. volgur.
teratogen see vansköpunarvaldur.
teratology see vanskapanafræði.
terbium see 1. terbín, 2. terbíum.
term see 1. liður, 2. tími, 3. tímabil, 4. tal, 5. nafn.
terminal see 1. endastæður, 2. tengill, 3. úttak, 4. útstöð, 5. tengipunktur.
termination see 1. endahólkur, 2. endamúffa, 3. endi, 4. uppsögn, 5. úttak.
terminator see 1. loki, 2. skuggaskil, 3. loktákn.
terms see 1. skilmálar, 2. tiðir.
terrace see hjalli.
terrain see 1. fold, 2. landsvæði.
terrestrial see jarðneskur.
terrible see 1. hræðilegur, 2. hryllilegur.
territory see 1. landsvæði, 2. óðal, 3. svæði, 4. yfirráðasvæði.
terror see 1. hræðsla, 2. ógn.
terrorism see 1. hermdarverk, 2. hermdarverkastarfsemi, 3. hryðjuverk, 4. hryðjuverkastarfsemi, 5. ógnarstjórn.
tertiary see 1. tertier, 2. tertiertímabil.
test see 1. prófa, 2. prófefni, 3. prófun, 4. rannsaka, 5. tilraun.
testis see 1. eista, 2. eistu.
testosterone see testósterón.
tetanus see 1. stifkrampi, 2. stjarfi.
tetany see 1. kalkkrampi, 2. kalkstjarfi, 3. stjarki.
tetrad see 1. einkennaferna, 2. ferna, 3 gróferna.
tetragonal see 1. ferhyrndur, 2. fjórhliða.
tetraploid see 1. ferlitna, 2. ferlitnungur.
tetrapod see ferfætlingur.
tetrasomy see ferstæða.
tetravalent see 1. fjórgildur, 2. fergildur.
tetrode see 1. ferskautalampi, 2. ferskauti, 3. tetróða.
text see 1. lesmál, 2. texti.
texture see áferð.
thalamus see 1. blómbotn, 2. heilastúka, 3. stúka.
thallium see 1. þallín, 2. þallíum.
thallus see þal.
thank see þakka.

thankful *see* þakklátur.
thankless *see* vanþakklátur.
thanks *see* þökk.
thaw *see* 1. bráðna, 2. hláka, 3. þíða, 4. þiðna.
theca *see* 1. frjóhnappshelmingur, 2. hula.
theme *see* 1. stef, 2. tema, 3. þema.
then *see* þá.
theocracy *see* 1. guðveldi, 2. klerkaveldi, 3. prestaveldi.
theodolite *see* hornmælir.
theorem *see* 1. kennisetning, 2. setning.
theoretical *see* 1. fræðilegur, 2. kennilegur.
theory *see* 1. fræðasvið, 2. kenning, 3. fræði, 4. fræðikenning.
therapeutic *see* læknandi.
therapist *see* 1. lækningamaður, 2. meðferðaraðili.
therapy *see* 1. meðferð, 2. lækning.
there *see* 1. þar, 2. þangað.
therefore *see* því.
thermal *see* 1. hitabóla, 2. hitauppstreymi.
thermistor *see* 1. heitleiðir, 2. hitamótstaða, 3. hitaviðnám, 4. termistor.
thermochemistry *see* 1. hitaefnafræði, 2. varmaefnafræði.
thermocouple *see* 1. snertispennunemi, 2. tvinn, 3. hitarafvaki, 4. hitapar, 5. hitatvinn.
thermodynamic *see* 1. varmaaflfræðilegur, 2. varmafræðilegur.
thermodynamics *see* 1. varmafræði, 2. hitaaflfræði, 3. varmaaflfræði.
thermogram *see* 1. hitarit, 2. hitasírit.
thermograph *see* hitariti.
thermoluminescence *see* 1. hitaljómun, 2. varmaljómun.
thermolysis *see* 1. hitaleysing, 2. varmasundrun.
thermometer *see* hitamælir.
thermophile *see* hitafíkill.
thermophilic *see* hitakær.
thermopile *see* tvinnhlaði.
thermoplastic *see* hitaþjáll.
thermosphere *see* 1. hitahvolf, 2. hithvolf.
thermostat *see* 1. hitastýring, 2. hitavökull, 3. hitastillir, 4. hitaliði, 5. vatnslás.
thesaurus *see* 1. hugtakabók, 2. hugtakasafn, 3. orðaskrín, 4. samheitaorðabók.
thiamine *see* þíamín.
thick *see* 1. þykkur, 2. seigfljótandi, 3. þykkfljótandi.
thickness *see* 1. gildleiki, 2. þykkt.
thief *see* þjófur.
thimble *see* 1. bikar, 2. björg, 3. festarauga.
thin *see* 1. mjór, 2. þunnur.
thing *see* objekto.
things *see* 1. objekto, 2. afero, 3. aĵo.
think *see* 1. þykja, 2. hugsa, 3. halda.

thinking *see* hugsun.
thinner *see* þynnir.
thinning *see* 1. grisjun, 2. þynning.
third *see* 1. þriðji, 2. þriðja.
thirst *see* þorsti.
thirteen *see* þrettán.
thirty *see* þrjátíu.
thither *see* þangað.
thole *see* 1. áraþollur, 2. þollur.
thorax *see* 1. brjósthol, 2. bringa, 3. frambolur, 4. brjóst, 5. brjóstgrind.
thorium *see* 1. þórín, 2. þóríum.
thorough *see* heill.
thoroughly *see* gagngert.
thou *see* 1. þú, 2. þér, 3. við.
though *see* þótt.
thought *see* hugsun.
thread *see* 1. snytti, 2. skrúfgangur, 3. þráður, 4. gengjur, 5. snitta.
threat *see* Hótun.
three *see* þrír.
threonine *see* 1. þre, 2. þreónín.
threshold *see* 1. þröskuldur, 2. viðmiðunarmörk, 3. þröskuldsgildi, 4. þröm, 5. markgildi.
thrift *see* 1. geldingahnappur, 2. ráðdeild, 3. sparsemi.
throb *see* sláttur.
thrombin *see* 1. blóðhleypir, 2. þrombín.
thromboplastin *see* þrombóplastín.
thrombosis *see* 1. æðasegamyndun, 2. segamyndun.
thrombus *see* 1. segi, 2. æðasegi, 3. blóðsegi.
throttle *see* 1. stýrifetill, 2. þrenging, 3. stýrihandfang, 4. kok, 5. eldsneytisgjafi.
through *see* 1. fyrir, 2. meðan, 3. tillbúinn.
throughput *see* afköst.
throw *see* 1. kasta, 2. sveifarlengd, 3. varpa.
thrush *see* þruska.
thrust *see* 1. knýr, 2. ýta, 3. troða, 4. þrýstikraftur, 5. risgengi.
thulium *see* 1. túlín, 2. túlíum.
thunder *see* 1. þruma, 2. skrugga.
thunderstorm *see* þrumuveður.
thus *see* því.
thymectomy *see* 1. hóstarkirtilsnám, 2. týmusnám.
thymidine *see* týmídín.
thymocyte *see* 1. týmusfruma, 2. hóstarkirtilsfruma.
thymus *see* 1. hóstarkirtill, 2. hóstill, 3. tímgill, 4. týmus.
thyroid *see* skjaldlaga.
thyroxine *see* 1. skjaldkirtilshormón, 2. þýroxín.
tibia *see* 1. langliður, 2. sköflungur.
tic *see* 1. skeytingarmerki, 2. viðmiðunarmerki, 3. mið, 4. merki, 5. vöðvakvik.
tick *see* 1. blóðmítill, 2. farmaur, 3. stórmaur.
ticker *see* sími.

ticket *see* 1. aðgöngumerki, 2. aðgöngumiði, 3. aðgönguspjald, 4. farmiði, 5. farseðill.
tide *see* 1. háflóð, 2. sjávarföll, 3. sjávarfall, 4. bylgja, 5. alda.
tidy *see* innrétta.
tie *see* binda.
tier *see* 1. flötur, 2. tengiflötur
tighten *see* 1. herða, 2. þétta.
tile *see* 1. reitur, 2. tigla, 3. gluggareitur, 4. flís, 5. tigull.
till *see* 1. jökulruðningur, 2. unz.
tiller *see* 1. stýrissveif, 2. stofnskot, 3. stofnteinungur.
tilt *see* 1. halli, 2. slagsíða.
timber *see* 1. skógur, 2. tré.
timberland *see* skógur.
timbre *see* hljómblær.
time *see* 1. tími, 2. tímabil, 3. tímalengd, 4. tíð, 5. stund.
timely *see* nákvæmur.
timer *see* 1. tímagisti, 2. tímastýring.
timing *see* 1. tímasetning, 2. tímastilling, 3. ventlastjórnun.
tin *see* 1. blikkdós, 2. dós, 3. þríhyrnunet, 4. tina, 5. tinhúða.
tinea *see* reformur.
tingle *see* náladofi.
tip *see* 1. halla, 2. hallast, 3. nafli, 4. tota.
tire *see* 1. dekk, 2. hjólbarði.
tissue *see* 1. tisja, 2. tissjú, 3. vefur.
tit *see* meisa.
titanium *see* 1. títan, 2. titan.
titer *see* 1. títer, 2. títri.
title *see* 1. eignarréttur, 2. titill, 3. eignaréttur, 4. heiti, 5. fyrirsögn.
titration *see* títrun.
titre *see* títri.
to *see* til.
to abdicate *see* yfirgefa.
to abduct *see* fráfæra.
to aberrate *see* víkja.
to abhor *see* hrylla.
to abnegate *see* neita.
to abominate *see* hrylla.
to achieve *see* afreka.
to activate *see* 1. vekja, 2. virkja, 3. örva, 4. orsaka, 5. espa
to adopt *see* 1. ættleiða, 2. samþykkja, 3. undirbúa.
to advise *see* ráða.
to algebra *see* bókstafareikningur.
to allocate *see* 1. ráðstafa, 2. skipta, 3. úthluta, 4. veita, 5. beina.
to amortize *see* afskrifa.
to asphyxiate *see* 1. kæfa, 2. kafna.
to assemble *see* smala.

to assess *see* 1. meta, 2. áætla.
to asymptotic *see* aðfelldur.
to attune *see* aðlagast.
to auscultation *see* hlustun.
to bake *see* baka.
to bisect *see* helminga.
to braze *see* 1. brasa, 2. harðlóða.
to byte *see* 1. bæti, 2. tölvustafur.
to camphor *see* 1. kamfóra, 2. kamfórutré.
to capitalize *see* 1. eignfæra, 2. hástafa.
to catalyze *see* hvetja.
to categorize *see* innrétta.
to caulk *see* 1. hampþétta, 2. stemma, 3. þétta.
to circulate *see* 1. hringrása, 2. hringsóla.
to come *see* koma.
to commence *see* 1. upphaf, 2. byrja, 3. byrjun.
to compel *see* 1. neyða, 2. þvinga.
to compensate *see* 1. jafna, 2. umbuna.
to compile *see* 1. vistþýða, 2. þýða.
to comply *see* 1. uppfylla, 2. hlíta.
to compute *see* reikna.
to computerize *see* tölvuvæða.
to concede *see* 1. játa, 2. viðurkenna.
to condone *see* þola.
to connect *see* tengja.
to construe *see* 1. túlka, 2. þýða.
to contemplate *see* 1. áforma, 2. hugleiða, 3. íhuga.
to corrode *see* 1. tærast, 2. æta, 3. ryðga, 4. tæra.
to debug *see* kemba.
to decode *see* afkóta.
to decompose *see* 1. sundra, 2. rotna.
to decontaminate *see* 1. afmenga, 2. hreinsa.
to decorticate *see* 1. barkarstýfa, 2. barkarstýfur.
to deflate *see* raunvirða.
to defrost *see* 1. affrysta, 2. þíða.
to delete *see* 1. eyða, 2. seinka, 3. eyðingarhamur, 4. eyðing.
to delude *see* svíkja.
to deny *see* neita.
to deplete *see* fullnýta.
to deploy *see* 1. nota, 2. nýta.
to depolarize *see* 1. afskauta, 2. umpóla.
to derive *see* fá.
to desensitize *see* 1. afnæma, 2. ónæma, 3. skynsvipta.
to detoxify *see* 1. afeitra, 2. afvatna.
to develop *see* 1. framkalla, 2. þróa, 3. þroska.
to differentiate *see* 1. deilda, 2. diffra.
to disassemble *see* 1. baksmala, 2. sundra.
to diversify *see* fjölþætta.
to dormouse *see* heslimús.
to dredger *see* 1. dýpkunarprammi, 2. dýpkunarskip.
to elucidate *see* 1. þýða, 2. útlista, 3. útskýra.
to embed *see* 1. innmúra, 2. innsteypa.

to emend *see* leiðrétta.
to emulsify *see* 1. fleyta, 2. þeyta, 3. blanda, 4. vatnsblanda.
to encapsulate *see* 1. húða, 2. hjúpa.
to encode *see* 1. kóta, 2. tákna, 3. kóða, 4. umtákna.
to endorse *see* 1. samþykkja, 2. styðja, 3. framselja, 4. aðhyllast, 5. ábekja.
to enquire *see* spyrja.
to epigenesis *see* 1. formaukning, 2. formmyndun, 3. síðbirting.
to equip *see* 1. búa, 2. útbúa.
to evaluate *see* 1. virða, 2. ráða, 3. meta, 4. ákvarða, 5. finna.
to evolve *see* þróa.
to execute *see* 1. aftaka, 2. framkvæma, 3. inna.
to expect *see* vænta.
to expectorate *see* hrækja.
to exude *see* 1. vætla, 2. vilsa.
to focalize *see* staðbinda.
to galvanize *see* 1. galva, 2. galvanhúða, 3. rafhúða.
to generalize *see* 1. algilda, 2. alhæfa, 3. hæfa.
to geodesy *see* 1. landmælingafræði, 2. landmælingar, 3. landmæling.
to geometry *see* 1. rúmfræði, 2. flatarmálsfræði, 3. hornafræði.
to identify *see* 1. auðkenna, 2. kenna, 3. samsama, 4. skilgreina.
to imbue *see* fylla.
to impart *see* gefa.
to imprest *see* 1. fyrirframgreiðsla, 2. smágreiðslusjóður.
to induce *see* 1. framkalla, 2. virkja, 3. vekja, 4. spana.
to infiltrate *see* 1. ífara, 2. ífarinn.
to inhibit *see* 1. hamla, 2. hindra, 3. banna.
to initialize *see* 1. frumgilda, 2. frumstilla.
to insure *see* 1. tryggja, 2. vátryggja.
to interact *see* 1. umgangast, 2. víxlverka.
to interrelate *see* umgangast.
to intersect *see* 1. skara, 2. skörun, 3. skerast.
to introduce *see* 1. byrja, 2. kynna.
to ionize *see* jóna.
to itemize *see* sundurliða.
to lactate *see* 1. laktat, 2. mjólka.
to loathe *see* hrylla.
to localize *see* 1. staðgreina, 2. staðmarka, 3. staðbinda, 4. afmarka, 5. staðsetja.
to lube *see* 1. smurefni, 2. olía.
to lubricate *see* smyrja.
to marmot *see* múrmeldýr.
to maximize *see* 1. besta, 2. hámarka, 3. fullstækka.
to minimize *see* lágmarka.
to mislead *see* svíkja.
to modify *see* 1. breyta, 2. endurnýja.
to modulate *see* 1. móta, 2. tempra, 3. stilla.

to narrate *see* segja.
to navigate *see* 1. rápa, 2. sigla, 3. stýra.
to necessitate *see* 1. þvinga, 2. neyða.
to neutralize *see* 1. hlutleysa, 2. afmagna.
to nippers *see* 1. naglbítur, 2. nagltöng, 3. töng.
to normalise *see* 1. norma, 2. staðla.
to normalize *see* staðla.
to noun *see* nafnorð.
to occlude *see* svæfa.
to oscillate *see* 1. snúa, 2. sveiflast, 3. titra.
to overdrive *see* yfirgír.
to oversee *see* stilla.
to overstress *see* 1. yfirálag, 2. ofurálag.
to overwhelm *see* kaffæra.
to oxidize *see* 1. oxa, 2. oxast.
to penetrate *see* 1. borast, 2. smjúga.
to persuade *see* sannfæra.
to preoccupy *see* gleypa.
to prolong *see* 1. framlengja, 2. lengja.
to provide *see* 1. útvega, 2. afla, 3. gefa.
to pursue *see* elta.
to qualify *see* 1. sérgreina, 2. skilgreina.
to quantify *see* 1. meta, 2. mæla, 3. tölubúa, 4. magnhæfa, 5. magngreina.
to quantize *see* 1. búta, 2. skammta.
to ragout *see* ragú.
to react *see* 1. hvarfast, 2. svara.
to reciprocate *see* 1. endurgjalda, 2. róla.
to recognise *see* 1. þekkja, 2. viðurkenna.
to recondition *see* endurbyggja.
to reconstruct *see* 1. endursemja, 2. endurgera, 3. endurbyggja.
to recover *see* 1. batna, 2. endurheimta, 3. endurrétta.
to recursive *see* endurkvæmur.
to recycle *see* 1. endurnýta, 2. endurvinna, 3. endurvinnsla.
to redeem *see* innleysa.
to reenact *see* kynna.
to reimburse *see* endurgreiða.
to reinforce *see* 1. efla, 2. styrkja.
to relate *see* 1. tengjast, 2. vensla, 3. samlæta, 4. segja, 5. tengja.
to renew *see* endurnýja.
to replace *see* 1. endurnýja, 2. umskipting, 3. umskiptingarhamur.
to resect *see* stýfa.
to resent *see* gremjast.
to restrict *see* 1. hamla, 2. hefta, 3. takmarka, 4. þrengja.
to restructure *see* 1. endurmóta, 2. ummóta, 3. umskipa.
to revalue *see* endurmeta.
to saccharify *see* 1. sæta, 2. sykra.
to sanitize *see* 1. hreinsa, 2. gjörhreinsa.

to scavenge *see* 1. hirða, 2. hreinsa, 3. snapa.
to seem *see* þykja.
to send *see* senda.
to sensitize *see* næma.
to solidify *see* harðna.
to stow *see* 1. fansa, 2. hlaða, 3. stafla, 4. stúa.
to stratify *see* lagskipta.
to striate *see* rákóttur.
to summon *see* 1. kalla, 2. stefna.
to synchronize *see* 1. samstilla, 2. samhraða.
to taxis *see* 1. rétting, 2. sækni.
to telefax *see* 1. símsending, 2. símriti, 3. bréfsími,
    4. myndsími, 5. símrit.
to thank *see* þakka.
to tighten *see* 1. herða, 2. þétta.
to transect *see* 1. snið, 2. þverskera, 3. þversnið.
to transform *see* 1. snara, 2. ummynd, 3. ummynda,
    4. umvarpa, 5. myndfall.
to translate *see* 1. þýða, 2. hliðra.
to transmit *see* senda.
to tritium *see* þrívetni.
to undershoot *see* 1. inndindill, 2. skammdindill, 3.
    skammlenda, 4. vandindill.
to underwrite *see* 1. tryggja, 2. vátryggja, 3.
    sölutryggja.
to undo *see* 1. ógilding, 2. afturkalla, 3. afturköllun,
    4. ógilda.
to unhook *see* afkrækja.
to unify *see* 1. jafna, 2. sameina, 3. sameinast, 4.
    samræma.
to validate *see* 1. löggilda, 2. staðfesta, 3.
    viðurkenna.
to warn *see* vara.
to yearn *see* þrá.
toddler *see* trítill.
toe *see* tá.
together *see* saman.
toggle *see* 1. víxla, 2. skipta.
toilet *see* hreinsun.
token *see* 1. kuml, 2. tóki.
tolerance *see* 1. málvik, 2. vikmörk, 3. þolvik, 4.
    þol, 5. þolmörk.
tolerant *see* umburðarlyndur.
tolerate *see* þola.
toll *see* skattur.
tomato *see* tómati.
tomography *see* 1. sneiðmyndagerð, 2.
    sneiðmyndataka.
ton *see* tonn.
tone *see* 1. vöðvaspenna, 2. litblær, 3.
    samdráttarástand, 4. þan, 5. tónn.
toner *see* 1. prentduft, 2. litskerpir.
tongs *see* 1. tengur, 2. töng.
tongue *see* 1. tunga, 2. fjöður.
tonic *see* stælingarlyf.

tonnage *see* 1. burðarmagn, 2. stærð.
tonne *see* tonn.
tonometer *see* spennumælir.
tonsil *see* 1. eitla, 2. hálskirtill.
tonus *see* 1. samdráttarástand, 2. vöðvaspenna.
too *see* 1. einnig, 2. líka, 3. of.
tool *see* 1. stál, 2. tæki, 3. tól, 4. verkfæri.
tooth *see* 1. tönn, 2. dento.
top *see* 1. topptala, 2. þak, 3. snúður, 4. efstur, 5.
    toppur.
tope *see* 1. stjörnuháfur, 2. sléttháfur, 3. músháfur, 4.
    gráháfur.
tophus *see* 1. steinefnahnútur, 2.
    þvagsýrugigtarhnútur, 3. þvagsýrugigtarsteinn.
topic *see* 1. kjarni, 2. umræðuefni, 3. efni, 4. atriði.
topical *see* 1. nútímalegur, 2. núverandi, 3.
    staðbundinn, 4. núgildandi.
topknot *see* skjálgi.
topography *see* 1. landslag, 2. svæðislýsing, 3.
    svæðalýsing, 4. staðfræði, 5. landslagsútlínur.
topology *see* grannfræði.
toponymy *see* 1. örnefnafræði, 2. örnefni, 3.
    staðarnafn.
topsoil *see* 1. gróðurmold, 2. mold.
torch *see* 1. kyndill, 2. logsuðulampi, 3. vasaljós.
tornado *see* 1. hvirfilbylur, 2. skýstrokkur, 3.
    skýstrókur.
toroid *see* 1. holhringsrör, 2. hringspóla.
torpid *see* sljór.
torpor *see* 1. mók, 2. sinnuleysi, 3. dvali, 4. dá, 5.
    sljóleiki.
torque *see* 1. vægi, 2. kraftvægi, 3. snúningsátak, 4.
    snúningsmætti, 5. snúningsvægi.
torsion *see* 1. vindingur, 2. augnvindingur, 3.
    snúningur.
torus *see* 1. blómbotn, 2. gatfláki, 3. hjólflötur, 4.
    hringfeldi.
toss *see* kasta.
total *see* 1. alger, 2. heild, 3. heildartala, 4.
    samanlagt, 5. samtala.
totalitarian *see* alræðishyggja.
totality *see* 1. almyrkvun, 2. heild.
totalizer *see* úrkomusafnmælir.
touch *see* 1. snerta, 2. snerting.
touchdown *see* brautarsnerting.
touching *see* tilfinningasamurlegur.
tough *see* 1. máttagur, 2. sterkur, 3. þungur, 4.
    vandur.
tourism *see* 1. ferðaþjónusta, 2. ferðamál, 3.
    ferðamannastraumur, 4. ferðaútvegur.
tournament *see* Mót.
tower *see* 1. mastur, 2. turn.
town *see* 1. bær, 2. borg, 3. borgarbúar, 4.
    kaupstaður, 5. miðbær.
toxic *see* 1. banvænn, 2. eitraður.

toxicant *see* 1. eitraður, 2. eitur.
toxicity *see* eiturvirkni.
toxin *see* 1. eiturefni, 2. eitur.
toxoid *see* afeitur.
trace *see* 1. endurvarp, 2. lóðning, 3. myndlína, 4. mynstur, 5. rakningur.
tracer *see* 1. merkiefni, 2. sporefni, 3. kenniefni.
trachea *see* 1. loftæð, 2. viðaræð, 3. barki.
tracing *see* rakning.
track *see* 1. kappreiðabraut, 2. sporvídd, 3. slóð, 4. skeiðvöllur, 5. siglingaleið.
tracking *see* 1. hjólasporun, 2. háspennuútslag, 3. fylgni, 4. elting, 5. sjónfylgd.
tract *see* 1. braut, 2. skák, 3. spilda, 4. svæði.
tractable *see* meðfærilegur.
traction *see* 1. grip, 2. spyrna, 3. tog, 4. togun.
trade *see* 1. siglingar, 2. viðskipti, 3. verzlun, 4. iðn, 5. iðngrein.
trademark *see* vörumerki.
traffic *see* 1. umferðarþungi, 2. farðþegafjöldi, 3. umferð.
trail *see* 1. slóð, 2. fylgja, 3. elta, 4. ferill.
trailer *see* 1. eftirvagn, 2. sporhundur, 3. tengivagn, 4. stikla, 5. aftanívagn.
train *see* 1. lest, 2. loftsteinsslóð, 3. rás, 4. þjálfa.
training *see* 1. æfing, 2. hæfing, 3. þjálfun.
trait *see* 1. einkenni, 2. eiginleiki.
trajectory *see* 1. ferill, 2. braut, 3. farbraut.
tramp *see* 1. leiguskip, 2. stapp.
trance *see* 1. dvali, 2. leiðsla, 3. trans.
tranquilizer *see* 1. kyrrilyf, 2. róarlyf.
transaction *see* 1. verk, 2. uppfærsla, 3. verzlun, 4. uppfærsluaðgerð, 5. hreyfing.
transamination *see* amínfærsla.
transceiver *see* sendiviðtæki.
transcendental *see* 1. torræður, 2. yfirskilvitlegur.
transcription *see* umritun.
transducer *see* 1. ferjald, 2. umbreytir, 3. merkjabreytir, 4. breytir, 5. boðbreytir.
transduction *see* 1. umbreyting, 2. umleiðsla, 3. veiruleiðsla.
transect *see* 1. snið, 2. þverskera, 3. þversnið.
transfection *see* 1. genaleiðsla, 2. genefnafærsla, 3. innleiðsla.
transfer *see* 1. millifærsla, 2. tilfærsla, 3. framselja, 4. flutningur, 5. flugskipti.
transferability *see* 1. flutningshæfni, 2. flytjanleiki.
transferable *see* 1. yfirfæranlegur, 2. framseljanlegur.
transference *see* gagnúð.
transform *see* 1. snara, 2. ummynd, 3. ummynda, 4. umvarpa, 5. myndfall.
transformation *see* 1. umbreyting, 2. umvörpun, 3. vörpun, 4. snörun, 5. færsla.
transformer *see* 1. spennir, 2. spennubreytir.

transfusion *see* blóðgjöf.
transhipment *see* umskipun.
transient *see* 1. skammvinnur, 2. svipull, 3. svipall, 4. skyndibreyting, 5. sveipur.
transistor *see* 1. trítill, 2. smári, 3. trasnsistor.
transit *see* 1. þverganga, 2. umflutningur, 3. flutningur, 4. gegnumflutningur.
transition *see* 1. ástandsbreyting, 2. breyting, 3. færsla, 4. formendasveiging, 5. hrökk.
transitory *see* 1. hverfull, 2. svipull, 3. brigðull.
translate *see* 1. þýða, 2. hliðra.
translation *see* 1. hliðrun, 2. hnik, 3. þýðing, 4. yfirfærsla.
translator *see* 1. breytir, 2. þýðandi.
translocation *see* 1. genayfirfærsla, 2. litningayfirfærsla, 3. tilfærsla, 4. yfirfærsla.
translucent *see* 1. hálfgagnsær, 2. hálfglær, 3. glær.
transmission *see* 1. flutningur, 2. framferð, 3. gegnför, 4. gegnskin, 5. gírkassi.
transmissivity *see* 1. Gegnfararhæfni, 2. leiðni, 3. leiðnistuðull.
transmit *see* senda.
transmittal *see* skilaflutningur.
transmittance *see* 1. framferðarhlutfall, 2. gegnfararhlutfall.
transmitter *see* 1. boðefni, 2. sendir, 3. senditæki, 4. skynjari.
transmutation *see* frumefnabreyting.
transom *see* 1. þverstag, 2. þverbiti.
transparency *see* gagnsæi.
transparent *see* 1. augljós, 2. gagnsær, 3. gegnsær, 4. auðskilinn.
transpiration *see* útgufun.
transplantation *see* 1. ágræðsla, 2. ígræðsla, 3. flutningur, 4. færsla.
transponder *see* 1. merkissvari, 2. ratsjársvari.
transport *see* 1. flutningar, 2. flutningur, 3. flytja, 4. reið.
transportation *see* 1. samgöngukerfi, 2. samgöngur, 3. reið, 4. flutningur, 5. flutningastarfsemi.
transpose *see* 1. bylta, 2. umhverfa, 3. yfirfæra.
transposition *see* 1. færsla, 2. upptaka, 3. umröðun, 4. tilfærsla, 5. stökk.
transposon *see* stökkull.
transshipment *see* 1. umskipun, 2. ferming.
transversal *see* þverlægur.
transverse *see* 1. þversnið, 2. þverstæður, 3. þversum.
transvestism *see* 1. fataskiptahneigð, 2. klæðskiptahneigð.
trap *see* 1. Gildra, 2. spjald, 3. hremma, 4. römmun, 5. skilja.
trapezium *see* 1. Trapisan, 2. hálfsamsíðungur, 3. trapisa.
trapezoid *see* 1. hálfsamsíðungur, 2. trapisa.

trash *see* 1. karfa, 2. Sorp.
trauma *see* 1. áfall, 2. áverki, 3. löskun, 4. meiðsli.
trawl *see* 1. botnvarpa, 2. troll, 3. varpa.
trawler *see* togari.
trawling *see* togveiðar.
tray *see* 1. geymabakki, 2. hólf, 3. bakki.
treasurer *see* 1. féhirðir, 2. fjárreiðustjóri, 3. gjaldkeri.
treasury *see* 1. fjármálaráðuneyti, 2. ríkissjóður.
treatment *see* 1. liður, 2. meðferð, 3. meðhöndlun, 4. tilraunaliður.
treaty *see* 1. ríkjasamningur, 2. samkomulag, 3. milliríkjasamningur, 4. sáttmáli.
tree *see* 1. tré, 2. hrísla, 3. hrísluskipan.
trek *see* 1. fjallaferð, 2. hike.
trematode *see* agða.
tremor *see* 1. titringur, 2. riða, 3. skjálfti.
trend *see* 1. tilhneiging, 2. hneigð, 3. langtímaþróun, 4. leitni, 5. stefna.
trepidation *see* 1. beygur, 2. uggur.
treponema *see* gyrmi.
trial *see* 1. tilraun, 2. prófun, 3. réttarhald.
triangle *see* 1. þríhyrningur, 2. þríhyrna.
triangulation *see* 1. þríhyrningamælingar, 2. hornamælingar, 3. þríhyrningamæling.
tribalism *see* 1. ættarbönd, 2. ættarsamfélag, 3. ættbálkahyggja.
tribe *see* 1. ætt, 2. kynþáttur, 3. kynkvísl, 4. hópur, 5. ættbálkur.
trichina *see* 1. fleskormur, 2. purkormur, 3. tríkína.
trick *see* svíkja.
trickle *see* 1. drjúpa, 2. leka, 3. seytla.
trigger *see* 1. gikkur, 2. ræsir, 3. rafmagnspúls, 4. ræsimerki, 5. afhleypir.
triglyceride *see* 1. þríglyseríð, 2. þríglýseríð.
trigonometry *see* hornafræði.
trim *see* 1. innrétting, 2. klæðning, 3. skreyta, 4. snyrta, 5. stafnhalli.
trimming *see* 1. gráðuhreinsun, 2. snyrting, 3. finstilling.
triode *see* 1. þrískauti, 2. þristur, 3. tríóða, 4. þrískautalampi.
trip *see* 1. ferð, 2. ferðalag, 3. ferðalög.
triplet *see* 1. grunnpunktur, 2. þrenna, 3. þrennd, 4. þríburi, 5. þrístig.
trisaccharide *see* þrísykra.
tritium *see* þrívetni.
trivalent *see* þrígildur.
trna *see* tRKS.
troop *see* sveit.
trophoblast *see* 1. næringarhýði, 2. næriþekja.
tropic *see* hvarfbaugur.
tropism *see* 1. leitni, 2. umhvarf.
tropopause *see* 1. veðrahvörf, 2. veðramörk.
troposphere *see* veðrahvolf.

trouble *see* 1. bilun, 2. galli.
troubleshooting *see* 1. bilanagreining, 2. truflanagreining.
trough *see* 1. lægðardrag, 2. öldudalur, 3. sigdalur, 4. trog, 5. lægð.
trout *see* 1. aurriði, 2. silungur, 3. sjóbirtingur, 4. sjóurriði, 5. urriði.
truck *see* 1. vöruvagn, 2. vörubíll, 3. vöruhifreið, 4. vagn.
true *see* 1. réttvísandi, 2. sannur, 3. réttur.
truing *see* afrétting.
truncate *see* 1. stýfa, 2. stytting, 3. þverstýfður.
truncated *see* 1. skorinn, 2. stýfður.
truncation *see* 1. stöðvun, 2. stýfing.
trunk *see* 1. farangursgeymsla, 2. tengilína, 3. skott, 4. farangursgeymla, 5. stofn.
trust *see* 1. einokunarhringur, 2. fyrirtækjahringur, 3. fyrirtækjasamteypa, 4. traust.
trustee *see* 1. fjárhaldsmaður, 2. fjárvörslumaður.
trustworthy *see* 1. áreiðanlegur, 2. traustur.
truth *see* 1. sannleikur, 2. topptala, 3. tryggð.
trypsin *see* 1. trypsín, 2. trýpsín.
tryptophan *see* 1. trý, 2. trýtófan.
tsunami *see* 1. sjávarskafl, 2. skjálftaflóðbylgja.
tub *see* 1. dallur, 2. ker.
tuba *see* trompet.
tube *see* 1. lampi, 2. pípa, 3. rör, 4. slanga, 5. útvarpslampi.
tubercle *see* 1. berkill, 2. hnjótur, 3. arða, 4. smáhnúður.
tuberculosis *see* 1. berklar, 2. berklaveiki.
tubular *see* 1. hólklaga, 2. pípulaga, 3. rörlaga.
tubule *see* pípla.
tuft *see* 1. þúfa, 2. toppur.
tularemia *see* hérasótt.
tummy *see* 1. kviður, 2. magi.
tumor *see* 1. hnútur, 2. fyrirferðaraukning, 3. æxli.
tuna *see* túnfiskur.
tundra *see* 1. freðmýri, 2. túndra.
tune *see* 1. aðlagast, 2. samstilling, 3. stilla, 4. tíðnistilla.
tungsten *see* 1. þungsteinn, 2. volfram, 3. wolfram.
tunneling *see* smug.
tup *see* hrútur.
tuple *see* 1. færsla, 2. lína.
turbid *see* 1. gruggugur, 2. morugur.
turbidity *see* 1. grugg, 2. gruggun, 3. mor.
turbine *see* 1. hverfill, 2. túrbína.
turbot *see* sandhverfa.
turbulence *see* 1. iðustreymi, 2. loftsveipir, 3. ókyrrð, 4. kvika, 5. iða.
turgid *see* 1. þrútinn, 2. tútinn, 3. tútnaður.
turkey *see* Kalkún.
turn *see* 1. snúa, 2. vafningar, 3. vöf, 4. vaf, 5. umbreyta.

turnbuckle *see* 1. strekkingarró, 2. strengiró, 3. stagherðir.
turnip *see* 1. næpukál, 2. fóðurnæpa, 3. næpa.
turnover *see* 1. viðskiptavelta, 2. velta, 3. heildartiðni, 4. umsetning.
turpentine *see* terpentína.
turtle *see* 1. skjaldbaka, 2. táta.
tusk *see* keila.
tweezers *see* 1. plokktöng, 2. flísatöng.
twelve *see* tólf.
twenty *see* tuttuga.
twig *see* kvistur.
twilight *see* 1. rökkur, 2. ljósaskipti.
twin *see* 1. ĝemela, 2. tví, 3. tvíburi.
twine *see* 1. seglgarn, 2. trollgarn.
twins *see* 1. ĝemela, 2. ĝemelo.
twist *see* snúðleiðir.
two *see* 1. tveir, 2. tveggja, 3. tvær, 4. tvö.
tympanum *see* 1. gaflflötur, 2. hljóðhimna.
type *see* 1. gerð, 2. manngerð, 3. rita, 4. tag, 5. tegund.
typed *see* 1. tagaður, 2. tagskiptur.
typewriter *see* ritvél.
typhoid *see* 1. taugaveikilegur, 2. taugaveiki.
typhoon *see* 1. hvirfilbylur, 2. fellibylur.
typhus *see* 1. flekkusótt, 2. taugaveiki.
typical *see* dæmigerður.
typology *see* 1. formgerðarflokkun, 2. gerðaflokkun, 3. gerðafræði, 4. manngerðaflokkun, 5. manngerðafræði.
tyre *see* hjólbarði.
tyrosine *see* 1. týr, 2. týrósín.

U

ugly *see* ljótur.
ulcer *see* 1. fleiður, 2. særi, 3. sár.
ullage *see* borð.
ultimate *see* endanlegur.
ultrasonic *see* örhljóðs.
ultrasound *see* 1. yfirhljóð, 2. örhljóð, 3. úthljóð.
ultraviolet *see* 1. útfjólublár, 2. útblámi, 3. útblár.
umbra *see* 1. alskuggi, 2. blettkjarni, 3. blettmiðja, 4. kjarni.
unaccompanied *see* 1. aleinn, 2. einn, 3. einmana.
unanimity *see* 1. samhljóða, 2. samstaða.
unassuming *see* hógvær.
unauthorized *see* 1. óheimilt, 2. ósamþykkt, 3. óviðkomandi.
unbalance *see* 1. misvægi, 2. ójafnvægi.
unbiased *see* 1. skakkalaus, 2. meðalgildisréttur, 3. óbjagaður, 4. óhlutdrægur, 5. óvilhallur.

uncertainty *see* óvissa.
uncle *see* 1. móðurbróðir, 2. föðurbróðir.
uncommon *see* sjaldgæfur.
unconformity *see* mislægi.
uncongenial *see* óviðkunnanlegur.
unconscious *see* 1. dulvitaður, 2. dulvitund, 3. meðvitundarlaus.
uncooked *see* hrár.
unction *see* makstur.
undamaged *see* 1. ólaskaður, 2. óskemmdur.
undercut *see* 1. úrsnörun, 2. skurður.
underemployment *see* atvinnuleysi.
underground *see* neðanjarðarlest.
underhand *see* óheiðarlegur.
underline *see* undirstrika.
underpants *see* kalsono.
underscore *see* undirstrik.
undershoot *see* 1. inndindill, 2. skammdindill, 3. skammlenda, 4. vandindill.
undersize *see* undirstærð.
understand *see* skilja.
understatement *see* vanskráning.
underwrite *see* 1. tryggja, 2. vátryggja, 3. sölutryggja.
underwriter *see* 1. sölutryggjandi, 2. tryggjandi, 3. vátryggjandi.
undo *see* 1. ógilding, 2. afturkalla, 3. afturköllun, 4. ógilda.
undoing *see* ógilding.
undoubted *see* óvís.
undoubtedly *see* vafalaust.
undulation *see* bylgjuhreyfing.
unemployment *see* atvinnuleysi.
unequal *see* 1. mislangur, 2. ójafn.
uneven *see* 1. grófur, 2. ósléttur, 3. ójafn.
unfortunate *see* óheppinn.
ungrateful *see* vanþakklátur.
ungulate *see* hófdýr.
unhappy *see* óhamingjusamur.
unhealthy *see* 1. heilsutæpur, 2. heilsuveill, 3. óhraustlegur.
unhook *see* afkrækja.
unicellular *see* einfruma.
unification *see* 1. sameining, 2. samræming, 3. jöfnun.
uniform *see* einkennisbúningur.
unify *see* 1. jafna, 2. sameina, 3. sameinast, 4. samræma.
unilateral *see* 1. einhliða, 2. einhliðmælt.
union *see* 1. sammengi, 2. sameining, 3. verkalýðsfélag, 4. samtök, 5. samruni.
unionism *see* 1. bandalagsstefna, 2. sameiningarstefna.
unipolar *see* einskauta.
unisexual *see* 1. einkynja, 2. sérkynja.

unit see 1. mælieining, 2. vörublendi, 3. vörublanda, 4. vörumengi, 5. eining.
unitary see 1. samræmdur, 2. einoka, 3. óskiptur.
united see Samstæð.
units see EININGAR.
univalent see 1. eingildur, 2. einstæður, 3. staklitningur.
universal see 1. almennur, 2. alþjóðlegur, 3. alkvæður, 4. altækur, 5. alhæfur.
universe see alheimur.
university see háskóli.
unkind see 1. óvænn, 2. óvingjarnlegur.
unload see afferma.
unloaded see 1. álagslaus, 2. óhlaðinn.
unloading see afferming.
unmarried see ógiftur.
unmistakable see óvís.
unmistakably see vafalaust.
unpalatable see óþægilegur.
unpleasant see 1. óþægilegur, 2. óvænn, 3. óviðkunnanlegur, 4. óvingjarnlegur.
unpretentious see hógvær.
unquestionable see óvís.
unquestionably see vafalaust.
unrecorded see 1. óbókfært, 2. óbókfærður.
unreliable see 1. óáreiðanlegur, 2. ótraustur.
unsaturated see ómettaður.
unselfishness see 1. örlæti, 2. rausnarskapur, 3. gjafmildi.
unsettled see óstöðugt.
unspecified see 1. óskilgreindur, 2. ótilgreindur.
unstable see 1. óstöðugur, 2. valtur.
untainted see hreinn.
unthankful see vanþakklátur.
untrue see ósannur.
untrustworthy see 1. óáreiðanlegur, 2. ótraustur.
unwell see 1. sjúkur, 2. veikur.
upbraid see átelja.
update see 1. dagrétting, 2. núrétting, 3. uppfæra, 4. núrétta, 5. leiðrétta.
upgrade see 1. stigbæta, 2. stigbót.
upkeep see viðhald.
uplift see landris.
upload see uppflutningur.
upright see 1. heiðarlegur, 2. uppréttur.
upset see 1. hnoða, 2. stytta.
upstream see rangsælis.
upward see upp.
uranium see 1. úran, 2. úraníum.
uranoschisis see gómklauf.
urbanization see 1. borgmyndun, 2. þéttbýlismyndun.
urea see 1. karbamíð, 2. þvagefni.
uremia see þvageitrun.

ureter see 1. nýraleiðari, 2. nýrnaleiðari, 3. þvagáll, 4. þvagpípa.
urine see þvag.
urology see þvagfærafræði.
urticaria see ofsakláði.
usage see 1. málnotkun, 2. málvenja, 3. not, 4. notkun, 5. siður.
use see 1. brúka, 2. nota.
user see 1. notandi, 2. nýtir.
usual see venjulegur.
usufruct see 1. nýtingarréttur, 2. afnotaréttur.
usurp see yfirtaka.
usury see 1. okur, 2. okurlán, 3. okurvextir.
uterus see leg.
utilitarianism see 1. gagnsemishyggja, 2. nytjahyggja, 3. nytjastefna, 4. nytsemishyggja.
utility see 1. nytjar, 2. nytsemi, 3. notkun, 4. notagildi, 5. not.
utilization see nýting.
utilize see 1. nota, 2. nýta.
utricle see 1. hvekkskjatti, 2. skjatti, 3. skjóða.
utterance see segð.
uvula see úfur.

V

vacancy see 1. eyða, 2. eyðuveila.
vaccination see 1. bólusetning, 2. kúabólusetning, 3. ónæming.
vaccine see 1. bóluefni, 2. ónæmingarefni, 3. kúabóluefni.
vaccinia see 1. kúabóla, 2. kúabóluveira.
vacuole see 1. frymisbóla, 2. safabóla.
vacuum see 1. lofttæmi, 2. sogkraftur, 3. tóm, 4. tómarúm, 5. undirþrýstingur.
vagina see 1. skeið, 2. slíður, 3. leggöng, 4. blaðslíður.
vaginitis see slíðurbólga.
vale see dalur.
valence see 1. gildi, 2. gildistala, 3. löð.
valency see 1. gildi, 2. hleðslutala.
valid see 1. réttmætur, 2. gildur.
validate see 1. löggilda, 2. staðfesta, 3. viðurkenna.
validation see 1. réttmæting, 2. staðfesting, 3. viðurkenning, 4. gilding.
validity see 1. gildi, 2. lögmæti, 3. réttmæti.
valine see 1. val, 2. valín.
valley see dalur.
valuable see sætur.
valuation see 1. mat, 2. matsgjörð, 3. virðing.
value see 1. virði, 2. verðgildi, 3. gildi, 4. verð, 5. verðmæti.

valve *see* 1. ventill, 2. lampi, 3. loka, 4. loki, 5. útvarpslampi.
van *see* 1. vagn, 2. sendiferðabíll, 3. sendibifreið, 4. sendibíll.
vanadium *see* 1. vanadín, 2. vanadíum.
vane *see* 1. spjald, 2. blað, 3. spaði.
vanity *see* 1. hégómi, 2. hégómaskapur.
vapor *see* 1. eimur, 2. gufa.
vaporization *see* 1. gufumyndun, 2. sundrun, 3. uppgufun.
vaporizer *see* eimir.
vapour *see* 1. eimur, 2. gufa.
variability *see* 1. breytileiki, 2. flökt.
variable *see* 1. breyta, 2. breytistærð, 3. breytilegur.
variance *see* 1. dreifni, 2. fervik, 3. frávik, 4. mismunur, 5. tvíveldisfrávik.
variant *see* 1. afbrigði, 2. gróðurtilbrigði, 3. tilbrigði.
variate *see* hending.
variation *see* 1. hnikun, 2. Varijanta, 3. tilbrigði, 4. segulskekkja, 5. hnik.
variety *see* 1. afbrigði, 2. stofn.
variola *see* bólusótt.
varistor *see* rafeindaviðnám.
varix *see* 1. æðahnútur, 2. bláæðaskúlk.
varnish *see* 1. lakk, 2. fernis, 3. glæra, 4. glærulakk.
vasectomy *see* sáðrásarúrnám.
vasoconstriction *see* 1. æðaþrenging, 2. æðasamdráttur.
vasodilator *see* 1. æðavíkkandi, 2. æðavíkkari.
vast *see* 1. rúmgóður, 2. víður.
veal *see* kálfskjöt.
vector *see* 1. vigur, 2. beind, 3. genaferja, 4. smitberi, 5. stefna.
veer *see* snúast.
vegetarian *see* 1. grænmetisæta, 2. jurtaæta.
vegetation *see* 1. gróandi, 2. gróður, 3. jurtir, 4. lokuhrúður, 5. ofvöxtur.
vegetative *see* 1. ómeðvitaður, 2. ósjálfráður, 3. viljalaus.
vehicle *see* 1. ökutæki, 2. reið, 3. burðarefni, 4. vagn.
vein *see* 1. æð, 2. bláæð, 3. strengur.
velocity *see* 1. hraðavektor, 2. hraðavigur, 3. hraði, 4. veltuhraði.
velum *see* 1. segl, 2. uppgómur.
venation *see* 1. íæðun, 2. æðasetning, 3. æðaskipan, 4. bláæðavæðing.
vend *see* selja.
vendor *see* seljandi.
veneer *see* 1. spónlögn, 2. viðarlögn, 3. viðarspónn.
venerable *see* gamall.
venesection *see* æðaskurður.
vent *see* 1. loftop, 2. útrás, 3. loftunarop, 4. loftgat, 5. öndunarop.

ventilate *see* 1. viðra, 2. blóðilda, 3. loftræsta.
ventilation *see* 1. Loftun, 2. öndun, 3. útloftun, 4. loftskipting, 5. loftræsing.
ventilator *see* 1. loftræstitæki, 2. vifta.
ventral *see* 1. aðhverfur, 2. kviðlægur.
ventricle *see* 1. heilahol, 2. hólf, 3. hvolf, 4. slegill.
venture *see* 1. þora, 2. áhættufyrirtæki, 3. áhætta, 4. vogun.
venue *see* 1. heimili, 2. staður, 3. vettvangur.
verb *see* sagnorð.
verbal *see* yrtur.
verdigris *see* 1. eirgræna, 2. spansgræna, 3. spanskgræna.
verge *see* egg.
verification *see* 1. staðfesting, 2. fylgiskjal, 3. sannprófun, 4. sönnun.
verify *see* 1. staðfesta, 2. sanna, 3. sannprófa.
vermicide *see* 1. ormadeyðir, 2. ormaeyðir, 3. ormalyf.
vermicular *see* 1. ormalegur, 2. ormlaga.
vermiform *see* ormlaga.
vermifuge *see* ormalyf.
vermin *see* meindýr.
vernier *see* 1. brotamælir, 2. níundarkvarði.
verruca *see* varta.
versatile *see* 1. fjölhæfur, 2. hreyfanlegur.
version *see* 1. augnsnúningur, 2. gerð, 3. þýðing, 4. útgáfa, 5. vending.
versus *see* gegn.
vertebrate *see* hryggdýr.
vertex *see* 1. tengipunktur, 2. brotpunktur, 3. hnútur, 4. hornpunktur, 5. oddpunktur.
vertical *see* 1. lóðréttur, 2. lóðlína, 3. lóðrétt.
vertigo *see* svimi.
very *see* 1. æði, 2. eigin, 3. mjög.
vesicant *see* blöðrulyf.
vesicle *see* 1. blaðra, 2. blöðrungur, 3. bóla.
vesicular *see* blöðrulaga.
vessel *see* 1. æð, 2. ílát.
vestibule *see* 1. forgarður, 2. önd.
vestige *see* 1. líffærisleif, 2. leif.
vestry *see* sóknarnefnd.
vet *see* dýralæknir.
veterinary *see* dýralæknir.
veto *see* 1. neitunarvald, 2. synjunarvald.
via *see* 1. gegnum, 2. um.
viability *see* 1. lífvæni, 2. lífvænleiki.
viable *see* lífvænn.
vibration *see* 1. titringur, 2. hristingur, 3. sveifla.
vibrator *see* 1. bifrari, 2. riðill, 3. titrari, 4. titurriðill.
vibrograph *see* titringsriti.
vice *see* skrúfstykki.
video *see* 1. sjá, 2. vídeó, 3. sjóngögn, 4. stokkur, 5. víðsjá.

view see 1. viðhverfa, 2. yfirlit, 3. útsýn, 4. töflusýn,
5. sýnd.
viewpoint see 1. álit, 2. skoðun.
vigilance see árvekni.
vigilant see 1. árvakur, 2. aðgætinn.
vigorous see 1. máttagur, 2. sterkur.
vigour see 1. athafsnemi, 2. kraftur, 3. þróttur, 4.
virkni.
vile see 1. hræðilegur, 2. viðbjóðslegur.
vilify see slúðra.
village see 1. þorpsbúar, 2. þorp.
villous see loðinn.
vine see 1. leiðaval, 2. vafningsjurt, 3. klifurjurt.
vinegar see edik.
violation see 1. brot, 2. rof.
violet see fjólublár.
virile see karlmannlegur.
virion see 1. veirueind, 2. veiruögn.
viroid see veirungur.
virology see veirufræði.
virtual see ímyndaður.
virtually see 1. nær, 2. næstum.
virulence see 1. meinvirkni, 2. smithæfni, 3.
sýkingarmáttur.
virulent see 1. meinvirkur, 2. vígur.
virus see 1. vírus, 2. veira.
viscera see 1. iður, 2. innyfli.
viscid see 1. klístraður, 2. líminn, 3. seigfljótandi.
viscometer see seigjumælir.
viscosity see 1. fljótanleiki, 2. þykkt, 3. seigla, 4.
seigja.
viscous see 1. seigfljótandi, 2. seigur.
visibility see 1. skyggni, 2. tilvísanleiki, 3.
vísunarsvið.
visible see 1. sjáanlegur, 2. sýnilegur.
vision see 1. sjón, 2. sýn.
visual see sjón.
visualization see 1. hugarsýn, 2. myndbirting.
vitalism see 1. lífhyggja, 2. lífsorkukenning.
vitality see 1. lífsfjör, 2. lífsorka, 3. lífsþróttur, 4.
táp, 5. fjör.
vitamin see 1. vítamín, 2. fjörefni.
vitiligo see skjallblettur.
vitreous see 1. glær, 2. gleıkenndur.
vivification see lífgun.
viviparous see 1. blaðgróinn, 2. fósturbær.
vivisection see kvikskurður.
vocabulary see orðabók.
vocation see 1. atvinna, 2. fag, 3. köllun, 4. starf, 5.
starfsgrein.
voice see 1. rödd, 2. mæli, 3. mynd, 4. rómur.
voicing see röddun.
void see 1. innfláki, 2. ógiltur, 3. tómur.
volatile see 1. rokgjarn, 2. sveiflukenndur.

volatility see 1. flökt, 2. hverfulleiki, 3. hviklyndi,
4. óstöðugleiki, 5. rokgirni.
volcano see 1. eldstöð, 2. eldfjall.
volcanology see 1. eldfjallafræði, 2. jarðeldafræði.
vole see vatnastúfa.
volition see vilji.
volleyball see blak.
voltage see 1. spennumunur, 2. rafspenna, 3. spenna.
voltameter see voltamælir.
voltmeter see 1. spennumælir, 2. voltmælir.
volume see 1. hljóðmagn, 2. hljóðstyrkur, 3. magn,
4. raunvirði, 5. rúmmál.
voluntary see 1. viljastýrður, 2. sjálfráður, 3.
viljafrjáls.
volvulus see garnaflækja.
vomit see 1. spýja, 2. æla, 3. gubba, 4. uppsala.
vomiting see 1. uppköst, 2. uppsala.
voracious see 1. átfrekur, 2. matgráðugur.
vortex see 1. iða, 2. straumsveipur, 3. sveipur, 4.
hvirfill.
vote see 1. atkvæðaseðill, 2. kosningaréttur, 3.
kosning, 4. atkvæði, 5. atkvæðisréttur.
voter see kjósandi.
voting see atkvæðagreiðsla.
voucher see 1. úttektarseðill, 2. ávísun, 3. fylgiskjal,
4. kvittun.
voyage see 1. ferð, 2. sigling.
voyeurism see gægjuhneigð.
vulcanization see 1. brennisteinsmeðferð, 2.
gúmmísuða.
vulgar see ókurteis.
vulnerability see 1. nerti, 2. veila, 3. varnarleysi, 4.
særanleiki, 5. tjónnæmi.
vulnerable see 1. berskjaldaður, 2. særanlegur.
vulture see 1. gæsagammur, 2. gammur.
vulva see kvensköp.

W

wage see 1. laun, 2. salajro.
wager see veðja.
wages see 1. laun, 2. vinnulaun, 3. salajro, 4.
laborpago, 5. konduki.
waggon see vagn.
waist see mitti.
wait see vænta.
waiter see thjónn.
waiver see 1. afsal, 2. tilslökun, 3. undanþága.
wake see kjölfar.
wakefulness see vökuvitund.
walk see ganga.
wall see 1. gerði, 2. veggur, 3. þil.
walleye see glæruvagl.

walnut see 1. valhneta, 2. hnotutré, 3. hnotviður, 4. valhnot.

walrus see rostungur.

wandering see 1. flakkandi, 2. sveimandi.

want see 1. ósk, 2. vilja.

war see ófriður.

ward see sjúkradeild.

wardrobe see skápur.

warehouse see 1. vöruhús, 2. vörugeymsla, 3. pakkhús.

warfare see ófriður.

warm see 1. heitur, 2. hjartanlegur, 3. hlýr, 4. varmur, 5. vinsamlegur.

warmonger see stríðsæsingamaður.

warn see vara.

warp see 1. bjagast, 2. verpast.

warping see 1. verping, 2. verpingur, 3. bjögun, 4. kast, 5. vindingur.

warrant see kaupheimild.

warranty see ábyrgð.

warship see herskip.

wart see 1. varta, 2. festiflötur.

wash see þvo.

washbowl see skál.

washer see 1. skífa, 2. þvottatæki.

washing see 1. sethraðagreining, 2. vatnsskolun.

waste see 1. úrgangur, 2. sorp, 3. tærast, 4. sóun, 5. rýrna.

watch see úr.

water see 1. vatn, 2. vatna, 3. vökva.

waterborne see sjóleiðis.

watercress see vætukarsi.

waterfall see foss.

waterlogged see 1. vatnssósa, 2. vatnsósa.

watermelon see 1. blóðmelóna, 2. vatnsmelóna.

waterproof see 1. vatnsheldur, 2. vatnsþétt, 3. vatnsþéttur, 4. vatnsþolið.

waters see 1. hafsvæði, 2. legvatn.

watershed see 1. blóðrásaskil, 2. vatnaskil, 3. vatnasvið.

waterspout see 1. rör, 2. skýstrokkur, 3. vatnsstrokkur, 4. pípa.

watertight see vatnsþéttur.

waterworks see 1. vatnsdælustöð, 2. vatnsveita.

watt see 1. afl, 2. vatt.

wattmeter see 1. aflmælir, 2. raunaflsmælir, 3. vattmælir, 4. wattmælir.

wave see 1. sveifla, 2. alda, 3. bára, 4. bylgja.

waveform see 1. bylgjuform, 2. bylgjulögun.

waveguide see 1. bylgjuleiðari, 2. ölduleiðir, 3. öldustokkur.

wavelength see 1. bylgjulengd, 2. öldulengd.

wax see 1. bón, 2. vax, 3. vaxa.

way see 1. vani, 2. vegur.

weak see veikur.

weaken see þynna.

weakening see veiking.

weakfish see doði.

wealth see 1. auðlegð, 2. auður.

wealthy see ríkur.

weapon see vopn.

wear see 1. slit, 2. slitna, 3. slitþol.

weasel see 1. hreysiköttur, 2. vesla.

weather see 1. veður, 2. illviðri, 3. óveður, 4. veðurfar.

weathering see 1. veðrun, 2. vegghetta.

web see 1. skref, 2. styrking, 3. þrep, 4. vefnaður, 5. vefur.

webbed see 1. fitjaður, 2. með, 3. veflíkur.

wed see giftast.

wedding see brúðkaup.

wedge see 1. fleygur, 2. misgengisfleygur, 3. kíll, 4. fleygjárn, 5. hæðarhryggur.

wedlock see hjónaband.

weed see illgresi.

week see vika.

weep see gráta.

weeping see 1. seytl, 2. vætl.

weighbridge see 1. bílavog, 2. hafnarvog.

weight see 1. þyngd, 2. vægi, 3. vigt, 4. vog, 5. lóð.

weird see 1. skrýtinn, 2. vitlaus.

weld see 1. logsjóða, 2. málmsuða, 3. rafsjóða, 4. sjóða, 5. suða.

weldable see 1. sjóðanlegt, 2. sjóðanlegur.

welding see 1. málmsuða, 2. spansuða, 3. suða, 4. spankveiking, 5. lóðun.

welfare see 1. farsæld, 2. velferð, 3. velmegun.

well see 1. brunnur, 2. uppspretta, 3. vatnsból, 4. mjög, 5. lind.

wench see 1. stelpa, 2. stúlka.

west see vestur.

westerlies see 1. vestanvindabelti, 2. vestanvindabeltið, 3. vestanvindar.

westward see vestur.

westwards see vestur.

wet see 1. blautur, 2. votur, 3. rakur.

wetland see votlendi.

whale see hvalur.

whaleback see 1. hvalbakur, 2. bakki.

whaling see hvalveiðar.

wharf see bryggja.

wheat see hveiti.

wheel see 1. hjól, 2. stíga, 3. felga.

wheelbase see 1. hjólahaf, 2. öxlaafstaða.

wheelhouse see 1. hjólhús, 2. hjólskál, 3. stýrishús.

when see hvenær.

whence see hvaðan.

where see 1. hvar, 2. hvert.

whereas see meðan.

whet see 1. brýna, 2. hvessa, 3. skarpa, 4. skerpa.

whetstone see 1. hverfisteinn, 2. steinbrýni, 3. brýni.
while see 1. tíð, 2. tími, 3. meðan.
whip see svipa.
whirl see 1. hvirfill, 2. þyrlast, 3. þeytingur, 4. iða, 5. snarsnúa.
whirlpool see 1. hringiða, 2. svelgur.
whirlwind see hvirfilvindur.
whisper see hvísla.
white see 1. hvítur, 2. Hvítt.
whitefish see bolfiskur.
whitewood see 1. hvítviður, 2. túlípanviður.
whiting see 1. lýsa, 2. lundaseiði, 3. jakobsfiskur.
who see 1. hver, 2. Alþjóðaheilbrigðismálastofnunin.
whole see heill.
wholesale see 1. heildsala, 2. heildverslun.
wholesaler see 1. heildsali, 2. stórkaupmaður.
whore see 1. hóra, 2. skækja.
whorl see 1. hvirfing, 2. sveipur.
wick see kveikur.
wide see 1. breiður, 2. víður, 3. rúmgóður.
widow see 1. einstæðingur, 2. ekkja, 3. hóruungi.
widower see ekkill.
width see 1. breidd, 2. vídd.
wife see 1. eiginkona, 2. kona.
wild see reiður.
wildcat see 1. skógarköttur, 2. villiköttur.
wilderness see 1. óbyggð, 2. öræfi, 3. auðn.
wildlife see náttúrulíf.
will see 1. vilji, 2. erfðaskrá.
willing see reiðubúinn.
willingness see vilji.
winch see 1. dráttarspil, 2. spil, 3. vinda.
wind see 1. vindur, 2. veður, 3. vinda.
windage see vindáhrif.
windbreak see 1. skjólbelti, 2. skjólgarður, 3. skjólveggur, 4. limgerði.
winding see 1. spóla, 2. sveigja, 3. vaf, 4. vafningur, 5. vefja.
windlass see 1. akkerisvinda, 2. spil, 3. vinda.
windmill see vindmylla.
window see 1. gluggi, 2. minnisgluggi, 3. skjár, 4. hlið.
windowpane see 1. kaliforníukoli, 2. slétthverfa, 3. deplahverfa.
windpipe see barki.
windscreen see framrúða.
windshield see framrúða.
windward see 1. kulborði, 2. vindborðsmegin, 3. vindborði, 4. kulborðsmegin, 5. vindátt.
wine see vin.
wing see 1. vængur, 2. skipssíða, 3. þunnildi, 4. bretti, 5. börð.
winter see 1. vetur, 2. vetrarlegur.

wipe see þurka.
wiper see 1. snertiarmur, 2. þurrka.
wire see 1. þáttur, 2. vír, 3. sími, 4. síma, 5. málmvír.
wireless see 1. þráðlaus, 2. útvarp, 3. geisli.
wiring see innitaugar.
wish see 1. ósk, 2. vilji, 3. óska, 4. vilja.
wishbone see 1. geislastengur, 2. klofajárn, 3. klofspyrna, 4. spyrna.
witch see 1. langlúra, 2. galdranorn.
with see 1. við, 2. með.
withdrawal see 1. afturköllun, 2. úrsögn, 3. úttekt.
wizard see 1. álfur, 2. gandálfur.
wobble see 1. reik, 2. skjögur.
wolf see 1. úlfur, 2. vargur.
wolffish see 1. flekkjaháfur, 2. steinbítur, 3. steinbítsgóna, 4. sladdi, 5. brúngrani.
woman see 1. kona, 2. kvenmaður.
womb see leg.
wonder see 1. furða, 2. undrast, 3. undrun.
wood see 1. skógur, 2. tré, 3. trjáviður, 4. Viður.
woodcutter see skógarhöggsmaður.
woodland see skógur.
woodpecker see spæta.
woodsman see skógarhöggsmaður.
woody see viðarkenndur.
wool see ull.
word see orð.
work see 1. verk, 2. vinna, 3. starfa, 4. verka, 5. verko.
workable see vinnanlegur.
workday see vinnudagur.
worker see 1. starfsmaður, 2. vinnumaur, 3. vinnudýr, 4. þerna, 5. verkamaður.
workforce see 1. mannafli, 2. starfslið.
workload see vinnuálag.
workman see verkamaður.
workmanship see 1. handbragð, 2. smíð.
works see 1. labori, 2. verko, 3. skulpti, 4. laboro, 5. funkciigi.
workshop see 1. vinnufundur, 2. smiðja, 3. verkstæði, 4. verkstofa, 5. hugmyndasmiðja.
workstation see vinnustöð.
world see 1. veröld, 2. heimur.
worm see 1. maðkur, 2. ormur, 3. snákur, 4. snigill.
wormwood see 1. eðalmalurt, 2. remmujurt, 3. malurt, 4. fjaðra.
worn see 1. jaskaður, 2. notaður, 3. slitinn.
worse see verri.
worst see verstur.
worth see 1. verð, 2. virði.
worthwhile see verður.
worthy see verður.
wound see 1. sár, 2. særi.
wounded see særður.

wrangle *see* 1. rifrildi, 2. rífast.
wraparound *see* 1. umhlaup, 2. kápa.
wrapper *see* lok.
wrasses *see* varafiskar.
wreck *see* 1. brotna, 2. flak, 3. flugvélarbrak, 4. flugvélarflak.
wrench *see* 1. lykill, 2. skrúflykill, 3. skrúfukraftur.
wrist *see* 1. hreifi, 2. úlnliður.
write *see* 1. skrifa, 2. rita.
wrong *see* 1. móðga, 2. Rangur.

X

xanthic *see* gulur.
xanthophyll *see* 1. sanþófýll, 2. vefjagula.
xanthous *see* 1. gulleitur, 2. gulur.
xenon *see* senón.
xiphoid *see* sverðlaga.
xylene *see* 1. sýlen, 2. sýlól, 3. xýlen.
xylose *see* 1. viðarsykur, 2. xýlósi.

Y

y *see* yttrín.
yacht *see* 1. snekkja, 2. lystiskúta.
yam *see* 1. jamrótarhnýði, 2. kínakartafla.
yard *see* 1. bæjarhlað, 2. hlað.
yarrow *see* 1. jarðhumall, 2. mellifolia, 3. vallhumall.
yaw *see* 1. geiga, 2. hliðarhreyfing, 3. svansa, 4. veltingur.
yaws *see* himberjasótt.
yeah *see* já.
year *see* ár.
yearn *see* þrá.
yearning *see* þrá.
yeast *see* 1. ger, 2. gersveppur.
yellow *see* gulur.
yes *see* já.
yesterday *see* gær.
yet *see* þó.
yew *see* 1. barrlind, 2. bogviður, 3. ýr, 4. ýviður.
yield *see* 1. ávöxtun, 2. eftirtekja, 3. afrakstur, 4. framlegð, 5. arður.
yoke *see* 1. klafi, 2. ok, 3. oki.
yolk *see* 1. blómi, 2. eggjarauða, 3. fósturnesti, 4. gula, 5. guluforði.
yonder *see* 1. þangað, 2. þar.
young *see* ungur.
youngster *see* 1. ungdómur, 2. barn.

youth *see* 1. æska, 2. ungdómur.
ytterbium *see* 1. ytterbín, 2. ytterbíum.
yttrium *see* 1. yttrín, 2. yttríum.

Z

zebra *see* sebrahestur.
zenith *see* 1. hvirfilpunktur, 2. himinhvirfill, 3. hápunktur.
zero *see* 1. núll, 2. núllstöð.
zinc *see* 1. sink, 2. zink.
zipper *see* rennilás.
zirconium *see* 1. sirkon, 2. sirkoníum.
zodiac *see* 1. dýrahringur, 2. dýrahringurinn.
zona *see* belti.
zonation *see* 1. gróðurbeltun, 2. beltun.
zone *see* 1. svæði, 2. svæða, 3. sérsvæði, 4. sérsvæða, 5. belti.
zoning *see* 1. sérsvæðing, 2. svæðisskipulag, 3. byggðaskipulag, 4. svæðing, 5. svæðaskipting.
zoogeography *see* dýralandafræði.
zoology *see* dýrafræði.
zoom *see* 1. þysja, 2. renna, 3. súma.
zoster *see* ristill.
zucchini *see* 1. kúrbítur, 2. dvergbítur.
zygote *see* okfruma.
zygotene *see* okþráðlufasi.
zymogen *see* 1. símógen, 2. forensím, 3. símogen.

Vocabulary Study Lists

Verbs (Icelandic - English)

áætla	assess
ábekja	endorse
aðfelldur	asymptotic
aðgreina	distinguish
aðhyllast	endorse
aðlaga	adapt
aðlagast	attune
aðskilja	segregate
æta	corrode
ætla	propose
ættleiða	adopt
afeitra	detoxify
afferma	unload
affrysta	defrost
afkóta	decode
afkrækja	unhook
afla	provide
afmagna	neutralize
afmarka	localize
afmenga	decontaminate
afnæma	desensitize
afnema	abolish
áforma	contemplate
afreka	achieve
afriða	rectify
afskauta	depolarize
afskrifa	amortize
aftaka	execute
aftengja	disconnect
afþakka	dismiss
afturkalla	undo
afturköllun	undo
afvatna	detoxify
ákvarða	evaluate
algilda	generalize
alhæfa	generalize
ásaka	accuse
ássnið	intercept
auðkenna	identify
bæla	repress
bæta	improve
bæti	byte
baka	bake
baksmala	disassemble
banna	inhibit
barkarstýfa	decorticate
barkarstýfður	decorticate
batna	recover
beina	allocate
besta	maximize
biðja	ask
bióða	invite
blanda	emulsify
bókstafareikningur	algebra
borast	penetrate
borða	eat
bræða	dissolve
brasa	braze
bréfsími	telefax
breyta	modify
búa	equip
búta	quantize
byrja	introduce
byrjun	commence
deilda	differentiate
deyfa	extinguish
diffra	differentiate
draga	absorb
drekka	eat
dýpkunarprammi	dredger
dýpkunarskip	dredger
efla	promote
eftirmynda	replicate
eignfæra	capitalize
einangra	segregate
einelta	intercept
elta	pursue
endurbæta	improve
endurbyggja	restore

Reference: Webster's Online Dictionary (www.websters-online-dictionary.org)

endurgera	reconstruct	fylla	imbue
endurgjalda	reciprocate	fyrirframgreiðsla	imprest
endurgreiða	reimburse	fyrirgefa	forgive
endurheimt	restore	galva	galvanize
endurheimta	recover	galvanhúða	galvanize
endurkvæmur	recursive	gefa	provide
endurmeta	revalue	gera	render
endurmóta	restructure	geyma	carry
endurnýja	renew	geymd	carry
endurnýta	recycle	gjörhreinsa	sanitize
endurrétta	recover	gleypa	preoccupy
endurrita	restore	greina	detect
endursemja	reconstruct	gremjast	resent
endurtaka	replicate	gruna	assume
endurteiknari	refresh	hæfa	generalize
endurtekning	replicate	hækka	promote
endurvinna	recycle	hafa	have
endurvinnsla	recycle	hafna	reject
espa	activate	halda	deem
éta	eat	halli	loll
eyða	delete	hámarka	maximize
eyðing	delete	hamla	inhibit
eyðingarhamur	delete	hampþétta	caulk
fá	get	harðlóða	braze
færa	enter	harðna	solidify
fansa	stow	hástafa	capitalize
fara	depart	hefja	elevate
fatra	frustrate	hefta	restrict
finna	evaluate	heimta	retrieve
fjölþætta	diversify	helminga	bisect
flatarmálsfræði	geometry	hengja	suspend
fleygja	reject	herða	tighten
fleyta	emulsify	heslimús	dormouse
formaukning	epigenesis	heyra	hear
formmyndun	epigenesis	hindra	inhibit
fráfæra	abduct	hirða	scavenge
framkalla	develop	hjúpa	encapsulate
framkvæma	execute	hlaða	stow
framlengja	prolong	hliðra	translate
framselja	endorse	hlíta	comply
frátengja	disconnect	hlotnast	receive
frumgilda	initialize	hlustun	auscultation
frumstilla	initialize	hlutleysa	neutralize
fullnýta	deplete	hornafræði	geometry
fullstækka	maximize	hrækja	expectorate
fylgja	accompany	hreinsa	sanitize

hringrása	circulate	látast	simulate
hringsóla	circulate	leiðrétta	emend
hrylla	abominate	lengja	prolong
húða	render	lesa	read
hugleiða	contemplate	liðka	mobilize
hugsa	think	löggilda	accredit
hvarfast	react	lögskipa	constitute
hvetja	catalyze	losa	mobilize
ífara	infiltrate	lyfta	elevate
ífarinn	infiltrate	mæla	detect
ígrip	interrupt	magnfesta	quantify
íhuga	contemplate	magngreina	quantify
inna	execute	magnhæfa	quantify
inndindill	undershoot	meta	evaluate
innheimta	collect	mjólka	lactate
innleysa	redeem	móðga	offend
innmúra	embed	móta	modulate
innrétta	categorize	múrmeldýr	marmot
innsteypa	embed	mynda	constitute
jafna	unify	myndfall	transform
játa	concede	myndsími	telefax
jóna	ionize	næma	sensitize
kæfa	asphyxiate	nafnorð	noun
kæra	accuse	naglbítur	nippers
kaffæra	overwhelm	nagltöng	nippers
kafna	asphyxiate	neita	abnegate
kalla	summon	nema	detect
kamfóra	camphor	neyða	require
kamfórutré	camphor	niðurlægja	abate
kanna	inspect	norma	normalise
kemba	debug	nota	deploy
kenna	identify	nýglæða	refresh
kjósa	constitute	nýglæðing	refresh
kóða	encode	nýta	deploy
koma	come	ofurálag	overstress
kóta	encode	ógilda	extinguish
kynna	promote	ógilding	undo
læra	learn	olía	lube
laga	improve	ónæma	desensitize
lagfæra	rectify	orsaka	activate
lágmarka	minimize	örva	promote
lagskipta	stratify	oxa	oxidize
laktat	lactate	oxast	oxidize
landmæling	geodesy	prófa	examine
landmælingafræði	geodesy	ráða	advise
landmælingar	geodesy	ráðstafa	allocate

rafhúða	galvanize	sigla	navigate
ragú	ragout	síglæðari	refresh
rákóttur	striate	símrit	telefax
rannsaka	examine	símriti	telefax
rápa	navigate	símsending	telefax
raunvirða	deflate	sitja	sit
reikna	calculate	skamma	offend
reisa	rotate	skammdindill	undershoot
reka	dismiss	skammlenda	undershoot
rétta	rectify	skammta	quantize
rétting	taxis	skara	intersect
ritla	edit	skerast	intersect
ritsetja	edit	skilgreina	identify
ritstýra	edit	skilja	realize
ritvinna	edit	skipa	constitute
rjúfa	disconnect	skipta	allocate
rof	interrupt	skoða	examine
róla	reciprocate	skörun	intersect
rotna	decompose	skurðpunktur	intercept
rúmfræði	geometry	skynja	detect
ryðga	corrode	skynsvipta	desensitize
sækja	retrieve	slagsíða	loll
sækni	taxis	slökkva	extinguish
sæta	saccharify	smágreiðslusjóður	imprest
safna	collect	smala	assemble
sameina	merge	smita	infect
sameinast	unify	smjúga	penetrate
samhraða	synchronize	smurefni	lube
samlæta	relate	smyrja	lubricate
samliðast	interfere	snapa	scavenge
samræma	unify	snara	transform
samsama	identify	snið	transect
samsniða	conform	snúa	rotate
samsníða	conform	snúast	rotate
samstilla	synchronize	sölutryggja	underwrite
samþykkja	endorse	spana	induce
sanna	verify	spyrja	enquire
sannfæra	convince	staðbinda	localize
sannprófa	verify	staðfesta	accept
sannreyna	ascertain	staðgreina	localize
segja	narrate	staðla	normalize
seinka	delete	staðmarka	localize
selja	vend	staðreyna	ascertain
senda	transmit	staðsetja	localize
sérgreina	qualify	stækka	enlarge
síðbirting	epigenesis	stafla	stow

stefna	summon	tölubúa	quantify
stemma	caulk	tölvustafur	byte
stilla	oversee	tölvuvæða	computerize
stjórna	supervise	töng	nippers
stofna	constitute	trúa	deem
stúa	stow	tryggja	underwrite
styðja	endorse	túlka	interpret
stýfa	resect	tvinna	merge
stýra	navigate	umbreyta	alter
styrkja	reinforce	umbuna	compensate
sundra	decompose	umgangast	interact
sundurliða	itemize	ummóta	restructure
svæfa	occlude	ummynd	transform
svara	react	ummynda	transform
sveiflast	oscillate	umpóla	depolarize
sveigja	deflect	umskipa	restructure
svigna	deflect	umskipting	replace
svíkja	delude	umskiptingarhamur	replace
sykra	saccharify	umtákna	encode
sýsl	edit	umvarpa	transform
tæra	seize	undirbúa	adopt
tærast	corrode	uppfylla	comply
takmarka	restrict	uppgötva	detect
tákna	encode	upphaf	commence
tempra	modulate	upphefja	extinguish
tengja	connect	útbúa	equip
tengjast	relate	úthluta	allocate
þakka	accept	útiloka	exclude
þekkja	recognise	útlista	elucidate
þétta	tighten	útnefna	constitute
þeyta	emulsify	útskýra	explain
þíða	defrost	útvega	provide
þola	condone	vænta	expect
þrá	yearn	vætla	exude
þrengja	restrict	vandindill	undershoot
þrívetni	tritium	vara	warn
þróa	evolve	vatnsblanda	emulsify
þroska	develop	vátryggja	insure
þverskera	transect	vaxa	accrue
þversnið	transect	veita	allocate
þvinga	compel	vekja	activate
þýða	construe	vensla	relate
þykja	think	verða	happen
þykjast	simulate	viðurkenna	concede
tilreiða	edit	víkja	aberrate
titra	oscillate	vilsa	exude

virða	evaluate
virkja	activate
vistþýða	compile
víxlast	interfere
víxlverka	interact
yfirálag	overstress
yfirfara	inspect
yfirgefa	exclude
yfirgír	overdrive
yfirtaka	usurp

Verbs (English - Icelandic)

abate	niðurlægja
abdicate	yfirgefa
abduct	fráfæra
aberrate	víkja
abhor	hrylla
abnegate	neita
abolish	afnema
abominate	hrylla
absorb	draga
accept	staðfesta
accompany	fylgja
accredit	löggilda
accrue	vaxa
accumulate	safna
accuse	ásaka
achieve	afreka
acknowledge	játa
activate	espa
adapt	aðlaga
admit	viðurkenna
adopt	ættleiða
advise	ráða
algebra	bókstafareikningur
allocate	veita
alter	umbreyta
amortize	afskrifa
appear	þykja
arrive	koma
ascertain	sannreyna
ask	spyrja

asphyxiate	kæfa
assemble	smala
assess	áætla
assume	gruna
asymptotic	aðfelldur
attune	aðlagast
auscultation	hlustun
bake	baka
become	verða
begin	byrja
bisect	helminga
braze	brasa
byte	bæti
calculate	áætla
camphor	kamfóra
capitalize	eignfæra
carry	geyma
catalyze	hvetja
categorize	innrétta
caulk	þétta
circulate	hringrása
collect	innheimta
come	koma
commence	byrja
compel	neyða
compensate	jafna
compile	þýða
comply	hlíta
compute	reikna
computerize	tölvuvæða
concede	viðurkenna
condone	þola
conform	samsniða
connect	tengja
constitute	skipa
construe	þýða
contemplate	íhuga
convince	sannfæra
corrode	ryðga
debug	kemba
decode	afkóta
decompose	rotna
decontaminate	afmenga
decorticate	barkarstýfður
deem	halda
deflate	raunvirða
deflect	sveigja
defrost	þíða

delete	seinka	forgive	fyrirgefa
delude	svíkja	frustrate	fatra
deny	neita	galvanize	galva
depart	fara	generalize	algilda
deplete	fullnýta	geodesy	landmæling
deploy	nýta	geometry	flatarmálsfræði
depolarize	umpóla	get	fá
derive	fá	grow	vaxa
desensitize	afnæma	happen	verða
detect	nema	have	fá
detoxify	afeitra	hear	heyra
develop	framkalla	identify	auðkenna
differentiate	diffra	imbue	fylla
disassemble	baksmala	impart	gefa
disconnect	aftengja	imprest	fyrirframgreiðsla
dismiss	afþakka	improve	laga
dissolve	sameina	induce	virkja
distinguish	skynja	infect	smita
diversify	fjölþætta	infiltrate	ífara
dormouse	heslimús	inhibit	hamla
dredger	dýpkunarprammi	initialize	frumgilda
eat	éta	inspect	kanna
edit	ritsetja	insure	vátryggja
elevate	lyfta	interact	umgangast
elucidate	útlista	intercept	ássnið
embed	innmúra	interfere	samliðast
emend	leiðrétta	interpret	túlka
emulsify	fleyta	interrelate	umgangast
encapsulate	hjúpa	interrupt	ígrip
encode	kóða	intersect	skara
endorse	ábekja	introduce	kynna
enlarge	stækka	invite	bióða
enquire	spyrja	ionize	jóna
enter	færa	itemize	sundurliða
epigenesis	síðbirting	lactate	laktat
equip	útbúa	learn	læra
evaluate	ákvarða	loathe	hrylla
evolve	þróa	localize	staðmarka
examine	prófa	loll	halli
exclude	útiloka	lube	olía
execute	aftaka	lubricate	smyrja
expect	vænta	marmot	múrmeldýr
expectorate	hrækja	maximize	hámarka
explain	þýða	merge	sameina
extinguish	deyfa	minimize	lágmarka
exude	vætla	mislead	svíkja
focalize	staðbinda	mobilize	losa

modify	endurnýja	reenact	kynna
modulate	móta	refresh	endurteiknari
narrate	segja	reimburse	endurgreiða
navigate	stýra	reinforce	styrkja
necessitate	neyða	reject	neita
neutralize	afmagna	relate	vensla
nippers	naglbítur	render	kynna
normalise	norma	renew	endurnýja
normalize	staðla	replace	endurnýja
noun	nafnorð	replicate	endurtekning
occlude	svæfa	repress	bæla
offend	móðga	require	þvinga
oscillate	snúa	resect	stýfa
overdrive	yfirgír	resent	gremjast
oversee	stilla	restore	endurrita
overstress	ofurálag	restrain	stilla
overwhelm	kaffæra	restrict	hamla
oxidize	oxa	restructure	endurmóta
penetrate	borast	retire	innleysa
permeate	fylla	retrieve	sækja
persuade	sannfæra	revalue	endurmeta
preoccupy	gleypa	rotate	reisa
presume	halda	saccharify	sykra
profess	játa	sanitize	hreinsa
prolong	framlengja	scavenge	hirða
promote	efla	seek	biðja
propose	ætla	seem	þykja
provide	útvega	segregate	aðskilja
provoke	orsaka	seize	tæra
pursue	elta	send	senda
qualify	sérgreina	sensitize	næma
quantify	magnhæfa	simulate	látast
quantize	búta	sit	sitja
ragout	ragú	solidify	harðna
react	svara	stow	fansa
read	lesa	straighten	laga
realize	skilja	stratify	lagskipta
receive	fá	strengthen	efla
reciprocate	endurgjalda	striate	rákóttur
recognise	þekkja	submit	senda
recondition	endurbyggja	suffer	þola
reconstruct	endurbyggja	summon	stefna
recount	segja	supervise	stjórna
recover	endurheimta	suppose	halda
rectify	lagfæra	suspend	hengja
recursive	endurkvæmur	synchronize	samhraða
recycle	endurvinnsla	taxis	rétting
redeem	innleysa	telefax	bréfsími

thank	þakka
think	hugsa
tighten	þétta
tolerate	þola
transect	snið
transform	myndfall
translate	hliðra
transmit	senda
tritium	þrívetni
undershoot	skammdindill
underwrite	sölutryggja
undo	ógilding
unhook	afkrækja
unify	jafna
unload	afferma
usurp	yfirtaka
validate	löggilda
veer	snúast
vend	selja
verify	sanna
warn	vara
yearn	þrá

Nouns (Icelandic - English)

áætlanagerð	planning
áætlunargerð	planning
áætlunarskip	liner
áætlunartala	estimator
áalíking	atavism
aangström	angstrom
áavísi	atavism
ábeking	endorsement
ábending	reminder
ábúandi	occupant
ábúð	occupancy
áburður	fertilizer
ábyrgð	liability
ábyrgðarskil	accountability
ábyrgðarskylda	accountability
ábyrgni	accountability
aðalbláber	bilberry

aðalbláberjalyng	bilberry
aðalbraut	highway
aðalhvatamaður	protagonist
aðalmerking	denotation
aðalskip	nave
adamsepli	larynx
aðdragandi	preamble
aðdráttarafl	attraction
aðdráttarkraftur	attraction
aðdráttur	attraction
adenín	adenine
adenosíneinfosfat	amp
aðfærir	adductor
aðfærsla	adduction
aðfallsfasi	diastole
aðfella	regression
aðferð	methodology
aðferðafræði	methodology
aðferðarlýsing	protocol
aðflugsgreining	briefing
aðflugshringviti	locator
aðföng	stores
aðgangur	admission
aðgát	precaution
aðgengi	accessibility
aðgengileiki	availability
aðgerð	operation
aðgerðarmaður	operator
aðgreining	resolution
aðhæfing	adjustment
aðhvarf	regression
aðild	involvement
aðili	member
aðkvæni	exogamy
aðleiðsla	induction
aðleiðsluaðferð	induction
aðlifun	acculturation
aðlífun	anabolism
aðloðun	adsorption
aðlögun	assimilation
aðlögunarhæfileiki	adaptability
aðlögunarhæfni	adaptability
aðlögunarörðugleikar	maladjustment
aðmíráll	admiral
adrenalín	adrenaline
aðrennslisrör	penstock

aðsetur	residence	afbrigðileiki	anomaly
aðskilnaðarstefna	separatism	afdragi	puller
aðskilnaður	disjunction	afdráttarþvinga	puller
aðskotaefni	contaminant	afdráttur	annealing
aðsog	adsorption	afeinangrunartæki	stripper
aðsóp	accretion	afeitrun	detoxification
aðstaða	facilities	afeitur	anatoxin
aðstæður	situation	áfengi	alcohol
aðstoð	assistance	afero	things
æð	vessel	afflæði	regression
æða	choroid	afglóðun	tempering
æðahimna	choroid	afgreiðsla	discharging
æðahnútur	varix	afhelgun	secularization
æðahýði	choroid	afhjúpun	exposure
æðasamdráttur	vasoconstriction	afhreistrun	descaling
æðasegamyndun	thrombosis	afhröðun	deceleration
æðasegi	thrombus	afi	grandfather
æðaskurður	venesection	afísingarbúnaður	defroster
æðaþrenging	vasoconstriction	afkóðun	decoding
æðavíkkandi	vasodilator	afkoma	survival
æðavíkkari	vasodilator	afköst	throughput
æðhnoðri	glomerulus	afkótari	decoder
æði	personality	afkúpling	decoupling
æðisgerðir	psychokinesis	afkynjun	castration
AEF	amp	afl	watt
æfi	life	aflauki	booster
æfing	training	afleiðsla	deduction
æfisaga	biography	aflestur	reading
æska	adolescence	aflfræði	mechanics
æting	corrosion	aflimun	amputation
ætiþistill	artichoke	aflögun	deformation
ætt	tribe	aflskiljun	centrifugation
ættbálkur	tribe	aflstýritæki	controller
ættfeðrastjórn	patriarchy	aflýsing	cancellation
ættflokkur	tribe	afmæli	birthday
ættgengi	heredity	afmælisdagur	birthday
ættgengisfræði	genetics	afmengun	decontamination
æxli	neoplasm	afmögnun	neutralization
æxlisgen	oncogene	afmörkun	cutoff
æxlismyndun	neoplasia	afmótari	demodulator
afæta	predator	afmótun	demodulation
áfall	trauma	afmyndun	skewness
áfangastaður	destination	afnæming	desensitization
áfangi	event	afnám	abolition
afborgun	amortization	afneitun	abjuration
afbrigði	anomaly	afnotagreiðsla	royalty

afnotaréttur	usufruct	áhættuvægi	leverage
afræningi	predator	áhersluatviksorð	intensifier
afrán	predation	áhleðsla	accretion
afrennsli	runoff	áhöfn	crew
afrennslishraði	runoff	áhrif	impression
afrétting	truing	áhrifasvæði	sphere
afriðill	converter	áhrifasvið	sphere
afritun	replication	áhrifsbreyting	analogy
afruglari	decoder	aĵo	things
afsal	waiver	ákæra	complaint
afseglun	demagnetisation	ákærandi	accuser
afsegulmögnun	demagnetisation	ákærði	accused
afsjálfgun	depersonalization	akcesora	accessories
afskautun	depolarization	akcesoraĵo	accessories
afskiljun	centrifugation	akiro	asset
afskráning	decoding	akkerisrauf	hawse
afskrift	amortization	aktín	actinium
afsláttarmiði	coupon	aktíníum	actinium
afsögn	resignation	akto	records
afstaða	alignment	akurhænsn	partridge
afstæði	relativity	akurhafri	oat
afstæðiskenning	relativity	ákvæði	statute
afsteypa	impression	ákvæðisvextir	coupon
afsýrir	reductant	ákvörðunarstaður	destination
aftanívagn	trailer	ál	aluminium
aftengsl	decoupling	álagning	markup
afþreying	recreation	albatrosi	albatross
afturbati	convalescence	albínismi	albinism
afturbolur	abdomen	albúmín	albumin
afturhvarf	reversion	aldabil	eon
afturhvarfsþörf	nostalgia	aldinsykur	fructose
afturkippur	recession	aldursákvörðun	dating
afurð	product	aldursgreining	dating
afvik	anomaly	aldurshópur	cohort
afvötnun	dehydration	álengd	elongation
afvöxtun	discounting	álestur	reading
áfylling	refuelling	alfa	alpha
agða	trematode	alfalfagras	alfalfa
ágeislun	insolation	algengi	prevalence
ágeislunarmagn	irradiation	algilding	generalization
ágeislunarstyrkur	irradiance	algildishyggja	absolutism
agnakerfi	system	algildiskenning	absolutism
agnúði	aerosol	alhæfing	generalization
ágræðsla	anchoring	alheimur	universe
ágreiningur	dissension	álit	contention
agúrka	cucumber	aljafna	identity

alkóhól	alcohol	andverkun	antagonism
allsherjaratkvæðagreiðsla	referendum	andvirkni	counteraction
allsherjarfundur	plenum	andvökur	insomnia
álma	ramus	aneksa	accessories
almiðill	multimedia	angalýja	ameba
almiðlun	multimedia	angan	odour
almynd	hologram	angíótensín	angiotensin
almyrkvun	totality	angist	agony
alnet	internet	anilín	aniline
álögur	duties	anker	rotor
alpafjóla	cyclamen	annattó	annatto
alpherbejo	alp	annóna	cherimoya
alræði	autarchy	anóða	anode
alræðisstjórn	autarchy	anorakkur	anorak
alræðisvald	sovereignty	antecedentoj	records
alrófsmælir	bolometer	antímon	antimony
alþjóðahyggja	internationalism	apabrauðstré	baobab
alþjóðarækni	internationalism	apótek	pharmacy
alúminíum	aluminium	apríkósa	apricot
álun	proliferation	ar	aerosol
alveldi	autarchy	ár	year
ályktun	recommendation	árásargirni	aggression
amaba	ameba	árásarhvöt	aggression
amapóstur	spam	áratta	compulsion
amba	ameba	árblinda	onchocerciasis
amín	amine	arða	tubercle
áminning	reminder	arðhleðsla	payload
amma	grandmother	arðmiði	coupon
amper	amp	arðrán	exploitation
amýlópektín	amylopectin	arðsemi	profitability
andardráttur	breath	áreiðanleiki	accuracy
andarteppa	asthma	áreitaval	selectivity
andi	breath	áreiti	stimulus
andkvistur	antinode	áreiting	stimulation
andlíf	antibiosis	áreitni	aggression
andlífi	antibiosis	arfbætur	eugenics
andlitsfall	physiognomy	arfberi	gene
andlyf	antagonist	arfgengi	heredity
andnauð	dyspnea	arfgerð	genotype
andoxunarefni	antioxidant	arfstofn	gene
andrafögn	positron	árgreiðsla	annuity
andrógen	androgen	arĥivo	archives
andrúmsloft	atmosphere	árhólmar	delta
andspyrna	rebellion	áriðill	oscillator
andstaða	antagonism	áritun	rating
andþrengsli	dyspnea	arkitekt	architect

armabúnaður	linkage	atburðarit	script
armaturo	braces	atburðasvið	setting
armband	bracelet	atburður	event
ármót	junction	atferði	behaviour
arsen	arsenic	atferli	behaviour
arsenik	arsenic	atferlisfræði	ethology
arta	acne	atferlishamla	barrier
artiskokkur	cardoon	atferlisstefna	behaviorism
árvekni	vigilance	átfruma	phagocyte
ás	spindle	átfrumnakerfi	res
ásælni	affinity	athafnamaður	entrepreneur
ásæta	epiphyte	athafnasvæði	premises
asatíðir	menorrhagia	athafsnemi	vigour
asbesteitrun	asbestosis	athöfn	activity
asbestveiki	asbestosis	athugasemd	reminder
asetat	acetate	athugasemdafrestur	deadline
aseton	acetone	athugun	investigation
asetón	acetone	athyglisvakning	arousal
asetýl	acetyl	átköst	bulimia
asetýlen	acetylene	atlag	impulse
asetýlkólínseytandi	cholinergic	atriði	event
áshorn	anomaly	atríum	atrium
askgró	ascospore	atrópín	atropine
askja	caldera	átthagabönd	localism
áskrifandi	subscriber	átthyrningur	octagon
askur	ascus	áttstig	octet
áskyn	awareness	áttun	orientation
asma	asthma	áttund	octet
asn	asparagine	atvik	event
asni	donkey	atviksbreyting	modification
ásog	adsorption	átvilla	pica
ásökun	accusal	atvinnugrein	industry
asparagín	asparagine	atvinnuleysi	unemployment
ástandsbreyting	transition	atvinnurekandi	employer
ástandslýsing	scenario	atvinnuvegur	industry
ástaræði	erotomania	auðfræði	economics
astat	astatine	auðgun	enrichment
astma	asthma	auðhringur	cartel
astmi	asthma	auðkenni	criterion
Ástralíusvertingi	aborigine	auðkenning	identification
ásvelta	precession	auðmýing	humiliation
ásýnd	projection	auðvaldsskipulag	capitalism
át	ingestion	auðveldun	facilitation
áta	krill	augabolti	eyebolt
átak	exertion	augabrún	eyebrow
atburðarás	scenario	augabrúnahár	eyebrow

auglýsing	announcement	bær	municipality
augnakarl	acetabulum	bæri	parity
augnalok	eyelid	bakari	baker
augnangur	conjunctivitis	bakflug	reentry
augnasíld	shad	bakhjarl	fulcrum
augngler	eyepiece	bakka	backspace
augnhár	cilium	bakkastokkar	shıpway
augnhvíta	sclera	bakland	hinterland
augnkvef	conjunctivitis	bakögn	electron
augnsnúningur	version	bakpoki	rucksack
augntin	nystagmus	bakrás	regression
augntinun	nystagmus	bakrauf	anus
augnvindingur	torsion	bakskaut	cathode
auka	increment	baksveifla	flyback
aukabiðdagaþóknun	demurrage	baksveip	flyback
aukabreyta	parameter	bakteríuæta	phage
aukabúnaður	accessories	bakteríueyðir	bactericide
aukahringur	epicycle	bakteríufræði	bacteriology
aukamerking	connotation	bakteríuhár	pilus
aukasól	parhelion	bakteríukólónía	colony
aukatæki	accessories	bakteríuleysi	asepsis
auki	neoplasm	bakteríuþyrping	colony
aukning	increment	bakteríuveira	phage
aurbreð	mudguard	ballett	ballet
aurbretti	mudguard	balsamínutré	balsam
aurhlíf	mudguard	bálstofa	crematory
aurriði	trout	band	ligament
ávali	convexity	bandalag	federation
ávanabinding	addiction	bandalagsstefna	unionism
ávanasýki	addiction	bandbreidd	bandwidth
ávani	habituation	bandormur	taenia
ávaxtasykur	fructose	bandvefsreifar	fascia
averaða	means	bandvídd	bandwidth
áverki	trauma	bankaleynd	confidentiality
ávísun	voucher	banki	reservoir
axlarvöðvi	deltoid	banko	banks
bað	bathroom	bannsetning	grounding
bæjarfélag	municipality	barako	barracks
bæjarþil	gable	barbitúrat	barbiturate
bæki	buckwheat	barbitúrsýrulyf	barbiturate
bækigrjón	buckwheat	barð	fin
bæklingur	leaflet	barðaháfur	monkfish
bæklunarlækningar	orthopedics	barín	barium
bæling	repression	baríum	barium
bælir	suppressor	barkablaðka	epiglottis
bæn	prayer	barkakvísl	bronchus

barkakýli	larynx	beinkímfruma	osteoblast
barkakýlislok	epiglottis	beinkröm	rickets
barkalok	epiglottis	beinkvilli	osteopathy
barkapípa	bronchus	beinlínuröðun	alignment
barkarenna	airway	beinmergsherðing	osteopetrosis
barkhúð	cortex	beinmóðir	osteoblast
barki	windpipe	beinmyndunarfruma	osteoblast
barksteri	corticosteroid	beinörshnútur	callus
barksýra	tannin	beinstillir	collimator
barn	youngster	beinútvöxtur	apophysis
barnaat	meconium	beitiland	grassland
barnabik	meconium	beitiskip	cruiser
barnaheimili	kindergarten	beitning	baiting
barnalækningar	pediatrics	beitusmokkur	squid
barnalæknir	pediatrician	bekkur	pew
barnasorta	meconium	belgbólga	bursitis
barnavagn	pram	belghýði	follicle
barrakúda	barracuda	belgkirtill	follicle
barsíli	capelin	belgmein	bursitis
basafruma	basophil	belgur	cyst
basíða	basidium	belti	zona
basilíka	basil	beltun	zonation
basilíkum	basil	bendill	cursor
basill	basil	bendir	pointer
bataskeið	convalescence	bendistál	reinforcement
bátsmaður	boatswain	bensín	petrol
bátsugla	davit	bensíngjöf	accelerator
bauganet	graticule	bensól	benzole
baugaskáu	psoriasis	ber	berry
baugmyndun	halation	berfrymingar	mycoplasma
baunarlaga	pisiform	bergamía	bergamot
báxít	bauxite	bergamóappelsína	bergamot
bazo	grounds	bergamótappelsína	bergamot
beð	beet	bergeitill	stocks
bein	os	berggrunnur	bedrock
beinæta	osteoclast	bergkvika	magma
beinafræði	osteology	bergminta	oregano
beinátfruma	osteoclast	bergmynta	oregano
beinbris	callus	beri	carrier
beinbrjótur	osteoclast	berkel	berkelium
beind	vector	berkelín	berkelium
beinfræði	osteology	berkelíum	berkelium
beinfruma	osteocyte	berkill	tubercle
beinherðing	osteosclerosis	berkja	bronchus
beining	deflection	berkjuasma	asthma
beinispóla	concentrator	berklar	tuberculosis

berklaveiki	tuberculosis	bíótín	biotin
berklín	berkelium	birgðasali	supplier
berskjöldun	exposure	Birgðastöð	storage
beryllín	beryllium	birgðatalning	stocktaking
beryllíum	beryllium	birgðir	stocks
bestun	optimization	birgir	supplier
betahraðall	betatron	birta	brilliance
betatrónn	betatron	birting	representation
beyging	inflection	birtingarupplausn	resolution
beygingardæmi	paradigm	birtustig	magnitude
beygir	flexor	bísamrotta	muskrat
beygivöðvi	flexor	bismút	bismuth
beygja	diffraction	biti	member
beygla	depression	bixín	annatto
beygur	trepidation	bjálki	girder
bið	latency	bjargræðisvegur	industry
biða	ampulla	bjögun	warping
biðdagar	demurrage	bjór	pediment
biðfæra	spool	bjórar	castor
biðgjald	demurrage	bjúgborð	meniscus
biðlari	client	bjúgflötur	meniscus
biðtími	latency	bjúglinsa	meniscus
bifhár	cilium	bjúglopi	edema
bifháraskúfur	cirrus	bjúgskekkja	astigmatism
bifrar	castor	bjúgur	edema
bifrari	vibrator	bláæðaskúlk	varix
bifreið	limousine	blað	lobe
bifreiðarstjóri	driver	blaðbeðja	chard
bikar	beaker	blaðgræna	chlorophyll
bíkarbónat	bicarbonate	blaðhvirfing	rosette
bikarglas	beaker	blaðka	membrane
bil	clearance	blaðra	cyst
bilanagreining	diagnosis	blaðselserí	celery
bílaverkstæði	garage	blaðsilla	celery
bilbreidd	bandwidth	blaðstæði	node
bílírúbín	bilirubin	blæðari	bleeder
bilkvæmi	periodicity	blæðingarstöðvun	hemostasis
bíll	car	blæjubíll	cabriolet
bílskúr	garage	blæti	fetish
bílslys	accident	bláhaus	wolffish
bílstjóri	driver	blak	volleyball
bilun	problem	blanda	mixture
bindefni	binder	blandari	mixer
bindiefni	emulsifier	blastúla	blastula
bindindi	abstinence	bleðill	lobe
binding	fixation	bleiklax	humpback

Reference: Webster's Online Dictionary (www.websters-online-dictionary.org)

blekfiskar	cuttlefish	blóðsegi	thrombus
blendingsmál	pidgin	blóðsifjar	consanguinity
blendingsstyrkur	heterosis	blóðsjúkdómafræði	hematology
blendingsþróttur	heterosis	blóðskortur	anemia
blettabryngedda	billfish	blóðskyldleiki	consanguinity
blettagreining	chromatography	blóðsótt	shigellosis
blettahreistur	psoriasis	blóðstorkuheftir	anticoagulant
blettaskán	psoriasis	blóðstreymi	circulation
blettur	macula	blóðsýring	acidosis
blíða	beauty	blóðtala	erythrocyte
blik	corona	blóðþurrð	ischemia
blika	cirrostratus	blóðvökvi	plasma
blikkræma	shim	blokki	antagonist
bliksjá	stroboscope	blómbikar	calyx
blikufjaðrir	cirrus	blómbotn	torus
blikuhnoðrar	cirrocumulus	blómhnoða	glomerulus
blikutrefjar	cirrus	blómi	yolk
blindhríð	blizzard	blómkál	cauliflower
blindsvæði	occlusion	blómkróna	corolla
blinduflekkur	scotoma	blómleggur	pedicel
blóðbönd	consanguinity	blómskipunarstöngull	rachis
blóðeitrun	septicemia	blöndun	mixing
blóðflaga	platelet	blöndunarstig	mixer
blóðfrumnamyndun	hematopoiesis	blöndungur	carburettor
blóðfrumumyndun	hematopoiesis	blótgripur	fetish
blóðgjöf	transfusion	blýeitrun	saturnism
blóðhlaup	ecchymosis	bobbingur	bobbin
blóðhreinsun	clearance	boð	message
blóðkornamyndun	hematopoiesis	boðbreytir	transducer
blóðkýli	furuncle	boddíhlutir	bodywork
blóðleysi	anemia	boðefni	transmitter
blóðmelóna	watermelon	boðritari	programmer
blóðnasir	nosebleed	boðritun	programming
blóðögðusótt	schistosomiasis	bogaeining	radian
blóðögðuveiki	schistosomiasis	bogagöng	arcade
blóðrásaskil	watershed	bogamælieining	radian
blóðrauðalos	hemolysis	bogamálseining	radian
blóðrauðamiga	hemoglobinuria	bogarið	arcade
blóðrauði	hemoglobin	bognun	deflection
blóðrek	embolus	boguggi	bowfin
blóðreki	embolus	bókari	bookkeeper
blóðreksstífla	embolism	bókasafn	library
blóðrennslisstöðvun	hemostasis	bókhveiti	buckwheat
blöðrufóstur	blastula	bókhveitigrjón	buckwheat
blöðrunám	cystectomy	bókun	minutes
blöðrustjórn	continence	bólfesta	nidation

bolfiskur	whitefish	Brasilía	brazil
bólga	inflammation	brask	speculation
bólgnun	intumescence	braut	runway
bolli	cups	brautarhorn	anomaly
bólómælir	bolometer	brautarhringur	orb
bölró	resignation	brautryðjandi	entrepreneur
bólstraský	cumulus	breidd	width
bólsturský	cumulus	breiddarbaugur	latitude
bólusetning	vaccination	breiddargráða	latitude
bólusótt	smallpox	breiðstræti	avenue
bóndi	farmer	bremsukjálki	shoe
bónuskerfi	incentive	bremsuskór	shoe
bór	boron	brenglari	scrambler
bora	crypt	brennari	burner
borald	unit	brennir	burner
borð	ullage	brennisteinn	brimstone
borðabreidd	bandwidth	brennisteinsmeðferð	vulcanization
borðganga	boarding	brennsluofn	incinerator
borði	lining	breyta	characterisation
bordo	banks	breytigen	mutagen
borg	municipality	breytileiki	variance
borgaraskilningur	citizenship	breyting	revision
borgarastétt	bourgeoisie	breytingar	modernization
borgaravitund	citizenship	breytir	converter
borgarstjórn	municipality	breytistykki	adapter
borgmyndun	urbanization	breytiviðnám	potentiometer
börkur	cortex	brímavaki	oestrogen
bot	baud	brimbrjótur	breakwater
bótaþegi	beneficiary	brimvarnargarður	breakwater
botnfall	sediment	bringa	thorax
botnfelling	sedimentation	bringubein	breastbone
botnlag	sediment	brislingur	sprat
botnlanganám	appendectomy	brjóst	chest
botnlangaskurður	appendectomy	brjóstbein	breastbone
botnskál	sump	brjóstgrind	thorax
botnstykki	transducer	brjósthimnubólga	pleurisy
botntala	beauty	brjósthol	thorax
bráðaofnæmi	anaphylaxis	brjóstkassi	chest
bráðaofnæmishneigð	atopy	broddkúmen	cumin
bráðavandi	crisis	broddmjólk	colostrum
bráðnun	fusion	broddur	colostrum
bræðsla	fusion	bróðir	brother
bræðsluofn	furnace	bróðurdóttir	niece
Bragð	gambit	bróðurflekkur	sibling
bragðskyn	gustation	bróðursonur	nephew
bragfræði	metrics	brókarsótt	nymphomania

brokkál	broccoli	búseta	population
brokkoli	broccoli	bústaður	residence
brokkólí	broccoli	bústjóri	administrator
bróm	bromine	búsvæði	habitat
brot	fragmentation	bútan	butane
brotamælir	vernier	bútasaumur	quilting
brotmark	boundary	bútun	segmentation
brotpunktur	vertex	bútýl	butyl
brottfall	deletion	bygg	barley
brottnám	removal	byggð	population
brottvísun	exclusion	byggðaskipulag	zoning
brú	pons	bygging	construction
brúðfruma	gamete	byggingajöfur	client
brúður	bride	byggingareining	subunit
brúngrani	wolffish	bylgjubeyging	diffraction
brúnkol	lignite	bylgjubeygja	diffraction
brunnur	source	bylgjuform	waveform
brúsi	canister	bylgjuhreyfingar	peristalsis
brutaro	stocks	bylgjuleiðari	waveguide
brutoj	stocks	bylgjulengd	wavelength
bryggja	quay	bylgjulögun	waveform
bryggjun	extrapolation	byrða	bunker
bryggjupláss	pier	byrði	liability
bryggjupolli	bollard	býretta	burette
bryti	steward	byrgir	suppressor
bú	estate	byrjun	commencement
búamalurt	mugwort	celi	means
buddubólga	bursitis	cirkonstanco	circumstances
búfé	livestock	dægrastytting	recreation
búgarður	estate	dæld	depression
bugða	curvature	dæmasafn	corpus
bugpunktur	antinode	dæmi	example
bugspjót	bowsprit	daggarber	dewberry
bugur	antinode	dagmaður	sweeper
búkhlaup	diarrhea	dagskrá	agenda
búkhreinsun	purgation	dagur	day
bulla	piston	daktíli	dactyl
búmalurt	mugwort	dáleiðsla	hypnosis
BÚNADUR	equipment	dalur	valley
búnaður	facilities	damdisko	checkers
bunga	prominence	dampeco	checkers
bunki	batch	dánarbú	estate
búpeningur	livestock	dans	saltation
búr	pantry	danssjónleikur	ballet
burðarefni	vehicle	dáraaldin	durian
búrót	mugwort	dauðbörkur	rhytidome

dauðhreinsun	sterilization	dómsaga	jurisdiction
dávaldur	hypnotist	dómsvald	jurisdiction
davíða	davit	doppa	caruncle
db	decibel	dór	arbor
deigla	crucible	doría	dory
deild	taxon	dóttir	daughter
deildarsérfræðingur	adviser	drag	fossa
deilibil	spacing	dragkló	puller
deilibox	hub	dramb	arrogance
deilikorn	centriole	dráttarskífa	sheave
deiling	segmentation	dráttur	demurrage
deilir	distributor	dreggjar	sediment
deilitegund	subspecies	dregill	taenia
deiltegund	subspecies	dreifa	suspension
deklari	rules	dreifari	diffuser
demókrati	democrat	dreifbýli	hinterland
deplaháfur	dogfish	dreifikerfi	grid
deplahverfa	windowpane	dreifilausn	suspension
deplasíld	alewife	dreifing	decentralization
depra	depression	dreifingaraðili	distributor
desibel	decibel	dreifir	diffuser
desíbel	decibel	dreifistýring	decentralization
dextrósi	dextrose	dreifkjörnungur	prokaryote
deyfð	drowsiness	dreifni	variance
deyfing	anesthesia	drekajurt	tarragon
deyfingarhylki	dashpot	drekamalurt	tarragon
deyfir	suppressor	drengur	boy
dígitalis	digitalis	dreypari	pipette
digull	crucible	dreyrasýki	hemophilia
dílaroði	roseola	drif	propulsion
dilkur	cell	drifhlutfall	gearing
díll	macula	drifrás	driver
dingull	hypophysis	drifrit	driver
díóða	diode	dröfnuskata	rocker
diplómat	diplomat	dröfnuský	cirrocumulus
dípóll	dipole	drómedari	dromedary
direkto	directions	drotning	queen
dísa	nozzle	Drottning	queen
disklingur	diskette	drottnun	domination
disko	records	drottnunargirni	dominance
diskur	disk	drullusokkur	plunger
djúphafsbotn	abyss	drýsill	cursor
doði	weakfish	dúan	fluctuation
dökkna	macula	duaranga	accessories
dokumento	papers	dugur	potency
dómnefnd	jury	dúkstyrking	doping

dul	latency	eðlisviðnám	resistivity
dulnefni	pseudonym	eðlisvísir	anlage
dulsálarfræði	parapsychology	eðun	disjunction
dulskyggni	clairvoyance	efiki	works
dumpning	dumping	efling	recruitment
dúnepli	loquat	eflir	booster
dúnfjöður	plumule	efnablanda	mixture
durianávöxtur	durian	efnabreyting	reaction
dvali	latency	efnaferli	pathway
dvergbítur	zucchini	efnaformúla	formula
dverggalangal	galangal	efnahagslægð	recession
dvergkráka	jackdaw	efnahagsmál	economics
dvergrásatækni	microelectronics	efnahemill	inhibitor
dvergvöxtur	dwarfism	efnahvarf	reaction
dyljun	masking	efnahvarfi	catalyst
dýna	mattress	efnahvati	activator
dýnamór	generator	efnalitsjá	colorimeter
dýpi	depth	efnanemi	chemoreceptor
dýpt	depth	efnasamtenging	synthesis
dýptarsýn	perspective	efnaskipti	metabolism
dyr	door	efnaskynjari	chemoreceptor
dyrafaldur	architrave	efnasmíð	synthesis
dýrafélag	colony	efnasmíði	synthesis
dýrafræði	zoology	efnastyrkur	concentration
dýrahringur	zodiac	efnaviðtaki	chemoreceptor
dýrahringurinn	zodiac	efnavísir	indicator
dýralæknir	veterinary	efnaviti	indicator
dýralandafræði	zoogeography	efnhvarfi	catalyst
dýramjölvi	glycogen	efni	topic
dýraríki	fauna	efnishyggja	materialism
dýrasambú	colony	efnismolun	catabolism
dýrasterkja	glycogen	efnisvísir	descriptor
dýrseðli	bestiality	eftirbrennari	afterburner
dysprósín	dysprosium	eftirbrennir	afterburner
dysprósíum	dysprosium	eftirburður	afterbirth
eðalmalurt	wormwood	eftirhrif	aftereffect
eðalvagn	limousine	eftirlaunaskeið	retirement
edik	vinegar	eftirlíking	simulation
eðjufiskur	bowfin	eftirlíkir	simulator
eðlisbreyting	denaturation	eftirlit	monitoring
eðlisfræði	physics	eftirlitsmaður	supervisor
eðlisgerð	constitution	eftirljóm	afterglow
eðlislíking	homology	eftirljómi	persistence
eðlismassi	density	eftirmyndun	modeling
eðlissvipting	denaturation	eftirskin	afterglow
eðlisþyngd	density	eftirskjálfti	aftershock

eftirsókn	affinity	einelti	interception
eftirvagn	trailer	einföldun	simplification
egg	edging	einindi	entity
eggbólstur	cumulus	eining	entity
eggbú	ovule	einingarhluti	subunit
eggbúsegg	ovule	einkaleyfi	monopoly
eggbússtig	oestrus	einkaleyfisþóknun	royalty
eggfruma	ovum	einkaréttargreiðsla	royalty
egghjúpur	integument	einkaréttur	monopoly
eggjagöng	oviduct	einkasala	monopoly
eggjakerfi	ovary	einkennagreining	diagnosis
eggjaleiðari	oviduct	einkennamynstur	syndrome
eggjarauða	yolk	einkenni	symptom
eggjastokkur	ovary	einkunnagjöf	rating
eggleg	ovary	einleiki	identity
eggrás	oviduct	einokun	monopoly
eggvarp	oviposition	einokunaraðstaða	monopoly
eigandi	owner	einokunarhringur	cartel
eigindarvídd	dimension	einræðisherra	dictator
eiginleiki	calibre	einræðisstjórn	absolutism
eign	asset	einræðisvald	sovereignty
eignahalli	insolvency	einslögun	similarity
eignaliðir	assets	einsömun	individuation
eignarhald	holdings	einstaklingshyggja	individualism
eignarleiga	leasing	einstaklingsmyndun	ontogeny
eignasafn	portfolio	einstaklingsþroskun	ontogenesis
eignast	occupancy	einstaklingsþróun	ontogenesis
eignastétt	bourgeoisie	einsteinín	einsteinium
eignfærsla	capitalization	einsteiníum	einsteinium
eignir	resources	eintak	specimen
eilífðargreiðslur	perpetuity	einvaldsríki	monarchy
eiming	distillation	einveldi	monarchy
eimir	vaporizer	einveldsríki	monarchy
eimsvali	condenser	einvetni	protium
eimþéttir	condenser	einyrki	amp
eimun	distillation	eir	copper
eimur	exhalation	eisa	plasma
einangrari	dielectric	eista	testis
einangri	insulator	eistu	testis
einangrun	insulation	eitilæxli	lymphoma
einangrunarefni	insulation	eitilbú	follicle
einangrunarlag	dielectric	eitilfruma	lymphocyte
einangur	insulator	eitilfrumukrabbamein	lymphoma
einbeiting	focusing	eitilkorn	lymphocyte
eindagi	deadline	eitla	tonsil
eindahraðall	accelerator	eitlaæxli	lymphoma

eitlafruma	lymphocyte	endi	apex
eitlingur	lymphocyte	ending	life
eitrun	intoxication	endingartími	life
eitur	toxin	endir	conclusion
eiturefni	toxin	endívusalat	endive
eitursveipur	hemlock	endurbætur	modernization
eiturúðun	fumigation	endurbót	improvement
eiturvirkni	toxicity	endurbygging	reconstruction
ekkill	widower	endurgerð	annealing
ekla	dearth	endurgerving	reconstruction
ekra	acre	endurgreiðsla	reimbursement
eldaldin	guava	endurhæfing	rehabilitation
eldfjallafræði	volcanology	endurhringrás	recirculation
eldhólf	hearth	endurhvarf	regression
eldhús	galley	endurkastari	reflector
eldi	culture	endurkastshlutfall	reflectance
eldkeila	cone	endurkastsskaut	reflector
eldsmíði	forging	endurkoma	recurrence
eldsmíðisgripur	forging	endurlífgun	resuscitation
eldsneytisgjöf	accelerator	endurmat	revaluation
eldsneytistaka	refuelling	endurminni	anamnesis
eldvarnarþil	firewall	endurmótun	restructuring
elektróna	electron	endurnýjun	renewal
elemento	element	endurnýun	renewal
elgsber	dewberry	endursemja	reconstruction
ellifjarsýni	presbyopia	endurskin	albedo
ellisjón	presbyopia	endurskinshæfni	albedo
elspezo	expenses	endurskinshlutfall	albedo
eltihalli	caster	endurskinsstuðull	reflectance
eltihjól	caster	endurskipulagning	reorganization
eltihorn	caster	endurskoðun	revision
elting	tracking	endursköpun	recreation
em	pica	endurstilling	readjustment
embættismaður	officer	endurtakanleiki	reproducibility
embættismannakerfi	bureaucracy	endurtekning	repetition
embættismannastétt	officialdom	endurtrygging	reinsurance
embættismenn	officialdom	enduruppbygging	reconstitution
enarhivigi	archives	endurvarpsflötur	reflector
enarkivigi	archives	endurvarpsskaut	reflector
enbankigi	banks	endurvarpsstuðull	reflectance
endaheftur	acrocentric	endurvinnsla	recycling
endahólkur	termination	enging	peristalsis
endalok	catastrophe	engispretta	grasshopper
endamúffa	termination	ensím	enzyme
endaþarmsop	anus	ensímhvarfefni	substrate
endheftur	acrocentric	enskribi	records

enskribo	records	fag	profession
eósinfíkinn	eosinophil	faga	phage
eósíntækur	eosinophil	fagrikeppur	reticulum
erbín	erbium	fágun	burnishing
erbíum	erbium	fagurlitleiki	chroma
erfð	heredity	faldur	architrave
erfðafar	genotype	fálki	gyrfalcon
erfðafræði	genetics	fall	descent
erfðagervi	genotype	fallbeyging	inflection
erfðamark	marker	fálmari	antenna
erfðavísir	gene	falur	socket
erfðir	heredity	fána	fauna
erfiði	severity	far	impression
ero	elements	farbreyta	parameter
ertanleiki	excitability	fareind	ion
erting	stimulation	fareindalækning	iontophoresis
ertir	stimulus	fareindaleysing	ionization
esdragon	tarragon	farmaður	seafarer
espir	activator	farmþungi	payload
espun	activation	farmur	payload
estragon	tarragon	farnaðarsaga	anamnesis
estrógen	estrogen	farskráning	reservation
eta	minutes	farsynjun	bumping
etanól	ethanol	farþegarými	cabin
etiko	ethics	farþegi	passenger
etýlen	ethylene	fashani	pheasant
evropín	europium	fasi	phase
evrópín	europium	fasismi	fascism
evrópíum	europium	fastanefnd	mission
eyðimerkurvin	oasis	fasteignasali	broker
eyðing	annihilation	fasti	parameter
eyra	pinna	fastmerki	benchmark
eyrnalokkur	earring	fastyrðing	assertion
eyrnamergur	cerumen	FAT	fad
eyrnamerking	earmarking	fataskiptahneigð	transvestism
eyrnatól	earphone	fé	livestock
eyrnavala	otolith	feðraveldi	patriarchy
eyrnavölur	otolith	fegrun	idealization
fæðingarblettur	birthmark	fegurð	beauty
fæðuinntaka	ingestion	féhirðir	treasurer
fælni	phobia	feigðarferli	apoptosis
færiband	conveyor	feitlagni	adiposity
færiboð	polling	feitletra	boldface
færibreyta	parameter	feitletraður	boldface
færsla	movement	félagi	member
fáfnisgras	tarragon	félagsfræði	sociology

félagsgjöld	dues	fíbrínógen	fibrinogen
félagshyggja	socialism	fiðrildislirfa	caterpillar
félagsmaður	member	fihelpanto	accessories
félagsmótun	socialization	fíkn	addiction
fell	fascia	fíkni	affinity
fellibylur	cyclone	fíkniávani	addiction
felling	convolution	filmo	movie
fellir	depressor	fimbulfamb	confabulation
feminismi	feminism	fimleikar	acrobatics
femínismi	feminism	fimmhyrningur	pentagon
fen	phenylalanine	fingrafar	fingerprint
fenging	conception	fingravettlingar	gloves
fengrani	wolffish	fingur	digit
fenílketónúría	phenylketonuria	fingurbjargarblóm	digitalis
fennika	fennel	fingurnögl	fingernail
fenníka	fennel	finkull	fennel
fennikka	fennel	firmamerki	logo
fennill	fennel	fiskeldi	aquaculture
fenýlalanín	phenylalanine	fiskigarður	barrier
fenýlketónmiga	phenylketonuria	fiskirækt	aquaculture
ferðamál	tourism	fitjuflokkur	category
ferðamannastraumur	tourism	fittni	fitness
ferðaþjónusta	tourism	fituefni	lipid
ferðaútvegur	tourism	fitungar	lipid
ferging	compression	fitusækni	adiposity
ferhyrningur	quadrangle	fjaðra	wormwood
ferilhorn	anomaly	fjaðurbrúun	spline
ferilris	kurtosis	fjaðurmagn	resilience
ferja	carrier	fjallarakki	ranger
ferjald	transducer	fjárfesting	investment
ferjustuðull	sensitivity	fjárfestir	investor
ferli	procedure	fjárhagshlið	economics
ferlishemill	inhibitor	fjárhagsskuldbinding	liability
fermín	fermium	fjárhagsstaða	finances
ferming	confirmation	fjárhagur	finances
fermíum	fermium	fjarhrif	psychokinesis
fervik	variance	fjármagnskerfi	capitalism
festa	constraint	fjármál	financing
festarhæll	bitt	fjármálaráðuneyti	treasury
festarkorn	mitochondrion	fjármálastjóri	controller
festibúnaður	clamping	fjarmiðlun	telecommunication
festiefni	fixative	fjármögnun	capitalization
festiflötur	wart	fjármögnunarleiga	leasing
festing	holder	fjármunaleiga	rental
festivökvi	fixative	fjármunir	resources
fíbrín	fibrin	fjárnám	execution

fjáröflun	revenue	flæðiengi	marsh
fjárreiðustjóri	treasurer	flæðiland	marsh
fjarriti	teleprinter	flæðirit	flowchart
fjarskiptafræði	telecommunication	flæðisstjórnun	logistics
fjarskiptatækni	telecommunication	flaga	lamella
fjarskipti	telecommunications	fláki	polygon
fjarskynjun	telepathy	flangi	flange
fjarstýring	telecontrol	fláning	exfoliation
fjarsýni	hypermetropia	flankafero	accessories
fjárveiting	allocation	flans	flange
fjarvera	absence	flasa	seborrhea
fjarvídd	perspective	flaska	ampulla
fjarvíddaráhrif	perspective	flatarfjórðungur	quadrant
fjarvinnsla	teleprocessing	flatbytna	flatboat
fjarvísi	telepathy	fleiðrubólga	pleurisy
fjarvist	absence	fleirrit	polygraph
fjarvistir	absenteeism	fleirriti	polygraph
fjöðrun	suspension	flekkblæðing	ecchymosis
fjöðurstafur	rachis	flekkjaháfur	wolffish
fjölbinding	overloading	flekkun	spotting
fjölbreytni	polymorphism	flekkusótt	typhus
fjölbrigðni	polymorphism	flesk	pork
fjöldahlutfall	abundance	fleskormur	trichina
fjöldi	frequency	flétta	lichen
fjölfingrun	polydactyly	fléttari	multiplexer
fjölfléttun	multiplexing	fléttun	convolution
fjölforritavinnsla	multiprogramming	fleygbogi	parabola
fjölgervi	allotropy	fleygdrep	infarct
fjölgjörvavinnsla	multiprocessing	fleytihæfni	buoyancy
fjölgun	proliferation	fleyting	flotation
fjölliða	polymer	fleytir	emulsifier
fjölliðun	polymerization	flipi	lobe
fjölmiðlar	media	fljótakrabbi	crayfish
fjölmótun	polymorphism	flóðslétta	floodplain
fjölrásari	multiplexer	flogaveikilyf	antiepileptic
fjölrásun	multiplexing	flogboði	aura
fjöltáun	polydactyly	flogleysandi	antiepileptic
fjórðungsbogi	quadrant	flögnun	exfoliation
fjórðungsgeiri	quadrant	flói	inlet
fjórðungskorthlöð	quadrangle	flokksþing	convention
fjórðungsmælir	quadrant	flokkun	categorization
fjórðungur	quadrant	flokkunareining	taxon
fjörður	cove	flokkunarheild	taxon
fjörudoppa	periwinkle	flokkunarvél	grader
fjörugrös	carragheen	flokkur	category
flæði	osmosis	flökt	fluctuation

flóra	flora	fóður	liner
flotaforingi	admiral	föðurbróðir	uncle
floteiginleiki	buoyancy	fóðurkál	kale
flothæfni	buoyancy	föðurlandsást	patriotism
flothylki	pontoon	föðurlandsvinur	patriot
flotkraftur	buoyancy	fóðurnæpa	turnip
flotmælir	hydrometer	fóðurrör	casing
flotþol	buoyancy	födursystir	aunt
flötur	facet	fógeti	magistrate
flotvog	hydrometer	fok	deflation
flugbann	grounding	fokjarðvegur	loess
flugbraut	runway	fokmold	loess
flugeldar	fireworks	fókspóla	concentrator
flugfarþegi	passenger	fókun	focusing
flugfélag	airline	fold	earth
flughæð	altitude	földun	folding
flughamur	configuration	fólksfjöldafræði	demography
flughöfn	airport	fólksfjöldi	population
flugleið	airline	fólksrými	cabin
fluglipurð	manoeuvrability	fön	fin
flugrekandi	operator	forðabúr	reservoir
flugskeyti	missile	fordæmi	paradigm
flugslóði	contrail	forðahneta	butternut
flugstöð	airport	forðun	avoidance
flugþjónn	steward	foreind	proton
flugvallarvirkt	facilitation	foreldrafjarvera	absenteeism
flugvél	aeroplane	foreldrar	parents
flugvöllur	airfield	forensím	zymogen
flúor	fluorine	forgarður	vestibule
flúr	fluorine	forgjöf	priming
flúra	megrim	forhleðsla	priming
flúreitrun	fluorosis	forhólf	atrium
flúrgeislun	fluorescence	forhúð	prepuce
flúrljóm	fluorescence	forhúðarstýfing	circumcision
flúrljómun	fluorescence	foringjafiskur	cobia
flúrskíma	fluorescence	form	morphology
flúrskin	fluorescence	formaður	president
flutningafræði	shipping	formaldehýð	methanal
flutningaprammi	flatboat	formalín	formalin
flutningaskip	freighter	formdeild	category
flutningur	displacement	formendasveiging	transition
flysjun	exfoliation	formengi	domain
flýtivísun	shortcut	formerkisbreytir	inverter
flytjanleiki	portability	formfræði	morphology
fóarn	gizzard	formgerðarflokkun	typology
fóðring	bushing	formgerðarstefna	structuralism

formúla	formula	fósturfræði	embryology
fornæmi	predisposition	fósturfylgja	afterbirth
fórnfýsi	altruism	fósturhár	lanugo
fornmenntastefna	humanism	fósturlát	abortion
fornmynd	archetype	fósturlífsvaki	progesterone
fornveðurfræði	paleoclimatology	fósturnesti	yolk
forögn	proton	fósturskúfur	cotyledon
forráð	hegemony	fósturþroskun	development
forræði	hegemony	fösun	chamfering
forritari	programmer	fótabúnaður	footwear
forritseining	module	fótfesta	holdfast
forritun	programming	fótliður	acetabulum
forröð	leader	fötlun	disability
forsenda	criterion	fótóna	photon
forseti	president	fótónunemi	photocell
forsjálni	precaution	fótsnyrting	podiatry
forskaut	anode	frábrigði	exception
forskilyrði	presupposition	frádráttur	deduction
forskoða	preview	fræ	semen
forskrift	script	fræðasvið	theory
forsmíð	prototype	fræði	theory
forsnið	formatting	fræðikenning	theory
forsögn	prognosis	fræfill	stamen
forsprengja	detonator	fræll	stamen
forstillimerki	preamble	frænmyndun	seeding
forstjóri	president	frænafli	hilum
forstöðumaður	administrator	frændfólk	relations
forsýn	preview	frændi	cousin
forþjappa	supercharger	frænka	cousin
föruhnöttur	planet	fræsæti	placenta
forvaxtareikningur	discounting	fræskurn	integument
forveri	precursor	fræva	pistil
forvígismaður	protagonist	frævill	stamen
forviska	precognition	frævísir	ovule
forvörn	prophylaxis	frævísishimna	integument
forysta	hegemony	fráfærir	abductor
fosfat	phosphate	fragtvél	freighter
fosfór	phosphor	fráhalli	divergence
fosfórljóm	phosphorescence	fráhrinding	repulsion
fósfórljóm	phosphorescence	fráhrindingarkraftur	repulsion
fosfórljómun	phosphorescence	fráhvarf	recession
fosfórskíma	phosphorescence	fráhverfa	divergence
fósfórskin	phosphorescence	frálífun	catabolism
foss	waterfall	frálíking	dissimilation
fóstur	fetus	frambolur	thorax
fóstureyðing	abortion	framdráttur	extraction

framdrif	propulsion	friðarhugsjón	pacifism
framdrift	propulsion	friðarstefna	pacifism
framfærlsueyrir	maintenance	friðarstillir	conciliator
framfærslufé	maintenance	friðdómari	magistrate
framfærslumeðlag	maintenance	friðhelgi	immunity
framferðarhlutfall	transmittance	fríðindi	immunity
framför	development	friðkauparstefna	appeasement
framgangsmáti	procedure	friðþæging	appeasement
framgómur	palate	friðun	preservation
framheili	prosencephalon	fríhæð	clearance
framhjátenging	jumper	frílitningur	autosome
framknúning	propulsion	frjálsræði	latitude
framkoma	behaviour	frjó	spermatozoon
framkvæmd	transaction	frjófruma	sperm
framkvæmdaaðili	operator	frjóhnappshelmingur	theca
framkvæmdastjóri	manager	frjókorn	pollen
framlag	contribution	frjómóðurfruma	spermatocyte
framleiðandi	manufacturer	fróð	information
framleiðsla	product	froskdýr	amphibia
framleiðslugrein	industry	froskur	frog
framleiðsluvara	product	frostþurrkun	lyophilization
framlenging	extension	frú	madam
frammistöðuviðmið	benchmark	frúktósi	fructose
framreikningur	extrapolation	fruma	cell
framrúða	windshield	frumbernska	infancy
framsal	delegation	frumbreyta	argument
framsetning	representation	frumbyggi	aborigine
framskögun	protrusion	frumdeild	somite
framsókn	precession	frumdýr	protozoon
framtak	enterprise	frumefnabreyting	transmutation
framþróun	development	frumefni	element
framtíðarsýn	scenario	frumeintak	prototype
framvinda	succession	frumflokkun	categorization
fransín	francium	frumflokkur	category
fransíum	francium	frumgerð	prototype
frárás	outlet	frumgildi	argument
frásog	absorption	frumhlutur	symbol
frásögn	storyline	fruminnlag	hypoblast
frávarp	projection	frumkvöðull	entrepreneur
frávik	exception	frumliður	somite
frávísun	refusal	frummynd	prototype
frekna	lentigo	frumregla	axiom
fremdardýr	primates	frumsenda	axiom
frestun	suspension	frumsetning	axiom
frestur	deadline	frumskjal	protocol
freyjublóm	aconite	frumsmíð	prototype

frumsögn	category	fylgni	correlation
frumstærð	argument	fylking	phylum
frumtryggjandi	insurer	fýll	fulmar
frumubörkur	cortex	fylli	filler
frumufræði	cytology	fylling	filler
frumuhlaup	cytosol	fyllir	filler
frumuhýði	pellicle	fyrirbæri	phenomenon
frumukrans	rosette	fyrirbrigði	phenomenon
frumulíffæri	organelle	fyrirgreiðsla	facilitation
frumuöndun	respiration	fyrirkomulag	layout
frumuræktun	culture	fyrirmæli	instructions
frumutenging	coupling	fyrirmunun	exclusion
frumvarp	proposal	fyrirmynd	template
frumvefur	parenchyma	fyrirsögn	heading
frumvera	protist	fyrirsvar	representation
frygð	libido	fyrirtæki	entity
frymi	protoplasm	fyrirvari	reservation
frymisbóla	vacuole	fyrning	amortization
frymisgrisjuhít	cistern	gaddur	fluorosis
frymisvökvi	cytosol	gadolín	gadolinium
frysting	refrigeration	gadólín	gadolinium
fuglasótt	psittacosis	gadólínium	gadolinium
fullgilding	ratification	gægjuhneigð	voyeurism
fullkomnunarárátta	perfectionism	gæsajurt	chamomile
fullnusta	ratification	gæslumaður	moderator
fullþroski	maturity	gætni	precaution
fulltrúahópur	representation	gafl	gable
fulltrúi	representation	gaflbrík	pediment
fullveldi	sovereignty	gaflhlað	pediment
fullvissa	assurance	gaflhlaðsþríhyrningur	pediment
fullyrðing	statement	gaflhyrna	pediment
fundamento	elements	gagnaðgerð	countermeasure
fundargerð	minutes	gagnahjúpun	encapsulation
fundarstjóri	moderator	gagnainnsetning	editing
fundo	grounds	gagnalind	source
fundur	conference	gagnamengun	contamination
funkcii	works	gagnasetning	editing
funkciigi	works	gagnauga	temple
furða	astonishment	gagnmiðlun	multimedia
fýlasótt	psittacosis	gagnráðstöfun	countermeasure
fylgdarfrumur	glia	gagnsæi	transparency
fylgibúnaður	accessories	gagnsæismælir	densitometer
fylgihlutir	accessories	gagnseglun	demagnetisation
fylgirit	enclosure	gagnsemishyggja	utilitarianism
fylgiskjal	voucher	gagntak	reaction
fylgja	placenta	gagnúð	transference

gagnverkun	antagonism	gaupa	lynx
gagnvirkni	interaction	gazeto	papers
gagnvirkun	reaction	geavo	grandparent
galaktósi	galactose	geðblær	mood
galangarót	galangal	geðdeyfð	neurasthenia
galari	gallery	geðdeyfðarleysandi	antidepressant
galeiða	galley	geðdeyfðarlyf	antidepressant
gálgi	gantry	geðhreinsun	catharsis
gall	bile	geðlægð	depression
gallabuxur	jeans	geðlægðarlyf	antidepressant
gallerí	gallery	geðlæknir	psychiatrist
galli	drawback	geðlæknisfræði	psychiatry
gallín	gallium	geðlausn	abreaction
gallíum	gallium	geðrof	psychosis
gallrauði	bilirubin	geðsjúkdómafræði	psychiatry
galvanhúðun	galvanization	geðsjúkdómalæknir	psychiatrist
gammaglóbúlínekla	agammaglobulinemia	geðstjarfi	catatonia
gámur	container	geðveiki	psychosis
gangbrú	catwalk	geðvilla	psychopathy
gangfræði	kinematics	geðvillingur	psychopath
gangráður	pacemaker	geðvonska	irritation
gangriti	logger	gefrata	siblings
gangsvalir	gallery	gefrato	siblings
gangverk	mechanism	gegndræpi	permeability
gangvirki	mechanism	gegnfararhlutfall	transmittance
garðahlynur	sycamore	gegnflæði	osmosis
garðajarðarber	strawberry	gegnsíun	filtration
garðnellíka	carnation	gegntak	bushing
garðrækt	horticulture	gegnumlýsing	radiography
garður	barrier	gegnumumferð	tandem
garðyrkja	horticulture	gegnvæting	imbibition
garðyrkjufræði	horticulture	geimfari	astronaut
garnarteppa	obturation	geimferðafræði	astronautics
gaseyðing	degassing	geimlíffræði	astrobiology
gasgríma	respirator	geimsiglingafræði	astronautics
gáshaukur	goshawk	geimský	nebula
gashylki	reservoir	geimþoka	nebula
gasmyndun	gassing	geiraskipting	segmentation
gat	perforation	geiraskurður	lobotomy
gatari	perforator	geiri	sector
gatfláki	torus	geirvarta	mamilla
gatnamót	intersection	geisl	radian
gátstaður	checkpoint	geislabaugar	halation
gátt	gateway	geislabeinir	collimator
gaukull	glomerulus	geisladeyfni	opacity
gaumun	monitoring	geislagjafi	radiator

geislaharka	hardness	gerandefni	agonist
geislakerfi	aster	gerandvöðvi	agonist
geislalækningar	radiology	gerð	version
geislalæknisfræði	radiology	gerðabók	minutes
geislaloft	emanation	gerðaflokkun	typology
geislamælir	dosimeter	gerðafræði	typology
geislameðferð	radiotherapy	gerðardómari	arbitrator
geislaónæmismæling	radioimmunoassay	gerðardómsmaður	arbitrator
geislar	aster	gerðardómsmeðferð	arbitration
geislari	radiator	gerðardómur	arbitration
geislaskammtamælir	dosimeter	gerðarlýsing	schema
geislaskammtur	exposure	gerðarmaður	moderator
geislastengur	wishbone	gerhvati	enzyme
geisli	radius	geri	operator
geislun	irradiation	gerilæta	phage
geislunarafl	luminosity	gerilhár	pilus
geislunarfræði	radiology	gerilsneyðing	pasteurization
geislunarmælingar	dosimetry	gerilveira	phage
geislunarmagn	exposure	gerlabani	bactericide
geit	goat	gerlafræði	bacteriology
gelding	castration	gerlaþyrping	colony
geldögn	neutron	german	germanium
gelgjubólur	acne	germaníum	germanium
gelgjuskeið	adolescence	gersveppur	saccharomyces
gelgjuþrymlar	acne	gervending	reversion
gellir	loudspeaker	gerviefni	polymer
gelsykra	agar	gervigúmmí	neoprene
ĝemela	twins	gervilíffæri	prosthesis
ĝemelo	twins	gerving	synthesis
gemsa	chamois	gervingur	artifact
gen	gene	gestur	guest
genaferja	vector	geta	qualifications
genasæti	locus	getnaðarfæri	genitalia
genasamsæta	allele	getnaðarvörn	contraception
genayfirfærsla	translocation	getnaður	conception
gengd	mechanism	getuleysi	impotence
gengi	success	geymd	storage
gengisfelling	devaluation	geyming	storing
gengishækkun	revaluation	geymir	receiver
gengislækkun	devaluation	geymsla	preservation
gengismunur	agio	geymsluhýsill	reservoir
genmögnun	amplification	gildi	valency
gensæti	locus	gilding	validation
genset	locus	gildisákvörðun	evaluation
gento	stocks	gildislok	expiration
gepatro	parents	gildisskömmtun	quantization

gildleiki	thickness	glóðarker	pumpkin
gingkó	ginkgo	glóðhitamælir	pyrometer
ginvarta	palate	glómælir	pyrometer
gips	gypsum	glompa	bunker
gírhlutfall	gearing	glufa	fissure
gíring	gearing	gluggaþykkni	altocumulus
gírkassi	gearbox	gluggi	window
gírskipting	gearshift	glúkósi	glucose
gírstöng	gearshift	gluteo	buttocks
gistihús	hotel	glý	glycine
gistilíf	commensalism	glýkógen	glycogen
gistilífi	commensalism	glýkógenmyndun	glycogenesis
gjá	fissure	glýserín	glycerin
gjafi	source	glýseról	glycerol
gjafmildi	unselfishness	glysín	glycine
gjald	agio	glýsín	glycine
gjaldfærni	solvency	gnægð	abundance
gjaldhæfi	solvency	gnótt	abundance
gjaldkeri	treasurer	goðadrottning	carnation
gjaldlagning	charging	góðkynjun	eugenics
gjaldskrá	tariff	goðsögn	myth
gjaldþrot	bankruptcy	göfgun	sublimation
gjöld	expenditure	goggur	rostrum
gjörvi	processor	gögn	documentation
glæpur	offence	gólari	howler
glæra	acetate	gólfræsi	gully
glærfrymi	cytosol	golþorskur	angler
glærumóða	nebula	gómur	palate
glæruvagl	walleye	göndull	rotor
glas	glasses	göng	duct
glaso	glasses	gormsýkill	spirillum
gleraugu	goggles	gortari	bragger
gleypifruma	scavenger	Gösun	gasification
gleyping	absorption	götun	fenestration
gleypir	collector	gráblika	altostratus
gleypni	absorptance	grábuska	mugwort
gleypnitala	absorptance	gráðubogi	protractor
gliðnun	dilation	gráðuhreinsun	burring
glimmer	mica	græðgi	bulimia
gljákol	anthracite	grænflekkur	scup
gljásteinn	mica	grænsíld	alewife
gljúpleiki	permeability	grænukorn	chloroplast
gló	incandescence	grafhvelfing	crypt
glóbrystingur	robin	grafit	graphite
glóð	incandescence	graftarbóla	pustule
glóðald	heater	graftarkýli	furuncle

graftarþrymlar	acne	gróandi	vegetation
gramm	gramme	grobbari	bragger
grannfræði	topology	gróðrarhópur	colony
grannfrumur	glia	gróður	vegetation
grannsvæðakennsl	contiguity	gróðuráburður	fertilizer
grasæta	herbivore	gróðurbeltun	zonation
grasalækningar	eclecticism	gróðurflokkur	classification
grasbítur	herbivore	gróðurfylki	alliance
graslendi	grassland	gróðurhúsanellíka	carnation
greiðsla	payment	gróðurmold	humus
greiðsluflæði	liquidity	gróðurríki	flora
greiðslufrestun	moratorium	gróðurskiki	facies
greiðslugeta	liquidity	gróf	fossa
greiðsluhæfi	liquidity	grófsía	strainer
greiðslumiðlun	clearing	grófþeyta	suspension
greiðslusending	remittance	gróhirsla	sporangium
greiðslustöðvun	moratorium	grókólfur	basidium
greiðsluþol	liquidity	grókylfa	basidium
greiðsluþrot	insolvency	grómyndun	sporulation
greifi	earl	grop	porosity
grein	bough	gropa	porosity
greinandi	analyst	grophlutfall	porosity
greinarmerki	punctuation	groppa	permeability
greinarmerkjasetning	punctuation	grósekkur	ascus
greinimark	threshold	gróstilkur	basidium
greinimörk	threshold	grotnun	decomposition
greining	resolution	grugg	turbidity
greiningarhæfni	resolution	grugglausn	suspension
greiningartæki	analyzer	gruggun	turbidity
greinir	analyst	grundo	grounds
greinisía	analyser	grundvallarregla	axiom
greip	grapefruit	grundvöllur	foundation
greipaldin	grapefruit	grunngerð	infrastructure
greipaldintré	grapefruit	grunnkerfi	infrastructure
greyping	incrustation	grunnlína	baseline
griðastaður	asylum	grunnmálun	priming
grimmd	abhorrence	grunnpunktur	triplet
grind	grid	grunntala	radix
grindarhol	pelvis	grunnungur	tench
grindarskaut	grid	grunnur	foundation
grindarvirki	framework	grunnvatn	groundwater
grindverk	balustrade	grunnvatnsgeymir	aquifer
gripla	acronym	grunnvefur	parenchyma
gripluþráður	dendrite	grunnviðmiðun	baseline
grisjun	pruning	guð	divinity
grjótskriða	talus	guðlax	opah

guðveldi	theocracy	hafnarbakki	quay
gufa	vapour	hafnargarður	breakwater
gufuhvolf	atmosphere	hafnargjaldagreiðsla	clearance
gufuketill	boiler	hafnín	hafnium
gufumyndun	vaporization	hafníum	hafnium
gula	yolk	hafnsaga	pilotage
gulbúshormón	progesterone	hafnsögugjald	pilotage
gulbúsvaki	progesterone	hafri	oat
gúll	intumescence	hafsbotn	abyss
gullgægir	orfe	hafsvæði	waters
gullmakríll	dolphin	haft	constriction
gúlpur	sinus	háfur	dogfish
gulrófa	rutabaga	hagfræði	economics
gulrót	carrot	háglansslípun	burnishing
guluforði	yolk	haglendi	grassland
gúmmíhamar	mallet	hagnaður	revenue
gúmmíkragi	grommet	hagnýting	implementation
gúmmílíki	elastomer	hagræðing	rationalization
gúmmísuða	vulcanization	hagtölur	statistics
gúmmítékki	bouncer	háhitamælir	pyrometer
gúrka	cucumber	hak	tang
gvatsekvi	tails	haladzi	fumes
gvava	guava	haladzo	fumes
gvöndargrös	carragheen	halastjarna	comet
gyðingahatur	anti-semitism	hald	clamping
gyðingahof	synagogue	haldari	retainer
gyðingaprestur	rabbi	halddepill	desmosome
gyllinæð	hemorrhoid	haldfesta	holdfast
H	hydrogen	haldsmaður	occupant
hæð	altitude	haldsréttur	lien
hæðarlína	contour	haldvilla	delusion
hæðarstilling	levelling	hálendi	highland
hæfi	qualifications	hálfdvali	stupor
hæfing	training	hálfhnöttur	hemisphere
hæfni	ability	hálfhvel	hemisphere
hæfnismat	rating	hálfkúla	hemisphere
hæging	deceleration	hálfleiðari	semiconductor
hægir	retarder	hálfpottur	pint
hækkun	elevation	hálfrið	alternation
hæli	asylum	hálfsamsíðungur	trapezium
hæringur	capelin	hálfstaða	dichotomy
hætta	danger	hálfviti	moron
hættumat	exposure	hallamælir	inclinometer
hafáll	conger	hallar	descent
hafdjúp	abyss	hallastefna	exposure
haffærni	navigability	háls	cervix

hálsband	necklace	háspennuútslag	tracking
hálskirtill	tonsil	hass	cannabis
hálsklútur	neckerchief	hassjurt	marijuana
hamar	malleus	hástafaritun	capitalization
hámark	summit	hástig	acme
hámarksflughæð	ceiling	hátalari	loudspeaker
hámeri	porbeagle	háþrýstingslyf	antihypertensive
hamingja	happiness	háþrýstingur	hypertension
hamla	constraint	hátindur	summit
hamlari	retarder	hátternisfræði	ethology
hamning	containment	hattur	pileus
hámörkun	optimization	háttur	procedure
hamskipti	ecdysis	háttvís	diplomat
hamskipting	metamorphosis	haus	heading
hamur	facies	hausamót	fontanelle
handarkriki	armpit	hausbor	perforator
handbor	gimlet	hauskúpa	cranium
handfæri	handline	haust	autumn
handfjöllun	manipulation	hausun	heading
handfjötlun	manipulation	háværð	loudness
handhöfn	holdings	hefta	constraint
handhverfa	isomer	hefti	leaflet
handiðn	handicraft	hegðun	behaviour
handlæknir	surgeon	hegðunarmynstur	norm
handlæknisaðgerð	operation	hegðunarreglur	norm
handlæknisfræði	surgery	hegning	punishment
hanskar	gloves	hégómaskapur	vanity
happ	success	hégómi	vanity
hápunktur	acme	hegri	heron
hár	pilus	heiðar	heathland
hárbelgur	follicle	heiðhvolf	stratosphere
harðgúmmí	ebonite	heiði	heath
harðkol	anthracite	heiðursmerkjaveiting	decoration
harðmálmur	carbide	heilabólga	encephalitis
harðstál	carbide	heilabörkur	cortex
harka	hardness	heilabrú	pons
harpeis	resin	heilabylur	brainstorming
harpeisar	resin	heiladingull	hypophysis
hárpest	sycosis	heilafelling	convolution
hárpípuhrif	capillarity	heilaferli	cerebration
hárpípukraftur	capillarity	heilahol	ventricle
hárpípuverkun	capillarity	heilahristingur	concussion
harpixar	resin	heilakúpa	cranium
hártap	baldness	heilaleysi	anencephaly
háseti	sailor	heilalínurit	electroencephalogram
háskólaráð	senate	heilarafrit	electroencephalogram

heilarit	electroencephalogram	hengi	suspension
heilastúka	thalamus	henging	suspension
heilaþvottur	brainwashing	hengivagn	trailer
heild	totality	hengja	cornice
heildarbreytileiki	variation	hengsli	suspension
heildarhyggja	holism	hentugleiki	convenience
heildari	integrator	heptan	heptane
heildarkerfi	system	hérað	region
heildarneysla	intake	hérasótt	tularemia
heildsali	wholesaler	herðakistill	humpback
heilfeldissveiflur	harmonics	herma	resonance
heilfrumutengi	desmosome	hermifall	spline
heili	cerebrum	herming	mimesis
heilkenni	syndrome	hermir	emulator
heilkjörnungur	eukaryote	hermireikningur	simulation
heilmynd	hologram	hermueind	resonance
heilsufræði	hygiene	hermuhol	cavity
heilsugestur	client	hermun	simulation
heilsuveðurfræði	climatology	herpanleiki	contractility
heiltala	integer	herping	shrinkage
heimild	authorization	herra	lord
heimildir	data	herskip	warship
heimili	venue	hersli	cirrhosis
heimilisfang	location	herts	hertz
heimilun	authorization	heslihneta	hazelnut
heimkynni	habitat	hestafl	horsepower
heimsfræði	cosmology	hetta	diaphragm
heimsmynd	system	hettusótt	parotitis
heimsmyndarfræði	cosmology	hettuvaki	adrenaline
heimsmyndunarfræði	cosmogony	hey	hay
heimsvaldastefna	imperialism	heyrnardeyfa	deafness
heitleiðir	thermistor	heyrnarleysi	deafness
helftarblinda	hemianopia	hildir	afterbirth
helftarhöfuðverkur	hemicrania	hilla	shelf
helgisaga	legend	himberjasótt	yaws
helín	helium	himinbjarmi	skylight
helíum	helium	himinhnöttur	orb
helmingun	bisection	himinhvel	orb
hemilefni	moderator	himinhvirfill	zenith
hemill	inhibitor	himinljós	skylight
hemiltaugafruma	inhibitor	himinn	heaven
hemiltaugungur	inhibitor	himinskin	skylight
hemlun	braking	himintungl	planet
hemóglóbín	hemoglobin	himna	acetate
hemoroido	haemorrhoid	himnuflæði	osmosis
hendi	handedness	himnusíun	dialysis

himnuskilja	dialyzer	hjartalínurit	electrocardiogram
himnuskiljun	dialysis	hjartarafrit	electrocardiogram
hindber	raspberry	hjartarit	cardiogram
hindri	inhibitor	hjartariti	cardiograph
hindrun	barrier	hjartastilling	defibrillation
hirðuleysi	carelessness	hjartslráttaróregla	arrhythmia
hít	cistern	hjartsláttarsprettur	tachycardia
hitaaflfræði	thermodynamics	hjartsláttartruflun	arrhythmia
hitaeining	calorie	hjásól	parhelion
hitaflutningur	crossover	hjátrú	superstition
hitageislunarmælir	bolometer	hjöðnun	subsidence
hitakassi	incubator	hjólahaf	wheelbase
hitalækkandi	antipyretic	hjólás	axle
hitaleysing	thermolysis	hjólasporun	tracking
hitaliði	thermostat	hjólbarðastofn	carcass
hitameðferð	tempering	hjólbarði	tyre
hitamótstaða	thermistor	hjólflötur	torus
hitapar	thermocouple	hjólhlíf	mudguard
hitarafvaki	thermocouple	hjólhús	wheelhouse
hitari	heater	hjólkróna	borage
hitarit	thermogram	hjólnöf	hub
hitariti	thermograph	hjólskál	wheelhouse
hitasírit	thermogram	hjöruliðskross	spider
hitaskápur	incubator	hjúpun	encapsulation
hitaslag	heatstroke	hjúpur	integument
hitasótt	fever	hlaðeindahraðandi	cyclotron
hitastillir	thermostat	hlass	epiphysis
hitastýring	thermostat	hlaun	hipbone
hitatæki	heater	hlaup	clearance
hitaþjáll	thermoplastic	hlaupabreyta	parameter
hitatvinn	thermocouple	hlé	interval
hitaviðnám	thermistor	hlébarði	leopard
hitavökull	thermostat	hlébil	diastole
hiti	fever	hleðsla	loading
hittni	accuracy	hleðslutala	valency
hjákróna	corona	hleifur	ingot
hjalli	terrace	hlerun	tapping
hjálmur	radome	hleypandi	coagulant
hjálp	assistance	hleypir	coagulant
hjálparkíkir	finder	hlið	hilum
hjálparsetning	lemma	hliðarljós	sidelight
hjálparsjónauki	finder	hliðarstýri	rudder
hjarðhvöt	gregariousness	hliðarsveigja	deflection
hjarni	cerebrum	hliðlægi	laterality
hjartaáfall	coronary	hliðrun	avoidance
hjartahlé	diastole	hliðsetning	juxtaposition

hliðstaða	analogy	hneta	nut
hliðstæða	correspondence	hnettla	coccus
hlíf	deflector	hnignun	devolution
hlífðargleraugu	goggles	hnik	variation
hlítarárátta	perfectionism	hnikun	variation
hljóðbein	ossicle	hnitakerfi	grid
hljóðdeyfir	muffler	hnítarris	kurtosis
hljóðfirring	dissimilation	hnitklukka	chronometer
hljóðgjafi	sounder	hnitun	encoding
hljóðhimna	eardrum	hnjáliður	knee
hljóðkútur	silencer	hnjótur	tubercle
hljóðmögnun	amplification	hnoða	glomerulus
hljóðrófsriti	spectrograph	hnoðri	glomerulus
hljóðsetning	dubbing	hnökri	nodule
hljóðsjá	sonar	hnöttur	sphere
hljóðstyrkur	loudness	hnúðkál	kohlrabi
hljóðvarp	mutation	hnúðlax	humpback
hljóðver	studio	hnúðselja	celeriac
hljómblær	timbre	hnúðsellerí	celeriac
hljómplata	album	hnúðsilla	celeriac
hljómspuni	improvisation	hnúður	node
hljómsveit	orchestra	hnúfa	condyle
hlust	receiver	hnúi	condyle
hlutafjáreigandi	shareholder	hnúta	node
hlutasamstæða	assembly	hnútamál	height
hlutavelta	lottery	hnútpunktur	node
hlutfall	ratio	hnútur	vertex
hlutfallstala	ratio	hnykill	cerebellum
hluthafi	stockholder	hnykkingar	osteopathy
hluthyggja	realism	hnykkir	osteopath
hluti	stratum	hnykksuða	bumping
hlutleysi	independence	hof	temple
hlutleysing	neutralization	höfði	promontory
hlutmengi	subset	höfnun	rejection
hlutmergð	abundance	hofstöpull	pylon
hluttekning	empathy	höft	constraint
hlutun	segmentation	höfuðbók	ledger
hlutverk	mission	höfuðkvef	coryza
hlýðni	compliance	höfuðlagsfræði	phrenology
hlynur	sycamore	höfuðlausn	disengagement
hnappaborð	keyboard	höfuðskepna	element
hnattlaukur	onion	höfuðsmaður	admiral
hné	node	höfuðstöðvar	headquarters
hnéliður	knee	höfundarlaun	royalty
hneppi	domain	höfundarréttargreiðsla	royalty
hnéskel	kneecap	höfundur	originator

högg	impulse	horngerð	keratinization
höggbor	jumper	hornhimna	cornea
höggormur	adder	hornmælir	theodolite
höggsuða	bumping	hornmyndun	keratinization
höggun	tectonics	hornpunktur	vertex
höggunarfræði	tectonics	hornsíli	stickleback
högnun	arbitrage	Hörpun	sizing
hol	lumen	hörund	integument
hola	sinus	hörundskröm	pellagra
holbor	perforator	hóstameðal	expectorant
hólf	cell	hóstarkirtill	thymus
holfósturmyndun	gastrulation	hóstastillandi	antitussive
holhönd	axilla	hóstill	thymus
holhringsrör	toroid	Hótun	threat
hólkur	liner	hraðaaukning	acceleration
höll	palace	hraðafræði	kinetics
holleggur	catheter	hraðall	accelerator
holmín	holmium	hraðaminnkun	deceleration
hólmín	holmium	hraði	ratio
hólmíum	holmium	hraðriti	tachograph
holrúm	cavity	hraðtaktur	tachycardia
holsepi	polyp	hrææta	scavenger
holsígerð	empyema	hræðsla	agony
holun	excavation	hrægammur	scavenger
hömlur	constraint	hræking	expectoration
hönnunarlýsing	specification	hræring	movement
hóp	lagoon	hráki	sputum
hopa	backspace	hráolía	petroleum
hópfelling	agglutination	hrapsteinn	meteor
hópmyndun	aggregation	hrávara	commodity
hópun	aggregation	hreðka	radish
hópur	tribe	hreiðrun	implantation
hóra	hooker	hreiður	nidus
horf	attitude	hreinlæti	hygiene
horfur	prognosis	hreinræktun	isolation
hörgull	dearth	hreinsari	cleaner
hormón	hormone	hreinsiefni	cleaner
hormóni	hormone	hreinsistöð	refinery
horn	argument	hreinsun	clearing
hornafræði	trigonometry	hreinsunarstöð	refinery
hornamælingar	triangulation	hremmir	raider
hornarit	polygon	hreppapólitík	localism
hornefni	keratin	hreppsfélag	municipality
horneining	radian	hreyfiglöp	ataxia
hornfiskur	garfish	hreyfihömlun	disability
horngæla	garfish	hreyfilaukatæki	accessories

hreyfimagn	momentum	hrunskriða	talus
hreyfing	movement	húð	integument
hreyfingafræði	kinematics	húðangur	pellagra
hreyfingarleysi	akinesis	húðdrafna	macule
hreyfiskyn	kinesthesia	húðkröm	pellagra
hreyfistol	apraxia	húðskæni	lichen
hríð	blizzard	húðskæningur	lichen
hríðahormón	oxytocin	húðþekja	epidermis
hríðarbylur	blizzard	húðun	encapsulation
hrifill	effector	hugarfar	mentality
hrifnæmi	affectivity	hugarflug	brainstorming
hrifnánd	exposure	hugarmisræmi	dissonance
hrifsari	raider	hugarró	sedation
hringekja	merry-go-round	hugarsýn	visualization
hringfari	dividers	hugbúnaður	software
hringfeldi	torus	hugerni	mentality
hringferill	circumference	huggrip	apperception
hringgeiri	sector	huggun	consolation
hringhraðall	cyclotron	hughyggja	idealism
hringiða	turbulence	huglægi	subjectivity
hringjaðar	circumference	huglægni	subjectivity
hringormur	nematode	hugmyndafræði	ideology
hringrás	circulation	hugmyndakerfi	ideology
hringrif	atoll	hugmyndaregn	brainstorming
hringspóla	toroid	hugmyndasaga	ideology
hringstallur	counterbore	hugmyndasmiðja	workshop
hringstreymi	circulation	hugrenningur	brainstorming
hringþétti	gland	hugrof	dissociation
hringur	cartel	hugsæl	intuition
hringvöðvi	sphincter	hugsanasamhengi	coherence
hrip	percolation	hugsjónastefna	idealism
hristingur	concussion	hugstol	stupor
hröðun	acceleration	hugsýki	neurosis
hröðunarrafskaut	accelerator	hugtak	concept
hrogn	roe	hugtakabók	thesaurus
hrognaseiði	capelin	hugtakamyndun	conception
hrognasíli	capelin	hugtakasafn	thesaurus
hroki	arrogance	hugvilla	delusion
hrökk	transition	hula	integument
hrörleiki	degeneracy	hulstur	cassette
hrörnun	degeneration	húmanismi	humanism
hrossaríkja	barnacle	húmus	humus
hrúðurkarl	barnacle	hundraðshlutamark	percentile
hrufur	fluting	hundraðshluti	percentile
hrúga	colony	hundraðsmark	percentile
hrun	implosion	hundraðstala	percentage

hundsspor	psoriasis	hvítfrumnafjölgun	leukocytosis
hurð	door	hvítfrumnaskortur	leukopenia
hús	nacelle	hvítfrumufæð	leukopenia
húsaþyrping	settlement	hvítingseðli	albinism
húsgafl	gable	hvítkorn	leukocyte
hússtyrja	beluga	hvítkornafæð	leukopenia
hústökumaður	squatter	hvítkornafjölgun	leukocytosis
hvalambur	spermaceti	hvítsveppasýking	candidiasis
hvaláta	krill	hvítukljúfur	protease
hvalsauki	spermaceti	hvítuskurður	lobotomy
hvalskutull	harpoon	hvítusundrun	proteolysis
hvarf	reaction	hvítviður	whitewood
hvarfafræði	kinetics	hvolf	ventricle
hvarfefni	reactant	hvoreind	neutron
hvarffræði	kinetics	hvörf	reaction
hvarfhraðafræði	kinetics	hvöt	incentive
hvarfi	reactor	hvötun	catalysis
hvarmur	eyelid	hýdrat	hydrate
hvassleiki	harshness	hýdríð	hydride
hvatamaður	initiator	hýdrókortisón	cortisol
hvatberi	mitochondrion	hýdrókortísón	hydrocortisone
hvati	incentive	hýdroxíð	hydroxide
hvatning	motivation	hyggja	conception
hvekkskjatti	utricle	hyldýpi	abyss
hvel	orb	hylki	canister
hvelaheili	cerebrum	hylla	shelf
hvelfing	concavity	hyrni	keratin
hvelkápa	pallium	hyrningur	polygon
hvellhetta	detonator	hyrnishúðun	keratinization
hverfa	isomer	hyrnismyndun	keratinization
hverfi	precinct	hýsing	outsourcing
hverfilbylur	cyclone	íbæting	doping
hverfileggur	radius	íblöndun	doping
hverfill	turbine	íbót	impurity
hverfisenditilboð	polling	íbúafjöldi	population
hvilft	cirque	íbúar	population
hvirfilbylur	cyclone	íbúatala	population
hvirfilpunktur	zenith	íbúi	occupant
hvirfilvindur	whirlwind	iða	turbulence
hvirfing	whorl	ídæling	injection
hvíta	sclera	ídælingarefni	injection
hvítagull	platinum	iðjuver	factory
hvítbörkur	albedo	iðnaður	industry
hvítfiskur	cisco	iðnbúskapur	agribusiness
hvítfruma	leukocyte	iðngrein	industry
hvítfrumnafæð	leukopenia	iðnnámstími	apprenticeship

iðnvæðing	industrialization	innfærsla	entry
iðrahreyfing	peristalsis	innfelling	embedding
iðrakveisa	colic	innflæði	influx
iðraskynfæri	interoceptor	innflutningsgjald	tariff
iðumyndun	turbulence	innganga	admission
iðustreymi	turbulence	inngangur	inlet
ífelling	implantation	inngrip	intrusion
íflekkur	child	innheimta	collection
ígræðsla	implantation	innherji	insider
ígulber	rambutan	innhvelfing	invagination
íhald	holdfast	innhverfa	introversion
íhaldsstefna	conservatism	innhverfing	invagination
íhrif	impression	innilokun	containment
íhvelft	concavity	innilokunarfælni	claustrophobia
íhvolfa	concavity	innilokunarstefna	containment
ílát	container	inning	execution
ildi	oxygen	innitaugar	wiring
ildisþurrð	anoxia	innkoma	entry
íle	isoleucine	innkýling	impaction
ílending	acclimatization	innlag	hypoblast
ílengd	elongation	innlagskím	hypoblast
ílifun	anabolism	innlán	deposits
ílimun	incorporation	innlausn	realization
illgresiseyðir	herbicide	innleggshólkur	collet
ilmappelsína	bergamot	innleiðing	institution
ilmkvoða	balsam	innleiðsla	transposition
ilmur	odour	innlendingur	autochthon
imperíalismi	imperialism	innlimum	incorporation
ímynd	imago	innlimun	incorporation
ímyndun	imagination	innöndun	inhalation
ímyndunarafl	imagination	innöndunarlyf	inhalation
indín	indium	innrækt	endogamy
indíum	indium	innrás	invasion
ingredienco	elements	innrauður	infrared
innæxlun	inbreeding	innrautt	infrared
innankönnun	exploration	innrennsli	inlet
innanrannsókn	exploration	innrétting	adjustment
innantaka	colic	innritun	registration
innanþreifing	exploration	innroði	infrared
innátenging	intrusion	innskeyti	intercalation
innblöndun	entrainment	innskeyting	intercalation
innborgun	reimbursement	innskot	intrusion
innbörkur	albedo	innsníkill	endoparasite
innbrotsþjófur	burglar	innsprautun	injection
innbyrðing	ingestion	innsprautunarventill	nozzle
inndæling	injection	innspýting	injection

innsteyping	embedding	jafnaðarmaður	democrat
innstilling	setting	jafnaðarstefna	socialism
innstreymi	inflow	jafnari	equalizer
innstunga	insertion	jafndægrapunktur	equinox
innsýn	perspective	jafndægri	equinox
inntak	inlet	jafndægur	equinox
inntaka	induction	jafngengi	parity
innvensl	endogamy	jafngildislína	isoline
innviðir	infrastructure	jafngreiðsla	annuity
innvirki	infrastructure	jafngreiðsluröð	annuity
intenci	means	jafni	potentiometer
interfasi	interphase	jafnkeypisviðskipti	clearing
interligiteco	relations	Jafnliðun	isomerization
interrilato	relations	jafnrétti	equality
inúlín	inulin	jafnréttisstefna	egalitarianism
iridín	iridium	jafnskipting	karyokinesis
iridíum	iridium	jafnstaða	inclusion
ísæi	insight	jafnþrýstiflötur	isobar
ísetning	installation	jafnþrýstilína	isobar
ísing	icing	jafnvægishneigð	homeostasis
ískuldi	frigidity	jafnvægiskorn	otolith
ísog	absorption	jafnvægismissir	disequilibrium
ísogshæfni	absorptance	jafnvægisskortur	disequilibrium
ísogshlutfall	absorptance	jafnvætting	equilibration
ísogstala	absorptance	jakobsfiskur	whiting
ísólefsín	isoleucine	japanspera	quince
ísóleusín	isoleucine	japansplóma	loquat
ísólevsín	isoleucine	jarðarber	strawberry
ísómer	isomer	jarðarbúar	earth
íspuni	confabulation	jarðarhálfhvel	hemisphere
ístað	stapes	jarðarkringlan	earth
ísvari	defroster	jarðeðlisfræði	geophysics
ítak	easement	jarðefnaleit	prospecting
ítaugun	innervation	jarðeign	estate
íþróttamaður	athlete	jarðeldafræði	volcanology
íþróttavöllur	arena	jarðfirð	apogee
ítónun	intonation	jarðfræði	geology
ítrekun	iteration	jarðhnik	tectonics
ítroðning	tamponade	jarðhniksfræði	tectonics
ítroðsla	tamponade	jarðhumall	yarrow
ítrun	iteration	jarðlag	stratum
ívaf	markup	jarðlagafræði	stratigraphy
jaðar	limb	jarðlagaskipan	stratigraphy
jaðarsvæði	periphery	jarðlagatenging	correlation
jáeind	positron	jarðnánd	perigee
jafna	equation	jarðolía	petroleum

jarðpera	groundnut	jurtasvif	phytoplankton
jarðrækt	agriculture	jurtir	vegetation
jarðræktarfræði	agronomy	jútarunni	jute
jarðræktunarfræði	agronomy	jútujurt	jute
jarðsamband	earth	kabyssa	caboose
jarðskjálftamælir	seismograph	kæfing	quenching
jarðskjálftariti	seismograph	káeind	kaon
jarðskorpa	lithosphere	kælibúnaður	refrigerator
jarðstöngulhnýði	corm	kæliefni	coolant
jarðtenging	earth	kælimiðill	coolant
jarðvatn	groundwater	kæling	refrigeration
jarðvegsfræði	agrology	kæliplata	lamella
jarðvegsjafnari	scraper	kælir	radiator
jarðyrkja	agriculture	kæliskápur	refrigerator
jarðýta	bulldozer	kælivökvi	coolant
járnbraut	railway	kæra	announcement
járnsmíði	forging	kæruleysi	carelessness
járnsmiðja	smithy	káeta	cabin
jáskaut	anode	kafaraverkir	bends
jeppi	jeep	kaffifífill	chicory
jepplingur	jeep	kaflahleðsla	segmentation
joð	iodine	kafli	episode
joðber	feijoa	kafmæði	asthma
jöfnuður	equality	kakó	cacao
jöfnun	unification	kakótré	cacao
jöfnunartenging	equalizer	kál	mustard
jökulalda	moraine	kaldbleyting	maceration
jökulgarður	moraine	kaldlæti	frigidity
jökulgjá	crevasse	kálfskjöt	veal
jökulkast	calving	kálfur	calf
jökulmelur	moraine	kalifornín	californium
jökulskál	cirque	kalífornín	californium
jökulskári	ogive	kaliforníukoli	windowpane
jökulsprunga	crevasse	kaliforníum	californium
jökulurð	moraine	kalín	potassium
jón	ion	kalínítrat	saltpetre
jónfærsla	electrophoresis	kalísaltpétur	saltpetre
jónun	ionisation	kalíum	potassium
jörð	earth	kalíumnítrat	saltpetre
Jörðin	earth	kalk	calcium
júðafiskur	jewfish	kalkkrampi	tetany
juĝi	rules	kalkspat	calcite
júl	joule	kalkstjarfi	tetany
jurtaæta	herbivore	kalómel	calomel
jurtagróður	flora	kaloría	calorie
jurtaríki	flora	kalsín	calcium

kalsít	calcite	kaupauðgistefna	mercantilism
kalsitónín	calcitonin	kaupleiga	leasing
kalsítónín	calcitonin	kaupleiguíbúð	condominium
kalsíum	calcium	kaupskaparstefna	mercantilism
kalsono	briefs	keðjuferill	catenary
kambabolla	cardoon	keðjuhnettla	streptococcus
kambás	camshaft	keðjukokkur	streptococcus
kambur	lobe	keðjun	condensation
kampasíld	capelin	kefli	spool
kandela	candela	keila	cusk
kanína	cony	keiluhólkur	socket
kannabis	cannabis	keiluþekjufruma	cone
kantalúpmelóna	cantaloupe	keipur	rowlock
kapítalismi	capitalism	keisarastjórn	imperialism
kapítlalismi	capitalism	kekkjun	agglutination
kappreiðabraut	runway	kembirannsókn	screening
kapteinn	commander	kennari	teacher
karbamíð	urea	kenni	identifier
karbíð	carbide	kennidæmi	paradigm
karbítur	carbide	kenniefni	tracer
kardimomma	cardamom	kennileitaflug	pilotage
kardimommujurt	cardamom	kennimark	logo
karfi	redfish	kennimerki	identifier
karlhormón	androgen	kenning	theory
karlmaður	bloke	kenningakerfi	ideology
karlveldi	patriarchy	kennisetning	theorem
karótín	carotene	kennistærð	parameter
kartafla	potato	kennitala	ratio
kartöflubaun	groundnut	kenniþekja	identity
kassava	cassava	kenniviðnám	resistivity
kassavamjöl	cassava	kennsl	identification
kassavarunni	cassava	kennslubók	reader
kassi	casing	kepalaukur	onion
kassía	cassia	keppni	competition
kassíakanell	cassia	keppur	reticulum
kassíukanill	cassia	keratín	keratin
kast	epiphysis	kerfi	system
kasthjól	flywheel	kerfiseining	taxon
kasthringur	slinger	kerfisfræði	cybernetics
Kastor	castor	kerfishyggja	holism
kasúhneta	cashew	kerra	car
katóða	cathode	kerti	candela
kaup	wages	ketill	boiler
kaupandi	buyer	ketónmiga	ketonuria
kaupauðgiskenning	mercantilism	kialo	grounds
kaupauðgisstefna	mercantilism	kíkir	binocular

kílókaloría	kilocalorie	kjarnakorn	nucleolus
kílómetri	kilometre	kjarnakvik	karyokinesis
kílóvatt	kilowatt	kjarnaofn	reactor
kílówatt	kilowatt	kjarnaögn	nucleon
kím	germ	kjarnasafi	nucleoplasm
kímblað	cotyledon	kjarnasamruni	fusion
kímblaðra	blastula	kjarnaskipting	karyokinesis
kímblöðrudiskur	blastoderm	kjarnasundrun	fission
kímblöðruveggur	blastoderm	kjarneind	nucleon
kímfruma	gamete	kjarni	kernel
kímmiðja	follicle	kjarnögn	nucleon
kímstöð	follicle	kjarnskipting	karyokinesis
kínín	kinin	kjarnviður	heartwood
kíníntré	quinine	kjarr	copse
kinnkjálki	maxilla	kjarrmæra	oregano
kippstýring	inching	kjarrminta	oregano
kippur	impulse	kjölfarssog	slipstream
kirkjupallur	gallery	kjörbýli	habitat
kirkjuskip	nave	kjördæmi	constituency
kirkjusvalir	gallery	kjörhæfni	selectivity
kirtilæxli	adenoma	kjörlendi	habitat
kirtilblaðra	acinus	kjörnungur	eucaryote
kirtilbólga	adenitis	kjörstilling	preference
kirtilhol	crypt	kjörvísi	selectivity
kirtilkrabbamein	adenocarcinoma	kjósandi	voter
kirtilkrabbi	adenocarcinoma	kjöt	meat
kirtill	gland	klæðaföll	menstruation
kirtilsafi	secretion	klæðning	lining
kirtilvaki	hormone	klæðskiptahneigð	transvestism
kísilflaga	microchip	klakskápur	incubator
kísilgúr	diatomite	klamydía	chlamydia
kísill	silicon	klasagerill	staphylococcus
kísiltvíoxíð	silica	klasahnettla	staphylococcus
kísl	silica	klasakokkur	staphylococcus
kista	chest	klefi	cabin
kítín	chitin	klemma	impaction
kíttisspaði	spatula	klerkaveldi	theocracy
kívíflétta	kiwi	klifun	repetition
kjaftagelgja	angler	klifurjurt	vine
kjalbakki	keelson	klifurplanta	scrambler
kjalband	keelson	klinkulæsing	latching
kjalsvín	keelson	klippir	clipper
kjarnablóðkorn	normoblast	klístrun	aggregation
kjarnaeind	nucleon	klofajárn	wishbone
kjarnafrymi	nucleoplasm	klofi	clevis
kjarnaklofnun	fission	klofning	dissociation

klofningur	dichotomy	kollur	condyle
klofnun	fission	kólónía	colony
klofspyrna	wishbone	koltvísýringsaukning	hypercapnia
klór	chlorine	koltvísýringshækkun	hypercapnia
klórflúrkolefni	chlorofluorocarbon	kólumbíum	niobium
klóríð	chloride	kolun	carbonization
klórófýl	chlorophyll	kolvatn	carbohydrate
klósigar	cirrus	kolvatnsefni	hydrocarbon
klukkustund	hour	kolvetni	carbohydrate
klukkutími	hour	kolvetnisgas	acetylene
klunguralpafjóla	cyclamen	kólvirkur	cholinergic
klungurfjóla	cyclamen	komplico	accessories
kluss	hawse	kon	gene
knastás	camshaft	kona	dame
knattgerill	coccus	konduki	wages
knattspyrna	football	kóngasalat	tarragon
knattspyrnumaður	footballer	köngull	cone
knattsýkill	coccus	konguló	spider
kné	knee	kónguló	spider
knippi	fascicle	köngur	spider
knýing	propulsion	kónn	cone
kódeín	codeine	könnun	exploration
kódín	codeine	könnunarleiðangur	exploration
kóðun	encoding	konsistigajo	elements
kofi	hut	konsúll	consul
köfnun	suffocation	kontraŭanto	opossum
köfnunarefni	n	kontraŭulo	opossum
Köggull	briquette	kontrolisto	checkers
kok	pharynx	konungdæmi	realm
kóka	coca	konungdómur	kingdom
kókarunni	coca	Konungsdæmið	monarchy
kokkur	coccus	konungsríki	realm
kókó	cacao	konungsveldi	kingdom
kókoshneta	coconut	Konungsveldið	monarchy
kókóshneta	coconut	kopar	copper
kokrenna	airway	kóraldýr	corals
kola	collier	kórallar	corals
kolamylsnuköggull	briquette	kóralrif	atoll
köldusótt	fever	körfukál	artichoke
kólera	cholera	körfuknattleikur	basketball
kólesteról	cholesterol	kóríander	coriander
kólfur	piston	kóríandrajurt	coriander
kolhýdrat	carbohydrate	kóríandri	coriander
kólínergur	cholinergic	kóríandur	coriander
kolkrabbi	squid	korka	dystrophy
kollektor	collector	korkudvergur	cretin

korndrjóli	ergot	krosspunktur	node
kóróna	corona	krosstengsl	chiasma
kortagerð	mapping	krossviður	plywood
kortavörpun	projection	krumpun	shrinkage
kortisól	cortisol	kúabóla	vaccinia
kortlagning	mapping	kúabólusetning	vaccination
kósínus	cosine	kúabóluveira	vaccinia
kostnaðaráætlun	quotation	kuðungur	cochlea
kostnaður	expenditure	kúla	sphere
kostoj	expenses	kúlomb	coulomb
kótangens	cotangent	kultivi	works
kotbóndi	peasant	kúlubaktería	coccus
kóti	height	kúluflötur	sphere
kótun	coding	kúlufrávik	flattening
krafa	requirement	kúlugerill	coccus
kraftfræði	mechanics	kúluskel	sphere
kraftmælir	ergometer	kúmen	caraway
kraftur	activity	kúmín	cumin
kraftvægi	torque	kummin	cumin
kragi	annulus	kunkulpa	accessories
krampaleysandi	anticonvulsant	kunkulpulo	accessories
krampaleysir	anticonvulsant	kúpa	sphere
krampi	braces	kúpling	coupling
krampo	braces	kúpni	convexity
krani	faucet	kuraĝiĝi	braces
krappi	curvature	kúrbítur	zucchini
kreppa	crisis	kúrín	curium
kretíndvergur	cretin	kúríum	curium
kríli	krill	kutimo	customs
kringla	disc	kvaðrant	quadrant
kristallslegur	crystalloid	kvaðrantur	quadrant
kristallslíki	crystalloid	kvæði	poem
kró	bifurcation	kvanti	quantum
kröfuhafi	creditor	kvarðabreyting	scaling
kröfukaup	factoring	kvarg	quark
kröfuskipti	clearing	kvark	quark
krókódíll	crocodile	kvarki	quark
króm	chromium	kvarkur	quark
króna	corolla	kvarnir	otolith
kross	spider	kvaronjaro	quarters
krossbrú	chiasma	kvarono	quarters
krossfiskar	starfish	kvartalo	quarters
krossfiskur	starfish	kvartil	phase
krossgáta	crossword	kvartmílubíll	slingshot
krosskúmen	cumin	kvashósti	croup
krossliður	sacrum	kveða	quince

kveði	quince	kynfruma	gamete
kveikibank	pinking	kyngingartregða	dysphagia
kveiking	welding	kynhneigð	sexuality
kveikir	igniter	kynhvörf	homosexuality
kveikja	ignition	kynjalyf	panacea
kveikjari	igniter	kynkirtill	gonad
kveikur	wick	kynkuldi	frigidity
kveisa	colic	kynkvísl	tribe
kvellislekja	neurasthenia	kynlöngun	erotism
kvenfrelsisstefna	feminism	kynnautn	erotism
kvengerð	feminism	kynning	demonstration
kvenhormón	estrogen	kynningarbæklingur	brochure
kvenmaður	dame	kynningarrit	brochure
kvenréttindastefna	feminism	kynningarskjal	prospectus
kvensjúkdómafræði	gynecology	kynningarspóla	trailer
kviðdómur	jury	kynningarstarf	promotion
kviðskjöldur	sternum	kynþáttaaðskilnaður	apartheid
kviður	abdomen	kynþáttaaðskilnarstefna	apartheid
kvika	magma	kynþáttafordómar	racism
kvikasilfursklóríð	calomel	kynþáttahatur	racism
kvikmæling	bioassay	kynþáttahroki	racism
kvísl	bough	kynþáttaraðskilnaðarstefna	apartheid
kvíslun	bifurcation	kynþáttarembingur	racism
kvistur	node	kynþáttastefna	racism
kvittun	voucher	kynþáttur	clan
kvöð	easement	kynþóttafórdomar	racism
kvoða	resin	kynþroska	imago
kvöðull	releaser	kynþroskaaldur	puberty
kvoðutré	sapodilla	kynþroskaskeið	puberty
kvörðun	scaling	kynþroski	puberty
kvos	excavation	kyntigla	gynandromorph
kvóti	quotient	kynvilla	homosexuality
kW	kilowatt	kynvís	heterosexual
kylfa	mallet	kynvísi	heterosexuality
kýli	furuncle	kýr	cattle
kynæði	erotomania	kýrauga	sidelight
kynbætur	eugenics	kyrkingur	cretinism
kynblöndun	hybridization	kyrkivöxtur	cretinism
kynbótafræði	eugenics	kyrningahrap	agranulocytosis
kynbótastefna	eugenics	kyrrahafsþorskur	dogfish
kyndiklefi	stokehold	kyrrðarstund	taps
kyndikorn	mitochondrion	kyrrsetning	sequestration
kyndill	flashlight	kyrrstaða	stasis
kyndirúm	stokehold	laborenspezo	wages
kynfæri	genitals	labori	works
kynferði	sexuality	laboro	works

laborpago	wages	landbúnaðarviðskipti	agribusiness
láð	earth	landbúnaður	agriculture
lægð	depression	landeyjar	delta
lægðardrag	trough	landgangur	gangway
lægðarsvæði	depression	landgöngubryggja	pier
læging	masking	landgönguliði	mariner
lækkar	descent	landhæð	elevation
lækkun	depression	landkönnun	exploration
læknamóttaka	surgery	landmælingamaður	surveyor
lækning	therapy	landmótunarfræði	geomorphology
lækningamaður	therapist	landnám	settlement
lækningastofa	surgery	landsig	subsidence
læknir	physician	landslag	morphology
læknisfræði	medication	landslagsútlínur	topography
lærlingsstaða	apprenticeship	landsvæði	terrain
læsi	literacy	landsýn	landfall
læsing	lockout	landtaka	landfall
lag	strata	landvistarleyfi	asylum
lagaboð	statute	langa	ling
lagabreyting	amendment	langeldur	hearth
lagarsíld	cisco	langhalar	grenadiers
lagasetning	legislation	langhlið	hypotenuse
lagatúlkun	construction	langliður	tibia
lagdeiling	stratification	langlífi	longevity
lagfæring	improvement	langljómun	phosphorescence
laggangur	sill	langrauf	spline
lágleggsstafur	descender	langsetill	stretcher
lágleggur	descender	langsýni	hypermetropia
lagskipting	stratification	langtímaleiga	leasing
lágský	stratus	langtímaverðbréf	investments
lagsverð	rapier	lántaka	borrowing
láhnit	abscissa	lántakandi	borrower
laki	psalterium	lantan	lanthanum
laktósi	lactose	lantaníð	lanthanide
lampi	valve	lanþan	lanthanum
lán	borrowing	lanþaníð	lanthanide
lánardrottinn	creditor	lánveitandi	creditor
land	earth	lárensín	lawrencium
landafræði	geography	lárensíum	lawrencium
landamæri	boundary	lásfleygur	cotter
landamerki	boundary	lati	inhibitor
landamerkjalýsing	delineation	lauf	sheet
landamerkjamæling	demarcation	lauffelling	defoliation
landareign	premises	laufgræna	chlorophyll
landauki	reclamation	laugardagur	sabbath
landbúnaðarverkamaður	peasant	laukur	corm

laun	salary	leigutaki	charterer
launagjöld	payroll	leigutekjur	rental
launaskrá	payroll	leikhús	playhouse
launþegi	employee	leikhverfing	dramatization
lausabeinsmyndun	sequestration	leikkona	actress
lausafjárstaða	liquidity	leirgedda	bowfin
lausafregn	grapevine	leit	prospecting
lausn	disengagement	leitarljós	searchlight
lausnarbeiðni	resignation	leitarljóskastari	searchlight
lax	salmon	leitarmaður	trailer
laxaseiði	parr	leitarsjónauki	finder
leður	corium	leki	leakage
leðurhúð	corium	lekt	permeability
leg	uterus	lén	domain
lega	attitude	lend	croup
legástunga	amniocentesis	lending	landing
legghöfuð	epiphysis	lengd	longitude
leggjarhöfuð	condyle	lengdarbaugur	longitude
leggur	crus	lengdargráða	longitude
legháls	cervix	lenging	dilation
leghetta	diaphragm	lénsskipulag	feudalism
legkaka	placenta	lénsveldi	feudalism
legkökutotur	cotyledon	les	lexeme
legstunga	amniocentesis	lesandi	reader
leguhús	casing	lesblinda	alexia
legvatn	waters	lesefni	reading
legvatnsástunga	amniocentesis	lesmál	text
leið	routing	lesstol	alexia
leiðamót	intersection	lestarými	stowage
leiðari	leader	lestun	loading
leiðarit	flowchart	lestur	reading
leiðarval	routing	letur	font
leiðaval	vine	leturborð	keyboard
leiðbeinandi	supervisor	leturgerð	font
leiðbeining	guideline	leturprentun	letterpress
leiðbeiningar	instructions	leyfishafi	subscriber
leiðing	implication	leyfisveiting	licensing
leiðni	conductance	leynd	confidentiality
leiðrétting	amendment	leynimakk	collusion
leiðsaga	navigation	leysiensím	lysozyme
leiðsögn	navigation	leysigeisli	laser
leiðsögumaður	navigator	leysing	solution
leifar	pickling	leysir	laser
leiga	rental	leysitæki	laser
leigubíll	cab	leysni	solubility
leigusali	lessor	liðband	ligament

liðdýr	arthropod	lífsundrun	biodegradation
liðfætla	arthropod	lífsviðurværi	subsistence
liðhlaup	luxation	lífsýki	diarrhea
liðhöfuð	epiphysis	líftækni	biotechnology
liðkun	mobilization	líftaktur	biorhythm
liðsforingi	officer	lífþyngd	biomass
liðskipting	segmentation	líftölfræði	biostatistics
liðun	polymerization	lifun	survival
liður	knee	lifur	liver
líf	life	lífvæni	viability
lífeðlisfræði	physiology	lífvænleiki	viability
lífefnafræði	biochemistry	lífvera	organism
lífefnamagn	biomass	lífverkfræði	bioengineering
lífefnamyndun	biosynthesis	lífvirkniprófun	bioassay
lífefnasmíð	biosynthesis	lígasi	ligase
lífefnasundrun	catabolism	lignín	lignin
lífefnatækni	biotechnology	lík	cadaver
lífeyrisgreiðsla	annuity	líkami	soma
líffæri	organ	líkamsbygging	constitution
líffærisbilun	insufficiency	líkamsfræði	morphology
líffærisleif	rudiment	líkamsgerð	somatotype
líffærisvísir	rudiment	líkanagerð	modelling
líffræði	biology	líkbrennsluofn	crematory
lífgreining	bioassay	líkfrumulitningur	autosome
lífgun	vivification	líkhár	lanugo
lífheimur	biosphere	líking	simulation
lífheldni	survival	líkingalæti	symbolism
lífhimnubólga	peritonitis	líkn	palliation
lífhrynjandi	biorhythm	líknarbelgur	amnion
lífhvati	enzyme	líkskurður	dissection
lífhvolf	biosphere	limgerði	windbreak
líflengd	life	límingasía	dialyzer
lífljómi	phosphorescence	límingasíun	dialysis
lífmælingar	biometry	límir	ligase
lífmagn	biomass	límmiði	sticker
lífmassi	biomass	limur	limb
lifraræxli	hepatoma	lind	source
lifrarfrumukrabbamein	hepatoma	lindarblettur	fontanelle
lifrarskorpnun	cirrhosis	línhvolf	asthenosphere
lífríki	biota	linsa	lentil
lífritmi	biorhythm	linsubaun	lentil
lífsbjörg	subsistence	linsufrekna	lentigo
lífshvöt	libido	linsusjónauki	refractor
lífsmáti	lifestyle	línuhlaupsbjögun	pairing
lífsstíll	lifestyle	línuröðun	alignment
lífsþægindagrædgi	materialism	línusamdragi	concentrator

línutvennd	doublet	litrófssamfella	continuum
lípíð	lipid	litrófssjá	spectroscope
lipurð	manoeuvrability	litsjá	spectrometer
lirfa	larva	litskiljun	chromatography
listbær	gallery	litstilling	chroma
listhús	gallery	litstökun	quantization
listskrubba	gallery	litukrampi	miosis
liststöð	gallery	litunarkollur	safflower
listval	gallery	litunarþistill	safflower
listvör	gallery	litvilla	dichromatism
lita	iris	litvísir	indicator
litamæling	colorimetry	ljóm	luminescence
litarleysi	albinism	ljómefni	phosphor
litbaugur	corona	ljómi	luminance
litblær	chroma	ljómstækkun	irradiation
litfestir	fixative	ljómun	luminescence
litgildi	chroma	ljóni	liner
litgreining	colorimetry	ljóri	skylight
lithimna	iris	ljörvi	laser
liþín	lithium	ljósafl	luminosity
lithvolf	chromosphere	ljósálfur	brownie
litillækkun	humiliation	ljósameðferð	phototherapy
litín	lithium	ljósáta	krill
litíum	lithium	ljósbeyging	diffraction
litkaaldin	litchi	ljósbrjótur	refractor
litkaber	litchi	ljósdeyfitala	opacity
litkaplóma	litchi	ljósdeyfni	opacity
litkjarni	karyosome	ljóseðlisfræði	optics
litleysi	achromasia	ljóseind	photon
litmælifræði	colorimetry	ljósfræði	optics
litmæling	colorimetry	ljósker	lantern
litmælir	colorimeter	ljóslækning	phototherapy
litni	chromatin	ljósleiðninemi	photocell
litningapörun	synapsis	ljósleitni	heliotropism
litningayfirfærsla	translocation	ljósleysir	laser
litningur	chromosome	ljósmælir	photometer
lítri	liter	ljósnæmishlutfall	luminosity
litritun	chromatography	ljósnemi	photocell
litrófsfræði	spectroscopy	ljósögn	photon
litrófsgreining	spectroscopy	ljósop	aperture
litrófsljósmælir	spectrophotometer	ljósopsstærandi	mydriatic
litrófsmælir	spectrometer	ljósopsstærir	mydriatic
litrófsmynd	spectrogram	ljósopsþrenging	miosis
litrófsrannsókn	spectroscopy	ljósopsþynna	diaphragm
litrófsrit	spectrogram	ljósröfunarnemi	photocell
litrófsriti	spectrograph	ljóssella	photocell

ljósskammtur	photon	löggilding	authorization
ljósspennunemi	photocell	löggjöf	legislation
ljósþéttir	condenser	löghald	sequestration
ljósþéttni	absorptivity	löghyggja	determinism
ljósturn	lantern	lögleiðing	transposition
ló	pubescence	lögmaður	attorney
lóð	location	lögmæti	validity
loðka	capelin	lögmál	law
loðna	pubescence	lögn	duct
loðsíld	capelin	lögregluðjónn	officer
loðsíli	capelin	lögreglumaður	constable
lóðun	welding	lögreglustjóri	commissioner
lófatak	acclamation	lögregluþjónn	bobby
loforð	assurance	lögsaga	jurisdiction
loft	ambience	lögsagnarumdæmi	jurisdiction
loftæð	trachea	lögskýring	construction
loftauga	stoma	lögstétt	estate
loftbólurek	aeroembolism	logsuða	welding
loftbraut	airway	logsuðugas	acetylene
loftfæla	anaerobe	lögtak	execution
lofthjúpur	atmosphere	lögun	morphology
loftlagsfræði	climatology	lok	conclusion
loftlíf	aerobiosis	loka	valve
loftlína	airline	lokasteinn	keystone
loftnet	antenna	loki	terminator
loftnetshlíf	radome	lökkun	lacquering
loftpoki	aerostat	loktákn	terminator
loftpressa	compressor	lokuhrúður	vegetation
loftpúðaskip	hovercraft	lokun	obturation
loftræsing	ventilation	lokuvöðvi	sphincter
loftræsting	ventilation	lömunarveiki	poliomyelitis
loftskipting	ventilation	lón	lagoon
loftskolun	injection	löndun	landing
loftskrúfa	propeller	longanber	longan
loftslagsfræði	climatology	lopi	edema
loftsog	suction	lorno	binocular
loftsteinn	meteor	löskun	trauma
loftsveipir	turbulence	löss	loess
loftþyngd	atmosphere	lostaböðull	sadist
lofttómshreinsun	degassing	lostakvalari	sadist
loftúði	aerosol	losun	clearing
Loftun	ventilation	losunaróhapp	episode
loftvera	aerobe	lota	batch
lög	statute	lotun	cutoff
lögfræði	law	lótusblóm	lotus
lögfræðingur	attorney	lúða	halibut

lúgugatsábreiða	tarpaulin	lystiskúta	yacht
lúmen	lumen	maður	homo
lummari	butterfish	mæða	modality
lundaseiði	whiting	mæði	dyspnea
lungnablaðra	alveolus	mægðir	affinity
lungnablöðruseyti	surfactant	mælaborð	fascia
lungnapípa	bronchus	mælahús	binnacle
lungnaþan	emphysema	mælandi	speaker
lungnaþemba	emphysema	mælieining	unit
lúsaegg	nit	mælikvarði	criterion
lúserna	alfalfa	mæling	measuring
lútesín	lutetium	mælipípa	burette
lútetín	lutetium	mælisálestur	reading
lútetíum	lutetium	mælistærð	parameter
lútfíkill	basophil	mælitæki	indicator
lýðfræði	demography	mælitækjavæðing	instrumentation
lýðnet	internet	mælitækni	instrumentation
lýðræðissinni	democrat	mælivídd	dimension
lyf	medicine	mænugránabólga	poliomyelitis
lyfjablanda	mixture	mænusótt	poliomyelitis
lyfjabúð	dispensary	mænuveiki	poliomyelitis
lyfjaforskrift	formula	mænuvisnun	tabes
lyfjafræði	pharmacology	mæri	boundary
lyfjagjöf	dosage	mætti	potency
lyfjameðferð	medication	máfuglar	lari
lyfjamisnotkun	habituation	magaverkur	gastralgia
lyfjaþol	habituation	magi	abdomen
lyflæknisfræði	medicine	magn	magnitude
lyfting	suspension	magnákvörðun	quantification
lyftispillir	spoiler	magnesín	magnesium
lykja	ampulla	magnesíum	magnesium
lykkja	jumper	magnetróna	magnetron
lyklaborð	keyboard	magnetrónn	magnetron
lykt	odour	magnfesting	quantification
lyktarskyn	olfaction	magnhæfing	quantification
lyndi	mood	magnín	magnesium
lyngheiði	heath	magníum	magnesium
lyngmói	heath	magnmæling	quantification
lýsa	whiting	magnsetja	quantification
lýsing	schema	maísíld	shad
lýsingarmagn	exposure	makríll	mackerel
lýsingur	descriptor	mál	dimension
lýsiorð	descriptor	málaflutningsmaður	lawyer
lýsir	descriptor	málamiðlari	conciliator
lýsitala	statistic	málamiðlun	mediation
lýsitölufall	statistic	malarás	esker

málari	painter	manngerðafræði	typology
malaríumý	anopheles	mannhatur	misanthropy
málboð	message	mannheimar	earth
málfærslumaður	lawyer	mannhyggja	humanism
málflutningur	representation	mannop	porthole
málflytjandi	lawyer	manntalsfræði	demography
málfræði	syntax	mannþróun	anthropogenesis
málgögn	data	mannúðarstefna	humanism
máilína	baseline	mannvirki	culture
mállýska	dialect	mannvistarfræði	demography
málmgrýti	ore	mánuður	month
málmhleifur	ingot	mappa	folder
málmsteypa	casting	mar	hematoma
málmsuða	welding	mara	incubus
málmþynna	shim	marantarót	arrowroot
málmur	metal	margfaldari	multiplier
malnobla	means	margfeldi	product
málraun	rating	margfeldni	degeneracy
málskipan	syntax	margföldun	proliferation
málskostnaður	expenses	marghyrningur	polygon
málsmeðferð	procedure	margleitni	polymorphism
málsskjöl	dossier	margmiðlun	hypermedia
málstærð	norm	margúll	hematoma
málstærðir	rating	maríúana	marijuana
málsvari	protagonist	maríutása	cirrocumulus
málþing	symposium	mark	marker
máltilfinning	intuition	markaðsfærsla	marketing
maltósi	maltose	markaðsfræði	marketing
maltsykur	maltose	markaðskerfi	capitalism
malurt	wormwood	markaðssamtök	cartel
málvik	tolerance	markaðssetning	marketing
málvísindi	linguistics	markari	marker
mandla	almond	markgildi	threshold
mangan	manganese	marki	marker
máni	meniscus	markmiðshugsjón	entelechy
manjók	cassava	marktækni	significance
manjokrunni	cassava	marktekt	significance
mannafli	manpower	markvirkni	effectiveness
mannakynbætur	eugenics	mastfruma	mastocyte
mannbætur	eugenics	mastur	mast
mannblendni	gregariousness	mat	appraisal
manndauði	lethality	mát	template
mannfélag	society	matarbúr	pantry
mannfjöldi	population	matarlaukur	onion
mannfræði	anthropology	materia	materials
manngerðaflokkun	typology	materiala	materials

materialo	materials	mendelevín	mendelevium
matgrægi	bulimia	mendelevíum	mendelevium
matlaukur	onion	mengari	polluter
maur	pismire	mengi	category
meðal	medicine	mengill	polluter
meðaldæmi	norm	mengun	impurity
meðalganga	mediation	mengunarefni	pollutant
meðferð	therapy	mengunarský	smog
meðferðaraðili	therapist	mengunarvaldar	pollutant
meðferðarheldni	compliance	mengunarvaldur	contaminant
meðferðarreglur	procedure	menn	homo
meðför	implication	menning	culture
meðgönguhormón	progesterone	menningaraðlögun	acculturation
meðlimur	member	menningarblöndun	acculturation
meðmæli	recommendation	menningarhættir	culture
meðsog	entrainment	menningarnám	acculturation
meðsveiflun	resonance	menntun	education
meðvitund	consciousness	menntunarbót	enrichment
megind	quantity	mergur	medulla
megindlegur	quantity	mergvaki	adrenaline
meginstofn	axis	merkantílismi	mercantilism
meginstöngull	axis	merki	pylon
megintölva	mainframe	merkiefni	tracer
mehanikisto	mechanics	merkigen	marker
meiðsli	trauma	merking	definition
meinafræði	pathology	merkingarauki	connotation
meinaleit	screening	merkingarblær	connotation
meindýr	vermin	merkingarháttur	modality
meinlætamunaður	masochism	merkingarkjarni	denotation
meinlíf	antibiosis	merkingarleysa	anomaly
meinrek	metastasis	merkingarskipti	metonymy
meinsáð	metastasis	merkiskjöldur	escutcheon
meinvaldur	pathogen	merkisspjald	badge
meinvarp	metastasis	merkjablöndun	crosstalk
meiósa	meiosis	merkjabreytir	transducer
meisa	tit	merski	marsh
mekantílismi	mercantilism	mesóna	meson
meldrjóli	ergot	met	methionine
mellifolia	yarrow	metakerfi	hierarchy
melóna	cantaloupe	metan	methane
melónuplanta	cantaloupe	metanól	methanol
melónutré	papaya	meþíónín	methionine
melting	assimilation	metill	estimator
membra	membrane	metíónín	methionine
memuaro	papers	metri	metre
mendelefín	mendelevium	mettun	satiation

meysir	maser	millistykki	adapter
meza	means	millitenging	jumper
meznombra	means	millitengsl	interconnection
mezo	means	milliverkun	interaction
miðbaugsbreidd	declination	milta	lien
miðbaugur	equator	milti	lien
miðeind	meson	minning	reminiscence
miðheili	midbrain	minnisbót	reminiscence
miðhvolf	mesosphere	minnisefling	mnemonics
miðill	media	minnisgeymd	retention
miðjarðarlína	equator	minnisgluggi	window
miðlari	mediator	minnishjálp	mnemonics
miðlun	brokerage	minnishylki	cartridge
miðögn	meson	minnisleysi	amnesia
miðpunktur	centroid	minnisspor	engram
miðskip	nave	minnistækni	mnemonics
miðskipan	concentration	minnistap	fugue
miðstétt	bourgeoisie	mínusskaut	cathode
miðstöð	forum	minuto	minutes
miðstöðvarketill	furnace	misáttun	disorientation
miðstöðvarofn	radiator	misgengishreyfing	faulting
miðstrengur	diameter	mishæfing	maladjustment
miðstýring	centralization	mishljómur	dissonance
miðtaugakerfishrörnun	degeneration	mishverfa	asymmetry
míeind	muon	mislægi	discordance
mikilmennskuæði	megalomania	mismunur	variance
milliás	countershaft	misræmi	discordance
millibil	interval	missætti	disagreement
millifasi	interphase	misseravindur	monsoon
milliganga	mediation	misserisvindar	monsoon
milligátt	gateway	misvægi	disequilibrium
millihaldari	adapter	misvirðiskaup	arbitrage
milliheili	diencephalon	misvísun	variation
milliheyrsla	crosstalk	mítósa	karyokinesis
millihimna	diaphragm	mjaðmagrind	pelvis
millikyn	intersex	mjaðmarbein	hipbone
millikynjungur	intersex	mjaðmarskál	acetabulum
millilegg	shim	mjak	inching
millileggsskífa	spacer	mjaltavaki	oxytocin
milliliður	mediator	mjölbanani	plantain
millinetagátt	gateway	mjólkurhormón	prolactin
milliplata	shim	mjólkurmyndun	lactation
millirifjaverkur	pleurodynia	mjólkurmyndunarvaki	prolactin
milliríkjasamningur	treaty	mjólkursafi	latex
milliskorageiri	internode	mjólkursykur	lactose
millistig	interphase	mjölrót	arrowroot

Reference: Webster's Online Dictionary (www.websters-online-dictionary.org)

mjölvakljúfur	ptyalin	motivo	grounds
mjósi	ling	mótlyf	antagonist
móar	heath	mótmæli	demonstration
móðgun	offence	mótsermi	antiserum
móðurborð	motherboard	mótsetning	contradistinction
móðurbróðir	uncle	Motspíspil	counterplay
móðurspjald	motherboard	mótstaða	resistor
móðursýki	hysteria	móttakandi	receiver
móðursystir	aunt	móttakari	receiver
mögnun	amplification	mótþrói	rebellion
mókol	lignite	möttulbaktería	chlamydia
mól	mol	möttulgerill	chlamydia
molar	pickling	mótun	modulation
mold	topsoil	mótvægisaðgerð	countermeasure
moldarefni	humus	mótvægismælir	compensator
mólendi	heath	mótverkun	antagonism
mólýbden	molybdenum	mRKS	mrna
mólýbdin	molybdenum	múffa	socket
möndull	axis	múkki	fulmar
möndulvelta	precession	munaðarhyggja	sensualism
mongólítagervi	mongolism	munni	aperture
mongólófðaháttur	mongolism	munnur	stoma
monsún	monsoon	munnvatn	saliva
monsúntími	monsoon	munnvatnsmyndun	salivation
monsúnvindur	monsoon	munnvatnsrennsli	salivation
montprik	bragger	munuðvíma	orgasm
mor	turbidity	munúðvíma	orgasm
Mór	peat	murkrampo	braces
morala	morals	murpapero	papers
moralajô	morals	mustarðar	mustard
moralinstruo	morals	musterishneta	ginkgo
mörður	marten	musteristré	ginkgo
mórena	moraine	mýeind	muon
morgunberkja	cherimoya	mýelín	myelin
mörk	boundary	mýkt	flexibility
mörkun	modification	myldi	humus
moro	customs	mýli	myelin
moskusmelóna	cantaloupe	mýlishimna	neurolemma
moskusrotta	muskrat	mylking	lactation
mót	template	mylla	chopper
mótefnaskortur	agammaglobulinemia	myndbirting	visualization
mótefnaþurrð	agammaglobulinemia	myndbreyting	metamorphosis
mótefnavaki	immunogen	myndbrigði	isomer
mótefni	immunoglobulin	myndefni	product
mótefnisvaki	antigen	myndeind	pixel
móteitur	antidote	myndeining	pixel

myndfærsla	imaging	nafarhlíf	spinner
myndfóstur	fetus	nafli	navel
myndgagnasafn	library	nafn	denomination
myndhermig	imaging	nafnauki	extension
myndhöndlun	imaging	nafnhvörf	metonymy
myndhús	gallery	nafnmerki	logo
myndhverfing	metaphor	nafnstol	anomia
myndhvörf	metaphor	nafnvextir	coupon
myndleif	afterimage	nagli	fingernail
myndlíking	metaphor	náhvalur	narwhal
myndlykill	decoder	nákvæmni	definition
myndsetning	rendering	nálægð	involvement
myndstilling	focusing	nálormur	nematode
myndtákn	icon	náma	reservoir
myndun	production	nánd	proximity
myndunarfræði	morphology	nándhrif	exposure
mynni	stoma	nár	cadaver
mynstrasafn	epoch	naríutása	altocumulus
mynstrun	masking	nasaop	nostrils
myntslátta	coining	nasir	nostrils
mýóglóbín	myoglobin	natrín	sodium
mýraköldumý	anopheles	natríum	sodium
mýraköldusýkill	plasmodium	náttblinda	hemeralopia
mýrakölduvaldur	plasmodium	náttföt	pyjamas
mýri	marsh	nátthús	binnacle
myrkur	obscurity	náttúruhamfarir	catastrophe
myrkvastig	magnitude	náttúrulíf	wildlife
nabbi	papilla	natur	sodium
náðarvald	charisma	nauðasamningar	composition
naðra	asp	nauðasamningur	composition
næmi	excitability	nauðhyggja	determinism
næming	sensitization	nauðþurftir	subsistence
næmir	sensitizer	nauðung	compulsion
næmisaukning	facilitation	nauðungarsamningur	composition
næmisstuðull	sensitivity	nauður	compulsion
næmleikastuðull	sensitivity	naut	cattle
næmni	affinity	nautgripaklafi	stanchion
næpa	turnip	neĉefa	accessories
næpukál	turnip	neðanjarðarlest	metro
nærbuxur	knickers	nefkvef	rhinitis
næringarferli	nutrition	nefnari	denominator
næringarfræði	nutrition	nefnd	committee
næringarskortur	malnutrition	nefndarmaður	commissioner
nærsifjar	inbreeding	nefni	identifier
nærsýni	myopia	nefnistol	anomia
næturgali	nightingale	nefrennsli	rhinorrhea

nefslímubólga	rhinitis	nifteind	neutron
nefstefna	heading	nikótínsýra	niacin
neftróna	neutron	nióbín	niobium
negling	fixation	nióbín	niobium
negravajo	accessories	nióbíum	niobium
neikvæði	negativism	nippill	nipple
neind	neutron	nítratmyndun	nitrification
neiskaut	cathode	nítrít	nitrite
neistadreifir	distributor	nítrun	nitrification
neitun	negation	nitur	nitrogen
nemandi	pupil	nítur	nitrogen
nemi	receptor	níundarkvarði	vernier
neodým	neodymium	njálgsýking	oxyuriasis
neódým	neodymium	njótandi	beneficiary
neptún	neptunium	njúton	newton
nerti	vulnerability	nóbelín	nobelium
nes	peninsula	nóbelíum	nobelium
nesjamennska	insularity	nöf	spider
net	grid	nögl	fingernail
netheimar	cyberspace	noradrenalín	noradrenaline
nethimna	retina	notahyggja	pragmatism
nethimnugróf	fovea	nudd	attrition
Netið	reticulum	núðlur	macaroni
netjuský	altocumulus	nukso	nut
netjuþykkni	altocumulus	nurta	papilla
netkorn	ribosome	nútímavæðing	modernization
netkort	grid	núvirðing	discounting
netlykkja	lobe	nýbreytni	innovation
netskoðari	navigator	nýburakassi	incubator
netvörn	firewall	nýbyggð	settlement
nevtróna	neutron	nýgengi	incidence
neysla	ingestion	nýjung	innovation
níasín	niacin	nýlenda	colony
niðurbrot	degradation	nýliðun	recruitment
niðurfærir	depressor	nýmæli	innovation
niðurfelling	suspension	nýmyndun	synthesis
niðurgangur	diarrhea	nýra	kidney
niðurrif	degradation	nýráðning	recruitment
niðurröðun	disposal	nýrahnoðrabólga	glomerulonephritis
niðursetning	installation	nýrakvilli	nephropathy
niðurseyðing	condensation	nýrapípnaskemmd	nephrosis
niðurskipan	classification	nýrilmergvaki	adrenaline
niðurstaða	conclusion	nýrlægur	adrenal
niðurstreymi	subsidence	nýrnahnoðrabólga	glomerulonephritis
niðurstreymisstrókur	chimney	nýskipan	restructuring
niðursuða	canning	nýsköpun	modernization

nýskráning	recruitment	ofurhiti	hyperthermia
nýsmíð	synthesis	ofurkvöl	hyperalgesia
nýsteinöld	neolithic	ofurmagni	squid
nýting	utilization	ofurmiðlun	hypermedia
nýtingarréttur	usufruct	ofurnæmi	hypersensitivity
nytjahyggja	utilitarianism	ofursársaukanæmi	hyperalgesia
nytjastefna	utilitarianism	ofurslef	salivation
nytsemishyggja	utilitarianism	ofurtölva	supercomputer
nýuppfinning	innovation	ofvirkni	hyperactivity
nýyrði	neologism	ofvöxtur	vegetation
óætisfíkn	pica	ógætni	carelessness
objekto	things	ógagnsæi	opacity
óðal	domain	ögðulirfa	redia
oddbogi	ogive	ógegnsæi	opacity
oddpunktur	vertex	ógilding	abolition
oddur	apex	ógjaldfærni	insolvency
óðjurt	hemlock	óhæði	independence
ódugur	impotence	óhapp	mishap
óendanlegt	infinity	óhreinindi	impurity
óendanleiki	infinity	óhreinkun	doping
ofanfall	fallout	ójafnvægi	imbalance
ofanvarp	projection	okfruma	zygote
ofanvörpun	projection	oki	cleat
ófarir	catastrophe	ökklabein	talus
ofbætur	overcompensation	okþráðlufasi	zygotene
ofbeit	overgrazing	ökumaður	driver
offita	adiposity	ökuriti	tachograph
offramleiðsla	overproduction	ökutæki	vehicle
offylli	engorgement	ókyrrð	turbulence
ófjósemi	infertility	ólæsi	illiteracy
ofkæling	hypothermia	öld	century
ofloðna	hirsutism	öldrunarfræði	gerontology
ofn	radiator	öldubeygja	diffraction
ofnæmi	allergy	öldubrjótur	breakwater
ofnæmistilhneiging	atopy	öldudalur	trough
ófreskigáfa	psi	ölduhreyfing	fluctuation
ófriður	warfare	ölduleiðir	waveguide
ófrjósemi	infertility	öldulengd	wavelength
ofsakláði	urticaria	öldungadeild	senate
ofskynjun	hallucination	öldungadeildin	senate
ofskynjunarefni	hallucinogen	öldungaráð	senate
ofstæling	hypertonia	öldusótt	brucellosis
ofþrýstingur	hypertension	öldustokkur	waveguide
öfugkjafta	megrim	ólga	turbulence
öfugþróun	devolution	ölgleymi	blackout
öfuguggaháttur	degeneracy	olíubiða	sump

olíugeymir	bunker	örbylgjuleysir	maser
olíugjöf	accelerator	örbylgjuvaki	magnetron
olíugöng	gallery	orða	decoration
olíupanna	sump	ordabóg	dictionary
Olíuskip	tanker	orðabók	dictionary
ölvíma	intoxication	orðasafn	lexicon
ölvun	intoxication	orðaskrín	thesaurus
óm	ohm	orðastæða	collocation
ómega	omega	orðhlutafræði	morphology
óminni	amnesia	orðmerki	logo
ómsjá	sonar	orðmyndunaratferli	neologism
ómskoðun	sonar	orðrómur	grapevine
ómur	resonance	orðstöðulykill	concordance
ónæmi	immunity	óreganó	oregano
ónæming	vaccination	óregla	anomaly
ónæmingargeta	antigenicity	óregluhreyfing	ataxia
ónæmingarmeðferð	immunotherapy	óreiða	entropy
ónæmisaðgerð	immunization	óreiðustig	entropy
ónæmisbæling	immunosuppression	öreigalýður	proletariat
ónæmisbælingarmeðferð	immunotherapy	öreigar	proletariat
ónæmisblóðvatn	antiserum	öreigastétt	proletariat
ónæmisflúrljóm	immunofluorescence	öreindafræði	microelectronics
ónæmisflúrljómun	immunofluorescence	örflóra	microflora
ónæmisflúrskíma	immunofluorescence	orgel	organ
ónæmisflúrskin	immunofluorescence	örgjörvi	microprocessor
ónæmisfræðingur	immunologist	örhljóð	ultrasound
ónæmisglóbúlín	immunoglobulin	órigan	oregano
ónæmissermi	antiserum	óriganó	oregano
ónæmisvaki	immunogen	orkubreytir	transducer
önd	vestibule	orkukorn	mitochondrion
öndun	ventilation	orkuleysing	neutralization
öndunarefnaflutningur	respiration	örlæti	unselfishness
öndunargríma	inhaler	örmagni	squid
öndunarvél	respirator	ormalyf	vermifuge
óneyti	impotence	orniþín	ornithine
öng	degeneracy	ornitín	ornithine
öngfælni	claustrophobia	örorka	disability
öngstig	degeneracy	orsakaflétta	nexus
ónotakennd	dysphoria	orsakalögmál	causality
op	orifice	orsakasamband	causality
opbreidd	aperture	orsakasamhengi	causality
opna	outcrop	orsakatrú	determinism
opnun	dehiscence	örtölva	microcomputer
oponanto	opossum	örtölvuflaga	microchip
opþvermál	aperture	örvari	activator
opvídd	aperture	örvarrót	arrowroot

örvera	microbe	papava	papaw
örverufræði	microbiology	papero	papers
örverugróður	flora	paprikuduft	paprika
örveruræktun	culture	parencino	relatives
örvi	inducer	parenco	relations
örvun	facilitation	paŝi	steps
ósamfellanleiki	incompatibility	páskar	passover
ósamhverfa	asymmetry	paŝo	steps
ósamlægi	nonconformity	patróna	collet
ósamleitni	divergence	pektín	pectin
ósamræmi	nonconformity	peningasending	remittance
ósamrýmanleiki	incompatibility	peptíð	peptide
ósérplægni	altruism	pera	pear
óseyrar	delta	persóna	personage
óseyri	delta	persono	persons
óshólmar	delta	persónugerð	personality
öskjubaugur	ellipse	persónukenni	identity
óskyldraæxlun	exogamy	persónuleikarof	dissociation
osmín	osmium	persónuleiki	personality
osmósa	osmosis	persónutöfrar	charisma
osmósuflæði	osmosis	perubróðir	quince
óson	ozone	perustæði	socket
ösp	poplar	pétursfiskur	dory
ostakúmen	cumin	peysa	sweater
osteopati	osteopath	piezorör	piezometer
óstjórn	anarchy	piltur	lad
óstöðugleiki	instability	pípa	conduit
östrógen	oestrogen	piparminta	peppermint
otur	otter	piparmynta	peppermint
óværi	irritation	piparrót	horseradish
óvinur	foe	pípetta	pipette
óvissa	uncertainty	pípla	tubule
oxíð	oxide	pípuhné	knee
öxlaafstaða	wheelbase	pípusetning	intubation
öxull	spindle	pláneta	planet
oxun	oxidation	plantekra	plantation
oxytósín	oxytocin	plasmi	plasma
paðreimur	stadium	plastíð	plastid
páfagaukasótt	psittacosis	plata	diskette
páfagaukaveiki	psittacosis	platína	platinum
pakki	packet	plöntuhormón	phytohormone
pakkning	gasket	plöntulandafræði	phytogeography
pall	pawl	plöntuör	callus
pallur	pallet	plöntur	vegetation
panna	sump	plönturíki	flora
papaja	papaya	plöntusvif	phytoplankton

plötupressun	stamping	próteasi	protease
plússkaut	anode	próþrombín	prothrombin
pokastrigi	burlap	prótín	protium
poki	sac	prótíninnkljúfur	endopeptidase
pökkun	packing	prótínkljúfur	protease
pökkur	puck	prótínleysing	proteolysis
pólering	burnishing	prótínrof	proteolysis
polli	bitt	prótínsundrun	proteolysis
pólon	polonium	prótóna	proton
pólriða	nutation	provizo	stocks
pólstefna	polarity	prufuleiðsla	jumper
pólun	polarization	psí	psi
pólunarmælir	polarimeter	psóríasis	psoriasis
pólvelta	precession	púlskveikjari	ignitor
pönnun	panning	púlsræsir	ignitor
port	hilus	punktafylki	bitmap
pörun	pairing	punktasíld	alewife
posi	saccule	púpa	chrysalis
pósitífismi	positivism	purkormur	trichina
pósitróna	positron	pussa	cunt
postaĵo	tails	puti	digit
postvango	buttocks	pylsa	sausage
prammi	hopper	rabbi	asp
praseodým	praseodymium	rabbíni	rabbi
praseódým	praseodymium	ráð	council
prentari	printer	ráðaleitun	consultation
prentmál	letterpress	raðbrigði	isomer
preskribo	regulations	raðbrögð	isomerization
pressa	compression	raddarmissir	aphonia
pressun	coining	raddleysi	aphonia
prestaveldi	theocracy	raddlömun	aphonia
prímatar	primates	raddstol	aphonia
prisma	prism	ráðgjafi	consultant
prófdómari	moderator	ráðgjöf	consultation
prófefni	reagent	raðgreiðsla	installment
prófunarefni	reagent	ráðherraembætti	portfolio
prófviðbragð	reaction	radíani	radian
prógesterón	progesterone	radísa	radish
prólaktín	prolactin	radíus	radius
prómeþín	promethium	ráðkænska	policy
prómetín	promethium	ráðning	evaluation
prómetíum	promethium	ráðningarstarfsemi	recruitment
prósent	percentile	ráðningartenging	linkage
prósenta	percentage	ráðstefna	convention
protaktín	protactinium	ráðstöfun	disposal
prótaktín	protactinium	ráðunautur	adviser

ráðuneyti	department	rafskaut	electrode
ræði	rowlock	rafskautun	polarization
ræðismaður	consul	rafspenna	voltage
ræðismannsbústaður	consulate	rafsvari	dielectric
ræðismannsskrifstofa	consulate	rafþegi	acceptor
ræðumaður	speaker	rafþéttir	capacitor
rækja	prawn	rafvæðing	electrification
rækt	culture	rakagleypir	desiccator
rækta	culture	rakamagn	humidity
ræktun	culture	rakariti	hygrograph
ræktunarfræði	agronomy	rakasíriti	hygrograph
rænuleysi	absence	rakastig	humidity
ræpa	diarrhea	rakaþétting	condensation
ræsiforrit	bootstrap	raki	humidity
ræsing	activation	rakning	tracing
ræsir	activator	rakstraumsrafali	dynamo
rafagnaslöngvir	betatron	rammi	bezel
rafali	generator	ramo	bough
rafall	generator	randbyggð	suburbia
rafberi	carrier	randhár	cilium
rafbúnaður	equipment	rándýr	predator
rafdráttur	electrophoresis	rangeygð	strabismus
rafeind	electron	ránlíf	predation
rafeindarstökk	transition	rannsókn	investigation
raferti	excitability	rannsóknarþýði	cohort
rafertimörk	threshold	rannsóknir	exploration
rafgas	plasma	rápari	browser
rafgeymamælir	hydrometer	rápforrit	browser
rafgeymir	accumulator	raporto	records
rafhlað	cell	rás	duct
rafhleðsla	capacitance	rásaskiptir	distributor
rafhlöðueining	cell	rásasmit	crosstalk
rafhúðun	electroplating	ráskerðingur	stockfish
rafi	ion	rass	buttocks
rafker	cell	rasskinnar	buttocks
raflækning	electrotherapy	ratsjá	radar
rafloki	rectifier	ratsjársvari	racon
rafmagnstafla	switchboard	ratsjársvarviti	racon
rafmeðferð	electrotherapy	ratsjártækni	radar
rafmögnun	electrification	rauða	yolk
rafnæmi	sensitivity	rauðalos	hemolysis
rafnemi	electrode	rauðauga	roach
rafögn	electron	rauðbeða	beetroot
rafpóll	electrode	rauðbeðja	beetroot
rafrýmd	capacitance	rauðber	cowberry
rafsegulspönun	inductance	rauðberjalyng	cowberry

Reference: Webster's Online Dictionary (www.websters-online-dictionary.org)

rauðfruma	erythrocyte	reikistjarna	planet
rauðfrumuforveri	erythroblast	reiknihending	statistic
rauðhundar	rubella	reikningshald	accountancy
rauðkorn	erythrocyte	reikningsyfirlit	statement
rauðkornamóðir	erythroblast	reimhjól	pulley
rauðkornarof	hemolysis	reimskífa	pulley
rauðkornskímfruma	erythroblast	rein	lane
rauðrófa	beetroot	reising	rotation
rauðspretta	plaice	reiti	stimulus
rauf	perforation	reiting	stimulation
raufaræðahnútur	hemorrhoid	reitur	beet
raufun	perforation	rekill	catkin
raunhorn	radian	rekki	fitness
raunhyggja	empiricism	rekorda	records
raunhyggjuaðferð	empiricism	rekordo	records
raunleiðni	conductance	rekstur	operation
raunsæi	pragmatism	relativa	relatives
raunsæishyggja	realism	remma	concentration
raunsæismaður	realist	remmujurt	wormwood
raunsæisstefna	realism	renín	rhenium
raunspeki	positivism	reníum	rhenium
raunviðnám	resistivity	renna	machine
rausnarskapur	unselfishness	rennibekkur	lathe
reagens	reagent	rennibraut	shipway
refasmári	alfalfa	rennimótstaða	rheostat
referaĵo	papers	rennipípa	pipette
reformur	tinea	renniviðnám	rheostat
refsing	punishment	rennivölur	mandrel
regado	regulations	rennslisop	orifice
regi	rules	rennslisstöðvun	stasis
registri	records	resín	resin
registro	records	réttarstaða	constitution
regla	law	rétthafi	beneficiary
reglugerð	regulations	rétthyrningur	rectangle
reglugerðir	regulations	rétting	extension
reglur	regulations	réttir	extensor
regluveldi	bureaucracy	réttivöðvi	extensor
regnbogahimna	iris	réttlæting	rationalization
regnfrakki	raincoat	réttlætng	rationalization
regnskógur	rainforest	réttmæti	validity
reguligo	regulations	réttmæting	validation
regulo	rules	réttur	easement
reið	vehicle	reykelsi	frankincense
reiða	availability	reykelsistré	frankincense
reiðufjárgeta	liquidity	reykháfur	chimney
reiðufjárhæfni	liquidity	reykjarmóða	smog

Reykþoka	smog	ritskoðun	censorship
reynd	praxis	ritstol	agraphia
reynslustefna	empiricism	ró	nut
reyrsykur	sucrose	Róari	moderator
ríbónúkleasi	ribonuclease	róbóti	robot
ríbósóm	ribosome	roðafræ	annatto
rið	hertz	roðafruma	erythrocyte
riðari	chopper	roðagægir	roach
riðill	inverter	roðarunnaaldin	quince
riðstraumsrafali	alternator	roðarunnaepli	quince
riðstraumsrafall	alternator	roðarunni	quince
riðstraumsviðnám	impedance	röddun	voicing
rifa	crevice	ródín	rhodium
rifflar	fluting	ródíum	rhodium
rifflur	fluting	röðun	sequencing
rifrildi	argument	röðunarmat	rating
ríki	domain	rofatafla	switchboard
ríkisborgararéttur	nationality	rófgreining	spectroscopy
ríkiserindreki	diplomat	rófgreinir	spectrometer
ríkisfang	nationality	rofi	interrupter
ríkissjóður	treasury	róflínuriti	spectrograph
ríkistekjur	revenue	rófljósmælir	spectrophotometer
ríkjabandalag	alliance	rófmynd	spectrogram
ríkjasamband	federation	rófrit	spectrogram
ríkjasamningur	treaty	rófriti	spectrograph
rikordo	records	rófsjá	spectroscope
ríla	spline	rófukál	chard
rilato	relations	röfun	ionization
rílur	fluting	röggvarský	altocumulus
rimlagirðing	balustrade	rökfærsla	rationalization
ringlun	confusion	rökhlið	gate
rípla	ribosome	rökleiðing	implication
risaborri	barramundi	rökleiðsla	argumentation
risagrasker	pumpkin	rökliður	argument
risasameind	macromolecule	röksemd	argument
risavöxtur	giantism	röksemdafærsla	argument
rispun	scarification	rönd	periphery
rissnál	scriber	rondo	quarters
rist	grid	röntgenmyndun	radiography
ristarhleri	louver	rör	conduit
ristill	shingles	rórmaður	helmsman
ritari	registrar	rót	radix
ritill	editor	rótarhnúður	corm
ritsetning	editing	róteind	proton
ritsímakerfi	telegraphy	rotnun	putrefaction
ritsími	telegraphy	rotplanta	saprophyte

rótsellerí	celeriac
rotvera	saprophyte
róun	sedation
rúbidín	rubidium
rúbidíum	rubidium
rúða	pane
ruglari	scrambler
rúmhornseining	steradian
rúmsýn	perspective
rumungur	asp
rúmvídd	dimension
runa	batch
runnabláber	blueberry
runnar	copse
runun	sequencing
rúten	ruthenium
rútenium	ruthenium
rúþeníum	ruthenium
rútur	roach
ryðgun	corrosion
ryðhreinsun	descaling
rýmari	reamer
rýmd	capacitance
rýmir	capacitor
rýriskipting	meiosis
rýrnun	degeneration
sablobenko	banks
sáð	sperm
sáðfall	ejaculation
sáðfruma	sperm
sáðfrumnadeyðir	spermicide
sáðfrumnaeyðir	spermicide
sáðfrumuvísir	spermatocyte
sáðgeymsla	spermatheca
sáðlát	ejaculation
sáðlaukur	onion
sáðmein	metastasis
sáðmóðurfruma	spermatocyte
saðning	satiation
sáðrásarúrnám	vasectomy
sæði	semen
sæðing	insemination
sæðisfruma	spermatozoon
sæðisfrumuvísir	spermatocyte
sæfari	mariner
sæfíflar	corals
sækni	affinity
sældarvilla	euphoria
særanleiki	vulnerability
sæstjarna	starfish
sæti	socket
sæúr	chronometer
safabóla	vacuole
saffismi	lesbianism
safflúr	safflower
safn	library
safnari	accumulator
safnplanta	accumulator
safnstútur	nozzle
safnvöllur	hub
safnvörður	librarian
safnvörsluforrit	librarian
sagnorð	verb
sagtenning	serration
sakaruppgjöf	immunity
sakborningur	accused
sakka	sinker
sakkarín	saccharin
sál	psyche
salajro	wages
sálarfræði	psychology
sálarlífeðlisfræði	psychophysiology
salatfífill	endive
salatþistill	cardoon
sáld	strainer
sáldvefur	bast
salerni	lavatory
sálfræði	psychology
sálfræðingur	psychologist
sálgreining	psychoanalysis
sálgreinir	psychoanalyst
sálkönnuður	psychoanalyst
sálkönnunarkenning	psychoanalysis
sállæknlng	psychotherapy
sálsýkisfræði	psychopathology
salt	acetate
saltpétur	saltpetre
saltsýrusalt	chloride
samanbuðartafla	nomogram
samanburðarhæfi	comparability
samanburðarhæfni	comparability
samantekt	superposition

samarín	samarium	samhengi	coherence
samaríum	samarium	samhjálp	symbiosis
samband	alliance	samhlekkjun	chaining
sambandsríki	federation	samhljóða	unanimity
sambeining	focusing	samhljómun	resonance
sambú	colony	samhljómur	agreement
sambúð	cohabitation	samhorf	symmetry
samdráttarástand	tonus	samhraðall	synchrotron
samdráttargeta	contractility	samhröðun	synchronization
samdráttarhæfni	contractility	samhrúgun	agglomeration
samdráttarskeið	recession	samhverfa	symmetry
samdráttur	contraction	samingsaðili	contractor
samdrykkja	symposium	samkennd	empathy
samefling	synergism	samkeppni	competition
sameignarfélag	partnership	samkeppnishæfi	competitiveness
sameignarstefna	collectivism	samkeppnishæfni	competitiveness
sameindasundrun	dissociation	samkjörnungur	eucaryote
sameining	unification	samkoma	assembly
sameiningarstefna	unionism	samkomulag	consonance
samfærsla	registration	samkunda	assembly
samfarablossi	orgasm	samkvæmni	concordance
samfas	synchronism	samkynhneigð	homosexuality
samfasa	synchronism	samkynmök	homosexuality
samfasari	synchronizer	samlægi	concordance
samfélag	society	samlagning	superposition
samfélagsvitund	citizenship	samlegð	synergy
samfella	continuum	samlegðaráhrif	synergy
samfelldni	continuity	samleggjari	adder
samfesta	cohesion	samleiðni	admittance
samfösun	synchronization	samleitni	allotropy
samfrumungur	plasmodium	samlíf	symbiosis
samfrysting	congelation	samlífi	symbiosis
samgangur	interconnection	samlíkir	simulator
samgengi	synchronism	samloðun	adhesion
samgepatrido	siblings	samlögun	assimilation
samgerð	configuration	samnefni	synonym
samgildi	degeneracy	samninganefnd	delegation
samgjörvi	coprocessor	samningaviðræður	conference
samgróning	adhesion	samningsaðili	contractor
samgróningur	adhesion	samningur	concurrence
samhæfi	comparability	samráð	collusion
samhæfing	harmonization	samræmi	concordance
samheildun	inclusion	samræming	coordination
samheitaorðabók	thesaurus	samrit	strainer
samheiti	synonym	samröðun	assembly
samheldni	cohesion	samruni	incorporation

samsækni	affinity	samtök	federation
samsæta	allele	samvægi	homeostasis
samsætuberi	carrier	samveldi	commonwealth
samsætuensím	isozyme	samverkan	interaction
samsætugerð	allotype	samverkun	synergy
samsafn	aggregation	samviðnám	impedance
samsemd	identity	samvinna	cooperation
samsetning	composition	samvirkni	synergy
samsíðungur	parallelogram	samvöxtur	concrescence
samskeyti	junction	samyrkja	synergy
samskeyting	splicing	sandbylur	blizzard
samskil	occlusion	sandeðla	lizard
samskipan	configuration	sandfláki	sandbank
samskiptaaðferð	protocol	sandhverfa	turbot
samskiptamáti	protocol	sandmaðkur	lugworm
samskiptareglur	protocol	sandrif	sandbank
samskipti	interaction	sandskel	gaper
samslíping	lapping	sandsteinn	sandstone
samslípun	lapping	sáning	seeding
samsnið	conformity	sannfæring	creed
samsöfnun	aggregation	sanngreining	identification
samsömun	identification	sanþófýll	xanthophyll
samspil	interaction	sapódilla	sapodilla
samstaða	unanimity	sapódillaplóma	sapodilla
samstæða	consolidation	sapódillatré	sapodilla
samstarf	interaction	sár	lesion
samstarfandi	synergist	sárasótt	syphilis
samstarfsmaður	colleague	sardína	pilchard
samsteypa	alliance	sarkmein	sarcoma
samstig	pacing	sarpur	economizer
samstilling	alignment	sátt	conciliation
samstjórn	condominium	sáttamaður	conciliator
samsveiflun	resonance	sáttargerð	agreement
samsvörun	correspondence	sáttasemjari	conciliator
samtak	synergy	sáttaumleitun	conciliation
samtal	conversation	sáttmáli	convention
samtengiafl	cohesion	sátur	stator
samtenging	synthesis	sauðkind	sheep
samþætting	annealing	sauður	sheep
samþjappari	compressor	saur	faeces
samþjöppun	compression	saurfræði	scatology
samþrýstingur	compaction	saurgun	contamination
samþykki	approval	saurhneigð	scatology
samþykkjandi	acceptor	saurteppa	impaction
samþykkt	convention	savanni	savanna
samþyrping	aggregation	saxari	chopper

sebrahestur	zebra	sendandi	originator
sefandi	neuroleptic	sendifulltrúi	diplomat
sefasýki	hysteria	sendiherra	ambassador
sefun	appeasement	sendinefnd	delegation
segamyndun	thrombosis	sending	submission
segavarnarefni	anticoagulant	sendir	transmitter
segavarnarlyf	anticoagulant	sendiráðsstarfsmaður	diplomat
segð	utterance	senditæki	transmitter
segi	thrombus	sennileiki	likelihood
segl	velum	senón	xenon
seglskip	clipper	sent	penny
segulbandsspóla	cassette	sentimetri	centimetre
segulkveikja	magneto	sepi	polyp
segull	magnet	séreignarskipan	capitalism
segulleiðni	permeability	sérfræðingur	consultant
segulmælir	magnetometer	sérfræðistarf	profession
segulmagnsvél	exciter	sérhæfing	specialization
segulmögnun	magnetization	sérhæfni	specificity
segulmögnunarkerfi	exciter	serín	cerium
segulmögnunarvél	exciter	seríum	cerium
segulrafagnarör	magnetron	sérleyfisgjald	royalty
segulrör	magnetron	serótónín	serotonin
segulskekkja	variation	sérréttindi	immunity
segulstál	magnet	sérrímóla	cherimoya
segulstefna	polarity	sérstaða	singularity
segulstuðull	permeability	sérstæða	singularity
segulsviðsmælir	magnetometer	sérstæði	identity
segulsviðsrör	magnetron	sérstöðupunktur	singularity
segulsvörunarstuðull	permeability	sérsvæðing	zoning
segulvaki	exciter	sértæki	specificity
segulviðnám	reluctance	sérvefur	parenchyma
seighersla	tempering	sérvirkni	specificity
seighvolf	asthenosphere	sesín	caesium
seigjumælir	viscometer	sess	niche
seigla	persistence	set	sediment
seilarmiðlag	chordamesoderm	seta	session
sekkgró	ascospore	setlag	sediment
sektor	sector	setmyndun	sedimentation
selen	selenium	setning	theorem
seleníum	selenium	setningafræði	syntax
selir	seals	setningarfræði	syntax
seljandi	seller	setur	setting
sella	cell	sexhyrningur	hexagon
sellerírót	celeriac	sexkantur	hexagon
selta	salinity	sextantur	sextant
selveiðiskip	sealer	sextungur	sextant

seyti	secretion	sími	ticker
seyting	secretion	símogen	zymogen
seytl	percolation	símógen	zymogen
síbeygjukrampar	spasticity	símskeyti	telegram
siðareglur	protocol	sin	tendon
siðblinda	psychopathy	sinarbólga	tendinitis
siðblindingi	psychopath	sinarhlaupbelgur	ganglion
siðfræði	ethics	sindra	sinter
siðgát	censorship	sindrun	sinter
siðir	mores	sink	zinc
síðmynd	afterimage	sínkrótrónn	synchrotron
sidvango	buttocks	sinna	involvement
siðvarsla	censorship	sinnep	mustard
siðvenja	convention	sinnepsjurtir	mustard
sífella	perpetuity	sinnuleysi	apathy
sífill	syphilis	sinnustig	involvement
sifjar	kinship	sínus	sine
sifjaspell	incest	síriti	polygraph
sig	descent	sirkill	dividers
sigdæld	graben	sirkon	zirconium
sigdalur	trough	sirkoníum	zirconium
sigg	callus	sísegull	magnet
sigketill	caldera	sísegulrafali	magneto
sigla	mast	sístaða	priapism
siglingafræði	navigation	sitjandi	buttocks
siglingar	shipping	síun	filtering
siglutré	mast	sjáaldur	pupil
signifi	means	sjáaldursjurt	belladonna
sígóð	fennel	sjáaldursrönd	areola
sígreiðslur	perpetuity	sjálf	ego
sigti	strainer	sjálfdrep	apoptosis
sigurkufl	caul	sjálfgengi	automatism
Síka	psyche	sjálfi	robot
síklíðar	cichlids	sjálflitningur	autosome
síklótrónn	cyclotron	sjálfsálit	self-esteem
síkoría	chicory	sjálfsást	narcissism
síld	herring	sjálfsfróun	masturbation
silfurgægir	dace	sjálfskilningur	insight
silfurkóngur	tarpon	sjálfsmyndun	autogenesis
silfurskjaddi	alewife	sjálfspíslahvöt	masochism
síling	percolation	sjálfssefjun	autosuggestion
silisíum	silicon	sjálfssemd	identity
síls	sill	sjálfssömun	identity
silungur	trout	sjálfsstjórn	sovereignty
símaliður	internode	sjálfstæði	independence
símasamskipti	telecommunications	sjálfstæðishreyfing	nationalism

sjálfstæðisstefna	nationalism	sjúkdómseinkenni	symptom
sjálfsþurftarbúskapur	autarky	sjúkdómsgreining	diagnosis
sjálfsþurftir	subsistence	sjúkdómsherming	simulation
sjálfstjórnarsvæði	sovereignty	sjúkdómsmynd	syndrome
sjálfstýrikerfi	servomechanism	sjúkdómsvaldur	pathogen
sjálfstýring	autopilot	sjúkdómsvörn	prophylaxis
sjálfstýriverk	servomechanism	sjúkrabíll	ambulance
sjálftamiðja	epicentre	sjúkrabörur	stretcher
sjálfþýða	bootstrap	sjúkrasaga	anamnesis
sjálfvirkjun	automation	sjúkraþjálfari	physiotherapist
sjálfvirkni	automation	skaðabætur	indemnity
sjálfvirkniaðgerð	automation	skaðabótaskylda	liability
sjalottulaukur	shallot	skaðleysi	indemnity
sjávargróður	seaweed	skækja	hooker
sjávarskafl	tsunami	skæni	pellicle
sjáver	gallery	skærð	magnitude
sjóbirtingur	trout	skærleiki	luminosity
sjófarandi	seafarer	skaf	attrition
sjóflutningar	shipping	skafa	scraper
sjóleið	seaway	skafgígur	palimpsest
sjóliðsforingi	commander	skagi	peninsula
sjómælingar	hydrography	skak	concussion
sjóna	retina	skakki	skewness
sjónarhorn	perspective	skál	fossa
sjónarmið	perspective	skáletur	italics
sjónauki	binocular	skáli	hut
sjónbeiting	fixation	skalotlaukur	shallot
sjónfesting	fixation	skalottlaukur	shallot
sjónfræði	optics	skammleiðsla	jumper
sjónfylgd	tracking	skammljómun	fluorescence
sjóngróf	fovea	skammstöfun	abbreviation
sjónhimna	retina	Skammtamæling	dosimetry
sjónhorf	perspective	skammtamælingar	dosimetry
sjónleiðsaga	pilotage	skammtamælir	dosimeter
sjónmyrkvi	blackout	skammtapípa	pipette
sjónnæmismælir	photometer	skammtari	hopper
sjónskekkja	astigmatism	skammtur	dosage
sjónsviðseyða	scotoma	skammyrði	acronym
sjónsviðsmælir	perimeter	skán	epistasis
sjóntenging	fusion	skandín	scandium
sjónugróf	fovea	skandíum	scandium
sjónukeila	cone	skann	scanning
sjónvarp	television	skanni	scanner
sjöttungsmælir	sextant	skansgluggi	oriel
sjóurriði	trout	skap	mood
sjúkdómafræði	pathology	skapahárastaða	escutcheon

skapalon	template	skilmálar	terms
skápur	wardrobe	skilning	centrifugation
skári	ogive	skilningarvit	modality
skarkoli	plaice	skilningur	realization
skarpskyggni	poignancy	skilorðsbinding	suspension
skattálagning	assessment	skilríki	credentials
skattlagning	taxation	skilrúm	separator
skattur	taxation	skiltákn	separator
skaut	electrode	skilviður	separator
skautari	polarizer	skilvinda	separator
skautnæmi	dichroism	skilyrði	constraint
skautsjá	polariscope	skilyrðing	conditioning
skautstefna	polarity	skíma	luminescence
skautun	polarization	skimari	scanner
skautunarefni	polarizer	skimrás	multiplexer
skautunarmælir	polarimeter	skimun	screening
skautunarsía	polarizer	skin	luminance
skefill	excavator	skinefni	phosphor
skeið	interval	skinfótur	pseudopodium
skeiðvöllur	runway	skinhreyfisjá	stroboscope
skeif	skewness	skinnflagningur	exfoliation
skekking	skewness	skinubólga	peritonitis
skellur	concussion	skip	nave
skema	schema	skipalægi	roadstead
skemmd	lesion	skipgengi	navigability
skepnuskapur	bestiality	skipherra	commander
skerðing	sinus	skipsbátur	dinghy
skerðingaraðferð	jackknife	skipsklukka	chronometer
skerfur	contribution	skipsskrúfa	propeller
skerjasteinbítur	butterfish	skipstjóri	commander
skerpa	definition	skipstjórn	navigation
skeyti	intersection	skipstjórnarmaður	navigator
skeyting	registration	skipta	toggle
skíði	ski	skiptaráðandi	administrator
skíðisfótur	pedestal	skiptiborð	switchboard
skífa	washer	skiptihæfi	interchangeability
skífumiðja	grommet	skipting	stratification
skilaboð	message	skiptir	exchanger
skilaflutningur	transmittal	skipulag	planning
skilaskylda	accountability	skipulagning	planning
skilgreining	identification	skipulagsbók	organizer
skili	separator	skipulagsbreyting	reorganization
skilja	separator	skipulagsgerð	infrastructure
skiljuhimna	dialyzer	skipun	appointment
skiljun	purification	skírteini	diploma
skillag	separator	skírteinisútgáfa	certification

skjáborð	desktop	skor	department
skjalahald	documentation	skorða	constraint
skjalamappa	portfolio	skorðun	fixation
skjalataska	briefcase	skorður	dunnage
skjalavistun	filing	skordýrafræði	entomology
skjalbúnaður	documentation	skorpnun	cirrhosis
skjaldkirtilsauki	goitre	skorpulifur	cirrhosis
skjaldkirtilshormón	thyroxine	skorpumyndun	incrustation
skjaldkyrkingsdvergur	cretin	skorsteinn	chimney
skjaldvakaeitrun	hyperthyroidism	skortítur	hemiptera
skjálftaflóðbylgja	tsunami	skortur	shortage
skjálftamælir	seismograph	skoruhjól	sheave
skjálftamiðja	epicentre	skörun	intersection
skjálftanemi	geophone	skorur	fluting
skjálgi	strabismus	skotrun	panning
skjálgur	strabismus	sköttun	taxation
skjár	window	skötuselur	angler
skjatti	sacculus	skrælnun	mummification
skjóða	utricle	skráning	recruitment
skjól	asylum	skráningarskírteini	registration
skjöl	documentation	skráningartæki	recorder
skjólbelti	windbreak	skrásetjari	registrar
skjólgarður	windbreak	skrásetning	registration
skjólstæðingur	client	skraut	decoration
skjólveggur	windbreak	skreið	stockfish
skoðari	browser	skreppa	pawl
skoðun	viewpoint	skreyting	decoration
skoðunarforrit	browser	skriða	talus
skoðunarmaður	surveyor	skriðbelti	caterpillar
skóf	lichen	skriðþungi	momentum
skófatnaður	footwear	skrifari	polygraph
skófluhjól	impeller	skrifborð	bureau
sköflungur	tibia	skriffinnska	bureaucracy
skógarhöggsmaður	woodcutter	skrifræði	bureaucracy
skógrækt	forestry	skrifstofa	secretariat
skögun	projection	Skrifstofan	bureau
skógur	timberland	skrifstofuveldi	bureaucracy
skolp	sewage	skrifstol	agraphia
skólp	sewage	skrokklanga	ling
skolun	circulation	skröltormur	rattlesnake
skölun	scaling	skróp	absenteeism
skömmtun	dosage	skrúfa	propeller
skömmtunarmiði	coupon	skrúfhólkur	bushing
skönnun	scanning	skrúfjárn	screwdriver
sköpulagsfræði	morphology	skrúflykill	spanner
sköpunargáfa	creativity	skrúfugraftarverkfæri	chaser

Reference: Webster's Online Dictionary (www.websters-online-dictionary.org)

skrúfuhringur	nozzle	skynjari	analyser
skrúfuröst	slipstream	skynjun	detection
skrúfuskeri	chaser	skynnemi	receptor
skrunskoðun	browsing	skynsemi	precaution
skrýfing	transposition	skyntak	percept
skrykkur	saltation	skyntúlkun	perception
skúffa	drawer	skynvilla	hallucination
skúfur	cirrus	skyrbjúgur	scorbutus
skuggamyndun	shading	skýrgreining	definition
skuggaskil	terminator	skýring	clarification
skuggsæi	symmetry	skýringar	legend
skuld	liability	skýringarmynd	schema
skuldabréf	debenture	skýringartexti	legend
skuldalúkning	settlement	skýrleiki	definition
skuldari	debtor	skýrsla	statement
skuldbinding	commitment	skyrta	shirt
skuldbindingar	liabilities	skýstrokkur	tornado
skuldir	liabilities	skýstrókur	tornado
skuldsetning	gearing	sladdi	wolffish
skuldunautur	debtor	slag	pulsation
skulpti	works	slagæð	artery
skúraflákar	cumulonimbus	slagæðlingur	arteriole
skúraský	cumulonimbus	slagbor	jumper
skurðaðgerð	operation	slagrými	displacement
skurðarpunktur	intersection	sláttarglapastillandi	antiarrhythmic
skurðlæknir	surgeon	sláttarglapastillir	antiarrhythmic
skurðlæknisfræði	surgery	sláttarglöp	arrhythmia
skurðpunktur	intersection	sláttur	pulsation
skutull	harpoon	slaufa	jumper
skvass	courgette	slef	salivation
skygging	shading	slefun	salivation
skyggnir	scanner	slegill	ventricle
skýjablika	cirrostratus	slekja	hypotonia
skýjabólstur	cumulus	slembifundur	serendipity
skýjahetta	pileus	slétta	mare
skýjaþekjuhæð	ceiling	slétthverfa	windowpane
skýla	deflector	sléttun	burnishing
skylda	commitment	slíðrun	invagination
skyldleiki	consanguinity	slíðurbaktería	chlamydia
skyldraæxlun	endogamy	slif	liner
skylduögun	conditioning	slíma	mucosa
skýling	screening	slímdýr	ameba
skylmingasverð	rapier	slímhimna	mucosa
skyndihvöt	impulse	slímlosandi	expectorant
skynfæri	sensorium	slingur	ataxia
skynform	modality	slippur	shipyard

slípun	leveling	smyrsl	balsam
sliskja	catwalk	snælda	spindle
slit	attrition	snapi	scavenger
slitgigt	osteoarthritis	snaralur	reamer
slóði	leader	snarkolla	spinner
slökun	modification	snarstefjun	improvisation
slöngvari	ejector	snasar	snooks
slúður	defamation	snati	gopher
slys	accident	snefilefni	micronutrient
smábein	ossicle	sneiðir	slicer
smáber	acinus	sneiðmyndagerð	tomography
smáblað	leaflet	sneiðmyndataka	tomography
smábóndi	peasant	snekkja	yacht
smæð	element	snepill	lobule
smáflóra	microflora	snerpir	booster
smáhnúður	tubercle	snerpivél	booster
smali	assembler	snertiarmur	wiper
smámagni	squid	snertispennunemi	thermocouple
smári	transistor	snið	intersection
smárit	prospectus	sniðmát	template
smásali	retailer	sniðmengi	intersection
smáseiði	parr	sniðmótun	formatting
smásjármynd	photomicrograph	sniðsetning	editing
smáverugróður	culture	sniðskurður	chamfering
smeyging	invagination	snigill	cochlea
smíði	construction	sníkjulíf	parasitism
smiðja	workshop	sníkjulífi	parasitism
smit	spillover	snjóplógur	snowplow
smitáhrif	spillover	snörun	transformation
smitberi	carrier	snúða	gyroscope
smiteyðing	disinfection	snúðáttaviti	gyrocompass
smitgát	asepsis	snúðkúla	orb
smitsæfing	sterilization	snúðsjá	stroboscope
smitun	contamination	snúðstjarna	spider
smitvörn	antisepsis	snúður	armature
smjörfiskur	butterfish	snúðvísir	gyroscope
smjörhneta	butternut	snúðviti	gyrocompass
smjörhnetutré	butternut	snúningsás	axis
smjörhnot	butternut	snúningsátak	torque
smokkfiskur	squid	snúningsmætti	torque
smokkur	squid	snúningssjá	stroboscope
smurefni	lubricator	snúningstala	periodicity
smurkoppur	lubricator	snúningsvægi	torque
smurnippill	lubricator	snúningur	rotation
smurtittur	sweeper	snyrting	pruning
smyrjari	oiler	sódómska	bestiality

sódómusaurlifnaður	bestiality	sonur	son
söðull	col	sori	impurity
söðulsvæði	col	sóri	psoriasis
söfnun	compilation	sorti	melanosis
sog	suction	sortnun	melanosis
sogabarnaveiki	croup	sortuæxli	melanoma
soggúlar	suckers	sortumiga	alkaptonuria
sogkarpar	suckers	sósíalismi	socialism
sogpípukraftur	capillarity	sóttbrigði	crisis
sograni	acetabulum	sótthiti	fever
sogskál	acetabulum	sótthræðsla	hypochondria
sogtrantar	suckers	sótthreinsun	disinfection
sogun	suction	sótthreinsunarefni	bactericide
sök	liability	sótthvörf	crisis
sökk	sedimentation	sóttkvíun	isolation
sökkull	foundation	sóttsýki	hypochondria
sóknarnefnd	vestry	sóttvarnarlyf	antisepsis
sóknarpunktur	apex	sóttvörn	antisepsis
sól	sol	spá	prognosis
söl	dulse	spaðabátur	hydrofoil
sólaldin	papaya	spaðastyrja	paddlefish
sólaldintré	papaya	spaði	spatula
sólarhringur	day	spælkross	spider
sólbaugur	ecliptic	spæringur	psoriasis
sólblettur	sunspot	spæta	woodpecker
sólborri	opah	spáfiskur	loach
sólbraut	ecliptic	spákaupmennska	speculation
sólflekkur	plage	span	induction
sólgeislun	insolation	spanald	inductor
sólhlíf	shading	spanali	armature
sólhorf	configuration	spankveiking	welding
sólhvarfapunktur	solstice	spanlóðun	welding
sólhvörf	solstice	spanrafmagn	induction
sólmark	apex	spanskreyrspálmi	rattan
sólmið	apex	spanspóla	inductor
sólnánd	perihelion	spanstuðull	inductance
sólskinslækning	heliotherapy	spansuða	welding
sólsproti	gnomon	sparri	spaccr
sólstingur	insolation	spasmi	spasm
sólstöðupunktur	solstice	spegilfesting	spider
sólstöður	solstice	spegill	reflector
sólstrókur	prominence	spegilsjónauki	reflector
sólþræðlingur	fibril	speglun	mirroring
sóltjald	awning	speglunartala	parity
sólúr	sundial	speldi	epiglottis
sölutryggjandi	underwriter	spendýr	mammal

spenna	voltage	staðfærsla	localization
spennihólkur	collet	staðfesting	affirmation
spennir	transformer	staðfræði	topography
spennitreyja	straitjacket	staðgreiðsla	payment
spennubreytir	transformer	staðgreining	localization
spennumælir	tonometer	staðhæfing	contention
spennumunur	voltage	staðreyndahyggja	positivism
spergilkál	broccoli	staðsetning	situation
spilliefnaflæði	loading	staðsetningarviti	locator
spilun	playback	staðtölur	statistics
spindilbolti	kingpin	staður	venue
spindill	spindle	staðvindur	monsoon
spíss	nozzle	staðvísir	marker
spjald	adapter	stæða	expression
spjaldbein	sacrum	stæði	socket
spjaldhryggur	sacrum	stækkun	expansion
spjaldliðir	sacrum	stærð	quantity
splæsifall	spline	stærðfræði	mathematics
splæsing	splicing	stærðtákn	expression
splitti	cotter	stærir	dilator
spóla	spindle	stærisýki	megalomania
spónaplata	fibreboard	stærivöðvi	dilator
spöng	jumper	stafagerð	font
spönnuður	generator	stafbaktería	bacillus
spönun	loading	staffylli	filler
spor	impression	stafgerill	bacillus
sporbaugur	ellipse	stafróf	fundamentals
sporefni	tracer	stagherðir	turnbuckle
sporhundur	trailer	stajo	braces
sprang	surfing	stak	element
sprettfiskur	butterfish	stakaskil	transition
sproti	gnomon	stakmótun	individualization
sprunga	fissure	staktrjáaslétta	savanna
spunamælir	spinner	stallbakur	sedan
spuni	improvisation	stallur	pedestal
spurning	enquiry	standliður	axis
spurningaeyðublað	questionnaire	standur	arrack
spurningalisti	questionnaire	stangveiðimaður	angler
spurningaskrá	questionnaire	stansaður	stamping
spyrna	wishbone	starfsbilun	insufficiency
staða	configuration	starfsbróðir	colleague
staðall	norm	starfsemi	operation
staðalloftþyngd	atmosphere	starfsfólk	personnel
staðalýsing	topography	starfsglöp	apraxia
staðarval	location	starfsgrein	profession
staðbinding	localization	starfshættir	procedure

Reference: Webster's Online Dictionary (www.websters-online-dictionary.org)

starfslið	workforce	stéttskipting	stratification
starfslok	retirement	steyping	embedding
starfsmaður	officer	steypumót	casting
starfsmögnun	synergy	steypumótun	casting
starfsreglur	regulations	steypustyrktarjárn	reinforcement
starfsstétt	profession	steyting	contention
starfssvæði	premises	Stía	bunker
starfstruflun	dysfunction	stífludrep	infarct
starfsvefur	parenchyma	stíflufleygsmyndun	infarction
startari	starter	stíflufleygun	infarction
stautur	ejector	stíflufleygur	infarct
steðji	incus	stíflun	occlusion
stef	theme	stífni	rigidity
stefja	subroutine	stigflokkun	staging
stefna	orientation	stiggreining	hierarchy
stefnufesta	commitment	stigsetning	staging
stefnufrávik	deflection	stigskipting	hierarchy
stefnugeiri	lobe	stigskipun	hierarchy
stefnuhneigð	anisotropy	stigun	staging
stefnuhorn	argument	stigveldi	hierarchy
stefnumál	policy	stigveldun	hierarchy
stefnusneyða	isotropy	stigvöxtur	hierarchy
stefnuvirkni	directivity	stiki	parameter
stego	braces	stikill	pedicel
steinaldin	drupe	stikla	trailer
steinber	drupe	stiklari	scaler
steinbítsbarn	wolffish	stikluleggur	hyperlink
steinbítsgóna	wolffish	stiklumiðlun	hypermedia
steinbítur	catfish	stílabók	notebook
steinefnahnútur	tophus	stilkselja	celery
steinefnaútfelling	mineralization	stilksellerí	celery
steingeit	ibex	stilkur	rachis
steinhvel	lithosphere	stillibreyta	parameter
steinhvolf	lithosphere	stilligen	operator
steinkvörn	concretion	stilligildi	setting
steinmyndun	concretion	stillimótstaða	rheostat
steinn	concretion	stilling	setting
steinsmuga	diarrhea	stillingar	adjustment
stelling	configuration	stillir	operator
stelpa	gal	stillisvæði	operator
ŝtelsekvi	tails	stilliviðnám	rheostat
stemmir	barrier	stimpill	piston
steradíani	steradian	stinnhvolf	lithosphere
sterkjukljúfur	ptyalin	stirðleiki	rigidity
sterkjurót	arrowroot	stirðnun	rigidity
stétt	estate	stjarki	tetany

stjarnfræði	astronomy	stöðlun	standardization
stjarnfræðingur	astronomer	stöðnun	stagnation
stjarnvísindi	astronomy	stöðugjafi	servomotor
stjórn	steerage	stöðugleiki	stability
stjórnandi	manager	stöðuhækkun	promotion
stjórnardeild	secretariat	stöðuhólkur	spacer
stjórnarerindreki	diplomat	stöðuskipti	transition
stjórnarfar	regime	stöðusteinn	otolith
stjórnarfyrirkomulag	regime	stöðvun	truncation
stjórnarnefndarmaður	commissioner	stöðvunarstefna	containment
stjórnarskrá	constitution	stöflun	stacking
stjórnarskrifstofa	secretariat	stofn	population
stjórnarstefna	policy	stofnfræði	demography
stjórnás	camshaft	stofnsamþykkt	statute
stjórnhæfi	controllability	stofntala	radix
stjórnhæfni	manoeuvrability	stofnun	institution
stjórnkænska	policy	ŝtofo	materials
stjórnleysi	anarchism	stoki	stocks
stjórnleysisstefna	anarchism	stökk	saltation
stjórnlög	constitution	stökkbreyting	mutation
stjórnskipulag	constitution	stökkbreytivaldur	mutagen
stjórnskipun	constitution	stökkull	transposon
stjörnualmanak	ephemeris	stokkur	sinus
stjörnuathugunarstöð	observatory	stoko	stocks
stjörnubreidd	declination	stöngulliðamót	node
stjörnubyggð	population	stöngulliður	internode
stjörnufífill	aster	stönsun	embossing
stjörnufræði	astronomy	stöplarit	histogram
stjörnufræðingur	astronomer	stöpull	pylon
stjörnuhæð	altitude	stórabóla	smallpox
stjörnuhæðarmælir	astrolabe	stórbóndi	rancher
stjörnuhnitatafla	ephemeris	stórbýli	estate
stjörnuhrap	meteor	stórgalangal	galangal
stjörnulíffræði	astrobiology	stórgró	megaspore
stjörnum	operation	stórheili	cerebrum
stjörnumát	horoscope	stórhesli	filbert
stjörnun	adjustment	stórheslihneta	filbert
stjörnuskífa	astrolabe	stórhríð	blizzard
stjörnuspáfræði	astrology	stórkaupmaður	wholesaler
stjörnuspeki	astrology	stórkjafta	megrim
stjörnustöð	observatory	storknun	setting
stjörnuturn	observatory	storkuvari	anticoagulant
stjörnvölur	joystick	stórmennskubrjálun	megalomania
stöð	cell	stormsveipur	cyclone
stoðband	ligament	stórnetja	caul
stoðfótur	outrigger	stórsameind	macromolecule

stórslys	catastrophe	sturlun	psychosis
stórtölva	mainframe	sturttæming	dumping
strákur	lad	stuttfrumuvefur	parenchyma
strammi	stroma	stútur	nozzle
strand	grounding	stýfing	pruning
strandblaðka	chard	stýranleiki	controllability
strandlengja	coastline	stýri	rudder
strandlón	lagoon	stýridór	arbor
strangleiki	severity	stýrifræði	cybernetics
straumbeinir	diode	stýrihreyfill	servomotor
straumbreytir	convertor	stýrikerfi	system
straumgægir	rudd	stýrikraftur	entelechy
straumhlaup	commutation	stýring	steering
straumleki	leakage	stýringardór	arbor
straumlína	curvature	stýripinni	joystick
straumrofi	interrupter	stýrisameind	effector
straumskipting	commutation	stýrisblað	rudder
straumskiptir	commutator	stýrisbúnaður	steering
straumstefna	polarity	stýrishús	cab
straumtækni	hydraulics	stýriskaut	gate
straumvending	commutation	stýrismaður	helmsman
straumvendir	commutator	stýristautur	joystick
strekking	dilation	stýristöng	joystick
strekkingarró	turnbuckle	stýrisvölur	kingpin
strendingur	prism	stýritækni	automation
strengiró	turnbuckle	stýriþræll	servomechanism
strengur	ligament	stýrivél	servomotor
stríðsæsingamaður	warmonger	styrking	consolidation
strigi	burlap	styrkt	concentration
strípun	stripping	styrktarvaf	reinforcement
strokka	displacement	styrkþegi	beneficiary
strönd	coastline	styrkur	magnitude
strontín	strontium	stytting	abbreviation
strontíum	strontium	suða	welding
strúktúralismi	structuralism	suðugleraugu	goggles
stuð	impulse	súkrósi	sucrose
stúdíó	studio	súla	crus
stuðlarit	histogram	súlfat	sulfate
stuðningsmaður	acolyte	súlnaás	architrave
stuðningur	endorsement	súlnagöng	colonnade
stuðull	multiplier	súlnarið	colonnade
stúka	thalamus	súlnarit	histogram
stúlka	girl	súlurit	histogram
stund	hour	sumardá	aestivation
stunga	injection	sumardvali	aestivation
štupo	stairs	summuferill	ogive

sund	narrows	svefnleysi	insomnia
sundrun	vaporization	sveif	radius
sundrunarferli	catabolism	sveifarás	crankshaft
sundurgreining	disjunction	sveifill	oscillator
sundurgreinir	discriminator	sveifla	hertz
sundurhvarf	divergence	sveiflugjafi	oscillator
sundurlausn	dissolution	sveifluhreyfing	oscillation
sundurleitni	divergence	sveiflunemi	geophone
sundurleitun	divergence	sveiflur	fluctuation
sundurleysing	decomposition	sveiflusjá	oscilloscope
sundurliðun	specification	sveifluvaki	oscillator
sundurtæting	laceration	sveifluvik	displacement
sundurvísun	divergence	sveigja	curvature
súrefni	oxygen	sveigjanleiki	flexibility
súrefniskassi	incubator	sveinmök	pederasty
súrefnisskortur	anoxia	sveipur	whorl
súrhey	silage	sveit	municipality
súrnun	acidification	sveitarfélag	municipality
surpapera	papers	sveitarstjórn	council
surtarbrandur	lignite	sveitasetur	estate
sút	dejection	sveppadeyðir	fungicide
sútunarsýra	tannin	sveppafræði	mycology
svæðalýsing	topography	sveppasýking	mycosis
svæðaskipting	zoning	sveppeyðir	fungicide
svæðavæðing	localism	svepphattur	pileus
svæði	territory	sveppir	fungi
svæðing	zoning	sveppsýki	mycosis
svæðislýsing	topography	sveppur	fungi
svæðisrammi	boundary	sverðfiskur	swordfish
svæðissklpting	sector	sverfing	attrition
svæðisskipulag	zoning	svið	realm
svæfing	anesthesia	sviðsetning	staging
svæling	fumigation	sviðsmynd	scenario
svaf	damping	svifbiti	cantilever
svalir	balcony	svifefnablanda	suspension
svarðarhneta	groundnut	svifefnasía	dialyzer
svari	effector	svifefnasíun	dialysis
svarthlutur	blackbody	sviflausn	suspension
svarthyrna	anglerfish	svifnökkvi	hovercraft
svartlyfting	pedestal	svig	deflection
svartþröstur	blackbird	svigar	parenthesis
svefnblik	rem	svigi	parenthesis
svefndá	sopor	svigrúm	latitude
svefnganga	somnambulism	svik	duplicity
svefngengill	somnambulist	svimi	vertigo
svefnhöfgi	drowsiness	svín	porker

svipa	flagellum	sýnistaka	sampling
svipbrigðafræði	physiognomy	synjun	refusal
svipfar	phenotype	sýri	oxide
svipgerð	phenotype	sýring	acidification
svipmót	similarity	sýringareitrun	acidosis
svipting	suspension	syrja	sediment
svipur	physiognomy	syrpa	member
sviputrekt	reservoir	sýruaukning	acidification
sviti	perspiration	sýrufíkill	acidophil
svitifall	ablative	sýrufruma	eosinophil
svitnun	sudation	sýrumyndun	acidification
svörður	peat	sýrustig	ph
svörun	reaction	sýruþvottur	pickling
sýanókóbalamín	cyanocobalamin	sýsla	county
sýfilis	syphilis	sýslari	driver
sýfílis	syphilis	sýslumaður	magistrate
syfja	drowsiness	systir	sister
sýkill	pathogen	systkin	siblings
sýkingarhreiður	nidus	systurdóttir	niece
sýklaeyðir	bactericide	systurefni	isomer
sýklavörn	asepsis	systurkjarni	isomer
sykra	carbohydrate	systursonur	nephew
sykrungur	carbohydrate	systurtegund	isomer
sykrusundrun	glycolysis	tá	digit
sykur	saccharose	tæki	machine
sykurleysing	glycolysis	tækjabeiting	instrumentation
sykurmelóna	cantaloupe	tækjabúnaður	apparatus
sykurrof	glycolysis	tækjakostur	equipment
sykursmælir	saccharimeter	tækjastilling	calibration
sykursundrun	glycolysis	tæknifrjóvgun	insemination
sykursýkileysandi	antidiabetic	tæknilýsing	specification
sykursýkislyf	antidiabetic	tæring	oxidation
sýlen	xylene	tafla	switchboard
sýlól	xylene	tag	taxon
sýnataka	sampling	tak	pleurodynia
sýnd	penetrance	takmarkanir	limitation
sýndarfótur	pseudopodium	takmarkari	limiter
sýndarleiðni	admittance	takmörk	boundary
sýndarviðnám	impedance	takmörkun	demarcation
sýngæfur	hallucinogen	tákn	icon
sýngjafi	hallucinogen	táknaraðarbútur	exon
sýni	specimen	táknfræði	semiotics
sýnihneigð	exhibitionism	tákngjafi	signifier
sýnikennsla	demonstration	táknkerfi	symbolism
sýning	demonstration	táknmerking	significance
sýnishorn	specimen	táknmynd	symbol

táknröð	exon	taugafruma	neuron
táknsetning	coding	taugahnoð	ganglion
táknun	symbolization	taugahnoða	ganglion
taktiko	tactic	taugarfruma	neuron
tala	puck	taugarslíður	neurolemma
talfælni	phonophobia	taugasími	axon
talk	talc	taugasjúkdómafræði	neurology
tálkn	branchia	taugaskipan	innervation
tálknahol	atrium	taugaskipun	innervation
tálknalok	operculum	taugaslíður	myelin
talkúm	talc	taugatrefja	fibril
tálmi	inhibitor	taugatróð	glia
tálmun	barrier	taugaveiki	typhus
talsímakerfi	telephony	taugaveiklun	neurosis
talsími	telephony	taugungur	neuron
tangerína	tangerine	tegund	category
tankbíll	tanker	tegundaklofnun	speciation
Tankskip	tanker	tegundamyndun	speciation
tannbogi	quadrant	tegundargreining	identification
tanndráttur	extraction	tegundarþróun	phylogenesis
tannfræði	odontology	teikn	icon
tanngerð	dentition	teiknari	plotter
tannhjól	cogwheel	teiknivél	plotter
tannhjólasett	gearing	teiknun	graphics
tannhjólatenging	gearing	teistufiskur	butterfish
tannhola	alveolus	tekjuliður	revenue
tannholubor	excavator	tekjulind	revenue
tannín	tannin	tekjur	income
tannkoma	dentition	tekjurafrakstur	revenue
tannsetning	dentition	teknetín	technetium
tannsíld	sprat	teknetíum	technctium
tanntaka	teething	tektóník	tectonics
tannteppa	retention	teljari	numerator
tantal	tantalum	tellúr	tellurium
tap	degeneration	tema	theme
tapeti	papers	temprun	homeostasis
tapíókagrjón	tapioca	tengi	coupling
tapíókamjöl	cassava	tengibraut	highway
tappasnittun	tapping	tengiensím	ligase
tappi	tampon	tengikragi	flange
tárabólga	conjunctivitis	tengildi	adapter
tarpúnn	tarpon	tengill	socket
tárubólga	conjunctivitis	tengimiðlun	hypermedia
taugaboð	impulse	tenging	junction
taugabraut	pathway	tengipunktur	vertex
taugafræði	neurology	tengir	ligase

tengispjald	adapter	þáttun	factoring
tengistétt	coupling	þáttur	diploma
tengistig	connectivity	þefskyn	olfaction
tengivagn	trailer	þefur	odour
tengjanleiki	connectivity	þegnskapur	citizenship
tengni	connectivity	þekja	hood
tengsl	affiliation	þekjuhúð	epidermis
tengslafasi	coupling	þekjustig	coverage
tengsli	coupling	þekjuvefur	epithelium
tengslkragi	coupling	þekkingargrind	schema
tenning	serration	þema	theme
teppa	retention	þenjari	expander
tepping	tamponade	þensla	dilation
terbín	terbium	þenslujafnari	compensator
terbíum	terbium	þermimök	sodomy
tereno	grounds	þerna	worker
terkonekti	grounds	þéttbýlismyndun	urbanization
termistor	thermistor	þétti	gasket
tero	grounds	þéttiefni	sealer
tersurfaco	grounds	þéttihringur	gland
textaröðun	alignment	þéttihvarf	condensation
textasafn	corpus	þéttikragi	gland
textastilling	alignment	þéttilinsa	condenser
texti	text	þétting	condensation
teyging	warping	þéttir	capacitor
teygja	elongation	þéttispegill	condenser
teygjudýr	ameba	þéttleikamælir	densitometer
þægindi	convenience	þéttleiki	consistency
þætting	fractionation	þéttni	concentration
þættun	fractionation	þéttun	condensation
þagnarskylda	confidentiality	þeytari	slinger
þak	ceiling	þeytiefni	emulsifier
þallín	thallium	þeytihjól	impeller
þallíum	thallium	þíamín	thiamine
þan	diastole	þíðingarbúnaður	defroster
þanbil	diastole	þiður	capercaillie
þang	tang	þiggjandi	receiver
þani	expander	þilfarspláss	steerage
þankahríð	brainstorming	þilfarspolli	bitt
þankaþeyr	brainstorming	þiljuljóri	skylight
þari	seaweed	þind	diaphragm
þarmastjórn	continence	þing	conference
þáttapörun	hybridization	þinglýsing	registration
þáttatenging	annealing	þingnefnd	committee
þátttaka	involvement	þjalakoli	megrim
þátttakandi	protagonist	þjálfun	training

þjappa	compressor	þörf	requirement
þjappi	compressor	þórín	thorium
þjarki	robot	þóríum	thorium
þjó	buttocks	þorp	settlement
þjóð	nation	þorskur	codfish
þjóðabandalag	alliance	þörungar	algae
þjóðarafkoma	economics	þráarhindri	antioxidant
þjóðaratkvæðagreiðsla	referendum	þráavari	antioxidant
þjóðarmorð	genocide	þráavarnarefni	antioxidant
þjóðerni	citizenship	þráðla	fibril
þjóðerniseinkenni	ethnicity	þráðormur	nematode
þjóðernisrembingur	nationalism	þráður	fibre
þjóðernisstefna	nationalism	þræðlingur	fibril
þjóðfélag	society	þræll	servomechanism
þjóðfélagsstéttir	estate	þráhyggja	obsession
þjóðfélagsstofnun	institution	þraut	problem
þjóðfræði	ethnography	þrávirkni	persistence
þjóðháttafræði	ethnology	þreifari	antenna
þjóðháttarfræði	ethnology	þreklyf	energizer
þjóðland	nation	þrenging	shrinkage
þjóðlýsing	ethnography	þrengir	sphincter
þjóðmegunarfræði	economics	þrengivöðvi	sphincter
þjóðmenning	culture	þrenna	triplet
þjóðnýting	nationalization	þrennd	triplet
þjóðræknisstefna	nationalism	þrep	interval
þjóðríki	nation	þrepræktun	fractionation
þjóðtunga	language	þrepun	induction
þjóhnappar	buttocks	þrepúttak	tapping
þjónn	server	þrepveldi	hierarchy
þjónusta	services	þreykur	smog
þjónustuhæfni	serviceability	þríburi	triplet
þjónustuleiga	leasing	þrif	cleaning
þjónustustjóri	purser	þríhyrna	triangle
þjónustuþegi	client	þríhyrndur	deltoid
þjöppun	packing	þríhyrningamæling	triangulation
þófi	disk	þríhyrningamælingar	triangulation
þökk	gratitude	þríhyrningur	triangle
þóknun	retainer	þrískautalampi	triode
þokuský	stratus	þrískauti	triode
þol	immunity	þrístig	triplet
þolandi	operand	þrístrendingur	prism
þolhjúpur	cyst	þristur	triode
þoli	operand	þrívídd	perspective
þöll	hemlock	þrívíddarmynd	stereogram
þolmörk	tolerance	þrívíddarrit	stereogram
þolvik	tolerance	þró	sump

þröm	threshold
þrombóplastín	thromboplastin
þröng	congestion
þröngsýni	insularity
þroski	development
þröskuldsgildi	threshold
þröskuldur	threshold
þroskun	development
þroskunarsaga	ontogenesis
þrot	deprivation
þroti	inflammation
þróttur	vigour
Þroun	development
þróun	development
þróunarferill	phylogeny
þrúgusykur	dextrose
þrumuský	cumulonimbus
þruska	thrush
þrútnun	intumescence
þrykking	stamping
þrýstifágun	burnishing
þrýstifall	depression
þrýstigeymir	accumulator
þrýstilína	isobar
þrýstimælir	manometer
þrýstingslækkandi	antihypertensive
þrýstingslína	isobar
þrýstingsmælir	manometer
þrýstingur	compression
þrýstiriti	barograph
þrýstivatnspípa	penstock
þumbaldaháttur	negativism
þungefni	metal
þunglyndislyf	antidepressant
þungsteinn	tungsten
þungunarvörn	contraception
þunnlífi	diarrhea
þurrð	dearth
þurrgufun	sublimation
þurrka	wiper
þurrkaskur	desiccator
þurrkskál	desiccator
Þurrkun	dehydration
þursaviður	peppermint
þvagblöðrunám	cystectomy
þvagefni	carbamide
þvageitrun	uremia
þvagfærafræði	urology
þvagleggur	catheter
þvagleysi	anuria
þvagsýrugigtarhnútur	tophus
þvagsýrugigtarsteinn	tophus
þvagtemprandi	antidiuretic
þvagþurrð	anuria
þveiti	excretion
þverbiti	transom
þverganga	culmination
þvermál	diameter
þverstag	transom
þvertré	cleat
þviti	briquette
þvottabjörn	raccoon
þvottatæki	washer
þýðandi	translator
þýði	population
þýðing	compilation
þýðistölur	parameter
þykkt	thickness
þykktarhólkur	spacer
þykktarskífa	spacer
þyngdarafl	gravitation
þyngdaráhrif	gravitation
þyngdarhlutfall	abundance
þyngdarhröðun	g
þyngdarpunktur	centroid
þyngdarverkun	gravitation
þynna	lamella
þynning	dilution
þynningur	dilution
þynnir	thinner
þyrill	rotor
þyrla	helicopter
þýroxín	thyroxine
þyrping	aggregation
tíðahvörf	menopause
tíðalok	menopause
tíðaþrautir	dysmenorrhea
tídd	frequency
tíðir	terms
tíðni	frequency
tíðniafmótari	discriminator
tíðnibil	bandwidth

tíðniskerpa	selectivity	tími	epoch
tíðnissvið	bandwidth	tindaknurri	piper
tignun	idealization	tirkesto	drawer
tigull	rhombus	titan	titanium
tígull	rhombus	títan	titanium
tilboð	proposal	títer	titer
tilbrigði	variation	titill	heading
tilefni	opportunity	titrari	vibrator
tilfæring	manipulation	títri	titer
tilfærsla	transposition	titringur	oscillation
tilfinningaleysi	anesthesia	tittlingur	penis
tilfinningaofsi	intoxication	titurriðill	vibrator
tilfinningarleysi	anesthesia	tíundarmark	decile
tilgangur	mission	tjaldhiminn	tarpaulin
tilgáta	hypothesis	tjaldþak	awning
tilhliðrun	modification	tjáning	expression
tilhneigð	predisposition	tjáningarröð	exon
tilhögun	procedure	tjáningarstig	penetrance
tilhvatning	motivation	tjáröð	exon
tilkoma	inclusion	tjón	losses
tilkynning	announcement	tjónnæmi	vulnerability
tillæti	plasticity	töf	latency
tillaga	proposal	töflureiknir	spreadsheet
tillífgun	anabolism	togari	trawler
tillífun	anabolism	toggálgi	gantry
tillíking	assimilation	tognun	dilation
tilmæli	recommendation	togsprunga	fissure
tilnefning	appointment	togtengi	desmosome
tilskipun	constitution	togveiðar	trawling
tilslökun	waiver	tól	device
tiltækileiki	availability	tólffótungur	caterpillar
tiltækt	availability	tölfræði	statistics
tilvik	event	tölfræðilegar	statistics
tilvistarstefna	existentialism	tölfræðilegur	statistic
tilvísun	referral	tollar	dues
tilvitnun	quotation	tollgæsla	customs
tilvitund	awareness	tollgæsluvöllur	gateway
tímabil	stadium	tollskrá	tariff
tímabundin	suspension	tollur	customs
tímagisti	timer	tölusamræmi	agreement
tímamörk	deadline	tölustafur	digit
tímarit	organ	tölutákn	digit
tímasetning	timing	tölvari	operator
tímastilling	timing	tölvubúnaður	hardware
tímastýring	timer	tölvugarpur	hacker
tímgill	thymus	tölvurefur	hacker

tölvuskeyti	message	trog	trough
tölvuþrjótur	hacker	tröllagrasker	pumpkin
tölvutorg	forum	tröllaldin	grapefruit
tölvuvæðing	computerization	tröllepli	cantaloupe
tombóla	lottery	tröllvöxtur	gigantism
tómstundaiðja	recreation	tromluás	countershaft
tómstundargaman	recreation	trompet	tuba
tónfall	intonation	trú	creed
tonn	tonne	truflanagreining	troubleshooting
töp	losses	truflanakæfir	suppressor
toppur	apex	trúlofun	betrothal
torleiðari	semiconductor	trúnaðarbréf	credentials
torleiði	dielectric	trúnaðarkvöð	confidentiality
torleiðiefni	dielectric	trúnaðarsamband	confidentiality
torleiðir	semiconductor	trúnaðarstaðfesting	accreditation
torleiðisfærsla	displacement	trúnaðarstig	confidentiality
torleiðnistuðull	permittivity	trúnaður	confidentiality
tota	papilla	trý	tryptophan
traf	fibrin	trygging	insurance
traktaĵo	papers	tryggingafræðingur	actuary
trapisa	trapezium	tryggingasali	insurer
Trapisan	trapezium	tryggjandi	insurer
trasnsistor	transistor	trýptófan	tryptophan
tratanto	drawers	túða	nozzle
tréefni	lignin	túlín	thulium
trefill	muffler	túlípanviður	whitewood
trefja	fibril	túlíum	thulium
trefjaefni	fibrin	túlkun	interpretation
trefjaplata	fibreboard	túlkur	interpreter
trefjar	fiber	tunga	projection
tregða	rigidity	tunglfiskur	opah
trenaĵo	tails	tunglflói	sinus
tréni	lignin	tunglhaf	mare
tréspíri	methanol	tunglmánuður	month
tréspíritus	methanol	tunglvik	libration
tríkína	trichina	tunguflúrur	soles
trimestro	quarters	tungumál	language
tríóða	triode	túrbína	turbine
trissa	sheave	turn	pylon
trítill	transistor	turnfálki	kestrel
trjóna	rostrum	tvenndargen	allele
tRKS	trna	tvenndarmynd	stereogram
troð	avenue	tvennun	synapsis
tróð	dunnage	tvíaugna	binocular
troðningur	congestion	tvíbrot	birefringence
troðsla	packing	tvíflokkun	dichotomy

tvígildistakmarkari	slicer	ulo	persons
tvíglerungur	doublet	umbjóðandi	consignor
tvígreining	dichotomy	umboðslaun	royalty
tvíhyggja	dualism	umboðsmaður	consignee
tvíklofnun	bifurcation	umbreyting	transduction
tvíkynhneigð	bisexuality	umbreytir	converter
tvíkynjun	bisexuality	umbrot	layout
tvílitni	dichroism	umbúðir	packaging
tvinn	thermocouple	umbun	retainer
tvinnhlaði	thermopile	umdæmi	precinct
tvinnleiðni	admittance	umfang	coverage
tvinnviðmnám	impedance	umferð	circulation
tvinnviðnám	impedance	umferðaræð	artery
tvípóla	dipole	umferðarbeining	routing
tvípóll	dipole	umferðarheildi	circulation
tvísæi	diplopia	umferðartegur	circulation
tvísær	binocular	umferill	periphery
tvískaut	dipole	umfrymi	cytoplasm
tvískautalampi	diode	umgjörð	circumference
tvískauti	diode	umhorf	milieu
tvískipting	dichotomy	umhverfi	environment
tvístig	doublet	umhverfisaðlögun	acclimatization
tvístringur	fragmentation	umhverfishyggja	environmentalism
tvístrun	fragmentation	umhverfiskerfi	ecosystem
tvistur	diode	umhverfislöghyggja	environmentalism
tvístur	fragmentation	umhverfisverndarsinni	environmentalist
tvísýni	diplopia	umleiðsla	transduction
tvítyngi	bilingualism	ummál	circumference
tvíveðrungur	ambivalence	ummótun	restructuring
tvíveldisfrávik	variance	ummyndun	transition
tvívetni	deuterium	umráð	occupancy
tyggigúmmítré	sapodilla	umráðasvæði	realm
tygjun	mobilization	umræðuefni	topic
týmídín	thymidine	umræðufundur	conference
týmus	thymus	umriðill	converter
typping	kurtosis	umritun	transcription
týtuber	cowberry	umröðun	rearrangement
úðari	nozzle	umröðunarhvarf	rearrangement
úðastútur	nozzle	umsjónarmaður	administrator
úðatæki	inhaler	umskiptanleiki	interchangeability
úðun	atomization	umskipti	alteration
ufsi	saithe	umskipting	commutation
uggi	fin	umskipun	transhipment
uggur	trepidation	umskurður	circumcision
ull	wool	umskurn	circumcision
úlnliðs	carpal	umtáknun	encoding

umvörpun	transformation	uppgufun	evaporation
undanfaraeinkenni	prodrome	upphafsefni	initiator
undanfari	precursor	upphafsmaður	initiator
undanhald	recession	upphafsstafaheiti	acronym
undantekning	exception	upphafsstafanafn	acronym
undanþága	immunity	upphafsstafaorð	acronym
undirboð	dumping	upphengja	suspension
undireining	subunit	upphengjulager	hanger
undirflokkur	subclass	uppistaða	stroma
undirgefni	submission	uppistöðuvefur	stroma
undirkæling	supercooling	uppkallsleitari	finder
undirklasi	subclass	uppkast	protocol
undirlag	carcass	uppköst	vomiting
undirlyfta	lifter	upplægi	exposure
undirlyftuarmur	lifter	upplag	anlage
undirlyftutappi	lifter	uppland	hinterland
undirsetning	hypostasis	upplausn	resolution
undirstaða	pedestal	uppleysing	dissolution
undirstæði	hypostasis	uppljóstrun	denunciation
undirstæðni	hypostasis	upplyfting	recreation
undirstöðuefni	substrate	upplýsingar	data
undirsvæðl	module	upplýsingaskjal	documentation
undirtegund	subspecies	uppörvun	incentive
undirvagn	chassis	upprakning	playback
undralyf	panacea	uppreisn	rebellion
undrun	astonishment	upprifjun	anamnesis
ungbarnakveisa	colic	upprunaferli	source
ungdómur	youngster	upprunafræði	cosmogony
unglingsár	adolescence	uppsala	vomiting
unnusta	bride	uppsetning	installation
uppbót	complementation	uppskafningsminni	palimpsest
uppbygging	development	uppsog	absorption
uppdrif	buoyancy	uppsögn	denunciation
uppeldi	education	uppsölulyf	antiemetic
uppfærsla	promotion	uppsölustillandi	antiemetic
uppfærsluaðgerð	transaction	uppspretta	source
uppfinning	invention	upptaka	absorption
uppflettimynd	lemma	upptekning	recurrence
uppflutningur	upload	uppþemba	flatulence
uppfylling	compliance	upptíningur	pickling
uppgangur	sputum	upptök	source
uppgerð	simulation	upptökusalur	studio
uppgjör	settlement	úrættun	degeneracy
uppgómur	velum	úrdráttur	extraction
uppgötvun	detection	úrfall	fallout
uppgröftur	excavation	úrfelling	deletion

úrgangsefni	excretion	úthverfing	eversion
úrgangslosun	excretion	úthýsing	outsourcing
úrhlutun	extraction	útilokun	exclusion
úrkomusafnmælir	totalizer	útjaðar	periphery
úrkynjun	degeneration	útjöfnun	neutralization
úrlausn	solution	útkast	ejection
úrlausnarefni	problem	útkastarahringur	ejector
úrrek	mandrel	útkastarastautur	ejector
urriði	trout	útkastari	ejector
úrskurður	arbitration	útlag	ectoderm
úrsnörun	counterbore	útleiðsla	deduction
úrtaka	sampling	útleiga	rental
úrvalsstefna	eclecticism	útlimur	limb
úrvötnun	dehydration	útlína	contour
útæð	artery	útlínur	contour
útæxlun	exogamy	útlistun	specification
utanæðablæðing	extravasation	útlitsfræði	morphology
utankaup	outsourcing	útlitsmynd	projection
utanmál	circumference	útloftun	ventilation
utanríkisstefna	policy	útmægðir	exogamy
útblástur	outlet	útmörk	periphery
útboðslýsing	prospectus	útnefning	appointment
útborg	suburb	útöndun	expiration
útbreiðsla	circulation	útprent	printout
útbreiðslustarf	promotion	útrás	outfall
útbúnaður	equipment	útrekstur	exclusion
útburður	eviction	útrennsli	outlet
útdráttur	extraction	útrennslisop	outlet
úteitur	exotoxin	útröð	exon
útensím	exoenzyme	útsetning	representation
úteyra	pinna	útskolun	leaching
útfærsla	extraction	útskot	protrusion
útferð	exudation	útskotsgluggi	oriel
útflæði	effusion	útskrift	printout
útfrymi	cortex	útskúfun	exclusion
útgáfa	flotation	útslag	deflection
útgangur	outlet	útsníkill	ectoparasite
útgiskun	extrapolation	útstandandi	protrusion
útgjöld	expenditure	útstreymi	effusion
útgufun	transpiration	útstrikun	deletion
úthelling	effusion	útsveim	effusion
úthjúpur	adventitia	útsýnisgreining	exposure
úthljóð	ultrasound	útsynningsklakkar	cumulonimbus
úthlutun	allocation	úttak	socket
úthverfa	extroversion	úttekt	assessment
úthverfi	suburbia	úttektarseðill	voucher

Reference: Webster's Online Dictionary (www.websters-online-dictionary.org)

útþekja	epithelium	vanviti	moron
útþensla	expansion	vara	commodity
útþensluaðgerð	dilatation	varafiskar	wrasses
útþrýsting	expression	varahljóð	labial
útþynning	dilution	varamæltur	labial
útvarp	radius	varanleiki	persistence
útvarpslampi	valve	varðveisla	preservation
útvíkkun	dilatation	varfærnisregla	conservatism
útvistun	outsourcing	Varijanta	variation
útvöxtur	apophysis	varkárnisregla	conservatism
vægi	torque	varmaaflfræði	thermodynamics
vændir	expectations	varmaeining	calorie
vængildi	aerofoil	varmafræði	thermodynamics
væntingar	expectations	varmagildi	enthalpy
vætl	seepage	varmahitamælir	bolometer
vafningsjurt	vine	varmamælir	calorimeter
vagn	car	varmaskiptamælir	calorimeter
váhrif	exposure	varmasundrun	thermolysis
vakahæfni	antigenicity	varnarbúnaður	armature
vaki	hormone	varnarleysi	vulnerability
vakning	activation	varp	oviposition
vala	talus	varsla	containment
valddreifing	devolution	varta	caruncle
valdframsal	delegation	varúð	precaution
valdsvið	domain	varúðarráðstöfun	precaution
vali	selector	vasi	stove
vallarmarki	marker	vatn	loch
vallhumall	yarrow	vatnableikja	trout
valllendi	grassland	vatnaflekkur	ling
valoraĵo	assets	vatnakrabbi	crayfish
valur	falcon	vatnamælingar	hydrography
valvísi	selectivity	vatnasíld	cisco
vanabinding	fixation	vatnaskeggi	barbel
vanadín	vanadium	vatnaskeggur	barbel
vanadíum	vanadium	vatnaskil	watershed
Vandamál	problem	vatnastúfa	vole
vandi	problem	vatnasvið	watershed
vaneldi	dystrophy	vatnaurriði	trout
vanfrjósemi	infertility	vatnavængildi	hydrofoil
vangakirtilsbólga	parotitis	vatnsberi	aquifer
vanilding	anoxia	vatnsbretti	sill
vannæring	malnutrition	vatnsdælustöð	waterworks
vanögn	neutron	vatnsefni	hydrogen
vansköpun	malformation	vatnsfælni	hydrophobia
vanskráning	understatement	vatnshaull	hydrocele
vanvirkni	dysfunction	vatnshöfði	hydrocephalus

vatnshöfðun	hydrocephalus	veggleysingi	protoplast
vatnshöfuð	hydrocephalus	veggrif	pier
vatnshræðsla	hydrophobia	veggskot	niche
vatnskassi	radiator	veggtafla	blackboard
vatnsklær	cirrus	veghefill	grader
vatnslás	thermostat	vegur	pathway
vatnsleiðsla	aqueduct	veiðistöðvun	moratorium
vatnsmelóna	watermelon	veiðiþjófur	poacher
vatnspýtingur	salivation	veifill	chopper
vatnsrás	aqueduct	veila	vulnerability
vatnsrýmd	storage	veira	virus
vatnsþró	cistern	veirubinding	lysogeny
vatnsveita	waterworks	veirueyðandi	antiviral
vatnsveitubrú	aqueduct	veirufræði	virology
vatnsveitustokkur	aqueduct	veiruhamlandi	antiviral
vátrygging	insurance	veiruhjúpur	capsid
vátryggingarskírteini	policy	veiruhylki	capsid
vátryggjandi	underwriter	veiruleiðsla	transduction
vatt	watt	veirungur	viroid
vébönd	domain	veiruskurn	capsid
veðrahvolf	troposphere	veising	excretion
veðrun	weathering	veisla	fiesta
veðurfarsfræði	climatology	veita	accreditation
veðurfarssaga	paleoclimatology	veitingahús	restaurant
veðurfræði	meteorology	veitir	aquifer
veðurfyrirbæri	meteor	veitur	facilities
veðurspjall	briefing	vektor	vector
vefildisþurrð	anoxia	vél	mechanism
vefjafláning	dissection	vélar	machinery
vefjafræði	histology	vélarhlíf	hood
vefjagula	xanthophyll	vélaþétti	gasket
vefjahrúður	vegetation	vélbúnaður	apparatus
vefjameinafræði	histopathology	veldi	domain
vefjaöndun	respiration	vélgengi	mechanism
vefjaskemmdir	histopathology	vélgerving	synthesis
vefjasýni	biopsy	vélhyggja	mechanism
vefjaþemba	emphysema	vélinda	esophagus
vefskemmd	lesion	veljari	selector
vefsprang	surfing	vélknúinn	motorization
vefsteyping	fixation	velli	secretion
vefsýni	biopsy	vellíðan	euphoria
vefsýnitaka	biopsy	vélmenni	robot
vegabréf	passport	vélþræll	robot
vegamót	intersection	veltiás	fulcrum
vegghetta	weathering	vélvæðing	mechanization
veggjahvilft	niche	vélvinna	machine

vembilsmyndun	gastrulation	verkstol	apraxia
vémynd	icon	verktaki	builder
vending	version	verkþáttur	activity
venja	convention	verkun	processing
vensl	relationship	verma	calorie
venslarit	nomogram	vermi	enthalpy
ventill	valve	vermibreyta	entropy
ventilsplitti	keeper	vernd	immunity
ventlastjórnun	timing	verndarríki	protectorate
venusvagn	aconite	verndarsvæði	protectorate
veraldarhyggja	materialism	verping	warping
verðbréfamiðlari	stockbroker	verpingur	warping
verðbréfamiðlun	brokerage	verslanamiðstöð	mall
verðbréfasafn	portfolio	verslunarvara	commodity
verðbréfasali	stockbroker	verufræði	ontology
verðbreytingarfærsla	revaluation	verzlun	transaction
verðhækkun	markup	vésögn	myth
verðhjöðnun	deflation	vespa	scooter
verðhrun	deflation	vessabjúgur	lymphedema
verði	ft	vessagrotnun	maceration
verðlækkun	deflation	vessaþurrð	dehydration
verðlagning	pricing	vessavökvi	plasma
verðmunarviðskipti	arbitrage	vetni	hydrogen
verðsamtök	cartel	vetniskol	hydrocarbon
verðskrá	tariff	vetniskolefni	hydrocarbon
vergirni	nymphomania	vetrarsalat	endive
verk	transaction	vettvangur	forum
verkalýður	proletariat	viðaræð	trachea
verkamaður	labourer	viðarkolahylki	canister
verkaskrá	agenda	viðarkvoða	resin
verkbann	lockout	viðarsykur	xylose
verkefni	problem	viðbein	clavicle
verkfæri	apparatus	viðbjóður	abhorrence
verkframkvæmd	construction	viðbót	increment
verkgangur	procedure	viðbragð	acceleration
verkgeta	praxis	viðbragðafjör	erethism
verklag	procedure	viðbragðafræði	reflexology
verklagsreglur	procedure	viðbragðahyggja	reflexology
verklýsing	specification	viðbragðshæfni	reactivity
verko	works	vídd	calibre
verkröðun	scheduling	víddartala	dimension
verkskömmtun	assignment	viðfangsefni	problem
verksmiðja	factory	viðhald	maintenance
verkstæði	workshop	viðhorf	attitude
verkstjóri	foreman	viðkoma	proliferation
verkstofa	workshop	viðkomugeta	resilience

viðkvæmni	excitability	viljastol	abulia
viðlegð	superposition	vilji	willingness
viðlegukantur	quay	vilsun	exudation
viðloðnun	adhesion	víma	intoxication
viðloðun	adhesion	vin	oasis
viðmælandi	addressee	vínandi	alcohol
viðmið	system	vínberjasykur	dextrose
viðmiðshæð	datum	vindáhrif	windage
viðmiðun	guideline	vindgangur	flatulence
viðmiðunarhæð	datum	vindingur	warping
viðmiðunarkerfi	system	vindkljúfur	spoiler
viðmiðunarmerki	benchmark	vindmylla	windmill
viðmiðunarmörk	threshold	vindriti	anemograph
viðmiðunarregla	guideline	vindrof	deflation
viðmiðunartími	epoch	vindsveipur	cyclone
viðnæmi	reactivity	vindþembingur	flatulence
viðnám	impedance	vingl	instability
viðnámskveikir	ignitor	vinkona	girlfriend
viðnámsstefna	containment	vínlandskarfi	rosefish
viðnámstæki	resistor	vinnsla	processing
viðræðufundur	consultation	vinnsluverk	microprocessor
viðræður	consultation	vinnuálag	workload
viðrini	intersex	vinnuborð	desktop
viðskiptakröfur	receivables	vinnudýr	worker
viðskiptamaður	customer	vinnuferill	operation
viðskiptavild	goodwill	vinnufundur	workshop
viðskiptavinur	client	vinnuhollustufræði	ergonomics
viðskipti	transaction	vinnulaun	wages
viðsnúningur	reversion	vinnumaur	worker
viðtæki	receiver	vinnustöð	workstation
viðtak	antenna	vinnuveitandi	employer
viðtakandi	addressee	vinnuvistfræði	ergonomics
viðtaki	receiver	vinstur	abomasum
viðtökuskoðun	acceptance	vinsun	screening
viðurkenning	approval	virðing	appraisal
viðvani	habituation	virðingaröð	hierarchy
vígahnöttur	meteor	virðuleiki	self-respect
vigur	vector	virki	equipment
vík	cove	virking	activation
vika	week	virkir	activator
víkkari	reamer	virkjun	activation
víkkun	dilatation	virkni	effectiveness
vikmörk	tolerance	virknisaukning	potentiation
vild	preference	vírus	virus
viljabeiting	conation	vísbending	indicator
viljadoði	abulia	vísbendir	indicator

vísir	indicator	vökvageymir	reservoir
vísitala	quotient	vökvahreyfifræði	hydraulics
vismút	bismuth	vökvakúpull	meniscus
visnun	tabes	vökvamyndun	liquefaction
vissustefna	positivism	vökvasókn	congestion
vist	habitat	vökvastöðufræði	hydraulics
vistarfirring	disorientation	vökvaþrútnun	imbibition
vistfræði	ecology	vökvun	hydration
vistir	provisions	volfram	tungsten
vistkerfi	ecosystem	voltamælir	voltameter
vistþýðandi	compiler	völur	spindle
vistþýðing	compilation	völvuauga	belladonna
vistun	outsourcing	vömb	rumen
vísun	indication	von	advertence
vit	gnosis	vonbrigði	disappointment
vitahús	lighthouse	vöntun	absence
viti	lighthouse	vönun	castration
vitneskja	information	vopn	weapon
vitra	glasses	vor	springtime
vitro	glasses	Vörn	defence
vitsmunir	intellect	vörpun	transformation
vitund	consciousness	vorsíld	capelin
víxill	commutator	vorsíli	capelin
víxl	alternation	vortími	springtime
víxla	toggle	vörtubaugur	areola
víxlstaða	repulsion	vörtuber	longan
víxlun	transposition	vörtuberjatré	longan
víxlverkun	interaction	vörubíll	lorry
vöðvafesta	insertion	vörublanda	unit
vöðvaglóbín	myoglobin	vörublendi	unit
vöðvahald	insertion	vörubretti	pallet
vöðvarauði	myoglobin	vöruferilsstjórn	logistics
vöðvaspenna	tonus	vöruferlisstjórnun	logistics
vöðvastífni	rigidity	vöruflutningaskip	freighter
vöðvaþráðla	myofibril	vöruflutningavél	freighter
vöðvatrefja	myofibril	vöruflytjandi	shipper
vöðvavisnun	dystrophy	vörumengi	unit
vogarafl	leverage	vörumerki	trademark
vogarás	fulcrum	vörumóttakandi	consignee
vögguljóð	berceuse	vörusendandi	consignor
vögguvísa	berceuse	vörustjórnun	logistics
vogris	stye	vosto	tails
vogun	leverage	vothey	silage
vogur	inlet	votlendi	wetland
vöktun	monitoring	vötnun	hydration
vökvagerð	liquefaction	vottun	certification

vöxtur	accretion
wolfram	tungsten
xýlen	xylene
xýlósi	xylose
yfirborðsbatn	runoff
yfirbreiðsla	tarpaulin
yfirbygging	superstructure
yfirbyggingarhlutir	bodywork
yfirbyggingarvinna	bodywork
yfirdráttur	overdraft
yfirfærsla	translocation
yfirflæði	spillover
yfirhalning	overhauling
yfirhitun	superheating
yfirhljóð	ultrasound
yfirhúð	epidermis
yfirlit	schema
yfirlýsing	statement
yfirmaður	officer
yfirráð	domination
yfirráðaréttur	sovereignty
yfirráðasvæði	territory
yfirráðasvið	domain
yfirrita	overwrite
yfirsetning	epistasis
yfirsjálf	superego
yfirstaða	epistasis
yfirstæði	epistasis
yfirstæðni	epistasis
yfirstýring	overloading
yfirsveiflur	harmonics
yfirtónn	overtone
yfirvald	magistrate
yfirvinna	overtime
yfrráðasvæði	realm
yggli	grapefruit
ygglingur	grapefruit
ýgi	aggression
ýlda	putrefaction
ylfingur	brownie
yrðing	statement
ýring	atomization
ýruefni	emulsifier
ytterbín	ytterbium
ytterbíum	ytterbium
yttrín	yttrium

yttríum	yttrium
zink	zinc

Nouns (English - Icelandic)

abbreviation	stytting
abdomen	afturbolur
abductor	fráfærir
abhorrence	grimmd
ability	hæfni
abjuration	afneitun
ablative	svitifall
abnormality	afbrigðileiki
abolition	ógilding
abomasum	vinstur
aborigine	Ástralíusvertingi
abortion	fóstureyðing
abreaction	geðlausn
abrogation	afnám
abscissa	láhnit
absence	vöntun
absenteeism	fjarvistir
absolutism	algildishyggja
absorptance	gleypnitala
absorption	frásog
absorptivity	ljósþéttni
abstinence	fráhvarf
abulia	viljadoði
abundance	fjöldahlutfall
abyss	hafsbotn
acceleration	hröðun
accelerator	bensíngjöf
acceptance	viðtökuskoðun
acceptor	rafþegi
accessibility	aðgengi
accession	vöxtur
accessories	flankafero
accident	bílslys
acclamation	lófatak
acclimation	ílending
acclimatization	umhverfisaðlögun
accordance	samhljómur
accountability	ábyrgð

accountancy	reikningshald	adjuster	stillir
accreditation	trúnaðarstaðfesting	adjustment	aðhæfing
accretion	aðsóp	administrator	forstöðumaður
acculturation	aðlifun	admiral	aðmíráll
accumulator	þrýstigeymir	admission	aðgangur
accuracy	hittni	admittance	samleiðni
accusal	ásökun	adolescence	æska
accused	ákærði	adrenal	nýrlægur
accuser	ákærandi	adrenaline	adrenalín
acetabulum	sograni	adsorption	aðloðun
acetate	asetat	adventitia	úthjúpur
acetone	aseton	advertence	von
acetyl	asetýl	adviser	deildarsérfræðingur
acetylene	asetýlen	aerobe	loftvera
achromasia	litleysi	aerobiosis	loftlíf
acidification	sýruaukning	aerodrome	flugvöllur
acidophil	sýrufíkill	aeroembolism	loftbólurek
acidosis	blóðsýring	aerofoil	vængildi
acinus	kirtilblaðra	aeroplane	flugvél
acme	hápunktur	aerosol	agnúði
acne	gelgjuþrymlar	aerostat	loftpoki
acolyte	stuðningsmaður	aestivation	sumardá
aconite	freyjublóm	affectivity	hrifnæmi
acre	ekra	affiliation	tengsl
acrimony	hvassleiki	affinity	ásælni
acrobatics	fimleikar	affirmation	staðfesting
acrocentric	endaheftur	afterbirth	hildir
acronym	upphafsstafanafn	afterburner	eftirbrennari
actinium	aktín	aftereffect	eftirhrif
activation	espun	afterglow	eftirljóm
activator	örvari	afterimage	myndleif
activity	þróttur	aftershock	eftirskjálfti
actress	leikkona	agammaglobulinemia	mótefnaþurrð
actuary	tryggingafræðingur	agar	gelsykra
adaptability	aðlögunarhæfileiki	agenda	dagskrá
adapter	tengildi	agglomeration	samhrúgun
adaptor	millistykki	agglutination	hópfelling
adder	höggormur	aggregation	samsteypa
addiction	ávanabinding	aggression	áreitni
addressee	viðtakandi	agio	gjald
adduction	aðfærsla	agonist	gerandvöðvi
adductor	aðfærir	agony	hræðsla
adenine	adenín	agranulocytosis	kyrningahrap
adenitis	kirtilbólga	agraphia	ritstol
adenocarcinoma	kirtilkrabbamein	agreement	tölusamræmi
adenoma	kirtilæxli	agribusiness	iðnbúskapur
adhesion	samgróning	agriculture	jarðrækt
adiposity	feitlagni	agrology	jarðvegsfræði

agronomy	jarðræktarfræði	amine	amín
aircraft	flugvél	amnesia	minnisleysi
airdrome	flugvöllur	amniocentesis	legvatnsástunga
airfield	flugvöllur	amnion	líknarbelgur
airline	flugleið	amortization	afskrift
airport	flughöfn	amp	adenosíneinfosfat
airway	barkarenna	ampere	amper
akinesis	hreyfingarleysi	amphibia	froskdýr
albatross	albatrosi	amplification	mögnun
albedo	hvítbörkur	ampulla	lykja
albinism	hvítingseðli	amputation	aflimun
album	hljómplata	amylopectin	amýlópektín
albumin	albúmín	anabolism	aðlífun
alcohol	áfengi	anaerobe	loftfæla
alewife	silfurskjaddi	analogy	samsvörun
alexia	lesstol	analyser	skynjari
alfalfa	alfalfagras	analyst	greinandi
algae	þörungar	analyzer	greiningartæki
alignment	textaröðun	anamnesis	endurminni
alkaptonuria	sortumiga	anaphylaxis	bráðaofnæmi
allele	tvenndargen	anarchism	stjórnleysi
allergy	ofnæmi	anarchy	stjórnleysi
alliance	gróðurfylki	anatoxin	afeitur
allocation	úthlutun	anchoring	ágræðsla
allotropy	fjölgervi	androgen	andrógen
allotype	samsætugerð	anemia	blóðleysi
almond	mandla	anemograph	vindriti
alp	alpherbejo	anencephaly	heilaleysi
alpha	alfa	anesthesia	deyfing
alphabet	stafróf	angiotensin	angíótensín
alteration	ummyndun	angler	golþorskur
alternation	víxl	anglerfish	svarthyrna
alternator	riðstraumsrafali	angstrom	aangström
altitude	flughæð	aniline	anilín
altocumulus	dröfnuský	anisotropy	misáttun
altostratus	gráblika	anlage	eðlisvísir
altruism	fórnfýsi	annatto	annattó
aluminium	alúmíníum	annealing	afdráttur
aluminum	ál	annihilation	eyðing
alveolus	kirtilblaðra	announcement	auglýsing
amalgamation	sameining	annuity	árgreiðsla
ambassador	sendiherra	annulus	liður
ambience	loft	anode	jáskaut
ambivalence	tvíveðrungur	anomaly	ferilhorn
ambulance	sjúkrabíll	anomia	nafnstol
ameba	teygjudýr	anopheles	malaríumý
amendment	lagabreyting	anorak	anorakkur

anoxia	ildisþurrð	appointment	setning
antagonism	andstaða	appraisal	mat
antagonist	blokki	apprenticeship	iðnnámstími
antenna	loftnet	approval	samþykki
anthracite	gljákol	apraxia	hreyfistol
anthropogenesis	einstaklingsþróun	apricot	apríkósa
anthropology	mannfræði	aquaculture	fiskeldi
antiarrhythmic	sláttarglapastillir	aqueduct	vatnsveitustokkur
antibiosis	meinlíf	aquifer	veitir
antibody	mótefni	arbitrage	högnun
anticoagulant	blóðstorkuheftir	arbitration	gerð
anticonvulsant	krampaleysandi	arbitrator	gerðardómsmaður
antidepressant	geðlægðarlyf	arbor	ás
antidiabetic	sykursýkislyf	arcade	bogagöng
antidiuretic	þvagtemprandi	archetype	fornmynd
antidote	móteitur	architect	arkitekt
antiemetic	uppsölulyf	architrave	faldur
antiepileptic	flogaveikilyf	archives	arhivo
antigen	vaki	arena	íþróttavöllur
antigenicity	vakahæfni	areola	reitur
antihypertensive	háþrýstingslyf	argument	horn
antimony	antímon	argumentation	rökleiðsla
antinode	andkvistur	armature	anker
antioxidant	þráavarnarefni	armpit	handarkriki
antipyretic	hitalækkandi	arousal	athyglisvakning
anti-semitism	gyðingahatur	arrack	standur
antisepsis	smitvörn	arrhythmia	hjartsláttaróregla
antiserum	mótsermi	arrogance	dramb
antitoxin	móteitur	arrowroot	marantarót
antitussive	hóstastillandi	arsenic	arsen
antiviral	veirueyðandi	arteriole	slagæðlingur
anuria	þvagleysi	artery	slagæð
anus	bakrauf	arthropod	liðdýr
anvil	steðji	artichoke	ætiþistill
apartheid	kynþáttaaðskilnaður	article	greinir
apathy	sinnuleysi	artifact	gervingur
aperture	opþvermál	asbestosis	asbesteitrun
apex	endi	ascospore	sekkgró
aphonia	raddarmissir	ascus	askur
apogee	jarðfirð	asepsis	bakteríuleysi
apophysis	beinútvöxtur	asp	naðra
apoptosis	feigðarferli	asparagine	asparagín
apparatus	tæki	ass	asni
appeasement	friðkauparstefna	assembler	smali
appellation	nafn	assembly	fundur
appendage	útlimur	assertion	staðhæfing
appendectomy	botnlanganám	assessment	úttekt
apperception	huggrip	asset	akiro

assets	akiro	avenue	troð
assignment	gilding	avoidance	forðun
assimilation	samlögun	awareness	áskyn
assistance	aðstoð	awning	sóltjald
assurance	fullvissa	axilla	handarkriki
astatine	astat	axiom	frumregla
aster	stjörnufífill	axis	öxull
asthenosphere	linhvolf	axle	ás
asthma	andarteppa	axon	sími
astigmatism	bjúgskekkja	azote	köfnunarefni
astonishment	furða	bacillus	stafgerill
astrobiology	stjörnulíffræði	backside	rass
astrolabe	stjörnuhæðarmælir	backspace	hopa
astrology	stjörnuspáfræði	bactericide	bakteríueyðir
astronaut	geimfari	bacteriology	bakteríufræði
astronautics	geimferðafræði	bacteriophage	gerilveira
astronomer	stjarnfræðingur	badge	merkisspjald
astronomy	stjarnfræði	bairn	barn
asylum	griðastaður	baiting	beitning
asymmetry	mishverfa	baker	bakari
atavism	áalíking	balcony	svalir
ataxia	hreyfiglöp	baldness	hártap
athlete	íþróttamaður	ballet	ballett
atmosphere	andrúmsloft	balsam	balsamínutré
atoll	hringrif	balustrade	grindverk
atomization	sundrun	bandwidth	bandvídd
atopy	bráðaofnæmishneigð	bankruptcy	gjaldþrot
atrium	forhólf	banks	banko
atropine	atrópín	baobab	apabrauðstré
attitude	afstaða	barbel	vatnaskeggi
attorney	málaflutningsmaður	barbiturate	barbitúrat
attraction	aðdráttarkraftur	barium	barín
attrition	nudd	barley	bygg
aunt	föðursystir	barnacle	hrossaraekja
aura	flogboði	barograph	þrýstiriti
autarchy	alræði	barracks	barako
autarky	sjálfsþurftarbúskapur	barracuda	barrakúda
authorization	heimild	barramundi	risaborri
autochthon	frumbyggi	barrier	garður
autogenesis	sjálfsmyndun	barrister	málfærslumaður
automation	stýritækni	baseline	grunnlína
automatism	sjálfvirkni	basics	stafróf
autopilot	sjálfstýring	basidium	gróstilkur
autosome	frílitningur	basil	basilíka
autosuggestion	sjálfssefjun	basin	lægð
autumn	haust	basis	grunnur
availability	aðgengileiki	basketball	körfuknattleikur

basophil	basafruma	biometry	líftölfræði
bast	sáldvefur	biopsy	vefjasýni
batch	runa	biorhythm	lífhrynjandi
bathroom	bað	biosphere	lífhvolf
baud	bot	biostatistics	lífmælingar
bauxite	báxít	biosynthesis	lífefnamyndun
beaker	bikar	biota	lífríki
beauty	blíða	biotechnology	líftækni
bedrock	berggrunnur	biotin	bíótín
beet	beð	birefringence	tvíbrot
beetroot	rauðbeða	birthday	afmæli
behaviorism	atferlisstefna	birthmark	fæðingarblettur
behaviour	atferði	bisection	helmingun
behaviourism	atferlisstefna	bisexuality	tvíkynhneigð
bel	desíbel	bismuth	bismút
belladonna	sjáaldursjurt	bitmap	punktafylki
beluga	hússtyrja	bitt	festarhæll
benchmark	fastmerki	blackbird	svartþröstur
bends	kafaraverkir	blackboard	veggtafla
beneficiary	njótandi	blackbody	svarthlutur
benzole	bensól	blackout	ölgleymi
berceuse	vögguljóð	blastoderm	kimblöðruveggur
bergamot	ilmappelsína	blastula	blaðra
berkelium	berklín	bleeder	blæðari
berry	ber	blizzard	hríð
beryllium	beryllín	bloke	karlmaður
bestiality	sódómska	blueberry	runnabláber
betatron	betatrónn	boarding	borðganga
betrothal	trúlofun	boatswain	bátsmaður
bezel	rammi	bobbin	bobbingur
bicarbonate	bíkarbónat	bobby	lögregluþjónn
bifurcation	tvíklofnun	bodywork	boddíhlutir
bilberry	aðalbláberjalyng	boiler	gufuketill
bile	gall	boldface	feitletra
bilingualism	tvítyngi	bollard	bryggjupolli
bilirubin	bílirúbín	bolometer	varmahitamælir
billfish	blettabryngedda	bookkeeper	bókari
binder	bindefni	booster	aflauki
binnacle	mælahús	bootstrap	ræsiforrit
binocular	kíkir	borage	hjólkróna
binoculars	lorno	boron	bór
bioassay	lífgreining	borrower	lántakandi
biochemistry	lífefnafræði	borrowing	lán
biodegradation	lífsundrun	bough	grein
bioengineering	líftækni	bouncer	gúmmítékki
biography	æfisaga	boundary	brotmark
biology	líffræði	bourgeoisie	borgarastétt
biomass	lífmassi	bowfin	boguggi

Reference: Webster's Online Dictionary (www.websters-online-dictionary.org)

bowsprit	bugspjót	burner	brennari
boy	strákur	burnishing	þrýstifágun
bracelet	armband	burring	gráðuhreinsun
braces	stajo	bursitis	belgmein
bragger	grobbari	bushing	fóðring
brainstorming	heilabylur	butane	bútan
brainwashing	heilaþvottur	butterfish	skerjasteinbítur
braking	hemlun	butternut	forðahneta
branchia	tálkn	buttock	gluteo
brazil	Brasilía	buttocks	sitjandi
breakwater	brimbrjótur	butyl	bútýl
breastbone	bringubein	buyer	kaupandi
breath	andardráttur	cab	leigubíll
bride	brúður	cabin	káeta
briefcase	skjalataska	caboose	kabyssa
briefing	veðurspjall	cabriolet	blæjubíll
briefs	kalsono	cacao	kakó
brilliance	birta	cadaver	lík
brimstone	brennisteinn	caesium	sesín
briquette	Köggull	calcite	kalsit
broadbill	sverðfiskur	calcitonin	kalsítónín
broccoli	spergilkál	calcium	kalk
brochure	kynningarbæklingur	caldera	askja
broker	fasteignasali	calf	kálfur
brokerage	miðlun	calibration	tækjastilling
bromine	bróm	calibre	eiginleiki
bronchus	lungnapípa	californium	kalifornín
brother	bróðir	callus	beinbris
brownie	ljósálfur	calomel	kalómel
browser	rápari	calorie	hitaeining
browsing	skrunskoðun	calorimeter	varmamælir
brucellosis	öldusótt	calving	jökulkast
buckwheat	bókhveitigrjón	calyx	bikar
builder	verktaki	camshaft	knastás
bulimia	grædgi	cancellation	aflýsing
bulla	blaðra	candela	kerti
bulldozer	jarðýta	candidiasis	hvítsveppasýking
bumping	höggsuða	canister	brúsi
bunker	byrða	cannabis	hass
bunny	kanína	canning	niðursuða
buoyancy	flotþol	cantaloupe	tröllepli
burbot	vatnaflekkur	cantilever	svifbiti
bureau	skrifborð	capacitance	rafrýmd
bureaucracy	embættismannakerfi	capacitor	rýmir
burette	býretta	capelin	kampasíld
burglar	innbrotsþjófur	capercaillie	þiður
burlap	pokastrigi	capillarity	hárpípukraftur

capitalism	auðvaldsskipulag	catheter	holleggur
capitalization	eignfærsla	cathode	katóða
capitulum	kollur	catkin	rekill
capsid	veiruhjúpur	cattle	kýr
car	vagn	catwalk	gangbrú
caraway	kúmen	caul	sigurkufl
carbamide	karbamíð	cauliflower	blómkál
carbide	harðmálmur	causality	orsakalögmál
carbohydrate	kolhýdrat	cavity	hol
carbonization	kolun	ceiling	hámarksflughæð
carburetor	blöndungur	celeriac	rótsellerí
carburettor	blöndungur	celery	stilksellerí
carcass	hjólbarðastofn	cell	rafhlöðueining
cardamom	kardimommujurt	censorship	ritskoðun
cardiogram	hjartarit	centile	hundraðshlutamark
cardiograph	hjartariti	centimetre	sentimetri
cardoon	ætiþistill	centralization	miðstýring
carelessness	hirðuleysi	centrifugation	aflskiljun
carnation	garðnellíka	centriole	miðögn
carotene	karótín	centroid	miðpunktur
carpal	úlnliðs	century	öld
carragheen	fjörugrös	cerebellum	hnykill
carrier	arfberi	cerebration	heilaferli
carrot	gulrót	cerebrum	heili
cartel	einokunarhringur	cerium	serín
cartography	kortagerð	certification	vottun
cartridge	minnishylki	cerumen	eyrnamergur
caruncle	sepi	cervix	háls
cashew	kasúhneta	cesium	sesín
casing	fóðurrör	chaining	keðjun
cassava	manjokrunni	chamfering	sniðskurður
cassette	segulbandsspóla	chamois	gemsa
cassia	kassía	chamomile	gæsajurt
caster	eltihalli	characterisation	breyta
casting	steypumót	chard	blaðbeðja
castor	bjórar	charging	gjaldlagning
castration	afkynjun	charisma	náðarvald
catabolism	efnismolun	charterer	leigutaki
catalysis	hvötun	chaser	skrúfugraftarverkfæri
catalyst	efnahvarfi	chasm	hyldýpi
catastrophe	endalok	chassis	undirvagn
catatonia	geðstjarfi	checkers	damdisko
categorization	flokkun	checkpoint	gátstaður
category	hópur	chemoreceptor	efnaviðtaki
catenary	keðjuferill	cherimoya	sérrímóla
caterpillar	fiðrildislirfa	chest	brjóst
catfish	steinbítur	chiasma	krossbrú
catharsis	geðhreinsun	chicory	kaffifífill

child	íflekkur	clearing	losun
chimney	skorsteinn	cleat	oki
chitin	kítín	clevis	klofi
chlamydia	klamydía	client	biðlari
chloride	klóríð	climatology	loftslagsfræði
chlorine	klór	clipper	klippir
chlorofluorocarbon	klórflúrkolefni	coagulant	hleypandi
chlorophyll	blaðgræna	coastline	strandlengja
chloroplast	grænukorn	cobia	foringjafiskur
cholera	kólera	coca	kóka
cholesterol	kólesteról	coccus	knattgerill
cholinergic	asetýlkólínseytandi	cochlea	kuðungur
chopper	veifill	coconut	kókoshneta
chordamesoderm	seilarmiðlag	codeine	kódeín
choroid	æðahimna	codfish	þorskur
chroma	fagurlitleiki	coding	táknsetning
chromatin	litni	cogwheel	tannhjól
chromatography	blettagreining	cohabitation	sambúð
chromium	króm	coherence	hugsanasamhengi
chromosome	litningur	cohesion	samloðun
chromosphere	lithvolf	cohort	hópur
chronometer	hnitklukka	coinage	myntslátta
chrysalis	púpa	coining	myntslátta
cichlids	síklíðar	col	söðulsvæði
cilium	augnhár	colic	ungbarnakveisa
circulation	blóðstreymi	colleague	samstarfsmaður
circumcision	forhúðarstýfing	collection	innheimta
circumference	ummál	collectivism	sameignarstefna
circumstances	cirkonstanco	collector	gleypir
cirque	hvilft	collet	spennihólkur
cirrhosis	hersli	collier	kola
cirrocumulus	dröfnuský	collimator	geislabeinir
cirrostratus	skýjablika	collocation	orðastæða
cirrus	bifháraskúfur	collusion	leynimakk
cisco	hvítfiskur	colonnade	súlnagöng
cistern	frymisgrisjuhít	colony	hrúga
citizenship	borgaraskilningur	colorimeter	efnalitsjá
clairvoyance	dulskyggni	colorimetry	litmæling
clamping	hald	colostrum	broddmjólk
clan	kynþáttur	comet	halastjarna
clarification	skýring	commander	kapteinn
classification	flokkun	commencement	byrjun
claustrophobia	innilokunarfælni	commensalism	gistilífi
clavicle	viðbein	commissioner	stjórnarnefndarmaður
cleaner	hreinsari	commitment	kvöð
cleaning	hreinsun	committee	fastanefnd
clearance	bil	commodity	verslunarvara

commonwealth	þjóðfélag	confusion	ringlun
commutation	straumhlaup	congelation	samfrysting
commutator	straumskiptir	conger	hafáll
compaction	þétting	congestion	vökvasókn
comparability	samanburðarhæfni	conjunctivitis	augnangur
compensator	mótvægismælir	connectivity	tengistig
competition	keppni	connector	leiðari
competitiveness	samkeppnishæfi	connotation	aukamerking
compilation	söfnun	consanguinity	blóðbönd
compiler	þýðandi	consciousness	vitund
complaint	ákæra	conservatism	varkárnisregla
complementation	uppbót	consignee	umboðsmaður
compliance	hlýðni	consignor	umbjóðandi
composition	nauðungarsamningur	consistency	samræmi
comprehension	skilningur	consolation	huggun
compression	ferging	consolidation	efling
compressor	loftpressa	consonance	samraemi
compulsion	árátta	consortium	samsteypa
computerization	tölvuvæðing	constable	lögreglumaður
conation	misvægi	constancy	festa
concavity	hvelfing	constituency	kjördæmi
concentration	miðskipan	constitution	stjórnskipulag
concentrator	beinispóla	constraint	skilyrði
concept	álit	constriction	haft
conception	fenging	construction	bygging
conciliation	samkomulag	consul	ræðismaður
conciliator	friðarstillir	consulate	ræðismannsbústaður
conclusion	ályktun	consultant	ráðgjafi
concordance	orðstöðulykill	consultation	ráðaleitun
concrescence	samleitni	container	gámur
concretion	steinn	containment	hamning
concurrence	samræmi	contaminant	aðskotaefni
concussion	áfall	contamination	gagnamengun
condensation	þétting	contention	staðhæfing
condenser	eimsvali	contiguity	grannsvæðakennsl
conditioning	Hæfing	continence	blöðrustjórn
condom	smokkur	continuity	samfella
condominium	kaupleiguíbúð	continuum	litrófssamfella
conductance	leiðni	contour	jafngildislína
conduit	pípa	contraception	getnaðarvörn
condyle	leggjarhöfuð	contractility	herpanleiki
cone	keila	contraction	herping
confabulation	fimbulfamb	contractor	samingsaðili
conference	ráðstefna	contradistinction	mótsetning
confidentiality	bankaleynd	contrail	flugslóði
configuration	samgerð	contribution	framlag
confirmation	ferming	controllability	stjórnhæfi
conformity	samræmi	controller	aflstýritæki

controversy	rifrildi	countermeasure	gagnráðstöfun
convalescence	afturbati	counterplay	Motspíspil
convenience	hentugleiki	countershaft	milliás
convention	sáttmáli	county	hérað
conversation	samtal	coupling	tengistétt
converter	afriðill	coupon	afsláttarmiði
convertor	umriðill	courgette	dvergbítur
convexity	ávali	cousin	frændi
conveyor	færiband	cove	fjörður
conviction	sannfæring	coverage	þekja
convolution	felling	cowberry	rauðber
cony	kanína	cowl	vélarhlíf
coolant	kæliefni	cradlesong	vögguljóð
cooler	kælir	cranium	hauskúpa
cooperation	samstarf	crankshaft	sveifarás
coordination	hnitun	crayfish	fljótakrabbi
copper	eir	creativity	sköpunargáfa
coprocessor	samgjörvi	credentials	skilríki
copse	kjarr	creditor	lánveitandi
corals	kórallar	creed	trú
coriander	kóríandrajurt	crematory	bálstofa
corium	leður	cretin	korkudvergur
corm	jarðstöngulhnýði	cretinism	kyrkivöxtur
cornea	glæra	crevasse	jökulgjá
cornice	hengja	crevice	rifa
corolla	blómkróna	crew	áhöfn
corona	blik	crisis	bráðavandi
coronary	hjartaáfall	criterion	viðmið
corpus	dæmasafn	crocodile	krókódíll
correlation	jarðlagatenging	crossover	hitaflutningur
correspondence	hliðstæða	crosstalk	merkjablöndun
corrosion	æting	crossword	krossgáta
cortex	barkhúð	croup	lend
corticosteroid	barksteri	crucible	digull
cortisol	kortisól	cruiser	beitiskip
coryza	höfuðkvef	crus	leggur
cosine	kósínus	crypt	bora
cosmogony	heimsmyndunarfræði	crystalloid	kristallslegur
cosmology	heimsfræði	cucumber	gúrka
cosmos	alheimur	culmination	þverganga
cotangent	kótangens	culture	smáverugróður
cotter	lásfleygur	cumin	krosskúmen
cotyledon	fósturskúfur	cumulonimbus	skúraflákar
coulomb	kúlomb	cumulus	bólsturský
council	ráð	cunt	pussa
counteraction	andvirkni	cups	bolli
counterbore	hringstallur	curium	kúrín

cursor	bendill	decoration	heiðursmerkjaveiting
curvature	straumlína	decoupling	aftengsl
cusk	keila	deduction	útleiðsla
customer	kaupandi	defamation	slúður
customs	kutimo	defence	Vörn
cutoff	afmörkun	defibrillation	hjartastilling
cuttlefish	blekfiskar	definition	skilgreining
cyanocobalamin	sýanókóbalamín	deflation	fok
cybernetics	kerfisfræði	deflection	bognun
cyberspace	netheimar	deflector	skýla
cyclamen	alpafjóla	defoliation	lauffelling
cyclone	hvirfilbylur	deformation	aflögun
cyclotron	hlaðeindahraðandi	defroster	ísvari
cyst	belgur	degassing	lofttómshreinsun
cystectomy	blöðrunám	degeneracy	úrættun
cytology	frumufræði	degeneration	hrörnun
cytoplasm	umfrymi	degradation	niðurbrot
cytosol	frumuhlaup	dehiscence	opnun
dace	silfurgægir	dehydration	vessaþurrð
dactyl	daktíli	dejection	sút
dale	dalur	delegation	sendinefnd
damages	skaðabætur	deletion	úrfelling
dame	kona	delineation	landamerkjalýsing
damping	svaf	dell	dalur
danger	hætta	delta	óseyrar
dashboard	mælaborð	deltoid	axlarvöðvi
dashpot	deyfingarhylki	delusion	hugvilla
data	gögn	demagnetisation	afseglun
dating	aldursákvörðun	demarcation	landamerkjamæling
datum	viðmiðshæð	democrat	demókrati
daughter	dóttir	demodulation	afmótun
davit	davíða	demodulator	afmótari
day	dagur	demography	stofnfræði
deadline	tímamörk	demonstration	sýning
deafness	heyrnardeyfa	demurrage	aukabiðdagagaþóknun
dearth	ekla	denaturation	eðlissvipting
debenture	skuldabréf	dendrite	gripluþráður
debt	skuld	denial	afneitun
debtor	skuldunautur	denomination	nafn
deceleration	hraðaminnkun	denominator	nefnari
decentralization	dreifistýring	denotation	merkingarkjarni
decibel	db	densitometer	þéttleikamælir
decile	tíundarmark	density	þéttleiki
declination	stjörnubreidd	dentition	tanntaka
decoder	afkótari	denunciation	uppljóstrun
decoding	afskráning	department	svið
decomposition	niðurbrot	depersonalization	afsjálfgun
decontamination	Hreinsun	depolarization	afskautun

deposits	innlán	digitalis	dígitalis
depression	lægðarsvæði	dilatation	útþensluaðgerð
depressor	niðurfærir	dilation	tognun
deprivation	svipting	dilator	stærivöðvi
depth	dýpi	dilution	þynning
derivation	afleiðsla	dimension	mælivídd
descaling	ryðhreinsun	dinghy	skipsbátur
descender	lágleggsstafur	diode	tvistur
descent	fall	diploma	skírteini
descriptor	efnisvísir	diplomat	sendifulltrúi
desensitization	afnæming	diplopia	tvísæi
desiccator	rakagleypir	dipole	tvískaut
desktop	skjáborð	directions	direkto
desmosome	halddepill	directivity	stefnuvirkni
destination	áfangastaður	disability	hreyfihömlun
detection	skynjun	disagreement	ágreiningur
detector	skynjari	disappointment	vonbrigði
determinism	löghyggja	disaster	stórslys
detonator	forsprengja	disc	kringla
detoxification	afeitrun	discharging	afgreiðsla
deuterium	tvívetni	disclosure	upplýsingar
devaluation	gengisfelling	discordance	mislægi
development	þroskun	discounting	núvirðing
device	búnaður	discrepancy	misræmi
devolution	valddreifing	discriminator	þröskuldur
dewberry	elgsber	disengagement	höfuðlausn
dextrose	dextrósi	disequilibrium	jafnvægismissir
diagnosis	greining	disillusionment	vonbrigði
dialect	mállýska	disinfection	sótthreinsun
dialysis	himnusíun	disjunction	aðskilnaður
dialyzer	límingasía	disk	diskur
diameter	þvermál	diskette	disklingur
diaphragm	millihimna	disorientation	misáttun
diarrhea	lífsýki	dispatching	verkröðun
diastase	sterkjukljúfur	dispensary	lyfjabúð
diastole	þanbil	displacement	torleiðisfærsla
diatomite	kísilgúr	disposal	ráðstöfun
dichotomy	skipting	dissection	vefjafláning
dichroism	skautnæmi	dissension	missætti
dichromatism	litvilla	dissimilation	hljóðfirring
dictator	einræðisherra	dissociation	persónuleikarof
dictionary	orðabók	dissolution	sundurlausn
dielectric	einangrari	dissonance	hugarmisræmi
diencephalon	milliheili	distillation	eimun
diffraction	öldubeygja	distraint	lögtak
diffuser	dreifir	distributor	rásaskiptir
digit	tölutákn	divergence	sundurleitun

divider	skilrúm	dystrophy	korka
dividers	sirkill	eardrum	hljóðhimna
divinity	guð	earl	greifi
documentation	skjalbúnaður	earmarking	eyrnamerking
dogfish	háfur	earphone	eyrnatól
dolphin	gullmakríll	earring	eyrnalokkur
domain	vettvangur	earth	jarðarbúar
dominance	yfirráð	easement	réttur
domination	yfirráð	ebonite	harðgúmmí
donkey	asni	ecchymosis	blóðhlaup
door	hurð	ecdysis	hamskipti
doping	íbæting	eclecticism	úrvalsstefna
dory	doría	ecliptic	sólbraut
dosage	skömmtun	ecology	vistfræði
dosimeter	geislaskammtamælir	economics	þjóðarafkoma
dosimetry	geislunarmælingar	economizer	sarpur
dossier	málsskjöl	ecosystem	vistkerfí
doublet	tvíglerungur	ectoderm	útlag
dramatization	leikhverfing	ectoparasite	útsníkill
drawback	galli	ectoplasm	útfrymi
drawer	tirkesto	edema	bjúgur
drawers	tratanto	edging	egg
dressing	umbúðir	editing	gagnainnsetning
driver	bifreiðarstjóri	edition	útgáfa
dromedary	drómedari	editor	ritill
drowsiness	syfja	education	menntun
drugstore	lyfjabúð	effectiveness	markvirkni
drupe	steinaldin	effector	hrifill
dualism	tvíhyggja	effusion	úthelling
dubbing	blöndun	egalitarianism	jafnréttisstefna
duct	lögn	ego	sjálf
dues	tollar	einsteinium	einsteinín
dulse	söl	ejaculation	sáðfall
dumping	sturttæming	ejection	útkast
dunnage	tróð	ejector	útkastari
duplicity	svik	elastomer	gúmmílíki
durability	ending	electrification	rafmögnun
duramen	kjarnviður	electrocardiogram	hjartalínurit
durian	dáraaldin	electrode	skaut
duties	álögur	electroencephalogram	heilarit
dwarfism	dvergvöxtur	electron	bakögn
dynamo	rakstraumsrafali	electrophoresis	jónfærsla
dysfunction	vanvirkni	electroplating	rafhúðun
dysmenorrhea	tíðaþrautir	electrotherapy	raflækning
dysphagia	kyngingartregða	element	elemento
dysphoria	ónotakennd	elements	ingredienco
dyspnea	andþrengsli	elevation	hæð
dysprosium	dysprósín	ellipse	öskjubaugur

elongation	álengd	eosinophil	eósíntækur
emanation	geislaloft	ephemeris	stjörnualmanak
embedding	steyping	epicentre	sjálftamiðja
embolism	blóðrek	epicycle	aukahringur
embolus	blóðrek	epidermis	húðþekja
embossing	stönsun	epiglottis	barkakýlislok
embryology	fósturfræði	epinephrine	adrenalín
emitter	eimir	epiphysis	hlass
empathy	hluttekning	epiphyte	ásæta
emphysema	vefjaþemba	episode	atvik
empiricism	raunhyggja	epistasis	skán
employee	starfsmaður	epistaxis	blóðnasir
employer	atvinnurekandi	epithelium	þekja
empyema	holsígerð	epoch	mynstrasafn
emulation	herming	equality	jafnrétti
emulator	hermir	equalizer	jafnari
emulsifier	þeytiefni	equation	líking
encapsulation	húðun	equator	miðbaugur
encephalitis	heilabólga	equilibration	jafnvætting
enclosure	fylgiskjal	equinox	jafndægrapunktur
encoding	umtáknun	equipment	tækjabúnaður
endive	endívusalat	era	öld
endogamy	skyldraæxlun	erbium	erbín
endoparasite	innsníkill	erethism	viðbragðafjör
endopeptidase	prótíninnkljúfur	ergometer	kraftmælir
endorsement	ábeking	ergonomics	vinnuhollustufræði
energizer	þreklyf	ergot	meldrjóli
engorgement	offylli	eroticism	kynnautn
engram	minnisspor	erotism	kynnautn
enquiry	spurning	erotomania	ástaræði
enrichment	auðgun	erythroblast	rauðfrumuforveri
entelechy	markmiðshugsjón	erythrocyte	blóðtala
enterprise	framtak	escutcheon	merkiskjöldur
enthalpy	varmagildi	esker	malarás
entitlement	réttur	esophagus	vélinda
entity	aðili	estate	bú
entomology	skordýrafræði	estimating	mat
entrainment	innblöndun	estimator	áætlunartala
entrepreneur	athafnamaður	estrogen	estrógen
entropy	óreiða	ethanol	etanól
entry	innfærsla	ethic	etiko
environment	umhverfi	ethics	etiko
environmentalism	umhverfishyggja	ethnicity	þjóðerniseinkenni
environmentalist	umhverfisverndarsinni	ethnography	þjóðfræði
envoy	sendiherra	ethnology	þjóðfræði
enzyme	lifhvati	ethology	atferlisfræði
eon	aldabil	ethylene	etýlen

eucaryote	samkjörnungur	extrapolation	útgiskun
eugenics	arfbætur	extravasation	utanæðablæðing
eukaryote	samkjörnungur	extremity	útjaðar
euphoria	sældarvilla	extroversion	úthverfa
europium	evropín	exudation	útferð
evaluation	gildisákvörðun	eyebolt	augabolti
evaporation	uppgufun	eyebrow	augabrún
evaporator	eimir	eyelid	augnalok
event	mót	eyepiece	augngler
eversion	úthverfing	facet	flötur
eviction	útburður	facies	ásýnd
exactitude	nákvæmni	facilitation	næmisaukning
example	dæmi	facilities	búnaður
excavation	holun	factoring	þáttun
excavator	tannholubor	factory	iðjuver
exception	undantekning	fad	FAT
exchanger	skiptir	faeces	saur
excitability	ertanleiki	falcon	fálki
exciter	segulmagnsvél	fallout	úrfall
exclusion	útilokun	farmer	stórbóndi
excretion	þveiti	fascia	fell
execution	fjárnám	fascicle	knippi
exertion	átak	fascism	fasismi
exfoliation	flögnun	faucet	krani
exhalation	eimur	faulting	misgengishreyfing
exhibitionism	sýnihneigð	fauna	dýraríki
existentialism	tilvistarstefna	federation	samtök
exobiology	geimlíffræði	feijoa	joðber
exoenzyme	útensím	feminism	kvenréttindastefna
exogamy	aðkvæni	fenestration	götun
exon	táknröð	fennel	finkull
exotoxin	úteitur	fermium	fermín
expander	þani	fertilizer	áburður
expansion	liðun	fetish	blæti
expectations	vændir	fetus	fóstur
expectorant	hóstameðal	feudalism	lénsveldi
expectoration	hræking	fever	hitasótt
expenditure	gjöld	fiber	þráður
expenses	elspezo	fibre	þráður
expiration	gildislok	fibreboard	spónaplata
explanation	skýring	fibril	taugatrefja
exploitation	hagnýting	fibrin	fíbrín
exploration	innankönnun	fibrinogen	fíbrínógen
exposure	geislunarmagn	fiesta	veisla
expression	pressun	filaria	þráðormur
extension	framlenging	filbert	stórheslihneta
extensor	réttir	filing	skjalavistun
extraction	tanndráttur	filler	fylli

filtering	síun	forestry	skógrækt
filtration	síun	forging	eldsmíði
fin	uggi	formalin	formalín
finances	fjárhagsstaða	formatting	forsnið
financing	fjármál	formula	lyfjaforskrift
finder	uppkallsleitari	forum	miðstöð
finding	leit	fossa	drag
fingernail	fingurnögl	foundation	grundvöllur
fingerprint	fingrafar	fovea	nethimnugróf
firewall	eldvarnarþil	fractionation	þrepræktun
fireworks	flugeldar	fragmentation	hlutun
fission	skipting	framework	grindarvirki
fissure	gjá	francium	fransín
fitness	rekki	frankincense	reykelsistré
fixation	skorðun	freighter	flutningaskip
fixative	festiefni	frequency	fjöldi
flagellum	svipa	friar	bróðir
flange	flans	frigidity	kaldlæti
flashlight	kyndill	frog	froskur
flatboat	flatbytna	fructose	aldinsykur
flattening	kúlufrávik	ft	verði
flatulence	vindþembingur	fugue	minnistap
flexibility	mýkt	fulcrum	bakhjarl
flexor	beygir	fulmar	fýll
floodplain	flóðslétta	fumes	haladzi
flora	örverugróður	fumigation	eiturúðun
flotation	fleyting	fundamentals	stafróf
flowchart	flæðirit	funding	fjármögnun
fluctuation	óstöðugleiki	fungi	sveppir
fluorescence	flúrljóm	fungicide	sveppadeyðir
fluorine	flúor	furnace	bræðsluofn
fluorosis	flúreitrun	furuncle	blóðkýli
fluting	rifflar	fusion	bráðnun
flyback	bakflug	g	þyngdarhröðun
flywheel	kasthjól	gable	gafl
focusing	sambeining	gadolinium	gadólín
foe	óvinur	gal	stelpa
foetus	fóstur	galactose	galaktósi
folder	mappa	galangal	dverggalangal
folding	földun	gallery	listskrubba
follicle	belgkirtill	galley	eldhús
font	letur	gallium	gallíum
fontanelle	lindarblettur	galvanization	galvanhúðun
football	knattspyrna	gambit	Bragð
footballer	knattspyrnumaður	gamete	brúðfruma
footwear	fótabúnaður	ganglion	hnoða
foreman	verkstjóri	gangway	landgangur

gantry	gálgi	glycine	glý
gaper	sandskel	glycogen	glýkógen
garage	bílaverkstæði	glycogenesis	glýkógenmyndun
garfish	hornfiskur	glycolysis	sykrusundrun
gasification	Gösun	gnomon	kambur
gasket	pakkning	gnosis	vit
gassing	gasmyndun	goat	geit
gastralgia	magaverkur	goggles	hlífðargleraugu
gastrulation	holfósturmyndun	goitre	skjaldkirtilsauki
gate	gátt	gonad	kynkirtill
gateway	tollgæsluvöllur	goodwill	álit
gearbox	gírkassi	gopher	snati
gearing	tannhjólatenging	goshawk	gáshaukur
gearshift	gírstöng	graben	sigdæld
gene	arfberi	grader	flokkunarvél
generalisation	hæfing	gramme	gramm
generalization	algilding	grandeur	stærð
generator	gjafi	grandfather	afi
genetics	ættgengisfræði	grandmother	amma
genitalia	getnaðarfæri	grandparent	geavo
genitals	kynfæri	grapefruit	greipaldin
genocide	þjóðarmorð	grapevine	lausafregn
genotype	erfðagervi	graphics	teiknun
geography	landafræði	graphite	grafít
geology	jarðfræði	grasshopper	engispretta
geomorphology	landmótunarfræði	grassland	beitiland
geophone	skjálftanemi	graticule	bauganet
geophysics	jarðeðlisfræði	gratitude	þökk
germ	kím	gravitation	aðdráttarafl
germanium	german	greatness	stærð
gerontology	öldrunarfræði	gregariousness	hjarðhvöt
giantism	risavöxtur	grenadiers	langhalar
gigantism	risavöxtur	grid	hnitakerfi
gimlet	handbor	grommet	gúmmíkragi
ginkgo	gingkó	grounding	strand
girder	biti	groundnut	svarðarhneta
girl	stelpa	grounds	kialo
girlfriend	vinkona	groundwater	jarðvatn
gizzard	fóarn	guava	eldaldin
gland	hringþétti	guest	gestur
glasses	glas	guideline	viðmiðunarregla
glia	taugatróð	gulf	hyldýpi
glomerulonephritis	nýrahnoðrabólga	gully	gólfræsi
glomerulus	æðhnoðri	gustation	bragðskyn
gloves	fingravettlingar	gynandromorph	kyntigla
glucose	þrúgusykur	gynecology	kvensjúkdómafræði
glycerin	glýserín	gypsum	gips
glycerol	glýseról	gyration	vindingur

gyrfalcon	fálki	hemianopia	helftarblinda
gyrocompass	snúðviti	hemicrania	helftarhöfuðverkur
gyroscope	snúðvísir	hemiptera	skortítur
h	vatnsefni	hemisphere	hálfhnöttur
habitat	bústaður	hemlock	eitursveipur
habituation	aðlögun	hemoglobin	blóðrauði
hacker	tölvugarpur	hemoglobinuria	blóðrauðamiga
haemorrhoid	hemoroido	hemolysis	blóðrauðalos
hafnium	hafnín	hemophilia	dreyrasýki
halation	baugmyndun	hemorrhoid	raufaræðahnútur
halibut	lúða	hemostasis	blóðrennslisstöðvun
hallucination	ofskynjun	hepatoma	lifraræxli
hallucinogen	sýngæfur	heptane	heptan
handedness	hendi	herbicide	illgresiseyðir
handicraft	handiðn	herbivore	grasbítur
handline	handfæri	heredity	ættgengi
hanger	upphengjulager	heron	hegri
happiness	hamingja	herring	síld
hardness	harka	hertz	herts
hardware	tölvubúnaður	heterosexual	kynvís
harmonics	heilfeldissveiflur	heterosexuality	kynvísi
harmonization	samræming	heterosis	blendingsþróttur
harpoon	hvalskutull	hexagon	sexhyrningur
harshness	hvassleiki	hidrosis	svitnun
hawse	akkerisrauf	hierarchy	stigvöxtur
hay	hey	highland	hálendi
hazelnut	heslihneta	highway	aðalbraut
heading	fyrirsögn	hilum	frænafli
headquarters	höfuðstöðvar	hilus	port
hearth	eldhólf	hinterland	bakland
heartwood	kjarnviður	hipbone	hlaun
heater	glóðald	hirsutism	ofloðna
heath	heiði	histogram	stuðlarit
heathland	heiðar	histology	vefjafræði
heatstroke	hitaslag	histopathology	vefjameinafræði
heaven	himinn	hives	ofsakláði
hegemony	forræði	holder	haldari
height	kóti	holdfast	fótfesta
helicopter	þyrla	holdings	eignarhald
heliotherapy	sólskinslækning	holism	kerfishyggja
heliotropism	ljósleitni	holmium	hólmín
helium	helín	hologram	almynd
helmsman	rórmaður	homeostasis	samvægi
hematology	blóðsjúkdómafræði	homo	maður
hematoma	mar	homogenization	jöfnun
hematopoiesis	blóðkornamyndun	homology	eðlislíking
hemeralopia	náttblinda	homosexuality	samkynmök

hood	vélarhlíf	hypnosis	dáleiðsla
hooker	hóra	hypnotist	dávaldur
hopper	hólkur	hypoblast	fruminnlag
hormone	hormón	hypochondria	sótthræðsla
horoscope	stjörnumát	hypophysis	dingull
horsepower	hestafl	hypostasis	undirsetning
horseradish	piparrót	hypotenuse	langhlið
horticulture	garðrækt	hypothermia	ofkæling
hotel	gistihús	hypothesis	tilgáta
hour	klukkustund	hypotonia	slekja
hovercraft	loftpúðaskip	hysteria	sefasýki
howler	gólari	ibex	steingeit
hub	safnvöllur	icing	ísing
humanism	fornmenntastefna	icon	vémynd
humidity	raki	idealism	hughyggja
humiliation	auðmýing	idealization	fegrun
humpback	herðakistill	identification	samsömun
humus	gróðurmold	identifier	kenni
hut	kofi	identity	einleiki
hybridization	kynblöndun	ideology	hugmyndakerfi
hydrate	hýdrat	igniter	kveikjari
hydration	vötnun	ignition	kveikja
hydraulics	straumtækni	ignitor	kveikja
hydride	hýdríð	illiteracy	ólæsi
hydrocarbon	kolvatnsefni	illuminance	lýsing
hydrocele	vatnshaull	imagination	ímyndunarafl
hydrocephalus	vatnshöfði	imaging	myndfærsla
hydrocortisone	hýdrókortísón	imago	kynþroska
hydrofoil	vatnavængildi	imbalance	misvægi
hydrogen	vetni	imbibition	ísog
hydrography	vatnamælingar	immunity	undanþága
hydrometer	rafgeymamælir	immunization	bólusetning
hydrophobia	vatnsfælni	immunofluorescence	ónæmisflúrskin
hydroxide	hýdroxíð	immunogen	mótefnavaki
hygiene	hreinlæti	immunoglobulin	ónæmisglóbúlín
hygrograph	rakariti	immunologist	ónæmisfræðingur
hyperactivity	ofvirkni	immunosuppression	ónæmisbæling
hyperalgesia	ofurkvöl	immunotherapy	ónæmingarmeðferð
hypercapnia	koltvísýringshækkun	impaction	saurteppa
hyperlink	stikluleggur	impedance	tvinnviðnám
hypermedia	ofurmiðlun	impeller	skófluhjól
hypermetropia	fjarsýni	imperialism	heimsvaldastefna
hyperopia	fjarsýni	implantation	ífelling
hypersensitivity	ofurnæmi	implementation	hagnýting
hypertension	háþrýstingur	implication	ályktun
hyperthermia	ofurhiti	implosion	hrun
hyperthyroidism	skjaldvakaeitrun	impotence	óneyti
hypertonia	ofstæling	impression	afsteypa

improvement	lagfæring	infrastructure	grunngerð
improvisation	spuni	ingestion	át
impulse	stuð	ingot	hleifur
impurity	mengun	inhalation	innöndun
inbreeding	skyldraæxlun	inhaler	öndunargríma
incandescence	glóð	inhibitor	hindrun
incentive	uppörvun	initiator	hvatamaður
incest	sifjaspell	injection	innspýting
inching	mjak	inlet	inntak
incidence	nýgengi	innervation	ítaugun
incinerator	brennsluofn	innovation	nýbreytni
inclinometer	hallamælir	inoculum	sáð
inclusion	skráning	insemination	sæðing
income	tekjur	insertion	festing
incompatibility	ósamfellanleiki	insider	innherji
incorporation	ílimun	insight	ísæi
increment	viðbót	insolation	ágeislun
incrustation	greyping	insolvency	eignahalli
incubator	klakskápur	insomnia	svefnleysi
incubus	mara	instability	vingl
incus	steðji	installation	ísetning
indemnity	skaðabætur	installment	afborgun
independence	sjálfstæði	instalment	afborgun
indication	vísbending	institution	innleiðing
indicator	mælitæki	instructions	leiðbeiningar
indium	indín	instrumentation	tækjabúnaður
individualism	einstaklingshyggja	insufficiency	líffærisbilun
individualization	stakmótun	insularity	nesjamennska
individuation	einsömun	insulation	einangrun
inducer	örvi	insulator	einangrari
inductance	rafsegulspönun	insurance	vátrygging
induction	spanrafmagn	insurer	vátryggjandi
inductor	spanald	intake	heildarneysla
industrialization	iðnvæðing	integer	heiltala
industry	atvinnugrein	integrator	heildari
infancy	frumbernska	integument	hula
infarct	fleygdrep	intellect	vitsmunir
infarction	fleygdrep	intensifier	áhersluatviksorð
inference	ályktun	interaction	samverkun
infertility	ófjósemi	intercalation	innskeyti
infinity	óendanlegt	interception	einelti
inflammation	þroti	interchangeability	umskiptanleiki
inflection	beyging	interconnection	Samtenging
inflow	innflæði	internationalism	alþjóðahyggja
influx	innflæði	internet	alnet
information	fróð	internode	stöngulliður
infrared	innrautt	interoceptor	iðraskynfæri

interphase	interfasi	jeans	gallabuxur
interpretation	túlkun	jeep	jeppi
interpreter	túlkur	jewfish	júðafiskur
interrupter	straumrofi	joule	júl
intersection	vegamót	joystick	stýripinni
intersex	millikyn	jumper	prufuleiðsla
interval	bil	junction	samskeyti
intonation	tónfall	jurisdiction	dómsaga
intoxication	víma	jury	dómnefnd
introversion	innhverfa	jute	jútarunni
intrusion	innátenging	juxtaposition	hliðsetning
intubation	pípusetning	kale	fóðurkál
intuition	máltilfinning	kaon	káeind
intumescence	bólgnun	karyokinesis	mítósa
inulin	inúlín	karyosome	litkjarni
invagination	innhverfing	keelson	kjalsvín
invasion	innrás	keeper	ventilsplitti
invention	uppfinning	keratin	hornefni
inverter	áriðill	keratinization	horngerð
investigation	rannsókn	kernel	kjarni
investment	fjárfesting	kestrel	turnfálki
investments	langtímaverðbréf	ketonuria	ketónmiga
investor	fjárfestir	keyboard	hnappaborð
involvement	aðild	keystone	lokasteinn
iodine	joð	kidney	nýra
ion	rafí	kilocalorie	kílókaloría
ionisation	jónun	kilometre	kílómetri
ionization	fareindaleysing	kilowatt	kW
iontophoresis	fareindalækning	kindergarten	barnaheimili
iridium	iridín	kinematics	gangfræði
iris	lithimna	kinesthesia	hreyfiskyn
irradiance	ágeislunarstyrkur	kinesthesis	hreyfiskyn
irradiation	ljómstækkun	kinetics	hvarfafræði
irritation	óværi	kingdom	konungsveldi
ischemia	blóðþurrð	kingpin	spindilbolti
isobar	jafnþrýstiflötur	kinin	kinín
isolation	hreinræktun	kinship	sifjar
isoleucine	íle	kitchen	eldhús
isoline	jafngildislína	kiwi	kívíflétta
isomer	ísómer	knee	liður
isomerization	Jafnliðun	kneecap	hnéskel
isopleth	jafngildislína	knickers	nærbuxur
isotropy	stefnusneyða	kohlrabi	hnúðkál
isozyme	samsætuensím	krill	ljósáta
italics	skáletur	kurtosis	ferilris
iteration	ítrekun	labial	varahljóð
jackdaw	dvergkráka	labourer	verkamaður
jackknife	skerðingaraðferð	laceration	sundurtæting

lacquering	lökkun	lethality	manndauði
lactation	mylking	letterpress	prentmál
lactose	mjólkursykur	leukocyte	hvítkorn
lad	piltur	leukocytosis	hvítfrumnafjölgun
lagoon	strandlón	leukopenia	hvítfrumnafæð
lamella	blað	leveling	hæðarstilling
landfall	landtaka	levelling	hæðarstilling
landing	lending	leverage	vogarafl
lane	rein	levulose	frúktósi
language	mál	lexeme	les
lantern	ljósker	lexicon	orðasafn
lanthanide	lantaníð	liabilities	skuldbindingar
lanthanum	lanþan	liability	ábyrgð
lanugo	líkhár	libido	frygð
lapping	samslíping	librarian	safnvörður
lari	máfuglar	library	bókasafn
larva	lirfa	libration	tunglvik
larynx	adamsepli	licensing	leyfisveiting
laser	leysir	lichen	flétta
lass	stelpa	lid	lok
latching	klinkulæsing	lien	milta
latency	dvali	life	ending
laterality	hliðlægi	lifestyle	lífsstíll
latex	mjólkursafi	lifter	undirlyftutappi
lathe	rennibekkur	ligament	liðband
latitude	breidd	ligase	límir
lavatory	salerni	lighthouse	vitahús
law	lög	lighting	lýsing
lawrencium	lárensín	lignin	tréni
lawyer	málfærslumaður	lignite	surtarbrandur
layout	umbrot	likelihood	sennileiki
leaching	útskolun	limb	jaðar
leader	forröð	limitation	fyrning
leaflet	bæklingur	limiter	takmarkari
leakage	leki	limousine	bifreið
leasing	fjármögnunarleiga	liner	ljóni
ledger	höfuðbók	ling	langa
legend	helgisaga	linguistics	málvísindi
legislation	lagasetning	liniment	áburður
legislature	þing	lining	fóður
lemma	hjálparsetning	linkage	armabúnaður
lentigo	frekna	lipid	fitungar
lentil	linsubaun	liquefaction	þétting
leopard	hlébarði	liquidation	gjaldþrot
lesbianism	saffismi	liquidity	greiðsluþol
lesion	löskun	litchi	litkaaldin
lessor	leigusali	liter	lítri

literacy	læsi	lysozyme	leysiensím
lithium	litíum	macaroni	núðlur
lithosphere	jarðskorpa	maceration	kaldbleyting
liver	lifur	machine	renna
livestock	fé	machinery	vélar
lizard	sandeðla	mackerel	makríll
loach	spáfiskur	macromolecule	risasameind
loading	hleðsla	macula	blettur
lobe	blað	macule	húðdrafna
lobotomy	hvítuskurður	madam	frú
lobule	snepill	magistrate	fógeti
localism	svæðavæðing	magma	bergkvika
localization	staðgreining	magnesium	magnesín
location	staður	magnet	segull
locator	staðsetningarviti	magnetization	segulmögnun
loch	vatn	magneto	kveikja
lockout	læsing	magnetometer	segulmælir
locus	staður	magnetron	örbylgjuvaki
loess	fokjarðvegur	magnification	stækkun
logger	skógarhöggsmaður	magnitude	magn
logistics	vörustjórnun	mainframe	megintölva
logo	kennimark	maintenance	framfærslufé
longan	longanber	maladjustment	aðlögunarörðugleikar
longevity	endingartími	malformation	vansköpun
longitude	lengdargráða	mall	verslanamiðstöð
loquat	japansplóma	mallet	kylfa
lord	herra	malleus	hamar
lorry	vörubíll	malnutrition	vannæring
losses	tap	maltose	maltósi
lottery	hlutavelta	mamilla	geirvarta
lotus	lótusblóm	mammal	spendýr
loudness	háværð	manager	framkvæmdastjóri
loudspeaker	gellir	mandrel	dór
louver	ristarhleri	manganese	mangan
lubricator	smurnippill	manhole	op
lugworm	sandmaðkur	manipulation	tilfæring
lumen	hol	manoeuvrability	fluglipurð
luminance	ljómi	manometer	þrýstingsmælir
luminescence	ljóm	manpower	mannafli
luminosity	ljósnæmishlutfall	manufacturer	framleiðandi
lutetium	lútesín	mapping	kortagerð
luxation	liðhlaup	mare	slétta
lymphedema	vessabjúgur	marijuana	hassjurt
lymphocyte	eitilfruma	mariner	landgönguliði
lymphoma	eitilfrumukrabbamein	markdown	verðlækkun
lynx	gaupa	marker	merki
lyophilization	frostþurrkun	marketing	markaðsfærsla
lysogeny	veirubinding	markup	verðhækkun

marsh	votlendi	merry-go-round	hringekja
marten	mörður	meson	miðeind
maser	meysir	mesosphere	miðhvolf
masking	dyljun	message	skilaboð
masochism	meinlætamunaður	metabolism	efnaskipti
mast	mastur	metal	málmur
mastocyte	mastfruma	metamerism	liðun
masturbation	sjálfsfróun	metamorphosis	hamskipting
materialism	veraldarhyggja	metaphor	myndhverfing
materials	materia	metastasis	meinrek
mathematics	stærðfræði	meteor	stjörnuhrap
mattress	dýna	meteorite	loftsteinn
maturation	þroskun	meteorology	veðurfræði
maturity	þroski	methanal	formaldehýð
maxilla	kinnkjálki	methane	metan
mayday	hjálp	methanol	tréspíritus
means	meza	methionine	meþíónín
measuring	mæling	methodology	aðferð
meat	kjöt	metonymy	nafnhvörf
mechanics	aflfræði	metre	metri
mechanism	gangverk	metrics	bragfræði
mechanization	vélvæðing	metro	neðanjarðarlest
meconium	barnaat	mica	glimmer
media	miðill	microbe	örvera
mediation	sáttaumleitun	microbiology	örverufræði
mediator	miðlari	microchip	kisilflaga
medication	læknisfræði	microcomputer	örtölva
medicine	lyf	microelectronics	dvergrásatækni
medulla	mergur	microflora	smáflóra
megalomania	mikilmennskuæði	micronutrient	snefilefni
megaspore	stórgró	microorganism	örvera
megrim	þjalakoli	microprocessor	örgjörvi
meiosis	meiósa	midbrain	miðheili
melanoma	sortuæxli	milieu	umhorf
melanosis	sorti	mimesis	herming
melon	melóna	mineralization	steinefnaútfelling
member	biti	minutes	bókun
membrane	himna	miosis	ljósopsþrenging
men	maður	mirroring	speglun
mendelevium	mendelefín	misanthropy	mannhatur
meniscus	bjúgflötur	mishap	óhapp
menopause	tíðahvörf	missile	flugskeyti
menorrhagia	asatíðir	mission	sendinefnd
menstruation	klæðaföll	missis	frú
mentality	hugerni	mistress	frú
mercantilism	merkantílismi	mitochondrion	festarkorn
merger	samruni	mixer	blöndunarstig

mixing	blöndun	municipality	bæjarfélag
mixture	blanda	muon	mýeind
mnemonics	minnisefling	muskrat	bísamrotta
mobilization	liðkun	mustard	kál
modality	mæða	mutagen	stökkbreytivaldur
modeling	eftirmyndun	mutation	stökkbreyting
modelling	líkanagerð	mutualism	samhjálp
moderator	hægir	mycology	sveppafræði
modernization	breytingar	mycoplasma	berfrymingar
modification	takmörkun	mycosis	sveppsýki
modulation	mótun	mydriatic	ljósopsstærandi
module	undirsvæði	myelin	mýelín
moisture	raki	myofibril	vöðvatrefja
mol	mól	myoglobin	mýóglóbín
molybdenum	mólýbden	myopia	nærsýni
momentum	hreyfimagn	myth	vésögn
monarchy	einvaldsríki	n	köfnunarefni
mongolism	mongólóíðaháttur	nacelle	hlíf
monitoring	gaumun	narcissism	sjálfsást
monkfish	barðaháfur	narrows	sund
monopoly	einokun	narwhal	náhvalur
monsoon	misseravindur	nation	þjóðland
month	tunglmánuður	nationalism	sjálfstæðishreyfing
mood	lyndi	nationality	ríkisborgararéttur
moonfish	tunglfiskur	nationalization	þjóðnýting
moraine	jökulurð	nave	skip
morals	moralajo	navel	nafli
moratorium	greiðslufrestun	navigability	haffærni
mores	siðir	navigation	skipstjórn
moron	hálfviti	navigator	netskoðari
morphology	formfræði	nebula	geimský
motherboard	móðurborð	neckerchief	hálsklútur
motivation	tilhvatning	necklace	hálsband
motorization	vélknúinn	negation	neitun
movement	hræring	negativism	þumbaldaháttur
movie	filmo	nematode	hringormur
mrna	mRKS	neodymium	neodým
mucosa	slíma	neolithic	nýsteinöld
mudguard	aurhlíf	neologism	nýyrði
muffler	hljóðdeyfir	neoplasia	æxlismyndun
mugwort	búamalurt	neoplasm	auki
multimedia	almiðlun	neoprene	gervigúmmí
multiplexer	fjölrásari	nephew	systursonur
multiplexing	fjölfléttun	nephropathy	nýrakvilli
multiplier	margfaldari	nephrosis	nýrapípnaskemmd
multiprocessing	fjölgjörvavinnsla	neptunium	neptún
multiprogramming	fjölforritavinnsla	neurasthenia	geðdeyfð
mummification	skorpnun	neurilemma	taugaslíður

neurolemma	mýlishimna	nystagmus	augntin
neuroleptic	sefandi	oasis	eyðimerkurvin
neurology	taugasjúkdómafræði	oat	akurhafri
neuron	taugungur	obscurity	myrkur
neurosis	hugsýki	observatory	stjörnuathugunarstöð
neutralization	afmögnun	obsession	þráhyggja
neutron	nevtróna	obturation	lokun
nevus	fæðingarblettur	occlusion	stíflun
newton	njúton	occupancy	ábúð
nexus	orsakaflétta	occupant	íbúi
niacin	níasín	octagon	átthyrningur
niche	veggjahvilft	octet	áttstig
nidation	bólfesta	odontology	tannfræði
nidus	hreiður	odour	þefur
niece	bróðurdóttir	oedema	bjúgur
nightingale	næturgali	oestrogen	estrógen
niobium	nióbíum	oestrus	eggbússtig
nipple	geirvarta	offence	glæpur
nit	lúsaegg	officer	starfsmaður
nitrification	nítratmyndun	officialdom	embættismannastétt
nitrite	nítrít	ogive	summuferill
nitrogen	köfnunarefni	ohm	óm
nobelium	nóbelín	oiler	smyrjari
node	hnúður	olfaction	lyktarskyn
nodule	hnúður	omasum	laki
nomogram	samanbuðartafla	omega	ómega
nonconformity	ósamlægi	onchocerciasis	árblinda
noradrenaline	noradrenalín	oncogene	æxlisgen
norm	fyrirmynd	onion	matlaukur
normalization	skipulagning	ontogenesis	einstaklingsþroskun
normoblast	kjarnablóðkorn	ontogeny	einstaklingsmyndun
nosebleed	blóðnasir	ontology	verufræði
nostalgia	afturhvarfsþörf	opacity	ógegnsæi
nostrils	nasaop	opah	sólborri
notebook	stílabók	operand	þolandi
notification	birting	operation	aðgerð
nozzle	úðastútur	operator	stjórnandi
nucleolus	kjarnakorn	operculum	hetta
nucleon	kjarnaeind	opossum	kontraŭanto
nucleoplasm	kjarnafrymi	opponent	kontraŭulo
nucleus	kjarni	opportunity	tilefni
numerator	teljari	optics	ljóseðlisfræði
nursery	barnaheimili	optimization	bestun
nut	nukso	orb	himinhvel
nutation	pólriða	orchestra	hljómsveit
nutrition	næringarferli	ore	málmgrýti
nymphomania	brókarsótt	oregano	bergminta

orfe	gullgægir	oviposition	varp
organ	tímarit	ovule	frævísir
organelle	frumulíffæri	ovum	eggfruma
organism	lífvera	owner	eigandi
organizer	stillir	oxidation	tæring
orgasm	samfarablossi	oxide	sýri
oriel	útskot	oxygen	ildi
orientation	áttun	oxytocin	hríðahormón
orifice	op	oxyuriasis	njálgsýking
originator	höfundur	ozone	óson
ornithine	ornitín	pacemaker	gangráður
orthopedics	bæklunarlækningar	pacifism	friðarhugsjón
os	bein	pacing	samstig
oscillation	sveifla	packaging	pökkun
oscillator	sveifill	packet	pakki
oscilloscope	sveiflusjá	packing	þétti
osmium	osmín	paddlefish	spaðastyrja
osmosis	flæði	painter	málari
ossicle	hljóðbein	pairing	línuhlaupsbjögun
osteoarthritis	slitgigt	palace	höll
osteoblast	beinkímfruma	palate	gómur
osteoclast	beinátfruma	paleoclimatology	fornveðurfræði
osteocyte	beinfruma	palimpsest	skafgígur
osteology	beinafræði	pallet	pallur
osteopath	osteopati	palliation	líkn
osteopathy	hnykkingar	pallium	hvelkápa
osteopetrosis	beinmergsherðing	panacea	kynjalyf
osteosclerosis	beinherðing	pane	rúða
otolith	kvarnir	panning	pönnun
otter	otur	pantry	matarbúr
outcrop	opna	papaw	papava
outfall	útrás	papaya	sólaldintré
outflow	útstreymi	papers	murpapero
outlet	útrennsli	papilla	tota
outrigger	stoðfótur	paprika	paprikuduft
outsourcing	utankaup	parabola	fleygbogi
ovary	eggleg	paradigm	viðmið
oven	ofn	parallelogram	samsíðungur
overcompensation	ofbætur	parameter	stillibreyta
overdraft	yfirdráttur	parapsychology	dulsálarfræði
overgrazing	ofbeit	parasitism	sníkjulífi
overhauling	yfirhalning	parenchyma	frumvefur
overloading	fjölbinding	parenthesis	svigi
overproduction	offramleiðsla	parents	foreldrar
overtime	yfirvinna	parhelion	hjásól
overtone	yfirtónn	parity	bæri
overwrite	yfirrita	parliament	þing
oviduct	eggjaleiðari	parotitis	vangakirtilsbólga

parr	smáseiði	perforator	holbor
partnership	sameignarfélag	perigee	jarðnánd
partridge	akurhænsn	perihelion	sólnánd
passenger	farþegi	perimeter	jaðar
passover	páskar	periodicity	bilkvæmi
passport	vegabréf	periphery	jaðarsvæði
pasteurization	gerilsneyðing	peristalsis	bylgjuhreyfingar
patella	hnéskel	peritonitis	lífhimnubólga
pathogen	sýkill	periwinkle	doppa
pathology	sjúkdómafræði	permeability	gleypni
pathway	efnaferli	permittivity	torleiðnistuðull
patriarchy	feðraveldi	perpetuity	sígreiðslur
patriot	föðurlandsvinur	persistence	eftirljóm
patriotism	föðurlandsást	persona	persóna
paunch	kviður	personage	persóna
pawl	skreppa	personality	persónuleiki
payload	arðhleðsla	personnel	starfsfólk
payment	staðgreiðsla	persons	persono
payroll	launagjöld	perspective	fjarvídd
pear	pera	perspiration	sviti
peasant	smábóndi	petrol	bensín
peat	svörður	petroleum	hráolía
pectin	pektín	pew	bekkur
pederasty	sveinmök	ph	sýrustig
pedestal	stallur	phage	gerilæta
pediatrician	barnalæknir	phagocyte	átfruma
pediatrics	barnalækningar	pharmacology	lyfjafræði
pedicel	blómleggur	pharmacy	lyfjabúð
pediment	gaflhlaðsþríhyrningur	pharynx	kok
pellagra	húðkröm	phase	kvartil
pellicle	frumuhýði	phasing	fösun
pelvis	mjaðmagrind	pheasant	fashani
penetrance	tjáningarstig	phenomenon	fyrirbæri
peninsula	skagi	phenotype	svipfar
penis	tittlingur	phenylalanine	fen
penny	sent	phenylketonuria	fenílketónúría
penstock	aðrennslisrör	phobia	fælni
pentagon	fimmhyrningur	phonophobia	talfælni
peppermint	piparminta	phosphate	fosfat
peptide	peptíð	phosphor	skinefni
percentage	prósenta	phosphorescence	lífljómi
percentile	hundraðshlutamark	phosphorus	fosfór
percept	skyntak	photocell	fótónunemi
perception	skynjun	photometer	sjónnæmismælir
percolation	seytl	photomicrograph	smásjármynd
perfectionism	fullkomnunarárátta	photon	fótóna
perforation	gat	photoreceptor	ljósnemi

phototherapy	ljósameðferð	plenum	allsherjarfundur
phrenology	höfuðlagsfræði	pleurisy	brjósthimnubólga
phylogenesis	tegundarþróun	pleurodynia	millirifjaverkur
phylogeny	þróunarferill	plotter	teiknivél
phylum	fylking	plumule	dúnfjöður
physician	læknir	plunger	drullusokkur
physics	eðlisfræði	plywood	krossviður
physiognomy	svipur	poacher	veiðiþjófur
physiology	lífeðlisfræði	podiatry	fótsnyrting
physiotherapist	sjúkraþjálfari	poem	kvæði
phytogeography	plöntulandafræði	poignancy	skarpskyggni
phytohormone	plöntuhormón	pointer	vísir
phytoplankton	jurtasvif	polarimeter	pólunarmælir
pica	óætisfíkn	polariscope	skautsjá
pickling	leifar	polarity	pólstefna
pidgin	blendingsmál	polarization	pólun
pier	veggrif	polarizer	skautunarefni
piezometer	piezorör	policy	utanríkisstefna
pilchard	sardína	poliomyelitis	mænugránabólga
pileus	svepphattur	pollen	frjó
pilotage	sjónleiðsaga	polling	hverfisenditilboð
pilus	þráður	pollutant	mengunarvaldur
pinking	kveikibank	polluter	mengari
pinna	smáblað	polonium	pólon
pint	hálfpottur	polydactyly	fjölfingrun
piper	tindaknurri	polygon	marghyrningur
pipette	skammtapípa	polygraph	skrifari
pisiform	baunarlaga	polymer	gerviefni
pismire	maur	polymerization	fjölliðun
pistil	fræva	polymorphism	fjölmótun
piston	stimpill	polyp	sepi
pixel	myndeining	pons	brú
placenta	fræsæti	pontoon	flothylki
plage	sólflekkur	poplar	ösp
plaice	rauðspretta	population	þýði
planet	reikistjarna	porbeagle	hámeri
planning	skipulagning	pork	flesk
plantain	mjölbanani	porker	svín
plantation	plantekra	porosity	gljúpleiki
plasma	vessavökvi	portability	flytjanleiki
plasmodium	samfrumungur	portfolio	verðbréfasafn
plasticity	tillæti	porthole	mannop
plastid	plastíð	positivism	pósitífismi
platelet	blóðflaga	positron	andrafögn
platinum	hvítagull	potassium	kalium
playback	spilun	potato	kartafla
playhouse	leikhús	potency	hæfni
plea	bæn	potentiation	efling

potentiometer	breytiviðnám	programmer	boðritari
pragmatism	gagnsemishyggja	programming	forritun
pram	barnavagn	projection	skögun
praseodymium	praseódým	prokaryote	dreifkjörnungur
prawn	rækja	prolactin	mjólkurhormón
praxis	framkvæmd	proletariat	öreigalýður
prayer	bæn	proliferation	álun
preamble	aðdragandi	promethium	prómetín
precaution	gætni	prominence	bunga
precession	ásvelta	promontory	höfði
precinct	hverfi	promotion	efling
precognition	forviska	promptness	nákvæmni
precursor	forveri	propeller	skrúfa
predation	át	prophylaxis	forvörn
predator	afæta	proposal	frumvarp
predisposition	fornæmi	propulsion	drif
preference	kjörstilling	prosencephalon	framheili
premises	athafnasvæði	prospecting	leit
prepuce	forhúð	prospectus	kynningarbæklingur
prerogative	einkaréttur	prosthesis	gerviliffæri
presbyopia	ellifjarsýni	protactinium	protaktín
preservation	friðun	protagonist	málsvari
president	forseti	protease	próteasi
presupposition	forsenda	protectorate	verndarríki
prevalence	algengi	proteolysis	hvítusundrun
preview	forskoða	prothrombin	próþrombín
priapism	sístaða	protist	frumvera
pricing	verðlagning	protium	einvetni
primates	fremdardýr	protocol	aðferðarlýsing
priming	forgjöf	proton	prótóna
printer	prentari	protoplasm	frymi
printout	útprent	protoplast	veggleysingi
prism	prisma	prototype	fyrirmynd
problem	Vandamál	protozoa	frumdýr
procedure	starfshættir	protozoon	frumdýr
processing	verkun	protractor	gráðubogi
processor	gjörvi	protrusion	framskögun
prodrome	undanfaraeinkenni	provisions	birgðir
producer	framleiðandi	proximity	nánd
product	framleiðsla	pruning	stýfing
production	framleiðsla	psalterium	laki
proenzyme	forensím	pseudonym	dulnefni
profession	fag	pseudopodium	skinfótur
profitability	arðsemi	psi	ófreskigáfa
progenitor	forveri	psittacosis	páfagaukaveiki
progesterone	gulbúshormón	psoriasis	baugaskán
prognosis	forsögn	psyche	Síka

psychiatrist	geðlæknir	questionnaire	spurningaeyðublað
psychiatry	geðlæknisfræði	quietness	ró
psychoanalysis	sálgreining	quill	broddur
psychoanalyst	sálgreinir	quilting	bútasaumur
psychokinesis	æðisgerðir	quince	kveða
psychologist	sálfræðingur	quinine	kínín
psychology	sálfræði	quotation	kostnaðaráætlun
psychopath	geðvillingur	quotient	kvóti
psychopathology	sálsýkisfræði	rabbi	gyðingaprestur
psychopathy	geðvilla	raccoon	þvottabjörn
psychophysiology	sálarlífeðlisfræði	rachis	blómskipunarstöngull
psychosis	geðrof	racism	kynþáttahatur
psychotherapy	sállækning	racon	ratsjársvarviti
ptyalin	mjölvakljúfur	radar	ratsjá
puberty	kynþroskaaldur	radian	bogaeining
pubescence	kynþroski	radiator	miðstöðvarofn
publication	útgáfa	radiography	gegnumlýsing
puck	tala	radioimmunoassay	geislaónæmismæling
puller	afdragi	radiology	geislalæknisfræði
pulley	reimhjól	radiotherapy	geislameðferð
pullover	peysa	radish	hreðka
pulsation	slag	radius	útvarp
pumpkin	risagrasker	radix	stofntala
punctuation	greinarmerki	radome	loftnetshlíf
punishment	hegning	raider	hrifsari
pupa	púpa	railway	járnbraut
pupil	ljósop	raincoat	regnfrakki
purchaser	kaupandi	rainforest	regnskógur
purgation	búkhreinsun	rambutan	ígulber
purification	hreinsun	ramus	álma
purser	bryti	rancher	stórbóndi
pustule	graftarbóla	ranger	fjallarakki
putrefaction	rotnun	rapier	lagsverð
pyjamas	náttföt	rarefaction	þynning
pylon	mastur	raspberry	hindber
pyrometer	glóðhitamælir	ratification	fullgilding
quadrangle	ferhyrningur	rating	einkunnagjöf
quadrant	fjórðungsmælir	ratio	hlutfall
qualifications	geta	rationalization	hagræðing
quantification	magnmæling	rattan	spanskreyrspálmi
quantity	megind	rattlesnake	skröltormur
quantization	gildisskömmtun	reactant	hvarfefni
quantum	kvanti	reaction	viðbragð
quark	kvarki	reactivity	Virkni
quarters	kvaronjaro	reactor	sátur
quay	bryggja	reader	kennslubók
queen	drotning	reading	aflestur
quenching	kæfing	readjustment	endurstilling

reagent	prófunarefni	reimbursement	endurgreiðsla
realism	raunhyggja	reinforcement	bendistál
realist	raunsæismaður	reinsurance	endurtrygging
realization	innlausn	rejection	höfnun
realm	yfrráðasvæði	relations	frændfólk
reamer	víkkari	relationship	samband
rearrangement	umröðun	relatives	frændfólk
rebellion	andspyrna	relativity	afstæði
receivables	viðskiptakröfur	releaser	kvöðull
receiver	viðtæki	reliability	áreiðanleiki
receptor	viðtaki	religion	trú
recession	undanhald	reluctance	segulviðnám
recirculation	endurhringrás	rem	svefnblik
reclamation	landauki	reminder	ábending
recommendation	tillaga	reminiscence	minning
reconstitution	enduruppbygging	remittance	greiðslusending
reconstruction	endurbygging	removal	afnám
recorder	síriti	rendering	myndsetning
records	akto	renewal	framlenging
recreation	upplyfting	rennin	hleypir
recruitment	skráning	rental	fjármunaleiga
rectangle	rétthyrningur	reorganization	skipulagsbreyting
rectifier	rafloki	repetition	klifun
recurrence	endurkoma	replication	afritun
recycling	endurvinnsla	representation	fyrirsvar
redfish	karfi	repression	bæling
redia	ögðulirfa	repressor	bælir
reductant	afsýrir	reproducibility	endurtakanleiki
reentry	endurkoma	repulsion	fráhrinding
referendum	allsherjaratkvæðagreiðsla	requirement	þörf
referral	tilvísun	res	átfrumnakerfi
refinery	hreinsistöð	resemblance	líking
reflectance	endurkastshlutfall	reservation	bókun
reflector	endurkastsskaut	reservoir	geymsluhýsill
reflexology	viðbragðafræði	residence	aðsetur
refractor	linsusjónauki	resignation	uppsögn
refrigeration	frysting	resilience	viðkomugeta
refrigerator	kælibúnaður	resin	harpeis
refuelling	áfylling	resistivity	eðlisviðnám
refusal	frávísun	resistor	viðnám
regime	stjórn	resolution	ályktun
region	umdæmi	resonance	herma
registrar	ritari	resorption	uppsog
registration	þinglýsing	resources	eignir
regression	endurhvarf	respiration	vefjaöndun
regulations	reguligo	respirator	gasgríma
rehabilitation	endurhæfing	restaurant	veitingahús

restructuring	endurmótun	rules	deklari
resuscitation	endurlífgun	rumen	vömb
retailer	smásali	runoff	afrennslishraði
retainer	umbun	runway	flugbraut
retarder	hamlari	rutabaga	gulrófa
retention	minnisgeymd	ruthenium	rúten
reticulum	fagrikeppur	s	brennisteinn
retina	nethimna	sabbath	laugardagur
retirement	eftirlaunaskeið	sac	poki
revaluation	gengishækkun	saccharimeter	sykursmælir
revenue	fjáröflun	saccharin	sakkarín
reversion	gervending	saccharomyces	gersveppur
revision	breyting	saccharose	sykur
rhenium	renín	saccharum	sykur
rheostat	rennimótstaða	saccule	posi
rhinitis	nefkvef	sacculus	posi
rhinorrhea	nefrennsli	sacrum	spjaldliðir
rhodium	ródín	sadist	lostaböðull
rhombus	tigull	safflower	litunarkollur
rhytidome	dauðbörkur	sailor	háseti
ribonuclease	ríbónúkleasi	saithe	ufsi
ribosome	netkorn	salary	laun
rickets	beinkröm	salinity	selta
rigging	stilling	saliva	munnvatn
rigidity	vöðvastífni	salivation	slef
roach	rauðauga	salmon	lax
roadstead	skipalægi	saloon	stallbakur
robin	glóbrystingur	saltation	dans
robot	vélmenni	saltpetre	kalíumnítrat
rocker	dröfnuskata	samarium	samaríum
roe	hrogn	sampling	sýnataka
rosefish	vínlandskarfi	sandbank	sandfláki
roseola	dílaroði	sandstone	sandsteinn
rosette	blaðhvirfing	sapodilla	sapódilla
rostrum	goggur	saprophyte	rotplanta
rotation	reising	sarcoma	sarkmein
rotor	göndull	satiation	mettun
routing	beining	saturation	mettun
rover	fjallarakki	saturnism	blýeitrun
rowlock	keipur	sausage	pylsa
royalty	einkaleyfisþóknun	savanna	staktrjáaslétta
rubella	rauðhundar	scaler	teljari
rubidium	rúbidín	scaling	skölun
rucksack	bakpoki	scandium	skandín
rudd	straumgægir	scanner	skanni
rudder	stýrisblað	scanning	skann
rudiment	líffærisvísir	scarification	rispun
rudiments	stafróf	scatology	saurhneigð

scavenger	hrægammur	semiotics	táknfræði
scenario	sviðsmynd	senate	háskólaráð
scheduling	verkröðun	sensitivity	næmisstuðull
schema	yfirlit	sensitization	næming
schistosomiasis	blóðögðusótt	sensitizer	næmir
sclera	hvíta	sensorium	skynfæri
scooter	vespa	sensualism	munaðarhyggja
scorbutus	skyrbjúgur	separatism	aðskilnaðarstefna
scotoma	blinduflekkur	separator	einangrari
scrambler	klifurplanta	septicemia	blóðeitrun
scraper	skafa	sequencing	runun
screening	hlíf	sequestration	kyrrsetning
screwdriver	skrúfjárn	serendipity	slembifundur
scriber	rissnál	serotonin	serótónín
script	forskrift	serration	sagtenning
scup	grænflekkur	servant	þjónn
scurf	flasa	server	þjónn
seaboard	strönd	serviceability	þjónustuhæfni
seafarer	farmaður	services	þjónusta
sealer	þéttiefni	servomechanism	sjálfstýrikerfi
sealing	þétting	servomotor	stýrivél
seals	selir	session	seta
seaman	háseti	setting	atburðasvið
searchlight	leitarljós	settlement	samkomulag
seaway	sjóleið	severity	erfiði
seaweed	sjávargróður	sewage	skólp
seborrhea	flasa	sextant	sextantur
secretariat	stjórnarskrifstofa	sexuality	kynhneigð
secretion	seyti	shad	maísíld
sector	geiri	shading	skuggamyndun
secularization	afhelgun	shallot	sjalottulaukur
sedan	stallbakur	shareholder	hlutafjáreigandi
sedation	róun	sheave	dráttarskífa
sediment	dreggjar	sheep	sauðkind
sedimentation	botnfelling	sheet	lauf
seeding	fræmyndun	shelf	hylla
seepage	seytl	shigellosis	blóðsótt
segmentation	liðun	shim	millilegg
seismograph	jarðskjálftamælir	shinbone	sköflungur
selectivity	valvísi	shingles	ristill
selector	vali	shipper	vöruflytjandi
selenium	seleníum	shipping	sjóflutningar
self-esteem	virðing	shipway	rennibraut
self-respect	virðing	shipyard	slippur
seller	seljandi	shirt	skyrta
semen	fræ	shoe	bremsuskór
semiconductor	hálfleiðari	shortage	skortur

shortcut	flýtivísun	sol	sól
shorts	kalsono	soles	tunguflúrur
shrinkage	þrenging	solicitor	málfærslumaður
sibling	systkin	solstice	sólstöður
siblings	gefrata	solubility	leysni
sibs	systkin	solution	lausn
sidelight	hliðarljós	solvency	gjaldfærni
significance	marktækni	soma	líkami
signifier	tákngjafi	somatotype	líkamsgerð
silage	súrhey	somite	frumliður
silencer	hljóðkútur	somnambulism	svefnganga
silica	kísl	somnambulist	svefngengill
silicon	kísill	son	sonur
sill	laggangur	sonar	ómskoðun
similarity	einslögun	sopor	svefndá
simplification	einföldun	sounder	hljóðgjafi
simulation	sjúkdómsherming	source	uppspretta
simulator	eftirlíkir	sovereignty	yfirráðaréttur
sine	sínus	spacer	þykktarskífa
singularity	sérstöðupunktur	spacing	deilibil
sinker	sakka	spam	amapóstur
sinter	sindra	spanner	skrúflykill
sinus	stokkur	spasm	krampi
sir	herra	spasticity	síbeygjukrampar
sister	systir	spatula	kíttisspaði
situation	aðstæður	speaker	mælandi
sizing	Hörpun	specialization	sérhæfing
skewness	skekking	speciation	tegundamyndun
ski	skíði	specification	verklýsing
skylight	himinskin	specificity	sérvirkni
slicer	sneiðir	specimen	eintak
slinger	kasthringur	spectrogram	litrófsmynd
slingshot	kvartmílubíll	spectrograph	róflínuriti
slipstream	kjölfarssog	spectrometer	litrófsmælir
smallpox	bólusótt	spectrophotometer	litrófsljósmælir
smithy	smiðja	spectroscope	litsjá
smog	mengunarský	spectroscopy	litrófsgreining
snooks	snasar	speculation	brask
snowplow	snjóplógur	sperm	sæðisfruma
socialism	sósíalismi	spermaceti	hvalambur
socialization	félagsmótun	spermatheca	sáðgeymsla
society	mannfélag	spermatocyte	frjómóðurfruma
sociology	félagsfræði	spermatozoon	frjó
socket	falur	spermicide	sáðfrumnadeyðir
sodium	natrín	sphere	hvolf
sodomy	sódómska	sphincter	lokuvöðvi
software	hugbúnaður	spider	köngur
sojourner	gestur	spillover	smit

spindle	völur	sticker	límmiði
spinner	nafarhlíf	stickleback	hornsíli
spirillum	gormsýkill	stimulation	erting
splicing	fléttun	stimulus	reiti
spline	hcrmifall	stipulation	ákvæði
spoiler	lyftispillir	stockbroker	verðbréfamiðlari
spool	biðfæra	stockfish	ráskerðingur
sporangium	gróhirsla	stockholder	hluthafi
sporulation	grómyndun	stocks	birgðir
spotting	flekkun	stocktaking	birgðatalning
sprat	brislingur	stokehold	kyndiklefi
spreadsheet	töflureiknir	stoma	munnur
sprig	kvistur	stopcock	krani
springtime	vor	storage	birgðir
sputum	uppgangur	stores	aðföng
squatter	hústökumaður	storing	geyming
squid	kolkrabbi	storyline	frásögn
stability	stöðugleiki	stove	vasi
stacking	stöflun	stowage	lestarými
stadium	íþróttavöllur	strabismus	skjálgur
staging	stigun	straightening	rétting
stagnation	stöðnun	strainer	sáld
stair	ŝtupo	straitjacket	spennitreyja
stairs	ŝtupo	stranding	strand
stamen	fræfill	strata	jarðlag
stamping	plötupressun	stratification	lagdeiling
stance	afstaða	stratigraphy	sneiðmyndataka
stanchion	nautgripaklafi	stratosphere	heiðhvolf
standardization	stöðlun	stratum	jarðlag
stapes	ístað	stratus	þokuský
staphylococcus	klasakokkur	strawberry	garðajarðarber
starfish	sæstjarna	streptococcus	keðjukokkur
starter	ræsir	stretcher	sjúkrabörur
stasis	kyrrstaða	stripper	afeinangrunartæki
statement	staðhæfing	stripping	strípun
statistic	tölfræði	stroboscope	snúningssjá
statistics	hagtölur	stroma	uppistaða
stator	sátur	strontium	strontíum
statute	samþykkt	structuralism	formgerðarstefna
steerage	stjórn	studio	upptökusalur
steering	stýring	stupor	hugstol
steps	paŝi	stye	vogris
steradian	rúmhornseining	subclass	undirflokkur
stereogram	þríviddarrit	subjectivity	huglægni
sterilization	dauðhreinsun	sublimation	göfgun
sternum	kviðskjöldur	submission	undirgefni
steward	bryti	subroutine	stefja

subscriber	áskrifandi	symbol	merki
subset	hlutmengi	symbolism	líkingalæti
subsidence	sig	symbolization	táknun
subsistence	lífsviðurværi	symmetry	samhorf
subspecies	undirtegund	symposium	málþing
substrate	ensímhvarfefni	symptom	einkenni
subunit	byggingareining	synagogue	gyðingahof
suburb	útborg	synapsis	tvennun
suburbia	úthverfi	synchronism	samgengi
success	happ	synchronization	samfösun
succession	framvinda	synchronizer	samfasari
suckers	sogkarpar	synchronizing	samfösun
sucrose	reyrsykur	synchrotron	sínkrótrónn
suction	sogun	syndrome	einkennamynstur
sudation	svitnun	synergism	starfsmögnun
suffocation	köfnun	synergist	samstarfandi
sulfate	súlfat	synergy	samlegðaráhrif
summit	hámark	synonym	samheiti
sump	botnskál	syntax	málskipan
sundial	sólúr	synthesis	gerving
sunspot	sólblettur	syphilis	sýfilis
sunstroke	sólstingur	system	agnakerfi
supercharger	forþjappa	tabes	mænuvisnun
supercomputer	ofurtölva	tachograph	hraðriti
supercooling	undirkæling	tachycardia	hjartsláttarsprettur
superego	yfirsjálf	tactic	taktiko
superheating	yfirhitun	taenia	dregill
superposition	viðlegð	tails	trenaĵo
superstition	hjátrú	talc	talk
superstructure	yfirbygging	talus	vala
supervisor	eftirlitsmaður	tampon	tróð
supplier	birgðasali	tamponade	tepping
suppressor	truflanakæfir	tandem	tengivagn
surfactant	lungnablöðruseyti	tang	hak
surfing	sprang	tangerine	tangerína
surgeon	handlæknir	tanker	Tankskip
surgery	handlæknisfræði	tannin	tannín
surveyor	landmælingamaður	tantalum	tantal
survival	lifun	tapioca	tapíókagrjón
suspension	henging	tapping	hlerun
sweater	peysa	taps	kyrrðarstund
sweeper	smurtittur	tariff	gjaldskrá
swine	svín	tarpaulin	lúgugatsábreiða
switchboard	tafla	tarpon	silfurkóngur
swordfish	sverðfiskur	tarragon	kóngasalat
sycamore	hlynur	taxation	skattur
sycosis	hárpest	taxon	kerfiseining
symbiosis	samhjálp	teacher	kennari

technetium	teknetín	thermograph	hitariti
tectonics	jarðhniksfræði	thermolysis	hitaleysing
teething	tanntaka	thermopile	tvinnhlaði
tegument	hula	thermoplastic	hitaþjáll
telecommunication	fjarmiðlun	thermostat	hitavökull
telecommunications	fjarskipti	thesaurus	hugtakasafn
telecontrol	fjarstýring	thiamine	þíamín
telegram	símskeyti	thickness	gildleiki
telegraphy	ritsímakerfi	thing	objekto
telepathy	fjarvísi	things	ajo
telephony	talsími	thinner	þynnir
teleprinter	fjarriti	thorax	bringa
teleprocessing	fjarvinnsla	thorium	þórín
teletypewriter	fjarriti	threat	Hótun
television	sjónvarp	threshold	rafertimörk
tellurium	tellúr	thromboplastin	þrombóplastín
tempering	seighersla	thrombosis	segamyndun
template	mát	thrombus	segi
temple	gagnauga	throughput	afköst
tench	grunnungur	thrush	þruska
tendinitis	sinarbólga	thulium	túlín
tendon	sin	thymidine	týmídín
tenet	trú	thymus	tímgill
terbium	terbín	thyroxine	skjaldkirtilshormón
termination	endahólkur	tibia	sköflungur
terminator	loktákn	ticker	sími
terms	tíðir	timberland	skógur
terrace	hjalli	timbre	hljómblær
terrain	fold	timer	tímagisti
territory	yfirráðasvæði	timing	tímasetning
testis	eistu	tinea	reformur
tetany	kalkkrampi	tit	meisa
text	lesmál	titanium	titan
thalamus	stúka	titer	títer
thallium	þallín	titre	títri
theca	frjóhnappshelmingur	toddler	trítill
theme	stef	toggle	skipta
theocracy	guðveldi	toilet	hreinsun
theodolite	hornmælir	tolerance	þol
theorem	kennisetning	tomography	sneiðmyndagerð
theory	fræðasvið	tonne	tonn
therapist	lækningamaður	tonometer	spennumælir
therapy	meðferð	tonsil	eitla
thermistor	termistor	tonus	vöðvaspenna
thermocouple	hitapar	tophus	steinefnahnútur
thermodynamics	varmaaflfræði	topic	umræðuefni
thermogram	hitarit	topography	landslagsútlínur

topology	grannfræði	treasury	fjármálaráðuneyti
topsoil	gróðurmold	treaty	ríkjasamningur
tornado	skýstrókur	trematode	agða
toroid	holhringsrör	trepidation	beygur
torque	snúningsmætti	triangle	þríhyrna
torsion	vindingur	triangulation	þríhyrningamælingar
torus	gatfláki	tribe	kynþáttur
totality	almyrkvun	trichina	fleskormur
totalizer	úrkomusafnmælir	trigonometry	hornafræði
tourism	ferðaþjónusta	triode	þrískauti
toxicity	eiturvirkni	triplet	þríburi
toxin	eiturefni	trna	tRKS
toxoid	afeitur	troposphere	veðrahvolf
tracer	sporefni	troubleshooting	bilanagreining
trachea	viðaræð	trough	trog
tracing	rakning	trout	aurriði
tracking	sjónfylgd	truing	afrétting
trademark	vörumerki	truncation	stöðvun
trailer	aftanívagn	tryptophan	trýptófan
training	hæfing	tsunami	sjávarskafl
transaction	framkvæmd	tuba	trompet
transcription	umritun	tubercle	arða
transducer	boðbreytir	tuberculosis	berklar
transduction	umbreyting	tubule	pípla
transference	gagnúð	tularemia	hérasótt
transformation	umskipti	tummy	kviður
transformer	spennir	tungsten	þungsteinn
transfusion	blóðgjöf	turbidity	mor
transhipment	umskipun	turbine	hverfill
transistor	smári	turbot	sandhverfa
transition	færsla	turbulence	iðustreymi
translator	breytir	turnbuckle	strekkingarró
translocation	yfirfærsla	turnip	næpukál
transmittal	skilaflutningur	twins	ĝemelo
transmittance	gegnfararhlutfall	typhus	flekkusótt
transmitter	skynjari	typology	gerðaflokkun
transmutation	frumefnabreyting	tyre	hjólbarði
transom	þverbiti	ullage	borð
transparency	gagnsæi	ultrasound	úthljóð
transpiration	útgufun	unanimity	samhljóða
transposition	skrýfing	uncertainty	óvissa
transposon	stökkull	uncle	föðurbróðir
transvestism	fataskiptahneigð	unconformity	mislægi
trapezium	hálfsamsíðungur	underpants	kalsono
trauma	áfall	understatement	vanskráning
trawler	togari	underwriter	tryggjandi
trawling	togveiðar	undoing	ógilding
treasurer	fjárreiðustjóri	unemployment	atvinnuleysi

unification	jöfnun	ventricle	slegill
unionism	bandalagsstefna	venue	staður
unit	eining	verb	sagnorð
universe	alheimur	vermifuge	ormalyf
unselfishness	örlæti	vermin	meindýr
upkeep	viðhald	vernier	brotamælir
upload	uppflutningur	verruca	varta
urbanization	þéttbýlismyndun	version	vending
urea	karbamíð	vertex	hnútur
uremia	þvageitrun	vertigo	svimi
urology	þvagfærafræði	vessel	ílát
urticaria	ofsakláði	vestibule	forgarður
usufruct	nýtingarréttur	vestry	sóknarnefnd
uterus	leg	veterinary	dýralæknir
utilitarianism	nytjastefna	viability	lífvæni
utilization	nýting	vibrator	titurriðill
utricle	hvekkskjatti	viewpoint	álit
utterance	segð	vigilance	árvekni
vaccination	ónæming	vigour	athafsnemi
vaccinia	kúabóla	vine	klifurjurt
vacuole	frymisbóla	vinegar	edik
vale	dalur	viroid	veirungur
valency	hleðslutala	virology	veirufræði
validation	viðurkenning	virus	vírus
validity	réttmæti	viscometer	seigjumælir
valley	dalur	visualization	hugarsýn
valve	loki	vivification	lífgun
vanadium	vanadíum	vocabulary	orðabók
vanity	hégómaskapur	voicing	röddun
vaporization	gufumyndun	volcanology	eldfjallafræði
vaporizer	eimir	vole	vatnastúfa
vapour	eimur	volleyball	blak
variability	breytileiki	voltage	rafspenna
variance	dreifni	voltameter	voltamælir
variation	tilbrigði	vomiting	uppsala
varix	æðahnútur	voter	kjósandi
vasectomy	sáðrásarúrnám	voucher	ávísun
vasoconstriction	æðasamdráttur	voyeurism	gægjuhneigð
vasodilator	æðavíkkari	vulcanization	brennisteinsmeðferð
veal	kálfskjöt	vulnerability	veila
vector	stefna	wages	laborpago
vegetation	jurtir	waggon	vagn
vehicle	vagn	waiter	thjónn
velum	segl	waiver	undanþága
vendor	seljandi	walleye	glæruvagl
venesection	æðaskurður	wardrobe	skápur
ventilation	loftræsing	warfare	ófriður

warmonger	stríðsæsingamaður	woodpecker	spæta
warping	bjögun	woodsman	skógarhöggsmaður
warranty	ábyrgð	wool	ull
warship	herskip	worker	vinnumaur
wart	festiflötur	workforce	mannafli
washbowl	skál	workload	vinnuálag
washer	skífa	workman	verkamaður
waterfall	foss	works	efiki
watermelon	blóðmelóna	workshop	smiðja
waters	hafsvæði	workstation	vinnustöð
watershed	vatnaskil	wormwood	eðalmalurt
waterworks	vatnsdælustöð	wrapper	lok
watt	vatt	wrasses	varafiskar
waveform	bylgjuform	xanthophyll	sanþófýll
waveguide	bylgjuleiðari	xenon	senón
wavelength	bylgjulengd	xylene	sýlen
weakfish	doði	xylose	xýlósi
weapon	vopn	yacht	lystiskúta
weathering	veðrun	yarrow	jarðhumall
week	vika	yaws	himberjasótt
welding	kveiking	year	ár
wetland	votlendi	yolk	fósturnesti
wheelbase	öxlaafstaða	youngster	barn
wheelhouse	hjólhús	ytterbium	ytterbín
whirlwind	hvirfilvindur	yttrium	yttríum
whitefish	bolfiskur	zebra	sebrahestur
whitewood	hvítviður	zenith	himinhvirfill
whiting	lundaseiði	zinc	sink
wholesaler	heildsali	zirconium	sirkon
whorl	hvirfing	zodiac	dýrahringur
wick	kveikur	zona	belti
widower	ekkill	zonation	beltun
width	vídd	zoning	svæðisskipulag
wildlife	náttúrulíf	zoogeography	dýralandafræði
willingness	vilji	zoology	dýrafræði
windage	vindáhrif	zoster	ristill
windbreak	limgerði	zucchini	dvergbítur
windmill	vindmylla	zygote	okfruma
window	hlið	zygotene	okþráðlufasi
windowpane	deplahverfa	zymogen	símógen
windpipe	barki		
windscreen	framrúða		
windshield	framrúða		
wiper	þurrka		
wiring	innitaugar		
wishbone	geislastengur		
wolffish	bláhaus		
woodcutter	skógarhöggsmaður		

westwards	vestur
whence	hvaðan

Adverbs (Icelandic - English)

antaŭa	forwards
antaŭen	forwards
avanulo	forwards
einnig	too
ekspedi	forwards
gagngert	radically
heldur	ideally
hvað	how
hvaðan	whence
hvernig	how
líka	too
nákvæmlega	punctually
of	too
oft	oftentimes
skyndilega	rudely
trudema	forwards
vafalaust	decidedly
vestur	westwards

Adverbs (English - Icelandic)

abruptly	skyndilega
commonly	oft
decidedly	vafalaust
exactly	nákvæmlega
forwards	antaŭa
frequently	oft
how	hvernig
ideally	heldur
offhandedly	skyndilega
oftentimes	oft
promptly	nákvæmlega
punctually	nákvæmlega
radically	gagngert
rudely	skyndilega
too	einnig

Adjectives (Icelandic - English)

ábyrgur	liable
aðalhringur	deferent
aðfærandi	afferent
aðfenginn	heterogenous
aðhverfur	ventral
aðkomandi	extrinsic
aðkominn	adventitious
aðlægur	contiguous
aðliggjandi	contiguous
aðverminn	endothermic
aðvífandi	exogenous
æfinlegur	perpetual
ær	manic
æstæður	stationary
ætandi	corrosive
ætiefni	corrosive
ættgengur	hereditary
afbrigðilegur	heterologous
aflvaxinn	athletic
aflvöxtur	athletic
afoxaður	reduced
afréttur	reduced
afsakið	sorry
afsýrður	reduced
aftengjanlegur	detachable
ágengur	invasive
ákjósanlegur	optimal
álagslaus	unloaded
alhliða	comprehensive
alkalí	alkaline
alkalískur	alkaline
allegóríkur	allegoric
altækur	global
alþjóðlegur	global
alvarlegur	meaningful
amöbulegur	ameboid
ánægður	gratified

Reference: Webster's Online Dictionary (www.websters-online-dictionary.org)

ánægjulegur	homy	biljafn	periodic
andfélagslegur	antisocial	bilkvæmur	periodic
andlegur	mental	bjagaður	biased
andstæður	refractory	blaðra	latent
andstyggilegur	gruesome	blaðskiptur	lobate
angandi	aromatic	blandanlegur	miscible
annar	different	blendinn	heterologous
árásargjarn	aggressive	blettóttur	punctate
arðbær	economic	blóðeitrun	sepsis
áreiðanlegur	reliable	blóðlaus	anemic
arfbætandi	eugenic	blóðrauðaleysandi	hemolytic
arfgengur	hereditary	blöðrulaga	vesicular
arfhreinn	homozygous	blóðsýking	sepsis
arfskapaður	innate	bogtenntur	crenate
arfskemmandi	dysgenic	bóla	latent
arfspillandi	dysgenic	bólgueyðandi	antiphlogistic
arómatískur	aromatic	bólgueyðir	antiphlogistic
ásfrálægur	abaxial	botnlangabólga	appendicitis
áslægur	axial	botnsætinn	sessile
ástalyf	aphrodisiac	bráðlyndur	choleric
átfrekur	voracious	bráður	stark
áþreifanlegur	tactile	bragðskyn	gustatory
átthyrndur	octagonal	breytilegur	adjustable
átthyrnt	octagonal	brigðull	transitory
augljós	explicit	brostinn	ruptured
augsær	macroscopic	brothættur	fragile
aukalegur	redundant	bundinn	latent
bældur	repressed	Celsíusstig	centigrade
bakteríueyðandi	bactericidal	daglegur	diurnal
bakteríulaus	aseptic	dapur	lugubrious
banvænn	toxic	dástjarfasjúklingur	cataleptic
barkaopshljóð	laryngeal	dástjarfi	catalepsy
barnalegur	infantile	dástjarfur	cataleptic
barnslegur	infantile	daufdumbur	dumb
basískur	alkaline	daufgerður	phlegmatic
baunarlaga	sesamoid	daufur	depressed
beinlaus	boneless	deildur	lobate
beinn	explicit	dekraður	spoiled
beiskur	acerbic	deplóttur	punctate
beittur	lurid	dormandi	dormant
bersýnilegur	overt	dreifbær	extensive
bestur	optimal	dulinn	latent
beygjanlegur	flexible	dulvitaður	unconscious
beyglaður	depressed	dulvitund	unconscious
bifhærður	ciliated	dumbur	dumb
bilfrjáls	aperiodic	dýr	pricey

eðlislægur	intrinsic	fitjaður	webbed
efnahagslegur	economic	fjær	distal
eigin	personal	fjandsamlegur	hostile
einfruma	unicellular	fjandsamur	hostile
eingerður	homogeneous	fjárhagslegur	financial
eingildur	monovalent	fjarlægur	distal
einhliða	unilateral	fjarri	distal
einhliðmælt	unilateral	fjartengdur	remote
einkynja	dioecious	fjölbreytilegur	polymorphic
einleitur	homogeneous	fjölbreytinn	polymorphic
einlitna	haploid	fjölgena	polygenic
einlitnungur	haploid	fjölhæfur	versatile
einlitur	monochromatic	fjölkerfa	systemic
einoka	unitary	fjöllitna	polyploid
einsátta	isotropic	fjöllitnungur	polyploid
einsheiti	homonym	fjölmóta	polymorphic
einskauta	unipolar	fjölþættur	multilateral
einslaga	isomorphic	fjórgildur	tetravalent
einsleitur	homogeneous	fjórhliða	tetragonal
einsmóta	isomorphic	fleirliða	polynomial
eitraður	noxious	flekklaus	stainless
eldfimur	flammable	flogaveikisjúklingur	epileptic
eldsmíðað	forged	flogaveikur	epileptic
elliær	senile	flúrljómandi	fluorescent
ellihrumur	senile	flúrskímandi	fluorescent
elskulegur	alluring	fólginn	implicit
endurmyndandi	regenerative	forklíniskur	preclinical
endurnýjandi	regenerative	formlaus	amorphous
endurnýjanlegur	regenerative	forskriftar	normative
erður	inherited	fortakslaus	implicit
erfiður	refractory	frábrigðilegur	anomalous
erlendur	foreign	frábrugðinn	exceptional
eyðileggjandi	destructive	fráfærandi	efferent
eymslalaus	indolent	fráhverfur	abaxial
fagur	handsome	frákennilegur	atypical
fáir	few	frálægur	efferent
fallegur	handsome	framandi	adventitious
falskur	fictitious	framleiðinn	productive
fáránlegur	nonsensical	framseljanlegur	negotiable
fátækur	impoverished	frátakanlegt	detachable
fatlaður	handicapped	freðinn	frozen
felli	functional	frosinn	frozen
fellir	precipitant	frumbernskur	infantile
fergildur	tetravalent	frumbjarga	autotrophic
ferhyrndur	tetragonal	frumbyggi	indigenous
fimlegur	acrobatic	frygðarauki	aphrodisiac

frygðarlyf	aphrodisiac	grunnlægur	superficial
frystur	frozen	grunnur	superficial
fúll	dismal	gull	golden
fullsterkur	concentrated	gulleitur	xanthous
fyrirframgreiddur	prepaid	gulur	xanthous
fyrirframgreitt	prepaid	háður	endogenous
fyrirgefðu	sorry	hæfilegur	adequate
gagnkvæmur	mutual	hægfara	indolent
gagnverkandi	reactive	hæglyndur	phlegmatic
gagnvirkur	interactive	hærður	pilose
gallaður	detrimental	hættulaus	innocuous
gallharður	adamantine	hættulegur	pernicious
gamall	old	haffær	navigable
gangviss	dependable	hagfræðilegur	economic
gaskenndur	gaseous	hagkvæmur	economic
gataður	perforated	hagnýttur	applied
geðbrigðinn	emotional	hagnýtur	functional
geðklofa	schizophrenic	hagrænn	economic
geðklofasjúklingur	schizophrenic	hagstæðastur	optimal
geðrænn	affective	hagstæður	economic
geðrættur	psychogenic	hagsýnn	economic
geðvefrænn	psychosomatic	haldbær	sustainable
geiraskiptur	segmental	hálfgagnsær	translucent
geislóttur	centric	hálfglær	translucent
gerlaeyðandi	bactericidal	hálfsárslegur	biannual
gervitvíkynja	androgynous	hamlandi	inhibitory
giftur	married	hamstola	manic
gigtarsjúklingur	rheumatic	handahófskenndur	arbitrary
gildandi	approved	hangandi	suspended
gildur	valid	hár	tall
gjaldfærsluhæfur	chargeable	harður	sclerous
gjaldfallinn	overdue	harkalegur	drastic
gjaldskyldur	chargeable	háttbundið	periodic
glaðlyndur	cheerful	heftur	centric
glaður	lighthearted	heiðarlegur	honest
glær	vitreous	heilagur	holy
glerharður	chilled	heildsær	macroscopic
glerkenndur	vitreous	heill	thorough
glúten	gluten	heillandi	alluring
gormlaga	acyclic	heilnæmur	salutary
gormraðaður	acyclic	heilsutæpur	unhealthy
graftarmyndandi	pyogenic	heilsuveill	unhealthy
graftarsótt	sepsis	heimafenginn	autogenous
greindur	arborescent	heittempraður	subtropical
greinóttur	ramose	hemjandi	inhibitory
gruggugur	cloudy	hertur	sclerous

hindraður	blocked	hugrænn	cognitive
hindrandi	inhibitory	hugstola	stuporous
hitabóla	thermal	hugsýnn	intuitive
hitauppstreymi	thermal	hugvíkkandi	psychedelic
hjálægur	adventitious	hulinn	latent
hjartagrófarverkur	cardialgia	hvapholda	flabby
hjartanlegur	cardiac	hvarfbaugur	tropic
hjartasjúklingur	cardiac	hvarfgjarn	reactive
hlaðinn	energized	hvarftregur	inactive
hlaupkenndur	gelatinous	hvatvís	impulsive
hliðstæður	analogous	hvellur	strident
hljómmikill	sonorous	hverfandi	negligible
hlutafélag	limited	hverflyndur	labile
hlutdrægur	biased	hverfull	transitory
hlutfallsbundinn	proportional	hvikull	chaotic
hlutfallslegur	proportional	hvíta	sclerotic
hlutlaus	passive	hvítleitur	albescent
hlutverkslegur	functional	hvítnaður	albescent
hlýtempraður	subtropical	hyrndur	angular
hnattlaga	globular	ífarandi	invasive
hnattrænn	global	ígróinn	inherent
hnöttóttur	spherical	illkynja	malignant
hnugginn	depressed	illkynjaður	malignant
höfuðlaus	acephalous	ilmandi	aromatic
hógvær	modest	ilmefni	aromatic
hol	latent	ilmjurt	aromatic
holefni	clathrate	ímyndaður	virtual
hólklaga	tubular	innanverður	internal
hornmyndaður	angular	innbyggður	structural
hræðilegur	gruesome	inndraganlegur	retractable
hrár	uncooked	innfæddur	autochthonous
hratt	expeditious	innkýldur	impacted
hreisturglæsir	bleak	innlendur	internal
hreyfanlegur	versatile	innrænn	endogenous
hreyfiafl	kinematic	innri	intrinsic
hreyfifræðilegur	kinematic	innsækinn	afferent
hreyfingarfræðilegur	kinematic	innstæður	medial
hreyfingarlaus	inert	innverminn	endothermic
hrífandi	alluring	innvortis	internal
hringlaga	annular	ítrekaður	recurrent
hringmyndaður	annular	jafn	homogeneous
hringtengdur	cyclic	jafnátta	isotropic
hrjúfur	lurid	jafnvægur	balanced
hrúðurkenndur	crustaceous	jarðlægur	procumbent
hryllilegur	dazzled	járnblandað	ferrous
huglægur	subjective	jórturdýr	ruminant

kældur	chilled	lágstafa	lowercase
kaffærður	engulfed	landfræðilegur	geographical
kaldur	bleak	langsum	longitudinal
kalkborinn	calcareous	langur	lengthy
kalkkenndur	calcareous	laskaður	damaged
kámugur	sticky	laus	removable
kappnógur	plentiful	lausataug	flexible
karbónýl	carbonyl	laust	aweigh
karlmannlegur	virile	leiftandi	acerbic
keilulaga	conical	lestaður	loaded
kerfislægur	structural	letjandi	inhibitory
kerfistengdur	systemic	leyndur	latent
kjálkahyrna	angular	leysanlegur	soluble
kjarnkleyfur	fissile	leysinn	soluble
kjörfrjáls	facultative	liðbólgusjúklingur	arthritic
kjörvís	selective	liðskiptur	segmental
klasakenndur	racemose	lifandi	alive
klasaleitur	racemose	lífbrotgjarn	biodegradable
klemmdur	impacted	lífeðlisfræðilegur	physiological
kleyfhuga	schizophrenic	liffræðilegur	biological
kleyfur	fissile	lífhverfur	biodegradable
klíniskur	clinical	lífræðilegur	biological
klístraður	viscid	lífrænn	biotic
kljúfanlegur	fissile	lífsprakur	biodegradable
kornóttur	granular	lífvænn	viable
krabbalíkur	cancerous	lífvirkur	biological
kringlóttur	orbicular	líkindasvæði	orbital
kúlulaga	globular	líklegur	liable
kurteis	polite	líminn	viscid
kvenkyn	feminine	límkenndur	sticky
kvenlegur	feminine	línulaga	linear
kviðlægur	ventral	línulegur	linear
kvíslóttur	ramose	lítið	few
kvoðulausn	colloid	litlaus	achromatic
kynferðislegur	sexual	ljósmælifræði	photometry
kynlaus	asexual	ljósmæling	photometry
kynnæmur	erogenous	ljósmælingar	photometry
kynorkuaukandi	aphrodisiac	ljótur	ugly
kynorkulyf	aphrodisiac	loðinn	hirsute
kyrr	stabile	lófalægur	palmar
Kyrrahaf	pacific	loftborinn	airborne
l	aerobic	loftfælinn	anaerobic
læknandi	therapeutic	loftfíkinn	aerobic
lagalegur	statutory	loftfirrður	anaerobic
lagskipt	laminated	loftfylltur	pneumatic
lagskiptur	laminar	lofthádur	aerobic

loftkenndur	gaseous	meðvitandi	conscious
loftknúíð	pneumatic	meðvitundarlaus	unconscious
loftknúinn	pneumatic	megindlegur	quantitative
loftkveikjandi	pyrophoric	megn	concentrated
loftsækinn	aerobic	meinafræðilegur	pathologic
loftþurfi	aerobic	meinlaus	innocuous
lögákveðinn	statutory	meinvaldandi	pathogenic
lögboðinn	statutory	meinvirkur	pathogenic
lögbundinn	statutory	merkingarlaus	anomalous
löggengur	deterministic	metaskiptur	hierarchic
löggiltur	statutory	miðlægur	medial
lögmæltur	statutory	miðleitinn	centripetal
lögskipaður	statutory	miðtækur	normative
lostavekjandi	aphrodisiac	mikill	substantial
lotubundinn	periodic	minnstur	minimal
lotukvæmur	cyclic	misátta	anisotropic
lotulaus	aperiodic	misgerður	discordant
lotutíminn	periodic	mislangur	unequal
lyktarskyn	olfactory	misleitur	heterologous
lystarleysi	anorexia	misserislegur	biannual
mæddur	depressed	misvísandi	magnetic
mælanlegur	quantitative	mjölvakenndur	amyloid
magn	quantitative	mjúkhærður	pilose
magnbundinn	quantitative	mjúkur	bland
málfræðilegur	grammatical	móðurlegur	maternal
mállaus	dumb	möndullægur	axial
mállýskubundinn	dialectal	mótsvarandi	complementary
málstola	aphasic	móttækilegur	susceptible
málstoli	aphasic	myndlaus	amorphous
manngerður	anthropogenic	myndrænn	graphical
mannmótað	anthropogenic	nægilegur	adequate
mannmótaður	anthropogenic	næmur	sensitive
margbreytilegur	polymorphic	nærandi	nutritive
marghliða	multilateral	nærlægur	proximal
marglaga	laminated	nærliggjandi	proximal
margleitur	polymorphic	nærri	proximal
margliða	polynomial	náinn	inmost
markaðshæfur	marketable	nakinn	naked
matgráðugur	voracious	nállaga	acicular
máttagur	forceful	nauðgengur	deterministic
máttlítill	flabby	nauðsynlegur	obligatory
með	webbed	nauðugur	involuntary
meðalgildisréttur	unbiased	niðurbældur	depressed
meðalgildisskakkur	biased	nógur	adequate
meðfæddur	inherent	notalegur	homy
meðvirkur	reactive	nothæfur	functional

nýtinn	economic	ólögmætur	illegal
óaðgætinn	inadvertent	ólotubundinn	aperiodic
óánægður	disgruntled	ölvaður	intoxicated
óáreiðanlegur	dicey	ömbulegur	ameboid
óbeinn	implicit	ómettaður	unsaturated
óbilkvæmur	aperiodic	ómótaður	amorphous
óbjagaður	unbiased	ónæmur	resistant
óblandaður	concentrated	opinber	overt
óblandanlegur	immiscible	óræður	irrational
óbrennanlegur	incombustible	orkugæfur	exothermic
óbreyta	invariant	orkukræfur	endothermic
óbreytanlegur	invariable	örlítill	minimal
óbreytilegur	invariant	ormalegur	vermicular
óbreytinn	invariant	ormlaga	vermicular
oddbaugóttur	elliptic	órökrænn	irrational
óður	manic	örsvif	colloid
óeðlilegur	abnormal	örþeyta	colloid
óeldfimur	incombustible	örvæntingarfullur	hopeless
óendanlegur	infinite	örvhendur	sinistral
ofaukið	redundant	ósamfasa	asynchronous
ófélagslegur	asocial	ósamhæfður	asynchronous
ófjaðrandi	inelastic	ósamkynja	heterogenous
ófrumbjarga	heterotrophic	ósamloka	asymmetrical
ófullnægjandi	deficient	ósamræmur	discordant
öfundarfullur	envious	ósamstæður	heterologous
öfundsjúkur	jealous	ósamstilltur	asynchronous
ofursætur	saccharine	ósannur	fictitious
ofvirkur	hyperactive	ósjálfráður	autonomic
ógiftur	unmarried	óskaðlegur	innocuous
ógnvekjandi	alarming	óskilgreindur	unspecified
óhamingjusamur	unhappy	óskiptur	unitary
óháttbundið	aperiodic	óstöðugur	labile
óheiðarlegur	dishonest	ósvífinn	impertinent
óheppinn	unfortunate	ótær	cloudy
óhlaðinn	unloaded	óteyginn	inelastic
óhlutdrægur	unbiased	óþægilegur	bleak
óhraustlegur	unhealthy	óþjáll	refractory
óhvarfgjarn	stabile	óþjappanlegur	incompressible
ójafn	unequal	óþolinmóður	impatient
ókristallaður	amorphous	óþroskaður	immature
ókurteis	impolite	ótilgreindur	unspecified
ólífrænn	inorganic	ótiltekinn	arbitrary
ólíkur	different	ótímabær	premature
ólita	achromatic	ótraustur	dodgy
óljós	implicit	óvænn	unkind
ólöglegur	illegal	óvanlegur	abnormal

óviðkunnanlegur	uncongenial	ryðfrír	rustproof
óvilhallur	unbiased	ryðfrítt	rustproof
óvingjarnlegur	brutal	ryðrauður	ferruginous
óvinveittur	hostile	rýrður	reduced
óvirkur	latent	særður	injured
óvís	undoubted	sætur	expensive
peningalegur	monetary	sagtenntur	serrated
pípulaga	tubular	sakarforræði	optional
pólstilltur	equatorial	saklaus	guiltless
ráðstöfunarvald	optional	sálrænn	psychogenic
ræður	rational	samása	coaxial
rafeindadrægur	electronegative	sambærilegur	comparable
rafeindagæfur	electropositive	sameiginlegur	concerted
rafeindajákvæður	electropositive	samfallandi	complementary
rafeindaneikvæður	electronegative	samfasa	coherent
rafeindastýrður	electronic	samfelldur	seamless
rafeindatæknilegur	electronic	samhangandi	coherent
rafeindavæddur	electronic	samheldinn	coherent
raftæknilegur	electronic	samhverfur	symmetric
rakur	moist	samkynja	homogeneous
randhærður	ciliated	samlægur	contiguous
randstæður	marginal	samleitur	homogeneous
rásaður	cyclic	samliggjandi	contiguous
rauðaleysandi	hemolytic	samloðandi	coherent
rauðkornarjúfandi	hemolytic	samloka	symmetrical
raunsær	realistic	sammiðja	axial
raunverulegur	realistic	samræmdur	unitary
reiður	angry	samstæður	homologous
rétthverfing	supination	samstilling	synchronous
réttlátur	equitable	samstilltur	synchronous
réttmætur	valid	samstunda	synchronous
riða	scrapie	samstundis	instantaneous
riðuveiki	scrapie	samsvarandi	homologous
rifgataður	perforated	samtaka	coherent
ríkjandi	prevailing	samtengdur	interactive
ríkulegur	plentiful	samþátta	homogeneous
rofinn	ruptured	samþykktur	approved
róflegur	spectral	samtíma	simultaneous
rófrænn	spectral	samtímis	synchronous
rökréttur	rational	samur	same
rólyndur	phlegmatic	sandborinn	arenaceous
rörlaga	tubular	sannfærður	convincing
rotinn	putrid	sanngjarn	equitable
rúmgóður	vast	sársaukalaus	indolent
runubundinn	sequential	saumlaus	seamless
rústrauður	ferruginous	saumlaust	seamless

sefjandi	suggestive	skilmerkilegur	explicit
sefnæmur	suggestible	skilvitlegur	cognitive
seglanlegur	magnetic	skilyrðislaus	implicit
segulmagnaður	magnetic	skipgengur	navigable
seigfljótandi	viscid	skiptisending	simplex
seinn	indolent	skiptital	simplex
seljanlegur	marketable	skörðóttur	serrated
sennilegur	probable	skorinn	truncated
sérbýlinn	dioecious	skorpukenndur	crustaceous
sérkynja	unisexual	skrækur	strident
sérstæður	exceptional	skrýtinn	peculiar
sextánskur	hexadecimal	skuggsær	symmetrical
síendurtekinn	recurring	skýjaður	cloudy
sigðlaga	falciform	skyldubundinn	compulsory
sístæður	stationary	skyldugur	liable
sívalningslaga	centric	skyldur	obligatory
sjaldgæfur	rare	skyndilegur	dismissive
sjálfbær	sustainable	skynjanlegur	sensible
sjálfbirgur	autotrophic	skynnæmur	perceptive
sjálfkveiktur	autogenous	skynsamlegur	rational
sjálfmyndaður	autogenous	skynsamur	reasonable
sjálfráður	autonomic	skýr	straightforward
sjálfsfrævandi	autogamous	slappur	flabby
sjálfsfrjóvgandi	autogamous	sligandi	exhaustive
sjálfskapaður	autogenous	slímkenndur	mucoid
sjálfsmyndaður	autogenous	slímlíki	mucoid
sjálfstæður	autonomic	sljór	torpid
sjálfvakinn	idiopathic	smækkaður	reduced
sjálfvirkur	autonomic	smæstur	minimal
sjúkdómsvaldandi	pathogenic	smágötóttur	clathrate
sjúklegur	pathological	smásær	microscopic
skaðlegur	destructive	smávægilegur	negligible
skaðsamur	destructive	smitaður	infectious
skaðvænn	noxious	smitandi	infectious
skæður	pernicious	smitlaus	aseptic
skakkalaus	unbiased	snældulaga	fusiform
skakkur	biased	snertiskyn	tactile
skammvinnur	ephemeral	snöggur	naked
skarpur	acerbic	sólar	solar
skátastarf	guiding	söluhæfur	marketable
skattskyldur	taxable	sóttnæmur	susceptible
skattskylt	taxable	spólulaga	fusiform
skemmdur	damaged	sporöskjulaga	elliptic
skerandi	snappy	staðbundinn	localized
skertur	reduced	staðlandi	normative
skilinn	cognitive	staðmarkaður	localized

staðvilltur	ectopic	sýkilvirkur	pathogenic
stæður	stationary	sýkinn	infectious
staflaga	bacillary	sýkjandi	pathogenic
stafnrið	prostyle	sýkladrepandi	bactericidal
stafnriðshof	prostyle	sykursjúkur	diabetic
starfandi	functional	sykursýkissjúklingur	diabetic
starfrænn	functional	sýrukær	acidophilic
stefnuháður	anisotropic	sýrusækinn	acidophilic
stefnuhneigður	anisotropic	sýrusólginn	acidophilic
stefnusnauður	isotropic	tæknifræðilegur	technological
sterkjulíki	amyloid	tæmandi	exhaustive
sterkur	concentrated	tærandi	corrosive
stigskipt	hierarchical	tærinn	corrosive
stigskiptur	hierarchical	tafarlaus	instantaneous
stilklaus	sessile	tagaður	typed
stillanlegur	adjustable	tagskiptur	typed
stirðnun	catalepsy	takmarkaður	limited
stjarnlaga	stellate	takmarkalaus	infinite
stjörnulaga	stellate	táknsögulegur	allegoric
stöðlunar	normative	taktbundinn	periodic
stöðugur	stationary	tálmandi	inhibitory
stökkur	fragile	tenginn	associative
stór	substantial	teningslaga	cubic
stórsær	macroscopic	tepptur	impacted
straumfræðilegur	hydrodynamic	teygjanlegt	ductile
strendur	angular	teygjanlegur	ductile
striklaga	linear	þægilegur	enjoyable
stúrinn	depressed	þakklátur	thankful
stýfður	truncated	þanþolinn	ductile
stýranlegur	navigable	þjóðernislegur	ethnic
sundurdraganlegur	telescopic	þjóðlegur	ethnic
sundurskiptur	fragmented	þolinn	resistant
súr	acidic	þolmyndarsetning	passive
svæðisbundinn	regional	þráðlaga	filiform
svarbúinn	responsive	þrepskiptur	fractional
svefnhöfugur	hypnagogic	þrígildur	trivalent
sveigjanlegur	flexible	þrykktur	forged
sveppadeyðandi	fungicidal	þungbúinn	cloudy
sveppasýktur	fungous	þunglyndur	depressed
sveppdeyðandi	fungicidal	þungur	onerous
sveppeyðandi	fungicidal	þvalur	moist
sverðlaga	xiphoid	þverlægur	transversal
svigrúm	orbital	þverlami	paraplegic
svipull	transitory	þýlundaður	subservient
svitaaukandi	diaphoretic	tilfallandi	accidental
svitalyf	diaphoretic	tilfinninganæmur	susceptible

tilfinningasamurlegur	emotional	útsækinn	efferent
tilraunalegur	experimental	útverminn	exothermic
tiltækur	quiescent	vænn	affable
tilviljunarkenndur	accidental	vætukarsi	watercress
tölfræðilegur	statistical	valbundinn	facultative
topplægur	apical	valfrjáls	optional
traustur	liable	valfrjálst	optional
trefjalíkur	fibrous	valkvæður	optional
trefjóttur	fibrous	vandur	inconvenient
tregur	inert	vanþakklátur	unthankful
trjábýll	arboreal	vanþroska	subnormal
trjákynjaður	arboraceous	varmaaflfræðilegur	thermodynamic
tungubroddshljóð	apical	varmadrægur	endothermic
tvíátta	ambivalent	varmafræðilegur	thermodynamic
tvíbentur	ambivalent	varmagæfur	exothermic
tvíbýlinn	dioecious	varmagleypinn	endothermic
tvígildur	divalent	vatna	aquatic
tvíhvolfur	biconcave	vatnaður	hydrated
tvíkynja	hermaphroditic	vatnafræði	hydrology
tvílíða	binomial	vatns	aquatic
tvínafn	binomial	vatnsfælinn	hydrophobic
Tvípeð	doubled	vatnsfirrtur	anhydrous
tvískiptur	dual	vatnsfræði	hydrology
tvístraður	fragmented	vatnsfrír	anhydrous
tvítala	dual	vatnsfrítt	anhydrous
tvíþættur	dual	vatnshaldinn	hydrated
tvítyngdur	bilingual	vatnsrænn	aquatic
tvöfaldur	dual	vatnsþéttur	watertight
úldinn	putrid	veðurfarslegur	climatic
umburðarlyndur	tolerant	veflíkur	webbed
umframur	redundant	veganlegur	quantitative
umlukinn	engulfed	venjubundið	conventional
umsemjanlegur	negotiable	venjulegt	conventional
umskiptanlegur	removable	venjulegur	conventional
undanskilinn	implicit	verður	worthwhile
undantekning	exceptional	vermandi	calefacient
undarlegur	remarkable	vermilyf	calefacient
undirskilinn	implicit	viðarkenndur	woody
uppíloft	supine	viðbjóðslegur	hideous
uppland	inland	víðfeðmur	global
upprunalegur	autochthonous	viðhaldsbær	sustainable
utanaðkomandi	adventitious	viðkunnanlegur	approachable
utanlands	offshore	viðkvæmur	sensitive
útbreiddur	systemic	víðtækur	global
útlendur	offshore	víður	spacious
útrænn	exogenous	viðurkenndur	approved

víðvær	global	acetous	súr
viðvarandi	prevailing	achromatic	litlaus
víkjandi	recessive	acicular	nállaga
vilhallur	biased	acidic	súr
villtur	ectopic	acidophilic	sýrukær
vindborinn	airborne	acrobatic	fimlegur
vingjarnlegur	affable	acyclic	gormlaga
vinnanlegur	workable	adamantine	gallharður
vinstri	sinistral	adequate	nægilegur
virkur	functional	adjustable	stillanlegur
vís	certain	adventitious	aðkominn
vissulegur	certain	aerobic	loftfíkinn
vistfræðilegur	ecological	affable	vænn
visthverfur	biodegradable	affecting	tilfinningasamurlegur
vistrænn	ecological	affective	geðrænn
vitlaus	odd	afferent	aðliggjandi
vitrænn	cognitive	aggressive	ýgur
víxlverkandi	interactive	agreeable	þægilegur
víxlvirkur	interactive	airborne	loftborinn
vöðvamikill	muscular	alarmed	hryllilegur
vökvaaflfræði	hydrodynamic	alarming	ógnvekjandi
vökvaaflfræðilegur	hydrodynamic	albescent	hvítnaður
vökvahreyfifræði	hydrodynamic	alive	lifandi
vökvakyrrstaða	hydrostatics	alkaline	alkalí
vökvastöðufræði	hydrostatics	allegoric	allegóríkur
volgur	lukewarm	allegorical	allegóríkur
yfirfæranlegur	transferable	alluring	heillandi
yfirgefinn	immoral	ambivalent	tvíbentur
yfirgripsmikill	comprehensive	ameboid	amöbulegur
yfirvofandi	imminent	amorphous	formlaus
ýgur	aggressive	ample	kappnógur
yrtur	verbal	amyloid	mjölvakenndur
ytri	extrinsic	anaerobic	loftfælinn
		analogous	hliðstæður
		androgynous	tvíkynja
		anemic	blóðlaus
		angry	reiður
		angular	hornmyndaður

Adjectives (English - Icelandic)

		anhydrous	vatnsfrítt
		anisotropic	stefnuhneigður
		annular	hringlaga
abaxial	fráhverfur	anomalous	afbrigðilegur
abnormal	afbrigðilegur	anorexia	lystarleysi
abysmal	hræðilegur	anthropogenic	manngerður
accidental	tilviljunarkenndur	antiphlogistic	bólgueyðandi
acephalous	höfuðlaus	antisocial	andfélagslegur
acerbic	beittur	aperiodic	ólotubundinn

aphasic	málstoli	brazen	ósvífinn
aphrodisiac	ástalyf	brutal	óvænn
apical	tungubroddshljóð	calcareous	kalkborinn
appealing	heillandi	calefacient	vermandi
appendicitis	botnlangabólga	cancerous	krabbalíkur
applied	hagnýttur	capacious	víður
approachable	viðkunnanlegur	carbonyl	karbónýl
approved	gildandi	cardiac	hjartasjúklingur
aquatic	vatns	cardialgia	hjartagrófarverkur
arbitrary	ótiltekinn	catalepsy	dástjarfi
arboraceous	trjákynjaður	cataleptic	dástjarfasjúklingur
arboreal	trjábýll	centigrade	Celsíusstig
arborescent	greindur	centric	geislóttur
arenaceous	sandborinn	centripetal	miðleitinn
aromatic	arómatískur	certain	vís
arthritic	liðbólgusjúklingur	chaotic	hvikull
articulated	liðskiptur	chargeable	gjaldfærsluhæfur
aseptic	bakteríulaus	charming	elskulegur
asexual	kynlaus	cheerful	glaðlyndur
asocial	ófélagslegur	cherished	sætur
associative	tenginn	chilled	glerharður
asymmetrical	ósamloka	choleric	bráðlyndur
asynchronous	ósamfasa	ciliated	bifhærður
athletic	aflvaxinn	clathrate	smágötóttur
atypical	frábrigðilegur	climatic	veðurfarslegur
autochthonous	innfæddur	clinical	klí…

crustaceous	hrúðurkenndur	electropositive	rafeindagæfur
cubic	teningslaga	elliptic	oddbaugóttur
curious	skrýtinn	emotional	geðbrigðinn
cyclic	hringlaga	endogenous	háður
damaged	laskaður	endothermic	varmagleypinn
dazzled	hryllilegur	energized	hlaðinn
deferent	aðalhringur	engulfed	kaffærður
deficient	ófullnægjandi	enjoyable	þægilegur
dependable	traustur	envious	öfundarfullur
depressed	stúrinn	ephemeral	skammvinnur
destructive	skaðsamur	epileptic	flogaveikisjúklingur
detachable	aftengjanlegur	equatorial	pólstilltur
deterministic	löggengur	equitable	réttlátur
detrimental	gallaður	erogenous	kynnæmur
diabetic	sykursýkissjúklingur	eternal	æfinlegur
dialectal	mállýskubundinn	ethnic	þjóðernislegur
diaphoretic	svitalyf	eugenic	arfbætandi
dicey	óáreiðanlegur	exceptional	frábrugðinn
different	annar	exhaustive	sligandi
dioecious	tvíbýlinn	exogenous	aðvífandi
discordant	ósamræmur	exothermic	orkugæfur
disgruntled	óánægður	expeditious	hratt
dishonest	óheiðarlegur	expensive	sætur
dismal	viðbjóðslegur	experimental	tilraunalegur
dismayed	hryllilegur	explicit	beinn
dismissive	skyndilegur	extensive	dreifbær
distal	fjær	extrinsic	aðkomandi
distasteful	óþægilegur	facultative	kjörfrjáls
diurnal	daglegur	falciform	sigðlaga
divalent	tvígildur	feminine	kvenkyn
dodgy	ótraustur	ferrous	járnblandað
dormant	dormandi	ferruginous	rústrauður
doubled	Tvípeð	few	lítið
drastic	harkalegur	fibrous	trefjalíkur
dreadful	hræðilegur	fictitious	falskur
dreary	viðbjóðslegur	filiform	þráðlaga
dual	tvöfaldur	financial	fjárhagslegur
ductile	teygjanlegt	fissile	kjarnkleyfur
dumb	mállaus	flabby	hvapholda
dumbfounded	hryllilegur	flammable	eldfimur
dysgenic	arfskemmandi	flexible	beygjanlegur
ecological	vistfræðilegur	fluorescent	flúrljómandi
economic	hagkvæmur	forceful	sterkur
ectopic	staðvilltur	foreign	erlendur
efferent	fráfærandi	forged	eldsmíðað
electronegative	rafeindadrægur	fortuitous	tilviljunarkenndur
electronic	rafeindastýrður	fractional	þrepskiptur

Reference: Webster's Online Dictionary (www.websters-online-dictionary.org)

fragile	brothættur	honest	heiðarlegur
fragmented	sundurskiptur	honourable	heiðarlegur
frozen	freðinn	hopeless	örvæntingarfullur
functional	hagnýtur	hostile	fjandsamlegur
fungicidal	sveppadeyðandi	humid	rakur
fungous	sveppasýktur	hydrated	vatnaður
fusiform	snældulaga	hydrodynamic	vökvaaflfræðilegur
gaseous	loftkenndur	hydrology	vatnsfræði
gelatinous	hlaupkenndur	hydrophobic	vatnsfælinn
generative	kynferðislegur	hydrostatics	vökvakyrrstaða
geographical	landfræðilegur	hyperactive	ofvirkur
ghastly	hræðilegur	hypnagogic	svefnhöfugur
glad	glaður	idiopathic	sjálfvakinn
global	altækur	illegal	ólögmætur
globose	hnöttóttur	immature	óþroskaður
globular	hnattlaga	imminent	yfirvofandi
gloomy	dapur	immiscible	óblandanlegur
gluten	glúten	immoral	yfirgefinn
golden	gull	immune	ónæmur
grammatical	málfræðilegur	impacted	tepptur
granular	kornóttur	impatient	óþolinmóður
graphical	myndrænn	impertinent	ósvífinn
gratified	ánægður	implicit	fólginn
grim	dapur	impolite	ókurteis
gruesome	hræðilegur	impoverished	fátækur
guiding	skátastarf	impulsive	hvatvís
guiltless	saklaus	inactive	hvarftregur
gustatory	bragðskyn	inadvertent	óaðgætinn
handicapped	fatlaður	incombustible	óbrennanlegur
handsome	fagur	incompressible	óþjappanlegur
haploid	einlitna	inconvenient	þungur
hemolytic	blóðrauðaleysandi	indigenous	frumbyggi
hereditary	ættgengur	indolent	eymslalaus
hermaphroditic	tvíkynja	inelastic	óteyginn
heterogenous	aðfenginn	inert	tregur
heterologous	blendinn	infantile	barnalegur
heterotrophic	ófrumbjarga	infectious	smitaður
hexadecimal	sextánskur	infective	næmur
hideous	andstyggilegur	infinite	takmarkalaus
hierarchic	stigskiptur	inflammable	eldfimur
hierarchical	stigskiptur	inherent	arfskapaður
hirsute	loðinn	inherited	erfður
holy	heilagur	inhibitory	hamlandi
homogeneous	samleitur	injured	særður
homologous	samstæður	inland	uppland
homonym	einsheiti	inmost	náinn
homozygous	arfhreinn	innate	arfskapaður
homy	ánægjulegur	innocuous	óskaðlegur

inorganic	ólífrænn	medial	innstæður
instantaneous	tafarlaus	mental	andlegur
interactive	gagnvirkur	mesial	miðlægur
internal	innri	microscopic	smásær
intoxicated	ölvaður	minimal	minnstur
intrinsic	eðlislægur	miscible	blandanlegur
intuitive	hugsýnn	modest	hógvær
invariable	óbreytanlegur	moist	rakur
invariant	óbreytilegur	monetary	fjárhagslegur
invasive	ífarandi	monochromatic	einlitur
involuntary	nauðugur	monovalent	eingildur
irrational	óræður	mucoid	slímkenndur
isomorphic	einslaga	multilateral	fjölþættur
isotropic	einsátta	muscular	vöðvamikill
jealous	öfundsjúkur	mutual	gagnkvæmur
joyful	glaður	naked	nakinn
joyous	glaður	navigable	haffær
kinematic	hreyfiafl	negligible	hverfandi
labile	hverflyndur	negotiable	framseljanlegur
laminar	lagskiptur	nonsensical	fáránlegur
laminated	lagskipt	normative	forskriftar
laryngeal	barkaopshljóð	noteworthy	undarlegur
latent	hulinn	noxious	eitraður
lengthy	langur	nutritive	nærandi
liable	traustur	obligatory	nauðsynlegur
lighthearted	glaður	octagonal	átthyrndur
likable	viðkunnanlegur	odd	skrýtinn
limited	hlutafélag	offshore	erlendur
linear	línulaga	old	gamall
loaded	lestaður	olfactory	lyktarskyn
loathsome	andstyggilegur	onerous	þungur
lobate	blaðskiptur	optimal	ákjósanlegur
localized	staðbundinn	optional	valfrjálst
longitudinal	langsum	orbicular	kringlóttur
lowercase	lágstafa	orbital	líkindasvæði
lugubrious	dapur	overdue	gjaldfallinn
lukewarm	volgur	overt	bersýnilegur
lurid	leiftandi	pacific	Kyrrahaf
macroscopic	heildsær	palmar	lófalægur
magnetic	misvísandi	paraplegic	þverlami
malignant	illkynja	passive	aðfenginn
manic	hamstola	pathogenic	sýkjandi
marginal	randstæður	pathologic	meinafræðilegur
marketable	markaðshæfur	pathological	sjúklegur
married	giftur	peculiar	skrýtinn
maternal	móðurlegur	perceptive	skynnæmur
meaningful	alvarlegur	perforated	gataður

periodic	biljafn	recurring	síendurtekinn
pernicious	hættulegur	reduced	afoxaður
perpetual	æfinlegur	redundant	aukalegur
personal	náinn	refractory	andstæður
phlegmatic	rólyndur	regenerative	endurmyndandi
photometry	ljósmælifræði	regional	svæðisbundinn
physiological	lífeðlisfræðilegur	reliable	áreiðanlegur
pilose	mjúkhærður	remarkable	undarlegur
pleasant	þægilegur	remote	fjarlægur
plentiful	kappnógur	removable	laus
pneumatic	loftfylltur	repressed	bældur
poisonous	eitraður	resistant	þolinn
polite	kurteis	responsive	svarbúinn
polygenic	fjölgena	retractable	inndraganlegur
polymorphic	fjölbreytilegur	rheumatic	gigtarsjúklingur
polynomial	fleirliða	ruminant	jórturdýr
polyploid	fjöllitna	ruptured	brostinn
practical	raunverulegur	rustproof	ryðfrír
precipitant	fellir	saccharine	ofursætur
preclinical	forklínískur	salutary	heilnæmur
premature	ótímabær	same	samur
prepaid	fyrirframgreiddur	schizophrenic	geðklofasjúklingur
prevailing	ríkjandi	sclerotic	hvíta
pricey	dýr	sclerous	harður
probable	sennilegur	scrapie	riða
procumbent	jarðlægur	seamless	samfelldur
productive	framleiðinn	segmental	geiraskiptur
proportional	hlutfallsbundinn	selective	kjörvís
prostyle	stafnrið	senile	elliær
proximal	nærlægur	sensible	skynjanlegur
psychedelic	hugvíkkandi	sensitive	viðkunnanlegur
psychogenic	sálrænn	sepsis	blóðeitrun
psychosomatic	geðvefrænn	sequential	runubundinn
punctate	blettóttur	serrated	skörðóttur
putrid	rotinn	sesamoid	baunarlaga
pyogenic	graftarmyndandi	sessile	botnsætinn
pyrophoric	loftkveikjandi	sexual	kynferðislegur
quantitative	magnbundinn	simplex	skiptisending
quiescent	óvirkur	simultaneous	samtíma
racemose	klasakenndur	sinistral	vinstri
ramose	greinóttur	slavish	þýlundaður
rare	sjaldgæfur	snappy	skerandi
rational	skynsamur	solar	sólar
reactive	gagnverkandi	soluble	leysanlegur
realistic	raunsær	sonorous	hljómmikill
reasonable	skynsamur	sorrowful	dapur
recessive	víkjandi	sorry	afsakið
recurrent	ítrekaður	spacious	rúmgóður

spectral	róflegur	thorough	heill
spherical	hnöttóttur	tolerant	umburðarlyndur
spoiled	dekraður	torpid	sljór
stabile	kyrr	toxic	banvænn
stainless	flekklaus	transferable	framseljanlegur
stark	heill	transitory	brigðull
stationary	æstæður	translucent	glær
statistical	tölfræðilegur	transversal	þverlægur
statutory	löggiltur	trivalent	þrígildur
stellate	stjarnlaga	tropic	hvarfbaugur
sticky	kámugur	truncated	skorinn
straightforward	skýr	tubular	hólklaga
stratified	lagskiptur	typed	tagaður
strident	skerandi	ugly	ljótur
structural	innbyggður	unassuming	hógvær
stuporous	hugstola	unbiased	skakkalaus
subjective	hugrænn	uncommon	sjaldgæfur
submissive	þýlundaður	uncongenial	óviðkunnanlegur
subnormal	vanþroska	unconscious	dulvitaður
subservient	þýlundaður	uncooked	hrár
substantial	mikill	undoubted	óvís
subtropical	heittempraður	unequal	ójafn
suggestible	sefnæmur	unfortunate	óheppinn
suggestive	sefjandi	ungrateful	vanþakklátur
superficial	grunnlægur	unhappy	óhamingjusamur
supination	rétthverfing	unhealthy	heilsutæpur
supine	uppíloft	unicellular	einfruma
susceptible	móttækilegur	unilateral	einhliðmælt
suspended	hangandi	unipolar	einskauta
sustainable	viðhaldsbær	unisexual	einkynja
symmetric	samhverfur	unitary	einoka
symmetrical	samhverfur	unkind	óvænn
synchronous	samtíma	unloaded	óhlaðinn
systemic	kerfistengdur	unmarried	ógiftur
tactile	áþreifanlegur	unpretentious	hógvær
tall	hár	unquestionable	óvís
taxable	skattskyldur	unreliable	óáreiðanlegur
technological	tæknifræðilegur	unsaturated	ómettaður
telescopic	sundurdraganlegur	unspecified	óskilgreindur
tensile	teygjanlegur	unthankful	vanþakklátur
terrible	hræðilegur	untrue	ósannur
tetragonal	ferhyrndur	valid	gildur
tetravalent	fergildur	vast	rúmgóður
thankful	þakklátur	venerable	gamall
therapeutic	læknandi	ventral	aðhverfur
thermal	hitabóla	verbal	yrtur
thermodynamic	varmaaflfræðilegur	vermicular	ormalegur

versatile	fjölhæfur
vesicular	blöðrulaga
viable	lífvænn
villous	loðinn
virile	karlmannlegur
virtual	ímyndaður
viscid	líminn
vitreous	glær
voracious	átfrekur
watercress	vætukarsi
watertight	vatnsþéttur
webbed	veflíkur
woody	viðarkenndur
workable	vinnanlegur
worthwhile	verður
xanthic	gulur
xanthous	gulleitur
xiphoid	sverðlaga

6594067R0

Made in the USA
Lexington, KY
05 September 2010